Vision in depth

Submarine Periscopes

Thermal Imaging

Night Vision

Laser Rangefinding

and other Optronic Systems

BARR AND STROUD

Glasgow and London

JANE'S FIGHTING SHIPS

Edited by Captain John E. Moore
RN, FRGS

Order of Contents

World Sales Distribution

Jane's Yearbooks,
Paulton House, 8 Shepherdess Walk
London N1 7LW, England

All the World
except

United States of America and Canada:
Franklin Watts Inc
730 Fifth Avenue
New York, NY 10019, USA

Editorial communication to:

The Editor, Jane's Fighting Ships
Jane's Yearbooks, Paulton House, 8 Shepherdess Walk
London N1 7LW, England
Telephone 01-251 1666

Advertisement communication to:

The Advertisement Manager
Jane's Yearbooks, Paulton House, 8 Shepherdess Walk
London N1 7LW, England
Telephone 01-251 1666

*Classified List of Advertisers
The various products available from the advertisers in this edition are listed alphabetically in about 350 different headings.

Cossor Naval IFF Systems

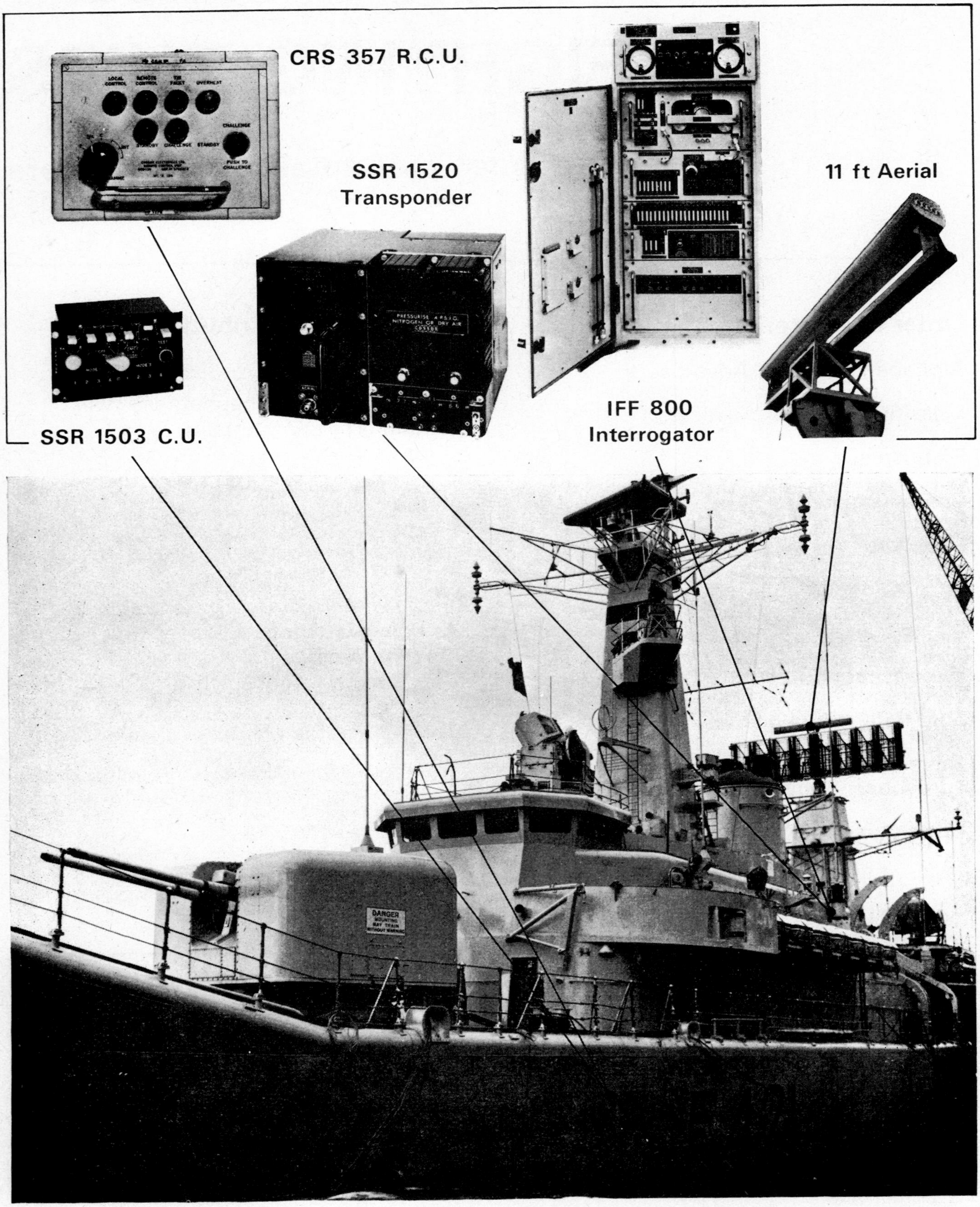

CRS 357 R.C.U.

SSR 1520
Transponder

11 ft Aerial

SSR 1503 C.U.

IFF 800
Interrogator

Cossor manufacture a range of IFF Systems to meet all Naval requirements ranging from the IFF 800 System, for Escort ships offering comprehensive facilities coupled with high reliability and ease of maintainance, to the newly introduced IFF 825 M – a miniature solid state rugged diesel equipment designed for Fast Patrol Boats.

COSSOR

Cossor Electronics Limited,
Sales Division — Aviation & Surface Electronics.
The Pinnacles, Harlow, Essex, England.
Telephone : Harlow 26862 Telex : 81228 Cables : Cossor, Harlow.

RBOC — RAPID BLOOM OFFBOARD COUNTERMEASURES
COUNTERMEASURE LAUNCHING SYSTEMS
FOR SHIPS OF ALL SIZES

SMALL : LIGHTWEIGHT : LOW COST : PROVEN

The MK 33 RBOC Countermeasure System is the most effective Anti-ship Missile Defense System now available. It is a very versatile system which can launch various types of payloads such as:

- o Radar Countermeasures (Chaff) Cartridges
- o Infrared Countermeasure Cartridges
- o Flares
- o Signals

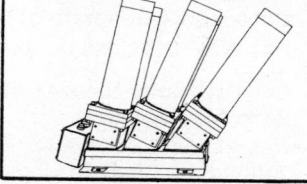
LAUNCHER (MK 135 MOD 0)

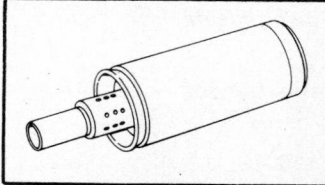
CHAFF CARTRIDGE (MK 171 MOD 0)

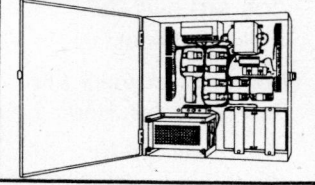
POWER SUPPLY (MK 160 MOD 0)

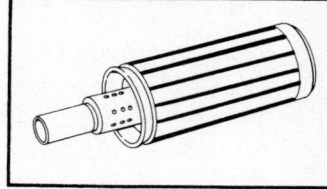
HIRAM DECOY CARTRIDGE

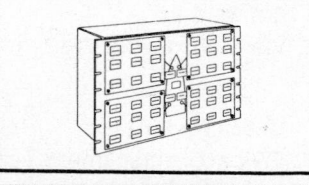
MASTER LAUNCHER CONTROL (MK 158 MOD 0)

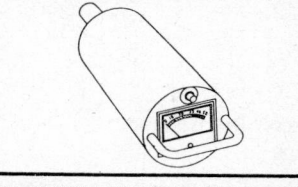
TEST CARTRIDGE (MK 173 MOD 0)

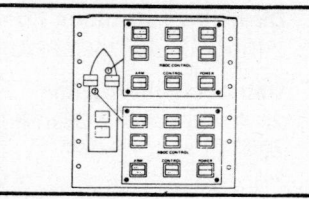
BRIDGE LAUNCHER CONTROL (MK 164 MOD 0)

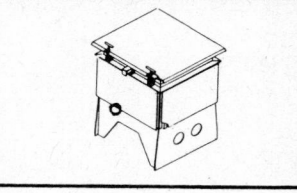
READY SERVICE LOCKER (MK 4 MOD 0)

HYCOR INC.
MILITARY SYSTEMS DIVISION
1 GILL STREET,
WOBURN, MASS. 01801,
U.S.A.
TEL. (617) 935 5956.
TELEX TWX 7103936345

FOR FURTHER INFORMATION
CALL COLLECT

EXPORT REPRESENTATIVES:-
MISCOTA
10 MONIS PETRAKI STR.
ATHENS, 140, GREECE.
TEL. 742 080: 742 081. TELEX 216499.

JANE'S FIGHTING SHIPS
ALPHABETICAL LIST OF ADVERTISERS
1976/77 EDITION

LM 2500

a marine gas turbine for navy
applications jointly developed
by Fiat and General Electric Co.

.low fuel consumption
.low weight
.reduced volume
.long life

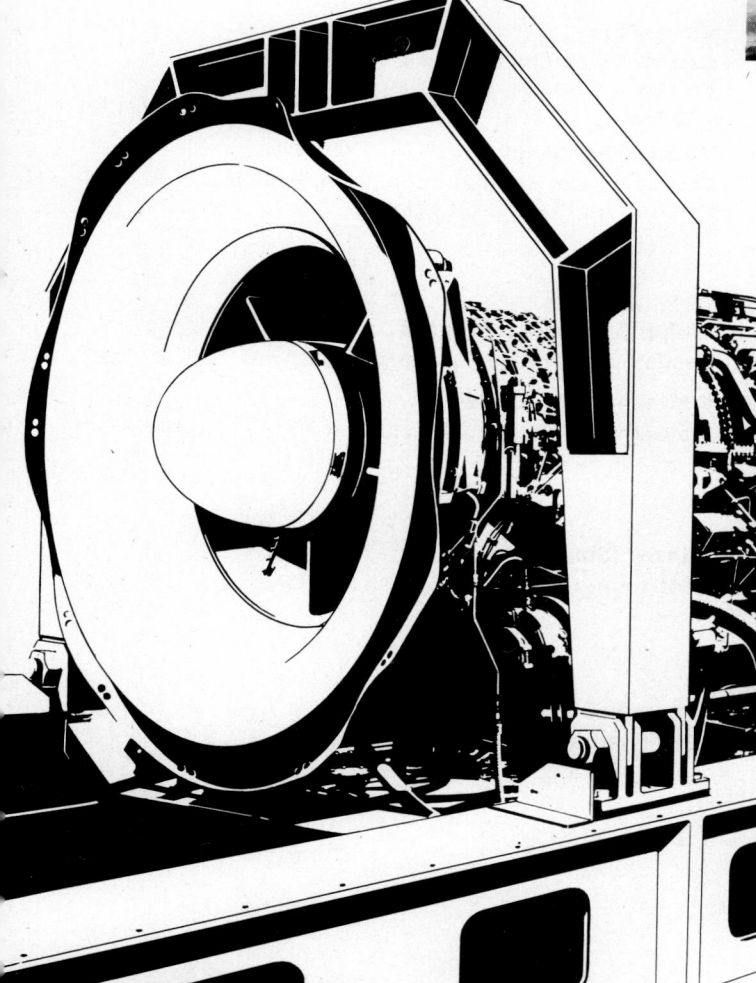

[7]

JANE'S FIGHTING SHIPS
CLASSIFIED LIST OF ADVERTISERS
1976-77 EDITION

The companies advertising in this publication have informed us
that they are involved in the fields of manufacture indicated
below:

ACTIVE INFORMATION SYSTEMS
D.T.C.N.
Ferranti
Plessey Radar
S.M.A.
Vickers

ACTIVE INFORMATION TRAINERS
Ferranti

AIR COMPRESSORS
CIT Alcatel
D.T.C.N.
Whitehead Moto Fides

AIRCRAFT, ANTI-SUBMARINE PATROL
Rinaldo Piaggio

AIRCRAFT ARRESTING GEAR
Aérospatiale
MacTaggart Scott

AIRCRAFT CARRIERS
Cantieri Navali Riuniti
D.T.C.N.
Fincantieri
Rhine-Schelde-Verolme
Vickers
Vosper Thornycroft

AIRCRAFT INSTRUMENTS
Cossor Electronic
D.T.C.N.
Edo Corporation
Ferranti
Sperry Gyroscope

AIRCRAFT, MARITIME RECONNAISSANCE
Rinaldo Piaggio

AIR CUSHION VEHICLES
Bell Aerospace Canada
British Hovercraft Corporation
D.T.C.N.
Vosper Thornycroft

AIRFRAME MANUFACTURERS
Aérospatiale
Agusta
British Hovercraft Corporation
Hawker Siddeley Aviation

ALIGNMENT EQUIPMENT
British Aircraft Corporation

AMMUNITION
Bofors
COS.MO.S
Snia Viscosa

AMMUNITION FUSES
Borletti Fratelli

AMMUNITION HOISTS
Blohm & Voss
MacTaggart Scott
Oto Melara
Vickers

ANTENNAE
S.G. Brown Communications

ANTI-SUBMARINE LAUNCHERS
Brooke Marine
D.T.C.N.
Plessey Marine
Vickers
Yarrow (Shipbuilders)

ANTI-SUBMARINE ROCKET LAUNCHERS
Bofors
D.T.C.N.
Vickers

ANTI-SUBMARINE ROCKETS
Bofors
CIT Alcatel
D.T.C.N.

ASSAULT CRAFT
Allday Aluminium
Bell Aerospace Canada
Blohm & Voss
British Hovercraft Corporation
Brooke Marine
Cantieri Baglietto
Cantieri di Pisa
Fairey Marine
Lambie (Boats)
Sofrexan
Supramar
Vosper Thorneycroft

ASSAULT SHIPS
Blohm & Voss
Brooke Marine
Cantieri Navali Riuniti
D.T.C.N.
Fincantieri
Lürssen Werft
Sofrexan
Vickers
Vosper Thornycroft
Yarrow (Shipbuilders)

ASW WEAPON CONTROL SYSTEMS
Singer Librascope

AUTOMATIC CONTROL SYSTEMS
CIT Alcatel
D.T.C.N.
Ferranti
Motoren-und Turbinen-Union
Singer Librascope
Sperry Gyroscope
Thomson CSF
Vosper Thornycroft

AUTOMATIC STEERING
Sperry Gyroscope

AUXILIARY MACHINERY
Blohm & Voss
Fincantieri
Motoren-und Turbinen-Union
Termomeccanica Italiana

BINOCULARS
Barr & Stroud
British Aircraft Corporation
Fincantieri
Officine Galileo

BOILERS
Blohm & Voss
Bremer Vulkan
Howaldtswerke-Deutsche Werft
Rhine-Schelde-Verolme
Ruston Paxman Diesels
Yarrow (Shipbuilders)

BOOKS (NAVAL)
D.T.C.N.
Vosper Thornycroft

BULK CARRIERS
Blohm & Voss
Bremer Vulkan
Cantieri Navali Riuniti
Dubigeon-Normandie
Fincantieri
Howaldtswerke-Deutsche Werft
Lürssen Werft
Rhine-Schelde-Verolme
Sippican Oceanographic Systems
Vickers

CABLE LOOMS (WITH OR WITHOUT CAISSONS)
Brooke Marine

CAPSTANS AND WINDLASSES
MacTaggart Scott
Riva Calzoni

CAR FERRIES
Ailsa Shipbuilding
Bell Aerospace Canada
Blohm & Voss
Bremer Vulkan
British Hovercraft Corporation
Brooke Marine
Cantieri Navali Riuniti
C.N.I.M.
D.T.C.N.
Dubigeon-Normandie
Fincantieri
Lürssen Werft
Rhine-Schelde-Verolme
Vickers
Yarrow (Shipbuilders)

CARGO HANDLING EQUIPMENT
Blohm & Voss
Bremer Vulkan
Fincantieri
MacTaggart Scott
Schat Davits

CARGO SHIPS
Ailsa Shipbuilding
Blohm & Voss
Bremer Vulkan
Cantieri Navali Riuniti
Dubigeon-Normandie
Fincantieri
Howaldtswerke-Deutsche Werft
Italcantieri
Lürssen Werft
Rhine-Schelde-Verolme
Vickers

CASTINGS—ALUMINIUM/BRONZE
Barr & Stroud
Rhine-Schelde-Verolme
Vickers

CASTINGS—HIGH DUTY IRON
Bremer Vulkan

CASTINGS—NON-FERROUS
Vickers

CASTINGS—SHELL MOULDED
Bremer Vulkan

CASTINGS—S.G. IRON
Bremer Vulkan

CASTINGS—STEEL
Bremer Vulkan
Rhine-Schelde-Verolme

CATHODIC PROTECTION EQUIPMENT
Marconi
Thomson CSF
Vickers

CENTRALISED AND AUTOMATIC CONTROL
CIT Alcatel
Thomson CSF

COASTAL AND INSHORE MINESWEEPERS
Ailsa Shipbuilding
Bell Aerospace Canada
British Hovercraft Corporation
Brooke Marine
Cantieri Baglietto
Cantieri Navali Riuiti
Fincantieri
Netherlands United Shipbuilders
Rhine-Schelde-Verolme
Sofrexan
Vickers
Vosper Thornycroft
Yarrow (Shipbuilders)

COMMAND/CONTROL/COMMUNICATIONS SYSTEMS
Singer Librascope

COMMAND(CONTROL REAL-TIME DISPLAYS
Singer Librascope

COMPRESSED AIR STARTERS FOR GAS TURBINES AND DIESEL ENGINES
D.T.C.N.
Hatch & Kirk

COMPRESSORS
CIT Alcatel
D.T.C.N.
Fincantieri
Rhine-Schelde-Verolme
Whitehead Moto Fides

COMPUTER SERVICES
Thomson CSF
Vickers
Yarrow (Shipbuilders)

COMPUTERS
CIT Alcatel
Ferranti
Hollandse Signaalapparaten
Sperry Gyroscope
Thomson CSF

CONDENSER TUBES
Fincantieri
Rhine-Schelde-Verolme

CONDENSERS
Blohm & Voss
Bremer Vulkan
Fincantieri

CONTAINER SHIPS
Ailsa Shipbuilding
Blohm & Voss
Bremer Vulkan
Brooke Marine
Cantieri Navali Riuniti
D.T.C.N.
Dubigeon-Normandie
Fincantieri
Howaldtswerke-Deutsche Werft
Italcantieri
Lürssen Werft
Rhine-Schelde-Verolme
Vickers

CONTROL DESKS (ELECTRIC)
D.T.C.N.
Vosper Thornycroft
Whipp & Bourne

CONTROL GEAR
Rhine-Schelde-Verolme
Ruston Paxman Diesels
Vosper Thornycroft

CORVETTES
Blohm & Voss
Bremer Vulkan
Cantieri Navali Riuniti
Crestitalia
D.T.C.N.
Dubigeon-Normandie
Fincantieri
Howaldtswerke-Deutsche Werft
Lürssen Werft
Netherlands United Shipbuilders
Rhine-Schelde-Verolme
Sofrexan
Vickers
Vosper Thornycroft
Yarrow (Shipbuilders)

CRANES—SHIPS'
D.T.C.N.
Dubigeon-Normandie
Fincantieri
Schat Davits

CRUISERS
Cantieri di Pisa
Cantieri Navali Riuniti
Crestitalia
D.T.C.N.
Dubigeon-Normandie
Fincantieri
Italcantieri
Netherlands United Shipbuilders
Rhine-Schelde-Verolme
Sofrexan
Vickers
Yarrow (Shipbuilders)

DATA RECORDING SYSTEMS
S.G. Brown Communications

DAVITS
Schat Davits

DECK MACHINERY
Cantieri Navali Riuniti
D.T.C.N.
Fincantieri
MacTaggart Scott
Standard Telephones & Cables

DESTROYERS
Blohm & Voss
Cantieri Navali Riuniti
D.T.C.N.
Dubigeon-Normandie
Fincantieri
Italcantieri
Netherlands United Shipbuilders
Rhine-Schelde-Verolme
Sofrexan
Vickers
Vosper Thornycroft
Yarrow (Shipbuilders)

DIESEL ENGINES—AUXILIARY
Blohm & Voss
Bremer Vulkan
Chantiers de l'Atlantique
D.T.C.N.
Fincantieri
Isotta Fraschini
Korody-Colyer
Motoren-und Turbinen-Union
Rhine-Schelde-Verolme
Ruston Paxman Diesels
S.A.C.M.
Vickers

DIESEL ENGINES—MAIN PROPULSION
Blohm & Voss
Bremer Vulkan
Chantiers de l'Atlantique
C.R.M.
D.T.C.N.
Fincantieri
Grandi Motori Trieste
Isotta Fraschini
Korody-Colyer
Motoren-und Turbinen-Union
Rhine-Schelde-Verolme
Ruston Paxman Diesels
S.A.C.M.
Vickers

DIESEL ENGINE SPARE PARTS
Blohm & Voss
Bremer Vulkan
Cantieri Navali Riuniti
C.R.M.
D.T.C.N.
Fincantieri
Hatch & Kirk
Korody-Colyer
Motoren-und Turbinen-Union
Rhine-Schelde-Verolme
Ruston Paxman Diesels
Vickers

DIESEL FUEL-INJECTION EQUIPMENT
D.T.C.N.
Fincantieri
Hatch & Kirk
Korody-Colyer

DISPLAY SYSTEMS
Plessey Radar

DOCK GATES
Ailsa Shipbuilding
Bremer Vulkan
D.T.C.N.
Dubigeon-Normandie
Rhine-Schelde-Verolme
Vickers

DREDGERS
Ailsa Shipbuilding
Brooke Marine
Dubigeon-Normandie
Fincantieri
Rhine-Schelde-Verolme

DRY CARGO VESSELS
Ailsa Shipbuilding
Blohm & Voss
Bremer Vulkan
Cantieri Navali Riuniti
Dubigeon-Normandie
Fincantieri
Howaldtswerke-Deutsche Werft
Italcantieri
Lürssen Werft
Rhine-Schelde-Verolme
Vickers

DRY DOCK PROPRIETORS
Blohm & Voss
CIT Alcatel
Fincantieri
Rhine-Schelde-Verolme

DYNAMIC POSITIONING
Thomson CSF

ECHO SOUNDERS
D.T.C.N.
Thomson CSF

ELECTRIC CABLES
Standard Telephones & Cables

ELECTRIC COUNTERMEASURES
Bofors
British Aircraft Corporation
Decca Radar
Sperry Gyroscope
Thomson CSF

ELECTRICAL AUXILIARIES
D.T.C.N.
Fincantieri
Rhine-Schelde-Verolme

ELECTRICAL EQUIPMENT
D.T.C.N.
Officine Panerai

ELECTRICAL FITTINGS
D.T.C.N.

ELECTRICAL INSTALLATIONS AND REPAIRS
Bremer Vulkan
Fincantieri
Lürssen Werft
Rhine-Schelde-Verolme
Vickers
Vosper Thornycroft

ELECTRICAL SWITCHGEAR
Lürssen Werft
Thomson CSF
Vosper Thornycroft
Whipp & Bourne

ELECTRO-HYDRAULIC AUXILIARIES
Fincantieri
MacTaggart Scott

ELECTRONIC COUNTERMEASURES
Plessey Radar

ELECTRONIC ENGINE ROOM TELEGRAPH
Officine Panerai

ELECTRONIC EQUIPMENT
British Aircraft Corporation
S.G. Brown Communications
CIT Alcatel
Decca Radar
D.T.C.N.
Edo Corporation
Ferranti
Montedel
Motoren-und Turbinen-Union
Officine Panerai
Oto Melara
Plessey Marine
Plessey Radar
Rhine-Schelde-Verolme
Sippican Oceanographic Systems
S.M.A.
Sperry Gyroscope
Thomson CSF
USEA
Vickers

ELECTRONIC EQUIPMENT REFITS
Ferranti
Plessey Marine
Plessey Radar
Sofrexan
Sperry Gyroscope

ENGINE MONITORS AND DATA LOGGERS
Decca Radar

We put you in the precise place at the precise time

S.G. Brown and Magnavox
advanced and proven integrated navigation systems

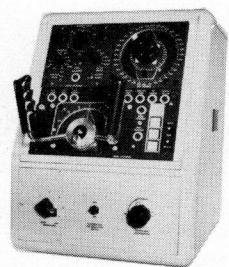

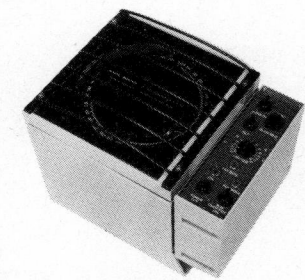

Satellite Navigation
Operational independence from shore based facilities. 24 hour day operation – up to 30 fixes per day. High accuracy fixes establishing position within 100 ft (static), 0.2 nm underway in all weather conditions anywhere in the world. Entirely automatic in operation – no operator intervention to achieve results.

Autopilot and Hand Steering
Fewer manual controls. Improved manoeuvring in autopilot mode. Weather helm automatically applied. Rudder positioning servo loop completely self-contained in steering flat. Helm demand fed to servo loop as analogue signals. Loss of any one helm demand does not affect overall rudder control.

Mk 12 Gyro Compass
Automatic start from single switching action. Low magnetic signature. Remote Control for North seeking/directional modes. Modular construction and solid-state circuitry. Fail-safe protection circuits. Electrically independent coarse/fine synchro transmission for integrating with retransmission units for radars, direction/finders, repeaters etc.

For further information contact the Marketing Manager.

 HAWKER SIDDELEY
S.G. BROWN LIMITED
GREYCAINE ROAD, WATFORD, HERTS. WD2 4XU, ENGLAND. Telephone: Watford 27241. Cables: Sidbrownix, Watford. Telex: 23408
Hawker Siddeley Group supplies mechanical, electrical and aerospace equipment with world-wide sales and service.

ENGINE PARTS—DIESEL
Bremer Vulkan
C.R.M.
Fincantieri
Grandi Motori Trieste
Hatch & Kirk
Rhine-Schelde-Verolme
Vickers

ENGINE SPEED CONTROLS
D.T.C.N.

**ENGINE START AND
SHUT-DOWN CONTROLS**
Lürssen Werft

ENGINES—AIRCRAFT
Avco Lycoming
D.T.C.N.
FIAT
Motoren-und Turbinen-Union
Rinaldo Piaggio

ENGINES—DIESEL
Blohm & Voss
Bremer Vulkan
Chantiers de l'Atlantique
C.R.M.
D.T.C.N.
Fincantieri
Isotta Fraschini
Motoren-und Turbinen-Union
Ruston Paxman Diesels
S.A.C.M.

ENGINES—GAS TURBINE
Avco Lycoming
CIT Alcatel
D.T.C.N.
FIAT
Motoren-und Turbinen-Union
Rhine-Schelde-Verolme
S.A.C.M.
Yarrow (Shipbuilders)

ENGINES—STEAM TURBINE
Blohm & Voss
Bremer Vulkan
Cantieri Navali Riuniti
Fincantieri
Yarrow (Shipbuilders)

EPICYCLIC GEARS
Fincantieri
Vickers

**EQUIPMENT FOR HELICOPTER
NIGHT DECK LANDING**
Officine Panerai

ESCORT VESSELS
Blohm & Voss
Bremer Vulkan
Brooke Marine
Cantieri Navali Riuniti
D.T.C.N.

Fincantieri
Italcantieri
Lürssen Werft
Netherlands United Shipbuilders
Sofrexan
Vickers
Vosper Thornycroft
Yarrow (Shipbuilders)

FAST PATROL CRAFT
Ailsa Shipbuilding
Allday Aluminium
Bell Aerospace Canada
Bianchi & Cecchi
British Hovercraft Corporation
Brooke Marine
Cantieri Baglietto
Cantieri di Pisa
Cantieri Navali Riuniti
Crestitalia
D.T.C.N.
Fairey Marine
Fincantieri
Lambie (Boats)
Lürssen Werft
Netherlands United Shipbuilders
Sofrexan
Supramar
Vosper Thornycroft
Yarrow (Shipbuilders)

FAST WARSHIP DESIGN SERVICE
Cantieri Navali Riuniti
D.T.C.N.
Fincantieri
Lüssen Werft
Sofrexan
Supramar
Vickers
Vosper Thornycroft

FEED WATER HEATERS
Blohm & Voss
Fincantieri

FERRIES
Ailsa Shipbuilding
Bell Aerospace Canada
Bremer Vulkan
British Hovercraft Corporation
Cantieri Navali Riuniti
Dubigeon-Normandie
Fincantieri
Hawaldtswerke-Deutsche Werft
Italcantieri
Lürssen Werft
Rhine-Schelde-Verolme
Vickers
Yarrow (Shipbuilders)

FIBRE OPTICS
Barr & Stroud
D.T.C.N.
Plessey Radar

**FIBREGLASS VESSELS AND
OTHER PRODUCTS**
Crestitalia
D.T.C.N.
Fairey Marine
Lambie (Boats)

Sofrexan
Vickers
Vosper Thornycroft

FIRE AND SALVAGE VESSELS
Bell Aerospace Canada
Brooke Marine
Cantieri Navali Riuniti
Crestitalia
Fincantieri

**FIRE CONTROL AND GUNNERY
EQUIPMENT**
Bofors
D.T.C.N.
Ferranti
Hollandse Signaalapparaten
Oto Melara
Plessey Marine
Singer Librascope
Sperry Gyroscope
Thomson CSF
Vickers

FIRE RESISTANT LIFEBOATS
Bianchi & Cecchi

FITTINGS—SHIPS
D.T.C.N.
Fincantieri
Rhine-Schelde-Verolme

FRIGATES
Blohm & Voss
Bremer Vulkan
Cantieri Navali Riuniti
D.T.C.N.
Dubigeon-Normandie
Fincantieri
Netherlands United Shipbuilders
Rhine-Schelde-Verolme
Sofrexan
Vickers
Vosper Thornycroft
Yarrow (Shipbuilders)

FUEL FILTRATION EQUIPMENT
Vickers

FUEL INJECTION—OIL
D.T.C.N.

GAS TURBINE BOATS
Avco Lycoming
Bell Aerospace Canada
Blohm & Voss
Cantieri Baglietto
Cantieri Navali Riuniti
D.T.C.N.
Fincantieri
Vickers
Vosper Thornycroft
Yarrow (Shipbuilders)

Pilot Boats for safety in the sea

MOTOMAR PILOT BOAT 40' FOR HARBOUR AUTHORITIES

MOTOMAR PILOT BOAT 40' FOR MARINE POLICE

POLIZIA

MAIN FEATURES
.O.A. (to outside of rubbing strake) 12.54 m
41'2").
EAM MAX (to outside of rubbing strake)
61 m (11'10").
ULL of GRP (Glass reinforced plastic) un-
er the supervision of Lloyd's Register of
hipping and certified accordingly.
NGINES AND SPEED: According to the re-
uested motorization, the maximum speed
aries from 21 to 25 knots.

EMPLOYERS
These patrol and pilot boats have been
adopted by:
— The Navy (Harbour Authorities)
— Marine Police
— Marine Carabinieri
— Marine Customs
Many other foreign customers too have been
using them and acknowledge their seakeeping
qualities, the seaworthiness and remarkable
capacity of speed.

 CANTIERI NAVALI *MOTOMAR*

GAS TURBINES
Avco Lycoming
CIT Alcatel
D.T.C.N.
FIAT
Motoren-und Turbinen-Union
Rhine-Schelde-Verolme
S.A.C.M.

GEAR CASINGS
Bremer Vulkan
Fincantieri
Vickers

GEARS
Isotta Fraschini

GEARS AND GEARING
FIAT
Fincantieri
Howaldtswerke-Deutsche Werft
Rhine-Schelde-Verolme
Vickers
Vosper Thornycroft

GEARS—HYPOID
Fincantieri

GEARS—SPIRAL BEVEL
Fincantieri

GEARS—REVERSE-REDUCTION
C.R.M.
Fincantieri
Motoren-und Turbine-Union
Vickers
Zahnradfabrik Friedrichshafen

GEARS—SPUR
Fincantieri

GEARS—VEE DRIVE
C.R.M.
Vosper Thornycroft
Zahnradfabrik Friedrichshafen

GENERATORS—ELECTRIC
Avco Lycoming
Ferranti

GOVERNORS
D.T.C.N.
Hatch & Kirk

GOVERNORS—ENGINE SPEED
D.T.C.N.
Hatch & Kirk

GUIDED MISSILE SERVICING EQUIPMENT
Aérospatiale
British Aircraft Corporation
D.T.C.N.
Oto Melara
Sofrexan
Thomson CSF

GUIDED MISSILE SHIPS
Blohm & Voss
Bremer Vulkan
Brooke Marine
Cantieri Navali Riuniti
D.T.C.N.
Fincantieri
Lürssen Werft
Netherlands United Shipbuilders
Rhine-Schelde-Verolme
Sofrexan
Supramar
Vickers
Vosper Thornycroft
Yarrow (Shipbuilders)

GUIDED MISSILES
Aérospatiale
Bofors
British Aircraft Corporation
Oto Melara
Sistel-Sistemi Elettronici
S.M.A.
Sofrexan
Sperry Gyroscope

GUN BOATS
Ailsa Shipbuilding
Allday Aluminium
Bell Aerospace Canada
Brooke Marine
Cantieri Baglietto
Cantieri Navali Riuniti
D.T.C.N.
Fairey Marine
Fincantieri
Lambie (Boats)
Lürssen Werft
Netherlands United Shipbuilders
Sofrexan
Vosper Thornycroft
Yarrow (Shipbuilders)

GUNS AND MOUNTINGS
Bofors
Breda Meccanica Bresciana
D.T.C.N.
Oerlikon Italiana
Oto Melara
Sofrexan
Vickers

GUN MOUNTS
Bofors
D.T.C.N.
Emerson Electric
Oto Melara
Vickers

GUN-SIGHTING APPARATUS AND HEIGHT FINDERS
Barr & Stroud
Officine Galileo
Thomson CSF
Vickers

GYROSCOPIC COMPASSES
D.T.C.N.
Sperry Gyroscope
Thomson CSF

HEADPHONES
S.G. Brown Communications

HEADSETS
S.G. Brown Communications

HEAT EXCHANGERS
Blohm & Voss
Bremer Vulkan
Fincantieri
Howaldtswerke-Deutsche Werft
Yarrow (Shipbuilders)

HEATED WINDOWS
Barr & Stroud

HEAVY DUTY MOORING MOTORBOATS
Bianchi & Cecchi

HIGH LEVEL LIQUID ALARM SYSTEM
Officine Panerai

HOVERCRAFT
Bell Aerospace Canada
British Hovercraft Corporation
D.T.C.N.
Vosper Thornycroft

HYDRAULIC EQUIPMENT
D.T.C.N.
Fincantieri
MacTaggart Scott
Officine Galileo
Oto Melara
Riva Calzoni
Vickers

HYDRAULIC MACHINERY
Cantieri Navali Riuniti
D.T.C.N.
Fincantieri
MacTaggart Scott
Riva Calzoni
Vickers

HYDRAULIC PLANT
Aerimpianti
Fincantieri
MacTaggart Scott
Riva Calzoni

[19]

HYDROFOILS
Aérospatiale
Blohm & Voss
Cantiere Navaltecnica
Cantieri Navali Riuniti
D.T.C.N.
Edo Corporation
Fincantieri
Lürssen Werft
Supramar
Vosper Thornycroft

HYDROGRAPHIC SURVEY EQUIPMENT
D.T.C.N.
Edo Corporation
Standard Telephones & Cables

I.F.F. RADAR
Bell Aerospace Canada
D.T.C.N.
Hollandse Signaalapparaten
Plessey Radar
Thomson CSF

I.F.F. Mk. 10 SYSTEMS
D.T.C.N.
Plessey Radar
Thomson CSF

INDICATORS, ELECTRIC
Thomson CSF

INERTIAL NAVIGATION SYSTEMS
D.T.C.N.
Sperry Gyroscope

INFRA-RED MATERIALS
Barr & Stroud
D.T.C.N.
Thomson CSF

INFRA-RED SYSTEMS
Barr & Stroud
D.T.C.N.
Officine Galileo
Vickers

INJECTORS
D.T.C.N.

INSTRUMENT CALIBRATION SERVICES
Vickers

INSTRUMENT COMPONENTS (MECHANICAL)
Thomson CSF

INSTRUMENTS—ELECTRONIC
Barr & Stroud
Bofors
S.G. Brown Communications
Ferranti
Howaldtswerke-Deutsche Werft
Sperry Gyroscope
Thomson CSF

INSTRUMENTS—NAUTICAL
D.T.C.N.
Sippican Oceanographic Systems
Sperry Gyroscope

INSTRUMENT PANELS
D.T.C.N.
Ferranti
Lürssen Werft
Thomson CSF
Vosper Thornycroft

INSTRUMENTS—PRECISION
D.T.C.N.
Ferranti
Sperry Gyroscope

INSTRUMENT TEST EQUIPMENT
British Hovercraft Corporation
S.G. Brown Communications
Cossor Electronics
D.T.C.N.
Ferranti
Hatch & Kirk
Sperry Gyroscope
Thomson CSF.
Vickers

INTERIOR DESIGN AND FURNISHING FOR SHIPS
Blohm & Voss
Bremer Vulkan
Brooke Marine
D.T.C.N.
Fincantieri
Lürssen Werft
Rhine-Schelde-Verolme
Vickers
Vosper Thornycroft

INVERTERS AND BATTERY CHARGERS
Ferranti

LANDING CRAFT
Ailsa Shipbuilding
Allday Aluminium
Bell Aerospace Canada
Bremer Vulkan
British Hovercraft Corporation
Brooke Marine
Cantieri Baglietto
C.N.I.M.
D.T.C.N.
Fincantieri
Lambie (Boats)
Lürssen Werft
Netherlands United Shipbuilders
Sofrexan
Yarrow (Shipbuilders)

LASER RANGEFINDERS
Barr & Stroud
Bofors
D.T.C.N.
Ferranti
Thomson CSF

LASER SYSTEMS
Barr & Stroud
Ferranti
Officine Galileo
Thomson CSF
Vickers

LIFEBOATS
Bianchi & Cecchi

LIFTS—HYDRAULIC
D.T.C.N.
MacTaggart Scott

LIGHTS AND LIGHTING
D.T.C.N.
Officine Panerai
Rhine-Schelde-Verolme

LIQUID PETROLEUM GAS CARRIERS
Bremer Vulkan
C.N.I.M.
Dubigeon-Normandie
Fincantieri
Lürssen Werft
Rhine-Schelde-Verolme
Vickers

LOUDSPEAKER EQUIPMENT
Rhine-Schelde-Verolme
Thomson CSF

MACHINED PARTS—FERROUS
Ailsa Shipbuilding
Blohm & Voss
Bremer Vulkan
Fincantieri
Vickers

MACHINED PARTS—NON-FERROUS
Ailsa Shipbuilding
Blohm & Voss
Vickers

MAINTENANCE AND REPAIR SHIPS
Ailsa Shipbuilding
Bremer Vulkan
Brooke Marine
Cantiere Navaltecnica
Dubigeon-Normandie
Fincantieri
Lürssen Werft
Rhine-Schelde-Verolme
Vickers

EMERLEC 30

30MM NAVAL GUN MOUNT

MARINE ARCHITECTS
Ailsa Shipbuilding
Bremer Vulkan
D.T.C.N.
Fincantieri
Ingenieurkontor Lübeck
Lürssen Werft
Netherlands United Shipbuilders
Rhine-Schelde-Verolme
Vickers

MARINE ENGINE MONITORING AND DATA RECORDING SYSTEMS
Decca Radar
Hatch & Kirk
Vosper Thornycroft

MARINE RADAR
Cossor Electronics
Decca Radar
D.T.C.N.
Hollandse Signaalapparaten
S.M.A.
Thomson CSF

MATERIALS HANDLING EQUIPMENT
D.T.C.N.
MacTaggart Scott
Schat Davits

MERCHANT SHIPS
Ailsa Shipbuilding
Blohm & Voss
Bremer Vulkan
Brooke Marine
Cantieri Navali Riuniti
D.T.C.N.
Dubigeon-Normandie
Fincantieri
Lürssen Werft
Rhine-Schelde-Verolme
Vickers

MICROPHONE EQUIPMENT
S.G. Brown Communications
D.T.C.N.
Thomson CSF

MINE COUNTERMEASURES
British Hovercraft Corporation
CIT Alcatel
D.T.C.N.
Fairey Marine
Plessey Marine
S.M.A.
Sperry Gyroscope
Vosper Thornycroft

MINELAYERS
Blohm & Voss
Bremer Vulkan
Brooke Marine
Cantieri Navali Riuniti
Dubigeon-Normandie
Fincantieri
Lürssen Werft
Netherlands United Shipbuilders
Rhine-Schelde-Verolme
Vickers
Vosper Thornycroft
Yarrow (Shipbuilders)

MINESWEEPERS
Ailsa Shipbuilding
Blohm & Voss
British Hovercraft Corporation
Brooke Marine
Cantieri Baglietto
Cantieri Navali Riuniti
D.T.C.N.
Dubigeon-Normandie
Edo Corporation
Fincantieri
Netherlands United Shipbuilders
Sofrexan
Thomson CSF
Vickers
Vosper Thornycroft
Yarrow (Shipbuilders)

MISSILE CONTROL SYSTEMS
Aérospatiale
British Aircraft Corporation
CIT Alcatel
D.T.C.N.
Ferranti
Officine Galileo
Oto Melara
Sistel-Sistemi Elettronici
Sofrexan
Sperry Gyroscope
Thomson CSF
Vickers

MISSILE INSTALLATIONS
Aérospatiale
British Aircraft Corporation
D.T.C.N.
Lürssen Werft
Oto Melara
Sistel-Sistemi Elettronici
Sofrexan
Thomson CSF
Vickers

MISSILE LAUNCHING SYSTEMS
Aérospatiale
British Aircraft Corporation
CIT Alcatel
D.T.C.N.
Lürssen Werft
Oto Melara
Sistel-Sistemi Elettronici
Sofrexan
Vickers

MISSILE SHIPS
Blohm & Voss
Bremer Vulkan
British Hovercraft Corporation
Cantiere Navaltecnica
Cantieri Baglietto
Cantieri Navali Riuniti
D.T.C.N.
Fincantieri
Lürssen Werft
Netherlands United Shipbuilders
Rhine-Schelde-Verolme
Sofrexan
Vickers
Vosper Thornycroft
Yarrow (Shipbuilders)

MODEL MAKERS AND DESIGNERS
Ailsa Shipbuilding
British Hovercraft Corporation

Fincantieri
Ingenieurkontor Lübeck
Lürssen Werft
Netherlands United Shipbuilders
Vickers
Vosper Thornycroft
Yarrow (Shipbuilders)

MODEL TEST TOWING TANK SERVICE
British Hovercraft Corporation
Vickers

MOTOR CONTROL GEAR
Bremer Vulkan
Thomson CSF

MOTOR STARTERS
Thomson CSF

MOTOR TORPEDO BOATS
Brooke Marine
Cantieri Baglietto
Cantieri Navali Riuniti
D.T.C.N.
Dubigeon-Normandie
Fincantieri
Lürssen Werft
Netherlands United Shipbuilders
Thomson CSF
Vosper Thornycroft
Yarrow (Shipbuilders)

MOTORS—ELECTRIC
D.T.C.N.
Thomson CSF

NAVAL GUNS
Bofors
D.T.C.N.
Emerson Electric
Oto Melara
Sofrexan
Vickers

NAVAL RADAR
Decca Radar
D.T.C.N.
Hollandse Signaalapparaten
Plessey Radar
S.M.A.
Sofrexan
Sperry Gyroscope
Thomson CSF

NAVIGATION AIDS
British Aircraft Corporation
S.G. Brown Communications
Decca Radar
D.T.C.N.
Sofrexan
Sperry Gyroscope
Thomson CSF
USEA

There are still some people who think that a heavier motor is a more powerful motor...

...Pity!

Yes a pity. A pity because they live in a wonderful old world where weight was important; powerful radios were heavy, powerful weapons were heavy, powerful marine engines were heavy.

Today engineering and science say the opposite.

Very few of man's modern instruments are heavy. In the field of marine engines, CRM has proved that the power — weight relationship is false. That is why we always find CRM engines when out of the ordinary performances are expected, where nautical science has to be ahead of the times and come up with new solutions.

For the adventures of modern seafarers CRM propose 415 HP - 9 cylinder diesel engines or 1350 HP - 18 cylinders (the latter complete with reverse gear weighs only 2075 kg.); or eight cycle engines from 1150 HP to 1800 HP (this one with 18 cylinders weighs 1600 kg. with reverse gear).

In order that these can be installed on any boat, CRM has also produced reduction units, corner joints and axle lines, all of which, it goes without saying, are designed and manufactured to achieve the same robust and lightweight characteristics.

20121 milano via manzoni 12 tel. 708326/708327 telegr.cremme

NIGHT VISION SYSTEMS
Barr & Stroud
D.T.C.N.
Officine Galileo
Thomson CSF

NON-MAGNETIC MINESWEEPERS
British Hovercraft Corporation
Cantieri Baglietto
D.T.C.N.
Dubigeon-Normandie
Fincantieri
Netherlands United Shipbuilders
Rhine-Schelde-Verolme
Sofrexan
Sperry Gyroscope
Vickers
Vosper Thornycroft

OCEANOGRAPHIC ELECTRONIC SYSTEMS
D.T.C.N.
Sippican Oceanographic Systems

OCEANOGRAPHIC SURVEY SHIPS
Bremer Vulkan
Brooke Marine
Cantieri Navali Riuniti
D.T.C.N.

Fairey Marine
Fincantieri
Lürssen Werft
Netherlands United Shipbuilders
Rhine-Schelde-Verolme
Vickers
Yarrow (Shipbuilders)

OIL DRILLING RIGS
Bremer Vulkan
CIT Alcatel
Fincantieri
Howaldtswerke-Deutsche Werft
Vickers

OIL FUEL HEATERS
Blohm & Voss
Fincantieri

OIL RIG SUPPLY VESSELS AND WORK BOATS
Bell Aerospace Canada
Brooke Marine
Cantieri Navali Riuniti
Dubigeon-Normandie
Fairey Marine
Fincantieri
Supramar
Yarrow (Shipbuilders)

OPTICAL EQUIPMENT
Barr & Stroud
D.T.C.N.
Officine Panerai
Vickers

OPTICAL FILTERS
Barr & Stroud
D.T.C.N.

OPTRONICS
Hollandse Signaalapparaten

ORDNANCE
Bofors
Borletti Fratelli
Vickers

PARTS FOR DIESEL ENGINES
Blohm & Voss
Fincantieri
Grandi Motori Trieste
Hatch & Kirk
Vickers

PASSENGER SHIPS
Ailsa Shipbuilding
Blohm & Voss
Bremer Vulkan
Brooke Marine
Cantiere Navaltecnica
Cantieri Navali Riuniti
Crestitalia
D.T.C.N.
Fincantieri
Howaldtswerke-Deutsche Werft
Lürssen Werft
Rhine-Schelde-Verolme
Supramar
Vickers

PATROL BOATS, LAUNCHES, TENDERS AND PINNACLES
Ailsa Shipbuilding
Allday Aluminium
Bell Aerospace Canada
British Hovercraft Corporation
Brooke Marine
Cantiere Navaltecnica
Cantieri Baglietto
Cantieri Navali Riuniti
Crestitalia
D.T.C.N.
Dubigeon-Normandie
Fairey Marine
Fincantieri
Lambie (Boats)
Lürssen Werft

Netherlands United Shipbuilders
Valtec Italiana
Vosper Thornycroft

PERISCOPE FAIRINGS
D.T.C.N.
Edo Corporation
MacTaggart Scott

PERISCOPES
Barr & Stroud
D.T.C.N.
Sofrexan

PIPES—COPPER AND BRASS
D.T.C.N.
Rhine-Schelde-Verolme
Vickers

PIPES—SEA WATER
D.T.C.N.
Rhine-Schelde-Verolme
Vickers

PISTONS, PISTON RINGS AND GUDGEON PINS
Bremer Vulkan
D.T.C.N.
Fincantieri
Rhine-Schelde-Verolme

PLOTTING TABLES
Plessey Radar
S.M.A.
Sofrexan

PLUGS AND SOCKETS
D.T.C.N.
Rhine-Schelde-Verolme
Thomson CSF

PONTOONS—SELF-PROPELLED
Allday Aluminium
Bremer Vulkan
Brooke Marine
D.T.C.N.
Fincantieri
Lambie (Boats)

PORTABLE EQUIPMENT FOR AIRCRAFT LANDING
Officine Panerai

PRESSURE VESSELS
Bremer Vulkan
D.T.C.N.
Vickers
Yarrow (Shipbuilders)

PROPELLANTS
Bofors
Snia Viscosa

PROPELLER SHAFT COUPLINGS— FLEXIBLE
Vickers

PROPELLERS—SHIPS'
Fincantieri
Vickers

PROPELLERS—SHIPS' RESEARCH
D.T.C.N.
Fincantieri
Vosper Thornycroft

PROPULSION MACHINERY
Avco Lycoming
Blohm & Voss
Bremer Vulkan
Cantieri Navali Riuniti
D.T.C.N.
Fincantieri
Motoren-und Turbinen-Union
Rhine-Schelde-Verolme
Ruston Paxman Diesels
Vickers

PUMPS
CIT Alcatel
MacTaggart Scott
Termomeccanica Italiana
Vickers

PUMPS—COMPONENT PARTS
Fincantieri
Termomeccanica Italiana

RADAR AERIALS
British Aircraft Corporation
Cossor Electronics
Decca Radar
D.T.C.N.
Hollandse Signaalapparaten
Plessey Radar
S.M.A.
Thomson CSF

RADAR FOR FIRE CONTROL
D.T.C.N.
Ferranti
Hollandse Signaalapparaten

Marconi
Plessey Radar
S.M.A.
Sperry Gyroscope
Thomson CSF

RADAR FOR HARBOUR SUPERVISION
Decca Radar
D.T.C.N.
Hollandse Signaalapparaten
S.M.A.
Thomson CSF

RADAR FOR NAVIGATION WARNING INTERCEPTION
Decca Radar
D.T.C.N.
Hollandse Signaalapparaten
S.M.A.
Thomson CSF

RADIO—AIR
D.T.C.N.
Thomson CSF

RADIO EQUIPMENT
S.G. Brown Communications
Cossor Electronics
D.T.C.N.
Marconi
Montedel
Sofrexan
Thomson CSF

RADIO TRANSMITTERS AND RECEIVERS
S.G. Brown Communications
Cossor Electronics
D.T.C.N.
Ferranti
Montedel
Sofrexan
Thomson CSF

RADOMES
British Aircraft Corporation
British Hovercraft Corporation
D.T.C.N.
Lürssen Werft
Thomson CSF
Vickers

RAMJETS
Aerospatiale

RANGEFINDERS
Barr & Stroud
S.M.A.
Thomson CSF

REFRIGERATION PLANTS
Termomeccanica Italiana

RELOCALISATION DEVICES
CIT Alcatel

REMOTE CONTROLS
Oto Melara
Thomson CSF

REMOTE LEVEL INDICATOR EQUIPMENT FOR SUBMARINE TRIM TANKS
Officine Panerai

REPLACEMENT PARTS FOR DIESEL ENGINES
Blohm & Voss
Bremer Vulkan
Fincantieri
MacTaggart Scott
Rhine-Schelde-Verolme
Vickers

RESEARCH SHIPS
Ailsa Shipbuilding
Bell Aerospace Canada
Bremer Vulkan
Brooke Marine
Cantieri Navali Riuniti
D.T.C.N.
Dubigeon-Normandie
Fincantieri
Lürssen Werft
Netherlands United Shipbuilders
Rhine-Schelde-Verolme
Vickers
Yarrow (Shipbuilders)

REVERSE REDUCTION GEARS— OIL OPERATED
Fincantieri
Vickers

REVERSING GEARS
C.R.M.
Fincantieri
Isotta Fraschini
Vickers

ROCKET LAUNCHERS
Bofors
Breda Meccanica Bresciana
C.N.I.M.
D.T.C.N.
Oto Melara
Vickers

ROLL DAMPING FINS
Blohm & Voss
D.T.C.N.
Vickers
Vosper Thornycroft

RUDDERS
Ailsa Shipbuilding
Bremer Vulkan
Fincantieri
Howaldtswerke-Deutsche Werft
Lürssen Werft
Rhine-Schelde-Verolme
Yarrow (Shipbuilders)

SALVAGE VESSELS
D.T.C.N.

SALVAGE AND BOOM VESSELS
Bremer Vulkan
Brooke Marine
Cantiere Navaltecnica
Cantieri Navali Riuniti
Fincantieri
Lürssen Werft
Netherlands United Shipbuilders
Yarrow (Shipbuilders)

SCIENTIFIC INSTRUMENTS
D.T.C.N.
Ferranti
Thomson CSF
Vickers

SHIP BUILDERS AND SHIP REPAIRERS
Ailsa Shipbuilding
Blohm & Voss
Bremer Vulkan
Brooke Marine
Cantiere Navaltecnica
Cantieri Navali Riuniti
D.T.C.N.
Dubigeon-Normandie
Fairey Marine
Fincantieri
Howaldtswerke-Deutsche Werft
Lürssen Werft
Netherlands United Shipbuilders
Rhine-Schelde-Verolme
Sofrexan
Vickers
Vosper Thornycroft
Yarrow (Shipbuilders)

SHIP AND SUBMARINE DESIGN
Ailsa Shipbuilding
Cantieri Navali Riuniti
D.T.C.N.
Dubigeon-Normandie
Fincantieri
Ingenieurkontor Lübeck
Netherlands United Shipbuilders
Rhine-Schelde-Verolme
Sofrexan
Vickers
Yarrow (Shipbuilders)

SHIP MACHINERY
Blohm & Voss
Bremer Vulkan
Cantieri Navali Riuniti
D.T.C.N.
Fincantieri
Motoren-und Turbinen-Union
Rhine-Schelde-Verolme
Vickers
Yarrow (Shipbuilders)

**SHIPBOARD AIR CONDITIONING
AND VENTILATING PLANT**
Aerimpianti

**SHIPS MAGNETIC COMPASS
TEST TABLES**
Barr & Stroud

SHIP STABILISERS
Blohm & Voss
Cantieri Navali Riuniti
D.T.C.N.
Fincantieri
Howaldtswerke-Deutsche Werft
Supramar
Vickers
Vosper Thornycroft

SHIP SYSTEMS ENGINEERING
Cantiere Navaltecnica
Cantieri Navali Riuniti
D.T.C.N.
Fincantieri
Netherlands United Shipbuilders
Rhine-Schelde-Verolme
Vickers

**SHIPS BRASS FOUNDRY FOR
SONAR AND RADAR**
D.T.C.N.

SIMULATORS
CIT Alcatel
D.T.C.N.
Ferranti
Vickers

SMOKE INDICATORS
Barr & Stroud

**SOCKETS AND PLUGS—
ELECTRIC WATERTIGHT**
Standard Telephones & Cables
Thomson CSF

**SOCKETS AND PLUGS—
MULTI-PIN PATTERNS**
Standard Telephones & Cables
Thomson CSF

SOCKET TERMINATIONS
Thomson CSF

SONAR EQUIPMENT
British Aircraft Corporation
CIT Alcatel
D.T.C.N.
Emerson Electric
Hollandse Signaalapparaten
Plessey Marine
Sippican Oceanographic Systems
Sofrexan
Thomson CSF
USEA

**SONAR EQUIPMENT (PASSIVE
ACTIVE-INTERCEPT)**
CIT Alcatel
D.T.C.N.
Edo Corporation
Hollandse Signaalapparaten
Plessey Marine
Sofrexan
Thomson CSF
USEA

**SONAR EQUIPMENT—HULL
FITTINGS AND HYDRAULICS**
CIT Alcatel
D.T.C.N.
Edo Corporation
Hollandse Signaalapparaten
Plessey Marine
Sofrexan
USEA

SPARE PARTS FOR DIESEL ENGINES
Blohm & Voss
Bremer Vulkan
C.R.M.
D.T.C.N.
Fincantieri
Grandi Motori Trieste
Rhine-Schelde-Verolme
Vickers

SPEED BOATS
Allday Aluminium
Bell Aerospace Canada
Brooke Marine
Cantieri Baglietto
Crestitalia
D.T.C.N.
Fincantieri
Lambie (Boats)
Sofrexan
Vosper Thornycroft

STABILISING EQUIPMENT
Blohm & Voss
D.T.C.N.
Ferranti
Vickers
Vosper Thornycroft

**STABILISING EQUIPMENT FOR
FIRE CONTROL**
D.T.C.N.
Ferranti
Vickers

**STEAM-RAISING PLANT,
CONVENTIONAL**
Blohm & Voss
Bremer Vulkan
D.T.C.N.
Fincantieri
Yarrow (Shipbuilders)

**STEAM-RAISING PLANT,
NUCLEAR**
D.T.C.N.
Vickers
Yarrow (Shipbuilders)

STEAM TURBINES
Blohm & Voss
Bremer Vulkan
Cantieri Navali Riuniti
D.T.C.N.
Fincantieri
Howaldtswerke-Deutsche Werft

From 0 to 40+ kts in 40 seconds: Avco-powered multi-mission patrol ship

Six Avco Lycoming TF35 gas turbines demonstrated this phenomenal acceleration in the first of a fleet of 165 foot multi-mission patrol ships (PSMM) built by Tacoma Boatbuilding Company, Inc.

Providing well over 15,000 shaft horsepower in combined drive, these reliable marine gas turbines will first see service in the Navy of an Asiatic country, and the performance they already have established assures the use of these turbines in many other fast patrol craft the free world over.

As demonstrated in acceptance tests, combinations of these versatile gas turbines can produce relatively inexpensive fighting ships with the top speed of the fastest destroyers.

For further information, please write on company letterhead.

For information, call or write Director Marine & Industrial Marketing, (203) 378-8211 Avco Lycoming Division, 550 South Main Street Stratford, Connecticut 06497

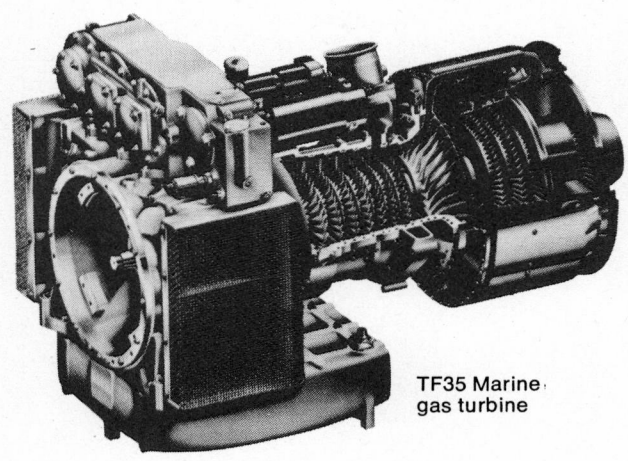

TF35 Marine gas turbine

LYCOMING DIVISION
STRATFORD, CONNECTICUT 06497

STEEL, ALLOY AND SPECIAL STEEL FORGINGS, PLATES AND SECTIONS, STAMPINGS
Bofors
Rhine-Schelde-Verolme

STEEL MANGANESE—WEAR-RESISTING
Bofors

STEERING GEAR
Fincantieri
Rhine-Schelde-Verolme
Vickers
Vosper Thornycroft

STRESS RELIEVING
Bremer Vulkan
Fincantieri
Vickers
Yarrow (Shipbuilders)

SUBMARINE DISTRESS BUOYS
Barr & Stroud
D.T.C.N.
Sofrexan
Thomson CSF

SUBMARINE FIRE CONTROL
CIT Alcatel
Singer Librascope
Sperry Gyroscope
Vickers
Whitehead Moto Fides

SUBMARINE PERISCOPES
Barr & Stroud
D.T.C.N.
Thomson CSF

SUBMARINES
COS.MO.S
D.T.C.N.
Fincantieri
Howaldtswerke-Deutsche Werft
Ingenieurkontor Lübeck
Italcantieri
Netherlands United Shipbuilders
Sofrexan
Vickers

SUBMARINES (CONVENTIONAL)
COS.MO.S
D.T.C.N.
Dubigeon-Normandie
Fincantieri
Ingenieurkontor Lübeck
Netherlands United Shipbuilders
Rhine-Schelde-Verolme
Sofrexan
Vickers

SUBMERSIBLES (WET)
COS.MO.S
D.T.C.N.
Sofrexan
Vickers

SUPERHEATERS
Blohm & Voss
Bremer Vulkan
Fincantieri
Yarrow (Shipbuilders)

SUPPORT SERVICES
Vickers
Vosper Thornycroft

SURVEY EQUIPMENT
D.T.C.N.

SWITCHBOARDS
Blohm & Voss
Lürssen Werft
Vosper Thornycroft
Whipp & Bourne

SWITCHBOARDS AND SWITCHGEAR
Lürssen Werft
Vosper Thornycroft
Whipp & Bourne

TACTICAL TRAINING SIMULATORS
D.T.C.N.
Ferranti
Marconi
Sofrexan
Vickers

TANKERS
Blohm & Voss
Bremer Vulkan
Cantieri Navali Riuniti
D.T.C.N.
Fincantieri
Howaldtswerke-Deutsche Werft
Italcantieri
Netherlands United Shipbuilders
Rhine-Schelde-Verolme
Sofrexan
Vickers
Yarrow (Shipbuilders)

TANKERS (SMALL)
Bremer Vulkan
Cantieri Navali Riuniti
D.T.C.N.
Dubigeon-Normandie
Fincantieri
Italcantieri
Lürssen Werft
Rhine-Schelde-Verolme
Yarow (Shipbuilders)

TANKS—OIL AND WATER STORAGE
Bremer Vulkan
Fincantieri
Howaldtswerke-Deutsche Werft

TECHNICAL PUBLICATIONS
Vickers
Vosper Thornycroft

TELECOMMUNICATION EQUIPMENT
S.G. Brown Communications
CIT Alcatel
Montedel
Thomson CSF

TELEGRAPH SYSTEMS
Montedel
Thomson CSF

TELEMOTORS
MacTaggart Scott

TENDERS
Allday Aluminium
Blohm & Voss
Bremer Vulkan
Brooke Marine
Howaldtswerke-Deutsche Werft
Lambie (Boats)
Lürssen Werft
Netherlands United Shipbuilders
Sofrexan
Yarrow (Shipbuilders)

TEST EQUIPMENT FOR FIRE CONTROL SYSTEMS
CIT Alcatel
Singer Librascope
Thomson CSF
Whitehead Moto Fides

TORPEDO CONTROL SYSTEMS
CIT Alcatel
D.T.C.N.
Plessey Marine
Sofrexan
Sperry Gyroscope
Thomson CSF
Vickers
Whitehead Moto Fides

TORPEDO DEPTH AND ROLL RECORDERS
D.T.C.N.
Sofrexan

TORPEDO ORDER AND DEFLECTION CONTROL
CIT Alcatel
D.T.C.N.
Vickers

TORPEDO SIDE-LAUNCHERS
D.T.C.N.

TORPEDOES AND TORPEDO TUBES
CIT Alcatel
D.T.C.N.
Plessey Marine
Sofrexan
Vickers
Whitehead Moto Fides

TRAINING EQUIPMENT
CIT Alcatel
D.T.C.N.
Ferranti
Fincantieri
Sofrexan
Vickers

TRAWLERS
Brooke Marine
Crestitalia
D.T.C.N.
Dubigeon-Normandie
Fincantieri
Howaldtswerke-Deutsche Werft
Lambie (Boats)
Yarrow (Shipbuilders)

TUGS
Ailsa Shipbuilding
Brooke Marine
D.T.C.N.
Dubigeon-Normandie
Fincantieri
Lambie (Boats)
Lürssen Werft
Sofrexan
Yarrow (Shipbuilders)

TURBINE GEARS
Bremer Vulkan
Cantieri Navali Riuniti
CIT Alcatel
D.T.C.N.
Fincantieri
Vickers

TURBINES
Avco Lycoming
Blohm & Voss
Bremer Vulkan
Cantieri Navali Riuniti
D.T.C.N.
FIAT
Fincantieri
Hatch & Kirk
S.A.C.M.
Yarrow (Shipbuilders)

TURBINES—EXHAUST
Avco Lycoming
Bremer Vulkan
Cantieri Navali Riuniti
D.T.C.N.

TURBINES—GAS MARINE
Avco Lycoming
D.T.C.N.
S.A.C.M.
Yarrow (Shipbuilders)

TURBINES—STEAM MARINE
Blohm & Voss
Cantieri Navali Riuniti
D.T.C.N.
Fincantieri
Yarrow (Shipbuilders)

VALVES AND COCKS
Cockburns

VALVES AND COCKS—HYDRAULICS
Cockburns
MacTaggart Scott

VALVES, AUTOMATIC PLATE OR DISC
Cockburns

VALVES, BUTTERFLY, FLUID AND VENTILATION
Cockburns

VOLTAGE REGULATORS—AUTOMATIC
Ferranti

WARSHIP REPAIRERS
Bremer Vulkan
Brooke Marine
Cantieri Navali Riuniti
D.T.C.N.
Fincantieri
Howaldtswerke-Deutsche Werft
Lürssen Werft
Netherlands United Shipbuilders
Plessey Radar
Rhine-Schelde-Verolme
Vosper Thornycroft
Yarrow (Shipbuilders)

WARSHIPS
Blohm & Voss
Cantieri Navali Riuniti
D.T.C.N.
Dubigeon-Normandie
Fincantieri
Lürssen Werft
Netherlands United Shipbuilders
Rhine-Schelde-Verolme
Sofrexan
Vickers
Vosper Thornycroft
Yarrow (Shipbuilders)

WATER TUBE BOILERS
Bremer Vulkan
Fincantieri
Rhine-Schelde-Verolme
Yarrow (Shipbuilders)

WEAPON CONTROL SYSTEMS
Singer Librascope

WEAPON SYSTEMS
Aérospatiale
Bofors
D.T.C.N.
Ferranti
Officine Galileo
Plessey Marine
Plessey Radar
Sippican Oceanographic Systems
Sistel-Sistemi Elettronici
Snia Viscosa
Sofrexan
Sperry Gyroscope
Thomson CSF
Vickers
Vosper Thornycroft

WEAPON SYSTEMS (SONAR COMPONENTS)
Ailsa Shipbuilding
CIT Alcatel
D.T.C.N.
Edo Corporation
Plessey Marine
Sofrexan
Thomson CSF

WELDING, ARC, ARGON ARC OR GAS
Fincantieri
Lürssen Werft
Rhine-Schelde-Verolme
Vickers
Yarrow (Shipbuilders)

WINCHES
Standard Telephones & Cables
Vickers

WRIST COMPASSES AND DEPTH METERS FOR UNDERWATER OPERATORS
Officine Panerai

YACHTS (POWERED)
Ailsa Shipbuilding
Cantiere Navaltecnica
Cantieri Baglietto
Crestitalia
D.T.C.N.
Dubigeon-Normandie
Fairey Marine
Lürssen Werft
Vosper Thornycroft
Yarrow (Shipbuilders)

X-RAY WORK
D.T.C.N.
Vickers

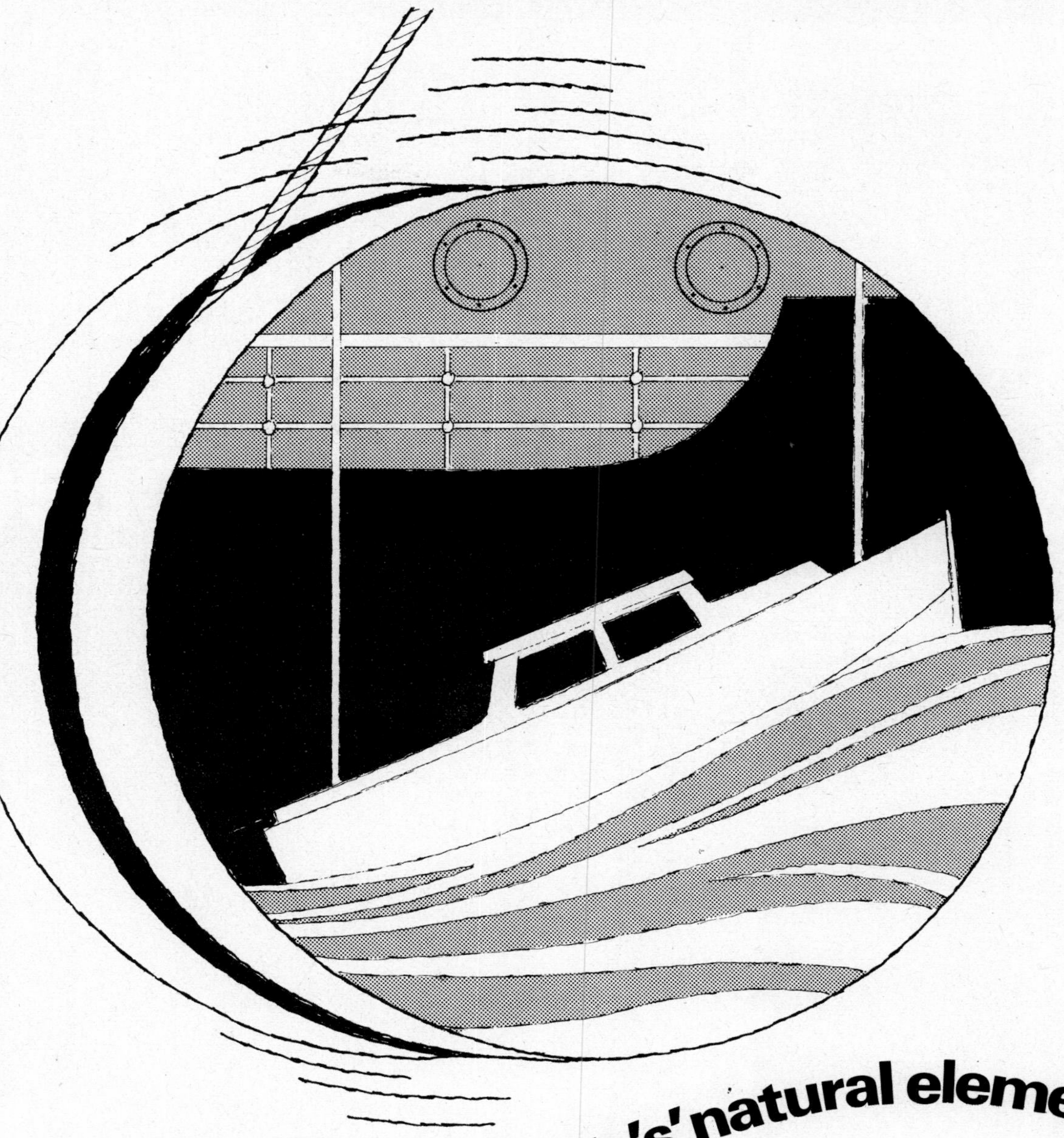

Foul weather is the 'Yo-Yo's' natural element

Lowering or hoisting a boat in rough weather is a tricky business. Specially when a wave lifts the boat and then lets it drop – putting a big strain on boat, falls, davits and winch. Not to mention crew.

But the Schat Yo-Yo automatic self-tensioning and rendering winch takes rough weather and boat work in its stride. It eliminates shocks in lowering or hoisting, eases the task of the crew and ensures maximum safety.

The 'Yo-Yo' winch maintains a constant tension on the wire falls.

This prevents the boat, or buoyant apparatus, from 'snatching' by allowing the craft to follow wave movements. During 'Yo-Yo-ing' the gearing in the winch allows the falls to be pulled off and recovered on the barrels at a speed equal to the vertical wave velocity. Hoisting begins on an upward movement of the boat and is accelerated by wave motion.

The Schat winch is particularly suitable for pilot vessels, sea rescue ships and other vessels whose business takes them to sea in rough

weather. It can be used with any modern winch-operated davits and represents an important contribution to marine safety. It has been adopted by the Royal Navy, the Royal Netherlands Navy, the Department of Trade (Canada) and the German Federal Navy among others.

For full information write or telephone Schat Davits Ltd., 'Ashley Mead', London Colney. Herts, A12 1BS, England (Tele: 0727 22244, Telex 21811) or contact either of the addresses given below.

SCHAT DAVITS

Schat Davits GmbH Hamburg
Tele: 040-278384. Telex: 214874

Schat Davit B.V. Utrecht
Tele: 030-310812. Telex: 47027

cantiere navale breda

construction of: tankers up to 250,000 tdw; ore-oil carriers and bulkcarriers up to 175,000 tdw; ore-bulk-oil carriers, completely double-skinned, up to 150,000 tdw; product carriers up to 80,000 tdw; liquid gas carriers up to 80,000 tdw; container-ships of all types and dimensions; general dry cargo and multipurpose vessels of all types and dimensions: merchant and/or passenger/merchant ferry boats; navy crafts: guided missile gun boats, corvettes, minesweepers. great jumboizing works. construction of industrial plants: refining towers, heat exchangers, electrical power station condensers.

230 T Standard displacement
260 T full load displacement

Guided missile gunboat

Dimensions	Max Engine Output	Speed	
49.80×7.50 (m)	20,000 HP	max	42 knots
		max continuous	40 knots
		cruising	20 knots

	Crew	Endurance	
	35 men	at 40 knots	500 miles
		at 20 knots	2,000 miles

Armament

4 missiles on fixed launching ramps
1 76/62 OTO MELARA compact gun
1 40/70 BREDA BOFORS twin gun

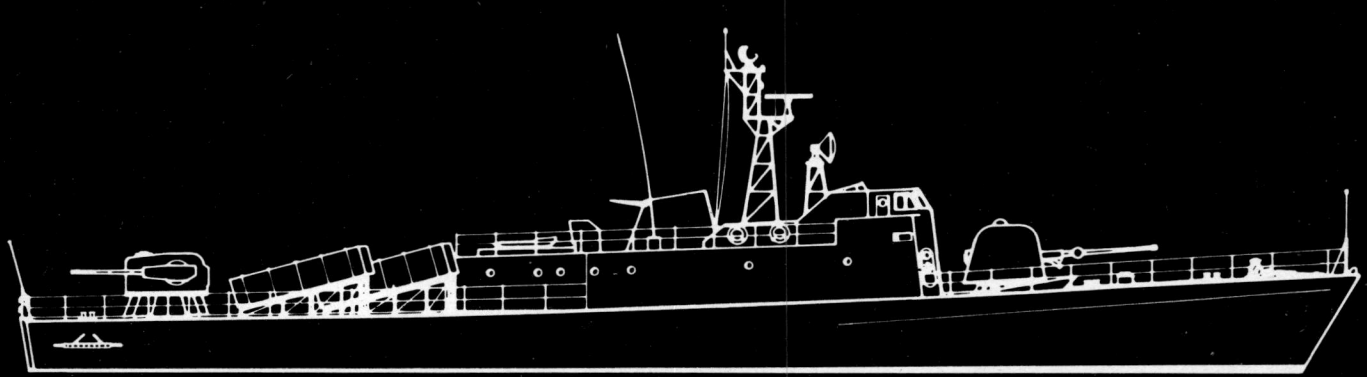

GRUPPO EFIM

cantiere navale breda spa

venice marghera italy
via delle industrie 18
phone (041) 59860
telex 41106 bredanav
cables cantbreda venice
postal address
p.o.b. 1043 (succ. 1) 30170 mestre

AB 212ASW
the self-contained killer that only needs the deck of a ship

Many Navies throughout the World have been looking out for an anti-submarine/anti-ship helicopter for immediate use, completely self-contained, and requiring only the minimum maintenance normally available aboard light vessels.

Agusta, with its long experience in designing naval helicopters, meets this requirement with its twin-engined AB 212ASW, which has a rugged, well-proven airframe and sophisticated avionics equipment optimized to provide a genuinely all-weather weapon system.

The AB 212ASW has integrated equipment for navigation, piloting, target acquisition, as well as for the transport and launching of missiles, torpedoes and sonobuoys over a wide radius.

AGUSTA
Cascina Costa - Gallarate - Italy - Telex 39569

sippican
ssxbt

SIPPICAN OCEANOGRAPHIC • MARION • MASSACHUSETTS

To survive in the Sea
You must know the Environment

Plessey Marine, Ilford, Essex, England • **Tsurumi Seiki Co., Ltd.,** Yokohama Japan • **L'electronique Appliquee,** Services Commerciaux, Montrouge, France

[41]

331/396

538

652

956

400 to 6000 horses mtu diesel power

mtu

Motoren- und Turbinen-Union Friedrichshafen GmbH · M. A. N. Maybach Mercedes-Benz · 799 Friedrichshafen · W.-Germany

[42]

Crestitalia S.p.A.

16.50 METRES HIGH-SPEED PATROL BOAT

CRESTITALIA builds a wide selection of g.r.p. fast patrol boats ranging from 7 to 21 metres.

The high speed patrol boat shown above is one of the most modern, efficient and rational boats yet built in the field of open sea planing hulls. The main features of the vessel are the hydrodynamic hull shape, the robustness of the hull and its proportions as well as the proportions and the reliability of the essential equipment (in particular the power plant and the control equipment) the stability, the safety, the manoeuvrability and, finally, the combination of the logistic, styling and functional characteristics.

The Deep-Vee hull has been developed from the well proven "CLIPPER 37" and "SENECA" line of power boats.

Open sea tests carried out on the prototype only served to confirm the parameters characteristic of this series and high-lighted the low water resistance, the very best performance in heavy seas even at low speed and when in a displacement condition, the excellent qualities of manoeuvrability and directional stability.

MAIN SPECIFICATIONS		GM powered	BREDA powered
LOA overall length .... mts.		16.5	16.5
LWL stationary water line .... mts.		13.75	13.75
width .... mts.		5.3	5.3
displacement, unloaded and dry .... tons		18.6	18.0
displacement, fully loaded .... tons		23.4	22.8
maximum speed, at full power with full load plus four (4) persons, in still waters and calm air .... knots		23	30
cruising speed with full load plus four (4) persons, in still waters and calm air .... knots		23	26

CRESTITALIA S.p.A. - Head office: 20151 Milano - Via Gallarate, 36 - tel. 364490 - telegr. Crestitalia-Milano
Yard: 19031 Ameglia (La Spezia) tel. 65746 - 65583 - 65584 - telex: Savid 38201

FOR SWIFTY INTERVENTIONS ON WATERS

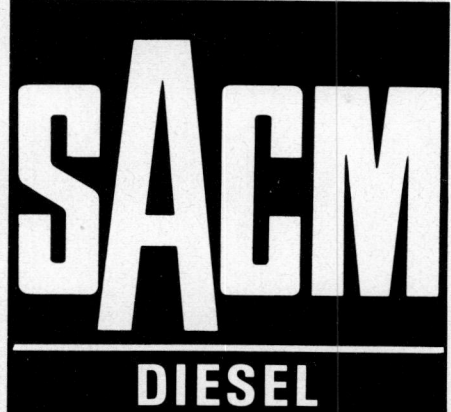

From 150 to 8 000 hp

Our range includes top high performance light weight engines to suit the requirements of the newest military fast patrol crafts.
SACM main engines and generating sets cover every aspect of power for naval applications.

H+H Conseil

SOCIÉTÉ ALSACIENNE DE CONSTRUCTIONS MÉCANIQUES DE MULHOUSE
1, rue de la Fonderie / BP 1319 / 68054 Mulhouse Cedex (France) / Tél. (89) 42.99.08 / Télex N° 881699 Mécalsa Mulhs

When in 1866 Roberto Whitehead
invented the first torpedo,
could he possibly have thought
that his name would still have
been the leading one in the torpedo
field to day? Perhaps not,
but nevertheless it is.

A-184

torpedo (ø 21″ - 533 mm). Wire guided
anti-submarine/anti-surface-ship torpedo,
launchable either by submarine or by surface vessel.
Equipped with an acoustic homing system
for the automatic search and attack of the target.

A-244

lightweight torpedo (ø 12″¾ - 324 mm).
Anti-submarine acoustic homing torpedo with
shallow water capabilities and anti-reverberation
and CCM characteristics. Launchable by
surface vessel, helicopter and aircraft.

A-244/S

lightweight torpedo (ø 12″¾ - 324 mm).
Same dimensions and operational characteristics
as the A-244 but with an improved homing
system specially intended for CCM and
shallow water capabilities.

WHITEHEAD - MOTO FIDES STABILIMENTI MECCANICI RIUNITI S.p.A.
VIA SALVATORE ORLANDO, 10 - TELEFONI: 21.554, 5, 6, 39.051, 39.054 - TELEX: 50271 WHITEMOT - LIVORNO

WHITEHEAD - MOTO FIDES
the torpedoes for the eighties

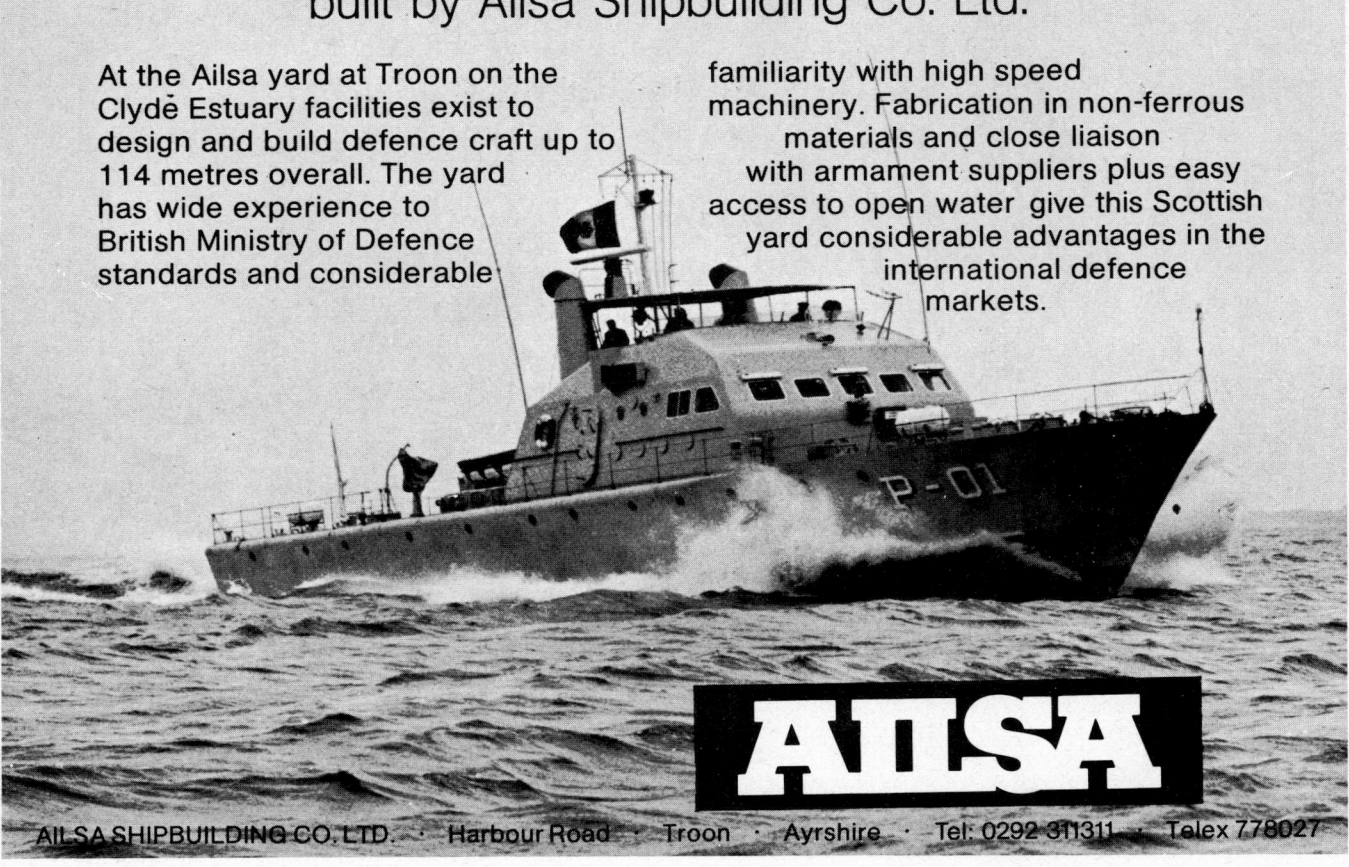

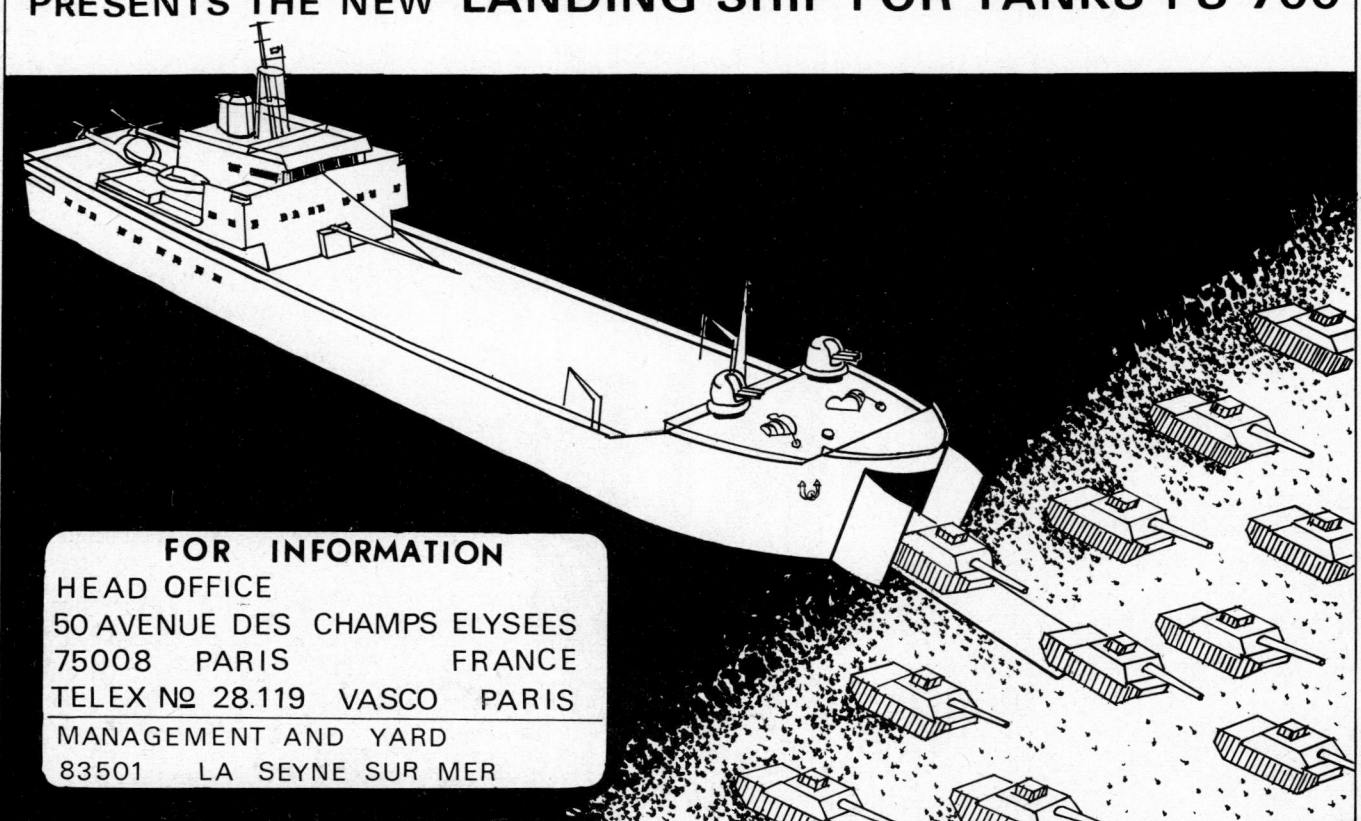

Now you'll
carrier when you

ANDREA DORIA – ITALY – 5000 TONS

VIKRANT – INDIA – 16000 TONS

PROVIDER – CANADA – 7300 TONS

ORAGE – FRANCE – 5800 TONS

BLAKE – UK – 9500 TONS

POOLSTER – NETHERLANDS – 16800 TONS

SKEENA – CANADA – 2260 TONS

GENERAL BELGRANO – ARGENTINA – 10800 TONS

MELBOURNE – AUSTRALIA – 16000 TONS

KATORI – JAPAN – 3372 TONS

Huge, expensive, often vulnerable, the modern jet aircraft carrier is today giving way to the Harrier Carrier – any ship, large or small, with deck-space enough to operate one or more V/STOL Sea Harrier strike aircraft.

The implications are enormous.

For the Harrier alone can instantly transform a whole range of mobile, pad-equipped ships into the naval equivalent of dispersed strike-jet airfields – giving unparalleled flexibility to naval air operations.

And, most important of all, even small navies, with vessels of only a few thousand tons, can now reap the operational advantages of their own organic seaborne jet strike force, large or small.

The Sea Harrier has changed everything.

know an aircraft
see one.

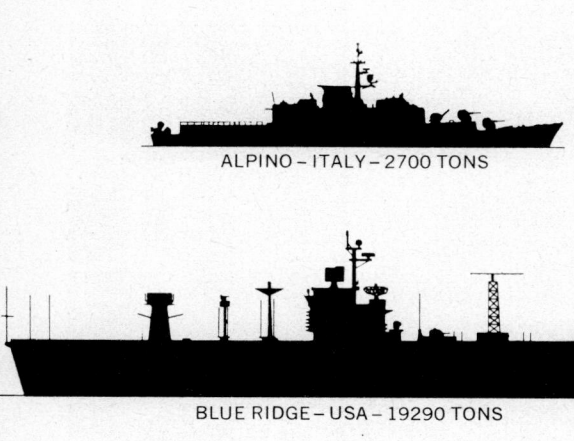

ALPINO – ITALY – 2700 TONS

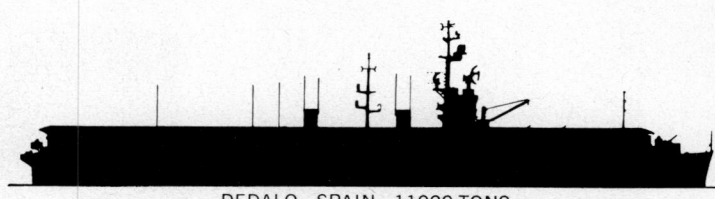

DEDALO – SPAIN – 11000 TONS

BLUE RIDGE – USA – 19290 TONS

GREEN ROVER – UK – 3185 TONS

STALWART – AUSTRALIA – 10000 TONS

LA SALLE – USA – 8040 TONS

HARUNA – JAPAN – 4700 TONS

JEANNE D'ARC – FRANCE – 10000 TONS

MINAS GERAIS – BRAZIL – 15890 TONS

VITTORIO VENETO – ITALY – 7500 TONS

Fast, powerfully armed and equipped with dual-mode radar, it can take off either vertically from heli-pad type decks on small vessels, or – with greater range and armament loads – make short take offs from through-deck cruisers or from small older carriers.

Now that the Sea Harrier is here, naval tactics will never be the same again.

The unique Sea Harrier by Hawker Siddeley Aviation, ordered for the Royal Navy.

HAWKER SIDDELEY AVIATION
Kingston upon Thames, England.
Hawker Siddeley Group supplies mechanical, electrical and aerospace equipment with world-wide sales and service.

[51]

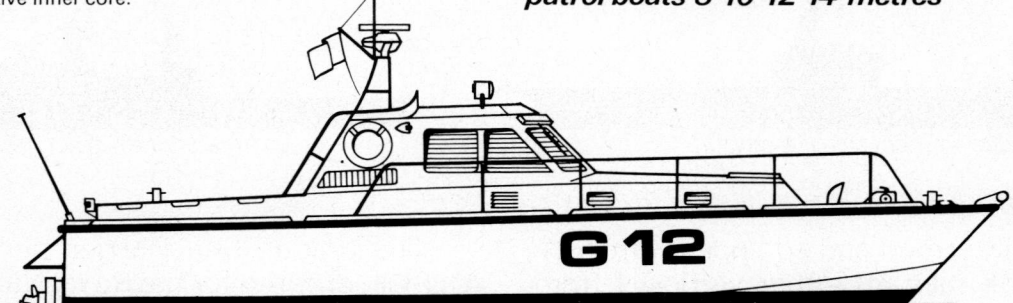

THE LARGEST SHIPBUILDING
AND SHIPREPAIRING GROUP
IN THE MEDITERRANEAN

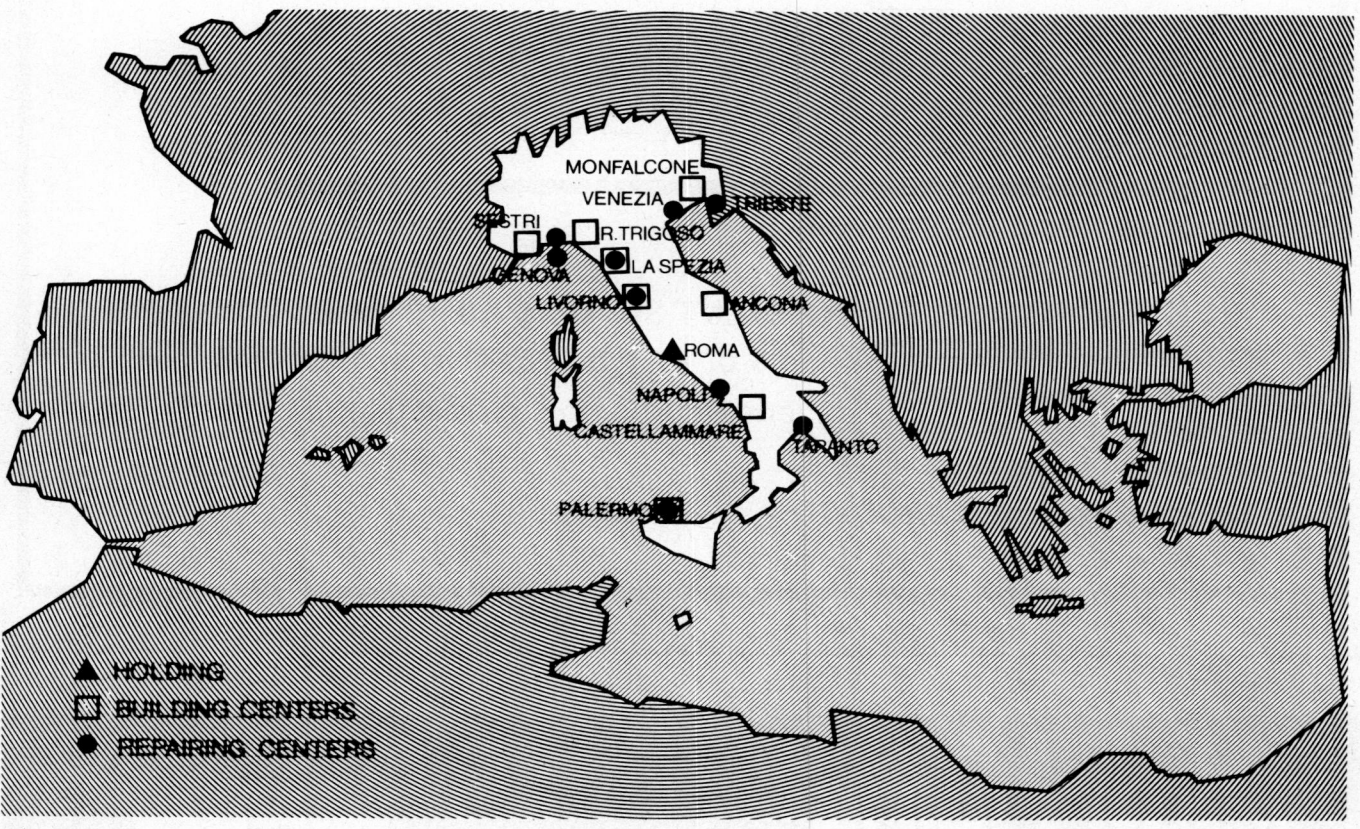

▲ HOLDING
☐ BUILDING CENTERS
● REPAIRING CENTERS

Shipbuilding system

8 yards with an annual production capacity of about
1 million grt. for any kind of ship up to over 300,000
dwt. Each yard is specialized in building the
ships most suitable for its own lay-out, equipment,
skills and traditions.

Shiprepairing system

9 yards with 26 graving docks for ships up to
350,000 dwt. (3 new graving docks for v.l.c.c. up
to 400,000 dwt. under construction), 10 floating
docks for ships up to 160,000 dwt. and about 15
kilometres of outfitting quays.

Mechanical products

3 factories for the production of main and auxiliary
Diesel engines, main and auxiliary turbines,
deck and E.R. machinery and marine propellers.

GROUP'S COMPANIES

ITALCANTIERI (Trieste)
CANTIERI NAVALI RIUNITI "C.N.R." (Genova)
CANTIERE NAVALE MUGGIANO (La Spezia)
CANTIERE NAVALE LUIGI ORLANDO "C.N.L.O."(Livorno)
**OFFICINE ALLESTIMENTO E RIPARAZIONE NAVI
"O.A.R.N." (Genova)**
**SOCIETÀ ESERCIZIO BACINI NAPOLETANI
"S.E.B.N." (Napoli)**
STABILIMENTI NAVALI (Taranto)
**CANTIERI NAVALI E OFFICINE MECCANICHE DI
VENEZIA "C.N.O.M.V." (Venezia)**
ARSENALE TRIESTINO S. MARCO (Trieste)
LIPS ITALIANA (Livorno)
GRANDI MOTORI TRIESTE "G.M.T." (Trieste)

FINCANTIERI

Società Finanziaria Cantieri Navali
via Sardegna n. 40 Roma
phone (06) 482241
telex 61180 FINCANT.

 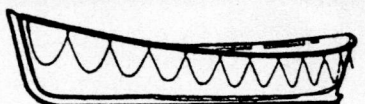
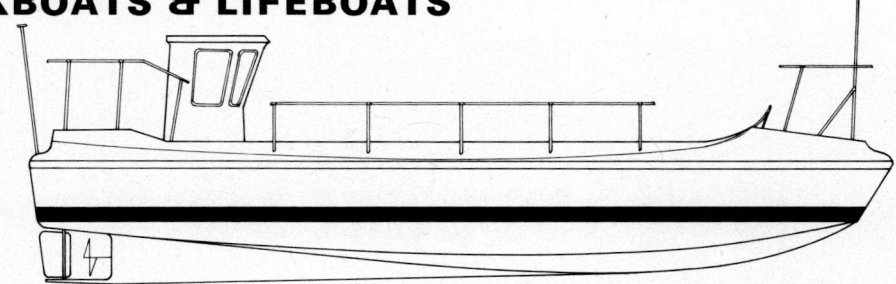

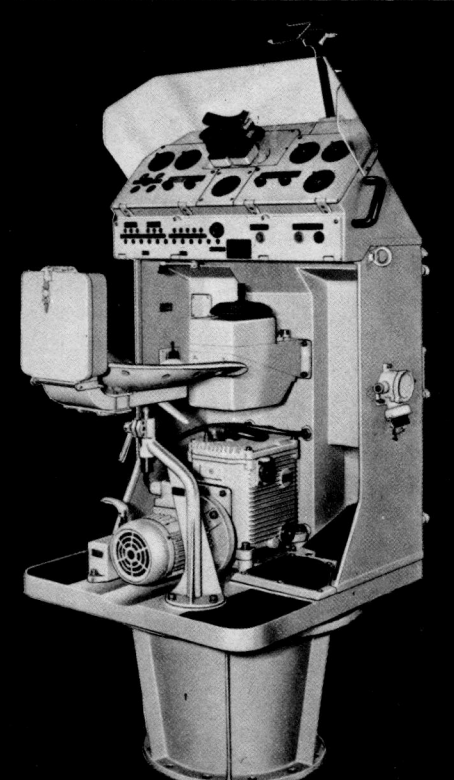

[55]

TRITON radar antenna surveillance,
radar of VEGA system.

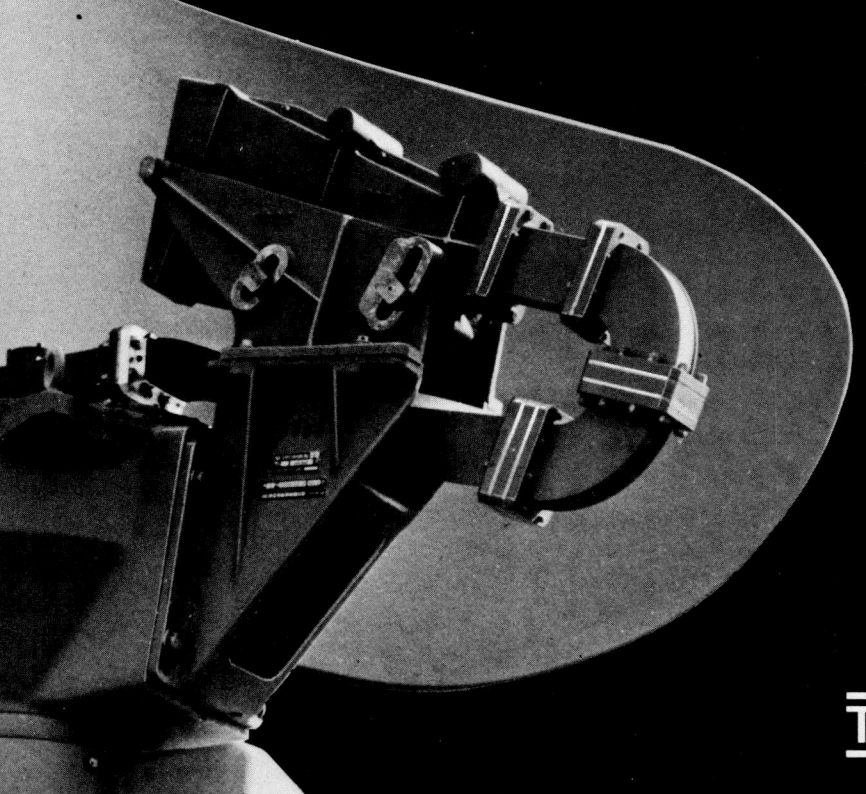

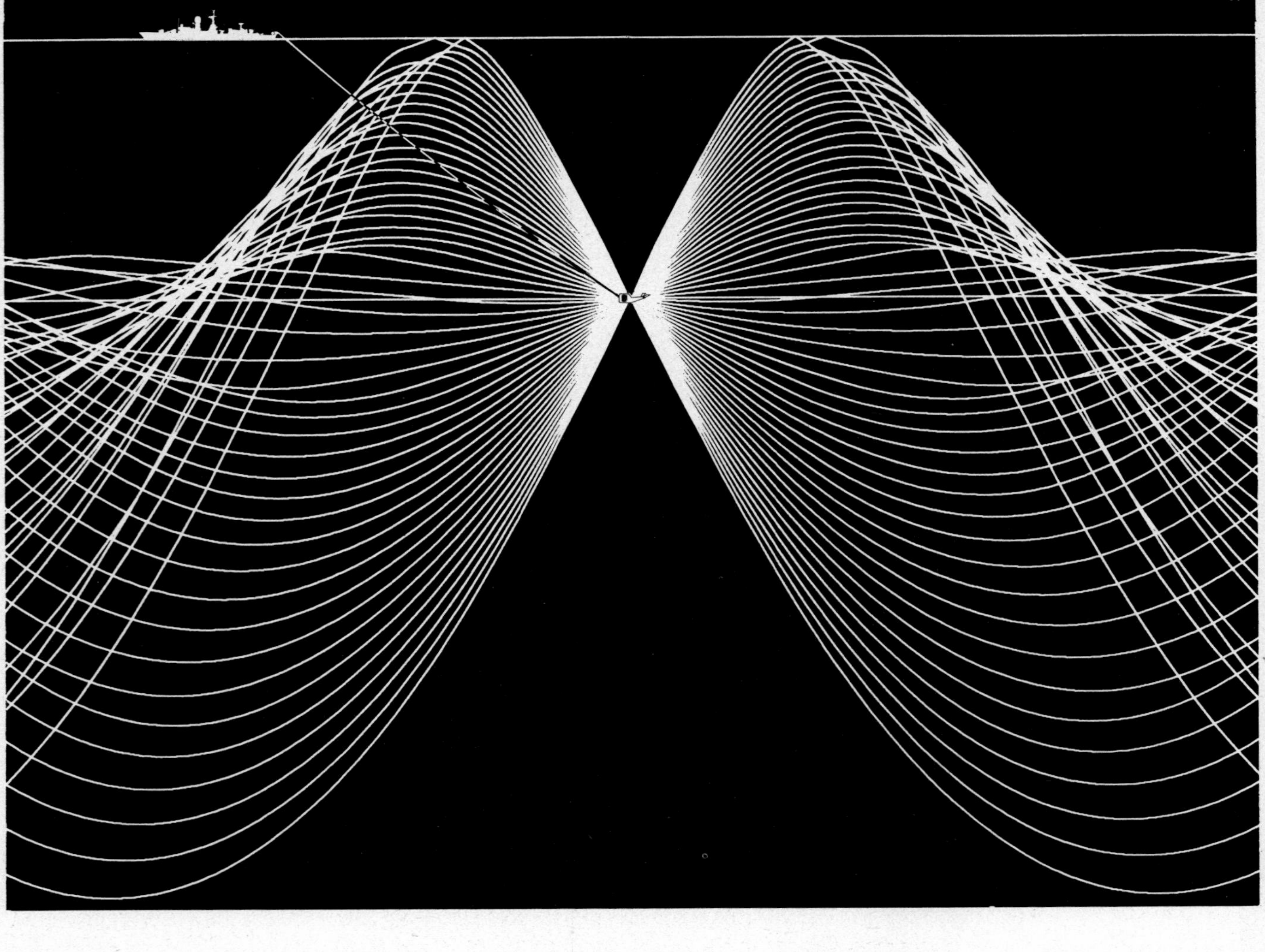

D'après photo Paris-Match/Saulnier.

Photo Soulard/Raoho.

UNRUFFLED
in any weather

Proof against the effect of the sea in any weather, even at very low altitudes, the electromagnetic proximity fuse will ensure destruction of the enemy even in the worst firing configurations.

Proximity fuses for naval artillery:
- electromagnetic with doppler effect, to NATO specs;
- quality guaranteed by acceptance trial firings;
- available for any caliber from 40 mm to 127 mm and for any type of gun (American, British, Italian, French...).

Proximity fuses for ground forces:
- impervious to the ground reflection coefficient;
- constant burst height;
- for AP and antitank use.

THOMSON-CSF
DIVISION EQUIPEMENTS AVIONIQUES
178, BOULEVARD GABRIEL PERI / 92240 MALAKOFF / FRANCE / TEL. (1) 655 44.22.

2668

[62]

Now-small ship displays get mini computers to speed tactical data

New Plessey A10/CIC systems for command and control.

Faster decision-making is aided by this entirely new concept from Plessey Radar; naval autonomous displays with individual minicomputers. These processors, with their firmware programs, enable the tactical picture to be compiled rapidly, then distributed and presented in the action information system. Integration of sensors and weapons is achieved without the need for a large central computer complex. And the firmware removes all on-board program handling problems, whilst retaining the ability to evolve new tactics and procedures.

Contact us at the address below for further information.

PLESSEY
electronic systems

PLESSEY RADAR
Addlestone Surrey England KT15 2PW
Telephone: Weybridge (0932) 47282

603 P166A

[63]

Operation and simulation. Ferranti have the hardware, the software and the experience.

Today there is hardly a branch of the armed forces where you might not find Ferranti systems or equipment making a contribution to efficiency.

For example, Ferranti action data systems are in service with most ships of the Royal Navy. An airborne digital computer has been developed for maritime reconnaissance aircraft. Digital data links have been supplied for air defence. A Ferranti naval tactical trainer at H.M.S. Dryad and submarine command team simulator/trainers are bringing a new realism to naval command training,

and weapon simulators are helping with operator training for the Sea King and Wessex helicopters. Ferranti equipment is measuring the velocity of shells for the Army, and a Ferranti Large Screen Display has been developed for briefing, tactical and demonstration uses.

The same sort of thing is happening in civilian fields, especially civil aviation. Ferranti telegraph message switching systems are speeding data communication for the Australian D.C.A. Air traffic control training

simulators are in use at several international airports. Ferranti have made operational ATC systems for Prestwick and the London ATC Centre. And police command and control systems are in operation.

All these systems are necessarily complex. But the software that goes with them is getting simpler. And Ferranti supply that too. Equally important, they supply experience. Their close involvement with the problems in each area of activity gives them a knowledge that 'rubs off' elsewhere.

FERRANTI

Ferranti Limited
Digital Systems Division,
Bracknell,
Berkshire RG12 1RA
Telephone: 0344 3232
Military Systems Division,
Wythenshawe,
Manchester M22 5LA
Telephone: 061-437 5291

DS 60 rb

Some things ...like Edo excellence ...never change

In 1935 Edo floats crossed Antarctica with Bernt Balchen on Lincoln Ellsworth's Polar Star. Today, Edo sonar routinely dives under the Polar ice cap aboard the nuclear submarines of the U.S. Navy. In 46 years our standard of excellence has never been lowered...in Edo systems developed for antisubmarine warfare, oceanography, mine countermeasures, strike warfare, airborne navigation, hydrodynamics and airframes, command and control. And speaking of sonar, sonar designed and built by Edo is standard equipment aboard all the nuclear-powered submarines of the U.S. Navy and many of our modern destroyers.

CANTIERI NAVALI DI PISA

56100 PISA - VIA AURELIA KM. 334 DARSENA PISANA - TEL. (050) 22072 - 22073
TELEGRAMMI: CNIPAM - PISA TELEX 58635 CANTPISA

TWO OF OUR FAST PATROL BOATS IN SERVICE

- **FAST PATROL BOAT of m. 46**
- Equipped with 3 engines MTU type MB20V538TB91 (HP 4500 x 3) knots 40

- **COAST-GUARD of m. 27**
- Equipped with 2 engines MTU type MB20V672TY (HP 3500 x 2) knots 42
- Equipped with 4 engines MTU type MB12V331TC81 (HP 1350 x 4) knots 35
- Equipped with 3 engines MTU type MB12V331TC81 (HP 1350 x 3) knots 30

- **COAST-GUARD of m. 23**
- Equipped with 3 engines MTU type MB12V331TC81 (HP 1350 x 3) knots 38
- Equipped with 2 engines MTU type MB12V331TC81 (HP 1350 x 2) knots 30

- **COAST-GUARD of m. 16,60**
- Equipped with 2 engines MTU type MB8V331TC80 (HP 900 x 2) knots 38
- Equipped with 2 engines MTU type 6V331TC80 (HP 675 x 2) knots 31
- Equipped with 2 engines G.M. type 12V71TI (HP 650 x 2) knots 30

- **COAST-GUARD of m. 14,00**
- Equipped with 2 engines G.M. type 8V71N (HP 350 x 2) knots 25
- Equipped with 2 engines G.M. type 8V71TI (HP 435 x 2) knots 30
- Equipped with 2 engines G.M. type 12V71TI (HP 675 x 2) knots 38

[69]

Special oil hydro-mechanical devices and complete systems for submarines and other warships

- extra noiseless pumps
- steering and diving gears
- antenna and periscope hoisting devices
- m.t.b. flood and vent valve controls
- remotely controlled hull valves

- windlass and capstan gears
- torpedo handling systems
- trim manifold (remote controlled)
- induction and exhaust snorkel
- etc.

- **noiseless**
- **compact**
- **tailor-made**
- **high shock resistant devices**

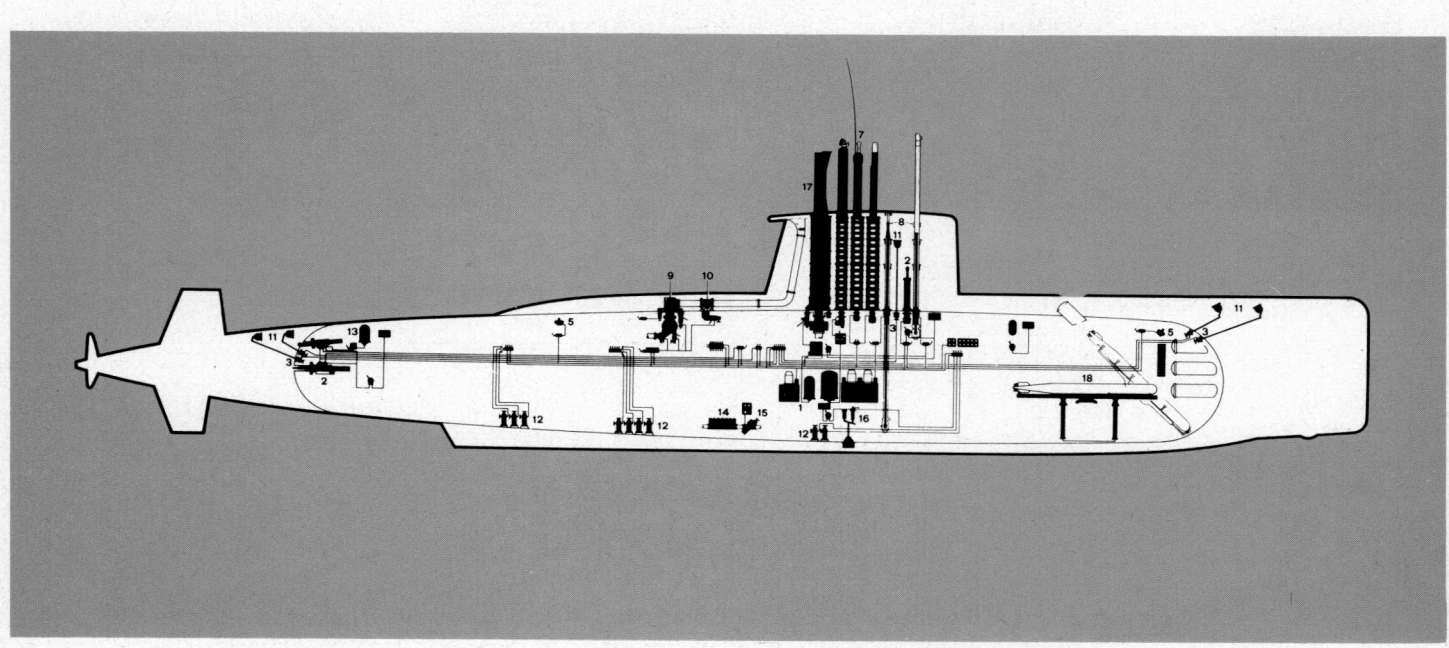

RIVA CALZONI S.p.A. — Via Emilia Ponente, 72-Bologna-Italy-Telex 51156

[72]

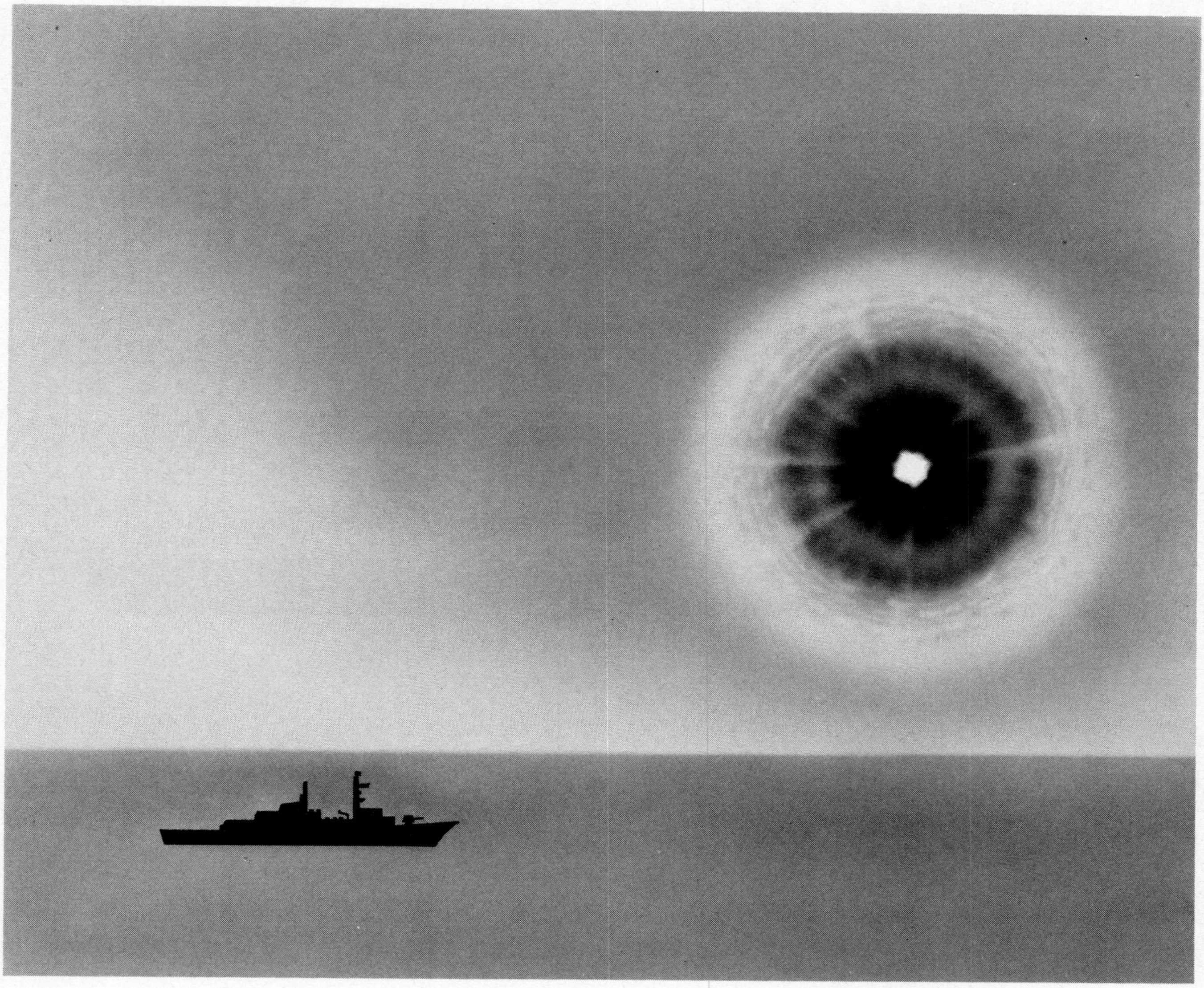

Ship Installed Radiac Systems

Plessey Ship Installed Radiac Systems are widely used by the British Royal Navy and other navies. The systems continuously and automatically provide early warning of radioactive contamination of the air and sea.

They enable the command to appreciate fully the nature and scale of the radiological hazard in which a ship must operate during the long period of contamination following a nuclear burst.

PLESSEY
NUCLEONICS

Features of the larger system (22 NRS) include:

- [ ] Seven detector units
- [ ] Automatic visual and audio alarms
- [ ] Automatic fault indication
- [ ] Built-in test facilities
- [ ] NATO codified
- [ ] Simulator with pre-recorded programmes for crew training.

The smaller system (23 NRS) is designed for submarines, small naval vessels and dockyard protection.

Full details are available on request from:
The Plessey Company Limited Sopers Lane Poole Dorset England BH17 7ER Telephone: Poole (020 13) 5161 Telex: 41272

600 P105A

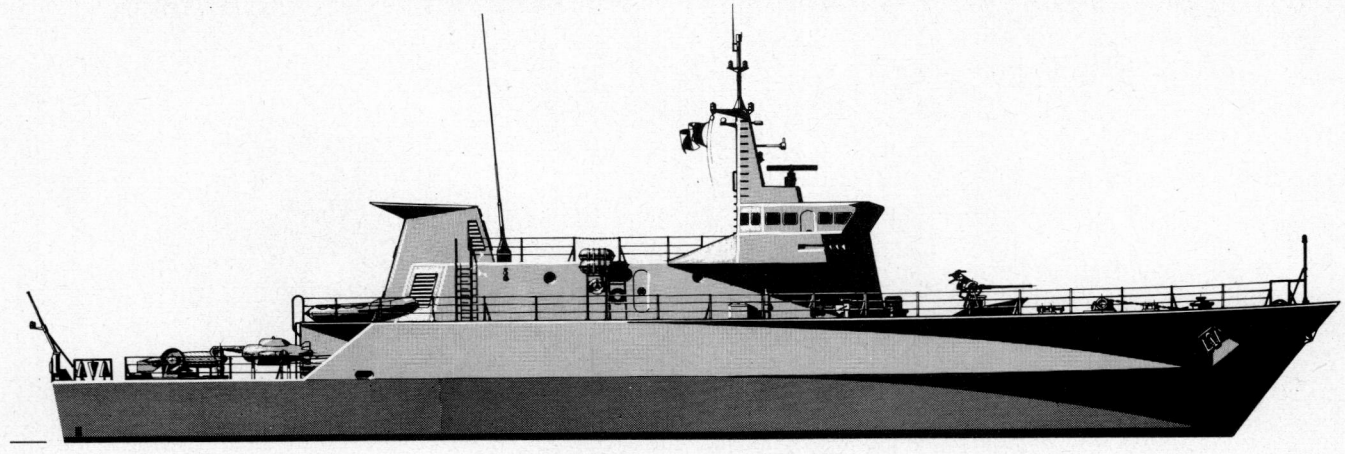

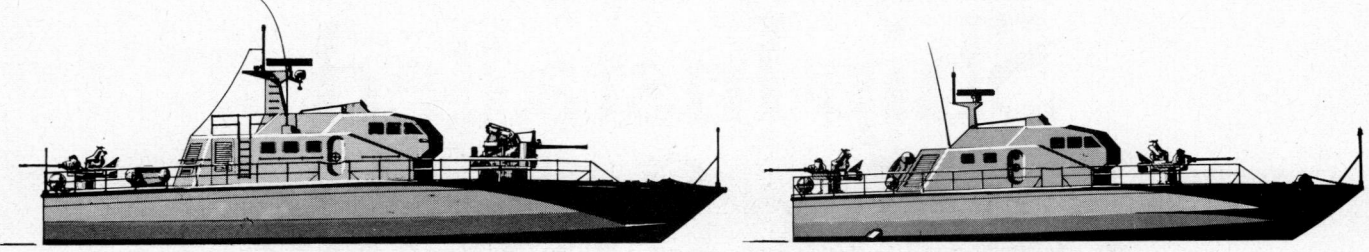

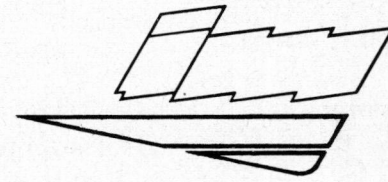

ITALIAN G.R.P. MINEHUNTER
BUILT BY INTERMARINE ACCORDING TO
ITALIAN NAVY GENERAL SPECIFICATION

intermarine
spa

SARZANA - LA SPEZIA - ITALY
TEL. 0187/61768 - TELEX 28062 I. MARINE

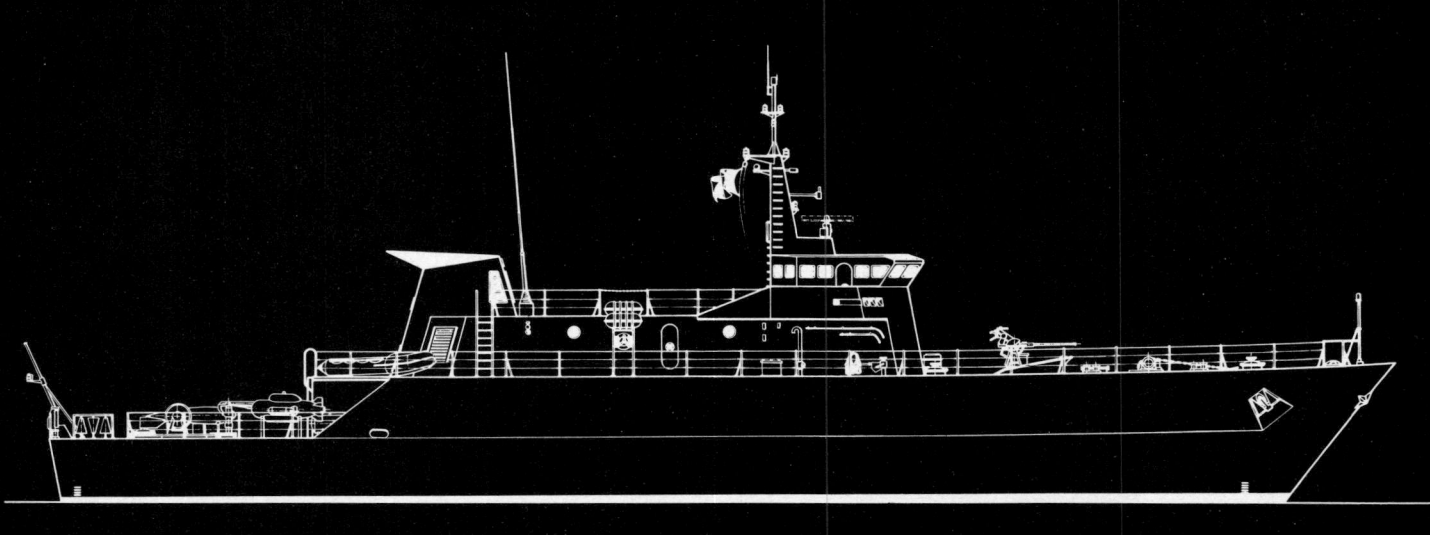

in collaboration with : **ATISA - CGE - DATAMAT - ELMER - GALEAZZI - GRANDI MOTORI TRIESTE - IFEN - RIVA CALZONI - SEPA - SIGNANI - SMA - VM.**

ITALCANTIERI

HEAD OFFICE: TRIESTE, CORSO CAVOUR 1

TELEPHONE: 7367 — TELEX: 46041 ITALCANT

CABLES: ITALCANT TRIESTE

SHIPYARDS
MONFALCONE
GENOVA SESTRI
CASTELLAMMARE DI STABIA

Submarine "1081 type,,
SAURO class

This type has been designed in accordance with the latest requirements of the evolution of underwater fighting means and their use.

Special stress has been put on those features and performances that, also in the near future, will undoubtedly represent the most essential factors for efficient undersea combat, mainly in ASK and attack tasks.

Main characteristics

Length overall	63.85 m
Beam	6.83 m
Height overall (masts in)	12.38 m
Light displacement	1250 tons
Surface displacement	1450 tons
Surface mean draught	5.70 m
Submerged displacement	1630 tons

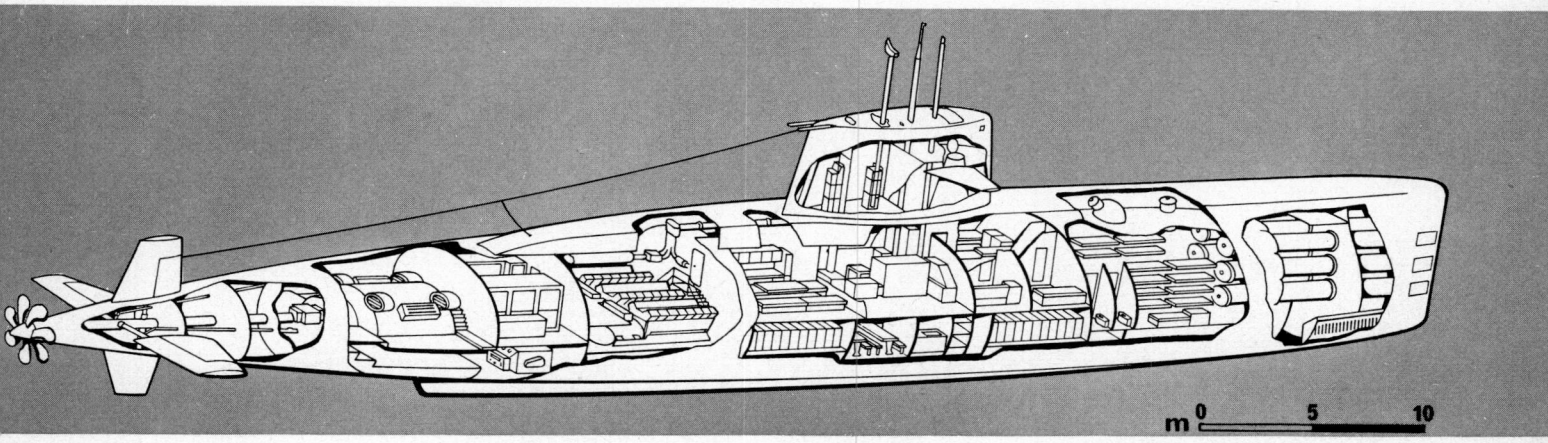

Submarine "1077 type,,
500 - ton class

This design has been developed to exploit to the utmost the operational possibilities of the 500-ton class submarines, simplifying as far as possible handling and service problems whilst keeping the cost comparatively low.

Main characteristics

Length overall	47.47 m
Beam	4.77 m
Height overall (masts in)	8.67 m
Light displacement	465 tons
Surface displacement	550 tons
Surface mean draught	4.00 m
Submerged displacement	610 tons

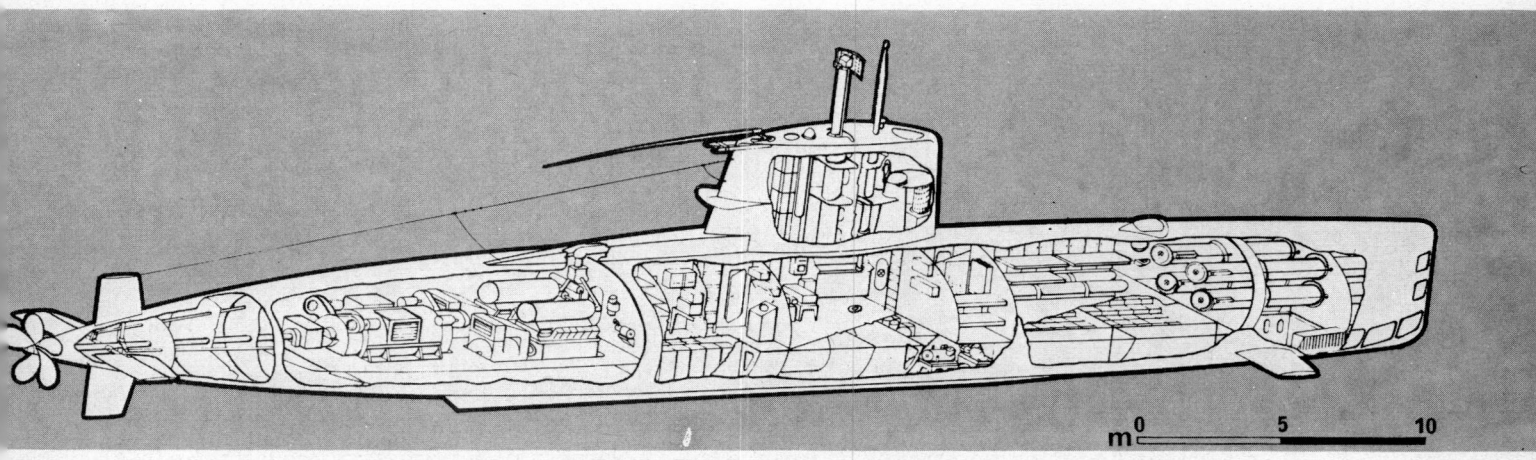

Italcantieri belongs to the Fincantieri Group, the largest shipbuilding and shiprepairing organization in the Mediterranean.

Brooke

SHIPBUILDERS · ENGINEE

100 YEARS OF ENGINEERING & SHIPBUILDING

A DOWSETT COMPANY

Lowestoft · Suffolk · England

TELEPHONE : LOWESTOFT 65221 · TELEX 97145 · CABLES BROOKCRAFT LOWESTOFT.

Marine Limited

AND CONSULTING NAVAL ARCHITECTS

ESTABLISHED 1874

Designers and builders of specialised ships and naval
vessels for British, Commonwealth and Foreign navies

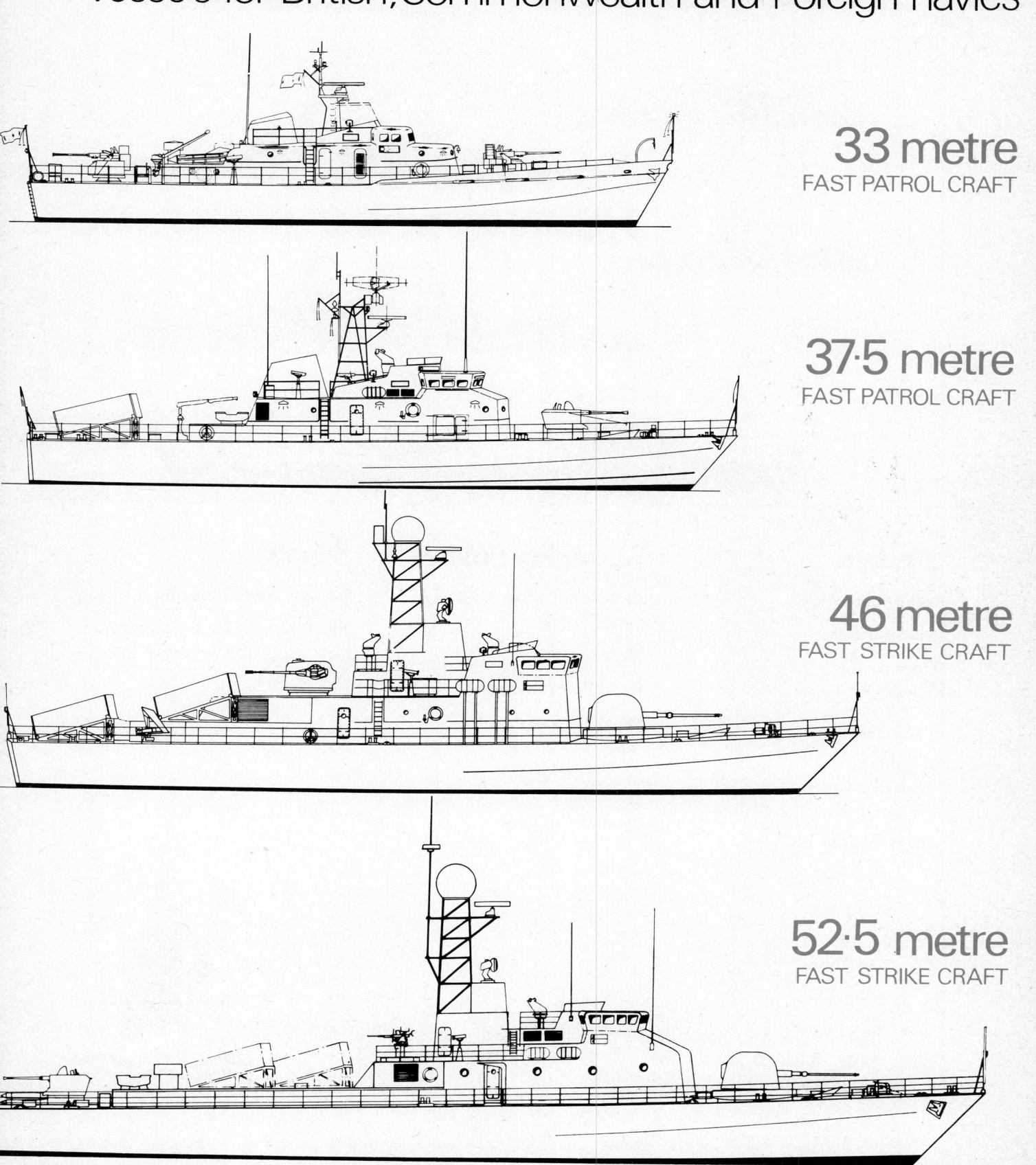

33 metre
FAST PATROL CRAFT

37·5 metre
FAST PATROL CRAFT

46 metre
FAST STRIKE CRAFT

52·5 metre
FAST STRIKE CRAFT

coastguard

BRITISH HOVERCRAFT

Patrol at 50 knots. Cover more
coastline than two conventional craft.
Operate from the nearest beach.
Cross sand, swamp, and reefs.
Intruders can't outrun or evade you.
How? Only by British Hovercraft.

british hovercraft corporation

East Cowes Isle of Wight England Telephone Cowes 4101 Telex 86190

*A Member of the Westland Group of Companies—
7 times winner of the Queen's Award to Industry.*

1975

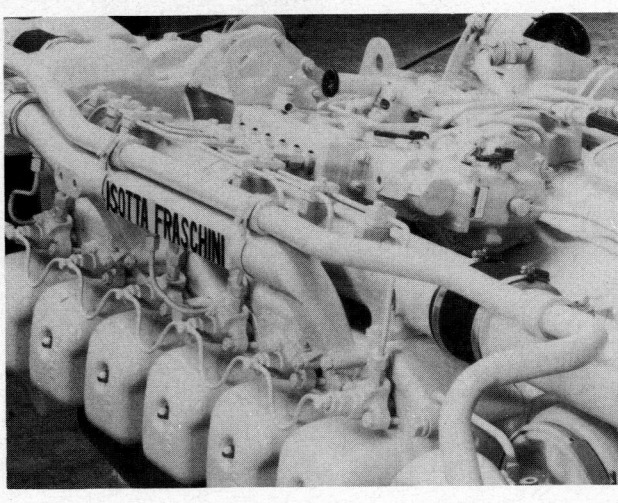

HMS Royal Sovereign

HMS Amazon

HMS Courageous

HMS Hermes

What's in a name?

The Royal Navy sets a special value on names.
Royal Sovereign, Amazon, Courageous, Hermes – they help to carry down its tradition from one generation to another.

These great old ships have their present day namesakes, whose purpose and duties are the same, though their methods and equipment are very different.

Each of them carries a Ferranti computer system.

The nuclear powered submarine Sovereign carries a Ferranti FM 1600B system for tactical purposes.

The Royal Navy's new frigate Amazon carries two computer systems – CAAIS for operations room display and WSA4 for control of her gun and Seacat armament. Each is based on an FM 1600B computer.

Courageous is today a nuclear powered Fleet submarine of the Churchill class. Units of this class are fitted with Ferranti FM 1600B computer systems to assist in tactical data handling display and appreciation. The present Hermes, built in 1953, was converted to a helicopter carrier in 1970 and her Operations Room is now fitted with a Ferranti CAAIS system.

In their own field, Ferranti too, are a great name.
At the end of the last century they were one of the pioneers in electrical engineering and in the early nineteen-fifties they were responsible for the first commercially available British computer.

Today they are recognised as leaders in the application of digital systems for naval, airborne, military and civil uses.

Ferranti Limited, Digital Systems Division, Western Road, Bracknell, Berkshire, RG12 1RA. Telephone: 0344 3232   Telex: 848117.

FERRANTI
Naval Digital Systems

DS 56 [rb]

Command, weapon control and sensor systems...

System integration results in the shortest possible reaction times and optimal weapon deployment. Advanced sensors and data-handling facilities enable the engagement of air, surface, subsurface and shore targets in a multi-target environment.

Signaal's 3-dimensional radar, micromin computer and human-engineered display consoles form this tightly knit system with its modest personnel requirements.

It performs the indispensable functions of warning, threat evaluation, weapon assignment and fire control. Moreover it features facilities for electronic warfare, tactical operations and simulation.

Interesting detailed information is available on request.

Hollandse Signaalapparaten BV
Hengelo, The Netherlands

SIGNAAL

...all in one hand on board the Royal Netherlands Navy's 'Tromp'-class frigates.

DECCA ELECTRONICS
The choice of the world's navies
Standard marine radar for navigational and
tactical roles–Special displays–Navigation and
Action Information Systems–EW Systems–
Marine automation
systems–Coastal
surveillance and
harbour radar.

The Decca Navigator Company Limited, Decca Radar Limited   9 Albert Embankment London SE1 7SW

INMA presents its constructions:

- **fast patrol boat**
- **training ship**
- **landing ship**
- **fleet support ship**

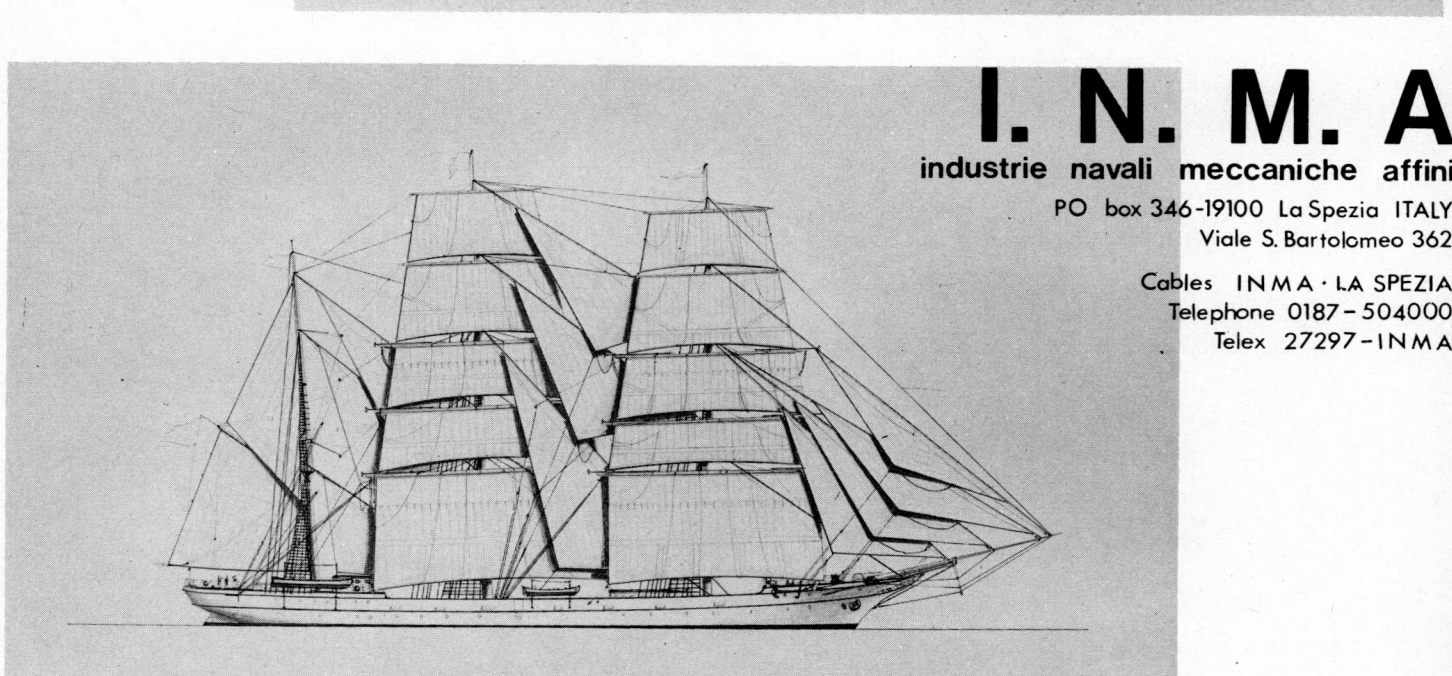

I. N. M. A
industrie navali meccaniche affini
PO box 346-19100 La Spezia ITALY
Viale S. Bartolomeo 362

Cables INMA · LA SPEZIA
Telephone 0187 - 504000
Telex 27297 - INMA

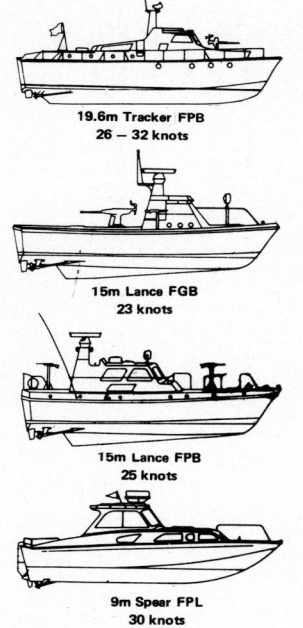
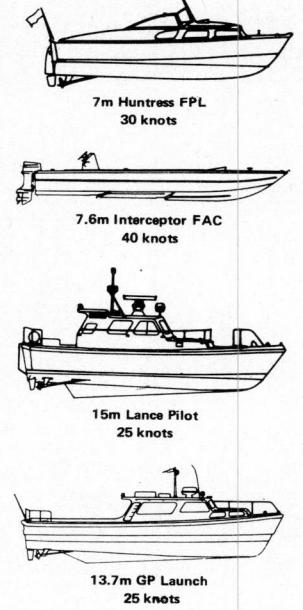
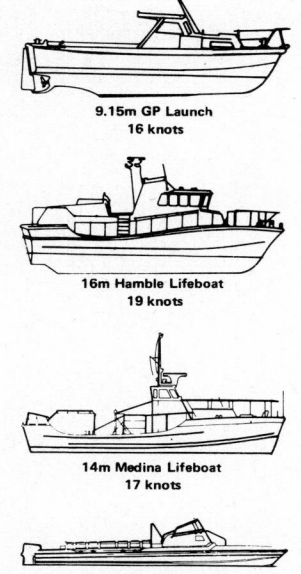

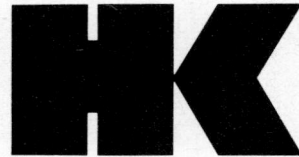

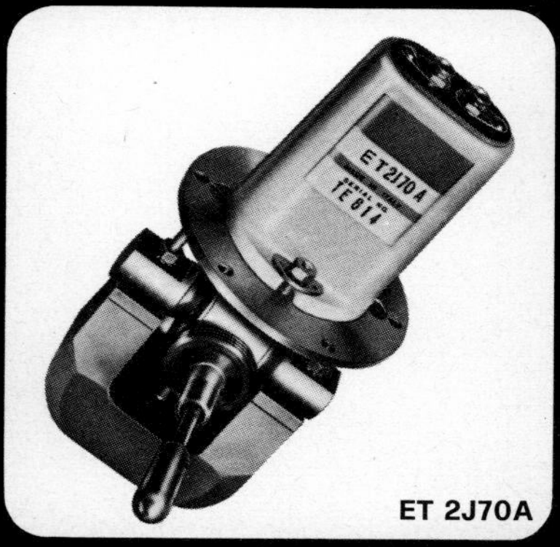

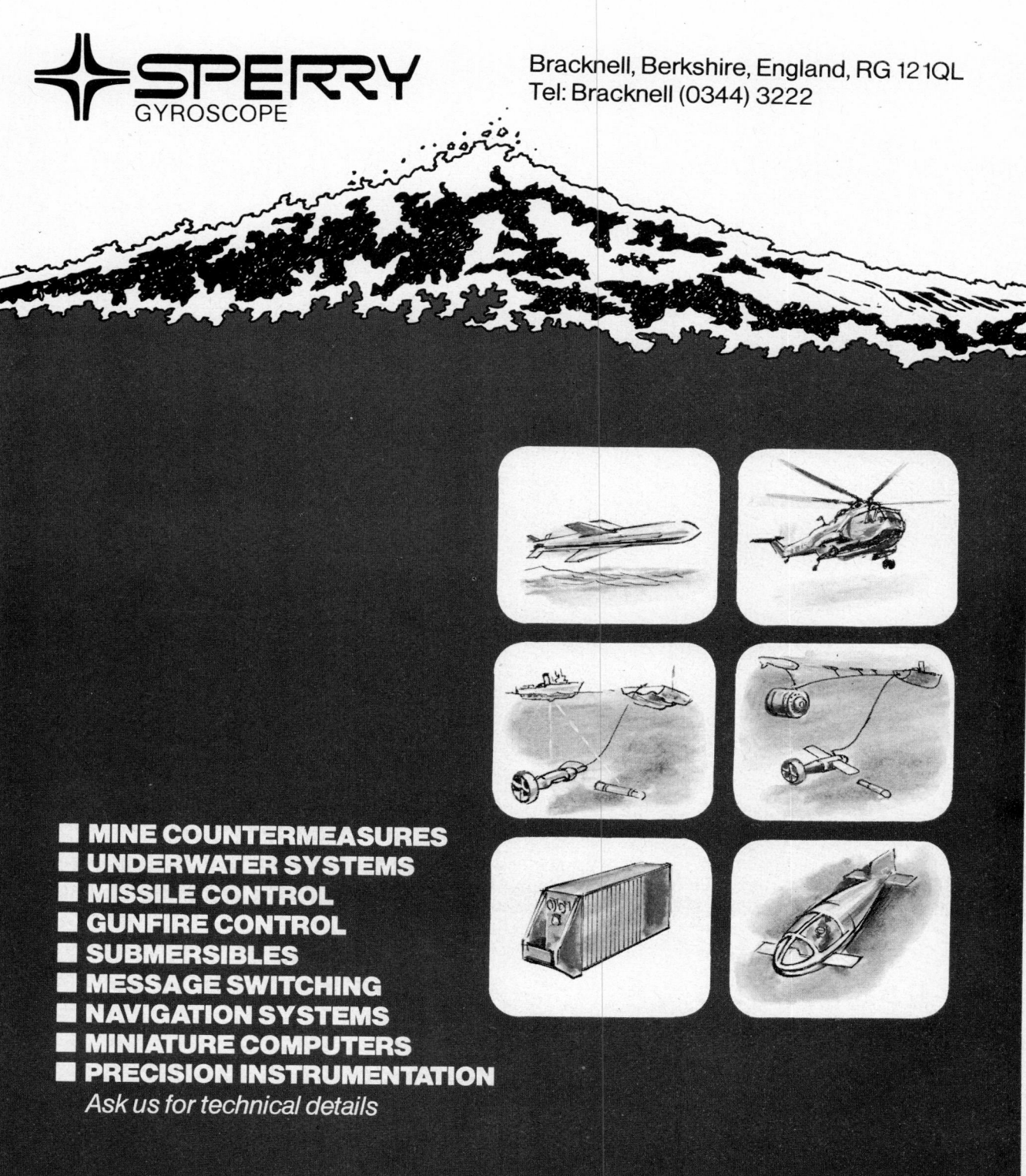

CANTIERI BAGLIETTO S.p.A.
17019 VARAZZE ITALY

BAGLIETTO 20 GC *FAST PATROL BOAT*

**67 UNITS BUILT AND UNDER CONSTRUCTION
FOR ITALIAN AND FOREIGN NAVAL FORCES
TO OUR DESIGN**

CANTIERI BAGLIETTO S.p.A.
17019 VARAZZE ITALY

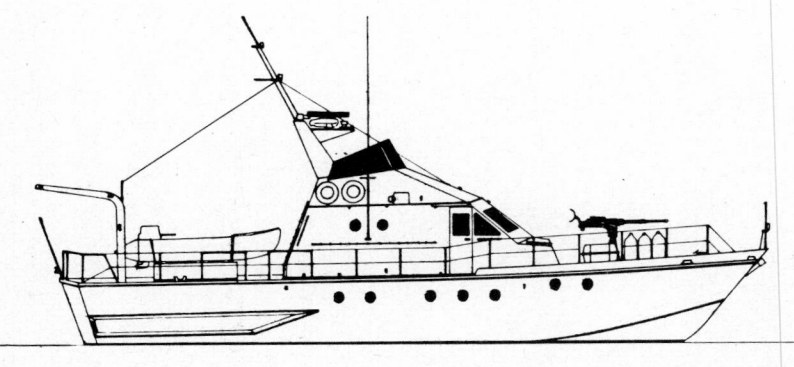

**18 CGA
Coastal Patrol Boat
32 Tons   28 Knots**

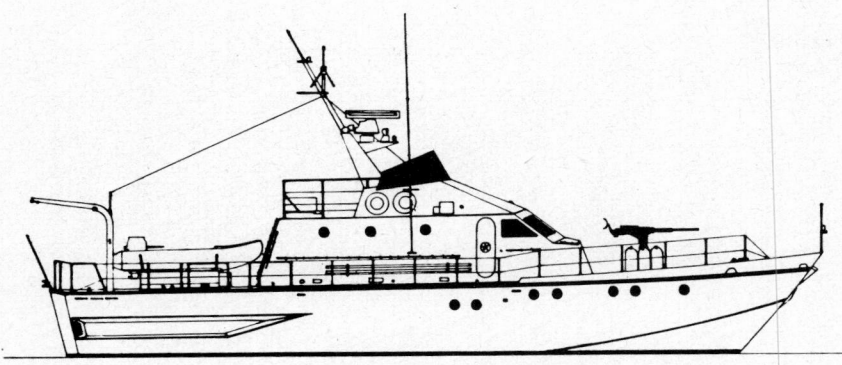

**20 GC
Fast Patrol Boat
40 Tons   35 Knots**

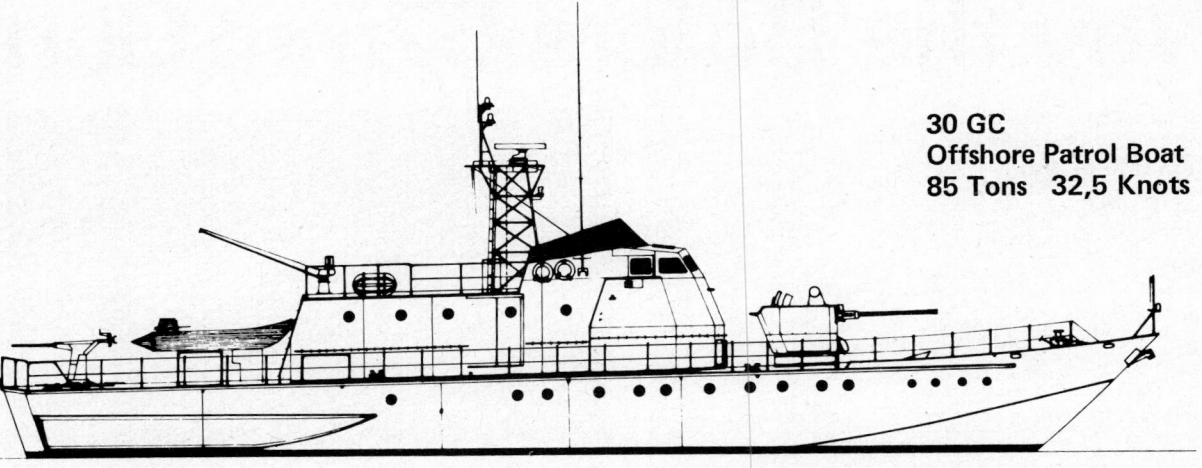

**30 GC
Offshore Patrol Boat
85 Tons   32,5 Knots**

Telegr. BAGLIETTO-VARAZZE   Telex 28214 CANABAG   Tel.(019) 95901-95902-95903

[95]

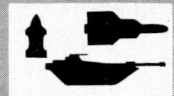

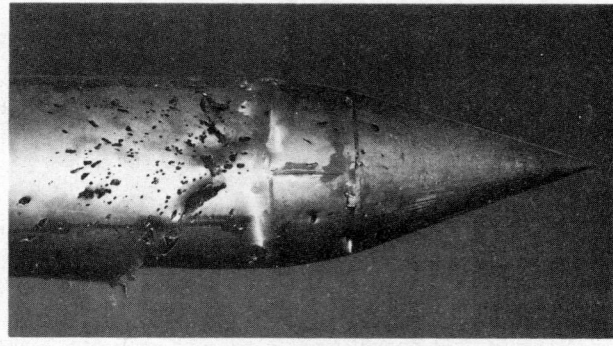

KNOW-HOW

We have decades of experience in research, development and design of all kind of hydrofoil vessels.

We offer standard types of military hydrofoils but also design to meet your specific needs.

We assist you in your local construction under the terms of technical assistance and license agreements.

We supply not only detailed construction drawings and specifications but also our experienced team of production engineers.

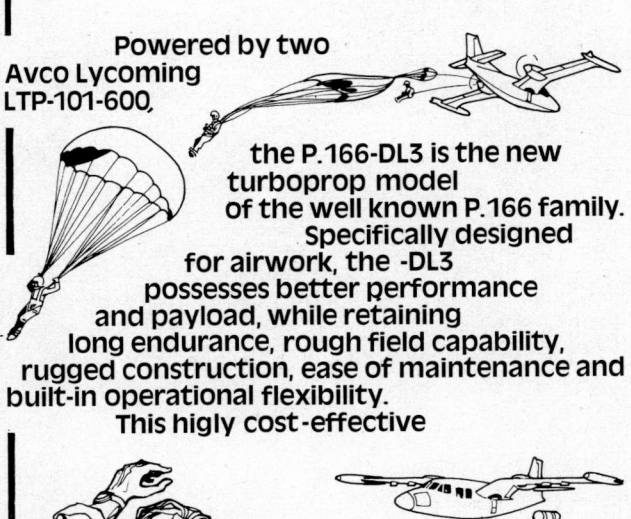

P. 166-DL3 : the versatile round-the-clock performer

Powered by two Avco Lycoming LTP-101-600, the P. 166-DL3 is the new turboprop model of the well known P.166 family. Specifically designed for airwork, the -DL3 possesses better performance and payload, while retaining long endurance, rough field capability, rugged construction, ease of maintenance and built-in operational flexibility. This higly cost-effective and reliable aircraft is an ideal tool for a variety of military and commercial missions. Maritime patrol SAR, light tactical transport, air command post, paratroop-dropping and ambulance

are just a few of the various tasks which have been field-proven by the P.166 family and which will be even better performed by this new turboprop.

 RINALDO PIAGGIO
Via Brigata Bisagno 14 - Genova - Italy - Telex 27695

Bendix Provides ASW Capability!

For more than 20 years Bendix has been a leader in providing the United States and Allied Navies with airborne ASW capability. We don't plan to give up that leadership! Since 1955 Bendix has continually upgraded the AN/AQS-13B series of helicopter dipping sonars. Performance and reliability have increased; size and weight decreased. Our systems are now being flown by twelve nations throughout the world. Today these systems feature the latest in hybrid microcircuit technology and digital processing techniques. Tomorrow an on-going program promises significant increases in range and area search rate. With all this experience to draw upon, we are confident we can increase the effectiveness of your ASW operations.

For further information, please contact: R.E. Garrison, Director of Aerospace Marketing, The Bendix Corporation, International Marketing Operations, 1633 Broadway, New York, New York 10019, U.S.A.

Bendix

RADAR SYSTEMS FOR SHIPS, HELICOPTERS AND GROUND STATIONS - RADARS FOR NAVIGATION AND AIR-NAVAL SEARCH - DISPLAYS - MISSILE ASSIGNMENT CONSOLLES - HOMING RADARS - SIGNAL PROCESSING AND DATA HANDLING TECHNIQUES.

SMA
SEGNALAMENTO MARITTIMO ED AEREO

P.O. BOX 200 - FIRENZE (ITALIA) - TELEPHONE: 705651 - TELEX: SMARADAR 57622 - CABLE: SMA FIRENZE

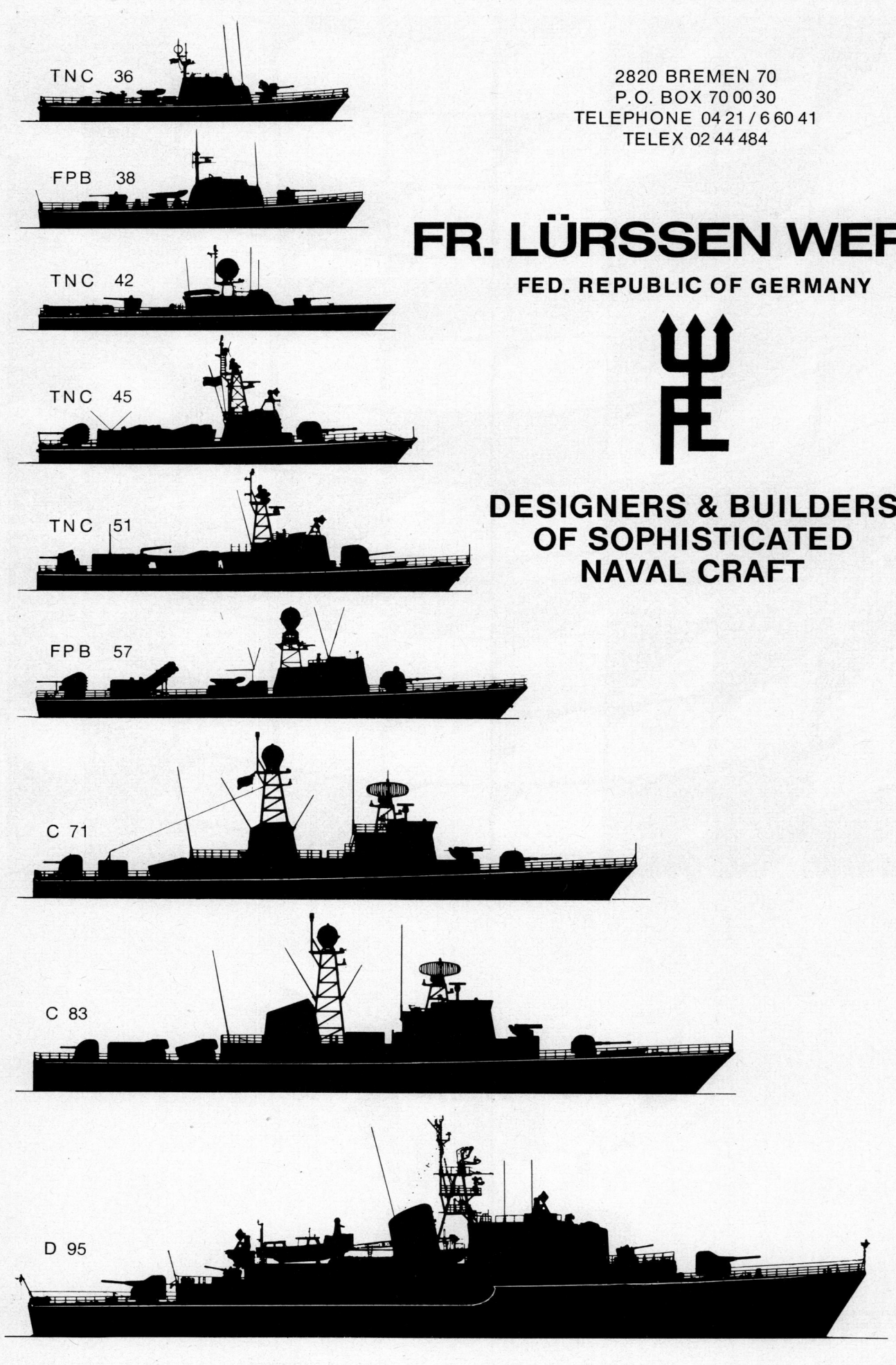

TNC 36

FPB 38

TNC 42

TNC 45

TNC 51

FPB 57

C 71

C 83

D 95

2820 BREMEN 70
P.O. BOX 70 00 30
TELEPHONE 04 21 / 6 60 41
TELEX 02 44 484

FR. LÜRSSEN WERFT

FED. REPUBLIC OF GERMANY

DESIGNERS & BUILDERS
OF SOPHISTICATED
NAVAL CRAFT

Judge us by the company we keep!

Some of the biggest names place their trust in Whipp & Bourne Switchgear—organisations like British Rail, The Central Electricity Generating Board, the Ministry of Defence, the British Steel Corporation; international companies like Shell, Mobil, Rio Tinto Zinc, Selection Trust. They know for heavy situations where reliability is essential, the reputation of Whipp & Bourne stands supreme. Rigorously tested to the most exacting standards, Whipp & Bourne equipment is specified with absolute confidence for applications in power, chemicals, steel, oil, traction, water, shipping and indeed throughout the whole of industry.

Write for technical literature:-
Switchgear · Switchboards · Switches · Circuit Breakers

Whipp & Bourne (1975) ltd

Castleton, Rochdale, England. Tel: Rochdale 32051 (10 lines)
Telex: 63442 (Whipborn, Casltn.)
Member of Babcock & Wilcox Ltd. (Electrical Group).

CANTIERE NAVALTECNICA S.p.A.

MILITARY HYDROFOILS

MAFIUS 600

– A NEW WORD IN THE FIELDS OF FAST LIGHT MILITARY SHIPS

– THE RIGHT HIGH-SPEED WARSHIP FOR TODAY'S AND TOMORROW'S NEEDS

CANTIERE NAVALTECNICA S.p.A.
22, Via S. Ranieri - 98100 MESSINA (ITALY) - Phone (090) 774862

are the right answer to
the new trends of the world's navies
as regards coast defence and attack

MAFIUS 600

– EQUIPPED WITH A HELICOPTER AND PARTICULARLY QUALIFIED

FOR MISSILE ATTACK, PATROLLING, LONG RANGE MISSIONS, ASW,

RECONNAISSANCE AND OTHER TASKS.

Cable: NAVALTECNICA MESSINA - Telex: 98030 RODRIKEZ

COUNTDOWN FOR TOMORROW

The U.S. Navy's SES-100B has proved the concept of launching a missile at high speed at sea, a technological breakthrough for tomorrow's Navy.

While traveling at 60 knots on a cushion of air over the Gulf of Mexico in April, the 100-ton Surface Effect Ship, developed by Bell Aerospace Textron, successfully launched a medium range guided missile. The missile hit its target positioned 5 nautical miles away, marking the first time an operational weapon was fired from an advanced high-speed marine vehicle and the first vertical launching from any Navy ship.

After the SES-100B set a world speed standard in 1975 (82.3 knots), the world has come to expect more "firsts" from this versatile U.S. Navy craft. And well they should. Because Bell Aerospace Textron is first in Air Cushion Vehicle and Surface Effect Ship technology.

Bell Aerospace TEXTRON
Division of Textron Inc.

New Orleans, Louisiana 70189 U.S.A.

Buffalo, New York 14240 U.S.A.

For all naval vessels and weapon-systems, new constructions, modernization, engineering, technical assistance, training

Shareholders :

French Navy
Dubigeon-Normandie
Constructions Mécaniques de Normandie
Société Française de Constructions Navales
Chantiers Navals de l'Estérel
Thomson-CSF
Creusot-Loire
Société Nationale Industrielle Aérospatiale
Compagnie Industrielle des Télécommunications CIT-Alcatel
Compagnie de Signaux et d'Entreprises Electriques
Electronique Marcel Dassault

sofrexan

SOCIETE FRANÇAISE D'EXPORTATION DE MATERIELS NAVALS MILITAIRES
30, rue d'Astorg, F - 75008 Paris, Tél.°265.47.47 / 265.12.11, Telex 640670 F

NAVAL SYSTEMS DIVISION

SELENIA
INDUSTRIE ELETTRONICHE ASSOCI
S.

via Tiburtina km 12,400
00131 ROMA (Italy)

ELETTRONICA SAN GIORGIO
ELSAG
S.

via Hermada, 6
16154 GENOVA-SESTRI (Italy)

SEARCH RADARS	RAN 3L	early warning radar for cruisers, destroyers and large frigates.
	RAN 10S	combined air and surface surveillance coded radar for medium tonnage warships.
	RAN 11 L/X	Dual purpose, dual frequency integrated radar system for air and surface search for application on small warships, or, as complementary sensor, on large vessels.
COAST SURVEILLANCE RADARS	RAT 8S	Transportable radars for coastal surveillance.
	RAT 10S	Long range, high resolution radar for fixed installations.
TRACKING RADARS	ORION SERIES	Multirole acquisition and tracking radars for missile and gun fire control.
WEAPON CONTROL SYSTEMS	NA10 mod. 2	fire control system for small and medium calibre guns and S/A missiles (Albatros system) used on frigates, destroyers and cruisers.
	NA10 mod. 3	fire control system for light naval vessels (hydrofoil and fast patrol boats).
	ALBATROS SYSTEM	combined missile and gun weapon system to counter the air threat both in the self-defence and mutual defence roles, and to perform conventional gunfire actions.
	DARDO SYSTEM	for short range defence.
	SCLAR	multi-role rockets launching system.
	ANTISUBMARINE SYSTEM	for A/S bomb and torpedo launching control.
DATA HANDLING	IPN10 SERIES	Computer assisted display systems for command and control functions.
INTEGRATED SHIPBORNE SYSTEMS		Design and Engineering activities for Combat system integration.

SHIPS EQUIPPED WITH SYSTEMS SUPPLIED BY NAVAL SYSTEMS DIVISION

VITTORIO VENETO

AUDACE class

ANDREA DORIA class

IMPETUOSO class

HAMBURG class

IMPAVIDO class

NITEROI class

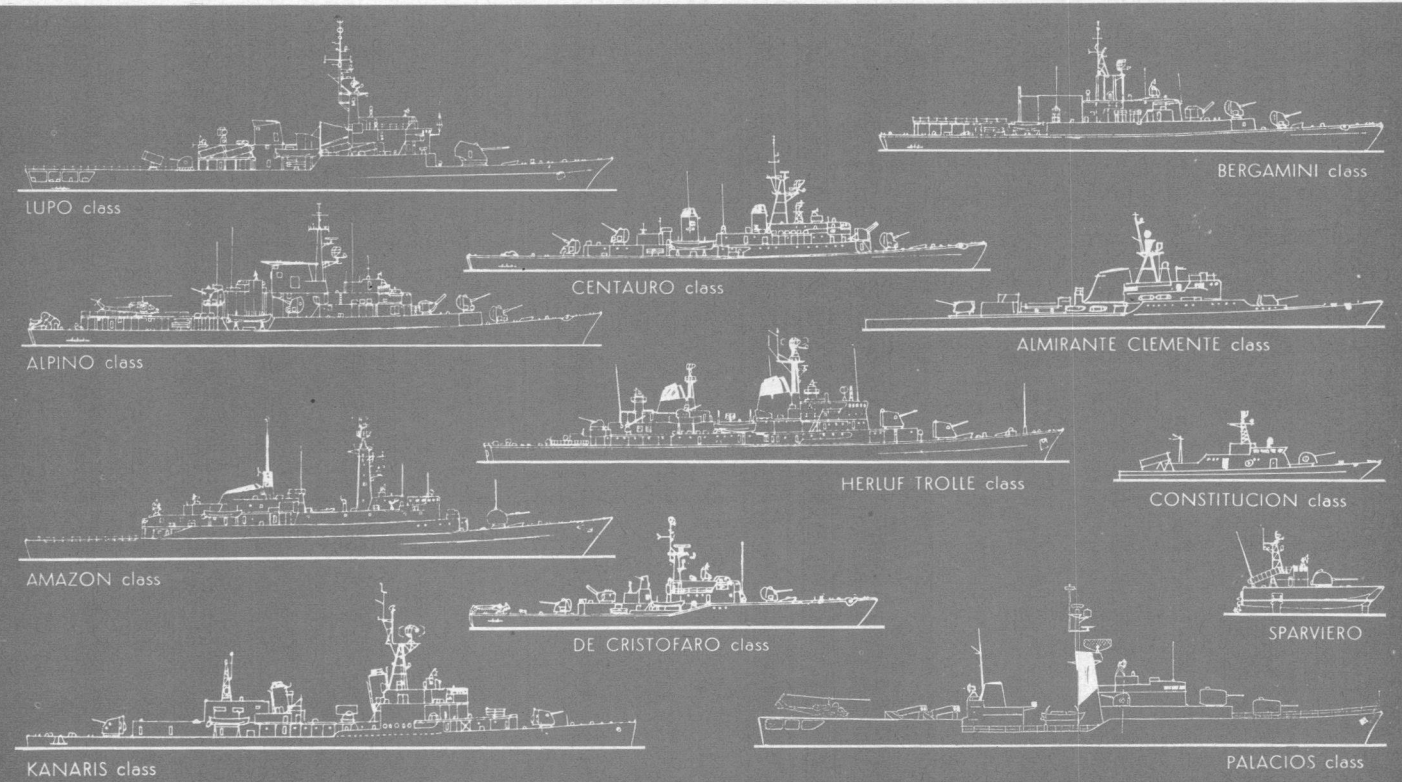

LUPO class

ALPINO class

AMAZON class

KANARIS class

CENTAURO class

HERLUF TROLLE class

DE CRISTOFARO class

BERGAMINI class

ALMIRANTE CLEMENTE class

CONSTITUCION class

SPARVIERO

PALACIOS class

USS Nimitz, at 91 400 tons the largest warship ever built

1976, United States Navy

JANE'S
FIGHTING SHIPS

FOUNDED IN 1897 BY FRED T. JANE

EDITED BY
CAPTAIN JOHN E. MOORE RN, FRGS

1976-77

I.S.B.N. 0 531 03261 2
L. of C. Cat No. 75-15172

JANE'S YEARBOOKS

FRANKLIN WATTS INC.
NEW YORK

ITALIAN NAVAL EXHIBITION

GENOA
20-26 September 1976

SHIPBUILDING
PROPULSION SYSTEMS
ELECTRICAL AND AUXILIARY ENGINES
WEAPON SYSTEMS AND AMMUNITION
ELECTRONICS
HELICOPTERS FOR NAVAL USES
SHIPBORNE EQUIPMENT FOR NAVAL DEFENCE

ENQUIRIES TO:

FIERA INTERNAZIONALE DI GENOVA - CONSORNAUTICA

16100 GENOVA - ITALY
PIAZZALE J. F. KENNEDY 1
PHONE: (010) 589371
TELEX: 28248 CONAUTIC

JANE'S FIGHTING SHIPS 1976-77

EDITED BY

CAPTAIN JOHN E. MOORE

The sections on United States of America, Philippines, Republic of Korea,
and Taiwan were edited and compiled by:

NORMAN POLMAR

CONTENTS

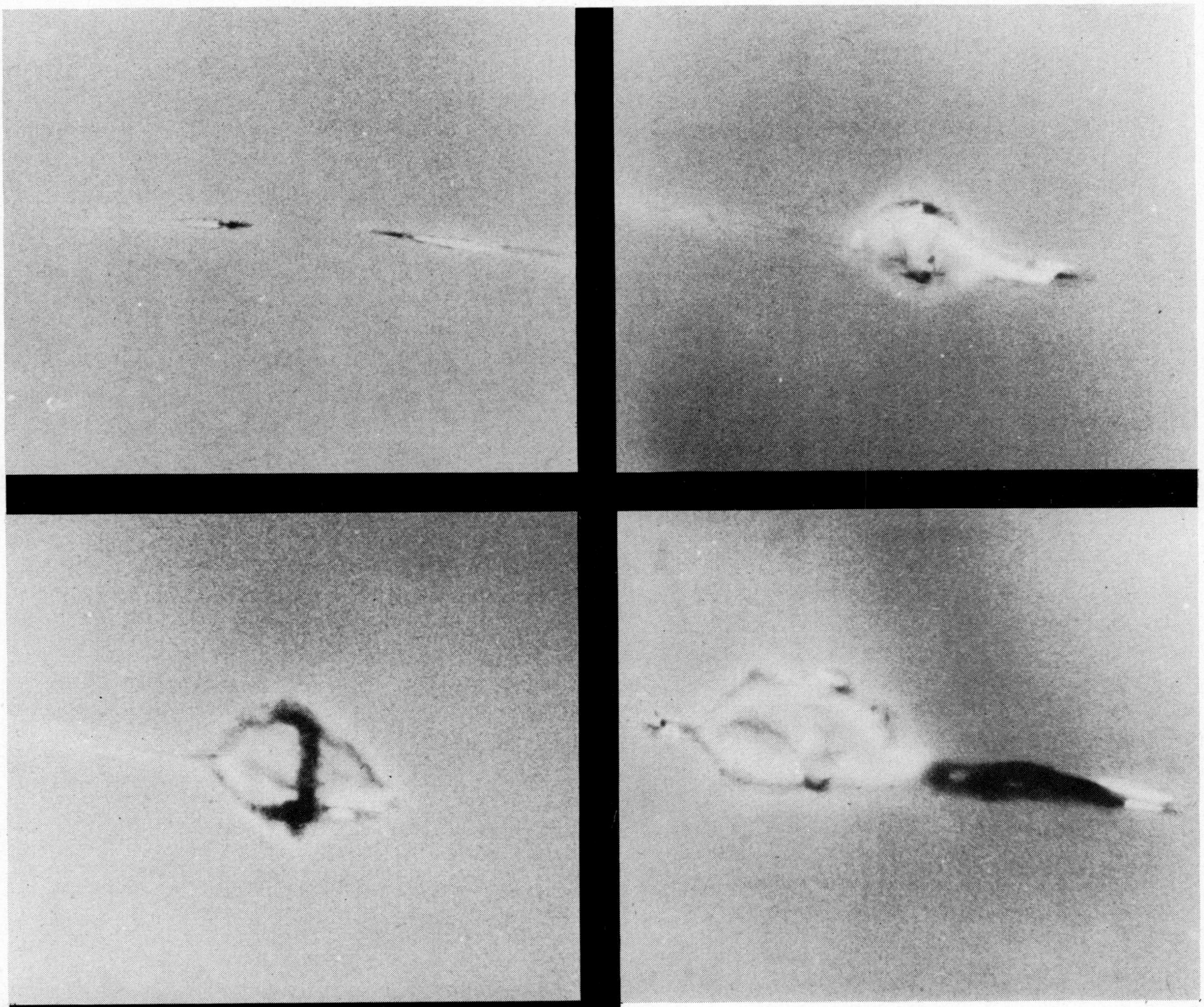

FOREWORD

The twelve months since the publication of the last edition of JANE'S FIGHTING SHIPS have been notable for a number of items of interest and importance both in the international scene and the more narrow subjects covered by this book.

INTERNATIONAL RELATIONS

From the international point of view the Conference on Security and Co-operation in Europe which concluded at Helsinki on 1st August 1975 could have been the starting point of a great improvement in international relations. Amidst the customary high-sounding expressions of principle and intent were those which spoke of the participating states refraining from the threat or use of force, acknowledged the need to respect the equal rights of peoples and their right to self determination, the fact that it was in the interest of all the signatories to aim at a lessening of military confrontation and the promotion of disarmament as well as the early publication of national budgets. Although many have waited with dwindling hope for some evidence of moves which might suggest that these principles were honestly and sincerely held little has been seen to give encouragement. The new methods of Soviet involvement in Angola, which is admittedly outside the boundaries of the participating states, and the announcement by the late Marshal Grechko in January of the necessity for the increase of Soviet armed forces are only two of the pointers to the future. We shall examine later the effects of current planning on Soviet naval force levels at a time when the situation of NATO is an unhappy one. While the naval forces of Britain and Iceland have been in confrontation over a fishery dispute and the future political alignment of Italy is in doubt, while Greece has withdrawn from the military alliance and with the problems arising between Turkey and the USA, not to mention the confusion that has existed for some time in Portugal, it is clear that this grouping of democratic states lacks the cohesion and the willpower of those of the Warsaw Pact. All these facts are indications of future trends. For the present the continuing terrorism, frequently nurtured from without, which threatens so many countries makes us very conscious that the words of Winston Churchill in the period of the Nazi tyranny are equally applicable to our own situation—"We are sunk in a barbarism that is all the deeper because it is tolerated by moral lethargy and covered with a veneer of scientific convenience".

NAVAL AFFAIRS

From the more parochial aspect of naval affairs there are continuing indications of a steady increase not only in the size of forces throughout the world but also in their capability. Amongst the larger navies the building programmes continue to advance although overall numbers are being reduced in certain categories as large batches of ships become over age. However, the improvement in missile capability now gives a single ship a capacity for destruction only equalled in the past by great fleets and squadrons of aircraft. The Western navies have been replacing a number of their ships by newer vessels which in all cases far outweigh the cost of their predecessors. In the USA certain ships now under construction are costing as much as a whole squadron of earlier classes. The Soviet naval building programme continues at a steady rate although there is little sign as yet of any important change in design pattern from that reported last year. However, amongst the smaller navies there has been considerable reinforcement and the proliferation of the comparatively small fast attack craft armed with missiles must inevitably change the balance of power in many important areas. The Chinese Navy continues to increase in numbers and remains primarily oriented towards defence of the long coastline of the People's Republic.

INCREASE IN MERCHANT FLEETS

One other point which comes clearly from the figures published in this book is the steady increase in numbers in the world's mercantile fleets in which the most numerous are those of Japan (9,932) and the USSR (7,652). The overall increase throughout the world is almost 10 per cent over last year's figure and double that of ten years ago. Of the thirty largest fleets today only two have shown a slight reduction in the last year and one of these is a flag of convenience. The doubling of the size of the world's fleets is in many cases reflected in the export/import trade of the nations concerned. For instance, that of the USA has very nearly doubled itself in the last ten years and in monetary terms is little short of treble the 1965 figures. These facts demonstrate a reliance on sea communications which notably increases the vulnerability of the trading countries.

The dependence of the USA on sea-borne trade is typical of the state of most of the major powers. The People's Republic of China now has trading links with one hundred and twenty-two countries, Japan relies almost entirely on imports for her raw materials while the condition of the European members of NATO, as well as of the non-aligned states of Europe, would deteriorate rapidly were their sea-lanes cut. The USSR, on the other hand, is not reliant on the import of foreign raw materials but depends in a large measure and in a very competitive field on cut-price freight for the support of her national hard currency balance. In addition she is dependent on the Western nations and other countries of the non-Communist area for a great deal of her heavy machinery and technical imports and also, as we have seen during the last two disastrous harvests, for a considerable quantity of her food. This is also true of the Soviet fishing fleet which provides vast amounts of protein food and fishmeal for agriculture.

SAFETY OF SEA ROUTES

It is therefore hardly surprising that the sea routes of the world are becoming more and more congested. There are some who are only too prepared to accept the situation and reject the argument of vulnerability. It is here that the age-old lessons of seapower must once again be put forward. Those who have the capacity to use those sea routes in safety will survive. Those who have the capacity to interrupt this international intercourse will remain, as always in the past, in a position to achieve their ends. The argument that war is unthinkable in this nuclear age applies less to the sea than to any other area. It must be remembered that the high seas are neutral ground, and that without any overt conflict, without the firing of any guns or missiles or torpedoes, great areas of the oceans can be declared dangerous: harassment may occur, mined areas declared or exercises conducted which can adversely affect the flow of shipping. Delays will result in increased prices; interference in increased insurance premiums. With 98 per cent of the bulk of the world's trade being carried in ships it needs little emphasis to show the disastrous effects of any or all of these acts, none of which reaches the definition of war. To conduct trade with security a country needs the manifest capability to defend its own, whether that be shipping lanes, fishing areas, its oil rigs or the coastal traffic upon which so much depends in so many areas.

AREAS OF INFLUENCE

The world has temporarily resolved itself into certain areas of influence: the NATO area, the Soviet dominated Communist bloc, China, Japan and the various geographical areas such as South East Asia, the Persian Gulf, Australasia, the Indian Ocean and both coasts of South America. In reviewing the state of the world's fighting ships today it is convenient to consider these and their problems.

NATO'S DEPENDENCE ON THE SEA

As has already been said NATO is in an unhappy state. This is no place to consider the political problems which confront the leaders of the various nations comprising the alliance. Today their reliance on ocean trade is evidenced by the fact that in the North Atlantic and Mediterranean areas at any one time there are just over four thousand merchant ships at sea plying between their ports, in addition to some three thousand within those ports. Oil comes to these nations in NATO tankers of which two hundred are daily at sea in the Indian Ocean. Of the British Merchant Navy over a quarter of its ships is east of the Suez at any one time. It is therefore totally illogical to apply geographical boundaries to the naval areas of concern to this alliance. That the southern boundary should be set at the Tropic of Cancer in the North Atlantic makes no sense when the above facts are considered.

You sometimes have to look beneath the surface to see our achievements.

STC Hydrospace Division has designed, developed and produced many types of cable and associated equipment for marine defence systems all over the world and is a major supplier to the British Ministry of Defence.

ELECTRICAL AND ELECTRO-MECHANICAL CABLES for:
Helicopter dipping and variable depth sonars
Sonobuoys and torpedoes
Towing and diving
Surveillance and tracking
Minesweeping-acoustic and magnetic
Submersibles and seafloor vehicles
Fixed underwater installations
Buoyant and neutrally buoyant systems

ELECTRICAL GLANDS AND PENETRATORS for:
Submarines and submersibles
Diving units
Underwater equipment housings
ELECTRICAL CONNECTORS for underwater connection and disconnection of low power and communications circuits.

SHIPBOARD CABLE HANDLING SYSTEMS AND RELATED EQUIPMENT for:
Towing and diving
Seafloor cable installation, including trans-oceanic systems
Oceanography and deep sea coring.

Look into STC for a proper *under*standing of what goes on below.
Standard Telephones and Cables Ltd.,
Hydrospace Division, Dept: J4,
Christchurch Way, Greenwich, London SE10 0AG.
Telephone: 01-858 3291. Telex: 23687

Standard Telephones and Cables Limited
A British Company of ITT

STANDARDISATION

It is now twenty-seven years since the Treaty inaugurating the North Atlantic Treaty Organisation came into force. In that time many committees have considered the problems of standardisation within the forces of NATO and yet today we see little advance in this respect. Particularly at a time when economic problems have caused the limitation of defence budgets the prevailing lack of standardisation is resulting in continued and gross waste. Several different designs of ship destined for the same purpose, a plenitude of various radars, missiles of many designs, the requirement for different types of fuel and spares, the need for some thirty different types of ammunition, and a regrettable lack of uniformity in doctrine and frequencies has resulted in an increasingly difficult task for the staffs required to plan co-ordinated operations and for those who provide the support for the fleets.

However, this situation is not surprising when one reflects on the national differences of opinion over the requirement for seapower and, when this is agreed, the methods by which it should be provided. During the last year there have been endless and vitriolic debates in the USA over what is required in her navy today. At a time when many politicians choose to view détente as a new method of achieving world peace instead of the prolongation of Khruschev's policy of peaceful co-existence leading to eventual Communist overlordship, this energetic debate causes little surprise. Allied with the generalities of the situation are the continued efforts of the "nuclear propulsion" faction whose proposed policies would result in the investment of great sums of money in a comparatively few nuclear-fuelled ships, while others seek to provide greater numbers for more extensive surveillance and protection of the areas of greatest concern to the USA. "Deterrence" is frequently a matter of presence and since presence requires sufficient numbers of ships this requirement means a very carefully computed balance between cost and efficiency. No matter how potent a ship is, it can never be in more than one geographical position at one time. It is at this point, however, that the situation is complicated by Congressional legislation dictating the use of nuclear propulsion for all new major combatants designed for strike forces.

UNITED STATES NAVY

The current operational strength of the US Navy includes thirteen aircraft carriers of which two are nuclear propelled and three of World War II design. The fourteenth carrier is used for training. Two more nuclear propelled carriers will come into active service over the next five years. In the wake of the debate which has been under way for so long alternative plans have been drawn up for smaller ships which could operate high performance aircraft as well as being nuclear powered. None of these can be considered particularly small, ranging from 65,000 tons full load to 85,000 tons and costing an estimated 1979 price between $2·1 billion and $2·25 billion. There is also a plan to supplement these very expensive ships with what are called VSTOL support ships (VSS) which would operate fixed-wing VTOL aircraft and helicopters. The need for this re-design has come as a result of the Congress turning down the Navy's plan for the sea control ship of 14,000 tons. The new design, which it is not planned to fund for another four years, varies between ships of 22,000 tons and 33,000 tons. In these cases their propulsion would be either by gas turbines or steam turbines.

In other categories of surface-ships the urge to "go big" appears again. Enough has already been said and written about the "Spruance" class—this year details of the proposed eight nuclear powered strike-cruisers are available, ships whose primary duty would be the protection of nuclear aircraft-carriers. Of some 17,000 tons, equipped with the AEGIS system and both surface-to-air and surface-to-surface missiles, carrying at least two and possibly six aircraft (helicopters, or perhaps VTOL) and with a speed of 28-30 knots, the official estimate of their cost reaches as high as $1·6 billion. These must be the most expensive screening ships ever envisaged and, if the cost increases in the same proportion as has that of the "Virginia" class of nuclear-powered cruisers, look set to be priced out of the programme. This cancellation would also seem to be encouraged by the development of anti-ship weapons in other navies and the USN's need to provide more numerous classes of ships for the manifold duties short of general war which are inherent in a fleet with world-wide responsibilities.

At the same time the "DDG47" class is proposed for the 1977 programme, the aim being to support the strike-cruisers in "the protection of high value forces (including carriers)" as the Secretary of Defense described it. These 9,000-ton ships would carry the same AEGIS system as the cruisers, linked to Standard surface-to-air launchers, surface-to-surface missiles, two helicopters and would be propelled by gas turbines. The lead ship cost requested is $858,500,000—although this could be less in later ships it is still much more than the $125,000,000 (1973 values) for the originally planned missile-armed variant of the "Spruance" class.

Size and cost increases apply also to the submarine fleet. The "Trident" class of ballistic-missile submarines, of which ten are currently planned, is designed for a dived displacement of 18,700 tons. This vast size is dictated by the requirement to fit twenty-four missile-tubes for the eventual 6,000 mile Trident SLBMs. This large hull has brought a need for greater power, a large reactor to provide it and, finally, an even bigger hull to take the reactor. Nevertheless the $791,500,000 request for the fifth in the class is still less than the first "DDG47" class estimate, whilst the estimated cost for the three submarines of the "Los Angeles" class of nuclear attack boats which are proposed for the 1977 programme is $320,000,000 per hull. These are 6,900 tons dived with, it is believed, a modified surface-ship reactor—perhaps indicating an omission in the design process and also, possibly, explaining the fact that the first of the class is two years behind schedule.

Having emphasised the cost of these increasingly large ships and submarines it is perhaps comforting to end this very brief review of the USN with two most important developments—the frigates of the "Oliver Hazard Perry" class and the trials of the new cruise-missile. The first of these carries both surface-to-air and surface-to-surface missiles, two helicopters and a gun armament on a 3,600-ton hull propelled by gas turbines. Although costs have risen steeply to $143 million for the 1977 programme it will be possible to provide a considerable number of these ships for the multiplicity of tasks such as surveillance, escort and patrol which make up such a large proportion of any navy's tasks.

Whilst discussions on SALT II creep on their interminable way the fact that a US cruise-missile with long range and a low altitude capability has now been given initial tests is of the greatest importance. This could be one of the most significant additions to the US naval arsenal and a powerful deterrent in future years. How this and all other programmes is handled rests in the political balance and in the long run with the people of the USA. How far the reputed remark of Admiral Yamamoto at the time of Pearl Harbour—"I fear we have awakened a sleeping giant and filled him with a terrible resolve"—would be applicable today is a matter of the greatest importance to the rest of the world.

SOVIET NAVY

A reasonably correct and objective analysis of the Soviet Navy today is very hard to achieve when criticism from that quarter heavily outweighs the facts given to support it. Such an analysis depends on three major factors—the current building programme, the training of those that man the ships and the deployment of the ships themselves. Admittedly there have been a wealth of statements by senior Soviet officers on their views of the proper operations for this fleet but these must be considered in the context of what has in fact happened. Admiral Gorshkov has made it quite clear that he considers the fleet which he commands as an essential element of the political advance of his country. At the same time he recognises that to carry out this duty the fleet must be capable of any form of naval operation and action which may come its way. It has become almost a tradition amongst some people to consider the Soviet Navy as a defensive force for the protection of Mother Russia. However, the armament of the new ships and the introduction of carrier-borne aircraft has suggested an extended outlook beyond that of pure defence. When in the past a country with few overseas financial or colonial interests has embarked on the building of a considerable fleet the true aims of the ships concerned have proved to be not only protection of the homeland and the sea lines of communications which run to it but also aggressive activities designed to support national policy. In the last twenty years the question of defence has also included the

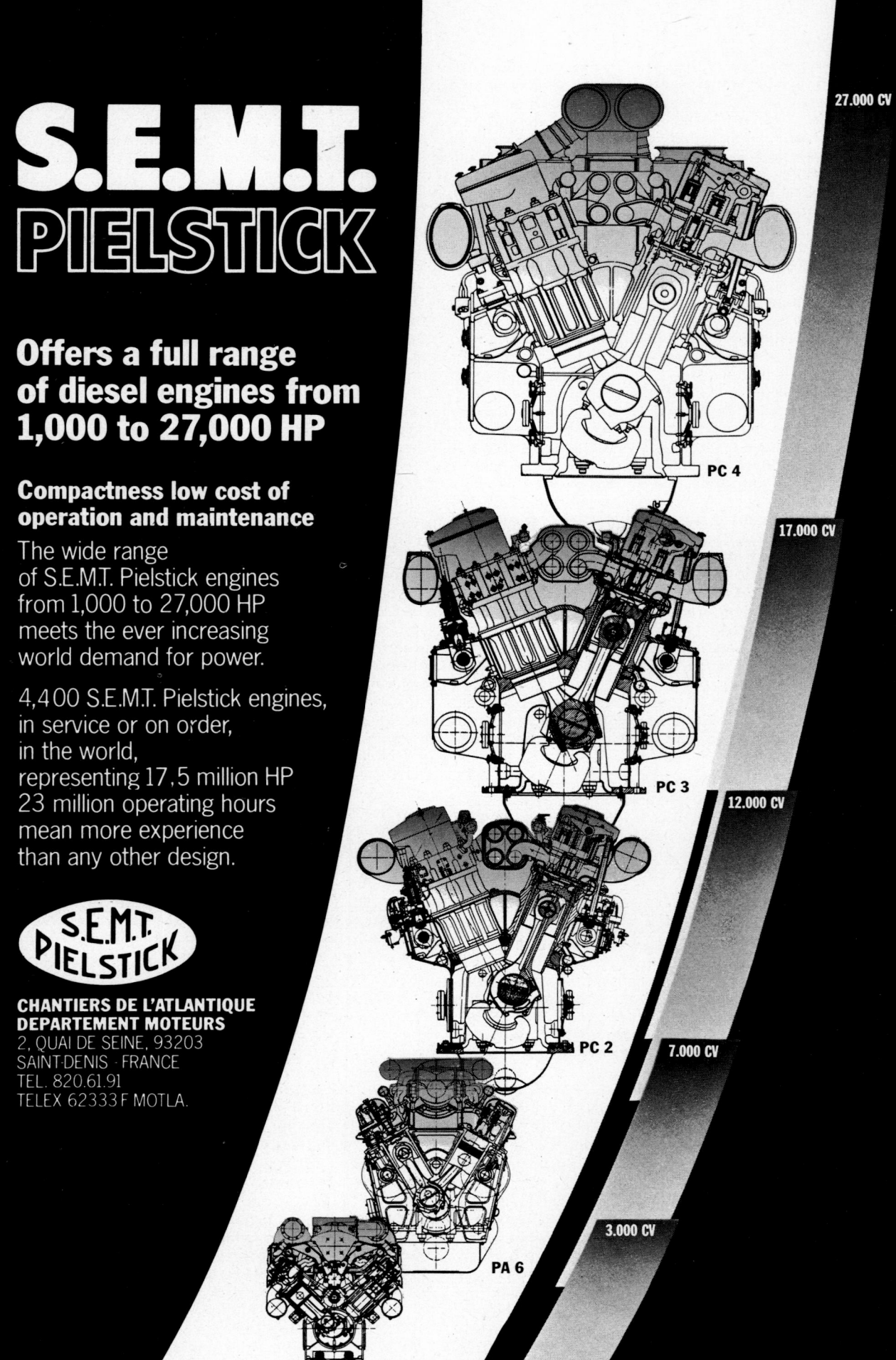

neutralisation of forces armed with strategic nuclear-headed weapons. It is therefore of value to consider the building programme of the Soviet Navy in the light of protection against these weapons, protection of its own coastlines and overseas aggrandisement.

During the last year it has become clear that both observers and politicians remain rooted to the argument of pure numbers. As a result, many false conclusions have been drawn and, in this respect, data can be twisted to meet a multitude of requirements. So far as strength of the fleet is concerned it has become apparent that the Soviet navy has reached a plateau of numbers. What is changing is the capabilities of the ships and submarines involved and, as a result, the operations which they are capable of undertaking. This plateau of numbers is governed by the active production lines in the Soviet shipyards, by the money which is available for shipbuilding and by the number of men who are available to man the fleet. Admittedly in a major crisis the building rates could be accelerated but it would appear that the provision of additional trained manpower is unlikely.

The young sailors who man the Soviet ships enter the navy in two groups of 50,000 to 60,000 each year. After six months training they may expect to spend the rest of their three years of conscript service in the same ship. At the end of this time they either return to their homes or, in a minority of cases, sign on for further service. In this case they become senior ratings of Petty Officer and Chief Petty Officer status at the age of 21—very much earlier than their opposite numbers in the Western navies could expect. As a result a considerable strain must be placed upon the junior officers who receive a five year training, primarily in technical matters. It is probably this concentration on technology which has resulted in the situation which Admiral Gorshkov criticised very strongly in his recent article in *Red Star.* In this he complained primarily of the narrow approach of too many officers in his fleet and also criticised the methods of selection for command. Where there is weakness amongst the officers the rest of the navy must suffer in proportion.

While the consideration of numbers is, as always, a dangerous exercise for the uninformed, the composition of the Soviet fleet is of considerable interest and gives certain clues to its future planned employment. Several classes of surface ships have already reached the end of their theoretical twenty-year hull life although, in a fashion well known in the Soviet Navy, many have been remodelled or reconstructed. These elderly ships include the "Sverdlov", "Kildin", "Kotlin", "Skory", "Riga", "Kola", "SO 1" and "Kronstadt" classes as well as a number of the light forces. Many of these have already been paid off and the main interest here centres on their future replacements. The "Kara" and "Kresta II" cruisers, the "Krivak" destroyers and the "Grisha" and "Nanuchka" corvettes all appear to have provided satisfaction and their construction is continuing. Added to the "Kiev" class aircraft carriers, of which a third and possibly a fourth are now under construction, these will probably provide the main surface force of the Soviet navy in the immediate future. However, with the proven ability of Soviet ship designers to produce new and fascinating concepts it is possible that other variants may be seen within the next few years.

From the submarine point of view there have been certain changes in the production of enlarged types of the "Victor" and "Charlie" classes while the "Delta" and "Delta II" have replaced the "Yankees" as the main ballistic missile carriers. Continuation of a diesel-driven programme with the "Tangos" suggests that the Soviets appreciate the need for such boats which can operate in shallower waters where the larger fleet submarines are inhibited in their use of speed, and which can also provide training facilities.

The continuation of building programmes of support and service forces shows a determination to continue the operations of the fleets away from home bases and this has clearly been reflected in the out-of-area deployments over the last twelve months.

The armament available to these ships and submarines is also a pointer to their employment. When the "Kiev" class will be equipped with VTOL aircraft is still uncertain but with a mixed complement of VTOL and helicopters these ships will provide a central point for independent squadrons. In the event of major hostilities it is possible that the main task of the "Kievs"

would be that given in their Russian type name—anti-submarine cruiser. The label "anti-submarine" appears in the majority of modern Soviet ships of both cruiser and destroyer varieties. This may appear somewhat surprising since the main anti-submarine armament appears to be either comparatively short range rocket launchers (MBUs), even shorter range depth-charge throwers, A/S torpedoes, or helicopters. However, the forward launcher (SUWN-1) in the "Moskvas" is apparently intended for long range A/S weapons and suggests an appreciation of the need for such missiles. The existence of the FRAS 1 launched from the SUWN-1 and SSN-14 weapons provides a means for engaging submarines out to a range of fifteen to twenty miles. In this event it would seem logical that the other larger surface ships would be provided with alternative weapons in what are normally considered as surface-to-surface launchers.

While the submarine remains one of the best detection platforms against other submarines we must look for a means of completing the weapons' system with an adequate long range missile. This, it is believed, is now available in the 25-mile SSN-15, similar in many respects to the US Navy's Subroc. Although further details of this missile are not available it would appear to be a logical advance to be used in the cruise missile and attack submarines. Further conjecture has been advanced that the SSN-13, a ballistic missile with a range of some 350 miles, could be used from the missile-tubes of the "Yankee" class submarines in an A/S role. While it is undoubtedly true that Soviet satellite reconnaissance by conventional and other means is most efficient and the command and control system exercised by Moscow extremely effective, there is insufficient evidence that this missile could be used against any target other than a force of surface ships. In fact even on this aspect the evidence is inconclusive, although the vast sums spent by the USSR on research and development must result in a cautious approach by any country not allied with the Soviet ideology.

With bases or friendly havens in such places as Cuba, North Africa, Guinea, Somalia, and Aden as well as anchorages in many places around the world the overseas deployment of the Soviet navy has continued over the last year. Backed by the activities of their Research and Survey fleet which comprises a very high proportion of the total of such ships in the world and by a meteorological forecasting service of huge proportions, experience of overseas operations is clearly building up at a great rate. That such areas are not basically part of the defence of the Soviet Union suggests, taking into account the unusual operations in Exercise Okean II in 1975, that this deployment is capable of use for other purposes. With the flexibility provided by afloat support and remembering the basic principles of sea-power, such deployments could well affect the maintenance of Western sea lines of communications if not by active hostilities then by the sheer presence of the ships and the introduction of such problems as oceanic danger areas. If the operations and intentions of this great fleet are to be understood by Western operators and politicians, ships and aircraft need to be deployed to observe their activities.

WESTERN NAVIES—GREAT BRITAIN

The question of numbers raises again the problem stated above—that of simple sums, the cost of ships and their deployment. It is in this regard that the composition of Western navies needs close inspection. The US Navy, as we have seen in the past, has already halved the total strength of its fleet by the elimination of out-of-date ships but is building new destroyers and frigates which will go some way to redress this cut. Great Britain's policy has been stated clearly in both the last Defence Review and in the more recent White Paper on Defence: an intention to withdraw the ships of the Royal Navy to an inner area, the Eastern Atlantic. As a result the Ministry of Defence will no longer be able to receive direct information on any activities further afield. The ships themselves are now reaching a standard of cost which prevents a country in difficult financial straits from building sufficient to provide for surveillance, normal operations and exercises and, at the same time, taking account of the unexpected and the unforeseen. Here again the character of future employment must be considered and, as the pattern of new construction is dictated primarily by the amount of money allocated rather than by the needs of the country's defence, this consideration is vital. While any ship built for the Royal Navy must be fully capable of operations in any foreseen

OTO MELARA

OTO MELARA S.p.A. 19100 - La Spezia (Italy) 15, Via Valdilocchi Tel. 504041 - Telex 27368 OTO

OTO Melara was estabilished in 1905 to manufacture guns for the Italian Army and Navy. Since then, except for brief periods immediately following the two world wars, it has continued to be one of the most important suppliers of weapons to the Italian Armed Forces and to more than 30 countries throughout the world.

35 mm OE/OTO TWIN MOUNTING

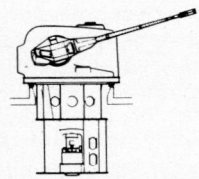

Rate of fire: 1,100 rds/min
Crew: none. Automatic fire: 800 rds
Training: unlimited
Weight (w/out ammo): 4,900 kg
Versions: remote control, local control, integrated F.C.S.
(Private venture OTO Melara-Oerlikon)

OTO 76/62 COMPACT MOUNTING (3-INCH)

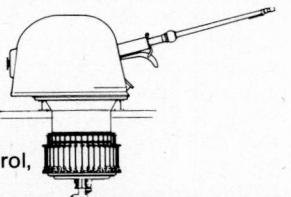

Rate of fire: 85 rds/min
Crew: none. Automatic fire: 80 rds
Training: unlimited
Weight (w/out ammo): 7,350 kg
Versions: remote control, local control, integrated F.C.S.

OTO 127/54 COMPACT MOUNTING (5-INCH)

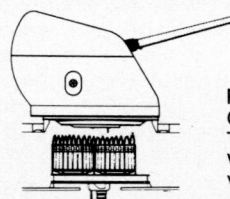

Rate of fire: 45 rds/min
Crew: none. Automatic fire: 66 rds
Training: 350°
Weight (w/out ammo): 32,500 kg
Versions: remote control, local control.

- Navy small and medium caliber automatic rapid fire guns. Remote control systems for naval armament. Anti-ship missiles. Research and development of army and naval ammunition.

- Handling and launching equipment for naval anti-ship and anti-aircraft medium and long range missiles. Army missiles handling and transport equipments.

OTOMAT ANTI-SHIP MISSILE SYSTEM

Speed: 0.9 mach.
Warhead: 250 kg
Effective range: > 80 km
Guidance: - target approach: inertial preset at launch
            - target attack: active homing
Attacking path: dive on target unaffected by sea state conditions.
(Private venture OTO Melara-Engins Matra).

ALBATROS SYSTEM S/A MISSILE LAUNCHER

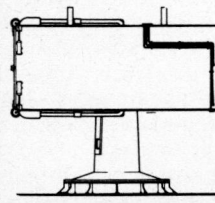

Training: ± 165°
Elevation: −5° to +65°
Weight: (without missiles) 7 tons
Missiles on launcher:
8 (Sparrow III)

105/14 PACK HOWITZER

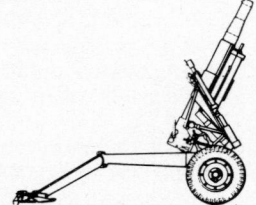

Ammunition: US M1
Shell weight: 14,9 kg
Range: max 10,575 m
Elevation: −5° to + 65°
Traverse: 36°
Total weight: 1,290 kg

INFANTRY ARMOURED FIGHTING VEHICLE

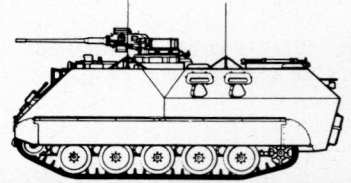

Crew: 9
Weight: 11,560 kg
Road speed: 64 km/h
Range: 550 km
Armament:
12.7 mm machine gun or
20 mm rapid fire gun.

6616 ARMOURED CAR

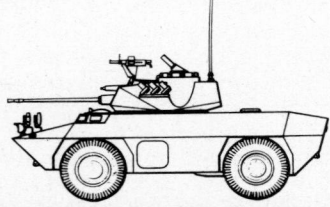

Crew: 3
Weight: 7,400 kg
Road speed: over 95 km/h
Range: 750 km
Armament:
20 mm, 7.62 mm guns;
40 mm grenade launcher.

- Mono-propellant and bi-propellant auxiliary propulsion systems for attitude and orbital control of artificial satellites.

- Tanks production. Track floating personnel carrier vehicles production, and special armed versions. Armament of self-propelled howitzers.

- Army medium caliber artillery. Automatic loading devices for field medium caliber guns and tanks.

LEOPARD MAIN BATTLE TANK

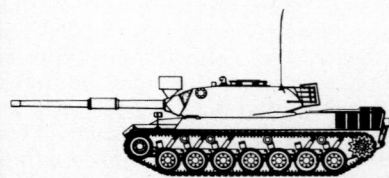

Crew: 4
Weight: 40 tons
Gun: 105/51
Road speed: 65 km/h
Range: 600 km
(Under licence)

SELF PROPELLED HOWITZER - SP70

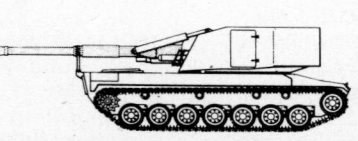

Crew: 5
Weight: 44 tons
Road speed: 67 km/h
Range: 450 km
Armament: 155/39 howitzer automatic loading system;
cal. 7.62 mm gun.

conflict there is, at the same time, a need to consider the construction of less expensive ships for the more mundane operations which occupy so much of a navy's attention in what is predominantly a peacetime setting.

The outbreak of a major war appears to be something which both the Soviet Communists and Western countries wish to avoid—the alternative of harassment and actions short of war requires a widespread presence which can be achieved only by the use of imaginative concepts which will, in the long run, provide more ships for the same budget. An instance of this is the problem raised by the need to protect not only oil-rigs but also the 200-mile Exclusive Economic Zone and the expanded fishery limits which, despite the failure so far to reach agreement at the Law of the Sea Conference, are being adopted with increasing rapidity throughout the world. This need has brought the realisation that the Royal Navy is inadequately equipped for such a task—the Type 14 frigates and considerable numbers of coastal minesweepers being paid off with nothing to replace them. The surface ship building programme, with one or two minor and unsatisfactory exceptions, is devoted to large, complex and expensive destroyers and frigates. Very little money has been made available to provide the ships needed to protect one of Great Britain's most valuable assets against terrorism, damage or destruction. The result has been the "Island" class offshore patrol vessel of a trawler design, presumably to save drawing-office effort, which has a speed inadequate to cope with a high proportion of foreign trawlers, is denied the helicopter needed for swift reaction and costs more than a fully-equipped freezer-trawler. The five ships of this class, backed in inshore waters by the "Bird" class of large patrol craft which has been years in production at a cost which is apparently too horrific to be revealed, will be all that bear the brunt of such operations. Admittedly the main force of surface-ships will be available as support in much the same way as has recently been seen off Iceland when some fifteen of NATO's category "A" ships were damaged, some seriously, at a cost which must eventually reach over the million pound mark. To have to send in the "heavy mob" when acceptance of at least one of the highly efficient commercial designs would have provided the force needed is surely an indication of inadequate provision.

At a time when the need for an abundance of helicopters is realised as clearly in the Royal Navy as elsewhere, and now that the British Government has tardily accepted the need for the Harrier VTOL aircraft at sea, the cost of achieving this end has doubled. Whereas £60 million was mentioned as the original estimate for the first "through-deck-cruiser" the order for the second of the "Invincible" class has been quoted as £120 million. With delays resulting from variations in design as well as from labour and sub-contracting problems this figure may turn out to be a minimum first-estimate. If the third ship is eventually ordered it will be interesting to compare unit cost against such ingenious alternatives as the Vosper Thornycroft "Harrier-carrier" and the conversion of mercantile designs for similar purposes.

SCANDINAVIA AND WEST GERMANY

Financial stringencies have affected nearly all the Western states. Norway, although possessing one of the world's largest merchant fleets, provides only a local defence force consisting of submarines, fast attack craft and mine warfare forces. Denmark possesses a considerable merchant navy and although her parliament has called a halt to party bickering on defence matters, naval plans are still restrained by the budget. The fleet is similarly constituted to that of Norway and is capable of operations only within her coastal waters.

West Germany, with a healthier economy than many countries is still concentrating on the defence of the Baltic and the North Sea. She is carrying out a replacement and modernisation programme which is aimed at the further improvement of quality without reduction in overall numbers. Eighteen new Type 206 submarines have brought this force to a total of twenty-four. Thirty fast attack craft (missile) will have entered service by the end of 1976, with ten missile hydrofoils apparently still planned for commissioning by the end of 1980.

The "Hamburg" class destroyers will have completed their modernisation with new missiles, sonar and radar by the end of 1976 and the new Type 122 frigates are planned to replace the "Köln" class. Modernisation is also taking place in the mine warfare forces where twelve minehunter conversions are planned to operate the French PAP system.

The Fleet Air Arm has a new stand-off night attack capability with Kormoran missiles and will so arm the 100 MRCAs which are planned to replace their F104Gs. Further replacements envisaged are those of the Breguet Atlantics by S3A Vikings.

All in all this seems a well-balanced navy with its fleet designed to fulfil the policies of its Government. There is little fat but much sinew.

NETHERLANDS AND STANDARDISATION

Cuts in defence expenditure have been proposed in the Netherlands but the overall programme will still provide the main bulk of the programme in which the "Tromp" class destroyers and the "Kortenaer" class frigates figure. With a sideways look to Belgium's programme of "E71" frigates, the "Lupos" in Italy and the "Berk" class in Turkey one cannot help feeling that this is a major sphere of design where NATO has once again failed to achieve any form of standardisation. In the last few years the countries of the Alliance have produced or are planning to produce four classes of destroyers and eleven classes of frigates. In contrast to this unco-ordinated proliferation the discovery that Belgium, France and the Netherlands have set up a combined planning centre in Paris to provide for the replacement programme of minehunters needed in all three countries comes as something of a surprise.

FRANCE

France has recently been subjected to a series of political tirades over the form her defence strategy is to take but this not unusual situation has made no impact on a naval building programme which has been affected more by financial problems than by fundamental changes in thought. With *De Grasse* and the three "Georges-Leygues" class as the main bulk of the larger surface ships programme, the fourteen "A69" avisos are unlikely to be joined by the "A70" class for some time. The submarine programme of three new ballistic-missile boats and four "Agosta" class will soon be strengthened by the first nuclear attack submarine (SNA) on the stocks. With this plan unchanged, the number of fast attack craft appears to have been reduced. The major material weakness of the French Navy, afloat support, is however being steadily rectified. With the solution of that problem and provided the difficulties over manpower are satisfactorily resolved there is every chance of this becoming the main fleet of Western Europe.

THE MEDITERRANEAN

In an Italy beset by financial and political problems a positive step towards stabilisation of the naval programme was taken in 1975 with the passing of the *Legge Navale*. This law, whose implementation presumably depends on future political alignments, allows for a considerable building programme (listed in the summary following) which is well-balanced except for the inclusion of only one replenishment tanker. With a number of bases along the Italian coastline it must be assumed that this fleet, the product of excellent and imaginative designers, will be primarily homebased, relying on external support if NATO deployments require any lengthy absence.

The same restriction on long-range movement is also true of the Royal Spanish Navy which has been forced by financial considerations to limit its new construction programme. The continued build-up of the Naval Air Arm with Harriers and extra helicopters, allied with the advanced years of *Dedalo* suggest that the previous plans for a new helicopter/VTOL carrier will be revived as soon as money allows and a design is available. The modernisation of this fleet must be acknowledged—the arming of new frigates and large patrol craft with surface-to-surface missiles, as well as the increase in new submarines will put Spain in a commanding position at the entrance to the Mediterranean.

At the eastern end of that sea the Hellenic Navy has made a significant increase in its light forces with a further four missile craft completing, as well as the acquisition of West German "Jaguar" class and other smaller types. To the four Type 209 submarines are to be added three, or possibly four more, while a start has been made on Greek-built vessels of the coastal patrol and auxiliary categories. Across the Aegean another significant advance has been started as the Turkish Navy continues

JANE'S

Published in the United States and Canada by

FW

FRANKLIN WATTS, INC.

730 Fifth Avenue
New York, N. Y. 10019
212-757-4050

Telex: 236537
Cable: FRAWATTS, NEW YORK

Franklin Watts, Inc., a subsidiary of Grolier Incorporated, is proud to announce its appointment as the American publisher of JANE'S comprehensive reference works. International in scope, each of these impressive volumes contains the most accurate and up-to-date information—information unparalleled by any other source—and describes its respective area of interest with a wealth of illustration and detail.

For those working or interested in each industry or service, JANE'S remains an essential and invaluable reference work. We shall be pleased to honor inquiries or orders at the address listed above.

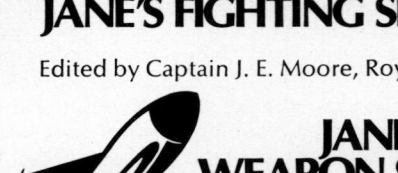

JANE'S ALL THE WORLD'S AIRCRAFT

Edited by John W. R. Taylor,
Fellow, Royal Historical Society,
Associate Fellow, Royal Aeronautical Society.

JANE'S FIGHTING SHIPS

Edited by Captain J. E. Moore, Royal Navy

JANE'S WEAPON SYSTEMS

Edited by Ronald Pretty

JANE'S INFANTRY WEAPONS

Edited by Denis H. R. Archer

JANE'S SURFACE SKIMMERS

Edited by Roy McLeavy

JANE'S OCEAN TECHNOLOGY

Edited by Robert L. Trillo

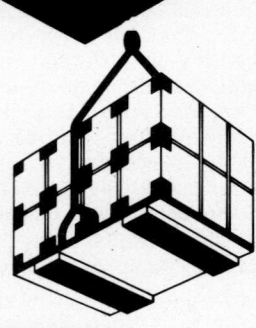

JANE'S FREIGHT CONTAINERS

Edited by Patrick Finlay

JANE'S WORLD RAILWAYS

Edited by Paul Goldsack

JANE'S MAJOR COMPANIES OF EUROPE

Edited by Jonathan Love

its programme of home building by the decision to build submarines at Gölcük after the successful completion of the "Berk" class frigates.

From the southern Turkish border to the Straits of Gibraltar, the Levantine and North African coasts are closely associated with the activities of the Soviet Union. Syrian "Osa" class missile-boats and the strong force of similar craft held by Egypt have brought the expected reaction from Israel of an expanded programme of "Saar IV" missile craft and "Dabur" patrol craft. Egypt has also built missile craft in her home yards—excellent facsimiles of Soviet "Komars". What the future holds for the maintenance of all the vessels originating in the USSR now that the break between that country and Egypt appears complete is hard to estimate, but must depend to a very large extent on the ability and ingenuity of local engineers. The Soviets, never renowned for their liberality in providing spare parts, have presumably left little behind.

Libya, however, has forecast a bonanza period with the Soviets: both "Foxtrot" class submarines and "Osas" appear to be on the list of planned acquisitions. At the same time missile corvettes from Italy and missile craft from France will combine with these ships to make the Libyan navy a powerful force in the area abutting on the Sicilian Narrows. Whether base facilities will be granted to the Russians; whether Mr. Mintoff will retain power in Malta and continue his flirtation with the Libyans; whether the unpredictable Colonel Qadaffi will use his new found sea-power for other than defence of his own coast-line; these are questions that only the future can answer.

The Tunisian Navy, with its increasing force of French-built ships, will be sandwiched between the Soviet-provided forces of Libya and Algeria. The latter, with no augmentation of its force of "Osa", "Komar" and "P6" classes, has apparently no intention of providing facilities for the USSR in the magnificent base at Mers-el-Kebir.

From Morocco down the western side of Africa there is a continual alternation of the sources of the various small navies' ships. Morocco, Mauritania, Senegal, Ivory Coast and Cameroon are primarily provided with French craft with some leavening of British. The latter have provided the main strength for Ghana and Nigeria whilst China is well represented in Sierra Leone and the Republic of Congo. With Guinea Bissau fully provided by the USSR, Guinea has shared her requirements between China and the USSR, Liberia is stocked from the USA and Zaire has impartially received deliveries from France, the USA and North Korea.

INDIAN OCEAN AND PERSIAN GULF

At the southern tip of Africa and in the most strategically important point in this area south of the Equator the Republic of South Africa has reacted to the increasing threats from without by increasing her 1976 defence budget by 40 per cent over the previous year's total. Included in this are allocations for six new frigates to be built in Durban, two new submarines and six Israeli fast attack craft (missile) similar to the "Saar IVs". How far this will go towards the protection of her more than 2,000 miles of coastline and the vital trade between the ports upon it is debatable but it shows a determination to guard her own which is lacking in a number of the critics of her system.

There is at present no information on what sea forces are to be provided to Mozambique or Angola but north of the Mozambique Channel Tanzania is primarily provided by China. Her neighbour, Kenya, has met her needs with British construction and further to the north, Somalia, with a major Soviet base at Berbera, is not surprisingly equipped entirely with Soviet craft. The addition of "Osa" missile craft to her force must pose a problem off the Straits of Bab el Mandeb should there be a conflict of views in this area. With Soviet light forces provided to both Yemeni countries and ports available to Soviet forces at Hodeida and Aden, access to the Red Sea and Suez Canal could easily be sealed off should policy so dictate. Within the Red Sea this could present a major problem to the Sudanese who, having had their original naval force provided by Yugoslavia, are now receiving ships from Iran. If this is an indication of alliance the western ally could very easily be marooned in a hostile sea.

Sudan's probable supporter, Iran, has led the great naval build-up in the Persian Gulf which suggests a resolve by the rulers of the Gulf states to ensure free passage in their own enclosed and congested waters. Saudi Arabia, faced with protection problems in both the Red Sea and the Gulf and with the

same threat of a throttle being placed on Bab-el-Mandeb, has embarked on a major naval expansion with the assistance of the USA. Within the Gulf her neighbours Oman, Sharjah, Ras Al Khaima, Dubai, Abu Dhabi, Qatar, Bahrain and Kuwait are all aware of possible threats to their coastline and to their increasing tanker tonnage. Expanding light forces mark this awareness while Iraq, slung between the Gulf State coastlines and Iran, still relies on a mixture of antique British craft and the products of the USSR, including six "Osas". The latter could have a major impact on Gulf trading but Iran with a programme including US "Spruance" class destroyers, submarines, French missile craft and US maritime patrol aircraft is clearly determined to carry out the Shah's intentions of taking care of Iranian waters, both within the Gulf and in the Arabian Sea beyond the Straits of Hhomuz.

Within an area flanked by the Arabian peninsula, Pakistan and India and with the southern boundary a line drawn westward from Sri Lanka the bulk of the Soviet squadron is normally deployed. On average this comprises a cruiser, a destroyer, two frigates, two to four ocean minesweepers, a submarine (nuclear or diesel-propelled) and a support group of some half-dozen ships such as an intelligence collector, a depot-ship, a tanker, a space-event ship and two harbour-based vessels (a barrack-ship and a floating workshop). This support group shows an intention to remain in the area, although, unless reinforced, this is a squadron which must be constrained in its operations by numbers and by insufficiency of service forces. With the re-opening of the Suez Canal, although the attitude of Egypt must remain in question, such reinforcements from the Black Sea would have to steam only 2,400 miles to reach Aden rather than 11,000 miles around South Africa. Within the normal operating area of this squadron little welcome can be expected in Pakistan where, with a mixed force of British, French and Chinese ships, there appears to be more inclination towards support from the United Kingdom despite the problems which have arisen over the two "Whitby" class frigates. The static size of the Pakistani fleet and the lack of any notable reinforcement over the last two to three years does little to support Indian charges of a "growing aggressive force".

India, however, at a time of both financial and political problems, is continuing to add to her fleet. Experiments with SSN-Z in *Talwar*, extra "Petyas" and "Polnocnys", the continued building of "Leander" class frigates, the promise of home-built submarines and the acquisition of "Nanuchka" class missile corvettes from the USSR will provide her with a navy which will be of over-mastering size and the only one, except the RAN, with an organic Fleet Air Arm in the Indian Ocean.

Despite this orientation towards Soviet-provided ships there is, as yet, no indication of Russian forces being allowed havens in Indian ports other than reports of a Soviet command centre at Vizagapatnam, which may be a hang-over from the Bangladesh clearance operations.

The latter country has shown no pro-Soviet bias in the choice of ships for its growing navy, having chosen both Yugoslavian and home-built vessels. Even the arrival in Sri Lanka of the variously labelled "Stenka"/"modified Osa" class has not been followed by the frequently forecast Soviet arrival in Trincomalee.

SOUTH EAST ASIA AND THE ANTIPODES

Not only is the garnering of bases in the Indian Ocean a difficult matter for the Soviet fleet—there could be problems not only with reinforcement through the Suez Canal but also via the Straits of Malacca, the shortest possible route from Vladivostock. Here both Malaysia and Singapore are building up effective forces of missile craft whilst Indonesia to the south and west is replacing her out-dated Soviet ships by more efficient Western vessels. Although at the moment a combination of these three navies could close the Malacca Straits, the advance of the Soviet-armed guerillas into Northern Malaysia might in the future nullify this advantage. Shore-action and politics must never be forgotten in considering the basic principles of sea-power—geographical advantage can be swiftly whittled away from within.

The coasts about the South China Sea are areas from which information is meagre—the state of the Khmer and Vietnamese navies is still obscure, Thailand has ordered new missile craft while the Philippines has considerably reinforced its forces in the wake of the Communist take-overs. But well to the south, in

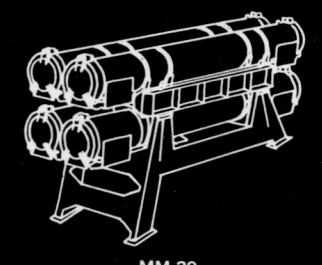
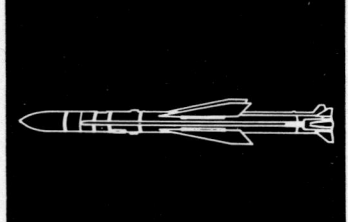

more temperate waters, a fresh attitude is to be seen. The Prime Ministers of the new governments in Australia and New Zealand are clearly aware that an ability to defend oneself is a necessary pre-requisite to the gathering of treaty partners. Both have spoken in recent months of maritime dangers in their quarter, although it is still far too early to record the steps likely to be taken to protect the sea-lanes on which both countries are totally dependent.

THE PACIFIC

A force which is occupying considerable attention in Australasia is the Soviet Pacific Fleet as well as the Indian Ocean squadron which receives certain of its reinforcements from Vladivostock. It is this very considerable group that the Chinese Navy looks on as its most likely threat, a fact underlined by the larger size of the North Sea Fleet, based at Tsingtao and Lu Shun, compared with the East and South Sea Fleets. Construction is still concentrated mainly on the defensive capability of submarines and light forces with some six diesel boats and twenty missile craft completed each year. This programme has given the Chinese the largest force of fast attack craft in the world and the third largest submarine branch. Beyond the confines of home waters the rapidly growing foreign trade of China has already been mentioned and this includes an increasing quantity of oil exports. With what appear to be vast reserves of oil both onshore and offshore their future as an exporting country depends on their continued adherence to Mao Tse-tung's policy of "self-reliance", the ability to tap their gigantic offshore reserves and the provision of the necessary ships and berthing facilities to handle the trade. From a point where oil production has risen by over 600 per cent in the last ten years and can now provide for all domestic needs, matters could advance to make China one of the world's great exporters with the implied question of whether her navy will expand to guard the movement of a commodity which could, as Chou En-lai promised, put China's economy into the "world's front-rank".

Oil is also of major importance in all Japanese calculations. Offshore exploration may ease the burden of the 98 per cent imports which, when OPEC prices were greatly increased, caused such an unwelcome shock to the Japanese economy. An increasing dependence on Chinese oil could also reduce the risks of interference with long range sea-borne trade. The recent Japanese White Paper on Defence, the first since 1970, skates delicately around a number of patches of thin ice, leaving the impression that the defence of such routes will be achieved by dependence on American nuclear capability as part of the overall deterrent to aggression. With a defence budget less than half that of Great Britain and about 5 per cent of that of the USA it is hard to see how much else can be achieved. The planned naval building programmes have been reduced and, although the provision of more missiles and helicopters at sea shows an appreciation of modern problems, the lack of adequate afloat support must limit any operations to home waters unless the USN is prepared to sustain them.

One point made in this White Paper is clearly stated—the instability inherent in the North-West Pacific where the interests of the USSR, USA and China converge and where North and South Korea stand ready for engagement. The former continues to build up her navy with new submarines, frigates and fast attack craft while the latter's considerable fleet of ex-US ships ranges from destroyers downwards and includes a considerable amphibious force. In many respects similar but with larger forces, including submarines, is the navy of Taiwan, the centre of another possible danger area.

Far removed are the navies of the western seaboard of the Americas. A proportion of the naval and coast-guard forces of Canada are deployed on this coast but there has been little change here since last year. Plans for a modern force of maritime patrol aircraft are hung up on the spikes of finance while decisions are still awaited on what type of ships are required to replace some fifteen ageing frigates.

SOUTH AMERICA

The southern neighbour of the USA, Mexico, has continued her programme of coastal protection with orders for ten more of the highly successful "Azteca" class. New orders have come, too, from Venezuela for six of the Italian designed "Lupo" class missile frigates, an addition which will make her the most powerful local naval power in the vicinity of the Panama Canal. Peru has also turned to "Lupos" for her replacement programme while new submarines figure not only in her navy but also in those of Colombia, Chile, Argentina, Brazil and Venezuela with Uruguay reported as showing a similar interest. New destroyers, frigates and missile craft now serve around the whole of South America but, in a continent of such vast distances, their numbers are comparatively small. Concentration in focal areas or at a point of anticipated action would be vital if these navies were to make a major impact on affairs.

THE FUTURE

From the foregoing it is very apparent that many people and governments have widely differing views on the necessity and employment of navies and their contribution to the overall equation of seapower. The urge to build big, complex and, therefore, very expensive ships sometimes ignores the tasks which those ships are likely to be given in the twenty-or-so years of their life—the result, very often, of a failure to consider the political background which is an essential feature of any study of seapower. In a world where instability and uncertainty are two of the major factors affecting such a consideration and where the present horrifying concentration of nuclear and thermonuclear weapons suggests that only an act of insanity or gross mismanagement could prompt a major nuclear exchange, the operations of navies and their deployment deserve more attention than they receive. A logical appreciation of such matters allied with the fundamental need for re-assigning to the human intellect the position it is rapidly losing to technology and the computer could well produce equal, if not greater, results at less cost than at present. What is to be done? Can it best be done by a ship, a fixed-wing aircraft or a helicopter? Are "full naval standards" essential for all tasks? Can more thoughtful use of sensors, or even silence, achieve the desired end with greater efficiency? Can the resources of allies be better deployed to save expense? These and a multitude of other questions come to mind as one turns the pages of this book. Human ingenuity knows few barriers and upon it the navies of the world must rely. The seas upon which they move are the lifelines of our existence.

John E. Moore

ACKNOWLEDGEMENTS

This edition, reset and largely re-written, has, as usual, been greatly assisted by advice of many kinds received in the hundreds of letters which have come in during the year. If acknowledgement of all this invaluable help has been slow in coming I hope I may be excused—the production of this book has meant a vast amount of work not only in producing the copy but in checking some 900 pages of galleys and proofs, a most time-consuming task. It has been a task, too, which could never have been completed without the continuing help of my honorary assistant-editor, who is also my wife, and the help with the copy given by David and Jean Parsons.

Many people ask, "How do you get your facts?" and to dispel any idea that Jane's is a government-sponsored espionage agency let me make it clear that there are three main sources of information. Firstly my wife keeps a continual watch on some thirty newspapers a week and nearly three dozen periodicals, in five languages, every month. This produces an invaluable background as well as much information which, when combined with the second source, my many friends and correspondents who voluntarily give a great deal of their time to Jane's, provides a solid data base. Amongst these it is so difficult to differentiate that it is only fair that I should list those without whose help my task would become almost impossible. With facts and photographs the following have given me every support, not only in revising last year's copy but in keeping matters up-to-date: Contre Amiral M. J. Adam CVO CBE, Dr. Giorgio Arra, Lieutenant Erminio Bagnasco, Herr Siegfried Breyer, Mr. John Callis, Commander A. Fraccaroli, Lieutenant-Commander A. Hague VRD, Mr. G. K. Jacobs, Captain F. de Blocq van Kuffeler, Mr. John Mortimer, Mr. S. L. Morison, Mr. J. S. Rowe, Mr. A. J. R. Risseeuw, Mr. C. W. E. Richardson, Lieutenant Toshio Tamura, Senor J. Taibo, Mr. and Mrs. C. Taylor, Mr. R. Winfield. Mr. Graeme Andrews has given invaluable help with the editing of the Australian and New Zealand sections. To all of them and to the many who are not mentioned by name, my very grateful thanks.

The third source is the Governments and Defence Ministries of the countries concerned who each receive annual requests for up-to-date information and illustrations. Some respond magnificently and to them and their attachés in London I am most grateful. Some prefer to reply that security prevents any assistance and I do hope that, in the future, these authorities will realise that the truth is more often to their advantage than silence. The countries of the last group maintain a churlish reticence and fail to reply in any form.

So far as timing is concerned I would remind people of the old staff aim of "the safe and timely arrival of the convoy". Items may reach me safely but if not "timely" (i.e. before 1st January) may not be available for inclusion. November and December are the period of Jane's main harvest.

What leaves my desk is dealt with most sympathetically by Macdonald and Janes where Mr. Ken Harris and his production team are ever ready to help. Mrs. Barbara Hessler and the Paulton House Girls have again shown uncanny ability in interpreting copy and pasting-up the result while Netherwood and Dalton Ltd, the printers, have shown a fine Yorkshire resilience in the face of all demands, particularly in this year of change.

The sections on South Korea, the Philippines, Taiwan and the USA have, for the ninth year, been the responsibility of Mr. Norman Polmar. I am very grateful for what he has done and he is, in his turn, particularly in debt to the following for their assistance: Captains Charles R. Smith, Gerald H. Barkalow, and G. B. Holcomb of the Office of the Deputy Chief of Naval Operations (Air Warfare); Captain Stuart D. Landersman, formerly of the Office of the DCNO (Surface Warfare); Lieutenant A. E. Norton, Mr. Robert Carlisle, Miss Anna Urban, and Journalist William Lane of the Office of Navy Information; Mr. Richard C. Bassett, Mr. William Branch, and Mrs. Eleanor Prentiss of the Naval Sea Systems Command; Mr. H. A. Taylor of the Bureau of Naval Personnel; Lieutenant-Commander Peter Litrenta of Naval Surface Forces, Pacific Fleet; Mr. J. J. Farriss III of the Office of the Oceanographer of the Navy; Mr. Larry C. Manning of the Military Sealift Command; Commander Ronald Black and Lieutenant Richard Merki of the Information Directorate of the Department of Defense; Captain Adrian Lonsdale and Miss Elizabeth Segedi of the Public Information Division, US Coast Guard; Mr. James Murray of the Philadelphia Naval Shipyard; Mr. Kohji Ishiwata, Editor of *Ships of the World;* Commander Ernesto M. Arzaga of the Philippine Navy; Messrs. William Whalen and William Whalen Jnr, John Mortimer, Edward Chuang and Alfred W. Harris; and most especially to Mr. Samuel L. Morison and Dr. Giorgio Arra.

Finally to the editors of the other naval annuals I send my thanks for the part they have played; *Almanacco Navale* edited by Dr. Giorgio Giorgerini and Signor Augusto Nani, *Flottentaschenbuch* edited by Herr Gerhard Albrecht, *Flottes de Combat* edited by M. J. Labayle-Couhat, and *Marinkalender* edited by Captain Allan Kull.

No illustrations from this book may be reproduced without the publishers' permission but the Press may reproduce information and governmental photographs provided JANE'S FIGHTING SHIPS is acknowledged as the source. Photographs credited to other than official organisations must not be reproduced without permission from the originator.

Contributions for the next edition, which is already in preparation, should be sent as soon as possible to:

Captain J. E. Moore, RN,
Editor, Jane's Fighting Ships,
Elmhurst,
Rickney,
Hailsham,
Sussex BN27 1SF,
England.

or, if concerned with South Korea, the Philippines, Taiwan or the USA directly to:

Mr. Norman Polmar,
4302 Dahill Place,
Alexandria,
Virginia 22312,
USA.

What does it take to make a ship that is also a good policeman?

It takes expertise in marine technology and an awareness that 'through-life costs' are more important than ever before.

Because policework at sea as on land is becoming a more and more expensive operation.

Vickers recognise these facts and build for them with a wide range of ships to meet all duties.

The Type 42 destroyers, for example. Vickers has already built the first two of these and is the lead yard for their construction. Or the nuclear-powered submarines for the Royal Navy for which Vickers is the sole builder.

Now there's a further notable example in the Vickers Vedette. A private venture design for a small, fast warship with an ocean-going capability which enables it to stand in for larger, more expensive units or work alongside them.

The vessel is adaptable and versatile. The emphasis throughout its design is on effectiveness, reliability and strict control of through-life costs.

The Vedette is a fine piece of ship-building. And a fine example of shipbuilding economics too.

We think it will be a credit to the force.

The 1,000-ton Vedette designed to fulfill wide-ranging tactical and strategic roles. The design shown here incorporates a helicopter.

VICKERS SHIPBUILDING GROUP

Vickers Ltd Shipbuilding Group Barrow-in-Furness Cumbria

SHIP DESIGNATIONS

In an effort to standardise the type designations in the various navies, despite somewhat idiosyncratic listing in some fleets, a regular formula has been used wherever possible in the majority of sections. This has caused some queries and comments, therefore a list is given below.

TYPE DESIGNATIONS

AIRCRAFT CARRIERS
Attack Carriers (Large)	Over 50,000 tons (all US ships)
Attack Carriers (Medium and Light)	*Essex, Ark Royal,* two French *et al*
Helicopter Carriers/ Cruisers	*Kiev* and *Moskva*

MAJOR SURFACE SHIPS
A/S Cruisers	"Invincible" class
Cruisers	Pre 1960 cruisers, including missile conversions
Light Cruisers	Above 5,000 tons
Destroyers	3,000 tons and over, plus original conventional destroyers
Frigates	1,100 to 3,000 tons
Corvettes	500 to 1,100 tons

LIGHT FORCES
Fast Attack Craft 25 and above 25 knots	FAC (Missile) FAC (Gun) FAC (Torpedo) FAC (Patrol)
Patrol Craft Below 25 knots	Large Patrol Craft (100 to 500 tons) Coastal Patrol Craft (below 100 tons)

SUBMARINES
Strategic Missile	Nuclear propelled and conventionally propelled
Fleet Submarines	Nuclear propelled
Patrol Submarines	Conventionally propelled

AMPHIBIOUS FORCES
Command Ships
Assault Ships
Landing Ships
Landing Craft
Transports

MINE WARFARE FORCES
Mine Layers
MCM Support Ships
Mine Sweepers (Ocean)
Mine Hunters
Mine Sweepers (Coastal)
Mine Sweepers (Inshore)
Mine Sweeping Boats

SURVEYING VESSELS
Surveying Ships
Coastal Surveying Craft
Inshore Surveying Craft

D.D.G.
"AUDACE.."

CANTIERI NAVALI RIUNITI

Head Office:

Via Cipro 11 - 16129 Genova (Italy) - Telex: CANTGE 27168 - Tel. 59951

Shipyards:

RIVA TRIGOSO – ANCONA – PALERMO

Repair Works:

GENOVA –PALERMO

1) 17.000 ton
SEA CONTROL AND ASSAULT SHIP

2) 6.000 ton
TRAINING, COMMAND AND ASSAULT SHIP

3) FLEET SUPPORT SHIP "STROMBOLI"
Italian Navy

4) 2.400 ton GUIDED MISSILE FRIGATE
4 Units for Italian Navy
4 Units for Peruvian Navy
6 Units for Venezuelan Navy

5) 1.700 ton HYDROGRAPHIC SURVEY SHIP
"Amm MAGNAGHI" Italian Navy

6) 1.000 ton CORVETTE

7) 550 ton GUIDED MISSILE CORVETTE
4 Units for Libyan Navy

8) 280 ton MISSILE FAST PATROL BOAT

9) 60 ton MISSILE HYDROFOIL "SPARVIERO"
6 Units for Italian Navy.

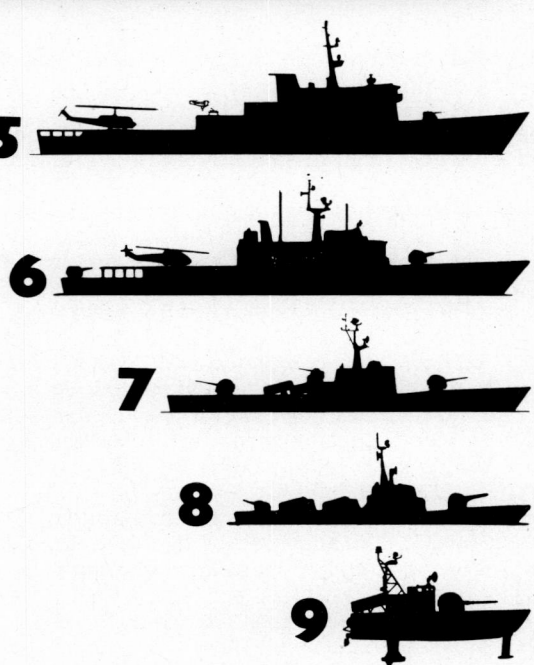

FINCANTIERI GROUP

MAJOR MATTERS

ABU DHABI
The last of a class of six 175-ton large patrol craft has been completed and two 27 ft coastal patrol craft have been purchased.

ARGENTINA
Six Type 21 frigates are to be built at AFNE with assistance from Vosper Thornycroft. In addition two new construction survey/oceanographic ships and a new Wärtsila icebreaker have been ordered.

AUSTRALIA
Two new frigates have been ordered from the US. A new large patrol craft design is under consideration and it is intended to build new fleet replenishment ships and a new research ship.

BANGLADESH
Two "Kraljevica" class have been received from Yugoslavia.

BELGIUM
The first "E71" frigate is to be commissioned in December 1976 and a new minehunter programme is under discussion.

BRAZIL
Niteroi ran trials early in 1976 and two more "Oberon" class are to commission in 1977.

BRUNEI
The last pair of "Perwira" class patrol craft were commissioned.

CAMEROON
A new large patrol craft has been acquired from France.

CHINA
Six new "Romeo" class submarines, ten new "Hola" class and ten new "Hoku" class missile craft have been built.

COLOMBIA
Two Type 209 submarines were commissioned.

CUBA
Five "Zhuk" class coastal patrol craft were acquired from the USSR.

DENMARK
The frigate *Beskytteren* was commissioned; four missile craft and five coastal patrol craft came into service; two new minelayers are commissioning.

ECUADOR
Two Type 209 submarines are completing and three missile craft have come into service.

EGYPT
Six "Komar" type have been built in Alexandria: extra missiles and rocket launchers have been mounted in the light forces.

ETHIOPIA
One "Kraljevica" class has been acquired from Yugoslavia.

FIJI
A navy has been formed with three ex-US "Bluebird" MSCs.

FINLAND
A class of six GRP inshore minesweepers has been completed.

FRANCE
Three Type A69 have been completed and Type A70 has been suspended. A sixth SNLE is building and the first SSN is to be laid down, but no date has been set for the nuclear helicopter carrier. The "Trident" class missile craft, of which two have been completed, is to be reduced in numbers.

GERMANY (FEDERAL REPUBLIC)
New Type 122 frigates and new aircraft are planned. The navy has thirty new missile craft and Boeing will provide ten Type 162 hydrofoils. All of the "Jaguar" class has been deleted.

GHANA
There is a new programme of large patrol craft.

GREECE
Three or four Type 209 submarines have been ordered. Four "Combattante III" class missile craft, two Esterel type and two ex-US "Asheville" class are in service and seven "Jaguar" class have been transferred from the Federal German Republic. There is also a new class of locally built patrol craft.

GUINEA
Four "Shanghai" class are now in service.

GUINEA BISSAU
This navy is newly founded, with one "P6" class and one "Poluchat" class from the USSR.

GUYANA
An order for three large patrol craft has been reported.

INDIA
Four "Leander" class were completed with two more to come. *Talwar* has been fitted with ex-"Osa" SSN-2 launchers. The new, larger "Abhay" class is under construction and there are reports of acquisition of some "Nanuchka" class from the USSR.

IRAN
The order for "Spruance" class destroyers was reduced to four. There is some question over the transfer of three "Tang" class submarines from the US, but twelve missile craft are building in France and all are to be completed by April 1979. A 20,000-ton tanker is to be delivered in 1977.

IRAQ
Four "Zhuk" class coastal patrol craft have been transferred from the USSR.

ISRAEL
A building programme of "Saar IV" ("Reshef" and "Dabur") classes is continuing.

ITALY
The *Legge Navale* covers a tentative programme of one helicopter cruiser, two missile destroyers, eight frigates, two submarines, ten minehunters, thirteen hydrofoils, one LPD, one tanker, one salvage ship, seventeen tugs, sixty-two AB212 and twelve SH3D helicopters.

JAPAN
The 1976 new construction programme consists of one improved "Haruna" class, one MSC, one survey ship and a tanker. This is a major reduction in the programme requested by the MSDF, including two submarines.

KENYA
Kenya has three new 145-ton large patrol craft.

KOREA, NORTH
Two "Romeo" class submarines are being constructed locally, in addition to "Najin" class frigates and "P6" class patrol craft.

KOREA, SOUTH
A further two "Gearing" class and one LSD were transferred by the USA. Seven "Asheville" type missile corvettes will be completed by 1977 and there are plans to fit Standard missiles in several larger ships.

LIBYA
There are doubts over the full extent of this programme which includes four missile corvettes from Italy, ten missile craft from France and could include twenty-four "Osa" class and a number of "Foxtrot" submarines from the USSR. There are also reports of a programme of French submarines.

MALAYSIA
Four more "Perdana" class and six Leong Lürssen missile craft were ordered. Two LSTs from the USA have joined this navy.

MEXICO
Ten more "Azteca" class are under construction with eighty as the possible target.

MOROCCO
A programme of two more "PR72" type corvettes, twenty "P92" class patrol craft and three "Batral" type has been agreed.

NETHERLANDS
Thirteen "Kortenaer" class frigates are to be built with Harpoon missiles which are also to be fitted in "Van Speijk" class. A new submarine design is in hand, a minehunter programme is under study with France and Belgium. A new survey ship is completing.

NEW ZEALAND
Four "Lake" class large patrol craft were completed.

NIGERIA
Two new 143-ton and two more 90-ton patrol craft have been ordered. A new survey ship *Lana* completed.

NORWAY
The construction programme consists of fourteen "Hauk" class missile craft and two minelayers as well as a depot ship and seven patrol craft for the newly created Coastguard. A design for Type 210 submarines is in hand with the Federal German Republic.

OMAN
Four large patrol craft are building.

PERU

Four modified "Lupo" class frigates, two Type 209 submarines to join the present pair, six 150-ton patrol craft, one 25 000-ton tanker and one 10 000-ton tanker are on order or building.

PHILIPPINES

Nine frigates, 12 LSTs and considerable light and service forces from S. Vietnam and Japan have been added to this force.

PORTUGAL

A large deletion list has followed the withdrawal from Africa.

ROMANIA

A programme of local variants of "Shanghai" and "Hu-chwan" classes continues in addition to locally built river patrol craft.

SAUDI ARABIA

Forty-three coastal patrol craft were delivered from the UK. Four "322" class MSCs were ordered from the USA with six large and two coastal patrol craft, four LCTs and three training ships to come.

SINGAPORE

All "TNC 48" class missile craft were completed. Eight extra US LSTs joined the fleet.

SOMALIA

Three "Osa II" class were transferred by the USSR.

SOUTH AFRICA

A construction programme of six frigates (building in Durban), two submarines and six "Saar IV" class missile craft is underway.

SPAIN

A reduced programme: cut to four frigates, two "Agosta" class submarines, six 400-ton and six 140-ton patrol craft. A replacement helicopter carrier is still under discussion.

SRI LANKA

Ex-Soviet "Modified Stenka" class was transferred.

SUDAN

The transfer of ex-Iranian large patrol craft was concluded.

SWEDEN

A construction programme of three submarines (with new design under consideration), three corvettes, sixteen missile craft (the first has been completed), one minelayer, nine minehunters and twenty-five LCUs is in hand or projected.

SYRIA

Two "Petya" class frigates were acquired from the USSR.

TAIWAN

Gabriel missiles were fitted in several destroyers and a number of "SX404" small submarines were reported to have been acquired.

TANZANIA

Possibly six more "Shanghai", four "Hu-chwan", "P6" and "P4" classes were acquired from China.

THAILAND

Three Lürssen missile craft were ordered.

TUNISIA

Two Vosper Thornycroft 103 ft patrol craft have been ordered.

TURKEY

One depot ship, seven "Jaguar" class and five MSCs were acquired from West Germany. A second "Type 209" submarine is building with two more to be built at Gölcük. Four missile craft are building (three at Istanbul).

UNITED KINGDOM

Hampshire, Rorqual and *Grampus* have been deleted prematurely, and *Hermes* is under conversion as an A/S carrier, and a second "Invincible" class has been ordered. Three Type 42 have been completed, with five on order or building and one projected. Five Type 21 have been completed with two building (the last four to have Exocet and Seawolf missiles). The "Leander" class conversions continue. Three SSNs are under construction and one new design is to be ordered; two MCM vessels of the "Brecon" class are building; five offshore patrol craft have been ordered; two new Fleet Replenishment ships are being built.

USA

The building programme consists of two "Nimitz" class nuclear carriers, four SSBNs, twenty-seven SSNs, four "Virginia" class CGN, twenty-seven "Spruance" class (eight of thirty to complete by the end of 1976), ten "Oliver Hazard Perry" class frigates, four LHA, five missile hydrofoils, and ten support ships.

USSR

The *Kiev* is now at sea and two more of this class are building. A programme of "Delta II", "Charlie" and "Charlie II", "Victor" and "Victor II" and "Tango" classes of submarines, "Kara" and "Kresta II" class cruisers, "Krivak" class destroyers, "Grisha" and "Nanuchka" class corvettes, "Ropucha" class LSTs, "Turya" and "Zhuk" classes of light forces, "Sonya" and "Natya" class minesweepers, "Amur", "Ugra", "Boris Chilikin" and several smaller classes in the support section is continuing.

VENEZUELA

One Type 209 submarine was completed and one is building. Six "Lupo" class frigates have been ordered.

YUGOSLAVIA

A home based programme of at least two 964-ton submarines, ten missile craft and at least one 3,000-ton LST with GRP hulled LCAs is underway.

THE USE OF JANES FIGHTING SHIPS

This edition has, like its editor, increased in girth. The reason for the latter is inertia at a desk but the reverse is true of the book itself. Thanks to new methods of printing it has been possible to recast all pages and this has allowed a reasonably standard format which gives the name, number, builder and, in the case of larger ships, laid down, launch and commissioning dates. Smaller ships have had to have these details confined to commissioning dates although, where known, the remainder has been included in the text and this is where all transfer dates are listed.

All deletions are now listed at the head of each country's section and the data on a navy is now placed above these in a similar order, where this is possible without undue pedantry, throughout. Pennant lists are now provided for major navies and the line drawings, at a standard scale of 1 : 1200, are largely new entries. Again, so far as possible, tonnages are included in both standard and full-load displacements—that of "standard" because it is the usage of international documents (eg. The London Naval Treaty of March 1936 and the Montreux Convention of July 1936) and is defined as "the displacement of the vessel, complete, fully manned, engined and equipped ready for sea— but without fuel or reserve feed-water on board".

The major matters relating to the fleets of the world are included after the foreword to relieve that section of the necessity for quantities of figures. Also intended as relief from such complexities, details of radars, sonars and torpedoes have been added at the end in addition to the tables of missiles and aircraft.

Once again I should be most grateful for any additions, corrections or suggestions which will improve the new layout.

IDENTIFICATION SILHOUETTES

Scale shown against each type or class as appropriate

BATTLESHIP

Scale: 177 Feet to 1 inch

IOWA CLASS (USA)

AIRCRAFT CARRIERS

Scale: 138 Feet to 1 Inch

COLOSSUS CLASS (ARGENTINA, BRAZIL)

NB Minas Gerais different island

Scale: 140 Feet to 1 Inch

MAJESTIC CLASS (AUSTRALIA, INDIA)

Scale: 173 Feet to 1 Inch

CLEMENCEAU CLASS (FRANCE)

AIRCRAFT CARRIERS

Scale: 169 Feet to 1 Inch   **ARK ROYAL (UK)**

Scale: 154 Feet to 1 Inch   **HERMES (UK)**

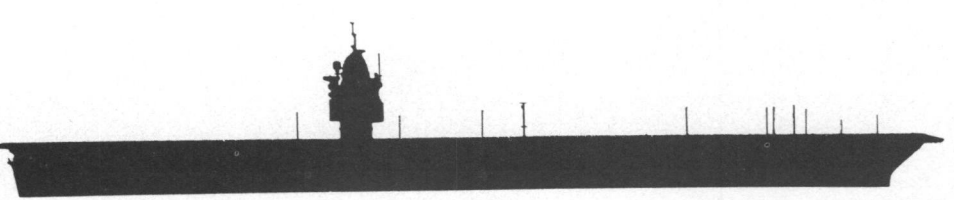

Scale: 225 Feet to 1 Inch   **ENTERPRISE CLASS (USA)**

Scale: 179 Feet to 1 Inch   **ESSEX AND HANCOCK CLASS (USA)**

AIRCRAFT CARRIERS

Scale: 207 Feet to 1 Inch   FORRESTAL CLASS (USA)

Scale: 118 Feet to 1 Inch   IWO JIMA CLASS (USA)

Scale: 212 Feet to 1 Inch   KITTY HAWK (USA)

Scale: 195 Feet to 1 Inch   MIDWAY CLASS (USA)

LONG RANGE BALLISTIC MISSILE SUBMARINES

Scale: 122 Feet to 1 Inch

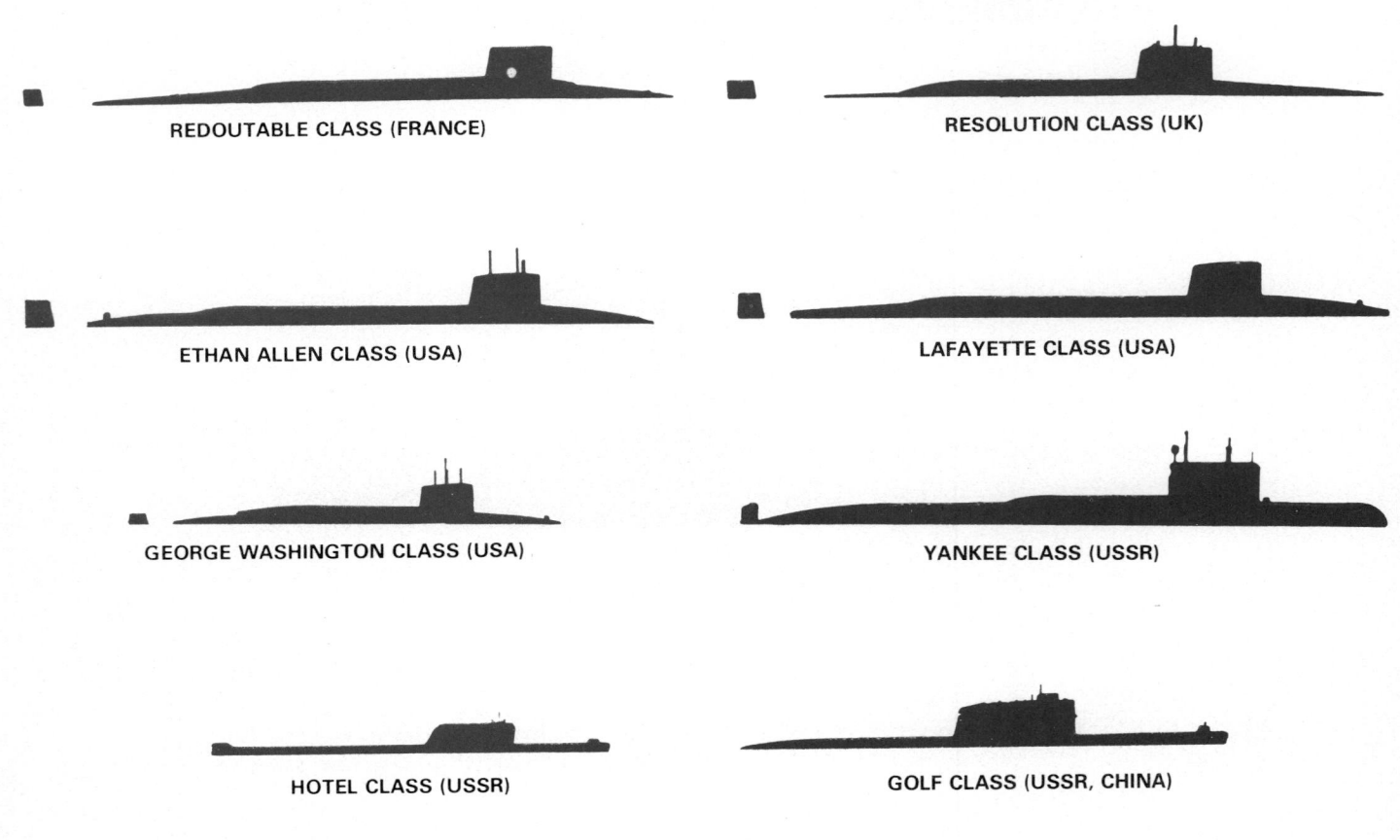

REDOUTABLE CLASS (FRANCE)

RESOLUTION CLASS (UK)

ETHAN ALLEN CLASS (USA)

LAFAYETTE CLASS (USA)

GEORGE WASHINGTON CLASS (USA)

YANKEE CLASS (USSR)

HOTEL CLASS (USSR)

GOLF CLASS (USSR, CHINA)

SUBMARINES

Scale: 80 Feet to 1 Inch

209 TYPE (ARGENTINA, COLOMBIA, GREECE, PERU, TURKEY, VENEZUELA)

206 TYPE (W. GERMANY, ISRAEL)

205 TYPE (W. GERMANY, DENMARK)

DAPHNE CLASS (FRANCE, PAKISTAN, PORTUGAL, S. AFRICA)

DELFINEN CLASS (DENMARK)

ARETHUSE CLASS (FRANCE)

QUEBEC CLASS (USSR)

KOBBEN CLASS (NORWAY)

TOTI CLASS (ITALY)

SUBMARINES

Scale: 166 Feet to 1 Inch

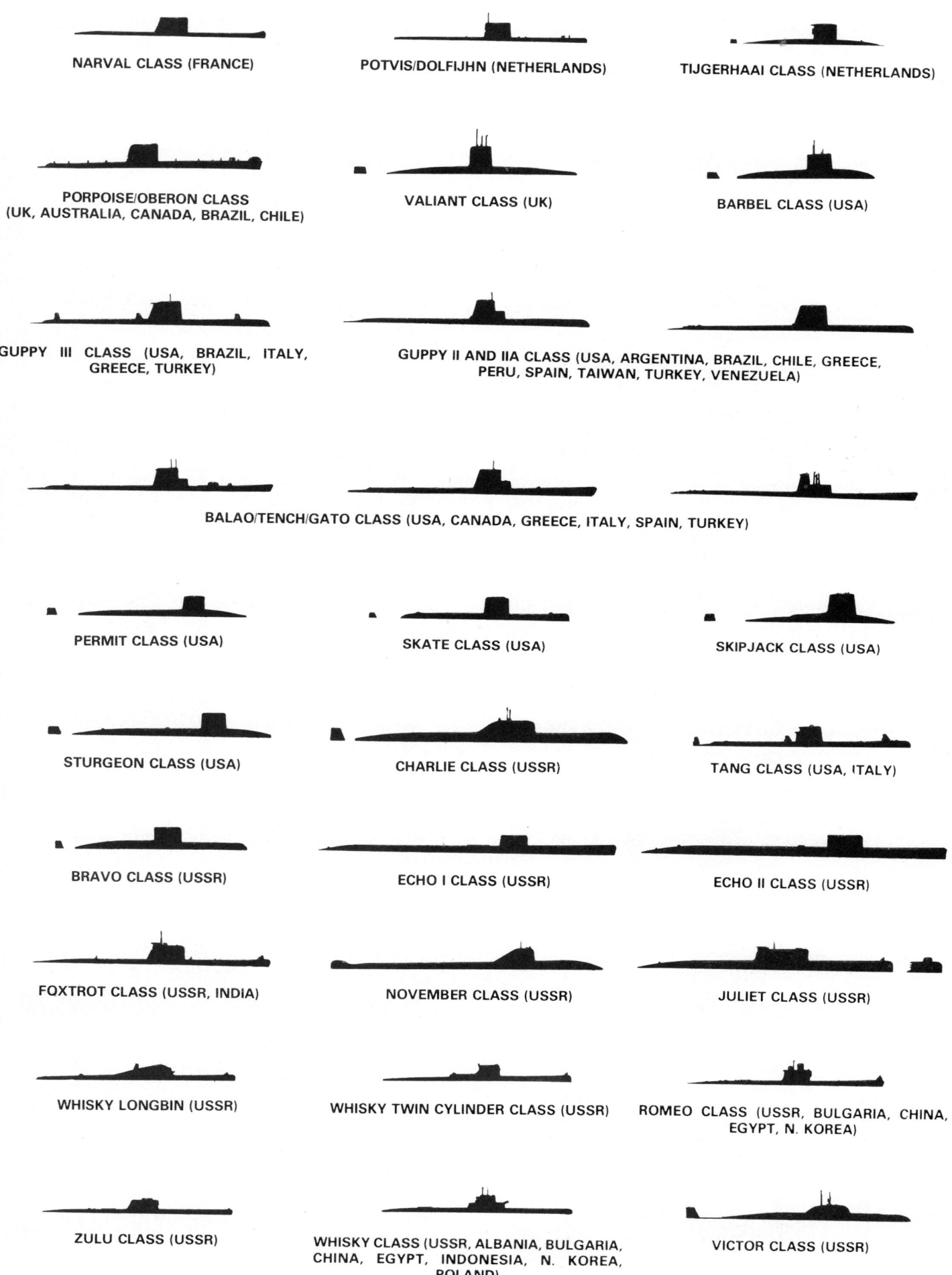

NARVAL CLASS (FRANCE)

POTVIS/DOLFIJHN (NETHERLANDS)

TIJGERHAAI CLASS (NETHERLANDS)

PORPOISE/OBERON CLASS
(UK, AUSTRALIA, CANADA, BRAZIL, CHILE)

VALIANT CLASS (UK)

BARBEL CLASS (USA)

GUPPY III CLASS (USA, BRAZIL, ITALY,
GREECE, TURKEY)

GUPPY II AND IIA CLASS (USA, ARGENTINA, BRAZIL, CHILE, GREECE,
PERU, SPAIN, TAIWAN, TURKEY, VENEZUELA)

BALAO/TENCH/GATO CLASS (USA, CANADA, GREECE, ITALY, SPAIN, TURKEY)

PERMIT CLASS (USA)

SKATE CLASS (USA)

SKIPJACK CLASS (USA)

STURGEON CLASS (USA)

CHARLIE CLASS (USSR)

TANG CLASS (USA, ITALY)

BRAVO CLASS (USSR)

ECHO I CLASS (USSR)

ECHO II CLASS (USSR)

FOXTROT CLASS (USSR, INDIA)

NOVEMBER CLASS (USSR)

JULIET CLASS (USSR)

WHISKY LONGBIN (USSR)

WHISKY TWIN CYLINDER CLASS (USSR)

ROMEO CLASS (USSR, BULGARIA, CHINA,
EGYPT, N. KOREA)

ZULU CLASS (USSR)

WHISKY CLASS (USSR, ALBANIA, BULGARIA,
CHINA, EGYPT, INDONESIA, N. KOREA,
POLAND)

VICTOR CLASS (USSR)

CRUISERS
Scale: 266 Feet to 1 Inch

COLBERT (FRANCE)

VITTORIO VENETO (ITALY)

ANDREA DORIA CLASS (ITALY)

DE ZEVEN PROVINCIEN (NETHERLANDS)

ALMIRANTE GRAU (PERU)

TIGER CLASS (UK)

ALBANY CLASS (USA)

CLEVELAND CLASS (USA)

LONG BEACH (USA)

CHAPAEV CLASS (USSR)

KARA CLASS (USSR)

KIROV CLASS (USSR)

KRESTA I CLASS (USSR)
(before modification)

KRESTA II CLASS (USSR)

KYNDA CLASS (USSR)

MOSKVA CLASS (USSR)

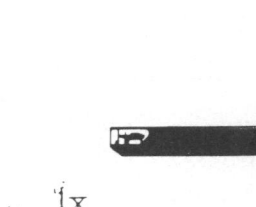

SVERDLOV CLASS (USSR)

ZHDANOV (USSR) CONVERTED SVERDLOV CLASS

DZERZHINSKI (USSR) MODIFIED SVERDLOV CLASS

CRUISERS

Scale: 160 Feet to 1 Inch

TRUXTON (USA)

CALIFORNIA CLASS (USA)

COUNTY CLASS (UK)

BRISTOL (UK)

DESTROYERS

Scale: 160 Feet to 1 Inch

IROQUOIS CLASS (CANADA)

ACONIT (FRANCE)

TYPE 53 (FRANCE)

SAN GIORGIO (ITALY)

TYPE 47 (ASW) (FRANCE)

TYPE 47 (DDG) (FRANCE)

SUFFREN CLASS (FRANCE)

TOURVILLE CLASS (FRANCE)

HAMBURG CLASS (W. GERMANY)

LÜTJENS CLASS (W. GERMANY)

AUDACE CLASS (ITALY)

IMPAVIDO CLASS (ITALY)

FLETCHER CLASS (USA, ARGENTINA, BRAZIL, CHILE, COLOMBIA, WEST GERMANY, GREECE, JAPAN, ITALY, SOUTH KOREA, MEXICO, PERU, SPAIN, TAIWAN, TURKEY)

DESTROYERS
Scale: 160 Feet to 1 Inch

ALLEN M. SUMNER CLASS (USA, ARGENTINA, COLOMBIA, GREECE, IRAN, SPAIN, TAIWAN, VENEZUELA)

CHARLES F. ADAMS (USA, AUSTRALIA and W. GERMANY similar)

SHEFFIELD CLASS (UK, ARGENTINA)

FORREST SHERMAN CLASS (CONVERTED) (USA)

FORREST SHERMAN CLASS (USA)

GEARING CLASS (USA, GREECE, SPAIN, TAIWAN, TURKEY)

GEARING CLASS (FRAM 2) (USA, GREECE, TAIWAN, TURKEY)

MITSCHER CLASS (USA)

SPRUANCE CLASS (USA)

KANIN CLASS (USSR)

KASHIN CLASS (USSR)

KILDIN CLASS (USSR)

KOTLIN CLASS (USSR) (WITH HELICOPTER PLATFORM)

KOTLIN CLASS (USSR)

SAM KOTLIN (USSR)

SKORY CLASS (USSR, EGYPT, INDONESIA, POLAND)

KRIVAK CLASS (USSR)

KRUPNY CLASS (USSR)

FRIESLAND/HOLLAND CLASS (NETHERLANDS)

DESTROYERS
Scale: 160 Feet to 1 Inch

IMPETUOSO CLASS (ITALY)

BELKNAP CLASS (USA)

COONTZ CLASS (USA)

LEAHY CLASS (USA)

FRIGATES
Scale: 160 Feet to 1 Inch

PEDER SKRAM CLASS (DENMARK)

HVIDBJÖRNEN CLASS (DENMARK)

COMMANDANT RIVIÈRE CLASS (FRANCE)

LE CORSE CLASS (FRANCE)

KÖLN CLASS (W. GERMANY)

ALPINO CLASS (ITALY)

LE NORMAND CLASS (FRANCE)

BERGAMINI CLASS (ITALY)

CENTAURO CLASS (ITALY)

VAN SPEIJK CLASS (NETHERLANDS)

OSLO CLASS (NORWAY)

DE SILVA CLASS (PORTUGAL)

ESCOBAR (PORTUGAL)

AMAZON CLASS (UK)

BLACKWOOD CLASS (UK, INDIA)

LEANDER CLASS (UK, AUSTRALIA, CHILE, INDIA, NEW ZEALAND)

LEOPARD CLASS (UK, INDIA)

ROTHESAY (UK)

SALISBURY CLASS (UK)

TRIBAL CLASS (UK)

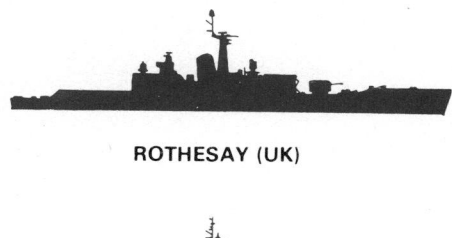

WHITBY CLASS (UK, INDIA)

FRIGATES

Scale: 160 Feet to 1 Inch

ANNAPOLIS CLASS (CANADA)

MACKENZIE CLASS (CANADA)

ST. LAURENT CLASS (CANADA)

RESTIGOUCHE CLASS (CANADA)

Scale: 125 Feet to 1 Inch

A69 (FRANCE)

KOLA CLASS (USSR)

**RIGA CLASS
(USSR, BULGARIA, CHINA, FINLAND, E. GERMANY, INDONESIA)**

BROOKE CLASS (USA)

KNOX CLASS (USA)

GARCIA CLASS (USA)

MIRKA CLASS (USSR)

PETYA CLASS (USSR)

CORVETTES

Scale: 110 Feet to 1 Inch

**ALBATROS/TRITON CLASS
(DENMARK, ITALY)**

THETIS CLASS (W. GERMANY)

DE CRISTOFARO CLASS (ITALY)

WOLF CLASS (NETHERLANDS)

COUTINHO CLASS (PORTUGAL)

POTI CLASS (USSR)

Scale: 125 Feet to 1 Inch

GRISHA CLASS (USSR)

NANUCHKA CLASS (USSR)

SOI CLASS (USSR)

AMPHIBIOUS FORCES

Scale: 170 Feet to 1 Inch

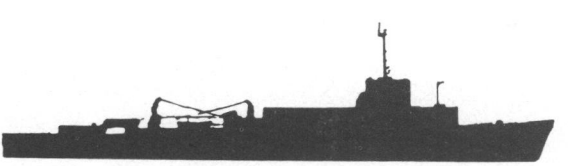

OURAGAN CLASS (FRANCE)

JEANNE D'ARC (FRANCE)

FEARLESS CLASS (UK)

AUSTIN CLASS (USA)

NEWPORT CLASS (USA)

THOMASTON CLASS (USA)

Scale: 117 Feet to 1 Inch

SIR LANCELOT CLASS (UK)

Scale: 148 Feet to 1Inch

RALEIGH CLASS (USA)

Scale: 157 Feet to 1Inch

ALLIGATOR CLASS (USSR)

**POLNOCNY CLASS
(USSR, POLAND, INDIA, EGYPT, S. YEMEN)**

MP8 CLASS (USSR)

LIGHT FORCES

Scale: as indicated

140 Feet to 1 inch

JAGUAR CLASS (GREECE INDONESIA, SAUDI
ARABIA, TURKEY)

200 Feet to 1 inch

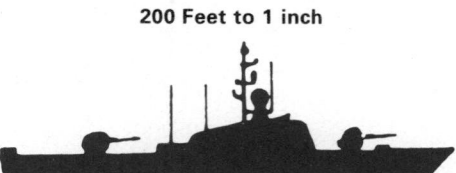

TYPE 143 (W. GERMANY)

88 Feet to 1 inch

TYPE 148 (W. GERMANY)

120 Feet to 1 inch

STÖRM CLASS (NORWAY)

80 Feet to 1 inch

TJELD CLASS (NORWAY, GREECE)

84 Feet to 1 inch

KOMAR CLASS (USSR)

129 Feet to 1 inch

OSA 1 and 2 CLASS (USSR, ALGERIA, BULGARIA, CHINA, CUBA,
EGYPT, EAST GERMANY, INDIA, IRAQ, POLAND, ROMANIA, SYRIA,
YUGOSLAVIA)

116 Feet to 1 inch

SHERSHEN CLASS
(USSR, EGYPT, E. GERMANY, YUGOSLAVIA)

84 Feet to 1 inch

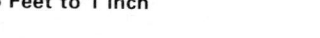

P. CLASS (P 6, 8 and 10—USSR, ALGERIA, CHINA, CUBA, EGYPT, E.
GERMANY, GUINEA, GUINEA BISSAU, INDONESIA, IRAQ, NIGERIA,
POLAND, SOMALIA, N. VIETNAM)

130 Feet to 1 inch

STENKA CLASS (USSR)

MINE WARFARE FORCES

Scale: 111 Feet to 1 Inch

FALSTER CLASS (DENMARK)

GOR CLASS (NORWAY)

ABDIEL (UK)

MINEWARFARE FORCES

Scale: 97 Feet to 1 Inch

CIRCE (FRANCE)

KRAKE (E. GERMANY)

KONDOR (E. GERMANY)

LINDAU CLASS (W. GERMANY)

SCHUTZE CLASS (W. GERMANY, BRAZIL)

KASADA (JAPAN)

DOKKUM, WILDERVANK (NETHERLANDS, ETHIOPIA)

KROGULEC (POLAND)

ALMANZORA (SPAIN)

TON (UK, ARGENTINA, AUSTRALIA, GHANA, INDIA, IRELAND, MALAYSIA, S. AFRICA)

AGILE (USA, BELGIUM, FRANCE, ITALY, NETHERLANDS, PORTUGAL, SPAIN, URUGUAY)

AUK (USA, S. KOREA, NORWAY, PERU, TAIWAN, PHILIPPINES, URUGUAY)

BLUEBIRD (USA, BELGIUM, DENMARK, FRANCE, FIJI, GREECE, IRAN, INDONESIA, ITALY, KOREA, JAPAN, NETHERLANDS, NORWAY, PAKISTAN, PORTUGAL, PHIL- IPPINES, TAIWAN, SPAIN, THAILAND, TURKEY, S. VIETNAM)

NATYA CLASS (USSR)

SASHA CLASS (USSR)

T-43 CLASS (USSR, ALBANIA, ALGERIA, BULGARIA, CHINA, EGYPT, INDONESIA, POLAND, SYRIA)

T-58 CLASS (USSR, INDIA)

T301 CLASS (USSR, ALBANIA, BULGARIA, EGYPT, ROMANIA)

VANYA CLASS (USSR, BULGARIA, SYRIA)

YURKA CLASS (USSR, EGYPT)

SUPPORT SHIPS

Scale: 156 Feet to 1 Inch

ZINNIA (BELGIUM)

GODETIA (BELGIUM)

RHEIN CLASS (W. GERMANY, GREECE, TUR-KEY)

PRESERVER CLASS (CANADA)

DON CLASS (USSR, INDONESIA)

LAMA CLASS (USSR)

UGRA CLASS (USSR, INDIA)

ENGADINE (UK)

Scale: 85 Feet to 1 Inch

ENDURANCE (UK)

Scale: 206 Feet to 1 Inch   **Scale: 152 Feet to 1 Inch**

DEUTSCHLAND (W. GERMANY)

BORIS CHILIKIN CLASS (USSR)

Scale: 200 Feet to 1 Inch

TRIUMPH (UK)

SHIP REFERENCE SECTION

ABU DHABI

The Naval Force of Abu Dhabi was formed in March 1968. The Force's function is to patrol territorial waters and oil installations in the UAE Marine Areas.

LIGHT FORCES

6 VOSPER THORNYCROFT TYPE (LARGE PATROL CRAFT)

Name	No.	Builders	Completed
ARDHANA	1101	Vosper Thornycroft	7 Mar 1975
ZURARA	1102	Vosper Thornycroft	13 June1975
MURBAN	1103	Vosper Thornycroft	15 Sep 1975
AL GHULIAN	1104	Vosper Thornycroft	16 Sep 1975
RADOOM	1105	Vosper Thornycroft	15 Dec 1975
GHANADHAH	1106	Vosper Thornycroft	1 Mar 1976

MURBAN   9/1975 John G. Callis

Displacement, tons: 110 standard; 175 full load
Dimensions, feet (metres): 110 oa × 21 × 6·6 *(33·5 × 6·4 × 1·7)*
Guns: 2—30 mm A32 (twin); 1—20 mm A41A
Main engines: 2 Paxman Valenta diesels; 5 400 hp = 30 knots
Range, miles: 1 800 at 14 knots
Complement: 26

A class of round bilge steel hull craft which have been transported to Abu Dhabi by heavy-lift ships.

3 KEITH NELSON TYPE (COASTAL PATROL CRAFT)

Name	No.	Builders	Completed
BANI YAS	P563	Keith Nelson, Bembridge	July 1969
KAWKAB	P561	Keith Nelson, Bembridge	Jan 1969
THOABAN	P562	Keith Nelson, Bembridge	Jan 1969

Displacement, tons: 32
Dimensions, feet (metres): 57 × 16·5 × 4·5 *(17·4 × 5·1 × 1·4)*
Guns: 2—20 mm (single)
Main engines: 2 Caterpillar diesels. 750 bhp = 19 knots
Range, miles: 300 at 10 knots
Complement: 11 (2 officers, 9 men)

Of glass fibre hull construction.

BANI YAS   1974, Abu Dhabi Naval Force

5 FAIREY MARINE "SPEAR" CLASS (COASTAL PATROL CRAFT)

Dimensions, feet (metres): 29·8 × 9·2 × 2·6 *(9·1 × 2·8 × ·8)*
Guns: 2—7·62 mm MGs
Main engines: 2 Perkins diesels of 290 hp = 25 knots
Complement: 3

Order placed in Feb 1974. Craft delivered between July 1974 and Jan 1975.

"SPEAR" CLASS   1974, Faireys

6 "DHAFEER" CLASS (COASTAL PATROL CRAFT)

Name	No.	Builders	Launched
DHAFEER	P401	Keith Nelson, Bembridge	Feb 1968
DURGHAM	P404	Keith Nelson, Bembridge	Sep 1968
GHADUNFAR	P402	Keith Nelson, Bembridge	May 1968
HAZZA	P403	Keith Nelson, Bembridge	May 1968
MURAYJIB	P406	Keith Nelson, Bembridge	Feb 1970
TIMSAH	P405	Keith Nelson, Bembridge	Sep 1968

Displacement, tons: 10
Dimensions, feet (metres): 40·3 × 11 × 3·5 *(12·3 × 3·4 × 1·1)*
Guns: 1—7·62 MG, 2 light MG
Main engines: 2 Cummins diesels; 370 bhp = 19 knots
Range, miles: 150 at 12 knots
Complement: 6 (1 officer, 5 men)

Of glass fibre hull construction.

HAZZA   1974, Abu Dhabi Naval Force

2 27 FT CHEVERTON TYPE

Of 33 tons and 15 knots. Acquired from Chevertons, Cowes, Isle of Wight in 1975.

ALBANIA

Personnel

(a) 1976: Total 3 000 including 300 coastal frontier guards.
(b) Ratings on 3 years military service.

Bases

Durazzo (Durresi) and Valona (Vlora)

Mercantile Marine

Lloyd's Register of Shipping:
  20 vessels of 57 368 tons gross.

Strength of the Fleet

Corvettes	4
Submarines	4
Fast Attack Craft (Torpedo)	42
Fast Attack Craft (Gun)	4
Minesweepers—Ocean	2
Minesweepers—Inshore	6
MSB	10
Tankers	4
Small Auxiliaries	approx 20

CORVETTES

4 Ex-SOVIET "KRONSTADT" CLASS

Displacement, tons: 310 standard; 380 full load
Dimensions, feet (metres): 170·6 × 21·5 × 9·0 *(52·0 × 6·5 × 2·7)*
Guns: 1—3·5 in *(85 mm)*; 2—37 mm (single); 6—12·7 MG (3 vertical twin)
A/S weapons: 2 depth charge projectors; 2 DC rails
Main engines: 3 Diesels; 3 shafts; 3 300 bhp = 24 knots
Range, miles: 1 500 at 12 knots
Complement: 65

Equipped for minelaying: 2 rails; about 40 mines. Four were transferred from the USSR in 1958. Albania sent two for A/S updating in 1960 and two others in 1961.

Radar: Surface search—Ball Gun. Navigation—Neptun. IFF—High Pole.

"KRONSTADT" Class

"KRONSTADT" Class

SUBMARINES

4 Ex-SOVIET "WHISKY" CLASS

Displacement, tons: 1 030 surfaced; 1 350 dived
Length, feet (metres): 249·3 *(76)*
Beam, feet (metres): 22·0 *(6·7)*
Draught, feet (metres): 15·0 *(4·6)*
Tubes: 6—21 in (4 bow, 2 stern); 18 torpedoes or 40 mines
Main machinery: Diesels; 4 000 bhp; 2 shafts = 17 knots surfaced
  Electric motors; 2 500 hp = 15 knots dived
Range, miles: 13 000 at 8 knots surfaced
Complement: 60

Three of the four "Whisky" class submarines are operational and one is now used as a stationary training hulk. All are based at Vlora. Two were transferred from the USSR in 1960, and two others were reportedly seized from the USSR in mid-1961 upon the withdrawal of Soviet ships from their Albanian base.

Radar: Snoop Plate.

"WHISKY" CLASS

LIGHT FORCES

32 Ex-CHINESE "HU CHWAN" CLASS (FAST ATTACK CRAFT—TORPEDO)

Displacement, tons: 45
Dimensions, feet (metres): 71 × 14·5 × 3·1 *(21·8 × 4·5 × 0·9)*
Guns: 2—14·5 mm (twin vertical)
Torpedo tubes: 2—21 inch
Main engines: 2 M50 Diesels; 2 shafts; 2 200 hp = 55 knots

Built in Shanghai and transferred as follows: 6 in 1968, 15 in 1969, 2 in 1970 and 7 in 1971.

Radar: Skinhead.

HU CHWAN   *1972*

4 Ex-CHINESE "SHANGHAI II" CLASS

Displacement, tons: 120 standard; 155 full load
Dimensions, feet (metres): 128 × 18 × 5·6 *(39 × 5·5 × 1·7)*
Guns: 1—57 mm (forward); 2 37 mm (twin, aft); 2—25 mm (twin, abaft bridge)
A/S armament: 8 DCs
Mines: Minerails can be fitted; probably only 10 mines
Main engines: 4 Diesels; 4 800 bhp = 30 knots
Complement: 25

Transferred in mid-1974.

Radar: Skinhead.

"SHANGHAI II" Class

12 Ex-SOVIET "P-4" CLASS (FAST ATTACK CRAFT—TORPEDO)

111   115   304   +9

Displacement, tons: 25
Dimensions, feet (metres): 62·3 × 11·5 × 5·6 *(19·0 × 3·5 × 1·7)*
Guns: 2 or 4—12·7 mm MG (see notes)
Tubes: 2—18 in *(450 mm)*
Main engines: 2 Diesels; 2 Shafts; 2 200 bhp = 50 knots

Six were transferred from the USSR in 1956 (with radar and 2-12·7 mm MG) and six from China, three in April 1965 and three in Sep 1965, without radar and with 4—12·7 mm MG (2 twin). Radar now fitted.

Albanian "P4" Class

MINE WARFARE FORCES

2 Ex-SOVIET "T 43" CLASS (MINESWEEPERS, OCEAN)

Displacement, tons: 500 standard; 610 full load
Dimensions, feet (metres): 190·2 × 28·2 × 6·9 *(58·0 × 8·6 × 2·1)*
Guns: 4—37 mm (2 twin); 4—25 mm
Main engines: 2 Diesels; 2 shafts; 2 000 bhp = 17 knots
Range, miles: 1 600 at 10 knots
Complement: 40

Transferred in Aug 1960.

"T 43" Class

10 Ex-SOVIET "PO 2" CLASS (MSB)

Displacement, tons: 40 to 45 standard; 45 to 50 full load
Dimensions, feet (metres): 82·0 × 16·7 × 5·6 *(25 × 5·1 × 1·7)*
Guns: 2—25 mm or 2—13 mm
Main engines: Diesels = 30 knots

There are reports of some 10 "PO 2" class in service and possibly 3 ex-Italian "MS 501" class. The "PO 2" class, though primarily minesweeping boats, are also general utility craft. They were transferred as follows: 4 in 1957, 3 in 1958-59, 4 in 1960.

6 Ex-SOVIET "T 301" CLASS (MINESWEEPERS—INSHORE)

343   344   +4

Displacement, tons: 150 standard; 180 full load
Dimensions, feet (metres): 128·0 × 18·0 × 4·9 *(39·0 × 5·5 × 1·5)*
Guns: 2—37 mm; 2—25 mm
Main engines: 2 diesels; 2 shafts; 1 440 bhp = 17 knots
Range, miles: 2 200 at 10 knots
Complement: 25

Transferred from USSR—two in 1957, two in 1959 and two in 1960.

"T 301" Class

DEGAUSSING SHIP

1 Ex-SOVIET "SEKSTAN" CLASS

354

Dimensions, feet (metres): 134·0 × 40·0 × 14·0 *(40·9 × 12·2 × 4·3)*
Main engines: Diesels; 400 bhp = 11 knots
Complement: 35

Built in Finland in 1956. Transferred from the USSR in 1960.

TANKERS

2 Ex- SOVIET "KHOBI" CLASS (PETROL TANKERS)

PATOS   SEMANI

Displacement, tons: 800
Measurement, tons: 1 600 deadweight; 1 500 oil
Dimensions, feet (metres): 220·0 × 33·0 × 15·0 *(67·1 × 10·1 × 4·6)*
Main engines: 2 diesels; 1 600 bhp = 12 knots

Launched in 1956. Transferred from the USSR in Sep 1958 and Feb 1959. *Semani* may be ex-Soviet M/V *Linda*.

Radar: Neptun.

"KHOBI" Class

1 Ex-SOVIET "TOPLIVO 1" CLASS (YARD TANKER)

Displacement, tons: 280

Transferred from the USSR in March 1960. Similar to "Khobi" class in appearance though smaller.

1 Ex-SOVIET "TOPLIVO 3" CLASS (YARD TANKER)

Displacement, tons: 275

Transferred from the USSR in 1960.

MISCELLANEOUS

1 Ex-SOVIET "POLUCHAT I" CLASS

SKENDERBEU A641

Displacement, tons: 86 standard; 91 full load
Dimensions, feet (metres): 98·0 pp × 15·0 × 4·8 *(29·9 × 4·6 × 1·5)*
Guns: 2—14·5 mm
Main engines: 2 Diesels; 2 Shafts; 1 200 bhp = 18 knots
Range, miles: 460 at 17 knots
Complement: 16

Probably used for torpedo recovery. Transferred in 1968.

TUGS

Several small tugs are employed in local duties or harbour service.

DIVING TENDER

1 Ex-SOVIET "NYRIAT" CLASS

There are reported to be a dozen or so harbour and port tenders including a water carrier and two small transports. The "Atrek" class submarine tender transferred from USSR in 1961 as a depot ship was converted into a merchant ship. With large lakes on both the Yugoslav and Greek borders a number of small patrol craft are stationed on these lakes.

ALGERIA

Personnel

(a) 1976: Total 3 500 (250 officers and cadets and 3 250 men)
(b) Voluntary service

Bases

Algiers, Annaba, Mers el Kebir

Mercantile Marine

Lloyd's Register of Shipping:
   78 vessels of 246 432 tons gross

Strength of the Fleet

Corvettes	6
Fast Attack Craft (Missile)	9
Fast Attack Craft (Torpedo)	10
Minesweepers—Ocean	2
Training Ship	1

CORVETTES

6 Ex-SOVIET "SO I" CLASS

P651-656

Displacement, tons: 215 light; 250 full load
Dimensions, feet (metres): 138·6 × 20·0 × 9·2 *(42·3 × 6·1 × 2·8)*
Guns: 4—25 mm (2 twin mounts)
A/S weapons: 4 MBU 1800 rocket launchers
Main engines: 3 diesels; 6 000 bhp = 29 knots
Range, miles: 1 100 at 13 knots
Complement: 30

Delivered by USSR on 7 and 8 Oct 1967, first two, and the other four since 1968. Two have subsequently been fitted with two torpedo tubes, possibly 16 inch.

"SO I" Class

LIGHT FORCES

3 Ex-SOVIET "OSA I" CLASS (FAST ATTACK CRAFT—MISSILE)

R167   R267   R367

Displacement, tons: 165 standard; 200 full load
Dimensions, feet (metres): 128·7 × 25·1 × 5·9 *(39·3 × 7·7 × 1·8)*
Missiles: 4 SSN 2A (Styx)
Guns: 4—30 mm (2 twin)
Main engines: 3 diesels; 13 000 bhp = 32 knots
Range, miles: 800 at 25 knots
Complement: 25

One boat was delivered by USSR on 7 Oct 1967. Two others transferred later in same year.

"OSA I" Class

6 Ex-SOVIET "KOMAR" CLASS (FAST ATTACK CRAFT—MISSILE)

671-676

Displacement, tons: 70 standard; 80 full load
Dimensions, feet (metres): 83·7 × 19·8 × 5·0 *(25·5 × 6·0 × 1·5)*
Missiles: 2 SSN 2A (Styx)
Guns: 2—25 mm (twin)
Main engines: 4 diesels, 4 shafts, 4 800 bhp = 40 knots
Range, miles: 400 at 30 knots
Complement: 20

Acquired in 1967 from USSR.

10 Ex-SOVIET "P6" CLASS (FAST ATTACK CRAFT—TORPEDO)

621-630

Displacement, tons: 66 standard; 75 full load
Dimensions, feet (metres): 84·2 × 20·0 × 6·0 *(25·7 × 6·1 × 1·8)*
Guns: 4—25 mm (twin)
Tubes: 2—21 inch (or mines or depth charges)
Main engines: 4 diesels, 4 shafts, 4 800 bhp = 43 knots
Range, miles: 450 at 30 knots
Complement: 25

Acquired from the USSR between 1963 and 1966. Four retain their original armament whilst the remainder, with tubes removed, are used for coast-guard duties. Two deleted 1975.

MINE WARFARE FORCES

2 Ex-SOVIET "T 43" CLASS (MINESWEEPERS, OCEAN)

M221   M222

Displacement, tons: 500 standard; 610 full load
Dimensions, feet (metres): 190·2 × 28·2 × 6·9 *(58·0 × 8·6 × 2·1)*
Guns: 4—37 mm (twin); 4—25 mm (twin)
Main engines: 2 diesels; 2 shafts; 2 000 hp = 17 knots
Range, miles: 1 600 at 10 knots
Complement: 40

Transferred in 1968.

"T 43" Class

MISCELLANEOUS

1 Ex-SOVIET "POLUCHAT" CLASS

A641

Operates as TRV.

1 Ex-SOVIET "SEKSTAN" CLASS

VASOUYA A640

Transferred in 1964. Operates as survey ship.

1 HARBOUR TUG

YAVDEZAN VP650

Completed in 1965.

2 FISHERY PROTECTION CRAFT

JEBEL ANTAR   JEBEL HONDA

1 TRAINING SHIP

SIDI FRADJ (ex-*Darfour*)

One of two ex-US BYMS given to Algeria by Egypt in 1962 as the start of the new navy. Sister ship *(Djebel Aures)* wrecked in 1963. *Sidi Fradj* probably ready for disposal.

ANGUILLA

1 FAIREY MARINE "HUNTSMAN" CLASS

A 28 ft launch supplied in 1974. She is unarmed and used for anti-smuggling operations and for Air-Sea Rescue. Belongs to the Royal St. Christopher, Nevis and Anguilla Police Force being based at Basseterre, St. Kitts under the supervision of Superintendent W. Galloway.

ARGENTINA

Headquarters Appointments

Commander of the Navy and Chief of Naval Operations:
  Rear Admiral E. E. Massera
Chief of Naval Staff:
  Rear Admiral A. Lambruschini

Diplomatic Representation

Head of Argentinian Training Mission Asunción, Paraguay:
  Captain Jorge E. Bocaccio
Naval Attaché in Bogota:
  Captain Luis Santiago Martella
Naval Attaché in Brasilia:
  Captain Mario E. Olmos
Naval Attaché in Cape Town:
  Captain Eldo Buzzo
Naval Attaché in London and The Hague and Head of the Argentine Naval Mission in Europe:
  Rear Admiral Jorge I. Anaya
Naval Attaché in Lima:
  Captain Horacio M. Goñi
Naval Attaché in Madrid:
  Captain Isidro A. Paradelo
Naval Attaché in Montevideo:
  Captain Pedro H. Dimenna
Naval Attaché in Paris:
  Captain J. C. Malugani
Naval Attaché in Rome:
  Captain Mario F. Robles
Naval Attaché in Santiago:
  Captain Niceto E. Ayerra
Naval Attaché in Tokyo:
  Captain Rafael J. Serra
Naval Attaché in Washington:
  Rear Admiral Antonio Vanek

Personnel

(a) 1976: 32 900 (2 890 officers, 18 010 petty officers and ratings and 12 000 conscripts)
  Marine Corps: 6 000 officers and men
(b) Volunteers plus 14 months national service

Note. Corpo de Infanteria de Marina (Marine Corps)
1st Marine Force: (3 battalions)
2nd Marine Force: (1 field artillery battalion, 1 air defence battalion, 1 anti-tank company, communication and amphibious craft units)
Based at or near naval bases and installations. Equipped with 20 LVTP-7, 15 LARC-5, 10 "Tigercat" SAM, 155 mm and 105 mm how., 30 mm guns, "Bantam" A-T missiles, 105 mm recoilless rifles.

Naval Bases

Buenos Aires (Darsena Norte): Dockyard, 3 Floating Docks, Schools.
Rio Santiago (La Plata): Naval Base, Schools, Naval shipbuilding yard (AFNE).
Mar de Plata: Submarine base with slipway.
Puerto Belgrano: Main Naval Base, Schools, 2 dry docks, 1 floating dock.
Ushaia: Small naval base.

Naval Aviation

15 A-4Q Skyhawk*
12 Aermacchi MB 326 GB
6 S-2A Tracker*

3 HU-16B Albatross maritime patrol
4 P2-H Neptune
— PBY-5A Catalina

4 Alouette III Helicopter
6 Bell 47 (Sioux) (2 with PNA)
6 Hughes 500M (Cayuse) (PNA)
4 Sikorsky S-61D (Sea King)
5 SH-34G (Seabat)
2 Sea Lynx
5 Sikorsky S-55 (Chickasaw)

3 DHC Beaver Transport
8 C-47 Dakota/Skytrain
3 C-54 Skymaster
1 FMA IA 50 GII
1 HS 125 Srs. 400A
3 Lockheed L-188 Electra
5 Short Skyvan (PNA)
30 T-28 Fennec Trainer
1 DHC-6 Twin Otter
2 Beech Super King Air 200
3 Fairchild-Hiller Porter
6 Beech C45-H
10 North American SNJ-5C/T-6

*Carrier-based.

Prefectura Naval Argentina (PNA)

PNA is responsible for coastguard and rescue duties. It also administers the Merchant Navy School at Buenos Aires.

Prefix to Ships' Names

ARA

Mercantile Marine

Lloyd's Register of Shipping:
  374 vessels of 1 447 165 tons gross

Strength of the Fleet

Type	Active	Building
Attack Carrier (Medium)	1	—
Cruisers	2	—
Destroyers	9	1
Frigates	—	(6)*
Corvettes	12	—
Patrol Submarine	4	—
Landing Ships (Tank)	4	1
Landing Craft (Tank)	1	—
Minor Landing Craft	19	—
Fast Attack Craft (Missile)	—	2
Fast Attack Craft (Gun)	2	—
Fast Attack Craft (Torpedo)	2	—
Large Patrol Craft	5	—
Minesweepers (Coastal)	4	—
Minehunters	2	—
Survey Ships	5	2
Survey Launches	2	—
Transports	2	—
Tankers (Fleet Support)	3	—
Icebreaker	1	1
Training Ship	1	—
Tugs	14	—

*Preliminary agreement was reached with Vosper Thornycroft in May 1975 for building at AFNE of six Type 21 Frigates.

DELETIONS

Attack Carrier (medium)

1971 *Independencia*

Cruiser

1973 *La Argentina*

Destroyers

1971 *Buenos Aires, Misiones, San Luis*
1973 *Entre Rios, San Juan, Santa Cruz*

Frigates

1973 *Juan B Azopardo, Piedrabuena, Azopardo*

Minesweeper Support Ship

1971 *Corrientes*

Submarines

1972 *Santa Fe (ex-Lamprey) Santiago del Estero (ex-Macabi),* scrapped for spares

Amphibious Forces

1971 *BDI 4, BDI 15, BDM 1, Cabo San Bartolome*
1973 *EDVP 4, 5, 6, 11, 20, 22, 27*

Survey Ships

1970 *Commodoro Augusto Lasserre*
1972 *Capitan Canepa* (scrap)
1973 *Ushuia* sunk in collision

Transport

1971 *La Patria* (sold)
1973 *Bahia Thetis*

Tankers

1971 *Punta Rasa, Punta Lara*

Salvage Ship

1974 *Guardiamarina Zicari*

Tugs

1971 *Querendi*
1974 *Mataco*

PENNANT LIST

Aircraft Carrier

V 2   25 de Mayo

Cruisers

C 4	Belgrano
C 5	9 de Julio

Destroyers

D 01	Hercules
D 02	Santissima Trinidad
D 20	Almirante Brown
D 21	Espora
D 22	Rosales
D 23	Almirante Domecq Garcia
D 24	Almirante Storni
D 25	Segui
D 26	Bouchard
D 27	Py

Corvettes

P 20	Murature
P 21	King
A 1	Com. G. Irigoyen
A 2	Com. G. Zapiola
A 3	Francisco de Churruca
A 4	Thompson
A 5	Diaguita
A 6	Yamana
A 7	Chiriguano
A 8	Sanavirón
A 9	Alferez Sobral
A 10	Comodoro Somellera

Submarines

S 21	Santa Fe
S 22	Santiago del Estero
S 31	Salta
S 32	San Luis

Mine Warfare Forces

M 1	Neuquen
M 2	Rio Negro
M 3	Chubut
M 4	Tierra del Fuego
M 5	Chaco
M 6	Formosa

Light Forces

P 55	Surubi
P 82	Alakush
P 84	Towara
ELPR 1	Intrepida
ELPR 2	Indomita
GC 21	Lynch
GC 22	Toll
GC 23	Erezcano
GC 31	—

Amphibious Forces

Q 42	Cabo San Antonio
Q 43	Candido De Lasala
Q 44	Cabo San Gonzalo
Q 46	Cabo San Isidro
Q 50	Cabo San Pio
Q 56	BDI

Miscellaneous

B 2	Bahia Aguirre
B 6	Bahia Buen Suceso
B 12	Punta Alta
B 16	Punta Delgada
B 1	Punta Médanos
Q 2	Libertad
Q 4	General San Martin
Q 7	El Austral
Q 9	Islas Orcadas
Q 15	Cormoran
R 3	Mataco
R 4	Toba
R 5	Mocovi
R 6	Calchaqui
R 10	Huarpe
R 12	Huarpe
R 16	Capayan
R 18	Chiquillan
R 19	Morcoyan
R 29	Pehuenche
R 30	Tonocote
R 32	Quilmes
R 33	Guaycuru

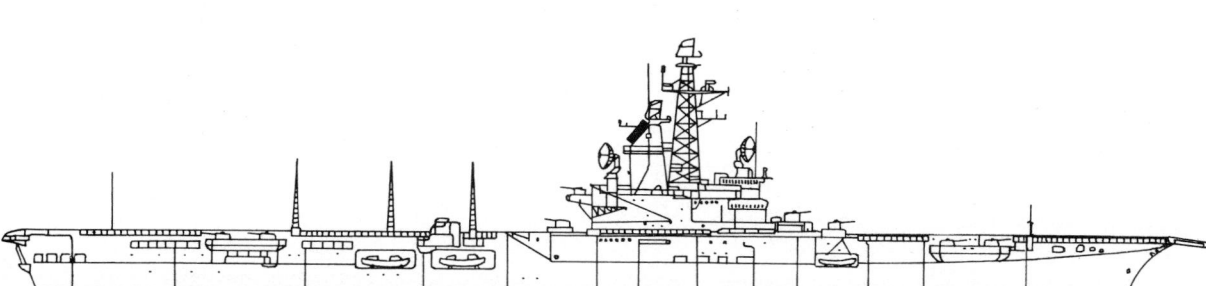

VEINTICINCO DE MAYO

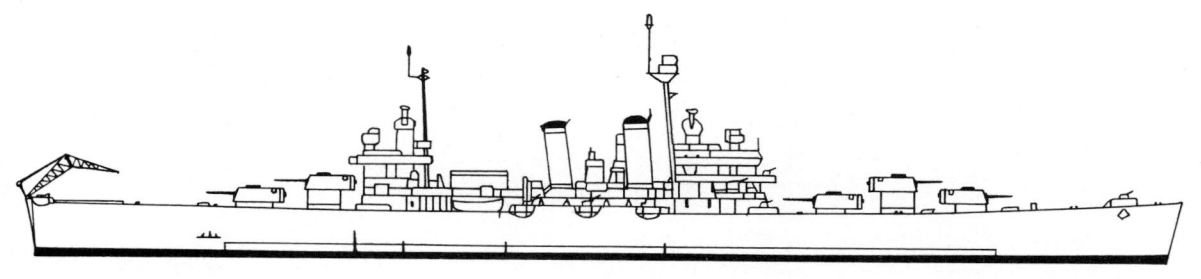

"BROOKLYN" Class

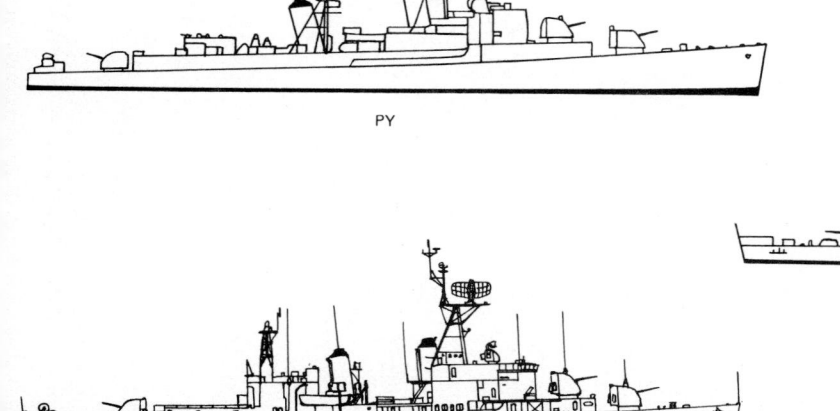

PY

"ALLEN M. SUMNER" Class

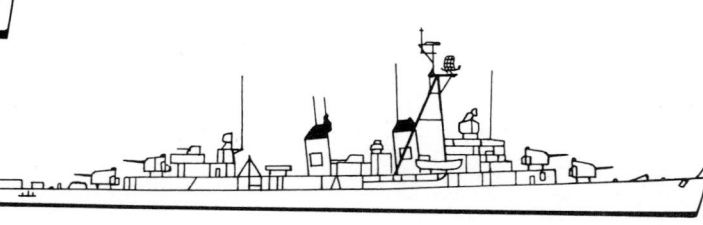

"FLETCHER" Class

AIRCRAFT CARRIER
1 Ex-BRITISH "COLOSSUS" CLASS

Name
VEINTICINCO DE MAYO
(ex-*HNMS Karel Doorman*, ex-*HMS Venerable*)

No.	Builders	Laid down	Launched	Commissioned
V 2	Cammell Laird & Co. Ltd., Birkenhead	3 Dec 1942	30 Dec 1943	17 Jan 1945

Displacement, tons: 15 892 standard; 19 896 full load
Length, feet (metres): 630 *(192·0)* pp 693·2 *(211·3)* oa
Beam, feet (metres): 80 *(24·4)*
Draught, feet (metres): 25 *(7·6)*
Width, feet (metres): 121·3 *(37·0)* oa
Hangar:
  Length, feet (metres): 455 *(138·7)*
  Width, feet (metres): 52 *(15·8)*
  Height, feet (metres): 17·5 *(5·3)*
Aircraft: Capacity 21; operates with variable complement of
  S-2A Trackers, A-4Q Skyhawks and S-61D Sea King ASW
  helicopters
Guns: 9—40 mm (single Bofors 40/70)
Main engines: Parsons geared turbines; 40 000 shp; 2 shafts
Boilers: 4 three-drum; working pressure 400 psi *(28·1 kg/cm²)*;
  Superheat 700°F *(371°C)*
Speed, knots: 24·25
Oil fuel, tons: 3 200
Range, miles: 12 000 at 14 knots, 6 200 at 23 knots
Complement: 1 500

25 DE MAYO

1969, Argentine Navy

Purchased from Great Britain on 1 Apr 1948 and commissioned in the Royal Netherlands Navy on 28 May 1948. Damaged by boiler fire on 29 Apr 1968. Sold to Argentina on 15 Oct 1968 and refitted at Rotterdam by N. V. Dok en Werf Mij Wilton Fijenoord. Commissioned in the Argentine Navy on 12 Mar 1969. Completed refit on 22 Aug 1969 and sailed for Argentina on 1 Sep 1969. With modified island superstructure and bridge lattice tripod radar mast, and tall raked funnel, she differs considerably from her former appearance and from her original sister ships in the British, Australian, Brazilian, French and Indian navies.

Engineering: The turbine sets and boilers are arranged *en echelon*, the two propelling-machinery spaces having two boilers and one set of turbines in each space, on the unit system. She was reboilered in 1965-1966 with boilers removed from HMS *Leviathan*. During refit for Argentina in 1968-1969 she received new turbines, also from HMS *Leviathan*.

Radar: *Search:* Two Philips LWO series early warning radars with associated height finders of VI series for air interception. *Tactical:* DA Series tactical and navigation radar.

Reconstruction: Underwent extensive refit modernisation in 1955-1958 including angled flight deck and steam catapult, rebuilt island, mirror sight landing system, and new anti-aircraft battery of ten 40 mm guns, at the Wilton-Fijenoord Shipyard, at a cost of 25 million guilders. Conversion completed in July 1958.

Electronics: Fitted with Ferranti CAAIS with Plessey Super-CAAIS displays. The system has been modified to provide control of carrier based aircraft and will be capable of direct computer-to-computer radio data links with the new Type 42 destroyers.

25 DE MAYO

1974, Argentine Navy

CRUISERS

2 Ex-US "BROOKLYN" CLASS

Name
GENERAL BELGRANO (ex-*17 de Octubre*, ex-*Phoenix*, CL 46)
NUEVE DE JULIO (ex-*Boise*, CL 47)

No.	Builders	Laid down	Launched	Commissioned
C 4	New York S.B. Corp, Camden	15 Apr 1935	12 Mar 1938	18 Mar 1939
C 5	Newport News S.B. & D.D. Co.	1 Apr 1935	3 Dec 1936	1 Feb 1939

Displacement, tons: *Gen. Belgrano:* 10 800 standard; 13 645 full load. *Nueve de Julio:* 10 500 standard; 13 645 full load
Length, feet (metres): 608·3 *(185·4)* oa
Beam, feet (metres): 69 *(21·0)*
Draught, feet (metres): 24 *(7·3)*
Aircraft: 2 helicopters
Missiles: 2 quadruple "Sea Cat" launchers *(General Belgrano only)*
Guns: *Gen. Belgrano:* 15—6 in *(153 mm)* 47 cal; 8—5 in *(127 mm)* 25 cal; 2 Twin—40 mm; 4—47 mm (saluting)
Nueve de Julio: 15—6 *(153 mm)* 47 cal; 6—5 in *(127 mm)* 25 cal; 4 Twin—40 mm; 4—47 mm (saluting)
Armour:
 Belt 4 in—1½ in *(102–38 mm)*
 Decks 3 in—2 in *(76–51 mm)*
 Turrets 5 in—3 in *(127–76 mm)*
 Conning Tower 8 in *(203 mm)*
Main engines: Parsons geared turbines; 100 000 shp; 4 shafts
Boilers: 8 Babcock & Wilcox Express type
Speed, knots: 32·5 (when new)
Range, miles: 7 600 at 15 knots
Oil fuel, tons: 2 200
Complement: 1 200

1973, Argentine Navy

Superstructure was reduced, bulges added, beam increased, and mainmast derricks and catapults removed before transfer. Purchased from the United States in 1951 at a cost of $7 800 000 and transferred to the Argentine Navy on 12 Apr 1951. *General Belgrano* was commissioned under the name *17 de Octubre* at Philadelphia on 17 Oct 1951. *9 de Julio* was commissioned into the Argentine Navy at Philadelphia on 11 Mar 1952. *9 de Julio* refers to 9 July 1816, when the Argentine provinces signed the Declaration of Independence. *17 de Octubre* was renamed *General Belgrano* in 1956 following the overthrow of President Peron the year before.

Radar: Search: LWO and DA Series (Signaal).

Hangar: The hangar in the hull right aft accommodates two helicopters together with engine spares and duplicate parts, though 4 aircraft was the original complement.

Gunnery: FCS 33 (2) (1 in *Belgrano*), FCS 34 (1), FCS 57 (2), FCS 63 (2), FCS NA9-D1 (1 in *Belgrano*), TDS (1)

9 DE JULIO

1971, Argentine Navy

DESTROYERS

1 + 1 BRITISH TYPE 42

Name
HERCULES
SANTISSIMA TRINIDAD

No.	Builders	Laid down	Launched	Commissioned
D 01	Vickers, Barrow-in-Furness	16 June1971	24 Oct 1972	Nov 1975
D 02	AFNE, Rio Santiago	11 Oct 1971	Mar 1974	1976 (?)

Displacement, tons: 3 150 standard; 3 500 full load
Length, feet (metres): 392·0 *(119·5)* wl; 410·0 *(125·0)* oa
Beam, feet (metres): 48 *(14·6)*
Draught, feet (metres): 17 *(5·2)*
Missile launchers: 1 "Sea Dart" (twin)
Aircraft: 1 Lynx helicopter
Guns: 1—4·5 in automatic; 2—20 mm Oerlikon
Main engines: Rolls Royce Olympus gas turbines for full power; Rolls Royce Tyne gas turbines for cruising; 2 shafts; 50 000 shp
Speed, knots: 30
Range, miles: 4 000 at 18 knots
Complement: 300

These two destroyers are of the British Type 42. On 18 May 1970 the signing of a contract between the Argentine Government and Vickers Ltd, Barrow-in-Furness was announced. This provided for the construction of these two ships, one to be built at Barrow-in-Furness and the second at Rio Santiago with British assistance and overseeing. *Santissima Trinidad* was sabotaged on 22 Aug 1975 whilst fitting-out and subsequently placed in floating-dock at AFNE. Completion date remains uncertain.

TYPE 42

5 Ex-US "FLETCHER" CLASS

Name
ALMIRANTE BROWN (ex-USS *Heermann*, DD 532)
ESPORA (ex-USS *Dortch*, DD 670)
ROSALES (ex-USS *Stembel*, DD 644)
ALMIRANTE DOMECQ GARCIA (ex-USS *Braine*, DD 630)
ALMIRANTE STORNI (ex-USS *Cowell*, DD 547)

No.	Builders	Laid down	Launched	Commissioned
D 20	Bethlehem Steel Co, San Francisco	8 May 1942	5 Dec 1942	6 July 1943
D 21	Federal S.B. & D.D. Co, Port Newark	2 Mar 1943	20 June1943	7 Aug 1943
D 22	Bath Iron Works Corporation, Bath, Maine	21 Dec 1942	8 May 1943	16 July 1943
D 23	Bath Iron Works Corporation, Bath, Maine	12 Oct 1942	7 Mar 1943	11 May 1943
D 24	Bethlehem Steel Co, San Pedro	7 Sep 1942	18 Mar 1943	23 Aug 1943

Displacement, tons: 2 100 standard; 3 050 full load
Length, feet (metres): 376·5 *(114·8)* oa
Beam, feet (metres): 39·5 *(12·0)*
Draught, feet (metres): 18 *(5·5)*
Guns: 4—5 in *(127 mm)* 38 cal; 6—3 in *(76 mm)* 50 cal
Torpedo tubes: 4—21 in *(533 mm)* quad (20, 21, 22);
6—Mk 32 (Triples) (23, 24)
A/S depth charges: 2 fixed Hedgehogs; 1 DC rack (Mk 3)
Main engines: 2 sets GE or AC geared turbines 60 000 shp;
2 shafts
Boilers: 4 Babcock & Wilcox
Speed, knots: 35
Range, miles: 6 000 at 15 knots
Oil fuel, tons: 650
Complement: 300

First three transferred to the Argentine Navy on 1 Aug 1961.
Espora is of the later "Fletcher" class. Last pair transferred 17
Aug 1971. *Almirante Brown* is division leader. USS *Knapp* (D
653) is also reported transferred as source of spare parts.

Gunnery: D20, 21, 22: FCS 37 (1), FCS 56 (1), FCS 63 (2),
FCS 105 (1), TDS 5 (1).
D23, 24: FCS 37 (1), FCS 56 (1), FCS 105 (1), TDS 5 (1).

Missiles: To be fitted with Exocet.

Radar: Search: C/D Band SPS 6.   Tactical: G Band SPS 10. Fire
Control: I Band, antenna on Director.

ESPORA   *1974, Argentine Navy*

2 Ex-US "ALLEN M. SUMNER" CLASS

Name
BOUCHARD (ex-USS *Borie* DD 704)
SEGUI (ex-USS *Hank* DD 702)

No.	Builders	Laid down	Launched	Commissioned
D 26	Federal SB & DD Co.	—	4 July 1944	21 Sep 1944
D 25	Federal SB & DD Co.	—	21 May 1944	28 Aug 1944

Displacement, tons: 2 200 standard; 3 320 full load
Length, feet (metres): 376·5 *(114·8)* oa
Beam, feet (metres): 40·9 *(12·5)*
Draught, feet (metres): 19 *(5·8)*
Guns: 6—5 in *(127 mm)* 38 cal; 8; DP (twin); 4—3 in *(Segui* only)
A/S Weapons: 6—Mk 32 (Triple); 2 ahead-firing Hedgehogs;
1 DCT. Facilities for small helicopter
Main engines: 2 geared turbines; 60 000 shp; 2 shafts
Boilers: 4
Speed, knots: 34
Range, miles: 3 865 at 11 knots; 990 at 31 knots
Complement: *Bouchard* 291; *Segui* 331

Transferred to Argentina 1 July 1972. *Bouchard* has been modernised with VDS, helicopter facilities and hangar. Two units,
ex-USS *Mansfield* DD 728 and ex-USS *Collet* DD 730, transferred June 1974 and Apr 1974 respectively for spares.

Gunnery: FCS 37 (1), FCS 36 (1 in *Segui*), FCS 105 (1), TDS 5 (1).

Missiles: To be fitted with Exocet.

Radar: *(Bouchard)*. SPS 10, SPS 40 and GFCS Mk 25.

Sonar: *(Bouchard)*. SQA 10A, SQS 30.

SEGUI (as USS BORIE)

1 FRAM II "GEARING" CLASS

Name
PY (ex-USS *Perkins* DD 877)

No.	Builders	Laid down	Launched	Commissioned
D 27	Consolidated Steel Corpn.	7 Dec 1944	—	5 Apr 1945

Displacement, tons: 2 425 standard; approx 3 500 full load
Length, feet (metres): 390·5 *(119·0)*
Beam, feet (metres): 40·9 *(12·4)*
Draught, feet (metres): 19·0 *(5·8)*
Guns: 6—5 inch *(127 mm)*, 38 cal. DP (twins)
A/S weapons: 2 Fixed Hedgehogs; 6—Mk 32 (triple).
Facilities for small helicopter
Main engines: 2 geared Westinghouse turbines
Boilers: 4 Babcock & Wilcox
Speed, knots: 31·5
Range, miles: 6 150 at 11 knots; 1 475 at 30 knots
Complement: 275

Transferred by sale 15 Jan 1973.

Gunnery: FCS 37 (1), FCS 106 (1).

Radar: SPS 10, SPS 40 and GFCS Mk 25.

Sonar: SQS 23.

PY (as USS PERKINS)

CORVETTES

Note. A 40 metre Aviso is reported as being ordered from an Argentine yard in 1975.

2 "KING" CLASS

Name	No.	Builders	Commissioned
KING	P 21	Astillero Nav. Rio Santiago	28 July 1946
MURATURE	P 20	Astillero Nav. Rio Santiago	18 Nov 1946

Displacement, tons: 913 standard; 1 000 normal; 1 032 full load
Length, feet (metres): 252·7 *(77·0)*
Beam, feet (metres): 29 *(8·8)*
Draught, feet (metres): 7·5 *(2·3)*
Guns: 3—4·1 *(105 mm);* 4—40 mm Bofors; 2—MG
A/S: 4—DCT
Main engines: 2—Werkspoor 4-stroke diesels; 2 500 bhp; 2 shafts
Speed, knots: 18
Oil fuel (tons): 90
Range, miles: 6 000 at 12 knots
Complement: 130

Named after Captain John King, an Irish follower of Admiral Brown, who distinguished himself in the war with Brazil, 1826-28; and Captain Murature, who performed conspicuous service against the Paraguayans at the Battle of Cuevas on Aug 6 1865. Used for cadet training.

MURATURE   *1974, Argentine Navy*

6 Ex-US ATA TYPE

Name	No.	Builders	Commissioned
ALFEREZ SOBRAL (ex-USS *Catawba,* ATA 210)	A 9	Levingstone Sb Co, Orange	1944
CHIRIGUANO (ex-US ATA 227)	A 7	,,	1945
COMODORO SOMELLERA (ex-USS *Salish* ATA 187)	A 10	,,	1945
DIAGUITA (ex-US ATA 124)	A 5	,,	1945
SANAVIRON (ex-US ATA 228)	A 8	,,	1945
YAMANA (ex-US ATA 126)	A 6	,,	1945

Displacement, tons: 689 standard; 800 full load
Dimensions, feet (metres): 134·5 wl; 143 oa × 34 × 12 *(43·4 × 10·4 × 3·6)*
Gun: 1—40/60 mm
Main engines: Diesel-electric; 1 500 bhp = 12·5 knots
Oil fuel (tons): 154
Range, miles: 16 500 at 8 knots
Complement: 49

Former US auxiliary ocean tugs. *Diaguita* and *Yamana* are fitted as rescue ships. A 5, A 6, A 7 and A 8 which were acquired in 1947 bear names of South American Indian tribes. Classified as ocean salvage tugs until 1966 when they were re-rated as patrol vessels. A 9 and A 10 were transferred on 10 Feb 1972. A 10 operated by Coast Guard.

YAMANA   *1969, Argentine Navy*

3 Ex-US ATF TYPE

Name	No.	Builders	Commissioned
COMMANDANTE GENERAL IRIGOYEN (ex-USS *Cahuilla* ATF 152)	A 1	Charleston SB and DD Co.	10 Mar 1945
COMMANDANTE GENERAL ZAPIOLA (ex-USS *Arapaho* ATF 68)	A 2	Charleston SB and DD Co.	20 Jan 1943
FRANCISCO DE CHURRUCA (ex-USS *Luiseno* ATF 156)	A 3	Charleston SB and DD Co.	17 Mar 1945 (launched)

Displacement, tons: 1 235 standard; 1 675 full load
Dimensions, feet (metres): 195 wl; 205 oa × 38·2 × 15·3 *(62·5 × 11·6 × 4·7)*
Guns: 6—40/60 mm (2 twin; 2 single)
Main engines: 4 sets diesels with electric drive; 3 000 bhp = 16 knots
Complement: 85

Former US fleet ocean tugs of the "Apache" class. Fitted with powerful pumps and other salvage equipment. First two transferred to Argentina at San Diego, California, in 1961. Classified as tugs until 1966 when they were re-rated as patrol vessels. *Francisco De Churruca* transferred 1 July 1975 by sale.

FRANCISCO DE CHURRUCA (as LUISENO)   *USN*

1 "BOUCHARD" CLASS

Name	No.	Builders	Commissioned
SPIRO	GC 12	Rio Santiago	1938

Displacement, tons: 560 normal; 650 full load
Dimensions, feet (metres): 197 oa × 24 × 11·5 *(60·1 × 7·3 × 3·5)*
Guns: 4—40 mm
Main engines: 2 MAN Diesels; 2 000 bhp = 13 knots
Range, miles: 3 000 at 10 knots
Complement: 77

Former minesweeper of the "Bouchard" class, now operated by the Prefectura Naval Argentina. Sister ships *Bouchard, Py* and *Seaver* were transferred to the Paraguayan Navy. This class, originally of 9, were the first warships built in Argentine yards.

SPIRO   *1969, Argentine Navy*

SUBMARINES

2 "SALTA" CLASS (TYPE 209)

Name	No.	Builders	Laid down	Launched	Commissioned
SALTA	S 31	Howaldtswerke, Kiel	—	22 Nov 1972	May 1974
SAN LUIS	S 32	Howaldtswerke, Kiel	—	2 May 1973	May 1974

Displacement, tons: 980 surfaced; 1 230 dived
Length, feet (metres): 183·4 *(55·9)*
Beam, feet (metres): 20·5 *(6·25)*
Draught, feet (metres): 17·9 *(5·4)*
Torpedo tubes: 8—21 in; bow tubes (with reloads)
Main machinery: Diesel electric; MTU Diesels, 4 generators;
1 shaft; 5 000 hp
Speed knots: 10 surfaced, 22 dived
Complement: 32

Built in sections by Howaldtswerke Deutsche Werft AG, Kiel
from the IK 68 design of Ingenieurkontor, Lübeck. Sections
were shipped to Argentina for assembly at Tandanor, Buenos
Aires.

SALTA   *1973, Argentine Navy*

2 "GUPPY (IA and II)" CLASS

Name	No.	Builders	Laid down	Launched	Commissioned
SANTE FE (ex-USS *Catfish* SS 339)	S 21	Electric Boat Co.	—	19 Nov 1944	19 Mar 1945
SANTIAGO DEL ESTERO (ex-USS *Chivo* SS 341)	S 22	Electric Boat Co.	—	14 Jan 1945	28 Apr 1945

Displacement, tons: 1 870 surfaced; 2 420 *(Santa Fe)*;
2 540 *(Santiago)* dived
Length, feet (metres): 307·5 *(93·8)* oa
Beam, feet (metres): 27·2 *(8·3)*
Draught, feet (metres): 18·0 *(5·5) (Santa Fe)*;
17·0 *(5·2) (Santiago)*
Torpedo tubes: 10—21 in *(533 mm)*; 6 fwd, 4 aft
Main machinery: 3 diesels; 4 800 shp; 2 electric motors;
5 400 shp; 2 shafts
Speed, knots: 18 surfaced; 15 dived
Range, miles: 12 000 at 10 knots
Oil fuel, tons: 300
Complement: 82-84

Both of the "Balao" class. *Catfish* was modified under the
Guppy II programme (1948-50) and *Chivo* under the Guppy 1A
programme (1951). Both transferred to Argentina at Mare
Island on 7 Jan 1971.

SANTA FE   *1972, Argentine Navy*

AMPHIBIOUS FORCES

1 Ex-US LANDING SHIP (DOCK)

Name	No.	Builders	Commissioned
CANDIDO DE LASALA (ex-USS *Gunston Hall* LSD 5)	Q 43	Moor Dry Dock Co, Oakland	10 Nov 1943

Displacement, tons: 5 480 standard; 9 375 full load
Dimensions, feet (metres): 457·8 oa × 72·2 × 18·0 *(139·6 × 22 × 6·3)*
Guns: 12—40 mm
Main engines: 2 Skinner Unaflow; 2 shafts; 7 400 shp = 15·4 knots
Boilers: 2 Two drum
Range, miles: 8 000 at 15 knots
Complement: Accommodation for 326 (17 officers and 309 men)

Arcticized in 1948/9. Transferred from the US Navy on 1 May 1970. Carries 14 LCA and has
helicopter facilities. Used as light forces tender.

CANDIDO DE LASALA   *1973, Argentine Navy*

1 LANDING SHIP (TANK)

Name	No.	Builder	Commissioned
CABO SAN ANTONIO	Q 42	AFNE, Rio Santiago	? 1976

Displacement, tons: 4 300 light; 8 000 full load
Dimensions, feet (metres): 445 oa × 62 × 16·5 *(135·7 × 18·9 × 5)*
Guns: 12—40/60 mm (3 quad)
Main engines: Diesels; 2 shafts; 13 700 bhp = 16 knots
Complement: 124

Designed to carry a helicopter and two landing craft. Launched 1968. Completion delayed—
fitting out continuing early 1976. Modified US "De Soto" Class.

Radar: Plessey AWS-1.

CABO SAN ANTONIO   *1974, Argentine Navy*

3 Ex-US LST TYPE

Name	No.	Builders	Commissioned
CABO SAN GONZALO (ex-USS LST 872)	Q 44	Puget Sound B and D Co, Seattle	1944
CABO SAN ISIDRO (ex-USS LST 919)	Q 46	Puget Sound B and D Co, Seattle	1944
CABO SAN PIO (ex-USS LST 1044)	Q 50	Puget Sound B and D Co, Seattle	1944

Displacement, tons: 2 366 beaching; 4 080 full load
Dimensions, feet (metres): 328 oa × 50 × 14 *(100 × 15·3 × 4·3)*
Main engines: 2 diesels; 2 shafts; 1 800 bhp = 11 knots
Oil fuel, tons: 700
Range, miles: 9 500 at 9 knots
Complement: 80

Transferred 1946-47. All ships have two rudders.

1 Ex-US LCT TYPE

BDI (ex-USS *LCIL* 583) Q 56

Displacement, tons: 230 light; 387 full load
Dimensions, feet (metres): 159 oa × 23·2 × 5 *(48·5 × 7·1 × 1·5)*
Guns: 2—20 mm
Main engines: 8 sets diesels; 3 200 bhp = 14 knots. Two reversible propellers
Oil fuel, tons: 110
Range, miles: 6 000 at 12 knots
Complement: 30

Used for training.

27 MINOR LANDING CRAFT

EDM 1, 2, 3, 4

It was stated in Jan 1971 that four LCMs of 195 tons and 11 knots built in the USA had been incorporated in the Fleet.

EDVP 1, 3, 7, 8, 9, 10, 12, 13, 17, 19, 21, 24, 28, 29, 30

Displacement, tons: 12
Dimensions, feet (metres): 39·5 × 10·5 × 5·5 *(12·1 × 3·2 × 1·7)*
Main engines: Diesels, 9 knots

Ex USN LCVPs. Transferred 1946.

8 EDVP

Incorporated at the end of 1970. Numbers not known. Vehicle and personnel landing craft.

LIGHT FORCES

2 GERMAN TYPE 148 (FAST ATTACK CRAFT—MISSILE)

Displacement, tons: 234 standard; 265 full load
Dimensions, feet (metres): 154·2 × 23·0 × 5·9 *(47 × 7 × 2)*
Missiles: Triple launcher for Gabriel missiles
Guns: 1—76 mm; 1—40 mm
Torpedo tubes: 2—21 in (or 8 mines)
Main engines: 4 Diesels = 38 knots
Range, miles: 600 at 30 knots
Complement: 30

Building in Argentina.

GERMAN TYPE 148   1974, Federal German Navy

2 "COMBATTANTE II" CLASS (FAST ATTACK CRAFT—GUN)

Name	No.	Builders	Commissioned
INTREPIDA	ELPR 1	Lürssen, Vegesack	20 July 1974
INDOMITA	ELPR 2	Lürssen, Vegesack	late 1974

Displacement, tons: 240
Dimensions, feet (metres): 164 × 24 × 8·2 *(50 × 7·3 × 2·5)*
Guns: 1—3 in *(76 mm)* Oto Melara; 2—40 mm
Torpedo tubes: 2—21 inch for wire-guided torpedoes
Main engines: 4 Diesels; 4 shafts; 12 000 hp = 40 knots
Complement: 35

These two vessels were ordered in 1970.

INTREPIDA   4/1974, Stefan Terzibaschitsch

3 "LYNCH" CLASS (LARGE PATROL CRAFT)

Name	No.	Builders	Commissioned
EREZCANO	GC 23	AFNE Rio Santiago	1967
LYNCH	GC 21	AFNE Rio Santiago	1964
TOLL	GC 22	AFNE Rio Santiago	1965

Displacement, tons: 100 normal; 117 full load
Dimensions, feet (metres): 90 × 19 × 6 *(27·5 × 5·8 × 1·8)*
Gun: 1—20 mm
Main engines: 2 Maybach Diesels; 2 700 bhp = 22 knots
Complement: 16

Patrol craft operated by the Prefectura Naval Argentina.

LYNCH   1969, Argentine Navy

1 LARGE PATROL CRAFT

Name	No.	Builders	Commissioned
SURUBI	P 55	Ast. Nav. del Estero	1951

Displacement, tons: 100
Guns: 2—20 mm
Speed, knots: 20

1 LARGE PATROL CRAFT

GC 31

Dimensions generally similar to US 63 ft AVR class but of slightly different silhouette.

GC 31   *1971*

2 EX-US "HIGGINS CLASS" (FAST ATTACK CRAFT—TORPEDO)

Name	No.	Builders	Commissioned
ALAKUSH	P 82	New Orleans SB	1946
TOWORA	P 84	New Orleans SB	1946

Displacement, tons: 45 standard; 50 full load
Dimensions, feet (metres): 78·7 × 9·8 × 4·6 *(24 × 3 × 1·4)*
Guns: 2—40/60 mm; 4—MG
Torpedo launchers: 4—21 inch racks
Rocket launchers: 2 sextuple sets 12·7 cm
Main engines: 3 Packard (Petrol); 4 500 hp = 42 knots
Range, miles: 1 000 at 20 knots
Complement: 12

The last of a class of nine. Given names in 1972.

Note. In addition the following are listed as operated by PNA: *Delfin* of 1 000 tons and 15 knots, *Robalo, Mandubi, Adhara, Albatross, Dorado,* LT 1 and 8, PAV 1, 2 and 3. PAM 1, 2 and 3, V 2 and 6, GN 1, 4, 38 and 42, PF 17, P 2, 5, 13, 22, 26, 39 and 41.

MINE WARFARE FORCES

6 Ex-BRITISH "TON" CLASS
(MINESWEEPERS—COASTAL and MINEHUNTERS)

Name	No.	Builders	Launched
CHACO (ex-HMS *Rennington*)	M 5	Richards	27 Nov 1958
CHUBUT (ex-HMS *Santon*)	M 3	Fleetlands	18 Aug 1955
FORMOSA (ex-HMS *Ilmington*)	M 6	Camper, Nicholson	8 Mar 1954
NEUQUEN (ex-HMS *Hickleton*)	M 1	Thornycroft	26 Jan 1955
RIO NEGRO (ex-HMS *Tarlton*)	M 2	Doig	10 Nov 1954
TIERRA DEL FUEGO (ex- HMS *Bevington*)	M 4	Whites	17 Mar 1953

Displacement, tons: 360 standard; 425 full load
Dimensions, feet (metres): 140 pp; 153 oa × 28·8 × 8·2 *(46·3 × 8·8 × 2·5)*
Gun: 1—40/60 mm
Main engines: 2 Diesels; 2 shafts; 3 000 bhp = 15 knots
Oil fuel, tons: 45
Range, miles: 2 300 at 13 knots; 3 000 at 8 knots
Complement: Minesweepers 27; Minehunters 36

Former British coastal minesweepers of the "Ton" class. Of composite wooden and non-magnetic metal construction. Purchased in 1967. In 1968 *Chaco* and *Formosa* were converted into minehunters in HM Dockyard, Portsmouth, and the other four were refitted and modernised as minesweepers by the Vosper Thornycroft Group with Vosper activated-fin stabiliser equipment.

NEUQUEN (SWEEPER)   *1974, Argentine Navy*

SURVEY SHIPS

1 NEW CONSTRUCTION SURVEY SHIP

Displacement, tons: 1 960 standard

Laid down in 1974 at Alianza, Avellaneda.

1 NEW CONSTRUCTION OCEANOGRAPHIC SHIP

Displacement, tons: 2 100 standard
Dimensions, feet (metres): 249 × 43·4 × 14·9 *(75·9 × 13·2 × 4·5)*
Engine: 1 Diesel; 2 600 hp = 12 knots

Laid down at Astarsa, San Fernando in 1974.

2 Ex-US TYPE V4 TUGS

Name	No.	Builders	Commissioned
GOYENA (ex-USS *Dry Tortuga*)	Q 17	Pendleton SY, New Orleans	1943
THOMPSON (ex-USS *Sombrero Key*)	A 4	Pendleton SY, New Orleans	1943

Displacement, tons: 1 863 full load
Dimensions, feet (metres): 191·3 × 37 × 18 *(58·3 × 11·3 × 5·5)*
Guns: 2—40 mm Bofors (twin); 2—20 mm (single)
Main engines: 2 Enterprise Diesels; 2 250 bhp = 12 knots
Oil fuel, tons: 532
Complement: 62

Leased to Argentina in 1965. Temporarily used as survey ships.

THOMPSON   *1973, Argentine Navy*

Name	No.	Builders	Commissioned
ISLAS ORCADAS (ex USS *Eltanin*, T-AGOR 8)	Q 9	Avondale, New Orleans	2 Aug 1957

Displacement, tons: 2 036 light; 4 942 full load
Dimensions, feet (metres): 262·2 oa × 51·5 × 18·7 *(80 × 15·7 × 5·7)*
Main engines: Diesel electric; 3 200 bhp; 2 shafts = 12 knots
Complement: 12 officers, 36 men, 38 scientists

Converted for Antarctic Research 1961. Operated in conjunction by Argentine Navy, US National Science Foundation and Argentine National Directorate of the Antarctic.

1 AUXILIARY SAILING SHIP

Name	No.	Builders	Commissioned
EL AUSTRAL (ex-USS *Atlantis*)	Q 7	Burmeister and Wain, Copenhagen	1931

Displacement, tons: 571
Dimensions, feet (metres): 110 pp; 141 oa × 27 × 20 *(33·6; 43 × 8·2 × 6·1)*
Main engines: Diesels; 400 bhp
Oil fuel, tons: 22
Complement: 19

Incorporated into the Argentine Navy on 30 April, 1966. Acquired from USA.

Name	No.	Builders	Commissioned
COMODORO RIVADAVIA	Q —	Mestrina, Tigre	Late 1974

Displacement, tons: 700
Dimensions, feet (metres): 167 × 28·9 × 8·5 *(50·9 × 8·8 × 2·6)*
Main engines: 2 Werkspoor Diesels = 12 knots
Complement: 27

Laid down 17 July 1971, launched 2 Dec 1972.

CORMORAN

Coastal survey launch of 102 tons with complement of 19, built in 1963. Speed 13 knots.

PETREL

Coastal survey launch of 50 tons with complement of 9, built in 1965.

TRANSPORTS

Note. 3 Transports of "Costa Sur" Type ordered in Argentina—reported 1975

Name	No.	Builders	Commissioned
BAHIA AGUIRRE	B 2	Canadian Vickers, Halifax	1950
BAHIA BUEN SUCESO	B 6	Canadian Vickers, Halifax	June 1950

Displacement, tons: 3 100 standard; 5 000 full load
Dimensions, feet (metres): 334·7 × 47 × 13·8 *(95·1 × 14·3 × 7·9)*
Main engines: 2 sets Nordberg diesels; 2 shafts; 3 750 bhp = 16 knots
Oil fuel, tons: 442 (B 6); 355 (B 2)
Complement: 100

Survivors of class of three.

BAHIA BUEN SUCESO

1974, Argentine Navy

TANKERS

1 LARGE FLEET TANKER (FLEET SUPPORT)

Name	No.	Builders	Commissioned
PUNTA MEDANOS	B 18	Swan Hunter	10 Oct 1950

Displacement, tons: 14 352 standard; 16 331 full load
Measurement, tons: 8 250 deadweight
Dimensions, feet (metres): 470 pp; 502 oa × 62 × 28·5 *(143·4; 153·1 × 18·9 × 8·7)*
Main engines: Double reduction geared turbines. 2 shafts; 9 500 shp = 18 knots
Boilers: 2 Babcock & Wilcox two-drum integral furnace water-tube
Oil fuel, tons: 1 500
Range, miles: 13 700 at 15 knots
Complement: 99

Available as a training vessel. She was, when completed, the finest equipped and fastest of her type afloat. Boilers built under licence by the Wallsend Slipway & Engineering Company. Steam conditions of 400 lb per sq in pressure and 750 deg F.

PUNTA MEDANOS

1973, Argentine Navy

1 ex-US MS TYPE (FLEET SUPPORT)

Name	No.	Builders	Commissioned
PUNTA DELGADA (ex-USS *Sugarland*, ex-*Nanticoke* AOG 66)	B 16	St. Johns River SB, Jacksonville	1945

Displacement, tons: 5 930 standard; 6 090 full load
Dimensions, feet (metres): 325 × 48·2 × 20 *(99·1 × 14·7 × 6·1)*
Main engines: Westinghouse diesel; 1 shaft; 1 400 bhp = 11·5 knots
Oil fuel, tons: 150
Range, miles: 9 000 at 11 knots
Complement: 72

USMS type T1-M-BT1. Launched on 7 Apr 1945.

1 TANKER (FLEET SUPPORT)

Name	No.	Builders	Commissioned
PUNTA ALTA	B 12	Puerto Belgrano	1938

Displacement, tons: 1 600 standard; 1 900 full load
Measurement, tons: 800 deadweight
Dimensions, feet (metres): 210 × 33·8 × 12·5 *(64 × 10·3 × 3·8)*
Main engines: Diesel; 1 shaft; 1 850 bhp = 8 knots
Oil fuel, tons: 146

TRAINING SHIP

Name	No.	Builders	Commissioned
LIBERTAD	Q 2	AFNE, Rio Santiago	1962

Displacement, tons: 3 025 standard; 3 765 full load
Dimensions, feet (metres): 262 wl; 301 oa × 47 × 21·8 *(92, 94·5 × 13·8 × 6·8)*
Guns: 1—3 in; 4—40 mm; 4—47 mm saluting
Main engines: 2 Sulzer diesels; 2 400 bhp = 13·5 knots
Complement: 370 (crew) plus 150 cadets

Launched on 20 June 1956. She is the largest sail training ship in the world and set up the fastest crossing of the N. Atlantic under sail in 1966, a record which still stands.

LIBERTAD   *10/1973, Reiner Nerlich*

ICEBREAKERS

1 NEW CONSTRUCTION WÄRTSILA TYPE

Dimensions, feet (metres): 392 × 82 × 31·2 *(119 × 25 × 9·5)*
Main engines: Diesel electric; 16 200 shp (4 Wärtsila-SEMT Pielstick 8PC2-5L diesels); 2 shafts
Speed, knots: 16·5
Complement: 133 ship's company; 100 passengers

Contract signed on 17 Dec 1975 with Wartsila (Helsinki) delivery to be in Autumn 1978. The ship is designed for Antartic support operations and will be able to remain in the polar regions throughout the winter with 210 people aboard. Fitted for helicopters and landing craft with two 16 ton cranes. Will have fin stabilisers, Wärtsila bubbling system and a 60 ton towing winch.

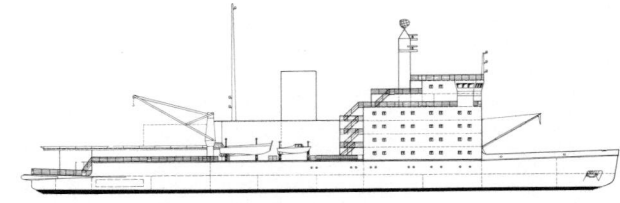

New Construction Wärtsila Icebreaker   1975

Name	No.	Builders	Commissioned
GENERAL SAN MARTIN	Q 4	Seebeck Yd-Weser AG	Oct 1954

Displacement, tons: 4 854 standard; 5 301 full load
Measurement, tons: 1 600 deadweight
Dimensions, feet (metres): 279 × 61 × 21 *(85·1 × 18·6 × 6·4)*
Aircraft: 1 reconnaissance aircraft and 1 helicopter
Guns: 1—4 in; 2—40 mm Bofors
Main engines: 4 diesel-electric; 2 shafts; 7 100 hp = 16 knots
Oil fuel, tons: 1 100
Range, miles: 35 000 at 10 knots
Complement: 160

Launched on 24 June 1954. Fitted for research. New second radar mast fitted on after end of the hangar in late 1972.

GENERAL SAN MARTIN (2nd radar mast now fitted)   *1970, Argentine Navy*

TUGS

GUAYCURU R 33   **QUILMES** R 32

Displacement, tons: 368 full load
Dimensions, feet (metres): 107·2 × 24·4 × 12·5 *(32·7 × 7·4 × 3·8)*
Main engines: Skinner Unaflow engines; 645 ihp = 9 knots
Boilers: Cylindrical
Oil fuel, tons: 52
Range, miles: 2 200 at 7 knots
Complement: 14

"Quilmes" class tugs built at Rio Santiago Naval Yard. Laid down on 23 Aug and 15 Mar 1956 respectively, launched on 27 Dec 1959 and 8 July 1957 and completed on 29 July and 30 Mar 1960.

PEHUENCHE R 29   **TONOCOTE** R 30

Displacement, tons: 330
Dimensions, feet (metres): 105 × 24·7 × 12·5 *(32 × 7·5 × 3·8)*
Main engines: Triple expansion; 600 ihp = 11 knots
Boilers: 2
Oil fuel, tons: 36
Range, miles: 1 200 at 9 knots
Complement: 13

Both built in Rio Santiago Naval Yard. Commissioned for service in 1954.

TOBA R 4

Displacement, tons: 600
Measurement, tons: 339 gross
Dimensions, feet (metres): 139 oa × 28.5 × 11.5 *(42.4 × 8.7 × 3.5)*
Main engines: Triple expansion; 2 shafts; 1 200 ihp = 12 knots
Boilers: 2
Oil fuel, tons: 95
Range, miles: 3 900 at 10 knots
Complement: 34

Built by Hawthorn Leslie, Ltd, Hebburn-on-Tyne. Launched on 23 Dec 1927 and completed in Mar 1928.

HUARPE R 12

Displacement, tons: 370
Dimensions, feet (metres): 107 × 27.2 × 12 *(32.2 × 8.3 × 3.7)*
Main engines: Triple expansion; 800 ihp
Boilers: 1 cylindrical (Howaldtwerke)
Oil fuel, tons: 58
Complement: 13

Built by Howaldtwerke in 1927. Entered service in the Argentine Navy in 1942.

CALCHAQUI	R 6 (ex-US 445)	**CHULUPI**	R 10 (ex-US 426)
CAPAYAN	R 16 (ex-US 443)	**MOCOVI**	R 5 (ex-US 441)
CHIQUILLAN	R 18 (ex-US 444)	**MORCOYAN**	R 19 (ex-US 448)

Displacement, tons: 70
Dimensions, feet (metres): 67 × 14 × 13 *(20.4 × 4.3 × 4)*
Main engines: Diesel; 310 bhp = 10 knots
Oil fuel, tons: 8.7
Complement: 5

YTL Type built in USA and transferred on lease in Mar 1965 R (16, 18 and 19), remainder in Mar 1969

Note. Two harbour tugs built by Vicente Forte entered service in 1974.

FLOATING DOCKS

Number	Dimensions, feet (metres)	Capacity, tons
Y 1 (ex-ARD 23)	492 × 88.6 × 56 *(150 × 27 × 17.1)*	3 500
2	300.1 × 60 × 41 *(91.5 × 18.3 × 12.5)*	1 000
ASD 40	215.8 × 46 × 45.5 *(65.8 × 14 × 13.7)*	750
—	215.8 × 46 × 45.5 *(65.8 × 14 × 13.7)*	750

First three are at Darsena Norte, Buenos Aires and the fourth at Puerto Belgrano.

MISCELLANEOUS

Four auxiliaries, *E 6*, *Fortuna*, *Itati* and *Juana* listed.
The ex-training ship *Presidente Sarmiento* is retained at Buenos Aires as a museum ship, as also is the 1874 Corvette *Uruguay*.

AUSTRALIA

Administration

Minister for Defence (and Navy):
Hon. D. J. Killen, MP

Chairman of the Chiefs of Staff:
General F. G. Hassett

Headquarters Appointments

Chief of Naval Staff:
Vice-Admiral H. D. Stevenson, CBE
Chief of Naval Personnel:
Rear-Admiral A. G. McFarlane
Chief of Naval Technical Services:
Rear-Admiral M. P. Reed
Chief of Supply and Works:
Commodore J. Davidson
Deputy Chief of the Naval Staff:
Rear-Admiral B. S. Murray
Special Deputy (Navy Office):
Mr. T. S. Philpott, OBE

Senior Appointments

Flag Officer Commanding Australian Fleet:
Rear-Admiral G. V. Gladstone DSC*
Flag Officer Commanding East Australian Area:
Rear-Admiral N. E. McDonald

Diplomatic Representation

Australian Naval Representative in London:
Commodore A. A. Willis, OBE
Naval Attaché in Washington:
Commodore R. Percy
Naval Attaché in Tokyo:
Captain P. M. Rees
Naval Attaché in Jakarta:
Captain M. A. McK. Clarke
Naval Representative Papua and New Guinea:
Commander C. H. C. Spurgeon

Personnel

1 January 1972: 17 000 officers and sailors
1 January 1973: 17 128 officers and sailors
1 January 1974: 16 743 officers and sailors
1 January 1975: 16 200 officers and sailors
1 January 1976: 16 800 officers and sailors
(including 1 200 WRANS)

Navy Estimates

$A
1971-72: 270 244 000*
1972-73: 293 094 000*
1973-74: 319 994 000*
1974-75: 375 014 000*
1975-76: 428 879 000*
(*Includes United States Credits)

Naval Bases

FOCEA—Sydney and Jervis Bay
NOC Queensland—Brisbane and Cairns (PCs)
NOC Northern Territory—Darwin (PCs)
NOC W. Australia—Cockburn Sound (estimated completion 1978-79)

Naval Shipyards

Building at Williamstown (Melbourne) and Cockatoo Island (Sydney). Refits at both and Garden Island (Sydney).

Fleet Air Arm

Squadron Aircraft
Ht	723	Iroquois and Bell 206B-1 helos
VC	724	A4G and TA4G Skyhawks, Macchi Trainers (Training, FRU and Trials)
HT	725	Wessex 31B helos (training and FRU)
VF	805	A4G Skyhawks (Front line fighter/strike)
VS	816	S2E Trackers (Front line A/S)
HS	817	Wessex 31B helos (Front line A/S)
VC	851	S2E Trackers, HS 748 (Training, communications and FRU)

Note: HS 817 to re-equip with Mk 50 Sea Kings during 1976.

Prefix to Ships' Names

HMAS. Her Majesty's Australian Ship

Mercantile Marine

Lloyd's Register of Shipping:
419 vessels of 1 205 248 tons gross

Army Craft

Army watercraft squadrons have been much reduced and, for the most part, been absorbed into the RAN. Two tugs, ten work-boats, several LCVPs and LCM8s and other small craft are still in Army use.

Strength of the Fleet

Type	Active	Building
Attack Carrier (Medium)	1	—
Destroyers	5 (3DDG)	
Frigates (GM)	—	2?
Frigates	6	—
Patrol Submarines	4	2
MCM Vessels	3	—
Large Patrol Craft	12	—
Survey Ships	4	1
Fleet Tanker	1	—
Destroyer Tender	1	—
Landing Craft (Heavy)	6	—
Training Ship	1	—
Others	14	—

Naval Procurement and Modernisation

In April 1974 the Australian Government decided to acquire two United States Patrol Frigates rather than proceed with the proposed DDL project, (see Jane's 1974). On Feb 18 1976 the Minister of Defence announced that a firm decision had been taken to order two US "Perry" class frigates and that further studies on destroyer replacements were under way.

On 6 May 1975 the Minister of Defence announced an invitation to register interest in the design and construction of a new class of Large Patrol Craft, the majority to be built in Australia.

On 28th Aug 1975 the Minister announced that the RAN would acquire a Landing Ship (Logistic) to be an improved version of the British "Sir Lancelot" class. The ship would be of 6 000 tons with a long-range lift capability of 2 000 tons and capable of disembarking tanks, equipment and men over beaches. Helicopter to be embarked. On the same day it was announced that the RAN had called for tenders for a new Fleet Replenishment Ship.

Tenders have also been called for a project definition study for a trials and research ship to replace *Kimbla*.

3 Destroyers (DDG's *Hobart*, *Perth* and *Brisbane*) being modernised (see class notes). Older frigates to have extended refits.

10 Sea King helicopters (in lieu of 20) at a cost of $A43 million. Delivery to be completed in 1976. A Sea King flight simulator costing $A2·5 million was operational in March 1976.

Papua-New Guinea Defence Force

The RAN base in the Admiralty Islands, HMAS *Tarangau*, was decommissioned 14.11.74 and handed over to the PNG Defence Force. It is now the PNG Defence Force Base, Lombrum. Five RAN "Attack" class patrol boats, *Aitape*, *Ladava*, *Lae*, *Madang* and *Samarai*, plus two LCH's *Buna* and *Salamaua* have been re-commissioned as PNG Ships and are fully or partially manned by PNG personnel with some RAN personnel as technical advisers.

DELETIONS

Ex-Carrier

Sydney	For disposal 20.7.73. Left Sydney for South Korean breakers 23.12.75

Destroyers

Arunta	Sank under tow to breaker 13.2.69
Tobruk	Left Sydney for Taiwan 10.4.72
Anzac	Left Sydney for Hong Kong 30.12.75

Frigates

Barcoo	Left Sydney for Taiwan 17.3.72
Culgoa	Left Sydney for Taiwan 17.3.72
Quickmatch	Left Sydney for Japan 10.4.72

Quiberon	Left Sydney for Japan 6.7.72
Gascoyne	Left Sydney for Taiwan 6.7.72
Queenborough	Left Sydney for Hong Kong 12.5.75

Landing Craft (Heavy)

Buna	To Papua New Guinea
Salamaua	Defence Force 14.11.74

MCM Vessels

Hawk	Sales List 1974
Gull	Sales List 1974
Popham	Disposal 30.8.74
Teal	Sales List 1975

Large Patrol Craft

Archer and *Bandolier*	To Indonesia 21.10.74 & 16.11.73
Arrow	Sunk Darwin (Cyclone Tracy) 25.12.74
Aitape, Ladava, Lae, Madang, Samarai	To Papua New Guinea Defence Force 16.9.75

Miscellaneous

SDBs 1321	1972
Kara Kara	Base Ship sunk as target 30.1.73
Paluma	Sold Commercial 1974
Otter	Sold as fishing boat 1974
Tortoise & *Turtle*	Sold Commercial 1975
Bronzewing (tug)	Sales List 1975

PENNANT LIST

Aircraft Carrier

21	Melbourne

Submarines

57	Oxley
59	Otway
60	Onslow
61	Orion
62	Otama
70	Ovens

Destroyers

08	Vendetta
11	Vampire
38	Perth
39	Hobart
41	Brisbane

Frigates

45	Yarra
46	Parramatta
48	Stuart
49	Derwent
50	Swan
53	Torrens

Minehunters

1102	Snipe
1121	Curlew

Minesweeper (Coastal)

1183	Ibis

Training Ship

154	Duchess

Survey Ships

73	Moresby
266	Diamantina
312	Flinders
314	Kimbla

Fleet Tanker

195	Supply

Destroyer Tender

215	Stalwart

General Purpose Ships

244	Banks
247	Bass

Large Patrol Craft

81	Acute
82	Adroit
83	Advance
87	Ardent
89	Assail
90	Attack
91	Aware
97	Barbette
98	Barricade
99	Bombard
100	Buccaneer
101	Bayonet

PNGDF (Numbers may soon be changed)

84	Aitape
85	Samarai
92	Ladava
93	Lae
94	Madang

Landing Craft

L126	Balikpapan
L127	Brunei
L128	Labuan
L129	Tarakan
L130	Wewak
L133	Betano

PNGDF

L131	Salamaua
L132	Buna

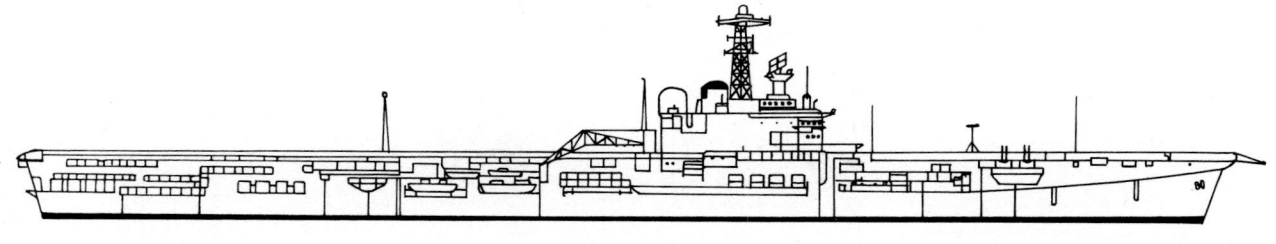

MELBOURNE

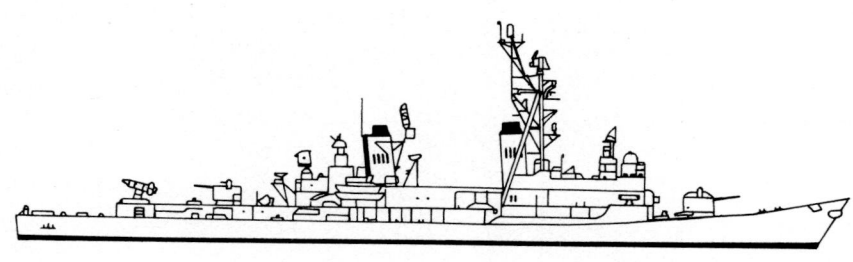

"PERTH" Class

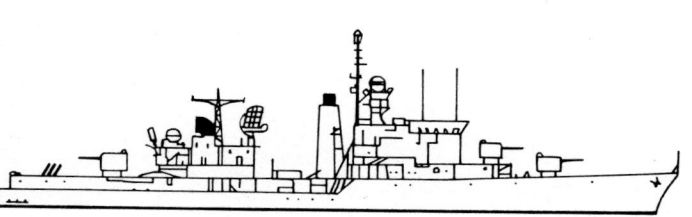

VAMPIRE and VENDETTA

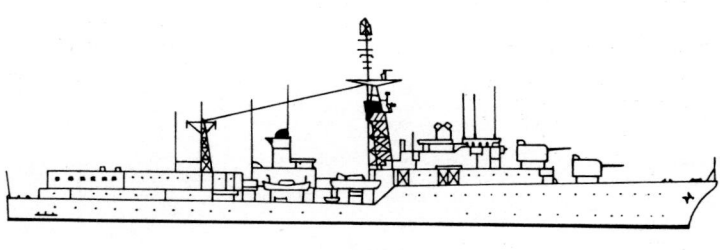

DUCHESS

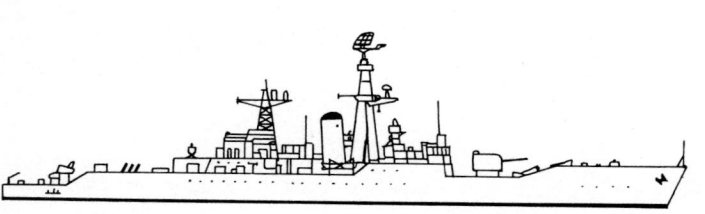

PARRAMATTA and YARRA

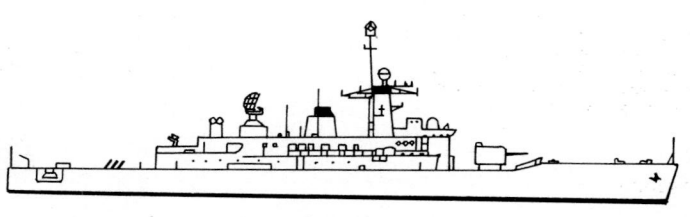

SWAN and TORRENS

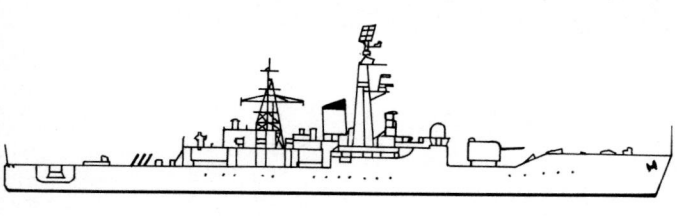

DERWENT and STUART

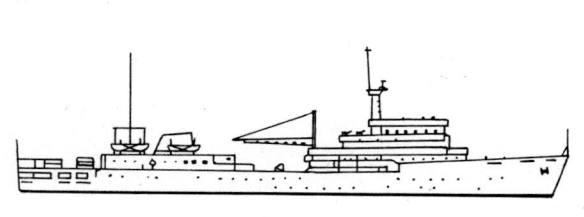

MORESBY

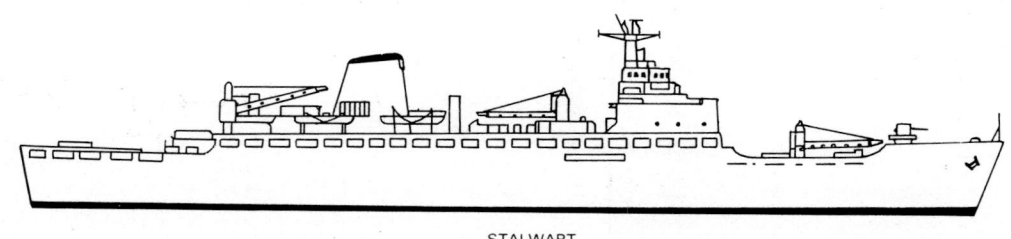

STALWART

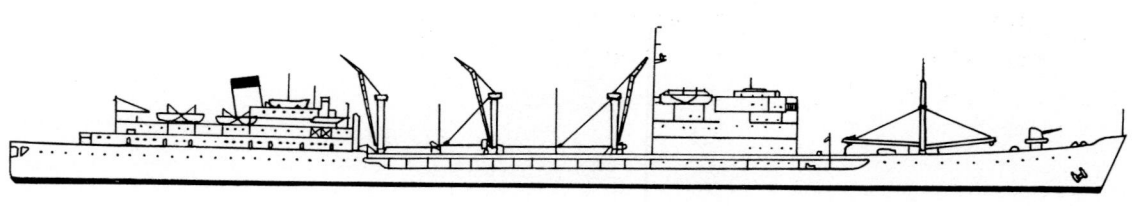

SUPPLY

AIRCRAFT CARRIER

1 MODIFIED "MAJESTIC" CLASS

Name	No.	Builders	Laid down	Launched	Commissioned
MELBOURNE (ex-*Majestic*)	21	Vickers-Armstrong, Barrow-in-Furness	15 Apr 1943	28 Feb 1945	28 Oct 1955

Displacement, tons: 16 000 standard; 19 966 full load
Length, feet (metres): 650·0 *(198·1)* wl; 701·5 *(213·8)* oa
Beam, feet (metres): 80·2 *(24·5)* hull
Draught, feet (metres): 25·5 *(7·8)*
Width, feet (metres): 80·0 *(24·4)* flight deck
126·0 *(38·4)* oa including 6 deg angled deck and mirrors
Hangar, feet (metres): 444 × 52 × 17·5 *(135·3 × 15·8 × 5·3)*
Aircraft: 8 Sky Hawk jet fighters; 6 Tracker aircraft; 10 Westland Wessex A/S helicopters (see *Aircraft* notes)
Guns: 12—40 mm (4 twin, 4 single) Bofors
Boilers: 4 Admiralty 3-drum type
Main engines: Parsons single reduction geared turbines; 2 shafts; 42 000 shp
Speed, knots: 23
Range, miles: 12 000 at 14 knots; 6 200 at 23 knots
Complement: 1 335 (includes 347 Carrier Air Group personnel); 1 070 (75 officers and 995 sailors) as Flagship

At the end of the Second World War, when she was still incomplete, work on this ship was brought to a standstill pending a decision as to future naval requirements. When full-scale work was resumed during 1949-55, and after her design had been re-cast several times, she underwent reconstruction and modernisation in Great Britain, including the fitting of the angled deck, steam catapult and mirror deck landing sights, and was transferred to the RAN on completion. She was commissioned and renamed at Barrow-in-Furness on 28 Oct 1955, sailed from Portsmouth on 5 Mar 1956, and arrived at Fremantle, Australia, on 23 April 1956. She became flagship of the Royal Australian Navy at Sydney on 14 May 1956. She cost £A8 309 000.

Aircraft: The aircraft complement formerly comprised 8 Sea Venom jet fighters, 17 Gannet turbo-prop anti-submarine aircraft, and 2 Sycamore helicopters, later 4 Sea Venom, 6 Gannet and 10 Wessex A/S helicopters. Fourteen S2E Tracker anti-submarine aircraft and ten A4G Skyhawk fighter/bombers were purchased in 1966 in the USA (in service 1967) at a cost of $A46 000 000. Another 10 A4G Skyhawk (including 2 TA4G Trainers) were delivered during 1971.
Melbourne now carries Skyhawks, Trackers and Wessex and embarked Sea Kings Mk 50 in lieu of Wessex from 2 Feb 1976.

Modernisation: *Melbourne* completed her extended refit during 1969 at a cost of over $A8 750 000 to enable her to operate with S2E Tracker and A4G Skyhawk aircraft, and to improve habitability. In 1971 the catapult was rebuilt and a bridle-catcher fitted, and the flight deck was strengthened. Under refit from November 1972 to July 1973.
On 9 Apr 1975 the Minister for Defence said that it was planned to give *Melbourne* an extended refit during which it would be assessed how far the ship's life could be extended.

Radar: Search: Philips LWO series early warning and associated height finders for aircraft direction.
Tactical: Type 293 Target Indication and surface warning.
EW: Electronic intelligence and warfare equipment also fitted.
Carrier controlled approach Radar. (Dome on island).

MELBOURNE

1973, Royal Australian Navy

MELBOURNE

10/1973, Royal Australian Navy

MELBOURNE

1974, Royal Australian Navy

DESTROYERS

3 "PERTH" CLASS (DDGs)

Name.	No.	Builders	Laid down	Launched	Commissioned
BRISBANE	41	Defoe Shipbuilding Co, Bay City, Mich.	15 Feb 1965	5 May 1966	16 Dec 1967
HOBART	39	Defoe Shipbuilding Co, Bay City, Mich.	26 Oct 1962	9 Jan 1964	18 Dec 1965
PERTH	38	Defoe Shipbuilding Co, Bay City, Mich.	21 Sep 1962	26 Sep 1963	17 July 1965

Displacement, tons: 3 370 standard; 4 618 full load
Length, feet (metres): 431·0 *(131·4)* wl; 437·0 *(132·2)* oa
Beam, feet (metres): 47·1 *(14·3)*
Draught, feet (metres): 20·1 *(6·1)*
Missile launchers: 1 single for "Tartar" (see Modernisation note)
Guns: 2—5 in *(127 mm)* 54 cal. dp, single-mount
A/S weapons: 2 single launchers for "Ikara" system
Torpedo-tubes: 6 (2 triple) for A/S torpedoes
Main engines: 2 GE double reduction turbines, 2 shafts; 70 000 shp
Boilers: 4 Foster Wheeler "D" type, 1 200 psi; 950°F
Speed, knots: 35
Range, miles: 6 000 at 14 knots; 1 600 at 30 knots
Complement: 333 (21 officers, 312 sailors)

On 6 Jan 1962, in Washington, US defence representatives and Australian military officials (on behalf of the Royal Australian Navy) and executives of the Defoe Shipbuilding Company, of Bay City, Michigan, signed a $A25 726 700 contract for the construction of two guided-missile destroyers (shipbuilding cost only). On 22 Jan 1963 it was announced by the Navy Minister in Canberra, Australia, that a third guided-missile destroyer was to be built in USA for Australia. The first of their kind for the Australian Navy, they constitute the 1st Destroyer Squadron, RAN. All three ships have been in action off Vietnam where they served with the US 7th fleet.

Cost: Original estimate $A12 800 000 to $A14 000 000 each (with missiles and electronics $A40 000 000 each). The total cost of *Perth* was reported to be $A50 000 000.

Design: Generally similar to the US "Charles F. Adams" class, but they differ by the addition of a broad deckhouse between the funnels enclosing the Ikara anti-submarine torpedo-carrying missile system, and the mounting of a single-arm launcher, instead of a twin, for the Tartar surface-to-air guided missiles. They have a new hull design with aluminium superstructures. The most recent habitability improvements have been incorporated into their construction, including air-conditioning of all living spaces.

Modernisation: *Perth* started a modernisation at the Long Beach Naval Shipyard on 3 Sep 1974, completing 2 Jan 1975. The work included the installation of a Naval Combat Data System, updating of the Tartar missile fire control system, replacing 5-inch gun mounts and modernising radars. The Australian Government has announced that *Hobart* and *Brisbane* would be given similar modernisations in Australia. This is a reversal of the previous Government's policy to have all modernisation completed in the United States. *Hobart's* gun mounts were modernised in the U.S. in 1972. *Brisbane's* gun mounts will be stripped and re-installed in Australia, with the gun mount re-engineering being done in the U.S.

Weapons: Ikara launcher temporarily removed from *Perth* after modification in USA.

HOBART

1974, Royal Australian Navy

BRISBANE

11/1975, John Mortimer

3 "DARING" CLASS (DD)

Name	No.	Builders	Laid down	Launched	Commissioned
VAMPIRE	11	Cockatoo Island Dockyard, Sydney	1 July 1952	27 Oct 1956	23 June 1959
VENDETTA	08	HMA Naval Dockyard, Williamstown	4 July 1949	3 May 1954	26 Nov 1958
DUCHESS	154	John I. Thornycroft & Co, Southampton	2 July 1948	9 Apr 1951	23 Oct 1952

Displacement, tons: 2 800 standard; 3 600 full load; 3 580 (*Duchess*)
Length, feet (metres): 366 *(111·3)* pp; 388·5 *(118·4)* oa
Beam, feet (metres): 43 *(13·1)*
Draught, feet (metres): 12·8 *(3·9)*
Guns: 6—4·5 in *(115 mm)* in 3 twin turrets, two forward and one aft (4 forward guns only in *Duchess*); 6—40 mm (2—40 mm in *Duchess*)
A/S weapons: 1 3-barrelled Limbo mortar (not *Duchess*) (see Design notes)
Main engines: English Electric geared turbines; 2 shafts; 54 000 shp
Boilers: 2 Foster Wheeler; 650 psi; 850°F
Speed, knots: 30·5
Range, miles: 3 700 at 20 knots; 3 000 at 20 knots *(Duchess)*
Oil fuel, tons: 584
Complement: 320 (14 officers, 306 sailors); 260 (*Duchess*, including Trainees)

Vampire and *Vendettà,* constitute the 2nd Destroyer Squadron, RAN, and are the largest destroyers ever built in Australia. They were ordered in 1946. Their sister ship, *Voyager,* the prototype of the class, collided with the aircraft carrier *Melbourne* and sank off the southern coast of New South Wales on the night of 10 Feb 1964. She was replaced by the British destroyer *Duchess*, lent to Australia by the United Kingdom for four years on 8 May 1964, later extended to 1971 and purchased by RAN in 1972.

Four large destroyers of this type were originally projected, to have been named after the Royal Australian Navy's famous "Scrap Iron Flotilla" of destroyers during the Second World War, but *Waterhen* was cancelled in 1954.

Design: *Vampire* and *Vendetta* were of similar design, including all welded construction to that of the "Daring" class, built in Great Britain, but were modified to suit Australian conditions and have "Limbo" instead of "Squid" anti-submarine mortars. The superstructure is of light alloy, instead of steel, to reduce weight.

Modernisation: *Vampire* completed in Dec 1971. *Vendetta* completed May 1973. The $A20 million programme for both ships included new Mk 22 fire-control systems, new LW-02 air-warning and navigation radars, new action-information centre, modernised communications, fitting modernised turrets, improved habitability, the fitting of an enclosed bridge and new funnels. The work was carried out by Williamstown Dockyard. These alterations afford an interesting comparison with the Peruvian "Darings" (ex-*Decoy* and *Diana*) with their eight Exocet SSMs and rebuilt forefunnel and radar.

Radar: Philips LW-02 early warning, (not *Duchess*).

Note: *Duchess* has been converted for training purposes, including the removal of X-turret and Squid to make way for new upper-deck classrooms. She retains her forward battery, radar (Type 293 and I-band fire control) and sonar (in maintenance). Completed November 1974.

VENDETTA (Front) VAMPIRE   *1975, Royal Australian Navy*

DUCHESS   *1975, Royal Australian Navy*

VAMPIRE   *1974, John Mortimer*

FRIGATES

6 "RIVER" CLASS

Name	No.	Builders	Laid down	Launched	Commissioned
YARRA	45	Williamstown Naval Dockyard, Melbourne	9 Apr 1957	30 Sep 1958	27 July 1961
PARRAMATTA	46	Cockatoo Island Dockyard, Sydney	3 Jan 1957	31 Jan 1959	4 July 1961
STUART	48	Cockatoo Island Dockyard, Sydney	20 Mar 1959	8 Apr 1961	28 June1963
DERWENT	49	Williamstown Naval Dockyard, Melbourne	16 June1958	17 Apr 1961	30 Apr 1964
SWAN	50	Williamstown Naval Dockyard, Melbourne	18 Aug 1965	16 Dec 1967	20 Jan 1970
TORRENS	53	Cockatoo Island Dockyard, Sydney	18 Aug 1965	28 Sep 1968	19 Jan 1971

Displacement, tons: 2 100 standard; 2 700 full load
Length, feet (metres): 360·0 *(109·7)* pp; 370·0 *(112·8)* oa
Beam, feet (metres): 41·0 *(12·5)*
Draught, feet (metres): 17·3 *(5·3)*
Missile launchers: 1 quadruple for "Seacat"
Guns: 2—4·5 in *(115 mm)*
A/S weapons: 1 launcher for "Ikara" system; 1 "Limbo" 3-barrelled DC mortar
Main engines: 2 double reduction geared turbines; 2 shafts; 30 000 shp
Boilers: 2 Babcock & Wilcox; 550 psi; 850°F
Speed, knots: 30
Range, miles: 4 500 at 12 knots
Complement: 247 (13 officers, 234 sailors) in *Swan* and *Torrens*; 250 (13 officers, 237 sailors) in other four ships

YARRA (PARRAMATTA similar)

11/1975, John Mortimer

The design of the first four is basically similar to that of British "Type 12", the last pair to that of the "Leander" frigates. All are modified by the Royal Australian Navy to incorporate improvements in equipment and habitability. *Stuart* was the first ship fitted with the "Ikara" anti-submarine guided missile; (trial ship for the system). *Derwent* was the first RAN ship to be fitted with "Seacat". The variable depth sonar has been removed from *Derwent* and *Stuart*. Note difference in sihouette between *Swan* and *Torrens* and the earlier ships of the class, the former pair having a straight-run upper deck.

Modernisation: *Parramatta, Stuart* and *Derwent* to begin half-life refits and modernisation in 1976 at Williamstown. These will include improved accommodation consequent on reduction in complement, installation of M22 gunnery direction system, the fitting of Australian Mulloka sonar, the conversion of the boilers to burn diesel fuel, installation of Mk 32 torpedo tubes in lieu of Limbo mortar and new navigation radar. *Yarra* has been fitted with Mulloka sonar, trials beginning in April

1975. She will subsequently receive a limited modernisation at Cockatoo Island.
The whole modernisation programme is due to be completed by 1981.

Radar: Search: All ships fitted with Philips LWO series of C Band early warning radars. Type 293 combined air and surface warning, except *Swan* and *Torrens* which have Philips/HSA I Band radar. Fire Control: MRS 3 or HSA systems, I Band radar.

DERWENT (STUART similar)

1975, Royal Australian Navy

SWAN (TORRENS similar)

11/1975, John Mortimer

SUBMARINES

4 + 2 "OXLEY" CLASS (BRITISH "OBERON" CLASS)

Name	No.	Builders	Laid down	Launched	Commissioned
ONSLOW	60	Scotts' Shipbuilding & Eng Co Ltd, Greenock	4 Dec 1967	3 Dec 1968	22 Dec 1969
OTWAY	59	Scotts' Shipbuilding & Eng Co Ltd, Greenock	29 June1965	29 Nov 1966	23 Apr 1968
OVENS	70	Scotts' Shipbuilding & Eng Co Ltd, Greenock	17 June1966	4 Dec 1967	18 Apr 1969
OXLEY	57	Scotts' Shipbuilding & Eng Co Ltd, Greenock	2 July 1964	24 Sep 1965	18 Apr 1967
ORION	61	Scotts' Shipbuilding & Eng Co Ltd, Greenock	6 Oct 1972	16 Sep 1974	Due mid 1977
OTAMA	62	Scotts' Shipbuilding & Eng Co Ltd, Greenock	25 May 1973	3 Dec 1975	Due late 1977

Displacement, tons: 1 610 standard; 2 196 surfaced; 2 417 dived
Length, feet (metres): 241 *(73·5)* pp; 295·5 *(90·1)* oa
Beam, feet (metres): 26·5 *(8·1)*
Draught, feet (metres): 18 *(5·5)*
Torpedo tubes: 8—21 in *(533 mm)* (6 bow, 2 stern)
Main machinery: 2 Admiralty Standard Range Diesels; 3 600 bhp; 2 shafts; 2 electric motors; 6 000 shp; electric drive
Speed, knots: 16 surfaced; 18 dived
Oil fuel, tons: 300
Range, miles: 12 000 at 10 knots
Complement: 62 (7 officers, 55 sailors)

It was announced by the Minister for the Navy on 22 Jan 1963 that four submarines of the "Oberon" class were to be built in British shipyards under Admiralty supervision at an overall cost of £A5 000 000 each. These were to constitute the 1st Submarine Squadron RAN based at HMAS Platypus, Neutral Bay, Sydney. Subsequently two more were ordered in October 1971 for delivery in 1975-76 later extended to 1977.

Dock: Slave Dock (Sydney) was first used in 1974, allowing submarine dockings to be carried out without occupying graving docks.

Modernisation: *Onslow, Otway, Ovens* and *Oxley* are to be fitted with new fire-control systems and passive ranging and attack sonars. *Orion* and *Otama* will be fitted whilst building.

Names: *Oxley* and *Otway* are named after two earlier RAN submarines, completed in 1927. *Otama* is the Queensland aboriginal word for Dolphin, *Onslow* is a town in Western Australia, *Ovens* was an early explorer and *Orion* is named after the constellation.

R.N. Squadron: The last unit of the Fourth Submarine Squadron of the Royal Navy, *Trump,* was withdrawn from Balmoral, Sydney in Jan 1969.
Odin arrived in Australian waters in Dec 1972 for attachment to the RAN, leaving on 16 Sep 1975.

OXLEY

1975, Royal Australian Navy

OVENS

1975, Royal Australian Navy

MINE WARFARE SHIPS

3 BRITISH "TON" CLASS (MODIFIED)

Name	No.
CURLEW (ex-HMS Cnediston)	1121
IBIS (ex-HMS Singleton)	1183
SNIPE (ex-HMS Alcaston)	1102

Builders	Laid down	Launched	Commissioned
Montrose SY	1952	6 Oct 1953	1954
Montrose SY	1952	23 Nov 1955	1956
Thornycroft	1952	5 Jan 1953	1953

Displacement, tons: 375 standard; 445 full load
Dimensions, feet (metres): 140 pp; 152 oa × 28·8 × 8·2 (42·7; 46·4 × 8·8 × 2·5)
Guns: Ibis 2—40 mm; Curlew and Snipe 1—40 mm
Main engines: Napier Deltic diesels; 2 shafts; 3 000 bhp = 16 knots
Range, miles: 2 300 at 13 knots; 3 000 at 8 knots
Complement: Ibis 34 (4 officers; 30 sailors); Curlew and Snipe 38 (3 officers, 35 sailors)

"Ton" class coastal minesweepers. Six purchased from the United Kingdom in 1961, and modified in British Dockyards to suit Australian conditions. Turned over to the Royal Australian Navy, commissioned and the survivors re-named on 21 Aug, 7 Sep and 11 Sep 1962, respectively. Mirlees diesels were replaced by Napier Deltic, and ships air-conditioned and fitted with stabilisers. Sailed from Portsmouth to Australia on 1 Oct 1962. Constitute the 1st Mine Countermeasures Squadron. Curlew and Snipe have been converted into minehunters—Curlew 26 June 1967 to 13 Dec 1968 and Snipe 10 Apr 1969 to 18 Dec 1970.

CURLEW

10/1975, Graeme Andrews

LIGHT FORCES

12 "ATTACK" CLASS (LARGE PATROL CRAFT)

ACUTE 81	ASSAIL 89	BARRICADE 98
ADROIT 82	ATTACK 90	BAYONET 101
ADVANCE 83	AWARE 91	BOMBARD 99
ARDENT 87	BARBETTE 97	BUCCANEER 100

Displacement, tons: 146 full load
Dimensions, feet (metres): 107·5 oa × 20 × 7·3 (32·8 × 6·1 × 2·2)
Guns: 1—40 mm; 2 medium MG (no guns in Aware)
Main engines: Paxman 16 YJCM Diesels 3 500 hp; 2 shafts 21·24 knots
Complement: 19 (3 officers, 16 sailors)

Steel construction. Builders: Evans Deakin & Co. Pty Ltd, Brisbane, and Walkers Ltd, Maryborough. Ordered in Nov 1965. First vessel was originally scheduled for delivery in Aug 1966, but was not launched until Mar 1967. Cost $A800 000 each. Aware does not carry armament but all have been employed in fishery protection and search and rescue off North Australia. These craft are expected to be replaced by a new class by 1980.

Disposals: Bandolier transferred to Indonesia after refit 16 Nov 1973. Archer transferred 21 Oct 1974. Aitape, Ladava, Lae, Madang, Samarai transferred to Papua-New Guinea Defence Force 16 Sep 1975.

Darwin Cyclone: On 25 Dec 1974 Arrow was lost during Cyclone Tracy at Darwin. Attack was beached and badly damaged at the same time but was salved and towed to Cairns for repairs.

BUCCANEER

1975, John Mortimer

OCEANOGRAPHIC AND SURVEY SHIPS

1 NEW CONSTRUCTION

Name	No.
COOK	291

Builders	Laid down	Launched	Commissioned
Williamstown Naval DY	30 Sep 1974	1976	1978

Displacement, tons: 1 910 standard; 2 650 full load
Length, feet (metres): 317·5 (91·2)
Beam, feet (metres): 44·0 (13·4)
Draught, feet (metres): 15·1 (4·6)
Main engines: Diesels; 2 shafts; 3 400 bhp
Speed, knots: 17
Oil fuel, tons: 640
Range, miles: 11 000 at 14 knots
Complement: 150 including 13 scientists

Intended to replace HMAS Diamantina. She will have dual hydrographic and oceanographic roles. The after part of the ship will contain research equipment and facilities. Accommodation for 13 scientists.

COOK

1972, Official, revised artist's impression

Name	No.	Builders	Laid down	Launched	Commissioned
MORESBY	73	State Dockyard, Newcastle NSW	June 1961	7 Sep 1963	6 Mar 1964

Displacement, tons: 1 714 standard; 2 351 full load
Length, feet (metres): 284·5 *(86·7)* pp; 314·0 *(95·7)* oa
Beam, feet (metres): 42·0 *(12·8)*
Draught, feet (metres): 15·0 *(4·6)*
Aircraft: 1 Bell 206B-1 (Kiowa) helicopter
Guns: 2—40 mm Bofors (single) (removed)
Main engines: Diesel-electric; 3 diesels; 3 990 bhp; 2 electric motors; 2 shafts; 5 000 shp = 19 knots
Complement: 135

The Royal Australian Navy's first specifically designed survey ship. Built at a cost of £A2 000 000 ($A4 000 000). Guns are not currently embarked.

Refit: During refit from 13 Aug 1973 to 18 Jan 1974 *Morseby's* funnel was heightened, her 40 mm guns removed and an exhaust outlet fitted on her forecastle.

MORESBY (new funnel cap—no guns)   *1974, Royal Australian Navy*

Name	No.	Builders	Laid down	Launched	Commissioned
DIAMANTINA	266 (ex-F 377)·	Walkers Ltd, Maryborough, Queensland	12 Apr 1943	6 Apr 1944	27 Apr 1945

Displacement, tons: 1 340 standard; 2 127 full load
Length, feet (metres): 283 *(86·3)* pp; 301·3 *(91·8)* oa
Beam, feet (metres): 36·7 *(11·2)*
Draught, feet (metres): 12·5 *(3·8)*
Gun: 1—40 mm
Main engines: Triple expansion 5 500 ihp; 2 shafts
Boilers: 2 Admiralty 3-drum
Speed, knots: 19·5
Range, miles: 7 700 at 12 knots
Complement: 125 (6 officers, 119 sailors)

Frigate converted in 1959-60 for survey and completed conversion for oceanographic research in June 1969. The conversion included the provision of special laboratories. Sister ship *Lachlan* was sold to the Royal New Zealand Navy, and was finally paid off in 1975. *Diamantina* is to be replaced by *Cook* in 1978.

Armament: The two 4-inch guns and two "Squid" A/S mortars in "B" position were removed.

DIAMANTINA   *1974, John Mortimer*

Name	No.	Builders	Laid down	Launched	Commissioned
FLINDERS	312	Williamstown Naval Dockyard	11 June1971	29 July 1972	27 Apr 1973

Displacement, tons: 750
Dimensions, feet (metres): 161 × 33 × 12 *(49·1 × 10 × 3·7)*
Main engines: 2 Paxman Ventura Diesels, bhp 1 680
Speed, knots: 13·5
Range, miles: 5 000 at 9 knots
Complement: 38 (4 officers, 34 sailors)

Similar in design to *Atyimba* built for the Philippines, she replaced *Paluma* in April 1973, the latter having been running steadily since her conversion from stores tender in 1959. *Flinders* is based at Cairns, with her primary responsibility in the Barrier Reef area.

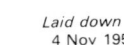

FLINDERS   *1975, Royal Australian Navy*

Name	No.	Builders	Laid down	Launched	Commissioned
KIMBLA	A314	Walkers Ltd, Maryborough, Queensland	4 Nov 1953	23 Mar 1955	26 Mar 1956

Displacement, tons: 762 standard; 1 021 full load
Dimensions, feet (metres): 150 pp; 179 oa × 32 × 12 *(45·8; 54·6 × 9·8 × 3·7)*
Main engines: Triple expansion; 1 shaft; 350 ihp
Speed, knots: 9·5
Complement: 40 (4 officers, 36 sailors)

Built as a boom defence vessel. Converted to trials vessel in 1959. Guns were removed (1—40 mm; 2—20 mm)

KIMBLA   *1969, Royal Australian Navy*

SERVICE FORCES

Note: On 22 August 1973, the Australian Government decided, amongst other things, not to continue with *Protector*—a ship basically similar to her Canadian namesake. Examination of cheaper alternatives is in hand.

1 DESTROYER TENDER

Name	No.	Builders	Laid down	Launched	Commissioned
STALWART	215	Cockatoo Island DY, Sydney	June 1964	7 Oct 1966	9 Feb 1968

Displacement, tons: 10 000 standard; 15 500 full load
Length, feet (metres): 515·5 *(157·1)* oa
Beam, feet (metres): 67·5 *(20·6)*
Draught, feet (metres): 29·5 *(9·0)*
Missiles: Provision for Seacat
Guns: 4—40 mm (2 twin)
Main engines: 2 Scott-Sulzer 6-cyl diesels 2 shafts; 14 400 bhp
Speed, knots: 20+
Complement: 396 (23 officers and 373 sailors)

Largest naval vessel designed and built in Australia. Ordered on 11 Sep 1963. Designed to maintain destroyers and frigates, and advanced weapons systems, including guided missiles. She has a helicopter flight deck. High standard of habitability. Formerly rated as Escort Maintenance Ship. Redesignated Destroyer Tender in 1968. Cost officially estimated at just under \$A15 000 000.

STALWART (*Curlew* alongside)   1974, Royal Australian Navy

1 FLEET TANKER

Name	No.	Builders	Laid down	Launched	Commissioned
SUPPLY (ex-*Tide Austral*)	195	—	—	1 Sep 1954	Mar 1955

Displacement, tons: 15 000 standard; 25 941 full load
Measurement, tons: 17 600 deadweight; 11 200 gross
Dimensions, feet (metres): 550 pp; 583 oa × 71 × 32 *(167·8; 177·8 × 21·7 × 9·8)*
Guns: 6—40 mm (2 twin, 2 single)
Main engines: Double reduction geared turbines; 15 000 shp = 17·25 knots
Complement: 205

British "Tide" Class. Lent to Great Britain until 1 Sep 1962, when *Tide Austral* was re-named HMAS *Supply* and commissioned in the Royal Australian Navy at Portsmouth 15 Aug 1962. Sailed for Australia 1 Oct 1962. Bridge was rebuilt in 1973-74.

SUPPLY (with new bridge)   1974, Royal Australian Navy

AMPHIBIOUS FORCES

6 LANDING CRAFT (HEAVY) (LCH)

Name	No.	Builders	Commissioned
BALIKPAPAN	L126	—	8 Dec 1971 (Army)
BETANO	L133	—	8 Feb 1974
BRUNEI	L127	—	5 Jan 1973
LABUAN	L128	—	9 Mar 1973
TARAKAN	L129	—	15 June 1973
WEWAK	L130	—	10 Aug 1973

Displacement, tons: 310 light; 503 full load
Dimensions, feet (metres): 146 × 33 × 6·5 *(44·5 × 10·1 × 1·9)*
Guns: 2—0·5 in MG
Main engines: 2 GM Diesels; twin screw = 10 knots
Complement: 13 (2 officers, 11 sailors)

Originally this class was ordered for the Army with whom *Balikpapan* remained until June 1974 being commissioned for naval service on 27 Sep 1974. All now transferred to RAN. Can carry three medium tanks.

PNG: *Buna* and *Salamaua* transferred to Papua-New Guinea Defence Force.

BRUNEI   1973, Royal Australian Navy
```
```

GENERAL PURPOSE VESSELS

Name	No.	Builders	Commissioned
BANKS	DG244	Walkers, Maryborough	16 Feb 1960
BASS	GS247	Walkers, Maryborough	25 May 1960

Displacement, tons: 207 standard; 255 and 260 full load respectively
Dimensions, feet (metres): 90 pp; 101 oa × 22 × 8 *(27·5; 30·8 × 6·7 × 2·4)*
Main engines: Diesels; speed = 10 knots
Complement: 14 (2 officers, 12 sailors)

"Explorer" class. Of all steel construction. *Banks* was fitted for fishery surveillance and *Bass* for surveying, but both were used for other duties, including reserve training. *Banks* based in Port Adelaide, *Bass* in Hobart.

TORPEDO RECOVERY VESSELS

TRV 253 254 255

Displacement, tons: 91·6
Dimensions, feet (metres): 88·5 × 20·9 × 4·5 *(27 × 6·4 × 1·4)*
Main engines: 3 GM diesels; 890 hp; triple screws = 13 knots.
Complement: 9 (1 officer, 8 men)

All built at Williamstown—completed between Jan 1970 and Apr 1971. TRV 254 used as diving tender.

TRV 802 (new pennant number)   *10/1975 Graeme Andrews*

DIVING TENDERS

Name	No.	Builders	Launched
PORPOISE (ex-*Neasham*)	Y280	White, Cowes	14 Mar 1956
SEAL (ex-*Wintringham*)	Y298	White, Cowes	24 May 1955

Displacement, tons: 120 standard; 159 full load
Dimensions, feet (metres): 100 pp × 22 × 5·8 *(30·7 × 6·7 × 1·8)*
Main engines: 2 Paxman diesels; 1 100 bhp = 14 knots
Range, miles: 2 000 at 9 knots; 1 500 at 12 knots
Complement: 7 (can accommodate 14 divers)

Purchased from the Royal Navy in 1966-67, these ex-inshore Minesweepers were converted to Diving Tenders and attached to the Diving School at Sydney. HMS *Popham* (Vospers, launched 11 Jan 1955) also purchased but not converted and now laid up for disposal. *Porpoise* and *Seal* carry recompression chambers.

PORPOISE   *1975, John Mortimer*

TUGS

BRONZEWING Y 290

Built in 1946—of 132 tons gross. Laid up.

501   502   503   504

Displacement, tons: 47·5
Dimensions, feet (metres): 50 × 15 × *(15·4 × 4·6 × —)*
Main engines: 2 GM Diesels; 340 bhp = 8-9 knots
Complement: 3

First pair with bipod mast funnel built by Stannard Bros, Sydney in 1969 and second pair with conventional funnel by Perrin Engineering, Brisbane in 1972.

501   *Royal Australian Navy*

SARDIUS TB9   +1

2 Ex-US ARMY TYPE

Of 29 tons and 10 knots. Complement 4. *Sardius* employed in Sydney as ammunition-lighter   tug, other at HMAS *Cerberus* (Victoria).

MISCELLANEOUS

1 TANK CLEANING VESSEL

Name	No.	Builders	Launched
COLAC	—	Mort's Dock Sydney	13 Aug 1941

Originally 1 025 ton "Bathurst" class minesweeper. Now a dumb craft, painted black, based in Sydney. Sister ship *Castlemaine*, given by D of D as museum ship to Melbourne in 1973.

1 AIR SEA RESCUE CRAFT

Name	No.	Builders	Commissioned
AIR SPRITE	Y256	Halvorsen, Sydney	1960

Displacement, tons: 23·5 standard
Dimensions, feet (metres): 63 × 15·5 × 3·3 *(19·2 × 4·7 × 1)*
Main engines: Two Scott Hall Defender (Petrol) = 25 knots
Complement: Up to 8

Used as rescue craft from Jervis Bay with TRV 253 and AWL 304.

AIR SPRITE   *Royal Australian Navy*

1 AIRCRAFT LIGHTER—CATAMARAN

AWL 304

Dimensions, feet (metres): 77·8 × 32 × 6·6 *(23·7 × 9·8 × 2)*

Built at Cockatoo Dockyard 1967-68. Coastal craft. Capacity one S2E Tracker or two A4D Skyhawks.

2 Ex ASR CRAFT

38101   38102

38 ft Bertram craft of little value except in harbour.

3 CRANE STORES LIGHTERS

CSL 01   02   03

Based on design of AWL 304 but with crane and after superstructure. Built from 1972.

WORK BOATS

More than 20 are in use all built to a basic 40 ft *(12·2 m)* design.

WORK BOATS

AM 400-415

ARMY WATERCRAFT

12 LCM8

AB 1050-1053   1055-1061

Of 70 ft oa and 70 tons.

LCM8

6 LCVP

AB 751   752   755   756   758   759

Of 56 ft. Can carry 120 people.

2 TUGS

JOE MANN   THE LUKE

Built in 1964. Of 60 tons with a range of 5 700 miles and fitted for firefighting.

AUSTRIA

Commanding Officer

Major Walter Slovacek

Diplomatic Representation

Defence Attache´ in London:
Brigadier General H. Wingelbauer

Personnel

1 officer, 13 NCOs, 13 ratings, plus a small shipyard unit

Base

Marinekaserne Tegetthof, Wien-Kuchelau (under command of Austrian School of Military Engineering)

Mercantile Marine

Lloyd's Register of Shipping:
15 vessels of 3 670 tons gross

RIVERINE PATROL CRAFT

NIEDERÖSTERREICH   **A604**

Displacement, tons: 75
Dimensions, ft (metres): 96·8 × 17·8 × 3·6 *(29·4 × 5·4 × 1·1)*
Guns: 1—20 mm SPz Mk 66 Oerlikon in a turret; 1—12·7 mm MG; 1—Mk 42 MG; 2—8·4 cm PAR 66 "Carl Gustav" AT rifles
Main engines: 2 V 16 Diesels; 1 600 hp = 22 knots
Complement: 9

Built by Korneuberg Werft AG. Fully welded. Only one built of a projected class of twelve.

NIEDERÖSTERREICH   1975, Austrian Government

OBERST BRECHT   **A 601**

Displacement, tons: 10
Dimensions, feet (metres): 40·3 × 8·2 × 2·5 *(12·3 × 2·5 × 0·75)*
Gun: 1—12·7 mm MG
Main engines: 2 Diesels; 107 hp = 10 knots
Complement: 5

Built by Korneuburg Werft AG. Welded.

OBERST BRECHT   1974, Heeres Film

10 Ex-US "M3" PATROL CRAFT

27 foot craft. Four with petrol engines, six with diesels. Unarmed, they form part of the "military floating bridge equipment".

BAHAMAS

Mercantile Marine

Lloyd's Register of Shipping:
119 vessels of 189 890 tons gross

PATROL CRAFT

4 60 ft GRP TYPE

ACKLINS   **ANDROS**   **GLENTHIRA**   **SAN SALVADOR**

Displacement, tons: 30 standard
Dimensions, feet (metres): 62·0 oa × 15·8 × 4·6 *(18·9 × 4·8 × 1·4)*
Guns: 1 MG forward; 2 LMG on bridge
Main engines: 2 Caterpillar diesels = 20 knots
Complement: 11

"60 ft" Keith Nelson patrol craft built by Vosper Thornycroft in glass reinforced plastic, delivered in 1970 as the first four units of the Bahamas Police Marine Division. With air-conditioned living spaces, these craft are designed for patrol amongst the many islands of the Bahamas Group. The foredeck is specially strengthened for a 20 mm MG with light MGs in sockets either side of the bridge.

ANDROS   1972, Vosper Thornycroft

BAHRAIN

Mercantile Marine

Lloyd's Register of Shipping:
15 vessels of 3 670 tons

1 FAIREY MARINE "TRACKER" CLASS

Displacement, tons: 26
Dimensions, ft (metres): 64 × 16 × 5 *(19.5 × 4.9 × 1.5)*
Gun: 1—20 mm
Main engines: 2 diesels; 1 120 bhp = 28 knots

Purchased 1974.

"TRACKER" Class   *1974, Fairey Marine*

2 FAIREY MARINE "INTERCEPTOR" CLASS

25 ft *(7.6 metres)* craft with catamaran hull. Can carry eight 25-man liferafts (as shown) or a platoon of soldiers. Powered by twin 135 hp outboard motors for a speed of 30 knots.

"INTERCEPTOR" Class   *1975, Fairey Marine*

2 FAIREY MARINE "SPEAR" CLASS

Dimensions, feet (metres): 29.8 × 9.2 × 2.6 *(9.1 × 2.8 × .8)*
Guns: 2 MG
Main engines: 2 Perkins diesels, 290 hp = 26 knots
Complement: 3

Purchased 1974.

2 PATROL CRAFT

HOWAR   JIDA

Displacement, tons: 15
Dimensions, feet (metres): 45.5 × 12 × 3 *(13.9 × 3.7 × 0.9)*
Main engines: 2 Diesels; 1 080 bhp = 23 knots

BANGLADESH

Headquarters Appointments

Chief of Naval Staff:
 Rear-Admiral Mosharraf Hussain Khan psn.
Administrative Authority, Dacca:
 Captain Mahboob Ali Khan

Senior Appointments

NOIC Chittagong
 Commander Sultan Ahmad
SNO Khulna
 Commander Mujibur Rahman

Personnel:
1976: 3 000 (150 officers, 2 850 ratings)

Naval Bases

Chittagong (BNS Issa Khan), Dacca (BNS Haji Mohsin), Khulna (BNS Titumir)

Prefix to Ships Names

BNS

Mercantile Marine

Lloyd's Register of Shipping:
 120 vessels of 133 016 tons gross

Formation

The Bangladesh Navy was the last of the three services to be formed, Commander Nurul Huq being appointed Chief of Staff at the end of March 1972. Commodore Khan took over in Nov 1973 when Nurul Huq became Chairman of the BIWT. The first ship was commissioned by General Osmani on 12 June 1972 as P101.

Strength of the Fleet

Large Patrol Craft	5
Riverine Patrol Craft	3
Training Ship	1

LIGHT FORCES

3 "PABNA" CLASS (RIVERINE PATROL CRAFT)

Name	No.	Builders	Commissioned
NOAKHALI	P102	DEW Narayangonj, Dacca	8 July 1972
PABNA	P101	DEW Narayangonj, Dacca	12 June 1972
PATUAKHALI	P103	DEW Narayangonj, Dacca	7 Nov 1974

Displacement, tons: 69.5
Dimensions, feet (metres): 75 × 20 × 3.5 *(22.9 × 6.1 × 1.1)*
Gun: 1—40/60 Bofors
Main engines: Cummins diesel = 10.8 knots
Range, miles: 700
Complement: 33 (3 officers, 30 ratings)

The first indigenous naval craft built in Bangladesh.

PATUAKHALI   *1975, Bangladesh Navy*

2 Ex-YUGOSLAV "KRALJEVICA" CLASS (LARGE PATROL CRAFT)

Name	No.	Builders	Commissioned
KARNAPHULI (ex-PBR 502)	P301	Yugoslavia	1956
TISTA (ex-PBR 505)	P302	Yugoslavia	1956

Displacement, tons: 190 standard; 202 full load
Dimensions, feet (metres): 134·5 × 20·7 × 7·2 *(41 × 6·3 × 2·2)*
Guns: 1—128 mm rocket launcher; 1—40/60 mm
Main engines: MAN diesels; 2 shafts; 3 300 bhp = 18 knots
Range, miles: 1 000 at 12 knots
Complement: 44 (4 officers, 40 ratings)

Transferred and commissioned on 6 June 1975.

TISTA   *1975, Bangladesh Navy*

3 Ex-INDIAN "AKSHAY" CLASS (LARGE PATROL CRAFT)

Name	No.	Builders	Commissioned
PADMA (ex-*Ins Akshay*)	P 201	Hooghly D & E Co, Calcutta	1962
SURMA (ex-*Ins Ajay*)	P 202	Hooghly D & E Co, Calcutta	1962

Displacement, tons: 120 standard; 150 full load
Dimensions, feet (metres): 117·2 × 20 × 5·5 *(35·7 × 6·1 × 1·7)*
Gun: 1—40/60 mm
Main engines: 2 Paxman diesels = 12·5 knots
Range, miles: 5 000 at 10 knots
Complement: 35 (3 officers, 32 ratings)

Generally similar to Royal Navy's "Ford" class. Transferred and commissioned on 12 Apr 1973 and 3 Oct 1974 respectively.

SURMA   *1975, Bangladesh Navy*

TRAINING SHIP

SHAHEED RUHUL AMIN *(ex-MS Anticosti)*

Displacement, tons: 710 full load
Dimensions, feet (metres): 155·8 × 36·5 × 10 *(47·5 × 11·1 × 3·1)*
Gun: 1—40/60 mm Bofors
Main engines: Caterpillar diesel; 1 shaft = 11·5 knots
Range, miles: 4 000
Complement: 80 (8 officers, 72 ratings)

After use in relief work was handed over to BN in 1972, modified at Khulna and commissioned 10 Dec 1974.

BARBADOS

Mercantile Marine

Lloyd's Register of Shipping: 30 vessels of 3 897 tons gross

Coastguard

This was formed early in 1973.

3 12 Metre "GUARDIAN" CLASS (COASTAL PATROL CRAFT)

COMMANDER MARSHALL CG 402   **TT LEWIS** CG 403   **J. T. C. RAMSAY** CG 404

Displacement, tons: 11
Dimensions, feet (metres): 41 × 12·1 × 3·3 *(12·5 × 3·7 × 1)*
Gun: 1—·76 mm MG
Main engines: 2 Caterpillar Diesels; 580 hp = 24 knots
Complement: 4

Same general notes as for 20 metre "Guardian" above. CG 402 delivered Dec 1973, 403 Feb 1974, 404 launched 16 Oct 1974.

1 20 Metre "GUARDIAN" CLASS (COASTAL PATROL CRAFT)

GEORGE FERGUSON CG 601

Displacement, tons: 60
Dimensions, feet (metres): 65·6 × 17·4 × 4·3 *(20 × 5·3 × 1·3)*
Guns: 2—·76 mm MG
Main engines: 2 GM diesels; 1 300 hp = 24 knots
Range, miles: 650 cruising
Complement: 11

GRP hull by Halmatic Ltd; fitted out by E. F. Elkins Ltd, Christchurch, England. Air conditioned and designed for coastguard/SAR duties. Launched 16 Oct 1974 for delivery in December.

1 Ex-US LST

— (ex-*Kemper County*)

Transferred 6 Jan 1976.

BELGIUM

Headquarters Appointment

Chief of Naval Staff:

Rear Admiral J. P. L. van Dyck

Diplomatic Representation

Naval, Military and Air Attaché in Bonn:
Colonel Derille
Naval, Military and Air Attaché in The Hague:
Lieutenant-Colonel de Brouchoven de Bergeyck
Naval, Military and Air Attaché in London:
Colonel (BEM) Jules Kaisin
Naval, Military and Air Attaché in Paris:
Colonel (BEM) Hugo Rel
Naval, Military and Air Attaché in Washington:
Brigadier-General de Wilde
1974 *Hasselt, Kortryk* (Belgian built "Herstal" class)

Personnel

(a) 1972: 330 officers and 4 085 men
    1973: 330 officers and 4 150 men
    1974: 330 officers and 4 125 men
    1975: 350 officers and 4 582 men
(b) 12 months Military Service

Naval Aviation

3 Alouette III helicopters
2 Sikorsky S58 helicopters

New Construction

It is reported that 15 French "Circe II" minehunters are to be built to replace ex-US MSOs and MSCs, the first unit to be completed in 1980.

Strength of the Fleet

Type	Active	Building
Frigates	—	4
Minehunters	7	—
Minesweepers (Coastal)	9	—
Minesweepers (Inshore)	12	—
Support Ships	2	—
River Patrol Boats	6	—
Research Ships	2	—
Auxiliary and Service Craft	12	—

Mercantile Marine
Lloyd's Register of Shipping:
252 vessels of 1 358 425 tons gross

Base

Ostend

DISPOSALS

Minesweepers (Inshore)

1974 Hasselt, Kortryk (Belgian built "Herstal" class)

PENNANT LIST

Frigates

F 910	Wielingen
F 911	Westdiep
F 912	Wandelaar
F 913	Westhinder

Minewarfare Forces

M 473	Lokeren
M 474	Turnhout
M 475	Tongeren
M 476	Merksem
M 477	Oudenaarde
M 478	Herstal
M 479	Huy
M 480	Seraing
M 482	Vise

Minewarfare Forces *(cont)*

M 483	Ougrée
M 484	Dinant
M 485	Andenne
M 902	Haverbeke
M 903	Dufour
M 904	De Brouwer
M 906	Breydel
M 907	Artevelde
M 908	Truffaut
M 909	Bovesse
M 927	Spa
M 928	Stavelot
M 929	Heyst
M 930	Rochefort
M 931	Knokke
M 932	Nieuwport
M 933	Koksijde
M 934	Verviers
M 935	Veurne

Support Ships and Auxiliaries

A 950	Valcke
A 951	Hommel
A 952	Wesp
A 953	Bij
A 956	Krekel
A 958	Zenobe Gramme
A 959	Mier
A 960	Godetia
A 961	Zinnia
A 962	Mechelen

River Patrol Boats

P 901	Leie
P 902	Liberation
P 903	Meuse
P 904	Sambre
P 905	Schelde
P 906	Semois

FRIGATES

4 "E-71" CLASS

No.	Builders	Laid down	Launched	Commissioning
F 910	Boelwerf, Temse	5 Mar 1974	—	Dec 1976
F 911	Cockerill, Hoboken	2 Sep 1974	—	June 1977
F 912	Boelwerf, Temse	1 Apr 1975	—	Dec 1977
F 913	Cockerill, Hoboken	8 Dec 1975	—	June 1978

Name
WIELINGEN
WESTDIEP
WANDELAAR
WESTHINDER

Displacement, tons: 1 940 standard; 2 340 full load
Length, feet (metres): 347·7 *(106)*
Beam, feet (metres): 39·4 *(12)*
Draught, feet (metres): 18·8 *(5·6)*
Guns: 1—3·9 in *(100 mm)* 1 CIWS
Missiles: 1 NATO Sea Sparrow SAM, (2 × 4); 4 Exocet SSM
Torpedo launchers: 2 for L-5 torpedos
A/S rocket launchers: 1—6 × 375 mm LR Bofors
Rocket Launchers: 2—8 barrelled Corvus dual-purpose Chaff/flare launchers
Main engines: CODOG—1 Rolls Royce Olympus TM3 gas turbine; 28 000 bhp; 2 Cockerill CO-240 diesels; 6 000 bhp. Twin vp propellers
Speed, knots: 28 (15 on 1 diesel, 18 on 2 diesels)
Range, miles: 4 500 at 18 knots
Complement: 14 officers; 146 men

This compact, well-armed class of frigate is the first class fully designed by the Belgian Navy and built in Belgian yards. All to be fitted with hull-mounted sonar and fin stabilisers.

Electronics: Fully integrated and automated weapons command and control system of HSA (SEWACO 4). ESM and ECM capability.

Missiles: Sea Sparrow RIM 7H-2 manufactured under licence by Selenia. Exocet MM 38.

Radar: Air and surface warning and target indication radar with Control System (HSA). Navigation radar by Raytheon.

"E 71" Class Model

WESTDIEP (on launch)

1975, E. G. Pieters

MINE WARFARE FORCES

7 U.S. MSO (Ex-AM) TYPE 498 (MINEHUNTERS)

Name	No.	Builders	Laid down	Launched	Commissioned
A. F. DUFOUR (ex-*Lagen* M 950, ex-*MSO 498*)	M 903	Bellingham Shipyard Inc, Wash.	1954	13 Aug 1954	27 Sep 1955
ARTEVELDE (ex-*MSO 503*, ex-*AM 503*)	M 907	Tacoma Boatbuilding Co, Tacoma, Wash.	1953	19 June1954	15 Dec 1955
BREYDELL (ex-*MSO 504*, ex-*AM 504*)	M 906	Tacoma Boatbuilding Co, Tacoma, Wash.	1954	25 Mar 1955	24 Jan 1956
DE BROUWER (ex-*Nansen*, M 951, ex-*MSO 499*)	M 904	Bellingham Shipyard Inc, Wash.	1954	15 Oct 1954	1 Nov 1955
F. BOVESSE (ex-*MSO 516*, ex-*AM 516*)	M 909	Tampa Shipbuilding Co, Inc. Tampa, Fla.	1954	8 Feb 1956	21 Dec 1956
G. TRUFFAUT (ex-*MSO 515*, ex-*AM 515*)	M 908	Tampa Shipbuilding Co, Inc, Tampa, Fla.	1955	1 Nov 1955	21 Sep 1956
VAN HAVERBEKE (ex-*MSO 522*)	M 902	Petersen Builders Inc, Sturgeon Bay, Wisc.	1959	25 Oct 1959	7 Nov 1960

Displacement, tons: 720 standard; 780 full load
Length, feet (metres): 165·0 *(50·3)* wl; 172·5 *(52·6)* oa
Beam, feet (metres): 35·0 *(10·7)*
Draught, feet (metres): 11·0 *(3·4)*
Gun: 1—40 mm (except *De Brouwer* and *Dufour*)
Main engines: 2 GM diesels; 2 shafts; 1 600 bhp
Speed, knots: 14
Oil fuel, tons: 50
Range, miles: 2 400 at 12 knots; 3 000 at 20 knots
Complement: 72 (5 officers, 67 men)

Wooden hulls and non-magnetic structure. Capable of sweeping mines of all types. Diesels of non-magnetic stainless steel alloy. Controllable pitch propellers.

Dufour and *De Brouwer* originally served in Royal Norwegian Navy (1955-66). *Artevelde* converted to Diving Vessel in 1972—all the remainder now fitted as minehunters.

Transfer dates: *M902* 9 Dec 1960, *M903* 14 Apr 1966, *M904* 14 Apr 1966, *M906* 15 Feb 1956, *M907* 16 Dec 1955, *M908* 12 Oct 1956, *M909* 25 Jan 1957.

BREYDEL

12 1974, C. and S. Taylor

9 U.S. MSC (ex-AMS) TYPE 60 (MINESWEEPERS—COASTAL)

Name	No.	Builders	Commissioned
HEIST	M 929	Boelwerf, Temse	Nov 1955
KNOKKE	M 931	Beliard, Ostend	Apr 1955
KOKSIJDE	M 933	Beliard, Ostend	Nov 1955
NIEUWPOORT	M 932	Beliard, Ostend	May 1955
ROCHEFORT	M 930	Beliard, Ostend	Feb 1955
SPA	M 927	Boelwerf, Temse	Mar 1955
STAVELOT	M 928	Boelwerf, Temse	July 1955
VERVIERS (ex-*MSC 259*)	M 934	Boston, USA	1956
VEURNE (ex-*MSC 260*)	M 935	Boston, USA	1956

Displacement, tons: 330 light; 390 full load
Dimensions, feet (metres): 139 pp; 144 oa × 27·9 × 8 *(42·4; 44·0 × 8·5 × 2·6)*
Gun: 1—40 mm
Main engines: 2 GM diesels; 2 shafts; 880 bhp = 13·5 knots
Oil fuel, tons: 28
Range, miles: 3 000 at economical speed (10·5 knots)
Complement: 39

Wooden hulls and constructed throughout of materials with the lowest possible magnetic signature. M 934 and 935 were built in USA, under MDAP, and M 926-933 of same type were built in Belgium with machinery and equipment from USA. M 934 (ex-*MSC 259*) transferred 19 June 1956, M 935 (ex-*MSC 260*) was transferred on 7 Sep 1956. *Verviers* and *Veurne* converted to minehunters with Voith-Schneider propellers.

Reclassification: *Mechelen*, M 926, former coastal minesweeper of this class, was re-rated as a research ship in 1964 and re-numbered A 962 in 1966 (see next page).

KNOKKE

8 1975 Wright and Logan

12 "HERSTAL" CLASS (MINESWEEPERS—INSHORE)

Name	No.	Builders	Launched
ANDENNE	M 485 (ex-*MSI 97*)	Mercantile Marine Yard, Kruibeke	May 1958
OUDENAARDE	M 477	Mercantile Marine Yard, Kruibeke	May 1958
DINANT	M 484 (ex-*MSI 96*)	Mercantile Marine Yard, Kruibeke	5 Apr 1958
OUGREE	M 483 (ex-*MSI 95*)	Mercantile Marine Yard, Kruibeke	16 Nov 1957
HERSTAL	M 478 (ex-*MSI 90*)	Mercantile Marine Yard, Kruibeke	6 Aug 1956
SERAING	M 480 (ex-*MSI 92*)	Mercantile Marine Yard, Kruibeke	Mar 1957
TONGEREN	M 475	Mercantile Marine Yard, Kruibeke	16 Nov 1957
LOKEREN	M 473	Mercantile Marine Yard, Kruibeke	18 May 1957
TURNHOUT	M 474	Mercantile Marine Yard, Kruibeke	7 Sep 1957
MERKSEM	M 476	Mercantile Marine Yard, Kruibeke	5 Apr 1958
VISÉ	M 482 (ex-*MSI 94*)	Mercantile Marine Yard, Kruibeke	7 Sep 1957

Displacement, tons: 160 light; 190 full load
Dimensions, feet (metres): 106·7 pp; 113·2 oa × 22·3 · 6 *(32·5; 34·5 · 6·9 · 1·8)*
Guns: 2 — ·5 (Twin)
Main engines: 2 diesels; 2 shafts; 1 260 bhp = 15 knots
Oil fuel, tons: 18
Range, miles: 2 300 at 10 knots
Complement: 17

Modified AMI "100-foot" class. Originally a class of sixteen. The first MSI *Herstal* was completed in June 1957 the last pair being completed in 1959.

The first group of eight (M 478 to 485) was a United States "off shore order", the remaining eight (M 470 to 477) being financed under the Belgian Navy Estimates.

OUDENAARDE

5/1974, C. and S. Taylor

SUPPORT SHIPS

Name	No.	Builders	Commissioned
ZINNIA	A 961	Cockerill, Hoboken	5 Sep 1967

Displacement, tons: 1 705 light; 2 685 full load
Length, feet (metres): 299·2 *(91·2)* pp; 309 *(94·2)* wl; 326·4 *(99·5)* oa
Beam, feet (metres): 49·9 *(14·0)*
Draught, feet (metres): 11·8 *(3·6)*
Guns: 3—40 mm (single)
Aircraft: 1 helicopter
Main engines: 2 Cockerill V 12 RT 240 CO diesels; 5 000 bhp; 1 Shaft
Speed, knots: 20
Oil fuel, tons: 500
Range, miles: 14 000 at 12·5 knots
Complement: 125

Launched on 6 May 1967. Controllable pitch propeller. Design includes a platform and a retractable hangar for one light liason-helicopter. Rated as Command and Logistic Support Ship.

ZINNIA   *1975 Dr. Giorgio Arra*

Name	No.	Builders	Commissioned
GODETIA	A 960	Boelwerf, Temse	23 May 1966

Displacement, tons: 1 700 light; 2 500 full load
Dimensions, feet (metres): 289 wl; 301 oa × 46 × 11·5 *(88·0; 91·8 × 14 × 3·5)*
Guns: 2—40 mm (twin)
Aircraft: Provision for light helicopter
Main engines: 4 ACEC—MAN diesels; 2 shafts; 5 400 bhp = 19 knots
Oil fuel, tons: 294
Range, miles: 8 700 at 12·5 knots
Complement: 100 plus 35 spare billets

Laid down on 15 Feb 1965, launched on 7 Dec 1965. Controllable pitch propellers. Provided with a platform which can take a light liason-helicopter.

GODETIA   *10 1974 Reiner Nerlich*

RIVER PATROL BOATS

LEIE P 901	**MEUSE** P 903	**SCHELDE** P 905
LIBERATION P 902	**SAMBRE** P 904	**SEMOIS** P 906

Displacement, tons: 25 light; 27·5 full load
Dimensions, feet (metres): 75·5 pp; 82 oa × 12·5 × 3 *(23·0; 25·0 × 3·8 × 0·9)*
Liberation 85·5 × 13·1 × 3·2 *(26·0 × 4·0 × 1·0)*
Guns: 2—13 mm (·50) MG
Main engines: 2 diesels; 2 shafts; 440 bhp = 19 knots
Complement: 7

Built by Hitzler, Regensburg, Germany, in 1953, except *Liberation* in 1954. *Semois* acts as base ship for divers.

MEUSE   *1974, Belgian Navy*

RESEARCH SHIPS

MECHELEN (ex-M 926) A926

Displacement, tons: 330 light; 390 full load
Dimensions, feet (metres): 139 pp; 144 oa × 27·9 × 7·5 *(42·4; 44·0 × 8·5 × 2·3)*
Main engines: 2 GM diesels; 2 shafts; 880 bhp ~ 13·5 knots
Oil fuel, tons: 28
Range, miles: 3 000 at economical speed (10·5 knots)
Complement: 39

Former coastal minesweeper built by Boelwerf, Temse and commissioned in Dec 1954. Used as a research ship since 1964 being renumbered as A 962 in 1966.

MECHELEN   *1974, Neptunus, Ostend*

ZENOBE GRAMME A 958

Displacement, tons: 149
Dimensions, feet (metres): 92 × 22·5 × 7 *(28·2 × 6·8 × 2·1)*
Main engines: 1 MWM diesel; 1 shaft; 200 bhp ~ 10 knots
Complement: 14

Auxiliary sail ketch. Built by Boelwerf, Temse, Belgium, commissioned 23 Oct 1961. Designed for scientific research.

TUGS

O/Lt VALCKE (ex-AT 1) A 950

Displacement, tons: 110
Dimensions, feet (metres): 78·8 pp; 95 oa × 21 × 5·5 *(24·0; 29·0 × 6·4 × 1·7)*
Main engines: 1 diesel; 1 shaft; 600 bhp = 12 knots
Complement: 14

Built by Holland Nautic NV, Haarlem, Netherlands in 1951 and served as Dutch mercantile tug *Elis* until purchased by Belgian Navy in 1953.

BIJ A 953   **KREKEL** A 956

Harbour tugs with fire-fighting facilities. Of 71 tons and twin shafts; 400 hp with Voith-Schneider propellers. *Bij* built by Akerboom 1959, *Krekel* by Ch. Navals de Rupelmonde 1961.

HOMMEL A 951   **WESP** A 952

Harbour tugs of 22 tons, 300 bhp diesels with Voith-Schneider propellers. Both built by Voith, Heidenheim in 1953.

MIER A 959

Harbour tug of 17·5 tons with 90 bhp diesel. Built Liége 1962.

AUXILIARY CRAFT

Harbour craft: There are three barges, namely **FN 4**, **FN 5** and **FN 6**, displacement 300 tons, length. 105 feet, built by Plaquet, Peronne-lez-Antoing in 1957; the ammunition ship *Ekster*, displacement 140 tons, length 118 feet, built at Niel (Germany) in 1953; a diving cutter ZM 4, displacement 8 tons, length 33 feet, built at Ostend in 1954; and the harbour transport cutter *Spin*, displacement 32 tons, length 47·8 feet, with 250 bhp diesels 8 knots and Voith-Schneider propeller, built in the Netherlands in 1958.

BELIZE

Personnel

(a) 50 approx
(b) Voluntary

Base

Belize

Mercantile Marine

Lloyd's Register of Shipping: 3 vessels of 620 tons gross

2 COASTAL PATROL CRAFT

Name	No.	Builders	Commissioned
BELIZE	PBM 01	Brooke Marine, Lowestoft	1972
BELMOPAN	PBM 02	Brooke Marine, Lowestoft	1972

Displacement, tons: 15
Dimensions, feet (metres): 40 × 12 × 2 *(12·2 × 3·6 × 0·6)*
Guns: 3 MG
Main engines: 2 Diesels; 370 hp × 22 knots

BOLIVIA

Headquarters Appointment

C in C replaced Jan 1976.

Personnel

(a) 1976: 1 500 officers and men
(b) 12 months selective military service

A small navy used for patrolling Lake Titicaca and the Beni River system. Most of the training of officers and senior ratings is carried out in Argentina.

Base

Tiquina

Prefix to Ships' Names

FNB

I TRANSPORT

CORONEL ABAROA M 08

16 PATROL CRAFT

Of various sizes.

BRAZIL

Headquarters Appointments

Chief of Naval Staff:
  Admiral Gualter Maria Menezes de Magalhães
Chief of Naval Material:
  Admiral Sylvio de Magalhães Figueiredo
Chief of Naval Personnel:
  Admiral Eddy Sampaio Espellet

Diplomatic Representation

Naval Attaché in Asunción:
  Captain Luiz Fernando da Silva e Souza
Naval and Defence Attaché in Athens:
  Captain Gerson Fleischauer
Naval and Defence Attaché in Buenos Aires:
  Captain Odilon Lima Cardoso
Naval and Defence Attaché in Lima:
  Captain Luis Carlos de Freitas
Naval Attaché in La Paz:
  Captain Paulo Demaria Serôa da Motta
Naval and Defence Attaché in Lisbon and Madrid:
  Captain Valbert Lisieux Medeiros de Figueiredo
Naval Attaché in London:
  Captain Mauricio Henrique Bittencourt de Carvalho
Naval Attaché in Paris:
  Captain Henrique Octávio Aché Pillar
Naval and Defence Attaché in Santiago:
  Captain Francisco Lafayette de Moraes
Naval and Defence Attaché in Tokyo:
  Captain Luiz Augusto Paraguassu de Sá
Naval Attaché in Washington:
  Rear Admiral Rafael de Azevedo Branco

Personnel

(a)
1972: 42 125 (3 264 officers and 38 861 men)
1973: 44 337 (3 591 officers and 40 746 men)
1974: 49 600 (3 887 officers and 45 713 men)
1975: 43 100 (3 800 officers and 39 300 men)
1976: 45 300 (3 800 officers and 41 500 men)
Figures include marines and auxiliary corps

(b) 1 year National service

Naval Bases

Rio de Janeiro (main base with 3 dry docks and 1 floating dock)
Aratu (Bahia) (major naval yard with 1 dry dock and 1 floating dock)
Belém (naval base and repair yard with 1 dry dock)
Recife (naval base and repair yard)
Natal (small naval base and repair yard with 1 floating dock)
Ladario (river base of *Mato Grosso* flotilla)
Sao Pedro (naval air station)

Maritime Aviation

A Fleet Air Arm was formed on 26 January 1965.

Navy
  5 Sikorsky SH-3D
  4 Sikorsky SH-34J (SH-1)
  5 Westland Whirlwind (UH-5)
  3 Westland Wasp HAS-1 (UH-2)
  18 Bell 206B Jetrangers
  9 Westland Lynx WG 13 to be provided for "Niteroi" class

Air Force
  3 Lockheed P2-E Neptunes (to be replaced by Brazilian EMB-111)
  13 Grumman HU-16A Albatross (SAR)
  8 Grumman S-2A Trackers (to be replaced by S-2E)
  14 Lockheed RC-130E Hercules (SAR/PR)
  9 Convair PBY-5A Catalinas (Transport)

Prefix to Ships' Names

These vary, indicating the type of ship e.g. N Ae L = Aircraft Carrier; CT = Destroyer.

Mercantile Marine

Lloyd's Register of Shipping:
  482 vessels of 2 691 408 tons gross

Strength of the Fleet

Type	Active	Building
Attack Carrier (medium)	1	—
Destroyers	12	6
Submarines (Patrol)	8	2
Landing Ships	2	—
Monitor and Gunboats	9	—
River Patrol Ships	5	—
Minesweepers (Coastal)	8	2
Survey Ships	6	—
Survey Launches	11	—
S/M Rescue Ships	1	—
Repair Ship	1	—
Tankers	2 (1 small)	—
Transports	4	—
Tugs	3	—
Floating Docks	3	—

Proposed New Construction

1 Helicopter Carrier
3 A-A Frigates
4 Coastal Patrol Craft
1 Replenishment Tanker

4 LCVP
10 LCM
1 Survey Ship
3 Tugs

DELETIONS

Cruiser

1973 *Barroso*
1975 *Tamandare* offered for auction (September)
(both ex-US "St Louis" class)

Destroyers

1973 *Amazonas, Mariz E. Barros*
1974 *Acre, Araguaia, Araguari*—(auction July for scrap)
(All Brazilian built 1949-51)

Frigates

1973 *Baependi, Bracui*
1975 *Benevente, Bocaina* (auction Feb for scrap)
(All ex-US "Bertioga" class)

Submarines

1972 *Rio Grande do Sul* (ex-*Sandlance*) for alongside training
Bahia (ex-*Plaice*)

Mine Warfare Forces

1974 *Jutai, Juruena* (paid off in Aug)
(ex-US AMS)

Patrol Forces

1971 *Piraju, Piranha*
1972 *Paraguaçu*
1973 *Pirague*

PENNANT LIST

Aircraft Carrier

A 11	Minas Gerais

Destroyers

F 40	Niteroi
F 41	Defensora
F 42	Independencia
F 43	União
F 44	Constituição
F 45	Liberal
D 25	Marcilio Dias
D 26	Mariz E. Barros
D 27	Para
D 28	Paraiba
D 29	Parana
D 30	Pernambuco
D 33	Maranhão
D 34	Mato Grosso
D 35	Sergipe
D 36	Alagoas
D 37	Rio Grande Do Norte
D 38	Espirito Santo

Submarines

S 10	Guanabara
S 11	Rio Grande Do Sul
S 12	Bahia
S 13	Rio De Janeiro
S 14	Ceara
S 15	Goiaz
S 16	Amazonas
S 20	Humaita
S 21	Tonelero
S 22	Riachuelo

Amphibious Forces

| G 26 | Duque De Caxias |
| G 28 | Garcia D'Avila |

Patrol Forces

P 20	Pedro Teixeira
P 21	Raposo Tavares
P 30	Roraima
P 31	Rondonia
P 32	Amapa
U 17	Parnaiba
V 15	Imperial Marinheiro
V 16	Iguatemi
V 17	Ipiranga
V 18	Forte De Coimbra
V 19	Cabocla
V 20	Angostura
V 21	Baiana
V 22	Mearim
V 23	Purus
V 24	Solimoes

Light Forces

P 10	Piratini
P 11	Piraja
P 12	Pampeiro
P 13	Parati
P 14	Penedo
P 15	Poti
R 54	Anchova
R 55	Arenque
R 56	Atum
R 57	Acara
R 58	Agulha
R 59	Aruana

Mine Warfare Forces

M 15	Aratu
M 16	Anhatomirim
M 17	Atalaia
M 18	Aracatuba
M 19	Abrolhos
M 20	Albardão

Survey Vessels and Tenders

H 11	Paraibano
H 12	Rio Branco
H 13	Mestre João Dos Santos
H 14	Nogueira Da Gama
H 15	Itacurussa
H 16	Camocim
H 17	Caravelas
H 21	Sirius
H 22	Canopus
H 24	Castelhanos
H 27	Faroleiro Areas
H 28	Faroleiro Santana
H 30	Faroleiro Nascimento
H 31	Argus
H 32	Orion
H 33	Taurus
H 34	Graça Aranha
H 41	Almirante Camara
U 10	Almirante Saldanha

Miscellaneous

G 15	Paraguassu
G 16	Barroso Pereira
G 17	Potengi
G 21	Ary Parreiras
G 22	Soares Dutra
G 24	Belmonte
G 25	Afonso Pena
G 26	Am. Jeronimo Gonçalves
G 27	Marajó
K 10	Gastao Moutinho
M 11	Javari
M 13	Jurua
R 21	Tritão
R 22	Tridente
R 23	Triunfo
U 20	Rio Doce
U 21	Rio Das Contas
U 22	Rio Formoso
U 23	Rio Real
U 24	Rio Turvo
U 25	Rio Verde
U 26	Custodio De Mello
U 40	Rio Pardo
U 41	Rio Negro
U 42	Rio Chui
U 43	Rio Oiapoque

AIRCRAFT CARRIER

1 Ex-BRITISH "COLOSSUS" CLASS

Name	No.	Builders	Laid down	Launched	Commissioned
MINAS GERAIS (ex-HMS *Vengeance*)	A 11	Swan, Hunter & Wigham Richardson, Ltd, Wallsend on Tyne	16 Nov 1942	23 Feb 1944	15 Jan 1945

Displacement, tons: 15 890 standard; 17 500 normal;
  19 890 full load (see *Displacement* note)
Length, feet (metres): 630 *(192·0)* pp; 695 *(211·8)* oa
Beam, feet (metres): 80 *(24·4)*
Draught, feet (metres): 24·5 *(7·5)*
Flight deck,
  Length, feet (metres): 690 *(210·3)*
  Width, feet (metres): 121 *(37·0)* oa as reconstructed
  Height, feet (metres): 39 *(11·9)* above water line
Catapults: 1 steam
Aircraft: 20 aircraft including 7 S2A Trackers, 4 Sea Kings
Guns: 10—40 mm (2 quadruple, 1 twin), 2—47 mm (saluting)
Main engines: Parsons geared turbines; 2 shafts; 40 000 shp
Boilers: 4 Admiralty 3-drum type; Working pressure 400 psi *(28 kg/cm²)*; max superheat 700°F (371°C)
Speed, knots: 24; 25·3 on trials after reconstruction
Oil fuel, tons: 3 200
Range, miles: 12 000 at 14 knots; 6 200 at 23 knots
Complement: 1 000 (1 300 with air group)

MINAS GERAIS
1971, Brazilian Navy

Served in the Royal Navy from 1945 onwards. Fitted out in late 1948 to early 1949 for experimental cruise to the Arctic. Lent to the Royal Australian Navy early in 1953, returned to the Royal Navy in Aug 1955. Purchased by the Brazilian Government on 14 Dec 1956. Reconstructed at Verolme Dock, Rotterdam from summer 1957 to Dec 1960. The conversion and overhaul included the installation of the angled deck, steam catapult, mirror-sight deck landing system, armament fire control and radar equipment. The ship was purchased for $9 000 000 and the reconstruction cost $27 000 000. Commissioned in the Brazilian Navy at Rotterdam on 6 Dec 1960. Left Rotterdam for Rio de Janeiro on 13 Jan 1961. Used primarily for anti-submarine aircraft and helicopters.

Displacement: Before reconstruction: 13 190 tons standard; 18 010 tons full load.

Engineering: The two units each have one set of turbines and two boilers installed side by side. Maximum speed at 120 rpm. Steam capacity was increased when the boilers were retubed during reconstruction in 1957-60.

Electrical: During reconstruction an alternating current system was installed with a total of 2 500 kW supplied by four turbogenerators and one diesel generator.

Hangar: Dimensions: length, 445 feet; width, 52 feet; clear depth, 17·5 feet. Aircraft lifts: 45 feet by 34 feet. During reconstruction in 1957-60 new lifts replaced the original units.

Radar: Air Surveillance SPS 12; Surface Search SPS 4; Fighter Direction SPS 8B; Air Control SPS 8A; Fire Control SPG 34; Navigation MP 1402.

Operational: Single track catapult for launching, and arrester wires for recovering, 30 000 lb aircraft at 60 knots. Catapult accelerator gear port side forward.

MINAIS GERAIS
1972, Brazilian Navy

MINAIS GERAIS
1972, Brazilian Navy

DESTROYERS

6 "NITEROI" CLASS

Name	No.	Builders	Laid down	Launched	Commissioning
CONSTITUIÇÃO	F 44	Vosper Thornycroft Ltd.	13 Mar 1974	Apr 1976	Feb 1978
DEFENSORA	F 41	Vosper Thornycroft Ltd.	14 Dec 1972	27 Mar 1975	April 1977
INDEPENDENCIA	F 42	Arsenal de Marinho, Rio de Janeiro	11 June 1972	2 Sep 1974	Mar 1978
LIBERAL	F 45	Vosper Thornycroft Ltd.	2 May 1975	Oct 1976	Aug 1978
NITEROI	F 40	Vosper Thornycroft Ltd.	8 June 1972	8 Feb 1974	July 1976
UNIÃO	F 43	Arsenal de Marinho, Rio de Janeiro	11 June 1972	14 Mar 1975	Oct 1978

Displacement, tons: 3 200 standard; 3 800 full load
Length, feet (metres): 400 *(121·9)* wl; 424 *(129·2)* oa
Beam, feet (metres): 44·2 *(13·5)*
Draught, feet (metres): 18·2 *(5·5)*
Aircraft: One WG 13 Lynx helicopter
Missile launchers: 2 twin Exocet MM 38 surface-to-surface in General Purpose version; 2 triple Seacat; Ikara in Anti-Submarine version
Guns: 2—4·5 inch Mark 8 in General Purpose version; 1—4·5 inch Mark 8 in Anti-Submarine version; 2—40 mm
A/S weapons: One Bofors 375 mm twin tube A/S rocket launcher; Two triple Mark 32 torpedo tubes; 1 DC rail
Main engines: CODOG system; 2 Rolls Royce Olympus gas turbines = 56 000 bhp; 4 MTU diesels, = 18 000 shp
Speed, knots: 30 on gas turbines; 22 on diesels
Range, miles: 5 300 at 17 knots (2 diesels); 4 200 at 19 knots (4 diesels); 1 300 at 28 knots (gas turbine)
Endurance: 45 days stores; 60 days provisions
Complement: 200·

A very interesting design of handsome appearance—Vosper Thornycroft Mark 10. The moulded depth is 28½ feet *(8·8 metres)*. Exceptionally economical in personnel, amounting to a fifty per cent reduction of manpower in relation to previous warships of this size and complexity. Require 80 fewer men than the British Type 42 of approximately similar characteristics.

Class: F 40, 41, 44 and 45 are of the A/S configuration. F 42 and 43 are General Purpose design.

Contract: A contract announced on 29 Sep 1970, valued at about £100 000 000, was signed between the Brazilian Government and Vosper Thornycroft Ltd, Portsmouth, England for the design and building of these six Vosper Thornycroft Mark 10 frigates comparable with the British Type 42 guided missile destroyers being built for the Royal Navy.

Construction: Materials, equipment and lead-yard services supplied by Vosper Thornycroft at Arsenal de Marinho.

Electronics: CAAIS equipment by Ferranti (FM 1600B computers). ECM by Decca.

Names: The names of the six ships as originally allocated in 1971 were: *Campista, Constituição, Defensora, Imperatriz, Isabel* and *Niteroi.*

Radar:
Air Warning:1 Plessey AWS-2 with Mk 10 IFF.
Surface Warning: 1 Signaal ZWO-6.
Weapon Control and Tracking: 2 Selenia RTN-10X.
Ikara Tracker: 1 set in A/S ships only.

Sonar: 1 EDO 610E medium range.
1 EDO 700E VDS (A/S ships only).

NITEROI on trials
1/1976, Vosper Thornycroft

NITEROI on trials
1/1976, Vosper Thornycroft

NITEROI on trials
1/1976, Vosper Thornycroft

5 Ex-US "FLETCHER" CLASS

Name	No.	Builders	Laid down	Launched	Commissioned
PARA (ex-USS *Guest*, DD 472)	D 27	Boston Navy Yard	27 Sep 1941	20 Feb 1942	15 Dec 1942
PARAIBA (ex-USS *Bennett*, DD 473)	D 28	Boston Navy Yard	10 Dec 1941	16 Apr 1942	9 Feb 1943
PARANA (ex-USS *Cushing*, DD 797)	D 29	Bethlehem Steel Co (Staten Island)	3 May 1943	30 Sep 1943	17 Jan 1944
PERNAMBUCO (ex-USS *Hailey*, DD 556)	D 30	Seattle-Tacoma S.B. Corpn, (Seattle)	1 Apr 1942	9 Mar 1943	30 Sep 1943
MARANHAO (ex-USS *Shields*, DD 596)	D 33	Puget Sound Navy Yard	10 Aug 1943	25 Sep 1944	8 Feb 1945

Displacement, tons: 2 050 standard; 3 050 full load
Length, feet (metres): 376·5 *(114·8)* oa
Beam, feet (metres): 39·3 *(12·0)*
Draught, feet (metres): 18 *(5·5)*
Missiles: 1 quadruple Seacat *(Maranhao* only)
Guns: 5—5 in *(127 mm)* 38 cal (except *Pernambuco:* 4—5 in);
6—3 in *(76 mm)* 50 cal (3 twin) *(Pernambuco* only);
10—40 mm (2 quad, 1 twin) *(Paraiba, Parana* and *Maranhão)*;
6—40 mm (3 twin) *(Para)*
Torpedo tubes: 5—21 in *(533 mm)*
A/S weapons: 2 Hedgehogs;
1 DC rack;
2 side launching torpedo racks;
2 triple Mk 32 torpedo launchers *(Maranhao* only)
Main engines: 2 GE geared turbines; 2 shafts; 60 000 shp
Boilers: 4 Babcock & Wilcox
Speed, knots: 35
Oil fuel, tons: 650
Range, miles: 5 000 at 15 knots; 1 260 at 30 knots
Complement: 260

Para was transferred on loan 5 June 1959; *Paraiba* on loan 15 Dec 1959 and subsequently by sale 1 Aug 1973. *Parana* on loan 20 July 1961 and subsequently by sale 8 Jan 1973; *Pernambuco* on loan 20 July 1961 and *Maranhao* by sale 1 July 1972. *Piaui* (ex-*Lewis Hancock* DD 675) was transferred on loan 2 Aug 1967 whilst *Santa Catarina* (ex-*Irwin* DD 794) was transferred on loan 10 May 1968, and both by sale 11 April 1973, being used subsequently for spare parts.

Radar: Search: SPS 6. Tactical: SPS 10. Fire Control: I Band.

PERNAMBUCO (four 5 inch guns)   1974, Brazilian Navy

PARANA (five 5 inch guns)
1970, Captain A. M. de Silva

1 Ex-US "ALLEN M. SUMNER" and 4 Ex-US "ALLEN M. SUMNER FRAM II" CLASSES

Name	No.	Builders	Laid down	Launched	Commissioned
ALAGOAS (ex-USS *Buck* DD 761)	D 36	Bethlehem (San Francisco)	—	11 Mar 1945	28 June1946
ESPIRITO SANTO (ex-USS *Lowry* DD 770)	D 38	Bethlehem (San Pedro)	—	6 Feb 1944	23 July 1944
RIO GRANDE DO NORTE (ex-USS *Strong* DD 758)	D 37	Bethlehem (San Francisco)	—	23 Apr 1944	8 Mar 1945
SERGIPE (ex-USS *James C. Owens* DD 776)	D 35	Bethlehem (San Pedro)	—	1 Oct 1944	17 Feb 1945
MATO GROSSO (ex-USS *Compton*, DD 705)	D 34	Federal S.B. & D.D. Co.	—	17 Sep 1944	4 Nov 1944

Displacement, tons: 2 200 standard; 3 320 full load
Length, feet (metres): 376·5 *(114·8)* oa
Beam, feet (metres): 40·9 *(12·4)*
Draught, feet (metres): 19 *(5·8)*
Guns: 6—5 in *(127 mm)* 38 cal DP (twins)
A/S weapons: 2 triple torpedo launchers; 2 ahead-firing Hedgehogs; facilities for small helicopter (Fram II). Depth charges *(Mato Grosso)*
Main engines: 2 geared turbines; 60 000 shp; 2 shafts
Boilers: 4
Speed, knots: 34
Range, miles: 4 600 at 15 knots, 1 260 at 30 knots
Complement: 274

Transferred to Brazil as follows: *Mato Grosso* 27 Sep 1972, *Sergipe* and *Alagoas* 16 July 1973, *Espirito Santo* 29 Oct 1973, *Rio Grande do Norte* 31 Oct 1973, the last four being FRAM II conversions, *Mato Grosso* being of the original "Sumner" class.

Gunnery: 3 inch guns in *Mato Grosso* removed before transfer.

MATO GROSSO   1974, Brazilian Navy

Radar: SPS 6 and 10 *(Mato Grosso)*.   **Sonar:** SQS 31 *(Mato Grosso)*.

2 Ex-US "GEARING" (FRAM I) CLASS

Name	No.	Builders	Laid down	Launched	Commissioned
MARCILIO DIAS (ex-USS *Henry W. Tucker* DD 875)	D 25	Consolidated Steel	—	8 Nov 1944	12 Mar 1945
MARIZ E. BARROS (ex-USS *Brinkley Bass* DD 887)	D 26	Consolidated Steel	—	26 May 1945	1 Oct 1945

Displacement, tons: 2 425 standard; 3 500 full load
Length, feet (metres): 390·5 *(119·0)*
Beam, feet (metres): 40·9 *(12·4)*
Draught, feet (metres): 19 *(5·8)*
Guns: 4—5 inch *(127 mm)* 38 cal DP (twin)
A/S weapons: 1 Asroc 8-tube launcher; 2 triple Mk 32 torpedo launchers; facilities for small helicopter
Main engines: 2 GE geared turbines; 60 000 shp; 2 shafts
Boilers: 4 Babcock & Wilcox
Speed, knots: 34
Range, miles: 5 800 at 15 knots
Complement: 274 (14 officers, 260 men)

Enlarged "Allen M. Sumner" class—14 feet longer.
Fitted with VDS. Transferred 3 Dec 1973.

"GEARING" (FRAM I) Class

Radar: SPS-10 and SPS-40.   **Sonar:** SQS-23.

SUBMARINES

3 BRITISH "OBERON" CLASS

Name	No.
HUMAITA	S 20
TONELERO	S 21
RIACHUELO	S 22

Builders	Laid down	Launched	Commissioned
Vickers, Barrow	3 Nov 1970	5 Oct 1971	18 June 1973
Vickers, Barrow	18 Nov 1971	22 Nov 1972	? 1977
Vickers, Barrow	26 May 1973	6 Sep 1975	Early 1977

Displacement, tons: 1 610 standard;
2 030 surfaced; 2 410 dived
Length, feet (metres): 295·5 *(90·1)* oa
Beam, feet (metres): 26·5 *(8·1)*
Draught, feet (metres): 18·0 *(5·5)*
Tubes: 8—21 in *(533 mm)* (6 bow and 2 stern)
Main machinery: 2 Admiralty Standard Range 1 16-cyl diesels;
3 680 bhp; 2 electric motors; 6 000 shp; 2 shafts; electric
drive
Speed, knots: 12 surfaced, 17 dived
Complement: 70 (6 officers and 64 men)

In 1969 it was announced that two submarines of the British
"Oberon" class were ordered from Vickers, Barrow. The third
boat was ordered in 1972. Completion of *Tonelero* has been
much delayed by a serious fire on board. She spent a period in
Chatham Dockyard, having been towed from Barrow, return-
ing in January 1976. Completion unlikely before early 1977.
Whilst in Chatham the centre 60 ft was replaced. Diesels by
Vickers Shipbuilding Group. Electric Motors by AEI-English
Electric. Sonar, modern navigational aids and provision for
modern fire control system developed by Vickers.

HUMAITA

1973, Vickers

2 Ex-US GUPPY III TYPE

Name	No.	Builder	Laid down	Launched	Commissioned
AMAZONAS (ex-USS *Greenfish* SS 351)	S 16	Electric Boat Co	29 June 1944	21 Dec 1945	7 June 1946
GOIAZ (ex-USS *Trumpetfish* SS 425)	S 15	Cramp SB Co	23 Aug 1943	13 May 1945	29 Jan 1946

Displacement, tons: 1 975 standard; 2 450 dived
Length, (metres): 326·5 *(99·4)*
Beam, feet (metres): 27 *(8·2)*
Draught, feet (metres): 17 *(5·2)*
Torpedo tubes: 10—21 in; 6 bow 4 stern
Main machinery: 4 diesels; 6 400 hp; 2 electric motors;
5 400 hp; 2 shafts
Speed, knots: 20 surfaced; 15 dived
Complement: 85

Converted in 1960-62. *Goiaz* transferred by sale 15 Oct 1973
and *Amazonas* by sale 19 Dec 1973.

Sonar: BQR-2 array, BQG-4 (PUFFS) fire control sonar (fins on
casing).

AMAZONAS

1969, USN

5 Ex-US GUPPY II TYPE

Name	No.	Builders	Laid down	Launched	Commissioned
GUANABARA (ex-USS *Dogfish* SS 350)	S 10	Electric Boat Co	22 June 1944	27 Oct 1945	29 Apr 1946
RIO GRANDE DO SUL (ex-USS *Grampus* SS 523)	S 11	Boston Navy Yard	8 Feb 1944	15 Dec 1944	26 Oct 1946
BAHIA (ex-USS *Sea Leopard* SS 483)	S 12	Portsmouth Navy Yard	7 Nov 1944	2 Mar 1945	11 June 1945
RIO DE JANEIRO (ex-Guanabara, ex-USS *Odax* SS 484)	S 13	Portsmouth Navy Yard	4 Dec 1944	10 Apr 1945	11 July 1945
CEARÁ (ex-USS *Amberjack* SS 522)	S 14	Boston Navy Yard	8 Feb 1944	15 Dec 1944	4 Mar 1946

Displacement, tons: 1 870 standard; 2 420 dived
Length, feet (metres): 307·5 *(93·8)* oa
Beam, feet (metres): 27·2 *(8·3)*
Draught, feet (metres): 18 *(5·5)*
Torpedoe tubes: 10—21 in (6 bow, 4 stern)
Main machinery: 3 diesels, 4 800 shp; 2 motors; 5 400 shp;
2 shafts
Speed, knots: 18 surfaced; 15 dived
Range, miles: 12 000 at 10 knots (surfaced)
Complement: 82

Modernised under Guppy II programme 1948-50 except *Rio de
Janeiro* which was first modernised to Guppy I standards and
later to Guppy II. Transferred 13 May 1972 *(Rio Grande do Sul)*,
8 July 1972 *(Rio de Janeiro)*, 28 July 1972 *(Guanabara)*, 27 Mar
1973 *(Bahia)*, 17 Oct 1973 *(Ceara)*. All by sale.

RIO GRANDE DO SUL

1972, Brazilian Navy

AMPHIBIOUS FORCES

1 Ex-US TANK LANDING SHIP

Name	No.	Builders	Commissioned
GARCIA D'AVILA	G 28	—	17 Apr 1945
(ex-USS *Outagamie County* LST 1073)			

Displacement, tons: 1 653 standard; 2 366 beaching; 4 080 full load
Dimensions, feet (metres): 328 oa × 50 × 14 *(100 × 15·3 × 3·4)*
Guns: 8—40 mm (2 twin, 4 single)
Main engines: GM diesels; 2 shafts; 1 700 bhp = 11·6 knots
Complement: 119
Troops: 147

Of LST 511-1152 Series. Transferred on loan to Brazil by USN 21 May 1971, purchased 1 Dec 1973.

GARCIA D'AVILA   *1973, Brazilian Navy*

1 Ex-US TANK LANDING SHIP

Name	No.	Builders	Commissioned
DUQUE DE CAXAIS	G 26	Avondale, New Orleans	8 Nov 1957
(ex-USS *Grant County* LST 1174)			

Displacement, tons: 3 828 light; 7 804 full load
Dimensions, feet (metres): 445 oa × 62 × 16·9 *(135·7 × 18·9 × 5·2)*
Guns: 2—3 in 50 cal (twins)
Main engines: Diesels; 13 700 shp; 2 shafts; CP propellers = 17·2 knots
Complement: 175 (11 officers, 164 men)
Troops: App. 575

"De Soto County" Class. Launched 12 Oct 1956 and transferred 15 Jan 1973. On lease.

28 LCV (P)

Built in Japan 1959-60.

7 EDVP

Fitted with Saab-Skania Diesels of 153 hp. 37 ft long and with glass-fibre hulls. Built in Brazil in 1971-73. Can carry 36 men or equivalent amount of equipment.

4 LCU TYPE

CAMBORIÁ   GUARAPARI   TIMBAN   TRAMANDAI

Built in Rio de Janeiro 1974-75.

9 LCM (6)

Also reported but not confirmed.

PATROL FORCES

10 "IMPERIAL MARINHEIRO" CLASS

Name	No.	Builders	Commissioned
IMPERIAL MARINHEIRO	V 15	Netherlands	1954
IGUATEMI	V 16	Netherlands	1954
IPIRANGA	V 17	Netherlands	1954
FORTE DE COIMBRA	V 18	Netherlands	1954
CABACLA	V 19	Netherlands	1954
ANGOSTURA	V 20	Netherlands	1955
BAIANA	V 21	Netherlands	1955
MEARIM	V 22	Netherlands	1955
PURUS	V 23	Netherlands	1955
SOLIMOES	V 24	Netherlands	1955

Displacement, tons: 911 standard
Dimensions, feet (metres): 184 × 30·5 × 11·7 *(55·7 × 9·6 × 4·6)*
Guns: 1—3 in 50 cal; 4—20 mm
Main engines: 2 Sulzer diesels; 2 160 bhp = 16 knots
Oil fuel, tons: 135
Complement: 60

SOLIMOES   *1972, Brazilian Navy*

Actually fleet tugs. Equipped for fire fighting. *Imperial Marinheiro* employed as submarine support ship.

2 "PEDRO TEIXEIRA" CLASS (RIVER PATROL SHIPS)

Name	No.	Builders	Commissioned
PEDRO TEIXEIRA	P 20	Arsenal de Marinha, Rio de Janeiro	17 Dec 1973
RAPOSO TAVARES	P 21	Arsenal de Marinha, Rio de Janeiro	17 Dec 1973

Displacement, tons: 700 standard
Dimensions, feet (metres): 203·4 × 30·7 × 6·3 *(62 × 9·4 ×1·7)*
Guns: 1—40 mm; 2—81 mm mortars 6—·50 cal MG
Main engines: 4 diesels; 2 shafts = 16 knots

Helicopter platform and hangar fitted. Carry one LCVP. *Pedro Teixeira* launched 14 Oct 1970—*Raposo Tavares* 11 June 1972.

PEDRO TEIXEIRA   *1975, Brazilian Navy*

1 THORNYCROFT TYPE (RIVER MONITOR)

Name	No.	Builders	Commissioned
PARNAIBA	U 17 (ex-P 2)	Arsenal de Marinha, Rio de Janeiro	Nov 1937

Displacement, tons: 620 standard; 720 full load
Dimensions, feet (metres): 180·5 oa · 33·3 · 5·1 *(54·5 × 10·2 × 1·5)*
Guns: 1—3 in, 50 cal; 2—47 mm; 2—40 mm, 6—20 mm
Armour: 3 in side and partial deck protection
Main engines: 2 Thornycroft triple expansion; 2 shafts; 1 300 ihp = 12 knots
Boilers: 2 three drum type, working pressure 250 psi
Oil fuel, tons: 70
Range, miles: 1 350 at 10 knots
Complement: 90

Laid down on 11 June 1936. Launched on 2 Sep 1937. In Mato Grosso Flotilla. Rearmed with the above guns in 1960.

PARNAIBA

1971, Brazilian Navy

3 "RORAIMA" CLASS (RIVER PATROL SHIPS)

Name	No	Builders	Commissioned
RORAIMA	P 30	Maclaren, Niteroi	Mar 1974
RONDONIA	P 31	Maclaren, Niteroi	1974
AMAPA	P 32	Maclaren, Niteroi	1975

Displacement, tons: 340 standard; 365 full load
Dimensions, feet (metres): 147·6 · 27·7 · 4·2 *(45 · 8·5 · 1·4)*
Guns: 1—40 mm; 2—81 mm mortars; 6—·50 cal MGs
Main engines: Diesels; 2 shafts 14·5 knots

Rondonia launched 10 Jan 1973, *Amapa* 9 Mar 1973.

LIGHT FORCES

6 "PIRATINI" CLASS (LARGE PATROL CRAFT)

Name	No.	Builders	Commissioned
PIRATINI (ex-PGM 109)	P 10	Arsenal de Marinha, Rio de Janeiro	Nov 1970
PIRAJA (ex-PGM 110)	P 11	Arsenal de Marinha, Rio de Janeiro	Mar 1971
PAMPEIRO (ex-PGM 118)	P 12	Arsenal de Marinha, Rio de Janeiro	May 1971
PARATI (ex-PGM 119)	P 13	Arsenal de Marinha, Rio de Janeiro	July 1971
PENEDO (ex-PGM 120)	P 14	Arsenal de Marinha, Rio de Janeiro	Sept 1971
POTI (ex-PGM 121)	P 15	Arsenal de Marinha, Rio de Janeiro	Oct 1971

Displacement, tons: 105 standard
Dimensions, feet (metres): 95 · 19 · 6·5 *(30·5 · 6·1 · 1·9)*
Guns: 3—·50 cal MG; 1—81 mm mortar
Main engines: 4 diesels; 1 100 bhp 17 knots
Range, miles: 1 700 at 12 knots
Complement: 15 officers and men

Built under offshore agreement with the USA.

POTI

1972, Brazilian Navy

6 "ANCHOVA" CLASS (RIVER PATROL CRAFT)

Name	No.	Builders	Commissioned
ANCHOVA	R 54	Brazil	1965
ARENQUE	R 55	Brazil	1965
ATUM	R 56	Brazil	1966
ACARA	R 57	Brazil	1966
AGULHA	R 58	Brazil	1967
ARUANA	R 59	Brazil	1967

Displacement, tons: 11
Dimensions, feet (metres): 42·6 · 12·5 · 3·9 *(13 · 3·8 · 1·2)*
Main engines: 2 Diesels; 280 hp 25 knots
Range, miles: 400 at 20 knots
Complement: 3 plus 12 passengers

4 RIVER PATROL CRAFT

Built in 1968. Of about 30 tons and 45 feet *(13·7 metres)* in length. Capable of 17 knots and with a range of 1 400 miles at 10 knots. Operate on the Upper Amazon.

MINE WARFARE FORCES

6 "ARATU" CLASS (MINESWEEPERS—COASTAL)

Name	No.	Builders	Commissioned
ARATU	M 15	Abeking and Rasmussen	5 May 1971
ANHATOMIRIM	M 16	Abeking and Rasmussen	30 Nov 1971
ATALAIA	M 17	Abeking and Rasmussen	13 Dec 1972
ARACATUBA	M 18	Abeking and Rasmussen	13 Dec 1972
ABROLHOS	M 19	Abeking and Rasmussen	16 Apr 1975
ALBARDÃO	M 20	Abeking and Rasmussen	21 July 1975

Displacement, tons: 230 standard; 280 full load
Dimensions, feet (metres): 154·9 · 23·6 · 6·9 *(47·2 · 7·2 · 2·1)*
Gun: 1—40 mm
Main engines: 4 Maybach diesels; 2 shafts; 4 500 bhp 24 knots
Range, miles: 710 at 20 knots
Complement: 39

Wooden hulled. First four ordered in April 1969 and another pair in Nov 1973. Same design as W. German "Schutze" class.

ABROLHOS

8/1975, Stefan Terzibaschitsch

SURVEY SHIPS

ALVARO ALBERTO

Dimensions, feet (metres): 196·8 × 3·7 × 14·1 *(60 × 12 × 4·3)*
Complement: 26 plus 17 scientists

A new oceanographic research ship ordered in 1973.

1 Ex-US "CONRAD" CLASS

Name	No.	Builders	Commissioned
ALMIRANTE CAMARA	H 41	Marietta Co, Point Pleasant	8 Feb 1965
(ex-USNS *Sands* T-AGOR 6)		West Va.	

Displacement, tons: 1 200 standard; 1 380 full load
Dimensions, feet (metres): 208·9 oa × 37·4 × 15·3 *(63·7 × 11·4 × 4·7)*
Main engines: Diesel electric; Caterpillar Tractor Co diesels; 10 000 bhp; 1 shaft = 13·5 knots
Range, miles: 12 000 at 12 knots
Complement: 26 (+15 scientists)

Built specifically for oceanographic research. Equipped for gravimetric, magnetic and geological research. Has bow thruster, 10 ton crane and 620 hp gas turbine for providing "quiet power". Transferred 1 July 1974.

ALMIRANTE CÀMARA   *USN*

2 "SIRIUS" CLASS

Name	No.	Builders	Commissioned
CANOPUS	H 22	Ishikawajima Co Ltd, Tokyo	15 Mar 1958
SIRIUS	H 21	Ishikawajima Co Ltd, Tokyo	1 Jan 1958

Displacement, tons: 1 463 standard; 1 800 full load
Dimensions, feet (metres): 255·7 oa × 39·3 × 12·2 *(78 × 12 × 3·7)*
Guns: 1—3 in; 4—20 mm MG
Main engines: 2 Sulzer diesels; 2 shafts; 2 700 bhp = 15·75 knots
Range, miles: 12 000 at cruising speed of 11 knots
Complement: 116

Laid down 1955-56. Helicopter platform aft. Special surveying apparatus, echo sounders, Raydist equipment, sounding machines installed, and helicopter, landing craft (LCVP), jeep, and survey launches carried. All living and working spaces are air-conditioned. Controllable pitch propellers.

SIRIUS   *1970, Brazilian Navy*

3 "ARGUS" CLASS

Name	No.	Builders	Commissioned
ARGUS	H 31	Arsenal da Marinha, Rio de Janeiro	29 Jan 1959
ORION	H 32	Arsenal da Marinha, Rio de Janeiro	11 June 1959
TAURUS	H 33	Arsenal da Marinha, Rio de Janeiro	23 Apr 1959

Displacement, tons: 250 standard; 343 full load
Dimensions, feet (metres): 147·7 oa × 20 × 6·6 *(45 × 6·1 × 2)*
Guns: 2—20 mm
Main engines: 2 diesels coupled to two shafts; 1 200 bhp = 15 knots
Oil fuel, tons: 35
Range, miles: 1 200 at 15 knots
Complement: 42

All laid down in 1955 and launched Dec 1957—Feb 1958.

TAURUS   *1972, Brazilian Navy*

Name	No.	Builders	Launched
ALMIRANTE SALDANHA	U 10 (ex-NE I)	Vickers Armstrong Ltd	19 Dec 1933

Displacement, tons: 3 325 standard; 3 825 full load
Dimensions, feet (metres): 307·2 oa × 52 × 18·2 *(93·7 × 15·9 × 5·6)*
Main engines: Diesel; 1 400 bhp = 11 knots
Range, miles: 12 000 at 10 knots
Complement: 218

Former training ship with a total sail area of 25 990 sq ft and armed with four 4 -inch guns, one 3-inch AA gun and four 3-pounders. Cost £314 500. Instructional minelaying gear was included in equipment. The single 21-inch torpedo tube was removed. Re-classified as an Oceanographic Ship (NOc) Aug 1959, and completely remodelled by 1964. A photograph as sailing ship appears in the 1952-53 to 1959-60 editions.

ALMIRANTE SALDANHA   *1972, Brazilian Navy*

1 LIGHTHOUSE TENDER

Name	No.	Builders	Commissioned
GRAÇA ARANHA	H 34	Elbin, Niteroi	Dec 1974

Displacement, tons: 1 250
Dimensions, feet (metres): 247·6 × 42·6 × 12·1 *(75·5 × 13 × 3·7)*
Aircraft: 1 Helicopter
Main engines: 1 Diesel; 2 000 hp; 1 shaft = 14 knots
Complement: 95

Laid down in 1971 and launched 23 May 1974. Fitted with collapsible helo-hangar.

2 "JAVARI" CLASS (BUOY TENDERS)

JAVARI (ex-USS *Cardinal*) M 11
JURUA (ex-USS *Jackdaw*) M 13

Displacement, tons: 270 standard; 350 full load
Dimensions, feet (metres): 136 × 24·5 × 8 *(41·5 × 7·5 × 2·5)*
Guns: 4—20 mm in two twin mountings
A/S weapons: 2 DCT
Main engines: 2 GM diesels; 2 shafts; 1 000 bhp = 15 knots
Oil fuel, tons: 16
Range, miles: 2 300 at 8·5 knots
Complement: 50

Of wooden construction, launched in 1942-43. Originally known in USA as Auxiliary Motor minesweepers (AMS). *Javari* was transferred to Brazil by USA at Charleston Naval Shipyard on 15 Aug 1960. *Juruá* was transferred in Jan 1963 and will probably be disposed of in 1976.

SURVEY LAUNCHES

CAMOCIM H 16
CARAVELAS H 17
ITACURUSSA H 15

NOGUEIRA DA GAMA (ex*Jaceguai*) H 14
PARAIBANO H 11
RIO BRANCO H 12

Displacement, tons: 32 standard; 50 full load
Dimensions, feet (metres): 52·5 × 15·1 × 4·3 *(16 × 4·6 × 1·3)*
Main engines: 1 diesel; 165 bhp = 11 knots
Range, miles: 600 at 11 knots
Complement: 11

First four launched 1968—last pair in 1972.

PARAIBANO   1974, Brazilian Navy

CASTELHANOS H 24
FAROLEIRO AREAS H 27
FAROLEIRO NASCIMENTO H 30

FAROLEIRO SANTANA H 28
MESTRE JOÀO DOS SANTOS H 13

Buoy Tenders. Taken over 1973.

CASTELHANOS   1974, Brazilian Navy

SUBMARINE RESCUE SHIP

Name	No.	Builders	Launched
GASTÀO MOUTINHO (ex-USS *Skylark* ASR 20)	K 10	Charleston SB & DD Co.	19 Mar 1946

Displacement, tons: 1 235 standard; 1 740 full load
Dimensions, feet (metres): 205 oa × 38·5 × 15·3 *(62·5 × 11·7 × 4·7)*
Main engines: Diesel electric; 1 shaft; 3 000 bhp = 14 knots
Complement: 85

Converted to present form in 1947. Fitted with special pumps, compressors and submarine rescue chamber. Fitted for oxy-helium diving. Transferred 30 June 1973.

GASTÀO MOUTINHO   1975, Brazilian Navy

REPAIR SHIP

Name	No.	Builders	Commissioned
BELMONTE (ex-USS *Helios* ARB 12, ex-LST 1127)	G 24	Maryland DD Co, Baltimore	26 Feb 1945

Displacement, tons: 1 625 light; 2 030 standard; 4 100 full load
Dimensions, feet (metres): 328 oa × 50 × 11 *(98·4 × 15·3 × 3·4)*
Guns: 8—40 mm
Main engines: GM diesels; 2 shafts; 1 800 bhp = 11·6 knots
Oil fuel, tons: 1 000
Range, miles: 6 000 at 9 knots

Former United States battle damage repair ship (ex LST). Laid down on 23 Nov 1944. Launched on 14 Feb 1945. Loaned to Brazil by USA in Jan 1962 under MAP.

TANKERS

Name	No.	Builders	Commissioned
MARAJO	G 27	Ishikawajima do Brasil-Estaleisos SA	22 Oct 1968

Measurements, tons: 10 500 deadweight
Dimensions, feet (metres): 440·7 × 63·3 × 24 *(134·4 × 19·3 × 7·3)*
Main engines: Diesel; one shaft = 13·6 knots
Capacity, (cu metres): 14 200
Range, miles: 9 200 at 13 knots
Complement: 80

Laid down on 13 Dec 1966 and launched on 31 Jan 1968.

MARAJO   *1972, Brazilian Navy*

Name	No.	Builders	Launched
POTENGI	G 17	Papendrecht, Netherlands	16 Mar 1938

Displacement, tons: 600
Dimensions, feet (metres): 178·8 oa × 24·5 × 6 *(54·5 × 7·5 × 1·8)*
Main engines: Diesels; 2 shafts ; 550 bhp = 10 knots
Oil fuel, tons: 450
Complement: 19

Employed in the Mato Grosso Flotilla on river service.

MARTINS DE OLIVEIRA (Ex-*Gastao Moutinho*) R 11

Displacement, tons: 588
Dimensions, feet (metres): 162 × 23·1 × 7·9 *(49·4 × 7 × 2·4)*
Speed, knots: 10·3

Taken over 1973.

TRANSPORTS

4 "PEREIRA" CLASS

Name	No.	Builders	Commissioned
ARY PARREIRAS	G 21	Ishikawajima Co Ltd, Tokyo	29 Dec 1956
BARROSO PEREIRA	G 16	Ishikawajima Co Ltd, Tokyo	1 Dec 1954
CUSTÓDIO DE MELLO	U 26	Ishikawajima Co Ltd, Tokyo	30 Dec 1954
SOARES DUTRA	G 22	Ishikawajima Co Ltd, Tokyo	23 Mar 1957

Displacement, tons: 4 800 standard; 7 300 full load
Measurement, tons: 4 200 deadweight; 4 879 gross (Panama)
Dimensions, feet (metres): 362 pp; 391·8 oa × 52·5 × 20·5 *(110·4; 119·5 × 16 × 6·3)*
Guns: 4—3 in (U 26); 2—3 in (others); 2/4—20 mm
Main engines: Ishikawajima double reduction geared turbines; 2 shafts; 4 800 shp = 17·67 knots (sea speed 15 knots)
Boilers: 2 Ishikawajima two drum water tube type, oil fuel
Complement: 127 (Troop capacity 497)

Transports and cargo vessels. Helicopter landing platform aft. Troop carrying capacity for 497, with commensurate medical, hospital and dental facilities. Working and living quarters are mechanically ventilated with partial air conditioning. Refrigerated cargo space 15 500 cubic feet. Can carry 4 000 tons of cargo. *Custódio de Mello* has been classified as a training ship since July 1961.

CUSTODIO DE MELLO   *5/1975, C and S. Taylor*

6 "RIO DOCE" CLASS (RIVER TRANSPORTS)

Name	No.	Builders	Commissioned
RIO DOCE	U 20	Netherlands	1954
RIO DAS CONTAS	U 21	Netherlands	1954
RIO FORMOSO	U 22	Netherlands	1954
RIO REAL	U 23	Netherlands	1955
RIO TURVO	U 24	Netherlands	1955
RIO VERDE	U 25	Netherlands	1955

Of 150 tons and 14 knots. Can carry 600 passengers. *Rio Doce* in collision in Rio Bay 13 Jan 1976.

4 NEW CONSTRUCTION (RIVER TRANSPORTS)

RIO PARDO U 40   **RIO NEGRO** U 41   **RIO CHUI** U 42   **RIO OIAPOQUE** U 43

Of 150 tons with 2 diesels = 14 knots. Capable of carrying 600 passengers. Completed by Inconav de Niteroi 1975-76.

PARAGUASSU (ex-*Guarapunava*) G 15 (RIVER TRANSPORT)

Of 285 tons. Acquired in 1971. Capable of 12 knots, with a range of 2 500 miles at 10 knots. Command ship of the Mato Grosso flotilla.

FLOATING DOCKS

3 FLOATING DOCKS

CIDADE DE NATAL (ex-AFDL 39)

Displacement, tons: 7 600
Length, feet (metres): 390·3 *(119)*
Beam, feet (metres): 86·9 *(26·5)*
Capacity, tons: 2 800

Concrete floating dock loaned to Brazil by USN, 10 Nov 1966.

ALMIRANTE JERONIMO GONÇALVES (ex-*Goiaz* AFDL 4) G 26

Displacement, tons: 3 000
Length, feet (metres): 200 *(61)*
Beam, feet (metres): 44 *(13·4)*
Capacity, tons: 1 000

Steel floating dock sold to Brazil by USN, 10 Nov 1966.

AFONSO PENA (ex-*Ceara*, ex-ARD 14) G 25

Displacement, tons: 5 200
Dimensions, feet (metres): 402·0 × 81·0 *(122·6 × 24·7)*

Transferred from the US Navy to the Brazilian Navy in 1963.

TUGS

3 Ex-US ATA TYPE

TRIDENTE (ex-ATA 235) R 22   **TRITÃO** (ex-ATA 234) R 21   **TRIUNFO** (ex-ATA 236 R 23

Displacement, tons: 534 standard; 835 full load
Dimensions, feet (metres): 143 oa × 33 × 13·2 *(43·6 × 10 × 4)*
Guns: 2—20 mm
Main engines: GM diesel-electric; 1 500 hp = 13 knots

All built by Gulfport Boiler & Welding Works, Inc, Port Arthur, Texas, and launched in 1944. Sold to Brazil 1947.

ISLAS DE NORONHA

Of 200 tons. Built 1972.

2 COASTAL TUGS

DNOG   LAHMEYER

Of 100 tons and 105 ft long, built in Brazil in 1972. Based at Aratu.

MISCELLANEOUS

(A number of ships previously included are, presumably merchant ships and have, therefore been deleted)

BAURU (ex-USS *McAnn* DE 179) U 28

An ex-US "Bostwick" class DE, last of eight transferred in 1944. Of 1 900 tons full load used as support vessel in Guanabara Bay.

BRUNEI

(Askar Melayu Diraja Brunei (Royal Brunei Malay Regiment) Flotilla)

Commanding Officer:
Commander David Wright RN

Personnel

(a) 1976: 240 (17 officers and 223 ratings)
(b) Voluntary

Base

Muara

Prefix to Ships' Names

KDB (Kapal Di-Raja Brunei)

Mercantile Marine

Lloyd's Register of Shipping:
1 vessel of 283 tons gross

LIGHT FORCES

1 "PALAHWAN" CLASS (FAST ATTACK CRAFT—MISSILE)

Name	No.	Builders	Commissioned
PALAHWAN	P 01	Vosper (UK)	19 Oct 1967

Displacement, tons: 95 standard; 114 full load
Dimensions, feet (metres): 99·0 oa × 25·2 × 7·0 *(30·3 × 7·3 × 2·2)*
Missiles: 8—SS 12 on 2 launchers
Guns: 1—40 mm; 1—20 mm Hispano Suiza
Main engines: 3 Bristol Siddeley Proteus gas turbines; 3 shafts; 12 750 bhp = 57 knots;
2 diesels for cruising and manoeuvring
Range, miles: 450 at full speed; 2 300 at 10 knots
Complement: 20

Ordered from Vosper Ltd, Portsmouth, England, on 10 Dec 1965. Launched on 5 Dec 1966. Constructed of resin bonded timber with aluminium alloy superstructure. Missile launchers fitted in May 1972.

PALAHWAN

1974, Royal Brunei Malay Regiment

3 "PERWIRA" CLASS (COASTAL PATROL CRAFT)

Name	No.	Builders	Commissioned
PERWIRA	P 14	Vosper Thornycroft (Singapore)	9 Sept 1974
PEMBURU	P 15	Vosper Thornycroft (Singapore)	April 1975
PENYARANG	P 16	Vosper Thornycroft (Singapore)	April 1975

Displacement, tons: 30
Dimensions, feet (metres): 71 × 20 × 5 *(21·7 × 6·1 × 1·2)*
Guns: 2—20 mm Hispano Suiza; 2—7·62 MG
Main engines: 2 MTU Diesels; 2 250 bhp
Speed, Knots: 32
Range, miles: 600 at 22 knots; 1 000 miles cruising
Complement: 12

Perwira launched 9 May 1974. Other two ordered June 1974. Of all wooden construction on laminated frames.

PERWIRA

1974, Royal Brunei Malay Regiment

3 "RAJA ISTERI" CLASS (COASTAL PATROL CRAFT)

Name	No.	Builders	Commissioned
MASNA	P 11	Vosper Thornycroft (Singapore)	1972
NORAIN	P 13	Vosper Thornycroft (Singapore)	Aug 1972
SALEHA	P 12	Vosper Thornycroft (Singapore)	1972

Displacement, tons: 25
Dimensions, feet (metres): 62·0 × 16·0 × 4·5 *(18·9 × 4·8 × 1·4)*
Guns: 2—20 mm Hispano-Suiza; 2 MG
Main engines: 2 GM diesels; 1 250 bhp = 26 knots
Range, miles: 600 at 23 knots
Complement: 8

Fitted with Decca 202 radar. Named after Brunei princesses.

NORAIN

1974, Royal Brunei Malay Regiment

3 PATROL CRAFT (RIVERINE)

Name	No.	Conversion
BENDAHARA	P 21	1974
KEMAINDERA	P 23	1975
MAHARAJALELA	P 22	1975

Displacement, tons: 10
Dimensions, feet (metres): 47·0 × 12·0 × 3·0 *(14·3 × 3·6 × 0·9)*
Guns: 2 twin MG 42, 7·62 cal
Main engines: 2 GM diesels; 334 bhp = 20 knots
Range, miles: 200
Complement: 6

Fitted with Decca 202 radar.

Conversion: *Kemaindera* was converted in July 1974 for riverine duties. Other pair were similarly converted during 1975.

BENDAHARA

1975, Royal Brunei Malay Regiment

AMPHIBIOUS FORCES

1 + 1 "CHEVERTON LOADMASTER"

Of 60 ft and 45 tons. Speed 10 knots. 2 MG. First delivered late 1975, second projected 1976.

24 FAST ASSAULT BOATS

Rigid Raider type with 1 MG.

BULGARIA

Headquarters Appointment

Commander-in-Chief, Navy:
Vice-Admiral VG Yanakiev

Diplomatic Representation

Naval, Military and Air Attaché in London:
Lt. Colonel Dimitar Toskov

Personnel

(a) 1976: 10 000 officers and ratings
(b) 3 years national service (6 000)

Bases

Varna, Burgas, Sozopol

Naval Aviation

6 Mi4 (Hound) Helicopters

Mercantile Marine

Lloyd's Register of Shipping:
179 vessels of 937 458 tons gross

Strength of the Fleet

No building programme available

Type	Active
Frigates	2
Corvettes	2
Patrol Submarines	4
Fast Attack Craft (Missile)	2
Fast Attack Craft (Patrol)	6
Fast Attack Craft (Torpedo)	12
Minesweepers (Ocean)	2
Minesweepers (Coastal)	4
Minesweepers (Inshore)	2
Minesweeping Boats	24
Landing Craft	20
Auxiliaries	several

FRIGATES

2 Ex-SOVIET "RIGA" CLASS

DRUZKI 31   **SMELI** 32

Displacement, tons: 1 200 standard; 1 600 full load
Length, feet (metres): 298·8 *(91·0)*
Beam, feet (metres): 33·7 *(10·2)*
Draught, feet (metres): 11·0 *(3·4)*
Guns: 3—3·9 in *(100 mm)*; 4—37 mm
A/S Weapons: 2 16 barrelled MBU 2 500, 4 DCT
Tubes: 3—21 in *(533 mm)*
Main engines: Geared turbines; 2 shafts; 25 000 shp
Speed, knots: 28
Range, miles: 2 500 at 15 knots
Complement: 150

Transferred from USSR in 1957-8.

Radar: Search; Slim Net. Navigation; Neptune.
IFF; Highpole A. Fire Control; Wasphead/Sunvisor A.

"RIGA" Class

SUBMARINES (PATROL)

2 Ex-SOVIET "ROMEO" CLASS

Displacement, tons: 1 000 surfaced; 1 600 dived
Length, feet (metres): 249·3 *(76)*
Beam, feet (metres): 24 *(7·3)*
Draught, feet (metres): 14·5 *(4·4)*
Torpedo tubes: 6—21 in *(533 mm)* (bow)
Main machinery: 2 Diesels; 4 000 hp; 2 main motors; 4 000 hp;
2 shafts
Speed, knots: 17 surfaced, 14 dived
Complement: 65

Transferred in 1972-73.

Radar. Snoop Plate.

"ROMEO" Class   *1974*

2 Ex-SOVIET "WHISKY" CLASS

POBEDA   **SLAVA**

Displacement, tons: 1 030 surfaced; 1 350 dived
Length, feet (metres): 249·3 *(76)*
Beam, feet (metres): 22 *(6·7)*
Draught, feet (metres): 15 *(4·6)*
Torpedo tubes: 6—21 in *(533 mm)*, (4 bow, 2 stern)
Main machinery: 2 Diesels 4 000 hp; 2 Main Motors 2 500 hp;
2 shafts
Speed knots: 17 surfaced; 15 dived
Range, miles: 13 000 at 8 knots (surface)
Complement: 60

Transferred from the USSR in 1958.

Radar: Snoop Plate.

"WHISKY" Class

CORVETTES

Note: Three "Poti" Class transferred by USSR in December 1975.

2 Ex-SOVIET "KRONSTADT" CLASS

"KRONSTADT" Class

33   34

Displacement, tons: 310 standard; 380 full load
Length, feet (metres): 170·6 (52·0)
Beam, feet (metres): 21·5 (6·6)
Draught, feet (metres): 9·0 (2·7)
Guns: 1—3·5 in (85 mm); 2—37 mm
A/S weapons: Depth charge throwers
Main engines: 3 Diesels; 3 shafts; 3 300 hp
Speed: 24 designed. Probably 18—20
Oil fuel, tons: 20
Range, miles: 1 500 at 12 knots
Complement: 65

Transferred from USSR in 1957.

Radar: Pot Drum.

6 Ex-SOVIET "SO I" CLASS

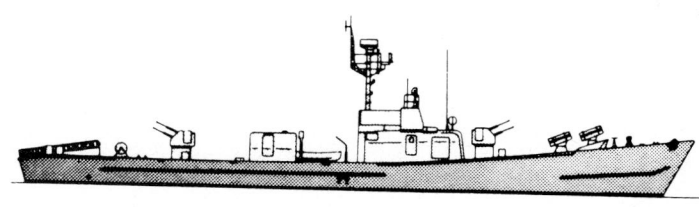

"SO 1" Class

41 to 46

Displacement, tons: 215 light; 250 full load
Length, feet (metres): 138·6 (42·3)
Beam, feet (metres): 20 (6·1)
Draught, feet (metres): 9·2 (2·8)
Guns: 4—25 mm (2 twin)
A/S weapons: 4 five-barrelled MBU 1800 launchers; DCs
Main engines: 3 diesels; 6 000 bhp = 26 knots
Range, miles: 1 100 at 13 knots
Complement: 30

Steel hulled vessels transferred from USSR in 1963.

Radar: Pot Head.

LIGHT FORCES

3 Ex-SOVIET "OSA I" CLASS (FAST ATTACK CRAFT—MISSILE)

"OSA 1" Class

21   22   23

Displacement, tons: 165 standard; 200 full load
Dimensions, feet (metres): 128·7 × 25·1 × 5·9 (39·3 × 7·7 × 1·8)
Missile launchers: 4 in two pairs abreast for SSN-2 system
Guns: 4—30 mm (2 twin, 1 forward, 1 aft)
Main engines: 3 diesels; 13 000 bhp = 36 knots
Range, miles: 800 at 25 knots
Complement: 25

Reported to have been transferred from USSR in 1970-71.

Radar: Drum Tilt and Square Tie.

4 Ex-SOVIET "SHERSHEN" CLASS (FAST ATTACK CRAFT—TORPEDO)

"SHERSHEN" Class

27   +3

Displacement, tons: 150 standard; 160 full load
Dimensions, feet (metres): 115·5 × 23·1 × 5·0 (35·2 × 7·1 × 1·5)
Guns: 4—30 mm (2 twin)
Tubes: 4—21 in (single)
A/S armament: 12 DCs
Main engines: 3 diesels; 3 shafts; 13 000 bhp = 41 knots
Range, miles: 700 at 20 knots
Complement: 25

Transferred from USSR in 1970.

Radar: Pot Drum, Drum Tilt. IFF; High Pole A.

8 Ex-SOVIET "P 4" CLASS (FAST ATTACK CRAFT—TORPEDO)

"P 4" Class

Displacement, tons: 22 full load
Dimensions, feet (metres): 62·7 × 11·6 × 5·6 (19·1 × 3·5 × 1·7)
Guns: 2—15 mm
Torpedo tubes: 2—18 in
Main engines: 2 diesels; 2 shafts; 2 200 bhp = 50 knots
Complement: 12

Transferred from USSR in 1956.

MINE WARFARE FORCES

2 Ex-SOVIET "T 43" CLASS (MINESWEEPERS—OCEAN)

Displacement, tons: 500 standard; 610 full load
Dimensions, feet (metres): 190·2 × 28·2 × 6·9 *(58·0 × 8·6 × 2·1)*
Guns: 4—37 mm (twin); 2—25 mm (twin)
Main engines: 2 Diesels; 2 shafts; 2 000 hp = 17 knots
Range, miles: 1 600 at 10 knots
Complement: 40

Three were transferred from USSR in 1953—One scrapped for spares.

1 Ex-SOVIET "T 301" CLASS (MINESWEEPER—INSHORE)

Displacement, tons: 150 standard; 180 full load
Dimensions, feet (metres): 128 × 18 × 4·9 *(39 × 5·5 × 1·5)*
Guns: 2—37 mm; 2—MG
Main engines: 2 diesels; 2 shafts; 1 440 hp = 17 knots
Range, miles: 2 200 at 10 knots
Complement: 30

Four were transferred from USSR in 1955. Three recently deleted.

4 Ex-SOVIET "VANYA" CLASS (MINESWEEPERS—COASTAL)

36   37   38   39

Displacement, tons: 250 standard; 275 full load
Dimensions, feet (metres): 130·7 × 24 × 6·9 *(39·9 × 7·3 × 2·1)*
Guns—2—30 mm (twin)
Main engines: 2 Diesels; 2 200 bhp = 18 knots
Complement: 30

Transferred from USSR in 1971-72.

24 "PO 2" CLASS (MSB)

Built in Bulgaria—first units completed in 1957 and last in early 1960s.

AMPHIBIOUS FORCES

10 Ex-SOVIET "VYDRA" CLASS

Displacement, tons: 300 standard; 500 full load
Dimensions, feet (metres): 157·4 × 24·6 × 7·2 *(48 × 7·5 × 2·2)*
Main engines: 2 diesels; 2 shafts; 400 bhp = 10 knots

Transferred from USSR in 1970.

"VYDRA" Class   1971

8 MFP TYPE

Dimensions, feet (metres): 164·0 oa × 20·0 × 6·6 *(50 × 6·1 × 2·0)*
Guns: 1—37 mm or none

Built in Bulgaria in 1954. Based on a German Second World War MFP design.

AUXILIARIES

3 Coastal Tankers, 5 Tugs, 2 "Varna" class Survey Ships (built in Bulgaria in 1959), 2 Salvage Craft and up to another 12 auxiliaries have been reported.

BURMA

Headquarters Appointment

Vice-Chief of Staff, Defence Services (Navy):
   Commodore Thaung Tin

Diplomatic Representation

Naval, Military and Air Attaché in London:
   Lieutenant-Colonel Soe Myint

Naval, Military and Air Attaché in Washington:
   Colonel Tin Htut

Strength of the Fleet

Type	Active	Building
Frigates	2	—
Corvettes	4	—
River Patrol Craft	35	—
Gunboats	37	—
Survey Vessels	2	—
Auxiliaries	11	—

Personnel

(a) 1976: 6 200 including 800 marines
(b) 2 years national service

Mercantile Marine

Lloyd's Register of Shipping:
   39 vessels of 54 548 tons gross

DELETIONS

Light Forces

1975   T201-205—Saunders-Roe convertibles

FRIGATES

1 Ex-BRITISH "RIVER" CLASS

Name	No.	Builders	Laid down	Launched	Commissioned
MAYU (ex-HMS *Fal*)	—	Smiths Dock Co Ltd, South Bank-on-Tees, Middlesborough, England	20 May 1942	9 Nov 1942	2 July 1943

Displacement, tons: 1 460 standard; 2 170 full load
Length, feet (metres): 283 *(86·3)* pp; 301·3 *(91·8)* oa
Beam, feet (metres): 36·7 *(11·3)*
Draught, feet (metres): 12 *(3·7)*
Guns: 1—4 in *(102 mm)*; 4—40 mm
Main engines: Triple expansion 5 500 ihp; 2 shafts
Boilers: 2—three drum type
Speed, knots: 19
Oil fuel, tons: 440
Range, miles: 4 200 at 12 knots
Complement: 140

"River" class frigate. Acquired from Great Britain and renamed in March 1948.

Radar: British Type 974.

MAYU

Burmese Navy

1 Ex-BRITISH "ALGERINE" CLASS

Name	No.	Builders	Laid down	Launched	Commissioned
YAN MYO AUNG (ex-HMS *Mariner*, ex-*Kincardine*)	—	Port Arthur Shipyards, Canada	26 Aug 1943	9 May 1944	23 May 1945

Displacement, tons: 1 040 standard; 1 335 full load
Length, feet (metres): 225 *(68·6)* pp; 235 *(71·6)* oa
Beam, feet (metres): 35·5 *(19·8)*
Draught, feet (metres): 11·5 *(3·5)*
Guns: 1—4 in *(102 mm)*; 4—40 mm
Main engines: Triple expansion; 2 000 ihp; 2 shafts
Boilers: 2 three-drum type
Speed, knots: 16·5
Range, miles: 4 000 at 12 knots
Complement: 140

Former ocean minesweeper in the British Navy, used as escort vessel. Handed over to Burma in London and renamed *Yan Myo Aung*, on 18 Apr 1958. Fitted for minelaying and can carry 16 mines, eight on each side.

Radar: Decca Type 202.

Sonar: British Type 144.

YAN MYO AUNG

1964, Burmese Navy

CORVETTES

1 Ex-US "PCE 827" CLASS

Name	No.	Builders	Commissioned
YAN TAING AUNG (ex-USS *Farmington* PCE 894)	PCE 41	Willamette Iron & Steel Co, Portland, Oregon	10 Aug 1943

Displacement, tons: 640 standard; 903 full load
Dimensions, feet (metres): 180 wl; 184 oa × 33 × 9·5 *(56 × 10·1 × 2·9)*
Guns: 1—3 in 50 cal dp; 2—40 mm (1 twin); 8—20 mm (4 twin)
A/S weapons: 1 hedgehog; 2 DCT; 2 DC racks
Main engines: GM diesels; 2 shafts; 1 800 bhp = 15 knots

Laid down on 7 Dec 1942, launched on 15 May 1943. Transferred on 18 June 1965.

1 Ex-US "ADMIRABLE" CLASS

Name	No.	Builders	Commissioned
YAN GYI AUNG (ex-USS *Craddock* MSF 356)	PCE 42	Willamette Iron & Steel Co, Portland, Oregon	1944

Displacement, tons: 650 standard; 945 full load
Dimensions, feet (metres): 180 wl; 184·5 oa × 33 × 9·8 *(56× 10·1 × 2·8)*
Guns: 1—3 in 50 cal single forward; 4—40 mm (2 twin); 4—20 mm (2 twin)
A/S weapons: 1 US Hedgehog; 2 DCT; 2 DC Racks
Main engines: Diesels; 2 shafts; 1 710 shp = 14·8 knots
Range, miles: 4 300 at 10 knots

Laid down on 10 Nov 1943 and launched on 22 July 1944. Transferred at San Diego on 31 Mar 1967.

2 "NAWARAT" CLASS

Name	No.	Builders	Commissioned
NAGAKYAY	—	Government Dockyard, Dawbon, Rangoon	3 Dec 1960
NAWARAT	—	Government Dockyard, Dawbon, Rangoon	26 Apr 1960

Displacement, tons: 400 standard; 450 full load
Dimensions, feet (metres): 163 × 26·8 × 5·8 *(49·7 × 8·2 × 1·8)*
Guns: 2—25 pdr QF; 2—40 mm
Main engines: 2 Paxman-Ricardo turbo-charged diesels; 2 shafts; 1 160 bhp = 12 knots
Complement: 43

NAGAKYAY

1962, Burmese Navy

LIGHT FORCES

10 BURMESE-BUILT RIVER PATROL CRAFT

Small craft, 50 feet long, built in Burma in 1951-52.

25 YUGOSLAV-BUILT RIVER PATROL CRAFT

Small craft, 52 feet long, acquired from Yugoslavia in 1965.

GUNBOATS

4 Ex-BRITISH LCG (M) TYPE

INDAW   **INLAY**   **INMA**   **INYA**

Displacement, tons: 381
Dimensions, feet (metres): 154 oa × 22·5 × 7·8 *(47·1 × 6·8 × 2·4)*
Guns: 2—25 pdr; 2—2 pdr
Main engines: Paxman Ricardo diesels; 2 shafts; 1 000 bhp = 13 knots
Complement: 39

Former British landing craft, gun (medium) LCG (M). Employed as gunboats.

Radar: British Type 974.

INMA   *Burmese Navy*

10 "Y 301" CLASS

Y 301   **Y 302**   **Y 303**   **Y 304**   **Y 305**   **Y 306**   **Y 307**   **Y 308**   **Y 309**   **Y 310**

Displacement, tons: 120
Dimensions, feet (metres): 100 pp; 104·8 oa × 24 × 3 *(32 × 7·3 × 0·9)*
Guns: 2—40 mm; 1—2 pdr
Main engines: 2 Mercedes-Benz (MTU) diesels; 2 shafts; 1 000 bhp = 13 knots
Complement: 29

All ten of these boats were completed in 1958 at the Uljanik Shipyard, Pula, Yugoslavia.

Y 310   *1964, Burmese Navy*

2 IMPROVED "Y 301" CLASS

Y 311   **Y 312**

Guns: 2—40 mm (single); 4—20 mm (single).

Dimensions approximately as "Y 301" Class (following). Built in Burma 1969.

8 GUNBOATS (Ex-TRANSPORTS)

SABAN   **SEINDA**   **SETYAHAT**   **SHWETHIDA**
SAGU   **SETKAYA**   **SHWEPAZUN**   **SINMIN**

Displacement, tons: 98
Dimensions, feet (metres): 94·5 × 22 × 4·5 *(28·8 × 6·7 × 1·4)*
Guns: 1—40 mm, 3—20 mm
Main engines: Crossley ERL—6 diesel; 160 bhp = 12 knots
Complement: 32

SHWEPAZUN   *1971, Burmese Navy*

6 Ex-US PGM TYPE

PGM 401   **PGM 402**   **PGM 403**   **PGM 404**   **PGM 405**   **PGM 406**

Displacement, tons: 100
Dimensions, feet (metres): 95 × 19 × 5 *(29 × 5·8 × 1·5)*
Guns: 2—40 mm (single); 2—0·5 Browning MG
Main engines: 4 GM diesels; 2 shafts; 1 000 bhp = 16 knots
Complement: 17

Built by the Marinette Marine Corporation, USA. Ex-US PGM 43-46, 51 and 52 respectively. Machinery comprises 2-stroke, 6-cylinder, tandem geared twin diesel propulsion unit—1 LH and 1 RH; 500 bhp per unit.

Radar: Raytheon 1 500 in PGM 405-6; EDO 320 in PGM 401-4.

PGM 401   *1962, Burmese Navy*

7 Ex-US CGC TYPE

MGB 101   **MGB 102**   **MGB 104**   **MGB 105**   **MGB 106**   **MGB 108**   **MGB 110**

Displacement, tons: 49 standard; 66 full load
Dimensions, feet (metres): 78 pp; 83 oa × 16 × 5·5 *(25·3 × 4·9 × 1·7)*
Guns: 1—40 mm; 1—20 mm
Main engines: 4 GM diesels; 2 shafts; 800 bhp = 11 knots
Complement: 16

Ex-USCG 83-ft type cutters with new hulls built in Burma. Completed in 1960. Three of this class are reported to have been sunk.

MGB 102   *1962, Burmese Navy*

SURVEY VESSELS

1 OCEAN SURVEY SHIP				1 COASTAL SURVEY SHIP			
Name	*No.*	*Builder*	*Commissioned*	*Name*	*No.*	*Builder*	*Commissioned*
THU TAY THI	—	Yugoslavia	1965	**YAY BO**	UBHL 807	Netherlands	1957

Displacement, tons: 1 059
Length, feet (metres): 204 oa *(62·2)*
Complement: 99

Displacement, tons: 108
Complement: 25

Fitted with helicopter platform. The Burmese Air Force operates Alouette III, Husky and Sioux helicopters.

SUPPORT SHIP

YAN LON AUNG

Light forces support ship of 520 tons, acquired from Japan in 1967.

TRANSPORTS

PYIDAWAYE

Measurement, tons: 2 217·31 gross
Dimensions, feet (metres): 270 × 47 × 15 *(82·3 × 14·3 × 4·6)*
Main engines: Fleming & Ferguson triple expansion 2 000 ihp
Boilers: 2 Scotch (return type)
Range, miles: 2 000
Complement: 88

Former passenger ship. In service since 1962.

PYIDAWAYE   *1964, Burmese Navy*

1 LCU TYPE

AIYAR LULIN (ex-USS LCU 1626) 603

Displacement, tons: 200 light; 342 full load
Dimensions, feet (metres): 135·2 oa × 29 × 5·5 *(41·2 × 8·8 × 1·7)*
Main engines: Diesels; 2 shafts; 1 000 bhp = 11 knots

US type utility landing craft 603 completed in Rangoon 1966. Transferred as Grant aid in Oct 1967. Used as transport.

8 Ex-US LCM 3 TYPE

LCM 701   LCM 702   LCM 703   LCM 704   LCM 705   LCM 706   LCM 707   LCM 708

Displacement, tons: 28
Dimensions, feet (metres): 56 × 14 × 4 *(17·0 × 4·3 × 1·2)*
Guns: 2—20 mm single
Main engines: 2 Gray Marine diesels; 225 bhp = 9 knots

US-built LCM type landing craft. Used as local transports for stores and personnel.

CAMEROON

Personnel

1976: 200 officers and men

Base

Douala

Mercantile Marine

Lloyd's Register of Shipping:
18 vessels of 3 199 tons gross

DELETIONS

1975   French VC Type—*Vigilant* (ex-VC 6), *Audacieux* (ex-VC 8)

LIGHT FORCES

1 LARGE PATROL CRAFT

Displacement, tons: 250 full load
Dimensions, feet (metres): 157·5 × 23·3 × 7·5 *(48 × 7·1 × 2·3)*
Guns: 2—40 mm
Main engines: 2 AGO Diesels; 4 000 hp = 20 knots
Range, miles: 2 000 at 16 knots

Ordered from Soc. Français Construction Naval in Sep 1974 for delivery in 1976. Similar to "Bizerte" class in Tunisia.

1 LARGE PATROL CRAFT

Name	No.	Builders	Commissioned
QUARTIER MAÎTRE ALFRED MOTTO	—	At. et Ch. de l'Afrique Equatoriale Libreville, Gabon	1974

Displacement, tons: 96
Dimensions, feet (metres): 95·4 × 20·3 × 6·3 *(29·1 × 6·2 × 1·9)*
Guns: 2—20 mm; 2 MG
Main engines: 2 Baudoin diesels; 1 290 bhp = 15·5 knots
Complement: 17

ALFRED MOTTO   *1973, Y. Betrand*

Name	No.	Builders	Commissioned
BRIGADIER M'BONGA TOUNDA	—	Ch. Navals d l'Esterel	1967

Displacement, tons: 20 full load
Dimensions, feet (metres): 60 × 13·5 × 4 *(18·3 × 4·1 × 1·2)*
Gun: 1—12·7 mm MG
Main engines: Caterpillar Diesel; 2 shafts; 540 bhp = 22·5 knots
Complement: 8

Customs duties. Sister of Mauritanian *Imrag 'ni.*

Name	No.	Builders	Commissioned
LE VALEUREUX	—	Ch. Navals de l'Esterel	1970

Displacement, tons: 45 full load
Dimensions, feet (metres): 78·1 × 16·3 × 5·1 *(26·8 × 5·0 × 1·6)*
Guns: 2—20 mm
Main engines: 2 diesels; 2 shafts; 960 hp = 25 knots
Complement: 9

2 HARBOUR LAUNCHES

SANAGA   BIMBIA

Of 10 tons.

1 LCM

BAKASI

Built by Carena, Abidjan, Ivory Coast. Of 57 tons and 56 feet long. 9 knots on 2 Baudoin diesels.

5 LCVP

INDÉPENDANCE   REUNIFICATION   SOUELLABA   MACHTIGAL   MANOKA

Built by Ateliers et Chantiers de l'Afrique Equatorile, Libreville, Gabon. Of 11 tons and 10 knots.

MISCELLANEOUS

Tornade and *Ouragan*—Built in 1966. *St. Sylvestre*—Built in 1967.
Four small outboard craft.
Mungo operated by Transport Ministry. *Dr. Jamot* operated by Health Ministry.

CANADA

Ministerial

Minister of National Defence:
   The Hon. James Richardson MP

Headquarters Appointments

Chief of Maritime Operation:
   Commodore J. M. Cutts, CD

Senior Appointments

Commander, Maritime Command:
   Vice-Admiral D. S. Boyle, CD
Commander, Maritime Forces, Pacific:
   Rear-Admiral A. L. Collier DSC, CD

Diplomatic Representation

Senior Liaison Officer (Maritime) London:
   Captain (N) J. W. Mason, CD
Canadian Forces Attaché and Maritime Liaison Officer, Washington:
   Commodore M. A. Martin, CD
Canadian Forces Attaché (Naval) Moscow:
   Commander H. R. Waddell, CD
Canadian Forces Attaché (Naval) The Hague:
   Commander W. G. Brown, CD

Establishment

The Royal Canadian Navy was officially established on 4 May 1910, when Royal Assent was given to the Naval Service Act. On 1 February 1968 the Canadian Forces Reorganisation Act unified the three branches of the Canadian Forces and the title "Royal Canadian Navy" was dropped.

Personnel

(a) 1971: 16 906 (2 379 officers, 14 527 men and women)
    1972: 15 223 (2 590 officers, 12 633 men and women)
    1973: 16 003 (1 985 officers, 14 018 men and women)
    1974: 14 000 (2 000 officers, 12 000 men and women)

Note: Canada no longer accounts for separate services in a unified command. Total armed forces 78 000

(b) Voluntary Service

Defence Estimates (Naval)

1971-72: $348 000 000
1972-73: $363 000 000
1973-74: $394 300 000
1975-76: $472 268 000
1976-77: $712 000 000

Bases

Halifax and Esquimalt

Air Arm

In an integrated force there is no specific Fleet Air Arm, but two squadrons of Sea King helicopters provide for ships' needs.

Prefix to Ships' Names

HMCS

Mercantile Marine

Lloyd's Register of Shipping:
   1 231 vessels of 2 459 998 tons gross

Strength of the Fleet

Type	Active	Building
Destroyers (DDH)	4	—
Frigates (some with helicopters)	19	—
Patrol Submarines	3	—
Replenishment Ships	3	—
Small Tankers	2	—
Patrol Escorts (Small)	7	—
Research Ships	5	—
Diving Support Ships and Tenders	2	—
Gate Vessels	5	—
Tugs (Large)	6	—
Tugs (Small)	11	—
Police Patrol Vessels	38	—
Hydrofoil	1	—

Reserve (Cat. C)

Frigates

1974 *Columbia, St. Croix, Chaudiere*

Research Vessels

1975 *Sackville*

DELETIONS

Attack Carrier (medium)

1970 *Bonaventure* paid off 1 April, towed to Taiwan for scrap, leaving Halifax 27 October.

Destroyers

1971 *Algonquin* left Victoria BC for Taiwan 21 April,
      Crescent left Victoria BC for Taiwan 21 May

Frigates

1974 *Granby*
1975 *St. Laurent.* Break-up at Halifax

Submarine

1974 *Rainbow* for disposal Jan 8

Maintenance Ships

1972 *Cape Breton* and *Cape Scott* decommissioned

Research Vessels

1972 *Fort Frances*

Tugs

1975 *Heatherton, Glendyne*

TRANSFERS

Patrol Escorts (Small)

1973 *Fort Steele* from RCMP to DND

Gate Vessels

1974 *Porte Dauphine* from MOT to DND

PENNANT NUMBERS

Destroyers

280	Iroquois
281	Huron
282	Athabaskan
283	Algonquin

Frigates

206	Saguenay
207	Skeena
229	Ottawa
230	Margaree
233	Fraser
234	Assiniboine
235	*Chaudiere
236	Gatineau
256	*St. Croix
257	Restigouche
258	Kootenay
259	Terra Nova
260	*Columbia
261	Mackenzie
262	Saskatchewan
263	Yukon
264	Qu'Appelle
265	Annapolis
266	Nipigon

Submarines

72	Ojibwa
73	Onondaga
74	Okanagan
75	*Rainbow

Replenishment Ships

AOR 508	Provider
AOR 509	Protecteur
AOR 510	Preserver
AOC 501	Dundalk
AOC 502	Dundurn

Research Vessels

AGOR 113	Sackville
AGOR 114	Bluethroat
AGOR 171	Endeavour
AGOR 172	Quest
AGOR 173	Kapuskasing
AGOR 516	Laymore

Patrol Escort (PFL)

140	Fort Steele
159	Fundy
160	Chignecto
161	Thunder
162	Cowichan
163	Miramichi
164	Chaleur

Gate Vessels

180	Porte St. Jean
183	Porte St. Louis
184	Porte de la Reine
185	Porte Quebec
186	Porte Dauphine

Tugs

ATA 528	Riverton
ATA 529	Clifton
ATA 531	St. Anthony
ATA 533	St. Charles
YTB 500	Glenside
YTB 501	Glenbrook
YTB 502	Glenevis
YTB 504	Glenlivet II
YMT 550	Eastwood
YMT 553	Wildwood
YTS 577	Mannville
YTS 582	Cree
YTS 583	Beamsville
YTS 586	Queensville
YTS 587	Plainsville
YTS 588	Youville
YTS 589	Loganville
YTS 590	Laurenceville
YTS 591	Parkesville
YTS 592	Listerville
YTS 593	Merrickville
YTS 594	Marysville

*Cat C Reserve 1974.

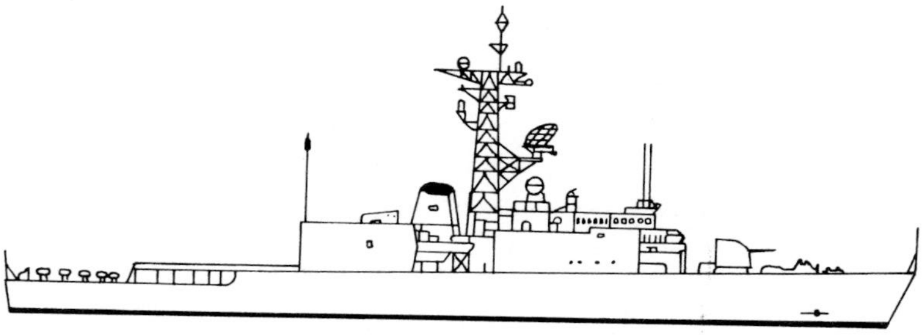

"TRIBAL" Class

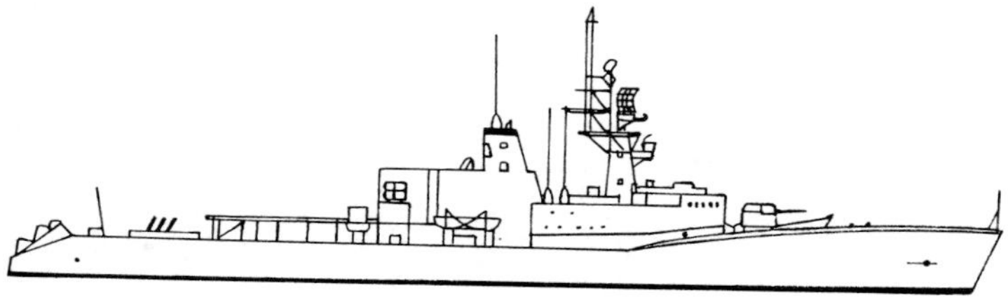

"ANNAPOLIS" Class

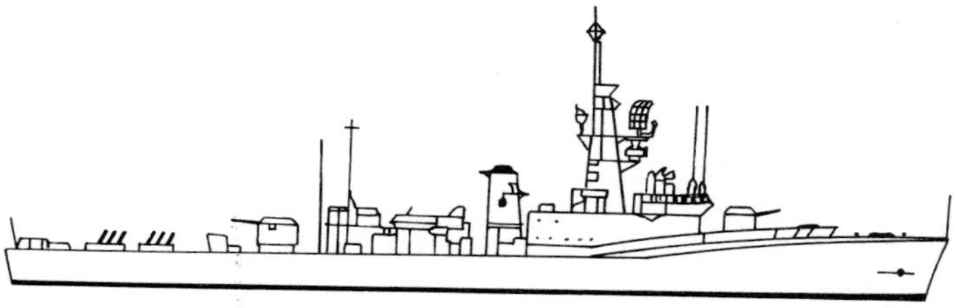

"MACKENZIE" Class

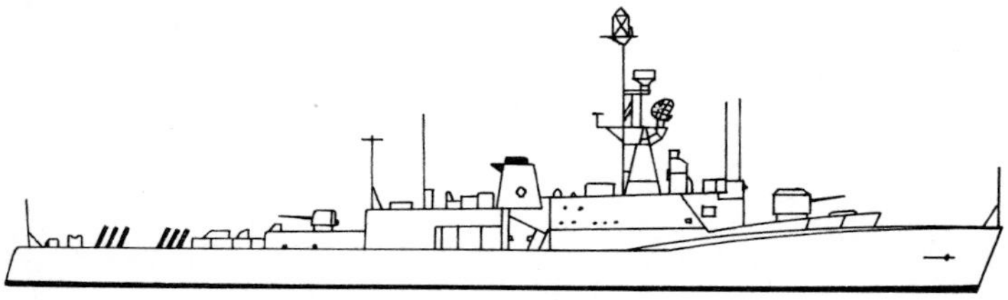

"RESTIGOUCHE" Class

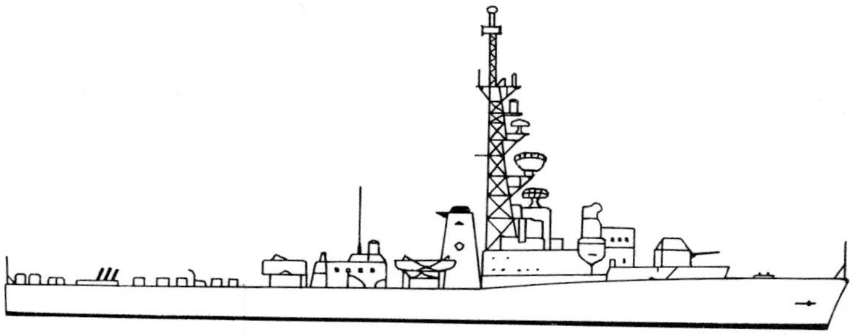

"IMPROVED RESTIGOUCHE" Class (GATINEAU)

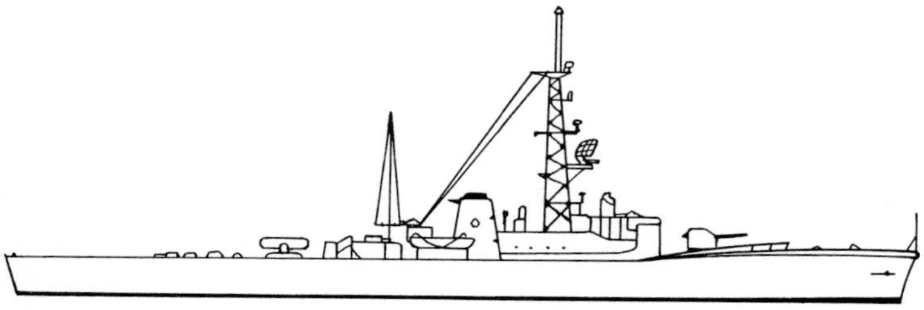

"IMPROVED RESTIGOUCHE" Class (RESTIGOUCHE)

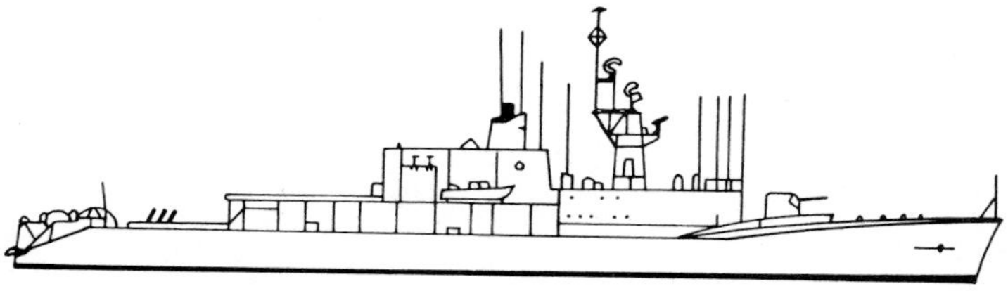

"ST. LAURENT" Class (except FRASER)

FRASER

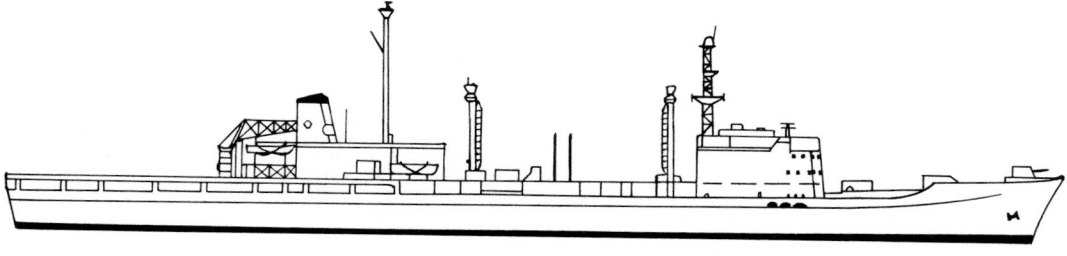

PROTECTEUR, PRESERVER

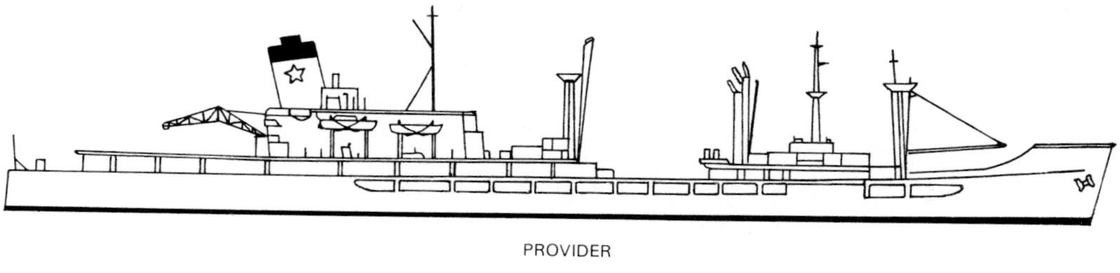

PROVIDER

DESTROYERS (DDH)

4 "TRIBAL" CLASS

Name	No.	Builders	Laid down	Launched	Commissioned
ALGONQUIN	283	Davie SB Co, Lauzon	1 Sep 1969	27 Nov 1971	30 Sep 1973
ATHABASKAN	282	Davie SB Co, Lauzon	1 June 1969	23 Apr 1970	30 Nov 1972
HURON	281	Marine Industries Ltd, Sorel	15 Jan 1969	3 Apr 1971	16 Dec 1972
IROQUOIS	280	Marine Industries Ltd, Sorel	15 Jan 1969	28 Nov 1970	29 July 1972

Displacement, tons: 4 200 full load
Length, feet (metres): 398 *(121·3)* pp; 426 *(129·8)* oa
Beam, feet (metres): 50 *(15·2)*
Draught, feet (metres): 14·5 *(4·4)*
Aircraft: 2 "Sea King" CHSS-2 A/S Helicopters
Missiles: (see note)
Gun: 1—5 in *(127 mm)* 54 cal single Oto-Melara
A/S: 1 Mk 10 "Limbo"
Torpedo tubes: 2 triple Mk 32 for A/S homing torpedoes
Main engines: Gas turbine; 2 Pratt & Whitney FT4A2 50 000 shp; 2 Pratt & Whitney FT12AH3 7 400 shp for cruising; 2 shafts
Speed, knots: 29 +
Range, miles: 4 500 at 20 knots
Complement: 245 (20 officers, 225 men) plus air unit, 7 officers + 33 men)

These ships have the same hull design, dimensions and basic characteristics as the large general purpose frigates cancelled at the end of 1963 (see particulars and illustration in the 1963-64 edition). Designed as anti-submarine ships, they are fitted with variable depth and hull sonar, landing deck equipped with double hauldown and Beartrap, flume type anti-rolling tanks to stabilise the ships at low speed, pre-wetting system to counter radio-active fallout, enclosed citadel, and bridge control of machinery.

Engineering: The gas turbines feed through a Swiss double reduction gearbox to two five bladed CP propellers.

Electronics: Mk 22 Weapon System Control by Hollandse Signaal.

Missiles: Launch system (GMLS) by Raytheon for Mk III Sea Sparrow missiles. Two quadruple launchers in forward end of the superstructure.

Radar: Surface warning and navigation; SPQ 2D.
Long range Warning; SPS 501 (SPS 12). Fire Control; M 22.

Sonar: Hull mounted; SQS 505 in 14 ft dome. VDS; 18 ft towed body aft. Bottomed target classification; SQS 501.

Torpedoes: The Mk 32 tubes are to be used with Mk 46 torpedoes.

HURON   *1975, Canadian Forces*

ALGONQUIN   *1975, Reiner Nerlich*

ATHABASKAN   *9/1975, Dr Giorgio Arra*

FRIGATES

2 "ANNAPOLIS" CLASS

Name	No.	Builders	Laid down	Launched	Commissioned
ANNAPOLIS	265	Halifax Shipyards Ltd, Halifax	July 1960	27 Apr 1963	19 Dec 1964
NIPIGON	266	Marine Industries Ltd, Sorel	Apr 1960	10 Dec 1961	30 May 1964

Displacement, tons: 2 400 standard; 3 000 full load
Length, feet (metres): 371·0 *(113·1)* oa
Beam, feet (metres): 42·0 *(12·8)*
Draught, feet (metres): 14·4 *(4·4)*
Aircraft: 1 CHSS-2 "Sea King" helicopter
Guns: 2—3 in *(76 mm)* 50 cal (1 twin)
A/S weapons: 1 Mk 10 "Limbo" in after well
Main engines: Geared turbines; 2 shafts; 30 000 shp
Boilers: 2 water tube
Speed, knots: 28 (30 on trials)
Range, miles: 4 570 at 14 knots
Complement: 210 (11 Officers, 199 ratings)

These two ships represented the logical development of the original "St. Laurent" class, through the "Restigouche" and "Mackenzie" designs. Due to the erection of a helicopter hangar and flight deck, and Variable Depth Sonar only one "Limbo" mounting could be installed. Also the 50 cal 3 inch mounting had to be moved forward to replace the 70 cal mounting in the original design.

Classification: Officially classified as DDH.

Construction: As these are largely prefabricated no firm laying down date is officially given. Work on hull units started under cover long before components were laid on the slip.

Radar: Search: SPS 12. Tactical: SPS 10. Fire Control: I Band.

ANNAPOLIS

6/1974, J. L. M. van der Burg

4 "MACKENZIE" CLASS

Name	No.	Builders	Laid down	Launched	Commissioned
MACKENZIE	261	Canadian Vickers Ltd, Montreal	15 Dec 1958	25 May 1961	6 Oct 1962
QU'APPELLE	264	Davie Shipbuilding & Repairing	14 Jan 1960	2 May 1962	14 Sep 1963
*SASKATCHEWAN	262	Victoria Machinery (and Yarrow)	16 July 1959	1 Feb 1961	16 Feb 1963
YUKON	263	Burrard DD & Shipbuilding	25 Oct 1959	27 July 1961	25 May 1963

Displacement, tons: 2 380 standard; 2 880 full load
Length, feet (metres): 366·0 *(111·5)* oa
Beam, feet (metres): 42·0 *(12·8)*
Draught, feet (metres): 13·5 *(4·1)*
Guns: 4—3 in *(76 mm)* (2 twin) (70 cal fwd, 50 cal aft);
(Qu'Appelle 2—3 in 50 cal (twin))
A/S weapons: 2 Mk 10 "Limbo" in well aft
Main engines: Geared turbines; 2 shafts; 30 000 shp
Boilers: 2 water tube
Speed, knots: 28
Range, miles: 4 750 at 14 knots
Complement: 210 (11 officers, 199 ratings)

Classification: Officially classified as DDE.

Radar: Search: SPS 12. Tactical: SPS 10. Fire Control: I Band.

Saskatchewan was launched by Victoria Machinery Depot Co Ltd, but completed by Yarrow's Ltd.

YUKON

5/1974, John G. Callis

3 "RESTIGOUCHE" CLASS

Name	No.	Builders	Laid down	Launched	Commissioned
CHAUDIERE	235	Halifax Shipyards Ltd	30 July 1953	13 Nov 1957	14 Nov 1959
COLUMBIA	260	Burrard DD and Shipbuilding	11 June 1953	1 Nov 1956	7 Nov 1959
ST. CROIX	256	Marine Industries Ltd, Sorel	15 Oct 1954	17 Nov 1957	4 Oct 1958

Displacement, tons: 2 370 standard; 2 880 full load
Length, feet (metres): 366·0 *(111·5)* oa
Beam, feet (metres): 42·0 *(12·8)*
Draught, feet (metres): 13·5 *(4·1)*
Guns: 4—3 in *(76 mm)* (2 twin)
A/S weapons: 2 Mk 10 "Limbo" in well aft
Main engines: Geared turbines; 2 shafts; 30 000 shp
Boilers: 2 water tube
Speed, knots: 28
Range, miles: 4 750 at 14 knots
Complement: 248 (12 officers, 236 ratings)

All three declared surplus and paid off into Category C Reserve in 1974.

Classification: Officially classified as DDE.

Radar: Search: SPS 12. Tactical: SPS 10. Fire Control: I Band.

CHAUDIERE

1970, Canadian Forces

4 "IMPROVED RESTIGOUCHE"

Name	No.	Builders	Laid down	Launched	Commissioned
GATINEAU	236	Davie Shipbuilding & Repairing	30 Apr 1953	3 June1957	17 Feb 1959
KOOTENAY	258	Burrard DD & Shipbuilding	21 Aug 1952	15 June1954	7 Mar 1959
RESTIGOUCHE	257	Canadian Vickers, Montreal	15 July 1953	22 Nov 1954	7 June1958
TERRA NOVA	259	Victoria Machinery Depot Co.	14 Nov 1952	21 June1955	6 June1959

Displacement, tons: 2 390 standard; 2 900 full load
Length, feet (metres): 371·0 (113·1)
Beam, feet (metres): 42·0 (12·8)
Draught, feet (metres): 14·1 (4·3)
Guns: 2—3 in (76 mm) 70 cal (twin forward)
A/S weapons: ASROC aft and 1 Mk 10 "Limbo" in after well
Torpedo tubes: 2 Triple Mk 32 for A/S torpedoes
Main engines: Geared turbines; 2 shafts; 30 000 shp
Boilers: 2 water tube
Speed, knots: 28 plus
Range, miles: 4 750 at 14 knots
Complement: 214 (13 officers, 201 ratings)

Classification: Officially classified as DDE.

Conversion: These four ships were refitted with ASROC aft and lattice foremast. Work included removing the after 3 inch 50 cal twin gun mounting and one "Limbo" A/S Mk 10 triple mortar, to make way for ASROC and Variable Depth Sonar. Dates of refits Terra Nova was completed on 18 Oct 1968: Gatineau completed in 1972 and Kootenay and Restigouche in 1973. Refit also included improvements to communications fit.

Radar: Search: SPS 12. Tactical: SPS 10. Fire Control: I Band.

GATINEAU   1972, Canadian Forces

6 "ST. LAURENT" CLASS

Name	No.	Builders	Laid down	Launched	Commissioned
SAGUENAY	206	Halifax Shipyards Ltd, Halifax	4 Apr 1951	30 July 1953	15 Dec 1956
SKEENA	207	Burrard Dry Dock & Shipbuilding	1 June1951	19 Aug 1952	30 Mar 1957
OTTAWA	229	Canadian Vickers Ltd, Montreal	8 June1951	29 Apr 1953	10 Nov 1956
MARGAREE	230	Halifax Shipyards Ltd, Halifax	12 Sep 1951	29 Mar 1956	5 Oct 1957
*FRASER	233	Yarrows Ltd, Esquimalt, B.C.	11 Dec 1951	19 Feb 1953	28 June1957
ASSINIBOINE	234	Marine Industries Ltd, Sorel, Quebec	19 May 1952	12 Feb 1954	16 Aug 1956

Displacement, tons: 2 260 standard; 2 858 full load
Length, feet (metres): 366·0 (111·5) oa
Beam, feet (metres): 42·0 (12·8)
Draught, feet (metres): 13·2 (4·0)
Aircraft: 1 CHSS-2 "Sea King" helicopter
Guns: 2—3 in (76 mm) 50 cal (1 twin)
A/S weapons: 1 Mk 10 "Limbo" in after well
Main engines: English Electric geared turbines; 2 shafts; 30 000 shp
Boilers: 2 water tube
Speed, knots: 28·5
Range, miles: 4 570 at 12 knots
Complement: 208 (11 officers, 197 ratings) (plus air unit of 7 officers and 13 ratings)

The first major warships to be designed in Canada. In design, much assistance was received from the Royal Navy (propelling machinery of British design) and the US Navy.
St. Laurent declared surplus in 1974.

*Fraser was launched by Burrard Dry Dock & Shipbuilding but completed by Yarrows Ltd.

Classification: Officially classified as DDH.

Gunnery: Original armament was 4—3 inch, 50 cal (2 twin), 2—40 mm (single), and 2 "Limbo" mortars.

Radars: Search: SPS 12. Tactical: SPS 10. Nav: Sperry. Fire Control: I band.

Reconstruction: All have helicopter platforms and VDS. Twin funnels were fitted to permit forward extension of the helicopter hangar.
Gunhouses are of glass fibre. In providing helicopter platforms and hangars it was possible to retain only one three barrelled "Limbo" mortar and only one twin 3-inch gun mounting. Dates of recommissioning after conversion: Assiniboine 28 June 1963, St. Laurent 4 Oct 1963, Ottawa 21 Oct 1964, Saguenay 14 May 1965, Skeena 15 Aug 1965, Margaree 15 Oct 1965, Fraser 31 Aug 1966.
Fraser has lattice radar-mast by the funnels.

SKEENA   1975, Canadian Forces

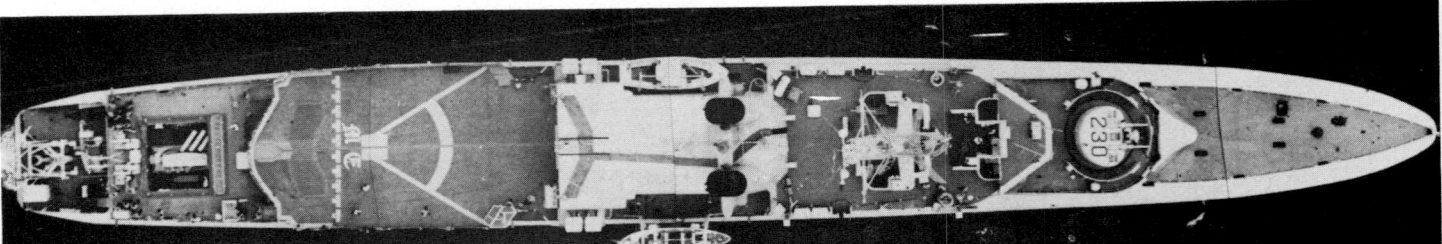

MARGAREE   1975, Commander R. E. George

SUBMARINES

3 "OBERON" CLASS (PATROL SUBMARINES)

Name	No.
OJIBWA (ex-Onyx)	72
OKANAGAN	74
ONONDAGA	73

Builders	Laid down	Launched	Commissioned
HM Dockyard, Chatham	27 Sep 1962	29 Feb 1964	23 Sep 1965
HM Dockyard, Chatham	25 Mar 1965	17 Sep 1966	22 June 1968
HM Dockyard, Chatham	18 June 1964	25 Sep 1965	22 June 1967

Displacement, tons: 2 060 full bouyancy surface; 2 200 normal surfaced; 2 420 dived
Length, feet (metres): 294·2 (90·0) oa
Beam, feet (metres): 26·5 (8·1)
Draught, feet (metres): 18 (5·5)
Torpedo tubes: 8—21 in (533 mm), 6 bow and 2 stern
Main machinery: 2 Admiralty Standard Range diesels; 3 680 bhp; 2 shafts; 2 electric motors; 6 000 hp
Speed, knots: 12 surfaced; 17 dived
Complement: 65 (7 officers, 58 ratings)

On 11 April 1962 the Ministry of National Defence announced that Canada was to buy three "Oberon" class submarines in UK. The first of these patrol submarines was obtained by the Canadian Government from the Royal Navy construction programme. She was laid down as Onyx but launched as Ojibwa. The other two were specific Canadian orders. There were some design changes to meet specific new needs including installation of RCN communications equipment and increase of air-conditioning capacity to meet the wide extremes of climate encountered in Canadian operating areas.

Electronics: The equipment includes sonar with fore casing mounted array and I band surveillance radar installations.

Nomenclature: The name Ojibwa is that of a tribe of North American Indians now widely dispersed in Canada and the USA and one of the largest remnants of aboriginal population. Okanagan and Onondaga are also Canadian Indian tribes.

OKANAGAN
10/1975 Dr. Giorgio Arra

OJIBWA
6/1973, Wright and Logan

REPLENISHMENT SHIPS

Name	No.
PRESERVER	AOR 510
PROTECTEUR	AOR 509

Builders	Laid down	Launched	Commissioned
Saint John Dry Dock Co Ltd, N.B.	17 Oct 1967	29 May 1969	30 July 1970
Saint John Dry Dock Co Ltd, N.B.	17 Oct 1967	18 July 1968	30 Aug 1969

Displacement, tons: 8 380 light; 24 700 full load
Measurement, tons: 22 100 gross; 13 250 deadweight
Length, feet (metres): 564 (172) oa
Beam, feet (metres): 76 (23·2)
Draught, feet (metres): 30 (9·1)
Aircraft: 3 CHSS-2 "Sea King" helicopters
Guns: 2—3 in (76 mm)
A/S launcher: 1 Sea Sparrow to be fitted
Main engines: Geared turbine; 21 000 shp; 1 shaft
Boilers: 2 forced draught water tube
Range, miles: 4 100 at 20, 7 500 at 11·5 knots
Complement: 227 (15 officers, 212 ratings)

Contract price $47 500 000 for both ships. In design they are an improvement on that of the prototype Provider. They could carry spare anti-submarine helicopters, military vehicles and bulk equipment for sealift purposes. 14 122 tons fuel, 1 048 tons dry cargo and 1 250 tons of ammunition.

PROTECTEUR
9/1974, Reiner Nerlich

Name	No.	Builders	Laid down	Launched	Commissioned
PROVIDER	AOR 508	Davie Shipbuilding Ltd, Lauzon	1 May 1961	5 July 1962	28 Sep 1963

Displacement, tons: 7 300 light; 22 000 full load
Measurement, tons: 20 000 gross; 14 700 deadweight
Length, feet (metres): 523 *(159·4)* pp; 555 *(169·2)* oa
Beam, feet (metres): 76 *(23·2)*
Draught, feet (metres): 32 *(9·8)*
Aircraft: 3 CHSS-2 "Sea King" helicopters
Main engines: Double reduction geared turbine 21 000 shp;
   1 shaft
Boilers: 2 water tube
Speed, knots: 20
Oil fuel, tons: 12 000
Range, miles: 3 600 at 20 knots
Complement: 166 (15 officers, 151 ratings)

Preliminary construction work was begun in September 1960.
Cost $15 700 000.
The helicopter flight deck is aft with the hangar at the same
level and immediately below the funnel. 3 Sea King Helicopters
can be accommodated in the hangar. The flight deck can
receive the largest and heaviest helicopters. A total of 20
electro-hydraulic winches are fitted on deck for ship-to-ship
movements of cargo and supplies, as well as shore-to-ship
requirements when alongside.

PROVIDER   1975, Canadian Forces

2 "DUN" CLASS TANKERS

DUNDALK AOC 501   **DUNDURN** AOC 502

Displacement, tons: 950
Dimensions, feet (metres): 178·8 × 32·2 × 13 *(54·5 × 9·8 × 3·9)*
Main engines: Diesel; 700 bhp = 10 knots

Small tankers, classed as fleet auxiliaries.

DUNDURN   1969, Mr. G. R. Hooper (Master)

MAINTENANCE SHIPS

2 "CAPE" CLASS

Name	No.	Builders	Laid down	Launched	Commissioned
CAPE BRETON	100	Burrard Dry Dock Co, Vancouver, BC	5 July 1944	7 Oct 1944	25 Apr 1945
CAPE SCOTT	101	Burrard Dry Dock Co, Vancouver, BC	8 June1944	27 Sep 1944	20 Mar 1945

Displacement, tons: 8 580 standard; 10 000 full load
Dimensions, feet (metres): 441·5 × 57 × 20 *(134·7 × 17·4 × 6·1)*

Alongside Base Ships for FMU's on each coast. They are
decommissioned and no further operational role is planned.
These ships, with a number of sisters, were originally built in
Canada for the R.N.

CAPE BRETON   Canadian Forces

RESEARCH VESSELS

Name	No.	Builders	Commissioned
BLUETHROAT	AGOR 114	Geo. T. Davie & Sons Ltd, Lauzon	28 Nov 1955

Displacement, tons: 785 standard; 870 full load
Dimensions, feet (metres): 157 oa × 33 × 10 (47 × 9·9 × 3)
Main engines: Diesel; 2 shafts; 1 200 bhp = 13 knots

Authorised under 1951 Programme. Laid down on 31 Oct 1952. Launched on 15 Sep 1955. Completed on 28 Nov 1955 as Mine and Loop Layer. In 1957 she was rated Controlled Minelayer, NPC 114. Redesignated as Cable Layer (ALC) in 1959, and as Research Vessel (AGOR) and GP craft in 1964.

BLUETHROAT
1975, Canadian Forces

Name	No.	Builders	Commissioned
KAPUSKASING	AGOR 173	Port Arthur SB Co, Ontario	23 July 1943

Displacement, tons: 1 040 standard; 1 335 full load
Dimensions, feet (metres): 225 oa × 35 × 11 (68·6 × 10·7 × 3·4)
Main engines: Triple expansion; 2 shafts; 2 000 ihp = 16·5 knots
Boilers: 2, of 3-drum type

Former "Algerine" class minesweeper—all this class was redesignated coastal escort (FSE) in 1953.
Refitted as survey ship (AGH) in 1959—redesignated AGOR 1964.

Name	No.	Builders	Commissioned
QUEST	AGOR 172	Burrard Dry Dock Co, Vancouver	21 Aug 1969

Displacement, tons: 2 130
Dimensions, feet (metres): 235 oa × 42 × 15·5 (77·2 × 12·8 × 4·6)
Aircraft: Light helicopter
Main engines: Diesel electric; 2 shafts; 2 950 shp = 16 knots; bow thruster propeller
Range, miles: 10 000 at 12 knots
Complement: 55

Built for the Naval Research Establishment of the Defence Research Board for acoustic, hydrographic and general oceanographic work. Capable of operating in heavy ice in the company of an icebreaker. Construction began in 1967. Launched on 9 July 1968. Completed on 21 Aug 1969. Based at Halifax.

QUEST
1972, Canadian Maritime Command

Name	No.	Builders	Commissioned
ENDEAVOUR	AGOR 171	Yarrows Ltd, Esquimalt, B.C.	9 Mar 1965

Displacement, tons: 1 560
Dimensions, feet (metres): 236 oa × 38·5 × 13 (71·9 ×-11·7 × 4)
Aircraft: 1 light helicopter
Main engines: Diesel electric; 2 shafts; 2 960 shp = 16 knots
Range, miles: 10 000 at 12 knots
Complement: 50 (10 officers, 13 scientists, 25 ratings plus helicopter pilot and engineer)

A naval research ship designed primarily for anti-submarine research. Flight deck 48 by 31 feet. Stiffened for operating in ice-covered areas. She is able to turn in 2·5 times her own length. Two 9-ton Austin-Weston telescopic cranes are fitted. There are two oceanographical winches each holding 5 000 fathoms of wire, two bathythermograph winches and a deep-sea anchoring and coring winch. She has acoustic insulation in her machinery spaces.

ENDEAVOUR
1970, Canadian Maritime Command

LAYMORE AGOR 516 (ex-AKS 516)

Measurement, tons: 560 gross, 262 net
Dimensions, feet (metres): 76·5 × 32 × 8 (53·6 × 9·8 × 2·5)
Main engines: GM diesels; 1 000 bhp = 10·8 knots

Former coastal supply vessel, rated as fleet auxiliary and designated AKS. Converted to research vessel 2 Aug 1965 to Mar 1966 and reclassified AGOR.

1 ANTI-SUBMARINE HYDROFOIL (FHE)

BRAS D'OR FHE 400

Displacement, tons: 180
Dimensions, feet (metres): 150·8 × 21·5 × 15 (hull depth) (46 × 6·6 × 5·1) = (7·5 (2·3) (60 knots) draught on foils) Foil base 90
Main engines: Pratt & Whitney FT4A-2 gas turbine on foils; 22 000 shp = 50-60 knots
Davey Paxman Diesel when hull borne; 2 000 shp = 12-15 knots
Pratt and Whitney ST 6A gas-turbine for hull-borne boost and foil-borne auxiliary power—390 shp

A prototype craft designed by De Havilland Aircraft (Canada). After very successful trials she was laid up ashore at Halifax in 1971 for 5 years.

BRAS D'OR
1971, Canadian Forces

TRAINING SHIPS

6 "BAY" CLASS Ex-MSC (PFL)

Name	No.	Builders	Commissioned
CHALEUR	164	Marine Industries Ltd, Sorel	12 Sep 1957
CHIGNECTO	160	Davie Shipbuilding Co, Lauzon	1 Aug 1957
COWICHAN	162	Yarrows Ltd, Esquimalt	19 Dec 1957
FUNDY	159	Davie Shipbuilding Co, Lauzon	27 Nov 1956
MIRAMICHI	163	Victoria Machinery Depot Co	28 Oct 1957
THUNDER	161	Port Arthur SB Co	3 Oct 1957

Displacement, tons: 390 standard; 464 full load
Dimensions, feet (metres): 152.0 oa × 28.0 × 7.0 (50 × 9.2 × 2.8)
Main engines: 2 GM V-12 diesels; 2 shafts; 2 400 bhp = 16 knots
Oil fuel, tons: 52
Range, miles: 3 290 at 12 knots
Complement: 18+ (2 officers, 16 ratings + trainees)

Extensively built of aluminium, including frames and decks. There were originally 14 vessels of this class of which four were transferred to Turkey and four sold commercially. Named after Canadian straits and bays. Designation changed from AMC to MCB in 1954. They were redesignated as Patrol Escorts (small) (PFL) in 1972 being used as training ships.

MIRAMICHI   1975, Canadian Forces

1 "FORT" CLASS PATROL ESCORT (PFL)

Name	No.	Builders	Commissioned
FORT STEELE	AGOR 140	Canadian SB and Eng. Co	Nov 1955

Displacement, tons: 85
Dimensions, feet (metres): 118 oa × 21 × 7 (36 × 6.4 × 2.1)
Main engines: 2 Paxman Ventura 12 YJCM diesels; 2 shafts; Kamewa cp propellers; 2 800 bhp = 18 knots
Complement: 16

Steel hull aluminium superstructure. Twin rudders. Acquired by DND in 1973 from RCMP—acts as Reserve Training ship based on Halifax.

FORT STEELE   1975, Canadian Forces

5 "PORTE" CLASS (GATE VESSELS)

Name	No.	Builders	Commissioned
PORTE DE LA REINE	184	Victoria Machinery	19 Sep 1952
PORTE QUEBEC	185	Burrard Dry Dock	7 Oct 1952
PORTE ST. JEAN	180	Geo T. Davie	4 June 1952
PORTE ST. LOUIS	183	Geo T. Davie	28 Aug 1952
PORTE DAUPHINE	186	Ferguson Ind.	12 Dec 1952

Displacement, tons: 429 full load
Dimensions, feet (metres): 125.5 × 26.3 × 13 (38 × 8.5 × 3.9)
Main engines: Diesel; A/C Electric; 1 shaft; 600 bhp = 11 knots
Complement: 23 (3 officers, 20 ratings)

Of trawler design. Multi-purpose vessels used for operating gates in A/S booms, fleet auxiliaries, anti-submarine netlayers for entrances to defended harbours. Can be fitted for minesweeping. Designation changed from YNG to YMG in 1954. First four used during summer for training Reserves. *Porte Dauphine* was reacquired from MOT in 1974 and employed in Reserve Training in Great Lakes area.

Note: Ex-Diving Tender YMT2 of 46 ft is used for sea-cadet training and the yacht *Oriole* QW3 has been used for officer cadet training since 1953.

PORTE ST. LOUIS   1972, Canadian Forces

DIVING SHIP AND TENDERS

1 FLEET DIVING SUPPORT SHIP

ASXL 20 (ex-*Aspa Quarto*)

Displacement, tons: 2 500
Dimensions, feet (metres): 236 × 39 × 16.5 (72 × 11.9 × 5)
Main engines: Diesel electric = 14 knots

Ex-Italian stern trawler bought in 1975 for conversion. When operational she will carry, launch and recover the Canadian submersible SDL/1, and support saturation diving operations.

2 DIVING TENDERS

Name	No.	Builders	Commissioned
YMT 11	—	Ferguson, Picton, NS	Jan 1962
YMT 12	—	Ferguson, Picton, NS	7 Aug 1963

Displacement, tons: 110
Dimensions, feet (metres): 125.5 × 26.3 × 13 (38.3 × 8 × 4)
Main engines: GM diesels; 228 bhp = 10.75 knots
Complement: 23 (3 officers, 20 ratings)

Can operate 4 divers at a time to 250 ft. Recompression chamber.

7 "VILLE" CLASS (OLD)

MANNVILLE YTS 577		**PLAINSVILLE** YTS 587	
CREE (ex-*Adamsville*) YTS 582		**YOUVILLE** YTS 588	
BEAMSVILLE YTS 583		**LOGANVILLE** YTS 589	
QUEENSVILLE YTS 586			

Dimensions, feet (metres): 40 × 10.5 × 4.8 (12.2 × 3.2 × 1.5)
Main engines: Diesel; 1 shaft; 150 bhp

Small harbour tugs now used for Reserve training.

There are small diving tenders YMT 6, YMT 8, YMT 9 and YMT 10, 70 tons, 75 × 18.5 × 8.5 feet, 2 diesels 165 bhp. YMT 1 (46 ft) was transferred to the Naval Research Establishment as a yard craft. Two new diving tenders, YSD 1 and YSD 2, entered service in 1965.

TUGS

2 "SAINT" CLASS

Name	No.	Builders	Commissioned
SAINT ANTHONY	ATA 531	St. John Dry Dock Co.	22 Feb 1957
SAINT CHARLES	ATA 533	St. John Dry Dock Co.	7 June1957

Displacement, tons: 840 full load
Dimensions, feet (metres): 151·5 × 33 × 17 *(46·2 × 10 × 5·2)*
Main engines: Diesel; 1 shaft; 1 920 bhp = 14 knots

Ocean tugs. Authorised under the 1951 Programme. Originally class of three.

ST. CHARLES   *1975, Canadian Forces*

2 "NORTON" CLASS

Name	No.	Builders	Commissioned
CLIFTON	ATA 529	—	Late 1944
RIVERTON	ATA 528	—	Late 1944

Displacement, tons: 462
Dimensions, feet (metres): 111·2 oa × 28 × 11 *(33·9 × 8·5 × 3·4)*
Main engines: Dominion Sulzer diesel; 1 000 bhp = 11 knots
Complement: 17

Large harbour tugs. *Clifton* was launched on 31 July 1944.

2 "GLEN" CLASS (HARBOUR/COASTAL)

Name	No.	Builders	Commissioned
GLENDYNE	ATA 640	Yarrows, Esquimalt	1975
GLENDALE	ATA 641	Yarrows, Esquimalt	1975

Displacement, tons: 255
Dimensions, feet (metres): 92·5 × 28 × 14·5 *(28·2 × 8·5 × 4·4)*
Main engines: 2 diesels with Voith-Schneider propellers = 11·5 knots
Complement: 6

Harbour/coastal tugs.

4 "GLEN" CLASS (HARBOUR)

Name	No.	Builders	Commissioned
GLENSIDE	YTB 500	—	1950
GLENBROOK	YTB 501	—	1950
GLENEVIS	YTB 502	—	1950
GLENLIVET II	YTB 504	—	1950

Dimensions, feet (metres): 80 × 20·7 × 7·2 *(24·4 × 6·3 × 2·2)*
Main engines: Diesel; 300 bhp = 9 knots

Large harbour tugs.

2 "WOOD" CLASS

EASTWOOD YMT 550   WILDWOOD YMT 553

Dimensions, feet (metres): 60 oa × 16 × 5 *(18·3 × 4·9 × 1·5)*
Main engines: 250 hp = 10 knots

Medium harbour tugs. Used as A/S Target Towing Vessels. Launched 1944.

Other medium harbour tugs are:
FT1, FT2. Employed as fire tugs, Hull numbers YMT 556 and 557 respectively.

5 "VILLE" CLASS (NEW)

Name	No.	Builders	Commissioned
LAWRENCEVILLE	YTS 590	Vito Steel & Barge Co.	1974
PARKSVILLE	YTS 591	Vito Steel & Barge Co.	1974
LISTERVILLE	YTS 592	Georgetown SY PEI	1974
MERRICKVILLE	YTS 593	Georgetown SY PEI	1974
MARYSVILLE	YTS 594	Georgetown SY PEI	1974

Dimensions, feet (metres): 64 × 15·5 × 9 *(19·5 × 4·7 × 2·7)*
Main engines: Diesel; 1 shaft; 365 bhp = 9·8 knots

Small harbour tugs employed at Esquimalt and Halifax.

PARKSVILLE   *1974, Canadian Forces*

2 TORPEDO RECOVERY VESSELS

SONGHEE YMR 1   NIMPKISH YMR 120

R.C.M.P. MARINE DIVISION

3 75 ft "DETACHMENT" CLASS

STAND OFF   **NICHOLSON**   **CENTENNIAL**

Displacement, tons: 69
Dimensions, feet (metres): 75 oa × 17 × 6·5 *(22·9 × 5·2 × 2)*
Main engines: 2 diesels; 1 018 bhp = 16 knots
Complement: 5

Of wood construction. First pair built by Smith and Rhuland Shipyard of Lunenburg, NS and completed in 1967 and 1968 respectively. *Centennial* built by A. F. Therault and Sons Meteghan River NS. Intended for service on the Atlantic coast.

STAND OFF   *1973, RCMP*

2 65 ft "DETACHMENT" CLASS

TOFINO   **GANGES**

Displacement, tons: 48
Dimensions, feet (metres): 65 × 15 × 4 *(19·8 × 4·6 × 1·2)*
Main engines: 1 Cummins diesel; 1 shaft; 410 bhp = 12 knots

Coastal patrol police boats for service on the east and west coasts.

2 52 ft PATROL VESSELS

RIVETT-CARNAC   **PEARKES**

Displacement, tons: 34
Dimensions, feet (metres): 52 × 14·75 × 3 *(15·9 × 4·5 × ·9)*
Main engines: 2 Cummins 903 (320 hp each); twin shafts = 20 knots

RIVETT-CARNAC   *1974, RCMP*

1 50 ft "DETACHMENT" CLASS

MOOSOMIN II

Dimensions, feet (metres): 50 × 13 × 3 *(15·3 × 4·1 × ·9)*
Main engines: 2 diesels; 600 bhp = over 17 knots

In service on the Great Lakes.

Valleyfield II, Outlook, Whitehorse, Yellowknife, Fort MacLeod and *Brule,* patrol craft varying from 26 to 41 ft in length, operate on the Great Lakes. *Advance, McLennan, Harvison* and *Mayberries* are located on the West coast together with *Duncan* (28 ft), *Dufferin* (41 ft) and *Regina* (41 ft).

CANADIAN COAST GUARD

Administration

Minister of Transport:
  Hon. Otto Lang, MP, PC
Deputy Minister of Transport:
  Mr. Sylvain Cloutier
Administrator, Marine Transportation Administration:
  Mr. R. Illing
Commissioner Canadian Coast Guard:
  Mr. W. A. O'Neil

Establishment

In January 1962 all ships owned and operated by the Federal Department of Transport with the exception of pilotage and canal craft, were amalgamated into the Canadian Coast Guard, a civilian service.

Ships

The Canadian Coast Guard comprises 146 ships and craft of all types (including 63 barges). They operate in Canadian waters from the Great Lakes to the northernmost reaches of the Arctic Archipelago.
There are heavy icebreakers, icebreaking ships for tending buoys and lighthouses, marine survey craft, weather-oceanographic ships, and many specialised vessels for tasks such as search and rescue, cable lifting and repair, marine research and shallow-draft operations in areas such as the Mackenzie River system and some parts of the Arctic.
The Ship Building and Heavy Equipment Branch of the Department of Defence Productions arranges for the design, construction and repair of Coast Guard ships and also provides this service for a number of other Canadian Government departments.
Principle bases for the ships are the department's 11 District offices, located at— St. John's, Newfoundland; Dartmouth, N.S.; Saint John, N.B.; Charlottetown, P.E.I.; Quebec and Sorel, Que; Prescott and Parry Sound, Ont.; Victoria and Prince Rupert, B.C.; and at Hay River, on Great Slave Lake.

Flag

The Canadian Coast Guard has its own distinctive jack, a red maple leaf on a white ground at the hoist and two gold dolphins on a blue ground at the fly.
Canadian Coast Guard vessels have white funnels with a red band at the top and the red maple leaf against the white.

Missions

The Canadian Coast Guard carries out the following missions:
1. Icebreaking and Escort. Icebreaking is carried out in the Gulf of St. Lawrence and River St. Lawrence and the Great Lakes in winter to assist shipping and for flood control, and in Arctic waters in summer.
2. Icebreaker-Aids to Navigation Tenders. Installation, supply and maintenance of fixed and floating aids-to-navigation in Canadian waters.
3. Organise and provide icebreaker support and some cargo vessels for the annual Northern sealift which supplies bases and settlements in the Canadian Arctic and Hudson Bay.
4. Provide and operate special patrol cutters and lifeboats for marine search and rescue.
5. Provide and operate survey and sounding vessels for the St. Lawrence River Ship Channel.
6. Provide and operate weatherships for Ocean Station "Papa" in the Pacific.
7. Provide and operate vessel for the repairing of undersea cables.
8. Provide and operate vessel for Marine Traffic Control on the St. Lawrence river.
9. Operate a small fleet of aircraft primarily for aids to navigation, ice reconnaissance, and pollution control work.

Fleet Strength

Weather ships	2
Cable ship	1
Heavy Icebreakers	5
Medium Icebreaker	1
Medium Icebreaking aid-to-navigation vessels	8
Light Icebreaking aid-to-navigation vessels	7
Ice strengthened aid-to-navigation vessels	4
Aid-to-navigation vessels	7
Offshore patrol cutters	2
Great Lakes Patrol Cutters	3
R Class cutters	5
Lifeboats	14
Hovercraft	1
Launches	6
St. Lawrence River vessels	4
Training vessels	2
Survey and sounding vessels	6
Mackenzie River navigation craft	5
Total	83

Aircraft

Fixed wing	1
Helicopters	33

WEATHER SHIPS

Name	No.	Builders	Commissioned
QUADRA	—	Burrard Dry Dock Co Ltd	Mar 1967
VANCOUVER	—	Burrard Dry Dock Co Ltd	4 July 1966

Displacement, tons: 5 600 full load
Dimensions, feet (metres): 404·2 oa × 50 × 17·5 *(121 × 15·5 × 5·3)*
Aircraft: 1 helicopter
Main engines: Turbo-electric; 2 shafts; 7 500 shp = 18 knots
Boilers: 2 automatic Babcock & Wilcox D type
Range, miles: 10 400 at 14 knots
Complement: 96

Turbo-electric twin screw weather and oceanographic vessels for Pacific Ocean service. *Quadra* laid down Feb 1965, launched 4 July 1966. *Vancouver* laid down Mar 1964, launched 29 June 1965. They have bow water jet reaction system to assist steering at slow speeds. Flume stabilisation systems are fitted. They are turbo-electric powered, with oil-fired boilers to provide the quiet operation needed for vessels housing much scientific equipment. Their complement includes 15 technical officers such as meteorologists, oceanographers and electronics technicians.

VANCOUVER

1975, Canadian Ministry of Transport

CABLE SHIP

Name	No.	Builders	Commissioned
JOHN CABOT	—	Canadian Vickers Ltd, Montreal	July 1965

Displacement, tons: 6 375 full load
Dimensions, feet (metres): 313·3 × 60 × 21·5 *(95·6 × 18·3 × 6·6)*
Aircraft: 1 helicopter
Main engines: Diesel-electric; 2 shafts; 9 000 shp = 15 knots
Range, miles: 10 000 at 12 knots
Complement: 85 officers and men

Laid down May 1963 and launched 15 April 1964. Combination cable repair ship and icebreaker. Designed to repair and lay cable over the bow only. For use in East Coast and Arctic waters. Bow water jet reaction manoeuvring system, heeling tanks and Flume stabilisation system. Three circular storage holds handle a total of 400 miles of submarine cable. Personnel include technicians and helicopter pilots.

JOHN CABOT   *1975, Canadian Ministry of Transport*

ICEBREAKERS

Name	No.	Builders	Commissioned
LOUIS ST. LAURENT	—	Canadian Vickers Ltd, Montreal	Oct 1969

Displacement, tons: 13 800 full load
Dimensions, feet (metres): 366·5 oa × 80 × 31 *(111·8 × 24·4 × 9·5)*
Aircraft: 2 helicopters
Main engines: Turbo-electric; 3 shafts; 24 000 shp = 17·75 knots
Range, miles: 16 000 miles at 13 knots cruising speed
Complement: Total accommodation for 216

She is larger than any of the former Coast Guard icebreakers. She has a helicopter hangar below the flight deck, with an elevator to raise the two helicopters to the deck when required. She was launched on 3 Dec 1966. She is officially rated as a heavy icebreaker.

LOUIS ST. LAURENT   *1971, Canadian Coast Guard*

Name	No.	Builders	Commissioned
NORMAN McLEOD ROGERS	—	Canadian Vickers Ltd, Montreal	Oct 1969

Displacement, tons: 6 320 full load
Dimensions, feet (metres): 295 oa × 62·5 × 20 *(90 × 19·5 × 6·1)*
Aircraft: 1 helicopter
Landing craft: 2
Main engines: 4 diesels and 2 gas turbines powering 2 electric motors; 2 shafts; 12 000 shp = 15 knots
Complement: 55

Built for use in the Gulf of St. Lawrence and East Coast waters. This is the world's first application of gas turbine/electric propulsion in an icebreaker. Officially rated as a heavy icebreaker.

NORMAN McLEOD ROGERS   *1975, Canadian Coastguard*

Name	No.	Builders	Commissioned
JOHN A. MACDONALD	—	Davie Shipbuilding Ltd, Lauzon	Sep 1960

Displacement, tons: 9 160 full load
Measurement, tons: 6 186 gross
Dimensions, feet (metres): 315 × 70 × 28 *(96 × 21·3 × 8·6)*
Aircraft: 2 helicopters
Main engines: Diesel-electric; 15 000 shp = 15·5 knots

Officially rated as a heavy icebreaker. Launched 3 Oct 1959.

JOHN A. MACDONALD   *1975, Canadian Coastguard*

Name	No.	Builders	Commissioned
MONTCALM	—	Davie Shipbuilding Ltd, Lauzon	June 1957
WOLFE	—	Canadian Vickers Ltd, Montreal	Nov 1959

Displacement, tons: 3 005 full load
Measurement, tons: 2 022 gross
Dimensions, feet (metres): 220 × 48 × 16 *(72·7 × 14·6 × 4·9)*
Aircraft: 1 helicopter
Main engines: Steam reciprocating; 4 000 ihp = 13 knots

Montcalm launched 23 Oct 1956. Officially rated as Medium Icebreaking Aid to Navigation Vessels.

WOLFE   *1975, Canadian Coastguard*

AID TO NAVIGATION VESSELS

Name	No.	Builders	Commissioned
CAMSELL	—	Burrard Dry Dock Co Ltd	Oct 1959

Displacement, tons: 3 072 full load
Measurement, tons: 2 020 gross
Dimensions, feet (metres): 223·5 × 48 × 16 *(68·2 × 14·6 × 4·9)*
Main engines: Diesel-electric; 4 250 shp = 13 knots

Launched 17 Feb 1959. Officially rated as Medium Icebreaking Aid to Navigation Vessel.

CAMSELL   *1975, Canadian Coast Guard*

Name	No.	Builders	Commissioned
SIR HUMPHREY GILBERT	—	Davie Shipbuilding Ltd, Lauzon	June 1959

Displacement, tons: 3 000 full load
Measurement, tons: 1 930 gross
Dimensions, feet (metres): 220 × 48 × 16·3 *(68 × 14·6 × 5·0)*
Main engines: Diesel-electric; 4 250 shp = 13 knots

Officially rated as Medium Icebreaking Aid to Navigation Vessel.

SIR HUMPHREY GILBERT   *1970, Canadian Coast Guard*

Name	No.	Builders	Commissioned
LABRADOR	—	Marine Industries Ltd, Sorel	8 July 1954

Displacement, tons: 6 490 full load
Measurement, tons: 3 823 gross
Dimensions, feet (metres): 290·0 oa × 63·5 × 29·0 *(88·5 × 19·4 × 8·8)*
Aircraft: Provision for 2 helicopters
Main engines: Diesel-electric; 10 000 shp = 16 knots

Ordered in Feb 1949, laid down on 18 Nov 1949, launched on 14 Dec 1951 and completed for the Royal Canadian Navy but transferred to the Department of Transport in Feb 1958. Officially rated as a Heavy Icebreaker. She was the first naval vessel to traverse the North West passage and circumnavigate North America, when she was Canada's largest and most modern icebreaker.

LABRADOR   *1975, Dept. of Transport*

Name	No.	Builders	Commissioned
d'IBERVILLE	—	Davie Shipbuilding Ltd, Lauzon	May 1953

Displacement, tons: 9 930 full load
Measurement, tons: 5 678 gross
Dimensions, feet (metres): 310 × 66·5 × 30·2 *(94·6 × 20·3 × 9·2)*
Main engines: Steam reciprocating; 10 800 ihp = 15 knots

Officially rated as a Heavy Icebreaker.

d'IBERVILLE   *1975 Canadian Coast Guard*

Name	No.	Builders	Commissioned
ERNEST LAPOINTE	—	Davie Shipbuilding Ltd, Lauzon	Feb 1941

Displacement, tons: 1 675 full load
Measurement, tons: 1 179 gross
Dimensions, feet (metres): 184 × 36 × 15·5 *(56·1 × 11 × 4·7)*
Main engines: Steam reciprocating; 2 000 ihp = 13 knots

Officially rated as St. Lawrence Ship Channel Icebreaking Survey and Sounding Vessel.

Name	No.	Builders	Commissioned
N. B. McLEAN	—	Halifax S.Y. Ltd	1930

Displacement, tons: 5 034 full load
Measurements, tons: 3 254 gross
Dimensions, feet (metres): 277 × 60·5 × 24·0 *(90 × 19·5 × 6·1)*
Main engines: Steam reciprocating; 6 500 ihp = 13 knots

Officially rated as Medium Icebreaker.

Name	No.	Builders	Commissioned
GRIFFON	—	Davie Shipbuilding Ltd, Lauzon	Dec 1970

Displacement, tons: 3 096
Dimensions, feet (metres): 234 × 49 × 15·5 *(71·4 × 14·9 × 4·7)*
Main engines: Diesel; 4 000 bhp; 13·5 knots

Officially rated as Medium Icebreaking Aid to Navigation Vessel.

Name	No.	Builders	Commissioned
SIMCOE	—	Canadian Vickers Ltd, Montreal	1962

Displacement, tons: 1 300 full load
Dimensions, feet (metres): 179·5 × 38 × 12 *(54·7 × 11·6 × 3·7)*
Main engines: Diesel-electric; 2 000 shp = 12 knots

Officially rated as Ice Strengthened Aid to Navigation Vessel.

GRIFFON
1975, Canadian Coast Guard

Name	No.	Builders	Commissioned
J. E. BERNIER	—	Davie Shipbuilding Ltd, Lauzon	Aug 1967

Displacement, tons: 3 096
Dimensions, feet (metres): 231 × 49 × 16 *(70·5 × 14·9 × 4·9)*
Aircraft: 1 helicopter
Main engines: Diesel Electric; 4 250 bhp = 13·5 knots (trial speed)

Officially rated as Medium Icebreaking Aid to Navigation Vessel.

J. E. BERNIER
1975, Ministry of Transport

Name	No.	Builders	Commissioned
SIMON FRASER	—	Burrard D. Y. Co. Ltd	Feb 1960
TUPPER	—	Marine Industries Ltd	Dec 1959

Displacement, tons: 1 876 full load
Measurements, tons: 1 357 gross
Dimensions, feet (metres): 204·5 × 42 × 14 *(62·4 × 12·8 × 4·3)*
Main engines: Diesel-electric; 2 900 shp = 13·5 knots

Simon Fraser was launched 18 Aug 1959. Both officially rated as Light Icebreaking Aid to Navigation Vessels.

Name	No.	Builders	Commissioned
THOMAS CARLETON	—	St. John Dry Dock Ltd	1960

Displacement, tons: 1 532 full load
Dimensions, feet (metres): 180 × 42 × 13 *(54·9 × 12·8 × 4)*
Main engines: Diesel; 2 000 bhp = 12 knots

Officially rated as Light Icebreaking Aid to Navigation Vessel.

Name	No.	Builder	Commissioned
EDWARD CORNWALLIS	—	Canadian Vickers Ltd, Montreal	Dec 1949

Displacement, tons: 3 700 full load
Measurement, tons: 1 965 gross
Dimensions, feet (metres): 259 × 43·5 × 18 *(79 × 13·3 × 5·5)*
Main engines: Steam reciprocating; 2 800 ihp = 13·5 knots

Launched 5 Aug 1949. In reserve. Officially rated as a Light Icebreaking Aid to Navigation Vessel.

EDWARD CORNWALLIS
1971, Canadian Coast Guard

Name	No.	Builders	Commissioned
ALEXANDER HENRY	—	Port Arthur SB Ltd	July 1959

Displacement, tons: 2 497 full load
Measurements, tons: 1 647 gross
Dimensions, feet (metres): 210 × 43·5 × 16 *(64 × 13·3 × 4·9)*
Main engines: Diesel; 3 550 bhp = 13 knots

Launched 18 July 1958. Officially rated as a Medium Icebreaking Aid to Navigation Vessel.

Name	No.	Builders	Commissioned
TRACY	—	Port Weller Drydocks	1968

Displacement, tons: 1 300
Dimensions, feet (metres): 251·5 × 42 × 12 *(76·7 × 12·8 × 3·7)*
Main engines: Diesel; 2 000 bhp = 11 knots

Officially rated as Light Icebreaking Aid to Navigation Vessel.

Name	No.	Builders	Commissioned
SIR WILLIAM ALEXANDER	—	Halifax Shipyards Ltd	June 1959

Displacement, tons: 3 555 full load
Measurements, tons: 2 153 gross
Dimensions, feet (metres): 227·5 × 45 × 17·5 *(69·4 × 13·7 × 5·3)*
Main engines: Diesel electric; 4 250 shp = 15 knots

Launched 13 Dec 1958. Equipped with Flume Stabilisation System. Officially rated as a Medium Icebreaking Aid to Navigation Vessel.

SIR WILLIAM ALEXANDER   1975, Dept. of Transport

Name	No.	Builders	Commissioned
WALTER E. FOSTER	—	Canadian Vickers Ltd, Montreal	Dec 1954

Displacement, tons: 2 715 full load
Measurement, tons: 1 672 gross
Dimensions, feet (metres): 229·2 × 42·5 × 16 *(69·9 × 12·9 × 4·9)*
Main engines: Steam reciprocating; 2 000 ihp = 12·5 knots

Officially rated as a light Icebreaking Aid to Navigation Vessel.

WALTER E. FOSTER   1975, Canadian Coast Guard

Name	No.	Builders	Commissioned
NARWHAL	—	Canadian Vickers Ltd, Montreal	July 1963

Measurement, tons: 2 064 gross
Dimensions, feet (metres): 251·5 × 42·0 × 12·0 *(76·7 × 12·8 × 3·7)*
Main engines: Diesel; 2 000 bhp
Range, miles: 9 200 cruising
Complement: 32

Originally rated as Sealift Stevedore Depot Vessel, now re-rated as Light Icebreaking Aid to Navigation Vessel.

NARWHAL   1975, Canadian Coast Guard

Name	No.	Builders	Commissioned
BARTLETT	—	—	1970
PROVO WALLIS	—	—	1970

Displacement, tons: 1 620
Dimensions, feet (metres): 189·3 × 42·5 × 12·5 *(57·7 × 13 × 3·8)*
Main engines: Diesel; 1 760 bhp = 12 knots

Classed as Ice Strengthened Aid to Navigation Vessels.

BARTLETT   1975, Ministry of Transport

Name	No.	Builders	Commissioned
MONTMORENCY	—	Davie Shipbuilding Ltd, Lauzon	Aug 1957

Displacement, tons: 1 006 full load
Measurement, tons: 750 gross
Dimensions, feet (metres): 163 × 34 × 11 *(49·7 × 10·2 × 3·4)*
Main engines: Diesel; 1 200 bhp

Officially rated as an Ice Strengthened Aid to Navigation Vessel.

MONTMORENCY   *1975, Canadian Coast Guard*

Name	No.	Builders	Commissioned
MONTMAGNY	—	Russel Bros, Owen Sound	May 1963

Displacement, tons: 565 full load
Dimensions, feet (metres): 148·0 × 29·0 × 8·0 *(45·1 × 10·2 × 2·4)*
Main engines: Diesels; 1 000 bhp

Officially rated as Aid to Navigation Tender.

MONTMAGNY   *1970, Canadian Coast Guard*

Name	No.	Builders	Commissioned
VERENDRYE	—	Davie Shipbuilding Ltd, Lauzon	Oct 1959

Displacement, tons: 400 full load
Dimensions, feet (metres): 125·0 × 26·0 × 7·0 *(38·1 × 7·9 × 2·1)*
Main engines: Diesels; 760 bhp

Officially rated as Aid to Navigation Tender.

Name	No.	Builders	Commissioned
ROBERT FOULIS	—	St John Drydock	1969

Displacement, tons: 260
Dimensions, feet (metres): 104 × 25 × 7 *(31·7 × 7·6 × 2·1)*
Main engines: Diesel; 960 bhp = 10 knots

Officially rated as Aid to Navigation Tender.

KENOKI

Displacement, tons: 270
Dimensions, feet (metres): 108 × 36 × 5 *(32·9 × 11 × 1·5)*
Main engines: Diesel; 940 bhp = 10 knots

Officially rated as Aid to Navigation Tender.

Name	No.	Builders	Commissioned
ALEXANDER MACKENZIE	—	Burrard Dry Dock Ltd	1950
SIR JAMES DOUGLAS	—	Burrard Dry Dock Ltd	Nov 1956

Displacement, tons: 720 full load
Dimensions, feet (metres): 150·0 × 30·0 × 10·3 *(45·8 × 9 × 3·1)*
Main engines: Diesels; 1 000 bhp

Officially rated as Aid to Navigation Tenders.

NOKOMIS

Displacement, tons: 64
Dimensions, feet (metres): 66 × 17 × 7 *(20·1 × 5·2 × 2·1)*
Main engines: Diesel; 120 bhp

Officially rated as Aid to Navigation Tender.

SEARCH AND RESCUE CUTTERS

Name	No.	Builders	Commissioned
ALERT	—	Davie Shipbuilding Ltd, Lauzon	Dec 1969

Displacement, tons: 2 025
Dimensions, feet (metres): 234·3 × 39·9 × 15·1 *(71·5 × 12·2 × 4·6)*
Aircraft: 1 helicopter
Main engines: Diesel electric; 7 716 hp = 18·75 knots
Range, miles: 6 000

Officially rated as Offshore Patrol Cutter.

ALERT   *1975, Canadian Coast Guard*

Name	No.	Builders	Commissioned
DARING (ex-*Wood*, MP 17)	—	Davie Shipbuilding Ltd, Lauzon	July 1958

Displacement, tons: 600 standard
Dimensions, feet (metres): 178 oa × 29 × 9·8 *(54·3 × 8·8 × 3·0)*
Main engines: 2 Fairbanks-Morse diesels; 2 shafts; 2 660 bhp = 16 knots

Used for patrol on the east coast of Canada, this ship is built of steel, strengthened against ice, with aluminium superstructure. Transferred from the Royal Canadian Mounted Police Marine Division to the Ministry of Transport in 1971, and renamed *Daring*. Offshore Patrol Cutter.

DARING (as *Wood*)   *1966, Director of Marine Services*

CG 101-109   CG 114-118

Displacement, tons: 18
Dimensions, feet (metres): 44 × 12 × 3 *(13·4 × 3·7 × 0·9)*
Main engines: Diesel; 294 bhp = 14 knots
Range, miles: 150

Lifeboats shore-based at Coast Guard Stations on both coasts.

Note. For search and rescue and patrol duties: six launches *(Mallard, Moorhen,* CG 110-113) and one Hovercraft (CG 021).

Name	No.	Builders	Commissioned
RACER	—	Yarrows Ltd, Esquimalt	1963
RALLY	—	Davie Shipbuilding Ltd	1963
RAPID	—	Ferguson Industries, Picton	1963
READY	—	Burrard Dry Dock	1963
RELAY	—	Kingston Shipyard	1963
RIDER	—	—	1963

Measurement, tons: 153 gross
Dimensions, feet (metres): 95·2 × 20 × 6·5 *(29 × 6·1 × 2)*
Main engines: Diesel; 2 400 bhp = 20 knots designed

Rider, completed for the Dept. of Fisheries, was taken over by the Coast Guard in Mar 1969.
Relay rerated as St. Lawrence River Marine Traffic Control Vessel.

RELAY

1975, Ministry of Transport

Name	No.	Builders	Commissioned
SPINDRIFT	—	Cliff Richardson Ltd, Meaford	1963
SPRAY	—	J. J. Taylor & Sons Ltd, Toronto	1963
SPUME	—	Grew Ltd, Penetanguishene	1964

Measurement, tons: 57 gross
Dimensions, feet (mwtres): 70 × 16·8 × 4·7 *(21·4 × 5·1 × 1·4)*
Main engines: 2 diesels; 1 050 bhp = 19 knots

Employed on Great Lakes Patrol.

SPINDRIFT

1975, Canadian Coast Guard

NORTHERN SUPPLY VESSELS

2 FORMER TANK LANDING CRAFT (LCT 8)

Name	No.	Builders	Commissioned
EIDER	—	Sir Wm Arrol & Co	1946
SKUA	—	Harland & Wolff	1946

Measurement, tons: 1 083 to 1 104 gross
Dimensions, feet (metres): 231·2 oa × 38 × 7 *(70·5 × 11·6 × 2·1)*
Main engines: Diesel; 1 000 shp = 9 knots

Converted LCT (8)s, acquired from Great Britain in 1957-61.

SKUA

Canadian Coast Guard

1 FORMER TANK LANDING CRAFT (LCT 4)

Name	No.	Builders	Commissioned
MINK	—	—	1944

Displacement, tons: 586 full load
Dimensions, feet (metres): 187·2 × 33·8 × 4 *(57·1 × 10·3 × 1·2)*
Main engines: Diesel; 920 shp = 8 knots

Converted LCT (4) acquired from Great Britain in 1958. Formerly officially rated as Steel Landing Craft for Northern Service, now re-rated as Aids to Navigation Tender, in reserve.

MINK

1963, Canadian Coast Guard

SURVEY AND SOUNDING VESSELS

BEAUPORT

Displacement, Tons: 767 full load
Dimensions, feet (metres): 167·5 × 24·0 × 9·0 *(51·1 × 7·3 × 2·7)*
Main engines: Diesels; 1 280 bhp

Completed in 1960.

DETECTOR

Displacement, tons: 584 full load
Dimensions, feet (metres): 140·0 × 35·0 × 10·0 *(42·7 × 10·7 × 3·1)*
Main engines: Steam reciprocating

VILLE MARIE

Displacement, tons: 493 full load
Dimensions, feet (metres): 134·0 × 28·0 × 9·5 *(40·9 × 8·5 × 2·9)*
Main engines: Diesel electric; 1 000 hp

Completed in 1960.

There are also two smaller vessels *Glendada* and *Jean Bourdon* for the St. Lawrence Ship Channel.

NICOLET

Displacement, tons: 935 full load
Dimensions, feet (metres): 166·5 × 35·0 × 9·6 *(50·8 × 10·7 × 2·9)*
Main engines: Diesels; 1 350 bhp

SHORE-BASED CRAFT

| DUMIT | ECKALOO | MISKANAW | TEMBAH | NAHIDIK |

Assist navigation in Mackenzie River operations. Small tug/buoy tender type.

TRAINING SHIPS

MIKULA

Displacement, tons: 617
Dimensions, feet (metres): 128 × 30 × 11 *(39 × 9·2 × 3·4)*
Main engines: Diesel; 150 bhp = 9 knots

Converted Light Vessel.

SKIDEGATE

Displacement, tons: 200
Dimensions, feet (metres): 87 × 22 × 8 *(26·5 × 6·7 × 2·4)*
Main engines: Diesel; 640 bhp = 11 knots

Formerly an Aid to Navigation Tender.

CHILE

Headquarters Appointments

Commander-in-Chief of the Navy:
Admiral José Toribio Merino Castro
Chief of the Naval Staff:
Rear-Admiral Carlos A. Le May Délano

Diplomatic Representation

Naval Attaché in Brasilia:
Captain Jorge Salugo Silva
Naval Attaché in Buenos Aires and Montevideo:
Commander Hernan Rivero Calderon
Naval Attaché in Lima:
Captain Jorge Grez Casarino
Naval Attaché in London, Paris, The Hague and Stockholm:
Rear Admiral R. Lopez Silva
Naval Attaché in Madrid:
Commander Ary Acuna Figueroa
Naval Attaché in Quito:
Captain Javier Gantes Salcedo
Naval Attaché in Tokyo:
Commander Francisco Ghilsofo Araya
Naval Attaché in Washington:
Rear Admiral Jorge Paredes Wetzer

Personnel

(a) 1976: 23 000 (1 320 officers, 19 000 ratings, 2 680 marines)
(b) 1 year National Service

Naval Bases

Talcahuano. Main Naval Base, Schools, major repair yard, (2 dry docks, 2 floating docks) 2 floating cranes.
Valparaiso. Naval Base, Schools, major repair yard.
Puerto Monti. Small naval base.
Punta Arenas. Small naval base. Repair yard with slipway.
Puerto Williams. Small naval base.

Maritime Air

(B) 4 Bell 206 A JetRangers
2 Bell 47
(C) 4 Lockheed SP-2E Neptunes (Air Force)
5 Grumman HU-16B Albatross (Air force)
3 Convair PBY-6A Catalina (SAR)
5 Douglas C 47
5 Beech C-45/D18s
1 Piper PA-31-310 Navajo
6 Beech T-34B Mentor

There is a requirement for 12 new maritime patrol aircraft but the UK and Netherlands Governments have vetoed the supply of HS. 748 or Fokker/VFW F.27 MP aircraft. It is possible that Brazilian EMB-111 may be bought instead.

Infanteria de Marina

1 Brigade and Coast Defence units (2 680 marines)

Strength of the Fleet

Type	Active	Building
Cruisers	2	—
Destroyers	6	—
Frigates	6	—
Corvettes	4	—
Patrol Submarines	2	—
Landing Ships (Tank)	4	—
Landing Craft	3	—
Fast Attack Craft (Torpedo)	4	—
Large Patrol Craft	2	—
Coastal Patrol Craft	3	—
Survey Ship	1	—
Sail Training Ship	1	—
Transports	4	—
Tankers	3	—
Floating Docks	2	—
Tugs	7	—

Mercantile Marine

Lloyd's Register of Shipping:
135 vessels of 364 364 tons gross

DELETIONS

Cruiser

1975 *O'Higgins* ("Brooklyn" Class) grounded in Aug 1974. Subsequently used as alongside accommodation ship.

Submarines

1973 *Thomson* (ex-US "Balao" Class)
1975 *Simpson* (ex-US "Balao" Class)

Landing Craft

1971 *Bolados* (LCU 95)
1973 *Grumete Tellez* (withdrawn from service)

Tugs

1971 *Cabrales, Ugarte*

PENNANT LIST

Cruisers

03 Prat
04 Latorre

Destroyers/Frigates

06 Condell
07 Lynch
14 Blanco Encalada
15 Cochrane
16 Ministero Zenteno
17 Ministero Portales
18 Almirante Riveros
19 Almirante Williams
26 Serrano
27 Orella
28 Riquelme
29 Uribe

Submarines

22 O'Brien
23 Hyatt

Corvettes

37 Papudo
60 Lientur
62 Lautaro
63 Sergento Aldea

Light Forces

75 Marinero Fuentealba
76 Cabo Odger
79 Contramaestro Ortiz
80 Guacolda
81 Fresia
82 Quidora
83 Tegualda

Survey Ship

64 Yelcho

Training Ship

43 Esmeralda

Amphibious Forces

88 Comandante Hemmerdinger
89 Comandante Araya
90 Elicura
91 Aguila
92 Aspirante Morel
94 Orompello
96 Grumete Diaz
97 Comandante Toro

Transports

45 Piloto Pardo
47 Aquiles
110 Meteoro
111 Cirujano Videla

Tankers

52 Al Jorge Montt
53 Araucano
54 Beagle

Tugs

63 S. Aldea
73 Colocolo
104 Ancud
105 Monreal
120 Reyes
127 Caupolican
128 Cortez

LATORRE

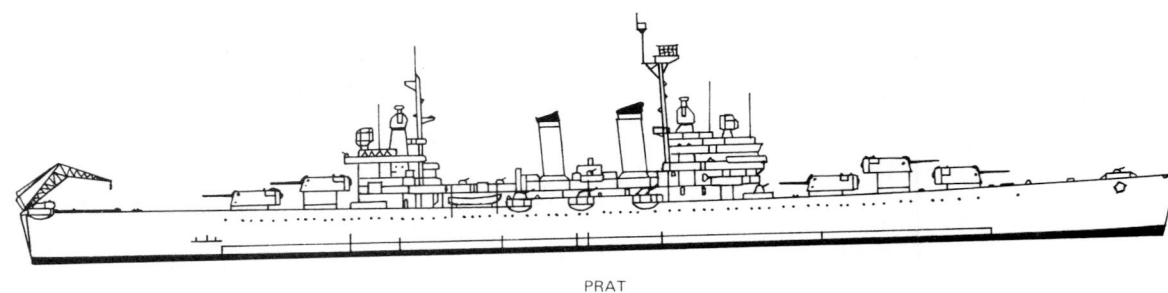

PRAT

"ALMIRANTE" Class

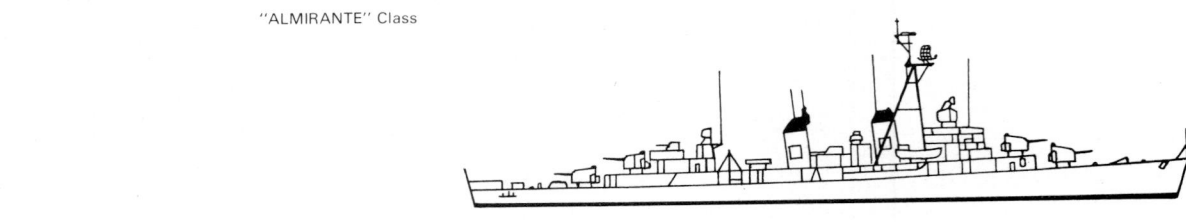

"FLETCHER" Class

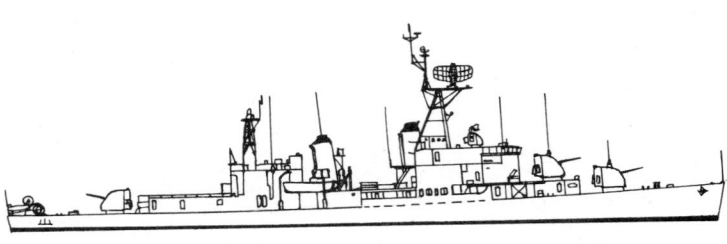

"ALLEN M. SUMNER" Class

CRUISERS

Name	No.	Builders	Laid down	Launched	Commissioned
LATORRE (ex-*Göta Lejon*)	04	Eriksberg Mekaniska Verkstad, Göteborg	27 Sep 1943	17 Nov 1945	15 Dec 1947

Displacement, tons: 8 200 standard; 9 200 full load
Length, feet (metres): 590·5 *(180·0)* wl; 597 *(182·0)* oa
Beam, feet (metres): 54 *(16·5)*
Draught, feet (metres): 21·5 *(6·6)*
Guns: 7—6 in *(150 mm)* 53 cal. 4—57 mm; 11—40 mm
Tubes: 6—21 inch
Armour: 3 in—5 in *(75—125 mm)*
Main engines: 2 sets De Laval geared turbines; 100 000 shp; 2 shafts
Boilers: 4 Swedish 4-drum type
Speed, knots: 33
Complement: 610

Radar control arrangements were installed for 6-inch guns. Fitted for minelaying with a capacity of 120 mines. Reconstructed in 1951-52, modernised in 1958, with new radar, 57 mm guns etc.

Gunnery: The 6 inch guns are high angle automatic anti-aircraft weapons with an elevation of 70 degrees.

Radar: Search: LW-03, Type 227. Tactical: Type 293. Fire Control: I band.

Transfer: Purchased by Chile from Sweden July 1971.

LATORRE

1973, Chilean Navy

1 "PRAT" CLASS

Name	No.	Builders	Laid down	Launched	Commissioned
PRAT (ex-USS *Nashville* CL 43)	03	New York S.B. Corp.	24 Jan 1935	2 Oct 1937	25 Nov 1938

Displacement, tons: 10 000 standard; 13 500 full load
Length, feet (metres): 608·3 *(185·4)* oa
Beam, feet (metres): 69 *(21·0)*
Draught, feet (metres): 24 *(7·3)*
Aircraft: 1 Bell helicopter
Guns: 15—6 in *(153 mm)* 47 cal (5 triple); 8—5 in *(127 mm)* 25 cal (single); 28—40 mm; 24—20 mm
Armour, inches (mm):
  Belt 4 in—1½ in *(102—38)*;
  Decks 3 in—2 in *(76—51)*;
  Turrets 5 in—3 in *(127—76)*; C.T. 8 in *(203)*
Main engines: Parsons geared turbines 100 000 shp; 4 shafts
Boilers: 8 Babcock & Wilcox Express type
Oil fuel, tons: 2 100
Speed, knots: 32·5
Range, miles: 14 500 at 15 knots
Complement: 888 to 975 (peace)

Former cruiser of the US "Brooklyn" Class. Purchased from the United States in 1951 at a price representing 10 per cent of original cost ($37 000 000) plus the expense of reconditioning.

Class: *O'Higgins* (ex-USS *Brooklyn*) was damaged by grounding in August 1974. She has subsequently been used as an alongside accommodation ship and is no longer considered operational.

Hangar: The hangar in the hull right aft could accommodate 6 aircraft if necessary together with engine spares and duplicate parts, though 4 aircraft was the normal capacity. Above the hangar two catapults were mounted as far outboard as possible, and a revolving crane was placed at the stern extremity overhanging the aircraft hatch.

Radar: Search: SPS 12. Tactical: SPS 10.

PRAT

1974, Chilean Navy

DESTROYERS

2 "ALMIRANTE" CLASS

Name	No.	Builders	Laid down	Launched	Commissioned
ALMIRANTE RIVEROS	18	Vickers-Armstrong Ltd, Barrow	12 Apr 1957	12 Dec 1958	31 Dec 1960
ALMIRANTE WILLIAMS	19	Vickers-Armstrong Ltd, Barrow	20 June 1956	5 May 1958	26 Mar 1960

Displacement, tons: 2 730 standard; 3 300 full load
Length, feet (metres): 402 *(122·5)* oa
Beam, feet (metres): 43 *(13·1)*
Draught, feet (metres): 13·3 *(4·0)*
Missiles: 4 Exocet MM 38 Launchers;
  2 Quadruple launchers for "Seacat"
Guns: 4—4 in *(102 mm)*; 4—40 mm (singles)
A/S weapons: 2 Squid 3-barrelled DC mortars;
  2 triple Mk 32 launchers
Main engines: Parsons Pametrada geared turbines; 54 000 shp; 2 shafts
Boilers: 2 Babcock & Wilcox
Speed, knots: 34·5
Range, miles: 6 000 at 16 knots
Complement: 266

Ordered in May 1955. Layout and general arrangements are conventional. Bunks fitted for entire crew. Both modernised by Swan Hunter, *Almirante Williams* in 1971-74 and *Almirante Riveros* in 1973-75.

Electrical: The electrical system is on alternating current. Galleys are all electric. There is widespread use of fluorescent lighting. Degaussing cables are fitted.

Gunnery: The four inch guns are in four single mountings, two superimposed forward and two aft. They are automatic with a range of 12 500 yards *(11 400 metres)* and an elevation of 75 degrees.

Missiles: British "Seacat" surface-to-air installations were fitted at the Chilean Navy Yard at Talcahuano in 1964. Exocet MM 38 fitted during modernisations.

Operational: The operations room and similar spaces are air-conditioned. Twin rudders. Ventilation and heating system designed to suit Chilean conditions, extending from the tropics to the Antarctic.

Radar: Plessey AWSI and Target Indication radar with AIO autonomous displays being fitted at refits.

ALMIRANTE WILLIAMS

1974, Swan Hunter

ALMIRANTE WILLIAMS

1974, Swan Hunter

2 Ex-US "FLETCHER" CLASS

	No.	Builders	Laid down	Launched	Commissioned
	14	Bath Iron Works Corpn, Bath	Mar 1943	7 Aug 1943	19 Oct 1943
	15	Todd Pacific Shipyards	Jan 1944	6 June1944	2 Sep 1944

Name
BLANCO ENCALADA (ex-USS *Wadleigh DD 689*)
COCHRANE (ex-USS *Rooks DD 804*)

1972, Chilean Navy

Displacement, tons: 2 100 standard; 2 750 full load
Length, feet (metres): 376·5 *(110·5)* oa
Beam, feet (metres): 39·5 *(12·0)*
Draught, feet (metres): 18 *(5·5)*
Guns: 4—5 in *(127 mm)* 38 cal; 6—3 in *(76 mm)* 50 cal
Torpedo tubes: 5—21 in (quintupled)
A/S weapons: 2 Hedgehogs; 2 side launching torpedo racks;
  1 DC rack; 6 "K" DCT
Main engines: 2 Westinghouse geared turbines; 60 000 shp;
  2 shafts
Boilers: 4 Babcock & Wilcox
Speed, knots: 35
Oil fuel, tons: 650
Range, miles: 5 000 at 15 knots; 1 260 at 30 knots
Complement: 250 (14 officers, 236 men). Accommodation for
  324 (24 officers, 300 men)

Transferred to Chile under the Military Aid Programme in 1963.
Three more destroyers were scheduled for transfer from the
United States Navy to the Chilean Navy under a new transfer
law signed by the President of the United States in 1966. The
ships were to have been refitted and modernised and adapted
to Chilean requirements before transfer to the new flag, but the
four Frigates of the US "Charles Lawrence" Class were transferred instead.

Radar: Search: SPS 6. Tactical: SPS 10. Fire control: I Band.

COCHRANE

2 Ex-US "ALLEN M. SUMNER FRAM II" CLASS

	No.	Builders	Laid down	Launched	Commissioned
	17	Federal SB and DD Co.	1943	13 Mar 1944	17 May 1944
	16	Todd (Pacific) Shipyards	1944	30 Sep 1944	26 Dec 1944

Name
MINISTRO PORTALES (ex-USS *Douglas H. Fox, DD 779*)
MINISTRO ZENTENO (ex-USS *Charles S. Sperry, DD 697*)

Displacement, tons: 2 200 standard; 3 320 full load
Length, feet (metres): 376·5 *(114·8)* oa
Beam, feet (metres): 40·9 *(12·4)*
Draught, feet (metres): 19 *(5·8)*
Guns: 6—5 in *(127 mm)* 38 cal
A/S weapons: 2 triple Mk 32 launchers; 2 Hedgehogs; Facilities
  for small helicopter
Main engines: 2 Geared Turbines; 60 000 shp; 2 shafts
Boilers: 4
Speed, knots: 34
Range, miles: 4 600 at 15 knots
Complement: 274

Transferred 8 Jan 1974.

MINISTRO PORTALES (as *Douglas H. Fox*)

1969, United States Navy

FRIGATES

2 BRITISH "LEANDER" CLASS

Name	No.	Builders	Laid down	Launched	Commissioned
CONDELL	06	Yarrow & Co. Ltd.	5 June 1971	12 June 1972	21 Dec 1973
LYNCH	07	Yarrow & Co. Ltd.	6 Dec 1972	6 Dec 1972	25 May 1974

Displacement, tons: 2 500 standard; 2 962 full load
Length, feet (metres): 360·0 *(109·7)* wl; 372·0 *(113·4)* oa
Beam, feet (metres): 43·0 *(13·1)*
Draught, feet (metres): 18·0 *(5·5)*
Aircraft: 1 light helicopter
Missile launchers: 4 Exocet launchers; 1 quadruple "Seacat"
Guns: 2—4·5 in (1 twin); 2—20 mm
Main engines: 2 geared turbines; 30 000 shp
Boilers: 2
Speed, knots: 30
Range, miles: 4 500 at 12 knots
Complement: 263

Ordered from Yarrow & Co Ltd, Scotstoun in the modernisation programme of the Chilean Navy. Until the Swedish cruiser was acquired, *Condell,* laid down on 5 June 1971, was to have been named *Latorre.* Renamed 1971. Both arrived in Chilean waters by February 1975.

LYNCH   10/1974, C. and S. Taylor

4 Ex-US "CHARLES LAWRENCE" CLASS

Name	No.	Builders	Laid down	Launched	Commissioned
SERRANO (ex-USS *Odum,* APD 71, ex-DE 670)	26	—	1943	19 Jan 1944	1944
ORELLA (ex-USS *Jack C. Robinson,* APD 72, ex-DE 671)	27	—	1943	8 Jan 1944	1944
RIQUELME (ex-USS *Joseph E. Campbell,* APD 49, ex-DE 70)	28	—	1943	26 June 1943	1944
URIBE (ex-USS *Daniel Griffin,* APD 38, ex-DE 54)	29	—	1942	25 Feb 1943	1943

Displacement, tons: 1 400 standard; 2 130 full load
Length, feet (metres): 300·0 *(91·4)* wl; 306·0 *(93·3)* oa
Beam, feet (metres): 37·0 *(11·3)*
Draught, feet (metres): 12·6 *(3·8)*
Guns: 1—5 in 38 cal; 6—40 mm
Main engines: GE turbo-electric; 2 shafts; 12 000 shp = 23·6
  knots; 2 turbines 6 000 hp each; 2 generators 4 500 kW each
Boilers: 2 Foster Wheeler "D" type
Range, miles: 5 000 at 15 knots; 2 000 at 23 knots
Complement: 209

These former high speed transports (APD) were purchased from the USA, transferred at Orange, Texas 25 Nov 1966 (first two) and Norfolk Va 1 Dec 1966 *(Uribe).* They have been modernised, *Riquelme* was also transferred but is reported as being used for provision of spare parts.

ORELLA   1974, Chilean Navy

SUBMARINES

2 BRITISH "OBERON" CLASS

Name	No.	Builders	Laid down	Launched	Commissioned
O'BRIEN	22	Scotts, Greenock	17 Jan 1971	21 Dec 1972	April 1976
HYATT (ex-*Condell*)	23	Scotts, Greenock	10 Jan 1972	26 Sep 1973	Aug 1976

Displacement, tons: 1 610 standard; 2 030 surfaced;
  2 410 dived
Length, feet (metres): 241·0 *(73·5)* pp; 295·2 *(90·0)* oa
Beam, feet (metres): 26·5 *(8·1)*
Draught, feet (metres): 18·1 *(5·5)*
Torpedo tubes: 8—21 in *(533 mm)*
Main machinery: 2 diesels 3 680 bhp; 2 electric motors
  6 000 shp; 2 shafts, electric drive
Speed, knots: 12 surfaced; 17 dived

Ordered from Scott's Shipbuilding & Engineering Co Ltd, Greenock, late 1969. Both have suffered delays in fitting out due to re-cabling and a minor explosion in *Hyatt* in Jan 1976. Original completion was due in July 1974 and Apr 1975 (see new commissioning dates above).

O'BRIEN   1974, W. Ralston

CORVETTES

Name	No.	Builders	Commissioned
PAPUDO	37	Asmar, Talcahuano	27 Nov 1971

Displacement, tons: 450
Dimensions, feet (metres): 173·0 × 23·0 × 12·0 (52·8 × 7 × 3·7)
Guns: 1—40 mm; 4—20 mm
A/S weapons: 1 Hedgehog; 4 "K" DCT; 1 DC rack
Complement: 69 (4 officers, 65 men)

Of similar design to the Turkish "Akhisar" class built to the US PC plan.

PAPUDO   *1972, Chilean Navy*

2 Ex-US "MARICOPA" CLASS

Name	No.	Builders	Commissioned
LAUTARO (ex-USS *ATA 122*)	62	Levingstone SB Co, Orange	1943
LIENTUR (ex-USS *ATA 177*)	60	Levingstone SB Co, Orange	1944

Displacement, tons: 534 standard; 835 full load
Dimensions, feet (metres): 134·5 wl; 143 oa × 33 × 13·2 (43·6 × 10·1 × 4)
Guns: 1—3 in; 2—20 mm
Main engines: GM diesel-electric; 1 500 shp = 12·5 knots
Oil fuel, tons: 187
Complement: 33

Launched— *Lautaro* 27 Nov 1942, *Lientur* 5 June 1944. Originally ocean rescue tugs (ATRs), transferred to the Chilean Navy and reclassified as patrol vessels.

LAUTARO   *1969, Chilean Navy*

1 Ex-US "APACHE" CLASS

Name	No.	Builders	Commissioned
SERGENTO ALDEA (ex-USS *Arikara, ATF 98*)	63	—	1943

Displacement, tons: 1 235 standard; 1 675 full load
Dimensions, feet (metres): 195·0 wl; 205·0 oa × 38·5 × 15·5 (62·5 × 11·7 × 4·7)
Guns: 1—3 in 50 cal
Main engines: Diesel Electric; 1 shaft; 3 000 bhp = 15 knots
Complement: 85

Launched on 22 June 1943. Transferred on 1 July 1971.

LIGHT FORCES

4 LÜRSSEN TYPE (FAST ATTACK CRAFT—TORPEDO)

Name	No.	Builders	Commissioned
GUACOLDA	80	Bazan, Cadiz	30 July 1965
FRESIA	81	Bazan, Cadiz	9 Dec 1965
QUIDORA	82	Bazan, Cadiz	1966
TEGUALDA	83	Bazan, Cadiz	1966

Displacement, tons: 134
Dimensions, feet (metres): 118·1 × 18·4 × 7·2 (36 × 5·6 × 2·2)
Guns: 2—40 mm
Tubes: 4—21 in
Main engines: Diesels; 2 shafts; 4 800 bhp = 32 knots
Range, miles: 1 500 at 15 knots
Complement: 20

Built to German Lürssen design.

FRESIA   *1974, Chilean Navy*

1 COASTAL PATROL CRAFT

CONTRAMAESTRO ORTIZ 79

Displacement, tons: 33
Length, feet (metres): 59·4 (18·1)
Guns: 2—20 mm
Speed, knots: 15

2 COASTAL PATROL CRAFT

Two 32 ft Equity Standard Craft delivered in 1968. Diesel; 400 hp = 35 knots.

2 LARGE PATROL CRAFT

Name	No.	Builders	Commissioned
MARINERO FUENTEALBAS	75	Asmar, Talcahuano	22 July 1966
CABO ODGER	76	Asmar, Talcahuano	21 Apr 1967

Displacement, tons: 215
Dimensions, feet (metres): 80 × 21 × 9 (24·4 × 6·4 × 2·7)
Gun: 1—20 mm
Main engines: One Cummins diesel 340 hp = 9 knots
Range, miles: 2 600 at 9 knots
Complement: 19

FUENTEALBAS

1972, Chilean Navy

AMPHIBIOUS FORCES

4 Ex-US LANDING SHIPS (TANK)

Name	No.	Builders	Commissioned
COMANDANTE HEMMERDINGER (ex-USS *New London County, LST 1066*)	88	—	1944
COMANDANTE ARAYA (ex-USS *Nye County, LST 1067*)	89	—	1944
AGUILA (ex-USS *Aventinus ARVE 3*, ex-*LST 1092*)	91	American Bridge Co, Ambridge	19 May 1945
COMANDANTE TORO (ex-USS *LST 277*)	97	—	1945

Displacement, tons: 1 653 standard; 4 080 full load
Dimensions, feet (metres): 328 × 50 × 14 (100 × 15·3 × 4·3)
Guns: Fitted for 8—40 mm
Main engines: GM Diesels; 1 700 shp; 2 shafts = 11·6 knots
Complement: approx 110

Nos 88 and 89 transferred 29 Aug 1973. No 91 was a conversion to Aircraft Repair Ship and was transferred to Chile in 1963 under MAP. No. 97 was transferred 2 Feb 1973. After various employments all are now available for amphibiuos duties. Dimensions of No 97 vary very slightly from the others.

Name	No.	Builders	Commissioned
ASPIRANTE MOREL (ex-USS *Aloto, LSM 444*)	92	—	1945

Displacement, tons: 743 standard; 1 095 full load
Dimensions, feet (metres): 196·5 wl; 203·5 oa × 34·5 × 7·3 (62·1 × 10·5 × 2·2)
Main engines: Diesel; 2 shafts; 2 800 bhp = 12 knots
Oil fuel (tons): 60
Range, miles: 2 500 at 9 knots
Complement: 60

ASPIRANTE MOREL

1972, Chilean Navy

Former United States medium landing ship launched in 1945. *Aspirante Morel* (ex-*Aloto*) was leased to Chile on 2 Sep 1960 at Pearl Harbour to replace the older LSM of the same name.

1 Ex-US LANDING CRAFT (TANK)

Name	No.	Builders	Commissioned
GRUMETE DIAZ (ex-*LCU 1396*)	96	–	1944

Displacement, tons: 143 to 160 light; 329 full load
Dimensions, feet (metres): 105 wl; 119 oa × 32·7 × 5 (36·3 × 10 × 1·5)
Main engines: Diesels; 3 shafts; 675 bhp = 10 knots
Oil fuel (tons): 11
Range, miles; 700 at 7 knots
Complement: 12

Former United States tank landing craft of the LCT (6) type. Transferred by sale June 1970, in use as harbour craft.

2 CHILEAN LANDING CRAFT

Name	No.	Builders	Commissioned
ELICURA	90	Talcahuano	10 Dec 1968
OROMPELLO	94	Dade Dry Dock Co, Miami	15 Sep 1964

Displacement, tons: 290 light; 750 full load
Dimensions, feet (metres): 138 wl; 145 oa × 34 × 12·8 (44·2 × 10·4 × 3·9)
Main engines: Diesels; 2 shafts; 900 bhp = 10·5 knots
Oil fuel (tons): 77
Range, miles: 2 900 at 9 knots
Complement: 20

Orompello was built for the Chilean Government in Miami, *Elicura* was launched on 21 April 1967.

OROMPELLO

1971, Chilean Navy

SURVEY SHIP

1 ex-US "CHEROKEE" CLASS

Name	No.	Builders	Commissioned
YELCHO (ex-USS *Tekesta, ATF 93*)	64	Commercial Iron Works, Portland, Oregon	16 Aug 1943

Displacement, tons: 1 235 standard; 1 675 full load
Dimensions, feet (metres): 195 wl; 205 oa × 38.5 × 15.3 *(62.5 × 11.7 × 4.7)*
Guns: 2—40 mm
Main engines: 4 diesels/Diesel electric; 1 shaft; 3 000 bhp = 16 knots
Complement: 85

Fitted with powerful pumps and other salvage equipment. *Yelcho* was laid down on 7 Sep 1942, launched on 20 Mar 1943 and loaned to Chile by the USA on 15 May 1960, having since been employed as Antarctic research ship and surveying vessel.

YELCHO

1972, Chilean Navy

TRAINING SHIP

Name	No.	Builders	Commissioned
ESMERALDA (ex-*Don John de Austria*)	43	Echevarietta, Cadiz	1952

Displacement, tons: 3 040 standard; 3 673 full load
Dimensions, feet (metres): 308.8 oa × 43 × 23 *(94.2 × 13.1 ×7)*
Guns: 2—57 mm
Sail area: Total 26 910 sq feet
Main engines: 1 Fiat Auxiliary diesel; 1 shaft; 1 400 bhp = 11 knots
Range, miles: 8 000 at 8 knots
Complement: 271 plus 80 cadets

Four-masted schooner originally intended for the Spanish Navy. Transferred to Chile on 12 May 1953. Near sister ship of *Juan Sebastian de Elcano* in the Spanish Navy. Replaced transport *Presidente Pinto* as training ship.

ESMERALDA

1974, Chilean Navy

TRANSPORTS

Name	No.	Builders	Commissioned
AQUILES (ex-*Tjaldur*)	47	Aalborg Vaerft, Denmark	1953

Measurement, tons: 2 660 registered; 1 462 net; 1 395 dw
Dimensions, feet (metres): 288 × 44 × 17 *(87.8 × 13.4 × 5.2)*
Main engines: 1 Slow Burmeister and Wain Diesel; 3 600 bhp = 16 knots
Range, miles: 5 500 at 16 knots
Complement: 60 crew plus 447 troops

Ex-Danish MV *Tjaldur* bought by Chile in 1967.

AQUILES

1968, Chilean Navy

Name	No.	Builders	Commissioned
PILOTO PARDO	45	Haarlemsche Scheepsbouw, Netherlands	1959

Displacement, tons: 1 250 light; 2 000 standard; 3 000 full load
Dimensions, feet (metres): 269 × 39 × 15 *(82 × 11.9 × 4.6)*
Aircraft: 1 helicopter
Guns: 1—101 mm 50 cal; 2—20 mm
Main engines: 2 diesel-electric; 2 000 hp = 14 knots
Range, miles: 6 000 at 10 knots
Complement: 44 (plus 24 passengers)

Antarctic patrol ship, transport and research vessel with reinforced hull to navigate in ice. Launched 11 June 1958.

PILOTO PARDO

1974, Chilean Navy

Name	No.	Builders	Commissioned
METEORO	110	Asmar, Talcahuano	1967

Displacement, tons: 205
Main engines: Diesel = 8 knots

Transport for 220 Troops.

Name	No.	Builders	Commissioned
CIRUJANO VIDELA	111	Asmar, Talcahuano	1964

Displacement, tons: 140
Dimensions, feet (metres): 101.7 × 21.3 × 6.6 *(31 × 6.5 × 2)*
Main engines: Diesel; 700 hp = 14 knots

Hospital and dental facilities are fitted.

TANKERS

1 ex-US "PATAPSCO" CLASS

Name	No.	Builders	Commissioned
BEAGLE (ex-USS *Genesee* AOG 8)	54	Cargill Inc., Savage, Minn.	27 May 1944

Displacement, tons: 4 240 standard
Dimensions, feet (metres): 310 × 48·7 × 16 *(94·6 × 14·9 × 4·9)*
Guns: 2—3 inch 50 cal; 4—20 mm
Range, miles: 6 690 at 10 knots

Transferred on loan 5 July 1972.

BEAGLE

1972, Chilean Navy

Name	No.	Builders	Commissioned
ARAUCANO	53	Burmeister & Wain, Copenhagen	10 Jan 1967

Displacement, tons: 17 300
Measurement, tons: 18 030 deadweight
Dimensions, feet (metres): 497·6 × 74·9 × 28·8 *(151·8 × 22·8 × 8·8)*
Guns: 4—40 mm
Main engines: B and W diesels; 10 800 bhp = 15·5 knots (17 on trial)
Range, miles: 12 000 at 15·5 knots

Launched on 21 June 1966.

ARAUCANO

1972, U.S. Navy

Name	No.	Builders	Commissioned
ALMIRANTE JORGE MONTT	52	Ateliers et Chantiers de la Seine Maritime, Le Trait	Mar 1956

Displacement, tons: 9 000 standard; 17 500 full load
Measurement, tons: 11 800 gross; 17 750 deadweight
Dimensions, feet (metres): 548 × 67·5 × 30 *(167·1 × 20·6 × 9·2)*
Main engines: Rateau Bretagne geared turbine; 1 shaft; 6 300 shp = 14 knots
Boilers: 2 Babcock & Wilcox
Range, miles: 16 500 at 14 knots

Laid down in 1954. Launched on 14 Jan 1956.

ALMIRANTE JORGE MONTT

1969, Chilean Navy

FLOATING DOCKS

2 Ex-US ARD

MUTILLA (ex-US *ARD 32*) 132   **INGENIERO MERY** (ex-US *ARD 25*) 131

Displacement, tons: 5 200
Capacity, tons: 3 000
Dimensions, feet (metres): 492 × 84 × 5·7 to 33·2 *(150·1 × 25·6 × 1·7 to 10·1)*

Mutilla leased to Chile 15 Dec 1960. *Ingeniero Mery* transferred 20 Aug 1973.
2 Floating Cranes of 30 and 180 tons lift are at Talcahuano.

TUGS

Name	No.	Builders	Commissioned
COLOCOLO	73	Bow, McLachlan & Co, Paisley	1930

Displacement, tons: 790
Dimensions, feet (metres): 126·5 × 27·0 × 12·0 *(38·6 × 8·2 × 3·7)*
Main engines: Triple expansion; 1 050 ihp = 11 knots
Oil fuel, tons: 155

Formerly classed as coastguard vessel. Rebuilt in 1962-63. Last of class of five.

Name	No.	Builders	Commissioned
GALVEZ	—	Southern Shipbuilders Ltd, Faversham, England	June 1975

Measurement, tons: 112 gross
Length, feet (metres): 75 *(22·9)*

Tug HMS *Samson* was reported sold to Chile in 1974 but is still laid up in Portsmouth (1976).

ANCUD 104
CAUPOLICAN 127

CORTEZ 128
MONREAL 105

REYES 120

MISCELLANEOUS

Notes: (a) *Huascar,* completed 1865, previously Peruvian, now harbour flagship at Talcahuano.
(b) Two new ships, *Castor* and *Sabenes,* now listed.

CHINA (People's Republic)

Administration

Minister of National Defence:
Yeh Chien-ying

Headquarters Appointments

Commander-in-Chief of the Navy:
Hsiao Ching Kuang
1st Political Commissar:
Su Chen-Hua
2nd Political Commissar:
Wang Hung-K'un

Fleet Commanders

North Sea Fleet:
Ma Chung-Ch'uan
East Sea Fleet:
Kao Chih-Jung
South Sea Fleet:
Kuei Shao-Pin

Diplomatic Representation

Defence and Naval Attaché in London:
Shih Hsin-jen

Personnel

(a) 1976: 172 000 officers and men, including 20 000 naval air force and 38 000 marines.

(b) 4 years National Service.

Bases

North Sea Fleet: Tsingtao, Lu Shun
East Sea Fleet: Shanghai, Chusan
South Sea Fleet: Huan Pu, Chan Chiang
(The fleet is split with the main emphasis on the North Sea Fleet).

Strength of the Fleet

Type	Active	Building
Destroyers (DDG)	8	3
Frigates	10	?1
Corvettes	35	4
Fleet Submarines	1	?
Missile Firing Submarines	1	—
Patrol Submarines	60	6
Fast Attack Craft (Missile)	120	20
Fast Attack Craft (Gun)	438	?20
Fast Attack Craft (Torpedo)	240	?10
Minesweepers (Ocean)	16	—
Minesweepers (Coastal)	6	—
Landing Ships (LST)	15	—
LSMs	18	?4
LSILs	15	—
LCTs	15	—
LCMs	450	—
Survey & Research Ships	9	—
Range Instrumentation Ships	4	?
Supply Ships	16 (+?12)	—
Tankers (small)	10	—
Boom Defence Vessels	6	—
Escorts (old)	13	—
Repair Ship	1	—
Misc. Small Craft	375	—

Mercantile Marine

Lloyd's Register of Shipping:
360 vessels of 1 870 567 tons gross

The Chinese Navy

Despite setbacks under the Manchus, the Chinese have possessed a navy in some force since 200 BC. In addition they have had the will and capability to use their fleet, as their expeditions to the Persian Gulf and Africa in the 15th Century bear witness. So today's navy has a tradition older than any other except the Greek and Italian and a modern, rapidly expanding force capable of operations abroad. While studying this section it must be remembered that not only is there a steady building programme of all classes in the modernised Chinese Yards but also the Chinese have an advanced nuclear and missile capability. This combination will make the Chinese navy, already twice as strong in manpower as the Royal Navy, an important element in the future balance of power East of Suez.

In the last year there has been evidence of delays in all the new building programmes except Light Forces. Whether this is due to problems of weapon production, faults discovered in new construction ships or a straight political decision is not known. It is of interest that these delays appear to date from 1972, shortly after the flight and death of Lin Piao, the Defence Minister under whom the programmes were presumably generated. This may be coincidence but the plain fact is that the main emphasis today is on defensive units rather than the long-range projection forces whose design must have started in the mid or early 1960s.

Naval Air Force

With 20 000 officers and men and over 450 aircraft, this is a considerable land-based naval air force. Equipped with about 400 MIG 17 and 19 (and possibly MIG 21) fighter aircraft and SA2-SAM, with 100 IL 28 Torpedo bombers, Tu-2 bombers, Madge flying boats, Hound M14 helicopters and transport and communication aircraft this is primarily a defensive force. Chinese ingenuity should find little difficulty in getting a proportion of these aircraft afloat, particularly in view of the increasing tempo of their shipbuilding programme.

"LUTA" Class

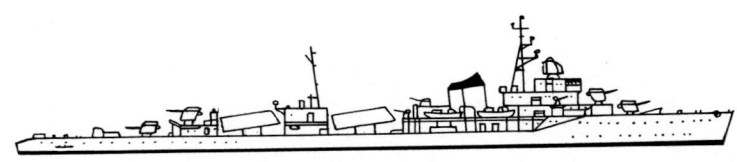

"GORDY" Class

"KIANGNAN" Class

"RIGA" Class

"KRONSTADT" Class

DESTROYERS

4 + 3 "LUTA" CLASS (DDG)

Name	No.	Builders	Laid down	Launched	Commissioned
—	240	Dairen (Luta)	—	—	1971
—	241	Dairen (Luta)	—	—	1972
—	242	Dairen (Luta)	—	—	1972
—	243	Dairen (Luta)	—	—	1973
—	—	—	—	—	—
—	—	—	—	—	—

Displacement, tons: 3 250 standard; 3 750 full load
Dimensions, feet (metres): 450 × 45 × 15 (137·3 × 13·7 × 4·6)
Missile launchers: 2 Twin SSN-2 type
Guns: 4—130 mm (2 twins) 8—57 mm 8—25 mm
A/S weapons: 2—A/S rocket launchers
Main engines: Geared turbines
Speed: 32+
Range, miles (estimated): 4 000 at 15 knots
Complement (approx): 300

Radar: Air search: Slim Net and Cross Slot.
Fire control, guns: Wasphead.
Fire control, missiles: Square Tie.
Navigation: Neptun.

"LUTA" Class

1972, Chinese

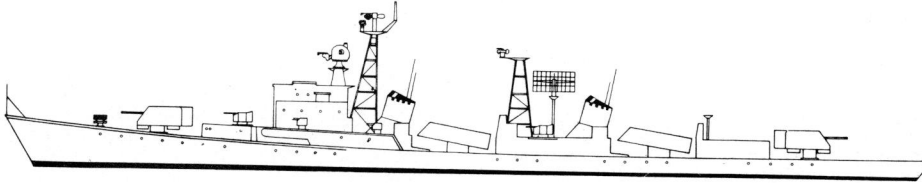

"LUTA" Class

1973

4 Ex-SOVIET "GORDY" CLASS

Name	No.	Builders	Laid down	Launched	Commissioned
ANSHAN	—	USSR	—	1936-41	1939-43
CHANG CHUN	—	USSR	—	1936-41	1939-43
CHI LIN	—	USSR	—	1936-41	1939-43
FU CHUN	—	USSR	—	1936-41	1939-43

Displacement, tons: 1 657 standard; 2 040 full load
Length, feet (meters): 357·7 (109·0) pp; 370 (112·8) oa
Beam, feet (metres): 33·5 (10·2)
Draught, feet (metres): 13 (4·0)
Missile launchers: 2 twin SSN—2
Guns: 4—5·1 in (130 mm); 8—37 mm (twins)
A/S weapons: 8 DCT
Main engines: Tosi geared turbines; 48 000 shp; 2 shafts
Boilers: 3-drum type
Speed, knots: 36
Oil fuel, tons: 540
Range, miles: 800 at 36 knots; 2 600 at 19 knots
Complement: 250

CHANG CHUN (before conversion)

Hajime Fukaya

Gordy Type 7 of Odero-Terni-Orlando design. Fitted for minelaying. Two transferred in Dec 1954 and two in July 1955.

Conversion: All converted between 1971 and 1974. The alterations consist of the replacement of the torpedo tubes by a pair of twin SSN-2 launchers and the fitting of twin 37 mm mounts in place of the original singles.

Radar: Air Search: Cross Bird. Fire Control: Square Tie. Navigation: Neptune. IFF Ski pole.

FRIGATES

1 + 1(?) "KIANGTUNG" CLASS

Name	No.	Builders	Laid down	Launched	Commissioned
CHUNG TUNG	—	Hutang-Shanghai	1971	1973	1974

Displacement, tons: 1 800 tons standard
Dimensions, feet (metres): 350 × 40 approx *(106 × 12)*
Missiles: 2 twin SAM
Guns: 4 3·9 in *(100 mm)* twin; 8—37 mm
A/S weapons: 2 A/S Mortars; 2 DCT
Main engines: Diesel = ? 28 knots

There have apparently been no further additions to this class—further evidence of the delays in new construction of major surface ships.

5 "KIANGNAN" CLASS

Name	No.	Builders	Laid down	Launched	Commissioned
—	230	Canton/Shanghai	1965	—	1967
—	231	Canton/Shanghai	1965	—	1967
—	232	Canton/Shanghai	1966	—	1968
—	233	Canton/Shanghai	1966	—	1968
—	234	Canton/Shanghai	1967	—	1969

Displacement, tons: 1 350 standard; 1 600 full load
Length, feet (metres): 298 *(90·8)*
Beam, feet (metres): 33·5 *(10·2)*
Draught, feet (metres): 11 *(3·4)*
Guns: 3—3·9 in *(100 mm)* 56 cal, 1 fwd, 2 aft;
6 or 8—37 mm (twin); 4 or 8—25 mm (twin)
A/S weapons: Depth charges
Main engines: Diesels; 9 000 shp
Speed, knots: 28
Complement: 175

"KIANGNAN" Class   1973

The Chinese Navy embarked on a new building programme in 1965 of which this class was the first.

Radar: Fire Control: Sun Visor.

4 "RIGA" CLASS

Name	No.	Builders	Laid down	Launched		Commissioned
CH'ENG TU	—	Hutang, Shanghai	1954	28 Apr	1956	1958
KUEI LIN	—		1955	26 Sept	1956	1958
KUEI YANG	—	Hutang, Shanghai	—	1957		1959
K'UN MING	—		—	1957		1959

Displacement, tons: 1 200 standard; 1 600 full load
Length, feet (metres): 298·8 *(91)* oa
Beam, feet (metres): 33·7 *(10·2)*
Draught, feet (metres): 10 *(3·0)*
Missile launchers: 1 twin SSN—2
Guns: 3—3·9 in *(100 mm)* (single); 4—37 mm
A/S weapons: 4 DC projectors
Mines: 50 capacity, fitted with rails
Main engines: Geared turbines; 2 shafts; 25 000 shp
Boilers: 2
Speed, knots: 28
Oil fuel, tons: 300
Range, miles: 2 500 at 15 knots
Complement: 150

First of the class had light tripod mast, but was later converted with heavier mast and larger bridge as in the other three. Similar to the Soviet "Riga" class frigates. Two were redesigned with modified superstructure.

Conversion: Two started conversion in 1971 for the replacement of the torpedo tubes by a twin SSN-2 launcher. All now converted.

Radar: Surface warning: Slim Net.
Fire Control: Sun Visor for Guns, Square Tie for missiles.
Navigation: Neptune.

"RIGA" Class (before conversion)   1971

SUBMARINES

Note: In 1973 the visit to West Germany from Peking of a party led by Professor Chang Wei highlighted Chinese interest in nuclear propulsion for ships. It also suggests that the Chinese may be meeting design problems as such visits are rare events.

However, reports suggest the construction of at least one nuclear submarine. This combined with the known Chinese capability to build liquid-fuelled rockets of the MRBM, IRBM and

ICBM types and the completion of a solid-propellant factory, suggests that the forecast of a Chinese ballistic-missile nuclear submarine in the early 1980s may not be out of the question.

1 "HAN" CLASS

This is the first report of a possible Chinese nuclear submarine. With an Albacore hull the first of this class was probably laid

down in 1971-72. Its construction may have been delayed if the problems mentioned in the note above have been encoun-

tered, but it appears to have run trials in 1974. Existence of a second "Han" class is reported but not confirmed. Built at Luta.

Displacement, tons: Possibly about 1 500 tons standard
Length, feet: Possibly about 250 feet
Armament: Possibly 6—21 in tubes
Main machinery: Probably diesels and main motors

2 "MING" CLASS

First believed to have been laid down in 1971-72 which would give an operational date around late 1974 or 1975.

1 SOVIET "GOLF" CLASS

(BALLISTIC MISSILE TYPE)

Displacement, tons: 2 350 surfaced; 2 800 dived
Length, feet (metres): 320·0 *(97·5)*
Beam, feet (metres): 25·1 *(7·6)*
Draught, feet (metres): 22·0 *(6·7)*
Missile launchers: 3 vertical tubes
Torpedo tubes: 10—21 in *(533 mm)* bow
Main machinery: 3 diesels, total 6 000 hp; 3 shafts
  3 electric motors, total 6 000 hp
Speed, knots: 20 surfaced; 17 dived
Range, miles: 22 700 surfaced; cruising
Complement: 86 (1 officers, 74 men)

Ballistic missile submarine similar to the Soviet "Golf" class. Built at Dairen in 1964. The missile tubes are fitted in the conning tower. It is not known whether this boat has been fitted with missiles, although it is possible and well within Chinese technical capability (see note above concerning SLBMs).

"GOLF" Class   1972

36 SOVIET "ROMEO" CLASS (PATROL TYPE)

Displacement, tons: 1 100 surfaced; 1 600 dived
Length, feet (metres): 246·0 *(75·0)*
Beam, feet (metres): 24 *(7·3)*
Draught, feet (metres): 14·5 *(4·4)*
Torpedo tubes: 6—21 in (bow) 18 torpedoes
Main machinery: 2 diesels; total 4 000 hp; 2 Electric motors;
  total 4 000 hp; 2 shafts
Speed, knots: 17 surfaced; 14 dived
Complement: 65

The Chinese are now building their own Soviet designed "Romeo" class submarines possibly at a rate of 6 a year.

"ROMEO" Class   1975

21 SOVIET "WHISKY" CLASS (PATROL TYPE)

Displacement, tons: 1 030 surfaced; 1 180 dived
Length, feet (metres): 240 *(73·2)*
Beam, feet (metres): 22 *(6·7)*
Draught, feet (metres): 15 *(4·6)*
Torpedo tubes: 6—21 in *(533 mm);* 4 bow 2 stern (20 torpedoes
  or 40 mines)
Main machinery: Diesel-electric; 2 shafts; 4 000 bhp diesels;
  2 500 hp electric motors
Speed, knots: 17 surfaced; 15 dived
Range, miles: 13 000 at 8 knots surfaced
Complement: 60

Equipped with snort. Assembled from Soviet components in Chinese yards between 1956 and 1964.

"WHISKY" Class   1972

1 Ex-SOVIET "M-V" CLASS

(COASTAL PATROL TYPE)

Displacement, tons: 350 surfaced; 420 dived
Length, feet (metres): 167·3 *(51·0)*
Beam, feet (metres): 16·0 *(4·9)*
Draught, feet (metres): 12·1 *(3·7)*
Guns: 1—45 mm; 1 MG
Torpedo tubes: 2—21 in *(533 mm)*
Main machinery: 1 000 hp diesels; 800 hp electric motors
Speed, knots: 13 surface; 10 submerged
Range, miles: 4 000 at 8·5 knots surfaced
Oil fuel, tons: 21
Complement: 24

Designed for coastal operations, latterly used for training and instruction but nearing the end of its life. Four were transferred from the USSR in 1954-55.

2 Ex-SOVIET "S-1" CLASS (PATROL TYPE)

Displacement, tons: 840 surfaced; 1 050 dived
Length, feet (metres): 256 *(78·0)*
Beam, feet (metres): 21 *(6·4)*
Draught, feet (metres): 13 *(4·0)*
Torpedo tubes: 6—21 in *(533 mm)*
Main machinery: 4 200 hp diesels; 2 200 hp electric motors
Speed, knots: 19 surface; 8·5 submerged
Range, miles: 9 800 at 9 knots surfaced
Oil fuel, tons: 105
Complement: 50

Launched in 1939. Transferred from the USSR in 1955.

ESCORTS

Note: It is reported that the majority of these escorts are, in fact, not only still in commission but have been refitted and rearmed.

Class	Total	Names	No.	Displacement tons, standard	Speed (knots)	Guns	Launched	Range, miles	Complement
Ex-Japanese "Ukuru"	1	HUI AN (ex-*Shisaka*)	218	940	19·5	3—3·9 in 4—37 mm	1943	5 000 at 16 knots	—
Ex-Japanese "Etorofu"	1	CHANG PAI (ex-*Oki*)	—	870	19·5	3—3·9 in 3—37 mm	1942	8 000 at 16 knots	—
Ex-Japanese "Uji"	1	NAN CHANG (ex-*Uji*)	—	950	20	2—5·1 in 5—37 mm	1940	3 460 at 14 knots	—
Ex-Japanese "C"	1	SHEN YANG	—	745	16·5	2—5·1 in 6—37 mm	1945	6 500 at 14 knots	150
Ex-Japanese "D"	5	TUNG AN CHANG SHA CHI NAN HSI AN WU CHANG	215 216 217 219 220	740	17·5	2—3 in or 5—37 mm	1944 to 1945	4 500 at 14 knots	150
Ex-Canadian "Castle"	1	KUANG CHOU (ex-*Bowmanville*)	—	1 100	16·5	2—5·1 in 10—37 mm	1944	5 400 at 9·5 knots	120
Ex-British "Flower"	2	KAI FENG (ex-*Clover*)	211						
		LIN I (ex-*Heliotrope*)	213	1 020	16	2—3·9 in	1941	—	—
Ex-Australian "Bathurst"	1	LOYANG (ex-*Bendigo*)	—	815	15	2—3·9 in 4—37 mm	1941	4 300 at 10 knots	100

HUI AN   *1974*

CORVETTES

20 "KRONSTADT" CLASS

Nos.   **251   252   253   261   262   263   264   265   266   286   +   10**

Displacement, tons: 310 standard; 380 full load
Dimensions, feet (metres): 170·6 × 21·5 × 9 *(52 × 6·5 × 2·7)*
Guns: 1—3·5 in; 2—37 mm; 6—12·7 mm
A/S weapons: 2 Rocket launchers; 2 DC racks
Mines: 2 rails for 8-10 mines
Main engines: Diesels; 2 shafts; 3 300 shp = 24 knots
Range, miles: 1 500 at 12 knots
Complement: 65

Six built in 1950-53 were received from USSR in 1956-57. Remainder were built at Shanghai and Canton, with 12 completed in 1956. The last was completed in 1957.

Radar: Ball Gun, Skinhead.

"KRONSTADT" Class firing Rocket Launchers   *1972*

15 "HAINAN" CLASS

Displacement, tons: 500 standard
Dimensions, feet (metres): 200 × 25 × 9 *(61 × 7·6 × 2·7)*
Guns: 2—3 in (fore and aft) (first pair); 4—57 mm (twins) (remainder); 4—25 mm (twins)
Main engines: Diesels; 3 300 shp (estimated)
Speed, knots: About 25

Chinese built. Low freeboard. The 25 mm guns are abaft the bridge. Programme started 1963-64 and continues—probably 4 per year.

Radar: Skinhead.

LIGHT FORCES

60 SOVIET "OSA" and CHINESE "HOLA" CLASS
(FAST ATTACK CRAFT—MISSILE)

Displacement, tons: 165 standard; 200 full load
Dimensions, feet (metres): 128·7 × 25·1 × 5·9 (39·3 × 7·7 × 1·8)
Missiles: 4 SSN-2 system launchers in two pairs abreast aft
Guns: 4—30 mm (2 twin, 1 forward and 1 aft)
Main engines: 3 Diesels; 13 000 bhp = 32 knots
Range, miles: 800 at 25 knots
Complement: 25

It was reported in Jan 1965 that one "Osa" class guided missile patrol boat had joined the Navy from the USSR. Four more were acquired in 1966-67, and two in 1968. A building programme of 10 boats a year in China is assumed. The first boat of the "Hola" class, a Chinese variant of the "Osa", has now joined the fleet. The chief difference is the fitting of a radome aft.

Radar: Square Tie and Drum Tilt in "Osas".

"OSA" Class   1972

60 SOVIET "KOMAR" and CHINESE "HOKU" CLASS
(FAST ATTACK CRAFT—MISSILE)

Displacement, tons: 70 standard; 80 full load
Dimensions, feet (metres): 83·7 oa × 19·8 × 5 (25·5 × 6 × 1·5)
Missiles: 2 SSN-2 system launchers
Guns: 2—25 mm (1 twin forward)
Main engines: Diesels; 2 shafts; 4 800 bhp = 40 knots

One "Komar" class was reported as joining the fleet in 1965. Two more were delivered in 1967 and seven in 1968 to 1971. A building programme of 10 a year is assumed. The first boat of the "Hoku" class, a Chinese variant of the "Komar", has now joined the fleet. The chief difference is the siting of the launchers clear of the bridge and further inboard, eliminating sponsons. A hydrofoil variant has also been reported.

"KOMAR" Class   1972

25 "SHANGHAI" CLASS TYPE I (FAST ATTACK CRAFT—GUN)

Displacement, tons: 100 full load
Dimensions, feet (metres): 115 × 18 × 5·5 (35·1 × 5·5 × 1·7)
Guns: 1—57 mm (forward); 2—37 mm (twin, aft)
Torpedo tubes: Twin 18 in
A/S armament: 8 DCs
Mines: Minerails can be fitted
Main engines: 4 diesels; 4 800 bhp = 28 knots
Complement: 25

The prototype of these boats appeared in 1959. Main difference from successors is lack of midships guns.

Radar: Skinhead.

320 "SHANGHAI" CLASS TYPES II, III and IV
(FAST ATTACK CRAFT—GUN)

Displacement, tons: 120 standard; 155 full load
Dimensions, feet (metres): 128 × 18 × 5·6 (39 × 5·5 × 1·7)
Guns: Type II: 1—57 mm (forward); 2—37 mm (twin, aft); 2—25 mm (twin, abaft bridge)
Types III and IV: 4—37 mm (twins, forward and aft); 2—25 mm (twin abaft bridge)
Note: In some boats a twin 75 mm recoilless rifle is mounted forward
Torpedo tubes: Some earlier boats had twin 18 in tubes mounted abaft the bridge
A/S weapons: 8 DCs
Mines: Minerails can be fitted but probably for no more than 10 mines
Main engines: 4 Diesels; 4 800 bhp = 30 knots
Complement: 25

"SHANGHAI III and IV Class" (with 75 mm forward)

Construction continues at Shanghai and other yards at rate of about 10 a year.

Appearance: The three types vary slightly in the outline of their bridges.

Radar: Skinhead.

Transfers: 4 to Albania, 3 to Congo, 4 to Guinea, 15 to North Korea, 12 to Pakistan, 10 to Romania, 5 to Sri Lanka in 1972, 2 to Sierra Leone in 1973, 6 to Tanzania in 1970-71, 4 to North Vietnam in May 1966.

"SHANGHAI IV" Class   1970

50 "SWATOW" CLASS (FAST ATTACK CRAFT—GUN)

Displacement, tons: 80 full load
Dimensions, feet (metres): 83·5 × 19 × 6·5 (25·5 × 5·8 × 2)
Guns: 4—37 mm, in twin mountings; 2—12·7 mm (some boats mount a twin 75 mm recoilless rifle forward)
A/S weapons: 8 DC
Main engines: 4 diesels; 4 800 bhp = 42 knots
Range, miles: 500 at 30 knots; 750 at 15 knots
Complement: 17

"P 6" class motor torpedo boat hulls with torpedo tubes removed. From 1958 "P-6" hulls were converted to "Swatow" class motor gunboats at Dairen, Canton, and Shanghai.

Transfers: 50 to North Vietnam.

100 "HU CHWAN" CLASS (FAST ATTACK CRAFT—TORPEDO)

Displacement, tons: 45
Dimensions, feet (metres): 70 × 16·6 oa × 7·9 (hullborne) *(21·3 × 5 × 2·5)*
Guns: 4—12·7 mm (2 twins)
Torpedo tubes: 2—21 inch
Main engines: Possibly 2 M50 12 cylinder Diesels; 2 shafts; 2 200 hp = 55 knots in calm conditions
Range, miles: 500 cruising

Hydrofoils designed and built by China, in the Hutang yard, Shanghai. Construction started in 1956. At least 25 hydrofoils were reported to be in the South China Fleet in 1968. Of all-metal construction with a bridge well forward and a low super-structure extending aft. The guns are mounted one pair on the main deck and one on the superstructure. Forward pair of foils can apparently be withdrawn into recesses in the hull. A continuing programme at possibly 10 per year.

Transfers: 30 to Albania, 4 to Pakistan, 1+ to Romania.

"HU CHWAN" Class

60 "P 4" CLASS (FAST ATTACK CRAFT—TORPEDO)

Displacement, tons: 25
Dimensions, feet (metres): 62·7 × 11·6 × 5·6 *(19·1 × 3·5 × 1·7)*
Guns: 2—25 mm
Torpedo tubes: 2—18 in
Main engines: 2 Diesels; 2 200 bhp; 2 shafts = 50 knots

This class has aluminium hulls. Numbers decreasing.

"P 4" Class

80 "P 6" CLASS (FAST ATTACK CRAFT—TORPEDO)

Displacement, tons: 66 standard; 75 full load
Dimensions, feet (metres): 84 × 20 × 6 *(25·7 × 6·1 × 1·8)*
Guns: 4—25 mm
Torpedo tubes: 2—21 in (or mines or DCs)
Main engines: Diesels 5 000 bhp = 43 knots
Range, miles: 450 at 30 knots
Complement: 25

This class has wooden hulls. Some were constructed in Chinese yards. All built since 1966.

Radar: Pothead or Skinhead.

Transfers: 6 to North Vietnam in 1967. 2 to Guinea in 1973.

"P 6" Class

40 "WHAMPOA" CLASS (FAST ATTACK CRAFT—GUN)

Displacement, tons: 40 standard
Length, feet (metres): 80 (approx) *(24·4)*
Guns: 1—37 mm (forward); 2—25 mm (twin, aft)
Main engines: 2 Diesels = 25 knots
Complement: 20

Entered service late 1950s, now probably decreasing in numbers.

3 "SHANTUNG" CLASS (FAST ATTACK CRAFT—GUN)

Displacement, tons: 75-85
Dimensions, feet (metres): 80 × 16 × 6 *(24·4 × 4·9 × 1·8)*
Guns: 4—37 mm (twins)
Speed, knots: 40

Numbers decreasing.

MINE WARFARE FORCES

Note. There are also some 60 auxiliary minesweepers of various types including trawlers.

16 SOVIET "T 43" CLASS (MINESWEEPERS—OCEAN)

Displacement, tons: 500 standard; 610 full load
Dimensions, feet (metres): 190·2 × 28·2 × 6·9 *(58·0 × 8·6 × 2·1)*
Guns: 4—37 mm (2 twin); 4—25 mm (2 twin)
Main engines: 2 diesels; 2 shafts; 2 000 bhp = 17 knots
Range, miles: 1 600 at 10 knots
Complement: 40

Two were acquired from USSR in 1954-55. Eighteen more were built in Chinese shipyards, the first two in 1956. The construction of "T 43" class fleet minesweepers was stopped at Wuchang, but continued at Canton. 3 converted for surveying.

Radar: Skinhead or Ballgun.

1972

"T 43" Class

4 Ex-US YMS TYPE (MINESWEEPERS—COASTAL)

Ex-YMS 346   Ex-YMS 367   Ex-YMS 393   Ex-YMS 2017

Displacement, tons: 270 standard; 350 full load
Dimensions, feet (metres): 136 × 24·5 × 6 *(41·5 × 7·5 × 1·8)*
Guns: 1—3 in; 2—20 mm
A/S weapons: 2 DCT
Main engines: 2 GM Diesels; 1 000 bhp = 13 knots

Built of wood in USA in 1942-43, and transferred to the Chinese Navy in 1948. Some are fitted as gunboats.
Two have one funnel, two have two.

2 Ex-JAPANESE AMS TYPE (MINESWEEPERS—COASTAL)

Ex-No. 4   No. 201 (ex-*No. 14*)

Displacement, tons: 222
Dimensions, feet (metres): 97·1 oa × 19·3 × 7·3 *(29·6 × 5·9 × 2·2)*
Guns: 1—3·1 in; 4—25 mm (No. 201; 1—40 mm; 1—25 mm; 2—13 mm; 3—7·7 mm)
Main engines: 1 Diesel; 300 bhp = 9·5 knots
Range, miles: 1 700 at 9·5 knots

Ex-Japanese auxiliary minesweepers. Trawler type No. 201, completed in 1943, was delivered to China at Tsingtau on 3 Oct 1947, and taken over by the Chinese Republic.

AMPHIBIOUS WARFARE FORCES

15 Ex-US LST 511-1152 SERIES

CHANG PAI SHAN
CH'ING KANG SHAN
I MENG SHAN (ex-*Chung 106*, ex-US *LST 589)*
TA PIEH SHAN
TAI HSING SHAN
SZU CH'ING SHAN
Ex-**CHUNG 100** (ex-US *LST 355)*
Ex-**CHUNG 101** (ex-US *LST 804)*

Ex-**CHUNG 102**
Ex-**CHUNG 107** (ex-US *LST 1027)*
Ex-**CHUNG 110**
Ex-**CHUNG 111** (ex/US *LST 805)*
Ex-**CHUNG 116** (ex-US *LST 406)*
Ex-**CHUNG 122** (ex-*Ch'ing Ling)*
Ex-**CHUNG 125**

Displacement, tons: 1 653 standard; 4 080 full load
Dimensions, feet (metres): 316 wl; 328 oa × 50 × 14 *(96·4; 100 × 15·3 × 4·4)*
Main engines: Diesel; 2 shafts; 1 700 bhp = 11 knots

Two transferred to N. Vietnam. Eleven other ex-US LSTs were in the merchant service.

US LST

1968, USN

13 Ex-US LSM TYPE

Ex-**HUA 201** (ex-US *LSM 112)*
Ex-**HUA 202** (ex-US *LSM 248)*
Ex-**HUA 204** (ex-US *LSM 430)*
Ex-**HUA 205** (ex-US *LSM 336)*
Ex-**HUA 207** (ex-US *LSM 282)*
Ex-**HUA 208** (ex-US *LSM 42)*
Ex-**HUA 209** (ex-US *LSM 153)*

Ex-**HUA 211**
Ex-**HUA 212**
Ex-**CHUAN SHIH SHUI**
Ex-**HUAI HO** (ex-Chinese *Wan Fu)*
Ex-**HUANG HO** (ex-Chinese *Mei Sheng*
  ex-US *LSM 433)*
Ex-**YUN HO** (ex-Chinese *Wang Chung)*

Displacement, tons: 743 beaching; 1 095 full load
Dimensions, feet (metres): 196·5 wl; 203·5 oa × 34·5 × 8·8 *(59·9; 62·1 × 10·5 × 2·7)*
Guns: 4—37 mm (twins)
Main engines: Diesel; 2 shafts; 2 800 hp = 12 knots

Built in USA in 1944-45. Some were converted for minelaying. Armament varies. Up to ten of these may be transferred temporarily to commercial operations.

15 Ex-US LSIL TYPE

| MIN 301 | 306 | 312 | 319 | |
| 303 | 311 | 313 | 321 | +7 |

Displacement, tons: 230 light; 387 full load
Dimensions, feet (metres): 159 × 23·7 × 5·7 *(48·5 × 7·2 × 1·7)*
Guns: 4—20 or 25 mm
Main engines: Diesel; 2 shafts; 1 320 bhp = 14 knots

Built in USA in 1943-45. Reported to be fitted with rocket launchers. Some are fitted as minesweepers. Armament varies.

10 Ex-US or BRITISH LCU (ex-LCT) TYPE

Displacement, tons: 160 light; 320 full load
Dimensions, feet (metres): 119 oa × 33 × 5 *(36·3 × 10 × 1·5)*
Main engines: Diesel; 3 shafts; 475 bhp = 10 knots
Oil fuel (tons): 80

Former United States Navy Tank Landing Craft later reclassified as Utility Landing Craft. There are reported to be ten utility landing craft comprising two of the ex-British LCT (3) class and eight of the ex-US LCT (5) and LCT (6) class.

4 or 5 "YU LING" CLASS (LSM)

250 ft *(76·3 mm)*—1 500 ton LSMs building in China since 1971. Continuing programme. ? 4 per year.

In addition a total of 450 LCMs is reported.

SUBMARINE SUPPORT SHIP

TA CHIH

Displacement, tons: 5 to 6 000
Dimensions, feet (metres): 350 × 50 × 20 *(106·8 × 15·3 × 6·1)*
Guns: 4—37 mm (twins); 4—25 mm (twins)

Reported in 1973.

REPAIR SHIP

TAKU SHAN (ex-*Hsing An*, ex-USS *Achilles*, ARL 41, ex-*LST 455)*

Displacement, tons: 1 625 light; 4 100 full load
Dimensions, feet (metres): 328 oa × 50 × 11 *(100 × 15·3 × 3·4)*
Guns: 1—3 in; 8—40 mm
Main engines: Diesel-electric; 2 shafts; 1 800 bhp = 11 knots

Launched on 17 Oct 1942. Burned and grounded in 1949, salvaged and refitted.

SURVEY AND RESEARCH SHIPS

2 "SHIH JIAN" CLASS (RESEARCH SHIPS)

Of about 400 feet. Completed 1974.

SHIH JIAN

1973

1 "FAN HUNG" CLASS (RESEARCH SHIP)

TUNG FAN HUNG

Completed in 1965, possibly at Shanghai. Similar to Soviet 3 000-ton "Zubov" class.

1 Ex-JAPANESE "KAIBOKAN" CLASS

Displacement, tons: 740
Speed, knots: 17·5

Believed built in 1945.

3 "SHU KUANG" CLASS (ex T-43)

For details see under Mine Warfare Forces. Converted from Minesweepers for use as Survey Ships.

1 COASTAL SURVEY CRAFT

Ex-**CHUNG NING** (ex-Japanese *Takebu Maru*)

Displacement, tons: 200 standard
Dimensions, feet (metres): 115 × 16 × 6 *(35 × 4·9 × 1·8)*
Speed, knots: 10

Former Japanese. Employed for hydrographic and general purpose duties.

1 COASTAL SURVEY CRAFT

Ex-**FUTING**

Displacement, tons: 160 standard
Dimensions, feet (metres): 90 × 20 × 8 *(27 × 6·1 × 2·4)*
Speed, knots: 11

BOOM DEFENCE VESSELS

1 Ex-BRITISH "BAR" CLASS

— (Ex-Japanese No. 101, ex-HMS *Barlight*)

Displacement, tons: 750 standard; 1 000 full load
Dimensions, feet (metres): 173·8 oa × 32·2 × 9·5 *(53 × 9·8 × 2·9)*
Guns: 1—3 in; 6 MG
Main engines: Triple expansion; 850 ihp = 11·75 knots
Boilers: 2 single-ended

Built by Lobnitz & Co Ltd, Renfrew. Launched on 10 Sep 1938. Captured by Japanese in 1941. Acquired by China in 1945.

5 Ex-US "TREE" CLASS

Displacement, tons: 560 standard; 805 full load
Dimensions, feet (metres): 163 oa × 30·5 × 11·8 *(49·7 × 9·3 × 3·6)*
Gun: 1—3 in
Main engines: Diesel-electric; 800 bhp = 13 knots

RANGE INSTRUMENTATION SHIPS (AGM)

4 CHINESE BUILT

HSIANG YANG HUNG WU

Completed Canton 1971-72.

HSIANG YANG HUNG WU

1974

HSIANG YANG HUNG SAN +**2** others, maybe more

These ships, of varying tonnage but all of an ocean-going size, operate in conjunction with the Academy of Science.

SUPPLY SHIPS

5 Ex-US ARMY FS 330 TYPE

Ex-US Army FS 146 (ex-*Clover*)
Ex-US Army FS 155 (ex-*Violet*)   +**3**

Displacement, tons: 1 000 standard
Dimensions, feet (metres): 175 oa × 32 × 10 *(53·4 × 9·9 × 2)*
Main engines: GM diesels; 1 000 bhp = 12 knots

Built in USA in 1944-45. Two are reported to be employed as fast attack craft.

2 "GALATZ" CLASS (AK)

From Romania.

1 "AN TUNG" CLASS

Chinese built AK.

2 Ex-MERCHANT SHIPS

HAI YUN 318   **HAI CHIU** 600

330 feet *(100·6 m)* long.

2 or 3 "TAN LIN" CLASS

1 500 ton AKLs.

There may be another 12 merchant ships operating under naval control.

TANKERS

3 (?) "LU CHOU" CLASS

The existence of these ships, reported as 2 500 tons, has not been confirmed.

3 "LEI CHOU" CLASS

LEI CHOU   **FOU CHOU**   **+1 (?)**

Ships of 1 000 to 1 500 tons, the number in the class not yet being confirmed.

2 ex-US "MATTAWEE" CLASS

Originally petrol tankers.

2 Ex-SOVIET "TM" CLASS

ICEBREAKERS

2 "HAI PING" CLASS

101   —

3 000 ton ships built for commercial use in 1970. Two others may be in service.

TRAINING SHIP

CH'ANG CHAING

Ex-coast defence vessel of 464 tons built in 1929, converted for training.

TUGS

7 "GROMOVOY" CLASS (SALVAGE TUG)

1 Ex-SOVIET "ROSLAVL" CLASS (SALVAGE TUG)

2 Ex-US 149' ATA

2 Ex-US 143' ATA

5 Ex-US ARMY 75' YTL

SERVICE CRAFT

There are also reported to be 125 armed motor junks, 100 armed motor launches and 150 service craft and miscellaneous boats.

COLOMBIA

Headquarters Appointments

Fleet Commander:
Admiral Jaime Barrera Larrarte
Chief of Naval Operations:
Vice Admiral Alfonso Diaz Osorio
Chief of Naval Staff:
Rear Admiral Héctor Calderón Salazar

Diplomatic Representative

Naval Attaché in Washington:
Captain Rafael Grau Arano

Personnel

(a) 1976: 700 officers and 6 500 men and 1 000 marines
(b) 1 year's national service

Base

Cartagena. Main naval base (floating dock, 1 slipway), schools.

Maritime Air Force

The Colombian Air Force with 50 helicopters and a number of attack/reconnaissance aircraft provides any support required by the navy.

Naval Infantry

Corpo de Infanteria de Marina is one battalion based at Cartagena, Buenaventura and Barranquilla.

Prefix to Ships' Names

ARC (Armada Republica de Colombia)

Strength of the Fleet

Type	Active	Building
Destroyers	4	—
Frigates	3	—
Submarines	2 + 4 (70 tons)	—
Coastal Patrol Craft	25	
Survey Vessels	4	—
Transports	6	—
Tanker	1	—
Training Ship	1	—
Tugs	12	—
Floating Docks	3	—
Floating Workshop	1	—

Mercantile Marine

Lloyd's Register of Shipping:
54 vessels of 211 083 tons gross

DELETIONS

Destroyer

1973 *Antioquia* ("Fletcher" class) (paid off 20 Dec)

Frigates

1972 *Almirante Brion* (ex-US APD type)
1973 *Almirante Padilla* (ex-US APD type)

Tankers

1970 *Tumaco, Barran Cabermeja*
1974 *Covenas, Mamonal, Sancho Jimeno*

Tug

1975 *Bahia Honda* (grounded and scrapped 13 Feb)

Light Forces

1974 *Gen. Rafael Reyes, Alberto Restrepo, Independiente, Palace, Tormentosa, Triunfante, Valerosa, Voladora*

Survey Ship

1974 *Bocas de Ceniza*

Transport

1974 *Bell Salter*

DESTROYERS

2 MODIFIED "HALLAND" CLASS

Name	No.	Builders	Laid down	Launched	Commissioned
SIETE DE AGOSTO	06	Götaverken, Göteborg	Nov 1955	19 June 1956	31 Oct 1958
VEINTE DE JULIO	05	Kockums Mek Verkstads A/B, Malmo	Oct 1955	26 June 1956	15 June 1958

Displacement, tons: 2 650 standard; 3 300 full load
Length, feet (metres): 380·5 *(116·0)* pp; 397·2 *(121·1)* oa
Beam, feet (metres): 40·7 *(12·4)*
Draught, feet (metres): 15·4 *(4·7)*
Guns: 6—4·7 in *(120 mm)* (3 twin turrets); 4—40 mm (single)
Torpedo tubes: 4—21 in *(533 mm)*
A/S weapons: 1 quadruple DC rocket launcher
Main engines: De Laval double reduction geared turbines;
  2 shafts; 55 000 shp
Boilers: 2 Penhöet, Motala Verkstad; 568 psi; 840°F
Speed, knots: 25 (16 economical)
Oil fuel, tons: 524
Range, miles: 445 at full power
Complement: 260 (20 officers, 240 men)

SIETE DE AGOSTO   *1971, Colombian Navy*

Ordered in 1954. The hull and machinery are similar to the Swedish class but they have different armament (six 4·7 inch instead of four, no 57 mm guns, four 40 mm guns instead of six, and four torpedo tubes instead of eight) and different accommodation arrangements. They have an anti-submarine rocket projector, more radar and communication equipment, and air-conditioned living spaces, having been designed·for the tropics.

Engineering: Although the designed speed was 35 knots, it is officially stated that the maximum sustained speed does not exceed 25 knots.

Radar: Search: HSA, LW-03/SGR 114.
Tactical: HSA DA-02/SGR 105.
Fire Control: I band, probably HSA M20 series.

Refit: *Siete de Agosto* returned to Colombia in 1975 after a lengthy refit in USA during which her engines were extensively overhauled.

SIETE DE AGOSTO   *1975, Dhr. J. van der Woude*

1 Ex-US "ALLEN M. SUMNER" CLASS, 1 Ex-US "ALLEN M. SUMNER FRAM II" CLASS

Name	No.	Builders	Laid down	Launched	Commissioned
CALDAS (ex-USS *Willard Keith, DD 775*)	D 02	Bethlehem (San Pedro)	—	29 Aug 1944	27 Dec 1944
SANTANDER (ex-USS *Waldron, DD 699*)	D 03	Federal SB Co	—	26 Mar 1944	8 June 1944

Displacement, tons: 2 200 standard; 3 320 full load
Length, feet (metres): 376 *(114·8)* oa
Beam, feet (metres): 40·9 *(12·4)*
Draught, feet (metres): 19 *(5·8)*
Guns: 6—5 in *(127 mm)* 38 cal (twins);
  4—3 in (twins) *(Caldas* only)
A/S weapons: 2 Fixed Hedgehogs; 2 triple torpedo tubes (Mk 32); Facilities for small helicopter *(Santander* only)
Main engines: 2 geared turbines; 2 shafts; 60 000 shp
Boilers: 4
Speed, knots: 34
Range, miles: 2 400 at 25 knots; 4 800 at 15 knots
Complement: 274

Caldas, an unmodified "Allen M. Sumner" class, was transferred on 1 July 1972 by sale.
Santander was modernised under the Fram II programme and transferred by sale on 30 Oct 1973.

CALDAS   1974

SANTANDER   *1975, Dhr. J. van der Woude*

FRIGATES

2 Ex-US APD TYPE

Name	No.	Builders	Commissioned
ALMIRANTE TONO (ex-USS *Basset APD 73*, ex-*DE 672*)	DT 04	Consolidated Steel Co, Orange	23 Feb 1945
CORDOBA (ex-USS *Ruchamkin LPR 89*, ex-*APD 89*, ex-*DE 228*)	DT 15	Philadelphia Navy Yard	June1945

Displacement, tons: 1 400 standard; 2 130 full load
Dimensions, feet (metres): 306 oa × 37 × 12·6 *(93·3 × 11·3 × 3·8)*
Guns: 1—5 in 38 cal; 4—40 mm
A/S weapons: 2 Mk 32 launchers *(Cordoba only)*
Main engines: GEC Turbines with electric drive; 2 shafts; 12 000 shp = 23 knots
Boilers: 2 "D" Express
Range, miles: 5 500 at 15 knots
Complement: 204 (plus accommodation for 162 troops)

Almirante Tono was laid down on 28 Nov 1943, launched on 15 Jan 1944, and transferred at Boston, Mass, on 6 Sep 1968. *Cordoba* was laid down on 14 Feb 1944, launched on 15 June 1944 and transferred on 24 Nov 1969. Modernised to Fram II standards.

CORDOBA   *1974*

1 Ex-US "COURTNEY" CLASS

Name	No.	Builders	Commissioned
BOYACA (ex-USS *Hartley DE 1029*)	DE 16	New York SB Corpn.	26 Jan 1957

Displacement, tons: 1 450 standard; 1 914 full load
Dimensions, feet (metres): 314·5 oa × 36·8 × 13·6 *(95·9 × 11·2 × 4·1)*
Guns: 2—3 in; 50 cal (twin)
A/S weapons: 2 triple torpedo tubes
Main engines: 1 De Laval geared turbine; 20 000 shp; 1 shaft
Boilers: 2 Foster Wheeler
Speed, knots: 25
Complement: 165

Transferred 8 July 1972, by sale. Helicopter platform in X position.

BOYACA   *1974*

SUBMARINES

2 TYPE 209 PATROL SUBMARINES

Name	No.	Builders	Commissioned
PIJAO	SS 28	Howaldtswerke, Kiel	17 Apr 1975
TAYRONA	SS 29	Howaldtswerke, Kiel	18 July 1975

Displacement, tons: 1 000 surfaced; 1 290 dived
Length, feet (metres): 183·4 *(55·9)*
Beam, feet (metres): 20·5 *(6·25)*
Torpedo tubes: 8—21 in bow with reloads
Main machinery: Diesel electric; 1 shaft; 5 000 hp
Speed, knots: 22 dived

Ordered in 1971.

PIJAO   *1975, Dhr J. van der Woude*

4 TYPE SX-506 SUBMARINES

Name	No.	Builders	Commissioned
INTREPIDO	SS 20	Cosmos Livorno	1972
INDOMABLE	SS 21	Cosmos Livorno	1972
RONCADOR	SS 23	Cosmos Livorno	1974
QUITA SUENO	SS 24	Cosmos Livorno	1974

Displacement, tons: 58 surfaced; 70 dived
Dimensions, feet (metres): 75·4 × 6·6 × 13·2 *(23 × 2 × 4)*
Main machinery: Diesel-electric; 300 bhp
Speed, knots: 8 surfaced; 6 dived; 7 snorting
Range, miles: 1 200 at 7 knots
Complement: 5

Delivered in sections for assembly in Cartagena. Can carry 8 attack swimmers with 2 tons of explosives, as well as two swimmer-delivery-vehicles (SDVs). Diving depth 330 ft *(100 ms)*.

LIGHT FORCES

Name	No.	Builders	Commissioned
GENERAL VASQUES COBO	AN 02	Lürssen	1955

Displacement, tons: 146
Dimensions, feet (metres): 124·7 oa × 23 × 5 *(38 × 7 × 1·5)*
Gun: 1—40 mm
Main engines: 2 Maybach (MTU) diesels; 2 500 bhp = 18 knots

Launched on 27 Sep 1955.

Name	No.	Builders	Commissioned
CARLOS ALBAN	—	—	1971
JORGE SOTO DEL CORVAL	—	—	1971
NITO RESTREPO	—	—	1971

Displacement, tons: 100
Main engines: 2 (MTU) Diesels; 2 450 bhp = 19 knots

CARLOS ALBAN

1971, Colombian Navy

Name	No.	Builders	Commissioned
PEDRO GUAL	AN 204	Schurenstedt KG Barden Fleth	1964
ESTEBAN JARAMILLO	AN 205	Schurenstedt KG Barden Fleth	1964
CARLOS E. RESTREPO	AN 206	Schurenstedt KG Barden Fleth	1964

Displacement, tons: 85
Dimensions, feet (metres): 107·8 pp × 18 × 6 *(32·9 × 5·5 × 1·8)*
Gun: 1—20 mm
Main engines: 2 Maybach (MTU) diesels; 2 450 bhp = 26 knots

PEDRO GUAL

1965, Colombian Navy

3 "ARAUCA" CLASS GUNBOATS

Name	No.	Builders	Commissioned
RIOHACHA	CF 35	Union Industrial de Barranquilla	1956
LETICIA	CF 36	Union Industrial de Barranquilla	1956
ARAUCA	CF 37	Union Industrial de Barranquilla	1956

Displacement, tons: 184 full load
Dimensions, feet (metres): 163·5 oa × 23·5 × 2·8 *(49·9 × 7·2 × 0·9)*
Gun: 2—3 in, 50 cal; 4—20 mm
Main engines: 2 Caterpillar diesels; 916 bhp = 14 knots
Range, miles: 1 890 at 14 knots
Complement: 43 (*Leticia* 39 and 6 orderlies)

Launched in 1955. *Leticia* has been equipped as a hospital ship with 6 beds.

RIOHACHA

1966, Colombian Navy

1 "BARRANQUILLA" CLASS GUNBOAT

Name	No.	Builders	Commissioned
CARTAGENA	CF 33	Yarrow & Co Ltd, Scotstoun	1930

Displacement, tons: 142
Dimensions, feet (metres): 137·8 oa × 23·5 × 2·8 *(42 × 7·2 × 0·9)*
Guns: 2—3 in; 1—20 mm; 4 MG
Main engines: 2 Gardner semi-diesels; 2 shafts working in tunnels; 600 hp = 15·5 knots
Oil fuel (tons): 24
Complement: 39

Launched on 22 Mar 1930. Sister ships *Santa Marta*, CF 32, withdrawn from service in Dec 1962, and *Barranquilla* in 1970.

CARTAGENA

1971, Colombian Navy

Name	No.	Builders	Commissioned
OLAYA HERRERA	AN 203	Ast. Magdalena Barranquilla	1960

Displacement, tons: 40
Dimensions, feet (metres): 68·8 pp × 12·8 × 3·5 *(21 × 3·9 × 1·1)*
Gun: 1—·50 mm Browning
Main engines: 2 Merbens diesels; 570 bhp = 20 knots

Name	No.	Builders	Commissioned
ESPARTANA	GC 100	Ast. Naval, Cartagena	1950

Displacement, tons: 50
Dimensions, feet (metres): 96 oa × 13·5 ×4 *(29·3 × 4·1 × 1·2)*
Gun: 1—20 mm
Main engines: 2 diesels; 300 bhp = 13·5 knots

Name	No.	Builders	Commissioned
CAPITAN R. D. BINNEY	GC 101	Ast. Naval, Cartagena	1947

Displacement, tons: 23
Dimensions, feet (metres): 67 × 10·7 × 3·5 *(20·4 × 3·3 × 1·1)*
Main engines: Diesels; 115 bhp = 13 knots

Buoy and lighthouse inspection boat. Named after first head of Colombian Naval Academy, Lt-Commander Ralph Douglas Binney, RN.

Name	No.	Builders	Commissioned
CARLOS GALINDO	LR 128	Ast. Naval, Cartagena	1954
HUMBERTO CORTES	LR 126	Ast. Naval, Cartagena	1953
JUAN LUCIO	LR 122	Ast. Naval, Cartagena	1953

Displacement, tons: 35
Dimensions, feet (metres): 81·8 oa × 12 × 2·8 *(24·6 × 3·7 × 0·8)*
Guns: 1—20 mm; 4 MG
Main engines: 2 GM diesels; 260 bhp = 13 knots
Complement: 13

Originally class of four.

Name	No.	Builders	Commissioned
ALFONSO VARGAS	LR 123	Ast. Naval, Cartagena	1952
FRITZ HAGALE	LR 124	Ast. Naval, Cartagena	1952

Displacement, tons: 33
Dimensions, feet (metres): 76 oa × 12 × 2·8 *(23·2 × 3·7 × 0·8)*
Guns: 1—20 mm; 4 MG
Main engines: 2 GM diesels 280 bhp = 13 knots
Complement: 10

Designed for operations on rivers. Named after naval officers.

Name	No.	Builders	Commissioned
DILIGENTE	LR 138	Ast. Naval, Cartagena	1952
VENGADORA	LR 139	Ast. Naval, Cartagena	1954

Originally a class of eight.

SURVEY VESSELS

Name	No.	Builders	Commissioned
SAN ANDRES (ex-USS *Rockville*, PCER 851)	BO 151	Pullman Standard Car Co, Chicago	15 May 1944

Displacement, tons: 674 standard; 968 full load
Dimensions, feet (metres): 184·5 oa × 33·6 × 7·0 *(56·3 × 10·2 × 2·1)*
Main engines: 2 diesels; 2 shafts; 1 800 bhp = 15 knots
Complement: 50

Former US patrol rescue escort vessel. Laid down on 18 Oct 1943, launched on 22 Feb 1944 Acquired on 5 June 1969 for conversion to a surveying vessel.

Name	No.	Builders	Commissioned
GORGONA	FB 161	Lidingoverken, Sweden	1955

Displacement, tons: 574
Dimensions, feet (metres): 135 × 29·5 × 9·3 *(41·2 × 9 × 2·8)*
Main engines: 2 Nohab diesels; 910 bhp = 13 knots
Complement: 45

Formerly classified as a tender.

GORGONA

1971, Colombian Navy

Name	No.	Builders	Commissioned
QUINDIO (ex-US *YPR 443)*	BO 153	—	1943

Displacement, tons: 380 light; 600 full load
Dimensions, feet (metres): 131 × 29·8 × 9 *(40 × 9·1 × 2·7)*
Main engines: 2 diesels; 300 hp = 10 knots
Complement: 17

Transferred by lease July 1964.

TANKER

1 Ex-US "PATAPSCO" CLASS (AOG)

Name	No.	Builders	Commissioned
TUMACO	BT 67	Cargill Inc, Savage, Minn	19 Feb 1945
(ex-USS *Chewaucan, AOG 50)*			

Displacement, tons: 1 850 light; 4 570
Dimensions, feet (metres): 310·8 × 48·5 × 16 *(94·8 × 14·8 × 4·9)*
Guns: 2—3 in *(76 mm)*
Main engines: Diesel electric; 2 shafts; 3 840 bhp = 15 knots
Range, miles: 4 740 at 15 knots; 8 350 at 11·5 knots
Complement: 95

Transferred 1975.

TUMACO (As USS *Chewaucan)*

1970, A. and J. Pavia

TRANSPORTS

Name	No.	Builders	Commissioned
CIUDAD DE QUIBDO	TM 43	Gebr Sander	1953
(ex-*Shamrock)*		Deltzijl	(see note)

Displacement, tons: 633
Dimensions, feet (metres): 165 × 23·5 × 9 *(49·9 × 7·2 × 2·7)*
Main engines: 1 Main diesel; 1 shaft; 390 bhp = 11 knots
Oil fuel, tons: 32
Complement: 12

Ex-Dutch coaster *Shamrock* sold to Colombia by commercial firm in Mar 1953.

CIUDAD DE QUIBDO

1971, Colombian Navy

Name	No.	Builders	Commissioned
MARIO SERPA	TF 51	Ast. Naval Cartagena	1954
HERNANDO GUTIERREZ	TF 52	Ast. Naval Cartagena	1955
SOCORRO (ex-*Alberto Gomez)*	BD 33	Ast. Naval Cartagena	1956

Displacement, tons: 70
Dimensions, feet (metres): 82 × 18 × 2·8 *(25 × 5·5 × 0·9)*
Main engines: 2 GM diesels; 260 bhp = 9 knots
Oil fuel, tons: 4
Range, miles: 650 at 9 knots
Complement: 12 (berths for 48 troops and medical staff)

River transports. Named after Army officers. *Socorro* was converted in July 1967 into a floating surgery. *Hernando Gutierrez* and *Mario Serpa* were converted into dispensary ships in 1970.

TRAINING SHIP

Name	No.	Builders	Commissioned
GLORIA	—	Bilbao	1968

Displacement, tons: 1 300
Dimensions, feet (metres): 212 × 34·8 × 21·7 *(64·7 × 10·6 × 6·6)*
Main engines: Auxiliary diesel; 500 bhp = 10·5 knots

Sail training ship. Barque rigged. Hull is entirely welded.
Sail area: 1 675 sq yards *(1 400 sq metres).*

GLORIA

1971, Colombian Navy

TUGS

PEDRO DE HEREDIA (ex-USS *Choctaw, ATF 70*) RM 72

Displacement, tons: 1 235 standard; 1 764 full load
Dimensions, feet (metres): 205 oa × 38·5 × 15·5 *(62·5 × 11·7 × 4·7)*
Main engines: 4 diesels; electric drive; 3 000 bhp = 16·5 knots

Former United States ocean tug of the "Cherokee" class. Launched on 18 Oct 1942.

PEDRO DE HEREDIA   8/1975, S. Terzibaschitsch

BAHIA UTRIA (ex-USS *Kalmia* ATA 184) RM 75

Displacement, tons: 534 standard; 858 full load
Dimensions, feet (metres): 143·0 oa × 33·9 × 8·0 *(43·6 × 10·3 × 2·4)*
Gun: 1—3 in
Main engines: 2 GM diesel-electric; 1 shaft; 1 500 bhp = 13 knots
Complement: 45

Launched 29 Aug 1944. Transferred from the United States Navy on 1 July 1971 on lease.

ANDAGOYA RM 71

Measurement, tons: 117 gross
Dimensions, feet (metres): 92·6 × 20 × 10 *(28·2 × 6·1 × 3·05)*
Main engines: Caterpillar diesel; 400 bhp = 10 knots

Launched in 1928. Re-engined in 1955.

CANDIDO LEGUIZAMO RR 82   **CAPITAN RIGOBERTO GIRALDO** RR 86
CAPITAN ALVARO RUIZ RR 84   **CAPITAN VLADIMIR VALEK** RR 87
CAPITAN CASTRO RR 81   **JOVES FIALLO** RR 90
                               TENIENTE LUIS BERNAL RR 88

Displacement, tons: 50
Dimensions, feet (metres): 63 × 14 × 2·5 *(19·2 × 4·3 × 0·8)*
Main engines: 2 GM diesels; 260 bhp = 9 knots

MAYOR ARIAS

Displacement, tons: 700
Capacity, tons: 165
Length, feet (metres): 140 *(42·7)*

TENIENTE SORZANO RM 73

Displacement, tons: 54
Dimensions, feet (metres): 65·7 oa × 17·5 × 9 *(20 × 5·3 × 2·7)*
Main engines: 6-cylinder diesel; 240 bhp

ABADIA MENDEZ

Displacement, tons: 39
Dimensions, feet (metres): 52·5 × 11 × 4 *((16 × 3·4 × 1·2)*
Main engines: Caterpillar diesel; 80 bhp = 8 knots

Built in Germany in 1924. Harbour tug. Existence now doubtful.

TENIENTE MIGUEL SILVA RR 89

Dimensions, feet (metres): 73·3 × 17·5 × 3 *(22·4 × 5·3 × 0·9)*
Main engines: 2 diesels; 260 bhp = 9 knots

River tug. Built by Union Industrial (Unial) of Barranquilla.

FLOATING DOCK

Note: It is reported that the 6 700 ton *Rodriguez Zamora*, the small floating dock *Manuel Lara*, the floating workshop *Mantilla* and the repair craft *Victor Cubillos* are probably under civil contract.

CONGO

The Republic of Congo, which became independent on 15 Aug 1960, formed a naval service, but the patrol vessel *Reine N' Galifowou* (ex-French P 754) which was transferred 16 Nov 1962 was returned to France on 18 Feb 1965 and then re-transferred to Senegal as *Siné Saloum*.

Personnel

(a) 1976: 180 officers and men
(b) Voluntary service

Mercantile Marine

Lloyd's Register of Shipping:
8 vessels of 1 846 tons gross

3 Ex-CHINESE "SHANGHAI" CLASS

Displacement, tons: 120 standard; 155 full load
Dimensions, feet (metres): 128 × 18 × 5·6 *(39 × 5·5 × 1·7)*
Guns: 4—37 mm; 2—25 mm
A/S armament: 8 DCs
Mines: Mine rails can be fitted for up to 10 mines
Main engines: 4 Diesels; 4 800 hp = 30 knots
Complement: 25

Probably transferred in 1974.

"Shanghai" Class

4 RIVER PATROL CRAFT

Reported as about 10 tons, transferred by China.

MISCELLANEOUS

It is reported that up to 12 small craft with outboard motors are employed on river patrol.

COSTA RICA

Personnel

(a) 1976: 50 officers and men
(b) Voluntary

Mercantile Marine

Lloyd's Register of Shipping:
14 vessels of 6 102 tons gross

3 COASTAL PATROL CRAFT

401   402   403

Displacement, tons: 10
Dimensions, feet (metres): 41 × 10 × 2·3 *(12·5 × 3·1 × 0·7)*
Gin: 1 MG

Built in early 1950s. Of the pre-war US Coastguard 40 ft type.

CUBA

Senior Appointment

Commander in Chief:
Commodore Aldo Santamaria

Personnel

(1976: 6 000 (380 officers, 220 petty officers and 5 400 men)
(3 years national service

Standard of Efficiency

The US embargo on exports to Cuba has been running for over a decade. As a result all ex-USN ships in the Cuban Navy must be suffering from lack of spares, though some may have been stripped to provide for others. Cuba has the highest estimated defence expenditure in Central America and the Caribbean at about £120 million, a fair proportion of this being on Soviet aid. The navy is the smallest of the three services but, with an adequate budget and Soviet assistance in training, must be assessed as having a reasonable level of tactical and material efficiency.

Naval Establishments

Naval Academy:
At Mariel, for officers and cadets

Naval School:
At Morro Castle, for petty officers and men

Naval Bases:
Mariel, Cienfuegos and Cabanas

Maritime Airforce

A helicopter force of 25 Mi-4 (Hound) and 30 Mi-1 (Hare) from USSR is in existence although these are probably all operated by the Air Force.

Strength of the Fleet

	Active	Building or (Reserve)
Frigates	—	(3)
Corvettes	19	—
Fast Attack Craft (Missile)	23	—
Fast Attack Craft (Torpedo)	24	—
Fast Attack Craft (Patrol)	7	—
Coastal Patrol Craft	22	—
LCMs	8	—
Survey Vessels	7	—
Miscellaneous	7	—

Mercantile Marine

Lloyd's Register of Shipping:
272 vessels of 442 547 tons gross

DELETIONS

Cruiser (so called)

1972 *Cuba* (built 1911—of 2 000 tons)

Corvette

1973 *Sibony* (ex-US PCER)

Light Forces

1973 *Donotivo, Matanzas*

FRIGATES

The three ex-US frigates of the PF type—*Antonio Maceo, Jose Marti, Maximo Gomez*—which were completed in 1944 and acquired in 1947 are still in existence as harbour hulks but have no operational value.

CORVETTES

12 Ex-SOVIET "SO I" CLASS

Displacement, tons: 215 standard; 250 full load
Dimensions, feet (metres): 138·6 × 20 × 9·2 *(42·3 × 6·1 × 2·8)*
Guns: 4—25 mm (2 twin)
A/S weapons: 4 five-barrelled rocket launchers
Main engines: 3 diesels; 6 000 bhp = 29 knots
Range, miles: 1 100 at 13 knots
Complement: 30

Six were transferred from the USSR by Sep 1964, and six more in 1967.

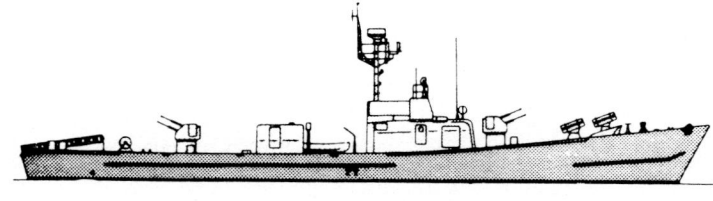

"SO I" Class

6 Ex-SOVIET "KRONSTADT" CLASS

Displacement, tons: 310 standard; 380 full load
Dimensions, feet (metres): 170·6 × 21·3 × 9 *(52·0 × 6·5 × 2·7)*
Guns: 1—3·5 in; 2—37 mm; 4—25 mm
A/S weapons: 1 DC thrower
Mines: 6 on two racks at the stern
Main engines: 3 diesels; 3 shafts; 3 030 hp = 24 knots
Range, miles: 1 500 at 12 knots
Complement: 65

Transferred from the USSR in 1962.

Radar: Surface: Skinhead or Ballgun. Navigation: Don. IFF; High Pole A.

"KRONSTADT" CLASS

1 Ex-US PCER TYPE

CARIBE (ex-USS PCER 872) PE 201

Displacement, tons: 640 standard; 903 full load
Dimensions, feet (metres): 180 wl; 184·5 oa × 33 × 9·5 *(54·9; 56·3 × 10·1 × 2·9)*
Guns: 1—3 in; 3—40 mm; 4—20 mm
A/S weapons: Hedgehog; DCT and racks
Main engines: 12 cylinder diesels; 2 shafts; 1 800 bhp = 14 knots
Complement: 99

Built in USA. Completed 1943-44. Refitted at Key West 1956.

CARIBE   *Cuban Navy*

LIGHT FORCES

5 Ex-SOVIET "OSA I" CLASS (FAST ATTACK CRAFT—MISSILE)

Displacement, tons: 165 standard; 200 full load
Dimensions, feet (metres): 128·7 × 25·1 × 5·9 (39·3 × 7·7 × 1·8)
Missiles: 4 SSN-2 launchers in two pairs
Guns: 4—30 mm (2 twin, 1 forward, 1 aft)
Main engines: 3 diesels; 13 000 bhp = 35 knots
Range, miles: 800 at 25 knots
Complement: 25

Two boats of this class were transferred to Cuba from the USSR in January 1972 and three in 1973. With the obvious rundown of the ex-USN ships in the Cuban Navy and the determination of the Cuban Government to maintain an independent Naval presence in the Caribbean, these could be the forerunners of further reinforcements. With the "Komar" class units there are now twenty-three hulls mounting 56 of the proven and effective "Styx" missiles in a highly sensitive area.

"OSA I" Class

18 Ex-SOVIET "KOMAR" CLASS (FAST ATTACK CRAFT—MISSILE)

Displacement, tons: 70 standard; 80 full load
Dimensions, feet (metres): 83·7 × 19·8 × 5·0 (25·5 × 6·0 × 1·8)
Missiles: 2 SSN-2 launchers
Guns: 2—25 mm
Main engines: 4 diesels; 4 shafts; 4 800 bhp = 40 knots
Range, miles: 400 at 30 knots

First twelve transferred in 1962. Last pair arrived in Dec 1966.

"KOMAR" Class   1970, US

12 Ex-SOVIET "P 6" CLASS (FAST ATTACK CRAFT—TORPEDO)

Displacement, tons: 66 standard; 75 full load
Dimensions, feet (metres): 84·2 × 20 × 6 (25·7 × 6·1 × 1·8)
Guns: 4—25 mm (two twin)
Tubes: 2—21 in (two single)
Main engines: 4 diesels; 4 shafts; 4 800 hp = 43 knots
Range, miles: 450 at 30 knots
Complement: 25

Transferred in 1962. Pothead or Skinhead Radar. Can carry mines or depth charges in place of torpedo tubes.

"P 6" Class

12 Ex-SOVIET "P 4" CLASS (FAST ATTACK CRAFT—TORPEDO)

Displacement, tons: 25
Dimensions, feet (metres): 62·7 × 11·6 × 5·6 (19·1 × 3·5 × 1·7)
Guns: 2—25 mm
Tubes: 2—18 in
Main engines: 2 diesels; 2 200 bhp; 2 shafts = 50 knots
Complement: 12

Transferred from the USSR in 1962-64.

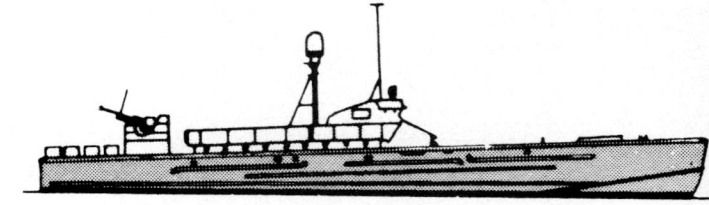

"P 4" Class

5 Ex-SOVIET "ZHUKH" CLASS (FAST ATTACK CRAFT—PATROL)

Displacement, tons: 60
Dimensions, feet (metres): 75 × 16 × 5 (22·9 × 4·9 × 1·5)
Guns: 2—14·5 mm (twin)
Main engines: Diesels = 34 knots (28 knots normal)
Complement: 18?

Transferred 1975.

"ZHUKH" Class

2 Ex-US PT TYPE (FAST ATTACK CRAFT—PATROL)

R 41 (ex-*PT* 715)   **R 42** (ex-*PT* 716)

Displacement, tons: 35
Dimensions, feet (metres): 71 × 19·2 × 5 *(21·7 × 5·9 × 1·5)*
Guns: 2 MG
Main engines: 2 Packard gas engines; 3 shafts; 3 600 bhp = 35 knots

Former US motor torpedo boats of the PT type. Built in the USA by Annapolis Yacht Yard Inc, Annapolis, Md. Launched on 9 July 1945 (R 41) and 17 July 1945 (R 42). Sunk during a hurricane on 5 Oct 1948, but were salvaged and put into service primarily as fast rescue craft.

4 Ex-US COASTAL PATROL CRAFT

HABANA (ex-*SC* 1291) GC 107   **ORIENTE** (ex-*SC* 1000) GC 104
LAS VILLAS (ex-*SC* 1290) GC 106   **PINAR DEL RIO** (ex-*SC* 1301) GC 108

Displacement, tons: 95
Dimensions, feet (metres): 107·5 wl; 111 oa × 17 × 6·6 *(33·7 × 5·7 × 2)*
Guns: 2—20 mm
Main engines: 2 GM diesels; 2 shafts; 1 000 bhp = 15 knots
Complement: 25

Built in the United States by Dingle Boat Works *(Oriente)*, W. A. Robinson, Inc, Ipswich, Mass. *(Havana* and *Las Villas)*, and Perkins & Vaughn Inc, Wickford, RI *(Pinar del Rio)* in 1942/43.

HABANA   *Cuban Navy*

1 COASTAL PATROL CRAFT

LEONCIO PRADO GC 101

Displacement, tons: 80
Dimensions, feet (metres): 110 × 17·7 × 6·2 *(33·5 × 5·4 × 1·9)*
Gun: 1—20 mm
Main engines: 2 8-cycle, 2 stroke diesels; 1 000 bhp = 15 knots
Oil fuel: 2 232 gallons

Built at Havana. Launched in 1946. Of wooden hulled construction.

LEONCIO PRADO

1966, Cuban Navy

3 Ex-US CG 56 ft TYPE (COASTAL PATROL CRAFT)

GC 32 (ex-USCGC 83351)   **GC 33** (ex-USCGC 83385)   **GC 34** (ex-USCGC 83395)

Length, feet (metres): 56 *(17·1)*
Guns: 1—20 mm
Main engines: 2 superior diesels; 460 bhp = 12 knots

Transferred 1943

3 Ex-US CG 83 ft TYPE (COASTAL PATROL CRAFT)

GC 11 (ex-USCGC 83351)   **GC 13** (ex-USCGC 83385)   **GC 14** (ex-USCGC 83395)

Displacement, tons: 45
Dimensions, feet (metres): 83 × 16 × 4·5 *(25·3 × 4·9 × 1·4)*
Gun: 1—20 mm
Main engines: 2 Sterling Viking petrol motors; 1 200 hp = 18 knots
Complement: 12

Built in USA. Ex-Coast Guard Cutters. Launched in 1942-43. Of wooden hulled construction. Received from US Navy in March 1943.

6 COASTAL PATROL CRAFT

SV 1   SV 2   SV 3   SV 4   SV 5   SV 6

Displacement, tons: 6·15
Dimensions, feet (metres): 32 × 10 × 2·8 *(9·8 × 3·1 × ·8)*
Main engines: 2 Chrysler Crown, 230 bhp = 18 knots

Auxiliary patrol boats for port patrol, launched in 1953.

6 COASTAL PATROL CRAFT

SV 7   SV 8   SV 9   SV 10   SV 12   SV 14

Length, feet (metres): 40 *(12·2)*
Gun: 1—50 cal MG
Main engines: 2 GM diesels = 25 knots

Later boats of the SV type equipped with radar. Completed 1958.

AMPHIBIOUS FORCES

7 T4 CLASS LCMs

Obtained 1967-74. Mainly employed as Harbour Craft.

1 SPANISH LCM

SURVEY VESSELS

H 101

Survey ship of 530 tons.

H 91   92   93   94   95   96

Survey craft of 125 tons.

MISCELLANEOUS

2 LIGHTHOUSE TENDERS

ENRIQUE COLLAZO (ex-*Joaquin Godoy*)

Displacement, tons: 815
Dimensions, feet (metres): 211 × 24 × 9 *(64 × 10·5 × 2·8)*
Main engines: Triple expansion; 2 shafts; 672 ihp = 8 knots

Built at Paisley, Scotland. Launched in 1906. Acquired in 1950 from Cuban Mercantile Marine.

BERTHA SF 10

Displacement, tons: 98
Dimensions, feet (metres): 104 × 19 × 11 *(31·5 × 5·8 × 3·4)*
Main engines: 2 Gray Marine diesels; 450 bhp = 10 knots

Launched in 1944.

1 OCEAN TUG

DIEZ DE OCTUBRE (ex-*ATR* 4) RS 210

Displacement, tons: 852 standard; 1 315 full load
Dimensions, feet (metres): 155 wl; 165·5 oa × 33·3 × 16 *(47·3; 50·4 × 10·2 × 4·9)*
Guns: 1—3 in *(76 mm)* 2—20 mm
Main engines: Triple expansion; 1 600 ihp 1 shaft = 12 knots
Boilers: 2 Babcock & Wilcox D-type; oil burning

Former US ocean rescue tug. Built in the USA. Launched in 1943. Largely of wooden construction. Purchased in 1948.

GRANMA A 11

Yacht which reached Cuba on 2 Dec 1956 with Dr Fidel Castro and the men who began the liberation war. Historic vessel incorporated into the Navy as an Auxiliary.

3 HARBOUR AUXILIARIES

A1   A2   A3

Displacement, tons: 60
Dimensions, feet (metres): 74 × 15 × 5 *(22·6 × 4·6 × 1·5)*
Gun: 1 MG
Main engines: 2 diesels

Built in USA 1949.

CYPRUS

Personnel

1976: 330 officers and men

Mercantile Marine

Lloyd's Register of Shipping:
  735 vessels of 3 221 070 tons gross

LIGHT FORCES

6 Ex-SOVIET "P 4" CLASS

Displacement, tons: 25
Dimensions, feet (metres): 62·7 × 11·6 × 6·5 *(19·1 × 3·5 × 1·7)*
Guns: 2—25 mm
Tubes: 2—18 in
Main engines: 2 diesels; 2 200 bhp; 2 shafts = 50 knots
Complement: 12

Four of these were transferred by USSR in Oct 1964 and two in Feb 1965. Also reported that two extra engines have been supplied since that time.

Radar: Skinhead.

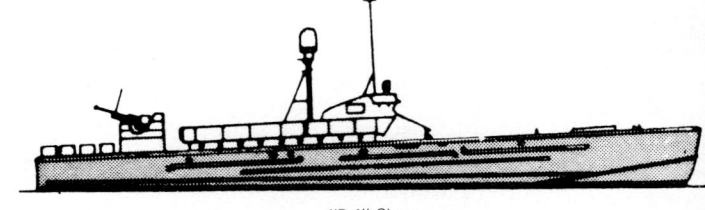

"P 4" Class

2 Ex-GERMAN "R" CLASS

Displacement, tons: 125
Dimensions, feet (metres): 124 × 19 × 4·5 *(37·8 × 5·8 × 1·4)*
Guns: 1—40 mm; 1—20 mm
Main engines: 2 MAN (MTU) diesels; 1 800 bhp = 18 knots

Built in 1943.

Originally three of this class were taken up from mercantile use and re-armed. One was destroyed by Turkish air attack on 8 Aug 1964 at Xeros.

It is reported that there are 10 small craft of about 50 tons, armed with one or two 20 mm guns.

"R" Class

1972, Dr. Giorgio Arra

CZECHOSLOVAKIA

Although a navy as such does not exist there is a river patrol force, the personnel of which wear naval-type uniforms.

DENMARK

Headquarters Appointment

Commander-in-Chief:
Vice-Admiral S. Thostrup

Diplomatic Representation

Defence Attaché, Bonn
Colonel P. E. M. O. Gruner
Defence Attaché, London:
Colonel H. H. Prince Georg of Denmark, KCVO
Assistant Defence Attaché, London:
Commander I. E. Eriksen, MVO
Defence Attaché, Washington:
Colonel P. B. Nissen

Personnel

(a) 1976: 5 800 officers and men
(Reserves of 3 100 Naval Home Guard)
(b) 9 months National service

Navy Estimates

1973-74: 583 600 000 Kr.
1974-75: 638 500 000 Kr.

Naval Bases

Copenhagen, Korsør, Frederikshavn, Grønnedal (Greenland)

Farvands Direktoratet

This Directorate of Waters (under the MOD) now controls the Pilot Service. Lighthouse Service, and Lifeboat service.

Naval Air Arm

8 Alouette III helicopters

Prefix to Ships' Names

HDMS

Strength of the Fleet

Type	Active	Building or Projected
Frigates	7	—
Corvettes	3	(3)
Submarines (Patrol)	6	—
Fast Attack Craft (Missile)	4	6
Fast Attack Craft (Torpedo)	10	—
Large Patrol Craft	23	—
Coastal Patrol Craft	15	—
Minelayers	4	2
Minesweepers (Coastal)	8	—
Depot Ship	1	—
Tankers (Small)	2	—
Icebreakers	4	—
Royal Yacht	1	—

Mercantile Marine

Lloyd's Register of Shipping:
1 371 vessels of 4 478 112 tons gross

New Construction

Programme includes 6 Corvettes, 6 Submarines, 2 Minelayers, 4 MCM Vessels, 3 Mine Transports, 24 Fast Attack Craft.

DELETIONS

Corvette

1974 *Diana* ("Triton" class)

Fast Attack Craft

1974 6 "Flyvefisken" Class

Large Patrol Craft

1972 *Alholm*

Coastal Patrol Craft

1975 Y 354, Y 359

Mine Warfare Forces

1974 2 "Lougen" Class Minelayers
4 "Vig" Class Inshore Minesweepers

Tenders

1970 *Hollaenderdybet, Kongedybet*

Icebreaker

1972 *Lillebjørn*

PENNANT LIST

Frigates and Corvettes

F 340	Beskytteren
F 344	Bellona
F 346	Flora
F 347	Triton
F 348	Hvidbjørnen
F 349	Vaedderen
F 350	Ingolf
F 351	Fylla
F 352	Peder Skram
F 353	Herluf Trolle

Submarines

S 320	Nahrvalen
S 321	Nordkaperen
S 326	Delfinen
S 327	Spaekhuggeren
S 328	Tumleren
S 329	Springeren

Light Forces

P 506	Falken
P 507	Glenten
P 508	Gribben
P 509	Høgen
P 510	Søloven
P 511	Søridderen
P 512	Søbjørnen
P 513	Søhesten
P 514	Søhunden
P 515	Søulven
P 530	Daphne
P 531	Dryaden
P 532	Havmanden
P 533	Havfruen
P 534	Najaden
P 535	Nymfen
P 536	Neptun
P 537	Ran
P 538	Rota
P 540	Bille

Light Forces

P 541	Bredal
P 542	Hammer
P 543	Huitfeldt
P 544	Krieger
P 545	Norby
P 546	Rodsteen
P 547	Sehested
P 548	Suenson
P 549	Willemoes
Y 300	Barsø
Y 301	Drejø
Y 302	Romsø
Y 303	Samsø
Y 304	Thurø
Y 305	Vejrø
Y 306	Farø
Y 307	Laesø
Y 308	Rømø
Y 371	Ertholm
Y 374	Lindholm

Light Forces

Y 383	Tejsten
Y 384	Maagen
Y 385	Mallemukken
Y 386	Agdleq
Y 387	Agpa

Minewarfare Forces

N 80	Falster
N 81	Fyen
N 82	Møen
N 83	Sjaelland
M 571	Aarøsund
M 572	Alssund
M 573	Egernsund
M 574	Grønsund
M 575	Guldborgsund
M 576	Omøsund
M 577	Ulvsund
M 578	Wilsund

Auxiliaries

A 540	Dannebrog
A 542	Henrik Gerner
A 568	Rimfaxe
A 569	Skinfaxe

Naval Home Guard

69	Faenø
81	Askø
82	Enø
83	Mano
84	Baagø
85	Hjortø
86	Lyø

"PEDER SKRAM" Class

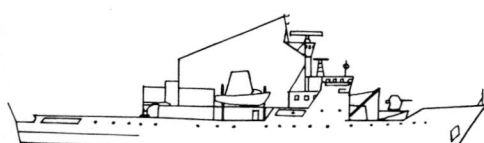

"HVIDBJORNEN" Class

"FALSTER" Class

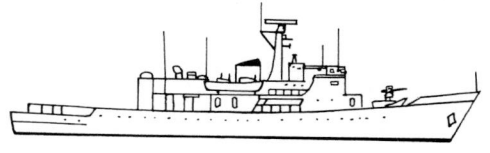

BESKYTTEREN

FRIGATES

2 "PEDER SKRAM" CLASS

Name	No.
HERLUF TROLLE	F 353
PEDER SKRAM	F 352

Builders	Laid down	Launched	Commissioned
Helsingörs J. & M.	18 Dec 1964	8 Sep 1965	16 Apr 1967
Helsingörs J. & M.	25 Sep 1964	20 May 1965	30 June 1966

Displacement, tons: 2 030 standard; 2 720 full load
Length, feet (metres): 354·3 (108) pp; 396·5 (112·6) oa
Beam, feet (metres): 39·5 (12)
Draught, feet (metres): 11·8 (3·6)
Missiles: 1 Sea Sparrow system on quarter-deck
Guns: 4—5 in (127 mm) 38 cal (twins); 4—40 mm
A/S weapons: DCs, A/S Torpedo launchers on each beam
Main engines: CODOG:—2 GM 16-567 D diesels; 4 800 hp; 2 Pratt & Whitney PWA GG 4A-3 gas turbines; 44 000 hp total output; 2 shafts
Speed, knots: 30, 18 economical
Complement: 112

Danish design. In addition to other armament they were originally designed for three 21 inch torpedo tubes and the "Terne" anti-submarine weapon.

Radar: Search: two E Band air and surface search.
Tactical: I Band. Fire Control: three I Band and Contraves.

PEDER SKRAM

1974, Royal Danish Navy

4 "HVIDBJØRNEN" CLASS

Name	No.
FYLLA	F 351
HVIDBJØRNEN	F 348
INGOLF	F 350
VAEDDEREN	F 349

Builders	Laid down	Launched	Commissioned
Aalborg Vaerft	27 June1962	18 Dec 1962	10 July 1963
Aarhus Flydedok	4 June1961	23 Nov 1961	15 Dec 1962
Svendborg Vaerft	5 Dec 1961	27 July 1961	27 July 1963
Aalborg Vaerft	30 Oct 1961	6 Apr 1962	19 Mar 1963

Displacement, tons: 1 345 standard; 1 650 full load
Length, feet (metres): 219·8 (67·0) pp; 238·2 (72·6) oa
Beam, feet (metres): 38·0 (11·6)
Draught, feet (metres): 16 (4·9)
Aircraft: 1 Alouette III helicopter
Gun: 1—3 in (76 mm)
Main engines: 4 GM 16—567C diesels; 6 400 bhp; 1 shaft
Speed, knots: 18
Range, miles: 6 000 at 13 knots
Complement: 75

Ordered in 1960-61. Of frigate type for fishery protection and surveying duties in the North Sea, Faroe Islands and Greenland waters. They are equipped with a helicopter platform aft.

Radar: Search: E Band combined air and surface.
Navigation: I Band.

INGOLF

1974, Royal Danish Navy

1 MODIFIED "HVIDBJØRNEN" CLASS

Name	No.
BESKYTTEREN	F 340

Builders	Laid down	Launched	Commissioned
Aalborg Vaerft	1970	1974	Oct 1975

Length, feet (metres): 244 (74·4) oa
Beam, feet (metres): 39 (11·8)
Draught, feet (metres): 15 (4·5)
Aircraft: 1 Alouette III helicopter
Gun: 1—3 in (76 mm)
Main engines: 4 B.W. Alpha diesels; 7 440 bhp; 1 shaft
Speed, knots: 18
Range, miles: 4 500 at 16 knots
Complement: 60

Cost approx £5 million

BESKYTTEREN

1975, Royal Danish Navy

CORVETTES

3 NEW CONSTRUCTION "KV 72" CLASS

Displacement, tons: 1 000
Dimensions, feet (metres): 270 approx × — ×— (82 approx × — ×—)
Missiles: Seasparrow; SSMs (?6)
Guns: 1—76 mm; 2—40 mm
Main engines: CODOG
Speed, knots: 30+

First of a class which may reach a total of 6. Designed to replace "Triton" Class.

"KV 72" Class

3 "TRITON" CLASS

Name	No.
BELLONA	F 344
FLORA	F 346
TRITON	F 347

Builders	Laid down	Launched	Commissioned
Naval Meccanicia, Castellammare	1954	9 Jan 1955	31 Jan 1957
Cantiere del Tirreno, Riva Trigoso	1953	25 June1955	28 Aug 1956
Cantiere Navali di Taranto	1953	12 Sep 1954	10 Aug 1955

Displacement, tons: 760 standard; 873 full load
Length, feet (metres): 242·8 (74·0) pp; 250·3 (76·3) oa
Beam, feet (metres): 31·5 (9·6)
Draught, feet (metres): 9 (2·7)
Guns: 2—3 in (76 mm); 1—40 mm
A/S: 2 Hedgehogs; 4 DCT
Main engines: 2 Ansaldo Fiat 409T diesels, 4 400 bhp; 2 shafts
Speed, knots: 20
Range, miles: 3 000 at 18 knots
Complement: 110

These were built in Italy for the Danish Navy under the United States "offshore" account. Sisters of the Italian "Albatros" class. *Diana* deleted 1974.

Radar: Search: Plessey AWS 1. Navigation: E Band.

Classification: Officially classified as corvettes in 1954, but have "F" pennant numbers.

FLORA   1974, Royal Danish Navy

SUBMARINES

2 "NARHVALEN" CLASS

Name	No.
NARHVALEN	S 320
NORDKAPEREN	S 321

Builders	Laid down	Launched	Commissioned
Royal Dockyard, Copenhagen	16 Feb 1965	10 Sep 1968	27 Feb 1970
Royal Dockyard, Copenhagen	20 Jan 1966	18 Dec 1969	22 Dec 1970

Displacement, tons: 370 surfaced; 450 dived
Length, feet (metres): 144·4 (44·3)
Beam, feet (metres): 15 (4·6)
Draught, feet (metres): 12·5 (3·8)
Torpedo tubes: 8—21 in (533 mm) bow
Main Machinery: 2 MB (MTU) diesels; 1 500 bhp surfaced; 2 electric motors; 1 500 bhp dived
Speed, knots: 12 surfaced; 17 dived
Complement: 22

These coastal submarines are similar to the German Improved Type 205 and were built under licence at the Royal Dockyard, Copenhagen with modifications for Danish needs. They are fitted with snort and radar.

NAHRVALEN   1974, Royal Danish Navy

4 "DELFINEN" CLASS

Name	No.
DELFINEN	S 326
SPAEKHUGGEREN	S 327
TUMLERIN	S 328
SPRINGEREN	S 329

Builders	Laid down	Launched	Commissioned
Royal Dockyard, Copenhagen	1 July 1954	4 May 1956	16 Sep 1958
Royal Dockyard, Copenhagen	1 Dec 1954	20 Feb 1957	27 June1959
Royal Dockyard, Copenhagen	22 May 1956	22 May 1958	15 Jan 1960
Royal Dockyard, Copenhagen	3 Jan 1961	26 Apr 1963	22 Oct 1964

Displacement, tons: 550 standard; 595 surfaced; 643 dived
Length, feet (metres): 117·2 (54·0)
Beam, feet (metres): 15·4 (4·7)
Draught, feet (metres): 13·1 (4·0)
Torpedo tubes: 4—21 in (533 mm)
Main Machinery: 2 Burmeister & Wain (MTU) diesels; 2 600 bhp surfaced; electric motors
Speed, knots: 15 surfaced and dived
Range, miles: 4 000 at 8 knots
Complement: 33

Equipped with snort and radar.

TUMLEREN   1975, Royal Danish Navy

LIGHT FORCES

2 "AGDLEQ" CLASS (LARGE PATROL CRAFT)

Name	No.	Builders	Commissioned
AGDLEQ	Y 386	Svendborg Vaerft	12 Mar 1974
AGPA	Y 387	Svendborg Vaerft	14 May 1974

Displacement, tons: 300
Dimensions, feet (metres): 101·7 × 25·3 × 10·9 *(31 × 7·7 × 3·3)*
Guns: 2—20 mm (twin)
Speed, knots: 12

Designed for service off Greenland.

AGDLEQ   *1974, Royal Danish Navy*

10 "WILLEMOES" CLASS (FAST ATTACK CRAFT—MISSILE)

Name	No.	Builders	Commissioned
BILLE	P 540	Frederikshavn V and F	1975
BREDAL	P 541	Frederikshavn V and F	1975
HAMMER	P 542	Frederikshavn V and F	1976
HUITFELDE	P 543	Frederikshavn V and F	1976
KRIEGER	P 544	Frederikshavn V and F	—
NORBY	P 545	Frederikshavn V and F	—
RODSTEEN	P 546	Frederikshavn V and F	—
SEHESTED	P 547	Frederikshavn V and F	—
SUENSON	P 548	Frederikshavn V and F	—
WILLEMOES	P 549	Frederikshavn V and F	—

Displacement, tons: 220
Dimensions, feet (metres): 151 × 24 × 8 *(46 × 7·4 × 2·4)*
Guided weapons: To be installed
Guns: 1—76 mm Oto Melara or 1—57 mm L 70 Bofors
Torpedo tubes: 4—21 in
Main engines: CODAG arrangement of 3 Rolls Royce Proteus gas turbines plus diesels for cruising on wing shafts
Speed, knots: 40

First four ordered in 1971. Lürssen Werft design. Controllable pitch propellers.

WILLEMOES Class   *1975, Royal Danish Navy*

4 "FALKEN" CLASS (FAST ATTACK CRAFT—TORPEDO)

Name	No.	Builders	Commissioned
FALKEN	P 506	R. Dockyard, Copenhagen	4 Oct 1962
GLENTEN	P 507	R. Dockyard, Copenhagen	15 Dec 1962
GRIBBEN	P 508	R. Dockyard, Copenhagen	26 Apr 1963
HØGEN	P 509	R. Dockyard, Copenhagen	6 June 1963

Displacement, tons: 119
Dimensions, feet (metres): 118 × 17·8 × 6 *(35·9 × 5·4 × 1·8)*
Guns: 1—40 mm; 1—20 mm
Torpedo Tubes: 2—41 in
Main engines: 3 MTU diesels; 3 shafts; 9 000 bhp = 40 knots
Complement: 23

Ordered under US offshore procurement in the Military Aid Programme. All laid down in 1961-62.

HØGEN   *1974, Royal Danish Navy*

6 "SØLØVEN" CLASS (FAST ATTACK CRAFT—TORPEDO)

Name	No.	Builders	Commissioned
SØLØVEN	P 510	Vosper	12 Feb 1965
SØRIDDEREN	P 511	Vosper	10 Feb 1965
SØBJORNEN	P 512	R. Dockyard, Copenhagen	Sep 1965
SØHESTEN	P 513	R. Dockyard, Copenhagen	June 1966
SØHUNDEN	P 514	R. Dockyard, Copenhagen	Dec 1966
SØULVEN	P 515	R. Dockyard, Copenhagen	Mar 1967

Displacement, tons: 95 standard; 114 full load
Dimensions, feet (metres): 90 pp; 96 wl; 99 oa × 25·5 × 7 *(30·3 × 7·3 × 2·2)*
Guns: 2—40 mm Bofors
Torpedo tubes: 4—21 in
Main engines: 3 Bristol Siddeley Proteus gas turbines; 3 shafts; 12 750 bhp = 54 knots
   GM diesels on wing shafts for cruising = 10 knots
Range, miles: 400 at 46 knots
Complement: 29

The design is a combination of the Vosper "Brave" class hull form and "Ferocity" type construction. *Søløven* and *Søridderen* were both completed in June 1964 and handed over to the RDN after 6 month's trials.

SØHUNDEN   *1974, Royal Danish Navy*

9 "BARSØ" CLASS (LARGE PATROL CRAFT)

Name	No.	Builders	Commissioned
BARSØ	Y 300	—	1969
DREJØ	Y 301	—	1969
ROMSØ	Y 302	—	1969
SAMSØ	Y 303	—	1969
THURØ	Y 304	—	1969
VEJRØ	Y 305	—	1969
FARØ	Y 306	—	1972
LAESØ	Y 307	—	1973
ROMØ	Y 308	—	1973

Displacement, tons: 155
Dimensions, feet (metres): 83·7 × 19·7 × 9·8 *(25·5 × 6 × 2·8)*
Speed: 11 knots

Rated as patrol cutters.

DREJØ   *1974, Royal Danish Navy*

2 "MAAGEN" CLASS (LARGE PATROL CRAFT)

Name	No.	Builders	Commissioned
MAAGEN	Y 384	Helsingør	May 1960
MALLEMUKKEN	Y 385	Helsingør	May 1960

Displacement, tons: 190
Dimensions, feet (metres): 88·5 × 21·7 × 9·5 *(37 × 6·6 × 2·9*
Gun: 1—40 mm
Main engines: 385 hp; 1 shaft = 11 knots

Of steel construction. Laid down 15 Jan 1960.

1 "TEJSTEN" CLASS (LARGE PATROL CRAFT)

Name	No.	Builders	Commissioned
TEJSTEN	Y 383	Holbaek Skibsbyggeri	1951

Displacement, tons: 130
Dimensions, feet (metres): 82 × 20·7 × 9·4 *(25 × 6·1 × 2·9)*
Gun: 1—37 mm
Main engines: Alfa Diesel; 180 bhp = 9 knots

Auxiliary ketch of wooden construction. Based in Faeroe Is.

TEJSTEN   *1973, Royal Danish Navy*

9 "DAPHNE" CLASS (LARGE PATROL CRAFT)

Name	No.	Builders	Commissioned
DAPHNE	P 530	R. Dockyard, Copenhagen	19 Dec 1961
DRYADEN	P 531	R. Dockyard, Copenhagen	4 Apr 1962
HAVFRUEN	P 533	R. Dockyard, Copenhagen	20 Dec 1962
HAVMANDEN	P 532	R. Dockyard, Copenhagen	30 Aug 1962
NAJADEN	P 534	R. Dockyard, Copenhagen	26 Apr 1963
NEPTUN	P 536	R. Dockyard, Copenhagen	18 Dec 1963
NYMFEN	P 535	R. Dockyard, Copenhagen	4 Oct 1963
RAN	P 537	R. Dockyard, Copenhagen	15 May 1964
ROTA	P 538	R. Dockyard, Copenhagen	20 Jan 1965

Displacement, tons: 170
Dimensions, feet (metres): 121·3 × 20 × 6·5 *(38 × 6·8 × 2)*
Gun: 1—40 mm
A/S weapons: 2—51 mm rocket launchers; depth charges
Main engines: Diesels; 2 shafts; 2 600 bhp = 20 knots (plus 1 cruising engine; 100 bhp)
Complement: 23

4 were built under US offshore programme.

NEPTUN   *1974, Royal Danish Navy*

2 LARGE BOTVED TYPE (COASTAL PATROL CRAFT)

Y 375   Y376

Displacement, tons: 12
Dimensions, feet (metres): 42·9 × 14·8 × 3·7 *(13·3 × 4·5 × 1·1)*
Main engines: Diesel; 2 shafts; 680 hp = 26 knots

Built in 1974 by Botved Boats

Y 376   *1975, Royal Danish Navy*

3 SMALL BOTVED TYPE (COASTAL PATROL CRAFT)

Y 377   Y 378   Y 379

Displacement, tons: 9
Dimensions, feet (metres): 32·1 × 10·4 × 3·1 *(9·8 × 3·3 × 0·9)*
Main engines: Diesels; 2 shafts; 500 hp = 27 knots

Built in 1975 by Botved Boats.

Small BOTVED Type   *1975, Royal Danish Navy*

1 "FYRHOLM" CLASS (COASTAL PATROL CRAFT)

Name	No.	Builders	Commissioned
LINDHOLM (ex-*MSK* 6)	Y 374	Sydhavns Vaerft	1945

Displacement, tons: 68
Dimensions, feet (metres): 65·7 × 16·8 × 7·5 *(20 × 5·1 × 2·3)*
Main engines: Diesel; 120 bhp = 9 knots

1 "ALHOLM" CLASS (COASTAL PATROL CRAFT)

Name	No.	Builders	Commissioned
ERTHOLM (ex-*MSK* 3)	Y 371	Frederiksund Vaerft	1945

Displacement, tons: 70
Dimensions, feet (metres): 69 × 17 × 9 *(24·6 × 6·2 × 2·8)*
Gun: 1—20 mm
Main engines: Diesel; 120 bhp = 10 knots

3 Y TYPE (COASTAL PATROL CRAFT)

Y 338   Y 339   Y 343

Miscellaneous patrol cutters (ex-fishing vessels) all built in 1944-45.

6 "MHV 90" CLASS

MHV 90   MHV 91   MHV 92   MHV 93   MHV 94   MHV 95

Displacement, tons: 90
Dimensions, feet (metres): 64·9 × 18·7 × 8·2 *(19·8 × 5·7 × 2·5)*
Gun: 1—20 mm
Main engines: Diesel; 1 shaft = 10 knots

Built in 1975. Manned by Naval Home Guard.

MHV 93   *1975, Royal Danish Navy*

7 "MHV 80" CLASS (COASTAL PATROL CRAFT)

Name	No.	Builders	Commissioned
ASKØ (ex-Y 386, ex-M 560, ex-MS 2)	MHV 81	Denmark	1941
BAAGØ (ex-Y 387, ex-M 561, ex-MS 3)	MHV 84	Denmark	1941
ENØ (ex-Y 388, ex-M 562, ex-MS 5)	MHV 82	Denmark	1941
FAENØ (ex-M 563, ex-MS 6)	MHV 69	Denmark	1941
HJORTØ (ex-Y 389, ex-M 564, ex- MS 7)	MHV 85	Denmark	1941
LYØ (ex-Y 390, ex-M 565, ex-MS 8)	MHV 86	Denmark	1941
MANØ (ex-Y 391, ex-M 566, ex-MS 9)	MHV 83	Denmark	1941

Displacement, tons: 74
Dimensions, feet (metres): 78·8 × 21 × 5 *(24·4 × 4·9 × 1·6)*
Gun: 1—20 mm
Main engines: Diesel; 1 shaft; 350 bhp = 11 knots

Of wooden construction. All launched in 1941. Former inshore minesweepers. Manned by the Naval Home Guard.

FAENO   *1974, Royal Danish Navy*

3 "MHV 70" CLASS (COASTAL PATROL CRAFT)

Name	No.	Builders	Commissioned
MHV 70	—	R. Dockyard, Copenhagen	1958
MHV 71	—	R. Dockyard, Copenhagen	1958
MHV 72	—	R. Dockyard, Copenhagen	1958

Displacement, tons: 76
Dimensions, feet (metres): 65·9 × 16·7 × 8·2 *(20·1 × 5·1 × 2·5)*
Gun: 1—20 mm
Main engines: 200 bhp = 10 knots

Patrol boats and training craft for the Naval Home Guard. Formerly designated DMH, but allocated MHV numbers in 1969.

In addition there are some 20 small vessels of the trawler and other types.

MHV 71   *1974, Royal Danish Navy*

MINE WARFARE FORCES

4 "FALSTER" CLASS MINELAYERS

Name	No.	Builders	Commissioned
FALSTER	N 80	Nakskov Skibsvaerft	7 Nov 1963
FYEN	N 81	Frederikshavn Vaerft	18 Sep 1963
MØEN	N 82	Frederikshavn Vaerft	29 Apr 1964
SJAELLAND	N 83	Nakskov Skibsvaerft	7 July 1964

Displacement, tons: 1 900 full load
Length, feet (metres): 238 *(72·5)* pp; 252·6 *(77·0)* oa
Beam, feet (metres): 41 *(12·5)*
Draught, feet (metres): 10 *(3·0)*
Missiles: Seasparrow
Guns: 4—3 in *(76 mm)*, 2 twin mountings
Mines: 400
Main engines: 2 GM—567D 3 diesels; 4 800 shp; 2 shafts
Speed, knots: 17
Complement: 120

Ordered in 1960-61 and launched 1962-63. All are named after Danish islands. The steel hull is flush-decked with a raking stem, a full stern and a prominent knuckle forward. The hull has been specially strengthened for ice navigation. Similar to Turkish *Nusret*.

Radar: Search: G Band low coverage. Navigation: E and I Band.

SJAELLAND

1972, Royal Danish Navy

2 NEW CONSTRUCTION MINELAYERS "N 43" CLASS

Name	No.	Builders	Commissioned
—	N 43	Svendborg Vaerft	1976
—	N 44	Svendborg Vaerft	1976

Displacement, tons: 570
Dimensions, feet (metres): 147·6 × 29·5 × 8·9 *(45 × 9 × 2·7)*
Guns: 2—20 mm
Main engines: Diesels = 14 knots
Complement: 27

Replacements for "Lougen" Class. Controlled Minelayers.

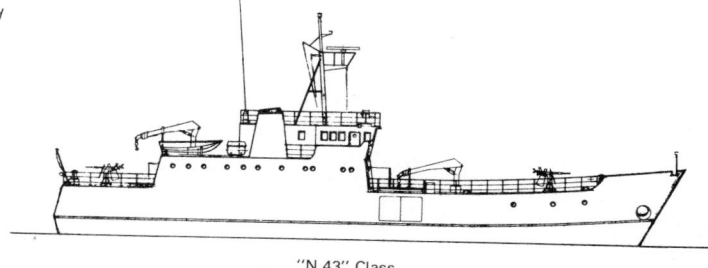

"N 43" Class

8 "SUND" CLASS (MINESWEEPERS—COASTAL)

AARØSUND (ex-*MSC* 127) M 571
ALSSUND (ex-*MCS* 128) M 572
EGERNSUND (ex-*MSC* 129) M 573
GRØNSUND (ex-*MSC* 256) M 574

GULDBORGSUND (ex-*MSC* 257) M 575
OMØSUND (ex-*MSC* 221) M 576
ULVSUND (ex-*MSC* 263) M 577
VILSUND (ex-*MSC* 264) M 578

Displacement, tons: 350 standard; 376 full load
Dimensions, feet (metres): 138 pp; 144 oa × 27 × 8·5 *(41·5; 43 × 8 × 2·6)*
Guns: 2—20 mm
Main engines: Diesels; 2 shafts; 1 200 bhp = 13 knots
Range, miles: 2 500 at 10 knots
Complement: 35

MSC (ex-*AMS*) 60 class NATO coastal minesweepers all built in USA. Completed in 1954-56. *Aarøsund* was transferred on 24 Jan 1955, *Alssund* on 5 Apr 1955, *Egernsund* on 3 Aug 1955, *Grønsund* on 21 Sep 1956, *Guldborgsund* on 11 Nov 1956, *Omøsund* on 20 June 1956, *Ulvsund* on 20 Sep 1956 and *Vilsund* on 15 Nov 1956, *Guldborgsund* has been fitted with a charthouse between bridge and funnel and is employed on surveying duties.

SLEIPNER

A 200 ton torpedo recovery/transporter.

ULVSUND

1975, Reiner Nerlich

SERVICE FORCES
DEPOT SHIP

Name	No.	Builder	Commissioned
HENRIK GERNER (ex-M/S *Hammershus*)	A 542	–	1936

Displacement, tons: 2 200 standard
Dimensions, feet (metres): 252·7 × 40 × 18·3 *(81 × 12 × 2·5)*
Main engines: Burmeister & Wain diesel; speed = 15 knots
Complement: 230

Former Danish passenger ship. Built in 1936. Transferred to the Royal Danish Navy on 8 Jan 1964, refitted at the Royal Dockyard, Copenhagen, and commissioned as a depot ship for submarines.

HENRIK GERNER

1971, Royal Danish Navy

TANKERS

Name	No.	Builders	Commissioned
RIMFAXE (ex-US YO 226)	A 568	USA	1945
SKINFAXE (ex-US YO 229)	A 569	USA	1945

Displacement, tons: 422 light; 1 390 full load
Dimensions, feet (metres): 174 oa × 32 × 13·2 *(53·1 × 9·8 × 4)*
Main engines: 1 GM diesel; 560 bhp = 10 knots
Complement: 23

Transferred to the Royal Danish Navy from the USA on 2 Aug 1962.

RIMFAXE

1971, Royal Danish Navy

ICEBREAKERS

Note: Icebreakers are controlled by the Ministry of Trade and Shipping, but are maintained by RDN at Frederikshavn in summer.

Name	No.	Builders	Commissioned
DANBJØRN	—	—	1965
ISBJØRN	—	—	1956

Displacement, tons: 3 685
Dimensions, feet (metres): 252 × 56 × 20 *(75·6 × 16·8 × 6)*
Main engines: Diesels; Electric drive; 11 880 bhp = 14 knots
Complement: 34

DANBJØRN   *1970, Royal Danish Navy*

Name	No.	Builders	Commissioned
ELBJØRN	—	—	1953

Displacement, tons: 893 standard; 1 400 full load
Dimensions, feet (metres): 156·5 × 40·3 × 14·5 *(47 × 12·1 × 4·4)*
Main engines: Diesels; electric drive; 3 600 bhp = 12 knots

Recently used by RDN for surveying in summer.

Name	No.	Builders	Commissioned
STOREBJØRN	—	—	1931

Displacement, tons: 2 540
Dimensions, feet (metres): 197 × 49·2 × 19 *(59·1 × 14·8 × 5·7)*

ROYAL YACHT

Name	No.	Builders	Commissioned
DANNEBROG	A 540	R. Dockyard, Copenhagen	1932

Displacement, tons: 1 130
Dimensions, feet (metres): 246 oa × 34 × 11·2 *(75 × 10·4 × 3·4)*
Guns: 2—37 mm
Main engines: 2 sets Burmeister & Wain 8 cylinder; 2 cycle diesels; 1 800 bhp = 14 knots
Complement: 57

Launched on 10 Oct 1931.

DANNEBROG   *1971, Royal Danish Navy*

DOMINICAN REPUBLIC

Headquarters Appointments

Chief of Naval Staff:
  Commodore Francisco J. Rivera Caminero
Vice-Chief of Naval Staff:
  Captain Francisco Ant. Marte Victoria

Personnel

(a) 1976: 4 100 officers and men
(b) Selective Military Service

Mercantile Marine

Lloyd's Register of Shipping:
  20 vessels of 9 920 tons gross

Maritime Air
(All operated by Dominican Air Force)

2 PBY-5A Catalinas
3 Alouette II/III helicopters
2 H-19 Chickasaws
7 OH-6A Cayuse
2 Hiller 12-E Ravens

Naval Bases

"27 Febrero": HQ of CNS. Naval School. Marine Training.
Haina: Naval Dockyard (Ast. Navales Dominicanos)
"Las Calderas": Naval Training Centre, Supply Base and 750-ton lift marine elevator.
San Pedro de Macoris.

Strength of the Fleet

Type	Active	Projected
Frigates	3	—
Corvettes	7	—
Large Patrol Craft	2	—
Coastal Patrol Craft	13	—
LSM	1	—
LCU	1	1
Survey Vessel	1	—
Tankers (Small)	2	—
Tugs (Large)	2	—
Tugs (Harbour)	6	—

DELETIONS

Destroyers

1972 *Duarte* (ex-HMS *Hotspur*)

Corvettes

1972 *Gerardo Jansen, Juan Bautista Cambiaso, Juan Bautista Maggiola* (all ex-Canadian "Flower" class)

Light Forces

1975 *Maymyon, Puerto Hemosa*

Tugs

1975 *Consuelo, Haina, Santana*

Survey Craft

1972 *Caonobo*

FRIGATES

2 Ex-US "TACOMA" CLASS

Name
CAP. GENERAL PEDRO SANTANA
(ex-*Presidente Peynado*, ex-USS *Knoxville*, PF 64)
GREGORIO LUPERON
(ex-*Presidente Troncoso*, ex-USS *Pueblo*, PF 13)

Displacement, tons: 1 430 standard; 2 415 full load
Length, feet (metres): 298·0 *(90·8)* wl; 304·0 *(92·7)* oa
Beam, feet (metres): 37·5 *(11·4)*
Draught, feet (metres): 13·7 *(4·2)*
Guns: 3—3 in *(76 mm)* single; 4—40 mm (2 twin);
6—20 mm; 4—0·5 in *(12·7 mm)* MG (2 twin)
Main engines: Triple expansion; 2 shafts; 5 500 ihp
Boilers: 2 of three-drum type
Speed, knots: 19
Oil fuel, tons: 760
Range, miles: 9 500 at 12 knots
Complement: 140

Formerly United States patrol frigates, PF of the "Tacoma" class similar to the contemporary British frigates of the "River" class. Transferred from the US Navy to the Dominican Republic Navy in July 1946 (453) and Sept 1947 (452). Renamed in 1962.

No.	Builders	Laid down	Launched	Commissioned
453 (ex-F 104)	Kaiser S.Y. Richmond, Cal.	14 Nov 1943	20 Jan 1944	27 May 1944
452 (ex-F 103)	Leatham D. Smith S.B. Co. Wis.	15 April 1943	10 July 1943	29 April 1944

GREGORIO LUPERON

1972, Dominican Navy

1 Ex-CANADIAN "RIVER" CLASS

Name
MELLA (ex-*Presidente Trujillo*, ex-HMCS *Carlplace*)

Displacement, tons: 1 400 standard; 2 125 full load
Length, feet (metres): 310·5 *(91·9)*
Beam, feet (metres): 36·7 *(11·2)*
Draught, feet (metres): 12·0 *(3·7)*
Guns: 1—4 in; 2—47 mm; 1—40 mm; 4—20 mm (2 twin)
Main engines: Triple expansion; 2 shafts; 5 500 ihp
Boilers: 2 of three-drum type
Speed, knots: 20
Oil fuel, tons: 645
Range, miles: 4 200 at 12 knots
Complement: 195 (15 officers, 130 ratings, 50 midshipmen)

Transferred to the Dominican Navy in 1946. Modified for use as Presidential yacht with extra accommodation and deck-houses built up aft. Pennant number as a frigate was F 101, but as the Presidential yacht it was no longer worn. Now carries pennant number 451 as training ship. Renamed *Mella* in 1962. Used for training midshipmen.

No.	Builders	Laid down	Launched	Commissioned
451	Davies SB & Repairing Co., Lauzon, Canada	—	6 July 1944	1944

MELLA

1972, Dominican Navy

CORVETTES

2 Ex-CANADIAN "FLOWER" CLASS

Name
CRISTOBAL COLON (ex-HMCS *Lachute*)
JUAN ALEJANDRO ACOSTA (ex-HMCS *Louisburg*)

Displacement, tons: 1 060 standard; 1 350 full load
Length, feet (metres): 193·0 *(58·8)* pp; 208·0 *(63·4)* oa
Beam, feet (metres): 33·0 *(10·0)*
Draught, feet (metres): 13·3 *(4·0)*
Guns: 1—4 in *(102 mm)*
C. Colon: 2—40 mm (twin); 6—20 mm; 4—0·5 in MG (2 twin)
J. A. Acosta: 1—40 mm; 6—20 mm; 2—0·5 in MG
Main engines: Triple expansion; 2 750 ihp
Boilers: 2 of three-drum type
Speed, knots: 16
Oil fuel, tons: 282
Range, miles: 2 900 at 15 knots
Complement: 53

Built in Canadian shipyards under the emergency construction programme during the Second World War. Five were transferred to the Dominican Navy in 1947. Pennant numbers were changed in 1968.

No.	Builders	Laid down	Launched	Commissioned
401 (ex-C 101)	Morton Ltd, Quebec City, P.Q.	—	9 June 1944	24 Oct 1944
402 (ex-C 102)	Morton Ltd, Quebec City, P.Q.	—	13 July 1943	13 Dec 1943

JUAN ALEJANDRO ACOSTA

1972, Dominican Navy

2 Ex-US "ADMIRABLE" CLASS

Name	No.	Builders	Commissioned
SEPARACIÓN	BM 454	Associated SB	16 Aug 1943
(ex-USS *Skirmish, MSF 303*)			
TORTUGERO	BM 455	Associated SB	16 Aug 1943
(ex-USS *Signet, MSF 302*)			

Displacement, tons: 650 standard; 900 full load
Dimensions, feet (metres): 180·0 wl; 184·5 oa × 33·0 × 14·5 *(56·3 × 9·9 × 4·4)*
Guns: 1—3 in; 2—40 mm; 6—20 mm
Main engines: 2 diesels; 2 shafts; 1 710 bhp = 14 knots
Range, miles: 5 600 at 9 knots
Complement: 90 (8 officers, 82 men)

Former US fleet minesweepers. Purchased on 13 Jan 1965.

SEPARACIÓN   *1972, Dominican Navy*

3 Ex-USCG WPC TYPE

Name	No.	Builders	Commissioned
INDEPENDENCIA	204	Bath Ironworks	1932
(ex-USCGC *Icarus*)	(ex-*P 105*)		
LIBERTAD	205	—	—
(ex-*Rafael Atoa*, ex-USCGC *Thetis*)	(ex-*P 106*)		
RESTAURACION	203	John H. Machis & Co,	1933
(ex-USCGC *Galathea*)	(ex-*P 104*)	Camden, N.J.	

Displacement, tons: 337 standard
Dimensions, feet (metres): 165·0 × 25·2 × 9·5 *(50·3 × 7·7 × 2·9)*
Guns: 1—3 in; 1—40 mm; 1—20 mm
Main engines: 2 Diesels; 1 280 bhp = 15 knots
Range, miles: 1 300 at 15 knots
Complement: 49 (5 officers, 44 men)

Ex-US Coastguard Cutters.

RESTAURACION   *1972, Dominican Navy*

LIGHT FORCES

1 US PGM TYPE (LARGE PATROL CRAFT)

Name	No.	Builders	Commissioned
BETELGEUSE (ex-US *PGM 77*)	GC 102	Peterson, USA	1966

Displacement, tons: 145·5
Dimensions, feet (metres): 101·5 × 21·0 × 5·0 *(40 × 6·4 × 1·5)*
Guns: 1—40 mm; 4—20 mm (2 twin); 2—0·5 in 50 cal MG
Main engines: 4 diesels; 2 shafts; 2 200 bhp = 21 knots
Range, miles: 1 500 at 10 knots
Complement: 20

Built in the USA and transferred to the Dominican Republic under the Military Aid Programme on 14 Jan 1966.

BETELGEUSE   *1972, Dominican Navy*

1 LARGE PATROL CRAFT

Name	No.	Builders	Commissioned
CAPITAN ALSINA (ex-*RL 101*)	GC 105	—	1944

Displacement, tons: 100 standard
Dimensions, feet (metres): 92·0 wl; 104·8 oa × 19·2 × 5·8 *(32 × 5·9 × 1·8)*
Guns: 2—20 mm
Main engines: 2 GM diesels; 2 shafts; 1 000 hp = 17 knots
Complement: 20

Of wooden construction. Launched in 1944. Named as above in 1957.

CAPITAN ALSINA

1 "ATLANTIDA" CLASS (COASTAL PATROL CRAFT)

ATLANTIDA BA 8

Probably employed on surveying duties.

4 "BELLATRIX" CLASS (COASTAL PATROL CRAFT)

Name	No.	Builders	Commissioned
BELLATRIX	GC 106	Sewart Seacraft Inc, Berwick, La.	—
PROCYON	GC 103	Sewart Seacraft Inc, Berwick, La.	—
CAPELLA	GC 108	Sewart Seacraft Inc, Berwick, La.	—
ALDEBARÁN	GC 104	Sewart Seacraft Inc, Berwick, La.	—

Displacement, tons: 60
Dimensions, feet (metres): 85 × 18 × 5 *(25·9 × 5·5 × 1·5)*
Guns: 3—5 MG
Main engines: 2 GM Diesels; 500 bhp = 18·7 knots

Transferred to the Dominican Navy by USA, *Bellatrix* on 18 Aug 1967, *Procyon* on 1 May 1967, *Capella* on 15 Oct 1968 and *Aldebarán* in May 1972.

BELLATRIX   *1970, Dominican Navy*

1 COASTAL PATROL CRAFT

Name	No.	Builders	Commissioned
GEL (ex-*US AVR*)	GC 101	—	1953

Displacement, tons: 27 standard; 32·2 full load
Dimensions, feet (metres): 63·0 × 15·5 × 5·0 *(19·2 × 4·7 × 1·5)*
Guns: 2—50 cal MG
Main engines: General Motors V8—71 diesels = 18·5 knots
Complement: 9

Originally built in 1953. Reconditioned by NAUSTA, Key West, USA.

6 COASTAL PATROL CRAFT

Name	No.	Builders	Commissioned
CARITE	—	Ast. Navales Dominicanos	1975
ALBACORA	—	Ast. Navales Dominicanos	1975
BONITO	—	Ast. Navales Dominicanos	1975
ATÚN	—	Ast. Navales Dominicanos	1975
PICÚA	—	Ast. Navales Dominicanas	1975
MERO	—	Ast. Navales Dominicanos	1975

Displacement, tons: Approx 30
Dimensions, feet (metres): 45 × 13 × 6 *(13·7 × 4 × 1·8)*
Gun: 1—30 mm
Main engines: GM Diesels; 200 hp

AMPHIBIOUS FORCES

1 Ex-US LSM

Name	No.	Builders	Commissioned
SIRIO (ex-US *LSM 483*)	BDM 301 (ex-*BA 104*)	Brown SB Co, Houston	13 April 1945

Displacement, tons: 734 standard; 1 100 full load
Dimensions, feet (metres): 196 wl; 203·5 oa × 34 × 10 *(62·1 × 10·4 × 3·1)*
Main engines: 2 General Motors diesels; 2 shafts; 1 800 bhp = 14 knots
Oil fuel, tons: 164
Complement: 30

Ex-United States LSM (Medium Landing Ship). Laid down on 17 Feb 1945, launched on 10 Mar 1945 and completed on 13 April 1945. Transferred to the Dominican Navy in Mar 1958. Refitted in Dominican Republic in 1970.

SIRIO   1968, Dominican Navy

1 LCU

Name	No.	Builders	Commissioned
AMANA (ex-*LA 2*)	LDM 302	Ast. Navales Dominicanos	1958

Displacement, tons: 150 standard; 310 full load
Dimensions, feet (metres): 105 wl; 119·5 oa × 36 × 3 *(36·4 × 11 × 0·9)*
Gun: 1—50 cal MG
Main engines: 3 General Motors diesels; 441 bhp = 8 knots
Oil fuel, tons: 80
Complement: 17

SAMANA   1972, Dominican Navy

1 PLANNED NEW CONSTRUCTION (LCU)

Name	No.	Builders	Commissioned
COA	LDM 303	—	—

Displacement, tons: —
Dimensions, feet (metres): 56·2 × 14 × 3·9 *(17·1 × 4·3 × 1·2)*
Main engines: 2—6 cyl Diesels 225 bhp = 9 knots
Range, miles: 130 at 9 knots

Capacity about 30 tons.

SURVEY VESSELS

(See also *Atlantida* under Light Forces)

Name	No.	Builders	Commissioned
APOTILLO (ex-*Camillia*)	FB 1	—	—

Displacement, tons: 337
Dimensions, feet (metres): 117 × 24 × 7·8 *(35·7 × 7·3 × 2·4)*
Main engines: 2 Diesels; 880 bhp = 10 knots
Complement: 29

Built in the United States in 1911. Acquired from the United States Coast Guard in 1949. Underwent a major refit in Dominican Republic in 1970.

Name	No.	Builders	Commissioned
NEPTUNO (ex-*Toro*)	BA 10	John H. Mathis Co, New Jersey	Feb 1954

Measurement, tons: 67·1 (net)
Dimensions, feet (metres): 64 × 18·7 × 8 *(19·5 × 5·7 × 2·4)*
Main engines: 2 Diesels = 12·5 knots

NEPTUNO   1975, Dominican Navy

TANKERS

2 Ex-US YO TYPE

Name	No.	Builders	Commissioned
APITAN W. ARVELO (ex-US *YO 213*)	—	Ira S. Bushey Inc, Brooklyn	1943
APITAN BEOTEGUI (ex-US *YO 215*)	—	Ira S. Bushey Inc, Brooklyn	1945

Displacement, tons: 370 light; 1 400 full load
Dimensions, feet (metres): 174·0 × 32·0 × 13·0 *(53·1 × 9·8 × 4)*
Gun: 1—20 mm
Main engines: 1 Fairbanks-Morse diesel; 525 bhp = 8 knots
Capacity: 6 570 barrels
Complement: 27

Former United States self-propelled fuel oil barges. Lent by the USA in April 1964.

TUGS

1 Ex-US "CHEROKEE" CLASS

Name	No.	Builders	Commissioned
MACORIX (ex-USS *Kiowa ATF 72)*	RM 21	—	1942

Displacement, tons: 1 235 standard; 1 675 full load
Dimensions, feet (metres): 195 wl; 205 oa × 38·5 × 15·5 *(62·5 × 11·7 × 4·7)*
Gun: 1—3 in 50 cal
Main engines: Diesel-electric; 1 shaft; 3 000 bhp = 15 knots
Complement: 85

Carries additional salvage equipment. Transferred 16 Oct 1972.

MACORIX   1975, Dominican Navy

1 Ex-US "SOTOYOMO" CLASS

Name	No.	Builders	Commissioned
CAONABO (ex-USS *Sagamore ATA 208)*	RM 18	—	1944

Displacement, tons: 534 standard; 835 full load
Dimensions, feet (metres): 143 oa × 33·9 × 13 *(43·6 × 10·3 × 4)*
Gun: 1—3 in 50 cal
Main engines: 2 GM diesel-electric; 1 shaft; 1 500 bhp = 13 knots

Transferred 1 Feb 1972.

CAONABO   1975, Dominican Navy

2 "HERCULES" CLASS

Name	No.	Builders	Commissioned
HERCULES (ex-*R 2)*	RP 12	Ast. Navales Dominicanos	1960
GUACANAGARIX (ex-*R 5)*	RP 13	Ast Navales Dominicanos	1960

Displacement, tons: 200 (approx)
Dimensions, feet (metres): 70·0 × 15·6 × 9·0 *(21·4 × 4·8 × 2·7)*
Main engines: 1 Caterpillar motor; 500 hp; 1 225 rpm
Complement: 8 to 11

4 HARBOUR TUGS

BOHECHIO RP 16   **MAGUANA** RP 14 (ex-*R 10)*
CALDERAS RP 19   **ISABELA** RP 20 (ex-*R 1)*

Small tugs for harbour and coastal use. Not all of uniform type and dimensions.
Bohechio of US YTL 600 type, transferred Jan 1971.

ECUADOR

Administration

Minister of Defence:
General Victor Aulestia

Headquarters Appointment

Commander-in-Chief of the Navy:
Vice Admiral Alfredo Poveda Burbano

Diplomatic Representation

Naval Attaché in London:
Rear Admiral G. Jarrin
Naval Attaché in Washington:
Commander M. Valviviezo

Personnel

(a) 1976. Total 3 800 (300 officers and 3 500 men)
(b) Two years selective National Service

Naval Bases

Guayaquil (main naval base).
San Lorenzo and Galapagos Island (small bases).

Establishments

The Naval Academy is in Salinas

Maritime Air

Air Force planes working with the Navy

2 Alouette III helicopters
1 IAI Arava
1 Cessna 320E
1 Cessna 177
2 Cessna T 337 F
2 Cessna T-41D

Naval Infantry

A small force of naval infantry exists of which a detachment is based on the Galapagos Islands.

Prefix to Ships' Names

BAE

Mercantile Marine

Lloyd's Register of Shipping:
44 vessels of 142 356 tons gross

Strength of the Fleet

Type	Active	Building
Frigates	3	—
Corvettes	2	—
Patrol Submarines	—	2
Fast Attack Craft (Missile)	3	—
Fast Attack Craft (Torpedo)	3	3
Large Patrol Craft	2	—
Coastal Patrol Craft	6	—
LSMs	2	—
Survey Vessels	2	—
Tugs	3	—
Supply Ship (Small)	1	—
Auxiliary Dock	1	—
Miscellaneous	5	—
Sail Training Ship	—	1

New Construction

The Ecuadorian Navy, after considering the purchase of two "Whitby" class frigates from UK is now investigating new construction frigates.

DELETION

Frigate

1972 *Guayas* (ex-US PF Type)

PENNANT LIST

Frigates

D	1	Veinticinco de Julio
D	2	Presidente Alfaro
D	3	Presidente Velasco Ibarra

Corvettes

P	22	Esmeraldas
P	23	Manabi

Tugs

R	101	Cayambe
R	102	Sangay
R	103	Cotopaxi

Light Forces

LC	61	Quito
LC	62	Guayaquil
LP	81	LSP 1
LP	82	LSP 2
LP	83	LSP 3
LP	84	LSP 4
LP	85	LSP 5
LP	86	LSP 6

Amphibious Forces

T	31	Jambel
T	32	Tarqui

Survey Vessels

O	111	Orion
—		Rigel

Miscellaneous

BT	62	Putu Mayor
T	33	Atahualpa
T	34	Calicuchima
UT111		Isla de la Plata
UT112		Isla de Puna

FRIGATES

1 Ex-US "CHARLES LAWRENCE" CLASS

Name	No.	Builders	Laid down	Launched	Commissioned
VEINTICINCO DE JULIO (ex-Enright, APD 66, ex-DE 216)	D 1 (ex-E 12)	Philadelphia Navy Yard	22 Feb 1943	29 May 1943	21 Sep 1943

Displacement, tons: 1 400 standard; 2 130 full load
Dimensions, feet (metres): 306·0 oa × 37·0 × 12·6 (93·3 × 11·3 × 3·8)
Guns: 1—5 in 38 cal; 4—40 mm
A/S weapons: DC racks
Main engines: GE geared turbines with electric drive; 2 shafts; 12 000 shp = 23 knots
Boilers: 2 "D" Express
Range, miles: 2 000 at 23 knots
Complement: 204

Former US high speed transport (APD, modified destroyer escort). Transferred to Ecuador on 14 July 1967 under MAP. Can carry 162 troops.

VEINTICINCO DE JULIO (Now D 1)   1968, Ecuadorian Navy

2 Ex-BRITISH "HUNT" CLASS (TYPE 1)

Name	No.	Builders	Laid down	Launched	Commissioned
PRESIDENTE ALFARO (ex-HMS Quantock)	D 2 (ex-D 01)	Scotts S.B. & Eng Co Ltd, Greenock	26 July 1939	22 Apr 1940	6 Feb 1941
PRESIDENTE VELASCO IBARRA (ex-HMS Meynell)	D 3 (ex-D 02)	Swan Hunter & Wigham Richardson, Wallsend	10 Aug 1939	7 June 1940	30 Dec 1940

Displacement, tons: 1 000 standard; 1 490 full load
Length, feet (metres): 272·3 (83·0) pp; 280 (85·4) oa
Beam, feet (metres): 29 (8·8)
Draught, feet (metres): 14 (4·3)
Guns: 4—4 in (102 mm); 2—40 mm (twin); 2—20 mm
A/S weapons: DC throwers, DC racks
Main engines: Parsons geared turbines (by Wallsend Slipway in Presidente Velasco Ibarra); 19 000 shp; 2 shafts
Boilers: 2 Admiralty 3-drum
Speed, knots: 23
Oil fuel, tons: 280
Range, miles: 2 000 at 12 knots
Complement: 146

"Hunt" class. Type 1, Purchased by Ecuador from Great Britain on 18 Oct 1954, and refitted by J. Samuel White & Co. Ltd, Cowes, Isle of Wight. Quantock was taken over by the Ecuadorian Navy in Portsmouth Dockyard on 16 Aug 1955, when she was renamed Presidente Alfaro. Sister ship Meynell was transferred to the Ecuadorian Navy and renamed Presidente Velasco Ibarra in Aug 1955.

PRESIDENTE ALFARO (now D 2)   1970, Ecuadorian Navy

CORVETTES

2 Ex-US PCE TYPE

Name	No.	Builders	Laid down	Launched	Commissioned
ESMERALDAS (ex-USS Eunice, PCE 846)	P 22 (ex-E 22, ex-E 03)	USA	—	—	4 Mar 1944
MANABI (ex-USS Pascagoula, PCE 874)	P 23 (ex-E 23, ex-E 02)	USA	—	—	31 Dec 1943

Displacement, tons: 640 standard; 903 full load
Dimensions, feet (metres): 180 wl; 184·5 oa × 33 × 9·5 (56·3 × 10 × 2·9)
Guns: 1—3 in; 6—40 mm
A/S weapons: 4 DCT; 2 DC Racks; Hedgehog
Main engines: GM diesels; 2 shafts; 1 800 bhp = 15·4 knots
Range, miles: 4 300 at 10 knots
Complement: 100 officers and men

Former United States patrol vessels (180 ft Escorts). Transferred on 29 Nov and 5 Dec 1960 respectively.

MANABI   1974

SUBMARINES

2 TYPE 209

Name	No.	Builders	Commissioning
—	—	Howaldtswerke, Kiel	1977
—	—	Howaldtswerke, Kiel	1977

Displacement, tons: 980 surfaced; 1 356 dived
Dimensions, feet (metres): 183·4 × 20·5 × 17·9 (55·9 × 6·3 × 5·4)
Torpedo tubes: 8—21 in (bow) with reloads
Main machinery: Diesel-electric; MTU diesels; 4 generators; 1 shaft; 5 000 shp
Speed, knots: 10 surfaced; 22 dived
Complement: 32

Ordered in 1974.

LIGHT FORCES

3 LÜRSSEN TYPE (FAST ATTACK CRAFT—MISSILE)

Name	No.	Builders	Commissioned
—	—	Lürssen, Vegesack	1976
—	—	Lürssen, Vegesack	1976
—	—	Lürssen, Vegesack	1976

Displacement, tons: 200?
Dimensions, feet (metres): 119·5 × 23 × 8·2 *(36 × 7 × 2·4)*
Missiles: 4—MM 38 Exocet
Guns: 1—76 mm; 2—35 mm
Main engines: 4 MTU Diesels; 14 000 hp; 4 shafts = 40 knots
Range, miles: 700 at 40 knots; 1 800 at 16 knots
Complement: 35

3 "MANTA" CLASS (FAST ATTACK CRAFT—TORPEDO)

Name	No.	Builders	Commissioned
MANTA	LT 91	Lürssen, Vegesack	11 June1971
TULCAN	LT 92	Lürssen, Vegesack	2 Apr 1971
TENA	LT 93	Lürssen, Vegesack	23 June1971

Displacement, tons: 119 standard; 134 full load
Dimensions, feet (metres): 119·4 × 19·1 × 6·0 *(36 × 5·8 × 1·7)*
Guns: 1—40 mm; 1—81 mm rocket launcher
Torpedo tubes: 2—21 inch
Main engines: 3 MTU diesels; 3 shafts; 9 000 bhp = 35 knots
Range, miles: 700 at 30 knots; 1 500 at 15 knots
Complement: 19

Similar design to the Chilean "Guacoida" Class. *Manta* launched 8 Sep 1970.

MANTA   *1972, Ecuadorian Navy*

2 Ex-US PGM TYPE (LARGE PATROL CRAFT)

Name	No.	Builders	Commissioned
GUAYAQUIL (ex-US *PGM 76,* ex-*LC 72)*	LC 62	USA	1965
QUITO (ex-US *PGM 75,* ex-*LC 71)*	LC 61	USA	1965

Displacement, tons: 130 standard; 147 full load
Dimensions, feet (metres): 101 oa × 21 × 6 *(30·8 × 6·4 × 1·9)*
Guns: 1—40 mm; 2—20 mm
Main engines: 4 diesels; 2 shafts; 2 200 bhp = 21 knots
Range, miles: 1 500 at crusing speed
Complement: 15

Transferred to the Ecuadorian Navy under MAP on 30 Nov 1965.

GUAYAQUIL   *1967, Ecuadorian Navy*

6 COASTAL PATROL CRAFT

Name	No.	Builders	Commissioned
LSP 1	LP 81	Schurenstedt, Barden Fleth	Aug 1954
LSP 2	LP 82	Schurenstedt, Barden Fleth	Aug 1954
LSP 3	LP 83	Schurenstedt, Barden Fleth	1955
LSP 4	LP 84	Schurenstedt, Barden Fleth	1955
LSP 5	LP 85	Schurenstedt, Barden Fleth	1955
LSP 6	LP 86	Schurenstedt, Barden Fleth	1955

Displacement, tons: 45 standard; 64 full load
Dimensions, feet (metres): 76·8 × 13·5 × 6·3 *(23·4 × 4·6 × 1·8)*
Guns: Light MGs
Main engines: Bohn & Kähler diesel; 2 shafts; 1 200 bhp = 22 knots
Range, miles: 550 at 16 knots
Complement: 9

Ordered in 1954.

Note: 1 40 ft CGB transferred by USA 1971.

LSP 6   *1963, Ecuadorian Navy*

AMPHIBIOUS SHIPS

2 Ex-US LSM

Name	No.	Builders	Commissioned
JAMBELI (ex-USS *LSM 539)*	T 31	Brown S.B. Co, Houston	1945
TARQUI (ex-USS *LSM 555)*	T 32	Charleston Navy Yard	1945

Displacement, tons: 743 beaching; 1 095 full load
Dimensions, feet (metres): 196·5 wl; 203·0 oa × 34·0 × 7·9 *(61·9 × 10·3 × 2·4)*
Guns: 2—40 mm
Range, miles: 2 500 at 12 knots
Main engines: Diesels; 2 shafts; 2 800 bhp = 12·5 knots

Former US Landing Ships. Medium. *Jambeli* was laid down on 10 May 1945, *Tarqui* was laid down on 3 Mar 1945 and launched on 22 Mar 1945. Transferred to the Ecuadorian Navy at Green Cove Springs, Florida in Nov 1958.

JAMBELI   *1967, Ecuadorian Navy*

SURVEY VESSELS

Name	No.	Builders	Commissioned
ORION	O 111	Commercial Iron Works,	1941
(ex-USS *Mulberry, AN 27*)	(ex-*A 101*)	Portland, Oregon	

Displacement, tons: 560 standard; 805 full load
Dimensions, feet (metres): 146 wl; 163 oa × 30·5 × 11·8 *(49·7 × 9·3 × 3·6)*
Gun: 1—3 in
Main engines: Diesel-electric; 800 bhp = 13 knots
Complement: 35

Former United States netlayer. Launched on 26 Mar 1941. Transferred to Ecuador in Nov 1965 as loan.

RIGEL

Of 50 tons, launched in 1975. Complement 10.

TUGS

1 Ex-US "CHEROKEE" CLASS

Name	No.	Builders	Commissioned
CAYAMBE (ex-USS *Cusabo, ATF 155*)	R 101 (ex-*R 51*, ex-*R 01*)	—	1945

Displacement, tons: 1 235 standard; 1 675 full load
Dimensions, feet (metres): 195 wl; 205 oa × 38·5 × 15·5 *(62·5 × 11·7 × 4·7)*
Guns: 1—3 in; 4—40 mm; 2—20 mm
Main engines: 4 diesels with electric drive; 3 000 bhp = 16·5 knots
Complement: 85

Launched on 26 Feb 1945. Fitted with powerful pumps and other salvage equipment. Transferred to Ecuador by lease on 2 Nov 1960 and renamed *Los Rios*. Again renamed *Cayambe* in 1966.

CAYAMBE   *1970, Ecuadorian Navy*

Name	No.	Builders	Commissioned
SANGAY (ex-*Loja*)	R 102 (ex-*R 52*)	—	1952

Displacement, tons: 295 light; 390 full load
Dimensions, feet (metres): 107 × 26 × 14 *(32·6 × 7·9 × 4·3)*
Main engines: Fairbanks Morse diesel; speed = 12 knots

Acquired by the Ecuadorian Navy in 1964. Renamed in 1966.

Name	No.	Builders	Commissioned
COTOPAXI (ex-USS *R. T. Ellis*)	R 103 (ex-*R 53*)	Equitable Building Corpn.	1945

Displacement, tons: 150
Dimensions, feet (metres): 82 × 21 × 8 *(25 × 6·4 × 2·4)*
Main engines: Diesel; 1 shaft; 650 bhp = 9 knots

Purchased from the United States in 1947.

MISCELLANEOUS

TRAINING SHIP

Name	No.	Builders	Commissioned
—	—	Ast. Celaya, Spain	Dec 1976

Measurement, tons: 934 gross
Dimensions, feet (metres): 249·9 × 34·8 ×13·4 *(76·2 × 10·6 × 4·2)*
Main engines: General Motors; 700 bhp = 10 knots

Sail training ship.

1 Ex-US SUPPLY SHIP

Name	No.	Builders	Commissioned
CALICUCHIMA (ex-US *FS 525*)	T 34 (ex-*T 42*)	USA	1944

Displacement, tons: 650 light; 950 full load
Dimensions, feet (metres): 176 × 32 × 14 *(53·7 × 9·8 × 4·3)*
Main engines: Diesels; 2 shafts; 500 bhp = 11 knots

Former United States small cargo ship of the Army FS type. Leased to Ecuador on 8 Apr 1963 and purchased in April 1969. Provides service to the Galapagos Islands.

2 Ex-US YP TYPE

Name	No.	Builders	Commissioned
ISLA DE LA PLATA	UT 111	USA	—
ISLA DE PUNA	UT 112	USA	—

Transferred 1962. Coastguard utility boats.

1 Ex-US YR TYPE

Name	No.	Builders	Commissioned
PUTU MAYOR (ex-US *YR 34*)	BT 62	USA	—

Repair barge leased July 1962.

1 Ex-US WATER CARRIER

Name	No.	Builders	Commissioned
ATAHUALPA (ex-US *YW 131*)	T 33 (ex-*T 41*, ex-*A 01*)	Leatham D. Smith SB Co.	1945

Displacement, tons: 415 light; 1 235 full load
Dimensions, feet (metres): 174·0 × 32·0 × 15·0 *(53·1 × 9·8 × 4·6)*
Main engines: GM diesels; 750 bhp = 11·5 knots

Acquired by the Ecuadorian Navy on 2 May 1963.

1 Ex-US FLOATING DOCK

Name	No.	Builders	Commissioned
AMAZONAS (ex-US *ARD 17*)	—	USA	1944

Measurement, tons: 3 500 lifting capacity
Dimensions, feet (metres): 491·7 oa × 81·0 oa × 32·9 *(149·9 × 24·7 × 10)*

Transferred on loan on 7 Jan 1961. Suitable for docking destroyers and landing ships. Dry dock companion craft YFND 20 was leased on 2 Nov 1961.

EGYPT

Headquarters Appointment

Commander Naval Forces:
Vice-Admiral Fuad Zikry

Diplomatic Representation

Defence Attaché in London:
Air Commodore Mohsen Hussein Ezzy

Personnel

(a) 1976: 17 500 officers and men, including the Coast Guard.
(Reserves of about 12 000)
(b) 3 years National Service

Bases

Alexandria, Port Said, Mersa Matru, Port Tewfik and Berenice (Ras Banas) on the Red Sea.

Coastal Defences

The Samlet missiles employed for Coastal Defence are Naval-manned.

Mercantile Marine

Lloyd's Register of Shipping:
143 vessels of 361 383 tons gross

Strength of the Fleet

Type	Active	Building
Destroyers	5	—
Frigates	3	—
Corvettes	12	—
Submarines (Patrol)	12	—
Fast Attack Craft (Missile)	18	—
Fast Attack Craft (Torpedo)	26	—
Coastal Patrol Craft	?	—
LCTs	3	—
LCUs	14	—
Minesweepers (Ocean)	10	—
Minesweepers (Inshore)	2	—
Training Ships	2	—
Tugs	4	—
Hovercraft	—	3

DELETIONS

Light Forces

1975 4 "P 6" Class
4 "108" Class

DESTROYERS

4 Ex-SOVIET "SKORY" CLASS

SUEZ   **DIAMIETTE**
AL ZAFFER   **6 OCTOBER** (ex-*Al Nasser*)

Displacement, tons: 2 600 standard; 3 500 full load
Length, feet (metres): 395·2 *(120·5)*
Beam, feet (metres): 38·7 *(11·8)*
Draught, feet (metres): 15·1 *(4·6)*
Guns: 4—5·1 in *(130 mm)* 50 cal; 2—3·4 in *(88 mm)*;
8—37 mm (unmodified);
4—57 mm (quad); 4—37 mm (twins) (modified)
A/S weapons: 4 DCT (unmodified);
2—12 barrelled MBU 2500A (modified)
Torpedo tubes: 10—21 in *(533 mm)* (quins) (unmodified); 1
mounting with 5 tubes (modified)
Mines: 80 can be carried
Main engines: Geared turbines; 2 shafts; 60 000 shp
Boilers: 3
Speed, knots: 35
Range, miles: 4 000 at 15 knots
Complement: 260

"SKORY" Class   *1966*

Former "Skory" class destroyers of the Soviet Navy. Launched in 1951. *Al Nasser* and *Al Zaffer* were delivered to the Egyptian Navy on 11 June 1956 at Alexandria. *Damiette* and *Suez* were delivered at Alexandria in Jan 1962. In April 1967 the original *Al Nasser* and *Damiette* were exchanged for ships with modified secondary and A/S armament which took the same names. *Al Nasser* was later renamed *6 October* to commemorate the Egyptian crossing of the Suez Canal in the 1973 Israeli war.

Radar: Search: Probably E/F Band.
Tactical: Probably G Band.
Fire Control: Hawkscreech.

1 Ex-BRITISH "Z" CLASS

Name	No.	Builders	Laid down	Launched	Commissioned
EL FATEH (ex-HMS *Zenith*)	—	Wm. Denny & Bros, Dumbarton	19 May 1942	5 June 1944	22 Dec 1944

Displacement, tons: 1 730 standard; 2 575 full load
Length, feet (metres): 350 *(106·8)* wl; 362·8 *(110·6)* oa
Beam, feet (metres): 35·7 *(10·9)*
Draught, feet (metres): 17·1 *(5·2)*
Guns: 4—4·5 in *(115 mm)*; 6—40 mm
A/S weapons: 4 DCT
Main engines: Parsons geared turbines; 2 shafts; 40 000 shp
Boilers: 2 Admiralty 3-drum
Speed, knots: 31
Oil fuel, tons: 580
Range, miles: 2 800 at 20 knots
Complement: 250

Purchased from Great Britain in 1955. Before being taken over by Egypt, *El Fateh* was refitted by John I. Thornycroft & Co Ltd, Woolston, Southampton in July 1956, subsequently modernised by J. S. White & Co Ltd, Cowes, completing July 1964.

Radar: Search: Type 960 Metric wavelength.
Tactical: Type 293. E/F Band. Fire Control: I Band.

EL FATEH

FRIGATES

1 Ex-BRITISH "BLACK SWAN" CLASS

Name
TARIK (ex-*Malek Farouq*, ex-HMS *Whimbrel*)

No. 555 (ex-42)	Builders Yarrow & Co Ltd, Glasgow	Laid down 31 Oct 1941	Launched 25 Aug 1942	Commissioned 13 Jan 1943

Displacement, tons: 1 490 standard; 1 925 full load
Length, feet (metres): 283 *(86·3)* pp; 299·5 *(91·3)* oa
Beam, feet (metres): 38·5 *(11·7)*
Draught, feet (metres): 14·0 *(4·3)*
Guns: 6—4 in *(102 mm)*; 4—40 mm; 2—20 mm
A/S weapons: 4 DCT
Main engines: Geared turbines; 2 shafts; 4 300 shp
Boilers: 2 three-drum type
Speed, knots: 19·75
Oil fuel, tons: 370
Range, miles: 4 500 at 12 knots
Complement: 180

Transferred from Great Britain in Nov 1949.

TARIK

1 Ex-BRITISH "RIVER" CLASS

Name **RASHID** (ex-HMS *Spey*)	*No.* 43

Builders Smith's Dock Co Ltd	Laid down 18 July 1941	Launched 10 Dec 1941	Commissioned 19 May 1942

Displacement, tons: 1 490 standard; 2 216 full load
Length, feet (metres): 283 *(86·3)* pp; 301·5 *(91·9)* oa
Beam, feet (metres): 36·7 *(11·2)*
Draught, feet (metres): 14·1 *(4·3)*
Guns: 1—4 in *(102 mm)*; 2—40 mm; 6—20 mm
A/S weapons: 4 DCT
Main engines: Triple expansion; 2 shafts; 5 500 ihp
Boilers: 2 Admiralty 3-drum type
Speed, knots: 18
Range, miles: 7 700 at 12 knots
Oil fuel, tons: 640
Complement: 180

Purchased in Dec 1949. Has been operated as Submarine Support Ship.

RASHID

1968

1 Ex-BRITISH "HUNT" CLASS

Name
PORT SAID (ex-*Mohamed Ali*, ex-*Ibrahim el Awal*, ex-HMS *Cottesmore*)

No. 525 (ex-11)	Builders Yarrow & Co Ltd, Scotstoun, Glasgow	Laid down 12 Dec 1939	Launched 5 Sep 1940	Commissioned 29 Dec 1940

Displacement, tons: 1 000 standard; 1 490 full load
Length, feet (metres): 273 *(83·2)* wl; 280 *(85·3)* oa
Beam, feet (metres): 29 *(8·8)*
Draught, feet (metres): 15·1 *(4·3)*
Guns: 4—4 in *(103 mm)* 2—37 mm; 2—50 cal (twin)
A/S weapons: 2DCT
Main engines: Parsons geared turbines; 2 shafts; 19 000 shp
Boilers: 2 three-drum type
Speed, knots: 25
Range, miles: 2 000 at 12 knots
Oil fuel, tons: 280
Complement: 146

Transferred from the Royal Navy to the Egyptian Navy in July 1950: Sailed for Egypt in April 1951, after a nine months refit by J. Samuel White & Co Ltd, Cowes.

PORT SAID (ex-*Mohamed Ali*) (old pennant number)

SUBMARINES

6 Ex-SOVIET "ROMEO" CLASS

744	745	765	766	+2

Displacement, tons: 1 000 surfaced; 1 600 dived
Length, feet (metres): 249·3 *(76·0)*
Beam, feet (metres): 24·0 *(7·3)*
Draught, feet (metres): 14·5 *(4·4)*
Torpedo tubes: 6—21 in *(533 mm)* bow
Main machinery: 2 Diesels; 4 000 bhp; 2 Electric motors; 4 000 hp; 2 shafts
Speed, knots: 17 surfaced; 14 dived
Complement: 65

One "Romeo" was transferred to Egypt in Feb 1966. Two more replaced "Whiskys" in May 1966 and another pair was delivered later that year. The sixth boat joined in 1969.

"ROMEO" Class

1968, Skyfotos

6 Ex-SOVIET "WHISKY" CLASS

415 418 421 455 +2

Displacement, tons: 1 030 surface; 1 350 dived
Length, feet (metres): 249·6 (76) oa
Beam, feet (metres): 22 (6·7)
Draught, feet (metres): 15 (4·6)
Torpedo tubes: 6—21 in (533 mm); 4 bow, 2 stern;
  18 torpedoes or 40 mines
Main machinery: 2 diesels; 4 000 bhp; 2 electric motors;
  2 500 hp
Speed, knots: 17 surfaced; 15 dived
Range, miles: 13 000 at 8 knots surfaced
Complement: 60

The first four "Whisky" class were transferred from the Soviet
Navy to the Egyptian Navy in June 1957. Three more arrived at
Alexandria on 24 Jan 1958. Another was transferred to Egypt at
Alexandria in Jan 1962. Two were replaced by "Romeos" in
Feb 1966.
Two "Whisky" class sailed from Alexandria to Leningrad in late
1971 under escort, being replaced the following year.

"WHISKY" Class   1974

CORVETTES

12 Ex-SOVIET "SO I" CLASS

211 217 222 229 233 236 244 255 +4

Displacement, tons: 215 light; 250 full load
Dimensions, feet (metres): 138·6 × 20 × 9·2 (42·3 × 6·1 × 2·8)
Guns: 4—25 mm (2 twin mountings)
A/S weapons: 4 five-barrelled MBU 1800
Main engines: 3 diesel; 6 000 bhp = 29 knots
Range, miles: 1 100 at 13 knots
Complement: 30

Eight reported to have been transferred by the USSR to Egypt in 1962 to 1967 and four others
later.
Reported as carrying SA-7 Grail missiles in some units and 2—21 inch torpedo tubes in others.

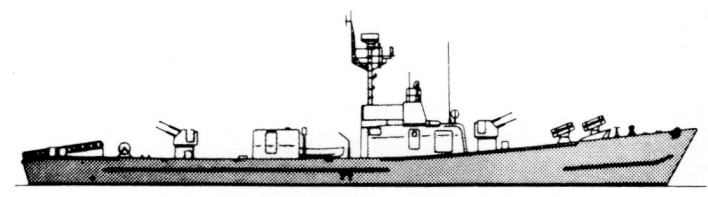

"SO I" Class

LIGHT FORCES

6 Ex-SOVIET "OSA I" CLASS (FAST ATTACK CRAFT—MISSILE)

312 324 378 +3

Displacement, tons: 165 standard; 200 full load
Dimensions, feet (metres): 128·7 × 25·1 × 5·9 (39·3 × 7·7 × 1·8)
Missiles: 4 launchers in two pairs abreast for SSN-2 system
Guns: 4—30 mm (2 twin, 1 forward, 1 aft)
Main engines: 3 diesels; 13 000 bhp = 35 knots
Complement: 25

Reported to have been delivered to Egypt by the Soviet Navy in 1966. Four reported sunk during
the Israeli War October 1973.

Missiles: Some carry SA7 Grail.

"OSA I" Class

4 Ex-SOVIET "KOMAR" CLASS
(FAST ATTACK CRAFT—MISSILE)

Displacement, tons: 70 standard; 80 full load
Dimensions, feet (metres): 83·7 × 19·8 × 5·0 (25·5 × 6 × 1·5)
Missiles: 2 launchers for SSN-2 system
Guns: 2—25 mm
Main engines: 4 diesels; 4 shafts; 4 800 hp = 40 knots
Range, miles: 400 at 30 knots
Complement: 20

Transferred from the USSR in 1962 to 1967. One of this type was sunk by Israeli jets on 16 May
1970. Two reported sunk in Israeli War October 1973.

"KOMAR" Class   1966, Col. Bjorn Borg

6 EGYPTIAN "KOMAR" TYPE (FAST ATTACK CRAFT—MISSILE)

Displacement, tons: 80 full load
Dimensions, feet (metres): 84 × 20 × 5 *(25·6 × 6 × 1·5)*
Missiles: ? Otomat
Guns: ? Twin 25 mm
Main engines: 4 diesels; 4 shafts; 4 800 hp = 40 knots
Range, miles: 400 at 30 knots
Complement: ? 20

Built in Alexandria 1975—76. Hull of same design as Soviet "Komar" class and fitted with Soviet diesels. The armament is of West European manufacture.

6 Ex-SOVIET "SHERSHEN" CLASS
(FAST ATTACK CRAFT—TORPEDO)

332   343   354   356   +2

Displacement, tons: 150 standard; 160 full load
Dimensions, feet (metres): 115·5 × 23 × 5 *(35·2 × 7·1 × 1·5)*
Guns: 4—30 mm (2 twin)
Torpedo tubes: 4—21 in (single)
A/S weapons: 12 DC
Main engines: 3 diesels; 3 shafts; 13 000 hp = 41 knots
Complement: 16

One delivered from USSR in Feb 1967, two more in Oct 1967, and three since. Four have had their guns and tubes removed to make way for multiple rocket-launchers and one SA-7 Grail.

"SHERSHEN" Class

20 Ex-SOVIET "P 6" CLASS
(FAST ATTACK CRAFT—TORPEDO)

Displacement, tons: 66 standard; 75 full load
Dimensions, feet (metres): 84·2 × 20 × 6 *(25·7 × 6·1 × 1·8)*
Guns: 2 or 4—25 mm
Tubes: 2—21 in
Main engines: 4 diesels; 4 shafts; 4 800 hp = 43 knots
Range, miles: 450 at 30 knots
Complement: 25

The first twelve boats arrived at Alexandria on 19 Apr 1956, 6 more in 1960. Two were destroyed by British naval aircraft on 4 Nov 1956, two were sunk by the Israeli destroyer *Elath* off Sinai on 2 July 1967, two by Israeli MTBs off Sinai coast on 11 July 1967, two by Israeli air attacks in 1969, and two in the Red Sea on 22 Jan 1970. Further reinforcements have been sent by USSR

"P 4" Class with 8-barrelled rocket launcher   *10/1974*

3 LARGE PATROL CRAFT

NISR 1, 2 and 3

Displacement, tons: 110
Gun: 1—20 mm

Built by Castro, Port Said and launched in May 1963.

4 Ex-SOVIET/SYRIAN "P 4" CLASS
(FAST ATTACK CRAFT—TORPEDO)

Transferred by Syria in 1970. Now armed with 8 barrelled 122 mm rocket launcher forward and twin 12·7 mm aft.

20 BERTRAM TYPE (COASTAL PATROL CRAFT)

of approximately 8 tons, now in service probably with the coastguard.

"BERTRAM" Type   *10/1974*

2 Ex-YUGOSLAVIAN "108" CLASS (FAST TARGET CRAFT)

Displacement, tons: 55 standard; 60 full load
Dimensions, feet (metres): 69 pp; 78 oa × 21·3 × 7·8 *(23·8 oa × 6·5 × 2·4)*
Main engines: 3 Packard motors; 3 shafts; 5 000 bhp = 36 knots
Complement: 14

Purchased from Yugoslavia in 1956. Similar to the boats of the US "Higgins" class. Originally a class of six. Remaining pair now fitted with reflectors and used as targets.

AMPHIBIOUS FORCES

3 Ex-SOVIET "POLNOCNY" CLASS (LCT)

Displacement, tons: 780 standard; 1 000 full load
Dimensions, feet (metres): 239·4 × 29·5 × 9·8 *(73 × 9 × 3)*
Guns: 2—30 mm (twin)
A/S weapons: 2—18 barrelled MBUs
Main engines: 2 diesels; 5 000 bhp = 18 knots

Can carry 6 tanks. Transferred early 1970s.

"POLNOCNY" Class   *1973, USN*

10 Ex-SOVIET "VYDRA" CLASS (LCU)

Displacement, tons: 300 standard; 500 full load
Dimensions, feet (metres): 157·4 × 24·6 × 7·2 (48 × 7·5 × 2·2)
Main engines: 2 diesels; 2 shafts; 400 bhp = 15 knots

Can carry and land up to 250 tons of military equipment and stores.

10 LCMs

Generally used as harbour-craft.

1 Ex-SOVIET "SMB 1" CLASS (LCU)

Displacement, tons: 200 standard; 420 full load
Dimensions, feet (metres): 157·5 × 21·3 × 5·6 (48 × 6·5 × 1·7)
Main engines: 2 diesels; 2 shafts; 400 hp = 11 knots

Delivered to the Egyptian Navy in 1965. Can carry 150 tons of military equipment.

MINEWARFARE FORCES

6 Ex-SOVIET "T 43" CLASS (MINESWEEPERS—OCEAN)

ASSIUT	CHARKIEH	GHARBIA
BAHAIRA	DAKHLA	SINAI

Displacement, tons: 500 standard; 610 full load
Dimensions, feet (metres): 190·2 × 28·2 × 6·9 (58·0 × 8·6 × 2·1)
Guns: 4—37 mm; 4—25 mm
Main engines: 2 diesels; 2 shafts; 2 000 hp = 17 knots
Range, miles: 1 600 at 10 knots
Complement: 40

Three were transferred from the Soviet Navy and delivered to Egypt 1956-59, and three since 1970. *Miniya* was sunk by Israeli air attack in the Gulf of Suez on 6 Feb 1970 but was later replaced.

"T 43" Class

4 Ex-SOVIET "YURKA" CLASS (MINESWEEPERS—OCEAN)

ASWAN 695	GIZA 690	SOHAG 699	QENA 696

Displacement, tons: 500 standard; 550 full load
Dimensions, feet (metres): 172 × 31 × 8·9 (52·5 × 9·5 × 2·7)
Guns: 4—30 mm (2 twin)
Main engines: 2 diesels; 4 000 bhp = 18 knots

Steel-hulled minesweepers transferred from USSR 1970-71.

"YURKA" Class   S. Breyer

2 Ex-SOVIET "T 301" CLASS (MINESWEEPERS—INSHORE)

Displacement, tons: 130 standard; 180 full load
Dimensions, feet (metres): 124·6 × 19·7 × 4·9 (39 × 5·5 × 1·5)
Guns: 2—37 mm; 2—MG
Main engines: 2 diesels; 2 shafts; 1 440 hp = 17 knots
Range, miles: 2 200 at 10 knots
Complement: 30

Reported to have been transferred by the USSR to Egypt in 1962; a third ship may have been transferred later.

2 E-x SOVIET "K 8" CLASS
(MINESWEEPERS—INSHORE)

Of 70 tons reported transferred in 1968.

MISCELLANEOUS

4 Ex-SOVIET "OKHTENSKY" CLASS TUGS

AL MAKAS	ANTAR	+2

A number of Soviet fleet tugs were reported transferred to the Egyptian Navy in 1966.

SWIMMER DELIVERY VEHICLES

There is a strong underwater team in the Egyptian navy who use, amongst other equipment, the 2-man SDVs shown here. Range could be 4 hours at 3-4 knots.

3 TRAINING SHIPS

El Horria (ex-*Mahroussa*) of 4 560 tons, built by Sanuda, Poplar in 1865 and once the Egyptian Royal Yacht, has been completely refitted and is used as a training ship.

Intishat, a smaller training ship.

1 Ex-SOVIET "SEKSTAN" CLASS

160 Used as cadet training ship.

1 AUXILIARY

Nasr (ex-HMS *Bude),* a "Bangor" class minesweeper of 900 tons is still in existence although probably only used for target-towing etc.

3 Winchester SRN-6 Hovercraft. Purchased 1975.

SDV   10/1974

EL SALVADOR

Personnel

(a) 1976: 130 officers and men
(b) Voluntary Service

Mercantile Marine

Lloyd's Register of Shipping:
2 vessels of 1 957 tons gross

DELETION

1975 GC 1

PATROL BOATS

1 Ex-BRITISH HDML

Name	No.	Builders	Commissioned
GC 2 (ex-*Nohaba*)	—	UK	1942

Displacement, tons: 46
Dimensions, feet (metres): 72 oa × 16 × 5·5 *(21·9 × 4·9 × 1·7)*
Gun: 1—20 mm
Main engines: 2 diesels; 2 shafts = 12 knots
Complement: 16

Purchased from commercial sources in 1959.

2 Ex-US CG TYPE

Name	No.	Builders	Commissioned
GC 3	—	USA	1950
GC 4	—	USA	1950

Displacement, tons: 14

1 SEWART 65 ft TYPE

Name	No.	Builders	Commissioned
GC 5	—	Sewart, USA	1967

Displacement, tons: 33
Dimensions, feet (metres): 65 × 16·3 × 5·0 *(19·8 × 4·9 × 1·5)*
Guns: 3 MG
Main engines: GM Diesels; 1 600 hp = 25 khots

Transferred Sep 1967.

ETHIOPIA

Administration

All command arrangements under review.

Commander-in-Chief:
—

Chief of Staff:
—

Personnel

(a) 1976: 1 500 officers and men
(b) Voluntary service

Naval Establishments

Massawa: Naval Base and College, established in 1956.
Embaticalla: Marine Commando Training School.
Assab: Naval Base, expanding to include a ship repair facility.

Mercantile Marine

Lloyd's Register of Shipping:
23 vessels of 24 953 tons gross

MINESWEEPER (COASTAL)

1 Ex-NETHERLANDS "WILDERVANK" CLASS

Name	No.	Builders	Commissioned
MS 41 (ex-*Elst*, M 829)	—	Netherlands	1956

Displacement, tons: 373 standard; 417 full load
Dimensions, feet (metres): 149·8 oa × 28·0 × 7·5 *(46·6 × 8·8 × 2·3)*
Guns: 2—40 mm
Main engines: 2 diesels; 2 shafts; 2 500 bhp = 14 knots
Oil fuel, tons: 25 tons
Range, miles: 2 500 at 10 knots
Complement: 38

Launched 21 Mar 1956. Purchased by Ethiopia and transferred from the Royal Netherlands Navy in 1971.

Missiles: It has been reported that MS 41 has been fitted for launching SS-12 missiles.

MS 41 (as *Elst*)

TRAINING SHIP

Name	No.	Builders	Commissioned
ETHIOPIA (ex-USS *Orca*, AVP 49)	A 01	Lake Washington SY	23 Jan 1944

Displacement, tons: 1 766 standard; 2 800 full load
Dimensions, feet (metres): 310·8 oa × 41 × 13·5 *(94·7 × 12·5 × 3·7)*
Guns: 1—5 in 38 cal; 5—40 mm
Main engines: 2 sets diesels; 2 shafts; 6 080 bhp = 18·2 knots
Complement: 215

Former United States small seaplane tender of "Barnegat" class. Laid down 13 July 1942, launched on 4 Oct 1942. Transferred from the US Navy in Jan 1962.

ETHIOPIA   *1972, Imperial Ethiopian Navy*

LIGHT FORCES

5 PGM TYPE (LARGE PATROL CRAFT)

Name	No.	Builders	Commissioned
PC 11 (ex-US CG WVP 95304)	—	Petersen, USA	1958
PC 12 (ex-US CG WVP 95310)	—	Petersen, USA	1958
PC 13 (ex-USN PGM 53)	—	Petersen, USA	1961
PC 14 (ex-USN PGM 54)	—	Petersen, USA	1961
PC 15 (ex-USN PGM 58)	—	Petersen, USA	1962

Displacement, tons: 145·5 full load
Dimensions, feet (metres): 95 × 19 × 5·2 (28·8 × 5·8 × 1·6)
Guns: 1—40 mm; 1—50 cal MG
Main engines: 4 diesels; 2 shafts; 2 200 bhp = 21 knots
Range, miles: 1 500 at cruising speed
Complement: 20

PC 12

1970, Imperial Ethiopian Navy

1 Ex-YUGOSLAV "KRALJEVICA" CLASS (LARGE PATROL CRAFT)

Name	No.	Builders	Commissioned
— (ex-509)	—	Yugoslavia	1953

Displacement, tons: 190·5 standard; 202 full load
Dimensions, feet (metres): 134·5 × 20·7 × 7·2 (41 × 6·3 × 2·2)
Guns: 1—3 in; 1—40 mm; 4—20 mm
A/S weapons: DCs
Main engines: MAN diesels; 2 shafts; 3 300 bhp = 18 knots

Transferred 1975.

4 "SEAWARD" CLASS (COASTAL PATROL CRAFT)

Name	No.	Builders	Commissioned
GB 21	—	Seward Inc, Berwick	1966
GB 22	—	Seward Inc, Berwick	1966
GB 23	—	Seward Inc, Berwick	1967
GB 24	—	Seward Inc, Berwick	1967

Displacement, tons: 15
Length, feet (metres): 40 (12·2)
Guns: 2—·50 calibre machine guns
Speed, knots: 20
Complement: 7

GB 21

1970, Imperial Ethiopian Navy

LANDING CRAFT

There are 2 of the US LCM type and 2 of the US LCVP type. Two were bought in 1962 and two in 1971.

LC 34

1972, Imperial Ethiopian Navy

FIJI

On 12 June 1975 a Fijian Naval Force was created for customs, coastguard, fishery protection, survey work and training of reservists.

Commanding Officer	Personnel	Base
Commander S. Brown	1976: 672 (10 officers, 62 petty officers, 600 ratings)	Suva.

3 Ex-US "BLUEBIRD" CLASS (MINESWEEPERS—COASTAL)

Name	No.	Builders	Commissioned
KULA (ex-USS Vireo, MSC 205)	—	USA	1955
KIRO (ex-USS Warbler, MSC 206)	—	USA	1955
— (ex-USS Woodpecker, MSC 209)	—	USA	1955

Displacement, tons: 370 full load
Dimensions, feet (metres): 144 oa × 28 × 8·5 (43·9 × 8·5 × 2·6)
Guns: 2—20 mm
Main engines: 2 GM Diesels; 2 shafts; 880 bhp = 13 knots
Range, miles: 2 500 at 10 knots
Complement: 39

First pair transferred 14 Oct 1975 and the third in early 1976.

"BLUEBIRD" Class

USN

FINLAND

Headquarters Appointment

Commander-in-Chief Finnish Navy:
Rear-Admiral S. O. Wikberg

Diplomatic Representation

Naval Attaché in London:
Captain Erik Wihtol

Naval Attaché in Moscow:
Colonel E. Pallasvirta

Naval Attaché in Paris:
Lieutenant-Colonel Erkki Palmujoki

Naval Attaché in Washington:
Colonel Erkki Kaira

Treaty Limitations

The Finnish Navy is limited by the Treaty of Paris (1947) to 10 000 tons of ships and 4 500 personnel. Submarines and motor torpedo boats are prohibited.

Personnel

(a)   1972: 2 000 (150 officers and 1 850 ratings)
1973: 2 500 (200 officers and 2 300 ratings)
1974: 2 500 (200 officers and 2 300 ratings)
1975: 2 500 (200 officers and 2 300 ratings)
1976: 2 500 (200 officers and 2 300 ratings)
(b)   8-11 months National Service

Hydrographic Department

This office and the survey ships come under the Ministry of Trade and Industry.

Coast Guard

All Coast Guard vessels come under the Ministry of the Interior.

Icebreakers

All these ships work for the Board of Navigation.

Mercantile Marine

Lloyd's Register of Shipping:
361 vessels of 1 989 807 tons gross

Strength of the Fleet

Type	Active	Building
Frigates	1	—
Corvettes	2	—
Fast Attack Craft (Missile)	4	—
Fast Attack Craft (Gun)	15	—
Large Patrol Craft	9	—
Coastal Patrol Craft	8	—
Minelayer	1	—
Minesweepers	6	—
HQ Ships	2	—
Transports (LCUs)	14	—
Tugs	3	—
Cable Ship	1	—
Icebreakers	9+1	—
Coastguard Vessels	14	—

DELETIONS

Frigates

1975   *Matti Kurki* (ex-British "Bay" Class)

Light Forces
1975   *Tursas* (Large Patrol Craft)

Minewarfare Forces
1975   *Ruotsinsalmi*

Coastguard Vessels
1970   VMV 11, 13, 19 and 20
1971   *Aura*

FRIGATES

2 "UUSIMAA" CLASS

HÄMEENMAA   UUSIMAA

Displacement, tons: 1 200 standard; 1 600 full load
Length, feet (metres): 298·8 *(91)*
Beam, feet (metres): 33·7 *(10·2)*
Draught, feet (metres): 11 *(3·4)*
Guns: 3—3·9 in *(100 mm)* single; 2—40 mm; 2—30 mm (twin) (in bow)
A/S weapons: 1 Hedgehog; 4 DC projectors
Torpedo tubes: 3—21 in *(533 mm)*
Mines: 50 (capacity)
Main engines: Geared turbines; 2 shafts; 25 000 shp
Speed, knots: 28
Boilers: 2
Range, miles: 2 500 at 15 knots
Complement: 150

Former Soviet frigates of the "Riga" class. Purchased from the USSR and transferred to the Finnish Navy on 28 April 1964 and 12 May 1964, respectively. Armament modified in 1971.

Radar: Search: Slimnet. Fire control: Wasphead, Sun Visor A. Navigation: Neptun. IFF: High Pole A.

UUSIMAA

1974, Finnish Navy–SA Kuva

CORVETTES

2 "TURUNMAA" CLASS

Name	No.
KARJALA	—
TURUNMAA	—

Builders	Laid down	Launched	Commissioned
Wärtsilä, Helsinki	Mar 1967	16 Aug 1967	21 Oct 1968
Wärtsilä, Helsinki	Mar 1967	11 July 1967	29 Aug 1968

Displacement, tons: 660 standard; 770 full load
Dimensions, feet (metres): 243·1 × 25·6 × 7·9 *(74·1 × 7·8 × 2·4)*
Guns: 1—4·7 in *(120 mm)* automatic forward; 2—40 mm; 2—30 mm (1 twin) aft
A/S weapons: Depth charge projectors
Main engines: CODOG. 3 Mercedes-Benz (MTU) diesels; 3 900 bhp; 1 Rolls Royce Olympus gas turbine; 22 000 hp = 35 knots. On diesels = 17 knots
Complement: 70

Ordered on 23 Feb 1965 from Wärtsilä, Helsinki. Flush decked. Rocket flare guide rails on sides of 4·7 in turret. Fitted with Vosper Thornycroft fin stabiliser equipment.

Radar: Search and Tactical: H/I Band. (HSA).

KARJALA

1975, Finnish Navy

LIGHT FORCES

4 "TUIMA" CLASS (FAST ATTACK CRAFT—MISSILE)

TUIMA   TUULI   TUISKU   TYRSKY

Displacement, tons: 165 standard; 200 full load
Dimensions, feet (metres): 128·7 × 25·1 × 5·9 (39·3 × 7·7 × 1·8)
Missiles: 4—SSN-2 system launchers
Guns: 4—30 mm (twin)
Main engines: 3 Diesels; 13 000 hp
Speed, knots: 36
Range, miles: 800 at 25 knots
Complement: 25

Ex-Soviet "Osa" class purchased from USSR. 1974—75.

TUIMA   *1975, Finnish Navy*

1 EXPERIMENTAL CRAFT—MISSILE

Name	No.	Builders	Commissioned
ISKU	—	Reposaaron, Konepaja	1970

Displacement, tons: 115
Dimensions, feet (metres): 86·5 × 28·6 × 6·6 (26 × 8·7 × 2)
Missile launchers: 4 SSN-2 system launchers
Guns: 2—30 mm (1 twin)
Main engines: 4 diesels; 4 800 bhp = 25 knots

Guided missile craft of novel design built for training and experimental work. The construction combines a missile boat armament on a landing craft hull.

ISKU   *1972, Finnish Navy*

13 "NUOLI" CLASS (FAST ATTACK CRAFT—GUN)

Name	No.	Builders	Commissioned
NUOLI 1—13	—	Laivateollisuus, Turku	1961—3

Displacement, tons: 45 standard; 64 full load
Dimensions, feet (metres): 72·2 × 21·7 × 5·0 (22 × 6·6 × 1·5)
Guns: 1—40 mm; 1—20 mm
A/S weapons: DCs
Main engines: 3 diesels; 2 700 bhp = 40 knots
Complement: 15

Designed by Laivateollisuus, Turku.

Radar: I-band.

NUOLI 13   *1968, Finnish Navy*

2 "VASAMA" CLASS (FAST ATTACK CRAFT—GUN)

Name	No.	Builders	Commissioned
VASAMA I	—	Saunders Roe (Anglesey) Ltd	1956
VASAMA 2	—	Saunders Roe (Anglesey) Ltd	1957

Displacement, tons: 50 standard; 70 full load
Dimensions, feet (metres): 67·0 pp; 71·5 oa × 19·5 × 6·0 (21·8 oa × 5·9 × 1·8)
Guns: 2—40 mm
Main engines: 2 Napier Deltic diesels; 5 000 bhp = 42 knots
Complement: 20

British "Dark" type.

VASAMA 2   *1970, Finnish Navy*

1 LARGE PATROL CRAFT

Name	No.	Builders	Commissioned
VALPAS	—	Laivateollisuus, Turku	1971

Displacement, tons: 540
Dimensions, feet (metres): 159·1 × 27·9 × 12·5 (48·5 × 8·5 × 3·8)
Main engines: Diesel; 1 800 bhp = 15 knots

Coastguard vessel.

VALPAS   *1975, Finnish Navy*

1 LARGE PATROL CRAFT

Name	No.	Builders	Commissioned
SILMÄ	—	Laivateollisuus, Turku	1963

Displacement, tons: 500
Dimensions, feet (metres): 160·8 × 27·2 × 11·8 *(49 × 8·3 × 3·6)*
Main engines: 1 800 bhp = 15 knots

Coast Guard vessel.

SILMÄ   *1975, Finnish Navy*

1 LARGE PATROL CRAFT

Name	No.	Builders	Commissioned
UISKO	—	Valmet, Helsinki	1959

Displacement, tons: 400
Dimensions, feet (metres): 141 × 24 × 12·8 *(43 × 7·3 × 3·9)*
Main engines: 3 MTU diesels; 4 050 bhp = 24 knots

Coast Guard vessel. Launched in 1958.

UISKO   *1975, Finnish Navy*

1 LARGE PATROL CRAFT

Name	No.	Builders	Commissioned
VIIMA	—	Laivatteollisuus, Turku	1964

Displacement, tons: 135
Dimensions, feet (metres): 118·1 × 21·7 × 7·5 *(36 × 6·6 × 2·3)*
Guns: 1—20 mm
Main engines: 3 diesels; 4 050 bhp = 24 knots

Coast guard patrol boat.

VIIMA   *1974, Finnish Navy*

8 "KOSKELO" CLASS (COASTAL PATROL CRAFT)

KAAKKURI	KOSKELO	KUIKKA	TAVI
KIISLA	KUOVI	KURKI	TELKKA

Displacement, tons: 75 standard; 97 full load
Dimensions, feet (metres): 95·1 × 16·4 × 4·9 *(29 × 5 × 1·5)*
Guns: 2—20 mm
Main engines: 2 Mercedes-Benz (MTU) diesels; 2 shafts; 1 000 bhp = 16 knots
Complement: 8

Built of steel and strengthened against ice, *Koskelo* and *Kuikka* were completed in 1956. Remaining six were completed in 1958—60. Some have been modified—more powerful engines and new bridge arrangement.

TELKKA   *1975, Finnish Navy*

3 LARGE PATROL CRAFT

Name	No.	Builders	Commissioned
RAISIO	4	Laivatteollisuus, Turku	1959
RÖYTTA	5	Laivatteollisuus, Turku	1959
RUISSALO	3	Laivatteollisuus, Turku	1959

Displacement, tons: 110 standard; 130 full load
Dimensions, feet (metres): 108·3 × 18·0 × 5·9 *(33 × 5·5 × 1·8)*
Guns: 1—40 mm; 1—20 mm
A/S weapons: 1 Squid mortar
Main engines: 2 Mercedes-Benz (MTU) diesels; 2 500 bhp = 17 knots

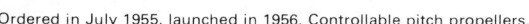

RAISIO   *1975, Finnish Navy*

2 LARGE PATROL CRAFT

Name	No.	Builders	Commissioned
RIHTNIEMI	1	Rauma Repola	20 May 1957
RYMÄTTYLÄ	2	Rauma Repola	20 May 1957

Displacement, tons: 90 standard; 110 full load
Dimensions, feet (metres): 101·7 × 18·7 × 5·9 *(31 × 5·6 × 1·8)*
Guns: 1—40 mm; 1—20 mm
Main engines: 2 Mercedes-Benz (MTU) diesels; 1 400 bhp = 15 knots

Ordered in July 1955, launched in 1956. Controllable pitch propellers.

RIHTNIEMI   *1968, Finnish Navy*

MINE WARFARE FORCES
1 MINELAYER

Name	No.	Builders	Commissioned
KEIHÄSSALMI	—	Valmet, Helsinki	1957

Displacement, tons: 360
Dimensions, feet (metres): 168× 23 × 6 *(52 × 7 × 1·9)*
Guns: 4—30 mm (twins); 2—20 mm
Mines: Up to 100 capacity
Main engines: 2 Wärtsilä diesels; 2 shafts; 2 000 bhp = 15 knots
Complement: 60

Of improved "Ruotsinsalmi" Class. Contract dated June 1955. Launched on 16 Mar 1957. Armament modified in 1972.

Radar: Search and Tactical: I band.

KEIHÄSSALMI *1974, Finnish Navy*

6 "KUHA" CLASS (MINESWEEPERS—INSHORE)

Name	No.	Builders	Commissioned
KUHA 21—26	—	Laivatteollisuus, Turku	1974—75

Displacement, tons: c. 90
Dimensions, feet (metres): 84 × 23 *(25·6 × 7)*
Guns: 1 or 2—20 mm
Main engines: 2 Diesels; 600 shp
Complement: 15

Kuha 21 completed 28 June 1974. Hulls are of Glass Reinforced Plastic (GRP).

KUHA 22 *1974, Finnish Navy—SA Kuva*

MISCELLANEOUS

KORSHOLM (HQ SHIP)

Displacement, tons: 650
Dimensions, feet (metres): 160·8 × 27·9 × 10·8 *(49 × 8·5 × 3·3)*
Speed, knots: 10·5

Converted merchant ship. Built in 1931.

1 Ex-ICEBREAKER (HQ SHIP)

Name	No.	Builders	Commissioned
LOUHI (ex-*Sisu*)	—	Wärtsilä, Helsinki	1939

Displacement, tons: 2 075
Dimensions, feet (metres): 210·2 oa × 46·5 × 16·8 *(64·1 × 14·2 × 5·1)*
Guns: 2—3·9 in
Main engines: 2 sets Atlas Polar Diesels with electric drive; 2 shafts and a bow propeller; 4 000 hp = 16 knots
Complement: 28

Launched on 24 Sep 1938. Used as submarine depot ship 1939—45. Transferred 1975 to be HQ and Logistics ship.

6 "KALA" CLASS (LCU TRANSPORTS)

KALA 1—6

Displacement, tons: 60
Dimensions, feet (metres): 81·8 × 26·2 × 6 *(24·9 × 8 × 1·8)*
Main engines: 2 diesels; 360 bhp = 9 knots

Launched in 1956. Completed in 1959.

KALA 2 *7/1974, Dittmair*

5 "KAVE" CLASS (LCU TRANSPORTS)

KAVE 1—4 and 6

Displacement, tons: 30
Dimensions, feet (metres): 75·8 × 16·4 × 5·9 *(23·1 × 5 × 1·8)*
Gun: 1—20 mm
Main engines: 2 Diesels; 370 hp = 9 knots

Built 1956-60.

KAVE 4 *1961, Finnish Navy*

3 "PANSIO" CLASS (TUG TYPE)

PANSIO   PORKKALA   PUKKIO

Displacement, tons: 162 standard
Dimensions, feet (metres): 92·0 × 21·5 × 9·0 *(28·1 × 6·6 × 2·7)*
Guns: 1—40 mm; 1—20 mm
Main engines: Diesels; 300 bhp = 9 knots

Built by Valmet, Turku. Launched 1947, 1940 and 1939 respectively. Vessels of the tug type used as transports, minesweeping tenders, minelayers and patrol vessels. Can carry 20 mines.

TUGS

3 "PIRTTISAARI" CLASS

PIRTTISAARI (ex-*DR* 7) **PYHTÄA** (ex-*DR* 2) **PURHA** (ex-*DR* 10)

Displacement, tons: 106
Dimensions, feet (metres): 69 × 20 × 8·5 *(21 × 6·1 × 2·6)*
Guns: 1—20 mm
Main engines: 1 diesel; 400 bhp = 9 knots

Former US Army Tugs. Launched in 1943-44. General purpose vessels used as minesweepers, minelayers, patrol vessels, tenders, tugs or personnel transports. *DR* 2 and *DR* 7, were adapted as the Coast Artillery Transports *Pyhtää* and *Pirttisaari* in 1958 and 1959, respectively.

PIRTTISAARI

1970, Finnish Navy

PUTSAARI (CABLE SHIP)

Displacement, tons: 430
Dimensions, feet (metres): 147·6 × 38·5 × 9·8 *(44·8 × 11·7 × 3)*
Main engines: Diesel; 450 bhp = 10 knots

Built by Rauma Repola, Rauma. Launched in Dec 1965.

ICEBREAKERS

2 "URHO" CLASS

Name	No.	Builders	Commissioned
URHO	—	Wärtsilä, Helsinki	Jan 1975
SISU	—	Wärtsilä, Helsinki	Jan 1976

Displacement, tons: 7 900 standard; 9 500 full load
Dimensions, feet (metres): 337·8 × 77·1 × 24·6 *(104·6 × 23·8 × 8·3)*
Aircraft: 1 helicopter
Main engines: Diesel-electric; 5 Wärtsila-SEMT Pielstick diesels 25 000 bhp. Electric Motors; 22 000 shp; 2 shafts forward, 2 aft; = 18 knots
Complement: 57

Ordered on 11 Dec 1970 and 10 May 1971 respectively. Fitted with two screws aft, taking 60% of available power and two forward, taking the remainder.

URHO

1975, Wärtsila

3 "TARMO" CLASS

Name	No.	Builders	Commissioned
TARMO	—	Wärtsilä, Helsinki	1963
VARMA	—	Wärtsilä, Helsinki	1968
APU	—	Wärtsilä, Helsinki	25 Nov 1970

Displacement, tons: 4 890
Dimensions, feet (metres): 281·0 × 71·0 × 22·5 *(85·7 × 21·7 × 6·8)*
Aircraft: 1 helicopter
Main engines: Wärtsilä-Sulzer diesels; electric drive; 4 shafts (2 screws forward 2 screws aft); 12 000 bhp = 17 knots

VARMA

1975, Finnish Navy

3 "KARHU" CLASS

Name	No.	Builders	Commissioned
KARHU	—	Wärtsilä, Helsinki	Dec 1958
MURTAJA	—	Wärtsilä, Helsinki	1959
SAMPO	—	Wärtsilä, Helsinki	1960

Displacement, tons: 3 540
Dimensions, feet (metres): 243·2 × 57 × 21 *(74·2 × 17·4 × 6·4)*
Main engines: Diesel-electric; 4 shafts; 7 500 bhp = 16 knots

Karhu was launched on 22 Oct 1957, *Murtaja* was launched on 23 Sep 1958.

KARHU

1975, Finnish Navy

1 "VOIMA" CLASS

Name	No.	Builders	Commissioned
VOIMA	—	Wärtsilä, Helsinki	1953

Displacement, tons: 4 415
Dimensions, feet (metres): 274 oa × 63·7 × 22·5 *(83·6 × 19·4 × 6·8)*
Main engines: Diesels with electric drive; 4 shafts; 14 000 bhp = 16·5 knots
Oil fuel, tons: 740

Launched in 1953. Two propellers forward and aft.

VOIMA

1975, Finnish Navy

There is also the West German owned, Finnish manned, icebreaker *Hansa*, of the "Karhu" class, completed on 25 Nov 1966, which operates off Germany in winter and off Finland at other times.

COASTGUARD VESSELS

VMV 1—10

10 ton craft of 20 knots built 1956—59.

VMV 11   13   19   20

35 ton craft with a 20 mm gun—first pair built 1935, second pair in 1943.

FRANCE

Headquarters Appointments

Conseil Supérieur de la Marine:
Amiraux Joire Noulens and Daille
Vice-Amiraux d'Escadre Le Front, Darvi, Banuls Lannuzel
Vice-Amiraux Wacrenier and Faure

Senior Appointments

Préfet Maritime de la Première Région (PREMAR UN):
Vice-Amiral Wacrenier
C in C Atlantic Theatre (CECLANT) and Préfet Maritime de la Deuxième Région (PREMAR DEUX):
Vice-Amiral d'Escadre Le Franc
C in C Mediterranean Theatre (CECMED) and Préfet Maritime de la Troisième Région (PREMAR TROIS):
Vice-Amiral d'Escadre Darvi
C in C French Naval Forces, Polynesia:
Vice-Amiral Tardy
C in C Atlantic Fleet:
Vice-Amiral de Gaulle
C in C Mediterranean Fleet:
Contre-Amiral

Diplomatic Representation

Naval Attaché in Bonn:
Capitaine de Frégate Boischot
Naval Attaché in Brasilia:
Capitaine de Corvette Clisson
Naval Attaché in the Hague:
Capitaine de Vaisseau Lamy
Naval Attaché in Kuala Lumpur:
Capitaine de Frégate Osmont
Naval Attaché in Lisbon:
Capitaine de Frégate Gicquel
Naval Attaché in London (& Defence Attaché):
Contre-Amiral François Flohic
Naval Attaché in Madrid:
Capitaine de Vaisseau Touzet de Vigier
Naval Attaché in Moscow:
Capitaine de Vaisseau Cahuac
Naval Attaché in Oslo:
Capitaine de Vaisseau Menes
Naval Attaché in Rome:
Capitaine de Vaisseau de Pouillous de Saint-Mars
Naval Attaché in Santiago:
Capitaine de Vaisseau Vasseur
Naval Attaché in Tokyo:
Capitaine de Vaisseau Laserre
Naval Attaché in Washington:
Contre-Amiral Gelinet

Personnel

(a) 1971: 68 586 (4 732 officers, 63 854 ratings)
1972: 68 308 (4 604 officers, 63 704 ratings)
1973: 67 600 (4 400 officers, 63 200 ratings)
1974: 67 700 (4 500 officers, 63 200 ratings)
1975: 68 000 (4 550 officers, 63 450 ratings)
1976: 68 315 (4 550 officers, 63 765 ratings)

(personnel to be increased by 5 000 under the 15-year re-equipment plan)

(b) National Service 12 months
(providing approx 16 000 ratings)

Bases

Cherbourg: Atlantic Fleet base. Prémar Un
Brest: Main Atlantic base. SSBN base. Prémar Deux
Lorient: Atlantic submarine base
Toulon: Main Mediterranean Fleet base. Prémar Trois

Fleet Dispositions

Atlantic: All new destroyers, frigates and one tanker. All SSBNs and 8 submarines
Mediterranean: *Colbert* (flag) *Foch, Clemenceau, Duquesne, Suffren,* older destroyers and frigates, one tanker and 11 submarines

Mercantile Marine

Lloyd's Register of Shipping:
1 393 vessels of 10 745 999 tons gross

Strength of the Fleet

Type	Active	Building or (Projected)
Attack Carriers (Medium)	2	—
Helicopter Carrier (Nuclear)	—	(1)
Cruisers	2	—
Destroyers	20	4
Frigates	27	11
Submarines (Strat Missile)	4	2
	1 (Diesel powered)	
Submarines (Fleet)	—	1
Submarines (Patrol)	20	3
Corvettes	22	—
Fast Attack Craft (Missile)	4	1
Large Patrol Craft	6	—
LPD	2	—
LST	5	—
LCT	13	—
LCM	16	—
Minesweepers (Ocean)	11	—
Minesweepers (Coastal)	29	—
Minehunters	7	—
Surveying Ships	6	—
Coastal Survey Ships	4	—
Inshore Survey Craft	1	—
Tankers (UR)	5	1
Tankers (Support)	5	—
Maintenance Ships	2	—
Depot Ships	5	—
Repair Ships (ex-LCT)	2	—
Trials Ships	4	—
Boom Defence Vessels	15	—
Torpedo Recovery Vessels	2	—
Victualling Stores Ships	2	—
Stores Ships	4	—
Light Transports	2	—
Small Transports	12	2
Tenders	14	—
Tugs	107	—
Training Ships	8	—

Naval Air Stations

St. Raphael, Lann Bihoue, Nimes Garon, Lanveox Poulmic Dax, Aspretto, Landvisiau, Hyères, St. Mandrier.

Shipyards (Naval)

Cherbourg: Submarines and Fast Attack Craft
Brest: Major warships and refitting
Lorient: Destroyers, frigates and avisos

Submarine Service

Known as Force Océanique Stratégique (FOST) with HQ at Houilles near Paris. SSBN *(SNLE)* force based at Ile Longue Brest with a training base at Roche-Douvres and VLFW/T station at Rosay. Patrol submarines are based at Lorient and Toulon. Plans for nuclear fleet submarines are included in the 15 year plan, with the first being laid down in 1976.

15-Year Re-equipment Plan

Note: All submarines laid down from 1976 onwards are to be nuclear-powered.

This programme ("Plan Bleu") was approved by Parliament on 29 Feb 1972 and provides for the following fleet by 1985:

2 Aircraft Carriers
2 Helicopter Carriers
30 Frigates or Corvettes
35 Avisos
6 SSBN
20 Patrol Submarines (or Fleet)
30 Fast Attack Craft
36 MHC and MSC
5 Replenishment Tankers
Logistic Support and Maintenance Ships
2 Assault Ships
Landing Ships and Craft
Transports
50 LRMP aircraft
Carrier borne craft
Helicopters

1971-75 New Construction Plan

Financial problems have necessitated the addition of an extra year to this plan. Financial allowance made for construction of ships listed below as well as a second Fleet Replenishment Ship, 1 Fleet Submarine (SSN), and the first new minehunter.

1 Helicopter Carrier (PH 75)
3 Guided Missile Destroyers ("Corvettes") "C 70" Type
3 Guided Missile Destroyers ("Corvettes") "C 67" Type
14 Escorts (officially rated as *Avisos)* "A 69" Type
3 Nuclear Powered Ballistic Missile Submarines
4 Patrol Submarines
4 Patrol Boats (for overseas service)
1 Fleet Support & Repair Ship (major conversion)
1 Fleet Replenishment Ship
2 Medium Landing Ships (Transports)

DELETIONS

Helicopter Carrier
1974 *Arromanches*

Cruiser
1973 *De Grasse*

Destroyers
1974 *Chevalier Paul, Cassard*

Frigates
1974 *Le Bordelais, Le Corse* (Type E 50)
1975 *Le Brestois* (Type E 50)

Corvettes
1975 *Le Fougueux, L'Opiniatre* and *L'Agile* ("Le Fougueux" class)

Light Forces
1974 M 691, VC 2, VC 10, P 9785, P 9786

Minewarfare Forces
1974 *Begonia,* and *Glaieul* deleted; *Aries* ("Sirius" class) (To Morocco)
1975 *Bellatrix, Dénébola, Pégase* ("Sirius" class) deleted; *Jacinthe, Liseron* and *Magnolia* ("Adjutant" class) as diving base ships.

Amphibious Forces
1974 LCT 9099 deleted; LCT 9095 to Senegal

Survey Ship
1973 *La Coquille*

Service Forces
1972 *Lac Chambon, Lac Tchad* (small Tankers)
1973 *Médoc* (Supply Ship)
1974 *Oasis* (Water Carrier)
1975 *Maurienne* (Fleet Support Ship)
L 9082 and 9083 (Repair Ships)
Trébéron (ex-German Transport)
Cataracte (Water Carrier)

Trials Ship
1973 *Arago*

BDV
1972 *Tarantule*
1974 *Scorpion, Locuste*

Miscellaneous

1974 M691 (ex-*SC 525),* FNRS 3
1975 *Belier, Pachyderme, Infatgable, Peuplier* (Tugs)

PENNANT LIST

R Aircraft and Helicopter Carriers

97 Jeanne d'Arc
98 Clemenceau
99 Foch

C Cruiser

611 Colbert

D Destroyers

602 Suffren
603 Duquesne
609 Aconit
610 Tourville
611 Duguay-Trouin
612 De Grasse
622 Kersaint
624 Bouvet
625 Dupetit Thouars
627 Maillé Brézé
628 Vauquelin
629 D'Estrées
630 Du Chayla
631 Casablanca
632 Guépratte
633 Duperré
634 La Bourdonnais
635 Forbin
636 Tartu
637 Jauréguiberry
638 La Galissonniere
640 Georges Leygues
641 Dupleix
642 Montcalm

S Submarines

610 Le Foudroyant
611 Le Redoutable
612 Le Terrible
613 L'Indomptable
614 Le Tonnant
620 Agosta
621 Bévéziers
622 La Praya
623 Ouessant
631 Narval
632 Marsouin
633 Dauphin
634 Requin
635 Aréthuse
636 Argonaute
637 Espadon
638 Morse
639 Amazone
640 Ariane
641 Daphné
642 Diane
643 Doris
645 Flore
646 Galatée
648 Junon
649 Venus
650 Psyche
651 Sirène
655 Gymnote

F Frigates and Corvettes

725 Victor Schoelcher
726 Commandant Bory
727 Amiral Charner
728 Doudart de Lagrée
729 Balny
733 Commandant Rivière
740 Commandant Bourdais
748 Protet
749 Enseigne de Vaisseau Henry
763 Le Boulonnais
765 Le Normand
766 Le Picard
767 Le Gascon
768 Le Lorrain
769 Le Bourguignon
770 Le Champenois
771 Le Savoyard
772 Le Breton
773 Le Basque
774 L'Agenais
775 Le Béarnais
776 L'Alsacien
777 Le Provençal
778 Le Vendéen
781 D'Estienne d'Orves
782 Amyot d'Inville
783 Drogou
784 Detroyat
785 Jean Moulin
786 Quartier Maitre Anquetil
787 Commandant de Pimodan
788 Seconde Maitre Le Bihan
789 Lieutenant de Vaisseau le Henaff
790 Lieutenant de Vaisseau Lavallée
791 Commandant l'Herminier
792 Premier Maitre l'Her
793 Commandant Blaison
794 Enseigne de Vaisseau Jacoubet

M Minewarfare Forces

609 Narvik
610 Ouistreham
612 Alençon
613 Berneval
615 Cantho
616 Dompaire
617 Garigliano
618 Mytho
619 Vinh-long
620 Berlaimont
622 Autun
623 Baccarat
624 Colmar
632 Pervenche
633 Pivoine
635 Réséda
638 Acacia
639 Acanthe
640 Marjolaine
668 Azalée
670 Bleuet
671 Camélia
672 Chrysantheme
674 Cyclamen
675 Eglantine
677 Giroflée
679 Glycine
681 Laurier
682 Lilas
684 Lobelia
687 Mimosa
688 Muguet
703 Antares
704 Algol
707 Véga
712 Cybele
713 Calliope
714 Clio
715 Circe
716 Ceres
737 Capricorne
740 Cassiopée
741 Eridan
743 Sagittaire
747 Bételgeuse
749 Phénix
755 Capella
756 Céphée
757 Verseau
759 Lyre
765 Mercure

P Light Forces

630 L'Intrépide
635 L'Ardent
637 L'Etourdi
638 L'Effronté
639 Le Frondeur
640 Le Fringant
644 L'Adroit
645 L'Alerte
646 L'Attentif
647 L'Enjoué
648 Le Hardi
650 Arcturus
651 La Malouine
652 La Lorientaise
653 La Dunkerquoise
654 La Bayonnaise
655 La Dieppoise
656 Altair
657 La Paimpolaise
658 Croix du Sud
659 Canopus
660 Etoile Polaire
661 Jasmin
662 Petunia
670 Trident
671 Glaive
672 Epée
673 Pertuisane
730 La Combattante
770 PB
771 PB
772 PB
774 PB
784 Geranium
787 Jonquille
788 Violette

L Amphibious Forces

9003 Argens
9004 Bidassoa
9007 Trieux
9008 Dives
9009 Blavet
9021 Ouragan
9022 Orage
9030 Champlain
9031 Francis Garnier
9061 LCT
9070 LCT
9071 LCT
9072 LCT
9073 LCT
9074 LCT
9081 Workshop

Amphibious Forces

9082 LCT
9083 LCT
9084 Workshop
9091 LCT
9092 LCT
9093 LCT
9094 LCT
9096 LCT

(CTM   LCMs 1-16)

A Auxiliaries and Support Ships

603 Henry Poincaré
608 Moselle
610 Ile d'Oléron
614 Falleron
615 Loire
617 Garonne
618 Rance
619 Aber Wrach
620 Jules Verne
621 Rhin
622 Rhône
623 Liseron
625 Papenoo
626 La Charente
627 La Seine
628 La Sâone
629 La Durance
630 Lac Tonlé Sap
632 Punaruu
638 Sahel
640 Origny
643 Aunis
644 Berry
646 Triton
648 Archimède
649 L'Etoile
650 La Belle Poule
652 Mutin
653 La Grande Hermine
660 Hippopotame
664 Malabar
665 Goliath
666 Eléphant
667 Hercules
668 Rhinocéros
669 Tenace
671 Le Fort
672 Utile
673 Lutteur
674 Centaure
675 Isère
682 Alidade
683 Octant
684 Coolie
685 Robuste
686 Actif
687 Laborieux
688 Valeureux
692 Travailleur
694 Efficace
695 Acharne
698 Petrel
699 Pelican
701 Ajonc
706 Courageux
710 Myosotis
711 Gardénia
716 Oiseau des Iles
722 Poseidon
727 Araignée
730 Libellule
731 Tianée
733 Saintonge
735 Hibiscus
736 Dahlia
737 Tulipe
738 Capucine
739 Oeillet
740 Hortensia
741 Armoise
742 Paquerette
753 La Découverte
755 Commandant Robert Giraud
756 Espérance
757 D'Entrecasteaux
758 La Recherche
759 Marcel Le Bihan
760 Cigale
761 Criquet
762 Fourmi
763 Grillon
764 Scarabée
766 Estafette
777 Luciole
780 L'Astrolabe
781 Boussole
789 Archéonaute
794 Corail

Y Auxiliaries

601 Acajou
602 Aigrette
604 Ariel
607 Balsa
608 Bambou
611 Bengali
612 Bouleau
613 Faune
616 Canari
617 Mouette
618 Cascade
620 Chataigner
621 Mésange
623 Charme
624 Chêne
628 Colibri
629 Cormier
630 Bonite
631 Courlis
632 Cygne
633 Délange
634 Rouget
635 Equeurdibille
636 Martinet
637 Fauvette
640 Fontaine
641 Forméne
644 Fréne
645 Gave
646 Geyser
647 Giens
648 Goeland
649 Grive
651 Hanneton
652 Haut Barr
653 Heron
654 Hêtre
655 Hévéat
657 Hirondelle
658 Ibis
659 Jonque
661 Korrigan
662 Dryade
663 Latanier
664 Lutin
666 Manguier
667 Tupa
668 Méléze
669 Merisier
670 Merle
671 Morgane
673 Moineau
675 Martin Pecheur
678 Moule
680 Muréne
682 Okoume
683 Ondée
684 Oued
685 Oursin
686 Palétuvier
687 Passereau
688 Peuplier
689 Pin
690 Pingouin
691 Pinson
694 Pivert
695 Platane
696 Alphée
699 Poulpe
702 Rascasse
704 Rossignol
706 Chimère
708 Saule
709 Sycamore
710 Sylphe
711 Farfadet
717 Ébene
718 Erable
719 Olivier
720 Santal
721 Alouette
722 Vauneau
723 Engoulevent
724 Surcelle
725 Marabout
726 Toucan
727 Macreuse
728 Grand Duc
729 Eider
730 Ara
735 Merlin
736 Mélusine
738 Marronier
739 Noyer
740 Papayer
741 Elfe
743 Palangrin
745 Aiguiére
746 Embrun
747 Loriot
748 Gelinotte
749 La Prudente
750 La Persévérante
751 La Fidéle
760 PB

NAVAL AIR ARM

NAVAL AIR ARM

Squadron Number	Base	Aircraft	Task
Embarked Squadrons			
4F	Lann Bihoue	BR1050 "Alize"	Patrol & A/S
6F	Nimes Garons	BR1050 "Alize"	Patrol & A/S
11F	Landivisiau	ETD IV M	Fighter Bomber
12F	Landivisiau	F8E "Crusader"	Interceptors
14F	Landivisiau	F8E "Crusader"	Interceptors
16F	Landivisiau	ETD IV P	Reconnaissance
17F	Hyeres	ETD IV M	Fighter Bomber
31F	St. Mandrier	HSS 1	A/S
32F	Lanveoc Poulmic	Super-Frelon	A/S
33F	St. Mandrier	HSS 1	Assault
J. d'Arc	J. d'Arc or St. Mandrier	HSS 1	Training
SRL	Landivisiau	MS 760 "Paris"	Support
Support Squadrons			
2S	Lann Bihoue	Navajo, Nord 262	Support 1st & 2nd Region
3S	Hyeres	Navajo, Nord 262	Support 3rd Region
10S	St. Raphael	Nord 2504, BR1050 Navajo, MS 733	Trials CEPA
20S	St. Raphael	AL 11, AL 111 AL 111 ASM HSS 1, Super Frelon	Trials CEPA
22S	Lanveoc Poulmic	AL 11, AL 111 AL 111 VSV	Support 2nd Region, SAR
23S	St. Mandrier	AL 11, AL 111	Support 3rd Region, SAR
SSD	Dugny	C 54, Nord 262 Navajo	Support

Squadron Number	Base	Aircraft	Task
Maritime Patrol Squadrons			
21F	Nimes Garons	BR 1150 "Atlantic"	MP
22F	Nimes Garons	BR 1150 "Atlantic"	MP
23F	Lann Bihoue	BR 1150 "Atlantic"	MP
24F	Lann Bihoue	BR 1150 "Atlantic"	MP
25F	Lann Bihoue	Neptune P2H	MP
Training Squadrons			
55S	Aspretto	Nord 262, SNB 5	Twin-engine conversion
56S	Nimes Garons	C 47	Flying School
59S	Hyeres	ET IV, BR 1050 CM 175 "Zephyr"	Fighter School
SVS	Lanveoc Poulmic	MS 733	Naval School Recreational
Esalat Dax	Dax	AL 11	Helicopter School
Overseas Detachments			
New Caledonia	Tontouta	C 54, C 47	Support and Liaison
Malagasy	Diego Suarez	C 47	Support and Liaison
CEP Formations			
Sectal Pac.	Hao	AL 111	Support
27S	Hao	Super-Frelon	Support
12S	Papeete	Neptune P2H	MP

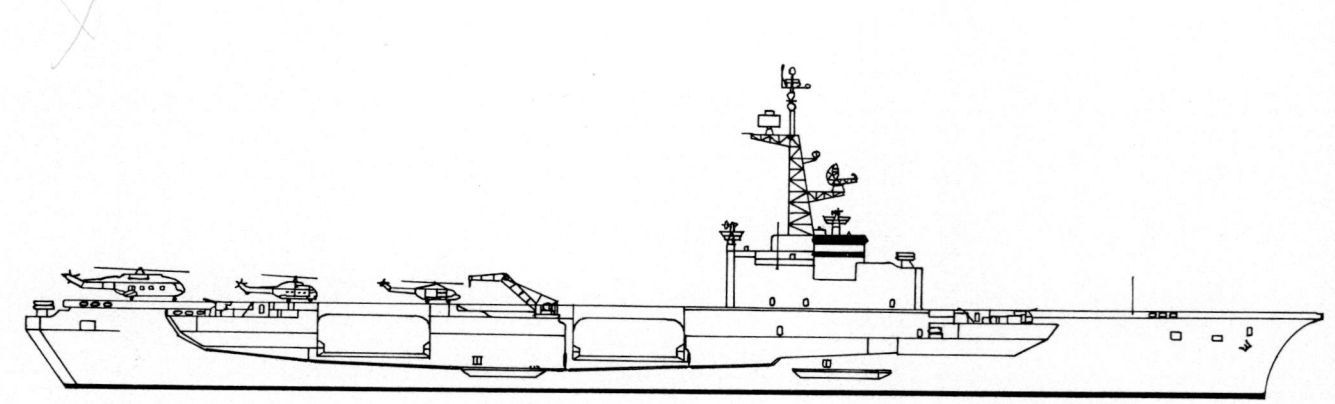

PH 75

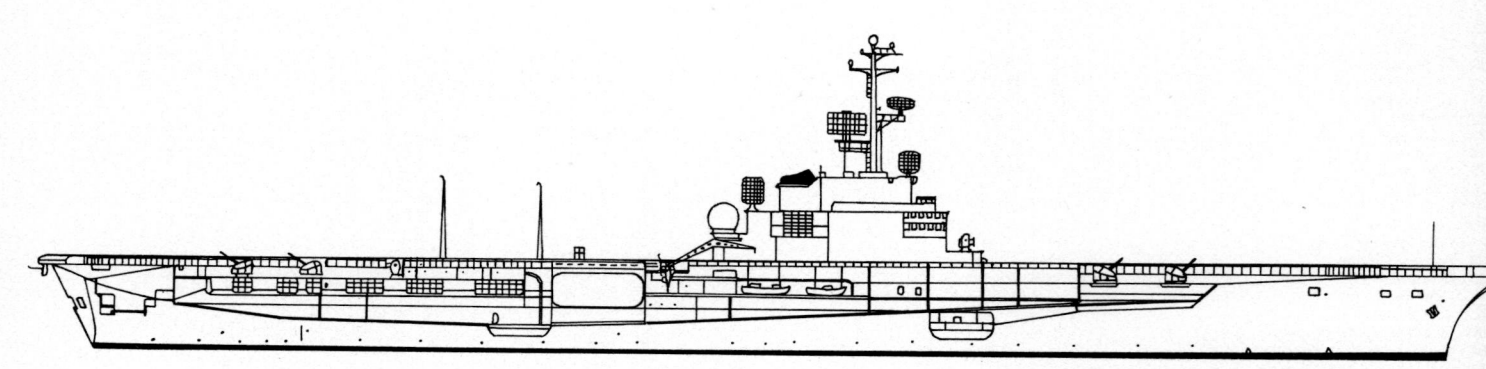

"CLEMENCEAU" Class

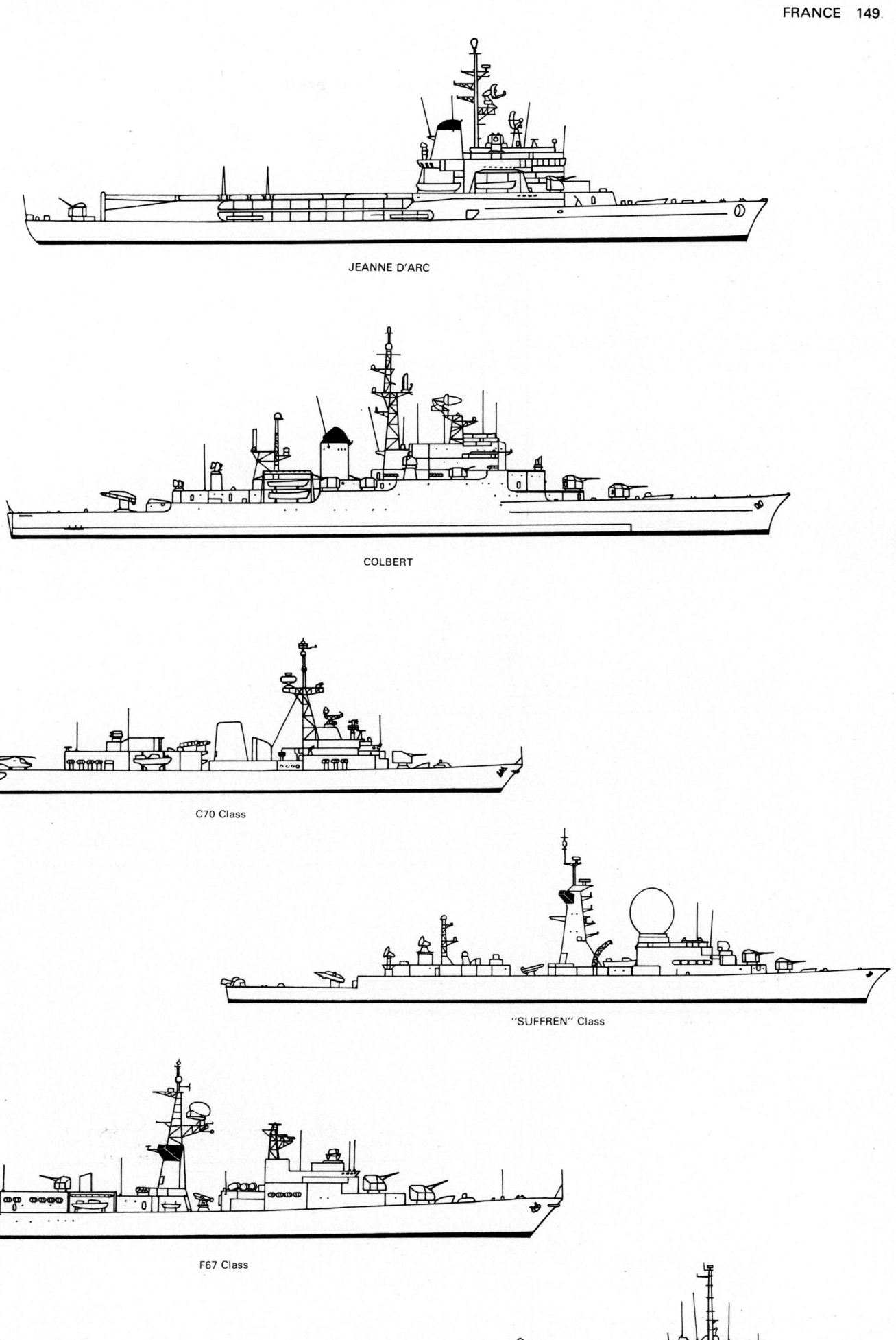

JEANNE D'ARC

COLBERT

C70 Class

"SUFFREN" Class

F67 Class

OURAGAN and ORAGE

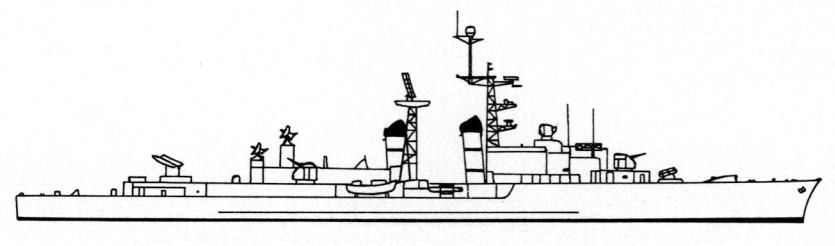

TYPE 47 (DDG)

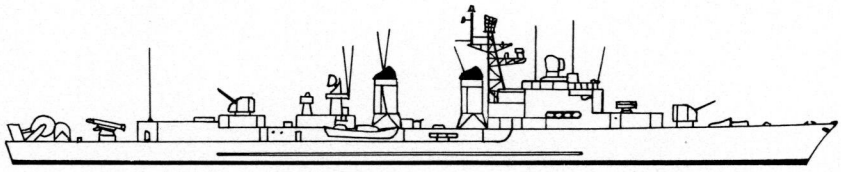

TYPE 47 (ASW)

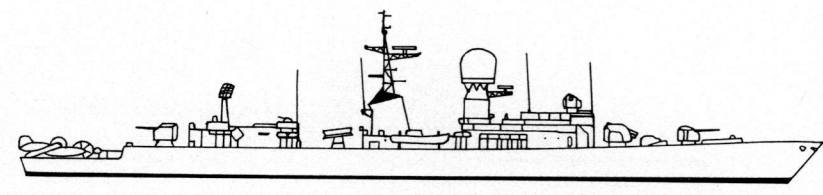

ACONIT

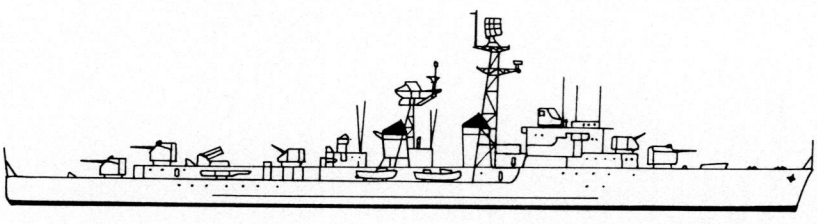

TYPE 53

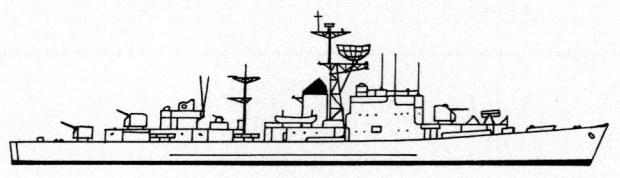

E52 TYPE

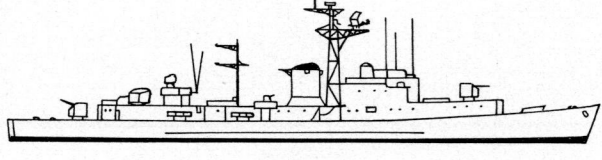

E52B TYPE

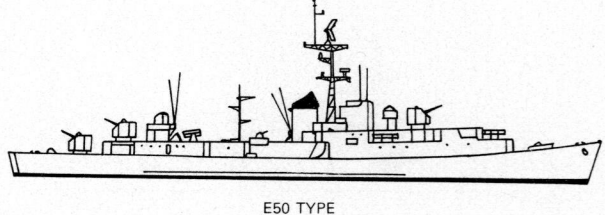

E50 TYPE

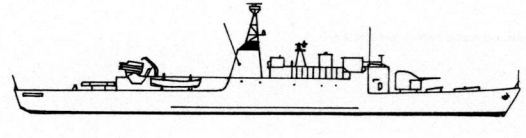

A69 TYPE

AIRCRAFT CARRIERS

1 PH 75 (NUCLEAR-PROPELLED HELICOPTER CARRIER)

Name	No.	Builders	Laid down	Launch	Commissioning
—	PH 75	DCAN, Brest	—	—	?1981

Displacement, tons: 16 400 trials; 18 400 full load
Length, feet (metres): 682·2 oa (208)
Length, feet (metres): 662·6 flight deck (202)
Beam, feet (metres): 86·6 wl (26·4)
Beam, feet (metres): 157·4 flight deck (46)
Aircraft: 25 WG 13 Lynx or 10 Super Frelon or 15 Puma helicopters
Missiles: 2 Crotale SAM systems; 4 SAM systems with a sea-skimming capability for anti-missile defence are eventually to replace the guns
Guns: 2—100 mm (singles—forward)
Main engines: 1—CAS 230 reactor to two turbines; 65 000 bhp; two emergency AGO diesels
Speed, knots: 28
Range, miles: Unlimited on reactor; 3 000 at 18 knots (diesels)
Endurance: Stores for 45 days; 30 days for passengers
Complement: 890 plus 1 500 passengers

Coming at a time of financial stringency, this is a bold design showing the French Navy's appreciation of the great and universal value of helicopters in both peace and war. While her wartime role in a force composed of both A/S and A/A ships is clear, she has been designed with an intervention role in mind as well. For peacetime duties in the event of natural disasters, her large passenger and hospital capacity will be of immense value. Construction by DCAN, Brest with a programme allowing for trials in 1980 and service in 1981.

Accommodation: A crew of 840 plus 50 staff and Ground Intervention Staff is provided for. Passenger accommodation is available for 1 000, with more austere conditions on portable bunks for an extra 500 in the garage (forward of the hangar).

Aircraft: Although designed primarily for helicopter operations the possibility of VTOL operations was also taken into account.

Electrical supply: A total of 9 400 kW from two turbines each driving a pair of 1 500 kW alternators and four diesel alternators of 850 kW each.

Flight Deck: The flight deck, 662 feet long, is 157 feet wide at its maximum and 102 feet at the island. Four spots are provided for Super Frelon helicopters and eight for Lynx or Puma.

Hangar: One hangar, 275 × 69 × 21 feet, is provided with two lateral lifts to starboard at the rear of the island. Storage for 1 000 cubic metres of TR5 fuel in tanks is available. One fixed crane and one mobile crane are provided.

Hospital: 3 main wards, 1 X-ray ward, 1 intensive care ward, 1 infectious diseases ward, 2 dental surgeries and a laboratory.

Operations Rooms: Normal Operations Room, ASW centre and Communication Offices are supplemented by an Operations Centre with facilities for Ground Intervention Forces and Air Intervention Forces. These include a Warfare Coordinating Centre, an Air Intervention Command Centre and a Helicopter Command Station.

Radar: 1 DRBV 26 long range air search set; 1 DRBV 51C combined search set; 2 Decca systems; 2DRBC 32 for missile guidance.

Main engines: The CAS 230 reactor of 230 megawatts is being constructed under the supervision of l'Etablissement des Constructions et Armes Navales d'Indret.

Replenishment: 1 250 tons of fuel is carried for replenishment of Escorts.

Sonar: 1 DUBA 25.

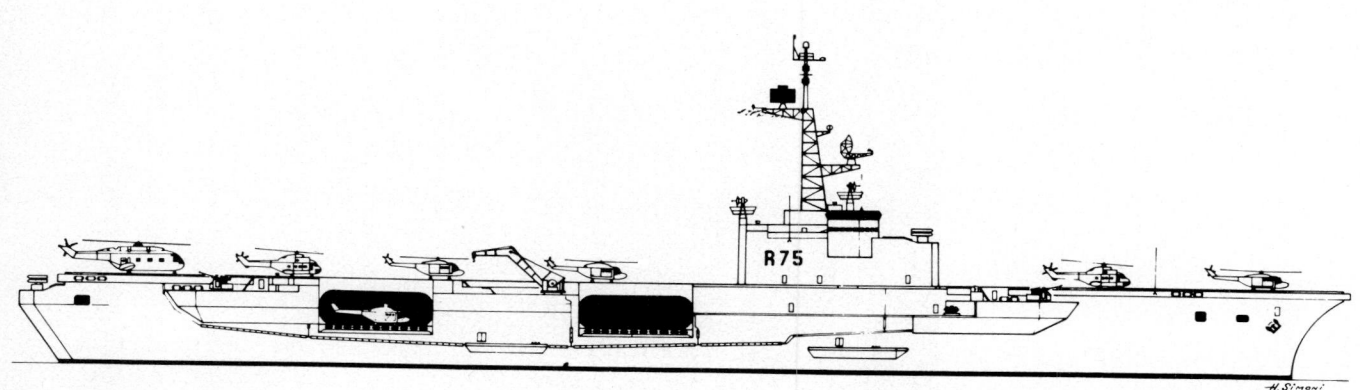

PH 75

1974, French Navy

2 "CLEMENCEAU" CLASS

Name	No.	Builders	Laid down	Launched	Commissioned
CLEMENCEAU	R 98	Brest Dockyard	Nov 1955	21 Dec 1957	22 Nov 1961
FOCH	R 99	Chantiers de L'Atlantique	Feb 1957	28 July 1960	15 July 1963

Displacement, tons: 27 307 normal; 32 780 full load
Length, feet (metres): 780·8 *(238·0)* pp; 869·4 *(265·0)* oa
Beam, feet (metres): 104·1 *(31·7)* hull (with bulges)
Width, feet (metres): 168·0 *(51·2)* oa
Draught, feet (metres): 28·2 *(8·6)*
Aircraft: Capacity 40. Each carries 3 Flights—1 of Etendard IV, 1 of Crusader, 1 of Breguet Alizé
Catapults: 2 Mitchell-Brown steam, Mk BS 5
Guns: 8—3·9 in *(100 mm)* automatic in single turrets
Armour Flight deck, island superstructure and bridges, hull (over machinery spaces and magazines)
Main engines: 2 sets Parsons geared turbines; 2 shafts; 126 000 shp
Boilers: 6; steam pressure 640 psi *(45 kg/cm²)*, superheat 842°F *(450°C)*
Speed, knots: 32
Oil fuel, tons: 3 720
Range, miles: 7 500 at 18 knots; 4 800 at 24 knots; 3 500 at full power
Complement: 1 228 (65 officers, 1 163 men)

First aircraft carriers designed as such and built from the keel to be completed in France. Authorised in 1953 and 1955, respectively. *Clemenceau* ordered from Brest Dockyard on 28 May 1954 and begun in Nov 1955. *Foch* begun at Chantiers de l'Atlantique at St. Nazaire, Penhoet-Loire, in a special dry dock (contract provided for the construction of the hull and propelling machinery) and completed by Brest Dockyard.

Bulges: *Foch* was completed with bulges. These having proved successful, *Clemenceau* was modified similarly on first refit, increasing her beam by 6 feet.

Electronics: Comprehensive DF and ECM equipment. Both fitted with SENIT 4 Tactical data automation system.

Flight Deck: Angled deck, two lifts, measuring 52·5 × 36 feet, one on the starboard deck edge, two steam catapults and two mirror landing aids. The flight deck measures 543 × 96·8 feet and is angled at 8 degrees.
Flight deck letters: F = *Foch*, U = *Clemenceau*.

Gunnery: Originally to have been armed with 24—2·25 inch guns in twin mountings, but the armament was revised to 12—3·9 inch *(100 mm)* in 1956 and to 8—3·9 inch *(100 mm)* in 1958. Rate of fire 60 rounds per minute.

Hangar: Dimensions of the hangar are 590·6 × 78·7 × 23·0 feet *(180 × 24 × 7 metres)*

Radar: One DRBV 20C; one DRBV 23B; two DRBI 10; one DRBV 50; one DRBC 31.

Sonar: One SQS 505.

FOCH

1974, Dr. Giorgio Arra

CLEMENCEAU

1972, French Navy

FOCH

7/1974 Wright & Logan

CRUISERS

Name	No.	Builders	Laid down	Launched	Commissioned
JEANNE D'ARC (ex-La Résolue)	R 97	Brest Dockyard	7 July 1960	30 Sep 1961	1 July 1963 (trials) 30 June 1964 (service)

Displacement, tons: 10 000 standard; 12 365 full load
Length, feet (metres): 564·2 (172) pp; 597·1 (182·0) oa
Beam, feet (metres): 78·7 (24·0) hull
Draught, feet (metres): 24·0 (7·3)
Flight deck, feet (metres): 203·4 × 68·9 (62·0 × 21·0)
Aircraft: Heavy A(S helicopters (4 in peace-time as training ship; 8 in wartime)
Missiles: 6—MM38 Exocet
Guns: 4—3·9 in (100 mm) single
Main engines: Rateau-Bretagne geared turbines; 2 shafts; 40 000 shp
Boilers: 4; working pressure 640 psi (45 kg/cm²); 842°F (450°C)
Speed, knots: 26·5
Oil fuel, tons: 1 360
Range, miles: 6 000 at 15 knots
Complement: 809 (30 officers, 587 ratings and 192 cadets)

Authorised under the 1957 estimates. Used for training officer cadets in peacetime in place of the old training cruiser *Jeanne d'Arc* (which was decommissioned on 28 July 1964 and sold for scrap in Dec 1965 at Brest). In wartime, after rapid modification, she would be used as a commando ship, helicopter carrier or troop transport with commando equipment and a battalion of 700 men. The lift has a capacity of 12 tons. The ship is almost entirely air-conditioned.

Missiles: Due to be fitted with Crotale.

Modifications: Between first steaming trials and completion for operational service the ship was modified with a taller funnel to clear the superstructure and prevent the smoke and exhaust gases swirling on to the bridges.

Radar: One DRBV 22D; one DRBV 50; one DRBN 32; one DRBI 10.

Sonar: One SQS 503.

JEANNE D'ARC

1975, French Navy

JEANNE D'ARC

1975, French Navy

Name	No.	Builders	Laid down	Launched	Commissioned
COLBERT	C 611	Brest Dockyard	Dec 1953	24 Mar 1956 (floated out of dry dock)	5 May 1959 (trials late 1957)

Displacement, tons: 8 500 standard; 11 300 full load
Length, feet (metres): 593·2 *(180·8)*
Beam, feet (metres): 66·1 *(20·2)*
Draught, feet (metres): 25·2 *(7·7)*
Missile launchers: 1 twin "Masurca" surface-to-air aft.
   4-MM38 Exocet to be fitted
Guns: 2—3·9 in *(100 mm)* single automatic;
   12—57 mm in 6 twin mountings, 3 on each side
Armour: 50—80 mm belt and 50 mm deck
Main engines: 2 sets CEM-Parsons geared turbines; 2 shafts;
   86 000 shp
Boilers: 4 Indret multitubular; 640 psi *(45 kg/cm²)*; 842°F *(450°C)*
Speed, knots: 31·5
Oil fuel, tons: 1 492
Range, miles: 4 000 at 25 knots
Complement: 560 (24 officers, 536 men)

She was equipped as command ship and for radar control of air strikes.

Electronics: Senit data automation system; Radar intercept equipment; wireless intercept equipment; two Knebworth Corvus dual-purpose launchers for CHAFF.

Gunnery: Prior to Apr 1970 the armament comprised sixteen 5 inch *(127 mm)* dual purpose guns in eight twin mountings, and twenty 57 mm Bofors anti-aircraft guns in ten twin mountings.

Missiles: *Colbert* carries 48 Masurca missiles (Mk 2 Mod 3 semi-active radar homing version). 4 Exocet to be shipped at a later refit.

Radar: Navigation: one Decca RM416.
Surveillance: one DRBV 50.
Air surveillance: one DRBV 23C
Warning: one DRBV 20.
Fire control: two DRBR 51; one DRBR 32C; two DRBC 31.
Height finder: one DRBI 10D.

Reconstruction: Between April 1970 and October 1972 she underwent a complete reconstruction and rearmament. The gunnery systems were altered to those given above, the "Masurca" surface-to-air missile system was fitted and helicopter facilities were installed on the quarter-deck. Reductions in the original armament schedule saved 80 mil francs from the original refit cost of 350 mil francs.

Sonar: Hull mounted set.

COLBERT   *1973, French Navy*

COLBERT   *1973, French Navy*

COLBERT   *1973, French Navy*

DESTROYERS

3 TYPE C70

Name	No.	Builders	Laid down	Launched	Commissioned
GEORGES LEYGUES	D 640	Brest Dockyard	June 1974	6 Sep 1975	1978
DUPLEIX	D 641	Brest Dockyard	Sep 1975	—	1979
MONTCALM	D 642	Brest Dockyard	Sep 1975	—	1979

Displacement, tons: 3 800 standard; 4 100 full load
Dimensions, feet (metres): 455·9 oa × 45·9 *(139 × 14)*
Aircraft: 2 WG 13 "Lynx" helicopters with Mk 44 or 46 torpedoes
Missile launchers: 4 MM 38 Exocet; 1 Crotale
Guns: 1—3·9 in *(100 mm);* 2—20 mm
Torpedoes: 10 tubes in 2 mountings for Mk L5
Main engines: CODOG; 2 Rolls Royce Olympus gas turbines
42 000 bhp; 2 SEMT-Pielstick 16PA6 diesels 10 000 bhp;
2 shafts; VP screws
Speed, knots: 29·75 (19·5 on diesels)
Range, miles: 9 000 at 18 knots on diesels
Complement: 242 (19 officers, 223 ratings)

A new C 70 type of so-called "corvette". Three are included in
the new construction programme.
A total of at least 24 is planned for completion by 1985, eighteen being of an A(S version like *G. Leygues* and six of an A(A
version.

Electronics: Senit action data automation system.

Helicopter: The Lynx, as well as its A(S role, can have an
anti-surface role when armed with 4 AS 12 missiles.

Missiles: AA version to carry Standard SM2 system.

Radar: one DRBV 26; one DRBV 51; one DRBV 32E; two Decca
1226.

Sonar: One DUBV 23 (hull-mounted); one DUBV 43 (VDS).

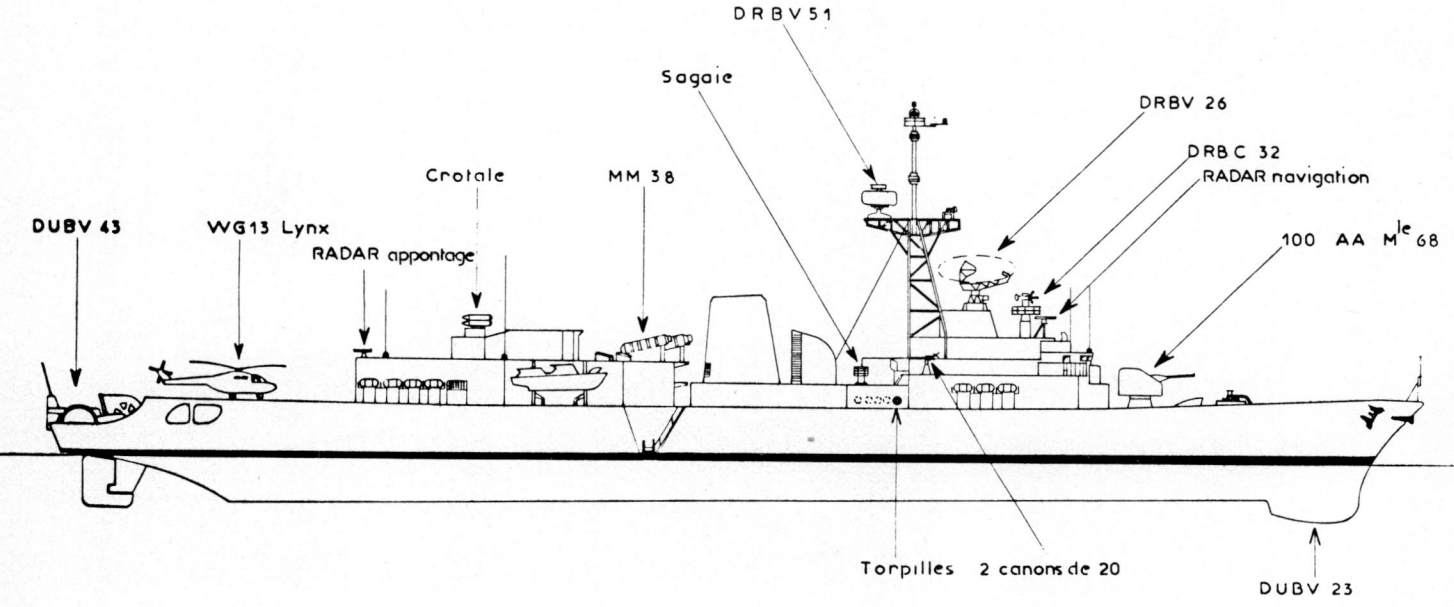

Type C 70   *1974, French Navy*

2 "SUFFREN" CLASS

Name	No.	Builders	Laid down	Launched	Commissioned
DUQUESNE	D 603	Brest Dockyard	Nov 1964	12 Feb 1966	Apr 1970
SUFFREN	D 602	Lorient Dockyard	Dec 1962	15 May 1965	July 1967

Displacement, tons: 5 090 standard; 6 090 full load
Length, feet (metres): 517·1 *(157·6)* oa
Beam, feet (metres): 50·9 *(15·5)*
Draught, feet (metres): 20·0 *(6·1)*
Missile launchers: Twin "Masurca" surface-air
Guns: 2—3·9 in *(100 mm)* (automatic, single)
   2—30 mm (automatic single)
A/S weapons: Malafon single launcher with 13 missiles; 4
   launchers (2 each side) for L5 A/S homing torpedoes
Main engines: Double reduction Rateau geared turbines;
   2 shafts; 72 500 shp
Boilers: 4 automatic; working pressure 640 psi *(45 kg/cm²)*;
   superheat 842°F *(450°C)*
Speed, knots: 34
Range, miles: 5 100 at 18 knots; 2 400 at 29 knots
Complement: 426 (23 officers, 332 men)

Ordered under the 1960 Programme. Equipped with gyro controlled stabilisers controlling three pairs of non-retractable
fins. Air-conditioning of accommodation and operational
areas. Excellent sea-boats and weapon platforms.

Electronics: Senit I action data automatic system. Two Syllex.

Missiles: Carry 48 Masurca missiles, a mix of Mk 2 Mod 2 beam
riders and Mk 2 Mod 3 semi-active homers. Eventually 4 Exocet
launchers will replace the 100 mm gun mountings.

Radar: Search and navigation: one DRBN 32.
Air surveillance and target designator (radome): one DRBI 23.
Surface surveillance: one DRBV 50.
Masurca fire-control: two DRBR 51.
Gun fire-control: one DRBC 32A.

Sonar: One DUBV 23 hull-mounted set and a DUBV 43 VDS.

DUQUESNE   8/1975, Stefan Terzibaschitsch

SUFFREN   11/1975, Dr. Giorgio Arra

SUFFREN   6/1974, Wright and Logan

Name	No.
TOURVILLE	D 610
DUGUAY-TROUIN	D 611
DE GRASSE	D 612

Displacement, tons: 4 580 standard; 5 745 full load
Length, feet (metres): 510·3 *(152·8)* oa
Beam, feet (metres): 50·2 *(15·3)*
Draught, feet (metres): 18·7 *(5·7)*
Aircraft: 2 WG 13 Lynx ASW helicopters
Missile launchers: 6 MM 38 Exocet;
  1—Crotale SAM *(De Grasse)*
Guns: 3—3·9 in *(100 mm)* (2 in *De Grasse)*
A/S weapons: 1 "Malafon" rocket/homing torpedo
  (13 missiles); 2 mountings for Mk L5 torpedoes
Main engines: Rateau geared turbines; 2 shafts; 54 400 shp
Boilers: 4 automatic
Speed, knots: 31
Range, miles: 5 000 at 18 knots
Complement: 303 (25 officers, 278 men)

Developed from the "Aconit" design. Originally rated as "Corvettes" but reclassified as "Frigates" on 8 July 1971 and given "D" pennant numbers like destroyers.

Electronics: Senit action data automatic system. Two Syllex.

Missiles: Crotale fitted in *De Grasse* in place of after 100 mm gun.

Radar: Surface/air surveillance: one DRBV 51
Fire control: one DRBC 32D
Navigation: two Decca type 1226
Air search: one DRBV 26

Sonars: One DUBV 23 hull-mounted; one DUBV 43 VDS.

TYPE F 67 (ex-C-67A)

Builders	Laid down	Launched	Commissioned
Lorient Naval Dockyard	Mar 1970	13 May 1972	21 June1974
Lorient Naval Dockyard	Jan 1971	1 June1973	Sep 1975
Lorient Naval Dockyard	1972	30 Nov 1974	Nov 1976

DUGUAY-TROUIN (Exocet abaft bridge)   1975, French Navy

DUGUAY-TROUIN (Exocet abaft bridge)   1975, French Navy

1 TYPE T 56

Name	No.
LA GALISSONNIÈRE	D 638

Displacement, tons: 2 750 standard; 3 740 full load
Length, feet (metres): 435·7 *(132·8)* oa
Beam, feet (metres): 41·7 *(12·7)*
Draught, feet (metres): 18·0 *(5·4)*
Aircraft: 1 A/S helicopter
A/S weapons: 1 "Malafon" rocket/homing torpedo launcher
Guns: 2—3·9 in *(100 mm)* automatic, single
Torpedo tubes: 6—21·7 in *(550 mm)* ASM, 2 triple for Mks K2 and L3
Main engines: 2 sets Rateau geared turbines; 2 shafts; 63 000 shp
Boilers: 4 A &C de B Indret; 500 psi *(35 kg/cm²)*; 617°F *(380°C)*
Speed, knots: 32
Oil fuel, tons: 800
Range, miles: 5 000 at 18 knots
Complement: 270 (15 officers, 255 men)

Same characteristics as regards hull and machinery as T 47 and T 53 types, but different armament. She has a hangar which hinges outwards and a platform for landing a helicopter. When first commissioned she was used as an experimental ship for new sonars and anti-submarine weapons.

Armament: First French combatant ship to be armed with Malafon. This is the reason for the two 3·9 in *(100 mm)* guns instead of the 3 or 4 previously planned. France's first operational guided missile ship.

Electronics: Tacan beacon and full DF and ECM fit.

Radar: Surface/air surveillance: one DRBV 50
Navigation: one DRBN 32
Air search: one DRBV 22
Gun fire-control: one DRBC 32A

Sonar: One hull mounted DUBV 23; one DUBV 43 VDS.

Builders	Laid down	Launched	Commissioned
Lorient Naval Dockyard	Nov 1958	12 Mar 1960	July 1962

LA GALISSONIÈRE   1974, Wright and Logan

1 TYPE T 53 (MODIFIED—ASW)

Name	No.	Builders	Laid down	Launched	Commissioned
DUPERRÉ	D 633	Lorient Naval Dockyard	Nov 1954	23 June 1956	8 Oct 1957

Displacement, tons: 2 800 standard; 3 900 full load
Length, feet (metres): 435·7 (132·8) oa
Beam, feet (metres): 41·7 (12·7)
Draught, feet (metres): 18·0 (5·5)
Aircraft: 1 WG 13 Lynx helicopter
Missiles: 4 MM 38 Exocet
Guns: 1—3·9 in (100 mm)
A/S weapons: Launcher for 8 torpedoes (Mk L5)
Main engines: 2 sets Rateau geared turbines; 2 shafts;
  63 000 shp
Boilers: 4 A & C de B Indret: 500 psi (35 kg/cm²); 617°F (380°C)
Speed, knots: 32
Oil fuel, tons: 800
Range, miles: 5 000 at 18 knots
Complement: 272 (15 officers, 257 men)

After serving as trial ship from 1967-71, she was converted at Brest to her present state in 1972-74. Recommissioned 21 May 1974.

Electronics: One Senit automatic data system; two Syllex.

Radar: Air search: one DRBV 22A
Navigation: one Decca
Helicopter: one Decca
Fire control: one DRBC 32E
Surface/air surveillance: one DRBV 51

Sonar: DUBV 23 hull-mounted; DUBV 43 VDS.

DUPERRÉ

6/1975, Dr. Giorgio Arra

4 TYPE T 53

Name	No.	Builders	Laid down	Launched	Commissioned
LA BOURDONNAIS	D 634	Brest Naval Dockyard	Aug 1954	15 Oct 1955	Mar 1958
FORBIN	D 635	Brest Naval Dockyard	Aug 1954	15 Oct 1955	1 Feb 1958
TARTU	D 636	At. Chantiers de Bretagne	Nov 1954	2 Dec 1955	5 Feb 1958
JAURÉGUIBERRY	D 637	Gironde	Sep 1954	5 Nov 1955	July 1958

Displacement, tons: 2 750 standard; 3 740 full load
Length, feet (metres): 421·3 (128·6)
Beam, feet (metres): 41·7 (12·7)
Draught, feet (metres): 18·0 (5·4)
Guns: 6—5 in (127 mm) (twins); (Forbin 4—5 in);
  6—57 mm (twins); 2—20 mm
A/S weapons: 2 triple mountings (550 mm) for Mk K2 and L3;
  375 mm Mk 54 projector
Main engines: 2 geared turbines; 63 000 shp; 2 shafts
Boilers: 4 A & C de B Indret
Speed, knots: 32
Oil fuel, tons: 800
Range, miles: 5 000 at 18 knots
Complement: 276 (15 officers, 261 men)

Air-direction ships—*Forbin* has helicopter platform aft in place of Y mount.
Forbin acts as a training ship for L'École d'Application des Enseignes de Vaisseau, being part of the *Jeanne d'Arc* group.
La Bourdonnais to reserve in 1976.

Electronics: Senit automatic data system.
Tacan Beacon.

Radar: Three dimensional air search: DRBI 10A
Air search: DRBV 22A
Navigation: DRBV 31

Sonar: One DUBA 1; one DUBV 24.

TARTU

11/1975, Dr. Giorgio Arra

FORBIN (with helo platform)

1973, French Navy

4 TYPE T 47 (DDG)

Name	No.	Builders	Laid down	Launched	Commissioned
KERSAINT	D 622	Lorient Naval Dockyard	June 1951	3 Oct 1953	20 Mar 1956
BOUVET	D 624	Lorient Naval Dockyard	Nov 1951	3 Oct 1953	13 May 1956
DUPETIT THOUARS	D 625	Brest Naval Dockyard	Mar 1952	4 Mar 1954	15 Sep 1956
DU CHAYLA	D 630	Brest Naval Dockyard	July 1953	27 Nov 1954	4 June 1957

Displacement, tons: 2 750 standard; 3 740 full load
Length, feet (metres): 421·3 (128·6)
Beam, feet (metres): 41·7 (12·7)
Draught, feet (metres): 18·0 (5·4)
Missiles: Single Mk 13 Tartar launcher (40 missiles—SMI or SMIA)
Guns: 6—57 mm (twins)
A/S weapons: 2 triple mountings (550 mm) for Mk K2 and L3; 375 mm Mk 54 projector
Main engines: 2 geared turbines; 63 000 shp; 2 shafts
Boilers: 4 A & C de B Indret
Speed, knots: 32
Oil fuel, tons: 800
Range, miles: 5 000 at 18 knots
Complement: 277 (17 officers, 260 men)

Electronics: Senit automatic data system.

Sonars: One DUBA 1; one DUBV 24.

Radar: Air-search: one DRBV 20 A
Tartar search (3D): one SPS 39
Tartar control: two SPG 51B
Navigation: one DRBV 31

DU CHAYLA

7/1973, Wright and Logan

5 TYPE T 47 (ASW)

Name	No.	Builders	Laid down	Launched	Commissioned
MAILLE BRÈZÈ	D 627	Lorient Naval Dockyard	Oct 1953	26 Sep 1954	4 May 1957
VAUQUELIN	D 628	Lorient Naval Dockyard	Mar 1953	26 Sep 1954	3 Nov 1956
D'ESTRÉES	D 629	Brest Naval Dockyard	May 1953	27 Nov 1954	19 Mar 1957
CASABIANCA	D 631	F. C. Gironde	Oct 1953	13 Nov 1954	4 May 1957
GUÉPRATTE	D 632	A. C. Bretagne	Aug 1953	8 Nov 1954	6 June 1957

Displacement, tons: 2 750 standard; 3 900 full load
Length, feet (metres): 434·6 (132·5)
Beam, feet (metres): 41·7 (12·7)
Draught, feet (metres): 18·3 (5·8)
Guns: 2—3·9 in (100 mm) (singles); 2—20 mm
A/S weapons: 1 Malafon; 1—375 mm Mk 54 projector; two triple mountings (550 mm) for Mk K2 and L3
Main engines: 2 geared turbines; 63 000 shp; 2 shafts
Boilers: 4 A & C de B Indret
Speed, knots: 32
Range, miles: 5 000 at 18 knots
Oil fuel, tons: 800
Complement: 260 (15 officers, 245 men)

Modernised between 1968-71 including air-conditioning of living spaces, replacement of electronic equipment and updating of damage control equipment.

Radar: Navigation: one DRBN 32
Air surveillance: one DRBV 22A
Air/surface search: one DRBV 50
Gun fire control: two DRBC 32A

VAUQUELIN

12/1975, Dr. Giorgio Arra

Electronics: Senit data handling.

Sonars: One DUBV 23 hull mounted; one DUBV 43 VDS.

MAILLE BRÈZÈ

6/1975, Dr. Giorgio Arra

1 TYPE C 65

Name	No.	Builders	Laid down	Launched	Commissioned
ACONIT	D 609 (ex-*F 703*)	Lorient Naval Dockyard	Jan 1966	7 Mar 1970	30 Mar 1973 (trials 15 May 1971)

Displacement, tons: 3 500 standard; 3 900 full load
Length, feet (metres): 416·7 *127·0)* oa
Beam, feet (metres): 44·0 *(13·4)*
Draught, feet (metres): 18·9 *(5·8)*
Missiles, A/S: "Malafon" rocket/homing torpedo;
 MM 38 Exocet to be fitted
Guns: 2—3·9 in *(100 mm)*
A/S weapons: 1 quadruple 12 in *(305 mm)* mortar;
 2 launchers for Mk L5 torpedoes
Main engines: 1 Rateau geared turbine; 1 shaft; 28 650 shp
Boilers: 2 automatic (450°C)
Speed, knots: 27
Range, miles: 5 000 at 18 knots
Complement: 228 (15 officers, 213 men)

Forerunner of the F67 Type. A one-off class ordered under 1965 programme. Has no helicopter or facilities for such.

Electronics: An early form of centralised data analysis. Two Syllex.

Radar: Pulse Doppler (E/F band surveillance): one DRBV 13
100 mm guns fire-control: one DRBC 32B
Navigation: one DRBN 32
Air surveillance: one DRBV 22A.

Sonar: One hull-mounted DUBV 23; one DUBV 43 VDS.

ACONIT

6/1975, Dr. Giorgio Arra

ACONIT

6/1975, Dr. Giorgio Arra

FRIGATES

9 "COMMANDANT RIVIÈRE" CLASS

Name	No.	Builders	Laid down	Launched	Commissioned
AMIRAL CHARNER	F 727	Lorient Naval Dockyard	Nov 1958	Mar 1960	Dec 1962
BALNY	F 729	Lorient Naval Dockyard	Mar 1960	Mar 1962	Feb 1971
COMMANDANT BORY	F 726	Lorient Naval Dockyard	Mar 1958	Oct 1958	Mar 1964
COMMANDANT BOURDAIS	F 740	Lorient Naval Dockyard	April 1959	April 1961	Mar 1963
COMMANDANT RIVIÈRE	F 733	Lorient Naval Dockyard	April 1957	Oct 1958	Dec 1962
DOUDART DE LAGRÉE	F 728	Lorient Naval Dockyard	Mar 1960	April 1961	Mar 1963
ENSEIGNE DE VAISSEAU HENRY	F 749	Lorient Naval Dockyard	Sep 1962	Dec 1963	Jan 1965
PROTET	F 748	Lorient Naval Dockyard	Sep 1961	Dec 1962	May 1964
VICTOR SCHOELCHER	F 725	Lorient Naval Dockyard	Oct 1957	Oct 1958	Dec 1962

Displacement, tons: 1 750 standard; 2 250 full load
 (*Balny* 1 650 standard; 1 950 full load)
Length, feet (metres): 321·5 *(98·0)* pp; 338 *(103)* oa
Beam, feet (metres): 37·8 *(11·5)*
Draught, feet (metres): 14·1 *(4·3)*
Aircraft: 1 light helicopter can land aft
Missiles: 4 MM 38 Exocet
Guns: 2—3·9 in *(100 mm)* automatic, singles; 2—30 mm
A/S weapons: 1—12 in *(305 mm)* quadruple mortar
Torpedo tubes: 6—21 in *(533 mm)* (triple) for Mk K2 and L3
Main engines: 4 SEMT-Pielstick diesels; 16 000 bhp; 2 shafts;
 (except *Balny:* CODAG; 2 diesels (16 cyl); one TG Turboméca
 M38; 1 shaft; VP screw)
Speed, knots: 25
Range, miles: 4 500 at 15 knots (*Balny* 8 000 at 12 knots)
Complement: 167 (10 officers, 157 men)

Built for world-wide operations—air-conditioned.

Accommodation: Can carry a senior officer and staff. If necessary a force of 80 soldiers can be carried as well as two 30 ft *(9 m)* LCPs with a capacity of 25 men at 11 knots.

Engines: Experimental CODAG arrangement in *Balny*. *Commandant Bory* was fitted with experimental machinery which was replaced with SEMT-Pielstick diesels in 1974-75.

Helicopter: In 1973 the after 100 mm mounting in *Commandant Bourdais* and *Enseigne Henry* was removed to make way for a helicopter platform. (See "Missile" note).

Missiles: All of this class except *Balny* are to be fitted with 4—MM 38 Exocet in place of B gun. *Bory* was the first to be fitted followed by *Doudart De Lagrée*. At the same time the 100 mm gun is replaced in X position.

Radar: Navigation: one DRBN 32
Fire control: one DRBC 32A
Air search: one DRBV 22A
Surface/air search: one DRBV 50
Exocet ships: one DRBC 32C.

Sonar: One DUBA 3; one SQS 17.

BALNY

1974, French Navy

COMMANDANT BORY (with Exocet)

11/1975, Dr. Giorgio Arra

14 TYPE E 52

Name	No.	Builders	Laid down	Launched	Commissioned
L'AGENAIS	F 774	Lorient Naval Dockyard	Aug 1955	23 June 1956	14 May 1958
L'ALSACIEN	F 776	Lorient Naval Dockyard	July 1956	26 Jan 1957	27 Aug 1960
LE BASQUE	F 773	Lorient Naval Dockyard	Dec 1954	25 Feb 1956	18 Oct 1957
LE BÉARNAIS	F 775	Lorient Naval Dockyard	Dec 1955	23 June 1956	18 Oct 1958
LE BRETON	F 772	Lorient Naval Dockyard	June 1954	2 April 1955	20 Aug 1957
LE BOURGUIGNON	F 769	Penhoet	Jan 1954	28 Jan 1956	11 July 1957
LE CHAMPENOIS	F 770	A. C. Loire	May 1954	12 Mar 1955	1 June 1957
LE GASCON	F 767	A. C. Loire	Feb 1954	23 Oct 1954	29 Mar 1957
LE LORRAIN	F 768	F. Ch. de la Medit	July 1953	13 Feb 1954	3 Nov 1956
LE NORMAND	F 765	F. Ch. de la Medit	July 1953	13 Feb 1954	3 Nov 1956
LE PICARD	F 766	A. C. Loire	Nov 1953	31 May 1954	20 Sep 1956
LE PROVENÇAL	F 777	Lorient Naval Dockyard	Feb 1957	5 Oct 1957	6 Nov 1959
LE SAVOYARD	F 771	F. Ch. de la Medit	Nov 1953	7 May 1955	14 June 1956
LE VENDÉEN	F 778	F. Ch. de la Medit	Mar 1957	27 July 1957	1 Oct 1960

Displacement, tons: 1 250 standard; 1 702 full load
Length, feet (metres): 311·7 (95·0) pp; 325·8 (99·8) oa
Beam, feet (metres): 33·8 (10·3)
Draught, feet (metres): 13·5 (4·1)
Guns: 6—2·25 in (57 mm) in twin mountings (4 only in F 771, 772, 773); 2—20 mm
A/S weapons: Sextuple Bofors ASM mortar forward (except F 776, 777, 778 with 1—12 in (305 mm) quadruple mortar); 2 DC mortars; 1 DC rack; 12 ASM (4 triple mountings aft) for Mk K2 and L3
Main engines: Parsons or Rateau geared turbines; 20 000 shp
Boilers: 2 Indret; pressure 500 psi (35·2 kg/cm²); superheat 725°F (385°C)
Speed, knots: 27
Range, miles: 4 500 at 15 knots
Oil fuel, tons: 310
Complement: 205 (13 officers, 192 men)

L'Agenais, L'Alsacien, Le Basque, Le Béarnais, Le Breton, Le Provencial and Le Vendéen have a different arrangement of bridges from the remainder. L'Alsacien, Le Provencal and Le Vendéen are of the E 52B type and have the Strombos-Velensi modified funnel cap.

Class: Le Lorrain was disarmed on 31 Dec 1975 and Le Champenois on 4 Aug 1975.
Le Breton and Le Bourguignon to reserve in 1976.

Radar: Navigation: one DRBV 31
Air search: one DRBV 22A
Fire control: one DRBC 31

Sonar: One DUBV 24; one DUBA 1 (except 771, 772, 773; one DUBV 1 and one DUBA 1).

Trials: Le Basque and Le Savoyard form a trials and experimental squadron for varying navigation and communication systems.

L'AGENAIS
6/1975, Dr. Giorgio Arra

LE PROVENÇAL
11/1975, Dr. Giorgio Arra

1 TYPE E 50

Name	No.	Builders	Laid down	Launched	Commissioned
LE BOULONNAIS	F 763	A. C. Loire	Mar 1952	12 May 1953	5 Aug 1955

Displacement, tons: 1 250 standard; 1 528 for trials; 1 702 full load
Length, feet (metres): 311·7 (95·0) pp; 327·3 (99·8) oa
Beam, feet (metres): 33·8 (10·3)
Draught, feet (metres): 13·5 (4·1)
Guns: 6—2·25 in (57 mm) (twins); 2—20 mm
A/S weapons: 1—375 mm Mk 54 rocket launcher;
Torpedo tubes: 12 tubes (four triple mounts forward) for Mk K2 and L3
Main engines: 2 Rateau A & C de B geared turbines; 20 000 shp; 2 shafts
Speed, knots: 27 (29 on trials); economical speed 14
Oil fuel, tons: 292
Range, miles: 4 500 at 15 knots
Complement: 205 (13 officers, 192 men)

Last survivor of a class of four

Radar: Air search: one DRBV 20
Navigation: one DRBN 32
Fire control: one DRBC 31

Sonar: One DUBV 1; one DUBA 1.

14 TYPE A 69

Name	No.	Builders	Laid down	Launched	Commissioned
D'ESTIENNE D'ORVES	F 781	Lorient Naval Dockyard	Aug 1972	1 June1973	Nov 1975
AMYOT D'INVILLE	F 782	Lorient Naval Dockyard	Sep 1973	Sep 1974	May 1976
DROGOU	F 783	Lorient Naval Dockyard	Oct 1973	Sep 1974	July 1976
DÉTROYAT	F 784	Lorient Naval Dockyard	1974	1975	Feb 1977
JEAN MOULIN	F 785	Lorient Naval Dockyard	15 Jan 1975	1 Feb 1976	Mar 1977
QUARTIER MAITRE ANQUETIL	F 786	Lorient Naval Dockyard	1 Aug 1975	15 Aug 1976	Sep 1977
COMMANDANT DE PIMODAN	F 787	Lorient Naval Dockyard	1 Sep 1975	15 Aug 1976	Oct 1977
SECOND MAITRE LE BIHAN	F 788	Lorient Naval Dockyard	15 Feb 1976	Mar 1977	Feb 1978
LIEUTENANT DE VAISSEAU LE HENAFF	F 789	Lorient Naval Dockyard	15 Mar 1976	Mar 1977	Mar 1978
LIEUTENANT DE VAISSEAU LAVALLÉE	F 790	Lorient Naval Dockyard	1 Sep 1976	Sep 1977	Oct 1978
COMMANDANT L'HERMINIER	F 791	Lorient Naval Dockyard	1 Oct 1976	Sep 1977	Nov 1978
PREMIER MAITRE L'HER	F 792	Lorient Naval Dockyard	15 Mar 1977	April1978	Mar 1979
COMMANDANT BLAISON	F 793	Lorient Naval Dockyard	15 April1977	April1978	April 1979
ENSEIGNE DE VAISSEAU JACOUBET	F 794	Lorient Naval Dockyard	—	—	—

Displacement, tons: 950 standard; 1 170 full load
Length, feet (metres): 262·5 *(80·0)* oa
Beam, feet (metres): 33·8 *(10·3)*
Draught, feet (metres): 9·8 *(3·0)*
Missiles: 2 MM 38 Exocet (see *Missile* note)
Guns: 1—3·9 in *(100 mm);* 2—20 mm
A/S weapons: 1—375 mm Mk 54 Rocket launcher; 4 fixed tubes
for Mk L3 and L5 torpedoes
Main engines: 2 SEMT-Pielstick PC2V diesels; 2 shafts;
controllable pitch propellers; 11 000 bhp
Speed, knots: 24
Range, miles: 4 500 at 15 knots
Endurance, days: 15
Complement: 75 (5 officers, 70 men)

Primarily intended for coastal A/S operations—officially classified as "Avisos". Also available for overseas patrols and can carry an extra detachment of 1 officer and 17 men. *D'Estienne D'Orves* commissioned for trials 26 Oct 1974. Construction of *Ens. de V. Jacoubet* has been delayed for financial reasons.

Missiles: 2—MM 38 Exocet will be fitted in those ships earmarked for foreign service—either side of the funnel.

Radar: Navigation: one Decca Type 202; one DRBN 32
Surface/air search: one DRBV 51
Fire control: one DRBC 32E

Sonar: One hull mounted sonar DUBA 25.

D'ESTIENNE D'ORVES after launching   *1973, French Navy*

D'ESTIENNE D'ORVES   *11/1975, French Navy*

NEW CONSTRUCTION TYPE A 70

Very similar to the type A 69, ships of this type are planned for building in the future with Lorient acting as the lead yard. The details and remarks listed for Type A 69 apply also to Type A70. The construction of this class was delayed indefinitely in 1975 due to financial restrictions.

SUBMARINES

6 NUCLEAR POWERED BALLISTIC MISSILE TYPE (SNLE)

Name	No.	Builders	Laid down	Launched	Trials	Operational
LE REDOUBTABLE	S 611	Cherbourg Naval Dockyard	30 Mar 1964	29 Mar 1967	July 1969	1 Dec 1971
LE TERRIBLE	S 612	Cherbourg Naval Dockyard	24 June1967	12 Dec 1969	1971	1 Jan 1973
LE FOUDROYANT	S 610	Cherbourg Naval Dockyard	1969	4 Dec 1971	May 1973	6 July 1974
L'INDOMPTABLE	S 613	Cherbourg Naval Dockyard	1971	17 Aug 1974	12 Jan 1975	Dec 1976
LE TONNANT	S 614	Cherbourg Naval Dockyard	1973	1975	1976	April 1979
L'INFLEXIBLE	— (Q 260)	Cherbourg Naval Dockyard	27 Mar 1975	—	—	1982

Displacement, tons: 7 500 surface; 9 000 dived
Length, feet (metres): 420 *(128·0)*
Beam, feet (metres): 34·8 *(10·6)*
Draught, feet (metres): 32·8 *(10·0)*
Missile launchers: 16 tubes amidships for MSBS
Torpedo tubes: 4—21·7 inch (18 torpedoes)
Nuclear reactor: 1 pressurised water-cooled
Main machinery: 2 turbo-alternators; 1 electric motor;
 15 000 hp; 1 shaft
Auxiliary propulsion: 1 diesel; fuel for 5 000 miles
Speed, knots: 20 on surface; 25 dived
Complement: Two alternating crews each of 135 (15 officers,
 120 men)
Diving depth: Over 700 ft

Le Redoubtable was the first French nuclear-powered, ballistic missile armed submarine and the prototype of the *"Force de dissuasion"* of six such vessels which the Navy plans to have in the early 1980s. The decision to build a fourth unit of this class was announced on 7 Dec 1967, the fifth in Feb 1972 and the sixth on 30 April 1974.

Missiles: First boats armed with MSBS M-1 of 18 tons launch weight. *Le Foudroyant* is armed with MSBS M-2 of 19·9 tons with a 1 300 n. mile range carrying a 500 KT head. *Le Redoutable* will be fitted with M-2 at her first refit. *L'Indomptable* will recieve the M-20 system with 1 500 n. mile range missiles carrying a megaton reinforced head. All of this class will later receive the M-4 system with a range reportedly in the 3 000 mile bracket and carrying MIRV warheads.

Radar: *Le Redoutable* is equipped with Calypso I Band radar for navigation and attack. Has passive ECM and DF systems.

Reactor: The reactor is a natural-water-cooled type running on enriched uranium, feeding twin turbines and two turbo-alternators.

LE TERRIBLE

1975, ECPA

LE REDOUTABLE, LE TERRIBLE, LE FOUDROYANT

1973, French Navy

1 EXPERIMENTAL MISSILE TYPE

Name	No.	Builders	Laid down	Launched	Commissione
GYMNOTE	S 655	Cherbourg Naval Dockyard	17 Mar 1963 (see **Hull** Note)	17 Mar 1964	17 Oct 1966

Displacement, tons: 3 000 surface; 3 250 dived
Length, feet (metres): 275·6 (84·0)
Beam, feet (metres): 34·7 (10·6)
Draught, feet (metres): 25 (7·6)
Missile launchers: 4 tubes for MSBS
Main machinery: 4 sets 620 kW diesel electric;
  2 electric motors; 2 shafts; 2 600 hp
Speed, knots: 11 surface; 10 dived
Complement: 78 (8 officers, 70 men)

An experimental submarine for testing ballistic missiles for the first French nuclear-powered deterrent submarines, and for use as an underwater laboratory to prove equipment and arms for nuclear-powered submarines.

Hull: Gymnote was the hull laid down in 1958 as the nuclea powered submarine Q 244 which was cancelled in 1959. Tl hull was still available when a trials vessel for the Fren "Polaris" type missiles was required and was completed Gymnote.

GYMNOTE

1970, French Na

FLEET SUBMARINES

1 NEW CONSTRUCTION FLEET SUBMARINE

Name	No.	Builders	Laid down	Launched	Commissior
—	SNA 72	Cherbourg Naval Dockyard	1976	—	1981

Displacement, tons: 2 385 surfaced; 2 670 dived
Dimensions, feet (metres): 236·5 × 24·9 × 21 (72·1 × 7·6 × 6·4)
Torpedo tubes: 4—21 in (533 mm) (14 torpedoes or mines)
Main machinery: 1 nuclear reactor; 48 MW;
  2 turbo alternators; 1 main motor; 1 shaft
Auxiliary machinery: 1 set diesel-electric
Speed, knots: 25
Complement: 66 (9 officers, 35 petty officers, 22 junior ratings)

A prototype for a new class of fleet-submarines included in the 1974 programme. The armament, sonar and fire control equipment will be similar to the "Agosta" class.

Machinery: Studies of the machinery are in progress at Cadarche.

Future: Two squadrons of these submarines are forecast, o to be stationed at Brest and the other at Toulon from 198:

PATROL SUBMARINES

4 "AGOSTA" CLASS

Name	No.	Builders	Laid down	Launched	Commissior
AGOSTA	S 620	Cherbourg Naval Dockyard	7 Feb 1972	19 Oct 1974	Sep 1976
BÉVÉZIERS	S 621	Cherbourg Naval Dockyard	17 May 1973	14 June 1975	Dec 1976
LA PRAYA	S 622	Cherbourg Naval Dockyard	1974	Oct 1975	June 1977
OUESSANT	S 623	Cherbourg Naval Dockyard	1974	Jan 1976	Oct 1977

Displacement, tons: 1 200 standard; 1 450 surfaced; 1 725 dived
Length, feet (metres): 221·7 (67·6)
Beam, feet (metres): 22·3 (6·8)
Draught, feet (metres): 17·7 (5·2)
Tubes: 4—21·7 in (550 mm) 20 reload torpedoes
Main machinery: Diesel-electric; 2 SEMT Pielstick 16 PA4 diesels 3 600 hp; 1 main motor (3 500 kW) 4 600 hp; 1 cruising motor (23 kW); 1 shaft
Speed, knots: 12 surfaced; 20 dived
Range, miles: 8 500 at 9 knots (snorting);
  350 at 3·5 knots (dived)
Endurance: 45 days
Complement: 50 (7 officers, 43 men)

Building of this class was announced in 1970 under the third five-year new construction plan 1971-75. Considerable efforts have been made to improve the silencing of this class, including a clean casing and the damping of internal noise.

Radar: Possibly I Band Calypso Th D 1030 or 1031 for search/navigation.

Sonar: DUUA 2 active sonar with transducers forward and aft; DSUV passive sonar with 36 hydrophones; passive ranging; intercept set.

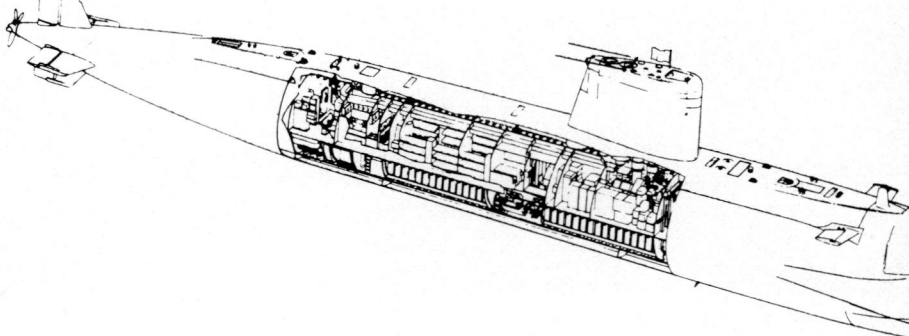

BÉVÉZIERS

1973, Cols Ble

Torpedo tubes: A new design allowing for Torpedo discharge at all speeds and down to full diving depth. Rapid reloading fitted.

Foreign orders: Two to be built at Cartagena for Spanish N and two for South Africa.

9 "DAPHNÉ" CLASS

Name	No.	Builders	Laid down	Launched	Commissioned
DAPHNÉ	S 641	Dubigeon	Mar 1958	20 June1959	1 June 1964
DIANE	S 642	Dubigeon	July 1958	4 Oct 1960	20 June 1964
DORIS	S 643	Cherbourg Naval Dockyard	Sep 1958	14 May 1960	26 Aug 1964
FLORE	S 645	Cherbourg Naval Dockyard	Sep 1958	21 Dec 1960	21 May 1964
GALATÉE	S 646	Cherbourg Naval Dockyard	Sep 1958	22 Sep 1961	25 July 1964
JUNON	S 648	Cherbourg Naval Dockyard	July 1961	11 May 1964	25 Feb 1966
VENUS	S 649	Cherbourg Naval Dockyard	Aug 1961	24 Sep 1964	1 Jan 1966
PSYCHÉ	S 650	Brest Naval Dockyard	May 1965	28 June1967	1 July 1969
SIRÈNE	S 651	Brest Naval Dockyard	May 1965	28 June1967	1 Mar 1970

Displacement, tons: 869 surfaced; 1 043 dived
Length, feet (metres): 189·6 *(57·8)*
Beam, feet (metres): 22·3 *(6·8)*
Draught, feet (metres): 15·1 *(4·6)*
Torpedo tubes: 12—21·7 in *(550 mm)* 8 bow 4 stern
Main machinery: SEMT-Pielstick diesel-electric;
  1 300 bhp surfaced; 1 600 bhp motors dived; 2 shafts
Range, miles: 2 700 at 12·5 knots (surfaced); 4 500 at 5 knots
  (snorting); 3 000 at 7 knots (snorting)
Speed, knots: 13·5 surfaced; 16 dived
Complement: 45 (6 officers, 39 men)

Improved "Arethusé" class with diving depth about 1 000 ft
(300 metres). Sirène sank at Lorient in 1972, and was subsequently salved.

Modernisation: In hand from 1971 to improve sonar and armament.

Radar: I Band Calypso II for search/navigation.

Sonar: DUUA 2 active sonar with transducers forward and aft;
passive ranging; intercept set.

Foreign orders: South Africa (1967) (3), Pakistan (1966) (3),
Portugal (1964) (4), Spain (built in Spain) (1965) (4).

SIRÈNE   *8I1975, Stefan Terzibaschitsch*

VENUS   *1975, Dr. Giorgio Arra*

4 "ARÉTHUSE" CLASS

Name	No.	Builders	Laid down	Launched	Commissioned
AMAZONE	S 639	Cherbourg Naval Dockyard	Dec 1955	3 April1958	1 July 1959
ARÉTHUSE	S 635	Cherbourg Naval Dockyard	Mar 1955	9 Nov 1957	23 Oct 1958
ARGONAUTE	S 636	Cherbourg Naval Dockyard	Mar 1955	29 June1957	11 Feb 1959
ARIANE	S 640	Cherbourg Naval Dockyard	Dec 1955	12 Sep 1958	16 Mar 1960

Displacement, tons: 400 standard; 543 surfaced;
  669 dived
Length, feet (metres): 162·7 *(49·6)*
Beam, feet (metres): 19 *(5·8)*
Draught, feet (metres): 13·1 *(4·0)*
Torpedo tubes: 4—21·7 in *(550 mm)* bow, 4 reloads
Main machinery: 12-cyl SEMT-Pielstick diesel-electric;
  1 060 bhp surfaced; 1 300 hp motors dived; 1 shaft
Speed, knots: 12·5 surfaced; 16 dived
Complement: 40 (6 officers, 34 men)

An excellent class of small submarines with a minimum
number of ballast tanks and a diving depth of about 600 feet.

ARGONAUTE   *1975, Dr. Giorgio Arra*

6 "NARVAL" CLASS

Name	No.	Builders	Laid down	Launched	Commissioned
NARVAL	S 631	Cherbourg Naval Dockyard	June 1951	11 Dec 1954	1 Dec 1957
MARSOUIN	S 632	Cherbourg Naval Dockyard	Sep 1951	21 May 1955	1 Oct 1957
DAUPHIN	S 633	Cherbourg Naval Dockyard	May 1952	17 Sep 1955	1 Aug 1958
REQUIN	S 634	Cherbourg Naval Dockyard	June 1952	3 Dec 1955	1 Aug 1958
ESPADON	S 637	Normand	Dec 1955	15 Sep 1958	2 April1960
MORSE	S 638	Seine Maritime	Feb 1956	10 Dec 1958	2 May 1960

Displacement, tons: 1 320 standard; 1 635 surfaced; 1 910
  dived
Length, feet (metres): 257·2 *(77·6)*
Beam, feet (metres): 25·6 *(7·8)*
Draught, feet (metres): 18·5 *(5·4)*
Torpedo tubes: 6—21·7 in *(550 mm)* bow; 14 reload torpedoes;
  capable of minelaying
Main machinery: Diesel electric, three 12-cyl SEMT-Pielstick
  diesels; two 2 400 hp electric motors; 2 shafts
Speed, knots: 15 surfaced; 18 dived
Range, miles: 15 000 at 8 knots (snorting)
Endurance: 45 days
Complement: 63 (7 officers, 56 men)

Improved versions based on the German Type XXI. *Dauphin,
Marsouin, Narval* and *Requin* were built in seven prefabricated
parts each of 10 metres in length.

Sonar: DUUA 1.

NARVAL   *1974, French Navy*

Engineering: New main propelling machinery installed on
reconstruction during 1965 to 1970 includes diesel-electric
drive on the surface with SEMT-Pielstick diesels. The original
main machinery was Schneider 4 000 bhp 7 cyl. 2 str. diesels
for surface propulsion and 5 000 hp electric motors dived.

Reconstruction: During a five-year reconstruction programme, announced in 1965 and completed by the end of 1970,
these submarines, *Requin* in Spring 1967 and *Espadon* and
Morse in succession at Lorient followed by the other three,
were given a new diesel electric power plant as well as new
weapon and detection equipment.

AMPHIBIOUS FORCES
NOTE—SEE "BATRAL" CLASS UNDER "TRANSPORTS"

2 LANDING SHIPS (DOCK) (TCD)

Name	No.	Builders	Laid down	Launched	Commissioned
OURAGAN	L 9021	Brest Dockyard	June 1967	9 Nov 1963	June 1965
ORAGE	L 9022	Brest Dockyard	June 1966	22 April 1967	Mar 1968

Displacement, tons: 5 800 light; 8 500 full load; 15 000 when fully immersed
Length, feet (metres): 488·9 *(149·0)*
Beam, feet (metres): 70·5 *(21·5)*
Draught, feet (metres): 16·1 *(4·9)*; 28·5 *(8·7)* (flooded)
Guns: 2—4·7 in *(120 mm)* mortars; 6—30 mm
Main engines: 2 diesels; 2 shafts; 8 640 bhp
Speed, knots: 17
Range, miles: 4 000 at 15 knots
Complement: 201 *(Orage)*; 207 *(Ouragan)*

Ouragan was completed for trials in 1964. Bridge is on the starboard side. Fitted with a platform for four heavy helicopters. Able to carry two EDICs loaded with eleven light tanks each, or 18 loaded LCMs Type VI. In the logistic role 1 500 tons of material and equipment can be carried and handled by two 35 ton cranes. *Orage* is allocated to the Pacific Nuclear Experimental Centre. Can carry 350 troops normally or 470 for short periods. Have command facilities for directing amphibious and helicopter operations.

Sonar: One SQS-17 in *Ouragan*

OURAGAN   *1975, Wright and Logan*

ORAGE   *1969, French Navy*

5 LANDING SHIPS (TANK) (BDC)

Name	No.	Builders	Commissioned
ARGENS	L 9003	Ch. de Bretagne	1960
BIDASSOA	L 9004	Ch. Seine Maritime	1961
BLAVET	L 9009	Ch. de Bretagne	1960
DIVES	L 9008	Ch. Seine Maritime	1961
TRIEUX	L 9007	Ch. de Bretagne	1960

Displacement, tons: 1 400 standard; 1 765 normal; 4 225 full load
Dimensions, feet (metres): 328 oa × 50 × 14 *(102·1 × 15·5 × 3·2)*
Guns: 2—40 mm; 4—20 mm *(Argens, Trieux)* 1—4·7 in mortar; 3—40 mm *(Bidassoa, Blavet, Dives)*
Main engines: SEMT-Pielstick diesels; 2 shafts; 2 000 bhp = 11 knots
Range, miles: 18 500 at 10 knots
Complement: 75 (6 officers and 69 men). Plus 170 troops (normal)

Launched on 7 April 1959, 30 Dec 1960, 15 Jan 1960, 29 June 1960 and 6 Dec 1958, respectively. Can carry: 4 LCVPs, 1 800 tons of freight, 335 troops (up to 807 in an emergency). *Blavet* and *Trieux* are fitted as light helicopter carriers with a hangar before the bridge and can carry two Alouette III.

ARGENS   *11/1975, Dr. Giorgio Arra*

12 LANDING CRAFT (TANK) (EDIC)

L 9070 (30 Mar 1967)	L 9074 (22 July 1969)	L 9092 (2 Dec 1958)
L 9071 (4 Nov 1967)	L 9082 (1964)	L 9093 (17 April 1958)
L 9072 (1968)	L 9083 (1964)	L 9094 (24 July 1958)
L 9073 (1968)	L 9091 (7 Jan 1958)	L 9096 (11 Oct 1958)

Displacement, tons: 250 standard; 670 full load
Dimensions, feet (metres): 193·5 × 39·2 × 4·5 *(59 × 12 × 1·3)*
Guns: 2—20 mm
Main engines: MGO diesels; 2 shafts; 1 000 bhp = 8 knots
Range, miles: 1 800 at 8 knots
Complement: 16 (1 officer, and 15 men)

EDIC L 9092   *1973, Dr. Giorgio Arra*

Seven were built by C. N. Franco Belges, three by Toulon Dockyard, two by La Perrière. Launch dates above. Can carry 11 lorries or 5 Light Fighting Vehicles.

Transfer: L 9095 transferred to Senegal 1 July 1974 as *La Falème*.

ISSOLE A 734

Displacement, tons: 610 full load
Dimensions, feet (metres): 160·8 × 32 × 7·2 *(49 × 9·7 × 2·2)*
Main engines: 2 diesels; 1 000 bhp = 12 knots

Built at Toulon in 1957-58. LCT type with bow doors and ramp.

ISSOLE   *1974, Michael D. J. Lennon*

16 LCMs

CTM 1 to 16

Displacement, tons: 56 standard; 150 full load
Dimensions, feet (metres): 92·8 × 21 × 3·9 *(28·3 × 6·4 × 1·2)*
Main engines: Hispano diesels; 2 shafts; 225 hp = 9·5 knots
Complement: 6

Can carry up to 90 tons in coastal or protected waters.

20 LCMs

Of varying displacements between 26 and 52 tons.

1 Ex-BRITISH LCT (8)

LCT 9061 (ex-HMS *Buttress, LCT (8) 4099)*

Displacement, tons: 657 standard; 1 000 full load
Dimensions, feet (metres): 231·2 × 39 × 5·9 *(70·5 × 11·9 × 1·8)*
Guns: 2—20 mm; 1—120 mm mortar
Main engines: 4 Paxman diesels; 2 shafts; 1 840 bhp = 9 knots
Complement: 29 (2 officers, 27 men)

Former British landing craft bought in July 1965. Lent to the Comoro Islands.

CORVETTES

11 "LE FOUGUEUX" CLASS

L'ADROIT P 644	L'ÉTOURDI P 637
L'ALERTE P 645	LE FRINGANT P 640
L'ATTENTIF P 646	LE FRONDEUR P 639
L'ARDENT P 635	LE HARDI P 648
L'EFFRONTÉ P 638	L'INTRÉPIDE P 630
L'ENJOUÉ P 647	

Displacement, tons: 325 standard; 400 full load
Dimensions, feet (metres): 170 pp × 23 × 6·5 *(53 × 7·3 × 3·1)*
Guns: 2—40 mm Bofors
A/S weapons: 1—120 mm A(S mortar; 2 DC mortars; 2 DC racks
Tubes: *L'Intrepide* has a tube mounted on the stern
Main engines: 4 SEMT-Pielstick diesel engines coupled 2 by 2; 3 240 bhp = 18·6 knots
Range, miles: 3 000 at 12 knots; 2 000 at 15 knots
Complement: 46 (4 officers, 42 men)

Five were built under the 1955 and six under the 1956 estimates. All launched 1957-59. Original 3 of this class of 14 deleted 1975.

Reserve: *L'Intrépide, L'Étourdi, L'Attentif* and *L'Enjoué* to reserve 1976.

Radar: One set Decca.

Sonar: One QCU2.

L'ALERTE   *6/1975, Dr. Giorgio Arra*

Similar classes: Four "Boavista" class (Portugal), one in Yugoslavia, one in W. Germany, one in Italy.

6 "LA DUNKERQUOISE" CLASS

Name	No.	Builders	Commissioned
LA DUNKERQUOISE (ex-*Fundy*)	P 653	Canada	1954
LA MALOUINE (ex-*Cowichan*)	P 651	Canada	1954
LA BAYONNAISE (ex-*Chignecto*)	P 654	Canada	1954
LA PAIMPOLAISE (ex-*Thunder*)	P 657	Canada	1954
LA DIEPPOISE (ex-*Chaleur*)	P 655	Canada	1954
LA LORIENTAISE (ex-*Miramichi*)	P 652	Canada	1954

Displacement, tons: 370 full load; 470 standard
Dimensions, feet (metres): 140 pp; 152 oa × 28 × 8·7 *(50 × 9·2 × 2·8)*
Gun: 1—40 mm
Main engines: General Motors diesels; 2 shafts; 2 500 bhp = 15 knots
Oil fuel, tons: 52
Range, miles: 4 500 at 11 knots
Complement: 35 (4 officers, 31 men)

La Bayonnaise (launched 12 May 1952), *La Malouine* (launched 12 Nov 1951) and *La Paimpolaise* (launched 17 July 1953) were transferred to the French flag at Halifax on 1 April 1954, *Dunkerquoise* (launched 17 July 1953) on 30 April 1954, and *La Dieppoise* (launched 21 June 1952) and *La Lorientaise* (launched in 1953) on 10 Oct 1954. All similar to the "Bay" class in the Canadian Forces. All transferred from minesweeping to overseas patrol operations 1973. They have been air conditioned.

LA DIEPPOISE   *1971, French Navy*

Reserve: *La Malouine* and *La Bayonnaise* to reserve 1976.

5 "SIRIUS" CLASS

ALTAIR P 656	CANOPUS P 659
ARCTURUS P 650	ÉTOILE POLAIRE P 660
CROIX DU SUD P 658	

All of "Sirius" class minesweepers (see Minewarfare Section for details) transferred for coastal patrol operations 1973. Minesweeping gear removed.

CANOPUS   *1975, J. van der Woude*

LIGHT FORCES

1 LA COMBATTANTE I TYPE
(FAST ATTACK CRAFT—MISSILE)

Name	No.	Builders	Commissioned
LA COMBATTANTE	P 730	C.M. de Normandie	1 Mar 1964

Displacement, tons: 180 standard; 202 full load
Dimensions, feet (metres): 147·8 × 24·2 × 6·5 (45 × 7·4 × 2·5)
Missiles: 1 quadruple launcher for SS 11
Guns: 1—30 mm; 1 launcher for 14 flares
Main engines: 2 SEMT-Pielstick diesels; 2 shafts; controllable pitch propellers;
   3 200 bhp = 23 knots
Range, miles: 2 000 at 12 knots
Complement: 25 (3 officers, 22 men)

Authorised under the 1960 Programme. Laid down in April 1962, launched on 20 June 1963. Of wooden and plastic laminated non-magnetic construction. Can carry a raiding force of 80 for a very short run.

LA COMBATTANTE   1974, Dr. Giorgio Arra

4 "TRIDENT" CLASS (FAST ATTACK CRAFT—MISSILE)

Name	No.	Builders	Commissioned
TRIDENT	P 670	Auroux, Arcachon	June 1976
GLAIVE	P 671	Auroux, Arcachon	Nov 1976
EPÉE	P 672	C.M.N. Cherbourg	July 1976
PERTUISANE	P 673	—	Sep 1976

Displacement, tons: 115 standard; 130 full load
Dimensions, feet (metres): 121·4 × 18 × 5·2 (37 × 5·5 × 1·6)
Missiles: 6—SS 12
Guns: 1—40 mm
Main engines: 2 Ago diesels; 2 shafts; 4 000 hp = 26 knots
Range, miles: 1 500 at 15 knots
Complement: 18 (1 officer and 17 men)

Trident laid down 1973. These were intended as lead boats for a class of 30 in "Plan Bleu" of which 16 were to be adapted for overseas service. Trials for Trident started 1 Oct 1975. Epée laid down 10 April 1975.

5 Ex-BRITISH "HAM" CLASS (LARGE PATROL CRAFT)

GÉRANIUM (ex-Tibenham ex-M 784) P784
JONQUILLE (ex-Sulham, ex-M 787) P 787
VIOLETTE (ex-Mersham, ex-M 773) P 788
JASMINE (ex-Stedham, ex-M 776) P 661
PETUNIA (ex-Pineham, ex-M 789) P 662

Displacement, tons: 140 standard; 170 full load
Dimensions, feet (metres): 100 pp; 106·5 oa × 21·2 × 5·5 (32·4 × 6·5 × 1·7)
Gun: 1—20 mm Oerlikon forward
Main engines: 2 Paxman diesels; 550 bhp = 14 knots
Oil fuel, tons: 15
Complement: 12 (2 officers, 10 men)

Former British inshore minesweepers of the "Ham" class transferred to France under the US "off-shore" procurement programme in 1955. Now used as patrol craft, the first three by Gendarmerie Maritime. Of these Violette is to be replaced by Paquerette A 742 in 1976, the former taking her place as a tender.

JONQUILLE   11/1975, Dr. Giorgio Arra

1 FAIRMILE ML TYPE (LARGE PATROL CRAFT)

OISEAU DES ILES A 716

Displacement, tons: 140 full load
Dimensions, feet (metres): 111·5 × 18·4 × 4·3 (34 × 5·6 × 1·3)
Speed, knots: 11·5

Former Fairmile motor launch used for training frogmen.

1 COASTAL PATROL CRAFT

Y 760 (ex-P 9786)

Displacement, tons: 45
Dimensions, feet (metres): 79·3 × 14·8 × 4·2 (24·2 × 4·5 × 1·3)
Guns: 8—0·5 MG (four twin mountings)
Main engines: 2 Daimler-Benz (MTU) diesels; 2 shafts; 1 000 bhp = 18 knots

Built by Bodenwerft-Kressbronn. Completed in 1954.

4 TECIMAR TYPE (COASTAL PATROL CRAFT)

P 770   P 771   P 772   P 774

Displacement, tons: 30
Dimensions, feet (metres): 43·6 × 13·4 × 3·5 (13·3 × 4·1 × 1·1)
Guns: 1—12·7 mm MG; 1—7·5 mm MG
Main engines: 2 GM diesels; 480 bhp = 25 knots

Hulls of moulded polyester. Built for gendarmerie in 1974.

1 COASTAL PATROL CRAFT

TOURMALINE A 714

Of 45 tons.

MINE WARFARE FORCES

5 "CIRCE" CLASS (MINEHUNTERS)

Name	No.	Builders	Commissioned
CYBELE	M 712	C.M. de Normandie	28 Sep 1972
CIRCE	M 715	C.M. de Normandie	18 May 1972
CALLIOPE	M 713	C.M. de Normandie	28 Sep 1972
CERES	M 716	C.M. de Normandie	8 Mar 1973
CLIO	M 714	C.M. de Normandie	18 May 1972

Displacement, tons: 460 standard; 495 normal; 510 full load
Dimensions, feet (metres): 167 oa × 29·2 × 11·15 (50·9 × 8·9 × 3·4)
Gun: 1—20 mm
Main engines: 1 MTU diesel; single axial screw; 1 800 bhp = 15 knots
Range, miles: 3 000 at 12 knots
Complement: 48 (4 officers, 44 men)

Ordered in 1968. *Circe* launched 15 Dec 1970; *Clio* launched 10 June 1971; *Calliope* launched 21 Nov 1971; *Cybèle* launched Jan 1972; *Ceres* launched 10 Aug 1972.

Minehunting: All ships are fitted with DUBM 20 minehunting sonar. The 9 foot long PAP is propelled by two electric motors at 6 knots and is wire-guided to a maximum range of 500 m. Fitted with a television camera, this machine detects the mine and lays its 100 kgm charge nearby. This is then detonated by an ultra-sonic signal.

Minesweeping: These ships carry no normal minesweeping equipment.

CLIO

1975, Dr. Giorgio Arra

13 Ex-US MSO "BERNEVAL" CLASS
(MINESWEEPERS—OCEAN and MINEHUNTERS)

NARVIK (ex-*MSO 512*) M 609
OUISTREHAM (ex-*MSO 513*) M 610
ALENCON (ex-*MSO 453*) M 612
BERNEVAL (ex-*MSO 450*) M 613
CANTHO (ex-*MSO 476*) M 615
DOMPAIRE (ex-*MSO 454*) M 616
GARIGLIANO (ex-*MSO 452*) M 617

MYTHO (ex-*MSO 475*) M 618
VINH LONG (ex-*MSO 477*) M 619
BERLAIMONT (ex-*MSO 500*) M 620
AUTUN (ex-*MSO 502*) M 622
BACCARAT (ex-*MSO 505*) M 623
COLMAR (ex-*MSO 514*) M 624

Displacement, tons: 700 standard; 780 full load
Dimensions, feet (metres): 165 wl; 171 oa × 35 × 10·3 (50·3 × 10·7 × 3·2)
Gun: 1—40 mm
Main engines: 2 GM diesels; 2 shafts; V.P. propellers; 1 600 bhp = 13·5 knots
Oil fuel, tons: 47
Range, miles: 3 000 at 10 knots
Complement: 58 (5 officers, 53 men)

The USA transferred these MSOs to France in three batches during 1953. *Bir Hacheim* M 614 (ex-MSO 451) was returned to the US Navy at Brest on 4 Sep 1970 and transferred to Uruguayan navy, being renamed *Maldonado*. *Origny* converted for survey duties in 1960.

Appearance: *Autun, Baccarat, Berlaimont, Colmar, Narvik* and *Ouistreham* have a taller funnel.

Minehunters: *Garigliano, Mytho, Cantho, Vinh Long* and *Dompaire* are being converted for minehunting between 1975 and 1977.

OUISTREHAM (tall funnel)

12/1974, Wright and Logan

GARIGLIANO (squat funnel)

12/1974, Wright and Logan

13 "SIRIUS" CLASS (MINESWEEPERS—COASTAL)

ALGOL (15 April 1953) M 704
ANTARES (21 Jan 1954) M 703
BETELGEUSE (12 July 1954) M 747
CAPELLA (6 Sep 1955) M 755
CAPRICORNE (8 Aug 1956) M 737
CASSIOPEE (16 Nov 1953) M 740
CÉPHÉE (3 Jan 1956) M 756

ÉRIDAN (18 May 1954) M 741
LYRE (3 May 1956) M 759
PHÉNIX (23 May 1955) M 749
SAGITTAIRE (12 Jan 1955) M 743
VEGA (14 Jan 1953) M 707
VERSEAU (26 April 1956) M 757

Displacement, tons: 400 standard; 440 full load
Dimensions, feet (metres): 140 pp; 152 oa × 28 × 8·2 (42·7; 46·4 × 8·6 × 2·5)
Guns: 1—40 mm Bofors; 1—20 mm Oerlikon (several have 2—20 mm)
Main engines: SIGMA free piston generators and Alsthom or Rateau-Bretagne gas turbines or SEMT-Pielstick 16-cyl diesels; 2 shafts; 2 000 bhp = 15 knots (11·5 knots when sweeping)
Oil fuel, tons: 48
Range, miles: 3 000 at 10 knots
Complement: 38 (3 officers, 35 men)

Of wooden and aluminium alloy construction. Of same general characteristics as the British "Ton" class, *Bételgeuse, Capella, Capricorne, Céphée, Lyre, Phénix* and *Verseau* have SEMT-Pielstick diesels. Launch dates above.
Antares, Algol and *Cassiopée* form a trials squadron but the latter pair will be disarmed and paid off to reserve in 1976.

Transfers: Three of this class, built in France and originally numbered D 25, 26 and 27 (now called *Hrabri, Smeli* and *Slobodnii*), were joined by *Snazni* (built in Yugoslavia) after their transfer to Yugoslavia in 1957. *Fomalhaut, Orion, Pollux* and *Procyon* were returned to the USN in 1970, *Achernar* and *Centaure* in 1971. *Aries* (M 758) loaned to Morocco for four years 1975

CASSIOPEE (40 mm gun)

7/1974, Wright and Logan

19 Ex-US "ADJUTANT" CLASS (MINESWEEPERS—COASTAL)

PERVENCHE (ex-*MSC 141)* M 632
PIVOINE (ex-*MSC 125)* M 633
RÉSÉDA (ex-*MSC 126)* M 635
ACACIA (ex-*MSC 69)* M 638
ACANTHE (ex-*MSC 70)* M 639
MARJOLAINE (ex-*Aconit,* ex-*MSC 66)* M 640
AZALEE (ex-*MSC 67)* M 668
BLEUÉT (ex-*MSC 116)* M 670
CAMÉLIA (ex-*MSC 68)* M 671
CHRYSANTHÈME (ex-*MSC 113)* M 672

CYCLAMEN (ex-*MSC 119)* M 674
EGLANTINE (ex-*MSC 117)* M 675
GIROFLÉE (ex-*MSC 85)* M 677
GLYCINE (ex-*MSC 118)* M 679
LAURIER (ex-*MSC 86)* M 681
LILAS (ex-*MSC 93)* M 682
LOBÉLIA (ex-*MSC 96)* M 684
MIMOSA (ex-*MSC 99)* M 687
MUGUET (ex-*MSC 97)* M 688

ACANTHE   *11/1975, Dr. Giorgio Arra*

Displacement, tons: 300 standard; 372 full load
Dimensions, feet (metres): 136·2 pp; 141 oa × 26 × 8·3 *(43 × 8 × 2·6)*
Guns: 2—20 mm
Main engines: 2 GM diesels; 2 shafts; 1 200 bhp = 13 knots (8 sweeping)
Oil fuel, tons: 40
Range, miles: 2 500 at 10 knots
Complement: 38 (3 officers, 35 men)

The USA agreed in Sep 1952 to allocate to France in 1953, 36 new AMS (later redesignated MSC) under the Mutual Defence Assistance Programme, but only 30 were finally transferred to France in 1953.

Transfers:
(a) Six of the class were not taken up by France—two (MSC 139 and 143) to Spain; two to Japan (MSC 95, 144) and two retained by USA.
(b) *Marguerite* (ex-*MSC 94)* M 686 returned to USA and transferred to Uruguay as *Rio Negro* 10 Nov 1969.
(c) *Pavot* (ex-*MSC 124)* M 631 and *Renoncule* (ex-*MSC 142)* M 634 returned to USA and transferred to Turkey on 24 Mar 1970 and 19 Nov 1970 respectively.
(d) *Coquelicot* (ex-*MSC 84)* M 673 to Tunisia in 1973.
(e) *Bégonia* (ex-*MSC 83)* M 669 and *Glaieul* (ex-*MSC 120)* M 678 returned to USA 1974.

Change of Task:
(a) *Ajonc* (ex-*M 667)* A 701 to diving training ship—1974.
(b) *Liseron* (ex-*M 683)* A 623 and *Gardénia* (ex-*M 676)* A 711 to clearance-diving base ship. *Magnolia* M 685 to join this task in 1976.
(c) *Jacinthe* M 680 to minelaying duties in 1968.
(d) *Acacia* M 638, *Marjolaine* M 640, *Azalée* M 668 and *Lobelia* M 684 scheduled for reserve 1976.

1 SPECIAL TYPE DBI (MINESWEEPER—COASTAL)

Name	No.	Builders	Commissioned
MERCURE	M 765	Mecaniques de Normandie	Dec 1958

Displacement, tons: 333 light; 365 normal; 400 full load
Dimensions, feet (metres): 137·8 pp; 145·5 oa × 27 × 8·5 *(44·4 × 8·3 × 4)*
Guns: 2—20 mm
Main engines: 2 Mercedes-Benz (MTU) diesels; 2 shafts; Kamewa variable pitch propellers; 4 000 bhp = 15 knots
Oil fuel, tons: 48
Range, miles: 3 000 at 15 knots
Complement: 48

MERCURE   *1968, French Navy*

Ordered in France under the "off-shore" programme. Laid down in Jan 1955. Launched on 21 Dec 1957.

Foreign sales: Six built for W. Germany.

SURVEY SHIPS

Note: (a) Survey ships are painted white. (b) A total of 20 officers and 74 technicians with oceanographic and hydrographic training is employed in addition to the ships' companies listed here. They occupy the extra billets marked as "scientists".

Name	No.	Builders	Commissioned
D'ENTRECASTEAUX	A 757	Brest	10 Oct 1970

Displacement, tons: 2 400 full load
Dimensions, feet (metres): 295·2 × 42·7 × 12·8 *(89 × 13 × 3·9)*
Main engines: 2 diesel-electric; 1 000 kW; 2 controllable pitch propellers; speed: 15 knots
Auxiliary engines: 2 Schottel trainable and retractable
Range, miles: 10 000 at 12 knots
Complement: 79 (6 officers, 73 men plus scientific staff)

This ship was specifically designed for oceanographic surveys. Accommodation for 38 scientists. Hangar for Alouette II helicopter. Carries one LCPS and three survey launches.

Radar: two sets.

Sonar: two sets.

D'ENTRECASTEAUX   *1975, Wright and Logan*

Name	No.	Builders	Commissioned
ESPÉRANCE (ex-*Jacques Coeur)*	A 756	Gdynia	see note
ESTAFETTE (ex-*Jacques Cartier)*	A 766	Gdynia	see note

Displacement, tons: 956 standard; 1 360 full load
Dimensions, feet (metres): 196·1 × 32·2 × 14·8 *(63·5 × 9·8 × 5·9)*
Main engines: MAN diesels; 1 850 bhp = 15 knots
Range, miles: 7 500 at 13 knots
Complement: 32 (3 officers, 29 men plus scientists)

Former trawlers built in 1962 at Gdynia and purchased in 1968-69. Adapted as survey ships commissioning in 1969 and 1972. Can carry 14 scientists.

Appearance: *Espérance* has a normal foremast in place of the crane in *Estafette.*

ESTAFETTE   *1973, French Navy*

Name	No.	Builders	Commissioned
LA RECHERCHE (ex-*Guyane*)	A 758	Chantiers Ziegler, Dunkirk	see note

Displacement, tons: 810 standard; 910 full load
Dimensions, feet (metres): 221·5 oa × 34·2 × 13 *(67·5 × 10·4 × 4·5)*
Main engines: 1 Werkspoor diesel; 1 535 bhp = 13·5 knots
Range, miles: 3 100 at 10 knots
Complement: 23 (2 officers, 21 men) (plus 43 scientists)

Former passenger motor vessel. Launched in April 1951. Purchased in 1960 and converted by Cherbourg Dockyard into a surveying ship. Commissioned into the French Navy in March 1961 and her name changed from *Guyane* to *La Recherche*. To improve stability she was fitted with bulges. Now comes under the Ministry for Overseas Affairs.

LA RECHERCHE   1975, Dr. Giorgio Arra

1 "BERNEVAL" CLASS

ORIGNY A 640

Displacement, tons: 700 standard; 795 full load
Dimensions, feet (metres): 171 × 35 × 10·5 *(52·2 × 10·7 × 3·2)*
Gun: 1—40 mm
Main engines: 2 GM diesels; 2 shafts; 1 600 bhp = 13·5 knots
Range, miles: 3 000 at 10 knots
Complement: 52

Launched Feb 1955 as a Minesweeper—Ocean of "Berneval" class. Converted for Oceanographic research 1961-62.

ORIGNY   1974, Wright and Logan

Name	No.	Builders	Commissioned
LA DÉCOUVERTE (ex-*Amalthée*, ex-*Plantagenet*, ex-*Barwood*)	A 753	Lobnitz, Renfrew	1939

Displacement, tons: 750 standard; 927 full load
Dimensions, feet (metres): 159·7 × 30·7 × 13 *(49 × 9·3 × 4·8)*
Main engines: Triple expansion; 720 ihp = 9·5 knots
Boilers: Cylindrical
Range, miles: 2 900 at 9 knots
Complement: 33 plus 25 surveyors

Formerly the British boom defence vessel HMS *Plantagenet* (ex-*Barwood*). Launched on 23 Feb 1939. She became the commercial oil research ship *Amalthée* under the French flag in 1960. She was purchased for the French Navy in 1969 and converted as a survey ship.

LA DÉCOUVERTE   1970, Admiral M. Adam

Name	No.	Builders	Commissioned
L'ASTROLABE	A 780	Chantiers de la Seine Maritime, Le Trait	1964
BOUSSOLE	A 781	Chantiers de la Seine Maritime, Le Trait	1964

Displacement, tons: 330 standard; 440 full load
Dimensions, feet (metres): 137·8 × 27 × 8·2 *(42·7 × 8·5 × 2·9)*
Guns: 1—40 mm; 2 MG (*L'Astrolabe* only)
Main engines: 2 Baudoin DV.8 diesels; 1 shaft; variable pitch propeller; 800 bhp = 13 knots
Range, miles: 4 000 at 12 knots
Complement: 33 (1 officer, 32 men)

Authorised under the 1961 Programme. Specially designed for surveys in tropical waters. Laid down in 1962, launched on 27 May and 11 April 1963 respectively. Each ship carries two 4·5 ton wireless-equipped survey craft with a crane on either side of the funnel.

l'ASTROLABE   1972, French Navy

ALIDADE (ex-*Evelyne Marie*) A 682   **OCTANT** (ex-*Michel Marie*) A 683

Displacement, tons: 128 standard; 133 full load
Dimensions, feet (metres): 78 × 20 × 10·5 *(24 × 6·1 × 3·2)*
Main engines: 2 diesels; 1 shaft; V.P propeller; 200 bhp = 9 knots
Range, miles: 2 000 at 7 knots
Endurance: 12 days
Complement: 13 (1 officer, 12 men)

Two small fishing trawlers purchased by the Navy and converted into survey craft by the Constructions Mécaniques de Normandie at Cherbourg as tenders to *La Recherche*. Wooden hull and steel upperworks. *Alidade* completed conversion on 15 Nov 1962 and *Octant* on 20 Dec 1962. Commissioned in 1963.

OCTANT   1973, Dr. Giorgio Arra

1 INSHORE SURVEY CRAFT

Name	No.	Builder	Commissioned
CORAIL (ex-*Marc Joly*)	A 794	Thuin, Belgium	1967

Displacement, tons: 54·8 light
Dimensions, feet (metres): 58·4 × 16·1 × 5·9 *(17·8 × 4·9 × 1·8)*
Main engines: 1 Caterpillar diesel; 250 bhp = 10·3 knots
Complement: 7

Operating in New Caledonia from 1974.

SERVICE FORCES

1 + 1 NEW CONSTRUCTION
(UNDERWAY REPLENISHMENT TANKERS)

Name	No.	Builders	Commissioned
DURANCE	A 629	Brest Naval Dockyard	July 1976
—	—	Brest Naval Dockyard	—

Displacement, tons: 17 800 full load
Dimensions, feet (metres): 515·9 × 69·5 × 28·5 *(157·3 × 21·2 × 8·7)*
Aircraft: 1 WG 13 Lynx helicopter
Guns: 2—40 mm
Main engines: 2 diesels SEMT-Pielstick 16 PC 2·5; 2 shafts; VP propellers 20 000 hp = 19 knots
Oil fuel, tons: 750
Range, miles: 9 000 at 15 knots
Complement: 150 (45 passengers)

Durance laid down 1973, launched 5 Sep 1975 for completion in July 1976. Beam fuelling both sides as well as astern. Helicopter hangar. Classed as P.R.E. (Pétrolier Ravitailleur d'Escadre). A second of this class is planned.

Capacity: To carry a total of 10 000 tonnes (7 500 FFO, 1 500 diesel, 500 TR5, 130 distilled water, 170 victuals, 150 munitions, 50 naval stores).

DURANCE (at launch)   9/1975, French Navy

1 UNDERWAY REPLENISHMENT TANKER and COMMAND SHIP

LA CHARENTE (ex-*Beaufort*) A 626

Displacement, tons: 7 440 light; 26 000 full load
Dimensions, feet (metres): 587·2 × 72 × 30·3 *(179 × 21·9 × 9·3)*
Guns: 4—40 mm
Main engines: 1 General Electric geared turbine; 1 screw = 17·5 knots
Boilers: 2
Complement: 100 (6 officers, 94 men)

Former Norwegian tanker built by Haldnes Mek. Verksted Tönsberg in 1957. Purchased by the French Navy in May 1964. Now converted for service as flagship of the Flag Officer commanding Indian Ocean forces. Fitted with helicopter platform and hangar and carries LCVP.

LA CHARENTE (after conversion)   1974, French Navy

1 UNDERWAY REPLENISHMENT TANKER

Name	No.	Builders	Commissioned
ISÈRE	A 675	Ch. Seine Maritime	see note
(ex-*La Mayenne*, ex-*Caltex Strasbourg*)			

Displacement, tons: 7 440 standard; 26 700 full load
Dimensions, feet (metres): 559 × 71·2 × 30·3 *(170·4 × 21·7 × 9·3)*
Main engines: 1 single geared Parsons turbine; 8 260 shp = 16 knots
Boilers: 2
Complement: 92 (6 officers, 86 men)

Launched on 22 June 1959. Former French tanker. Purchased in 1965. Fitted for beam fuelling as well as stern rig.

ISÈRE   11/1975, Dr. Giorgio Arra

2 UNDERWAY REPLENISHMENT TANKERS

LA SAONE A 628   **LA SEINE** A 627

Displacement, tons: 8 550 light; 24 200 full load
Dimensions, feet (metres): 525 × 72·5 × 33 *(160 × 22·1 × 10)*
Guns: 3—40 mm
Main engines: Parsons geared turbines; 2 shafts; 15 800 shp = 18 knots
Boilers: 3 Penhoet
Complement: 177 (9 officers, 168 men)

Ordered as fleet tankers. Completed as merchant tankers in 1948. Returned to the French Navy from charter company in Sep 1953. *La Seine* was fitted as a fleet replenishment ship in 1961, *La Saône* in 1962. They carry 9 000 tons of fuel, 750 tons of diesel fuel, 275 tons of food and wine tanks holding 82 000 litres. Fitted with automatic tensioning.

LA SEINE   11/1975, Dr. Giorgio Arra

1 SUPPORT TANKER

LAC TONLÉ SAP A 630

Displacement, tons: 800 light; 2 700 full load
Dimensions, feet (metres): 235 × 37 × 15·8 *(71·7 × 11·3 × 4·8)*
Guns: 3—20 mm
Main engines: 2 Fairbanks-Morse diesels; 1 150 bhp = 11 knots
Range, miles: 6 300 at 11 knots
Complement: 37 (2 officers, 35 men)

Ex-US Oil Barge acquired in 1945.

LAC TONLÉ SAP   *1973, French Navy*

2 SUPPORT TANKERS

PAPENOO (ex-Norwegian *Bow Queen*) A 625
PUNARUU (ex-Norwegian *Bow Cecil*) A 632

Displacement, tons: 1 195 standard; 2 927 full load
Dimensions, feet (metres): 272·2 × 45·6 × 18·0 *(83 × 13·9 × 5·5)*
Main engines: 2 diesels; 1 vp screw; 2 050 hp = 12 knots (bow screw in addition)

Two small tankers added to the navy in late 1969. Capacity 2 500 cu. m. (ten tanks).

PUNARUU   *1975, French Navy*

1 SUPPORT TANKER

Name	No.	Builders	Commissioned
ABER—WRACH (ex-*CA 1*)	A 619	Cherbourg	1966

Displacement, tons: 1 220 standard; 3 500 full load
Dimensions, feet (metres): 284 oa × 40 × 15·8 *(86·6 × 12·2 × 4·8)*
Gun: 1—40 mm
Main engines: 1 diesel; vp propeller; 3 000 bhp = 12 knots
Range, miles: 5 000 at 12 knots
Complement: 48 (3 officers, 45 men)

Authorised in 1956. Ordered in 1959. Laid down in 1961. The after part with engine room was launched on 24 April 1963. The fore part was built on the vacated slip, launched and welded to the after part. Complete hull floated up on 21 Nov 1963. Carries white oil, lubricating oil and petrol.

ABER—WRACH   *1970, French Navy*

5 "RHIN" CLASS (DEPOT SHIPS)

Name	No.	Builders	Commissioned
GARONNE	A 617	—	1 Sep 1965
LOIRE	A 615	—	10 Oct 1967
RANCE	A 618	—	5 Feb 1966
RHIN	A 621	—	1 Mar 1964
RHÔNE	A 622	—	1 Dec 1964

Displacement, tons: 2 075 standard; 2 445 full load *(Rhin, Rance and Rhône)*
  2 320 standard *(Garonne and Loire)*
Dimensions, feet (metres): 302·0 pp; 331·5 oa × 43·0 × 12·1 *(92·1; 101·1 × 13·1 × 3·7)*
Guns: 3—40 mm (except *Garonne*)
Aircraft: 1 to 3 Alouette helicopters (except *Garonne* and *Loire*)
Landing craft: 2 LCP
Main engines: 2 SEMT-Pielstick diesels (16PA2V in *Rhin* and *Rhône*, 12PA4 in *Rance*, *Loire* and *Garonne*); 1 shaft; 3 300 bhp = 16·5 knots
Range, miles: 13 000 at 13 knots
Complement: *Rhin* and *Rhône* 148 (6 officers, 142 men); *Rance* 150 (10 officers, 140 men) and about 118 passengers; *Garonne* 221 (10 officers, 211 men); *Loire* 140 (9 officers, 131 men)

Designed for supporting various classes of ships. Have a 5 ton crane, carry two LCPs and have a helicopter platform (except *Garonne*). *Rhin* and *Rhône* have a hangar and carry an Alouette helicopter. *Rance* carries three in her hangar and *Loire* has only the helicopter platform. *Garonne* is designed as a Repair Workshop, *Loire* for minesweeper support. *Rance* for laboratory and radiological services, *Rhin* for electronic maintenance. *Loire* and *Rhône* are currently operating in support of North Atlantic fishery patrols.

Radar: One DRBV 50 (in *Rhin* and *Rhône*).

RHÔNE (RHIN and LOIRE similar)   *1974, Michael D. J. Lennon*

GARONNE   *French Navy*

RANCE   *11/1975, Dr. Giorgio Arra*

1 SUPPORT TANKER

Name	No.	Builders	Commissioned
SAHEL	A 638	Chartiers Naval de Caen	Aug 1951

Displacement, tons: 630 light; 1 450 full load
Measurement, tons: 650 deadweight
Dimensions, feet (metres): 176·2 × 29·5 × 14·5 *(53·7 × 9 × 4·5)*
Guns: 2—20 mm
Main engines: 2 diesels; 1 400 bhp = 12 knots

SAHEL   *1972, Dr. Giorgio Arra*

1 MAINTENANCE SHIP

Name	No.	Builders	Commissioned
MOSELLE	A 608	Swan, Hunter & Wigham Richardson Ltd,	1948
(ex-*Foucauld*)		Wallsend-on-Tyne	

Displacement, tons: 8 200 standard; 8 700 full load
Dimensions, feet (metres): 480 oa × 62 × 22·3 *(146·3 × 18·9 × 6·9)*
Main engines: 2 Doxford diesels; 2 shafts; 8 800 bhp = 15 knots
Complement: 177 (7 officers, 170 men)

Former motor passenger ship of the Chargeurs Réunis (West Africa Coast Service). Launched on 17 July 1947. *Moselle* was converted in 1967. Used as Base Ship in Pacific Trial Centre. Can carry 500 passengers.

MOSELLE   *1972, Dr. Giorgio Arra*

1 MAINTENANCE and REPAIR SHIP

JULES VERNE (ex-*Achéron*) A 620

Displacement, tons: 6 485 standard; 10 250 full load
Dimensions, feet (metres): 482·2 × 70·5 × 21·3 *(147 × 21·5 × 6·5)*
Aircraft: 2 Helicopters
Main engines: 2 diesels SEMT-Pielstick; 1 shaft; 21 500 hp = 18 knots
Range, miles: 9 500 at 18 knots
Complement: 323 (20 officers, 303 men)

Ordered in 1961 budget, originally as an Armament Supply Ship. Role and design changed—now rated as Engineering and Electrical Maintenance Ship. Launched 30 May 1970. In service March 1976.

2 REPAIR SHIPS (Ex-LCT)

L 9081   **L9084**

Displacement, tons: 310 standard; 685 full load
Dimensions, feet (metres): 193·5 × 39 × 5 *(59 × 11·9 × 1·6)*
Main engines: 2 Diesels MGO; 1 000 bhp = 8 knots
Range, miles: 1 800 at 8 knots
Complement: 15

Built in 1964-65 by Ch. N. Franco-Belge. Repair facilities grafted onto LCT hulls. 9081 is fitted with mechanical workshops, and 9084 is primarily an electrical stores ship.

Ex-LCT   *1972, Dr. Giorgio Arra*

1 VICTUALLING STORES SHIP

BERRY (ex-M/S *Médoc*) A 644

Displacement, tons: 1 148 standard; 2 700 full load
Dimensions, feet (metres): 284·5 oa × 38 × 15 *(86·7 × 11·6 × 4·6)*
Main engines: 2 MWM diesels coupled on one shaft; 2 400 bhp = 15 knots
Range, miles: 7 000 at 15 knots

Built by Roland Werft, Bremen. Launched on 10 May 1958. Purchased in Oct 1964 and refitted in 1964-66.

BERRY   *1969, French*

3 STORES SHIPS

Name	No.	Builders	Commissioned
CHAMOIS	A —	La Perrière, Lorient	1975
—	—	La Perrière, Lorient	1976
—	—	La Perrière, Lorient	1976

Displacement, tons: 400
Dimensions, feet (metres): 136·1 × 24·6 × 10·5 *(41·5 × 7·5 × 3·2)*
Main engines: 2 Diesels SACM AGO V-16; 2 VP propellers; 2 200 hp = 14·5 knots
Complement: 14

Similar to the standard FISH oil rig support ships. Fitted with hydraulic crane for torpedo recovery. Can act as Tugs. Bow thruster and twin rudders.

1 VICTUALLING STORES SHIP

SAINTONGE (ex-*Santa Maria*) A 733

Measurement, tons: 300 standard; 990 full load
Dimensions, feet (metres): 177 × 28 × 10·5 *(54 × 8·5 × 3·2)*
Main engines: 1 diesel; 1 shaft; 760 bhp = 10 knots
Complement: 15

Built by Chantiers Duchesne et Bossière, Le Havre, for a Norwegian owner under the name of *Sven Germa*. Launched on 12 July 1956. Purchased in April 1965 from the firm of H. Beal & Co, Fort de France for the Pacific Nuclear Experimental Centre.

TRIALS RESEARCH SHIPS

Name	No.	Builders	Commissioned
HENRI POINCARÉ	A 603	Cantieri Riuniti de Adriaticos,	—
(ex-*Maina Marasso*)		Monfalcone	

Displacement, tons: 24 000 full load
Dimensions, feet (metres): 565·0 pp; 590·6 oa × 72·8 × 28·9 *(180 × 22·2 × 9·4)*
Guns: 2—20 mm
Main engines: 1 Parsons geared turbine; 1 shaft; 10 000 shp = 15 knots
Boilers: 2 Foster Wheeler high pressure water tube
Range, miles: 11 800 at 13·5 knots
Complement: 214 + 9 (11 officers, 9 civilians, 203 men)

Launched in Oct 1960. Former Italian tanker. Purchased in Sep 1964. Converted in Brest dockyard from 1 Oct 1964 to 1967. To work with the experimental guided missile station in the Landes (SW France). Named after the mathematician and scientist.

Aircraft: Can land heavy helicopters and has space for two large or five light helicopters in her hangar.

Operations: She is primarily a missile-range-ship and acts as Flagship of Force M, the trials squadron of the French Navy. To enable her to plot the trajectory etc of missiles fired from land or sea she is equipped with three tracking radars, a telemetry station, transit nav-aid, cinetheodolite, infra-red tracking as well as an up-to-date fit of hull-mounted sonar, meteorological and oceanographic equipment.

Radar: One Savoie, two Bearn, one DRBV 22D.

HENRI POINCARÉ   *1969, French Navy*

ILE d'OLÉRON (ex-*Munchen*, ex-*Mur*) A 610

Displacement, tons: 5 500 standard; 6 500 full load
Dimensions, feet (metres): 350·0 pp; 377·5 × 50·0 × 21·3 *(106·7 pp; 115·2 oa × 15·2 × 6·5)*
Main engines: MAN 6-cylinder diesels; 1 shaft; 3 500 bhp
Speed, knots: 14·5
Oil fuel, tons: 340
Range, miles: 7 200 at 12 knots
Complement: 195 (12 officers, 183 men)

Launched in Germany in 1939. Taken as a war prize. Formerly rated as a transport. Converted to experimental guided missile ship in 1957-58 by Chantiers de Provence and l'Arsenal de Toulon. Commissioned early in 1959. Equipped with stabilisers.

Experimental: When converted, was designed for experiments with two launchers for ship-to-air missiles, the medium range "Masurca" and the long range "Masalca", and one launcher for ship to shore missiles, the "Malaface". Latterly fitted with one launcher for target planes. Now fitted for trials on MM 38 ("Exocet").

Radar: One DRBV 22C, one DRBV 50, one DRBI 10.
The missile system tracking radar operates in G band.

ILE d'OLÉRON   *1974, Wright and Logan*

1 TRIALS SHIP

Name	No.	Builders	Commissioned
AUNIS (ex-*Regina Pacis*)	A 643	Roland Werft, Bremen	see note

Displacement, tons: 2 900 full load
Dimensions, feet (metres): 284·5 × 38 × 15 *(86·5 × 11·6 × 4·6)*
Main engines: MAN diesels geared to 1 shaft; 2 400 bhp = 12 knots
Range, miles: 4 500 at 12 knots

Launched on 3 July 1956. Purchased in Nov 1966 from Scotto Ambrosino & Pugliese and converted in Toulon 1972-73. Employed as trials ship in Operation Cormoran with deep sonar.

AUNIS   *1975, Wright and Logan*

1 TRIALS SHIP

Name	No.	Builders	Commissioned
TRITON	A 646	Lorient	1972

Displacement, tons: 1 410 standard; 1 510 full load
Dimensions, feet (metres): 242·7 × 38·9 × 12 *(74 × 11·8 × 3·7)*
Main engines: 2 MGO V Diesels driving a Voith Schneider screw aft; 2 electric motors driving a Voith Schneider forward
Speed, knots: 13
Range, miles: 4 000 at 13 knots
Complement: 65 (4 officers, 44 men + 5 officers and 12 men for diving)

Under sea recovery and trials ship to replace *Elie Monnier*. Equipped with a helicopter platform. Launched on 7 Mar 1970. Support ship for the 2-man submarine *Griffon*.

Operations: Operated by G.E.R.S. (Groupe d'Etude et de Recherches Sousmarins) for trials of submarines and deep-sea diving equipment. Underwater TV, recompression chamber, 4 man diving bell and laboratories are fitted. Available as submarine rescue ship.

Radar: Navigational.

Sonar: Special equipment for deep operations.

Submarine: The submarine *Griffon* is carried amidships on the starboard side of *Triton*. She is 25 feet *(7·8 metres)* long, displaces 16 tons and is driven by an electric motor. Her diving depth is 2 000 feet *(600 metres)* and her endurance 24 miles at 4 knots. Can be used for deep recovery operations.

TRITON (with *Griffon* amidships)   *6/1975, Dr. Giorgio Arra*

1 TRIALS SHIP

Name	No.	Builders	Commissioned
MARCEL LE BIHAN (ex-*Greif*)	A 759	Lubecker Fleudewerke	1937

Displacement, tons: 800 standard; 1 250 full load
Dimensions, feet (metres): 236·2 × 34·8 × 10·5 *(72 × 10·6 × 3·2)*
Guns: 4—20 mm (twins)
Main engines: 2 GM diesels; 2 shafts; 4 400 bhp = 13 knots
Range, miles: 2 500 at 13 knots
Complement: 50 (3 officers, 47 men), accommodation for 22 extra hands

Former German aircraft tender. Launched in 1936. Transferred by USA in Feb 1948. 4·1 in gun and 2—40 mm removed. Tender for DSV *Archimède*.

MARCEL LE BIHAN   *1974, Wright and Logan*

1 DEEP SUBMERGENCE VEHICLE

ARCHIMÈDE A 648

Built in Toulon. 68·9 feet long with surface displacement of 60 tons. Diving depth 36 000 feet *(11 000 metres)*. *Marcel le Bihan* acts as tender. FNRS 3 deleted 1974.

ARCHIMÈDE   *1974, Wright and Logan*

1 ARCHAEOLOGICAL RESEARCH CRAFT

L'ARCHÉONAUTE A 789

Built by Auroux, Arcachon August 1967. 120 tons full load and 96 feet long *(29·3 metres)* with two Baudoin diesels; 600 hp; twin VP propellers; 12 knots. For underwater archaeological research carries a complement of 2 officers, 4 men, 3 archaeologists and 6 divers.

L'ARCHÉONAUTE   *1975, Wright and Logan*

1 RADIOLOGICAL RESEARCH CRAFT

PALANGRIN Y 743

Acquired 1969. Of 44 tons with single diesel of 220 hp.

BOOM AND MOORING VESSELS

LA FIDÈLE Y 751   **LA PERSÉVÉRANTE** Y 750   **LA PRUDENTE** Y 749

Displacement, tons: 446 standard; 626 full load
Dimensions, feet (metres): 142·8 × 32·8 × 9·2 *(43·5 × 10 × 2·8)*
Main engines: 2 Baudoin diesels; Diesel-electric; 1 shaft; 620 bhp=10 knots
Range, miles: 4 000 at 10 knots
Complement: 30 (1 officer, 29 men)

Net layers and tenders built by Atel. Ch. La Manche, Dieppe, *(La Fidèle and La Prudente)* and Atel. Ch. La Rochelle *(La Persévérante)*. Launched on 26 Aug 1968 *(La Fidéle)*, 14 May 1968 *(La Persévérante)* and 13 May 1968 *(La Prudente)*. 25 ton lift.

LA PERSÉVÉRANTE   *11/1975, Dr Giorgio Arra*

TIANÉE A 731

Displacement, tons: 842 standard; 905 full load
Dimensions, feet (metres): 178·1 × 34·8 (54·3 × 10·6)
Main engines: Diesel-electric; 2 diesels; 1 shaft = 12 knots
Range, miles: 5 200 at 12 knots
Complement: 37 (1 officer, 36 men)

Built at Brest. Launched 17 Nov 1973. For service in the Pacific. Fitted with lateral screws in bow tunnel.

TIANÉE   1974, French Navy

CIGALE (ex-AN 98) A 760   **FOURMI** (ex-AN 97) A 762
CRIQUET (ex-AN 96) A 761   **GRILLON** (ex-AN 95) A 763
                                     SCARABÉE (ex-AN 94) A 764

Displacement, tons: 770 standard; 850 full load
Dimensions, feet (metres): 151·9 oa × 33·5 × 10·5 (46·3 × 10·2 × 3·2)
Guns: 1—40 mm Bofors; 4—20 mm
Main engines: 2, 4-stroke diesels, electric drive, 1 shaft; 1 600 bhp = 12 knots
Range, miles: 5 200 at 12 knots
Complement: 37 (1 officer, 36 men)

US off-shore order. Sister ship G 6 was allocated to Spain. *Cerberus* transferred to Netherlands and subsequently to Turkey as AG 6. *Criquet* was launched on 3 June 1954, *Cigale* on 23 Sep 1954, *Fourmi* on 6 July 1954, *Grillon* on 18 Feb 1954 and *Scarabée* on 21 Nov 1953.

FOURMI   1975, Wright and Logan

3 Ex-US AN TYPE NETLAYERS

ARAIGNÉE (ex-*Hackberry*, ex-*Maple*) A 727
LIBELLULE (ex-*Rosewood*) A 730
LUCIOLE (ex-*Sandalwood*) A 777

Displacement, tons: 560 standard; 850 full load
Dimensions, feet (metres): 146·0 wl; 163·0 oa × 30·5 × 11·7 (50 × 9·3 × 4·8)
Guns: 1—3 in; some MG
Main engines: 2 GM diesels; diesel-electric; 1 shaft; 1 300 bhp = 13 knots
Range, miles: 7 200 at 12 knots
Complement: 39 (2 officers, 37 men)

Launched on 6 Mar 1941, 1 Apr 1941, 6 Mar 1941 respectively. *Luciole* was purchased in 1967, *Libellule* in 1969. *Libellule* to reserve 1976.

LUCIOLE   1974, Wright and Logan

3 MOORING VESSELS

COMMANDANT ROBERT GIRAUD (ex-*Immelmann*) A 755 (ex-*F 755*)

Displacement, tons: 1 142 standard; 1 220 full load
Length, feet (metres): 239·0 (72·9) pp; 256·0 (78·0) oa
Beam, feet (metres): 36·0 (11·0)
Draught, feet (metres): 12·0 (3·7)
Main engines: 4 MAN diesels; 2 shafts; 5 720 bhp
Range, miles: 9 000 at 10 knots
Oil fuel, tons: 236
Complement: 54 (1 officer, 53 men)

Ex-German aircraft tender. Built by Norderwerft, Hamburg. Launched in Dec 1941. Transferred by Great Britain in Aug 1946, with *Paul Goffeny*. The diesels are coupled two by two with hydraulic transmission on two shafts. Crane lift 18 tons. To reserve 1976.

COMMANDANT ROBERT GIRAUD   1975, Dr Giorgio Arra

TUPA Y 667   **CALMAR** Y 688

292 tons with 210 hp diesel.

TORPEDO RECOVERY VESSELS

PÉLICAN (ex-*Kerfany*) A 699

Displacement, tons: 362 standard; 425 full load
Dimensions, feet (metres): 121·4 × 28·0 × 13·1 (37 × 8·6 × 4)
Torpedo tube: One
Main engines: 1 Burmeister and Wain diesel; 1 shaft; 650 bhp = 11 knots
Complement: 19

Built in USA in 1951. Purchased in 1965 and converted from tunny fisher into torpedo recovery craft in 1966.

PÉLICAN   11/1975, Dr Giorgio Arra

PÊTREL (ex-*Cap Lopez* ex-*Yvon Loic II*) A 698

Displacement, tons: 277 standard; 318 full load
Dimensions, feet (metres): 98·4 × 25·6 × 11·5 *(30 × 7·8 × 3·5)*
Main engines: 2 Baudoin diesels; 1 vp screw; 600 bhp = 10 knots
Complement: 19

Built by Daubigeon 1960. Purchased 1965 and converted from tunny fisher to torpedo recovery craft.

TRANSPORTS

2 BATRAL TYPE (LIGHT TRANSPORTS)

Name	No.	Builders	Commissioned
CHAMPLAIN	L 9030	Brest	5 Oct 1974
FRANCIS GARNIER	L 9031	Brest	21 June1974

Displacement, tons: 750 standard; 1 250 full load
Dimensions, feet (metres): 262·4 × 42·6 × 7·5 *(80 × 13 × 2·3)*
Guns: 2—40 mm; 2—81 mm Mortars
Main engines: 2 Diesels; 2 shafts; 1 800 hp = 16 knots
Range, miles: 3 500 at 13 knots
Complement: 39

Fitted with bow doors, and stowage for vehicles above and below decks. Helicopter landing platform. Can carry a landing company (Guépard) of 5 officers and 133 men with 12 vehicles. Both launched 17 Nov 1973.

CHAMPLAIN   1974, DCAN Brest

8 SMALL TRANSPORTS

ALPHÉE Y 696	**ELFE** Y 741	**KORRIGAN** Y 661
ARIEL Y 604	**FAUNE** Y 613	**Y—**
DRYADE Y 662		**Y—**

Displacement, tons: 195 standard; 225 full load
Dimensions, feet (metres): 132·8 × 24·5 × 10·8 *(40·5 × 7·5 × 3·3)*
Main engines: 2 diesels; 2 shafts; 1 640 bhp;/1 730 bhp = 15 knots
Complement: 9

Ariel was launched on 27 April 1964. *Korrigan* on 6 March 1964. *Alphée* on 10 June 1969. *Elfe* on 14 April 1970, *Faune* on 8 Sept 1971, *Dryade* in 1973. All built by Societe Française de Construction Naval (ex-Franco-Belge). Can carry 400 passengers (250 seated).

ALPHÉE   1972, Admiral M. Adam

6 SMALL TRANSPORTS

SYLPHE Y 710

Displacement, tons: 171 standard; 189 full load
Dimensions, feet (metres): 126·5 × 22·7 × 8·2 *(38·5 × 6·9 × 2·5)*
Main engines: One MGO diesel; 1 shaft; 425 bhp = 12 knots
Complement: 9

Small transport for passengers, built by Chantiers Franco-Belge in 1959-60.

LUTIN (ex-*Georges Clemenceau*) Y 664

Displacement, tons: 68
Main engines: 400 hp = 10 knots

Purchased in 1965. Ex-vedette. Detection school, Toulon.

MÉLUSINE Y 736   **MERLIN** Y 735   **MORGANE** Y 671

Displacement, tons: 170
Dimensions, feet (metres): 103·3 × 23·2 × 7·9 *(31·5 × 7·1 × 2·4)*
Main engines: MGO diesels; 2 shafts; 960 bhp = 11 knots

Small transports for 400 passengers built by Chantiers Navals Franco-Belge at Chalon sur Saône *(Mélusine* and *Merlin)* and Ars. de Mourillon *(Morgane)*. Laid down in Dec 1966 and accepted June 1968. Their home port is Toulon.

FALLERON (ex-German *Welle*) A 614

Displacement, tons: 200 standard; 429 full load
Dimensions, feet (metres): 128·0 × 22·0 × 7·8 *(39 × 6·7 × 2·3)*
Main engines: 1 Sulzer diesel; 280 bhp = 8 knots
Range, miles: 1 600 at 8 knots
Complement: 11

MORGANE   11/1975, Dr. Giorgio Arra

DIVING TENDERS

4 Ex-US "ADJUTANT" CLASS (MSC)

AJONC (ex-*M 667*) A 701
GARDÉNIA (ex-*M 676*) A 711
LISERON (ex-*M683*) A 623
MAGNOLIA (ex-*M 685*) —

Details as in same class under Minewarfare Forces except for complement, now 11. *Ajonc* employed as diving training ship, remainder as clearance-diving base ships. *Magnolia* transferred 1976.

GARDÉNIA   6/1975, Dr. Giorgio Arra

1 Ex-BRITISH "HAM" CLASS (MSI)

MYOSOTIS (ex-*M 788*) A 710

Details as in same class under Light Forces. Employed as diving-tender.

TENDERS

8 Ex-BRITISH "HAM" CLASS (MSI)

ARMOISE (ex-*Vexham*, ex-*M 772*) A 741
CAPUCINE (ex-*Petersham*, ex-*M 782*) A 738
DAHLIA (ex-*Whippingham*, ex-*M 786*) A 736
HIBISCUS (ex-*Sparham*, ex-*M 785*) A 735
HORTENSIA (ex-*Mileham*, ex-*M 783*) A 740
OEILLET (ex-*Isham*, ex-*M 774*) A 739
PAQUERETTE (ex-*Kingham*, ex-*M 775*) A 742
TULIPE (ex-*Frettenham*, ex-*M 771*) A 737

Details as in same class under Light Forces. Now general purpose tenders.

ARMOISE   11/1975, Dr. Giorgio Arra

POSEIDON A 722

Displacement, tons: 220
Dimensions, feet (metres): 132·9 × 23·6 × — *(40·5 × 7·2 × —)*
Main engines: 1 diesel; 600 bhp = 13 knots
Endurance: 8 days
Complement: 42

Base ships for assault swimmers.

POSEIDON   1975, French Navy

SSBN TENDER. A 1 200-ton service lighter of 1 000 hp for nuclear fuel elements of SSBNs was launched on 26 Oct 1967 for delivery in May 1968.

TRAINING SHIPS

CHIMÈRE Y 706   **FARFADET** Y 711

Displacement, tons: 100
Main engines: 1 diesel; 200 hp = 11 knots

Auxiliary sail training ships built at Bayonne in 1971. Tenders to the Naval School.

LA GRANDE HERMINE (ex-*La Route Est Belle*, ex-*Ménestral*) A 653

Ex-sailing fishing boat built in 1932. Purchased in 1964 in replacement for *Dolphin* (ex-*Simone Marcelle*) as the Navigation School (E.O.R.) Training ship. Length 46 feet.

— (ex-*Kayolle*)   — (ex-*Isaren*)

Ex-motor trawlers built by At. et Ch. de la Rochelle-Pallice in 1964. Bought in 1975 for conversion as training ships for the Naval College. Of 156 tons with a single diesel engine giving 11 knots.

LA BELLE-POULE A 650   **L'ÉTOILE** A 649

Displacement, tons: 227
Dimensions, feet (metres): 128 oa × 23·7 × 11·8 *(32·3 × 7 × 3·2)*
Main engines: Sulzer diesels; 125 bhp = 6 knots

Auxiliary sail vessels. Built by Chantiers de Normandie (Fécamp) in 1932. Accommodation for 3 officers, 30 cadets, 5 petty officers, 12 men. Attached to Naval School.

MUTIN A 652

A small 57 ton coastal tender built in 1927. Auxiliary diesel and sails. Attached to the Navigation School.

TUGS

3 OCEAN TUGS

CENTAURE A 674   **MALABAR** A 664   **TENACE** A 669

Displacement, tons: 1 080 light; 1 454 full load
Dimensions, feet (metres): 167·3 oa × 37·8 × 18·6 *(51 × 11·5 × 5·7)*
Main engines: 2 diesels; Kort engines 4 600 hp; 1 shaft = 15 knots
Range, miles: 9 500 at 15 knots
Complement: 42

Tenace built by Joelkers, Hamburg, *Centaure* built at La Pallice 1972-74. *Malabar* commissioned 7 Oct 1975.

TENACE   *1973, Reiner Nerlic*

1 OCEAN TUG

ÉLÉPHANT (ex-*Bar*) A 666

Displacement, tons: 880 standard; 1 180 full load
Main engines: Triple expansion 2 000 ihp = 11 knots

2 OCEAN TUGS

HIPPOPOTAME (ex-*Utrecht*) A 660   **RHINOCEROS** A 668

Displacement, tons: 640 standard; 940 full load
Main engines: Diesel-electric; 1 850 shp = 12 knots

A 660 built as USN ATA of "Sotoyomo" class. Former Netherlands Ocean tug. Built in 194
Purchased by the French Navy in Jan 1964 to be used at the Experimental Base in the Pacifi

1 COASTAL TUG

GOLIATH A 665

Displacement, tons: 380
Main engines: 900 hp

1 COASTAL TUG

COOLIE A 684

Displacement, tons: 300
Main engines: 1 000 hp

12 COASTAL TUGS

ACHARNÉ A 693   **HERCULE** A 667   **ROBUSTE** A 685
ACTIF A 686   **LE FORT** A 671   **TRAVAILLEUR** A 692
COURAGEUX A 706   **LABORIEUX** A 687   **VALEUREUX** A 688
EFFICACE A 694   **LUTTEUR** A 673   **UTILE** A 672

Displacement, tons: 230
Dimensions, feet (metres): 92 × 26 × 13 *(28·1 × 7·9 × 4)*
Main engines: 1 MGO diesel; 1 050 bhp = 11 knots
Range, miles: 2 400
Complement: 15

Courageux, Hercule, Robuste and *Valeureux* were completed in 1960, four more in 1962-63, two more in late 60s and *Acharné* and *Efficace* in 1974.

HERCULE   *11/1975, Dr. Giorgio Arr*

81 HARBOUR TUGS

Acajou Y 601, *Aigrette* Y 602, *Balsa* Y 607, *Bambou* Y 608, *Bengali* Y 611, *Bouleau* Y 612, *Canari* Y 616, *Mouette* Y 617, *Chataigner* Y 620, *Mésange* Y 621, *Charme* Y 623, *Chêne* Y 624, *Colibri* Y 628, *Cormier* Y 629, *Bonite* Y 630, *Courlis* Y 631, *Cygne* Y 632, *Délange* Y 633, *Rouget* Y 634, *Equeurdiville* Y 635, *Martinet* Y 636, *Fauvette* Y 637, *Fontaine* Y 640, *Forméne* Y 641, *Fréne* Y 644, *Giens* Y 647, *Goeland* Y 648, *Grive* Y 649, *Hanneton* Y 651, *Haut-Barr* Y 652, *Heron* Y 653, *Hétre* Y 654, *Hévéat* Y 655, *Hirondelle* Y 657, *Ibis* Y 658, *Jonque* Y659, *Latanier* Y 663, *Manguier* Y 666, *Tupa* Y 667, *Méléze* Y 668, *Merisier* Y 669, *Merle* Y 670, *Moineau* Y 673, *Martin Pécheur* Y 675, *Moule* Y 678, *Muréne* Y 680, *Okoume* Y 682, *Ondée* Y 683, *Oursin* Y 685, *Palétuvier* Y 686, *Passereau* Y 687, *Pin* Y 689, *Pingouin* Y 690, *Pinson* Y 691, *Pivert* Y 694, *Platane* Y 695, *Calmar* Y 698, *Poulpe* Y 699, *Rascasse* Y 702, *Rossignol* Y 704, *Saule* Y 708, *Sycomore* Y 709, *Ébène* Y 717, *Erable* Y 718, *Olivier* Y 719, *Santal* Y 720, *Alouette* Y 721, *Vauneau* Y 722, *Engoulevent* Y 723, *Sarcelle* Y 724, *Marabout* Y 725, *Toucan* Y 726, *Macreuse* Y 727, *Grand Duc* Y 728, *Eider* Y 729, *Ara* Y 730, *Marronier* Y 738, *Noyer* Y 739, *Papayer* Y 740, *Loriot* Y 747, *Gelinotte* Y 748.

BAMBOU   *11/1975, Dr. Giorgio Arra*

6 PUMP-TUGS

Aiguière Y 745, *Cascade* Y 618, *Embrun* Y 746, *Gave* Y 645, *Geyser* Y 646, *Oued* Y 684.

GABON

rsonnel

1976: 75 officers and men
Volunteers

Mercantile Marine

Lloyd's Register of Shipping: 15 vessels of 106 738 tons gross

Bases

Libreville, Port Gentil

DELETION

1975 *Bouet-Willaumez (ex-HDML 102)*

LIGHT FORCES

me	No.	Builders	Commissioned
RESIDENT ALBERT BERNARD BONGO	—	Chantiers Navals de l'Esterel	Mar 1972

splacement, tons: 80
mensions, feet (metres): 104 × 19 × 5 *(32 × 5·8 × 1·5)*
uns: 2—20 mm
ain engines: 2 MTU diesels; 2 700 hp = 30 knots
nge, miles: 1 500 at 15 knots
mplement: 17 (3 officers, 14 ratings)

tted with radar and echo sounder.

PRESIDENT ALBERT BERNARD BONGO   *1972, Chantiers Navals de L'Esterel*

me	No.	Builders	Commissioned	Name	No.	Builders	Commissioned
RESIDENT LEON M'BA	GCO 1	Gabon	1968	N'GUENE	GCO 3	Swift, USA	April 1975

splacement, tons: 85 standard
mensions, feet (metres): 92 × 20·5 × 5 *(28 × 6·3 × 1·5)*
uns: 1—75 mm; 1—12·7 mm MG
ain engines: Diesel = 12·5 knots
mplement: 16

unched on 16 Jan 1968.

Displacement, tons: 118
Dimensions, feet (metres): 105·6 × — × 7·5 *(32·2 × — × 2·3)*
Guns: 2—40 mm (twin); 2—20 mm (twin); 2—12·7 mm MG
Main engines: 3 Diesels; 3 shafts = 27 knots
Range, miles: 825 at 25 knots
Complement: 21

GAMBIA

Mercantile Marine

Lloyd's Register of Shipping:
3 vessels of 1 337 tons

LIGHT FORCES

MANSA KILA IV

isplacement, tons: 40
imensions, feet (metres): 74·5 × 19·7 × 5·0 *(22·7 × 6·0 × 1·5)*
ain engines: 2 Cummins diesels; 750 bhp × 20 knots

uilt by Camper and Nicholson Ltd. Gosport, England to Keith Nelson 75 ft design for a private
rder—eventually purchased by Gambia in 1974.

GERMANY (Federal Republic)

Headquarters Appointment

Chief of Naval Staff, Federal German Navy:
Vice-Admiral Gunter Luther

Senior Appointment

Commander-in-Chief of the Fleet:
Vice Admiral H. H. Klase

Diplomatic Representation

Naval Attaché in Ankara:
Commander J. von Rodbertus
Naval Attaché in The Hague:
Commander E. Kollenbaum
Defence Attaché in Lisbon:
Commander K. Perlich
Naval Attaché in London:
Rear Admiral Dr. W. Schünemann
Commander P. Laabs (ANA)
Naval Attaché in Oslo (and Stockholm):
Commander K. Hersche
Naval Attaché in Paris:
Captain C. Hoffman
Naval Attaché in Rome:
Commander L. Gabriel
Naval Attaché in Washington:
Captain E. Wiese

Personnel

(a) 1971: 35 000 (3 200 officers, 31 800 men)
1972: 35 900 (4 500 officers, 31 400 men)
1973: 36 000 (4 550 officers, 31 450 men)
1974: 36 000 (4 550 officers, 31 450 men)
1975: 35 900 (4 775 officers, 31 125 men)
1976: 35 900 (5 100 officers, 30 800 men)

(Includes Naval Air Arm)

(b) 15 months National Service

Bases

Flensburg, Wilhelmshaven, Kiel, Olpenitz.
The administration of these bases is vested in the Naval Support Command at Wilhelmshaven (Rear-Admiral Feindt)

Naval Air Arm

(See Future Developments)

6 000 men total
2 LRMP squadrons (15 Breguet Atlantic)
4 Fighter bomber squadrons (60 F104G)
1 Helicopter squadron (re-equipping with
22 Sea King Mk 41 for SAR.)
20 Liaison aircraft (DO28)

Prefix to Ships' Names

Not normally used but in British waters prefix FGS is used.

Mercantile Marine

Lloyd's Register of Shipping:
1 964 vessels of 8 516 567 tons gross

Future Development

Interest is being shown by the Naval Staff in various and varied projects.
(a) Development of more powerful ship-to-ship missiles.
(b) Development of SAMs and ASMs with the Franco German Kormoran ASM being introduced in 1976.
(c) Construction of 230 ton hydrofoils of USS Pegasus type. (Type 162)
(d) New frigates of 2 500 tons standard, 3 800 tons full load with guided weapons to replace "Köln" Class—12 are planned, first batch possibly similar to Netherlands "Kortenaer" class.
(e) Replacement of F104G aircraft by MRCAs.
(f) Replacement of Breguet Atlantics by S3A Vikings.
(g) Minewarfare forces to be improved by conversion of 12 MSCs to Minehunters and replacement of "Schütze" class by remotely controlled unmanned systems.

Hydrographic Service

This service is under the direction of the Ministry of Transport, is civilian manned with HQ at Hamburg. Survey ships are listed at the end of the section.

Strength of the Fleet

Type	Active	Building (Projected)
Destroyers	11	—
Frigates	6	(12)
Corvettes	6	
Submarines—Patrol	24	—
Fast Attack Craft (Missile)	30	4 (6) (hydrofoil)
Fast Attack Craft (Torpedo)	10	
LCUs	22	—
LCMs	28	—
Minesweepers— Coastal and Minehunter	40	—
Minesweepers—Inshore	18	—
Depot Ships	11	—
Repair Ships	3 (1 small)	—
Replenishment Tankers	6	—
Support Tankers	5	—
Support Ships	4	—
Supply Ships	9	—
Ammunition Transports	2	—
Mine Transports	2	—
Training Ship	1	—
Sail Training Ships	2	—
Misc. Tenders	5	—
Rescue Launches	7	—
Tugs—Ocean	16	—
Tugs—Harbour	9	—
*Icebreakers	3	—
*Coastguard Craft	8+	—
*Survey Ships	6	—
*Fishery Protection Ships	7	—
*Experimental Ships	10	—

*Non-naval

DELETIONS

Destroyers
1972 Z1

Frigates
1972 *Scharnhorst* and *Gneisenau*

Submarines
1974 U4, 5, 6, 7, 8, (Type 205)

Fast Attack Craft (Torpedo)
1972 *Marder*
1973 *Jaguar, Kranich, Leopard, Luchs, Panther*
1974 *Dommel, Elster*
1975 20 "Jaguar" class transferred (*Alk, Fuchs, Häher, Löwe, Pelikan, Pinguin, Reiher, Storch, Tiger* and *Wolf* to Turkey and *Albatros, Bussard, Falke, Geier, Greif, Habicht, Kondor, Kormoran, Seeadler* and *Sperber* to Greece).

Coastal Patrol Craft
1974 TM 1, KW 2, KW 8, FW 2, FW 3

Minelayers
1972 *Bochum, Bottrop* transferred to Turkey.

Minesweepers Coastal
1972 *Algol* ("Schütze" class) scrapped.
1973 *Capella, Krebs, Mira, Orion, Pegasus, Steinbock, Uranus* ("Schütze" class).
1975 *Vegesack, Hampeln, Siegen, Detmold, Worms* ("Vegesack" class) transferred to Turkey, Sept

Depot Ships
1974 *Ruhr* (paid off)
1975 *Weser* transferred to Greece.

Supply Ships
1972 *Angeln* transferred to Turkey.
1974 *Schwarzwald*
1975 *Dithmarschen*

Auxiliaries
1975 FW 6 to Turkey, *Karl Kolls* (sold).

PENNANT LIST

Destroyers

D 171	Z 2
D 172	Z 3
D 178	Z 4
D 179	Z 5
D 181	Hamburg
D 182	Schleswig-Holstein
D 183	Bayern
D 184	Hessen
D 185	Lütjens
D 186	Mölders
D 187	Rommel

Frigates

F 220	Köln
F 221	Emden
F 222	Augsburg
F 223	Karlsruhe
F 224	Lübeck
F 225	Braunschweig

Submarines

S 170	U 21
S 171	U 22
S 172	U 23
S 173	U 24
S 174	U 25
S 175	U 26
S 176	U 27
S 177	U 28
S 178	U 29
S 179	U 30
S 180	U 1
S 181	U 2
S 188	U 9
S 189	U 10
S 190	U 11
S 191	U 12
S 192	U 13
S 193	U 14
S 194	U 15
S 195	U 16
S 196	U 17
S 197	U 18
S 198	U 19
S 199	U 20

Light Forces

6092	Zobel
6093	Wiesel
6094	Dachs
6095	Hermelin
6096	Nerz
6097	Puma
6098	Gepard
6099	Hyäne
6100	Frettchen
6101	Ozelot
6111	S 61
6112	S 62
6113	S 63
6114	S 64
6115	S 65
6116	S 66

6117	S 67
6118	S 68
6119	S 69
6120	S 70
6141	S 41
6142	S 42
6143	S 43
6144	S 44
6145	S 45
6146	S 46
6147	S 47
6148	S 48
6149	S 49
6150	S 50
6151	S 51
6152	S 52
6153	S 53
6154	S 54
6155	S 55
6156	S 56
6157	S 57
6158	S 58
6159	S 59
6160	S 60

Minewarfare Forces

1051	Castor
1054	Pollux
1055	Sirius
1056	Rigel
1057	Regulus
1058	Mars
1059	Spica
1060	Skorpion
1062	Schütze
1063	Waage
1064	Deneb
1065	Jupiter
1067	Atair
1069	Wega
1070	Göttingen
1071	Koblenz
1072	Lindau
1073	Schleswig
1074	Tübingen
1075	Wetzlar
1076	Paderborn
1077	Weilheim
1078	Cuxhaven
1079	Düren
1080	Marburg
1081	Konstanz
1082	Wolfburg
1083	Ulm
1084	Flensburg
1085	Minden
1086	Fulda
1087	Völklingen
1090	Perseus
1092	Pluto
1093	Neptun
1094	Widder
1095	Herkilles
1096	Fischer
1097	Gemma
1099	Uranus
2650	Ariadne
2651	Freya
2652	Vineta
2653	Hertha
2654	Nymphe
2655	Nixe
2656	Amazone
2657	Gazelle
2658	Frauenlob
2659	Nautilus
2660	Gefion
2661	Medusa
2662	Undine
2663	Minerva
2664	Diana
2665	Loreley
2666	Atlantis
2667	Acheron

Patrol Craft

P 6052	Thetis
P 6053	Hermes
P 6054	Najade
P 6055	Triton
P 6056	Theseus

Amphibious Forces

L 760	Flunder
L 761	Karpfen
L 762	Lachs
L 763	Plötze
L 764	Rochen
L 765	Schleie
L 766	Stör
L 767	Tümmler
L 768	Wels
L 769	Zander
L 788	Butt
L 789	Brasse
L 790	Barbe
L 791	Delphin
L 792	Dorsch
L 793	Felchen
L 794	Forelle
L 795	Inger
L 796	Makrele
L 797	Müräne
L 798	Renke
L 799	Salm

Support Ships and Auxiliaries

A 50	Alster
A 52	Oste
A 53	Oker
A 54	Isar
A 55	Lahn
A 56	Lech
A 58	Rhein
A 59	Deutschland
A 60	Gorch Fock
A 61	Elbe
A 63	Main
A 65	Saar
A 66	Neckar
A 67	Mosel
A 68	Werra
A 69	Donau
A 512	Odin
A 513	Wotan
A 1401	Eisvogel
A 1402	Eisbär
A 1406	Bodensee
A 1407	Wittensee
A 1411	Lüneburg

A 1412	Coburg
A 1413	Freiburg
A 1414	Glücksburg
A 1415	Saarburg
A 1416	Nienburg
A 1417	Offenburg
A 1418	Meersburg
A 1424	Walchensee
A 1425	Ammersee
A 1426	Tegernsee
A 1427	Westensee
A 1428	Harz
A 1429	Eifel
A 1435	Westerwald
A 1436	Odenwald
A 1437	Sachsenwald
A 1438	Steigerwald
A 1439	Frankenland
A 1440	Emsland
A 1441	Münsterland
A 1449	Hans Bürkner
A 1450	Planet
A 1451	Wangerooge
A 1452	Spiekeroog
A 1453	Langeoog
A 1454	Baltrum
A 1455	Norderney
A 1456	Juist
A 1457	Helgoland
A 1458	Fehmarn
Y 801	Pellworm
Y 802	Plon
Y 803	Blauort
Y 804	Wieland
Y 805	Memmert
Y 806	Hansa
Y 809	Arcona
Y 811	Knurrhahn
Y 812	Lütje Hörn
Y 813	Mellum
Y 814	Knechtsand
Y 815	Schärhorn
Y 816	Vogelsand
Y 817	Nordstrant
Y 818	Trieschen
Y 819	Langeness
Y 820	Sylt
Y 821	Föhr
Y 822	Amrum
Y 823	Neuwerk
Y 827	KW 15
Y 829	KW 3
Y 830	KW 16
Y 832	KW 18
Y 833	KW 19
Y 834	Nordwind
Y 836	Holnis
Y 837	SP 1
Y 838	Wilhelm Pullwer
Y 841	Walther van Ledebur

Y 845	KW 17
Y 846	KW 2O
Y 847	OT 2
Y 849	Stier
Y 851-56	TF 101-106
Y 857-859	FL 5-7
Y 862	FL 10
Y 863	FL 11
Y 864-69	FW 1-6
Y 871	Heinz Roggenkamp
Y 872-74	TF 106-108
Y 877	H.C. Oersted
Y 878	H. von Helmholtz
Y 880	Wilhelm Bauer
Y 881	Adolf Bestelmeyer
Y 882	Otto Meycke
Y 887	Karl Kolls
Y 888	Friedrich Voge
Y 889	Rudolf Diesel
Y 1641	Förde
Y 1642	Jade
Y 1643	Niobe
Y 1662	Ems
Y 1663	Eider

Coastguard

BG 11	Neustadt
BG 12	Bad Bramstedt
BG 13	Uelzen
BG 14	Duderstadt
BG 15	Eschwege
BG 16	Alsfeld
BG 17	Bayreuth
BG 18	Rosenheim

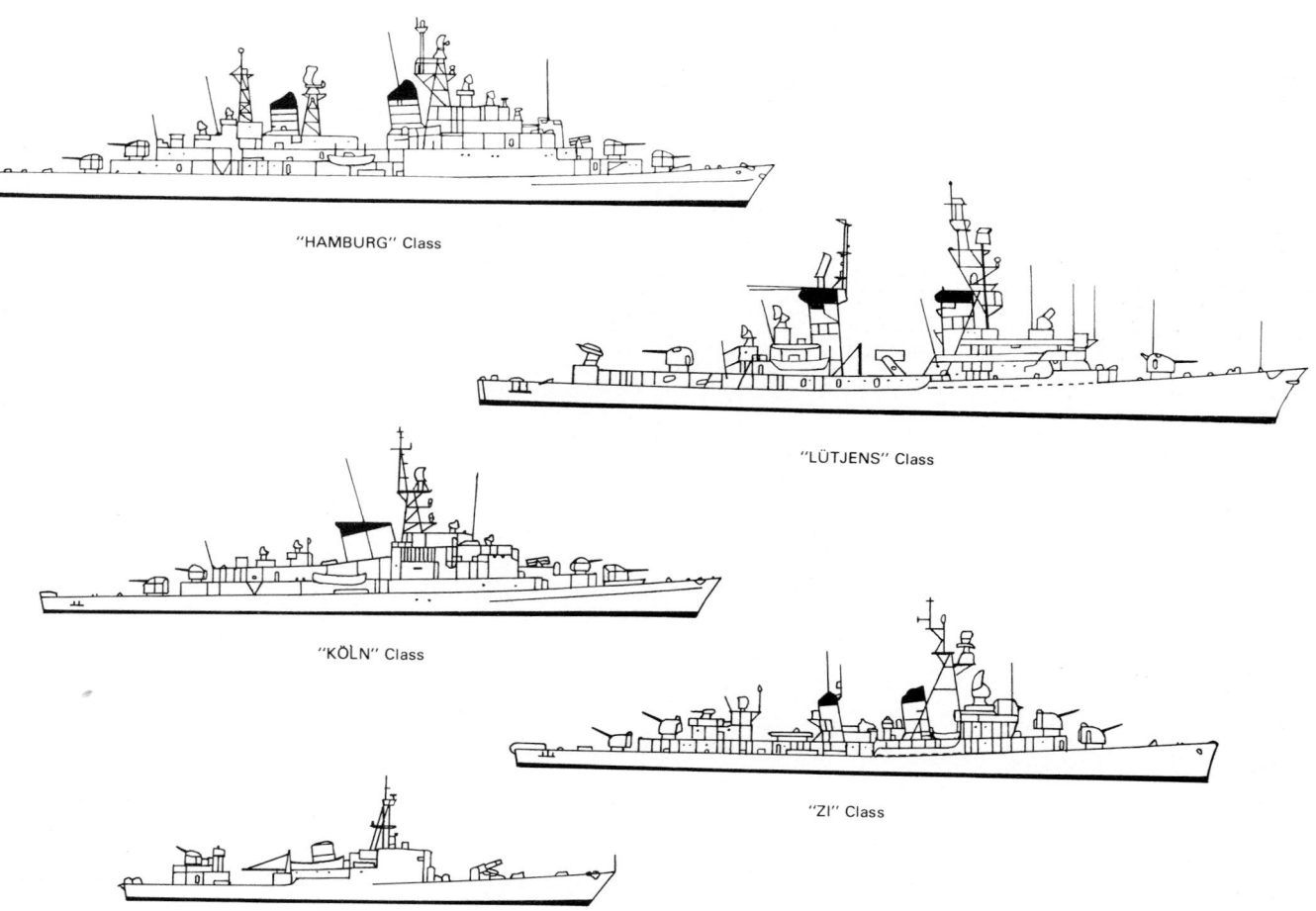

"HAMBURG" Class

"LÜTJENS" Class

"KÖLN" Class

"ZI" Class

"THETIS" Class

DESTROYERS

3 MODIFIED "CHARLES F. ADAMS" CLASS (DDGs)

Name	No.	Builders	Laid down	Launched	Commissioned
LÜTJENS (ex-US DDG 28)	D 185	Bath Iron Works Corp	1 Mar 1966	11 Aug 1967	12 Mar 1969
MÖLDERS (ex-US DDG 29)	D 186	Bath Iron Works Corp	12 April 1966	13 April 1968	12 Sep 1969
ROMMEL (ex-US DDG 30)	D 187	Bath Iron Works Corp	22 Aug 1967	1 Feb 1969	24 April 1970

Displacement, tons: 3 370 standard; 4 500 full load
Length, feet (metres): 431 *(131·4)* wl; 440 *(134·1)* oa
Beam, feet (metres): 47 *(14·3)*
Draught, feet (metres): 20 *(6·1)*
Missile launchers: 1 Tartar single
Guns: 2—5 in *(127 mm)* single
A/S weapons: Asroc; 2 triple torpedo; 1 DCT
Main engines: Geared steam turbines 70 000 shp; 2 shafts
Boilers: 4 Combustion Engineering; 1 200 psi *(84·4 kg cm²)*
Speed, knots: 35
Oil fuel, tons: 900
Range, miles: 4 500 at 20 knots
Complement: 340 (21 officers, 319 men)

Destroyers basically of the "Charles F. Adams" type; but modified to suit Federal German requirements and practice and presenting a different silhouette. 1965 contract.
Cost $43 754 000.

Electronics: SATIR I (similar to SENIT 2) automatic data system. TACAN beacon.

Radar: Three dimensional air search and target designator: one SPS 52 (after funnel)
Air surveillance: one SPS 40 (main-mast)
Tartar fire control: two SPG 51 (abaft after funnel)
Surface warning: one SPS 10.
Gun fire control: one GFCS 68.

Sonar: One SQS 23.

LÜTJENS   8/1975, Stefan Terzibaschitsch

LÜTJENS   1973, Stefan Terzibaschitsch

LÜTJENS   1974, Federal German Navy

4 "HAMBURG" CLASS

Name	No.	Builders	Laid down	Launched	Commissioned
BAYERN	D 183	H. C. Stülcken Sohn, Hamburg	1961	14 Aug 1962	6 July 1965
HAMBURG	D 181	H. C. Stülcken Sohn, Hamburg	1959	26 Mar 1960	23 May 1964
HESSEN	D 184	H. C. Stülcken Sohn, Hamburg	1962	4 May 1963	8 Oct 1968
SCHLESWIG-HOLSTEIN	D 182	H. C. Stülcken Sohn, Hamburg	1959	20 Aug 1960	12 Oct 1964

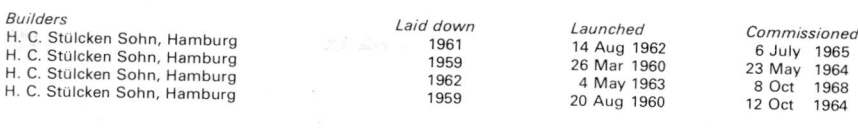

Displacement, tons: 3 400 standard; 4 400 full load
Length, feet (metres): 420 *(128)* wl; 439·7 *(134·0)* oa
Beam, feet (metres): 44 *(13·4)*
Draught, feet (metres): 17 *(5·2)*
Guns: 4—3·9 in *(100 mm)* (single); 8—40 mm (4 twin)
A/S weapons: 2 Bofors 4-barrel DC Mortars; 1 DCT
Torpedo tubes: 4—12 in for A/S torpedoes
Boilers: 4 Wahodag, 910 psi *(64 kg/cm²)*, 860°F (460°C)
Main engines: 2 Wahodag dr geared turbines; 68 000 shp;
  2 shafts
Speed, knots: 35·8; 18 economical
Range, miles: 6 000 at 13 knots; 920 at 35 knots
Complement: 280 (17 officers, 263 men)

All named after countries of the German Federal Republic.
Capable of minelaying.

Electronics: FCS for Bofors A/S launcher, torpedoes and DC
from Hollandsesignaalapparaten. ECM fitted.

Modernisation: Plans in hand for replacement of 100 mm in X
position by four MM 38 Exocet, replacement of 40 mm Bofors
by Bredas and addition of two extra A/S torpedo tubes. Modernisation started in 1975 with *Hessen* to be followed by *Hamburg, Schleswig-Holstein* and *Bayern,* all completing by 1977.
Hessen completed Nov 1975. *Hamburg* taken in hand by Blohm
and Voss 18 Aug 1975. *Schleswig-Holstein* taken in hand April
1976. *Bayern* to be started early in 1977.

Radar: All by Hollandse Signaalapparaten.
Navigation/surface warning: one set
Air warning: one LW.02/3
Target designator: one DAO 2
100 mm fire control: two M 45 series
40 mm fire control: two M 45 series

Sonar: One German M/F hull-mounted.

HESSEN (with MM 38 Exocet launchers in X position)   *11/1975, Reiner Nerlich*

HESSEN (after conversion—MM 38 Exocet not shipped)   *10/1975, Reiner Nerlich*

SCHLESWIG-HOLSTEIN

1975, Federal German Navy

4 Ex-US "FLETCHER" CLASS

Name	No.
Z 2 (ex-USS *Ringgold, DD 500)*	D 171
Z 3 (ex-USS *Wadsworth, DD 516)*	D 172
Z 4 (ex-USS *Claxton, DD 571)*	D 178
Z 5 (ex-USS *Dyson, DD 572)*	D 179

Builders	Laid down	Launched	Commissioned
Federal SB & DD Co, Port Newark	25 June1942	11 Nov 1942	24 Dec 1942
Bath Iron Works Corporation, Maine	18 Aug 1942	10 Jan 1943	16 Mar 1943
Consolidated Steel Corporation, Orange	25 June1941	1 April1942	8 Dec 1942
Consolidated Steel Corporation, Orange	25 June1941	15 April1942	30 Dec 1942

Displacement, tons: 2 100 standard; 2 750 full load
Length, feet (metres): 368·4 *(112·3)* wl; 376·5 *(114·8)* oa
Beam, feet (metres): 39·5 *(12)*
Draught, feet (metres): 18 *(5·5)*
Guns: 4—5 in *(127 mm)* 38 cal
  6—3 in *(76 mm)* 50 cal (twins)
A/S weapons: 2 Hedgehogs; 1 DC rack
Torpedo tubes: 5—21 in *(533 mm)* (quintuple); 2 ASW tubes
Main engines: 2 sets GE geared turbines; 60 000 shp; 2 shafts
Boilers: 4 Babcock & Wilcox, 569 psi *(40 kg/cm²)*; 851°F (455°C)
Speed, knots: 32; 17 economical
Oil fuel, tons: 540
Range, miles: 6 000 at 15 knots
Complement: 250

Former US "Fletcher" class destroyers. The original loan from the United States of a class of five for five years was extended. First ship arrived at Bremerhaven on 14 April 1958. Commissioned in FGN as follows: Z 2, 14 July 1959; Z 3, 6 Oct 1959; Z 4, 15 Dec 1959; Z 5, 23 Feb 1960. Capable of minelaying.

Gunnery: Z 4 carried out trials of a containerised 3-in *(76 mm)* Oto Melara gun in 1975 in place of after 3-in mounting. On completion of trials Oto Melara mounting was removed but original twin 3-in was not replaced.

Radar: Air and surface search: one SPS 6
Surface surveillance: one SPS 10
Fire control: one GFCS 56 and 68.

Z 5   1975, Federal German Navy

FRIGATES

Note: Twelve 3 800 ton (full load) frigates with SSM are planned.

6 "KÖLN" CLASS

Name	No.
AUGSBURG	F 222
BRAUNSCHWEIG	F 225
EMDEN	F 221
KARLSRUHE	F 223
KÖLN	F 220
LÜBECK	F 224

Builders	Laid down	Launched	Commissioned
H. C. Stülcken Sohn, Hamburg	—	15 Aug 1959	7 April 1962
H. C. Stülcken Sohn, Hamburg	—	3 Feb 1962	16 June 1964
H. C. Stülcken Sohn, Hamburg	—	21 Mar 1959	24 Oct 1961
H. C. Stülcken Sohn, Hamburg	—	24 Oct 1959	15 Dec 1962
H. C. Stülcken Sohn, Hamburg	—	6 Dec 1958	15 April 1961
H. C. Stülcken Sohn, Hamburg	—	23 July 1960	6 July 1963

Displacement, tons: 2 100 standard; 2 550 full load
Length, feet (metres): 360·9 *(110)*
Beam, feet (metres): 36·1 *(11·0)*
Draught, feet (metres): 11·2 *(3·4)*
Guns: 2—3·9 in *(100 mm)*
  6—40 mm (2 twin and 2 single)
A/S weapons: 2 Bofors 4-barrel DC mortars (72 charges)
Torpedo tubes: 4—21 in *(533 mm)* (twins) for A/S torpedoes
Mines: Can carry 80
Main engines: Combined diesel and gas turbine plant; 4 MAN 16-cyl diesels; total 12 000 bhp; 2 Brown Boveri gas turbines, 24 000 bhp; total 36 000 bhp; 2 shafts
Speed, knots: 32; 23 economical
Oil fuel, tons: 333
Range, miles: 920 at 32 knots
Complement: 200

Ordered in Mar 1957. All ships of this class are named after towns of West Germany.

Electronics: Hollandse Signaalapparaten FCS for Bofors A/S launchers. M9 torpedo fire control.

Engineering: Each of the two shafts is driven by two diesels coupled and geared to one BBC gas turbine. Controllable pitch propellers. A speed of 32 knots is reported to have been attained on full power trials.

Radar: All by Hollandse Signaalapparaten.
Navigation/surface search: one set.
Target designator: one DA 02.
Fire control *(100 mm)*: two M 45 series.
Fire control *(40 mm)*: two M 45 series.

Sonar: One German M/F set, hull-mounted.

LÜBECK   3/1975, Wright and Logan

SUBMARINES

TYPE 210

A development project is in hand by the Norwegian and Federal German navies for a 750 ton class to replace the Type 205 (FGN) and Type 207 (Norway) in the 1980s.

18 TYPE 206

Name	No.
U 13	S 192
U 14	S 193
U 15	S 194
U 16	S 195
U 17	S 196
U 18	S 197
U 19	S 198
U 20	S 199
U 21	S 170
U 22	S 171
U 23	S 172
U 24	S 173
U 25	S 174
U 26	S 175
U 27	S 176
U 28	S 177
U 29	S 178
U 30	S 179

Builders	Laid down	Launched	Commissioned
Howaldtswerke, Kiel	—	28 Sep 1971	1973
Reinstahl Nordseewerke, Emden	—	1 Dec 1972	1973
Howaldtswerke, Kiel	—	—	1973
Reinstahl Nordseewerke, Emden	—	22 Aug 1972	1973
Howaldtswerke, Kiel	—	—	1973
Reinstahl Nordseewerke, Emden	—	—	1973
Howaldtswerke, Kiel	—	—	1973
Reinstahl Nordseewerke, Emden	—	16 Jan 1973	1974
Howaldtswerke, Kiel	—	9 Mar 1973	1974
Reinstahl Nordseewerke, Emden	—	27 Mar 1973	1974
Reinstahl Nordseewerke, Emden	—	22 May 1974	1975
Reinstahl Nordseewerke, Emden	—	24 June1973	1974
Howaldtswerke, Kiel	—	23 May 1973	1974
Reinstahl Nordseewerke, Emden	—	20 Nov 1973	1975
Howaldtswerke, Kiel	—	21 Aug 1973	1975
Reinstahl Nordseewerke, Emden	—	22 Jan 1974	1975
Howaldtswerke, Kiel	—	5 Sep 1973	1975
Reinstahl Nordseewerke, Emden	—	26 Mar 1974	1975

Displacement, tons: 400 surfaced; 600 dived
Length, feet (metres): 159·4 *(48·6)*
Beam, feet (metres): 15·4 *(4·7)*
Draught, feet (metres): 13·1 *(4·0)*
Torpedo tubes: 8—21 in *(533 mm)* (bow)
Main machinery: (MTU) diesel-electric; 1 shaft; 1 800 hp
Speed, knots: 10 surfaced; 17 dived
Range, miles: 4 500 at 5 knots (surfaced)
Complement: 22

Authorised on 7 June 1969 from Howaldtswerke Deutsche Werft (8) and Rheinstahl Nordseewerke Emden, (10).

Squadrons: First: U 25-30 U 1 and 2, 9-12. Third: U 13-24.

U 24   10/1975, Reiner Nerlich

6 TYPE 205

Name	No.
U 1	S 180
U 2	S 181
U 9	S 188
U 10	S 189
U 11	S 190
U 12	S 191

Builders	Laid down	Launched	Commissioned
Howaldtswerke, Kiel	—	21 Oct 1961	—
Howaldtswerke, Kiel	—	25 Jan 1962	—
Howaldtswerke, Kiel	—	20 Oct 1966	—
Howaldtswerke, Kiel	—	20 July 1967	—
Howaldtswerke, Kiel	—	9 Feb 1968	21 June 1968
Howaldtswerke, Kiel	—	10 Sep 1968	14 Jan 1969

Displacement, tons: 370 surfaced; 450 dived
Length, feet (metres): 142·7 *(43·5)* oa
Beam, feet (metres): 15·1 *(4·6)*
Draught, feet (metres): 12·8 *(3·8)*
Torpedo tubes: 8—21 in *(533 mm)* (bow)
Main machinery: 2 Maybach (MTU) diesels; total 1 200 bhp
  2 Siemens electric motors, total 1 700 bhp; single screw
Speed, knots: 10 surfaced; 17 dived
Complement: 21

All built in floating docks. Fitted with snort mast. First submarines designed and built by Germany since the end of the Second World War. U 4-12 were built to a heavier and improved design. U 1 and U 2 were modified accordingly and refloated on 17 Feb 1967 and 15 July 1966 respectively. U 1 was reconstructed late 1963 to 4 Mar 1965. (See original appearance in the 1962-63 and 1963-64 editions.) U 9-12 have hulls of different steel alloys of non-magnetic properties. U 3 of this class lent to Norway on 10 July 1962 and temporarily named *Kobben* (S 310), was returned to Germany in 1964 and decommissioned on 15 Sep 1967 for disposal.

Radar: French Thomson-CSF Calypso, nav/attack set. Passive DF.

Torpedo equipment: The boats are trimmed by the stern to load through the bow caps. Also fitted for minelaying. Fire control by Hollandse. Mk 8.

U 9   1975, Reiner Nerlich

1 CONVERTED TYPE XXI

Name	No.
WILHELM BAUER (ex-*U 2540*)	Y 880

Builders	Laid down	Launched	Commissioned
Blohm and Voss, Hamburg	1943	1944	1944

Displacement, tons: 1 620 surfaced; 1 820 dived
Length, feet (metres): 252·7 *(77·0)* pp
Beam, feet (metres): 21·7 *(6·6)*
Draught, feet (metres): 20·3 *(6·2)*
Torpedo tubes: 4—21 in *(533 mm)* (bow)
Main machinery: (MTU) diesel-electric drive;
  2 diesels total 4 200 bhp; 2 electric motors total 5 000 hp
Speed, knots: 15·5 surfaced; 17·5 dived

Scuttled after air attack off Flensburg on 4 May 1945. Raised in 1957. Rebuilt in 1958-59 at Howaldtswerke, Kiel. Commissioned on 1 Sep 1960. Used for experiments on submarine equipment. Conning tower was modified.

WILHELM BAUER   1973, Howaldtswerke, Kiel

CORVETTES

5 "THETIS" CLASS

Name	No.	Builders	Commissioned
HERMES	P 6053	Rolandwerft, Bremen	16 Dec 1961
NAJADE	P 6054	Rolandwerft, Bremen	12 May 1962
THESEUS	P 6056	Rolandwerft, Bremen	15 Aug 1963
THETIS	P 6052	Rolandwerft, Bremen	1 July 1961
TRITON	P 6055	Rolandwerft, Bremen	10 Nov 1962

Displacement, tons: 564 standard; 650 full load
Dimensions, feet (metres): 229·7 × 27 × 14 *(70 × 8·5 × 4·2)*
Guns: 2—40 mm (twin mounting) (To be replaced by 1—3 in Oto Melara)
A/S weapons: Bofors DC mortar
Torpedo tubes: 4—21 in *(533 mm)*
Main engines: 2 MAN diesels; 2 shafts; 6 800 bhp = 24 knots
Complement: 48

Some have computer house before bridge.

Electronics: HSA M9 series torpedo control.

Radar: Combined nav/surface warning set.

NAJADE (forebridge type)   *1975, Federal German Navy*

THETIS (blockbridge type)   *1975, Federal German Navy*

Name	No.	Builders	Commissioned
HANS BÜRKNER	A 1449	Atlaswerke, Bremen	18 May 1963

Displacement, tons: 950 standard; 1 000 full load
Dimensions, feet (metres): 265·2 oa × 30·8 × 10 *(81 × 9·4 × 2·8)*
Guns: 2—40 mm (twin mounting)
A/S weapons: 1 DC mortar (four-barrelled) 2 DC racks
Torpedo tubes: 2—21 in *(533 mm)*
Main engines: 4 MAN diesels; 2 shafts; 13 600 shp = 24 knots
Complement: 50

Launched on 16 July 1961. Named after designer of German First World War battleships (1909-18). General purpose utility vessel.

HANS BÜRKNER   *1975, Federal German Navy*

LIGHT FORCES

10 NEW CONSTRUCTION TYPE 162
(FAST ATTACK HYDROFOIL—MISSILE)

Displacement, tons: 202 standard; 235 full load
Dimensions, feet (metres): 131·9 × 29·2 × 6·2 *(40·2 × 8·9 × 1·9)*
Missiles: 4 launchers for Exocet MM 38
Gun: 1—76 mm
Main engines: Gas turbines; 26 200 bhp; 2—MTU diesels; 1 340 bhp
Speed, knots: 50 on turbines; 12 on diesels
Complement: 21

First four ordered from Boeing, Seattle in May 1975. To be similar to USN "Pegasus" class and to replace "Zobel" class in 1980s.

10 TYPE 143 (FAST ATTACK CRAFT—MISSILE)

Name	No.	Builders	Commissioned
S 61	P 6111	Lürssen, Vegesack	Dec 1974 (trials)
S 62	P 6112	Lürssen, Vegesack	1975
S 63	P 6113	Lürssen, Vegesack	1975
S 64	P 6114	Lürssen, Vegesack	1975
S 65	P 6115	Kröger, Rendsburg	1976
S 66	P 6116	Lürssen, Vegesack	1976
S 67	P 6117	Kröger, Rendsburg	1976
S 68	P 6118	Lürssen, Vegesack	1977
S 69	P 6119	Kroger, Rendsburg	1977
S 70	P 6120	Lürssen, Vegesack	1977

Displacement, tons: 295 nominal, 378 full load
Dimensions, feet (metres): 200·0 × 24·6 × 8·5 *(57 × 7·8 × 2·4)*
Missiles: 4 launchers for Exocet MM 38
Guns: 2—76 mm Oto Melara
Torpedoes: 2—21 in wire guided aft
Main engines: 4 MTU diesels; 16 000 hp; 4 shafts = 38 knots
Range, miles: 1 300 at 30 knots
Complement: 40

Ordered in 1972 as replacements for last ten boats of the "Jaguar" class from 1976 onwards. Final funds allocated 13 July 1972. First laid down late 1972. The first boat, S 61, started trials in Dec 1974. Wooden-hulled craft. Launch dates—S 61, 22 Oct 1973; S 62, 21 March 1974; S 63, 18 Sep 1974; S 64, 10 Dec 1974; S 65, 10 Dec 1974; S 66, 5 Sep 1975; S 67, 6 March 1975; S 68, —; S 69, 5 June 1975; S 70, —.

Electronics: Believed that data automation system AGIS is being fitted to permit use of Type 143 as control ship for concerted operation as Type 148 boats.

Radar: All by Hollandse Signaal. WM 27 in radome for Exocet, gun and torpedo control.

S 61

3/1975, Reiner Nerlich

20 TYPE 148 (FAST ATTACK CRAFT—MISSILE)

Name	No.	Builders	Commissioned	
		(see note re Lürssen)		
S 41	P 6141	C. M. de Normandie, Cherbourg	30 Oct	1972
S 42	P 6142	C. M. de Normandie, Cherbourg	8 Jan	1973
S 43	P 6143	C. M. de Normandie, Cherbourg	9 April	1973
S 44	P 6144	C. M. de Normandie, Cherbourg	14 June	1973
S 45	P 6145	C. M. de Normandie, Cherbourg	21 Aug	1973
S 46	P 6146	C. M. de Normandie, Cherbourg	17 Oct	1973
S 47	P 6147	C. M. de Normandie, Cherbourg	13 Nov	1973
S 48	P 6148	C. M. de Normandie, Cherbourg	9 Jan	1974
S 49	P 6149	C. M. de Normandie, Cherbourg	26 Feb	1974
S 50	P 6150	C. M. de Normandie, Cherbourg	27 Mar	1974
S 51	P 6151	C. M. de Normandie, Cherbourg	12 June	1974
S 52	P 6152	C. M. de Normandie, Cherbourg	17 July	1974
S 53	P 6153	C. M. de Normandie, Cherbourg	24 Sep	1974
S 54	P 6154	C. M. de Normandie, Cherbourg	27 Nov	1974
S 55	P 6155	C. M. de Normandie, Cherbourg	7 Jan	1975
S 56	P 6156	C. M. de Normandie, Cherbourg	12 Feb	1975
S 57	P 6157	C. M. de Normandie, Cherbourg	3 April	1975
S 58	P 6158	C. M. de Normandie, Cherbourg	22 May	1975
S 59	P 6159	C. M. de Normandie, Cherbourg	24 June	1975
S 60	P 6160	C. M. de Normandie, Cherbourg	6 Aug	1975

Displacement, tons: 234 standard; 265 full load
Dimensions, feet (metres): 154·2 × 23·0 × 5·9 *(47 × 7 × 2)*
Missiles: 4 launchers for Exocet MM 38
Guns: 1—76 mm (Oto Melara); 1—40 mm (Bofors)
Main engines: 4 MTU diesels; 4 shafts; 12 000 bhp = 35·5 knots
Oil fuel, tons: 39
Range, miles: 600 at 30 knots
Complement: 30 (4 officers, 26 men)

S 44

1974, Federal German Navy

Ordered in Oct 1970. For completion from 1973 onwards to replace the first 20 of the "Jaguar" class. Eight hulls contracted to Lürssen but all fitted out in France. Steel-hulled craft. Launch dates: S 41, 27 Sep 1972; S 42, 12 Dec 1972; S 43, 7 Mar 1973; S 44, 5 May 1973; S 45, 3 July 1973; S 46, 21 May 1973; S 47, 20 Sep 1973; S 48, 10 Sep 1973; S 49 11 Jan 1974; S 50, 10 Dec 1973; S 51, 11 June 1974; S 52, 25 May 1974; S 53, 4 July 1974; S 54, 8 July 1974; S 55, 15 Nov 1974; S 56, 30 Oct 1974; S 57, 18 Feb 1975; S 58, 26 Feb 1975; S 59, 15 May 1975; S 60, 26 May 1975.

Electronics: Thomson-CSF, Vega-Pollux PCET control system, controlling missiles, torpedoes and guns.

Radar: Navigation: I band
Air and surface search/target designator: Triton G-band
Tracking: Pollux I band.

Squadrons: Third: S 41-50. Fifth: S 51-60.

10 "ZOBEL" CLASS (TYPE 142 FAST ATTACK CRAFT—TORPEDO)

Name	No.	Builders	Commissioned
DACHS	P 6094	Lürssen, Vegesack	1961
FRETTCHEN	P 6100	Lürssen, Vegesack	1963
GEPARD	P 6098	Kröger, Rendsburg	1962
HERMELIN	P 6095	Lürssen, Vegesack	1962
HYANE	P 6099	Kröger, Rendsburg	1963
NERZ	P 6096	Lürssen, Vegesack	1962
OZELOT	P 6101	Kröger, Rendsburg	1963
PUMA	P 6097	Lürssen, Vegesack	1962
WIESEL	P 6093	Lürssen, Vegesack	1961
ZOBEL	P 6092	Lürssen, Vegesack	1961

Displacement, tons: 225 full load
Dimensions, feet (metres): 139·4 × 23·4 × 7·9 *(42·5 × 7·2 × 2·4)*
Guns: 2—40 mm Bofors L 70 (single)
Tubes: 2—21 in for Seal wire-guided torpedoes
Main engines: 4 Mercedes-Benz (MTU) 20 cyl diesels; 4 shafts; 12 000 bhp = 40·5 knots
Complement: 39

Originally units of the "Jaguar" class, but, after conversion, known as the "Zobel" class. Form 7th Squadron.

Radar: Fire control: two M 20 series in radome

DACHS

5/1975, Reiner Nerlich

AMPHIBIOUS FORCES

22 TYPE 520 (LCUs)

BARBE L 790	FELCHEN L 793	LACHS L 762	SALM L 799
BRASSE L 789	FLUNDLER L 760	MAKRELE L 796	SCHLEI L 765
BUTT L 788	FORELLE L 794	MURÄNE L 797	STÖR L 766
DELPHIN L 791	INGER L 795	PLOTZE L 763	TÜMMLER L 767
DORSCH L 792	KARPFEN L 761	RENKE L 798	WELS L 768
		ROCHEN L 764	ZANDER L 769

FORELLE   9/1975, Reiner Nerlich

Displacement, tons: 200 light; 403 full load
Dimensions, feet (metres): 136·5 × 28·9 × 6·9 *(41·6 × 8·8 × 2·1)*
Guns: 1 or 2—20 mm (see *Gunnery* notes)
Main engines: GM diesels; 2 shafts; 1 380 bhp = 12 knots
Complement: 17

Similar to the United States LCU (Landing Craft Utility) type. Provided with bow and stern ramp. Built by Howaldtswerke, Hamburg, 1964-67. To carry 160 tons load. *Inge* employed for seamanship training. *Renke* and *Salm* in reserve.

Gunnery: Are being rearmed with two modern 20 mm.

28 LCM TYPE

LCM 1-28

Displacement, tons: 116 standard; 140 full load
Dimensions, feet (metres): 77·1 × 21·4 × — *(23·5 × 6·5 × —)*
Main engines: 2 diesels; 1 320 hp = 10 knots

Similar to US LCM 8 type. Built 1965-67. Can carry 60 tons.

LCM 11   1975, Reiner Nerlich

MINE WARFARE FORCES

18 "LINDAU" CLASS (TYPE 320)
(MINESWEEPERS—COASTAL and MINEHUNTERS)

Name	No.	Builders	Commissioned
CUXHAVEN	M 1078	Burmester, Bremen	1959
DÜREN	M 1079	Burmester, Bremen	1959
FLENSBURG	M 1084	Burmester, Bremen	1960
FULDA	M 1086	Burmester, Bremen	1960
GÖTTINGEN	M 1070	Burmester, Bremen	1958
KOBLENZ	M 1071	Burmester, Bremen	1958
KONSTANZ	M 1081	Burmester, Bremen	1959
LINDAU	M 1072	Burmester, Bremen	1958
MARBURG	M 1080	Burmester, Bremen	1959
MINDEN	M 1085	Burmester, Bremen	1960
PADERBORN	M 1076	Burmester, Bremen	1958
SCHLESWIG	M 1073	Burmester, Bremen	1958
TÜBINGEN	M 1074	Burmester, Bremen	1958
ULM	M 1083	Burmester, Bremen	1958
VÖLKLINGEN	M 1087	Burmester, Bremen	1961
WEILHEIM	M 1077	Burmester, Bremen	1959
WETZLAR	M 1075	Burmester, Bremen	1958
WOLFSBURG	M 1082	Burmester, Bremen	1960

PADERBORN (Sweeper)   8/1975, C. and S. Taylor

Displacement, tons: 370 standard; 420 full load
Dimensions, feet (metres): 137·8 pp; 147·7 oa × 27·2 × 8·5 *(49·7 × 8·3 × 2·5)*
Guns: 1—40 mm; 2—20 mm
Main engines: Maybach (MTU) diesels; 2 shafts; 4 000 bhp = 16·5 knots
Range, miles: 850 at 16·5 knots
Complement: 46

Lindau, first German built vessel for the Federal German Navy since the Second World War, launched on 16 Feb 1957. Basically of NATO WU type but modified for German requirements. The hull is of wooden construction, laminated with plastic glue. The engines are of non-magnetic materials. The first six, *Göttingen, Koblenz, Lindau, Schleswig, Tubingen* and *Wetzlar*, were modified with lower bridges in 1958-59. *Schleswig* was lengthened by 6·8 feet in 1960—all others in 1960-64. *Fulda* and *Flensburg* were converted into minehunters in 1968-69 as part of a total of twelve ships to be so converted, with the second group started in 1975 with *Lindau, Tübingen* and *Minden*. These will be fitted with Plessey sonar and French PAP exploders. The remaining six will be fitted with Troika during 1978-80.

FULDA (Hunter)   1975, Reiner Nerlich

22 "SCHÜTZE" CLASS (TYPE 340-341)
(MINESWEEPERS—COASTAL (FAST))

Name	No.	Builders	Commissioned
ATAIR	M 1067	Schlichting, Travemünde	1962
CASTOR	M 1051	Abeking and Rasmussen	1963
DENEB	M 1064	Schürenstedt	1962
FISCHE	M 1096	Abeking and Rasmussen	1960
GEMMA	M 1097	Abeking and Rasmussen	1960
HERKULES	M 1095	Schlichting, Travemünde	1961
JUPITER	M 1065	Schürenstedt	1962
MARS	M 1058	Abeking and Rasmussen	1962
NEPTUN	M 1093	Schlichting, Travemünde	1961
PERSEUS	M 1090	Schlichting, Travemünde	1961
POLLUX	M 1054	Abeking and Rasmussen	1961
PLUTO	M 1092	Schrenstedt	1961
REGULUS	M 1057	Abeking and Rasmussen	1963
RIGEL	M 1056	Abeking and Rasmussen	1963
SCHÜTZE	M 1062	Abeking and Rasmussen	1959
SIRIUS	M 1055	Abeking and Rasmussen	1962
SKORPION	M 1060	Abeking and Rasmussen	1964
SPICA	M 1059	Abeking and Rasmussen	1961
STIER	Y 849	Abeking and Rasmussen	1959
WAAGE	M 1063	Abeking and Rasmussen	1960
WEGA	M 1089	Abeking and Rasmussen	1963
WIDDER	M 1094	Schürenstedt	1960

Displacement, tons: 204 standard; 230 full load
Dimensions, feet (metres): 124·7 × 27·2 × 6·6 *(43·8 × 8·2 × 2)*
Gun: 1—40 mm
Main engines: (MTU) diesels = 14 knots
Range, miles: 2 000 at 13 knots
Complement: 24

HERKULES   *1975, Federal German Navy*

40 originally built between 1959 and 1964. (Ex-*Uranus* is now German Navy league ship in Trier). The design is a development of the "R" boats of World War II. *Stier,* former number M 1061, carries no weapons, but has a recompression chamber, being a clearance diving vessel. Formerly classified as inshore minesweepers, but re-rated as fast minesweepers in 1966.

Transfer: Five transferred to Greece, deleted in 1974.

STIER (with recompression chamber)   *5/1974, Reiner Nerlich*

10 "FRAUENLOB" CLASS (TYPE 344)
(MINESWEEPERS—INSHORE)

Name	No.	Builders	Commissioned
ACHERON	M 2667	Krögerwerft, Rendsburg	1968
ATLANTIS	M 2666	Krögerwerft, Rendsburg	1968
DIANA	M 2664	Krögerwerft, Rendsburg	1967
FRAUENLOB	M 2658	Krögerwerft, Rendsburg	1966
GEFION	M 2660	Krögerwerft, Rendsberg	1966
LORELEY	M 2665	Krögerwerft, Rendsburg	1968
MEDUSA	M 2661	Krögerwerft, Rendsburg	1967
MINERVA	M 2663	Krögerwerft, Rendsburg	1967
NAUTILUS	M 2659	Krögerwerft, Rendsburg	1966
ONDINE	M 2662	Krögerwerft, Rendsburg	1967

Displacement, tons: 230 standard; 280 full load
Dimensions, feet (metres): 154·5 oa × 22·3 × 7·2 *(47·2 × 7·2 × 2·2)*
Gun: 1—40 mm (except *Stier*)
Mines: Laying capability
Main engines: Maybach (MTU) diesels; 2 shafts; Escher Wyss propellers; 3 600 bhp = 24·5 knots
Complement: 39

Launched in 1965-67. Originally designed coastguard boats with "W" numbers. Rated as inshore minesweepers in 1968 with the "M" numbers. All subsequently allocated Y numbers and later reallocated M numbers.

MINERVA (old pennant number)   *Federal Germany Navy*

8 "ARIADNE" CLASS (TYPE 343)
(MINESWEEPERS—INSHORE)

Name	No.	Builders	Commissioned
AMAZONE	M 2656	Krögerwerft, Rendsburg	1964
ARIADNE	M 2650	Krögerwerft, Rendsburg	1961
FREYA	M 2651	Krögerwerft, Rendsburg	1967
GAZELLE	M 2657	Krögerwerft, Rendsburg	1964
HERTHA	M 2653	Krögerwerft, Rendsburg	1962
NIXE	M 2655	Krögerwerft, Rendsburg	1963
NYMPHE	M 2654	Krögerwerft, Rendsburg	1963
VINETA	M 2652	Krögerwerft, Rendsburg	1961

Displacement, tons: 184 standard; 210 full load
Dimensions, feet (metres): 124·3 × 27·2 × 6·6 *(37·9 × 8·3 × 2)*
Gun: 1—40 mm
Mines: Laying capability
Main engines: 2 Mercedes-Benz (MTU) diesels; 2 shafts; 2 000 bhp = 14 knots
Range, miles: 740 at 14 knots
Complement: 23

All launched between April 1960 *(Ariadne)* and June 1966 *(Freya).* All named after cruisers of 1897-1900. Formerly classified as patrol boats but re-rated as inshore minesweepers in 1966, and given new M numbers in Jan 1968, Y numbers in 1970, and M numbers once more in 1974.

HERTHA   *8/1974, Reiner Nerlich*

1 TRIALS MINESWEEPER

Name	No.	Builders	Commissioned
HOLNIS	Y 836 (ex-*M 2651*)	Abeking and Rasmussen	1966

HOLNIS

1975, Federal German Navy

Displacement, tons: 180
Dimensions, feet (metres): 116·8 × 24·3 × 6·9 *(35·6 × 7·4 × 2·1)*
Gun: 1—20 mm
Main engines: 2 Mercedes-Benz (MTU) diesels; 2 shafts; 2 000 bhp = 14·5 knots
Complement: 21

Now serving for trials and evaluation. *Holnis* was launched on 22 May 1965 as the prototype of a new design projected as a class of 20 such vessels but she is the only unit of this type, the other 19 boats having been cancelled. Hull number changed from M 2651 to Y 836 in 1970.

2 "NIOBE" CLASS (MINESWEEPERS—INSHORE)

Name	No.	Builders	Commissioned
HANSA	Y 806	Krögerwerft, Rendsburg	1958
NIOBE	Y 1643	Krögerwerft, Rendsburg	1958

HANSA

1975, Federal German Navy

Displacement, tons: 150 standard; 180 full load
Dimensions, feet (metres): 115·2 × 21·3 × 5·6 *(35·1 × 6·5 × 1·7)*
Gun: 1—40 mm
Mines: Laying capability
Main engines: *Hansa:* 1 Mercedes-Benz (MTU) diesel; 1 shaft; 950 bhp = 14 knots
  Niobe: 2 Mercedes-Benz (MTU) diesels; 2 shafts; 1 900 bhp = 16 knots
Range, miles: 1 100 at max speed
Complement: *Hansa* 19; *Niobe* 22

Hansa serves as support ship for clearance divers. *Niobe* is test and trials ship.

SERVICE FORCES

11 "RHEIN" CLASS (DEPOT SHIPS)

Name	No.	Builders	Commissioned
DONAU	A 69	Schlichting, Travemünde	1962
ELBE	A 61	Schliekerwerft, Hamburg	1961
ISAR	A 54	Blöhm and Voss	1963
LAHN	A 55	Flender, Lübeck	1963
LECH	A 56	Flender, Lübeck	1963
MAIN	A 63	Lindenau, Kiel	1961
MOSEL	A 67	Schliekerwerft, Hamburg	1962
NECKAR	A 66	Lürssen, Vegesack	1962
RHEIN	A 58	Schliekerwerft, Hamburg	1961
SAAR	A 65	Norderwerft, Hamburg	1962
WERRA	A 68	Lindenau, Kiel	1964

MOSEL

1974, Reiner Nerlich

Displacement, tons: 2 370 standard; 2 540 full load
  except *Lahn* and *Lech* 2 460 standard; 2 680 full load
Length, feet (metres): 304·5 *(92·8)* wl; 323·5 *(99)* oa
Beam, feet (metres): 38·8 *(11·8)*
Draught, feet (metres): 11·2 *(3·4)*; 12·2 *(3·7)* in *Lahn* and *Lech*
Guns: 2—3·9 in *(100 mm)*; none in *Lahn, Lech;* 4—40 mm
Main engines: 6 Maybach or Daimler (MTU) diesels; Diesel-electric drive in *Isar, Lahn, Lech, Mossel, Saar* 11 400 bhp; 2 shafts
Speed, knots: 20·5, 15 economical
Range, miles: 1 625 at 15 knots
Oil fuel, tons: 334
Complement: 110 (accommodation for 200); 198 *(Lahn and Lech)*

Originally a class of 13. Rated as depot ships for minesweepers *(Isar, Mosel, Saar)*, submarines *(Lahn, Lech)*, Type 206 submarines *(Rhein)*, and motor torpedo boats (others) but these ships with their 3·9 in *(100 mm)* guns could obviously be used in lieu of frigates.

Conversion: *Lahn* major conversion in 1975.

Radar: All by Hollandse. Search: HSA DA 02.
Fire control: Two HSA M 45 for 100 mm and 40 mm.

Status: Five of these comparatively new ships, namely *Donau, Isar, Lahn, Lech* and *Weser* (now deleted) were placed in reserve by July 1968. This was part of the economy programme announced by the Federal German Navy in Sep 1967 but all have subsequently been recommissioned or transferred.

Transfer: *Weser* to Greece 1975. *Rühr* to Turkey 1975.

2 Ex-US LST (REPAIR SHIPS)

ODIN (ex-USS *Diomedes*, ARB 11, ex-*LST 1119*) A 512
WOTAN (ex-USS *Ulysses*, ARB 9, ex-*LST 967*) A 513

WOTAN

1975, Federal German Navy

Displacement, tons: 1 625 light; 3 455 full load
Dimensions, feet (metres): 328 oa × 50 × 9·2 *(100 × 15·2 × 2·8)*
Guns: 4—20 mm
Main engines: 2 GM diesels, 2 shafts; 1 800 bhp = 11·6 knots
Oil fuel, tons: 600
Range, miles: 2 000 at 9 knots
Complement: 187

Repair ships. Transferred under MAP in June 1961.
Odin commissioned in Jan 1966 and *Wotan* on 2 Dec 1965. *Wotan* now civilian-manned.

MEMMERT Y 805

The small repair ship *Memmert* Y 805 (ex-USN *106*, ex-*India*, ex-*BP 34*), 165 tons and 8 knots, rated as torpedo repair ship, salvage vessel with a derrick.

1 REPLENISHMENT TANKER

Name	No.	Builders	Commissioned
FRANKENLAND	A 1439 (ex-Y 827)	Lithgow, Greenock	29 April 1959
(ex-*Münsterland*, ex-*Powell*)			

Displacement, tons: 11 708 standard; 16 060 full load
Dimensions, feet (metres): 521·8 × 70·2 × 37·5 *(167 × 21·4 × 9·1)*
Main engines: Diesels; 5 800 bhp = 13·5 knots

Launched in 1950.

FRANKENLAND   1972

2 "EMSLAND" CLASS (REPLENISHMENT TANKERS)

Name	No.	Builders	Commissioned
EMSLAND	A 1440 (ex-Y 828)	CRDA Monfalcone	7 Nov 1961
(ex-*Antonio Zotti*)			
MÜNSTERLAND	A 1441 (ex-Y 829)	Ansaldo, Genoa	16 Oct 1961
(ex-*Angela Germona*)			

Displacement, tons: 6 200 gross *(Emsland)*; 6 191 *(Münsterland)*
Dimensions, feet (metres): 461 × 54·2 × 25·8 *(141 × 16·5 × 7·8)*
Main engines: Diesels; CRDA, 4 800 bhp *(Emsland)*; Fiat 5 500 bhp *(Münsterland)* = 12·5 knots

Both launched in 1943. Completed in 1947 and 1946 respectively. Purchased in 1960 from Italian owners. Converted in 1960-61 by Schliekerwerft, Hamburg, and Howaldtswerke, Hamburg, respectively. Civilian crew.

EMSLAND   1975, Reiner Nerlich

2 "BODENSEE" CLASS (REPLENISHMENT TANKERS)

Name	No.	Builders	Commissioned
BODENSEE (ex-*Unkas*)	A 1406 (ex-A 54)	Lindenau, Kiel	26 Mar 1959
WITTENSEE (ex-*Sioux*)	A 1407	Lindenau, Kiel	26 Mar 1959

Measurement, tons: 1 238 deadweight; 985 gross
Dimensions, feet (metres): 208·3 × 32·5 × 15 *(61·2 × 9·8 × 4·3)*
Main engines: Diesels; 1 050—1 250 bhp = 12 knots
Complement: 21

Launched on 19 Nov 1955 and on 23 Sep 1958, respectively.
Details above for *Bodensee*—*Wittensee* slightly larger.

WITTENSEE   5/1975, Reiner Nerlich

1 REPLENISHMENT TANKER

Name	No.	Builders	Commissioned
EIFEL (ex-*Friedrich Jung*)	A 1429	Norderwerft, Hamburg	27 May 1963

Displacement, tons: 4 720
Dimensions, feet (metres): 334 × 47·2 × 23·3 *(102 × 14·4 × 7·1)*
Main engines: 3 360 hp = 13 knots

Launched on 29 Mar 1958. Purchased in 1963 for service in the Federal German Navy.

EIFEL   1970, Federal German Navy

4 "WALCHENSEE" CLASS (TYPE 703) (SUPPORT TANKERS)

Name	No.	Builders	Commissioned
AMMERSEE	A 1425	Lindenau, Kiel	2 Mar 1967
TEGERNSEE	A 1426	Lindenau, Kiel	23 Mar 1967
WALCHENSEE	A 1424	Lindenau, Kiel	29 June 1966
WESTENSEE	A 1427	Lindenau, Kiel	6 Oct 1967

Displacement, tons: 2 174
Dimensions, feet (metres): 233 × 36·7 × 13·5 *(74·2 × 11·2 × 4·1)*
Main engines: Diesels; 2 shafts; 1 400 bhp = 12·6 knots

Launched on 22 Sep 1966, 22 Oct 1966, 10 July 1965 and 25 Feb 1966 respectively.

WALCHENSEE   1975, Reiner Nerlich

1 SUPPORT TANKER

Name	No.	Builders	Commissioned
HARZ (ex-*Claere Jung*)	A 1428	Norderwerft, Hamburg	27 May 1963 (see note)

Displacement, tons: 3 696 deadweight
Dimensions, feet (metres): 303·2 × 43·5 × 21·7 *(92·4 × 13·2 × 6·6)*
Main engines: 2 520 hp = 12 knots

Built in 1953 and purchased in 1963 for service as a tanker.

HARZ   *1970, Federal German Navy*

8 "LÜNEBURG" CLASS (SUPPORT SHIPS)

Name	No.	Builders	Commissioned
COBURG	A 1412	Flensburger Schiffbau	9 July 1968
FREIBURG	A 1413	Blöhm and Voss	27 May 1968
GLÜCKSBURG	A 1414	Flensburger, Schiffbau	9 July 1968
LÜNEBURG	A 1411	Flensburger, Schiffbau	9 July 1968
MEERSBURG	A 1418	Vulkan, Bremen	25 June 1968
NIENBURG	A 1416	Vulkan, Bremen	1 Aug 1968
OFFENBURG	A 1417	Blöhm and Voss	27 May 1968
SAARBURG	A 1415	Blöhm and Voss	30 July 1968

Displacement, tons: 3 254
Dimensions, feet (metres): 341·2 × 43·3 × 13·8 *(104 × 13·2 × 4·2)*
Guns: 4—40 mm
Main engines: 2 Maybach (MTU) diesels; 2 shafts; 5 600 bhp = 17 knots
Complement: 103

Modernisation: Four of this class are being lengthened and modernised to serve the new classes of Fast Attack Craft, including MM 38 Exocet maintenance. *Saarburg* completed 1975—*Lüneburg* now in hand.

GLÜCKSBURG   *5/1975, Reiner Nerlich*

2 "WESTERWALD" CLASS (AMMUNITION TRANSPORTS)

Name	No.	Builders	Commissioned
ODENWALD	A 1436	Lübecker, Masch	23 Mar 1967
WESTERWALD	A 1435	Lubecker, Masch	1 Feb 1967

Displacement, tons: 3 460
Dimensions, feet (metres): 347·8 × 46 × 12·2 *(106 × 14 × 3·7)*
Guns: 4—40 mm
Main engines: MTU diesel; 5 600 bhp = 17 knots
Complement: 60

Odenwald was launched on 5 May 1966 and *Westerwald* was launched on 25 Feb 1966.

WESTERWALD   *Federal German Navy*

2 "SACHSENWALD" CLASS (MINE TRANSPORTS)

Name	No.	Builders	Commissioned
SACHESENWALD	A 1437	Blöhm and Voss, Hamburg	20 Aug 1969
STEIGERWALD	A 1438	Blöhm and Voss, Hamburg	20 Aug 1969

Displacement, tons: 3 850 full load
Dimensions, feet (metres): 363·5 × 45·6 × 11·2 *(111 × 13·9 × 3·4)*
Guns: 4—40 mm (two twin mountings)
Mines: Laying capacity
Main engines: 2 MTU diesels; 2 shafts; 5 600 hp = 17 knots
Range, miles: 3 500
Complement: 65

Built as mine transports. Laid down on 1 Aug 1966 and 9 May 1966. Launched on 10 Dec 1966 and 10 Mar 1967. Have mine ports in the stern and can be used as minelayers.

SACHSENWALD   *5/1975, Reiner Nerlich*

5 "FW" CLASS (WATER BOATS)

FW 1 Y 864   **FW 2** Y 865   **FW 3** Y 866   **FW 4** Y 867   **FW 5** Y 868

Measurement, tons: 350 deadweight
Dimensions, feet (metres): 144·4 × 25·6 × 8·2 *(44·1 × 7·8 × 2·5)*
Main engines: MWM diesel; 230 bhp = 9·5 knots

Built in pairs by Schiffbarges, Unterweser, Bremerhaven; H. Rancke, Hamburg and Jadewerft, Wilhelmshaven, in 1963-64. *FW 6* to Turkey 1975.

TRAINING SHIPS

1 "DEUTSCHLAND" CLASS

Name	No.	Builders	Commissioned
DEUTSCHLAND	A 59	Nobiskrug, Rendesburg	25 May 1963

Displacement, tons: 4 880 normal; 5 400 full load
Length, feet (metres): 452·8 *(138·0)* pp; 475·8 *(145·0)* oa
Beam, feet (metres): 59 *(18)*
Draught, feet (metres): 15·7 *(4·8)*
Aircraft: 1 A/S helicopter
Guns: 4—3·9 in *(100 mm)* (single); 6—40 mm (2 twin and 2 single)
A/S weapons: 2 Bofors 4-barrel rocket launchers
Torpedo tubes: 2—21 in *(533 mm)* (surface targets); 4—21 in *(533 mm)* (A/S)
Mines: Laying capacity
Main engines: 6 800 bhp MTU diesels (2 Daimler-Benz and 2 Maybach); 2 shafts with VP propellers; 8 000 shp double reduction MAN geared turbines; 1 shaft
Boilers: 2 Wahodag; 768 psi *(54 km/cm²)*; 870°F (465°C)
Speed, knots: 22 (3 shafts); 17 (2 shafts) 14 economical (1 shaft)
Oil fuel, tons: 230 furnace; 410 diesel
Range, miles: 6 000 at 17 knots
Complement: 554 (33 officers, 271 men, 250 cadets)

First West German naval ship to exceed the post-war limit of 3 000 tons. Designed with armament and machinery of different types for training purposes. The name originally planned for this ship was *Berlin*. Ordered in 1956. Laid down in 1959 and launched 5 Nov 1960. Carried out her first machinery sea trials on 15 Jan 1963.

Electronics: HSA fire control for Bofors A/S launchers and Torpedoes.

Sonar: 1 M/F hull-mounted set.

DEUTSCHLAND   1975, Federal German Navy

Radar: All by Hollandse Signaalapparaten.
Navigation/surface warning: one set.
Air warning: one LW-02/3
Target designator: one DA 02.
Fire control: two M 45 series.

1 SAIL TRAINING SHIP

Name	No.	Builders	Commissioned
GORCH FOCK	A 60	Blöhm and Voss, Hamburg	17 Dec 1958

Displacement, tons: 1 760 standard; 1 870 full load
Dimensions, feet (metres): 257 oa × 39·2 × 15·8 *(81·3 × 12 × 4·8)*
Main engines: Auxiliary MAN diesel; 880 bhp = 11 knots
Sail area, sq ft: 21 141
Range, miles: 1 990 on auxiliary diesel
Complement: 206 (10 officers, 56 ratings, 140 cadets)

Sail training ship of the improved "Horst Wessel" type. Barque rig. Launched on 23 Aug 1958.

GORCH FOCK   8/1975, Reiner Nerlich

1 SAIL TRAINING SHIP

Name	No.	Builders	Commissioned
NORDWIND	Y 834	—	1944

Displacement, tons: 110
Dimensions, feet (metres): 78·8 × 22 × 9 *(24 × 6·4 × 2·5)*
Main engines: Diesel; 150 bhp = 8 knots (Sail area 2 037·5 sq ft)

Ketch rigged.

There are over 70 other sailing vessels of various types serving for sail training and recreational purposes. *Achat, Alarich, Amsel, Argonaut, Borasco, Brigant, Dankwart, Diamont, Dietrich, Drossel, Dompfaff, Fafnir, Fink, Flibustier, Freibeuter, Gernot, Geiserich, Geuse, Giselher, Gödicke, Gunnar, Gunter, Hadubrand, Hagen, Hartnaut, Hilderbrand, Horand, Hunding, Jaspis, Kaper, Klipper, Korsar, Kuchkuch, Lerche, Likendeeler, Magellan, Michel, Mime, Meise, Mistral, Monsun, Nachtigall, Ortwin, Ostwind, Pampero, Pirol, Ruediger, Samum, Saphir, Schirocco, Seeteufel, Siegfried, Siegmund, Siegura, Smaragd, Star, Stieglitz, Storetbecker, Taifun, Teja, Topas, Tornadon, Totila, Vitalienbrüder, Volker, Walter, Wate, Westwind, Wiking, Wittigo, Zeisig.*

1 S.A.R. LAUNCH

Name	No.	Builders	Commissioned
FL 11	Y 863 (ex-D 2766)	Kröger, Rendsburg	1955

Displacement, tons: 70
Dimensions, feet (metres): 95·2 × 15·6 × 4·2 *(29 × 5 × 1·3)*
Main engines: Maybach (MTU) diesels; 2 shafts; 3 200 bhp = 30 knots
Range, miles: 600 at 25 knots

FL 10 (FL 11 similar)   1972

13 TORPEDO RECOVERY VESSELS

TF 1-6 (Y 851-856)   **TF 101-104** (Y 883-886)   **TF 106-108** (Y 872-874)

All of approximately 30-40 tons. TF 1-6 and 106-108 built in 1966, the remainder a deal older.

TF 108   1974, Reiner Nerlich

COASTAL PATROL CRAFT

KW 15 Y 827		**KW 18** Y 832	
KW 16 Y 830		**KW 19** Y 833	
KW 17 Y 845		**KW 20** Y 846	

Displacement, tons: 45 standard; 60 full load
Dimensions, feet (metres): 93·5 oa × 15·5 × 4·0 *(28·9 × 4·9 × 1·5)*
Main engines: 2 Mercedes-Benz (MTU) diesels; 2 000 bhp = 25 knots
Complement: 14

Built in 1951-53.

KW 3 Y 829. Of 112 tons and 8 knots built in 1943.

KW 18   *5/1975, Reiner Nerlich*

TUGS

6 SALVAGE TUGS

Name	No.	Builders	Commissioned	
BALTRUM	A 1454	Schichau, Bremerhaven	8 Oct	1968
JUIST	A 1456	Schichau, Bremerhaven		1968
LANGEOOG	A 1453	Schichau, Bremerhaven	14 Aug	1968
NORDERNEY	A 1455	Schichau, Bremerhaven		1968
SPIEKEROOG	A 1452	Schichau, Bremerhaven	14 Aug	1968
WANGEROOGE	A 1451	Schichau, Bremerhaven	9 April	1968

Displacement, tons: 854 standard; 1 024 full load
Dimensions, feet (metres): 170·6 × 39·4 × 12·8 *(52·0 × 12·1 × 3·9)*
Gun: 1—40 mm
Main engines: Diesel-electric; 2 shafts; 2 400 hp = 14 knots
Range, miles: 5 000 at 10 knots
Complement: 24-35

Wangerooge, prototype salvage tug, was launched on 4 July 1966, *Baltrum* on 8 Oct 1968. *Baltrum* diving training ship (1974).

SPIEKEROOG   *2/1976, Reiner Nerlich*

2 SALVAGE TUGS

Name	No.	Builders	Commissioned	
FEHMARN	A 1458	Unterweser, Bremerhaven	1 Feb	1967
HELGOLAND	A 1457	Unterweser, Bremerhaven	8 Mar	1966

Displacement, tons: 1 310 standard; 1 643 full load
Dimensions, feet (metres): 223·1 × 41·7 × 14·4 *(68·0 × 12·7 × 4·4)*
Guns: 2—40 mm
Main engines: Diesel-electric; 4 MWM diesels; 2 shafts; 3 800 hp = 17 knots
Range, miles: 6 000 at 10 knots
Complement: 36-45

Launched on 25 Nov 1965 and 8 April 1965. Carry firefighting equipment.

FEHMARN   *1974, Federal German Navy—Marineamt*

4 HARBOUR TUGS

Name	No.	Builders	Commissioned
AMRUM	Y 822	Schichau, Bremerhaven	1963
FÖHR	Y 821	Schichau, Bremerhaven	1962
NEUWERK	Y 823	Schichau, Bremerhaven	1963
SYLT	Y 820	Schichau, Bremerhaven	1962

Displacement, tons: 266 standard
Dimensions, feet (metres): 100·7 oa × 25·2 *(30·6 × 7·5)*
Main engines: 1 Deutz diesel 800 bhp = 12 knots
Complement: 10

Launched in 1961.

SYLT   *1974, Federal German Navy*

1 COASTAL TUG

me	No.	Builders	Commissioned
LLWORM	Y 801	Schichau, Königsberg	1939

splacement, tons: 437 standard; 500 full load
mensions, feet (metres): 138·7 × 27·9 × 3·6 (38·7 × 8·5 × 1·2)
ain engines: 1—MWM-DM Diesel; 1 shaft; 800 hp = 12 knots
nge, miles: 2 900 at 8 knots

3 HARBOUR TUGS

me	No.	Builders	Commissioned
LERBEK	Y 1682	Schichau, Bremerhaven	1971
PPENS	Y 1681	Schichau, Bremerhaven	1971
UENDE	Y 1680	Schichau, Bremerhaven	1971

splacement, tons: 122
mensions, feet (metres): 87·2 × 24·3 × 8·5 (26·6 × 7·4 × 2·6)
ain engines: 1 MWM diesel; 1 shaft; 800 hp
eed, knots: 12
mplement: 6

ELLERBEK   1975, Federal German Navy

rbour Type: There are also ten small harbour tugs all completed in 1958-60:—*Blauort* Y 803, *echtsand* Y 814, *Langeness* Y 819, *Lütje Horn* Y 812, *Mellum* Y 813, *Nordstrand* Y 817, *Plon* Y *2, Scharhörn* Y 815, *Trischen* Y 818 and *Vogelsand* Y 816.

ICEBREAKERS

me	No.	Builders	Commissioned
NSE	—	Wärtsilä, Helsinki	13 Dec 1966

splacement, tons: 3 700
mensions, feet (metres): 243·2 × 57 × 20 (74·2 × 17·4 × 6·1)
ain engines: Diesel-electric; 4 shafts; 7 500 bhp = 16 knots

d down on 12 Jan 1965. Launched on 17 Oct 1966. Completed on 25 Nov 1966. Although rned by West Germany she sails under the Finnish flag, manned by a Finnish crew. Only when winter is so severe that icebreakers are needed in the southern Baltic will she be transferred der the German flag and command. She is of improved "Karhu" class. She does not belong to e Bundesmarine.

me	No.	Builders	Commissioned
SBAR	A 1402	J. G. Hitzler, Lauenburg	1 Nov 1961
SVOGEL	A 1401	J. G. Hitzler, Lauenburg	11 Mar 1961

splacement, tons: 560 standard
mensions, feet (metres): 125·3 × 31·2 × 15·1 (38·2 × 9·5 × 4·6)
ın: 1—40 mm
ain engines: 2 Maybach diesels; 2 shafts; 2 000 bhp = 14 knots

unched on 9 June and 28 April 1960 respectively.

EISVOGEL   5/1975, Reiner Nerlich

AUXILIARY SHIPS

1 Ex-BRITISH "ISLES" CLASS MSC (MC TRAINING SHIP)

me	No.	Builders	Commissioned
DER	Y 1663	Davie & Sons	1942
(ex-*Catherine*, ex-*Dochet*)	(ex-*A 50*)	Lauzon, Canada	

splacement, tons: 480 standard; 750 full load
mensions, feet (metres): 164·0 pp; 177·2 oa × 27·5 × 14·0 (53·9 × 8·4 × 4)
ıns: 1—40 mm; 1—20 mm
ain engines: Triple expansion; 1 shaft; 750 ihp = 12 knots
nge, miles: 3 700
l fuel, tons: 130
mplement: 45

nployed as a mine clearance training vessel. She has been civilian manned since 1 Jan 1968.

EIDER   5/1975, Reiner Nerlich

1 RADAR TRIALS SHIP

Name	No.	Builders	Commissioned
OSTE (ex-*Puddefjord*, ex-USN *101*)	A 52	Akers Mekaniske V, Oslo	1943

Displacement, tons: 567 gross
Dimensions, feet (metres): 160 × 29·7 × 17 *(48·8 × 9 × 5·2)*
Main engines: 1 Akers diesel; 1 shaft; 1 600 bhp = 12 knots

Taken over from the US Navy. Converted in 1968.

OSTE (as radar testing ship)   1970, Stefan Terzibaschitsc

2 RADAR TRIALS SHIPS

Name	No.	Builders	Commissioned
ALSTE (ex-*Mellum*)	A 50	Unterweser, Bremen	1972
OKER (ex-*Hoheweg*)	A 53	Unterweser, Bremen	1972

Measurement, tons: 1 187
Dimensions, feet (metres): 237·8 × 34·4 × 16·1 *(72·5 × 10·5 × 4·9)*
Main engines: Diesel-electric; 1 screw = 15 knots
Complement: 30

1 DIVING TENDER

Name	No.	Builders	Commissioned
EMS (ex-*Harle*, ex-USN *104*)	Y 1662 (ex-*A 53*)	Kremer, Elmshorn	1941

Measurement, tons: 660 gross
Dimensions, feet (metres): 185·7 oa × 29 × 15·5 *(56·6 × 8·8 × 4·7)*
Guns: 4—20 mm
Main engines: Sulzer diesels; 1 000 bhp = 12 knots
Range, miles: 2 400 at 12 knots

EMS   2/1976, Reiner Nerlic

1 DEGAUSSING SHIP

Name	No.	Builders	Commissioned
WALTHER VON LEDEBUR	Y 841	Burmester, Bremen	1966

Displacement, tons: 725
Dimensions, feet (metres): 219·8 × 34·8 × 8·9 *(63 × 10·6 × 2·7)*
Main engines: Maybach (MTU) diesels; 2 shafts; 5 000 bhp = 19 knots
Complement: 11 + 10

Wooden hulled vessel. Trials ship. Launched on 30 June 1966.

WALTHER VON LEDEBUR   10/1975, Reiner Nerlic

5 Ex-COASTAL MINESWEEPERS

ADOLF BESTELMEYER (ex-*BYMS 2213*) Y 881
H.C. OERSTED (ex-*Vinstra*, ex-*NYMS 247*) Y 877
HERMAN VON HELMOLTZ Y 878
RUDOLF DIESEL (ex-*BYMS 2279*) Y 889
OT 2 Y 847

Displacement, tons: 270 standard; 350 full load
Dimensions, feet (metres): 136 × 24·5 × 8 *(41·5 × 7·5 × 2·4)*
Main engines: 2 MTU diesels; 2 shafts; 1 000 bhp = 15 knots

Of US YMS type. Built in 1943. *Adolf Bestelmeyer* and *Rudolf Diesel* are used for gunnery trials.
H. C. Oersted was acquired from the Royal Norwegian Navy and with *Herman von Helmholtz*,
commissioned on 18 Dec 1962, used as degaussing ships.

ADOLF BESTELMEYER

PLANET A 1450 of 1 943 tons and 13·5 knots. Built in 1965. Weapons research ship.

WILHELM PULLWER Y 838, **SP 1** Y 837 of 160 tons and 12·5 knots. Built in 1966. Trials ships.

HEINZ ROGGENKAMP Y 871. Of 785 tons and 12 knots. Built in 1952. Trials ship.

FRIEDRICH VOGE Y 888. Of 179 tons. Trials ship.

OTTO MEYCKE Diving Trials.

EF 3 Y 840 of 100 tons and 13·4 knots, ex-FPB built in 1943. Trials ship.

TB 1 Y 1678 of 70 tons and 14 knots. Diving boat built in 1972.

LP 1, 2 and **3**. Battery workshop craft of 180 tons built in 1963-73.

FÖRDE Y 1641   **JADE** Y 1642

Tank cleaning vessels. Of 600 tons, completed in 1967.

FÖRDE

8/1975, Stefan Terzibaschitsch

KNURRHAHN Y 811 of 261 tons.
ARCONA (ex-*Royal Prince*) Y 809

Both accommodation ships. *Arcona* ex-liner.

BARBARA Y 844, lifting ship of 3 500 tons.

GRIEP Y 876, **HIEV** Y 875, Floating cranes.

SURVEY SHIPS

1 "VEGESACK" CLASS

PASSAU

Displacement, tons: 362 standard; 378 full load
Dimensions, feet (metres): 144·3 oa × 26·2 × 9 *(44·2 × 8 × 2·7)*
Main engines: 2 Mercedes-Benz (MTU) diesels; 1 500 hp; 2 shafts; CP propellers = 15 knots

The last of 6 "Vegesack" class minesweepers built in Cherbourg 1959-60. Converted for oceanographic research. Other five transferred to Turkey.

The following ships operate for the Deutsches Hydrographisches Institut, under the Ministry of Transport.

METEOR (research ship) 3 085 tons, launched 1964, complement 55
KOMET (survey and research) 1 595 tons, launched 1969, complement 42
GAUSS (survey and research) 1 074 tons, launched 1949, complement 40
SÜDEROOG (survey ship) 211 tons, launched 1956, complement 16
ATAIR (survey and wrecks) 148 tons, launched 1962, complement 13
WEGA (survey and wrecks) 148 tons, launched 1962, complement 12

GAUSS

1974, Reiner Nerlich

COASTGUARD VESSELS
(BUNDESGRENZSCHUTZ—SEE)

Note: This paramilitary force consists of about 1 000 men who operate the craft below as well as helicopters.

8 LARGE PATROL CRAFT

ALSFELD BG 16
BAD BRAMSTEDT BG 12
BAYREUTH BG 17
DUDERSTADT BG 14

ESCHWEGE BG 15
NEUSTADT BG 11
ROSENHEIM BG 18
UELTZEN BG 13

Displacement, tons: 203
Length, feet (metres): 127·1 *(38·5)*
Guns: 2—40 mm
Main engines: 3 MTU diesels; 4 500 hp = 30 knots

All built between 1969 and late 1970—BG 13 by Schlichting, Travemünde, the remainder by Lürssen, Vegesack. Form two flotillas: BG 11-14 the 1st and BG 15-18 the 2nd. A third flotilla of smaller craft has been formed.

ROSENHEIM

8/1974, Dittmair

1 TUG

A 600 hp tug was ordered autumn 1975 from Mützelfeldtwerft, Cuxhaven to complete in 1976. Voight-Schneider propeller.

FISHERY PROTECTION SHIPS

Operated by Ministry of Agriculture and Fisheries.

ANTON DOHRN of 1 950 tons and 15 knots
FRITHJOF of 2 150 tons and 15 knots.
MEERKATZE of 1 000 tons and 12 knots.
MINDEN of 973 tons and 16 knots.
NORDENHAM of 975 tons and 16 knots.
POSEIDON of 935 tons and 12 knots.
ROTERSAND of 1 000 tons. Built in 1974.
SOLEA of 340 tons and 12 knots.
UTHÖRN of 110 tons and 9 knots.
WALTHER HERTWIG of 2 500 tons and 15 knots.

GERMANY (Democratic Republic)

Headquarters Appointments

Commander-in-Chief, Volksmarine:
Vice Admiral Willi Ehm
Chief of Naval Staff:
Rear Admiral Gustav Hesse

Personnel

(a) 1973: 1 700 officers and 15 200 men (including GBK)
1974: 1 750 officers and 15 300 men (including GBK)
1975: 1 800 officers and 15 500 men (including GBK)
1976: 1 850 officers and 16 000 men (including GBK)

(b) 18 months National Service

Mercantile Marine

Lloyd's Register of Shipping:
437 vessels of 1 389 000 tons gross

Bases

Rostock/Gehlsdorf: Navy Headquarters;
Peenemunde: HQ 1st Flotilla;
Warnemunde: HQ 4th Flotilla;
Dranske-Bug: HQ 6th Flotilla;
Sassuitz: Minor base;
Wolgast: Minor base;
Tarnewitz: minor base.

Naval Air

1 squadron with 8 Mi-4 helicopters

Grenzbrigade Kuste (GBK)

The seaborne branch of the Frontier Guards, this is a force of about 3 000 men. Their various craft are difficult to disentangle from those of the Navy, many being taken from that list. Where possible, mention of this is made in the notes.

Strength of the Fleet

Type	Active	Building
Frigates	2	—
Corvettes	18	—
Fast Attack Craft—Missile	12	—
Fast Attack Craft—Torpedo	58	—
Fast Attack Craft—Patrol	4 (GBK)	—
Coastal Patrol Craft	18	—
Landing Ships and Craft	18	—
Minesweepers—Coastal	52	3
Intelligence Ships	3	—
Survey Ships	4	—
Supply Ships	4	—
Support Tankers	4	—
Buoy Tenders	17	—
Ice Breakers	3	—
Tugs	13	—
Tenders	4	—
Training Ships and Craft	10	—
Cable Layer	1	—
Torpedo Recovery Vessels	2	—

FRIGATES

2 Ex-SOVIET "RIGA" CLASS

ERNEST THÄLMANN 141   **KARL MARX** 142

Displacement, tons: 1 200 standard; 1 600 full load
Dimensions, feet (metres): 298·8 × 33·7 × 11 *(91 × 10·2 × 3·4)*
Guns: 3—3·9 in (single); 4—37 mm (twin)
Tubes: 2—21 in
A/S weapons: 4 depth charge projectors; 2 MBUs
Mines: Can carry 50
Main engines: Geared turbines; 2 shafts; 25 000 shp = 28 knots
Oil fuel, tons: 300
Range, miles: 2 500 at 15 knots
Complement: 150

Sister ships *Friedrich Engels* 124 and *Karl Liebnecht* 123 were scrapped in 1971. A fifth ship of this type was burnt out at the end of 1959 and became a total wreck. Two of these hulks are beached at Warnemünde.

Radar: Slim Net; Sun Visor; Neptun.

Torpedo tubes: The triple 21 in tubes were replaced by a modern twin mounting in 1974.

KARL MARX   *1965, Werner Kähling*

CORVETTES

4 Ex-SOVIET "SO-I" CLASS

421   422   423   424

Displacement, tons: 215 standard; 250 full load
Dimensions, feet (metres): 138 × 20 × 9·2 *(42·3 × 6·1 × 2·8)*
Guns: 4—25 mm (2 twin mounts)
A/S weapons: 4 MBU 1 800 5 barrelled launchers; 2 DCT
Main engines: 3 diesels; 6 000 bhp = 29 knots
Range, miles: 1 100 at 13 knots
Complement: 30

Fitted with mine rails. These vessels belonged to the coast guard (GBK) but have now been returned to the navy.

"SO-I" Class   *1970, Niels Gartig*

14 "HAI" CLASS

BAD DOBERAN	LÜBZ	RIBNITZ-DAMGARTEN
BÜTZOW	LUDWIGSLUST	STERNBERG
GREVESMÜHLEN	PARCHIM	TETEROW
GADEBUSCH	PERLEBERG	WISMAR + 2

Displacement, tons: 300 standard; 370 full load
Dimensions, feet (metres): 174 pp; 187 oa × 19 × 10 *(53·1, 57 × 5·8 × 3·1)*
Guns: 4—30 mm (2 twin)
A/S weapons: 2 MBU 1 800 5 barrelled launchers
Main engines: 2 gas turbines; diesels; 8 000 bhp = 25 knots
Complement: 45

Built by Peenewerft, Wolgast. The prototype vessel was completed in 1963. All were in service by the end of 1969, and the programme is now completed.
Pennant numbers are: 411-414, 431-434, 451-454, V 81 and 1 unknown.

"HAI" Class (above)   *1974*

"HAI" Class (left)   *1973*

LIGHT FORCES

12 Ex-SOVIET "OSA" CLASS (FAST ATTACK CRAFT—MISSILE)

ARVID HARNACK
AUGUST LUTTGENS
FRITZ GAST
HEINRICH DORRENBACH
JOSEF SCHARES
KARL MESEBERG

MAX REICHPIETSCH
OTTO TOST
PAUL EISENSCHNEIDER
PAUL WIECZOREK
RICHARD SORGE
RUDOLF EGELHOFER

Displacement, tons: 165 standard; 200 full load
Dimensions, feet (metres): 128·7 × 25·1 × 5·9 *(39·3 × 7·7 × 1·8)*
Missiles: 4 mountings in 2 pairs for SSN-2 system
Guns: 4—30 mm (2 twin, 1 forward, 1 aft)
Main engines: 3 diesels; 13 000 hp = 36 knots

Pennant numbers: 711-714, 731-734, 751-754.

"OSA I" Class

1965, Reinecke

15 Ex-SOVIET "SHERSHEN" CLASS
(FAST ATTACK CRAFT—TORPEDO)

ADAM KUCKHOFF
ANTON SAEFKOW
ARTHUR BECKER
BERNHARD BÄSTLEIN
BRUNO KÜHN
EDGAR ANDRÉ
ERNST GRUBE
ERNST SCHNELLER

FIETE SCHULZE
FRITZ BEHN
FRITZ HECKERT
HANS COPPI
HEINZ KAPELLE
RUDOLF BREITSCHEID
WILLI BANSCH

Displacement, tons: 150 standard; 160 full load
Dimensions, feet (metres): 115·5 × 23·1 × 5 *(35·2 × 7·1 × 1·5)*
Guns: 4—30 mm (2 twin)
A/S weapons: 12 DC
Tubes: 4—21 in (single)
Main engines: 3 Diesels; 13 000 bhp; 3 shafts = 41 knots
Complement: 16

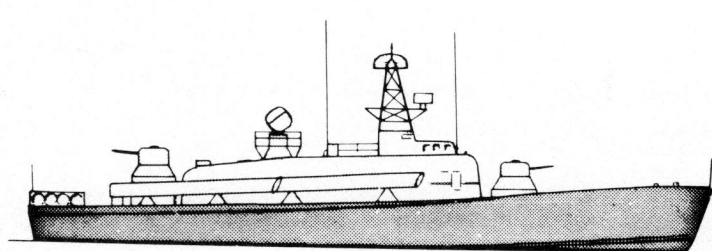

"SHERSHEN" Class

Acquired from the USSR. Four were delivered in 1968-69, the first installment of a flotilla. They do not differ from the Soviet boats of the class.
Pennant numbers 811-5, 831-5, 851-5.

3 "LIBELLE" CLASS (FAST ATTACK CRAFT—TORPEDO)

Displacement, tons: 20
Dimensions, feet (metres): 52·5 × 11·5 × 3·6 *(16 × 3·5 × 1·1)*
Guns: 2—12·7 mm
Torpedo tubes: 2—21 inch (stern launching)
Main engines: Diesels = 45 knots

A new class first reported in 1975.

40 "ILTIS" CLASS (FAST ATTACK CRAFT—TORPEDO)

Displacement, tons: 20
Dimensions, feet (metres): 55·8 × 10·5 × 2·5 *(17 × 3·2 × 0·8)*
Tubes: 2—21 in (torpedoes fired over stern). Some have three tubes (Type 3)
Mines can be carried in place of torpedo tubes
Main engines: Diesels; 3 000 bhp = 30 knots

No guns. Several different types of this class exist, varying in hull material and silhouette, eg Type 1 are flush-decked and Type 2 have a raised forecastle. With the torpedo tubes removed these boats are used to land frogmen and raiding parties. Displacement and dimensions given are for Type 2. Others vary slightly. Built by Mitteldeutschland, starting in 1962. Some pennant numbers in 970, 980, 990 series.

"ILTIS" Class

1971, S. Breyer

4 Ex-SOVIET "P 6" CLASS (FAST ATTACK CRAFT—PATROL)

Displacement, tons: 66 standard; 75 full load
Dimensions, feet (metres): 84·2 × 20 × 6 *(25·7 × 6·1 × 1·8)*
Guns: 4—25 mm (2 twin mountings) (removed in target boats)
Main engines: 4 diesels; 4 800 bhp; 4 shafts = 43 knots
Range, miles: 450 at 30 knots
Complement: 25

Acquired in 1957-60 from the USSR. Originally there were 27. Wooden hull. Most of this class has been scrapped or converted. Four have had their tubes removed and been transferred to the GBK with pennant Nos G81-84. Pot Head radar.

18 "KB 123" CLASS (COASTAL PATROL CRAFT)

Displacement, tons: about 25
Dimensions, feet (metres): 74 × 16·4 × — *(23 × 5 × —)*
Main engines: 2 Diesels = 14 knots

This class (total uncertain) was introduced in 1971 for operations on rivers and inland waterways by the GBK. It appears to be fast and unarmed, though small arms are certainly carried.

"KB 123" Class

1972

AMPHIBIOUS FORCES

6 "ROBBE" CLASS (LST)

EBERSWALDE	GRIMMEN	LÜBBEN
ELSENHÜTTENSTADT	HOYERSWERDA	SCHWEDT

Displacement, tons: 600 standard; 800 full load
Dimensions, feet (metres): 196·8 × 32·8 × 6·6 *(60 × 10 × 2·0)*
Guns: 2—57 mm (1 twin); 4—25 mm (2 twin)
Main engines: Diesels = 12 knots

Launched in 1962-64. Can carry 500 tons stores and vehicles.

"ROBBE" Class   1971, S. Breyer

12 "LABO" CLASS (LCT)

GERHARD PRENZLER	HEINZ WILKOWSKI	ROLF PETERS + 9

Displacement, tons: 150 standard; 200 full load
Dimensions, feet (metres): 131·2 × 27·9 × 5·9 *(40·0 × 8·5 × 1·8)*
Guns: 4—25 mm (2 twin)
Main engines: Diesels = 10 knots

Built by Peenewerft, Wolgast. Launched in 1961-63.

"LABO" Class   1969, S. Breyer

MINE WARFARE FORCES

52 "KONDOR I" and "II" CLASS
(MINESWEEPERS—COASTAL)

AHRENSHOOP	GUBEN	ROSSLAU
ALTENTREPTOW	GREIFSWALD	SCHÖNEBECK
ANKLAM	KAMENZ	STRALSUND
BANSIN	KLÜTZ	STRASBURG
BERGEN	KUHLUNGSBORN	TANGERHÜTTE
BITTERFELD	KYRITZ	TEMPLIN
BERNAU	NEURUPPIN	UCKERMÜNDE
BOLTENHAGEN	NEUSTRELITZ	VITTE
DEMMIN	ORANIENBURG	WARNEMÜNDE
DESSAU	PASEWALK	WEISSWASSER
EILENBURG	PREROW	WITTSTOCK
EISLEBEN	PRITZWALK	WOLGAST
GENTHIN	RATHENOW	ZERBST
GRAAL-MÜRITZ	RIESA	ZINGST
GRIMMA	ROBEL	+8

Displacement, tons: 245 standard; 280 full load
Dimensions, feet (metres): 154·2 × 23·0 × 6·6 *(47 × 7 × 2)* (Kondor II plus 2 metres)
Guns: 2—25 mm or 2—30 mm (Kondor I); 6—25 mm (twins) (Kondor II)
Main engines: 2 diesels; 2 shafts; 4 000 bhp = 21 knots

"KONDOR II" Class   1973, S. Breyer

Built by Peenewerft Wolgast. Five units were operational in 1970 and 15 by the end of 1971. They replace the small minesweepers of the "Schwalbe" class. Type II has additional length and extra MGs. First appeared in 1971. Production continues.

PENNANT NUMBERS

These have been changed with some frequency. At present the following is as near as can be offered;

Type I (Total 22)   Prototype-V31. S24-26. Attached to GBK;-G11-16. G21-26, G41-46. Conversion for torpedo recovery—B73 and B74. Conversion to AGIs Meteor and Komet.

Type II (Total 30)   Prototype—V32. Active minesweepers 311-316, 321-327, 331-336 341-347. S21-23.

INTELLIGENCE SHIPS

2 "KONDOR I" CLASS

METEOR	KOMET

Displacement, tons: 245 standard; 280 full load
Dimensions, feet (metres): 154·2 × 23·0 × 6·6 *(47 × 7 × 2)*
Guns: 2—30 mm
Main engines: 2 diesels; 2 shafts; 4 000 bhp
Speed, knots: 21

Conversions from standard "Kondor" class Coastal Minesweepers.

HYDROGRAPH

Displacement, tons: 500
Dimensions, feet (metres): 167 × 28·8 × — *(50·9 × 8·7 ×—)*
Main engines: Diesel; 540 hp = 11 knots

Built in 1960 by Volkswerft, Stralsund.

SURVEY SHIPS

KARL F. GAUS

Built in 1952-55. Of 200 tons and 9·5 knots. Seiner type.

PROFESSOR KRÜMMEL

Built in 1954. Of 135 tons and 10 knots.
Civilian Research Ship.

JORDAN

Of 100 tons and 9 knots.

FLAGGTIEF

Built in 1953. Of 50 tons and 8 knots.

SERVICE FORCES

1 "BASKUNCHAK" CLASS (SUPPLY SHIP)

USEDOM

Displacement, tons: 2 500
Dimensions, feet (metres): 227 × 29 × 12·3 *(70 × 8·9 × 3·8)*
Speed, knots: 13

Tanker converted to act as supply ship.

USEDOM   *1973, S. Breyer*

3 TYPE 600 (SUPPORT TANKERS)

HIDDENSEE   POEL   RIEMS

Displacement, tons: 600 DWT
Dimensions, feet (metres): 195 oa × 29·5 × 12·5 *(59·5 × 9·0 × 3·8)*
Main engines: 2 diesels; 2 800 bhp = 14 knots
Complement: 26

Built by Peenewerft, Wolgast, in 1960-61.

RIEMS   *1971, S. Breyer*

5 "KUMO" CLASS

E 18   E 44   RUDEN   RUGEN V 71   **VILM**

Displacement, tons: 400
Dimensions, feet (metres): 118 × 24 × 8·9 *(36 × 7·3 × 2·7)*
Speed, knots: 10

Built in mid-1950s. *Rugen* is a torpedo Trials Ship, *Vilm* a tanker and the other three employed as Supply Ships.

1 Ex-SOVIET "KAMENKA" CLASS (BUOY LAYER)

BUK

Displacement, tons: 1 000 standard
Dimensions, feet (metres): 180·5 × 31·2 × 11·5 *(55 × 9·5 × 3·4)*
Main engines: Diesels = 16 knots

BUK   *1970*

1 CABLE LAYER

DORNBUSCH

Cable layer of 700 tons with bow rollers.

DORNBUSCH   *1967*

2 "KONDOR I" CLASS (TRVs)

B 73   B 74

Details under Minewarfare Forces. Converted for Torpedo Recovery.

4 "TAUCHER" CLASS (DIVING TENDERS)

Displacement, tons: 310 full load
Dimensions, feet (metres): 98·4 × 21·3 × 9 *(30 × 6·5 × 3)*
Main engines: 2 diesels = 12 knots

LUMME

Small diving tender. Tug type.

FREESENDORF

Built in 1963. Buoy-layer.

Small diving tenders with recompression chamber.

8 BUOY TENDERS

BREITLING	GOLWITZ	LANDTIEFF	RAMZOW
ESPER ORT	GRASS ORT	PALMER ORT	ROSEN ORT

Displacement, tons: 158
Dimensions, feet (metres): 97 × 20·3 × 6·2 *(29·6 × 6·2 × 1·9)*
Main engines: 1 diesel; 580 hp = 11·5 knots

Delivered 1970-72. Civilian manned under the Naval Hydrographic Service.

BREITLING   *1972*

3 BUOY TENDERS

ARKONA   DASSER ORT   STUBBEN KAMMER

Built in 1956. Of 55 tons and 10 knots.

TRAINING SHIPS

3 "KRAKE" CLASS (ex-MINESWEEPERS—OCEAN)

BERLIN   POTSDAM   ROSTOCK

Displacement, tons: 650 standard
Dimensions, feet (metres): 229·7 × 26·5 × 12·2 *(70 × 8·1 × 3·7)*
Guns: 1—3·4 in; 10—25 mm (vertical twins)
A/S weapons: 4 DCT
Mines: Can carry 30
Main engines: Diesels; 2 shafts; 3 400 bhp = 18 knots
Complement: 90

Built in 1956-58 by Peenewerft, Wolgast. Of the original ten, four completed in 1958, were originally for Poland. Appearance is different compared with the first type, the squat wide funnel being close to the bridge with lattice mast and radar. Fitted for minelaying. On 1 May 1961 they were given the names of the capitals of districts etc. of East Germany. Pennant numbers are S11-13. All used for training and will probably be deleted before long.

"KRAKE" Class   *1970, Niels Gartig*

6 "KONDOR I" CLASS

Details in Minewarfare Forces, being part of that total.

ICEBREAKERS

STEPHAN JANTZEN

Of 2 500 tons and 13 knots built in 1965. Of Soviet "Dobrynya Nikitch" class. Civilian manned.

EISBAR   EISVOGEL

Of 550 tons and 12 knots built in 1957. Civilian manned.

TUGS

1 "700" CLASS

A 14

Of 800 tons and 12 knots.

WISMAR

Of 700 tons and 14 knots. Possibly civilian manned.

11 HARBOUR TUGS

Of varying classes.

Note: Gesellschaft für Sport und Technik (GST) (Association for Sport and Technical Science) controls several training ships—*Ernst Thälman,* a retired "Habicht I" Class minesweeper; *Ernst Schneller,* "Tummler" class; *Partisan,* and *Pionier* of 80 tons; *Freundschaft* of 200 tons; *F. L. Jahn* of 100 tons; and the sail training ships *Wilhelm Pieck, Seid Bereil, Jonny Scheer, Max Reichpietsch II* and *Knechtsand II.*

GHANA

Administration

Commander of the Navy: Commodore P. F. Quaye

Personnel

(a) 1976: 1 300 (150 officers, 1 150 ratings)
(b) Voluntary Service

Naval Base

Tema, near Accra

Deletions

1973: 3 ex-Soviet "Poluchat I" Class Patrol Craft

Mercantile Marine

Lloyd's Register of Shipping: 82 vessels of 180 351 tons gross

---

CORVETTES

2 "KROMANTSE" CLASS (VOSPER MARK I TYPE)

Name	No.	Builders	Commissioned
KROMANTSE	F 17	Vosper Ltd.	27 July 1964
KETA	F 18	Vickers Ltd (Tyne)	18 May 1965

Displacement, tons: 380 light; 440 standard; 500 full load
Dimensions, feet (metres): 162 wl; 177 oa × 28·5 × 13 *(49·4, 54 × 8·7 × 4)*
Guns: 1—4 in; 1—40 mm (see notes)
A/S weapons: 1 Squid triple-barrelled depth charge mortar
Main engines: 2 Bristol Siddeley Maybach (MTU) diesels; 2 shafts; 390 rpm; 7 100 bhp = 20 knots
Oil fuel, tons: 60
Range, miles: 2 000 at 16 knots; 2 900 at 14 knots
Complement: 54 (6 + 3 officers, 45 ratings)

Designed by Vosper Ltd, Portsmouth, a joint venture with Vickers-Armstrong's Ltd, one ship being built by each company. Vosper roll damping fins, and air conditioning throughout excepting machinery spaces. Generators 360 kW. The electrical power supply is 440 volts, 60 cycles ac. A very interesting patrol vessel design, an example of what can be achieved on a comparatively small platform to produce an inexpensive and quickly built anti-submarine vessel. *Kromantse* was launched at the Camber Shipyard, Portsmouth, on 5 Sep 1963. *Keta* was launched at Newcastle on 18 Jan 1965.

Radar: Search: Plessey AWS 1.

KROMANTSE

9/1975, Vosper Thornycroft

Refit: Both were fully refitted by Vosper Thornycroft Ltd (a £1·2 million contract) in 1974-75—*Keta* completed in April 1975 and *Kromantse* in Sep 1975.

Sonar: Both fitted with hull-mounted set.

LIGHT FORCES

2 LARGE PATROL CRAFT

Name	No.	Builders	Commissioned
DIELA	—	Ruthof Werft, Mainz	1974
SAHENE	—	Ruthof Werft, Mainz	1974

Displacement, tons: 160
Dimensions, feet (metres): 115·5 × 21·3 × 5·9 *(35·2 × 6·5 × 1·8)*
Guns: 2—40 mm

Ordered from Ruthof Werft (Mainz) BRG in 1973 as part of a class of six. Only these two had been delivered when the builders went bankrupt in 1975—no further decisions known.

2 "FORD" CLASS (LARGE PATROL CRAFT)

ELMINA P 13 **KOMENDA** P 14

Displacement, tons: 120 standard; 142 full load
Dimensions, feet (metres): 110 wl; 117·5 oa × 20 × 7 *(33·6; 35·8 × 6·1 × 2·1)*
Gun: 1—40 mm, 60 cal Bofors
A/S weapons: Depth charge throwers
Main engines: 2 Davey Paxman diesels; 2 shafts; 1 000 bhp = 18 knots
Complement: 19

KOMENDA

1969, Ghana Navy

MINEWARFARE FORCES

1 Ex-BRITISH "TON" CLASS (MINESWEEPER—COASTAL)

Name	No.	Builders	Commissioned
EJURA (ex-HMS *Aldington*)	M 16	Camper and Nicholson	1955

Displacement, tons: 360 standard; 425 full load
Dimensions, feet (metres): 140 pp; 153 oa × 28·8 × 8·2 *(42·7; 46·7 × 8·6 × 2·4)*
Guns: 1—40 mm forward; 2—20 mm aft
Main engines: Deltic diesels; 2 shafts; 3 000 bhp = 15 knots
Oil fuel, tons: 45
Range, miles: 2 300 at 13 knots
Complement: 27

Lent to Ghana by Britain in 1964.

2 Ex-BRITISH "HAM" CLASS (MINESWEEPERS—INSHORE)

Name	No.	Builders	Commissioned
AFADZATO (ex-HMS *Ottringham*)	M 12	Ailsa (Clyde)	30 Oct 1959
YOGAGA (ex-HMS *Malham*)	M 11	Fairlie Yacht Co.	2 Oct 1959

Displacement, tons: 120 standard; 159 full load
Dimensions, feet (metres): 100 pp; 107·5 oa × 22 × 5·8 *(30·5; 32·8 × 6·7 × 1·8)*
Gun: 1—15 mm
Main engines: 2 Paxman diesels; 1 100 = 14 knots
Oil fuel, tons: 15
Range, miles: 2 000 at 9 knots
Complement: 22

Yogaga and *Afadzato* sailed for Ghana on 31 Oct 1959 under original names, and were transferred from the Royal Navy to the Ghana Navy at Takoradi at the end of Nov 1959 and renamed after hills in Ghana. Fitted with funnel.

YOGAGA

1966, Ghana Navy

SERVICE CRAFT

ASUANTSI (ex-*MRC* 1122)

Displacement, tons: 657
Dimensions, feet (metres): 225 pp; 231·3 oa × 39 × 5 *(68·6; 70·5 × 11·9 × 1·5)*
Main engines: 4 Paxman; 1 840 bhp = 9 knots cruising

Acquired from Britain in 1965 and arrived in Ghana waters in July 1965. Used as a base workshop at Tema Naval Base. Is kept operational, and does a fair amount of seatime in general training and exercise tasks.

GREECE

Headquarters Appointments

Chief Hellenic Navy:
Vice-Admiral Egolfopoulos
Deputy Chief:
Rear-Admiral S. Kapsalis

Fleet Command

Commander of the Fleet:
Vice-Admiral S. Konofaos

Diplomatic Representation

Naval Attaché in London:
Captain Papas
Naval Attaché in Washington:
Captain O. Kapetos
Naval Attaché in Bonn:
Captain T. Alicampiotis
Naval Attaché in Cairo:
Captain P. Vossos
Naval Attaché in Ankara:
Captain G. Tsakonas

Personnel

(a) 1976: 17 600 (1 900 officers and 15 700 ratings)
(b) 2 years National Service

Naval Bases

Salamis and Suda Bay.

Naval Aviation

1 Squadron Alouette III helicopters with naval crews formed on 7 Aug 1975.
14 HU-16B Albatross are operated under naval command by mixed Air Force and Navy crews.

Harbour Corps

This force is equipped with coastal patrol craft and charged with harbour policing and coast-guard duties.

Prefix to Ships' Names

H.S. (Hellenic Ship)

Mercantile Marine

Lloyd's Register of Shipping:
2 743 vessels of 22 527 156 tons gross

Strength of the Fleet

Type	Active	Building
Destroyers	11	—
Frigates	4	—
Corvettes	5	—
Patrol Submarines	6	3
Fast Attack Craft—Missile	10	—
Fast Attack Craft—Torpedo	19	—
Large Patrol Craft	7	—
Landing Ships	14	—
LCUs	6	—
Minor Landing Craft	47	—
Minelayers—Coastal	2	—
Minesweepers—Coastal	15	—
Survey Vessels	6	—
Depot Ship	1	—
Support Tankers	2	—
Harbour Tankers	6	—
Salvage Ship	1	—
Repair Ship	1	—
Lighthouse Tenders	4	—
Tugs	12	—
Netlayer	1	—
Water Boats	5	—
Auxiliary Transports	2	—

DELETIONS

Destroyers

1972 *Doxa, Niki* (Gleaves Class)

Submarines

1975 *Poseidon*
1976 *Triaina* returned to USA for disposal.

Light Forces

1971 *Antiploiarkhos Laskos, Ploiarchos Meletopoulos*
1972 *Inionos* ("Nasty") Class.

Minesweepers—Coastal

1972 *Paxi*
1973 *Afroessa, Kalymnos, Karteria, Kerkyra, Papalos, Zakynthos*

Amphibious Forces

1971 *Nafkratoussa* (ex-*Hyperion*, ex-*LSD 9*)
1972 *Ipopliarkhos Merlin* (ex-US *LSM 557*) sunk in collision with a supertanker (15 Nov).
1975 *Skopelos* and *Kea* (ex-US *LCT 6*)

Survey Vessel

1973 *Ariadne*

Minesweeper Depot Ship

1973 *Hermes*

Tugs

1972 *Aegeus, Adamastos*

Water Boat

1972 *Kaliroe*

PENNANT NUMBERS

Destroyers and Frigates

01	Aetos
06	Aspis
16	Velos
28	Thyella
31	Ierax
54	Leon
56	Lonchi
63	Navarinon
67	Panthir
85	Sfendoni
210	Themistocles
211	Miaoulis
212	Kanaris
213	Kontouriotis
214	Sachtouris

Submarines

110	Glavkos
111	Nereus
112	Triton
113	Proteus
114	Papanikolis
115	Katsonis

Minelayers

N04	Aktion
N05	Amvrakia

Minesweepers

M12	Armatolos
M58	Mahitis
M64	Navmachos
M74	Polemistis
M76	Pyrpolitis

Minesweepers

M202	Atalanti
M205	Antiopi
M206	Faedra
M210	Thalia
M211	Alkyon
M213	Argo
M214	Avra
M240	Pleias
M241	Kichli
M242	Kissa
M245	Doris
M246	Aigli
M247	Dafni
M248	Aedon
M254	Niovi

Light Forces

P14	Arslanoglou
P15	Dolphin
P16	Draken
P17	Polikos
P18	Polidefkis
P19	Aiolos
P20	Astrapi
P21	Andromeda
P23	Kastor
P24	Kyknos
P25	Pigassos
P26	Toxotis
P27	Foinix
P53	Kymothoi
P54	Calypso
P55	Evniki
P56	Navsithoi
P70	A. Pezopoulos
P94	P. Maridakis
P95	P. Vlachavas
P96	P. Chadzikonstandis

Amphibious Forces

L144	Syros
L145	Kassos
L146	Karpathos
L147	Kimonos
L149	Kithos
L150	Sifnos
L152	Skiathos
L153	Nafkratoussa
L154	Ikaria
L157	Rodos
L158	Limnos
L161	I. Grigoropoulos
L162	I. Tournas
L163	I. Daniolos
L164	I. Roussen
L165	I. Krystalidis
L171	Kriti
L172	Lesbos
L179	Samos
L195	Chios

Service Forces

A307	Thetis
A329	Sakipis
A345	Sirios
A372	Zeus
A373	Kronos
A374	Prometheus
A376	Orion
A377	Arethousa
A384	Sotir
A413	Hephestos
A414	Ariadni
A469	Anemos
A471	Vivies
A478	Vegas
A481	St. Lykoudis
A485	Skyros

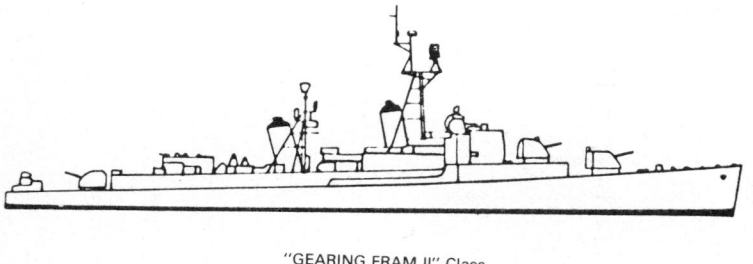

"GEARING FRAM II" Class

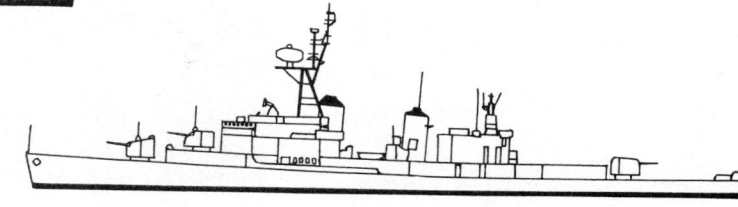

"GEARING FRAM I" Class

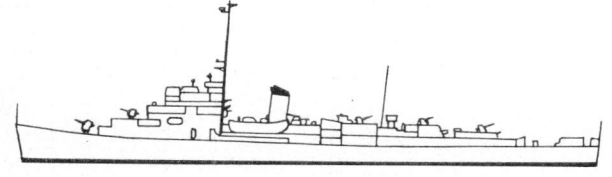

"BOSTWICK" Class

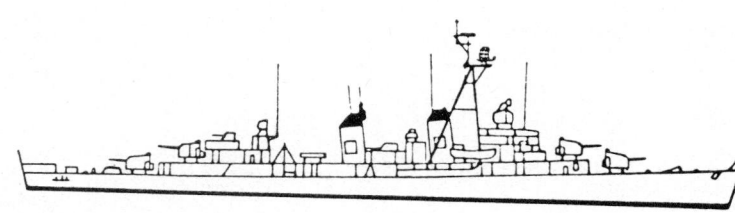

"FLETCHER" Class (4 Guns)

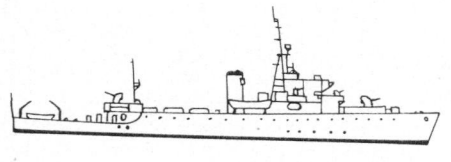

"ALGERINE" Class

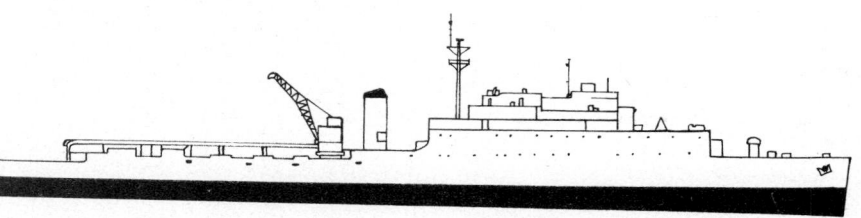

NAFKRATOUSSA

DESTROYERS

1 Ex-US "GEARING FRAM II" CLASS
3 Ex-US "GEARING FRAM I" CLASS

Name	No.	Builders	Laid down	Launched	Commissioned
SACHTOURIS (ex-USS *Arnold J. Isbell, DD 869*)	214	Bethlehem (Staten Island)	—	6 Aug 1945	5 Jan 1946
KANARIS (ex-USS *Stickell, DD 888*)	212	Consolidated Steel Corp	—	16 June1945	26 Sep 1945
KONTOURIOTIS (ex-USS *Rupertus, DD 851*)	213	Bethlehem (Quincy)	—	21 Sep 1945	8 Mar 1946
THEMISTOCLES (ex-USS *Frank Knox, DD 742*)	210	Bath Iron Works	—	17 Sep 1944	11 Dec 1944

Displacement, tons: 2 425 standard; 3 500 full load
Length, feet (metres): 390·5 *(119·0)* oa
Beam, feet (metres): 40·9 *(12·4)*
Draught, feet (metres): 19·0 *(5·8)*
Guns: 6—5 in *(127 mm)* 38 cal (twin) *(Themistocles)*;
  4—5 in (twin) (remainder)
A/S weapons: 2 fixed Hedgehogs, *(Themistocles)*; 1 ASROC
  8-barrelled launcher and facilities for small helicopter in
  remainder
Torpedo tubes: 2 triple (Mk 32)
Main engines: 2 Westinghouse geared turbines; 2 shafts;
  60 000 shp
Boilers: 4 Babcock & Wilcox
Speed, knots: 34
Range, miles: 4 800 at 15 knots
Complement: 269 (16 officers, 253 men)

Themistocles was a Fram II Radar Picket conversion, remainder
are Fram I DD conversions. It is reported that another "Gearing" class is to be taken over in 1976.

Transfers: From USA: *Sachtouris,* 4 Dec 1973; *Kanaris,* 1 July
1972; *Kontouriotis,* 10 July 1973; *Themistocles* 30 Jan 1971.

THEMISTOCLES (FRAM II)

1972, Hellenic Navy

KANARIS (FRAM I)

1973, Hellenic Navy

1 ex-US "ALLEN M. SUMNER" CLASS

Name	No.	Builders	Laid down	Launched	Commissioned
MIAOULIS (ex-USS Ingraham, DD 694)	211	Federal SB & DD Co	1943	16 Jan 1944	10 Mar 1944

Displacement, tons: 2 200 standard; 3 320 full load
Length, feet (metres): 376·5 (114·8) oa
Beam, feet (metres): 40·9 (12·4)
Draught, feet (metres): 19·0 (5·8)
Guns: 6—5 in (127 mm) 38 cal
A/S weapons: 2 triple torpedo launchers, Mk 32;
 2 ahead throwing hedgehogs
Main engines: 2 geared turbines; 2 shafts; 60 000 shp
Boilers: 4
Speed, knots: 34
Range, miles: 4 600 at 15 knots
Complement: 269 (16 officers, 94 POs, 159 men)

Former fleet destroyer of the "Allen M. Sumner" class which
had been modernised under the FRAM II programme.
Transferred by USA July 1971.

MIAOULIS   1973, Hellenic Navy

6 Ex-US "FLETCHER" CLASS

Name	No.	Builders	Laid down	Launched	Commissioned
ASPIS (ex-USS Conner, DD 582)	06	Boston Navy Yard	16 Apr 1942	18 July 1942	8 June 1943
LONCHI ((ex-USS Hall, DD 583)	56	Boston Navy Yard	16 Apr 1942	18 July 1942	6 July 1943
NAVARINON (ex-USS Brown, DD 546)	63	Bethlehem (S. Pedro)	27 June1942	22 Feb 1943	10 July 1943
SFENDONI (ex-USS Aulick, DD 569)	85	Consolidated Steel Corp. Texas	14 May 1941	2 Mar 1942	27 Oct 1942
THYELLA (ex-USS Bradford, DD 545)	28	Bethlehem (S. Pedro)	28 Apr 1942	12 Dec 1942	12 June 1943
VELOS (ex-USS Charette, DD 581)	16	Boston Navy Yard	20 Feb 1941	3 June1942	18 May 1943

Displacement, tons: 2 100 standard; 3 050 full load
Length, feet (metres): 376·5 (114·7) oa
Beam, feet (metres): 39·5 (12·0)
Draught, feet (metres): 18 (5·5)
Guns: 4—5 in (127 mm) 38 cal. in Aspis, Lonchi, Sfendoni and
 Velos, 5 in Navarinon and Thyella
 6—3 in (76 mm), 3 twin, in Aspis, Lonchi, Sfendoni and Velos.
 10—40 mm (2 quadruple, 1 twin) in Navarinon and Thyella
A/S weapons: Hedgehogs; DCs
Torpedo tubes: 5—21 in (533 mm), quintuple bank, in Aspis,
 Lonchi, Sfendoni and Velos, none in Navarinon and Thyella
Torpedo racks: Side-launching for A/S torpedoes
Boilers: 4 Babcock & Wilcox; 615 psi (43·5 km/cm²) 800°F
 (427°C)
Main engines: 2 sets GE geared turbines; 2 shafts; 60 000 shp
Speed, knots: 32
Range, miles: 6 000 at 15 knots; 1 260 at full power
Oil fuel, tons: 506
Complement: 250

Transferred from USA, Aspis, Lonchi and Velos at Long Beach,
Cal, on 15 Sep 1959, 9 Feb 1960 and 15 June 1959, respectively,
Sfendoni at Philadelphia on 21 Aug 1959, Navarinon and
Thyella at Seattle, Wash, on 27 Sep 1962. All purchased 1976.

Radar: Search: SPS 6, SPS 10.
Fire control: GFC 56 and 63 systems.

VELOS   1973, Dr Giorgia Arra

FRIGATES

Note: It is reported that replacement frigates including a possible purchase of two FFG 7 from Bath Iron Works, are under consideration. No confirmation to hand.

4 Ex-US "CANNON" CLASS

Name	No.	Builders	Laid down	Launched	Commissioned
AETOS (ex-USS Slater, DE 766)	01	Tampa SB Co.	9 Mar 1943	13 Feb 1944	1 May 1944
IERAX (ex-USS Elbert, DE 768)	31	Tampa SB Co.	1 Apr 1943	23 May 1944	12 July 1944
LEON (ex-USS Eldridge, DE 173)	54	Federal SB & DD Co.	22 Feb 1943	25 June1943	27 Aug 1943
PANTHIR (ex-USS Garfield Thomas, DE 193)	67	Federal SB & DD Co.	23 Sep 1943	12 Dec 1943	24 Jan 1944

Displacement, tons: 1 240 standard; 1 900 full load
Length, feet (metres): 306 (93·3) oa
Beam, feet (metres): 36·7 (11·2)
Draught, feet (metres): 14 (4·3)
Guns: 3—3 in (76 mm) 50 cal. 6—40 mm, (3 twin)
 14—20 mm (7 twin)
A/S weapons: Hedgehog; 8 DCT; 1 DC rack
Torpedo racks: Side launching for A/S torpedoes
Main engines: 4 sets GM disel-electric 6 000 bhp; 2 shafts
Speed, knots: 19·25
Oil fuel, tons: 316
Range, miles: 9 000 at 12 knots
Complement: 220

Aetos and Ierax were transferred on 15 Mar 1951 and Leon and
Panthir on 15 Jan 1951. Their 3—21 inch torpedo tubes in a
triple mount were removed.

LEON   1972, Hellenic Nav

CORVETTES

5 Ex-BRITISH "ALGERINE" CLASS

ame	No.	Builders	Laid down	Launched	Commissioned
RMATOLOS (ex-HMS *Aries*)	M 12	Toronto Shipyard	1942	19 Sep 1942	1943
AHITIS (ex-HMS *Postillion*)	M 58	Redfern Construction Co	1942	14 Nov 1942	1943
AVMACHOS (ex-HMS *Lightfoot*)	M 64	Redfern Construction Co	1942	31 Aug 1942	1943
)LEMISTIS (ex-HMS *Gozo*)	M 74	Redfern Construction Co	1942	18 Mar 1943	1943
*RPOLITIS (ex-HMS *Arcturus*)	M 76	Redfern Construction Co	1942	27 Jan 1943	1943

splacement, tons: 1 030 standard; 1 325 full load
ngth, feet (metres): 225 *(68·6)* oa
am, feet (metres): 35·5 *(10·8)*
aught, feet (metres): 11·5 *(3·5)*
ins: 2—3 in *(76 mm)* (US Mark 21) (1 in *Pirpolitis*, none in
Mahitis); 4—20 mm (US), 2 MG
S weapons: 2 to 4 DCT
ain engines: 2 triple expansion, 2 shafts; 2 700 ihp
eed, knots: 16
ilers: 2 Yarrow, 250 psi *(17·6 kg cm²)*
 fuel, tons: 235
nge, miles: 5 000 at 10 knots; 2 270 at 14·5 knots
mplement: 85

rmer British ocean minesweepers. Acquired from the Execu-
e Committee of Surplus Allied Material. Latterly employed
Corvettes. The armament of *Mahitis* was removed when she
came a training ship. *Armatolos* now used as a light house
der and the others as personnel transports.

POLEMISTIS   *1974, Hellenic Navy*

SUBMARINES

4 + 3 TYPE 209 "GLAVKOS" CLASS

ame	No.	Builders	Laid down	Launched	Commissioned
.AVKOS	S 110	Howaldtswerke, Kiel	—	Sep 1970	5 Nov 1971
EREUS	S 111	Howaldtswerke, Kiel	—	Sep 1971	10 Feb 1972
*OTEUS	S 113	Howaldtswerke, Kiel	—	Dec 1971	8 Aug 1972
*ITON	S 112	Howaldtswerke, Kiel	—	1971	23 Nov 1972

splacement, tons: 990 surfaced; 1 290 dived
ngth, feet (metres): 177·1 *(54·0)*
am, feet (metres): 20·3 *(6·2)*
rpedo tubes: 8—21 in (with reloads) bow
ain machinery: Diesel-electric; 4 MTU; Siemens diesel-
generators; 1 Siemens electric motor; 1 shaft
eed, knots: 10 surfaced; 22 dived
nge: 50 days
mplement: 31

signed by Ingenieurkontor, Lübeck for construction by
waldtswerke, Kiel and sale by Ferrostaal Essen all acting as a
nsortium.
single-hull design with two ballast tanks and forward and
er trim tanks. Fitted with snort and remote machinery con-
l. The single screw is slow revving. Very high capacity bat-
ies with GRP lead-acid cells and battery cooling—by Wilh.
gen and VARTA. Active and passive sonar, sonar detection
uipment, sound ranging and underwater telephone. Fitted
th two periscopes, radar and Omega receiver. Fore-planes
ract.

GLAVKOS   *1973, Hellenic Navy*

TRITON   *1973, Hellenic Navy*

NEW CONSTRUCTION

A further three (with an option on a fourth) of this class were
ordered from Howaldtswerke in a contract signed 1 Nov 1975
for delivery late 1976-77.

1 Ex-US "GUPPY III" CLASS

Name	No.	Builders	Laid down	Launched	Commissione
KATSONIS (ex-USS Remora, SS 487)	S 115	Portsmouth Navy Yard	5 Mar 1945	12 July 1945	3 Jan 1946

Displacement, tons: 1 975 standard; 2 450 dived
Dimensions, feet (metres): 326 × 27 × 17 (99·4 × 8·2 × 5·2)
Torpedo tubes: 10—21 in; 6 bow, 4 stern
Main machinery: 4 diesels; 6 400 hp;
  2 electric motors; 5 400 shp; 2 shafts
Speed, knots: 20 surfaced; 15 dived
Range, miles: 12 000 at 10 knots (surfaced)
Complement: 85

Originally of the wartime "Tench" class, subsequently converted under the Guppy II programme and, in 1961-62 to Guppy III. Amongst other modifications this involved the fitting of BQG-4 Sonar (Puffs) for dived fire-control, in addition to the BQR-2 array sonar. Transferred 29 Oct 1973.

KATSONIS   1974, Commander Aldo Fraccar

1 Ex-US "GUPPY IIA" CLASS

Name	No.	Builders	Laid down	Launched	Commissione
PAPANIKOLIS (ex-USS Hardhead, SS 365)	S 114	Manitowoc SB Co	7 July 1943	12 Dec 1943	April 1944

Displacement, tons: 1 840 standard; 2 445 dived
Length, feet (metres): 306 (93·2)
Beam, feet (metres): 27 (8·3)
Draught, feet (metres): 17 (5·2)
Torpedo tubes: 10—21 inch; 6 bow, 4 stern
Main engines: 3 diesels; 4 800 shp;
  2 Motors, 5 400 shp; 2 shafts
Speed, knots: 17 surfaced; 15 dived
Range, miles: 12 000 at 10 knots (surface)
Complement: 84

Transferred 26 July 1972.

PAPANIKOLIS   1973, Hellenic Nav

LIGHT FORCES

4 "LA COMBATTANTE III" CLASS (FAST ATTACK CRAFT—MISSILE)

Name	No.	Builders	Commissioned
IPOPLIARKHOS KONIDIS	—	Construction M. de Normandie	1976
IPOPLIARKHOS BATSIS	—	Construction M. de Normandie	1976
IPOPLIARKHOS ARLIOTIS	—	Construction M. de Normandie	1976
IPOPLIARKHOS ANNINOS	—	Construction M. de Normandie	1976

Displacement, tons: 385 standard; 418 full load
Dimensions, feet (metres): 184 × 26 × 7 (56 × 7·9 × 2·1)
Missiles: 4 MM 38 Exocet surface-to-surface
Guns: 2—76 mm; 4—30 mm (2 twin)
Torpedo tubes: 2—21 inch aft for wire-guided torpedoes
Main engines: 4 Diesels; 18 000 bhp = 34 knots
Range, miles: 700 at 25 knots
Complement: 38

Ordered in September 1974. I. Konidis laid down 28 June 1975; I. Batsis 5 Nov 1975.

4 "LA COMBATTANTE II" CLASS (FAST ATTACK CRAFT—MISSILE)

Name	No.	Builders	Commissioned
CALYPSO	P 54	C. M. de Normandie, Cherbourg	April 1972
EVNIKI	P 55	C. M. de Normandie, Cherbourg	June 1972
KYMOTHOI	P 53	C. M. de Normandie, Cherbourg	Dec 1971
NAVSITHOI	P 56	C. M. de Normandie, Cherbourg	July 1972

Displacement, tons: 234 standard; 255 full load
Dimensions, feet (metres): 154·2 × 23·3 × 8·2 (47 × 7·1 × 2·5)
Missiles: 4 MM 38 Exocet surface-to-surface
Guns: 4—35 mm (2 twin)
Torpedo tubes: 2 aft for wire-guided torpedoes
Main engines: 4 MTU diesels; 4 shafts; 12 000 bhp = 36·5 knots
Oil fuel, tons: 39
Range, miles: 850 at 25 knots
Complement: 40 (4 officers, and 36 men)

Ordered in 1969 from Constructions Mécaniques de Normandie, Cherbourg.
Fitted with Thomson CSF Triton radar and Plessey IFF Mk 10.
Calypso launched 26 April 1971. Evniki launched 8 Sep 1971. Kymothoi launched 26 Jan 1971.
Navsithoi launched 20 Dec 1971.

NAVSITHOI   1973, Hellenic Na

2 Ex-US "ASHEVILLE" CLASS (LARGE PATROL CRAFT)

Name	No.	Builders	Commissioned
— (ex-USS *Beacon, PG 99)*	—	Peterson Builders	21 Nov 1969
— (ex-USS *Green Bay, PG 101)*	—	Peterson Builders	5 Dec 1969

Displacement, tons: 225 standard; 245 full load
Dimensions, feet (metres): 164·5 × 23·5 × 9·5 *(50·2 × 7·2 × 2·9)*
Guns: 1—3 in *(76 mm)* 50 cal forward; 1—40 mm; 4—50 cal MG
Main engines: Codag; 2 Cummins diesels; 1 450 hp; 2 shafts = 16 knots.
    1 GE gas turbine; 13 300 hp; 2 shafts = 40+ knots
Complement: 27

Transferred 30 June 1976.

Ex-*BEACON*   9/1975, Dr. Giorgio Arra

5 "SILBERMÖWE" CLASS (FAST ATTACK CRAFT—TORPEDO)

Name	No.	Builders	Commissioned
DOLPHIN (ex-*Sturmmöwe)*	P 15	Lurrsen, Vegesack	1951-1956
DRAKON (ex-*Silbermöwe)*	P 16	Lurssen, Vegesack	1951-1956
FOINIX (ex-*Eismöwe)*	P 27	Lurssen, Vegesack	1951-1956
POLIKOS (ex-*Raubmöwe)*	P 17	Lurssen, Vegesack	1951-1956
POLIDEFKIS(ex-*Wildschwan)*	P 18	Lurssen, Vegesack	1951-1956

Displacement, tons: 119 standard; 155 full load
Dimensions, feet (metres): 116·1 × 16·7 × 5·9 *(35·5 × 5·1 × 1·8)*
Torpedo tubes: 2—21 in
Guns: 1—40 mm; 2—20 mm (1 twin)
Main engines: 3 diesels; 3 shafts; 9 000 bhp = 38 knots

Old S-Boote taken over from Germany 17 Dec 1968.

2 FAST ATTACK CRAFT (MISSILE)

Name	No.	Builders	Commissioned
KELEFSTIS STAMOU	—	Ch. N. de l'Esterel	1975
DIOPOS ANTONIOU	—	Ch. N. de l'Esterel	1976

Displacement, tons: 115
Dimensions, feet (metres): 105 × 19 × 5 *(32 × 5·8 × 1·5)*
Missiles: 4—SS 12
Guns: 2—20 mm
Main engines: 2 diesels; 2 700 hp = 30 knots
Range, miles: 1 500 at 15 knots
Complement: 17

Wooden hulls.

5 "NASTY" CLASS (FAST ATTACK CRAFT—TORPEDO)

Name	No.	Builders	Commissioned
ANDROMEDA	P 21	Mandal, Norway	Feb 1967
KASTOR	P 23	Mandal, Norway	1967
KYKNOS	P 24	Mandal, Norway	1967
PIGASSOS	P 25	Mandal, Norway	1967
TOXOTIS	P 26	Mandal, Norway	1967

Displacement, tons: 69 standard; 76 full load
Dimensions, feet (metres): 75 pp; 80·4 oa × 24·6 × 6·9 *(22·9; 24·5 × 7·5 × 2·1)*
Torpedo tubes: 4—21 in
Guns: 2—40 mm
Main engines: 2 Napier Deltic T 18-37 K diesels; 3 100 bhp = 43 knots
Complement: 22

Andromeda and *Inionos* (deleted 1972) were taken over in Feb 1967 from Mandal, Norway.
Kastor and *Kyknos,* and the third pair, *Pigassos* and *Toxotis,* were delivered in succession in
1967.

ANDROMEDA   1974, Hellenic Navy

7 Ex-GERMAN "JAGUAR" CLASS
(FAST ATTACK CRAFT—TORPEDO)

Name	No.	Builders	Commissioned
—(ex-*Falke P 6072)*	—	FDR	1958
—(ex-*Geier P 6073)*	—	FDR	1958
—(ex-*Greif P 6071)*	—	FDR	1958
—(ex-*Habicht P 6075)*	—	FDR	1958
—(ex-*Kondor P 6070)*	—	FDR	1958
—(ex-*Kormoran P 6077)*	—	FDR	1958
—(ex-*Seeadler P 6068)*	—	FDR	1958

Displacement, tons: 160 standard; 190 full load
Dimensions, feet (metres): 139·4 × 23·4 × 7·9 *(42·5 × 7·2 × 2·4)*
Guns: 2—40 *mm* Bofors L70 (single)
Torpedo tubes: 4—21 inch
Main engines: 4 Diesels; 4 shafts; 12 000 bhp—42 knots
Complement: 39

Transferred 1975-76. Three others (ex-*Albatros,* ex-*Bussard* and ex-*Sperber)* transferred at
same time for spares. Built by Lürssen Vegesack or Kroger Rendsburg.

GEIER (before transfer)   1975, Reiner Nerlich

1 VOSPER "BRAVE" CLASS
(FAST ATTACK CRAFT—TORPEDO)

Name	No.	Builders	Commissioned
ASTRAPI (ex-*Strahl P6194*)	P 20	Vosper, Portsmouth	21 Nov 1962

Displacement, tons: 95 standard; 110 full load
Dimensions, feet (metres): 99 oa × 25 × 7 *(30·2 × 7·6 × 2·1)*
Torpedo chutes: 4—21 in side launching
Guns: 2—40 mm
Main engines: 3 Bristol Siddeley Marine Proteus gas turbines; 3 shafts; 12 750 bhp = 55·5 knots

Launched on 10 Jan 1962. Commissioned in Federal German Navy on 21 Nov 1962. Transferred to Royal Hellenic Navy in Apr 1967. Refitted by Vosper in 1968. Of similar design to British "Brave" class.

ASTRAPI   *1972, Hellenic Navy*

1 VOSPER "FEROCITY" CLASS
(FAST ATTACK CRAFT—TORPEDO)

Name	No.	Builders	Commissioned
AIOLOS (ex-*Pfeil P 6193*)	P 19	Vosper, Portsmouth	27 June 1962

Displacement, tons: 75 standard; 80 full load
Dimensions, feet (metres): 92 wl; 95 oa × 23·9 × 6·5 *(28·1; 29 × 7·3 × 2)*
Torpedo chutes: 4—21 in side launching
Guns: 2—40 mm
Main engines: 2 Bristol Siddeley Marine Proteus gas turbines; 2 shafts; 8 500 bhp = 50 knots

Launched on 26 Oct 1961. Commissioned in German Navy on 27 June 1962. Transferred to Royal Hellenic Navy in Apr 1967. Refitted by Vosper in 1968. Based on design of Vosper prototype *Ferocity*.

AIOLOS   *1972, Hellenic Navy*

3 PGM TYPE (LARGE PATROL CRAFT)

ANTIPLOIARKHOS PEZOPOULOS (ex-*PGM 21*, ex-*PC 1552*) P 70
PLOTARKHIS ARSLANOGLOU (ex-*PGM 25*, ex-*PC 1565*) P 14
PLOTARKHIS CHADZIKONSTANDIS (ex-*PGM 29*, ex-*PC 1565*) P 96

Displacement, tons: 335 standard; 439 full load
Dimensions, feet (metres): 170 wl; 174·7 oa × 23 × 10·8 *(51·8; 53·3 × 7 × 3·3)*
Guns: 1—3 in; 6—20 mm
A/S weapons: Hedgehog; side launching torpedo racks; depth charges
Main engines: 2 GM diesels; 2 shafts; 3 600 bhp = 19 knots

All launched in 1943-44. Acquired from USA in Aug 1947. The two 40 mm guns were removed and a Hedgehog was installed in 1963.

ANTIPLOIARKHOS PEZOPOULOS   *1973, Hellenic Navy*

2 LSSL TYPE (LARGE PATROL CRAFT)

Name	No.	Builders	Commissioned
PLOTARKHIS MARIDAKIS (ex-USS *LSSL 65*)	L 94 (ex-*P 94*)	Albina Engine & Machinery Works Inc	—
PLOTARKHIS VLACHAVAS (ex-USS *LSSL 35*)	L 95 (ex-*P 95*)	Commercial Iron Works Portland	—

Displacement, tons: 257 standard; 395 full load
Dimensions, feet (metres): 157·0 × 23·2 × 5·7 *(47·9 × 7·1 × 1·7)*
Guns: 1—3 in; 4—40 mm (2 twin); 4—20 mm
Main engines: Diesels; 2 shafts; 1 600 bhp = 14·4 knots

Launched on 14 Nov and 17 Sep 1944, respectively. *Plotarkhis Vlachavas* was transferred from USA on 12 Aug 1957 and *Plotarkhis Maridakis* in June 1958. Given L instead of P pennant numbers in 1971.

1 + ? COASTAL PATROL CRAFT

Name	No.	Builders	Commissioned
N. I. GOULANDRIAS I	—	Syros Shipyard	June 25 1975

Displacement, tons: 38·5
Dimensions, feet (metres): 78·7 × 20·3 × 3·4 *(24 × 6·2 × 1·1)*
Speed, knots: 25
Range, miles: 1 600 at cruising speed

The first of these craft was donated to the Hellenic Navy by the wealthy shipowner after whom she is named. She is lead craft of a number of the same type, most of them donated by Greek shipowners.

AMPHIBIOUS FORCES

1 Ex-US "CABILDO" CLASS (LSD)

Name	No.	Builders	Commissioned
NAFKRATOUSSA	L 153	Boston Navy Yard	31 Oct 1945
(ex-USS *Fort Mandan, LSD 21*)			

Displacement, tons: 4 790 light; 9 357 full load
Dimensions, feet (metres): 457·8 oa × 72·2 × 18 *(139·6 × 22 × 5·5)*
Guns: 8—40 mm
Main engines: Geared turbines; 2 shafts; 7 000 shp = 15·4 knots
Boilers: 2

Laid down on 2 Jan 1945. Launched on 22 May 1945. Taken over from USA in 1971 replacing the previous *Nafkratoussa* (ex-*Hyperion*, ex-*LSD 9*) out of service in 1971 as Headquarters ship of Captain, Landing Forces.

NAFKRATOUSSA

1973, Hellenic Navy

8 Ex-US LSTs
(2 of 511—1152 series, 6 of 1—510 series)

511—1152 Series

IKARIA (ex-USS *Potter County, LST 1086*) L 154
KRITI (ex-USS *Page County, LST 1076*) L 171

1—510 Series

CHIOS (ex-USS *LST 35*) L 195
LESBOS (ex-USS *Boone County, LST 389*) L 172
LIMNOS (ex-USS *LST 36*) L 158
RODOS (ex-USS *Bowman County, LST 391*) L 157
SAMOS (ex-USS *LST 33*) L 179
SYROS (ex-USS *LST 325*) L 144

Displacement, tons: 1 653 standard; 2 366 beaching; 4 080 full load
Dimensions, feet (metres): 328 × 50 × 14 *(100 × 15·3 × 2·9)*
Guns: 8—40 mm; 6—20 mm *(Rodos 10—40 mm)*
Main engines: 2 GM diesels; 2 shafts; 1 700 bhp = 11·6 knots
Range, miles: 9 500 at 9 knots
Complement: 93 (8 officers, 85 men)

LIMNOS

1972, Hellenic Navy

Former United States tank landing ships. Cargo capacity 2 100 tons. *Ikaria*, *Lesbos* and *Rodos* were transferred to the Royal Hellenic Navy on 9 Aug 1960. *Syros* was transferred on 29 May 1964 at Portsmouth, Virginia, under MAP. *Kriti* was transferred in Mar 1971. Others under lease-lend in 1943.

5 Ex-US LSMs

IPOPLIARKHOS KRISTALIDIS (ex-USS *LSM 541*) L 165
IPOPLIARKHOS DANIOLOS (ex-USS *LSM 227*) L 163
IPOPLIARKHOS GRIGOROPOULOS (ex-USS *LSM 45*) L 161
IPOPLIARKHOS ROUSSEN (ex-USS *LSM 399*) L 164
IPOPLIARKHOS TOURNAS (ex-USS *LSM 102*) L 162

Displacement, tons: 743 beaching; 1 095 full load
Dimensions, feet (metres): 196·5 wl; 203·5 oa × 34·2 × 8·3 *(59·9; 62·1 × 10·4 × 2·5)*
Guns: 2—40 mm; 8—20 mm
Main engines: Diesel direct drive; 2 shafts; 3 600 bhp = 13 knots

LSM 541 was handed over to Greece at Salamis on 30 Oct 1958 and *LSM 45*, *LSM 102*, *LSM 227* and *LSM 399* at Portsmouth, Virginia on 3 Nov 1958. All were renamed after naval heroes killed during World War 2.

IPOPLIARKHOS KRISTALIDIS

1974, Hellenic Navy

6 Ex-US LCUs (Ex-LCT 6)

Name	No.	Builders	Commissioned
KARPATHOS (ex-*LCU 1379*)	L 146	—	1944
KASSOS (ex-*LCU 1382*)	L 145	—	1944
KIMONOS (ex-*LCU 971*)	L 147	—	1944
KITHNOS (ex-*LCU 763*)	L 149	—	1944
SIFNOS (ex-*LCU 677*)	L 150	—	1944
SKIATHOS (ex-*LCU 827*)	L 152	—	1944

Displacement, tons: 143 standard; 309 full load
Dimensions, feet (metres): 105 wl; 119 oa × 32·7 × 5 *(32; 36·3 × 10 × 1·5)*
Guns: 2—20 mm
Main engines: Diesel; 3 shafts; 440 bhp = 8 knots
Complement: 13

Former US Utility Landing Craft of the *LCU* (ex-*LCT 6*) type. *Skiathos* acquired in 1959. *Kithnos* and *Sifnos* were transferred from USA in 1961, and *Karpathos*, *Kassos* and *Kimonos* in 1962.

KITHNOS

1971, Hellenic Navy

13 LCMs

Transferred from USA.

34 LCVPs

Transferred from USA.

MINE WARFARE FORCES

2 COASTAL MINELAYERS

Name	No.	Builders	Commissioned
AKTION (ex-*LSM 301*, ex-*MMC 6*)	N 04	Charleston Naval Shipyard	1945
AMVRAKIA (ex-*LSM 303*, ex-*MMC 7*)	N 05	Charleston Naval Shipyard	1945

Displacement, tons: 720 standard; 1 100 full load
Dimensions, feet (metres): 203·5 oa × 34·5 × 8·3 *(62·1 × 10·5 × 2·5)*
Guns: 8—40 mm (4 twin); 6—20 mm (single)
Mines: Capacity 100 to 130
Main engines: 2 diesels; 2 shafts; 3 600 bhp = 12·5 knots
Range, miles: 3 000 at 12 knots
Complement: 65

Former US Medium Landing Ships. *Aktion* was launched on 1 Jan 1945 and *Amvrakia* on 14 Nov 1944. Converted in the USA into minelayers for the Royal Hellenic Navy. Underwent extensive rebuilding from the deck up. Twin rudders. Transferred on 1 Dec 1953.

AMVRAKIA   *1974, Hellenic Navy*

10 Ex-US "FALCON" CLASS (MINESWEEPERS—COASTAL)

Name	No.	Builders	Commissioned
AEDON (ex-*MSC 310*)	M 248	USA	1964-65
AIGLI (ex-*MSC 299*)	M 246	USA	1964-65
ALKYON (ex-*MSC 319*)	M 211	USA	1969-70
ARGO (ex-*MSC 317*)	M 213	USA	1968
AVRA (ex-*MSC 318*)	M 214	USA	1968
DAFNI (ex-*MSC 307*)	M 247	USA	1964-65
DORIS (ex-*MSC 298*)	M 245	USA	1964-65
KICHLI (ex-*MSC 308*)	M 241	USA	1964-65
KISSA (ex-*MSC 309*)	M 242	USA	1964-65
PLEIAS (ex-*MSC 314*)	M 240	USA	1969-70

Displacement, tons: 320 standard; 370 full load
Dimensions, feet (metres): 138 pp; 144 oa × 28 × 8·2 *(42·1; 43·3 × 8·5 × 2·5)*
Guns: 2—20 mm (twin)
Main engines: 2 GM diesels; 2 shafts; 880 bhp = 13 knots
Complement: 39

Built in USA for Greece. Wooden hulls.

AVRA   *1974, Hellenic Navy*

5 Ex-US "ADJUTANT" CLASS (MINESWEEPERS—COASTAL)

ANTIOPI (ex-Belgian *Herve*, M 921, ex-USS *MSC 153*) M 205
ATALANTI (ex-Belgian *St. Truiden*, M 919, ex-USS *MSC 169*) M 202
NIOVI (ex-Belgian *Laroche*, M 924, ex-USS *MSC 171*) M 254
FAEDRA (ex-Belgian *Malmedy*, M 922, ex-USS *MSC 154*) M 206
THALIA (ex-Belgian *Blankenberge*, M 923, ex-USS *MSC 170*) M 210

Displacement, tons: 330 standard; 402 full load
Dimensions, feet (metres): 145·0 oa × 27·9 × 8·0 *(44·2 × 8·5 × 2·4)*
Guns: 2—20 mm Oerlikon (1 twin)
Main engines: 2 GM diesels; 2 shafts; 900 bhp = 14 knots
Complement: 38 officers and men

Originally supplied to Belgium under MDAP. Subsequently returned to USA and simultaneously transferred to Greece as follows:— 29 July 1969 (*Herve* and *St. Truiden*) and 26 Sep 1969 (*Laroche*, *Malmedy* and *Blankenberge*).

ANTIOPI   *1973, Dr. Giorgio Arra*

SURVEY AND RESEARCH VESSELS

Name	No.	Builders	Commissioned
NAFTILOS	—	Greece	1976

Displacement, tons: 1 400
Complement: 74 (8 officers, 66 men)

ATALANTI

Of 383 tons, launched in 1954 with a complement of 35.

VEGAS (ex-*BYMS 2078*) A 748

Of 350 tons and with a complement of 33.
Former coastal minesweeper of the wooden hulled BYMS type.

ANEMOS (ex-German *KFK KW7*) A 469

Displaces 112 tons, was launched in 1944 and has a complement of 16. Added to the Navy List in 1969.

1 Ex-US "BARNEGAT" CLASS

Name	No.	Builders	Commissioned
HEPHESTOS (ex-USNS *Josiah Willard Gibbs*, T-AGOR 1, ex-USS *San Carlos*, AVP 51)	A 413	Lake Washington Shipyard, Houghton, Wash.	21 Mar 1944

Displacement, tons: 1 750 standard; 2 800 full load
Dimensions, feet (metres): 300·0 wl; 310·8 oa × 41·2 × 13·5 *(91·5; 94·8 × 12·6 × 4·1)*
Main engines: 2 Fairbanks-Morse diesels; 2 shafts; 6 080 bhp = 18 knots
Range, miles: 10 000 at 14 knots
Endurance: 30 days
Complement: 82 (8 officers and 74 men)

Former US seaplane tender converted for oceanographic research. Laid down on 7 Sep 1942, launched on 20 Dec 1942. Transferred to the Hellenic Navy on 7 Dec 1971.

HEPHESTOS   *1974, Hellenic Navy*

1 SURVEYING LAUNCH

Of 25 tons, launched in 1940. Complement 9.

SERVICE FORCES

1 Ex-FDR DEPOT SHIP

Name	No.	Builders	Commissioned
— (ex-*Weser A 62*)	—	Elsflether Werft	1960

Displacement, tons: 2 370
Dimensions, feet (metres): 323·5 × 38·8 × 11·2 *(99 × 11·8 × 3·4)*
Guns: 2—3·9 in *(100 mm)*; 4—40 mm
Main engines: 6 Diesels; 12 000 hp
Speed, knots: 20·5
Range, miles: 1 625 at 15 knots (economical)
Complement: 110

Transferred 1974.

2 ex-US "PATAPSCO" CLASS (SUPPORT TANKERS)

Name	No.	Builders	Commissioned
ARETHOUSA (ex-USS *Natchaug, AOG 54*)	A 377	Cargill Inc, Savage, Minn.	1945
ARIADNI (ex-USS *Tombigbee, AOG 11*)	A 414	—	1945

Displacement, tons: 1 850 light; 4 335 full load
Measurement, tons: 2 575 deadweight; cargo capacity 2 040
Dimensions, feet (metres): 292 wl; 310·8 oa × 48·5 × 15·7 *(89·1; 93·2 × 14·8 × 4·8)*
Guns: 4—3 in; 50 cal
Main engines: GM diesels; 2 shafts; 3 300 bhp = 14 knots
Complement: 43 (6 officers, 37 men)

Former US petrol carriers. *Arethousa* laid down on 15 Aug 1944. Launched on 16 Dec 1944. Transferred from the USA to Greece under the Mutual Defense Assistance Program in July 1959 and *Ariadni* transferred 7 July 1972, both at Pearl Harbor.

ARETHOUSA

1972, Hellenic Navy

1 PETROL CARRIER

ZEUS (ex-*YOG 98*) A 372

Dimensions, feet (metres): 165 × 35 × 10 *(50·3 × 10·2 × 3·2)*

Former US yard petrol carrier. Launched in 1944. Capacity 900 tons.

1 HARBOUR TANKER

SIRIOS (ex-*Poseidon*, ex-*Empire Faun*) A 345

Formerly on loan from Great Britain, but purchased outright in 1962. This ship was renamed *Sirios* when the name *Poseidon* was given to the submarine *Lapon* acquired from the USA in 1958. Capacity 850 tons.

1 HARBOUR TANKER

VIVIES A 471

Originally a water carrier. Capacity 687 tons.

1 HARBOUR TANKER

PROMETHEUS A 374

Launched in 1959. Capacity 520 tons.

1 HARBOUR TANKER

KRONOS (ex-*Islay*, ex-*Dresden*) A 373

Displacement, tons: 311
Capacity: 110 tons

1 HARBOUR TANKER

ORION (ex-US tanker Y 126) A 376

Formerly small United States yard tanker. Capacity 700 tons.

ORION

1969, Hellenic Navy

1 SALVAGE SHIP

SOTIR (ex-*Salventure*) A 384

Displacement, tons: 1 440 standard; 1 700 full load
Measurement, tons: 1 112 gross
Dimensions, feet (metres): 216 oa × 37·8 × 13 *(65·9 × 11·5 × 4)*
Main engines: Triple expansion; 2 shafts; 1 500 ihp = 12 knots
Oil fuel, tons: 310
Complement: 60

Former British Royal Fleet Auxiliary ocean salvage vessel of the "Salv" class. On loan from Great Britain. Equipped with a recompression chamber.

SOTIR

1972, Dr. Giorgio Arra

1 REPAIR SHIP

Name	No.	Builders	Commissioned
SAKIPIS (ex-*HNoMS Ellida*, ex-USS *ARB 18*, ex-USS *LST 50*)	A 329	Dravo Corporation, Pittsburgh	27 Nov 1943

Displacement, tons: 3 800 standard; 5 000 full load
Dimensions, feet (metres): 316 wl; 328 oa × 50 × 11 *(96·4; 100 × 15·3 × 3·4)*
Guns: 12—40 mm; 12—20 mm
Main engines: GM diesels; 2 shafts; 1 800 bhp = 10 knots
Complement: 200

Laid down on 29 Aug 1943, launched on 16 Oct 1943. Converted to a repair ship in 1952 by Puget Sound Bridge & Dry Dock Co. Taken over by the Royal Norwegian Navy at Seattle on 14 Nov 1952. Returned to the US Navy on 1 July 1960. Transferred to Greece on 16 Sep 1960 at Bergen.

SAKIPIS   *1972, Hellenic Navy*

1 NETLAYER

Name	No.	Builders	Commissioned
THETIS (ex-USS *AN 103*)	A 307	Krüger, Rendsburg	April 1960

Displacement, tons: 680 standard; 805 full load
Dimensions, feet (metres): 146 wl; 169·5 oa × 33·5 × 11·8 *(44·5; 51·7 × 10·2 × 3·6)*
Guns: 1—40 mm; 4—20 mm
Main engines: MAN diesels; 1 shaft; 1 400 bhp = 12 knots
Complement: 48

US offshore order. Launched in 1959.

THETIS   *1971, Hellenic Navy*

2 AUXILIARY TRANSPORTS

Name	No.	Builders	Commissioned
PANDORA	—	Perama Shipyard	1973
PANDROSOS	—	Perama Shipyard	1974

Displacement, tons: 350
Length, feet (metres): 212·2 *(64·6)*
Speed, knots: 13

Launched 1972 and 1973. Transport capacity for 500 people.

2 LIGHTHOUSE TENDERS (NEW CONSTRUCTION)

Displacement, tons: 1 350
Length, feet (metres): 207·3 *(63·2)*

Under construction (1976) at Perama Shipyard. Have facilities for small helicopter.

1 Ex-BRITISH "FLOWER" CLASS (LIGHTHOUSE TENDER)

Name	No.	Builders	Commissioned
ST. LYKOUDIS (ex-*Cania*, ex-HMS *Nasturtium*)	A 481	Smiths Dock Ltd	1940

Displacement, tons: 1 020 standard; 1 280 full load
Dimensions, feet (metres): 190 pp; 205 oa × 33 × 14·5 *(58; 62·5 × 10 × 4·4)*
Main engines: Triple expansion; 2 750 ihp = 14 knots
Boilers: 2 SE
Oil fuel, tons: 230

Former corvette originally planned for France but taken over on the stocks. Launched in 1940. Sold to Greece as a merchant ship in 1948 and bought by the Navy.

ST. LYKOUDIS   *1969, Hellenic Navy*

1 LIGHTHOUSE TENDER

SKYROS A 485

Displacement, tons: 350

12 TUGS

ACCHILEUS (ex-*Confident*)	ATROMITOS A 410	PERSEUS (ex-*ST 772*)
AIAS	CIGAS	ROMALEOS
ANKACHAK (ex-*YTM 767*)	MINOTAVROS	TITAN
ANTAIOS (ex-*Busy*)	(ex-*Theseus*, ex-*ST 539*)	SAMSON (ex-*F 16*)
ATLAS (ex-*F 5*)		

Ankachak transferred on lease 1972.

5 WATER BOATS

ILIKI	KASTORIA	STYMFALIA	TRICHONIS	VOLVI

Capacity: *Iliki* and *Stymfalia* 120 tons, *Trihonis* 300 tons, *Volvi* 350 tons, *Kastoria* 520 tons.

GRENADA

Grenada was granted self-government, in association with Great Britain (who was responsible for her defence) on 3 March 1967.

Full self-government was achieved in February 1973.

Mercantile Marine

Lloyd's Register of Shipping: 2 vessels of 226 tons gross

1 COASTAL PATROL CRAFT

Displacement, tons: 15
Dimensions, feet (metres): 40 × 12 × 2 *(12·2 × 3·7 × 0·6)*
Guns: 3 MG
Main engines: 2 Diesels; 370 hp = 22 knots

Delivered by Brooke Marine, Lowestoft early in 1972.

GUATEMALA

On 5 Jan 1959 Guatemala announced the establishment of a navy for coastguard work. Subsequently the navy was assigned missions of search and rescue and the support of amphibious operations. The commissioning of a Marine Elevator (Synchrolift) at Santo Tomás on 23 June 1973 (230 ton lift) has greatly improved this navy's repair facilities.

Personnel

(a) 1976: 400 (50 officers and 350 men, including 10 officers and 200 men of the Marines)
(b) 2 years National Service

Bases

Santo Tomás de Castillas (Atlantic); Sipacate (Pacific)

Mercantile Marine

Lloyd's Register of Shipping: 7 vessels of 9 584 tons gross

2 85 ft COASTAL PATROL CRAFT

Name	No.	Builders	Commissioned
USORIO SARAVIA	P 852	Sewart, Florida	1972
UTATLAN	P 851	Sewart, Florida	May 1967

Displacement, tons: 42
Dimensions, feet (metres): 85 × 18·7 × 3 *(25·9 × 5·7 × 0·9)*
Guns: 2 MG
Main engines: 2 GM Diesels; 2 200 bhp = 23 knots
Range, miles: 400 at 12 knots
Complement: 12 (2 officers, 10 ratings)

Built to "Commercial Cruiser" design.

UTATLAN   *1973, Guatemalan Navy*

3 65 ft COASTAL PATROL CRAFT

Name	No.	Builders	Commissioned
AZUMANCHE	P 653	Halter, USA	1972
KAIBILBALAM	P 652	Halter, USA	1972
TECUNUMAN	P 651	Halter, USA	1972

Displacement, tons: 32
Dimensions, feet (metres): 64·5 × 17 × 3 *(19·7 × 5·2 × 0·9)*
Guns: 2 MG
Main engines: 2 GM Diesels = 25 knots
Complement: 10 (2 officers, 8 ratings)

2 63 ft COASTAL CRAFT (ex-USCGS)

Name	No.	Builders	Commissioned
CABRAKAN	P 631	USA	—
HUNAHPU	P 632	USA	—

Displacement, tons: 32
Dimensions, feet (metres): 63·3 × 15·4 × 3 *(19·3 × 4·7 × 0·9)*
Guns: 2 MG
Main engines: 2 GM Diesels 8V71 = 25 knots
Complement: 10 (2 officers, 8 men)

Transferred from USA—*Hunahpu,* 1964; *Cabrakan,* 1965.

2 Ex-USCG UTILITY BOATS MK IV

TIKAL P 401   IXINCHE P 402

Of 40 ft. Transferred Aug 1963.

2 28 ft COASTAL PATROL CRAFT

XUCUXUY P 281   CAMALOTE P 282

Striker Utility Patrol Craft modified for one GM 6-53 Diesel. 28 ft, 6½ tons with 1 MG. Transferred in 1961.

1 Ex-US LCM 6 MK VI

CHINALTENANGO 561

Transferred Dec 1965.

6 Ex-US LCUs

Transferred in late 1960s.

1 Ex-US REPAIR BARGE

Ex-US YR 40. Transferred in 1952.

1 TUG

Note: Three other names listed—*Escuintla, Mazatenango, Retalhuleu*—in addition to two yachts—*Mendieta* and one other.

GUINEA

Personnel	Base	Mercantile Marine
1976: 350 officers and men	Conakry	*Lloyd's Register of Shipping:* 10 vessels of 15 054 tons gross

---

LIGHT FORCES

4 Ex-CHINESE "SHANGHAI" CLASS (FAST ATTACK CRAFT—GUN)

P 733   P 734   P 735   P 736

Displacement, tons: 120 standard; 155 full load
Dimensions, feet (metres): 128 × 18 × 5·6 *(39 × 5·5 × 1·7)*
Guns: 4—37 mm; 2—25 mm
A/S weapons: 8 DCs
Mines: Minerails can be fitted for some 10 mines
Main engines: 4 Diesels; 4 800 hp = 30 knots
Complement: 25

Transferred 1973-74.

"SHANGHAI" Class

4 Ex-SOVIET "P 6" CLASS (FAST ATTACK CRAFT—TORPEDO)

Displacement, tons: 66 standard; 75 full load
Dimensions, feet (metres): 84·2 × 20·0 × 6·0 *(25·7 × 6·1 × 1·8)*
Guns: 4—25 mm
Tubes: 2—21 in (or mines or depth charges)
Main engines: 4 Diesels; 4 shafts; 4 800 bhp = 43 knots
Range, miles: 450 at 30 knots
Complement: 25

It seems unlikely that the torpedo armament is operational.

2 Ex-SOVIET "POLUCHAT I" CLASS (COASTAL PATROL CRAFT)

Displacement, tons: 86 standard; 91 full load
Dimensions, feet (metres): 98·0 pp × 15·0 × 4·8 *(29·9 × 4·6 × 1·5)*
Guns: 2—14·5 mm (1 twin)
Main engines: 2 diesels; 2 shafts; 1 200 bhp = 18 knots
Oil fuel, tons: 9·25
Range, miles: 460 at 17 knots
Complement: 16 (2 officers, 14 ratings)

2 Ex-SOVIET "MO VI" CLASS (COASTAL PATROL CRAFT)

Displacement, tons: 64 standard; 73 full load
Dimensions, feet (metres): 83·6 × 19·7 × 4·0 *(25·5 × 6 × 1·2)*
Guns: 4—25 mm (twin)
A/S weapons: DC mortars and racks
Main engines: 4 Diesels; 4 shafts; 4 800 hp = 40 knots

Transferred 1972-73. Radar—Pot Head.

LANDING CRAFT

2 SMALL UTILITY TYPE

Recent visits by considerable numbers of Soviet ships may have increased these numbers.

GUINEA BISSAU

Personnel

(a) 1976: 100 officers and men.
(b) Voluntary service.

Base

Bissau.

LIGHT FORCES

1 Ex-SOVIET "P 6" CLASS (FAST ATTACK CRAFT TORPEDO)

Details as above under Guinea. Transferred 1974.

1 Ex-SOVIET "POLUCHAT I" CLASS (COASTAL PATROL CRAFT

Details as above under Guinea. Transferred 1974.

GUYANA

Mercantile Marine

Lloyd's Register of Shipping: 63 vessels of 16 828 tons gross

Bases

Georgetown, New Amsterdam

LARGE PATROL CRAFT

There are unconfirmed reports of the ordering of up to three 33 metre craft for delivery in Nov 1976.

3 VOSPER 12·2 METRE TYPE
(COASTAL PATROL CRAFT)

Name	No.	Builders	Commissioned
JAGUAR	—	Vospers	28 April 1971
MARGAY	—	Vospers	21 May 1971
OCELOT	—	Vospers	22 June 1971

Displacement, tons: 10
Dimensions, feet (metres): 40 × 12 × 3·5 *(12·2 × 3·7 × 1·1)*
Gun: 1—7·62 mm MG
Main engines: 2 Cummins diesels; 370 hp = 19 knots
Range, miles: 150 at 12 knots
Complement: 6

They have glass fibre hulls with aluminium superstructures.

1 or 2 Ex-US LSTs

Reported that these will shortly be transferred.

1 LIGHTER

YFN 960 transferred from US 1 Aug 1975.

JAGUAR   *1971, C. and S. Taylor*

HAITI

Personnel

(a) 1976: Total 300 (40 officers and 260 men)
(b) Voluntary service

Base

Port Au Prince

COAST GUARD VESSELS

1 Ex-US "COHOES" CLASS (ex-NETLAYER)

Name	No.	Builders	Commissioned
JEAN JACQUES DESSALINES (ex-USS *Tonawanda, AN 89*)	GC10	Leatham D. Smith SB Co	1944

Displacement, tons: 650 standard; 785 full load
Dimensions, feet (metres): 168·5 × 33 × 10·8 *(51·4 × 10 × 3·3)*
Guns: 1—76 mm; 3—20 mm
Main engines: Busch-Sulzer diesel-electric; 1 200 shp = 12 knots
Complement: 48

Launched on 14 Nov 1944. Loaned to Haiti in 1960.

1 ex-US WAGL TYPE

Name	No.	Builders	Commissioned
AMIRAL KILLICK (ex-USCG *Black Rock, WAGL 367*)	GC 7	—	Jan 1956 (Haiti)

Displacement, tons: 160
Length feet (metres): 114 *(35)*

Former buoy tender purchased from the US Coast Guard in 1955, commissioned in Jan 1956.

1 ex- USCG 95 ft CUTTER

Name	No.	Builders	Commissioned
LA CRETE A PIERROT (ex-USCG *953 15*)	GC 8	US Coast Guard Yard, Curtiss Bay, Maryland	—

Displacement, tons: 100
Dimensions, feet (metres): 95 × 19 × 5 *(29 × 5·8 × 1·5)*
Guns: 3—20 mm
Main engines: 4 diesels; 2 shafts; 2 200 bhp = 21 knots
Range, miles: 1 500
Complement: 15

Former US Coast Guard steel cutter. Acquired on 26 Feb 1956.

1 ex-US SC TYPE

SEIZE AOUT 1946 (ex-*SC 453*) GC 2

Displacement, tons: 110 standard; 138 full load
Dimensions, feet (metres): 110·5 × 18·8 × 6·5 *(33·7 × 5·7 × 2)*
Guns: 2—40 mm; 2—20 mm
Main engines: Diesels; 2 shafts; 1 000 hp = 15 knots

Of the SC type acquired during 1947 from the US Navy. Launched in 1943. Laid up in reserve.

1 Ex-USCG 56 ft CUTTER

Name	No.	Builders	Commissioned
SAVANNAH (ex-USCG *563200*)	GC 1	Wheeler Shipyard, Brooklyn, USA	1944

Displacement, tons: 47
Dimensions, feet (metres): 56 × 16 × 4·2 *(17·1 × 4·9 × 1·3)*
Main engines: Diesels; 2 shafts; 200 bhp = 9 knots
Complement: 12

1 Ex-US LCT

ARTIBONITE (ex-US *LCT)* GC 5

Displacement, tons: 134 standard; 285 full load
Dimensions, feet (metres): 120·3 oa × 32 × 4·2 *(36·7 × 9·8 × 1·3)*
Main engines: 3 diesels; 675 bhp = 8 knots
Range, miles: 700 at 7 knots
Complement: 12

Former US tank landing craft. Transferred 1944. Salvaged by Haitian Coast Guard after grounding and converted.

6 Ex-USCG 83 ft CUTTERS

Displacement, tons: 45
Dimensions, feet (metres): 83 × 16 × 4·5 *(25·3 × 4·9 × 1·4)*
Gun: 1—20 mm
Main engines: 2 Petrol; 1 200 hp = 20 knots

Built in 1942.

1 PRESIDENTIAL YACHT

SANS SOUCI (ex-*Captain James Taylor)*

Displacement, tons: 161
Main engines: 2 diesels; 2 shafts; 300 bhp × 10 knots

Employed, when required, as the Presidential Yacht. Built in USA.

HONDURAS

Mercantile Marine

Lloyd's Register of Shipping: 60 vessels of 67 923 tons gross

3 COASTAL PATROL CRAFT

Employed on coastguard duties.

1 ex-US LST

Reported as being transferred.

HONG KONG

All the following craft are operated by the Marine District of the Royal Hong Kong Police Force.

Personnel

(a) 1976: 71 officers, 330 NCOs, 891 constables
(b) Voluntary service

Mercantile Marine

Lloyd's Register of Shipping: 104 vessels of 418 512 tons gross

Deletion

1975: Logistic Craft No 24
45 ft Patrol Craft No 5 and 8

2 COMMAND VESSELS

No. 1   No. 2

Displacement, tons: 222·5
Dimensions, feet (metres): 111·3 × 24 × 10·5 *(33·9 × 7·3 × 3·2)*
Main engines: 2 diesels of 337 bhp = 11·8 knots
Range, miles: 5 200 at 11·8 knots
Complement: 25

Built at Taikoo 1965 (now Hong Kong United Dockyard). Can carry two platoons in addition to complement. Cost $HK 1 778 550.

POLICE LAUNCH No. 2   *1974, RHKP*

7 78 ft PATROL CRAFT

Nos. 50-56

Displacement, tons: 82
Dimensions, feet (metres): 78·5 oa × 17·2 × 5·6 *(23·9 × 5·2 × 1·7)*
Gun: 1—50 cal MG
Main engines: Two Cummins diesels; 1 500 hp = 20·7 knots
Range, miles: 4 000 at 20 knots
Complement: 16

Steel hulled craft built by Vosper Thornycroft Private Ltd, Singapore. Delivered May 1972 to May 1973 to the Royal Hong Kong Police. Can carry an extra Platoon. Cost $HK 1 873 800.

POLICE LAUNCH No. 51   *1974, RHKP*

1 78 ft PATROL CRAFT

No. 4

Slightly smaller than the above with 3 diesels, a speed of 15·5 knots and a range of 600 miles at that speed.

1 65 ft PATROL CRAFT

No. 6

Slightly smaller than Nos. 26-34 with single diesel and 48 tons. Complement 12. Range 1 400 miles at 9 knots.

Nos. 20-22

Displacement, tons: 17
Dimensions, feet (metres): 40·3 × 11·6 × 2 *(12·3 × 3·5 × 0·6)*
Main engines: 2 diesels of 370 bhp = 24 knots
Range, miles: 380 at 24 knots
Complement: 5

Built in Choy Lee in 1971.

POLICE LAUNCH No. 22

No. 3

Of 37 tons and 16 knots with a range of 240 miles at 15 knots. Complement 8. Built by Thornycroft Singapore in 1958.

POLICE LAUNCH No. 3

1 LOGISTIC CRAFT

No. 7

Of 18·5 tons and 23·5 knots. Range 200 miles at 20 knots. Complement of 5—can carry 25 passengers. Built by Hip Hing Cheung Shipyard in 1975.

9 70 ft PATROL CRAFT

Nos. 26-34

Displacement, tons: 52
Dimensions, feet (metres): 70 × 17 × 5·2 *(24·5 × 5·2 × 1·6)*
Main engines: 2 Diesels of 215 bhp = 10 knots
Range, miles: 1 600 at 10 knots
Complement: 12

8 45 ft PATROL CRAFT

Nos. 9-16

Displacement, tons: 27·7
Dimensions, feet (metres): 45 × 15 × 7 *(13·7 × 4·6 × 2·1)*
Main engines: 1 diesel; 144 bhp = 9 knots
Range, miles: 1 700 at 8 knots
Complement: 5

Built in Australia—1944.

3 40 ft PATROL CRAFT

1974, RHKP

1 58 ft LOGISTIC CRAFT

1974, RHKP

11 22 ft LAUNCHES

Nos. 35-45

Of 4·8 tons and 20 knots with a range of 160 miles at full speed. Built in Choy Lee in 1970.

HUNGARY

Diplomatic Representation

Military and Air Attaché London: Lieut Colonel Károly Mészáros

Personnel

(a) 1976: 500 officers and men
(b) 2 years national service

Mercantile Marine

Lloyd's Register of Shipping: 16 vessels of 47 943 tons gross

The Navy was dissolved by 1969 but a maritime wing of the Army is still very active on the Danube.

10 100 ton PATROL CRAFT

Displacement, tons: 100
Gun: 1—14·7 mm
Main engines: 2 diesels

5 LCUs

100 ton Patrol Craft

1972, Hungarian River Guard

ICELAND

Personnel

1976: 170 officers and men

Duties

The Coast Guard Service (Landhelgisgaezlan) deals with fishery protection, salvage, rescue, hydrographic research, surveying and lighthouse duties.

Bases

Reykjavik
Akurreyri

Aircraft

2 Bell helicopter
(1 helicopter on order)
1 Fokker Friendship (1 more on order)

Research Ships

A number of Research Ships bearing RE pendant number operate off Iceland.

Mercantile Marine

Lloyd's Register of Shipping:
363 vessels of 154 381 tons gross

COAST GUARD PATROL VESSELS

Name	No.	Builders	Commissioned
AEGIR	—	Aalborg Vaerft, Denmark	1968
TYR	—	Aarhus Flyedock AS, Aalborg, Denmark	15 Mar 1975

Displacement, tons: 1 150 *(Tyr 1500)*
Dimensions, feet (metres): 204 × 33 × 14·8 *(62·2 × 10 × 4·6) Aegir*
229·6 × 32·8 × 19 *(70 × 10 × 5·8) Tyr*
Gun: 1—57 mm
Main engines: 2 MAN diesels; 2 shafts; 8 000 bhp = 19 knots (8 600 hp = 20 knots *Tyr*)
Complement: 22

Aegir was the first new construction patrol vessel for the Icelandic Coast Guard Service for about eight years. Projected in Feb 1965. Laid down in May 1967. *Tyr*, basically similar to *Aegir*, but a slightly improved design with higher speed was launched by Aarhus Flyedock AS, Aalborg, Denmark on 10 October 1974. Both have helicopter deck.

AEGIR   1969, Icelandic Coast Guard

Name	No.	Builders	Commissioned
ODINN	—	Aalborg Vaerft, Denmark	Jan 1960

Measurement, tons: 1 000
Dimensions, feet (metres): 187 pp × 33 × 13 *(57 × 10 × 4)*
Gun: 1—157 mm
Main engines: 2 B and W diesels; 2 shafts; 5 050 bhp = 18 knots
Complement: 22

Laid down in Jan 1959. Launched in Sep 1959. Refitted in Denmark by Aarhus Flydedock late 1975, with twin funnels and helicopter hanger.

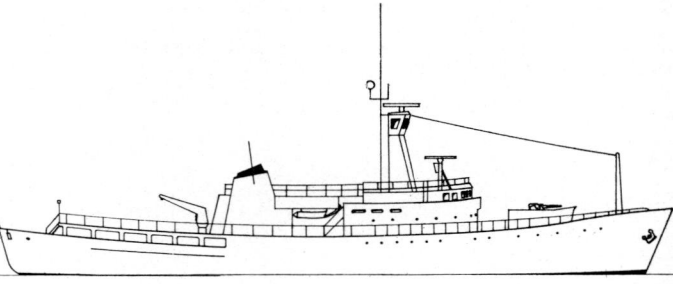

ODINN (after 1975 refit)   1975, Icelandic Coast Guard

Name	No.	Builders	Commissioned
ALBERT	—	Stalsmidjan, Reykjavik	Apr 1957

Measurement, tons: 200 gross
Dimensions, feet (metres): Length: 111·2 *(33·9)*
Gun: 1—47 mm
Main engines: 1 Nohab diesel; 650 bhp = 12·5 knots
Complement: 15

Launched in 1956. Refitted in 1972.

ALBERT   1975, Icelandic Coast Guard

Name	No.	Builders	Commissioned
ARVAKUR	—	Netherlands	1962

Displacement, tons: 716
Dimensions, feet (metres): 106 × 33 G 13 *(32·3 × 10 × 4)*
Gun: 1 MG
Main engine: 1 diesel; 1 000 bhp = 12 knots
Complement: 12

Built as a lighthouse tender in the Netherlands. Acquired by Iceland for duty in the Coast Guard Service in 1969.

ARVAKUR   1969, Icelandic Coast Guard

Name	No.	Builders	Commissioned
THOR	—	Aalborg Vaerft, Denmark	Late 1951

Displacement, tons: 920
Dimensions, feet (metres): 183·3 pp; 206 oa × 31·2 × 13 *(55·8; 62·8 × 9·5 × 4)*
Gun: 1—57 mm
Main engines: 2 8 cyl. Crossley diesels; 3 200 bhp = 17 knots
Complement: 22

Launched in 1951. Fitted with helicopter platform during refit in 1972. Now has twin funnels and hanger.

THOR

1975, Icelandic Coast Guard

Name	No.	Builders	Commissioned
BALDUR	—	Stoeznia Im. Kommuny Paryskiez, Gdynia, Poland	1974

Displacement, tons: 740
Dimensions, feet (metres): 201 × 37 × 15 *(62 × 11·3 × 4·6)*
Gun: 1—57 mm
Main engines: 6 cyl Sulzer diesel; 3 000 bhp; 3 000 bhp = 15 knots; single shaft
Complement: 20

Stern trawler taken over on charter in 1975 from Adalsteinn Loftssohn, Dalvik.

BALDUR

2/1976

INDIA

Headquarters Appointment

Chief of the Naval Staff:
Admiral J. Cursetji

Senior Appointments

Flag Officer C in C, Western Naval Command:
———

Flag Officer Commanding Western Fleet:
Rear Admiral N. P. Datta
Flag Officer C in C Eastern Naval Command:
Vice-Admiral K. L. Kulkarni
Flag Officer Commanding Eastern Fleet:
Rear-Admiral R. K. S. Ghandi
Flag Officer, Southern Naval Area:
Rear-Admiral R. L. Pereira

Diplomatic Representation

Naval Attaché in Bonn:
Captain L. Ramdas
Naval Adviser, Dacca:
Captain R. B. Mukherjee
Naval Attaché in Djakarta:
Captain R. Vir
Naval Adviser in London:
Commodore C. L. Sachdeva
Naval Attaché in Moscow:
Commodore G. K. Nadkar
Defence Attaché in Washington:
Brigadier Srendra Singh MC

Personnel

(a) 1976: 46 000 officers and ratings (including Naval Air Arm)
(b) Voluntary service

Naval Bases and Establishments

Bombay (C in C Western Fleet, barracks and main Dockyard);
Vishakapatnam (C in C Eastern Command, submarine base, dockyard and barracks);
Cochin (FO Southern Area Naval Air Station, barracks and professional schools);
Lonavala and Jamnagar (professional schools);
Calcutta, Goa and Port Blair (small bases only).

Naval Air Arm

Squadron No.	Aircraft	Role
300	Seahawk FGA6	Strike
310	Alize 1050	ASW
321	Alouette III	SAR
330	Sea Kings	ASW
331	Alouette III	ASW
550	Alize, Alouette	Training
561	HTZ16, Devon Hughes 300, Alouette III	Training

Prefix to Ships' Names

IS (Indian Ship)

Mercantile Marine

Lloyd's Register of Shipping:
471 vessels of 3 869 187 tons gross

Strength of the Fleet

Type	Active	Building
Attack Carrier (Medium)	1	—
Cruisers	2	—
Destroyers	3	—
Frigates	25	2
Patrol Submarines	8	—
Fast Attack Craft—Missile	8	—
Large Patrol Craft	1	—
Coastal Patrol Craft	7	—
Landing Ship	1	—
Landing Craft	6	—
Minesweepers—Coastal	4	—
Minesweepers—Inshore	4	—
Survey Ships	3	—
Submarine Tender	1	—
Submarine Rescue Ship	1	—
Replenishment Tanker	1	—
Support Tankers	3	—
Harbour Tankers	2	—
Repair Ship	1	—
Ocean Tug	1	—
Harbour Craft	5	—

DELETIONS

Frigates

1971 *Khukri* sunk in war with Pakistan (9 Dec)
1975 *Ganga* and *Gomati* ("Hunt" Class) paid off.

Survey Ship

1975 *Investigator* ("River" class) paid off.

Light Forces

1974 *Ajay* and *Akshay* to Bangladesh, *Amar* to Mauritius (April).
1975 *Savitri, Sharayu, Subhadra, Suvarna* paid off.

Minewarfare Forces

1973 *Konkan* (last of 6 "Bangor" class) paid off.

PENNANT LIST

Aircraft Carrier

R	11	Vikrant

Cruisers

C	60	Mysore
C	74	Delhi

Destroyers

D	92	Godavari
D	115	Rana
D	141	Ranjit
D	209	Rajput

Frigates

F	11	Jamuna (Survey)
F	31	Brahmaputra
F	33	Nilgiri
F	34	Himgiri
F	35	Udaygiri
F	36	Dunagiri
F	46	Kistna
F	95	Sutlej
F	110	Kaveri
F	137	Beas
F	139	Betwa
F	140	Talwar
F	143	Trishul
F	144	Kirpan
F	146	Kuthar
F	256	Tir

Submarines

S	40	Vela
S	41	Vagir
S	42	Vagli
S	43	Vagsheer
S	121	Kalvari
S	122	Kanderi
S	123	Karanj
S	124	Karsula

Light Forces
(including "Petya" class)

P	68	Arnala
P	69	Androth
P	73	Anjadip
P	74	Andaman
P	75	Amini
P	77	Kamorta
P	78	Kadmath
P	79	Kiltan
P	80	Kavaratti
P	81	Katchal
P	246	Panvel
P	247	Pamban
P	248	Puri
P	249	Panaji
P	250	Pulicat
P	684	Nashak
P	685	Nirbhik
P	686	Veer
P	690	Nirghat
P	691	Nipat
P	692	Vinash
P	693	Vigeta
P	694	Vidyut
SPB	3132	Sukanya
SPB	3133	Sharada
P	3135	Abhay

Minewarfare Forces

M	89	Bhaktal
M	90	Bulsar
M	1190	Kuddalore
M	1191	Cannanore
M	1197	Karwar
M	1201	Kakinada
M	2705	Bimlipitan
M	2707	Bassein

Amphibious Forces

L	3011	Magar
L	3032	Gharial
L	3033	Guldar
L	3034	Ghorpad
L	—	Kesari
L	—	Shardul
L	—	Sharab

Service Forces

A	14	Amba
A	15	Nistar
A	136	Shakti
A	139	Darshak
A	306	Dharini
A	1750	Deepak

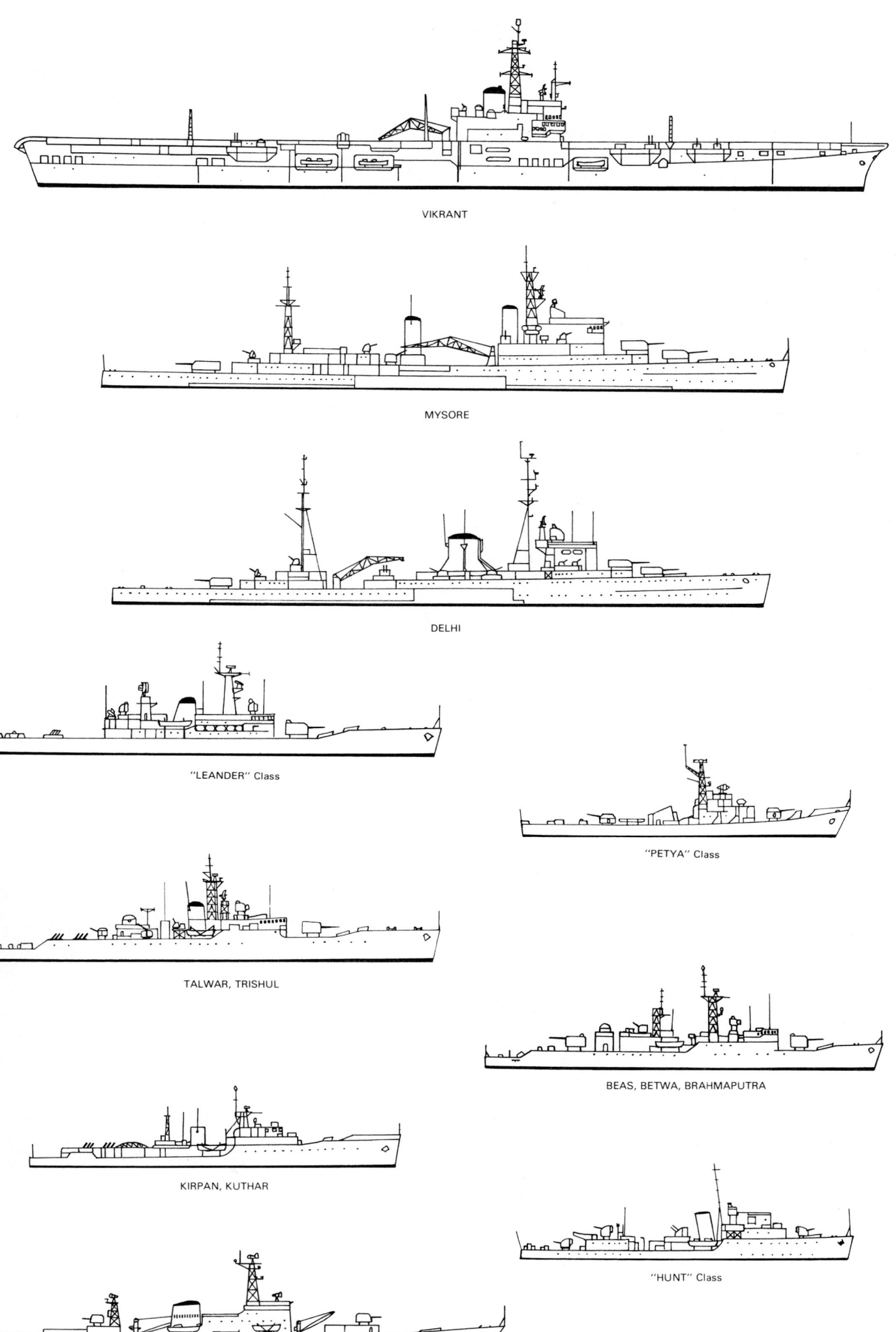

VIKRANT

MYSORE

DELHI

"LEANDER" Class

"PETYA" Class

TALWAR, TRISHUL

BEAS, BETWA, BRAHMAPUTRA

KIRPAN, KUTHAR

"HUNT" Class

AMBA

AIRCRAFT CARRIER (ATTACK MEDIUM)

1 Ex-BRITISH "MAJESTIC" CLASS

Name	No.	Builders	Laid down	Launched	Commissioned
VIKRANT (ex-HMS *Hercules*)	R 11	Vickers-Armstrong Ltd, Tyne	14 Oct 1943	22 Sep 1945	4 Mar 1961

Displacement, tons: 16 000 standard; 19 500 full load
Length, feet (metres): 630 *(192·0)* pp; 700 *(213·4)* oa
Beam, feet (metres): 80 *(24·4)* hull
Width, feet (metres): 128 *(39·0)*
Draught, feet (metres): 24 *(7·3)*
Aircraft: 22 capacity (18 Seahawk, 4 Alize)
Guns: 15—40 mm (4 twin, 7 single)
Main engines: Parsons single reduction geared turbines; 40 000 shp; 2 shafts
Boilers: 4 Admiralty 3-drum; 400 psi; 700°F
Speed, knots: 24·5
Oil fuel, tons: 3 200
Range, miles: 12 000 at 14 knots; 6 200 at 23 knots
Complement: 1 075 (peace); 1 345 (war)

Acquired from Great Britain in Jan 1957 after having been suspended in May 1946 when structurally almost complete and 75% fitted out. Taken in hand by Harland & Wolff Ltd, Belfast, in April 1957 for completion in 1961. Commissioned on 4 Mar 1961 and renamed *Vikrant*.
Completed extensive overhaul—1973 to Aug 1974.

Aircraft: Still equipped with Seahawks although re-equipment is planned. Harrier trials in mid-1972 showed promise, but subsequently the IN is understood to have preferred Soviet Yakovlev VTOL aircraft due to problems in purchasing the Harrier.

Engineering: One set of turbines and two boilers are installed side by side in each of the two propelling machinery spaces, on the unit system, so that the starboard propeller shaft is longer than the port.

Flight deck: The aircraft, including strike and anti-submarine aircraft, operate from an angled deck with steam catapult, landing sights and two electrically operated lifts.

Habitability: Partially air-conditioned and insulated for tropical service, the ship's sides being sprayed with asbestos cement instead of being lagged. Separate messes and dining halls.

Radar: Search: Type 960, Type 277.
Tactical: Type 293.
Miscellaneous: Type 963 Carrier Controlled Approach.

1971, John G. Callis

VIKRANT

CRUISERS
1 Ex-BRITISH "FIJI" CLASS

Name	No.	Builders	Laid down	Launched	Commissioned
MYSORE (ex-HMS *Nigeria*)	C 60	Vickers-Armstrong Ltd, Tyne	8 Feb 1938	18 July 1939	23 Sep 1940

Displacement, tons: 8 700 standard; 11 040 full load
Length, feet (metres): 538·0 *(164·0)* pp; 549·0 *(176·3)*wl
555·5 *(169·3)* oa
Beam, feet (metres): 62·0 *(18·9)*
Draught, feet (metres): 21·0 *(6·4)*
Guns: 9—6 in *(152 mm)*, (3 triple); 8—4 in *(102 mm)*, (4 twin); 12—40 mm (5 twin, 2 single)
Armour: Side 4½ in—3 in *(114—76 mm)*; Deck 2 in *(51 mm)*; Conning tower 4 in *(102 mm)*; Turrets 2 in *(51 mm)*
Main engines: Parsons geared turbines; 4 shafts; 72 500 shp
Boilers: 4 Admiralty 3-drum type
Speed, knots: 31·5
Complement: 800

MYSORE

1971, Roland Rodwell

Flagship at the Battle of Porsanger Fjord Sep 1941. Purchased from Great Britain on 8 April 1954 for £300 000. Extensively refitted and reconstructed by Cammell Laird & Co Ltd, Birkenhead, before commissioning. Formally handed over to the Indian Navy at Birkenhead and renamed *Mysore* on 29 Aug 1957. Involved in two serious collisions, the second in late 1972 with *Beas*, resulting in two months of repairs.

Radar: Search: Type 960, Type 277.
Tactical: Type 293.
Fire control: I Band.

Reconstruction: Ship formerly had tripod masts. During reconstruction the triple 6 inch turret in "X" position and the 6—21 inch torpedo tubes (tripled) were removed, the bridge was modified, two lattice masts were stepped, all electrical equipment was replaced and the engine room and other parts of the ship were refitted.

1 Ex-BRITISH "LEANDER" CLASS

Name	No.
DELHI (ex-HMS *Achilles*)	C 74

Builders	Laid down	Launched	Commissioned
Cammell Laird & Co Ltd, Birkenhead	11 June 1931	1 Sep 1932	5 Oct 1933

Displacement, tons: 7 114 standard; 9 740 full load
Length, feet (metres): 522·0 *(159·1)* pp; 544·5 *(166·0)* oa
Beam, feet (metres): 55·2 *(16·8)*
Draught, feet (metres): 20·0 *(6·1)*
Guns: 6—6 in *(152 mm)* (3 twins); 8—4 in *(102mm)* (twins);
14—40 mm (4 twin, 6 single); 4—3 pdr saluting
Armour: 4 in-2 in side; 1 in gunhouses; 1 in bridge; 2 in deck
Main engines: Parsons geared turbines; 4 shafts 72 000 shp
Boilers: 4 Admiralty 3-drum type
Oil fuel, tons: 1 800
Speed, knots: 32
Complement: 800

As HMS *Achilles*, then lent to the Royal New Zealand Navy, this
ship, with HMS *Ajax* and HMS *Exeter*, defeated the German
battleship *Admiral Graf Spee* in the Battle of the River Plate on
13 Dec 1939. Purchased from Great Britain and delivered on 5
July 1948. Refitted in 1955. Now used for training.

Radar: Search: Type 960, Type 277.
Tactical: Type 293.
Fire control: Early design.

Torpedo Tubes: In 1958 the original eight 21 inch torpedo
tubes, in two quadruple banks, were removed, and the forecastle deck plating was consequently extended aft to the twin 40
mm gun mounting abreast the boat stowage.

DELHI

1969, Graeme Andrews

DESTROYERS

3 Ex-BRITISH "R" CLASS

Name	No.
RANA (ex-HMS *Raider*)	D 115
RAJPUT (ex-HMS *Rotherham*)	D 209
RANJIT (ex-HMS *Redoubt*)	D 141

Builders	Laid down	Launched	Commissioned
Cammell Laird & Co Ltd, Birkenhead	16 April 1941	1 April 1942	16 Nov 1942
John Brown & Co Ltd, Clydebank	10 April 1941	21 Mar 1942	27 Aug 1942
John Brown & Co Ltd, Clydebank	19 June 1941	2 May 1942	1 Oct 1942

Displacement, tons: 1 725 standard; 2 424 full load
Length, feet (metres): 339·5 *(103·5)* wl; 362·0 *(110·3)* oa
Beam, feet (metres): 35·7 *(10·9)*
Draught, feet (metres): 17·1 *(5·2)*
Guns: 4—4·7 in *(120 mm)* (singles); 4—40 mm
A/S weapons: 4 DCT
Torpedo tubes: 8—21 in (2 quadruple) in *Rana*
Main engines: Parsons geared turbines; 2 shafts 40 000 shp
Boilers: 2 Admiralty 3-drum type
Oil fuel, tons: 490
Speed, knots: 32
Range, miles: 2 500 at 20 knots
Complement: 240

First British destroyers with officers accommodation forward
instead of aft. Refitted and modernised before transfer. Arrived
in Indian waters in Jan 1950. Constitute 11th Destroyer Squadron of which *Rajput* is Leader. *Rana* now in reserve.

Radar: Search: Type 293.

Transfers: *Rana* 9 Sep 1949; *Rajput* 29 July 1949;
Ranjit 4 July 1949.

RAJPUT

FRIGATES

4 + 2 "LEANDER" CLASS

Name	No.
DUNAGIRI	F 36
HIMGIRI	F 34
NILGIRI	F 33
UDAYGIRI	F 35
—	—
—	—

Builders	Laid down	Launched	Commissioned
Mazagon Docks Ltd, Bombay	Jan 1973	9 Mar 1974	1976
Mazagon Docks Ltd, Bombay	1967	6 May 1970	23 Nov 1974
Mazagon Docks Ltd, Bombay	Oct 1966	23 Oct 1968	3 June 1972
Mazagon Docks Ltd, Bombay	14 Sep 1970	24 Oct 1972	1975
Mazagon Docks Ltd, Bombay	—	—	—
Mazagon Docks Ltd, Bombay			

Displacement, tons: 2 450 standard; 2 800 full load
Length, feet (metres): 360 *(109·7)* wl; 372 *(113·4)* oa
Beam, feet (metres): 43 *(13·1)*
Draught, feet (metres): 18 *(5·5)*
Aircraft: 1 Wasp helicopter
Missiles: 2 "Seacat" quadruple launchers
Guns: 2—4·5 in *(115 mm)* (1 twin); 2—40 mm
A/S weapons: 1 "Limbo" 3 barrelled DC mortar
Main engines: 2 geared turbines; 30 000 shp
Boilers: 2
Oil fuel, tons: 460
Speed, knots: 30
Range, miles: 4 500 at 12 knots
Complement: 263

First major warships built in Indian yards. Of similar design to
later (broad beam) "Leander" class in the Royal Navy.

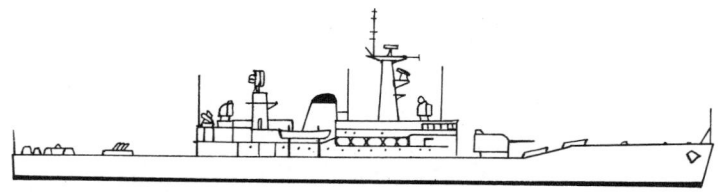

"LEANDER" Class

10 ex-SOVIET "PETYA" CLASS

AMINI P 75	KADMATH P 78	
ANDAMAN P 74	KAMORTA P 77	
ANDROTH P 69	KATCHAL P 81	
ANJADIP P 73	KAVARATTI P 80	
ARNALA P 68	KILTAN P 79	

Displacement, tons: 950 standard; 1 150 full load
Length, feet (metres): 250·0 (76·2) wl; 270 (82·3) oa
Beam, feet (metres): 29·9 (9·1)
Draught, feet (metres): 10·5 (3·2)
Guns: 4—3 in (76 mm) (2 twin)
A/S weapons: 4 MBU 2 500 (16 barrelled rocket launchers)
Torpedo tubes: 5—16 in ("K" names); 3—21 in ("A" names)
Main engines: 2 gas turbines; 30 000 hp;
  2 diesels; 2 shafts; 6 000 hp
Speed, knots: 30
Complement: 100

"PETYA" Class   Ex-Soviet

Transferred to the Indian Navy since 1969. *Andaman* delivered Mar 1974, *Amini* late 1974.
Ships with "K" names are of "Petya I" class.

Radar: Air surveillance: Head Net A ("K" names).
Surface Search: Slim Net ("A" names).

2 Ex-BRITISH "WHITBY" CLASS

Name	No.	Builders	Laid down	Launched	Commissioned
TALWAR	F 140	Cammell Laird & Co Ltd, Birkenhead	1957	18 July 1958	1960
TRISHUL	F 143	Harland & Wolff Ltd, Belfast	1957	18 June 1959	1960

Displacement, tons: 2 144 standard;
  2 545 full load *(Talwar)*, 2 557 *(Trishul)*
Length, feet (metres): 360 (109·7) pp 369·8 (112·7) oa
Beam, feet (metres): 41 (12·5)
Draught, feet (metres): 17·8 (5·4)
Missiles: see note
Guns: 2—4·5 in (115 mm) (see missile note);
  4—40 mm (1 twin before "Limbos", 2 singles abaft funnel)
A/S weapons: 2 "Limbo" 3-barrelled DC mortars
Main engines: 2 sets geared turbines; 30 000 shp; 2 shafts
Boilers: 2 Babcock & Wilcox
Oil fuel, tons: 400
Speed, knots: 30
Range, miles: 4 500 at 12 knots
Complement: 231 (11 officers, 220 men)

TALWAR   A. & J. Pavia

Generally similar to the British frigates of the "Whitby" class, but slightly modified to suit Indian conditions. *Trishul* acts as Squadron commander.

Missiles: In late 1975 *Talwar* was fitted with three SSN-2 missile launchers from an "OSA" class in place of the 4·5 inch turret.

Radar: Tactical: Type 293 and 277.
Fire control: I Band.

3 Ex-BRITISH "LEOPARD" CLASS

Name	No.	Builders	Laid down	Launched	Commissioned
BEAS	F 137	Vickers-Armstrong Ltd, Newcastle-on-Tyne	1957	9 Oct 1958	24 May 1960
BETWA	F 139	Vickers-Armstrong Ltd, Newcastle-on-Tyne	1957	15 Sep 1959	8 Dec 1960
BRAHMAPUTRA (ex-*Panther*)	F 31	John Brown & Co Ltd, Clydebank	1956	15 Mar 1957	28 Mar 1958

Displacement, tons: 2 251 standard; 2 515 full load
Length, feet (metres): 320·0 (97·5) pp; 330·0 (100·6) wl;
  339·8 (103·6) oa
Beam, feet (metres): 40·0 (12·2)
Draught, feet (metres): 16·0 (4·9)
Guns: 4—4·5 in (114 mm) (2 twin); 2—40 mm
A/S weapons: 1 Squid 3-barrelled DC motar
Main engines: Admiralty standard range diesels 2 shafts;
  12 380 bhp
Speed, knots: 25
Range, miles: 7 500 at 16 knots
Complement: 210

Brahmaputra, originally ordered as *Panther* for the Royal Navy on 28 June 1951, was the first major warship to be built in Great Britain for the Indian Navy since India became independent. All three ships are generally similar to the British frigates of the "Leopard" class, but modified to suit Indian conditions.

Radar: Search: Type 960
Tactical: Type 293.
Fire control: I Band forward and aft.

BRAHMAPUTRA   1971, Indian Navy

2 Ex-BRITISH "BLACKWOOD" CLASS

Name	No.
KIRPAN	F 144
KUTHAR	F 146

Displacement, tons: 1 180 standard; 1 456 full load
Length, feet (metres): 300 (91·4) pp; 310 (94·5) oa
Beam, feet (metres): 33 (10·0)
Draught, feet (metres): 15·5 (4·7)
Guns: 3—40 mm (single)
A/S weapons: 2 "Limbo" 3-barrelled DC mortars
Main engines: 1 set geared turbines; 15 000 shp; 1 shaft
Boilers: Babcock & Wilcox
Speed, knots: 27·8
Oil fuel, tons: 300
Range, miles: 4 000 at 12 knots
Complement: 150

Builders	Laid down	Launched	Commissioned
Alex Stephen & Sons Ltd, Govan, Glasgow	1957	19 Aug 1958	July 1959
J. Samuel White & Co Ltd, Cowes, Isle of Wight	1957	14 Oct 1958	1959

Generally similar to the British frigates of the "Blackwood" class, but slightly modified to suit Indian requirements. *Khukri* of this class was sunk in the Pakistan war on 9 Dec 1971.

Radar: Fitted with E Band air and surface surveillance radar.

KUTHAR

A & J Pavia

1 Ex-BRITISH "HUNT" CLASS TYPE II

Name
GODAVARI (ex-HMS *Bedale*, ex-ORP *Slazak*, ex-HMS *Bedale*)

Displacement, tons: 1 050 standard; 1 610 full load
Length, feet (metres): 264·2 (80·5) pp; 280·0 (85·3) oa
Beam, feet (metres): 31·5 (9·6)
Draught, feet (metres): 14·0 (4·3)
Guns: 6—4 in (102 mm) (twins); 4—20 mm
Main engines: Parsons geared turbines; 2 shafts; 19 000 shp
Boilers: 2 Admiralty 3-drum
Oil fuel, tons: 280
Speed, knots: 25
Range, miles: 3 700 at 14 knots
Complement: 150

No.	Builders	Laid down	Launched	Commissioned
D 92	R. & W. Hawthorn, Leslie & Co Ltd, Hebburn	25 May 1940	23 July 1941	9 May 1942

Former "Hunt" class, Type II destroyer. Transferred from Great Britain in May 1953. Lent to the Indian Navy for three years, subject to extension by agreement. Now used for training. Lent to Poland Apr 1942—Nov 1946.

GANGA (Godavari similar)

2 Ex-BRITISH "BLACK SWAN" CLASS

Name	No.
KAVERI	F 110
KISTNA	F 46

Displacement, tons: 1 470 standard; 1 925 full load
Length, feet (metres): 283·0 (86·3) pp; 295·5 (90·1) wl; 299·5 (91·3) oa
Beam, feet (metres): 38·5 (11·7)
Draught, feet (metres): 11·2 (3·4)
Guns: 4—4 in (102 mm); 4—40 mm
A/S weapons: 2 DCT
Main engines: Parsons geared turbines; 2 shafts; 4 300 shp
Boilers: 2 three-drum type
Speed, knots: 19
Oil fuel, tons: 370
Range, miles: 4 500 at 12 knots
Complement: 210

Builders	Laid down	Launched	Commissioned
Yarrow & Co Ltd, Scotstoun, Glasgow	28 Oct 1942	15 June 1943	21 Oct 1943
Yarrow & Co Ltd, Scotstoun, Glasgow	14 July 1942	22 April 1943	23 Aug 1943

Former sloops of the British "Black Swan" class built for India and modified to suit Indian conditions. *Cauvery* was renamed *Kaveri* in 1968.

Radar: Fitted with E band air and surface surveillance radar and ranging radar for the gunfire control systems.

KISTNA

1 Ex-BRITISH "RIVER" CLASS

Name	No.
TIR (ex-HMS *Bann*)	F 256

Displacement, tons: 1 463 standard; 1 934 full load
Length, feet (metres): 283·0 (86·3) pp; 303 (92·4) oa
Beam, feet (metres): 37·6 (11·2)
Draught, feet (metres): 14·5 (4·4)
Guns: 1—4 in (102 mm); 1—40 mm; 2—20 mm
Main engines: Triple expansion; 2 shafts; 5 500 ihp
Boilers: 2 Admiralty 3-drum type
Speed, knots: 18
Oil fuel, tons: 385
Range, miles: 4 200 at 12 knots
Complement: 120

Builders	Laid down	Launched	Commissioned
Charles Hill & Sons Ltd, Bristol	18 June 1942	29 Dec 1942	7 May 1943

Transferred on 3 Dec 1945. Converted to a Midshipman's Training Frigate by Bombay Dockyard in 1948.

TIR

1971, Indian Navy

SUBMARINES

Note: India is still discussing plans to build her own submarines though no details have been released.

8 Ex-SOVIET "FOXTROT" CLASS

KALVARI S 121	**VELA** S 40
KANDERI S 122	**VAGIR** S 41
KARANJ S 123	**VAGLI** S 42
KURSURA S 124	**VAGSHEER** S 43

Displacement, tons: 2 000 surfaced; 2 300 dived
Length, feet (metres): 296·8 (90·5)
Beam, feet (metres): 42·1 (7·3)
Draught, feet (metres): 19·0 (5·8)
Torpedo tubes: 10—21 in (20 torpedoes carried)
Main machinery: 3 diesels; 3 shafts; 6 000 bhp;
3 electric motors; 6 000 hp
Speed, knots: 20 surfaced; 15 dived
Complement: 70

Kalvari arrived in India on 16 July 1968, *Kanderi* in Jan 1969. *Karanj* in Oct 1970 and *Kursura* in Dec 1970. *Vela* Nov 1973, *Vagir* Dec 1973, *Vagli* Sep 1974, *Vagsheer* May 1975.

Additions: There are reports, so far unconfirmed, that a further pair may be transferred later.

VAGSHEER

1974, Contre Amiral M. Adam

LIGHT FORCES

Notes:
(a) Reliably reported that a number of "Nanuchka" class missile corvettes are to be transferred from USSR. This would present problems over the release of a new type of missile but, if confirmed would give the Indians a notable increase in aggressive capacity.
(b) The first of a new class of Large Patrol Craft, believed to be slightly larger edition of *Abhay*, is under construction at Garden Reach, Calcutta.

8 Ex-SOVIET "OSA" CLASS (FAST ATTACK CRAFT—MISSILE)

NASHAK P 684	**VEER** P 686
NIPAT P 691	**VIDYUT** P 694
NIRBHIK P 685	**VIJETA** P 693
NIRGHAT P 690	**VINASH** P 692

Displacement, tons: 165 standard; 200 full load
Dimensions, feet (metres): 128·7 × 25·1 × 5·9 (37 × 7 × 1·8)
Missiles: 4 in two pairs for SSN-2
Guns: 4—30 mm (2 twin)
Main engines: 3 diesels; 3 shafts; 13 000 bhp = 36 knots
Complement: 25

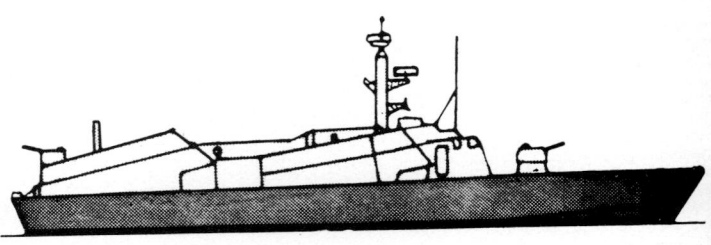

"OSA" Class

Some of these craft took part in a night attack with Styx off Karachi on 4-5 Dec 1971. They sank the PNS *Khaibar,* damaged *Badr* and a CMS as well as one Panamanian m/s without damage to themselves.
Further reinforcement reported.

Missiles: One craft had three SSN-2 launchers transferred to I. S. *Talwar* in late 1975.

Radar: Square Tie and Drum Tilt. IFF—Ski Pole.

5 Ex-SOVIET "POLUCHAT" CLASS (COASTAL PATROL CRAFT)

PAMBAN P 247	**PANVEL** P 246	**PURI** P 248
PANAJI P 249	**PULICAT** P 250	

Displacement, tons: 86 standard; 91 full load
Dimensions, feet (metres): 98 × 15 × 4·8 (29·9 × 4·6 × 1·5)
Guns: 2—14·5 mm (twin)
Main engines: 2 Diesels; 2 shafts; 1 200 bhp = 18 knots
Range, miles: 460 at 17 knots
Complement: 16

One transferred to Bangladesh in 1973 but returned.

1 "ABHAY" CLASS (LARGE PATROL CRAFT)

Name	No.	Builders	Commissioned
ABHAY	P 3135	Hoogly Docking & Engineering Co Ltd, Calcutta	13 Nov 1961

Displacement, tons: 120 standard; 151 full load
Dimensions, feet (metres): 110 pp; 117·2 oa × 20 × 5 (33·6; 35·7 × 6·1 × 1·5)
Gun: 1—40 mm
Main engines: 2 diesels; speed = 18 knots

Generally similar to the "Ford" class in the Royal Navy. Originally a class of six. *Ajay* and *Akshay* transferred to Bangladesh 1974, *Amar* to Mauritius April 1974.

2 "SHARADA" CLASS (COASTAL PATROL CRAFT)

Name	No.	Builders	Commissioned
SHARADA	SPB 3133	Yugoslavia	5 Dec 1959
SUKANYA	SPB 3132	Yugoslavia	5 Dec 1959

Displacement, tons: 86
Dimensions, feet (metres): 103·2 (31·5) length
Guns: Small arms
Main engines: 2 MTU diesels

AMPHIBIOUS FORCES

6 Ex-SOVIET "POLNOCNY" CLASS (LCT)

GHARIAL L 3032   **GHORPAD** L 3034   **SHARDUL**
GULDAR L 3033   **KESARI**   **SHARAB**

Displacement, tons: 780 standard; 1 000 full load
Dimensions, feet (metres): 246 × 29·5 × 9·8 *(75 × 9 × 3)*
Guns: 2—30 mm
A/S weapons: 2—18 barrelled MBU
Main engines: 2 diesels; 5 000 bhp = 18 knots

First pair transferred from USSR in 1966, *Ghorpad* in 1975, *Kesari* Sep 1975, *Shardul* Dec 1975 and *Sharab* Mar 1976.

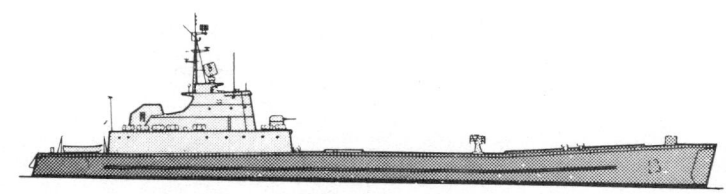

"POLNOCNY" Class

1 Ex-BRITISH LST (3)

MAGAR (ex-HMS *Avenger*) L 3011

Displacement, tons: 2 256 light; 4 980 full load
Dimensions, feet (metres): 347·5 oa × 55·2 × 11·2 *(106 × 16·8 × 3·4)*
Guns: 2—40 mm; 6—20 mm; (2 twin, 2 single)
Main engines: Triple expansion; 2 shafts; 5 500 ihp = 13 knots

There is also LCT 4294 (ex-1294), yard craft of 200 tons, speed 9·5 knots

MAGAR

1964, A. & J. Pavia

MINE WARFARE FORCES

4 Ex-BRITISH "TON" CLASS (MINESWEEPERS—COASTAL)

Name	No.	Builders	Commissioned
CANNANORE (ex-HMS*Whitton*)	M 1191	Fleetlands Shipyard Ltd, Gosport	1956
KUDDALORE (ex-HMS*Wennington*)	M 1190	J. S. Doig Ltd, Grimsby	1955
KAKINADA (ex-HMS*Durweston*)	M 1201	Dorset Yacht Co Ltd, Hamworthy	1955
KARWAR (ex-HMS*Overton*)	M 1197	Camper & Nicholson Ltd, Gosport	1956

Displacement, tons: 360 standard; 425 full load
Dimensions, feet (metres): 140·0 pp; 153·0 oa × 28·8 × 8·2 *(46·7 × 8·8 × 2·5)*
Guns: 2—20 mm
Main engines: Napier Deltic diesels; 2 shafts; 1 250 bhp = 15 knots
Oil fuel, tons: 45
Range, miles: 3 000 at 8 knots
Complement: 40

"Ton" class coastal minesweepers of wooden construction built for the Royal Navy, but transferred from Great Britain to the Indian Navy in 1956. *Cannanore* was launched 30 Jan 1956, *Karwar* was launched 30 Jan 1956. *Kuddalore* and *Kakinada* were taken over in Aug 1956, and sailed for India in Nov-Dec 1956. Named after minor ports in India. Constitute the 18th Mine Counter Measures Squadron, together with the inshore minesweepers.

KARWAR

1971, Wright & Logan

4 "HAM" CLASS (IMS)

Name	No.	Builders	Commissioned
BASSEIN (ex-HMS*Littleham*)	M 2707	Brooke Marine Ltd, Oulton Broad, Lowestoft	1954
BHAKTAL	M 89	Magazon Dockyard, Bombay	1968
BIMLIPITAN (ex-HMS*Hildersham*)	M 2705	Vosper Ltd, Portsmouth	1954
BULSAR	M 90	Magazon Dockyard, Bombay	1970

Displacement, tons: 120 standard; 170 full load
Dimensions, feet (metres): 98·0 pp; 107·0 oa × 22·0 × 6·7 *(32·6 × 6·7 × 1·6)*
Gun: 1—20 mm
Main engines: 2 Paxman diesels; 550 bhp = 14 knots (9 knots sweeping)
Oil fuel, tons: 15
Complement: 16

Of wooden construction two of which were built for the Royal Navy but transferred from Great Britain to the Indian Navy in 1955. *Bassein* was launched on 4 May 1954; *Bimlipitan* was launched on 5 Feb 1954. *Bhaktal* was launched in April 1967, and *Bulsar* on 17 May 1969.

BASSEIN

1971, A & J Pavia

SURVEY SHIPS

Name	No.	Builders	Commissioned
DARSHAK	A 139	Hindustan Shipyard, Vishakapatnam	28 Dec 1964

Displacement, tons: 2 790
Length, feet (metres): 319 *(97·2)* oa
Beam, feet (metres): 49 *(14·9)*
Draught, feet (metres): 28·8 *(8·8)*
Main engines: 2 diesel-electric units; 3 000 bhp
Speed, knots: 16
Complement: 150

First ship built by Hindustan Shipyard for the Navy. Launched on 2 Nov 1959. Provision was made to operate a helicopter. The ship is all welded.

DARSHAK

1967

2 "SUTLEJ" CLASS

Name	No.	Builders	Laid down	Launched	Commissioned
JAMUNA (ex-*Jumna*)	F 11	Wm. Denny & Bros Ltd, Dumbarton	20 Feb 1940	16 Nov 1940	13 May 1941
SUTLEJ	F 95	Wm. Denny & Bros Ltd, Dumbarton	4 Jan 1940	10 Oct 1940	23 Apr 1941

Displacement, tons: 1 300 standard; 1 750 full load
Length, feet (metres): 276 *(84·1)* wl; 292·5 *(89·2)* oa
Beam, feet (metres): 37·5 *(11·4)*
Draught, feet (metres): 11·5 *(3·5)*
Main engines: Parsons geared turbines 3 600 shp; 2 shafts
Boilers: 2 Admiralty 3-drum
Speed, knots: 18
Oil fuel, tons: 370
Range, miles: 5 600 at 12 knots
Complement: 150

Former frigates employed as survey ships since 1957 and 1955 respectively. Both ships are generally similar to the former British frigates of the "Egret" class.

JAMUNA   *11/1975, P. Elliott*

SERVICE FORCES

1 Ex-SOVIET "UGRA" CLASS

AMBA A 14 (SUBMARINE TENDER)

Displacement, tons: 6 000 light; 9 000 full load
Length, feet (metres): 370 pp; 420 oa × 65 × 20 *(138 × 16·8 × 6·5)*
Guns: 4—3 in *(76 mm)* (twins)
Main engines: Diesels; 2 shafts; 7 000 bhp = 17 knots

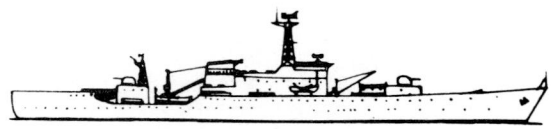

AMBA

Acquired from the USSR in 1968. Provision for helicopter. Can accommodate 750. Two cranes, one of 6 tons and one of 10 tons.

Radar: One Slim Net; two Hawk Screech.

DHARINI (ex-*Hermine*) A 306

Displacement, tons: 4 600 (oil capacity 1 000)
Dimensions, feet (metres): 324·7 × 45·6 × 13·3 *(99 × 13·9 × 4)*
Main engines: Triple expansion; 809 ihp = 9 knots
Oil fuel, tons: 621

Cargo ship converted to a tender. Commissioned in May 1960.

1 REPAIR SHIP

DHARINI   *1964, Indian Navy*

1 Ex-SOVIET "T58" (Mod.) CLASS (SUBMARINE RESCUE SHIP)

NISTAR A 15

Displacement, tons: 790 standard; 900 full load
Dimensions, feet (metres): 220·0 × 29·5 × 7·9 *(67·7 × 9·1 × 2·3)*
Main engines: 2 diesels; 2 shafts; 5 000 bhp = 18 knots

Converted from a fleet minesweeper to a submarine rescue ship and transferred from USSR late-1971. Carries diving-bell and recompression chamber.

1 REPLENISHMENT TANKER

DEEPAK A 1750

Displacement, tons: 1 500

On charter to Indian Navy from Mogul Lines. Fitted with a helicopter landing platform aft, but no hangar. Automatic tensioning fitted to replenishment gear. Also carries dry cargo. Built by Bremer-Vulkan.

SHAKTI A 136

Displacement, tons: 3 500
Dimensions, feet (metres): 323 × 44 × 20 *(97 × 13·5 × 6·6)*
Main engines: Diesel; speed = 13 knots

1 SUPPORT TANKER

Acquired from Italy in Nov 1953.

1 SUPPORT TANKER

HOOGHLY

Formerly "*Baqir*" of Gulf Shipping Corp. Ltd. Acquired in 1972.

1 SUPPORT TANKER

DESH DEEP

Ex-merchant tanker taken over in 1972.

2 HARBOUR TANKERS

Name	No.	Builders	Commissioned
CHILKA	—	Blythwood Shipbuilding Co, Scotstoun	1942
SAMBHAR	—	A. & J. Inglis Ltd, Glasgow	1942

Displacement, tons: 1 530 (oil capacity 1 000)
Dimensions, feet (metres): 202 × 30·7 × 13 *(61 × 9·2 × 4)*
Main engines: Triple expansion; 809 ihp = 9 knots

Both acquired in 1948. Engined by David Rowan & Co. Two steam dynamos, two steam pumps, ballast pump. Rated as yard craft.

1 TUG (OCEAN)

Name	No.	Builders	Commissioned
HATHI	—	Taikoo Dock & Engineering Company, Hong Kong	1933

Displacement, tons: 668
Dimensions, feet (metres): 147·5 × 23·7 × 15 *(45 × 7·2 × 4·6)*
Main engines: Triple expansion; speed = 13 knots

Launched in 1932.

4 Ex-BRITISH HDML TYPE

SPC 3110 (ex-*HDML 1110*)   SPC 3117 (ex-*HDML 1117*)
SPC 3112 (ex-*HDML 1112*)   SPC 3118 (ex-*HDML 1118*)

Displacement, tons: 48 standard; 54 full load
Dimensions, feet (metres): 72 oa × 16 × 4·7 *(22 × 4·9 × 1·4)*
Guns: 2—20 mm
Main engines: Diesels; 2 shafts; 320 bhp = 12 knots
Complement: 14

Used as harbour craft.

Barq (ex-*MMS 132*), *MMS 130* and *MMS 154*, former British motor minesweepers of the "105 ft" type of wooden construction, transferred from Great Britain, are employed as yard craft. *MMS 1632* and *MMS 1654* are yard craft in Bombay.

INDONESIA

Administration

Chief of the Naval Staff:
Admiral R. Subiyakto
Deputy Chief of the Naval Staff Operations:
Rear-Admiral Wulujo Sugito
Inspector General of the Navy:
Commodore M. Wibowo
Chief for Naval Material:
Commodore Urip Subiyanto
Chief for Naval Personnel:
Commodore Imem Muharam
Commander of Navy Marine Corps:
Major General Moch Anwar
Commander-in-Chief Indonesian Fleet:
Rear-Admiral Rudy Purwana

Diplomatic Representation

Naval Attaché in Bangkok:
Lt. Colonel Purnomo
Naval Attaché in Canberra:
Colonel Eddy Tumengkol
Naval Attaché in Delhi:
Lt. Colonel B. Sumitro
Naval Attaché and Naval Attaché for Air in London:
Lt. Colonel Abu
Naval Attaché in Moscow:
Colonel Priyonggo
Naval Attaché in Tokyo:
Colonel Agus Subroto
Naval Attaché and Naval Attaché for Air in Washington:
Colonel Ariffin Roesady

Personnel

(a) 1976: 39 000 including 5 000 Marine Commando Corps and Naval Air Arm
(b) Selective National Service

Ex-Soviet Ships

Indonesia obtained 104 ships from the USSR. Of these half have now been deleted and all will have gone in the near future.

Future Plans

It is planned, over the next 20 years, to provide a Navy of some 25 000 seamen and 5 000 marines to man a Fleet including 4 fast A/S Frigates, some Submarines, Light Forces of Fast Attack Craft—Missile and—Torpedo, Minelayers, Minesweepers, a fast HQ ship and a fast Supply Ship. Tender for 3 Corvettes has been served by the Netherlands.

Naval Air Arm

6—C 47 and 3—Alouette III helicopters.

Strength of the Fleet

Note: This is a formidable if rapidly depleting total of ships but the number truly operational is probably a fairly small proportion of that total.

Type	Active	Building
Frigates	11	—
Corvettes	11	—
Patrol Submarines	3	—
Fast Attack Craft—Missile	12	—
Fast Attack Craft—Torpedo	5	—
Large Patrol Craft	14	—
Coastal Patrol Craft	2	—
LSTs	9	—
LCUs	2	—
Minesweepers—Ocean	6	—
Minesweepers—Coastal	11	—
Survey Ships	4	—
Submarine Tenders	3	—
Destroyer Depot Ship	1	—
Repair Ship	1	—
Replenishment Tanker	1	—
Support Tankers	8	—
Harbour Tankers	3	—
Cable Ship	1	—
Tugs	4	—
Auxiliary Patrol Craft	16	—
Training Ship	1	—

DELETIONS

Cruiser

1972 *Irian*

Destroyers

1973 *Brawidjaja, Sandjaja, Sultan Babarudin*

Frigates

1973 *Lambung Mangkurat, Slamet Rijadi*
1974 *Ngurah Rai* ("Riga" class)

Corvettes

1974 *Palu, Tenggiri*
1975 *Landjuru, Lapai, Lumba Lumba, Madidihang, Tongkol, Tjutjut* ("Kronstadt" class)

Submarines

1974 *Alugoro, Hendradjala, Nagarangsang, Tjandrasa, Tjundmani, Trisula, Widjajadanu* (all "Whisky" class)

Amphibious Forces

1974 3 ex-Yugoslav LCTs, *Tandjung Nusanive* (es-US LST); 3 ex-US LCI Type

Minewarfare Forces

1974 4 ex-Dutch CMS, 5 "R" Class

Light Forces

1970 *310, 314, 315, 316* (Kraljevica), *Dorang, Lajang, Rubara*
1974 2 "Jaguar" class, 25 HDMLs, 10 Motor Launches
1975 14 "P 6" class, 18 "BK" class

Survey Ships

1972 *Hidral*
1973 *Dewa Kembar*

Auxiliaries

1974 2 Transports, 1 Salvage Vessel, 1 Tug, 37 Patrol Craft

Prefix to Ships' Names

KRI (Kapal di Republik Indonesia)

Mercantile Marine

Lloyd's Register of Shipping:
616 vessels of 762 278 tons gross

PENNANT LIST

Frigates

250	Iman Bondjol
251	Surapati
252	Pattimura
253	Sultan Hasanudin
341	Samadikun
342	Martadinata
343	Mongisidi
344	Ngurah Rai
351	Jos Sudarso
359	Kakiali
360	Nuku

Corvettes

313	Tjakalang
317	Torani
318	Hiu
811	Katula
814	Pandrong
815	Sura
816	Kakap
817	Barakuda
829	Tohok
?	Momare
?	Sembilang

Submarines

403	Nagabanda
410	Pasopati
412	Bramastra

Light Forces

570	Bentang Kalakuang
571	Bentang Waitatire
572	Bentang Silunkang
602	Anoa
603	Biruang
604	Harimau
605	Matjan Kumbang
607	Serigala
830	Sibarau
831	Silinan
DKN 901-911	Auxiliary Patrol Craft

Amphibious Forces

501	Teluk Langsa
502	Teluk Bajur
504	Teluk Kau
505	Teluk Manado
510	Teluk Saleh
511	Teluk Bone
?	Teluk Tomini
?	Teluk Rati
869	Teluk Amboina

Minewarfare Forces

717	Pulau Alor
718	Pulau Aruan
719	Pulau Anjer
720	Pulau Impalasa
721	Pulau Antang
722	Pulau Aru

Support Ships

561	Multatuli
?	Ratulangi
?	Thamrin

Service Forces

901	Tjepu
903	Sambu
904	Bunju
911	Sorong
921	Jaya Widjaja
928	Rakata
934	Lampo Batang
935	Tambora
936	Bromo
AD 31	Dumai

RATULANGI

"RIGA" Class

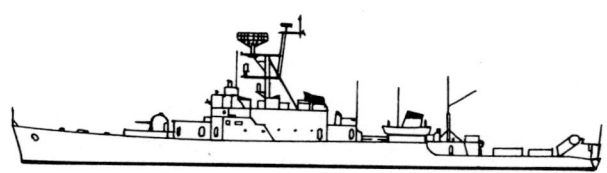

"CLAUD JONES" Class

"SURAPATI" Class

FRIGATES

4 Ex-US "CLAUD JONES" CLASS

Name	No.	Builders	Laid down	Launched	Commissioned
SAMADIKUN (ex-USS *John R. Perry DE 1034*)	341	Avondale Marine Ways	1 Oct 1957	29 July 1958	5 May 1959
MARTADINATA (ex-USS *Charles Berry DE 1035*)	342	American SB Co, Toledo, Ohio	29 Oct 1958	17 Mar 1959	25 Nov 1959
NGURAH RAI (ex-USS *McMorris DE 1036*)	344	American SB Co, Toledo, Ohio	5 Nov 1958	26 May 1959	4 Mar 1960
MONGISIDI (ex-USS *Claud Jones DE 1033*)	343	Avondale Marine Ways	1 June 1957	27 May 1958	10 Feb 1959

Displacement, tons: 1 450 standard; 1 750 full load
Length, feet (metres): 310 *(95)* oa
Beam, feet (metres): 37 *(11·3)*
Draught, feet (metres): 18 *(5·5)*
Gun: 1—3 in 50 cal
A/S weapons: 2 triple Torpedo Tubes (Mk 32)
Main engines: 4 diesels; 9 200 hp; 1 shaft
Speed, knots: 22
Complement: 175

Samadikun acts as fleet flagship.

Radar: SPS 6 and 10.

Sonar: SQS 29.

Transfer: *Samadikun*, 20 Feb 1973; *Martadinata*, 31 Jan 1974; *Mongisidi* and *Ngurah Rai* 16 Dec 1974.

SAMADIKUN   *1975, Indonesian Navy*

3 Ex-SOVIET "RIGA" CLASS

JOS SUDARSO 351   NUKU 360
KAKIALI 359

Displacement, tons: 1 200 standard; 1 600 full load
Length, feet (metres): 298·8 *(91)*
Beam, feet (metres): 33·7 *(10·2)*
Draught, feet (metres): 11 *(3·4)*
Guns: 3—3·9 in *(100 mm)* (single); 4—37 mm
A/S weapons: 4 DC projectors
Torpedo tubes: 3—21 in *(533 mm)*
Mines: Fitted with mine rails
Main engines: Geared steam turbines; 2 shafts; 25 000 shp
Boilers: 2
Speed, knots: 28
Range, miles: 2 500 at 15 knots
Complement: 150

Transferred in 1964.

Radar: Slim Net search and warning; Fire control Sun Visor A with Wasp Head director; Navigation Neptun; IFF, High Pole A.

JOS SUDARSO   *1974, John Mortimer*

2 "SURAPATI" CLASS

Name	No.	Builders	Laid down	Launched	Commissioned
IMAN BONDJOL	250	Ansaldo, Genoa	8 Jan 1956	5 May 1956	19 May 1958
SURAPATI	251	Ansaldo, Genoa	8 Jan 1956	5 May 1956	28 May 1958

Displacement, tons: 1 150 standard; 1 500 full load
Dimensions, feet (metres): 325 × 36 × 8·5 *(99 × 11 × 2·6)*
Guns: 4—4 in *(102 mm)* (twins); 6—30 mm (twins);
  6—20 mm (twins)
A/S weapons: 2 Hedgehogs; 4 DCT
Torpedo tubes: 3—21 in *(533 mm)*
Boilers: 2 Foster Wheeler
Main engines: 2 sets Parsons geared turbines, 2 shafts;
  24 000 shp
Speed, knots: 32
Oil fuel, tons: 350
Range, miles: 2 800 at 22 knots
Complement: 200

Near sisters of the "Almirante Clemente" class of Venezuela.

IMAN BONDJOL   *Dr Ing Luigi Accorsi*

2 "PATTIMURA" CLASS

Name	No.	Builders	Laid down	Launched	Commissioned
PATTIMURA	252	Ansaldo, Leghorn	8 Jan 1956	1 July 1956	28 Jan 1958
SULTAN HASANUDIN	253	Ansaldo, Leghorn	8 Jan 1957	24 Mar 1957	8 Mar 1958

Displacement, tons: 950 standard; 1 200 full load
Length, feet (metres): 246 *(75·0)* pp; 270·2 *(82·4)* oa
Beam, feet (metres): 34 *(10·4)*
Draught, feet (metres): 9 *(2·7)*
Guns: 2—3 in *(76 mm)* 40 cal. 2—30 mm 70 cal (twin)
A/S weapons: 2 Hedgehogs; 4 DCT
Main engines: 3 Ansaldo-Fiat diesels; 3 shafts; 6 900 bhp
Speed, knots: 22
Range, miles: 2 400 at 18 knots
Oil fuel, tons: 100
Complement: 110

Similar to Italian "Albatros" class.

PATTIMURA

Dr Ing Luigi Accorsi

CORVETTES

8 Ex-SOVIET "KRONSTADT" CLASS

BARAKUDA 817	**MOMARE**	**SURA** 815
KAKAP 816	**PANDRONG** 814	**TOHOK** 829
KATULA 811	**SEMBILANG**	

Displacement, tons: 310 standard; 380 full load
Dimensions, feet (metres): 170·6 × 21·5 × 9 *(52·0 × 6·5 × 2·7)*
Guns: 1—3·5 in; 2—37 mm; 4—25 mm
A/S weapons: Depth charge projectors
Mines: 2 mine rails for 10 mines
Main engines: 3 Diesels; 3 shafts; 3 300 bhp = 24 knots
Oil fuel, tons: 20
Range, miles: 1 500 at 12 knots
Complement: 65

Built in 1951-54. Transferred to the Indonesian Navy on 30 Dec 1958.

Radar: Ball Gun or Don 2; IFF, High Pole A

"KRONSTADT" Class

3 Ex-US PC TYPE

HIU (ex-USS *Malvern*, PC 580) 318
TJAKALANG (ex-USS *Pierre*, PC 1141) 313
TORANI (ex-USS *Manville*, PC 581) 317

Displacement, tons: 280 standard; 450 full load
Dimensions, feet (metres): 170 wl; 173·7 oa × 23 × 10·8 *(55·7; 53 × 7 × 3·3)*
Guns: 1—3 in; 1—40 mm; 2—20 mm
A/S weapons: 4 DCT
Main engines: 2 GM diesels; 2 shafts; 2 880 bhp = 20 knots
Oil fuel, tons: 60
Range, miles: 5 000 at 10 knots
Complement: 54 (4 officers, 50 men)

Built in 1942-43. *Pierre* transferred from the US Navy at Pearl Harbor, Hawaii in Oct 1958 and *Malvern* and *Manville* in Mar 1960.

PC TYPE

1966, Indonesian Navy

SUBMARINES

3 Ex-SOVIET "WHISKY" CLASS

BRAMASTRA 412 **PASOPATI** 410
NAGABANDA 403

Displacement, tons: 1 030 surfaced; 1 350 dived
Length, feet (metres): 249·3 *(76)*
Beam, feet (metres): 22 *(6·7)*
Draught, feet (metres): 15 *(4·6)*
Torpedo tubes: 6—21 in *(533 mm)* 4 forward, 2 aft; 18 torpedoes carried
Mines: 40 in lieu of torpedoes
Main machinery: 4 000 bhp diesels; 2 500 hp electric motors, diesel-electric drive; 2 shafts
Speed, knots: 17 surfaced; 15 dived
Range, miles: 13 000 at 8 knots surfaced
Complement: 60

"WHISKY" Class

The four Soviet submarines of the "Whisky" class, which arrived in Indonesia on 28 June 1962, brought the total number of this class transferred to Indonesia to 14 units, but it was reported that only six would be maintained operational, while six would be kept in reserve and two used for spare parts. Now reduced to three operational boats of which two have been refitted and have received new batteries from UK.

LIGHT FORCES

12 Ex-SOVIET "KOMAR" CLASS
(FAST ATTACK CRAFT—MISSILE)

GUAWIDJAJA	KATJABOLA	SUROTAMA
HARDADALI	KELAPLINTAH	SARPAMINA
KALAMISANI	PULANGGENI	SARPAWASESA
KALANADA	NAGAPASA	TRITUSTA

Displacement, tons: 70 standard; 80 full load
Dimensions, feet (metres): 83·7 × 19·8 × 5 *(25·5 × 6·0 × 1·8)*
Guns: 2—35 mm (1 twin)
Guided weapons: 2 launchers for SSN-2
Main engines: 4 diesels; 4 800 hp = 40 knots
Range, miles: 400 at 30 knots
Complement: 20

Six were transferred to Indonesia in 1961-63, four more in Sep 1964 and two in 1965. Missiles probably of doubtful capability.

Indonesian "Komar" Class   1967

5 GERMAN-BUILT "JAGUAR" CLASS
(FAST ATTACK CRAFT—TORPEDO)

Name	No.	Builders	Commissioned
ANOA	602	Lürssen, Bremen-Vegesack	1959
BIRUANG	603	Lürssen, Bremen-Vegesack	1959
HARIMAU	604	Lürssen, Bremen-Vegesack	1960
MATJAN KUMBANG	605	Lürssen, Bremen-Vegesack	1960
SERIGALA	607	Lürssen, Bremen-Vegesack	1960

Displacement, tons: 160 standard; 190 full load
Dimensions, feet (metres): 131 pp; 138 oa × 22 × 7·5 *(42·9; 42·1 × 6·7 × 2·3)*
Guns: 2—40 mm (single)
Torpedo tubes: 4—21 in
Main engines: 4 Daimler-Benz (MTU) diesels; 4 shafts; 12 000 bhp = 42 knots
Complement: 39

The first four boats had wooden hulls. Some reported as refitting in Singapore.

HARIMAU   Indonesia

3 Ex-US "PGN 53" CLASS (LARGE PATROL CRAFT)

BENTANG SILUNGKANG (ex-*PGM 55)* 572
BENTANG WAITATIRE (ex-*PGM 56)* 571
BENTANG KALAKUANG (ex-*PGM 57)* 570

Displacement, tons: 122 full load
Dimensions, feet (metres): 100 × 21 × 8·5 *(30·5 × 6·4 × 2·6)*
Guns: 2—20 mm; 2 MG
Main engines: 2 diesels; 2 shafts = 17 knots

Used as Amphibious Control Craft. All transferred Jan 1962.

2 Ex-AUSTRALIAN "ATTACK" CLASS
(LARGE PATROL CRAFT)

SIBARAU (ex-HMAS *Bandolier)* 830
SILINAN (ex-HMAS *Archer)* 831

Displacement, tons: 146 full load
Dimensions, feet (metres): 107·5 × 20 × 7·3 *(32·8 × 6·1 × 2·2)*
Guns: 1—40 mm; 2 medium MGs
Main engines: 2 Paxman diesels; 2 shafts = 21 knots
Complement: 19 (3 officers, 16 men)

Transferred from RAN after refit—*Bandolier* 16 Nov 1973, *Archer* in 1974. It is reported, though not confirmed, that another six may be transferred.

SIBARAU   1973, Graeme Andrews

6 Ex-YUGOSLAVIAN "KRALJEVICA" CLASS
(LARGE PATROL CRAFT)

BUBARA	KRAPU	LEMADANG
DORANG	LAJANG	TODAK

Displacement, tons: 190 standard; 245 full load
Dimensions, feet (metres): 134·5 × 20·8 × 7 *(41 × 6·3 × 2·1)*
Guns: 1—3 in; 1—40 mm; 6—20 mm
A/S weapons: DC
Main engines: 2 MAN diesels; 2 shafts; 3 300 bhp = 20 knots
Oil fuel, tons: 15
Range, miles: 1 500 at 12 knots
Complement: 54

Purchased and transferred on 27th Dec 1958.

DORANG   1968, Indonesian Navy

3 "KELABANG" CLASS (LARGE PATROL CRAFT)

KALAHITAM   KELABANG   KOMPAS

Displacement, tons: 147
Guns: 40 mm
Main engines: 2 diesels; speed 21 knots

Built in Indonesia in 1960.

KALAHITAM

1968, Indonesian Navy

2 FAIREY MARINE "SPEAR" CLASS
(COASTAL PATROL CRAFT)

Dimensions, feet (metres): 29·8 × 9·2 × 2·6 *(9·1 × 2·8 × ·8)*
Main engines: Twin 180 hp diesels
Speed, knots: 30
Range, miles: 200 at 26 knots

AMPHIBIOUS FORCES
6 + 2(?) Ex-US "LST 511" CLASS

Name	No.	Builders	Commissioned
TELUK BAJUR (ex-USS *LST 616*)	502	—	—
TELUK KAU (ex-USS *LST 652*)	504	—	—
TELUK SALEH (ex-USS *Clark County, LST 601*)	510	—	—
TELUK MANADO (ex-USS *LST 657*)	505	—	—
TELUK BONE (ex-USS *Iredell County, LST 839*)	511	—	—
TELUK LANGSA (ex-USS *LST 1128*)	501	—	—

Purchased in 1973-74.

Displacement, tons: 1 653 standard; 4 080 full load
Dimensions, feet (metres): 316 wl; 328 oa × 50 × 14 *(103·6; 100 × 15·3 × 4·3)*
Guns: 7—40 mm; 2—20 mm
Main engines: GM diesels; 2 shafts; 1 700 bhp = 11·6 knots
Oil fuel, tons: 600
Range, miles: 7 200 at 10 knots
Cargo capacity: 2 100 tons
Complement: 119 (accommodation for 266)

Transfers: 505 in Mar 1960, 502, 510 and 511 in June 1961. 504 and 501 in July 1970. *Teluk Tomini* and *Teluk Rati* also reported as transferred.

1 JAPANESE TYPE LST

Name	No.	Builders	Commissioned
TELUK AMBOINA	LST 869	Japan	1961

Displacement, tons: 2 200 standard; 4 800 full load
Dimensions, feet (metres): 327 × 50 × 15 *(99·7 × 15·3 × 4·6)*
Guns: 2—85 mm; 4—40 mm
Main engines: MAN diesels; 2 shafts; 3 000 bhp = 13·1 knots
Oil fuel, tons: 1 200
Range, miles: 4 000 at 13·1 knots
Complement: 88 (accommodation for 300)

Launched on 17 Mar 1961 and transferred in June 1961. A copy of US "LST 511" class.

2 LCU TYPE

DORE   AMURANG

Displacement, tons: 182 standard; 275 full load
Dimensions, feet (metres): 125·7 × 32·8 × 5·9 *(38·3 × 10 × 1·8)*
Main engines: Diesels; 210 hp = 8 knots
Complement: 17

Built in Japan.

MINE WARFARE FORCES

6 Ex-SOVIET "T 43" CLASS (MINESWEEPERS—OCEAN)

PULAU RANI	PULAU RATENO	PULAU ROON
PULAU RADJA	PULAU RONDO	PULAU RORBAS

Displacement, tons: 500 standard; 610 full load
Dimensions, feet (metres): 190·2 × 28·2 × 6·9 *(58 × 8·6 × 2·1)*
Guns: 4—37 mm; 4—25 mm
Main engines: 2 diesels; 2 shafts; 2 000 bhp = 17 knots
Range, miles: 1 600 at 10 knots
Complement: 40

Transferred to Indonesia by the USSR, four in 1962 and two in 1964. *Pulau Rondo* is in reserve.

6 Ex-US "FALCON" CLASS (MINESWEEPERS—COASTAL)

PULAU ALOR (ex-USS *Meadowlark*) 717
PULAU ANJER (ex-USS *Limpkin*) 719
PULAU ANTANG (ex-USS *Frigate Bird*) 721
PULAU ARU (ex-USS *Falcon*) 722
PULAU ARUAN (ex-USS *Jacina*) 718
PULAU IMPALASA (ex-USS *Humming Bird*) 720

Displacement, tons: 320 light; 370 full load
Dimensions, feet (metres): 138·0 pp; 144·0 oa × 28·0 × 8·2 *(45·2; 43·9 × 8·5 × 2·5)*
Guns: 2—20 mm (1 twin)
Main engines: Packard diesels; 2 shafts; 1 200 bhp = 12·5 knots
Complement: 39

Transferred from the USN in 1971; *Falcon* (24 June), *Frigate Bird* (11 Aug), *Humming Bird* (12 July), *Jacana* (12 July), *Limpkin* (24 June), *Meadowlark* (11 Aug). All have wooden hulls with low magnetic signature.

5 "R" CLASS (MINESWEEPERS—COASTAL)

Name	No.	Builders	Commissioned
PULAU RAU	—	Abeking & Rasmussen Jacht-und Bootswerft, Lermwerder	—
PULAU RENGAT	—	Abeking & Rasmussen Jacht-und Bootswerft, Lemwerder	—
PULAU RINDJA	—	Abeking & Rasmussen Jacht-und Bootswerft, Lemwerder	—
PULAU RUPAT	—	Abeking & Rasmussen Jacht-und Bootswerft, Lemwerder	—
PULAU RUSA	—	Abeking & Rasmussen Jacht-und Bootswerft, Lemwerder	—

Displacement, tons: 139·4 standard
Dimensions, feet (metres): 129 × 18·7 × 5 *(39·3 × 5·7 × 1·5)*
Guns: 1—40 mm; 2—20 mm
Main engines: 2 MAN diesels; 12 cyl; 2 800 bhp = 24·6 knots
Complement: 26

"R" Class

Indonesian Navy

Originally a class of ten. These boats have a framework of light metal covered with wood.

SURVEY SHIPS

Name	No.	Builders	Commissioned
BURUDJULASAD	1006	—	1967

Displacement, tons: 2 150 full load
Dimensions, feet (metres): 269·5 × 37·4 × 11·5 (82·2 × 11·4 × 3·5)
Main engines: 4 MAN diesels; 2 shafts; 6 850 bhp = 19·1 knots
Complement: 113

Burudjulasad was launched in 1966; her equipment includes laboratories for oceanic and meteorological research, a cartographic room, and a helicopter.

JALANIDHI

Displacement, tons: 985
Dimensions, feet (metres): 159·1 × 31·2 × 14·1 (48·5 × 9·5 × 4·3)
Speed, knots: 11·5
Complement: 58

Launched in 1962.

Name	No.	Builders	Commissioned
BURDJAMHAL	—	Scheepswerf De Waal, Zaltbommel	6 July 1953

Displacement, tons: 1 500 full load
Dimensions, feet (metres): 211·7 oa; 192 pp × 33·2 × 10 (58·6 × 10·1 × 3·3)
Main engines: 2 Werkspoor diesels; 1 160 bhp = 10 knots
Complement: 90

Launched on 6 Sep 1952.

ARIES

Displacement, tons: 35
Dimensions, feet (metres): 68·9 × 12·5 × 6·6 (21 × 3·8 × 2)
Main engines: Werkspoor diesel engines; 450 bhp
Complement: 13

Launched 1960.

COMMAND AND SUPPORT SHIPS

1 SUBMARINE TENDER

Name	No.	Builders	Commissioned
MULTATULI	561	Ishikawajima-Harima Heavy Industries Co Ltd	Aug 1961

Displacement, tons: 3 220
Dimensions, feet (metres): 338 pp; 365·3 oa × 52·5 × 23 (103; 111·4 × 16 × 7)
Guns: 1—85 mm; 4—40 mm (single mountings)
Main engines: B & W diesel; 5 500 bhp = 18·5 knots
Oil fuel, tons: 1 400
Range, miles: 6 000 at 16 knots cruising speed
Complement: 134

Built as a submarine tender. Launched on 15 May 1961. Delivered to Indonesia Aug 1961. Flush decker. Capacity for replenishment at sea (fuel oil, fresh water, provisions, ammunition, naval stores and personnel). Medical and hospital facilities. Equipment for supplying compressed air, electric power and distilled water to submarines. Air-conditioning and mechanical ventilation arrangements for all living and working quarters.

1 Ex-SOVIET "ATREK" CLASS (SUBMARINE TENDER)

THAMRIN

Displacement, tons: 3 500 standard; 6 700 full load
Measurement, tons: 3 258 gross
Dimensions, feet (metres): 336 × 49 × 20 (102·5 × 14·9 × 6·1)
Main engines: Steam expansion and exhaust turbine; 2 450 bhp = 13 knots
Boilers: 2
Range, miles: 3 500 at 13 knots

Built in 1955-57 and converted to naval use from a mercantile freighter. Arrived in Indonesia on 28 June 1962.

1 Ex-SOVIET "DON" CLASS (SUBMARINE TENDER)

RATULANGI

Displacement, tons: 6 700 standard; 9 000 full load
Dimensions, feet (metres): 458·9 × 57·7 × 22·3 (140 × 17·6 × 6·8)
Guns: 4—3·9 in; 8—57 mm
Main engines: Diesels; 14 000 bhp = 21 knots
Complement: 300

A submarine support ship, escort vessel and maintenance tender transferred from the USSR to Indonesia in 1962, arriving in Indonesia in July. Fitted with Slim Net search and warning radar and with fire control radar.

RATULANGI — 1968, Indonesian Navy

SERVICE FORCES

1 Ex-US LCT (REPAIR SHIP)

JAYA WIDJAJA (ex-USS *Askari* 9109, ex-*ARL 30*, ex-*LST 1131*) 921

Displacement, tons: 1 625 light; 4 100 full load
Dimensions, feet (metres): 316·0 wl; 328·0 oa × 50·0 × 11·0 (96·4; 100 × 15·3 × 3·4)
Guns: 8—40 mm (2 quadruple)
Main engines: General Motors diesels; 2 shafts; 1 800 bhp = 11·6 knots
Complement: 280

Of wartime construction this ship was in reserve from 1956-66. She was recommissioned and reached Vietnam in 1967 to support River Assault Flotilla One. She was used by the USN and Vietnamese Navy working up the Mekong in support of the Cambodian operations in May 1970. Transferred on lease to Indonesia at Guam on 31 Aug 1971.

1 Ex-US "SHENANDOAH" CLASS (DESTROYER DEPOT SHIP)

DUMAI (ex-USS *Tidewater*) AD31

Displacement, tons: 8 165 standard; 16 635 full load
Dimensions, feet (metres): 465 wl; 492 oa × 69·5 × 27·2 (141·8; 150·1 × 21·2 × 8·3)
Gun: 1—5 in; 38 cal
Main engines: Geared turbines; 1 shaft; 8 500 shp = 18·4 knots
Boilers: 2 Babcock & Wilcox
Complement: 778

Transferred Feb 1971 as destroyer depot ship. Also used to maintain off-shore drilling rigs.

1 REPLENISHMENT TANKER

SORONG 911

Measurement, tons: 5 100 dead weight
Dimensions, feet (metres): 367·4 × 50·5 × 21·6 (112 × 15·4 × 6·6)
Speed, knots: 15 (10 economical)

Built in Yugoslavia in 1965. Has underway replenishment facilities. Capacity 3 000 tons fuel and 300 tons water.

SORONG — 1974, John Mortimer

2 Ex-SOVIET TYPE (SUPPORT TANKERS)

BUNJU 904   **SAMBU** 903

Displacement, tons: 2 170 standard; 6 170 full lad
Dimensions, feet (metres): 350·5 × 49·2 × 20·2 *(106·9 × 15 × 6·2)*
Guns: 2—20 mm
Main engines: Polar diesel; 1 shaft; 2 650 bhp = 10 knots
Oil fuel, tons: 390
Cargo capacity: 4 739 tons
Complement: 71

Transferred to the Indonesian Navy on 19 June 1959. Both laid up in 1969.

5 Ex-SOVIET "UDA" CLASS (SUPPORT TANKERS)

BALIKPAPAN   **PANGKALAN BRANDAN**   **WONOKROMO**   +2

Displacement, tons: 5 500 standard; 7 200 full load
Dimensions, feet (metres): 400·3 × 51·8 × 20·3 *(122·1 × 15·8 × 6·2)*
Main engines: Diesels; 2 shafts; 8 000 bhp = 17 knots

1 HARBOUR TANKER

PAKAN BARU

Displacement, tons: 1 500 full load
Dimensions, feet (metres): 63 × 11·5 × 4·5 *(19·2 × 3·5 × 1·2)*
Main engines: Diesels; 2 shafts; 800 bhp = 11 knots

1 SUPPORT TANKER

TJEPU (ex-*Scandus*, ex-*Nordhem*) 901

Displacement, tons: 1 372
Measurement, tons: 1 042 gross
Dimensions, feet (metres): 226·5 × 34 × 14·2 *(69·1 × 10·4 × 6·3)*
Main engines: Polar diesel; 1 shaft; 850 bhp = 11 knots

Built in Sweden in 1949. Acquired in 1951. Laid up in 1969.

2 HARBOUR TANKERS

TARAKAN   **BULA**

Displacement, tons: 1 340 full load
Dimensions, feet (metres): 352·0 × 37·7 × 14·8 *(107·4 × 11·5 × 4·5)*
Main engines: Diesels; 1 shaft; 1 500 bhp = 13 knots

CABLE SHIP

RAKATA (ex-USS *Menominee, ATF 73*) 928

Displacement, tons: 1 235 standard; 1 675 full load
Dimensions, feet (metres): 195 wl; 205 oa × 38·5 × 15·5 *(59·5; 62·5 × 11·7 × 4·7)*
Guns: 1—3 in; 4—40 mm; 2—20 mm
Main engines: 4 diesels with electric drive; 3 000 bhp = 16·5 knots
Complement: 85

Cable Layer, Lighthouse Tender, and multi-purpose naval auxiliary. Launched on 30 Oct 1951.

TUGS

Name	No.	Builders	Commissioned
BIDUK	—	J & K Smit, Kinderijk	30 July 1952

Displacement, tons: 1 250 standard
Dimensions, feet (metres): 213·2 oa × 39·5 × 11·5 *(65 × 12 × 3·5)*
Main engines: 1 Triple expansion engine; 1 600 ihp = 12 knots
Complement: 66

Former American fleet ocean tug of the "Apache" class. Launched on 14 Feb 1942. Transferred from the United States Navy to the Indonesian Navy at San Diego in Mar 1961.

Name	No.	Builders	Commissioned
LAMPO BATANG	934	Japan	Nov 1961
TAMBORA	935	Japan	Nov 1961

Displacement, tons: 250
Dimensions, feet (metres): 86·7 pp; 92·3 oa × 23·2 × 11·3 *(26·4; 28·2 × 7·1 × 3·4)*
Main engines: 2 diesels; 1 200 bhp = 11 knots
Oil fuel, tons: 18
Range, miles: 1 000 at 11 knots
Complement: 43

Ocean tugs. Launched in April 1961. Delivered in Nov 1961.

Name	No.	Builders	Commissioned
BROMO	936	Japan	Aug 1961

Displacement, tons: 150
Dimensions, feet (metres): 71·7 wl; 79 oa × 21·7 × 9·7 *(21·9; 24·1 × 6·6 × 3)*
Main engines: MAN diesel; 2 shafts; 600 bhp = 10·5 knots
Oil fuel, tons: 9
Range, miles: 690 at 10·5 knots
Complement: 15

Harbour tug. Launched in June 1961. Delivered in Aug 1961.

AUXILIARY PATROL CRAFT

10 DKN TYPE

Name	No.	Builders	Commissioned
—	DKN 901	Lürssen, Vegesack	1958
—	DKN 902	Lürssen, Vegesack	1958
—	DKN 903	Abeking & Rasmussen Lemwerder	1958
—	DKN 904	Lürssen, Vegesack	1959
—	DKN 905	Abeking & Rasmussen Lemwerder	1959
—	DKN 906	Abeking & Rasmussen Lemwerder	1959
—	DKN 908	Soerabaya	1960
—	DKN 909	Soerabaya	1960
—	DKN 910	Soerabaya	1960
—	DKN 911	Soerabaya	1960

Displacement, tons: 140
Dimensions, feet (metres): 128 × 19 × 5·2 *(39 × 5·8 × 1·6)*
Guns: 4—20 mm
Main engines: Maybach (MTU) diesels; 2 shafts; 3 000 bhp = 24·5 knots

Patrol craft and police boats. Indonesian built craft carry 1—40 mm only.

6 "PAT" CLASS

PAT 01   **PAT 02**   **PAT 03**   **PAT 04**   **PAT 05**   **PAT 06**

Dimensions, feet (metres): 91·9 pp; 100 oa × 17 × 6 *(28; 30·5 × 5·2 × 1·8)*
Main engines: 2 Caterpillar diesels; 340 bhp

TRAINING SHIP

Name	No.	Builders	Commissioned
DEWARUTJI	—	H. C. Stülcken & Sohn, Hamburg	9 July 1953

Displacement, tons: 810 standard; 1 500 full load
Dimensions, feet (metres): 136·2 oa, 191·2 pp × 31·2 × 13·9 *(41·5; 58·3 × 9·5 × 4·2)*
Main engines: MAN diesels; 600 bhp = 10·5 knots
Complement: 110 (32 + 78 midshipmen)

Barquentine of iron construction. Sail area, 1 305 sq yds *(1 091 sq metres)*. Launched on 24 Jan 1953.

IRAN

Headquarters Appointments

Commander-in-Chief Imperial Iranian Navy:
Vice Admiral Habibelahi
Deputy Commander-in-Chief:
Rear-Admiral Biglari

Fleet Command

Commander Fleet
Rear-Admiral Azadhi

Diplomatic Representation

Naval Attaché in London, Brussels and The Hague:
Commander F. Fiuzi
Naval Attaché in Rome and Paris:
Captain H. Keshvardoust
Naval Attaché in Washington and Ottawa:
Captain S. Baharmast

Personnel

(a) 1976: 22 000 officers and men
(b) 2 years National Service

Note: A Marine Battalion is being formed.

Bases

Persian Gulf
  Bandar Abbas (MHQ)
  Booshehr
  Kharg Island
  Khorramshar (Light Forces)
Indian Ocean
  Chah Bahar (under construction)
Caspian Sea
  Bandar—Pahlavi (Training)

Naval Air

8 Sikorsky SH-3D
7 Bell AB-212
2 Lockheed P-3C Orions (Maritime Patrol)
4 Fokker F-27 (Transport)
4 Aero Commanders (Flag officers)

Prefix

IIS

Mercantile Marine

Lloyd's Register of Shipping:
135 vessels of 479 718 tons

Strength of the Fleet

Type	Active	Building (Planned)
Destroyers	3	4
Frigates	4	—
Corvettes	4	—
Submarines	—	(3)
Fast Attack Craft (Missile)	—	12
Large Patrol Craft	7	—
Coastal Patrol Craft	3	—
Hovercraft	14	—
Landing Ships	2	(4 poss.)
Landing Craft	1	—
Minesweepers—Coastal	3	—
Minesweepers—Inshore	2	—
Fleet Tanker	—	1
Supply Ships	2	—
Repair Ships	2	—
Harbour Tanker	1	—
Water Boat	1	—
Tugs	3	—
Yachts	2	—
Floating Docks	1	—

Missile Purchase

222 Harpoon missiles recently purchased.

DELETIONS

(see Addendum)

Mine Warfare Forces

1974 *Shahbaz* (ex-US *MSC*) after collision damage.

Service Forces

1974 *Sohrab* (ex-US *ARL 36*) sunk as A/S target.

PENNANT NUMBERS

Destroyers

D	5	Artemiz
D	7	Babr
D	9	Palang

Frigates

DE	12	Saam
DE	14	Zaal
DE	16	Rostam
DE	18	Faramarz

Corvettes

F	25	Bayandor
F	26	Naghdi
F	27	Milanian
F	28	Khanamuie

Light Forces

01-08	"Winchester" class hovercraft
61	Kayvan
62	Mehran
63	Tiran
64	Mahan
65	Parvin
66	Bahram
67	Nahid
101-106	"Wellington" class hovercraft
P 221	Kaman
P 222	Zoubin
P 223	Khadang
P 224	Peykan
P 225	Joshan
P 226	Falakhon
P 227	Shamshir
P 228	Gorz
P 229	Gardouneh
P 230	Khanjar
P 231	Neyzeh
P 232	Tabarzin

Minewarfare Forces

31	Shahrokh
33	Simorgh
34	Karkas
301	Harischi
302	Riazi

Service and Auxiliary Forces

A	41	Chahbahar
A	42	Bandar Abbas
A	43	Hormuz
A	44	Booshehr
	45	Bahmanshir
A	46	Lengeh
LCU	47	Quesm
	51	Larak
	52	Hengam

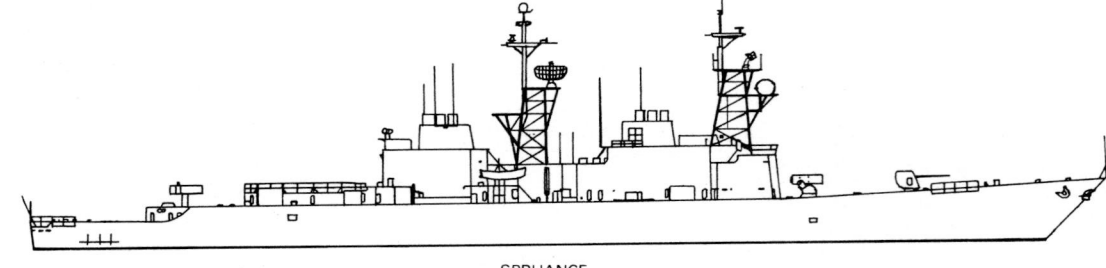

SPRUANCE

BABR and PALANG

ARTEMIZ

"SAAM" Class

"BAYANDOR" Class

DESTROYERS

4 US "SPRUANCE" CLASS

Name	No.	Builders	Laid down	Launched	Commissioned
KHOUROOSH	—	Litton Industries, USA	—	—	—
—	—	Litton Industries, USA	—	—	—
—	—	Litton Industries, USA	—	—	—
—	—	Litton Industries, USA	—	—	—

Displacement, tons: 7 800 full load
Dimensions, feet (metres): 563·3 oa × 55 × 29 (171·1 × 17·6 × 8·8)
Aircraft: 1 helicopter
Missiles: Standard SS/SAM
Gun: 1—5 in Mk 45, 54 cal
A/S weapons: 1 Asroc; 2 triple Mk 32 torpedo tubes
Main engines: 4 gas turbines; 80 000 shp; 2 shafts
Speed, knots: 30+
Complement: 250

Ordered from Litton Industries, USA, in 1974, first to be delivered in 1980. Original order was for six ships, reduced in 1976.

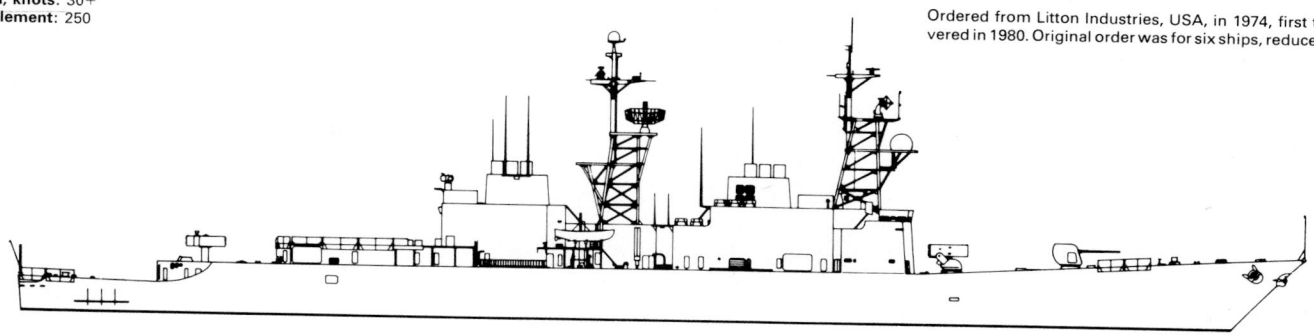

"SPRUANCE" class (modified)

1 Ex-BRITISH "BATTLE" CLASS

Name	No.	Builders	Laid down	Launched	Commissioned
ARTEMIZ (ex-HMS *Sluys*, D 60)	D 5	Cammell Laird & Co Ltd, Birkenhead	24 Nov 1943	28 Feb 1945	30 Sep 1946

Displacement, tons: 2 325 standard; 3 360 full load
Length, feet (metres): 355·0 (108·2) pp; 379·0 (115·5) oa
Beam, feet (metres): 40·5 (12·3)
Draught, feet (metres): 17·5 (5·2)
Missiles: 4 standard launchers with 8 missiles; 1 quadruple "Seacat" aft
Guns: 4—4·5 in (115 mm) (2 twin forward); 8—40 mm Bofors
A/S weapons: 1 "Squid" 3-barrelled DC mortar
Main engines: Parsons geared turbines; 2 shafts; 50 000 shp
Boilers: 2 Admiralty 3-drum type
Speed, knots: 35·5
Oil fuel, tons: 680
Range, miles: 3 000 at 20 knots
Complement: 270

Transferred to Iran at Southampton on 26 Jan 1967, and handed over to the Imperial Iranian Navy after a 3-year modernisation refit by the Vosper Thornycroft Group.

Radar: Search: Plessey AWS 1. Air surveillance with on-mounted IFF; Contraves Sea-Hunter fire control; Decca RDL 1 radar intercept; Racal DF equipment.

ARTEMIZ

1975, Imperial Iranian Navy

2 Ex-US "ALLEN M. SUMNER" CLASS

Name	No.	Builders	Laid down	Launched	Commissioned
BABR (ex-USS *Zellers*, DD 777)	D 7	Todd Pacific Shipyards	—	19 July 1944	25 Oct 1944
PALANG (ex-USS *Stormes*, DD 780)	D 9	Todd Pacific Shipyards	—	4 Nov 1944	27 Jan 1945

Displacement, tons: 2 200 standard; 3 320 full load
Length, feet (metres): 376·5 (114·8) oa
Beam, feet (metres): 40·9 (12·4)
Draught, feet (metres): 19 (5·8)
Aircraft: 1 A/S helicopter
Missiles: 4 Standard launchers with 8 missiles
Guns: 4—5 in (127 mm) 38 calibre (twin)
A/S weapons: 2 fixed Hedgehogs; depth charges; 2 triple torpedo launchers (Mk 32)
Main engines: 2 geared turbines; 60 000 shp; 2 shafts
Boilers: 4
Speed, knots: 34
Complement: 274 (14 officers, 260 ratings)

Two "FRAM II" conversion destroyers of the "Allen M. Sumner" class nominally transferred to Iran from the USN in March 1971 for delivery in 1972.

Conversion: Both ships received a full refit as well as conversion at Philadelphia NSY before sailing for Iran. This included a much-improved air-conditioning layout, the removal of B gun-mount with its magazine, altered accommodation, the fitting of a Canadian telescopic hangar, the siting of the four Standard missile launchers beside the new torpedo stowage between the funnels and the rigging of VDS.

Radar: SPS 10 search; SPS 37 air-surveillance with on-mounted IFF; Gun fire control system Mk 56 with radar on director.

Sonar: SQS 23/SQS 29; VDS.

Spares: USS *Gainard* (DD 706) was to have been taken over in Mar 1971, but, being beyond repair, was replaced by USS *Stormes* (DD 780). Ex-USS *Kenneth D. Bailey* (DD 713) ("Gearing" class) purchased 13 Jan 1975 for spares.

PALANG

1975, Imperial Iranian Navy

FRIGATES

4 "SAAM" CLASS

Name	No.
FARAMARZ	DE 18
ROSTAM	DE 16
SAAM	DE 12
ZAAL	DE 14

Builders	Laid down	Launched	Commissioned
Vosper Thornycroft, Woolston	25 July 1968	30 July 1969	28 Feb 1972
Vickers, Newcastle & Barrow	10 Dec 1967	4 Mar 1969	June 1972
Vosper Thornycroft, Woolston	22 May 1967	25 July 1968	20 May 1971
Vickers, Barrow	3 Mar 1968	4 Mar 1969	1 Mar 1971

Displacement, tons: 1 110 standard; 1 290 full load
Length, feet (metres): 310·0 (94·4) oa
Beam, feet (metres): 34·0 (10·4)
Draught, feet (metres): 11·2 (3·4)
Missile launchers: 1 quintuple "Seakiller"; 1 triple "Seacat"
Guns: 1—4·5 in (115 mm) Mk 8
 2—35 mm Oerlikon (1 twin)
A/S weapons: 1 "Limbo" 3-barrelled DC mortar
Main engines: 2 Rolls-Royce "Olympus" gas turbines; 2 Pax-
man diesels; 2 shafts; 46 000 + 3 800 shp
Speed, knots: 40
Complement: 125 (accommodation for 146)

It was announced on 25 Aug 1966 that Vosper Ltd, Portsmouth
had received an order for four vessels for the Iranian Navy.
Air-conditioned throughout. Fitted with Vosper stabilisers.
Rostam was towed to Barrow for completion.

Radar: Plessey AWS 1 air surveillance with on-mounted IFF.
Two Contraves Seahunter systems for control of 35 mm, Sea-
killers and Seacats. Decca RDL 1 passive DF equipment.

Refit: *Saam* and *Zaal* taken in hand by HM Dockyard Devonport
July/Aug 1975 for major refit including replacement of Mk 5 4·5
in gun by Mk 8.

ZAAL

1975, Imperial Iranian Navy

CORVETTES

4 Ex-US PF 103 TYPE

Name	No.
BAYANDOR (ex-US PF 103)	F 25
KAHNAMUIE (ex-US PF 106)	F 28
MILANIAN (ex-US PF 105)	F 27
NAGHDI (ex-US PF 104)	F 26

Builders	Laid down	Launched	Commissioned
Levingstone Shipbuilding Co, Orange, Texas	20 Aug 1962	7 July 1963	18 May 1964
Levingstone Shipbuilding Co, Orange, Texas	12 June 1967	4 April 1968	13 Feb 1969
Levingstone Shipbuilding Co, Orange, Texas	1 May 1967	4 Jan 1968	13 Feb 1969
Levingstone Shipbuilding Co, Orange, Texas	12 Sep 1962	10 Oct 1963	22 July 1964

Displacement, tons: 900 standard; 1 135 full load
Length, feet (metres): 275·0 (83·8) oa
Beam, feet (metres): 33·0 (10·0)
Draught, feet (metres): 10·2 (3·1)
Guns: 2—3 in (76 mm); 2—40 mm
A/S weapons: 1 Hedgehog; 4 DCT
Main engines: F-M diesels; 2 shafts; 6 000 bhp
Speed, knots: 20
Complement: 140

Built as two pairs, five years apart. Transferred from the USA to
Iran under the Mutual Assistance programme in 1964 (*Bayandor* and *Naghdi*) and 1969 (*Kahnamuie* and *Milanian*).

Radar: SPS 12 search and navigation.

BAYANDOR

1975, Imperial Iranian Navy

SUBMARINES

3 Ex-US "TANG" CLASS (PATROL SUBMARINES)

Name	No.
— (ex-USS *Wahoo, SS 565*)	—
— (ex-USS *Trout, SS 566*)	—
— (ex-USS *Gudgeon, SS 567*)	—

Builders	Laid down	Launched	Commissioned
Portsmouth Navy Yard	24 Oct 1949	16 Oct 1951	30 May 1952
Electric Boat Co, Groton	1 Dec 1949	21 Aug 1951	27 June 1952
Portsmouth Navy Yard	20 May 1950	11 June 1952	21 Nov 1952

Displacement, tons: 2 100 surfaced; 2 700 dived
Dimensions, feet (metres): 287 × 27·3 × 19 (87·4 × 8·3 × 6·2)
Torpedo tubes: 8—21 in (533 mm) (6 forward, 2 aft)
Main machinery: 3 Diesels; 4 500 bhp; 2 electric motors; 5 600
shp; 2 shafts
Speed, knots: 16 surfaced; 16 dived
Complement: 87 (8 officers, 79 men)

Agreement on transfer from USN reached in 1975 to provide
training for the establishment of a larger submarine force.

Ex-USS *Gudgeon*

1970, USN

LIGHT FORCES

12 "KAMAN" CLASS (FAST ATTACK CRAFT—MISSILE)

Name	No.	Builders	Commissioned
KAMAN	P 221	Construction de Mécanique, Normandie	—
ZOUBIN	P 222	Construction de Mécanique, Normandie	—
KHADANG	p 223	Construction de Mécanique, Normandie	—
PEYKAN	P 224	Construction de Mécanique, Normandie	—
JOSHAN	P 225	Construction de Mécanique, Normandie	—
FALAKHON	P 226	Construction de Mécanique, Normandie	—
SHAMSHIR	P 227	Construction de Mécanique, Normandie	—
GORZ	P 228	Construction de Mécanique, Normandie	—
GARDOUNEH	P 229	Construction de Mécanique, Normandie	—
KHANJAR	P 230	Construction de Mécanique, Normandie	—
NEYZEH	P 231	Construction de Mécanique, Normandie	—
TABARZIN	P 232	Construction de Mécanique, Normandie	—

Displacement, tons: 249 standard; 275 full load
Dimensions, feet (metres): 154·2 × 23·3 × 6·4 *(47 × 7·1 × 1·9)*
Missiles: 2 Twin Harpoon launchers
Guns: 1—76 mm Oto Melara; 1—40 mm Bofors
Main engines: 4 MTU diesels; 4 shafts; 14 400 bhp = 36 knots
Oil fuel, tons: 41
Range, miles: 700 at 30+ knots
Complement: 30

Ordered in Feb 1974. For completion by April 1979. *Kaman* laid down 5 Feb 1975, launched 8 Jan 1976; *Zoubin* laid down 4 April 1975; *Khadang* laid down 20 June 1975; *Peykan* laid down 15 Oct 1975.

Radar: Tactical and Fire control: WM 28 (Hollandse Signaalapparaten)

"KAMAN" Class

1975, Imperial Iranian Navy

3 IMPROVED PGM TYPE (LARGE PATROL CRAFT)

Name	No.	Builders	Commissioned
BAHRAAM (ex-US *PGM 112)*	66	Tacoma Boatbuilding Co, Tacoma	1967
NAHID (ex-US *PGM 122)*	67	Tacoma Boatbuilding Co, Tacoma	1968
PARVIN (ex-US *PGM 103)*	65	Peterson Builders Inc, Sturgeon Bay, Wisconsin	1970

Displacement, tons: 105 standard; 146 full load
Dimensions, feet (metres): 100 × 22 × 10 *(30·5 × 6·7 × 3·1)*
Guns: 1—40 mm; 2—20 mm; 2—50 cal MG
Main engines: 8 MG diesels; 2 000 bhp = 15 knots

See Addendum

PARVIN (original number)

'1971

6 40 ft TYPE (COASTAL PATROL CRAFT)

MAHNAVI-HAMRAZ	MAHNAVI-VAHEDI	MORVARID
MAHNAVI-TAHERI	MARDJAN	SADAF

Displacement, tons: 10 standard
Dimensions, feet (metres): 40·0 × 11·0 × 3·7 *(12·2 × 3·4 × 1·1)*
Guns: Light MG
Main engines: 2 General Motors diesels = 30 knots

Small launches for port duties of Sewart (USA) standard 40 ft type. All transferred June 1953. Pennant numbers 5001 and above. Some serve in the Caspian Sea.

4 US COASTGUARD "CAPE" CLASS

Name	No.	Builders	Commissioned
KAYVAN	61	USA	14 Jan 1956
MAHAN	64	USA	1959
TIRAN	63	US Coast Guard, Curtis Bay, Maryland	1957
MEHRAN	62	USA	1959

Displacement, tons: 85 standard; 107 full load
Dimensions, feet (metres): 90 pp; 95 oa × 20·2 × 6·8 *(27·5; 28·9 × 6·2 × 2)*
Gun: 1—40 mm
A/S weapons: 8-barrelled 7·2 in projector, 8—300 lb depth charges
Main engines: 4 Cummins diesels; 2 shafts; 2 200 bhp = 20 knots
Range, miles: 1 500 cruising
Complement: 15

See Addendum

MAHAN

1975, Imperial Iranian Navy

3 PATROL BOATS (COASTAL PATROL CRAFT)

Name	No.	Builders	Commissioned
GOHAR	—	Abeking and Rasmussen	1970
SHAHPAR	—	Abeking and Rasmussen	1970
SHAHRAM	—	Abeking and Rasmussen	1970

Displacement, tons: 70
Dimensions, feet (metres): 75·2 × 16·5 × 6 *(22·9 × 5·0 × 1·8)*
Main engines: 2 diesels; 2 200 hp; 2 shafts = 27 knots
Complement: 19

Gohar launched 22 Jan 1970. *Shahpar* on 19 Mar 1970. Transferred to Iranian Coastguard 1975.

6 "WELLINGTON" (BH.7) CLASS (HOVERCRAFT)

Name	No.	Builders	Commissioned	
—	101	British Hovercraft Corporation	Nov	1970
—	102	British Hovercraft Corporation	Mar	1971
—	103	British Hovercraft Corporation	Mid	1974
—	104	British Hovercraft Corporation	Mid	1974
—	105	British Hovercraft Corporation	Late	1974
—	106	British Hovercraft Corporation	Early	1975

Displacement, tons: 50 max weight, 33 empty
Dimensions, feet (metres): 76 × 45 ×42 *(23·2 × 13·7 × 12·8)*
Missiles: SSMs in last four (see note)
Guns: 2 Browning MG
Main engines: 1 Proteus 15 M/541 gas turbine = 60 knots
Oil fuel, tons: 10

First pair are BH 7 Mk 4 (delivered Nov 70 and Mar 71) and the next four are Mk 5 craft (two in mid 1974, one in late 1974, and one in early 1975). Mk 5 craft fitted for, but not with, surface-to-surface missiles.

"Wellington" Hovercraft 101   *1975, Imperial Iranian Navy*

8 "WINCHESTER" (SR.N6) CLASS (HOVERCRAFT)

Name	No.	Builders	Commissioned
—	01	British Hovercraft Corporation	1973
—	02	British Hovercraft Corporation	1973
—	03	British Hovercraft Corporation	1973
—	04	British Hovercraft Corporation	1974
—	05	British Hovercraft Corporation	1974
—	06	British Hovercraft Corporation	1975
—	07	British Hovercraft Corporation	1975
—	08	British Hovercraft Corporation	1975

Displacement, tons: 10 normal gross weight (basic weight 14 200 lbs; disposable load 8 200 lbs)
Dimensions, feet (metres): 48·4 × 25·3 × 15·9 (height) *(14·8 × 7·7 × 4·8)*
Guns: 1 or 2 50 cal MGs
Main engines: 1 Gnome Model 1050 gas turbine = 58 knots
1 Peters diesel as auxiliary power unit

Ordered 1970-72. The Imperial Iranian Navy has the world's largest fully operational hovercraft squadron, which is used for coastal defence and logistic duties.

"Winchester" Hovercraft 03   *1971*

LANDING CRAFT

QUESM (ex-US *LCU 1431)* LCU 47

Displacement, tons: 160 light; 320 full load
Dimensions, feet (metres): 119 × 32 × 5·7 *(36·3 × 9·8 × 1·7)*
Guns: 2—20 mm
Main engines: Diesels; 675 bhp = 10 knots
Complement: 14

LCU 1431 was transferred to Iran by US in Sep 1964 under the Military Aid Programme.

QUESM   *1971*

MINE WARFARE FORCES

3 Ex-US MSC TYPE (MINESWEEPERS—COASTAL)

Name	No.	Builders	Commissioned
KARKAS (ex-USS *MSC 292)*	34	Petersen Builders Inc	1959
SHAHROKH (ex-USS *MSC 276)*	31	Bellingham Shipyards Co	1960
SIMORGH (ex-USS *MSC 291)*	33	Tacoma Boatbuilding Co	1962

Displacement, tons: 320 light; 378 full load
Dimensions, feet (metres): 138 pp; 145·8 oa × 28 × 8·3 *(42·1; 44·5 × 8·5 × 2·5)*
Guns: 1—20 mm (double-barrelled)
Main engines: 2 GM diesels; 2 shafts; 890 bhp = 12·8 knots
Oil fuel, tons: 27
Range, miles: 2 400 at 11 knots
Complement: 40 (4 officers, 2 midshipmen, 34 men)

Originally class of four. Of wooden construction. Launched in 1958-61 and transferred from US to Iran under MAP in 1959-62. *Shahrokh* now in the Caspian Sea.

SIMORGH   *1975, Imperial Iranian Navy*

2 US MSI TYPE (MINESWEEPERS—INSHORE)

Name	No.	Builders	Commissioned
HARISCHI (ex-*Kahnamuie*, ex-*MSI 14*)	301	Tacoma Boatbuilding Co	3 Sep 1964
RIAZI (ex-*MSI 13*)	302	Tacoma Boatbuilding Co	15 Oct 1964

Displacement, tons: 180 standard; 235 full load
Dimensions, feet (metres): 111 × 23 × 6 *(33·9 × 7·0 × 1·8)*
Gun: 1 50 cal MG
Main engines: Diesels; 650 bhp = 13 knots
Oil fuel, tons: 20
Range, miles: 1 000 at 9 knots
Complement: 23 (5 officers, 18 men)

Delivered to Iran under MAP. Laid down on 22 June 1962 and 1 Feb 1963, and transferred at Seattle, Washington, on 3 Sep 1964 and 15 Oct 1964, respectively. In Aug 1967 *Kahnamuie* was renamed *Harischi* as the name was required for one of the new US PFs (see Light Forces).

RIAZI

1975, Imperial Iranian Navy

SERVICE FORCES

1 FLEET TANKER

Name	No.	Builders	Commissioned
—	—	Swan Hunter Ltd, Wallsend	1977

Measurement, tons: 20 000 dwt
Main engines: Geared steam turbines; 26 870 hp

Ordered Oct 1974.

2 LANDING SHIPS (LOGISTIC)

Name	No.	Builders	Commissioned
HENGAM	52	Yarrow, Clyde	12 Aug 1974
LARAK	51	Yarrow, Clyde	12 Nov 1974

Displacement, tons: 2 500
Length, feet (metres): 300 *(91·5)*
Aircraft: 1 helicopter
Guns: 4—40 mm (single)
Main engines: Diesels; 2 shafts; 5 600 bhp
Speed, knots: 16

Similar in many respects to British *Sir Lancelot* but smaller with bridge amidships. Ordered 1972. *Hengam* laid down late 1972, launched 24 Sep 1973. *Larak* laid down 1973, launched 7 May 1974.

LARAK

5/1975, C. & S. Taylor

2 FLEET SUPPLY SHIPS

Name	No.	Builders	Commissioned
BANDAR ABBAS	A 42	C. Lühring Yard, Brake, W. Germany	Apr 1974
BOOSHEHR	A 44	C. Lühring Yard, Brake, W. Germany	Nov 1974

Measurement, tons: 3 250 deadweight
Dimensions, feet (metres): 354·2 × 54·4 × 14·8 *(108 × 16·6 × 4·5)*
Aircraft: 1 helicopter
Main engines: 2 MAN (MTU) diesels; 2 shafts; 6 000 bhp
Speed, knots: 16
Complement: 60

Combined tankers and store-ships carrying victualling, armament and general stores. *Bandar Abbas* launched 11 Aug 1973, *Booshehr* launched 23 Mar 1974.

BANDAR ABBAS

1975, Imperial Iranian Navy

1 Ex-US "AMPHION" CLASS (REPAIR SHIP)

Name	No.	Builders	Commissioned
CHAHBAHAR (ex-USS *Amphion*, ex-*AR 13*)	A 41	Tampa Shipbuilding Co	30 Jan 1946

Displacement, tons: 7 826 standard; 14 490 full load
Dimensions, feet (metres): 456·0 wl; 492·0 oa × 70·0 × 27·5 *(139; 150·1 × 21·4 × 8·4)*
Guns: 2—3 in 50 cal
Main engines: Westinghouse turbines; 1 shaft; 8 500 shp = 16·5 knots
Boilers: 2 Foster-Wheeler
Complement: Accommodation for 921

Launched on 15 May 1945. Transferred to IIN on 1 Oct 1971. Based at Bandar Abbas as permanent repair facility.

CHAHBAHAR

1972, Imperial Iranian Navy

1 HARBOUR TANKER

Name	No.	Builders	Commissioned
HORMUZ (ex-*YO 247*)	A 43	Cantiere Castellamàre di Stabia	1956

Displacement, tons: 1 250 standard; 1 700 full load
Dimensions, feet (metres): 171·2 wl; 178·3 oa × 32·2 × 14 *(52·2; 54·4 × 9·8 × 4·3)*
Guns: 2—20 mm
Main engines: 1 Ansaldo Q 370, 4 cycle diesel
Oil fuel, tons: 25

Cargo oil capacity: 5 000 to 6 000 barrels.

HORMUZ

1970, Imperial Iranian Navy

1 Ex-US YW TYPE (WATER BOAT)

LENGEH (ex-US *YW 88)* A 46

Displacement, tons: 1 250 standard
Dimensions, feet (metres): 178 × 32 × 14 *(54·3 × 9·8 × 4·3)*
Main engines: Diesels; speed = 10 knots

Transferred to Iran by US in 1964. Similar to tanker *Hormuz*.

LENGEH   *1975, Imperial Iranian Navy*

1 TUG

BAHMANSHIR 45

Harbour tug (ex-US Army *ST 1002)*, 150 tons, transferred in 1962.

2 HARBOUR TUGS

No. 1 (ex-German *Karl)*   **No. 2** (ex-German *Ise)*

Sister ships of 134 tons taken over from W. Germany 17 June 1974. Both built 1962-63.

No. 1 and No. 2   *4/1974, Reiner Nerlich*

IMPERIAL YACHTS

Name	No.	Builders	Commissioned
KISH	—	Yacht und Bootswerft, Burmester, Germany	1970

Displacement, tons: 178
Dimensions, feet (metres): 122 × 25 × 7 *(37·2 × 7·6 × 2·1)*
Main engines: MTU diesels; 2 920 hp

A smaller and more modern Imperial Yacht. In the Persian Gulf.

KISH   *1971*

Name	No.	Builders	Commissioned
SHAHSAVAR	—	N.V. Boele's Scheepwerven, Bolnes, Netherlands	1936

Displacement, tons: 530
Dimensions, feet (metres): 176 × 25·3 × 10·5 *(53·7 × 7·7 × 3·2)*
Main engines: 2 sets diesels; 1 300 bhp

Launched in 1936. In the Caspian Sea.

SHAHSAVAR   *1971, Imperial Iranian Navy*

FLOATING DOCK

FD 4 (ex-US *ARD 29)*

Dimensions, feet (metres):
Lift: 3 000 tons

Transferred Sep 1971. Of steel construction.

CUSTOMS VESSELS

TOUFAN   TOUSAN

Built by CN Inmar, La Spezia in 1954-55. Of 65 tons with twin diesels. 22 knots.

SURVEY VESSELS

(Operated by the Ministry of Finance)

MEHR

Of 422 tons. Launched in 1964. Complement 22.

HYDROGRAPH SHAHPOUR

Of 9 tons. Launched in 1965.

HYDROGRAPH PAHLAVI

Of 9 tons. Launched in 1966.

IRAQ

Administration

Commander-in-Chief:
Rear-Admiral Abd Al Diri
Chief of Staff:
Commander Samad Sat Al Mufti

Personnel

(a) 1976: 3 000 officers and men
(b) 2 years National Service

Mercantile Marine

Lloyd's Register of Shipping:
56 vessels of 310 594 tons gross

SOVIET-IRAQI TREATY

Under this treaty, signed in April 1972, the Soviet fleet will have access to the Iraqi base of Umm Qasr. In return Soviet assistance will be given to strengthen Iraq's defences. From the naval aspect, taking into account the small number of personnel, this is most likely to be confined to Light Forces.

CORVETTES

3 Ex-SOVIET "SO I" CLASS

Displacement, tons: 215 light; 250 full load
Dimensions, feet (metres): 138·6 × 20 × 9·2 *(42·3 × 6·1 × 2·8)*
Guns: 4—25 mm
A/S weapons: 4 five-barrelled ahead-throwing rocket launchers
Main engines: 3 diesels; 6 000 bhp = 29 knots
Complement: 30

Delivered by the USSR to Iraq in 1962.

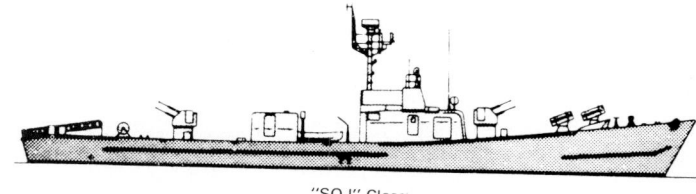

"SO I" Class

LIGHT FORCES

10 Ex-SOVIET "OSA" CLASS (FAST ATTACK CRAFT—MISSILE)

Displacement, tons: 165 standard; 200 full load
Dimensions, feet (metres): 128·7 × 25·1 × 5·9 *(39·3 × 7·7 × 1·8)*
Missiles: 4 launchers for SS-N-2
Guns: 4—30 mm (twin)
Main engines: 3 Diesels; 13 000 hp = 32 knots
Range, miles: 800 at 25 knots
Complement: 25

A combination of 6 "OSA I" and 4 "OSA II" classes. This increase in the Iraqi navy must make a major impact on naval affairs in the Persian Gulf. Other navies have shown the effectiveness of the Styx missiles, even in comparatively untrained hands, against unalerted forces. It will be a surprise if this Soviet incursion does not accelerate the build up of high-effectiveness forces in this area.

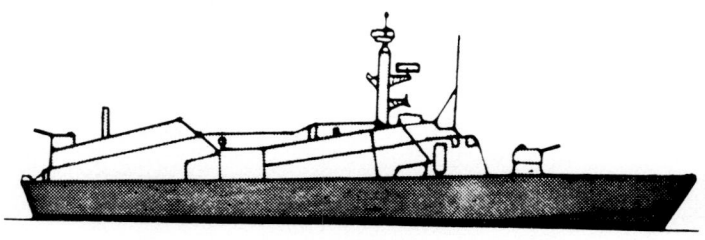

"OSA I" Class

12 Ex-SOVIET "P 6" CLASS
(FAST ATTACK CRAFT—TORPEDO)

Displacement, tons: 66 standard; 75 full load
Dimensions, feet (metres): 84·2 × 20 × 6 *(25·7 × 6·1 × 1·8)*
Guns: 4—25 mm
Tubes: 2—21 in
Main engines: Diesels; 4 800 bhp = 45 knots
Complement: 25

Transferred from the USSR. Two were received in 1959, four in Nov 1960, and six in Jan 1961. Some remain non-operational.

2 Ex-SOVIET "POLUCHAT" CLASS (LARGE PATROL CRAFT)

Displacement, tons: 100 standard
Dimensions, feet (metres): 98·4 × 19·0 × 5·9 *(30·0 × 5·8 × 1·8)*
Guns: 2—25 mm

Transferred by USSR in late 1960s.

4 Ex-SOVIET "ZHUK" CLASS
(COASTAL PATROL CRAFT)

Displacement, tons: 50
Dimensions, feet (metres): 75 × 16 × — *(22·9 × 4·9 × —)*
Guns: 2—14·5 MM MG; 1—12·7 mm MG
Main engines:
Speed, knots: 30

Transferred in 1975.

4 COASTAL PATROL CRAFT

Name	No.	Builders	Commissioned	
—	1	John I. Thornycroft & Co Ltd, Woolston, Southampton	1937	Protected by bullet-proof plating. All built by John I. Thornycroft & Co Ltd, Woolston, Southampton. All launched, completed and delivered in 1937.
—	2	John I. Thornycroft & Co Ltd, Woolston, Southampton	1937	
—	3	John I. Thornycroft & Co Ltd, Woolston, Southampton	1937	
—	4	John I. Thornycroft & Co Ltd, Woolston, Southampton	1937	

Displacement, tons: 67
Dimensions, feet (metres): 100 × 17 × 3 *(30·5 × 5·2 × 0·9)*
Guns: 1—3·7 in howitzer; 2—3 in mortars; 4 MG
Main engines: 2 Thornycroft diesels; 2 shafts; 280 bhp = 12 knots

4 THORNYCROFT 21 ft TYPE

Length, feet (metres): 21 *(6·4)*
Main engines: 1 diesel; 40 bhp

Pilot despatch launches built by John I. Thornycroft & Co for the Iraqi Ports.

8 THORNYCROFT 36 ft TYPE

Length, feet (metres): 36 *(11·0)*
Main engines: 1 diesel; 125 bhp

Patrol boats built by John I. Thornycroft & Co for the Iraqi Ports Administration.

4 COASTAL PATROL CRAFT

Reported as ex-Soviet "Nyriat" Class used as diving craft.

TUG

ALARM (ex-*St. Ewe*)

Displacement, tons: 570 standard; 820 full load
Dimensions, feet (metres): 135 × 30 × 14·5 *(41·2 × 9·2 × 4·4)*
Main engines: Triple expansion; 1 shaft; 1 200 ihp = 12 knots
Boilers: 2 oil-fired

Former British Rescue type tug of the "Saint" class. Built by Murdock & Murray. Launched in 1919.

LIGHTHOUSE TENDER

— (ex-*Sans Peur*, ex-*Restless*)

Displacement, tons: 1 025
Dimensions, feet (metres): 186 × 29·5 × 14·5 *(56·7 × 9·0 × 4·4)*
Main engines: Triple expansion; 2 shafts; 850 ihp = 13 knots
Boilers: 1 oil-fired

Former Royal Yacht. Designed by G. L. Watson Ltd. Built by John Brown & Co Ltd, Clydebank. Launched in 1923.

PRESIDENTIAL YACHT

AL THAWRA (ex-*Malike Aliye*)

Displacement, tons: 746
Main engines: Diesels; 2 shafts; 1 800 shp = 14 knots

Royal Yacht before assassination of King Faisal II in 1958, after which she was renamed *Al Thawra (The Revolution)* instead of *Malike Aliye (Queen Aliyah)*.

AL THAWRA   *1966, Aldo Fraccaroli*

IRELAND (REPUBLIC of)

Minister for Defence: Mr. P. S. Donegan, TD
Commanding Officer and Director Naval Service: Captain P. Kavanagh, NS

The Irish Naval Service is administered from Naval Headquarters, Department of Defence, Dublin, by the Commanding Officer and Director Naval Service. The naval base and dockyard are on Haulbowline island in Cork Harbour.

Personnel

1976: Approximately 500 officers and men

Disposals

Cliona (ex-HMS *Bellwort*) and *Macha* (ex-HMS *Borage*), both built by George Brown, & Co (Marine) Ltd, Greenock, were sold for breaking up in 1970-71. *Maev* (ex-HMS *Oxlip*) deleted 1972. Tender *Wyndham* sold in 1968 and *General McHardy* in 1971.

Mercantile Marine

Lloyd's Register of Shipping:
   88 vessels of 208 700 tons gross

CORVETTES

Name	No.	Builders	Commissioned	
DEIRDRE	P 20	Verolme, Cork	May	1972
—	P 21	Verolme, Cork	Nov	1977

Displacement, tons: 972
Dimensions, feet (metres): 184·3 pp × 34·1 × 14·4 *(56·2 × 10·4 × 4·4)*
Gun: 1—40 mm Bofors
Main engines: 2 British Polar diesels coupled to 1 shaft; 4 200 bhp = 18 knots
Oil fuel, tons: 17
Range, miles: 10 000 at 12 knots
Complement: 46 (5 officers, 41 men)

Controllable pitch propeller, stabilisers and sonar. *Deirdre* was the first vessel ever built for the Naval Service in the Republic of Ireland. Launched on 29 Dec 1971. A second vessel of this class has been ordered from Verolme for delivery Nov 1977. Improvements in design will result in an increase of 6·5 ft *(2 metres)* in the overall length of this ship.

DEIRDRE   *1974, Irish Naval Service*

COASTAL MINESWEEPERS

3 Ex-BRITISH "TON" CLASS

BANBA (ex-HMS *Alverton, M 1104*) CM 11
FÓLA (ex-HMS *Blaxton, M 1132*) CM 12
GRÁINNE (ex-HMS *Oulston, M 1129*) CM 10

Displacement, tons: 360 standard; 425 full load
Dimensions, feet (metres): 140·0 pp; 153·0 oa × 28·8 × 8·2 *(42·7; 46·7 × 8·8 × 2·5)*
Guns: 1—40 mm; 2—20 mm
Main engines: 2 diesels; 2 shafts; 3 000 bhp = 15 knots
Oil fuel, tons: 45
Range, miles: 2 300 at 13 knots
Complement: 33

Former British "Ton" class coastal minesweepers. Built in 1954-59. Double mahogany hulls and otherwise constructed of aluminium alloy and other materials with the lowest possible magnetic signature. Purchased from Great Britain in 1971. Acquired for fishery protection duties as replacements for the corvettes. Arrived in Irish waters in spring 1971.

FOLA   *1972, Irish Naval Service*

TENDER

JOHN ADAMS

Measurement, tons: 94 gross
Dimensions, feet (metres): 85 × 18·5 × 7 *(25·9 × 5·6 × 2·1)*
Main engines: Diesel; 216 bhp = 10 knots

Built by Richard Dunston, Ltd, Thorne, Doncaster, Yorks. Launched in 1934. New engine fitted in 1976.

ITALY

Headquarters Appointment

Chief of Naval Staff:
Admiral Gino di Giorgio

Principal Flag Officers

Commander, Allied Naval Forces, Southern Europe (Naples) and Commander-in-Chief Dipartimento Basso Tirreno:
Admiral Luigi Tomasuolo
Commander-in-Chief of Fleet (and Comedcent):
Vice-Admiral Aldo Baldini
Commander-in-Chief Dipartimento Alto Tirreno:
Vice-Admiral Giuseppe Oriana
Commander-in-Chief Dipartimento Adriatico:
Vice-Admiral Enzo Consolo
Commander-in-Chief Dipartimento dello Jonio e Canale d'Otranto:
Vice-Admiral Mario Bini
Commander 1st Naval Division:
Vice-Admiral Giuliano Martinelli
Commander 2nd Naval Division:
Rear-Admiral Romualdo Balzano
Commander 3rd Naval Division:
Vice-Admiral Giuseppe Di Giovanni
Commander 4th Naval Division:
Rear-Admiral Aldo Macchiavelli
Chief of Naval Personnel:
Vice-Admiral Giovanni Torrisi

Diplomatic Representation

Naval Attaché in London:
Rear-Admiral F. Mottolese
Naval Attaché in Moscow:
Captain Armando Vigliano
Naval Attaché in Paris:
Captain P. Della Croce di Dojola
Naval Attaché in Washington:
Captain Carlo A. Vandini

Personnel

(a) 1976: 42 000 (including Naval Air Arm and an expanding Force of Marines)
(b) 1½ years National Service

Bases

Main—La Spezia, Taranto
Secondary—Brindisi, Augusta, Messina, La Maddalena, Cagliari, Napoli, Venezia

Mercantile Marine

Lloyd's Register of Shipping:
1 732 vessels of 10 136 989 tons gross

Naval Air Arm

2 LRMP Squadrons—18 Breguet Atlantics (BR 1150)
1 SRMP Squadron—Grumman S2F
2 Shore-based helicopter Squadrons (24 SH 3D)

Strength of the Fleet

Type	Active	Building (Planned)
Cruisers	3	—
Destroyers	8	—
Frigates	11	4
Corvettes	13	—
Submarines	9	2
Hydrofoil—Missile	1	(6)
Fast Attack Craft—Torpedo	6	—
Fast Attack Craft (Convertible)	4	—
LSTs	2	—
Minesweepers—Ocean	4	—
Minesweepers—Coastal	31	—
Minesweepers—Inshore	10	—
Survey Vessels	3	—
Replenishment Tanker	1	—
Transport	1	—
Fleet Support Ship	1	—
Coastal Transports	10	—
Transports (LCM)	20	—
Transports (LCVP)	39	—
Sail Training Ships	4	—
Netlayers	2	—
Lighthouse Tenders	4	—
Salvage Ship	1	—
Repair Craft	7	—
Water Carriers	15	—
Tugs—Large	29	—
Tugs—Small	31	—

Shipbuilding and Conversion Programme

In 1975 a law (Legge Navale) was approved which provided 1 000 billion lire for the next ten years (1975-84), for the provision of new and converted ships and aircraft over and above the normal annual expenditure.
The tentative new-construction programme is as follows:
1 Helicopter Cruiser
2 Guided Missile Destroyers
8 Frigates
2 Submarines
10 Minehunters
9 "Sparviero" class Hydrofoils
4 NATO Hydrofoils
1 LPD
1 Replenishment Tanker
1 Salvage Ship
17 Tugs
62 AB212 Helicopters
12 SH3D Helicopters
The conversion programme (1977-80) is: 10 MSCs to MSHs.

DELETIONS

Cruiser

1971 *Giuseppe Garibaldi*

Destroyers

1971 *San Marco, Artigliere, Lanciere*
1975 *Geniere, Altair*

Corvettes

1970-72 12 "Ape" Class

Submarines

1972 *Pietro Calvi*
1973 *Leonardo da Vinci, Enrico Tazzoli*
1974 *Francesco Morosini* ("Balao" Class)
1975 *Evangelista Torricelli* ("Balao" Class)

Minesweepers (Coastal)

1966-67 17 ships of "Azalea" and "Anemone" classes
1974 *Rovere, Acacia, Betulla, Ciliegio*

Minesweepers (Inshore)

1974 *Arsella, Attinia, Calamaro, Conchiglia, Dromia, Ostrica, Paguro, Seppia, Tellina, Totano*

Amphibious Forces

1974 *Anteo, MTM 9903, 9904, 9906, 9921. MTP 9701, 9702, 9704-6, 9709, 9712, 9717, 9718, 9721, 9722, 9724, 9731*
1975 *Etna*

Light Forces

1974 *MS 472* (ex-*813*)
1975 *MS 452* (ex-*852*) *MS 473* (ex-*813*)

Miscellaneous

1974 *Aviere* (experimental ship), *Po, Flegetonte, Isonzo, Sesia, Metauro, Arno, Leno* and *Sprugola* (water carriers). 24 tugs
1975 *Sterope* (repl. tanker), *Frigido* (water carrier), *MTM 9916-7, Porto Vecchio* (tug)

PENNANT NUMBERS

Cruisers

C550	Vittorio Veneto
C553	Andrea Dorea
C554	Caio Duilio

Destroyers

D550	Ardito
D551	Audace
D558	Impetuoso
D559	Indomito
D561	Fante
D562	San Giorgio
D570	Impavido
D571	Intrepido

Frigates

F551	Canopo
F553	Castore
F554	Centauro
F555	Cigno
F580	Alpino
F581	Carabiniere
F590	Aldebaran
F593	Carlo Bergamini
F594	Virginio Fasan
F595	Carlo Margottini
F596	Luigi Rizzo

Corvettes

F540	Pietro De Cristofaro
F541	Umberto Grosso
F542	Aquila
F543	Albatros
F544	Alcione
F545	Airone
F546	Licio Visintini
F549	Bombarda
F550	Salvatore Todaro

F567	Ape
F569	Chimera
F579	Sfinge
F597	Vedetta

Submarines

S501	Primo Longobardo
S502	Gianfranco Gazzana Priaroggia
S505	Attilio Bagnolini
S506	Enrico Toti
S507	Alfredo Cappellini
S513	Enrico Dandolo
S514	Lazzaro Mocenigo
S515	Livio Piomarta
S516	Romeo Romei

Light Forces

P420	Sparviero
P490	Folgore
P491	Lampo
P492	Baleno
P493	Freccia
P494	Saetta
—	MS441
—	MS443
—	MS453
—	MS474
—	MS481

Minesweepers

M5430	Salmone
M5431	Storione
M5432	Sgombro
M5433	Squalo
M5450	Aragosta
M5452	Astice
M5457	Gambero
M5458	Granchio
M5459	Mitilo
M5462	Pinna
M5463	Polipo
M5464	Porpora
M5465	Riccio
M5466	Scampo
M5501	Abete
M5504	Castagno
M5505	Cedro
M5507	Faggio
M5508	Frassino
M5509	Gelso
M5510	Larice
M5511	Noce
M5512	Olmo
M5513	Ontano
M5514	Pino
M5516	Platano
M5517	Quercia
M5519	Mandorlo
M5521	Bambù
M5522	Ebano
M5523	Mango
M5524	Mogano
M5525	Palma
M5527	Sandalo
M5531	Agave
M5532	Alloro
M5533	Edera
M5534	Gaggia
M5535	Gelsomino
M5536	Giaggiolo
M5537	Glicine
M5538	Loto
M5540	Timo
M5541	Trifolgio
M5542	Vischio

Amphibious Forces

L9871	Andrea Bafile
L9881	Quarto
L9890	Grado
L9891	Caorle

Service Forces

A5301	Pietro Cavezzale
A5303	Ammiraglio Magnaghi
A5304	Alicudi
A5305	Filicudi
A5306	Mirto
A5307	Pioppo
A5309	Rampino
A5310	Proteo
A5311	Palinuro
A5312	Amerigo Vespucci
A5313	Stella Polare
A5316	Corsaro II
A5319	Ciclope
A5320	Colosso
A5321	Forte
A5322	Gagliardo
A5323	Robusto
A5324	Ustica
A5326	S. Giusto
A5327	Stromboli 1201
A5331-5338	MOC 1201-1208
A5354	Piave
A5355	Tevere
A5356	Basento
A5357	Bradano
A5358	Brenta
A5359	Bormida
A5361-5363	MTF 1301-1303
A5366	Volturno
A5369	Adige
A5374	Mincio
A5376	Tanaro
A5377	Ticino
A5378	Porto d'Ischia
A5379	Riva Trigoso
A5381	Caprera
A5382	Pantelleria
A5385	Favignana
A5386	Porto Pisano
A5387	Porto Recanati
A5388	
A5391	Salvore
A5392	Tino
A5394	Vigoroso
A5396	Pianova
A5397	Levanzo

CRUISERS

1 HELICOPTER CRUISER

Name	No.	Builders	Laid down	Launched	Commissioned
VITTORIO VENETO	C 550	Navalmeccanica, Castellammare di Stabia	10 June 1965	5 Feb 1967	12 July 1969

Displacement, tons: 7 500 standard; 8 850 full load
Length, feet (metres): 589 *(179·6)* oa
Beam, feet (metres): 63·6 *(19·4)*
Draught, feet (metres): 19·7 *(6)*
Aircraft: 9 AB-204B helicopters
Missiles: 1 Terrier/Asroc twin launcher forward
Guns: 8—3 in *(76 mm)* 62 cal
Torpedo tubes: 2 triple for A/S torpedoes
Main engines: 2 Tosi double reduction geared turbines; 73 000 shp; 2 shafts
Boilers: 4 Foster-Wheeler; 711 psi *(50 kg/cm²)*; 842°F *(450°C)*
Speed, knots: 32
Oil fuel, tons: 1 200
Range, miles: 6 000 at 20 knots
Complement: 560 (60 officers, 500 men)

Developed from the "Andrea Doria" class but with much larger helicopter squadron and improved facilities for anti-submarine operations. Projected under the 1959-60 New Construction Programme, but her design was recast several times. Started trials 30 April 1969. Flagship of C-in-C Fleet.

Radar: Air search and target designator (3D on fore funnel): one SPS 48.
Long-range search (after funnel): one SPS 40.
Search and navigation: one SMA/SPQ-2.
Terrier fire control: two SPG 55B.
Gun fire control: four Orion radars in Argo/Elsag NA9 systems.

Sonar: One SQS 23.

VITTORIO VENETO   1974, Dr. Giorgio Arra

VITTORIO VENETO   1973, Italian Navy

VITTORIO VENETO   1973, Dr. Giorgio Arra

Cruisers—*continued*

2 "ANDREA DORIA" CLASS

ame	No.	Builders	Laid down	Launched	Commissioned
NDREA DORIA	C 553	Cantieri del Tirreno, Riva Trigoso	11 May 1958	27 Feb 1963	23 Feb 1964
AIO DUILIO	C 554	Navalmeccanica di Stabia	16 May 1958	22 Dec 1962	30 Nov 1964

splacement, tons: 5 000 standard; 6 500 full load
ngth, feet (metres): 489·8 *(149·3)* oa
am, feet (metres): 56·4 *(17·2)*
aught, feet (metres): 16·4 *(5·0)*
rcraft: 4 AB-204B helicopters
ssiles: 1 Terrier twin launcher forward
ns: 8—3 in *(76 mm)* 62 cal.
rpedo tubes: 2 triple for 12 in *(305 mm)* A/S torpedoes
ain engines: 2 double reduction geared turbines 60 000 shp; 2 shafts
ilers: 4 Foster-Wheeler 711 psi *(50 kg/cm²)*; 842°F *(450°C)*
eed, knots: 31
nge, miles: 6 000 at 20 knots
l fuel, tons: 1 100
mplement: 485 (45 officers, 440 men)

cort cruisers of novel design with a good helicopter capacity relation to their size. *Enrico Dandolo* was the name originally ocated to *Andrea Doria*.

ectronics: ECM and DF. Tacan beacon.

unnery: The anti-aircraft battery includes eight 3-inch fully tomatic guns of a new pattern, disposed in single turrets, ur on each side amidships abreast the funnels and the bridge.

licopter platform: Helicopters operate from a platform aft easuring 98·5 feet by 52·5 feet *(30 by 16 metres)*. The Harrier, signed and built by Hawker Siddeley, demonstrated its pabilities of operating from shipborne platforms when it mpleted a two-day demonstration with a vertical landing on e comparatively small helicopter flight deck of the *Andrea ria*.

ll damping: Both ships have Gyrofin-Salmoiraghi stabilis-s.

dar: Air surveillance and target designator (3D on main-ast): one SPS 39
ng range search: one SPS 40.
vigation: one set.
rrier fire-control: two SPG 55A.
un fire control: four Orion radars in Argo/Elsag NA9 systems

nar: One SQS 23.

ANDREA DORIA   1973, Dr. Giorgio Arra

CAIO DUILIO   1972, Commander Aldo Fraccarali

NDREA DORIA   11/1975, Dr. Giorgio Arra

DESTROYERS

2 "AUDACE" CLASS (DDG)

Name	No.	Builders	Laid down	Launched	Commissione
ARDITO	D 550	Navalmeccanica, Castellammare	19 July 1968	27 Nov 1971	5 Dec 1973
AUDACE	D 551	Cantieri del Tirreno, Riva Trigoso	27 April 1968	2 Oct 1971	16 Nov 1972

Displacement, tons: 3 600 standard; 4 400 full load
Length, feet (metres): 446·4 *(136·6)*
Beam, feet (metres): 47·1 *(14·5)*
Draught, feet (metres): 15 *(4·6)*
Aircraft: 2 AB-204B helicopters
Missile launcher: 1 Tartar
Guns: 2—5 in *(127 mm)* 54 cal single; 4—3 in *(76 mm)* 62 cal
Torpedo tubes: 6 A/S (two tripled) 4 fixed tubes
Main engines: 2 geared turbines; 73 000 shp; 2 shafts
Boilers: 4 Foster Wheeler type
Speed, knots: 33
Complement: 380 (30 officers, 350 men)

It was announced in April 1966 that two new guided missile destroyers would be built. They are basically similar to, but an improvement in design on that of the "Impavido" class.

Aircraft: Originally planned to carry two AB-204B helicopters carrying two A/S torpedoes. These may be replaced by two Sea King SH3Ds.

Radar: Air Surveillance (3D on after funnel): one SPS 52
Tracking and missile guidance: two SPG 51
Surface Search: one SPS 12
Gun fire control: Three Orion RTN 10X for Argo 10/Elsag NA 10 systems

Sonar: one CWE 610

SCLAR: fitted with SCLAR control and launch units for 105 mm rockets which can be fitted with chaff dispensers, flares or HE heads and have a range of 7 miles.

Torpedo Tubes: The two triple Mk 32 launchers for Mk 44 torpedoes are on either beam amidships. The four fixed torpedo tubes (A 184 System) for A/S or anti-ship torpedoes are built into the transom, a pair being fitted high on either quarter.

AUDACE   11/1975, Dr Giorgio Ar

ARDITO   1974, Commander Aldo E. Fraccaro

AUDACE (with new MAD pod on bridge)   11/1975, Dr Giorgio Arr

Destroyers—*continued*

2 "IMPAVIDO" CLASS (DDG)

Name	No.
IMPAVIDO	D 570
INTREPIDO	D 571

Builders	Laid down	Launched	Commissioned
Cantieri del Tirreno, Riva Trigoso	10 June1957	25 May 1962	16 Nov 1963
Ansaldo, Leghorn	16 May 1959	21 Oct 1962	30 Oct 1964

Displacement, tons: 3 201 standard; 3 851 full load
Length, feet (metres): 429·5 *(131·3)*
Beam, feet (metres): 44·7 *(13·6)*
Draught, feet (metres): 14·8 *(4·5)*
Aircraft: 1 AB-204 B helicopter
Missiles: 1 Tartar launcher, aft
Guns: 2—5 in *(127 mm)* 38 cal. forward; 4—3 in *(76 mm)* 62 cal
Torpedo tubes: 2 triple for A/S torpedoes
Boilers: 4 Foster Wheeler; 711 psi *(50 kg/cm²)*; 842°F *(450°C)*
Main engines: 2 double reduction geared turbines 70 000 shp; 2 shafts
Speed, knots: 34
Range, miles: 3 300 at 20 knots; 2 900 at 25 knots
Oil fuel, tons: 650
Complement: 335 (23 officers, 312 men)

Built under the 1956-57 and 1958-59 programmes respectively. Both ships have stabilisers. In 1974-75 *Intrepido* underwent modernisation which included the improvement of the missile system and the replacement of the original gun fire-control system by Argo 10/Elsag NA 10 system. *Impavido* in hand 1975-76 for same modifications.

Engineering; On first full power trials *Impavido,* at light displacement, reached 34·5 knots (33 knots at normal load).

Radar: Search: SPS 12 and SPS 39 (3-D)
Fire control: SPG 51 for Tartar; Argo 10/Elsag NA 10 for guns.

Sonar: One SQS 23

IMPAVIDO

1974, Dr Giorgio Arra

INTREPIDO (after refit, with new radar installation)

6/1975, Dr Giorgio Arra

1 "SAN GIORGIO" CLASS (DD)

Name	No.
SAN GIORGIO (ex-*Pompeo Magno*)	D 562

Builders	Laid down	Launched	Commissioned
Cantieri N. Riuniti Ancona	23 Sep 1939	28 Aug 1941	24 June 1943

Displacement, tons: 3 950 standard; 4 350 full load
Length, feet (metres): 455·2 *(138·8)* wl; 466·5 *(142·3)* oa
Beam, feet (metres): 47·2 *(14·4)*
Draught, feet (metres): 21·0 *(4·5)*
Guns: 4—5 in *(127 mm)* 38 cal; 3—3 in *(76 mm)* 62 cal
A/S weapons: 1 three-barrelled motar; 2 triple torpedo tubes
Main engines: 2 Tosi Metrovick gas turbines; 15 000 bhp; 4 Fiat diesels; 16 600 hp; 2 shafts
Speed, knots: 20 (diesels), 28 (diesel and gas)
Range, miles: 4 800 at 20 knots
Oil fuel, tons: 500 (diesel oil)
Complement: 295 (15 officers, 280 men) plus 130 cadets

Converted into fleet destroyer in 1951 by Cantieri del Tirreno, Genova, being completed 1 July 1955. Underwent complete re-construction at the Naval Dockyard, La Spezia, in 1963-65. The modernisation included her adaptation as a Training Ship for 130 cadets of the Accademia Navale. Changes were made in the armament and new machinery was fitted, gas turbines and diesels replacing steam turbines and boilers.

Radar: Search: SPS 6.
Fire control: Four I Band sets.
Navigation: One set.

Sonar: One SQS 10.

SAN GIORGIO

1975, Dr Giorgio Arra

Destroyers—*continued*

2 "IMPETUOSO" CLASS

Name	No.
IMPETUOSO	D 558
INDOMITO	D 559

Builders	Laid down	Launched	Commissioned
Cantieri del Tirreno, Riva Trigosa	7 May 1952	16 Sep 1956	25 Jan 1958
Ansaldo, Leghorn (formerly OTO)	24 April 1952	7 Aug 1955	23 Feb 1958

Displacement, tons: 2 755 standard; 3 800 full load
Length, feet (metres): 405 *(123·4)* pp; 418·7 *(127·6)* oa
Beam, feet (metres): 43·5 *(13·3)*
Draught, feet (metres): 17·5 *(4·5)*
Guns: 4—5 in *(127 mm)* 38 cal. 16—40 mm 56 cal
A/S weapons: 1 three-barrelled mortar; 4 DCT; 1 DC rack
Tubes: 6 (2 triple) for A/S torpedoes
Main engines: 2 double reduction geared turbines; 2 shafts; 65 000 shp
Boilers: 4 Foster-Wheeler; 711 psi *(50 kg/cm²)* working pressure; 842°F *(450°C)* superheat temperature
Speed, knots: 34 (see *Engineering* notes)
Oil fuel, tons: 650
Range, miles: 3 400 at 20 knots
Complement: 315 (15 officers, 300 men)

Italy's first destroyers built since Second World War.

Engineering: On their initial sea trials these ships attained a speed of 35 knots at full load.

Radar: Search: one SGS 6B.
Fire control: one SFS 60.

Sonar: One SQS 4 or 11.

IMPETUOSO   6/1975, Dr. Giorgio Arra

INDOMITO   5/1974, Commander Aldo Fraccaroli

1 Ex-US "FLETCHER" CLASS

Name	No.
FANTE (ex-USS *Walker, DD 517)*	D 561

Builders	Laid down	Launched	Commissioned
Bath Iron Works Corp.	31 Aug 1942	31 Jan 1943	2 April 1943

Displacement, tons: 2 080 standard; 2 940 full load
Length, feet (metres): 376·5 *(114·3)* oa
Beam, feet (metres): 39·5 *(12·0)*
Draught, feet (metres): 18 *(5·5)*
Guns: 2—5 inch, 38 cal; 4—3 inch, 50 cal in twin mountings
A/S weapons: 1 DC rack, 2 side-launching torpedo racks, 2 fixed Hedgehogs
Main engines: GE geared turbines; 2 shafts; 60 000 shp
Boilers: 4 Babcock & Wilcox
Speed, knots: 35
Oil fuel, tons: 650
Range, miles: 6 000 at 15 knots
Complement: 250 (10 officers, 240 men)

Walker was transferred from the United States and commissioned as *Fante* on 2 July 1969.

Radar: Search: SPS 6 and SPS 10.
Fire control: US Mk 37 forward.

Sonar: One hull mounted set.

Torpedo tubes: The five 21-inch torpedo tubes (originally ten, in two quintuple banks) were removed.

FANTE (after removal of weapon Able)   1973, Dr. Giorgio Arra

FRIGATES

4 "LUPO" CLASS

Name	No.
LUPO	—
SAGITTARIO	—
PERSEO	—
ORSA	—

Builders	Laid down	Launched	Commission
Riva Trigoso	11 Oct 1974	June 1976	April 1977
Riva Trigoso	4 Feb 1975	April 1976	Jan 1978
Riva Trigoso	Dec 1976	Nov 1977	Aug 1978
Riva Trigoso	May 1977	April 1978	April 1979

Displacement, tons: 2 208 standard; 2 500 full load
Dimensions, feet (metres): 355·6 × 37·1 × 12·1 *(108·4 × 11·3 × 3·7)*
Aircraft: 1 helicopter
Missiles: 8 Oto-Melara surface-to-surface; Sea-Sparrow NATO PDMS
Guns: 1—5 in (127/54) Oto-Melara Compact; 4—40 mm (twin Dardo systems)
Torpedo tubes: 6—for Mk 46 A/S torpedoes (triples)
Main engines: CODOG—2 Fiat LM 2 500 gas turbines; 50 000 hp; 2 GMP 2320 ss diesels; 8 000 hp; 2 shafts
Speed, knots: 35 on turbines; 21 on diesels
Complement: 185 (15 officers, 170 ratings)

First of class named after the most famous Italian torpedo-boat of 2nd World War.

Radar: Air search: one Selenia.
Surface search: one SPQ-2F (SMA)
Gun fire control: Orion in Argo 10/Elsag NA10 system.

Sonar: One M/F hull-mounted set.

Foreign sales: Similar ships being built for Peru and Venezuela.

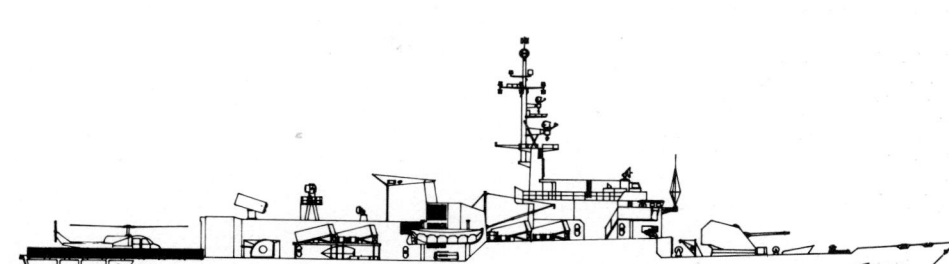

"LUPO" Class

1976, Italian Navy

2 "ALPINO" CLASS

Name	No.
ALPINO (ex-*Circe*)	F 580
CARABINIERE (ex-*Climene*)	F 581

Builders	Laid down	Launched	Commissioned
Cantieri Navali del Tirreno, Riva Trigoso	27 Feb 1963	10 June1967	14 Jan 1968
Cantieri Navali del Tirreno, Riva Trigoso	9 Jan 1965	30 Sep 1967	28 April 1968

Displacement, tons: 2 700 full load
Length, feet (metres): 349·0 *(106·4)* pp; 352·0 *(107·3)* wl; 371·7 *(113·3)* oa
Beam, feet (metres): 43·6 *(13·3)*
Draught, feet (metres): 12·7 *(3·9)*
Aircraft: 2 AB-204B helicopters
Guns: 6—3 in *(76 mm)* 62 cal (single)
A/S weapons: 1 single depth charge mortar
Tubes: 6 (2 triple) 12 in *(305 mm)* for A/S torpedoes
Main engines: 4 Tosi diesels = 16 800 hp; 2 Tosi Metrovick gas turbines = 15 000 hp; 2 shafts
Speed, knots: 22 (diesel), 29 (diesel and gas)
Oil fuel, tons: 275
Range, miles: 4 200 at 18 knots
Complement: 253 (20 officers, 233 men)

The design is an improved version of that of the "Centauro" class combined with that of the "Bergamini" class.

Electronics: MAD aerial fitted in *Alpino* 1975.

Radar: Combined search: one SPS 12.
Air/surface search/navigation: one SPQ2.
Fire control: 3 Orion radars in Elsag/Argo "O" control systems.
Radar intercept: MM/SPR A.

Sonar: One SQS 29. One SQA 10 VDS.

ALPINO (with MAD aerial)

6/1975, Dr. Giorgio Arra

4 "BERGAMINI" CLASS

Name	No.
CARLO BERGAMINI	F 593
CARLO MARGOTTINI	F 595
LUIGI RIZZO	F 596
VIRGINIO FASAN	F 594

Builders	Laid down	Launched	Commissioned
San Marco, CRDA Trieste	19 May 1959	16 June1960	23 June 1962
Navalmeccanica, Castellammare	26 May 1957	12 June1960	5 May 1962
Navalmeccanica, Castellammare	26 May 1957	6 Mar 1960	15 Dec 1961
Navalmeccanica, Castellammare	6 Mar 1960	9 Oct 1960	10 Oct 1962

Displacement, tons: 1 650 full load
Length, feet (metres): 311·7 *(95·0)* oa
Beam, feet (metres): 37·4 *(11·4)*
Draught, feet (metres): 10·5 *(3·2)*
Aircraft: 1 AB-204B helicopter
Guns: 2—3 in *(76 mm)* 62 cal single
A/S weapons: 1 single depth charge mortar
Tubes: 6 (2 triple) 12 in *(305 mm)* for A/S torpedoes
Main engines: 4 diesels (Fiat in *Fasan* and *Margottini*, Tosi in others); 2 shafts; 15 000 bhp
Speed, knots: 24·5
Range, miles: 4 000 at 18 knots
Complement: 158 (19 officers, 139 men)

Modernisation: A slightly enlarged helicopter platform was fitted and a telescopic hangar shipped to allow for embarkation of one AB-204B helicopter. The after 3-inch gun was removed. *Carlo Margottini*, 1968; *Virginio Fasan*, 1969; *Carlo Bergamini*, 1970; *Luigi Rizzo*, 1971.

Radar: Combined search: one SPS 12.
Air/surface search/navigation: one SPQ2.
Fire control: two Orion radars in Elsag/Argo control systems.
Radar intercept: MM/SPR A.

Roll damping: Two Denny-Brown stabilisers reduce inclination in heavy seas from 20 to 5 degrees.

Sonar: One SQS 11.

CARLO BERGAMINI

5/1974, Commander Aldo Fraccaroli

Frigates—continued

4 "CENTAURO" CLASS

Name	No.	Builders	Laid down	Launched	Commissioned
CANOPO	F 551 (ex-D 570)	Cantieri Navali di Taranto	15 May 1952	20 Feb 1955	1 April 1958
CASTORE	F 553 (ex-D 573)	Cantieri Navali di Taranto	14 Mar 1955	8 July 1956	14 July 1957
CENTAURO	F 554 (ex-D 571)	Ansaldo, Leghorn	31 May 1952	4 April 1954	5 May 1957
CIGNO	F 555 (ex-D 572)	Cantieri Navali di Taranto	10 Feb 1954	20 Mar 1955	7 Mar 1957

Displacement, tons: 1 807 standard; 2 250 full load
Length, feet (metres): 308·4 (94) pp; 338·4 (103·1) oa
Beam, feet (metres): 39·5 (12)
Draught, feet (metres): 12·6 (3·8)
Guns: 3—3 in (76 mm) 62 cal (single)
A/S weapons: 1 three-barrelled depth charge mortar
Tubes: 6 (2 triple) 12 in (305 mm) for A/S torpedoes
Main engines: 2 double reduction geared turbines 2 shafts; 22 000 shp
Boilers: 2 Foster Wheeler; 626 psi (44 kg/cm²) working pressure; 842°F (450°C) superheat temperature
Speed, knots: 25
Oil fuel, tons: 400
Range, miles: 3 660 at 20 knots
Complement: 225 (16 officers, 209 men)

Built to Italian plans and specifications under the US off-shore programme.

Conversion: Carried out as follows: *Castore*—1966-67, *Canopo*—1968-69, *Centauro*—1970-71, *Cigno*—1972-73. This provided the new 3 in (76 mm) armament.

Radar: Search: one SPS 6.
Combined search and navigation: one SMA/SPQ 2.
Fire control: I band.
Radar Intercept: MM/SPR A.

Sonar: SQS-11.

CENTAURO

6/1975, Dr. Giorgio Arra

1 Ex-US "CANNON" CLASS

Name	No.	Builders	Laid down	Launched	Commissioned
ALDEBARAN (ex-USS *Thornhill, DE 195*)	F 590	Federal SB & DD Co, Newark	7 Oct 1943	30 Dec 1943	1 Feb 1944

Displacement, tons: 1 900 full load
Length, feet (metres): 306 (93·3) oa
Beam, feet (metres): 36·7 (11·2)
Draught, feet (metres): 14 (4·3)
Guns: 3—3 in (76 mm) 50 cal; 6—40 mm; 18—20 mm
A/S weapons: 1 Hedgehog; 8 DCT; 2 DC racks
Main engines: GM diesel-electric; 2 shafts; 6 000 hp
Speed, knots: 21
Oil fuel, tons: 300
Range, miles: 11 500 at 11 knots
Complement: 113 (10 officers, 103 men)

Transferred on 10 Jan 1951. In 1956 a tripod foremast was stepped in place of the former polemast.

Class: Sister ship *Aviere* now used as target for underwater demolition training in place of other sister ship *Altair* which was used from 1971-75.

Radar: Search: SPS 6.
Fire control: I band.

ALDEBARAN

1973, Italian Navy

CORVETTES

4 "DE CRISTOFARO" CLASS

Name	No.	Builders	Laid down	Launched	Commissioned
LICIO VISINTINI	F 546	CRDA Monfalcone	30 Sep 1963	30 May 1965	25 Aug 1966
PIETRO DE CRISTOFARO	F 540	Cantiere Navali de Tirreno, Riva Trigoso	30 Apr 1963	29 May 1965	19 Dec 1965
SALVATORE TODARO	F 550	Cantiere Ansaldo, Leghorn	21 Oct 1962	24 Oct 1964	25 Apr 1966
UMBERTO GROSSO	F 541	Cantiere Ansaldo, Leghorn	21 Oct 1962	12 Dec 1964	25 Apr 1966

Displacement, tons: 850 standard; 1 020 full load
Length, feet (metres): 246 (75·0) pp; 263·2 (80·2) oa
Beam, feet (metres): 33·7 (10·3)
Draught, feet (metres): 9 (2·7)
Guns: 2—3 in (76 mm) 62 cal, (single)
A/S weapons: 1 single-barrelled DC mortar
Tubes: 2 triple for A/S torpedoes
Main engines: 2 diesels = 8 400 bhp; 2 shafts
Speed, knots: 23·5
Oil fuel, tons: 100
Range, miles: 4 000 at 18 knots
Complement: 131 (8 officers, 123 men)

The design is an improved version of the "Albatros" class.

Radar: Air and surface surveillance radar with antenna mounted at top of foremast. Gunfire control system has director mounted aft, above compass platform, with I band tracker radar.

Sonar: SQS/36. ELSAG DLB-1 fire control system.

LICIO VISINTINI

6/1975, Dr Giorgio Arr

Corvettes—*continued*

4 "ALBATROS" CLASS

Name	No.	Builders	Laid down	Launched	Commissioned
AIRONE	F 545	Navalmeccanica, Castellammare di Stabia	1953	21 Nov 1954	29 Dec 1955
ALBATROS	F 543	Navalmeccanica, Castellammare di Stabia	1953	18 July 1954	1 June 1955
ALCIONE	F 544	Navalmeccanica, Castellammare di Stabia	1953	19 Sep 1954	23 Oct 1955
AQUILA	F 542	Breda Marghera, mestre, Venezia	25 July 1953	31 July 1954	2 Oct 1956

Displacement, tons: 800 standard; 950 full load
Length, feet (metres): 250·3 *(76·3)* oa
Beam, feet (metres): 31·5 *(9·6)*
Draught, feet (metres): 9·2 *(2·8)*
Guns: 4—40 mm 70 cal Bofors (see *Gunnery*)
A/S weapons: 2 Hedgehogs Mk II; 2 DCT; 1 DC rack
Tubes: 2 triple A/S
Main engines: 2 Fiat diesels; 2 shafts; 5 200 bhp
Speed, knots: 19
Oil fuel, tons: 100
Range, miles: 3 000 at 18 knots
Complement: 109

Eight ships of this class were built in Italy under US offshore MDAP orders. 3 for Italy, 4 for Denmark and 1 for the Netherlands. *Aquila*, laid down on 25 July 1953, was transferred to the Italian Navy on 18 Oct 1961 at Den Helder.

Gunnery: The two 3-inch guns originally mounted, one forward and one aft, were temporarily replaced by two 40 mm guns in 1963. The ultimate armament will include two 3-inch Oto Melara guns.

Radar: Combined search and navigation: one SMA/SPQ-2. Fire control: radar control for Elsag NA-2 system.

ALBATROS

1974, Dr. Giorgio Arra

4 "APE" CLASS

Name	No.	Builders	Laid down	Launched	Commissioned
APE	F 567	Navalmeccanica, Castellamare	1942	1942	1943
BOMBARDA	F 549	Breda, Venezia	1942	1944	1951
CHIMERA	F 569		—	—	1942
SFINGE	F 579	CRDA, Trieste	1942	1942	1943

Displacement, tons: 670 standard; 771 full load
Length, feet (metres): 192·8 *(58·8)* wl; 212·6 *(64·8)* oa
Beam, feet (metres): 28·5 *(8·7)*
Draught, feet (metres): 8·9 *(2·7)*
Guns: 4—40 mm 56 cal in *Chimera* and *Sfinge*; 2—40 mm 56 cal and 2—20 mm 70 cal in *Bombarda*
A/S weapons: 1 Hedgehog Mk 10
Main engines: 2 Fiat diesels; 2 shafts; 3 500 bhp
Speed, knots: 15
Oil fuel, tons: 64
Range, miles: 2 450 at 15 knots
Complement: 56 (6 officers, 50 men)

Originally fitted for minesweeping. Modified with navigating bridge. *Ape* is now support ship for frogmen and commandos. Remainder fitted for target work.

Radar: Search: SPS 6 in *Sfinge*.

CHIMERA

1973, Dr Giorgio Arra

1 US PC TYPE

Name	No.	Builders	Laid down	Launched	Commissioned
VEDETTA (ex-*Belay Deress*, ex-US PC 1616)	F 597	Arsenal Naval, Brest	1953	1954	1955

Displacement, tons: 325 standard; 450 full load
Dimensions, feet (metres): 170 pp; 174 oa × 23 × 10 *(51·9; 53·1 × 7 × 3·1)*
Guns: 2—40 mm 56 cal Bofors; 2—20 mm
A/S weapons: 1 Hedgehog; 4 DCT; 2 DC racks
Main engines: 4 diesels; 2 shafts; 3 500 bhp = 19 knots
Range, miles: 6 350 at 12 knots
Complement: 60 (6 officers, 54 men)

Originally allocated to Germany and then to Ethiopia (1957-59). She was sold to Italy, being transferred on 3 Feb 1959. Air-conditioning equipment is installed. Refitted in La Spezia Navy Yard in 1959. Employed as a Fishery Protection Vessel.

VEDETTA

1974, Dr Giorgio Arra

SUBMARINES

2 "SAURO" CLASS

Name	No.	Builders	Laid down	Launch	Commission
NAZARIO SAURO	—	CRDA Monfalcone	15 July 1974	Mar 1977	Dec 1977
DI COSSATO	—	CRDA Monfalcone	15 Nov 1975	Nov 1977	Oct 1978

Displacement, tons: 1 456 surfaced; 1 631 dived
Length, feet (metres): 210 *(64)*
Beam, feet (metres): 22·5 *(6·8)*
Draught, feet (metres): 18·9 *(5·7)*
Torpedo tubes: 6—21 in (bow) (6 reloads)
Main machinery: 3 diesel generators; 1 electric motor; 1 shaft
Speed, knots: 11 surfaced; 20 dived
Range, miles: 7 000 miles surfaced; 12 500 snorting at 4 knots; 250 miles dived at 4 knots; 20 miles dived at 20 knots
Endurance: 45 days
Complement: 45

Two of this class were originally ordered in 1967 but were cancelled in the following year. Reinstated in the building programme in 1972. To be fitted with Selenia passive and active sonars, search/navigation radar. ECM, Velox and IFF.

4 "TOTI" CLASS

Name	No.	Builders	Laid down	Launched	Commissioned
ATTILIO BAGNOLINI	S 505	CRDA Monfalcone	15 April 1965	26 Aug 1967	16 June 1968
ENRICO DANDOLO	S 513	CRDA Monfalcone	10 Mar 1967	16 Dec 1967	25 Sep 1968
LAZZARO MOCENIGO	S 514	CRDA Monfalcone	12 June 1967	20 April 1968	11 Jan 1969
ENRICO TOTI	S 506	CRDA Monfalcone	15 April 1965	12 Mar 1967	22 Jan 1968

Displacement, tons: 460 standard; 524 surfaced; 582 dived
Length, feet (metres): 151·5 *(46·2)*
Beam, feet (metres): 15·4 *(4·7)*
Draught, feet (metres): 13·1 *(4·0)*
Torpedo tubes: 4—21 in
Main machinery: 2 Fiat MB 820 N/I diesels, 1 electric motor, Diesel-electric drive; 2 200 hp; 1 shaft
Speed, knots: 14 surfaced; 15 dived
Range, miles: 3 000 at 5 knots (surfaced)
Complement: 26 (4 officers, 22 men)

Italy's first indigenously-built submarines since the Second World War. The design was recast several times.

Electronics: WT, HF, UHF and VLF equipment. Computer based fire control.

Radar: Search/nav set. IFF, ECM.

Sonar: Passive set in stem. Active set in bow dome. Passive range finding. Ray path analyzer.

ENRICO DANDOLO   *6/1975, Dr. Giorgio Arra*

2 Ex-US "TANG" CLASS

Name	No.	Builders	Laid down	Launched	Commissioned
ROMEO ROMEI (ex-USS *Harder, SS 568*)	516	General Dynamics (Electric Boat Div)	30 June 1950	14 June 1951	31 Mar 1952
LIVIO PIOMARTA (ex-USS *Trigger, SS 564*)	515	General Dynamics (Electric Boat Div)	24 Feb 1949	3 Dec 1951	19 Aug 1952

Displacement, tons: 2 100 surfaced; 2 700 dived
Length, feet (metres): 287 *(87·4)*
Beam, feet (metres): 27·3 *(8·3)*
Draught, feet (metres): 19 *(6·2)*
Torpedo tubes: 8—21 in; 6 bow, 2 stern
Main machinery: 3 Diesels 4 500 shp; 2 electric motors 5 600 hp
Speed, knots: 20 surfaced; 18 dived
Complement: 83 (8 officers, 75 men)

Transferred as follows: *Romeo Romei* 20 Feb 1974, *Livio Piomarta* 10 July 1973. Subsequently refitted at Philadelphia Navy Yard.

ROMEO ROMEI   *11/1975, Dr. Giorgio Arra*

2 Ex-US "GUPPY III" CLASS

Name	No.	Builders	Laid down	Launched	Commissioned
PRIMO LONGOBARDO (ex-USS *Volador, SS 490*)	S 501	Boston Navy Yard	8 Feb 1944	15 Dec 1944	4 April 1949
GIANFRANCO GAZZANA PRIAROGGIA (ex-USS *Pickerel, SS 524*)	S 502	Portsmouth Navy Yard	15 June 1945	17 Jan 1946	10 Jan 1948

Displacement, tons: 1 975 standard; 2 450 dived
Length, feet (metres): 326·5 *(99·4)* oa
Beam, feet (metres): 27 *(8·2)*
Draught, feet (metres): 17 *(5·2)*
Torpedo tubes: 10—21 in; 6 bow, 4 stern
Main machinery: 4 diesels; 6 400 bhp; 2 electric motors; 5 400 shp; 2 shafts
Speed, knots: 20 surfaced; 15 dived
Oil fuel, tons: 300
Range, miles: 12 000 at 10 knots (surfaced)
Complement: 85 (10 officers, 75 men)

Both transferred 18 Aug 1972.

GIANFRANCO GAZZANA PRIAROGGIA   *1973, Dr. Giorgio Arra*

1 Ex-US "BALAO" CLASS

Name	No.	Builders	Laid down	Launched	Commissioned
ALFREDO CAPPELLINI (ex-USS *Capitaine, SS 336*)	S 507	General Dynamics (Electric Boat Div)	1944	1 Oct 1944	26 Jan 1945

Displacement, tons: 1 600 standard; 1 855 surfaced; 2 455 dived
Length, feet (metres): 311·5 *(95·0)*
Beam, feet (metres): 27 *(8·2)*
Draught, feet (metres): 17 *(5·2)*
Torpedo tubes: 10—21 in *(533 mm)* 6 bow and 4 stern
Main machinery: 4 GM 16/278 diesels; 6 000 hp; 4 electric motors; 2 750 hp
Speed, knots: 18 surfaced; 10 dived
Oil fuel, tons: 300
Range, miles: 14 000 at 10 knots (surfaced)
Complement: 75 (7 officers, 68 men)

Transferred 5 Mar 1966.

ALFREDO CAPPELLINI   1974, Dr. Giorgio Arra

LIGHT FORCES

1 + (6) "SPARVIERO" CLASS (HYDROFOIL—MISSILE)

Name	No.	Builders	Commissioned
SPARVIERO	P 420	Alinavi, La Spezia	15 July 1974

Displacement, tons: 62·5
Dimensions, feet (metres): 80·7 × 39·7 × 14·4 *(24·6 × 12·1 × 4·4)* (length and beam foils extended, draught hullborne)
Missile launchers: 2 fixed for Otomat ship-to-ship missiles
Gun: 1 Oto Melara 76 mm automatic anti-aircraft
Main engines: Rolls Royce "Proteus" gas turbine driving waterjet pump; 4 500 bhp; diesel and retractable propeller unit for hullborne propulsion
Range, miles: 400 at 45 knots; 1 200 at 8 knots
Speed, knots: 50 max, 42 cruising (sea state 4)
Complement: 10 (2 officers, 8 men)

Completed for trials 9 May 1973. Missiles made by Oto Melara/Matra. Fitted with Elsag NA-10 Mod 1 fire control system with Orion RTN-10X radar. Delivered to the Navy as class prototype on 15 July 1974. Six more hydrofoils planned.

SPARVIERO   1974, Italian Navy

2 "FRECCIA" CLASS (FAST ATTACK CRAFT—CONVERTIBLE)

Name	No.	Builders	Commissioned
FRECCIA (ex-*MC 590*)	P 493	Cantiere del Tirreno, Riva Trigoso	6 July 1965
SAETTA (ex-*MC 591*)	P 494	CRDA, Monfalcone	1966

Displacement, tons: 188 standard; 205 full load
Dimensions, feet (metres): 150 × 23·8 × 5·5 *(45·8 × 7·3 × 1·7)*
Guns: *As Gunboat:* 3—40 mm, 70 cal or 2—40 mm, 70 cal. *As Fast Minelayer:* 1—40 mm with 8 mines. *As Torpedo Boat:* 1—40 mm, 70 cal
Tubes: *As Torpedo Boat:* 2—21 in
Main engines: 2 diesels; 7 600 bhp; 1 Bristol Siddeley Proteus gas turbine, 4 250 shp; Total hp 11 850 = 40 knots
Complement: 37 (4 officers, 33 men)

Freccia was laid down on 30 Apr 1963 and launched on 9 Jan 1965. *Saetta* was laid down on 11 June 1963, launched on 11 Apr 1965. Can be converted in 24 hours to gunboat, torpedo boat, fast minelayer, or missile boat. Fitted with E band navigation and tactical radar. The gunfire control system has a director with I band tracker radar. *Saetta* has been armed with Sea Killer Mk 1 system with 5 round trainable launcher, Contraves fire control, including target-tracking radar, with TV camera mounted on top.

SAETTA experimentally armed with 5 Sea Killer I missiles   1970, Italian Navy

FRECCIA   1974, Italian Navy

Light Forces—*continued*

2 "LAMPO" CLASS (FAST ATTACK CRAFT—CONVERTIBLE)

Name	No.	Builders	Commissioned
LAMPO (ex-*MC 491*)	P 491	Arsenale MM, Taranto	July 1963
BALENO (ex-*MC 492*)	P 492	Arsenale MM, Taranto	16 July 1965

Displacement, tons: 170 standard; 196 full load
Dimensions, feet (metres): 131·5 × 21 × 5 *(40·1 × 6·4 × 1·5)*
Guns: *As Gunboat:* 3—40 mm, 70 cal or 2—40 mm, 70 cal; *As Torpedo Boat:* 1—40 mm, 70 cal
Tubes: *As Torpedo Boat:* 2—21 in
Main engines: 2 Fiat diesels; 1 Metrovick gas turbine; 3 shafts; total 11 700 hp = 39 knots
Complement: 33 (5 officers, 28 men)

Convertible gunboats, improved versions of the *Folgore* prototype. *Lampo* was laid down on 4 Jan 1958 and launched on 22 Nov 1960. *Baleno* was laid-down on the same slip on 22 Nov 1960, launched on 10 May 1964. She has been converted to an improved design.

LAMPO   6/1975, Dr Giorgio Arra

1 FAST ATTACK CRAFT —TORPEDO

Name	No.	Builders	Commissioned
FOLGORE (ex-*MC 490*)	P 490	CRDA Monfalcone	21 July 1955

Displacement, tons: 160 standard; 190 full load
Dimensions, feet (metres): 129·5 × 19·7 × 5 *(39·5 × 6 × 1·5)*
Guns: 2—40 mm
Tubes: 2—21 in
Main engines: 4 MTU diesels; 4 shafts; 10 000 bhp = 38 knots (accelerating from 20 knots to full speed very rapidly)
Complement: 39 (9 officers, 30 men)

Authorised in Nov 1950, launched on 21 Jan 1954. Two rudders.

FOLGORE   1972, Dr Giorgio Arra

3 Ex-US "HIGGINS" CLASS (FAST ATTACK CRAFT—TORPEDO)

MS 441 (ex-841)   **MS 443** (ex-843)   **MS 453** (ex-853)

Displacement, tons: 64 full load
Dimensions, feet (metres): 78 × 20 × 6 *(23·8 × 6·1 × 1·8)*
Guns: 1—40 mm, 56 cal; 2 or 3—20 mm, 70 cal
Torpedoes: 2—17·7 in (no tubes)
Main engines: 3 petrol motors; 3 shafts; 4 500 bhp = 34 knots
Range, miles: 1 000 at 20 knots
Complement: 24 (3 officers, 21 men)

MS 441 and 453 converted for frogmen support with after weapons removed. Refitted in Italy in 1949-53. New radar installed.

M 453 (modified for frogmen support)   6/1975, Dr Giorgio Arra

2 FAST ATTACK CRAFT—TORPEDO

Name	No.	Builders	Commissioned
—	MS 474 (ex-*614*)	CRDA, Monfalcone	1942
—	MS 481 (ex-*615*)	CRDA, Monfalcone	1942

Displacement, tons: 72 full load
Dimensions, feet (metres): 92 × 15 × 5 *(28·1 × 4·6 × 1·5)*
Guns: 1 or 2—40 mm, 56 cal
Torpedoes: 2—17·7 in
Main engines: Petrol motors; 3 shafts; 3 450 bhp = 27 knots
Range, miles: 600 at 16 knots
Complement: 24 (3 officers, 21 men)

Converted as MV (motovedette) with no tubes under the Peace Treaty. Reconverted in 1951-53. MS 473 and MS 481 were refitted as convertible boats in 1960 and MS 474 in 1961. Originally class of four. Further refits 1965-69.

MS 481   1974, Italian Navy

AMPHIBIOUS FORCES

2 Ex-US "DE SOTO COUNTY" CLASS (LSTs)

Name	No.	Builders	Commissioned
GRADO (ex-USS De Soto County, LST 1171)	L 9890	Avondale, New Orleans	1957
CAORLE (ex-USS York County, LST 1175)	L 9891	Newport News SB & DD Co.	1957

Displacement, tons: 4 164 light; 8 000 full load
Dimensions, feet (metres): 444 × 62 × 16·5 (133·4 × 18·9 × 5)
Guns: 6—3 inch (76 mm)
Main engines: Diesels; 1 440 shp; 2 shafts; (CP propellers) = 17·5 knots
Complement: 165 (10 officers, 155 men)
Troops: Approx 575

Both completed 1957 and transferred 17 July 1972.

GRADO　　　　　　　　　　　　　　　　1974, Dr. Giorgio Arra

1 Ex-US "KENNETH WHITING" CLASS (TRANSPORT)

Name	No.	Builders	Commissioned
ANDREA BAFILE (ex-USS St. George, AV 16, ex-A 5314)	L 9871	—	1944

Displacement, tons: 8 510 standard; 14 000 full load
Dimensions, feet (metres): 492 oa × 69·5 × 26 (163 × 23 × 8·5)
Aircraft: 1 or 2 helicopters
Guns: 2—5 in 38 cal
Main engines: Allis-Chalmers geared turbines; 1 shaft; 8 500 shp = 17 knots
Boilers: 2 Foster-Wheeler
Range, miles: 13 400 at 13 knots
Complement: 58 (10 officers, 48 men)

Former USN seaplane carrier, launched on 14 Feb 1944. Purchased and commissioned in the Italian Navy on 11 Dec 1968 and modified. Depot ship for "Special Forces". In reserve at Taranto.

ANDREA BAFILE　　　　　　　　　　　　1974, Italian Navy

MINE WARFARE FORCES

4 "SALMONE" CLASS (Ex-US MSO TYPE)
(MINESWEEPERS—OCEAN)

Name	No.	Builders	Commissioned
SALMONE (ex-MSO 507)	M 5430	Martinolich SB Co	17 June 1956
SGOMBRO (ex-MSO 517)	M 5432	—	June 1957
SQUALO (ex-MSO 518)	M 5433	—	June 1957
STORIONE (ex-MSO 506)	M 5431	Martinolich SB Co	23 Feb 1956

Displacement, tons: 665 standard; 750 full load
Dimensions, feet (metres): 173 oa × 35 × 13·6 (52·7 × 10·7 × 4)
Gun: 1—40 mm, 56 cal
Main engines: 2 diesels; 2 shafts; 1 600 bhp = 14 knots
Oil fuel, tons: 46
Range, miles: 3 000 at 10 knots
Complement: 51 (7 officers, 44 men)

Former US "Agile" class. Wooden hulls and non-magnetic diesels of stainless steel alloy. Controllable pitch propellers. Storione, launched on 13 Nov 1954, Salmone, launched on 19 Feb 1955 transferred at San Diego, on 17 June 1956.

STORIONE　　　　　　　　　　　　　　6/1975, Dr Giorgio Arra

14 "ABETE" CLASS (MINESWEEPERS—COASTAL)

ABETE M 5501	GELSO M 5509	ONTANO M 5513
CASTAGNO M 5504	LARICE M 5510	PINO M 5514
CEDRO M 5505	MANDORLO M 5519	PLATANO M 5516
FAGGIO M 5507	NOCE M 5511	QUERCIA M 5517
FRASSINO M 5508	OLMO M 5512	

Displacement, tons: 378 standard; 405 full load (Mandorlo 360)
Dimensions, feet (metres): 138 pp; 144 oa × 26·5 × 8·5 (42·1; 43·9 × 8·1 × 2·6)
Guns: 2—40 mm, 70 cal
Main engines: 2 diesels; 2 shafts; 1 200 bhp = 13·5 knots
Oil fuel, tons: 25
Range, miles: 2 500 at 10 knots
Complement: 38 (5 officers, 33 men)

Wooden hulled and constructed throughout of anti-magnetic materials. All transferred by the US in 1953-54. Originally class of 18. Pioppo used for surveying.

CASTAGNO　　　　　　　　　　　　　6/1975, Dr Giorgio Arra

17 "AGAVE" CLASS (MINESWEEPERS—COASTAL)

BAMBU M 5521	AGAVE M 5531	GLICINE M 5537
EBANO M 5522	ALLORO M 5532	LOTO M 5538
MANGO M 5523	EDERA M 5533	TIMO M 5540
MOGANO M 5524	GAGGIA M 5534	TRIFOGLIO M 5541
PALMA M 5525	GELSOMINO M 5535	VISCHIO M 5542
SANDALO M 5527	GIAGGIOLO M 5536	

Displacement, tons: 375 standard; 405 full load
Dimensions, feet (metres): 144 oa × 25·6 × 8·5 *(43 × 8 × 2·6)*
Guns: 2—20 mm 70 cal
Main engines: 2 diesels; 2 shafts; 1 200 bhp = 13·5 knots
Oil fuel, tons: 25
Range, miles: 2 500 at 10 knots
Complement: 38 (5 officers, 33 men)

Non-magnetic minesweepers of composite wooden and alloy construction similar to those transferred from the US but built in Italian yards. First six were built by CRDA, Monfalcone, and launched in 1956. Originally class of nineteen. *Mirto* now used for surveying.

AGAVE   6/1975, Dr Giorgio Arra

10 "ARAGOSTA" CLASS (MINESWEEPERS—INSHORE)

ARAGOSTA M 5450	GRANCHIO M 5458	POLIPO M 5463
ASTICE M 5452	MITILO M 5459	PORPORA M 5464
GAMBERO M 5457	PINNA M 5462	RICCIO M 5465
		SCAMPO M 5466

Displacement, tons: 188 full load
Dimensions, feet (metres): 106 × 21 × 6 *(32·5 × 6·4 × 1·8)*
Main engines: 2 diesels; 1 000 bhp = 14 knots
Oil fuel, tons: 15
Range, miles: 2 000 at 9 knots
Complement: 16 (4 officers, 12 men)

Similar to the British "Ham" class. All constructed in Italian yards to the order of NATO in 1955-57. All names of small sea creatures. Designed armament of one 20 mm gun mounted. Originally class of twenty.

SCAMPO   6/1975, Dr Giorgio Arra

SURVEY VESSELS

Name	No.	Builders	Commissioned
AMMIRAGLIO MAGNAGHI	A 5303	Cantieri Navali di Tirreno é Riuniti	1975

Displacement, tons: 1 700
Dimensions, feet (metres): 271·3 × 44·9 × 11·5 *(82·7 × 13·7 × 3·5)*
Aircraft: 1—AB 204 helicopter
Gun: 1—40 mm
Main engines: 2 Fiat diesels = 3 000 hp; 1 shaft; Auxiliary electric motor—240 hp = 4 knots
Speed, knots: 16
Range, miles: 6 000 at 12 knots (1 diesel); 4 200 at 16 knots (2 diesels)
Complement: 140 (15 officers, 15 scientists, 110 men)

Ordered under 1972 programme. Laid down 13 June 1973. Launched 8 Oct 1974. Fitted with flight-deck and hangar, bow thruster, full air-conditioning, bridge engine controls, flume-type stabilisers and fully equipped for oceanographical studies.

AMMIRAGLIO MAGNAGHI   6/1975, Dr. Giorgio Arra

MIRTO A 5306   **PIOPPO** A 5307

Mirto of the "Agave" class and *Pioppo* of the "Abete" class (see Minewarfare section for details) have been converted for surveying duties.

MIRTO   1973, Dr. Giorgio Arra

SERVICE FORCES

1 REPLENISHMENT TANKER

Name	No.	Builders	Commissioned
STROMBOLI	A 5327	Cantiere del Tirreno, Riva Trigoso	1975

Displacement, tons: 3 556 light; 8 706 full load
Dimensions, feet (metres): 423·1 oa × 59 × 21·3 (120 oa × 18 × 6·5)
Guns: 1—76 mm/62 cal Oto Melara; 2—40 mm
Main engines: 2 Fiat diesels C 428 SS; 4 800 hp; 1 shaft; 4-bladed LIPS propeller
Complement: 115 (9 officers, 106 men)

Laid down on 1 Oct 1973. Launched early 1975.

STROMBOLI _1975, Italian Navy_

1 EXPERIMENTAL SHIP

Name	No.	Builders	Commissioned
QUARTO	L 9881	Taranto Naval Shipyard	1967

Displacement, tons: 764 standard; 980 full load
Dimensions, feet (metres): 226·4 × 31·3 × 6 (69·1 × 9·5 × 1·8)
Guns: 4—40 mm (2 twin)
Main engines: 3 diesels; 2 300 bhp = 13 knots
Range, miles: 1 300 at 13 knots

Laid down on 19 Mar 1966 and launched on 18 Mar 1967. The design is intermediate between that of LSM and LCT. She is now being used as experimental ship for new weapon-systems trials and evaluation.

QUARTO (old pennant number) _1971, Commander Aldo Fraccaroli_

1 Ex-US "BARNEGAT" CLASS (SUPPORT SHIP)

Name	No.	Builders	Commissioned
PIETRO CAVEZZALE (ex-USS Oyster Bay, AVP 28, ex-AGP 6)	A 5301	Lake Washington Shipyard	1943

Displacement, tons: 1 766 standard; 2 800 full load
Dimensions, feet (metres): 311·8 oa × 41 × 13·5 (95 × 12·5 × 3·7)
Guns: 1—76 mm; 2—40 mm, 56 cal
Main engines: 2 sets diesels; 2 shafts; 6 080 bhp = 16 knots
Oil fuel, tons: 400
Range, miles: 10 000 at 11 knots
Complement: 143 (12 officers, 131 men)

Former United States seaplane tender (previously motor torpedo boat tender). Launched on 7 Sep 1942. Transferred to the Italian Navy on 23 Oct 1957 and renamed.

PIETRO CAVEZZALE _1975, Dr. Giorgio Arra_

10 Ex-GERMAN MFP TYPE (COASTAL TRANSPORTS)

MTC 1001	MTC 1004	MTC 1006	MTC 1008	MTC 1010
MTC 1003	MTC 1005	MTC 1007	MTC 1009	MTC 1102

Displacement, tons: 240 standard
Dimensions, feet (metres): 164 × 21·3 × 5·7 (50 × 6·5 × 1·7)
Guns: 2 or 3—20 or 37 mm
Main engines: 2 or 3 diesels; 500 bhp = 10 knots
Complement: 19 (1 officer, 18 men)

Moti-Trasporti Costieri, MTC 1001 to 1010 are Italian MZ _(Motozattere)._ MTC 1102 and 1103 are ex-German built in Italy. MTC 1002 was removed from the effective list in 1964, MTC 1101 and MTC 1104 in 1970, and MTC 1103 in 1971.

MTC 1006 _1974, Italian Navy_

20 Ex-US LCM TYPE

MTM 9901	MTM 9909	MTM 9914	MTM 9920	MTM 9925
MTM 9902	MTM 9911	MTM 9915	MTM 9922	MTM 9926
MTM 9905	MTM 9912	MTM 9918	MTM 9923	MTM 9927
MTM 9908	MTM 9913	MTM 9919	MTM 9924	MTM 9928

Displacement, tons: 20 standard
Dimensions, feet (metres): 49·5 × 14·8 × 4·2 (15·1 × 4·5 × 1·3)
Guns: 2—20 mm
Main engines: Diesels; speed 10 knots

39 US LCVP TYPE

MTP 9703	MTP 9715	MTP 9730	MTP 9739	MTP 9747
MTP 9707	MTP 9719	MTP 9732	MTP 9740	MTP 9748
MYP 9708	MTP 9720	MTP 9733	MTP 9741	MTP 9749
MTP 9710	MTP 9723	MTP 9734	MTP 9742	MTP 9750
MTP 9711	MTP 9726	MTP 9735	MTP 9743	MTP 9751
MTP 9713	MTP 9727	MTP 9736	MTP 9744	MTP 9752
MTP 9714	MTP 9728	MTP 9737	MTP 9745	MTP 9753
	MTP 9729	MTP 9738	MTP 9746	MTP 9754

Displacement, tons: 10 standard
Dimensions, feet (metres): 36·5 × 10·8 × 3 (11·1 × 3·3 × 0·9)
Guns: 2 MG
Main engines: Diesels; Speed 12 knots

MTP 9703 to 9723 are former US landing craft of the LCVP type. MTP 9726 and following craft of similar characteristics are of Italian construction.

TRAINING SHIPS

Name	No.	Builders	Commissioned
AMERIGO VESPUCCI	A 5312	Castellammare	1931

Displacement, tons: 3 543 standard; 4 146 full load
Dimensions, feet (metres): 229·5 pp; 270 oa hull; 330 oa bowsprit × 51 × 22 *(70; 82·4; 100 × 15·5 × 7)*
Guns: 4—3 in, 50 cal; 1—20 mm
Main engines: Two Fiat diesels with electric drive to 2 Marelli motors, 1 shaft; 2 000 hp = 10 knots
Sail area: 22 604 square feet
Endurance: 5 450 miles at 6·5 knots
Complement: 67 (7 officers, 60 men)

Launched on 22 March 1930. Hull, masts and yards are of steel. Extensively refitted at La Spezia Naval Dockyard in 1964.

AMERIGO VESPUCCI   *1974, Wright and Logan*

Name	No.	Builders	Commissioned
PALINURO (ex-*Commandant Louis Richard*)	A 5311	France	1921

Displacement, tons: 1 042 standard; 1 450 full load
Measurement, tons: 858 gross
Dimensions, feet (metres): 204 pp; 226·3 oa × 32 × 18·7 *(59 × 10 × 4·8)*
Main engines: 1 diesel; 1 shaft; 450 bhp = 7·5 knots
Endurance, miles: 5 390 at 7·5 knots
Sail area, square feet: 1 152

Barquentine launched in 1920. Purchased in 1950. Rebuilt and commissioned in Italian Navy on 16 July 1955.

PALINURO   *1968, Italian Navy*

Name	No.	Builders	Commissioned
CORSARO II	A 5316	Costaguta Yard, Voltri	1960

Measurement, tons: 47
Dimensions, feet (metres): 69 × 15·4 × 9·8 *(21 × 4·7 × 3)*
Sail area, square feet: 2 200
Complement: 13 (7 officers, 6 men)

Special yacht for sail training and oceanic navigation. RORC class.

Name	No.	Builders	Commissioned
STELLA POLARE	A 5313	Sangermani, Chiavari	1965

Measurement, tons: 41
Dimensions, feet (metres): 68·6 × 15·4 × 9·5 *(20·9 × 4·7 × 2·9)*
Auxiliary engines: 1 Mercedes-Benz diesel, 96 bhp
Sail area: 2 117 square feet
Complement: 14 (8 officers, 6 men)

Yawl rigged built as a sail training vessel for the Italian Navy.

NETLAYERS

2 "ALICUDI" CLASS

Name	No.	Builders	Commissioned
ALICUDI (ex-USS *AN 99*)	A 5304	Ansaldo, Leghorn	1955
FILICUDI (ex-USS *AN 100*)	A 5305	Ansaldo, Leghorn	1955

Displacement, tons: 680 standard; 834 full load
Dimensions, feet (metres): 151·8 pp; 165·3 oa × 33·5 × 10·5 *(46·3 × 10·2 × 3·2)*
Guns: 1—40 mm, 70 cal; 4—20 mm, 70 cal
Main engines: Diesel-electric; 1 200 shp = 12 knots
Complement: 51 (5 officers, 46 men)

Built to the order of NATO. Laid down on 22 April 1954 and 19 July 1954, respectively, and launched on 11 July 1954 and 26 Sep 1954.

ALICUDI   *6/1975, Dr. Giorgio Arra*

LIGHTHOUSE TENDERS

Name	No.	Builders	Commissioned
RAMPINO	A 5309	Osaka	1912

Displacement, tons: 350 standard; 645 full load
Dimensions, feet (metres): 158·8 × 24·2 × 13 *(48·4 × 7·4 × 4)*
Main engines: Triple expansion = 7 knots
Complement: 40 (3 officers, 37 men)

Buoy tender. Of netlayer type.

3 Ex-BRITISH LCT (3) TYPE

MTF 1301 A 5361   **MTF 1302** A 5362   **MTF 1303** A 5363

Displacement, tons: 296 light; 700 full load
Dimensions, feet (metres): 192 × 31 × 7 *(58·6 × 9·5 × 2·1)*
Guns: 1—40 mm, 56 cal; 2—20 mm, 70 cal
Main engines: Diesel; 1 shaft; speed = 8 knots
Complement: 23 (3 officers, 20 men)

Converted landing craft of the British LCT (3) type. Lighthouse motor transports.

MTF 1301   *1968, Italian Navy*

SALVAGE SHIP

Name	No.	Builders	Commissioned
PROTEO (ex-*Perseo*)	A 5310	Cantieri Navali Riuniti, Ancona	1950

Displacement, tons: 1 865 standard; 2 147 full load
Dimensions, feet (metres): 220·5 pp; 248 oa × 38 × 21 *(67·3; 75·6 × 11·6 × 6·4)*
Main engines: 2 diesels; 4 800 bhp; single shaft = 16 knots
Range, miles: 7 500 at 13 knots
Complement: 130 (10 officers, 120 men)

Laid down at Cantieri Navali Riuniti, Ancona, in 1943. Suspended in 1944. Seized by Germans and transferred to Trieste. Construction re-started at Cantieri Navali Riuniti, Ancona, in 1949. Formerly mounted one 3·9 inch gun and two 20 mm.

PROTEO

1975, Italian Navy

REPAIR CRAFT

7 Ex-BRITISH LCT 3s

MOC 1201	MOC 1203	MOC 1205	MOC 1208
MOC 1202	MOC 1204	MOC 1207	

Displacement, tons: 350 standard; 640 full load
Dimensions, feet (metres): 192 × 31 × 7 *(58·6 × 9·5 × 2·1)*
Guns: 2—40 mm; 2—20 mm (2 ships have 2—40 mm and 1 ship has 3—20 mm)
Main engines: Diesel = 8 knots
Complement: 24 (3 officers, 21 men)

Originally converted as repair craft. Other duties have been taken over—MOC 1207 and 1208 are ammunition transports and MOC 1201 has been used for torpedo trials.

MOC 1201 (with torpedo tube)

1973, Dr Giorgio Arra

WATER CARRIERS

PIAVE A 5354   **TEVERE** A 5355

4 973 tons full load—built 1971-73. Complement 55 (7 officers, 48 men).

PIAVE

1974, Commander Aldo Fraccaroli

Name	No.	Builders	Commissioned
BASENTO	A 5356	Inma di La Spezia	1970
BRADANO	A 5357	Inma di La Spezia	1971
BRENTA	A 5358	Inma di La Spezia	1972

1 914 tons. Laid down in 1969-70. Complement 24 (3 officers, 21 men).

ADIGE (ex-*YW 92*) A 5369   **TANARO** (ex-*YW 99*) A 5376
TICINO (ex-*YW 79*) A 5377

Ex-US Army YW type. 1 470 tons full load. Complement 35 (4 officers, 31 men).

VOLTURNO A 5366

Complement 67 (7 officers, 60 men)

MINCIO A 5374

645 tons. Launched in 1929. Complement 19 (1 officer, 18 men).

BORMIDA A 5359

Complement 11 (1 officer, 10 men)

BASENTO

1974, Commander Aldo Fraccaroli

TIMAVO

645 tons. Built by COMI, Venezia, 1926.

OFANTO

250 tons. Built 1913-14.

SIMETO   STURA

Small water carriers of 167 and 126 tons displacement, respectively.

TUGS

CICLOPE A 5319

Displacement, tons: 1 200
Dimensions, feet (metres): 157·5 × 32·5 × 13 *(48 × 9·8 × 4)*
Main engines: Triple expansion; 1 shaft; 1 000 ihp = 8 knots

Launched in 1944.

Name	No.	Builders	Commissioned
ATLANTE	A 5317	Visentini-Donada	14 Aug 1975
PROMETEO	A 5318	Visentini-Donada	14 Aug 1975

Displacement, tons: 750 full load
Dimensions, feet (metres): 116·7 × 28·8 × 14·8 *(39 × 9·6 × 4·1)*
Main engines: Diesel; 1 shaft; cp propeller; 2670 hp

Both launched 1974.

COLOSSO (ex-*LT 214*) A 5320   **FORTE** (ex-*LT 159*) A 5321

Displacement, tons: 525 standard; 835 full load
Dimensions, feet (metres): 142·8 × 32·8 × 11 *(43·6 × 10 × 3·4)*
Main engines: 2 diesel-electric; 690 hp = 11 knots

Ex-US Army.

SAN GIUSTO A 5326

Displacement, tons: 486 standard
Main engines: 900 hp = 12 knots

ERCOLE A 5388 (1971)   **GAGLIARDO** A 5322 (1938)
ROBUSTO A 5323 (1939)   **VIGOROSO** A 5394 (1971)

Displacement, tons: 389 standard; 506 full load
Main engines: 1 000 ihp = 8 knots

PORTO D'ISCHIA A 5378   **RIVA TRIGOSO** A 5379

Displacement, tons: 296 full load
Dimensions, feet (metres): 83·7 × 23·3 × 10·8 *(25·5 × 7·1 × 3·3)*
Main engines: Diesel; 1 shaft; 850 bhp = 12·1 knots

Both launched in Sep 1969. Controllable pitch propeller.

MISENO   **MONTE CRISTO**

Displacement, tons: 285

Former United States Navy harbour tugs.

CAPRERA A 5381 (1972)   **PORTO PISANO** A 5386 (1937)
LEVANZO A 5397 (1973)   **PORTO RECANATI** A 5387 (1937)
PANTELLERIA A 5382 (1972)   **SALVORE** A 5391 (1927)
PIANOVA A 5396 (1914)   **TINO** A 5392 (1930)

Displacement, tons: 270
Dimensions, feet (metres): 88·8 × 22 × 10 *(27·1 × 6·7 × 3·1)*
Main engines: 600 ihp = 9 knots

Principally employed as harbour tugs.

FAVIGNANA A 5385 (1973)   **USTICA** A 5324 (1973)

Displacement, tons: 270 standard
Dimensions, feet (metres): 114·8 × 29·5 × 13 *(35 × 9 × 4)*
Main engines: 1 200 hp

AUSONIA   **PANARIA**

Displacement, tons: 240

Both launched in 1948. Coastal tugs for general duties.

VENTIMIGLIA

Displacement, tons: 230 standard
Dimensions, feet (metres): 108·2 × 23 × 7·2 *(33 × 7 × 2·2)*
Main engines: 550 hp = 10 knots

PASSERO Y 439 (1934)   **RIZZUTO** Y 473 (1956)   **CIRCEO** Y 433 (1956)

Principally employed as ferry tugs.

ABBAZIA Y 411 (1968)   **MESCO** Y 435 (1933)
ALBENGA Y 412 (1973)   **NISIDA** Y 437 (1943)
ARZACHENA Y 414 (1931)   **PIOMBINO** Y 440 (1969)
ASINARA Y 415 (193¾)   **POZZI** Y 422 (1912)
BOEO Y 417 (1943)   **SAN BENEDETTO** Y 446 (1941)
CARBONARA Y 419 (1936)   **SPERONE** Y 454 (1965)
CHIOGGIA Y 421 (1919)   **TAVOLARA** Y 455 (1955)
CORDEVOLE Y 423 (1915)   **No 78** Y 469 (1965)
LAMPEDUSA Y 416 (1972)   **No 96** Y 474 (1962)
LINARO Y 430 (1913)

Small tugs for harbour duties.

RP 101 Y 403 (1972)   **RP 105** Y 408 (1974)   **RP 109** Y 456 (1975)
RP 102 Y 404 (1972)   **RP 106** Y 410 (1974)   **RP 110** Y 458 (1975)
RP 103 Y 406 (1974)   **RP 107** Y 413 (1974)   **RP 111** Y 460 (1975)
RP 104 Y 407 (1974)   **RP 108** Y 452 (1975)   **RP 112** Y 462 (1975)

Displacement, tons: 36 standard
Dimensions, feet (metres): 61·6 × 14·6 × 5·9 *(18·8 × 4·5 × 1·8)*
Main engines: 1 diesel; 500 hp

Built by Cantiere Navale Visentini-Donado (Rovigo).

IVORY COAST

Bases

Use made of ports at Abidjan, Sassandra, Tabou and San Pedro

Personnel

1976: 240 officers and men

Mercantile Marine

Lloyd's Register of Shipping: 49 vessels of 119 215 tons gross

Future Programme

A sister-ship to *Vigilant* is planned as well as French Batral type transport. Eventually it is intended to organise the navy into two coastal patrol squadrons.

LIGHT FORCES

1 + 1 FRANCO-BELGE TYPE

Name	No.	Builders	Commissioned
VIGILANT	—	SFCN	1968

Displacement, tons: 235 standard
Dimensions, feet (metres): 149·3 pp; 155·8 oa × 23·6 × 8·2 *(45·5; 47·5 × 7 × 2·6)*
Missiles: 8—SS12
Guns: 2—40 mm
Main engines: 2 AGO diesels; 2 shafts; 4 220 bhp = 18·5 knots
Range, miles: 2 000 at 15 knots
Complement: 25 (3 officers, and 22 men)

Laid down in Feb 1967. Launched on 23 May 1967. Sister ship to *Malaika* of Malagasy Navy and to *Saint Louis* and *Popenguine* of Senegal and similar craft in Tunisia and Cameroons. See Future Programme note above.

1 Ex-FRENCH VC TYPE

ame	No.	Builders	Commissioned
RSEVERANCE (ex-*VC 9, P 759*)	—	Constructions Mécaniques de Normandie, Cherbourg	25 feb 1958

splacement, tons: 75 standard; 82 full load
mensions, feet (metres): 104·5 × 15·5 × 5·5 *(31·8 × 4·7 × 1·7)*
uns: 2—20 mm
ain engines: 2 Mercedes-Benz (MTU) diesels; 2 shafts; 2 700 bhp = 28 knots
l fuel, tons: 10
ange, miles: 1 100 at 16·5 knots; 800 at 21 knots
omplement: 15

rmer French seaward defence motor launch. Transferred from France to Ivory Coast 26 April 63.

PERSEVERANCE   *1964, Ivory Coast Armed Forces*

5 RIVER PATROL CRAFT

Of varying sizes from 24—34 feet. Used for river and lake patrols.

LANDING CRAFT

LCVP

isplacement, tons: 7
uns: 2 MG
ain engines: Mercedes diesels
eed, knots: 9

uilt in Abidjan in 1970.

MISCELLANEOUS

LOKODJO

Displacement, tons: 450

Now used as a training and supply ship. Built in West Germany in 1953 and purchased in 1970. Trawler type.

1 SMALL TRANSPORT

Capable of carrying 25 men.

JAMAICA

efence Force Coast Guard

amaica, which became independent within the Commonwealth on 6 Aug 1962, formed the oast Guard as the Maritime Arm of the Defence Force. This is Based at HMJS Cagway, Port yal.

he Jamaican Government signed an agreement with the USA for the transfer of a small umber of coastguard vessels for the new navy.

reat Britain lent several RN petty officers for technical assistance. The British Mission included technical team to survey sites for the establishment of local naval bases.

Administration

Officer Commanding Jamaican Defence Force Coast Guard:
Lieutenant-Commander L. E. Scott

Personnel

1976: 17 officers, 106 petty officers and ratings *(Coast Guard Reserve:* 16 officers, 30 men)

Mercantile Marine

Lloyd's Register of shipping: 5 vessels of 6 740 tons gross

LIGHT FORCES

ame	No.	Builders	Commissioned
SCOVERY BAY	P 4	Teledyne Sewart Seacraft Inc, Berwick, La, USA	3 Nov 1966
OLLAND BAY	P 5	Teledyne Sewart Seacraft Inc, Berwick, La, USA	4 April 1967
ANATEE BAY	P 6	Teledyne Sewart Seacraft Inc, Berwick, La, USA	9 Aug 1967

splacement, tons: 60
imensions, feet (metres): 85 × 18·8 × 5·9 *(25·9 × 5·7 × 1·8)*
uns: 3—50 cal Browning
ain engines: 3 GM 12 V71 diesels; 3 shafts; 2 000 shp = 26·5 knots
l fuel, tons: 13
ange, miles: 1 000 at 20 knots
omplement: 10

ll aluminium construction. *Discovery Bay,* the prototype was launched in Aug 1966. *Holland ay* and *Manatee Bay* were supplied under the US Military Assistance Programme. All three oats were extensively refitted and modified in 1972-73 by the builders with GM 12V 71 urbo-injected engines to give greater range, speed and operational flexibility.

ame	No.	Builders	Commissioned
ORT CHARLES	P 7	Teledyne Sewart Seacraft Inc, Berwick, La, USA	1974
-	P 8	Teledyne Sewart Seacraft Inc, Berwick, La, USA	1975

imensions, feet (metres): 105 × 19 × 7 *(31·5 × 5·7 × 2·1)*
uns: 1—20 mm; 3—·50 cal MG;
ain engines: 2 Maybach (MTU) MB 16V 538 TB90; 6 000 shp = 32 knots
omplement: 15

oats have accommodation for 24 soldiers and may be used as mobile hospitals in an mergency.

DISCOVERY BAY   *1973, Jamaica CG*

FORT CHARLES   *1975, Jamaican CG*

JAPAN

Naval Board

Chief of the Maritime Staff, Defence Agency:
Admiral Hiroichi Samejima
Commander-in-Chief, Self-Defence Fleet:
Vice-Admiral Teiji Nakamura
Chief, Administration Division, Maritime Staff Office:
Rear-Admiral Fumio Sato

Diplomatic Representation

Defence (Naval) Attaché in London:
Captain Hideo Sato
Defence (Naval) Attaché in Washington:
Captain Tameo Oki
Naval Attaché in Moscow:
Captain Tsyneo Fujikawa
Defence Attaché in Paris:
Colonel Ryuzo Yabunaka

Personnel

1976: 39 000 (including Naval Air)

Bases

Naval—Yokosuka, Kure, Sasebo, Maizuru, Oominato
Naval Air—Atsugi, Hachinohe, Iwakuni, Kanoya, Komatsujima, Okinawa, Ozuki, Oominato, Oomura, Shimofusa, Tateyama, Tokushima.

Fleet Air Arm

14 Air ASW Sqns, P2-J, P2V-7, PS-1, S2F-1, HSS-2
4 Air Training Sqns, P2-J, P2V-7, YS-11, B-65, KM-2, Mentor, Bell-47, OH-6, HSS-2
1 Transport Sqn, YS-11
1 MCM Sqn

Names

The practice of painting the ships' names on the broadsides of the hulls was discontinued in 1970.

Mercantile Marine

Lloyd's Register of Shipping:
9 932 vessels of 39 739 958 tons gross

Five-Year Defence Plan

The fourth 5-year defence programme (1972-76) announced 9 October 1972 provides for the building of the following:

2 Haruna class DDH of 5 200 tons
1 SAM DDG of 3 900 tons
1 SSM DDG of 3 600 tons
3 DDs of 2 500 tons
3 Frigates of 1 450 tons
3 Frigates of 1 500 tons
3 Isoshio class submarines of 1 800 tons
2 Submarines of 2 200 tons
19 Minesweepers
3 Missile Boats of 160 tons
3 Torpedo Boats of 100 tons
2 LSTs of 1 500 tons
3 LSTs of 2 000 tons
1 Supply Ship of 5 000 tons
1 Submarine Tender of 2 700 tons
1 Oceanographic Research Ship of 2 000 tons
3 Patrol Boats
Plus miscellaneous craft

At the end of this programme the fleet should consist of 170 modern ships totalling 214 000 tons.

New Construction Programme

1973 1 DD, 1 DDE, 1 SS, 2 MSC, 2 MSB, 1 PT, 1 LST
1974 1 DDK, 2 MSC, 1 LST
1975 1 DDH, 1 SS, 3 MSC, 1 LST
1976 Possible programme: 1 DDH, 1 MSC, 1 AGS, 1 AOE (though MSDF request was for 1 DDH, 1 DDK or DDE, 1 SS, 3 MSC, 1 PT, 1 AOE, 1 AGS)

Strength of the Fleet

Type	Active	Building (Projected)
Destroyers	29	2 (2)
Frigates	16	1
Corvettes	20	—
Submarines—Patrol	16	1 (1)
Fast Attack Craft—Torpedo	5	(1)
Patrol Craft—Coastal	10	—
LSTs	4	1 (1)
Minelayer	1	—
M/S Support Ships	3	—
Minesweepers—Coastal	30	2 (3)
MSBs	6	—
Training Ships	4	—
S/M Rescue Vessels	2	—
Support Tanker	1	(1)
Icebreaker	1	—
Tugs	31 (2 large)	(1)
Auxiliaries	18	—
Survey Ships	5	1

DELETIONS

Light Forces

1972 PT 2, 3, 4 and 9. *Kosoku* 1, 22-28, 30
1973 PT 7 and 8, *Kosoku* 3
1974 *Kosoku* 4 and 5
1975 PT 10 (15 Apr)

LST

1972 *Hayatomo*
1974 *Osumi*
1975 *Shimokita*
1976 *Shiretoko* (returned to US in Mar)

LSM

1973 3001 (paid off 30 Mar 1974)

Destroyers

1974 *Ariake*, *Yugure* (Transferred to S. Korea for spares in 1976).

Frigates

1970 *Kiri, Keyaki, Nire, Sugi, Shii* to US
1972 *Kaya, Bura, Kashi, Moni, Tochi, Ume, Maki, Kusu,. Matsu, Nata, Sakura,* (All ex-US PFs). *Wakaba*
1975 *Ikazuchi, Achebono* scrapped. *Asahi* and *Hatsuhi* (ex-"Bostwick" class) returned to US for disposal

Submarines

1971 *Kuroshio* to US

Minewarfare Forces

1974 MSB 05, 06 deleted (10 Dec). *Koozu*

Tenders

1974 YAS 45 *(Suma)*, YAS 48, YAS 49 *(Miho)*

Maritime Safety Agency (Coast Guard)

10 Large Patrol Vessels
50 Medium Patrol Vessels
31 Small Patrol Vessels
9 Fire Fighting Craft
209 Patrol Craft
6 Surveying Vessels
21 Surveying Launches
5 Tenders
1 Underwater Research Vessel
2 Salvage Craft
14 Utility Launches

PENNANT LIST

Destroyers

DD 101	Harukaze
102	Yukikaze
103	Ayanami
104	Isonami
105	Uranami
106	Shikinami
107	Murasame
108	Yudachi
109	Harusame
110	Takanami
111	Oonami
112	Makinami
113	Yamagumo
114	Makigumo
115	Asagumo
116	Minegumo
117	Natsugumo
118	Murakumo
119	Aokumo
120	Akigumo
141	Haruna
142	Hiei
143	New Construction
144	New Construction
161	Akizuki
162	Teruzuki
163	Amatsukaze
164	Takatsuki
165	Kikuzuki
166	Mochizuki
167	Nagatsuki
168	Tachikaze
169	New Construction

Frigates

DE 203	Inazuma
211	Isuzu
212	Mogami
213	Kitakami
214	Ooi
215	Chikugo
216	Ayase
217	Mikuma
218	Tokachi
219	Iwase
220	Chitose
221	Niyodo
222	Teshio
223	Yoshino
224	Kumano
225	New Construction

Corvettes

PC 301	Kari
302	Kiji
303	Taka
304	Washi
305	Kamome
306	Tsubame
307	Misago
308	Hayabusa
309	Umitaka
310	Ootaka
311	Mizutori
312	Yamadori
313	Ootori

Corvettes

314	Kasasagi
315	Hatsukari
316	Umidori
317	Wakataka
318	Kumataka
319	Shiratori
320	Hiyodori

Submarines—Patrol

SS 511	Oyashio
521	Hayashio
522	Wakashio
523	Natsushio
524	Huyushio
561	Ooshio
562	Asashio
563	Harushio
564	Michishio
565	Arashio
566	Uzushio
567	Makishio
568	Isoshio
569	Narushio
570	Kuroshio
571	Takashio
572	New Construction

Minesweepers—Coastal

MSC 611	Tsukumi (Training)
612	Mikura (Training)
613	Shikine
616	Hotaka
617	Karato
618	Hario
619	Mutsure
620	Chiburi
621	Ootsu
622	Kudako
623	Rishiri
624	Rebun
625	Amami
626	Urume
627	Minase
628	Ibuki
629	Katsura
630	Takami
631	Iou
632	Miyake
633	Utone
634	Awaji
635	Toushi
636	Teuri
637	Murotsu
638	Tashiro
639	Miyato
640	Takane
641	Muzuki
642	Yokose
643	Sakate
644	Oumi
645	Fukue
646	New Construction
647	New Construction
648	New Construction

Minesweeper Tender

MST 462	Hayase

Light Forces

PT 11-15	—
PB 19-27	—
ASH 06	Kosoku 6

Mine Layer

MMC 951	Sooya

Amphibious Forces

LST 4101	Atsumi
4102	Motobu
4103	New Construction
4151	Miura
4152	Ozika
4153	Satsuma

Salvage Vessel

41	Shobo

Submarine Rescue Ships

ASR 401	Chihaya
402	Fushimi

Tanker

AO 411	Hamana

Training Ship

TV 3501	Katori

Training Support Ship

ATS 4201	Azuma

Cable Layer

ARC 481	Tsugaru

Icebreaker

AGB 5001	Fuji

Surveying Ships

AGS 5101	Akashi
5111	Ichi-GO
5112	Yi-GO
5113	San-GO
5114	Yon-GO

Tenders

YAS 46	Yashima
47	Hashima
56	Atada
57	Itsuki
58	Yashiro
60	Tsushima
61	Toshima
62	Shisaka
63	Koshiki
64	Sakito
65	Kanawa
69	Erimo

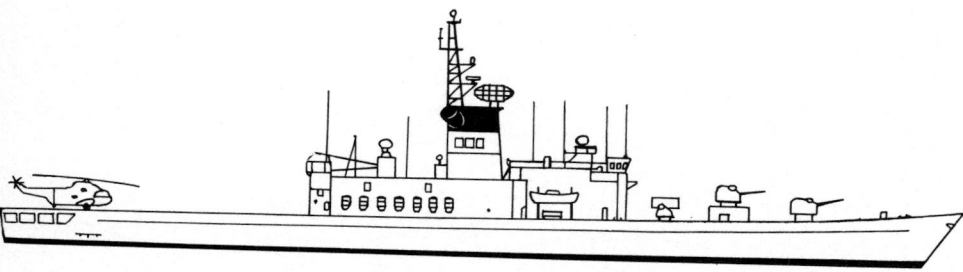

"HARUNA" Class

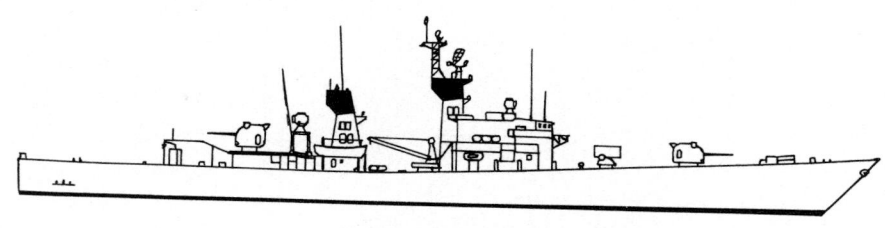

"TAKATSUKI" Class

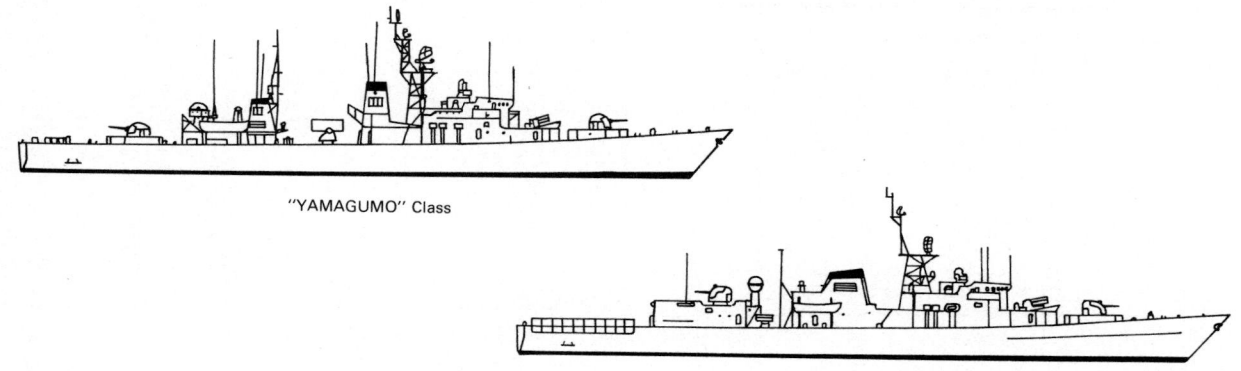

"YAMAGUMO" Class

"MINEGUMO" Class

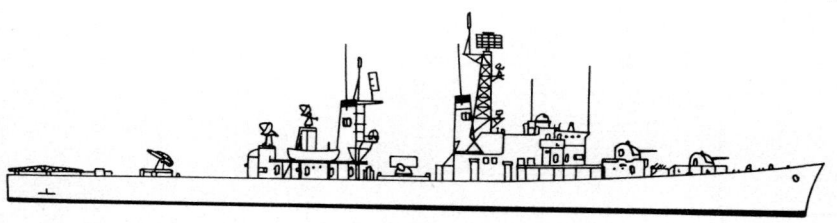

AMUTSUKAZE

"AKIZUKI" Class

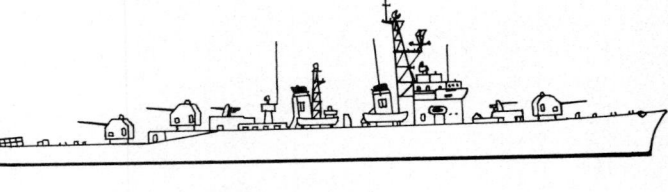

"MURASAME" Class

"AYANAMI" Class

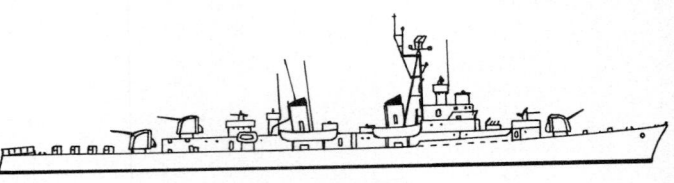

"HARUKAZE" Class

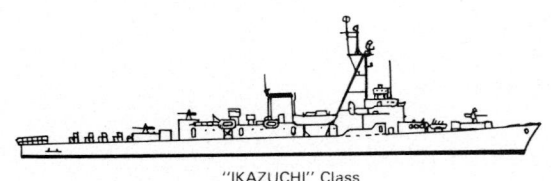

"CHIKUGO" Class

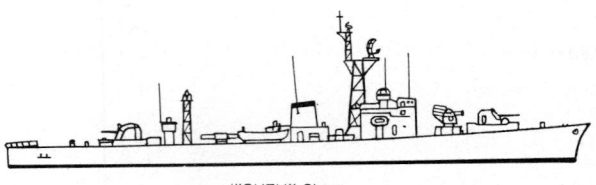

"ISUZU" Class

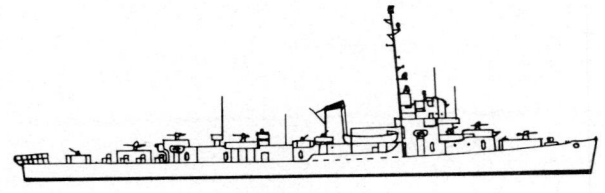

"IKAZUCHI" Class

"AKEBONO" Class

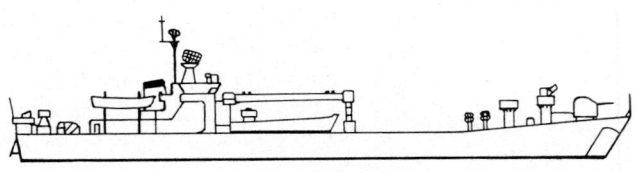

"ASAKI" Class

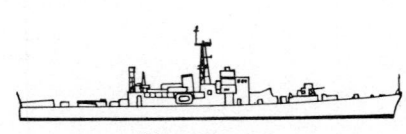

"MIZUTORI" Class

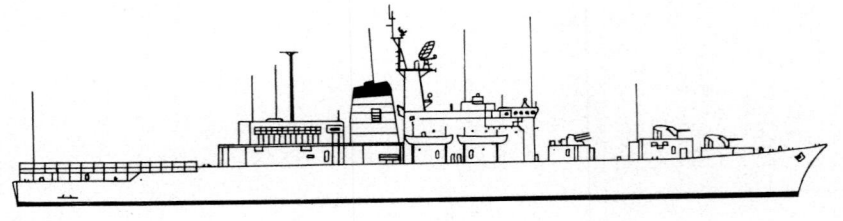

"MIURA" Class

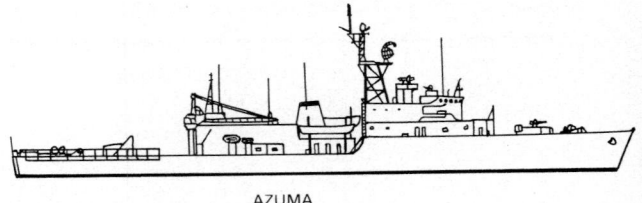

AZUMA

KATORI

DESTROYERS

2 "TACHIKAZE" CLASS

Name	No.	Builders	Laid down	Launched	Commissioned
TACHIKAZE	DD 168	Mitsubishi, Nagasaki	19 June1973	17 Dec 1974	26 Mar 1976
—	DD 169	Mitsubishi, Nagasaki	April1976	Nov 1977	Mar 1979

Displacement, tons: 3 850
Dimensions, feet (metres): 443 × 47 × 15 *(143 × 14·3 × 4·6)*
Missiles: Standard RIM 60A SAM
Guns: 2—5 in (singles)
A/S weapons: 8 tube ASROC and 2 triple A/S torpedo tubes
Main engines: 2 turbines; 2 shafts; 60 000 hp
Speed, knots: 33

Sonar: VDS.

TACHIKAZE

1975, Japanese Maritime Self-Defence Force

2 "HARUNA" CLASS

Name	No.	Builders	Laid down	Launched	Commissioned
HARUNA	DD 141	Mitsubishi, Nagasaki	19 Mar 1970	1 Feb 1972	22 Feb 1973
HIEI	DD 142	Ishikawajima, Tokyo	8 Mar 1972	13 Aug 1973	27 Nov 1974

Displacement, tons: 4 700
Length, feet (metres): 502·0 *(153·0)*
Beam, feet (metres): 57·4 *(17·5)*
Draught, feet (metres): 16·7 *(5·1)*
Aircraft: 3 anti-submarine helicopters
Guns: 2—5 in *(127 mm)* (single)
A/S weapons: Asroc launcher; 6—12·7 in (2 triple) tubes
Torpedo tubes: 6—21 in *(533 mm)* (2 triple)
Main engines: 2 turbines; 70 000 shp; 2 shafts
Speed, knots: 32
Range, miles: 7 000 at 20 knots
Complement: 364

Ordered under the third five-year defence programme (from 1967-71).

HARUNA

1975, Japanese Maritime Self-Defence Force

2 "IMPROVED HARUNA" CLASS

Name	No.	Builders	Laid down	Launched	Commissioned
—	DD 143	—	1976	—	1980
—	DD 144	—	1977	—	1981

Displacement, tons: 5 200
Aircraft: 3 anti-submarine helicopters
Missiles: 1 Sea Sparrow launcher
Guns: 2—5 in *(127 mm)* 54 cal (singles); 2—35 mm
A/S weapons: 1 Asroc launcher; 6—12·7 in tubes (triples)
Main engines: 2 turbines; 75 000 shp; 2 shafts
Speed, knots: 32

One in 1975 Programme and one in 1976 Programme.

4 "TAKATSUKI" CLASS

Name	No.	Builders	Laid down	Launched	Commissioned
KIKUZUKI	DD 165	Mitsubishi Jyuko Co, Nagasaki	15 Mar 1966	25 Mar 1967	27 Mar 1968
MOCHIZUKI	DD 166	Ishikawajima Jyuko Co, Tokyo	25 Nov 1966	15 Mar 1968	25 Mar 1969
NAGATSUKI	DD 167	Mitsubishi Jyuko Co, Nagasaki	2 Mar 1968	19 Mar 1969	12 Feb 1970
TAKATSUKI	DD 164	Ishikawajima Jyuko Co, Tokyo	8 Oct 1964	7 Jan 1966	15 Mar 1967

Displacement, tons: 3 100
Length, feet (metres): 446·2 *(136·0)* oa
Beam, feet (metres): 44·0 *(13·4)*
Draught, feet (metres): 14·5 *(4·4)*
Aircraft: 3 Dash helicopters
A/S weapons: Octuple Asroc; 1 four barrelled rocket launcher
Guns: 2—5 in *(127 mm)* 54 cal (single)
Torpedo launchers: 2 triple for A/S homing torpedoes
Main engines: 2 Mitsubishi WH geared turbines; 60 000 shp; 2 shafts
Boilers: 2 Mitsubishi CE
Speed, knots: 32
Range, miles: 7 000 at 20 knots
Complement: 270

Takatsuki was provided under the 1963 programme. Equipped with helicopter hangar.

Radar: Search: metric wavelength.
Tactical: probably C band.
Fire control: GFCS 56 with I Band.

Sonars: Hull mounted sonar. VDS in *Takatsuki* (1970), *Kikuzuki* (1972). Remainder not so fitted though planned.

KIKUZUKI   *1975, Japanese Maritime Self-Defence Force*

6 "YAMAGUMO" CLASS

Name	No.	Builders	Laid down	Launched	Commissioned
AKIGUMO	DD 120	Sumitomo, Uraga	7 July 1972	23 Oct 1973	24 July 1974
AOKUMO	DD 119	Sumitomo, Uraga	2 Oct 1970	30 Mar 1972	25 Nov 1972
ASAGUMO	DD 115	Maizuru	24 June 1965	25 Nov 1966	29 Aug 1967
MAKIGUMO	DD 114	Uraga	10 June 1964	26 July 1965	19 Mar 1966
YAMAGUMO	DD 113	Mitsui, Tamano	23 Mar 1964	27 Feb 1965	29 Jan 1966
—	DD 121	Sumitomo, Uraga	4 Feb 1976	June 1977	Mar 1978

Displacement, tons: 2 100
Length, feet (metres): 377 *(115)*
Beam, feet (metres): 38·7 *(11·8)*
Draught, feet (metres): 13·1 *(4)*
Guns: 4—3 in; 50 cal (2 twin)
A/S weapons: 1 Asroc ; 1 four barrelled rocket launcher 2 triple mountings for A/S torpedoes
Main engines: 6 Diesels; 26 500 bhp; 2 shafts
Speed, knots: 27
Range, miles: 7 000 at 20 knots
Complement: 210

Radar: Search: metric set
Tactical: G band set
Fire control: I band control of GFCS 56.

Sonar: *Yamagumo*, *Akigumo* and *Makigumo* fitted with VDS.

AKIGUMO   *1975, Japanese Maritime Self-Defence Force*

3 "MINEGUMO" CLASS

Name	No.	Builders	Laid down	Launched	Commissioned
MINEGUMO	DD 116	Mitsui, Tamano	14 Mar 1967	16 Dec 1967	21 Aug 1968
MURAKUMO	DD 118	Maizuru	19 Oct 1968	15 Nov 1969	21 Aug 1970
NATSUGUMO	DD 117	Uraga	26 June 1967	25 July 1968	25 April 1969

All details as for "Yamagumo" class except:

Aircraft: 2 Dash helicopter in place of Asroc

Note difference in silhouettes between this and the "Yamagumo" class.

Sonar: VDS in *Murakumo*.

NATSUGUMO   *1972, Japanese Maritime Self-Defence Force*

1 "AMATSUKAZE" CLASS

Name	No.	Builders	Laid down	Launched	Commissioned
AMATSUKAZE	DD 163	Mitsubishi, Nagasaki	29 Nov 1962	5 Oct 1963	15 Feb 1965

Displacement, tons: 3 050 standard; 4 000 full load
Length, feet (metres): 429·8 *(131·0)*
Beam, feet (metres): 44 *(13·4)*
Draught, feet (metres): 13·8 *(4·2)*
Aircraft: Helicopter
Missile launchers: 1 single Tartar
Guns: 4—3 in *(76 mm)* 50 cal, (2 twin)
A/S weapons: Asroc; 2 Hedgehogs
6 Short A/S tubes (triples)
Main engines: 2 Ishikawajima GE geared turbines 2 shafts;
60 000 shp
Boilers: 2 Ishikawajima Foster Wheeler
Speed, knots: 33
Oil fuel, tons: 900
Range, miles: 7 000 at 18 knots
Complement: 290

Ordered under the 1960 programme. Refitted in 1967 when A/S
Tubes and new Sonar were fitted.

Radar: Search: SPS 37 and SPS 39 (3 D).
Fire control: SPS 51 for Tartar: I band for guns.

Sonar: SQS 23.

AMATSUKAZE   1975, Japanese Maritime Self-Defence Force

2 "AKIZUKI" CLASS

Name	No.	Builders	Laid down	Launched	Commissioned
AKIZUKI	DD 161	Mitsubishi Zoosen Co, Nagasaki	31 July 1958	26 June1959	13 Feb 1960
TERUZUKI	DD 162	Shin Mitsubishi Jyuko Co, Kobe	15 Aug 1958	24 June1959	29 Feb 1960

Displacement, tons: 2 350 standard; 2 890 full load
Length, feet (metres): 387·2 *(118·0)* oa
Beam, feet (metres): 39·4 *(12·0)*
Draught, feet (metres): 13·1 *(4·0)*
Guns: 3—5 in *(127 mm)* 54 cal (single)
4—3 in *(76 mm)* 50 cal, (2 twin)
A/S weapons: 1—US model Mk 108 rocket launcher; 2
hedgehogs; 2 Short A/S tubes
Torpedo tubes: 4—21 in *(533 mm)* (quadrupled)
Main engines: 2 geared turbines:— *Akizuki:* Mitsubishi
Escher-Weiss. *Teruzuki:* Westinghouse 45 000 shp, 2 shafts
Boilers: 2 Mitsubishi CE type
Speed, knots: 32
Complement: 330

Built under the 1957 Military Aid Programme.

Radar: Search: SPS 6.
Tactical: SPS 10.
Fire control: I Band.

Sonar: Hull mounted sonar. VDS fitted in *Teruzuki* (1967) and
Akizuki (1968).

TERUZUKI   1974, Japanese Maritime Self-Defence Force

3 "MURASAME" CLASS

Name	No.	Builders	Laid down	Launched	Commissioned
HARUSAME	DD 109	Uraga Dock Co	17 June1958	18 June1959	15 Dec 1959
MURASAME	DD 107	Mitsubishi Zoosen Co, Nagasaki	17 Dec 1957	31 July 1958	28 Feb 1959
YUDACHI	DD 108	Ishikawajima Jyuko Co, Tokyo	16 Dec 1957	29 July 1958	25 Mar 1959

Displacement, tons: 1 800 standard; 2 500 full load
Length, feet (metres): 354·3 *(108·0)* oa
Beam, feet (metres): 36 *(11·0)*
Draught, feet (metres): 12·2 *(3·7)*
Guns: 3—5 in *(127 mm)* 54 cal
4—3 in *(76 mm)* 50 cal, (2 twin)
A/S weapons: 2 tubes for Short torpedoes; 1 Hedgehog; 1 DC
rack; 1 Y-gun (see note)
Main engines: 2 sets geared turbines; 30 000 shp; 2 shafts
Boilers: 2 (see *Engineering* notes)
Speed, knots: 30
Range, miles: 6 000 at 18 knots
Complement: 250

Murasame and *Yudachi* were built under the 1956 Programme,
Harusame 1957 Programme.

A/S weapons: *Murasame* fitted Sep 1975 with two triple tubes
in place of those above. DC rack and Y-gun removed.

Engineering: *Murasame* has Mitsubishi Jyuko turbines and
Mitsubishi CE boilers; and the other two have Ishikawajima
Harima Jyuko turbines and Ishikawajima FW-D boilers.

Radar: Search: SPS 6.
Tactical: SPS 10.
Fire control: I Band.

Sonar: VDS fitted in *Harusame* in 1968.

HARUSAME   1975, Japanese Maritime Self-Defence Force

7 "AYANAMI" CLASS

Name	No.
AYANAMI	DD 103
ISONAMI	DD 104
MAKINAMI	DD 112
OONAMI	DD 106
SHIKINAMI	DD 110
TAKANAMI	DD 105
URANAMI	DD 105

Builders	Laid down	Launched	Commissioned
Mitsubishi Zoosen Co, Nagasaki	20 Nov 1956	1 June 1957	12 Feb 1958
Shin Mitsubishi Jyuko Co, Kobe	14 Dec 1956	30 Sep 1957	14 Mar 1958
Iino Jyuko Co, Maizuru	20 Mar 1959	25 April 1960	30 Oct 1960
Ishikawajima Jyuko Co, Tokyo	20 Mar 1959	13 Feb 1960	29 Aug 1960
Mitsui Zoosen Co, Tamano	24 Dec 1956	25 Sep 1957	15 Mar 1958
Mitsui Zoosen Co, Tamano	8 Nov 1958	8 Aug 1959	30 Jan 1960
Kawasaki Jyuko Co, Tokyo	1 Feb 1957	29 Aug 1957	27 Feb 1958

Displacement, tons: 1 700 standard; 2 500 full load
Length, feet (metres): 357·6 (109·0) oa
Beam, feet (metres): 35·1 (10·7)
Draught, feet (metres): 12 (3·7)
Guns: 6—3 in (76 mm) 50 cal (3 twin)
A/S weapons: 2 triple mountings for A/S torpedoes (103, 104, 105, 106, 112); 2 fixed tubes for A/S torpedoes (110, 111); 2 US Mk 15 Hedgehogs
Torpedo tubes: 4—21 in (533 mm) (quadruple) (see *Training Ship* note)
2 fixed, for A/S homing torpedoes
Main engines: 2 Mitsubishi Escher-Weiss geared turbines; 2 shafts; 35 000 shp
Boilers: 2 (see *Engineering*)
Speed, knots: 32
Range, miles: 6 000 at 18 knots
Complement: 230

Anti-submarine: Trainable Hedgehogs forward of the bridge.

Engineering: Types of boilers installed are as follows: Mitsubishi CE in *Ayanami*, *Isonami*, and *Uranami*. Hitachi, Babcock & Wilcox in *Oonami*, *Shikinami* and *Takanami*. Kawasaki Jyuko BD in *Makinami*.

Radar: Search: SPS 12.
Tactical: SPS 10. Fire control: I Band.

Training Ships: *Isonami* and *Shikinami* converted 1975-76 to training ships in place of *Asahi* and *Hatsuhi*. 21 inch torpedo tubes removed and lecture hall built in the space.

MAKINAMI   1975, Japanese Maritime Self-Defence Force

2 "HARUKAZE" CLASS

Name	No.
HARUKAZE	DD 101
YUKIKAZE	DD 102

Builders	Laid down	Launched	Commissioned
Mitsubishi Zosen Co, Nagasaki	15 Dec 1954	20 Sep 1955	26 Apr 1956
Shin Mitsubishi Co, Kobe	17 Dec 1954	20 Aug 1955	31 July 1965

Displacement, tons: 1 700 standard; 2 340 full load
Length, feet (metres): 347·8 (106·0) wl; 358·5 (190·3) oa
Beam, feet (metres): 34·5 (10·5)
Draught, feet (metres): 12·0 (3·7)
Guns: 3—5 in (127 mm) 38 cal; 8—40 mm (2 quadruple)
A/S weapons: 2 Tubes for Short A/S torpedoes; 2 Hedgehogs;
Main engines: 2 sets geared turbines; *Harukaze*; 2 Mitsubishi Escher Weiss; *Yukikaze*; 2 Westinghouse; 2 shafts; 30 000 shp
Boilers: *Harukaze*: 2 Hitachi-Babcock; *Yukikaze*: 2 Combustion Engineering
Speed, knots: 30
Range, miles: 6 000 at 18 knots
Oil fuel, tons: 557
Complement: 240

Authorised under the 1953 programme. First destroyer hulled vessels built in Japan after the Second World War. Electric welding was extensively used in hull construction; development of weldable high tension steel in main hull and light alloy in superstructure were also new.
Nearly all the armament was supplied from the USA under the MSA clause.

Anti-Submarine: Armament was modified in Jan. 1959 when 2 torpedo tubes for A/S torpedoes were mounted and depth charges and K guns removed.

Radar: Search: L Band.
Tactical: SPS 10.
Fire control: I Band.

HARUKAZE   1975, Japanese Maritime Self-Defence Force

YUKIKAZE   1972, Toshio Tamura

FRIGATES

11 + 1 "CHIKUGO" CLASS

ame	No.	Builders	Laid down	Launched	Commissioned
ʹASE	DE 216	Ishikawajima Harima	5 Dec 1969	16 Sep 1970	20 May 1971
ᴵIKUGO	DE 215	Mitsui Zoosen, Tamano	9 Dec 1968	13 Jan 1970	31 July 1970
ᴵITOSE	DE 220	Hitachi Zoosen, Maizuru	7 Oct 1971	25 Jan 1973	31 Aug 1973
ʹASE	DE 219	Mitsui Zoosen, Tamano	6 Aug 1971	29 June1972	12 Dec 1972
ᴵKUMA	DE 217	Mitsui Zoosen, Tamano	17 Mar 1970	16 Feb 1971	26 Aug 1971
ʹYODO	DE 221	Mitsui Zoosen, Tamano	20 Sep 1972	28 Aug 1973	8 Feb 1974
ᴵKACHI	DE 218	Mitsui Zoosen, Tamano	11 Dec 1970	25 Nov 1971	17 May 1972
ᴵSHIO	DE 222	Hitachi Zoosen, Maizuru	11 July 1973	29 May 1974	10 Jan 1975
ᴵSHINO	DE 223	Mitsui Zoosen, Tamano	28 Sep 1973	22 Aug 1974	6 Feb 1975
ᴵMANO	DE 224	Hitachi Zoosen, Maizuru	29 May 1974	24 Feb 1975	19 Nov 1975
ᴵSHIRO	DE 225	Mitsui Zoosen, Tamano	Apr 1976	Feb 1977	Aug 1977
	DE 226	—	—	—	—

splacement, tons: 1 470 (216, 217-219,221); 1 480 (216, 220); 1 500 (222 onwards)
ngth, feet (metres): 305·5 (93·0) oa
am, feet (metres): 35·5 (10·8)
aught, feet (metres): 11·5 (3·5)
ins: 2—3 in (76 mm) 50 cal, (1 twin); 2—40 mm (1 twin)
ᴵ weapons: 8 tube Asroc
rpedo launchers: 2 triple 12·7 in (324 mm)
ain engines: 4 Mitsui B & W diesels (215, 217, 218, 219, 221, 223, 225); 4 Mitsubishi UEV 30/40 N diesels (remainder); 2 shafts; 16 000 shp
eed, knots: 25
mplement: 165

dar: Search: D Band.
ctical: SPS 10.
e control: I Band.

nar: Fitted with VDS.

MIKUMA   1972, Toshio Tamura

4 "ISUZU" CLASS

me	No.	Builders	Laid down	Launched	Commissioned
ᴵZU	DE 211	Mitsui Zoosen Co, Tamano	16 Apr 1960	17 Jan 1961	29 July 1961
ᴵAKAMI	DE 213	Ishikawajima-Harima Co, Tokyo	7 June1962	21 June1963	27 Feb 1964
ᴵGAMI	DE 212	Mitsubishi Zoosen Co, Nagasaki	4 Aug 1960	7 Mar 1961	28 Oct 1961
ᴵI	DE 214	Maizuru Co	10 June1962	15 June1963	22 Jan 1964

splacement, tons: 1 490 standard; 1 700 full load
ngth, feet (metres): 309·5 (94) oa
am, feet (metres): 34·2 (10·4)
aught, feet (metres): 11·5 (3·5)
ins: 4—3 in (76 mm) 50 cal, (2 twin)
ᴵ weapons: 4 Barrelled Bofors rocket launcher; 2 Triple ᴵShort A/S tubes (Isuzu and Mogami); 1 Mk 108 launcher; 2 ᴵShort A/S tubes (Kitakami and Ooi); 1 Y-gun; 1 DC rack (Ooi)
rpedo tubes: 4—21 in (533 mm) (quadrupled)
ain engines: 4 diesels, Mitsui in Ooi, Isuzu, Mitsubishi in ᴵKitakami, Mogami, 16 000 hp; 2 shafts
eed, knots: 25
mplement: 180

odernisation: In 1966 (Mogami) and 1968 (Kitakami) 1 Y-gun ᴵd DC racks removed for VDS. Isuzu (1974-75) and Mogami ᴵ74) modified for new A/S weapon fit.

dar: Search: SPS 6
ctical: SPS 10.

nar: VDS in Mogami and Kitakami.

KITAKAMI   1975, Japanese Maritime Self-Defence Force

1 "IKAZUCHI" CLASS

me	No.	Builders	Laid down	Launched	Commissioned
ᴵAZUMA	DE 203	Mitsui Zoosen Co, Tamano	15 Dec 1954	4 Aug 1955	5 Mar 1956

splacement, tons: 1 070 standard; 1 300 full load
ngth, feet (metres): 287 87·5) wl; 288·7 (88·0) oa
am, feet (metres): 28·5 (8·7)
aught, feet (metres): 10·2 (3·1)
ins: 2—3 in (76 mm) 50 cal; 2—40 mm
ᴵ weapons: 1 Hedgehog; 8 K-guns; 2 DC racks
ain engines: 2 Mitsui B & W diesels; 12 000 hp; 2 shafts
eed, knots: 25
nge, miles: 5 500 at 15 knots
mplement: 160

dar: Search: SPS 6.

ctical:SPS 10.
e Control: I Band.

INAZUMA   1974, Japanese Maritime Self-Defence Force

CORVETTES

8 "MIZUTORI" CLASS (PC)

Name	No.	Builders	Laid down	Launched	Commissioned
HATSUKARI	315	Sasebo Shipyard	25 Jan 1960	24 June1960	15 Nov 1960
HIYODORI	320	Sasebo Shipyard	26 Feb 1965	25 Sep 1965	28 Feb 1966
KASASAGI	314	Fujinagata, Osaka	18 Dec 1959	31 May 1960	31 Oct 1960
MIZUTORI	311	Kawasaki, Kobe	13 Mar 1959	22 Sep 1959	27 Feb 1960
OTORI	313	Kure Shipyard	16 Dec 1959	27 May 1960	13 Oct 1960
SHIRATORI	319	Sasebo Shipyard	29 Feb 1964	8 Oct 1964	26 Feb 1965
UMIDORI	316	Sasebo Shipyard	15 Feb 1962	15 Oct 1962	30 Mar 1963
YAMADORI	312	Fujinagata, Osaka	14 Mar 1959	22 Oct 1959	15 Mar 1960

Displacement, tons: 420 to 440 standard
Dimensions, feet (metres): 197·0 × 23·3 × 7·5 *(60·1 × 7·1 × 2·3)*
Guns: 2—40 mm (1 twin)
A/S weapons: 1 Hedgehog; 1 DC rack; 6 A/S torpedo tubes (triple) (316, 319, 320); 2 A/S torpedo tubes (remainder)
Main engines: 2 MAN diesels; 2 shafts; 3 800 bhp = 20 knots
Range, miles: 2 000 at 12 knots
Complement: 80

OTORI
1972, Toshio Tamura

4 "UMITAKA" CLASS (PC)

Name	No.	Builders	Laid down	Launched	Commissioned
OTAKA	310	Kure Shipyard	18 Mar 1959	3 Sep 1959	14 Jan 1960
UMITAKA	309	Kawasaki, Kobe	13 Mar 1959	25 July 1959	30 Nov 1959
KUMATAKA	318	Fujinagata, Osaka	20 Mar 1963	21 Oct 1963	25 Mar 1964
WAKATAKA	317	Kure Shipyard	5 Mar 1962	13 Nov 1962	30 Mar 1963

Displacement, tons: 440 to 460 standard
Dimensions, feet (metres): 197·0 × 23·3 × 8·0 *(60·1 × 7·1 × 2·4)*
Guns: 2—40 mm (1 twin)
A/S weapons: 1 Hedgehog, 1 DC rack; 2 triple A/S torpedo tubes (317, 318); 2 A/S torpedo tubes (309, 310)
Main engines: 2 B & W diesels; 2 shafts; 4 000 bhp = 20 knots
Complement: 80

OTAKA
1972, Japanese Maritime Self-Defence Force

1 "HAYABUSA" CLASS (PC)

Name	No.	Builders	Laid down	Launched	Commissioned
HAYABUSA	308	Mitsubishi Shipbuilding & Engineering Co. Ltd, Nagasaki	23 May 1956	20 Nov 1956	10 June 1957

Displacement, tons: 380 standard
Dimensions, feet (metres): 190·2 × 25·7 × 7 *(58 × 7·8 × 2·1)*
Guns: 2—40 mm (1 twin)
A/S weapons: 1 Hedgehog; 2 Y Guns; 2 DC racks
Main engines: 2 diesels; 4 000 bhp; 2 shafts = 20 knots
Complement: 75

Built under the 1954 fiscal year programme.
A gas turbine was installed in Mar 1962 and removed in 1970.

HAYABUSA
1974, Japanese Maritime Self-Defence Force

7 "KARI" and "KAMOME" CLASS (PC)

Name	No.	Builders	Laid down	Launched	Commissioned
KAMOME	305	Uraga	27 Jan 1956	3 Sep 1956	14 Jan 1957
KARI	301	Fujinagata, Osaka	18 Jan 1956	26 Sep 1956	8 Feb 1957
KIJI	302	Iino, Maizuru	14 Dec 1955	11 Sep 1956	29 Jan 1957
MISAGO	307	Uraga	27 Jan 1956	1 Nov 1956	11 Feb 1957
TAKA	303	Fujinagata, Osaka	18 Jan 1956	17 Nov 1956	11 Mar 1957
TSUBAME	306	Kure Shipyard	15 Mar 1956	10 Oct 1956	31 Jan 1957
WASHI	304	Iino, Maizuru	14 Dec 1955	12 Nov 1956	20 Mar 1957

Displacement, tons: 330 standard (305-307); 310 standard (301-304)
Dimensions, feet (metres): 177·1 × 21·6 × 6·8 *(54 × 6·6 × 2·1)* (305-307)
  183·7 × 21·3 × 6·6 *(56 × 6·5 × 2)* (301-304)
Guns: 2—40 mm (1 twin)
A/S weapons: 1 Hedgehog; 2-Y guns; 2 DC racks
Main engines: 2 diesels *(Kari, Kiji, Taka* and *Washi* Kawasaki-MAN; others Mitsui-Burmeister & Wain). 2 shafts; 4 000 bhp = 20 knots
Oil fuel, tons: 21·5
Range, miles: 2 000 at 12 knots
Complement: 70

Authorised under the 1954 programme. At the time they were an entirely new type of fast patrol vessels, reminiscent of the United States PC type but modified and improved in many ways. "Kari" class (301-304). "Kamome" class (305-307).

KAMOME
1975, Japanese Maritime Self-Defence Force

MISAGO
1970, Japanese Maritime Self Defence Force

SUBMARINES

5 + 1 "UZUSHIO" CLASS

Name	No.	Builders	Laid down	Launched	Commissioned
UZUSHIO	SS 566	Kawasaki Jyuko, Kobe	25 Sep 1968	11 Mar 1970	21 Jan 1971
MAKISHIO	SS 567	Mitsubishi Jyuko, Kobe	21 June1969	27 Jan 1971	2 Feb 1972
ISOSHIO	SS 568	Kawasaki Jyuko, Kobe	9 July 1970	18 Mar 1972	25 Nov 1972
NARUSHIO	SS 569	Mitsubishi Jyuko, Kobe	8 May 1971	22 Nov 1972	28 Sep 1973
KUROSHIO	SS 570	Kawasaki Jyuko, Kobe	5 July 1972	22 Feb 1974	27 Nov 1974
TAKASHIO	SS 571	Mitsubishi Jyuko, Kobe	6 July 1973	30 June1975	30 Jan 1976
—	SS 572	Kawasaki Jyuko, Kobe	14 April 1975	April 1977	Mar 1978

Displacement, tons: 1 850 standard
Length, feet (metres): 236·2 (72·0)
Beam, feet (metres): 32·5 (9·9)
Draught, feet (metres): 24·6 (7·5)
Torpedo tubes: 6—21 in (533 mm); amidships
Main machinery: 2 Kawasaki MAN diesels; 3 400 bhp; 1 shaft; 1 electric motor; 7 200 hp
Speed, knots: 12 surfaced; 20 dived
Complement: 80

Of double-hull construction and "tear-drop" form, built of HT steel to increase diving depth. New bow sonar fitted.
An enlarged version of 2 200 tons with an extra 13 feet (4 metres) length and increased diving depth is to be built. SS 573 to be laid down at Mitsubishi, Kobe in Mar 1979.

NARUSHIO   1973, Japanese Maritime Self-Defence Force

5 "OOSHIO" CLASS

Name	No.	Builders	Laid down	Launched	Commissioned
ARASHIO	SS 565	Mitsubishi Jyuko, Kobe	5 July 1967	24 Oct 1968	25 July 1969
ASASHIO	SS 562	Kawasaki Jyuko Co, Kobe	5 Oct 1964	27 Nov 1965	13 Oct 1966
HARUSHIO	SS 563	Mitsubishi Jyuko Co, Kobe	12 Oct 1965	25 Feb 1967	1 Dec 1967
MICHISHIO	SS 564	Kawasaki Jyuko, Kobe	26 July 1966	5 Dec 1967	29 Aug 1968
OOSHIO	SS 561	Mitsubishi Jyuko Co, Kobe	29 June1963	30 April1964	31 Mar 1965

Displacement, tons: 1 650 standard; Ooshio 1 600
Length, feet (metres): 288·7 (88·0)
Beam, feet (metres): 26·9 (8·2)
Draught, feet (metres): 16·2 (4·9) Ooshio 15·4 (4·7)
Torpedo tubes: 6—21 in (533 mm) (bow); 2—12·7 in A/S torpedoes in swim-out tubes
Main machinery: 2 diesels; 2 900 bhp; 2 shafts; 2 electric motors; 6 300 hp
Speed, knots: 14 surfaced; 18 dived
Complement: 80

Double-hulled boats. A bigger design to obtain improved seaworthiness, a larger torpedo capacity and more comprehensive sonar and electronic devices. Ooshio was built under the 1961 programme, Asashio 1963. Cost $5 600 000.

MICHISHIO   1975, Japanese Maritime Self-Defence Force

4 "HAYASHIO" and "NATSUSHIO" CLASS

Name	No.	Builders	Laid down	Launched	Commissioned
FUYUSHIO	SS 524	Kawasaki Jyuko Co, Kobe	6 Dec 1961	14 Dec 1962	17 Sep 1963
HAYASHIO	SS 521	Shin Mitsubishi Jyuko Co, Kobe	6 June1960	31 July 1961	30 June 1962
NATSUSHIO	SS 523	Shin Mitsubishi Jyuko Co, Kobe	5 Dec 1961	18 Sep 1962	29 June 1963
WAKASHIO	SS 522	Kawasaki Jyuko Co, Kobe	7 June1960	28 Aug 1961	17 Aug 1962

Displacement, tons: 750 standard; (SS 521, 522); 790 standard (SS 523, 524)
Length, feet (metres): 193·6 (59·0) oa (SS 521, 522); 200·1 (61·0) oa (SS 523, 524)
Beam, feet (metres): 21·3 (6·5)
Draught, feet (metres): 13·5 (4·1)
Torpedo tubes: 3—21 in (533 mm) (bow)
Main machinery: 2 diesels; total 900 hp; 2 shafts; 2 electric motors, total 2 300 hp
Speed, knots: 11 surfaced; 15 dived (14 dived "Hayashio" class)
Complement: 40

Very handy and successful boats, with a large safety factor, complete air-conditioning and good habitability.

"Hayashio" class   SS 521-522
"Natsushio" class   SS 523-524

NATSUSHIO   1973, Japanese Maritime Self-Defence Force

1 "OYASHIO" CLASS

Name	No.	Builders	Laid down	Launched	Commissioned
OYASHIO	SS 511	Kawasaki Jyuko Co, Kobe	25 Dec 1957	25 May 1959	30 June 1960

Displacement, tons: 1 100 surfaced; 1 420 dived
Length, feet (metres): 258·5 (78·8)
Beam, feet (metres): 23 (7·0)
Draught, feet (metres): 15·2 (4·6)
Torpedo tubes: 4—21 in (533 mm); 10 torpedoes
Main machinery: 2 diesels, total 2 700 hp; 2 electric motors, total 5 900 hp
Speed, knots: 13 surfaced; 19 dived
Range, miles: 5 000 at 10 knots
Complement: 65

Ordered under the 1956 Programme. The first submarine built in a Japanese shipyard after the Second World War. First estimated to cost £2 718 000, but this figure was exceeded. Of double-hull construction.

OYASHIO   1972, Japanese Maritime Self-Defence Force

LIGHT FORCES

5 FAST ATTACK CRAFT—TORPEDO

Name	No.	Builders	Commissioned	
—	PT 11	Mitsubishi, Shimonoseki	27 Mar	1971
—	PT 12	Mitsubishi, Shimonoseki	28 Mar	1972
—	PT 13	Mitsubishi, Shimonoseki	16 Dec	1972
—	PT 14	Mitsubishi, Shimonoseki	15 Feb	1974
—	PT 15	Mitsubishi, Shimonoseki	10 July	1975

Displacement, tons: 100
Dimensions, feet (metres): 116·4 × 30·2 × 3·9 (35·5 × 9·2 × 1·2)
Guns: 2—40 mm
Tubes: 4—21 inch
Main engines: CODAG 2 Mitsubishi diesels; 2 IHI gas turbines; 3 shafts; 11 000 hp (PT 11; 10 500 hp) = 40 knots
Complement: 26-28

Laid down on 17 Mar 1970, 22 Apr 1971, 28 Mar 1972, 23 Mar 1973, and 23 Apr 1974 respectively. One more projected.

PT 13   1972, Ships of the World

9 COASTAL PATROL CRAFT

Name	No.	Builders	Commissioned
—	PB 19	Ishikawajima, Yokohama	31 Mar 1971
—	PB 20	Ishikawajima, Yokohama	31 Mar 1971
—	PB 21	Ishikawajima, Yokohama	31 Mar 1971
—	PB 22	Ishikawajima, Yokohama	31 Mar 1971
—	PB 23	Ishikawajima, Yokohama	31 Mar 1972
—	PB 24	Ishikawajima, Yokohama	31 Mar 1972
—	PB 25	Ishikawajima, Yokohama	29 Mar 1973
—	PB 26	Ishikawajima, Yokohama	29 Mar 1973
—	PB 27	Ishikawajima, Yokohama	29 Mar 1973

Displacement, tons: 18
Dimensions, feet (metres): 55·8 × 14·1 × 2·7 (17 × 4·3 × 0·8)
Gun: 1—20 mm
Main engines: 2 diesels; 760 hp = 20 knots
Complement: 6

GRP hulls.

PB 22   11/1975, Toshio Tamura

Name	No.	Builders	Commissioned
KOSOKU 6	ASH 06	Mitsubishi Shimonoseki	20 Mar 1967

Displacement, tons: 40
Dimensions, feet (metres): 75·9 × 18·2 × 3·3 (23·1 × 5·6 × 1)
Main engines: 3 diesels; 2 800 bhp = 30 knots

Of aluminium construction. Laid down on 28 June 1966 under the 1965 Programme. Launched 22 Nov 1966.

KOSOKU 6   1974, Japanese Maritime Self-Defence Force

AMPHIBIOUS FORCES

3 "MIURA" CLASS (LST)

Name	No.	Builders	Commissioned	
MIURA	4151	Ishikawajima, Tokyo	29 Jan	1975
OJIKA	4152	Ishikawajimi, Tokyo	22 Mar	1976
SATSUMA	4153	Ishikawajimi, Tokyo	Feb	1977

Displacement, tons: 2 000
Dimensions, feet (metres): 321·4 × 45·9 × 9·8 (98 × 14 × 3)
Guns: 2—3 in (76 mm) (twin); 2—40 mm (twin)
Main engines: 2 diesels; 2 shafts 4 400 hp = 14 knots
Complement: 115

Fitted with bow doors. Miura laid down 26 Nov 1973, launched 13 Aug 1974. Ojika laid down 10 June 1974, launched Sep 1975. Satsuma laid down 26 May 1975, launched May 1976. Carry 2 LCMs and 2 LCVPs.

OJIKA   1976

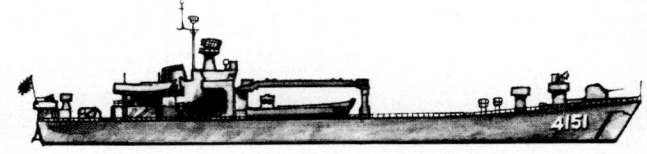

MIURA   1974, Japanese Maritime Self-Defence Force

3 "ATSUMI" CLASS (LST)

Name	No.	Builders	Commissioned
ATSUMI	4101	Sasebo Jyuko Co, Sasebo	27 Nov 1972
MOTOBU	4102	Sasebo Jyuko Co, Sasebo	21 Dec 1973
—	4103	Sasebo Jyuko Co, Sasebo	Oct 1977

Displacement, tons: 1 480 *(Atsumi)*; 1 550 *(Motobu)*
Dimensions, feet (metres): 291·9 × 42·6 × 8·5 *(89 × 13 × 2·7)*
Guns: 4—40 mm (twins)
Main engines: 2 diesels; 4 400 hp = 13 knots
Complement: 100 *(Atsumi)*; 95 *(Motobu)*

Atsumi laid down 7 Dec 1971, launched 13 June 1972. *Motobu* laid down 23 April 1973, launched 3 Aug 1973.

MOTOBU   *1974, Japanese Maritime Self-Defence Force*

MINE WARFARE FORCES

1 "SOUYA" CLASS MINELAYER

Name	No.	Builders	Laid down	Launched	Commissioned
SOUYA	951	Hitachi Zoosen, Maizuru	9 July 1970	31 Mar 1971	30 Sep 1971

Displacement, tons: 2 150 standard; 3 050 full load
Length, feet (metres): 324·8 *(99·0)*
Beam, feet (metres): 49·5 *(15·0)*
Draught, feet (metres): 13·9 *(4·2)*
Guns: 2—3 in *(76 mm)* 50 cal (1 twin); 2—20 mm
Torpedo tubes: 6 anti-submarine (2 triple)
Main engines: 4 diesels; 4 000 bhp; 2 shafts
Speed, knots: 18
Complement: 185

With twin rails can carry 200 buoyant mines. Has helicopter platform aft and acts at times as command ship for MCM forces.

SOUYA   *1974, Japanese Maritime Self-Defence Force*

1 MINESWEEPER SUPPORT SHIP

Name	No.	Builders	Commissioned
HAYASE	462	Ishikawajima, Haruna	6 Nov 1971

Displacement, tons: 2 000 standard
Length, feet (metres): 324·8 *(99·0)*
Beam, feet (metres): 42·7 *(13·0)*
Draught, feet (metres): 12·5 *(3·8)*
Guns: 2—3 in *(76 mm)* 50 cal, (1 twin); 2—20 mm
Torpedo tubes: 6 anti-submarine (2 triple)
Main engines: 2 diesels; 4 000 bhp; 2 shafts
Speed, knots: 18
Complement: 185

Laid down 16 Sep 1970, launched 21 June 1971. Has helicopter platform aft.

HAYASE   *1972, Japanese Maritime Self Defence Force*

NEW CONSTRUCTION MINESWEEPERS—COASTAL

Displacement, tons: 440 standard
Dimensions, feet (metres): 177·1 × 30·8 × 13·8 *(54 × 9·4 × 4·2)*
Gun: 1—20 mm
Main engines: 2 diesels; 2 shafts; 1 440 bhp = 14 knots

To be fitted with new S4 mine detonating equipment, a remote-controlled counter-mine charge.
First of class ordered under 1976 programme.

15 "KASADO" CLASS (MINESWEEPERS—COASTAL)

Name	No.	Builders	Commissioned
AMAMI	MSC 625	Nippon Steel Tube Co.	6 Mar 1967
CHIBURI	MSC 620	Hitachi, Kanagawa	25 Mar 1964
HARIO	MSC 618	Hitachi, Kanagawa	23 Mar 1963
HOTAKA	MSC 616	Hitachi, Kanagawa	24 Feb 1962
IBUKI	MSC 628	Hitachi, Kanagawa	27 Feb 1968
KARATO	MSC 617	Nippon Steel Tube Co	23 Mar 1963
KATSURA	MSC 629	Nippon Steel Tube Co	15 Feb 1968
KUDAKO	MSC 622	Hitachi, Kanagawa	24 Mar 1965
MINASE	MSC 627	Nippon Steel Tube Co.	25 Mar 1967
MUTSURE	MSC 619	Nippon Steel Tube Co.	24 Mar 1964
OOTSU	MSC 621	Nippon Steel Tube Co.	24 Feb 1965
REBUN	MSC 624	Hitachi, Kanagawa	24 Mar 1966
RISHIRI	MSC 623	Nippon Steel Tube Co	5 Mar 1966
SHIKINE	MSC 613	Nippon Steel Tube Co	15 Nov 1960
URUME	MSC 626	Hitachi, Kanagawa	30 Jan 1967

Displacement, tons: 330 standard; (380 later ships)
Dimensions, feet (metres): 150·9 × 28 × 7·5 *(46 × 8·5 × 2·3)*; 171·6 × 28·9 × 7·9 *(52·3 × 8·8 × 2·4)*
 later ships
Gun: 1—20 mm
Main engines: 2 diesels; 2 shafts; 1 200 bhp (1 440 later ships) = 14 knots

Originally a class of 28 ships. Hull is of wooden construction. Otherwise built of non-magnetic materials.

Surveying vessels: *Tatara* (ex-*MSC 610)* AGS 5113 and *Hirado* (ex-*MSC 614)* AGS 5114 transferred to surveying duties after conversion Mar 1976 as well as *Kasado* and *Habushi.*

Training ships: *Tsukumi* (ex-*MSC 611)* YAS 65 and *Mikura* (ex-*MSC 612)* YAS 66 transferred to training duties after conversion Mar 1976. Both originally commissioned April-May 1960.

SHIKINE   1972, Toshio Tamura

17 + 2 "TAKAMI" CLASS (MINEHUNTERS)

Name	No.	Builders	Commissioned
AWAJI	MSC 634	Hitachi, Kanagawa	29 Mar 1971
IOU	MSC 631	Nippon Steel Tube Co	22 Jan 1970
MIYAKE	MSC 632	Hitachi, Kanagawa	19 Nov 1970
MIYATO	MSC 639	Nippon Steel Tube Co	24 Aug 1973
MUROTSU	MSC 637	Nippon Steel Tube Co	3 Mar 1972
TAKAMI	MSC 630	Hitachi Kanagawa	15 Dec 1969
TASHIRO	MSC 638	Hitachi Kanagawa	30 July 1973
TEURI	MSC 636	Hitachi Kanagawa	10 Mar 1972
TOUSHI	MSC 635	Nippon Steel Tube Co	18 Mar 1971
UTONE	MSC 633	Nippon Steel Tube Co	3 Sep 1970
TAKANE	MSC 640	Hitachi Kanagawa	28 Aug 1974
MUZUKI	MSC 641	Nippon Steel Tube Co	28 Aug 1974
YOKOSE	MSC 642	Hitachi Kanagawa	15 Dec 1975
SAKATE	MSC 643	Nippon Steel Tube Co	17 Dec 1975
OUMI	MSC 644	Hitachi Kanagawa	Feb 1977
FUKUE	MSC 645	Nippon Steel Tube Co	Feb 1977
—	MSC 646	Hitachi Kanagawa	Sep 1977
—	MSC 647	Nippon Steel Tube Co	1977
—	MSC 648	Hitachi Kanagawa	1978

Of similar dimensions to "Kasado" class but of slightly different construction and with a displacement of 380 tons.
As minehunters fitted with mine-detecting sonar and carry four clearance divers.
Laid down dates: 646 in Sep 1976, 647 in Mar 1978, 648 in Mar 1978.

YOKOSE   12/1975, Hitachi, Kanagawa

MIYATO   1975, Toshio Tamura

1 "KOUZU" CLASS

Similar to "Kasado" class but has had minesweeping gear removed and was fitted as MCM command ship in June 1972.

4 "YASHIMA" CLASS

HASHIMA (ex-USS *AMS 95)* YAS 47
TOSHIMA (ex-USS *MSC 258)* YAS 61
TSUSHIMA (ex-USS *MSC,* ex-*AMS 255)* YAS 60
YASHIMA (ex-USS *AMS 144)* YAS 46

Displacement, tons: 335 standard; 375 full load
Dimensions, feet (metres): 138 pp; 144 oa × 26·5 × 8·3 *(42·1; 43·9 × 8·1 × 2·5)*
Gun: 1—20 mm
Main engines: 2 GM diesels; 880 bhp = 13 knots
Range, miles: 2 500 at 10 knots

Former US auxiliary minesweepers, *Hashima* and *Yashima* now used as accommodation ships. *Tsushima* and *Toshima* now act as auxiliaries.

6 "NANA-GO" CLASS (MSBs)

Name	No.	Builders	Commissioned
NANA-GO	707	Hitachi, Kanagawa	30 Mar 1973
HACHI-GO	708	Nippon Kokan, Tsurumi	27 Mar 1973
KYUU-GO	709	Hitachi, Kanagawa	28 Mar 1974
JYUU-GO	710	Nippon Kokan,Tsurumi	29 Mar 1974
JYUU-ICHI-GO	711	Hitachi, Kanagawa	10 May 1975
JYUU-NI-GO	712	Nippon Kokan, Tsurumi	22 Apr 1975

Displacement, tons: 53
Dimensions, feet (metres): 73·8 × 17·7 × 3·3 *(22·5 × 5·4 × 1)*
Main engines: 2 Mitsubishi diesels; 2 shafts; 480 hp = 11 knots
Complement: 10

Laid down 26 May 1972, 3 Aug 1972, 5 July 1973, 7 June 1973, 2 July 1974, respectively. 712 launched 27 Jan 1975.

JYUU-GO   3/1974, Toshio Tamura

SERVICE FORCES

Name	No.	Builders	Commissioned
AZUMA	ATS 4201	Maizuru Jyuko Co, Maizuru	26 Nov 1969

Displacement, tons: 1 950 standard; 2 500 full load
Length, feet (metres): 323·4 *(98·6)*
Beam, feet (metres): 42·7 *(13·0)*
Draught, feet (metres): 12·5 *(3·8)*
Aircraft: 1 helicopter, 3 jetdrones, 7 propeller drones
Gun: 1—3 in *(76 mm)* 50 cal
A/S weapons: 2 A/S Short Torpedo launchers
Main engines: 2 diesels; 2 shafts; 4 000 bhp
Speed, knots: 18
Complement: 185

Laid down on 15 July 1968, launched on 14 Apr 1969. Has drone hangar amidships.

AZUMA — *1974, Japanese Maritime Self-Defence Force*

Name	No.	Builders	Commissioned
KATORI	3501	Ishikawajima Harima, Tokyo	10 Sep 1969

Displacement, tons: 3 350 standard; 4 000 full load
Length, feet (metres): 422·4 *(128·0)*
Beam, feet (metres): 49·5 *(15·0)*
Draught, feet (metres): 14·6 *(4·3)*
Guns: 4—3 in *(76 mm)* 50 cal
A/S weapons: 1 four barrelled rocket launcher
Torpedo launchers: 6 (2 triple mounts) for homing torpedoes
Main engines: Geared turbines; 2 shafts; 20 000 shp
Range, miles: 7 000 at 18 knots
Speed, knots: 25
Complement: 460 (295 ship's company and 165 trainees)

Laid down 8 Dec 1967, launched on 19 Nov 1968. Provided with a landing deck aft for a helicopter and large auditorium for trainees amidships.

Radar: Search: SPS 12 Tactical: SPS 10

KATORI — *9/1975, Dr Giorgio Arra*

1 TRAINING SHIP

Name	No.	Builders	Commissioned
ERIMO	YAS 69	Uraga Dock Co.	28 Dec 1955

Displacement, tons: 630 standard
Dimensions, feet (metres): 210 × 26 × 8 *(64·1 × 7·9 × 2·4)*
Guns: 2—40 mm; 2—20 mm
A/S weapons: 1 Hedgehog; 2 K-guns; 2 DC racks
Main engines: Diesel; 2 shafts; 2 500 bhp = 18 knots
Complement: 80

Conversion to training Ship for EOD completed Mar 1976.

ERIMO (old pennant number) — *1970, Japanese Maritime Self-Defence Force*

2 Ex-"KASADO" CLASS

TSUKUMI (ex-*MSC 611*) YAS 65   **MIKURA** (ex-*MSC 612*) YAS 66

Both of "Kasado" class (see minewarfare section for details). Transferred to Training duties after conversion Mar 1976.

1 SUBMARINE RESCUE SHIP

Name	No.	Builders	Commissioned
FUSHIMI	ASR 402	Sumnitorno SB & Machinery Co	10 Feb 1970

Displacement, tons: 1 430 standard
Dimensions, feet (metres): 249·5 × 41 × 12 *(76·1 × 12·5 × 3·7)*
Main engines: 2 diesels; 1 shaft; 3 000 bhp = 16 knots
Complement: 100

Laid down on 5 Nov 1968, launched 10 Sep 1969. Has a rescue chamber and two recompression chambers.

FUSHIMI — *1972, Japanese Maritime Self-Defence Force*

1 SUBMARINE RESCUE SHIP

Name	No.	Builders	Commissioned
CHIHAYA	ASR 401	Mitsubishi Nippon Heavy Industries Co, Yokohama	15 Mar 1961

Displacement, tons: 1 340 standard
Dimensions, feet (metres): 239·5 × 39·3 × 12·7 *(73 × 12 × 3·9)*
Main engines: Diesels; 2 700 bhp = 15 knots
Complement: 90

Authorised under the 1959 programme. The first vessel of her kind to be built in Japan. Laid down on 15 Mar 1960. Launched on 4 Oct 1960. Has rescue chamber, 2 recompression chambers, four-point mooring equipment and a 12 ton derrick.

CHIHAYA — *1972, Japanese Maritime Self-Defence Force*

1 SALVAGE VESSEL

Name	No.	Builders	Commissioned
SHOBO	41	Azumo Zoosen, Yokosuka	28 Feb 1964

Displacement, tons: 45
Dimensions, feet (metres): 75 × 18 × 3·3 *(22·9 × 5·5 × 1)*
Main engines: 4 diesels; 3 shafts; Speed = 19 knots
Complement: 8

Four fixed fire hoses fitted.

1 CABLE LAYER

Name	No.	Builders	Commissioned
TSUGARU	ARC 481	Yokohama Shipyard & Engine Works	15 Dec 1955

Displacement, tons: 2 150 standard
Dimensions, feet (metres): 337·8 × 40·7 × 16 *(103 × 12·4 × 4·9)*
Guns: 2—20 mm
Main engines: 2 diesels; 2 shafts; 3 200 bhp = 13 knots
Complement: 103

Dual purpose cable layer and coastal minelayer. Built under the 1953 programme. Laid down on 18 Dec 1954. Launched on 19 July 1955. Converted to cable-layer 10 July 1969-30 April 1970 by Nippon Steel Tube Co.

TSUGARU   *1972, Toshio Tamura*

1 SUPPORT TANKER

Name	No.	Builders	Commissioned
HAMANA	411	Uraga Dock Co	10 Mar 1962

Displacement, tons: 2 900 light; 7 550 full load
Dimensions, feet (metres): 420 × 51·5 × 20·5 *(128·1 × 15·7 × 6·3)*
Guns: 2—40 mm
Main engines: 1 diesel; 5 000 bhp 1 shaft = 16 knots
Complement: 100

Built under the 1960 programme. Laid down on 17 Apr 1961, launched on 24 Oct 1961.

1 NEW CONSTRUCTION FLEET SUPPORT SHIP

Displacement, tons: 5 000
Dimensions, feet (metres): 459·3 × 62·3 × 35·4 *(140 × 19 × 10·8)*
Main engines: 2 diesels; 2 shafts; 20 000 bhp
Speed, knots: 22

Merchant type hull.

SURVEYING SHIPS

1 "AKASHI" CLASS (AGS)

Name	No.	Builders	Commissioned
AKASHI	5101	Nippon Steel Tube Co	25 Oct 1969

Displacement, tons: 1 420
Dimensions, feet (metres): 244·2 × 42·2 × 14·2 *(74·0 × 13·0 × 4·3)*
Main engines: 2 diesels; 2 shafts; 3 200 bhp
Speed, knots: 16
Range, miles: 16 500 at 14 knots
Complement: 65

Laid down 21 Sep 1968. Launched 30 May 1969.

AKASHI   *1974, Japanese Maritime Self-Defence Force*

1 NEW CONSTRUCTION

Displacement, tons: 2 000
Dimensions, feet (metres): 295·3 × 49·2 × 24·9 *(90 × 15 × 7·6)*
Main engines: 2 diesels; 2 shafts; 4 400 hp
Speed, knots: 16

Similar (but larger) to "Akashi" class.

4 Ex-"KASADO" CLASS (AGS)

ICHI-GO (ex-*Kasado*) 5111   **SAN-GO** (ex-*Tatara*) 5113
NI-GO (ex-*Habushi*) 5112   **YON-GO** (ex-*Hirado*) 5114

Displacement, tons: 340
Dimensions, feet (metres): 150·9 × 28 × 7·5 *(46 × 8·5 × 2·3)*
Main engines: 2 diesels; 2 shafts; 1 200 bhp = 14 knots

Converted MSCs.

TENDERS

5 "500 TON" CLASS

Name	Laid down	Launched	Commissioned
YAS 101	10 Oct 1967	18 Jan 1968	30 Mar 1968
YAS 102	25 Sep 1968	20 Dec 1968	31 Mar 1969
YAS 103	2 Apr 1971	24 May 1971	30 Sep 1971
YAS 104	4 Feb 1972	15 June1972	13 Sep 1972
YAS 105	20 Feb 1973	16 July 1973	19 Sep 1973

Displacement, tons: 500
Dimensions, feet (metres): 171·6 × 33·0 × 8·3 *(52·3 × 10·1 × 2·5)*
Main engines: 2 diesels; 2 shafts; 1 600 bhp = 14 knots

Training support and rescue.

YAS 101

1975, Japanese Maritime Self-Defence Force

7 Ex-"KASADO" CLASS

Name	No.	Builders	Commissioned
ATADA (ex-*MSC 601*)	YAS 56	Hitachi, Kanagawa	30 Apr 1956
ITSUKI (ex-*MSC 602*)	YAS 57	Hitachi, Kanagawa	20 June 1956
YASHIRO (ex-*MSC 603*)	YAS 58	Nippon Steel Tube Co	10 July 1956
SHISAKA (ex-*MSC 605*)	YAS 62	Nippon Steel Tube Co	16 Aug 1958
KOSHIKI (ex-*MSC 615*)	YAS 63	Nippon Steel Tube Co	29 Jan 1962
SAKITO (ex-*MSC 607*)	YAS 64	Nippon Steel Tube Co	25 Aug 1959
KANAWA (ex-*MSC 606*)	YAS 65	Hitachi, Kanagawa	24 July 1959

Details as for "Kasado" class under Minewarfare Forces.

ICEBREAKER

Name	No.	Builders	Commissioned
FUJI	5001	Nippon Steel Tube Co	15 July 1965

Displacement, tons: 5 250 standard; 7 760 normal; 8 838 full load
Dimensions, feet (metres): 328 × 72·2 × 29 *(100 × 22 × 8·8)*
Aircraft: 3 helicopters
Main engines: 4 diesel-electric; 2 shafts; 12 000 bhp = 17 knots
Oil fuel, tons: 1 900
Range, miles: 15 000 at 15 knots
Complement: 200 plus 35 scientists and observers

Antarctic Support Ship. Laid down on 28 Aug 1964, launched on 18 Mar 1965. Hangar and flight deck aft. Can cope with ice up to 8·5 feet *(2·5 metres)*.

FUJI

1975, Japanese Maritime Self-Defence Force

MARITIME SAFETY AGENCY

Establishment

Established in May 1948 to carry out patrol and rescue duties as well as hydrographic and research tasks.

Commandant: Yasuhiko Sonomura

Personnel:

1976: 11 203

Strength of the Fleet

	Active
Large Patrol Vessels	10
Medium Patrol Vessels	50
Small Patrol Vessels	31
Patrol Craft	209
Survey Vessels	6
Surveying Launches	21
Tenders	5
Underwater Research Vessel	1
Firefighting Craft	9
Salvage Craft	2
Utility Launches	14

DELETIONS

1975 *Abukuma, Fuji, Ishikari, Isuzu, Kikuchi, Kuzuryu, Oyodo, Tenryu* ("Fuji", later "Sagami" class small patrol vessels)
Suzunami, Hayanami, Hatagumo, Makigumo, Tatsugumo (Patrol Craft)
CS 57, 58, 115 (harbour patrol craft)
FS 01, 02, 04, 05, 06 (Salvage Craft)

LARGE PATROL VESSELS

2 "IZU" CLASS

Name	No.	Builders	Commissioned
IZU	PL 31	—	July 1967
MIURA	PL 32	Maizuru Jukogyo Ltd	Mar 1969

Displacement, tons: 2 080 normal
Dimensions, feet (metres): 313·3 oa × 38 × 12·8 (95·6 × 11·6 × 3·9)
Main engines: 2 diesels; 2 shafts; 10 400 bhp = 21·6 knots
Range, miles: 14 500 at 12·7 knots; 5 000 at 21 knots
Complement: 72

Izu was laid down in Aug 1966, launched in Jan 1967. *Miura* was laid down in May 1968, launched in Oct 1968. Employed in long range rescue and patrol and weather observation duties. Equipped with weather observation radar, various types of marine instruments. Ice strengthened hull.

MIURA   1970, Japanese Maritime Safety Agency

4 "ERIMO" CLASS

Name	No.	Builders	Commissioned
DAIO	PL 15	Hitachi Maizuru	28 Sep 1973
ERIMO	PL 13	Hitachi Zoosen Co Ltd	30 Nov 1965
MUROTO	PL 16	Naikai Zoosen Co Ltd	30 Nov 1974
SATSUMA	PL 14	Hitachi Zoosen Co Ltd	30 July 1966

Displacement, tons: 1 009 normal (1 206 *Daio*)
Dimensions, feet (metres): 251·3 oa × 30·2 × 9·9 (31·5 × 10·7 *Daio*) (76·6 × 9·2 × 3) (9·6 × 3·3 *Daio*)
Guns: 1—3 in 50 cal; 1—20 mm (1—40 mm; 1—20 mm *Daio*)
Main engines: Diesels; 2 shafts; 4 800 bhp = 19·78 knots (7 000 bhp CP propellers = 20 knots, *Daio*)
Range, miles: 5 000 at 17 knots

Erimo was laid down on 29 Mar 1965 and launched on 14 Aug 1965. Her structure is strengthened against ice. Employed as a patrol vessel off northern Japan. *Satsuma*, is assigned to guard and rescue south of Japan. *Daio* was laid down 18 Oct 1972 and launched 19 June 1973. *Muroto* was laid down 15 Mar 1974 and launched 5 Aug 1974.

DAIO   1973, Japanese Maritime Safety Agency

Name	No.	Builders	Commissioned
KOJIMA	PL 21	Kure Zoosen	21 May 1964

Displacement, tons: 1 206
Dimensions, feet (metres): 228·3 oa × 33·8 × 10·5 (69·6 × 10·3 × 3·2)
Guns: 1—3 in; 1—40 mm; 1—20 mm
Main engines: Diesels; 2 600 hp = 17 knots
Range, miles: 6 000 at 13 knots
Complement: 17 officers, 42 men, 47 cadets

Maritime Safety Agency training ship.

KOJIMA   1965, Japanese Maritime Safety Agency

2 "NOJIMA" CLASS

Name	No.	Builders	Commissioned
NOJIMA	PL 11	Uraga Dock Co Ltd	30 April 1962
OJIKA	PL 12	Uraga Dock Co Ltd	10 June 1963

Displacement, tons: 950 standard; 1 009 normal; 1 113 full load
Dimensions, feet (metres): 208·8 pp; 226·5 oa × 30·2 × 10·5 (63·7; 69·1 × 9·2 × 3·2)
Main engines: 2 sets diesels; 3 000 bhp = 17·5 knots
Complement: 51

Nojima laid down on 27 Oct 1961, launched on 12 Feb 1962. Both employed as patrol vessels and weather ships.

OJIKA   1972, Japanese Maritime Safety Agency

SOYA PL 107

Displacement, tons: 4 364 normal; 4 818 full load
Dimensions, feet (metres): 259·2 wl × 51·9 (including bulge) × 18·9 (79·1 × 15·8 × 5·8)
Main engines: 2 sets diesels; 4 800 bhp = 12·5 knots on trials
Range, miles: 10 000 at 12 knots
Complement: 96

Assigned to guard and rescue service.

SOYA   1970, Japanese Maritime Safety 7

MEDIUM PATROL VESSELS

10 "BIHORO" CLASS

Name	No.	Builders	Commissioned
ABUKUMA	PM 79	Tohoku Zoosen	Jan 1976
BIHORO	PM 73	Tohoku Zoosen	28 Feb 1974
FUJI	PM 75	Usuki Tekko	Feb 1975
ISHIKARI	PM 78	Tohoku Zoosen	Mar 1976
ISUZU	PM 80	Naikai Zoosen	Mar 1976
KABASHIMA	PM 76	Usuki Tekko	Mar 1975
KIKUCHI	PM 81	Usuki Tekko	Feb 1976
KUMA	PM 74	Usuki Tekko	28 Feb 1974
KUZURYU	PM 82	Usuki Tekko	Mar 1976
SADO	PM 77	Tohoku Zoosen	Feb 1975

Displacement, tons: 636 standard; 657 full load
Dimensions, feet (metres): 208 × 25·6 × 8·3 (63·4 × 7·8 × 2·5)
Gun: 1—20 mm
Main engines: Diesels; 2 shafts; 3 000 hp = 18 knots
Range, miles: 3 200 at 18 knots
Complement: 34

KUMA

1974, Japanese Maritime Safety Agency

3 "MIYAKE" CLASS

Name	No.	Builders	Commissioned
AWAJI	PM 71	—	25 Jan 1973
MIYAKE	PM 70	—	25 Jan 1973
YAEYAMA	PM 72	—	20 Dec 1972

Displacement, tons: 530 standard; 574 full load
Dimensions, feet (metres): 190·4 oa × 24·2 × 8·2 (58·1 × 7·4 × 2·5)
Gun: 1—20 mm
Main engines: Diesels; 2 shafts; cp propellers; 3 200 hp = 17·8 knots
Range, miles: 3 580 at 16 knots
Complement: 40

Of similar hull design to "Kunashiri" class.

MIYAKE

1973, Japanese Maritime Safety Agency

4 "KUNASHIRI" CLASS

Name	No.	Builders	Commissioned
KAMISHIMA	PM 68	—	1972
KUNASHIRI	PM 65	Maizuru Jukogyo Ltd	Mar 1969
MINABE	PM 66	—	Mar 1970
SAROBETSO	PM 67	—	1971

Displacement, tons: 498 normal
Dimensions, feet (metres): 190·4 oa × 24·2 × 7·9 (58·1 × 7·4 × 2·4)
Gun: 1—20 mm
Main engines: 2 sets diesels; 2 600 bhp = 17·6 knots
Range, miles: 3 000 at 16·9 knots
Complement: 40

Kunashiri was laid down in Oct 1968 and launched in Dec 1968. *Minabe* was laid down in Oct 1969.

KUNASHIRI

1970, Japanese Maritime Safety Agency

5 "CHIFURI" CLASS

CHIFURI PM 18   KOZU PM 20   SHIKINE PM 21
DAITO PM 22   KUROKAMI PM 19

Displacement, tons: 465 standard; 483 normal
Dimensions, feet (metres): 182·7 oa × 25·2 × 8·5 (55·9 × 7·7 × 2·6)
Guns: 1—3 in 50 cal; 1—20 mm
Main engines: 2 sets diesels; 1 300 bhp = 15·8 knots
Range, miles: 3 000 at 12 knots

DAITO

1970, Japanese Maritime Safety Agency

14 "REBUN" CLASS

AMAKUSA PM 09   HIRADO PM 17   NOTO PM 13
GENKAI PM 07   IKI PM 05   OKI PM 06
HACHIJO PM 08   KOSHIKI PM 16   OKUSHIRI PM 10
HEKURA PM 14   KUSAKAKI PM 11 REBUN PM 04
                 MIKURA PM 15   RISHIRI PM 12

Displacement, tons: 450 standard; 488 trials; 495 normal
Dimensions, feet (metres): 155·2 pp; 164 wl; 171·9 oa × 26·5 × 8·5 (47·3; 50; 52·4 × 8·1 × 2·6)
Guns: 1—3 in 50 cal; 1—20 mm
Main engines: 2 sets diesels; 1 300 bhp = 15 knots
Range, miles: 3 000 at 12 knots

A development of the original "Awaji" class design. All completed in 1951.

HIRADO

1972, Japanese Maritime Safety Agency

5 "MATSUURA" CLASS

Name	No.	Builders	Commissioned
AMAMI	PM 62	Hitachi Zoosen Co Ltd	29 Mar 1965
KARATSU	PM 64	Hitachi Zoosen Co Ltd	31 Mar 1967
MATSUURA	PM 60	Osaka Shipbuilding Co Ltd	18 Mar 1961
NATORI	PM 63	Hitachi Zoosen Co Ltd	1966
SENDAI	PM 61	Osaka Shipbuilding Co Ltd	21 April 1962

MATSUURA   1970, Japanese Maritime Safety Agency

Displacement, tons: 420 standard; 425 normal
Dimensions, feet (metres): 163·3 pp; 181·5 oa × 23 × 7·5 *(49·8; 55·4 × 7 × 2·3)*
Gun: 1—20 mm
Main engines: 2 sets diesels; 1 400 bhp = 16·5 knots *(Matsuura, Sendai)*;
  1 800 bhp = 16·8 knots *(Amami, Natori)*; 2 600 bhp *(Karatsu)*
Range, miles: 3 500 at 12 knots
Complement: 37

Matsuura was laid down on 16 Oct 1960, launched on 24 Dec 1960. *Sendai* was laid down on 23 Aug 1961, launched on 18 Jan 1962.

7 "YAHAGI" CLASS

Name	No.	Builders	Commissioned
CHITOSE	PM 56	Niigata Engineering Co Ltd	30 April 1958
HORONAI	PM 59	Niigata Engineering Co Ltd	4 Feb 1961
OKINAWA	PM 69	Niigata Engineering Co Ltd	—
SORACHI	PM 57	Niigata Engineering Co Ltd	Mar 1959
SUMIDA	PM 55	Niigata Engineering Co Ltd	30 June 1957
YAHAGI	PM 54	Niigata Engineering Co Ltd	31 July 1956
YUBARI	PM 58	Niigata Engineering Co Ltd	15 Mar 1960

SORACHI   1972, Japanese Maritime Safety Agency

Displacement, tons: 333·15 standard; 375·7 normal
Dimensions, feet (metres): 147·3 pp; 164·9 oa × 24 × 7·4 *(44·9; 50·3 × 7·3 × 2·3)*
Gun: 1—40 mm
Main engines: 2 sets diesels; 1 400 bhp = 15·5 knots
Range, miles: 3 500 at 12 knots
Complement: 37

Yahagi was laid down on 9 Dec 1955, launched on 19 May 1956. *Chitose* was laid down on 20 Sep 1957, launched on 24 Feb 1958.

Name	No.	Builders	Commissioned
TESHIO	PM 53	Uraga Dock Co Ltd	19 Mar 1955

Displacement, tons: 421·5 normal
Dimensions, feet (metres): 149·4 pp; 165 oa × 23 × 8·2 *(45·6; 50·3 × 7 × 2·5)*
Gun: 1—40 mm
Main engines: 2 sets diesels; 1 400 bhp = 15·71 knots
Range, miles: 3 800 at 12 knots
Complement: 37

Laid down on 15 Sep 1954, launched on 12 Jan 1955.

2 "TOKACHI" CLASS

Name	No.	Builders	Commissioned
TATSUTA	PM 52	—	10 Sep 1954
TOKACHI	PM 51	Harima Dockyard, Kure	31 July 1954

TOKACHI   1972, Japanese Maritime Safety Agency

Displacement, tons: 336 standard; 381 normal *(Tokachi)*
  324 standard; 369 normal *(Tatsuta)*
Dimensions, feet (metres): 157·5 pp; 164 wl; 170 oa × 21·9 × 11·2 *(48; 50; 51·9 × 6·7 × 3·4)*
Gun: 1—40 mm
Main engines: 2 sets of 4 cycle single acting diesels
  1 500 bhp = 16 knots *(Tokachi)*
  1 400 bhp = 15 knots *(Tatsuta)*
Range, miles: 3 800 at 12 knots
Complement: 37

Tokachi was laid down on 14 Nov 1953, launched on 8 May 1954.

SMALL PATROL VESSELS

3 "NAGARA" CLASS

KITAKAMI PS 20   **NAGARA** PS 18   **TONE** PS 19

Displacement, tons: 296
Dimensions, feet (metres): 133·4 oa × 23 × 7·2 *(40·7 × 7 × 2·2)*
Gun: 1—40 mm
Main engines: 2 diesels; 2 shafts; 800 bhp = 13·5 knots
Range, miles: 2 000 at 12 knots
Complement: 35

Improved versions of the "Sagami" class. All launched and completed in 1952.

NAGARA   1970, Japanese Maritime Safety Agency

8 "SAGAMI" CLASS

CHIKUGO PS 16	MOGAMI PS 11	SHINANO PS 15
KISO PS 14	NOSHIRO PS 13	YOSHINO PS 12
KUMANO PS 17	SAGAMI PS 05	

Displacement, tons: 258 standard; 275 normal
Dimensions, feet (metres): 122 pp; 126·3 wl; 132·2 oa × 23 × 7·5 *(37·2; 38·5; 40·3 × 7 × 2·3)*
Gun: 1—40 mm
Main engines: 2 sets diesels; 800 bhp = 13·6 knots
Range, miles: 2 000 at 12 knots
Complement: 35

Built in the early 1950s.

MOGAMI

1970, Japanese Maritime Safety Agency

14 "HIDAKA" CLASS

Name	No.	Builders	Commissioned
ASHITAKA	PS 43	—	1967
AKIYOSHI	PS 37	—	1965
HIDAKA	PS 32	Azuma Shipbuilding Co	23 April 1962
HIYAMA	PS 33	Hitachi Shipbuilding Co	Mar 1963
IBUKI	PS 45	—	1967
KAMUI	PS 41	—	1966
KUNIMI	PS 38	Hayashikane Shipbuilding & Engineering Co, Shimoneseki	15 Feb 1965
KURAMA	PS 44	—	1967
NOBARU	PS 49	—	1968
ROKKO	PS 35	—	1965
TAKANAWA	PS 36	—	1965
TAKATSUKI	PS 39	—	1966
TOUMI	PS 46	—	1968
TSURUGI	PS 34	Hitachi Shipbuilding Co	Mar 1963

Displacement, tons: 166·2 to 164·4 standard; 169·4 normal
Dimensions, feet (metres): 100 pp; 111 oa × 20·8 × 5·5 *(30·5; 33·8 × 6·3 × 1·7)*
Main engines: 1 set diesels; 1 shaft; 690 to 700 bhp = 13·5 knots
Range, miles: 1 200 at 12 knots

ASHITAKA

1972, Japanese Maritime Safety Agency

Hidaka was laid down on 4 Oct 1961, launched on 2 Mar 1962. *Kunimi* was built under the 1964 programme, laid down on 15 Nov 1964, launched on 19 Dec 1964.

COASTAL PATROL CRAFT

Name	No.	Builders	Commissioned
TSUKUBA	PS 31	Hitachi Zoosen, Kanagawa	30 May 1962

Displacement, tons: 65
Dimensions, feet (metres): 80·5 × 21·5 × 3·7 *(24·6 × 6·6 × 1·1)*
Main engines: 2 Niigata diesels; 1 800 bhp = 18 knots
Range, miles: 230 at 15 knots

Name	No.	Builders	Commissioned
ASAMA	PS 47	Shimonoseki Shipyard & Engine Works	Feb 1969
BIZAN	PS 42	Shimonoseki Shipyard & Engine Works	Mar 1966
SHIRAMINE	PS 48	Shimonoseki Shipyard & Engine Works	Dec 1969

Displacement, tons: 40 normal; *Shiramine* 48 normal
Dimensions, feet (metres): 85·3 oa × 18·3 × 2·8 *(26 × 5·6 × 0·9)*
Gun: 1 MG aft
Main engines: 2 Mitsubishi diesels; 1 140 bhp = 21·6 knots. *Shiramine*, 2 Benz (MTU) diesels; 2 200 bhp = 25 knots
Range, miles: 400 at 18 knots; *Shiramine* 250 at 25 knots

Of light metal construction.

SHIRAMINE

1972, Japanese Maritime Safety Agency

Name	No.	Builders	Commissioned
AKAGI	PS 40	Hitachi Zoosen, Kanagawa	1965

Displacement, tons: 42
Dimensions, feet (metres): 78·8 oa × 17·8 × 3·2 *(24·0 × 5·4 × 1)*
Main engines: 2 Mercedes Benz diesels; 2 200 bhp = 28 knots
Range, miles: 350 at 21 knots

3 "YAEGUMO" CLASS

ASAGUMO PC 34   NATSUGUMO PC 35   YAEGUMO PC 33

Displacement, tons: 42
Dimensions, feet (metres): 69 × 17·2 × 3·2 (21 × 5·2 × 1)
Main engines: 2 Diesels; 1 400 bhp = 20·5 knots

Completed in 1954-55. Wooden hulls.

3 "HANAYUKI" CLASS

Name	No.	Builders	Commissioned
HANAYUKI	PC 37	—	Mar 1959
MINEYUKI	PC 38	—	Mar 1959
ISOYUKI	PC 39	—	Feb 1960

Displacement, tons: 46
Dimensions, feet (metres): 72 oa × 17·6 × 3·2 (22 × 5·4 × 1)
Main engines: 3 diesels; 1 500 bhp = 20·7 knots (Hanayuki)
2 diesels; 1 800 bhp = 21·3 knots (Isoyuki)

Of light wooden hulls.

6 "AKIZUKI" CLASS

Name	No.	Builders	Commissioned
AKIZUKI	PC 64	Mitsubishi Heavy Industries Co Ltd	28 Feb 1974
HATAGUMO	PC 76	Mitsubishi Heavy Industries Co Ltd	Feb 1976
ISEYUKI	PC 73	Mitsubishi Heavy Industries Co Ltd	July 1975
MAKIGUMO	PC 75	Mitsubishi Heavy Industries Co Ltd	Mar 1976
SHINONOME	PC 65	Mitsubishi Heavy Industries Co Ltd	28 Feb 1974
YURAYUKI	PC 72	Mitsubishi Heavy Industries Co Ltd	May 1975

Displacement, tons: 74
Dimensions, feet (metres): 83·5 oa × 20·7 × 9·8 (26 × 8·2 × 3)
Main engines: 3 Mitsubishi diesels; 3 000 bhp = 22·1 knots
Range, miles: 220 at 22 knots
Complement: 10

AKIZUKI   1974, Japanese Maritime Safety Agency

14 "MATSUYUKI" CLASS

Name	No.	Builders	Commissioned
MATSUYUKI	PC 40	Hitachi Kanagawa	1964
SHIMAYUKI	PC 41	Hitachi Kanagawa	1964
TAMAYUKI	PC 42	Hitachi Kanagawa	1965
HAMAYUKI	PC 43	Hitachi Kanagawa	1965
YAMAYUKI	PC 44	Hitachi Kanagawa	1966
KOMAYUKI	PC 45	Hitachi Kanagawa	1966
UMIGIRI	PC 46	Hitachi Kanagawa	1967
ASAGIRI	PC 47	Hitachi Kanagawa	1967
HAMAGIRI	PC 48	Hitachi Kanagawa	1968
SAGIRI	PC 49	Hitachi Kanagawa	1968
SETOGIRI	PC 50	Hitachi Kanagawa	1969
HAYAGIRI	PC 51	Hitachi Kanagawa	1969
HAMANAMI	PC 52	Hitachi Kanagawa	1970
MATSUNAMI	PC 53	Hitachi Kanagawa	1970

Displacement, tons: 40-60 tons
Dimensions, feet (metres): 69 oa × 16·6 × 3·2 (21 × 5·1 × 1)
Gun: 1—13 mm
Main engines: 2 Mercedes Benz (MTU) diesels; 2 200 bhp = 26·3 knots;
PC 48 1 140 bhp = 14·6 knots; PC 52 = 21·8 knots; PC 53 = 20·8 knots
Range, miles: About 300 miles at near maximum speed
Complement: 10

Since 1964 two or three craft of this type have been built per year by Hitachi Kanagawa Dockyard; PCs 40-47 and 49-51 were built of light alloy frames with wooden hulls. PCs 48 and 52 were built of steel; PC 53 was built completely of light alloy.

17 "SHIKINAMI" CLASS

Name	No.	Builders	Commissioned
ASOYUKI	PC 74	Hitachi Kanagawa	1975
HARUZUKI	PC 61	Hitachi Kanagawa	1972
ISENAMI	PC 57	Mitsubishi Shimonoseki	1971
KIYONAMI	PC 69	Mitsubishi Shimonoseki	1974
KIYOZUKI	PC 62	Hitachi Kanagawa	1973
MINEGUMO	PC 68	Mitsubishi Shimonoseki	1973
MOCHIZUKI	PC 60	Hitachi Kanagawa	1972
MUTSUKI	PC 59	Mitsubishi Shimonoseki	1972
OKINAMI	PC 70	Hitachi Kanagawa	1974
SHIKINAMI	PC 54	Mitsubishi Shimonoseki	1971
TAKANAMI	PC 58	Mitsubishi Shimonoseki	1972
TAMANAMI	PC 67	Hitachi Kanagawa	1973
TOMONAMI	PC 55	Hitachi Kanagawa	1971
URANAMI	PC 66	Mitsubishi Shimonoseki	1973
URAZUKI	PC 63	Hitachi Kanagawa	1973
WAKAGUMO	PC 71	Mitsubishi Shimonoseki	1974
WAKANAMI	PC 56	Hitachi Kanagawa	1971

Displacement, tons: 44
Dimensions, feet (metres): 69 oa × 17·4 × 3·2 (21 × 5·3 × 1)
Main engines: 2 Mercedes Benz (MTU) Diesels; 2 200 bhp = 26·5 knots
Range, miles: 280 miles at near maximum speed
Complement: 10

Built completely of light alloy.

KIYONAMI   1973, Japanese Maritime Safety Agency

CL 21—154, 301—319

Displacement, tons: 20·2 full load
Dimensions, feet (metres): 49·2 × 13·5 × 3·1 (15 × 4·1 × 1)
Main engines: Diesels; 2 shafts; 520 bhp = 19 knots
Range, miles: 160 at 15 knots

For coastal patrol and rescue duties. Since 1971 about 20 of this class, built of high tensile steel, have been delivered each year.

14 HARBOUR PATROL CRAFT

CS 100, 105, 107, 108, 116—120, 122—126

153 15 METRE MOTOR LAUNCH TYPE

CL 127   1973, Japanese Maritime Safety Agency

SURVEYING VESSELS

Name	No.	Builders	Commissioned
SHOYO	HL 01	Hitachi Zoosen, Maizuru	Mar 1972

Displacement, tons: 2 000
Dimensions, feet (metres): 262·4 × 40·3 × 13·8 *(80 × 12·3 × 4·2)*
Main engines: 2 Fuji V-12; 4 800 hp; 1 shaft = 17·4 knots
Complement: 73

Launched 18 Sep 1971. Fully equipped for all types of hydrographic and oceanographic work.

SHOYO

1973, Japanese Maritime Safety Agency

Name	No.	Builders	Commissioned
TENYO	HM 05	—	—

Displacement, tons: 171
Dimensions, feet (metres): 99·1 oa × 19·2 × 9·2 *(30·2 × 5·9 × 2·8)*
Main engines: Diesels; 230 bhp = 10 knots
Range, miles: 3 160 at 10 knots

Name	No.	Builders	Commissioned
HEIYO	HM 04	Shimuzu Dockyard, Nipponkokan Kabushiki Kaisha	Mar 1955

Displacement, tons: 69
Dimensions, feet (metres): 76·5 oa × 14·5 × 8 *(23·3 × 4·4 × 2·4)*
Main engines: Diesel; 150 bhp = 9 knots
Range, miles: 670 at 9 knots

Name	No.	Builders	Commissioned
MEIYO	HL 03	Nagoya Shipbuilding & Engineering Co, Nagoya	15 Mar 1963

Displacement, tons: 486 normal
Measurement, tons: 360 gross
Dimensions, feet (metres): 133 wl; 146 oa × 26·5 × 9·5 *(40·6; 44·5 × 8·1 × 2·9)*
Main engines: 1 set diesel; 700 bhp = 12 knots
Range, miles: 5 000 at 11 knots
Complement: 40

Laid down on 14 Sep 1962, launched 22 Dec 1962. Controllable pitch propeller.

MEIYO

1971, Japanese Maritime Safety Agency

Name	No.	Builders	Commissioned
TAKUYO	HL 02	Niigata Engineering Co Ltd	March 1957

Displacement, tons: 880 standard
Dimensions, feet (metres): 204·7 oa × 31·2 × 10·7 *(62·4 × 9·5 × 3·3)*
Main engines: 2 sets diesels; 1 300 bhp = 14 knots
Range, miles: 8 000 at 12 knots

Laid down on 19 May 1956, launched on 19 Dec 1956.

TAKUYO

1971, Japanese Maritime Safety Agency

Name	No.	Builders	Commissioned
KAIYO	HM 06	Nagoya Shipbuilding & Engineering Co, Nagoya	14 Mar 1964

Displacement, tons: 378 normal
Dimensions, feet (metres): 132·5 wl; 146 oa × 26·5 × 7·8 *(40·4; 44·5 × 8·1 × 2·4)*
Main engines: 1 set diesels; 450 bhp = 12 knots
Range, miles: 6 100 at 11 knots

Controllable pitch propeller.

KAIYO

1972, Japanese Maritime Safety Agency

Note. There are 21 surveying launches of 5-8 tons.

TENDERS

Name	No.	Builders	Commissioned
MYOJO	LM 11	—	Mar 1974

Displacement, tons: 318 normal
Dimensions, feet (metres): 88·6 oa × 39·4 × 8·8 *(27 × 12 × 2·7)*
Main engines: 2 sets diesels; 600 bhp = 11·1 knots
Range, miles: 1 360 at 10 knots

Completed in Mar 1974 to replace an identical ship of the same name, completed in 1967, which was lost in collision April 1972. Catamaran type buoy tender, propelled by controllable pitch propeller, this ship is employed in maintenance and position adjustment service to floating aids to navigation.
There are also 8 LMs for the same maintenance service, 87 LSs and 18 HSs.

Name	No.	Builders	Commissioned
WAKASUKA	LL 01	Hitachi Inoshima Dockyard	Mar 1946

Displacement, tons: 1 760 normal
Dimensions, feet (metres): 226·4 oa × 32·2 × 19·1 *(69·1 × 9·8 × 5·8)*
Main engines: 2 100 hp

Purchased from Osaka Shosen Kaisha in Jan 1956. Rated as Navigation Aid Vessel (Lighthouse Supply Ship).

WAKASUKA   *1971, Japanese Maritime Safety Agency*

Name	No.	Builders	Commissioned
GINGA	LL 12	Osaka Shipbuilding Co Ltd	30 June 1954

Displacement, tons: 500
Dimensions, feet (metres): 135·5 oa × 31·2 × 13·9 *(41·3 × 9·4 × 4·2)*
Main engines: 2 diesels; 420 bhp = 11·26 knots
Range, miles: 2 800 at 10 knots

Ginga was laid down on 11 Nov 1953 and launched on 6 May 1954. Equipped with 15 ton derrick for laying buoys. Rated as Navigation Aid Vessel (Buoy Tender).

GINGA   *1971, Japanese Maritime Safety Agency*

2 NAVIGATION AID VESSELS (BUOY TENDERS)

HOKUTO LL 11   **KAIO** LL 13

There are also 9 LMs (LM 101 to LM 109) and 15 navigation and buoy tenders for miscellaneous service.

UNDERWATER RESEARCH VESSEL

Name	No.	Builders	Commissioned
SHINKAI	HU 06	Kawasaki Heavy Industries Ltd	Mar 1969

Displacement, tons: 91
Dimensions, feet (metres): 54·2 oa × 18·1 × 13 *(16·5 × 5·5 × 4)*
Main engines: 1 set electric motors; 11 kW
Range, miles: 4·6 at 2·3 knots
Complement: 4

SHINKAI   *1970, Japanese Maritime Safety Agency*

Laid down in Sep 1967, launched in Mar 1968. An underwater vehicle designed for carrying out research on biological and underground resources of the continental shelves. With a main propeller and two auxiliary ones installed on each side of the hull, this ship can dive to 2 000 feet and stay on the sea bed for sampling, observing and photographing.

FIRE FIGHTING CRAFT

3 "HIRYU" CLASS

Name	No.	Builders	Commissioned
HIRYU	FL 01	Nippon Kokan Kabushiki Kaisha, Asano Dockyard	4 Mar 1969
NANRYU	FL 03	Nippon Kokan Kabushiki Kaisha, Asano Dockyard	4 Mar 1971
SHORYU	FL 02	Nippon Kokan Kabushiki Kaisha, Asano Dockyard	4 Mar 1970

Displacement, tons: 251 normal
Dimensions, feet (metres): 90·2 oa × 34·1 × 7·2 *(27·5 × 10·4 × 2·2)*
Main engines: 2 sets diesels; 2 200 bhp = 13·5 knots
Range, miles: 395 at 13·4 knots
Complement: 14

Hiryu, a catamaran type fire boat, was laid down in Oct 1968, launched 21 Jan 1969. Designed and built for firefighting services to large tankers. *Shoryu* was launched on 18 Jan 1970, and *Nanryu* was launched on 16 Jan 1971.

HIRYU   *1970, Japanese Maritime Safety Agency*

6 "NUNOBIKI" CLASS

Name	No.	Builders	Commissioned	
KOTOBIKI	FM 05	Yokohama Yacht Co Ltd	Jan	1976
NACHI	FM 06	Sumidagawa Zoosen	Feb	1976
NUNOBIKI	FM 01	Yokohama Yacht Co Ltd		1974
OTOWA	FM 03	Sumidagawa Zoosen	Dec	1974
SHIRAITO	FM 04	Yokohama Yacht Co Ltd	Feb	1975
YODO	FM 02	Yokohama Yacht Co Ltd	Mar	1975

Displacement, tons: 87
Dimensions, feet (metres): 75·4 oa × 19·7 × 10·5 *(23 × 6 × 3·2)*
Main engines: 1 Mercedes-Benz (MTU) diesel plus 2 Nissan diesels; 1 100 bhp + 500 bhp = 14 knots
Range, miles: 180 at 14 knots
Complement: 12

SALVAGE CRAFT

FS 03 and **FS 07** for fire-fighting service, rescue and salvage duties.

UTILITY LAUNCHES

There are 14 local and miscellaneous boats of various sizes and employment.

JORDAN

Coastal Guard

It was officially stated in 1969 that Jordan had no naval force known as such, but the Jordan Coastal Guard, sometimes called the Jordan Sea Force, took orders directly from the Director of Operations at General Headquarters. There is no longer a flotilla in the Dead Sea.

Base

Aqaba

Personnel

1976: 300 officers and men

Mercantile Marine

Lloyd's Register of Shipping: 1 vessel of 200 tons gross

LIGHT FORCES

HUSSEIN ABDALLAH

Wooden hulled of 40 ft *(12 m)* acquired in Aug 1974.

1 BERTRAM TYPE (COASTAL PATROL CRAFT)

Displacement, tons: 7
Dimensions, feet (metres): 30·4 × 10·8 × 1·6 *(9·2 × 3·3 × 0·5)*
Guns: 1—12·7 mm; 1—7·2 mm
Main engines: Diesels = 24 knots
Complement: 8

Glass fibre hull.

4 25 ft TYPE (COASTAL PATROL CRAFT)

Aluminium hulls.

4 PATROL CRAFT

Wooden-hulled craft of about 18 ft—unarmed.

KENYA

Establishment

The Kenya Navy, which is based in Mombasa, was inaugurated on 12 Dec 1964, the first anniversary of Kenya's independence.

Administration

Commander, Kenya Navy: Lieut. Col. J. C. J. Kimaro

Personnel

(a) 1976: 350 officers and men
(b) Volunteers

Mercantile Marine

Lloyd's Register of Shipping: 19 vessels of 17 331 tons gross

Prefix to Ships' Names

KNS

LIGHT FORCES

3 BROOKE MARINE 32·6 metre TYPE
(LARGE PATROL CRAFT)

Name	No.	Builders	Commissioned
MADARAKA	P 3121	Brooke Marine, Lowestoft	16 June 1975
JAMHURI	P 3122	Brooke Marine, Lowestoft	16 June 1975
HARAMBE	P 3123	Brooke Marine, Lowestoft	22 Aug 1975

Displacement, tons: 120 standard; 145 full load
Dimensions, feet (metres): 107 × 20 × 5·6 *(32·6 × 6·1 × 1·7)*
Guns: 2—40 mm
Main engines: 2 Ruston-Paxman Valenta diesels; 5 400 bhp; 2 shafts = 25·5 knots
Range, miles: 2 500 at 12 knots
Complement: 21 (3 officers, 18 men)

Ordered 10 May 1973. *Madaraka* launched 28 Jan 1975, *Jamhuri* 14 Mar 1975, *Harambe* 2 May 1975.

JAMHURI

9/1975, *John G. Callis*

BROOKE MARINE 37·5 metre TYPE
(LARGE PATROL CRAFT)

Name	No.	Builders	Commissioned
MAMBA	P 3100	Brooke Marine, Lowestoft	7 Feb 1974

Displacement, tons: 125 standard; 160 full load
Dimensions, feet (metres): 123 × 22·5 × 5·2 *(37·5 × 6·9 × 1·6)*
Guns: 2—40 mm Bofors
Main engines: 2—16 cylinder Rustons diesels; 4 000 hp = 25 knots
Range, miles: 3 300 at 13 knots
Complement: 25 (3 officers, 22 men)

Laid down 17 Feb 1972.

MAMBA

1974

3 VOSPER 31 metre TYPE (LARGE PATROL CRAFT)

Name	No.	Builders	Commissioned
CHUI	P 3112	Vosper Ltd, Portsmouth	7 July 1966
NDOVU	P 3117	Vosper Ltd, Portsmouth	27 July 1966
SIMBA	P 3110	Vosper Ltd, Portsmouth	23 May 1966

Displacement, tons: 96 standard; 109 full load
Dimensions, feet (metres): 95 wl; 103 oa × 19·8 × 5·8 *(28·8; 31·4 × 6 × 1·8)*
Guns: 2—40 mm Bofors
Main engines: 2 Paxman Ventura diesels; 2 800 bhp = 24 knots
Range, miles: 1 000 at economical speed; 1 500 at 16 knots
Complement: 23 (3 officers and 20 ratings)

The first ships specially built for the Kenya Navy. Ordered on 28 Oct 1964. *Simba* was launched on 9 Sep 1965. All three left Portsmouth on 22 Aug 1966 and arrived at their base in Mombasa on 4 Oct 1966. Air-conditioned. Fitted with modern radar communications equipment and roll damping fins.

SIMBA

1973, Kenyan Navy

KHMER REPUBLIC

The Marine Royale Khmer was established on 1 March 1954 and became Marine Nationale Khmer on 9 October 1970. With the imminent victory of the forces of Khmer Rouge in April-May 1975, several ships (listed in Deletions section) escaped from Khmer waters.

Personnel

(a) 1975: 11 000 officers and men including Marine Corps (4 000 officers and men) (current situation not known)
(b) 18 months National Service

Mercantile Marine

Lloyd's Register of Shipping:
2 vessels of 1 208 tons gross

DELETIONS

Corvettes

1975 E 311 to Thailand (16 May), E312 to Subic Bay, Philippines (2 May). P111 and P112 to Subic Bay (17 Apr).

Light Forces

1975 VR1 and VR2 (ex-Yugoslav "101" class) believed sunk by US aircraft during *Mayaguez* incident (13 May).

LIGHT FORCES

19 Ex-US "SWIFT" CLASS (COASTAL PATROL CRAFT)

Displacement, tons: 22·5
Dimensions, feet (metres): 50× 13 × 3·5 *(15 × 4 × 1·1)*
Guns: 1—81 mm mortar; 3—50 cal MG
Main engines: 2 diesels; 960 hp; 2 shafts = 28 knots
Complement: 6

Transferred in 1972-73

2 Ex-US AVR TYPE (COASTAL PATROL CRAFT)

VR 3   VR 4

Displacement, tons: 30
Dimensions, feet (metres): 63 × 13 × 4·6 *(19·1 × 4 × 1·4)*
Guns: 4—12·7 mm MG
Main engines: GM Diesel 500 bhp = 15 knots
Complement: 12

65 Ex-US PBR MARK 1 and II (RIVER PATROL CRAFT)

Displacement, tons: 8
Dimensions, feet (metres): 32 × 11 × 2·6 *(9·8 × 3·4 × 0·8)*
Guns: 3—·50 cal MG; 1 grenade launcher
Main engines: 2 geared diesels; water jets = 25 knots
Complement: 5

Transferred 1973-74.

PBR Mk II Type

United States Navy

3 Ex-CHINESE CPB TYPE (COASTAL PATROL CRAFT)

VP 1   VP 2   VP 3

Displacement, tons: 7·7 standard; 9·7 full load
Dimensions, feet (metres): 42 × 9 × 3·9 *(12·8 × 2·7 × 1·2)*
Guns: 2—12·7 mm MG
Main engines: Diesel, 300 bhp = 20 knots
Complement: 10

Transferred from the People's Republic of China in Jan 1968.

1 Ex-HDML TYPE (COASTAL PATROL CRAFT)

VP 212 (ex-*VP 748*, ex-*HDML 1223*)

Displacement, tons: 46 standard; 54 full load
Dimensions, feet (metres): 72 oa × 16 × 5·5 *(22 × 4·9 × 1·7)*
Guns: 2—20 mm; 4—7·5 mm MG
Main engines: 2 diesels; 2 shafts; 300 bhp = 10 knots
Complement: 8

Former British harbour defence motor launch of the HDML type. Transferred from the British Navy to the French Navy in 1950 and again transferred from the French Navy to the MNK in 1956.

AMPHIBIOUS VESSELS

4 Ex-US LCU TYPE

SKILAK (ex-US *YFU 73*) T 920
T 919 (ex-US *YFU 68*, ex-*LCU 1385*)
T 918 (ex-US *YFU 56*, ex-*LCU 646*)
T 917 (ex-US *YFU*, ex-*LCU 1577*)

Displacement, tons: 320 full load
Dimensions, feet (metres): 119 oa × 32·7 × 5 *(36·3 × 10 × 1·5)*
Guns: 2—20 mm
Main engines: Diesels; 675 bhp; 3 shafts = 10 knots
Complement: 13

Landing craft transferred as follows; 917 Oct 1969, 918 and 919 Nov 1972, 920 Nov 1973.

US LCU Type

1970, Defoe Shipbuilding

1 EDIC TYPE

T 916 (ex-*EDIC 606*)

Displacement, tons: 292 standard; 650 full load
Dimensions, feet (metres): 193·5 × 39·2 × 4·5 *(59 × 12 × 1·4)*
Guns: 1—81 mm mortar; 2—12·7 mm MG
Main engines: 2 MGO diesels; 2 shafts; 1 000 bhp = 10 knots
Complement: 16 (1 officer, 15 men)

Completed and transferred from the French Government in Aug 1969.

2 Ex-US LCU TYPE

T 914 (ex-USS *LCU 783*)   **T 915** (ex-USS *LCU 1421*)

Displacement, tons: 180 standard; 360 full load
Dimensions, feet (metres): 115 wl; 119 oa × 34 × 6 *(35·1; 36·3 × 10·4 × 1·8)*
Guns: 2—20 mm
Main engines: 3 diesels; 3 shafts; 675 bhp = 8 knots
Complement: 12

Former US utility landing craft of the LCU type. LCU 783 and LCU 1421 were transferred on 31 May 1962. T919 (ex-USS *LCU 1577*) was sunk by a mine on 5 May 1970.

LCU Type

1969, Marine Nat. Khmere

TUG

PINGOUIE R 911 (ex-USS *YTL 556*)

KOREA (North)

Administration

Commander of the Navy: Rear Admiral Yu Chang Kwon

Personnel

(a) 1976: 18 Q00 officers and men
(b) National Service; 3-4 years

Bases

Ch'ongjin, Haeju, Nampo, Najin, Munchon, Wonson, Pipa-got, Cha-ho, Mayang Do, Sagon-ni.

Mercantile Marine

Lloyd's Register of Shipping:
17 vessels of 81 782 tons gross

Strength of the Fleet

Type	Active
Submarines—Patrol	13
Frigates	3
Corvettes	19
Fast Attack Craft—Missile	18
Fast Attack Craft—Torpedo	157
Fast Attack Craft—Gun	44
Large Patrol Craft	2
Coastal Patrol Craft	30
LCMs	30
Trawlers etc.	5/10

SUBMARINES

9 Ex-CHINESE "ROMEO" CLASS (PATROL TYPE)

Displacement, tons: 1 000 surfaced; 1 600 dived
Dimensions, feet (metres): 249·3 × 24 × 14·5 *(76 × 7·3 × 4·4)*
Tubes: 6—21 in (bow); 18 torpedoes
Main machinery: 2 diesels—4 000 bhp; 2 electric motors—4 000 hp; 2 shafts
Speed, knots: 17 surfaced; 14 dived
Complement: 65

Two transferred from China 1973, two in 1974 and three in 1975. Local building at Mayang Do provided two more in 1976. Continuing programme with slightly different dimensions etc. Stationed on West coast (Yellow Sea).

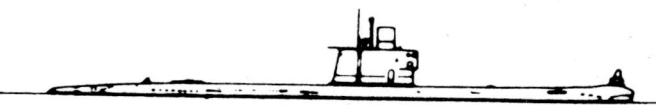

"ROMEO" Class

4 Ex-SOVIET "WHISKY" CLASS (PATROL TYPE)

Displacement, tons: 1 030 surfaced; 1 350 dived
Dimensions, feet (metres): 249·3 × 22 × 15 *(76 × 6·7 × 4·6)*
Tubes: 6—21 in (4 bow, 2 stern); 18 torpedoes carried normally (or up to 40 mines)
Main machinery: 2 diesels; 4 000 bhp; 2 electric motors; 2 500 hp; 2 shafts
Speed, knots: 17 surfaced; 15 dived
Range, miles: 13 000 at 8 knots
Complement: 60

"WHISKY" Class

Stationed on East Coast (Sea of Japan).

FRIGATES

2 + 1 "NAJIN" CLASS

Displacement, tons: 1 200
Dimensions, feet (metres): 230 × 26 × 9 *(70·2 × 7·9 × 2·7)*
Guns: 3—3·9 in *(100 mm)*, 56 cal; 4—57 mm (twin); 4—25 mm (twin vertical)
A/S weapons: 4 DC racks
Mines: 30 (estimated)
Main engines: 2 diesels; 5 000 bhp; 2 shafts
Speed, knots: 25 (estimated)
Complement: 90 (estimated)

Enlarged edition of "Sariwan" class built in North Korea. First laid down 1971-72, completed 1973, second completed 1975, third probably to be launched in 1977.

Radar: Skinhead, surface search; possible Ski Pole; IFF.

CORVETTES

1 or 2 Ex-SOVIET "TRAL" CLASS

Displacement, tons: 475
Dimensions, feet (metres): 203·5 × 23·8 × 7·8 *(62 × 7·2 × 2·4)*
Guns: 1—3·9 in *(100 mm)* 56 cal; 3—37 mm (singles); 4—12·7 mm MG
A/S weapons: 2 DC racks
Mines: 30
Main engines: 2 diesels; 2 800 hp; 2 shafts
Speed, knots: 18
Complement: 55

"TRAL" Class

An elderly class of Fleet Minesweepers of which some 4-5 were transferred by USSR in mid 1950s. Used for escort purposes.

Radar: Surface search: Skinhead. IFF: Yard Rake.

3 "SARIWAN" CLASS

Displacement, tons: 600-650
Dimensions, feet (metres): 203·5 × 24 × 7·8 *(62·1 × 7·3 × 2·4)*
Guns: 1—3·9 in *(100 mm)* 56 cal; 4—37 mm (twin); 4—25 mm (twin vertical)
A/S weapons: 2/4 DC Racks
Mines: 30
Main engines: 2 diesels; 3 000 bhp; 2 shafts
Speed, knots: 21 (estimated)
Complement: 65-70

Built in North Korea in the mid 1960s.

Radar: Surface search: Skinhead. IFF: Ski Pole or Yard Rake.

15 SOVIET "SO 1" CLASS

Displacement, tons: 215 light; 250 normal
Dimensions, feet (metres): 138·6 × 20·0 × 9·2 *(42·3 × 6·1 × 2·8)*
Guns: 4—25 mm (2 twin)
A/S weapons: 4 five barrelled launchers
Main engines: 3 diesels; 6 000 bhp = 29 knots
Range, miles: 1 100 at 13 knots
Complement: 30

"SO 1" Class   1972

6 transferred by USSR in 1957-58. Remainder built in North Korea.

LIGHT FORCES

8 Ex-SOVIET "OSA I" CLASS (FAST ATTACK CRAFT—MISSILE)

Displacement, tons: 165 standard; 200 full load
Dimensions, feet (metres): 128·7 × 25·1 × 5·9 *(39·3 × 7·7 × 1·8)*
Missile launchers: 4 in two pairs abreast for Styx missiles
Guns: 4—30 mm (1 twin forward, and aft)
Main engines: 3 diesels; 13 000 bhp = 32 knots
Range, miles: 800 at 25
Complement: 25

The combination of the "Osa" flotilla and the "Komar" units (below), both armed with the very potent 23 mile range Styx missile, provides a powerful striking force on the South Korean border and within 250 miles of Japan.

"OSA I" Class   1970

10 Ex-SOVIET "KOMAR" CLASS (FAST ATTACK CRAFT—MISSILE)

Displacement, tons: 70 standard; 80 full load
Dimensions, feet (metres): 83·7 × 19·8 × 5·0 *(25·5 × 6·0 × 1·8)*
Missile launchers: 2 for Styx missiles
Guns: 2—25 mm (1 twin forward)
Main engines: 4 diesels; 4 shafts; 4 800 bhp = 40 knots
Range, miles: 400 at 30 knots

See note under "Osa" class above.

"KOMAR" Class

8 Ex-CHINESE "SHANGHAI" CLASS (FAST ATTACK CRAFT—GUN)

Displacement, tons: 120 standard; 155 full load
Dimensions, feet (metres): 128 × 18 × 5·6 *(39 × 5·5 × 1·7)*
Guns: 4—37 mm (twin); 4—25 mm (abaft bridge);
2—3 in *(75 mm)* recoilless rifles (bow)
A/S weapons: 8 DC
Main engines: 4 diesels; 4 800 bhp = 30 knots
Mines: Rails can be fitted for 10 mines
Range, miles: 800 at 17 knots
Complement: 25

Acquired from China since 1967. Skinhead radar.

"SHANGHAI" Class

1970

8 Ex-CHINESE "SWATOW" CLASS (FAST ATTACK CRAFT—GUN)

Displacement, tons: 80
Dimensions, feet (metres): 83·5 × 19 × 6·5 *(25·5 × 5·8 × 2)*
Guns: 4—37 mm; 2—12·7 mm
A/S weapons: 8 DC
Main engines: 4 diesels; 4 800 bhp = 42 knots
Range, miles: 500 at 30 knots
Complement: 17

Transferred from China in 1968.

4 "CHODO" CLASS (FAST ATTACK CRAFT—GUN)

Displacement, tons: 130 (estimated)
Dimensions, feet (metres): 140 × 19 × 8·5 *(42·7 × 5·8 × 2·6)*
Guns: 1—3 in *(76 mm)* 50 cal (forward); 3—37 mm (single); 4—25 mm (twin, vertical)
Main engines: Diesels; 2 shafts; 6 000 bhp
Speed, knots: 24 (estimated)
Complement: 40 (estimated)

Built in North Korea in mid 1960s.

Radar. Skin Head.

4 "K-48" CLASS (FAST ATTACK CRAFT—GUN)

Displacement, tons: 110 (estimated)
Dimensions, feet (metres): 125 × 18 × 5 *(38·1 × 5·5 × 1·5)*
Guns: 1—3 in *(76 mm)* 50 cal (forward); 3—37 mm (single); 4—25 mm (twin, vertical); 4/6—14·5 mm MG (twin)
Main engines: Diesels; 4/5 000 bhp; 2 shafts
Speed, knots: 24 (estimated)

Probably built in North Korea in late 1950s.

Radar: Skin Head.

20 Ex-SOVIET "MO IV" CLASS (FAST ATTACK CRAFT—GUN)

Displacement, tons: 56
Dimensions, feet (metres): 88·5 × 13·2 × 5 *(27 × 4 × 1·5)*
Guns: 1—37 mm; 1/2—14·5 mm MG
Main engines: Diesels; 2 600 hp = 25 knots
Complement: 20

Transferred in 1950s.

4 Ex-SOVIET "SHERSHEN" CLASS
(FAST ATTACK CRAFT—TORPEDO)

Displacement, tons: 150 standard; 160 full load
Dimensions, feet (metres): 115·5 × 23 × 5 *(35·2 × 7·1 × 1·5)*
Guns: 4—30 mm (2 twin)
Torpedo tubes: 4—21 (single)
A/S weapons: 12 DC
Main engines: 3 diesels; 3 shafts; 13 000 bhp = 41 knots
Complement: 16

Transferred in 1973-74.

"SHERSHEN" Class

60 Ex-SOVIET "P 6" CLASS
(FAST ATTACK CRAFT—TORPEDO)

Displacement, tons: 66 standard; 75 full load
Dimensions, feet (metres): 84·2 × 20 × 6 *(25·7 × 6·1 × 1·8)*
Guns: 4—25 mm
Torpedo tubes: 2—21 in (or mines or DC)
Main engines: 4 diesels; 4 800 hp; 4 shafts = 43 knots
Range, miles: 450 at 30 knots

There is a growing number of these craft in N. Korea with local building programme in hand. About fifteen of this class have a different armament including 2—37 mm (single) and 4—25 mm (twin, vertical).

Radar: Pothead or Skinhead.

"P 6" Class

12 Ex-SOVIET "P 4" CLASS
(FAST ATTACK CRAFT—TORPEDO)

Displacement, tons: 25
Dimensions, feet (metres): 62·7 × 11·6 × 5·6 *(19·1 × 3·5 × 1·7)*
Guns: 2—MG
Torpedo tubes: 2—18 in
Main engines: 2 diesels; 2 200 bhp = 50 knots.

Built in 1951-57. Aluminium hulls. Some locally built.

"P 4" Class
1971

15 "IWON" CLASS (FAST ATTACK CRAFT—TORPEDO)

Displacement, tons: 40
Dimensions, feet (metres): 63 × 12 × 5 *(19·2 × 3·7 × 1·5)*
Guns: 4—25 mm (twin, vertical)
Torpedo tubes: 2—21 in

Built in North Korea in late 1950s. Similar to older Soviet "P 2" class.

Radar: Skinhead.

"CHAHO" CLASS (FAST ATTACK CRAFT—TORPEDO)

Reported as building in North Korea.

6 "AN JU" CLASS (FAST ATTACK CRAFT—TORPEDO)

Displacement, tons: 35
Dimensions, feet (metres): 65 × 12 × 6 *(19·8 × 3·7 × 1·8)*
Guns: 2—25 mm (twin, vertical)
Torpedo tubes: 2—21 in

Built in North Korea in 1960s.

60 "SIN HUNG" and "KOSONG" CLASSES
(FAST ATTACK CRAFT—TORPEDO)

Displacement, tons: 35
Dimensions, feet (metres): 60 × 11 × 5·5 *(18·3 × 3·4 × 1·7)*
Guns: 2—14·5 mm (twin)
Torpedo tubes: 2—18 in or 2—21 in

Built in North Korea mid 1950s to 1970. Frequently operated on South Korean border. All resemble the Soviet "D-3" class of 25 years ago.

1 or 2 Ex-SOVIET "ARTILLERIST" CLASS
(LARGE PATROL CRAFT)

Displacement, tons: 240
Dimensions, feet (metres): 160·8 × 19 × 6·5 *(49 × 5·8 × 2)*
Guns: 1—3·9 in *(100 mm)*; 2—37 mm (singles); 4/6—25 mm (twin, vertical)
Main engines: 2 diesels; 3 300 bhp; 2 shafts
Speed, knots: 25
Complement: 30

Transferred in mid 1950s.

10 Ex-SOVIET "KM 4" CLASS
(COASTAL PATROL CRAFT)

Displacement, tons: 10
Dimensions, feet (metres): 46 × 10·5 × 3 *(14 × 3·2 × ·9)*
Guns: 1—36 mm; 1—14·5 mm MG
Main engines: Petrol; 146 shp; 2 shafts
Complement: 10

20 LIGHT GUNBOATS

Believed to be for inshore patrols. Locally built.

AMPHIBIOUS FORCES

30 LCM now in service with others building in North Korea. Used on South Korean border.

SERVICE FORCES

5-10 Large Trawlers and small cargo vessels used as store ships. Some of the trawlers operate on South Korean border where several have been sunk in the last few years.

KOREA (REPUBLIC OF)

Senior Flag Officers

Chief of Naval Operations:
Rear Admiral Kyu-Sup Kim
Vice Chief of Naval Operations:
Vice-Admiral Yun-Kyong Oh
Commander-in-Chief of Fleet:
Rear-Admiral Chong-Yon Hwang

Diplomatic Representation

Naval Attaché in London:
Colonel Yull-Sec Dong (Air Force)
Naval Attaché in Paris:
Colonel Ock-Sup Yoon (Army)
Naval Attaché in Washington:
Captain Choong Hah Choi (Navy)

Personnel

Approx 20 000 in Navy.

Bases

Chinhae, Cheju, Inchon, Mokpo, Mukho, Pusan, Pohang.

Marine Corps

Over 20 000 organised into one division and one brigade plus smaller and support units. Since October 1973 the ROK Marine Force has been placed directly under the ROK Navy command with a Vice Chief of Naval Operations for Marine Affairs replacing the Commandant of Marine Corps.

Naval Aviation

The ROK Navy operates 20+ S-2 Tracker anti-submarine aircraft. Approximately ten utility aircraft and several helicopters are operated by the ROK Marine Corps. Additional Tracker aircraft are being acquired.

Mercantile Marine

Lloyd's Register of Shipping:
828 vessels of 1 623 532 tons gross

Strength of the Fleet

7	Destroyers
3	Frigates
6	Escort Transports
18+	Patrol Vessels (over 100 ft)
30+	Patrol Boats
12	Minesweepers
1	Dock Landing Ship
8	Tank Landing Ships
11	Medium Landing Ships
1	Survey Ship
13	Auxiliary Ships

Guided Missiles

Several large ships of the Korean Navy have been armed with US Standard surface-to-surface missiles as well as the new-construction PSMM and possibly CPIC types. Some reports also cite the Israeli Gabriel missile being in ROK service.

DESTROYERS

2 + 2 Ex-US "GEARING" CLASS

Name	No.	Builders	Launched	US Comm.	Transferred
CHUNG BUK (ex-USS *Chevalier*, DD 805)	DD 95	Bath Iron Works Corp, Bath, Maine	29 Oct 1944	9 Jan 1945	5 July 1972
JEONG BUK (ex-USS *Everett F. Larson*, DD 830)	DD 96	Bath iron Works Corp, Bath, Maine	28 Jan 1945	6 April 1945	30 Oct 1972

Displacement, tons: 2 425 standard; approx 3 500 full load
Length, feet (metres): 383 *(116·7)* wl; 390·5 *(119·0)* oa
Beam, feet (metres): 40·9 *(12·4)*
Draught, feet (metres): 19 *(5·8)*
Guns: 6—5 inch *(127 mm)* 38 cal DP (twin) (Mk 38)
A/S weapons: 6—12·75 inch *(324 mm)* torpedo tubes (Mk 32 triple); 2 fixed hedgehogs (Mk 11)
Main engines: 2 geared turbines (General Electric); 60 000 shp; 2 shafts
Boilers: 4 (Babcock & Wilcox)
Speed, knots: 34
Complement: approx 275

Former US "Gearing" class destroyers.
These ships were converted to radar picket destroyers (DDR) in 1949; subsequently modernised under the US Navy's Fleet Rehabilitation and Modernisation (FRAM II) programme. Fitted with small helicopter hangar and flight deck. Anti-ship torpedo tubes and secondary gun armament have been removed.
Two additional destroyers were expected to be transferred from the US Navy to South Korea in 1976-1977. The USS *Richard E. Kraus* (DD 849) and USS *Stribling* (DD 867) were initially indicated for transfer; both ships are FRAM I type.

Electronics: These ships have SPS-40 and SPS-10 search radar antennae on the tripod mast; SQS-29 series hull mounted sonar.

JEONG BUK

1973

2 Ex-US "ALLEN M. SUMNER" CLASS

Name	No.	Builders	Launched	US Comm.	Transferred
DAE GU (ex-USS *Wallace L. Lind*, DD 703)	DD 97	Bath Iron Works Corp, Bath, Maine	14 June1944	8 Sep 1944	3 Dec 1973
IN CHEON (ex-USS *De Haven*, DD 727)	DD 98	Federal SB & DD Co, Kearney, New Jersey	9 Jan 1944	31 Mar 1944	4 Dec 1973

Displacement, tons: 2 200 standard; 3 320 full load
Length, feet (metres): 376·5 *(114·8)* oa
Beam, feet (metres): 40·9 *(12·4)*
Draught, feet (metres): 19 *(5·8)* (Mk 38)
Guns: 6—5 inch *(127 mm)* 38 calibre DP (twin) (Mk 38)
A/S weapons: 6—12·75 inch *(324 mm)* torpedo tubes (Mk 32 triple); 2 fixed hedgehogs (Mk 11)
Main engines: 2 geared turbines (General Electric); 60 000 shp; 2 shafts
Boilers: 4 (Babcock & Wilcox)
Speed, knots: 34
Complement: approx 275

Former US "Allen M. Sumner" class destroyers.
Both ships were modernised under the US Navy's Fleet Rehabilitation and Modernisation (FRAM II) programme. Fitted with small helicopter deck and hangar. Anti-ship torpedo tubes and secondary gun armament have been removed.

Electronics: *Dae Gu* fitted with SPS-40 and SPS-10 search radar antennae; *In Cheon* has SPS-37 and SPS-10 antennae. Fitted with SQS-29 series hull-mounted sonar and SQA-10 variable depth sonar (VDS) on stern.

Photographs: The ex-"Gearing" class destroyers can be distinguished from the ex-"Sumner" class by the wider spacing of the funnels in the former ships. The basic configuration and equipment are the same in both classes.

DAE GU (as USS *Wallace L. Lind*)

1967, United States Navy

3 Ex-US "FLETCHER" CLASS

Name		No.
CHUNG MU (ex-USS *Erben, DD 631*)		DD 91
SEOUL (ex-USS *Halsey Powell, DD 686*)		DD 92
PUSAN (ex-USS *Hickox, DD 673*)		DD 93

Builders	Launched	US Comm	Transferred
Bath Iron Works, Bath, Maine	21 Mar 1943	28 May 1943	1 May 1963
Bethlehem Steel, Staten Island, New York	30 June 1943	25 Oct 1943	27 Apr 1968
Federal Shipbuilding, Kearny, New Jersey	4 July 1943	10 Sep 1943	15 Nov 1968

Displacement, tons: 2 050 standard; 3 050 full load
Length, feet (metres): 360 *(110·3)* wl; 376·5 *(114·8)* oa
Beam, feet (metres): 39·6 *(12·0)*
Draught, feet (metres): 18 *(5·5)*
Guns: 5—5 inch *(127 mm)* 38 calibre DP (single) (Mk 30); 10—40 mm AA (2 quad, 1 twin) except *Seoul* (none)
A/S weapons: 6—12·75 inch *(324 mm)* torpedo tubes (Mk 32 triple); 2 hedgehogs (Mk 10/11); depth charges
Main engines: Geared turbines (General Electric) 60 000 shp; 2 shafts
Boilers: 4 (Babcock & Wilcox)
Speed, knots: 35
Complement: approx 250

Former US "Fletcher" class destroyers.
Tripod masts have been fitted to support larger radar antennae; the two 21 inch quintuple torpedo tube mounts originally fitted have been removed as have the 20 mm light anti-aircraft guns.

Electronics: SPS-10 and SPS-6 search radar antennae are fitted.

SEOUL   *1968, United States Navy*

FRIGATES

1 Ex-US "RUDDEROW" CLASS

Name		No.
CHUNG NAM (ex-USS *Holt, DE 706*)		DE 73

Builders	Launched	US Comm.	Transferred
Defoe Shipbuilding, Bay City, Michigan	15 Feb 1944	9 June 1944	19 June 1963

Displacement, tons: 1 450 standard; 1 890 full load
Length, feet (metres): 300 *(91·5)* wl; 306 *(83·2)* oa
Beam, feet (metres): 37 *(11·3)*
Draught, feet (metres): 14 *(4·3)*
Guns: 2—5 inch *(127 mm)* 38 cal DP; 4—40 mm AA (twin)
A/S weapons: 6—12·75 inch *(324 mm)* torpedo tubes (Mk 32 triple); 1 hedgehog; depth charges
Main engines: Turbo-electric drive (General Electric geared turbines); 12 000 shp; 2 shafts
Boilers: 2 (Combustion Engineering)
Speed, knots: 24
Complement: approx 210

Former US destroyer escort of the TEV design. Triple 21 inch torpedo tube mount originally fitted was removed shortly after completion.

Electronics: SPS-5 and SPS-6 search radars are fitted.

CHUNG NAM   *1971, Korean Navy*

2 Ex-US "BOSTWICK" CLASS

Name		No.
KYONG KI (ex-USS *Muir, DE 770*)		DE 71
KANG WON (ex-USS *Sutton, DE 771*)		DE 72

Builders	Launched	US Comm.	Transferred
Tampa Shipbuilding, Tampa, Florida	4 June 1944	30 Aug 1944	2 Feb 1956
Tampa Shipbuilding, Tampa, Florida	6 Aug 1944	22 Dec 1944	2 Feb 1956

Displacement, tons: 1 265 standard; 1 700 full load
Length, feet (metres): 300 *(91·5)* wl; 306 *(93·3)* oa
Beam, feet (metres): 36·6 *(11·2)*
Draught, feet (metres): 14 *(4·3)*
Guns: 3—3 inch *(76 mm)* 50 cal AA; 6—40 mm AA (twin); 4—20 mm AA (single)
A/S weapons: 6—12·75 inch *(324 mm)* torpedo tubes (Mk 32 triple); 1 hedgehog; depth charges
Main engines: Diesel-electric (4 General Motors diesels); 6 000 bhp; 2 shafts
Speed, knots: 21
Complement: approx 210

Former US destroyer escorts of DET design. Triple 21 inch torpedo tube mount originally fitted was removed shortly after completion. Refitted at Pearl Harbor, Hawaii, in 1964, being provided with tripod masts to support improved radar antennae; also fitted with more modern sonar and anti-submarine weapons.

Electronics: Fitted with SPS-6 and SPS-5 search radars.

KYONG KI   *Korean Navy*

ESCORT TRANSPORTS

6 Ex-US APD TYPE

Name	No.	Builders	Launched	US Comm.	Transferred
KYONG NAM (ex-USS *Cavallaro*, APD 128)	APD 81	Defoe Shipbuilding Co, Bay City, Michigan	15 June1944	13 Mar 1945	Oct 1959
AH SAN (ex-USS *Harry L. Corl*, APD 108)	APD 82	Bethlehem Shipbuilding Co, Higham, Massachusetts	1 Mar 1944	5 June1945	June 1966
UNG PO (ex-*Julius A. Raven*, APD 110)	APD 83	Bethlehem Shipbuilding Co, Higham, Massachusetts	3 Mar 1944	28 June1945	June 1966
KYONG PUK (ex-USS *Kephart*, APD 61)	APD 85	Charleston Navy Yard, South Carolina	6 Sep 1943	7 Jan 1944	Aug 1967
JONNAM (ex-USS *Hayter*, APD 80)	APD 86	Charleston Navy Yard, South Carolina	11 Nov 1943	16 Mar 1944	Aug 1967
CHR JU (ex-*William M. Hobby*, APD 95)	APD 87	Charleston Navy Yard, South Carolina	11 Feb 1944	4 April1945	Aug 1967

Displacement, tons: 1 400 standard; 2 130 full load
Length, feet (metres): 300 *(91·4)* wl; 306 *(93·3)* oa
Beam, feet (metres): 37 *(11·3)*
Draught, feet (metres): 12·6 *(3·2)*
Guns: 1—5 inch *(127 mm)* 38 cal DP 6—40 mm AA (twin)
A/S weapons: depth charges
Main engines: Turbo-electric (General Electric turbines); 12 000 shp; 2 shafts
Boilers: 2 (Foster Wheeler "D" Express)
Speed, knots: 23·6
Complement: approx 200
Troop capacity: approx 160

All begun as destroyers escorts (DE), but converted during construction or after completion to high-speed transports (APD).

In Korean service four latter ships originally rated as gunboats (PG); changed in 1972 to APD. All are fitted to carry approximately 160 troops.

Photographs: Note davits aft of funnel for carrying four LCVP-type landing craft or other small boats. Two different configurations; ex-APD 37 class with high bridge and lattice mast supporting 10-ton capacity boom; ex-APD 87 class with low bridge and tripod mast supporting 10-ton capacity boom. One twin 40 mm gun mount is forward of bridge; two others aft, on either side of boom.

KYONG NAM

PATROL VESSELS

7 PATROL MISSILE SHIPS

Name	No.	Builders	Commissioned
PAEK KU 12	PGM 12	Tacoma Boatbuilding Co, Tacoma, Washington	1975
PAEK KU 13	PGM 13	Tacoma Boatbuilding Co, Tacoma, Washington	1975
PAEK KU 15	PGM 15	Tacoma Boatbuilding Co, Tacoma, Washington	1976
PAEK KU 16	PGM 16	South Korea	
PAEK KU 17	PGM 17	South Korea	1976-77
PAEK KU 18	PGM 18	South Korea	
PAEK KU 19	PGM 19	South Korea	

Displacement, tons: approx 250 full load
Dimensions, feet (metres): 165 oa × 24 *(50·3 × 7·3)*
Missile launchers: 4 launchers for Standard surface-to-surface missile
Guns: 1—3 inch *(76 mm)* 50 cal AA (forward)
1—40 mm AA (aft; may have been removed with missile installation)
2—·50 cal MG
Main engines: 6 gas turbines (Avco Lycoming); 2 shafts (controllable pitch propellers) = 40+ knots
Complement: 32 (5 officers, 27 enlisted men)

PAEK KU 12   1975, Alfred W. Harris

These are multi-purpose patrol and attack ships based on the US Navy's *Asheville* (PG 84) design. Tacoma design designation was PSSM for multi-mission patrol ship. The Korean designation *Paek Ku* means seagull.

Engineering: The six TF 35 gas turbines turn two propeller shafts; the "Asheville" class ships have combination gas turbine-diesel power plants. In the Korean units one, two, or three turbines can be selected to provide each shaft with a variety of power settings.

Photographs: The *Paek Ku 12* is shown in bow view after launching on 17 Feb 1975; she and the *Paek Ku 13* were commissioned by the ROK Navy on 14 Mar 1975.

PAEK KU 12 firing standard missile

PAEK KU 12   1975, Alfred W. Harris

1 Ex-US "ASHEVILLE" CLASS

Name	No.	Builders	Launched
PAEK KU 11	PGM 101	Tacoma Boatbuilding Co,	20 Dec 1969
(ex-USS *Benicia, PG 96*)	(ex-*PGM 11*)	Tacoma, Washington	

Displacement, tons: 225 standard; 245 full load
Dimensions, feet (metres): 164·5 oa × 23·8 × 9·5 *(50·1 × 7·3 × 2·9)*
Guns: 1—3 inch *(76 mm)* 50 cal AA (forward); 1—40 mm AA (aft); 4—·50 cal MG (twin)
Main engines: CODAG; 2 diesels (Cummins); 1 450 bhp; 2 shafts = 16 knots; 1 gas turbine
(General Electric); 13 300 shp; 2 shafts = 40+ knots
Complement: approx 25

Former US "Asheville" class patrol gunboat. Commissioned in US Navy on 25 April 1970; transferred to ROK Navy on 15 Oct 1971 and arrived in Korea in January 1972. See United States section for design, engineering, and gunnery notes. No anti-submarine sensors or weapons are fitted. Designation believed changed from PGM 11 to PGM 101 during 1975.

Missiles: During 1971, while in US Navy service, this ship was fitted experimentally with one launcher for the Standard surface-to-surface missile. The box-like container/launcher held two missiles. See 1971-1972 edition for additional photo of *Benicia* in missile configuration (page 706). It is assumed that South Korea has fitted the ship with surface-to-surface missiles.

PAEK KU 11   *1972*

Several COASTAL PATROL and INTERDICTION CRAFT (CPIC)

Name	No.	Builders	Launched
GIREOGI	PKM 123	Tacoma Boatbuilding Co, Tacoma, Washington	1974
	PKM		
	PKM		
	PKM		
	PKM		

Displacement, tons: 71·25 full load
Dimensions, feet (metres): 100 oa × 18·5 × 6 *(30·5 × 5·6 × 1·8)*
Guns: 2—30 mm MG (twin) (Mk 74) (see *Gunnery* notes)
Main engines: 3 gas turbines (Avco Lycoming); 6 750 shp; 3 shafts = 45 knots; 2 auxiliary
diesels (Volvo); 500 bhp
Complement: approx 11 (varies with armament)

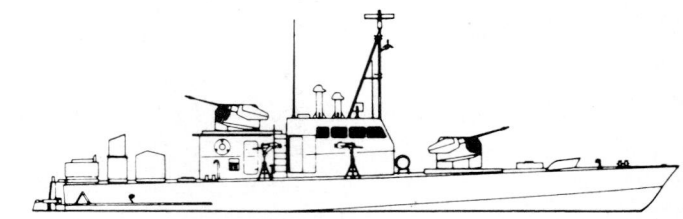

These are high-speed patrol and interdiction craft designed by the US Navy specifically for foreign sales and as a successor to PTFs in the US Navy. The CPIC is capable of operating in rougher waters than PTFs and is more adaptable for cold and hot weather operating areas. Fitted with fin stabilisers.
The lead craft, after extensive Navy trials, was transferred to South Korea on 1 Aug 1975. At least four additional craft of this type are under construction in South Korean yards.

Gunnery: The lead craft was completed with a twin rapid-fire 30 mm mount forward of the bridge structure. As shown in the drawing, light machine guns can be fitted along the sides and a second 30 mm gun mount or missile launchers can be installed aft of the bridge. Up to 20 000 pounds of weapons can be carried.

CPIC on trials   *1974, United States Navy*

3 Ex-US "AUK" CLASS

Name	No.	Builders	Launched
SHIN SONG (ex-USS *Ptarmigan, MSF 376)*	PCE 1001	Savannah Machine & Foundry Co, Savannah, Georgia	15 July 1944
SUNCHON (ex-USS *Speed, MSF 116)*	PCE 1002	American SB Co, Lorain, Ohio	18 April 1942
KOJE (ex-USS *Dextrous, MSF 341)*	PCE 1003	Gulf SB Corp, Madisonville, Texas	17 Jan 1943

Displacement, tons: 890 standard; 1 250 full load
Dimensions, feet (metres): 215 *(61·3)* wl; 221·2 oa × 32·2 × 10·8 *(63·2 × 9·2 × 3)*
Guns: 2—3 inch *(76 mm)* 50 cal AA (single); 4—40 mm AA (twin); 4—20 mm AA (twin)
A/S weapons: 3—12·75 inch *(324 mm)* torpedo tubes (Mk 32 triple); 1 hedgehog; depth charges
Main engines: Diesel-electric (General Motors diesels); 3 532 bhp; 2 shafts = 18 knots
Complement: approx 110

Former US Navy minesweepers (originally designated AM). Launch dates above; PCE 1001 commissioned in US Navy on 15 Jan 1944, PCE 1002 on 15 Oct 1942, and PCE 1003 on 8 Sep 1943; PCE 1001 transferred to ROK Navy in July 1963, PCE 1002 in Nov 1967, and PCE 1003 in Dec 1967.
The minesweeping gear was removed prior to transfer and a second 3 inch gun fitted aft; additional anti-submarine weapons also fitted. See 1973-1974 edition for broadside views.

SHIN SONG

7 Ex-US 185-ft PCE TYPE

Name	No.	Launched
RO RYANG (ex-USS *PCEC 882*)	PCEC 51	3 Dec 1943
MYONG RYANG (ex-USS *PCEC 896*)	PCEC 52	22 May 1943
HAN SAN (ex-USS *PCEC 873*)	PCEC 53	5 May 1943
OK PO (ex-USS *PCEC 898*)	PCEC 55	3 Aug 1943
PYOK PA (ex-USS *Dania, PCE 870*)	PCE 57	27 Feb 1943
RYUL PO (ex-USS *Somerset, PCE 892*)	PCE 58	1 May 1943
SA CHON (ex-USS *Batesburg, PCE 903*)	PCE 59	6 Sep 1943

Displacement, tons: 640 standard; 950 full load
Dimensions, feet (metres): 180 *(51·4)* wl; 184·5 oa × 33 × 9·5 *(52·7 × 9·4 × 2·7)*
Guns: 1—3 inch *(76 mm)* 50 cal AA; 6—40 mm AA (twin) except *Ko Jin* only 4—40 mm; 4 or 8—20 mm AA (single or twin)
A/S weapons: 1 hedgehog (except *Ko Jin*); depth charges
Main engines: Diesels (General Motors); 2 000 bhp; 2 shafts = 15 knots
Complement: approx 100

OK PO   1969

Former US Navy patrol craft. Launch dates above. Four units had been modified in US service as "control" ships (PCEC) for operation with landing craft, being fitted with additional communications equipment in an enlarged bridge area.
Ro Ryang and *Myong Ryang* transferred to South Korea in Feb 1955; *Han San* and *Ok Po* in Sep 1955; *Pyok Pa, Ryul Po,* and *Sa Chon* in Dec 1961.

8 Ex-US COAST GUARD 95-ft TYPE

PB 3 (ex-USCGC *Cape Rosier, WPB 95333*)
PB 5 (ex-USCGC *Cape Sable, WPB 95334*)
PB 6 (ex-USCGC *Cape Providence, WPB 95335*)
PB 8 (ex-USCGC *Cape Porpoise, WPB 95327*)
PB 9 (ex-USCGC *Cape Falcon, WPB 95330*)
PB 10 (ex-USCGC *Cape Trinity, WPB 95331*)
PB 11 (ex-USCGC *Cape Darby, WPB 95323*)
PB 12 (ex-USCGC *Cape Kiwanda, WPB 95329*)

Displacement, tons: 98 full load
Dimensions, feet (metres): 95 oa × 19 × 6 *(31·1 × 6·2 × 1·9)*
Guns: 1—·50 cal MG/1—81 mm mortar; several ·30 cal MG
Main engines: 4 diesels (General Motors); 2 200 bhp; 2 shafts = 20 knots
Complement: 13

PB 5

Former US Coast Guard steel-hulled patrol craft. Built in 1958-1959. Nine units transferred to South Korea in Sep 1968. PB 7 (ex-USCGC *Cape Florida,* WPB 95325) stricken after grounding in May 1971.
Combination machinegun/mortar mount is forward; single light machineguns are mounted aft.
See US Coast Guard listings for additional details.

PB 11

2 100-ft PATROL TYPE

PK 10   **PK 11**

Displacement, tons: 120
Dimensions, feet (metres): 100 oa *(32·7)*
Guns: 1—40 mm AA; 1—20 mm AA
Main engines: Diesels (Mercedes Benz-MTU); 10 200 bhp; 3 shafts = 35 knots

Two patrol craft reported built in Korea in 1971-1972.

10+ 72-ft PATROL TYPE

Displacement, tons: 30
Dimensions, feet (metres): 72 oa × 11·5 × 3·6 *(23·6 × 3·8 × 1·2)*
Guns: 2—20 mm AA (single)
Main engines: Diesels; 1 600 bhp; 2 shafts

At least 10 and possibly as many as 20 patrol craft of this type are being built in Korea, with the first units completed in 1973. Believed to be designated in the PB series.

9 65-ft SEWART TYPE

FB 1	FB 3	FB 6	FB 8	FB 10
FB 2	FB 5	FB 7	FB 9	

Displacement, tons: 33 full load
Dimensions, feet (metres): 65 oa × 16 *(21·3 × 5·2)*
Guns: 2—20 mm (single)
Main engines: 3 diesels (General Motors); 1 590 bhp; 3 shafts = 25 knots
Complement: 5

These craft were built in the United States by Sewart. The design is adapted from a commercial 65-foot craft. Referred to as "Toksuuri" No. 1 through 10 by the South Koreans (with the No. 4 being considered unlucky and not assigned). Transferred to South Korea in August 1967.

FB 10 on marine railway

4 US 40-ft SEWART TYPE

SB 1   SB 2   SB 3   SB 5

Displacement, tons: 9·25 full load
Dimensions, feet (metres): 40 oa × 12 × 3 *(13·1 × 3·9 × 0·9)*
Guns: 1—·50 cal MG; 2—·30 cal MG
Main engines: 2 diesels (General Motors); 500 bhp; 2 shafts = 31 knots
Complement: 7

These are aluminium-hulled craft built in the United States by Sewart. Transferred to South Korea in 1964. No. 4 not assigned.

MINESWEEPERS

8 Ex-US MSC TYPE

Name	No.	Builders
KUM SAN (ex-US *MSC 284*)	MSC 522	Peterson Builders, Sturgeon Bay, Wisconsin
KO HUNG (ex-US *MSC 285*)	MSC 523	Peterson Builders, Sturgeon Bay, Wisconsin
KUM KOK (ex-US *MSC 286*)	MSC 525	Peterson Builders, Sturgeon Bay, Wisconsin
NAM YANG (ex-US *MSC 295*)	MSC 526	Peterson Builders, Sturgeon Bay, Wisconsin
NA DONG (ex-US *MSC 296*)	MSC 527	Peterson Builders, Strugeon Bay, Wisconsin
SAM CHOK (ex-US *MSC 316*)	MSC 528	Peterson Builders, Sturgeon Bay, Wisconsin
YONG DONG (ex-US *MSC 320*)	MSC 529	Peterson Builders, Sturgeon Bay, Wisconsin
OK CHEON (ex-US *MSC 321*)	MSC 530	Peterson Builders, Sturgeon Bay, Wisconsin

Displacement, tons: 320 light; 370 full load
Dimensions, feet (metres): 144 oa × 28 × 8·2 *(117·2 × 9·2 × 2·7)*
Guns: 2—20 mm AA
Main engines: Diesels; 1 200 bhp; 2 shafts = 14 knots
Complement: approx 40

KUM KOK

"Bluebird" class coastal minesweepers built by the United States specifically for transfer under the Military Aid Programme. Wood hulled with non-magnetic metal fittings.
Kum San transferred to South Korea in June 1959, *Ko Hung* in Sep 1959, *Kum Kok* in Nov 1959, *Nam Yang* in Sep 1963, *Ha Dong* in Nov 1963, *Sam Chok* in July 1968, *Yong Dong* and *Ok Cheon* on 1 Oct 1975.

3 Ex-US YMS TYPE

Name	No.
KUM HWA (ex-USS *Curlew*, MSCO 8, ex-*AMS 8*, ex-*YMS 218*)	MSC 519
KIM PO (ex-USS *Kite*, MSCO 22, ex-*AMS 22*, ex-*YMS 375*)	MSC 520
KO CHANG (ex-USS *Mockingbird*, MSCO 27, ex-*AMS 27*, ex-*YMS 419*)	MSC 521

Displacement, tons: 270 standard; 350 full load
Dimensions, feet (metres): 136 oa × 24·5 × 8 *(44·6 × 8·1 × 2·6)*
Guns: 1—40 mm AA; 2—20 mm AA
Main engines: Diesels; 1 000 bhp = 15 knots
Complement: approx 50

KO CHANG   *1969, Korean Navy*

Former US Navy auxiliary motor minesweepers built in 1941-1942. Wood hulled. *Kum Hwa, Kim Po,* and *Ko Chang* transferred to South Korea in Jan 1956. *Kwang Chu* MSC 503 (ex-USS *YMS 413*) scrapped in 1974.
See 1974-1975 and previous editions for disposals of other ex-US YMS type minesweepers transferred to South Korea.

1 MINESWEEPING BOAT

Name	No.
PI BONG (ex-US *MSB 2*)	MSB 1

Displacement, tons: 30 light; 39 full load
Dimensions, feet (metres): 57·2 oa × 15·3 × 4 *(18·7 × 5 × 1·3)*
Guns: machine guns
Main engines: 2 geared diesels (Packard); 600 bhp; 2 shafts = 12 knots

Former US Navy minesweeping boat transferred on 1 Dec 1961. Wood hulled.

PI BONG   *1969, Korean Navy*

LANDING SHIPS

8 Ex-US LST TYPE

Name	No.	Launched
UN PONG (ex-USS LST 1010)	LST 807	29 Mar 1944
DUK BONG (ex-USS LST 227)	LST 808	21 Sep 1943
BI BONG (ex-USS LST 218)	LST 809	20 July 1943
KAE BONG (ex-USS Berkshire County, LST 288)	LST 810	7 Nov 1943
WEE BONG (ex-USS Johnson County, LST 849)	LST 812	30 Dec 1944
SU YONG (ex-USS Kane County, LST 853)	LST 813	17 Nov 1944
BUK HAN (ex-USS Lynn County, LST 900)	LST 815	9 Dec 1944
HWA SAN (ex-USS Pender County, LST 1080)	LST 816	2 May 1945

Displacement, tons: 1 653 standard; 2 366 beaching; 4 080 full load
Dimensions, feet (metres): 316 wl; 328 oa × 50 × 14 *(103·6; 107·5 × 16·4 × 4·6)*
Guns: 10 or 8—40 mm AA
Main engines: Diesels; 1 700 bhp; 2 shafts = 11·6 knots
Complement: approx 110

Former US Navy tank landing ships. Cargo capacity 2 100 tons. Launch dates above. *Un Bong* transferred to South Korea in Feb 1955, *Duk Bong* in Mar 1955, *Bi Bong* in May 1955, *Kae Bong* in Mar 1956, *Wee Bong* in Jan 1959, *Su Yong* and *Buk Han* in Dec 1958, and *Hwa San* in Oct 1958. LSTs previously operated by South Korea and stricken were: ex-USS LST 120, ex-USS LST 213, *Tan Yang* ex-USS LST 343, ex-USS LST 378, ex-USS LST 380, *Ryong Pi* LST 806 ex-USS LST 388, *In Tong* LST 803 ex-USS LST 491 sunk in 1952, ex-USS LST 536, ex-USS LST 594, *Chon Po* LST 805; ex-USS LST 595, ex-USS LST 624, *Ryong Hwa* LST 801 ex-USS LST 659, *Lyung Wha* ex-USS LST 805.

HWA SAN

DUK BONG

1 Ex-US LSD TYPE

Name	Builders	Commissioned
(ex-USS Fort Marion, LSD 22)	Gulf Shipbuilding Corp, Chickasaw, Alabama	29 Jan 1946

Displacement, tons: 4 790 standard; 9 375 full load
Dimensions, feet (metres): 475·4 oa × 76·2 × 18
Guns: 12—40 mm AA (2 quad, 2 twin)
Main engines: Geared turbines; 9 000 shp; 2 shafts = 15·4 knots
Boilers: 2

Former US Navy dock landing ship of the "Casa Grande" class. Launched on 22 May 1945, and transferred to South Korea in 1976.
Docking well is 392 × 44 feet; can accommodate 3 LCUs or 18 LCMs or 32 LVTs (amphibious tractors) in docking well. Fitted with helicopter platform (which can be used to transport trucks or equipment for loading into landing craft).

Ex-USS FORT MARION ballasted down at stern

1969, United States Navy

1 Ex-US LSMR TYPE

Name	No.	Builders
SI HUNG (ex-USS St Joseph River LSMR 527)	LSMR 311	Brown Shipbuilding Co, Houston, Texas

Displacement, tons: 944 standard; 1 084 full load
Dimensions, feet (metres): 204·5 wl; 206·2 oa × 34·5 × 10 *(67·1; 67·6 × 11·3 × 3·3)*
Guns: 1—5 inch *(127 mm)* 38 cal DP; 2—40 mm AA; 4—20 mm AA
Rocket launchers: 8 twin rapid-fire launchers for 5 inch rockets
Main engines: 2 diesels (General Motors); 2 800 bhp; 2 shafts = 12·6 knots
Complement: approx 140

Former US Navy landing ship completed as a rocket-firing ship to support amphibious landing operations. Launched on 19 May 1945, transferred to South Korea on 15 Sep 1960. Configuration differs from conventional LSM type with "island" bridge structure and 5 inch gun aft; no bow doors.

SI HUNG

1967, Korean Navy

10 Ex-US LSM TYPE

Name	No.
TAE CHO (ex-USS *LSM 546*)	LSM 601
TYO TO (ex-USS *LSM 268*)	LSM 602
KA TOK (ex-USS *LSM 462*)	LSM 605
KO MUN (ex-USS *LSM 30*)	LSM 606
PIAN (ex-USS *LSM 96*)	LSM 607
WOL MI (ex-USS *LSM 57*)	LSM 609
KI RIN (ex-USS *LSM 19*)	LSM 610
NUNG RA (ex-USS *LSM 84*)	LSM 611
SIN MI (ex-USS *LSM 316*)	LSM 612
UL RUNG (ex-USS *LSM 17*)	LSM 613

Displacement, tons: 743 beaching; 1 095 full load
Dimensions, feet (metres): 196·5 wl; 203·5 oa × 34·6 × 8·5 *(64·4; 66·7 × 11·3 × 2·8)*
Guns: 2—40 mm AA (twin); several 20 mm AA
Main engines: 2 diesels (direct drive; Fairbanks Morse except *Tyo To* General Motors); 2 800 bhp; 2 shafts = 12·5 knots
Complement: approx 60

TYO TO   1969

Former US Navy medium landing ships. Built 1944-1945. LSM 601, 602, and 605 transferred to South Korea in 1955; others in 1956. *Sin Mi* served in Indochina as French L 9014 and *Ul Rung* as French L 9017 during 1954-1955; returned to United States in Oct 1955 and retransferred to South Korea in autumn 1956.

Pung To serves as mine force flagship fitted with mine-laying rails and designated LSML. Arrangement of 20 mm guns differs; some ships have two single mounts adjacent to forward 40 mm mount on forecastle; other 20 mm guns along sides of cargo well. *Tok To* LSM 603 (ex-USS *LSM 419*) scrapped in 1963. *Pung To* LSML 608 (ex-USS *LSM 54*) scrapped in 1974. *Pong Song Man* LSSL 109 (ex-USS LSSL 54), *Yung Hung Man* LSSL 107 (ex-USS LSSL 77), *Yong Il Man* LSSL 110 (ex-USS LSSL 84), and *Kang Hwa Man* LSSL 108 (ex-USS LSSL 91) have been scrapped.

1 Ex-US LCU TYPE

LCU 1 (ex-USS *LCU 531*)

Displacement, tons: 309 full load
Dimensions, feet (metres): 105 wl; 119·1 oa × 32·66 × 5 *(34·4; 39 × 10·7 × 1·6)*
Main engines: Diesels (Gray Marine); 675 bhp; 3 shafts = 10 knots

Former US Navy utility landing craft. Built in 1943 as LCT(6) 531. Transferred to South Korea in Dec 1960. No name assigned.

AUXILIARY SHIPS

1 REPAIR SHIP: Ex-US ARL TYPE

Name	No.	Builders	Commissioned
DUK SU (ex-USS *Minotaur*, ARL 15, ex-*LST 645*)	ARL 1	Chicago Bridge & Iron Co, Seneca, Illinois	30 Sep 1944

Displacement, tons: 2 366 standard; 4 100 full load
Dimensions, feet (metres): 316 wl; 328 oa × 50 × 11·2 *(103·6; 107·5 × 16·4 × 3·7)*
Guns: 8—40 mm AA; 12—10 mm AA
Main engines: Diesels (General Motors); 1 800 bhp; 2 shafts = 11·6 knots
Complement: approx 250

DUK SU

Former US Navy landing craft repair ship. Converted during construction from an LST. Launched on 20 Sep 1944, transferred to South Korea in Oct 1955.

6 SUPPLY SHIPS: Ex-US ARMY FS TYPE

Name	No.	Builders
IN CHON (ex-US Army *FS 198*)	AKL 902	Higgins Industries
CHI NAM PO (ex-US Army *FS 356*)	AKL 905	J. K: Welding
MOK PO (ex-USCGC *Trillium*, WAK 170, ex-US Army *FS 397*)	AKL 907	Ingalls, Decatur, Alabama
KU SAN (ex-USS *Sharps*, AKL 10, ex-*AG 139*, ex-US Army *FS 385*)	AKL 908	Ingalls, Decatur, Alabama
MA SAN (ex-USS *AKL 35*, ex-US Army *FS 383*)	AKL 909	Ingalls, Decatur, Alabama
UL SAN (ex-USS *Brule*, AKL 28, ex-US Army *FS 370*)	AKL 910	Sturgeon Bay

Displacement, tons: approx 700
Dimensions, feet (metres): 176·5 oa × 32·8 × 10 *(57·9 × 10·7 × 3·3)*
Guns: 2—20 mm AA (single) in most ships
Main engines: Diesel; 1 000 bhp; 1 shaft = 10 knots
Complement: approx 20

MA SAN   1957

Originally US Army freight and supply ships built in World War II for coastal operation. *In Chon* and *Chin Nam Po* transferred to South Korea in 1951; *Mok Po, Kin San,* and *Ma San* in 1956; *Ul San* on 1 Nov 1971.
Many subsequently served in US Navy and Military Sea Transportation Service (later Military Sealift Command). Details and configurations differ. *Chin Nam Po* placed in reserve in 1971.
Pusan AKL 901 (ex-US Army FS 162), *Wonsan* AKL 903 (ex-US Army FS 254), *Song Chin* AKL 906 (ex-US Army FS 285) scrapped in 1958.

1 OILER: NORWEGIAN TYPE

Name	No.	Builders	Launched
CHUN JI (ex-*Birk*)	AO 2	A/S Berken Mek Verks, Bergen	1951

Displacement, tons: 1 400 standard; 4 160 full load
Dimensions, feet (metres): 297·5 oa × 44·5 × 18·2 *(97·5 × 14·6 × 5·9)*
Guns: 1—40 mm AA; several 20 mm AA
Main engines: 2 diesels; 1 800 bhp; 1 shaft = 12 knots
Complement: approx 70

Former Norwegian tanker. Transferred to South Korea in Sep 1953. Sister ship *Pujon* AO 3 (ex-*Hassel*) ran aground and was lost on 24 May 1971.

CHUN JI   1969

1 OILER: Ex-US 235-ft YO TYPE

Name	No.
HWA CHON (ex-*Paek Yeon AO 5*, ex-USS *Derrick YO 59*)	AO 5

Displacement, tons: 890 standard; 2 700 full load
Dimensions, feet (metres): 235 oa × 37 × 15 *(77 × 12·1 × 4·9)*
Guns: several 20 mm AA
Main engines: Diesel (Fairbanks Morse); 1 150 bhp; 1 shaft = 10·5 knots
Complement: approx 45

Former US Navy self-propelled fuel barge. Transferred to South Korea on 14 Oct 1955. Capacity 10 000 barrels petroleum. The ship has been laid up in reserve since 1974; to be scrapped.

HWA CHON

1969

2 OILERS: Ex-US 174-ft YO TYPE

KU YONG (ex-USS *YO 118*) YO 1   — (ex-US *YO 179*) YO 6

Displacement, tons: 1 400 full load
Dimensions, feet (metres): 174 oa × 32 *(57 × 10·5)*
Guns: several 20 mm AA
Main engines: Diesel (Union); 500 bhp; 1 shaft = 7 knots
Complement: approx 35

Former US Navy self-propelled fuel barges. Transferred to South Korea on 3 Dec 1946 and 13 Sep 1971, respectively. Cargo capacity 6 570 barrels.

2 AUXILIARY TUGS: Ex-US ATA TYPE

Name	No.	Builders	Launched
YONG MUN (ex-USS *Keosanqua, ATA 198*)	ATA 2	Levingston SB Co, Orange, Texas	17 Jan 1945
DO BONG (ex-USS *Pinola, ATA 206*)	ATA (S) 3	Gulfport Boiler & Welding Works, Port Arthur, Texas	14 Dec 1944

Displacement, tons: 538 standard; 835 full load
Dimensions, feet (metres): 133·66 wl × 143 oa × 33·8 *(43·8; 46·9 × 11·1)*
Guns: 1—3 inch *(76 mm)* 50 cal AA; 4—20 mm AA
Main engines: Diesel (General Motors); 1 500 bhp; 1 shaft = 13 knots
Complement: approx 45

Former US Navy auxiliary ocean tugs. Both transferred to South Korea in February 1962. *Do Bong* modified for salvage work.

The South Korean Navy also operates nine small harbour tugs (designated YTL). These are one ex-US Navy craft (YTL 550) and five ex-US Army craft.

SERVICE CRAFT

The South Korean Navy operates approximately 35 small service craft in addition to the YO-type oilers listed above and the harbour tugs noted above. These craft include open lighters, floating cranes, diving tenders, dredgers, ferries, non-self-propelled fuel barges, pontoon barges, and sludge removal barges. Most are former US Navy craft.

HYDROGRAPHIC SERVICE

The following craft are operated by the Korean Hydrographic Service and are not rated as Navy. All are engaged in surveying operations.

1 Ex-US ATA TYPE

Name	Launched
TAN YUNG (ex-USS *Tillamook, ATA 192*)	15 Nov 1944

Characteristics similar to the two ex-US ocean tugs listed above. Transferred to South Korea on 25 July 1971 for use as surveying ship. Reportedly to be disposed of in 1976.

2 Ex-BELGIAN MSI TYPE

SURO 5 (ex-Belgian *Temse*)   SURO 6 (ex-Belgian *Tournai*, ex-US *MSI 93*)

Displacement, tons: 160 light; 190 full load
Dimensions, feet (metres): 113·2 oa × 22·3 × 6 *(37·1 × 7·3 × 1·9)*
Main engines: Diesels; 1 260 bhp; 2 shafts = 15 knots

Former Belgian inshore minesweepers. Built in Belgium, the *Tournai* being financed by United States. Launched on 6 Aug 1956 and 18 May 1957, respectively. Transferred to South Korea in March 1970.

1 Ex-US YMS TYPE

SURO 3 (ex-USC&GS *Hodgson*)

Displacement, tons: 289 full load
Dimensions, feet (metres): 136 oa × 24·5 × 9·25 *(44·6 × 8·1 × 3)*
Main engines: Diesels; 1 000 bhp; 2 shafts = 15 knots

YMS type transferred to South Korea from US Coast & Geodetic Survey in 1968.

COAST GUARD

The Korean Coast Guard operates about 25 small ships and craft including several tugs and rescue craft.

KUWAIT

Personnel

1976: 200 (Coastguard) Administered by Ministry of the Interior

Mercantile Marine

Lloyd's Register of Shipping: 172 vessels of 990 857 tons gross

LIGHT FORCES

10 THORNYCROFT 78 ft TYPE (COASTAL PATROL CRAFT)

AL SALEMI	AMAN	MASHHOOR	MURSHED
AL SHURTI	INTISAR	MAYMOON	WATHAH
AL MUBARAKI	MARZOOK		

INTISAR

1972, Vosper Thornycroft

Displacement, tons: 40
Dimensions, feet (metres): 78 oa × 15·5 × 4·5 *(23·8 × 4·7 × 1·4)*
Gun: 1 MG
Main engines: 2 Rolls Royce V8 marine diesels; 1 340 shp at 1 800 rpm; 1 116 shp at 1 700 rpm = 20 knots
Range, miles: 700 at 15 knots
Complement: 12 (5 officers, 7 men)

Two were built by Thornycroft before the merger and eight by Vosper Thornycroft afterwards. *Al Salemi* and *Al Mubaraki* were shipped to Kuwait on 8 Sep 1966.
Hulls are of welded steel construction, with superstructures of aluminium alloy. Twin hydraulically operated rudders, Decca type D 202 radar. The later boats are slightly different in appearance with modified superstructure and no funnel, see photograph of *Intisar.*

2 VOSPER THORNYCROFT 56 ft TYPE
(COASTAL PATROL CRAFT)

Name	No.	Builders	Commissioned
DASTOOR	—	Vosper Thornycroft Private Ltd, Singapore	June 1974
KASAR	—	Vosper Thornycroft Private Ltd, Singapore	June 1974

KASAR (guns not fitted)

1974, Vosper Thornycroft

Displacement, tons: 25
Length, feet (metres): 56 *(1781)*
Guns: 1—20 mm; 2 MG
Main engines: 2 MTU MB6 V.331 diesels; 1 350 hp = 26 knots
Range, miles: 320 at 20 knots
Complement: 8 (2 officers, 6 men)

Ordered September 1973. Both laid down 31 Oct 1973. Steel hulls and aluminium superstructure.

7 THORNYCROFT 50 ft TYPE (COASTAL PATROL CRAFT)

Built by the Singapore Yard of Thornycroft (Malaysia) Limited, now the Tanjong Rhu, Singapore Yard of Vosper Thornycroft Private Ltd.

1 VOSPER THORNYCROFT 46 ft TYPE
(COASTAL PATROL CRAFT)

Name	No.	Builders	Commissioned
MAHROOS	—	Vosper Thornycroft Private Ltd, Singapore	Nov 1975

Length, feet (metres): 46 *(14)*
Guns: Can mount 2—20 mm
Main engines: 2 Rolls-Royce C8M-410 diesels; 780 hp = 21+ knots
Complement: 5

Ordered in Oct 1974. Hull is of welded steel construction with aluminium superstructure.

8 VOSPER THORNYCROFT 35 ft TYPE
(COASTAL PATROL CRAFT)

Length, feet (metres): 35 *(10·3)*
Main engines: 2 turbocharged Perkins Diesels = 25 knots

Ordered July 1972 from Vosper Thornycroft Private Ltd, Singapore. Built of double-skinned teak with Cascover sheathing. First four delivered late 1972, second four in May 1973.

MAHROOS (guns not fitted)

1975, Singapore Hilton

LANDING CRAFT

3 VOSPER THORNYCROFT 88 ft TYPE

Name	No.	Builders	Commissioned
WAHEED	—	Vosper Thornycroft Private Ltd, Singapore	May 1971
FAREED	—	Vosper Thornycroft Private Ltd, Singapore	May 1971
REGGA	—	Vosper Thornycroft Private Ltd, Singapore	Nov 1975

Dimensions, feet (metres): 88 × 22·6 × 4·3 *(27 × 6·9 × 1·3)*
Main engines: 2 Rolls-Royce C8M-410 diesels; 752 bhp = 10 knots
Complement: 9 (can carry 8 passengers)

First pair ordered in 1970 and third in Oct 1974 by Kuwait Ministry of the Interior. Can carry 6 400 gals oil-fuel, 9 400 gals water and 40 tons deck cargo, the last being handled by a 2·5 ton derrick. Used to support landing-parties working on Kuwait's off-shore islands.

WAHEED

1974, Vosper Thornycroft

LAOS

The situation in this force is uncertain.

Personnel

1976: 550 officers and men

RIVER PATROL CRAFT

7	LCM (6) Type	28 tons	4 in commission, 3 in reserve
6	Cabin Type	21 tons	2 in commission, 4 in reserve
2	Chris Craft Type	15 tons	2 in commission
12	11 metre Type	10 tons	5 in commission, 7 in reserve
8	8 metre Type	6 tons	8 in reserve
7	Cargo Transport	50 tons	1 in commission, 6 in reserve

The above craft are formed into four squadrons, although at least half of them must be considered non-operational.

LEBANON

Diplomatic Representation

Naval Military and Air Attaché in London:
  Colonel F. El Hussami

Personnel

1976: 250 officers and men

Mercantile Marine

Lloyd's Register of Shipping:
  123 vessels of 167 490 tons gross

DELETION

1975   Djounieh (ex *Fairmile B. ML*)

LIGHT FORCES

3 LARGE PATROL CRAFT

Name	No.	Builders	Commissioned
TARABLOUS	31	Ch. Navals de l'Estérel	1959

Displacement, tons: 105 standard
Dimensions, feet (metres): 124·7 × 18 × 5·8 *(38 × 5·5 × 1·8)*
Guns: 2—40 mm
Main engines: 2 Mercedes-Benz (MTU) diesels; 2 shafts; 2 700 bhp = 27 knots
Range, miles: 1 500
Complement: 19 (3 officers, 16 men)

Laid down in June 1958. Launched in June 1959. Completed in 1959.

TARABLOUS

1968, Lebanese Navy

1 LARGE PATROL CRAFT

Displacement, tons: 135
Length, feet (metres): 118·1 *(36)*
Guns: 2—30 mm
Speed, knots: 29

Ordered from Hamelin SY, West Germany on 9 Jan 1974.

3 "BYBLOS" CLASS (COASTAL PATROL CRAFT)

Name	No.	Builders	Commissioned
BYBLOS	11	Ch. Navals de l'Estérel	1955
SIDON	12	Ch. Navals de l'Estérel	1955
BEYROUTH (ex-*Tir*)	13	Ch. Navals de l'Estérel	1955

Displacement, tons: 28 standard
Dimensions, feet (metres): 66 × 13·5 × 4 *(20·1 × 4·1 × 1·2)*
Guns: 1—20 mm; 2 MG
Main engines: General Motors diesels; 2 Shafts; 530 bhp = 18·5 knots

French built ML type craft. Launched in 1954-55.

LANDING CRAFT

SOUR (ex-*LCU 1474*)

Displacement, tons: 180 standard; 360 full load
Dimensions, feet (metres): 115 × 34 × 6 *(35·1 × 10·4 × 1·8)*
Guns: 2—20 mm
Main engines: 3 diesels; 3 shafts; 675 bhp = 10 knots

Former United States utility landing craft built in 1957, transferred in Nov 1958.

LIBERIA

Personnel

1976: about 150 officers and men

Mercantile Marine

Lloyd's Register of Shipping:
2 520 vessels of 65 820 414 tons gross

MOTOR GUNBOAT

ALERT (ex-US *PGM 102*) 102

Displacement, tons: 100
Dimensions, feet (metres): 95 oa × 19 × 5 *(29 × 5·8 × 1·5)*
Gun: 1—40 mm
Main engines: 4 diesels; 2 shafts; 2 200 bhp = 21 knots
Complement: 15

PGM 102 (US number) was built in the United States for transfer under the Military Aid Programme in 1967.

PRESIDENTIAL YACHT

LIBERIAN (ex-*Virginia*)

Measurement, tons: 692·27 gross; 341·6 net
Dimensions, feet (metres): 173 wl; 209 oa × 29·7 × 13·1 *(52·8; 63·7 × 9·1 × 4)*

Motor yacht of 742 tons (yacht measurement) built in 1930 by William Beardmore & Co Ltd, Dalmuir. Purchased by Liberia for use as the Presidential Yacht in 1957. Extensively refitted by Cammell Laird & Co Ltd, Birkenhead, at the end of 1962.

PATROL BOATS

ML 4001

ML 4002

Displacement, tons: 11·5
Dimensions, feet (metres): 40·5 oa × 11·5 × 3·5 *(12·3 × 3·5 × 1·1)*
Guns: 2 MG
Main engines: 2 GM diesels; 2 shafts; 380 bhp = 23 knots

Coastguard cutters built at the United States Coast Guard Yard, Curtis Bay, Maryland, presented by the USA and transferred during 1957.

ML 4002   *Dr Giorgio Arra*

LANDING CRAFT

Landing craft reported to be used for transport and general utility purposes.

LIBYA

Establishment

The Libyan Navy was established in Nov 1962 when a British Naval Mission was formed and first recruits were trained at HMS *St. Angelo*, Malta. Cadets were also trained at the Britannia Royal Navy College, Dartmouth, and technical ratings at HMS *Sultan*, Gosport, and HMS *Collingwood*, Fareham, England.

Headquarters Appointment

Senior Officer, Libyan Navy: Captain A. Shaksuki

Personnel

(a) 1976: Total 2 000 officers and ratings, including Coast Guard
(b) Voluntary service

Mining Capability

Although none of the listed Libyan ships is credited with a mining capability the fact that, in June 1973, two minefields were laid off Tripoli harbour, some eight miles out, suggests that a stock of mines is available.

Base

Tripoli. Operating Ports at Benghazi, Darna, Tobruk.

Mercantile Marine

Lloyd's Register of Shipping:
27 vessels of 241 725 tons gross

Strength of the Fleet

Type	Active	Building
Frigate	1	—
Submarines	—	?3-4
LSD	1	—
Corvettes	1	4 (missiles)
Fast Attack Craft—Missile	3	10
Large Patrol Craft	10	—
Coastal Patrol Craft	1	—
MRC	1	—

DELETIONS

Inshore Minesweepers

1973 *Brak* and *Zura* ("Ham" Class)

FRIGATE

1 VOSPER THORNYCROFT MARK 7

Name	No.	Builders	Laid down	Launched	Commissioned
DAT ASSAWARI	F 01	Vosper Thornycroft	27 Sep 1968	Sep 1969	1 Feb 1973

Displacement, tons: 1 325 standard; 1 625 full load
Length, feet (metres): 310·0 *(94·5)* pp; 330·0 *(100·6)* oa
Beam, feet (metres): 36·0 *(11·0)*
Draught, feet (metres): 11·2 *(3·4)*
A/S weapons: 1 Mortar Mk 10
Missile launchers: 6 (2 triple) Seacat close range ship-to-air
Guns: 1—4·5 in; 2—40 mm (singles); 2—35 mm (twin)
Main engines: CODOG arrangement; 2 shafts; with Kamewa cp propellers; 2 Rolls Royce gas turbines; 23 200 shp = 37·5 knots; 2 Paxman diesels; 3 500 bhp = 17 knots economical cruising speed
Range, miles: 5 700 at 17 knots

Mark 7 Frigate ordered from Vosper Thornycroft on 6 Feb 1968. Generally similar in design to the two Iranian Mark Vs built by this firm, but larger and with different armament. After trials she carried out work-up at Portland, England, reaching Tripoli autumn 1973.

Radar: AWS-1 air surveillance set; fire control radar and RDL-1 radar direction finder.

DAT ASSAWARI   *1973, John G. Callis*

SUBMARINES

There are reports of orders being placed for submarines. An enquiry made in Great Britain was turned down at Governmental level and now the most likely choice lies between 3 or 4 "Daphne" class built in France or the same number of French "Agosta" class built in Spain. A further unconfirmed report of Soviet submarines being supplied to be manned by Libyans trained in the USSR shows the uncertainty now existing.

LOGISTIC SUPPORT SHIP

1 LSD TYPE

Name	No.	Builders	Laid down	Launched	Commissioned
ZELTIN	—	Vosper Thornycroft, Woolston	1967	29 Feb 1968	23 Jan 1969

Displacement, tons: 2 200 standard; 2 470 full load
Length, feet (metres): 300·0 *(91·4)* wl; 324·0 *(98·8)* oa
Beam, feet (metres): 48·0 *(14·6)*
Draught, feet (metres): 10·2 *(3·1)*; 19·0 *(5·8)* aft when flooded
Dock:
Length, feet (metres): 135·0 *(41·1)*
Width, feet (metres): 40·0 *(12·2)*
Guns: 2—40 mm
Main engines: 2 Paxman 16 cyl diesels; 3 500 bhp; 2 shafts
Speed, knots: 15
Range, miles: 3 000 at 14 knots
Complement: As Senior Officer Ship: 101 (15 officers and 86 ratings)

ZELTIN   1969

The ship provides full logistic support, including mobile docking maintenance and repair facilities for the Libyan fleet. Craft up to 120 ft can be docked. Used as tender for Light Forces. The Vosper-Thornycroft Group received the order for this ship in Jan 1967 for delivery in late 1968.

Fitted with accommodation for a flag officer or a senior officer and staff. Operational and administrative base of the squadron. Workshops with a total area of approx 4 500 sq ft are situated amidships with ready access to the dock, and there is a 3-ton travelling gantry fitted with outriggers to cover ships berthed alongside up to 200 feet long.

CORVETTES

4 550 TON MISSILE CORVETTES

Displacement, tons: 550 full load
Dimensions, feet (metres): 202·4 oa × 30·5 × 8·9 *(61·7 oa × 9·3 × 2·7)*
Missiles: 4 Otomat
Guns: 2—76/62 mm (see note)
Main engines: Diesel engines
Complement: 54

Ordered from Cantieri Navali del Tirreno e Riuniti in 1974. Completion presumed to be 1977-78. As this corvette can be provided with two, three or four diesels, the performance is very variable. The data given above is basic information for the missile variant (schedule 1).

Electronics: ECM equipment.

Gunnery: A twin Bofors 40 mm can be fitted if required.

Radar: Air and surface search: Selenia RAN 11 LX
Navigation: Decca TM 1226.   Fire control: Elsag NA 10.

Sonar: An EDO 700E can be fitted.

550 ton Corvette   1975, CNTR

Name	No.	Builders	Commissioned
TOBRUK	—	Vosper Ltd, Portsmouth and Vickers Ltd	20 April 1966

Displacement, tons: 440 standard; 500 full load
Dimensions, feet (metres): 162 wl 177 oa × 28·5 × 13 *(49·4; 54 × 8·7 × 4)*
Guns: 1—4 in; 4—40 mm (single)
Main engines: 2 Paxman Ventura 16 YJCM diesels; 2 shafts; 3 800 bhp = 18 knots
Range, miles: 2 900 at 14 knots
Complement: 63 (5 officers and 58 ratings)

Launched on 29 July 1965, completed on 30 Mar 1966, commissioned for service at Portsmouth on 20 Apr 1966, and arrived in Tripoli on 15 June 1966. Fitted with surface warning radar, Vosper roll damping fins and air-conditioning. A suite of State apartments is included in the accommodation.

TOBRUK   1971, A. & J. Pavia

LIGHT FORCES

It is reported that 24 "Osa" class are to be transferred by USSR in 1976-77.

10 PR 72S TYPE (FAST ATTACK CRAFT—MISSILE)

Displacement, tons: 536
Dimensions, feet (metres): 207·3 oa × 29·5 × 7·9 *(63·2 oa × 9 × 2·4)*
Missiles: 4 MM 38 Exocet
Guns: 1—76 mm Oto Melara (forward); 2—40 mm Bofors Breda turret (see note) (aft); 2—20 mm Oerlikon
Main engines: 4 SACM V16-240 diesels; 20 000 bhp = 33·5 knots
Range, miles: 2 000 at 16 knots; 700 at 30 knots
Complement: 44

Ordered from France (SFCN) in 1975. This type is an advance on the PR 72 (two building for Morocco) and can be provided in a number of versions. Figures given are for the missile type.

Gunnery: The twin 40 mm aft can be replaced by a single 76 mm. CSEE optical directors for fire control.

Radar: Navigation: Decca TM 1226
Air and surface search: Thomson CSF Triton (G-Band)
Tracking: Thomson CSF Pollux (I-Band). IFF.

PR 72S   1974, SFCN

Sonar: Hull-mounted or towed sonar can be fitted.

Torpedoes: Two wire-guided torpedoes or two A/S torpedo launchers can be fitted.

3 "SUSA" CLASS (FAST ATTACK CRAFT—MISSILE)

Name	No.	Builders	Commissioned	
SEBHA (ex-*Sokna*)	—	Vosper Ltd, Portsmouth		1969
SIRTE	—	Vosper Ltd, Portsmouth	23 Jan	1969
SUSA	—	Vosper Ltd, Portsmouth	23 Jan	1969

Displacement, tons: 95 standard; 114 full load
Dimensions, feet (metres): 90·0 pp; 96·0 wl; 100·0 oa × 25·5 × 7·0 *(27·5; 29·3; 30·5 × 7·8 × 2·1)*
Missiles: 8—SS 12
Guns: 2—40 mm (single)
Main engines: 3 Bristol Siddeley "Proteus" gas turbines; 3 shafts; 12 750 bhp = 54 knots
Complement: 20

SEBHA

1969, Wright & Logan

The order for these three fast patrol boats was announced on 12 Oct 1966. They are generally similar to the "Soloven" class designed and built by Vosper for the Royal Danish Navy. Fitted with air-conditioning and modern radar and radio equipment. *Suza* was launched on 31 Aug 1967, *Sirte* on 10 Jan 1968 and *Sokna* (renamed *Sebha*) on 29 Feb 1968. First operational vessels in the world to be armed with Nord-Aviation SS 12(M) guided weapons with sighting turret instalation and other equipment developed jointly by Vosper and Nord.

4 "GARIAN" CLASS (LARGE PATROL CRAFT)

Name	No.	Builders	Commissioned	
KHAWLAN	—	Brooke Marine, Lowestoft	30 Aug	1969
MERAWA	—	Brooke Marine, Lowestoft	early	1970
SABRATHA	—	Brooke Marine, Lowestoft	early	1970
GARIAN	—	Brooke Marine, Lowestoft	30 Aug	1969

Displacement, tons: 120 standard; 159 full load
Dimensions, feet (metres): 100 pp; 106 oa × 21·2 × 5·5 *(30·5; 32·3 × 6·5 × 1·7)*
Gun: 1—20 mm
Main engines: 2 Paxman diesels; 1 100 bhp = 14 knots
Range, miles: 1 500 at 12 knots
Complement: 15 to 22

Launched on 21 April 29, May, 25 Oct and 30 Sep 1969, respectively.

KHAWLAN

1970, Brooke Marine

6 THORNYCROFT TYPE (LARGE PATROL CRAFT)

Name	No.	Builders	Commissioned	
AKRAMA	—	Vosper Thornycroft	early	1969
AR RAKIB	—	John I. Thornycroft, Woolston	4 May	1967
BENINA	—	Vosper Thornycroft	29 Aug	1968
FARWA	—	John I. Thornycroft, Woolston	4 May	1967
HOMS	—	Vosper Thornycroft	early	1969
MISURATA	—	Vosper Thornycroft	29 Aug	1968

Displacement, tons: 100
Dimensions, feet (metres): 100 × 21 × 5·5 *(30·5 × 6·4 × 1·7)*
Gun: 1—20 mm
Main engines: 3 Rolls-Royce DV8TLM Diesels; 1 740 bhp = 18 knots
Range, miles: 1 800 at 14 knots

Welded steel construction. Slight difference in silhouette between first pair and the remainder.

FARWA

1969, Thornycroft

1 THORNYCROFT TYPE (COASTAL PATROL CRAFT)

Dimensions, feet (metres): 78 × 15 × 4·5 *(23·8 × 4·6 × 1·4)*
Gun: 1 MG
Main engines: 3 Rolls-Royce diesels; 3 shafts; 945 bhp = 22·5 knots
Range, miles: 400 at 15 knots

Built by John I. Thornycroft, Singapore in 1962. Two similar but smaller boats transferred to Malta in 1974.

MAINTENANCE REPAIR CRAFT

ZLEITEN (ex-*MRC 1013*, ex-*LCT*)

Displacement, tons: 657 standard; 900 approx full load
Dimensions, feet (metres): 225·0 pp; 231·3 oa × 39·0 × 5·0 *(68·6; 70·5 × 11·9 × 1·5)*
Main engines: 4 Paxman diesels; 2 shafts; 1 840 bhp × 9 knots cruising

Built in 1944-45. Purchased from Great Britain on 5 Sep 1966. Now a hulk.

MALAWI

Three small patrol-boats are deployed on Lake Nyasa; the first was bought in 1968.

MALAYSIA

SEE ALSO SABAH

Administration

Minister of Defence:
Hon. Tun Haji Abdul Razak Bin Hussain SMN

Headquarters Appointments

Chief of the Naval Staff:
Rear-Admiral Datuk K. Thanabalasingam, DPMJ, JMN, SMJ
Deputy Chief of the Naval Staff:
Commodore Mohd. Zain Bin Mohd. Salleh, KMN

Senior Commands

Commander Naval Forces Naval Area 1:
Colonel (N) Mohd Sidek Bin Shabudin, KMN
Commander Naval Forces Naval Area 2:
Colonel (N) P. K. Nettur, KMN

Diplomatic Representation

Services Adviser in London:
Colonel M. Shah Bin Yahaya

Personnel

(a) 1976: 5 500 officers and ratings (Reserves about 1 000)
(b) Voluntary service

Bases

KD *Malaya*, Johore Straits; Port Swettenham; Penang; Labuan.

Prefix to Ships' Names

The names of Malaysian warships are prefixed by KD, (Kapal Diraja).

Mercantile Marine

Lloyd's Register of Shipping:
129 vessels of 358 798 tons gross

Strength of the Fleet

Type	Active	Building
Frigates	2	—
Fast Attack Craft—Missile	8	10
Large Patrol Craft	24	—
Minesweepers—Coastal	6	—
Diving Tender	1	—
Survey Vessel	1	—
LSTs	3	—
Police Launches	27	3

PENNANT LIST

Frigates

F 24	Rahmat
F 433	Hang Tuah

Light Forces

P 34	Kris
P 36	Sundang
P 37	Badek
P 38	Renchong
P 39	Tombak
P 40	Lembing
P 41	Serampang
P 42	Panah
P 43	Kerambit
P 44	Beledau
P 45	Kelewang
P 46	Rentaka
P 47	Sri Perlis

Light Forces

P 49	Sri Johor
P 150	Perkasa
P 151	Handalan
P 152	Gempita
P 153	Pendekar
P 3138	Sri Kedah
P 3139	Sri Selangor
P 3140	Sri Perak
P 3141	Sri Pahang
P 3142	Sri Kelantan
P 3143	Sri Trengganu
P 3144	Sri Sabah
P 3145	Sri Sarawak
P 3146	Sri Negri Sembilan
P 3147	Sri Melaka
P 3501	Perdana
P 3502	Serang
P 3503	Ganas
P 3504	Ganyang

Minewarfare Forces

M 1127	Mahamiru
M 1134	Kinabalu
M 1143	Ledang
M 1163	Tahan
M 1168	Jerai
M 1172	Brinchang

Support Forces

A 151	Perantau
A 1109	Duyong
A 1500	Sri Langkawi

Police Craft

PX 1-30	Coastal Patrol Craft

FRIGATES

1 YARROW TYPE

Name	No.	Builders	Laid down	Launched	Commissioned
RAHMAT (ex-*Hang Jebat*)	F 24	Yarrow	Feb 1966	18 Dec 1967	Mar 1971

Displacement, tons: 1 250 standard; 1 600 full load
Length, feet (metres): 300·0 *(91·44)* pp; 308 *(93·9)* oa
Beam, feet (metres): 34·1 *(10·4)*
Draught, feet (metres): 14·8 *(4·5)*
Aircraft: 1 helicopter
Missile launchers: 1 quadruple Seacat surface-to-air
Guns: 1—4·5 in *(114 mm)*; 2—40 mm
A/S weapon: 1 Limbo three-barrelled mortar
Main engines: 1 Bristol Siddeley Olympus gas turbine; 19 500 shp; Crossley Pielstick Diesel; 3 850 bhp; 2 shafts
Speed, knots: 26 boosted by gas turbine; 16 on diesel alone
Range, miles: 6 000 at 16 knots; 1 000 at 26 knots
Complement: 140

General purpose frigate of new design developed by Yarrow. Fully automatic with saving in complement. Ordered on 11 Feb 1966.

Radar: Air Surveillance: HSA LW 02. Fire control: M 20 with radar in spherical radome for guns; M 44 for Seacat.

RAHMAT

1972, Wright & Logan

1 Ex-BRITISH "LOCH" CLASS

Name	No.	Builders	Laid down	Launched	Commissioned
HANG TUAH (ex-HMS *Loch Insh*)	F 433	Henry Robb Ltd, Leith	17 Nov 1943	10 May 1944	20 Oct 1944

Displacement, tons: 1 575 standard; 2 400 full load
Length, feet (metres): 297·2 *(90·6)* wl; 307·0 *(93·6)* oa
Beam, feet (metres): 38·5 *(11·7)*
Draught, feet (metres): 14·8 *(4·5)*
Guns: 6—40 mm
Main engines: 2 triple expansion; 5 500 ihp; 2 shafts
Boilers: 2 Admiralty 3-drum
Speed, knots: 19·5
Range, miles: 6 400 at 10 knots
Complement: 140

On transfer, refitted (in Portsmouth Dockyard) with helicopter deck, air-conditioning, modern radar and extra accommodation. Re-commissioned on 12 Oct 1964. Sailed on 12 Nov 1964. Converted into a training ship in April 1971, the two 4-inch guns and the two Squid mortars having been removed. *Hang Tuah* was the name of a Malay Admiral of the 15th century.

Radar: Search: Type 272.

HANG TUAH

1972, Royal Malaysian Navy

LIGHT FORCES

4 + 4 "PERDANA" CLASS (FAST ATTACK CRAFT—MISSILE)

Name	No.	Builders	Commissioned	
PERDANA	P 3501	Constructions Mécaniques de Normandie	Dec	1972
GANAS	P 3503	Constructions Mécaniques de Normandie	28 Feb	1973
SERANG	P 3502	Constructions Mécaniques de Normandie	31 Jan	1973
GANYANG	P 3504	Constructions Mécaniques de Normandie	20 Mar	1973

GANAS   4/1973, Wright & Logan

Displacement, tons: 234 standard; 265 full load
Dimensions, feet (metres): 154·2 × 23·1 × 12·8 (47·0 × 7·0 × 3·9)
Missile launchers: 2 MM38 Exocet
Guns: 1—57 mm Bofors; 1—40 mm 70 cal Bofors
Main engines: 4 MTU diesels; 4 shafts; 14 000 bhp = 36·5 knots
Range, miles: 800 at 25 knots

Perdana launched 31 May 1972 and *Ganas* launched 26 Oct 1972, *Serang* launched 22 Dec 1971, and *Ganyang* launched 16 March 1972. All of basic "La Combattante II" design. Left Cherbourg for Malaysia 2 May 1973. Additional four ordered early 1976.

6 FAST ATTACK CRAFT—MISSILE

150 ft craft ordered from Leong-Lürssen Yard, Butterworth, Malaysia late 1975 for completion late 1976-1977.

4 "PERKASA" CLASS (FAST ATTACK CRAFT—MISSILE)

Name	No.	Builders	Commissioned
GEMPITA	P 152	Vosper Ltd, Portsmouth	1967
HANDALAN	P 151	Vosper Ltd, Portsmouth	1967
PENDEKAR	P 153	Vosper Ltd, Portsmouth	1967
PERKASA	P 150	Vosper Ltd, Portsmouth	1967

Displacement, tons: 95 standard; 114 full load
Dimensions, feet (metres): 90 pp; 96 wl; 99 oa × 25·5 × 7 (27·5; 29·3; 30·2 × 7·8 × 2·1)
Missiles: 8—SS 12 (M) in 2 quadruple launchers
Guns: 1—40 mm; 1—20 mm
Main engines: 3 Rolls Royce Proteus gas turbines; 3 shafts; 12 750 bhp = 54 knots; GM diesels on wing shafts for cruising = 10 knots

The design is a combination of the "Brave" class hull form and Ferocity type construction. Ordered on 22 Oct 1964. They can also operate in the gunboat role or a minelaying role. *Perkasa* (Valiant) was launched on 26 Oct 1965, *Handalan* (Reliant) on 18 Jan 1966, *Gempita* (Thunderer) on 6 Apr 1966 and *Pendekar* (Champion) on 24 June 1966. The hull is entirely of glued laminated wooden construction, with upperworks of aluminium alloy. Equipment includes Rover gas turbine generating sets, full air-conditioning, Decca radar and comprehensive navigation and communications system. The craft were shipped to Malaysia in mid-1967. They were re-armed with eight SS.12 missiles in place of four 21-inch torpedoes in 1971.

GEMPITA (Firing SS 12 missile)   1972, Royal Malaysian Navy

6 "KEDAH" CLASS (LARGE PATROL CRAFT)

Name	No.	Builders	Commissioned	
SRI KEDAH	P 3138	Vosper Ltd, Portsmouth	6 Feb	1963
SRI KELANTAN	P 3142	Vosper Ltd, Portsmouth	12 Nov	1963
SRI PAHANG	P 3141	Vosper Ltd, Portsmouth	2 Aug	1963
SRI PERAK	P 3140	Vosper Ltd, Portsmouth	June	1963
SRI SELANGOR	P 3139	Vosper Ltd, Portsmouth	25 Mar	1963
SRI TRENGGANU	P 3143	Vosper Ltd, Portsmouth	16 Dec	1963

4 "SABAH" CLASS (LARGE PATROL CRAFT)

Name	No.	Builders	Commissioned	
SRI MELAKA	P 3147	Vosper Ltd, Portsmouth	2 Nov	1964
SRI NEGRI SEMBILAN	P 3146	Vosper Ltd, Portsmouth	28 Sep	1964
SRI SABAH	P 3144	Vosper Ltd, Portsmouth	2 Sep	1964
SRI SARAWAK	P 3145	Vosper Ltd, Portsmouth	30 Sep	1964

14 "KRIS" CLASS (LARGE PATROL CRAFT)

Name	No.	Builders	Commissioned	
BADEK	P 37	Vosper Ltd, Portsmouth	15 Dec	1966
BELEDAU	P 44	Vosper Ltd, Portsmouth	12 Sep	1967
KELEWANG	P 45	Vosper Ltd, Portsmouth	4 Oct	1967
KERAMBIT	P 43	Vosper Ltd, Portsmouth	28 July	1967
KRIS	P 34	Vosper Ltd, Portsmouth	1 Jan	1966
LEMBING	P 40	Vosper Ltd, Portsmouth	12 Apr	1967
PANAH	P 42	Vosper Ltd, Portsmouth	27 July	1967
RENCHONG	P 38	Vosper Ltd, Portsmouth	17 Jan	1967
RENTAKA	P 46	Vosper Ltd, Portsmouth	22 Sep	1967
SERAMPANG	P 41	Vosper Ltd, Portsmouth	19 May	1967
SRI JOHOR	P 49	Vosper Ltd, Portsmouth	14 Feb	1968
SRI PERLIS	P 47	Vosper Ltd, Portsmouth	24 Jan	1968
SUNDANG	P 36	Vosper Ltd, Portsmouth	29 Nov	1966
TOMBAK	P 39	Vosper Ltd, Portsmouth	2 Mar	1967

BADEK ("Kris" Class)   1972, Royal Malaysian Navy

Displacement, tons: 96 standard; 109 full load
Dimensions, feet (metres): 95 wl; 103 oa × 19·8 × 5·5 (29; 31·4 × 6 × 1·7)
Guns: 2—40 mm; 70 cal
Main engines: 2 Bristol Siddeley/Maybach (MTU) MD 655/18 diesels; 3 500 bhp = 27 knots
Range, miles: 1 400 (*Sabah* class 1 660) at 14 knots
Complement: 22 (3 officers, 19 ratings)

The first six boats, constituting the "Kedah" class were ordered in 1961 for delivery in 1963. The four boats of the "Sabah" class were ordered in 1963 for delivery in 1964. The remaining 14 boats of the "Kris" class were ordered in 1965 for delivery between 1966 and 1968. All are of prefabricated steel construction and are fitted with Decca radar, air-conditioning and Vosper roll damping equipment. The differences between the three classes are minor, the later ones having improved radar, communications, evaporators and engines of Maybach (MTU), as opposed to Bristol Siddeley construction. *Sri Johor*, the last of the 14 boats of the "Kris" class, was launched on 22 June 1967.

MINE WARFARE FORCES

6 Ex-BRITISH "TON" CLASS (MINESWEEPERS—COASTAL)

Name	No.	Builders	Commissioned
BRINCHANG (ex-HMS *Thankerton*)	M 1172	Camper and Nicholson	1957
JERAI (ex-HMS *Dilston*)	M 1168	Cook, Welton and Gemmell	1955
KINABALU (ex-HMS *Essington*)	M 1134	Camper and Nicholson	1955
LEDANG (ex-HMS *Hexton*)	M 1143	Cook, Welton and Gemmell	1954
MAHAMIRU (ex-HMS *Darlaston*)	M 1127	Cook, Welton and Gemmell	1954
TAHAN (ex-HMS *Lullington*)	M 1163	Harland and Wolff	1956

Displacement, tons: 360 standard; 425 full load
Dimensions, feet (metres): 140 pp; 152 oa × 28·8 × 8·2 *(42·7; 46·4 × 8·8 × 2·5)*
Guns: 1 —40 mm forward; 2—20 mm aft
Main engines: Diesels; 2 shafts; 2 500 bhp = 15 knots
Oil fuel, tons: 45
Range, miles: 2 300 at 13 knots
Complement: 39

MAHAMIRU

1972, Royal Malaysian Navy

Mahamiru transferred from the Royal Navy on May 1960. *Ledang*, refitted at Chatham Dockyard before transfer, commissioned for Malaysia in Oct 1963. *Jerai* and *Kinabalu*, refitted in Great Britain, arrived in Malaysia summer 1964. *Brinchang* and *Tahan*, refitted in Singapore, transfer- red to Malaysian Navy in May and Apr 1966, respectively. All six underwent a 9-month refit by Vosper Thornycroft, Singapore during 1972-73 which will extend their availability by some years.

AMPHIBIOUS FORCES

3 Ex-US 511-1152 SERIES LSTs

SRI LANGKAWI (ex-USS *Hunterdon County LST 838, AGP 838*) A 1500
— (ex-USS *Henry County LST 824*)
— (ex-USS *Sedgewick County LST 1123*)

Displacement, tons: 1 653 standard; 2 366 beaching; 4 080 full load
Dimensions, feet (metres): 316·0 wl; 328·0 oa × 50·0 × 14·0 *(96·4; 100 × 15·3 × 4·3)*
Guns: 8—40 mm (2 twin, 4 single)
Main engines: GM diesels; 2 shafts; 1 700 bhp = 11·6 knots
Complement: 138 (11 officers, 127 ratings)

Built in 1945. *Sri Langkawi* transferred from the US Navy and commissioned in the Royal Malaysian Navy on 1 July 1971. Other two transferred 1976. All used as cargo support ships. Cargo capacity 2 100 tons.

SRI LANGKAWI

1972, Royal Malaysian Navy

SURVEY VESSEL

1 Ex-BRITISH "TON" CLASS

Name	No.	Builders	Commissioned
PERANTAU (ex-HMS *Myrmidon*, ex-HMS *Edderton*)	A 151	Doig	20 July 1964

Displacement, tons: 360 standard; 420 full load
Dimensions, feet (metres): 152 oa × 28·8 × 8·2 *(46·4 × 8·8 × 2·5)*
Main engines: Diesels; 2 shafts; 3 000 bhp = 15 knots
Range, miles: 2 300 at 13 knots
Complement: 35

A former coastal minesweeper of the "Ton" type, converted by the Royal Navy into a survey ship, renamed *Myrmidon* in Apr 1964, and commissioned for service on 20 July 1964. Paid off in 1968 and purchased by Malaysia in 1969. Service in Malaysian waters since 1970.

Replacement: A contract was placed in early 1975 for a replacement new-design survey ship to be built in Malaysia with assistance from Lürssen, Vegesack.

PERANTAU

1972, Royal Malaysian Navy

DIVING TENDER

Name	No.	Builders	Commissioned
DUYONG	A 1109	Kall Teck (Pte) Ltd, Singapore	5 Jan 1971

Displacement, tons: 120 standard; 140 full load
Dimensions, feet (metres): 99·5 wl; 110·0 oa × 21·0 × 5·8 *(30·3; 33·6 × 6·4 × 1·8)*
Gun: 1—20 mm
Main engines: 2 Cummins diesels; 1 900 rpm; 500 bhp = 10 knots
Complement: 23

Launched on 18 Aug 1970.

DUYONG

1973

ROYAL MALAYSIAN POLICE

18 PX CLASS

MAHKOTA PX 1	**BENTARA** PX 7	**PEKAN** PX 13	
TEMENGGONG PX 2	**PERWIRA** PX 8	**KELANG** PX 14	
HULUBALANG PX 3	**PERTANDA** PX 9	**KUALA KANGSAR** PX 15	
MAHARAJASETIA PX 4	**SHAHBANDAR** PX 10	**ARAU** PX 16	
MAHARAJALELA PX 5	**SANGSETIA** PX 11	**SRI GUMANTONG** PX 17	
PAHLAWAN PX 6	**LAKSAMANA** PX 12	**SRI LABUAN** PX 18	

Displacement, tons: 85
Dimensions, feet (metres): 87·5 oa × 19 × 4·8 *(26·7 × 5·8 × 1·5)*
Guns: 2—20 mm
Main engines: 2 Mercedes Benz (MTU) diesels; 2 shafts; 2 700 hp = 25 knots
Range, miles: 700 at 15 knots
Complement: 15

6 IMPROVED PX CLASS

ALOR STAR PX 19　**KUALA TRENGGANU** PX 21　**SRI MENANTI** PX 23
KOTA BAHRU PX 20　**JOHORE BAHRU** PX 22　**KUCHING** PX 24

Displacement, tons: 92
Dimensions, feet (metres): 91 oa *(27·8)*
Guns: 2—20 mm
Main engines: 2 (MTU) diesels; 2 460 hp = 25 knots
Range, miles: 750 at 15 knots
Complement: 18

All 24 boats built by Vosper Thornycroft Private, Singapore; PX class between 1963 and 1970, Improved PX class 1972-73. *Sri Gumantong* and *Sri Labuan* operated by Sabah Government, remainder by Royal Malaysian Police.

SRI MENANTI

1972, Yam Photos, Singapore

3 + 3 LÜRSSEN PATROL CRAFT

SRI — PX 25　　**SRI KUDAT** PX 26　　**SRI TAWAU** PX 27

Of 62·5 tons and 25 knots with 1—20 mm. Completed mid-1973. Three more building.

MALAGASY

Personnel

1976: 300 officers and men (including Marine Company)

Mercantile Marine

Lloyd's Register of Shipping: 50 vessels of 44 273 tons gross

LIGHT FORCES

1 LARGE PATROL CRAFT

Name	No.	Builders	Commissioned
MALAIKA	—	Chantiers Navals Franco-Belges	Dec 1967

Displacement, tons: 235 light
Dimensions, feet (metres): 149·3 pp; 155·8 oa × 23·6 × 8·2 *(45·5; 47·5 × 7·1 × 2·5)*
Guns: 2—40 mm
Main engines: 2 MGO diesels; 2 shafts; 2 400 bhp = 18·5 knots
Range, miles: 4 000 at 18 knots
Complement: 25

Ordered by the French Navy for delivery to Madagascar. Laid down in Nov 1966, launched on 22 Mar 1967.

5 PATROL BOATS

Displacement, tons: 46
Gun: 1—40 mm
Main engines: 2 diesels = 22 knots

Used by the Maritime Police. Built by Küstenwache in 1962.

AMPHIBIOUS FORCE

1 "BATRAM" CLASS

Name	No.	Builders	Commissioned
TOKY	—	Arsenal de Diego Suarez	Oct 1974

Displacement, tons: 810
Dimensions, feet (metres): 217·8 × 41 × 6·2 *(66·4 × 12·5 × 1·9)*
Missiles: 8—SS12
Guns: 2—40 mm
Main engines: 2 MGO diesels; 2 400 hp; 2 shafts = 13 knots
Complement: 27
Range, miles: 3 000 at 12 knots

Similar to French EDIC. Bow doors. Can carry 250 tons stores and 30 passengers or 120 troops over short distances. Paid for by the French Government as military assistance.

TRAINING SHIP

Name	No.	Builders	Commissioned
FANANTENANA (ex-*Richelieu*)	—	A. G. Weser, Bremen, Germany	1959

Displacement, tons: 1 040 standard; 1 200 full load
Dimensions, feet (metres): 183·7 pp; 206·4 oa × 30 × 14·8 *(56; 62·9 × 9·2 × 4·5)*
Guns: 2—40 mm
Main engines: 2 Deutz diesels; 1 shaft; 1 060 + 500 bhp = 12 knots

Trawler purchased and converted in 1966-67 to Coast Guard and training ship. 691 tons gross.

TENDER

JASMINE (ex-*D 385*, ex-*D 211*, ex-*YMS 31*)

Displacement, tons: 280 standard; 325 full load
Dimensions, feet (metres): 134·5 × 24·5 × 12 *(41 × 7·5 × 3·7)*
Main engines: 2 diesels; 2 shafts; 1 000 bhp = 12 knots
Oil fuel, tons: 22

Former coastal minesweeper of the ex-US YMS type launched on 10 April 1942 acquired by France in 1954 and Malagasy in 1965.

MALTA

A coastal patrol force of small craft was formed in 1973. It is manned by the Maltese Regiment and primarily employed as a coastguard.

Mercantile Marine

Lloyd's Register of Shipping: 31 vessels of 45 950 tons gross

2 Ex-US "SWIFT" CLASS

C 23   C 24

Displacement, tons: 22·5
Dimensions, feet (metres): 50 × 13 × 3·5 *(15·6 × 4 × 1·2)*
Guns: 3—12·7 cal MG
Main engines: 2 Gray diesels = 25 knots
Endurance: 24 hours
Complement: 6

Built in 1967. Bought in Jan 1971.

C 23 and 24   *1975, D. Bateman*

3 Ex-GERMAN CUSTOMS LAUNCHES

C 27 (ex-*Brunsbuttel*)

Of 90 tons and 104 feet *(31·7 m)*
Gun—1 MG. Built by Buschmann, Hamburg.

C 27   *1975, D. Bateman*

C 28 (ex-*Geier*)

Of 115 tons and 92 feet *(28 m)*.
Gun—1 MG.

C 28   *1975, D. Bateman*

C 29 (ex-*Kondor*)

Of 100 tons and 92 feet *(28 m)*.
Gun—1 MG. Built by Lürssen, Vegesack 1952.

C 29   *1975, D. Bateman*

2 Ex-LIBYAN CUSTOMS LAUNCHES

Dimensions, feet (metres): 58 × 12·5 × 3·5 *(17·7 × 3·8 × 1·2)*
Gun: 1 Light MG
Main engines: 2 RR Diesels; 2 shafts; 630 bhp = 21 knots
Range, miles: 350 at 12 knots

Wooden hulled boats built by John I. Thornycroft & Co, Hampton in 1963. First transferred 16 Jan 1974.

1 CUSTOMS LAUNCH

C 21

Built by Malta Drydocks 1969 and purchased 1973.

MALDIVES

A series of widely separated atolls where fishing has been interrupted by foreign craft and the small communities can be reached only by sea.

Mercantile Marine

Lloyd's Register of Shipping: 37 vessels of 95 154 tons gross.

1 FAIREY MARINE 45 ft TYPE

Provided for patrol and intercommunication duties in 1975.

FAIREY 45 ft TYPE   1975, Brian Manby

MALI

Personnel

1976: 50 officers and men

Patrol Craft

A small river patrol service with 3 craft.

MAURITANIA

Mercantile Marine

Lloyd's Register of Shipping: 4 vessels of 1 681 tons gross

Personnel

(a) 1976: 200 officers and men
(b) Voluntary service

PATROL BOATS

Name	No.	Builders	Commissioned	Name	No.	Builders	Commissioned
DAR EL BARKA	—	Chantiers Navales de l'Estérel	June 1969	IM RAQ NI	—	Chantiers Navales de l'Estérel	Nov 1965
TICHITT	—	Chantiers Navales de l'Estérel	April 1969	SLOUGHI	—	Chantiers Navales de l'Estérel	May 1968

Displacement, tons: 75 standard; 80 full load
Dimensions, feet (metres): 105 × 18·9 × 5·5 *(31·4 × 5·8 × 1·7)*
Guns: 1—20 mm; 1 MG
Main engines: 2 Mercedes Maybach (MTU) diesels; 2 shafts; 2 700 bhp = 28 knots
Range, miles: 1 500 at 15 knots
Complement: 19

Displacement, tons: 20
Dimensions, feet (metres): 59 × 13·5 × 3·8 *(18 × 4·1 × 1·1)*
Gun: 1—12·7 mm
Main engines: 2 GM diesels; 512 bhp = 21 knots
Range, miles: 860 at 12 knots

CHINGUETTI

Small patrol craft reaching the end of her life.

MAURITIUS

Mercantile Marine

Lloyd's Register of Shipping: 12 vessels of 33 105 tons gross

1 Ex-INDIAN "ABHAY" CLASS (LARGE PATROL CRAFT)

Displacement, tons: 120 standard; 151 full load
Dimensions, feet (metres): 110 pp; 117·2 oa × 20 × 5 *(33·6 pp; 35·7 oa × 6·1 × 1·5)*
Gun: 1—40 mm
Main engines: 2 diesels = 18 knots

Built by Hooghly D & E Co, Calcutta 1961. Transferred April 1974.

MEXICO

Headquarters Appointments

Secretary of the Navy:
Admiral C. G. Demn. Luis M. Bravo Carrera
Under-Secretary of the Navy:
Rear-Admiral Ing M. N. Ricardo Chazaro Lara
Commander-in-Chief of the Navy:
Vice-Admiral C. G. Demn. Humberto Uribe Escandon
Chief of the Naval Staff:
Rear-Admiral C. G. Demn. Miguel A. Gomez Ortega
Director Naval Air Services:
Rear Admiral Blanco Peyrefitte
Director of Services:
Rear-Admiral C. G. Demn. Mario Artigas Fernandez

Diplomatic Representation

Naval Attaché in London:
Rear-Admiral C. Lopez Sotelo
Naval Attaché in Washington:
Vice-Admiral Miguel Manzarraga

Personnel

a) 1976: Total 11 000 officers and men (including Naval Air Force and Marines)
b) Voluntary Service

Mercantile Marine

Lloyd's Register of Shipping:
274 vessels of 574 857 tons gross

Naval Air Force

Naval air bases at Mexico City, Las Bajadas, Puerto Cortes, Isla Mujeres, Ensenada.

4 Hu-16 Albatros
2 Bell 47G helicopters
1 Bell 47J helicopter
4 Alouette III helicopters
5 Hughes 269A
4 DC 3 (Dakota)
1 Riley Turbo-Rocket
1 Cessna 402B
3 Beechcraft C45H
4 Cessna 150
1 Cessna 180-D
1 Cessna 337
1 Cessna 402B
1 Stearman
3 Mentor T-43B

Naval Bases

The Naval Command is split between the Pacific and Gulf areas and each subdivided into Naval Zones and, subsequently, Naval Sectors.

Gulf Command: (odd numbered zones):
Veracruz (HQ 3rd Naval Zone and Command HQ)
Tampico (1st Naval Zone)
Ciudad del Carmen (5th Naval Zone)
Isla Mujeres (7th Naval Zone)
Tuxpan, Coatzacoalcos, Progreso, Chetumal (Naval Sector HQs)

Pacific Command: (even numbered zones):
Acapulco (HQ 8th Naval Zone and Command HQ)
Puerto Cortes (2nd Naval Zone)
Guaymas (4th Naval Zone)
Manzanillo (6th Naval Zone)
Ensenada, La Paz, Mazatlan, Salina Cruz (Naval Sector HQs)

Strength of the Fleet

Type	Active	Building
Destroyers	2	—
Frigates	7	—
Corvettes	18	—
Minesweepers Ocean (some as escorts)	17	—
Large Patrol Craft	21	10
Survey Vessel	1	—
Coastal and River Patrol Craft	12	—
Transport	1	—
LSTs (1 repair ship)	3	—
Tankers-Harbour	2	—
Tugs	6	—
Floating Dock	1	—
Training Ship	1	—
Floating Cranes	7	—

Frigates

1972 *Potosi, Queretaro* ("Guanajato" class). *California* (APD type) standard (16 Jan)
1975 *Guanajato*

DELETIONS

Survey Ships

1973 *Sotavento*
1975 *Virgilio Uribe*

Tug

1974 *R4*

DESTROYERS

2 Ex-US "FLETCHER" CLASS

Name	No.	Builders	Laid down	Launched	Commissioned
CUAUTHEMOC (ex-USS *Harrison, DD 573*)	F 1	Consolidated Steel	25 July 1941	7 May 1942	25 Jan 1943
CUITLAHUAC (ex-USS *John Rodgers, DD 574*)	F 2	Consolidated Steel	25 July 1941	7 May 1942	9 Feb 1943

Displacement, tons: 2 100 standard; 3 050 full load
Length, feet (metres): 376·5 *(114·7)* oa
Beam, feet (metres): 39·5 *(12·0)*
Draught, feet (metres): 18·0 *(5·5)*
Guns (original): 5—5 in *(127 mm)*; 5—40 mm; 7—20 mm
Torpedo tubes: 5—21 in *(533 mm)* (quintuple)
A/S weapons: 8 DCT, 2 Hedgehogs
Main engines: 2 geared turbines; 2 shafts; 60 000 shp
Boilers: 4
Speed, knots: 36; 14 economical
Oil fuel, tons: 650
Range, miles: 5 000 at 14 knots
Complement: 197

Former US destroyers of the original "Fletcher" class. Transferred to the Mexican Navy in Aug 1970.

CUAUTHEMOC

1972, Mexican Navy

FRIGATES

1 Ex-US "EDSALL" CLASS

Name	No.	Builders	Laid down	Launched	Commissioned
MANUEL AZUETA (ex-USS *Hurst, DE 250*)	IA 06	Brown SB Co, Houston	1942	14 April 1943	30 Aug 1943

Displacement, tons: 1 200 standard; 1 850 full load
Dimensions, feet (metres): 306 × 36·6 × 13 *(93·3 × 11·3 × 4)*
Guns: 3—3 in *(76 mm)*, 50 cal
A/S weapons: 2 Hedgehogs; DC racks
Main engines: 4 diesels; 6 000 shp; 2 shafts
Speed, knots: 20; 12 economical
Complement: 149

Transferred to Mexico 1 Oct 1973.

"EDSALL" Class

USN

1 "DURANGO" CLASS

Name	No.	Builders	Laid down	Launched	Commissioned
DURANGO	B-1 (ex-128)	Union Naval de Levante, Valencia	1934	28 June 1935	1936

Displacement, tons: 1 600 standard; 2 000 full load
Length, feet (metres): 256·5 (78·2) oa
Beam, feet (metres): 36·6 (11·2)
Draught, feet (metres): 10·5 (3·1)
Guns: 2—4 in (102 mm); 2—2·24 in (57 mm); 4—20 mm
Main engines: 2 Enterprise DMR-38 diesels electric drive; 2 shafts; 5 000 bhp
Speed, knots: 18; 12 economical
Oil fuel, tons: 140
Range, miles: 3 000 at 12 knots
Complement: 149 (24 officers and 125 men)

Originally designed primarily as an armed transport with accommodation for 20 officers and 450 men. The two Yarrow boilers and Parsons geared turbines of 6 500 shp installed when first built were replaced with two 2 500 bhp diesels in 1967 when the ship was re-rigged with remodelled funnel. *Durango* replaced *Zaragoza* as training ship in March 1964.

DURANGO
1972, Mexican Nav

5 Ex-US APD TYPE

Name	No.	Builders	Laid down	Launched	Commissioned
CHIHUAHUA (ex-USS *Rednour*, APD 102, ex-*DE 592*)	IB-08	Bethlehem SB Co, Hingham	9 Jan 1944	1 Mar 1944	15 Mar 1945
COAHUILA (ex-USS *Barber*, LPR, ex-*APD 57*, ex-*DE 161*)	IB-02	Norfolk Navy Yard, Norfolk, Va	27 Apr 1943	20 May 1943	10 Oct 1943
PAPALOAPAN (ex-USS *Earhart*, APD 113, ex-*DE 603*)	IB-04 (ex-*H 4*)	Bethlem SB Co, Hingham	20 Mar 1945	12 May 1945	26 July 1945
TEHUANTEPEC (ex-USS *Joseph M. Auman*, APD 117, ex-*DE 674*)	IB-05 (ex-*H 5*)	Consolidated Steel Corp, Orange	8 Nov 1943	5 Feb 1944	25 Apr 1945
USUMACINTA (ex-USS *Don O. Woods*, APD 118, ex-*DE 721*)	IB-06 (ex-*H 6*)	Consolidated Steel Corp, Orange	1 Dec 1943	19 Feb 1944	28 May 1945

Displacement, tons: 1 400 standard; 2 130 full load
Length, feet (metres): 300·0 (91·5) wl; 306·0 (93·3) oa
Beam, feet (metres): 37·0 (11·3)
Draught, feet (metres): 11·3 (3·4)
Guns: 1—5 in (127 mm) 38 cal dp; 6—40 mm (3 twin); 6—20 mm (single)
Main engines: GE turbo-electric; 2 shafts; 12 000 shp
Speed, knots: 20; 13 economical
Boilers: 2 Foster Wheeler "D" with superheater
Range, miles: 5 000 at 15 knots
Oil fuel, tons: 350
Complement: 204 plus 162 troops

IB 4-6 were purchased by Mexico in December 1963 and IB 2 and 8 on 17 Feb 1969. The first four replaced the four ex-US "Tacoma" type frigates bearing the same names, which were deleted in June and Aug 1964. *California* (ex-USS *Belet* APD 109) stranded and lost 16 Jan 1972 on Bahia Peninsula.

TEHUANTEPEC
1975, Mexican Navy

CORVETTES

18 Ex-USS "AUK" Class

Name	No.
FRANCISCO ZARCO (ex-USS *Threat*, MSF 124)	IG-13
GUILLERMO PRIETO (ex-USS *Symbol*, MSF 123)	IG-02
HERMENEGILDO GALEANA (ex-USS *Sage*, MSF 111)	IG-19
IGNACIO ALTAMIRANO (ex-USS *Sway*, MSF 120)	IG-12
IGNACIO L. VALLARTA (ex-USS *Velocity*, MSF 128)	IG-14
IGNACIO DE LA LLAVE (ex-USS *Spear*, MSF 322)	IG-08
JESUS G. ORTEGA (ex-USS *Chief*, MSF 315)	IG-15
JUAN ALDARMA (ex-USS *Pilot*, MSF 104)	IG-18
JUAN N. ALVARES (ex-USS *Ardent*, MSF 340)	IG-09
LEANDRO VALLE (ex-USS *Pioneer*, MSF 105)	IG-01
MANUAL G. ZAMORA (ex-USS *Scoter*, MSF 381)	IG-16
MANUAL DOBLADO (ex-USS *Defense*, MSF 317)	IG-05
MARIANO ESCOBEDO (ex-USS *Champion*, MSF 314)	IG-03
MELCHOR OCAMPO (ex-USS *Roselle*, MSF 379)	IG-10
PONCIANO ARRIAGA (ex-USS *Competent*, MSF 316)	IG-04
SANTOS DEGOLLADO (ex-USS *Gladiator*, MSF 319)	IG-07
SEBASTIAN L. DE TEJADA (ex-USS *Devastator*, MSF 318)	IG-06
VALENTIN G. FARIAS (ex-USS *Starling*, MSF 64)	IG-11

Displacement, tons: 890 standard; 1 250 full load
Dimensions, feet (metres): 215 wl; 221·2 oa × 32·2 × 10·8 (65·6; 67·5 × 10 × 3·3)
Guns: 1—3 in 50 cal; 4—40 mm (twins); 8—20 mm (twins)
Main engines: Diesel electric; 2 shafts; 3 500 bhp
Speed, knots: 17; 10 economical
Complement: 9 officers and 96 ratings

IGNACIO DE LA LLAVE
1975, Mexican Navy

Transferred—6 in Feb 1973, 4 in Apr 1973, 9 in Sep 1973. Employed on patrol duties—*Mariano Matamoros* of this class employed on surveying duties. (see Survey section)

MINESWEEPERS

17 Ex-US "ADMIRABLE" CLASS

Name	No.
DM 01 (ex-USS *Jubilant AM 255*)	ID-1
DM 02 (ex-USS *Hilarity AM 241*)	ID-2
DM 03 (ex-USS *Execute AM 232*)	ID-3
DM 04 (ex-USS *Specter AM 306*)	ID-4
DM 05 (ex-USS *Scuffle AM 298*)	ID-5
DM 06 (ex-USS *Eager AM 224*)	ID-6
DM 10 (ex-USS *Instill AM 252*)	ID-0
DM 11 (ex-USS *Device AM 220*)	ID-11
DM 12 (ex-USS *Ransom AM 283*)	IE-2
DM 13 (ex-USS *Knave AM 256*)	IE-3
DM 14 (ex-USS *Rebel AM 284*)	IE-4
DM 15 (ex-USS *Crag AM 214*)	IE-5
DM 16 (ex-USS *Dour AM 223*)	IE-6
DM 17 (ex-USS *Diploma AM 221*)	IE-7
DM 18 (ex-USS *Invade AM 254*)	IE-8
DM 19 (ex-USS *Intrigue AM 253*)	IE-9
DM 20 (ex-USS *Harlequin AM 365*)	IE-0

Displacement, tons: 650 standard; 945 full load
Dimensions, feet (metres): 184·5 oa × 33 × 9 *(56·3 × 10·1 × 3·1)*
Guns: 1—3 in, 50 cal 4—40 mm (twin); 6—20 mm (twins)
Main engines: 2 diesels; 2 shafts; 1 710 bhp = 15 knots
Range, miles: 4 300 at 10 knots
Complement: 104

Former US steel-hulled "180-ft" fleet minesweepers. All completed in 1943-44. Of the twenty vessels transferred at Orange, Texas, on 2 Oct 1962 ten were designated *dragaminas* for minesweeping duties, with D pennant numbers, and ten *escoltas* for escort and general purpose duties with E pennant numbers. 5 previous members of this class deleted and to be used for spare parts. DM 04 (ex-USS *Specter*) acquired Feb 1973.

DM 14   *1975, Mexican Navy*

LIGHT FORCES

21 + 10 "AZTECA" CLASS (LARGE PATROL CRAFT)

Name	No.	Builders	Commissioned
ANDRES QUINTANA ROOS	P 01	Ailsa Shipbuilding Co Ltd	1 Nov 1974
MATIAS DE CORDOVA	P 02	Scott & Sons, Bowling	22 Oct 1974
MIGUEL RAMOS ARIZPE	P 03	Ailsa Shipbuilding Co Ltd	23 Dec 1974
JOSE MARIA IZAZGU	P 04	Ailsa Shipbuilding Co Ltd	19 Dec 1974
JUAN BAUTISTA MORALES	P 05	Scott & Sons, Bowling	19 Dec 1974
IGNACIO LOPEZ RAYON	P 06	Ailsa Shipbuilding Co Ltd	19 Dec 1974
MANUEL CRECENCIO REJON	P 07	Ailsa Shipbuilding Co Ltd	4 July 1975
ANTONIO DE LA FUENTE	P 08	Ailsa Shipbuilding Co Ltd	4 July 1975
LEON GUZMAN	P 09	Scott & Sons, Bowling	7 April 1975
IGNACIO RAMIREZ	P 10	Ailsa Shipbuilding Co Ltd	17 July 1975
IGNACIO MARISCAL	P 11	Ailsa Shipbuilding Co Ltd	23 Sep 1975
HERIBERTO JARA CORONA	P 12	Ailsa Shipbuilding Co Ltd	7 Nov 1975
JOSE MARIA MAJA	P 13	J. Lamont & Co Ltd	13 Oct 1975
FELIX ROMERO	P 14	Scott & Sons, Bowling	23 June 1975
FERNANDO LIZARDI	P 15	Ailsa Shipbuilding Co Ltd	Dec 1975
FRANCISCO J. MUJICA	P 16	Ailsa Shipbuilding Co Ltd	Dec 1975
PASTOR ROUAIX	P 17	Scott & Sons, Bowling	7 Nov 1975
JOSE MARIA DEL CASTILLO VELASCO	P 18	Lamont & Co Ltd	14 Jan 1975
LUIS MANUEL ROJAS	P 19	Lamont & Co Ltd	3 April 1976
JOSE NATIVIDAD MACIAS	P 20	Lamont & Co Ltd	June 1976
ESTEBAN BACA CALDERON	P 21	Lamont & Co Ltd	June 1976
	P 22	Vera Cruz	1976

Displacement, tons: 130
Dimensions, feet (metres): 111·8 oa × 28·1 × 6·8 *(34·1 × 8·6 × 2·0)*
Guns: 1—40 mm; 1—20 mm; 2—2 in rocket launchers
Main engines: 2—12 cyl Paxman Ventura diesels; 3 600 bhp = 24 knots

JOSE MARIA IZAZGU   *1975, Mexican Navy*

Ordered by Mexico, for Fishery Protection duties, on 27 Mar 1973 from Associated British Machine Tool Makers Ltd.
HM Queen Elizabeth II went to sea in *Andres Quintana Roos* during her visit to Mexico in Mar 1975—an intention to place further orders for this class was announced shortly afterwards. Ten have been ordered for building in Mexican yards with ABMTM assistance and a final total of 80 is planned.

4 "POLIMAR" CLASS (COASTAL PATROL CRAFT)

Name	No.	Builders	Commissioned
POLIMAR 1	G 1	Astilleros de Tampico	1 Oct 1962
POLIMAR 2	G 2	Icacas Shipyard, Guerrero	1966
POLIMAR 3	G 3	Icacas Shipyard, Guerrero	1966
POLIMAR 4	G 4	Astilleros de Tampico	1968

Displacement, tons: 37 standard; 57 full load
Dimensions, feet (metres): 60·1 × 15·1 × 4·0 *(20·1 × 5·3 × 3·3)*
Gun: 1—20 mm
Main engines: 2 diesels; 456 bhp = 11 knots

Of steel construction.

POLIMAR 3   *1972, Mexican Navy*

2 "AZUETA" CLASS (COASTAL PATROL CRAFT)

Name	No.	Builders	Commissioned
AZUETA	G 9	Astilleros de Tampico	1959
VILLAPANDO	G 6	Astilleros de Tampico	1960

Displacement, tons: 80 standard; 85 full load
Dimensions, feet (metres): 85·3 × 16·4 × 7·0 *(26 × 5 × 2·1)*
Guns: 2—13·2 mm (1 twin)
Main engines: Superior diesels; 600 bhp = 12 knots

Of all steel construction.

7 RIVER TYPE (RIVER PATROL CRAFT)

AM 4	AM 5	AM 6	AM 7	AM 8	AM 9	AM 10

Displacement, tons: 37
Dimensions, feet (metres): 56·1 × 16·4 × 8·2 *(17·1 × 5 × 2·5)*
Main engines: Diesel; speed = 6 knots

Of steel construction. Built in Tampico and Veracruz. Entered service from 1960 to 1962.

TRANSPORT

Name	No.	Builders	Commissioned
ZACATECAS	B 2	Ulua Shipyard, Veracruz	1960

Displacement, tons: 785 standard
Dimensions, feet (metres): 158 × 27·2 × 10 *(48·2 × 8·3 × 2·7)*
Guns: 1—40 mm; 2—20 mm (single)
Main engines: 1 MAN diesel; 560 hp = 8 knots
Complement: 50 (13 officers and 37 men)

Launched in 1959. Cargo ship type. The hull is of welded steel construction. Cargo capacity 400 tons.

SURVEY VESSEL

1 Ex-US "AUK" CLASS

MARIANO METAMOROS (ex-USS *Herald, MSF 101*)

Details given in "Auk" class under Corvettes. Took over surveying duties from *Virgilio Uribe*.

SERVICE FORCES

2 Ex-US LST (511-1152 SERIES)

RIO PANUCO (ex-USS *Park County, LST 1077*) IA 01
MANZANILLO (ex-USS *Clearwater County, LST 602*) IA 02

Displacement, tons: 1 653 standard; 2 366 beaching; 4 080 full load
Dimensions, feet (metres): 316 wl; 328 oa × 50 × 14 *(96·4; 100 × 15·3 × 4·3)*
Guns: 6—40 mm (1 twin; 4 singles)
Main engines: 2 GM diesels; 2 shafts; 1 700 bhp = 10·5 knots
Range, miles: 6 000 at 11 knots
Complement: 130
Troop capacity: 147

Transferred to Mexico on 20 Sep 1971 and 25 May 1972 respectively. Both employed as rescue ships.

RIO PANUCO   1975, Mexican Navy

1 Ex-US "FABIUS" CLASS (ex-LST REPAIR SHIP)

VICENTE GUERRERO (ex-USS *Megara, ARVA-6*)

Displacement, tons: 1 625 light; 4 100 full load
Dimensions, feet (metres): 328 oa × 50 × 14 *(100 × 15·3 × 4·3)*
Guns: 8—40 mm
Main engines: 2 GM diesels; 2 shafts; 1 800 bhp = 14·6 knots
Range, miles: 10 000 at 10 knots
Complement: 250

Ex-aircraft repair ship sold to Mexico 1 Oct 1973.

2 Ex-US YOG TYPE (HARBOUR TANKERS)

Name	No.	Builders	Commissioned
AGUASCALIENTES (ex-*YOG 6*)	A-5	Geo H. Mathis Co Ltd, Camden, N.J.	1943
TLAXCALA (ex-*YO 107*)	A-6	Geo Lawley & Son, Neponset, Mass	1943

Displacement, tons: 440 light; 1 480 full load
Dimensions, feet (metres): 159·2 × 30 × 8·2 *(48·6 × 9·2 × 2·5)*
Guns: 2—20 mm (singles)
Main engines: Union diesel; 1 shaft; 500 bhp = 8 knots
Capacity: 6 570 barrels
Complement: 26 (5 officers and 21 ratings)

Former US self-propelled fuel oil barges. Purchased in 1964. Entered service in Nov 1964.

AGUASCALIENTES   1975, Mexican Navy

TUGS

4 Ex-US YTM TYPE

R-1 (ex-*Farallon*) A 11
R-2 (ex-*Montauk*) A 12
R-3 (ex-*Point Vicente*) A 13
R-5 (ex-*Burnt Island*) A 15

Acquired in 1968.

PRAGMAR   PATRON

Acquired in 1973.

1 FLOATING DOCK

Ex-US ARD 11

Lift capacity of 3 000 tons. Built of steel. Transferred June 1974.

7 FLOATING CRANES

Ex-US YDs 156, 157, 179, 180, 183, 194 and 203, transferred Sep 1964 to July 1971.

1 PILE DRIVER

Ex-US YPD 43 leased Aug 1968.

TRAINING SHIP

Spanish merchant ship *Monte Anaga* purchased in late 1973 for conversion into a training ship. Of 6 813 tons and built in 1959.

MONTSERRAT

Marine Police

The following craft is employed on general patrol duties under control of Montserrat Police Force.

Mercantile Marine

Lloyd's Register of Shipping: 2 vessels of 949 tons gross

1 BROOKE MARINE 12 metre TYPE

EMERALD STAR

Displacement, tons: 15
Length, feet (metres): 40 *(12)*
Guns: Can mount 3 MGs
Main engines: 2 diesels; 370 hp = 22 knots
Complement: 4

Purchased in 1971.

EMERALD STAR

1975, Montserrat Government

MOROCCO

Diplomatic Representation

Defence Attaché in London:
Colonel Benomar Sbay

Personnel

(a) 1976: 2 000 officers and ratings (including 500 Marines)
(b) 18 months National Service

Bases

Casablanca, Safi, Agadir, Kenitra, Tangier

Mercantile Marine

Lloyd's Register of Shipping:
53 vessels of 79 863 tons gross

New Construction Programme 1973-77

4—PR 72 Corvettes
20—32 metre Coastal Patrol Craft
3—"Batral" Type Landing Ships (Logistics)

Strength of the Fleet

Type	Active	Building (Projected)
Corvettes	2	1
MSC	1	—
Large Patrol Craft	2	—
Coastal Patrol Craft	2	4 (14)
Landing Ships	2	1
LCT	1	—
Customs Craft	12	—

DELETION

Frigate

1975 *Al Maouna*

CORVETTES

2 FRENCH PR 72 TYPE

Name	No.	Builders	Commissioned
OKBA	—	Soc. Francaise de Construction Navale	1976
TRIKI	—	Soc. Francaise de Construction Navale	1977

Displacement, tons: 375 standard; 445 full load
Dimensions, feet (metres): 188·8 × 25 × 7·1 *(57·5 × 7·6 × 2·1)*
Guns: 1—76 mm Oto-Melara; 1—40 mm Breda Bofors
Main engines: 4 AGO V16 diesels; 4 shafts; 11 040 hp
Speed, knots: 28
Range, miles: 2 500 at 16 knots
Complement: 53 (5 officers; 48 ratings)

Ordered June 1973. This type can be fitted with Exocet—as the Vega control system will be installed this would be a simple operation. *Okba* launched 10 Oct 1975, *Triki* 1 Feb 1976. Two more in the New Construction Programme.

Name	No.	Builders	Commissioned
LIEUTENANT RIFFI	32	Constructions Mécaniques de Normandie, Cherbourg	May 1964

Displacement, tons: 311 standard; 374 full load
Dimensions, feet (metres): 174 × 23 × 6·6 *(53 × 7 × 2)*
Guns: 1—76 mm; 2—40 mm
A/S weapons: 2—A/S mortars
Main engines: 2 SEMT Pielstick diesels; 2 cp propellers; 3 600 bhp = 19 knots
Range, miles: 3 000 at 12 knots
Complement: 49

Of modified "Fougeux" design. Laid down May 1963.

MINE WARFARE SHIP

1 MINESWEEPER—COASTAL

TAWFIC (ex-*Aries M 758*)

Displacement, tons: 365 standard; 424 full load
Dimensions, feet (metres): 152 oa × 28 × 8·2 *(46·3 × 8·5 × 2·1)*
Guns: 1—40 mm; 1—20 mm
Main engines: 2 diesels; 2 shafts; 2 000 bhp = 15 knots
Range, miles: 3 000 at 15 knots
Complement: 38

Launched 31 Mar 1956 of the French "Sirius" class. Transferred on loan by France on 28 Nov 1974 for 4 years.

LIGHT FORCES

1 LARGE PATROL CRAFT

Name	No.	Builders	Commissioned
AL BACHIR	22 (ex-*12*)	Constructions Mécaniques de Normandie, Cherbourg	30 Mar 1967

Displacement, tons: 125 light; 154 full load
Dimensions, feet (metres): 124·7 pp; 133·2 oa × 20·8 × 4·7 *(38; 40·6 × 6·4 × 1·4)*
Guns: 2—40 mm; 2—MG
Main engines: 2 SEMT-Pielstick diesels; 2 shafts; 3 600 bhp = 25 knots
Oil fuel, tons: 21
Range, miles: 2 000 at 15 knots
Complement: 23

Ordered in 1964. Launched 25 Feb 1967.

AL BACHIR   1967, Royal Moroccan Navy

6 + 14 P 92 TYPE (COASTAL PATROL CRAFT)

Name	No.	Builders	Commissioned
EL WACIL	—	Constructions Mécaniques de Normandie, Cherbourg	9 Oct 1975
EL JAIL	—	Constructions Mécaniques de Normandie, Cherbourg	3 Dec 1975
EL MIKDAM	—	Constructions Mécanques de Normandie, Cherbourg	Feb 1976
EL HARRIS	—	Constructions Mécaniques de Normandie, Cherbourg	April 1976
EL KHAFIR	—	Constructions Mécaniques de Normandie, Cherbourg	June 1976
ESSEHIR	—	Constructions Mécaniques de Normandie, Cherbourg	Aug 1976

Displacement, tons: 90
Dimensions, feet (metres): 105 oa × 17·6 × 9·8 *(32 × 5·3 × 2·9)*
Guns: 2—20 mm
Main engines: 2 MGO-12V BZSHR Diesels; 2 540 bhp; 2 shafts = 28 knots
Range, miles: 1 200 at 15 knots

Wooden hull sheathed in plastic.
The first six of these patrol craft were ordered in Feb 1974. Launch dates—*El Wacil* 12 June 1975, *El Jail* 10 Oct 1975, *El Mikdam* 26 Nov 1975, *El Harris* Feb 1976, *El Khafir* Apr 1976, *Essehir* June 1976. Fourteen more in the New Construction Programme.

Radar: 1 set Decca

1 Ex-FRENCH LARGE PATROL CRAFT

Name	No.	Builders	Commissioned
EL SABIQ (ex-*P 762, VC 12*)	11	Chantiers Navals de l'Estérel	1958

Displacement, tons: 60 standard; 82 full load
Dimensions, feet (metres): 104·5 × 15·5 × 5·5 *(31·8 × 4·7 × 1·7)*
Guns: 2—20 mm
Main engines: 2 Mercedes-Benz diesels; 2 shafts; 2 700 bhp = 28 knots
Range, miles: 1 500 at 15 knots
Complement: 17

Former French seaward defence motor launch of the VC type. Launched on 13 Aug 1957. Transferred from the French Navy to the Moroccan Navy on 15 Nov 1960 and renamed *El Sabiq*.

AMPHIBIOUS FORCES

2 + 1 BATRAL TYPE

Displacement, tons: 750 standard; 1 250 full load
Dimensions, feet (metres): 262·4 × 42·6 × 7·5 *(80 × 13 × 2·3)*
Guns: 2—40 mm; 2—81 mm mortars
Main engines: 2 Diesels; 2 shafts; 1 800 hp = 16 knots
Range, miles: 3 500 at 13 knots
Complement: 37

Fitted with helicopter landing platform and with vehicle-stowage above and below decks. Can carry an extra 140 men and twelve vehicles. Two ordered from Dubigeon on 12 Mar 1975. Third ordered 19 Aug 1975.

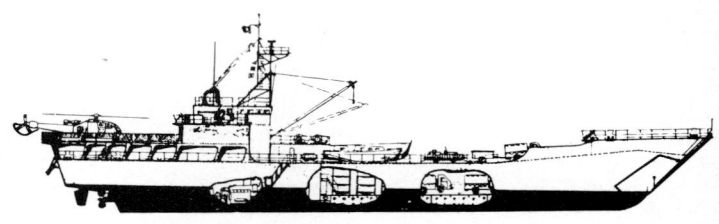

BATRAL TYPE   1974, French Navy

Name	No.	Builders	Commissioned
LIEUTENANT MALGHAGH	21	Chantiers Navals Franco-Belges	1964

Displacement, tons: 292 standard; 642 full load
Dimensions, feet (metres): 193·6 × 39·2 × 4·3 *(59 × 12 × 1·3)*
Guns: 2—20 mm; 1—120 mm mortar
Main engines: 2 MGO diesels; 2 shafts; 1 000 bhp = 8 knots
Complement: 16 (1 officer, 15 men)

Ordered early in 1963. Similar to the French landing craft of the EDIC type built at the same yard.

MISCELLANEOUS

There are also the yacht *Essaouira,* 60 tons, from Italy in 1967, used as a training vessel for watchkeepers; and twelve customs boats, four of 40 tons, 82 feet, diesels 940 bhp = 23 knots, and eight 42·7 feet; all built in 1963. The *Murene,* Coast Guard Cutter, has also been reported.

NETHERLANDS

Administration

Minister of Defence:
Ir. H. Vredeling
State Secretary of Defence (Personnel):
C. L. J. van Lent
State Secretary of Defence (Equipment):
A. Stemerdink
Chief of the Defence Staff:
Lt-Gen. A. J. W. Wijting

Headquarters Appointments

Chief of the Naval Staff:
Vice-Admiral B. Veldkamp
Vice Chief of the Naval Staff:
Rear-Admiral F. Poldermans
Flag Officer Naval Personnel:
Vice-Admiral F. H. Heckman
Flag Officer Naval Material:
Rear-Admiral J. L. Langenberg

Commands

Admiral Netherlands Home Command:
Rear-Admiral H. E. Rambonnet
Commander Netherlands Task Group:
Rear-Admiral H. L. van Beek
Commandant General Royal Netherlands Marine Corps:
Major-General A. C. Lamers
Flag Officer Netherlands Antilles:
Commodore W. G. Landzaat

Diplomatic Representation

Naval Attaché in Bonn:
Captain R. H. Berts
Naval Attaché in London:
Captain J. R. Roele
Naval Attaché in Paris:
Captain A. J. M. Stoffels
Naval Attaché in Washington and NLR SACLANT:
Rear-Admiral J. J. Binnendijk

Personnel

(a) 1 January 1976: 18 100 officers and ratings (including the Navy Air Service, Royal Netherlands Marine Corps and about 360 officers and women of the (W.R.NI.NS.)
(b) 17-20 months National Service

Bases

Main Base: Den Helder
Minor Bases: Flushing and Curacao
Fleet Air Arm: NAS Valkenburgh (main),
NAS De Kooy (helicopters)
R. Neth. Marines: Rotterdam
Training Bases: Amsterdam and Hilversum

Naval Air Force

Personnel: 2 000

3 MR Squadrons with 7 Atlantics, 15 Neptunes
12 Wasps and 7 AB-204B helicopters
(new MR aircraft by late 70s—Lynx replacements by mid-70s)

Prefix to Ships' Names

HNMS

Mercantile Marine

Lloyd's Register of Shipping:
1 348 vessels of 5 679 413 tons gross

Future New Construction Programme

1 Frigate (Command and Air Defence)
12 Frigates (ASW)
1 Oceanographic Ship
16 Lynx Helicopters

Strength of the Fleet

	Active	Building (Projected)
Cruiser	1	—
Destroyers	12	—
Frigates	6	4 (9)
Corvettes	11	—
Submarines (Patrol)	6	—
MCM Support Ships	5	—
Minehunters	4	(15)
Minesweepers—Coastal	11	—
Diving Ships	3	—
Minesweepers—Inshore	16	—
LCAs	11	—
Surveying Vessels	3	1
Combat Support Ships	2	—
Training Ships	2	—
Tugs	13	—
Tenders	5	—

Planned Strength in 1980s

2 ASW Groups each of 6 ASW frigates, 1 DLG, 1 Support Ship (helicopters in all ships) to operate in Eastlant Area
1 ASW Group of 6 ASW frigates and 1 DLG to operate in Channel Approaches
1 ASW Group of 4 frigates to operate in Channel Command
6 Patrol Submarines
21 LRMP Aircraft in 3 squadrons (1 training)
2 MCM Groups of 12 ships each operating off Dutch ports
1 MCM Group of 7 ships for Channel command
2 R. Neth. Marine Commando Groups and 1 Cold Weather Reinforced Company

DELETIONS

Cruiser

Oct 1972 *De Ruyter* to Peru as *Almirante Grau*

Destroyers

1973 *Gelderland* for harbour training
1974 *Noord Brabant* (after collision 9 Jan 1974)

Submarines

Nov 1970 *Zeeleuw* (ex-*Hawkbill*) — returned to US
Nov 1971 *Walrus* (ex-*Icefish*) — and scrapped

Minesweepers

1972 *Onvermoeid, Bolsward, Breukelen, Bruinisse* returned to USN
1973 *Grijpskerk* for harbour training
1974 *Wildervank, Meppel, Goes, Brummen, Brouwershaven* to disposal
Axel, Aalsmeer to Oman
1975 *Waalwijk, Leersum* ("Wildervank" class)
Beemster, Bedum, Beilen, Borculo, Borne, Blaricum, Brielle, Breskens, Boxtel ("Beemster" class MSC)

Survey Ships

1972 *Luymes* to disposal
1973 *Snellius* as accommodation ship

Amphibious Forces

1975 L 9515, 9521

Storeships

1972 *Woendi*
1973 *Pelikaan*

Netlayer

Sept 1970 *Cerberus* returned to US for transfer to Turkey

PENNANT NUMBERS

Cruiser

C 802	De Zeven Provincien

Destroyers

F 801	Tromp
F 806	De Ruyter
D 808	Holland
D 809	Zeeland
D 812	Friesland
D 813	Groningen
D 814	Limburg
D 815	Overijssel
D 816	Drenthe
D 817	Utrecht
D 818	Rotterdam
D 819	Amsterdam

Frigates

F 802	Van Speijk
F 803	Van Galen
F 804	Tjerk Hiddes
F 805	Van Nes
F 814	Isaac Sweers
F 815	Evertsen

Submarines

S 804	Potvis
S 805	Tonijn
S 806	Zwaardvis
S 807	Tijgerhaai
S 808	Dolfijn
S 809	Zeehond

Corvettes

F 817	Wolf
F 818	Fret
F 819	Hermelijn
F 820	Vos
F 821	Panter
F 822	Jaguar

MCM Command/Support and Escort Ships

A 854	Onversaagd
A 855	Onbevreesd
A 856	Mercuur
A 858	Onvervaard
A 859	Onverdroten

Mine Hunters

M 801	Dokkum
M 818	Drunen
M 828	Staphorst
M 842	Veere

Coastal Minesweepers

M 802	Hoogezand
M 809	Naaldwijk
M 810	Abcoude
M 812	Drachten
M 813	Ommen
M 815	Giethoorn
M 817	Venlo
M 823	Naarden
M 827	Hoogeveen
M 830	Sittard
M 841	Gemert

Inshore Minesweepers

M	868	Alblas
M	869	Bussemaker
M	870	Lacomblé
M	871	Van Hamel
M	872	Van Straelen
M	873	Van Moppes
M	874	Chömpff
M	875	Van Well-Groeneveld
M	876	Schuiling
M	877	Van Versendaal
M	878	Van Der Wel
M	879	Van 't Hoff
M	880	Mahu
M	881	Staverman
M	882	Houtepen
M	883	Zomer

Diving Vessels

M	806	Roermond
M	820	Woerden
M	844	Rhenen

Patrol Vessels

P	802	Balder
P	803	Bulgia
P	804	Freijer
P	805	Hadda
P	806	Hefring

Amphibious Forces

L 9510-14
L 9516-18
L 9520
L 9522
L 9526

Auxiliary Ships

A	832	Zuiderkruis
A	835	Poolster
A	847	Argus
A	848	Triton
A	849	Nautilus
A	850	Hydra
A	870	Wamandai
A	871	Wambrau
A	872	Westgat
A	873	Wielingen
A	903	Zeefakkel
A	904	Buyskes
A	905	Blommendal
A	923	Van Bochove
Y	8014	Harbour Tug
Y	8016	Harbour Tug
Y	8017	Harbour Tug
Y	8020	Dreg IV
Y	8022	Harbour Tug
Y	8028	Harbour Tug
Y	8037	Berkel
Y	8038	Dintel
Y	8039	Dommel
Y	8040	Ijssel
Y	8050	Urania

DE ZEVEN PROVINCIEN

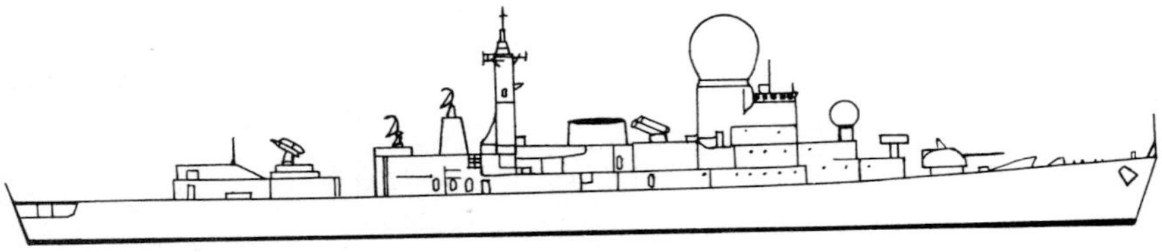

"TROMP" Class

"FRIESLAND" Class

"HOLLAND" Class

"KORTENAER" Class

"VAN SPEIJK" Class

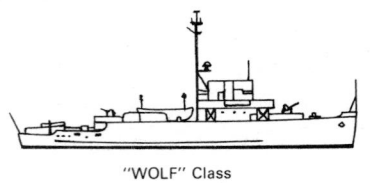
"WOLF" Class

"BALDER" Class

CRUISER

Name		No.	Builders	Laid down	Launched	Commissioned
DE ZEVEN PROVINCIEN (ex-De Ruyter, ex-Eendracht, ex-Kijkduin)		C 802	Rotterdam Drydock Co.	19 May 1939	22 Aug 1950	17 Dec 1953

Displacement, tons: 9 529 standard; 11 850 full load
Length, feet (metres): 590·5 *(180·0)* pp; 614·5 *(190·3)* oa
Beam, feet (metres): 56·7 *(17·3)*
Draught, feet (metres): 22·0 *(6·7)*
Missiles: 1 twin Terrier aft
Guns: 4—6 in *(152 mm)* (twin turrets); 6—57 mm (twin turrets); 4—40 mm
Main engines: 2 De Schelde-Parsons geared turbines; 85 000 shp; 2 shafts
Boilers: 4 Werkspoor-Yarrow
Speed, knots: 32
Complement: 940

Machinery by K. M. de Schelde. Construction resumed in 1946. In reserve 17 Oct 1975—disposal will follow commissioning of both *De Ruyter* and *Tromp*.

Gunnery: Main armament has 60 degrees elevation. All guns are fully automatic and radar controlled. The 6 inch guns have a rate of fire of 15 rounds per minute.

Missile conversion: *De Zeven Provincien* was converted in 1962-64 by Rotterdamsche Droogdoik Mij, Rotterdam with Terrier installation by NV Dok en Werf Mij Wilton-Fijenoord Schiedam. She was again refitted and modernised in 1971-72.

Radar: Search: LW 01, SPS 39 (3-D), SGR 104 Height Finder. Tactical: DA 02.
Fire Control: HSA M 20 series for larger guns. 2 SPG 55 for Terrier. 2 M 45 for 40 mm guns.

DE ZEVEN PROVINCIEN

9/1974, Ian S. Pearsall

DESTROYERS

2 "TROMP" CLASS (DLG)

Name	No.	Builders	Laid down	Launched	Commissioned
DE RUYTER	F 806	Koninklijke Maatschappij De Schelde, Flushing	22 Dec 1971	9 Mar 1974	June 1976
TROMP	F 801	Koninklijke Maatschappij De Schelde, Flushing	4 Sep 1971	4 June1973	3 Oct 1975

Displacement, tons: 4 300 standard; 5 400 full load
Length, feet (metres): 429·5 *(130·9)* pp; 454·1 *(138·4)* oa
Beam, feet (metres): 48·6 *(14·8)*
Draught, feet (metres): 15·1 *(4·6)*
Aircraft: 1 Lynx helicopter
Missile launchers: 1 Tartar aft; Seasparrow Point defence missile system; Harpoon (2 quadruple)
Guns: 2—4·7 in (twin turret)
A/S weapons: ASW torpedo tubes
Main engines: 2 Olympus gas turbines; 50 000 hp; 2 Tyne cruising gas turbines, 8 000 hp
Speed, knots: 30
Complement: 306

First design allowance was voted for in 1967 estimates. Ordered (announced on 27 July 1970) for laying down in 1971. Hangar and helicopter spot landing platform aft. Fitted as flag-ships.

ECM: 2 Knebworth Corvus Chaff projectors (and illuminators).

Electronics: SEWACO I automated AIO.

Engineering: Each ship carries 4-1 000 KW Diesel generators by Ruston Paxman, England.

Gunnery: Turrets from *Gelderland* with considerable modifications.

Radar: Search and designator; One HSA 3D in radome. Search, tracker and fire control for Seasparrow and 4·7 in guns; one HSA WM 25.
Tartar control: Two SPG-51.
Navigation: Two Decca.

Sonar: One CWE 610. One Type 162.

Trials: *De Ruyter*—Jan 1976. *Tromp*—Mar 1975.

TROMP

3/1975

TROMP

3/1975

8 "FRIESLAND" CLASS

Name	No.	Builders	Laid down	Launched	Commissioned
FRIESLAND	D 812	Nederlandse Dok en Scheepsbouw Mij, Amsterdam	17 Dec 1951	21 Feb 1953	22 Mar 1956
GRONINGEN	D 813	Nederlandse Dok en Scheepsbouw Mij, Amsterdam	21 Feb 1952	9 Jan 1954	12 Sep 1956
LIMBURG	D 814	Koninklijke Maatschappij De Schelde, Flushing	28 Nov 1953	5 Sep 1955	31 Oct 1956
OVERIJSSEL	D 815	Dok-en-Werfmaatschappij Wilton-Fijenoord	15 Oct 1953	8 Aug 1955	4 Oct 1957
DRENTHE	D 816	Nederlandse Dok en Scheepsbouw Mij, Amsterdam	9 Jan 1954	26 Mar 1955	1 Aug 1957
UTRECHT	D 817	Koninklijke Maatschappij De Schelde, Flushing	15 Feb 1954	2 June 1956	1 Oct 1957
ROTTERDAM	D 818	Rotterdamse Droogdok Mij, Rotterdam	7 Jan 1954	26 Jan 1956	28 Feb 1957
AMSTERDAM	D 819	Nederlandse Dok en Schepsbouw Mij, Amsterdam	26 Mar 1955	25 Aug 1956	10 Aug 1958

Displacement, tons: 2 497 standard; 3 070 full load
Length, feet (metres): 370 (112·8) pp; 380·5 (116·0) oa
Beam, feet (metres): 38·5 (11·7)
Draught, feet (metres): 17 (5·2)
Guns: 4—4·7 in (120 mm) (twin turrets) 4—40 mm
A/S weapons: 2 four-barrelled depth charge mortars. Bofors
  rocket launchers
Main engines: 2 Werkspoor geared turbines, 60 000 shp; 2
  shafts
Boilers: 4 Babcock
Speed, knots: 36
Complement: 284

These ships have side armour as well as deck projection.
"Bofors" type anti-submarine rocket throwers. Twin rudders.
Propellers 370 rpm. Named after provinces of the Netherlands,
and the two principal cities. To be replaced by "Kortenaer"
class of frigates.

Gunnery: The 4·7 inch guns are fully automatic with a rate of
fire of 42 rounds per minute. All guns are radar controlled.
Originally six 40 mm guns were mounted.

Radar: Search: LW 03.
Tactical: DA 05.
Fire Control: HSA M 45 for 4·7 in.
HSA fire control for 40 mm and A/S rockets.

Torpedo tubes: *Utrecht* was equipped with eight 21 inch A/S
torpedo tubes (single, four on each side) in 1960 and *Overijssel*
in 1961, and the others were to have been, but the project was
dropped and tubes already fitted were removed.

DRENTHE   9/1974, Ian S. Pearsall

OVERIJSSEL   11/1975, Dr. Giorgio Arra

2 "HOLLAND" CLASS

Name	No.	Builders	Laid down	Launched	Commissioned
HOLLAND	D 808	Rotterdamse Droogdok Mij, Rotterdam	21 April 1950	11 April 1953	31 Dec 1954
ZEELAND	D 809	Koninklijke Maatschappij De Schelde, Flushing	12 Jan 1951	27 June 1953	1 Mar 1955

Displacement, tons: 2 215 standard; 2 765 full load
Length, feet (metres): 360·5 (109·9) pp; 371·1 (113·1) oa
Beam, feet (metres): 37·5 (11·4)
Draught, feet (metres): 16·8 (5·1)
Guns: 4—4·7 in (120 mm); 1—40 mm
A/S weapons: 2 four-barrelled DC mortars, Bofors rocket laun-
  chers
Main engines: Werkspoor Parsons geared turbines; 2 shafts;
  45 000 shp
Boilers: 4 Babcock
Speed, knots: 32
Complement: 247

Two ships of this class were equipped with engines of the
pre-war "Callenburgh" class design and the other two with
engines of German construction. (The four "Callenburgh"
class destroyers were being built in 1940. *Isaac Sweers* was
towed to England and completed there, *Tjerk Hiddes* was completed by the Germans as ZH 1. The other two, *Callenburgh* and
Van Almonde, were too severely damaged for further use and
were scrapped, the engines being installed in the "Holland"
class).

Gunnery: The 4·7 inch guns are fully automatic with a rate of
fire of 42 rounds per minute. All guns are radar controlled.

Radar: Search: LW 03.
Tactical: DA 02.
Fire Control: HSA M 45 for 4·7 in.
HSA fire control for A/S rocket launcher.

Sisterships: *Gelderland* now a harbour-training hulk in Amsterdam. *Noord Brabant* too severely damaged in collision 9 Jan
1974 for repair. To be replaced by "Kortenaer" class.

HOLLAND   1973, Royal Netherlands Navy

FRIGATES

8 + 5 "KORTENAER" CLASS

Name	No.
KORTENAER	F 807
CALLENBURGH	F 808
VAN KINSBERGEN	F 809
BANCKERT	F 810
PIET HEYN	F 811
PIETER FLORISZ	F 812
WITTE DE WITH	F 813
ABRAHAM CRIJNSSEN	F 816

Builders	Laid down	Launched	Commissioned
Koninklijke Maatschappij De Schelde, Flushing	8 Apr 1975	Late 1976	Autumn 1978
Koninklijke Maatschappij De Schelde, Flushing	30 June 1975	1977	Autumn 1979
Koninklijke Maatschappij De Schelde, Flushing	2 Sep 1975	1977	Summer 1980
Koninklijke Maatschappij De Schelde, Flushing	25 Feb 1976	1978	Spring 1981
Koninklijke Maatschappij De Schelde, Flushing	1977	—	Late 1981
Koninklijke Maatschappij De Schelde, Flushing	1977	—	Autumn 1982
Koninklijke Maatschappij De Schelde, Flushing	1977	—	Summer 1983
Koninklijke Maatschappij De Schelde, Flushing	1978		Spring 1984

Displacement, tons: 3 500
Dimensions, feet (metres): 419·8 × 47·2 × — (128 × 14·4 × —)
Aircraft: 1 Lynx helicopter
Missiles: Harpoon surface-to-surface; NATO Seasparrow PDMS
Gun: 1—76 mm Oto Melara
Torpedo tubes: 4 single mountings for Mk 46 in after deckhouse (2 each side)
Main engines: 2 Rolls Royce Olympus gas turbines = 50 000 shp; 2 Rolls Royce Tyne gas turbines = 8 000 shp; 2 variable pitch propellers
Speed, knots: 30
Range, miles: 4 000 on Tyne cruising turbines
Complement: 185

First four of class ordered 31 Aug 1974, second four 28 Nov 1974. *Kortenaer* to be ready for trials 1 Apr 1978. Funds in 1976 estimates provide for five more in 1976-77, including the flagship (SAM version). *Callenburgh* to commission in Autumn 1979 and thereafter at 9 monthly intervals. These ships are to replace the "Holland" and "Friesland" classes. Cost at 1974 prices £37 m.

Complement: Reduced to 185 by adaption of large amount of automation.

Radar: Hollandse Signaal for radar and fire-control.

Sonar: SQS 505.

"KORTENAER" Class

1974, Royal Netherlands Navy

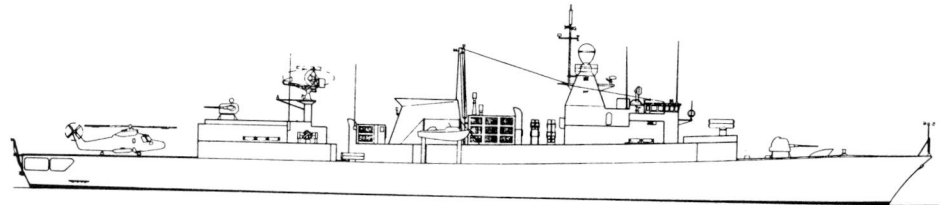

"KORTENAER" Class

1973, Royal Netherlands Navy

6 "VAN SPEIJK" CLASS

Name	No.
EVERTSEN	F 815
ISAAC SWEERS	F 814
TJERK HIDDES	F 804
VAN GALEN	F 803
VAN NES	F 805
VAN SPEIJK	F 802

Builders	Laid down	Launched	Commissioned
Koninklijke Maatschappij De Schelde, Flushing	6 July 1965	18 June 1966	21 Dec 1967
Nederlandse Dok en Scheepsbouw Mij, Amsterdam	5 May 1965	10 Mar 1967	15 May 1968
Nederlandse Dok en Scheepsbouw Mij, Amsterdam	1 June 1964	17 Dec 1965	16 Aug 1967
Koninklijke Maatschappij De Schelde, Flushing	25 July 1963	19 June 1965	1 Mar 1967
Koninklijke Maatschappij De Schelde, Flushing	25 July 1963	26 Mar 1966	9 Aug 1967
Nederlandse Dok en Scheepsbouw Mij, Amsterdam	1 Oct 1963	5 Mar 1965	14 Feb 1967

Displacement, tons: 2 200 standard; 2 850 full load
Dimensions, feet (metres): 360 wl, 372 oa × 41 × 18 (109·8; 113·4 × 12·5 × 5·8)
Aircraft: 1 lightweight helicopter
Missile: 2 quadruple Seacat anti-aircraft (see note)
Guns: 2—4·5 in (twin turret)
A/S weapons: 1 Limbo three-barrelled depth charge mortar
Main engines: 2 double reduction geared turbines; 2 shafts; 30 000 shp
Boilers: 2 Babcock & Wilcox
Speed, knots: 30
Complement: 254

Four ships were ordered in Oct 1962 and two later. Ships of this class will undergo mid-life conversion from 1976 to 1980, consisting of the replacement of the turret by a Harpoon mounting, considerable improvement of the Seacat system, electronic equipment and accommodation.

Design: Although in general these ships are based on the design of the British Improved Type 12 ("Leander" class), there are a number of modifications to suit the requirements of the Royal Netherlands Navy. As far as possible equipment of Netherlands manufacture was installed. This resulted in a number of changes in the ship's superstructure compared with the British "Leander" class. To avoid delay these ships were in some cases fitted with equipment already available, instead of going through long development stages.

Electronics: ECM equipment.

Radar: LW 02 air surveillance on mainmast
DA 05 target indicator on foremast
Surface-warning/nav set on foremast
1-M45 for 4·5 in guns
2-M44 for Seacat

Sonar: Hull-mounted and VDS stets.

Missiles: All are to be converted to launch Harpoon missiles.

VAN SPEIJK

11/1975, Dr Giorgio Arra

VAN SPEIJK

9/1974, Ian S. Pearsall

CORVETTES

6 "WOLF" CLASS

Name	No.	Builders	Commissioned
FRET (ex-PCE 1604)	F 818	General Shipbuilding and Engineering Works, Boston	4 May 1954
HERMELIJN (ex-PCE 1605)	F 819	General Shipbuilding and Engineering Works, Boston	5 Aug 1954
JAGUAR (ex-PCE 1609)	F 822	Avondale Marine Ways, Inc, New Orleans, Louisiana	11 June 1954
PANTER (ex-PCE 1608)	F 821	Avondale Marine Ways, Inc, New Orleans, Louisiana	11 June 1954
VOS (ex-PCE 1606)	F 820	General Shipbuilding and Engineering Works, Boston	2 Dec 1954
WOLF (ex-PCE 1607)	F 817	Avondale Marine Ways, Inc, New Orleans, Louisiana	26 Mar 1954

Displacement, tons: 870 standard; 975 full load
Dimensions, feet (metres): 180 pp; 184·5 oa × 33 × 14·5 *(54·9; 56·2 × 10 × 4·4)*
Guns: 1—3 in *(76 mm)*; 6—40 mm *(Jaguar, Panter: 4—40 mm)*; 8—20 mm
A/S weapons: 1 Hedgehog; 2 DCT *(Jaguar, Panter:* 4); 2 DC racks
Main engines: 2 GM diesels; 1 800 bhp; 2 shafts
Speed, knots: 15
Range, miles: 4 300 at 10 knots
Complement: 96

Built as part of the US "off-shore" agreement—all laid down 1952-53. 20 mm guns not fitted in peacetime.

HERMELIJN   7/1973, Wright and Logan

5 "BALDER" CLASS

Name	No.	Builders	Commissioned
BALDER	P 802	Rijkswerf Willemsoord	6 Aug 1954
BULGIA	P 803	Rijkswerf Willemsoord	9 Aug 1954
FREYR	P 804	Rijkswerf Willemsoord	1 Dec 1954
HADDA	P 805	Rijkswerf Willemsoord	3 Feb 1955
HEFRING	P 806	Rijkswerf Willemsoord	23 Mar 1955

Displacement, tons: 169 standard; 225 full load
Dimensions, feet (metres): 114·9 pp; 119·1 oa × 20·2 × 5·9 *(35; 36·3 × 6·2 × 1·8)*
Guns: 1—40 mm; 3—20 mm
A/S weapons: 2 DGT, Mousetrap
Main engines: Diesels; 2 shafts; 1 300 shp = 15·5 knots
Range, miles: 1 000 at 13 knots
Complement: 27

Built on US "off-shore" account.

HEFRING   1971, Royal Netherlands Navy

SUBMARINES

Note: A sum was set aside in the 1975 Estimates to start design work on an "Improved Zwaardvis" class to be ordered in 1979.

2 "ZWAARDVIS" CLASS

Name	No.	Builders	Laid down	Launched	Commissioned
TIJGERHAAI	S 807	Rotterdamse Droogdok Mij, Rotterdam	14 July 1966	25 May 1971	20 Oct 1972
ZWAARDVIS	S 806	Rotterdamse Droogdok Mij, Rotterdam	14 July 1966	2 July 1970	18 Aug 1972

Displacement, tons: 2 350 surfaced; 2 640 dived
Length, feet (metres): 217·2 *(66·2)*
Beam, feet (metres): 33·8 *(10·3)*
Draught, feet (metres): 23·3 *(7·1)*
Torpedo tubes: 6—21 in *(533 mm)*
Main machinery: Diesel-electric; 3 diesel generators; 1 shaft
Speed, knots: 13 surfaced; 20 dived
Complement: 67

In the 1964 Navy Estimates a first instalment was approved for the construction of two conventionally powered submarines of tear-drop design. HSA M8 Fire Control.

ZWAARDVIS   1972, Royal Netherlands Navy

2 "POTVIS" CLASS

2 "DOLFIJN" CLASS

Name	No.
POTVIS	S 804
TONIJN	S 805
DOLFIJN	S 808
ZEEHOND	S 809

Builders	Laid down	Launched	Commissioned
Wilton-Fijenoord, Schiedam	17 Sep 1962	12 Jan 1965	2 Nov 1965
Wilton-Fijenoord, Schiedam	27 Nov 1962	14 June1965	24 Feb 1966
Rotterdamse Droogdok Mij, Rotterdam	30 Dec 1954	20 May 1959	16 Dec 1960
Rotterdamse Droogdok Mij, Rotterdam	30 Dec 1954	20 Feb 1960	16 Mar 1961

Displacement, tons: 1 140 standard; 1 494 surfaced; 1 826 dived
Length, feet (metres): 260·9 *(79·5)*
Beam, feet (metres): 25·8 *(7·8)*
Draught, feet (metres): 15·8 *(4·8)*
Torpedo tubes: 8—21 in *(533 mm)*
Main machinery: 2 MAN diesels; total 3 100 bhp Electric motors; 4 200 hp; 2 shafts
Speed, knots: 14·5 surfaced; 17 dived
Complement: 64

These submarines are of a triple-hull design, giving a diving depth 980 feet *(300 metres)*. *Potvis* and *Tonijn*, originally voted for in 1949 with the other pair, but suspended for some years, had several modifications compared with *Dolfijn* and *Zeehond* and were officially considered to be a separate class; but modernisation of both classes has been completed, and all four boats are now almost identical. HSA M8 Fire control.

TONIJN

6/1975, John G. Callis

Construction: The hull consists of three cylinders arranged in a triangular shape. The upper cylinder accommodates the crew, navigational equipment and armament. The lower two cylinders house the propulsion machinery comprising diesel engines, batteries and electric motors, as well as store-rooms.

MINE WARFARE FORCES

Future Construction: Agreement reached with France and Belgium to develop an improved "Circe" class minehunter to be fitted with PAP mine-destructor. Combined planning centre set up in Paris—France will build the first ship of fifteen to replace "Onversaagd" and "Dokkum" classes. To complete about 1980.

5 "ONVERSAAGD" CLASS
(MCM SUPPORT SHIPS and ESCORTS)

Name	No.	Builders	Commissioned
MERCUUR (ex-Onverschrokken, ex-AM 483)	A 856	Peterson Builders, Wisconsin	22 July 1954
ONBEVREESD (ex-AM 481)	A 855 (ex-M 885)	Astoria Marine Construction Co	21 Sep 1954
ONVERDROTEN (ex-AM 485)	A 859 (ex-M 889)	Peterson Builders, Wisconsin	22 Nov 1954
ONVERSAAGD (ex-AM 480)	A 854 (ex-M 884)	Astoria Marine Construction Co	27 May 1954
ONVERVAARD (ex-AM 482)	A 858 (ex-M 888)	Astoria Marine Construction Co.	31 Mar 1955

Displacement, tons: 735 standard; 790 full load
Dimensions, feet (metres): 165·0 pp; 172·0 oa × 36·0 × 10·6 *(50·3; 52·5 × 11 × 3·2)*
Gun: 1—40 mm
A/S weapons: 2 DC
Main engines: Diesels; 1 600 bhp = 15·5 knots
Oil fuel, tons: 46
Range, miles: 2 400 at 12 knots
Complement: 70

ONVERVAARD (MCM support type)

1972, Royal Netherlands Navy

Built in USA for the Netherlands. Of wooden and non-magnetic construction. Originally designed as Minesweepers—Ocean—reclassified in 1966 and in 1972. *Onbevreesd, Onverdroten* and *Onvervaard* are MCM Command/Support Ships. *Mercuur* (ex-Onverschrokken) was converted into a Torpedo Trials Ship in 1972. *Onversaagd* has been converted for temporary duty as survey ship until the new construction Oceanographic Ship is delivered in 1976.

18 "DOKKUM" CLASS
(MINESWEEPERS, COASTAL and MINEHUNTERS)

ABCOUDE M 810	HOOGEZAND M 802	ROERMOND M 806 (D)
DOKKUM M 801 (H)	HOOGEVEEN M 827	SITTARD M 830
DRACHTEN M 812	NAALDWIJK M 809	STAPHORST M 828 (H)
DRUNEN M 818 (H)	NAARDEN M 823	VEERE M 842 (H)
GEMERT M 841	OMMEN M 813	VENLO M 817
GIETHOORN M 815	RHENEN M 844 (D)	WOERDEN M 820 (D)

Displacement, tons: 373 standard; 453 full load
Dimensions, feet (metres): 149·8 oa × 28 × 6·5 *(45·7 × 8·5 × 2)*
Guns: 2—40 mm
Main engines: 2 diesels; Fyenoord MAN; 2 500 bhp = 16 knots
Range, miles: 2 500 at 10 knots
Complement: 38

Of 32 Western Union type coastal minesweepers built in the Netherlands, 18 were under offshore procurement as the "Dokkum" class, with MAN engines, and 14 on Netherlands account as the "Wildervank" class, with Werkspoor diesels. All launched in 1954-56 and completed in 1955-56.
Of the "Dokkum" class four have been converted to minehunters (H), (1968-73) and three to diving vessels (D) (1962-68). The remaining eleven minesweepers of this class are subject to a fleet rehabilitation and modernisation programme by 1977. All "Wildervank" class deleted by 1976.

GIETHOORN (sweeper)

10/1975, D. Bateman

DRUNEN (hunter)

4/1975, John G. Callis

RHENEN (diving craft)

10/1975, D. Bateman

16 "VAN STRAELEN" CLASS (MINESWEEPERS—INSHORE)

Name	No.	Builders	Commissioned
ALBLAS	M 868	Werf de Noord, Albasserdam	12 Mar 1960
BUSSEMAKER	M 869	G. de Vries Lentsch Jr, Amsterdam	1960
CHÖMPFF	M 874	Werf de Noord, Albasserdam	1961
HOUTEPEN	M 882	N.V. de Arnhemse Scheepsbouw Maatschappij	1962
LACOMBLE	M 870	N.V. de Arnhemse Scheepsbouw Maatschappij	1960
MAHU	M 880	Werf de Noord, Albasserdam	1962
SCHUILING	M 876	G. de Vries Lentsch Jr, Amsterdam	1961
STAVERMAN	M 881	G. de Vries Lentsch Jr, Amsterdam	1962
VAN DER WEL	M 878	G. de Vries Lentsch Jr, Amsterdam	1961
VAN HAMEL	M 871	G. de Vries Lentsch Jr, Amsterdam	1960
VAN 'T HOFF	M 879	Werf de Noord, Albasserdam	1961
VAN MOPPES	M 873	Werf de Noord, Albasserdam	1960
VAN STRAELEN	M 872	N.V. de Arnhemse Scheepsbouw Maatschappij	1960
VAN VERSENDAAL	M 877	Werf de Noord, Albasserdam	1961
VAN WELL GROENVELD	M 875	N.V. de Arnhemse Scheepsbouw Maatschappij	1961
ZOMER	M 883	N.V. de Arnhemse Scheepsbouw Maatschappij	1962

LACOMBLÉ   10/1975, D. Bateman

Displacement, tons: 151 light; 169 full load
Dimensions, feet (metres): 90 pp; 99·3 oa × 18·2 × 5·2 *(27·5; 30·3 × 5·6 × 1·6)*
Gun: 1—20 mm
Main engines: Werkspoor diesels; 2 shafts; 1 100 bhp = 13 knots
Complement: 14

Eight were built under the offshore procurement programme, with MDAP funds, and the remaining eight were paid for by Netherlands. All ordered in mid-1957. Built of non-magnetic materials. *Alblas,* the first, was laid down on 26 Feb 1958, launched on 29 June 1959, started trials on 15 Jan 1960.

AMPHIBIOUS FORCES

L 9526

Displacement, tons: 20
Dimensions, feet (metres): 50 × 11·8 × 5·8 *(15·3 × 3·6 × 1·8)*
Main engines: 2 Kromhout diesels; 75 bhp = 8 knots
Complement: 3

Now officially rated as LCA Type.

L 9510	L 9512	L 9514	L 9517	L 9520
L 9511	L 9513	L 9516	L 9518	L 9522

Displacement, tons: 13·6
Dimensions, feet (metres): 46·2 × 11·5 × 6 *(14·1 × 3·5 × 1·8)*
Main engines: Rolls Royce diesel; Schottel propeller; 200 bhp = 12 knots
Complement: 3

Landing craft made of polyester, all commissioned in 1962-63, except L 9520 in 1964.

SURVEY SHIPS

1 NEW CONSTRUCTION
HYDROGRAPHIC/OCEANOGRAPHIC SHIP

Name	No.	Builders	Commissioned
TYDEMAN	—	Scheepswerf En Machine Fabrik	Dec 1976

Displacement, tons: 2 950
Dimensions, feet (metres): 295 × 47·2 × 15·7 *(90 × 14·4 × 4·8)*
Main engines: Diesel-electric
Speed, knots: 15
Complement: 64 plus 15 scientists

TYDEMAN   1974, Royal Netherlands Navy

Ordered in Oct 1974. Cost £6·7 m. Will be able to operate down to 7 000 m. Fitted with eight laboraties. Supplied with two bow propellers. Laid down 29 Apr 1975, launched 18 Dec 1975. Until she is completed the converted Minesweeper—Ocean *Onversaagd* will serve in her place.

2 "BUYSKES" CLASS

Name	No.	Builders	Commissioned
BLOMMENDAL	A 905	Boele's Scheepswerven en Machinefabriek BV, Bolnes	22 May 1973
BUYSKES	A 904	Boele's Scheepswerven en Machinefabriek BV, Bolnes	9 Mar 1973

Displacement, tons: 967 standard; 1 033 full load
Dimensions, feet (metres): 196·6 oa × 36·4 × 12 *(60 × 11·1 × 3·7)*
Main engines: Diesel electric; 2 100 hp (3 × 700) = 13·5 knots
Complement: 43

Both designed primarily for hydrographic work but have also limited oceanographic and meteorolgical capability. They will operate mainly in the North Sea. A data logging system is installed as part of the automatic handling of hydrographic data. They carry two 22 ft survey launches capable of 15 knots and two work-boats normally used for sweeping. Both ships can operate two floats, each housing an echo-sounding transducer, one streaming on each beam. This will enable the running of three simultaneous sounding lines 100m. apart.

BLOMMENDAL   1973, Royal Netherlands Navy

DREG IV Y 8020

Displacement, tons: 46 standard; 48 full load
Dimensions, feet (metres): 65·7 × 15·1 × 4·9 *(20 × 4·6 × 1·5)*
Main engines: 120 hp = 9·5 knots
Complement: 10

SERVICE FORCES

2 "POOLSTER" CLASS (FAST COMBAT SUPPORT SHIPS)

Name	No.	Builders	Commissioned
POOLSTER	A 835	Rotterdam se Droogdok Mij	10 Sep 1964
ZUIDERKRUIS	A 832	Verolme Shipyards, Albasserdam	27 June 1975

Displacement, tons: 16 800 full load; 16 900 *(Zuiderkruis)*
Measurement, tons: 10 000 deadweight
Dimensions, feet (metres): 515 pp; 556 oa × 66·7 × 27 *(157·1 pp; 169·6 × 20·3 × 8·2)*
  (Zuiderkruis 561 oa (171·1))
Aricraft: Capacity: 5 helicopters
Guns: 2—40 mm
Main engines: 2 Turbines; 22 000 shp = 21 knots *(Poolster)*
  2 Werkspoor diesels; 21 000 hp = 21 knots *(Zuiderkruis)*
Complement: 200

Poolster laid down on 18 Sep 1962.
Launched on 16 Oct 1963. Trials mid-1964. Helicopter deck aft. Funnel heightened by 4·5 m.
Zuiderkruis ordered Oct 1972. Laid down 16 July 1973, launched 15 Oct 1974.

ZUIDERKRUIS   *11/1975, Dr Giorgio Arra*

TRAINING SHIPS

Name	No.	Builders	Commissioned
ZEEFAKKEL	A 903	J. & K. Smit, Kinderdijk	22 May 1951

Displacement, tons: 355 standard; 384 full load
Dimensions, feet (metres): 149 oa × 24·7 × 6·9 *(45·4 × 7·6 × 2·1)*
Guns: 1—3 in; 1—40 mm
Main engines: 2 Smit/MAN 8 cyl diesels; 2 shafts; 640 bhp = 12 knots
Complement: 29

Laid down Sep 1949, launched 21 July 1950. Former surveying vessel. Now used as local training ship at Den Helder.

Name	No.	Builders	Commissioned
URANIA (ex-*Tromp*)	Y 8050	—	23 April 1938

Displacement, tons: 38
Dimensions, feet (metres): 72 × 16·3 × 10 *(22 × 5 × 3·1)*
Main engines: Diesel; 65 hp
Complement: 15

Schooner used for training in seamanship.

Note: *Gelderland* (ex-destroyer) and *Grypskerk* (ex-minesweeper) are used at Amsterdam as harbour training and accommodation ships for the Technical Training establishment. *Soemba* (ex-sloop) used at Den Oever as harbour training and accommodation ship for divers and underwater-swimmers.

TUGS

Name	No.	Builders	Commissioned
WESTGAT	A 872	Rijkswerf, Willemsoord	10 Jan 1968
WIELINGEN	A 873	Rijkswerf, Willemsoord	4 April 1968

Displacement, tons: 185
Dimensions, feet (metres): 90·6 × 22·7 × 7·7 *(27·6 × 6·9 × 2·3)*
Guns: 2—20 mm
Main engines: Bolnes diesel; 750 bhp = 12 knots

Launched on 22 Aug 1967 and 6 Jan 1968, respectively. Equipped with salvage pumps and fire fighting equipment. Stationed at Den Helder.

Name	No.	Builders	Commissioned
WAMANDAI	A 870 (ex-*Y 8035*)	Rijkswerf, Willemsoord	1960

Displacement, tons: 159 standard; 201 full load
Dimensions, feet (metres): 89·2 × 21·3 × 7·5 *(27·2 × 6·5 × 2·3)*
Guns: 2—20 mm
Main engines: Diesel; 500 bhp = 11 knots

Launched on 28 May 1960. Equipped with salvage pumps and fire fighting equipment. In the Netherlands Antilles since 1964.

Name	No.	Builders	Commissioned
WAMBRAU	A 871	Rijkswerf Willemsoord	8 Jan 1957

Displacement, tons: 154 standard; 179 full load
Dimensions, feet (metres): 86·5 oa × 20·7 × 7·5 *(26·4 × 6·3 × 2·3)*
Guns: 2—20 mm
Main engines: Werkspoor diesel and Kort nozzle; 500 bhp = 10·8 knots

Launched on 27 Aug 1956. Equipped with salvage pumps and fire fighting equipment. Stationed at Den Helder.

Name	No.	Builders	Commissioned
BERKEL	Y 8037	H. H. Bodewes, Millingen	1956
DINTEL	Y 8038	H. H. Bodewes, Millingen	1956
DOMMEL	Y 8039	H. H. Bodewes, Millingen	1957
IJSSEL	Y 8040	H. H. Bodewes, Millingen	1957

Displacement, tons: 139 standard; 163 full load
Dimensions, feet (metres): 82 oa × 20·5 × 7·3 *(25 × 6·3 × 2·2)*
Main engines: Werkspoor diesel and Kort nozzle; 500 bhp

Harbour tugs specially designed for use at Den Helder.
There are also five small harbour tugs—Y 8014, Y 8016, Y 8017, Y 8022, Y 8028.

ACCOMMODATION SHIPS

(See note under Training Ships)

Cornelis Drebbel is the name of the "Boatel"—775 tons, length 206·7 feet, beam 38·7 feet, draught 3·6 feet, complement 200, cost 3m guilders. Ordered in 1969 from Scheepswerft Voorwaarts at Hoogezand, launched on 19 Nov 1970 and completed in 1971. Serves as accommodation vessel for crews of ships refitting at private yards in the Rotterdam area. *Snellius* (ex-survey ship) is used for accommodation for R. Neth. N. personnel at the RN Submarine Base, Faslane.

TENDER

Name	No.	Builders	Commissioned
VAN BOCHOVE	A 923	Zaanlandse Scheepsbouw Mij, Zaandam	Aug 1962

Displacement, tons: 140
Dimensions, feet (metres): 97·2 × 18·2 × 6 *(29·6 × 5·6 × 1·8)*
Main engines: Kromhout diesel; Schottel propeller; 140 bhp = 8 knots
Complement: 8

Torpedo trials vessel. Ordered Oct 1961. Launched on 20 July 1962.

4 DIVING TENDERS

ARGUS A 847
HYDRA A 850
NAUTILUS A 849
TRITON A 848

NEW ZEALAND

Headquarters Appointments

Chief of Naval Staff:
Rear-Admiral J. F. McKenzie, CBE
Deputy Chief of Naval Staff:
Commodore D. Cheney

The three New Zealand Service Boards were formally abolished in 1971 as part of the Defence Headquarters reorganisation. The former three Service Headquarters and Defence Office have been reorganised into functional branches and offices.
On 1 June 1970 the command and control of the three New Zealand Services was vested in the Chief of Defence Staff who exercises this authority through the three Service Chiefs of Staff.

Diplomatic Representation

Head of New Zealand Defence Liaison Staff, London and Senior Naval Liaison Officer:
Commodore F. H. Bland, OBE
Deputy Head of New Zealand Defence Staff, Washington and Naval Attaché:
Captain E. R. Ellison

Personnel

(a) January 1973: 2 966 officers and ratings
January 1974: 2 730 officers and ratings
January 1975: 2 690 officers and ratings
January 1976: 2 800 officers and ratings
(b) Voluntary
Reserve; 290 RNZNVR

Base

Auckland (HMNZS *Philomel*)

Prefix to Ships' Names

HMNZS

Mercantile Marine

Lloyd's Register of Shipping:
109 vessels of 162 520 tons gross

Strength of the Fleet

Type	Active	Building
Frigates	4	—
Corvettes	2	—
Patrol Craft	11	—
Survey Ship	1 (converting)	—
Research Vessel	1	—
Tenders	2	—

Note: Construction of 10 000 ton Support Ship under discussion.

DELETIONS

Cruiser

Dec 1971   *Black Prince*

Frigate

April 1971   *Blackpool* returned to Royal Navy

Patrol Craft

1972   *Maroro* (HDML)
1975   *Kahawai, Mako, Parore, Tamure* (HDMLs)

Survey Ships

June 1971   *Endeavour* (ex-US *Namakagon*) returned to USN for transfer to Taiwan. (now *Lung Chuan*)

1975   *Lachlan*

PENNANT LIST

Frigates

F 55	Waikato
F 111	Otago
F 148	Taranaki
F 421	Canterbury

Corvettes

M 233	Inverell
M 353	Kiama

Light Forces

P 3563	Kuparu
P 3564	Koura
P 3565	Haku
P 3568	Pukaki
P 3569	Rotoiti
P 3570	Taupo
P 3571	Hawea

Surveying Vessels

P 3552	Paea
P 3556	Takapu
P 3566	Tarapunga

Research Vessel

A 2	Tui

FRIGATES

2 "LEANDER" CLASS

Name	No.	Builders	Laid down	Launched	Commissioned
CANTERBURY	F 421	Yarrow Ltd, Clyde	12 April 1969	6 May 1970	22 Oct 1971
WAIKATO	F 55	Harland & Wolff Ltd, Belfast	10 Jan 1964	18 Feb 1965	16 Sep 1966

Displacement, tons: 2 450 standard; 2 860 full load *Waikato*; 2 470 standard; 2 990 full load *Canterbury*
Length, feet (metres): 360·0 *(109·7)* pp; 372·0 *(113·4)* oa *Waikato*; 370·0 *(112·8)* pp *Canterbury*
Beam, feet (metres): 41·0 *(12·5)* *Waikato*; 43·0 *(13·1)* *Canterbury*
Draught, feet (metres): 18 *(5·5)*
Aircraft: 1 Wasp helicopter
Missiles: 1 quadruple Seacat
Guns: 2—4·5 in *(155 mm)* in twin turret; 2—20 mm
A/S weapons: 1 Limbo 3-barrelled DC mortar *Waikato*; 2—TF Mk 32 Mod 5 torpedo tubes *Canterbury*
Main engines: 2 sets d.r. geared turbines; 2 shafts; 30 000 shp
Boilers: 2 Babcock & Wilcox
Speed, knots: 30 *Waikato*; 28 *Canterbury*
Complement: 248 (14 officers, 234 ratings) *Waikato*; 243 (14 officers, 229 ratings) *Canterbury*

Waikato, ordered on 14 June 1963. Commissioned on 16 Sep 1966, trials in the United Kingdom until spring 1967, arrived in New Zealand waters in May 1967. *Canterbury* was ordered in Aug 1968, arrived in New Zealand in Aug 1972.

Radar: Search: Type 965.
Tactical: Type 993.
Fire Control: MRS 3 System and I Band.

CANTERBURY

1974, Royal New Zealand Navy

2 "ROTHESAY" CLASS TYPE 12

Name	No.	Builders	Laid down	Launched	Commissioned
OTAGO (ex-HMS *Hastings*)	F 111	J. I. Thornycroft & Co Ltd, Woolston, Southampton	1957	11 Dec 1958	22 June 1960
TARANAKI	F 148	J. Samuel White & Co Ltd, Isle of Wight	1958	19 Aug 1959	28 Mar 1961

Displacement, tons: 2 144 standard; 2 557 full load
Length, feet (metres): 360·0 *(109·7)* pp; 370·0 *(112·8)* oa
Beam, feet (metres): 41·0 *(12·5)*
Draught, feet (metres): 17·3 *(5·3)*
Missiles: 1 quadruple Seacat
Guns: 2—4·5 in *(115 mm)* in twin turret; 2—40 mm *(Taranaki only)*
A/S weapons: 2 Limbo 3-barrelled DC mortars
Main engines: 2 sets d.r. geared turbines; 2 shafts; 30 000 shp
Boilers: 2 Babcock & Wilcox
Speed, knots: 30
Complement: 240 (13 officers, 227 ratings)

Taranaki was ordered direct (announced by J. Samuel White & Co on 22 Feb 1957). For *Otago* New Zealand took over the contract (officially stated on 26 Feb 1957) for *Hastings* originally ordered from John I. Thornycroft & Co in Feb 1956 for the Royal Navy. Both vessels are generally similar to those in the Royal Navy, but were modified to suit New Zealand conditions. *Otago* has had enclosed foremast since 1967 refit; *Taranaki* was similarly fitted during 1969.

Radar: Search; Type 993 and Type 277.
Fire Control; I Band.

Tubes: The original twelve 21 in *(533 mm)* A/S torpedo tubes (8 single and 2 twin) were removed.

OTAGO   1974, Royal New Zealand Navy

CORVETTES

2 "BATHURST" CLASS

Name	No.	Builders	Laid down	Launched	Commissioned
INVERELL	M 233	Mort's Dock, Sydney	7 Dec 1941	2 May 1942	2 May 1943
KIAMA	M 353	Evans Deakins, Brisbane	2 Nov 1942	3 July 1943	26 Jan 1944

Displacement, tons: 790 standard; 1 025 full load
Length, feet (metres): 162·0 *(49·4)* pp; 186·0 *(56·7)* oa
Beam, feet (metres): 31·0 *(9·4)*
Draught, feet (metres): 9·5 *(2·9)*
Guns: 2—40 mm
Main engines: Triple expansion; 2 shafts; 1 800 ihp
Boilers: 2 Admiralty 3-drum small tube
Speed, knots: 15
Complement: 71

Originally four vessels of this class were given to New Zealand by Australia in 1952, *Echuca* and *Stawell* being deleted in 1968. *Kiama* was recommissioned on 15 Mar 1966 for training and fishery protection duties, her 4-inch gun being replaced by a 40 mm gun, and a deckhouse being built aft. *Inverell* was recommissioned on 15 Aug 1965 as a training ship for new entry ratings, replacing the frigate *Rotoiti*. Her sweeping gear was removed and her deckhouse extended further aft. 4-inch gun replaced by 40 mm.

INVERELL   1974, Royal New Zealand Navy

SURVEY VESSELS

MONOWAI (ex-*Moana Roa*)

Measurement, tons: 2 893 gross; 1 318 net
Dimensions, feet (metres): 296·5 oa × 36 × 17 *(90·4 × 11 × 5·2)*
Main engines: 2 7-cyl Sulzer diesels; 3 080 hp = 13·5 knots
Oil fuel, tons: 300
Complement: 120 approx

Previously employed on the Cook Is. service. Taken over 1974—put out to tender in early 1975 for conversion which will include an up-rating of the engines, provision of a helicopter deck and hangar and fitting of cp propellers and a bow thruster. Due for service late 1976. Conversion undertaken by Scott Lithgow Drydocks Ltd.

MONOWAI (as *Moana Roa*)   1975, Graeme Andrews

3 HDML TYPE

MAEA P 3552 (ex-*Q 1184*)
TAKAPU P 3556 (ex-*Q 1188*)
TARAPUNGA P 3566 (ex-*Q 1387*)

Of similar description as those listed under Light Forces.

MONOWAI (after conversion)   1975, Royal New Zealand Navy

LIGHT FORCES

4 "LAKE" CLASS (LARGE PATROL CRAFT)

Name	No.	Builders	Commissioned
HAWEA	P 3571	Brooke Marine, Lowestoft, England	29 July 1975
PUKAKI	P 3568	Brooke Marine, Lowestoft, England	24 Feb 1975
ROTOITI	P 3569	Brooke Marine, Lowestoft, England	24 Feb 1975
TAUPO	P 3570	Brooke Marine, Lowestoft, England	29 July 1975

Displacement, tons: 105 standard; 134 full load
Dimensions, feet (metres): 107 oa × 20 × 11·8 *(32·8 × 6·1 × 3·6)*
Guns: 1—·5 in MG; 2—7·62 mm MGs, 1—81 mm mortar
Main engines: 2 Paxman 12YJCM Diesels; 3 000 bhp = 25 knots
Complement: 21 (3 officers, 18 ratings)

The first to complete, *Pukaki,* was finished on 20 July 1974. She and *Rotoiti* were shipped to New Zealand in Nov 1974. Launch dates—*Hawea,* 9 Sep 1974; *Pukaki,* 1 March 1974; *Rotoiti,* 8 March 1974; *Taupo,* 25 July 1974.

PUKAKI   1974

ROTOITI   *1975, Royal New Zealand Navy*

"LAKE" Class   *1973, Brooke Marine*

4 HDML TYPE

HAKU P 3565 (ex-*Wakefield,* ex-*Q 1197)*
KOURA P 3564 (ex-*Toroa,* ex-*Q 1350)*
KUPARU P 3563 (ex-*Pegasus,* ex-*Q 1349)*
MANGA P 3567 (ex-*Q 1185)*

Displacement, tons: 46 standard; 54 full load
Dimensions, feet (metres): 72 × 16 × 5·5 *(22 × 4·9 × 1·7)*
Guns: Armament temporarily removed
Main engines: Diesel; 2 shafts; 320 bhp = 12 knots
Complement: 9

All built in various yards in the United States and Canada and shipped to New Zealand. All have been converted with lattice masts surmounted by a radar aerial.
Attached to RNZNVR divisions;
   Auckland: *Kuparu.*
   Canterbury: *Haku.*
   Otago: *Koura.*
   Wellington: *Manga.*

HAKU   *1973, Royal New Zealand Navy*

RESEARCH VESSEL

Name	No.	Builders	Commissioned
TUI (ex-USS *Charles H. Davis,* T-AGOR 5)	A 2	Christy Corp, Sturgeon Bay, Wis.	25 Jan 1963

Displacement, tons: 1 200 standard; 1 380 full load
Dimensions, feet (metres): 208·9 × 37·4 × 15·3 *(63·7 × 11·3 × 4·7)*
Main engines: Diesel-electric; 1 shaft; 10 000 hp = 12 knots
Complement: 8 officers, 16 ratings, 15 scientists

Oceanographic research ship. Laid down on 15 June 1961, launched on 30 June 1962. On loan from US since 28 July 1970 for 5 years. Commissioned in the Royal New Zealand Navy on 11 Sep 1970. Announced that she will remain in RNZN until at least 1980. Operates for NZ Defence Research Establishment on acoustic research. Bow propeller 175 hp.

TUI   *1971, Royal New Zealand Navy*

TUGS

ARATAKI   MANAWANUI

Dimensions, feet (metres): Length: 75 *(22·9)*
Main engines: Diesel; 1 shaft; 320 hp

Steel tugs. *Arataki* is used as a dockyard tug and *Manawanui* as a diving tender. Built by Steel Ships Ltd, Auckland in 1947.

NICARAGUA

Mercantile Marine

Lloyd's Register of Shipping:
26 vessels of 37 220 tons gross

Personnel

1976: 200 officers and men

All craft operated by Marine Section of the Guardia Naçional

PATROL CRAFT

1 SEWART TYPE

Displacement, tons: 60
Dimensions, feet (metres): 85 × 18·8 × 5·9 *(25·9 × 5·6 × 1·8)*
Guns: 3—50 cal MG
Main engines: 3 GM diesels; 3 shafts; 2 000 shp = 26·5 knots
Range, miles: 1 000 at 20 knots
Complement: 10

Delivered July 1972.

RIO CRUTA

Dimensions, feet (metres): Length: 85 *(25·9)*
Gun: 1—20 mm (bow)
Main engines: Diesels; speed = 9 knots
Complement: 11

Wooden-hulled.

4 90 ft LARGE PATROL CRAFT

Wooden-hulled (27·5 metres).

2 80 ft LARGE PATROL CRAFT

Wooden hulled (24·4 metres)

1 75 ft LARGE PATROL CRAFT

Built in 1925 so present existence doubtful. Was used for training. (22·9 metres).

1 26 ft COASTAL PATROL CRAFT

Armed with a 20 mm gun, capable of 25 knots and with a crew of 6. (7·9 metres).

NIGERIA

Headquarters Appointments

Chief of the Naval Staff:
Rear Admiral Michael Ayinde Adelanwa
Chief of Staff:
Captain Hussaini Abdullahi

Commands

Naval Flotilla:
Captain I. A. Wright
Western Naval Command:
Captain Edwin Kentebe
Eastern Naval Command:
Commander Raheem Adisa Adegbite

Diplomatic Representation

Naval Adviser in Delhi:
Captain Akintunde Aduwo

Personnel

(a) 1976: 300 officers and 2 500 ratings
(b) Voluntary Service

Bases

Apapa—Lagos:
Western Naval Command.
Dockyard Training Schools.
Port Harcourt:
Eastern Naval Command

Prefix to Ships' Names

NNS.

Mercantile Marine

Lloyd's Register of Shipping:
84 vessels of 142 050 tons gross

Strength of the Fleet

Type	Active	Building
Frigate	1	—
Corvettes	2	2
Large Patrol Craft	8	4
Landing Craft	1	—
Survey Ships	1	1
Tug	1	—
Police Craft	8	—

DELETIONS

Light Forces

1975 3 ex-Soviet "P 6" class; *Kaduna, Ibadan II* ("Ford" class)

Survey Ship

1975 *Pathfinder*

FRIGATE

Name	No.	Builders	Laid down	Launched	Commissioned
NIGERIA	F 87	Wilton, Fijenoord NV, Netherlands	9 April 1964	12 April 1965	16 Sep 1965

Displacement, tons: 1 724 standard; 2 000 full load
Length, feet (metres): 341·2 *(104·0)* pp; 360·2 *(109·8)* oa
Beam, feet (metres): 37·0 *(11·3)*
Draught, feet (metres): 11·5 *(3·5)*
Guns: 2—4 in *(102 mm)* (1 twin); 5—40 mm (single)
A/S weapons: 1—triple-barrelled DC mortar
Main engines: 4 MAN Diesels; 2 shafts; 16 000 bhp
Speed, knots: 26
Range, miles: 3 500 at 15 knots
Complement: 216

Cost £3 500 000. Helicopter platform aft.
Refitted at Birkenhead, 1973.

NIGERIA

3/1976, Wright and Logan

CORVETTES

2 Mk 9 VOSPER THORNYCROFT TYPE

Length, feet (metres): 235 *(71·6)* approx
Missiles: 1 Seacat launcher
Gun: 1—76 mm Oto Melara
A/S weapons: 1 Bofors rocket launcher
Main engines: 2 diesels
Speed, knots: 29

Ordered from Vosper Thornycroft in 1975. First to be launched Summer 1976. Above details await official confirmation.

2 Mk 3 VOSPER THORNYCROFT TYPE

Name	No.	Builders	Commissioned
DORINA	F 81	Vosper Thornycroft	June 1972
OTOBO	F 82	Vosper Thornycroft	Nov 1972

Displacement, tons: 500 standard; 650 full load
Dimensions, feet (metres): 202 oa × 31 × 11·33 *(61·6 × 9·5 × 3·5)*
Guns: 2—4 in (1 twin); 2—40 mm Bofors (single) 2—20 mm
Main engines: 2 MAN diesels; = 23 knots
Range, miles: 3 500 at 14 knots
Complement: 66 (7 officers and 59 ratings)

Ordered on 28 Mar 1968. *Dorina* laid down 26 Jan 1970, launched 16 Sep 1970, *Otobo* laid down 28 Sep 1970, launched 25 May 1971. Both refitted by Vosper Thornycroft 1975.

Radar: Air Search: Plessey AWS 1.
Fire Control: HSA M20.
Navigation: Decca TM626.

OTOBO   4/1975, John G. Callis

LIGHT FORCES

2 + 2 BROOKE MARINE TYPE (LARGE PATROL CRAFT)

Name	No.	Builders	Commissioned
HADEJIA	P 168	Brooke Marine, Lowestoft	14 Aug 1974
MAKURDI	P 167	Brooke Marine, Lowestoft	14 Aug 1974
+2			

Displacement, tons: 115 standard; 143 full load
Dimensions, feet (metres): 107 × 20 × 11·5 *(32·6 × 6·1 × 3·5)*
Guns: 2—40 mm; 2 Rocket flare launchers
Main engines: 2 Ruston Paxman YJCM diesels; 3 000 bhp; 2 shafts = 20·5 knots
Complement: 21

First pair ordered in 1971. Two more ordered 30 Oct 1974. Launch dates—*Hadejia,* 25 May 1974. *Makurdi,* 21 March 1974.

MAKURDI   1974

4 Ex-BRITISH "FORD" CLASS (LARGE PATROL CRAFT)

Name	No.	Builders	Commissioned
BENIN (ex-HMS *Hinksford)*	—	Richards, Lowestoft	1955
BONNY (ex-HMS *Gifford)*	—	Scarr, Hessle	1954
ENUGU	—	Camper & Nicholson's, Gosport	14 Dec 1961
SAPELE (ex-HMS *Dubford)*	P 09	J. Samuel White, Cowes	1953

Displacement, tons: 120 standard; 160 full load
Dimensions, feet (metres): 110 pp; 117·2 oa × 20 × 5 *(33·6; 35·7 × 6·1 × 1·5)*
Guns: 1—40 mm Bofors; 2—20 mm Oerlikon
Main engines: Davey Paxman diesels; Foden engine on centre shaft; 1 100 bhp = 18 knots
Complement: 26

Enugu was the first warship built for the Nigerian Navy. Ordered in 1960. Sailed from Portsmouth for Nigeria on 10 April 1962. Fitted with Vosper roll damping fins. *Hinksford* purchased from Great Britain on 1 July 1966 and transferred at Devonport on 9 Sep 1966. *Dubford* and *Gifford* were purchased from Great Britain during 1967-68.

Ex-British "Ford" Class   1970, Nigerian Navy

2 + 2 ABEKING AND RASMUSSEN TYPE (LARGE PATROL CRAFT)

Name	No.	Builders	Commissioned
ARGUNGU	P 165	Abeking & Rasmussen	Aug 1973
YOLA	P 166	Abeking & Rasmussen	Aug 1973

Displacement, tons: 90
Dimensions, feet (metres): 95·1 × 18·0 × 5·2 *(29 × 5·5 × 1·6)*
Guns: 1—40 mm Bofors 60 cal in Mk 3 mtg; 1—20 mm
Main engines: 2 Paxman Diesels; 2 200 hp; 2 shafts = 20 knots
Complement: 25

Two more ordered 1975. Launch dates—*Argungu,* 9 July 1973. *Yola,* 12 June 1973.

YOLA   10/1974, Michael D. J. Lennor

SURVEY SHIPS

1 NEW CONSTRUCTION

Displacement, tons: 800 standard; 1 100 full load
Dimensions, feet (metres): 189 × 37·5 × 12 *(57·8 × 11·4 × 3·7)*
Main engines: 4 diesels; 2 shafts; 3 000 bhp = 16 knots
Range, miles: 4 500 at 12 knots
Complement: 38

Ordered from Brooke Marine, Lowestoft in late 1973, laid down 5 April 1974.

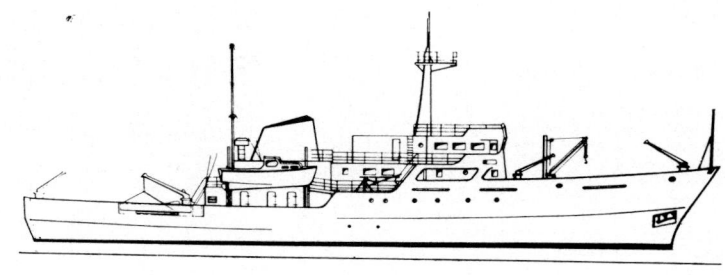

New Survey Ship

1975

Name	No.	Builders	Commissioned
PENELOPE	P 11	Aldous Successors, Brightlingsea	1958

Measurement, tons: 79 gross
Dimensions, feet (metres): 79·5 × 7·8 × 4·5 *(24·2 × 2·4 × 1·4)*
Main engines: 2 Gardner diesels = 10 knots

Used for local survey duties.

TUG

Name	No.	Builders	Commissioned
RIBADU	—	Oelkers, Hamburg	19 May 1973

Displacement, tons: 147
Dimensions, feet (metres): 93·5 × 23·6 × 12·1 *(28·5 × 7·2 × 3·7)*
Main engines: Diesel; 800 shp = 12 knots

Fitted for firefighting and salvage work.

RIBADU

1973, Reiner Nerlich

LANDING CRAFT

LOKOJA (ex-*LCT (4) 1213*)

Displacement, tons: 350 standard; 586 full load
Dimensions, feet (metres): 187·5 × 38·8 × 4·5 *(57·2 × 11·8 × 1·4)*
Guns: 2—20 mm
Main engines: 2 Paxman diesels; 920 bhp = 10 knots

Purchased from Great Britain in 1959. Allocated the name *Lokoja* in 1961. Underwent a major refit in 1966-67, including complete replating of the bottom, but currently in poor condition.

1 SUPPLY SHIP

KWA RIVER

1 000-ton ex-Dutch coaster captured while running army stores to the Biafrans.

1 or 2 ex-US LSTs (511-1152 SERIES)

To be transferred in near future.

POLICE CRAFT

8 VOSPER THORNYCROFT TYPE
(COASTAL PATROL CRAFT)

Displacement, tons: 15
Dimensions, feet (metres): 34 oa × 10 × 2·8 *(10·4 × 3·1 × 0·9)*
Guns: 1 machine gun
Main engines: 2 diesels; 290 hp = 19 knots
Complement: 6

Ordered for Nigerian Police March 1971, completed 1971-72. GRP hulls.

NORWAY

Ministerial

Minister of Defence:
Mr. Fostervoll

Headquarters Appointments

Inspector General:
Rear-Admiral O. P. Aakenes
Commander Naval Logistics Services:
Rear-Admiral N. A. Owren
Commodore Sea Training:
Commodore Rolf Henningsen

Diplomatic Representation

Defence Attaché in Bonn:
Lt. Colonel Rolf Kristiansen
Defence Attaché in Helsinki:
Lt. Colonel C. D. Gravdal
Assistant Defence Attaché (Naval) in London:
Commander J. C. Bøgh-Tobiassen
Defence Attaché in Moscow:
Lt. Colonel A. V. W. Lerheim
Defence Attaché in Stockholm:
Captain Paul H. Roest
Defence Attaché in Washington (for USA and Canada):
Rear-Admiral Magne Braadland, CVO

Personnel

(a)
1973: 8 500 officers and ratings
1974: 8 400 officers and ratings
1975: 8 400 officers and ratings
1976: 8 000 officers and ratings
(All above figures include 1 600 Coast Artillery)

(b)
15 months National Service (5 000)

Naval Bases

Karljohansvern (Horten), Haakonsvern (Bergen), Ramsund and Ramfjordnes (N. Norway)

Prefix to Ships' Names

KNM

Mercantile Marine

Lloyd's Register of Shipping:
2 706 vessels of 26 153 682 tons gross

Strength of the Fleet

Type	Active	Building
Frigates	5	—
Corvettes	2	—
Submarines—Coastal	15	—
Fast Attack Craft—Missile	26	14
Fast Attack Craft—Torpedo	20	—
Minelayers	5	2
Minesweepers—Coastal	10	—
LCTs	7	—
Depot Ship	1	1
Royal Yacht	1	—
Research Ship	1	—
Coast Guard Vessels	6	8

DELETIONS

Training Ship	LCT
1974 *Haakon VII*	1975 *Tjeldsund*

PENNANT LIST

F (Frigates and Corvettes)		M (Minesweepers)		S (Submarines)		P (Light Forces)		P (Light Forces)		P (Light Forces)		A (Amphibious Forces)	
300	Oslo	315	Ogna	300	Ula	343	Tjeld	387	Lyr	971	Tross	31	Kvalsund
301	Bergen	316	Vosso	301	Utsira	344	Skarv	388	Gribb	972	Hvass	32	Raftsund
302	Trondheim	317	Glomma	302	Utstein	345	Teist	389	Geir	973	Traust	33	Reinsøysund
303	Stavanger	331	Tista	303	Utvaer	346	Jo	390	Erle	974	Brott	34	Sorøysund
304	Narvik	332	Kvina	304	Uthaug	347	Lom	960	Storm	975	Odd	35	Maursund
310	Sleipner	334	Utla	305	Sklinna	348	Stegg	961	Blink	976	Pil	36	Rotsund
311	Aeger			306	Skolpen	349	Hauk	962	Glimt	977	Brask	37	Borgsund
		N (Minelayers)		307	Stadt	350	Falk	963	Skjold	978	Rokk		
		47	Tyr	308	Stord	357	Ravn	964	Trygg	979	Gnist		
M (Minesweepers)		48	Gor	309	Svenner	380	Skrei	965	Kjekk	980	Snögg	**A (Service Forces)**	
		49	Brage	315	Kaura	381	Hai	966	Djerv	981	Rapp		
311	Sauda	50	Uller	316	Kinn	382	Sel	967	Skudd	982	Snar	531	NordKapp
312	Sira	51	Borgen	317	Kya	383	Hval	968	Arg	983	Rask	533	Norge
313	Tana			318	Kobben	384	Laks	969	Steil	984	Kvikk	535	Valkyrien
314	Alta			319	Kunna	385	Knurr	970	Brann	985	Kjapp	536	Senja
						386	Delfin						

FRIGATES

5 "OSLO" CLASS

Name	No.	Builders	Laid down	Launched	Commissioned
BERGEN	F 301	Marinens Hovedverft, Horten	1964	23 Aug 1965	15 June 1967
NARVIK	F 304	Marinens Hovedverft, Horten	1964	8 Jan 1965	30 Nov 1966
OSLO	F 300	Marinens Hovedverft, Horten	1963	17 Jan 1964	29 Jan 1966
STAVANGER	F 303	Marinens Hovedverft, Horten	1965	4 Feb 1966	1 Dec 1967
TRONDHEIM	F 302	Marinens Hovedverft, Horten	1963	4 Sep 1964	2 June 1966

Displacement, tons: 1 450 standard; 1 745 full load
Length, feet (metres): 308 *(93·9)* pp; 317 *(96·6)* oa
Beam, feet (metres): 36·7 *(11·2)*
Draught, feet (metres): 17·4 *(5·3)*
Missile launchers: Penguin, Nato Seasparrow in some
Guns: 4—3 in *(76 mm)* (2 twin mounts)
A/S weapons: Terne system; 2 launchers for ASW Torpedoes
Main engines: 1 set De Laval Ljungstrom double reduction geared turbines; 1 shaft; 20 000 shp
Boilers: 2 Babcock & Wilcox
Speed, knots: 25
Complement: 151 (11 officers, 140 ratings)

Built under the five-year naval construction programme approved by the Norwegian *Storting* (Parliament) late in 1960. Although all the ships of this class were constructed in the Norwegian Naval Dockyard, half the cost was borne by Norway and the other half by the United States. The design of these ships is based on that of the "Dealey" class destroyer escorts in the United States Navy, but considerably modified to suit Norwegian requirements.

Engineering: The main turbines and auxiliary machinery were all built by De Laval Ljungstrom, Sweden at the company's works in Stockholm-Nacka.

Radar: Search: DRBV 22.
Tactical and Fire Control: HSA M 24 system.

Missiles: All fitted with Terne and Penguin. Seasparrow being retrofitted—all to be completed in 1976.

BERGEN

1975, Reiner Nerlich

NARVIK

6/1974, J. L. M. van der Burg

CORVETTES

2 "SLEIPNER" CLASS

Name	No.	Builders	Laid down	Launched	Commissioned
AEGER	F 311	Akers, Oslo	1964	24 Sep 1965	31 Mar 1967
SLEIPNER	F 310	Nylands Verksted Shipyard	1963	9 Nov 1963	29 April 1965

Displacement, tons: 600 standard; 780 full load
Dimensions, feet (metres): 227·8 oa × 26·2 × 8·2 *(69 × 8 × 2·4)*
Guns: 1—3 in; 1—40 mm
A/S weapons: Terne ASW system
Main engines: 4 Maybach (MTU) diesels; 2 shafts; 9 000 bhp = over 20 knots
Complement: 62

Under the five-year programme only two instead of the originally planned five new Corvettes were built. Temporarily employed as training ships until new construction is available.

SLEIPNER   4/1975, Reiner Nerlich

SUBMARINES

TYPE 210

A design contract for a new class of 750 ton patrol submarines has been placed with IKL (Lübeck). This is being carried out in conjunction with the navy of the Federal Republic of Germany.

15 TYPE 207

Name	No.	Builders	Laid down	Launched	Commissioned
KAURA	S 315	Rheinstahl-Nordseewerke, Emden, West Germany	1961	16 Oct 1964	5 Feb 1965
KINN	S 316	Rheinstahl-Nordseewerke, Emden, West Germany	1960	30 Nov 1963	8 April 1964
KOBBEN	S 318	Rheinstahl-Nordseewerke, Emden, West Germany	1961	25 April 1964	17 Aug 1964
KUNNA	S 319	Rheinstahl-Nordseewerke, Emden, West Germany	1961	16 July 1964	1 Oct 1964
KYA	S 317	Rheinstahl-Nordseewerke, Emden, West Germany	1961	20 Feb 1964	15 June 1964
SKLINNA	S 305	Rheinstahl-Nordseewerke, Emden, West Germany	1963	21 Jan 1966	27 May 1966
SKOLPEN	S 306	Rheinstahl-Nordseewerke, Emden, West Germany	1963	24 Mar 1966	17 Aug 1966
STADT	S 307	Rheinstahl-Nordseewerke, Emden, West Germany	1963	10 June 1966	15 Nov 1966
STORD	S 308	Rheinstahl-Nordseewerke, Emden, West Germany	1964	2 Sep 1966	9 Feb 1967
SVENNER	S 309	Rheinstahl-Nordseewerke, Emden, West Germany	1965	27 Jan 1967	1 July 1967
ULA	S 300	Rheinstahl-Nordseewerke, Emden, West Germany	1962	19 Dec 1964	7 May 1965
UTHAUG	S 304	Rheinstahl-Nordseewerke, Emden, West Germany	1962	8 Oct 1965	16 Feb 1966
UTSIRA	S 301	Rheinstahl-Nordseewerke, Emden, West Germany	1963	11 Mar 1965	1 July 1965
UTSTEIN	S 302	Rheinstahl-Nordseewerke, Emden, West Germany	1962	19 May 1965	9 Sep 1965
UTVAER	S 303	Rheinstahl-Nordseewerke, Emden, West Germany	1962	30 June 1965	1 Dec 1965

Displacement, tons: 370 standard; 435 dived
Length, feet (metres): 149 *(45·2)*
Beam, feet (metres): 15 *(4·6)*
Draught, feet (metres): 14 *(4·3)*
Torpedo tubes: 8—21 in *(533 mm)* (bow)
Main machinery: 2 MB 820 Maybach-Mercedes-Benz (MTU) diesels; 1 200 bhp; electric drive; 1 200 hp; 1 shaft
Speed, knots: 10 surfaced; 17 dived
Complement: 18 (5 officers, 13 men)

It was announced in July 1959 that the USA and Norway would share equally the cost of these submarines. These are a development of IKL Type 205 (West German U4-U8) with increased diving depth. *Svenner* has a second periscope for COs training operations.

Names: *Kobben* was the name of the first submarine in the Royal Norwegian Navy. Commissioned on 28 Nov 1909.

KINN   1970, Royal Norwegian Navy

SVENNER (with second periscope)   1972, Royal Norwegian Navy

LIGHT FORCES

(N.B. Armament varies in "Snögg" and "Storm" classes as Penguin SSM is installed)

14 "HAUK" CLASS (FAST ATTACK—MISSILE)

P 986-999

Displacement, tons: 120 standard; 150 full load
Dimensions, feet (metres): 119·7 oa × 20·3 × 5·5 (36·5 × 6·2 × 1·6)
Missiles: 4—Penguin
Gun: 1—40 mm
Torpedo tubes: 4—21 in
Main engines: 2 MTU diesels; 7 000 hp = 34 knots
Range, miles: 440 at 34 knots
Complement: 22

Ordered 12 June 1975—ten from Bergens Mek. Verksteder (Lakeseväg) and four from Westermöen (Alta).

Control system: Weapon control by MSI-80S developed by Kongsberg Vappenfabrikk.

Missiles: Of a longer-range version developed in collaboration with the Royal Swedish Navy.

6 "SNÖGG" CLASS (FAST ATTACK CRAFT—MISSILE)

Name	No.	Builders	Commissioned
KJAPP	P 985	Batservice Werft, A/S, Mandal, Norway	1971
KVIKK	P 984	Batservice Werft, A/S, Mandal, Norway	1971
RAPP	P 981	Batservice Werft, A/S, Mandal, Norway	1970
RASK	P 983	Batservice Werft, A/S, Mandal, Norway	1971
SNAR	P 982	Batservice Werft, A/S, Mandal, Norway	1970
SNÖGG (ex-*Lyr*)	P 980	Batservice Werft, A/S, Mandel, Norway	1970

Displacement, tons: 100 standard; 125 full load
Dimensions, feet (metres): 120·0 × 20·5 × 5·0 (36·5 × 6·2 × 1·3)
Missile launchers: 4 Penguin
Gun: 1—40 mm
Torpedo tubes: 4—21 in
Main engines: 2 Maybach (MTU) diesels; 2 shafts; 7 200 bhp = 32 knots
Complement: 18

These steel hulled fast attack craft ordered from Batservice Werft, A/S, Mandal, Norway, started coming into service in 1970. Hulls are similar to those of the "Storm" class gunboats.

RAPP   1973, Royal Norwegian Navy

20 "STORM" CLASS (FAST ATTACK CRAFT—MISSILE)

Name	No.	Builders	Commissioned
ARG	P 968	Bergens MV	1966
BLINK	P 961	Bergens MV	18 Dec 1965
BRANN	P 970	Bergens MV	1967
BRASK	P 977	Bergens MV	1967
BROTT	P 974	Bergens MV	1967
DJERV	P 966	Westermoen, Mandal	1966
GLIMT	P 962	Bergens MV	1966
GNIST	P 979	Bergens MV	1968
HVASS	P 972	Westermoen, Mandal	1967
KJEKK	P 965	Bergens MV	1966
ODD	P 975	Westermoen, Mandal	1967
PIL	P 976	Bergens MV	1967
ROKK	P 978	Westermoen, Mandal	1968
SKJOLD	P 963	Westermoen, Mandal	1966
SKUDD	P 967	Bergens MV	1966
STEIL	P 969	Westermoen, Mandal	1967
STORM	P 960	Bergens MV	1968
TRAUST	P 973	Bergens MV	1967
TROSS	P 971	Bergens MV	1967
TRYGG	P 964	Bergens MV	1966

Displacement, tons: 100 standard; 125 full load
Dimensions, feet (metres): 120·0 oa × 20·5 × 5·0 (36·5 × 6·2 × 1·5)
Missile launchers: 6 Penguin
Guns: 1—3 in; 1—40 mm
A/S weapons: DC throwers
Main engines: 2 Maybach (MTU) diesels; 2 shafts; 7 200 bhp = 32 knots

TRAUST with 6 Penguins fitted   1971, A/S Kongsbergvappenfabrikk

The first of 20 (instead of the 23 originally planned) gunboats of a new design built under the five-year programme was *Storm*, launched on 8 Feb 1963, and completed on 31 May 1963, but this prototype was eventually scrapped and replaced by a new series construction boat as the last of the class. The first of the production boats was *Blink*, launched on 28 June 1965 and completed on 18 Dec 1965. The introduction of Penguin surface-to-surface guided missile launchers started in 1970, in addition to originally designed armament.

20 "TJELD" CLASS (FAST ATTACK CRAFT—TORPEDO)

Name	No.	Builders	Commissioned
DELFIN	P 386	Båtservis, Mandal	20 May 1966
ERLE	P 390	Båtservis, Mandal	1966
FALK	P 350	Båtservis, Mandal	1961
GEIR	P 389	Båtservis, Mandal	1965
GRIBB	P 388	Båtservis, Mandal	1965
HAI	P 381	Båtservis, Mandal	1962
HAUK	P 349	Båtservis, Mandal	1961
HVAL	P 383	Båtservis, Mandal	1963
JO	P 346	Båtservis, Mandal	1961
KNURR	P 385	Båtservis, Mandal	1964
LAKS	P 384	Båtservis, Mandal	1964
LOM	P 347	Båtservis, Mandal	1961
LYR	P 387	Båtservis, Mandal	1966
RAVN	P 357	Båtservis, Mandal	1962
SEL	P 382	Båtservis, Mandal	1963
SKARV	P 344	Båtservis, Mandal	1960
SKREI	P 380	Båtservis, Mandal	1962
STEGG	P 348	Båtservis, Mandal	1961
TEIST	P 345	Båtservis, Mandal	1960
TJELD	P 343	Båtservis, Mandal	June 1960

Displacement, tons: 70 standard; 82 full load
Dimensions, feet (metres): 80·3 oa × 24·5 × 6·8 (24·5 × 7·5 × 2·1)
Guns: 1—40 mm; 1—20 mm
Torpedo tubes: 4—21 in
Main engines: 2 Napier Deltic Turboblown diesels; 2 shafts; 6 200 bhp = 45 knots
Range, miles: 450 at 40 knots; 600 at 25 knots
Complement: 18

SKARV   1973, Royal Norwegian Navy

Built of mahogany to Båtservis design, known generally as "Nasty" class.

Transfers: 2 to Turkey via West Germany, 2 to USA and 6 to Greece.

MINEWARFARE FORCES

2 COASTAL MINELAYERS

VALE   VIDAR

Displacement, tons: 1 673 full load
Dimensions, feet (metres): 212·6 × 39·4 × 29·5 *(64·8 × 12 × 9)*
Guns: 2—40 mm (twin)
Main engines: 2 Wichman 7AX diesels; 4 200 bhp; 2 shafts = 15 knots
Complement: 50

Ordered from Msellm and Karlsen (Bergen) and Skaaluren Skibsbyggeri, Rosendal for completion in 1977. One to be used for training duties originally carried out by *Haakon VII* and now by *Sleipner* and *Aeger*.

Mines: To carry 320 on three decks with an automatic lift between. Loaded through hatches forward and aft each served by two cranes.

1 CONTROLLED MINELAYER

Name	No.	Builders	Commissioned
BORGEN	N 51	Marinens Hovedverft, Horten	1961

Displacement, tons: 282 standard
Dimensions, feet (metres): 102·5 ao × 26·2 × 11 *(31·2 × 8 × 3·4)*
Main engines: 2 GM diesels; 2 Voith-Schneider propellers; 330 bhp = 9 knots

Launched 29 April 1960.

BORGEN
1972, Royal Norwegian Navy

4 Ex-US "AUK" CLASS (MINELAYERS—COASTAL)

Name	No.	Builders	Commissioned
BRAGE (ex-USS *Triumph, MMC 3*)	N 49	Associated Shipbuilders	1944
GOR (ex-USS *Strive, MMC 1*)	N 48	American Shipbuilding Co	1942
TYR (ex-USS *Sustain, MMC 2*)	N 47	American Shipbuilding Co	1942
ULLER (ex-USS *Seer, MMC 5*)	N 50	American Shipbuilding Co	1942

Displacement, tons: 890 standard; 1 250 full load
Dimensions, feet (metres): 221·2 oa × 32·2 × 16 *(67 × 9·8 × 3·4)*
Guns: 1—3 in, 50 cal; 4—20 mm (2 twin) *(Brage, Gor, Tyr)*
  1—3 in, 50 cal; 1—40 mm *(Uller)*
A/S weapons: 2 Hedgehogs; 3 DCT *(Brage, Gor, Tyr)*
  Terne ASW system; 1 DCT *(Uller)*
Mines: Laying capability
Main engines: GM diesels; electric drive; 2 shafts; 2 070 bhp = 16 knots
Complement: 83

Former US Coastal Minelayers (MMC) converted from "Auk" class MSOs. *Gor* and *Tyr* converted 1959 and *Brage* 1960 into coastal minelayers at Charleston Naval Shipyard, but *Uller* was converted in Norway. All transferred 1959-1960.

BRAGE
1972, Royal Norwegian Navy

10 "SAUDA" CLASS (MINESWEEPERS—COASTAL)

Name	No.	Builders	Commissioned
ALTA (ex-*Arlon M 915*, ex-*MSC 104*)	M 314	USA	1954
GLOMMA (ex-*Bastogne, M 916*, ex-*MSC 151*)	M 317	USA	1954
KVINA	M 332	Båtservis, Mandal	12 July 1955
OGNA	M 315	Båtservis, Mandal	5 Mar 1955
SAUDA (ex-USS *MSC 102*)	M 311	Hodgeson Bros, Gowdy & Stevens, East Boothbay, Maine	25 Aug 1953
SIRA (ex-USS *MSC 132*)	M 312	Hodgeson Bros, Gowdy & Stevens, East Boothbay, Maine	28 Nov 1955
TANA (ex-*Roeselaere, M 914*, ex- *MSC 103*)	M 313	USA	1954
TISTA	M 331	Forende Batbyggeriex, Risør	27 April 1955
UTLA	M 334	Båtservis, Mandal	15 Nov 1955
VOSSO	M 316	Skaaluren Skibsbyggeri, Rosendal	16 Mar 1955

Displacement, tons: 333 standard; 384 full load
Dimensions, feet (metres): 144 × 28 × 8·5 *(44 × 8·1 × 2·6)*
Guns: 2—20 mm
Main engines: GM diesels; 880 bhp = 13·5 knots
Oil fuel, tons: 25
Complement: 38

Hull of wooden construction. Five coastal minesweepers were built in Norway with US engines. *Alta, Glomma* and *Tana* were taken over from the Royal Belgian Navy in May, Sep and Mar 1966, respectively, having been exchanged for two Norwegian ocean minesweepers of the US MSO type, *Lagen* (ex-MSO 498) and *Nansen* (ex-MSO 499).

TISTA
7/1975, J. L. M. van der Burg

1 SWEDISH "GASSTEN" CLASS
(MINESWEEPER—INSHORE)

Displacement, tons: 135 full load
Dimensions, feet (metres): 75·5 × 21·7 × 6·5 *(23 × 6·6 × 2)*
Gun: 1—40 mm
Main engines: Diesels = 11 knots

GRP hull. Ordered from Sweden to be used in tests and evaluation.

AMPHIBIOUS FORCES

2 "KVALSUND" CLASS (LCT)

Name	No.	Builders	Commissioned
KVALSUND	A 31	Mjellem & Karlsen, Bergen	1970
RAFTSUNDA	A 32	Mjellem & Karlsen, Bergen	1970

5 "REINØYSUND" CLASS (LCT)

Name	No.	Builders	Commissioned
BORGSUND	A 37	Mjellem & Karlsen, Bergen	1973
MAURSUND	A 35	Mjellem & Karlsen, Bergen	Sep 1972
REINØYSUND	A 33	Mjellem & Karlsen, Bergen	Jan 1972
ROTSUND	A 36	Mjellem & Karlsen, Bergen	1973
SØRØYSUND	A 34	Mjellem & Karlsen, Bergen	June 1972

REINØYSUND   1973, Royal Norwegian Navy

Displacement, tons: 590 ("Reinoysund" class 596)
Dimensions, feet (metres): 167·3 × 33·5 × 5·9 *(50 × 10·2 × 1·8)*
Guns: 2—20 mm (3 in "Reinoysund" class)
Speed, knots: 11

All capable of carrying 7 tanks. Both classes of same dimensions.

DEPOT SHIPS

1 NEW CONSTRUCTION

Name	No.	Builders	Commission
HORTEN	—	A/S Horten Verft	1979?

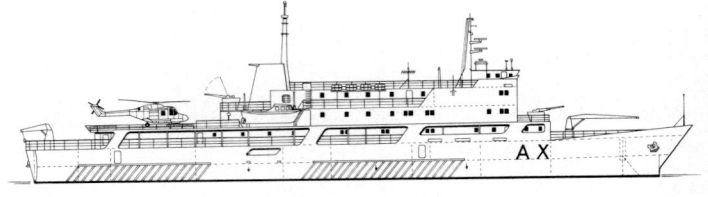

HORTEN   1976, Horten Verft

Displacement, tons: 2 500
Dimensions, feet (metres): 285·5 × 42·6 × 23 *(87 × 13 × 7)*
Complement: 85

Contract signed 30 Mar 1976. Cost approx £8 mill. To serve both submarines and fast attack craft. Quarters for 60 extra and cater for 190 extra.

1 Ex-CANADIAN FRIGATE TYPE

Name	No.	Builders	Commissioned
VALKYRIEN	A 535	Davie Shipbuilding Co, Lauzon,	6 May 1944
(ex-*Garm*, ex-*Toronto*)	(ex-*F 315*)	Port Quebec, Canada	

VALKYRIEN   1972, Royal Norwegian Navy

Displacement, tons: 1 570 standard; 2 240 full load
Dimensions, feet (metres): 301·3 × 36·5 × 16 *(91·9 × 11·1 × 4·9)*
Guns: 2—4 in, 2—40 mm
Main engines: Triple expansion; 2 shafts; 5 500 ihp = 19 knots
Complement: 104

Former Canadian modernised "River" class frigate. Loaned to Norway on 10 Mar 1956 and finally converted as depot ship for Light Forces.

Name	No.	Builders	Commissioned
DRAUG	—	Nielsen, Harstad	1972
SARPEN	—	Nielsen, Harstad	1972

Small depot ships of 250 tons for frogmen and divers.

ROYAL YACHT

Name	No.	Builders	Commissioned
NORGE (ex-*Philante*)	A 533	Camper & Nicholson's Ltd, Gosport, England	1937

Measurement, tons: 1 686 *(Thames yacht measurement)*
Dimensions, feet (metres): 263 oa × 28 × 15·2 *(80·2 × 8·5 × 4·6)*
Main engines: 8-cyl diesels; 2 shafts; 3 000 bhp = 17 knots

Built to the order of the late Mr. T. O. M. Sopwith as an escort and store vessel for the yachts *Endeavour I* and *Endeavour II*. Launched on 17 Feb 1937. Served in the Royal Navy as an anti-submarine escort during the Second World War, after which she was purchased by the Norwegian people for King Haakon at a cost of nearly £250,000 and reconditioned as a Royal Yacht at Southampton. Can accommodate about 50 people in addition to crew.

NORGE   1971, Royal Norwegian Navy

RESEARCH SHIP

Name	No.	Builders	Commissioned
H. U. SVERDRUP	—	Orens Mekaniske Verkstad, Trondheim	1960

Displacement, tons: 400
Measurement, tons: 295 gross
Dimensions, feet (metres): 127·7 × 25 × 13 *(38·9 × 7·6 × 4)*
Main engines: Wichmann diesel; 600 bhp = 11·5 knots
Oil fuel, tons: 65
Range, miles: 5 000 at 10 knots cruising speed
Complement: 10 crew; 9 scientists

Operates for Norwegian Defence Research Establishment.

COASTGUARD

Set up in 1976 for combined duties of Fishery Protection and Oil Rig Patrol.

Name	No.	Builders	Commissioned
O/S NORNEN	—	Mjellem & Karlsen, Bergen	1963

Measurement, tons: 930 gross
Dimensions, feet (metres): 201·8 × 32·8 × 15·8 *(61·5 × 10 × 4·8)*
Gun: 1—3 in *(76 mm)*
Main engines: 4 diesels; 3 500 bhp = 17 knots
Complement: 32

Launched 20 Aug 1962.

NORNEN

1970, Royal Norwegian Navy

Name	No.	Builders	Commissioned
O/S FARM	—	Ankerlokken Verft	1962
O/S HEIMDAL	—	Bolsones Verft, Molde	1962

Measurement, tons: 600 gross
Dimensions, feet (metres): 177 × 26·2 × 16·5 *(54·3 × 8·2 × 4·9)*
Gun: 1—3 in *(76 mm)*
Main engines: 2 diesels; 2 700 bhp = 16 knots
Complement: 29

Farm launched 22 Feb 1962 and *Heimdal* 7 Mar 1962.

Name	No.	Builders	Commissioned
O/S ANDENES	—	Netherlands	1957
O/S NORDKAPP	A 531	Netherlands	1957
O/S SENJA	—	Netherlands	1957

Measurement, tons: 500 gross
Dimensions, feet (metres): 186 × 31 × 16 *(56·7 × 9·5 × 4·9)*
Gun: 1—3 in *(76 mm)*
Main engines: MAN diesel; 2 300 bhp = 16 knots
Complement: 29

All three built in 1957 as whalers. Acquired by Norway in 1965 and converted into Fishery Protection Ships.

NORDKAPP

1974, Royal Norwegian Navy, Foto FRO

7 NEW CONSTRUCTION PATROL VESSELS

A new class of 15 knots ships (with a burst speed of 25) fitted with recompression chamber, helicopter, fire-fighting and anti-oil pollution equipment.

1 NEW CONSTRUCTION SUPPORT SHIP

A new class designed to operate deep-diving vehicles capable of operations at 1 600 feet *(500 metres)*.

OMAN, SULTANATE OF

Personnel

(a) 1976: 450 officers and men
(b) Voluntary service

Mercantile Marine

5 vessels of 3 149 tons gross

Bases

Qa'Adat Sultan Bin Ahmed Al Bahryya, Muscat (Main base and slipway). Raysut (advanced naval base).

Prefix to Ships' Names

SNV (Sultanate Naval Vessel)

CORVETTES

Name	No.	Builders	Commissioned
AL SAID	—	Brooke Marine, Lowestoft	1971

Displacement, tons: 900
Dimensions, feet (metres): 203·4 × 35·1 × 9·8 *(62 × 10·7 × 3)*
Gun: 1—40 mm
Main engines: 2 Paxman Ventura 12 cyl diesels; 2 shafts; 2 470 bhp
Complement: 32 + 7 staff + 32 troops

Built by Brooke Marine, Lowestoft. Launched 7 Apr 1970 as a yacht for the Sultan of Muscat and Oman, she was converted for a dual purpose role with a gun on her forecastle as flagship of the Sultanate Navy. Carried on board is one Fairey Marine Spear patrol craft. Completed in 1971.

AL SAID

1971, Brooke Marine

2 Ex-NETHERLANDS "WILDERVANK" CLASS

Name	No.	Builders	Commissioned
AL NASIRI (ex-*Aalsmeer, M 811*)	P 1	Netherlands	1955
AL SALIHI (ex-*Axel, M 808*)	P 2	Netherlands	1955

Displacement, tons: 373 standard; 417 full load
Dimensions, feet (metres): 149·8 oa × 28 × 6·5 *(46·6 × 8·8 × 2)*
Guns: 2—40 mm
Main engines: 2 Werkspoor diesels; 2 500 bhp
Speed, knots: 16
Range, miles: 2 500 at 10 knots
Complement: 38

Acquired in March 1974 and converted for patrol duties at van der Giessen/de Noord in 1974-75.

AL SALIHI

1976, Omani Dept. of Defence

LIGHT FORCES

3 + 4 BROOKE MARINE 37·5 metre TYPE

Name	No.	Builders	Commissioned
AL BUSHRA	B 1	Brooke Marine, Lowestoft	22 Jan 1973
AL MANSUR	B 2	Brooke Marine, Lowestoft	26 Mar 1973
AL NEJAH	B 3	Brooke Marine, Lowestoft	13 May 1973
—	B 4-7	Brooke Marine, Lowestoft	1976-77

Displacement, tons: 135 standard; 153 full load
Dimensions, feet (metres): 123 oa × 22·5 × 5·5 *(37·5 × 6·9 × 1·7)*
Guns: 2—40 mm (B 1-3); 1—76 mm Oto Melara; 1—20 mm (B 4-7)
Main engines: 2 Paxman Ventura diesels; 4 800 bhp = 29 knots
Range, miles: 3 300 at 15 knots
Complement: 25

First three ordered 5 Jan 1971.
4 more (B 4-7) ordered from Brooke Marine 26 Apr 1974, 2 for delivery Sept 1976 and 2 more in early 1977.

AL BUSHRA

1974, Omani Dept. of Defence

2 27 ft CHEVERTON TYPE (COASTAL PATROL CRAFT)

Displacement, tons: 3·5
Dimensions, feet (metres): 27 × 9 × 2·8 *(8·2 × 2·7 × 0·8)*
Main engines: Twin diesels = 15 knots

Purchased Apr 1975.

AMPHIBIOUS FORCES

2 60 ft CHEVERTON "LOADMASTERS"

Name	No.	Builders	Commissioned
AL SANSOOR	—	Cheverton's, Cowes	Jan 1975
KINZEER AL BAHR	—	Cheverton's, Cowes	Jan 1975

Measurement, tons: 60 deadweight
Dimensions, feet (metres): 60 oa × 20 × 3·5 *(18·3 × 6·1 × 1·1)*
Main engines: 2 × 120 hp = 8·5 knots

Delivered Jan 1975.

AL SANSOOR

1975, Roger Smith

1 45 ft CHEVERTON "LOADMASTER"

Name	No.	Builders	Commissioned
SULHAFA AL BAHR	—	Cheverton's, Cowes	1975

Measurement, tons: 45
Dimensions, feet (metres): 45 × 15 × 3 *(13·7 × 4·6 × 0·9)*
Main engines: Twin Perkins 4 236 = 8·5 knots

SULHAFA AL BAHR

1975, Cheverton Workboats

AUXILIARIES

Name	No.	Builders	Commissioned
AL SULTANA	—	Conoship, Gröningen	4 June 1975

Measurement, tons: 1 380 dw
Dimensions, feet (metres): 214·3 oa × 35 × 13·5 *(65·4 × 10·7 × 4·2)*
Main engines: Mirrlees Blackstone diesel; 1 150 bhp = 11 knots

Launched 18 May 1975.

AL SULTANA

1975, Dick van der Heijde Jnr.

1 TRAINING SHIP

DHOFAR

Displacement, tons: 1 500 full load
Dimensions, feet (metres): 219 oa × 34 × 13 *(66·8 × 10·4 × 4)*
Main engines: MAK diesel; 1 500 bhp = 10 5 knots
Complement: 22

Ex-Logistic ship now used for new entry training.

DHOFAR

1974, Omani Dept. of Defence

PAKISTAN

Headquarters Appointments

Chief of the Naval Staff:
  Vice-Admiral M. Shariff HJ
Vice Chief of the Naval Staff:
  Rear-Admiral Leslie Norman Mungavin SK

Command Appointment

Commander Pakistan Fleet:
  Commodore S. I. H. Rizvi

Diplomatic Representation

Naval Attaché in London:
  Captain T. K. Khan
Naval Attaché in Paris:
  Captain Y. H. Malik
Naval Attaché in Teheran:
  Captain Ahmed Wali Ullah
Naval Attaché in Washington:
  Captain M. Saeed

Personnel

(a) 1976: 11 000 (950 officers; 10 050 ratings)
(b) Voluntary Service

Naval Base and Dockyard

Karachi

Naval Air Arm

3 Breguet Atlantic BR 1150
6 Sea King helicopters
4 Alouette III helicopters
2 UH 19 Chickasaw helicopters
2 Cessna

Prefix to Ships' Names

PNS

Mercantile Marine

Lloyd's Register of Shipping:
  84 vessels of 479 358 tons gross

Strength of the Fleet

(No building programme announced)

Type	Active
Cruiser	1
Destroyers	4
Frigates	2 (+2)
Submarines—Patrol	3
Submarines—40 tons	6
Fast Attack Craft—Gun	12
Fast Attack Craft—Torpedo	6
Large Patrol Craft	1
Minesweepers—Coastal	7
Survey Ship	1
Tankers	2
Tugs—Ocean	2
Tugs—Harbour	2
Water-boat	1
Floating Docks	2

DELETIONS

Destroyer

1971 *Khaibar* (sunk in Indo-Pakistan War Dec 1971)

Submarine

1971 *Ghezi* (ex-US "Tench" class) (sunk in Indo-Pakistan War 4 Dec 1971)

Large Patrol Craft

1971 *Comilla, Jessore* and *Sylhet* (sunk in Indo-Pakistan War Dec 1971)

Minewarfare Forces

1971 *Muhafiz* (ex-US *MSC*) (sunk in Indo-Pakistan War Dec 1971)

PENNANT LIST

C (Cruiser)

84	Babur

D (Destroyers)

160	Alamgir
161	Badr
162	Jahangir
164	Shah Jahan

F (Frigates)

260	Tippu Sultan
261	Tughril

S (Submarines)

131	Hangor
132	Shushuk
133	Mangro

M (Minesweepers)

160	Mahmood
161	Momin
162	Murabak
164	Mujahid
165	Mukhtar
166	Munsif
167	Moshal

P (Light Forces)

140	Rajshahi
141	Lahore
142	Multan
143	Gilgit
144	Sehwan
145	Pishin
146	Kalat
147	Sukkur
148	Quetta
149	Sahiwal
150	Bannu
151	Larkana
152	Bahawalpur

HDF

01-06	"Shanghai" Class

A (Service Forces)

41	Dacca
42	Madadgar
262	Zulfiquar
298	Attock

YW

15	Zum Zum

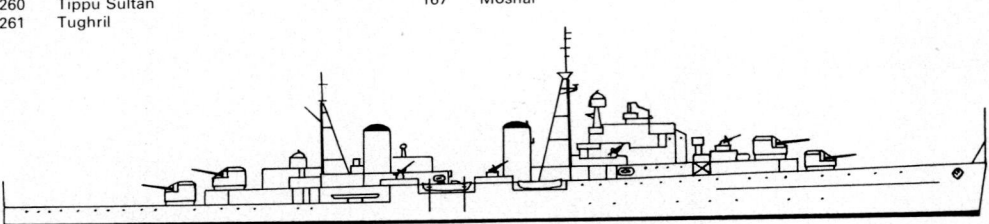

BABUR

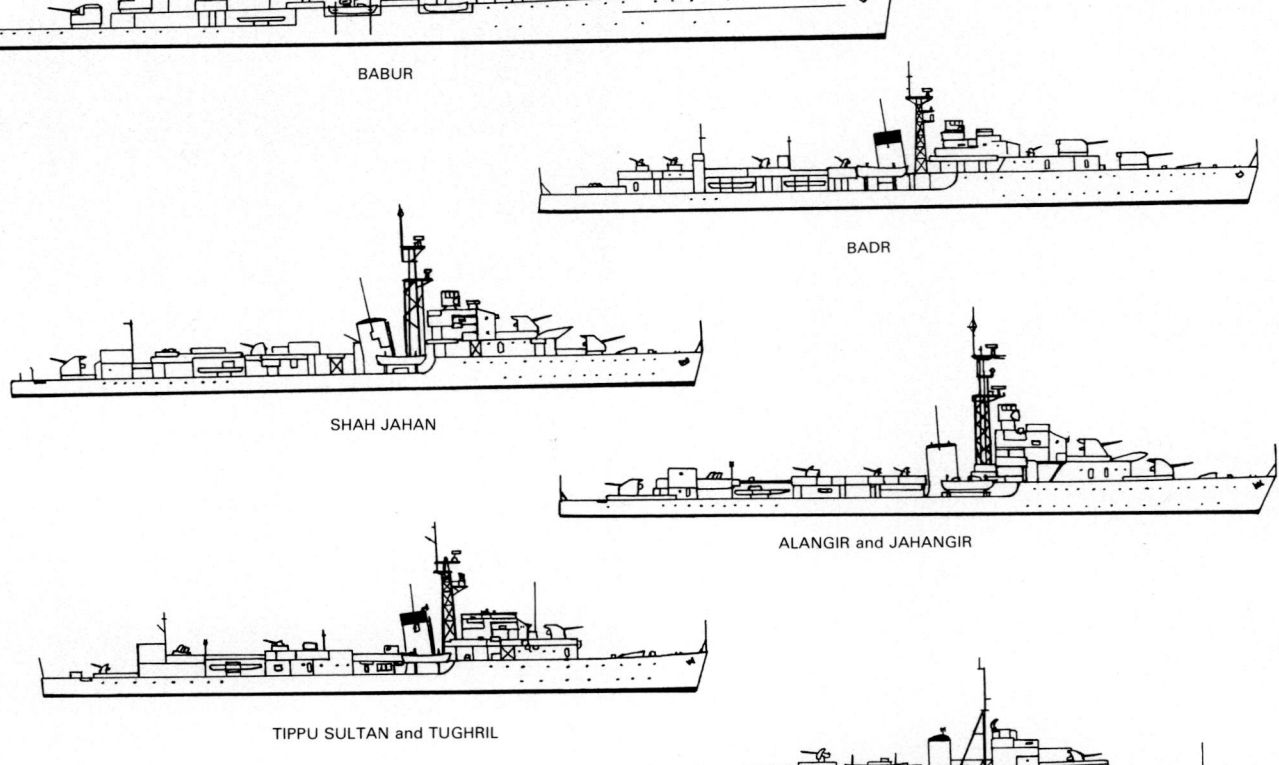

BADR

SHAH JAHAN

ALANGIR and JAHANGIR

TIPPU SULTAN and TUGHRIL

ZULFIQUAR

CRUISER *(Cadet Training Ship)*

1 Ex-BRITISH "MODIFIED DIDO" CLASS

Name	No.	Builders	Laid down	Launched	Commissioned
BABUR (ex-HMS *Diadem*)	84	R. & W. Hawthorn Leslie & Co. Ltd., Hebburn-on-Tyne	15 Nov 1939	26 Aug 1942	6 Jan 1944

Displacement, tons: 5 900 standard; 7 560 full load
Length, feet (metres): 485 *(147·9)* pp; 512 *(156·1)* oa
Beam, feet (metres): 52·0 *(15·8)*
Draught, feet (metres): 18·5 *(5·6)*
Guns: 8—5·25 in *(133 mm)* (4 twin); 14—40 mm
Torpedo tubes: 6—21 in *(533 mm)* (2 triple)
Armour: 3 in *(76 mm)* sides; 2 in *(51 mm)* decks and turrets
Main engines: Parsons s.r. geared turbines; 4 shafts; 62 000 shp
Boilers: 4 Admiralty 3-drum
Speed, knots: 20
Oil fuel, tons: 1 100
Range, miles: 4 000 at 18 knots
Complement: 588

Purchased on 29 Feb 1956. Refitted at HM Dockyard, Portsmouth and there transferred to Pakistan and renamed *Babur* on 5 July, 1957. Adapted as Cadet Training Ship in 1961.

Radar: Search: Type 960, Type 293.
Fire Control: Early British design.

BABUR
1966, Pakistan Navy

DESTROYERS

1 Ex-BRITISH "BATTLE" CLASS

Name	No.	Builders	Laid down	Launched	Commissioned
BADR (ex-HMS *Gabbard*, D 47)	161	Swan, Hunter & Wigham Richardson Ltd, Wallsend-on-Tyne	2 Feb 1944	16 Mar 1945	10 Dec 1946

Displacement, tons: 2 325 standard; 3 361 full load
Length, feet (metres): 355·0 *(108·2)* pp; 379·0 *(115·5)* oa
Beam, feet (metres): 40·2 *(12·3)*
Draught, feet (metres): 17·0 *(5·2)*
Guns: 4—4·5 in *(115 mm)* ; 10—40 mm
A/S weapons: Squid triple DC mortar
Torpedo tubes: 8—21 in *(533 mm)* (quadrupled)
Main engines: Parsons geared turbines; 2 shafts; 50 000shp
Boilers: 2 Admiralty 3-drum type
Speed, knots: 35·75
Oil fuel, tons: 680
Range, miles: 6 000 at 20 knots
Complement: 270

Purchased from Britain on 29 Feb 1956. Modernised with US funds under MDAP. Refitted at Palmers Hebburn, Yarrow, transferred to Pakistan on 24 Jan 1957 and sailed from Portsmouth for Karachi on 17 Feb 1957.

Loss: Sister ship *Khaibar* (ex-HMS *Cadiz*) was sunk during the Indo-Pakistan War in Dec 1971.

Radar: Search: Type 277, Type 293
Fire Control: I Band.

BADR
1972, Pakistan Navy

1 Ex-BRITISH "CH" CLASS

Name	No.	Builders	Laid down	Launched	Commissioned
SHAH JAHAN (ex-HMS *Charity*, D 29)	164	John I. Thornycroft Co Ltd, Woolston	9 July 1943	30 Nov 1944	19 Nov 1945

Displacement, tons: 1 710 standard; 2 545 full load
Length, feet (metres): 350·0 *(106·7)* wl; 362·7 *(110·5)* oa
Beam, feet (metres): 35·7 *(10·9)*
Draught, feet (metres): 17·0 *(5·2)*
Guns: 3—4·5 in *(115 mm)*; 6—40 mm
A/S weapons: 2 Squid triple DC mortars
Torpedo tubes: 4—21 in *(533 mm)* (quadrupled)
Main engines: Parsons geared turbines; 2 shafts; 40 000 shp
Boilers: 2 Admiralty 3-drum type
Speed, knots: 36·75
Range, miles: 5 600 at 20 knots
Complement: 200

Purchased by USA and handed over to Pakistan on 16 Dec 1958, under MDAP, at yard of J. Samuel White & Co Ltd, Cowes, who refitted her. Sister ship *Taimur* (ex-HMS *Chivalrous*) was returned to the Royal Navy and scrapped in 1960-61.

Radar: Search: Type 293.
Fire Control: I Band.

SHAH JAHAN
1972, Pakistan Navy

2 Ex-BRITISH "CR" CLASS

Name	No.	Builders	Laid down	Launched	Commissioned
ALAMGIR (ex-HMS *Creole, D 82*)	160	J. Samuel White & Co Ltd, Cowes	3 Aug 1944	22 Nov 1945	14 Oct 1946
JAHANGIR (ex-HMS *Crispin*, ex-*Craccher, D 168*)	162	J. Samuel White & Co Ltd, Cowes	1 Feb 1944	23 June1945	10 July 1946

Displacement, tons: 1 730 standard; 2 560 full load
Length, feet (metres): 350·0 *(106·7)* wl; 362·8 *(110·5)* oa
Beam, feet (metres): 35·7 *(10·9)*
Draught, feet (metres): 17·0 *(5·2)*
Guns: 3—4·5 in *(115 mm)*; 6—40 mm
A/S weapons: 2 Squid triple DC mortars
Torpedo tubes: 4—21 in *(533 mm)* (quadrupled)
Main engines: Parsons geared turbines; 2 shafts 40 000 shp
Boilers: 2 Admiralty 3-drum type
Speed, knots: 36·75
Oil fuel, tons: 580
Range, miles: 5 600 at 20 knots
Complement: 200

Purchased by Pakistan in Feb 1956. Refitted and modernised in Great Britain by John I. Thornycroft & Co Ltd, Woolston, Southampton, in 1957-58 with US funds under MDAP. Turned over to the Pakistan Navy at Southampton in 1958 (*Crispin* on 18 Mar and *Creole* 20 June) and renamed.

Radar: Search: Type 293.
Fire Control: I Band.

ALAMGIR   *1973, Pakistan Navy*

JAHANGIR   *1972, Pakistan Navy*

FRIGATES

2 Ex-BRITISH "WHITBY" CLASS

Tenby and *Scarborough* were acquired by Pakistan and were due to be refitted by Swan, Hunter Ltd. *Scarborough* was towed to the Tyne in November 1975 whilst *Tenby* remained at Plymouth.

2 Ex-BRITISH TYPE 16

Name	No.	Builders	Laid down	Launched	Commissioned
TIPPU SULTAN (ex-HMS *Onslow*, ex-*Pakenham, F 249*)	260	John Brown & Co Ltd, Clydebank	1 July 1940	31 Mar 1941	8 Oct 1941
TUGHRIL (ex-HMS *Onslaught*, ex-*Pathfinder, F 204*)	261	Fairfield SB & Eng Co Ltd, Glasgow	14 Jan 1941	9 Oct 1941	19 June 1942

Displacement, tons: 1 800 standard; 2 300 full load
Length, feet (metres): 328·7 *(100·2)* pp; 345·0 *(107·2)* oa
Beam, feet (metres): 35·0 *(10·7)*
Draught, feet (metres): 15·7 *(4·8)*
Guns: 2—4 in *(102 mm)*; 5—40 mm
A/S weapons: 2 Squid triple DC mortars
Torpedo tubes: 4—21 in *(533 mm)*
Main engines: Parsons geared turbines; 2 shafts; 40 000 shp
Boilers: 2 Admiralty 3-drum type
Speed, knots: 34
Complement: 170

Originally three "O" class destroyers were acquired from Great Britain, *Tippu Sultan* being handed over on 30 Sep 1949; *Tariq* on 3 Nov 1949; and *Tughril* on 6 Mar 1951. An agreement was signed in London between Great Britain and USA for refit and conversion in the United Kingdom of *Tippu Sultan* and *Tughril* (announced 29 April 1957) with US funds. All three ships were scheduled for conversion into fast anti-submarine frigates. *Tippu Sultan* and *Tughril* were converted at Liverpool by Grayson Rolls & Clover Docks Ltd, Birkenhead, and C. & H.

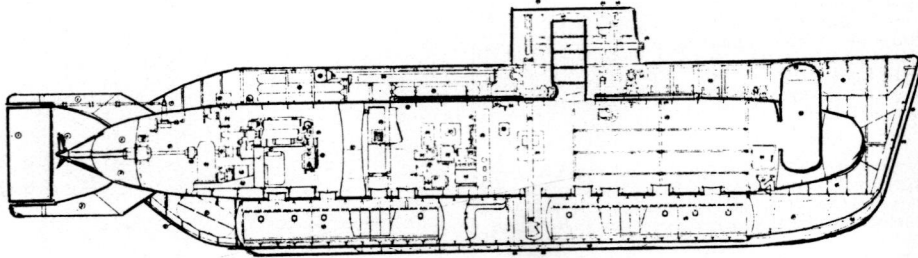

TUGHRIL   *1972, Pakistan Navy*

Crighton Ltd, respectively. *Tariq* was not converted. She was handed back to Great Britain at Portsmouth on 10 July 1959 and broken up at Sunderland, arriving there in Oct 1959.

Tughril employed on training duties.

Radar: Equipped with Type 293 search radar.

SUBMARINES

6 "SX 404" CLASS

Displacement, tons: 40
Dimensions, feet (metres): 52·4 × 6·6 × — *(16 × 2 × —)*
Speed, knots: 11 surfaced; 6·5 dived
Range, miles: 1 200 surfaced; 60 dived
Complement: 4

Purchased 1972-73 from Cosmos, Livorno. With a diving depth of 330 ft *(100 metres)* and capable of carrying 12 passengers these submarines are valuable craft for clandestine raids, reconnaissance and a multitude of shallow-water tasks.

Drawing of "SX 404" Class   *1973*

3 "HANGOR" CLASS (FRENCH "DAPHNE" CLASS)

Name	No.	Builders	Laid down	Launched	Commissioned
HANGOR	S 131	Arsenal de Brest	1 Dec 1967	28 June 1969	12 Jan 1970
MANGRO	S 133	C. N. Ciotat (Le Trait)	8 July 1968	7 Feb 1970	8 Aug 1970
SHUSHUK	S 132	C. N. Ciotat (Le Trait)	1 Dec 1967	30 July 1969	12 Jan 1970

Displacement, tons: 700 standard; 869 surfaced; 1 043 dived
Length, feet (metres): 189·6 *(57·8)*
Beam, feet (metres): 22·3 *(6·8)*
Draught, feet (metres): 15·1 *(4·6)*
Torpedo tubes: 12—21 in *(550 mm)* 8 bow, 4 stern (external)
Main machinery: Diesel electric; 1 300 bhp (surfaced); electric
motors 1 600 hp (dived); 2 shafts
Speed, knots: 13 surfaced; 15·5 dived
Complement: 45

These are the first submarines built for the Pakistan Navy. They
are basically of the French "Daphne" class design, but slightly
modified internally to suit Pakistan requirements and naval
conditions. They are broadly similar to the submarines built in
France for Portugal and South Africa and the submarines being
constructed to the "Daphne" design in Spain.

MANGRO

1971, Contre Amiral M. J. Adam

SHUSHUK

1972

LIGHT FORCES

12 Ex-CHINESE "SHANGHAI II" CLASS
(FAST ATTACK CRAFT—GUN)

BAHAWALPUR P 152	LARKANA P 151	QUETTA P 148
BANNU P 150	LAHORE P 141	SAHIWAL P 149
GILGIT P 143	MULTAN P 142	SEHWAN P 144
KALAT P 146	PISHIN P 145	SUKKUR P 147

Displacement, tons: 120 full load
Dimensions, feet (metres): 130 × 18 × 5·6 *(39·6 × 5·5 × 1·7)*
Guns: 4—37 mm; 4—25 mm
Main engines: 4 diesels; 5 000 bhp = 30 knots
Complement: 25

Transferred early 1972 (first eight) and remaining four in 1974.

PAKISTAN "SHANGHAI" Class

1973, Pakistan Navy

6 Ex-CHINESE "HU CHWAN" CLASS
(FAST HYDROFOIL ATTACK CRAFT—TORPEDO)

HDF 01, 02, 03, 04, 05, 06

Displacement, tons: 45
Dimensions, feet (metres): 70 × 16·5 × 3·1 *(21·4 × 5·0 × 0·9)*
Torpedo tubes: 2—21 inch
Guns: 4—12·7 mm (twins)
Main engines: 2—12 cyl diesels; 2 shafts; 2 200 hp = 55 knots (calm)

Hydrofoil craft transferred by China in 1973.

PAKISTAN "HU CHWAN" Class

1973, Pakistan Navy

1 "TOWN" CLASS (LARGE PATROL CRAFT)

Name	No.	Builders	Commissioned
RAJSHAHI	P 140	Brooke Marine	1965

Displacement, tons: 115 standard; 143 full load
Dimensions, feet (metres): 107 oa × 20 × 11 *(32·6 × 6·1 × 3·4)*
Guns: 2—40 mm; 70 cal Bofors
Main engines: 2 Maybach/Mercedes (MTU) MD 655/18 diesels; 3 400 bhp = 24 knots
Complement: 19

The last survivor of a class of four built by Brooke Marine in 1965 (see "Deletions"). Steel hull
and aluminium superstructure.

RAJSHAHI

1973, Pakistan Navy

MINE WARFARE FORCES

7 US MSC TYPE (MINESWEEPERS—COASTAL)

MAHMOOD (ex-*MSC 267*) M 160
MOMIN (ex-*MSC 293*) M 161
MOSHAL (ex-*MSC 294*) M 167
MURABAK (ex-*MSC 262*) M 162

MUJAHID (ex-*MSC 261*) M 164
MUKHTAR (ex-*MSC 274*) M 165
MUNSIF (ex-*MSC 273*) M 166

Displacement, tons: 335 light; 375 full load
Dimensions, feet (metres): 144 oa × 27 × 8·5 *(43·9 × 8·2 × 2·6)*
Guns: 2—20 mm
Main engines: GM diesels; 2 shafts; 880 bhp = 14 knots
Complement: 39

Transferred to Pakistan by the US under MAP. *Mukhtar* and *Munsif* on 25 June 1959, *Muhafiz* on 25 Feb 1955, *Mujahid* in Nov 1956, *Mahmood* in May 1957, *Murabak* in 1957, *Momin* in Aug 1962 and *Moshal* on 13 July 1963. *Muhafiz* sunk during Indo-Pakistan War Dec 1971.

MUNSIF

1972, Pakistan Navy

SURVEY SHIP

Name	No.	Builders	Commissioned
ZULFIQUAR (ex-*Dhanush*, ex-*Deveron F 265*)	262	Smith's Dock Co Ltd, South Bank-on-Tees	2 Mar 1943

Displacement, tons: 1 370 standard; 2 100 full load
Dimensions, feet (metres): 301·5 oa × 36·7 × 12·5 *(91·9 × 11·2 × 3·8)*
Guns: 1—4 in *(102 mm)*; 2—40 mm
Main engines: Triple expansion; 5 500 ihp
Boilers: 2 Admiralty 3-drum type
Speed, knots: 20
Range, miles: 6 000 at 12 knots
Complement: 150

Former British frigate of the "River" class converted into a survey ship, additional charthouse aft. She has strengthened davits and carries survey motor boats. The after 4-inch gun was removed.

TANKERS

1 Ex-US "MISSION" CLASS

DACCA (ex-USNS *Mission Santa Cruz, AO 132*) A 41

Displacement, tons: 5 730 light; 22 380 full load
Dimensions, feet (metres): 523·5 oa × 68 × 30·9 *(159·7 × 20·7 × 9·4)*
Main engines: Turbo-electric; 6 000 shp = 15 knots
Boilers: 2 Babcock & Wilcox
Oil capacity: 20 000 tons
Complement: 160 (15 officers and 145 men)

Transferred on loan to Pakistan under MDAP. Handed over from the US on 17 Jan 1963. Purchased 31 May 1974.

DACCA

1 US YO TYPE

Name	No.	Builders	Commissioned
MADADGAR (ex-USS *Yuma*, ATF 94)	A 42	Commercial Iron Works, Portland, Oregon	31 Aug 1943

Displacement, tons: 1 235 standard; 1 675 full load
Dimensions, feet (metres): 205 oa × 38·5 × 15·3 *(62·5 × 11·7 × 4·7)*
Main engines: 4 GM diesels; electric drive; 1 shaft; 3 000 bhp = 16·5 knots
Complement: 85

A harbour oiler of 6 500 barrels capacity built for the Pakistan Navy, under the Mutual Defence Assistance Programme of USA.

RESCUE SHIP

Name	No.	Builders	Commissioned
ATTOCK (ex-USS *YO 249*)	A 298	Trieste	1960

Displacement, tons: 600 standard; 1 255 full load
Dimensions, feet (metres): 177·2 oa × 32 × 15 *(54 × 9·8 × 4·6)*
Main engines: Direct coupled diesel; speed 8·5 knots
Complement: 26

Ocean-going salvage tug. Laid down on 13 Feb 1943. Launched on 17 July 1943. Transferred from the US Navy to the Pakistan Navy on 25 Mar 1959 under MDAP. Fitted with powerful pumps and other salvage equipment.

TUGS

Name	No.	Builders	Commissioned
BHOLU (ex-US *YTL 755*)	—	Costaguta-Voltz	Sept 1958
GAMA (ex-US *YTL 754*)	—	Costaguta-Voltz	Sept 1958

Small harbour tugs built under an "off-shore" order.

RUSTOM

Dimensions, feet (metres): 105 × 30 × 11 *(32 × 9·1 × 3·3)*
Main engines: Crossley diesel; 1 000 bhp = 9·5 knots
Range, miles: 3 000 at economic speed
Complement: 21

General purpose tug for the Pakistan Navy originally ordered from Werf-Zeeland at Hansweert, Netherlands, in August 1952, but after the liquidation of this yard the order was transferred to Worst & Dutmer at Meppel. Launched on 29 Nov 1955.

MISCELLANEOUS

1 WATER CARRIER

ZUM ZUM YW 15

Built in Italy under MDA programme.

2 FLOATING DOCKS

PESHAWAR (ex-US *ARD 6*)

Transferred June 1961. 3 000 tons lift.

FD II

Built 1974. 1 200 tons lift.

PANAMA

Personnel

A Coastguard service split between both coasts.

(a) 1976: approx 100
(b) Voluntary

Mercantile Marine

Lloyd's Register of Shipping:
2 418 ships of 13 667 123 tons gross

2 VOSPER TYPE (LARGE PATROL CRAFT)

Name	No.	Builders	Commissioned
PANQUIACO	GC 10	Vospers, Porchester, Portsmouth	Mar 1971
LIGIA ELENA	GC 11	Vospers, Porchester, Portsmouth	Mar 1971

Displacement, tons: 96 standard; 123 full load
Dimensions, feet (metres): 90·5 wl; 103·0 oa × 18·9 × 5·8 *(30; 31·4 × 5·8 × 1·8)*
Guns: 2—20 mm
Main engines: 2 Paxman Ventura 12 cyl diesels; 2 800 bhp = 24 knots
Complement: 23

Hull of welded mild steel and upperworks of welded or buck-bolted aluminium alloy. Vosper fin stabiliser equipment. *Panquiaco* was launched on 22 July 1970 and *Ligia Elena* on 25 Aug 1970.

2 Ex-US CG UTILITY TYPE (COASTAL PATROL CRAFT)

Displacement, tons: 35
Dimensions, feet (metres): 69 × 14 × 5 *(21 × 4·3 × 1·5)*
Gun: 1 MG
Main engines: 400 hp = 13 knots
Complement: 10

Transferred to Panama by the USA at the US Naval Station, Rodman, Canal Zone, in June 1962.

Note: Five additional small craft transferred by USA, three being Coastal Patrol Craft delivered 1965-66, and two handed over in 1947.

PAPUA—NEW GUINEA

The Australian base at Manus in the Admiralty Islands, HMAS *Tarangau* was de-commissioned on 14 Nov 1974 and handed over to the PNG Defence Force. It is now the PNG Patrol Boat Base Lombrun. The following ships were handed over to the PNGDF by the RAN.

LIGHT FORCES

5 "ATTACK" CLASS (LARGE PATROL CRAFT)

Name	No.	Builders	Commissioned
AITAPE	—	Walkers Ltd, Maryborough	13 Nov 1967
LADAVA	—	Walkers Ltd, Maryborough	21 Oct 1968
LAE	—	Evans Deakin & Co, Queenborough	3 April 1968
MADANG	—	Evans Deakin & Co, Queenborough	28 Nov 1968
SAMARAI	—	Evans Deakin & Co, Queenborough	1 Mar 1968

Displacement, tons: 146 full load
Dimensions, feet (metres): 107·5 × 20 × 7·3 *(32·8 × 6·1 × 2·2)*
Guns: 1—40 mm; 2 MG
Main engines: 2 Paxman 16 YJCM diesels; 2 shafts; 3 500 bhp = 24 knots
Complement: 18

Steel hulls with aluminium superstructure. Can lay mines.

"ATTACK" Class

1974

AMPHIBIOUS FORCES

Name	No.	Builders	Commissioned
BUNA	—	—	1973
SALAMAUA	—	—	1973

Displacement, tons: 310 light; 503 full load
Dimensions, feet (metres): 146 × 33 × 6·5 *(44·5 × 10·1 × 1·9)*
Guns: 2—0·5 in MG
Main engines: 2 V12 GM diesels; twin screw = 10 knots
Complement: 13

PARAGUAY

Personnel

1976   1 900 officers and men including coastguard and 500 marines

Naval Air Arm

2 H-13 Sioux helicopters

Strength of the Fleet

2 River Defence Vessels
3 Corvettes
1 Large Patrol Craft
8 Coastal Patrol Craft
2 Tugs
1 Tender
2 LCUs
1 Floating Dock
2 Service Craft

Mercantile Marine

Lloyd's Register of Shipping:
26 vessels of 21 930 tons gross

RIVER DEFENCE VESSELS

2 "HUMAITA" CLASS

Name	No.	Builders	Commissioned
HUMAITA (ex-*Capitan Cabral*)	C 2	Odero, Genoa	May 1931
PARAGUAY (ex-*Commodor Meza*)	C 1	Odero, Genoa	May 1931

Displacement, tons: 636 standard; 865 full load
Dimensions, feet (metres): 231 × 35 × 5·3 *(70 × 10·7 × 1·7)*
Guns: 4—4·7 in; 3—3 in; 2—40 mm
Mines: 6
Armour: ·5 in side amidships; ·3 in deck; ·8 in CT
Main engines: Parsons geared turbines; 2 shafts; 3 800 shp = 17 knots
Boilers: 2
Oil fuel, tons: 150
Range, miles: 1 700 at 16 knots
Complement: 86

PARAGUAY   *1974, A. J. Englis*

CORVETTES

3 "BOUCHARD" CLASS

Name	No.	Builders	Commissioned
CAPITAN MEZA (ex-*Parker*)	—	Sanchez Shipyard, San Fernando	1938
TENIENTE FARINA (ex-*Py*)	—	Rio Santiago Naval Yard	1937
NANAVA (ex-*Bouchard*)	—	Hansen & Puccini, San Fernando	1939

Displacement, tons: 450 standard; 620 normal; 650 full load
Dimensions, feet (metres): 197 oa × 24 × 8·5 *(60 × 7·3 × 2·6)*
Guns: 4—40 mm Bofors; 2 MG
Main engines: 2 sets MAN 2-cycle diesels; 2 000 bhp = 16 knots
Oil fuel, tons: 50
Range, miles: 6 000 at 12 knots
Complement: 70

Former Argentinian minesweepers of the "Bouchard" class.
Launched on 2 May 1937, 20 Mar 1936 and 18 Aug 1938. Can carry mines.
Transferred from the Argentinian Navy to the Paraguayan Navy in April 1964 onward.

CAPITAN MEZA

LIGHT FORCES

Name	No.	Builders	Commissioned
CAPITAN CABRAL (ex-*Adolfo Riquelme*)	A 1	Werf-Conrad, Haarlem	1908

Displacement, tons: 180 standard; 206 full load
Dimensions, feet (metres): 107·2 oa × 23·5 × 9·8 *(32·7 × 7·2 × 3)*
Guns: 1—3 in Vickers; 2—37 mm Vickers; 4 MG
Main engines: Triple expansion; 1 shaft; 300 ihp = 9 knots
Complement: 47

Former tug. Launched in 1907. Of wooden construction.

2 CG TYPE (COASTAL PATROL CRAFT)

P1 (ex-USCGC 20417)   P2 (ex-USCGC 20418)

Displacement, tons: 16
Dimensions, feet (metres): 45·5 oa × 13·5 × 3·5 *(13·9 × 4·1 × 1·1)*
Guns: 2—20 mm
Main engines: 2 petrol motors; 2 shafts; 190 hp = 20 knots
Complement: 10

Of wooden construction. Built in the United States in 1944. Acquired from the United States Coast Guard in 1944.

6 "701" CLASS (COASTAL PATROL CRAFT)

P 101   102   103   104   105   106

Patrol craft of 40 ft and 10 tons transferred by USA—2 in Dec 1967, 3 in Sep 1970 and 1 in Mar 1971.

TENDER

TENIENTE PRATT GILL (ex-Argentine *Corrientes*, ex-US *LSM 86*)

Displacement, tons: 1 095
Guns: 4—40 mm
Speed, knots: 13

Transferred as a gift from Argentina 13 Jan 1972. Light Forces Tender.

TUGS

Name	No.	Builders	Commissioned
YLT 559 (ex-US *YTL 211*)	A 4	Everett Pacific SB & DD Co, Wash	—
— (ex-US *YTL 567*)	A 5	Everett Pacific SB & DD Co, Wash	—

Dimensions, feet (metres): 66·2 × 17 × 5 *(20·2 × 5·2 × 1·5)*
Main engines: Diesel; 300 bhp

Small harbour tugs transferred to Paraguay by the USA under the Military Aid Programme in March 1967. YTL 567 loaned April 1974.

MISCELLANEOUS

1 FLOATING DOCK

Ex-US *AFDL 26*

Transferred March 1965. Lift 1 000 tons.

1 DREDGER

TENIENTE O CARRERAS SAGUIER

1 FLOATING WORKSHOP

Ex-US *YR 37*

Transferred March 1965.

2 Ex-US LCUs

— (ex-US *YFB 82*)   — (ex-US *YFB 86*)

Leased by US in June 1970. Used as ferries.

PERU

Headquarters Appointments

Minister of Marine and Chief of Naval Operations:
 Vice-Admiral Jorge Parodi Galliani
Chief of Naval Staff:
 Vice-Admiral Guillermo Villa Pazos

Command

Commander-in-Chief of the Fleet:
 Rear-Admiral Juan Egúsquiza Babilonia

Diplomatic Representation

Naval Attaché in London and Paris:
 Rear-Admiral Daniel Masias
Naval Attaché in Washington:
 Vice-Admiral Rafael Durán Rey

Personnel

a) 1976: 14 000 (1 200 officers, 12 800 men)
b) 2 years National Service

Bases

Callao—Main naval base; dockyard with ship-building capacity, 1 dry dock, 2 floating docks, 1 floating crane; naval academy; training schools.
Iquitos—River base for Amazon flotilla; small building yard, repair facilities.

Naval Air Arm

2 Fokker 27 FPA MP aircraft (on order for 1/1977)
2 Alouette III helicopters
10 Bell 206 Jetrangers
2 Bell 47G
6 Bell UH-1D
9 Grumman S-2A (ASW)
6 Douglas C-47 (Transport)
1 Piper Aztec C (Liaison)
2 Beech T-34 Mentor (Training)

Following operated in maritime role by Peruvian Air Force.

4 Grumman HU-16B Albatros (ASW/SAR)
4 Lockheed PV-2 Neptunes (MP)

Marines

There is one battalion of 1 000 men, additionally armed with vehicle-mounted missiles.

Prefix to Ships' Names

BAP (Baque Armada Peruana)

Mercantile Marine

Lloyd's Register of Shipping:
 675 vessels of 513 875 tons gross

Strength of the Fleet

Type	Active	Building
Cruisers	3	—
Destroyers	4	—
Frigates	2	4
Corvettes	2	—
Submarines—Patrol	8	2
Large Patrol Craft	8	6
Coastal Patrol Craft	7	—
Lake Patrol Craft	4	—
River Gunboats	5	—
Landing Ships	4	—
Transports	2	—
Tankers	5	1
Floating Docks	2	—
Survey Vessels	2	—
Tugs	2	—
Water Boat	1	—

DELETIONS

Frigate

1974 *Aguirre* (target for Exocet tests)

Minewarfare Forces

1974 *Bondy, San Martin* (ex-YMS)

Transports

Sept 1972 *Callao*
1975 *Rimac* (transferred to mercantile use)

Tanker

1973 *Talara*

Amphibious Forces

1975 3 LCUs, 10 LCAs

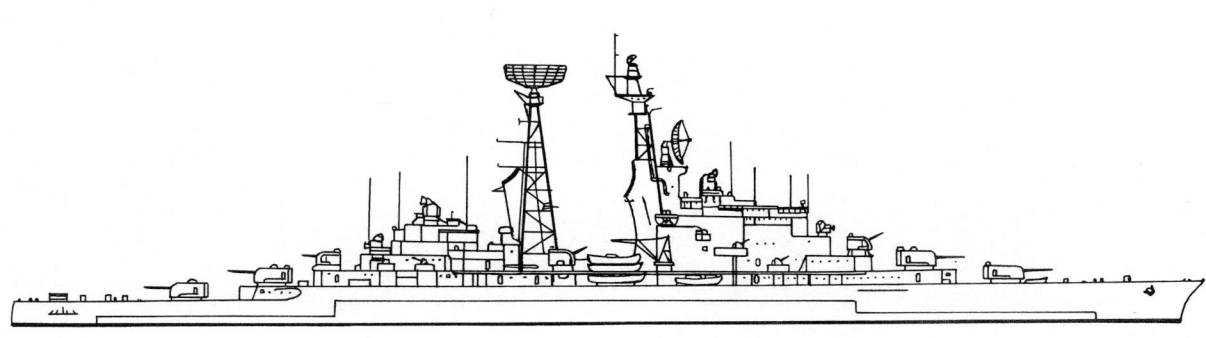

ALMIRANTE GRAU

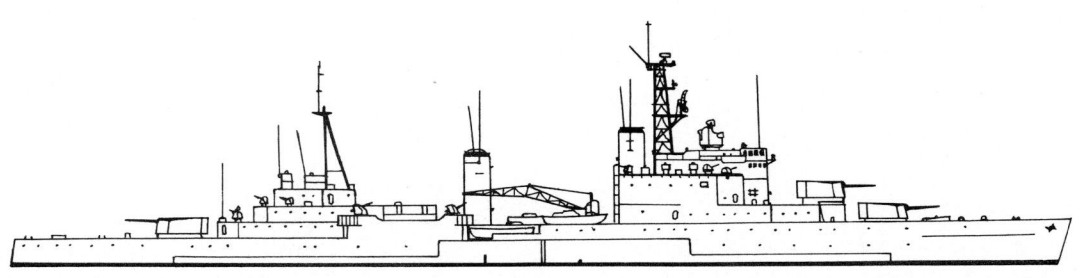

Ex-"CEYLON" Class

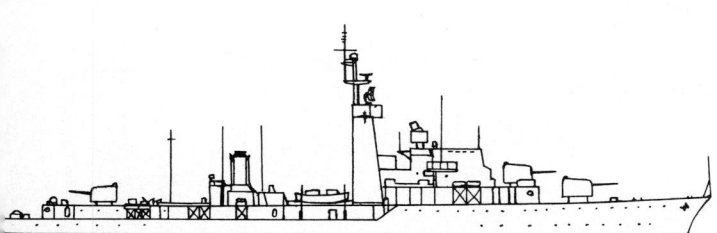

Ex-"DARING" Class

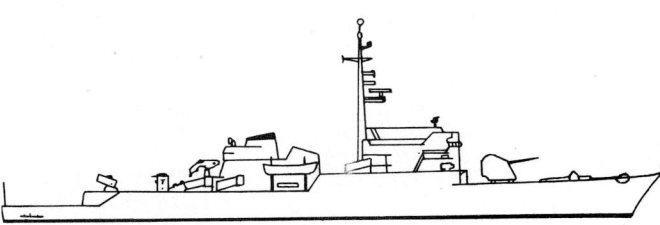

"LUPO" Class

CRUISERS

1 Ex-NETHERLANDS "DE RUYTER" CLASS

Name	No.	Builders	Laid down	Launched	Commissioned
ALMIRANTE GRAU (ex-HNMS De Ruyter)	81	Wilton-Fijenoord, Schiedam	5 Sep 1939	24 Dec 1944	18 Nov 1953

Displacement, tons: 9 529 standard; 11 850 full load
Dimensions, feet (metres): 950·5 pp; 614·5 oa × 56·7 × 22
(180 pp; 190·3 oa × 17·3 × 6·7)
Guns: 8—6 in (twin turrets); 8—57 mm (twins); 8—40 mm
Main engines: 2 De Schelde-Parsons geared turbines;
85 000 shp; 2 shafts
Boilers: 4 Werkspoor-Yarrow
Speed, knots: 32
Complement: 926

Transferred by purchase 7 March 1973.

Radar: Search: LWO 1; SPS 39(3D).
Heightfinder: SGR 104.
Tactical: DA 02.
Fire control: HSA M20 for 6 in guns and M45 for secondary
battery.

ALMIRANTE GRAU

1973, Peruvian Navy

ALMIRANTE GRAU

1975, Peruvian Navy

2 Ex-BRITISH "CEYLON" CLASS

Name	No.	Builders	Laid down	Launched	Commissioned
CAPITAN QUIÑONES (ex-Almirante Grau, ex-HMS Newfoundland)	83	Swan, Hunter & Wigham Richardson Ltd, Wallsend-on-Tyne	9 Nov 1939	19 Dec 1941	31 Dec 1942
CORONEL BOLOGNESI (ex-HMS Ceylon)	82	Alexander Stephen & Sons Ltd, Govan, Glasgow	27 Apr 1939	30 July 1942	13 July 1943

Displacement, tons:
  Capitan Quiñones: 8 800 standard; 11 090 full load
  Col. Bolognesi: 8 781 standard; 11 110 full load
Length, feet (metres): 538 *(164·0)* pp; 549 *(167·4)* wl; 555·5
(169·3) oa
Beam, feet (metres): 63·6 *(19·4)*
Draught, feet (metres): 20·5 *(6·2)*
Guns: 9—6 in *(152 mm)* (triple turrets); 8—4 in (4 twin)
  12—40 mm *Capitan Quiñones*
  18—40 mm *Col. Bolognesi*
Armour: 4 in *(102 mm)* sides and CT; 2 in *(51 mm)* turrets and
deck
Main engines: Parsons s.r. geared turbines; 72 500 shp; 4
shafts
Boilers: 4 Admiralty 3-drum; 400 psi *(28 km/cm²)*; 720°F *(382°C)*
Speed, knots: 31·5
Oil fuel, tons: 1 620
Range, miles: 6 000 at 13 knots; 2 800 at full power
Complement: *Capitan Quiñones:* 743; *Col. Bolognesi:* 766

83 was transferred as *Almirante Grau* in December 1959, being
renamed *Capitan Quiñones* on 15 May 1973. 82 was transferred
as *Coronel Bolognesi* on 9 Feb 1960.

Radar: Search: Types 960, 277 and 293.
Fire Control: E band surface, I band AA.

Reconstruction: 83 was reconstructed in 1951-53 at HM Dockyard, Devonport, with two lattice masts, new bridge and
improved AA armaments, her torpedo tubes being removed.
82 was similarly modified in 1955-56.

CAPITAN QUIÑONES

1975, Peruvian Navy

DESTROYERS

2 Ex-BRITISH "DARING" CLASS

Name
FERRÉ (ex-HMS *Decoy*) — No. 74
PALACIOS (ex-HMS *Diana*) — No. 73

Builders	Laid down	Launched	Commissioned
Yarrow Co Ltd, Scotstoun	22 Sep 1946	29 Mar 1949	28 Apr 1953
Yarrow Co Ltd, Scotstoun	3 April 1947	8 May 1952	29 Mar 1954

Displacement, tons: 2 800 standard; 3 600 full load
Length, feet (metres): 366 *(111·7)* pp; 375 *(114·3)* wl; 390 *(118·9)* oa
Beam, feet (metres): 43 *(13·1)*
Draught, feet (metres): 18 *(5·5)*
Missiles: 8 MM 38 Exocet launchers abaft after funnel
Guns: 6—4·5 *(115 mm)*; (2 twin fwd; 1 twin aft (Mk VI)); 2—40 mm
A/S weapons: 1 Squid 3 barrelled DC mortar
Torpedo tubes: 5—21 in *(533 mm)*
Main engines: English Electric dr geared turbines; 2 shafts
Boilers: 2 Forster Wheeler; Pressure 650 psi *(45·7 kg/cm²)*; Superheat 850°F *(454°C)*
Oil fuel, tons: 580
Speed, knots: 34
Range, miles: 3 000 at 20 knots
Complement: 297

Purchased by Peru in 1969 and refitted by Cammel Laird (Ship Repairers) Ltd, Birkenhead, for further service.

Refit: A second major refit was carried out in 1971-73. The main points after this refit are the reconstructed and enclosed foremast carrying Plessey AWS-1 radar and the Exocet launcher positions in place of the Close Range Blind Fire Director forward of X Turret.
Commissioned after refit—*Palacios* Feb 1973, *Ferré* April 1973.

Radar: TSF fire control on fore-funnel; Plessey AWS-1.

FERRÉ

10/1973, Wright and Logan

FERRÉ

1973, Peruvian Navy

2 Ex-US "FLETCHER" CLASS

Name
GUISE (ex-USS *Isherwood*, DD 520) — No. 72
VILLAR (ex-USS *Benham*, DD 796) — No. 71

Builders	Laid down	Launched	Commissioned
Bethlehem Steel Co, Staten Island	12 May 1942	24 Nov 1942	10 April 1943
Bethlehem Steel Co, Staten Island	Jan 1943	29 Aug 1943	20 Dec 1943

Displacement, tons: 2 120 standard; 2 715 normal; 3 050 full load
Length, feet (metres): 360·2 *(109·8)* pp; 370 *(112·8)* wl; 376·2 *(114·7)* oa
Beam, feet (metres): 39·7 *(12·1)*
Draught, feet (metres): 18 *(5·5)*
Guns: 4—5 in *(127 mm)* 38 cal; (5—5 in *Guise*); 6—3 in *(76 mm)* 50 cal (3 twin)
A/S weapons: 2 fixed Hedgehogs; 1 DC rack
Torpedo tubes: 5—21 in *(533 mm)* (quintupled)
Torpedo racks: 2 side-launching for A/S torpedoes
Main engines: 2 GE impulse reaction geared turbines; 60 000 shp; 2 shafts
Boilers: 4 Babcock & Wilcox; 600 psi *(42 kg/cm²)*; 850°F *(455°C)*
Speed, knots: 34
Oil fuel, tons: 650
Range, miles: 5 000 at 15 knots; 900 at full power
Complement: 245 (15 officers and 230 men)

Former United States destroyers of the later "Fletcher" class *(Villar)* and "Fletcher" class *(Guise)*.

Radar: Search: SPS 6, SPS 10.
Fire Control: GFCS 68 system forward, GFCS 56 system aft.

Transfer: Transferred from the United States Navy to the Peruvian Navy at Boston, Massachusetts, on 15 Dec 1960, and at San Diego, California, on 8 Oct 1961 respectively.

VILLAR

1975, Peruvian Navy

FRIGATES

4 ITALIAN "MODIFIED LUPO" CLASS

Displacement, tons: 2 208 standard; 2 500 full load
Dimensions, feet (metres): 347·7 × 39·5 × 12 *(106 × 12 × 3·7)*
Aircraft: 1 helicopter
Missiles: 2 Otomat twin-missile launchers; 1 Octuple Albatros (Aspide missiles) launcher for Point Defence
Guns: 1—127 mm Oto Melara; 2—35 mm Oto-Oerlikon (twin)
Rocket launchers: 2—105 mm Breda ELSAG multi-purpose 20-barrelled launchers
Torpedo tubes: 6 tubes in triple mountings (port and starboard)
Main engines: CODOG with 2 GE Fiat LM 2500 gas turbines; 50 000 hp; 2 Fiat 20 cyl A 230 diesels; 7 800 hp
Speed, knots: 35 knots

Two to be built by Cantiero Navale di Tireno e Riuniti (CNTR), the first being laid down on 8 Aug 1974. The second pair are to be built at Servicio Industrial de la Marina at Callao with technical assistance from CNTR. The design is similar to the "Lupo" class of Italy with a major modification in the inclusion of an A/S helicopter at the expense of four surface-to-surface missiles.

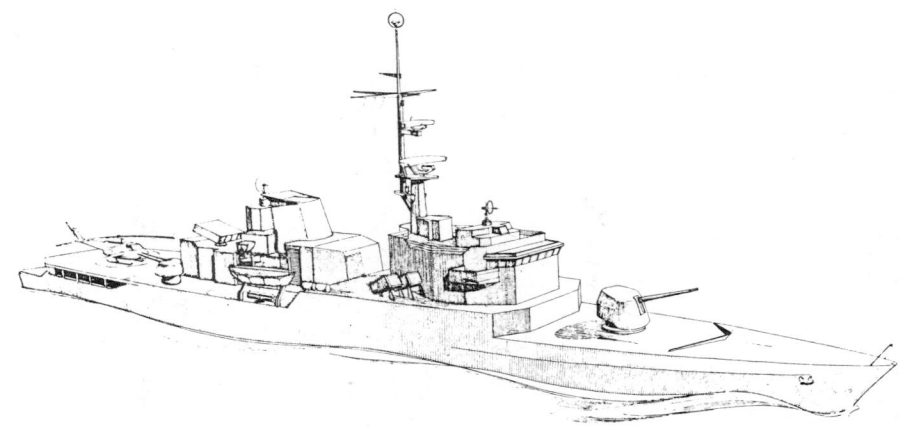

"MODIFIED LUPO" Class

1975, Peruvian Navy

2 Ex-US "CANNON" CLASS

Name	No.	Builders	Laid down	Launched	Commissioned
CASTILLA (ex-USS *Bangust, DE 739*)	61	Western Pipe & Steel Co, San Pedro, California	Jan 1943	6 June 1943	30 Oct 1943
RODRIQUEZ (ex-USS *Weaver, DE 741*)	63	Western Pipe & Steel Co, San Pedro, California	Jan 1943	20 June 1943	30 Nov 1943

Displacement, tons: 1 240 standard; 1 900 full load
Dimensions, feet (metres): 306 oa × 36·9 × 14·1 *(93·3 × 11·2 × 4·3)*
Guns: 3—3 in *(76 mm)* 50 cal; 6—40 mm (3 twin); 10—20 mm
A/S weapons: 1 Mk 10 ahead-throwing mortar; 8 K mortars; 2 DC racks aft
Main engines: 4 GM diesel-electric sets 60 000 hp; 2 shafts
Speed, knots: 21
Range, miles: 10 500 at 12 knots
Complement: 172 (12 officers and 160 men)

Transferred to Peru on 26 Oct 1951, under the Mutual Defence Assistance Programme. Reconditioned and modernised at Green Cove Springs and Jacksonville, Florida Arrived in Peru on 24 May 1952. Due for retirement.
Castilla now used as a training ship on the Amazon with home port Iquitos and *Rodriquez* as submarine accommodation ship.

Torpedo tubes: The original three 21 inch torpedo tubes in a triple mounting were removed.

RODRIQUEZ

1975, Peruvian Navy

CORVETTES

2 Ex-US "AUK" CLASS

Name	No.	Builders	Laid down	Launched	Commissioned
DIEZ CANSECO (ex-USS *Shoveler, MSF 382*)	69	Gulf Shipbuilding Corp	1 Apr 1944	10 Dec 1944	28 June 1945
GALVEZ (ex-USS *Ruddy, MSF 380*)	68	Gulf Shipbuilding Corp	24 Feb 1944	29 Oct 1944	28 Apr 1945

Displacement, tons: 890 standard; 1 250 full load
Dimensions, feet (metres): 221·2 oa × 32·2 × 11 *(67·5 oa × 9·8 × 3·4)*
Guns: 1—3 in 50 cal; 2—40 mm
A/S weapons: 1 Hedgehog
Main engines: Diesel electric; 2 shafts; 3 532 bhp = 18 knots
Range, miles: 4 300 at 10 knots
Complement: 100

Recommissioned at San Diego, California, and transferred to the Peruvian Navy under the Mutual Defence Assistance Programme on 1 Nov 1960. Sonar equipment was fitted so that they could be used as patrol vessels. The 3 inch gun director was removed. Both purchased by Peru in 1974. Transferred to the Coast Guard Service in 1975.

GALVEZ

1970, Peruvian Navy

SUBMARINES

2 + 2 TYPE 209

Name	No.	Builders	Laid down	Launched	Commissioned
ISLAY	S 45	Howaldtswerke, Kiel	1971	1973	28 Aug 1974
ARICA	S 46	Howaldtswerke, Kiel	1972	17 Apr 1974	21 Jan 1975
—	S 47	Howaldtswerke, Kiel	—	—	—
—	S 48	Howaldtswerke, Kiel	—	—	—

Displacement, tons: 990 surfaced; 1 290 dived
Length, feet (metres): 177·1 (54·0)
Beam, feet (metres): 20·3 (6·2)
Torpedo tubes: 8—21 in (with reloads)
Main machinery: Diesel Electric; 4 MTU Siemens diesel-
    generators; 1 Siemens electric motor; 1 shaft
Speed, knots: 10 surfaced; 22 dived
Range: 50 days
Complement: 31

Designed by Ingenieurkontor, Lübeck for construction by
Howaldtswerke, Kiel and sale by Ferrostaal Essen all acting as a
consortium.
A single-hull design with two ballast tanks and forward and
after trim tanks. Fitted with snort and remote machinery control. The single screw is slow revving, very high capacity batteries with GRP lead-acid cells and battery cooling—by Wilh.
Hagen and VARTTA. Active and passive sonar, sonar detection
equipment, sound ranging gear and underwater telephone.
Fitted with two periscopes, radar and Omega reciever. Fore-
planes retract.
Islay ran trials in June 1974. Arica launched 17 Apr 1974.
Two further boats ordered.

ISLAY   1975, Peruvian Navy

2 Ex-US "GUPPY 1A" CLASS

Name	No.	Builders	Laid down	Launched	Commissioned
LA PEDRERA (ex-Pabellon de Pica, ex-USS Sea Poacher SS 406)	47	Portsmouth Navy Yard	23 Feb 1944	20 May 1944	31 July 1944
PACOCHA (ex-USS Atule SS 403)	48	Portsmouth Navy Yard	2 Dec 1943	6 Mar 1944	21 June 1944

Displacement, tons: 1 870 standard; 2 440 dived
Dimensions, feet (metres): 308 oa × 27 × 17 (93·8 × 8·2 × 5·2)
Torpedo tubes: 10—21 in; 6 forward 4 aft
Main machinery: 3 diesels; 4 800 hp—2 electric motors; 5 400
    shp; 2 shafts
Speed, knots: 18 surfaced; 15 dived
Complement: 85

Modernised under the 1951 Guppy programme. Purchased by
Peru—La Pedrera on 1 July 1974, Pacocha on 31 July 1974. The
name of La Pedrera was changed a fortnight after purchase.
Both became operational in 1975 after refit.

LA PEDRERA (as SEA POACHER)   1966, Dr Giorgio Arra

4 "ABTAO" CLASS

Name	No.	Builders	Laid down	Launched	Commissioned
ABTAO (ex-Tiburon)	42	General Dynamics (Electric Boat), Groton, Connecticut	12 May 1952	27 Oct 1953	20 Feb 1954
ANGAMOS (ex-Atun)	43	General Dynamics (Electric Boat), Groton, Connecticut	27 Oct 1955	5 Feb 1957	1 July 1957
DOS DE MAYO (ex-Lobo)	41	General Dynamics (Electric Boat), Groton, Connecticut	12 May 1952	6 Feb 1954	14 June 1954
IQUIQUE (ex-Merlin)	44	General Dynamics (Electric Boat), Groton, Connecticut	27 Oct 1955	5 Feb 1957	1 Oct 1957

Displacement, tons: 825 standard; 1 400 dived
Length, feet (metres): 243 (74·1) oa
Beam, feet (metres): 22 (6·7)
Draught, feet (metres): 14 (4·3)
Guns: 1—5 in (127 mm) 25 cal (Abtao and Dos de Mayo)
Torpedo tubes: 6—21 in (533 mm); 4 bow, 2 stern
Main machinery: 2 GM 278A diesels; 2 400 bhp; Electric
    motors; 2 shafts
Speed, knots: 16 surfaced, 10 dived
Oil fuel, tons: 45
Range, miles: 5 000 at 10 knots (surfaced)
Complement: 40

They are of modified US "Mackerel" class. Refitted at Groton
as follows—Dos de Mayo and Abtao in 1965, other pair in 1968.

IQUIQUE   1975, Peruvian Navy

MINEWARFARE FORCES

2 Ex-US "AGGRESSIVE" CLASS (MINESWEEPERS—OCEAN)

— (ex-USS *Aggressive*)   — (ex-USS *Embattle*)

Transferred 1975.

LIGHT FORCES

6 LARGE PATROL CRAFT

PCGC 50-55

Displacement, tons: 150
Speed, knots: 25

Building by Servicio Industrial de Marina, Callao for the Coast Guard Service. First due for completion 1976—launched 8 Aug 1974.

6 VOSPER TYPE (LARGE PATROL CRAFT)

Name	No.	Builders	Commissioned
RIO CHICAWA	224	Vosper Ltd, Portsmouth	1965
(ex-*De Los Heros*)	(ex-*23*)		
RIO PATIVILCA	225	Vosper Ltd, Portsmouth	1965
(ex-*Herrera*)	(ex-*24*)		
RIO HUAORA	226	Vosper Ltd, Portsmouth	1965
(ex-*Larrea*)	(ex-*25*)		
RIO LOCUMBA	227	Vosper Ltd, Portsmouth	1965
(ex-*Sanchez Carrion*)	(ex-*26*)		
RIO ICA	228	Vosper Ltd, Portsmouth	1965
(ex-*Santillana*)	(ex-*27*)		
RIO VITOR	229	Vosper Ltd, Portsmouth	1965
(ex-*Velarde*)	(ex-*21*)		

Displacement, tons: 100 standard; 130 full load
Dimensions, feet (metres): 109·7 oa × 21 × 5·7 *(33·5 oa × 6·4 × 1·7)*
Guns: 2—20 mm
A/S weapons: DC racks
Main engines: 2 Napier Deltic 18 cyl, turbocharged diesels; 6 200 bhp = 30 knots
Range, miles: 1 100 at 15 knots
Complement: 25 (4 officers and 21 ratings)

SANCHEZ CARRION (now RIO LOCUMBA)   *1971, Peruvian Navy*

Of all-welded steel construction with aluminium upperworks. Equipped with Vosper roll damping fins, Decca Type 707 true motion radar, comprehensive radio, up-to-date navigation aids, sonar, and air-conditioning. The first boat, *Velarde*, was launched on 10 July 1964, the last, *Sanchez Carrion*, on 18 Feb 1965. Can be armed as gunboat, torpedo boat (four side-launched torpedoes) or minelayer. A twin rocket projector can be fitted forward instead of gun. All transferred to the Coast Guard Service in 1975 and renamed.

2 US PGM TYPE (LARGE PATROL CRAFT)

RÍO SAMA (ex-US *PGM 78)* 222 (ex-*PC 11*)
RÍO CHIRA (ex-US *PGM 111*) 223 (ex-*PC 12*)

Displacement, tons: 130 standard; 147 full load
Dimensions, feet (metres): 101 × 21 × 6 *(30·8 × 6·4 × 1·8)*
Guns: 1—40 mm; 4—20 mm; 2—0·5 cal MG
Main engines: 2 diesels; 2 shafts; 1 800 hp = 18·5 knots
Range, miles: 1 500 at 10 knots
Complement: 15

Rio Sama built by Servicio Industrial de la Marina Callao, completed Sep 1966 under the US Military Aid Programme. *Rio Chira* transferred by US 30 June 1972. Transferred to the Coast Guard Service in 1975.

RIO SAMA   *1971, Peruvian Navy*

3 "RIO" CLASS (RIVER PATROL CRAFT)

Name	No.	Builders	Commissioned
RIO PIURA	252 (ex-*04*)	Viareggio, Italy	5 Sep 1960
RIO TUMBES	251 (ex-*02*)	Viareggio, Italy	5 Sep 1960
RIO ZARUMILLA	250 (ex-*01*)	Viareggio, Italy	5 Sep 1960

Displacement, tons: 37 full load
Dimensions, feet (metres): 65·7 × 17 × 3·2 *(20 × 5·2 × 1)*
Guns: 2—40 mm
Main engines: 2 GM diesels; 2 shafts; 1 200 bhp = 18 knots

Ordered in 1959 as a class of four laid down on 15 July 1959. Stationed at El Salto on Ecuadorian border.

RIO PIURA   *1975, Peruvian Navy*

2 "MARAÑON" CLASS (RIVER GUNBOATS)

Name	No.	Builders	Commissioned
MARAÑON	13	John I. Thornycroft & Co Ltd	July 1951
UCAYALI	14	John I. Thornycroft & Co Ltd	June 1951

Displacement, tons: 365 full load
Dimensions, feet (metres): 154·8 wl × 32 × 4 (47·2 × 9·7 × 1·2)
Guns: 2—3 in 50 cal; 7—20 mm (2 twin, 3 single)
Main engines: British Polar M 441 diesels; 800 bhp = 12 knots
Range, miles: 6 000 at 10 knots
Complement: 40

Ordered early in 1950 and both laid down in early 1951. Employed on police duties in Upper Amazon. Superstructure of aluminium alloy. Based at Iquitos.

UCAYALI

1975, Peruvian Navy

2 "LORETO" CLASS (RIVER GUNBOATS)

Name	No.	Builders	Commissioned
AMAZONAS	11	Electric Boat Co, Groton	1935
LORETO	12	Electric Boat Co, Groton	1935

Displacement, tons: 250 standard
Dimensions, feet (metres): 145 × 22 × 4 (44·2 × 6·7 × 1·2)
Guns: 1—3 in; 2—47 mm; 2—20 mm
Main engines: Diesel; 750 bhp = 15 knots
Range, miles: 4 000 at 10 knots
Complement: 35

Launched in 1934.

LORETO

1973, Peruvian Navy

1 RIVER GUNBOAT

Name	No.	Builders	Commissioned
NAPO	301	Yarrow Co Ltd, Scotstoun, Glasgow	1921

Displacement, tons: 98
Dimensions, feet (metres): 101·5 oa × 18 × 3 (31 × 5·5 × 0·9)
Main engines: Triple expansion; 250 ihp = 12 knots
Boilers: Yarrow
Complement: 22

Launched in 1920. Built of steel. Converted from wood to oil fuel burning. In the Upper Amazon Flotilla. Converted to a Dispensary Vessel in 1968.

NAPO

1975, Peruvian Navy

1 RIVER GUNBOAT

Name	No.	Builders	Commissioned
AMERICA	15	Tranmere Bay Development Co Ltd, Birkenhead	1904

Displacement, tons: 240
Dimensions, feet (metres): 133 × 19·5 × 4·5 (40·6 × 5·9 × 1·4)
Guns: 2—3 pdr; 4—12·7 mm
Main engines: Triple expansion; 350 ihp = 14 knots
Complement: 26

Built of steel. Converted from coal to oil fuel burning. In the Upper Amazon Flotilla. The river gunboat *Iquitos* was discarded in 1967 and after 92 years service.

AMERICA

1975, Peruvian Navy

4 COASTAL PATROL CRAFT

LA PUNTA 230
RÍO SANTA 232

RÍO CHILLÓN 231
RÍO MAJES 233

Of 16 tons with light MGs. Complement 4.

RÍO RAMIS 290   **RÍO LLAVE** 291

Of 12 tons with light MGs. Complement 4.

RÍO COATA 292   **RÍO HUANCANÉ** 293

Of 10 tons with light MGs. Complement 4. All stationed on Lake Titicaca.

4 LAKE PATROL CRAFT

Patrol craft on Lake Titicaca

1973, Peruvian Navy

AMPHIBIOUS FORCES

Name	No.	Builders	Commissioned
CHIMBOTE (ex-M/S *Rawhiti*, ex-US LST 283)	34	American Bridge Co, Ambridge, Pennsylvania	18 Nov 1943

Displacement, tons: 1 625 standard; 4 050 full load
Dimensions, feet (metres): 328 oa × 50 × 14·1 *(100 × 15·3 × 4·3)*
Gun: 1—3 in
Main engines: GM diesels; 2 shafts; 1 700 bhp = 10 knots
Oil fuel, tons: 600 oil tanks; 1 100 ballast tanks
Range, miles: 9 500 at 9 knots
Complement: Accommodation for 16 officers and 130 men

Former US tank landing ship of the 1-510 Series. Laid down on 2 Aug 1943, launched on 10 Oct 1943. Sold to Peru by a British firm in Mar 1947. Served commercially until 1951 when she was transferred to the Peruvian Navy.

1 ex-US LST

Name	No.	Builders	Commissioned
PAITA (ex-USS *Burnett County*, LST 512)	35 (ex-*AT 4*)	Chicago Bridge & Iron Co	8 Jan 1944

Displacement, tons: 1 653 standard; 4 080 full load
Dimensions, feet (metres): 328 oa × 50 × 14·5 *(100 × 15·3 × 4·4)*
Guns: 6—40 mm; 6—20 mm
Main engines: GM diesels; 2 shafts; 1 700 bhp = 10 knots
Range, miles: 9 500 at 9 knots
Complement: 13 officers, 106 men

Former US tank landing ship of the 511-1152 Series. Laid down on 29 July 1943. Launched on 10 Dec 1943. Purchased by Peru in Sep 1957.

PAITA

1972, Peruvian Navy

2 ex-US LSMs

Name	No.	Builders	Commissioned
ATICO (ex-US *LSM*)	37	Charleston Navy Yard	14 Sep 1945
LOMAS (ex-US *LSM*)	36	Charleston Navy Yard	23 Mar 1945

Displacement, tons: 513 standard; 913 full load
Dimensions, feet (metres): 203·5 oa × 34·5 × 7 *(62·1 × 10·5 × 2·1)*
Guns: 2—40 mm; 4—20 mm
Main engines: Diesels; 800 rpm; 2 shafts; 3 600 bhp = 12 knots
Range, miles: 5 000 at 7 knots
Complement: Accommodation for 116 (10 officers and 106 men)

Former US medium landing ships of the LSM type. Purchased in 1959.

LOMAS

1975, Peruvian Navy

SURVEY VESSELS

UNANUE

For details, see "Tug" section.

CARDENAS

Of 19 tons, launched in 1950, with a complement of 4.

WATER CARRIER

Name	No.	Builders	Commissioned
MANTILLA	141	Henry C. Grebe & Co Inc, Chicago, Illinois	1945

Displacement, tons: 1 235 full load
Dimensions, feet (metres): 174 × 32 × — *(52·3 × 9·8 × —)*
Gun: 1 MG forward
Speed, knots: 8
Capacity, gallons: 200 000

Former US water barge. Lent to Peru in July 1963.

TRANSPORTS

Name	No.	Builders	Commissioned
INDEPENDENCIA (ex-USS	31	Tampa Shipbuilding Co,	1941
Bellatrix, AKA 3, ex-Raven, SKA 20) (ex-21)		Tampa, Florida	

Displacement, tons: 6 194 light
Dimensions, feet (metres): 459 oa × 63 × 26·5 *(140 × 19·2 × 8·1)*
Guns: 1—5 in 38 cal; 3—3 in 50 cal; 10—20 mm
Main engines: 1 Nordberg diesel; 1 shaft; 6 000 bhp = 16·5 knots

Former US attack cargo ship. Transferred to Peru at Bremerton, Washington on 20 July 1963 under the Military Aid Programme. Training ship for the Peruvian Naval Academy.

INDEPENDENCIA   *1975, Peruvian Navy*

Name	No.	Builders	Commissioned
ILO	131	Servicio Industrial de la Marina, Callao	Dec 1971

Displacement, tons: 18 400 full load
Measurement, tons: 13 000 deadweight
Dimensions, feet (metres): 507·7 × 67·3 × 27·2 *(154·8 × 20·5 × 8·3)*
Main engines: Diesels; Speed = 15·6 knots

The *Ilo* completed in Dec 1971 at Servicio Industrial de la Marina, Callao.
Her sister ship *Rimac* was launched at the same yard on 12 Dec 1971 and transferred from the navy for commercial use in 1974.

ILO   *1973, Peruvian Navy*

TANKERS

1 FLEET TANKER

Measurement, tons: 25 000 dw
Dimensions, feet (metres): 561·5 × 82 × 31·2 *(171·2 × 25 × 9·5)*
Main engines: Diesels; 12 000 hp
Speed, knots: 15·5

Building by Servicio Industrial de la Marina, Callao for completion in 1977. Cargo space 35 662 cu metres.

2 + 1 "PARINAS" CLASS

Name	No.	Builders	Commissioned
PARINAS	155	Servicio Industrial de la Marina, Callao	13 June 1968
PIMENTEL	156	Servicio Industrial de la Marina, Callao	27 June 1969

Displacement, tons: 3 434 light; 13 600 full load
Measurement, tons: 10 000 deadweight
Dimensions, feet (metres): 410·9 × 63·1 × 26 *(125·3 × 19·2 × 7·9)*
Main engines: Burmeister and Wain Type 750 diesel; 5 400 bhp = 14·5 knots

Third laid down in 1975.

PIMENTEL   *1975, Peruvian Navy*

2 "SECHURA" CLASS

Name	No.	Builders	Commissioned
LOBITOS	159	Servicio Industrial de la Marina, Callao	1966
ZORRITOS	158	Servicio Industrial de la Marina, Callao	1959

Displacement, tons: 8 700 full load
Measurement, tons: 4 300 gross; 6 000 deadweight
Dimensions, feet (metres): 385·0 oa × 52·0 × 21·2 *(117·4 × 15·9 × 6·4)*
Main engines: Burmeister & Wain diesels; 2 400 bhp = 12 knots
Boilers: 2 Scotch with Thornycroft oil burners for cargo tank cleaning

Zorritos launched 8 Oct 1958, *Lobitos* May 1965.

LOBITOS   1975, Peruvian Navy

Name	No.	Builders	Commissioned
MOLLENDO (ex-*Amalienborg*)	ATP 151	Japan	Sep 1962

Displacement, tons: 6 084 standard; 25 670 full load
Dimensions, feet (metres): 534·8 oa × 72·2 × 30 *(164·3 × 22 × 9·2)*
Main engines: 674-VTFS-160 diesels; 7 500 bhp = 14·5 knots

This Japanese built tanker, completed Sep 1962, was acquired by Peru in Apr 1967.

ABA 001

800 ton tanker employed on the Amazon—built in Peru 1972.

ABA 113

300 ton harbour tanker built in Peru 1972.

MOLLENDO   1975, Peruvian Navy

TUGS

Name	No.	Builders	Commissioned
RIOS (ex-USS *Pinto*, ATF 90)	123	USA	1943

Displacement, tons: 1 235 standard; 1 675 full load
Dimensions, feet (metres): 205 oa × 38·5 × 15·5 *(62·5 × 11·7 × 4·7)*
Main engines: 4 GM diesel electric; 3 000 bhp = 16·5 knots

Former United States fleet ocean tug of the "Apache" class. Launched on 5 Jan 1943. Transferred to Peru in 1960 and delivered in Jan 1961. Fitted with powerful pumps and other salvage equipment.

Name	No.	Builders	Commissioned
UNANUE (ex-USS *Wateree*, ATA 174)	136	Levingston SB Co, Orange, Texas	20 July 1944

Displacement, tons: 534 standard; 852 full load
Dimensions, feet (metres): 143 oa × 33·9 × 13·2 *(43·6 × 9 × 4)*
Main engines: GM diesel-electric; 1 500 bhp = 13 knots

Former United States auxiliary ocean tug of the "Maricopa" class. Laid down on 5 Oct 1943, launched on 18 Nov 1943. Purchased from the USA in Nov 1961 under MAP. Temporarily employed as a Survey Ship.

CONTRAESTRE NAVARRO

50 ton tug for Amazon flotilla built in Peru in 1973.

FLOATING DOCKS

The former US auxiliary floating dry dock *ARD 8* now *ADF 112* was transferred to Peru in Feb 1961; displacement 5 200 tons; length 492 feet; beam 84 feet; draught 5·7 to 33·2 feet.
The former US floating dock *AFDL 33* now *ADF 111* launched in Oct 1964 was transferred to Peru in July 1969; displacement 1 900 tons; length 288 feet; beam 64 feet; draught 8·2 to 31·5 feet.

PHILIPPINES

Senior Flag Officers

Flag Officer in Command:
Rear-Admiral Hilario M. Ruiz
Commander, Naval Operating Forces:
Captain Simeon M. Alejandro

Diplomatic Representation

Armed Forces Attaché London:
Captain Artemio A. Tadiar, Jr (Navy)
Naval Attaché Washington:
Commander Ernesto M. Arzaga

Personnel

approx 2 000 officers and 15 000 enlisted men

Strength of the Fleet

10 Frigates	4 Minesweepers
22 Patrol Vessels	2 Command Ships
4 Hydrofoil Patrol Boats	33 Landing Ships
24 Patrol Boats	28 Auxiliary Ships

During 1976 the Philippine Navy assumed control of a large number of former South Vietnamese naval units that escaped from Indochina when the Saigon government fell in 1975. Most if not all these ships will be placed in active service as soon as trained personnel are available. (HQ was South Vietnamese ship designation).

Ships

Most ships are named for geographic locations and are prefixed by the letters RPS for Republic of Philippines Ship.

Marine Corps

Commandant: Captain Rodolfo Punsalang
Personnel: 500 officers and 5 000 enlisted men (organised into a single brigade)

Coast Guard

Commandant: Commodore Ernesto R. Ogbinar
Personnel: 300 officers and 1 700 enlisted men

Mercantile Marine

Lloyd's Register of Shipping:
413 vessels of 879 043 tons gross

FRIGATES
1 Ex-US DER TYPE

No.	Builders	Launched	US Navy Comm.	Trans. Vietnam
ex-HQ 01	Brown SB & Co, Houston	16 Apr 1943	16 Sep 1943	6 Feb 1971

Name
ex-*Tran Hung Dao*, ex-USS *Camp*, DER 251

Displacement, tons: 1 590 standard; 1 850 full load
Length, feet (metres): 300 wl; 306 oa *(93·3)*
Beam, feet (metres): 36·6 *(11·2)*
Draught, feet (metres): 14 *(4·3)*
Guns: 2—3 inch *(76 mm)* 50 cal AA (single)
A/S weapons: 6—12·75 inch *324 mm)* torpedo tubes (Mk 32 triple); 1 trainable hedgehog (Mk 15); depth charge rack
Main engines: Diesel (Fairbanks Morse); 6 000 bhp; 2 shafts
Speed, knots: 21
Complement: approx 170

Former US Navy destroyer escort, of the FMR design group. After World War II this ship was extensively converted to radar picket configuration to serve as seaward extension of US aircraft attack warning system; redesignated DER with original DE hull number. Large SPS-8 search radar and TACAN (tactical aircraft navigation) "pod" removed after radar picket barrier ended in 1965, but retained DER designation. Subsequently employed during 1960s in Indochina for coastal patrol and interdiction by US Navy (Operation MARKET TIME). Transferred to South Vietnamese Navy in 1971. Acquired by the Philippines in 1975 and formally transferred on 5 Apr 1976. This ship is second in firepower in the Philippine Navy only to the ex-US Coast Guard cutters with respect to gun calibre.

Electronics: SPS-28 and SPS-10 search radars on forward tripod mast. Apparently most electronic warfare equipment was removed prior to transfer.

Ex-TRAN HUNG DAO

Vietnamese Navy

6 Ex-US 311 ft COAST GUARD CUTTERS

No.	Builders	Launched	US Navy Comm.	Trans. Vietnam
ex-HQ 02	Lake Washington SY	15 Jan 1944	19 July 1944	1 Jan 1971
ex-HQ 03	Associated Shipbuilders	2 July 1942	31 Mar 1944	1 Jan 1971
ex-HQ 05	Lake Washington SY	11 Mar 1944	8 Oct 1944	21 Dec 1971
ex-HQ 06	Lake Washington SY	13 May 1944	5 Nov 1944	21 Dec 1971
ex-HQ 16	Lake Washington SY	15 Apr 1942	12 Apr 1943	21 June 1972
ex-HQ 17	Lake Washington SY	10 July 1943	17 May 1944	21 June 1972

Name
ex-*Tran Quang Khai* ex-USCGC *Bering Strait*, WHEC 382, ex-*AVP 34*
ex-*Tran Nhat Duat* ex-USCGC *Yakutat*, WHEC 380, ex-*AVP 32*
ex-*Tran Binh Trong* ex-USCGC *Castle Rock*, WHEC 383, ex-*AVP 35*
ex-*Tran Quoc Toan* ex-USCGC *Cook Inlet*, WHEC 384, ex-*AVP 36*
ex-*Ly Thuong Kiet* ex-USCGC *Chincoteague*, WHEC 375, ex-*AVP 24*
ex-*Ngo Kuyen* ex-USCGC *McCulloch*, WHEC 386, ex-USS *Wachapreague*, AGP 8, AVP 56

Displacement, tons: 1 766 standard; 2 800 full load
Length, feet (metres): 300 wl; 310·75 oa *(94·7)*
Beam, feet (metres): 41·1 *(12·5)*
Draught, feet (metres): 13·5 *(4·1)*
Guns: 1—5 inch *(127 mm)* 38 cal DP; 1 or 2—81 mm mortars in some ships; several MG
Main engines: Diesels (Fairbanks Morse); 6 080 bhp; 2 shafts
Speed, knots: approx 18
Complement: approx 200

Built as seaplane tenders of the "Barnegat" class for the US Navy; *Tran Nhat Duat* by Associated Shipbuilders, Seattle, Washington; others by Lake Washington Shipyard, Houghton, Washington.
All transferred to US Coast Guard in 1946-1948, initially on loan designated WAVP and then on permanent transfer except ex-*McCulloch* transferred outright from US Navy to Coast Guard; subsequently redesignated as high endurance cutters (WHEC). Transferred from US Coast Guard to South Vietnamese Navy in 1971-1972. Acquired by the Philippines in 1975 and formally transferred on 5 Apr 1976.
These ships are the largest combatants in the Philippine Navy and the only ones to mount a 5 inch gun battery. All anti-submarine weapons are believed to have been removed prior to transfer to South Vietnam.

Photographs: These ships are distinguished from the former US Navy radar picket frigate of similar size by their pole masts forward, open side passages amidships, and radar antenna on second mast. Note combination ·50 cal MG/81 mm mortar forward of bridge in "B" position.

Ex-TRAN NHAT DUAT

1971, Vietnamese Navy

Ex-TRAN QUANG KHAI

1971, Vietnamese Navy

3 Ex-US "BOSTWICK" CLASS

Name	No.	Builders	Launched	US Comm.	Transferred
DATU KALANTIAW (ex-USS *Booth, DE 170*)	PS 76	Federal Shipbuilding & Dry Dock Co, Newark, New Jersey	21 June 1943	21 July 1943	15 Dec 1967
ex-*Asahi, De 262,* ex-USS *Amick, DE 168*		Federal Shipbuilding & Dry Dock Co, Newark, New Jersey	27 May 1943	26 July 1943	1976
ex-*Hatsuhi, DE 263,* ex-USS *Atherton, DE 169*		Federal Shipbuilding & Dry Dock Co, Newark, New Jersey	27 May 1943	29 Aug 1943	1976

Displacement, tons: 1 220 standard; 1 620 full load
Length, feet (metres): 300 *(91·5)* wl; 306 *(93·2)* 0a
Beam, feet (metres): 36·6 *(11·2)*
Draught, feet (metres): 14 *(4·3)*
Guns: 3—3 inch *(76 mm)* 50 cal AA (single); 6—40 mm AA (twin); 2—20 mm AA (single)
A/S weapons: 1 hedgehog; 6—12·75 inch *(324 mm)* torpedo tubes (Mk 32 triple) in PS 76; depth charges
Main engines: Diesel-electric drive (General Motors diesels); 6 000 bhp; 2 shafts
Speed, knots: 21
Complement: Approx 165

Former US Navy destroyer escorts of the DET design. The USS *Booth* was completed by the Norfolk Navy Yard. Ex-USS *Booth* transferred directly to the Philippines Navy in 1967; two other ships originally transferred to the Japanese Navy on 14 June 1955 and were stricken in June 1975 for scrapping, but acquired by the Philippine Navy for service.

Electronics: The *Datu Kalantiaw* has been refitted with SPS-5 and SPS-6 radars with antennae mounted on tripod mast; ex-Japanese ships retain pole mast.

DATU KALANTIAW *Philippine Navy*

Ex-ASAHI *1972, Toshio Tamura*

PATROL VESSELS

2 Ex-US "AUK" CLASS MSF TYPE

Name	No.	Builders	Launched
RIZAL (ex-USS *Murrelet, MSF 372*)	PS 69	Savannah Machine & Foundry Co, Georgia	29 Dec 1944
QUEZON (ex-USS *Vigilance, MSF 324*)	PS 70	Associated Shipbuilders, Seattle, Washington	5 April 1943

Displacement, tons: 890 standard; 1 250 full load
Dimensions, feet (metres): 215 wl; 221·2 oa × 32·2 × 10·8 *(70·5; 72·5 × 10·5 × 3·5)*
Guns: 2—3 inch *(76 mm)* 50 cal AA (single); 4—40 mm AA (twin); 4—20 mm AA (twin)
A/S weapons: 3—12·75 inch *(324 mm)* torpedo tubes (Mk 32 triple); 1 hedgehog; depth charges
Main engines: Diesel-electric (General Motors diesels); 3 532 bhp; 2 shafts = 18 knots
Complement: approx 100

Former US Navy minesweepers (originally designated AM). Launch dates above. PS 69 commissioned in US Navy on 21 Aug 1945 and PS 70 on 28 Feb 1944; PS 69 transferred to the Philippines on 18 June 1965 and PS 70 on 19 Aug 1967.
Upon transfer the minesweeping gear was removed and a second 3 inch gun fitted aft; additional anti-submarine weapons also fitted.

RIZAL

8 Ex-US 185-ft PCE TYPE

Name	No.	Launched
CEBU (ex-USS *PCE 881*)	PS 28	10 Nov 1943
NEGROS OCCIDENTAL (ex-USS *PCE 884*)	PS 29	24 Feb 1944
LEYTE (ex-USS *PCE 885*)	PS 30	30 April 1945
PANGASINAN (ex-USS *PCE.891*)	PS 31	15 June 1944
ILOILO (ex-USS *PCE 897*)	PS 32	3 Aug 1943
ex-*Dong Da II* ex-USS *Crestview, PCE 895*	ex-HQ 07	18 May 1943
ex-*Ngoc Hoi* ex-USS *Brattleboro, EPCER 852*	ex-HQ 12	1 Mar 1944
ex-*Van Kiep II* ex-USS *Amherst, PCER 853*	ex-HQ 14	18 Mar 1944

Displacement, tons: 640 standard; 850 full load
Dimensions, feet (metres): 180 wl; 184·5 oa × 33·1 × 9·5 *(59; 60·5 × 10·8 × 3·1)*
Guns: 1—3 inch *(76 mm)* 50 cal AA; 3 or 6—40 mm AA (single or twin) in PS units; 2—40 mm AA (single) in HQ units; 4—20 mm AA (single) in PS units; 8—20 mm AA (twin) in HQ units
A/S weapons: 2—12·75 inch *(324 mm)* torpedo tubes (Mk 32 single) in PS units; 1 fixed hedgehog in some; depth charges
Main engines: Diesels (General Motors); 2 000 bhp; 2 shafts = 15 knots
Complement: approx 90-100

CEBU *Philippine Navy*

Ex-PCE TYPE—*continued*

former US Navy Patrol Craft—Escort (PCE), two of which were fitted as rescue ships (PCER) to rescue survivors of convoy sinkings. PS 28, 29, and 30 built by Albina Engineering & Machine Works, Portland, Oregon; PS 31, 32, and HQ 07 by Willamette Iron & Steel Corp, Portland, Oregon; HQ 12 and 14 by Pullman Standard Car Manufacturing Co, Chicago, Illinois. Launch dates above.

Five units transferred to the Philippines in July 1948; HQ 07 to South Vietnam on 29 Nov 1961, HQ 12 on 11 July 1966, and HQ 14 in June 1970. Last three acquired by the Philippines in 1976.

Ex-NGOC HOI   *1971, Vietnamese Navy*

2 Ex-US MSF TYPE

Name	No.	Builders	Launched
Ex-*Chi Lang II*	ex-HQ 08	Winslow Marine Railway	19 Mar 1944
ex-USS *Gayety*, MSF 239		& SB Co, Seattle, Wash	
Ex-*Chi Linh*	ex-HQ 11	Winslow Marine Railway	14 Nov 1943
ex-USS *Shelter*, MSF 301		& SB Co, Seattle, Wash	

Displacement, tons: 650 standard; 945 full load
Dimensions, feet (metres): 180 wl; 184·5 oa × 33 × 9·75 *(59; 60·5 × 10·8 × 3·2)*
Guns: 1—3 inch *(76 mm)* 50 cal AA; 2—40 mm AA (single); up to 8—20 mm AA (twin)
A/S weapons: 1 fixed hedgehog; depth charges
Main engines: Diesel (Cooper Bessemer); 1 710 bhp; 2 shafts = 14 knots
Complement: approx 80

former US Navy minesweepers of the "Admirable" class (originally designated AM). Ex-*Chi Lang II* transferred to South Vietnam in Apr 1962, and ex-*Chi Linh* transferred to Jan 1964. Minesweeping equipment has been removed and two depth charge racks fitted on fantail. These ships are believed to have two 20 mm twin mounts at after end of bridge and one or two 20 mm twin mounts on fantail.

Ex-CHI LANG II   *1962, Vietnamese Navy*

5 Ex-US 173 ft PC TYPE

Name	No.	Builders	Launched
BATANGAS (ex-USS PC 1134)	PS 24	Defoe SB Corp	18 Jan 1943
NUEVA ECIJA (ex-USS PC 1241)	PS 25	Nashville Bridge Co	24 Dec 1942
CAPIZ (ex-USS PC 1564)	PS 27	Leathem D. Smith SB Co	19 Apr 1944
NUEVA VISCAYA	PS 80	Brown SB Co	25 Apr 1942
(ex-USAF *Altus*, ex-USS PC 568)			
ex-*E 312*, ex-*L'Inconstant*, P 636,		Leathem D. Smith SB Co	15 May 1943
ex-USS PC 1171			

Displacement, tons: 280 standard; 450 full load
Dimensions, feet (metres): 170 wl; 173·66 oa × 23 × 10·8 *(55·7; 56·9 × 7·5 × 3·5)*
Guns: 1—3 inch *(76 mm)* 50 cal AA; 1—40 mm AA; several—20 mm AA (single or twin)
A/S weapons: depth charges
Main engines: Diesels (General Motors); 2 800 bhp; 2 shafts = 20 knots
Complement: Approx 70

former US Navy patrol craft. Launch dates above; completed 1942-1944. *Batangas* and *Capiz* transferred to the Philippines in July 1948; *Nueva Ecija* in Oct 1958; and *Nueva Viscaya* in Mar 1968. The *Nueva Viscaya* was stricken from the US Navy on 15 Mar 1963 and subsequently served with the US Air Force until transferred to the Philippines in March 1968. Ex-*E 312* transferred to France in 1951 for service in Indochina; again transferred to Khmer Republic (Cambodia) in 1956; fled to the Philippines in 1975 and acquired for service in 1976.

CAPIZ   *Philippine Navy*

Ex-E 312

5 100 ft PGM TYPE

Name	No.	Builders
AGUSAN	G 61 (PGM 39)	Tacoma Boatbuilding Co, Washington
CATANDUANES	G 62 (PGM 40)	Tacoma Boatbuilding Co, Washington
ROMBLON	G 63 (PGM 41)	Tacoma Boatbuilding Co, Washington
PALAWAN	G 64 (PGM 42)	Tacoma Boatbuilding Co, Washington
ex-*HonTroc*	ex-HQ 618 (PGM 83)	Petersen Builders, Wisconsin

Displacement, tons: 122 full load
Dimensions, feet (metres): 100·3 × 21·1 × 6·9 *(32·9 × 6·9 × 2·3)*
Guns: 1—40 mm AA in ex-*Hoc Troc*; 2—20 mm AA; 2—·50 cal MG
Main engines: Diesels; 1 900 bhp; 2 shafts = 17 knots
Complement: approx 15

Steel-hulled patrol gunboats built under US military assistance programmes; G 61-64 for the Philippines, ex-*Hoc Troc* for South Vietnam. Assigned US PGM-series numbers while under construction. G 61 and G 62 transferred upon completion in Mar 1960. G 63 and G 64 in June 1960; ex-*Hoc Troc* transferred to South Vietnam in Apr 1967 and acquired by the Philippines in 1976.

These craft are lengthened versions of the US Coast Guard 85-foot "Cape" class patrol boat design. Heavier armament is provided in ex-Vietnamese unit. No A/S weapons. The *Catanduanes* is operated by the Philippine Coast Guard.

ROMBLON   *1968, Philippine Navy*

HYDROFOIL PATROL BOATS

2 ITALIAN DESIGN

Name	No.	Builders	Completed
CAMIGUIN	HB 77	Cantiere Navale Leopoldo Rodriquez, Messina	April 1965
SIQUIJOR	HB 76	Cantiere Navale Leopoldo Rodriquez, Messina	April 1965

Displacement, tons: 28
Dimensions, feet: 15·3 (24·3 over foils) × 3·8 (8·9 foilborne)
Guns: MG
Main engines: Diesel (Mercedes Benz-MTU); 1 250 bhp; 2 shafts = 38 knots
Complement: 9

Laid down on 26 May and 28 Oct 1964. For military and police patrol.

CAMIGUIN Type on foils   1965

CAMIGUIN   *Philippine Navy*

2 JAPANESE DESIGN

Name	No.	Builders	Completed
BALER	HB 75	Hitachi Zosen, Kanagawa	Dec 1966
BONTOC	HB 74	Hitachi Zosen, Kanagawa	Dec 1966

Displacement, tons: 32 full load
Dimensions, feet (metres): 68·9 × 15·7 (24·6 over foils) *(21 × 4·8, 7·5)*
Guns: MG can be mounted fore and aft; normally unarmed
Main engines: Ikegai-Mercedes Benz (MTU) diesel; 3 200 bhp = 37·8 knots (32 cruising). Also
auxiliary engine
Complement: 14

For smuggling prevention. Also used as inter-island ferries.

BALER on foils   *Philippine Navy*

INSHORE PATROL CRAFT

De HAVILLAND TYPE

Additional small patrol boats of a De Havilland type are reported being constructed for the
Philippine Navy in Australia.

18 "SWIFT" TYPE

PCF 300	PCF 306	PCF 312
PCF 301	PCF 307	PCF 313
PCF 302	PCF 308	PCF 314
PCF 303	PCF 309	PCF 315
PCF 304	PCF 310	PCF 316
PCF 305	PCF 311	PCF 317

Displacement, tons: 22·5 full load
Dimensions, feet (metres): 51·3 × 13·6 *(16·8 × 4·5)*
Guns: 2—·50 cal MG (twin)
Main engines: 2 geared diesels (General Motors); 860 bhp; 2 shafts = 28 knots

Inshore patrol craft of the "Swift" type built in the United States. PCF 302-305 served in US Navy
prior to transfer to the Philippines; others built for US military assistance programmes. PCF 300
and 301 transferred to Philippines in Mar 1966, PCF 302-305 in Aug 1966, PCF 306-313 in Feb
1968, PCF 314-316 in July 1970. PCF 317 built in 1970 in the Philippines (ferro concrete).

PCF 310   *1969, Philippine Navy*

6 IMPROVED "SWIFT" TYPE

PCF 332	PCF 335
PCF 333	PCF 336
PCF 334	PCF 337

Displacement, tons: 33 full load
Dimensions, feet (metres): 65 oa × 16 × 3·4 *(21·3 × 5·2 × 1·1)*
Guns: 2—·50 cal MG (twin); 2—·30 cal MG (single)
Main engines: 3 diesels (General Motors); 1 590 bhp; 3 shafts = 25 knots
Complement: 8

Improved "Swift" type inshore patrol boats built by Sewart for the Philippine Navy.

PATROL MINESWEEPERS

2 Ex-US MSO TYPE

Name	No.	Builders	Launched
DAVAO DEL NORTE (ex-USS *Energy, MSO 436*)	PM 91	J. M. Martinac Shipbuilding Corp, Tacoma	13 Feb 1953
DAVAO DEL SUR (ex-USS *Firm, MSO 444*)	PM 92	J. M. Martinac Shipbuilding Corp, Tacoma	15 April 1953

Displacement, tons: 665 light; 750 full load
Dimensions, feet (metres): 165 wl; 172 oa × 36 × 13·6 *(54; 56·4 × 11·8 × 44·6)*
Guns: 2—20 mm AA (twin)
Main engines: 4 diesels (Packard); 2 280 bhp; 2 shafts (controllable-pitch propellers) = 15·5 knots
Complement: approx 70

Former US Navy ocean minesweepers of the "Agile" class. Commissioned in US Navy on 16 July 1954 and 12 Oct 1954, respectively. Wood-hulled with non-magnetic engines and fittings. Both ships transferred to the Philippine Navy on 5 July 1972; designated PM for patrol minesweepers.

DAVAO DEL NORTE (as USS *Energy*)　　　　　　　　1968, US Navy

2 Ex-US MSC TYPE

Name	No.	Builders
ZAMBALES (ex-USS *MSC 218*)	PM 55	Bellingham Shipyard, Washington
ZAMBOANGA DEL NORTE (ex-USS *MSC 219*)	PM 56	Bellingham Shipyard, Washington

Displacement, tons: 320 light; 385 full load
Dimensions, feet (metres): 144 oa × 28 × 8·2 *(47·2 × 9·2 × 2·7)*
Guns: 2—20 mm AA (twin)
Main engines: 2 diesels; 880 bhp; 2 shafts = 12 knots
Complement: approx 40

"Bluebird" class coastal minesweepers built by the United States specifically for transfer under the military aid programme. Transferred on 7 Mar 1956 and 23 April 1956, respectively. Wood hull with non-magnetic metal fittings.

ZAMBALES

COMMAND SHIPS

1 JAPANESE BUILT

Name	No.	Builders	Completed
THE PRESIDENT (ex-*Roxas*, ex-*Lapu-Lapu*)	TP 777	Ishikawajima, Japan	1959

Dimensions, feet (metres): 275 oa × 42·6 × 21 *((90 × 13·9 × 6·9)*
Guns: 2—20 mm AA
Main engines: Diesels; 5 000 bhp; 2 shafts = 18 knots
Complement: approx 90

Built as war reparation; launched in 1958. Used as presidential yacht and command ship. Originally named *Lapu-Lapu* after the chief who killed Magellan; renamed *Roxas* on 9 Oct 1962 after the late Manuel Roxas, the first President of the Philippines Republic, and again renamed *The President* in 1967.

THE PRESIDENT　　　　　　　　1968, Philippine Navy

1 Ex-US AM TYPE

Name	No.	Builders	Launched
MOUNT SAMAT (ex-*Pagasa*, ex-*Santa Maria*, ex-*Pagasa*, ex-*APO 21*, ex-USS *Quest, AM 281*)	TK 21	Gulf Shipbuilding Corp	16 Mar 1944

Displacement, tons: 650 standard; 945 full load
Dimensions, feet (metres): 184·5 wl; 180 oa × 33 × 9·8 *(60·8; 59 × 10·8 × 3·2)*
Main engines: Diesels (Cooper Bessemer); 1 710 bhp; 2 shafts = 14·8 knots
Complement: approx 60

Former US Navy minesweeper (AM). Commissioned on 25 Oct 1944. Transferred to the Philippines in July 1948. Used as presidential yacht and command ship. A sister ship serves as a surveying ship in the Coast & Geodetic Service as the *Samar*.

MOUNT SAMAT　　　　　　　　1971

LANDING SHIPS

22 Ex-US LST TYPE

Name	No.	Launched
BULACAN (ex-USS *LST 843*)	LT 38	29 Nov 1944
ALBAY (ex-USS *LST 865*)	LT 39	22 Nov 1944
MISAMIS ORIENTAL (ex-USS *LST 875*)	LT 40	29 Nov 1944
BATAAN (ex-USS *Caddo Parish, LST 515*)	LT 85	31 Dec 1943
CAGAYAN (ex-USS *Hickman County, LST 825*)	LT 86	11 Nov 1944
ILCOS NORTE (ex-USS *Madera County, LST 905*)	LT 87	30 Dec 1944
OCCIDENTAL MINDORO (ex-USNS *T-LST 222*)	LT 93	17 Aug 1943
SURIGAO DEL NORTE (ex-USNS *T-LST 546*)	LT 94	16 Feb 1944
SURIGAO DEL SUR (ex-USNS *T-LST 488*)	LT 95	5 Mar 1942
ex-*Cam Ranh*, ex-USS *Marion County,LST 975*	ex-HQ 500	6 Jan 1945
ex-*Thi Nai*, ex-USS *Cayuga County, LST 529*	ex-HQ 502	17 Jan 1944
ex-*Nha Trang*, ex-USS *Jerome County, LST 848*	ex-HQ 505	2 Jan 1943
ex-USNS *T-LST 47*		24 Sep 1943
ex-USNS *T-LST 230*		12 Oct 1943
ex-USNS *T-LST 287*		31 Oct 1943
ex-USNS *T-LST 491*		23 Sep 1943
ex-USNS *T-LST 566*		11 May 1944
ex-USNS *T-LST 607*		7 Apr 1944
ex-USNS *Daviess County, T-LST 692*		31 Mar 1944
ex-USNS *Harris County, T-LST 822*		1 Nov 1944
ex-USNS *Orleans Parish, T-LST 1069*, ex-*MSC 6*		7 Mar 1945
ex-USNS *T-LST 1072*		20 Mar 1945

MISAMIS ORIENTAL
1968, Philippine Navy

Ex-NHA TRANG (tripod mast)

Displacement, tons: 1 620 standard; 2 366 beaching; 4 080 full load
Dimensions, feet (metres): 316 wl; 328 oa × 50 × 14 *(103·6; 107·5 × 19 × ·7 × 4·9)*
Guns: 7 or 8—40 mm AA (1 or 2 twin, 4 or 5 single); several 20 mm AA in former Vietnamese ships; former USNS ships are unarmed
Main engines: Diesels (General Motors); 1 700 bhp; 2 shafts = 11·6 knots
Complement: varies; approx 60 to 110 (depending upon employment)

Former US Navy tank landing ships. Cargo capacity 2 100 tons. Launch dates above. Many of these ships served as cargo ships in the Western Pacific under the US Military Sealift Command (USNS/T-LST); they were civilian manned by Korean and Japanese crews. LT 38-40 transferred to the Philippines in July 1948; LT 85-87 on 29 Nov 1969; LT 93-95 on 15 July 1972; HQ 500, 502, 505 transferred from US Navy to South Korean Navy in Apr 1962, Dec 1963, and Apr 1070, respectively, and acquired by the Philippines in 1976; final ten ships transferred from US Navy to the Philippines in 1976.
The HQ 505 and some of the later USNS ships have tripod masts; other have pole masts. The USNS ships lack troop accommodations, landing craft davits, and other amphibious warfare features. Many of these ships are used for general cargo work in Philippine service.

5 Ex-US LSM TYPE

Name	No.	Launched
ISABELA (ex-USS *LSM 463*)	LP 41	3 Feb 1945
ORIENTAL MINDORO (ex-USS *LSM 320*)	LP 68	20 July 1944
ex-*Hat Giang*, ex-*LSM 9011*, ex-USS *LSM 335*	ex-HQ 400	10 Nov 1944
ex-*Han Giang*, ex-*LSM 9012*, ex-USS *LSM 110*	ex-HQ 401	28 Oct 1944
ex-*Huong Giang*, ex-USS *Oceanside, LSM 175*)	ex-HQ 404	3 Aug 1944

Displacement, tons: 743 beaching; 1 095 full load
Dimensions, feet (metres): 196·5 wl; 203·5 oa × 34·5 × 8·5 *(60·4; 66·7 × 11·3 × 2·7)*
Guns: 2—40 mm AA (twin); several 20 mm AA
Main engines: Diesels; 2 800 bhp; 2 shafts = 11·6 knots
Complement: approx 70

Ex-HAT GIANG (LSM-H)
Vietnamese Navy

Former US Navy medium landing ships. LP 41 transferred to the Philippines in Mar 1961 and LP 68 in Apr 1962; HQ 400 and HQ 401 originally transferred from US Navy to French Navy for use in Indochina in Jan 1954; both subsequently transferred to South Vietnam in Dec 1955; HQ 404 transferred from US Navy to South Vietnam on 1 Aug 1961. All three former South Vietnamese LSMs acquired by the Philippines in 1976.
HQ 400 and HQ 401 were fitted as hospital ships (LSM-H) for treating casualties; all were armed.

3 Ex-US LSSL TYPE

Name	No.	Launched
ex-*Doan Ngoc Tang*, ex-USS *LSSL 9*	ex-HQ 228	17 Aug 1944
ex-*Lulu Phu Tho*, ex-USS *LSSL 101*	ex-HQ 229	27 Jan 1945
ex-*Niguyen Duc Bong*, ex-USS *LSSL 129*	ex-HQ 231	13 Dec 1944

Displacement, tons: 227 standard; 383 full load
Dimensions, feet (metres): 158 oa × 23·7 × 5·7 *(51·8 × 7·8 × 1·8)*
Guns: 1—3 inch AA; 4—40 mm AA; 4—20 mm AA; 4 MG
Main engines: Diesel; 1 600 bhp; 2 shafts = 14 knots
Complement: 60

Ex-NIGUYEN DUC BONG
Vietnamese Navy

Former US Navy landing ships support; designed to provide close-in-fire support for amphibious assaults, but suitable for general gunfire missions.
HQ 228 was transferred to France in 1951 *(Hallebarde L. 9023)* transferred to Japan 1956-1964; returned and transferred to South Vietnam in 1965. Two other ships served in Japanese Navy 1953 to 1964; retransferred to South Vietnam in 1965 and 1966. All acquired by the Philippines in 1976.

3 Ex-US LSIL TYPE

Name	No.	Launched
ex-*Thien Kich* ex-L 9038, ex-USS *LSIL 872*	ex-HQ 329	4 Oct 1944
ex-*Loi Cong* ex-L 9034, ex-USS *LSIL 699*	ex-HQ 330	21 June1944
ex-*Tam Set* ex-L 9033, ex-USS *LSIL 871*	ex-HQ 331	3 Oct 1944

Displacement, tons: 227 standard; 383 full load
Dimensions, feet (metres): 158 oa × 22·7 × 5·3 *(51·8 × 7·6 × 1·7)*
Guns: 1—3 inch AA; 1—40 mm AA; 2—20 mm; 4 MG; and up to 4 army mortars (2—81 mm; 2—60 mm)
Main engines: Diesel; 1 600 bhp; 2 shafts = 14·4 knots
Complement: 55

Former US Navy landing ships infantry. Designed to carry 200 troops. HQ 331 originally transferred to France in 1951 and others in 1953 for use in Indochina; subsequently retransferred in 1956 to South Vietnam. All three acquired by the Philippines in 1976.

Ex-THIEN KICH

AUXILIARY SHIPS

4 REPAIR SHIPS: Ex-US ARL/AGP TYPES

Name	No.
KAMAGONG ex-*Aklan* (ex-USS *Romulus*, ARL 22, ex-*LST 926)*	AR 67
NARRA (ex-USS *Krishna*, ARL, 38, ex-*LST 1149)*	AR 88
Ex-*My Tho*, ex-USS *Harnett County*, AGP 821, ex-*LST 821*	ex-HQ 800
Ex-*Can Tho* ex-USS *Garrett County*, AGP 786, ex-*LST 786*	ex-HQ 801

Displacement, tons: AGP type: 4 080 full load; ARL type: 4 100 full load
Dimensions, feet (metres): 316 wl; 328 oa × 50 × 14 *(103·6; 107·5 × 16·4 × 4·6)*
Guns: AGP type: 8—40 mm (2 twin, 4 single); ARL type: 8—40 mm AA (2 quad)
Main engines: Diesels (General Motors); 1 700 bhp except *Vinh Long* 1 800 bhp; 2 shafts = 11·6 knots
Complement: approx 220

Former US Navy harbour oilers (YO) and gasoline tankers (YOG). Cargo capacity 6 570 barrels. small patrol craft (AGP). The ARLs were converted during construction and the AGPs during the Vietnam War while in service with the US Navy; note that the latter ships retained their LST hull numbers after conversion to auxiliaries. Both types have extensive machine shop, spare parts stowage, supplies, etc. Launched in 1944 except AR 88 in 1945. HQ 800 and HQ 801 reclassified as AGP on 25 Sep 1970. AR 67 transferred to the Philippines in Nov 1961 and AR 88 on 31 Oct 1971; HQ 800 transferred to South Vietnam on 12 Oct 1970 and HQ 801 on 23 April 1971, with both being acquired by the Philippines in 1976.
The HQ 800 and HQ 801 have tripod masts; the other ships have pole masts aft. Note the *Kamagong's* main deck clutter of small deck house, boats, and booms; the AGP-type ships have clear decks for helicopter operations.

KAMAGONG

1968, Philippine Navy

Ex-MY THO

1971, Vietnamese Navy

7 OILERS: Ex-US YO/YOG TYPES

Name	No.	Completed
LAKE MAUJAN (ex-US *YO 173)*	YO 43	
LAKE BOHI (ex-US *YOG 73)*	YO 78	
Ex-*L'Aulne*, ex-US *YOG 80*	ex-HQ 470	1943-44
Ex-US *YOG 33*	ex-HQ 471	
Ex-US *YO 115*		
Ex-US *YO 116*		
Ex-US *YOG 61*		

Displacement, tons: 520 standard; approx 1 400 full load
Dimensions, feet (metres): 174 oa × 32 *(57 × 10·5)*
Guns: several 20 mm AA
Main engines: Diesels; 560 bhp; 1 shaft = 8 knots

Former US Navy harbour oiler (YO) and gasoline tankers (YOG). Cargo capacity 6 570 barrels. YO 43 carries fuel oil and the YO 78 gasoline and diesel oil. YO 43 transferred to the Philippines in July 1948 and YO 78 in July 1967; HQ 470 transferred to France in Jan 1951 and then to South Vietnam; HQ 471 transferred to South Vietnam in Aug 1963; latter ships acquired by the Philippines in 1976. YO 115, YO 116, and YOG 61 transferred from US Navy to the Philippines on 16 July 1975.

Ex-HQ 471

Vietnamese Navy

Ex-HQ 470

1971, Vietnamese Navy

4 WATER CARRIERS: Ex-US YW TYPE

LAKE LANAO (ex-US YW 125)   YW 42
LAKE BULAN (ex-US YW 111)   YW 33
LAKE PAOAY (ex-US YW 130)   YW 34
Ex-US YN 103

Displacement, tons: 1 235 full load
Dimensions, feet (metres): 174 oa × 32 × 15 *(57 × 10·5 × 4·9)*
Guns: 2—20 mm AA
Main engines: Diesel; 560 bhp; 1 shaft = 8 knots

Former US Navy harbour water carriers. Cargo capacity 200 000 gallons fresh water. *Lake Lanao* transferred to the Philippines in July 1948; others on 16 July 1975.

1 TENDER: Ex-US COAST GUARD TENDER

Name	No.	Builders	Completed
KALINGA (ex-USCGC *Redbud*, WLB 398, ex-USNS *Redbud*, T-AKL 398)	TK 89	Marine Iron & Shipbuilding Co, Duluth	11 Sep 1943

Displacement, tons: 935 standard
Dimensions, feet (metres): 180 oa × 37 × 13 *(59 × 12·1 × 4·3)*
Guns: Unarmed
Main engines: Diesel-electric; 1 200 bhp; 1 shaft = 13 knots

Originally US Coast Guard buoy tender (WAGL 398). Transferred to US Navy on 25 Mar 1949 as AG 398; redesignated AKL 398 on 31 Mar 1949; transferred to Military Sea Transportation Service on 20 Feb 1952 (T-AKL 398); reacquired by Coast Guard on 20 Nov 1970; transferred to Philippines on 1 Mar 1972.

3 TENDERS: Ex-US ARMY FS TYPE

Name	No.
BOJEADOE (ex-US Army *FS 203*)	TK 46
LAUIS LEDGE (ex-US Army *FS 185*)	TK 45
LIMASAWA (ex-USCGC *Nettle* WAK 169, ex-US Army *FS 169*)	TK 79

Displacement, tons: 470 standard; 811 full load
Dimensions, feet (metres): 180 oa × 23 × 10 *(60 × 7 × 3)*
Main engines: Diesels; 1 000 shp; 1 shaft = 11 knots

Former US Army freight and supply ships. Employed as tenders for buoys and lighthouses.

LAUIS LEDGE   *1969, Philippine Navy*

1 TUG: Ex-US ATR TYPE

Name	No.	Launched
IFUGAO (ex-US Army *LO 4*, ex-Australian *MSL*)	AQ 44	27 Jan 1944

Displacement, tons: 783 full load
Dimensions, feet (metres): 134·6 wl; 143 oa × 33·8 × 13·5 *(44·1; 46·9 × 11 × 4·4)*
Guns: 1—3 inch *(76 mm)* 50 cal AA; 2—20 mm AA
Main engines: Diesel; 1 500 bhp; 1 shaft = 13 knots

US-built rescue tug transferred to Royal Navy upon launching; subsequently returned to US Navy and retransferred to the Philippines in July 1948.

IFUGAO

6 TUGS: Ex-US HARBOUR TYPE

MARANAO (ex-*YTL 554*) YQ 221   AETA (ex-*YTL 449*) YQ 224
IGOROT (ex-*YTL 572*) YQ 222   ILONGOT (ex-*YTL 427*) YQ 225
TAGBANUA (ex-*YTL 429*) YQ 223   TASADAY (ex-*YTL 425*) YQ 226

Former US Navy 66-foot harbour tugs.

1 CARGO SHIP: Ex-US C1-M-AV1 TYPE

Name	No.	Builders	Launched
MACTAN (ex-USCGC *Kukui*, WAK 186, ex-USS *Colquitt*, AK 174)	TK 90	Froemming Brothers, Milwaukee	21 Jan 1945

Displacement, tons: 4 900 light; 5 636 full load
Dimensions, feet (metres): 320 wl; 338·5 oa × 50 × 18 *(104·9; 110·9 × 16·4 × 5·9)*
Guns: Unarmed
Main engines: Diesel (Nordberg); 1 750 bhp; 1 shaft = 11·5 knots

Commissioned in US Navy on 22 Sep 1945; transferred to the US Coast Guard two days later. Subsequently served as Coast Guard supply ship in Pacific until transferred to Philippines on 1 March 1972. Used to supply military posts and lighthouses in the Philippine archipelago.

Commissioned in US Navy on 22 Sep 1945; transferred to the US Coast Guard two days later.

1 TENDER: Ex-AUSTRALIAN TYPE

PEARL BANK (ex-US Army *LO 4*, ex-Australian *MSL*)

Displacement, tons: 160 standard; 300 full load
Dimensions, feet (metres): 120 oa × 24·5 × 8 *(39·3 × 8 × 2·6)*
Main engines: Diesels (Fairbanks Morse); 240 bhp; 2 shafts = 7 knots

Originally an Australian motor stores lighter; subsequently transferred to the US Army and then to the Philippines. Employed as a lighthouse tender.

5 FLOATING DRY DOCKS

YD 200 (ex-*AFDL 24*)   YD 203   YD 205 (ex-*AFDL 44*)
YD 201   YD 204 (ex-*AFDL 20*)

Floating dry docks built in the United States; three are former US Navy units with YD 200 transferred in July 1948, YD 204 in Oct 1961, and YD 205 in Sep 1969; two other units built specifically for Philippine service were completed in May 1952 and Aug 1955, respectively.

COAST AND GEODETIC SERVICE

Name	No.	Builders	Launched
SAMAR (ex-USS *Project*, AM 278)	M 33	Gulf Shipbuilding Corp	20 Nov 1943

Former US Navy minesweeper, similar to the *Mount Samat*. Transferred to the Philippines in July 1948. Subsequently adapted for surveying and now operated by the Coast & Geodetic Service.

COAST GUARD

2 PATROL BOATS

Name	No.
ABRA	FB 83
BUKINDON	FB 84

Displacement, tons: 40 standard
Dimensions, feet (metres): 87·5 oa × 19 × 4·75 *(28·6 × 6·2 × 1·9)*
Guns: 2—20 mm AA
Main engines: Diesels (Mercedes-Benz/MTU); 2 460 bhp; 2 shafts = approx 25 knots
Complement: 15 (3 officers, 12 enlisted men)

One acquired from Singapore in late 1969. Wood hulls and aluminium superstructure.

The Coast Guard also has 14 40-foot utility boats, all transferred from the US Coast Guard except for the *CGC 127*, a 40-foot, 11-ton craft built in the Philippines with a ferro-concrete hull.

POLAND

Headquarters Appointments

Commander-in-Chief of the Polish Navy:
Vice-Admiral Ludwik Janczyszyn

Chief of the Naval Staff:
Rear-Admiral Henryk Pietraszkiewicz

Diplomatic Representation

Naval, Military and Air Attaché in London:
Colonel Henryk Krzeszowski
Naval, Military and Air Attaché in Washington:
Colonel Henryk Nowaczyk
Naval, Military and Air Attaché in Moscow:
Brigadier General Waclaw Jagas
Naval, Military and Air Attaché in Paris:
Colonel Marian Bugaj

Personnel

a) 1976: 25 000 (2 800 officers and 22 200 men)
b) 3 years National Service

Bases

Gdynia, Hel, Swinoujscie.

Naval Aviation

There is a Fleet Air Arm of about 50 fixed-wing aircraft (mainly MiG-17 and IL-28) and helicopters.

Prefix to Ships' Names

ORP, standing for *Okrety Polska Rzeczpospolita*

Mercantile Marine

Lloyd's Register of Shipping:
696 vessels of 2 817 129 tons gross

Strength of the Fleet

Including WOP (Coastguard)

Type	Active
Destroyer	1
Submarines—Patrol	4
Fast Attack Craft—Missile	12
Fast Attack Craft—Torpedo	18
	(some as targets)
Large Patrol Craft	26
Coastal Patrol Craft	23
Minesweepers—Ocean	24
Minesweeping Boats	20
LCTs	23
LCPs	15+
Surveying Vessels	1
AGIs	2
Training Ships	5
Salvage Ships	2
Tankers	6
TRVs	Several
Tugs	20
DGVs	2

DELETIONS

Destroyers

974 *Blyskawica* (museum ship in Gdynia in place of *Burza*)
975 *Grom* and *Wicher* (ex-"Skory" class) now immobile AA batteries at Gdynia.

Corvettes

1973 *Czuiny, Wytrwaly, Zawziety, Zrezczny, Zwinny, Zwrotny*
1974 *Grozny, Nieugiety* ("Kronstadt" class)

Fast Attack Craft—Torpedo

1973 3 "P 6" class
1974 6 "P 6" class
1975 4 "P 6" class

DESTROYERS

1 Ex-SOVIET "SAM KOTLIN" CLASS

WARSZAWA (ex-*Spravedlivy*) 275

Displacement, tons: 2 850 standard; 3 885 full load
Length, feet (metres): 415·0 *(126·5)* oa
Beam, feet (metres): 42·3 *(12·9)*
Draught, feet (metres): 16·1 *(4·9)*
Missile launchers: 1 twin SAN-1 (Goa) aft
Guns: 2—5·1 in (1 twin); 4—45 mm (quad); 4—30 mm (twin)
A/S weapons: 2—16 barrelled MBU; 4 side launch DC projectors
Main engines: Geared turbines; 2 shafts; 72 000 shp
Oil fuel, tons: 800
Range, miles: 5 500 at 16 knots
Speed, knots: 36
Complement: 285

Transferred from the USSR to the Polish Navy in 1970.

Radar: Air Search: Head Net C.
Fire Control: Peel Group (SAN-1), Wasp Head/Sun Visor B (main armament), Egg Cup (45 mm), 2 Drum Tilt (30 mm).
IFF: High Pole B.

WARSZAWA

5/1975, C. and S. Taylor

SUBMARINES

4 Ex-SOVIET "WHISKY" CLASS

BIELIK 295	ORZEL 292
KONDOR 294	SOKOL 293

Displacement, tons: 1 030 surfaced; 1 350 dived
Length, feet (metres): 249·3 *(76)*
Beam, feet (metres): 22 *(6·7)*
Draught, feet (metres): 15 *(4·6)*
Torpedo tubes: 6—21 in *(533 mm)*, (4 bow, 2 stern) 18 torpedoes carried
Mines: 40 mines in lieu of torpedoes
Main machinery: Diesel-electric; 2 diesels; 4 000 hp; 2 shafts; Electric motors; 2 500 hp
Speed, knots: 17 surfaced; 15 dived
Range, miles: 13 000 at 8 knots (surfaced)
Complement: 60

Built in the USSR and transferred to the Polish Navy.

Radar: Snoop Plate.

SOKOL

1971, Polish Navy

KONDOR

1972

LIGHT FORCES

12 SOVIET "OSA" CLASS
(FAST ATTACK CRAFT—MISSILE)

Displacement, tons: 165 standard; 200 full load
Dimensions, feet (metres): 128·7 × 25·1 × 5·9 *(39·3 × 7·7 × 1·8)*
Missiles: 4 launchers for SSN-2
Guns: 4—30 mm (2 twin, 1 forward, 1 aft)
Main engines: 3 diesels; 13 000 bhp = 32 knots
Range, miles: 800 at 25 knots
Complement: 25

Most pennant numbers are in the 140-150 series and are carried on side-boards on the bridge.

Radar: Search: Square Tie and Strut Curve. Fire control: Drum Tilt.

"OSA" Class   1969

12 "WISLA" CLASS (FAST ATTACK CRAFT—TORPEDO)

Displacement, tons: 70 full load
Dimensions, feet (metres): 82·0 × 18·0 × 6·0 *(25 × 5·5 × 1·8)*
A/S weapons: 4 DC
Guns: 2—30 mm (twin)
Tubes: 4—21 in *(533 mm)*
Main engines: Diesels; speed 30 knots

Polish built in a continuing programme. Most pennant numbers in 490 series but include 463.

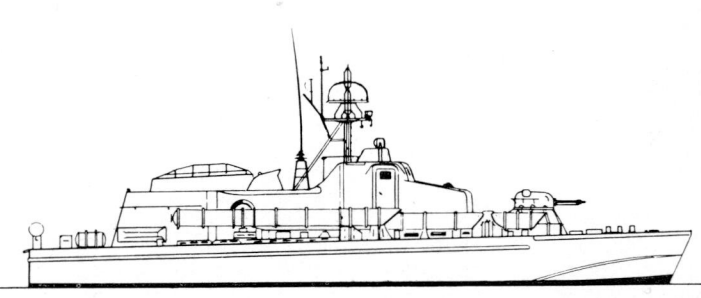

"WISLA" Class   1973, S. Breyer

WISLA   1973

6 Ex-SOVIET "P 6" CLASS
(FAST ATTACK CRAFT—TORPEDO)

Displacement, tons: 66 standard; 75 full load
Dimensions, feet (metres): 84·2 × 20 × 6 *(25·7 × 6·1 × 1·8)*
Guns: 4—25 mm; 8 DC
Tubes: 2—21 in
Main engines: 4 diesels; 4 800 bhp = 45 knots
Complement: 25

Acquired from the USSR in 1957-58. Torpedo tubes removed in some. At least two have been converted to target craft with reflectors similar to E. German variant.

Radar: Skin Head surface search.

"P 6" Class   1971, Polish Navy

5 "OBLUZE" CLASS (LARGE PATROL CRAFT)

Name	No.	Builders	Commissioned
—	349	Oksywie Shipyard	1965
—	350	Oksywie Shipyard	1965
—	351	Oksywie Shipyard	1965
—	352	Oksywie Shipyard	1966
—	353	Oksywie Shipyard	1966

Displacement, tons: 170
Dimensions, feet (metres): 143·0 × 19·0 × 7·0 *(42 × 6 × 2·1)*
A/S weapons: DC throwers
Guns: 4—30 mm (2 twins)
Main engines: 2 diesels = 20 knots

Belong to WOP (Coastguard).

OBLUZE (old number)   1969

8 "MODIFIED OBLUZE" CLASS (LARGE PATROL CRAFT)

301   302   303   304   305   306   307   308

Displacement, tons: 150
Dimensions, feet (metres): 137·8 × 19 × 6·6 (41 × 6 × 2)
Guns: 2 or 4—30 mm
A/S weapons: DC throwers
Main engines: 2 diesels = 20 knots

Slightly smaller than original "Obluze" class.

"OBLUZE" Class   1972, S. Breyer

4 "OKSYWIE" CLASS (LARGE PATROL CRAFT)

336   337   338   339

Displacement, tons: 170 standard
Dimensions, feet (metres): 134·5 × 19·0 × 6·9 (41 × 6 × 2)
Guns: 4—37 mm (2 twin)
A/S weapons: DC throwers; DC racks
Main engines: Diesels; speed = 20 knots

This class and the other Polish-built large patrol craft are all based on German R-boat hull design with variations in the superstructure.

OKSYWIE (old pennant number)   1972

"OKSYWIE" Class   M. Soroka

9 "GDANSK" CLASS (LARGE PATROL CRAFT)

340-348

Displacement, tons: 120
Dimensions, feet (metres): 124·7 × 19·2 × 5·0 (35 × 5·8 × 1·5)
Guns: 2—37 mm
A/S weapons: DC rails
Main engines: Diesels = 20 knots

Built in Poland in 1960. Belong to WOP (Coastguard).

"GDANSK" Class (old pennant number)   1970

"GDANSK" Class   M. Soroka

20 "K 8" CLASS (COASTAL PATROL CRAFT)

KP 118	KP 120	KP 122	KP 124	KP 126
KP 119	KP 121	KP 123	KP 125	KP 126 +11

Displacement, tons: 50 standard; 70 full load
Dimensions, feet (metres): 92 × 13·5 × 2·3 (28 × 4·1 × 0·7)
Guns: 2 MG (in twin mounting)
Main engines: 2 diesels; speed 14 knots

Converted MSBs. Belong to WOP (Coastguard). Now obsolescent and due for replacement.

3 "PILICA" CLASS (COASTAL PATROL CRAFT)

701	702	703

Displacement, tons: 100 (approx)
Guns: 2—25 mm (twin)
Main engines: 2 diesels = 15 knots

Built in Poland in 1973. Belong to WOP (Coastguard).

MINE WARFARE FORCES

12 "KROGULEC" CLASS (MINESWEEPERS—OCEAN)

Name	No.	Builders	Commissioned
ORLIK	643	Stocznia Yard, Gdynia	1964
KROGULEC	644	Stocznia Yard, Gdynia	1963
JASTRAB	645	Stocznia Yard, Gdynia	1964
KORMORAN	646	Stocznia Yard, Gdynia	1963
CZAPLA	647	Stocznia Yard, Gdynia	1964
ALBATROS	648	Stocznia Yard, Gdynia	1965
PELIKAN	649	Stocznia Yard, Gdynia	1965
TUKAN	650	Stocznia Yard, Gdynia	1966
KANIA	651	Stocznia Yard, Gdynia	1966
JASKOLKA	652	Stocznia Yard, Gdynia	1966
ZURAW	653	Stocznia Yard, Gdynia	1967
CZALPA	654	Stocznia Yard, Gdynia	1967

Displacement, tons: 500
Dimensions, feet (metres): 190·3 × 24·6 × 8·2 (58 × 8·4 × 2·5)
Guns: 6—25 mm (twins)
Main engines: Diesels = 16 knots

PELIKAN (old Pennant number)　　　5/1975, C. and S. Taylor

12 SOVIET "T 43" CLASS (MINESWEEPERS—OCEAN)

Name	No.	Builders	Commissioned
BIZON	635	Stocznia, Gdynia	1958
BOBR	636	Stocznia, Gydnia	1959
DELFIN	638	Stocznia, Gdynia	1960
DZIK	634	Stocznia, Gdynia	1958
FOKA	639	Stocznia, Gdynia	1960
LOS	633	Stocznia, Gdynia	1957
MORS	640	Stocznia, Gdynia	1961
ROSOMAK	637	Stocznia, Gdynia	1959
RYS	641	Stocznia, Gdynia	1961
TUR	632	Stocznia, Gdynia	1957
ZBIK	642	Stocznia, Gdynia	1962
ZUBR	631	Stocznia, Gdynia	1957

Displacement, tons: 500 standard; 610 full load
Dimensions, feet (metres): 190·2 × 28·2 × 6·9 (58 × 8·6 × 2·1)
Guns: 4—37 mm (twins); 4—25 mm (twins)
Main engines: 2 diesels; 2 shafts; 2 000 hp = 17 knots
Range, miles: 1 600 at 10 knots
Complement: 40

DELFIN (old pennant number)　　　1969, Polish Navy

20 "K 8" CLASS (MSBs)

Displacement, tons: 50 standard; 70 full load
Dimensions, feet (metres): 92 × 13·5 × 2·3 (28 × 4·1 × 0·7)
Guns: 2 MG
Main engines: 2 diesels = 14 knots

AMPHIBIOUS FORCES

23 "POLNOCNY" CLASS (LST)

BALAS	JANOW	NARWIK	+ 17
GRUNWALD	LENIN	WARTA	

Displacement, tons: 780 standard; 1 000 full load
Dimensions, feet (metres): 239·4 × 29·5 × 9·98 (73 × 9 × 3)
Guns: 2—30 mm (twin); 2 rocket launchers
Main engines: 2 diesels; 5 000 bhp = 18 knots

Polish built in Gdansk, but same as the Soviet "Polnocny" class—can carry six tanks. Of various types including Polish variations. Pennant numbers—811/832 and 882.

"POLNOCNY" Class　　　1971

15 NEW CONSTRUCTION LCPs

Length, feet (metres): 70 (21·3) approx
Gun: 1—30 mm

Pennant numbers in 500 series. Introduced 1975.

NEW CONSTRUCTION LCP　　　8/1975

SURVEYING VESSEL

1 "MOMA" CLASS

KOPERNIK

Displacement, tons: 1 240 standard; 1 800 full load
Dimensions, feet (metres): 219·8 × 32·8 × 13·2 *(67 × 10 × 4)*
Main engines: Diesels = 16 knots

INTELLIGENCE VESSELS

1 "MOMA" CLASS

NAVIGATOR

Details as for *Kopernik* above. Commissioned June 1975.

1 B 10 TYPE

BALTYK

Displacement, tons: 1 200
Measurements, tons: 658 gross; 450 deadweight
Dimensions, feet (metres): 194·3 oa × 29·5 × 14 *(59·2 × 9·0 × 4·3)*
Main engines: Steam; 1 000 hp = 11 knots

Trawler of B-10 type. Built in 1954 in Gdansk. Converted and structure altered.

BALTYK 1968

TRAINING SHIPS

3 "BRIZA" CLASS

ELEW   **KADET**   **PODCHORAZY**

Displacement, tons: 150
Dimensions, feet (metres): 98·4 × 9·8 × 6·4 *(30 × 7 × 2)*
Main engines: Diesels = 10 knots
Complement: 11 plus 26 cadets

Podchorazy commissioned 30 Nov 1974, *Elew* 5 March 1975 and *Kadet* July 1975.

Name	No.	Builders	Commissioned
GRYF (ex-*Zetempowiec*, ex-*Opplem*, ex-*Omsk* ex-*Empire Contees*, ex-*Irene Oldendorf*)	—	Burmeister & Wain	1944

Measurements, tons: 1 959 gross
Dimensions, feet (metres): 282·2 × 44·2 × 18·8 *(86 × 13·5 × 5·7)*
Guns: 2—3·9 in; 4—37 mm
Main engines: Steam; 1 200 hp = 10 knots

Former German "Hansa" class ship. Launched in 1944. Taken over in 1947. Transferred to the Navy in 1949. The name was changed from *Zetempowiec* to *Gryf* in 1957. Used as a cadet training ship.

GRYF 1969

Name	No.	Builders	Commissioned
ISKRA (ex-*Pigmy*, ex-*Iskra*, ex-*St. Blanc*, ex-*Vlissingen*)	—	Muller, Foxhol, Holland	1917

Displacement, tons: 560
Dimensions, feet (metres): 128 × 25 × 10 *(39 × 7·6 × 3·0)*
Main engines: Diesels; 250 bhp = 7·5 knots
Complement: 30, plus 40 cadets

A three masted schooner with auxiliary engines. Launched in 1917. Cadet training ship.

ISKRA 1969

TANKERS

3 "MOSKIT" CLASS

KRAB Z 3   **MEDUSA Z 8**   **SLIMAK Z 9**

Displacement, tons: approx 700
Guns: 2—30 mm (Twin)

Z 5   **Z 6**   **Z 7**

Lighters of 300 tons gross with diesels, converted into tankers for coastal service.

SALVAGE SHIPS

Name	No.	Builders	Commissioned
PIAST	—	Stocznia, Gdansk	26 Jan 1974
LECH	—	Stocznia, Gdansk	30 Nov 1974

Displacement, tons: 1 560 standard; 1 732 full load
Dimensions, feet (metres): 236 × 39·4 × 13·1 *(72 × 12 × 4)*
Guns: 8—25 mm (twins)
Main engines: 2 ZGODA diesels; 3 800 shp; 2 shafts
Speed, knots: 16·5
Range, miles: 3 000 at 12 knots

Carry a diving bell.

TORPEDO RECOVERY VESSELS

Some of a new class, including K 11, have been reported.

TUGS

Some 20 of various classes with H pennant numbers.

DEGAUSSING VESSELS

SD 11/13

A new class of d.g.vs of which details are not yet available.

AUXILIARIES

Ex-AGI *Kompas* now used as a barrack ship. Some 15 small diving craft.
Hydrograf and *Kontroller,* of 30 and 80 tons are civilian-operated survey craft.
Icebreaker *Perkun* of 800 is civilian-operated but available for naval use.

PORTUGAL

Headquarters Appointment

Chief of Naval Staff:
    Admiral A. S. Silva Cruz

Diplomatic Representation

Naval Attaché in London:
    Captain P. M. Carujo
Naval Attaché in Washington:
    Captain Jose L. Ferreira Lamas
Naval Attaché in Paris:
    Captain Pedro Azevedo Coutinho

Personnel

(a) 1976: 12 000(?) including marines
(b) 3 years National Service

Naval Bases

Main Base: Lisbon
Dockyard: Arsenal do Alfeite

Maritime Reconnaissance Aircraft

Whilst there are no aircraft belonging to the Navy, P2V Neptunes of the Portuguese Air Force are placed under naval operational control for specific maritime operations.

Prefix to Ships' Names

NRP

Mercantile Marine

Lloyd's Register of Shipping:
    440 vessels of 1 209 701 tons gross

Strength of the Fleet

Type	Active	Building
Frigates	17	—
Corvettes	11	—
Submarines (Patrol)	3	—
Large Patrol Craft	5	—
Coastal Patrol Craft	11	—
Minesweepers (Coastal)	4	—
LCTs	3	—
LCMs	8	—
LCA	1	—
Survey Ships and Craft	5	—
Replenishment Tanker	1	—
Sail Training Ship	1	—
Fishery Protection Vessel	1	—
Ocean Tug	1	—
Harbour Tugs	2	—
Harbour Tanker	1	—
Logistic Ship	1	—

DELETIONS

Frigates

1970 Francisco de Almeida, Pacheco Pereira
1971 Alvares Cabral, Vasco da Gama
1975 Pero Escobar

Corvettes

1971 Cacheu
1973 Porto Sante, Fogo, Maio ("Maio" class)
1975 Boavista, Brava, Santa Luzia ("Maio" class)

Submarine

1975 Cachalote ("Daphne" class)

Minesweepers

1973 Angra do Heroismo, Ponta Delgada, S. Pedro (MSC),
        Corvo, Pico, Graciosa, S. Jorge (MSO)
1975 Lajes, Santa Cruz (MSC)
1976 Horta, Velas, Vila do Porto

Light Forces

1975 Cassiopeia, Escorpião, Lira, Orion, Pegaso ("Argos"
        class)
        Sabre (River patrol craft)
        Albufeira, Aljezur, Alvor ("Alvor" class)
        Aldebaran, Altair, Arcturus, Bellatrix, Espiga,
        Fomalhaut, Pollux, Rigel, Sirius and Vega ("Bellatrix"
        class)
        Jupiter, Marte, Mercurio, Saturno, Urano and Venus
        ("Jupiter" class)
        Antares (Coastal patrol craft)
        Azevia, Corvina, Dourada ("Azevia" class)

Amphibious Forces

1975 Alfanage, Ariete, Cimitarra ("Alfange" class LCTs)
        LDM 401-411, 413-417 ("400" class LCMs)
        LDM 304, 309 ("300" class LCMs)
        LDM 204 ("200" class LCM)
        LDM 101, 102, 105-118 ("100" class LCMs)
        LDP 301-303, 201, 203-217, 107, 108 (21 LCAs)

Survey Ships

1975 Almirante Lacerda, Cavalho Araujo, Cruzeiro do Sul

Service Forces

1975 Sam Bras (Fleet Supply Ship), Santo André

PENNANT LIST

F (Frigates)

F 471	Antonio Enes
F 472	Almirante Pereira Da Silva
F 473	Almirante Gago Coutinho
F 474	Almirante Magalhaes Correia
F 475	João Coutinho
F 476	João Candido
F 477	Gen. Pereira d'Eca
F 480	Comandante João Belo
F 481	Comandante Hermenegildo Capelo
F 482	Comandante Roberto Ivens
F 483	Comandante Sacadura Cabral
F 484	Augusto de Castilho
F 485	Honorio Barreto
F 486	Baptista de Andrade
F 487	João Roby
F 488	Afonso Cerqueira
F 489	Oliveira Ecarmo

S (Submarines)

S 163	Albacora
S 164	Barracuda
S 166	Delfin

M (Minewarfare Forces)

M 401	Sao Roque
M 402	Ribeira Grande
M 403	Lagoa
M 404	Rosario

P (Light Forces and Corvettes)

P 369	Regulus
P 370	Rio Minho
P 372	Argos
P 374	Dragao

P 376	Hidra
P 580	Castor
P 589	Sao Nicolau
P 596	Bicuda
P 1130	Centauro
P 1131	Sagittario
P 1140	Cacine
P 1141	Cunene
P 1142	Mandovi
P 1143	Rovuma
P 1144	Cuanza
P 1145	Geba
P 1146	Zaire
P 1147	Zambese
P 1148	Dom Aleixo
P 1149	Dom Jeremias
P 1160	Limpopo
P 1161	Save
P 1162	Albatroz
P 1163	Acor
P 1164	Andorinha
P 1165	Aguia
P 1166	Condor
P 1167	Cisne

LDG (Amphibious Forces)

LDG 104	Montanee
LDG 105	Bacamarte
LDG 201	Bombarda
LDG 202	Alabarda

A (Service Forces)

A 520	Sagres
A 521	Xavier Schultz
A 526	Afonso de Albuquerque
A 527	Comandante Almeida Carvalho
A 528	Pedro Nunes
A 5200	Mira
A 5206	São Gabriel
A 5214	São Rafael

"COMANDANTE JOAO BELO" Class

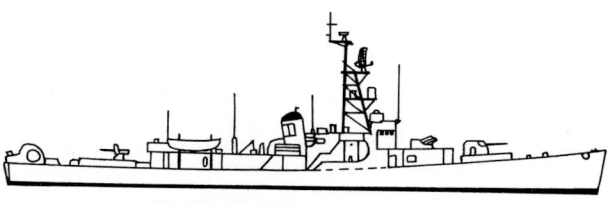

"ALMIRANTE PEREIRA DA SILVA" Class

"JOAO COUTINHO" Class

PERO ESCOBAR

AFONSO DE ALBUQUERQUE

FRIGATES

4 "COMANDANTE JOÃO BELO" CLASS

Name	No.	Builders	Laid down	Launched	Commissioned
COMANDANTE HERMENEGILDO CAPELO	F 481	At et Ch de Nantes	13 May 1966	29 Nov 1966	26 April 1968
COMANDANTE JOÃO BELO	F 480	At et Ch de Nantes	6 Sep 1965	22 Mar 1966	1 July 1967
COMANDANTE ROBERTO IVENS	F 482	At et Ch de Nantes	13 Dec 1966	8 Aug 1967	23 Nov 1968
COMANDANTE SACADURA CABRAL	F 483	At et Ch de Nantes	18 Aug 1967	15 Mar 1968	25 July 1969

Displacement, tons: 1 990 standard; 2 230 full load
Length, feet (metres): 321·5 (98) pp; 338 (103·0) oa
Beam, feet (metres): 37·7 (11·5)
Draught, feet (metres): 14·5 (4·42)
Guns: 3—3·9 in (100 mm) single; 2—40 mm
A/S weapons: 1—12 in quadruple mortar
Torpedo tubes: 6—21·7 in (550 mm) A/S (triple)
Main engines: SEMT/Pielstick diesels; 2 shafts; 18 760 bhp
Speed, knots: 25
Range, miles: 4 500 at 15 knots; 2 300 at 25 knots
Complement: 200 (14 officers, 186 men)

Construction: The prefabricated construction of these frigates was begun on 1 Oct 1964.

Design: They are similar to the French "Commandant Rivière" class except for the 30 mm guns which were replaced by 40 mm guns.

Radar: Search: DRBV 22.
Tactical: Probably E Band.
Fire Control: DRBC 32 radar director.

COMANDANTE ROBERTO IVENS   1970, Portuguese Navy

COMANDANTE SACADURA CABRAL   1972, Portuguese Navy

3 "ALMIRANTE PEREIRA DA SILVA" CLASS

Name	No.	Builders	Laid down	Launched	Commissioned
ALMIRANTE GAGO COUTINHO	F 473 (ex-US DE 1042)	Estaleiros Navais (Lisnave), Lisbon	2 Dec 1963	13 Aug 1965	29 Nov 1967
ALMIRANTE MAGALHÃES CORREA	F 474 (ex-US DE 1046)	Estaleiros Navais de Viana do Castelo	30 Aug 1965	26 April 1966	4 Nov 1968
ALMIRANTE PEREIRA DA SILVA	F 472 (ex-US DE 1039)	Estaleiros Navais (Lisnave), Lisbon	14 June 1962	2 Dec 1963	20 Dec 1966

Displacement, tons: 1 450 standard; 1 914 full load
Length, feet (metres): 314·6 (95·9)
Beam, feet (metres): 36·68 (11·18)
Draught, feet (metres): 17·5 (5·33)
Guns: 4—3 in (76 mm) 50 cal
A/S weapons: 2 Bofors 4-barrelled mortars 2 DC throwers
Torpedo tubes: 6 (2 triple) for A/S torpedoes
Main engines: De Laval dr geared turbines; 1 shaft; 20 000 shp
Boilers: 2 Foster Wheeler, 300 psi, 850°F
Speed, knots: 27
Oil fuel, tons: 400
Range, miles: 3 220 at 15 knots
Complement: 166 (12 officers, 154 men)

Construction: The prefabrication of Almirante Pereira da Silva and Almirante Gago Coutinho was begun in 1961 at Lisnave (formerly Navais Shipyard, Lisbon) and of Almirante Magalhães Correa in 1962.

Radar: Search: SPS 6.
Tactical: I Band.
Surface warning and navigation, Air Surveillance: E band.
Extensive EW.

Design: Similar to the United States destroyer escorts of the "Dealey" class, but modified to suit Portuguese requirements.

Sonar: Probably DUBV-43.

ALMIRANTE GAGO COUTINHO   1973, Dr. Giorgio Arra

10 "JOÃO COUTINHO" CLASS

Name	No.	Builders	Laid down	Launched	Commissioned
ANTONIO ENES	F 471	Empresa Nacional Bazan, Spain	April 1968	16 Aug 1969	18 June 1971
AUGUSTO DE CASTILHO	F 484	Empresa Nacional Bazan, Spain	Aug 1968	4 July 1969	14 Nov 1970
GENERAL PEREIRA D'ECA	F 477	Blöhm and Voss AG, Hamburg, Germany	Oct 1968	26 July 1969	10 Oct 1970
HONORIO BARRETO	F 485	Blöhm and Voss AG, Hamburg, Germany	July 1968	11 April 1970	15 April 1971
JACINTO CANDIDO	F 476	Blöhm and Voss AG, Hamburg, Germany	April 1968	16 June 1969	16 June 1970
JOÃO COUTINHO	F 475	Blöhm and Voss AG, Hamburg, Germany	Sep 1968	2 May 1969	7 Mar 1970
JOÃO ROBY	F 487	Empresa Nacional Bazan, Spain	1972	3 June 1973	18 Mar 1975
OLIVEIRA E. CARMO	F 489	Empresa Nacional Bazan, Spain	1972	Feb 1974	Feb 1975
AFONSO CERQUEIRA	F 488	Empresa Nacional Bazan, Spain	1973	6 Oct 1973	26 June 1975
BAPTISTA DE ANDRADE	F 486	Empresa Nacional Bazan, Spain	1972	Mar 1973	19 Nov 1974

Displacement, tons: 1 203 standard; 1 380 full load
Length, feet (metres): 227·5 *(84·6)*
Beam, feet (metres): 33·8 *(10·3)*
Draught, feet (metres): 11·8 *(3·6)*
Missiles: 2 MM 38 Exocet in 486-489
Guns: 2—3 in *(76 mm)* (twin); 2—40 mm (first six);
1—3·9 in *(100 mm)* 50 cal; 2 Bofors 40 mm (single) (486-489)
A/S weapons: 1 Hedgehog; 2 DC throwers (first six); 2 DC
racks; (2 triple Mk 32 torpedo tubes in 486-489)
Main engines: 2 OEW 12 cyl Pielstick diesels; 10 560 bhp
Speed, knots: 24·4
Range, miles: 5 900 at 18 knots
Complement: 100 (9 officers, 91 men) plus marine detachment
of 34

Radar: In first six:
Air Search: MLA-1B.
Navigation: Decca TM 626.
Main guns: On-mounted radar.
In 486-489:
Air Search: Plessey AWS-2.
Navigation: Decca TM 626.
Gun Fire Control: Thomson CSF Pollux.

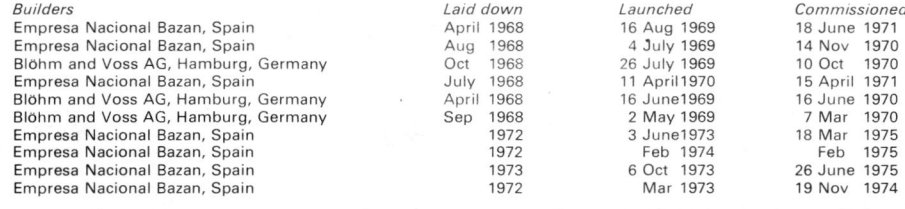

BAPTISTA DE ANDRADE   *8/1975, Wright and Logan*

CORVETTES

1 FRENCH BUILT "MAIO" CLASS

Name	No.	Builders	Commissioned
SAO NICOLAU (ex-*P 8*)	P 589	Normand, Le Havre	1959

Displacement, tons: 366 standard; 400 full load
Dimensions, feet (metres): 170 pp; 173·7 oa × 23 × 10 *(55·7; 56·9 × 7·5 × 3·3)*
Guns: 2—40 mm; 2—20 mm
A/S weapons: 1 Hedgehog; 4 DCT; 2 depth charge racks
Main engines: 4 SEMT-Pielstick diesels; 2 shafts; 3 240 bhp = 18 knots
Range, miles: 4 500 at 18 knots
Complement: 62 (5 officers, 57 men)

Of PC design, but built in France as a US offshore procurement order under the Mutual Defense
Assistance Program in 1954-55. Originally class of three. Fitted with two mine rails.

SAO NICOLAU   *1973, Portuguese Navy*

10 "CACINE" CLASS

Name	No.	Builders	Commissioned
CACINE	P 1140	Arsenal do Alfeite	1969
CUNENE	P 1141	Arsenal do Alfeite	1969
CUANZA	P 1144	Estaleiros Navais do Mendogo	May 1969
GEBA	P 1145	Estaleiros Navais do Mendogo	May 1969
LIMPOPO	P 1160	Arsenal do Alfeite	April 1973
MANDOVI	P 1142	Arsenal do Alfeite	1969
ROVUMA	P 1143	Arsenal do Alfeite	1969
SAVE	P 1161	Arsenal do Alfeite	May 1973
ZAIRE	P 1146	Estaleiros Navais do Mendogo	Nov 1970
ZAMBEZE	P 1147	Estaleiros Navais do Mendogo	1971

Displacement, tons: 292·5 standard; 310 full load
Dimensions, feet (metres): 144·0 oa × 25·2 × 7·1 *(44 × 7·7 × 2·2)*
Guns: 2—40 mm; 1—32 barrelled rocket launcher 37 mm
Main engines: 2 MTU 12V 538 Maybach (MTU) diesels; 4 000 bhp = 20 knots
Range, miles: 4 400 at 12 knots
Complement: 33 (3 officers, 30 men)

CACINE   *1973, Portuguese Navy*

SUBMARINES

3 "ALBACORA" CLASS (FRENCH "DAPHNE" CLASS)

Name	No.	Builders	Laid down	Launched	Commissioned
ALBACORA	S 163	Dubigeon-Normandie	6 Sep 1965	13 Oct 1966	1 Oct 1967
BARRACUDA	S 164	Dubigeon-Normandie	19 Oct 1965	24 Apr 1967	4 May 1968
DELFIN	S 166	Dubigeon-Normandie	14 May 1967	23 Sep 1968	1 Oct 1969

Displacement, tons: 700 standard; 869 surfaced; 1 043 dived
Length, feet (metres): 189·6 *(57·8)*
Beam, feet (metres): 22·3 *(6·8)*
Draught, feet (metres): 15·1 *(4·6)*
Torpedo tubes: 12—21·7 in *(550 mm)*; (8 bow, 4 stern)
Main machinery: SEMT-Pielstick diesels, 1 300 bhp; Electric
motors; 450 kW, 1 600 hp; 2 shafts
Speed, knots: 13·2 surfaced; 16 dived
Oil fuel, tons: 90
Range, miles: 2 710 at 12·5 knots surfaced; 2 130 at 10 knots
snorting
Complement: 50 (5 officers; 45 men)

The prefabricated construction of these submarines was
begun between 1 Oct 1964 and 6 Sep 1965 at the Dubigeon-
Normandie Shipyard. They are basically similar to the French
"Daphne" type, but slightly modified to suit Portuguese
requirements.

DELFIN   *1972, Portuguese Navy*

LIGHT FORCES

5 "ARGOS" CLASS (LARGE PATROL CRAFT)

Name	No.	Builders	Commissioned
ARGOS	P 372	Arsenal do Alfeite, Lisbon	1965
CENTAURO	P 1130	Arsenal do Alfeite, Lisbon	1965
DRAGÃO	P 374	Arsenal do Alfeite, Lisbon	1965
HIDRA	P 376	Arsenal do Alfeite, Lisbon	1965
SAGITARIO	P 1131	Arsenal do Alfeite, Lisbon	1965

Displacement, tons: 180 standard; 210 full load
Dimensions, feet (metres): 136·8 oa × 20·5 × 7 *(41·6 × 6·2 × 2·2)*
Guns: 2—40 mm
Main engines: 2 Maybach (MTU) diesels; 1 200 bhp = 17 knots
Oil fuel, tons: 16
Complement: 24 (2 officers, 22 men)

Argos and *Centauro* probably due for disposal.

DRAGÃO   *1973, Portuguese Navy*

2 "DOM ALEIXO" CLASS (COASTAL PATROL CRAFT)

Name	No.	Builders	Commissioned
DOM ALEIXO	P 1148	S. Jacintho Aveiro	7 Dec 1967
DOM JEREMIAS	P 1149	S. Jacintho Aveiro	22 Dec 1967

Displacement, tons: 62·6 standard; 67·7 full load
Dimensions, feet (metres): 82·1 oa × 17·0 × 5·2 *(25 × 5·2 × 1·6)*
Gun: 1—20 mm
Main engines: 2 Cummins diesels; 1 270 bhp = 16 knots
Complement: 10 (2 officers, 8 men)

Dom Aleixo in use as survey craft.

DOM JEREMIAS   *1973, Portuguese Navy*

6 "ALBATROZ" CLASS (COASTAL PATROL CRAFT)

Name	No.	Builders	Commissioned
ACOR	P 1163	Arsenal do Alfeite	1974
AGUIA	P 1165	Arsenal do Alfeite	1975
ALBATROZ	P 1162	Arsenal do Alfeite	1974
ANDORINHA	P 1164	Arsenal do Alfeite	1975
CISNE	P 1167	Arsenal do Alfeite	1974
CONDOR	P 1166	Arsenal do Alfeite	1975

Displacement, tons: 45
Dimensions, feet (metres): 72 × 17 × 5 *(23·6 × 5·6 × 1·6)*
Guns: 1—20 mm; 2—50 cal MGs
Speed, knots: 20

1 COASTAL PATROL CRAFT

Name	No.	Builders	Commissioned
CASTOR	P 580	Estaleiros Navais do Mondego	3 Feb 1964

Displacement, tons: 22
Dimensions, feet (metres): 58 oa × 13·1 × 3·3 *(17·7 × 4 × 1)*
Gun: 1—20 mm Oerlikon
Main engines: 2 Cummins diesels; 500 bhp = 15 knots
Complement: 7

1 COASTAL PATROL CRAFT

Name	No.	Builders	Commissioned
REGULUS	P 369	Navais Shipyard	27 Jan 1962

Displacement, tons: 18
Dimensions, feet (metres): 56 oa × 15·2 × 4 *(18 × 4·6 × 1·2)*
Gun: 1—20 mm Oerlikon
Main engines: 2 Cummins diesels; 2 shafts; 460 bhp = 18·2 knots
Complement: 7

The hull is of Deborine resin glass fibre moulding. *Regulus* was completed in Portugal by Navais Shipyard, the hull being imported from England.

1 COASTAL PATROL CRAFT

Name	No.	Builders	Commissioned
RIO MINHO	P 370	Arsenal do Alfeite	1957

Displacement, tons: 14
Dimensions, feet (metres): 49·2 × 10·5 × 2·3 *(15 × 3·2 × 0·7)*
Guns: 2 light MG
Main engines: 2 Alfa Romeo; 130 bhp = 9 knots
Complement: 7

Built for the River Minho on the Spanish border.

MINE WARFARE FORCES

4 "SAO ROQUE" CLASS (MINESWEEPERS—COASTAL)

Name	No.	Builders	Commissioned
LAGOA	M 403	CUF Shipyard, Lisbon	10 Aug 1956
RIBEIRA GRANDE	M 402	CUF Shipyard, Lisbon	8 Feb 1957
ROSARIO	M 404	CUF Shipyard, Lisbon	8 Feb 1956
SAO ROQUE	M 401	CUF Shipyard, Lisbon	6 June 1956

Displacement, tons: 394·4 standard; 451·9 full load
Dimensions, feet (metres): 140·0 (42·7) pp; 152·0 oa × 28·8 × 7·0 (46·3 × 8·8 × 2·3)
Guns: 2—20 mm (twin)
Main engines: 2 Mirrlees diesels; 2 shafts; 2 500 bhp = 15 knots
Complement: 47 (4 officers, 43 men)

Similar to British "Ton" class coastal minesweepers, laid down on 7 Sep 1954, under the OSP-MAP. *Lagoa* and *Sao Roque* were financed by USA and other two by Portugal. 40 mm gun removed 1972.

LAGOA (Before change of armament)   1972, Portuguese Navy

FISHERY PROTECTION VESSELS

1 "AZEVIA" CLASS

Name	No.	Builders	Commissioned
BICUDA	P 596	Arsenal do Alfeite	1942

Displacement, tons: 230 standard; 275 full load
Dimensions, feet (metres): 134·5 pp; 139·8 oa × 21·3 × 7·0 (39·8; 42 × 6·5 × 2·3)
Guns: 2—20 mm
Main engines: 2 MAN 10-cyl 4-stroke diesels; 2 shafts; 2 400 bhp = 17 knots
Oil fuel, tons: 25
Range, miles: 2 250 at 12·8 knots; 1 080 at 17·3 knots
Complement: 30 (2 officers, 28 men)

Last of class of four.

AZEVIA (BICUDA similar)   1968, Portuguese Navy

AMPHIBIOUS FORCES

2 "BOMBARDA" CLASS LDG (LCT)

Name	No.	Builders	Commissioned
ALABARDA	LDG 202	Estaleiros Navais do Mondego	1970
BOMBARDA	LDG 201 (ex-105)	Estaleiros Navais do Mondego	1971

Displacement, tons: 510 standard; 652 full load
Dimensions, feet (metres): 184·3 × 38·7 × 6·2 (56·2 × 11·8 × 1·9)
Main engines: 2 Maybach-Mercedes Benz (MTU) diesels; 910 hp = 9·5 knots
Complement: 20 (2 officers, 18 men)

BOMBARDA   1972, Portuguese Navy

2 "ALFANGE" CLASS LDG (LCT)

Name	No.	Builders	Commissioned
MONTANEE	LDG 104	Estaleiros Navais do Mondego	1965
ACAMARTE	LDG 105	Estaleiros Navais do Mondego	1965

Displacement, tons: 500
Dimensions, feet (metres): 187 × 39 × 6·2 (57 × 12 × 1·9)
Main engines: 2 diesels; 1 000 bhp
Complement: 20

ALFANGE (MONTANEE similar)   1968, Portuguese Navy

5 LDM 400 CLASS (LCM)

LDM 412   LDM 419   LDM 420   LDM 421   LDM 422

1 LDP 100 (Ex-LD) CLASS (LCA)

Name	No.	Builders	Commissioned
—	LDP 105	Estaleiros Navais do Mondego	22 Feb 1963

Displacement, tons: 12 light; 18 full load
Dimensions, feet (metres): Length: 46 oa (14)
Main engines: 2 diesels; 180 bhp

3 LDM 100 CLASS (LCM)

LDM 119   LDM 120   LDM 121

Displacement, tons: 50 full load
Dimensions, feet (metres): Length: 50 (15·25)
Main engines: 2 diesels; 450 bhp

All built at the Estaleiros Navais do Mondego in 1965.

SURVEY SHIPS

Name	No.	Builders	Commissioned
ALFONSO DE ALBUQUERQUE (ex-HMS *Dalrymple*, ex-HMS *Luce Bay*)	A 526	Wm. Pickersgill & Sons Ltd, Sunderland and HM Dockyard, Devonport	10 Feb 1949

Displacement, tons: 1 590 standard; 2 230 full load
Length, feet (metres): 286·0 (87·2) pp; 307·0 (93·6) oa
Beam, feet (metres): 38·5 (11·7)
Draught, feet (metres): 14·2 (4·3)
Main engines: 4-cylinder triple expansion; 2 shafts; 5 500 ihp
Speed, knots: 19·5
Boilers: 2 Admiralty 3-drum type
Range, miles: 7 055 at 9·1 knots
Complement: 109 (9 officers, 100 men)

Modified "Bay" class frigate. Built by Wm. Pickersgill & Sons Ltd, Sunderland, but completed at HM Dockyard, Devonport. Laid down on 29 April 1944. Launched on 12 April 1945. Purchased from Great Britain in April 1966.

1 "PEDRO NUNES" CLASS

Name	No.	Builders	Commissioned
PEDRO NUNES	A 528	Lisbon Naval Yard	11 April 1935

Displacement, tons: 1 162 standard; 1 217 full load
Dimensions, feet (metres): 234·3 oa × 32·8 × 10·2 *(71·4 × 10 × 3·1)*
Guns: 4—20 mm (see Notes)
Main engines: 2 sets MAN 8 cyl diesels; 2 400 bhp = 16·5 knots
Oil fuel, tons: 110
Range, miles: 6 400 at 13·4 knots
Complement: 48 (7 officers, 41 men)

Built as a second class sloop at Lisbon Naval Yard. Laid down on 5 Nov 1931, launched on 17 Mar 1934. Converted into a survey ship in 1956, when the forward 4·7 inch gun was removed.

DOM ALEIXO

See Light Forces section for details.

1 Ex-US "KELLAR" CLASS

Name	No.	Builders	Commissioned
COMANDANTE ALMEIDA CARVALHO (ex-USNS *Kellar*, T-AGS 25)	A 527	Marietta Shipbuilding Co.	31 Jan 1969

Displacement, tons: 1 200 standard; 1 400 full load
Dimensions, feet (metres): 190 oa × 39·0 × 15·0 *(58 × 11·7 × 4·5)*
Main engines: Diesel-electric; 1 shaft; 1 200 hp = 15 knots
Complement: 30 (5 officers, 25 men)

Laid down on 20 Nov 1962, launched on 30 July 1964. On loan from the US Navy since 21 Jan 1972.

MIRA (ex-*Fomalhaut*, ex-*Arrabida*) A 5200

Displacement, tons: 30 standard
Dimensions, feet (metres): 62·9 × 15·2 × 4 *(19·2 × 4·6 × 1·2)*
Main engines: 3 Perkins diesels; 300 bhp = 15 knots
Range, miles: 650 at 8 knots (economical speed)
Complement: 6 men

Launched 1961.

SERVICE FORCES

1 REPLENISHMENT TANKER

Name	No.	Builders	Commissioned
SÃO GABRIEL	A 5206	Estaleiros de Viana do Castelo	27 Mar 1963

Displacement, tons: 9 000 standard; 14 200 full load
Measurement, tons: 9 854 gross; 9 000 deadweight
Dimensions, feet (metres): 452·8 pp; 479·0 oa × 59·8 × 26·2 *(138; 146 × 18·2 × 8)*
Main engines: 1 Pametrada-geared turbine; 1 shaft; 9 500 shp = 17 knots
Boilers: 2
Range, miles: 6 000 at 15 knots
Complement: 98 (10 officers, 88 men)

SÃO GABRIEL   *1973, Portuguese Navy*

1 Ex-US ARC/LSM TYPE

Name	No.	Builders	Commissioned
SÃO RAFAEL (ex-*Medusa*, ex-USS *Portunus*, ARC 1, ex-LSM 275, ex-*LCT (7) 1773*)	A 5214	Federal Shipbuilding & Drydock Co, Newark, New Jersey	6 Oct 1944

Displacement, tons: 743 standard; 1 220 full load
Dimensions, feet (metres): 221·1 oa × 34·5 × 10·5 *(67·4 × 10·5 × 3·2)*
Guns: 2—40 mm; 2—20 mm
Main engines: GM direct drive diesel; 2 shafts; 2 800 bhp = 12 knots
Range, miles: 5 240 at 10 knots
Complement: 56 (6 officers, 50 men)

Former US medium landing ship, LSM type. Laid down on 1 Aug 1944, launched on 11 Sep 1944. Converted to a cable repairing or laying ship by the US Navy in 1952. Transferred to the Portuguese Navy under MAP in 1959. Delivered to Portugal on 16 Nov and commissioned on 18 Nov as a diving tender. Converted to a logistic ship in 1969 and guns mounted as above.

1 TRAINING SHIP

Name	No.	Builders	Commissioned
SAGRES (ex-*Guanabara*, ex-*Albert Leo Schlageter*)	A 520	Blöhm & Voss, Hamburg	1 Feb 1938

Displacement, tons: 1 725 standard; 1 869 full load
Dimensions, feet (metres): 293·5 oa × 39·3 × 17·0 *(89·5 × 12 × 4·6)*
Main engines: 2 MAN auxiliary diesels; 1 shaft; 750 bhp = 10 knots
Oil fuel, tons: 52
Range, miles: 3 500 at 6·5 knots
Complement: 153 (10 officers, 143 men)

Former German sail training ship. Built by Blöhm & Voss, Hamburg. Launched in June 1937 and completed on 1 Feb 1938. Sister of US Coast Guard training ship *Eagle* (ex-German *Horst Wessel*) and Soviet *Tovarisch*. Taken by USA as a reparation after the Second World War in 1945 and sold to Brazil in 1948. Purchased from Brazil and commissioned in the Portuguese Navy on 2 Feb 1972 at Rio de Janeiro and renamed *Sagres*.
Sail area 20 793 sq ft. Height of main-mast 142 ft.

SAGRES   *1973, Portuguese Navy*

1 HARBOUR TANKER

BC 3 (ex-US *YO 194*)

Transferred April 1962.

TUGS

1 OCEAN TUG

Name	No.	Builders	Commissioned
XAVIER SCHULTZ	A 521	Alfeite Naval Yard	14 July 1972

Displacement, tons: 900
Main engines: 2 Diesels; 2 shafts; 2 400 hp = 14·5 knots
Range, miles: 3 000 at 12·5 knots

A dual purpose ocean tug and buoy/lighthouse tender ordered late in 1968.

2 HARBOUR TUGS

RB 1 (ex-*ST 1994*)   **RB 2** (ex-*ST 1996*)

Transferred from US Navy—RB 1 Dec 1961, RB 2 March 1962.

QATAR

Now possesses an expanding Naval Force, generally described as "Coastguard". The geographical position of the state, dividing the Persian Gulf and covering Bahrain, gives this force added importance. The main oil-terminal is at Umm-Said.

Mercantile Marine

Lloyd's Register of Shipping:
6 vessels of 1 389 tons gross

Personnel

(a) 400 officers and men
(b) Voluntary

Base

Doha

6 VOSPER THORNYCROFT 103 ft TYPE
(LARGE PATROL CRAFT)

Name	No.	Builders	Commissioned	
AL KHATAB	Q 15	Vosper-Thornycroft Ltd	22 Jan	1976
AL WUSAAIL	Q 14	Vosper-Thornycroft Ltd	28 Oct	1975
BARZAN	Q 11	Vosper-Thornycroft Ltd	13 Jan	1975
HWAR	Q 12	Vosper-Thornycroft Ltd	30 Apr	1975
TARIQ	Q 16	Vosper-Thornycroft Ltd	1 Mar	1976
THAT ASSUARI	Q 13	Vosper-Thornycroft Ltd	3 Oct	1975

Displacement, tons: 120
Dimensions, feet (metres): 103·7 pp; 109·7 oa × 21 × 5·5 *(31·1; 32·4 × 6·3 × 1·6)*
Guns: 2—20 mm
Main engines: 2 Diesels; 4 000 hp = 27 knots
Complement: 25

Ordered in 1972-73. All laid down between Sept 1973 and Nov 1974.

AL WUSAAIL

12/1974, C and S Taylor

2 75 ft COASTAL PATROL CRAFT

Length, feet (metres): 75 *(22·5)*
Guns: 2—20 mm
Main engines: 2 Diesels; 1 420 hp

Built by Whittingham and Mitchell, Chertsey 1969.

3 KEITH NELSON 45 ft TYPE
(COASTAL PATROL CRAFT)

Displacement, tons: 13
Dimensions, feet (metres): 44 × 12·3 × 3·8 *(13·5 × 3·8 × 1·1)*
Guns: 1—12·7 mm; 2—7·62 mm (singles)
Main engines: 2 Caterpillar diesels; 800 hp = 26 knots
Complement: 6

15 FAIREY MARINE "SPEAR" CLASS
(COASTAL PATROL CRAFT)

Displacement, tons: 4·3
Dimensions, feet (metres): 29·8 × 9 × 2·8 *(9·1 × 2·8 × 0·8)*
Guns: 3—7·62 mm
Main engines: 2 Diesels; 290 hp; 2 shafts = 26 knots
Complement: 4

First seven ordered early 1974. Delivered 19 June 1974, 16 Sept 1974, 18 Sept 1974, 2 Nov 1974, Dec 1974, Jan 1975, Feb 1975. Contract for further five signed December 1975. Second contract for three fulfilled with delivery of two on 30 June 1975 and one on 14 July 1975.

FAIREY MARINE SPEARS

1974, Fairey Marine

2 FAIREY MARINE "INTERCEPTOR" CLASS
(FAST ASSAULT/RESCUE CRAFT)

Displacement, tons: 1¼
Dimensions, feet (metres): 25 × 8 × 2·5 *(7·9 × 2·4 × 0·8)*
Main engines: 2 Johnson outboard motors; 270 bhp = 35 knots
Range, miles: 150 at 30 knots
Complement: 3

In assault role can carry 10 troops. In rescue role carry number of life rafts. GRP catamaran hull. Delivered 28 Nov 1975.

RAS AL KHAIMAH

It is reported that up to five small patrol craft have been acquired recently.

ROMANIA

Headquarters Appointment

Commander in Chief of the Navy:
Rear Admiral Sebastian Ulmeanu

Diplomatic Representation

Naval Attaché in London:
Captain 1st Rank A. A. Dusa
Naval, Military and Air Attaché in Washington:
Colonel Nicolae Gheorghe Plesa

Bases

Mangalia, Constanta, Dulcea (Danube base)

Strength of the Fleet

(No details of building programme available)

Type	Active
Corvettes	6
Fast Attack Craft (Missile)	5
Fast Attack Craft (Gun and Patrol)	23
Fast Attack Craft (Torpedo)	12
River Patrol Craft	7
Coastal Patrol Craft	19
Minesweepers (Coastal)	4
Minesweepers (Inshore)	10
MSBs	8
Training Ships	1
Tugs	2

(Other unconfirmed vessels listed at end of section).

Personnel

(a) 1976: 9 000 officers and ratings
(b) 2 Years National Service

Mercantile Marine

Lloyd's Register of Shipping:
122 vessels of 777 309 tons gross

CORVETTES

3 Ex-SOVIET "POTI" CLASS

V 31   V 32   V 83

Displacement, tons: 550 standard; 600 full load
Dimensions, feet (metres): 193·5 × 26·2 × 9·2 *(59 × 8 × 2·8)*
Guns: 2—57 mm (twin)
Tubes: 4—16 in anti-submarine
A/S weapons: 2—12 barrelled MBUs
Main engines: 2 gas turbines; 2 diesels; 4 shafts; total 20 000 hp = 28 knots

Transferred from the USSR in 1970.

"POTI" Class   1971

3 Ex-SOVIET "KRONSTADT" CLASS

V-1   V-2   V-3

Displacement, tons: 310 standard; 380 full load
Dimensions, feet (metres): 170·6 × 21·5 × 9 *(52 × 6·5 × 2·7)*
Guns: 1—3·4 in; 2—37 mm (single); 4—25 mm (twin)
A/S weapons: 2 DC throwers; 2 depth charge racks
Main engines: 3 diesels; 3 shafts; 3 300 bhp = 24 knots
Range, miles: 1 500 at 12 knots
Complement: 65

Transferred by USSR in 1956.

Radar: Pothead.

"KRONSTADT" Class

LIGHT FORCES

16 Ex-CHINESE "SHANGHAI" CLASS
(FAST ATTACK CRAFT—GUN and PATROL)

VP 20-29   VS 41-46

Displacement, tons: 120 standard; 155 full load
Dimensions, feet (metres): 128 × 18 × 5·6 *(39 × 5·5 × 1·7)*
Guns: VP type: 1—57 mm; 2—30 mm (twin). VS type: 1—37 mm; 2—14·5 MG
A/S weapons: VS type: 2—5 barrelled MBU 1800
Main engines: 4 diesels; 4 800 bhp = 30 knots
Complement: 25

Two variants of the "Shanghai" class of which the VS type (patrol A/S) is a new departure. Built at Mangalia since 1973 in a continuing programme. There are reports that the dimensions given above (which are for standard "Shanghai" class) may have been altered as follows: VP type 112 × 18 and VS type 106 × 16. Unconfirmed figures.

"SHANGHAI" Class—VS Type   8/1974

5 Ex-SOVIET "OSA" CLASS
(FAST ATTACK CRAFT—MISSILE)

194 to 198

Displacement, tons: 165 standard; 200 full load
Dimensions, feet (metres): 128·7 × 25·1 × 5·9 *(39·3 × 7·7 × 1·8)*
Missile launchers: 4 for SSN 2
Guns: 4—30 mm (2 twin, 1 forward, 1 aft)
Main engines: 3 diesels; 13 000 bhp = 32 knots
Range, miles: 800 at 25 knots
Complement: 30

Transferred by USSR in 1964.

13 Ex-SOVIET "P 4" CLASS
(FAST ATTACK CRAFT—TORPEDO and GUN)

87 to 92 + 7

Displacement, tons: 25
Dimensions, feet (metres): 62·7 × 11·6 × 5·6 *(19·1 × 3·5 × 1·7)*
Guns: 4—14·5 mm (twins) (Gun version); 2—12·7 mm MG (twin) (Torpedo version)
Torpedo tubes: 2—18 in (Torpedo version)
Main engines: 2 diesels; 2 200 bhp = 50 knots
Complement: 12

Built in 1955-56. Now in two versions—six (87-92) with torpedo armament and other seven with heavier guns and no torpedoes.

6 Ex-CHINESE "HU CHWAN" CLASS
(FAST ATTACK CRAFT—TORPEDO)

VT 51-53 + 3

Displacement, tons: 45
Dimensions, feet (metres): 70 × 16·5 × 3·1 *(21·4 × 5 × 1)*
Guns: 4—25 mm (twins)
Torpedo tubes: 2—21 in *(533 mp)*
Main engines: 2 Diesels; 2 200 hp = 55 knots ((foilborne in calm conditions)
Range, miles: 500 cruising

Hydrofoils of the same class as the Chinese which were started in 1956. Three with unknown pennant numbers imported from China. Further three (VT 51-53) locally built in a continuing programme which started 1973-74.

"HU CHWAN" Class
8/1974

7 RIVER PATROL CRAFT

VB 76-82

Dimensions, feet (metres): 105 × 16 × 3 *(32 × 4·8 × 0·9)*
Guns: 1—3·9 in; 1—37 mm; 2—14·5 mm; 2 Grenade Throwers
Complement: about 25

Built in Romania from 1973 in continuing programme.

RIVER PATROL CRAFT
8/1974

10 "VG" CLASS (COASTAL PATROL CRAFT)

Displacement, tons: 40
Dimensions, feet (metres): 52·5 × 14·4 × 4 *(16 × 4·4 × 1·2)*
Gun: 1—20 mm
Main engines: 2 Diesels; 600 hp = 18 knots
Complement: 10

Steel-hulled craft built at Galata in 1954. Obsolescent.

9 "SM165" CLASS (COASTAL PATROL CRAFT)

SM 161-169

Locally built from 1954-56.

MINE WARFARE FORCES

4 Ex-GERMAN "M" CLASS (MINESWEEPERS—COASTAL)

DESCATUSARIA DB 13	**DEMOCRATIA** DB 15
DESROBIREA DB 14	**DREPTATEA** DB 16

Displacement, tons: 543 standard; 775 full load
Dimensions, feet (metres): 206·5 oa × 28 × 7·5 *(62·3 × 8·5 × 2·6)*
Guns: 2—3·4 in; 2—37 mm (twin); 3—20 mm (singles)
A/S weapons: 2 DCT
Main engines: Triple expansion; 2 shafts; 2 400 ihp = 17 knots
Boilers: 2 three-drum water tube
Range, miles: 1 200 at 17 knots
Complement: 80

German "M Boote"—designed as coal-burning minesweepers. Probably German-built, taken by USSR and handed over to Romania. Converted to oil in 1951.

DEMOCRATIA and DREPTATEA
1968

10 Ex-SOVIET "T 301" CLASS (MINESWEEPERS—INSHORE)

Displacement, tons: 150 standard; 180 full load
Dimensions, feet (metres): 128 × 18 × 4·9 *(39 × 5·5 × 1·5)*
Guns: 2—37 mm; 4—12·7 mm MG (twins)
Main engines: 2 diesels; 1 440 bhp; 2 shafts = 17 knots
Complement: 30

Transferred to Romania by the USSR in 1956-60. Probably half of these are non-operational. Two deleted 1975.

8 Ex-POLISH "TR-40" CLASS (MSBs)

VD-241   VD-242   VD-243   VD-244   VD-245   VD-246   VD-247   VD-248

Displacement, tons: 40 standard; 60 full load
Dimensions, feet (metres): 55·8 × 11·5 × 4 *(17 × 3·5 × 1·2)*
Guns: 2—25 mm (twin); 2 MG (twin)
Main engines: 2 Diesels; 2 shafts; 600 hp = 18 knots
Complement: 18

Employed on shallow water and river duties. These were originally a Polish class begun in 1955 but completed in Romania in late 1950s.

TUGS

2 "ROSLAVL" CLASS

VITEAZUL RM 101   **VOINICUL** —

Displacement, tons: 450
Dimensions, feet (metres): 135 × 29·3 × 11·8 *(41·2 × 8·9 × 3·6)*
Main engines: Diesels; 1 250 hp = 12·5 knots
Complement: 28

Built in Galata shipyard 1953-54.

TRAINING SHIP

Name	No.	Builders	Commissioned
MIRCEA	—	Blohm & Voss, Hamburg	29 Mar 1939

Displacement, tons: 1 604
Dimensions, feet (metres): 239·5 oa; 267·3 (with bowsprit) × 39·3 × 16·5 *(73; 81·5 × 12 × 5)*
Sail area: 18 830 sq ft
Main engines: Auxiliary MAN 6-cylinder Diesel; 500 bhp = 9·5 knots
Complement: 83 + 140 midshipmen for training

Laid down on 30 April 1938. Launched on 22 Sep 1938. Refitted at Hamburg in 1966.

MIRCEA

1970, Michael D. J. Lennon

MISCELLANEOUS

Although details are not available the following have been reported—two survey craft, three tankers, ten transports and twelve LCUs of "Braila" class.

SABAH

In addition to two PX-class 87 ft patrol boats on detachment from the Royal Malaysian Police the following have been provided direct to Sabah—based at Labuan.

2 91 ft PATROL BOATS

Name	No.	Builders	Commissioned
SRI GUMANTONG	—	Vosper Thornycroft Ltd, Singapore	8 April 1970
SRI LABUAN	—	Vosper Thornycroft Ltd, Singapore	6 April 1970

Sri Gumantong launched 18 Aug 1969.

1 YACHT

Name	No.	Builders	Commissioned
PUTRI SABAH	—	Vosper Thornycroft Ltd, Singapore	11 July 1971

Displacement, tons: 117
Dimensions, feet (metres): 91 × 19 × 5·5 *(27·8 × 5·8 × 1·7)*
Main engines: 1 diesel = 12 knots
Complement: 22

2 55 ft PATROL BOATS

Name	No.	Builders	Commissioned
SRI SEMPORNA	—	Chevertons, Isle of Wight	Feb 1975
SRI BANGJI	—	Chevertons, Isle of Wight	Feb 1975

Displacement, tons: 50
Dimensions, feet (metres): 55 × 15 × 3 *(16·8 × 4·6 × 0·9)*
Gun: 1—MG
Main engines: Diesels; 1 200 hp = 20 knots
Range, miles: 300 at 15 knots
Complement: 11

ST. KITTS

Mercantile Marine

Lloyd's Register of Shipping: 2 vessels of 405 tons

1 FAIREY MARINE "SPEAR" CLASS

Displacement, tons: 4·3
Dimensions, feet (metres): 29·8 × 9 × 2·8 *(9·1 × 2·8 × 0·8)*
Guns: 2—7·62 mm
Main engines: 2 diesels; 360 hp = 30 knots
Complement: 2

Ordered for the Police in June 1974—delivered 10 Sep 1974.

ST. LUCIA

Mercantile Marine

Lloyd's Register of Shipping: 2 vessels of 904 tons gross

1 BROOKE MARINE PATROL CRAFT

CHATOYER

Displacement, tons: 15
Dimensions, feet (metres): 40 × 12 × 2 *(12·2 × 3·7 × 0·6)*
Guns: 3 MG
Main engines: 2 Diesels; 370 hp = 22 knots

ST. VINCENT

Mercantile Marine

Lloyd's Register of Shipping: 17 vessels of 5 507 tons gross

1 BROOKE MARINE PATROL CRAFT

HELEN

Details as *Chatoyer* in St. Lucia section above.

SAUDI ARABIA

Diplomatic Representation

Defence Attaché in London:
  Brigadier Abdullah Al-Saheal

Personnel

(a) 1976: 1 500 officers and men
(b) Voluntary Service

Bases

Jiddah (Red Sea)
Az Zahran (Dhahran) (Persian Gulf)

Mercantile Marine

Lloyd's Register of Shipping:
  55 vessels of 180 246 tons gross

New Construction

In January 1972 an agreement was signed with the USA for a ten-year programme to provide 4 MSC, 6 large patrol craft, 2 coastal patrol craft, 4 LCTs, 3 training ships and 2 tugs. The first and last of these are listed in this section.

MINEWARFARE FORCES
4 "322" CLASS (MINESWEEPERS—COASTAL)

Ordered from Peterson Builders, Sturgeon Bay, Wisconsin on 30 Sept 1975 under the International Logistics Programme. All to be delivered 1978

LIGHT FORCES

3 GERMAN "JAGUAR" CLASS
(FAST ATTACK CRAFT—TORPEDO)

Name	No.	Builders	Commissioned
DAMMAM	—	Lürssen Vegesack	1969
KHABAR	—	Lürssen Vegesack	1969
MACCAH	—	Lürssen Vegesack	1969

Displacement, tons: 160 standard; 190 full load
Dimensions, feet (metres): 139·4 × 23·4 × 7·9 *(42·5 × 7 × 2·4)*
Guns: 2—40 mm
Torpedo tubes: 4—21 in *(533 mm)*
Main engines: 4 MTU diesels; 12 000 bhp = 42 knots
Complement: 33 (3 officers, 30 men)

1974, Reiner Nerlich

"JAGUAR" Class

1 USCG TYPE (LARGE PATROL CRAFT)

RYADH

Displacement, tons: 100 standard
Dimensions, feet (metres): 95·0 × 19·0 × 6·0 *(29 × 5·8 × 1·9)*
Gun: 1—40 mm
Main engines: 4 diesels; 2 shafts; 2 200 bhp = 21 knots
Complement: 15

Steel-hulled patrol boat transferred to Saudi Arabia in 1960.

20 45 ft PATROL BOATS

Built by Whittingham and Mitchell, Chertsey, England. Armed with one ·5 cal MG and powered with two 362 hp diesels.

2 Ex-US 40 ft UTILITY BOATS

Transferred late 1960s.

43 30 ft "C-80" CLASS (COASTAL PATROL CRAFT)

Dimensions, feet (metres): 29·3 oa × 9·3 × 1·5 *(8·9 × 2·9 × 0·6)*
Main engines: 1 Caterpillar diesel; 210 bhp; Castoldi pump jet unit = 20 knots
Gun: 1 MG

All delivered 1975 to Saudi Coastguard. Built by Northshore Yacht Yards under sub-contract to Planning Associates Ltd (London). Contract 1974.

1975, Northshore

C-80 Class

10 23 ft "HUNTRESS" PATROL BOATS

Built by Fairey Marine, Hamble, England. Capable of 20 knots with a cruising range of 150 miles and a complement of four.

20 ft PATROL BOATS

Smaller editions of the 45 ft craft above. By the same builder.

8 SRN-6 HOVERCRAFT

Displacement, tons: 10 normal (load 8 200 lbs)
Dimensions, feet (metres): 48·4 × 25·3 × 15·9 (height) *(14·8 × 7·7 × 4·8)*
Main machinery: 1 Gnome model 1050 gas turbine.
Speed, knots: 58

Acquired from British Hovercraft Corporation Ltd, between Feb and Dec 1970.

1971

SRN-6 hovercraft

2 AIR SEA-RESCUE LAUNCHES

ASR 1   ASR 2

With two diesels of 1 230 hp and capable of 25 knots. Belong to Ministry of Transportation.

SERVICE FORCES

1 ROYAL YACHT

Dimensions, feet (metres): 212 oa × 32 × 10 *(69·5 × 10·5 × 3·3)*
Main engines: 2 Diesels; 6 300 hp = 26 knots
Complement: 26 (accommodation for 18 passengers)

Ordered from "Van Lent" (de Kaag) Netherlands in October 1975.

2 Ex-US YTB TYPE (HARBOUR TUGS)

EN 111 (ex-*YTB 837*)   **EN 112** (ex-*YTB 838*)

Displacement, tons: 350 full load
Dimensions, feet (metres): 109 oa × 30 × 13·8 *(31·1 × 9·8 × 4·5)*
Main engines: 2 Diesels; 2 000 bhp; 2 shafts
Complement: 12

Transferred by USN 15 Oct 1975.

SENEGAL

Personnel	Base	Mercantile Marine
1976: approx 250 officers and men	Dakar	*Lloyd's Register of Shipping:* 56 vessels of 23 261 tons gross

DELETION

Light Forces

1974 *Sénégal*

LIGHT FORCES

2 + 1 "P 48" CLASS (LARGE PATROL CRAFT)

Name	No.	Builders	Commissioned
SAINT LOUIS	—	Ch. Navales Franco-Belges	1 Mar 1971
POPENGUINE	—	Soc. Francais de Constructions Navales	10 Aug 1974
PODOR	—	Soc. Francais de Constructions Navales	Mar 1977

Displacement, tons: 250 full load
Dimensions, feet (metres): 149·3 pp; 156 oa × 23·3 × 8·1 *(45·5; 47·5 × 7·1 × 2·5)*
Missiles: 8—SS 12
Guns: 2—40 mm
Main engines: 2 MGO diesels; 1 shaft; 2 400 bhp = 18·5 knots
Range, miles: 2 000 at 18 knots
Complement: 25

Saint Louis laid down on 20 April 1970, launched on 5 Aug 1970. *Popenguine* laid down in Dec 1973, launched 22 Mar 1974. Sisters to *Malaika* of Malagasy, *Vigilant* of Ivory Coast and "Bizerte" Class of Tunisian Navy. *Podor* ordered Aug 1975.

"P 48" Class   *1972*

1 TRAWLER TYPE

S ALMADIES

...u previously on fishery protection.

12 VOSPER 45 ft TYPE

Dimensions, feet (metres): 45 × 13·2 × 3·5 *(13·7 × 4 × 1·1)*
Guns: 1—12·7 mm; 2—7·62 mm
Main engines: 2 diesels; 920 hp = 25 knots
Complement: 6

2 Ex-FRENCH VC TYPE

Name	No.	Builders	Commissioned
CASAMANCE (ex-*VC 5*, ex-*P 755)*	—	Constructions Mécaniques de Normandie, Cherbourg	1958
SINE-SALOUM (ex-*Reine N'Galifourou*, ex-*VC 4*, ex-*P 754)*	—	Constructions Mécaniques de Normandie, Cherbourg	1958

Displacement, tons: 75 standard; 82 full load
Dimensions, feet (metres): 104·5 × 15·5 × 5·5 *(31·8 × 4·7 × 1·7)*
Guns: 2—20 mm
Main engines: 2 Mercedes-Benz (MTU) diesels; 2 shafts; 2 700 bhp = 28 knots
Complement: 15

Former French patrol craft (Vedettes de Surveillance Côtière). *Casamance* was transferred from France to Senegal in 1963. *Sine-Saloum* was given to Senegal on 24 Aug 1965 after having been returned to France by the Congo in Feb 1965.

SINE-SALOUM   *1967, Senegalese Navy*

1 FAIREY MARINE "SPEAR" CLASS

Displacement, tons: 4·3
Dimensions, feet (metres): 29·8 × 9 × 2·8 *(9·1 × 2·8 × 0·8)*
Guns: 1—12·7 mm; 2—7·62 mm
Main engines: 2 diesels; 360 hp = 30 knots
Complement: 2

Completed 28 Feb 1974 for Senegal Customs.

2 FAIREY MARINE "HUNTRESS" CLASS

Dimensions, feet (metres): 23·2 × 8·8 × 2·8 *(7·1 × 2·7 × 0·8)*
Main engines: 1 diesel; 180 hp; 29 knots
Complement: 2

Completed Mar 1974 for Senegal Customs.

AMPHIBIOUS FORCES

1 Ex-FRENCH EDIC

LA FALENCE (ex-*9095*) (LCT)

Displacement, tons: 250 standard; 670 full load
Dimensions, feet (metres): 193·5 × 39·2 × 4·5 *(59 × 12 × 1·3)*
Guns: 2—20 mm
Main engines: 2 MGO diesels; 2 shafts; 1 000 bhp = 8 knots
Complement: 6

Launched 7 April 1958. Transferred 1 July 1974.

2 Ex-US LCM 6

DIOU LOULOU   DIOMBOS

Transferred July 1968. Of 26 tons.

1 TENDER

CRAME JEAN

18 ton fishing boat used as training craft.

SHARJAH

Craft belong to Marine Division of the Sharjah Police Force

2 50 ft CHEVERTON TYPE

Name	No.	Builders	Commissioned
AL SHAHEEN	—	Chevertons, Cowes	Feb 1975
AL AQAB	—	Chevertons, Cowes	Feb 1975

Displacement, tons: 20
Dimensions, feet (metres): 50 × 14 × 4·5 *(15·2 × 4·3 × 1·4)*
Gun: 1 MG
Main engines: 2 GM diesels; 2 shafts; 850 bhp = 23 knots
Range, miles: 1 000 at 20 knots
Complement: 8

GRP Hull.

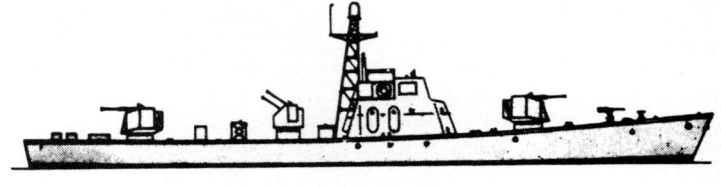

AL SHAHEEN   *1975, Roger M. Smith*

SIERRA LEONE

Personnel

(a) 1976: 150 officers and men
(b) Voluntary service

Base

Freetown

Mercantile Marine

Lloyd's Register of Shipping:
13 vessels of 17 200 tons gross

2 Ex-CHINESE "SHANGHAI II" CLASS
(FAST ATTACK CRAFT—GUN)

Displacement, tons: 120 standard; 155 full load
Dimensions, feet (metres): 128 × 18 × 5·6 *(39·6 × 5·5 × 1·7)*
Guns: 4—37 mm; 4—25 mm
A/S weapons: 8 DC
Mines: Mine rails can be fitted
Main engines: 4 Diesels; 4 800 hp = 30 knots
Complement: 25

Transferred by China June 1973.

"SHANGHAI II" Class

SINGAPORE

Headquarters Appointments

Commander of the Republic of Singapore Navy:
Lieutenant Colonel Khoo Eng An

Prefix to Ships' Names

RSS

Personnel

(a) 1976: 3 000 officers and men
(b) 2-3 years National Service and regular volunteers

Mercantile Marine

Lloyd's Register of Shipping: 610 vessels of 3 891 902 tons gross

---

LIGHT FORCES

6 LÜRSSEN VEGESACK "TNC 48" CLASS
(FAST ATTACK CRAFT—MISSILE)

Name	No.	Builders	Commissioned
SEA WOLF	P 76	Lürssen Werft, Vegesack	1972
SEA LION	P 77	Lürssen Werft, Vegesack	1972
SEA TIGER	P 79	Singapore Shipbuilding & Engineering Co	1974
SEA DRAGON	P 78	Singapore Shipbuilding & Engineering Co	1974
SEA HAWK	P 80	Singapore Shipbuilding & Engineering Co	1975
SEA SCORPION	P 81	Singapore Shipbuilding & Engineering Co	1975

Displacement, tons: 230
Dimensions, feet (metres): 158 × 23 × 7·5 *(48 × 7 × 2·3)*
Missiles: 5 Gabriel
Guns: 1—57 mm; 1—40 mm
Main engines: 4 MTU diesels; 4 shafts; 14 400 hp = 34 knots
Complement: 40

Designed by Lürssen Werft who built the first pair, *Sea Wolf* and *Sea Lion,* which arrived
Autumn 1972.

SEA SCORPION   *1975, Singapore Navy*

6 VOSPER THORNYCROFT DESIGN
3 "TYPE A" (FAST ATTACK CRAFT—GUN)

Name	No.	Builders	Commissioned
INDEPENDENCE	P 69	Vosper Thornycroft Ltd, UK	8 July 1970
FREEDOM	P 70	Vosper Thornycroft Private Ltd, Singapore	11 Jan 1971
JUSTICE	P 72	Vosper Thornycroft private Ltd, Singapore	23 Apr 1971

Displacement, tons: 100 standard
Dimensions, feet (metres): 103·6 wl; 109·6 × 21·0 × 5·6 *(31·6; 33·5 × 6·4 × 1·8)*
Guns: 1—40 mm (forward); 1—20 mm (aft)
Main engines: 2 Maybach (MTU 16 V538) diesels; 7 200 bhp = 32 knots
Range, miles: 1 100 at 15 knots
Complement: 19 to 22

On 21 May 1968 the Vosper Thornycroft Group announced the receipt of an order for six of their 110-foot fast patrol boats for the Republic of Singapore. Two sub-types, the first of each *(Independence* and *Sovereignty)* built in UK, the remainder in Singapore. *Independence* was launched 15 July 1969. *Freedom* 18 Nov 1969 and *Justice* 20 June 1970.

INDEPENDENCE

1971, Vosper Thornycroft

3 "TYPE B" (FAST ATTACK CRAFT—GUN)

Name	No.	Builders	Commissioned
DARING	P 73	Vosper Thornycroft Private Ltd, Singapore	18 Sep 1971
DAUNTLESS	P 74	Vosper Thornycroft Private Ltd, Singapore	1971
SOVEREIGNTY	P 71	Vosper Thornycroft Ltd, Portsmouth, England	Feb 1971

Displacement, tons: 100 standard; 130 full load
Dimensions, feet (metres): 103·6 wl; 109·6 × 21·0 × 5·6 *(31·6; 33·5 × 6·4 × 1·8)*
Guns: 1—76 mm Bofors; 1—20 mm Oerlikon
Main engines: 2 Maybach (MTU 16 V538) diesels; 7 200 bhp = 32 knots
Range, miles: 1 100 at 15 knots
Complement: 19 (3 officers, 16 ratings)

Sovereignty was launched 25 Nov 1969. *Dauntless* launched 6 May 1971. Steel hulls of round bilge form. Aluminium alloy superstructure.

SOVEREIGNTY

1971, Vosper Thornycroft

MINEWARFARE FORCES

2 Ex-US "BLUEBIRD" CLASS (MINESWEEPERS—COASTAL)

JUPITER (ex-USS *Thrasher MSC 203*)
MERCURY (ex-USS *Whippoorwill MSC 207*)

Displacement, tons: 370 full load
Dimensions, feet (metres): 144 × 28 × 8·2 *(43·9 × 8·5 × 2·5)*
Guns: 2—20 mm (twin)
Main engines: 2 GM diesels; 1 760 bhp; 2 shafts = 12 knots
Range, miles: 2 500 at 10 knots
Complement: 39

Transferred by sale 5 Dec 1975.

TRAINING SHIPS

1 "FORD" CLASS (LARGE PATROL CRAFT)

Name	No.	Builders	Commissioned
PANGLIMA	P 68	United Engineers, Singapore	May 1956

Displacement, tons: 119 standard; 134 full load
Dimensions, feet (metres): 117·0 × 20·0 × 6·0 *(35·7 × 6·1 × 1·8)*
Gun: 1—40 mm; 60 cal forward
Main engines: Paxman YHAXM supercharged B 12 diesels (MTU) = 14 knots
Oil fuel, tons: 15
Complement: 15 officers and men

Laid down in 1954. Launched on 14 Jan 1956. Similar to the British seaward defence boats of the "Ford" class. Transferred to the Royal Malaysian Navy on the formation of Malaysia. Transferred to the Republic of Singapore in 1967.

PANGLIMA

1975, Singapore Navy

ENDEAVOUR

Displacement, tons: 250
Dimensions, feet (metres): 35 × — × — *(41·2 × — × —)*
Guns: 2—20 mm

Former Netherlands ship built in 1955.

AMPHIBIOUS FORCES

6 Ex-US "501-1152" CLASS (LSTs)

ENDURANCE A 81   (ex-USS *Holmes County, LST 836*)
   —   (ex-US *LST 579*)
   —   (ex-US *LST 613*)
   —   (ex-US *LST 623*)
   —   (ex-US *LST 629*)
   —   (ex-US *LST 649*)

Displacement, tons: 1 653 light; 4 080 full load
Dimensions, feet (metres): 316·0 wl; 328 ·0 oa × 50·0 × 14·0 *(96·3; 100 × 15·2 × 4·3)*
Guns: 8—40 mm (4 twin)
Main engines: GM diesels; 2 shafts; 1 700 bhp = 11·6 knots
Complement: 120

Endurance loaned from the United States Navy on 1 July 1971 and transferred 5 Dec 1975. Remainder transferred 1976.

Note: there are also six small landing craft.

SERVICE FORCES

3 Ex-US LST TYPE

   —   (ex-USNS *117*)
   —   (ex-USNS *276*)
   —   (ex-USNS *Chase County LST 532*)

Displacement and other details similar to "501-1152" class above, although 117 and 276 of the "1-501" class are of slightly less tonnage. These two were unnamed and employed as transports in the US MSTS in Japan, being locally manned. All three now used as cargo ships.

POLICE PATROL CRAFT

4 VOSPER THORNYCROFT TYPE

Name	No.	Builders	Commissioned
—	PX 10	Vosper Thornycroft Ltd, Portsmouth, England	1969
—	PX 11	Vosper Thornycroft Ltd, Portsmouth, England	1969
—	PX 12	Vosper Thornycroft Ltd, Portsmouth, England	1969
—	PX 13	Vosper Thornycroft Ltd, Portsmouth, England	1969

Displacement, tons: 40 standard
Length, feet (metres): 87·0 *(26·5)*
Guns: 2—20 mm

Built for marine police duties.

SOMALI REPUBLIC

Personnel

(a) 1976: 350 officers and men
(b) Voluntary service

Bases

Berbera and Mogadishu

Mercantile Marine

Lloyd's Register of Shipping:
  273 vessels of 1 813 313 tons gross

LIGHT FORCES

3 Ex-SOVIET "OSA II" CLASS (FAST ATTACK CRAFT—MISSILE)

Displacement, tons: 165 standard; 200 full load
Dimensions, feet (metres): 128·7 × 25·1 × 5·9 *(39·3 × 7·7 × 1·8)*
Missiles: 4—SSN-2
Guns: 4—30 mm (twins)
Main engines: 3 diesels; 1 300 bhp = 32 knots
Range, miles: 800 at 25 knots
Complement: 30

Transferred in mid-1975.

4 Ex-SOVIET "P6" CLASS (FAST ATTACK CRAFT—TORPEDO)

Displacement, tons: 66 standard; 75 full load
Dimensions, feet (metres): 84·2 × 20·0 × 6·0 *(27·6 × 6·5 × 2)*
Guns: 4—25 mm
Torpedo tubes: 2—21 inch
Main engines: 4 diesels; 4 shafts; 4 800 hp = 43 knots
Range, miles: 450 at 30 knots
Complement: 25

Transferred in 1967.

6 Ex-SOVIET "POLUCHAT I" CLASS (LARGE PATROL CRAFT)

Displacement, tons: 100 standard; 120 full load
Dimensions, feet (metres): 98·4 × 20·0 × 5·9 *(32·3 × 6·5 × 1·9)*
Guns: 2—25 mm
Main engines: Diesels = 15 knots

Transferred in 1968.

SOUTH AFRICA

Headquarters Appointments

Chief of South African Defence Force:
Admiral H. H. Biermann SSA, OBE
Chief of the Navy:
Vice-Admiral J. Johnson, SM, DSC
Chief of Naval Staff:
Rear-Admiral S. C. Biermann, SM

Diplomatic Representation

Armed Forces Attaché in London:
Maj Gen H. R. Meintjes, SM
Naval Attaché in London:
Captain D. F. Silberbauer
Defence Attaché in W. Germany:
Brigadier P. E. K. Bosman
Naval Attaché in Washington:
Captain R. L. Shelver
Naval Attaché in Paris:
Captain J. A. de Kock
Armed Forces Attaché in Buenos Aires:
Captain F. C. Ferris

Personnel

(a) 1973: Total 4 665 (427 officers, 3 038 ratings and 1 200 National Service ratings)
1974: Total 4 204 (475 officers, 2 329 ratings and 1 400 National Service ratings)
1975: Total 4 250 (475 officers, 2 375 ratings and 1 400 National Service ratings)
1976: Total 4 700 (500 officers, 2 800 ratings and 1 400 National Service ratings)
(b) Voluntary plus 18 months National Service

Naval Bases

HM Dockyard at Simonstown was transferred to the Republic of South Africa on 2 April 1957. The new submarine base at Simonstown, SAS *Drommedaris*, incorporating offices, accommodation and operations centre alongside a Synchrolift marine elevator, capable of docking all South African ships except the *Tafelberg*, was opened in July 1972.
A new Maritime Headquarters was opened in March 1973 at Silvermine on the Cape Peninsula.

Air Sea Rescue Base

The SAAF Maritime Group base at Langebaan was transferred to the South African Navy on 1 Nov 1969, becoming SAN Sea Rescue Base (SAS *Flamingo*). The ASR launches were given Naval Coastal Forces numbers to replace SAAF "R" numbers.

Maritime Air

The SAAF operates an MP group consisting of 18 Piaggio P166s and 7 Shackleton MR 3. In addition 11 Wasp helicopters are available for embarkation in the frigates.

Prefix to Ships' Names

SAS (Suid Afrikaanse Skip)

Mercantile Marine

Lloyd's Register of Shipping:
286 vessels of 565 575 tons gross

Strength of the Fleet

Type	Active	Building
Destroyers	2	—
Frigates	7	6
Submarines Patrol	3	2
Fast Attack Craft—Missile	—	6
Large Patrol Craft	5	—
Minesweepers (Coastal)	10	—
Survey Ship	1	—
Fleet Replenishment Ship	1	—
BDV	1	—
TRV	1	—
Training Ships	1	—
Tugs	2	—
SAR Launches	4	—

New Construction

The South African defence budget announced on March 31 1976 showed an increase of 40% over the previous year, resulting in a budget which has nearly doubled in the last two years. The six new frigates, 2 submarines and 6 fast attack craft (missile) will have a proportion of their costs included in the total of 1·35 billion Rands (£880 mill).

DELETIONS

Survey Ship

1972 *Natal* (sunk as target 19 Sep)

Training Ship

1975 HDML 1204

PENNANT LIST

D (Destroyers)

237	Simon Van Der Stel
278	Jan Van Riebeeck

F (Frigates)

145	President Pretorius
147	President Steyn
150	President Krüger
157	Vrystaat
432	Good Hope
602	Transvaal

S (Submarines)

97	Maria Van Riebeeck
98	Emily Hobhouse
99	Johanna Van der Merwe

P (Light Forces)

285	Somerset (BDV)
3105	Gelderland
3120	Nautilus
3125	Reijger
3126	Haerlem
3127	Oosterland
3148	Fleur (TRV)

M (Minewarfare Forces)

291	Pietermaritzburg
1142	Kaapstad
1144	Pretoria
1207	Johannesburg
1210	Kimberley
1212	Port Elizabeth
1213	Mosselbaai
1214	Walvisbaai
1215	East London
1498	Windhoek
1499	Durban

A (Service Force)

243	Tafelberg

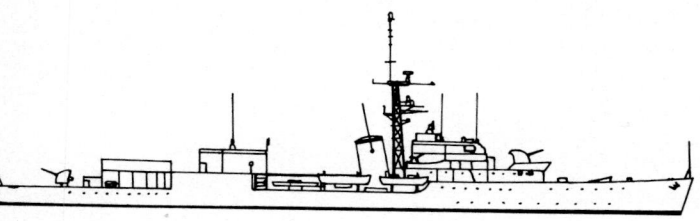

Ex-British "W" Class

"PRESIDENT" Class

VRYSTAAT

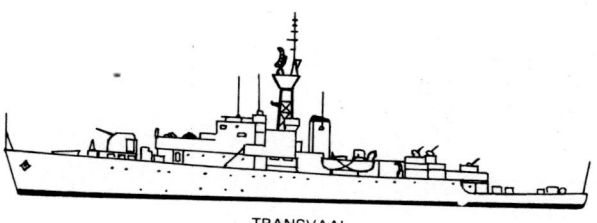

TRANSVAAL

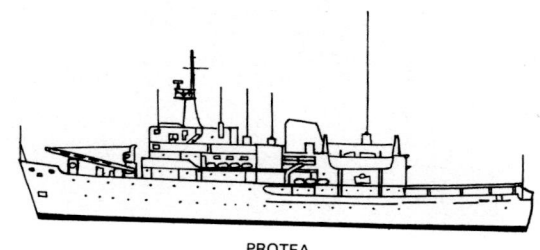

PROTEA

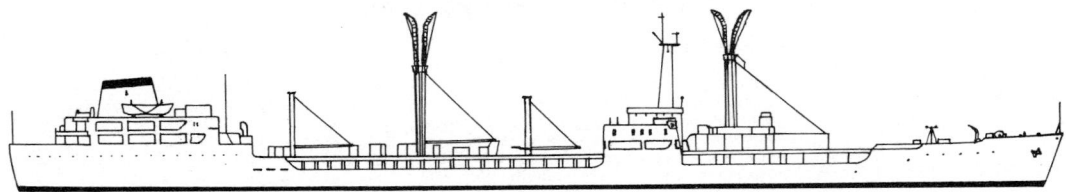

TAFELBERG

DESTROYERS

2 Ex-BRITISH "W" CLASS

Name	No.	Builders	Laid down	Launched	Commissioned
JAN VAN RIEBEECK(ex-HMS *Wessex*, ex-*Zenith*)	D 278	Fairfield SB & Eng Co Ltd, Govan, Glasgow	20 Oct 1942	2 Sep 1943	11 May 1944
SIMON VAN DER STEL (ex-HMS *Whelp*)	D 237	R. & W. Hawthorn Leslie & Co Ltd	1 May 1942	3 June1943	25 April 1944

Displacement, tons: 2 205 standard; 2 850 full load
Length, feet (metres): 339·5 *(103·6)* pp; 362·8 *(110·6)* oa
Beam, feet (metres): 35·7 *(10·9)*
Draught, feet (metres): 17·1 *(5·2)*
Aircraft: 2 Westland Wasp helicopters
Guns: 4—4 in *(102 mm)* (twin); 2—40 mm (single); 4—3 pdr (saluting)
Torpedo tubes: 4—21 in (quadruple)
Torpedo tubes, A/S: 6 (2 triple)
A/S weapons: 2 DCT; 2 DC racks
Boilers: 2 Admiralty 3-drum type; 300 psi; 670°F
Main engines: 2 Parsons sr geared turbines; 2 shafts; 40 000 shp
Speed, knots: 36
Range, miles: 3 260 at 14 knots; 1 000 at 30 knots
Oil fuel, tons: 579 (95%)
Complement: 192 (11 officers, 181 men)

Purchased from Great Britain. *Jan van Riebeeck* was transferred to South Africa on 29 Mar 1950, and *Simon van der Stel* early in 1952.

Gunnery: The main armament formerly comprised four 4·7 inch guns.

JAN VAN RIEBEECK   *1973, South African Navy*

Modernisation: *Simon van der Stel* was modernised in 1962-64 and *Jan van Riebeeck* in 1964-66.

Radar: Search: Type 293.
Fire Control: I Band (NSG NA 9 system).

FRIGATES

6 NEW CONSTRUCTION

In February 1975 it was announced that 6 frigates, to be armed with Gabriel missiles, were to be built in Durban.

3 "PRESIDENT" CLASS

Name	No.	Builders	Laid down	Launched	Commissioned
PRESIDENT KRUGER	F 150	Yarrow & Co, Scotstoun	6 April1959	20 Oct 1960	1 Oct 1962
PRESIDENT PRETORIUS	F 145	Yarrow & Co, Scotstoun	21 Nov 1960	28 Sep 1962	4 Mar 1964
PRESIDENT STEYN	F 147	Alex Stephen & Sons, Govan	20 May 1960	23 Nov 1961	25 April 1963

Displacement, tons: 2 250 standard; 2 800 full load
Dimensions, feet (metres): 370 oa × 41·1 × 17·1 *(112·8 × 12·5 × 5·2)*
Aircraft: 1 Wasp helicopter
Guns: 2—4·5 in *(115 mm)* (1 twin); 2—40 mm Bofors; 4—3 pdr (saluting)
A/S weapons: 1 Limbo 3-barrel DC mortar
Torpedo tubes: 6 A/S tubes (2 triple)
Main engines: 2 sets d.r. geared turbines; 2 shafts; 30 000 shp
Boilers: 2 Babcock & Wilcox 550 psi; 850°F
Speed, knots: 30
Oil fuel, tons: 430
Range, miles: 4 500 at 12 knots
Complement: 203 (13 officers, 190 men)

Originally "Rothesay" Type 12 frigates, *President Kruger* arrived in South Africa on 27 Mar 1963.

Modernisation: Refitted to carry a Wasp A/S helicopter, with hangar and landing deck. To accommodate this, one "Limbo" A/S mortar was removed and the two single 40 mm remounted on the hangar roof. *President Kruger* completed refit and recommissioned on 5 Aug 1969, *President Steyn* completed refit in 1971, when *President Pretorius* was taken in hand although delayed to take advantage gained from the previous conversions. The refits were carried out at S.A. Naval Dockyard, Simonstown and included replacement of the lattice foremast by a truncated pyramid tower. *Kruger* retained her original GDS5 director but will later be brought into line with the other pair. Small differences exist between all three ships.

Radar: Surveillance: Thomson CSF Jupiter.
Air/Surface search: Type 293.
Fire control: Elsag NA9C.

PRESIDENT KRUGER   *1973, South African Navy*

PRESIDENT KRUGER   *1974, Michael D. J. Lennon*

1 FORMER BRITISH TYPE 15

Name	No.
VRYSTAAT (ex-HMS *Wrangler*)	F 157

Builders	Laid down	Launched	Commissioned
Vickers-Armstrong, Barrow	23 Sep 1942	30 Dec 1943	14 June 1944

Displacement, tons: 2 240 standard; 2 880 full load
Length, feet (metres): 339·5 *(103·5)* pp; 362·8 *(110·6)* oa
Beam, feet (metres): 35·7 *(10·9)*
Draught, feet (metres): 17·1 *(5·2)*
Guns: 2—4 in *(102 mm)* (twin); 2—40 mm Bofors;
   4—3 pdr
A/S weapons: 2 Limbo 3-barrel DC Mortar
Main engines: Parsons single reduction geared turbines; 2
   shafts; 40 000 shp
Boilers: 2 Admiralty 3-drum; 300 psi; 675°F
Speed, knots: 36
Oil fuel, tons: 505
Range, miles: 3 200 at 14 knots; 1 300 at full power
Complement: 195 (13 officers, 182 men)

Fully converted into a Type 15 fast anti-submarine frigate from fleet destroyer of the "W" class in 1951-52 by Harland & Wolff Ltd, Belfast. Refitted by the Mount Stewart Dry Dock Ltd, Cardiff, and taken over from the Royal Navy on 29 Nov 1956 and renamed *Vrystaat*. Sailed for South Africa at the end of Jan 1957. Now in reserve.

VRYSTAAT   *1972, South African Navy*

Radar: Search: Type 277, Type 293. ECM and DF.

2 FORMER BRITISH "LOCH" CLASS

Name	No.
GOOD HOPE (ex-HMS *Loch Boisdale*)	F 432
TRANSVAAL (ex-HMS *Loch Ard*)	F 602

Builders	Laid down	Launched	Commissioned
Blyth Dry Docks & SB Co Ltd	8 Nov 1943	5 July 1943	1 Dec 1944
Harland & Wolff Ltd, Belfast	20 Jan 1944	2 Aug 1944	21 May 1945

Displacement, tons: 1 610 standard; 2 450 full load
Length, feet (metres): 286 *(87·2)* pp; 307 *(93·6)* oa
Beam, feet (metres): 38·5 *(11·7)*
Draught, feet (metres): 15·1 *(4·6)*
Guns: 2—4 in *(102 mm)* (1 twin)
   Transvaal: 6—40 mm Bofors
   Good Hope: 2—40 mm Bofors; 4—3 pdr
A/S weapons: 2 Squid triple DC mortars
Main engines: 2 sets triple expansion; 2 shafts; 5 500 ihp
Boilers: 2 Admiralty 3-drum; 225 psi
Speed, knots: 19
Oil fuel, tons: 720
Range, miles: 9 500 at 12 knots
Complement: 165 (10 officers, 155 men)

These two frigates, and a sister ship, *Natal*, were presented to South Africa by Great Britain in 1944-45.

Construction: *Transvaal* was completed by Lobnitz & Co Ltd, Renfrew.

Conversion: *Good Hope* was converted into a despatch vessel in 1955 as Administrative Flagship of the South African Navy. She has deckhouse superstructure for extra cabins, and reception platform above built on aft, and mainmast. Refitted in 1961.

TRANSVAAL   *1971, South African Navy*

Modification: When *Transvaal* was modernised she had her forecastle deck extended aft to provide extra accommodation (see photograph).

Radar: Equipment includes Type 277 search radar.

1 Ex-BRITISH "ALGERINE" CLASS

Name	No.
PIETERMARITZBURG (ex-HMS *Pelorus*)	M 291

Builders	Laid down	Launched	Commissioned
Lobnitz & Co Ltd, Renfrew	8 Oct 1942	18 June 1943	7 Oct 1943

Displacement, tons: 1 040 standard; 1 330 full load
Length, feet (metres): 212·5 *(64·8)* pp; 225 *(68·6)* oa
Beam, feet (metres): 35·5 *(10·8)*
Draught, feet (metres): 11·5 *(3·5)*
Guns: 2—4 in *(102 mm)* (twin); 2—40 mm Bofors
A/S weapons: 4 DCT
Main engines: 2 sets triple expansion; 2 shafts; 2 400 ihp
Boilers: 2 three-drum type; 250 psi
Speed, knots: 16
Oil fuel, tons: 270
Range, miles: 5 500 at 10 knots
Complement: 115 (8 Officers, 107 men)

Built as ocean minesweeper. Laid down on 8 Oct 1942, launched on 18 June 1943. Purchased from Great Britain in 1947 Re-commissioned as midshipmen's training ship on 30 Aug 1962. Refitted in 1971.

PIETERMARITZBURG   *1969, South African Navy*

SUBMARINES

2 FRENCH "AGOSTA" CLASS

Name	No.	Builders	Laid down	Launched	Commissioned
—	—	Dubigeon—Normandie (Nantes)	—	—	Nov 1978
—	—	Dubigeon—Normandie (Nantes)	—	—	Aug 1979

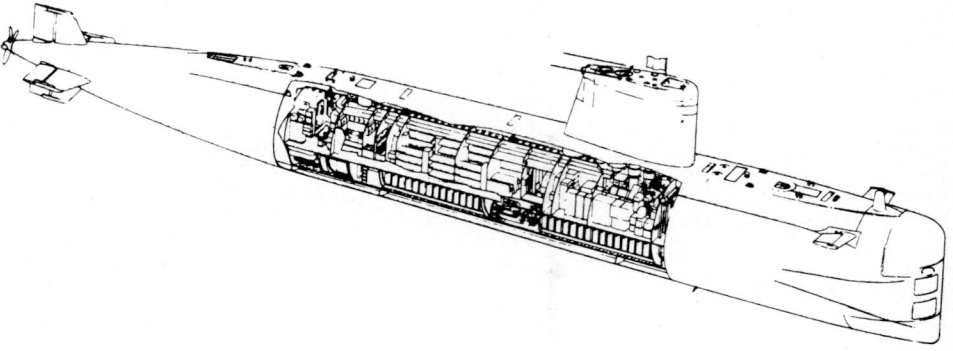

Displacement, tons: 1 470 surfaced; 1 790 dived
Dimensions, feet (metres): 221·7 × 22·3 × 17·7 (67·9 × 6·8 × 5·2)
Torpedo tubes: 4—21·7 (550 mm); 20 reload torpedoes
Main machinery: Diesel Electric; 2 SEMT Pielstick diesels; 3 600 bhp; 1 Main motor; 4 600 bhp; 1 cruising motor; 1 shaft
Speed, knots: 12 surfaced; 20 dived
Range, miles: 9 000 at 9 knots (surfaced); 350 at 3·5 knots (dived)
Complement: 50

Ordered June 1975.

3 FRENCH "DAPHNE" CLASS

Name	No.	Builders	Laid down	Launched	Commissioned
EMILY HOBHOUSE	S 98	Dubigeon—Normandie, Nantes-Chantenay	18 Nov 1968	24 Oct 1969	25 Jan 1971
JOHANNA VAN DER MERWE	S 99	Dubigeon—Normandie, Nantes-Chantenay	24 April 1969	21 July 1970	21 July 1971
MARIA VAN RIEBEECK	S 97	Dubigeon—Normandie, Nantes-Chantenay	14 Mar 1968	18 Mar 1969	22 June 1970

Displacement, tons: 850 surfaced; 1 040 dived
Length, feet (metres): 190·3 (58)
Beam, feet (metres): 22·3 (6·8)
Draught, feet (metres): 15·4 (4·7)
Torpedo tubes: 12—21·7 in (550 mm) (8 bow, 4 stern)
Main machinery: SEMT-Pielstick diesel electric; 1 300 bhp surfaced; 1 600 hp dived; 2 shafts
Speed, knots: 16 surfaced and dived
Range, miles: 4 500 at 5 knots (snorting)
Complement: 47 (6 officers, 41 men)

First submarines ordered for the South African Navy. They are of the French "Daphne" design, similar to those built in France for that country, Pakistan and Portugal and also built in Spain.

EMILY HOBHOUSE

1973, South African Navy

LIGHT FORCES

6 "RESHEF" CLASS (FAST ATTACK CRAFT—MISSILE)

Displacement, tons: 430 full load
Dimensions, feet (metres): 190 × 25 × 8 (58 × 7·8 × 2·4)
Missiles: 4—Gabriel (Selenia control)
Guns: 2—76 mm
Main engines: 4 Maybach diesels; 2 shafts; 5 340 hp = 32 knots
Range, miles: ? 1 500 at 30 knots
Complement: 45

Contract signed with Israel in late 1974; first three under construction at Haifa and at least one begun in Durban. Completion of order expected 1978.

5 BRITISH "FORD" CLASS (LARGE PATROL CRAFT)

Name	No.	Builders	Commissioned
GELDERLAND (ex-Brayford)	P 3105	A. & J. Inglis Ltd, Glasgow	30 Aug 1954
HAERLEM	P 3126	Vosper Ltd, Portsmouth	1959
NAUTILUS (ex-Glassford)	P 3120	Dunston, Thorne	23 Aug 1955
OOSTERLAND	P 3127	Vosper Ltd, Portsmouth	1959
REIJGER	P 3125	Vosper Ltd, Portsmouth	1958

Displacement, tons: 120 standard; 160 full load
Dimensions, feet (metres): 110·0 wl; 117·2 oa × 20·0 × 4·5 (35; 38·4 × 6·5 × 1·3)
Gun: 1—40 mm
A/S weapons: 2 DCT in Oosterland and Reijger
Main engines: 2 Davey Paxman diesels; Foden engine on centre shaft; 1 100 bhp = 18 knots

Gelderland was purchased from Britain, and handed over to South Africa at Portsmouth on 30 Aug 1954. Second ship, Nautilus was handed over 23 Aug 1955, Reijger was launched on 6 Feb 1958, Haerlem on 18 June 1958, Oosterland on 27 Jan 1959. All three of these later ships are fitted with Vosper roll damping fins. Haerlem had a charthouse added aft as an inshore survey craft.

REIJGER

1971

MINE WARFARE FORCES

10 BRITISH "TON" CLASS (MINESWEEPERS COASTAL)

Name	No.	Builders	Commissioned
DURBAN	M 1499	Camper & Nicholson, Gosport	1957
EAST LONDON (ex-HMS *Chilton*)	M 1215	Cook Welton and Gemmell	1958
JOHANNESBURG (ex-HMS *Castleton*)	M 1207	White, Southampton	1958
KAAPSTAD (ex-HMS *Hazleton*)	M 1142	Cook Welton and Gemmell	1954
KIMBERLEY (ex-HMS *Stratton*)	M 1210	Dorset Yacht Co	1958
MOSSELBAAI (ex-HMS *Oakington*)	M 1213	Harland & Wolff, Belfast	1959
PORT ELIZABETH (ex-HMS *Dumbleton*)	M 1212	Harland & Wolff, Belfast	1958
PRETORIA (ex-HMS *Dunkerton*)	M 1144	Goole Shipbuilding Co	1954
WALVISBAAI (ex-HMS *Packington*)	M 1214	Harland & Wolff, Belfast	1959
WINDHOEK	M 1498	Thornycroft, Southampton	1959

Displacement, tons: 360 standard; 425 full load
Dimensions, feet (metres): 140·0 pp; 152·0 oa × 28·8 × 8·2 *(45·9; 49·8 × 9·4 × 2·7)*
Guns: 1—40 mm Bofors; 2—20 mm
Main engines: Mirrlees diesels in *Kaapstad* and *Pretoria*, 2 500 bhp; Deltic diesels in remainder; 3 000 bhp = 15 knots
Range, miles: 2 300 at 13 knots

Kaapstad and *Pretoria*, open bridge and lattice mast, were purchased in 1955. *Windhoek*, frigate bridge and tripod mast, was launched by Thornycroft, Southampton, on 27 June 1957. *Durban*, covered bridge and tripod mast, was launched at Camper & Nicholson, Gosport, on 12 June 1957. *East London* and *Port Elizabeth*, transferred from the Royal Navy at Hythe on 27 Oct 1958, sailed for South Africa in Nov 1958. *Johannesburg, Kimberley* and *Mosselbaai* were delivered in 1959. *Walvisbaai* was launched by Harland & Wolff, Belfast on 3 July 1958 and delivered in 1959.

DURBAN   1971

SURVEY SHIP

Name	No.	Builders	Commissioned
PROTEA	—	Yarrow (Shipbuilders) Ltd.	23 May 1972

Displacement, tons: 1 930 standard; 2 750 full load
Length, feet (metres): 235 *(71·6)* pp; 260·1 *(79·3)* oa
Beam, feet (metres): 49·1 *(15·0)*
Draught, feet (metres): 15·1 *(4·6)*
Aircraft: 1 helicopter
Main engines: 4 Paxman/Ventura diesels geared to 1 shaft and controllable pitch propeller; 4 880 bhp
Speed, knots: 16
Range, miles: 12 000 at 11 knots
Oil fuel, tons: 560
Complement: Total 123 (12 officers, 104 ratings plus 7 scientists)

An order was placed with Yarrow (Shipbuilders) Ltd, for a "Hecla" class survey ship on 7 Nov 1969. Equipped for hydrographic survey with limited facilities for the collection of oceanographical data and for this purpose fitted with special communications equipment, naval surveying gear, survey launches and facilities for helicopter operations. Hull strengthened for navigation in ice and fitted with a transverse bow thrust unit and passive roll stabilisation system. Laid down 20 July 1970. Launched 14 July 1971.

PROTEA   1973, South African Navy

FLEET REPLENISHMENT SHIP

Name	No.	Builders	Commissioned
TAFELBERG (ex-*Annam*)	A 243	Nakskovs Skibsvaert, Denmark	1959

Measurement, tons: 12 500 gross; 18 430 deadweight
Main engines: B & W diesels; 8 420 bhp = 15·5 knots
Complement: 100

Built as Danish East Asiatic Co tanker. Launched on 20 June 1958. Purchased by the Navy in 1965. Accommodation rehabilitated by Barens Shipbuilding & Engineering Co, Durban with extra accommodation, air conditioning, re-wiring for additional equipment, new upper RAS (replenishment at sea) deck to contain gantries, re-fuelling pipes. Remainder of conversion by Jowies, Brown & Hamer, Durban. A helicopter flight-deck was added aft during refit in 1975.

TAFELBERG   1973, South African Navy

TORPEDO RECOVERY VESSEL

Name	No.	Builders	Commissioned
FLEUR	P 3148	Dorman Long (Africa) Ltd.	3 Dec 1969

Displacement, tons: 220 standard; 257 full load
Dimensions, feet (metres): 115·0 wl; 121·5 oa × 27·5 × 11·1 *(37·7; 39·8 × 9·0 × 3·6)*
Main engines: 2 Paxman Ventura diesels; 1 400 bhp

Combined Torpedo Recovery Vessel and Diving Tender.

FLEUR   1973 South African Navy

TRAINING VESSEL

Name	No.	Builders	Commissioned
NAVIGATOR	—	Fred Nicholls (Pty) Ltd, Durban	1964

Navigational Training Vessel. 75 tons displacement; 63 × 20 feet; 2 Foden diesels, 200 bhp = 9·5 knots. Based at Naval College, Gordon's Bay. Round bilge fishing boat wooden hull.

BOOM DEFENCE VESSEL

Name	No.	Builders	Commissioned
SOMERSET (ex-HMS *Barcross*)	P 285	Blyth Dry Dock & SB Co Ltd	14 April 1942

Displacement, tons: 750 standard; 960 full load
Dimensions, feet (metres): 150·0 pp; 182·0 oa × 32·2 × 11·5 *(49·2; 59 × 10·5 × 3·8)*
Main engines: Triple expansion; 850 hp = 11 knots
Boilers: 2 single ended
Oil fuel, tons: 186

Originally two in the class. Laid down on 15 April 1941, launched on 21 Oct 1941. Engined by Swan, Hunter & Wigham Richardson Ltd, Tyne.

NAVAL TUGS

1 NEW CONSTRUCTION

Displacement, tons: 392
Dimensions, feet (metres): 68·4 pp × 18·7 × 8·6 *(32·3 × 8·9 × 4·1)*
Main engines: Voith-Schneider propulsion = 12 knots

Delivery 1977. Bollard pull 25 tons.

Name	No.	Builders	Commissioned
DE NEYS	—	Globe Engineering Works Ltd, Cape Town	23 July 1969
DE NOORDE	—	Globe Engineering Works Ltd, Cape Town	Dec 1961

Displacement, tons: 180 and 170 respectively
Dimensions, feet (metres): 94·0 × 26·5 × 15·75 and 104·5 × 25·0 × 15·0 *(30·8 × 8·7 × 5·2, 34·2 × 8·2 × 4·9)*
Main engines: 2 Lister Blackstone diesels; 2 shafts; 608 bhp = 9 knots
Complement: 10

De Neys fitted with Voith-Schneider screws.

AIR SEA RESCUE LAUNCHES

2 FAIREY MARINE "TRACKER" CLASS

Name	No.	Builders	Commissioned
—	P 1554	Groves and Gutteridge, Cowes	1973
—	P 1555	Groves and Gutteridge, Cowes	1973

Displacement, tons: 26
Dimensions, feet (metres): 64 × 16 × 5 *(19·5 × 4·9 × 1·5)*
Main engines: 2 diesels; 1 120 bhp = 28 knots

Built by subsidiary of Fairey Marine.

P 1554

1973, South African Navy

2 KROGERWERFT TYPE

Name	No.	Builders	Commissioned
—	P 1551 (ex-*R 31*)	Krogerwerft, Rendsburg	1962
—	P 1552 (ex-*R 30*)	Krogerweft, Rendsburg	1961

Displacement, tons: 87
Dimensions, feet (metres): 96 × 19 × 4 *(29·3 × 5·8 × 1·2)*
Main engines: 2 diesels; 4 480 bhp = 30 knots

There are also 2 ex-seaplane tenders, 41 ft, and 2 ex-marine tenders, 24 ft.

DEPARTMENT OF TRANSPORT

1 NEW CONSTRUCTION (ANTARCTIC SURVEY AND SUPPLY VESSEL)

Displacement, tons: 1 400
Main engines: Two diesels; one shaft

Tenders invited 1975.

SPAIN

Headquarters Appointments

Minister of the Navy:
Admiral Excmo Sr Don Gabriel Pita da Veiga
Chief of the Naval Staff:
Admiral Excmo Sr Don Carlos Buhigas
Chief of Fleet Support:
Admiral Excmo Sr Don Pedro Durán
Vice Chief of the Naval Staff:
Vice-Admiral Excmo Sr Don Guillermo Mateu

Commands

Commander-in-Chief of the Fleet:
Vice-Admiral Excmo Sr Don Luis Arrévalo
Captain General, Cantabrian Zone:
Admiral Excmo Sr Don Pedro Español Iglesias
Captain General, Straits Zone:
Admiral Excmo Sr Don Felipe Pita da Veiga
Captain General, Mediterranean Zone:
Admiral Excmo Sr Don Francisco J de Elizalde
Commandant General, Marines:
Lieut-General Excmo Sr Don Carlos Arriaga

Diplomatic Representation

Naval Attaché in London:
Captain Don Gabino Aranda
Naval Attaché in Washington:
Captain Sr Don Adolfo Gregorio Alvarez

Personnel

(a) 1976: Total 51 200 (4 550 officers, 33 000 ratings, 4 650 civil branch, 9 000 marines)
(b) 18 months National Service

Bases

El Ferrol del Caudillo (Cantabrian Zone)
San Fernando, Cádiz (Straits Zone)
Cartagena (Mediterranean Zone)

Naval Air Service

 2 Harrier AV-8 (see note)
11 Bell 47G helicopters
 8 AB 204B and AB 212
11 Sikorsky SH-3D (see note)
11 Hughes 369 HM
 6 Bell AH-1G "Hueycobra" (see note)
 4 Sikorsky S-55 (phasing out)

Notes:

(a) Harrier AV-8 aircraft ordered from US Marine Corps in 1973. Initial order of 8 with possible follow-up of 12 and an additional 4. First two delivered early 1976.
(b) It is reported that an additional 12 SH-3D and 12 AH-1G (Hueycobras) are to be ordered.

US Agreement

Under an Agreement of 6 Aug 1970 the USA agreed to supply 2 submarines, 5 destroyers, 4 MSOs, 3 LSTs, 1 AE and 1 AO. Of this list an LSD was substituted for the AE and the AO was in too poor condition for further service. All now transferred.
Under 1976 Agreement US is to provide 4 Minesweepers—Ocean and 1 Repair Ship.

Mercantile Marine

Lloyd's Register of Shipping:
2 667 vessels of 5 433 354 tons gross

Strength of the Fleet

Type	Active	Building	Proposed
Helicopter Carrier	1	—	1
Destroyers	13	—	—
Frigates	16	4	7
Submarines—Patrol	8	2	2
Submarines—Small	2	—	—
Fast Attack Craft—Torpedo	2	—	—
Large Patrol Craft	11	1	—
Coastal Patrol Craft	11	—	—
LSD	1	—	—
Attack Transports	2	—	—
LST	3	—	—
LSM	2	—	—
LCT	8	—	—
Minor Landing Craft	93	—	—
Minesweepers—Ocean	10	—	—
Minesweepers—Coastal	12	—	—
Survey Ships	6	—	—
Transport	1	—	—
Replenishment Tanker	1	—	—
Harbour Tankers	13	—	—
Training Ship	1	—	—
Auxiliary Patrol Craft	16	—	—
Tugs (Ocean, Coastal and Harbour)	25	—	—
Miscellaneous	38	—	—

New Construction

Because of financial considerations last year's programme has been cut to the following: 4 Frigates (PF), 2 "Agosta" class submarines, 6 400-ton Large Patrol Craft, 6 140-ton Large Patrol Craft.

Of the above the following are under construction:
4 Frigates
2 Submarines
6 Large Patrol Craft (400 tons)
6 Large Patrol Craft (140 tons)

DELETIONS

Cruiser

1975 *Canarias* (17 Dec)

Destroyers

1970 *Almirante Miranda* ("Churruca" Class)

Frigates

1971 *Magallanes, Vasco Nunez de Balboa, Hernan Cortes* ("Pizarro" Class) *Marte* ("Jupiter" Class)
1972 *Eolo, Triton* ("Elol" Class), *Neptuno* ("Jupiter" Class)
1973 *Osado* ("Audaz" Class)
1974 *Audaz, Furor, Rayo* ("Audaz" Class), *Jupiter* ("Jupiter" Class), *Sarmiento de Gamboa* ("Pizarro" Class)
1975 *Meteoro, Relampago, Temerario,* ("Audaz" Class)

Corvettes

1971 *Descubierta* ("Atrevida" Class)
1973 *Diana* ("Atrevida" Class)

Submarines

1971 D 2 (S 21), D 3 (S 22), G 7 (ex-U573 VII C)
Midget submarines SA 41 (F 1), SA 42 (F 2)

Minewarfare Forces

1971 *Lerez* ("Bidasoa" Class)
1972 *Bidasoa, Nervion, Segura, Tambre, Ter* ("Bidasoa" Class)
1976 *Tinto* ("Guardioro" Class) (31 Jan)

Amphibious Forces

1974 LSM 3

Light Forces

1970 *Arcila, Xauen* (ex-trawlers)
1971 *Javier Quiroga* (ex-US PC)
1973 *Ciés* (Fishery Protection)
1974 *V 2, V 12, V 13, V 18, Candido Pérez, AR 10* (Coastal Launches)

Survey Ships

1971 *Malaspina*
1975 *Tofiño, Juan de la Cosa* (30 Apr)

Service Forces

1974 *PP 1, 3, 4, PB 5, 6, 17* (tankers)

LIST OF PENNANT NUMBERS

Helicopter Carrier PH

01 – Dédalo

Destroyers D

21 Lepanto
22 Almirante Ferrandiz
23 Almirante Valdes
24 Alcala Galiano
25 Jorge Juan
41 Oquendo
42 Roger de Lauria
43 Marques de la Ensenada
61 Churruca
62 Gravina
63 Mendez Nuñez
64 Langara
65 Blas de Lezo

Frigates D and F

D 38 Intrépido
51 Liniers
52 Alava
F 12 Vulcano
41 Vicente Yáñez Pinzon

Frigates D and F

42 Legazpi
61 Atrevida
62 Princesa
64 Nautilus
65 Villa de Bilbao
71 Baleares
72 Andalucia
73 Cataluña
74 Asturias
75 Extremadura
81 Descubierta
82 Diana
83-5 New Construction
91-5 Proposed New Construction

Submarines S

31 Almirante Garcia de los Reyes
32 Isaac Peral
33 Narciso Monturiol
34 Cosme Garcia
61 Delfin
62 Tonina
63 Marsopa
64 Narval
71-72 New Construction
SA 51-52 "Tiburon" class

Light Forces P

01 Lazaga
02 Alsedo
03 Cadarso
04 Villamil
05 Bonifaz
06 Recalde
11 Barceló
12 Laya
13 Javier Quiroga
14 Ordóñez
15 Acevedo
16 Candido Pérez
LT 30-31
LP 1-5
LAS 10, 20, 30
W 21 Pegaso
22 Procyon
32 Salvora
33 Centinela
34 Serviola
V 1, 4, 5, 6, 9, 10, 11, 17, 21

PENNANT LIST—*continued*

Amphibious Forces

TA 11	Aragon
TA 21	Castilla
TA 31	Galicia
L 11	Velasco
L 12	Martin Alvarez
L 13	C. de Venadito
LSM 1-2	
K 1-8	BDK 1-8

Minewarfare Forces M

11	Guadiaro
13	Eume
14	Almanzora
15	Navia
16	Guadalhorce
17	Eo
21	Nalón
22	Llobregat
23	Jucar

Minewarfare Forces M

24	Ulla
25	Miño
26	Ebro
27	Turia
28	Duero
29	Sil
30	Tajo
31	Genil
32	Odiel
41	Guadalete
42	Guadalmedina
43	Guadalquivir
44	Guadiana

Survey Ships A

21	Castor
22	Pollux
23	Antares
24	Rigel
31	Malaspina
32	Tofiño
—	Juan de la Cosa

Service Forces

A 41	Al Lobo
BP 11	Teide

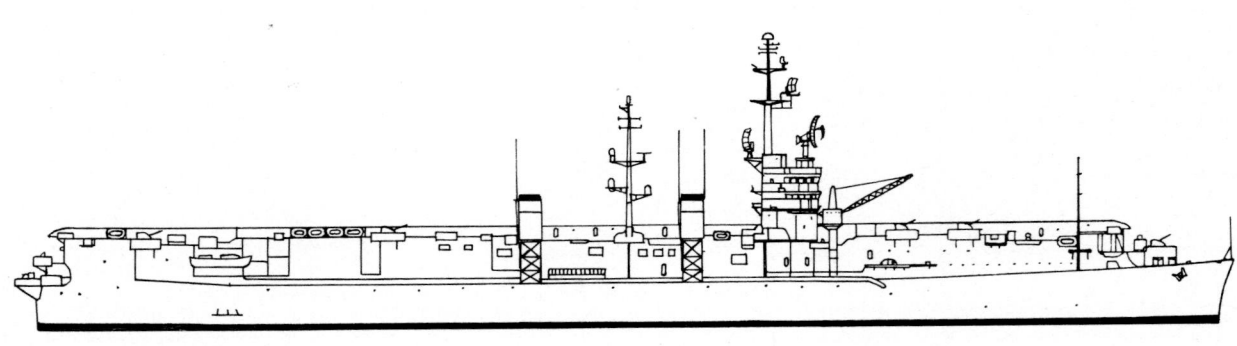

DEDALO

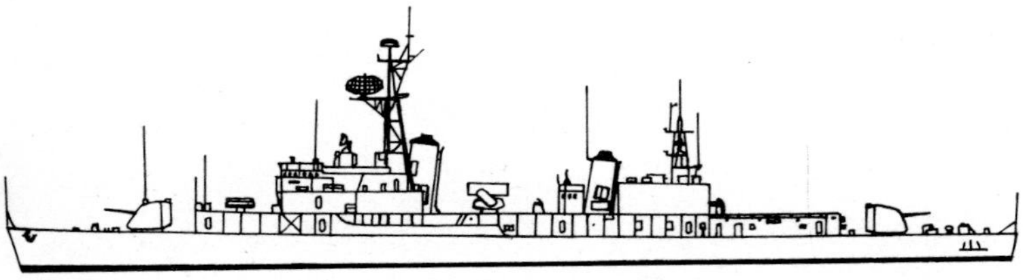

"D 60" Class

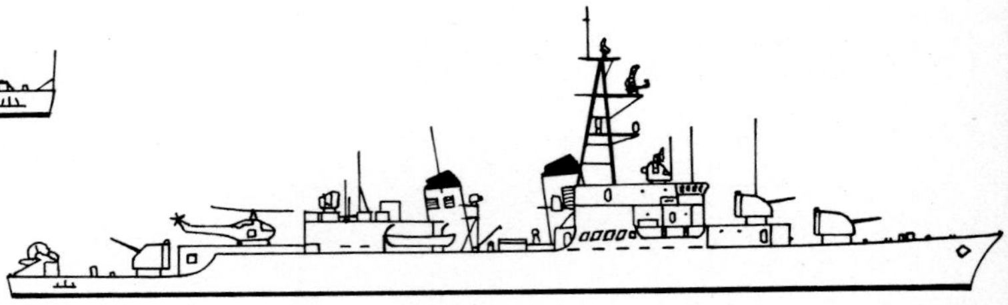

"MOD OQUENDO" Class

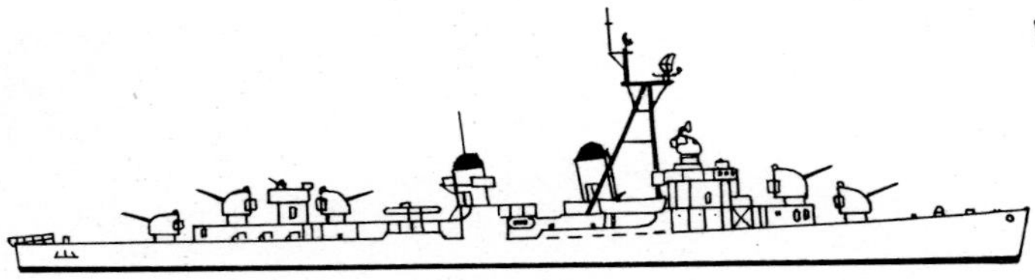

ALM. FERRANDIZ, LEPANTO and VALDES

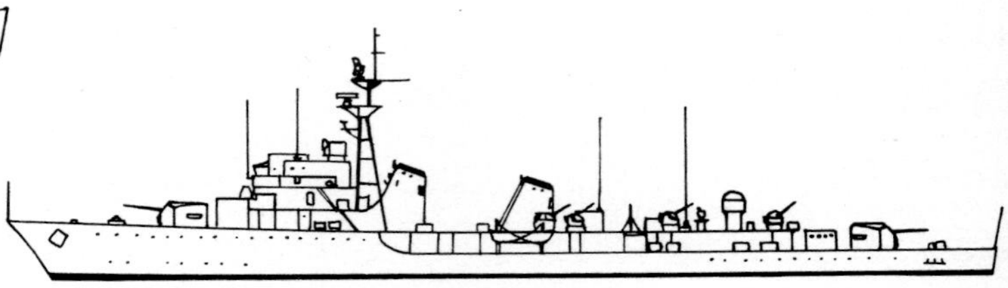

OQUENDO

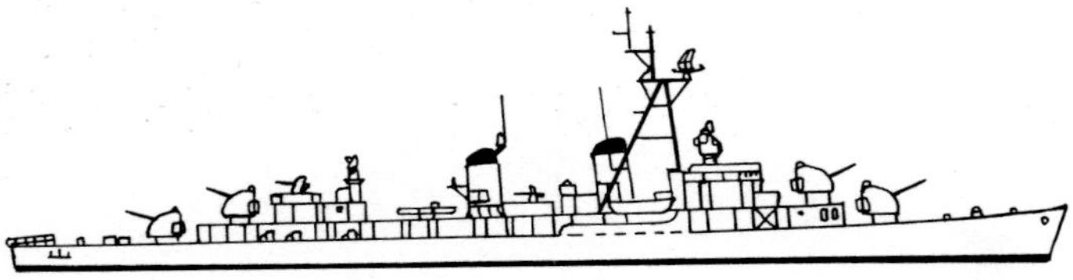

ALCALA GALIANO and JORGE JUAN

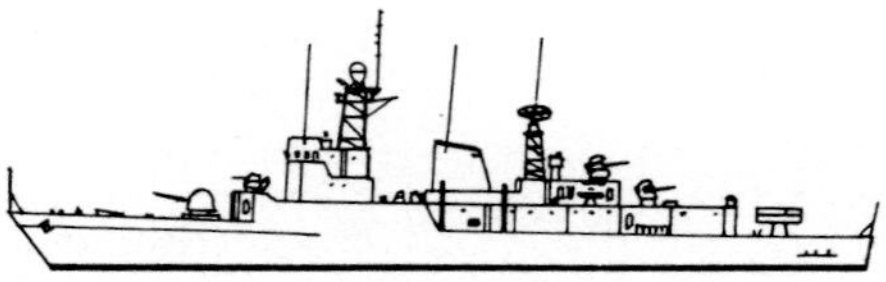

"F 80" Class

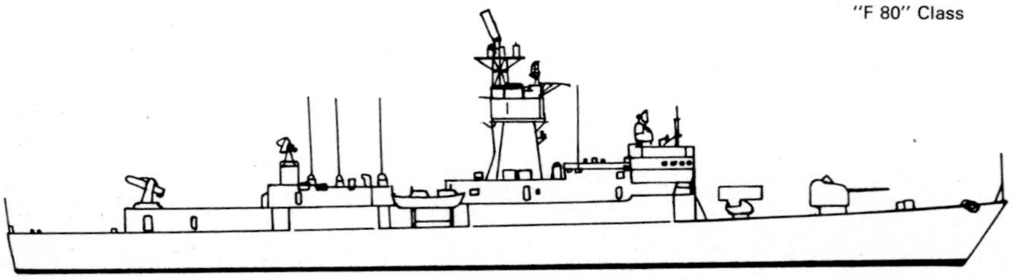

"F 70" ("BALEARES") Class

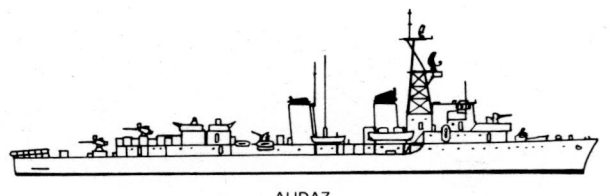

AUDAZ

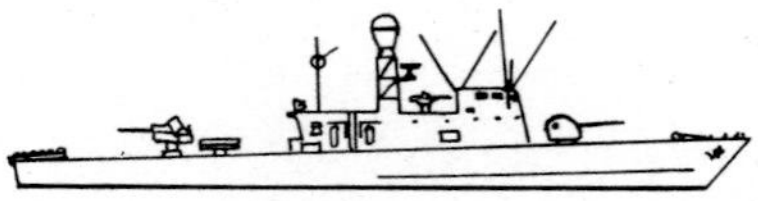

"P 00" Class

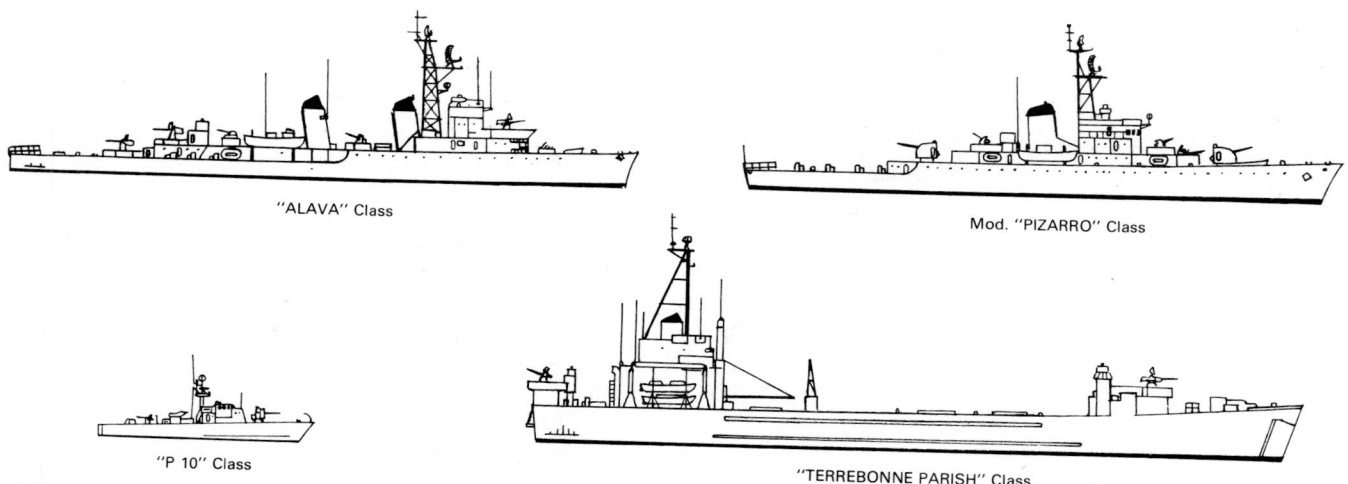

"ALAVA" Class

Mod. "PIZARRO" Class

"P 10" Class

"TERREBONNE PARISH" Class

HELICOPTER CARRIER

ALMIRANTE CARRERO

The future design of this ship, the eventual successor to *Dedalo,* is still in the planning stage and no definite decision has yet been reached.

1 Ex-US "INDEPENDENCE" CLASS (CVL)

Name		No.	Builders	Laid down	Launched	Commissioned
DÉDALO (ex-USS *Cabot*, AVT 3, ex-CVL 28, ex-*Wilmington, CL 79*)		PH 01	New York Shipbuilding Corporation	16 Aug 1942	4 Apr 1943	24 July 1943

Displacement, tons: 13 000 standard; 16 416 full load
Length, feet (metres): 600·0 *(182·8)* wl; 623·0 *(189·9)* oa
Beam, feet (metres): 71·5 *(21·8)* hull
Width, feet (metres): 109·0 *(33·2)*
Draught, feet (metres): 26·0 *(7·9)*
Aircraft: 8 Harriers (6 AV-8A, 2 TAV-8A)
  20 helicopters (ASW/Sea Kings—Combat/Huey Cobras—
  Landings/specially embarked S55s or Bell 212s)
Guns: 26—40 mm (2 quadruple, 9 twin)
Armour: 2 to 5 in sides; 2 to 3 in deck
Main engines: GE geared turbines; 4 shafts; 100 000 shp
Boilers: 4 Babcock & Wilcox
Speed, knots: 32
Range, miles: 7 200 at 15 knots
Oil fuel, tons: 1 800
Complement: 1 112 (without Air Groups)

Completed as an aircraft carrier from the hull of a "Cleveland" class cruiser. Originally carried over 40 aircraft. Converted with strengthened flight and hangar decks, large port side catapult, revised magazine arrangements, new electronic gear, with stability corrected to offset the added top-weight. Hangar capacity altered to take 20 aircraft. Flight deck: 545 × 108 feet *(166·1 × 32·9 metres)*.
Reactivated and modernised at Philadelphia Naval Shipyard, where she was transferred to Spain on 30 Aug 1967, on loan for five years. Purchased Dec 1973. Fleet flagship.

Radar: Air search: SPS 6 and SPS 40 (SPS 52B to be fitted 12/1976)
Heightfinder: SPS 8
Tactical: SPS 10
Fire control: 4 Sets
Tacan

DÉDALO

1974, Michael D. J. Lennon

DÉDALO

1974, Michael D. J. Lennon

DESTROYERS

5 "D 60" CLASS (Ex-US "GEARING" FRAM I CLASS)

Name	No.	Builders	Laid down	Launched	Commissioned
BLAS DE LEZO (ex-USS *Noa, DD 841*)	D 65	Bath Iron Works Corpn	1945	30 July 1945	2 Nov 1945
CHURRUCA (ex-USS *Eugene A. Greene, DD 711*)	D 61	Federal SB & DD Co.	1944	18 Mar 1945	8 June 1945
GRAVINA (ex-USS *Furse, DD 882*)	D 62	Consolidated Steel Corpn	1944	9 Mar 1945	10 July 1945
LANGARA (ex-USS *Leary, DD 879*)	D 64	Consolidated Steel Corpn	1944	20 Jan 1945	7 May 1945
MENDEZ NUÑEZ (ex-USS *O'Hare, DD 889*)	D 63	Consolidated Steel Corpn	1945	22 June1945	29 Nov 1945

Displacement, tons: 2 425 standard; 3 480 full load
Length, feet (metres): 390·5 *(119·0)* oa
Beam, feet (metres): 40·9 *(12·4)*
Draught, feet (metres): 19 *(5·8)*
Guns: 4—5 in *(127 mm)* 38 cal (twin)
A/S weapons: 1 Asroc launcher; 2 Triple Mk 32 tubes; Facilities for Hughes 369 HM helicopter
Main engines: 2 geared turbines (GE or Westinghouse) 60 000 shp; 2 shafts
Boilers: 4 Babcock and Wilcox
Speed, knots: 34
Fuel, tons: 650
Range, miles: 4 800 at 15 knots (economical)
Complement: 264 (17 officers, 247 ratings)

Radar: Air Search: D61 and 62, SPS 40—remainder, SPS 37; Surface Search: SPS 10; Fire Control: Mk 37.

Refits: The first pair were refitted at El Ferrol on transfer. The remainder arrived at El Ferrol on July 23 1974 after refit in the USA.

CHURRUCA

1974, Spanish Navy

Sonar: SQS 23 (hull mounted).

Transfers: All finally purchased 1975.

2 "MODIFIED OQUENDO" CLASS

Name	No.	Builders	Laid down	Launched	Commissioned
MARQUÉS DE LA ENSENADA	D 43	Ferrol	4 Sep 1951	15 July 1959	10 Sep 1970
ROGER DE LAURIA	D 42	Ferrol	4 Sep 1951	12 Nov 1958	30 May 1969

Displacement, tons: 3 370 standard; 3 785 full load
Length, feet (metres): 391·5 *(119·3)*
Beam, feet (metres): 42·7 *(13·0)*
Draught, feet (metres): 18·4 *(5·6)*
Aircraft: 1 Hughes 369 HM ASW helicopter
Guns: 6—5 in *(127 mm)* 38 cal (3 twin)
A/S weapons: 2 triple Mk 32 tubes for Mk 44 A/S torpedoes
Torpedo tubes: 2—21 in *(533 mm)* fixed single Mk 25 tubes for Mk 37 torpedoes
Main engines: 2 Rateau-Bretagne geared turbines; 2 shafts; 60 000 shp
Boilers: 3 three-drum type
Speed, knots: 31
Oil fuel, tons: 673
Range, miles: 4 500 at 15 knots
Complement: 318 (20 officers, 298 men)

Ordered in 1948. Originally of the same design as *Oquendo*. Towed to Cartegena for reconstruction to a new design. *Roger de Lauria* was re-launched after being lengthened and widened on 29 Aug 1967 and *Marqués de la Ensenada* on 2 Mar 1968. Weapons and electronics identical to Gearing Fram II.

Radar: Search: SPS 40.
Tactical: SPS 10.
Fire Control: One Mk 37 and one Mk 56.

Sonar: One hull mounted, probably SQS 29; one VDS, probably SQA 10.

ROGER DE LAURIA

8/1973, Commander Aldo Fraccaroli

1 "OQUENDO" CLASS

Name	No.	Builders	Laid down	Launched	Commissioned
OQUENDO	D 41	Ferrol	15 June 1951	5 Sep 1956	13 Sep 1960

Displacement, tons: 2 582 standard; 3 005 full load
Length, feet (metres): 382 *(116·4)*
Beam, feet (metres): 36·5 *(11·1)*
Draught, feet (metres): 12·5 *(3·8)*
Guns: 4—4·7 *(120 mm)* 50 cal (2 twin); 6—40 mm, 70 cal (single)
A/S weapons: 2 Hedgehogs
Torpedo tubes: 2 Mk 4 with 3 Mk 32 homing torpedoes each
Main engines: 2 Rateau-Bretagne geared turbines; 2 shafts; 60 000 shp
Boilers: 3 three-drum type
Speed, knots: 32·4
Oil fuel, tons: 659
Range, miles: 5 000 at 15 knots
Complement: 250 (17 officers, 233 men)

Ordered in 1947. Initially completed on 13 Sep 1960. Completed modernisation on 22 April 1963.

Construction: Designed as a conventional destroyer but modified during construction. Seven 21-inch torpedo tubes and two depth charge throwers were replaced by different antisubmarine weapons.

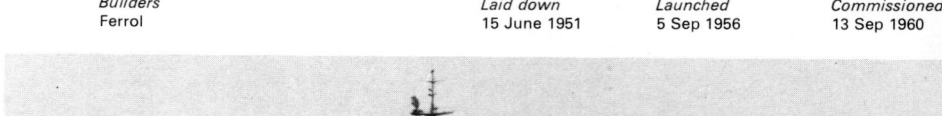

OQUENDO

1974, Spanish Navy

Radar: Search: British 293 type.
Air Search: Marconi SNW 10.
Nav: 1 set.
Fire Control: British type 275 on Mark 6 DCT and British Type 262 on CRBFD.

5 "D 20" CLASS (Ex-US "FLETCHER" CLASS)

Name	No.	Builders	Laid down	Launched	Commissioned
ALCALA GALIANO (ex-USS *Jarvis*, DD 799)	D 24	Todd Pacific Shipyards	7 June1943	14 Feb 1944	3 June 1944
ALMIRANTE FERRANDIZ (ex-USS *David W. Taylor*, DD 551)	D 22	Gulf SB Corpn, Chickasaw, Ala	12 June1941	4 July 1942	18 Sep 1943
ALMIRANTE VALDES (ex-USS *Converse*, DD 509)	D 23	Bath Iron Works Corp, Maine	23 Feb 1942	30 Aug 1942	8 June 1943
JORGE JUAN (ex-USS *McGowan*, DD 678)	D 25	Federal SB & DD Co	May 1943	14 Nov 1943	20 Dec 1943
LEPANTO (ex-USS *Capps*, DD 550)	D 21	Gulf SB Corpn, Chickasaw, Ala.	12 June1941	31 May 1942	23 June 1943

Displacement, tons: 2 080 standard; 2 750 normal; 3 050 full load
Length, feet (metres): 376·5 *(114·8)* oa
Beam, feet (metres): 39·5 *(12·0)*
Draught, feet (metres): 18·0 *(5·5)*
Guns: D21, D22: 5—5 in *(127 mm)* 38 cal; Others: 4—5 in *(127 mm)* single
D21, D22: 6—40 mm, 60 cal, (3 twin); 6—20 mm, 70 cal, (single); Others: 6—3 in *(76 mm)* 50 cal, (3 twin)
A/S weapons: 2 Hedgehogs; 6 DCT in D21 and D22, 4 in D23; 2 DC racks in D21, D22, 1 in others
Torpedo tubes: 3—21 in *(533 mm)* in D 21, 22 and 23 only
Torpedo racks: 2 side launching Mk 4 each with 3 Mk 32 A/S torpedoes
Main engines: Geared turbines; Westinghouse in D21, D22, GE in others; 2 shafts; 60 000 shp
Boilers: 4 Babcock & Wilcox
Speed, knots: 35
Oil fuel, tons: 650
Range, miles: 5 000 at 15 knots
Complement: 290 (17 officers, 273 men)

Lepanto, and *Almirante Ferrandiz*, were reconditioned at San Francisco, Cal, and there turned over to the Spanish Navy on 15 May 1957, sailing for Spain on 1 July 1957. *Valdes* was transferred at Philadelphia on 1 July 1959, *Jorge Juan*, was transferred at Barcelona on 1 Dec 1960 and *Alcala Galiano*, at Philadelphia on 3 Nov 1960, both being of the later "Fletcher" class. Modernisation of A/S equipment is planned. All purchased from US on 1 Oct 1972.

Radar: Search: SPS 6C.
Tactical: SPS 10.
Fire Control: D 23, 24 and 25—Mk 37 and Mk 56, 2 Mk 63 for 3 inch guns; D 21 and 22—Mk 37.

Sonar: One hull mounted set. SQS-29.

ALMIRANTE VALDES

1974, Wright and Logan

FRIGATES

5 "F 90" CLASS (NEW CONSTRUCTION)

This is a projected class of frigates, similar to the USN "Oliver Hazard Perry" class, planned to be built at El Ferrol. Reported as a fully-automated class with possibility of Westinghouse-Canada VDS and of Elettronica-San Giorgio ECM.

4 + 4 + 2 "F 80" CLASS (NEW CONSTRUCTION)

Name	No.	Builders	Laid down	Launched	Commissioned
DESCUBIERTA	F 81	Bazán, Cartagena	16 Nov 1974	8 July 1975	1976
DIANA	F 82	Bazán, Cartagena	8 July 1975	26 Jan 1976	—
—	F 83	Bazán, Cartagena	—	—	—
—	F 84	Bazán, Cartagena	—	—	—
—	F 85	Bazán, Cartagena	—	—	—

Displacement, tons: 1 200 standard; 1 400 full load
Dimensions, feet (metres): 291·3 × 34 × 11·5 *(88·8 × 10·5 × 3·5)*
Missiles: 1 Octuple Seasparrow mounting (16 reloads) (see note)
Guns: 1—3 in *(76 mm)* 62 cal Oto Melara; 2—40 mm 70 cal (singles); 1 or 2 Meroka 20 mm 120 cal (6 barrels non-rotating)
A/S weapons: 1—375 mm Bofors twin-barrelled rocket launcher
Torpedo tubes: 6 (2 triple) Mk 32 for Mk 44 torpedoes
Main engines: 4 MTU-Bazan 16V956 diesels; 16 000 bhp; 2 shafts; cp propellers
Speed, knots: 27
Complement: approx 100

Similar to the Portuguese "João Coutinho" class being built by Bazán with modifications to the armament and main engines. Officially rated as corvettes. Reported as designed to carry 30 marines.

Class: Four were ordered from Bazán, Cartagena in 1973. Approval for four more received whilst two more are planned.

Electronics: ECM probably Elettronica de San Georgio co-produced in Spain.

Missiles: Selenia system (Albatros) for Seasparrow. This will be built partly in Spain. SSMs will probably be fitted (Exocet or Harpoon).

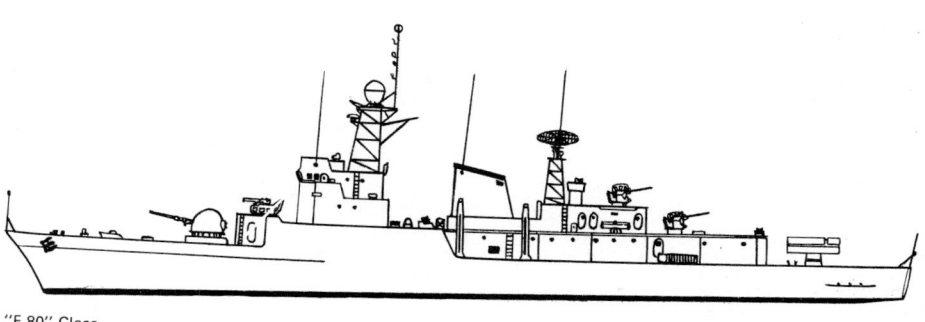

"F 80" Class

1974

Radar: Search and fire control: 1 Hollandse Signaal M 22.
Air Search: 1 Hollandse Signaal LW-04.
Navigation: 1 set.

Sonar: Possibly Raytheon.

5 "BALEARES (F 70)" CLASS

Name	No.
ANDALUCIA	F 72
ASTURIAS	F 74
BALEARES	F 71
CATALUÑA	F 73
EXTREMADURA	F 75

Builders	Laid down	Launched	Commissioned
Empresa Nacional Bazán, El Ferrol	2 July 1969	30 Mar 1971	23 May 1974
Empresa Nacional Bazán, El Ferrol	30 Mar 1971	13 May 1972	2 Dec 1975
Empresa Nacional Bazán, El Ferrol	31 Oct 1968	20 Aug 1970	24 Sep 1973
Empresa Nacional Bazán, El Ferrol	20 Aug 1970	3 Nov 1971	9 Dec 1974
Empresa Nacional Bazán, El Ferrol	3 Nov 1971	21 Nov 1972	1976

Displacement, tons: 3 000 standard; 4 177 full load
Length, feet (metres): 415·0 *(126·5)* pp; 438·0 *(133·5)* oa
Beam, feet (metres): 46·9 *(14·3)*
Draught, feet (metres): 25·9 *(7·9)*
Missile launchers: 1 single for Standard missiles
Guns: 1—5 in *(127 mm)* 54 cal Mk 42
A/S weapons: 1 eight-tube ASROC launcher
Torpedo tubes: 4 Mk 32 for Mk 44 torpedoes; 2 Mk 25 for Mk 37 torpedoes (stern)
Main engines: 1 set geared turbines; 1 shaft; 35 000 shp
Boilers: 2 high pressure V2M type; 1 200 psi *(84·4 kg/cm²)*
Speed, knots: 28
Range: Over 4 000 miles at 20 knots
Complement: 256 (15 officers, 241 men)

In June 1966 Spain and USA signed an agreement for the construction of five frigates by Empresa Nacional Bazán at El Ferrol with technical and material assistance by USA. Generally similar in appearance to the US escort ships of the "Knox" class but with modified weapons system and other characteristics to meet the requirements of the Spanish Navy. Equipped with weapons and electronic equipment furnished by USA. 2 or 3 more might be built before the "F 90" class.

Anti-Submarine: 8 Reloads carried for ASROC.

Gunnery: 600—5 inch rounds carried

Missile system: Mk 22 launcher with stowage for 16 missiles. Single director with two lines of fire against different targets with MR68 operating.

Radar: Search: SPS 52 (3D).
Tactical: SPS 10.
Fire control: SPS 51 continuous wave for missiles; Mk 68 for guns with continuous wave injection for limited use with missiles.

Torpedoes and tubes: All are fitted internally. Total of 41 torpedoes carried.

Sonar: SQS 23 bow mounted; SQS 35 VDS.

ANDALUCIA (firing Asroc) *1974, J. Taibo*

CATALUÑA *9/1975, Dr Giorgio Arra*

1 "AUDAZ" CLASS

Name	No.
INTRÉPIDO	D 38

Builders	Laid down	Launched	Commissioned
Ferrol	14 July 1945	15 Feb 1961	25 Mar 1965

Displacement, tons: 1 227 standard; 1 550 full load
Length, feet (metres): 295·2 *(90·0)* pp; 308·2 *(94·0)* oa
Beam, feet (metres): 30·5 *(9·3)*
Draught, feet (metres): 17·1 *(5·2)*
Guns: 2—3 in *(76 mm)* 50 cal; 2—40 mm 70 cal
A/S weapons: 2 hedgehogs; 8 mortars; 2 DC racks
Torpedo tubes: 2 side launching for Mk 32 A/S torpedoes (6 torpedoes)
Main engines: Rateau-Bretagne geared turbines; 2 shafts; 28 000 shp
Boilers: 2 La Seine 3-drum type
Speed, knots: 32
Oil fuel, tons: 290
Range, miles: 3 800 at 15 knots, 900 at 32 knots
Complement: 199 (13 officers, 186 men)

Based on the French "Le Fier" design. Allocated D Pennant number in 1961.

Engineering: The boilers are in two compartments separated by the engine rooms.

Radar: Surface search, SPS 5B.
Air search: MLA-1B.
Fire control: one Mk 63.

Sonar: One hull mounted-set.

INTRÉPIDO *1969, Spanish Navy*

2 "ALAVA" CLASS

Name	No.	Builders	Laid down	Launched	Commissioned
ALAVA	D 52 (ex-23)	Bazán, Cartagena	21 Dec 1944	19 May 1947	21 Dec 1950
LINIERS	D 51 (ex-21)	Bazán, Cartagena	1 Jan 1945	1 May 1946	27 Jan 1951

Displacement, tons: 1 842 standard; 2 287 full load
Length, feet (metres): 336·3 (102·5)
Beam, feet (metres): 31·5 (9·6)
Draught, feet (metres): 19·7 (6·0)
Guns: 3—3 in (76 mm) 50 cal, Mk 22; 3—40 mm, 70 cal
A/S weapons: 2 Hedgehogs; 8 DC mortars; 2 DC racks
Torpedo racks: 2 side launching for Mk 32 A/S torpedoes (6 torpedoes)
Main engines: Parsons geared turbines; 2 shafts; 31 500 shp
Boilers: 4 Yarrow 3-drum type
Speed, knots: 29
Oil fuel, tons: 370
Range, miles: 4 100 at 15 knots
Complement: 222 (15 officers, 207 men)

Ordered in 1936, but construction was held up by the Civil War. After being resumed in 1940, but restarted at Empresa Nacional Bazán in 1944.

Radar: Air search: MLA 1B. One surface-search set.
Fire control: 2-Mk 63.

Sonar: One hull-mounted set, probably SQS-4.

ALAVA   1974, Spanish Navy

2 MODERNISED "PIZARRO" CLASS

Name	No.	Builders	Laid down	Launched	Commissioned
LEGAZPI	F 42	Ferrol	1943	8 Aug 1944	8 Aug 1951
VICENTE YAÑEZ PINZON	F 41	Ferrol	1943	3 Aug 1944	5 Aug 1949

Displacement, tons: 1 924 standard; 2 228 full load
Length, feet (metres): 279·0 (85·0) pp; 312·5 (95·3) oa
Beam, feet (metres): 39·5 (12·0)
Draught, feet (metres): 17·7 (5·4)
Guns: 2—5 in (127 mm) 38 cal; 4—40 mm, 70 cal
A/S weapons: 2 Hedgehogs; 8 mortars; 2 racks
Torpedo racks: 2 side launching for Mk 32 torpedoes
Main engines: 2 sets Parsons geared turbines; 2 shafts; 6 000 shp
Boilers: 2 Yarrow type
Speed, knots: 18·5
Range, miles: 3 000 at 15 knots
Oil fuel, tons: 390
Complement: 255 (16 officers, 239 men)

Originally designed to carry 30 mines. Completed modernisation on 14 Jan and 25 Mar 1960 respectively.

Radar: Surface search: SPS 5B.
Air Search: MLA-1B.
Fire Control: Mk 52.

VICENTE YAÑEZ PINZON   1974, Spanish Navy

1 "JUPITER" CLASS

Name	No.	Builders	Laid down	Launched	Commissioned
VULCANO	F 12	Sociedad Española de Construccion Naval, El Ferrol	—	12 Oct 1935	1937

Displacement, tons: 2 103 standard; 2 360 full load
Length, feet (metres): 302·8 (92·3) pp; 328·1 (100·0) oa
Beam, feet (metres): 41·5 (12·6)
Draught, feet (metres): 11·5 (3·5)
Guns: 4—3 in (76 mm) Mk 26 (single); 4—40 mm, 70 cal
A/S weapons: 2 Hedgehogs; 8 mortars; DC racks
Mines: 238
Main engines: 2 sets Parsons geared turbines; 2 shafts; 5 000 shp
Boilers: 2 Yarrow type
Speed, knots: 17·4
Oil fuel, tons: 340
Range, miles: 5 700 at 12 knots
Complement: 255 (16 officers, 239 men)

Vulcano completed modernisation on 28 Feb 1961. Allocated F pennant number in 1961.

Radar: Air Search: MLA-IB.
Fire Control: MK 51.
Tactical: SG/6B.

VULCANO   1971, Spanish Navy

4 "ATREVIDA - F 60" CLASS

Name	No.	Builders	Laid down	Launched	Commissioned
ATREVIDA	F 61	Bazán, Cartagena	26 June1950	2 Dec 1952	19 Aug 1954
NAUTILUS	F 64	Bazán, Cadiz	27 July 1953	23 Aug 1956	1957
PRINCESA	F 62	Bazán, Cartagena	18 Mar 1953	31 Mar 1956	1957
VILLA DE BILBAO	F 65	Bazán, Cadiz	18 Mar 1953	19 Feb 1958	1959

Displacement, tons: 1 031 standard; 1 135 full load
Length, feet (metres): 247·8 (75·5) oa
Beam, feet (metres): 33·5 (10·2)
Draught, feet (metres): 9·8 (3·0)
Guns: 1—3 in (76 mm) 50 cal; 3—40 mm, 70 cal
A/S weapons: 2 Hedgehogs; 8 mortars; 2 DC racks
Mines: 20 can be carried
Main engines: Sulzer diesels; 2 shafts; 3 000 bhp
Speed, knots: 18·5
Oil fuel, tons: 100
Range, miles: 8 000 at 10 knots
Complement: 132 (9 officers, 123 men)

All have been modernised since 1959. No funnel, the diesel exhaust being on the starboard side waterline. Allocated F pennant numbers in 1961.

Modernisation: Completed: *Atrevida* 14 June 1960; *Nautilus* 15 Dec 1959; *Princesa* 3 Oct 1959; *Villa de Bilbao* 2 July 1960.

Radar: Modified SPS-5B combined air/surface search.

PRINCESA   *1974, Spanish Navy*

SUBMARINES

2 "S 70" CLASS (FRENCH "AGOSTA" CLASS)

S 71   S 72

Displacement, tons: 1 450 surfaced; 1 725 dived
Dimensions, feet (metres): 221·7 × 22·3 × 17·7 (67·6 × 6·8 × 5·4)
Tubes: 4—21·7 in (550 mm) (16 reloads)
Main machinery: Diesel-electric; 2 diesels; 3 600 hp; 1 Main motor; 6 400 hp; 1 cruising motor; 1 shaft
Speed, knots: 12 surfaced; 20 dived
Range, miles: 9 000 at 9 knots (snorting); 350 at 3·5 knots (dived)
Endurance: 45 days
Complement: 50

Ordered April 1974. To be built by Bazán Cartagena with some French advice. Both laid down 1975, and therefore, probably not operational until 1979. Two more orders are under consideration.

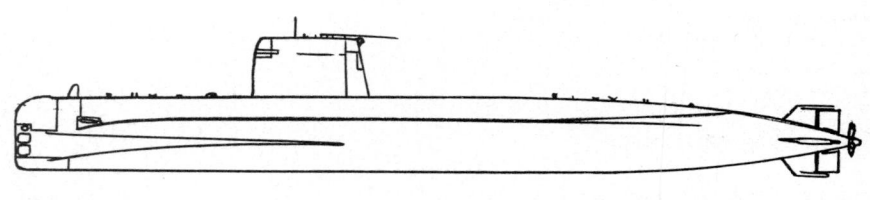

"S 70" Class   1974

3 "S 30" CLASS (Ex-US GUPPY IIA TYPE)

Name	No.	Builders	Laid down	Launched	Commissioned
ISAAC PERAL (ex-USS *Ronquil, SS 396*)	S 32	Portsmouth Navy Yard	9 Sep 1943	27 Jan 1944	22 April 1944
NARCISO MONTURIOL (ex-USS *Picuda, SS 382*)	S 33	Portsmouth Navy Yard	15 Mar 1943	12 July 1943	16 Oct 1943
COSME GARCIA (ex-USS *Bang, SS 385*)	S 34	Portsmouth Navy Yard	30 April1943	30 Aug 1943	4 Dec 1943

Displacement, tons: 1 840 surfaced; 2 445 dived
Length, feet (metres): 306·0 (93·3) oa
Beam, feet (metres): 27·0 (8·2)
Draught, feet (metres): 17·0 (5·2)
Torpedo tubes: 10—21 in (533 mm) 6 bow, 4 stern
Main machinery: 3 Fairbanks-Morse diesels; total 4 800 bhp; 2 shafts; 2 Elliot electric motors; 5 400 shp
Speed, knots: 18 surfaced; 15 dived
Range, miles: 12 000 at 10 knots
Complement: 74

Built by Portsmouth Navy Yard. Transferred to Spain on 1 July 1971 (*Ronquil*) 1 Oct 1972 (*Bang* and *Picuda*). All finally purchased 18 Nov 1974. *Narciso Monturiol* had mechanical defects in 1975 which resulted in *Almirante Garcia de los Reyes* being retained in service with the former's crew. These defects may result in *Narciso Monturiol* being paid off.

Appearance: S 33 has stepped section at forward end of fin.

NARCISO MONTURIOL   *1974, Spanish Navy*

COSME GARCIA (PERAL similar)   *1973, J. Taibo*

4 "S 60" CLASS (FRENCH "DAPHNE" CLASS)

Name	No.	Builders	Laid down	Launched	Commissioned
DELFIN	S 61	E. N. Bazán, Cartagena	13 Aug 1968	25 Mar 1972	3 May 1973
TONINA	S 62	E. N. Bazán, Cartagena	1969	3 Oct 1972	10 July 1973
MARSOPA	S 63	E. N. Bazán, Cartagena	1971	15 Mar 1974	12 April 1975
NARVAL	S 64	E. N. Bazán, Cartagena	1971	14 Dec 1974	22 Nov 1975

Displacement, tons: 870 surfaced; 1 040 dived
Length, feet (metres): 189·6 *(57·8)*
Beam, feet (metres): 22·3 *(6·8)*
Draught, feet (metres): 15·1 *(4·6)*
Tubes: 12—21·7 in *(550 mm)* (8 bow, 4 stern)
Main machinery: SEMT-Pielstick diesel-electric; 1 300 bhp surfaced; 1 600 hp dived; 2 shafts
Speed, knots: 16 surfaced and dived
Range, miles: 4 500 at 5 knots (snorting)
Complement: 47 (6 officers, 41 men)

Basically similar to the French "Daphne" class and built with extensive French assistance in the Cartagena Yard.

Radar: Thompson CSF "Calypso II" plus ECM.

Sonar: Active, DUUA 1; Passive with rangefinding, DSUV.

DELFIN

1973, J. Taibo

2 "TIBURON" CLASS

SA 51   SA 52

Displacement, tons: 78 surfaced; 81 dived
Length, feet (metres): 70·5 *(21·5)*
Beam, feet (metres): 9 *(2·7)*
Draught, feet (metres): 9 *(2·7)*
Torpedo tubes: 2—21 in *(533 mm)*
Main engines: Pegaso diesels; 400 hp. Electric motors; 400 hp
Speed, knots: 10 surfaced; 14·5 dived
Range, miles: 2 000 at 6 knots (surfaced); 150 at 7 knots (dived)
Complement: 8

Engineering: The diesels were built by ENASA (formerly Hispano-Suiza) Barcelona, 200 hp each at 2 000 rpm, with reduction gear on the single screw disposed in a nozzle in continuation of the conic after hull.

Launched in 1958. Originally rated as *Submarinos Experimentales,* but in 1963 designated Assault Submarines with "SA" numbers.

1 Ex-US "BALAO" CLASS

Name	No.	Builders	Laid down	Launched	Commissioned
ALMIRANTE GARCIA DE LOS REYES (ex-USS *Kraken,* SS 370)	S 31	Manitowoc SB Co.	—	30 April 1944	8 Sep 1944

Displacement, tons: 1 880 surfaced; 2 160 dived
Dimensions, feet (metres): 311·5 × 27·2 × 17·2 *(95 × 8·3 × 5·2)*
Torpedo tubes: 10—(6—21 in *(533 mm)* and 4 for A/S torpedoes)
Main machinery: 4 diesels; 6 400 bhp; 2 main motors; 4 600 shp; 2 shafts
Speed, knots: 20 surfaced; 10 dived
Oil fuel, tons: 300
Range, miles: 12 000 at 10 knots (surfaced)
Complement: 80

Transferred 24 October 1959 after modernisation at Pearl Harbor. Although due to be paid off in 1975 retained in service (see note under "S 30" class).

ALMIRANTE GARCIA DE LOS REYES

1969, Spanish Navy

LIGHT FORCES

6 "LAZAGA (P-OO)" CLASS (LARGE PATROL CRAFT)

Name	No.	Builders	Commissioned
LAZAGA	P 01	Lürssen Vegesack	16 July 1975
ALSEDO	P 02	Bazán, La Carraca	Oct 1975
CADARSO	P 03	Bazán, La Carraca	Oct 1975
VILLAMIL	P 04	Bazán, La Carraca	Feb 1976
BONIFAZ	P 05	Bazán, La Carraca	Feb 1976
RECALDE	P 06	Bazán, La Carraca	Aug 1976

Displacement, tons: 400 full load
Dimensions, feet (metres): 190·2 × 24·9 × 8·5 *(58 × 7·6 × 2·6)*
Guns: 1—3 in 62 cal Oto Melara; 1—40 mm 70 cal; 2—20 mm
A/S weapons: DC racks
Torpedo tubes: 2 triple Mk 32 mountings
Main engines: 2 MTU-Bazan diesels; 9 000 bhp
Speed, knots: 29·5
Range, miles: 6 100 at 17 knots
Complement: 30

Ordered in 1972, primarily for Fishery Protection duties. Although all will be operated by the Navy half the cost is being borne by the Ministry of Commerce. *Lazaga* launched on 30 Sep 1974. She was steamed to Spain in April 1975 for equipping and arming. Launch dates—02 and 03, 8 Jan 1975; 04 and 05 24 May 1975; 06, 9 Nov 1975.

Missiles: Provision has been made for fitting four surface-to-surface missiles (Exocet or Harpoon), involving a change of gun armament.

Radar: Surface search and Navigation; Hollandse Signaal M-20 ECM and IFF

Fire Control: Optical director CSEE.

Sonar: One hull-mounted set.

LAZAGA

7/1975, Spanish Navy

6 "BARCELO (P 10)" CLASS (LARGE PATROL CRAFT)

Name	No.	Builders	Commissioned
BARCELO	P 11	Lürssen Vegesack	Feb 1976
LAYA	P 12	Bazán, La Carraca	Apr 1976
JAVIER QUIROGO	P 13	Bazán, La Carraca	Apr 1976
ORDÓÑEZ	P 14	Bazán, La Carraca	1976
ACEVEDO	P 15	Bazán, La Carraca	1976
CANDIDO PÉREZ	P 16	Bazán, La Carraca	1977

Displacement, tons: 139
Dimensions, feet (metres): 118·7 × 19 × 8·2 (36·2 × 5·8 × 2·5)
Guns: 1—40 mm; 2—20 mm
Speed, knots: 40; 20 cruising
Range, miles: 1 200 at 20 knots

Ordered 5 Dec 1973, the prototype, *Barcelo,* to be built by Lürssen, Vegesack with MTU engines. Laid down 1974 for launch in Nov 1975. *Laya* and *Javier Quiroga* launched 18 Dec 1975. All to be manned by the Navy although the cost is being borne by the Ministry of Commerce.

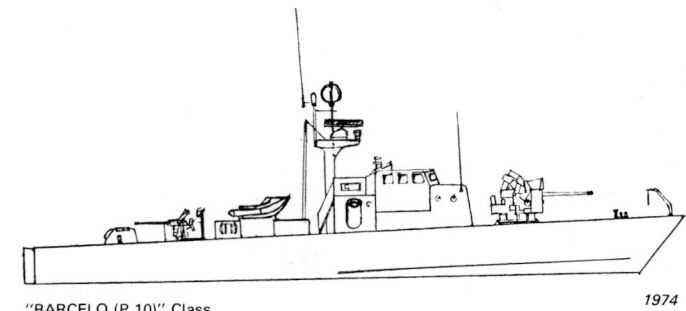

"BARCELO (P 10)" Class   1974

2 LÜRSSEN TYPE (FAST ATTACK CRAFT—TORPEDO)

Name	No.	Builders	Commissioned
—	LT 30	La Carraca, Cadiz	1956
—	LT 31	La Carraca, Cadiz	21 July 1956

Displacement, tons: 100 standard; 116 full load
Dimensions, feet (metres): 114 × 16·8 × 5 (34·8 × 5·1 × 1·5)
Gun: 1—20 mm
Tubes: 2—21 in
Main engines: 3 MTU diesels; 3 shafts; 7 500 bhp = 41 knots
Oil fuel, tons: 20
Range, miles: 650 at 30 knots
Complement: 26

Built to the design of Lürssens of Bremen. LT 32 of this class converted into target vessel for helicopters in Aug 1974, with sea-going capability at 12 knots.

Radar: Decca RM-914.

LT 31   1970, Spanish Navy

5 "LPI" CLASS (COASTAL PATROL CRAFT)

LPI 1   LPI 2   LPI 3   LPI 4   LPI 5

Displacement, tons: 25
Dimensions, feet (metres): 46 × 15·4 × 3·3 (14 × 4·7 × 1)
Guns: 2—7·62 mm

3 USCG 83 ft TYPE (COASTAL PATROL CRAFT)

Name	No.	Builders	Commissioned
—	LAS 10 (ex-*LAS 1*)	E. N. Bazán, Cadiz	1963
—	LAS 20 (ex-*LAS 2*)	E. N. Bazán, Cadiz	1963
—	LAS 30 (ex-*LAS 3*)	E. N. Bazán, Cadiz	1964

Displacement, tons: 49 standard; 63 full load
Dimensions, feet (metres): 78·0 pp; 83·3 oa × 16·1 × 6·6 (23·8; 25·4 × 4·9 × 2)
Guns: 1—20 mm; 2—7 mm (single)
A/S launchers: 2 Mousetrap Mk 20 (4 rockets each)
Main engines: 800 bhp = 15 knots
Complement: 15

Of wooden hull construction.

LAS 30   1974, Spanish Navy

3 "AGUILUCHO" CLASS (COASTAL PATROL CRAFT)

Name	No.	Builders	Commissioned
AGUILUCHO	—	J. Roberto Rodriguez e Hijos, Vigo	1973
GAVILAN I	—	J. Roberto Rodriguez e Hijos, Vigo	1975
GAVILAN II	—	J. Roberto Rodriguez e Hijos, Vigo	1976

Displacement, tons: 45
Dimensions, feet (metres): 85·5 oa × 16·7 × 4·3 (26·1 × 5·1 × 1·3)
Main engines: Diesels; 2 shafts; 2 750 bhp = 30 knots
Range, miles: 750 at 30 knots

Aguilucho launched 19 Feb 1973 for Coastguard duties. *Gavilan I* launched 22 July 1975. Transferred to Naval control.

2 FISHERY PROTECTION VESSELS

Name	No.	Builders	Commissioned
CENTINELA	W 33	Ferrol	1953
SERVIOLA	W 34	Ferrol	1953

Displacement, tons: 255 standard; 282 full load
Dimensions, feet (metres): 117·5 × 22·5 × 9·8 (36 × 6·8 × 3)
Guns: 2—37 mm
Main engines: 1 diesel; 430 bhp = 12 knots

Given pennant numbers as above in 1972.

SERVIOLA   1974, Spanish Navy

1 FISHERY PROTECTION VESSEL

SALVORA W 32

Displacement, tons: 180 standard; 275 full load
Dimensions, feet (metres): 107·0 × 20·5 × 9·0 *(31 × 6·1 × 2·5)*
Gun: 1—20 mm MG
Main engines: 1 Sulzer diesel; 400 bhp = 12 knots
Complement: 24

Purchased in Dec 1952.

Radar: Decca RM 914.

3 PATROL VESSELS

RR 19   RR 20   RR 29

Displacement, tons: 364 standard; 498 full load
Dimensions, feet (metres): 124·0 × 29·0 × 10·0 *(38 × 8·4 × 3)*
Guns: 1—1·5 in, 85 cal or 1—47 mm; 1—20 mm
Main engines: Triple expansion; 1 shaft; 800 ihp = 11·5 knots
Boilers: 1 cylindrical, (13 kg/cm)
Fuel, tons: 200 coal
Range, miles: 620 at 10 knots

Former tugs. All launched in 1941-42. Some have navigation radar.

10 PATROL LAUNCHES

V 4 Displacement: 65 tons. Speed: 9 knots
V 5 Displacement: 4·5 tons. Speed: 5 knots
V 6 Displacement: 42 tons. Guns: 2—20 mm. Speed: 19·2 knots
V 9 Displacement: 15·6 tons. Speed: 9 knots
V 10 Displacement: 11·6 tons. Speed: 9·5 knots
V 11 Displacement: 11·6 tons. Speed: 9·5 knots
V 17 Displacement: 110·9 tons. Gun: 1—20 mm. Speed: 10·5 knots
V 21 Displacement: 16 tons. Speed 17·6 knots

There is also **V 1**, yacht, ex-*Azor*. Coastal launches employed on surveillance and fishery protection duties. **V 4** is named *Alcatraz*.

GAVIOTA V 4

Of 104·2 tons. Taken over by Navy on 26 Nov 1970 being a confiscated smuggling craft.

CABO FRADERA

Of 28 tons with 1—7·62 mm gun.

CUSTOMS SERVICE

There are, in addition to the above, a large number of customs launches of similar size operating off the Spanish coast.

AMPHIBIOUS FORCES

1 Ex-US "CABILDO" CLASS (LSD)

Name	*No.*	*Builders*	*Commissioned*
GALICIA (ex-USS *San Marcos*, LSD 25)	TA 31	Philadelphia Navy Yard	1945

Displacement, tons: 4 790 standard; 9 375 full load
Dimensions, feet (metres): 475·4 oa × 72·6 × 18·0 *(139 × 21·9 × 4·9)*
Guns: 12—40 mm, 60 cal (2 quadruple, 2 twin)
Main engines: Geared turbines; 2 shafts; 7 000 shp = 15·4 knots
Boilers: 2
Range, miles: 8 000 at 15 knots
Complement: 265 (15 officers, 250 men)

Transferred to Spain on 1 July 1971. Fitted with helicopter platform. Can carry 3 LCUs or 18 LCMs. 1 347 tons of cargo or 100 2½ ton trucks or 27 M-48 tanks or 11 heavy helicopters. Accommodation for 137 troops (overnight) or 500 for short haul. Surface-search radar.

GALICIA

1972, Spanish Navy

1 Ex-US "HASKELL" CLASS (ATTACK TRANSPORT)

Name	*No.*	*Builders*	*Commissioned*
ARAGON (ex-USS *Noble*, APA 218)	TA 11	USA	1945

Displacement, tons: 6 720 light; 12 450 full load
Dimensions, feet (metres): 455 oa × 63·5 × 24 *(133 × 18·9 × 8·6)*
Guns: 12—40 mm 60 cal (1 quad, 4 twin)
Main engines: Geared turbines; 8 500 shp = 17 knots
Boilers: 2 Babcock & Wilcox
Range, miles: 14 700 at 16 knots

Former US Attack Transport, transferred at San Francisco on 19 Dec 1964. Can carry 1 190 men and 680 tons cargo (or 11 2½ ton trucks and 49 ¾ ton trucks). 24 landing craft.

Radar: Air Search SPS 6; surface search.

ARAGON

1971, Michael D. J. Lennon

1 Ex-US "ANDROMEDA" CLASS

Name	*No.*	*Builders*	*Commissioned*
CASTILLA (ex-USS *Achernar*, AKA 53)	TA 21	USA	1944

Displacement, tons: 7 430 light; 11 416 full load
Dimensions, feet (metres): 457·8 oa × 63 × 24 *(140 × 19·2 × 7·4)*
Guns: 1—5 in 38 cal; 8—40 mm 60 cal (twins)
Main engines: 2 GE geared turbines; 12 000 shp = 16 knots
Boilers: 2 Foster-Wheeler

Former US Attack Cargo Ship transferred at New York on 2 Feb 1965. Can carry 98 men, 6 M-48 tanks, 36 2½ ton trucks and 267 Jeeps. 24 landing craft.

Radar: Surface-search.

CASTILLA

1970, Spanish Navy

2 Ex-BRITISH LCT (4)

BDK 1 K 1 **BDK 2** K 2

Displacement, tons: 440 standard; 868 full load
Dimensions, feet (metres): 185·3 × 38·7 × 6·2 *(56·5 × 11·8 × 1·9)*
Guns: 2—20 mm (single)
Main engines: 2 Paxman diesels; 2 shafts; 920 bhp = 10 knots
Range, miles: 1 100 at 8 knots

Can carry 350 tons or 500 men.

3 Ex-US "TERREBONNE PARISH" CLASS (LST)

Name	No.	Builders	Commissioned
CONDE DE VENADITO	L 13	Bath Iron Works	12 Sep 1953
(ex-USS *Tom Green County, LST 1159*)			
MARTIN ALVAREZ	L 12	Christy Corpn	15 June 1954
(ex-USS *Wexford County, LST 1168*)			
VELASCO	L 11	Bath Iron Works	21 Nov 1952
(ex-USS *Terrebonne Parish, LST 1156*)			

Displacement, tons: 2 590 standard; 5 800 full load
Dimensions, feet (metres): 384·0 oa × 55·0 × 17·0 *(117·4 × 16·7 × 3·7)*
Guns: 6—3 in, 50 cal (3 twin, 2 forward, 1 aft)
Main engines: 4 GM diesels; 2 shafts; 6 000 bhp = 15 knots
Range, miles: 15 000 at 9 knots
Complement: 116 (troops 395)

LST 1156 and 1168 transferred on 29 Oct 1971, LST 1159 on 5 Jan 1972. Can carry 395 men, 10 M-48 tanks or 17 LVTP. 4 landing craft.

CONDE DE VENADITO   *1974, Spanish Navy*

2 Ex-US LSMs

LSM 1 (ex-USS *LSM 329*) L 01
LSM 2 (ex-USS *LSM 331*) L 02

Displacement, tons: 930 standard; 1 094 full load
Dimensions, feet (metres): 196·5 wl; 203·5 oa × 34·5 × 8·3 *(59·9; 62·1 × 10·5 × 2·5)*
Main engines: 2 diesels; 2 shafts; 3 600 bhp = 12·5 knots

Medium landing ships transferred at Bremerton, Washington, on 25 Mar 1960. In early 1976 both converted for use as alongside accommodation ships.

LSM 2   *1974, Spanish Navy*

3 SPANISH BUILT LCTs

Name	No.	Builders	Commissioned
BDK 3	K 3	Bazán, El Ferrol	15 June 1959
BDK 4	K 4	Bazán, El Ferrol	15 June 1959
BDK 5	K 5	Bazán, El Ferrol	15 June 1959

Displacement, tons: 902 full load
Dimensions, feet (metres): 186 × 38·4 × 6 *(56·6 × 11·6 × 1·7)*
Guns: 2—20 mm (singles)
Main engines: 2 M60 V8 AS diesels; 2 shafts; 1 000 hp = 8½ knots
Range, miles: 1 000 at 7 knots
Complement: Complement 20 (1 officer, 19 men)

All commissioned 15 June 1959. Can carry 300 tons or 400 men.

BDK 5   *1971, Spanish Navy*

3 EDIC TYPE (LCT)

Name	No.	Builders	Commissioned
BDK 6	K 6	Bazán, La Carraca	Dec 1966
BDK 7	K 7	Bazán, La Carraca	Dec 1966
BDK 8	K 8	Bazán, La Carraca	Dec 1966

Displacement, tons: 315 standard; 665 full load
Dimensions, feet (metres): 193·5 oa × 39·0 × 5·0 *(59 × 11·9 × 1·3)*
Guns: 1—20 mm; 2—12·7 mm MG
Main engines: 2 diesels; 2 shafts; 1 040 bhp = 9·5 knots
Range, miles: 1 500 at 9 knots

Landing craft of the French EDIC type built at La Carraca. Completed in Dec 1966.

6 SPANISH BUILT LCM (8) MODEL I

E 81   **E 82**   **E 83**   **E 84**   **E 85**   **E 86**

This new class was ordered from three Spanish yards in 1974. All commissioned in 1975.

Note: Total of landing craft (including those attached to *Aragón, Castilla, Galicia* and LSTs): 14 LCM (3) and (6), 43 LCVP, 21 LCP (L), 1 LCP (R), 2 LCU, 12 various.
All of US origin except 8 LCP (L), built at Cartagena.

MINE WARFARE FORCES

4 Ex-US "AGGRESSIVE" CLASS (MINESWEEPERS—OCEAN)

Name	No.	Builders	Commissioned
GUADALETE (ex-USS *Dynamic, MSO 432*)	M 41	USA	15 Dec 1953
GUADALMEDINA (ex-USS *Pivot, MSO 463*)	M 42	USA	12 July 1954
GUADALQUIVIR (ex-USS *Persistant, MSO 491*)	M 43	USA	3 Feb 1956
GUADIANA (ex-USS *Vigor, MSO 473*)	M 44	USA	8 Nov 1954

Displacement, tons: 665 standard; 750 full load
Dimensions, feet (metres): 165·0 wl; 172·0 oa × 36·0 × 13·6 *(52·3 × 10·4 × 4·2)*
Guns: 2—20 mm (twin)
Main engines: 4 Packard diesels; 2 shafts; controllable pitch propellers; 2 280 bhp = 15·5 knots
Range, miles: 3 000 at 10 knots
Complement: 71 (6 officers, 65 men)

The first three were transferred and commissioned on 1 July 1971. The fourth unit was delivered 4 April 1972. Surface search radar. VDS SQQ 14 with mine classification capability.

GUADALETE   *1973, J. Taibo*

12 "NALON" (M 20) CLASS (Ex-US AMS TYPE)
(MINESWEEPERS—COASTAL)

Name	No.	Builders	Commissioned
DUERO (ex-*Spoonbill, MSC 202*)	M 28	USA	1956
EBRO (ex-*MSC 269*)	M 26	Bellingham SY	1958
GENIL (ex-*MSC 279*)	M 31	USA	1958
JUCAR (ex-*MSC 220*)	M 23	USA	1956
LLOBREGAT (ex-*MSC 143*)	M 22	USA	1953
MIÑO (ex-*MSC 266*)	M 25	USA	1953
NALÓN (ex-*MSC 139*)	M 21	USA	1953
ODIEL (ex-*MSC 288*)	M 32	USA	1959
SIL (ex-*Redwing, MSC 200*)	M 29	USA	1956
TAJO (ex-*MSC 287*)	M 30	USA	1959
TURIA (ex-*MSC 130*)	M 27	USA	1953
ULLA (ex-*MSC 265*)	M 24	USA	1958

Displacement, tons: 355 standard; 384 full load
Dimensions, feet (metres): 138·0 pp; 144·0 oa × 27·2 × 8·0 *(41·5; 43 × 8 × 2·6)*
Guns: 2—20 mm (1 twin)
A/S weapons: 2 Mouse Trap Mk 20 rocket launchers
Main engines: 2 diesels; 2 shafts; 900 bhp = 14 knots
Oil fuel, tons: 30
Range, miles: 2 700 at 10 knots
Complement: 39

EBRO, Class B, small crane   *1974, Dr. Giorgio Arra*

Transferred from the USA, *Nalón* on 16 Feb 1954, *Llobregat* on 5 Nov 1954, *Turia* on 1 June 1955, *Jucar* on 22 June 1956, *Ulla* on 24 July 1956, *Miño* on 25 Oct 1956, *Sil* and *Duero* on 16 June 1959, *Ebro* on 19 Dec 1958, *Genil* on 11 Sep 1959, *Tajo* on 9 July 1959 and *Odiel* on 9 Oct 1959.

Two sub-types: (a) with derrick on mainmast: M 21, 22, 23, 24, 25, 27, 28, 29, (b) with no mainmast but crane abreast the funnel: M 26, 30, 31, 32.
Tactical radar of various types. AN/UQS-1 sonar.

ULLA, Class A, with mainmast   *1973, Dr. Giorgio Arra*

6 "GUADIARO" CLASS
(MINESWEEPERS—OCEAN AS PATROL VESSELS)

Name	No.	Builders	Commissioned
ALMANZORA	M 14	Cartagena	Nov 1954
EO	M 17	Cadiz	Mar 1955
EUME	M 13	Cartagena	Dec 1953
GUADALHORCE	M 16	Cartagena	Dec 1953
GUADIARO	M 11	Cartagena	Apr 1953
NAVIA	M 15	Cadiz	Mar 1955

Displacement, tons: 671 standard; 770 full load
Dimensions, feet (metres): 243·8 × 33·5 × 12·3 *(74·3 × 10·2 × 3·7)*
Guns: 2—20 mm
Main engines: Triple expansion and exhaust turbines; 2 shafts; 2 400 hp = 13 knots after modernisation
Boilers: 2 Yarrow
Oil fuel, tons: 90
Range, miles: 1 000 at 6 knots
Complement: 79

ALMANZORA   *1971, Cdr Aldo Fraccaroli*

Modernised in 1959-61. Currently employed on patrol duties. Will be paid off when replaced by "Lazaga" class.

Radar: Decca MTM 626 or RM 914.

SURVEY SHIPS

4 "CASTOR" CLASS

Name	No.	Builders	Commissioned
CASTOR	A 21	E. N. Bazán, La Carraca	10 Nov 1966
POLLUX	A 22	E. N. Bazán, La Carraca	6 Dec 1966
ANTARES	A 23	E. N. Bazán, La Carraca	21 Nov 1974
RIGEL	A 24	E. N. Bazán, La Carraca	21 Nov 1974

Displacement, tons: 327 standard; 383 full load
Dimensions, feet (metres): 111 pp; 125·9 oa × 24·9 × 8·9 *(33·8; 38·4 × 3·9 × 2·8)*
Main engines: 1 Sulzer 4TD-36 diesel; 720 hp = 11·7 knots
Range, miles: 3 620 at 8 knots
Complement: 39 (A 23 and 24) 37 (A 21 and 22)

Antares and *Rigel* ordered summer 1972, launched 1973. Fitted with Raydist, Omega and digital presentation of data.

CASTOR   *1974, Spanish Navy*

2 "MALASPINA" CLASS (OCEANOGRAPHIC SHIPS)

Name	No.	Builders	Commissioned
MALASPINA	A 31	E. N. Bazán, La Carraca	21 Feb 1975
TOFIÑO	A 32	E. N. Bazán, La Carraca	1 May 1975

Displacement, tons: 820 standard; 1 090 full load
Dimensions, feet (metres): 188·9 × 38·4 × 11·8 *(57·6 × 11·7 × 3·6)*
Guns: 2—20 mm (single)
Main engines: 2 diesels; 3 240 bhp; 2 VP propellers = 15 knots
Range, miles: 4 000 at 12 knots; 3 140 at 14·5 knots
Complement: 63 (9 officers, 54 men)

Malaspina laid down early 1973, launched 15 Aug 1973. *Tofiño* launched 22 Dec 1973. Both named after their immediate predecessors.

TOFIÑO   *1975, Royal Spanish Navy*

SERVICE FORCES

1 TRANSPORT

Name	No.	Builders	Commissioned
ALMIRANTE LOBO (ex-*Torrelaguna*)	A 41	Astilleros Echevarrieta, Cadiz	4 Oct 1954

Displacement, tons: 5 662 standard; 8 038 full load
Dimensions, feet (metres): 362·5 × 48·2 × 25·7 *(103 × 14·6 × 6·8)*
Gun: 1—1·5 in, 85 cal
Main engines: 1 triple expansion; 2 000 ihp = 12 knots

Ex-cargo vessel.

Radar: Navigation: Decca 12.

ALMIRANTE LOBO

1 REPLENISHMENT TANKER

Name	No.	Builders	Commissioned
TEIDE	BP 11	Factoria de Bazán, Cartagena	Oct 1956

Displacement, tons: 2 747 light; 8 030 full load
Oil capacity, tons: 5 350
Dimensions, feet (metres): 385·5 × 48·5 × 20·3 *(117·5 × 14·8 × 6·2)*
Gun: 1—4·1 in (not mounted)
Main engines: 2 diesels; 3 360 bhp = 12 knots

Ordered in December 1952. Laid down on 11 Nov 1954. Launched on 20 June 1955. Modernised in 1962 with refuelling at sea equipment.

Radar: Navigation: Decca TM 707.

TEIDE   *1968, Spanish Navy*

1 HARBOUR TANKER

PP 1

Displacement, tons: 470
Dimensions, feet (metres): 147·5 oa × 25 × 9·5 *(45 × 7·6 × 2·9)*
Main engines: Deutz diesel; 220 bhp = 10 knots
Complement: 12

Built at Santander and launched in 1939.

3 HARBOUR TANKERS

PP 3   PP 4   PP 5

Follow on class of harbour tankers.

9 HARBOUR TANKERS

PB 1, 2, 3, 4, 5, 6, 20, 21, 22

Small harbour tankers with capacity between 100 and 300 tons. All built by Bazán between 1960 and 1965.

1 SAIL TRAINING SHIP

Name	No.	Builders	Commissioned
JUAN SEBASTIAN DE ELCANO	—	Echevarrieta Yard, Cadiz	1928

Displacement, tons: 3 420 standard; 3 754 full load
Dimensions, feet (metres): 269·2 pp; 308·5 oa × 43 × 23 *(94·1 × 13·6 × 7)*
Guns: 2—37 mm
Main engines: 1 Sulzer diesel; 1 shaft; 1 500 bhp = 9·5 knots
Oil fuel, tons: 230
Endurance, miles: 10 000 at 9·5 knots
Complement: 224 + 80 cadets

Four masted top sail schooner—sister of Chilean *Esmeralda*. Named after the first circum-navigator of the world (1519-26) who succeeded to the command of the expedition led by Magellanas after the latter's death. Launched on 5 Mar 1927.

Radar: 2 Decca TM 626.

JUAN SEBASTIAN DE ELCANO   *1972, US Navy*

1 ROYAL YACHT

Name	No.	Builders	Commissioned
AZOR	—	E. N. Bazán, El Ferrol	20 July 1949

Displacement, tons: 442 standard; 486 full load
Dimensions, feet (metres): 153·0 × 25·2 × 12·5 *(47 × 7·7 × 3·8)*
Main engines: 2 diesels; 1 200 bhp = 12 knots
Range, miles: 4 000

Built as the Caudillo's yacht. Launched on 9 June 1949. Underwent an extensive refit, her hull being cut to admit an extension in length.

Radar: Decca TM 626.

AZOR   *1970, J. I. Taibo*

1 BOOM DEFENCE VESSEL

Name	No.	Builders	Commissioned
—	CR 1 (ex-G 6)	Penhoët, France	1955

Displacement, tons: 630 standard; 831 full load
Dimensions, feet (metres): 165·5 × 34 × 10·5 (44·5 × 10·2 × 3·2)
Guns: 1—40 mm; 4—20 mm (single)
Main engines: 2 diesels; electric drive; 1 shaft; 1 500 bhp = 12 knots
Range, miles: 5 200 at 12 knots

US off-shore order. Launched on 28 Sep 1954. Transferred from the US in 1955 under MDAP. Sister ship of French "Cigale" class.

PBP 1, 2 and 3

Gate Vessels.

PR 1-5

Net laying barges.

PRA 1-8

Tugs for PBPs and PRs.

1 OCEAN TUG

RA 3 ((ex-Metinda III)

Displacement, tons: 762 standard; 1 080 full load
Dimensions, feet (metres): 137 × 33·1 × 15·5 (41·8 × 10·1 × 4·5)
Main engines: Triple expansion; 12 knots

2 OCEAN TUGS

RA 1   RA 2

Displacement, tons: 757 standard; 1 039 full load
Dimensions, feet (metres): 184 × 33·5 × 12 (56·1 × 10·1 × 3·9)
Guns: 2—20 mm (singles)
Main engines: 2 Sulzer diesels; 3 200 bhp = 15 knots

Radar: Decca 12.

RA 2

1974, Reiner Nerlich

3 OCEAN TUGS

Name	No.	Builders	Commissioned
POSEIDON	BS 1	La Carraca	1963
—	RA 4	La Carraca	1963
—	RA 5	La Carraca	1963

Displacement, tons: 951 standard; 1 069 full load
Dimensions, feet (metres): 183·5 × 32·8 × 15·8 (55·9 × 10 × 4·5)
Main engines: 2 Sulzer diesels; 3 200 bhp = 15 knots

RA 6 was renumbered BS 1 when she became a frogman support ship, known as *Poseidon*.

Radar: Decca 707.

POSEIDON

1973, Dr. Giorgio Arra

6 COASTAL TUGS

Name	No.	Builders	Commissioned
—	RR 50	Cartagena	1963
—	RR 51	Cartegena	1963
—	RR 52	Cartagena	1963
—	RR 53	Cartagena	1967
—	RR 54	Cartagena	1967
—	RR 55	Cartagena	1967

Displacement, tons: 205 standard; 227 full load
Dimensions, feet (metres): 91·2 × 23 × 11 (27·8 × 7 × 3·4)
Main engines: Diesels; 1 shaft; 1 400 bhp (53 to 55), 800 bhp (50 to 52)

Radar: Pilot 7D 20 in RR 53, 54 and 55.

RR 53

1975, Dr. Giorgio Arra

18 HARBOUR TUGS

NOTE. 5 tug-launches of less than 50 tons:→ LR 47, 51, 67, 68, 69.

RP 1-12

Of 65 tons and 200 bhp (diesel). Commissioned 1965-67.

RP 40

Of 150 tons and 600 bhp (diesel). Commissioned 1961.

14 WATER CARRIERS

AB 1, 2, 3, 10, 17, 18

All of less than 400 tons. Harbour water boats with 200 tons or less capacity.

A1   A 2   A 6   A 8   A 9

A 1 and A 2 built in 1936, A 6 in 1949, A 8 in 1952, A 9 in 1963. Of 1 785 tons full load with 1 000 tons capacity. Ocean going.

A 7   A 10   A 11

Of 610 tons full load with 350 tons capacity. A 10 and 11, completed in 1963, A 7 completed 1949. Have radar Pilot 7 D 20. All oceangoing.

A 11

1973, Spanish Navy

9 TORPEDO RECOVERY CRAFT

BTM 1-6

Built by Bazán 1961-63 of 100-300 tons. To carry torpedoes and mines and, in emergency, can act as minelayers.

ST 5

Torpedo tracking craft on range at Alcudia, Majorca.

LRT 3 and 4

TRVs built in 1956. Can carry 6 torpedoes. Have stern ramp and crane.

6 DIVING CRAFT

BZL 1, 3, 9   NEREIDA (BZL 10)

Small self-propelled craft of less than 50 tons.

BL 10 and 13

Dumb barges for diving.

8 FLOATING CRANES

SANSÒN GRI (100 tons lift)
GR 3, 4 and 5 (30 tons lift)
GR 6, 7, 8, 9 (15 tons lift)

SRI LANKA

Formation

The Royal Ceylon Navy was formed on 9 Dec 1950 when the Navy Act was proclaimed. Called the Sri Lanka Navy since Republic Day 22 May 1972.

Headquarters Appointment

Commander of the Navy:
Commodore D. B. Goonesekera

Diplomatic Representation

Services Attaché in London:
Withdrawn from 1 November 1970

Personnel

(a) 1976: 2 310 (189 officers and 2 121 sailors)
(b) Voluntary Service

Naval Bases

A Naval Base established at Trincomalee, which was a British base from 1795 until 1957.
Minor bases at Karainagar, Colombo, Welisara, Tangale, Kalpitiya and Talaimannar.

Defence Expenditure and Policy

Since the Indo-Pakistan war visits by US, British, French, Indian and Russian ships have taken place. It is reported that defence spending has been doubled.

Mercantile Marine

Lloyd's Register of Shipping:
35 vessels of 80 862 tons gross

Strength of the Fleet

Type	Active	Building
Frigate	1	—
Fast Attack Craft—Patrol	1	—
Fast Attack Craft—Gun	5	—
Coastal Patrol Craft	22	—
Survey Craft	4	—

Prefix to Ships' Names

SLNS

Deletions

1974   Short hydrofoil and 1 Thornycroft Patrol Craft (101)
1975   Tug *Aliya*

FRIGATE

1 Ex-CANADIAN "RIVER" CLASS

Name	No.	Builders	Laid down	Launched	Commissioned
GAJABAHU (ex-*Misnak*, ex-HMCS *Hallowell*)	F 232	Canadian Vickers Ltd, Montreal	1944	8 Aug 1944	Jan 1945

Displacement, tons: 1 445 standard; 2 360 full load
Length, feet (metres): 282 *(86·3)* pp; 295·5 *(90·1)* wl; 310·5 *(91·9)* oa
Beam, feet (metres): 36·5 *(11·1)*
Draught, feet (metres): 13·8 *(4·2)*
Guns: 1—4 in *(102 mm)*; 3—40 mm
Main engines: Triple expansion; 5 500 ihp; 2 shafts
Boilers: 2 three-drum type
Speed, knots: 20
Range, miles: 4 200 at 12 knots
Oil fuel, tons: 585
Complement: 160

Acquired from Canada by Israel in 1950 and sold by Israel to Ceylon in 1959. Guns above replaced 3—4·7 inch, 8—20 mm in 1965.

GAJABAHU

1971, Royal Ceylon Navy

LIGHT FORCES

5 "SOORAYA" CLASS
(FAST ATTACK CRAFT—GUN)

ALAWATHA   SOORAYA
AKSAYA   WEERAYA
AMAKAMI

Displacement, tons: 120 full load
Dimensions, feet (metres): 130 × 18 × 5·6 *(42·6 × 5·9 × 1·8)*
Guns: 4—37 mm (2 twin); 4—25 mm (2 twin abaft the bridge)
Main engines: 4 Diesels; 5 000 bhp = 30 knots
Complement: 25

Of the "Shanghai IV" class.

The first pair was transferred by China in Feb 1972, the second
pair in July 1972 and the last in December 1972. In monsoonal
conditions off the coast of Sri Lanka these boats are lively and
uncomfortable.

Radar: Pothead.

SOORAYA   *1974, Sri Lanka Navy*

1 Ex-SOVIET "STENKA" CLASS

Name	No.	Builders	Commissioned
SAMUDRA DEVI	—	USSR	31 Dec 1975

Displacement, tons: 170 standard; 210 full load
Dimensions, feet (metres): 130·7 × 25·1 × 6 *(39·9 × 7·6 × 1·8)*
Guns: 4—30 mm (twin)
A/S weapons: 2 DC racks
Torpedo tubes: 4—16 in *(406 mm)* A/S
Main engines: 3 diesels; 10 000 bhp
Speed, knots: 40
Complement: 25

Built 1968. Has certain variations from standard Soviet craft. The after radar pedestal mounts
only a Kolonka optical sight and the torpedo tubes have been unshipped although the sponsons
remain. An additional section of superstructure has been added abaft the after pedestal.

SAMUDRA DEVI   *12/1975, Sri Lanka Navy*

20 THORNYCROFT TYPE (COASTAL PATROL CRAFT)

Name	No.	Builders	Commissioned	Name	No.	Builders	Commissioned
—	102	Thornycroft (Malaysia) Ltd, Singapore	1966	—	202	Thornycroft (Malaysia) Ltd, Singapore	1967
	103	Thornycroft (Malaysia) Ltd, Singapore	1966	—	203	Thornycroft (Malaysia) Ltd, Singapore	1968
	104	Thornycroft (Malaysia) Ltd, Singapore	1967	—	204	Thornycroft (Malaysia) Ltd, Singapore	1968
	105	Thornycroft (Malaysia) Ltd, Singapore	1967	—	205	Thornycroft (Malaysia) Ltd, Singapore	1968
	106	Thornycroft (Malaysia) Ltd, Singapore	1967	—	206	Thornycroft (Malaysia) Ltd, Singapore	1968
	107	Thornycroft (Malaysia) Ltd, Singapore	1967	—	207	Thornycroft (Malaysia) Ltd, Singapore	1968
	108	Thornycroft (Malaysia) Ltd, Singapore	1967	—	208	Thornycroft (Malaysia) Ltd, Singapore	1968
	109	Thornycroft (Malaysia) Ltd, Singapore	1967	—	209	Thornycroft (Malaysia) Ltd, Singapore	1968
	110	Thornycroft (Malaysia) Ltd, Singapore	1967	—	210	Thornycroft (Malaysia) Ltd, Singapore	1968
	201	Thornycroft (Malaysia) Ltd, Singapore	1967	—	211	Thornycroft (Malaysia) Ltd, Singapore	1968

Displacement, tons: 15
Dimensions, feet (metres): 45·5 × 12 × 3 *(14·9 × 3·9 × 0·9)*
Main engines: 2 boats: Thornycroft K6SMI engines; 500 bhp; 2 shafts = 25 knots. 7 boats:
General Motors 6 71-Series; 500 bhp; 2 shafts = 25 knots

The hulls are of hard chine type with double skin teak planking. Equipped with radar, radio,
searchlight etc. Two ordered in 1965. Seven ordered in 1966. 12 more assembled in Sri Lanka
and completed by Sep 1968. Originally 21 boats.
They are based, as two squadrons, at Kalpitiya and Karainagar.

2 HARBOUR PATROL LAUNCHES

Name	No.	Builders	Commissioned
DIYAKAWA	—	Italy	1955
KORAWAKKA	—	Italy	1955

Displacement, tons: 13
Dimensions, feet (metres): 46 pp; 48 oa × 12 × 3 *((15; 15·7 × 3·9 × 0·9)*
Main engines: 2 Foden FD 6 diesels; 240 bhp = 15 knots

Built in Italy in 1955.

SURVEY CRAFT

2 ITALIAN TYPE (COASTAL SURVEY CRAFT)

Name	No.	Builders	Commissioned	Name	No.	Builders	Commissioned
ANSAYA	—	Korody Marine Corp, Venice	1956	SERUWA	—	Italy	1955
HINIYA	—	Korody Marine Corp, Venice	1956	TARAWA	—	Italy	1955

Displacement, tons: 36
Dimensions, feet (metres): 63·5 pp; 66 oa × 14 × 4 *(20·8; 21·6 × 4·6 × 1·3)*
Main engines: 3 General Motors diesels; 450 bhp = 16 knots

Originally patrol craft. Employed on Survey duties.

Of similar characteristics to *Diyakawa* and *Korawakka* above.

SUDAN

Establishment

The navy was established in 1962 to operate on the Red Sea coast and on the River Nile. The original training staff was from Yugoslavian Navy, but this staff left in 1972.

Diplomatic Representation

Naval, Military and Air Attaché in London:
Col. M. T. Khalil

Bases

Port Sudan for Red Sea operations with a separate riverine unit on the Nile.

Personnel

(a) 1976: 600 officers and men
(b) Voluntary service

Mercantile Marine

Lloyd's Register of Shipping: 14 vessels of 45 578 tons gross

---

LIGHT FORCES

2 Ex-YUGOSLAV "KRALJEVICA" CLASS
(LARGE PATROL CRAFT)

Name	No.	Builders	Commissioned
FASHER	PBR 1	Yugoslavia	1954
KHARTOUM	PBR 2	Yugoslavia	1955

Displacement, tons: 190 standard; 245 full load
Dimensions, feet (metres): 134·5 × 20·7 × 7·2 *(41 × 6·3 × 2·2)*
Guns: 2—40 mm; 2—20 mm
Main engines: Diesel; 2 shafts; 3 300 bhp = 20 knots
Range, miles: 1 500 at 12 knots

Transferred from the Yugoslavian Navy during 1969.

3 Ex-IRANIAN IMPROVED PGM TYPE
(LARGE PATROL CRAFT)

Name	No.	Builders	Commissioned
GADEER (ex-*Battraam*, PGM 66)	—	Tacoma SB Co	1968
GOHAR (ex-*Nahid*, PGM 67)	—	Peterson, Sturgeon Bay	1969
SHAHPAR (ex-*Parvin*, PGM 65)	—	Peterson, Sturgeon Bay	1967

Displacement, tons: 105 standard; 146 full load
Dimensions, feet (metres): 100 × 22 × 10 *(31·1 × 4·9 × 3)*
Guns: 1—40 mm; 2—20 mm; 2 MG
Main engines: Diesels; 2 shafts; 2 000 bhp = 20 knots
Complement: 15

Built for Iran under MDAP and transferred to Sudan 1975.

4 Ex-YUGOSLAV PBR TYPE (LARGE PATROL CRAFT)

Name	No.	Builders	Commissioned
GIHAD	PB 1	Mosor Shipyard, Trogir, Yugoslavia	1961
HORRIYA	PB 2	Mosor Shipyard, Trogir, Yugoslavia	1961
ISTIQLAL	PB 3	Mosor Shipyard, Trogir, Yugoslavia	1962
SHAAB	PB 4	Mosor Shipyard, Trogir, Yugoslavia	1962

Displacement, tons: 100
Dimensions, feet (metres): 115 × 16·5 × 5·2 *(35 × 5 × 1·7)*
Guns: 1—40 mm; 1—20 mm; 2—7·6 mm MG
Main engines: Mercedes-Benz (MTU 12V 493) diesels; 2 shafts; 1 800 bhp = 20 knots
Range, miles: 1 400 at 12 knots
Complement: 20

Of steel construction. First craft acquired by the newly established Sudanese Navy.

HORRIYA   *Sudanese Na*

4 Ex-IRANIAN "CAPE" CLASS (LARGE PATROL CRAFT)

Name	No.	Builders	Commissioned
— (ex-*Kayvau*)	—	USA	1955
— (ex-*Mahan*)	—	USA	1959
— (ex-*Mehran*)	—	USA	1959
— (ex-*Tiran*)	—	Coast Guard, Curtis Bay, Maryland	1957

Displacement, tons: 85 standard; 107 full load
Dimensions, feet (metres): 95 × 20·2 × 6·8 *(29 × 4·1 × 2·1)*
Guns: 1—40 mm; 1—7·2 in grenade thrower
Main engines: 4 diesels; 2 shafts; 2 200 bhp = 20 knots
Complement: 15

Transferred by Iran in 1975.

6 Ex-YUGOSLAV "101" CLASS
(FAST ATTACK CRAFT—GUN)

Displacement, tons: 55 standard; 60 full load
Dimensions, feet (metres): 78 × 21·3 × 7·8 *(23·8 × 6·5 × 2·4)*
Guns: 2—40 mm; 2—20 mm (single)
Main engines: 3 Packard petrol motors; 3 shafts; 5 000 bhp = 36 knots
Complement: 14

Transferred in this "Gun" version of the class in 1970. Same characteristics as US "Higgin class.

AMPHIBIOUS FORCES

2 Ex-YUGOSLAV "DTK 221" CLASS (LCTs)

SOBAT   DINDER

Displacement, tons: 410
Dimensions, feet (metres): 144·3 × 19·7 × 7 *(44 × 6 × 2·1)*
Guns: 1—20 mm; 2—12·7 mm
Speed, knots: 10
Complement: 15

Transferred during 1969.

3 LCUs

Transferred by Yugoslavia 1970—of 40 tons.

SERVICE FORCES

1 SUPPORT TANKER

FASHODA (ex-PN 17)

Displacement, tons: 420 standard; 650 full load
Dimensions, feet (metres): 141·5 × 22·8 × 13·6 *(43·2 × 7 × 4·2)*
Main engines: 300 bhp = 7 knots

Former Yugoslavian Tanker rehabilitated and transferred to the Sudanese Navy in 1969.

1 SURVEY SHIP

TIENGA

A small vessel, converted into a hydrographic ship, acquired from Yugoslavia in 1969.

1 WATER BOAT

BARAKA (ex-PV 6)

A small water carrier, transferred from Yugoslavia to the Sudanese Navy in 1969.

SURINAM

Formerly Dutch Guyana—granted independence in 1975.

3 PATROL CRAFT

Of unspecified class ordered from Netherlands in 1975.

SWEDEN

Headquarters Appointments

Commander-in-Chief:
  Vice-Admiral Bengt Lundvall
Chief of Naval Material Department:
  Rear-Admiral Gunnar Grandin
Chief of Naval Staff:
  Major-General Bo Varenius (Coastal Artillery)

Senior Command

Commander-in-Chief of Coastal Fleet:
  Rear-Admiral Christer Kierkegaard

Diplomatic Representation

Naval Attaché in London:
  Commodore N. U. Rydström
Naval Attaché in Washington:
  Captain N. L. Lindgren

Personnel

(a) 1976: 15 100 officers and men of Navy and Coast Artillery made up of 4 500 regulars, 2 900 Reservists and 7 700 National Servicemen. In addition 7 000 conscripts receive annual training.
(b) 9-18 months

Bases

Stockholm, Karlskrona, Göteborg.
Minor base at Härnösand

Composition of the Navy

In addition to seagoing personnel the Navy includes the Coastal Artillery, manning 20 mobile and 45 coastal batteries of both major guns and SSMs. A number of amphibious and patrol craft are also controlled by the Coastal Artillery.

Naval Air Arm

10 Alouette II helicopters
10 Jet Ranger helicopters
10 Vertol 107 (Hkp-4B)

Mercantile Marine

Lloyd's Register of Shipping:
  775 vessels of 7 486 196 tons gross

Strength of the Fleet

Type	Active	Building (Planned)
Destroyers	6	—
Frigates	6	—
Submarines—Patrol	20	2
Corvettes—Light Forces	—	(3)
Fast Attack Craft—Missile	1	(16)
Fast Attack Craft—Torpedo	45	—
Large Patrol Craft	1	—
Coastal Patrol Craft	22	—
Minelayers	3	1
Minelayers—Coastal	9	—
Minelayers—Small	37	—
Minehunters	—	(9)
Minesweepers—Coastal	18	—
Minesweepers—Inshore	20	—
LCMs	9	—
LCUs	60	(25)
LCAs	54	—
Mine Transports	2	—
Survey Ships	5	—
Tankers—Support	1	—
Supply Ship	1	—
Command Ship	1	—
Tugs	7	—
Salvage Ship	1	—
Sail Training Ships	2	—
Ice Breakers	7	1
TRVs	3	—
Tenders	5	—
Water Boats	2	—

DELETIONS

Cruiser

1971 *Göta Lejon* to Chile *(Latorre)*

Frigate

1974 *Karlskrona*

Submarines

1975 *Gäddan, Siken* ("Abborren" class)

Light Forces

1973 *TV 101-106*
1975 *T 38, 39, 40*

Depot Ship

1972 *Patricia*

Surveying Vessels

1972 *Johen Nordenankar, Petter Gedda*
1973 *Anden*
1975 *Lederen*

Miscellaneous

1973 *Gälnan* (water carrier)
1974 *Ymer* (Icebreaker)
1975 *Urd* (experimental ship)

PENNANT LIST

Destroyers

J 18	Halland
J 19	Smaaland
J 20	Ostergotland
J 21	Södermanland
J 22	Gästrikland
J 23	Hälsingland

Frigates

F 11	Visby
F 12	Sundsvall
F 13	Hälsingborg
F 14	Kalmar
F 16	Öland
F 17	Uppland

Submarines

Abb	Abboren
Bäv	Bävern
Del	Delfinen
Dra	Draken
Gri	Gripen
Haj	Hajen
Iln	Illern
Lax	Laxen
Mak	Makrillen
Näc	Näcken
Naj	Najad
Nor	Nordkaperen
Nep	Neptun
Säl	Sälen
Sbj	Sjöbjörnen
Shu	Sjöhunden
Shä	Sjöhästen
Sle	Sjölejonet
Sor	Sjöormen
Spr	Springaren
Utn	Uttern
Val	Valen
Vgn	Vargen

Light Forces

R 01	Flotilla Leader
R 02	Flotilla Leader
R 03	Flotilla Leader
P 151	Jägaren
P 152-167	"Jägaren" class
T 41-56	"T 42" class
T 102	Plejad
T 103	Polaris
T 104	Pollux
T 105	Regulus
T 106	Rigel
T 107	Aldebaran
T 108	Altair
T 109	Antares
T 110	Arcturus
T 111	Argo
T 112	Astrea
T 121	Spica
T 122	Sirius
T 123	Capella
T 124	Castor
T 125	Vega
T 126	Virgo
T 131	Norrköping
T 132	Nynäshamn
T 133	Norrtälje
T 134	Varberg
T 135	Västerås
T 136	Västervik
T 137	Umea
T 138	Pitea
T 139	Lulea
T 140	Halmstad
T 141	Strömstad
T 142	Ystad

Amphibious Forces

A 333	Skagul
A 335	Sleipner
L 51-56	LCUs
201-255	LCUs
256-265	LCUs

Minewarfare Forces

M 01	Alvsnabben
M 02	Alvsborg
M 03	Visborg
M 04	New Construction
MUL 11-19	Coastal Minelayers
M 15-16, 21-26	MSI
M 31	Gässten
M 32	Norsten
M 33	Viksten
M 41	Orust
M 42	Tjörn
M 43	Hisingen
M 44	Blackan
M 45	Dämman
M 46	Galten
M 47	Gillöga
M 48	Rödlöga
M 49	Svartlöga
M 51	Hanö
M 52	Tärnö
M 53	Tjurkö
M 54	Sturkö
M 55	Ornö
M 56	Utö
M 57	Arkö
M 58	Spärö
M 59	Karlsö
M 60	Iggö
M 61	Styrsö
M 62	Skaftö
M 63	Aspö
M 64	Hasslö
M 65	Vinö
M 66	Jällo
M 67	Nämdö
M 68	Blidö

Support Forces

S 01	Gladen
S 02	Falken
A 201	Mariaholm
A 211	Belos
A 216	Unden
A 217	Fryken
A 221	Freja
A 228	Brännaren
A 231	Lommen
A 232	Spoven
A 236	Fällaren
A 237	Minören
A 242	Skuld
A 246	Hagern
A 247	Pelikanen
A 248	Pingvinen
A 251	Achilles
A 252	Ajax
A 253	Hermes
A 256	Sigrun
A 321	Hector
A 322	Hercules
A 323	Heros
A 324	Hera
A 333	Skagul
A 335	Sleipner

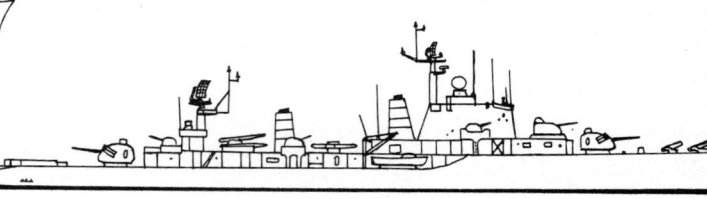

"OSTERGOTLAND" Class

"HALLAND" Class

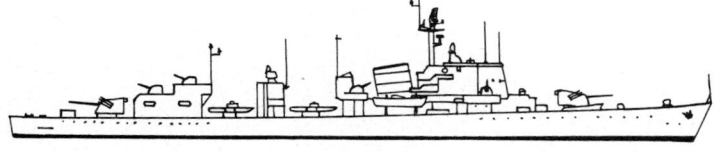

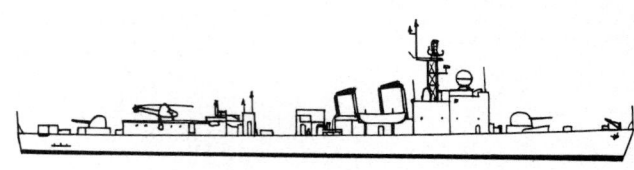

"ÖLAND" Class

"VISBY" Class

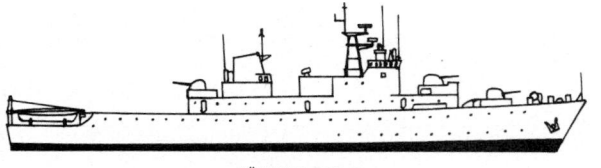

"ÄLVSBORG" Class

DESTROYERS

4 "ÖSTERGÖTLAND" CLASS

Name	No.	Builders	Laid down	Launched	Commissioned
GÄSTRIKLAND	J 22	Götaverken, Göteborg	1 Oct 1955	6 June1956	14 Jan 1959
HÄLSINGLAND	J 23	Kockums Mek Verkstads A/B	1 Oct 1955	14 Jan 1957	17 June 1959
ÖSTERGÖTLAND	J 20	Götaverken, Göteborg	1 Sep 1955	8 May 1956	3 Mar 1958
SÖDERMANLAND	J 21	Eriksberg Mekaniska Verkstad	1June 1955	28 May 1956	27 June 1958

Displacement, tons: 2 150 standard; 2 600 full load
Length, feet (metres): 367·5 (112·0) oa
Beam, feet (metres): 36·8 (11·2)
Draught, feet (metres): 12·0 (3·7)
Missile launchers: 1 quadruple Seacat (RB 07) surface-to-air
Guns: 4—4·7 in (120 mm), (2 twin); 4—40 mm (single)
A/S weapons: 1 Squid (triple-barrelled)
Torpedo tubes: 6—21 in (533 mm) (1 mount)
Mines: 60 can be carried
Main engines: De Laval turbines; 2 shafts; 47 000 bhp
Boilers: 2 Babcock & Wilcox
Speed, knots: 35
Oil fuel, tons: 330
Range, miles: 2 200 at 20 knots
Complement: 244 (18 officers, 226 men)

Modernisation: *Gästrikland* in 1965, *Södermanland* in 1967, *Hälsingland* in 1968, *Östergötland* in 1969.

Radar: Search and target designator: Thomson CSF Saturn.
Fire control: HSA M 44 for Seacat—M 45 series for guns.

HÄLSINGLAND

1975, Royal Swedish Navy

2 "HALLAND" CLASS

Name	No.
HALLAND	J 18
SMÅLAND	J 19

Displacement, tons: 2 800 standard; 3 400 full load
Length, feet (metres): 380·5 *(116·0)* wl; 397·2 *(121·0)* oa
Beam, feet (metres): 41·3 *(12·6)*
Draught, feet (metres): 14·8 *(4·5)*
Missiles: 1 RB 08A (Mk 20) launcher
Guns: 4—4·7 in *(120 mm)* (2 twin); 2—57 mm; 6—40 mm
A/S weapons: 2 four-barrelled rocket-launcher (Bofors)
Torpedo tubes: 8—21 in *(533 mm)* (1 triple; 1 quintuple)
Mines: Can be fitted for minelaying
Main engines: De Laval double reduction geared turbines; 2 shafts; 58 000 bhp
Boilers: 2 Penhöet
Speed, knots: 35
Oil fuel, tons: 500
Range, miles: 3 000 at 20 knots
Complement: 290 (18 officers, 272 men)

Both ordered in 1948. The first Swedish destroyers of post-war design. Fully automatic gun turrets forward and aft. Both modernised in 1962.

Radar: Search and target designator: Thomson CSF Saturn (foremast).
Air warning: LW 02/03 (mainmast).
Fire control, search and tracking: M 22 and associated sets (radome).
ECM.

Builders	Laid down	Launched	Commissioned
Götaverken, Göteborg	1951	16 July 1952	8 June 1955
Eriksberg Mekaniska Verkstad, Göteborg	1951	23 Oct 1952	12 Jan 1956

SMÅLAND   1975, Royal Swedish Navy

HALLAND   1973, Wright and Logan

FRIGATES

2 "ÖLAND" CLASS

Name	No.
ÖLAND	F 16
UPPLAND	F 17

Displacement, tons: 2 000 standard; 2 400 full load
Length, feet (metres): 351 *(107·0)* pp; 367·5 *(112·0)* oa
Beam, feet (metres): 36·8 *(11·2)*
Draught, feet (metres): 11·2 *(3·4)*
Guns: 4—4·7 in *(120 mm)* (2 twin); 6—40 mm (single)
A/S weapons: 1 triple-barrelled DC mortar
Torpedo tubes: 6—21 in *(533 mm)* (2 triple)
Mines: 60 capacity
Main engines: De Laval geared turbines; 2 shafts; 44 000 bhp
Boilers: 2 Penhöet
Speed, knots: 35
Oil fuel, tons: 300
Range, miles: 2 500 at 20 knots
Complement: 210

Builders	Laid down	Launched	Commissioned
Kockums Mek Verkstads A/B, Malmö	1943	15 Dec 1945	5 Dec 1947
Karlskrona Dockard	1943	5 Nov 1946	31 Jan 1949

Superstructure and machinery spaces lightly armoured.

Gunnery: 4·7 inch guns semi-automatic with 80° elevation. 40 mm gun near jackstaff was removed in 1962, and eight 20 mm guns in 1964.

Radar: Search and target designator: Thomson CSF Saturn.
Fire Control: Two M 45 series.
Navigation: One set.

Reconstruction: *Öland* was modernised with new bridge in 1960 and again in 1969; and *Uppland* with new bridge and helicopter platform in 1963.

ÖLAND (now F 16)
                                                1970, Royal Swedish Navy

4 "VISBY" CLASS

Name	No.	Builders	Laid down	Launched	Commissioned
HÄLSINGBORG	F 13	Götaverken	1942	23 Mar 1943	30 Nov 1943
KALMAR	F 14	Eriksberg	1942	20 July 1943	3 Feb 1944
SUNDSVALL	F 12	Eriksberg	1941	20 Oct 1942	17 Sep 1943
VISBY	F 11	Götaverken	1941	16 Oct 1942	10 Aug 1943

Displacement, tons: 1 150 standard; 1 320 full load
Length, feet (metres): 310·0 *(94·5)* wl; 321·5 *(98·0)* oa
Beam, feet (metres): 30 *(9·1)*
Draught, feet (metres): 12·5 *(3·8)*
Aircraft: 1 helicopter pad (F 11 and F 12)
Guns: 3—4·7 in *(120 mm)*; 3—40 mm (2—57 mm only in F 11 and F 12)
A/S weapons: 1—4 barrelled DC mortar (*Sundsvall* and *Visby*); DCT (*Hälsingborg* and *Kalmar*)
Main engines: De Laval geared turbines; 2 shafts; 36 000 shp
Boilers: 3 three-drum type
Speed, knots: 39
Range, miles: 1 600 at 20 knots
Oil fuel, tons: 150
Complement: 140

All were originally fitted for minelaying. All four will be paid off for disposal in the near future.

Radar: Thompson CSF Saturn S-band long-range search and target designator
M 24 fire control systems with co-mounted radars for search and tracking for guns.

SUNDSVALL

1972, Royal Swedish Navy

VISBY

1975, Royal Swedish Navy

SUBMARINES

NEW CONSTRUCTION A 17 CLASS

In design stage for completion mid 1980s.

3 "NÄCKEN" CLASS (A14)

Name	No.	Builders	Laid down	Launched	Commissioned
NÄCKEN	NÄC	Kockums, Malmö	—	—	1977
NAJAD	NAJ	Karlskrona	—	—	1978
NEPTUN	NEP	Kockums, Malmö	—	—	1978

Displacement, tons: 980 surfaced; 1 125 dived
Length, feet (metres): 135 *(41)*
Beam, feet (metres): 20·0 *(6·1)*
Draught, feet (metres): 16·7 *(5·1)*
Torpedo tubes: 4—21 in *(533 mm)* (8 reloads)
Main machinery: Diesels; electric motors; 1 shaft with large 5-bladed propeller
Speed, knots: 20 surfaced and dived
Complement: 25

The very high beam to length ratio is notable in this Albacore hull design. Have large bow mounted sonar. Main accommodation space is abaft the control room with machinery spaces right aft.

5 "SJÖORMEN" CLASS (A11B)

Name	No.	Builders	Laid down	Launched	Commissioned
SJÖORMEN	SOR	Kockums	1965	25 Jan 1967	31 July 1967
SJÖLEJONET	SLE	Kockums	1966	29 June 1967	16 Dec 1968
SJÖHUNDEN	SHU	Kockums	1966	21 Mar 1968	25 June 1969
SJÖBJÖRNEN	SBJ	Karlskrona	1967	6 Aug 1968	28 Feb 1969
SJÖHÄSTEN	SHÄ	Karlskrona	1966	9 Jan 1968	15 Sep 1969

Displacement, tons: 1 125 standard; 1 400 dived
Length, feet (metres): 167·3 *(50·5)*
Beam, feet (metres): 20·0 *(6·1)*
Draught, feet (metres): 16·7 *(5·1)*
Torpedo tubes: 4—21 in *(533 mm)* 2 A/S tubes
Main machinery: 2 Pielstick diesels; 1 large 5-bladed propeller; 2 200 bhp; 1 electric motor
Speed, knots: 15 surfaced; 20 dived
Endurance: 3 weeks
Complement: 23

Albacore hull. Twin-decked. Diving depth 500 ft.
Distinctive letters in place of pennant numbers are painted on the conning tower.

SJÖHUNDEN

1972, Royal Swedish Navy

SJÖBJÖRNEN (see previous page)   *1971, Royal Swedish Navy*

6 "DRAKEN" CLASS (A 11)

Name	No.
DELFINEN	DEL
DRAKEN	DRA
GRIPEN	GRI
NORDKAPAREN	NOR
SPRINGAREN	SPR
VARGEN	VGN

Builders	Laid down	Launched	Commissioned
Karlskrona	1959	7 Mar 1961	7 June 1962
Kockums	1958	1 Apr 1960	4 Apr 1962
Karlskrona	1959	31 May 1960	28 Apr 1962
Kockums	1959	8 Mar 1961	4 Apr 1962
Kockums	1960	31 Aug 1961	7 Nov 1962
Kockums	1958	20 May 1960	15 Nov 1961

Displacement, tons: 770 standard; 835 surfaced; 1 110 dived
Length, feet (metres): 226·4 *(69·0)*
Beam, feet (metres): 16·7 *(5·1)*
Draught, feet (metres): 17·4 *(5·3)*
Torpedo tubes: 4—21 in *(533 mm)* bow
Main machinery: 2 Pielstick diesels; 1 660 bhp; 1 large 5-bladed propeller; 1 electric motor
Speed, knots: 17 surfaced; 20 dived
Complement: 36

Distinctive letters are painted on the conning tower in place of pennant numbers.

NORDKAPAREN   *1971, Royal Swedish Navy*

6 "HAJEN" CLASS

Name	No.
BÄVERN	BAV
HÄJEN	HAJ
ILLERN	ILN—
SÄLEN	SAL—
UTTERN	UTN
VALEN	VAL

Builders	Laid down	Launched	Commissioned
Kockums	1956	3 Feb 1958	29 May 1959
Kockums	1953	11 Dec 1954	28 Feb 1957
Kockums	1956	15 Nov 1957	31 Aug 1959
Kockums	1954	3 Oct 1955	8 Apr 1957
Kockums	1957	14 Nov 1958	15 Mar 1960
Karlskrona	1953	24 Apr 1955	4 Mar 1957

Displacement, tons: 720 standard; 785 surfaced; 1 000 dived
Length, feet (metres): 216·5 *(66·0)*
Beam, feet (metres): 16·7 *(5·1)*
Draught, feet (metres): 16·4 *(5·0)*
Torpedo tubes: 4—21 in *(533 mm)* bow (8 torpedoes)
Main machinery: 2 SEMT-Pielstick diesels; 1 660 bhp; 2 Electric motors; 2 shafts
Speed, knots: 16 surfaced; 17 dived
Complement: 44

Distinctive letters are painted on the conning tower in place of pennant numbers.

HAJEN (old lettering)   *1970, Royal Swedish Navy*

ILLERN (old lettering)   *1972, Royal Swedish Navy*

3 "ABBORREN" CLASS

Name	No.	Builders	Laid down	Launched	Commissioned
ABBORREN (ex-U5)	ARB	Kockums	1942	8 July 1943	1944
LAXEN (ex-U8)	LAX	Karlskrona	1942	25 Apr 1944	1945
MAKRILLEN (ex-U9)	MAK	Karlskrona	1942	23 May 1944	1945

Displacement, tons: 420 standard; 430 surfaced; 460 dived
Length, feet (metres): 164·0 (50·0)
Beam, feet (metres): 14·1 (4·3)
Draught, feet (metres): 12·5 (3·8)
Torpedo tubes: 4—21 in (533 mm) (3 bow and 1 stern)
Main machinery: 1 MAN diesel; 800 bhp; 1 large 5-bladed propeller; 1 Electric motor; 750 hp
Speed, knots: 14 surfaced; 9 dived
Complement: 23

Distinctive letters are painted on the conning tower in place of pennant numbers.
Reconstructed 1960-63. Last of class of nine—probably to be deleted in 1976.

Note: A submarine-escape vehicle of French design was ordered from Kockums in mid-1974.

Displacement, tons: 49
Dimensions, feet (metres): 44·3 × 14·1 × 9·5 (14·5 × 4·6 × 3·1)
Complement: 5

With a diving depth of 1 500 ft it will be capable of operating and conducting rescues throughout the Baltic. Can lift up to 25 men at one time.

MAKRILLEN (old lettering)   1969, Royal Swedish Navy

LAXEN (old lettering)   1972, Royal Swedish Navy

LIGHT FORCES

3 PROJECTED FLOTILLA LEADERS

RO 1   RO 2   RO 3

Displacement, tons: 700
Dimensions, feet (metres): 246·0 × 26·2 × 8·0 (80·6 × 8·6 × 2·6)
Missiles: 2 SSM
Guns: 2—57 mm forward
A/S weapons: 1 single barrelled depth charge mortar forward
Main engines: Gas turbines for power; diesels for cruising = 35 knots
Complement: 70

A new type of corvette planned to fill the need for ships to act as flotilla leaders for fast attack craft and for escort duties.

RO 1   1973

1 + 16 "JÄGAREN" CLASS
(FAST ATTACK CRAFT—MISSILE)

Name	No.	Builders	Commissioned
JÄGAREN	P 151	Norway	8 June 1972
—	P 152	Norway	—
—	P 153	Norway	—
—	P 154	Norway	—
—	P 155	Norway	—
—	P 156	Norway	—
—	P 157	Norway	—
—	P 158	Norway	—
—	P 159	Norway	—
—	P 160	Norway	—
—	P 161	Norway	—
—	P 162	Norway	—
—	P 163	Norway	—
—	P 164	Norway	—
—	P 165	Norway	—
—	P 166	Norway	—
—	P 167	Norway	—

Displacement, tons: 140
Dimensions, feet (metres): 118 × 20·3 × 4·9 (36 × 6·2 × 1·5)
Missile launchers: 6 Penguin Mark 2 (4 in Jägaren)
Gun: 1—57 mm Bofors L 70
Torpedo tubes: Fitted for 4—21 inch (533 mm)
Main engines: 2 MTU MB20V 672 TY90 diesels; 2 shafts; 7 000 bhp = 35 knots
Complement: 20

Instead of the motor gunboats projected for several years a choice was made of fast attack craft similar to the Norwegian "Hauk" class armed with Penguin missiles.
She then underwent extensive trials and, on 15 May 1975, an order for a further eleven was placed with Bergens Mekaniske Verksted, Norway and five from Westermoen. Guns and electronics are being provided from Sweden. Fitted for alternative minelaying capability aft.

JÄGAREN   1975, Royal Swedish Nav

12 "REPEAT SPICA" CLASS
(FAST ATTACK CRAFT—TORPEDO)

Name	No.	Builders	Commissioned
HALMSTAD	T 140	Karlskronavarvet AB	1976
LULEA	T 139	Karlskronavarvet AB	1976
NORRKÖPING	T 131	Karlskronavarvet AB	5 Nov 1973
NORRTÄLJE	T 133	Karlskronavarvet AB	1 Feb 1974
NYNÄSHAMN	T 132	Karlskronavarvet AB	Sep 1973
PITEA	T 138	Karlskronavarvet AB	Oct 1975
STRÖMSTAD	T 141	Karlskronavarvet AB	1976
UMEÅ	T 137	Karlskronavarvet AB	June 1975
VARBERG	T 134	Karlskronavarvet AB	13 June 1974
VÄSTERÅS	T 135	Karlskronavarvet AB	25 Oct 1974
VÄSTERVIK	T 136	Karlskronavarvet AB	15 Jan 1975
YSTAD	T 142	Karlskronavarvet AB	1976

Displacement, tons: 230 standard
Dimensions, feet (metres): 134·5 × 23·3 × 5·2 *(41 × 7·1 × 1·6)*
Gun: 1—57 mm Bofors L 70
Rocket launchers: 8 for 57 mm flare rockets
Torpedo tubes: 6—21 in *(533 mm)* for wire-guided torpedoes
Main engines: 3 Rolls Royce Proteus gas turbines; 3 shafts; 12 900 bhp = 40·5 knots

Similar to the original "Spica" class from which they were developed. Guided missiles are not included in the design to date. Launched—*Norrköping* 16 Nov 1972, *Nynäshamn* 24 April 1973, *Norrtalje* 18 Sep 1973, *Varberg* 2 Feb 1974, *Västeräs* 15 May 1974, *Vastervik* 2 Sep 1974, *Umea* 13 Jan 1975, *Pitea* 12 May 1975. Laid down—*Lulea* 6 Sep 1974, *Halmstad* 7 Feb 1975.

Radar: Philips Teleindustrie 9 LV 200-simultaneous air and surface search in I band with tracking in separate band.

VÄSTERVIK

1975, Kapten Goran Frisk

6 "SPICA" CLASS (FAST ATTACK CRAFT—TORPEDO)

Name	No.	Builders	Commissioned
CAPELLA	T 123	Götaverken, Göteborg	1966
CASTOR	T 124	Karlskronavervarvet	1967
SIRIUS	T 122	Götaverken, Göteborg	1966
SPICA	T 121	Götaverken, Göteborg	1966
VEGA	T 125	Karlskronavervarvet	1967
VIRGO	T 126	Karlskronavervarvet	1967

Displacement, tons: 200 standard; 230 full load
Dimensions, feet (metres): 134·5 × 23·3 × 5·2 *(41 × 7·1 × 1·6)*
Gun: 1—57 mm Bofors
Torpedo tubes: 6—21 in *(533 mm)* (single, fixed)
Rocket launchers: 6—57 mm flare rockets; 4—10·3 mm flare rockets
Main engines: 3 Bristol Siddeley Proteus 1 274 gas turbines; 3 shafts; 12 720 shp = 40 knots
Complement: 28 (7 officers, 21 ratings)

The 57 mm gun is in a power operated turret controlled by a radar equipped director.

Radar: M 22 fire control system with co-mounted radars in radome for guns and torpedoes.

CAPELLA

1975, Royal Swedish Navy

11 "PLEJAD" CLASS (FAST ATTACK CRAFT—TORPEDO)

Name	No.	Builders	Commissioned
ALDEBARAN	T 107	Lurssen, Vegesack	1956
ALTAIR	T 108	Lurssen, Vegesack	1956
ANTARES	T 109	Lurssen, Vegesack	1957
ARCTURUS	T 110	Lurssen, Vegesack	1957
ARGO	T 111	Lurssen, Vegesack	1957
ASTREA	T 112	Lurssen, Vegesack	1956
PLEJAD	T 102	Lurssen, Vegesack	1955
POLARIS	T 103	Lurssen, Vegesack	1955
POLLUX	T 104	Lurssen, Vegesack	1955
REGULUS	T 105	Lurssen, Vegesack	1956
RIGEL	T 106	Lurssen, Vegesack	1956

Displacement, tons: 155 standard; 170 full load
Dimensions, feet (metres): 147·6 × 19 × 5·2 *(45 × 5·8 × 1·6)*
Guns: 2—40 mm Bofors
Rocket launchers: 4—57 mm flare rockets
Torpedo tubes: 6—21 in *(533 mm)*
Main engines: 3 Mercedes-Benz (MTU 20 V 672) diesels; 3 shafts; 9 000 bhp = 37·5 knots
Range, miles: 600 at 30 knots
Complement: 33

Launched between 1954 and 1957.

ALTAIR

1975, Royal Swedish Navy

16 "T 42" CLASS (FAST ATTACK CRAFT—TORPEDO)

Name	No.	Builders	Commissioned
—	T 41	Kockums Mekaniska Verkstads Aktiebolag, Malmo	1952
—	T 42	Kockums Mekaniska Verkstads Aktiebolag, Malmo	1956
—	T 43	Kockums Mekaniska Verkstads Aktiebolag, Malmo	1956
—	T 44	Kockums Mekaniska Verkstads Aktiebolag, Malmo	1956
—	T 45	Kockums Mekaniska Verkstads Aktiebolag, Malmo	1957
—	T 46	Kockums Mekaniska Verkstads Aktiebolag, Malmo	1957
—	T 47	Kockums Mekaniska Verkstads Aktiebolag, Malmo	1957
—	T 48	Kockums Mekaniska Verkstads Aktiebolag, Malmo	1957
—	T 49	Kockums Mekaniska Verkstads Aktiebolag, Malmo	1957
—	T 50	Kockums Mekaniska Verkstads Aktiebolag, Malmo	1958
—	T 51	Kockums Mekaniska Verkstads Aktiebolag, Malmo	1958
—	T 52	Kockums Mekaniska Verkstads Aktiebolag, Malmo	1958
—	T 53	Naval Dockyard, Stockholm	1958
—	T 54	Naval Dockyard, Stockholm	1959
—	T 55	Naval Dockyard, Stockholm	1959
—	T 56	Naval Dockyard, Stockholm	1959

T 56   1975, Royal Swedish Navy

Displacement, tons: 40 standard
Dimensions, feet (metres): 75·5 × 19·4 × 4·6 *(23 × 5·9 × 1·4)*
Gun: 1—40 mm Bofors
Rocket launchers: 4—57 mm flare launchers
Torpedo tubes: 2—21 in *(533 mm)*
Main engines: 3 Isotta Fraschini Petrol engines; 4 500 bhp = 45 knots

T 41 is the last of the "T 32" class, an earlier group of same dimensions as "T 42".

1 LARGE PATROL CRAFT

V 57

Displacement, tons: 115 standard
Dimensions, feet (metres): 98 × 17·3 × 7·5 *(30 × 5·3 × 2·3)*
Gun: 1—20 mm
Main engines: Diesel; 500 bhp = 13·5 knots
Complement: 12

Built at Stockholm. Launched in 1953. Fitted for minelaying. Attached to Coastal Artillery.

5 COASTAL PATROL CRAFT

SVK 1	SVK 2	SVK 3	SVK 4	SVK 5

Displacement, tons: 19 standard
Dimensions, feet (metres): 52·5 × 12·1 × 3·9 *(16 × 3·7 ×1·2)*
Gun: 1—20 mm
Main engines: Diesels; 100 to 135 bhp = 10 knots

Patrol craft of the Sjövarnskarens (RNVR). All launched in 1944.

17 COASTAL PATROL CRAFT

61-77

Displacement, tons: 28 standard
Dimensions, feet (metres): 69 × 15 × 5 *(21 × 4·6 × 1·5)*
Gun: 1—20 mm
Main engines: Diesel; speed = 18 knots

These are attached to the Coastal Artillery. "60" series launched in 1960-61 and "70" series in 1966-67.

Patrol craft 66   1975, Royal Swedish Navy

MINE WARFARE FORCES

2 + 1"ALVSBORG" CLASS (MINELAYERS)

Name	No.	Builders	Commissioned
ÄLVSBORG	M 02	Karlskrona Naval DY	10 April 1971
VISBORG	M 03	Karlskrona Naval DY	1976
—	M 04	—	—

Displacement, tons: 2 700
Length, feet (metres): 301·8 *(92)*
Beam, feet (metres): 48·2 *(14·7)*
Draught, feet (metres): 13·2 *(4·0)*
Aircraft: 1 Helicopter
Guns: 3—40 mm Bofors
Main engines: 2 Nohab-Polar 12 cyl diesels; 1 shaft; 4 200 bhp
Speed, knots: 15
Complement: 95 (accommodation for 205 more)

The *Alvsborg* was ordered in 1968 and launched on 11 Nov 1969. She replaced the submarine depot ship *Patricia* which was sold in 1972.
Visborg, laid down on 16 Oct 1973 and launched 22 Jan 1975 will succeed *Marieholm* as Command Ship for C-in-C Coastal Fleet.

M 04

This ship will be slightly larger at 328 ft *(100 m)* length and 3 000 tons. Not yet laid down. When eventually completed is planned to relieve *Alvsnabben* as Cadet Training Ship as well as serving as a minelayer.

ALVSBORG   1975, Royal Swedish Navy

1 MINELAYER/TRAINING SHIP

Name	No.	Builders	Commissioned
ÄLVSNABBEN	M 01	Eriksberg Mekaniska Verkstad Göteborg	8 May 1943

Displacement, tons: 4 250 standard
Length, feet (metres): 317·6 *(96·8)* wl; 334·7 *(102·0)* oa
Beam, feet (metres): 44·6 *(13·6)*
Draught, feet (metres): 16·4 *(5·0)*
Guns: 2—6 in *(152 mm);* 2—57 mm Bofors;
  2—40 mm; 4—37 mm saluting
Main engines: Diesels; 1 shaft; 3 000 bhp
Speed, knots: 14
Complement: 255 (63 cadets)

Built on a mercantile hull. Laid down on 31 Oct 1942, launched on 19 Jan 1943. Employed as a training ship during 1953-58. Relieved the anti-aircraft cruiser *Gotland* as Cadets' Seagoing Training Ship in 1959. Re-armed in 1961. Formerly carried 4—6 inch, 8—40 mm, 6—20 mm.

Radar: Search and Target designator: Thomson CSF Saturn.
Fire control: M45 series.

ÄLVSNABBEN

1975, J. Fama

Note: A new construction coastal minelayer MUL 20 projected.

1 COASTAL MINELAYER

MUL 11

Displacement, tons: 200 full load
Dimensions, feet (metres): 98·8 × 23·7 × 11·8 *(32·4 × 7·8 × 3·9)*
Guns: 2—20 mm
Main engines: 2 Atlas diesels; 300 bhp = 10 knots

Launched in 1946.

MUL 11

1971, Royal Swedish Navy

8 COASTAL MINELAYERS

MUL 12 (1952)	**MUL 14** (1953)	**MUL 16** (1956)	**MUL 18** (1956)
MUL 13 (1952)	**MUL 15** (1953)	**MUL 17** (1956)	**MUL 19** (1956)

Displacement, tons: 245 full load
Dimensions, feet (metres): 95·1 × 24·3 × 10·2 *(29 × 7·4 × 3·1)*
Gun: 1—40 mm
Main engines: 2 Nohab diesel-electric; 460 bhp = 10·5 knots

Launch dates in brackets. All completed in 1957.

MUL 12

1975, Royal Swedish Navy

37 SMALL MINELAYERS

501-537

Ordered in 1969. Of 15 tons and 14 knots with Diesel engines. Mines are laid from single traps on either beam.

SMALL MINELAYER 502

1975, Royal Swedish Navy

9 GRP MINEHUNTERS

Displacement, tons: 270
Dimensions, feet (metres): 141 × 30 × — *(43 × 8·5 × —)*
Gun: 1—20 mm
Main engines: 4 Diesels
Complement: 24

Ordered 1976. GRP hulls.

PROJECTED MINEHUNTER   *Captain Allan Kull*

6 "HANÖ" CLASS (MINESWEEPERS—COASTAL)

Name	No.	Builders	Commissioned
HANÖ	M 51	Karlskrona	1954
ORNÖ	M 55	Karlskrona	1954
STURKÖ	M 54	Karlskrona	1954
TÄRNÖ	M 52	Karlskrona	1954
TJURKÖ	M 53	Karlskrona	1954
UTÖ	M 56	Karlskrona	1954

Displacement, tons: 275 standard
Dimensions, feet (metres): 131·2 × 23 × 8 *(40 × 7 × 2·4)*
Guns: 2—40 mm (except *Utö;* 1—40mm)
Main engines: 2 Nohab Diesels; 2 shafts; 910 bhp = 14·5 knots

Steel hulls.

TJÜRKO   *1975, Royal Swedish Navy*

12 "ARKÖ" CLASS (MINESWEEPERS—COASTAL)

Name	No.	Builders	Commissioned
ARKÖ	M 57	Karlskrona	1958
ASPÖ	M 63	Karlskrona	1962
BLIDÖ	M 68	Hälsingborg	1964
HASSLÖ	M 64	Hälsingborg	1962
IGGÖ	M 60	Hälsingborg	1961
KARLSÖ	M 59	Karlskrona	1958
NÄMDÖ	M 67	Karlskrona	1964
SKAFTÖ	M 62	Hälsingborg	1962
SPÄRÖ	M 58	Hälsingborg	1958
STYRSÖ	M 61	Karlskrona	1962
VÄLLÖ	M 66	Hälsingborg	1963
VINÖ	M 65	Karlskrona	1962

Displacement, tons: 285 standard; 300 full load
Dimensions, feet (metres): 131 pp; 144·5 oa × 23 × 8 *(42 × 7 × 2·4)*
Gun: 1—40 mm
Main engines: 2 Mercedes-Benz (MTU 12V 493) diesels; 2 shafts; 1 600 bhp = 14·5 knots

Of wooden construction. There is a small difference in the deck-line between M 57-59 and M 60-68. *Arkö* was launched on 21 Jan 1957.

ASPÖ   *1975, Royal Swedish Navy*

3 "M 47" CLASS (MINESWEEPERS—INSHORE)

GILLÖGA M 47   **RÖDLÖGA** M 48   **SVARTLÖGA** M 49

Detalis same as "M 44" class. Built in 1964. Trawler type.

SVARTLOGA   *1970, Royal Swedish Navy*

3 "M 31" CLASS (MINESWEEPERS—INSHORE)

Name	No.	Builders	Commissioned
GÅSSTEN	M 31	Karlskrona	1973
NORSTEN	M 32	Karlskrona	1973
VIKSTEN	M 33	Karlskrona	1974

Displacement, tons: 120 standard; 135 full load
Dimensions, feet (metres): 79 oa × 21·7 × 12·2 *(24 × 6·6 × 3·7)*
Gun: 1—40 mm
Main engines: 1 Diesel; 460 bhp = 11 knots

Ordered 1972. *Viksten* built of glass reinforced plastic as a forerunner to new minehunters to be built at Karlskrona. *Gåssten* launched Nov 1972. *Norsten* Apr 1973, *Viksten* Apr 1974.

VIKSTEN

1975, Royal Swedish Navy

4 "M 44" CLASS (MINESWEEPERS—INSHORE)

BLACKAN M 44   GALTEN M 46
DÄMMAN M 45   HISINGEN M 43

Displacement, tons: 140
Dimensions, feet (metres): 72·2 × 21 × 11·2 *(22× 6·4 × 3·4)*
Gun: 1—40 mm
Main engines: 1 Diesel; 380 bhp = 9 knots

Built in 1960. Trawler type.

2 "M 41" CLASS (MINESWEEPERS—INSHORE)

ORUST M 41   TJÖRN M 42

Displacement, tons: 110
Dimensions, feet (metres): 62·3 × 19·7 × 8·5 *(19 × 6 × 2·4)*
Gun: 1—20 mm
Main engines: 1 Diesel; 210 bhp = 9 knots

Built in 1948. Trawler type.

8 "M 15" CLASS (MINESWEEPERS—INSHORE)

M 15   M 16   M 21   M 22   M 23   M 24   M 25   M 26

Displacement, tons: 70 standard
Dimensions, feet (metres): 85·3 × 16·5 × 4·5 *(26 × 5 × 1·4)*
Gun: 1—20 mm
Main engines: 2 Diesels; 320-430 bhp = 12-13 knots

All launched in 1941. M 17, M 18 and M 20 of this class were re-rated as tenders and renamed *Lommen, Spoven* and *Skuld* respectively: see later page.

M 25

1975, Royal Swedish Navy

2 MINE TRANSPORTS

FÄLLAREN A 236   MINÖREN A 237

Displacement, tons: 165 standard
Dimensions, feet (metres): 97 × 19 × 6·7 *(31·8 × 6·2 × 2·2)*
Main engines: 2 Diesels; 1 shaft; 240 bhp = 9 knots

Launched in 1941 and 1940 respectively.

AMPHIBIOUS FORCES

3 LCM

Name	No.	Builders	Commissioned
BORE	—	Åsigeverken	1967
GRIM	—	Åsigeverken	1962
HEIMDAL	—	Åsigeverken	1967

Displacement, tons: 340 full load
Dimensions, feet (metres): 118·1 × 27·9 × 8·5 *(36 × 8·5 × 2·6)*
Guns: 2—20 mm
Main engines: Diesels; 800 bhp = 12 knots

Launched in 1961 *(Grim)* and other two in 1966. Attached to Coastal Artillery.

BORE

1969, Royal Swedish Navy

2 LCM

Name	No.	Builders
SKAGUL	A 333	—
SLEIPNER	A 335	—

Displacement, tons: 335 standard
Dimensions, feet (metres): 114·8 × 27·9 × 9·5 *(35 × 8·5 × 2·9)*
Main engines: Diesels; 640 bhp = 10 knots

Sleipner was launched in 1959 and *Skagul* in 1960. Attached to Coastal Artillery.

4 "ANE" CLASS (LCM)

	Commissioned
	1960
	1960

ANE J 324	BALDER J 325	LOKE J 326	RING J 327

Displacement, tons: 135 standard
Dimensions, feet (metres): 91·9 × 26·2 × 6·0 *(28 × 8 × 1·2)*
Gun: 1—20 mm; 1 or 2 MG
Main engines: Speed = 8·5 knots

Built in 1943-45. Attached to Coastal Artillery.

10 + 9 + 5 "256" CLASS (LCU)

Nos. 256-265

Of same specifications as the "201" class. Completed 1975. 266-274 laid down 1975 onwards. 275-279 planned.

14 "242" CLASS (LCU)

Nos. 242-255

Of same specifications as the "201" class. Built in 1971-73.

LCU 245 ("242" Class)   *1975, Royal Swedish Navy*

41 "201" CLASS (LCU)

Nos. 201-241

Displacement, tons: 31
Dimensions, feet (metres): 69 × 13·8 × 4·2 *(20 × 4·2 × 1·3)*
Guns: 2—6·5 mm MG
Main engines: Diesels; 600 hp = 17 knots

Launched 1957-1960.

LCU 227 ("201" Class)   *1975, Royal Swedish Navy*

5 "L 51" CLASS (LCU)

L 51	L 52	L 53	L 54	L 55

Displacement, tons: 32 standard
Dimensions, feet (metres): 50·8 × 16 × 3·2 *(14 × 4·8 × 1)*
Main engines: Diesel; 140 bhp = 7 knots

Launched in 1947-48.

54 LCAs

337-354 of 6 tons and 21 knots. Built 1970-73.
332-336 of 5·4 tons and 25 knots. Built in 1967.
331 of 6 tons and 20 knots. Built in 1965.
301-330 of 4 tons and 9·5 knots. Built in 1956-59.

SURVEY SHIPS

(Operated by Ministry of Transport)

1 NEW CONSTRUCTION

Projected but not yet laid down.

ANDERS BURE (ex-*Rali*)

Displacement, tons: 54
Dimensions, feet (metres): 82·0 × 19·4 × 6·9 *(25 × 5·9 × 2·1)*
Main engines: Diesels = 15 knots
Complement: 11

Built in 1968 as *Rali*. She was purchased in 1971 and renamed.

RAN

Displacement, tons: 285 standard
Dimensions, feet (metres): 98·4 × 23·0 × 8·5 *(30 × 7 × 2·6)*
Main engines: Diesels; 260 bhp = 9 knots
Complement: 37

Ran was launched in 1945 and commissioned for service in 1946.

JOHAN MÅNSSON

Displacement, tons: 977 standard; 1 030 full load
Dimensions, feet (metres): 183·7 × 36·1 × 11·5 (56 × 11 × 3·5)
Main engines: Diesels; 3 300 bhp = 15 knots
Complement: 85

Launched on 14 Jan 1966. Her surveying launches are lowered and recovered over a stern ramp.

JOHAN MÅNSSON   1975, Royal Swedish Navy

GUSTAF AF KLINT

Displacement, tons: 750 standard
Dimensions, feet (metres): 170·6 × 36·2 × 15·4 (52 × 11 × 4·7)
Main engines: Diesels; 640 bhp = 10 knots
Complement: 66

Launched in 1941. Reconstructed in 1963. She formerly displaced 650 tons with a length of 154 feet (47 metres).

GUSTAV AF KLINT   1970, Royal Swedish Navy

NILS STRÖMCRONA

Displacement, tons: 140 standard
Dimensions, feet (metres): 88·6 × 17·0 × 8·2 (27 × 5·2 × 2·5)
Guns: None in peacetime
Main engines: Diesels; 300 bhp = 9 knots
Complement: 14

Launched in 1894, and reconstructed in 1952.

SERVICE FORCES

1 SUPPLY SHIP

Name	No.	Builders	Commissioned
FREJA	A 221	Kroger, Rendsburg	1954

Displacement, tons: 415 standard; 465 full load
Dimensions, feet (metres): 160·8 × 27·9 × 12·1 (49 × 8·5 × 3·7)
Main engines: Diesels; 600 bhp = 11 knots

Launched in 1953. Employed as a provision ship.

1 SUPPORT TANKER

BRÄNNAREN A 228

Displacement, tons: 857
Dimensions, feet (metres): 203·4 × 28·2 × 12·1 (62 × 8·6 × 3·7)
Speed, knots: 11

Ex-German merchant tanker *Indio* purchased early 1972. Built 1965.

1 COMMAND SHIP

Name	No.	Builders	Commissioned
MARIEHOLM	A 201	—	1934

Displacement, tons: 1 400 standard
Dimensions, feet (metres): 210 × 32·5 × 11·5 (64 × 10 × 3·5)
Aircraft: 1 helicopter
Guns: 2 MG (1—40 mm removed, see notes below)
Main engines: Steam reciprocating; 950 ihp = 12 knots

Former passenger ship. Converted during the Second World War to serve as a Base Communication Centre for the Commander-in-Chief of the Coastal Fleet. Recently used as a Staff Ship for the Commander-in-Chief in winter time, flying his flag. The ship had her mainmast removed and a helicopter platform installed aft in 1959 for employment as flagship of the Coastal Fleet. The 40 mm Bofors on the forecastle has been landed for the time being. To be relieved by *Visborg* 1976-77.

MARIEHOLM   1972, Royal Swedish Navy

1 SALVAGE SHIP

Name	No.	Builders	Commissioned
BELOS	A 211	—	29 May 1963

Displacement, tons: 1 000 standard
Dimensions, feet (metres): 204·4 × 37·0 × 12·0 (58 × 11·2 × 3·8)
Aircraft: 1 helicopter
Main engines: Diesels; 2 shafts; 1 200 bhp = 13 knots

Launched on 15 Nov 1961. Equipped with decompression chamber.

BELOS   1972, Wright & Logan

2 SAIL TRAINING SHIPS

Name	No.	Builders	Commissioned
FALKEN	S 02	—	1948
GLADAN	S 01	—	1947

Displacement, tons: 220 standard
Dimensions, feet (metres): 93 wl; 129·5 oa × 23·5 × 13·5 *(30·5; 42·5 × 7·7 × 4·4)*
Main engines: Auxiliary diesel; 120 bhp

Sail training ships. Two masted schooners. Launched 1947 and 1946 respectively. Sail area 5 511 square feet (512 square metres).

TENDERS

3 TRVs

Name	No.	Builders	Commissioned
PINGVINEN	A 248	Lundevarv-Ooverkstads AB, Kramfors	Mar 1975

Displacement, tons: 191
Dimensions, feet (metres): 108·2 × 20 × 6 *(33 × 6·1 × 1·8)*
Main engines: 2 diesels; 1 100 hp = 13 knots

Ordered 1972. Torpedo recovery and rocket trials ship. Launched 6 Sep 1973.

Name	No.	Builders	Commissioned
PELIKANEN	A 247	—	26 Sep 1963

Displacement, tons: 130 standard
Dimensions, feet (metres): 108·2 × 19·0 × 6·0 *(33 × 5·8 × 1·8)*
Main engines: 2 Mercedes Benz diesels; 1 040 bhp = 15 knots

Torpedo recovery and rocket trials vessel.

HÄGERN A 246

Displacement, tons: 50 standard
Dimensions, feet (metres): 88·6 × 16·4 × 4·9 *(29 × 5·4 × 1·6)*
Main engines: 2 diesels; 240 bhp = 10 knots

Launched in 1951.

5 TENDERS

SIGRUN A 256

Displacement, tons: 250 standard
Dimensions, feet (metres): 105·0 × 22·3 × 11·8 *(32 × 6·8 × 3·6)*
Main engines: Diesels 320 bhp = 11 knots

Launched in 1961. Laundry ship.

URD (ex-*Capella*) A 241

Displacement, tons: 63 standard; 90 full load
Dimensions, feet (metres): 73·8 × 18·3 × 9·2 *(22 × 5·6 × 2·8)*
Main engines: Diesels; 200 bhp = 8 knots

Experimental vessel added to the official list in 1970. Launched in 1969.

LOMMEN (ex-*M 17*) A 231

SKULD (ex-*M 20*) A 242
SPOVEN (ex-*M 18*) A 232

Displacement, tons: 70 standard
Dimensions, feet (metres): 85·3 × 16·5 × 4·5 *(26 × 5 × 1·4)*
Main engines: 2 diesels; 410 bhp = 13 knots

Former inshore minesweepers of the "M 15" Class. All launched in 1941.

TUGS

ACHILLES A 251   **AJAX A 252**

Displacement, tons: 450
Dimensions, feet (metres): 108·2 × 28·9 × 12 *(35·5 × 9·5 × 3·9)*
Main engines: Diesel; 1 650 bhp = 12 knots

Achilles was launched in 1962 and *Ajax* in 1963. Both are icebreaking tugs.

AJAX   *1970, Royal Swedish Navy*

HECTOR A 321   **HERMES A 253**   **HEROS A 323**

Displacement, tons: 185 standard
Dimensions, feet (metres): 75·5 × 22·6 × 11·1 *(24·5 × 7·4 × 3·6)*
Main engines: Diesels; 600 bhp = 11 knots

Launched in 1953-57. Icebreaking tugs.

HERA A 324   **HERCULES A 322**

Displacement, tons: 127 tons
Dimensions, feet (metres): 65·3 × 21·3 × 12·5 *(21·4 × 6·9 × 4·1)*
Main engines: Diesels; 615 bhp = 11·5 knots

Launched 1969 and 1971. Icebreaking Tugs.

WATER CARRIERS

FRYKEN A 217

Displacement, tons: 307 standard
Dimensions, feet (metres): 105·0 × 18·7 × 8·9 *(34·4 × 6·1 × 2·9)*
Main engines: Diesels; 370 bhp = 10 knots

A naval construction water carrier. Launched in 1959 and completed in 1960.

UNDEN A 216

Displacement, tons: 540 standard
Dimensions, feet (metres): 121·4 × 23·3 × 9·8 *(39·8 × 7·6 × 3·2)*
Main engines: Steam reciprocating; 225 ihp = 9 knots

Launched in 1946.

ICEBREAKERS

2 + 1 FINNISH "URHO" CLASS

Name	No.	Builders	Commissioned
ATLE	—	Wärtsilä, Helsinki	21 Oct 1974
FREJ	—	Wärtsilä, Helsinki	30 Sep 1974
YMER	—	Wärtsilä, Helsinki	1977

Displacement, tons: 7 900
Dimensions, feet (metres): 337·8 × 77·1 × 24·6 *(104·6 × 23·8 × 7·3)*
Aircraft: 1 helicopter
Main engines: 5 Wärtsilä-Pielstick diesels of 25 000 bhp; 4 Stromberg electric motors; 4 shafts (2 for'd, 2 aft); 22 000 shp = 18 knots
Complement: 54 (16 officers, 38 men)

Atle laid down 10 May 1973, launched 27 Nov 1973. *Frej* launched 3 June 1974. *Ymer* ordered 24 Mar 1975. Sister ships of Finnish "Urho" class.

FREJ

1974, Wärtsilä

Name	No.	Builders	Commissioned
NJORD	—	Wärtsilä, Finland	Dec 1969

Displacement, tons: 5 150 standard; 5 686 full load
Dimensions, feet (metres): 283·8 oa × 69·6 × 20·3 *(81 × 20·5 × 6·2)*
Main engines: Wärtsilä diesel-electric; 4 shafts, (2 forward, 2 aft); 12 000 hp = 18 knots

Launched on 20 Oct 1968. Near sister ship of *Tor*.

NJORD

1971, Royal Swedish Navy

Name	No.	Builders	Commissioned
TOR	—	Wärtsilä, Crichton-Vulcan Yard, Turku	31 Jan 1964

Displacement, tons: 4 980 standard; 5 290 full load
Dimensions, feet (metres): 283·8 oa × 69·6 × 20·3 *(81 × 20·5 × 6·2)*
Main engines: Wärtsilä-Sulzer diesel-electric; 4 shafts; (2 for'd; 2 aft); 12 000 hp = 18 knots

Launched on 25 May 1963. Towed to Sandvikens Skeppsdocka, Helsingfors, for completion. Larger but generally similar to *Oden,* and a near-sister to *Tarmo* built for Finland.

TOR

1972, Royal Swedish Navy

Name	No.	Builders	Commissioned
ALE	—	Wärtsilä, Helsinki	12 Dec 1973

Displacement, tons: 1 488
Dimensions, feet (metres): 150·9 × 42·6 × 16·4 *(46 × 13 × 5)*
Main engines: Diesels; 4 750 hp; 2 shafts = 14 knots
Complement: 21

Built for operations on Lake Vänern. Launched 1 June 1973.

Name	No.	Builders	Commissioned
THULE	—	Naval Dockyard, Karlskrona	1953

Displacement, tons: 2 200 standard; 2 280 full load
Dimensions, feet (metres): 204·2 oa × 52·8 × 19·4 *(57 × 16·1 × 5·9)*
Main engines: Diesel-electric; 3 shafts (1 for'd); 4 800 bhp = 14 knots
Complement: 43

Launched in Oct 1951.

Name	No.	Builders	Commissioned
ODEN	—	Sandviken, Helsingfors	1958

Displacement, tons: 4 950 standard; 5 220 full load
Dimensions, feet (metres): 273·5 oa × 63·7 × 22·7 *(78 × 19·4 × 6·9)*
Main engines: Diesel-electric; 4 shafts (2 for'd); 10 500 shp = 16 knots
Oil fuel, tons: 740
Complement: 75

Similar to the Finnish *Voima* and 3 Soviet icebreakers. Launched on 16 Oct 1956.

ODEN

1972, Royal Swedish Navy

SWITZERLAND

Diplomatic Representation

Defence Attaché in London: Colonel H. W. Fischer

The Swiss Army operates ten Coastal Patrol Craft on the lakes. These were originally built in 1942 against possible German operations and have been modernised. Fitted with machine guns and radar. New construction would seem imminent. There are also water-transport detachments and other detachments with smaller patrol craft.

SWISS PATROL CRAFT   *1966, Swiss Arm*

SYRIA

Personnel

(a) 1976: 2 500 officers and men
(b) 2½ years national service

Bases

Latakia, Baniyas

Mercantile Marine

Lloyd's Register of Shipping: 14 vessels of 7 531 tons gross

FRIGATES

2 Ex-SOVIET "PETYA I" CLASS

Displacement, tons: 950 standard; 1 150 full load
Dimensions, feet (metres): 270 × 29·9 × 10·5 *(82·3 × 9·1 × 3·2)*
Guns: 4—3 in *(76 mm)* (twin)
A/S weapons: 4—16 barrelled MBU 2500
Torpedo tubes: 5—16 in *(406 mm)* tubes
Main engines: 2 diesels; 6 000 hp; 2 gas-turbines; 30 000 hp; 2 shafts
Speed, knots: 30
Complement: 100

Transferred by USSR in 1975.

LIGHT FORCES

6 Ex-SOVIET "OSA" CLASS
(FAST ATTACK CRAFT—MISSILE)

Displacement, tons: 165 standard; 200 full load
Dimensions, feet (metres): 128·7 × 25·1 × 5·9 *(42·2 × 8·2 × 1·9)*
Missile launchers: 4, two pairs abreast, for SSN-2 (Styx)
Guns: 4—30 mm (twins; 1 forward, 1 aft)
Main engines: 3 diesels; 13 000 bhp = 32 knots
Range, miles: 800 at 25 knots
Complement: 25

Original pair sunk in Oct 1973 war. Up to six replacements reported.

SYRIAN "OSA" Class   *Dec, 197*

6 Ex-SOVIET "KOMAR" CLASS
(FAST ATTACK CRAFT—MISSILE)

Displacement, tons: 70 standard; 80 full load
Dimensions, feet (metres): 83·7 × 19·8 × 5 *(27·4 × 6·5 × 1·6)*
Missile launchers: 2 for SSN-2 (Styx)
Guns: 2—25 mm
Main engines: 4 diesels; 4 shafts; 4 800 bhp = 40 knots
Range, miles: 400 at 30 knots

Transferred between 1963 and 1966. Three reported lost in Israeli war October 1973, but were replaced.

"KOMAR" Class

8 Ex-SOVIET "P 4" CLASS
(FAST ATTACK CRAFT—TORPEDO)

Displacement, tons: 25 standard
Dimensions, feet (metres): 62·7 × 11·6 × 5·6 *(20·5 × 3·8 × 1·8)*
Torpedo tubes: 2—18 in
Guns: 2—MG (twin)
Main engines: 2 diesels; 2 200 bhp; 2 shafts = 50 knots

Five torpedo boats were transferred from the USSR at Latakia on 7 Feb 1957, and at least twelve subsequently. One reported lost in Israeli War October 1973. Four transferred to Egypt in 1970. Only eight of the remainder considered operational.

"P 4" Class

3 Ex-FRENCH CH TYPE (LARGE PATROL CRAFT)

ABABEH IBN NEFEH   ABDULLAH IBN ARISSI   TAREK IBN ZAYED

Displacement, tons: 107 standard; 131 full load
Dimensions, feet (metres): 116·5 pp; 121·8 oa × 17·5 × 6·5 *(38·2; 39·9 × 5·7 × 2·1)*
Guns: 1—3 in; 2—20 mm
A/S weapons: Depth charges
Main engines: MAN diesels; 2 shafts; 1 130 bhp = 16 knots
Oil fuel, to..s: 50
Range, miles: 1 200 at 8 knots; 680 at 13 knots
Complement: 28

All built in France and completed in 1940. Rebuilt in 1955-56 when the funnels were removed. These were transferred in 1962 to form the nucleus of the Syrian Navy. Two of these ships are probably non-operational.

MINE WARFARE FORCES

1 Ex-SOVIET "T 43" CLASS (MINESWEEPER—OCEAN)

YARMOUK

Displacement, tons: 500 standard; 610 full load
Dimensions, feet (metres): 191·5 × 28·1 × 6·9 *(62·8 × 9·2 × 2·3)*
Guns: 4—37 mm; 4—25 mm
Main engines: 2 diesels motors; 2 shafts; 2 000 hp = 17 knots
Range, miles: 1 600 at 10 knots
Complement: 40

Reported in 1962 to have been transferred from the Soviet Navy. The second of this class was sunk in the Israeli War October 1973.

2 Ex-SOVIET "VANYA" CLASS (MINESWEEPERS—COASTAL)

Displacement, tons: 225 standard; 250 full load
Dimensions, feet (metres): 130·7 × 24 × 6·9 *(39·9 × 7·3 × 2·1)*
Guns: 2—30 mm (twin)
Main engines: 2 diesels; 2 200 bhp = 18 knots
Complement: 30

Transferred Dec 1972.

MISCELLANEOUS

1 Ex-SOVIET "NYRIAT" CLASS

Displacement, tons: 145
Main engines: Diesel = 12·5 knots
Complement: 15

Used as divers' base-ship.

TAIWAN

Commander-in-Chief:
Admiral Soong Chang-chih
Deputy Commanders-in-Chief:
Vice-Admiral Chih Meng-ping
Vice-Admiral Tsou Chien
Chief of Staff:
Vice-Admiral Chen Tung-hai
Commander, Fleet Command:
Vice-Admiral Li Pei-chou
Commandant of Marine Corps:
Lieutenant-General Kung Lin-cheng

Diplomatic Representation

Naval Attaché in Washington:
Rear-Admiral Chiu Hua-ku

Bases

Tsoying, Makung (Pescadores), Keelung.

Personnel

7 100 officers and 28 000 enlisted in Navy
3 000 officers and 26 000 enlisted in Marine Corps

Naval Aviation

One squadron of Air Force S-2A tracker ASW aircraft is under
Navy operational control.
The Marine Corps operates several observation aircraft and
helicopters.

Mercantile Marine

Lloyd's Register of Shipping:
428 vessels of 1 449 957 tons gross

Guided Missiles

The Israeli Gabriel surface-to-surface missile has been fitted to
several Taiwan destroyers. Reportedly, some ships also may
be armed with a surface-to-air variant of the Sidewind-
er/Chaparral missile.

Strength of the Fleet

3 Midget Submarines (?)
18 Destroyers
12 Frigates
1 Frigate/Transport
3 Patrol Vessels
9 Torpedo Boats
2 Ocean Minesweepers
14 Coastal Minesweepers
9 Mine Boats & Launches
1 Amphibious Flagship
28 Landing Ships
22 Utility Landing Craft
21 Auxiliary Ships
5 Floating Dry Docks

Pennant Numbers

A major revision of warship pennant numbers was reported to
have taken place early in 1976.

SUBMARINES

2 Ex-US GUPPY II TYPE

Name	No.
HAI SHIH (ex-USS *Cutlass*, SS 478)	SS 91
HAI PAO (ex-USS *Tusk*, SS 426)	SS 92

Builders	Launched	US Comm	Transferred
Portsmouth Navy Yard	5 Nov 1944	17 Mar 1945	12 Apr 1973
Federal SB & DD Co, Kearney, New Jersey	8 July 1945	11 April 1946	18 Oct 1973

Displacement, tons: 1 870 standard; 2 420 submerged
Length, feet (metres): 307·5 *(93·6)* oa
Beam, feet (metres): 27·2 *(8·3)*
Draught, feet (metres): 18 *(5·5)*
Torpedo tubes: 10—21 inch *(533 mm)*; 6 fwd; 4 aft
Main engines: 3 diesels (Fairbanks Morse); 4 800 bhp; 2 elec-
tric motors (Elliott); 5 400 shp; 2 shafts
Speed, knots: 18 surface; 15 submerged
Complement: 81 (11 officers, 70 enlisted men)

Originally fleet-type submarines of the US Navy "Tench" class;
extensively modernised under the GUPPY II programme.
These submarines each have four 126-cell electric batteries;
fitted with snorkel.
Taiwan is the only nation in the Western Pacific currently to
operate former US Navy submarines.

HAI SHIH   *1972, United States Navy*

3 (?) MIDGET SUBMARINES: "SX 404" CLASS

Displacement, tons: 70 submerged
Dimensions, feet (metres): 52·4 oa × 6·6 *(17·2 × 2·2)*
Armament: Explosive charges carried externally for delivery
by divers
Main engines: Diesel-electric propulsion; 1 shaft = 11 knots
surfaced; 6·5 submerged
Complement: 5 + 8 passengers

Reportedly, Taiwan operates three midget submarines of this
design built by Costruzioni Motoscafi Sottomarini (COSMOS)
of Livorno, Italy. The "SX-404" design, first produced in 1955, is
known to be in service with the Colombian and Pakistani
navies. There are reports that more than 60 of these craft have
been built.
These submarines are fitted with snorkel devices, sonar
equipment, and have a lock-out trunk for divers or swimmers.
A pair of underwater "chariots" can be transported externally.
Operating depth is believed to be 330 feet.

HAI SHIH   *1973, US Navy*

DESTROYERS

5 Ex-US "GEARING" CLASS

Name	No.	Builders	Launched	US Comm	Transferred
DANG YANG (ex-USS *Lloyd Thomas*, DD 764)	DD 11	Bethlehem Steel (San Francisco)	5 Oct 1945	21 Mar 1947	12 Oct 197
CHIEN YANG (ex-USS *James E. Kyes*, DD 787)	DD 12	Todd Pacific Shipyards (Seattle, Wash)	4 Aug 1945	8 Feb 1946	18 Apr 197
HAN YANG (ex-USS *Herbert J. Thomas*, DD 833)	DD 15	Bath Iron Works Corp	25 Mar 1945	29 May 1945	6 May 197
LAO YANG (ex-USS *Shelton*, DD 790)	DD 20	Todd Pacific Shipyards (Seattle, Wash)	8 Mar 1946	21 June 1946	18 Apr 197
LIAO YANG (ex-USS *Hanson*, DD 832)	DD 21	Bath Iron Works Corp	11 Mar 1945	11 May 1945	18 Apr 197

Displacement, tons: 2 425 standard; approx 3 500 full load
Length, feet (metres): 390·5 *(119·0)* oa
Beam, feet (metres): 40·9 *(12·4)*
Draught, feet (metres): 19 *(5·8)*
Guns: 4—5 inch *(127 mm)* 38 cal (twin) (Mk 38)
Several ·50 cal MG fitted in several ships
A/S weapons: 1 ASROC 8-tube launcher except in *Dang Yang*
which has trainable hedgehog (Mk 15)
6—12·75 inch *(324 mm)* torpedo tubes (Mk 32 triple)
Main engines: 2 geared turbines (General Electric); 60 000 shp;
2 shafts
Boilers: 4
Speed, knots: 34
Complement: approx 275

Former US Navy destroyers of the "Gearing" class. The *Dang
Yang* was modified to a special anti-submarine configuration
and reclassified as an escort destroyer (DDE) in 1950; changed
again to "straight" DD upon modernisation in 1962. These
ships have been extensively modernised under the Fleet
Rehabilitation and Modernisation programme, all to FRAM I
standard except *Dang Yang* which was FRAM II (no ASROC). All
have helicopter platform and hangar.
Armament listed above was at time of transfer. The *Lao Yang*
has twin 5 inch gun mounts in "A" and "B" positions with A/S
torpedo tubes alongside second funnel; other ships have the
"A" and "Y" gun mounts with torpedo tubes in "B" position
except *Dang Yang* has torpedo tubes between funnels.

In 1963-1964 the *Herbert J. Thomas* was modified for protection against biological, chemical, and atomic attack; the ship
could be fully "Sealed" with enclosed lookout and control
positions, special air-conditioning. Upon transfer to Taiwan the
Herbert J. Thomas assumed name and pennant number of a
ex-US "Benson" class destroyer in Taiwan service.
Three of the FRAM I ships were initially scheduled for transfer
to Spain; however, they were declined by Spain and allocated
to Taiwan.
Electronics: At time of transfer three of these ships had SPS-3
and SPS-10 search radar antennae on their tripod mast; *Dang
Yang* had older SPS-6 and SPS-10 antennae; *Chien Yang* ha
SPS-40 and SPS-10 (correction to previous edition). Fitted wit
SQS-23 sonar except *Dang Yang* which has SQS-29 series.

LIAO YANG (as USS *Hanson*)   *1971, US Navy*   DANG YANG (as USS *Lloyd Thomas*)   *1970, US Navy*

1 Ex-US "GEARING" CLASS RADAR PICKET

Name	No.	Builders	Launched	US Comm	Transferred
FU YANG (ex-USS *Ernest G. Small, DD 838*)	DD 7	Bath Iron Works Corp	14 June 1945	21 Aug 1945	19 Feb 1971

Displacement, tons: 2 425 standard; approx 3 500 full load
Length, feet (metres): 390·5 *(119·0)* oa
Beam, feet (metres): 40·8 *(12·4)*
Draught, feet (metres): 19 *(5·8)*
Guns: 6—5 inch *(127 mm)* 38 calibre DP (twin) (Mk 38); 8—40 mm (twin); 4—·50 cal MG (single)
A/S weapons: 6—12·75 inch *(324 mm)* torpedo tubes (Mk 32 triple); 2 fixed hedgehogs
Main engines: 2 geared turbines; (General Electric); 60 000 shp; 2 shafts
Boilers: 4 Babcock & Wilcox
Speed, knots: 34
Complement: approx 275

Former US Navy radar picket destroyer of the "Gearing" class. Converted to a radar picket destroyer (DDR) during 1952 and subsequently modernised under the Fleet Rehabilitation and Modernisation (FRAM II) programme; redesignated as a "straight" destroyer (DD), but retained specialised electronic equipment. Not fitted with helicopter flight deck or hangar. The 40 mm guns were installed after transfer to Taiwan.

Electronics: At time of transfer the *Fu Yang* had SPS-37 and SPS-10 search radars on forward tripod mast, and large TACAN (tactical aircraft navigation) "beehive" antenna on second tripod mast. Fitted SQS-29 series hull-mounted sonar and SQA-10 variable depth sonar.

FU YANG

8 Ex-US "ALLEN M. SUMNER" CLASS

Name	No.	Builders	Launched	US Comm	Transferred
HSIANG YANG (ex-USS *Brush, DD 745*)	DD 1	Bethlehem Steel, Staten Island	28 Dec 1943	17 April 1944	9 Dec 1969
HENG YANG (ex-USS *Samuel N. Moore, DD 747*)	DD 2	Bethlehem Steel, Staten Island	23 Feb 1944	24 June 1944	9 Dec 1969
HUA YANG (ex-USS *Bristol, DD 857*)	DD 3	Bethlehem Steel, San Pedro	29 Oct 1944	17 Mar 1945	9 Dec 1969
YUEH YANG (ex-USS *Haynsworth, DD 700*)	DD 5	Federal SB & DD Co	15 Apr 1944	22 June 1944	12 May 1970
HUEI YANG (ex-USS *English, DD 696*)	DD 6	Federal SB & DD Co	27 Feb 1944	4 May 1944	11 Aug 1969
PO YANG (ex-USS *Maddox, DD 731*)	DD 10	Bath Iron Works Corp	19 Mar 1944	2 June 1944	6 July 1972
LO YANG (ex-USS *Taussig, DD 746*)	DD 14	Bethlehem Steel, Staten Island	25 Jan 1944	20 May 1944	6 May 1974
NAN YANG (ex-USS *John W. Thomason, DD 760*)	DD 17	Bethlehem Steel, San Francisco	30 Sep 1944	11 Oct 1945	6 May 1974

Displacement, tons: 2 200 standard; 3 320 full load
Length, feet (metres): 376·5 *(114·8)* oa
Beam, feet (metres): 40·9 *(12·4)*
Draught, feet (metres): 19 *(5·8)*
Missile launchers: *Heng Yang* and others reported being fitted with Gabriel surface-to-surface missile
Guns: 6—5 inch *(127 mm)* 38 calibre DP (twin) (Mk 38)
Up to 6—3 inch *(76 mm)* 50 calibre AA (2 twin, 2 single) in most ships; others, including *Heng Yang* and *Yueh Yang*, have 8—40 mm (1 quad, 2 twin) several ·50 cal MG (single) in most ships
A/S weapons: 6—12·75 inch *(324 mm)* torpedo tubes (Mk 32 triple); 2 fixed hedgehogs; depth charges in some ships
Main engines: 2 geared turbines (General Electric or Westinghouse); 60 000 shp; 2 shafts
Boilers: 4 Babcock & Wilcox
Speed, knots: 34
Complement: approx 275

HSIANG YANG   *1971, United States Navy*

"SUMNER" CLASS—*continued*

Former US Navy destroyers of the "Allen M. Sumner" class. These ships have not been modernised under the FRAM programmes, but retain their original configurations with removal of original torpedo tubes, and 40 mm and 20 mm AA guns, and installation of improved electronic equipment. Secondary gun battery now varies; during the 1950s most of these ships were rearmed with six 3 inch AA guns (two single alongside forward funnel and two twin amidships); number retained apparently varies from ship to ship, with some ships retaining original 40 mm guns. Tripod mast fitted.
Lo Yang and *Nan Yang* have names and numbers previously assigned to older ex-US destroyers.

Electronics: Most ships have SPS-6 and SPS-10 search radars on their tripod mast; *Po Yang* has SPS-40 and SPS-10 while *Nan Yang* has SPS-37 and SPS-10.

Photographs: The *Fu Yang* can be distinguished from the other six-gun destroyers operated by Taiwan by the former ship's additional space between funnels and the after tripod mast supporting large TACAN dome. The photographs of the *Heng Yang* and *Yueh Yang* show the 40 mm twin mounts, their directors, and stern depth charge racks.

HENG YANG   *Courtesy "Ships of the World"*

Ex-US "BENSON" CLASS

Lo Yang DD 14 (ex-USS *Benson, DD 421*), **Han Yang** DD 15 (ex-USS *Hilary P Jones, DD 427*) stricken in 1975 with names and numbers assigned to later ships. See 1974-1975 and previous editions for characteristics and photographs.

4 Ex-US "FLETCHER" CLASS

Name		No.
KWEI YANG (ex-USS *Twining, DD 540*)		DD 8
CHING YANG (ex-USS *Mullany, DD 528*)		DD 9
AN YANG (ex-USS *Kimberly, DD 521*)		DD 18
KUEN YANG (ex-USS *Yarnall, DD 541*)		DD 19

Builders	Launched	US Comm.	Transferred
Bethlehem Steel Co, San Francisco	11 July 1943	1 Dec 1943	16 Aug 1971
Bethlehem Steel Co, San Francisco	12 Oct 1942	23 Apr 1943	6 Oct 1971
Bethlehem Steel Co, Staten Island	4 Feb 1943	22 May 1943	2 June 1967
Bethlehem Steel Co, San Francisco	25 July 1943	30 Dec 1943	10 June 1968

Displacement, tons: 2 100 standard; 3 050 full load
Length, feet (metres): 376·5 *(114·7)* oa
Beam, feet (metres): 35·9 *(11·9)*
Draught, feet (metres): 18 *(5·5)*
Guns: 5—5 inch *(127 mm)* 38 calibre DP (single) except 4 guns in *Ching Yang* (Mk 30); 6—3 inch *(76 mm)* 50 calibre AA (twin) in *Kwei Yang* and *Ching Yang*; 6—40 mm AA (twin) in *An Yang* and *Kuen Yang*
A/S weapons: 6—12·75 inch *(324 mm)* torpedo tubes (Mk 32 triple) in *Kwei Yang* and *Ching Yang*; 2 fixed hedgehogs depth charges in some ships
Torpedo tubes: 5—21 inch *(533mm)* (quintuple) in *Kuen Yang*
Main engines: 2 geared turbines (General Electric in *An Yang*, Allis Chalmers in *Kuen Yang*, Westinghouse in others); 60 000 shp; 2 shafts
Boilers: 4 Babcock & Wilcox
Speed, knots: 36
Complement: approx 250

CHING YANG (four guns)

Former US "Fletcher" class destroyers. All now have tripod mast. Only *Kuen Yang* retains anti-ship torpedo tubes installed between second funnel and third 5 inch gun mount. Reportedly, the ship has been fitted for minelaying.

KUEN YANG (five guns and torpedo tubes)

1 TRAINING SHIP: Ex-US "GLEAVES" CLASS

Name	No.	Builders	Launched	US Comm.	Transferred
HSIEN YANG (ex-*Hatakaze*, ex-USS *Macomb, DMS 23*, ex-*DD 458*)	DD 1016	Bath Iron Works Corp	23 Sep 1941	26 Jan 1942	6 Aug 1970

Displacement, tons: 1 700 standard; 2 575 full load
Length, feet (metres): 341 *(104·0)* 348·33 *(106·2)* oa
Beam, feet (metres): 36 *(11·0)*
Draught, feet (metres): 18 *(5·5)*
Guns: 3—5 inch *(127 mm)* 38 calibre DP (single); several 40 mm AA; several 20 mm AA
A/S weapons: depth charges
Main engines: 2 geared turbines (Westinghouse); 50 000 shp; 2 shafts
Boilers: 4 Babcock & Wilcox
Speed, knots: 34
Complement: 250

HSIEN YANG (ex-Hatakaze)

The *Hsien Yang* is a former US destroyer of the "Gleaves" class; converted to a high speed minesweeper (DMS) in 1944 with removal of one (of five) 5 inch guns and torpedo tubes, and minesweeping gear fitted. Transferred to Japan on 19 Oct 1954 for service with the Maritime Self-Defence Force; subsequently transferred to Taiwan on 6 Aug 1970. Decommissioned in 1974 for use as a dockside training ship. Future status is in question.

DISPOSALS

Nan Yang DD 17 (ex-USS *Plunkett, DD 431*) stricken in 1975 with name and number assigned to later ship; **Hsien Yang** DD 16 (ex-USS *Rodman, DMS 21, DD 456*) stricken in 1969 after running aground; name and number assigned to ex-USS *Macomb* (above).

FRIGATES

All frigates of the US "Bostwick" class have been stricken: *Tai Ho* DE 23 (ex-USS *Thomas, DE 102*), *Tai Chong* DE 24 (ex-USS *Breeman, DE 104*), *Tai Cho* DE 26 (ex-USS *Carter, DE 112*) stricken in 1972-1973 for scrapping; *Tai Hu* DE 25 (ex-USS *Bostwick, DE 103*) stricken in 1975. See 1975-1976 and previous editions for characteristics.

The "short-hull" frigate *Tai Kang* DE 21 (ex-USS *Wyffel, DE 6*) was scrapped in 1972. See 1971-1972 and previous editions for description.

1 Ex-US "RUDDEROW" CLASS

Name	No.
TAI YUAN (ex-USS *Riley*, DE 579)	PF 27

Builders	Launched	US Comm.	Transferred
Bethlehem Steel Co, Higham, Massachusetts	29 Dec 1943	13 Mar 1944	10 July 1968

Displacement, tons: 1 450 standard; approx 2 000 full load
Length, feet (metres): 300 *(91·4)* wl; 306 *(93·3)* oa
Beam, feet (metres): 37 *(11·3)*
Draught, feet (metres): 14 *(4·3)*
Guns: 2—5 inch *(127 mm)* 38 calibre DP (single); 4—40 mm AA (twin); 4—20 mm AA (single)
A/S weapons: 6—12·75 inch *(324 mm)* torpedo tubes (Mk 32 triple); 1 hedgehog; depth charge
Main engines: Geared turbines (General Electric) with electric drive; 12 000 shp; 2 shafts
Boilers: 2 Foster Wheeler
Speed, knots: 24
Complement: approx 200

Former US Navy destroyer escort. Refitted with tripod mast and platforms before bridge for 20 mm guns. (Hedgehog is on main deck, behind forward 5 inch mount). SPS-6 and SPS-10 search radars are installed.
Designation changed from DE to PF in 1975.

TAI YUAN

Iain G. B. Lovie

11 FRIGATES } Ex-US APD TYPE
1 TRANSPORT

Name
Yu SHAN (ex-USS *Kinzer*, APD91|DE 232)
HWA SHAN (ex-*Donald W. Wolf* APD 129|DE 713)
WEN SHAN (ex-*Gantner*, APD 42|DE 60)
FU SHAN (ex-*Truxton*, APD 98|DE 282)
LU SHAN (ex-USS *Bull*, APD 78|DE 693)
SHOA SHAN (ex-*Kline*, APD 120|DE 687)
TAI SHAN (ex-*Register*, APD 92|DE 233)
HENG SHAN (ex-*R. W. Herndon*, APD 121|DE 688)
KANG SHAN (ex-*G. W. Ingram*, APD 43|DE 62)
CHUNG SHAN (ex-*Blessman*, APD 48|DE 69)
LUNG SHAN (ex-*Schmitt*, APD 76|DE 676)
TIEN SHAN (ex-*Kleinsmith*, APD 132|DE 718)

No.	Builders	Launched	US Comm.	Transferred
PF 32	Charleston Navy Yard, South Carolina	9 Dec 1943	1 Nov 1944	Apr 1965
PF 33	Defoe SB Co, Bay City, Michigan	22 July 1944	13 Apr 1945	May 1965
PF 34	Bethlehem SB Co, Higham, Massachusetts	17 Apr 1943	23 July 1943	May 1966
PF 35	Charleston Navy Yard, South Carolina	9 Mar 1944	9 July 1954	Mar 1966
PF 36	Defoe SB Co, Bay City, Michigan	25 Mar 1943	12 Aug 1943	Aug 1966
PF 37	Bethlehem, Quincy, Massachusetts	27 June1944	18 Oct 1944	Mar 1966
PF 38	Charleston Navy Yard, South Carolina	20 Jan 1944	11 Jan 1945	Oct 1966
PF 39	Bethlehem, Quincy, Massachusetts	15 July 1944	3 Nov 1944	Oct 1966
PF 42	Bethlehem SB Co, Higham, Massachusetts	8 May 1943	11 Aug 1943	July 1967
PF 43	Bethlehem SB Co, Higham, Massachusetts	19 June1943	19 Sep 1943	July 1967
PF 44	Bethlehem, Quincy, Massachusetts	29 May 1943	24 July 1943	Feb 1969
APD 215	Defoe SB Co, Bay City, Michigan	27 Jan 1945	12 June1945	May 1960

Displacement, tons: 1 400 standard; 2 130 full load
Length, feet (metres): 300 *(91·4)* wl; 306 *(93·3)* oa
Beam, feet (metres): 37 *(11·3)*
Draught, feet (metres): 12·6 *(3·2)*
Guns: 2—5 inch *(127 mm)* 38 cal DP; 6—40 mm AA (twin); 4—20 m AA (single) except *Hwa Shan* and possibly others have eight guns (twin mounts)
A/S weapons: 6—12·75 inch *(324 mm)* torpedo tubes (Mk 32 triple) except *Heng Shan* and possibly others have two hedgehogs; depth charges
Main engines: Geared turbines (General Electric) with electric drive; 12 000 shp; 2 shafts
Boilers: 2 Foster Wheeler
Speed, knots: 23·6
Complement: approx 200

Former US Navy high speed transports (APD) employed as frigates. All designated PF except *Tien Shan* which is designated APD.

All begun as destroyer escorts (DE), but converted during construction or after completion to high speed transports carrying 160 troops, commandoes, or frogmen.

The ex-USS *Walter B Cobb* (APD 106|DE 596) transferred to Taiwan in 1966 was lost at sea while under tow to Taiwan; replaced by ex-USS *Bull*.

Configurations differ: APD 37 class has high bridge; APD 87 class has low bridge. Radars and fire control equipment vary. The *Heng Shan, Chung Shan* and *Lung Shan* were decommissioned in 1974 and laid up in reserve. Others are active.

Gunnery: All ships are now believed to have been refitted with a second 5 inch gun aft. One twin 40 mm gun mount is forward of bridge and two twin mounts are amidships. Note after 5 inch mount and depth charge racks in photo of *Lung Shan*. Davits amidships can hold four LCVP-type landing craft.

FU SHAN

courtesy "Ships of the World"

LUNG SHAN

1973

PATROL VESSELS

3 Ex-US MSF TYPE

Name	No.	Builders	US Comm
WU SHENG (ex-USS *Red Start, MSF 378)*	PCE 66	Savannah Machine & Foundry Co, Georgia	4 Apr 1945
CHU YUNG (ex-USS *Waxwing, MSF 389)*	PCE 67	American SB Co, Cleveland, Ohio	6 Aug 1945
MO LING (ex-USS *Steady, MSF 118)*	PCE 70	American SB Co, Cleveland, Ohio	16 Nov 1942

Displacement, tons: 890 standard; 1 250 full load
Dimensions, feet (metres): 215 wl; 221·1 oa × 32·1 × 10·8 *(70·4; 61·4 × 10·5 × 3·5)*
Guns: 2—3 inch *(76 mm)* 50 cal AA (single); 4—40 mm AA (twin); 4—20 mm AA (twin)
A/S weapons: 1 hedgehog; 3—12·75 inch *(324 mm)* torpedo tubes (Mk 32 triple); depth charges
Main engines: Diesel-electric (General Motors diesels); 3 530 bhp; 2 shafts = 18 knots
Complement: approx 80

WU SHENG

Former US Navy minesweepers of the "Auk" class; originally designated AM. *Wu Sheng* transferred to Taiwan in July 1965, *Chu Yung* in Nov 1965 and *Mo Ling* in Mar 1968. Minesweeping equipment removed and second 3 inch gun fitted aft in Taiwan service. *Chein Men* PCE 45 (ex-USS *Toucan, MSF 387)* sunk by Communist Chinese warships south of Quemoy Island on 6 Aug 1965.

MO LING

14 PATROL BOATS (PB)

Displacement, tons: approx 30 tons
Guns: 1—40 mm

Small patrol boats designated PB. Constructed in Taiwan with the first of a reported 14 units completed about 1971. These are believed the first warships of indigenous Taiwan construction.

PB 1

TORPEDO BOATS

At least three additional torpedo boats are known to be in service; details are not available.

2 79-ft TYPE

Name	No.	Builders	Commissioned
FU KWO	—	Hutchins Yacht Corp, Jacksonville, Florida	—

Displacement, tons: 46 light; 53 full load
Dimensions, feet (metres): 79 oa × 23·25 × 5·5 *(25·9 × 7·6 × 1·8)*
Guns: 1—40 mm AA; 2—50 cal MG (single)
Torpedo launchers: 2
Main engines: 3 gasoline engines; 3 shafts = 39 knots max; 32 knots cruising
Complement: 12

Transferred to Taiwan on 1 Sep 1957. Their current pennant numbers are unknown.

2 71-ft TYPE

Name	No.	Builders	Commissioned
FAAN KONG	—	Annapolis Yacht Yard, Annapolis, Maryland	—
SAO TANG	—	Annapolis Yacht Yard, Annapolis, Maryland	—

Displacement, tons: 39 light; 46 full load
Dimensions, feet (metres): 71 oa × 19 × 5 *(23·3 × 6·3 × 1·6)*
Guns: 1—20 mm AA; 4—50 cal MG (twin)
Torpedo launchers: 2 (?)
Main engines: 3 gasoline engines; 3 shafts = 42 knots max; 32 knots cruising
Complement: 12

Transferred to Taiwan on 19 Aug 1957 and 1 Nov 1957, respectively.

2 JAPANESE TYPE

Name	No.	Builders	Commissioned
FUH CHOW	—	Mitsubishi SB Co	—
HSUEH CHIH	—	Mitsubishi SB Co	—

Displacement, tons: 33 light; 40 full load
Dimensions, feet (metres): 69 oa × 19·9 *(22·6 × 6·5)*
Guns: 1—40 mm AA; 2—20 mm AA (twin)
Torpedo launchers: 2—18 inch *(457 mm)*
Main engines: 3 gasoline engines; 3 shafts = 40 knots max; 27 knots cruising
Complement: 12

Transferred to Taiwan on 1 June 1957 and 6 Nov 1957, respectively. The 40 mm gun is not mounted in the adjacent photograph (can be fitted forward of bridge).

FUH CHOW

MINESWEEPERS

2 Ex-US "AGILE" CLASS

Name	No.	Builders	US Comm
Ex-USS *Bold*, MSO 424	—	Norfolk Naval Shipyard	25 Sep 1953
Ex-USS *Bulwark*, MSO 425	—	Norfolk Naval Shipyard	12 Nov 1953

Displacement, tons: 665 light; 750 full load
Dimensions, feet (metres): 165 wl; 172 oa × 36 × 13·6 *(54; 56·4 × 11·8 × 4·5)*
Guns: Unknown
Main engines: 4 diesels; 2 280 bhp; 2 shafts (controllable-pitch propellers) = 15 knots

Former US Navy ocean minesweepers. Wood hulls with non-magnetic engines and fittings; UQS-1 mine detecting sonar. Launched on 14 Mar 1953; transferred to Taiwan in Mar 1976. See United States "Agile" class listing for additional data and photographs.

14 US MSC TYPE

Name	No.
YUNG PING (ex-US *MSC 140*)	MSC 155
YUNG AN (ex-US *MSC 123*)	MSC 156
YUNG NIEN (ex-US *MSC 277*)	MSC 157
YUNG CHOU (ex-US *MSC 278*)	MSC 158
YUNG HSIN (ex-US *MSC 302*)	MSC 159
YUNG JU (ex-US *MSC 300*)	MSC 160
YUNG LO (ex-US *MSC 306*)	MSC 161
YUNG FU (ex-*Diest*, ex-US *MSC 77*)	MSC 162
YUNG CHENG (ex-*Maasieck*, ex-US *MSC 78*)	MSC 165
YUNG SHAN (ex-*Lier*, ex-US *MSC 63*)	MSC 164
YUNG CHING (ex-*Eekloo*, ex-US *MSC 101*)	MSC 163
YUNG LO (ex-US *Msc 306*)	MSC 161
YUNG CHI (ex-*Charleroi*, ex-US *MSC 152*)	MSC 166
YUNG SUI (ex-*Diksmude*, ex-US *MSC 65*	MSC 168

Displacement, tons: approx 380 full load
Dimensions, feet (metres): 144 oa × 28 × 8·5 *(47·2 × 9·2 × 2·8)*
Guns: 2—20 mm AA (twin)
Main engines: Diesels (General Motors); 2 shafts = 13·5 knots
Complement: 40 to 50

YUNG SHAN (pole mast aft)

YUNG CHOU (no pole mast aft)

Non-magnetic, wood-hulled minesweepers built in the United States specifically for transfer to allied navies. First seven units listed above transferred to Taiwan upon completion: MSC 155 and 156 in June 1965, MSC 157 in Dec 1958, MSC 158 in July 1959, MSC 159 in Mar 1965, MSC 160 in April 1965, and MSC 161 in June 1966. The seven other units were transferred to Belgium upon completion in 1953-1955; retransferred to Taiwan in Nov 1969.
All are of similar design; the ex-Belgium ships have a small boom aft on a pole mast. They carried a single 40 mm gun forward in Belgian service.

1 MINESWEEPING BOAT

MSB 12 (ex-US *MSB 4*)

Former US Army minesweeping boat; assigned hull number MSB 4 in US Navy and transferred to Taiwan in Dec 1961.

8 MINESWEEPING LAUNCHES

MSML 1	MSML 5	MSML 7	MSML 11
MSML 3	MSML 6	MSML 8	MSML 12

Fifty-foot minesweeping launches built in the United States and transferred to Taiwan in March 1961.

AMPHIBIOUS FLAGSHIP

1 Ex-US LST TYPE

Name	No.	Builders	US Comm
KAO HSIUNG (ex-*Chung Hai*, LST 219, ex-USS *Dukes County*, LST 735)	AGC1	Dravo Corp, Neville Island, Pennsylvania	26 Apr 1944

Displacement, tons: 316 wl; 328 oa × 50 × 14 *(103·6; 107·5 × 16·4 × 4·6)*
Guns: Several 40 mm AA (twin)
Main engines: Diesel (General Motors); 1 700 bhp; 2 shafts = 11·6 knots

Former US Navy tank landing ship launched on 11 Mar 1944. Transferred to Taiwan in May 1957 for service as an LST. Converted to a flagship for amphibious operations and renamed and redesignated (AGC) in 1964.
Note lattice mast atop bridge structure, modified bridge levels, and antenna mountings on main deck.

KAO HSIUNG

LANDING SHIPS

1 Ex-US "ASHLAND" CLASS

Name	No.	Builders	US Comm
CHUNG CHENG (ex-*Tung Hai*, ex-USS *White Marsh*, LSD 8)	LSD 639 (ex-LSD 191)	Moore Dry Dock Co, Oakland, California	2 July 1945

Displacement, tons: 4 790 standard; 8 700 full load
Dimensions, feet (metres): 454 wl; 457·8 oa × 72 × 18 *(148·8; 150 × 23·6 × 5·9)*
Guns: 12—40 mm AA (2 quad and 2 twin)
Main engines: Skinner Unaflow; 7 400 ihp; 2 shafts = 15 knots
Boilers: 2

Launched on 19 July 1943. Designed to serve as parent ship for landing craft and coastal craft. Transferred from the US Navy to Taiwan on 17 Nov 1960.
Renamed to honour the late President Chiang Kai-Shek on 18 Feb 1976; pennant numbers also changed.

CHUNG CHENG (as LSD 191)

1 Ex-US "CASA GRANDE" CLASS

Name	No.	Builders	Commissioned
Ex-USS *Comstock, LSD 19*	—	Newport News SB & DD Co, Newport News, Virginia	2 July 1945

Displacement, tons: 4 790 standard; 9 375 full load
Dimensions, feet (metres): 475·4 oa × 76·2 × 18 *(155·8 × 24·9 × 5·9)*
Guns: 12—40 mm AA (2 quad and 2 twin)
Main engines: Geared turbines; 7 000 shp; 2 shafts = 15·4 knots
Boilers: 2

Former US Navy dock landing ship. Launched on 28 April 1945 and transferred to Taiwan in 1976.
Docking well is 392 × 44 feet; can accommodate 3 LCUs or 18 LCMs or 32 LVTs (amphibious tractors) in docking well. Fitted with helicopter platform over well (which also can be used for truck parking; see photograph).

COMSTOCK (LSD 19) with LCU   *1965, United States Navy*

22 Ex-US LST TYPE

Name	No. LST	Transferred
CHUNG HAI (ex-USS *LST 755*)	201	April 1946
CHUNG TING (ex-USS *LST 537*)	203	Mar 1946
CHUNG HSING (ex-USS *LST 557*)	204	Mar 1946
CHUNG CHIEN (ex-USS *LST 716*)	205	June 1946
CHUNG CHI (ex-USS *LST 1017*)	206	Dec 1946
CHUNG SHUN (ex-USS *LST 732*)	208	Mar 1946
CHUNG LIEN (ex-USS *LST 1050*)	209	Jan 1947
CHUNG YUNG (ex-USS *LST 574*)	210	Mar 1959
CHUNG KUANG (ex-USS *LST 503*)	216	June 1960
CHUNG SUO (ex-USS *Bradley County, LST 400*)	217	Sep 1958
CHUNG CHIE (ex-USS *Berkley County, LST 279*)	218	June 1960
CHUNG CHUAN (ex-*LST 1030*)	221	Feb 1948
CHUNG SHENG (ex-*LST 211*, ex-USS *LST 1033*)	222	Dec 1947
CHUNG FU (ex-USS *Iron County, LST 840*)	223	July 1958
CHUNG CHENG (ex-USS *Lafayette County, LST 859*)	224	Aug 1958
CHUNG CHIANG (ex-USS *San Bernadino County, LST 1110*)	225	Aug 1958
CHUNG CHIH (ex-USS *Sagadahoc County, LST 1091*)	226	Oct 1958
CHUNG MING (ex-USS *Sweetwater County, LST 1152*)	227	Oct 1958
CHUNG SHU (ex-USS *LST 520*)	228	Sep 1958
CHUNG WAN (ex-USS *LST 535*)	229	Sep 1958
CHUNG PANG (ex-USS *LST 578*)	230	Sep 1958
CHUNG YEH (ex-USS *Sublette County, LST 1144*)	231	Sep 1961

Displacement, tons: 1 653 standard; 4 080 full load
Dimensions, feet (metres): 316 wl; 328 oa × 50 × 14 *(103·6; 107·5 × 16·4 × 4·6)*
Guns: Varies; up to 10—40 mm AA (2 twin, 6 single) with some modernised ships rearmed with
  2—3 inch AA (single) and 6—40 mm AA (twin)
  Several 20 mm AA (twin or single)
Main engines: Diesel (General Motors); 1 700 bhp; 2 shafts = 11·6 knots
Complement: Varies: 100 to 125 in most ships

CHUNG YUNG

Former US Navy tank landing ships constructed during World War II. Dates transferred to Taiwan are listed above. These ships have been rebuilt in Taiwan.
In the photographs note that the *Chung Yung* has landing craft davits forward and aft.
LST 211 ex-USS *LST 1033* changed to LST 222 on 13 Nov 1957. Other Taiwan pennant numbers in the LST series may have been assigned to more than one ship.
Hull numbers of LSTs are being changed to 600 series.
Several LSTs have been stricken: ex-USS *LST 717* (no name assigned; acquired in 1946 and reported sunk in 1948); *Chung Cheng* LST 207 ex-USS *LST 1075*, *Chung Hsun* LST 208 ex-USS *LST 993*, *Chung Kung* LST 213 ex-USS *LST 945*, *Chung Yu* LST 215 ex-USS *LST 330*. One of these ships is believed to have been sunk by Communist Chinese torpedo boats off Quemoy Island on 25 Aug 1958.

CHUNG SHUN

4 Ex-US LSM TYPE

Name	No.	Transferred
MEI CHIN (ex-USS *LSM 155*)	LSM 341	May 1946
MEI SUNG (ex-USS *LSM 457*)	LSM 347	June 1946
MEI PING (ex-USS *LSM 471*)	LSM 353	Nov 1956
MEI LO (ex-USS *LSM 362*)	LSM 356	May 1962

Displacement, tons: 1 095 full load
Dimensions, feet (metres): 196·5 wl; 203·5 oa × 34·5 × 7·3 *(66·4; 66·7 × 11·3 × 2·4)*
Guns: 2—40 mm AA (twin); 4 or 8—20 mm AA (4 single or 4 twin)
Main engines: Diesels; 2 800 bhp; 2 shafts = 12·5 knots
Complement: 65 to 75

Former US Navy medium landing ships constructed during World War II. Originally numbered in the 200-series in Taiwan service, but changed to 300-series as above. Some numbers may have been assigned to more than one ship. These ships are being rebuilt in Taiwan.

MEI PING

LANDING CRAFT

22 Ex-US LCU TYPE

Name	No. LCU	Name	No. LCU
HO CHUN (ex-*LCU 892*)	481	HO CHUN (ex-*LCU 1225*)	494
HO CH'UNG (ex-*LCU 1213*)	482	HO YUNG (ex-*LCU 1271*)	495
HO CHUNG (ex-*LCU 849*)	484	HO CHIEN (ex-*LCU 1278*)	496
HO CHANG (ex-*LCU 512*)	485	HO CHI (ex-*LCU 1212*)	501
HO CHENG (ex-*LCU 1145*)	486	HO HOEI (ex-*LCU 1218*)	502
HO SHAN (ex-*LCU 1596*)	488	HO YAO (ex-*LCU 1244*)	503
HO CHUAN (ex-*LCU 489*)	489	HO DENG (ex-*LCU 1367*)	504
HO SENG (ex-*LCU 1598*)	490	HO FENG (ex-*LCU 1397*)	505
HO MENG (ex-*LCU 1599*)	491	HO CHAO (ex-*LCU 1429*)	506
HO MOU (ex-*LCU 1600*)	492	HO TENG (ex-*LCU 1452*)	507
HO SHOU (ex-*LCU 1601*)	493	HO CHIE (ex-*LCU 700*)	SB1

LCU 501 Series:

Displacement, tons: 158 light; 268 full load
Dimensions, feet (metres): 115·1 oa × 32 × 4·2 *(37·7 × 10·5 × 1·4)*
Guns: 2—20 mm AA (single); some units also may have 2—·50 cal MG
Main engines: 3 diesels; 675 bhp; 3 shafts = 10 knots
Complement: 10 to 25 assigned

LCU 1466 SERIES:

Displacement, tons: 130 light; 280 full load
Dimensions, feet (metres): 115·1 oa × 34 × 4·1 *(37·7 × 10·5 × 1·4)*
Guns: 3—20 mm AA (single); some units may also have 2—·50 cal MG
Main engines: 3 diesels; 675 bhp; 3 shafts = 10 knots
Complement: 15 to 25 assigned

Ex-US LCU Type—*continued*

The LCU 501 series formerly were built in the United States during World War 11; initially designated LCT(6) series. LCU 1466 series built by Ishikawajima Heavy Industries Co, Tokyo, Japan, for transfer to Taiwan; completed in 1955. All originally numbered in 200-series; subsequently changed to 400 and 500 series numbers.

HO MOU (LCU 492 ex-*LCU 292*)

AUXILIARY SHIPS

1 REPAIR SHIP: Ex-US C-3 TYPE

Name	*No.*	*Builders*	*US Comm*
YU TAI	AR 521	Tampa Shipbuilding Co,	23 Apr 1946
(ex-USS *Cadmus, AR 14*)		Tampa, Florida	

Displacement, tons: 7 826 standard; 14 490 full load
Dimensions, feet (metres): 456 wl; 492 oa × 70 × 27·5 *(149·5; 161·3 × 22·9 × 9)*
Guns: 1—5 inch *(127 mm)* 38 calibre DP
Main engines: Turbines (Westinghouse); 8 500 shp; 1 shaft = 16·5 knots
Boilers: 2 (Foster Wheeler)

Former US Navy repair ship, launched on 5 Aug 1945. Transferred to Taiwan on 15 Jan 1973. A sister ship (ex-USS *Amphion, AR 13*) serves with the Iranian Navy.
Reported in reduced operational status.

1 TRANSPORT: Ex-US ARL TYPE

Name	*No.*	*Builders*	*US Comm*
TAI WU (ex-*Sung Shan, ARL 336*,	AP 520	Kaiser Co, Vancouver,	20 Aug 1943
ex-USS *Agenor, ARL 3*, ex-*LST 490*)		Washington	

Displacement, tons: 1 625 light; 4 100 full load
Dimensions, feet (metres): 316 wl; 328 oa × 50 × 11 *(103·6; 107·5 × 16·4 × 3·6)*
Guns: 8—40 mm AA (quad)
Main engines: Diesels (General Motors); 1 800 bhp; 2 shafts = 11·6 knots
Troops: 600

TAI WU (as repair ship)

Begun for the US Navy as an LST completed as a repair ship for landing craft (ARL). Launched on 3 Apr 1943. Transferred to France in 1951 for service in Indochina; subsequently returned to United States and retransferred to Taiwan on 15 Sep 1957
Employed as a repair ship (ARL 336, subsequently ARL 236) until converted in 1973-1974 to troop transport.

1 SURVEYING SHIP: Ex-US C1-M-AV1 TYPE

Name	*No.*	*Builders*	*Commissioned*
CHU HWA (ex-USNS *Sgt. George D. Keathley,*	AGS 564	—	—
T-AGS 35, ex-*T-APC 117*)			

Displacement, tons: 6 090 tons
Dimensions, feet (metres): 338·8 oa × 50·3 × 17·5 *(111·1 × 16·5 × 5·7)*
Guns: (current armament unknown)
Main engines: Diesel; 1 750 bhp; 1 shaft = 11·5 knots

Built in 1945 as merchant ship; subsequently acquired by US Army for use as transport, but assigned to Navy's Military Sea Transportation Service in 1950 and designated as coastal transport (T-APC 117). Refitted for oceanographic survey work in 1966-1967 and redesignated T-AGS 35. Transferred to Taiwan on 29 Mar 1972.

1 SURVEYING SHIP: Ex-US AUXILIARY TUG

Name	*No.*	*Builders*	*US Comm*
CHIU LIEN	AGS 563	Gulfport Boiler &	1 Mar 1945
(ex-USS *Geronimo, ATA 207*)		Welding Works,	
		Port Arthur, Texas	

Displacement, tons: 835
Dimensions, feet (metres): 143 oa × 33·9 × 13·2 *(46·9 × 11·1 × 4·3)*
Main engines: Diesel (General Motors); 1 500 bhp; 1 shaft = 13 knots

CHIU LIEN

Former US Navy auxiliary tug. Launched 4 Jan 1945. Transferred to Taiwan in Feb 1969 and converted to surveying ship. Currently employed as research ship for the Institute of Oceanology; Navy manned.

1 SURVEYING SHIP: Ex-US LSIL TYPE

Name	*No.*	*Builders*	*US Comm*
LIEN CHANG	AGSC 466	Albina Engineering & Machinery	12 Apr 1944
(ex-USS *LSIL 1017*)		Works, Portland, Oregon	

Dimensions, feet (metres): 153 wl; 159 oa × 23·6 × 5·6 *(50·2; 52·1 × 7·7 × 1·8)*
Guns: 2—40 mm AA (twin); several 20 mm AA
Main engines: Diesel (General Motors); 2 320 bhp; 2 shafts = 14 knots

Former US Navy Infantry Landing Ship (large). Launched on 14 Mar 1944. Transferred to Taiwan in Mar 1958. Employed as surveying ship; retains basic LSIL appearance. Not stricken in 1972 as previously reported.

1 OILER: JAPANESE TYPE

Name	No.	Builders	Commissioned
WAN SHOU	AOG 512	Ujina Shipbuilding Co, Hiroshima, Japan	1 Nov 1969

Displacement, tons: 1 049 light; 4 150 full load
Dimensions, feet (metres): 283·8 oa × 54 × 18 *(93·1 × 17·7 × 5·9)*
Guns: 2—40 mm AA (single); 2—20 mm AA
Main engines: Diesel; 2 100 bhp; 1 shaft = 13 knots
Complement: 70
Cargo: 73 600 gallons fuel; 62 000 gallons water

Employed in resupply of offshore islands.

Disposals: *Kuichi* AOG 506 (ex-*AOG 306*, ex-Soviet *Tuapse*) scrapped in 1975-1976. See 1975-1976 and previous editions for characteristics and photograph.

WAN SHOU

3 OILERS: Ex-US "PATASPCO" CLASS

Name	No.	Builders	Commissioned
CHANG PEI (ex-USS *Pecatonica* AOG 57)	AOG 507	Cargill, Inc, Savage Minnesota	—
LUNG CHUAN (ex-HMNZS *Endeavour*, ex-USS *Namakagon*, AOG 53)	AOG 515	Cargill, Inc, Savage, Minnesota	—
HSIN LUNG (ex-USS *Elkhorn* AOG 7)	AOG 517	Cargill, Inc, Savage, Minnesota	—

Displacement, tons: 1 850 light; 4 335 full load
Dimensions, feet (metres): 292 wl; 310·75 oa × 48·5 × 15·7 *(95·7; 101·9 × 15·9 × 5·1)*
Main engines: Diesels (General Motors); 3 300 bhp; 2 shafts = 14 knots

Former US gasoline tankers of the "Patapsco" class. The *Chang Pei* was launched on 17 Mar 1945 and transferred to Taiwan on 24 Apr 1961. The ex-USS *Namakagon* was launched on 4 Nov 1944 and transferred to New Zealand on 5 Oct 1962 for use as an Antarctic resupply ship; stengthened for polar operations and renamed *Endeavour*; returned to the US Navy on 29 June 1971 and retransfered to Taiwan the same date. The *Hsin Lung* was launched on 15 May 1943 and was transferred to Taiwan on 1 July 1972.
The smaller (220·5 ft) *Yu Chaun* AOG 303 ex-USS *Wantanga* AOG 22 stricken in 1959 after running aground; *Hsin Kao* AOG 502 (ex-*AOG 302*), ex-USS *Towalgia* AOG 42 stricken in 1973.

CHANG PEI

SZU MING (as AOG 304)

1 OILER: Ex-US YO TYPE

Name	No.	Builders	Commissioned
SZU MING (ex-US YO 198)	AOG 504 (ex-*AOG 304*)	Manitowoc SB Co, Manitowoc, Wisconsin	—

Displacement, tons: 650 light; 1 595 full load
Dimensions, feet (metres): 174 oa × 32 *(57·1 × 10·5)*
Guns: 1—40 mm AA; 5—20 mm AA (single)
Main engines: Diesel (Union); 560 bhp; 1 shaft = 10·5 knots
Complement: approx 65

Former US Navy self-propelled fuel oil barge built in 1945. Transferred to Taiwan in Dec 1949. Reportedly placed in reserve in 1976.

2 OILERS: JAPANESE TYPE

Two small oilers of Japanese construction are also reported to be in service.

Disposals: *Ho Lan* AO 305, formerly the Polish *Praca* scrapped in 1964; *O Mei* AO 509 (ex-*AO 309*), formerly the USS *Maumee* AG 124 (ex-*AO 2*) scrapped in 1967; *Tai Yun* AOG 510 formerly the US YO 175 scrapped in 1972.

1 CARGO SHIP: Ex-US AKL TYPE

Name	No.	Builders	Commissioned
YUNG KANG (ex-USS *Mark*, AKL 12, ex-AG 143 ex-US Army *FS 214*)	AKL 514	Higgins	—

Displacement, tons: approx 700
Dimensions, feet (metres): 176·5 oa × 32·8 × 10 *(57·8 × 10·7 × 3·3)*
Guns: (current armament unknown)
Main engines: Diesel; 1 000 bhp; 1 shaft = 10 knots

Built in 1944 as a small cargo ship (freight and supply) for the US Army. Transferred to US Navy on 30 Sep 1947; operated in Indochina area from 1963 until transferred to Taiwan on 1 July 1971.

YUNG KANG   1972

2 TUGS: Ex-US ATA TYPE

Name	No.	Builders	US Comm
TA TUNG (ex-USS *Chickasaw*, ATF 83)	ATF 548	United Engineering Co, Alameda, California	4 Feb 1943
TA WAN (ex-USS *Apache*, ATF 67)	ATF 550	Charleston SB & DD Co, South Carolina	12 Dec 1942

Displacement, tons: 1 235 standard; 1 675 full load
Dimensions, feet (metres): 195 wl; 205 oa × 38·5 × 15·5 *(63·9; 67·2 × 12·6 × 5·1)*
Guns: 1—3 inch *(76 mm)* 50 cal AA; several light AA
Main engines: Diesels (electric drive); 3 000 bhp; 1 shaft = 15 knots

Former US Navy "Apache" class fleet tugs. Launched on 23 July 1942 and 8 May 1942 respectively. *Ta Tung* transferred to Taiwan in January 1966 and *Ta Wan* on 30 June 1974.

3 TUGS: Ex-US ATA TYPE

Name	No.	Builders	US Comm
TA SUEH (ex-USS *Tonkawa, ATA 176)*	ATA 547	Levingston SB Co, Orange, Texas	19 Aug 1944
TA AN (ex-USS *Cahokia, ATA 186)*	ATA 550	Levingston SB Co, Orange, Texas	24 Nov 1944
TA TENG (ex-USS *Mahopac, ATA 196)*	ATA 549	Levingston SB Co, Orange, Texas	21 Dec 1944

Displacement, tons: 435 standard; 835 full load
Dimensions, feet (metres): 134·5 wl; 143 oa × 33·9 × 13 *(44·1; 46·9 × 11·1 × 4·3)*
Guns: 1—3 inch *(76 mm)* 50 cal AA; several light AA
Main engines: Diesel-electric (General Motors diesels); 1 500 bhp; 1 shaft = 13 knots

Former US Navy auxiliary ocean tugs. *Ta Sueh* launched on 1 Mar 1944 and transferred to Taiwan in April 1962. *Ta An* launched on 18 Sep 1944; assigned briefly to US Air Force in 1971 until transferred to Taiwan on 29 Mar 1972, (correction to previous edition). *Ta Teng* transferred on 1 July 1971. A third tug of this type serves as a surveying ship.

7 TUGS: Ex-US HARBOUR TYPES

YTL 3 (ex-US Army *ST 846)*
YTL 8 (ex-US Army *ST 2002)*

YTL 9 (ex-US Army *ST 2004)*
YTL 10 (ex-US Army *ST 2008)*

Former US Army 76-foot harbour tugs.

YTL 11 (ex-USN *YTL 454)*
YTL 12 (ex-USN *YTL 584)*

YTL 13 (ex-USN *YTL 585)*

Former US Navy 66-foot harbour tugs. Several other harbour tugs have been stricken; see 1975-1976 edition for details.

5 Ex-US FLOATING DRY DOCKS

Name	No.	Builders	Transferred
HAY TAN (ex-USN *AFDL 36)*	AFDL 1	—	Mar 1947
KIM MEN (ex-USN *AFDL 5)*	AFDL 2	—	Jan 1948
HAN JIH (ex-USN *AFDL 34)*	AFDL 3	—	July 1959
FO WU 5 (ex-USN *ARD 9)*	ARD 5	—	Oct 1967
FO WU 6 (ex-USS *Windsor, ARD 22)*	ARD 6	—	June 1971

Former US Navy floating dry docks; see United States section for characteristics.

SERVICE CRAFT

Approximately 25 non-self propelled service craft are in use; most are former US Navy service craft.

CUSTOMS SERVICE

Several small ships and small craft are in service with the Customs Service of Taiwan, an agency of the Ministry of Finance. The larger ships include two former minesweepers and three former submarine chasers, listed below.

2 Ex-US AM TYPE

Name	No.	Builders	US Comm
HUNG HSING (ex-USS *Embattle, AM 226)*	A 7	American Shipbuilding Co, Lorain, Ohio	25 Apr 1945
— (ex-USS *Improve, AM 247)*	—	Savannah Machine & Foundry Co, Georgia	29 Feb 1944

Dimensions, feet (metres): 180 wl; 184·5 oa × 33 × 9·75 *(59; 60·5 × 10·8 × 3·2)*
Guns: 1—3 inch *(76 mm)* 50 cal AA; several lighter guns
Main engines: Diesel (Cooper Bessemer); 1 710 bhp; 2 shafts = 14 knots

Former US Navy minesweepers (AM). Launched on 17 Sep 1944 and 26 Sep 1943 respectively.

3 Ex-US PC TYPE

Name	No.	Builders	Launched
Ex-*Tung Kiang* (ex-USS *Placerville, PC 1087)*	PC 119	—	21 Aug 1943
Ex-*Hsi Kiang* (ex-USS *Susanville, PC 1149)*	PC 120	—	11 Jan 1944
Ex-*Pei Chang* (ex-USS *Hanford, PC 1142)*	PC 122	—	20 Aug 1943

Displacement, tons: 450 full load
Dimensions, feet (metres): 173·66 oa × 23 × 10·8 *(56·9 × 7·5 × 3·5)*
Guns: 1—3 inch *(76 mm)* 50 cal AA; several lighter guns
Main engines: Diesels (General Motors); 2 880 bhp; 2 shafts = 20 knots

Former US Navy steel-hulled submarine chasers. Originally transferred to Taiwan for naval use; subsequently allocated to the Customs Service. PC 1087 and PC 1149 transferred in July 1957. Armament believed to have been retained.

TANZANIA

Mercantile Marine

Lloyd's Register of Shipping: 17 vessels of 33 449 tons gross

Base

Dar Es Salaam. A new base area built under Chinese supervision.

LIGHT FORCES

6 (?) Ex-CHINESE "SHANGHAI"CLASS
(FAST ATTACK CRAFT—GUN)

JW 9861-6

Displacement, tons: 100 full load
Dimensions, feet (metres): 120·0 × 18·0 × 6·0 *(39·3 × 5·9 × 1·9)*
Guns: 4—37 mm (twin fore and aft)
Main engines: 4 diesels; 4 800 bhp = 28 knots

Transferred by the Chinese People's Republic in 1970-71. A further six may now be held.

"SHANGHAI" Class

4 Ex-CHINESE "HU CHWAN" CLASS
(FAST ATTACK CRAFT—HYDROFOIL (TORPEDO))

Displacement, tons: 45
Dimensions, feet (metres): 70 × 16·5 × 3·1 *(22·9 × 5·4 × 1)*
Guns: 4—12·7 mm (twins)
Torpedo tubes: 2—21 in (533 mm)
Main engines: 2 diesels; 2 200 bhp = 55 knots (calm)
Range, miles: 500 at cruising speed

Transferred 1975.

"HU CHWAN" Class

3 Ex-CHINESE "P6" CLASS
(FAST ATTACK CRAFT—TORPEDO)

Displacement, tons: 75 full load
Dimensions, feet (metres): 84 × 20 × 6 *(25·7 × 6·1 × 1·8)*
Guns: 4—25 mm
Torpedo tubes: 2—21 in (533 mm)
Main engines: 4 diesels; 4 shafts; 4 800 bhp = 43 knots
Range, miles: 450 at 30 knots
Complement: 25

Transferred 1974-75.

4 Ex-CHINESE "P4" CLASS
(FAST ATTACK CRAFT—TORPEDO)

Displacement, tons: 22
Dimensions, feet (metres): 62·7 × 11·6 × 5·6 *(19·1 × 3·5 × 1·7)*
Guns: 2—14·5 mm MG (twin)
Torpedo tubes: 2—18 in
Main engines: 2 diesels; 2 shafts; 2 200 bhp = 50 knots
Complement: 12

2 Ex-EAST GERMAN "SCHWALBE" CLASS
(COASTAL PATROL CRAFT)

ARAKA   **SALAAM**

Displacement, tons: 70 full load
Dimensions, feet (metres): 85·2 × 14·8 × 4·6 *(26 × 4·5 × 1·4)*
Guns: 2—37 mm; 2 MG
Main engines: Diesel; 300 hp = 17 knots

Launched 1955-56. Transferred 1966-67.

"SCHWALBE" Class

2 Ex-EAST GERMAN COASTAL PATROL CRAFT

RAFIKI   **UHURU**

Displacement, tons: 50
Dimensions, feet (metres): 78·7 × 16·4 × 4·3 *(24 × 5 × 1·3)*
Guns: 1—40 mm; 4 MG

Purchased 1967.

4 Ex-CHINESE COASTAL PATROL CRAFT

Displacement, tons: 27
Dimensions, feet (metres): 42·6 × 13 × 4·2 *(13 × 4 × 1·2)*
Gun: 1—12·7 mm MG
Speed, knots: 20
Complement: 10

Transferred late 1966.

THAILAND

Administration

Commander-in-Chief of the Navy:
  Admiral Sa-Ngad Chaloryoo
Deputy Commander-in-Chief:
  Admiral Chanien Ruchibhan
Chief of Staff (RTN):
  Admiral Amorn Sirigaya
Commander-in-Chief, Fleet:
  Admiral Ching Chullasukum

Diplomatic Representation

Naval Attaché in London:
  Captain A. Iamsuro
Naval Attaché in Washington:
  Captain Kasem Rakcharcon

Personnel

(a) 1976: *Navy,* 20 000 (2 000 officers and 18 000 ratings)
  including *Marine Corps:* 7 000 (500 officers and 6 500 men)
(b) 2 years National Service

Bases

Bangkok, Sattahip, Songkhla. A new base on the West coast has been reported.

Prefix to Ships' Names

HTMS.

Mercantile Marine

Lloyd's Register of Shipping:
  80 vessels of 176 315 tons gross

New Construction

There is a reported interest in further new construction.

Strength of the Fleet

Type	Active
Frigates	8
Corvettes	14
Large Patrol Craft	14
Fast Attack Craft	3
Coastal Patrol Craft	16
Coastal Minelayers	6
MW Support Ship	1
MSBs	10
LSTs	4
LSMs	3
LCG	1
LCIs	2
LCTs	6
LCMs	26
LCVPs	6
Survey Vessels	3
Support Tankers	2
Harbour Tankers	4
Water Boats	2
Tugs	4

DELETIONS

Frigate

1973 *Bangpakong*

Large Patrol Craft

1973 *SC 7*

Coastal Patrol Craft

1973 *CGC1* and *11, T 31, 33, 34* and *35*

FRIGATES

1 YARROW TYPE

Name **MAKUT RAJAKUMARN**	No. 7	Builders Yarrow & Co Ltd, Scotstoun	Laid down 11 Jan 1970	Launched 18 Nov 1971	Commissioned 7 May 1973

Displacement, tons: 1 650 standard; 1 900 full load
Length, feet (metres): 305 *(93)* wl; 320·0 *(97·6)* oa
Beam, feet (metres): 36·0 *(11·0)*
Draught, feet (metres): 18·1 *(5·5)*
Missile launchers: 1 quadruple Seacat
Guns: 2—4·5 in Mk 8 *(114 mm)* (single)
  2—40 mm 60 cal Bofors (single)
A/S weapons: 1 triple barrelled Limbo mortar; 1 DC rack; 2 depth charge throwers
Main engines: 1 Rolls-Royce Olympus gas turbine; 23 125 shp; 1 Crossley-Pielstick 12 PC2V diesel; 6 000 bhp
Speed, knots: 26, 18 on diesel
Range, miles: 5 000 at 18 knots (diesel); 1 200 at 26 knots
Complement: 140 (16 officers, 124 ratings)

An order was placed on 21 Aug 1969 for a general purpose frigate. The ship is largely automated with a consequent saving in complement, and has been most successful in service. Fitted as flagship.

Electronics: HSA CIC system. Racal DF.

Radar: Surveillance: one LW 04 (amidships)
Fire Control: one M 20 series (radome)
Seacat Control: one M 44 Series (aft)
Navigation: one Decca Type 626
IFF: UK Mk 10.

Sonar: UK Type 170 and Plessey Type MS 27.

MAKUT RAJAKUMARN   *9/1973, Wright and Logan*

2 US PF TYPE

Name **KHIRIRAT** **TAPI**	No. 6 5	Builders Norfolk SB & DD Co American SB Co, Toledo, Ohio	Laid down 18 Feb 1972 1 April 1970	Launched 2 June 1973 17 Oct 1970	Commissioned 10 Aug 1974 1 Nov 1971

Displacement, tons: 900 standard; 1 135 full load
Length, feet (metres): 275 *(83·8)* oa
Beam, feet (metres): 33 *(10·0)*
Draught, feet (metres): 10 *(3·0)*
Guns: 2—3 in *(76 mm)*; 2—40 mm
A/S weapons: DCs, Hedgehogs; 2 triple A/S torpedo tubes *(Khirirat)*
Main engines: 2 FM Diesels; 6 000 bhp
Speed, knots: 20
Complement: 150

Of similar design to the Iranian ships of the "Bayandor" class. *Tapi* was ordered on June 27 1969. *Khirirat* was ordered on 25 June 1971.

TAPI   *1975, Royal Thai Navy*

10 US LARGE PATROL CRAFT

Name	No.	Builders	Commissioned
—	T 11 (ex-US *PGM 71*)	Peterson Builders Inc	1 Feb 1966
—	T 12 (ex-US *PGM 79*)	Peterson Builders Inc	1967
—	T 13 (ex-US *PGM 107*)	Peterson Builders Inc	28 Aug 1967
—	T 14 (ex-US *PGM 116*)	Peterson Builders Inc	18 Aug 1969
—	T 15 (ex-US *PGM 117*)	Peterson Builders Inc	18 Aug 1969
—	T 16 (ex-US *PGM 115*)	Peterson Builders Inc	12 Feb 1970
—	T 17 (ex-US *PGM 113*)	Peterson Builders Inc	12 Feb 1970
—	T 18 (ex-US *PGM 114*)	Peterson Builders Inc	12 Feb 1970
—	T 19 (ex-US *PGM 123*)	Peterson Builders Inc	25 Dec 1970
—	T 110 (ex-US *PGM 124*)	Peterson Builders Inc	Oct 1970

Displacement, tons: 130 standard; 147 full load
Dimensions, feet (metres): 101·0 oa × 21·0 × 6·0 *(30·8 × 6·4 × 1·9)*
Guns: 1—40 mm; 4—20 mm; 2—·50 cal MG
Main engines: Diesels; 2 shafts; 1 800 bhp = 18·5 knots
Range, miles: 1 500 at 10 knots
Complement: 30

T 11 was launched on 5 May 1965.

T 12   *1969, Royal Thai Navy*

1 Ex-US SC TYPE (LARGE PATROL CRAFT)

SC 8 (ex-SC *32,* ex-US SC *162*)

Displacement, tons: 110 light; 125 full load
Dimensions, feet (metres): 111 × 17 × 6 *(36·4 × 5·5 × 1·9)*
Guns: 1—40 mm; 3—20 mm
A/S weapons: Depth charges, Mousetrap
Main engines: High-speed diesel = 18 knots
Range, miles: 2 000 at 10 knots

Wooden hulled. Non-operational.

3 THAI BUILT (COASTAL PATROL CRAFT)

Name	No.	Builders	Commissioned
—	T 91	Royal Thai Naval Dockyard, Bangkok	1971
—	T 92	Royal Thai Naval Dockyard, Bangkok	1971
—	T 93	Royal Thai Naval Dockyard, Bangkok	1971

Displacement, tons: 87·5 standard
Dimensions, feet (metres): 104·3 × 17·5 × 5·5 *(30·8 × 6·4 × 1·9)*
Guns: 1—40 mm; 1—20 mm
Main engines: Diesels; 1 600 bhp = 25 knots
Complement: 21

T 91   *1970, Royal Thai Navy*

5 Ex-US "95 ft" CLASS CGC

CGC 11   **CGC 13**   **CGC 14**   **CGC 15**   **CGC 16**

Displacement, tons: 95 standard; 105 full load
Dimensions, feet (metres): 95 × 20·2 × 5 *(29 × 5·8 × 1·6)*
Gun: 1—20 mm
A/S weapons: 2 DC racks; 2 Mousetraps
Main engines: 4 diesels; 2 shafts; 2 200 bhp = 21 knots
Range, miles: 1 500 at 14 knots
Complement: 15

US coastguard cutters transferred in 1954. Similar to those built for USCG by US Coast Guard Yard, Curtis Bay in 1953. Cost £475 000 each.

CGC 14   *Royal Thai Navy*

7 Ex-US "SWIFT" CLASS (COASTAL PATROL CRAFT)

T 21   **T 22**   **T 23**   **T 24**   **T 25**   **T 26**   **T 27**

Displacement, tons: 20 standard; 22 full load
Dimensions, feet (metres): 50 × 13 *(16·4 × 4·3)*
Guns: 2—0·50 cal (1 twin)
Main engines: Diesels; 2 shafts; 480 bhp = 25 knots
Complement: 5

"Swift" class patrol craft transferred from USN; T22 in Aug 1968, T23-25 in Feb 1970. T21 in May 1970, T26 in Mar 1970, T27 in Apr 1970.

6 Ex-US RPC TYPE (COASTAL PATROL TYPE)

T 31   **T 32**   **T 33**   **T 34**   **T 35**   **T 36**

Displacement, tons: 10·4 standard; 13·05 full load
Dimensions, feet (metres): 35 × 10 *(11·5 × 3·2)*
Guns: 2—0·50 cal (1 twin); 2—0·30 cal
Main engines: Diesels; 2 shafts; 225 bhp = 14 knots
Complement: 7

Transferred Mar 1967.

There are reports that a patrol of Riverine Craft is maintained on the Upper Mekong although details are not available.

1 Ex-US "CANNON" CLASS

Name	No.
PIN KLAO (ex-USS *Hemminger DE 746*)	3 (ex-1)

Builders	Laid down	Launched	Commissioned
Western Pipe & Steel Co.	1943	12 Sep 1943	30 May 1944

Displacement, tons: 1 240 standard; 1 900 full load
Length, feet (metres): 306·0 *(93·3)* oa
Beam, feet (metres): 37·0 *(11·3)*
Draught, feet (metres): 14·1 *(4·3)*
Guns: 3—3 in *(76 mm)* 50 cal; 6—40 mm
A/S weapons: 8 DCT
Torpedo tubes: 6 (2 triple) for A/S torpedoes
Main engines: GM diesels with electric drive; 2 shafts; 6 000 bhp
Speed, knots: 20
Oil fuel, tons: 300
Range, miles: 11 500 at 11 knots
Complement: 220

Transferred from US Navy to Royal Thai Navy at New York Navy Shipyard in July 1959 under MDAP. The 3—21 in torpedo tubes were removed and the 4—20 mm guns were replaced by 4—40 mm. The six A/S torpedo tubes were fitted in 1966. Finally purchased 6 June 1975.

PIN KLAO   1975

2 Ex-US "TACOMA" CLASS

Name	No.
PRASAE (ex-USS *Gallup, PF 47*)	2
TAHCHIN (ex-USS *Glendale, PF 36*)	1

Builders	Laid down	Launched	Commissioned
Consolidated Steel Corpn, Los Angeles	18 Aug 1943	17 Sep 1943	29 Feb 1944
Consolidated Steel Corpn, Los Angeles	6 Apr 1943	28 May 1943	1 Oct 1943

Displacement, tons: 1 430 standard; 2 100 full load
Length, feet (metres): 304·0 *(92·7)* oa
Beam, feet (metres): 37·5 *(11·4)*
Draught, feet (metres): 13·7 *(4·2)*
Guns: 3—3 in *(76 mm)* 50 cal; 2—40 mm; 9—20 mm
A/S weapons: 8 DCT
Main engines: Triple expansion; 2 shafts; 5 500 ihp
Boilers: 2 small water tube 3-drum type
Speed, knots: 19
Oil fuel, tons: 685
Range, miles: 7 800 at 12 knots
Complement: 180

Delivered to the Royal Thai Navy on 29 Oct 1951. *Prasae* partially non-operational after collision in Jan 1972 and *Tahchin* may also be non-operational.

PRASAE   1971

1 Ex-BRITISH "ALGERINE" CLASS

Name
PHOSAMTON (ex-HMS *Minstrel*)

No.	Builders	Laid down	Launched	Commissioned
MSF 1	Redfern Construction Co	1943	5 Oct 1944	1945

Displacement, tons: 1 040 standard; 1 335 full load
Length, feet (metres): 225·0 *(68·6)* oa
Beam, feet (metres): 35·5 *(10·8)*
Draught, feet (metres): 10·5 *(3·2)*
Guns: 1—4 in *(102 mm)* ; 6—20 mm
A/S weapons: 4 DCT
Main engines: Triple expansion; 2 shafts; 2 000 ihp
Boilers: 2 three-drum type
Speed, knots: 16
Oil fuel, tons: 270
Range, miles: 5 000 at 10 knots
Complement: 103

Transferred in Apr 1947. The 20 mm guns were increased from 3 to 6, and the DCTs from 2 to 4 in 1966. Marginally operational—now used for training.

PHOSAMTON   1965, Royal Thai Navy

Name	No.
MAEKLONG	4

Builders	Laid down	Launched	Commissioned
Uraga Dock Co, Japan	1936	27 Nov 1936	June 1937

Displacement, tons: 1 400 standard; 2 000 full load
Length, feet (metres): 269·0 *(82·0)*
Beam, feet (metres): 34·0 *(10·4)*
Draught, feet (metres): 10·5 *(3·2)*
Guns: 4—3 in *(76 mm)* 50 cal (singles); 3—40 mm; 3—20 mm
Main engines: Triple expansion; 2 shafts; 2 500 ihp
Boilers: 2 water tube
Speed, knots: 14
Oil fuel, tons: 487
Range, miles: 8 000 at 12 knots
Complement: 155 as training ship

Employed as training ship. The 4—18 inch torpedo tubes were removed. Sister ship *Tachin,* heavily damaged on 1 June 1945, was scrapped.

Armament: 4—4·7 in guns replaced by 3 in guns in 1974.

MAEKLONG   1967, Royal Thai Navy

CORVETTES

7 "TRAD" CLASS

Name	No.	Builders	Commissioned
CHANDHABURI	22	Cantieri Riunti dell' Adriatico, Monfalcone	1937
CHUMPORN	31	Cantieri Riunti dell' Adriatico, Monfalcone	1938
PATTANI	13	Cantieri Riunti dell' Adriatico, Monfalcone	1937
PHUKET	12	Cantieri Riunti dell' Adriatico, Monfalcone	1936
RAYONG	23	Cantieri Riunti dell' Adriatico, Monfalcone	1938
SURASDRA	21	Cantieri Riunti dell' Adriatico, Monfalcone	1937
TRAD	11	Cantieri Riunti dell' Adriatico, Monfalcone	1936

Displacement, tons: 318 standard; 470 full load
Dimensions, feet (metres): 223 oa × 21 × 7 *(68 × 6·4 × 2·1)*
Guns: 2—3 in; 1—40 mm; 2—20 mm; *Chumporn, Phuket* and *Trad* 2—40 mm
Torpedo tubes: 4—18 in (2 twin); *Chumporn, Phuket* and *Trad* 2—18 in (twin)
Main engines: Parsons geared turbines; 2 shafts; 9 000 hp = 31 knots
Boilers: 2 Yarrow
Oil fuel, tons: 102
Range, miles: 1 700 at 15 knots
Complement: 70

Phuket and *Trad* were laid down on 8 Feb 1935. Armament was supplied by Vickers-Armstrong Ltd. First boat reached 32·34 knots on trials with 10 000 hp. 2 single 18 inch torpedo tubes and the 4—8 mm guns were removed.

TRAD

7 "LIULOM" CLASS (EX-US PCs)

LIULOM (ex-PC *1253*) PC 7   SUKRIP (ex-PC *1218*) PC 5
LONGLOM (ex-PC *570*) PC 8   THAYANCHON (ex-PC *575*) PC 2
PHALI (ex-PC *1185*) PC 4   TONGPLIU (ex-PC *616*) PC 6
SARASIN (ex-PC *495*) PC 1

Displacement, tons: 280 standard; 400 full load
Dimensions, feet (metres): 174 oa × 23·2 × 6·5 *(53 × 7 × 2)*
Guns: 1—3 in; 1—40 mm; 5—20 mm
A/S weapons: 2 ASW torpedo tubes (except *Sarasin*)
Main engines: Diesel; 2 shafts; 3 600 bhp = 19 knots
Oil fuel, tons: 60
Range, miles: 6 000 at 10 knots
Complement: 62 to 71

Launched in 1941-43. All transferred between Mar 1947 and Dec 1952.

THAYANCHON   1975

LIGHT FORCES

3 LÜRSSEN 45 METRE TYPE (FAST ATTACK CRAFT—MISSILE)

Name	No.	Builders	Commissioned
HANHAKSATTRU	2	Hong-Leong/Lürssen, Butterworth	Nov 1976
PRABPARAPAK	1	Hong-Leong/Lürssen, Butterworth	Aug 1976
SUPHAIRIN	3	Hong-Leong/Lürssen, Butterworth	Feb 1977

Displacement, tons: 224 standard; 260 full load
Dimensions, feet (metres): 147·6 oa × 23 × 8·2 *(48·4 × 7·5 × 2·7)*
Missiles: 5 Gabriel launchers (1 triple, 2 single)
Guns: 1—57 mm 70 Bofors (forward); 1—40 mm 70 Bofors (aft)
Main engines: 4 Maybach (MTU) diesels = 34 knots
Range: 2 000 cruising
Complement: 41

Ordered June 1973. Launch dates—*Prabparapak* 29 July 1975, *Hanhaksattru* 28 Oct 1975, *Suphairin* Jan 1976. Unconfirmed report of a fourth ordered.

PRABPARAPAK (model)   1975, Royal Thai Navy

3 "KLONGYAI" CLASS (LARGE PATROL CRAFT)

Name	No.	Builders	Commissioned
KANTANG	7	Ishikawajima Co, Japan	21 June 1937
KLONGYAI	5	Ishikawajima Co, Japan	21 June 1937
SATTAHIP	8	Royal Thai Naval Dockyard, Bangkok	1958

Displacement, tons: 110 standard; 135 full load
Dimensions, feet (metres): 131·5 × 15·5 × 4 *(42 × 4·6 × 1·5)*
Guns: 1—3 in; 1—20 mm
Torpedo tubes: 2—18 in
Main engines: Geared turbines = 2 shafts; 1 000 shp = 19 knots
Boilers: 2 water-tube
Range, miles: 480 at 15 knots
Oil fuel, tons: 18
Complement: 31

Sattahip was laid down on 21 Nov 1956, launched on 28 Oct 1957. The other two were both launched on 26 Mar 1937.

MINE WARFARE FORCES

2 "BANGRACHAN" CLASS (COASTAL MINELAYERS)

Name	No.	Builders	Commissioned
BANGRACHAN	MMC 1	Cantiere dell'Adriatico, Monfalcone	1937
NHONG SARHAI	MMC 2	Cantiere dell'Adriatico, Monfalcone	1936

Displacement, tons: 368 standard; 408 full load
Dimensions, feet (metres): 160·8 × 25·9 × 7·2 (52·7 × 8·5 × 2·4)
Guns: 2—3 in; 2—20 mm
Mines: 142
Main engines: Burmeister & Wain diesels; 2 shafts; 540 bhp = 12 knots
Oil fuel, tons: 180
Range, miles: 2 700 at 10 knots
Complement: 55

Launched in 1936.

BANGRACHAN

2 Ex-US "AGILE" CLASS (MINESWEEPERS—OCEAN)

— (ex-USS *Prime*, MSO 466)
— (ex-USS *Reaper*, MSO 467)

Displacement, tons: 665 light; 750 full load
Dimensions, feet (metres): 172 × 36 × 13·6 (56·4 × 11·8 × 4·5)
Guns: 1—40 mm; 2—20 mm
Main engines: 4 diesels; 2 shafts; 2 280 hp = 15·5 knots
Complement: 78

Transferred in 1974-75.

4 US "BLUEBIRD" CLASS (MINESWEEPERS—COASTAL)

Name	No.	Builders	Commissioned
BANGEKO (ex-USS MSC 303)	6	Dorchester SB Corpn, Camden	9 July 1965
DONCHEDI (ex-USS MSC 313)	8	Peterson Builders Inc, Sturgeon Bay, Wisc	17 Sep 1965
LADYA (ex-USS MSC 297)	5	Peterson Builders Inc, Sturgeon Bay, Wisc	14 Dec 1963
TADINDENG (ex-USS MSC 301)	7	Tacoma Boatbuilding Co, Tacoma, Wash	26 Aug 1965

Displacement, tons: 330 standard; 362 full load
Dimensions, feet (metres): 145·3 oa × 27 × 8·5 (43 × 8 × 2·6)
Guns: 2—20 mm
Main engines: 4 GM diesels; 2 shafts; 1 000 bhp = 13 knots
Range, miles: 2 500 at 10 knots
Complement: 43 (7 officers, and 36 men)

New construction for Thailand. USS *Bluebird* was to have been transferred in 1976 but this has been delayed.

TADINDENG   1975

1 MCM SUPPORT SHIP

Name	No.	Builders	Commissioned
RANG KWIEN (ex-*Umihari Maru*)	MSC 11	Mitsubishi Co.	1944

Displacement, tons: 586 standard
Dimensions, feet (metres): 162·3 × 31·2 × 13·0 (49 × 9·5 × 4)
Main engines: Triple expansion steam; speed = 10 knots

Originally built as a tug. Acquired by Royal Thai Navy on 6 Sep 1967.

RANG KWIEN   1969, Royal Thai Navy

5 MSB

MSML 6-10

Thai built. 50 ft, 30 tons with 2—20 mm guns.

5 MSB

MSML 1-5

Thai built. 40 ft, 25 tons with 2—20 mm guns.

AMPHIBIOUS FORCES

5 Ex-US LST TYPE (1-510 and 511-1152 SERIES)

Name	No.	Builders	Commissioned
ANGTHONG (ex-USS LST 294)	LST 1	USA	1944
CHANG (ex-USS Lincoln County, LST 898)	LST 2	Dravo Corp	29 Dec 1944
LANTA (ex-USS Stone County, LST 1141)	LST 4	USA	1945
PANGAN (ex-USS Stark County, LST 1134)	LST 3	USA	1945
— (ex-USS Dodge County, LST 722)	LST 5	USA	1944

Displacement, tons: 1 625 standard; 4 080 full load
Dimensions, feet (metres): 328 oa × 50 × 14 (100 × 15·2 × 4·4)
Guns: 6—40 mm; 4—20 mm
Main engines: GM diesels; 2 shafts; 1 700 bhp = 11 knots
Range, miles: 9 500 at 9 knots
Complement: 80
Cargo capacity: 2 100 tons

CHANG   1965, Royal Thai Navy

Angthong is employed as training ship. *Chang,* transferred to Thailand in 1962, was laid down on 15 Oct 1944. *Pangan* was transferred on 16 May 1966, *Lanta* on 12 Mar 1970 and *LST 5* on 17 Dec 1975.

3 Ex-US LSM TYPE

Name	No.	Builders	Commissioned
KRAM (ex-USS *LSM 469*)	LSM 3	Brown SB Co, Houston, Tex	17 Mar 1945
KUT (ex-USS *LSM 338*)	LSM 1	USA	1945
PHAI (ex-USS *LSM 333*)	LSM 2	USA	1945

Displacement, tons: 743 standard; 1 095 full load
Dimensions, feet (metres): 203·5 oa × 34·5 × 8·3 *(62 × 10·5 × 2·4)*
Guns: 2—40 mm
Main engines: Diesel direct drive; 2 shafts; 2 800 bhp = 12·5 knots
Range, miles: 2 500 at 12 knots
Complement: 55

Former United States landing ships of the LCM, later LSM (Medium Landing Ship) type. *Kram* was transferred to Thailand under MAP at Seattle, Wash, on 25 May 1962.

2 Ex-US LCI TYPE

PRAB (ex-LCMI 670) LSIL 1   **SATAKUT** (ex-LCMI 739) LSIL 2

Displacement, tons: 230 standard; 387 full load
Dimensions, feet (metres): 157 × 23 × 6 *(47 × 7 × 1·7)*
Guns: 2—20 mm
Main engines: Diesel; 2 shafts; 1 320 bhp = 14 knots
Complement: 54

Prab non-operational.

6 LCU Ex-US LCT (6) TYPE

ARDANG LCU 3   **MATAPHON** LCU 1   **RAWI** LCU 2
KOLUM LCU 5   **PHETRA** LCU 4   **TALIBONG** LCU 6

Displacement, tons: 134 standard; 279 full load
Dimensions, feet (metres): 112 × 32 × 4 *(37 × 9·7 × 1·2)*
Guns: 2—20 mm
Main engines: Diesel; 3 shafts; 675 bhp = 10 knots
Complement: 37

Employed as transport ferries.

1 Ex-US LCG TYPE

NAKHA (ex-USS *LSSL* 102) LSSL 3

Displacement, tons: 233 standard; 287 full load
Dimensions, feet (metres): 158 oa × 23 × 4·25 *(47·5 × 7 × 1·4)*
Guns: 1—3 inch; 4—40 mm; 4—20 mm; 4—81 mm mortars
Main engines: Diesels; 2 shafts; 1 320 bhp = 15 knots
Range, miles: 4 700 at 10 knots

Transferred in 1966. Acquired when Japan returned her to USA.

26 Ex-US LCM 6

14-16, 61-68, 71-78, 81-82, 85-87

First 21 delivered 1969.

6 Ex-US LCVP

LCAs

There is also a large but unknown number of Thai-built LCAs.

SURVEY SHIPS

Name	No.	Builders	Commissioned
CHANDHARA	AGS 11	C. Melchers & Co, Bremen, Germany	1961

Displacement, tons: 870 standard; 996 full load
Dimensions, feet (metres): 229·2 oa × 34·5 × 10 *(71 × 10·5 × 3)*
Gun: 1—20 mm
Main engines: 2 diesels; 2 shafts; 1 000 bhp = 13·25 knots
Range, miles: 10 000 (cruising)
Complement: 72

Laid down on 27 Sep 1960. Launched on 17 Dec 1960.

CHANDHARA   *1962, Royal Thai Nav*

---

2 OCEANOGRAPHIC CRAFT

Of 90 tons, with a crew of 8 launched in 1955.

SERVICE FORCES

1 SUPPORT TANKER

CHULA AO 2

Displacement, tons: 2 395 standard
Dimensions, feet (metres): 328 × 43·2 × 25 *(100 × 13·2 × 7·6)*
Main engines: Steam turbines

CHULA   *1969, Royal Thai Nav*

1 SUPPORT TANKER

MATRA AO 3

Displacement, tons: 4 744
Dimensions, feet (metres): 328 × 45·2 × 20 *(100 × 14 × 6·1)*
Main engines: Steam turbine

Employed as a freighting and fleet replenishment tanker and naval supply ship.

1 HARBOUR TANKER

Name	No.	Builders	Commissione
SAMED	—	Royal Thai Naval Dockyard, Bangkok	15 Dec 1970

Displacement, tons: 360 standard; 485 full load
Dimensions, feet (metres): 120 × 20 × 10 *(39 × 6·1 × 3·1)*
Main engines: Diesel; 500 bhp = 9 knots

Launched on 8 July 1966.

1 HARBOUR TANKER

PRONG YO 5

Displacement, tons: 150 standard
Dimensions, feet (metres): 95 × 18 × 7·5 *(29 × 5 × 2·5)*
Main engines: Diesel; 150 bhp = 10 knots
Complement: 14

Launched in 1938.

1 HARBOUR TANKER

SAMUI (ex-USS *YOG 60*) YO 4

Displacement, tons: 422 standard
Dimensions, feet (metres): 174·5 × 32 × 15 *(53·2 × 9·7 × 4·6)*
Main engines: Diesel; 2 shafts; 600 bhp = 8 knots
Complement: 29

1 HARBOUR TANKER

Name	No.	Builders	Commissioned
PROET	YO 6	Royal Thai Naval Dockyard, Bangkok	16 Jan 1970

Displacement, tons: 360
Dimensions, feet (metres): 122·7 × 19·7 × 8·7 *(37·4 × 6 × 2·7)*
Main engines: Diesels; 500 bhp = 9 knots

1 TRANSPORT

Name	No.	Builders	Commissioned
SICHANG	AKL 1	Harima Co, Japan	Jan 1938

Displacement, tons: 815 standard
Dimensions, feet (metres): 160 × 28 × 16 *(48·8 × 8·5 × 4·9)*
Main engines: Diesel; 2 shafts; 550 bhp = 16 knots
Complement: 30

Sichang was launched on 10 Nov 1937. Completed in Jan 1938.

1 TRANSPORT

KLED KEO AF 7

Displacement, tons: 382 standard; 450 full load
Dimensions, feet (metres): 154·9 × 25·4 × 14 *(46 × 7·6 × 4·3)*
Guns: 3—20 mm
Main engines: 1 diesel; 600 hp = 12 knots
Complement: 54

Operates with patrol boat squadron.

2 WATER CARRIERS

Name	No.	Builders	Commissioned
CHUANG	YW 8	Royal Thai Naval Dockyard, Bangkok	1965
CHARN	YW 6	Royal Thai Naval Dockyard, Bangkok	1965

Displacement, tons: 305 standard; 485 full load
Dimensions, feet (metres): 136 × 25 × 10 *(42 × 7·5 × 3·1)*
Main engines: GM diesel; 500 bhp = 11 knots
Complement: 29

Chuang launched on 14 Jan 1965.

TUGS

Name	No.	Builders	Commissioned
SAMAE SAN (ex-*Empire Vincent*)	YTM 1	Cochrane & Sons Ltd, Selby, Yorks, England	—

Displacement, tons: 503 full load
Dimensions, feet (metres): 105·0 × 26·5 × 13·0 *(32 × 8·1 × 4)*
Main engines: Triple expansion; 850 ihp = 10·5 knots
Complement: 27

3 Ex-US "YTL 422" CLASS

KLUENG BADEN YTL 2   **RAD** (ex-USN YTL 340) YTL 4
MARN VICHAI YTL 3

Displacement, tons: 63 standard (*Rad* 52 standard)
Dimensions, feet (metres): 64·7 × 16·5 × 6·0 *(18·6 × 4·5 × 1·8)*
  Rad 60·7 × 17·5 × 5·0 *(18·3 × 5·3 × 1·5)*
Main engines: Diesels; speed = 8 knots (*Rad* 6 knots)

Rad transferred May 1955 from US, the other pair bought from Canada 1953.

TOGO

Togo, which proclaimed independence on 27 April 1960 and has a port at Lomé operates one 130 ft patrol vessel, three 100 ft patrol vessels, and one 95 ft river gunboat.
Personnel is 250 officers and men.

TONGA

On 10 Mar 1973 King Taufa 'ahau Tupou IV commissioned the first craft of Tonga's Maritime Force, a necessary service in a Kingdom of seven main groups of islands spread over 270 square miles.

Mercantile Marine

Lloyd's Register of Shipping: 10 vessels of 9 644 tons gross

Name	*No.*	*Builders*	*Commissioned*
NGAHAU KOULA	P 101	—	10 Mar 1973

Length, feet (metres): 40 *(15·1)*
Gun: 1—·50 Browning MG
Main engines: 2 Cummins V8 diesels = 29 knots
Complement: 5

Fitted with Decca Super 100 radar, DF and echo-sounder (Ferrograph). Manned by volunteers from the Royal Guard and Tongan Defence Force.

NGAHAU KOULA   *1973, Statham*

TRINIDAD AND TOBAGO

COAST GUARD

Ministerial	**Headquarters Appointment**	**Personnel**	**Mercantile Marine**
Minister of National Security: Mr Victor Campbell	*Commanding Officer, T. & T. Coast Guard:* Commander M. O. Williams, MOM	(a) 1976: 264 (28 officers, 236 ratings) (b) Voluntary	*Lloyd's Register of Shipping:* 30 vessels of 13 864 tons gross

PATROL CRAFT

2 LATER VOSPER TYPE

Name	*No.*	*Builders*	*Commissioned*
BUCCO REEF	CG 4	Vosper Ltd, Portsmouth	18 Mar 1972
CHAGUARAMUS	CG 3	Vosper Ltd, Portsmouth	18 Mar 1972

Displacement, tons: 100 standard; 125 full load
Dimensions, feet (metres): 103·0 × 19·8 × 5·8 *(31·5 × 5·9 × 1·6)*
Gun: 1—20 mm Hispano Suiza
Main engines: 2 Paxman Ventura diesels; 2 900 bhp = 24 knots
Oil fuel, tons: 20
Range, miles: 2 000 at 13 knots
Complement: 19 (3 officers, 16 ratings)

Chaguaramus was laid down on 1 Feb 1971 and launched on 29 Mar 1971. Fitted with modern navigational equipment, air-conditioning and roll-damping.

CHAGUARAMUS   *1975, Trinidad and Tobago Coast Guard*

2 VOSPER TYPE

Name	*No.*	*Builders*	*Commissioned*
COURLAND BAY	CG 2	Vosper Ltd, Portsmouth	20 Feb 1965
TRINITY	CG 1	Vosper Ltd, Portsmouth	20 Feb 1965

Displacement, tons: 96 standard; 123 full load
Dimensions, feet (metres): 102·6 oa × 19·7 × 5·5 *(31·4 × 5·9 × 1·7)*
Gun: 1—40 mm Bofors
Main engines: 2 12 cyl Paxman Ventura YJCM turbo-charged diesels; 2 910 bhp = 24·5 knots
Oil fuel, tons: 18
Range, miles: 1 800 at 13·5 knots
Complement: 17 (3 officers, 14 ratings)

Designed by Vosper Limited, Portsmouth. Of steel construction with aluminium alloy superstructure. Up-to-date radar and navigational equipment is fitted, and the boats are air-conditioned throughout except the engine room. Vosper roll-damping equipment is fitted. Laid down Oct 1963. *Trinity* was launched on 14 April 1964. *Trinity* is named after Trinity Hills, so named by Columbus on making his landfall in 1498, and *Courland Bay* after a bay in Tobago where a settlement was founded by the Duke of Courland in the 17th century.

TRINITY   *1975, Trinidad and Tobago Coast Guard*

4 INSHORE TYPE

CG 6   CG 7   CG 8   CG 9

Three Glastron glass fibre runabouts and one locally built (also of glass fibre), all capable of 27 knots, are used for inshore patrol work, mainly in the Gulf of Paria.

TUNISIA

Headquarters Appointment

Chief of Naval Staff:
   Capitaine de Fregate Jedidi Bechir

Personnel

(a)   1976: 2 100 officers and men
(b)   1 year National Service

Mercantile Marine

Lloyd's Register of Shipping:
   28 vessels of 40 827 tons gross

Strength of the Fleet

Type	Active	Building
Frigate	1	—
Corvette	1	1
MSC	1	—
Large Patrol Craft	3	—
Coastal Patrol Craft	10	—
Tugs	3	—

FRIGATE

1 Ex-US "SAVAGE" CLASS

Name	No.	Builders	Commissioned
PRÉSIDENT BOURGUIBA (ex-USS *Thomas J. Gary DER 326*, ex-*DE 326*)	E 7	Consolidated Steel Corpn	27 Nov 1943

Displacement, tons: 1 590 standard; 2 100 full load
Dimensions, feet (metres): 306 oa × 36·6 × 14 *(93·3 × 11·1 × 4·3)*
Guns: 2—3 in *(76 mm)* 50 cal; 2—20 mm
Torpedo tubes: 2 triple MK 32
A/S weapon: 1 Hedgehog
Main engines: 4 diesels; 6 000 bhp; 2 shafts = 19 knots
Range, miles: 11 500 at 11 knots
Complement: 169

Completed as "Edsall" class DE. Converted to Radar Picket "Savage" class in 1958. Transferred 27 Oct 1973.

Radar: SPS 28 and SPS 10.

PRÉSIDENT BOURGUIBA   *1974, Tunisian Navy*

CORVETTES

1 FRENCH A69 TYPE AVISO

Displacement, tons: 950 standard; 1 260 full load
Dimensions, feet (metres): 262·5 oa × 33·8 × 9·8 *(80 × 10·3 × 3)*
Guns: 1—3·9 in *(100 mm)* 1—40 mm; 4—20 mm
A/S weapons: 1 sextuple Mk 64 rocket launcher *(375 mm)* 4 fixed torpedo launchers for homing torpedoes
Main engines: 2 SEMT Pielstick PC2V Diesels; 2 shafts; c-p propellers; 1 100 shp = 24 knots
Range, miles: 4 500 at 15 knots
Complement: 62

Reported as ordered from France in 1972 although this is still not confirmed.

TYPE A69

1 Ex-FRENCH "FOUGEUX" CLASS

Name	No.	Builders	Commissioned
SAKIET SIDI YOUSSEF (ex-*UW 12*)	P 303	Dubigeon, Nantes	1956

Displacement, tons: 325 standard; 440 full load
Dimensions, feet (metres): 170 pp × 23 × 6·5 *(53 × 7·3 × 2)*
Guns: 1—40 mm; 2—20 mm
A/S weapons: 1 Hedgehog; 4 DCT; 2 DC racks
Main engines: 4 SEMT-Pielstick diesels; 3 240 bhp = 18·7 knots
Range, miles: 2 000 at 15 knots
Complement: 4 officers, 59 men

Built in France, under US off-shore order. Purchased by Federal Germany in 1957 and served as A/S trials vessel. Transferred to Tunisia in Dec 1969.

SAKIET SIDI YOUSSEF   *1974, Tunisian Navy*

COASTAL MINESWEEPER

1 Ex-US "ACACIA" CLASS

Name	No.	Builders	Commissioned
HANNIBAL (ex-*Coquelicot*, ex-USN *MSC 84*)	—	USA	1953

Displacement, tons: 320 standard; 372 full load
Dimensions, feet (metres): 141 oa × 26 × 8·3 *(43 × 8 × 2·6)*
Guns: 2—20 mm
Main engines: 2 GM diesels; 2 shafts; 1 200 bhp = 13 knots
Oil fuel, tons: 40
Range, miles: 2 500 at 10 knots
Complement: 38

Built for France under MDAP and delivered in 1953—to Tunisia in 1973.

HANNIBAL   *1974, Tunisian Navy*

LIGHT FORCES

3 "P 48" CLASS (LARGE PATROL CRAFT)

Name	No.	Builders	Commissioned	
BIZERTE	P 301	Ch. Franco-Belges (Villeneuve, la Garenne)	10 July	1970
HORRIA (ex-*Liberté*)	P 302	Ch. Franco-Belges (Villeneuve, la Garenne)	Oct	1970
MONASTIR	P 304	Soc. Francaise Constructions Navale	Feb	1975

Displacement, tons: 250
Dimensions, feet (metres): 157·5 × 23·3 × 7 *(48 × 7·1 × 2·3)*
Missiles: 8—SS 12
Guns: 2—40 mm
Main engines: 2 MTU diesels; 4 800 bhp = 20 knots
Range, miles: 2 000 at 16 knots

Ordered in 1968. *Bizerte* was launched on 20 Nov 1969. *Horria* launched 12 Feb 1970. *Monastir* ordered in Aug 1973, laid down Jan 1974, launched 25 June 1974.

BIZERTE   *1974, Tunisian Nav*

4 32-metre COASTAL PATROL CRAFT

Name	No.	Builders	Commissioned	
AL JALA	P 203	Ch. Navale d'Esterel	Nov	1963
ISTIKLAL (ex-*VC 11, P 761*)	P 201	Ch. Navale d'Esterel		1957
JOUMHOURIA	P 202	Ch. Navale d'Esterel	Jan	1969
REMADA	P 204	Ch. Navale d'Esterel	July	1967

Displacement, tons: 60 standard; 82 full load
Dimensions, feet (metres): 104·5 × 15·5 × 5·6 *(31·5 × 5·8 × 1·7)*
Gun: 1—20 mm
Main engines: 2 Mercedes-Benz (MTU) diesels; 2 shafts; 2 700 bhp = 28 knots
Range, miles: 1 400 at 15 knots
Complement: 17

Istiklal transferred from France Mar 1959.

ISTIKLAL   *1971, Tunisian Nav*

6 25-metre COASTAL PATROL CRAFT

Name	No.	Builders	Commissioned
—	V 101	Ch. Navale d'Esterel	1961
—	V 102	Ch. Navale d'Esterel	1961
—	V 103	Ch. Navale d'Esterel	1962
—	V 104	Ch. Navale d'Esterel	1962
—	V 105	Ch. Navale d'Esterel	1963
—	V 106	Ch. Navale d'Esterel	1963

Displacement, tons: 38
Dimensions, feet (metres): 83 × 15·6 × 4·1 *(25 × 4·8 × 1·3)*
Gun: 1—20 mm
Main engines: 2 twin GM diesels; 2 400 hp = 23 knots
Range, miles: 900 at 16 knots
Complement: 11

Two further craft of the same design (V 107 and V 108) but unarmed were supplied to the Fisheries Administration in 1971.

V 104   *1970, Tunisian Nav*

2 VOSPER THORNYCROFT 103 ft TYPE

(FAST ATTACK CRAFT)

Reported as ordered in 1974.

V 105   *1974, Tunisian Navy*

TUGS

Name	No.	Builders	Commissioned	Name	No.	Builders	Commissioned
RAS ADAR (ex-*Zeeland*, ex-*Pan American*, ex-*Ocean Pride*, ex-HMS *Oriana, BAT 1*)	—	Gulfport Boilerworks & Eng Co.	1942	JAOUEL EL BAHR	T 1	Ch. Navale d'Esterel	—
				SABBACK EL BAHR	T 2	Ch. Navale d'Esterel	—

Displacement, tons: 540 standard
Dimensions, feet (metres): 144·4 × 33 × 13·5 *(43 × 10 × 4)*

Built in 1942 and lend leased to the Royal Navy in that year as BAT 1 HMS *Oriana*, returned and sold in 1946 as *Ocean Pride*, then *Pan America* in 1947, then *Zeeland* in 1956.

TURKEY

Headquarters Appointment

Commander in Chief, Turkish Naval Forces:
   Admiral Hilmi Firat

Senior Command

Fleet Commander:
   Vice-Admiral Arif Akdoganlar

Diplomatic Representation

Naval Attaché in Athens:
   Captain Y. Günçer
Naval Attaché in Bonn:
   Captain T. Özkan
Naval Attaché in Cairo:
   Commander Y. Erel
Naval Attaché in London:
   Captain Y. Özesen
Naval Attaché in Moscow:
   Captain R. Maldemir
Naval Attaché in Oslo:
   Captain T. Erdinç
Naval Attaché in Rome:
   Captain E. Akman
Naval Attaché in Tokyo:
   Commander E. Erdilek
Naval Attaché in Washington:
   Commander E. Gürsal

Personnel

(a) 1976: 45 000 officers and ratings
(b) 20 months national service

Naval Bases

Headquarters: Ankara
Main Naval Base: Gölçük
Senior Flag Officers: Istanbul, Izmir
Other Flag Officers: Eregli, Bosphorus,
   Heybeliada (Training), Dardanelles, Iskenderun
Dockyards: Gölçük, Taşkizak (Istanbul)

Naval Air Arm

 3 AB-204B Helicopters
16 S2E ASW Aircraft

Mercantile Marine

Lloyd's Register of Shipping:
   387 vessels of 994 668 tons gross

Strength of the Fleet

Type	Active	Building
Destroyers	13	—
Frigates	2	—
Submarines—Patrol	14	3
Fast Attack Craft—Missile	4	4
Fast Attack Craft—Torpedo	12	—
Large Patrol Craft	41	1
Coastal Patrol Craft	4	—
Minelayer—Large	1	—
Minelayers—Coastal	8	—
Minesweepers—Coastal	21	—
Minesweepers—Inshore	4	—
Minehunting Boats	9	—
LSTs	2	—
LCTs	17	—
LCUs	16	—
LCMs	20	—
Support Tankers	4	—
Harbour Tanker	1	—
Water Tankers	2	—
Repair Ships	3	—
Transports	5	—
Submarine Rescue Ships	2	—
BDVs	4	—
Gate Vessels	3	—
Tug—Ocean	1	—
Tugs—Harbour	5	—
Floating Docks	7	—
Training Ships	2	—
Survey Vessels	4	—

DELETIONS

Destroyers

1973 *Gaziantep, Giresun*
1974 *Kocatepe* (ex-USS *Harwood*) sunk on 22 July. *Gemlik.*

Corvettes

1973 *Edremit, Eregli*
1974 *Çardak, Çesme, Edinicik*
1975 *Alanya, Ayvalik*

Submarines

(Most replaced by submarines of same name).

1973 *Birinci Inönü, Çanakkale, Çerbe, Ikinci, Inönü, Pirireis*
1974 *Gür* (ex-*Chub*), *Sakarya* (ex-*Boarfish*)

Fast Attack Craft

1973 *Dogan, Marti* ("Nasty" class), *AB 1-4, 6-7*

Support Tanker

1975 *Akar*

Boom Defence Vessels

1975 *AG 2, AG 3, Kaldaray*

Survey Craft

1975 *Mesaha 3* and *4*

PENNANT LIST

Destroyers

D 340	Istanbul
D 341	Izmir
D 342	Izmit
D 343	Iskenderun
D 344	Içel
D 346	Gelibolu
D 351	M. Fevzi Çakmak
D 352	Gayret
D 353	Adatepe
D 354	Kocatepe
D 355	Tinaztepe
D 356	Zafer
D 357	Muavenet

Frigates

D 358	Berk
D 359	Peyk

Submarines

S 333	Ikinci Inönü
S 335	Burak Reis
S 336	Murat Reis
S 337	Oruc Reis
S 338	Uluçali Reis
S 339	Dumlupinar
S 340	Çerbe
S 341	Çanakkale
S 342	Turgut Reis
S 344	Hizir Reis
S 345	Preveze
S 346	Birinci Inönü
S 347	Atilay
S 348	Saldiray

Minewarfare Forces (Sweepers)

M 500	Foça
M 501	Fethiye
M 502	Fatsa
M 503	Finike
M 507	Seymen
M 508	Selcuk
M 509	Seyhan
M 510	Samsun
M 511	Sinop
M 512	Sumene
M 513	Seddulbahir
M 514	Silifke
M 515	Saros
M 516	Sigacik
M 517	Sapanca
M 518	Sariyer
M 520	Karamürsel
M 521	Kerempe
M 522	Kilimli
M 523	Kozlu
M 524	Kuşadasi
M 530	Trabzon
M 531	Terme
M 532	Tirebolu
M 533	Tekirdag

Minewarfare Forces (Layers)

N 101	Mordogan
N 102	Meriç
N 103	Marmaris
N 104	Mersin
N 105	Mürefte
N 110	Nusret
N 111	Mehemedcik
N 112	Bayraktar
N 115	Sancaktar

Light Forces

P 111	Sultanhisar
P 112	Demirhisar
P 113	Yarhisar
P 114	Akhisar
P 115	Sivrihisar
P 116	Koçhisar
P 301	AG 1 (BDV)
P 304	AG 4 (BDV)
P 305	AG 5 (BDV)
P 306	AG 6 (BDV)
P 311-4	MTB 1-4
P 316-20	MTB 6-10
P 321	Denizkuzu
P 322	Atmaca
P 323	Sahin
P 324	Kartal
P 325	Melten
P 326	Pelikan
P 327	Albatros
P 328	Şimşek
P 329	Kasirga
P 330	Firtina
P 331	Tufan
P 332	Kiliç
P 333	Mizrak
P 334	Yildiz
P 335	Kalkan
P 336	Karayel
P 338	Yildirim
P 339	Bora
P 340	Dogan
P 341	Marti
P 342	Tayfun
P 343	Volkan
P 1209-12	LS 9-12
P 1221-34	AB 21-34
J 12-30	Large Patrol Craft

Service Forces

A 571	Yuzbaşi Tolunay
A 572	Albay Hakki Burak
A 573	Binbaşi Saadettin Gürçan
A 574	Akpina
A 575	Savarona
A 581	Onaran
A 582	Başaran
A 583	Donatan
A 584	Kurtaran
A 585	Akin
A 586	Ülkü
A 587	Gazal
A 591	Erkin
A 593	Çandarli (survey)
A 594	Çarşamba (survey)
Y 1081-1087	Floating Docks
Y 1118	Akbas
Y 1119	Kepez
Y 1122	Kuvvet
Y 1123	Öncu
Y 1129	Kudret
Y 1155	Kanaria
Y 1156	Sarköy
Y 1163	Lapseki
Y 1164	Erdek
Y 1166	Kilya
Y 1168	Tuzla
Y 1207	Gölçük
Y 1208	Van
Y 1209	Ulabat
Y 1217	Sogut

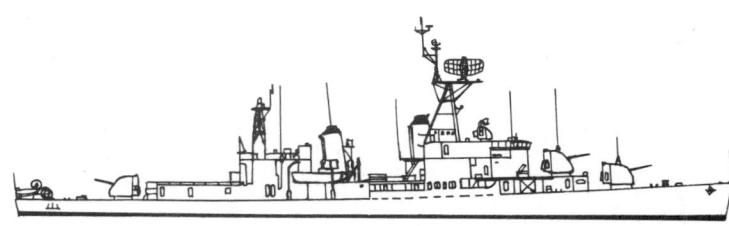

"TEPE" Class

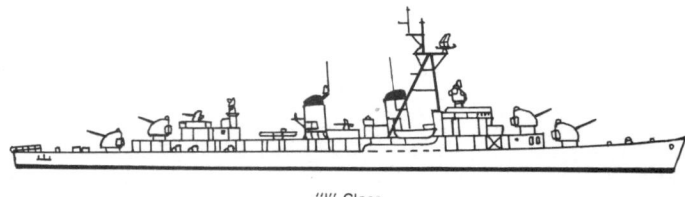

ZAFER

"I" Class

DESTROYERS

(Present status of *Gelibolu* uncertain)

5 "TEPE" CLASS (Ex-US "GEARING" CLASS)

Name	No.	Builders	Laid down	Launched	Commissioned
ADATEPE (ex-USS *Forrest Royal, DD 872*)	D 353	Bethlehem (Staten Is.)	1945	17 Jan 1946	28 June 1946
GAYRET (ex-USS *Eversole, DD 789*)	D 352	Todd Pacific Shipyard	1945	8 Jan 1946	10 July 1946
KOCATEPE (ex-USS *Norris, DD 859*)	D 354	Bethlehem (San Pedro)	1944	25 Feb 1945	9 June 1945
M. FEVZI ÇAKMAK (ex-USS *Charles H. Roan, DD 853*)	D 351	Bethlehem Steel Co, Quincy	1944	15 May 1945	12 Sep 1946
TINAZTEPE (ex-USS *Keppler, DD 765*)	D 355	Bethlehem (San Francisco)	1944	24 June1945	23 May 1947

Displacement, tons: 2 425 standard; 3 500 full load
Length, feet (metres): 390·5 *(119·0)* oa
Beam, feet (metres): 40·9 *(12·5)*
Draught, feet (metres): 19·0 *(5·8)*
Guns: 4—5 in *(127 mm)* 38 cal (2 twin)
A/S weapons: Fram I; 1 Asroc 8-tube launcher; 2 triple torpedo tubes (Mk 32); Facilities for small helicopter
Fram II; 1 Trainable Hedgehog; 2 Triple Torpedo tubes (Mk 32); 2 Fixed Torpedo tubes (Mk 28); Facilities for small helicopter
Main engines: 2 geared turbines; 2 shafts; 60 000 shp
Boilers: 4 Babcock & Wilcox
Speed, knots: 34
Oil fuel, tons: 650
Range, miles: 4 800 at 15 knots; 2 400 at 25 knots
Complement: 275 (15 officers, 260 ratings)

Adatepe, Gayret and *Çakmak* FRAM I conversions and *Kocatepe* and *Tinaztepe* FRAM II. They were transferred to Turkey on 27 Mar 1971 (*Adatepe*) 30 June 1972 (*Tinaztepe*) 11 July 1973 (*Gayret*) and 21 Sep 1973 (*Çakmak*), *Adatepe* purchased 15 Feb 1973 and *Kocatepe* 7 July 1974, commissioned 24 July 1975.

Replacement: The previous *Kocatepe* D 354 was sunk 22 July 1974. USS *Norris* had been purchased for spares on 7 July 1974 and has been re-activated to replace *Kocatepe*.

Radar: Long range air search: SPS 40 (FRAM I) SPS 6 (FRAM II).
Surface search: SPS 10.
Gunfire control: Mk 68.

Sonar: FRAM I, SQS 23; FRAM II, SQS 29.

ADATEPE   *1973, Dr. Giorgio Arra*

TINAZTEPE   *1975, Turkish Navy*

1 Ex-US "ROBERT H. SMITH" CLASS

Name
MUAVENET (ex-USS *Gwin,* ex-DM 33, ex-DD 772)

No.	Builders	Laid down	Launched	Commissioned
D 357	Bethlehem, San Pedro	1943	9 Apr 1944	30 Sep 1944

Displacement, tons: 2 250 standard; 3 375 full load
Dimensions, feet (metres): 376·5 × 41 × 19 *(114·8 × 12·5 × 5·8)*
Guns: 6—5 in *(127 mm)* 38 cal (twins); 12—40 mm; 11—20 mm
Mines: 80
Main engines: Geared turbines; 60 000 shp; 2 shafts
Boilers: 4 Babcock & Wilcox
Speed, knots: 34
Range, miles: 4 600 at 15 knots
Complement: 274

Modified "Allen M. Sumner" class converted for minelaying.
After modernisation at Philadelphia she was transferred on 22
Oct 1971.

Radar: Air search: SPS 6.
Director: Mk 68.

Sonar: SQS 29.

MUAVENET (As *Gwin*)   *Godfrey H. Walker*

1 Ex-US "ALLEN M. SUMNER (FRAM II)" CLASS

Name
ZAFER (ex-USS *Hugh, Purvis* ex-DD 709)

No.	Builders	Laid down	Launched	Commissioned
D 356	Federal SB and DD Co	1944	17 Dec 1944	1 Mar 1945

Displacement, tons: 2 200 standard; 3 320 full load
Length, feet (metres): 376·5 *(114·8)*
Beam, feet (metres): 40·9 *(12·5)*
Draught, feet (metres): 19·0 *(5·8)*
Guns: 6—5 in 38 cal (twins)
A/S weapons: 2 Triple torpedo launchers Mk 32; 2 Hedgehogs,
 2 Mk 25 torpedo tubes
Main engines: 2 geared turbines; 2 shafts; 60 000 shp
Boilers: 4 Babcock & Wilcox
Speed, knots: 34
Oil fuel, tons: 650
Range, miles: 4 600 at 15 knots
Complement: 275 (15 officers, 260 ratings)

Zafer is a standard FRAM II "Allen M. Sumner" class purchased
15 Feb 1973.

Radar: Air search: SPS 40.
Surface search: SPS 10.

Sonar: SQS 29.

5 "I" CLASS (Ex-US "FLETCHER" CLASS)

Name
İÇEL (ex-USS *Preston, DD 795)*
ISKENDERUN (ex-USS *Boyd, DD 544)*
ISTANBUL (ex-USS *Clarence K. Bronson, DD 668)*
IZMIR (ex-USS *Van Valkenburgh, DD 656)*
IZMIT (ex-USS *Cogswell, DD 651)*

No.	Builders	Laid down	Launched	Commissioned
D 344	Bethlehem Co, San Pedro	1943	12 Dec 1943	20 Mar 1944
D 343	Bethlehem Co, San Pedro	1942	29 Oct 1942	8 May 1943
D 340	Federal SB & DD Co, Newark	1942	18 Apr 1943	11 June 1943
D 341	Gulf Shipbuilding Corp	1943	19 Dec 1943	2 Aug 1944
D 342	Bath Iron Works, Corpn	1942	5 June 1943	17 Aug 1943

Displacement, tons: 2 050 standard; 3 000 full load
Length, feet (metres): 376·5 *(114·8)* oa
Beam, feet (metres): 39·5 *(12·1)*
Draught, feet (metres): 18·0 *(5·5)*
Guns: 4—5 in *(127 mm)* 38 cal; 6—3 in *(76 mm)*
A/S weapons: 2 Hedgehogs
Torpedo tubes: 5—21 in *(533 mm)* (quintuple)
Main engines: GE geared turbines; 2 shafts; 60 000 shp
Boilers: 4 Babcock & Wilcox
Speed, knots: 34
Oil fuel, tons: 650
Range, miles: 5 000 at 15 knots
Complement: 250

Transfers: Transferred as follows: *Istanbul* 14 Jan 1967, *Izmir*
28 Feb 1967, *Iskenderun* and *Ismit* on 1 Oct 1969, and *Icel* on 15
Nov 1969.

Radar: Search: SPS 6.
Tactical: SPS 10.
Fire Control: GFCS 68.

ISTANBUL   *1975, Turkish Navy*

FRIGATES

2 "BERK" CLASS

Name	No.	Builders	Laid down	Launched	Commissioned
BERK	D 358	Gölcük Naval Yard	9 Mar 1967	25 June1971	12 July 1972
PEYK	D 359	Gölcük Naval Yard	18 Jan 1968	7 June1972	24 July 1975

Displacement, tons: 1 450 standard; 1 950 full load
Length, feet (metres): 311·7 *(95·0)*
Beam, feet (metres):38·7 *(11·8)*
Draught, feet (metres): 18·1 *(5·5)*
Aircraft: 1 helicopter
Guns: 4—3 in *(76 mm)* (2 twin)
Torpedo tubes: 6—12·6 in *(320 mm)* (2 triple)
Main engines: 4 Fiat diesels; 2 shafts; 24 000 bhp
Speed, knots: 25

First major warships built in Turkey, the start of a most important era in the Eastern Mediterranean. Both are named after famous ships of the Ottoman Navy.

BERK   *1975, Turkish Navy*

SUBMARINES

3 + 2 TYPE 209 (HOWALDTSWERKE)

Name	No.	Builders	Laid down	Launched	Commissioned
ATILAY	S 347	Howaldtswerke, Kiel	2 Aug 1972	23 Oct 1974	29 July 1975
SALDIRAY	S 348	Howaldtswerke, Kiel	1973	14 Feb 1975	21 Oct 1975
—	S 349	Howaldtswerke, Kiel	11 June1975	1977	1978

Displacement, tons: 990 surfaced; 1 290 dived
Length, feet (metres): 183·7 *(56·0)*
Beam, feet (metres): 20·3 *(6·2)*
Torpedo tubes: 8—21 inch (with reloads)
Main machinery: Diesel electric; 4 MTU Siemens diesel-generators; 1 Siemens electric motor; 1 shaft
Speed, knots: 10 surfaced; 22 dived
Range: 50 days
Complement: 31

Designed by Ingenieurkontor, Lübeck for construction by Howaldtswerke, Kiel and sale by Ferrostaal, Essen all acting as a consortium.
A single-hull design with two ballast tanks and forward and after trim tanks. Fitted with snort and remote machinery control. The single screw is slow revving. Very high capacity batteries with GRP lead-acid cells and battery cooling—by Wilh. Hagen and VARTA. Active and passive sonar, sonar detection equipment, sound ranging gear and underwater telephone. Fitted with two periscopes, radar and Omega receiver. Foreplanes retract.

Future Construction: Two more of this class are to be built at Gölcük, the first submarines ever built in Turkey. If this class is to replace the ex-USN boats a considerable programme must be planned.

2 Ex-US "GUPPY III" CLASS

Name	No.	Builders	Laid down	Launched	Commissioned
ÇANAKKALE (ex-USS *Cobbler* SS 344)	S 341	Electric Boat Co	3 Apr 1944	1 Apr 1945	8 Aug 1945
IKINCI INONÜ (ex-USS *Corporal* SS 346)	S 333	Electric Boat Co	27 Apr 1944	10 June1945	9 Nov 1945

Displacement, tons: 1 975 standard; 2 540 dived
Dimensions, feet (metres): 326·5 × 27 × 17 *(99·4 × 8·2 × 5·2)*
Torpedo tubes: 10—21 inch *(533 mm)* 6 bow, 4 stern
Main machinery: 4 diesels; 6 400 shp; 2 electric motors 5 400 bhp; 2 shafts
Speed: 20 surfaced; 15 dived
Complement: 86

Transferred 21 Nov 1973.

Future Additions: When the US Congress imposed an arms embargo on exports to Turkey in 1975 arrangements were well-advanced for the transfer of the two "Guppy III" class, *Clamagore* and *Tiru*. It has yet to be seen whether these will be completed now that a relaxation of the embargo has taken place in April 1976.

IKINCI INONÜ (ex-US number)   *Turkish Navy*

1 Ex-US "GUPPY I A" CLASS

Name	No.	Builders	Laid down	Launched	Commissioned
DUMLUPINAR (ex-USS *Caiman*, SS 323)	S 339	Electric Boat Co	—	30 Mar 1944	17 July 1944

Displacement, tons: 1 840 standard; 2 445 dived
Dimensions, feet (metres): 306 × 27 × 17 *(93·2 × 8·2 × 5·2)*
Torpedo tubes: 10—21 in *(533 mm)* (6 bow, 4 stern); 24 torpedoes carried
Main machinery: 3 GM diesels; 4 800 hp; 2 electric motors; 5 400 hp
Speed, knots: 17 surfaced; 15 dived
Range, miles: 12 000 at 10 knots surfaced
Complement: 85

7 Ex-US "GUPPY II A" CLASS

Name	No.	Builders	Laid down	Launched	Commissioned
BIRINCI INÖNÜ (ex-USS *Threadfin*, SS 410)	S 346	Portsmouth Navy Yard	18 Mar 1944	26 June1944	30 Aug 1944
BURAK REIS (ex-USS *Seafox*, SS 402)	S 335	Portsmouth Navy Yard	2 Nov 1943	28 Mar 1944	13 June 1944
ÇERBE (ex-USS *Trutta*, SS 421)	S 340	Portsmouth Navy Yard	22 May 1944	22 May 1944	16 Nov 1944
MURAT REIS (ex-USS *Razorback*, SS 394)	S 336	Portsmouth Navy Yard	9 Sep 1943	27 Jan 1944	3 Apr 1944
ORUC REIS (ex-USS *Pomfret*, SS 391)	S 337	Portsmouth Navy Yard	14 July 1943	27 Oct 1943	19 Feb 1944
PREVEZE (ex-USS *Entemedor*, SS 340)	S 345	Electric Boat Co	3 Feb 1944	17 Dec 1944	6 Apr 1945
ULUÇALI REIS (ex-USS *Thornback*, SS 418)	S 338	Portsmouth Navy Yard	5 Apr 1944	7July 1944	13 Oct 1944

Displacement, tons: 1 840 standard; 2 445 dived
Dimensions, feet (metres): 306 × 27 × 17 *(93·2 × 8·2 × 5·2)*
Torpedo tubes: 10—21 in *(533 mm)* (6 bow, 4 stern); 24 torpedoes carried
Main machinery: 3 GM diesels; 4 800 hp; 2 electric motors; 5 400 hp
Speed, knots: 17 surfaced; 15 dived
Range, miles: 12 000 at 10 knots surfaced
Complement: 15

The fact that the same names are used for replacement submarines as for their predecessors can be confusing. eg "Cerbe" was used for both ex-USS *Hammerhead* and now for ex-USS *Trutta*.

Transfers: *Burak Reis* 25 June 1971, *Murat Reis* 17 Dec 1971, *Oruç Reis* 3 May 1972, *Çerbe, Dumlupinar, Preveze, Ulucali Reis* 24 Aug 1972, *Birinci Inönü* 15 Aug 1973.

5 HARBOUR TRAINING SUBMARINES

Ex-*Çanakkale* (ex-USS *Bumper*, SS 333) Y 1240
Ex-*Çerbe* (ex-USS *Hammerhead*, SS 364) Y 1242
Ex-*Ikinci Inönü* (ex-USS *Blueback*, SS 326) Y 1241
Ex-*Piri Reis* (ex-USS *Mapiro*, SS 376) Y 1244
Ex-*Preveze* (ex-USS *Guitarro*, SS 363) Y 1243

Classified as non-operational harbour training boats with new pennant numbers in 1974.

ULUÇALI REIS

1975, Turkish Navy

2 Ex-US MODIFIED FLEET TYPE (Ex-"BALAO" CLASS)

Name	No.	Builders	Laid down	Launched	Commissioned
HIZIR REIS (ex-USS *Mero*, SS 378)	S 344	Manitowoc SB Co.	1944	17 Jan 1945	17 Aug 1945
TURGUT REIS (ex-USS *Bergall*, SS 320)	S 342	Electric Boat Co.	1943	16 Feb 1944	12 June 1944

Displacement, tons: 1 562 standard; 1 829 surfaced; 2 424 dived
Dimensions, feet (metres): 311·8 × 27·2 × 13·8 *(95 × 8·3 × 4·2)*
Torpedo tubes: 10—21 inch *(533 mm)*; (6 bow, 4 stern) 24 torpedoes carried
Main machinery: 4 GM diesels; 6 400 shp; 2 electric motors; 5 400 shp
Speed, knots: 20 surfaced; 10 dived
Range, miles: 12 000 at 10 knots
Complement: 85

Streamlined boats of "Balao" class. Now becoming obsolescent. *Turgut Reis* purchased 15 Aug 1973 probably for spare parts eventually.

Transfers: *Hizir Reis*, 20 April 1960; *Turgut Reis*, 17 Oct 1958.

LIGHT FORCES

4 LÜRSSEN TYPE (FAST ATTACK CRAFT—MISSILE)

Name	No.	Builders	Commissioned
DOĞAN	P 340	Lürssen, Vegesack	1976
MARTI	P 341	Taşkizak Yard, Istanbul	1977
TAYFUN	P 342	Taşkizak Yard, Istanbul	1977
VOLKAN	P 343	Taşkizak Yard, Istanbul	—

Displacement, tons: 410
Dimensions, feet (metres): 190·6 × 25 × 8·8 *(58·1 × 7·6 × 2·7)*
Missiles: 8—Harpoon
Gun: 1—76 mm Oto Melara; 2—35 mm (twin)
Main engines: 4—16 cyl MTU diesels; 18 000 hp = 38 knots
Range, miles: 700 at 35 knots

Ordered 3 Aug 1973. *Dogan* laid down 2 June 1975, *Marti* 1 July 1975, *Tayfun* 1 Dec 1975.

9 "KARTAL" CLASS
(FAST ATTACK CRAFT—MISSILE/TORPEDO)

Name	No.	Builders	Commissioned
ALBATROS	P 327 (ex-*P 325*)	Lürssen, Vegesack	1968
ATMACA	P 322 (ex-*P 335*)	Lürssen, Vegesack	1967
DENIZKUSU	P 321 (ex-*P 336*)	Lürssen, Vegesack	1967
KARTAL	P 324 (ex-*P 333*)	Lürssen, Vegesack	1967
KASIRGA	P 329 (ex-*P 338*)	Lürssen, Vegesack	1967
MELTEM	P 325 (ex-*P 330*)	Lürssen, Vegesack	1968
PELIKAN	P 326	Lürssen, Vegesack	1968
SAHIN	P 323 (ex-*P 334*)	Lürssen, Vegesack	1967
ŞIMŞEK	P 328 (ex-*P 332*)	Lürssen, Vegesack	1968

Displacement, tons: 160 standard; 180 full load
Dimensions, feet (metres): 140·5 × 23·5 × 7·2 *(42·8 × 7·1 × 2·2)*
Missiles: (see note)
Guns: 2—40 mm
Torpedo tubes: 4—21 inch
Main engines: 4 Maybach (MTU) diesels; 4 shafts; 12 000 bhp = 42 knots
Complement: 39

Of the German "Jaguar" type. Launch dates—*Atmaca* 6 May 1966, *Kartal* 4 Nov 1965, *Meltem* 28 Dec 1966.

Missiles: Surface-to-surface missiles embarked in *Albatros, Meltem, Pelikan* and *Şimşek* during 1975.

DENIZKUSU

1975, Turkish Navy

7 Ex-FDR "JAGUAR" CLASS
(FAST ATTACK CRAFT—TORPEDO)

Name	No.	Builders	Commissioned
FIRTINA (ex-FDR Pelikan, P 6086)	P 330	Lürssen, Vegesack	1962
KALKAN	P 335	Lürssen, Vegesack	—
KARAYEL	P 336	Lürssen, Vegesack	—
KILIÇ	P 332	Lürssen, Vegesack	—
MIZRAK	P 333	Lürssen, Vegesack	—
TUFAN (ex-FDR Storch, P 6085)	P 331	Lürssen, Vegesack	1962
YILDIZ	P 334	Lürssen, Vegesack	—

Displacement, tons: 160 standard; 190 full load
Dimensions, feet (metres): 139·4 × 23·4 × 7·9 (42·5 × 7·2 × 2·4)
Guns: 2—40 mm L 70 Bofors (single)
Torpedo tubes: 4—21 inch (2 tubes can be removed to embark 4 mines)
Main engines: 4 Maybach (MTU) diesels; 4 shafts; 12 000 bhp = 42 knots
Complement: 39

In late 1975-early 1976 seven "Jaguar" class were transferred by the FDR to Turkey— *Häher* P 6087, *Löw* P 6065, *Pelikan* P 6086, *Pinguin* P 6090, *Storch* P 6085, *Tiger* P 6063, and *Wolf* P 6062. In addition three more were transferred for spare parts—*Alk* P 6084, *Fuchs* P 6066 and *Reiher* P 6089.

2 Ex-US "ASHEVILLE" CLASS (LARGE PATROL CRAFT)

Name	No.	Builders	Commissioned
BORA (ex-USS Surprise, PG 97)	P 339	Petersons, Wisconsin	17 Oct 1969
YILDIRIM (ex-USS Defiance, PG 95)	P 338	Petersons, Wisconsin	24 Sep 1969

Displacement, tons: 225 standard; 245 full load
Dimensions, feet (metres): 164·5 oa × 23·8 × 9·5 (50·1 × 7·3 × 2·9)
Guns: 1—3 in 50 cal; 1—40 mm; 4—50 cal MG
Main engines: CODAG; 2 Cummins Diesels; 1 450 hp = 16 knots; 1 GE gas turbine; 13 300 shp = 40 knots
Complement: 25

These vessels belong to the largest Patrol Type built by the USN since World War II and the first of that Navy to have gas turbines. Transferred to Turkey on 28th Feb 1973 and 11 June 1973 respectively.

BORA   1975, Turkish Navy

1 LARGE PATROL CRAFT

GIRNE P —

Details not available but reported as building.
Ex-FDR KW 2 and 8 also reported as transferred.

6 "HISAR" CLASS (LARGE PATROL CRAFT)

Name	No.	Builders	Commissioned
AKHISAR (ex-PC 1641)	P 114	Gunderson Bros Engineering Co, Portland, Oregon	1943
DEMIRHISAR (ex-PC 1639)	P 112	Gunderson Bros Engineering Co, Portland, Oregon	1943
KOCHISAR (ex-PC 1643)	P 116	Gölcük Dockyard, Turkey	1965
SIVRIHISAR (ex-PC 1642)	P 115	Gunderson Bros Engineering Co, Portland, Oregon	1943
SULTAN HISAR (ex-PC 1638)	P 111	Gunderson Bros Engineering Co, Portland, Oregon	1943
YARHISAR (ex-PC 1640)	P 113	Gunderson Bros Engineering Co, Portland, Oregon	1943

Displacement, tons: 280 standard; 412 full load
Dimensions, feet (metres): 173·7 oa × 23 × 10·2 (54 × 7 × 3·1)
Guns: 1—3 inch; 1—40 mm
A/S weapons: 4 DCT
Main engines: 2 FM diesels; 2 shafts; 2 800 bhp = 19 knots
Range, miles: 6 000 at 10 knots
Complement: 65 (5 officers, and 60 men)

Similar to US 173 ft class submarine chasers. Transferred on 3 Dec 1964, 22 April 1965, 22 April 1965, 2 May 1964, 24 Sep 1964 and 22 April 1965 respectively.

DEMIRHISAR   1975, Turkish Navy

10 LARGE PATROL CRAFT

Name	No.	Builders	Commissioned
AB 25	P 1225	Taskizak Naval Yard	1967
AB 26	P 1226	Taskizak Naval Yard	1967
AB 27	P 1227	Taskizak Naval Yard	1967
AB 28	P 1228	Taskizak Naval Yard	1968
AB 29	P 1229	Taskizak Naval Yard	1968
AB 30	P 1230	Taskizak Naval Yard	1969
AB 31	P 1231	Taskizak Naval Yard	1969
AB 32	P 1232	Taskizak Naval Yard	1970
AB 33	P 1233	Taskizak Naval Yard	1970
AB 34	P 1234	Taskizak Naval Yard	1970

Displacement, tons: 170
Dimensions, feet (metres): 132 × 21 × 5·5 (40·2 × 6·4 × 1·7)
Guns: 2—40 mm
Speed, knots: 22

AB 28   1970, Turkish Navy

First was launched on 9 Mar 1967. Six similar launches are operated by the Gendarmerie.

4 US PGM TYPE (LARGE PATROL CRAFT)

Name	No.	Builders	Commissioned
AB 21 (ex-*PGM 104*)	P 1221	Peterson, Sturgeon Bay, USA	Aug 1967
AB 22 (ex-*PGM 105*)	P 1222	Peterson, Sturgeon Bay, USA	Sep 1967
AB 23 (ex-*PGM 106*)	P 1223	Peterson, Sturgeon Bay, USA	Oct 1967
AB 24 (ex-*PGM 108*)	P 1224	Peterson, Sturgeon Bay, USA	May 1968

Displacement, tons: 130 standard; 147 full load
Dimensions, feet (metres): 101 × 21 × 7 *(30·8 × 6·4 × 1·9)*
Guns: 1—40 mm; 4—20 mm
Main engines: 2 diesels; 2 shafts; 1 850 hp = 18·5 knots
Range, miles: 1 500 at 10 knots
Complement: 15

AB 23

1970, Turkish Navy

19 LARGE PATROL CRAFT

Name	No.	Builders	Commissioned
—	J 12	Schweers, Bardenfleth	1961
—	J 13	Schweers, Bardenfleth	1961
—	J 14	Schweers, Bardenfleth	1961
—	J 15	Schweers, Bardenfleth	1961
—	J 16	Schweers, Bardenfleth	1962
—	J 17	Schweers, Bardenfleth	1962
—	J 18	Schweers, Bardenfleth	1962
—	J 19	Schweers, Bardenfleth	1962
—	J 20	Schweers, Bardenfleth	1962
—	J 21	Gölcük Navy Yard	1968
—	J 22	Gölcük Navy Yard	1968
—	J 23	Taskizak Naval Yard	1969
—	J 24	Taskizak Naval Yard	1969
—	J 25	Taskizak Naval Yard	1969
—	J 26	Taskizak Naval Yard	1969
—	J 27	Taskizak Naval Yard	1969
—	J 28	Taskizak Naval Yard	1970
—	J 29	Taskizak Naval Yard	1971
—	J 30	Taskizak Naval Yard	1971

Displacement, tons: 150
Dimensions, feet (metres): 129·3 × 20·6 × 4·9 *(34·4 × 6·3 × 1·5)*
Guns: 2—40 mm
Main engines: 4 MB (MTU) diesels; 2 shafts; 3 200 bhp = 22 knots

J 21

1972, Dr. Giorgio Arra

4 Ex-US COASTGUARD "83 ft" CLASS
(COASTAL PATROL CRAFT)

LS 9 P 1209   **LS 10** P 1210   **LS 11** P 1211   **LS 12** P 1212

Displacement, tons: 63 standard
Dimensions, feet (metres): 83·0 × 14·0 × 5·0 *(25·3 × 4·3 × 1·6)*
Gun: 1—20 mm
A/S weapons: 2 Mousetrap
Main engines: 2 Cummins diesels; 1 100 bhp = 20 knots

Ex-US type, transferred on 25 June 1953.

MINE WARFARE FORCES

1 MINELAYER

Name	No.	Builders	Commissioned
NUSRET	N 110 (ex-*N 108*)	Frederikshaven Dockyard, Denmark	16 Sep 1964

Displacement, tons: 1 880 standard
Length, feet (metres): 246 *(75·0)* pp; 252·7 *(77·0)* oa
Beam, feet (metres): 41 *(12·6)*
Draught, feet (metres): 11 *(3·4)*
Guns: 4—3 in *(76 mm)* (2 twin)
Mines: 400
Main engines: GM diesels; 4 800 hp; 2 shafts
Speed, knots: 18
Complement: 146

Laid down in 1962, launched in 1964. Similar to Danish "Falster" class.

Radar: Search: RAN 7S.
Fire Control: I Band.
Navigation Radar.

NUSRET

1975, Turkish Navy

2 Ex-US LST TYPE (COASTAL MINELAYERS)

SANCAKTAR
(ex-German *Bochum,* ex-USS *Rice County L 1089*) N 112
BAYRAKTAR
(ex-German *Bottrop,* ex-USS *Saline County L 1101*) N 111

Displacement, tons: 1 653 standard; 4 080 full load
Dimensions, feet (metres): 328 oa × 50 × 14 *(100 × 15·2 × 4·3)*
Guns: 6—40 mm (2 twin, 2 single)
Main engines: 2 GM diesels; 2 shafts; 1 700 bhp = 11 knots
Range, miles: 15 000 at 9 knots
Complement: 125

Formerly USN LSTs, transferred to Germany in 1961 and thence to Turkey on 13 Dec 1972.
Converted into minelayers in Germany 1962-64.

SANCAKTAR

1973, Reiner Nerlich

5 Ex-US LSM TYPE (COASTAL MINELAYERS)

Name	No.	Builders	Commissioned
MARMARIS (ex-LSM 481)	N 103	U.S.A.	1945
MERIÇ (ex-LSM 490)	N 102	U.S.A.	1945
MERSIN (ex-LSM 492)	N 104	U.S.A.	1945
MORDOĞAN (ex-LSM 484)	N 101	U.S.A.	1945
MÜREFTE (ex-LSM 493)	N 105	U.S.A.	1945

Displacement, tons: 743 standard; 1 100 full load
Dimensions, feet (metres): 203·2 oa × 34·5 × 8·5 (61·9 × 10·5 × 2·4)
Guns: 2—40 mm; 2—20 mm
Main engines: Diesels; 2 shafts; 2 880 bhp = 12 knots
Oil fuel, tons: 60
Range, miles: 2 500 at 12 knots
Complement: 89

Ex-US Landing Ships Medium. All launched in 1945, converted into coastal minelayers by the US Navy in 1952 and taken over by the Turkish Navy (LSM 481, 484 and 490) and the Norwegian Navy (LSM 492 and 493) in Oct 1952 under MAP. LSM 492 (Vale) and LSM 493 (Vidar) were retransferred to the Turkish Navy on 1 Nov 1960 at Bergen, Norway.

MERIÇ   1975, Turkish Navy

1 Ex-US YMP TYPE (COASTAL MINELAYEER)

Name	No.	Builders	Commissioned
MEHMETCIK (ex-US YMP 3)	N 115	Higgins Inc, New Orleans	1958

Displacement, tons: 540 full load
Dimensions, feet (metres): 130 × 35 × 6 (39·6 × 10·7 × 1·9)
Main engines: Diesels; 2 shafts; 600 bhp = 10 knots
Complement: 22

Former US motor mine planter. Steel hulled. Transferred under MAP in 1958. For harbour defence.

MEHMETCIK

12 Ex-US MSC TYPE (MINESWEEPERS—COASTAL)

SAMSUN (ex-USS MSC 268) M 510		SEYHAN (ex-MSC 142) M 509	
SAPANCA (ex-USS MSC 312) M 517		SEYMEN (ex-MSC 131) M 507	
SARIYER (ex-USS MSC 315) M 518		SIGACIK (ex-USS MSC 311) M 516	
SAROS (ex-USS MSC 305) M 515		SILIFKE (ex-USS MSC 304) M 514	
SEDDULBAHIR (ex-MSC 272) M 513		SINOP (ex-USS MSC 270) M 511	
SELCUK (ex-MSC 124) M 508		SURMENE (ex-USS MSC 271) M 512	

Displacement, tons: 320 standard; 370 full load
Dimensions, feet (metres): 138·0 pp; 144·0 oa × 28·0 × 9·0 (41·5; 43 × 8 × 2·6)
Guns: 2—20 mm
Main engines: 2 diesels; 2 shafts; 1 200 bhp = 14 knots
Oil fuel, tons: 25
Range, miles: 2 500 at 10 knots
Complement: 38 (4 officers, 34 men)

Transferred on 30 Sep 1958, 26 July 1965, 8 Sep 1967, 8 Nov 1965, 9 July 1959, 24 Mar 1970, 24 Mar 1970, 19 Nov 1970, 29 May 1965, 25 Oct 1965, 30 Jan 1959, 27 Mar 1959, respectively. Selcuk and Seyhan were transferred from France (via USA) and Seyman from Belgium (via USA).

SURMENE   1975, Turkish Navy

4 Ex-CANADIAN MCB TYPE (MINESWEEPERS—COASTAL)

TIREBOLU (ex-HMCS Comax) M 532		TERME (ex-HMCS Trinity) M 531	
TEKIRDAG (ex-HMCS Ungave) M 533		TRABZON (ex-HMCS Gaspe) M 530	

Displacement, tons: 390 standard; 412 full load
Dimensions, feet (metres): 152·0 oa × 20·8 × 7·0 (50 × 9·2 × 2·8)
Gun: 1—40 mm
Main engines: Diesels; 2 shafts; 2 400 bhp = 16 knots
Oil fuel, tons: 52
Range, miles: 4 500 at 11 knots
Complement: 44

Sailed from Sydney, Nova Scotia, to Turkey on 19 May 1958.

TIREBOLU   1970, Turkish Navy

5 Ex-FDR "VEGESACK" CLASS (MINESWEEPERS—COASTAL)

Name	No.	Builders	Commissioned
KARAMÜRSEL (ex-Worms M 1253)	M 520	Cherbourg	1960
KEREMPE (ex-Detmold M 1252)	M 521	Cherbourg	1960
KILIMLI (ex-Siegen M 1254)	M 522	Cherbourg	1960
KOZLU (ex-Hameln M 1251)	M 523	Cherbourg	1960
KUŞADASI (ex-Vegesack M 1250)	M 524	Cherbourg	1960

Displacement, tons: 362 standard; 378 full load
Dimensions, feet (metres): 144·3 × 26·2 × 9 (47·3 × 8·6 × 2·9)
Guns: 2—20 mm
Main engines: 2 Mercedes Benz (MTU) diesels; 2 shafts; 1 500 bhp = 15 knots (cp propellers)

Of similar class to French Mercure. Transferred by FDR to Turkey late 1975-early 1976.

KARAMÜRSEL (as Worms)   1972

4 Ex-US MINESWEEPERS—INSHORE

Name	No.	Builders	Commissioned
FATSA (ex-*MSI 17*)	M 502	USA	Sep 1967
FETHIYE (ex-*MSI 16*)	M 501	USA	Aug 1967
FINIKE (ex-*MSI 18*)	M 503	Peterson Builders Inc	8 Nov 1967
FOÇA (ex-*MSI 15*)	M 500	USA	Aug 1967

Displacement, tons: 180 standard; 235 full load
Dimensions, feet (metres): 111·9 × 23·5 × 7·9 *(34× 7·1 × 2·4)*
Gun: 1—·50 cal
Main engines: 4 diesels; 2 shafts; 960 bhp = 13 knots
Complement: 30

Built in USA and transferred under MAP at Boston, Mass, Aug-Sep 1967.

FOÇA

1970, Turkish Navy

9 MINEHUNTING BOATS

MTB 1 P 311	**MTB 3** P 313	**MTB 6** P 316	**MTB 8** P 318	
MTB 2 P 312	**MTB 4** P 314	**MTB 7** P 317	**MTB 9** P 319	
			MTB 10 P 320	

Displacement, tons: 70 standard
Dimensions, feet (metres): 71·5 × 13·8 × 8·5 *(21·8 × 4·2 × 2·6)*
Main engines: Diesel; 2 000 bhp = 20 knots

All launched in 1942. Now employed as minehunting base ships.

LS 9 (old pennant number)

1972, Turkish Navy

AMPHIBIOUS FORCES

2 Ex-US LSTs

Name	No.	Builders	Commissioned
ERTUĞRUL (ex-USS *Windham County, LST 1170*)	L 401	Christy Corp	1954
SERDAR (ex-USS *Westchester County, LST 1169*)	L 402	Christy Corp	1954

Displacement, tons: 2 590 light; 5 800 full load
Dimensions, feet (metres): 384 oa × 55 × 17 *(117·4 × 16·8 × 3·7)*
Guns: 6—3 in 50 cal (twins)
Main engines: 4 GM diesels; 2 shafts (cp propellers); 6 000 bhp = 15 knots
Complement: 116
Troops: 395

Transferred by US June 1973. (L 401) and 27 Aug 1974 (L 402).

ERTUĞRUL

1975, Turkish Navy

C 101 and 103-106

Displacement, tons: 500 light; 700 full load
Dimensions, feet (metres): 180·9 × 27·7 × 5·4 *(55·2 × 8·4 × 1·6)*
Guns: 2—20 mm
Complement: 15

Built in USA in 1942. Transferred 25 Sep 1967.

5 Ex-US LCTs

C 104

1975, Turkish Navy

C 107-118

Displacement, tons: 400 light; 600 full load
Dimensions, feet (metres): 180·9 × 36·8 × 4·8 *(55·2 × 11·2 × 1·4)*
Guns: 2—20 mm
Speed, knots: 10·5
Complement: 15

12 TURKISH-BUILT LCTs

Built in Turkey 1966-1973. Of French EDIC type.

12 TURKISH-BUILT LCUs

C 205-216

Displacement, tons: 320 light; 405 full load
Dimensions, feet (metres): 142 × 28 × 5·7 *(43·3 × 8·5 × 1·7)*
Guns: 2—20 mm
Main engines: GM diesels; 2 shafts; 600 bhp = 10 knots

Built in Turkey 1965-66. Of US LCU type.

C 207

1975, Turkish Navy

4 Ex-US LCU 501 SERIES

C201-204 (ex-US *LCU 588, 608, 666* and *667*)

Displacement, tons: 160 light; 320 full load
Dimensions, feet (metres): 119 oa × 32·7 × 5 *(36·3 × 10 × 1·5)*
Guns: 2—20 mm
Main engines: 3 diesels; 675 bhp = 10 knots
Complement: 13

Transferred from USA Oct-Dec 1966.

C 204   *1975, Turkish Navy*

20 TURKISH-BUILT LCM 8 TYPE

C 301-320

Displacement, tons: 58 light; 113 full load
Dimensions, feet (metres): 72 × 20·5 × 4·8 *(22 × 6·3 × 1·4)*
Guns: 2—12·7 mm
Main engines: GM diesels; 2 shafts; 660 bhp = 9·5 knots
Complement: 9

Built in Turkey in 1965.

C 302   *1975, Turkish Navy*

SURVEY SHIPS

2 "CANDARLI" CLASS

ÇANDARLI A 593   **ÇARSAMBA** A 594

Displacement, tons: 1 125 full load
Dimensions, feet (metres): 221 oa × 32 × 10·8 *(67·4 × 9·8 × 3·3)*
Main engines: Diesel electric; 2 shafts; 3 500 bhp
Speed, knots: 18
Complement: 98 (8 officers, 90 ratings)

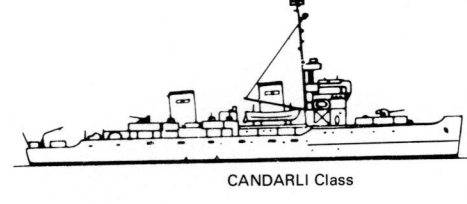

CANDARLI Class

Ex-US "Auk" class minesweepers. Both launched in 1942, they are the survivors of a class of five transferred via UK in 1947.

MESAHA 1 and 2

Of 45 tons with a complement of 8—built in 1966.

SERVICE FORCES

1 Ex-FDR DEPOT SHIP

Name	No.	Builders	Commissioned
— (ex-FDR *Ruhr*)	—	Schiekerwerft, Hamburg	1963

Displacement, tons: 2 370 standard; 2 540 full load
Dimensions, feet (metres): 323·5 oa × 38·8 × 11·2 *(99 × 11·8 × 3·4)*
Guns: 2—3·9 in *(100 mm)*
Main engines: 6 diesels; 11 400 bhp; 2 shafts
Speed, knots: 20·5
Range, miles: 1 625 at 15 knots
Complement: 110 (accommodation for 200)

Radar: Search: HSA DA 02.
Fire Control: Two HSA M 45.

Transfer: Late 1975.

1 SUPPORT TANKER

Name	No.	Builders	Commissioned
BINBASI SAADETTIN GÜRÇAN	A 573	Taskizak Naval DY, Istanbul	1970

Displacement, tons: 1 505 standard; 4 460 full load
Dimensions, feet (metres): 299 × 39·4 × 18 *(89·7 × 11·8 × 5·4)*
Main engines: Diesels; 4 400 bhp

Launched 1 July 1969.

BINBASI SAADETTIN GÜRÇAN   *1975, Turkish Navy*

1 SUPPORT TANKER

ALBAY HAKKI BURAK A 572

Displacement, tons: 3 800 full load
Dimensions, feet (metres): 274·7 oa × 40·2 × 18 *(83·7 × 12·3 × 5·5)*
Main engines: 2 GM diesels; electric drive; 4 400 bhp = 16 knots
Complement: 88

Built in 1964.

ALBAY HAKKI BURAK   *1975, Turkish Navy*

1 SUPPORT TANKER

Name	No.	Builders	Commissioned
YUZBASI TOLUNAY	A 571	Taşkizak, Naval DY, Istanbul	1951

Displacement, tons: 2 500 standard; 3 500 full load
Dimensions, feet (metres): 260 × 41 × 19·5 *(79 × 12·4 × 5·9)*
Main engines: Atlas-Polar diesels; 2 shafts; 1 920 bhp = 14 knots

Launched on 22 Aug 1950.

YUZBASI TOLUNAY   *1975, Turkish Navy*

1 Ex-US SUPPORT TANKER

Name	No.	Builders	Commissioned
AKPINAR (ex-*Chiwankum*)	A 574	East Coast S.Y. Inc, Bayonne	22 July 1944

Displacement, tons: 700 light; 2 700 full load
Measurement, feet (metres): 1 453 deadweight
Dimensions, feet (metres): 212·5 wl; 220·5 oa × 37 × 12·8 *(64·8; 67·3 × 11·3 × 3·9)*
Main engines: Diesel; 800 bhp = 10 knots

Formerly the United States oiler *AOG 26*. Laid down on 2 April 1944. Launched on 5 May 1944. Transferred to Turkey in 1949.

AKPINAR   *1975, Turkish Navy*

1 Ex-US REPAIR SHIP

DONATAN (ex-USS *Anthedon, AS 24)* A 583

Displacement, tons: 8 100 standard
Dimensions, feet (metres): 492 × 69·5 × 26·5 *(150 × 21·8 × 8·1)*
Main engines: Geared turbines; 1 shaft; 8 500 shp = 14·4 knots
Boilers: 2

Former US submarine tender of the "Aegir" class transferred to Turkey on 7 Feb 1969.

DONATAN   *1972, Turkish Navy*

2 Ex-US REPAIR SHIPS

Name	No.	Builders	Commissioned
BAŞARAN (ex-*Patroclus, ARL 19*, ex-*LST 955)*	A 582	Bethlehem Hingham Shipyard	1945
ONARAN (ex-*Alecto, AGP 14*, ex-*LST 558)*	A 581	Missouri Valley Bridge & Iron Co.	1945

Displacement, tons: 1 625 standard; 4 080 full load
Dimensions, feet (metres): 328 oa × 50 × 14 *(100 × 15·2 × 4·4)*
Guns: 2—40 mm; 8—20 mm
Main engines: Diesel; 2 shafts; 1 700 bhp = 11 knots
Oil fuel, tons: 1 000
Range, miles: 9 000 at 9 knots
Complement: 80

Former US repair ship and MTB tender, respectively of the LST type. *Basaran* was launched on 22 Oct 1944, *Onaran* on 14 April 1944. Acquired from the USA in 1952 and 1947, respectively.

ONARAN   *1973, Dr. Giorgio Arra*

1 HARBOUR TANKER

Name	No.	Builders	Commissioned
GÖLCÜK (ex-A 573)	Y 1207	Gölcük Dockyard	1954

Displacement, tons: 1 255
Measurement, feet: 750 deadweight
Dimensions, feet (metres): 185 × 31·1 × 10 (56·4 × 9·5 × 3·1)
Main engines: B & W diesel; 700 bhp = 12·5 knots

Launched on 4 Nov 1953.

KURTARAN (ex-Bluebird, ASR 19, ex-Yurak AT 165) A 584

Displacement, tons: 1 294 standard; 1 675 full load
Dimensions, feet (metres): 205·0 oa × 38·5 × 11·0 (62·5 × 12·2 × 3·5)
Guns: 1—3 inch; 2—40 mm
Main engines: Diesel-electric; 3 000 bhp = 16 knots

Former salvage tug adapted as a submarine rescue vessel in 1947. Transferred from the US Navy on 15 Aug 1950.

Name	No.	Builders	Commissioned
AKIN (ex-Greenlet, ASR 10)	A 585	Moore SB & DD Co.	1942

Displacement, tons: 1 770 standard; 2 321 full load
Dimensions, feet (metres): 251·3 × 42·2 × 14·7 (75·5 × 12·7 × 4·3)
Guns: 1—40 mm; 2—20 mm (twin)
Main engines: Diesel-electric; 1 shaft; 3 000 bhp = 15 knots
Complement: 85

Name	No.	Builders	Commissioned
ULKU (ex-Angeln)	A 586	A. C. de Bretagne	1955
KANARYA (ex-Dithmarschen)	Y 1155	A. C. de Bretagne	1956

Displacement, tons: 2 600 full load
Dimensions, feet (metres): 296·9 × 43·6 × 20·3 (90·5 × 13·3 × 6·2)
Main engines: Pielstick Diesel; 1 shaft; 3 000 bhp = 17 knots
Complement: 57

Ex-cargo ships bought by FDR in 1959. Transferred 22 March 1972.

4 TRANSPORTS

ERDEK Y 1164	**KILYA** Y 1166	**LAPSEKI** Y 1163	**TUZLA** Y 1168

Measurement, tons: 700
Dimensions, feet (metres): 183·7 × 37·2 × 8·9 (56 × 12·2 × 2·7)
Main engines: Steam; 700 hp = 9·5 knots

Have a minelaying capability. Survivors of a class of eleven car-ferries built in UK. 1940-1942.

2 WATER TANKERS

Name	No.	Builders	Commissioned
ULABAT	Y 1209	Gölcük Dockyard	1969
VAN	Y 1208	Gölcük Dockyard	1970

Displacement, tons: 1 200
Main engines: Designed for a speed of 14·5 knots

Two small tankers for the Turkish Navy built in 1968-70.

1 SUBMARINE DEPOT SHIP

ERKIN (ex-Trabzon, ex-Imperial) A 591

Displacement, tons: 10 900
Dimensions, feet (metres): 441 × 58·5 × 23 (133 × 17·5 × 7)
Guns: 2—40 mm
Speed, knots: 16
Complement: 128

Built in 1938. Purchased in 1968 and placed on the Navy list in 1970.

1 SUBMARINE RESCUE SHIP

KURTARAN   1971, A. & J. Pavia

1 SUBMARINE RESCUE SHIP

Submarine rescue vessel, ex-USN "Chanticleer" class. Transferred 12 June 1970 and purchased 15 Feb 1973.

2 TRANSPORTS

ULKU   1975, Turkish Navy

2 TRANSPORTS

Y 1204 (ex-US YPL 47)
Y 1205 (ex-US YPL 53)

Transferred: Y 1204 on 1 Dec 1971 and Y 1205 on 6 Dec 1974.

1 WATER TANKER

SOGUT (ex-FDR FW 6) Y 1217

Measurement, tons: 350 dw
Dimensions, feet (metres): 144·4 × 25·6 × 8·2 (44·1 × 7·8 × 2·5)
Main engines: MWM diesels; 230 bhp = 9·5 knots

Transferred by W. Germany late 1975.

BOOM DEFENCE VESSELS

Name	No.	Builders	Commissioned
AG 6 (ex-Cerberus, A 895)	P 306	Bethlehem Steel Co, Staten Island	10 Nov 1952

Displacement, tons: 780 standard; 902 full load
Dimensions, feet (metres): 165·0 × 33·0 × 10·0 (50·8 × 10·4 × 3·1)
Guns: 1—3 in; 4—20 mm
Main engines: Diesel-electric; 1 shaft; 1 500 bhp = 12·8 knots

Netlayer. Launched in May 1952. Transferred from USA to Netherlands in Dec 1952. Used first as a boom defence vessel and latterly as salvage and diving tender since 1961 but retained her netlaying capacity. Handed back to USN on 17 Sep 1970 but immediately turned over to the Turkish Navy.

Name	No.	Builders	Commissioned
AG 5 (ex-AN 104)	P 305	Kröger, Rendesburg	5 Feb 1961

Displacement, tons: 680 standard; 860 full load
Dimensions, feet (metres): 148·7 pp; 173·8 oa × 35·0 × 13·5 (52·5 × 10·5 × 4·1)
Guns: 1—40 mm; 3—20 mm
Main engines: 4 MAN diesels; 2 shafts; 1 450 bhp = 12 knots

AG 6   1975, Turkish Navy

Netlayer AN 104 built in US off-shore programme for Turkey. Launched on 20 Oct 1960.

Name	No.	Builders	Commissioned
AG 4 (ex-*Larch*, ex-*AN 21*)	P 304	American SB Co, Cleveland	1941

Displacement, tons: 560 standard; 805 full load
Dimensions, feet (metres): 163·0 oa × 30·5 × 10·5 *(50× 9·3 × 3·2)*
Gun: 1—3 inch
Main engines: Diesel-electric; 800 bhp = 12 knots

Former US netlayer of the "Aloe" class. Laid down in 1940. Launched on 2 July 1941. Acquired in 1947.

AG 4

1969

1 "BAR" CLASS

Name	No.	Builders	Commissioned
AG 1 (ex-*Barbarian*)	P 301	Blyth SB Co	1938

Displacement, tons: 750 standard; 1 000 full load
Dimensions, feet (metres): 150·0 pp; 173·8 oa × 32·2 × 9·5 *(52·9 × 9·4 × 2·7)*
Gun: 1—3 inch
Main engines: Triple expansion; 850 ihp = 11·5 knots
Boilers: 2 SE

Former British boom defence vessel.

3 GATE VESSELS

KAPI, I, II, III (Y 1201, 1202, 1203)

Displacement, tons: 360
Dimensions, feet (metres): 102·7 × 34 × 4·7 *(30·8 × 10·2 × 1·3)*

These gate vessels were built by US for Turkey under MAP. Transferred Mar 1961.

TUGS

1 OCEAN TUG

GAZAL (ex-USS *Sioux ATF 75*) A 587

Displacement, tons: 1 235 standard; 1 675 full load
Dimensions, feet (metres): 205 oa × 38·5 × 16 *(60·7 × 11·6 × 4·7)*
Gun: 1—3 inch
Main engines: Diesel electric; 3 000 bhp = 16 knots
Complement: 85

Transferred 30 Oct 1972. Purchased 15 Aug 1973.

1 HARBOUR TUG

ÖNCU Y 1123

Displacement, tons: 500
Speed, knots: 12

US harbour tug ex-*YTL 155*, transferred under MAP.

1 HARBOUR TUG

KUVVET Y 1122

Displacement, tons: 390
Dimensions, feet (metres): 107 × 26·5 × 12 *(32·1 × 8 × 3·6)*

2 HARBOUR TUGS

AKBAS Y 1118   **KEPEZ** Y 1119

Displacement, tons: 971
Dimensions, feet (metres): 149 × 33·9 × 14 *(44·7 × 10·2 × 4·3)*
Speed, knots: 12

1 HARBOUR TUG

KUDRET Y 1129

Displacement, tons: 128
Dimensions, feet (metres): 65 × 19·6 × 9 *(21·3 × 6·4 × 2·9)*

FLOATING DOCKS

Y 1081	**Y 1082**	**Y 1083** (ex-US *AFDL*)	**Y 1084**	**Y 1085**	**Y 1086**	**Y 1087** (ex-US *ARD 12*)
16 000 tons lift.	12 000 tons lift.	2 500 tons lift.	4 500 tons lift.	400 tons lift.	3 000 tons lift.	3 500 tons lift. Transferred Nov 1971.

MISCELLANEOUS

1 SMALL TRANSPORT

SARKÖY Y 1156

1 NAVAL DREDGER

TARAK Y 1209

Of 200 tons.

1 HARBOUR PATROL CRAFT

Y 1223

Y 1023

1 FLOATING CRANE

TRAINING SHIPS

Name	No.	Builders	Commissioned
SAVARONA	A 575	Blohm & Voss, Hamburg	1932

Displacement, tons: 5 100
Length, feet (metres): 349·5 *(106·5)* wl; 408·5 *(124·5)* oa
Beam, feet (metres): 53 *(16·2)*
Draught, feet (metres): 20·5 *(6·2)*
Guns: 4—3 in *(76 mm)* 2—40 mm; 2—20 mm
Main engines: 6 geared turbines; 2 shafts; 10 750 shp
Boilers: 4 watertube (400 psi)
Speed, knots: 18
Oil fuel, tons: 2 100
Range, miles: 9 000 at 15 knots
Complement: 132 + 81 midshipmen

Launched on 28 Feb 1931. Formerly probably the most sumptuously fitted yacht afloat. Equipment includes Sperry gyro-stablisers. Converted into a training ship in 1952, the saloons and dining rooms being adapted as classrooms, workshops and libraries for midshipmen.

CEZAYIRLI GAZI HASAN PAŞA

General training ship.

SAVARONA

1975, Turkish Navy

UNITED KINGDOM

Admiralty Board

Secretary of State for Defence (Chairman):
  The Right Honourable Mr Roy Mason, MP
Minister of State: Ministry of Defence (Vice-Chairman) and Minister of State for Defence Procurement:
  Mr William Rodgers, MP
Parliamentary Under-Secretary of State for Defence for the Royal Navy:
  Dr Patrick Duffy, MP
Chief of the Naval Staff and First Sea Lord:
  Admiral Sir Edward Ashmore, GCB, DSC
Chief of Naval Personnel and Second Sea Lord:
  Admiral Sir David Williams, KCB
Controller of the Navy:
  Vice-Admiral R. P. Clayton
Chief of Fleet Support:
  Vice-Admiral Sir Peter White, KBE
Vice-Chief of the Naval Staff:
  Vice-Admiral R. D. Lygo
Chief Scientist (Royal Navy): Mr Basil Wilfred Lythall, CB, MA
Deputy Under Secretary of State (Navy): Mr Sydney Redman, CB
Second Permanent Under-Secretary for Administration: Mr J. M. Wilson, CBE
Second Permanent Under-Secretary for Equipment: Sir Martin Flett, KCB

Commanders-in-Chief

Commander-in-Chief, Naval Home Command:
  Admiral Sir Terence Lewin, KCB, MVO, DSC
Commander-in-Chief, Fleet:
  Admiral Sir John Treacher, KCB

Flag Officers

Flag Officer, 1st Flotilla:
  Vice-Admiral A. S. Morton
Flag Officer, 2nd Flotilla:
  Rear-Admiral J. D. E. Fieldhouse
Flag Officer, Submarines:
  Vice-Admiral Sir Iwan Raikes, KCB, CBE, DSC
Flag Officer, Naval Air Command:
  Vice-Admiral P. M. Austin
Flag Officer, Carriers and Amphibious Ships:
  Rear-Admiral J. H. F. Eberle
Flag Officer, Scotland and Northern Ireland:
  Vice-Admiral J. A. R. Troup, DSC and Bar
Flag Officer, Medway:
  Rear-Admiral C. M. Bevan, ADC
Flag Officer, Plymouth:
  Vice-Admiral A. G. Tait DSC
Flag Officer, Sea Training:
  Rear-Admiral
Flag Officer, Malta:
  Rear Admiral O. N. A. Cecil
Flag Officer, Gibraltar:
  Rear-Admiral R. S. Sandford
Flag Officer, Spithead:
  Rear-Admiral: E. J. W. Flower

General Officers, Royal Marines

Commandant-General, Royal Marines:
  Lieutenant General P. J. F. Whiteley, OBE
Chief of Staff to Commandant-General, Royal Marines:
  Major General P. Wall
Major General Training Group, Royal Marines:
  Major-General D. C. Alexander
Major-General Commando Forces, Royal Marines:
  Major-General E. G. D. Pounds

Diplomatic Representation

British Naval Attaché in Bonn:
  Captain B. J. Williams
British Naval Attaché in Moscow:
  Captain R. J. F. Turner
British Naval Attaché in Paris:
  Captain V. M. Howard
British Naval Attaché in Rome:
  Captain M. A. George
British Naval Attaché in Washington:
  Rear-Admiral R. W. Halliday DSC

Personnel (including Royal Marines)

(a) 1973: 84 000
    1974: 81 000
    1975: 77 100
    1976: 76 200
(b) Voluntary Service

Mercantile Marine

Lloyd's Register of Shipping: 3 622 vessels of 33 157 422 tons gross

Fleet Air Arm

Aircraft	Role	Deployment	No. of squdns or flights
Buccaneer 2	Strike	Carrier	1 Squdn
Gannet 3	AEW	Carrier	1 Squdn
Gannet 3	AEW	Lossiemouth	1 Squdn
Phantom FG1	FGA	Carrier	1 Squdn

Helicopters

Sea King	ASW	Carrier	1 Squdn
Sea King	ASW	ASW Carrier	1 Squdn
Sea King	ASW	Cruiser	1 Squdn
Sea King	ASW	Prestwick	1 Squdn
Sea King	Aircrew Training	Culdrose	1 Squdn
Wasp	ASW	"Leander" Class	
Wasp	ASW	"Rothesay" Class	
Wasp	ASW	"Tribal" Class	40 flights
Wasp	ASW	Type 21	
Wasp	ASW	Type 42	
Wasp	Aircrew Training	Portland	1 Squdn
Wessex 3	ASW	"County" Class	7 Flights
Wessex 3	Aircrew Training	Portland	1 Squdn
Wessex 5	Commando Assault	Yeovilton/HMS *Hermes*	2 Sqdns
Wessex 5	Aircrew Training	Yeovilton	1 Squdn
Wessex 5	Fleet Requirements	Portland	1 Squdn

Strength of the Fleet

Type	Active	Building (Projected)
Aircraft Carrier	1+1 (A/S)	—
A/S Carriers (Cruisers)	—	2
Helicopter Cruisers	2	—
Light Cruisers	8	—
Destroyers	3	5 (1)
Frigates	61	6
Sonar Trials Ship	1	—
SSBNs	4	—
Submarines—Fleet	9	3 (1)
Submarines—Patrol	19	—
Commando Ships	1 (Res)	—
Assault Ships (LPD)	2	—
LSLs	6	—
LST	1	—
LCTs	3	2
LCMs	27	—
LCVPs	26	—
LCPLs	3	—
Offshore Patrol Craft	2	4
Fast Attack Craft—Patrol	1	—
Large Patrol Craft	8	3
Fast Training Boats	3	—
MCM Support Ship	1	—
Minehunters	16	2
Minesweepers—Coastal	21	—
Minesweepers—Inshore	6	—
Maintenance Ships	2	—
Submarine Depot Ships	2	—
Survey Ships	4	—
Coastal Survey Ships	4	—
Inshore Survey Craft	5	—
Ice Patrol Ship	1	—
Royal Yacht	1	—
Hovercraft	5	—
Diving Support Ship	1	—
Large Fleet Tankers	6	—
Support Tankers	4	—
Mobile Reserve Tanker	1	—
Small Fleet Tankers	6	—
Helicopter Support Ship	1	—
Stores Support Ships	3	—
Fleet Replenishment Ships	4	2
Store Carriers	2	1
MSBVs	12	—
Trials Ship	5	—
TRVs	9	—
Cable Ship	1	—
Armament Carriers	6	—
Water Carriers	15	—
Ocean Tugs	13	—
Harbour Tugs	59	—
Tenders	54	—
RNXS Craft	10	—
MFVs	30	—
DG Vessels	3	—
TCVs	6	—

DELETIONS

(Note following Disposal List)

Carriers (of all kinds)

1972 *Centaur* and *Albion*

Light Cruiser

1976 *Hampshire*

Destroyers

1970 *Aisne, Trafalgar, Camperdown*
1971 *Daring, Delight, Scorpion, Cambrian*
1972 *Crossbow, Defender, Saintes*
1974 *Agincourt* (1 Nov Milford Haven)

Frigates

1970 *Loch Killisport, Loch Fada, Ulysses, Zest, Murray*
1971 *Urania, Relentless, Pellew, Wakeful, Alert, Grafton*
1972 *Verulam, Venus*
1974 *Tenby, Scarborough* to Pakistan
1975 *Whitby, Leopard*

Submarines

1970 *Talent, Thermopylae, Anchorite, Astute*
1971 *Ambush, Alaric, Trump, Taciturn, Auriga*

Submarines

1972 *Artemis, Acheron, Alderney, Aeneas, Alcide, Alliance*
1975 *Andrew*
1976 *Rorqual, Grampus*

MCM Vessels

1970- *Dalswinton, Invermoriston, Maddiston, Puncheston, Quainton, Wilkieston*
71
1975 *Chawton, Boulston* (scrapped)
1976 *Highburton, Arlingham*

Service Forces

1974 *Wave Chief, Derwentdale* (returned to owners), *Brown Ranger* (Tankers). *Barmond* (MSBV), *Miner III*
1975 *Tideflow, Tidesurge* (Tankers), *Dispenser, Barfoot* (MSBVs), *Reliant,* (Air Stores ship), *Robert Middleton* (Stores Carrier), *Icewhale* (Trials Ship), *Bullfinch* (Cable Ship), *Freshmere* (Water boat), *Bowstring* (Armament Carrier).

Tugs

1975 *Diver, Driver, Eminent, Empire Ace, Empire Demon, Empire Fred, Empire Rosa, Fidget, Foremost, Freedom, Frisky, Grinder, Handmaid, Impetus, Integrity, (Lilian* and *May*—existence doubted), *Prompt, Security, Tampeon, Trunnion, Vagrant, Weasel.*

DISPOSAL LIST

The following ships not on the Active or Reserve list are held in the ports shown pending disposal by sale or scrap.

Aircraft Carrier

Eagle RO 5 (Plymouth)

Cruiser

Lion C 34 (Rosyth)

Light Cruiser

Hampshire DO 6

Destroyers

Caprice DO1 (Plymouth)
Cavalier D 73 (Chatham)
Barrosa D 68 (Portsmouth)

Fast Attack Craft

Brave Borderer (Pembroke Dock)
Brave Swordsman (Pembroke Dock)
Dark Gladiator (Portsmouth)
Dark Hero (Portsmouth)

Frigates

Blackpool F 77 (Portsmouth-Target ship)
Blackwood F 78 (Portsmouth)
Leopard F 14
Grenville F 197 (Portsmouth)
Palliser F 94 (Portsmouth)
Puma F 34 (Chatham)
Rapid F 138 (Chatham)
Undaunted F 53 (Gibraltar-Target)
Volage F 41
Whitby F 36
Whirlwind F 187 (Target)

Minesweepers—Coastal

Ashton (Rosyth)
Belton (Rosyth)
Boulston (Portsmouth)
Dufton (Portsmouth)
Maddiston (Porstmouth)

LSTs

Lofoten (Rosyth)
Messina (Plymouth)
Stalker (Rosyth)
Zeebrugge (Plymouth)

Survey Ship

Vidal (Chatham)

Immoblie Tenders

Diamond D 35. Attached to *Sultan* for engineering training at Portsmouth
Ulster F83. Accommodation ship at Portsmouth
Girdleness A 387. Accommodation ship at Rosyth

LIST OF PENNANT NUMBERS

*Disposal List

Aircraft Carriers

R	05	Eagle*
R	08	Bulwark (Reserve)
R	09	Ark Royal
R	12	Hermes

Submarines

S	01	Porpoise
S	03	Narwhal
S	05	Finwhale
S	06	Cachalot
S	07	Sealion
S	08	Walrus
S	09	Oberon
S	10	Odin
S	11	Orpheus
S	12	Olympus
S	13	Osiris
S	14	Onslaught
S	15	Otter
S	16	Oracle
S	17	Ocelot
S	18	Otus
S	19	Opossum
S	20	Oportune
S	21	Onyx
S	22	Resolution
S	23	Repulse
S	26	Renown
S	27	Revenge
S	46	Churchill
S	48	Conqueror
S	50	Courageous
S	63	Andrew*
S	101	Dreadnought
S	102	Valiant

Submarines—continued

S	103	Warspite
S	104	Sceptre
S	108	Sovereign
S	109	Superb
S	111	Spartan
S	112	Severn
S	113	—
S	126	Swiftsure

Cruisers

C	20	Tiger
C	34	Lion*
C	99	Blake

Light Cruisers and Destroyers

D	01	Caprice*
D	02	Devonshire
D	06	Hampshire*
D	12	Kent
D	16	London
D	18	Antrim
D	19	Glamorgan
D	20	Fife
D	21	Norfolk
D	23	Bristol
D	35	Diamond
D	43	Matapan
D	73	Cavalier*
D	80	Sheffield
D	86	Birmingham
D	87	Newcastle
D	88	Glasgow
D	108	Cardiff
D	118	Coventry

Frigates

F	10	Aurora
F	12	Achilles
F	14	Leopard*
F	15	Euryalus
F	16	Diomede
F	18	Galatea
F	27	Lynx
F	28	Cleopatra
F	32	Salisbury
F	34	Puma*
F	36	Whitby*
F	37	Jaguar
F	38	Arethusa
F	39	Naiad
F	40	Sirius
F	42	Phoebe
F	43	Torquay
F	45	Minerva
F	47	Danae
F	48	Dundas
F	52	Juno
F	53	Undaunted*
F	54	Hardy
F	56	Argonaut
F	57	Andromeda
F	58	Hermione
F	59	Chichester
F	60	Jupiter
F	61	Llandaff
F	69	Bacchante
F	70	Apollo
F	71	Scylla
F	72	Ariadne
F	73	Eastbourne
F	75	Charybdis
F	76	Mermaid
F	77	Blackpool*

Frigates—continued

F	80	Duncan
F	83	Ulster
F	84	Exmouth
F	85	Keppel
F	94	Palliser*
F	97	Russell
F	99	Lincoln
F	101	Yarmouth
F	103	Lowestoft
F	104	Dido
F	106	Brighton
F	107	Rothesay
F	108	Londonberry
F	109	Leander
F	113	Falmouth
F	114	Ajax
F	115	Berwick
F	117	Ashanti
F	119	Eskimo
F	122	Gurkha
F	124	Zulu
F	125	Mohawk
F	126	Plymouth
F	127	Penelope
F	129	Rhyl
F	131	Nubian
F	133	Tartar
F	138	Rapid*
F	169	Amazon
F	170	Antelope
F	171	Active
F	172	Ambuscade
F	173	Arrow
F	174	Alacrity
F	175	Ardent
F	176	Avenger
F	197	Grenville*

List of pennant numbers—continued

Assault Ships

L	10	Fearless
L	11	Interpid

Logistic Landing Ships and LCTs

L	3004	Sir Bedivere
L	3005	Sir Galahad
L	3027	Sir Geraint
L	3029	Sir Lancelot
L	3036	Sir Percivale
L	3505	Sir Tristram
L	4002	Agheila
L	4041	Abbeville
L	4061	Audemer
L	4062	Aachen
L	4097	Andalnes

Helicopter Support Ship

K	07	Lofotea
K	08	Engadine

Minelayer

N	21	Abdiel

Support Ships and Auxiliaries

A	00	Britannia
A	70	Echo
A	71	Enterprise
A	72	Egeria
A	75	Tidespring
A	76	Tidepool
A	77	Pearleaf
A	78	Plumleaf
A	80	Orangeleaf
A	82	Cherryleaf
A	84	Reliant
A	85	Faithful
A	86	Forceful
A	87	Favourite
A	88	Agile
A	89	Advice
A	90	Accord
A	91	Griper
A	92	Grinder
A	93	Dexterous
A	94	Director
A	95	Typhoon
A	96	Tidereach
A	97	Tideflow
A	98	Tidesurge
A	108	Triumph
A	111	Cyclone
A	122	Olwen
A	123	Olna
A	124	Olmeda
A	127	Torrent
A	128	Torrid
A	133	Hecla
A	134	Rame Head

Support Ships and Auxiliaries—continued

A	135	Nordenfelt
A	137	Hecate
A	144	Hydra
A	171	Endurance
A	176	Bullfinch
A	179	Whimbrel
A	185	Maidstone
A	187	Forth
A	191	Berry Head
A	200	Vidal*
A	219	Dewdale
A	220	Loyal Moderator
A	222	Spapool
A	224	Spabrook
A	231	Reclaim
A	232	Kingarth
A	241	Robert Middleton
A	257	Spaburn
A	259	St. Margarets
A	260	Spalake
A	261	Eddyfirth
A	264	Reward
A	268	Green Rover
A	269	Grey Rover
A	270	Blue Rover
A	271	Gold Rover
A	273	Black Rover
A	280	Resurgent
A	281	Kinbrace
A	288	Sea Giant
A	289	Confiance
A	290	Confident
A	310	Invergorden
A	311	Ironbridge
A	312	Ixworth
A	329	Retainer
A	332	Caldy
A	333	Coll
A	334	Bern
A	336	Lundy
A	338	Skomer
A	339	Lyness
A	340	Graemsay
A	344	Stromness
A	345	Tarbatness
A	346	Switha
A	364	Whitehead
A	377	Maxim
A	378	Kinterbury
A	382	Loyal Factor
A	385	Fort Grange
A	386	Fort Austin
A	404	Bacchus
A	406	Hebe
A	480	Resource
A	482	Kinloss
A	486	Regent
A	507	Uplifter
A	510	Loyal Governor

Auxiliaries

Y	—	Watercourse
Y	—	Waterfowl
Y	17	Waterfall

Auxiliaries—continued

Y	18	Watershed
Y	19	Waterspout
Y	20	Waterside
Y	21	Oilpress
Y	22	Oilstone
Y	23	Oilwell
Y	24	Oilfield
Y	25	Oilbird
Y	26	Oilman

Boom Defence Vessels

P	190	Laymoor
P	191	Layburn
P	192	Mandarin
P	193	Pintail
P	194	Garganey
P	195	Goldeneye
P	196	Goosander
P	197	Pochard
P	202	Barfoot
P	228	Moorsman

Light Forces

P	260	Kingfisher
P	261	Cygnet
P	262	Peterel
P	263	Sandpiper
P	271	Scimitar
P	274	Cutlass
P	275	Sabre
P	276	Tenacity
P	1007	Beachampton
P	1055	Monkton
P	1089	Wasperton
P	1093	Wolverton
P	1096	Yarnton
P	3104	Dee (Beckford)
P	3113	Droxford

Coastal Minesweepers

M	1103	Kilmorey (Alfriston)
M	1109	Killcrankie (Bickington)
M	1110	Bildeston
M	1113	Breeton
M	1114	Brinton
M	1115	Bronington
M	1124	St. David (Crichton)
M	1125	Cuxton
M	1130	Highburton
M	1133	Bossington
M	1136	Curzon (Fittleton)
M	1140	Gavinton
M	1141	Glasserton
M	1146	Venturer (Hodgeston)
M	1147	Hubberston
M	1151	Iveston
M	1153	Kedleston
M	1154	Kellington
M	1157	Kirkliston
M	1158	Laleston

Coastal Minesweepers—continued

M	1165	Maxton
M	1166	Nurton
M	1167	Clyde (Repton)
M	1173	Mersey (Pollington)
M	1180	Shavington
M	1181	Sheraton
M	1182	Shoulton
M	1187	Upton
M	1188	Walkerton
M	1194	Wollaston
M	1195	Wotton
M	1198	Ashton*
M	1199	Belton*
M	1200	Soberton
M	1204	Montrose (Stubbington)
M	1205	Northumbria (Wiston)
M	1208	Lewiston
M	1209	Chawton
M	1216	Solent (Crofton)

Inshore Minesweepers

M	2002	Aveley
M	2010	Isis (Cradley)
M	2603	Arlingham
M	2611	Bottisham R
M	2614	Bucklesham TRV
M	2616	Chelsham R
M	2621	Dittisham
M	2622	Downham TRV
M	2626	Everingham TRV
M	2628	Flintham
M	2630	Fritham TRV
M	2635	Haversham TRV
M	2636	Lasham TRV
M	2716	Pagham RNXS
M	2717	Fordham DGV
M	2720	Waterwitch (Powderham)
M	2726	Shipham RNXS
M	2733	Thakeham RNXS
M	2735	Tongham RNXS
M	2737	Warmingham DGV
M	2780	Woodlark (Yaxham)
M	2781	Portisham RNXS
M	2783	Odiham RNXS
M	2784	Puttenham RNXS
M	2785	Birdham RNXS
M	2790	Thatcham DGV
M	2793	Thornham

DGV =	*Degaussing Vessels*
PAS =	*Port Auxiliary Service*
RNXS =	*Royal Naval Auxiliary Service*
TRV =	*Torpedo Recovery Vessels*
R =	*Reserve (ex-RAF)*

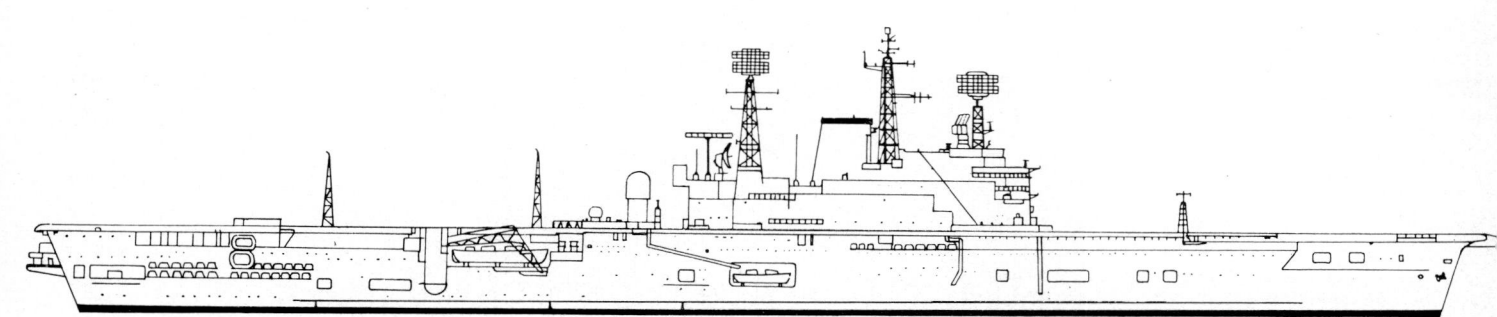

ARK ROYAL (scale =1:1300)

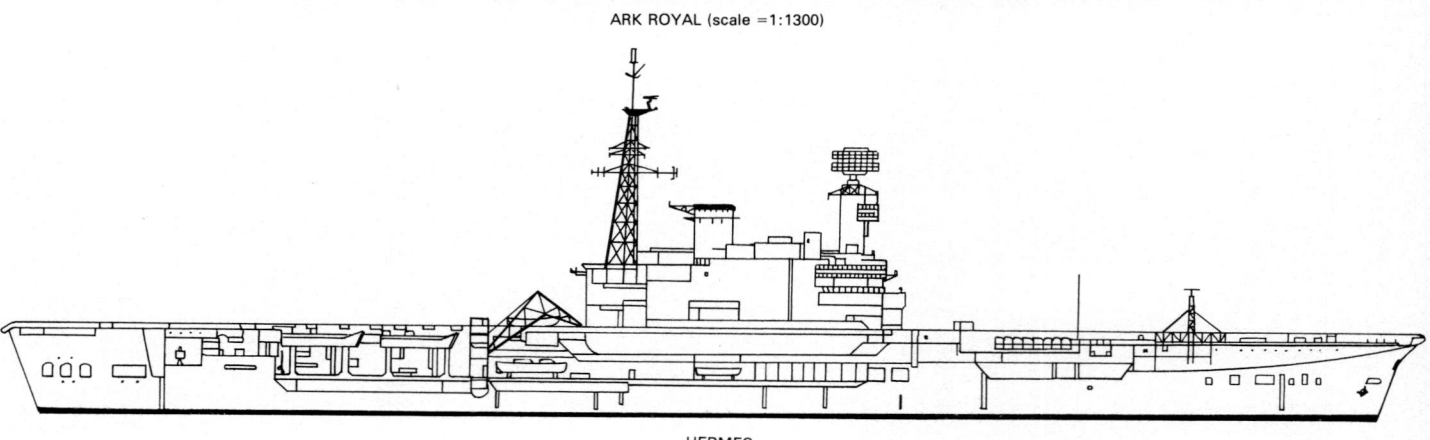

HERMES

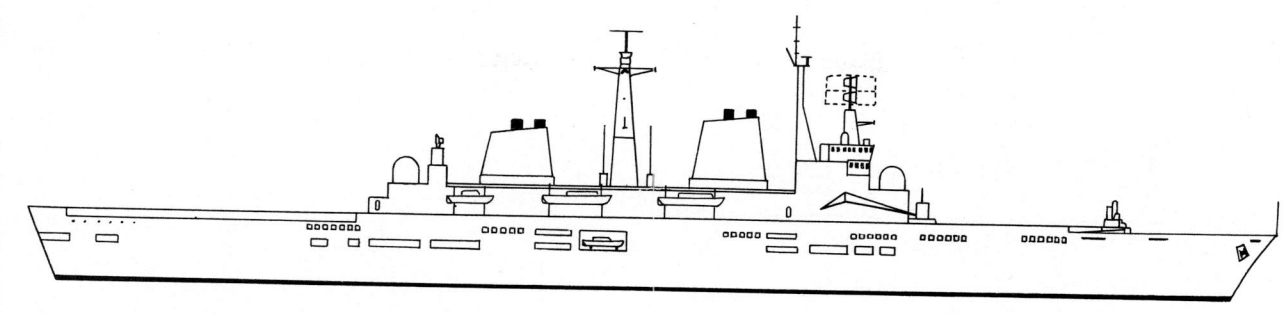

INVINCIBLE

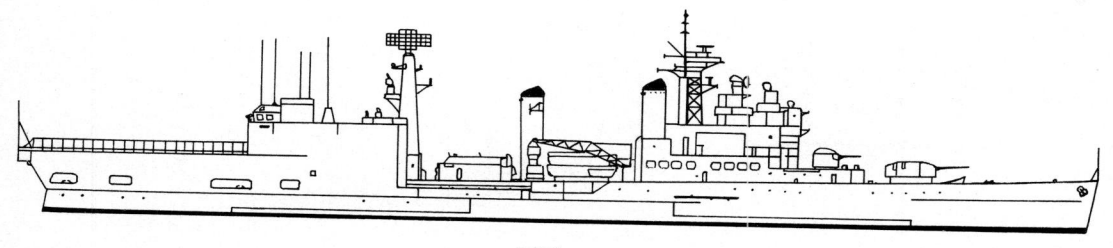

TIGER

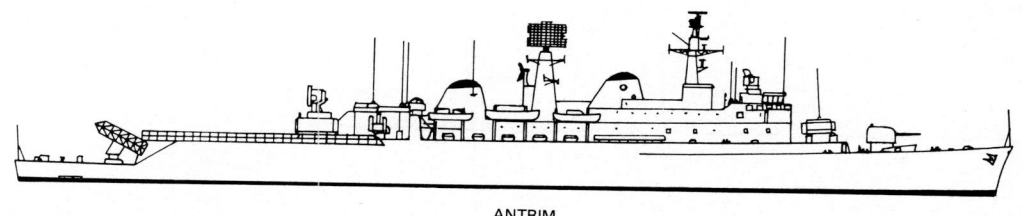

ANTRIM

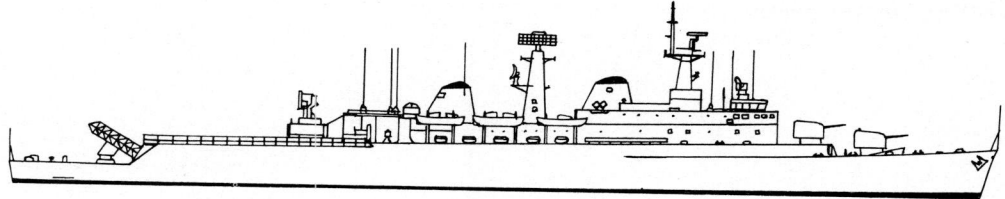

KENT

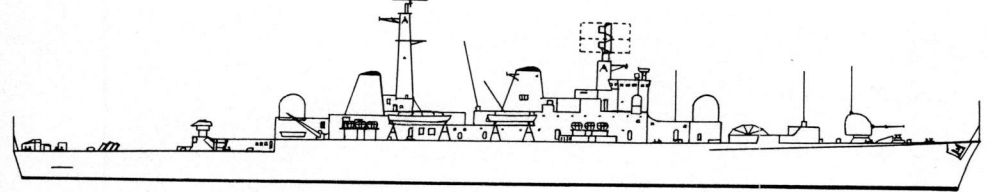

DEVONSHIRE

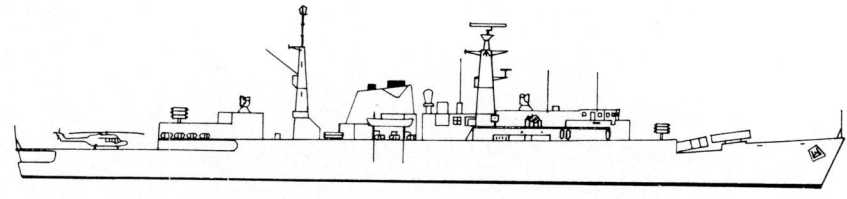

BRISTOL

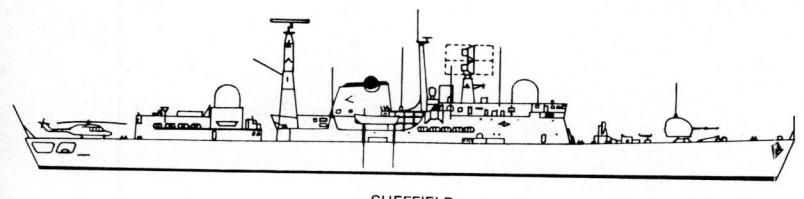

TYPE 22

SHEFFIELD

"LEANDER" Class (Ikara)

"LEANDER" Class (Exocet)

"ROTHESAY" Class

TORQUAY

MATAPAN

AMAZON

"TRIBAL" Class

"LEOPARD" Class

"SALISBURY" Class

"BLACKWOOD" Class

EXMOUTH

MERMAID

AIRCRAFT CARRIERS

Note: Eagle, see Disposal List.

1 "ARK ROYAL" CLASS

Name	No.	Builders	Laid down	Launched	Commissioned
ARK ROYAL	R 09	Cammell Laird, Birkenhead	3 May 1943	3 May 1950	25 Feb 1955

Displacement, tons: 43 060 standard; 50 786 full load
Length, feet (metres): 720·0 *(219·5)* pp; 845·0 *(257·6)* oa
Beam, feet (metres): 112·8 *(34·4)* hull
Draught, feet (metres): 36·0 *(11·0)*
Width, feet (metres): 166·0 *(50·6)*
Catapults: 2 improved steam
Aircraft: 30 fixed wing + 6 helicopters
Missile launchers: Fitted for four quadruple Seacat (not fitted)
Armour: 4·5 in belt; 4 in flight deck; 2·5 in hangar deck; 1·5 in hangar side
Main engines: Parsons single reduction geared turbines; 4 shafts; 152 000 shp
Boilers: 8 Admiralty 3-drum type; pressure 400 psi *(28·1 kg/cm²);* superheat 600°F (316°C)
Speed, knots: 31·5
Oil fuel, tons: 5 500 capacity
Complement: 260 officers (as Flagship); 2 380 ratings (with Air Staff)

First British aircraft carrier with steam catapults. Had first side lift in a British aircraft carrier, situated amidships on the port side and serving the upper hangar, but in 1959 this was removed, the deck park provided by the angled deck having obviated its necessity, leaving her with two centre lifts. In 1961, the deck landing projector sight, "Hilo" long range guidance system, and more powerful steam catapults were installed. Ship originally cost £21 428 000. Due for disposal in late 1970s.

Aircraft: Phantom FG1, 1 Squadron (12).
Buccaneer 2, 1 Squadron (14).
Gannet AEW, 1 Squadron (4).
Sea King ASW, 1 Squadron (7).
Wessex 3, —(2).

Corvus: Two eight barrelled launchers fitted. Has multi-purpose use including launching of illuminants and "Chaff".

Electronics: Fitted with Skynet and Tacan.

Modernisation: A three-years "special refit" and modernisation costing £32 500 000, from Mar 1967 to Feb 1970, enables her to operate both Phantom and Buccaneer Mk 2 aircraft. A fully angled deck 8·5 degrees off the centre line was fitted, involving two large extensions to the flight deck and the size of the island was increased. A new waist catapult with an increased launching speed allows her to operate aircraft at almost "nil" wind conditions. A new direct acting gear was installed to enable bigger aircraft to be landed at greater speeds.

Radar: Search: Two Type 965.
Aircraft Direction: One Type 982.
Heightfinder: Two Type 983.
CCA: 1 set.
Navigation: One Type 975.

ARK ROYAL   2/1976, MOD(N)

ARK ROYAL   4/1975, MOD(N)

ARK ROYAL (*Antrim* alongside)   2/1976, MOD(N)

1 HELICOPTER/VSTOL CARRIER

Name	No.	Builders	Laid down	Launched	Commissioned
HERMES	R 12	Vickers-Armstrong Ltd, Barrow-in-Furness	21 June 1944	16 Feb 1953	18 Nov 1959

Displacement, tons: 23 900 standard; 28 700 full load
Length, feet (metres): 650·0 *(198·1)* pp; 744·3 *(226·9)* oa
Beam, feet (metres): 90·0 *(27·4)* hull
Draught, feet (metres): 29·0 *(8·8)*
Width, feet (metres): 160·0 *(48·8)* overall
Aircraft: 20 Wessex Sea King, and Sioux helicopters
Armour: Reinforced flight deck
Missiles: 2 quadruple Seacat launchers either side abaft the after lift
Main engines: Parsons geared turbines; 2 shafts; 76 000 shp
Boilers: 4 Admiralty 3-drum type
Speed, knots: 28
Oil fuel, tons: 3 880 furnace; 320 diesel
Complement: 980. In emergency a Commando can be embarked

Originally name ship of a class including *Albion*, *Bulwark* and *Centaur*, but design was modified to a more advanced type, incorporating new equipment and improved arrangements, including five post-war developments— angled deck, steam catapult, landing sight, 3-D radar, and deck edge-lift. Air-conditioned. Embarked air squadrons and joined the Fleet summer 1960. Long refit 1964 to 1966, costing £10 000 000.

Conversion: *Hermes* was taken in hand for conversion to a Commando Carrier on 1 Mar 1971, commissioning for this role on 17 Aug 1973. Fixed wing facilities such as catapults and arrester gear were removed. The whole performance cost over £25 million.
In 1976, as a result of the Defence Review and pressure from other NATO countries, *Hermes'* role was altered to that of A/S carrier with the retention of a capability for commando support. How long she continues in this role depends on how much extra delay is experienced on the "Invincible" class but it seems likely that she will continue to run until at least 1980. When the "Harriers" are eventually in naval service they will fly from this ship amongst others.

Flight deck: Angled 6·5 deg off centre line of ship, the biggest angle that could be contrived in an aircraft carrier of this size. Strengthened to take Harrier aircraft.

HERMES   3/1976, Wright and Logan

Radar: Surveillance: One Type 965 with single AKE-1 array.
Search: One Type 993.
Navigation: One Type 975.
Fire Control: Two GWS 22.
Tacan beacon.

HERMES   1973, C. and S. Taylor

1 RESERVE HELICOPTER CARRIER

Name	No.	Builders	Laid down	Launched	Commissioned
BULWARK	R 08	Harland & Wolff Ltd, Belfast	10 May 1945	22 June 1948	4 Nov 1954

Displacement, tons: 23 300 standard; 27 705 full load
Length, feet (metres): 650 *(198·1)* pp; 737·8 *(224·9)* oa
Beam, feet (metres): 90 *(27·4)* hull
Draught, feet (metres): 28 *(8·5)*
Width, feet (metres): 123·5 *(37·7)* overall
Aircraft: 20 Wessex and Sioux helicopters
Landing craft: 4 LCVP
Guns: 8—40 mm (twins) Bofors Mk V
Main engines: Parsons geared turbines; 76 000 shp; 2 shafts
Boilers: 4 Admiralty 3 drum
Speed, knots: 28
Oil fuel, tons: 3 880 furnace; 320 diesel
Complement: 980 plus 750 Royal Marine Commando and troops

Former fixed-wing aircraft carrier. Converted into commando ship in Portsmouth Dockyard, Jan 1959 to Jan 1960. Her arrester gear and catapults have been removed but, with a helicopter and VSTOL capability she was placed in reserve in April 1976 as a result of the 1975 Defence Review. Her sale as a "package-deal" with eight Harriers to another navy is rumoured but would seem unwise in view of doubts about the delivery dates for the "Invincible" class.

BULWARK   1973, C. and S. Taylor

0 + 2 ANTI-SUBMARINE CRUISERS

Name	No.	Builders	Laid down	Launched	Commissioned
INVINCIBLE	CAH 1	Vickers Ltd, Barrow	20 July 1973	—	?1979
ILLUSTRIOUS	CAH 2	Swan Hunter Ltd, Wallsend	—	—	?1980

Displacement, tons: 19 500
Length, feet (metres): 632 pp *(192·9)*; 677 oa *(206·6)*
Beam, feet (metres): 90 wl *(27·5)*; 104·6 deck *(31·9)*
Draught, feet (metres): ?24 *(7·3)*
Flight deck length, feet (metres): 550 *(167·8)*
Aircraft: Total of 15: 10 Sea King helicopters (could carry 5 Harriers)
Missile launchers: Twin Sea Dart
Main engines: 4 "Olympus" gas turbines; 112 000 shp; 2 shafts (reversible gear box)
Speed, knots: 28
Range, miles: 5 000 at 18 knots
Complement: 900 (31 officers, 265 senior ratings, 604 junior ratings) (excluding aircrew)

The history of this class is a long and complex one starting almost sixteen years ago. The first of class, the result of many compromises, was ordered from Vickers on 17 April 1973. At that time completion might have been expected in 1977-8 but changes in design and labour problems have delayed this by probably two years. The results of this must be the running-on of the "Tiger" class and *Hermes* to provide the necessary aircraft platforms at sea. The order for the second ship to be named *Illustrious* was placed on 14 May 1976, whilst no decision has yet been reached on the third.

The primary task of this class, apart from providing a command centre for maritime air forces, is the operation of both helicopters and VTOL/STOL aircraft. Provision has been made for sufficiently large lifts and hangars to accommodate the next generation of both these aircraft.

The design allows for an open foc'sle head and a slightly angled deck which will allow the Sea Dart launcher to be set almost amidships.

Cost: Although originally estimated at approximately £60 million the final bill per ship is likely to be nearer £150 million.

Radar: Surveillance: One Type 966 with double AKE 1 array. Search: One Type 992 R. Fire Control; Two Type 909 for Sea Dart. Navigation: One Type 1006.

Sonar: Type 184.

INVINCIBLE   1973

INVINCIBLE   1973, Vickers Ltd.

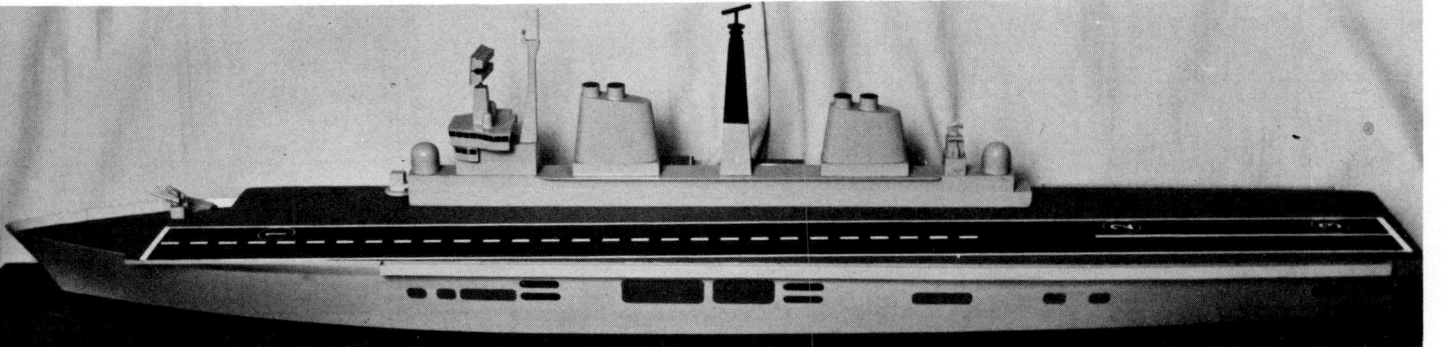

INVINCIBLE model   1973, MOD

CRUISERS

2 "TIGER" CLASS (HELICOPTER CRUISERS)

Name	No.	Builders	Laid down	Launched	Commissioned
BLAKE (ex-*Tiger*, ex-*Blake*)	C 99	Fairfield SB & Eng, Govan	17 Aug 1942	20 Dec 1945	8 Mar 1961
TIGER (ex-*Bellerophon*)	C 20	John Brown, Clydebank	1 Oct 1941	25 Oct 1945	18 Mar 1959

Displacement, tons: 9 500 standard; 12 080 full load
Length, feet (metres): 538·0 *(164·0)* pp; 550·0 *(167·6)* wl; 566·5 *(172·8)* oa
Beam, feet (metres): 64·0 *(19·5)*
Draught, feet (metres): 23·0 *(7·0)*
Aircraft: 4 Sea King helicopters
Missile launchers: 2 quadruple Seacat
Guns: 2—6 in *(152 mm)* (1 twin); 2—3 in *(76 mm)* (twin)
Armour: Belt 3·5 in—3·2 in *(89–83 mm)*; deck 2 in *(51 mm)*; turret 3 in—1 in *(76—25 mm)*
Main engines: 4 Parsons geared turbines; 4 shafts; 80 000 shp
Boilers: 4 Admiralty 3-drum type
Speed, knots: 30
Range, miles: 2 000 at 30 knots; 4 000 at 20 knots; 6 500 at 13 knots
Oil fuel, tons: 1 850
Complement: 85 officers, 800 ratings

This design was originally an improvement on that of *Superb/Swiftsure. Bellerophon* and *Hawke* of a similar design were cancelled in 1945-46 as were the projected ships *Centurion, Edgar, Mars* and *Neptune.* There was much juggling of names between ships; *Blake* was renamed *Tiger* in Dec 1944 and back to *Blake* in Feb 1945.

Defence was renamed *Lion* in Oct 1957. *Bellerophon* was renamed *Tiger* in Feb 1945. Work on all three of the surviving ships was suspended in July 1946, the decision to complete them being announced on 15 Oct 1954. Subsequent redesign delayed work even further and it was not completed until 1959-61. By this time *Tiger* had cost £13 113 000 and *Blake* £14 940 000. The next stage was conversion to command helicopter cruisers (official title). *Lion* was not converted and was eventually sent for scrap in April 1975. *Blake* was transformed by Portsmouth Dockyard at a cost of £5 500 000 from early 1965 until recommissioning on 23 April 1969. *Tiger* was in hand from 1968 to 1972 at Devonport Dockyard, her cost reaching the staggering sum of £13 250 000.(As a considerable amount of equipment from *Lion* was used in *Tiger's* conversion the latter was unofficially known for a time as "Liger").

Appearance: *Tiger's* funnels are taller than those in *Blake.*

Electrical: 4 turbo-generators provide 4 000 kW a/c, the first time this type of power had been used in British cruisers.

Engineering: Main machinery is largely automatic and can be remotely controlled. Steam conditions 400 psi pressure and 640°F. Propellers 11 ft dia, 285 rpm.

Radar: Search: One Type 965 and one Type 993.
Height Finder: One Type 277 or 278.
Fire Control: 4 MRS 3 fire control directors.
Navigation: One Type 975.

TIGER   *8/1975, Stefan Terzibaschitsch*

TIGER   *4/1975, John G. Callis*

BLAKE   *1/1976, Dr. Giorgio Arra*

LIGHT CRUISERS

1 TYPE 82

Name	No.	Builders	Laid down	Launched	Commissioned
BRISTOL	D 23	Swan Hunter & Tyne Shipbuilders Ltd.	15 Nov 1967	30 June 1969	31 Mar 1973

Displacement, tons: 6 100 standard; 7 100 full load
Beam, feet (metres): 490·0 *(149·4)* wl; 507·0 *(154·5)* oa
Beam, feet (metres): 55·0 *(16·8)*
Draught, feet (metres): 16·8 *(5·2)*
Aircraft: Landing platform for 1 Wasp helicopter
Missile launchers: 1 twin Sea Dart GWS 30 launcher aft
A/S weapons: 1 Ikara single launcher forward; 1 Limbo three-barrelled depth charge mortar (Mark 10) aft
Gun: 1—4·5 in *(115 mm)* Mark 8 forward
Main engines: COSAG arrangement (combined steam and gas turbines) 2 sets Standard Range geared steam turbines, 30 000 shp; 2 Bristol-Siddeley marine "Olympus" TMIA gas turbines, 30 000 shp; 2 shafts
Boilers: 2
Speed, knots: 30
Fuel, tons: 900
Range, miles: 5 000 at 18 knots
Complement: 407 (29 officers, 378 ratings)

Designed around Sea Dart GWS 30 weapons system. Fully stabilised to present a steady weapon platform. The gas turbines provide emergency power and high speed boost. The machinery is remotely-controlled from a ship control centre. Automatic steering, obviating the need for a quartermaster. Many labour-saving items of equipment fitted to make the most efficient and economical use of manpower resulting in a smaller ship's company for tonnage than any previous warship. Fitted with Action Data Automation Weapon System. Started trials 10 April 1972. Remainder of class cancelled owing to high cost and cancellation of aircraft-carrier building programme for which they were intended as A/A escorts. Officially listed as "destroyer".

Appearance: Three funnels, one amidships and two aft abreast the mainmast.

Communications: By GEC-Marconi to include SCOT satellite system compatible with both SKYNET and the US Defence satellites.

Cost: £22 500 000 (£27 000 000 overall). GEC-Marconi equipment for radar, weapons and communications cost over £3 000 000.

Missiles: The Sea Dart ship missile system; has a reasonable anti-ship capability.

Radar: Surveillance: One Type 965 with double AKE array and IFF.
Search: One Type 992.
Fire Control: One Type 909 (Sea Dart)
Navigation: One Type 1006; One Type 978.

BRISTOL

4/1975, MOD(N)

BRISTOL

4/1975, MOD(N)

7 "COUNTY" CLASS

Name	No.
ANTRIM	D 18
DEVONSHIRE	D 02
FIFE	D 20
GLAMORGAN	D 19
KENT	D 12
LONDON	D 16
NORFOLK	D 21

Builders	Laid down	Launched	Commissioned
Fairfield SB & Eng Co Ltd, Govan	20 Jan 1966	19 Oct 1967	14 July 1970
Cammell Laird & Co Ltd, Birkenhead	9 Mar 1959	10 June 1960	15 Nov 1962
Fairfield SB & Eng Co Ltd, Govan	1 June 1962	9 July 1964	21 June 1966
Vickers-Armstrong Ltd, Newcastle-on-Tyne	13 Sep 1962	9 July 1964	11 Oct 1966
Harland & Wolff Ltd, Belfast	1 Mar 1960	27 Sep 1961	15 Aug 1963
Swan, Hunter & Wigham Richardson, Wallsend	26 Feb 1960	7 Dec 1961	4 Nov 1963
Swan, Hunter & Wigham Richardson, Wallsend	15 Mar 1966	16 Nov 1967	7 Mar 1970

Displacement, tons: 5 440 standard; 6 200 full load
Length, feet (metres): 505·0 *(153·9)* wl; 520·5 *(158·7)* oa
Beam, feet (metres): 54·0 *(16·5)*
Draught, feet (metres): 20·0 *(6·1)*
Aircraft: 1 Wessex helicopter
Missile launchers: 4 Exocet in four ships (see *Missile* note) 1 twin Seaslug aft; 2 quadruple Seacat either side abreast hangar
Guns: 4—4·5 in *(115 mm)*, 2 twin turrets forward; 2—20 mm, (single) (2—4·5 only in ships with Exocet)
Main engines: Combined steam and gas turbines, 2 sets geared steam turbines, 30 000 shp
Boilers: 2 Babcock & Wilcox; 4 gas turbines, 30 000 shp; 2 shafts
Speed, knots: 30
Complement: 471 (33 officers and 438 men)

Fife, Glamorgan, Antrim and *Norfolk,* have the more powerful Seaslug II systems. All fitted with stablisers and are fully air-conditioned. *Hampshire* paid off April 1976. Original cost varied from £13·8 million *(Hampshire)* to £16·8 million *(Antrim)*. Officially rated as "destroyers" although they are the only "destroyers" in the world which carry no ship-borne A/S weapon.

Appearance: *Kent* and *London* have mainmast stepped further aft than remainder. The last four of the class have distinctive tubular foremast and twin AKE radar aerial.

Disposal: As a result of the Defence Review *Hampshire* was paid off in April 1976—at least seven years before she might have been expected on the disposal list.

Electrical: Two 1 000 kW turbo-alternators and three gas tur-bines alternators total 3 750 kW, at 440 V a/c SCOT fitted in *London.*

Engineering: These are the first ships of their size to have COSAG (combined steam and gas turbine machinery). Boilers work at a pressure of 700 psi and a temperature of 950 deg F. The steam and gas turbines are geared to the same shaft. Each shaft set consists of a high pressure and low pressure steam turbine of 15 000 shp combined output plus two G.6 gas turbines each of 7 500 shp. The gas turbines are able to develop their full power from cold within a few minutes, enabling ships lying in harbour without steam to get under way instantly in emergency.

Gunnery: The 4·5 inch guns are radar controlled fully automatic dual-purpose. The 20 mm guns were added for picket duties in S. E. Asia, but have been retained for general close range duties.

Missiles: Four Exocet fitted in *Norfolk, Antrim* and *Glamorgan* and being fitted in *Fife* in place of B turret. No reloads carried. *Norfolk* Exocet trials on French missile range (Mediterranean) in April 1974.

Radar: Air Search: One type 965 (double AKE-2 array in *Norfolk, Glamorgan, Antrim* and *Fife*–remainder single AKE-1).
Surveillance; One Type 992.
Height Finder; One Type 277.
Seaslug fire control; One Type 901.
Gunnery fire control; MRS 3 (forward).
Search fire control; GWS 22 in *Kent, Norfolk, Antrim, Fife* and *Glamorgan* (remainder optical)
Navigation; One Type 975.

NORFOLK
1/1976, C and S Taylor

DEVONSHIRE
9/1975, John G Callis

GLAMORGAN
3/1975, Dr Giorgio Arra

LONDON
11/1975, Dr Giorgio Arra

LONDON
1/1976, MOD

DESTROYERS

3 + 5 + 1 "SHEFFIELD" (TYPE 42) CLASS

Name	No.
SHEFFIELD	D 80
BIRMINGHAM	D 86
COVENTRY	D 118
CARDIFF	D 108
NEWCASTLE	D 87
GLASGOW	D 88
EXETER	—
No. 8	—

Builders	Laid down	Launched	Commissioned
Vickers Ltd SB Group, Barrow	15 Jan 1970	10 June 1971	16 Feb 1975
Cammell Laird & Co Ltd, Birkenhead	28 Mar 1972	30 July 1973	1976
Cammell Laird & Co Ltd, Birkenhead	22 Mar 1973	21 June 1974	1977
Vickers Ltd SB Group, Barrow	3 Nov 1972	22 Feb 1974	1976
Swan Hunter Ltd, Wallsend on Tyne	21 Feb 1973	24 Apr 1975	1977
Swan Hunter Ltd, Wallsend on Tyne	7 Mar 1974	14 Apr 1976	
Swan Hunter Ltd, Wallsend on Tyne	—	—	—
Vosper Thornycroft Ltd	—	—	—

Displacement, tons: 3 150 standard; 3 500 full load
Length, feet (metres): 392·0 (119·5) wl; 410·0 (125·0) oa
Beam, feet (metres): 46 (14)
Draught, feet (metres): 14 (4·3)
Aircraft: 1 Lynx helicopter (see note)
Missile launchers: 1 twin Sea Dart medium range surface-to-air (surface-to-surface capability) GWS 30 system
Guns: 1—4·5 in automatic, Mark 8, 2—20 mm Oerlikon; 2 saluting
A/S weapons: Helicopter-launched Mk 44 torpedoes (6 A/S torpedo tubes (triples) for Mk 46 to be fitted at 1st refit)
Main engines: COGOG arrangement of Rolls Royce Olympus gas turbines for full power 50 000 shp; 2 Rolls Royce Tyne gas turbines for cruising 8 000 shp; cp propellers; 2 shafts
Speed, knots: 30
Range: 4 500 miles at 18 knots
Complement: 299 (26 officers, 80 senior rates, 193 junior rates) (accommodation for 312)

This is a class of all gas-turbine ships fitted with four sets of stabilisers and twin rudders. The helicopter will carry the Skua (CK 834) air-to-surface weapon for use against lightly defended surface ship targets such as fast patrol boats. Advantages include ability to reach maximum speed with great rapidity, reduction in space and weight and 25 per cent reduction in technical manpower. To cost approximately £23 000 000 per ship, although this may well be increased by delays and rising costs of raw materials and labour.
Exeter ordered 22 Jan 1976. Eighth ship ordered 18 Mar 1976. Ninth ship to be ordered in 1976.

Completion: *Cardiff,* whose completion was delayed by lack of man-power at Vickers Ltd, Barrow, was towed to Swan Hunters, Ltd, Wallsend in Feb 1976.

Electronics: Twin SCOT Skynet satellite communication aerials; ADAWS 4 for coordination of action information. ECM D/F.

Engineering: Considerable automation has allowed a cut in engine-room staff required, a number of machinery spaces operating unmanned. Propellers by Stone Manganese (Type XX).

Helicopter: First ships provided with Wasp until Lynx becomes available.

Radar: Search; One Type 965 with double AKE-2 array and IFF. Surveillance and Target indication; One Type 992Q. Sea Dart fire control and Target; Two Type 909 Navigation, HDWS and helicopter control; One Type 1006

Sonar: Type 184 hull mounted. Type 162 classification.

SHEFFIELD　　　　　　　　　　　　　　　　11/1975, Dr Giorgio Arra

SHEFFIELD　　　　　　　　　　　　　　　　4/1975, John G Callis

SHEFFIELD　　　　　　　　　　　　　　　　11/1975, Dr Giorgio Arra

FRIGATES

5 + 3 "AMAZON" (TYPE 21) CLASS

Name	No.	Builders	Laid down	Launched	Commissioned
AMAZON	F 169	Vosper Thornycroft, Woolston	6 Nov 1969	26 April 1971	11 May 1974
ANTELOPE	F 170	Vosper Thornycroft, Woolston	23 Mar 1971	16 Mar 1972	19 July 1975
ACTIVE	F 171	Vosper Thornycroft, Woolston	23 July 1971	23 Nov 1972	1976
AMBUSCADE	F 172	Yarrow & Co Ltd, Glasgow	July 1971	18 Jan 1973	5 Sep 1975
ARROW	F 173	Yarrow & Co Ltd, Glasgow	June 1972	5 Feb 1974	1976
ALACRITY	F 174	Yarrow & Co Ltd, Glasgow	Feb 1973	18 Sep 1974	1977
ARDENT	F 175	Yarrow & Co Ltd, Glasgow	26 Feb 1974	9 May 1975	1977
AVENGER	F 176	Yarrow & Co Ltd, Glasgow	30 Oct 1974	20 Nov 1975	1978

Displacement, tons: 2 000 standard; 2 500 full load
Length, feet (metres): 360·0 *(109·7)* wl; 384·0 *(117·0)* oa
Beam, feet (metres): 41·8 *(12·7)*
Draught, feet (metres): 12·3 *(3·7)*
Aircraft: 1 Lynx helicopter
Missile launchers: 1 quadruple Seacat surface-to-air (later ships will have Seawolf); 2 Twin Exocet MM 38 (see Missile note)
Guns: 1—4·5 in Mark 8; 2—20 mm Oerlikon (singles)
A/S weapons: Helicopter launched torpedoes
Torpedo tubes: 6 (2 triple) for Mk 46 (to be fitted)
Main engines: COGOG arrangement of 2 Rolls Royce "Olympus" gas turbines 56 000 bhp; 2 Rolls Royce "Tyne" gas turbines for cruising 8 500 shp; 2 shafts; controllable pitch, 5-bladed propellers
Speed, knots: 32; 17 on Tyne GTs
Range, miles: 4 500 at 18 knots
Complement: 170 (11 officers, and 159 ratings)

A contract was awarded to Vosper Thornycroft, on 27 Feb 1968 for the design of a patrol frigate to be prepared in full collaboration with Yarrow Ltd. This is the first custom built gas turbine frigate (designed and constructed as such from the keel up, as opposed to conversion) and the first warship designed by commercial firms for many years. All eight were planned for completion by end 1977 but the building of the later ships has been delayed by lack of technical information and equipment from beyond the shipyards.

Electronics: SCOT satellite communication to be fitted in last four ships, CAAIS fitted.

Helicopter: First ships provided with Wasp until Lynx is available.

Missiles: It is planned to fit Exocet MM 38 and Seawolf in *Active, Alacrity, Ardent* and *Avenger.*

Radar: Surveillance and Target Indicator: One Type 992Q.
Navigation: One Type 978.
Seacat Control: Two GWS 24.
Gun Fire Control: Orion RTN-10X WSA 4 system.
IFF Interrogator: Cossor Type 1010.
IFF Transponder: Plessey PTR 461.

Sonar: Type 184M hull mounted.
Type 162M classification.

AMAZON
10/1975, Dr. Giorgio Arra

EXOCET fitted Type 21
9/1975, Vosper-Thornycroft model

AMBUSCADE
12/1975, Wright and Logan

0 + 3 "WEAPON" CLASS (TYPE 22)

Name	No.	Builders	Laid down	Launched	Commission
BROADSWORD	—	Yarrow Ltd, Glasgow	7 Feb 1975	12 May 1976	Late 1978?
BATTLEAXE	—	Yarrow Ltd, Glasgow	—	—	—
—	—		—	—	—

BROADSWORD model

1974, MOD

Displacement, tons: 3 500 standard; 4 000 full load
Dimensions, feet (metres): 430 oa × 48·5 × 14 *(131·2 × 14·8 × 4·3)*
Aircraft: 2 Lynx helicopters
Missile launchers: 2 Sea Wolf surface-to-air systems; 4 Exocet launchers forward
Guns: 2—40 mm
A/S weapons: 6 (2 triple) Mk 32 torpedo tubes for Mk 44 or Mk 46
Main engines: COGOG arrangement of 2 Rolls Royce "Olympus" gas turbines; 56 000 bhp and 2 Rolls Royce "Tyne" gas turbines; 8 500 bhp; 2 shafts
Speed, knots: 30+ (18 on Tynes)
Range, miles: 4 500 at 18 knots (on Tynes)
Complement: 250 (approx)

Designed as successors to the "Leander" class, the construction of which ceased with the completion of the scheduled programme of 26 ships. Order for the first of class, *Broadsword*, was placed on 26 Feb 1974, *Battleaxe* ordered 5 Sep 1975. Order for third ship due in 1976. This class is primarily designed for A/S operations and is capable of acting as OTC and helicopter control ship. These are the first major ships for the RN which have no main gun armament.

Radar: Surveillance: Two Type 967/8.
Navigation: One Type 1006.

Sonar: Type 2016.

16 "LEANDER" CLASS

Name	No.	Builders	Laid down	Launched	Commissioned
AJAX	F 114	Cammell Laird & Co Ltd, Birkenhead	12 Oct 1959	16 Aug 1962	10 Dec 1963
DIDO	F 104	Yarrow & Co Ltd, Scotstoun, Glasgow	2 Dec 1959	22 Dec 1961	18 Sep 1963
LEANDER	F 109	Harland & Wolff Ltd, Belfast	10 April 1959	28 June 1961	27 Mar 1963
PENELOPE	F 127	Vickers-Armstrong Ltd, Tyne	14 Mar 1961	17 Aug 1962	31 Oct 1963
AURORA	F 10	John Brown & Co (Clydebank) Ltd	1 June 1961	28 Nov 1962	9 April 1964
EURYALUS	F 15	Scotts Shipbuilding & Eng Co, Greenock	2 Nov 1961	6 June 1963	16 Sep 1964
GALATEA	F 18	Swan Hunter & Wigham Richardson, Tyne	29 Dec 1961	23 May 1963	25 April 1964
ARETHUSA	F 38	J. Samuel White & Co Ltd, Cowes	7 Sep 1962	5 Nov 1963	24 Nov 1965
NAIAD	F 39	Yarrow & Co Ltd, Scotstoun, Glasgow	30 Oct 1962	4 Nov 1963	15 Mar 1965
CLEOPATRA	F 28	HM Dockyard, Devonport	19 June 1963	25 Mar 1964	4 Jan 1966
SIRIUS	F 40	HM Dockyard, Portsmouth	9 Aug 1963	22 Sep 1964	15 June 1966
MINERVA	F 45	Vickers-Armstrong Ltd, Tyne	25 July 1963	19 Dec 1964	14 May 1966
PHOEBE	F 42	Alex Stephen & Sons Ltd, Glasgow	3 June 1963	8 July 1964	15 April 1966
DANAE	F 47	HM Dockyard, Devonport	16 Dec 1964	31 Oct 1965	7 Sep 1967
JUNO	F 52	John I. Thornycroft Ltd, Woolston	16 July 1964	24 Nov 1965	18 July 1967
ARGONAUT	F 56	Hawthorn Leslie Ltd, Hebburn-on-Tyne	27 Nov 1964	8 Feb 1966	17 Aug 1967

AURORA (with Ikara)

4/1976, C and S Taylor

10 "BROAD-BEAMED LEANDER" CLASS

Name	No.	Builders	Laid down	Launched	Commissioned
ANDROMEDA	F 57	HM Dockyard, Portsmouth	25 May 1966	24 May 1967	2 Dec 1968
JUPITER	F 60	Yarrow & Co Ltd, Scotstoun, Glasgow	3 Oct 1966	4 Sep 1967	9 Aug 1969
HERMIONE	F 58	Alex Stephen & Sons Ltd, Glasgow	6 Dec 1965	26 April 1967	11 July 1969
BACCHANTE	F 69	Vickers-Armstrong Ltd, Tyne	27 Oct 1966	29 Feb 1968	17 Oct 1969
SCYLLA	F 71	HM Dockyard, Devonport	17 May 1967	8 Aug 1968	12 Feb 1970
CHARYBDIS	F 75	Harland & Wolff Ltd, Belfast	27 Jan 1967	28 Feb 1968	2 June 1969
ACHILLES	F 12	Yarrow & Co Ltd, Scotstoun, Glasgow	1 Dec 1967	21 Nov 1968	9 July 1970
DIOMEDE	F 16	Yarrow & Co Ltd, Scotstoun, Glasgow	30 Jan 1968	15 April 1969	2 April 1971
APOLLO	F 70	Yarrow & Co Ltd, Scotstoun, Glasgow	1 May 1969	15 Oct 1970	28 May 1972
ARIADNE	F 72	Yarrow & Co Ltd, Scotstoun, Glasgow	1 Nov 1969	10 Sep 1971	10 Feb 1973

Displacement, tons: 2 450 standard; 2 860 full load (Leanders) 2 500 standard; 2 962 full load (Broad-beamed)
Length, feet (metres): 360 (109·7) wl; 372 (113·4) oa
Beam, feet (metres): 41 (12·5) (Leanders) 43 (13·1) (Broad-beamed)
Draught, feet (metres): 18 (5·5)
Aircraft: 1 Wasp helicopter
Missiles: Exocet in some and Seacat (see Notes)
Guns: 2—4·5 in (115 mm) (twin); 2—40 mm (varies); 2—20 mm (Seacat ships) (see Notes)
A/S weapons: Ikara in some (see Notes); 1 Limbo 3 barrelled mortar except in Exocet-fitted ships which carry triple A/S torpedo tubes instead
Main engines: 2 double reduction geared turbines; 2 shafts; 30 000 shp (see Notes)
Boilers: 2
Speed, knots: 30
Oil fuel, tons: 460
Complement: 251 (Leanders); 260 (Broad-beamed)

This class, whose construction extended over ten years, was an improvement on the Type 12. As originally designed there were several significant improvements—a helicopter, VDS and long-range air warning radar being the most important. Recently a number of conversions have been put in hand (see Notes below).

Electrical: 440 volts, 60 cycle AC. 1 900 kw in earlier ships, 2 500 kw in later ones.

Electronics: SCOT satellite communications being fitted at later conversions.

Engineering: The first ten have Y-100 machinery, the remainder of the "Leanders" Y-136. "Broad-beamed Leanders" have Y-160 machinery.

Gunnery: 4·5 in turret removed in Exocet and Ikara conversions and in Penelope. 40 mm are not fitted in unconverted ships mounting Seacat. Conversions mount 2 single 40 mm abaft the bridge.

Missiles: A series of rearmament programmes is in progress and some ships have already been completed.
(a) Exocet—Mounted forward in place of 4·5 inch turret. Cleopatra (Devonport) completed 28 Nov 1975; Phoebe (Devonport) started Aug 1974, completion Oct 1977; Sirius (Devonport) started Mar 1975, completion Oct 1977. Dido (Devonport) started July 1975, completion Dec 1977; Argonaut (Devonport) started Nov 1975, completion Oct 1978; Minerva (Chatham) started Dec 1975, completion Oct 1978; Juno (Portsmouth) started May 1976, completion Oct 1978; Danae (Devonport) started June 1976, completion Oct 1978; plus the ten "Broad-Beamed" ships.
(b) Ikara—Mounted forward in place of 4·5 inch turret. Radar Type 965 removed.
Leander (Devonport) completed Dec 1972; Ajax (Devonport) completed Sep 1973; Galatea (Devonport) completed Sep 1974; Naiad (Devonport) completed July 1975; Euryalus (Devonport) completed Dec 1975; Aurora (Chatham) completed Mar 1976; Arethusa (Portsmouth) completion Nov 1976; Penelope on completion of Seawolf trials.
(c) Seacat—Single Seacat first fitted in Naiad and subsequently in all but conversions which carry two Seacat mounts.
(d) Seawolf—Subsequent fitting in place of Seacat. Trials in Penelope continuing during 1976.

Radar: Air surveillance: One Type 965 with single AKE array (except in Ikara ships)
Combined air/surface warning: One Type 993.
Fire Control: MRS 3/GWS 22.
Navigation; One Type 975.

Sonar: VDS was originally fitted in all but Diomede. In some the VDS has been removed leaving the well—in others the well has been plated over to provide extra accommodation for RMs. Can be replaced.

PENELOPE (with Seawolf)   1975, MOD(N)

BACCHANTE   3/1976, MOD(N)

CLEOPATRA (with Exocet)

1/1976, MOD (N)

SCYLLA

5/1975, C and S Taylor

9 "ROTHESAY" CLASS (MODIFIED TYPE 12)

Name	No.	Builders	Laid down	Launched	Commissioned
BERWICK	F 115	Harland & Wolff Ltd, Belfast	16 June 1958	15 Dec 1959	1 June 1961
BRIGHTON	F 106	Yarrow & Co Ltd, Scotstoun	23 July 1957	30 Oct 1959	28 Sep 1961
FALMOUTH	F 113	Swan Hunter, Wigham Richardson	23 Nov 1957	15 Dec 1959	25 July 1961
LONDONDERRY	F 108	J. Samuel White & Co Ltd, Cowes	15 Nov 1956	20 May 1958	22 July 1960
LOWESTOFT	F 103	Alex Stephen & Sons Ltd, Govan	9 June 1958	23 June 1960	18 Oct 1961
PLYMOUTH	F 126	HM Dockyard, Devonport	1 July 1958	20 July 1959	11 May 1961
RHYL	F 129	HM Dockyard, Portsmouth	29 Jan 1958	23 Apr 1959	31 Oct 1960
ROTHESAY	F 107	Yarrow & Co Ltd, Scotstoun	6 Nov 1956	9 Dec 1957	23 Apr 1960
YARMOUTH	F 101	John Brown & Co Ltd, Clydebank	29 Nov 1957	23 Mar 1959	26 Mar 1960

Displacement, tons: 2 380 standard; 2 800 full load
Length, feet (metres): 360·0 (109·7) wl; 370·0 (112·8) oa
Beam, feet (metres): 41·0 (12·5)
Draught, feet (metres): 17·3 (5·3)
Aircraft: 1 Wasp helicopter
Missile launchers: 1 quadruple Seacat
Guns: 2—4·5 in (115 mm) (1 twin); 2—20 mm (single)
A/S weapons: 1 Limbo 3-barrelled DC mortar
Main engines: 2 double reduction geared turbines; 2 shafts; 30 000 shp
Boilers: 2 Babcock & Wilcox
Speed, knots: 30
Oil fuel, tons: 400
Complement: 235 (15 officers and 220 ratings)

Provided under the 1954-55 programme. Originally basically similar to the "Whitby" class but with modifications in layout.

Electrical: Two turbo generators and two diesel generators in all ships. Total 1 140 kW. Alternating current, 440 volts, three phase, 60 cycles per second.

Engineering: Two Admiralty Standard Range turbines each rated at 15 000 shp. Propeller revolutions 220 rpm. Boilers 550 psi (38·7 kg/cm²) pressure and 850°F (450°C) temperature.

Modernisation: The "Rothesay" class was reconstructed and modernised from 1966-72 during which time they were equipped to operate a Wessex Wasp helicopter armed with homing torpedoes. A flight deck and hangar were built on aft, necessitating the removal of one of their anti-submarine mortars. A Seacat replaced the 40 mm gun.

Radar: Search; One Type 993
Fire Control; MRS 3
Navigation; One Type 975

Refits: *Londonderry* started refit at Rosyth in Nov 1975 to become trials ship for Admiralty Surface Weapons Establishment.
Rothesay to have similar refit in mid-1977.

Seacat: Optical Director—GWS 20

RHYL

2 I 1976, Dr Giorgio Arra

FALMOUTH

10 I 1975, Dr Giorgio Arra

PLYMOUTH (in Johore Straits)

1975, MOD (N)

LOWESTOFT

4 I 1976, C and S Taylor

2 "WHITBY" CLASS (TYPE 12)

Name	No.	Builders	Laid down	Launched	Commissioned
EASTBOURNE	F 73	Vickers-Armstrong Ltd, Tyne	13 Jan 1954	29 Dec 1955	9 Jan 1958
TORQUAY	F 43	Harland & Wolff Ltd, Belfast	11 Mar 1953	1 July 1954	10 May 1956

Displacement, tons: 2 150 standard; 2 560 full load
Length, feet (metres): 360·0 (109·7) wl; 369·8 (112·7) oa
Beam, feet (metres): 41·0 (12·5)
Draught, feet (metres): 17 (5·2)
Guns: 2—4·5 in (115 mm) (twin) (not in Eastbourne)
A/S weapons: 1 Limbo 3-barrelled DC mortar (in Torquay only)
Main engines: 2 sets d.r. geared turbines; 2 shafts; 30 430 shp
Boilers: 2 Babcock & Wilcox; Pressure 550 psi (38·7 kg/cm²);
  Temperature 850°F (454°C)
Speed, knots: 31
Oil fuel, tons: 370
Complement: 225 (12 officers, and 213 ratings)

Ordered in 1951. Twin-rudders. They are all-welded. Originally class of six.

Class: Torquay used as Navigation/Direction training and trials ship at Portsmouth, having a large deck-house aft and carrying the first CAAIS (Computer Assisted Action Information System) to go to sea. Eastbourne, stripped of her gun and A/S armament, is based at Rosyth for engine-room trainees from HMS Caledonia. Blackpool now in use as target ship. Tenby and Scarborough sold to Pakistan in 1974. Still in UK waters (mid 1976) awaiting decision on form of refit.

Electrical: System is alternating current, 440 volts, three phase, 60 cycles per second. Two turbo alternators and two diesel alternators. Total 1 140 kilowatts.

Engineering: Y 100 turbines with double reduction gearing giving low propeller revolutions of 220 rpm at high power.

Radar: Search: One Type 293.
Navigation: Type 975 (Torquay Type 978)
Fire Control: Type 275 (Mk 6 MDCT)

Sonar: Types 174, 170 and 162.

EASTBOURNE   5/1975, Wright and Logan

TORQUAY   1/1976, Dr. Giorgio Arra

1 YARROW TYPE

Name	No.	Builders	Laid down	Launched	Commissioned
MERMAID	F 76	Yarrow Shipbuilders & Co Ltd	1965	29 Dec 1966	16 May 1973 (see notes)

Displacement, tons: 2 300 standard; 2 520 full load
Dimensions, feet (metres): 320 pp; 330 wl; 339·3 oa × 40 × 12
  (97·6; 100·7; 103·5 × 12·2 × 3·7)
Guns: 2—4 inch (twin); 2—40 mm
A/S weapons: 1 Squid
Main engines: 8 Diesels; 2 shafts; 2 cp propellers
Oil fuel, tons: 230
Range, miles: 4 800 at 15 knots

Similar in hull and machinery to "Leopard" and "Salisbury" classes. Originally built for Ghana as a display ship for ex-President Nkrumah at a cost of £5m but put up for sale after his departure. She was launched without ceremony on 29 Dec 1966 and completed in 1968. She was transferred to Portsmouth Dockyard in April 1972 being acquired by the Royal Navy. Refit started October 1972 at Chatham. Commissioned in Royal Navy 16 May 1973. She was based at Singapore 1974-75 returning to UK early 1976.

MERMAID

7 "TRIBAL" CLASS (TYPE 81)

Name	No.	Builders	Laid down	Launched	Commissioned
ASHANTI	F 117	Yarrow & Co Ltd, Scotstoun	15 Jan 1958	9 Mar 1959	23 Nov 1961
ESKIMO	F 119	J. Samuel White & Co Ltd, Cowes	22 Oct 1958	20 Mar 1960	21 Feb 1963
GURKHA	F 122	J. I. Thornycroft & Co Ltd, Woolston	3 Nov 1958	11 July 1960	13 Feb 1963
MOHAWK	F 125	Vickers-Armstrong Ltd, Barrow	23 Dec 1960	5 April 1962	29 Nov 1963
NUBIAN	F 131	HM Dockyard, Portsmouth	7 Sep 1959	6 Sep 1960	9 Oct 1962
TARTAR	F 133	HM Dockyard, Devonport	22 Oct 1959	19 Sep 1960	26 Feb 1962
ZULU	F 124	Alex Stephen & Sons Ltd, Govan	13 Dec 1960	3 July 1962	17 April 1964

Displacement, tons: 2 300 standard; 2 700 full load
Length, feet (metres): 350·0 *(106·7)* wl; 360·0 *(109·7)* oa
Beam, feet (metres): 42·3 *(12·9)*
Draught, feet (metres): 17·5 *(5·3)*
Aircraft: 1 Wasp helicopter
Missile launchers: 2 quadruple Seacats
Guns: 2—4·5 in (singles); 2—20 mm
A/S weapons: 1 Limbo 3-barrelled mortar
Main engines: Combined steam and gas turbine; Metrovick steam turbine; 12 500 shp; Metrovick gas turbine; 7 500 shp; 1 shaft
Boilers: 1 Babcock & Wilcox (plus 1 auxiliary boiler)
Speed, knots: 28
Oil fuel, tons: 400
Complement: 253 (13 officers and 240 ratings)

Ashanti, Eskimo and *Gurkha* were ordered under the 1955-56 estimates, *Nubian* and *Tartar* 1956-57, and *Mohawk* and *Zulu* 1957-58. Designed as self-contained units for service in such areas as the Persian Gulf. *Ashanti* cost £5 220 000.

Construction: All-welded prefabrication. Denny Brown stabilisers fitted. Enclosed bridge and twin rudders.

Electrical: Generator capacity of 1 500 kW.

Engineering: The gas turbine is used to boost the steam turbines for sustained bursts of high speed and also enables the ship lying in harbour without steam up to get under way instantly in emergency. The machinery is remotely controlled. The main boiler works at a pressure of 550 psi and a temperature of 850 deg F. Five-bladed propeller, 11·75 ft diameter, 280 rpm. The forward funnel serves the boiler, the after one the gas turbine.

Gunnery: Optical Seacat directors fitted.
Radar: Search: One Type 965 with single AKE 1 array and IFF. Air and surface warning: One Type 293.
Navigation: One Type 975.
Fire control: MRS 3 system.

Sonar: Types 177, 170 and 162. Type 199. VDS fitted in *Ashanti* and *Gurkha* in 1970.

TARTAR

8/1975, C. and S. Taylor

ASHANTI

1/1976, Dr. Giorgio Arra

TARTAR off Bear Island

11/1975, MOD(N)

2 "LEOPARD" CLASS (TYPE 41)

Name	No.
JAGUAR	F 37
LYNX	F 27

Builders	Laid down	Launched	Commissioned
Wm. Denny & Bros Ltd, Dumbarton	2 Nov 1953	30 July 1957	12 Dec 1959
John Brown & Co Ltd, Clydebank	13 Aug 1953	12 Jan 1955	14 Mar 1957

Displacement, tons: 2 300 standard; 2 520 full load
Length, feet (metres): 320 *(97·5)* pp; 330 *(100·6)* wl; 339·8 *(103·6)* oa
Beam, feet (metres): 40 *(12·2)*
Draught, feet (metres): 16 *(4·9)*
Guns: 4—4·5 in *(115 mm)* (twin turrets); 1—40 mm
A/S weapons: 1 Squid 3-barrelled DC mortar
Main engines: 8 ASR 1 diesels in three engine rooms; 14 400 bhp; 2 shafts; 4 engines geared to each shaft
Speed, knots: 24
Oil fuel, tons: 220
Range, miles: 2 300 at full power; 7 500 at 16 knots
Complement: 235 (15 officers, 220 ratings)

Originally a class of four, a fifth ship having been cancelled for a "Leander" class. Designed primarily for anti-aircraft protection. All welded. *Jaguar* and *Lynx* were ordered on 28 June 1951. Both now in reserve. Fitted with stabilisers.

Electronics: ECM and D/F.

Engineering: The propelling machinery comprises Admiralty Standard Range 1 diesels coupled to the propeller shafting through hydraulic gear boxes. These diesels are of light weight, about 17 lb/shp. *Jaguar* is the only ship of this class to be fitted with controllable pitch propellers, 12 ft diameter 200 rpm. The fuel tanks have a compensating system, so that sea water replaces oil fuel as it is used.

Radar: Air Search: One Type 965 with single AKE 1 array and IFF.
Fire Control: Mk 6 M I-band. Type 275.
Navigation: One Type 975.

Reconstruction: *Lynx* was extensively refitted in 1963 with new mainmast. *Jaguar* similarly refitted in 1966-7.

Sonar: Types 174 and 170.

Transfer: Another ship of this class, *Panther*, was transferred to India while building and renamed *Brahmaputra*.

JAGUAR

1974, John Mortimer

JAGUAR

1973, Wright and Logan

LYNX

1973

4 "SALISBURY" CLASS (TYPE 61)

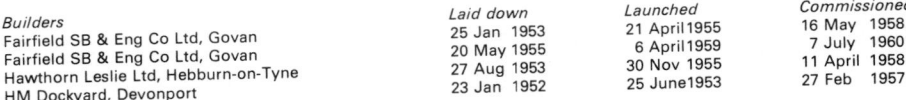

Name	No.	Builders	Laid down	Launched	Commissioned
CHICHESTER	F 59	Fairfield SB & Eng Co Ltd, Govan	25 Jan 1953	21 April 1955	16 May 1958
LINCOLN	F 99	Fairfield SB & Eng Co Ltd, Govan	20 May 1955	6 April 1959	7 July 1960
LLANDAFF	F 61	Hawthorn Leslie Ltd, Hebburn-on-Tyne	27 Aug 1953	30 Nov 1955	11 April 1958
SALISBURY	F 32	HM Dockyard, Devonport	23 Jan 1952	25 June 1953	27 Feb 1957

Displacement, tons: 2 170 standard; 2 408 full load
Length, feet (metres): 320·0 *(97·5)* pp; 330·0 *(100·6)* wl; 339·8 *(103·6)* oa
Beam, feet (metres): 40·0 *(12·2)*
Draught, feet (metres): 15·5 *(4·7)*
Missile launchers: 1 quadruple "Seacat" in *Lincoln* and *Salisbury* which also have 2 sextuple 3 in rocket launchers
Guns: 2—4·5 in *(115 mm)*; 2—40 mm *(Llandaff)*; 1—40 mm *(Chichester)*; 2—20 mm (remainder)
A/S weapons: 1 Squid triple-barrelled DC mortar
Main engines: 8 ASR 1 diesels in three engine rooms; 2 shafts; 14 400 bhp; 4 engines geared to each shaft
Speed, knots: 24
Oil fuel, tons: 230
Range, miles: 2 300 at full power; 7 500 at 16 knots
Complement: 237 (14 officers and 223 ratings)

Designed primarily for the direction of carrier-borne and shore-based aircraft. Ordered on 28 June 1951 except *Salisbury*, the prototype ship. Construction was all welded and largely prefabricated. The construction of three other ships *Exeter*, *Gloucester* and *Coventry* cancelled in 1957 being replaced by first three "Leander" class. Fitted with stabilisers (except *Lincoln*). Original lattice masts replaced by tower masts during 1960s. *Lincoln* and *Chichester* in reserve.

Engineering: Powered by Admiralty Standard Range 1 diesel engines coupled to the propeller shafts through hydraulic couplings and oil operated reverse and reduction gear boxes. *Llandaff* is the only Type 61 frigate to have a 500 kW gas-turbine alternator and three diesel generators. *Lincoln* is fitted with controllable pitch propellers, rotating at 200 rpm, which are 12 feet in diameter, manufactured by Stone Marine & Engineering Co Ltd. The fuel tanks are fitted with compensating system.

Hong Kong Guardship: In 1973 *Chichester* was re-equipped for service as permanent HK Guardship. This involved removal of Type 965. *Chichester* returned to UK early 1976 to reserve.

Radar: Long range surveillance: One Type 965 with double AKE 2 array with IFF (except *Chichester*).
Combined warning: One Type 993.
Height-finder: One Type 277Q.
Target indication: One Type 982.
Fire control: Mk 6M director with Type 275.
Seacat control (only *Salisbury* and *Lincoln*): GWS 22.
Navigation: One Type 975.

Sonar: Types 174 and 170B.

LINCOLN
1975, MOD(N)

CHICHESTER as Hong Kong guardship
1974, Wright and Logan

LLANDAFF
4/1976, C. and S. Taylor

4 "BLACKWOOD" CLASS (TYPE 14)

TWO ACTIVE SHIPS

Name	No.
DUNDAS	F 48
KEPPEL	F 85

Builders	Laid down	Launched	Commissioned
J. Samuel White & Co Ltd	17 Oct 1952	25 Sep 1953	16 Mar 1956
Yarrow & Co Ltd	27 Mar 1953	31 Aug 1954	6 July 1956

TWO HARBOUR TRAINING SHIPS

Name	No.
RUSSELL	F 97
DUNCAN	F 80

Builders	Laid down	Launched	Commissioned
Swan Hunter & Wigham Richardson	11 Nov 1953	10 Dec 1954	7 Feb 1957
John I. Thornycroft & Co Ltd	17 Dec 1953	30 May 1957	21 Oct 1958

Displacement, tons: 1 180 standard; 1 456 full load
Length, feet (metres): 300 *(91·4)* wl; 310 *(94·5)* oa
Beam, feet (metres): 33·0 *(10·1)*
Draught, feet (metres): 15·5 *(4·7)*
Guns: 2—40 mm Bofors
A/S weapons: 2 Limbo 3-barrelled DC mortars
Main engines: 1 set geared turbines; 1 shaft; 15 000 shp
Boilers: 2 Babcock & Wilcox; Pressure 550 psi *(38·7 kg/cm²)*;
   Temperature 850°F (454°C)
Speed, knots: 27·8
Oil fuel, tons: 275
Range, miles: 4 000 at 12 knots
Complement: 140 (8 officers, and 132 ratings)

Originally a class of twelve.

Of comparatively simple construction. Built in prefabricated sections. In 1958-59 their hulls were strengthened to withstand severe and prolonged sea and weather conditions on fishery protection in Icelandic waters.

Class: The first two are currently operational. *Duncan* is at Rosyth for harbour training and *Russell* at Portsmouth for similar duties with HMS *Sultan*.

Engineering: All engined by their builders, except *Russell*, by Wallsend Slipway & Eng Co Ltd. Four-bladed, 12 ft diameter propeller, 220 rpm.

DUNDAS   *5/1975, C. and S. Taylor*

Radar: Navigation: One Type 975.
General search: One Type 978.

Sonar: Types 174, 170 and 162.

1 TYPE 14 CONVERSION

Name	No.
EXMOUTH	F 84

Builders	Laid down	Launched	Commissioned
J. Samuel White & Co Ltd	24 Mar 1954	16 Nov 1955	20 Dec 1957

Details of displacement, dimensions and armament as for "Blackwood" Class Type 14 above.

Main engines: 1 Olympus Gas Turbine; 22 500 hp; 2 Proteus Gas Turbines; 6 500 hp; 1 shaft; cp propeller
Speed, knots: 28

The conversion of *Exmouth* to gas-turbine propulsion was completed in Chatham Dockyard on 20 July 1968. She was the first all gas-turbine major warship in the Royal Navy.

Engineering: She can be propelled on only one system at a time, either the Olympus or the pair of Proteus engines.

Radar: Navigation: One Type 975.
General Search: One Type 978.

EXMOUTH   *11/1975, Dr Giorgio Arra*

TYPE 15

For *Grenville* and *Undaunted* see Disposal List. With *Ulster*, acting as accommodation ship at Portsmouth, these are the sole survivors of the wartime "R", "T", "U", "V", "W", and "Z" classes of destroyers, launched in 1942-43. Of the 48 ships of these classes 33 were converted into Type 15 frigates and 7 ("T" Class) into Type 16 (limited conversion) frigates. A number have been transferred to other navies.

SONAR TRIALS SHIP

Name	No.
MATAPAN	D 43

Builders	Laid down	Launched	Commissioned
John Brown, Clydebank	11 Mar 1944	30 Apr 1945	5 Sep 1947

Displacement, tons: 3 835 full load
Length, feet (metres): 388 *(118·3)* oa
Beam, feet (metres): 40·5 *(12·3)*
Draught, feet (metres): 27 *(8·2)*
Main engines: Parsons geared turbines; 50 000 shp; 2 shafts
Boilers: 2 Admiralty 3-drum; 400 psi *(28·1 kg/cm²)*; 650°F *(343°C)*
Oil fuel, tons: 680
Speed, knots: 31
Range, miles: 1 300 at full power; 3 000 at 20 knots; 4 400 at 12 knots

A former standard "Battle Class" destroyer which went into reserve almost immediately after being completed. Attached to the Admiralty Underwater Weapons Establishment at Portland after conversion.

Conversion: Taken in hand at HM Dockyard, Portsmouth in Jan 1971 for conversion into a Sonar Trials Ship. The rebuilding involved a new clipper bow, different bridge, remodelled superstructure, extension of the forecastle deck aft all the way to the counter, thus converting her into a flushdecker, adding a second funnel, and a helicopter landing deck. Commissioned 2 Feb 1973 after a £2½m conversion.

MATAPAN   *5/1975, C. and S. Taylor*

SUBMARINES
Nuclear Powered Ballistic Missile Submarines (SSBN)

4 "RESOLUTION" CLASS

Name	No.	Builders	Laid down	Launched	Commissioned
RENOWN	S 26	Cammell Laird & Co Ltd, Birkenhead	25 June1964	25 Feb 1967	15 Nov 1968
REPULSE	S 23	Vickers (Shipbuilding) Ltd, Barrow-in-Furness	12 Mar 1965	4 Nov 1967	28 Sep 1968
RESOLUTION	S 22	Vickers (Shipbuilding) Ltd, Barrow-in-Furness	26 Feb 1964	15 Sep 1966	2 Oct 1967
REVENGE	S 27	Cammell Laird & Co Ltd, Birkenhead	19 May 1965	15 Mar 1968	4 Dec 1969

Displacement, tons: 7 500 surfaced; 8 400 dived
Length, feet (metres): 360 *(109·7)* pp; 425 *(129·5)* oa
Beam, feet (metres): 33 *(10·1)*
Draught, feet (metres): 30 *(9·1)*
Missiles, surface: 16 tubes amidships for "Polaris" A—3 SLBMs
Torpedo tubes: 6—21 in *(533 mm)* (bow)
Nuclear reactors: 1 pressurised water cooled
Main machinery: Geared steam turbines; 1 shaft
Speed, knots: 20 surfaced; 25 dived
Complement: 143 (13 officers, 130 ratings); 2 crews (see *Personnel*)

In Feb 1963 it was officially stated that it was intended to order four or five 7 000 ton nuclear powered submarines, each to carry 16 "Polaris" missiles, and it was planned that the first would be on patrol in 1968. Their hulls and machinery would be of British design. As well as building two submarines Vickers (Shipbuilding) would give lead yard service to the builder of the other two. Four "Polaris" submarines were in fact ordered in May 1963. The plan to build a fifth Polaris submarine was cancelled on 15 Feb 1965. Britain's first SSBN, *Resolution,* put to sea on 22 June 1967 and completed 6 weeks trial in the Firth of Clyde and Atlantic on 17 Aug 1967.

Cost: *Resolution,* £40 240 000; *Renown,* £39 950 000; *Repulse,* £37 500 000; *Revenge,* £38 600 000; completed ships excluding missiles.

Personnel: Each submarine, which has accommodation for 19 officers and 135 ratings, is manned on a two-crew basis, in order to get maximum operational time at sea.

Radar: Search; I-band
Periscope radar.

Sonar: Types 2001 and 2007.

REVENGE at Faslane

3/1976, Wren Veronica Evans (MOD(N))

REPULSE

1971

REVENGE at Faslane

3/1976, Wren Veronica Evans (MOD(N))

3 + 3 "SWIFTSURE" CLASS

Name	No.	Builders	Laid down	Launched	Commissioned
SWIFTSURE	S 126	Vickers Ltd (SB Group), Barrow	15 April 1969	7 Sep 1971	17 April 1973
SOVEREIGN	S 108	Vickers Ltd (SB Group), Barrow	17 Sep 1970	17 Feb 1973	11 July 1974
SUPERB	S 109	Vickers Ltd (SB Group), Barrow	16 Mar 1973	30 Nov 1974	1976
SCEPTRE	S 104	Vickers Ltd (SB Group), Barrow	25 Oct 1973	—	—
SPARTAN	S 111	Vickers Ltd (SB Group), Barrow	1974	—	—
SEVERN	S 112	Vickers Ltd (SB Group), Barrow	1976	—	—

Displacement, tons: 3 500 standard; 4 500 dived
Length, feet (metres): 272·0 *(82·9)*
Beam, feet (metres): 33·2 *(10·1)*
Draught, feet (metres): 27 *(8·2)*
Torpedo tubes: 5—21 in
Nuclear reactor: 1 pressurised water-cooled
Main machinery: English Electric geared steam turbines;
  1 shaft
Speed, knots: 30 dived
Complement: 97 (12 officers, 85 men)

In many respects similar to the "Valiant" class submarines
these are slightly shorter with the fore-planes set further forward and with one less torpedo tube. It is noticeable that whilst
Churchill took three years from the date of laying down to
commissioning the average now is about four years—over a
year longer than the time taken for the later boats of the

"Sturgeon" class in the USN. This much shorter building
period presumably results from a considerable and continuing
programme.

Design: The pressure hull in the "Swiftsures" maintains its
diameter for much greater length than previously. As a result
the fore-planes are mounted even further forward.

Engineering: Whilst the basic reactor design remains similar to
previous types core-life has probably increased.

Orders: *Swiftsure,* 3 Nov 1967; *Sovereign,* 16 May 1969;
Superb, 20 May 1970; *Sceptre,* 1 Nov 1971; *Spartan,* 17 Feb
1973; *Severn,* 1974.

Radar: Search; I-band.

Sonar: Type 2001 in "chin" position, Type 2007.

SOVEREIGN   9/1975, John G. Callis

SOVEREIGN   9/1975, John G. Callis

SUPERB   6/1976, Mod(N)

Fleet Submarines

5 "VALIANT" CLASS

Name	No.	Builders	Laid down	Launched	Commissioned
VALIANT	S 102	Vickers Ltd (SB Group), Barrow	22 Jan 1962	3 Dec 1963	18 July 1966
WARSPITE	S 103	Vickers Ltd (SB Group), Barrow	10 Dec 1963	25 Sep 1965	18 April 1967
CHURCHILL	S 46	Vickers Ltd (SB Group), Barrow	30 June 1967	20 Dec 1968	15 July 1970
CONQUEROR	S 48	Cammell Laird & Co Ltd, Birkenhead	5 Dec 1967	28 Aug 1969	9 Nov 1971
COURAGEOUS	S 50	Vickers Ltd (SB Group), Barrow	15 May 1968	7 Mar 1970	16 Oct 1971

Displacement, tons: 3 500 standard; 4 500 dived
Length, feet (metres): 285 *(86·9)*
Beam, feet (metres): 33·2 *(10·1)*
Draught, feet (metres): 27 *(8·2)*
Torpedo tubes: 6—21 in *(533 mm)*
Nuclear reactor: 1 pressurised water cooled
Main machinery: English Electric Geared steam turbines; 1 shaft
Speed, knots: 28 dived
Complement: 103 (13 officers, 90 men)

It was announced on 31 Aug 1960 that the contract for a second nuclear powered submarine *(Valiant)* had been awarded to Vickers Ltd, the principal sub-contractors being Vickers-Armstrong (Engineers) Ltd, for the machinery and its installation, and Rolls Royce and Associates for the nuclear steam raising plant. The class, of which she is the first, is broadly of the same design as that of *Dreadnought,* but slightly larger. She was originally scheduled to be completed in Sep 1965, but work was held up by the "Polaris" programme.

Orders: *Valiant,* 31 Aug 1960—*Warspite,* 12 Dec 1962—*Churchill,* 21 Oct 1965—*Conqueror,* 9 Aug 1966—*Courageous,* 1 Mar 1967.

Cost: Vary from £24 mill *(Warspite)* to £30 mill *(Conqueror).*

Endurance: On 25 April 1967 *Valiant* completed the 12 000-mile homeward voyage from Singapore, the record submerged passage by a British submarine, after 28 days non-stop.

Engineering: *Valiant's* reactor core was made in Great Britain, with machinery of British design and manufacture similar to the shore prototype installed in the Admiralty Reactor Test Establishment at Dounreay. The main steam turbines and condensers were designed and manufactured by the English Electric Company, Rugby, and the electrical propulsion machinery and control gear by Laurence, Scott & Electromotors Ltd.

Radar: Search; I-band.

Refits: *Conqueror* and *Courageous* refitting 1976.

Sonar: Type 2001 in "chin" position; Type 2007.

CHURCHILL 3/1976, MOD(N)

CONQUEROR 8/1975, C. and S. Taylor

1 NEW CONSTRUCTION

Name	No.	Builders	Laid down	Launched	Commissioned
—	S 113	Vickers Ltd (Shipbuilding Group), Barrow	? 1976	—	—

The first of an improved class of Fleet Submarines is due to be ordered in 1976.

1 "DREADNOUGHT" CLASS (FLEET SUBMARINE)

Name	No.	Builders	Laid down	Launched	Commissioned
DREADNOUGHT	S 101	Vickers-Armstrong, Barrow	12 June 1959	21 Oct 1960	17 April 1963

Displacement, tons: 3 000 standard; 3 500 surfaced; 4 000 dived
Length, feet (metres): 265·8 *(81·0)*
Beam, feet (metres): 32·2 *(9·8)*
Draught, feet (metres): 26 *(7·9)*
Torpedo tubes: 6—21 in *(533 mm)* (bow)
Nuclear reactor: 1 S5W pressurised water-cooled
Main machinery: Geared steam turbines; 1 shaft
Speed, knots: 28 dived
Complement: 88 (11 officers, 77 men)

As originally planned *Dreadnought* was to have been fitted with a British designed and built nuclear reactor, but in 1958 an agreement was concluded with the United States Government for the purchase of a complete set of propulsion machinery of the type fitted in USS *Skipjack*. This agreement enabled the submarine to be launched far earlier. The supply of this machinery was made under a contract between the Westinghouse Electric Corporation and Rolls-Royce. The latter were also supplied with design and manufacturing details of the reactor and with safety information and set up a factory in this country to manufacture similar cores. *Dreadnought* has a hull of British design both as regards structural strength and hydrodynamic features, although the latter are based on the pioneering work of the US Navy in *Skipjack* and *Albacore*. From about amidships aft, the hull lines closely resemble *Skipjack* to accommodate the propulsion machinery. The forward end is wholly British in concept. In the Control Room and Attack Centre the instruments are fitted into consoles.

The improved water distilling plant for the first time provides unlimited fresh water for shower baths and for washing machines in the fully equipped laundry.

She is fitted with an inertial navigation system and with means of measuring her depth below ice and was the first British submarine to surface at the North Pole, in 1970.

Radar: Search; I-band.

Sonar: Type 2001 in "chin" position; Type 2007.

DREADNOUGHT   *1974, Michael D. J. Lennon*

DREADNOUGHT   *1971, C. and S. Taylor*

Patrol Submarines

13 "OBERON" CLASS   6 "PORPOISE" CLASS

"OBERON" CLASS

Name	No.	Builders	Laid down	Launched	Commissioned
OBERON	S 09	HM Dockyard, Chatham	28 Nov 1957	18 July 1959	24 Feb 1961
OCELOT	S 17	HM Dockyard, Chatham	17 Nov 1960	5 May 1962	31 Jan 1964
ODIN	S 10	Cammell Laird & Co Ltd, Birkenhead	27 April 1959	4 Nov 1960	3 May 1962
OLYMPUS	S 12	Vickers-Armstrong Ltd, Barrow	4 Mar 1960	14 June 1961	7 July 1962
ONSLAUGHT	S 14	HM Dockyard, Chatham	8 April 1959	24 Sep 1960	14 Aug 1962
ONYX	S 21	Cammell Laird & Co Ltd, Birkenhead	16 Nov 1964	18 Aug 1966	20 Nov 1967
OPOSSUM	S 19	Cammell Laird & Co Ltd, Birkenhead	21 Dec 1961	23 May 1963	5 June 1964
OPPORTUNE	S 20	Scotts SB & Eng Co Ltd, Greenock	26 Oct 1962	14 Feb 1964	29 Dec 1964
ORACLE	S 16	Cammell Laird & Co Ltd, Birkenhead	26 April 1960	26 Sep 1961	14 Feb 1963
ORPHEUS	S 11	Vickers-Armstrong Ltd, Barrow	16 April 1959	17 Nov 1959	25 Nov 1960
OSIRIS	S 13	Vickers-Armstrong Ltd, Barrow	26 Jan 1962	29 Nov 1962	11 Jan 1964
OTTER	S 15	Scotts SB & Eng Co Ltd, Greenock	14 Jan 1960	15 May 1961	20 Aug 1962
OTUS	S 18	Scotts SB & Eng Co Ltd, Greenock	31 May 1961	17 Oct 1962	5 Oct 1963

"PORPOISE" CLASS

Name	No.	Builders	Laid down	Launched	Commissioned
CACHALOT	S 06	Scotts SB & Eng Co Ltd, Greenock	1 Aug 1955	11 Dec 1957	1 Sep 1959
FINWHALE	S 05	Cammell Laird & Co Ltd, Birkenhead	18 Sep 1956	21 July 1959	19 Aug 1960
NARWHAL	S 03	Vickers-Armstrong Ltd, Barrow	15 Mar 1956	25 Oct 1957	4 May 1959
PORPOISE	S 01	Vickers-Armstrong Ltd, Barrow	15 June1954	25 April1956	17 April 1958
SEALION	S 07	Cammell Laird & Co Ltd, Birkenhead	5 June1958	31 Dec 1959	25 July 1961
WALRUS	S 08	Scotts SB & Eng Co Ltd, Greenock	12 Feb 1958	22 Sep 1959	10 Feb 1961

Displacement, tons: 1 610 standard; 2 030 surfaced; 2 410 dived

Length, feet (metres): 241 *(73·5)* pp; 295·2 *(90·0)* oa

Beam, feet (metres): 26·5 *(8·1)*

Draught, feet (metres): 18 *(5·5)*

Torpedo tubes: 8—21 in *(533 mm)* (6 bow, 2 stern); 30 torpedoes carried

Main machinery: 2 Admiralty Standard Range 1, 16 VMS diesels; 3 680 bhp; 2 electric motors; 6 000 shp; 2 shafts

Speed, knots: 12 surfaced; 17 dived

Complement: 68 (6 officers, 62 men) in "Oberon" class
71 (6 officers, 65 men) in "Porpoise" class

As a result of the 1975 Defence Review the following have been retired some years before the end of hull life:—
Rorqual to disposal 1976
Grampus to reserve 1976, probably for disposal

Construction: For the first time in British submarines plastic was used in the superstructure construction of the "Oberon" class. Before and abaft the bridge the superstructure is mainly of glass fibre laminate in most units of this class. The superstructure of *Orpheus* is of light alloy aluminium.

Gunnery: "O" class submarines serving in the Far East carried a 20 mm Oerlikon gun during Indonesian Confrontation.

Modification: *Oberon* has been modified with deeper casing to house equipment for the initial training of personnel for nuclear powered submarines. Others of this class are currently undergoing modification.

Radar: Search; I-band.

Sonar: Types 186 and 187.

Transfer: The submarine of the Oberon class laid down on 27 Sep 1962 at HM Dockyard, Chatham, as *Onyx* for the Royal Navy was launched on 29 Feb 1964 as *Ojibwa* for the Royal Canadian Navy. She was replaced by another "Oberon" class submarine named *Onyx* for the Royal Navy built by Cammell Laird, Birkenhead.

OSIRIS   5/1975, C. and S. Taylor

ONSLAUGHT   10/1975, Dr Giorgio Arra

FINWHALE   10/1975, Wren Kathy Todd (MOD(N))

AMPHIBIOUS WARFARE FORCES

2 ASSAULT SHIPS (LPD)

Name	No.	Builders	Laid down	Launched	Commissioned
FEARLESS	L 10 (ex-L 3004)	Harland & Wolff Ltd, Belfast	25 July 1962	19 Dec 1963	25 Nov 1965
INTREPID	L 11 (ex-L 3005)	John Brown & Co (Clydebank) Ltd	19 Dec 1962	25 June1964	11 Mar 1967

Displacement, tons: 11 060 standard; 12 120 full load; 16 950 ballasted
Length, feet (metres): 500 *(152·4)* wl; 520 *(158·5)* oa
Beam, feet (metres): 80 *(24·4)*
Draught, feet (metres): 20·5 *(6·2)*
Draught, ballasted: 32 *(9·8)* aft; 23 *(7·0)* fwd; 27·5 *(8·4)* mean
Landing craft: 4 LCM(9) in dock; 4 LCVP at davits
Vehicles: Specimen load: 15 tanks, 7 three-ton and 20 quarter-ton trucks
Aircraft: Flight deck facilities for 5 Wessex helicopters
Missiles: 4 Seacat systems
Guns: 2—40 mm Bofors
Main engines: 2 EE turbines; 22 000 shp; 2 shafts
Boilers: 2 Babcock & Wilcox
Speed, knots: 21
Range, miles: 5 000 at 20 knots
Complement: 580 (see Troops note)

INTREPID

5/1975, Wright and Logan

These assault ships replace the former ships of the Amphibious Warfare Squadron. They carry landing craft which are floated through the open stern by flooding compartments of the ship and lowering her in the water; are able to deploy tanks, vehicles and men; have seakeeping qualities much superior to those of tank landing ships, and greater speed and range. Capable of operating independently. Another valuable feature is a helicopter platform which is also the deckhead of the dock from which the landing craft are floated out. Officially estimated building cost: *Fearless* £11 250 000; *Intrepid* £10 500 000.
Intrepid to reserve in 1976.

Countermeasures: Mount 2 Knebworth Corvus launchers.

Electrical: Power at 440V 60c/s 3-phase a/c is supplied by four 1 000 kW AE1 turbo-alternators.

Electronics: Fitted with CAAIS.

Engineering: The two funnels are staggered across the beam of the ship, indicating that the engines and boilers are arranged *en echelon,* two machinery spaces having one turbine and one boiler installed in each space. The turbines were manufactured by the English Electric Co, Rugby, the gearing by David Brown & Co, Huddersfield. Boilers work at a pressure of 550 lbs per sq in and a temperature of 850 deg F. Two 5-bladed propellers, 12·5 feet diameter, 200 rpm in *Fearless.*

Operational: Each ship is fitted out as a Naval Assault Group/Brigade Headquarters with an Assault Operations Room from which naval and military personnel, can mount and control the progress of an assault operation.

Radar: Air and surface search: One Type 993.
Navigation: One Type 975.

Satellite system: The Royal Navy fitted its first operational satellite communications system in *Intrepid* in 1969, the contract having been awarded to Plessey Radar—now removed.

Training: *Fearless* used for the sea training of officers from the Britannia Royal Naval College, Dartmouth, retaining full amphibious capabilities.

Troops: Each ship can carry 380 to 400 troops at ship's company standards, and an overload of 700 marines and military personnel can be accommodated for short periods.

FEARLESS

8/1975, C. and S. Taylor

INTREPID flooded down

1973, C. and S. Taylor

6 LOGISTIC LANDING SHIPS
(RFA MANNED)

Name	No.	Builders	Laid down	Launched	Commissioned
SIR LANCELOT	L 3029	Fairfield	Mar 1962	June1963	Jan 1964
SIR GALAHAD	L 3005	Alex Stephen	Feb 1965	19 April1966	17 Dec 1966
SIR GERAINT	L 3027	Alex Stephen	June 1965	26 Jan 1967	12 July 1967
SIR BEDIVERE	L 3004	Hawthorn Leslie	Oct 1965	20 July 1966	18 May 1967
SIR PERCIVALE	L 3036	Hawthorn Leslie	April 1966	4 Oct 1967	23 Mar 1968
SIR TRISTRAM	L 3505	Hawthorn Leslie	Feb 1966	12 Dec 1966	14 Sep 1967

Displacement, tons: 3 270 light; 5 674 full load (3 370 and 5 550 in *Sir Lancelot*)
Dimensions, feet (metres): 366·3 pp; 412·1 oa × 59·8 × 13·0 (120; 135·1 × 19·6 × 4·3)
Guns: Fitted for 2—40 mm—not normally carried
Main engines: 2 Mirrlees Diesels; 9 400 bhp; 2 shafts; (2 Denny/Sulzer diesels; 9 520 bhp in *Sir Lancelot*)
Speed, knots: 17
Oil fuel, tons: 815
Range, miles: 8 000 at 15 knots
Complement: 68 (18 officers, 50 ratings)
Military lift: 340

Sir Lancelot was the prototype of this class which was originally built for the Army but transferred to RFA in Jan and Mar 1970. Fitted for bow and stern loading with drive-through facilities and deck-to-deck ramps. Facilities provided for on-board maintenance of vehicles and for laying out pontoon equipment.

Aircraft: Helicopters can be operated from the well-deck and the after platform by day or night in the later ships. In *Sir Lancelot* well-deck operations are limited to fair weather-day conditions. If required to carry helicopters 11 can be stowed on the Tank Deck and 9 on the Vehicle Deck.

SIR BEDIVERE   6/1975, C. and S. Taylor

SIR PERCIVALE   7/1975, C. and S. Taylor

14 LCM (9) TYPE

Name	No.	Builders	Commissioned
—	L 700	Brooke Marine Ltd	1964
—	L 701	Brooke Marine Ltd	1964
—	L 702	Brooke Marine Ltd	1965
—	L 703	Brooke Marine Ltd	1965
—	L 704	R. Dunston (Thorne)	1964
—	L 705	R. Dunston (Thorne)	1965
—	L 706	R. Dunston (Thorne)	1965
—	L 707	R. Dunston (Thorne)	1965
—	L 708	R. Dunston (Thorne)	1966
—	L 709	R. Dunston (Thorne)	1966
—	L 710	J. Bolson (Poole)	1965
—	L 711	J. Bolson (Poole)	1965
—	L 3507	Vosper Ltd	1963
—	L 3508	Vosper Ltd	1963

Displacement, tons: 75 light; 176 loaded
Dimensions, feet (metres): 85 oa × 21·5 × 5·5 (25·7 × 6·5 × 1·7)
Capacity: 2 tanks or 100 tons of vehicles
Main engines: 2 Paxman 6 cyl YHXAM diesels; 2 shafts; 624 bhp = 10 knots. Screws enclosed in Kort nozzles to improve manoeuvrability

LCM (9) 3507 and LCM (9) 3508 were the first operational minor landing craft to be built since the Second World War. Ramped in the traditional manner forward, a completely enclosed radar-fitted wheelhouse is positioned aft. Upon completion they carried out familiarisation trials to perfect the new techniques required in launching and recovering LCMs from the flooded sterns of the parent assault ships. Now operated by RCT. Four each of the 700 Series allocated to assault ships.

LCM 707 (HMS *Intrepid*)   5/1975, Wright and Logan

LCM 3507 (RCT)   4/1975, John G. Callis

2 LOGISTIC LANDING CRAFT (RCT)

Name	No.	Builders	Commissioned
ARDENNES	L 4001	Brooke Marine, Lowestoft	1977
—	L 4002	Brooke Marine, Lowestoft	—

Displacement, tons: 870 standard; 1 413 full load
Dimensions, feet (metres): 237·5 oa × 46 × 5·8 (72·4 × 14 × 1·8)
Main engines: 2 diesels; 2 000 bhp = 10·3 knots
Range, miles: 4 000 at 10 knots
Complement: 35 (plus 34 troops)

Ordered in October 1974. *Ardennes* laid down 27 Aug 1975.

2 LCM (7)

7037   7100

Displacement, tons: 28 light; 63 loaded
Dimensions, feet (metres): 60·2 × 16 × 3·7 (18·4 × 4·9 × 1·2)
Main engines: 290 bhp = 9·8 knots

Employed as naval servicing boats and store carriers. Re-engined with Gray Marine diesels.

AVON RPL 01
BUDE RPL 02
CLYDE RPL 03
DART RPL 04
EDEN RPL 05
FORTH RPL 06

GLEN RPL 07
HAMBLE RPL 08
KENNET RPL 10
LODDON RPL 11
MEDWAY RPL 12

Diesel-driven LCMs manned by RCT and available for short coastal hauls.

11 LCM (RCT)

AVON

10/1973, John G. Callis

3 LCP (L) (3)

LCP (L) (3) 501, 503, 556

Displacement, tons: 6·5 light; 10 loaded
Dimensions, feet (metres): 37 × 11 × 3·2 *(11·3 × 3·4 × 1)*
Main engines: 225 bhp = 12 knots

**LCVP (1) 102, 112, 118, 120, 123, 127, 128, 134, 136
LCVP (2) 142-149
LCVP (3) 150-158**

Displacement, tons: 8·5 light; 13·5 full load
Dimensions, feet (metres): 41·5 (LCVP (2)); 43 (LCVP (3)) × 10 × 2·5 *(12·7; 13·1 × 3·1 × 0·8)*
Main engines: 130 bhp = 8 knots; 2 Foden diesels; 200 bhp = 10 knots (LCVP (2))

26 LCVP (1) (2) and (3)

LCVP (2)s carried by *Intrepid* and *Fearless* can carry 35 troops or 2 Land Rovers. Crew 4. LCA (2)s were redesignated LCVPs (Landing Craft Vehicle and Personnel) in 1966.
There were also a number of variations and prototypes of about the same length (43 feet).

Note: Raiding Landing Craft, including LCR 5507 and 5508, and Navigational Landing Craft, including LCN 604 (ex-LCR 5505).

3 LCT (8) TYPE (RCT)

ABBEVILLE L 4041
AGHEILA L 4002
AUDEMER L 4061

Displacement, tons: 657 light; 895 to 1 017 loaded
Dimensions, feet (metres): 231·2 oa × 39 × 3·2 forward; 5 aft *(70·5 × 11·9 × 1 forward; 1·8 aft)*
 Beaching draughts
Main engines: 4 Paxman engines; 1 840 bhp = 12·6 knots
Complement: 33 to 37

All transferred to the Army's Royal Corps of Transport from the Royal Navy. Originally nine of these ships were operated by the RCT.

AGHEILA

5/1975, C. and S. Taylor

1 LST (3) (RFA)

EMPIRE GULL (ex-*Trouncer*) L 3513

Measurement, tons: 4 257·9 gross
Dimensions, feet (metres): 347 × 54·1 × 12 *(105·8 × 16·5 × 3·7)*
Main engines: 2 Triple Expansion; 2 shafts; 5 500 shp
Boilers: 2 Water Tube
Oil fuel, tons: 950
Complement: 63 officers and men
Troop accommodation: 8 officers, 72 ORs

Launched 9 July 1945.

EMPIRE GULL

4/1975, John G. Callis

HELICOPTER SUPPORT SHIP

Name	No.	Builders	Commissioned
ENGADINE	K 08	Henry Robb Ltd, Leith	15 Dec 1967

Displacement, tons: 8 000 full load
Measurement, tons: 6 384 gross; 2 848 net
Dimensions, feet (metres): 424·0 oa × 58·4 × 22·1 *(129·3 × 17·8 × 6·7)*
Aircraft: 4 Wessex and 2 Wasp or 2 Sea King helicopters
Main engines: 1 Sulzer two stroke, 5 cyl turbocharged 5RD68 diesel; 5 500 bhp = 16 knots
Complement: RFA: 63 (15 officers, 48 men); RN: 14 (2 officers, 12 ratings)
 Accommodation for a further RN 113 (29 officers and 84 ratings)

Projected under the 1964-65 Navy Estimates. Ordered on 18 Aug 1964. Laid down on 9 Aug 1965. Officially named on 15 Sep 1966. Accepted into service on 15 Dec 1967. Largest ship then built by the company. Intended for the training of helicopter crews in deep water operations. She does not carry her own flight but embarks aircraft as necessary. Fitted with Denny Brown stabilisers, the only RFA vessel so equipped.

ENGADINE

10/1975, MOD(N)

MINE WARFARE FORCES

Name	No.	Builders	Commissioned
ABDIEL	N 21	John I. Thornycroft Ltd, Woolston, Southampton	17 Oct 1967

Displacement, tons: 1 375 standard; 1 500 full load
Dimensions, feet (metres): 244·5 pp; 265 oa × 38·5 × 10 *(80·2; 86·8 × 12·6 × 3·3)*
Mines: 44 carried
Main engines: 2 Paxman Ventura 16 cyl pressure charged diesels; 1 250 rpm; 2 690 bhp = 16 knots
Complement: 77

Exercise minelayer ordered in June 1965. Laid down on 23 May 1966. Launched on 27 Jan 1967. Completed on 17 Oct 1967. Main machinery manufactured by Davey Paxman, Colchester. Main gearing supplied by Messrs Wisemans. Her function is to support mine countermeasure forces, maintain these forces when they are operating away from their shore bases and minelaying. Cost £1 500 000.

ABDIEL   *9/1975, John G. Callis*

0 + 2 "BRECON" CLASS
(MINESWEEPERS/MINEHUNTERS—COASTAL)

Name	No.	Builders	Commissioned
BRECON	—	Vosper-Thornycroft Ltd.	1978
—	—	Yarrow Ltd	—

Displacement, tons: 615 standard; 725 full load
Dimensions, feet (metres): 197 × 32·3 × 7·3 *(60 × 9·9 × 2·2)*
Main engines: 2 Diesels; 3 540 bhp = 17 knots
Complement: 45

A new class of MCM Vessels combining both hunting and sweeping capabilities. The cost of these ships is likely to be in the region of £4-5 million. Will be fitted with the French PAP mine destructor. Second ship ordered 1976.

Artist's Impression of "BRECON" Class   *1974, MOD (N)*

1 MINESWEEPER/MINEHUNTER (COASTAL)

Name	No.	Builders	Commissioned
WILTON	M 1116	Vosper Thornycroft, Woolston	14 July 1973

Displacement, tons: 450 standard
Dimensions, feet (metres): 153·0 oa × 28·8 × 8·5 *(46·3 × 8·8 × 2·5)*
Gun: 1—40 mm Mark VII
Main engines: 2 English Electric Deltic 18 diesels; 2 shafts; 3 000 bhp = 16 knots
Complement: 37 (5 officers and 32 ratings)

The world's first GRP warship. Contract signed on 11 Feb 1970. Laid down 16 Nov 1970 and launched on 18 Jan 1972. Prototype built of glass reinforced plastic to the existing minehunter design by Vosper Thornycroft at Woolston. Similar to the "Ton" class and fitted with reconditioned machinery and equipment from the scrapped *Derriton*.

WILTON (in Suez Canal)   *8/1974, S. Taylor*

36 "TON" CLASS

15 MINEHUNTERS

Name	No.	Builders	Commissioned
BILDESTON	M 1110	J. S. Doig (Grimsby) Ltd	28 April 1953
BOSSINGTON	M 1133	J. I. Thornycroft & Co, Southampton	11 Dec 1956
BRERETON	M 1113	Richards Ironworks	9 July 1954
BRINTON	M 1114	Cook Welton and Gemmell	4 Mar 1954
BRONINGTON	M 1115	Cook Welton and Gemmell	4 June 1954
GAVINGTON	M 1140	J. S. Doig (Grimsby) Ltd	14 July 1954
HUBBERSTON	M 1147	Fleetlands Shipyards Ltd, London	14 Oct 1955
IVESTON	M 1151	Philip & Sons Ltd, Dartmouth	29 June 1955
KEDLESTON	M 1153	William Pickersgill & Son	2 July 1955
KELLINGTON	M 1154	William Pickersgill & Son	4 Nov 1955
KIRKLISTON	M 1157	Harland & Wolff Ltd, Belfast	21 Aug 1954
MAXTON	M 1165	Harland & Wolff Ltd, Belfast	19 Feb 1957
NURTON	M 1166	Harland & Wolff Ltd, Belfast	21 Aug 1957
SHERATON	M 1181	White's Shipyard Ltd, Southampton	24 Aug 1956
SHOULTON	M 1182	Montrose Shipyard Ltd	16 Nov 1955

12 MINESWEEPERS—CCASTAL

Name	No.	Builders	Commissioned
CUXTON	M 1125	Camper and Nicholson	1953
GLASSERTON	M 1141	J. S. Doig (Grimsby) Ltd	31 Dec 1954
HIGHBURTON	M 1130	J. I. Thornycroft & Co, Southampton	8 June 1955
LALESTON	M 1158	Harland and Wolff	1954
LEWISTON	M 1208	Herd & Mackenzie, Buckie, Banff	16 June 1960
SHAVINGTON	M 1180	White's Shipyard Ltd, Southampton	1 Mar 1956
STUBBINGTON	M 1204	Camper & Nicholsons Ltd, Gosport	30 July 1957
SOBERTON	M 1200	Fleetlands Shipyards Ltd, Gosport	17 Sep 1957
UPTON	M 1187	J. I. Thornycroft & Co, Southampton	24 July 1956
WALKERTON	M 1188	J. I. Thornycroft & Co, Southampton	10 Jan 1958
WOTTON	M 1195	Philip & Sons Ltd, Dartmouth	13 June 1957
WOOLASTON	M 1194	Herd and Mackenzie, Buckie, Banff	10 Oct 1958

9 MINESWEEPERS—COASTAL (RNR)

Name	No.	Builders	Commissioned
CLYDE (ex-Repton)	M 1167	Harland & Wolff Ltd, Belfast	12 Dec 1957
CURZON (ex-Fittleton)	M 1136	White's Shipyard Ltd, Southampton	28 Jan 1955
KILLIECRANKIE (ex-Bickington)	M 1109	White's Shipyard Ltd, Southampton	27 May 1954
KILMOREY (ex-Alfriston)	M 1103	J. I. Thornycroft & Co, Southampton	16 Mar 1954
MERSEY (ex-Pollington)	M 1173	Camper & Nicholsons Ltd, Gosport	5 Sep 1958
NORTHUMBRIA (ex-Wiston)	M 1205	Wivenhoe Shipyard Ltd, Wivenhoe	17 Feb 1960
ST. DAVID (ex-Crichton)	M 1124	J. S. Doig (Grimsby) Ltd	23 April 1954
SOLENT (ex-Crofton)	M 1216	J. I. Thornycroft & Co, Southampton	26 Aug 1958
VENTURER (ex-Hodgeston)	M 1146	Fleetlands Shipyards Ltd, London	17 Dec 1954

Displacement, tons: 360 standard; 425 full load
Dimensions, feet (metres): 140·0 pp; 153·0 oa × 28·8 × 8·2 (42·7; 46·3 × 8·8 × 2·5)
Guns: Vary in different ships, some sweepers having no 40 mm, some 1—40 mm whilst hunters have 1 or 2—40 mm; 2—20 mm
Main engines: 2 diesels; 2 shafts; 2 500 bhp (JVSS 12 Mirrlees), 3 000 bhp (18A-7A Deltic)
Speed, knots: 15
Oil fuel, tons: 45
Range, miles: 2 300 at 13 knots
Complement: 29 (38 in minehunters, 5 officers and 33 ratings)

The survivors of a class of 118 built between 1953 and 1960, largely as a result of lessons from the Korean War. John I. Thornycroft & Co Ltd, Southampton were the lead yard for these ships which have double mahogany hull and incorporate a considerable amount of non-magnetic material. Fitted with Vospers stabilisers. The majority has now been fitted with nylon in place of copper sheathing. *Cuxton* commissioned finally in Oct 1975 after 22 years in "moth-balls".

Appearance: Enclosed bridges in *Bildeston, Brereton, Brinton, Iveston, Kellington, Kirkliston, Lewiston, Solent, Bossington, Bronington, Clyde, Gavington, Hubberston, Kedleston, Maxton, Mersey, Northumbria, Nurton, Sheraton, Shoulton, Soberton, Stubbington, Walkerton.*

Conversions: *Beachampton, Monkton, Wasperton, Wolverton* and *Yarnton* were converted into coastal patrol vessels late in 1971, (see Lights Forces). *Laleston* was converted into diving trials ship in 1966-67. *Walkerton* used by Dartmouth RN College as Navigation Training Ship, to be relieved by *Alfriston* in early 1977. *Shoulton* was the original minehunter conversion, fitted with pump-jet and bow thruster.

Engineering: Earlier vessels had Mirrlees diesels, but later units had Napier Deltic lightweight diesels. *Highburton,* the first with Deltic diesels, was accepted on 21 April 1955. All minehunters have Deltics and active rudders. Generators for electrical power are in a separate engine room in Mirrlees, Deltic-conversions and minehunters. Deltic built minesweepers have a generator in the main engine-room and two generators in the generator-room. Mirrlees still fitted in *Glasserton, Laleston, Cuxton* and *Clyde.* Three-bladed propellers, 6 ft diameter, 400 rpm. *Shoulton,* refitted 1965-67, has pump-jet propulsion.

Fishery protection: Carried out by *Brereton, Brinton, Highburton, Kedleston, Shavington, Soberton. Cuxton* and *Stubbington* refitting for Fishery Duties. *Highburton* due for disposal 1976.

Osbourne sweep: *Glasserton* is fitted with derricks for Osbourne sweep. *Highburton* used in initial trials.

Royal Naval Reserve: Eleven units were renamed and attached to Royal Naval Reserve Division Headquarters as follows (Division under *Name*):—

Thames	Curzon	Solent	Venturer	St. David	Mersey
London	Sussex	Solent	Severn	S. Wales	Mersey
Kilmorey	Clyde	Montrose	Killiecrankie	Northumbria	
Ulster	Clyde	Tay	Forth	Tyne	

It is intended to reduce the total to six in the future. *Kellington* and *Upton* are to be transferred to the RNR to replace withdrawals.

Transfers: Argentine (6 in 1968), Australia (6 in 1962), Ghana (1 in 1964), India (4 in 1956), Ireland (3 in 1971), Malaysia (7 in 1960-68), South Africa (10 in 1958-59).

CURZON (ex-*Fittleton*) (Sussex RNR)   6/1975, John G. Callis

NURTON (Minehunter with 40 mm gun)   10/1975, Dr. Giorgio Arra

GLASSERTON (Sweeper—Osbourne and no 40 mm gun)   12/1975, MOD(N)

SHOULTON (Minehunter with no 40 mm gun)   1973, C. and S. Taylor

CUXTON (Sweeper with 40 mm gun)   10/1975, MOD(N)

LEWISTON (Sweeper with 40 mm gun)   5/1975, C. and S. Taylor

4 "HAM" CLASS (MINESWEEPERS—INSHORE)

Name	No.	Builders	Commissioned
ARLINGHAM	M 2603	Camper and Nicholson	1953
DITTISHAM	M 2621	Fairlie Yacht Slip	1954
FLINTHAM	M 2628	Bolson & Co	1955
THORNHAM (Aberdeen)	M 2793	Taylor, Shoreham	1957

Displacement, tons: 120 standard; 159 full load
Dimensions, feet (metres): 2601 Series: 100 pp; 106·5 oa × 21·2 × 5·5 (30·5; 32·4 × 6·5 × 1·7).
2793 Series: 100 pp; 107·5 oa × 22 × 5·8 (30·5; 32·1 × 6·6 × 1·8)
Gun: 1—20 mm Oerlikon forward
Main engines: 2 Paxman diesels; 1 100 bhp = 14 knots
Oil fuel, tons: 15
Complement: 15 (2 officers, 13 ratings)

DITTISHAM   1973, John G. Callis

The first inshore minesweeper, *Inglesham*, was launched by J. Samuel White & Co Ltd, Cowes, on 23 April 1952. The 2601 series were of composite construction. In all 95 of this class were built.
Arlingham is permanent guardship at Gibraltar. Due for disposal 1976. *Thornham* attached to Aberdeen University RNU.

Transfers: Australia (3 in 1966-68), France (15 in 1954-55), Ghana (2 in 1959), India (2 in 1955), Libya (2 in 1963), Malaysia (4 in 1958-59), South Yemen (3 in 1967). Ships subsequently returned are not listed.

2 "LEY" CLASS M 2001 SERIES (MINEHUNTERS—INSHORE)

Name	No.	Builders	Commissioned
AVELEY	M 2002	J. S. White & Co Ltd, Cowes	1953
ISIS (ex-*Cradley*)	M 2010	Saunders Roe Ltd	1955

Displacement, tons: 123 standard; 164 full load
Dimensions, feet (metres): 100 pp; 107 oa × 21·8 × 5·5 (30·5; 32·3 × 6·5 × 1·7)
Gun: 1—40 mm or 1—20 mm (forward)
Main engines: 2 Paxman diesels; 700 bhp = 13 knots
Complement: 15 (2 officers, 13 ratings)

The "Ley" class, originally of ten ships, differed from the "Ham" class. They were of composite (non-magnetic metal and wooden) construction, instead of all wooden construction. Their superstructure and other features also differed. They had no winch or sweeping gear, as they were minehunters, not sweepers. *Aveley* is attached to Plymouth. *Isis*, renamed in 1963, was transferred to Southampton University RNU on 1 April 1974.

ISIS   5/1975, C. and S. Taylor

MAINTENANCE SHIPS

Name	No.	Builders	Laid down	Launched	Commissioned
TRIUMPH	A 108 (ex-R 16)	R & W Hawthorn Leslie, Hebburn	27 Jan 1943	2 Oct 1944	9 April 1946

Displacement, tons: 13 500 standard; 17 500 full load
Length, feet (metres): 630·0 (192·0) pp; 650·0 (198·1) wl; 699·0 (213·1) oa
Beam, feet (metres): 80·0 (24·4)
Draught, feet (metres): 23·7 (7·2)
Width, feet (metres): 112·5 (34·3) overall
Aircraft: 3 helicopters in flight deck hangar
Guns: 4—40 mm; 3 saluting
Main engines: Parsons geared turbines; 2 shafts; 40 000 shp
Boilers: 4 Admiralty 3-drum type
  Pressure 400 psi (28·1 kg/cm²)
  Temperature 700°F (371°C)
Speed, knots: 24·25
Oil fuel, tons: 3 000
Range, miles: 10 000 at 14 knots; 5 500 at full speed
Complement: 500 (27 officers, 473 men) plus 285 (15 officers, 270 men) on maintenance staff

TRIUMPH   9/1974, Dr Giorgio Arra

Originally an aircraft carrier of the "Colossus" class. Converted for present role at a cost of £10·2 mill. at Portsmouth between 1958 and 1965. Now in reserve at Chatham in preservation.

1 "HEAD" CLASS

Name	No.	Builders	Laid down	Launched	Commissioned
RAME HEAD	A 134	Burrard DD Co, Vancouver	12 July 1944	22 Nov 1944	18 Aug 1945

Displacement, tons: 9 000 standard; 11 270 full load
Length, feet (metres): 416·0 (126·8) pp; 441·5 (134·6) oa
Beam, feet (metres): 57·5 (17·5)
Draught, feet (metres): 22·5 (6·9)
Guns: 11—40 mm

Main engines: Triple expansion; 2 500 ihp
Boilers: 2 Foster Wheeler
Speed, knots: 10 approx
Oil fuel, tons: 1 600 capacity
Complement: 425

Escort Maintenance Ship. In reserve in 1972. Accommodation ship at Londonderry.

ROYAL YACHT

Name	No.	Builders	Laid down	Launched	Commissioned
BRITANNIA	A 00	John Brown & Co Ltd, Clydebank	July 1952	16 April 1953	14 Jan 1954

Displacement, tons: 3 990 light; 4 961 full load
Measurement, tons: 5 769 gross
Dimensions, feet (metres): 360·0 pp; 380·0 wl; 412·2 oa × 55·0 × 17·0 (109·8; 115·9; 125·7 × 16·8 × 5·2)
Main engines: Single reduction geared turbines; 2 shafts; 12 000 shp = 21 knots
Boilers: 2
Oil fuel, tons: 330 (490 with auxiliary fuel tanks)
Range, miles: 2 100 at 20 knots; 2 400 at 18 knots; 3 000 at 15 knots
Complement: 270

Designed as a medium sized naval hospital ship for use by Her Majesty The Queen in peacetime as the Royal Yacht. Construction conformed to mercantile practice. Fitted with Denny-Brown single fin stabilisers to reduce roll in bad weather from 20 deg to 6 deg. Cost £2 098 000. To pass under the bridges of the St. Lawrence Seaway when she visited Canada, the top 20 feet of her mainmast and the radio aerial on her foremast were hinged in Nov 1958 so that they could be lowered as required.

BRITANNIA   8/1975, C. and S. Taylor

SUBMARINE DEPOT SHIPS

Name	No.	Builders	Laid down	Launched	Commissioned
FORTH	A 187	John Brown, Clydebank	30 June1937	11 Aug 1938	14 May 1939
MAIDSTONE	A 185	John Brown, Clydebank	17 Aug 1936	21 Oct 1937	5 May 1938

Displacement, tons: 10 000 standard; 13 000 full load
Length, feet (metres): 497·0 *(151·5)* pp; 531·0 *(161·8)* oa
Beam, feet (metres): 73·0 *(22·3)*
Draught, feet (metres): 21·2 *(6·5)*
Guns: 5—40 mm Bofors
Main engines: Geared turbines (Brown Curtis in *Forth;* Parsons in *Maidstone);* 2 shafts; 7 000 shp
Boilers: 4 Admiralty 3-drum type
Speed, knots: 16
Oil fuel, tons: 2 300
Complement: 695 (45 officers and 650 men)
   Accommodation for 1 159 (119 officers and 1 040 men)

Equipment includes foundry, coppersmiths', plumbers', carpenters'; heavy and light machine, electrical and torpedo repair shops and plant for charging submarine batteries. Designed for maintaining nine operational submarines, and supplying over 140 torpedoes and a similar number of mines. Repair facilities on board for all purposes in attached submarines, and extensive diving and salvage equipment. There are steam laundry, hospital, chapel, two canteens, bakery, barber shops, operating theatre and dental surgery.
In Oct 1969, *Maidstone* was restored and recommissioned as an accommodation ship for 2 000 troops and sent to Belfast.

As the Fleet Maintenance Base, Devonport and parent ship of the 2nd Submarine Squadron *Forth* is the depot ship of HMS *Defiance.*

Reconstruction: *Maidstone* was extensively reconstructed in HM Dockyard, Portsmouth in 1958-62 as support ship for nuclear powered submarines with a lattice foremast and additional superstructure amidships. *Forth* was similarly modernised and converted into a support ship for nuclear powered submarines in HM Dockyard Chatham, in 1962-66.

FORTH   1973, John G. Callis

ICE PATROL SHIP

Name	No.	Builders	Laid down	Launched	Commissioned
ENDURANCE (ex-*Anita Dan)*	A 171	Krögerwerft, Rendsburg	1955	May 1956	Dec 1956

Displacement, tons: 3 600
Measurement, tons: 2 641 gross
Length, feet (metres): 273·5 *(89·7)* pp; 300 *(91·44)* oa; 305 *(92·96);* including helicopter deck extension
Beam, feet (metres): 46 *(14·02)*
Draught, feet (metres): 18 *(5·5)*
Aircraft: 2 Whirlwind Mk IX helicopters
Guns: 2—20 mm
Main engines: 1 B & W 550 VTBF diesel; 3 220 ihp; 1 shaft
Speed, knots: 14·5
Range, miles: 12 000 at 14·5 knots
Complement: 119 (13 officers, 106 men, including a small Royal Marine detachment) plus 12 spare berths for scientists

Purchased from J. Lauritzen Lines, Copenhagen (announced on 20 Feb 1967). Strengthened for operation in ice. Converted by Harland & Wolff, Belfast 1967-68 into an ice patrol ship for southern waters to replace *Protector,* undertaking hydrographic and oceanographic surveys and acting as support ship for the British Antarctic Survey and guard vessel. Original cost £1·8 million.
An unusual feature for one of HM ships is her hull painted a vivid red for easy identification in the ice.

ENDURANCE   3/1976, MOD(N)

HOVERCRAFT

Notes: (a) The RN Hovercraft Trials Unit was established at Lee-on-the-Solent in 1974.
(b) 1 "Mountbatten" class large hovercraft chartered by MOD in 1976.

2 WINCHESTER (SRN-6) TYPE

Displacement, tons: 10 normal gross weight
Dimensions, feet (metres): 48·4 × 23·0 × 15·0 oa (height); 4·0 (skirt) *(14·8 × 7 × 4·6; 1·3)*
Main engines: 1 Rolls Royce Gnome gas turbine; 900 shp = 50 knots
Range, miles: 200

Modified with radar and military communications equipment for its primary role of a fast amphibious communication craft to support Royal Marine units.

SRN6   1971

1 WELLINGTON (BHN7) TYPE

Displacement, tons: 50 max weight; 33 light
Dimensions, feet (metres): 78·3 × 45·5 × 34·0 oa (height); 5·5 (skirt) *(23·9 × 13 × 10·4; 1·7)*
Main engines: 1 Rolls Royce Proteus gas turbine; 4 250 shp = 60 knots
Complement: 14 plus trials crew

First "hover warship" costing about £700 000, delivered to the inter-Service Hovercraft Trials Unit at the Royal Naval Air Station, Lee-on-Solent, in April 1970. She could be used as a missile armed fast patrol craft or amphibious assault craft. Winter trials in Swedish waters in Feb 1972. Records established: longest open sea voyage, furthest north, and sustained speeds of over 55 knots in the Baltic.

1 SRN-5 TYPE

This small hovercraft is used for crew training.

BHN7 Hovercraft

1975, J. P. Thompson

CHARTER

The Vosper Thornycroft VT2 helicopter is to be chartered for trials in 1976 by MOD.

DIVING SHIP

Name	No.	Builders	Commissioned
RECLAIM (ex-*Salverdant*)	A 231	Wm Simons & Co Ltd, Renfrew	Oct 1948

Displacement, tons: 1 200 standard; 1 800 full load
Dimensions, feet (metres): 200 pp; 217·8 oa × 38 × 15·5 *(61; 66·4 × 11·6 × 4·7)*
Main engines: Triple expansion; 2 shafts; 1 500 ihp = 12 knots
Oil fuel, tons: 310
Range, miles: 3 000
Complement: 100

Engined by Aitchison Blair Ltd. Laid down on 9 April 1946. Launched on 12 Mar 1948. Construction based on the design of a "King Salvor" class naval ocean salvage vessel. First deep diving and submarine rescue vessel built as such for the Royal Navy. Fitted with sonar, radar, echo-sounding apparatus for detection of sunken wrecks, and equipped for submarine rescue work. Due for replacement although no decision yet made concerning her successor.

RECLAIM

5/1975, C. and S. Taylor

LIGHT FORCES

(See Deletion List for "Dark" and "Brave" Classes).
(See last page of UK for "Alert" patrol craft and "Jura" photo).

1 OFFSHORE PATROL CRAFT

Name	No.	Builders	Commissioned
JURA	P 296	Hall Russell & Co	1973

Displacement, tons: 1 285 full load
Dimensions, feet (metres): 195·3 × 35 × 14·4 *(64 × 11·7 × 4·7)*
Gun: 1—40 mm
Main engines: 2 Polar diesels; 1 shaft; 4 200 bhp = 17 knots
Complement: 28

Owing to a lack of suitable ships or the numbers required for oil-rig patrols etc. *Jura* was chartered by the MOD from the Scottish Home Department in 1975 to whom she will be returned when *Jersey* commissions.

5 "ISLAND" CLASS (OFFSHORE PATROL CRAFT)

Name	No.	Builders	Commissioned
GUERNSEY	P 297	Hall Russell & Co Ltd	1976
JERSEY	P 295	Hall Russell & Co Ltd	1976
LINDISFARNE	P 300	Hall Russell & Co Ltd	1977
ORKNEY	P 299	Hall Russell & Co Ltd	1977
SHETLAND	p 298	Hall Russell & Co Ltd	1977

Displacement, tons: 925 standard; 1 250 full load
Dimensions, feet (metres): 195·3 oa × 35·8 × 14 *(59·6 × 10·9 × 4·3)*
Gun: 1—40 mm
Main engines: 2 diesels; 1 shaft; 4 380 hp = 16 knots
Range, miles: 7 000 at 15 knots
Complement: 24

Order announced 11 Feb 1975, to be in service 1976-77. *Jersey* launched 18 Mar 1976. Can handle a helicopter and carry small RM detachment.

JERSEY at launching

3/1976, Studio Morgan, Aberdeen

4 "BIRD" CLASS (LARGE PATROL CRAFT)

Name	No.	Builders	Commissioned
CYGNET	P 261	R. Dunston Ltd, Hessle	1976
KINGFISHER	P 260	R. Dunston Ltd, Hessle	8 Oct 1975
PETEREL	P 262	R. Dunston Ltd, Hessle	1976
SANDPIPER	P 263	R. Dunston Ltd, Hessle	1977

Displacement, tons: 190
Dimensions, feet (metres): 120 oa × 21·8 × 6·5 *(36·6 × 6·6 × 2)*
Guns: 2—40 mm; 2 MG
Main engines: 2 Ruston diesels; 3 750 bhp = 25 knots
Oil fuel, tons: 35
Complement: 24

Of similar type to "Seal" class RAF rescue launches with improved sea-keeping qualities and fitted with stabilisers. To be used initially for coastal Fishery Protection duties. *Kingfisher* launched 20 Sep 1974. *Cygnet* laid down June 1975 and launched 6 Oct 1975. *Peterel* was launched 14 May 1976.

KINGFISHER   10/1975, MOD(N)

3 FAST TRAINING BOATS

Name	No.	Builders	Commissioned
CUTLASS	P 274	Vosper Thornycroft Group, Porchester Shipyard	12 Nov 1970
SABRE	P 275	Vosper Thornycroft Group, Porchester Shipyard	5 Mar 1971
SCIMITAR	P 271	Vosper Thornycroft Group, Porchester Shipyard	19 July 1970

Displacement, tons: 102 full load
Dimensions, feet (metres): 90·0 wl; 100·0 oa × 26·6 × 6·4 *(27·4; 30·5 × 8·1 × 1·9)*
Main engines: 2 Rolls Royce Proteus gas turbines = 40 knots (2 Foden diesels for cruising in CODAG arrangement)
Range, miles: 425 at 35 knots; 1 500 at 11·5 knots
Complement: 12 (2 officers, 10 ratings)

Hull of glued laminated wood construction. Design developed from that of "Brave" class fast patrol boats. Design permits fitting of third gas-turbine and a gun armament if required. Launch dates:— *Cutlass* 19 Feb 1970, *Sabre* 21 April 1970, *Scimitar* 4 Dec 1969.

SABRE   5/1975, C. and S. Taylor

1 VOSPER THORNYCROFT (FAST ATTACK CRAFT—PATROL)

Name	No.	Builders	Commissioned
TENACITY	P 276	Vosper Thornycroft Ltd	17 Feb 1973

Displacement, tons: 165 standard; 220 full load
Dimensions, feet (metres): 144·5 oa × 26·6 × 7·8 *(44·1 × 8·1 × 2·4)*
Guns: 2 MGs
Main engines: 3 Rolls Royce Proteus gas turbines; 3 shafts; 12 750 bhp = 40 knots; 2 Paxman Ventura 6 cyl diesels on wing shafts for cruising = 16 knots
Range, miles: 2 500 at 15 knots
Complement: 32 (4 officers, 28 ratings)

Built as a private venture and launched on 18 Feb 1969 at Camber Shipyard, Portsmouth. Steel hull and aluminium alloy superstructure. Purchased by the Ministry of Defence (Navy) on 25 Jan 1972 for approximately £750 000 "as lying" and refitted with minor alterations and additions to meet naval requirements. To be used for exercises and fishery protection. Decca nav, radar.

TENACITY   1974, Michael D. J. Lennon

5 MODIFIED "TON" CLASS

Name	No.	Builders	Commissioned
BEACHAMPTON	P 1007 (ex-M 1107)	Goole SB Co	1953
MONKTON	P 1055 (ex-M 1155)	Herd & Mackenzie, Buckie	1956
WASPERTON	P 1089 (ex-M 1189)	J. Samuel White & Co Ltd	1956
WOLVERTON	P 1093 (ex-M 1193)	Montrose SY Co	1957
YARNTON	P 1096 (ex-M 1196)	Pickersgill	1956

Displacement, tons: 360 standard; 425 full load
Dimensions, feet (metres): 140·0 pp; 153·0 oa × 28·8 × 8·2 *(42·7; 46·3 × 8·8 × 2·5)*
Guns: 2—40 mm Bofors (single, 1 forward, 1 aft)
Main engines: 2 diesels; 2 shafts; 3 000 bhp = 15 knots
Oil fuel, tons: 45
Range, miles: 2 300 at 13 knots
Complement: 30 (5 officers and 25 ratings, but varies)

Former coastal minesweepers of the "Ton" class, refitted at the end of 1971, re-designated as coastal patrol vessels. Fitted with limited armour in bridge area. Form 6th Patrol Squadron Hong Kong.

MONKTON   1974, Michael D. J. Lennon

2 "FORD" CLASS (SDBs)

Name	No.	Builders	Commissioned
DEE (ex-*Beckford*)	P 3104	Wm. Simons, Renfrew	1953
DROXFORD	P 3113	Pimblott, Northwich	1954

Displacement, tons: 120 standard; 142 full load
Dimensions, feet (metres): 110·0 wl; 117·2 oa × 20·0 × 7·0 *(33·6; 35·7 × 6·1 × 2·1)*
Gun: 1—40 mm Bofors
A/S weapons: DC rails; large and small DC
Main engines: Davey Paxman diesels. Foden engine on centre shaft. 1 100 bhp = 18 knots
Oil fuel, tons: 23
Complement: 19

Built in 1953-57. Last survivors of a class of 20. *Dee* attached to Liverpool University RNU (administered by RNR Mersey) and *Droxford* to Glasgow University RNU (administered by RNR Clyde). *Dee* renamed 1965, this name having been used for *Droxford* 1955-1965.

DROXFORD   1972, Wright & Logan

SURVEY SHIPS

3 "HECLA" CLASS

Name	No.	Builders	Commissioned
HECATE	A 137	Yarrow & Co Ltd, Scotstoun	20 Dec 1965
HECLA	A 133	Yarrow & Co, Blythswood	9 Sep 1965
HYDRA	A 144	Yarrow & Co, Blythswood	5 May 1966

Displacement, tons: 1 915 light; 2 733 full load
Measurement, tons: 2 898 gross
Length, feet (metres): 235 (71·6) pp; 260·1 (79·3) oa
Beam, feet (metres): 49·1 (15·0)
Draught, feet (metres): 15·6 (4·7)
Aircraft: 1 Wasp helicopter
Main engines: Diesel-electric drive; 1 shaft; 3 Paxman "Ventura" 12-cyl Vee turbocharged diesels; 3 840 bhp; 1 electric motor; 2 000 shp
Speed, knots: 14
Oil fuel, tons: 450
Range, miles: 20 000 at 9 knots
Complement: 118 (14 officers, 104 ratings)

The first RN ships to be designed with a combined oceanographical and hydrographic role. Of merchant ship design and similar in many respects to the Royal Research ship *Discovery*, they have range and endurance to fit them for their specialised work. The hull is strengthened for navigation in ice, and a propeller built into a transverse tunnel in the bow for good manoeuvrability. The fore end of the superstructure incorporates a Landrover garage and the after end a helicopter hangar with adjacent flight deck. Equipped with chartroom, drawing office and photographic studio; two laboratories, dry and wet; electrical, engineering and shipwright workshops, large storerooms and two surveying motor-boats. Capable of operating independently of shore support for long periods. Air-conditioned throughout.
Average cost £1·25 million. *Hecate* laid down 26 Oct 1964, launched 31 Mar 1965. *Hecla;* 6 May 1964, 21 Dec 1964; *Hydra* 14 May 1964, 14 July 1965.

1 IMPROVED "HECLA" CLASS

Name	No.	Builders	Commissioned
HERALD	—	Robb Caledon, Leith	31 Oct 1974

Displacement, tons: 2 000 standard; 2 945 full load
Dimensions, feet (metres): 260·1 oa × 49·1 × 15·6 (79·3 × 15 × 4·7)
Aircraft: 1 Wasp helicopter
Main engines: Diesel-electric drive; 1 shaft
Speed, knots: 14
Range, miles: 12 000 at 11 knots
Complement: 128

A later version of the "Hecla" class design. Ordered under the 1972-73 Supply (Ministry of Defence) Estimates. Fitted with Hydroplot Satellite navigation system, computerised data logging, gravimeter, magnetometer, sonars, echo-sounders, coring and oceanographic winches, passive stabilisation tank, bow thruster and two surveying motor-boats.
Laid down 9 Nov 1972. Launched by Mrs Mary Hall, wife of the Hydrographer, on 4 Oct 1973.

HERALD   5/1975, C. and S. Taylor

COASTAL SURVEY SHIPS

4 "BULLDOG" CLASS

Name	No.	Builders	Commissioned
BEAGLE	A 319	Brooke Marine Ltd, Lowestoft	1968
BULLDOG	A 317	Brooke Marine Ltd, Lowestoft	21 Mar 1968
FAWN	A 325	Brooke Marine Ltd, Lowestoft	1968
FOX	A 320	Brooke Marine Ltd, Lowestoft	1968

Displacement, tons: 800 standard; 1 088 full load
Dimensions, feet (metres): 189 oa × 37·5 × 12 (60·1 × 11·4 × 3·6)
Main engines: 4 Lister Blackstone ERS8M, 8 cyl, 4 str diesels, coupled to 2 shafts; cp propellers; 2 000 bhp = 15 knots
Range, miles: 4 000 at 12 knots
Complement: 38 (4 officers, 34 ratings)

Designed for duty overseas, working in pairs. Launch dates: *Bulldog* on 12 July 1967, *Beagle* on 7 Sep 1967, *Fox* on 6 Nov 1967 and *Fawn* on 29 Feb 1968. Built to commercial standards. Fitted with passive tank stabilizer, precision ranging radar, Decca "Hifix" system, automatic steering. Air-conditioned throughout. Carry 28·5 ft surveying motor-boat.

FAWN   5/1975, Wright and Logan

INSHORE SURVEY CRAFT

3 "E" CLASS

Name	No.	Builders	Commissioned
ECHO	A 70	J. Samuel White & Co Ltd, Cowes	12 Sep 1958
EGERIA	A 72	Wm. Weatherhead & Sons Ltd, Cockenzie	1959
ENTERPRISE	A 71	M. W. Blackmore & Sons Ltd, Bideford	1959

Displacement, tons: 120 standard; 160 full load
Dimensions, feet (metres): 106·8 oa × 22·0 × 6·8 (32·6 × 7 × 2·1)
Main engines: 2 Paxman diesels; 2 shafts; controllable pitch propellers; 700 bhp = 14 knots
Oil fuel, tons: 15
Range, miles: 1 600 at 10 knots
Complement: 18 (2 officers, 16 ratings); accommodation for 22 (4 officers, 18 ratings)

Echo, the first Inshore Survey Craft, was launched on 1 May 1957. Equipped with two echo sounding machines, sonar, radar, wire sweep gear and surveying motor boat.

EGERIA   10/1974, C. and S. Taylor

2 "HAM" CLASS

MODIFIED INSHORE MINESWEEPERS

Name	No.	Builders	Commissioned
WATERWITCH (ex-*Powderham*)	M 2720	J. Samuel White & Co Ltd, Cowes	1959
WOODLARK (ex-*Yaxham*)	M 2780	J. Samuel White & Co Ltd, Cowes	1958

Displacement, tons: 120 standard; 160 full load
Dimensions, feet (metres): 107·5 oa × 22 × 5·5 (32·4 × 6·5 × 1·7)
Main engines: Diesels; 2 shafts; 1 100 bhp = 14 knots
Endurance, miles: 1 500 at 12 knots
Complement: 18 (2 officers, 16 ratings)

Former inshore minesweepers of the "Ham" class converted to replace the old survey motor launches *Meda* and *Medusa* for operation in inshore waters at home. *Waterwitch,* ex-M 2720, was seconded to Port Auxiliary Service in 1968.

WATERWITCH   1974, Michael D. J. Lennon

ROYAL FLEET AUXILIARY SERVICE

LARGE FLEET TANKERS (AOF(L))

3 "OL" CLASS

Name	No.	Builders	Commissioned
OLMEDA (ex-*Oleander*)	A 124	Swan Hunter, Wallsend	18 Oct 1965
OLNA	A 123	Hawthorn Leslie, Hebburn	1 April 1966
OLWEN (ex-*Olynthus*)	A 122	Hawthorn Leslie, Hebburn	21 June 1965

Displacement, tons: 10 890 light; 36 000 full load
Measurement, tons: 25 100 deadweight; 18 600 gross
Dimensions, feet (metres): 611·1 pp; 648·0 oa × 84·0 × 34·0 *(185·9; 197·5 × 25·6 × 10·5)*
Aircraft: 2 Wessex helicopters (can carry 3)
Main engines: Pametrada double reduction geared turbines; 26 500 shp = 19 knots
Boilers: 2 Babcock & Wilcox, (750 psi; 950°F)
Complement: 87 (25 officers and 62 ratings)

Largest and fastest ships when they joined the Royal Fleet Auxiliary Service. *Olmeda* was launched on 19 Nov 1964, while *Olna* and *Olwen* were launched on 28 July 1965 and 10 July 1964, respectively.
Designed for underway replenishment of the Fleet. A helicopter landing platform and hangar enable ships to collect stores by air. Specially strengthened for operations in ice, fully air-conditioned. *Olna* has a transverse bow thrust unit for improved manoeuvrability in confined waters and a new design of replenishment-at-sea systems.

OLNA (replenishment of *Lowestoft*)   4/1976, C. and S. Taylor

OLNA   4/1976, C. and S. Taylor

2 LATER "TIDE" CLASS

Name	No.	Builders	Commissioned
TIDESPRING	A 75	Hawthorn Leslie, Hebburn	18 Jan 1963
TIDEPOOL	A 76	Hawthorn Leslie, Hebburn	28 June 1963

Displacement, tons: 8 531 light; 27 400 full load
Measurement, tons: 18 900 deadweight; 14 130 gross
Dimensions, feet (metres): 550·0 pp; 583·0 oa × 71·0 × 32·0 *(167·7; 177·6 × 21·6 × 9·8)*
Main engines: Double reduction geared turbines; 15 000 shp = 18·3 knots
Boilers: 2 Babcock & Wilcox
Complement: 110 (30 officers and 80 ratings)

Highly specialised ships for fuelling (13 000 tons cargo fuel) and storing naval vessels at sea, helicopter platform and hangar. *Tidespring* was laid down on 24 July 1961, launched on 3 May 1962. *Tidepool* was laid down on 4 Dec 1961, launched on 11 Dec 1962.

TIDESPRING   5/1975, C. and S. Taylor

1 "TIDE" CLASS

Name	No.	Builders	Commissioned
TIDEREACH	A 96	Swan Hunter & Wigham Richardson Ltd, Wallsend-on-Tyne	30 Aug 1955

Displacement, tons: 9 040 light; 27 300 full load
Measurement, tons: 17 900 deadweight; 13 000 gross
Dimensions, feet (metres): 550 pp; 583 oa × 71 × 32 *(167·7; 177·6 × 21·6 × 9·8)*
Main engines: Double reduction geared turbines; 15 000 shp = 19 knots

Tidereach, launched on 2 June 1954, was the first of three Fleet Replenishment Tankers. A fourth ship of this class, *Tide Austral,* built for Australia, was renamed *Supply* on 7 Sep 1962.

TIDEREACH   11/1975, Dr Giorgio Arra

SUPPORT TANKERS (AOS)

(Note: Majority under long-term charter)

Name	No.	Builders	Commissioned
ORANGELEAF	A 80	Furness Shipbuilding Co Ltd,	June 1955
(ex-M.V. *Southern Satellite*)		Haverton Hill on Tees	

Measurement, tons: 18 222 deadweight; 12 146 gross; 6 800 net
Dimensions, feet (metres): 525 pp; 556·5 oa × 71·7 × 30·5 *(160·1; 169·7 × 21·9 × 9·3)*
Main engines: Doxford 6-cyl diesel; 6 800 bhp = 14 knots
Oil fuel, tons: 1 610

Launched on 8 Feb 1955. Chartered from South Georgia Co Ltd, 25 May 1959. Astern and abeam fuelling.

ORANGELEAF   1975, MOD(N)

Name	No.	Builders	Commissioned
CHERRYLEAF	A 82	Rheinstahl Nordseewerke	1963
(ex-*Overseas Adventurer*)			

Measurement, tons: 19 700 deadweight; 13 700 gross; 7 648 net
Dimensions, feet (metres): 559 × 72 × 30 *(170·5 × 22 × 9·2)*
Machinery: 7 cyl MAN diesel; 8 400 bhp = 16 knots

Ordered and completed in 1963. Transferred to RFA march 1973.

CHERRYLEAF   8/1975, C. and S. Taylor

Name	No.	Builders	Commissioned
PLUMLEAF	A 78	Blyth DD & Eng Co Ltd	July 1960

Displacement, tons: 26 480 full load
Measurement, tons: 19 430 deadweight; 12 459 gross
Dimensions, feet (metres): 534 pp; 560 oa × 72 × 30 *(162·9; 170·8 × 22 × 9·2)*
Main engines: N.E. Doxford 6-cyl diesels; 9 500 bhp = 15·5 knots

Launched 29 Mar 1960. Astern and abeam fuelling.

PLUMLEAF   3/1975, Dr. Giorgio Arra

Name	No.	Builders	Commissioned
PEARLEAF	A 77	Blythswood Shipbuilding Co Ltd, Scotstoun	Jan 1960

Displacement, tons: 25 790 full load
Measurement, tons: 18 711 deadweight; 12 353 gross; 7 215 net
Dimensions, feet (metres): 535 pp; 568 oa × 71·7 × 30 *(162·7; 173·2 × 21·9 × 9·2)*
Main engines: Rowan Doxford 6-cyl diesels; 8 800 bhp = 16 knots

Chartered from Jacobs and Partners Ltd, London on completion. Launched on 15 Oct 1959. Can carry three different grades of cargo. Astern and abeam fuelling.

PEARLEAF   1970, MOD (N)

MOBILE RESERVE TANKER (AOM)

Name	No.	Builders	Commissioned
DEWDALE (ex-M.V. *Edenfield*)	A 219	Harland and Wolff, Belfast	1965

Measurement, tons: 63 588 deadweight; 35 640 gross; 24 504 net
Dimensions, feet (metres): 747·0 pp; 774·5 oa × 107·8 × 41·5 *(227·8; 236·2 × 32·9 × 12·7)*
Main engines: B. & W. 9 cyl diesels; 1 shaft; 17 000 bhp = 15 knots
Complement: 51

In July 1967 the Ministry of Defence chartered three large tankers for service East of Suez. After limited modifications the ships operated in the Indian Ocean area. But *Ennerdale* sank on 1 June 1970 after striking a submerged hazard in the Indian Ocean. *Derwentdale* (ex-*Halcyon Breeze*) was returned to owners. *Dewdale* is the largest RFA tanker at present in service.

DEWDALE   1974, Michael D. J. Lennon

SMALL FLEET TANKERS (AOF(S))

5 "ROVER" CLASS

Name	No.	Builders	Commissioned
BLACK ROVER	A 273	Swan Hunter, Hebburn-on-Tyne	23 Aug 1974
BLUE ROVER	A 270	Swan Hunter, Hebburn-on-Tyne	Oct 1970
GOLD ROVER	A 271	Swan Hunter, Hebburn-on-Tyne	Jan 1974
GREEN ROVER	A 268	Swan Hunter, Hebburn-on-Tyne	Nov 1969
GREY ROVER	A 269	Swan Hunter, Hebburn-on-Tyne	Feb 1970

Displacement, tons: 4,700 light; 11 522 full load
Measurement, tons: 7 060 deadweight; 7 510 gross; 3 185 net
Dimensions, feet (metres): 461·0 oa × 63·0 × 24·0 (140·6 × 19·2 × 7·3)
Main engines: 2 Pielstick 16 cyl diesels; 1 shaft; controllable pitch propeller; 15 300 bhp = 18 knots
Complement: 47 (16 officers and 31 men)

Small fleet tankers designed to replenish HM ships at sea with fuel, fresh water, limited dry cargo and refrigerated stores under all conditions while underway. A helicopter landing platform is provided served by a stores lift, to enable stores to be transferred at sea by "vertical lift". *Green Rover* was launched on 19 Dec 1968, *Grey Rover* on 17 April 1969, *Blue Rover* on 11 Nov 1969. *Gold Rover* on 7 Mar 1973 and *Black Rover* on 30 Oct 1973. The cost of *Black Rover* was £7 mill. an increase of £4 mill. on the price of the original ships. Cargo capacity 6 600 tons fuel.

GREEN ROVER

7/1975, Wright and Logan

COASTAL TANKER (AO(H))

1 "EDDY" CLASS

Name	No.	Builders	Commissioned
EDDYFIRTH	A 261	Lobnitz & Co Ltd, Renfrew	10 Feb 1954

Displacement, tons: 1 960 light; 4 160 full load
Measurement, tons: 2 200 deadweight; 2 222 gross
Dimensions, feet (metres): 270 pp; 286 oa × 44 × 17·2 (82·4; 87·2 × 13·4 × 5·2)
Main engines: 1 set triple expansion; 1 shaft; 1 750 ihp = 12 knots
Boilers: 2 oil burning cylindrical

The last of a class of eight, all completed 1952-54. Cargo capacity: 1 650 tons oil.

EDDYFIRTH

6/1975, C. and S. Taylor

FLEET REPLENISHMENT SHIPS (AEFS)

Name	No.	Builders	Commissioned
FORT AUSTIN	A 386	Scott-Lithgow	1978
FORT GRANGE	A 385	Scott-Lithgow	1976

Displacement, tons: 17 200
Measurement, tons: 9 843 dw
Dimensions, feet (metres): 603 × 79 × 29·5 (183·9 × 24·1 × 9)
Aircraft: 1 Wessex helicopter
Main engines: Diesel; 23 300 hp single screw = 20 knots

Ordered in Nov 1971. To be fitted with a helicopter flight-deck and hangar, thus allowing not only for vertical replenishment but also a fuelling point for Force A/S helicopters. *Fort Grange* laid down 9 Nov 1973. *Fort Austin* laid down 9 Dec 1975.

New Construction FORT GRANGE

1972, MOD (N) Drawing

Name	No.	Builders	Commissioned
REGENT	A 486	Harland & Wolff, Belfast	1967
RESOURCE	A 480	Scotts Shipbuilding & Eng Co, Greenock	1967

Displacement, tons: 22 890 full load
Measurements, tons: 18 029 gross
Dimensions, feet (metres): 600·0 pp; 640·0 oa × 77·2 × 26·1 (182·8; 195·1 × 23·5 × 8)
Aircraft: 1 Wessex helicopter
Guns: Fitted for 2—40 mm Bofors (single) which are not carried in peacetime
Main engines: AEI steam turbines; 20 000 shp = 21 knots
Complement: 119 R.F.A. officers and ratings; 52 Naval Dept industrial and non-industrial civil servants; 11 Royal Navy (1 officer and 10 ratings) for helicopter flying and maintenance

RESOURCE

1973, John Mortimer

Ordered on 24 Jan 1963. They have lifts for armaments and stores, and helicopter platforms for transferring loads at sea. Designed from the outset as Fleet Replenishment Ships (previous ships had been converted merchant vessels). Air-conditioned. *Resource* was launched at Greenock on 11 Feb 1966, *Regent* at Belfast on 9 Mar 1966. Official title is Ammunition, Explosives, Food, Stores Ship (AEFS).

ARMAMENT SUPPORT SHIPS (AE)

Name	No.	Builders	Commissioned
RESURGENT (ex-*Changchow*)	A 280	Scotts Shipbuilding & Engineering Co Ltd, Greenock	1951
RETAINER (ex-*Chungking*)	A 329	Scotts Shipbuilding & Engineering Co Ltd, Greenock	1950

Displacement, tons: 14 400
Measurement, tons: *Resurgent* 9 357 gross; *Retainer* 9 498 gross
Dimensions, feet (metres): 477·2 oa × 62 × 29 (145·8 × 18·9 × 8·8)
Main engines: Doxford diesel; 1 shaft; 6 500 bhp = 16 knots
Oil fuel, tons: 925
Complement: 107

Retainer was purchased in 1952 and converted into a naval storeship during autumn 1954-April 1955 by Palmers Hebburn Co Ltd, where further conversion was carried out Mar-Aug 1957 to extend her facilities as a stores ship, including the fitting out of holds to carry naval stores, the installation of lifts for stores, the provision of extra cargo handling gear and new bridge wings. *Resurgent* was taken over on completion.

RESURGENT

9/1972, C. and S. Taylor

STORES SUPPORT SHIPS (AVS/AFS)

Name	No.	Builders	Commissioned
LYNESS	A 339	Swan Hunter & Wigham Richardson Ltd, Wallsend-on-Tyne	22 Dec 1966
STROMNESS	A 344	Swan Hunter & Wigham Richardson Ltd, Wallsend-on-Tyne	21 Mar 1967
TARBATNESS	A 345	Swan Hunter & Wigham Richardson Ltd, Wallsend-on-Tyne	10 Aug 1967

Displacement, tons: 9,010 light; 16 792 full load
Measurement, tons: 7 782 deadweight; 12 359 gross; 4 744 net
Dimensions, feet (metres): 490 pp; 524 oa × 72 × 25·5 *(149·4; 159·7 × 22 × 7·7)*
Aircraft: Helicopter deck
Main engines: Wallsend-Sulzer 8-cyl RD.76 diesel; 11 520 bhp = 18 knots
Complement: 105

Lifts and mobile appliances provided for handling stores internally, and a new replenishment at sea system and a helicopter landing platform for transferring loads at sea. A novel feature of the ships is the use of close circuit television to monitor the movement of stores. All air-conditioned. *Lyness* was launched on 7 April 1966, *Stromness* on 16 Sep 1966, and *Tarbatness* 22 Feb 1967. *Lyness* is an Air-Stores Support Ship and cost £3·5 million.

STROMNESS   *1972, C. and S. Taylor*

NEW CONSTRUCTION STORE CARRIER (AK)

Name	No.	Builders	Commissioned
—	—	Cleland SB Co, Wallsend	1977

Measurement, tons: 1 150 dw
Dimensions, feet (metres): 210·9 × 39 × 15 *(64·3 × 11·9 × 4·6)*
Main engines: 2 Mirrlees-Blackstone diesels; 3 000 bhp; 1 shaft = 14 knots

Ordered Dec 1975. To carry armament stores in two holds. Two 5 tonne derricks.

STORE CARRIERS (AK)

Name	No.	Builders	Commissioned
BACCHUS	A 404	Henry Robb Ltd, Leith	Sep 1962
HEBE	A 406	Henry Robb Ltd, Leith	May 1962

Displacement, tons: 2 740 light; 8 173 full load
Measurement, tons: 5 312 deadweight; 4 823 gross; 2 441 net
Dimensions, feet (metres): 379 oa × 55 × 22 *(115·6 × 16·8 × 6·4)*
Main engines: Swan Hunter Sulzer diesel; 1 shaft; 5 500 bhp = 15 knots
Oil fuel, tons: 720
Complement: 57

Built for the British India Steam Navigation Co. Taken over by the Royal Navy on completion on long term "bare-bones" charter. Crew accommodation and engines aft as in tankers. In 1973 both purchased by P and O SN Co, remaining on charter to MOD (N).

BACCHUS   *1972, C. and S. Taylor*

ROYAL MARITIME AUXILIARY SERVICE AND PORT AUXILIARY SERVICE

Note: To avoid over complication the ships and vessels of the Royal Naval Auxiliary Service and some of the Royal Corps of Transport are included here

---

MOORING, SALVAGE AND BOOM VESSELS

Note: *Salvador* and *Salveda* (Ocean Salvage vessels) laid up.

2 "WILD DUCK" CLASS

2 "IMPROVED WILD DUCK" CLASS

2 "LATER WILD DUCK" CLASS

Name	No.	Builders	Commissioned
MANDARIN (RMAS)	P 192	Cammell Laird & Co Ltd, Birkenhead	5 Mar 1964
PINTAIL (PAS)	P 193	Cammell Laird & Co Ltd, Birkenhead	Mar 1964
GARGANEY (RMAS)	P 194	Brooke Marine Ltd, Lowestoft	Sep 1966
GOLDENEYE (PAS)	P 195	Brooke Marine Ltd, Lowestoft	Dec 1966
GOOSANDER (RMAS)	P 196	Robb Caledon Ltd	10 Sep 1973
POCHARD (RMAS)	P 197	Robb Caledon Ltd	11 Dec 1973

Displacement, tons: 950 standard; 1 125 full load *(Goosander* and *Pochard)*
Dimensions, feet (metres): 198·3 *(60·5)* including horns *(Goosander* and *Pochard)*
190 *(58)* including horns *(Garganey* and *Goldeneye)*
182 *(55·5)* including horns *(Mandarin* and *Pintail)* × 40 × 11·3 *(12·2 × 3·4)*
Main engines: 1 Davey Paxman 16 cyl diesel; 1 shaft; controllable pitch propeller; 550 bhp = 10 knots
Range, miles: 3 000 at 10 knots
Complement: 24 (6 officers, 6 petty officers, 12 ratings)
32 (including salvage party) *(Goosander* and *Pochard)*

Mandarin was the first of a new class of marine service vessels. Launched on 17 Sep 1963. *Pintail* was launched on 3 Dec 1963. *Garganey* and *Goldeneye* were built in 1965-67. *Goosander* and *Pochard* of the later "Later Wild Duck" class were launched 12 April 1973 and 21 June 1973 respectively. Previously their three tasks were separately undertaken by specialist vessels. Capable of laying out and servicing the heaviest moorings used by the Fleet and also maintaining booms for harbour defence. Heavy lifting equipment enables a wide range of salvage operations to be performed, especially in harbour clearance work. The special heavy winches have an ability for tidal lifts over the apron of 200 tons.

GOLDENEYE   *9/1974, Dr. Giorgio Arra*

4 "KIN" CLASS

Name	No.	Builders	Commissioned
KINBRACE (PAS)	A 281	A. Hall, Aberdeen	1945
KINGARTH (RMAS)	A 232	A. Hall, Aberdeen	1944
KINLOSS (PAS)	A 482	A. Hall, Aberdeen	1945
UPLIFTER (RMAS)	A 507	Smith's Dock Co Ltd	1944

Displacement, tons: 950 standard; 1 050 full load
Measurement, tons: 262 deadweight; 775 gross
Dimensions, feet (metres): 179·2 oa × 35·2 × 12·0 *(54 × 10·6 × 3·6)*
Main engines: 1 British Polar Atlas M44M diesel; 630 bhp = 9 knots
Complement: 34

Originally classified as Coastal Salvage Vessels, but re-rated Mooring, Salvage and Boom Vessels in 1971. Equipped with horns and heavy rollers. Can lift 200 tons deadweight over the bow. *Kinbrace, Kingarth* and *Uplifter* were refitted with diesel engines in 1966-67, and *Kinloss* in 1963-64.

KINBRACE

1974, Michael D. J. Lennon

2 "LAY" CLASS

Name	No.	Builders	Commissioned
LAYBURN (RMAS)	P 191	Wm. Simons & Co Ltd (Simons-Lobnitz Ltd)	7 June 1960
LAYMOOR (RN)	P 190	Wm. Simons & Co Ltd (Simons-Lobnitz Ltd)	9 Dec 1959

Displacement, tons: 800 standard; 1 050 full load
Dimensions, feet (metres): 192·7 oa × 34·5 × 11·5 *(59 × 10·3 × 3·4)*
Main engines: Triple expansion; 1 shaft; 1 300 ihp = 10 knots
Boilers: 2 Foster Wheeler "D" type; 200 psi
Complement: 26 (4 officers; 22 ratings)

Layburn, cost £565 000. Designed for naval or civilian manning. Lifting capacity is greater than that of predecessors; improvement in accommodation enables them to be operated in any climate. Oil-fuelled.

LAYBURN

1973, John G. Callis

COASTAL TANKERS

6 "OILPRESS" CLASS (PAS)

Name	No.	Builders	Commissioned
OILBIRD	Y 25	Appledore Shipbuilders Ltd	1969
OILFIELD	Y 24	Appledore Shipbuilders Ltd	1969
OILMAN	Y 26	Appledore Shipbuilders Ltd	1969
OILPRESS	Y 21	Appledore Shipbuilders Ltd	1969
OILSTONE	Y 22	Appledore Shipbuilders Ltd	1969
OILWELL	Y 23	Appledore Shipbuilders Ltd	1969

Displacement, tons: 280 standard; 530 full load
Dimensions, feet (metres): 130·0 wl; 139·5 oa × 30·0 × 8·3 *(39·6; 41·5 × 9 × 2·5)*
Main engines: 1 Lister Blackstone ES6 diesel; 1 shaft; 405 shp at 900 rpm
Complement: 11 (4 officers and 7 ratings)

Ordered on 10 May 1967. Three are diesel oil carriers and three FFO carriers. Launched:— *Oilbird* 21 Nov 1968, *Oilfield* 5 Sep 1968, *Oilman* 18 Feb 1969, *Oilpress* 10 June 1968, *Oilstone* 11 July 1968, *Oilwell* 20 Jan 1969.

OILWELL

1/1976, Dr. Giorgio Arra

TRIALS SHIPS

Name	No.	Builders	Commissioned
NEWTON	A 367	Scott Lithgow Ltd	1976

Displacement, tons: 3 940
Dimensions, feet (metres): 323·5 × 53 × 15·4 *(98·6 × 16 × 4·7)*
Main engines: Diesel electric; 3 Mirrlees Blackstone diesels; 1 shaft; 4 350 bhp = 15 knots
Range, miles: 5 000 at 13 knots
Complement: 61 (including 12 scientists)

Ordered Nov 1971. Laid down 19 Dec 1973. Launched 25 June 1975. Fitted with bow thruster and Kort nozzle. Propulsion system is very quiet. Passive tank stabilisation. Prime duty sonar propagation trials. Can serve as cable-layer with large cable tanks. Special winch system.

Name	No.	Builders	Commissioned
WHITEHEAD (RMAS)	A 364	Scotts Shipbuilding Co Ltd, Greenock	1971

Displacement, tons: 3 040 full load
Dimensions, feet (metres): 291·0 wl; 319·0 oa × 48·0 × 17·0 *(88·8; 97·3 × 14·6 × 5·2)*
Main engines: 2 Paxman 12 YLCM diesels; 1 shaft; 3 400 bhp = 15·5 knots
Range, miles: 4 000 at 12 knots
Complement: 10 officers, 32 ratings, 15 trials and scientific staff

Designed to provide mobile preparation, firing and control facilities for weapons and research vehicles. Launched on 5 May 1970. Named after Robert Whitehead, the torpedo development pioneer and engineer. Fitted with equipment for tracking weapons and target and for analysing the results of trials.

WHITEHEAD

1972

Name	No.	Builders	Commissioned
CRYSTAL	RDV 01	HM Dockyard, Devonport	30 Nov 1971

Displacement, tons: 3 040
Dimensions, feet (metres): 413·5 × 56·0 × 5·5 *(126·1 × 17·1 × 1·7)*
Complement: 60, including scientists

Unpowered floating platform for Sonar Research and Development. Ordered in Dec 1969. Launched 22 Mar 1971. A harbour-based laboratory without propulsion machinery or steering which provides the Admiralty Underwater Weapons Establishment at Portland with a stable platform on which to carry out acoustic tests and other research projects. Under Dockyard Control.

CRYSTAL   10/1975, Dr. Giorgio Arra

2 "MINER" CLASS (PAS)

Name	No.	Builders	Commissioned
BRITANNIC	—	Philip & Son Ltd, Dartmouth	26 June 1941
STEADY	—	Philip & Son Ltd, Dartmouth	31 Mar 1944

Displacement, tons: 300 standard; 355 full load
Dimensions, feet (metres): 110·2 × 26·5 × 8·0 *(33·6 × 8·1 × 2·4)*
Main engines: Ruston & Hornsby diesels; 2 shafts; 360 bhp = 10 knots

Last of a class of eight small controlled-minelayers. *Miner V* was converted into a cable lighter and renamed *Britannic* in 1960 with PAS as store carrier. *Miner VII* was adapted as a stabilisation trials ship at Portsmouth and renamed *Steady* in 1960 with PAS.

BRITANNIC   1974, Michael D. J. Lennon

TORPEDO RECOVERY VESSELS (PAS)

Name	No.	Builders	Commissioned
TORRENT	A 127	Cleland SB Co, Wallsend	10 Sep 1971
TORRID	A 128	Cleland SB Co, Wallsend	Jan 1972

Measurement, tons: 550 gross
Dimensions, feet (metres): 151·0 × 31·5 × 11 *(46·1 × 9·6 × 3·4)*
Main engines: Paxman diesels; 700 bhp = 12 knots
Complement: 19

Torrent was launched on 29 Mar 1971 and *Torrid* on 7 Sep 1971. These ships have a stern well for torpedo recovery—can carry 22 torpedoes in hold and 10 on deck.

TORRID   3/1975, Dr. Giorgio Arra

Name	No.	Builders	Commissioned
THOMAS GRANT	—	Charles Hill & Sons Ltd, Bristol	July 1953

Displacement, tons: 209 light; 461 full load
Measurement, tons: 252 deadweight; 218 gross
Dimensions, feet (metres): 113·5 × 25·5 × 8·8 *(34·6 × 7·8 × 2·7)*
Main engines: 2 diesels; Speed = 9 knots

Built as a local store carrier. Launched on 11 May 1953. Converted into torpedo recovery vessel in 1968.

THOMAS GRANT   1969

6 "HAM" CLASS (PAS)

BUCKLESHAM M 2614	**EVERINGHAM** M 2626	**HAVERSHAM** M 2635	Details similar to other "Ham" class in Mine Warfare section but converted for TRV in 1964 onwards. Now fitted with stern well.
DOWNHAM M 2622	**FRITHAM** M 2630	**LASHAM** M 2636	

TRV 72 TYPE (PAS)

A number of this SAR type are still in use.

TRV 72   4/1975, Wright and Logan

EXPERIMENTAL SHIP

WHIMBREL (ex-LCT) A 179

Displacement, tons: 300
Dimensions, feet (metres): 187 × 29·5 × 5 *(57 × 9 × 1·5)*
Main engines: Diesels; 2 shafts

Employed for weapon research by Underwater Weapons Establishment, Portland.

WHIMBREL

1974, Michael D. J. Lennon

CABLE SHIP

Name	No.	Builders	Commissioned
ST. MARGARETS (RMAS)	A 259	Swan Hunter & Wigham Richardson Ltd.	1944

Displacement, tons: 1 300 light; 2 500 full load
Measurement, tons: 1 524 gross; 1 200 deadweight
Dimensions, feet (metres): 228·8 pp; 252 oa × 36·5 × 16·3 *(76 × 10·9 × 4·8)*
Main engines: Triple expansion; 2 shafts; 1 250 ihp = 12 knots

Provision was made for mounting one 4 inch gun and four 20 mm guns but no armament is fitted.

ST. MARGARETS

1972, Dittmair

TARGET SHIP

WAKEFUL (ex-*Dan*, ex-*Heracles*)

Displacement, tons: 492
Dimensions, feet (metres): 145·8 oa × 35 × 15·5 *(44·5 × 10·7 × 4·7)*
Complement: 18

Purchased from Sweden in 1974. Built as a tug and now operated as Submarine Target Ship in the Clyde.

ARMAMENT CARRIERS

Name	No.	Builders	Commissioned
KINTERBURY	A 378	Philip & Son Ltd	4 Mar 1943
THROSK	—	Philip & Son Ltd	22 Dec 1943

Displacement, tons: 1 490 standard; 1 770 full load
Measurement, tons: 600 deadweight
Dimensions, feet (metres): 199·8 × 34·3 × 13 *(60·9 × 10·2 × 4)*
Main engines: Triple expansion; 1 shaft; 900 ihp = 11 knots
Coal, tons: 154

Launched on 14 Nov 1942 and in 1943, respectively. Rated as naval armament carriers. Converted in 1959 with hold stowage and a derrick for handling guided missiles.

KINTERBURY

1972, Wright & Logan

Name	No.	Builders	Commissioned
MAXIM (PAS)	A 377	Lobnitz & Co Ltd, Renfrew	1944

Displacement, tons: 604
Measurement, tons: 340 deadweight
Dimensions, feet (metres): 144·5 × 25 × 8 *(44·1 × 7·6 × 2·3)*
Main engines: Reciprocating; 500 ihp = 9 knots
Complement: 13

CATAPULT   FLINTLOCK (PAS)

Of differing displacements and data.

WATER CARRIERS

6 "WATER" CLASS (PAS)

Name	No.	Builders	Commissioned
WATERFALL	Y 17	Drypool Engineering & Drydock Co, Hull	1967
WATERSHED	Y 18	Drypool Engineering & Drydock Co, Hull	1967
WATERSIDE	Y 20	Drypool Engineering & Drydock Co, Hull	1968
WATERSPOUT	Y 19	Drypool Engineering & Drydock Co, Hull	1967
WATERCOURSE	Y 22	Drypool Engineering & Drydock Co, Hull	1974
WATERFOWL	Y 21	Drypool Engineering & Drydock Co, Hull	25 May 1974

Measurement, tons: 285 gross
Dimensions, feet (metres): 131·5 oa × 24·8 × 8 *(40·1 × 7·5 × 2·3)*
Main engines: 1 Diesel; 1 shaft; 600 bhp = 11 knots
Complement: 11

Launched on 30 Mar 1966, 3 Aug 1966, 20 June 1967 and 29 Dec 1966, respectively and the last pair in 1973. Last pair have after deck-house extended forward.

WATERFALL

1972, Wright & Logan

4 "SPA" CLASS (PAS)

Name	No.	Builders	Commissioned
SPALAKE	A 260	Charles Hill & Sons Ltd, Bristol	1947
SPAPOOL	A 222	Charles Hill & Sons Ltd, Bristol	1947
SPABROOK	A 224	Philip & Son Ltd, Dartmouth	1945
SPABURN	A 257	Philip & Son Ltd, Dartmouth	1947

Displacement, tons: 1 219 full load
Measurement, tons: 630 deadweight; 672 to 719 gross
Dimensions, feet (metres): 172 oa × 30 × 12 (52·5 × 9·2 × 3·6)
Main engines: Triple expansion; 675 ihp = 9 knots
Coal, tons: 90

SPAPOOL   1967, MOD (N)

5 "FRESH" CLASS (PAS)

FRESHBURN	FRESHPOND	FRESHSPRING
FRESHLAKE	FRESHPOOL	

Displacement, tons: 594
Dimensions, feet (metres): 126·2 × 25·5 × 10·8 (38·5 × 7·8 × 3·3)
Main engines: Triple expansion; 450 ihp = 9 knots

Freshspring was converted from coal to oil fuel, in 1961. *Freshpool* is in reserve.

FRESHPOOL   1966, Dr. Giorgio Arra

TUGS

3 OCEAN TUGS

Name	No.	Builders	Commissioned
ROBUST (PAS)	—	Charles D. Holmes, Beverley Shipyard, Hull	6 April 1974
ROLLICKER	A 502	Charles D. Holmes, Beverley Shipyard, Hull	Feb 1973
ROYSTERER (RMAS)	—	Charles D. Holmes, Beverley Shipyard, Hull	26 April 1972

Displacement, tons: 1 630 full load
Dimensions, feet (metres): 162·0 pp; 179·7 oa × 38·5 × 18·0 (54 × 11·6 × 5·5)
Main engines: 2 Mirrlees KMR 6 diesels (by Lister Blackstone Mirrlees Marine Ltd); 2 shafts; 4 500 bhp at 525 rpm = 15 knots
Range, miles: 13 000 at 12 knots
Complement: 31 (10 officers and 21 ratings) (and able to carry salvage party of 10 RN officers and ratings)

These are the biggest and most powerful ocean tugs ever built for the Royal Navy. Bollard pull—50 tons. Designed principally for salvage and long range towage but can be used for general harbour duties, which *Robust* now undertakes. Cost well over £2 million apiece. *Robust* now at Gibraltar. Ordered Nov 1968 *(Rollicker, Roysterer)* and May 1970 *(Robust)*. Launch dates:— *Robust* 7 Oct 1971, *Rollicker* 29 Jan 1971, *Roysterer* 20 April 1970.

ROYSTERER   9/1975, John G. Callis

Name	No.	Builders	Commissioned
TYPHOON (RMAS)	A 95	Henry Robb & Co Ltd, Leith	1960

Displacement, tons: 800 standard; 1 380 full load
Dimensions, feet (metres): 200·0 oa × 40·0 × 13·0 (60·5 × 12 × 4)
Main engines: 2 turbocharged vee type 12-cyl diesels; 1 shaft; 2 750 bhp = over 16 knots

Launched on 14 Oct 1958. The machinery arrangement of two diesels geared to a single shaft was an innovation for naval ocean tugs in the RN. Controllable pitch propeller, 150 rpm. Fitted for fire fighting, salvage and ocean rescue, with a heavy mainmast and derrick attached. Bollard pull 32 tons.

TYPHOON   1973, Wright and Logan

5 "CONFIANCE" CLASS (PAS)

Name	No.	Builders	Commissioned
ACCORD	A 90	A. & J. Inglis Ltd, Glasgow	Sep 1958
ADVICE	A 89	A. & J. Inglis Ltd, Glasgow	Oct 1959
AGILE	A 88	Goole SB Co.	July 1959
CONFIANCE	A 289	A. & J. Inglis Ltd, Glasgow	27 Mar 1956
CONFIDENT	A 290	A. & J. Inglis Ltd, Glasgow	Jan 1956

Displacement, tons: 760 full load
Dimensions, feet (metres): 140·0 pp; 154·8 oa × 35·0 × 11·0 (42·7; 47·2 × 10·7 × 3·4)
Main engines: 4 Paxman HAXM diesels; 2 shafts; 1 800 bhp = 13 knots
Complement: 29 plus 13 salvage party

Fitted with 2·50 m diam. Stone Kamewa controllable pitch propellers. *Accord, Advice* and *Agile*, formerly rated as dockyard tugs were officially added to the "Confiance" class in 1971 as part of the Royal Maritime Auxiliary Service ocean towing force. Fitted for 1—40 mm gun.

AGILE   1974, Wright and Logan

3 "SAMSON" CLASS (PAS)

Name	No.	Builders	Commissioned
SEA GIANT	A 288	Alexander Hall & Co Ltd, Aberdeen	1955
SUPERMAN	—	Alexander Hall & Co Ltd, Aberdeen	1954
SAMSON	—	Alexander Hall & Co Ltd, Aberdeen	1954

Displacement, tons: 1 200 full load
Measurement, tons: 850 gross
Dimensions, feet (metres): 180 oa × 37 × 14 *(54 × 11·2 × 4·3)*
Main engines: Triple expansion; 2 shafts; 3 000 ihp = 15 knots

Samson was to have been sold to Chile in 1974 but is still in UK waters.

SEA GIANT

1972, John G. Callis

2 "BUSTLER" CLASS

Name	No.	Builders	Commissioned
CYCLONE (ex-*Growler*) (RMAS)	A 111	Henry Robb Ltd, Leith	Sep 1943
REWARD (RN)	A 264	Henry Robb Ltd, Leith	Oct 1945

Displacement, tons: 1 118 light; 1 630 full load
Dimensions, feet (metres): 190·0 pp; 205·0 oa × 40·2 × 16·8 *(58; 62·5 × 12·3 × 5·1)*
Main engines: 2 Atlas Polar 8-cyl diesels; 1 shaft; 4 000 bhp = 16 knots
Oil fuel, tons: 405
Range, miles: 17 000
Complement: 42 (29 in *Reward*)

Last of class of four. *Reward* taken out of reserve in 1975 to take part in oil-rig patrols and fitted with one 40 mm gun. Launch dates:— *Cyclone* 10 Sep 1942, *Reward* 30 Oct 1944.

REWARD (fitted for North Sea Patrol)

1975, MOD(N)

6 "DIRECTOR" CLASS (PAS)

Name	No.	Builders	Commissioned
DEXTROUS	A 93	Yarrow & Sons Ltd	1957
DIRECTOR	A 94	Yarrow & Sons Ltd	1957
FAITHFUL	A 85	Yarrow & Sons Ltd	1958
FORCEFUL	A 86	Yarrow & Sons Ltd	1958
FAVOURITE	A 87	Ferguson & Co Ltd	1959
GRIPER	A 91	Simons & Co Ltd	1958

Displacement, tons: 710 full load
Dimensions, feet (metres): 157·2 oa × 30 (60 over paddle boxes) × 10 *(47·9 × 9·2 (18·4) × 3·1)*
Main engines: Paxman diesels and BTH motors; diesel electric; 2 shafts; 2 paddle wheels; 2 000 bhp = 13 knots
Complement: 21

Modern paddlers. *Dextrous* at Gibraltar.

FORCEFUL

1973, Wright and Logan

19 "DOG" CLASS (PAS)

AIREDALE A 102	CAIRN A 126	ELKHOUND A 162	SALUKI A 182
ALSATION A 106	COLLIE A 328	HUSKY A 169	SEALYHAM A 187
BASSET A 327	CORGI A 330	LABRADOR A 168	SETTER A 189
BOXER A 394	DALMATION A 129	MASTIFF A 180	SHEEPDOG A 250
	DEERHOUND A 155	POINTER A 188	SPANIEL A 201

Displacement, tons: 170 full load
Dimensions, feet (metres): 94 × 24·5 × 12 *(28·7 × 7·5 × 3·7)*
Main engines: Lister Blackstone diesels; 1 320 bhp = 12 knots
Complement: 8

Harbour berthing tugs. *Airedale* and *Sealyham* at Gibraltar. Bollard pull 16 tons. Completed 1962-72.

SETTER

11/1974, C. and S. Taylor

8 "GIRL" CLASS (PAS)

AGATHA A 116	ALICE A 113	BARBARA A 324	BRENDA A 335
AGNES A 121	AUDREY A 117	BETTY A 232	BRIDGET A 322

The first of four new classes of harbour berthing tugs. Of 40 tons. 495 bhp = 10 knots. "A" names built by P. K. Harris, "B" names by Dunstons. Completed 1962-1972.

AUDREY

1972, C. and S. Taylor

9 "MODIFIED GIRL" CLASS (PAS)

CELIA A 206	CHRISTINE A 217	DAISY A 145	DORIS A 252
CHARLOTTE A 210	CLARE A 288	DAPHNE	DOROTHY
			EDITH A 177

Of 38 tons. 495 bhp = 10 knots. *Dorothy* in Hong Kong. *Edith* at Gibraltar.
"C" names built by Pimblott and "D" and "E" names by Dunstons. Completed 1972.

EDITH   *1974, Michael D. J. Lennon*

12 "SMALL GIRL" CLASS (PAS)

IRENE	JOYCE	LESLEY	MYRTLE
ISABEL	KATHLEEN	LILAH	NANCY
JOAN	KITTY	MARY	NORAH

All completed by August 1974 by Dunstons. Small "water-tractors" with small wheelhouse and adjoining funnel.

5 "LARGE GIRL" CLASS (PAS)

FELICITY	GEORGINA	HELEN
FIONA	GWENDOLINE	

Large "water tractors". Of 80 tons. 600 bhp = 10 knots. *Felicity* built by Dunstons and remainder by Hancocks. Completed 1973.

HELEN   *10/1975, Dr. Giorgio Arra*

FLEET TENDERS

7 "INSECT" CLASS (PAS)

Name	No.	Builders	Commissioned
BEE	—	C. D. Holmes Ltd, Beverley, Yorks	1970
CICALA	—	C. D. Holmes Ltd, Beverley, Yorks	1971
COCKCHAFER	—	C. D. Holmes Ltd, Beverley, Yorks	1971
CRICKET	—	C. D. Holmes Ltd, Beverley, Yorks	1972
GNAT	—	C. D. Holmes Ltd, Beverley, Yorks	1972
LADYBIRD	—	C. D. Holmes Ltd, Beverley, Yorks	1973
SCARAB (RMAS)	—	C. D. Holmes Ltd, Beverley, Yorks	1973

Displacement, tons: 450 full load
Dimensions, feet (metres): 111·8 oa × 28 × 11 *(34·1 × 8·5 × 3·4)*
Main engines: Lister-Blackstone Diesels; 1 shaft; 660 bhp = 10·5 knots
Complement: 10

First three built as stores carriers, two as armament carriers and *Scarab*, as mooring vessel capable of lifting 10 tons over the bows.

CICALA   *1971, Wright and Logan*

12 "ABERDOVEY" CLASS (PAS)

Name	No.	Builders	Commissioned
ABERDOVEY	—	Isaac Pimblott & Sons, Northwich	1963
ABINGER	—	Isaac Pimblott & Sons, Northwich	1964
ALNESS	—	Isaac Pimblott & Sons, Northwich	1965
ALNMOUTH	—	Isaac Pimblott & Sons, Northwich	1966
APPLEBY	—	Isaac Pimblott & Sons, Northwich	1967
ASHCOTT	—	Isaac Pimblott & Sons, Northwich	1968
BEAULIEU	A 99	J. S. Doig, Grimsby	1966
BEDDGELERT	A 100	J. S. Doig, Grimsby	1967
BEMBRIDGE	A 101	J. S. Doig, Grimsby	1968
BIBURY	A 103	J. S. Doig, Grimsby	1969
BLAKENEY	A 104	J. S. Doig, Grimsby	1970
BRODICK	A 105	J. S. Doig, Grimsby	1971

Displacement, tons: 117·5 full load
Dimensions, feet (metres): 79·8 oa × 18 × 5·5 *(24 × 5·4 × 2·4)*
Main engines: 1 Lister-Blackstone Diesel; 1 shaft; 225 bhp = 10·5 knots
Complement: 6

Multi-purpose for stores (25 tons), passengers (200 standing) plus a couple of torpedoes. *Ashcott* at Gibraltar.

APPLEBY   *1973, Wright and Logan*

4 DIVING TENDERS

Name	No.	Builders	Commissioned
CLOVELLY	A 389	I. Pimblott & Sons, Northwich	1972
ILCHESTER	—	Gregson Ltd, Blyth	1974
INSTOW	—	Gregson Ltd, Blyth	1974
INVERGORDON	A 310	Gregson Ltd, Blyth	1974

Of similar characteristics to "Cartmel" class. All completed 1974.

6 "HAM" CLASS (RNXS)

PAGHAM M 2716		SHIPHAM M 2726	
PORTISHAM M 2781		THAKEHAM M 2733	
PUTTENHAM M 2784		TONGHAM M 2735	

Details in Minewarfare Section.

31 "CARTMEL" CLASS (PAS)

Name	No.	Builders	Commissioned
CARTMEL	—	I. Pimblott & Sons, Northwich	1971
CAWSAND	—	I. Pimblott & Sons, Northwich	1971
CRICCIETH	—	I. Pimblott & Sons, Northwich	1972
CRICKLADE	—	C. D. Holmes, Beverley	1971
CROMARTY	—	J. Lewis, Aberdeen	1972
DATCHET	—	Vospers	1972
DENMEAD	—	C. D. Holmes, Beverley	1972
DORNOCH	—	J. Lewis, Aberdeen	1972
DUNSTER	A 393	R. Dunston, Thorne	1972
ELKSTONE	A 353	J. Cook, Wivenhoe	1971
ELSING	A 277	J. Cook, Wivenhoe	1971
EPWORTH	A 352	J. Cook, Wivenhoe	1972
ETTRICK	A 274	J. Cook, Wivenhoe	1972
FELSTED (RMAS)	A 384	R. Dunston, Thorne	1972
FINTRY	—	J. Lewis, Aberdeen	1972
FOTHERBY	—	R. Dunston, Thorne	1972
FROXFIELD	A 354	R. Dunston, Thorne	1972
FULBECK	—	C. D. Holmes, Beverley	1972
GLENCOVE	—	I. Pimblott & Sons, Northwich	1972
GRASMERE	—	J. Lewis, Aberdeen	1972
HAMBLEDON	—	R. Dunston, Thorne	1973
HARLECH	—	R. Dunston, Thorne	1973
HEADCORN	—	R. Dunston, Thorne	1973
HEVER	—	R. Dunston, Thorne	1973
HOLMWOOD	A 1772	R. Dunston, Thorne	1973
HORNING	A 1773	R. Dunston, Thorne	1973
IXWORTH	A 318	Gregson Ltd, Blyth	Sep 1974
LAMLASH	—	R. Dunston, Thorne	1974
LECHLADE	—	R. Dunston, Thorne	1974
LLANDOVERY	—	R. Dunston, Thorne	1974
LOYAL CHANCELLOR	—	—	—

Displacement, tons: 143 full load
Dimensions, feet (metres): 80 oa × 21 × 6·6 (24·1 × 6·4 × 3)
Main engines: 1 Lister-Blackstone diesel; 1 shaft; 320 bhp = 10·5 knots
Complement: 6

All fleet tenders as "Aberdovey" class except *Datchet,* diving tender with Gray diesels, 2 shafts, 450 bhp = 12 knots and *Felsted* with RMAS. *Elsing* and *Ettrick* at Gibraltar.
Of three types—A. Cargo only; B. Passengers or cargo; C. Training tenders (complement 12).

FROXFIELD   5/1973, Wright and Logan

DATCHET as Diving Tender   9/1974, Dr Giorgio Arra

4 "LOYAL" CLASS (RNXS)

LOYAL MODERATOR A 220	ALERT (ex-*Loyal Governor*) A 510
LOYAL PROCTOR A 1771	VIGILANT (ex-*Loyal Factor*) A 382

Details as for "Cartmel" class. *Loyal Proctor* employed by RNXS and *Loyal Moderator* used for PAS training. *Alert* and *Vigilant* classified as "Patrol Craft" in the Defence White Paper 1976 as they have , from time to time, carried out patrols off Ulster.

LOYAL MODERATOR   5/1974, John G Callis

30 MFV TYPES (PAS)

MFV 7, 15, 63, 93, 96, 119, 139, 140, 175, 205, 256, 278, 289

Length: 61·5 feet

MFV 642, 658, 686, 715, 740, 767, 775, 816, 911

Length: 45 feet

MFV 1021, 1033, 1037, 1048, 1062, 1077, 1190, 1256

Length: 75 feet

MFV 642   11/1973, Wright and Logan

TANK CLEANING VESSELS

6 "ISLES" CLASS (PAS)

Name	No.	Builders	Commissioned
BERN	A 334	Cook Welton and Gemmell	1942
CALDY	A 332	John Lewis and Sons	1943
GRAEMSAY	A 340	Ardrossan Dockyard Co	1943
LUNDY	A 366	Cook Welton and Gemmell	1943
SKOMER	A 338	John Lewis and Sons	1943
SWITHA	A 346	A. and J. Inglis Ltd	1942

Displacement, tons: 770 full load
Dimensions, feet (metres): 164 oa × 27·5 × 14 *(49 × 8·4 × 4·2)*
Main engines: Triple expansion; 1 shaft; 850 ihp = 12 knots
Boiler: 1 cylindrical
Coal, tons: 183

Last survivors, with *Mull* of RCT, in UK service of a class of 145 built for minesweeping during the war, most of them were employed on wreck dispersal after the war until conversion to their present role in 1951-57.

BERN   5/1973, Wright and Logan

DEGAUSSING VESSELS

3 "HAM" CLASS (PAS)

FORDHAM M 2717   **THATCHAM** M 2790   **WARMINGHAM** M 2737

Of the "Ham" class of Inshore Minesweepers. For details see Mine Warfare Section.

WARMINGHAM   10/1974, C. and S. Taylor

NUCLEAR DECONTAMINATION VESSELS

Name	No.	Builders	Commissioned
MAC 1012	—	Chatham	—
MAC 1013	—	Devonport	—

1012 launched at Chatham early in 1971. 1013 built at Devonport 1973. Length 180 feet, beam 30 feet. To be used in connection with the disposal of radio active waste from the Chatham nuclear submarine refitting complex.

SCOTTISH FISHERY PROTECTION VESSELS

2 "JURA" CLASS

Name	No.	Builders	Commissioned
JURA	P 296	Hall, Russell & Co, Aberdeen	1973
WESTRA	—	Hall, Russell & Co, Aberdeen	1975

Displacement, tons: 778 light; 1 285 full load
Measurement, tons: 942 gross
Dimensions, feet (metres): 195·3 oa × 35 × 14·4 *(59·6 × 10·7 × 4·4)*
Main engines: 2 British Polar SP112VS-F diesels; 4 200 bhp; 1 shaft = 17 knots
Complement: 28

Jura has been leased by the Ministry of Defence for oil-rig patrol and armed with 1—40 mm. *Westra* was launched on 6 Aug 1974. Three other craft are operated by Scottish Home Dept.

JURA (fitted for North Sea Patrol)   1975, MOD (N)

ROYAL CORPS OF TRANSPORT

As well as the "Avon" class listed in the Amphibious Warfare Section the following craft are operated by the RCT.

5 GENERAL DUTIES LAUNCHES

BREAM WB 03   **PERCH** WB 06
BARBEL WB 04   **PIKE** WB 07
ROACH WB 05

Generally of about 40 ft.

1 "ISLES" CLASS TRAWLER

MULL

Of 770 tons. For details see Tank Cleaning Vessels. Laid up in reserve.

7 MFV TYPE

MARTIN	SMIKE
NEWMAN BLOGGS	YARMOUTH NAVIGATOR
OLIVER TWIST	YARMOUTH SEAMAN
SKUA	

Distinguishable from naval MFVs by their dark blue hulls and white superstructure.

YARMOUTH SEAMAN   *5/1974, Wright and Logan*

FISHERY PATROL SHIPS

EUROMAN   LLOYDSMAN

Included here as a well-known pair which were originally chartered to patrol the British fishing fleet off Iceland in 1975-76, being "non-provocative". Even when this requirement was outdated they remained as invaluable support for the inadequate numbers of HM Ships available for this duty.

EUROMAN   *2/1976, MOD (N)*

LLOYDSMAN   *2/1976, MOD (N)*

UNITED STATES OF AMERICA

COMPILED AND EDITED BY NORMAN POLMAR

Administration

Secretary of the Navy:
  J. William Middendorf, II

There are one Under Secretary and four Assistant Secretaries.

Principal Flag Officers

Chief of Naval Operations:
  Admiral James Holloway, III, USN
Vice Chief of Naval Operations:
  Admiral Harold E. Shear, USN
Deputy Chief of Naval Operations (Manpower):
  Vice-Admiral James D. Watkins, USN
Deputy Chief of Naval Operations (Submarine Warfare):
  Vice-Admiral Robert L. J. Long, USN
Deputy Chief of Naval Operations (Surface Warfare):
  Vice-Admiral James H. Doyle, Jnr, USN
Deputy Chief of Naval Operations (Air Warfare):
  Vice-Admiral Forrest S. Peterson
Deputy Chief of Naval Operations (Logistics):
  Vice-Admiral Edward W. Cooke USN
Deputy Chief of Naval Operations (Plans, Policy and Operations):
  Vice-Admiral Joseph P. Moorer, USN
**Commander-in-Chief Atlantic and Commander-in-Chief Atlantic Fleet:*
  Admiral Isaac C. Kidd, Jnr, USN
Commander-in-Chief Pacific:
  Admiral Maurice F. Weisner, USN
Commander-in-Chief Pacific Fleet:
  Thomas B. Hayward, USN
Commander Second Fleet (Atlantic):
  Vice-Admiral John J. Shanahan, Jnr, USN
Commander Third Fleet (Eastern Pacific):
  Vice-Admiral Robert P. Coogan, USN
Commander Sixth Fleet (Mediterranean) and Commander Strike Force South (NATO):
  Vice-Admiral Harry D. Train, II, USN
Commander Seventh Fleet (Western Pacific):
  Vice-Admiral Robert B. Baldwin, USN
Commander Military Sealift Command:
  Rear-Admiral Sam H. Moore, USN
Chief of Naval Education and Training:
  Vice-Admiral James Wilson, USN
Chief of Naval Reserve:
  Vice-Admiral Pierre N. Charbonnet, Jnr, USN

Marine Corps

Commandant:
  General Louis H. Wilson, Jnr, USMC
Assistant Commandant:
  General Samuel Jaskilka, USMC
Chief of Staff:
  Lieutenant-General L. E. Brown, USMC

Materiél

Chief of Naval Material:
  Admiral F. H. Michaelis, USN
Vice Chief of Naval Material:
  Vice-Admiral Vincent A. Lascara
Commander Naval Air Systems Command:
  Vice-Admiral Kent L. Lee, USN
Commander Naval Electronic Systems Command:
  Rear-Admiral Earl B. Fowler, Jnr, USN
Commander Naval Facilities Engineering Command:
  Rear-Admiral Albert R. Marschall, USN
***Commander Naval Sea Systems Command:*
  Vice-Admiral Robert C. Gooding, USN
Commander Naval Supply Systems Command:
  Rear-Admiral Wallace R. Dowd, Jnr, USN

Notes: *Unified Command with the Commander-in-Chief directing all US Army, Navy, and Air Force activities in the area. Only naval officers serving as Unified Commanders-in-Chief are listed. **In addition to Unified Commander, also Supreme Allied Commander Atlantic (NATO position). ***In July 1974 the Naval Ordnance Systems Command and Naval Ship Systems Command were merged into the new Naval Sea Systems Command.

Diplomatic Representation

Defense Attaché and Naval Attaché in London:
  Rear-Admiral Francis T. Brown, USN
Naval Attaché and Naval Attaché for Air in Moscow:
  Captain Ronald J. Kurth, USN
Naval Attaché and Naval Attaché for Air in Paris:
  Captain George N. La Rocque, USN

Personnel

	30 June 1975 (Actual)	30 June 1976 (Planned)	30 Sep 1977 (Planned)
Navy			
Officers	65 680	63 871	63 650
Enlisted	466 121	456 477	476 000
Marine Corps			
Officers	18 591	18 552	18 552
Enlisted	177 360	177 448	177 448

Strength of the Fleet

The following table provides a tabulation of the ship strength of the United States Navy and an index to the ship listings within the United States section of this edition. Ship arrangement is based on function and employment; the official arrangement of ship types is contained in the "List of classifications of naval ships and service craft" which appears on a later page in this section. Numbers of ships listed in the table are estimated as of 1 July 1976, based on official and unofficial sources.

Category-Type		Active (a)	Building (b)	Reserve
STRATEGIC MISSILE SUBMARINES				
SSBN	Ballistic Missile Submarines	41	4	—
SUBMARINES				
SSN	Attack Submarines (nuclear)	64	27	1
SSN	Research Submarines (nuclear)	1	—	1
SS	Attack Submarines (diesel)	9	—	—
SSG	Guided Missile Submarines (diesel)	—	—	1
LPSS/SS	Transport Submarines (diesel)	1	—	1
AGSS	Research Submarines (diesel)	2	—	1
AIRCRAFT CARRIERS				
CVN	Aircraft Carriers (nuclear)	2	2	—
CV/CVA	Aircraft Carriers	11	—	2
CVS	Anti-Submarine Carriers	—	—	4
CVT	Training Carriers	1	—	—
CRUISERS				
CGN	Guided Missile Cruisers (nuclear)	5	4	—
CG	Guided Missile Cruisers	21(c)	—	3
CA	Heavy Cruisers	—	—	5
DESTROYERS				
DDG	Guided Missile Destroyers	39	—	—
DD	Destroyers	62(a)	26	—
FRIGATES				
FFG	Guided Missile Frigates	6	10	—
FF	Frigates	58	—	—
AGFF	Frigate Research Ships	1	—	—
BATTLESHIPS				
BB	Battleships	—	—	4
COMMAND SHIPS				
AGF	Miscellaneous Flagships	1	—	—
CC	National Command Ships	—	—	2
AMPHIBIOUS WARFARE SHIPS				
LCC	Amphibious Command Ships	2	—	4
LHA	Amphibious Assault Ships	1	4	—
LPH	Amphibious Assault Ships	7	—	—
LKA	Amphibious Cargo Ships	6(a)	—	12
LPA	Amphibious Transports	2(a)	—	7
LPD	Amphibious Transport Docks	14	—	—
LSD	Dock Landing Ships	13	—	7
LST	Tank Landing Ships	20	—	7
PATROL SHIPS AND CRAFT				
PHM	Patrol Combatants—Missile	1	5	—
PGH	Patrol Gunboats (hydrofoil)	1	—	—
PCH	Patrol Craft (hydrofoil)	1	—	—
PG	Patrol Combatants	11(a)	—	—
PTF	Fast Patrol Craft	17(a)	—	—
MINE WARFARE SHIPS				
MSO	Ocean Minesweepers	25(a)	—	12
UNDERWAY REPLENISHMENT SHIPS		49	2	14
FLEET SUPPORT SHIPS		78	8	19
SEALIFT SHIPS		28	—	13
EXPERIMENTAL, RESEARCH AND SURVEYING SHIPS		39	—	6

Note: (a) Includes ships undergoing overhaul and refuelling in the case of nuclear-powered ships; also includes 30 destroyers, 3 amphibious ships, 22 minesweepers, 17 fast patrol craft, and 5 patrol combatants assigned to the Naval Reserve Force and manned by composite reserve and active duty crews. (b) Generally includes ships authorised through the Fiscal Year 1976 new construction programme although actual construction may not have begun. (c) Does *not* include cruiser *Belknap* (CG 26) severely damaged in collision; to be rebuilt.

Mercantile Marine

US Maritime Administration: 533 vessels of 10 065 000 tons gross (14 993 000 tons deadweight) as of 1 Apr 1976. Another 260 vessels are laid up in reserve of which 71 are to be scrapped.

Lloyd's Register of Shipping: 4 346 vessels of 14 586 616 tons gross

SHIPBUILDING PROGRAMMES

Planned Five-Year Shipbuilding Programme (Fiscal Years 1977-1981)

7 Nuclear-Powered FBM Submarines (Trident/SSBN 726)
11 Nuclear-Powered Attack Submarines (SSN 688)
2 Nuclear-Powered Aircraft Carriers (CVNX)
1 VSTOL Support Ship (VSS)
2 Nuclear-Powered Strike Cruisers (CSGN)
8 Guided Missile Destroyers (DDG47)
40 Guided Missile Frigates (FFG 7)
1 Amphibious Ship (LX)
10 Mine Countermeasure Ships (MCM)
3 Destroyer Tenders (AD)
12 Ocean Surveillance Ships (AGOS)
6 Oilers (AO)
1 Fast Combat Support Ship (AOE)
1 Repair Ship (ARX)
1 Salvage Ship (ARSX)
1 Submarine Tender (AS)
4 Fleet Tugs (ATF)

Supplemental Fiscal Year 1977 Shipbuilding Programme
(Presented to the Congress in May 1976)

4 Guided Missile Frigates (FFG 7)
1 Oiler (AO)

Proposed Fiscal Year 1977 Shipbuilding Programme

1 Nuclear-Powered FBM Submarine (Trident/SSBN 726)
3 Nuclear-Powered Attack Submarines (SSN 688)
1 Guided Missile Destroyer (DDG 47)
8 Guided Missile Frigates (FFG 7)
1 Destroyer Tender (AD)
1 Oiler (AO)
1 Submarine Tender (AS)

Approved Fiscal Year 1976 Shipbuilding Programme

1 Nuclear-Powered FBM Submarine (Trident/SSBN 726)
2 Nuclear-Powered Attack Submarines (SSN 688)
*6 Guided Missile Frigates (FFG 7)
1 Destroyer Tender (AD)
2 Oilers (AO)
3 Fleet Tugs (ATF)

(*9 frigates were approved by Congress but the authorisation could fund only 6)

Naval Aviation

US Naval Aviation currently consists of approx 7 000 aircraft flown by the Navy and Marine Corps. The principal naval aviation organisations are 13 carrier air wings, 24 maritime reconnaissance/patrol squadrons, and three Marine Aircraft Wings. In addition, the Naval Reserve and Marine Corps Reserve operate 7 fighter squadrons, 11 attack squadrons, and 12 patrol squadrons, plus various reconnaissance, electrical warfare, tanker, helicopter and transport units.

Fighter: 26 Navy squadrons with F-4 Phantom and F-14 Tomcat aircraft; 12 Marine squadrons with F-4 Phantoms.
Attack: 39 Navy squadrons with A-6 Intruder and A-7 Corsair aircraft; 13 Marine squadrons with A-4 Skyhawk, A-6 Intruder, AV-8 Harrier aircraft.
Reconnaissance: 10 Navy RA-5C Vigilante and RF-8G Crusader aircraft; 3 Marine squadrons with RF-4B Phantoms.
Airborne Early Warning: 12 Navy squadrons with E-2 Hawkeye aircraft.
Electronic Warfare: 8 Navy squadrons with EA-6B Prowler aircraft (Marines operate EA-6A Intruder aircraft in composite reconnaissance squadrons).
Anti-Submarine: 9 Navy squadrons with S-3 Viking aircraft replacing S-2 Trackers.
Maritime Patrol: 24 Navy squadrons with P-3 Orion aircraft.
Helicopter Anti-Submarine: 16 Navy squadrons with SH-3 Sea King and SH-2 LAMPS helicopters.
Helicopter Mine Countermeasures: 1 Navy squadron with RH-53 Sea Stallion.
Helicopter Support: 4 Navy squadrons with UH-46 Sea Knight helicopters.
Electronic Reconnaissance: 2 Navy squadrons with EP-3E Orion and EC-121 Warning Star aircraft.
Communications Relay: 2 Navy squadrons with EC-130 Hercules aircraft.
Observation: 3 Marine squadrons with OV-10 Bronco aircraft.
Helicopter Gunship: 3 Marine squadrons with AH-1 Sea Cobra helicopters.
Helicopter Transport: 21 Marine squadrons with UH-1 Iroquois (Huey), CH-46 Sea Knight, and CH-53 Sea Stallion helicopters.

BASES

Naval Air Stations and Air Facilities (44)

NAS Alameda, Calif; NAF China Lake, Calif; NAF El Centro, Calif; NAS Los Alamitos, Calif; NAS Mirimar, Calif; NAS Moffett Field (San Jose), Calif; NAS Point Mugu, Calif; NAS North Island (San Diego), Calif; NAF Andrews, Washington DC; NAS Cecil Field (Pensacola), Fla; NAS Jacksonville, Fla; NAS Key West, Fla; NAS Whiting Field (Milton), Fla; NAS Saufley Field (Pensacola), Fla; NAS Pansacola, Fla; NAS Atlanta (Marietta), Ga; NAS Glenview, Ill; NAS Barbers Point (Oahu), Hawaii; NAS New Orleans, La; NAS Brunswick, Me; NAS Paxtuxent River, Md; NAS South Weymouth, Mass; NAF Detroit, Mich; NAS Meridan, Miss; NAS Fallon, Nev; NAS Lakehurst, NJ; NAF Warminster, Penna; NAS Willow Grove, Penna; NAS Memphis (Millington), Tenn; NAS Chase Field (Beeville), Texas; NAS Corpus Christi, Texas; NAS Dallas, Texas; NAS Kingsville, Texas; NAS Norfolk, Va; NAS Whidbey Island (Oak Harbor), Wash; NAF Lajes, Azores; NAS Bermuda; NAS Guantanamo Bay, Cuba; NAF Naples, Italy; NAF Atsugi, Japan; NAS Agana, Guam; NAF Okinawa; NAS Subic Bay, Philippines; NAF Mildenhall (Suffolk), England.

BASES—continued

Naval Amphibious Bases (2)

Coronado (San Diego), Calif; Little Creek (Norfolk), Va.

Naval Stations and Naval Bases (20)

Adak, Alaska; Long Beach, Calif; San Diego, Calif; Treasure Island (San Francisco), Calif; Mayport, Fla; Pearl Harbor, Hawaii; Boston, Mass; Brooklyn, NY; Philadelphia, Pa; Newport, RI; Charleston, SC; Norfolk, Va; Guantanmo Bay, Cuba; Keflavik, Iceland; Agana, Guam; Midway Island; Argentia, Newfoundland; Roosevelt Roads, Puerto Rico; Subic Bay, Philippines; Rota, Spain.

Naval Submarine Bases (2)

New London (Groton), Conn; Pearl Harbor, Hawaii.

Strategic Missile Submarine Anchorages (1)

Holy Loch, Scotland.*

Navy Yards (1)

Washington, DC.**

Naval Ship Repair Facilities (2)

Subic Bay, Philippines; Yokosuka, Japan.

Marine Air Stations and Air Facilities (7)

El Toro (Santa Ana), Calif; Kaneohe Bay (Oahu), Hawaii; Cherry Point, NC; New River (Jacksonville), Fla; Quantico, Va; Iwakuni, Japan; Futema, Okinawa.

Marine Corps Bases (5)

Camp Pendleton, Calif; Twentynine Palms, Calif; Camp H.M. Smith (Oahu), Hawaii; Camp Lejeune, NC; Camp Smedley D. Butler (Kawasaki), Okinawa.

*Polaris/Poseidon submarines also operate from Rota, Spain; Apra harbour, Guam; and Charleston, South Carolina. Trident submarines will be based in Seattle, Washington.
**Primarily administration and historical activities; no ship construction or repair activities.

MAJOR SHIPYARDS

Naval Shipyards

Boston Naval Shipyard, Boston, Massachusetts; closed in 1973-1974
Charleston Naval Shipyard, Charleston, South Carolina
Hunters Point Naval Shipyard, San Francisco, California (formerly a division of the San Francisco Bay Naval Shipyard and before that the San Francisco Naval Shipyard) closed 1973-1974
Long Beach Naval Shipyard, Long Beach, California
Mare Island Naval Shipyard, Vallejo, California (formerly a division of the San Francisco Bay Naval Shipyard)
Norfolk Naval Shipyard, Portsmouth, Virginia
Pearl Harbor Naval Shipyard, Pearl Harbor, Hawaii
Philadelphia Naval Shipyard, Philadelphia, Pennsylvania
Portsmouth Naval Shipyard, Portsmouth, New Hampshire (located in Kittery, Maine)
Puget Sound Naval Shipyard, Bremerton, Washington

(Note: None of the above shipyards is now engaged in new construction, but are used for the overhaul and conversion of warships and auxiliaries).

Commercial Shipyards

Avondale Shipyards, Inc, New Orleans, Louisiana
Bath Iron Works Corp, Bath, Maine
Bethlehem Steel Corp, Sparrows Point, Maryland
General Dynamics Corp, Electric Boat Division, Groton, Connecticut (formerly Electric Boat Company)
General Dynamics Corp, Quincy Shipbuilding Division, Quincy, Massachusetts (formerly Bethlehem Steel Corp Yard)
Ingalls Shipbuilding Division (Litton Industries), East Bank Yard, Pasagoula, Mississippi
Ingalls Shipbuilding Division (Litton Industries), West Bank Yard, Pasagoula, Mississippi
Lockheed Shipbuilding & Construction Co, Seattle, Washington
National Steel & Shipbuilding Co, San Diego, California
Newport News Shipbuilding & Dry Dock Co, Newport News, Virginia
Todd Shipyards Corp, San Pedro, California
Todd Shipyards Corp, Seattle, Washington

(Note: All of the above yards have engaged in naval and commercial shipbuilding, overhaul, or modernisation except for the General Dynamics/Electric Boat yard which is engaged only in submarine work).

CLASSIFICATION OF NAVAL SHIPS AND SERVICE CRAFT

The following is the official US Navy list of classifications of naval ships and service craft as promulgated by the Secretary of the Navy on 6 Jan 1975.

In actual usage, symbols preceded by the letter "E" indicate that the ship or craft is a prototype in an experimental or developmental status; the prefix "T" indicates that the ship is assigned to the Navy's Military Sealift Command and is civilian manned; and the prefix "F" indicates a ship being constructed by the United States for a foreign government.

The US Navy regularly develops additional ship classifications which do not appear in the official list, primarily to indicate new ship types under consideration. Current non-standard classifications include VSS for VSTOL support ship, CSGN for nuclear-propelled strike cruiser, and AGOS for ocean surveillance ship. In addition, the letter "X" is often added to existing classifications to indicate a new class whose characteristics have not yet been decided, as in LX, ARX, and ARSX.

COMBATANT SHIPS

(1) Warships

Aircraft Carriers:

Aircraft Carrier	CV
Attack Aircraft Carrier	CVA
Attack Aircraft Carrier (nuclear propulsion)	CVAN
Aircraft Carrier (nuclear propulsion)	CVN
ASW Aircraft Carrier	CVS

Surface Combatants:

Battleship	BB
Heavy Cruiser	CA
Guided Missile Cruiser	CG
Guided Missile Cruiser (nuclear propulsion)	CGN
Destroyer	DD
Guided Missile Destroyer	DDG
Frigate	FF
Guided Missile Frigate	FFG
Radar Picket Frigate	FFR

Patrol Combatants:

Patrol Combatant	PG
Patrol Combatant Missile (hydrofoil)	PHM
Patrol Escort	PCE

Command Ship	CC

Submarines:

Submarine	SS
Submarine (nuclear propulsion)	SSN
Fleet Ballistic Missile Submarine (nuclear propulsion)	SSBN
Guided Missile Submarine	SSG

(2) Amphibious Warfare Ships

Amphibious Command Ship	LCC
Inshore Fire Support Ship	LFR
Amphibious Assault Ship (general purpose)	LHA
Amphibious Cargo Ship	LKA
Amphibious Transport	LPA
Amphibious Transport Dock	LPD
Amphibious Assault Ship	LPH
Amphibious Transport (small)	LPR
Amphibious Transport Submarine	LPSS
Dock Landing Ship	LSD
Tank Landing Ship	LST

(3) Mine Warfare Ships

Mine Countermeasures Ship	MCS
Minesweeper, Coastal (non-magnetic)	MSC
Minesweeper, Ocean (non-magnetic)	MSO

COMBATANT CRAFT

(1) Patrol Craft

Coastal Patrol Boat	CPC
Coastal Patrol and Interdiction Craft	CPIC
Patrol Boat	PB
Patrol Craft (fast)	PCF
Patrol Craft (hydrofoil)	PCH
Patrol Gunboat (hydrofoil)	PGH
Fast Patrol Craft	PTF

(2) Landing Craft

Amphibious Assault Landing Craft	AALC
Landing Craft, Mechanised	LCM
Landing Craft, Personnel, Large	LCPL
Landing Craft, Personnel, Ramped	LCPR
Landing Craft, Utility	LCU
Landing Craft, Vehicle, Personnel	LCVP
Amphibious Warping Tug	LWT

(3) Mine Countermeasures Craft

Minesweeping Boat	MSB
Minesweeper, Drone	MSD
Minesweeper, Inshore	MSI
Minesweeper, River	MSM
Minesweeper, Patrol	MSR

(4) Riverine Warfare Craft

Assault Support Patrol Boat	ASPB
Mini-Armoured Troop Carrier	ATC
River Patrol Boat	PBR
Shallow Water Attack Craft, Medium	SWAM
Shallow Water Attack Craft, Light	SWAL

(5) SEAL Support Craft

Landing Craft Swimmer Reconnaissance	LCSR
Light SEAL Support Craft	LSSC
Medium SEAL Support Craft	MSSC
Swimmer Delivery Vehicle	SDV

(6) Mobile Inshore Undersea Warfare (MIUW) Craft

MIUW Attack Craft	MAC

AUXILIARY SHIPS

Destroyer Tender	AD
Degaussing Ship	ADG
Ammunition Ship	AE
Store Ship	AF
Combat Store Ship	AFS
Miscellaneous	AG
Auxiliary Deep Submergence Support Ship	AGDS
Frigate Research Ship	AGFF
Hydrofoil Research Ship	AGEH
Environmental Research Ship	AGER
Miscellaneous Command Ship	AGF
Patrol Combatant Support Ship	AGHS
Missile Range Instrumentation Ship	AGM
Major Communications Relay Ship	AGMR
Oceanographic Research Ship	AGOR
Patrol Craft Tender	AGP
Surveying Ship	AGS
Auxiliary Submarine	AGSS
Hospital Ship	AH
Cargo Ship	AK
Light Cargo Ship	AKL
Vehicle Cargo Ship	AKR
Oiler	AO
Fast Combat Support Ship	AOE
Gasoline Tanker	AOG
Replenishment Oiler	AOR
Transport	AP
Self-propelled Barracks Ship	APB
Repair Ship	AR
Battle Damage Repair Ship	ARB
Cable Repairing Ship	ARC
Internal Combustion Engine Repair Ship	ARG
Landing Craft Repair Ship	ARL
Salvage Ship	ARS
Submarine Tender	AS
Submarine Rescue Ship	ASR
Auxiliary Ocean Tug	ATA
Fleet Ocean Tug	ATF
Salvage and Rescue Ship	ATS
Guided Missile Ship	AVM
Training Aircraft Carrier	CVT
Surface Effects Ship	SES

SERVICE CRAFT*

Large Auxiliary Floating Dry Dock	AFDB
Small Auxiliary Floating Dry Dock	AFDL
Medium Auxiliary Floating Dry Dock	AFDM
Barracks Craft (non-self-propelled)	APL
Auxiliary Dry Dock	ARD
Medium Auxiliary Repair Dry Dock	ARDM
Deep Submergence Rescue Vehicle	DSRV
Deep Submergence Vehicle	DSV
Unclassified Miscellaneous	IX
Submersible Research Vehicle (nuclear propulsion)	NR
Miscellaneous Auxiliary (self-propelled)	YAG
Open Lighter	YC
Car Float	YCF
Aircraft Transportation Lighter	YCV
Floating Crane	YD
Diving Tender	YDT
Covered Lighter (self-propelled)	YF
Ferryboat or Launch (self-propelled)	YFB
Yard Floating Dry Dock	YFD
Covered Lighter	YFN
Large Covered Lighter	YFNB
Dry Dock Companion Craft	YFND
Lighter (special purpose)	YFNX
Floating Power Barge	YFP
Refrigerated Covered Lighter (self-propelled)	YFR
Refrigerated Covered Lighter	YFRN
Covered Lighter (Range Tender) (self-propelled)	YFRT
Harbour Utility Craft (self-propelled)	YFU
Garbage Lighter (self-propelled)	YG
Garbage Lighter (non-self-propelled)	YGN
Salvage Lift Craft, Heavy	YHLC
Dredge (self-propelled)	YM
Salvage Lift Craft, Medium	YMLC
Gate Craft	YNG
Fuel Oil Barge (self-propelled)	YO
Gasoline Barge (self-propelled)	YOG
Gasoline Barge	YOGN
Fuel Oil Barge	YON
Oil Storage Barge	YOS
Patrol Craft (self-propelled)	YP
Floating Pile Driver	YPD
Floating Workshop	YR
Repair and Berthing Barge	YRB
Repair, Berthing and Messing Barge	YRBM
Floating Dry Dock Workshop (Hull)	YRDH
Floating Dry Dock Workshop (Machine)	YRDM
Radiology Repair Barge	YRR
Salvage Craft Tender	YRST
Seaplane Wrecking Derrick (self-propelled)	YSD
Sludge Removal Barge	YSR
Large Harbour Tug (self-propelled)	YTB
Small Harbour Tug (self-propelled)	YTL
Medium Harbour Tug (self-propelled)	YTM
Water Barge (self-propelled)	YW
Water Barge	YWN

*Self-propelled barges are indicated in parenthesis. The final letter "N" generally indicates non-self-propelled.

CLASSIFICATION OF MARITIME COMMISSION SHIP DESIGNS

Ships constructed under the jurisdiction of the US Maritime Commission by private shipyards are assigned Maritime Commission design classifications. These classifications consist of three groups of letters and numbers.

First group letter(s) indicate type of ship and number indicates size class. The letters of Maritime Commission ship classifications now on the US Navy List are:

Cargo	C
Passenger	P
Refrigerator	R
Special Purpose	S
Tanker	T
Victory Cargo	VC

Second group letter(s) indicate type of propulsion and number "2" indicates twin shaft ship and "4" quadruple shaft ship.

Motor (diesel)	M
Motor (diesel) Electric	ME
Steam (reciprocating or turbine)	S
Steam Electric	SE

Third group of letters and numbers indicates the design of a particular type of ship, beginning with A1.

ELECTRONIC EQUIPMENT CLASSIFICATION

Major electronic equipment in US Navy ships is identified by the Joint Army-Navy Nomenclature System, with a series of letters indicating the installation, type of equipment, and purpose, with numerals indicating the particular model. This letter-numeral combination is prefixed with the letters AN to indicate that the designation is part of the joint service system. The AN prefix is deleted from the ship electronic listings in the United States section.

The first letter indicates the installation:

Airborne	A
Underwater (submarine)	B
Surface ship	S
Multiple-platform	U
Surface ship and underwater	W

The second letter indicates the type of equipment:

Countermeasures	L
Radar	P
Sonar and underwater sound	Q
Radio	R
Special type (eg, magnetic)	S
Data processing (eg, computer)	Y

The third letter indicates the purpose:

Part of other equipment	A
Fire control	G
Maintenance and test	M
Navigation	N
Special or combination	Q
Receiving/passive detection	R
Detecting	S
Computing	U

STRATEGIC MISSILE SUBMARINES

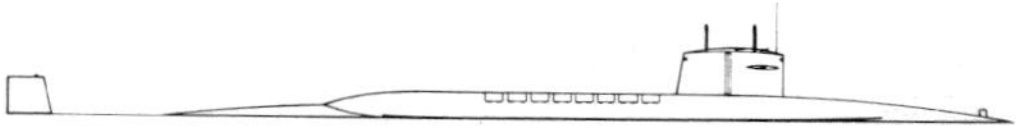

LAFAYETTE (SSBN 616)

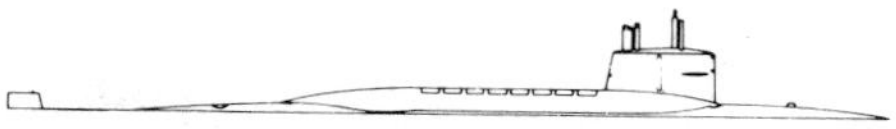

GEORGE WASHINGTON (SSBN 598)

SUBMARINES

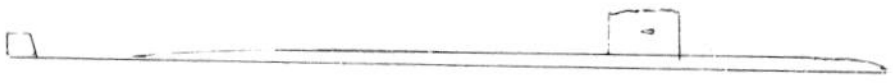

LOS ANGELES (SSN 688)

GLENARD P. LIPSCOMB (SSN 685)

NARWHAL (SSN 671)

STURGEON (SSN 637)

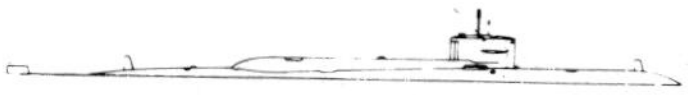

TULLIBEE (SSN 597)

PERMIT (SSN 594)

HALIBUT (SSN 587)

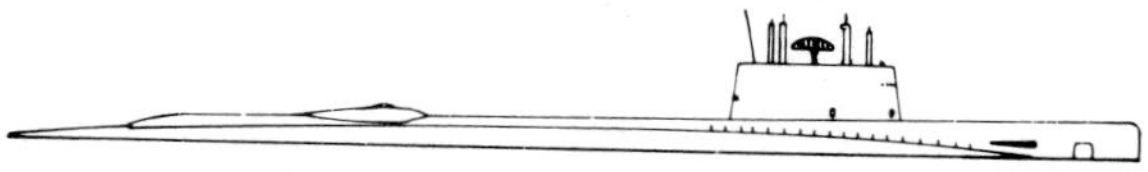

TRITON (SSN 586)

SKIPJACK (SSN 585)

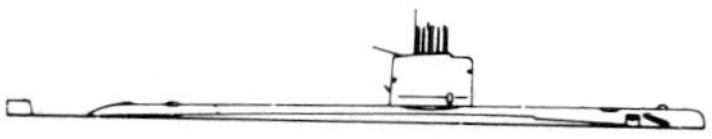

SWORDFISH (SSN 579)

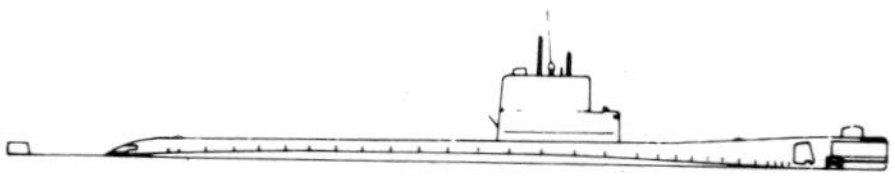

SEAWOLF (SSN 575)

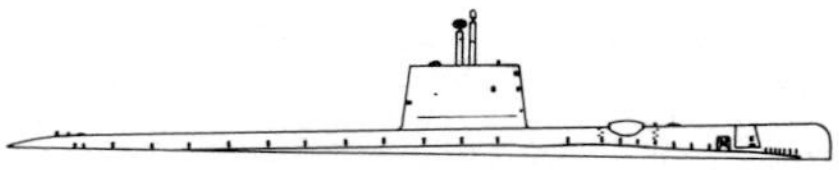

NAUTILUS (SSN 571)

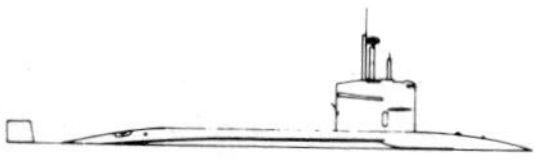

BARBEL (SS 580)

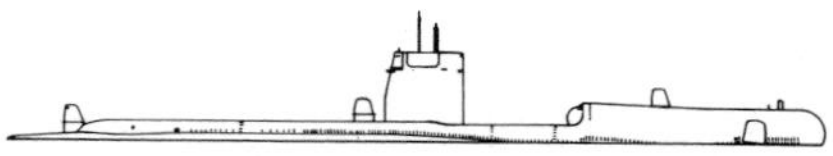

GRAYBACK (SS/LPSS 574)

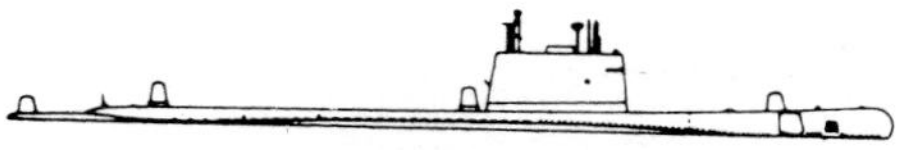

SAILFISH (SS 572)

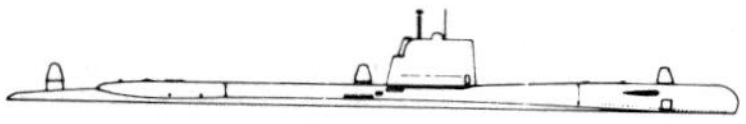

WAHOO (SS 565) "Tang" Class

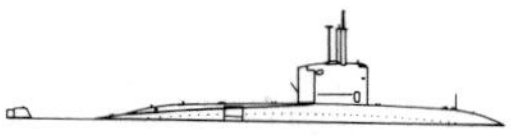

ALBACORE (AGSS 569)

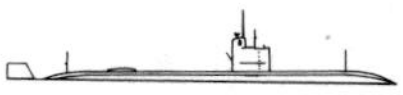

DOLPHIN (AGSS 555)

AIRCRAFT CARRIERS

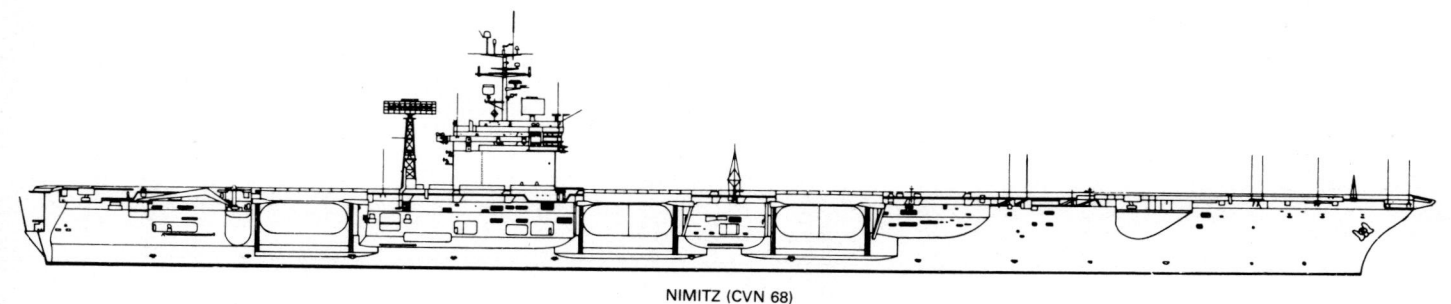

NIMITZ (CVN 68)

Scale: 1 inch = 150 feet (1 : 1 800)
Drawings by A. D. Baker

Aircraft Carriers—*continued*

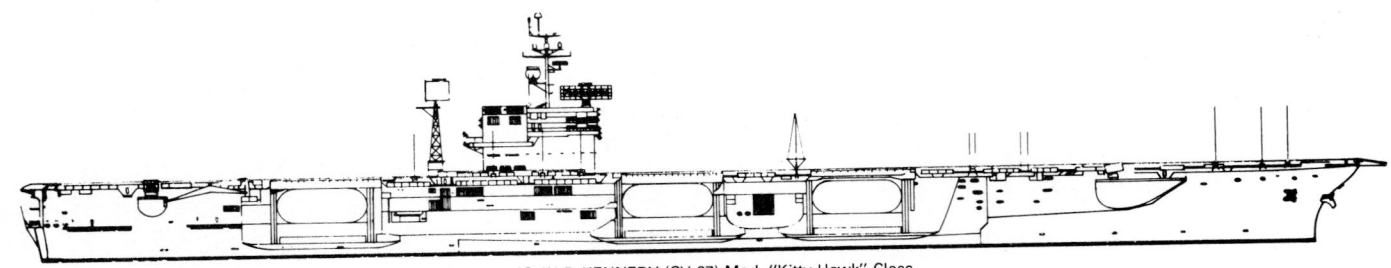

JOHN F. KENNEDY (CV 67) Mod. "Kitty Hawk" Class

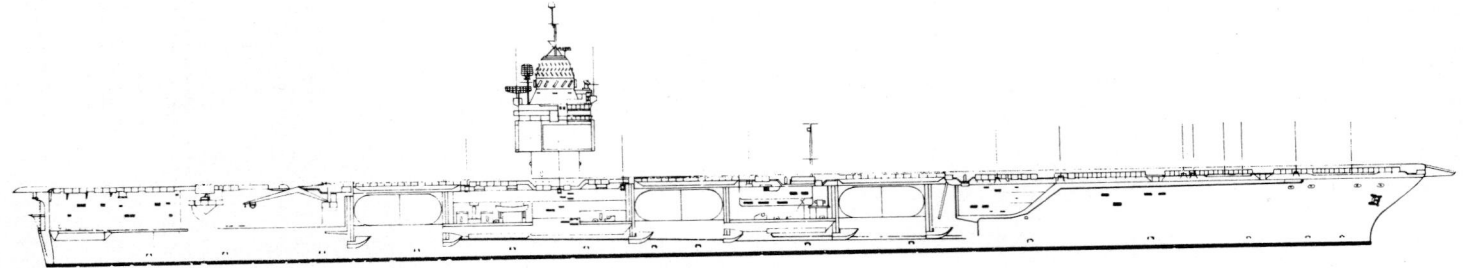

ENTERPRISE (CVN 65)

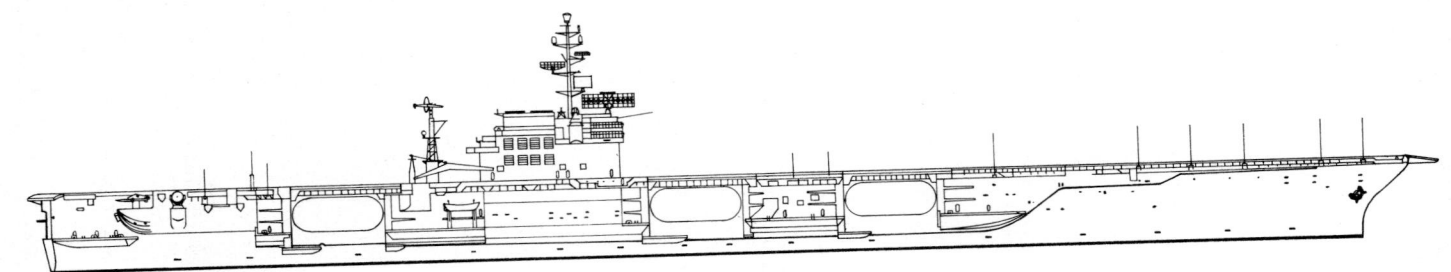

KITTY HAWK (CV 63)

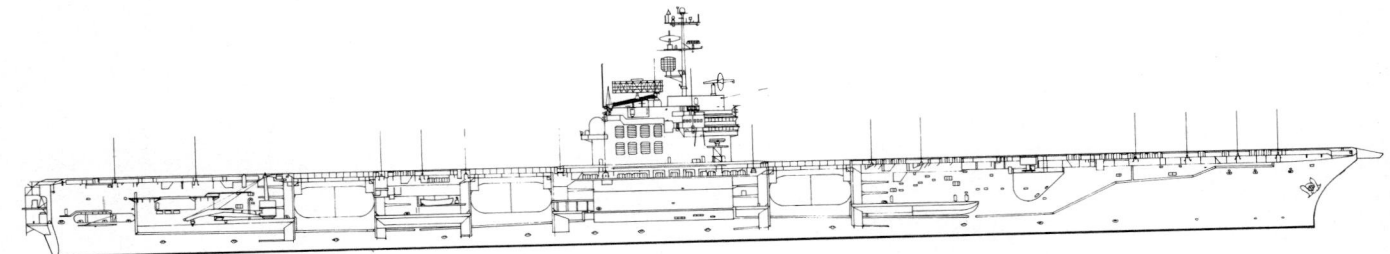

INDEPENDENCE (CV 62) "Forrestal" Class

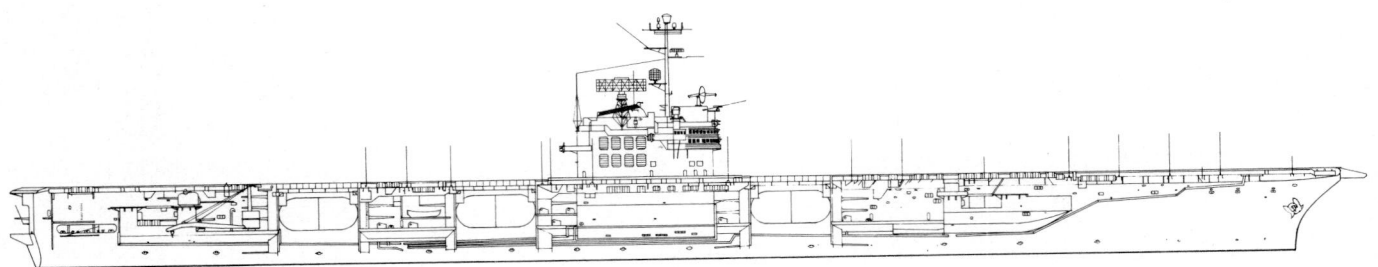

RANGER (CV 61) "Forrestal" Class

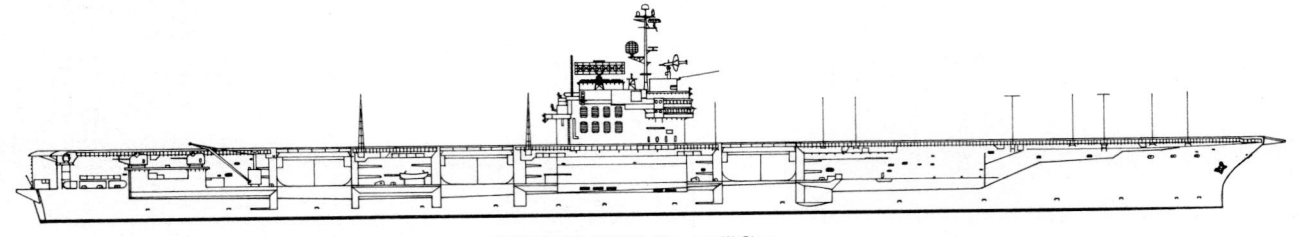

SARATOGA (CV 60) "Forrestal" Class

Scale: 1 inch = 150 feet (1 : 1 800)

Aircraft Carriers—*continued*

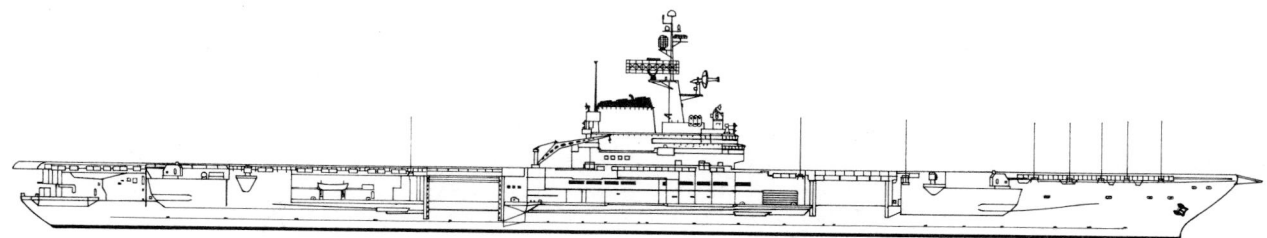

CORAL SEA (CV 43) "Midway" Class (ROOSEVELT similar)

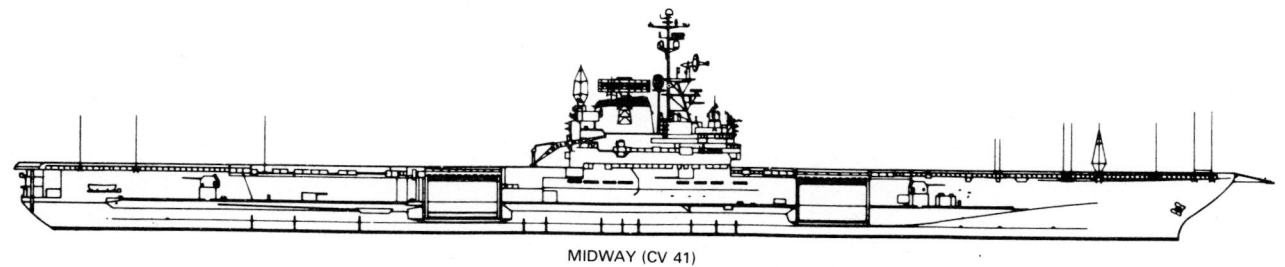

MIDWAY (CV 41)

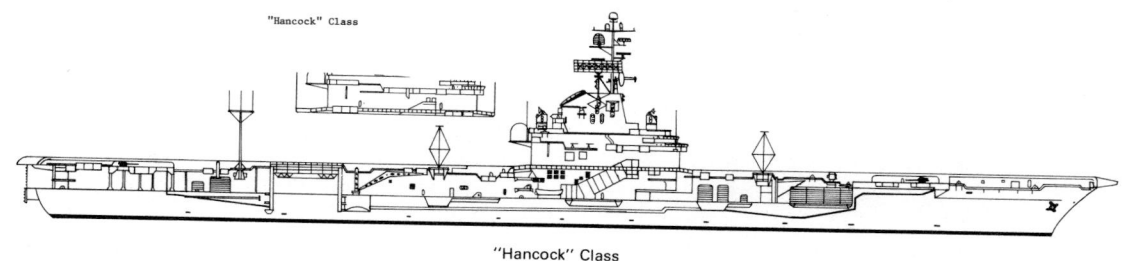

"Hancock" Class

"Hancock" Class

CRUISERS

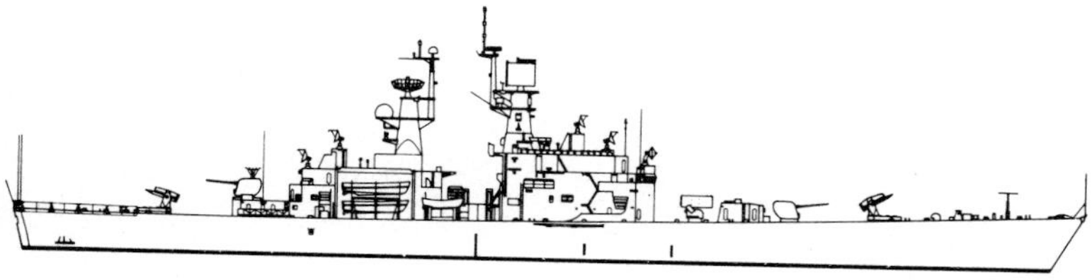

CALIFORNIA (CGN 36)

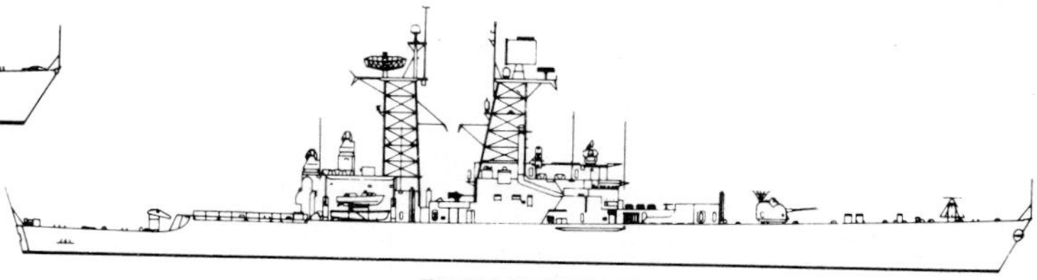

TRUXTUN (CGN 35)

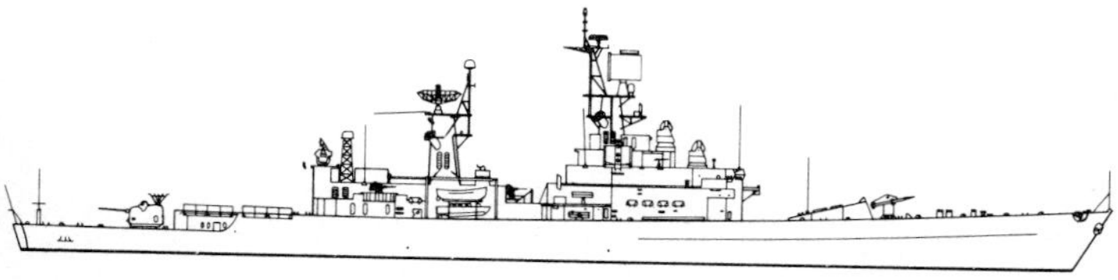

FOX (CG 33) "Belknap" Class

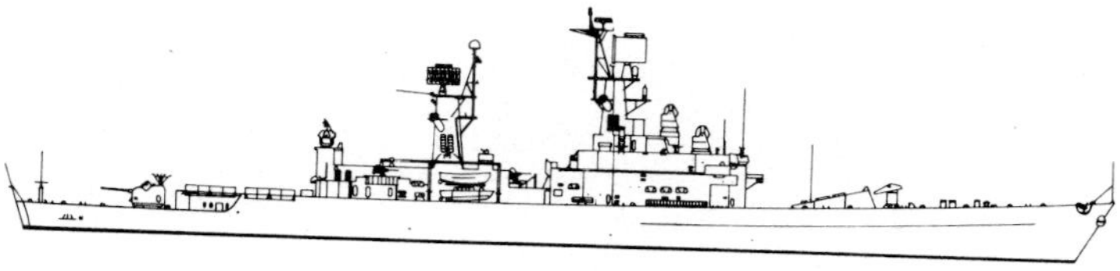

WAINWRIGHT (CG 28) "Belknap" Class

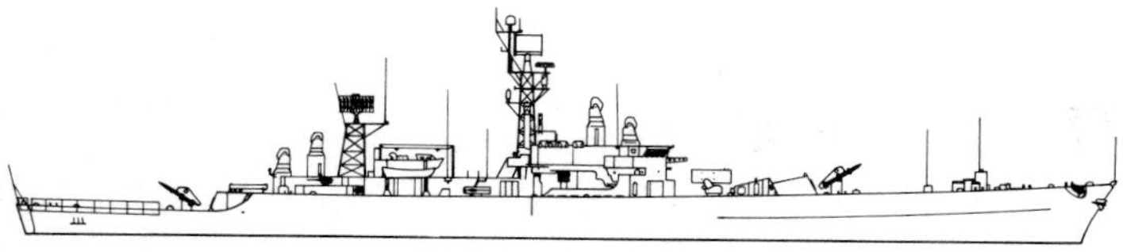

BAINBRIDGE (CGN 25)

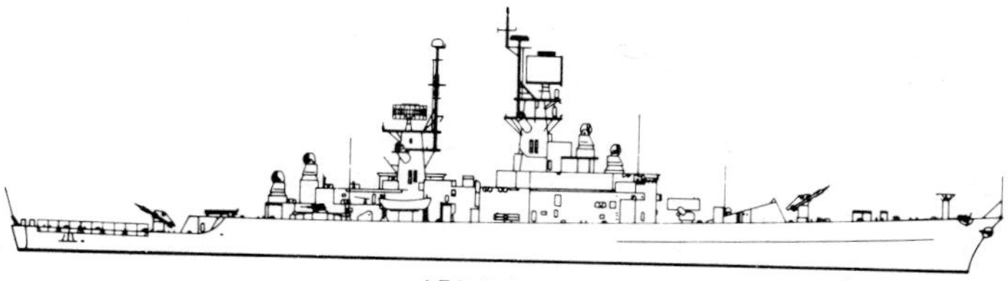

LEAHY (CG 16)

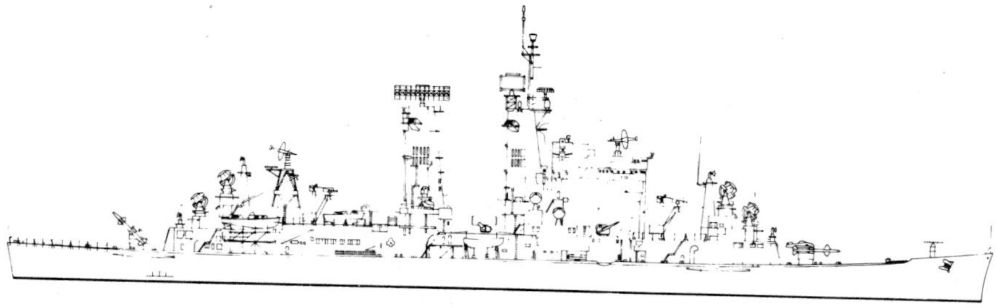

CHICAGO (CG 11) "Albany" Class

Cruisers—*continued*

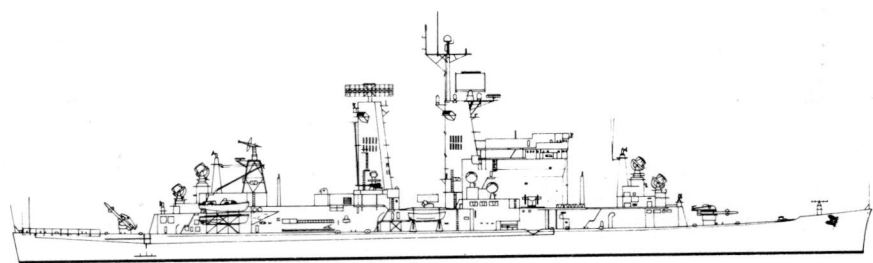

ALBANY (CG 10)

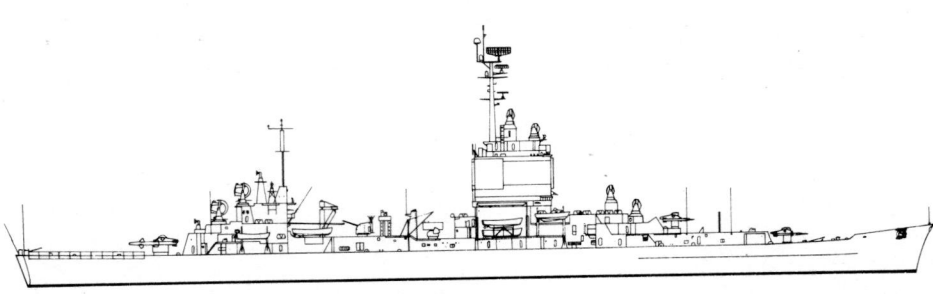

LONG BEACH (CGN 9)

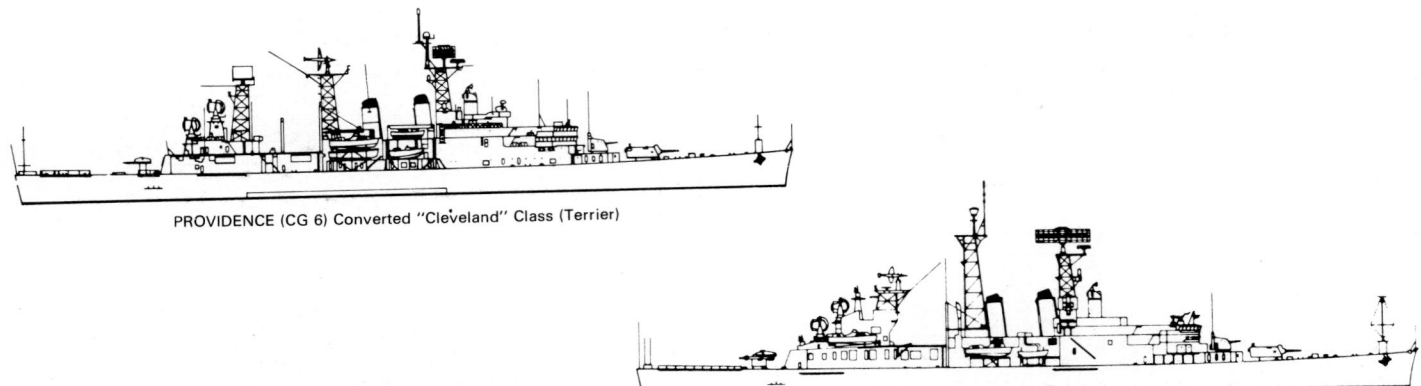

PROVIDENCE (CG 6) Converted "Cleveland" Class (Terrier)

OKLAHOMA CITY (CG 5) Converted "Cleveland" Class (Talos)

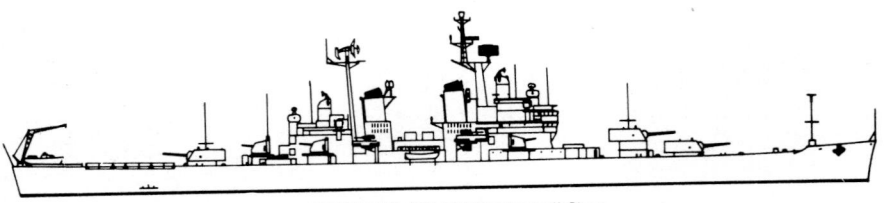

NEWPORT NEWS (CA 148) "Salem" Class

SAINT PAUL (CA 73) "Baltimore" Class

DESTROYERS

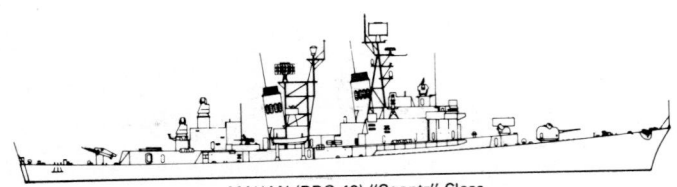

MAHAN (DDG 42) "Coontz" Class

FARRAGUT (DDG 37) "Coontz" Class

Destroyers—*continued*

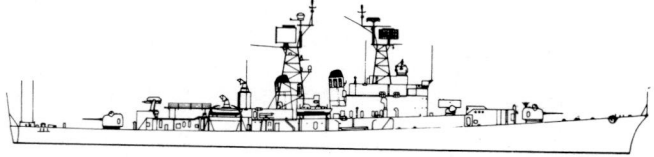

MITSCHER (DDG 35)

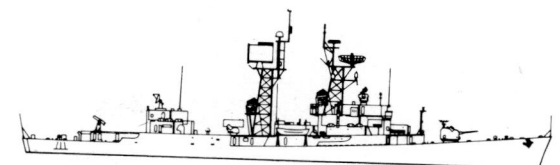

SOMERS (DDG 34) Converted "Forrest Sherman" Class

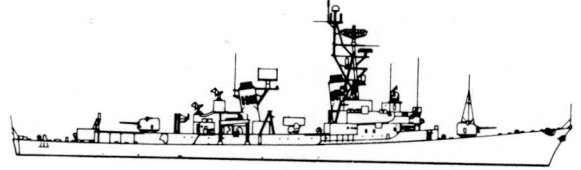

WADDELL (DD 940) "Forrest Sherman" Class

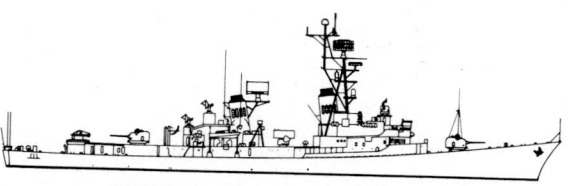

BARNEY (DDG 6) "Charles F. Adams" Class

SPRUANCE (DD 963)

MANLEY (DD 940) "Forrest Sherman" Class

JONAS INGRAM (DD 938) "Forrest Sherman" Class (ASW)

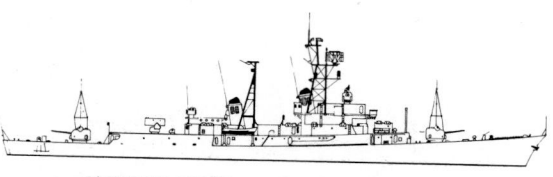

BARRY (DD 933) "Forrest Sherman" Class (ASW)

"Gearing" Class FRAM I (guns forward and aft)

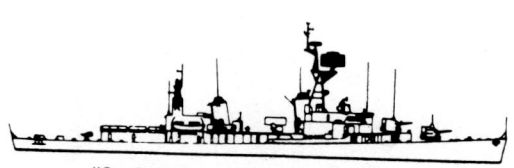

"Gearing" Class FRAM I (all guns forward)

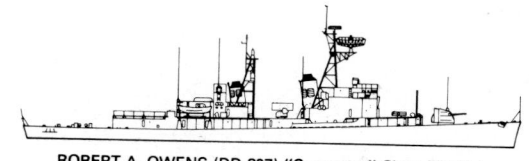

ROBERT A. OWENS (DD 827) "Carpenter" Class FRAM I

FRIGATES

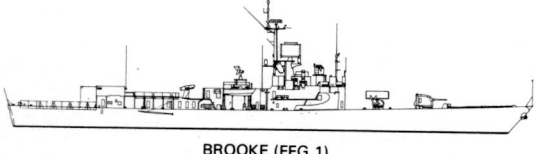

BROOKE (FFG 1)

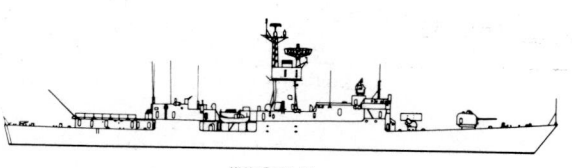

JULIUS A. FURER (FFG 6) "Brooke" Class

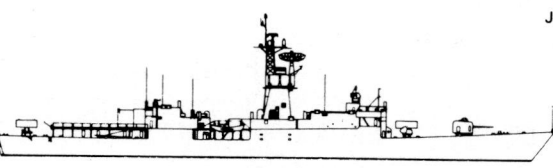

"Knox" Class (improved)

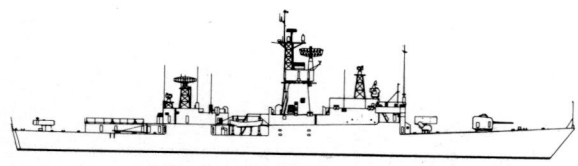

DOWNES (FF 1070) NATO Sea Sparrow

"KNOX" Class

Scale: 1 inch = 150 feet (1 : 1 800)

Frigates—*continued*

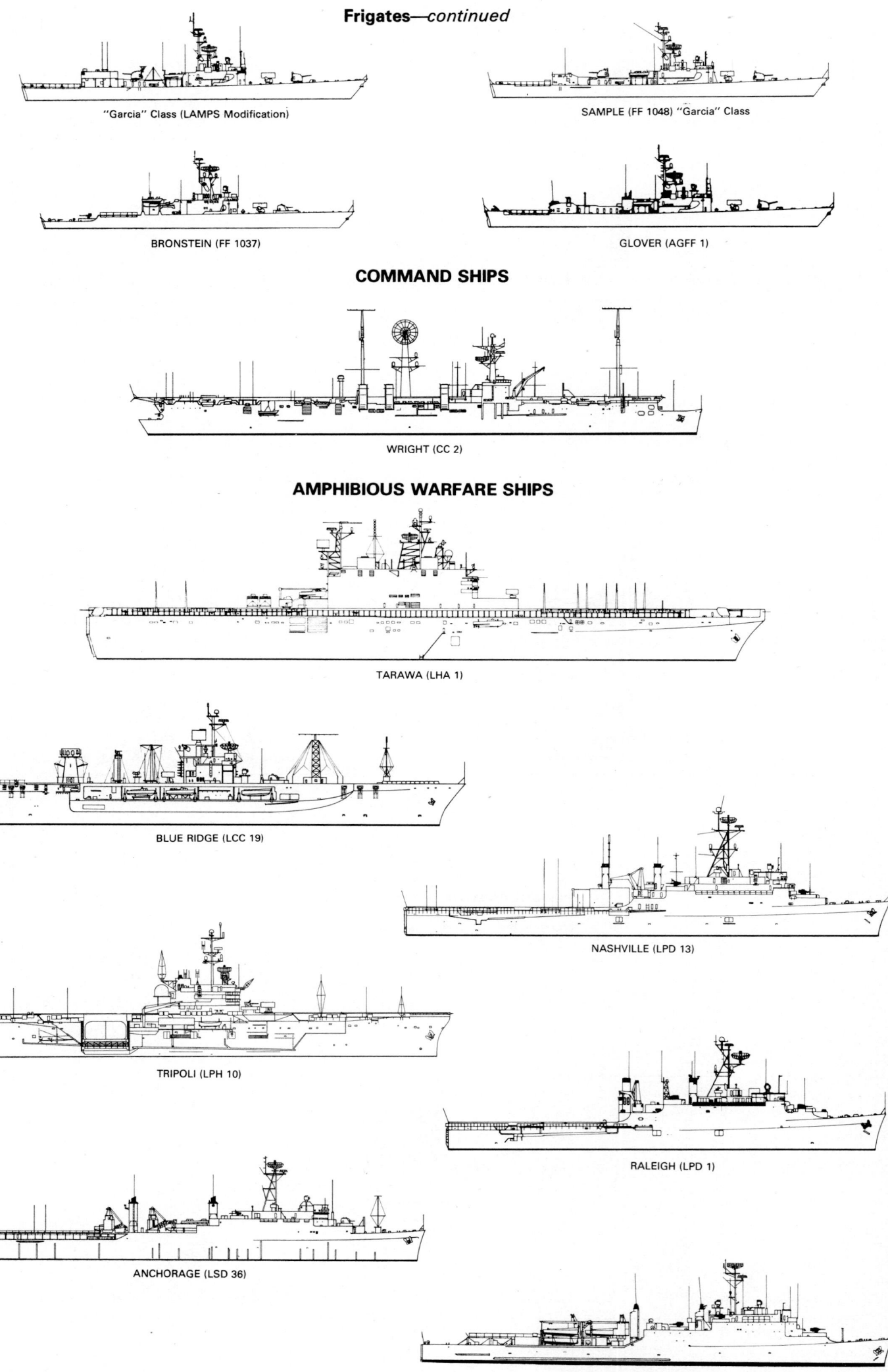

"Garcia" Class (LAMPS Modification)

SAMPLE (FF 1048) "Garcia" Class

BRONSTEIN (FF 1037)

GLOVER (AGFF 1)

COMMAND SHIPS

WRIGHT (CC 2)

AMPHIBIOUS WARFARE SHIPS

TARAWA (LHA 1)

BLUE RIDGE (LCC 19)

NASHVILLE (LPD 13)

TRIPOLI (LPH 10)

RALEIGH (LPD 1)

ANCHORAGE (LSD 36)

HERMITAGE (LSD 34) "Thomaston" Class

Amphibious Warfare Ships—*continued*

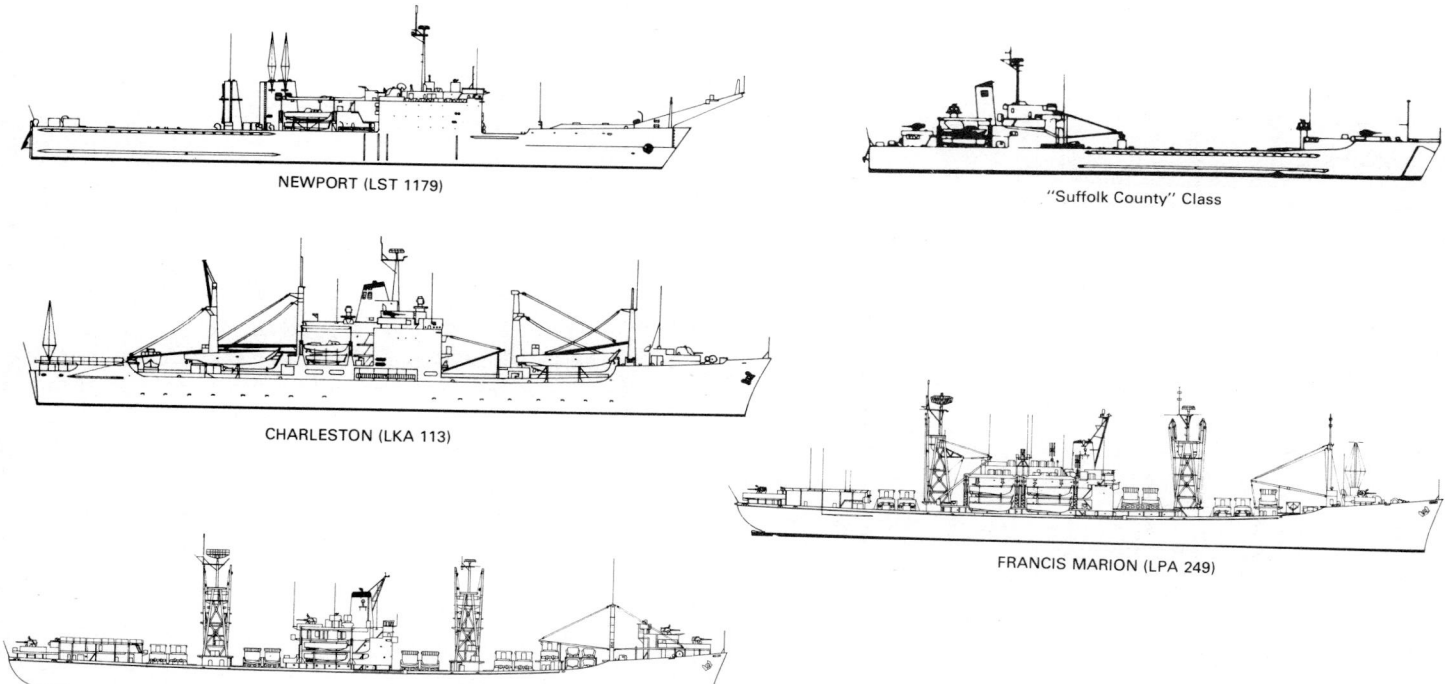

NEWPORT (LST 1179)

"Suffolk County" Class

CHARLESTON (LKA 113)

FRANCIS MARION (LPA 249)

TULARE (LKA 112)

AUXILIARY SHIPS

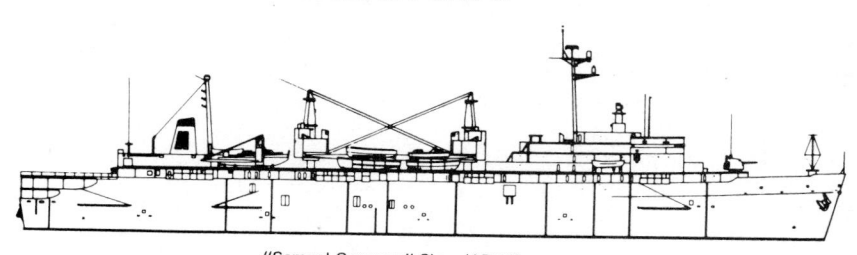

"Samuel Gompers" Class (AD 37)

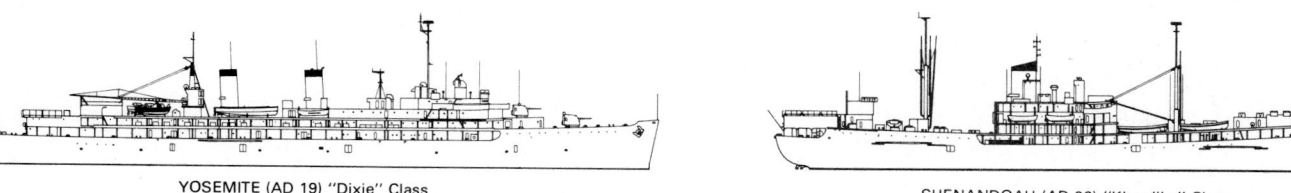

YOSEMITE (AD 19) "Dixie" Class

SHENANDOAH (AD 26) "Klondike" Class

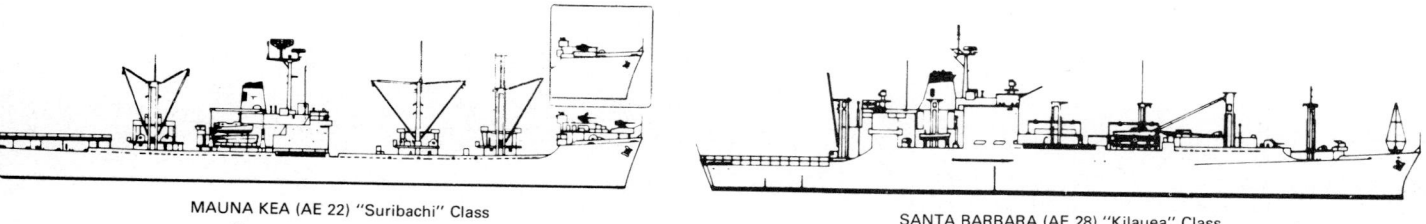

MAUNA KEA (AE 22) "Suribachi" Class
(inset shows gun variation)

SANTA BARBARA (AE 28) "Kilauea" Class

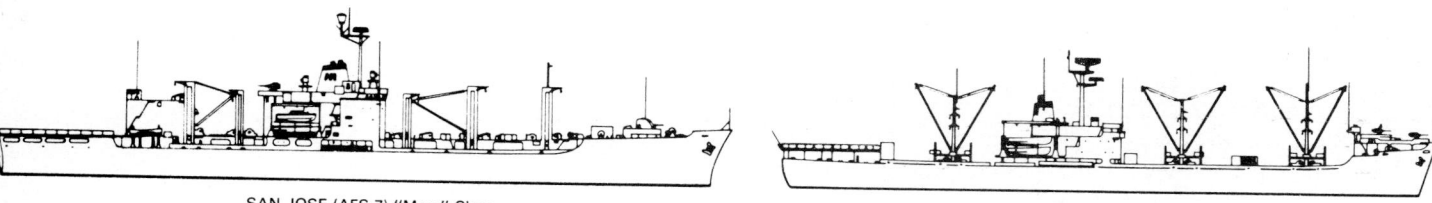

SAN JOSE (AFS 7) "Mars" Class

RIGEL (T-AF 58) R3-S-A4 Type

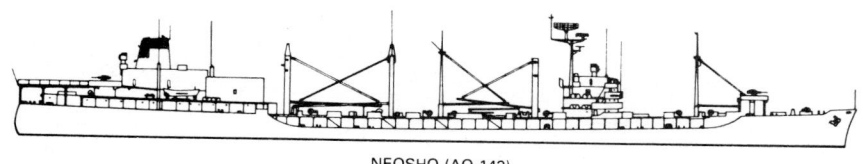

NEOSHO (AO 143)

Auxiliary Ships—*continued*

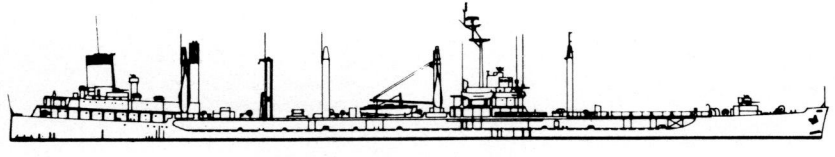

MISPILLION (T-AO 105) Jumboised T3-S2-A3

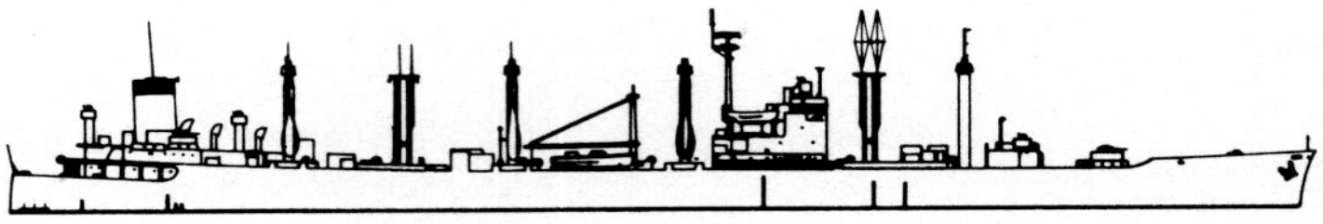

CANISTEO (AO 99) Jumboised T3-S2-A1

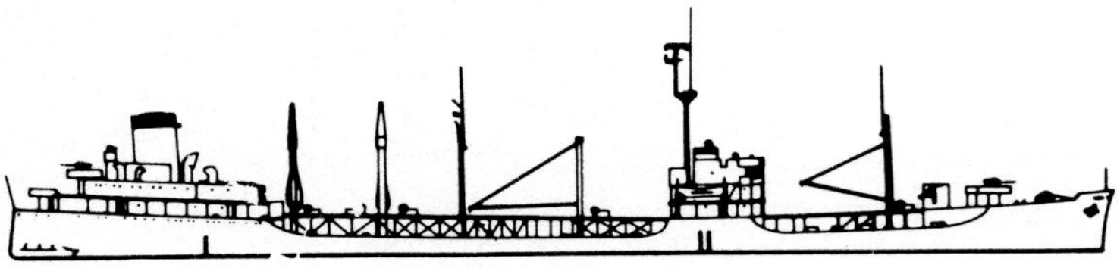

T-AO T3-S2-A1 Type

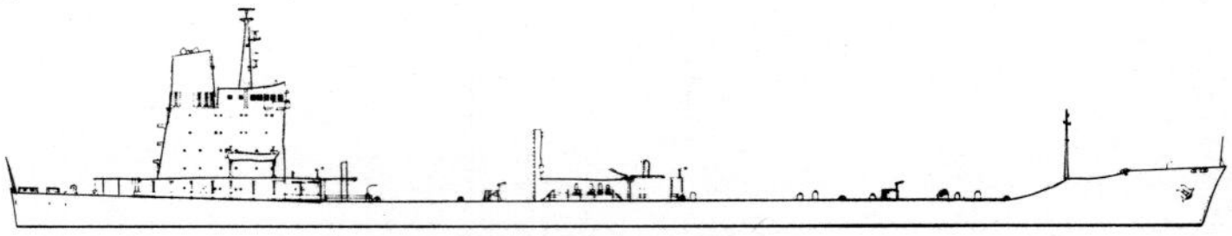

"Sealift" Class (T-AO 168)

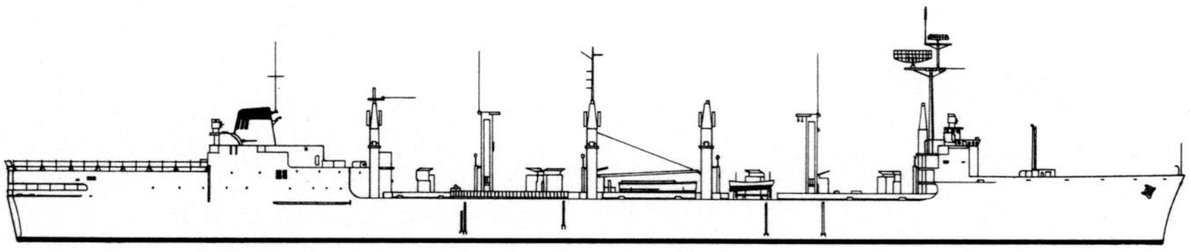

WABASH (AOR 5) "Wichita" Class

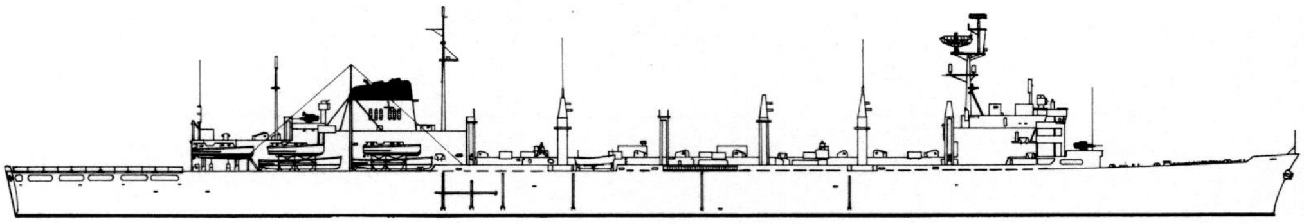

CAMDEN (AOE 2) "Sacremento" Class

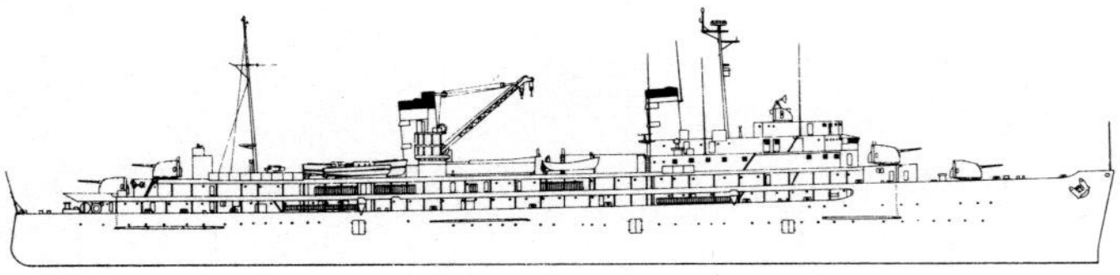

VULCAN (AR 5)

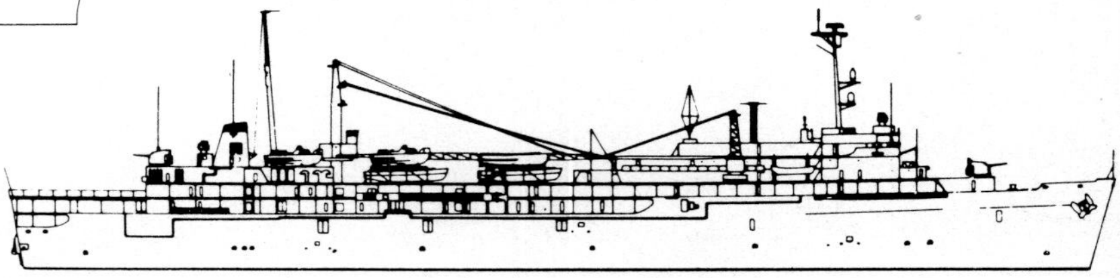

L. Y. SPEAR (AS 36)

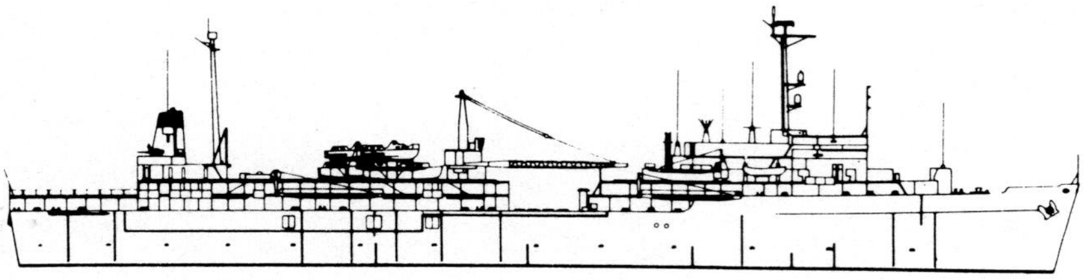

CANOPUS (AS 34) "Simon Lake" Class

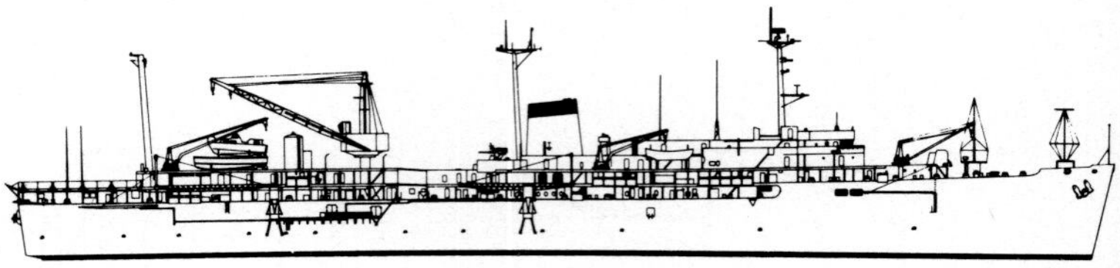

HUNLEY (AS 31)

Scale: 1 inch = 150 feet (1 : 1 800)

Auxiliary Ships—*continued*

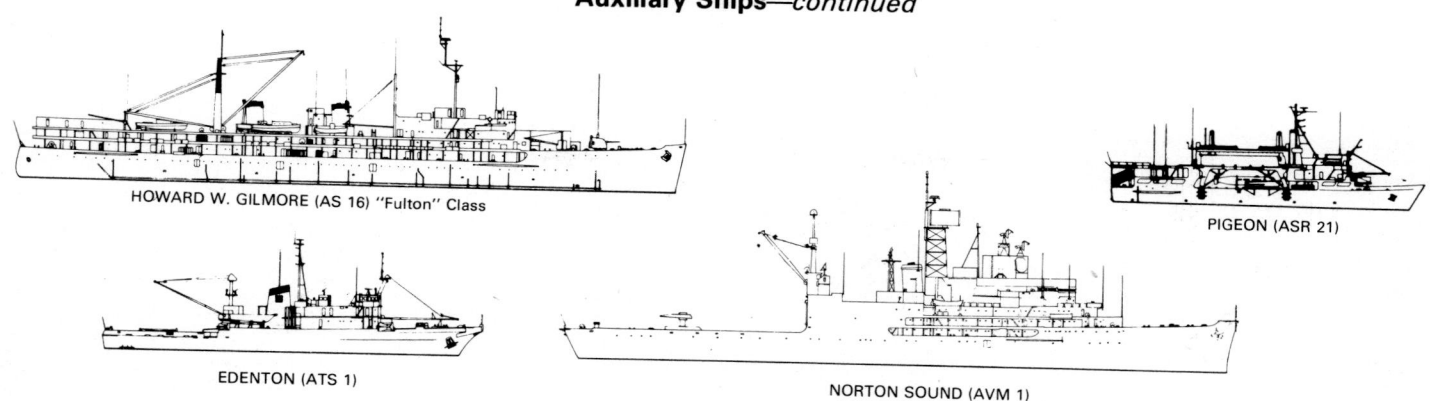

HOWARD W. GILMORE (AS 16) "Fulton" Class

PIGEON (ASR 21)

EDENTON (ATS 1)

NORTON SOUND (AVM 1)

Scale: 1 inch = 150 feet (1 : 1 800)

PATROL SHIPS AND CRAFT

PEGASUS (PHM 1)

ANTELOPE (PG 86) "Asheville" Class

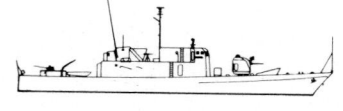

"Asheville" Class

FLAGSTAFFF (PGH 1)

Scale: 1 inch = 100 feet (1 : 1 200)

UNITED STATES SHIP HULL NUMBERS

(Type designations in order of arrangement within this volume; ships are in numerical sequence)

Strategic Missile Submarines

SSBN—Fleet Ballistic Missile Submarines

"Geo. Washington" Class
598 George Washington
599 Patrick Henry
600 Theodore Roosevelt
601 Robert E. Lee
602 Abraham Lincoln

"Ethan Allen" Class
608 Ethan Allen
609 Sam Houston
610 Thomas A. Edison
611 John Marshall

"Lafayette" Class
616 Lafayette
617 Alexander Hamilton

"Ethan Allen" Class (Cont'd)
618 Thomas Jefferson

"Lafayette" Class (Cont'd)
619 Andrew Jackson
620 John Adams
622 James Monroe
623 Nathan Hale
624 Woodrow Wilson
625 Henry Clay
626 Daniel Webster
627 James Madison
628 Tecumseh
629 Daniel Boone
630 John C. Calhoun
631 Ulysses S. Grant
632 Von Steuben
633 Casimir Pulaski
634 Stonewall Jackson
635 Sam Rayburn
636 Nathanael Greene
640 Benjamin Franklin
641 Simon Bolivar
642 Kamehameha
643 George Bancroft
644 Lewis and Clark
645 James K. Polk
654 George C. Marshall
655 Henry L. Stimson
656 George Washington Carver
657 Francis Scott Key
658 Mariano G. Vallejo
659 Will Rogers

"Ohio" Class
726 Ohio
727 Michigan

Submarines

SS SSN—Attack Submarines
AGSS—Auxiliary Submarines
LPSS—Amphibious Transport Submarines
SSG—Guided Missile Submarines

"Sealion" Type
315 Sealion LPSS

"Dolphin" Type
555 Dolphin AGSS

"Tang" Class
563 Tang AGSS
565 Wahoo
566 Trout
567 Gudgeon

"Albacore" Type
569 Albacore AGSS

"Nautilus" Type (SSN)
571 Nautilus

"Sailfish" Class
572 Sailfish
573 Salmon

"Grayback" Type
574 Grayback SS (LPSS)

"Seawolf" Type (SSN)
575 Seawolf

"Darter" Type
576 Darter

"Grayback" Type
577 Growler SSG

"Skate" Class (SSN)
578 Skate
579 Swordfish

"Barbel" Class
580 Barbel
581 Blueback
582 Bonefish

"Skate" Class (SSN) (Cont'd)
583 Sargo
584 Seadragon

"Skipjack" Class (SSN)
585 Skipjack

"Triton" Type (SSN)
586 Triton

"Halibut" Type (SSN)
587 Halibut

"Skipjack" Class (SSN) (Cont'd)
588 Scamp
590 Sculpin
591 Shark
592 Snook

"Permit" Class (SSN)
594 Permit
595 Plunger
596 Barb

"Tullibee" Type (SSN)
597 Tullibee

"Permit" Class (SSN) (Cont'd)
603 Pollack
604 Haddo
605 Jack
606 Tinosa
607 Dace
612 Guardfish
613 Flasher
614 Greenling
615 Gato
621 Haddock

"Sturgeon" Class (SSN)
637 Sturgeon
638 Whale
639 Tautog
646 Grayling
647 Pogy
648 Aspro
649 Sunfish
650 Pargo
651 Queenfish
652 Puffer
653 Ray
660 Sand Lance
661 Lapon
662 Gurnard
663 Hammerhead
664 Sea Devil
665 Guitarro
666 Hawkbill
667 Bergall
668 Spadefish
669 Seahorse
670 Finback

"Narwhal" Type (SSN)
671 Narwhal

"Sturgeon" Class (SSN) (Cont'd)
672 Pintado
673 Flying Fish
674 Trepang
675 Bluefish
676 Billfish
677 Drum
678 Archerfish
679 Silversides
680 William H. Bates
681 Batfish
682 Tunny
683 Parche
684 Cavalla

"Lipscomb" Type (SSN)
685 Glenard P. Lipscomb

"Sturgeon" Class (SSN) (Cont'd)
686 L. Mendel Rivers
687 Richard B. Russell

"Los Angeles" Class (SSN)
688 Los Angeles
689 Baton Rouge
690 Philadelphia
691 Memphis
692 Omaha
693 Cincinnati
694 Groton
695 Birmingham
696 New York City
697 Indianapolis
698 Bremerton
699 Jacksonville

Aircraft Carriers

CV CVA CVN—Attack Aircraft Carriers
CVS—ASW Aircraft Carriers
CVT—Training Aircraft Carriers

"Hancock" Class
11 Intrepid CVS

Modernised "Essex" Class
12 Hornet CVS

"Hancock" Class (Cont'd)
16 Lexington CVT
19 Hancock CV

Modernised "Essex" Class (Cont'd)
20 Bennington CVS

"Hancock" Class (Cont'd)
31 Bon Homme Richard (CVA)
34 Oriskany CV
38 Shangri-La CVS

"Midway" Class (CV)
41 Midway
42 Franklin D. Roosevelt
43 Coral Sea

"Forrestal" Class (CV)
59 Forrestal
60 Saratoga
61 Ranger
62 Independance

"Kitty Hawk" Class (CV)
63 Kitty Hawk
64 Constellation

"Enterprise" Type (CVN)
65 Enterprise

"Kitty Hawk" Class (Cont'd)
66 America
67 John F. Kennedy

"Nimitz" Class (CVN)
68 Nimitz
69 Dwight D. Eisenhower
70 Carl Vinson

Cruisers

CG CGN—Guided Missile Cruisers

Converted "Cleveland" Class
4 Little Rock
5 Oklahoma City
6 Province
7 Springfield

"Long Beach" Type (CGN)
9 Long Beach

"Albany" Class
10 Albany
11 Chicago
12 Columbus

"Leahy" Class
16 Leahy
17 Harry E. Yarnell
18 Worden
19 Dale
20 Richmond K. Turner
21 Gridley
22 England
23 Halsey
24 Reeves

"Bainbridge" Type (CGN)
25 Bainbridge

"Belknap" Class
26 Belknap
27 Josephus Daniels
28 Wainwright
29 Jouett
30 Horne
31 Sterett
32 William H. Standley
33 Fox
34 Biddle

"Truxtun" Type (CGN)
35 Truxtun

"California" Class (CGN)
36 California
37 South Carolina

"Virginia" Class (CGN)
38 Virginia
39 Texas
40 Mississippi
41 Arkansas

CA—Heavy Cruisers

"Baltimore" Class
70 Canberra
73 St. Paul

"Salem" Class
134 Des Moines

"Baltimore" Class (Cont'd)
135 Los Angeles

"Salem" Class (Cont'd)
139 Salem
148 Newport News

BB—Battleships

"Iowa" Class
61 Iowa
62 New Jersey
63 Missouri
64 Wisconsin

Destroyers

DDG—Guided Missile Destroyers

"Chas F. Adams" Class
2 Charles F. Adams
3 John King
4 Lawrence
5 Claude V. Ricketts
6 Barney
7 Henry B. Wilson
8 Lynde McCormack
9 Towers
10 Sampson
11 Sellers
12 Robinson
13 Hoel
14 Buchanan
15 Berkeley
16 Joseph Strauss
17 Conyngham
18 Semmes
19 Tattnall
20 Goldsborough
21 Cochrane
22 Benjamin Stoddert
23 Richard E. Byrd
24 Waddell

Converted "Sherman" Class
31 Decatur
32 John Paul Jones
33 Parsons
34 Somers

Converted "Mitscher" Class
35 Mitscher
36 John S. McCain

"Coontz" Class
37 Farragut
38 Luce
39 MacDonough
40 Coontz
41 King
42 Mahan
43 Dahlgren
44 William V. Pratt
45 Dewey
46 Preble

DD—Destroyers

"Gearing" Class
714 William R. Rush
715 William M. Wood
718 Hammer
743 Southerland
763 William C. Lawe
784 McKean
785 Henderson
788 Hollister
806 Highbee
817 Corry
818 New
819 Holder
820 Rich
821 Johnson
822 Robert H. McCard
824 Basilone

"Carpenter" Type
825 Carpenter

"Gearing" Class (Cont'd)
826 Agerholm

"Carpenter" Type (Cont'd)
827 Robert A. Owens

"Gearing" Class (Cont'd)
829 Myles C. Fox
835 Charles P. Cecil
836 George K. Mackenzie
837 Sarsfield
839 Power
840 Glennon
842 Fiske
844 Perry
847 Robert L. Wilson
849 Richard E. Kraus
850 Joseph P. Kennedy Jr.
852 Leonard F. Mason

858 Fred T. Berry
862 Vogelgesang
863 Steinaker
864 Harold J. Ellison
866 Cone
868 Brownson
871 Damato
873 Hawkins
876 Rogers
877 Perkins
878 Vesole
880 Dyess
881 Bordelon
883 Newman K. Perry
885 John F. Craig
886 Orleck
888 Stickell
890 Meredith

"Forrest Sherman" Class
931 Forrest Sherman
933 Barry
937 George F. Davis
938 Jonas Ingram
940 Manley
941 Dupont
942 Bigelow
943 Blandy
944 Mullinnix
945 Hull
946 Edson
948 Morton
950 Richard S. Edwards
951 Turner Joy

"Spruance" Class
963 Spruance
964 Paul F. Foster
965 Kinkaid
966 Hewitt
967 Elliot
968 Arthur W. Radford
969 Peterson
970 Caron
971 David R. Ray
972 Oldendorf
973 John Young
974 Comte de Grasse
975 O'Brien
976 Merrill
977 Briscoe
978 Stump
979 Conolly
980 Moosbrugger
981 John Hancock
982 Nicholson
983 John Rogers
984 Leftwich
985 Cushing
986 Harry W. Hill
987 O'Bannon
988 Thorn

Frigates

FFG—Guided Missile Frigates

"Brooke" Class
1 Brooke
2 Ramsey
3 Schofield
4 Talbot
5 Richard L. Page
6 Julius A. Furer

"Perry" Class
7 Oliver Hazard Perry

FF—Frigates

"Bronstein" Class
1037 Bronstein
1038 McCloy

"Garcia" Class
1040 Garcia
1041 Bradley
1043 Edward McDonnell
1044 Brumby
1045 Davidson
1047 Voge
1048 Sample
1049 Koelsch
1050 Albert David
1051 O'Callahan

"Knox" Class
1052 Knox
1053 Roark
1054 Gray
1055 Hepburn
1056 Connole
1057 Rathburne
1058 Mayerkord
1059 W. S. Sims
1060 Lang
1061 Patterson
1062 Whipple
1063 Reasoner
1064 Lockwood
1065 Stein
1066 Marvin Shields
1067 Francis Hammond
1068 Vreeland
1069 Bagley

1070 Downes
1071 Badger
1072 Blakely
1073 Robert E. Peary
1074 Harold E. Holt
1075 Trippe
1076 Fanning
1077 Ouellet
1078 Joseph Hewes
1079 Bowen
1080 Paul
1081 Aylwin
1082 Elmer Montgomery
1083 Cook
1084 McCandless
1085 Donald B. Beary
1086 Brewton
1087 Kirk
1088 Barbey
1089 Jesse L. Brown
1090 Ainsworth
1091 Miller
1092 Thomas C. Hart
1093 Capodanno
1094 Pharris
1095 Truitt
1096 Valdez
1097 Moinester

AGFF—Frigate Research Ship

"Glover" Type
1 Glover

Command Ships

AGF—Miscellaneous Flagships

"La Salle" Type

CC—Command Ships

"Northampton" Type
"Wright" Type

Amphibious Warships

LCC—Amphibious Command Ships (ex-AGC)

"Mount McKinley" Class
7 Mount McKinley
12 Estes
16 Pocono
17 Taconic

"Blue Ridge" Class
19 Blue Ridge
20 Mount Whitney

LHA—Amphibious Assault Ships

1 Tarawa
2 Saipan
3 Belleau Wood
4 Nassau
5 Da Nang

LPH—Amphibious Assault Ships

"Iwo Jima" Class
2 Iwo Jima
3 Okinawa
7 Guadalcanal
9 Guam
10 Tripoli
11 New Orleans
12 Inchon

LKA—Amphibious Cargo Ships

"Andromeda" Class
19 Thoban
54 Algol
57 Capricornus
61 Muliphen
93 Yancey
94 Winston
97 Merrick

"Rankin" Class
103 Rankin
104 Seminole
106 Union
107 Vermilion
108 Washburn

"Tulare" Type
112 Tulare

"Charleston" Class
113 Charleston
114 Durham
115 Mobile
116 St. Louis
117 El Paso

LPA—Amphibious Transports

"Haskell" Class
194 Sandoval
199 Maggoffin
208 Talladega
213 Mountrail
215 Navarro
222 Pickaway
237 Bexar

"Paul Revere" Class
248 Paul Revere
249 Francis Marion

LPD—Amphibious Transport Docks

"Raleigh" Class
1 Raleigh
2 Vancouver

"Austin" Class
4 Austin
5 Ogden
6 Duluth
7 Cleveland
8 Dubuque
9 Denver
10 Juneau
11 Coronado
12 Shreveport
13 Nashville
14 Trenton
15 Ponce

LSD—Dock Landing Ships

"Casa Grande" Class
13 Casa Grande
14 Rushmore
15 Shadwell
16 Cabildo
18 Colonial
20 Donner
26 Tortuga
27 Whetstone

"Thomaston" Class
28 Thomaston
29 Plymouth Rock
30 Fort Snelling
31 Point Defiance
32 Speigel Grove
33 Alamo
34 Hermitage
35 Monticello

"Anchorage" Class
36 Anchorage
37 Portland
38 Pensacola
39 Mt Vernon
40 Fort Fisher

LST—Tank Landing Ships

511-1152 series
758 Duval County
1148 Sumner County

"Terrebonne Parish" Class
1157 Terrell County
1169 Whitfield County

"Suffolk County" Class
1173 Suffolk County
1177 Lorain County
1178 Wood County

"Newport" Class
1179 Newport
1180 Manitowoc
1181 Sumter
1182 Fresno
1183 Peroria
1184 Frederick
1185 Schenectady
1186 Cayuga
1187 Tuscaloosa
1188 Saginaw
1189 San Bernardino
1190 Boulder
1191 Racine
1192 Spartanburg County
1193 Fairfax County
1194 Lamour County
1195 Barbour County
1196 Harlan County
1197 Barnstable County
1198 Bristol County

Patrol Ships and Craft

PHM—Patrol Combatants—Missile (Hydrofoil)

"Pegasus" Class
1 Pegasus
2 Hercules

PGH—Hydrofoil Gunboats

"Flagstaff" Type
1 Flagstaff

PCH—Hydrofoil Patrol Craft

"High Point" Type
1 High Point

PG—Patrol Combatants

"Asheville" Class
84 Asheville
85 Gallup
86 Antelope
87 Ready
88 Crockett
89 Marathon
90 Canon
92 Tacoma
93 Welch
98 Grand Rapids

Mine Warfare Ships

MSO—Ocean Minesweepers

"Agile" Class
421 Agile
427 Constant
428 Dash
429 Detector
430 Direct
431 Dominant
433 Engage
437 Enhance
438 Esteem
439 Excel
440 Exploit
441 Exultant
442 Fearless
443 Fidelity
446 Fortify
448 Illusive
449 Impervious
455 Implicit
456 Inflict
458 Lucid
459 Nimble
461 Observer
462 Pinnacle
464 Pluck
471 Skill
474 Vital
488 Conquest
489 Gallant
490 Leader
492 Pledge
494 Sturdy
495 Swerve
496 Venture

"Acme" Class
508 Acme
509 Adroit
510 Advance
511 Affray

AE—Ammunition Ships

"Lassen" Class
8 Mauna Loa

"Wrangell" Class
12 Wrangell
14 Firedrake

"Suribachi" Class
21 Suribachi
22 Mauna Kea
23 Nitro
24 Pyro
25 Haleakala

"Kilauea" Class
26 Kilauea
27 Butte
28 Santa Barbara
29 Mount Hood
32 Flint
33 Shasta
34 Mount Baker
35 Kiska

AF—Store Ships

C2-S-B1 Type
28 Hyades

R2-S-BV1 Type
49 Zelima
52 Arcturus
54 Pictor
55 Aludra

"Victory" Class
56 Denebola

R3-S-A4 Type
58 Rigel
59 Vega

R2-S-BV1 Type
61 Procyon

AFS—Combat Store Ships

"Mars" Class
1 Mars
2 Sylvania
3 Niagara Falls
4 White Plains
5 Concord
6 San Diego
7 San Jose

AO—Oilers

T3-S2-A1 Type
25 Sabine

T2-A Type
36 Kennebec
43 Tappahannock

"Jumboised" T3-S2-A1 Type
51 Ashtabula

T3-S2-A1 Type (Cont'd)
54 Chikaskia
56 Aucilla
57 Marias
62 Taluga
98 Caloosahatchee
99 Canisteo

"Jumboised" T3-S2-A3 Type
105 Mispillion
106 Navasota
107 Passumpsic
108 Pawcatuck
109 Waccamaw

"Neosho" Class
143 Neosho
144 Mississinewa
145 Hassayampa
146 Kawishiwi
147 Truckee
148 Ponchatoula

AOE—Fast Combat Support Ships

"Sacramento" Class
1 Sacramento
2 Camden
3 Seattle
4 Detroit

AOR—Replenishment Oilers

"Wichita" Class
1 Wichita
2 Milwaukee
3 Kansas City
4 Sabannah
5 Wabash
6 Kalamazoo
7 Roanoke

Fleet Support Ships

AD—Destroyer Tenders

"Dixie" Class
14 Dixie
15 Prairie
17 Piedmont
18 Sierra
19 Yosemite

"Klondike" Class
24 Everglades
26 Shenandoah
29 Isle Royal
36 Bryce Canyon

"Gompers" Class
37 Samuel Gompers
38 Puget Sound

AGP—Gunboat Support Ship

1176 Graham County

AH—Dependent Support Ship

17 Sanctuary

APB/IX—Self-Propelled Barracks Ships

37 Echols/IX 504
39 Mercer/IX 502

40 Nueces/IX 503
47 Kingman

AR—Repair Ships

"Vulcan" Class
5 Vulcan
6 Ajax
7 Hector
8 Jason

"Delta" Class
9 Delta
12 Briareus

"Grand Canyon" Type
28 Grand Canyon

ARC—Cable Ships

"Neptune" Class
2 Neptune

"Aeolus" Class
3 Aeolus
4 Thor

"Neptune" Class (Cont'd)
6 Albert J. Myer

ARL—Landing Craft Repair Ships

8 Egeria
24 Sphinx
37 Indra

ARS—Salvage Ships

"Diver" Class
6 Escape
7 Grapple
8 Preserver
23 Deliver
24 Grasp
25 Safeguard
33 Clamp
34 Gear
38 Bolster
39 Conserver
40 Hoist
41 Opportune
42 Reclaimer
43 Recovery

AS—Submarine Tenders

"Fulton" Class
11 Fulton
12 Sperry
15 Bushnell
16 Howard W. Gilmore
17 Nereus
18 Orion
19 Proteus

"Hunley" Class
31 Hunley
32 Holland

"Simon Lake" Class
33 Simon Lake
34 Canopus

"L.Y. Spear" Class
36 L.Y. Spear
37 Dixon
39 Emory S. Land
40 Frank Cable

ASR—Submarine Rescue Ships

"Chanticleer" Class
8 Coucal
9 Florikan
13 Kittiwake
14 Petrel
15 Sunbird
16 Tringa

"Pigeon" Class
21 Pigeon
22 Ortolan

ATA—Auxiliary Tugs

"Maricopa" Class
181 Accokeek
190 Samoset
193 Stallion
195 Tatnuck
213 Keywadin

ATF—Fleet Tugs

"Apache" Class
76 Ute
84 Cree
85 Lipan
86 Mataco
91 Seneca
96 Abnaki
100 Chowanoc
101 Cocopa
103 Hitchiti
105 Moctobi
106 Molala
110 Quapaw
113 Takelma
114 Tawakoni
149 Atakapa
156 Luiseno
157 Nipmuc
158 Mosospelea
159 Paiute
160 Papago
161 Salinan
162 Shakori

ATS—Salvage and Rescue Ships

"Edenton" Class
1 Edenton
2 Beaufort
3 Brunswick

Sealift Ships

AK—Cargo Ships

"Victory" Class
237 Greenville Victory
240 Pvt. John R. Towle
242 Sgt. Andrew Miller
254 Sgt. Truman Kimbro

"Brostrom" Type
255 Pvt. Leonard C. Brostrom

"Eltanin" Class
271 Mirfak

"Victory" Class
274 Lieut. James E. Robinson

"Bland" Type
277 Schuyler Otis Bland

"Victory" Class (cont'd)
279 Norwalk
280 Furman
281 Victoria
282 Marshfield

"Andromeda" Class
283 Wyandot

AKR—Vehicle Cargo Ships

"Comet" Type
7 Comet

"Meteor" Type
9 Meteor

AO—Tankers

"Mission" Class
50 Tullulah
73 Millicoma
75 Saugatuck
76 Schuylkill
134 Mission Santa Ynez

"Maumee" Class
149 Maumee
151 Shoshone
152 Yukon

"Sealift" Class
168 Sealift Pacific
169 Sealift Arabian Sea
170 Sealift China Sea
171 Sealift Indian Ocean
172 Sealift Atlantic
173 Sealift Mediterranean
174 Sealift Caribbean
175 Sealift Arctic
176 Sealift Antarctic

"Potomac" Type
181 Potomac

"Falcon" Class
182 Columbia
183 Neches
184 Hudson
185 Susquehanna

AOG—Gasoline Tankers

"Peconic" Class
77 Rincon
78 Nodaway
79 Petaluma

SHIPBOARD SYSTEMS

ASROC (Anti-Submarine Rocket) Anti-Submarine missile launched from surface ships with homing torpedo or nuclear depth charge as warhead. Launcher is Mk 10 or Mk 26 combination ASROC/surface-to-air missile launcher or Mk 16 eight-cell "pepper box". Installed in US Navy cruisers, destroyers, and frigates; Japanese, Italian, West German, and Canadian destroyer-type ships.
Weight of missile approximately 1 000 lbs; length 15 ft; diameter 1 ft; span of fins 2·5 ft.
Payload: Mk 44 or Mk 46 acoustic-homing torpedo or nuclear depth charge; range one to six miles.
Designation: RUR-5. Status: Operational.

AEGIS (formerly Advanced Surface Missile System) Advanced surface-to-air missile system intended for use in planned strike cruisers (CSGN) and guided missile destroyers (DDG 47 class) scheduled for construction during the 1980s. To have a capability against high-performance aircraft and air-launched, anti-ship missiles. Launcher is Mk 26 (with combined surface-to-air and surface-to-surface missile capability). Aegis will have an electronic scanning radar with fixed antenna, and will be capable of controlling friendly aircraft as well as detection. Additional components will include the UYK-7 computer (a component of the Naval Tactical Data System) and SPY-1 radar "illuminators" for missile guidance. Status: Development (radars only; for use with Standard surface-to-air-missile). Planned for strike cruisers (CSGN) and DDG 47 class destroyers. Being evaluated in *Norton Sound* (AVM 1).

BPDMS (Basic Point Defence Missile System) Close-in-air-defence system employing the Sparrow AIM-7E or 7F series missile designated Sea Sparrow and a modified ASROC-type "pepper box" launcher. Installed in aircraft carriers, ocean escorts, and amphibious ships. Status: Operational.

CAPTOR (Encapsulated Torpedo). Mk 46 torpedo inserted in mine casing. Can be launched by aircraft or submarine. Status: Operational.

CIWS (Close-in Weapon System) "Family" of advanced gun and missile systems to provide close-in or "point" defence for ships against anti-ship missiles and aircraft. Specific weapons being developed or evaluated under this programme include the Chaparral, Hybrid launcher, Pintle, Vulcan Air Defence, Phalanx, and OTO Melara 35 mm twin gun mount.

LAMPS (Light Airborne Multi-Purpose System) Ship-launched helicopter intended for anti-submarine and missile-defence missions, with secondary roles of search-and-rescue and utility (e.g., parts and personnel transfer). For use aboard destroyer-type ships with hangars and certain amphibious warfare ships. Sensors include Magnetic Airborne Detection (MAD), and sonobuoys with digital relays to permit control and attack direction by launching ship. Radar provided to extend detection range vis-a-vis hostile surface missile ships. Weapons: 2 Mk 46 ASW torpedoes. Crew: pilot and 2 operators.
Status: 105 Kaman Seasprite helicopters being modified to SH-2 configuration as interim LAMPS. Deployed on cruisers, destroyers, and frigates.

LAMPS III Improved Light Airborne Multi-Purpose System based on Army Utility Tactical Transport Aircraft System (UTTAS) helicopter. Status: Development.

MCLWG (Major Calibre Light-Weight Gun). Light-weight 8-inch gun (Mk 71) planned for advanced surface combatants including the strike cruiser (CSGN). Status: Evaluation in destroyer *Hull* (DD 945); see photograph below.

NTDS (Naval Tactical Data System) Combination of digital computers, displays, and transmission links to increase an individual ship commander's capability to assess tactical data and take action by integrating input from various sensors (e.g., radars) and providing display of tactical situation and the defence or offence options available. Data can be transmitted among NTDS-equipped ships. An automatic mode initiates action to respond to greatest threats in a tactical situation. Also can be linked to airborne Tactical Data System (ATDS) in E-2 Hawkeye aircraft. Fitted in US Navy aircraft carriers, missile-armed cruisers, destroyers ("Coontz" class), amphibious command ships, and two frigates (*Voge* [FF 1047] and *Koelsch* [FF 1049]).
Status: Operational.

NATO SEA SPARROW Follow-on to BPDMS with a Target Acquisition System (TAS), powered director, smaller launcher, and control console combined with the Sea Sparrow missile. Planned for US amphibious and auxiliary ships.
Status: Under development; also a NATO co-operative programme with Belgium, Denmark, Italy, Netherlands and Norway. Being evaluated in *Downes* (FF 1070).

QUICKSTRIKE Advanced mine system; details classified. Status: Development.

SINS (Ships' Inertial Navigation System) Navigation system providing exact navigation information without active input from terrestrial sources. Prime components are gyroscopes and accelerometers that relate movement of the ship in all directions, ship speed through water and over ocean floor, and true north to give a continuous report of the ship's position.
Status: Operational.

SIRCS (Shipboard Intermediate Range Combat System). Programme to integrate shipboard self-defence systems (existing and planned). Status: Development.

SUBROC (Submarine Rocket) Anti-submarine missile launched from submarines with nuclear warhead. Launched from 21-inch torpedo tube. Carried in US Navy submarines of "Permit" and later classes with amidships torpedo tubes, BQQ-2 or BQQ-5 sonar and Mk 113 or later torpedo fire control systems. The missile is fired from the submerged submarine, rises up through the surface, travels through air towards the hostile submarine, and then re-enters the water to detonate.
Weight of missile approximately 4 000 lbs, length 21 ft; diameter 1·75 ft (maximum); estimated range 25 to 30 miles.
Designation: UUM-44A. Status: Operational.

TACTAS (Tactical Towed Array Sonar). Ship-towed long-range acoustic detection system.

PHALANX Rapid-fire, close-in gun system being developed to provide "last-ditch" defence against anti-ship missiles. Fires 20 mm ammunition from six-barrel "gatling" gun with "dynamic gun aiming" with fire control radar tracking projectiles and target(s). Theoretical rate of fire 3 000 rounds-per-minute. Initially planned for "Spruance" class destroyers, frigates, and some auxiliary ships; tentative programme calls for approx 360 units in 220 ships. Status: Development. See 1975-1976 edition (page 402) for photographs of experimental Phalanx installation in *King* (DDG 47); subsequently removed.

HULL (DD 945) with 8-inch Major Calibre Light-Weight Gun

1975, United States Navy, PH1 Carl R. Begg

NAVAL MISSILES

Type(a)	Designation	Name	Launch Platform (tubes/launchers)	Range n. miles (km)	Length feet (metres)	Weight lbs (kg)	Notes(b)
FBM	UGM-27B	Polaris A-2	"Lafayette" submarines (16)	1 500 *(2 775)*	31 *(9·5)*	30 000 *(13 500)*	Thermo-nuclear; being replaced by Poseidon
FBM	UGM-27C	Polaris A-3	"Ethan Allen", "George Washington" submarines (16)	2 500 *(4 625)*	32 *(9·8)*	30 000 *(13 500)*	Thermo-nuclear; MRV warhead
FBM	UGM-73A	Poseidon C-3	"Lafayette" submarines (16)	approx 2 500 *(4 625)*	34 *(10·4)*	65 000 *(29 250)*	Thermo-nuclear; MIRV warhead
FBM	UGM-96A	Trident (I) C-4	"Ohio" submarines (24)	approx 4 000 *(7 400)*	34·1 *(10·4)*	70 000 *(31 500)*	Thermo-nuclear; MIRV and MARV warhead
FBM	UGM	Trident (II) D-5	Trident submarines (24)	approx 6 000 *(11 100)*	45·75 *(13·9)*	126 000 *(56 700)*	Proposed

NAVAL MISSILES—continued

NAVAL MISSILES—continued

Type(a)	Designation	Name	Launch Platform (tubes/launchers)	Range n. miles (km)	Length feet (metres)	Weight lbs (kg)	Notes(b)
SLCM	BGM-109	Tomahawk (c)	Attack submarines (torpedo tubes)	approx 1 500 (2 775)	20·5 (6·3)	2 400-2 700 (10 800-12 150)	Nuclear; under development; tactical 300 mile version proposed
SSM	RGM-66D/E	Standard-ARM	"Asheville" gunboats (4) some surface ships (ASROC launcher)	15 (27·75)	15 (4·6)	1 400 (630)	HE
SSM	RGM-84	Harpoon	Surface ships	60 (111)	15 (4·6)	1 425 (641·25)	Development; HE
SSM	RGM-84	Encapsulated Harpoon	Attack submarines (torpedo tubes)	60 (111)	21 (6·4)		Development; HE
SAM	RIM-2	Terrier	Cruisers (1 or 2 twin); "Coontz" destroyers (1 twin); "Kitty Hawk", "America" carriers (2 twin)	20+ (37)	26·1 (7·9)	3 000 (1 350)	Nuclear or HE
SAM	RIM-7	Sea Sparrow	Surface ships	8 (14·8)	12 (3·7)	380 (171)	HE; Mk 25 or Mk 29 (NATO) multiple launcher; Basic Point Defence Missile System
SAM	RIM-8	Talos	"Albany", "Long Beach" cruisers (2 twin)	65+ (120·2)	31·2 (9·5)	7 000 (3 510)	Nuclear or HE
SAM	RIM-24	Tartar	"Albany" cruisers (2 twin); "Chas. Adams" destroyers (1 twin or single); "Brooke" frigates (1 single); later cruisers	10+ (18·5)	15 (4·6)	1 425 (641·25)	HE
SAM	RIM-66	Standard-MR (SM-1)	Tartar replacement	20+ (37)	14·4 (4·5)	1 200-1 400 (540-630)	HE
SAM	RIM-66C	Standard (SM-2)	Talos replacement	60+ (110+)			Long range with mid-course guidance; development
SAM	RIM-67	Standard-ER (SM-1)	Terrier replacement	35+ (64·7)	26·2 (7·9)	2 900 (1 305)	HE
AAM	AIM-7	Sparrow III	F-4/F-14 fighters	9-16 (16·6-29·6)	12 (3·7)	500 (225)	
AAM	AIM-9C/D	Sidewinder-1B	F-4/F-14 fighters	8-15 (14·8-27·75)	9·5 (2·9)	185 (83·25)	
AAM	AIM-54	Phoenix	F-14 fighter (6)	60+ (14)	13 (3·9)	985 (443·25)	
AAM	AIM-95	Agile	Fighters	2 (3·7)	7·8 (2·4)		Development; close-in missile
ASM	AGM-12B	Bullpup-A	Attack/patrol aircraft	7 (12·9)	10 (3)	571 (156·95)	
ASM	AGM-12C/D	Bullpup-B	Attack/patrol aircraft	10 (18·5)	13·5 (4·1)	1 785 (803·25)	Nuclear or HE
ASM	AGM-45	Shrike	Attack/patrol aircraft	8-10 (14·8-18·5)	10 (3)	390 (175·5)	Anti-radiation
ASM	AGM-53	Condor	Attack/patrol aircraft	40-60 (74-111)	13·8 (4·2)	2 130 (958·5)	Nuclear or HE; production planned
ASM	AGM-62	Walleye	Attack/patrol aircraft	16 (29·6)	11·2 (3·4)	1 100 (495)	Nuclear or HE; larger Walleye II has 35-mile range (2 400 lbs)
ASM	AGM-78	Standard-ARM	Attack/patrol aircraft	35 (64·7)	15 (4·6)		Anti-radiation
ASM	AGM-83	Bulldog	Attack/patrol aircraft	35 (64·7)	9·8 (2·9)	600 (270)	Modified Bullpup
ASM	AGM-84	Harpoon	Attack/patrol aircraft	60 (111)	12·6 (3·8)	1 115 (501·75)	Development; HE
ASM	AGM-88	Harm	Attack/patrol aircraft				Development; High-speed Anti-Radiation Missile; larger than Shrike
ASW	RUR-5	ASROC	Cruisers, destroyers, frigates	1-6 (1·8-11·1)	15 (4·6)	1 000 (450)	Nuclear depth charge, Mk 44, or Mk 46 torpedo; multiple launcher in most ships; Mk 26 launcher in later ships; 570 lbs (256·5 kg) with Mk 46
ASW	UUM-44	SUBROC	"Permit" and later attack submarines (torpedo tubes)	25-30 (46·25-55·5)	21 (6·4)	4 000 (1 800)	Nuclear

(a) FBM = Fleet Ballistic Missile; SLCM = Submarine-Launched Cruise Missile; SSM = Surface-to-Surface Missile; SAM = Surface-to-Air Missile; AAM = Air-to-Air Missile; ASM = Air-to-Surface Missile; ASW = Anti-Submarine Warfare.
(b) MRV = Multiple Re-entry Vehicle; MIRV = Multiple Independently targeted Re-entry Vehicle; MaRV = Maneuvering Re-entry Vehicle; HE = High Explosive.
(c) Winner of SLCM competition between General Dynamics Convair BGM-109 and Vought (LTV) BGM-110 configurations.

TORPEDOES

Designation	Launch Platform	Weight lbs (kg)	Length feet (metres)	Diameter, in (mm)	Propulsion	Guidance	Notes
Mk 37 Mod 2	Submarines	1 690 (760·5)	13·4 (4·1)	19 (484·5)	Electric	Wire; active-passive acoustic homing	Anti-submarine
Mk 37 Mod 3	Submarines	1 430 (643·5)	11·25 (3·4)	19 (484·5)	Electric	Active-passive acoustic homing	Anti-submarine
Mk 37C	Submarines				Liquid mono-propellant	Active-passive acoustic homing	Anti-submarine; modified Mk 37-2/3 for allied navies; in production
Mk 44 Mod 1	Surface ships (Mk 32 tubes and ASROC); aircraft	433 (194·8)	8·4 (2·6)	12·75 (323·8)	Electric	Active acoustic homing	Anti-submarine
Mk 45 Mod 1 & Mod 2 (ASTOR)	Submarines	2 213 (995·8)	18·9 (5·7)	19 (484·5)	Electric	Wire	Anti-submarine; nuclear warhead; 10+ mile range; being replaced by Mk 48
Mk 46 Mod 0	Surface ships (Mk 32 tubes and ASROC); aircraft	568 (255·6)	8·5 (2·6)	12·75 (484·5)	Solid-propellant	Active-passive acoustic homing	Anti-submarine; successor to Mk 44
Mk 46 Mod 1 & Mod 2	Surface ships (Mk 32 tubes and ASROC); aircraft	508 (228·6)	8·5 (2·6)	12·75 (484·5)	Liquid mono-propellant	Active-passive acoustic homing	Anti-submarine; successor to Mk 44; Mod 4 used in CAPTOR (Encapsulated Torpedo) mine
Mk 48 Mod 1 & Mod 3	Submarines	3 480 (1 566)	19·1 (5·8)	21 (533·6)	Liquid mono-propellant	Wire/terminal acoustic homing	Anti-submarine and anti-shipping; in production; range approx 20 miles
ALWT	Aircraft; submarines						Advanced Light-Weight Torpedo; to replace Mk 46; in development

STRATEGIC MISSILE SUBMARINES

The US Navy's 41 nuclear-propelled submarines armed with Poseidon and Polaris missiles are a primary component of the nation's strategic offensive forces. The current submarine force will, with the completion of the last Poseidon conversion in 1977, provide over 5 000 separate warheads or "re-entry" vehicles, or about 55 percent of US strategic warheads. (Each Poseidon missile is believed normally to carry ten separately targetable RVs, while the Polaris A-3 missile delivers three RVs on the same target, thus the latter weapon is considered to deliver only one warhead).

The Trident strategic missile submarine programme has been initiated to replace the older Polaris/Poseidon submarines from about 1980 onwards. All 41 existing submarines will reach their 20th year of active service between 1981 and 1987. Their operations have been particularly arduous in some respects because of the two-crew concept which has kept them at sea for a greater part of their life than other submarines. In addition, there is increasing concern over the potential effectiveness of Soviet anti-submarine measures against these older undersea craft.

Trident Programme: The Trident programme provides for an improved nuclear-propelled submarine and longer-range missiles. The Trident submarine is described below; the Trident I missile now under development will have a nominal range of approximately 4 000 nautical miles. This missile will be installed in the new construction submarines and possibly retrofitted in ten of the Poseidon-armed submarines. The longer range (cica 6 000-mile) Trident II missile is under study. This weapon, which could be available in the mid-1980s, would also have a greater throw weight and accuracy than the Trident I.

When the Trident programme was initiated, the Navy planned to construct the first submarine with Fiscal Year 1974 funding and three submarines each year thereafter for the initial ten-SSBN class. However, in 1974 the Department of Defense slowed the rate to 1-2-2-2-2-1; in 1975 this was again revised to 1-2-1-2-1-2-1, and in 1976 it was further slowed to 1-2-1-1-2-1-2. Also in early 1976, Secretary of Defense Donald H. Rumsfeld announced that for planning purposes additional submarines beyond the ten-submarine force would be procured at the 1-2-1-2 rate continuously consistent with Strategic Arms Limitation Talks (SALT) agreements.

Narwhal Programme: Proposals to develop a smaller Trident-armed submarine than the SSBN 726 class described below led to preliminary studies of employing a modified "Narwhal" or "Los Angeles" design to carry the Trident missile. The smaller SSBN would have only 16 missiles. Under current Department of Defense planning, 45 of the smaller, 16-missile submarines would have been required to provide the planned force of 720 Submarine-Launched Ballistic Missiles (SLBMs) compared to only 30 of the larger SSBN 726-class submarines with 24 missiles each. The smaller number of SSBN 726-class units would have lower life-cycle costs, especially in personnel, training, and maintenance. Accordingly, the Department of Defense has dropped proposals for the smaller Trident submarines.

Strategic Cruise Missiles: The US Navy is in advanced development of a strategic Sea-Launched Cruise Missile (SLCM). This is an underwater-launched weapon with ram-jet propulsion which could deliver nuclear warheads to a range of approximately 1 500 nautical miles. With modification, the SLCM could also be carried by manned strategic bomber air-

WILL ROGERS (SSBN 659) in Holy Loch, Scotland

1972, United States Navy

craft (ie, B-52 and B-1). A shorter-range (circa 300-mile) version of the weapon with a conventional warhead is planned for use as an over-the-horizon anti-ship weapon.

According to a 1972 statement by the Director Defense Research & Engineering: "Informal Navy studies with respect to the development of sea-based strategic cruise missiles have led us to the conclusion that such a missile could effectively diversify our strategic forces. Development of a strategic cruise missile system is within the state of the art and is technically feasible without major new developments".

The strategic cruise missile would have a low-level, terrain following flight path over land, much like that of a manned bomber in contrast to the ballistic trajectory of a Polaris/Poseidon/Trident missile.

Nomenclature: US ballistic missile submarines (SSBN) have

been named for "distinguished Americans who were known for their devotion to freedom" since 1958 when the Polaris submarine programme was initiated. Included as "Americans" were Latin American and Hawaiian leaders, and several Europeans who supported the American fight for independence. In 1976 the SSBN name source was changed to States of the Union with the first Trident submarine (SSBN 726) being named Ohio. This move thoroughly confuses the US ship nomenclature scheme because since 1971 guided missile cruisers have been assigned state names and four state-named battleships of the "Iowa" class remain on the Navy List (in reserve).

Photographs: Above, the last US Polaris/Poseidon submarine in Holy Loch. The bitts, capstan, and other "deck hardware" retract when the submarine is at sea.

(10+) FLEET BALLISTIC MISSILE SUBMARINES (SSBN): TRIDENT PROGRAMME

Name	No.	Builders	Laid down	Launch	Commission
OHIO	**SSBN 726**	General Dynamics (Electric Boat)	10 Apr 1976	Mid-1977	Mid-1978
	SSBN 727	General Dynamics (Electric Boat)	—	Mid-1978	Mid-1979
	SSBN 728	General Dynamics (Electric Boat)	—	Mid-1979	Mid-1980
	SSBN 729	Fiscal Year 1976 programme			
	SSBN 730	Proposed FY 1977 programme			
	SSBN 731	Planned FY 1978 programme			
	SSBN 732	Planned FY 1978 programme			
	SSBN 733	Planned FY 1979 programme			
	SSBN 734	Planned FY 1980 programme			
	SSBN 735	Planned FY 1980 programme			

Displacement, tons: 18 700 submerged
Length, feet (metres): 560 *(170·7)* oa
Beam, feet (metres): 42 *(12·8)*
Draught, feet (metres): 35·5 *(10·8)*
Missiles: 24 tubes for Trident I Submarine-Launched Ballistic Missile (SLBM)
Torpedo tubes: 4—21 inch *(533 mm)* amidships
Main engines: Geared turbines; 1 shaft
Nuclear reactors: 1 pressurised-water cooled S8G (General Electric)
Complement: 150 (14 officers, 136 enlisted men)

These submarines will be the largest undersea craft yet constructed, being significantly larger than the Soviet "Delta" class missile submarines which are now the largest afloat. The lead submarine was contracted to the Electric Boat Division of the General Dynamics Corp (Groton, Connecticut) on 25 July 1974. The only other US shipyard currently capable of building submarines of this class is the Newport News SB & DD Co in Virginia.

According to the Navy, "in recognition of the high national priority assigned to the Trident programme the contractor has promised to use his best effort to support a December 1977 delivery date for the lead ship".

Design: The size of the Trident submarine is dictated primarily by the larger size missile required for 6 000-mile range and the larger reactor plant to drive the ship. The submarine will have 24 tubes in a vertical position penetrating the main submarine pressure hull. Early studies had indicated several advantages

would accrue from advanced design concepts, such as housing the missiles in a horizontal position external to the main pressure hull. However, a conservative submarine design was adopted, to a large extent a modification of the previous Polaris/Poseidon submarine classes.

The principle characteristics of the Trident concept as proposed were: (1) long-range missile (circa 6 000 miles) to permit targeting the Soviet Union while the submarine cruises in remote areas, making effective ASW virtually impossible for the foreseeable future, (2) extremely quiet submarines, (3) a high at-sea to in-port ratio, (4) high systems reliability, (5) dedicated systems design to provide the most effective submarine, and (6) underwater launch capability. Modular construction techniques could greatly facilitate maintenance, overhaul, and subsequent modernisation.

Designation: Initially the hull number SSBN 711 was planned for the first Trident submarine. However, on 21 Feb 1974 the designation SSBN 1 was assigned, confusing the Navy's submarine designation system which goes back to the USS Holland (SS 1), commissioned in 1900. Subsequently, the designation was again changed on 10 Apr 1974, with the "block" SSBN 726-735 being reserved for the Trident programme.

Electronics: These submarines have the BQQ-5 sonar system (with only passive components). UYK-7 computer is provided to support electronic and weapon systems. Mk 118 digital torpedo fire control system is installed.

Engineering: These submarines will have a nuclear core life of

about nine years between refuellings. A prototype of the S8G reactor plant has been constructed at West Milton, New York.

Fiscal: Costs of the first four SSBNs have increased over the initial appropriations. See 1975-1976 edition for initial costs. The SSBN 730 in Fiscal Year 1977 is funded at $791 500 000.

Missiles: The Trident submarines will be armed initially with the Trident I missile, scheduled to become operational late in 1978. This missile is expected to have a range of 3 000 to 4 000 nautical miles, a range already exceeded by the SS-N-8 missile in the Soviet "Delta" class submarines. However, the US missile will have a MIRV warhead, while at this writing, no statements by US officials have indicated that the SS-N-8 has a multiple warhead (the SS-N-6 missile associate with the "Yankee" class submarine has been fitted with a MRV warhead). The Trident missile is expected to carry more than the 10 to 14 re-entry vehicles that the Poseidon can lift. In addition, the Mk 500 MaRV (Manoeuvering Re-entry Vehicle) is under development for the purpose of demonstrating its compatability with the Trident I missile. This re-entry vehicle intended to evade ABM interceptor missiles and is not terminally guided to increase its accuracy. The Mk 500 MaRV is expected to be less accurate than previous submarine-launched ballistic missile warheads, according to official statements.

Navigation: Each submarine will have two Mk 2 Ships Inertial Navigation Systems; to be fitted with satellite navigation receivers.

31 FLEET BALLISTIC MISSILE SUBMARINES (FBM): "LAFAYETTE" CLASS

Name	No.	Builders	Laid down	Launched	Commissioned
*LAFAYETTE	SSBN 616	General Dynamics (Electric Boat Div)	17 Jan 1961	8 May 1962	23 Apr 1963
*ALEXANDER HAMILTON	SSBN 617	General Dynamics (Electric Boat Div)	26 June 1961	18 Aug 1962	27 June 1963
*ANDREW JACKSON	SSBN 619	Mare Island Naval Shipyard	26 Apr 1961	15 Sep 1962	3 July 1963
*JOHN ADAMS	SSBN 620	Portsmouth Naval Shipyard	19 May 1961	12 Jan 1963	12 May 1964
*JAMES MONROE	SSBN 622	Newport News Shipbuilding & DD Co	31 July 1961	4 Aug 1962	7 Dec 1963
*NATHAN HALE	SSBN 623	General Dynamics (Electric Boat Div)	2 Oct 1961	12 Jan 1963	23 Nov 1963
*WOODROW WILSON	SSBN 624	Mare Island Naval Shipyard	13 Sep 1961	22 Feb 1963	27 Dec 1963
*HENRY CLAY	SSBN 625	Newport News Shipbuilding & DD Co.	23 Oct 1961	30 Nov 1962	20 Feb 1964
*DANIEL WEBSTER	SSBN 626	General Dynamics (Electric Boat Div)	28 Dec 1961	27 Apr 1963	9 Apr 1964
*JAMES MADISON	SSBN 627	Newport News Shipbuilding & DD Co	5 Mar 1962	15 Mar 1963	28 July 1964
*TECUMSEH	SSBN 628	General Dynamics (Electric Boat Div)	1 June 1962	22 June 1963	29 May 1964
*DANIEL BOONE	SSBN 629	Mare Island Naval Shipyard	6 Feb 1962	22 June 1963	23 Apr 1964
*JOHN C. CALHOUN	SSBN 630	Newport News Shipbuilding & DD Co	4 June 1962	22 June 1963	15 Sep 1964
*ULYSSES S. GRANT	SSBN 631	General Dynamics (Electric Boat Div)	18 Aug 1962	2 Nov 1963	17 July 1964
*VON STEUBEN	SSBN 632	Newport News Shipbuilding & DD Co	4 Sep 1962	18 Oct 1963	30 Sep 1964
*CASIMIR PULASKI	SSBN 633	General Dynamics (Electric Boat Div)	12 Jan 1963	1 Feb 1964	14 Aug 1964
*STONEWALL JACKSON	SSBN 634	Mare Island Naval Shipyard	4 July 1962	30 Nov 1963	26 Aug 1964
*SAM RAYBURN	SSBN 635	Newport News Shipbuilding & DD Co	3 Dec 1962	20 Dec 1963	2 Dec 1964
*NATHANAEL GREENE	SSBN 636	Portsmouth Naval Shipyard	21 May 1962	12 May 1964	19 Dec 1964
*BENJAMIN FRANKLIN	SSBN 640	General Dynamics (Electric Boat Div)	25 May 1963	5 Dec 1964	22 Oct 1965
*SIMON BOLIVAR	SSBN 641	Newport News Shipbuilding & DD Co	17 Apr 1963	22 Aug 1964	29 Oct 1965
*KAMEHAMEHA	SSBN 642	Mare Island Naval Shipyard	2 May 1963	16 Jan 1965	10 Dec 1965
*GEORGE BANCROFT	SSBN 643	General Dynamics (Electric Boat Div)	24 Aug 1963	20 Mar 1965	22 Jan 1966
*LEWIS AND CLARK	SSBN 644	Newport News Shipbuilding & DD Co	29 July 1963	21 Nov 1964	22 Dec 1965
*JAMES K. POLK	SSBN 645	General Dynamics (Electric Boat Div)	23 Nov 1963	22 May 1965	16 Apr 1966
*GEORGE C. MARSHALL	SSBN 654	Newport News Shipbuilding & DD Co	2 Mar 1964	21 May 1965	29 Apr 1966
*HENRY L. STIMSON	SSBN 655	General Dynamics (Electric Boat Div)	4 Apr 1964	13 Nov 1965	20 Aug 1966
*GEORGE WASHINGTON CARVER	SSBN 656	Newport News Shipbuilding & DD Co	24 Aug 1964	14 Aug 1965	15 June 1966
*FRANCIS SCOTT KEY	SSBN 657	General Dynamics (Electric Boat Div)	5 Dec 1964	23 Apr 1966	3 Dec 1966
*MARIANO G. VALLEJO	SSBN 658	Mare Island Naval Shipyard	7 July 1964	23 Oct 1965	16 Dec 1966
*WILL ROGERS	SSBN 659	General Dynamics (Electric Boat Div)	20 Mar 1965	21 July 1966	1 Apr 1967

Displacement, tons: 6 650 light surface; 7 250 standard surface; 8 250 submerged
Length, feet (metres): 425 *(129·5)* oa
Beam, feet (metres): 33 *(10·1)*
Draught, feet (metres): 31·5 *(9·6)*
Missile launchers: 16 tubes for Polaris A-3 or Poseidon C-3 SLBM (see *Missile* notes)
Torpedo tubes: 4—21 inch *(533 mm)* bow
Main engines: 2 geared turbines; 15 000 shp; 1 shaft
Nuclear reactors: 1 pressurised-water cooled S5W (Westinghouse)
Speed, knots: 20 surface; approx 30 submerged
Complement: 145 (17 officers, 128 enlisted men)

These Fleet Ballistic Missile (FBM) submarines are the largest undersea craft to be completed in the West. The first four submarines (SSBN 616, 617, 619, 620) were authorised in the Fiscal Year 1961 shipbuilding programme with five additional submarines (SSBN 622-626) authorised in a supplemental FY 1961 programme; SSBN 627-636 (ten) in FY 1962, SSBN 640-645 (six) in FY 1963, and SSBN 654-659 (six) in FY 1964. Cost for the earlier ships of this class was approximately $109 500 000 per submarine.

Design: The *Daniel Webster* has diving planes mounted on bow in lieu of sail-mounted planes, the only "16-tube" FBM submarine of any navy with this configuration. (See photograph in 1974-1975 and previous editions).
The *Benjamin Franklin* and later submarines are officially considered a separate class; however, differences are minimal (eg, quieter machinery) and all 31 submarines are generally considered as a single class.

Electronics: Fitted with Mk 113 Mod 9 torpedo fire control system.

Engineering: The *Benjamin Franklin* and subsequent submarines of this class have been fitted with quieter machinery. All SSBNs have diesel-electric stand-by machinery, snorkels, and "outboard" auxiliary propeller for emergency use.
The nuclear cores inserted in refuelling these submarines during the late 1960s and early 1970s cost approximately $3 500 000 and provide energy for approximately 400 000 miles.

Missiles: The first eight ships of this class were fitted with the Polaris A-2 missile (1 500 nautical mile range) and the 23 later ships with the Polaris A-3 missile (2 500 nautical mile range). The SSBN 620 and SSBN 622-625 (5 ships) were rearmed with the Polaris A-3 missile during overhaul-refuellings from 1968 to 1970. Subsequently, all converted to carry the Poseidon C-3 missile.
The *Andrew Jackson* launched the first Polaris A-3 missile to be fired from a submarine on 26 Oct 1963. The *Daniel Webster* was the first submarine to deploy with the A-3 missile, beginning her first patrol on 28 Sep 1964. The *Daniel Boone* was the first Polaris submarine to deploy to the Pacific, beginning her patrol with the A-3 missile on 25 Dec 1964. The *James Madison* launched the first Poseidon C-3 missile from a submarine on 3 Aug 1970; the submarine began the first Poseidon deployment on 31 Mar 1971.
The *James Madison* was the first submarine to undergo conversion to carry the Poseidon missile. She began conversion in February 1969 and was completed in June 1970. (See conversion table on following page).
Poseidon conversion, overhaul, and reactor refuelling are conducted simultaneously. In addition to changes in missile tubes to accommodate larger Poseidon, the conversion provides replacement of Mk 84 fire control system with Mk 88 system. The Poseidon conversion programme was scheduled to complete in 1977.
Some of the options for the Trident missile programme include rearming submarines of this class with an advanced missile, providing a longer range capability than is available with the Poseidon missile. Current planning provides for the first of ten "Lafayette" class SSBNs to be refitted with the Trident I missile in 1979.

ULYSSES S. GRANT (SSBN 631)   1969, United States Navy

ULYSSES S. GRANT (SSBN 631) in floating dry dock   1974, US Navy, PH1 Bob Woods

MARIANO C. VALLEJO (SSBN 658)

1974, United States Navy

POSEIDON CONVERSION SCHEDULE

Navigation: FBM submarines are equipped with an elaborate Ship's Inertial Navigation System (SINS), a system of gyroscopes and accelerometers which relates movement of the ship in all directions, true speed through the water and over the ocean floor, and true north to give a continuous report of the submarine's position. The system includes the capability of both optical and electronic checks. Navigation data produced by SINS can be provided to each missile's guidance package until the instant the missile is fired.

The Polaris-armed submarines have two Mk 2 Mod 3 SINS inertial navigation systems; as converted, all Poseidon submarines have three Mk 2 Mod 4 SINS; all fitted with navigational satellite receivers.

Personnel: Each FBM submarine is assigned two alternating crews designated "Blue" and "Gold". Each crew mans the submarine during a 60-day patrol and partially assists during the intermediate 28-day refit alongside a Polaris tender. Beginning in January 1975 the submarines began making brief port visits mid-way through the 60-day patrol to break the monotony of the patrols. The "off-duty" crew is undergoing training or is on leave. All FBM submarines are fully airconditioned and the newer ships have elaborate crew study and recreation facilities.

Photographs: Fleet ballistic missile submarines converted to Poseidon are virtually indistinguishable from pre-conversion appearance. FBM submarines rarely operate on the surface and photographs are difficult to obtain. On the previous page the *Ulysses S. Grant* is seen steaming out of Pearl Harbor, Hawaii, and in a floating dry dock in Holy Loch, Scotland. Note the landing craft and tug assisting the *Tecumseh* (below) at Apra Harbor, Guam.

No.	Programme	Conversion Yard	Start		Complete	
SSBN 616	FY 1973	General Dynamics Corp (Electric Boat)	Oct	1972	Nov	1974
SSBN 617	FY 1973	Newport News SB & DD Co	Jan	1973	Mar	1975
SSBN 619	FY 1973	General Dynamics Corp (Electric Boat)	Mar	1973	Aug	1975
SSBN 620	FY 1974	Portsmouth Naval Shipyard	Feb	1974	Mar	1975
SSBN 622	FY 1975	Newport News SB & DD Co	Jan	1975		1976
SSBN 623	FY 1973	Puget Sound Naval Shipyard	June	1973	June	1975
SSBN 624	FY 1974	Newport News SB & DD Co	Oct	1973	Oct	1975
SSBN 625	FY 1975	Portsmouth Naval Shipyard	Apr	1975		1977
SSBN 626	FY 1975	General Dynamics Corp (Electric Boat)		1976		1977
SSBN 627	FY 1968	General Dynamics Corp (Electric Boat)	Feb	1969	June	1970
SSBN 628	FY 1970	Newport News SB & DD Co	Nov	1969	Feb	1971
SSBN 629	FY 1968	Newport News SB & DD Co	May	1969	Aug	1970
SSBN 630	FY 1969	Mare Island Naval Shipyard	Aug	1969	Feb	1971
SSBN 631	FY 1970	Puget Sound Naval Shipyard	Oct	1969	Dec	1970
SSBN 632	FY 1969	General Dynamics Corp (Electric Boat)	July	1969	Nov	1970
SSBN 633	FY 1970	General Dynamics Corp (Electric Boat)	Jan	1970	Apr	1971
SSBN 634	FY 1971	General Dynamics Corp (Electric Boat)	July	1970	Oct	1971
SSBN 635	FY 1970	Portsmouth Naval Shipyard	Jan	1970	Sep	1971
SSBN 636	FY 1971	Newport News SB & DD Co	July	1970	Sep	1971
SSBN 640	FY 1971	General Dynamics Corp (Electric Boat)	Feb	1971	May	1972
SSBN 641	FY 1971	Newport News SB & DD Co	Feb	1971	May	1972
SSBN 642	FY 1972	General Dynamics Corp (Electric Boat)	July	1971	Oct	1972
SSBN 643	FY 1971	Portsmouth Naval Shipyard	Apr	1971	Aug	1972
SSBN 644	FY 1971	Puget Sound Naval Shipyard	Apr	1971	July	1972
SSBN 645	FY 1972	Newport News SB & DD Co	July	1971	Nov	1972
SSBN 654	FY 1972	Puget Sound Naval Shipyard	Sep	1971	Feb	1973
SSBN 655	FY 1972	Newport News SB & DD Co	Nov	1971	Mar	1973
SSBN 656	FY 1972	General Dynamics Corp (Electric Boat)	Nov	1971	Apr	1973
SSBN 657	FY 1972	Puget Sound Naval Shipyard	Feb	1972	Apr	1973
SSBN 658	FY 1973	Newport News SB & DD Co	Aug	1972	Dec	1973
SSBN 659	FY 1973	Portsmouth Naval Shipyard	Oct	1972	Feb	1974

THOMAS A. EDISON (SSBN 610), in rear, passing FRANCIS SCOTT KEY (SSBN 657) in Panama Canal

1973, United States Navy

TECUMSEH (SSBN 628) approaching HUNLEY (AS 19)

United States Navy

5 FLEET BALLISTIC MISSILE SUBMARINES (SSBN): "ETHAN ALLEN" CLASS

Name	No.	Builders	Laid down	Launched	Commissioned
*ETHAN ALLEN	SSBN 608	General Dynamics (Electric Boat Div, Groton)	14 Sep 1959	22 Nov 1960	8 Aug 1961
*SAM HOUSTON	SSBN 609	Newport News Shipbuilding & DD Co	28 Dec 1959	2 Feb 1961	6 Mar 1962
*THOMAS A. EDISON	SSBN 610	General Dynamics (Electric Boat Div, Groton)	15 Mar 1960	15 June 1961	10 Mar 1962
*JOHN MARSHALL	SSBN 611	Newport News Shipbuilding & DD Co	4 Apr 1960	15 July 1961	21 May 1962
*THOMAS JEFFERSON	SSBN 618	Newport News Shipbuilding & DD Co	3 Feb 1961	24 Feb 1962	4 Jan 1963

Displacement, tons: 6 955 standard surface; 7 900 submerged
Length, feet (metres): 410·5 *(125·1)* oa
Beam, feet (metres): 33 *(10·1)*
Draught, feet (metres): 30 *(9·1)*
Missile launchers: 16 tubes for Polaris A-3 SLBM
Torpedo tubes: 4—21 inch *(533 mm)* bow
Main engines: 2 geared turbines (General Electric); 15 000 shp; 1 shaft
Nuclear reactors: 1 pressurised-water cooled S5W (Westinghouse)
Speed, knots: 20 surface; approx 30 submerged
Complement: 140 (12 officers, 128 enlisted men)

These submarines were designed specifically for the FBM role and are larger and better arranged than the earlier "George Washington" class submarines. The first four ships of this class were authorised in the Fiscal Year 1959 programme; the *Thomas Jefferson* (which is out of numerical sequence) was in the FY 1961 programme. These submarines and the previous "George Washington" class will not be converted to carry the Poseidon missile because of materiel limitations and the age they would be after conversion. Also the "George Washington" class submarines are depth limited compared to the later FBM classes which, according to official statements, are based on the "Permit" SSN design.

Design: These submarines and the subsequent "Lafayette" class are deep-diving submarines with a depth capability similar to the "Permit" class attack submarines; pressure hulls of HY-80 steel.

Missiles: These ships were initially armed with the Polaris A-2 missile (1 500 nautical mile range). The *Ethan Allan* launched the first A-2 missile fired from a submarine on 23 Oct 1961. She was the first submarine to deploy with the A-2 missile, beginning her first patrol on 26 June 1962. The *Ethan Allen* fired a Polaris A-2 missile in the Christmas Island Pacific Test Area on 6 May 1962 in what was the first complete US test of a ballistic missile including detonation of the nuclear warhead. All five of these ships have been modified to fire the A-3 missile (2 880 statute mile range). They will not be fitted with the advanced Poseidon missile.
Originally fitted with Mk 80 fire control system and compressed air missile ejectors; provided with Mk 84 fire control systems and gas-steam missile ejectors with A-3 missile.

Navigation: Fitted with two Mk 2 Mod 3 Ship's Inertial Navigation Systems (SINS) and navigational satellite receiver.

Personnel: Alternating "Blue" and "Gold" crews are assigned to these submarines as in "Lafayette" class submarines.

Photographs: Note sail number is painted out in view of *Ethan Allen* underway off Rota, Spain.

JOHN MARSHALL (SSBN 611)   1967, United States Navy

ETHAN ALLEN (SSBN 608)   1971, United States Navy

ETHAN ALLEN (SSBN 608)   1971, United States Navy

5 FLEET BALLISTIC MISSILE SUBMARINES (SSBN): "GEORGE WASHINGTON" CLASS

Name	No.	Builders	Laid down	Launched	Commissioned
*GEORGE WASHINGTON	SSBN 598	General Dynamics (Electric Boat Div, Groton)	1 Nov 1957	9 June1959	30 Dec 1959
*PATRICK HENRY	SSBN 599	General Dynamics (Electric Boat Div, Groton)	27 May 1958	22 Sep 1959	9 Apr 1960
*THEODORE ROOSEVELT	SSBN 600	Mare Island Naval Shipyard	20 May 1958	3 Oct 1959	13 Feb 1961
*ROBERT E. LEE	SSBN 601	Newport News Shipbuilding & DD Co	25 Aug 1958	18 Dec 1959	16 Sep 1960
*ABRAHAM LINCOLN	SSBN 602	Portsmouth Naval Shipyard	1 Nov 1958	14 May 1960	11 Mar 1961

Displacement, tons: 6 000 standard surface; 6 700 submerged
Length, feet (metres): 381·7 (116·3) oa
Beam, feet (metres): 33 (10·1)
Draught, feet (metres): 29 (8·8)
Missile launchers: 16 tubes for Polaris A-3 SLBM
Torpedo tubes: 6—21 inch (533 mm) bow
Main engines: 2 geared turbines (General Electric); 15 000 shp; 1 shaft
Nuclear reactors: 1 pressurised-water cooled S5W (Westinghouse)
Speed, knots: 20 surface; approx 30 submerged
Complement: 140 (12 officers, 128 enlisted men)

ABRAHAM LINCOLN (SSBN 602)

United States Navy

The *George Washington* was the West's first ship to be armed with ballistic missiles. A supplement to the Fiscal Year 1958 new construction programme signed on 11 Feb 1958 provided for the construction of the first three Fleet Ballistic Missile (FBM) submarines. The Navy had already ordered the just-begun attack submarine *Scorpion* (SSN 589) to be completed as a missile submarine on 31 Dec 1957, the hull was redesignated SSBN 598 and completed as the *George Washington*. The *Patrick Henry* similarly was re-ordered on the last day of 1957, her materials having originally been intended for the not-yet started SSN 590. These submarines and three sister ships (two authorised in FY 1959) were built to a modified "Skipjack" class design with almost 130 feet being added to the original design to accommodate two rows of eight missile tubes, fore control and navigation equipment, and auxiliary machinery.

Engineering: The *George Washington* was the first FBM submarine to be overhauled and "refuelled". During her 4½ years of operation on her initial reactor core she carried out 15 submerged missile patrols and steamed more than 100 000 miles.

Missiles: These ships were initially armed with the Polaris A-1 missile (1 200 nautical mile range). The *George Washington* successfully fired two Polaris A-1 missiles while submerged off Cape Canaveral (Kennedy) on 20 July 1960 in the first underwater launching of a ballistic missile from a US submarine. She departed on her initial patrol on 15 Nov 1960 and remained submerged for 66 days, 10 hours. All five submarines of this class have been refitted to fire the improved Polaris A-3 missile (2 880 statute mile range). Missile refit and first reactor refuelling were accomplished simultaneously during overhaul. *George Washington* from 20 June 1964 to 2 Feb 1966, *Patrick Henry* from 4 Jan 1965 to 21 July 1966, *Theodore Roosevelt* from 28 July 1965 to 14 Jan 1967, *Robert E. Lee* from 23 Feb 1965 to 2 July 1966, and *Abraham Lincoln* from 25 Oct 1965 to 3 June 1967, four at Electric Boat yard in Groton, Connecticut, and *Robert E. Lee* at Mare Island Naval Shipyard (California). These submarines all have Mk 84 fire control systems and gas-steam missile ejectors (originally fitted with Mk 80 fire control systems and compressed air missile ejectors, changed during A-3 missile refit).

These submarines will not be modified to carry and launch the advanced Poseidon ballistic missile.

Navigation: Fitted with three Mk 2 Mod 4 Ship's Inertial Navigation System (SINS) and navigational satellite receiver.

Personnel: Alternating "Blue" and "Gold" crews are assigned to these submarines as in "Lafayette" class submarines.

Photographs: Note that "hump" of hull extension for housing missile tubes is more pronounced in these submarines than later classes. Note the bitts and capstans visible in view of *Abraham Lincoln* while mooring; as in SSNs, most hull projects are removable or retractable to provide a "clean" hull and reduce noise as submarine passes through water.

GEORGE WASHINGTON (SSBN 598)

United States Navy

ROBERT E. LEE (SSBN 601)

1966, United States Navy

SUBMARINES

The US Navy's submarine forces consist of two principal categories: strategic missile submarines (SSBN), listed in the previous section, and attack submarines (SS and SSN).

The Navy's attack submarine force is almost entirely nuclear. The few remaining diesel-electric submarines are all of post-World War II construction; their age and the demand of foreign transfers to US allies will result in an all-nuclear submarine force by the mid-1980s, if not earlier. At that time the Navy will have some 85 to 90 SSNs ("Skipjack" class and later).

A construction rate of two SSNs per year for the foreseeable future has been proposed by the Department of Defense.

Construction of the submarines that have been funded as of 1 January 1976 was being slowed by the late delivery of component equipment and problems in the hiring of shipyard workers. Further complicating the situation has been the start-up of the Trident missile submarine programme and the loss of the Litton/Ingalls yard at Pascagoula, Mississippi, which delivered its last nuclear submarine in 1974. This leaves only two shipyards in the United States building nuclear submarines. (No diesel-propelled submarines have been built in the United States since 1959).

Advanced nuclear attack submarine designs are being investigated by the US Navy for programmes beyond the "Los Angeles" class. A follow-on to the "Los Angeles" class can be expected to be developed by the late 1970s when about 40 of that design have been ordered. Early in 1975, Secretary of Defense Schlesinger stated that: "Looking to the longer term, we are examining the feasibility and desirability of building a new class of SSNs. We are particularly interested in a less costly SSN". The design may include a wide-aperture array sonar for rapid passive localisation of targets.

Current SSN construction is limited to the "Los Angeles" class, a large submarine intended in part to counter the high-speed submarines of the Soviet Navy. US nuclear submarine size had grown steadily since the "Skipjack" class of 1959 while retaining the same S5W reactor plant; accordingly, submarine performance has deteriorated. In contrast, Soviet attack submarine speeds appear to have steadily increased.

Unofficial sources indicate that the lack of US progress in submarine reactor development required modification of a surface ship nuclear reactor plant for use in the "Los Angeles" class which, in turn, necessitated a larger submarine.

Missions: Nuclear-powered attack submarines are primarily considered anti-submarine platforms because of their ability to operate covertly, especially in waters which are otherwise under the control of enemy surface and air forces where other US anti-submarine forces could not operate.

The US Navy is investigating the use of SSNs in other roles, including the open-ocean escorting of high-value surface ships such as aircraft carriers. Also, the increasing capabilities and oceanic operations of Soviet surface forces have caused renewed US Navy interest in the employment of the submarines in the anti-ship role, armed with torpedoes and anti-ship missiles.

Anti-ship Missiles: An encapsulated version of the Harpoon anti-ship missile is being developed for launching from submarines. The Harpoon, also capable of surface ship and aircraft launch, is a 15-foot weapon carrying a conventional high-explosive warhead. In the encapsulated version, the Harpoon is launched from a torpedo tube and travels to the surface where the protective capsule is discarded, the missile's fins extend, and the rocket engine ignites. The Harpoon has a range of about 60 nautical miles.

Conventional Submarines: The US Navy now operates only nine diesel-electric attack submarines. In addition, one diesel transport submarine and two diesel research submarines are in service.

Deep Submergence Vehicles: The US Navy's Deep Submergence Vehicles (DSV), including the nuclear-propelled *NR-1*, are listed at the end of the United States Navy section of this edition.

Midget Submarines: The US Navy's only "midget" submarine, the 50-foot-long *X-1*, was stricken on 16 Feb 1973. See 1972-1973 edition for characteristics and photographs.

Nomenclature: US submarines generally have been named for fish and other marine life except that fleet ballistic missile submarines have been named for famous Americans. The tradition of naming "fleet" and "attack" submarines for fish was broken in 1971 when three submarines of the "Sturgeon" class and the one-of-a-kind SSN 685 were named for deceased members of the Congress. Previously US destroyer-type ships have honoured members of the Congress.

Later in 1971 the SSN 688, lead ship for a new class of attack submarines, was named *Los Angeles*, introducing "city" names to US submarines. This was the third name source applied to US submarines within a year, indicating the considerable confusion in ship nomenclature within the Navy.

(Of late, several types of auxiliary ships also have been named for cities, a name source traditionally applied to cruisers in the US Navy).

Transfers: The three "Tang" class attack submarines remaining on the Navy List are scheduled for transfer to the Imperial Iranian Navy in 1977-1978. The Iranians have tentatively assigned the following names and pennant numbers, which will probably be assigned in the order of transfer *vice* US hull number sequence: *Kusseh* (SS 101), *Nahang* (SS 102), and *Dolphin* (SS 103).

1 + 38 NUCLEAR-POWERED ATTACK SUBMARINES (SSN): "LOS ANGELES" CLASS

Name	No.	Builders	Laid down	Launched	Commissioned
*LOS ANGELES	SSN 688	Newport News SB & DD Co	8 Jan 1972	6 Apr 1974	June 1976
BATON ROUGE	SSN 689	Newport News SB & DD Co	18 Nov 1972	26 Apr 1975	Early 1977
PHILADELPHIA	SSN 690	General Dynamics (Electric Boat)	12 Aug 1972	19 Oct 1974	Sep 1976
MEMPHIS	SSN 691	Newport News SB & DD Co	23 June1973	3 Apr 1976	Early 1977
OMAHA	SSN 692	General Dynamics (Electric Boat)	27 Jan 1973	21 Feb 1976	Late 1977
CINCINNATI	SSN 693	Newport News SB & DD Co	6 Apr 1974	1976	Late 1977
GROTON	SSN 694	General Dynamics (Electric Boat)	3 Aug 1973	1976	Late 1977
BIRMINGHAM	SSN 695	Newport News SB & DD Co	26 Apr 1975	1976	Late 1977
NEW YORK CITY	SSN 696	General Dynamics (Electric Boat)	15 Dec 1973	1976	Late 1977
INDIANAPOLIS	SSN 697	General Dynamics (Electric Boat)	19 Oct 1974	1976	1978
BREMERTON	SSN 698	General Dynamics (Electric Boat)	Apr 1976	1977	1978
JACKSONVILLE	SSN 699	General Dynamics (Electric Boat)	21 Feb 1976	1977	1978
Six submarines	SSN 700-705	General Dynamics (Electric Boat)		1977-1978	1978-1980
Five submarines	SSN 706-710	General Dynamics (Electric Boat)		1979-1980	1980-1981
Three submarines	SSN 711-713	Newport News SB & DD Co		1979-1980	1980-1982
Two submarines	SSN 714-715	Newport News SB & DD Co			1983
Three submarines	SSN 716-718	Proposed FY 1977 programme			1985
Eight submarines	SSN	Planned FY 1978- 1981 programme			

Displacement, tons: 6 000 standard; 6 900 submerged
Length, feet (metres): 360 *(109·7)* oa
Beam, feet (metres): 33 *(10·1)*
Draught, feet (metres): 32·3 *(9·85)*
Torpedo tubes: 4—21 inch *(533 mm)* amidships
A/S weapons: SUBROC and Mk 48 A/S torpedoes
Main engines: 2 geared turbines; 1 shaft
Nuclear reactors: 1 pressurised-water cooled
Speed, knots: 30+ submerged
Complement: 127 (12 officers, 115 enlisted men)

These are "high-speed" attack submarines intended to counter the new Soviet classes of submarines that went to sea during the late 1960s and early 1970s.

The SSN 688-690 (3 ships) were authorised in the Fiscal Year 1970 new construction programme, SSN 691-694 (4 ships) in FY 1971, SSN 695-699 (5 ships) in FY 1972, SSN 700-705 (6 ships) in FY 1973, SSN 706-710 (5 ships) in FY 1974, SSN 711-713 (3 Ships) in FY 1975, and SSN 714-715 (2 ships) in the FY 1976 programme. Additional submarines are planned at the rate of two units per year at least into the early 1980s.

Detailed design of the SSN 688 class as well as construction of the lead submarine was contracted to the Newport News Shipbuilding & Dry Dock Company, Newport News, Virginia; the follow-on ships were awarded to Newport News and to the General Dynamics Electric Boat Division yard at Groton, Connecticut.

These ships are considerably behind schedule with the lead ship being completed approximately two years behind the original schedule. Thus, the *Los Angeles* is 4½ years from keel laying to completion.

Design: These submarines are considerably larger than the previous "Sturgeon" class. All construction features, including sail size, hull shape, propulsion plant design, machinery mounting technique, auxiliary machinery, etc, are designed to provide the maximum degree of quietness possible. Their sound level is similar to the "Sturgeon" class when both submarines are travelling at comparable speeds.

Electronics: Electronic equipment in these submarines includes BQQ-5 (formerly BQS-13DNA) long-range detection sonar, BQS-15 close contact avoidance sonar, and BPS-15 sur-

PHILADELPHIA (SSN 690)

1974, General Dynamics, Electric Boat Division

face search radar. A towed sonar array is fitted.
UYK-7 computer is installed to assist command and control functions: Mk 113 Mod 10 torpedo fire control system fitted in SSN 688-699; Mk 117 in later submarines.

Engineering: Unofficial sources indicate that a modified surface ship nuclear reactor plant may be used in this class. The "smallest" surface ship reactor now available for submarine use is the D2G type used in the frigates *Bainbridge* and *Trux-*

tun; these reactors each produce approximately 30 000 shp. Reactor core life between "refuellings" is estimated at ten years.

Fiscal: The costs of these submarines have increased in every fiscal year programme. In FY 1976 an average cost of $221 250 000 per unit was estimated for a 38-submarine class. However, the FY 1977 units are estimated to cost approximately $320 000 000 each.

1 NUCLEAR-POWERED ATTACK SUBMARINE (SSN): "LIPSCOMB" TYPE

Name	No.	Builders	Laid down	Launched	Commissioned
*GLENARD P. LIPSCOMB	SSN 685	General Dynamics (Electric Boat)	5 June 1971	4 Aug 1973	21 Dec 1974

Displacement, tons: 5 800 standard; 6 480 submerged
Length, feet (metres): 365 oa (111·3)
Beam, feet (metres): 31·7 (9·7)
Torpedo tubes: 4—21 inch (533 mm) amidships
A/S weapons: SUBROC and A/S torpedoes
Main engines: Turbine-electric drive (General Electric); 1 shaft
Nuclear reactors: 1 pressurised-water cooled S5Wa (Westinghouse)
Speed, knots: approx 25 submerged
Complement: 120 (12 officers, 108 enlisted men)

The Turbine-Electric Drive Submarine (TEDS) was constructed to test "a combination of advanced silencing techniques" involving "a new kind of propulsion system, and new and quieter machinery of various kinds", according to the Department of Defense. The noise level produced by an operating submarine is an important factor in its ability to remain undetected by an opponent's passive listening devices and its own ability to detect the opponent. The TEDS project will permit an at-sea evaluation of improvements in ASW effectiveness due to noise reduction.

No class of turbine-electric nuclear submarines has been proposed. Rather, quieting features developed in the SSN 685 which do not detract from speed will probably be incorporated in the SSN 688 design and subsequent SSN classes. (The TEDS design was several years ahead of the SSN 668 design).

Authorised in the Fiscal Year 1968 new construction programme, estimated construction cost was approximately $200 000 000.

Design of an advanced submarine specifically intended for quiet operation began with Navy studies which commenced in October 1964. Approval to construct the submarine was revoked on at least one occasion by the Department of Defense in an effort to combine several desired characteristics in a single submarine design. However, high speed and silent operation are apparently not compatible with available technology.

Final Department of Defense approval for construction of the turbine-electric drive submarine was announced on 25 Oct 1968. A contract was awarded to General Dynamics (Electric Boat Division) for construction of the SSN 685 on 16 Dec 1968.

Engineering: Turbine-electric drive eliminates the noisy reduction gears of standard steam turbine power plants, the major source of noise in a nuclear-powered submarine. The turbine-electric power plant is larger and heavier than comparable steam turbine submarine machinery.

The *Tullibee* (SSN 597) was an earlier effort at noise reduction through a turbine-electric nuclear plant.

GLENARD P. LIPSCOMB (SSN 685)   1974, General Dynamics, Electric Boat Division

1 NUCLEAR-POWERED ATTACK SUBMARINE (SSN): "NARWHAL" TYPE

Name	No.	Builders	Laid down	Launched	Commissioned
*NARWHAL	SSN 671	General Dynamics (Electric Boat)	17 Jan 1966	9 Sep 1967	12 July 1969

Displacement, tons: 4 450 standard; 5 350 submerged
Length, feet (metres): 314 (95·7) oa
Beam, feet (metres): 38 (11·5)
Draught, feet (metres): 26 (7·9)
Torpedo tubes: 4—21 inch (533 mm) amidships
A/S weapons: SUBROC and A/S torpedoes
Main engines: 2 steam turbines; approx 17 000 shp; 1 shaft
Nuclear reactors: 1 pressurised water-cooled S5G (General Electric)
Speed, knots: approx 20 surface; approx 30 submerged
Complement: 120 (12 officers, 108 enlisted men)

The *Narwhal* is a large attack submarine with an improved propulsion system. Authorised in the Fiscal Year 1964 new construction programme.

Design: The *Narwhal* is similar to the "Sturgeon" class submarines in hull design.

Electronics: Fitted with BQQ-2 sonar system. See "Sturgeon" and "Permit" classes for general notes. Fitted with Mk 113 Mod 6 torpedo fire control system.

Engineering: The *Narwhal* is fitted with the prototype sea-going S5G natural circulation reactor plant. According to Admiral H. G. Rickover the natural circulation reactor "offers promise of increased reactor plant reliability, simplicity, and noise reduction due to the elimination of the need for large reactor coolant pumps and associated electrical and control equipment by taking maximum advantage of natural convection to circulate the reactor coolant".

Natural circulation eliminates the requirement for primary coolant pumps, the second noisiest component of a pressurised-water propulsion system after the steam turbines. The Atomic Energy Commission's Knolls Atomic Power Laboratory was given prime responsibility for development of the power plant. Construction of a land-based prototype plant began in May 1961 at the National Reactor Testing Station in Idaho. The reactor achieved initial criticality on 12 Sep 1965.

Photographs: Note safety track on submarine deck to permit men to move on the low-lying deck without railings; the small deck fins are for BQS-8 upward-looking sonar for under-ice operation.

NARWHAL (SSN 671)   1969, General Dynamics, Electric Boat Division

NARWHAL (SSN 671)—see previous page

1969, General Dynamics, Electric Boat Division

37 NUCLEAR-POWERED ATTACK SUBMARINES (SSN): "STURGEON" CLASS

Name	No.	Builders	Laid down	Launched	Commissioned
*STURGEON	SSN 637	General Dynamics (Electric Boat)	10 Aug 1963	26 Feb 1966	3 Mar 1967
*WHALE	SSN 638	General Dynamics (Quincy)	27 May 1964	14 Oct 1966	12 Oct 1968
*TAUTOG	SSN 639	Ingalls Shipbuilding Corp	27 Jan 1964	15 April 1967	17 Aug 1968
*GRAYLING	SSN 646	Portsmouth Naval Shipyard	12 May 1964	22 June 1967	11 Oct 1969
*POGY	SSN 647	Ingalls Shipbuilding Corp	4 May 1964	3 June 1967	15 May 1971
*ASPRO	SSN 648	Ingalls Shipbuilding Corp	23 Nov 1964	29 Nov 1967	20 Feb 1969
*SUNFISH	SSN 649	General Dynamics (Quincy)	15 Jan 1965	14 Oct 1966	15 Mar 1969
*PARGO	SSN 650	General Dynamics (Electric Boat)	3 June 1964	17 Sep 1966	5 Dec 1967
*QUEENFISH	SSN 651	Newport News SB & DD Co	11 May 1965	25 Feb 1966	6 Dec 1966
*PUFFER	SSN 652	Ingalls Shipbuilding Corp	8 Feb 1965	30 Mar 1968	9 Aug 1969
*RAY	SSN 653	Newport News SB & DD Co	1 April 1965	21 June 1966	12 April 1967
*SAND LANCE	SSN 660	Portsmouth Naval Shipyard	15 Jan 1965	11 Nov 1969	25 Sep 1971
*LAPON	SSN 661	Newport News SB & DD Co	26 July 1965	16 Dec 1966	14 Dec 1967
*GURNARD	SSN 662	San Francisco NSY (Mare Island)	22 Dec 1964	20 May 1967	6 Dec 1968
*HAMMERHEAD	SSN 663	Newport News SB & DD Co	29 Nov 1965	14 April 1967	28 June 1968
*SEA DEVIL	SSN 664	Newport News SB & DD Co	12 April 1966	5 Oct 1967	30 Jan 1969
*GUITARRO	SSN 665	San Francisco NSY (Mare Island)	9 Dec 1965	27 July 1968	9 Sep 1972
*HAWKBILL	SSN 666	San Francisco NSY (Mare Island)	12 Sep 1966	12 April 1969	4 Feb 1971
*BERGALL	SSN 667	General Dynamics (Electric Boat)	16 April 1966	17 Feb 1968	13 June 1969
*SPADEFISH	SSN 668	Newport News SB & DD Co	21 Dec 1966	15 May 1968	31 July 1969
*SEAHORSE	SSN 669	General Dynamics (Electric Boat)	13 Aug 1966	15 June 1968	19 Sep 1969
*FINBACK	SSN 670	Newport News SB & DD Co	26 June 1967	7 Dec 1968	4 Feb 1970
*PINTADO	SSN 672	San Francisco NSY (Mare Island)	27 Oct 1967	16 Aug 1969	29 Apr 1971
*FLYING FISH	SSN 673	General Dynamics (Electric Boat)	30 June 1967	17 May 1969	29 April 1970
*TREPANG	SSN 674	General Dynamics (Electric Boat)	28 Oct 1967	27 Sep 1969	14 Aug 1970
*BLUEFISH	SSN 675	General Dynamics (Electric Boat)	13 Mar 1968	10 Jan 1970	8 Jan 1971
*BILLFISH	SSN 676	General Dynamics (Electric Boat)	20 Sep 1968	1 May 1970	11 Sep 1971
*DRUM	SSN 677	San Francisco NSY (Mare Island)	20 Aug 1968	23 May 1970	15 April 1972
*ARCHERFISH	SSN 678	General Dynamics (Electric Boat)	19 June 1969	16 Jan 1971	17 Dec 1971
*SILVERSIDES	SSN 679	General Dynamics (Electric Boat)	13 Oct 1969	4 June 1971	5 May 1972
*WILLIAM H. BATES	SSN 680	Ingalls Shipbuilding (Litton)	4 Aug 1969	11 Dec 1971	12 April 1973
*BATFISH	SSN 681	General Dynamics (Electric Boat)	9 Feb 1970	9 Oct 1971	1 Sep 1972
*TUNNY	SSN 682	Ingalls Shipbuilding (Litton)	22 May 1970	10 June 1972	26 Jan 1974
*PARCHE	SSN 683	Ingalls Shipbuilding (Litton)	10 Dec 1970	13 Jan 1973	17 Aug 1974
*CAVALLA	SSN 684	General Dynamics (Electric Boat)	4 June 1970	19 Feb 1972	9 Feb 1973
*L. MENDEL RIVERS	SSN 686	Newport News SB & DD Co	26 June 1971	2 June 1973	1 Feb 1975
*RICHARD B. RUSSELL	SSN 687	Newport News SB & DD Co	19 Oct 1971	12 Jan 1974	16 Aug 1975

Displacement, tons: 3 640 standard; 4 640 submerged
Length, feet (metres): 292·2 *(89·0)* oa
Beam, feet (metres): 31·7 *(9·5)*
Draught, feet (metres): 26 *(7·9)*
Torpedo tubes: 4—21 inch *(533 mm)* amidships
A/S weapons: SUBROC and A/S torpedoes
Main engines: 2 steam turbines; approx 15 000 shp; 1 shaft
Nuclear reactors: 1 pressurised-water cooled S5W (Westinghouse)
Speed, knots: approx 20 surface; approx 30 submerged
Complement: 120 (12 officers, 108 enlisted men)

The 37 "Sturgeon" class attack submarines comprise the largest US Navy group of nuclear-powered ships built to the same design (followed by the 31 "Lafayette" class ballistic missile submarines; the Soviet Navy has built 34 submarines of the same design in the "Yankee" class.

These submarines are intended to seek out and destroy enemy submarines. They are similar in design to the previous "Permit" (ex-"Thresher") class but are slightly larger. SSN 637-639 (3 ships) were authorised in the Fiscal Year 1962 new construction programme. SSN 646-653 (8 ships) in FY 1963, SSN 660-664 (5 ships) in FY 1964, SSN 665-670 (6 ships) in FY 1965, SSN 672-677 (6 ships) in FY 1966, SSN 678-682 (5 ships) in FY 1967, SSN 683-684 (2 ships) in FY 1968, and SSN 686-687 (2 ships) in FY 1969.
Some of these ships required seven years for construction (keel laying to completion).

Construction: The *Pogy* was begun by the New York Shipbuilding Corp (Camden, New Jersey), but was towed to Ingalls Shipbuilding Corp for completion; contract with the New York Shipbuilding Corp was terminated on 5 June 1967; contract for completion awarded to Ingalls Shipbuilding Corp on 7 Dec 1967.
The *Guitarro* sank in 35 feet of water on 15 May 1969 while being fitted out at the San Francisco Bay Naval Shipyard. According to a congressional report, the sinking, caused by Shipyard workers, was "wholly avoidable". Subsequently raised; damage estimated at $25 000 000 to repair damage due to interior flooding. Completion delayed more than two years.

Design: These submarines are slightly larger than the previous "Permit" (ex-"Thresher") class and can be identified by their

RICHARD B. RUSSELL (SSN 687)

1975, Newport News SB & DD Co.

taller sail structure and the lower position of their diving planes on the sail (to improve control at periscope depth). Sail height is 20 feet, 6 inches above deck. Sail-mounted diving planes rotate to vertical for breaking through ice when surfacing in arctic regions.
These submarines probably are slightly slower than the previous "Permit" and "Skipjack" classes because of their increased size with the same propulsion system as in the earlier classes.

Electronics: These submarines are fitted with the advanced BQQ-2 sonar system. Principal components of the BQQ-2 include the BQS-6 active sonar, with transducers mounted in a 15-foot diameter sonar sphere, and BQR-7 passive sonar, with hydrophones in a conformal array on sides of forward hull. The active sonar sphere is fitted in the optimum bow position, requiring placement of torpedo tubes amidships. These submarines also have BQS-8 and BQS-12 (first 16 units) or BQS-13 active/passive sonars. Transducers for the BQS-8, intended primarily for under-ice navigation, are in two small domes aft of the sail structure.

Sonar suites of the *Guitarro* and *Cavalla* have been modified. All "Sturgeon" class submarines are to be refitted with upgrading of the BQQ-2 to BQQ-5 configuration during regular overhauls.

Also fitted with BPS-14 surface search radar and Mk 113 torpedo fire control system (Mod 6 through SSN 677; Mod 8 in SSN 678-683; Mod 10 in later units).

Missiles: Compatability tests were conducted during 1972-1973 with several submarines of this class and the encapsulated Harpoon anti-ship missile.

Nomenclature: *William H. Bates,* ex-*Redfish,* re-named 25 June 1971 to honour a deceased member of Congress.

Operational: The *Whale, Pargo,* and older nuclear submarine *Sargo* conducted exercises in the Arctic ice pack during March-April 1969. The *Whale* surfaced at the geographic North Pole on April 6, the 60th anniversary of Rear Admiral Robert E. Peary's reaching the North Pole. This was believed the first instance of single-screw US nuclear submarines surfacing in the Arctic ice.

The *Hammerhead* and the older nuclear submarine *Skate* conducted excercises in the Arctic during November-December 1970, with the *Hammerhead* surfacing at the North Pole on 20 Nov 1970.

The *Trepang* operated in the Arctic with the *Skate* during the spring of 1971.

Submersibles: The *Hawkbill* has been modified to carry and support the Navy's Deep Submergence Rescue Vehicles (DSRV). The *Hawkbill* can transport a 50-foot DSRV "piggyback" on her after deck and, while submerged, can launch and recover the DSRV. The DSRV can also "land" on the submarine's forward hatch as well as the after hatch to transfer personnel. See section on Deep Submergence Vehicles for additional DSRV details. The research submarines *Halibut* (SSN 587) and *Seawolf* (SSN 575) are also fitted to carry submersibles. The modifications do not affect the *Hawkbill's* combat capabilities.

Photographs: These submarines have streamlined hulls with few deck projections to interrupt their clean lines; the two small fins on the main deck aft of the sail structure are BQS-8 sonar transducers and the darker "windows" on the sail structure (forward of diving planes) are BQS-8 hydrophones. Capstans and cleats are retractable.

The *Hawkbill* is shown carrying the submersible DSRV-1. The markings on the submarine's sail and around her forward hatch are luminescent to assist underwater "mating" operations.

RICHARD B. RUSSELL (SSN 687)   *1975, Newport News SB & DD Co*

POGY (SSN 647)   *1973, United States Navy*

HAWKBILL (SSN 666) with DSRV-1   *1971, United States Navy*

PERMIT (SSN 594)—see following page   *1970, United States Navy*

13 NUCLEAR-POWERED ATTACK SUBMARINES (SSN): "PERMIT" CLASS

Name	No.	Builders	Laid down	Launched	Commissioned
*PERMIT	SSN 594	Mare Island Naval Shipyard	16 July 1959	1 July 1961	29 May 1962
*PLUNGER	SSN 595	Mare Island Naval Shipyard	2 Mar 1960	9 Dec 1961	21 Nov 1962
*BARB	SSN 596	Ingalls Shipbuilding Corp	9 Nov 1959	12 Feb 1962	24 Aug 1963
*POLLACK	SSN 603	New York Shipbuilding Corp	14 Mar 1960	17 Mar 1962	26 May 1964
*HADDO	SSN 604	New York Shipbuilding Corp	9 Sep 1960	18 Aug 1962	16 Dec 1964
*JACK	SSN 605	Portsmouth Naval Shipyard	16 Sep 1960	24 Apr 1963	31 Mar 1967
*TINOSA	SSN 606	Portsmouth Naval Shipyard	24 Nov 1959	9 Dec 1961	17 Oct 1964
*DACE	SSN 607	Ingalls Shipbuilding Corp	6 June1960	18 Aug 1962	4 Apr 1964
*GUARDFISH	SSN 612	New York Shipbuilding Corp	28 Feb 1961	15 May 1965	20 Dec 1966
*FLASHER	SSN 613	General Dynamics (Electric Boat)	14 Apr 1961	22 June1963	22 July 1966
*GREENLING	SSN 614	General Dynamics (Electric Boat)	15 Aug 1961	4 Apr 1964	3 Nov 1967
*GATO	SSN 615	Ingalls Shipbuilding Corp	15 Dec 1961	14 May 1964	25 Jan 1968
*HADDOCK	SSN 621	Ingalls Shipbuilding Corp	24 Apr 1961	21 May 1966	22 Dec 1967

Displacement, tons: 3 750 standard; *Flasher, Greenling* and *Gato* 3 800; 4 300 submerged except *Jack* 4 500 submerged, *Flasher, Greenling* and *Gato* 4 600 submerged
Length, feet (metres): 278·5 *(84·9)* oa except *Jack* 296·7 *(89·5)*, *Flasher, Greenling* and *Gato* 292·2 *(89·1)*
Beam, feet (metres): 31·7 *(9·6)*
Draught, feet (metres): 25·2 *(7·6)*
Torpedo tubes: 4—21 inch *(533 mm)* amidships
A/S weapons: SUBROC and A/S torpedoes
Main engines: 2 steam turbines, approx 15 000 shp; 1 shaft
Nuclear reactors: 1 pressurised-water cooled S5W (Westinghouse)
Speed, knots: approx 20 surface; approx 30 submerged
Complement: 120 (12 officers, 108 enlisted men)

BARB (SSN 596)

1973, United States Navy

These submarines were the first of a series of advanced attack submarines intended to seek out and destroy enemy submarines. They have a greater depth capability than previous nuclear-powered submarines and are the first to combine the SUBROC anti-submarine missile capability with the advanced BQQ-2 sonar system. The lead ship of the class, the ill-fated *Thresher* (SSN 593), was authorised in the Fiscal Year 1957 new construction programme, the SSN 594-596 (3 ships) in FY 1958. SSN 603-607 (5 ships) in FY 1959, SSN 612-615 (4 ships) in FY 1960, and SSN 621 in FY 1961.
The *Thresher* (SSN 593) was lost off the coast of New England on 10 Apr 1963 while on post-overhaul trials. She went down with 129 men on board (108 crewmen plus four naval officers and 17 civilians on board for trials).

Class: These submarines were originally listed as belonging to the "Thresher" class; now referred to as the "Permit" class after loss of the *Thresher* in 1963.

Construction: *Greenling* and *Gato* were launched by the Electric Boat Division of the General Dynamics Corp (Groton, Connecticut); towed to Quincy Division (Massachusetts) for lengthening and completion.

Design: The *Jack* was built to a modified design to test a modified power plant (see *Engineering* notes).
The *Flasher, Gato* and *Greenling* were modified during construction; fitted with SUBSAFE features, heavier machinery, and larger sail structures.

These submarines have a modified "tear-drop" hull design. Their bows are devoted to sonar and their four torpedo tubes are amidships, angled out, two to port and two to starboard. The sail structure height of these submarines is 13 feet 9 inches to 15 feet above the deck, with later submarines of this class having a sail height of 20 feet.

Electronics: These submarines are fitted with the advanced BQQ-2 sonar system (first installed in the *Tullibee* SSN 597). Principal components of the BQQ-2 include the BQS-6 active sonar, with transducers mounted in a 15-foot diameter sonar sphere, and BQR-7 passive sonar, with hydrophones on a conformal array along sides of forward hull. The active sonar sphere is fitted in the optimum bow position, requiring placement of torpedo tubes amidships. The advanced BQS-13DNA active/passive sonar will be fitted in these submarines as well as other equipment to provide them the BQQ-5 sonar system (vice BQQ-2) during regular overhauls.

These submarines have the Mk 113 Mod 6 torpedo fire control system.

Engineering: The *Jack* is fitted with two propellers on essentially one shaft (actually a single shaft within a sleeve-like shaft) and a counter-rotating turbine-without a reduction gear. Both innovations are designed to reduce operating noises. To accommodate the larger turbine, the engine spaces were lengthened ten feet and the shaft structure was lengthened seven feet to mount the two propellers. The propellers are of different size and are smaller than in the other submarines of this class. Also eliminated in *Jack* was a clutch and secondary-propulsion electric motor.
The *Jack's* propulsion arrangement provides a ten per cent increase in power efficiency, but no increase in speed.

Nomenclature: Names changed during construction: *Plunder* ex-*Pollack: Barb* ex-*Pollack* ex-*Plunger: Pollack* ex-*Barb.*

1 NUCLEAR-POWERED ATTACK SUBMARINE (SSN): "TULLIBEE" TYPE

Name	No.	Builders	Laid down	Launched	Commissioned
*TULLIBEE	SSN 597	General Dynamics (Electric Boat)	26 May 1958	27 April1960	9 Nov 1960

Displacement, tons: 2 317 standard; 2 640 submerged
Length, feet (metres): 273 *(83·2)* oa
Beam, feet (metres): 23·3 *(7·1)*
Draught, feet (metres): 21 *(6·4)*
Torpedo tubes: 4—21 inch *(533 mm)* amidships
A/S weapons: A/S torpedoes
Main engines: Turbo-electric drive with steam turbine (Westinghouse); 2 500 shp; 1 shaft
Nuclear reactors: 1 pressurised- water cooled S2C (Combustion Engineering)
Speed, knots: approx 15 surface; 15+ submerged
Complement: 87 (7 officers, 80 enlisted men)

The *Tullibee* was designed specifically for anti-submarine operations and was the first US submarine with the optimum bow position devoted entirely to sonar. No additional submarines of this type were constructed because of the success of the larger, more-versatile "Permit" class. The *Tullibee* was authorised in the Fiscal Year 1958 new construction programme. She is no longer considered a "first line" submarine.

Design: The *Tullibee* has a modified, elongated "tear-drop" hull design. Originally she was planned as a 1 000-ton craft, but reactor requirements and other considerations increased her size during design and construction.
The *Tullibee* has four amidships torpedo tubes angled out from the centreline two to port and two to starboard. However, she is not fitted to fire the SUBROC anti-submarine missile. She cannot match the "Thresher" and later SSN classes in underwater speed or manoeuvrability.

Electronics: The *Tullibee* was the first submarine fitted with the integrated BQQ-2 system (see "Permit" class listing for details). The fin-like sonar domes are PUFFs for BQG-4 passive fire control sonar; in the earlier photograph only two PUFF domes are installed (not to be confused with fin-like rudder); later photograph shows three PUFF domes with second dome (aft of sail structure) painted light colour.
PUFF is an acronym for Passive Underwater Fire-control Feasibility system. Fitted with Mk 112 Mod 1 torpedo fire control system.

Engineering: The *Tullibee* has a small nuclear power plant designed and developed by the Combustion Engineering Company.

TULLIBEE (SSN 597)

1960, United States Navy

The *Tullibee* propulsion system features turbo-electric drive rather than conventional steam turbines with reduction gears in an effort to reduce operating noises.

Navigation: The *Tullibee* is fitted with Ships Inertial Navigation System (SINS).

1968, United States Navy

TULLIBEE (SSN 597)—see previous page

5 NUCLEAR-POWERED ATTACK SUBMARINES (SSN): "SKIPJACK" CLASS

Name	No.	Builders	Laid down	Launched	Commissioned
*SKIPJACK	SSN 585	General Dynamics (Electric Boat)	29 May 1956	26 May 1958	15 April 1959
*SCAMP	SSN 588	Mare Island Naval Shipyard	23 Jan 1959	8 Oct 1960	5 June 1961
*SCULPIN	SSN 590	Ingalls Shipbuilding Corp	3 Feb 1958	31 Mar 1960	1 June 1961
*SHARK	SSN 591	Newport News SB & DD Co	24 Feb 1958	16 Mar 1960	9 Feb 1961
*SNOOK	SSN 592	Ingalls Shipbuilding Corp	7 April 1958	31 Oct 1960	24 Oct 1961

Displacement, tons: 3 075 standard; 3 500 submerged
Length, feet (metres): 251·7 *(76·7)* oa
Beam, feet (metres): 31·5 *(9·6)*
Draught, feet (metres): 28 *(8·5)*
Torpedo tubes: 6—21 inch *(533 mm)* bow
A/S weapons: A/S torpedoes
Main engines: 2 steam turbines (Westinghouse in *Skipjack*; General Electric in others); approx 15 000 shp; 1 shaft
Nuclear reactors: 1 pressurised-water cooled S5W (Westinghouse)
Speed, knots: approx 20 surface; 30+ submerged
Complement: 112 (10 officers, 102 enlisted men)

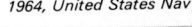

The "Skipjack" class combines the high-speed endurance of nuclear propulsion with the high-speed "tear-drop" hull design tested in the conventionally powered submarine *Albacore* (AGSS 569) (see *Design* and *Engineering* notes). The *Skipjack* was authorised in the Fiscal Year 1956 new construction programme and the five other submarines of this class were authorised in FY 1957.

These submarines are still considered suitable for "first line" service. Officially described as fastest US nuclear submarines in service.

Each cost approximately $40 000 000.

The *Scorpion* (SSN 589) of this class was lost some 400 miles southwest of the Azores while *en route* from the Mediterranean to Norfolk, Virginia, in May 1968. She went down with 99 men on board.

Construction: The *Scorpion's* keel was laid down twice; the original keel laid down on 1 Nov 1957 was renumbered SSBN 598 and became the Polaris submarine *George Washington*; the second SSN 589 keel became the *Scorpion*. The *Scamp's* Keel laying was delayed when materiel for her was diverted to the SSBN 599. This class introduced the Newport News Shipbuilding and Dry Dock Company and the Ingalls Shipbuilding Corporation to nuclear submarine construction. Newport News had not previously built submarines since before World War I; Ingalls previously had built only one submarine, the *Blueback* (SS 581) launched in 1959.

Design: The *Skipjack* was the first US nuclear submarine built to the "tear-drop" or modified spindle hull design for improved underwater performance. These submarines have a single propeller shaft (vice two in earlier nuclear submarines) and their diving planes are mounted on sail structures to improve underwater manoeuvrability. No after torpedo tubes are fitted because of their tapering sterns.

Electronics: Original BQS-4 sonar modified to provide improved anti-submarine capabilities. *Skipjack* fitted with Mk 101 Mod 20 torpedo fire control system; others with Mk 101 Mod 17.

Engineering: The "Skipjack" class introduced the S5W fast attack submarine propulsion plant which has been employed in all subsequent US attack and ballistic missile submarines until the "Los Angeles" class (SSN 688) except the *Narwhal* (SSN 671) and *Glenard P. Lipscomb* (SSN 685). The plant was developed by the Bettis Atomic Power Laboratory.

Photographs: Note streamlined shape and lack of topside projections; most equipment outside of the hull is either recessed or retractable. The *Sculpin* is shown at right during a rare high-speed surface run; her diving planes are mounted lower on the sail than later SSN classes.

SNOOK (SSN 592)   1964, United States Navy

SCULPIN (SSN 590)   1967, United States Navy

1 NUCLEAR-POWERED RESEARCH SUBMARINE (SSN): "HALIBUT" TYPE

Name	No.	Builders	Laid down	Launched	Commissioned
HALIBUT	SSN 587 (ex-SSGN 587)	Mare Island Naval Shipyard, Vallejo, Calif.	11 April 1957	9 Jan 1959	4 Jan 1960

Displacement, tons: 3 850 standard; 5 000 submerged
Length, feet (metres): 350 *(106·6)* oa
Beam, feet (metres): 29·5 *(8·9)*
Draught, feet (metres): 21·5 *(6·5)*
Torpedo tubes: 6—21 inch *(533 mm)* 4 bow; 2 stern
Main engines: 2 steam turbines (Westinghouse); approx 6 000 shp; 2 shafts
Nuclear reactors: 1 pressurised-water cooled S3W (Westinghouse)
Speed, knots: 15·5 surface; 15+ submerged
Complement: 120 (12 officers, 108 enlisted men)

HALIBUT (SSN 587)   1970, United States Navy

The *Halibut* is believed to have been the first submarine designed and constructed specifically to fire guided missiles. She was originally intended to have diesel-electric propulsion but on 27 Feb 1956 the Navy announced she would have nuclear propulsion. She was the US Navy's only nuclear-powered guided missile submarine (SSGN) to be completed. Authorised in the Fiscal Year 1956 new construction programme and built for an estimated cost of $45 000 000.

The *Halibut* was reclassified as an attack submarine on 25 July 1965 after the Navy discarded the Regulus submarine-launched missile force. Her missile equipment was removed, she is no longer considered a "first line" submarine and is employed in experimental work. The submarine's large missile compartment makes her an excellent ship for underwater projects.

The Navy has stated that the *Halibut* and earlier *Seawolf* have been designated as "mother" submarines for the deep submergence research programmes. Reportedly the *Halibut* has been fitted with a ducted bow thruster to permit precise control and manoeuvring.

She can carry the 50-foot Deep Submergence Rescue Vehicle (DSRV) and other submersibles on her after deck; the submersible can "take off" from and "land on" the *Halibut* while the larger craft is submerged.

The *Halibut* was being decommissioned in June 1976. Now in reserve.

Design: The *Halibut* was built with a large missile hangar faired into her bow. Her hull was intended primarily to provide a stable surface launching platform rather than for speed or manoeuvrabilty.

Electronics: Fitted with BQS-4 sonar. Mk 101 Mod 12 torpedo fire control system installed.

Engineering: Fitted with same reactor propulsion plant as *Skate* and *Sargo*. Submerged speed of *Halibut* is less than "Skate" class because of larger hull volume and shape.

Missiles: The *Halibut* was designed to carry two Regulus II surface-to-surface missiles. The Regulus II was a transonic missile which could carry a nuclear warhead and had a range of 1 000 miles. The Regulus II was cancelled before becoming operational and the *Halibut* operated from 1960 to 1964 carrying five Regulus I missiles, subsonic cruise missiles which could deliver a nuclear warhead on targets 575 nautical miles from the launching ship or submarine.

During this period the US Navy operated a maximum of five Regulus guided (cruise) missile submarines, the *Halibut,* the post-war constructed *Grayback* (SSG 574 now LPSS 574) and *Growler* (SSG 577), and the World War II-built *Tunny* (SSG 282 subsequently LPSS 282) and *Barbero* (SSG 317). The *Grayback* and *Growler* each could carry four Regulus I missiles and the older submarines each carried two missiles.

As SSGN carried a complement of 11 officers and 108 enlisted men.

Navigation: The *Halibut* is fitted with Ship's Inertial Navigation System (SINS).

Photographs: Both views of the *Halibut* presented here show the submarine carrying a submersible simulator on deck. Note the "bulge" of missile hangar door forward of the sail structure and wide forward hull shape for former missile hangar. On later pages the ex-Regulus missile submarines *Grayback* and *Growler* are shown with their more predominant hangar structures.

HALIBUT (SSN 587)   1970, United States Navy

TRITON (SSN 586)—see following page   1959, United States Navy

1 NUCLEAR-POWERED ATTACK SUBMARINE (SSN): "TRITON" TYPE

Name	No.	Builders	Laid down	Launched	Commissioned
TRITON	SSN 586 (ex-SSRN 586)	General Dynamics (Electric Boat)	29 May 1956	19 Aug 1958	10 Nov 1959

Displacement, tons: 5 940 standard; 6 670 submerged
Length, feet (metres): 447·5 (136·3) oa
Beam, feet (metres): 37 (11·3)
Draught, feet (metres): 24 (7·3)
Torpedo tubes: 6—21 inch (533 mm) 4 bow; 2 stern
Main engines: 2 steam turbines (General Electric); approx 34 000 shp; 2 shafts
Nuclear reactors: 2 pressurised-water cooled S4G (General Electric)
Speed, knots: 27 surface; 20+ submerged
Complement as SSRN: 172 (16 officers, 156 enlisted men)

The Triton was designed and constructed to serve as a radar picket submarine to operate in conjunction with surface carrier task forces.
Authorised in the Fiscal Year 1956 new construction programme and built for an estimated cost of $109 000 000.

The Triton circumnavigated the globe in 1960, remaining submerged except when her sail structure broke the surface to enable an ill sailor to be taken off near the Falkland Islands. The 41 500-mile cruise took 83 days and was made at an average speed of 18 knots.
The underwater giant was reclassified as an attack submarine (SSN) on 1 Mar 1961 as the Navy dropped the radar picket submarine programme. She is no longer considered a "first line" submarine and was decommissioned on 3 May 1969 to become the first US nuclear submarine to be relegated to the "mothball fleet". She has been followed into mothballs by the Halibut (SSN 587).
There had been proposals to operate the Triton as an underwater national command post afloat, but no funds were provided. See subsequent listings for Northampton (CC 1) and Wright in this edition.

Design: The Triton was designed to operate as a surface radar picket, submerging when in danger of enemy attack. She was fitted with an elaborate combat information centre and large radar antenna which retracted into the sail structure. Until the Trident SSBN programme the Triton was the longest US submarine ever constructed.

Electronics: Fitted with BQS-4 sonar. Mk 101 Mod 11 torpedo fire control system installed.

Engineering: The Triton is the only US submarine with two nuclear reactors. The Atomic Energy Commission's Knolls Atomic Power Laboratory was given prime responsibility for development of the power plant. After 2½ years of operation, during which she steamed more than 110 000 miles, the Triton was overhauled and refuelled from July 1962 to March 1964.

Photographs: Note on the previous page the opening in the Triton's sail structure for a large search radar antenna.

4 NUCLEAR-POWERED ATTACK SUBMARINES (SSN): "SKATE" CLASS

Name	No.	Builders	Laid down	Launched	Commissioned
*SKATE	SSN 578	General Dynamics (Electric Boat)	21 July 1955	16 May 1957	23 Dec 1957
*SWORDFISH	SSN 579	Portsmouth Naval Shipyard	25 Jan 1956	27 Aug 1957	15 Sep 1958
*SARGO	SSN 583	Mare Island Naval Shipyard	21 Feb 1956	10 Oct 1957	1 Oct 1958
*SEADRAGON	SSN 584	Portsmouth Naval Shipyard	20 June 1956	16 Aug 1958	5 Dec 1959

Displacement, tons: 2 570 standard; 2 861 submerged
Length, feet (metres): 267·7 (81·5) oa
Beam, feet (metres): 25 (7·6)
Draught, feet (metres): 21 (6·4)
Torpedo tubes: 8—21 inch (533 mm) 6 bow; 2 stern (short)
Main engines: 2 steam turbines (Westinghouse); approx 6 600 shp; 2 shafts
Nuclear reactors: 1 pressurised-water cooled S3W (Westinghouse) in Skate and Sargo, 1 pressurised-water cooled S4W (Westinghouse) in Swordfish and Seadragon
Speed, knots: 15·5 surface; 20+ submerged
Complement: 108 (9 officers, 99 enlisted men)

The "Skate" class submarines were the first production model nuclear-powered submarines. They are similar in design to the Nautilus but smaller. The Skate and Swordfish were authorised in the Fiscal Year 1955 new construction programme and the Sargo and Seadragon in FY 1956.
The Skate was the first submarine to make a completely submerged transatlantic crossing. In 1958 she established a (then)

record of 31 days submerged with a sealed atmosphere, on 11 Aug 1958 she passed under the North Pole during a polar cruise, and on 17 Mar 1959 she became the first submarine to surface at the North Pole. The Sargo undertook a polar cruise during January-February 1960 and surfaced at the North Pole on 9 Feb 1960.
The Seadragon transited from the Atlantic to the Pacific via the Northwest Passage (Lancaster Sound, Barrow and McClure Straits) in August 1960. The Skate, operating from New London, Connecticut and the Seadragon, based at Pearl Harbour, rendezvoused under the North Pole on 2 Aug 1962 and then conducted anti-submarine exercises under the polar ice pack and surfaced together at the North Pole.
The Skate also operated in the Arctic Ocean during April-May 1969, conducting exercises under the Arctic ice pack with the later nuclear-powered attack submarines Pargo and Whale; and again during the spring of 1971 with the nuclear attack submarine Trepang.

Design: The "Skate" design is similar to the Nautilus-Seawolf

design with GUPPY hull, bow diving planes, and twin propellers.

Electronics: Skate and Seadragon fitted with Mk 101 Mod 19 torpedo fire control system; Swordfish and Sargo have Mk 101 Mod 15. Fitted with BQS-4 sonar.

Engineering: The reactors for this class were developed by the Atomic Energy Commission's Bettis Atomic Power Laboratory, the new propulsion system was similar to that of the Nautilus but considerably simplified with improved operation and maintenance. The propulsion plant developed under this programme had two arrangements, the S3W configuration in the Skate, Sargo and Halibut and the S4W configuration in the Swordfish and Seadragon. Both arrangements proved satisfactory. The Skate began her first overhaul and refuelling in January 1961 after steaming 120 862 miles on her initial reactor core during three years of operation. The Swordfish began her first overhaul and refuelling in early 1962 after more than three years of operation in which time she steamed 112 000 miles.

SWORDFISH (SSN 579)   1970, United States Navy

SKATE (SSN 578)   United States Navy

1 NUCLEAR-POWERED RESEARCH SUBMARINE (SSN): "SEAWOLF" TYPE

Name	No.	Builders	Laid down	Launched	Commissioned
*SEAWOLF	SSN 575	General Dynamics (Electric Boat)	15 Sep 1953	21 July 1955	30 Mar 1957

Displacement, tons: 3 720 standard; 4 280 submerged
Length, feet (metres): 337·5 (102·9) oa
Beam, feet (metres): 27·7 (8·4)
Draught, feet (metres): 22 (6·7)
Torpedo tubes: 6—21 inch (533 mm) bow
Main engines: 2 steam turbines (General Electric), approx 15 000 shp; 2 shafts
Nuclear reactors: 1 pressurised-water cooled S2Wa (Westinghouse)
Speed, knots: 19 surface; 20+ submerged
Complement: 120 (12 officers, 108 enlisted men)

The *Seawolf* was the world's second nuclear-propelled vehicle; she was constructed almost simultaneously with the *Nautilus* to test a competitive reactor design. Funds for the *Seawolf* were authorised in the Fiscal Year 1952 new construction programme.
She is no longer considered a "first line" submarine and has been engaged primarily in research work since 1969.

Electronics: Fitted with Mk 101 Mod 8 torpedo fire control system. BQS-4 sonar installed.

Engineering: Initial work in the development of naval nuclear propulsion plants investigated a number of concepts, two of which were of sufficient interest to warrant full development: the pressurised water and liquid metal (sodium). The *Nautilus* was provided with a pressurised-water reactor plant and the *Seawolf* was fitted initially with a liquid-metal reactor. Originally known as the Submarine Intermediate Reactor (SIR), the liquid-metal plant was developed by the Atomic Energy Commission's Knolls Atomic Power Laboratory.
The SIR Mark II/S2G reactor in the *Seawolf* achieved initial criticality on 25 June 1956. Steam leaks developed during the dockside testing. The plant was shut down and it was determined that the leaks were caused by sodium-potassium alloy which had entered the super-heater steam piping. After repairs and testing the *Seawolf* began sea trials on 21 Jan 1957. The trials were run at reduced power and after two years of operation the *Seawolf* entered the Electric Boat yard for removal of her sodium-cooled plant and installation of a pressurised-water plant similar to that installed in the *Nautilus* (designated S2Wa). When the original *Seawolf* plant was shut down in December 1958 the submarine had steamed a total of 71 611

SEAWOLF (SSN 575)
1974, William Whalen, Jr.

miles. She was recommissioned on 30 Sep 1960. The pressurised-water reactor was refuelled for the first time between May 1965 and August 1967, having propelled the *Seawolf* for more than 161 000 miles on its initial fuel core.

SEAWOLF (SSN 575)
1967, United States Navy

1 NUCLEAR-POWERED ATTACK SUBMARINE (SSN): "NAUTILUS" TYPE

Name	No.	Builders	Laid down	Launched	Commissioned
*NAUTILUS	SSN 571	General Dynamics (Electric Boat)	14 June 1952	21 Jan 1954	30 Sep 1954

Displacement, tons: 3 530 standard; 4 040 submerged
Length, feet (metres): 323·7 (98·6) oa
Beam, feet (metres): 27·6 (8·4)
Draught, feet (metres): 22 (6·7)
Torpedo tubes: 6—21 inch (533 mm) bow
Main engines: 2 steam turbines (Westinghouse), approx 15 000 shp; 2 shafts
Nuclear reactors: 1 pressurised-water cooled S2W (Westinghouse)
Speed, knots: 18 surface; 20+ submerged
Complement: 120 (12 officers, 108 enlisted men)

The *Nautilus* was the world's first nuclear-propelled vehicle. She predated the first Soviet nuclear-powered submarine by an estimated five years.
The funds for construction of the *Nautilus* were authorised in the Fiscal Year 1952 budget. The *Nautilus* put to sea for the first time on 17 Jan 1955 and signalled the historic message: "Underway on nuclear power".
On her shakedown cruise in May 1955 the *Nautilus* steamed submerged from London, Connecticut, to San Juan, Puerto Rico, travelling more than 1 300 miles in 84 hours at an average speed of almost 16 knots; she later steamed submerged from Key West, Florida, to New London, a distance of 1 397 miles, at an average speed of more than 20 knots.
During 1958 the *Nautilus* undertook extensive operations under the Arctic ice pack and in August she made history's first polar transit from the Pacific to the Atlantic, steaming from Pearl Harbour to Portland, England. She passed under the geographic North Pole on 3 Aug 1958.

NAUTILUS (SSN 571)
1975, General Dynamics, Electric Boat Division

During 1972-74 the *Nautilus* underwent a 30-month overhaul and modification at the Electric Boat yard in Groton, Connecticut, where the submarine was built. Modified for submarine communications research.

Design: The *Nautilus* and *Seawolf* have GUPPY-type hull configurations. The *Seawolf* has a stepped sail and a slight rise at the bow.

Electronics: Fitted with Mk 101 Mod 6 torpedo fire control system. BQS-4 sonar installed.

Engineering: In January 1948 the Department of Defense requested the Atomic Energy Commission to undertake the design, development, and construction of a nuclear reactor for submarine propulsion. Initial research and conceptual design of the Submarine Thermal Reactor (STR) was undertaken by the Argonne National Laboratory. Subsequently the Atomic Energy Commission's Bettis Atomic Power Laboratory, operated by the Westinghouse Electric Corporation, undertook development of the first nuclear propulsion plant.
The *Nautilus* STR Mark II nuclear plant (redesignated S2W) was first operated on 20 Dec 1954 and first developed full power on 3 Jan 1955.
After more than two years of operation, during which she steamed 62 562 miles, the *Nautilus* began an overhaul which included refuelling in April 1957. She was again refuelled in 1959 after steaming 91 324 miles on her second fuel core, and again in 1964 after steaming approximately 150 000 miles on her third fuel core. (The prototype Mark I/S1W plant was refuelled in 1955, 1958 1960 and 1967; it remains in operation as an experimental and training facility).

NAUTILUS (SSN 571)

1975, General Dynamics, Electric Boat Division

3 ATTACK SUBMARINES (SS): "BARBEL" CLASS

Name	No.	Builders	Laid down	Launched	Commissioned
*BARBEL	SS 580	Portsmouth Naval Shipyard	18 May 1956	19 July 1958	17 Jan 1959
*BLUEBACK	SS 581	Ingalls Shipbuilding Corporation	15 April 1957	16 May 1959	15 Oct 1959
*BONEFISH	SS 582	New York Shipbuilding Corp	3 June 1957	22 Nov 1958	9 July 1959

Displacement, tons: 2 145 standard; 2 895 submerged
Length, feet (metres): 219·5 *(66·8)* oa
Beam, feet (metres): 29 *(8·8)*
Draught, feet (metres): 28 *(8·5)*
Torpedo tubes: 6—21 inch *(533 mm)* bow
Main engines: 3 diesels 4 800 bhp (Fairbanks Morse); 2 electric motors (General Electric) 3 150 shp; 1 shaft
Speed, knots: 15 on surface; 25 submerged
Complement: 78 (8 officers, 70 men)

These submarines were the last non-nuclear combatant submarines built by the US Navy. All three were authorised in the Fiscal Year 1956 new construction programme.

Construction: The *Blueback* was the first submarine built by the Ingalls Shipbuilding Corp at Pascagoula, Mississippi, and the *Bonefish* was the first constructed at the New York Shipbuilding Corp yard in Camden, New Jersey. None of the three shipyards that built this class is now employed in submarine construction.

Design: These submarines have the "tear drop" or modified spindle hull design which was tested in the experimental submarine *Albacore*. As built, their diving planes were bow-mounted; subsequently relocated to the sail structure.
These submarines introduced a new concept in centralised arrangement of controls in an "attack centre" to increase efficiency; the concept has been adapted for all later US combat submarines.

Electronics: Fitted with Mk 101 Mod 20 torpedo fire control system. BQS-4 sonar installed.

BLUEBACK (SS 581)

1967, United States Navy

Photographs: Note forward position of diving planes on sail structure, bow configuration for maximum underwater performance, and clear decks that are void of projections.

BONEFISH (SS 582)

1969, United States Navy

1 ATTACK SUBMARINE (SS): "DARTER" TYPE

Name	No.	Builders	Laid down	Launched	Commissioned
*DARTER	SS 576	General Dynamics (Electric Boat)	10 Nov 1954	28 May 1956	20 Oct 1956

Displacement, tons: 1 720 surface; 2 388 submerged
Length, feet (metres): 268·6 (81·9) oa
Beam, feet (metres): 27·2 (8·3)
Draught, feet (metres): 19 (5·8)
Torpedo tubes: 8—21 inch (533 mm) 6 bow; 2 stern
Main engines: 3 diesels (Fairbanks Morse); 4 500 bhp electric motors (Elliott); 2 shafts
Speed, knots: 19·5 surface; 14 submerged

Complement: 87 (8 officers, 79 men)

Designed for high submerged speed with quiet machinery. Planned sister submarines *Growler* and *Grayback* were completed to missile-launching configuration.
Basic design of the *Darter* is similar to the "Tang" class described on a later page.

Authorised in Fiscal Year 1954 shipbuilding programme. No additional submarines of this type were built because of shift to high-speed hull design and nuclear propulsion.

Electronics: Fitted with Mk 106 Mod 11 torpedo fire control system. BQG-4 passive fire control sonar (note three fin-like PUFF sonar domes).

DARTER (SS 576)

1967, Giorgio Arra

1 GUIDED MISSILE SUBMARINE (SSG): "GROWLER" TYPE

Name	No.	Builders	Laid down	Launched	Commissioned
GROWLER	SSG 577	Portsmouth Naval Shipyard	15 Feb 1955	5 April 1959	30 April 1958

Displacement, tons: 2 540 standard; 3 515 submerged
Length, feet (metres): 317·6 (96·8) oa
Beam, feet (metres): 27·2 (8·2)
Draught, feet (metres): 19 (5·8)
Torpedo tubes: 4—21 inch (533 mm) 4 bow; 2 stern
Main engines: 3 diesels (Fairbanks Morse); 4 600 bhp/2 electric motors (Elliott); 5 600 shp; 2 shafts
Speed, knots: 20 surface; approx 12 submerged
Complement: 84 officers and enlisted men

The *Growler* was authorised in the Fiscal Year 1955 new construction programme; completed as a guided missile submarine to fire the Regulus surface-to-surface cruise missile (see *Halibut*, SSN 587, for *Missile* notes).

When the Regulus submarine missile programme ended in 1964, the *Growler* and her near-sister *Grayback* were withdrawn from service with both submarines being decommissioned on 25 May 1964. The *Grayback* was subsequently converted to an amphibious transport submarine (LPSS). The *Growler* was scheduled to undergo a similar conversion when the *Grayback* was completed, but the second conversion was deferred late in 1968 because of rising ship conversion costs. The *Growler* is in reserve as an SSG.

Design: The *Grayback* and *Growler* were initially designed as attack submarines similar to the *Darter*. Upon redesign as missile submarines they were cut in half on the building ways and were lengthened approximately 50 feet, two cylindrical hangars, each 11 feet high and 70 feet long, were superimposed on

their bows, a missile launcher was installed between the hangars and sail structure, and elaborate navigation and fire control systems were fitted. The height of the sail structure on the *Growler* is approximately 30 feet above the deck; the *Grayback's* lower sail structure was increased during LPSS conversion.

Electronics: Fitted with BQS-4 sonar; Mk 106 Mod 13 torpedo fire control system.

Photographs: The *Growler* has large, twin missile hangars faired into her bow which are clearly visible; the Regulus missile launcher is between the hangars and sail structure. A side-by-side view of the *Grayback* and *Growler* appears in the 1974-1975 and previous editions.

GROWLER (SSG 577)

1958, United States Navy

GRAYBACK (SS 574)—see following page

1969, United States Navy

1 AMPHIBIOUS TRANSPORT SUBMARINE (SS/LPSS): "GRAYBACK" TYPE

Name	No.	Builders	Laid down	Launched	Commissioned	LPSS Comm.
*GRAYBACK	SS 574 (ex-LPSS 574, ex-SSG 574)	Mare Island Naval Shipyard	1 July 1954	2 July 1957	7 Mar 1958	9 May 1969

Displacement, tons: 2 670 standard; 3 650 submerged
Length, feet (metres): 334 (101·8) oa
Beam, feet (metres): 30 (9·0)
Draught, feet (metres): 19 (5·8)
Torpedo tubes: 8—21 inch (533 mm) 6 bow; 2 stern
Main engines: 3 diesels (Fairbanks Morse); 4 500 bhp/2 electric
    motors (Elliott); 5 600 shp; 2 shafts
Speed, knots: 20 surface; approx 12 submerged
Complement: 88 (10 officers, 78 enlisted men)
Troops: 67 (7 officers, 60 enlisted men)

The Grayback has been fully converted to a transport submarine and is officially classified as an amphibious warfare ship. She was originally intended to be an attack submarine, being authorised in the Fiscal Year 1953 new construction programme, but redesigned in 1956 to provide a Regulus missile launching capability; completed as SSG 574 in 1958, similar in design to the Growler (SSG 577). See Growler listing for basic design notes.

Classification: The Grayback was reclassified as an attack submarine (SS) on 30 June 1975 although she retains her transport configuration and capabilities. The reclassification was an administrative change associated with funding support.

Conversion: The Grayback began conversion to a transport submarine at the San Francisco Bay Naval Shipyard (Mare Island) in November 1967. The conversion was originally estimated at $15 200 000 but was actually about $30 000 000. She was reclassified from SSG to LPSS on 30 Aug 1968 (never officially designated APSS).
During conversion the Grayback was fitted to berth and mess 67 troops and carry their equipment including landing craft or swimmer delivery vehicles (SDV). Her torpedo tubes and hence attack capability are retained. As completed (SSG) the Grayback had an overall length of 322 ft 4 in; lengthened 12 ft during LPSS conversion. Conversion was authorised in Fiscal Year 1965 programme and completed in June 1969; delayed because of higher priorities being allocated to other submarine projects.

Electronics: Fitted with BQS-4 sonar and BQG-4 passive fire control sonar (note three fin-like PUFF sonar domes). See "Tang" class listing for details.
Mk 106 Mod 12 torpedo fire control system installed.

Photographs: In the upper photograph note the port hangar clamshell door is in the raised position. The doors are shown closed in the lower photograph; Marine reconnaissance personnel are shown handling rubber boats on the Grayback's deck just aft of the twin hangar doors. Note the PUFF sonar dome forward between the hangars; tracks on deck are for safety lines for men working on deck in rougher seas.

GRAYBACK (SS 574)   1975, US Navy, PH3 S. Halbert

GRAYBACK (SS 574) hangar doors   1975, United States Marine Corps

2 ATTACK SUBMARINES (SS): "SAILFISH" CLASS

Name	No.	Builders	Laid down	Launched	Commissioned
*SAILFISH	SS 572 (ex-SSR 572)	Portsmouth Naval Shipyard	8 Dec 1953	7 Sep 1955	14 April 1956
*SALMON	SS 573 (ex-AGSS 573, ex-SSR 573)	Portsmouth Naval Shipyard	10 Mar 1954	25 Feb 1956	25 Aug 1956

Displacement, tons: 2 625 standard; 3 168 submerged
Length, feet (metres): 350·4 (106·8) oa
Beam, feet (metres): 28·4 (8·8)
Draught, feet (metres): 18 (5·5)
Torpedo tubes: 6—21 inch (533 mm) bow
Main engines: 4 diesels (Fairbanks Morse); 6 000 bhp/2 electric
    motors (Elliott); 8 200 shp; 2 shafts
Speed, knots: 19·5 surface; 14 submerged
Complement: 87 (8 officers, 79 enlisted men)

The Sailfish and Salmon were built as radar picket submarines (SSR) with air search radars on their decks and elaborate aircraft control centres. Subsequently modified for "straight" attack operations. They were the largest non-nuclear submarines built by the US Navy since 1930 and are believed to tbe the largest conventional submarines now operated by any navy
Both authorised in the Fiscal Year 1952 programme; both have been modernised under the FRAM II programme.

Classification: Reclassified from radar picket submarines (SSR) to SS on 1 Mar 1961; Salmon reclassified AGSS on 29 June 1968 to serve as test and evaluation submarine for Navy's Deep Submergence Rescue Vehicle (DSRV). However, the DSRV programme was delayed and the Salmon reverted to the

SAILFISH (SS 572)   1966, United States Navy

SS designation on 30 June 1969.
All ten of the World War II-built submarines that had been converted to radar picket configurations have been stricken. Radar picket submarines were to operate ahead of carrier task forces to provide early warning of air attack; upon coming under attack themselves they would submerge for safety. The Soviet Navy operates several modified "W" class submarines in the radar picket role. They are designated "canvas bag" by NATO.

Electronics: Fitted with BQG-4 passive fire control sonar (note three fin-like PUFF sonar domes). The fourth "FIN" at stern is the upper rudder. See "Tang" class listing for details.
Fitted with Mk 106 Mod 21 torpedo fire control system.

Photographs: Note size of PUFF fins in comparison to men in photograph of the *Salmon*.

SALMON (SS 573)

United States Navy

3 ATTACK SUBMARINES (SS) } "TANG" CLASS
01 RESEARCH SUBMARINE (AGSS) }

Name	No.	Builders	Laid down	Launched	Commissioned
*TANG	AGSS 563	Portsmouth Naval Shipyard	18 April 1949	19 June 1951	25 Oct 1951
*WAHOO	SS 565	Portsmouth Naval Shipyard	24 Oct 1949	16 Oct 1951	30 May 1952
*TROUT	SS 566	Electric Boat Co, Groton	1 Dec 1949	21 Aug 1951	27 June 1952
*GUDGEON	SS 567	Portsmouth Naval Shipyard	20 May 1950	11 June 1952	21 Nov 1952

Displacement, tons: 2 100 standard; 2 700 submerged
Length, feet (metres): 287 *(87·4)* oa
Beam, feet (metres): 27·3 *(8·3)*
Draught, feet (metres): 19 *(6·2)*
Torpedo tubes: 8—21 inch *(533 mm)* 6 bow; 2 stern
Main engines: 3 diesels (Fairbanks Morse); 4 500 bhp/2 electric motors; 5 600 shp; 2 shafts
Speed, knots: 16 surface; 16 submerged
Complement: 87 (8 officers, 79 men)

Six submarines of this class were constructed, incorporating improvements based on German World War II submarine developments. The *Tang* was authorised in the Fiscal Year 1947 new construction programme, *Wahoo* and *Trout* in FY 1948, and *Gudgeon* in FY 1949. The *Gudgeon* was the first US submarine to circumnavigate the world during Sep 1957-Feb 1958. All modernised under FRAM II programme.
All remaining submarines of this class are active.

Classification: The *Tang* was reclassified as a research submarine (AGSS) on 30 June 1975 for use in acoustic research. She replaces the *Tigrone* (AGSS 419) which had served in that role for two decades. The *Tang* was modified at the Mare Island Naval Shipyard from July 1975 to mid-1976.

Electronics: BQG-4 fire control sonar is fitted in these submarines; the small, fin-like structures are antenna domes for the sonar (referred to as PUFFS—an acronym for Passive Underwater Fire Control Feasibility System).
Fitted with Mk 106 Mod 18 torpedo fire control system.

Engineering: *Tang, Trout* and *Wahoo* were originally powered by a compact, radial type engine produced after five years of development work, comprising a 16-cylinder 2-cycle plant, mounted vertically with four rows of cylinders radially arranged. These new engines were half the weight and two-thirds the size of the engines previously available for submarines. They proved to be unsatisfactory and were replaced by machinery similar to that in *Gudgeon* which has Fairbanks Morse high speed lightweight engines mounted horizontally. The electric motors are Elliott in *Tang*, General Electric in *Wahoo* and *Trout*, Westinghouse in *Gudgeon*.
Snorkel fitted as in all later US nuclear and conventionally propelled submarines.

Reconstruction: All six submarines of this class were built with an overall length of 269 ft 2 in. The units had their original diesel engines replaced during the late 1950s, were cut in half and a 9 ft section inserted amidships. All six submarines were modernised during the 1960s with the installation of improved electronics equipment and other features; additional sections were added to give an overall length of 287 ft.

Transfers: *Trigger* (SS 564) transferred to Italy on 10 July 1973; *Harder* (SS 568) transferred to Italy on 15 Mar 1974.
(These were the first US submarines of post-World War II construction to be transferred to foreign navies; four smaller submarines were built in the United States during the 1950s specifically for transfer to Peru).

GUDGEON (SS 567)

1970, United States Navy

WAHOO (SS 565)

1968, United States Navy

"TANG" Class

1974, William Whalen Jr.

1 RESEARCH SUBMARINE (AGSS): "ALBACORE" TYPE

Name	No.	Builders	Laid down	Launched	Commissioned
ALBACORE	AGSS 569	Portsmouth Naval Shipyard	15 Mar 1952	1 Aug 1953	5 Dec 1953

Displacement, tons: 1 500 standard; 1 850 submerged
Length, feet (metres): 210·5 *(63·6)* oa
Beam, feet (metres): 27·5 *(8·4)*
Draught, feet (metres): 18·5 *(5·6)*
Torpedo tubes: None
Main engines: 2 diesels; radial pancake type (General Motors) electric motor (Westinghouse) 15 000 shp; 1 shaft
Speed, knots: 25 on surface; 33 submerged
Complement: 52 (5 officers, 47 men)

The *Albacore* was built as a high-speed experimental submarine to test an advanced hull form. Officially described as a hydrodynamic test vehicle. Streamlined, whale shaped without the flat-topped superstructure deck. Conning tower resembles a fish's dorsal fin.

The *Albacore* was decommissioned and placed in reserve on 1 Sep 1972.

Experimental: The *Albacore* has been extensively modified to test advanced submarine design and engineering concepts. Phase I modifications were made from July 1954 to February 1955 to eliminate the many "bugs" inherent with completely new construction and equipment.
Phase II modifications from Dec 1955 to Mar 1956 during which conventional propeller-rudder-stern diving plane arrangement was modified; the new design provided for the propeller to be installed *aft* of the control surfaces. (At this time a small auxiliary rudder on the sail was removed.)
A concave bow sonar dome was fitted for tests in 1960. Phase III modifications from Nov 1960 to Aug 1961 during which an entirely new stern was installed featuring the stern planes in an

"X" configuration, a system of ten hydraulic operated dive brakes around the hull amidships, a dorsal rudder, and a new bow sonar dome. Phase IV modifications from Dec 1962 to Mar 1965 during which a silver-zinc battery was installed and counter-rotating stern propellers rotating around the same axis were fitted.
The *Albacore* conducted trials with towed sonar arrays from May to July 1966.
All modifications were made at the Portsmouth Naval Shipyard.

Photograph: Note stern rudder configuration; rounded hull without superstructure deck common to previous and contemporary submarines. Round electronic "ball" antenna on sail structure. Deck cleats and other equipment are recessed into hull.

ALBACORE (AGSS 569)

United States Navy

1 RESEARCH SUBMARINE (AGSS): "DOLPHIN" TYPE

Name	No.	Builders	Laid down	Launched	Commissioned
***DOLPHIN**	AGSS 555	Portsmouth Naval Shipyard	9 Nov 1962	8 June 1968	17 Aug 1968

Displacement, tons: 800 standard; 930 full load
Length, feet (metres): 152 *(46·3)*
Beam, feet (metres): 19·3 *(5·9)*
Draught, feet (metres): 18 *(5·5)* (maximum)
Torpedo tubes: Removed
Main engines: Diesel/electric (2 Detroit 12 V71 diesels), 1 500 hp; 1 shaft
Speed, knots: 12+ submerged
Complement: 24 (3 officers, 21 enlisted men) plus 4 to 7 scientists

The *Dolphin* is an auxiliary submarine specifically designed for deep-diving operations. Authorised in Fiscal Year 1961 new construction programme but delayed because of changes in mission and equipment coupled with higher priorities being given to other submarine projects. The *Dolphin* is fitted for deep-ocean sonar and oceanographic research. She is highly automated and has three computer-operated systems, a safety system, hovering system, and one that is classified. The digital-computer submarine safety system monitors equipment and provides data on closed-circuit television screens; malfunctions in equipment or trends towards potentially dangerous situations set off an alarm and if they are not corrected within the prescribed time the system, unless overridden by an operator, automatically brings the submarine to the surface. There are several research stations for scientists in the *Dolphin* and she is fitted to take water samples down to her operating (test) depth. The single, experimental torpedo tube was removed in 1970.
Underwater endurance is limited (endurance and habitability were considered of secondary importance in design). On 24 Nov 1968 the *Dolphin* "descended to a depth greater than that recorded by any other operational submarine" according to official statements.
Assigned to Submarine Development Group 1 at San Diego.

Classification: The *Dolphin's* number was taken from a block (551-562) authorised but cancelled late in World War II with no construction being assigned. (Submarines built in Norway and Denmark were assigned the hull numbers SS 553 and SS 554, respectively, for financial accounting purposes; hull numbers SS 551 and SS 552 in this series were assigned to the late hunter-killer submarines *Bass*, ex-SSK 2 and *Bonita* ex-SSK 3 respectively).

Design: The *Dolphin* has a constant diameter cylindrical pressure hull approximately 15 feet in outer diameter closed at both ends with hemispherical heads. Pressure hull fabricated of HY-80 steel with aluminium and fibre-glass used in secondary structures to reduce weight, a critical factor in retaining buoyancy at deep depths. No conventional diving planes are mounted, improved rudder design and other features provide

DOLPHIN (AGSS 555)

United States Navy

manoeuvring control and hovering capability. Access is through a single hatch in the pressure hull (opening into sail structure).

Engineering: Fitted with 330 cell silver zinc battery. Submerged endurance is approximately 24 hours with an at-sea endurance of 14 days.

Status: Completed in early 1969, approximately five years behind official schedule at time of keel laying. The *Dolphin* is in commission and has a commanding officer.

Photographs: On the following page note the *Dolphin's* large sonar dome faired into the bow. An earlier configuration without the sonar is shown here; note crewmen on narrow deck.

DOLPHIN (AGSS 555)—see previous page

United States Navy

1 AMPHIBIOUS TRANSPORT SUBMARINE (LPSS): "SEALION" TYPE

Name	No.	Builders	Laid down	Launched	Commissioned
SEALION	LPSS 315	Electric Boat Company, Groton	25 Feb 1943	31 Oct 1943	8 Mar 1944

Displacement, tons: 2 145 standard; 2 500 submerged
Length, feet (metres): 311·5 *(95·0)*
Beam, feet (metres): 27 *(8·2)*
Draught, feet (metres): 17 *(5·2)*
Torpedo tubes: Removed
Guns: Removed
Main engines: 2 diesels (General Motors), 2 305 bhp/4 electric
motors (General Electric); 2 shafts
Speed, knots: 13 surface; 10 submerged
Complement: 74 (6 officers, 68 men)
Troops: 160

Originally a "Balao" class submarine converted to underwater transport for carrying Marines, commandos or frogmen in covert operations where surface ships would be too vulnerable. The *Sealion* was to have been replaced by conversion of the *Growler* (SSG 577) to a transport submarine; however, conversion of *Growler* was cancelled.
The *Sealion* is the sole survivor of the US Navy's large World War II submarine construction programme.
The *Sealion* was decommissioned and placed in reserve in Feb 1970.

Classification: *Sealion* changed from SS to transport submarine (SSP) in March 1948; changed to auxiliary transport submarine (ASSP) in January 1950; changed to APSS in October 1956; changed again to amphibious transport submarine (LPSS) on 1 Jan 1969.

Conversion: The *Sealion* was converted to a transport submarine at the San Francisco Naval Shipyard in 1948. All torpedo tubes and half of her diesel propulsion plant were removed to provide berthing for 160 troops; stowage provided for rubber rafts and other equipment in enlarged superstructure deck aft of conning tower.

Engineering: Fitted with snorkel installation.

Gunnery: The two 40 mm single guns shown on conning tower steps were removed prior to the *Sealion* being decommissioned.

SEALION (LPSS 315)

1965, United States Navy

Status: In 1960 the *Sealion* was assigned to operational reserve training duties; recommissioned late in 1961 with increase of US conventional warfare capabilities. See 1971-1972 edition for disposals of earlier transport submarines.

Photographs: Note safety track on deck, "bulge" aft of conning tower for raft stowage compartments, and propeller guards at stern. The single 40 mm guns shown on the conning tower were removed after the photo was taken.

"TIGRONE" TYPE

The research submarine *Tigrone* (AGSS 419) was stricken on 30 June 1975 after several delays in her demise. The former "Tench" class submarine had been employed for more than two decades in acoustic research. See 1974-1975 and previous editions for characteristics. She was to be outfitted as a submerged target for advanced torpedo testing.

GUPPY SUBMARINES

All 52 submarines modernised to the GUPPY (Greater Underwater Propulsion Project) configurations have been stricken or transferred to other navies. The last GUPPY submarines to serve with the US Navy were the *Clamagore* (SS 343) stricken on 27 June 1975 and *Tiru* (SS 416) stricken on 1 July 1975. They were not transferred to Turkey, as planned, but at this writing the transfer was still pending.
Corrections to the comprehensive list if GUPPY submarine disposals and transfers provided in the 1974-1975 edition include: *Blenny* (SS 324) stricken on 15 Aug 1973 (sunk as target); *Sea Poacher* (SS 406) transferred to Peru on 1 July 1974; *Atule* (SS 403) transferred to Peru on 31 July 1974.

TRAINING SUBMARINES (SST)

All specifically designated target and training submarines have been stricken. See 1973-1974 and previous editions for characteristics.

The former "hunter-killer" type submarine *Barracuda* (SST 3/SST 3/SSK 1) stricken on 1 Oct 1973.

The built-for-the-purpose training submarine *Mackerel* (SST 1/AGSS 570) and *Marlin* (SST 2) stricken on 31 Jan 1973.

MIDGET SUBMARINES

The US Navy's only "midget" submarine, the 50-foot long *X-1* was stricken on 16 Feb 1973; see 1972-1973 edition for characteristics.

DEEP SUBMERGENCE VEHICLES

The US Navy's Deep Submergence Vehicles (DSV) are listed in a separate section at the end of the United States Navy portion of this edition.

AIRCRAFT CARRIERS

The US Navy currently operates 13 aircraft carriers: ten ships of post-World War II construction (including two nuclear powered) and three "Midway" class ships completed shortly after the war. In addition, an obsolescent "Hancock" class ship serves as a training carrier.

Two additional nuclear carriers are under construction, the *Dwight D. Eisenhower* (CVN 69), to commission in 1977, and the *Carl Vinson* (CVN 70), to commission in 1980. To maintain a 12-carrier force until the latter ship is fully operational in 1981, the *Midway* (CV 41) would not be retired until she has served more than 35 years. If a 13-carrier force were continued, the *Midway* would remain operational at least into the mid-1980s, past her 40th anniversary.

More aircraft carriers will have to be constructed if the Navy is to operate even a 12-ship force beyond the mid-1980s, when the early "Forrestal" class ships begin reaching their 30th year of service. The currently planned carrier construction programme provides for a fifth nuclear carrier to be funded in Fiscal Year 1979 and a sixth in FY 1981. Also being studied is a Ship Life Extension Programme (SLEP) for the "Forrestal" class ships which could extend their individual effective service lives to as much as 45 years.

There is considerable controversy within the Department of Defense and the Congress with respect to additional large carrier construction, with debates over the number and size/configuration of the carriers. A Navy study group has, at the request of the Secretary of Defense, developed a series of alternative designs to the current "Nimitz" class for consideration in future carrier programmes. These designs, collectively referred to as the CVNX concept, are described below. All

would be capable of operating fixed-wing, high-performance aircraft.

The US Navy's long-range plan provides for 14 or 15 CV/CVN aircraft carriers plus 8 VSTOL support ships. It is considered highly unlikely that the former force level can be achieved.

VSTOL Support Ships (VSS): The Navy also plans to construct a series of smaller carrier-type ships configured to operate Vertical/Short Take-Off and Landing (VSTOL) aircraft and helicopters. The first ship of this programme is planned for the FY 1980 budget. The VSS designs are described on the following page.

Training Carrier: The "Hancock" class carrier *Lexington* (CVT 16) operates as a training ship and is based at Pensacola, Florida. The ship has no aircraft maintenance or arming capabilities, and hence cannot be considered as a combat ship. In an emergency, aircraft could be embarked on a very restricted operational basis.

It is anticipated that the *Franklin D. Roosevelt* (CV42) or *Coral Sea* (CV 43) will replace the *Lexington* in the training role during the late 1970s.

Nomenclature: US aircraft carriers traditionally have been named for American battles and earlier Navy ships. However, during the past few years they have increasingly been named for statesmen and naval leaders (see individual class notes). The current confusion over ship name sources in the US Navy could lead to aircraft carriers also being named for states of the Union, the present name source for Trident ballistic missile

submarines (SSBN) and missile cruisers (CGN/CSGN); these, like aircraft carriers, are considered to be "capital ships".

Air Wings: Each large aircraft carrier (CV/CVN) normally operates an air wing of some 85 to 95 aircraft: two fighter squadrons of 24 F-4 Phantom or F-14 Tomcats; two light attack squadrons of 24 A-7 Corsairs; one medium attack squadron of 12 A-6 Intruders; one anti-submarine squadron of 10 S-3 Viking aircraft; one A/S squadron of 8 SH-3 Sea King helicopters; and smaller squadrons or detachments of 3 RA-5C Vigilante reconnaissance aircraft, 4 EA-6B Prowler electronic warfare aircraft, 4 KA-6 Intruder tankers, and 4 E-2 Hawkeye early-warning/control aircraft.

The "Midway" class carriers cannot accommodate the full wing described above, and normally would not operate the Vigilante and Viking aircraft.

The carriers generally also embark a Carrier On-board Delivery (COD) aircraft in addition to the air wing.

Classification: From 1972 onward several attack aircraft carriers (CVA) were reclassified as aircraft carriers (CV) upon being fitted with anti-submarine control centres and facilities to support A/S aircraft and helicopters (in addition to fighter/attack aircraft). The multi-purpose configuration was dictated by the phasing out of dedicated anti-submarine aircraft carriers (CVS), the last being decommissioned in 1974.

All active ships still classified as attack aircraft carriers (CVA/CVAN) on 30 June 1975 were changed to CV/CVN regardless of their ability to support anti-submarine aircraft.

NIMITZ (CVN 68) and SOUTH CAROLINA (CGN 37)

1975, US Navy, PH 1, Richard B. Clinton

ADVANCED NUCLEAR POWERED AIRCRAFT CARRIER (CVNX): PROPOSED

The Navy proposes the continued construction of large, "Nimitz" class ships to provide a force level of 12 or 13 first-line aircraft carriers into the 1990s. However, in July 1975 then-Secretary of Defense Dr. James R. Schlesinger directed the Navy to examine the feasibility of constructing "medium"-size aircraft carriers of approximately 50 000 tons *standard* displacement as an alternative to the "Nimitz" class ships. Nuclear propulsion was dictated as a result of previous Congressional legislation (Title VIII) which requires nuclear power plants for all new major combatants for strike forces.

Subsequently, from Aug 1975 to Jan 1976 the Navy conducted an extensive study of nuclear-propelled carrier options (with the designation CVNX being applied to the various candidate designs). The principal CVNX designs are described in the adjacent table. Three "model" configurations were developed by the CVNX Study Group:

● Model A: minimum size nuclear-propelled carrier capable of supporting modern naval aircraft across all the Navy's mission areas; propelled by a four-reactor D2G power plant (using D2W nuclear fuel cores) which delivers about one-half the propulsive power of a "Nimitz" class ship.

● Model B: minimum size nuclear-propelled carrier capable of supporting about two-thirds of a "Nimitz" air wing with a four-reactor D2W (D2W) power plant which delivers slightly more propulsive power than the Model A plant.

● Model D: minimum size nuclear-propelled carrier capable of supporting about two-thirds of a "Nimitz" air wing with a two-reactor A4W plant that delivers the full propulsive power of a "Nimitz" class carrier.

Drawings of the three flight deck arrangements also are provided. All three have conventional angled flight decks, an island structure on the starboard side, and two or more deck-edge elevators. Similarly, all three designs have armoured flight decks as well as extensive side protection (to defend against anti-ship cruise missiles) and internal sub-division and damage-limiting features to reduce the affects of mines and torpedoes. The A/B/D model designs would have less endurance on the basis of food stowage and slightly smaller crews. On the basis of the CVNX analysis, the Navy has requested funding of a fourth "Nimitz" class ship as the optimum means of maintaining 12 or 13 first-line aircraft carriers. On the basis of constructing three additional carriers, the cost of "Nimitz" size carriers is approximately the same as the cost of the smaller, less-capable ships because of the consid rable engineering design effort required for a new class. (If more than three additional smaller carriers were procured during the next decade the costs would be less for the A/B/D models).

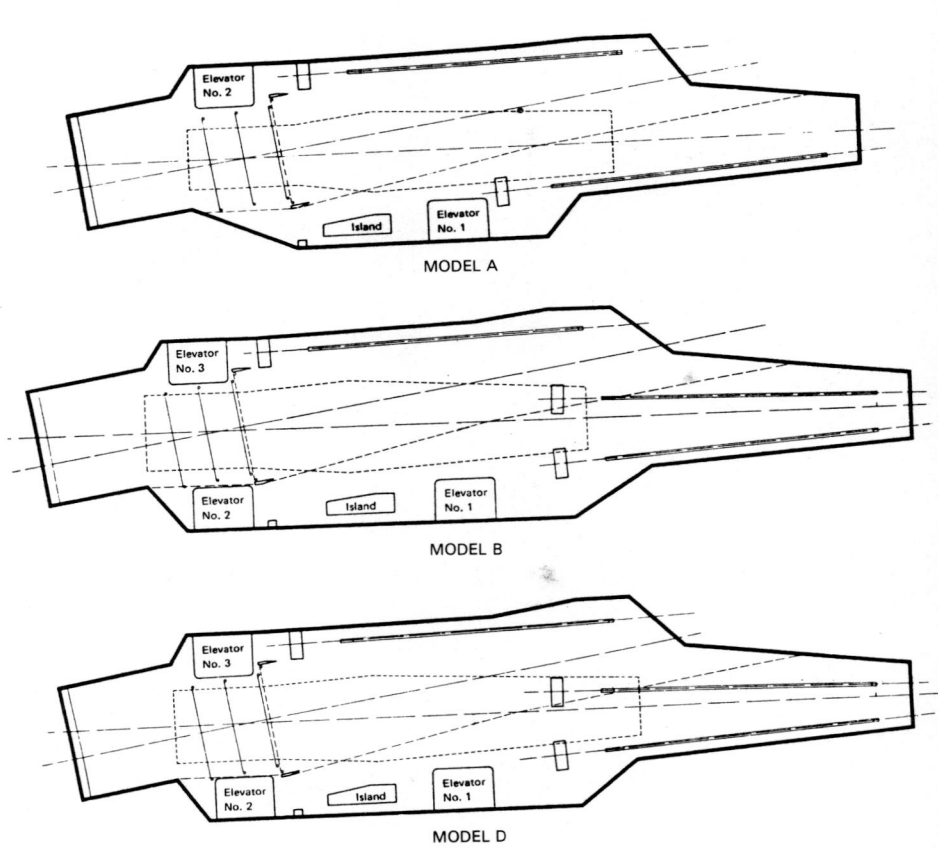

Scale: 1 inch = 225 feet

CVNX—continued

Aircraft: All three models would be capable of operating all fixed-wing, first-line aircraft envisioned for carrier operation through the year 2000.

Dimensions: The A/B/D models have been developed with length on waterline and beam on waterline characteristics. Length overall and maximum beam would vary on the basis of detailed design. By comparison, the *Nimitz* is 1 040 feet long.

Fiscal: Based on Fiscal Year 1976 dollars for research and development costs, and Fiscal Year 1979 dollars for construction (the year in which the ship would be started), the following are estimated costs of the alternative designs based on a three-ship programme: A model $2·1 *billion*; B model $2·25 *billion*; D model $2·2 *billion*, and a modified "Nimitz" class ship $2·1 *billion*.

Missiles: These ships would be armed with the NATO Sea Sparrow Basic Point Defence Missile System (BPDMS).

	Model A	Model B	Model D
Displacement, tons:	51 900 light	59 700 light	68 200 light
	55 900 standard	65 300 standard	73 700 standard
	64 600 full load	74 800 full load	84 800 full load
Length, feet *(metres)*	860 wl *(262·1)*	940 wl *286·5)*	970 wl *(295·7)*
Beam, feet *(metres)*	121 *(36·9)*	130 *(39·6)*	135 *(41·2)*
Aircraft:	48 to 53	59 to 65	59 to 65
Catapults:	2 C-13-1 steam	3 C-13-1 steam	3 C-13-1 steam
Elevators:	2	3	3
Missile launchers:	NATO Sea Sparrow	NATO Sea Sparrow	NATO Sea Sparrow
Main engines:	steam turbines	steam turbines	steam turbines
Nuclear reactors:	2 D2G (with D2W core)	2 D2G (with D2W core)	4 A4W
Complement:	2 004 ship	2 209 ship	2 200 ship
	1 296 air wing	1 580 air wing	1 580 air wing

VSTOL SUPPORT SHIPS (VSS): PROPOSED

The Navy seeks to supplement the larger aircraft carriers with a class of "light" aircraft carriers now designated as VSTOL Support Ships (VSS). These ships would operate fixed-wing Vertical/Short Take-Off and Landing aircraft and helicopters. The lead ship is planned for the Fiscal Year 1980 shipbuilding programme with possibly as many as a dozen ships being constructed over a ten-year period.

Congress refused to fund a VSTOL carrier known as the Sea Control Ship (SCS) that the Navy had planned for the FY 1975 shipbuilding programme. This ship was opposed on the basis of limited size, capability, and speed. Accordingly, the Navy has examined a number of designs that would provide a more flexible employment of sea-based tactical aircraft in a wide range of "low threat" situations as well as being able to conduct anti-submarine operations.

The adjacent table provides the characteristics of the aborted SCS design, of a 22 000-ton VSS design which is now the principal candidate for this class of ship, and those of a larger ship of some 33 000 tons, which would be able to operate conventional fixed-wing aircraft in limited numbers as well as VSTOL aircraft and helicopters.

Current Navy-Department of Defense planning provides for a VSS configuration suitable for sea control, amphibious assault, close air support, mine countermeasures, and low-intensity Anti-Air Warfare (AAW) operations. The last would be primarily against long-range reconnaissance and missile guidance aircraft, and not to counter high-performance fighter or attack aircraft. This multi-mission concept overcomes many of the objections which led to Congressional refusal to fund the smaller Sea Control Ship previously proposed by the Navy. In addition, the VSS would have sufficient speed (approximately 28-30 knots) to accompany carrier task forces or fast merchant ships.

The feasibility of the Sea Control Ship/VSS concept was demonstrated from 1972 to 1974 by the amphibious assault ship *Guam* (LPH 9) which operated as an interim SCS. The *Guam* carried AV-8 Harrier VSTOL fighter-attack aircraft, SH-3 Sea King helicopters, and SH-2 LAMPS helicopters during several exercises. She subsequently reverted to the amphibious role. (Photographs of the *Guam* with her SCS aircraft appear in the editions published during that period).

Aircraft: "Notional" air groups are indicated for the Sea Control Ship and 22 000-ton VSS design. The VSTOL strike aircraft is the AV-8 Harrier or its successor; the large anti-submarine

	Sea Control Ship (SCS) Design	22 000 ton VSS Design	33 000 ton VSS Design
Displacement, tons:	14 300 full load	22 000 full load	32 800 full load
Length, feet *(metres)*:	640 oa *(195·1)*	750 oa *(228·6)*	780 oa *(237·7)*
Beam, feet *(metres)*:	80 *(24·4)*	87 *(26·5)*	100 *(30·5)*
Draught, feet *(metres)*:	30 *(9·1)*	24 *(7·3)*	25 *(7·6)*
Aircraft:	3 VSTOL strike aircraft	4 VSTOL strike aircraft	approx 50+ (see notes)
	14 large A/S helicopters	16 large A/S helicopters	
	2 LAMPS helicopters	6 LAMPS helicopters	
Catapults:	none	none	2 C-13 steam
Elevators:	2	2	2
Guns:	2—20 mm CIWS	2—20 mm CIWS	2—20 mm CIWS
Main engines:	2 gas turbines; 40 000 shp; 1 shaft	4 gas turbines; 90 000 shp; 2 shafts	steam turbines; 100 000 shp; 2 shafts
Speed, knots:	approx 26	28+	26+

helicopter is the SH-3 Sea King or SH-53 Sea Stallion (in an A/S configuration); the LAMPS (Light Airborne Multi-Purpose System) is actually a medium-size helicopter primarily configured for A/S search and attack. The current LAMPS helicopter is the SH-2, while a later aircraft based on the Army's Utility Tactical Transport Aircraft System (UTTAS) programme will be developed as the LAMPS III.

A VSTOL carrier over 25 000 tons could operate a small number of conventional fixed-wing aircraft, particularly the S-3 Viking and A-7 Corsair II. These aircraft require catapults and arresting wires. The large VSS design described here would have two C-13 steam catapults and could operate an air group of 50 or more fixed-wing aircraft and helicopters, the exact number depending upon the type assigned.

Several advanced VSTOL aircraft are under development in the United States for ship-based use, with the more promising candidates being the Hawker Siddeley-McDonnell Douglas AV-16 Advanced Harrier, the Rockwell XFV-12 Thrust-Augmented Wing (TAW) aircraft, and the Grumman "Nutcracker" design.

Fiscal: Current cost estimates provide for a VSS of about 22 000 tons having an average cost of $270 000 000 in FY 1976 dollars.

Gunnery: All of the SCS/VSS designs provide for the installation of at least two Close-In Weapon Systems (CIWS), probably

the rapid-fire, multi-barrel 20 mm Phalanx gun system. This would be used as a final defence against incoming anti-ship cruise missiles.

Missiles: Harpoon anti-ship missiles in storage/launcher cannisters could be fitted in all of these ships.

Propulsion: Despite the Title VIII legislation passed by Congress which encourages nuclear propulsion for surface combatants, all SCS/VSS designs provide for fossil-fuel propulsion because of the high development and procurement costs of nuclear power plants. The Navy-Department of Defense decision not to seek nuclear propulsion for these ships accounts in part for their classification as VSTOL Support Ships vice "carriers".

Troops: Multi-mission features for the VSS include being able to accommodate 500 troops in the amphibious contingency role for limited periods with minimum modifications.

Photographs: A photograph and scale drawings of the proposed 14 300 ton Sea Control Ship appear in the 1974-1975 edition. The proposed 22 000 ton VSS would to a large extent be a scaled up SCS configuration.

NIMITZ (CVN 68)—see following page

1975, United States Navy, PH1 Harold Phillips

1 + 2 NUCLEAR POWERED AIRCRAFT CARRIERS (CVN): "NIMITZ" CLASS

Name	No.	Builders	Laid down	Launched	Commissioned
*NIMITZ	CVN 68	Newport News Shipbuilding & Dry Dock Co	22 June1968	13 May 1972	3 May 1975
DWIGHT D. EISENHOWER	CVN 69	Newport News Shipbuilding & Dry Dock Co	14 Aug 1970	11 Oct 1975	1977
CARL VINSON	CVN 70	Newport News Shipbuilding & Dry Dock Co	11 Oct 1975	Mar 1979	1981

Displacement, tons: 81 600 standard; 91 400 full load; 93 400 combat load
Length, feet (metres): 1 040 *(317·0)* wl; 1 092 *(332·0)* oa
Beam, feet (metres): 134 *(40·8)*
Draught, feet (metres): 37 *(11·3)*
Flight deck width, feet (metres): 252 *(76·8)*
Catapults: 4 steam (C13-1)
Aircraft: approx 100
Missiles: 3 Basic Point Defence Missile System (BPDMS) launchers with Sea Sparrow missiles (Mk 25)
Main engines: Geared steam turbines; 260 000 shp; 4 shafts
Nuclear reactors: 2 pressurised-water cooled (A4W)
Speed, knots: 30+
Complement: 3 300 plus approx 2 800 assigned to air wing for a total of 6 100 per ship

The lead ship for this class and the world's second nuclear-powered aircraft carrier was ordered 9½ years after the first such ship, the USS *Enterprise* (CVN 65). The *Nimitz* was authorised in the Fiscal Year 1967 new construction programme; the *Dwight D. Eisenhower* in the FY 1970 programme; and the *Carl Vinson* in the FY 1974 programme. All three ships are being constructed by the Newport News Shipbuilding & Dry Dock Co (Virginia), the only US shipyard now capable of constructing large, nuclear-propelled warships.
The completion of the first two ships has been delayed almost two years because of delays in the delivery and testing of nuclear plant components. The *Eisenhower* is contracted for delivery to the Navy 21 months after the *Nimitz*. However, the official Navy construction schedule notes that past underman-

ning by shipbuilder will probably result in slippage beyond contract delivery date.

Classification: *Nimitz* and *Eisenhower* were ordered as attack aircraft carriers (CVAN): reclassified as multi-mission aircraft carriers (attack and anti-submarine) on 30 June 1975. First two ships will be refitted with A/S control centre and facilities for A/S aircraft and helicopters after completion. The *Vinson* will be completed with these facilities.

Design: These ships strongly resemble the previous "Kitty Hawk" or improved "Forrestal" designs. However, their superstructure is significantly smaller because of the absence of fossil-engine exhausts. Full load displacement indicates maximum loading for port entry; "combat loading" indicates maximum aviation fuel and ordnance levels that can be provided with at-sea replenishment.

Electronics: These ships have the Naval Tactical Data System (NTDS) and the following radars: SPS-10 surface search, SPS-43A two-dimensional air search, and SPS-48 three-dimensional air search, and SPN-42, SPN-43, and SPN-44 navigation equipment. These ships will not have sonar.

Engineering: These carriers have only two nuclear reactors compared to the eight reactors required for the carrier *Enterprise*. The nuclear cores for the reactors in these ships are expected to provide sufficient energy for the ships each to steam for at least 13 years, an estimated 800 000 to 1 million miles between "refuelling". The two cores in one of these carriers will have the energy equivalent to 462 000 000 gallons (US) or 1 620 000 long tons of fuel oil.

Fiscal: A number of cost growth factors have had an impact on these ships, including the high rate of US economic inflation and delays in schedule. The cost of the *Nimitz* in Fiscal Year 1976 dollars is equivalent to $1·881 *billion;* the two later ships will cost in excess of $2 *billion* each in equivalent dollars.

Nomenclature: The *Nimitz* honours Fleet Admiral Chester W. Nimitz who was Commander-in-Chief Pacific Fleet and Commander-in-Chief Pacific Ocean Areas during World War II, and Chief of Naval Operations from December 1945 to December 1947.
The *Dwight D. Eisenhower* is believed to be the first major US surface warship to be named for an Army officer; General of the Army Eisenhower commanded Allied Forces in Western Europe in 1944-1945, subsequently was first Supreme Allied Commander in NATO, and the President of the United States from January 1953 to January 1961. The CVN 69 was named *Eisenhower* on 21 Feb 1970; renamed *Dwight D. Eisenhower* on 25 May 1970, but Secretary of Defense Laird dedicated the ship as the "USS *Eisenhower*" at the keel laying on 15 Aug 1970. The *Carl Vinson* is believed to be the first US naval ship to be named for a living person since the American Revolution when a small naval craft was named *Franklin* for American patriot Benjamin Franklin. Carl Vinson was a member of the House of Representatives from Georgia from 1914 to 1965; he served as Chairman of the House Naval Affairs Committee and later the House Armed Services Committee.

Photographs: The *Nimitz* and *America* have similar hull forms and lift arrangements. Note their differing island structures and the missile launchers on the starboard quarter, aft of the aircraft and boat crane.

1975, United States Navy, PH3 D. E. Patton

NIMITZ (CVN 68)

NIMITZ (CVN 68)

Drawing by A. D. Baker

4 AIRCRAFT CARRIERS (CV): "KITTY HAWK" CLASS

Name	No.	Builders	Laid down	Launched	Commissioned
*KITTY HAWK	CV 63	New York Shipbuilding Corp, Camden, NJ	27 Dec 1956	21 May 1960	29 April 1961
*CONSTELLATION	CV 64	New York Naval Shipyard	14 Sep 1957	8 Oct 1960	27 Oct 1961
*AMERICA	CV 66	Newport News Shipbuilding & Dry Dock Co	9 Jan 1961	1 Feb 1964	23 Jan 1965
*JOHN F. KENNEDY	CV 67	Newport News Shipbuilding & Dry Dock Co	22 Oct 1964	27 May 1967	7 Sep 1968

Displacement, tons:
  Kitty Hawk: 60 100 standard; 80 800 full load
  Constellation: 60 100 standard; 80 800 full load
  America: 60 300 standard; 80 800 full load
  John F. Kennedy: 61 000 standard; 87 000 full load
Length, feet (metres): 990 *(301·8)* wl
  Kitty Hawk: 1 062·5 *(323·9)* oa
  Constellation: 1 072·5 *(326·9)* oa
  America, J.F.K.: 1 047·5 *(319·3)* oa
Beam, feet (metres):
  Kitty Hawk, Constellation: 129·5 *(38·5)*
  America, J.F.K.: 130 *(39·6)*
Draught, feet (metres): 35·9 *(10·9)*
Flight deck width, feet (metres): 249 *(76·0)* maximum except *John F. Kennedy* 252 *(76·9)*
Catapults: 4 steam
Aircraft: approx 85 in *Kitty Hawk* and *Constellation;* approx 95 in *America* and *John F. Kennedy*
Missile launchers: 2 twin Terrier surface-to-air launchers (Mk 10) in *Kitty Hawk, Constellation, America*
3 Basic Point Defence Missile System (BPDMS) launchers (Mk 25) with Sea Sparrow missiles in *John F. Kennedy*
Main engines: 4 geared turbines (Westinghouse) 280 000 shp; 4 shafts
Boilers: 8 (Foster Wheeler)
Speed, knots: 30+
Complement: 2 800 (150 officers, approx 2 645 enlisted men) plus approx 2 150 assigned to attack air wing for a total of 4 950 officers and enlisted men per ship

These ships were built to an improved "Forrestal" design and are easily recognised by their smaller island structure which is set farther aft than the superstructure in the four "Forrestal" class ships. Lift arrangements also differ (see design notes). The *Kitty Hawk* was authorised in Fiscal Year 1956 new construction programme, the *Constellation* in FY 1957, the *America* in FY 1961, and the *John F. Kennedy* in FY 1963. Completion of the *Constellation* was delayed because of a fire which ravaged her in the New York Naval Shipyard in December 1960. Construction of the *John F. Kennedy* was delayed because of debate over whether to provide her with conventional or nuclear propulsion.
Construction costs were $265 200 000 for *Kitty Hawk,* $264 500 000 for *Constellation,* $248 800 000 for *America,* and $277 000 000 for *John F. Kennedy.*

Classification: Officially known as the "Kitty Hawk" class; generally referred to as improved "Forrestals". The *John F. Kennedy* is officially a separate one-ship class.
As completed, all four ships were classified as attack aircraft carriers (CVA); first two changed to multi-mission aircraft carriers (attack and anti-submarine) when modified with A/S command centres and facilities for S-3 Viking fixed-wing aircraft and SH-3 Sea King helicopters. *Kitty Hawk* to CV vice CVA on 29 April 1973; *John F. Kennedy* to CV vice CVA on 1 Dec 1974; *Constellation* and *America* from CVA to CV on 30 June 1975, prior to A/S modifications.

Design: These ships are officially considered to be of a different design from the "Forrestal" class. The island structure is smaller and set farther aft in the newer ships with two deck-edge lifts forward of the superstructure, a third lift aft of the structure, and the port-side lift on the after quarter (compared with two lifts aft of the island and the port-side lift at the forward end of the angled deck in the earlier ships). This lift arrangement considerably improves flight deck operations. All four of these ships also have a small radar mast aft of the island structure. Four C13 catapults (with one C13-1 in each of later ships). The *John F. Kennedy* and *America* have stern anchors because of their bow sonar domes.

CONSTELLATION (CV 64)

1974, US Navy, PHCS Robert L. Lawson

CONSTELLATION (CV 64)

1974, US Navy, PHCS Robert L. Lawson

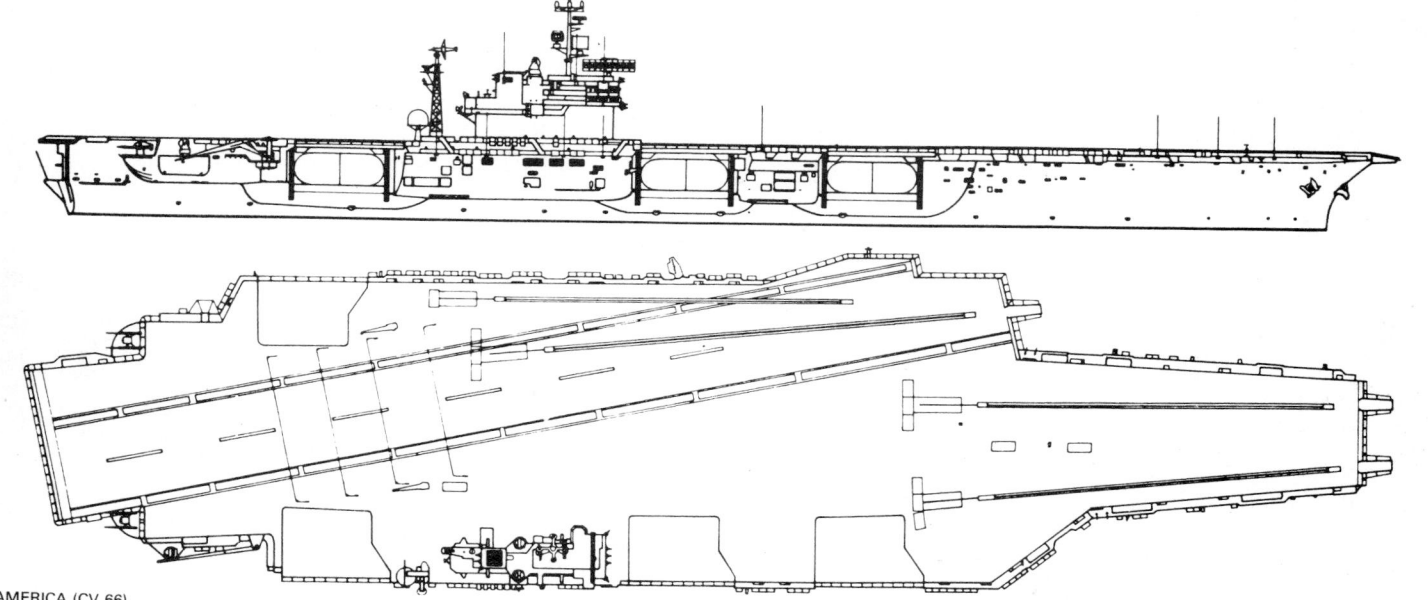

AMERICA (CV 66)

Drawing by A. D. Baker

"KITTY HAWK" CLASS—continued

Electronics: All four ships of this class have highly sophisticated electronic equipment including the Naval Tactical Data System (NTDS). The *America* has bow-mounted SQS-23 sonar, the only US attack carrier with anti-submarine sonar (several ASW carriers have been fitted with sonar during modernisations). Similar installation was planned for the *Kennedy,* but not installed because of operational limitations of sonar in an attack carrier.

All four ships have SPS-43 search radar antenna on island structure; three ships also have a three-dimensional SPS-52 search radar antenna on island and an SPS-30 search radar antenna on second mast while the *John F. Kennedy* has SPS-48 antenna on second mast; being fitted with SPS-58 radar to detect low-flying aircraft and missiles. All ships have TACAN navigation pods or "bee-hives".

The *Kitty Hawk* and *Constellation* have four Mk 76 guided missile control systems with an SPG-55A radar associated with each control system; the *America* has three Mk 76 systems with three associated SPG-55B radars.

Missiles: The three Terrier-armed ships have a Mk 10 Mod 3 launcher on the starboard quarter and a Mod 4 launcher on the port quarter.

The *America* has updated Terrier launchers and guidance system that can accommodate Standard missiles; the *Constellation* and *Kitty Hawk* retain older Terrier HT systems which will be replaced by three NATO Sea Sparrow launchers (Mk 29). Three Sea Sparrow BPDMS launchers were fitted in the *John F. Kennedy* early in 1969.

Nomenclature: US aircraft carriers are generally named after battles and historic ships. However, the *Kitty Hawk* better honours the site where the Wright brothers made their historic flights than the converted aircraft ferry of that name which served in World War II. The *Constellation* remembers a frigate built in 1797 and a later ship still afloat at Baltimore, Maryland, although no longer in Navy commission. The name *America* was previously carried by a 74-gun ship of the line launched in 1782, and presented to France, by the racing schooner which gave her name to the America's Cup, and by the German liner *Amerika* which was taken over by the US Navy in World War I, renamed, and used as a troop transport. The *John F. Kennedy* commemorates the president who was assassinated in 1963.

Photographs: Note the angled funnel and Sea Sparrow BPDMS launchers of the *John F. Kennedy.* These ships can be distinguished from the earlier "Forrestal" class carriers by the position of the island structure and the small radar mast aft of the superstructure. In the photograph of the *Enterprise* note the distinctive shape of the F-14 Tomcat fighters with their variable-sweep wings "tucked in" to save deck space. In flight, the wings are swept back to improve high-speed performance.

JOHN F. KENNEDY (CV 67)

1973, United States Navy, PH1 D. D. Deverman

AMERICA (CV 66)

1972, United States Navy

ENTERPRISE (CVN 65) —see following page

1975, United States Navy, PH1 James Lumzer

1 NUCLEAR-POWERED AIRCRAFT CARRIER (CVN): "ENTERPRISE" TYPE

Name	No.	Builders	Laid down	Launched	Commissioned
*ENTERPRISE	CVN 65	Newport News Shipbuilding & Dry Dock Co.	4 Feb 1958	24 Sep 1960	25 Nov 1961

Displacement, tons: 75 700 standard; 89 600 full load
Length, feet (metres): 1 040 *(317·0)* wl; 1 123 *(341·3)* oa
Beam, feet (metres): 133 *(40·5)*
Draught, feet (metres): 35·8 *(10·8)*
Flight deck width, feet (metres): 257 *(78·3)* maximum
Aircraft: approx 95
Catapults: 4 steam (C 13)
Missile launchers: 2 Basic Point Defence Missile Systems
  (BPDMS) launchers (Mk 25) with Sea Sparrow missiles
Main engines: 4 geared steam turbines (Westinghouse);
  approx 280 000 shp; 4 shafts
Nuclear reactors: 8 pressurised-water cooled A2W (Westing-
  house)
Speed, knots: approx 35
Complement: 3 100 (162 officers, approx 2 940 enlisted men)
  plus 2 400 assigned to attack air wing for a total of 5 500)

At the time of her construction, the *Enterprise* was the largest
warship ever built and is rivalled in size only by the nuclear-
powered "Nimitz" class ships. The *Enterprise* was authorised
in the Fiscal Year 1958 new construction programme. She was
launched only 19 months after her keel was laid down.
The cost of the *Entrprise* was $451 300 000.
The Fiscal Year 1960 budget provided $35 000 000 to prepare
plans and place orders for components of a second nuclear-
powered carrier, but the project was deferred.

Armament: The *Enterprise* was completed without any arma-
ment in an effort to hold down construction costs. Space for
Terrier missile system was provided. Short-range Sea Sparrow
BPDMS subsequently was installed in late 1967.

Classification: Originally classified as CVAN 65; reclassified as
multi-purpose carrier (CV) on 30 June 1975.

Design: Built to a modified "Forrestal" class design. The most
distinctive feature is the island structure. Nuclear propulsion
eliminated requirement for smoke stack and boiler air intakes,
reducing size of superstructure, and reducing vulnerability to
battle damage, radio-activity and biological agents. Rectangu-
lar fixed-array radar antennae ("billboards") are mounted on
sides of island; electronic countermeasure (ECM) antennae
ring cone-shaped upper levels of island structure. Fixed antennae have increased range and performance (see listing for
cruiser *Long Beach*). The *Enterprise* has four deck-edge lifts,
two forward of island and one aft on starboard side and one aft
on port side (as in "Kitty Hawk" class).

Electronics: Fitted with the Naval Tactical Data System (NTDS).
In addition to SPS-32 and SPS-33 "billboard" radar systems,
the *Enterprise* has SPS-10 and SPS-12 search radars and various navigation radar antennae atop her island structure; SPS-
58 radar fitted to detect low-flying aircraft and missiles. TACAN
(Tactical Aircraft Navigation) navigation pod caps mast.

Engineering: The *Enterprise* was the world's second nuclear-
powered warship (the cruiser *Long Beach* was completed a few
months earlier). Design of the first nuclear-powered aircraft
carrier began in 1950 and work continued until 1953 when the
programme was deferred pending further work on the submarine reactor programme. The large ship reactor project was
reinstated in 1954 on the basis of technological advancements
made in the previous 14 months. The Atomic Energy Commission's Bettis Atomic Power Laboratory was given prime
responsibility for developing the nuclear power plant.
The first of the eight reactors installed in the *Enterprise*
achieved initial criticality on 2 Dec 1960, shortly after the carrier

ENTERPRISE (CVN 65)

1974, United States Navy, PHAN L. Hayes

was launched. After three years of operation during which she
steamed more than 207 000 miles, the *Enterprise* was overhauled and refuelled from November 1964 to July 1965. Her
second set of cores provided about 300 000 miles steaming.
The eight cores initially installed in the *Enterprise* cost
$64 000 000; the second set cost about $20 000 000.
The *Enterprise* underwent an extensive overhaul from October
1969 to January 1971, which included installation of a new set
of uranium cores in the ship's eight nuclear reactors. The overhaul and refuelling took place at the Newport News shipyard.
Estimated cost of the overhaul was approximately $30 000 000,
with $13 000 000 being for non-nuclear repairs and alterations,
and $17 000 000 being associated with installation of the new
nuclear cores (the latter amount being in addition to the
$80 000 000 cost of the eight cores).
This third set of cores is expected to fuel the ship for 10 to 13
years, according to Admiral H. G. Rickover.
There are two reactors for each of the ship's four shafts. The

eight reactors feed 32 heat exchangers. The *Enterprise*
developed more horsepower during her propulsion trials than
any other ship in history (officially "in excess of 200 000 shaft
horsepower"; subsequently Navy officials stated that she can
generate 280 000 shp).

Nomenclature: Eight US Navy ships have carried the name
Enterprise. The first was a British supply sloop captured in 1775
and armed for use on Lake Champlain. The seventh *Enterprise*
(CV 6) was the most famous US carrier of World War II. She
earned 20 battle stars. That "Big E" was sold in 1958 and
scrapped.

Photographs: The *Enterprise* can be distinguished from all
other aircraft carriers by her "square" island structure with
fixed "billboard" radar antennae topped by an antenna-
studded dome (see *Design* notes). Lower-angle port and starboard views of the *Enterprise* appear in the 1975-1976 edition.

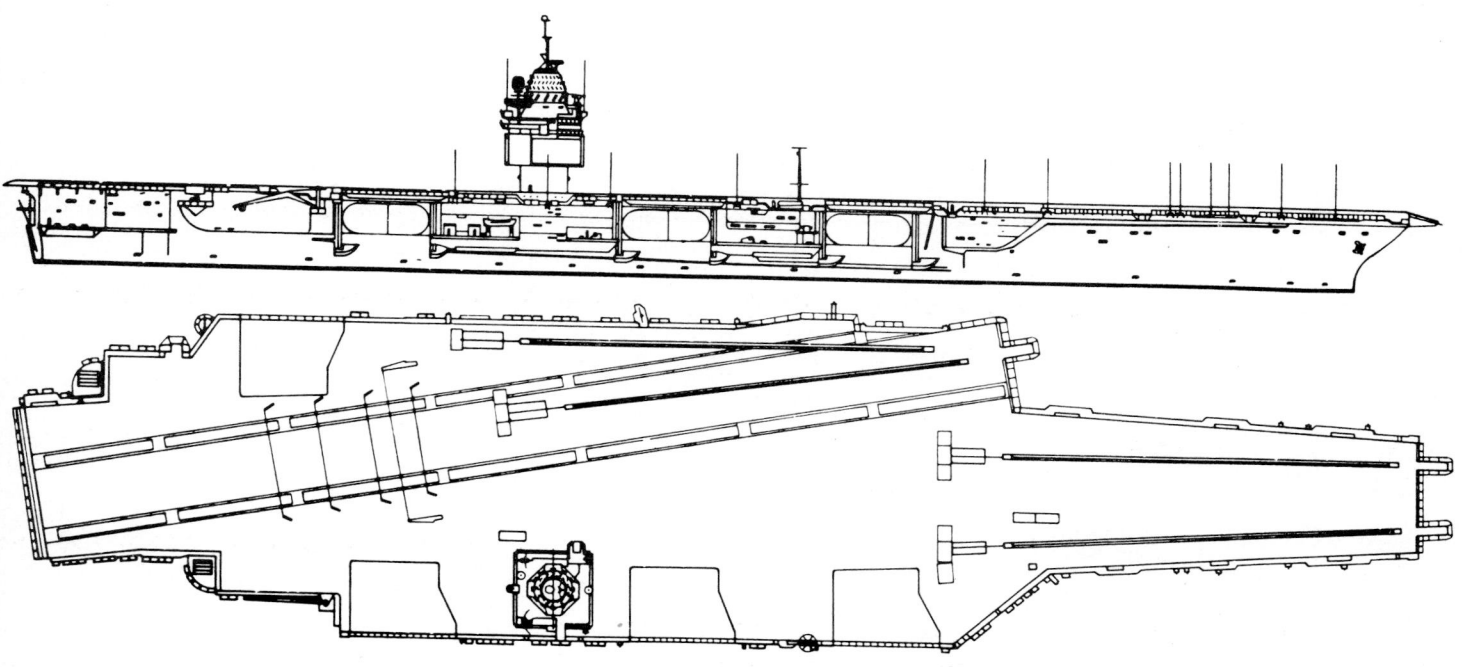

ENTERPRISE (CVN 65)

Drawing by A. D. Baker

4 AIRCRAFT CARRIERS (CV): "FORRESTAL" CLASS

Name	No.	Builders	Laid down	Launched	Commissioned
*FORRESTAL	CV 59	Newport News SB & DD Co	14 July 1952	11 Dec 1954	1 Oct 1955
*SARATOGA	CV 60	New York Naval Shipyard	16 Dec 1952	8 Oct 1955	14 April 1956
*RANGER	CV 61	Newport News SB & DD Co	2 Aug 1954	29 Sep 1956	10 Aug 1957
*INDEPENDENCE	CV 62	New York Naval Shipyard	1 July 1955	6 June 1958	10 Jan 1959

Displacement, tons:
 Forrestal: 59 650 standard; 78 000 full load
 Others: 60 000 standard; 78 000 full load
Length, feet (metres):
 Forrestal, Saratoga: 990 *(301·8)* wl
 Ranger: 1 039 *(316·7)* oa
 Independence: 1 046·5 *(319·0)* oa
Beam, feet (metres): 129·5 *(38·5)*
Draught, feet (metres): 37 *(11·3)*
Flight deck width, feet (metres): 252 *(76·8)* maximum except
 Ranger 260 *(79·2)*
Catapults: 4 steam
Aircraft: Approx 85
Guns: 4—5 inch *(127 mm)* 54 cal (Mk 42) DP (single) in *Ranger*
Missile launchers: 2 Basic Point Defence Missile Systems
 (BPDMS) launchers (Mk 25) with Sea Sparrow missiles in all
 except *Ranger*
Main engines: 4 geared turbines (Westinghouse) 4 shafts;
 26 000 shp in *Forrestal;* 280 000 shp in others
Boilers: 8 (Babcock & Wilcox)
Speed, knots:
 Forrestal: 33
 Others 35
Complement: 2 790 (145 officers, approx 2 645 enlisted men)
 plus approx 2 150 assigned to attack air wing for a total of
 4 940+ per ship

FORRESTAL (CV 59)   *1975, US Navy, PH2 James P. Kiser*

The *Forrestal* was the world's first aircraft carrier designed and
built after World War II. The *Forrestal* design drew heavily from
the aircraft carrier *United States* (CVA 58) which was cancelled
immediately after being laid down in April 1949. The *Forrestal*
was authorised in the Fiscal Year 1952 new construction programme; the *Saratoga* followed in the FY 1953 programme, the
Ranger in the FY 1954 programme, and the *Independence* in
the FY 1955 programme.
Construction costs were $188 900 000 for *Forrestal*,
$213 900 000 for *Saratoga,* $173 300 000 for *Ranger,* and
$225 300 000 for *Independence.*
All ships of this class are active.

Classification: The *Forrestal* and *Saratoga* were initially classified as Large Aircraft Carriers CVB 59 and 60, respectively;
reclassified as Attack Aircraft Carriers (CVA) in October 1952 to
reflect their purpose rather than size. The ill-fated *United States*
was a "heavy" carrier (CVA).
Saratoga redesignated CV 60 vice CVA 60 on 30 June 1972;
Independence to CV 62 on 28 Feb 1973; *Forrestal* and *Ranger*
on 30 June 1975.

Design: The "Forrestal" Class ships were the first aircraft carriers designed and built specifically to operate jet-propelled
aircraft. The *Forrestal* was redesigned early in construction to
incorporate British-developed angled flight deck and steam
catapults. These were the first US aircraft carriers built with an
enclosed bow area to improve seaworthiness. Four large
deck-edge lifts are fitted, one forward of island structure to
starboard, two aft of island structure to starboard and one at
forward edge of angled flight deck to port. Other features
include armoured flight deck and advanced underwater protection and internal compartmentation to reduce effects of conventional and nuclear attack. Mast configurations differ; the
Forrestal originally had two masts, one of which was removed
in 1967.
The first two ships have two C7 and two C11 catapults; the
others have four C7.

INDEPENDENCE (CV 62)   *1974, US Navy, JOCS R. P. Benjamin*

Electronics: The primary radars installed in these ships are
SPS-43, SPS-30, and SPS-10 search radars, and SPN-10 navigation radar.

SPS-58 radar being installed to detect low-flying aircraft and
missiles.
Naval Tactical Data System (NTDS) and TACAN (Tactical Air-

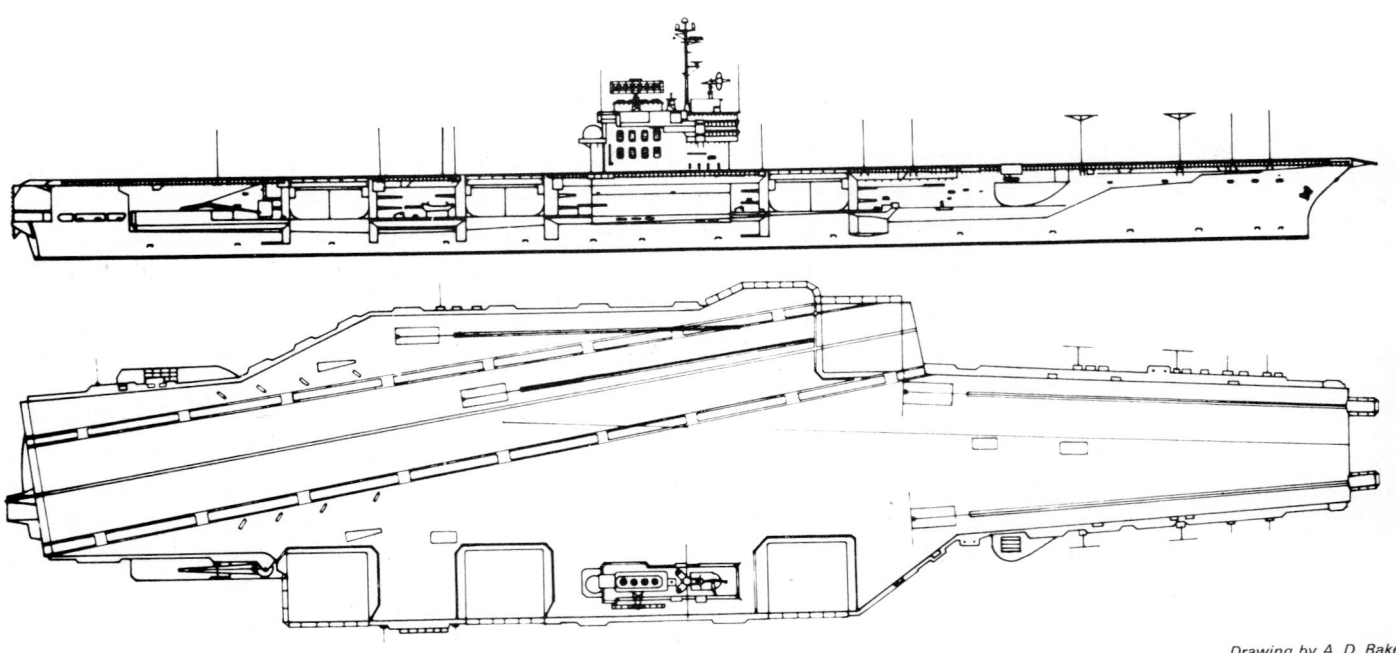

FORRESTAL (CV 59)   *Drawing by A. D. Baker*

"FORRESTAL" CLASS—continued

craft Navigation) are installed in all four ships.
Ranger has two Mk 56 gunfire control systems; other ships have two Mk 115 guided missile control systems.

Engineering: The *Saratoga* and later ships have an improved steam plant, increased machinery weight of the improved plant is more than compensated for by increased performance and decreased fuel consumption. *Forrestal* boilers are 615 psi *(42·7 kg/cm²);* 1 200 psi *(83·4 kg/cm²)* in other ships.

Gunnery: All four ships initially mounted 8—5 inch guns (Mk 42) in single mounts, two on each quarter. The forward sponsons carrying the guns interfered with ship operations in rough weather, tending to slow the ships down. The forward sponsons and guns were subsequently removed (except in *Ranger*), reducing armament to four guns per ship. The after guns were removed with installation of BPDMS launchers (see below).

Missiles: The four after 5 inch guns were removed from the *Forrestal* late in 1967 and a single BPDMS launcher for Sea Sparrow missiles was installed forward on the starboard side. An additional launcher was provided aft on the port side in 1972. Two BPDMS launchers fitted in *Independence* in 1973 and two launchers in *Saratoga* in 1974; the *Ranger* was to receive three NATO Sea Sparrow launchers (Mk 29) in FY 1977.

Nomenclature: The *Forrestal* honours James V. Forrestal, Secretary of the Navy from 1944 until he was appointed the first US Secretary of Defense in 1947, a post he held until shortly before his death in 1949. The *Saratoga* commemorates the battle at Saratoga, New York, in the American Revolution and five earlier US warships including a carrier of World War II fame (CV 3). The first USS *Ranger* was a sloop built in 1777 and a later ship of that name was the first US built-for-the-purpose carrier (CV 4). The first USS *Independence* was a sloop built in 1775 and a later ship of that name was a light carrier (CVL 22) that saw extensive combat in World War II.

SARATOGA (CV 60)

1975, United States Navy

FRANKLIN D. ROOSEVELT (CV 42)—see following page

1973, United States Navy

3 AIRCRAFT CARRIERS (CV): "MIDWAY" CLASS

Name	No.	Builders	Laid down	Launched	Commissioned
*MIDWAY	CV 41	Newport News SB & DD Co	27 Oct 1943	20 Mar 1945	10 Sep 1945
*FRANKLIN D. ROOSEVELT	CV 42	New York Navy Yard	1 Dec 1943	29 April 1945	3 Nov 1945
*CORAL SEA	CV 43	Newport News SB & DD Co	10 July 1944	2 April 1946	1 Oct 1947

Displacement, tons: *Midway:* 51 000 standard; *F. D. Roosevelt:* 51 000 standard; *Coral Sea:* 52 500 standard; all approx 64 000 full load
Length, feet (metres): 900 *(274·3)* wl; 979 *(298·4)* oa
Beam, feet (metres): 121 *(36·9)*
Draught, feet (metres): 35·3 *(10·8)*
Flight deck width, feet (metres): 238 *(72·5)* maximum
Catapults: 2 steam except 3 in *Coral Sea*
Aircraft: approx 75
Guns: 4—5 inch *(127 mm)* 54 cal (Mk 39) DP (single) in *F. D. Roosevelt;* 3 guns in *Midway* and *Coral Sea* (see Gunnery notes)
Main engines: 4 geared turbines (Westinghouse in *Midway* and *Coral Sea;* General Electric in *F. D. Roosevelt*); 212 000 shp; 4 shafts
Boilers: 12 (Babcock & Wilcox)
Speed, knots: 30+
Complement: 2 615 (140 officers, approx 2 475 enlisted men) except *Coral Sea* 2 710 (165 officers, approx 2 545 enlisted men) plus approx 1 800 assigned to attack air wing for a total of 4 400 to 4 500 per ship

These carriers were the largest US warships constructed during World War II. Completed too late for service in that conflict, they were the backbone of US naval strength for the first decade of the Cold War. The entire class has been in active service (except for overhaul and modernisation) since the ships were completed.
The *Midway* was homeported at Yokosuka, Japan, in October 1973; she is the only US aircraft carrier to be based overseas. One "Midway" class carrier will be decommissioned when the *Dwight D. Eisenhower* is completed and one when the *Vinson* is completed. Or, one of these ships may replace the *Lexington* (CVT 16) as a training carrier. The *Midway* will probably be retained in service into the 1980s to provide a 13 carrier force level.
Construction cost of *Midway* was $85 600 000, *F. D. Roosevelt* $85 700 000, and *Coral Sea* $87 600 000.

Classification: These ships were initially classified as large Aircraft Carriers (CVB); reclassified as Attack Aircraft Carriers (CVA) in October 1952. All three ships reclassified as Aircraft Carriers (CV) on 30 June 1975.

Design: These ships were built to the same design with a standard displacement of 45 000 tons, full load displacement of 60 100 tons, and an overall length of 968 feet. They have been extensively modified since completion (see notes below). These ships were the first US aircraft carriers with an armoured flight deck and the first US warships with a designed width too large to enable them to pass through the Panama Canal.
The unnamed CVB 44, 56 and 57 of this class were cancelled prior to the start of construction.

Electronics: Naval Tactical Data System (NTDS) in *Midway* and *Coral Sea.*
The principal radars installed on these ships are SPS-10, SPS-30, SPS-43, SPN-6, and SPN-10. *Midway* fitted with SPS-58 radar to detect low-flying aircraft and missiles. All have TACAN (Tactical Aircraft Navigation) pods; one Mk 37 and two or three Mk 56 gunfire control systems provided.

Gunnery: As built, these ships mounted 18—5 inch guns (14 in *Coral Sea),* 84—40 mm guns, and 28—20 mm guns. Armament reduced periodically with 3 inch guns replacing lighter weapons. Minimal 5 inch armament remains. The 5 inch guns are 54 calibre Mk 39, essentially modified 5 inch/38 calibre with a longer barrel for greater range; not to be confused with rapid-fire 5 inch/54s of newer US warships.

1971, United States Navy

MIDWAY

1973, United States Navy

FRANKLIN D. ROOSEVELT (CVA 43)

1971, United States Navy

CORAL SEA (CV 43)

"MIDWAY" CLASS—continued

Missiles: The *Midway* was scheduled to be fitted with three Basic Point Defense Missile launchers (Mk 25) for the Sea Sparrow missile during Fiscal Year 1977.

Modernisation: All three "Midway" Class carriers have been extensively modernised. Their most extensive conversion "package" gave them angled flight decks, steam catapults, enclosed "hurricane" bows, new electronics, and new lift arrangement (*Franklin D. Roosevelt* from 1953 to 1956, *Midway* from 1954 to 1957, and *Coral Sea* from 1956 to 1960; all at Puget Sound Naval Shipyard). Lift arrangement was changed in *Franklin D. Roosevelt* and *Midway* to one centreline lift forward, one deck-edge lift aft of island on starboard side, and one deck-edge lift at forward end of angled deck on port side. The *Coral Sea* has an improved arrangement with one lift forward and one aft of island on starboard side and third lift outboard

on port side aft. The *Midway* began another extensive modernisation at the San Francisco Bay Naval Shipyard in February 1966; she was recommissioned on 31 Jan 1970 and went to sea in March 1970.
Her modernisation included provisions for handling newer aircraft, new catapults, new lifts (arranged as in *Coral Sea*), and new electronics. A similar modernisation planned for the *Franklin D. Roosevelt*, to have begun in Fiscal Year 1970, has been cancelled because the *Midway* modernisation is taking longer and costing more than originally estimated (24 months and $88 000 00 was planned; actual work required approximately 52 months and $202 300 000). The *Franklin D. Roosevelt* completed an austere overhaul in June 1969 which enables her to operate newer aircraft; cost of overhaul was $46 000 000. The *Midway* is now the most capable of the three ships (for example, her lifts can handle aircraft weights to 100 000

pounds compared to 74 000 pounds for the *Coral Sea* and *Franklin D. Roosevelt*.
The *Midway* has C13 catapults; C11 catapults in the other ships.

Photographs: The unusual flight deck configuration of the *Midway* can be easily compared with the *Franklin D. Roosevelt* in the above views. Note the *Midway's* port-quarter lift, an arrangement not found in the following "Forrestal" class but returned to in later US aircraft carrier designs. Aircraft visible on flight decks include saucer-topped E-2 Hawkeye early warning aircraft alongside the *Midway's* island and the earlier E-1B Tracer AEW aircraft in the same position on the *F.D.R.* When built these ships could accommodate 137 contemporary aircraft.

MIDWAY (CV 41)

1970, United States Navy

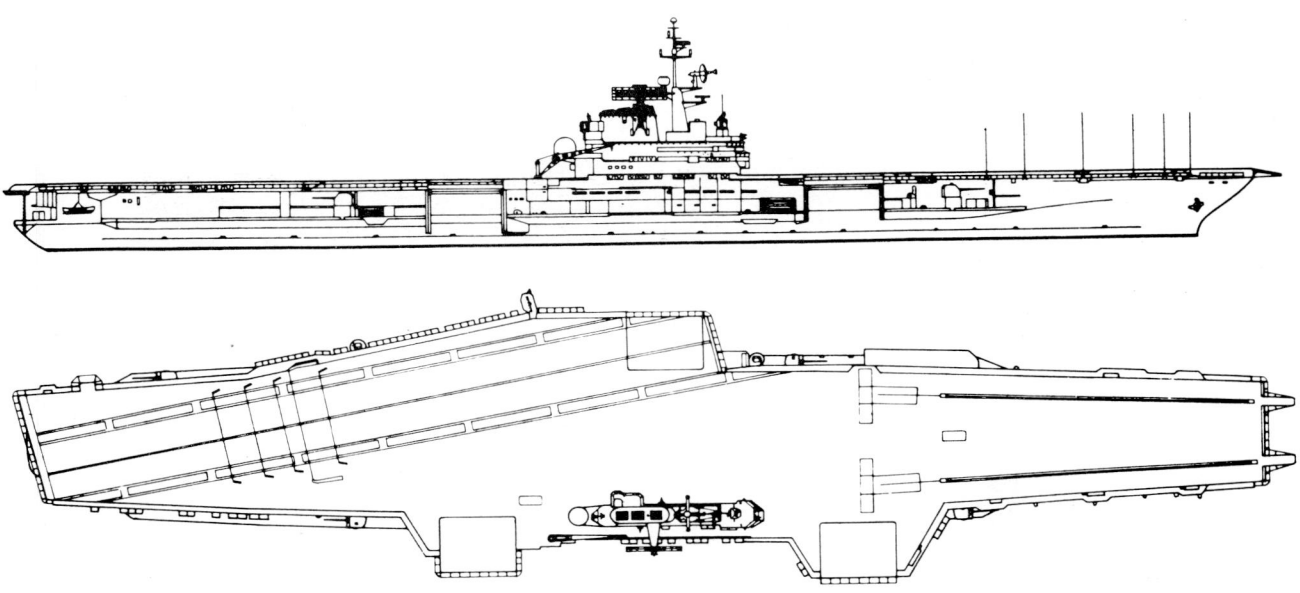

FRANKLIN D. ROOSEVELT (CV 42)

Drawing by A. D. Baker

ORISKANY (CV 34)—see following page

1970, United States Navy

2 ATTACK AIRCRAFT CARRIERS (CVA/CV)
2 ASW AIRCRAFT CARRIERS (CVS)   } "HANCOCK" CLASS
1 TRAINING CARRIER (CVT)

Name	No.	Builders	Laid down	Launched	Commissioned
INTREPID	CVS 11	Newport News Shipbuilding & Dry Dock Co	1 Dec 1941	26 April 1943	16 Aug 1943
*LEXINGTON	CVT 16	Bethlehem Steel Co, Quincy, Mass	15 July 1941	26 Sep 1942	17 Feb 1943
BON HOMME RICHARD	CVA 31	New York Navy Yard	1 Feb 1943	29 April 1944	26 Nov 1944
ORISKANY	CV 34	New York Navy Yard	1 May 1944	13 Oct 1945	25 Sep 1950
SHANGRI-LA	CVS 38	Norfolk Navy Yard	15 Jan 1943	24 Feb 1944	15 Sep 1944

Displacement, tons: approx 32 800 standard, except *Oriskany* 33 250; CVA type: approx 44 700 full load; others approx 42 000 full load except *Lexington* 39 000

Length, feet (metres): 894·5 *(272·6)* oa except *Oriskany* 890 *(271·3)*; 820 *(249·9)* wl

Beam, feet (metres): 103 *(30·8)* except *Oriskany* 106·5 *(32·5)*

Draught, feet (metres): 31 *(9·4)*

Flight deck width, feet (metres): 192 *(58·5)* maximum except *Oriskany* 195 *(59·5)*

Catapults: 2 steam

Aircraft: 70 to 80 for CVA type; approx 45 for CVS type; none assigned to *Lexington*

Guns: 2—5 inch *(127 mm)* 38 cal (Mk 24) dual-purpose (single) in *Oriskany*; 4 guns in other ships except all removed from *Lexington*

Main engines: 4 geared turbines (Westinghouse) 150 000 shp; 4 shafts

Boilers: 8 (Babcock & Wilcox)

Speed, knots: 30+

Complement:
CVA type: *Oriskany* 2 090 (110 officers, 1 980 enlisted men); plus approx 1 185 (135 officers, 1 050 enlisted men) in air wing for a total of approx 3 200 per ship
CVS type: 1 615 (115 officers, approx 1 500 enlisted men) plus approx 800 assigned to ASW air group for a total of 2 400 per ship
Lexington: 1 440 (75 officers, 1 365 enlisted men); no air unit assigned

These ships originally were "Essex" class aircraft carriers; extensively modernised during 1950s, being provided with enclosed, hurricane-bow, angled flight deck, improved elevators, increased aviation fuel storage, and steam catapults (last feature permits operation of more advanced aircraft that can be flown from modernised "Essex" class). Construction of *Oriskany* suspended after World War II and she was completed in 1950 to a modified "Essex" design. See "Essex" class listing for additional notes.

Bon Homme Richard decommissioned on 2 July 1971, *Shangri-La* on 30 July 1971, and *Intrepid* on 15 March 1974; *Oriskany* decommissioned in June 1976; *Lexington* remains in commission as a training carrier (with no aircraft support capability).

Classification: All "Essex" class ships originally were designated as Aircraft Carriers (CV); reclassified as Attack Aircraft Carriers (CVA) in Oct 1952. *Intrepid* reclassified as ASW Support Aircraft Carrier (CVS) on 31 Mar 1962, *Lexington* on 1 Oct 1962, *Shangri-La* on 30 June 1969. The *Lexington* became the Navy's training aircraft carrier in the Gulf of Mexico on 29 Dec 1962; reclassified CVT on 1 Jan 1969.
Oriskany redesignated as CV on 30 June 1975 (as was now-stricken *Hancock*).

Electronics: The *Oriskany* conducted the initial sea trials of the Naval Tactical Data System (NTDS) in 1961-1962.
The principal radars in these ships are SPS-43, SPS-30, and SPS-10 search radars, and SPN-10 navigation radar, except *Lexington* has SPS-43, SPS-12, SPS-10 and SPN-10 (the SPS-8 formerly mounted has been removed). TACAN aircraft navigation pods stop their masts.
These ships are generally fitted with one Mk 37 gunfire control system and one or more Mk 56 GFCS.

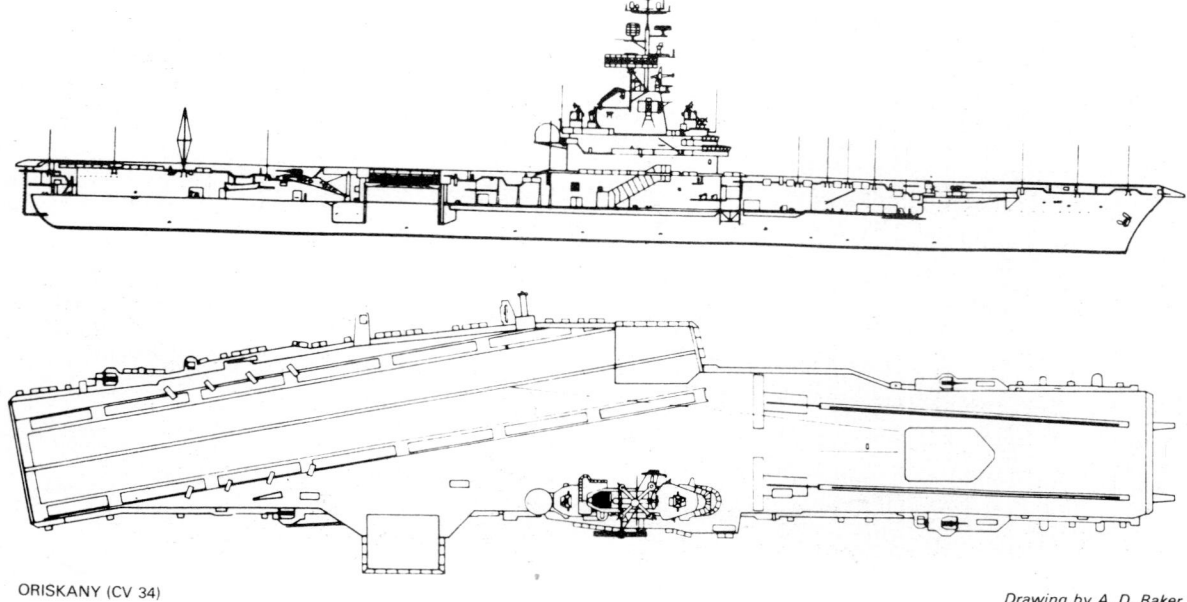

BON HOMME RICHARD (CVA 31)

1970, United States Navy

Modernisation: These ships have been modernised under several programmes to increase their ability to operate more-advanced aircraft. The *Oriskany* was completed with some post-war ("jet age") features incorporated. The most prominent difference from their original configuration is angled flight deck and removal of twin 5-inch gun mounts from flight deck forward and aft of island structure. Three elevators fitted; "Pointed" centreline lift forward between catapults, deckedge lift on port side at leading edge of angled deck, and deckedge lift on starboard side of island structure. Minimal gun battery retained (see description of original armament under "Essex" class listings). Remaining guns removed from *Lexington* in 1969; by 1975 the *Oriskany* had only 2—5 inch guns fitted.

Operational: As of early 1975 the *Lexington* had recorded 340 000 arrested aircraft landings during her operational career (1943-1947, 1955-present). The *Lexington* is expected to be relieved as a training carrier based at Pensacola, Florida, during the late 1970s by one of the "Midway" class ships.

Nomenclature: All 24 "Essex" class carriers were named for early American ships or battles except for *Shangri-La*, which is named for the imaginary locale in James Hilton's novel which President Roosevelt told the press was the base for the Doolittle-Halsey raid against Japan in 1942. Several ships renamed during construction to carry on names of carriers lost in battle.

Disposals: (since 1 Jan 1975) *Hancock* (CV 19) stricken on 31 Jan 1975.

ORISKANY (CV 34)

Drawing by A. D. Baker

4 NUCLEAR-POWERED GUIDED MISSILE CRUISERS (CGN): "VIRGINIA" CLASS

Name	No.	Builders	Laid down	Launched	Commission
VIRGINIA	CGN 38 (ex-DLGN 38)	Newport News Shipbuilding & Dry Dock Co	19 Aug 1972	14 Dec 1974	Mid 1976
TEXAS	CGN 39 (ex-DLGN 39)	Newport News Shipbuilding & Dry Dock Co	18 Aug 1973	9 Aug 1975	Mid 1977
MISSISSIPPI	CGN 40 (ex-DLGN 40)	Newport News Shipbuilding & Dry Dock Co	22 Feb 1975	July 1976	Mid 1978
ARKANSAS	CGN 41	Newport News Shipbuilding & Dry Dock Co			1980

Displacement, tons: 11 000 full load
Length, feet (metres): 585 (177·3) oa
Beam, feet (metres): 63 (18·9)
Draught, feet (metres): 29·5 (9·0)
Helicopters: 2 (see Helicopter notes)
Missile launchers: 2 combination twin Tartar-D/ASROC launchers firing Standard MR surface-to-air missile (Mk 26)
Guns: 2—5 inch (127 mm) 54 calibre dual-purpose (Mk 45) (single)
A/S weapons: ASROC (see above); 2 triple torpedo tubes (Mk 32)
Main engines: 2 geared turbines; 2 shafts
Reactors: 2 pressurised-water cooled D2G (General Electric)
Speed, knots: 30+
Complement: 442 (27 officers, 415 enlisted men)

The *Virginia* was authorised in the Fiscal Year 1970 new construction programme, the *Texas* in FY 1971, the *Mississippi* in FY 1972, and the *Arkansas* in FY 1975.
The CGN 42 was proposed in the FY 1976 new construction programme but was not funded by the Congress.
Construction of this class has been delayed because of a shortage of skilled labour in the shipyard. Newport News SB & DD Co (Virginia) is the only shipyard in the United States now

engaged in the construction of nuclear surface ships. The first three ships of the class are more than one year behind their original construction schedules. Additional delays are anticipated.

Classification: These ships were originally classified as guided missile frigates (DLGN); subsequently reclassified as guided missile cruisers (CGN) on 30 June 1975.

Design: The principal differences between the "Virginia" and "California" classes are the improved anti-air warfare capability, electronic warfare equipment, and anti-submarine fire control system. The deletion of the ASROC "pepper-box" Mk 16 launcher permitted the later ships to be ten feet shorter.

Electronics: These ships will have bow-mounted SQS-53A sonar (improved SQS-26 series); also to have Naval Tactical Data System (NTDS), SPS-48A three-dimensional radar, SPS-40B and SPS-55 radar antennae.

Fiscal: These ships have incurred major cost growth/escalation during their construction. Fiscal data on the earlier ships were in the 1974-1975 and earlier editions.
The CGN 42 was estimated to cost $368 000 000 ($257 000 000 proposed in FY 1976 and $111 000 000 in FY 1970-1975).

Gunnery: These ships will have Mk 86 gunfire control directors.

Helicopters: A hangar for helicopters is installed beneath the fantail flight-deck with a telescoping hatch cover and an electro-mechanical elevator provided to transport helicopters between the main deck and hangar. These are the first US post-World War II destroyer/cruiser ships with a hull hangar.

Missiles: The initial design for this class provided for a single surface-to-air missile launcher; revised in 1969 to provide two Mk 26 launchers that will fire the Standard-Medium Range (MR) surface-to-air missile and the ASROC anti-submarine missile. "Mixed" Standard/ASROC magazines are planned for each launcher. The digital Mk 116 ASW fire control system will simplify weapon system interfaces compared to previous US missile-armed warships. Mk 74 missile control directors.

Drawing: Chaff-rocket (CHAFROC) launchers are shown forward of bridge and aft of boat davits with triple anti-submarine torpedo tubes also aft of boat davits; "California" design on the following page has the torpedo tubes built into superstructure. Note enclosed radar towers, similar to "California" class.
For the photographs of the *South Carolina* the helicopter markings forward indicate helicopter vertical replenishment (VERT-REP) station; markings aft are for helicopter landing area.

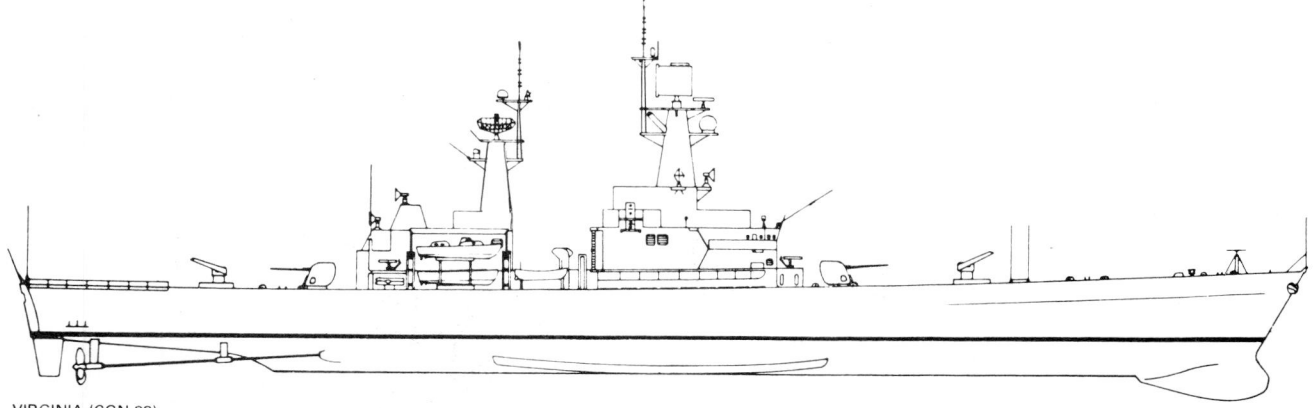

VIRGINIA (CGN 38)   *Drawing by A. D. Baker*

SOUTH CAROLINA (CGN 37)—see following page

1974, Newport News SB & DD Co.

2 NUCLEAR-POWERED GUIDED MISSILE CRUISERS (CGN): "CALIFORNIA" CLASS

Name	No.	Builders	Laid down	Launched	Commissioned
*CALIFORNIA	CGN 36	Newport News Shipbuilding & Dry Dock Co	23 Jan 1970	22 Sep 1971	16 Feb 1974
*SOUTH CAROLINA	CGN 37	Newport News Shipbuilding & Dry Dock Co	1 Dec 1970	1 July 1972	25 Jan 1975

Displacement, tons: 10 150 full load
Length, feet (metres): 596 *(181·7)* oa
Beam, feet (metres): 61 *(18·6)*
Draught, feet (metres): 31·5 *(9·6)*
Missile launchers: 2 single Tartar-D surface-to-air launchers firing Standard MR (Mk 13 Mod 3)
Guns: 2—5 inch *(127 mm)* 54 calibre dual-purpose (Mk 45) (single)
A/S weapons: 4 torpedo tubes (Mk 32); 1 ASROC 8-tube launcher
Main engines: 2 geared turbines; 2 shafts
Nuclear reactors: 2 pressurised-water cooled D2G (General Electric)
Speed, knots: 30+
Complement: 540 (28 officers, 512 enlisted men)

These are large, multi-purpose warships intended primarily to operate with fast carrier forces. Their high-speed and endurance capabilities also make them suitable for independent operations.

The *California* was authorised in the Fiscal Year 1967 new construction programme and the *South Carolina* in the FY 1968 programme. The construction of a third ship of this class (DLGN 38) was also authorised in FY 1968, but the rising costs of these ships and development of the DXGN/DLGN 38 design (now "Virginia" class) caused the third ship to be deferred. Both ships are active.

Classification: These ships were originally classified as guided missile frigates (DLGN); subsequently reclassified as guided missile cruisers (CGN) on 30 June 1975.

Design: These ships have tall, enclosed towers supporting radar antennae in contrast to the open lattice masts of the previous nuclear frigates *Truxtun* and *Bainbridge*.
No helicopter support facilities are provided.

Electronics: Fitted with bow-mounted SQS-26CX sonar and the Naval Tactical Data System (NTDS). These ships have SPS-48 three-dimensional, SPS-10 and SPS-40 search radars. Also provided with two Mk 74 Mod 4 missile fire control systems, one Mk 86 Mod 3 gunfire control system, one Mk II Mod 3 weapons direction system, and four SPG-51D, one SPG-60, and one SPQ-9A weapon control radars.

Engineering: Estimated nuclear core life for these ships provides 700 000 miles "range"; estimated cost is $11 500 000 for the two initial nuclear cores in each ship.

Fiscal: Estimated cost is $200 000 000 for *California* and $180 000 000 for *South Carolina*. See 1971-1972 edition for funding history.

Missiles: Reportedly, these ships carry some 80 surface-to-air missiles divided equally between a magazine beneath each launcher.

Photographs: The "California" class can be distinguished from the subsequent "Virginia" class cruisers by the ASROC launcher and "reload house" forward of the bridge and the after 5 inch gun being one level above the main deck in the earlier ships. Note the tower-like mast structures in both US classes; similar to the Soviet missile cruiser designs.

SOUTH CAROLINA (CGN 37)   *1974, United States Navy*

CALIFORNIA (CGN 36)   *1975, United States Navy, PH1 W. J. Pointer*

CALIFORNIA (CGN 36)   *1975, United States Navy*

1 NUCLEAR-POWERED GUIDED MISSILE CRUISER (CGN): "TRUXTUN" TYPE

Name	No.	Builders	Laid down	Launched	Commissioned
*TRUXTUN	CGN 35	New York Shipbuilding Corp (Camden, New Jersey)	17 June 1963	19 Dec 1964	27 May 1967

Displacement, tons: 8 200 standard; 9 200 full load
Length, feet (metres): 564 (117·9) oa
Beam, feet (metres): 58 (17·7)
Draught, feet (metres): 31 (9·4)
Missile launchers: 1 twin Standard ER/ASROC launcher (Mk 10 Mod 7)
Guns: 1—5 inch (127 mm) 54 calibre dual purpose (Mk 42)
2—3 inch (76 mm) 50 calibre anti-aircraft (Mk 34) (single)
A/S weapons: ASROC (see above)
4 fixed torpedo tubes (Mk 32)
facilities for helicopter
Main engines: 2 geared turbines; approx 60 000 shp; 2 shafts
Nuclear reactors: 2 pressurised-water cooled D2G (General Electric)
Speed, knots: 30+
Complement: approx 500 (35 officers, 455 enlisted men)
Flag accommodations: 18 (6 officers, 12 enlisted men)

The *Truxtun* was the US Navy's fourth nuclear-powered surface warship. The Navy had requested seven oil-burning frigates in the Fiscal Year 1962 shipbuilding programme, the Congress authorised seven ships; but stipulated that one ship must be nuclear-powered.
Although the *Truxtun* design is adapted from the "Belknap" class design, the nuclear ship's gun-missile launcher arrangement is reversed from the non-nuclear ships.
Construction cost was $138 667 000.

Classification: The *Truxtun* was originally classified as a guided missile frigate (DLGN); subsequently reclassified as a guided missile cruiser (CGN) on 30 June 1975.

Electronics: The *Truxtun* has bow-mounted SQS-26 sonar and the Naval Tactical Data System (NTDS). Fitted with SPS-48 three-dimensionsl and SPS-10 search radars on forward mast and an SPS-40 search radar and TACAN (Tactical Aircraft Navigation) "pod" on after mast.
Also provided with the Mk 76 Mod 4 missile control system, one Mk 68 Mod 8 gunfire control system, two Mk 51 Mod 3 gun directors, one Mk 11 Mod 1 weapon direction system, one SPG-53A and two SPG-55B weapon control radars.

Engineering: Power plant is identical to that of the cruiser *Bainbridge*.

TRUXTUN (CGN 35)

1970, United States Navy

Missiles: The twin missile launcher aft can fire Standard ER anti-aircraft missiles and ASROC anti-submarine rockets.

Nomenclature: The *Truxtun* is the fifth ship to be named for Commodore Thomas Truxton (sic) who commanded the frigate *Constellation* (38 guns) in her successful encounter with the French frigate *L'Insurgente* (44) in 1799.

Torpedoes: Fixed Mk 32 tubes are below 3-inch gun "tubs", built into superstructure. The two Mk 25 torpedo tubes built into her stern are not used.

Photographs: The *Truxtun* can be readily identified by her squared lattice radar masts, empty "B" gun position and lack of funnel. Two chaff rocket (CHAFROC) launchers subsequently have been fitted in the "B" position.

TRUXTUN (CGN 35)

1970, United States Navy

JOSEPHUS DANIELS (CG 27)—see following page

1973, Giorgio Arra

9 GUIDED MISSILE CRUISERS (CG): "BELKNAP" CLASS

Name	No.	Builders	Laid down	Launched	Commissioned
*BELKNAP	CG 26	Bath Iron Works Corp	5 Feb 1962	20 July 1963	7 Nov 1964
*JOSEPHUS DANIELS	CG 27	Bath Iron Works Corp	23 April1962	2 Dec 1963	8 May 1965
*WAINWRIGHT	CG 28	Bath Iron Works Corp	2 July 1962	25 April1964	8 Jan 1966
*JOUETT	CG 29	Puget Sound Naval Shipyard	25 Sep 1962	30 June1964	3 Dec 1966
*HORNE	CG 30	San Francisco Naval Shipyard	12 Dec 1962	30 Oct 1964	15 Apr 1967
*STERETT	CG 31	Puget Sound Naval Shipyard	25 Sep 1962	30 June1964	8 Apr 1967
*WILLIAM H. STANDLEY	CG 32	Bath Iron Works Corp	29 July 1963	19 Dec 1964	9 July 1966
*FOX	CG 33	Todd Shipyard Corp	15 Jan 1963	21 Nov 1964	8 May 1966
*BIDDLE	CG 34	Bath Iron Works Corp	9 Dec 1963	2 July 1965	21 Jan 1967

Displacement, tons: 6 570 standard; 7 930 full load
Length, feet (metres): 547 (166·7) oa
Beam, feet (metres): 54·8 (16·7)
Draught, feet (metres): 28·8 (8·7)
Helicopters: 1 SH-2D LAMPS helicopter
Missile launchers: 1 twin Standard ER/ASROC launcher (Mk 10 Mod 7)
Guns: 1—5 inch (127 mm) 54 cal dual-purpose (Mk 42)
2—3 inch (76 mm) 50 cal anti-aircraft (Mk 34) (single)
A/S weapons: ASROC (see above); 2 triple torpedo tubes (Mk 32)
Main engines: 2 geared turbines (General Electric in CG 26-28, 32, 34; De Laval in CG 29-31, 33): 85 000 shp; 2 shafts
Boilers: 4 (Babcock & Wilcox in CG 26-28, 32, 34; Combustion Engineering in CG 29-31, 33)
Speed, knots: 34
Complement: 418 (31 officers, 387 enlisted men) including squadron staff
Flag accommodations: 18 (6 officers; 12 enlisted men)

These ships were authorised as guided missile frigates; DLG 26-28 in the Fiscal Year 1961 shipbuilding programme; DLG 29-34 in the FY 1962 programme.
All ships of this class are active except the *Belknap*, which was severely damaged in a collision with the carrier *John F. Kennedy* (CV 67) on 22 Nov 1975 near Sicily; the cruiser was towed back to the United States for rebuilding, estimated to take about two years.

Classification: These ships were originally classified as guided missile frigates (DLG); reclassified as guided missile cruisers (CG) on 30 June 1975.

Design: These ships are distinctive by having their single missile launcher forward and 5 inch gun mount aft. This arrangement allowed missile stowage in the larger bow section and provided space aft of the superstructure for a helicopter hangar and platform. The reverse gun-missile arrangement, preferred by some commanding officers, is found in the *Truxtun*. The "Belknap" class ships have their masts and stacks combined into "mack" structures.

Electronics: SQS-26 bow-mounted sonar installed. These ships have the Naval Tactical Data System (NTDS). Fitted with SPS-48 three-dimensional and SPS-10 search radars on their forward "mack" and an SPS-37 (first three ships) or SPS-40 search radar and small TACAN (Tactical Aircraft Navigation) pod on their after "mack".
Also provided with two Mk 76 Mod 4 missile control systems, one Mk 68 Mod 8 gunfire control system, two Mk 51 Mod 3 gun directors, one Mk 11 Mod 0 weapon direction system, one SPG-53A and two SPG-55B weapon control radars.

Gunnery: The 5 inch guns were installed previously on forward The *Belknap* will be fitted with the Phalanx 20 mm Close-In Weapon System (CIWS) during rebuilding.

Helicopters: These ships are the only conventionally powered US cruisers with a full helicopter support capability. All fitted with the Light Airborne Multi-Purpose System, now the SH-2D helicopter. The *Belknap* embarked the first operational SH-2D/LAMPS in December 1971. Note built up structure atop hangar in *Josephus Daniels* on previous page.

Missiles: The *Truxtun* and "Belknap" class ships have a twin Terrier/ASROC Mk 10 missile launcher. A "triple-ring" rotating magazine stocks both Terrier anti-aircraft missiles and ASROC anti-submarine rockets, feeding either weapon to the launcher's two firing arms. The rate of fire and reliability of the launcher provide a potent AAW/ASW capability to these ships.

Torpedoes: As built, these ships each had two 21 inch tubes for anti-submarine torpedoes installed in the structure immediately forward of the 5 inch mount, one tube angled out to port and one to starboard; subsequently removed.

STERETT (CG 31)   1972, United States Navy

WILLIAM H. STANDLEY (CG 32)   1975, Giorgio Arra

JOSEPHUS DANIELS (CG 27)   1972, Giorgio Arra

1 NUCLEAR-POWERED GUIDED MISSILE CRUISER (CGN): "BAINBRIDGE" TYPE

Name	No.	Builders	Laid down	Launched	Commissioned
*BAINBRIDGE	CGN 25	Bethlehem Steel Co (Quincy, Mass)	15 May 1959	15 April 1961	6 Oct 1962

Displacement, tons: 7 600 standard; 8 580 full load
Length, feet (metres): 550 *(167·6)* wl; 565 *(172·5)* oa
Beam, feet (metres): 57·9 *(17·6)*
Draught, feet (metres): 29 *(7·9)*
Missile launchers: 2 twin Standard ER surface-to-air launchers
Guns: 4—3 inch *(76 mm)* 50 calibre anti-aircraft (Mk 33) (twin)
A/S weapons: 1 ASROC 8-tube launcher; 2-triple torpedo tubes (Mk 32)
Main engines: 2 geared turbines, approx 60 000 shp; 2 shafts
Nuclear reactors: 2 pressurised-water cooled D2G (General Electric)
Speed, knots: 30+
Complement: approx 450 (26 officers, approx 425 enlisted men)
Flag accommodations: 18 (6 officers, 12 enlisted men)

The *Bainbridge* was the US Navy's third nuclear powered surface warship (after the cruiser *Long Beach* and the aircraft carrier *Enterprise*). The *Bainbridge* was authorised in the Fiscal Year 1956 shipbuilding programme. Construction cost was $163 610 000.
The ship is active.

Classification: The *Bainbridge* was originally classified as a guided missile frigate (DLGN); reclassified as a guided missile cruiser (CGN) on 30 June 1975.

Design: The ship is similar in basic arrangements to the "Leahy" class cruisers; however, the nuclear ship has two heavy lattice radar masts in place of the "mack" structures of the conventional ships.

Electronics: Fitted with SQS-23 bow-mounted sonar.
The *Bainbridge* has SPS-52 three-dimensional search radar and SPS-10 search radar on her forward mast, and an SPS-37 search radar antenna on her after mast.
Also provided with two Mk 76 Mod 1 missile control systems, two Mk 63 Mod 28 gunfire control systems, one Mk 7 Mod 0 weapons direction system, two SPG-50 and four SPG-55A weapon control radars.

Engineering: Development of a nuclear power plant suitable for use in a large "destroyer type" warship began in 1957. The Atomic Energy Commission's Knolls Atomic Power Laboratory undertook development of the destroyer power plant (designated D1G/D2G).

Missiles: The *Bainbridge* has a Terrier Mk 10 Mod 5 launcher forward and a Mk 10 Mod 6 launcher aft. Reportedly, the ship Carries 80 missiles divided between the forward and aft rotating magazines.

Modernisation: The *Bainbridge* underwent an Anti-Air Warfare (AAW) modernisation at the Puget Sound Naval Shipyard in 1974-1976. The ship was fitted with the Naval Tactical Data System (NTDS) and improved guidance capability for missiles. Estimated cost of modernisation $103 000 000.

BAINBRIDGE (CGN 25)

1971, United States Navy

9 GUIDED MISSILE CRUISERS (CG): "LEAHY" CLASS

Name	No.	Builders	Laid down	Launched	Commissioned
*LEAHY	CG 16	Bath Iron Works Corp	3 Dec 1959	1 July 1961	4 Aug 1962
*HARRY E. YARNELL	CG 17	Bath Iron Works Corp	31 May 1960	9 Dec 1961	2 Feb 1963
*WORDEN	CG 18	Bath Iron Works Corp	19 Sep 1960	2 June1962	3 Aug 1963
*DALE	CG 19	New York SB Corp	6 Sep 1960	28 July 1962	23 Nov 1963
*RICHMOND K. TURNER	CG 20	New York SB Corp	9 Jan 1961	6 Apr 1963	13 June1964
*GRIDLEY	CG 21	Puget Sound Bridge & Dry Dock Co	15 July 1960	31 July 1961	25 May 1963
*ENGLAND	CG 22	Todd Shipyards Corp	4 Oct 1960	6 Mar 1962	7 Dec 1963
*HALSEY	CG 23	San Francisco Naval Shipyard	26 Aug 1960	15 Jan 1962	20 July 1963
*REEVES	CG 24	Puget Sound Naval Shipyard	1 July 1960	12 May 1962	16 May 1964

Displacement, tons: 5 670 standard; 7 800 full load
Length, feet (metres): 533 *(162·5)* oa
Beam, feet (metres): 54·9 *(16·6)*
Draught, feet (metres): 24·5 *(7·4)*
Missile launchers: 2 twin Standard-ER surface-to-air launchers (Mk 10 Mod 5 and Mod 6)
Guns: 4—3 inch *(76 mm)* 50 cal anti-aircraft (Mk 33) (twin)
A/S weapons: 1 ASROC 8-tube launcher; 2 triple torpedo tubes (Mk 32)
Main engines: 2 geared turbines (see *Engineering* notes); 85 000 shp; 2 shafts
Boilers: 4 (Babcock & Wilcox in CG 16-18, Foster Wheeler in 19-24)
Speed, knots: 34
Complement: 396 (31 officers, 365 enlisted men)
Flag accommodations: 18 (6 officers, 12 enlisted men)

These ships are "double-end" missile cruisers especially designed to screen fast carrier task forces. They are limited in only having 3 inch guns in comparison with 5 inch or larger calibre guns in other US missile cruisers. This class was authorised as DLG 16-18 in the Fiscal Year 1958 new construction programme and DLG 19-24 in the FY 1959 programme. All nine ships are active.

Classification: These ships were originally classified as guided missile frigates (DLG); reclassified as guided missile cruisers (CG) on 30 June 1975.

Design: These ships are distinctive in having twin missile launchers forward and aft with ASROC "pepper box" launcher between the forward missile launcher and bridge on main deck level. Masts and stacks are combined into "macks".
There is a helicopter landing area aft but only limited support facilities are provided; no hangar.

HARRY E. YARNELL (CG 17)

1971, United States Navy

Electronics: These ships were fitted with the Naval Tactical Data System (NTDS) during AAW modernisation. SQS-23 bow mounted sonar installed. These ships have SPS-10 and SPS-48 search radars on forward mast (the latter replacing SPS-39 or SPS-52 in some ships) and an SPS-37 search radar on their after mast.

"LEAHY" CLASS—*continued*

Also provided with four Mk 76 Mod 5 missile control systems (except two in *Halsey,* two Mk 63 Mod 28 gunfire control systems), one Mk 11 Mod 2 weapon direction system, two SPG-50 and four SPG-55B weapon control radars.

Engineering: General Electric turbines in CG 16-18, De Laval turbines in CG 19-22, and Allis-Chalmers turbines in CG 23 and CG 24.

Missiles: Reportedly, each ship carries 80 missiles divided between the two magazines.

Modernisation: These ships were modernised between 1967 and 1972 to improve their Anti-Air Warfare (AAW) capabilities. Superstructure enlarged to provide space for additional electronic equipment, including NTDS; improved TACAN fitted and improved guidance system for Terrier/Standard missiles installed, and larger ship's service turbo generators provided. All ships modernised at Bath Iron Works except *Leahy* at Philadelphia Naval Shipyard.
Cost of *Leahy* modernisation was $36 100 000.

Nomenclature: The *England* is the second US warship to honour a sailor killed at Pearl Harbor on 7 Dec 1941; the first *England* (DE 635) sank six Japanese submarines in just 12 days during May of 1944.

Photographs: These ships can be distinguished from other non-nuclear missile cruisers by having twin surface-to-air missile launchers forward and aft, and from all other new missile cruisers by the absence of distinctive 5 inch gun mounts.

HARRY E. YARNELL (CG 17)   *1972, Giorgio Arra*

DALE (CG 19)   *1973, Giorgio Arra*

COLUMBUS (CG 12)—see following page   *1972, Giorgio Arra*

3 GUIDED MISSILE CRUISERS (CG): "ALBANY" CLASS

Name	No.	Builders	Laid down	Launched	Commissioned	CG Comm.
*ALBANY	CG 10 (ex-CA 123)	Bethlehem Steel Co (Quincy)	6 Mar 1944	30 June1945	15 June1946	3 Nov 1962
*CHICAGO	CG 11 (ex-CA 136)	Philadelphia Navy Yard	28 July 1943	20 Aug 1944	1 Jan 1945	2 May 1964
COLUMBUS	CG 12 (ex-CA 74)	Bethlehem Steel Co (Quincy)	28 June1943	30 Nov 1944	8 June1945	1 Dec 1962

Displacement, tons: 13 700 standard; 17 500 full load
Length, feet (metres): 664 *(202·4)* wl; 673 *(205·3)* oa
Beam, feet (metres): 70 *(21·6)*
Draught, feet (metres): 27 *(8·2)*
Missile launchers:
 2 twin Talos surface-to-air launchers (Mk 12 Mod 1)
 2 twin Tartar surface-to-air launchers (Mk 11 Mod 1 and Mod 2)
Guns: 2—5 inch *(127 mm)* 38 calibre dual-purpose (Mk 24) (single)
A/S weapons: 1 ASROC 8-tube launcher; 2 triple torpedo tubes (Mk 32)
Helicopters: Utility helicopters carried
Main engines: 4 geared turbines (General Electric); 120 000 shp; 4 shafts
Boilers: 4 (Babcock & Wilcox)
Speed, knots: 33
Complement: 1 000 (60 officers, approx 940 enlisted men)
Flag accommodations: 68 (10 officers, 58 enlisted men)

These ships were fully converted from heavy cruisers, the *Albany* having been a unit of the "Oregon City" class and the *Chicago* and *Columbus* of the "Baltimore" class. Although the two heavy cruiser classes differed in appearance they had the same hull dimensions and machinery. These three missile ships form a new, homogeneous class.

The cruiser *Fall River* (CA 131) was originally scheduled for missile conversion, but was replaced by the *Columbus.* Proposals to convert two additional heavy cruisers (CA 124 and CA 130) to missile ships (CG 13 and CG 14) were dropped, primarily because of high conversion costs and improved capabilities of newer missile-armed frigates.

The *Columbus* was decommissioned on 31 January 1975 and placed in reserve; other ships are active.

Conversion: During conversion to missile configuration these ships were stripped down to their main hulls with all cruiser armament and superstructure being removed. New superstructures make extensive use of aluminium to reduce weight and improve stability. Former masts and stacks were replaced by "macks" which support electronic antennae and have machinery exhausts vented from sides near top. The *Albany* was converted at the Boston Naval Shipyard between January 1959 and November 1962; the *Columbus* at Puget Sound Naval Shipyard from June 1959 to March 1963; and *Chicago* at San Francisco Naval Shipyard from July 1959 to September 1964.

Electronics: These ships are fitted with SQS-23 sonar which is linked to the ASROC fire control system. The Naval Tactical Data System (NTDS) is fitted in the *Albany* and *Chicago.*

The radar arrangements differ slightly; the *Albany* has SPS-48 three-dimensional and SPS-10 search radars on her forward "mack", an SPS-43 radar on her second "mack", and an SPS-30 on the after platform; the *Chicago* has SPS-30 aft, SPS-52 and SPS-10 on her forward "mack", and an SPS-43 on her after "mack"; the *Columbus* had SPS-30 forward and aft, and an SPS-10 search radar on her forward "mack", and an SPS-43 on her after "mack".

Also provided with two Mk 77 Mod 3 missile fire control systems, four Mk 74 Mod 1 missile fire control systems, two Mk 56 Mod 43 gunfire control systems, one Mk 6 Mod 2 or Mod 3 weapon direction system, four SPG-49B and four SPG-51C weapon control radars.

Gunnery: No guns were fitted when these ships were converted to missile cruisers. Two single open-mount 5 inch guns were fitted subsequently to provide minimal defence against low-flying, subsonic aircraft or torpedo boat attacks.

Missiles: One twin Talos launcher is forward and one aft, a twin Tartar launcher is on each side of the main bridge structure. During conversion, space was allocated amidships for installation of eight Polaris missile tubes, but the plan to install ballistic missiles in cruisers was cancelled in mid-1959. Reportedly 92 Talos and 80 Tartar missiles are carried.

CHICAGO (CG 11)

1975, United States Navy

Modernisation: The *Albany* underwent an extensive anti-air warfare modernisation at the Boston Naval Shipyard; "conversion" began in February 1967 and was completed in August 1969. She was formally recommissioned on 9 Nov 1968. The *Chicago* and *Columbus* will not have AAW modernisations. The *Albany's* AAW conversion included installation of NTDS, a digital Talos fire-control system which provides faster and more reliable operation, and improved radars.

ALBANY (CG 10)

1972, Giorgio Arra

1 NUCLEAR-POWERED GUIDED MISSILE CRUISER (CGN): "LONG BEACH" TYPE

Name	No.	Builders	Laid down	Launched	Commissioned
*LONG BEACH	CGN 9 (ex-CGN 160, CLGN 160)	Bethlehem Steel Co. (Quincy, Massachusetts)	2 Dec 1957	14 July 1959	9 Sep 1961

Displacement, tons: 14 200 standard; 17 350 full load
Length, feet (metres): 721·2 *(219·8)* oa
Beam, feet (metres): 73·2 *(22·3)*
Draught, feet (metres): 29 *(8·8)*
Missile launchers: 1 twin Talos surface-to-air launcher (Mk 12 Mod 0); 2 twin Standard-ER surface-to-air launchers (Mk 10 Mod 1 and 2)
Guns: 2—5 inch *(127 mm)* 38 calibre dual-purpose (Mk 30) (single)
A/S weapons: 1 ASROC 8-tube launcher; 2 triple torpedo tubes (Mk 32)
Helicopter: Utility helicopter carried
Main engines: 2 geared turbines (General Electric); approx 80 000 shp; 2 shafts
Nuclear reactors: 2 pressurised water cooled C1W (Westinghouse)
Speed, knots: approx 35
Complement: 1 060 (60 officers, approx 1 000 enlisted men)
Flag accommodations: 68 (10 officers, 58 enlisted men)

The *Long Beach* was the first ship to be designed and constructed from the keel up as a cruiser for the United States since the end of World War II. She is the world's first nuclear-powered surface warship and the first warship to have a guided missile main battery. She was authorised in the Fiscal Year 1957 new construction programme. Estimated construction cost was $332 850 000. Construction was delayed because of a shipyard strike.

Classification: The *Long Beach* was ordered as a guided missile light cruiser (CLGN 160) on 15 Oct 1956; reclassified as a guided missile cruiser (CGN 160) early in 1957 and renumbered (CGN 9) on 1 July 1957. Through 1975 all US guided missile cruisers were numbered in a single series: CAG 1-2, CLG 3-8, CGN 9, and CG 10-12.

Design: The *Long Beach* was initially planned as a large destroyer or "frigate" of about 7 800 tons (standard displacement) to test the feasibility of a nuclear-powered surface warship. Early in 1956 the decision was made to capitalise on the capabilities of nuclear propulsion and her displacement was increased to 11 000 tons and a second Terrier missile launcher was added to the design. A Talos missile launcher was also added to the design which, with other features, increased displacement to 14 000 tons by the time the contract was signed for her construction on 15 October 1956.

Electronics: The *Long Beach* has fixed-array ("billboard") radar which provides increased range over rotating antennae. Horizontal antennae on bridge superstructure are for SPS-32 bearing and range radar; vertical antennae are for SPS-33 target tracking radar. The SPS-33 uses an "S" band frequency and the SPS-32 is VHF; both frequency scan in elevation. Developed and produced by Hughes Aircraft, they are believed the first operational fixed-array radar systems in the Western world. Also installed in the nuclear-powered aircraft carrier *Enterprise* (CVN 65).
SPS-12 and SPS-10 search radars are mounted on the forward mast. Four Mk 76 Mod 1 missile fire control systems, one Mk 77

Mod 4 missile fire control system, two Mk 56 gunfire control systems, one Mk 6 weapon direction system, two SPG-49B and four SPG-55A weapon-control radars.
The SPS-32/33 "Scanfar" radars and the associated computers were modified in 1970 to improve performance. She is equipped with Naval Tactical Data System (NTDS) and SQS-23 sonar.

Engineering: The reactors are similar to those of the nuclear-powered aircraft carrier *Enterprise* (CVN 65). The *Long Beach* first got underway on nuclear power on 5 July 1961. After four years of operation and having steamed more than 167 700 miles she underwent her first overhaul and refuelling at the Newport News Shipbuilding and Dry Dock Company from August 1965 to February 1966.

Gunnery: Completed with an all-missile armament. Two single 5 inch mounts were fitted during 1962-1963 year period to provide defence against low-flying subsonic aircraft and torpedo boats.

Missiles: The *Long Beach* has two Terrier twin missile launchers stepped forward and one Talos twin missile launcher aft. Reportedly, her magazines hold 120 Terrier missiles and approx 46 Talos missiles.

Modernisation: A "mid-life" modernisation is planned for the late 1970s; under consideration is installation of the Aegis electronics/missile system. The estimated Aegis installation cost in FY 1976 dollars is $400 000 000.

LONG BEACH (CGN 9)

1968, United States Navy

SPRINGFIELD (CG 7)—see following page

1973, United States Navy, PH2 H. E. Deffenbaugh

4 GUIDED MISSILE CRUISERS (CG): CONVERTED "CLEVELAND" CLASS

Name	No.	Builders	Laid down	Launched	Commissioned	CLG Comm.
*LITTLE ROCK	CG 4 (ex-CLG 4, ex-CL 92)	Cramp Shipbuilding (Philadelphia)	6 Mar 1943	27 Aug 1944	17 June1945	3 June1960
*OKLAHOMA CITY	CG 5 (ex-CLG 5, ex-CL 91)	Cramp Shipbuilding (Philadelphia)	8 Mar 1942	20 Feb 1944	22 Dec 1944	7 Sep 1960
PROVIDENCE	CG 6 (ex-CLG 6, ex-CL 82)	Bethlehem Steel Co. (Quincy)	27 July 1943	28 Dec 1944	15 May 1945	17 Sep 1959
SPRINGFIELD	CG 7 (ex-CLG 7, ex-CL 66)	Bethlehem Steel Co. (Quincy)	13 Feb 1943	9 Mar 1944	9 Sep 1944	2 July 1960

Displacement, tons: 10 670 standard; 14 600 full load
Length, feet (metres): 600 *(182·9)* wl; 610 *(185·9)* oa
Beam, feet (metres): 66·3 *(20·2)*
Draught, feet (metres): 25 *(7·6)*
Missile launchers:
CG 4, 5: 1 twin Talos surface-to-air launcher (Mk 7 Mod 0)
CG 6, 7: 1 twin Terrier surface-to-air launcher (Mk 9 Mod 1)
Guns: 3—6 inch *(152 mm)* 47 cal (triple); 2—5 inch *(127 mm)* 38 cal dual-purpose (Mk 32) (twin)
Helicopters: Utility helicopter carried
Main engines: 4 geared turbines (General Electric); 100 000 shp; 4 shafts
Boilers: 4 Babcock & Wilcox)
Speed, knots: 31·6 knots
Complement: approx 1 200
Flag accommodations: 216 (50 officers; 166 enlisted men) in CG 4 and CG 5)

Originally a series of six ships converted from light cruisers of the "Cleveland" class; three ships converted to Terrier missile configuration aft and three ships to Talos missile, with two ships of each missile type configured to serve as fleet flagships. The surviving ships are the *Little Rock* and *Oklahoma City* armed with the Talos missile, and the *Providence* and *Springfield* armed with the Terrier missile; all are fitted as fleet flagships.
The *Providence* was decommissioned on 31 Aug 1973 and the *Springfield* on 15 June 1974; both are in reserve. The *Little Rock* is active as flagship of the US Sixth Fleet in the Mediterranean (homeported in Gaeta, Italy) and the *Oklahoma City* as flagship of the US Seventh Fleet in the Western Pacific (homeported in Yokosuka, Japan).

Classification: Upon conversion to missile configuration these ships were reclassified as guided missile light cruisers (CLG). On 30 June 1975 the four ships were reclassified as guided missile cruisers (CG). (Correction to previous edition).

Conversion: All six of these ships had their two after 6 inch gun turrets replaced by a twin surface-to-air missile launcher, superstructure enlarged to support missile fire control equipment, lattice masts fitted to carry antennae, 5 inch battery reduced from original 12 guns and all 40 mm and 20 mm light anti-aircraft guns removed. The four ships fitted as fleet flagships additionally had their No. 2 turret of 6 inch guns removed and their forward superstructure enlarged to provide command and communications spaces. The *Little Rock* began conversion at the New York Shipbuilding Corp (Camden, New Jersey) in January 1957 and was completed in June 1960; the *Oklahoma City* began conversion at the Bethlehem Steel shipyard in San Francisco in May 1957 and was completed in September 1960; the *Providence* began conversion at the Boston Naval Shipyard in June 1957 and was completed in September 1959; the *Springfield* began conversion at the Bethlehem Steel shipyard in Quincy, Massachusetts, in August 1957, but was moved to the Boston Naval Shipyard in March 1960 for completion in July 1960. There is a helicopter landing area on the fantail, but only limited support facilities are provided; no hangar.

Electronics: Antenna arrangements differ in these ships. Three ships have SPS-43 and SPS-10 radar antennae on forward mast, with *Providence* having SPS-37 and SPS-10; all have SPS-30 antennae on second mast or after antennae support. *Providence* and *Springfield* have SPS-52 three-dimensional radar antennae on third lattice mast.
The Talos ships have Mk 77 missile fire control systems and the Terrier ships Mk 73; all had one Mk 34 gun director (removed from some ships) and one Mk 37 gunfire control system; Talos ships have one Mk 2 weapon direction system and two SPG-49A weapon control radars; Terrier ships one Mk 3 weapon direction system and two SPQ-5A radars.
No sonar is fitted.

Missiles: Reportedly, the cruisers armed with Terrier each carry 120 missiles and the ships armed with Talos each carry 46 missiles.

Photographs: In the above photographs of the *Providence* and *Little Rock* the differences in mast and radar antenna configurations of the Terrier and Talos ships are clearly evident. Note that the *Little Rock* does not have an SPS-52 three dimensional radar antenna (empty platform on second mast) and retains the older, "bee-hive" TACAN antenna; a UH-2 Sea Sprite utility helicopter is on her stern.

Disposals: *Topeka* (CLG 8, ex-CL 67) stricken on 1 Dec 1973; *Galveston* (CLG 3, ex-CL 93) stricken on 21 Dec 1973.

PROVIDENCE (CG 6)

United States Navy

LITTLE ROCK (CG 4)

1973, R. Nerlich

OKLAHOMA CITY (CG 5)

1975, United States Navy, PH1 S. Harris

3 HEAVY CRUISERS (CA): "SALEM" CLASS

Name	No.	Builders	Laid down	Launched	Commissioned
DES MOINES	CA 134	Bethlehem Steel Co (Quincy)	28 May 1945	27 Sep 1946	17 Nov 1948
SALEM	CA 139	Bethlehem Steel Co (Quincy)	4 June 1945	25 Mar 1947	9 May 1949
NEWPORT NEWS	CA 148	Newport News SB & DD Co	1 Oct 1945	6 Mar 1947	29 Jan 1949

Displacement, tons: 17 000 standard; 21 500 full load
Length, feet (metres): 700 *(213·4)* wl; 716·5 *(218·4)* oa
Beam, feet (metres): 76·3 *(23·3)*
Draught, feet (metres): 26 *(7·9)*
Guns: 9—8 inch *(203 mm)* 55 cal (triple) except 8—8 inch guns in *Newport News* (see *Gunnery* notes); 12—5 inch *(127 mm)* 38 cal DP (Mk 32) twin; 20—3 inch *(76 mm)* 50 cal AA (Mk 32) (twin), removed from *Newport News*
Main engines: 4 geared turbines (General Electric); 120 000 shp; 4 shafts
Boilers: 4 (Babcock & Wilcox)
Speed, knots: 33
Complement: approx 1 300 in *Newport News*
Flag accommodations: 267 (65 officers, 206 enlisted men) in *Newport News*

These ships were the largest and most powerful 8 inch gun cruisers ever built. Completed too late for World War II, they were employed primarily as flagships for the Sixth Fleet in the Mediterranean and the Second Fleet in the Atlantic. The *Salem* was decommissioned on 30 Jan 1959 and the *Des Moines* on 14 July 1961. The *Newport News* long served as flagship of the US Second Fleet in the Atlantic. Her decommissioning was delayed several times to retain the ship's "big guns" to support amphibious operations. Decommissioned on 27 June 1975, the last active all-gun cruiser of the US Navy.

Aircraft: As completed the *Des Moines* had two stern catapults and carried four floatplanes; catapults removed.

Design: These ships are an improved version of the previous "Oregon City" class. The newer cruisers have automatic main batteries, larger main turrets, taller fire control towers, and larger bridges. The *Des Moines* and *Newport News* are fully air-conditioned.
Additional ships of this class were cancelled: the *Dallas* (CA 140) and the unnamed CA 141-142, CA 149-153.

Electronics: The *Newport News* has an SPS-37 search radar antenna and TACAN on her forward mast, and SPS-8 and SPS-6 antennae on her after mast. (The small antenna on the forward mast is an SPS-10).
Newport News also provided with four Mk 56 and two Mk 54 gunfire control directors.

Gunnery: These cruisers were the first ships to be armed with fully automatic 8 inch guns firing cased ammunition. The guns can be loaded at any elevation from −5 to +41 degrees; rate of fire is four times faster than earlier 8 inch guns. Mk XVI 8-inch guns in these ships; other heavy cruisers remaining on Navy List have Mk XV guns.
As built, these ships mounted 12—5 inch guns, 24—3 inch guns (in twin mounts), and 12—20 mm guns (single mounts). The 20 mm guns were removed almost immediately and the 3 inch battery was reduced gradually as ships were overhauled. Last 3-inch guns removed from *Newport News* in 1973 (two twin mounts amidships). With full armament the designed wartime complement was 1 860.
The No. 2 main gun turret of the *Newport News* was severely damaged by an accidental explosion in October 1972; not repaired and centre gun subsequently removed. The turret is not operable (see photo).

Modernisation: The *Newport News* has been extensively modified to provide improved flagship facilities; note elaborate antennae on masts, forecastle, atop turrets, and on stern crane.

Photographs: Note the built-up amidships structure of the *Newport News*. As a fleet flagship she required additional working, communication, and accommodation spaces. Note absence of 3 inch guns in *Newport News* and two-gun main battery turret in "B" position.

1974, Wright & Logan

NEWPORT NEWS (CA 148)

United States Navy

SALEM (CA 139)

United States Navy

DES MOINES (CA 134)

1 HEAVY CRUISER (CA): "BALTIMORE" CLASS

Name	No.	Builders	Laid down	Launched	Commissioned
SAINT PAUL	CA 73	Bethlehem Steel Co (Quincy, Mass)	3 Feb 1943	16 Sep 1944	17 Feb 1945

Displacement, tons: 13 600 standard; 17 200 full load
Length, feet (metres): 664 *(204·4)* wl; 673·5 *(205·3)* oa
Beam, feet (metres): 70·9 *(21·6)*
Draught, feet (metres): 26 *(7·9)*
Guns: 9—8 inch *(203 mm)* 55 cal (triple); 10—5 inch *(127 mm)* 38 cal DP (Mk 32) (twin); 12—3 inch *(76 mm)* 50 cal AA (Mk 33) (twin)
Main engines: 4 geared turbines (General Electric); 120 000 shp; 4 shafts
Boilers: 4 (Babcock & Wilcox)
Speed, knots: 33
Complement: 1 146 (61 officers, 1 085 enlisted men); designed wartime complement 1 969
Flag accommodations: 217 (37 officers, 180 enlisted men)

The *Saint Paul* is the last all-gun cruiser of the "Baltimore" class. Fourteen of these ships were completed 1943-1945. This was the largest class of heavy (8-inch gun) cruisers built by any navy. Three missile ship conversions remain on the Navy List (see *Conversion* notes). The *Saint Paul* was the US Navy's last all-gun cruiser in commission except for the *Newport News*; the former ship was decommissioned in 1971 and placed in reserve.

Aircraft: As completed the "Baltimore" class ships had two stern catapults and carried four floatplanes; catapults removed after World War II. Hangar under fantail.

Conversions: Two ships of this class were converted to partial missile configurations, the *Boston* (CA 69/CAG 1) and *Canberra* (CA 70/CAG 2); and two ships were converted to all-missile configurations, the *Columbus* (CA 74 now CG 12) and *Chicago* (CA 136 now CG 11). The *Canberra* and the two later ships remain on the Navy List.

Electronics: The *Saint Paul's* principal radar antennae when decommissioned were an SPS-37 on the forward pylon mast and an SPS-8 on the after mast; a "bee-hive" TACAN (Tactical Air Navigation) was installed atop the forward mast.

Gunnery: As built the "Baltimore" class cruisers were armed with nine 8 inch guns, 12—5 inch DP guns, 48—40 mm AA guns, and 23—20 mm AA guns. After World War II all 20 mm weapons were removed and the 40 mm guns were replaced by 20—3 inch AA guns (except in one ship). Subsequently the 5 inch twin mount forward of the bridge was removed from the *Saint Paul* and the number of 3 inch twin gun mounts was reduced.

Modernisation: The *Saint Paul* was extensively modified to serve as flagship for the Seventh Fleet in the western Pacific; advanced communications equipment installed and amidships structure built up to provide more office space.

Nomenclature: The *Saint Paul* was renamed during construction; ex-*Rochester*.

SAINT PAUL (CA 73)   *United States Navy*

1 HEAVY CRUISER (CA): "CANBERRA" TYPE (Ex-CAG)

Name	No.	Builders	Laid down	Launched	Commissioned	CAG Comm.
CANBERRA	CA 70 (ex-CAG 2)	Bethlehem Steel Co (Quincy, Mass)	3 Sep 1941	19 April 1943	14 Oct 1943	15 June 1956

Displacement, tons: 13 300 standard; 17 500 full load
Length, feet (metres): 664 *(222·3)* wl; 673·5 *(205·3)* oa
Beam, feet (metres): 70·9 *(21·6)*
Draught, feet (metres): 26 *(7·9)*
Missile launchers: 2 twin Terrier surface-to-air launchers
Guns: 6—8 inch *(203 mm)* 55 cal (triple); 10—5 inch *(127 mm)* 38 DP (Mk 32) (twin); 8—3 inch *(76 mm)* 50 cal AA (Mk 33) (twin)
Main engines: 4 geared turbines (General Electric), 120 000 shp; 4 shafts
Boilers: 4 (Babcock & Wilcox)
Speed, knots: 33
Complement: 1 273 (73 officers; 1 200 enlisted men)
Flag accommodations: 72 (10 officers, 62 enlisted men)

The *Canberra* and her sister ship *Boston* (CA 69 ex-CAG 1) were the US Navy's first guided missile surface ships. They originally were heavy cruisers (CA) of the "Baltimore" class. The *Canberra* was converted 1952-1956 to a combination gun-missile configuration and reclassified CAG 2 on 4 Jan 1952.

Subsequently reverted to original classification of CA 70 on 1 May 1968; as a CA the *Canberra* retained the Terrier missile systems.
Retention of 8 inch guns forward made the *Boston* and *Canberra* valuable in the fire support role during the Vietnam War. The *Canberra* was decommissioned on 16 Feb 1970 and placed in reserve.

Conversion: The *Canberra* was converted to a missile configuration at the New York Shipbuilding Corp, Camden, New Jersey. Conversion included removal of after 8-inch gun turret (143 tons) and after twin 5-inch gun mount; all 40 mm and 20 mm guns replaced by six 3-inch twin mounts (subsequently reduced to four mounts). Original superstructure modified and twin funnels replaced by single large funnel as in "Oregon City" class. Forward pole mast replaced by lattice radar mast and radar platform fitted aft of pole mast. Missile systems include rotating magazine below decks, loading and check-out equipment, two large directors, and two launchers.

Electronics: The *Canberra* has an SPS-43 search radar antenna atop the pole mast and an SPS-30 antenna on the platform aft of the pole mast. The experimental radar atop the lattice mast has been removed (see photograph of *Boston* in the 1973-1974 and previous editions). TACAN antenna is mounted on the forward mast.
Also provided with one Mk 37 Mod 91 and four Mk 56 Mod 15 gunfire control systems, one Mk 34 Mod 16 gun director, and one Mk 1 weapon direction system.

Missiles: Reportedly, the *Canberra* carries 144 Terrier missiles in two rotating magazines. Each launcher can load and fire two missiles every 30 seconds; loading is completely automatic with the missiles sliding up onto the launchers when in the vertical position.

Nomenclature: The *Canberra* was originally named *Pittsburgh*; renamed while under construction to honour an Australian cruiser of that name which was sunk at the Battle of Savo Island with several US Navy ships in August 1942. She is the only US warship named for a foreign capital city.

CANBERRA (CA 70)   *1968, United States Navy*

DESTROYERS

Into 1976 the US Navy's destroyer force continued at a post-World War II nadir. However, the downward trend began to slow in September 1975 when the first of 30 "Spruance" class destroyers was commissioned. These ships will be completed at regular intervals through 1979. At this time the Navy plans to follow the "Spruance" class with a guided missile destroyer based on the same hull and machinery, but employing the Aegis missile system.

The US Navy destroyer force in mid-1976 consisted of some 70 ships (including 10 former "frigates") plus 30 ships assigned to the Naval Reserve Force (NRF) and manned partially by reservists.

Increasingly the Navy is using frigates (formerly escort ships/destroyer escorts) for operations that previously required destroyers. Although the frigates have modern anti-submarine weapons and sensors similar to destroyers, and in some classes superior, the frigates lack the guns, electronics, 30-knot speeds, and in most cases the surface-to-air missiles considered necessary for modern anti-air warfare and surface warfare operations.

Soon after the last of the "Spruance" class ships are completed in 1979, the destroyer force is expected to consist of 69 ships:

the 39 missile-armed DDG type and the 30 "Spruance" class non-missile DD type. Most or all of the "Forrest Sherman" class destroyers and the few surviving "Gearing" class ships will probably be assigned to the Naval Reserve Force by that time.

DXG PROGRAMME

These ships were a planned variation of the "Spruance" class all-gun destroyers but with an improved anti-aircraft capability afforded by a Tartar-D surface-to-air missile system.

Initial Department of Defense planning called for 28 ships of this design. However, construction of these ships was not proposed in the Fiscal Year 1971 shipbuilding programme as previously expected. In view of the increasing cost estimates of the non-missile "Spruance" class ships prior to the start of their construction, and probable new destroyer concepts, this class will apparently not be built. (The missile-armed DDG ships would of course have been more expensive than the "straight" DD ships).

The planned DDG/DXG programme provided for a ship similar in many respects to the "Spruance" class ships to reduce

design and construction costs. The missile-armed design would be similar to the DD type, but somewhat larger.

FRIGATES

All guided missile frigates (DLG/DLGN) on the Navy List as of 30 June 1975 were reclassified as guided missile cruisers (CG/CGN) except for the ten ships of the "Coontz" class which were reclassified as guided missile destroyers (DDG).

Previously two all-gun frigates had been reclassified as guided missile destroyers upon conversion to a missile configuration: Mitscher DDG 35 (ex-DL 2, ex-DD 927) and John S. McCain DDG 36 (ex-DL 3, ex-DD 928).

Three other all-gun frigates have been stricken: Willis A. Lee (DL 4) and Wilkinson (DL 5) of the "Mitscher" class stricken on 15 May 1972 and 1 May 1974, respectively; Norfolk (DL 1, ex-CLK 1), the only ship of that design, stricken on 1 Nov 1973.

Nomenclature: Destroyer-type ships of the US Navy have traditionally been named for officers and enlisted personnel of the Navy and Marine Corps, Secretaries of the Navy, members of Congress who have influenced naval affairs, and inventors.

(8+) GUIDED MISSILE DESTROYERS (DDG): AEGIS TYPE

	No.	Programme	Commission
One ship	DDG 47	Proposed Fiscal Year 1977	1982
Two Ships	DDG	Planned FY 1979	
Three Ships	DDG	Planned FY 1980	
Two Ships	DDG	Planned FY 1981	

Displacement, tons: 9 055 full load
Length, feet (metres): 563·3 (171·1) oa
Beam, feet (metres): 55 (17·6)
Missile launchers: 2 twin Standard-MR/ASROC launchers (Mk 26); Harpoon surface-to-surface cannisters
Guns: 2—5 inch (127 mm) 54 cal dual purpose; 2—20 mm Phlanx Close-In Weapon Systems
A/S weapons: 2 LAMPS helicopters; ASROC; torpedo tubes (Mk 32)
Main engines: 4 gas turbines; 80 000 shp; 2 shafts
Speed, knots: 30
Complement: 316 (27 officers, 289 enlisted men)

These ships are planned to complement the Aegis-armed, nuclear-propelled strike cruiser (CSGN) programme. According to Secretary of Defense Donald Rumsfeld: "The military value of an all-nuclear-powered Aegis programme does not warrant the increased costs or, alternatively, the reduced force

levels. Accordingly, we propose a mixed propulsion programme . . . . (including) conventional-powered DDG 47s to supplement the CSGNs in protection of high value forces including carriers)".

The DDG 47 class thus fulfils the proposal for a non-nuclear Aegis-armed ship as proposed in the early 1970s with the designation DG, but subsequently dropped to avoid conflict with the Navy's nuclear-propelled cruiser programme. The proposed DG was to have been a ship of 6 000 to 8 000 tons full load with gas turbine propulsion. The follow-on ships were to have had a target goal of $125 000 000 per unit in Fiscal Year 1973 dollars.

The DDG 47 budget request is for $858 500 000 for the lead ship; follow-on ships are expected to cost slightly less, but still many times that of the late DG proposal. The high cost of these ships and the view that all high-capability Aegis ships should have nuclear propulsion have made the class the target of intensive Congressional criticism. The Navy-Department of Defense five-year plan provides for eight of these ships. A total of 20 to 30 DDG/CSGN Aegis ships is envisioned by the Navy.

Design: The DDG 47 design is a modification of the "Spruance" class (DD 963). The same basic hull will be used with the same gas turbine propulsion system. The design calls for one-inch steel armour plate to protect the magazines.

Electronics: The Aegis advanced fleet air defence system is described earlier in this edition under the listing for the strike cruiser (CSGN). The DDG 47 will have the full Aegis electronics suite, including SPY-1 paired radar arrays (two sets, one forward and one amidships to provide 360° coverage), Mk 110 radar control system with UYK-7 computers to control radar phasing, SPS-49 search radar, Mk 86 gunfire control system, four Mk 99 missile guidance illuminators, and SPQ-9 weapon radar.
Bow-mounted SQS-53 sonar and TACTAS towed passive array sonar are planned.

Missiles: Two launchers will be provided for the Standard-MR surface-to-air missile. The Harpoon surface-to-surface missiles would be carried in two eight-tube deck cannisters.

10 GUIDED MISSILE DESTROYERS (DDG): "COONTZ" CLASS

Name	No.	Builders	Laid down	Launched	Commissioned
*FARRAGUT	DDG 37 (ex-DLG 6)	Bethlehem Co, Quincy	3 June1957	18 July 1958	10 Dec 1960
*LUCE	DDG 38 (ex-DLG 7)	Bethlehem Co, Quincy	1 Oct 1957	11 Dec 1958	20 May 1961
*MACDONOUGH	DDG 39 (ex-DLG 8)	Bethlehem Co, Quincy	15 April1958	9 July 1959	4 Nov 1961
*COONTZ	DDG 40 (ex-DLG 10)	Puget Sound Naval Shipyard	1 Mar 1957	6 Dec 1958	15 July 1960
*KING	DDG 41 (ex-DLG 10)	Puget Sound Naval Shipyard	1 Mar 1957	6 Dec 1958	17 Nov 1960
*MAHAN	DDG 42 (ex-DLG 11)	San Francisco Naval Shipyard	31 July 1957	7 Oct 1959	25 Aug 1960
*DAHLGREN	DDG 43 (ex-DLG 12)	Philadelphia Naval Shipyard	1 Mar 1958	16 Mar 1960	8 April1961
*WM V PRATT	DDG 44 (ex-DLG 13)	Philadelphia Naval Shipyard	1 Mar 1958	16 Mar 1960	4 Nov 1961
*DEWEY	DDG 45 (ex-DLG 14)	Bath Iron Works, Maine	10 Aug 1957	30 Nov 1958	7 Dec 1959
*PREBLE	DDG 46 (ex-DLG 15)	Bath Iron Works, Maine	16 Dec 1957	23 May 1959	9 May 1960

Displacement, tons: 4 700 standard; 5 800 full load
Length, feet (metres): 512·5 (156·2) oa
Beam, feet (metres): 52·5 (15·9)
Draught, feet (metres): 25 (7·6)
Missile launchers: 1 twin Terrier Standard-ER surface-to-air launcher (Mk 10 Mod 0)
Guns: 1—5 inch (127 mm) 54 cal dual-purpose (Mk 42)
A/S weapons: 1 ASROC 8-tube launcher; 2 triple torpedo tubes (Mk 32)
Main engines: 2 geared turbines; 85 000 shp; 2 shafts
Boilers: 4 (Foster Wheeler in DLG 6-8; Babcock & Wilcox in DLG 9-15)
Speed, knots: 34
Complement: 377 (21 officers, 356 enlisted men)
Flag accommodations: 19 (7 officers, 12 enlisted men)

These destroyers (formerly designated frigates) are an improvement of the "Mitscher" class (DL/DDG). The DDG 37-42 were authorised in the Fiscal Year 1956 shipbuilding programme; DDG 43-46 in FY 1957 programme. Average cost per ship was $52 000 000.

Although now classified as "destroyers", these ships have many of the capabilities of the larger US cruiser classes, including the Terrier/Standard-ER missile system and Naval Tactical Data System (NTDS).

All of these ships are active.

Classification: The Farragut, Luce and McDonough were initially classified as frigates (DL 6-8, respectively); changed to guided missile frigate (DLG) 6-8 on 14 Nov 1956. The first ship ordered as a missile frigate was the Coontz which became the

name ship for the class. All ten ships were classified as guided missile frigates (DLG 6-15) from completion until 30 June 1975 when reclassified as guided missile destroyers (DDG 37-46).

Design: These ships were the only US guided missile "frigates" with separate masts and funnels. They have aluminium superstructures to reduce weight and improve stability. Early designs for this class had a second 5 inch gun mount in the "B" position; design revised when ASROC "pepper box" launcher was developed.
Helicopter landing area on stern, but no hangar and limited support capability.

Electronics: The King and Mahan along with the aircraft carrier Oriskany (CV 34) 34 were the first ships fitted with the Naval

WILLIAM V. PRATT (DDG 44, ex-DLG 13)

1972, Giorgio Arra

"COONTZ" CLASS—*continued*

Tactical Data System (NTDS), conducting operational evaluation of the equipment in 1961-1962.

As completed these ships had an SPS-10 and three-dimensional SPS-39 search radars on their forward mast, and an SPS-37 search radar and TACAN (Tactical Aircraft Navigation) "bee hive" antenna on second mast. Prior to AAW modernisation some ships had the SPS-39 replaced with the SPS-52 radar. During modernisation SPS-48 three-dimensional search radar fitted on the forward mast (except SPS-52 in *King* and *Pratt*), an improved TACAN "pod" fitted on the second mast, and NTDS installed. These ships have SQS-23 sonar.

Also installed are two Mk 76 missile fire control systems, one Mk 68 gunfire control system, one SPG-53A and two SPG-55B weapon control radars.

Engineering: De Laval turbines in DDG 37-39 and DDG 46; Allis-Chalmers turbines in DDG 40-45.

Gunnery: These ships have a Mk 42 single 5 inch gun forward; along with the converted "Sherman" class DDGs they are the only US destroyers with one 5 inch gun. As-built, each ship of this class had 4—3 inch 50 cal AA guns in twin mounts amidships; removed during modernisation. Note 3 inch gun "tubs" are visible between second funnel and hangar structure in photo of *Pratt*.

The *King* was fitted with the 20 mm Phalanx Close-In Weapon System (CIWS) for at-sea evaluation from August 1973 to March 1974. The rapid-fire, six-barrel cannon was fitted on the *King's* fantail. See photos on page 402 of 1975-1976 edition.

Missiles: The first five ships of this class were built with Terrier BW-1 beam-riding missile systems; five later ships built with Terrier BT-3 homing missile systems. See *Modernisation* notes for conversion of earlier ships to improve missile capability. Reportedly, each ship carries 40 missiles.

Modernisation: These ships were modernised between 1968 and 1975 to improve their Anti-Air Warfare (AAW) capabilities. Superstructure enlarged to provide space for additional electronic equipment, including NTDS (previously fitted in *King* and *Mahan*); improved TACAN installed, first five ships given improved guidance system for Terrier/Standard missiles (SPG-55 fire control radar), and larger ship's service turbo generators fitted. The *Farragut* also had improved ASROC reload capability provided (with additional structure forward of bridge and second mast increased in height. (Other ships are not believed to carry ASROC reloads).

All ships modernised at Philadelphia Naval Shipyard, except *Mahan* at Bath Iron Works, Bath, Maine, and *King* at Boland Machine & Manufacturing Co, New Orleans, Louisiana.

Cost of modernisation was $39 000 000 per ship in FY 1970 conversion programme.

Nomenclature: The *Luce* was to have been named *Dewey*; renamed in 1957.

DEWEY (DDG 45, ex-DLG 14)

1974, Stefan Terzibaschitsch

COONTZ (DDG 40, ex-DLG 6)

1973, Giorgio Arra

DAHLGREN (DDG 43, ex-DLG 12)

1973, United States Navy, PH 2 W. J. Dupuis

2 GUIDED MISSILE DESTROYERS (DDG): CONVERTED "MITSCHER" CLASS

Name	No.	Builders	Laid down	Launched	DL Comm.	DDG Comm.
*MITSCHER	DDG 35 (ex-DL 2, ex-DD 927)	Bath Iron Works	3 Oct 1949	26 Jan 1952	15 May 1953	29 June1968
*JOHN S. McCAIN	DDG 36 (ex-DL 3, ex-DD 928)	Bath Iron Works	24 Oct 1949	12 July 1952	12 Oct 1953	21 June1969

Displacement, tons: 5 200 full load
Length, feet (metres): 493 (150·3) oa
Beam, feet (metres): 50 (15·2)
Draught, feet (metres): 21 (6·7)
Missile launchers: 1 single Tartar surface-to-air launcher (Mk 13 Mod 2)
Guns: 2—5 inch (127 mm) 54 calibre (Mk 42) dual-purpose (single)
A/S weapons: 1 ASROC 8-tube launcher; 2 triple torpedo tubes (Mk 32)
Main engines: 2 geared turbines (General Electric); 80 000 shp; 2 shafts
Boilers: 4 (Combustion Engineering)
Speed, knots: 33
Complement: 377 (28 officers, 349 enlisted men)

These ships are former "Mitscher" class all-gun frigates which have been converted to a guided missile and improved ASW configuration.
Both ships are active.

Classification: These ships were originally classified as destroyers (DD); reclassified as destroyer leaders (DL) on 9 Feb 1951 while under construction. The DL symbol was changed to "frigate" on 1 Jan 1955. Both ships were changed to DDG on 15 Mar 1967 during Tartar missile conversion.

Conversion: Both ships were converted to DDG at the Philadelphia Naval Shipyard. The Mitscher began conversion in March 1966 and the John S. McCain in June 1966. Superstructure was modified with ASROC launcher installed forward of the bridge in "B" position; two heavy lattice masts fitted; triple Mk 32 torpedo tubes retained amidships; and single Tartar launcher installed aft (system weighs approximately 135 000 pounds).

Electronics: SQS-23 hull-mounted sonar installed; SPS-10 and SPS-37 search radar antennae on forward mast and SPS-48 three-dimensional search radar antenna on the after mast. Also provided are Mk 74 gun/missile fire control system, Mk 67 gunfire control system, and two SPG-51C missile control radars.

Missiles: Tartar magazine capacity is reported to be 40 missiles.

Photographs: Both ships now have the smaller TACAN (Tactical Air Navigation) antenna on the after mast, as shown here in the more recent photo of the Mitscher. The Tartar missile launcher is in the vertical position for loading; note the cylindrical structure below the launcher which houses the rotating missile magazine.
These ships can be easily distinguished from the "Forrest Sherman" class destroyers by their larger size, forward position of ASROC, and second 5 inch gun aft.

JOHN S. McCAIN (DDG 36)   1975, United States Navy

MITSCHER (DDG 35)   1971, United States Navy

1973, Giorgio Arra

MITSCHER (DDG 35)

4 GUIDED MISSILE DESTROYERS (DDG): CONVERTED "FORREST SHERMAN" CLASS

Name	No.	Builders	Laid down	Launched	DD Comm.	DDG Comm.
*DECATUR	DDG 31 (ex-DD 936)	Bethlehem Steel Co (Quincy)	13 Sep 1954	15 Dec 1955	7 Dec 1956	29 Apr 1967
*JOHN PAUL JONES	DDG 32 (ex-DD 932)	Bath Iron Works	18 Jan 1954	7 May 1955	5 Apr 1956	23 Sep 1967
*PARSONS	DDG 33 (ex-DD 949)	Ingalls Shipbuilding Corp	17 June 1957	19 Aug 1958	29 Oct 1959	3 Nov 1967
*SOMERS	DDG 34 (ex-DD 947)	Bath Iron Works	4 Mar 1957	30 May 1958	3 Apr 1959	10 Feb 1968

Displacement, tons: 4 150 full load
Length, feet (metres): DDG 31-32: 418·4 *(127·5)* oa;
  DDG 33-34: 418 *(127·4)* oa
Beam, feet (metres): DDG 31-32: 45·2 *(13·8)*;
  DDG 33-34: 45 *(13·7)*
Draught, feet (metres): 20 *(6·1)*
Missile launchers: 1 single Tartar surface-to-air launcher
  (Mk 13 Mod 1)
Guns: 1—5 inch *(127 mm)* 54 calibre (Mk 42) dual-purpose
A/S weapons: 1 ASROC 8-tube launcher; 2 triple torpedo tubes
  (Mk 32)
Main engines: 2 geared turbines (Westinghouse in *John Paul
  Jones;* General Electric in others); 70 000 shp; 2 shafts
Boilers: 4 (Foster Wheeler in *Decatur* and *Parsons;* Babcock &
  Wilcox in *John Paul Jones* and *Somers)*
Speed, knots: 32·5 knots
Complement: 335 (22 officers, 313 enlisted men)

These four ships are former "Forrest Sherman" class
destroyers that have been converted to a guided missile and
improved ASW configuration. Plans for additional DDG conversions of this class were dropped. The *Decatur* was reclassified as DDG 31 on 15 Sep 1966; the *John Paul Jones, Somers*
and *Parsons* became DDG on 15 Mar 1967. See "Forrest Sherman" class for additional notes.
All ships are active.

Conversion: The *Decatur* began conversion to a DDG at the
Boston Naval Shipyard on 15 June 1965, the *John Paul Jones* at
the Philadelphia Naval Shipyard on 2 Dec 1965, the *Parsons* at
the Long Beach (California) Naval Shipyard on 30 June 1965,
and the *Somers* at the San Francisco Bay Naval Shipyard on 30
Mar 1966.
During conversion all existing armament was removed except
the forward 5 inch gun; two triple ASW torpedo tubes were
installed forward of the bridge; two heavy lattice masts fitted;
ASROC launcher mounted aft of second stack; single Tartar Mk
13 launcher installed aft (on 01 level; system weighs approximately 135 000 pounds).
Original DDG conversion plans provided for Drone Anti-
Submarine Helicopter (DASH) facilities; however, ASROC was
substituted in all four ships as DASH lost favour in the Navy.

Electronics: SQS-23 sonar installed. SPS-10 and SPS-37 search
radars on forward mast except *Somers* has SPS-40 in lieu of
SPS-37; all have SPS-48 three-dimensional search radar on
after mast.
Also provided with Mk 74 gun/missile fire control system, Mk
68 gunfire control system, and SPG-51C and SPG-53B weapon
control radars.

Gunnery: These ships and the "Coontz" class are the only US
destroyers with one 5 inch gun.

Missiles: Reportedly Tartar magazine capacity is 40 missiles.

Nomenclature: The *John Paul Jones* honours the Scottish-
born father of the American Navy who later served as a rear-
admiral in the Russian Navy (1788).

PARSONS (DDG 33)   *1975, United States Navy*

JOHN PAUL JONES (DDG 32)   *1970, United States Navy*

PARSONS (DDG 33)

1975, J. Mortimer

23 GUIDED MISSILE DESTROYERS (DDG): "CHARLES F. ADAMS" CLASS

Name	No.	Builders	Laid down	Launched	Commissioned
*CHARLES F. ADAMS	DDG 2	Bath Iron Works	16 June1958	8 Sep 1959	10 Sep 1960
*JOHN KING	DDG 3	Bath Iron Works	25 Aug 1958	30 Jan 1960	4 Feb 1961
*LAWRENCE	DDG 4	New York Shipbuilding Corp	27 Oct 1958	27 Feb 1960	6 Jan 1962
*CLAUDE V. RICKETTS	DDG 5	New York Shipbuilding Corp	18 May 1959	4 June1960	6 Jan 1962
*BARNEY	DDG 6	New York Shipbuilding Corp	18 May 1959	10 Dec 1960	11 Aug 1962
*HENRY B. WILSON	DDG 7	Defoe Shipbuilding Co	28 Feb 1958	23 April1959	17 Dec 1960
*LYNDE McCORMICK	DDG 8	Defoe Shipbuilding Co	4 April1958	9 Sep 1960	3 June1961
*TOWERS	DDG 9	Todd Shipyards Inc, Seattle	1 April 1958	23 April 1959	6 June1961
*SAMPSON	DDG 10	Bath Iron Works	2 Mar 1959	9 Sep 1960	24 June1961
*SELLERS	DDG 11	Bath Iron Works	3 Aug 1959	9 Sep 1960	28 Oct 1961
*ROBISON	DDG 12	Defoe Shipbuilding Co	23 April1959	27 April1960	9 Dec 1961
*HOEL	DDG 13	Defoe Shipbuilding Co	1 June1960	4 Aug 1960	16 June1962
*BUCHANAN	DDG 14	Todd Shipyards Inc, Seattle	23 April1959	11 May 1960	7 Feb 1962
*BERKELEY	DDG 15	New York Shipbuilding Corp	1 June1960	29 July 1961	15 Dec 1962
*JOSEPH STRAUSS	DDG 16	New York Shipbuilding Corp	27 Dec 1960	9 Dec 1961	20 April1963
*CONYNGHAM	DDG 17	New York Shipbuilding Corp	1 May 1961	19 May 1962	13 July 1963
*SEMMES	DDG 18	Avondale Marine Ways Inc	18 Aug 1960	20 May 1961	10 Dec 1962
*TATTNALL	DDG 19	Avondale Marine Ways Inc.	14 Nov 1960	26 Aug 1961	13 April1963
*GOLDSBOROUGH	DDG 20	Puget Sound Bridge & Dry Dock Co	3 Jan 1961	15 Dec 1961	9 Nov 1963
*COCHRANE	DDG 21	Puget Sound Bridge & Dry Dock Co	31 July 1961	18 July 1962	21 Mar 1964
*BENJAMIN STODDERT	DDG 22	Puget Sound Bridge & Dry Dock Co	11 June1962	8 Jan 1963	12 Sep 1964
*RICHARD E. BYRD	DDG 23	Todd Shipyards Inc, Seattle	12 Apr 1961	6 Feb 1962	7 Mar 1964
*WADDELL	DDG 24	Todd Shipyards Inc, Seattle	6 Feb 1962	26 Feb 1963	28 Aug 1964

Displacement, tons: 3 370 standard; 4 500 full load
Length, feet (metres): 437 *(133·2)* oa
Beam, feet (metres): 47 *(14·3)*
Draught, feet (metres): 20 *(6·1)*
Missile launchers: DDG 2-14: 1 twin Tartar surface-to-air launcher (Mk 11 Mod 0)
 DDG 15-24: 1 single Tartar surface-to-air launcher (Mk 13 Mod 0)
 DDG 4 and 13: 1 multiple launcher for Chaparral (see *Missile notes*)
Guns: 2—5 inch *(127 mm)* 54 calibre DP (Mk 42) (single)
A/S weapons: 1 ASROC 8-tube launcher; 2 triple torpedo tubes (Mk 32)
Main engines: 2 geared steam turbines (General Electric in DDG 2, 3, 7, 8, 10-13, 15-22; Westinghouse in DDG 4-6, 9, 14, 23, 24; 70 000 shp; 2 shafts
Boilers: 4 (Babcock & Wilcox in DDG2, 3, 7, 8, 10-13, 20-22; Foster Wheeler in DDG 4-6, 9, 14; Combustion Engineering in DDG 15-19)
Speed, knots: 31+
Complement: 354 (24 officers, 330 enlisted men)

These destroyers are considered excellent multi-purpose ships. The DDG 2-9 were authorised in the Fiscal Year 1957 new construction programme, DDG 10-14 in FY 1958, DDG 15-19 in FY 1959, DDG 20-22 in FY 1960, DDG 23 and DDg 24 in FY 1961. Three additional ships of this design have been built in US shipyards for Australia (DDG 25-27) and three for West Germany (DDG 28-30). All US ships are active.

Classification: The first eight ships were initially assigned hull numbers in the standard DD series (DDG 952-959); renumbered while under construction. The DDG 1 was the *Gyatt* (ex-DD 712), which operated as a missile destroyer from 1956 to 1962 armed with a twin Terrier launcher.

Design: These ships were built to an improved "Forrest Sherman" class design with aluminium superstructures and a high level of habitability including air conditioning in all living spaces. They do not have the second radar trellis mast nor secondary gun battery of the earlier class. DDG 20-24 have stem anchors because of sonar arrangement. The later ships with bow sonar are about one-half knot slower than the earlier ships.
Several ships have been modified with an extension of the bridge structure on the starboard side on the 02 level, providing additional space for storage.

Electronics: DDG 20-24 have bow mounted SQS-23 sonar; earlier ships have SQS-23 sonar with hull domes.
DDG 2-14 haveSPS-37 and SPS-10 search radars on tripod mast; DDG 15-24 have SPS-40 and SPS-10. All ships apparently being fitted with antenna associated with SPS-52 radar, but the ships retain SPS-39 system (three-dimensional search antenna on second stack); these ships were completed with SPS-39 radar antenna aft.
Mk 68 gunfire control system, Mk 4 weapon control system, SPG-51C and SPG-53A weapon control radars are provided.

Missiles: The DDG 2-14 have a twin Mk 11 Tartar missile launcher while the DDG 15-24 have a single Mk 13 Tartar launcher. The Mk 11 launcher installation weighs 165 240 pounds while the Mk 13 weighs only 132 561 pounds. Reportedly, their magazine capacities are 42 and 40 missiles, respectively, and ships equipped with either launcher can load, direct, and fire about six missiles per minute. (The twin Mk 11 launcher is installed in the cruisers CG 10-12; the "Mitscher" and "Forest Sherman" DDG conversions have a similar Mk 13 launcher which weighs approximately 135 000 pounds).
Lawrence and *Hoel* fitted in 1972-1973 with multiple launcher for Chaparral (MIM-72A) and other point-defence missiles in addition to their Tartar launcher.
All are being fitted to fire the Standard surface-to-surface missile (launched from Mk 11 or Mk 13 launcher).

Modernisation: These ships will be modernised during the late 1970s; to be fitted to launch Standard-MR surface-to-air and anti-ship missiles. The weight of additional electronics and other equipment related to their Anti-Air Warfare (AAW) mission may require removal of their ASROC launcher.

Nomenclature: The DDG 5 was originally named *Biddle*; renamed *Claude V. Ricketts* on 28 July 1964 to honour the late Vice Chief of Naval Operations who had supported mult-

BENJAMIN STODDERT (DDG 22)   *1974, United States Navy, PH3 D. J. Tyree*

JOHN KING (DDG 3)   *1974, United States Navy, PHAN C. R. Watkins*

national NATO manning of ballistic missile surface ships. (The name *Biddle* subsequently was assigned to the DLG 34). The DDG 23 honours the famed polar explorer and naval aviator.

Photographs: Note difference in radars on tripod mast and missile launchers on DDG 2-14 and DDG 15-24 series of this class.

4 + 26 DESTROYERS (DD): "SPRUANCE" CLASS

Name	No.	Laid down	Launched	Commissioned
*SPRUANCE	DD 963	17 Nov 1972	10 Nov 1973	20 Sep 1975
*PAUL F. FOSTER	DD 964	6 Feb 1973	23 Feb 1974	21 Feb 1976
*KINKAID	DD 965	19 April1973	25 May 1974	May 1976
*HEWITT	DD 966	23 July 1973	24 Aug 1974	June1976
ELLIOTT	DD 967	15 Oct 1973	19 Dec 1974	July 1976
ARTHUR W. RADFORD	DD 968	14 Jan 1974	1 Mar 1975	1976
PETERSON	DD 969	29 April1974	21 June1975	1976
CARON	DD 970	1 July 1974	24 June1975	1976
DAVID R. RAY	DD 971	23 Sep 1974	23 Aug 1975	1977
OLDENDORF	DD 972	27 Dec 1974	21 Oct 1975	1977
JOHN YOUNG	DD 973	17 Feb 1975	7 Feb 1976	1977
COMTE DE GRASSE	DD 974	4 April1975	1976	1977
O'BRIEN	DD 975	9 May 1975	1976	1977
MERRILL	DD 976	16 June1975	1976	1977
BRISCOE	DD 977	21 July 1975	1976	1977
STUMP	DD 978	25 Aug 1975	1976	1978
CONOLLY	DD 979	29 Sep 1975	1976	1978
MOOSBURGGER	DD 980	1975	1976	1978
JOHN HANCOCK	DD 981	1975	1976	1978
NICHOLSON	DD 982	1976	1976	1978
JOHN RODGERS	DD 983	1976	1976	1978
LEFTWICH	DD 984	1976	1976	1978
CUSHING	DD 985	1976	1977	1979
HARRY W. HILL	DD 986	1976	1976	1979
O'BANNON	DD 987	1976	1977	1979
THORN	DD 988	1976	1977	1979
Four ships	**DD 989-992**	1976	1977	1979

Displacement, tons: 7 800 full load
Length, feet (metres): 529 *(161·2)* wl; 563·3 *(171·1)* oa
Beam, feet (metres): 55 *(17·6)*
Draught, feet (metres): 29 *(8·8)*
Guns: 2—5 inch *(127 mm)* 54 calibre DP (Mk 45) (single)
A/S weapons:
  1 SH-3 Sea King or 2 SH-2D LAMPS helicopters
  1 ASROC 8-tube launcher
  2 triple torpedo tubes (Mk 32)
Main engines: 4 gas turbines (General Electric); 80 000 shp; 2 shafts
Speed, knots: 30+
Complement: approx 250 (18 officers, 232 enlisted men)

SPRUANCE (DD 963)   *1974, Litton Industries*

These ships were intended as replacements for the large number of World War II-built destroyers that have undergone extensive modernisation (FRAM) to enable them to serve into the 1970s. According to official statements. "The primary mission of these ships is anti-submarine warfare including operations as an integral part of attack carrier task forces. They also have the capability for shore bombardment and for surface warfare, and will have short range missiles for defence against airborne threats, including enemy missiles. Their effectiveness against submarines is expected to be far greater, particularly at high speeds, than that of current Navy ships due to ship silencing techniques and improved sea-keeping capabilities".

The Fiscal Year 1969 new construction programme proposed by the Department of Defense requested funding for the first five ships of this class, however, funds were denied by the Congress because of the design status. In the FY 1970 programme the Congress approved funds for five ships, but increasing costs forced the Department of Defense to construct only three ships under the FY 1970 programme (DD 963-965); six ships were authorised in the FY 1971 programme (DD 966-971); seven ships (DD 972-978) in the FY 1972 programme; seven ships (DD 979-985) in the FY 1974 programme, and seven ships (DD 986-992) in the FY 1975 programme.

These ships have been the subject of severe criticism because of their large size and limited anti-air/anti-ship capabilities. They are believed to be the largest surface warships of contemporary design except for aircraft carriers which do not have a major surface-to-air missile system.

The Imperial Iranian Navy ordered two ships of a modified "Spruance" design on 15 Dec 1973; the agreement was amended on 27 Aug 1974 to provide four additional ships, but two units were cancelled on 3 Feb 1976. The Iranian ships will have twin-rail Mk 26 launchers for the Standard surface-to-air and surface-to-surface missiles. The Iranian ships were assigned US hull numbers DD 993-998 for accounting puroposes (to have IIN hull numbers DD 11-16).

Construction: All ships of this class are being constructed by the Litton Ship Systems Division of Litton Industries in Pascagoula, Mississippi. The "production facility" is a new shipyard which launched its first ship (a commercial freighter) in 1971. Advanced production techniques including modular assembly of large ship components are featured. A contract for the development and production of the entire DD 963 class was awarded to Litton on 23 June 1970; that award also provided construction go-ahead for the first three ships.

Classification: During the early proposal stage these ships were designated as the DX project, the letter "X" signifying that the characteristics were not fully defined. They were ordered with DD hull numbers.

SPRUANCE (DD 963)   *1975, United States Navy, PH1 Lonnie MacKay*

"SPRUANCE" CLASS—*continued*

Design: Extensive use of the modular concept is used to facilitate initial construction and block modernisation of the ships. The ships are highly automated, resulting in about 20 per cent reduction in personnel over a similar ship with conventional systems.

Electronics: These ships have SPG-60 and SPQ-9 (radome) weapon control radars on the forward lattice mast; SPS-40 search radar antenna and URN-20B TACAN (Tactical Aircraft Navigation) pod on after lattice mast; SPS-55 radar is planned. Fitted with SQS-53 bow-mounted sonar (improved SQS-26). High performance of SQS-53 led to decision not to install SQS-35 Independent Variable Depth Sonar (IVDS) planned earlier.
Also provided with Mk 116 digital underwater fire control system and Mk 86 Mod 3 gunfire control system.

Engineering: These ships are the first large US warships to employ gas turbine propulsion. Each ship has four General Electric LM2500 marine gas turbine engines, a shaft-power version of the TF39 turbofan aircraft engine. The LM2500 is rated at approximately 20 000 horsepower. The gas turbine was selected because of comparatively low operating costs, smaller space requirements, rapid replacement capability, and cold-start capability (the engines can go from "cold iron" to full power in 12 minutes).
These ships have controllable-pitch propellers, because gas turbine engines cannot use a reversible shaft, fitted with advanced self-noise reduction features.
During normal operations these ships "steam" on two engines, going to three and then four engines for higher speeds. Range is estimated at 6 000 miles at 20 knots.

Gunnery: These ships have the 5 inch 54 calibre, light-weight Mk 45 gun which has a limited rate-of-fire (approx 20 rounds-per-minute) but reduced manning requirements. An improved 5 inch 54 calibre Mk 65 gun is being considered for use in later ships of the class. The "Spruance" design can accommodate the 8-inch Major Calibre Light-Weight Gun (MCLWG) (Mk 71), but there are now plans to install that weapon in the near future.
The 20 mm Phalanx rapid-fire Close-In Weapon System (CIWS) is planned for installation in these ships as a terminal defence against cruise missile attack.

Helicopters. Full helicopter facilities are provided to accommodate the Light Airborne Multi-Purpose System (LAMPS), now the SH-2D helicopter. However, the ship can handle the larger SH-3 Sea King series.

Missiles: The NATO Sea Sparrow multiple missile launcher (Mk 29) is planned for installation in these ships (between helicopter deck and after 5 inch gun mount).

Nomenclature: The *Spruance* is named for Admiral Raymond A. Spruance, who had tactical command of the US carriers in the Battle of Midway (June 1942) and of the US fleet in the

SPRUANCE (DD 963)   *1975, Litton Industries*

Battle of the Marianas (June 1944), two of the major engagements of the Pacific War. He was also considered one of the leading intellectuals of the US Navy.
Comte de Grass honours the French admiral who helped assure the American victory at Yorktown in 1781 by moving his fleet into Chesapeake Bay.

Torpedoes: The triple Mk 32 torpedo tubes are inside the superstructure to facilitate maintenance and reloading; they

are fired through side ports. The ASROC reload magazine is located *under* the launcher with the twin-cell launcher nacelles depressing to a vertical position to reload (see photograph; this is similar to the Soviet RBU/MBU-4500A and -2500A systems).

Photographs: Several "Spruance" class ships under construction are shown in the 1975-1976 edition.

HULL (DD 945)—"Forest Sherman" Class with 8 inch gun forward   *1975, United States Navy, PHAN V. M. Sundseth*

MANLEY (DD 940)—see following page   *1973, Giorgio Arra*

14 DESTROYERS (DD): "FORREST SHERMAN" CLASS

Name	No.	Builders	Laid down	Launched	Commissioned
*FORREST SHERMAN	DD 931	Bath Iron Works	27 Oct 1953	5 Feb 1955	9 Nov 1955
*BIGELOW	DD 942	Bath Iron Works	6 July 1955	2 Feb 1957	8 Nov 1957
*MULLINNIX	DD 944	Bethlehem Steel Co (Quincy, Mass)	5 April 1956	18 Mar 1957	7 Mar 1958
*HULL	DD 945	Bath Iron Works	12 Sep 1956	10 Aug 1957	3 July 1958
*EDSON	DD 946	Bath Iron Works	3 Dec 1956	1 Jan 1958	7 Nov 1958
*TURNER JOY	DD 951	Puget Sound Bridge & Dry Dock Co	30 Sep 1957	5 May 1958	3 Aug 1959

ANTI-SUBMARINE MODERNISATION

Name	No.	Builders	Laid down	Launched	Commissioned
*BARRY	DD 933	Bath Iron Works	15 Mar 1954	1 Oct 1955	31 Aug 1956
*DAVIS	DD 937	Bethlehem Steel Co (Quincy, Mass)	1 Feb 1955	28 Mar 1956	28 Feb 1957
*JONAS INGRAM	DD 938	Bethlehem Steel Co (Quincy, Mass)	15 June1955	8 July 1956	19 July 1957
*MANLEY	DD 940	Bath Iron Works	10 Feb 1955	12 April 1956	1 Feb 1957
*DU PONT	DD 941	Bath Iron Works	11 May 1955	8 Sep 1956	1 July 1957
*BLANDY	DD 943	Bethlehem Steel Co (Quincy, Mass)	29 Dec 1955	19 Dec 1956	26 Nov 1957
*MORTON	DD 948	Ingalls Shipbuilding Corp	4 Mar 1957	23 May 1958	26 May 1959
*RICHARD S. EDWARDS	DD 950	Puget Sound Bridge & Dry Dock Co	20 Dec 1956	24 Sep 1957	5 Feb 1959

Displacement, tons: approx 2 800 standard; approx 4 050 full load
Length, feet (metres):
  DD 931-944: 418·4 *(127·5)* oa
  Except DD 953: 425 *(129·5)*
  DD 945-951: 418 *(127·4)* oa
Beam, feet (metres):
  DD 931-944: 45·2 *(13·8)*
  DD 945-951: 45 *(13·7)*
Draught, feet (metres): 20 *(6·1)*
Guns A/S Mod: 2—5 inch *(127 mm)* 54 calibre DP (Mk 42) (single)
Others: 3—5 inch *(127 mm)* 54 calibre DP (Mk 42) (single) except *Hull* (see *Gunnery* notes); 1—8 inch *(203 mm)* (Mk 71) in *Hull*
A/S weapons: 2 triple torpedo tubes (Mk 32); 1 ASROC 8-tube launcher in A/S modified ships
Main engines: 2 geared turbines (Westinghouse in DD 931 and 933; General Electric in others); 70 000 shp; 2 shafts
Boilers: 4 (Babcock & Wilcox in DD 931 and 933, 940-942, 945, 946, 950, 951; Foster Wheeler in others)
Speed, knots: 32·5 knots
Complement: 292 (17 officers, 275 enlisted men) in unmodified ships; 304 in A/S Mod ships (17 officers, 287 enlisted men)

These ships were the first US destroyers of post-World War II design and construction to be completed with the DD designation (see *Classification* notes below). Four have been converted to a guided missile configuration and are listed separately. They were authorised in the Fiscal Year 1952-1956 new construction programmes. These ships each cost approximately $26 000 000.
All of these ships are active; they are expected to be assigned to the Naval Reserve Force during the late 1970s. The *Edson* was to be assigned to the NRF in Oct 1976 for employment as school ship for officer training at Newport, Rhode Island, and for reservist training.

Armament: As built all 18 ships of this class had three single 5 inch guns, two twin 3 inch mounts, four fixed 21 inch ASW torpedo tubes (amidships); two ASW hedgehogs (forward of bridge), and depth charge racks.

Classification: The destroyer hull numbers of the Second World War programmes ended with DD 926; the "Mitscher" class (DD 927-930) were completed with "frigate" (DL) hull numbers, with two ships subsequently being redesignated as guided missile destroyers (DDG 35 and DDG 36).
Hull numbers DD 934, 935, and 939 were assigned to former German and Japanese war prizes of 1945; DDG 952-959 originally were given to "Charles F. Adams" class destroyers (later DDG 2-9); DD 960 and DD 961 were assigned for administrative purposes to post-war destroyers built in Japan, and DD 962 to HMS *Charity* transferred to Pakistan in 1958 under US military assistance programmes.

Design: The entire superstructure of these ships is of aluminium to obtain maximum stability with minimum displacement. All living spaces are air conditioned. The *Decatur* and later ships have higher bows; the *Hull* and later ships have slightly different bow designs. The *Barry* had her sonar dome moved forward in 1959 and a stem anchor fitted.

Electronics: SQS-23 sonar installed with the *Barry* being the first US warship fitted with bow mounted sonar. Variable depth sonar installed on stern of A/S modified ships.
All of these ships have an SPS-10 search radar antenna and most also have SPS-40; a few retain older SPS-37. Several of the unmodified ships have elaborate electronic warfare pods on the after mast.

Gunnery: With original armament of one 5 inch mount forward and two 5 inch mounts aft, these were the first US warships with more firepower aft than forward. Note that *Barry* and later ships have their Mk 68 gunfire control director forward and Mk 56 director aft; positions reversed in earlier ships.
During 1974-1975 the *Hull* was fitted with an 8 inch gun forward to determine feasibility of installing a Major Calibre Light Weight Gun (MCLWG) in destroyer-type ships for shore bombardment. Forward 5 inch gun removed. There are no plans to remove the gun.

Modernisation: Eight ships of this class were extensively modified in 1967-1971 to improve their anti-submarine capabilities: *Barry, Davis, Du Pont* at the Boston Naval Shipyard; *Jonas Ingram, Manley, Blandy* at the Philadelphia Naval Shipyard; and *Morton, Richard S. Edwards* at the Long Beach (California) Naval Shipyard. During modernisation the anti-submarine torpedo tubes installed forward of bridge (on 01 level), deckhouse aft of second funnel extended to full width of ship, ASROC

HULL (DD 945) with 8 inch gun forward

1975, United States Navy

MULLINNIX (DD 944)

1975, US Navy, PH1 L. M. MacKay

launcher installed in place of after gun mounts on 01 level, and variable depth sonar fitted at stern. Six ships of this class were not provided with improved A/S capabilities because of increased costs.

Photographs: The photographs of the *Mullinnix* and *Hull* shows the ships' SPS-40 radar antenna on her forward tripod mast; the modernised *Manley* has the older SPS-37 antenna. The after masts hold Electronic Warfare (EW) pods. Note the outsize turret for the light-weight 8 inch gun in the *Hull;* a small deckhouse was added just forward of the after gun mounts to compensate for the loss of space forward.

42 DESTROYERS (DD): MODERNISED "GEARING" CLASS (FRAM I)

Name	No.	Builders	Laid down	Launched	Commissioned
*WILLIAM R. RUSH (NRF)	DD 714	Federal SB & DD Co	19 Oct 1944	8 July 1945	21 Sep 1945
*WILLIAM M. WOOD	DD 715	Federal SB & DD Co	2 Nov 1944	29 July 1945	24 Nov 1945
*HAMNER (NRF)	DD 718	Federal SB & DD Co	23 April 1945	24 Nov 1945	11 July 1946
*SOUTHERLAND (NRF)	DD 743	Bath Iron Works Corp	27 May 1944	5 Oct 1944	22 Dec 1944
*WILLIAM C. LAWE (NRF)	DD 763	Bethlehem (San Francisco)	12 Mar 1944	21 May 1945	18 Dec 1946
*McKEAN (NRF)	DD 784	Todd Pacific Shipyards	15 Sep 1944	31 Mar 1945	9 June 1945
*HENDERSON (NRF)	DD 785	Todd Pacific Shipyards	27 Oct 1944	28 May 1945	26 Mar 1946
*HOLLISTER (NRF)	DD 788	Todd Pacific Shipyards	27 Dec 1944	9 Oct 1945	27 Jan 1946
*HIGBEE (NRF)	DD 806	Bath Iron Works Corp	26 June 1944	12 Nov 1944	26 Feb 1946
*CORRY (NRF)	DD 817	Consolidated Steel Corp	5 April 1945	28 July 1945	5 April 1946
*NEW	DD 818	Consolidated Steel Corp	14 April 1945	18 Aug 1945	18 May 1946
*HOLDER (NRF)	DD 819	Consolidated Steel Corp	23 April 1945	25 Aug 1945	4 July 1946
*RICH (NRF)	DD 820	Consolidated Steel Corp	16 May 1945	5 Oct 1945	10 Oct 1946
*JOHNSTON (NRF)	DD 821	Consolidated Steel Corp	6 May 1942	19 Oct 1945	26 Oct 1946
*ROBERT H. McCARD (NRF)	DD 822	Consolidated Steel Corp	20 June 1945	9 Nov 1945	26 July 1949
*BASILONE	DD 824	Bath Iron Works Corp	7 July 1945	21 Dec 1945	20 June 1946
*AGERHOLM	DD 826	Bath Iron Works Corp	10 Sep 1945	30 Mar 1946	20 Mar 1945
*MYLES C. FOX (NRF)	DD 829	Bath Iron Works Corp	14 Aug 1944	13 Jan 1945	29 June 1945
*CHARLES P. CECIL (NRF)	DD 835	Bath Iron Works Corp	2 Dec 1944	22 April 1945	13 July 1945
*GEORGE K. MacKENZIE	DD 836	Bath Iron Works Corp	21 Dec 1944	13 May 1945	31 July 1945
*SARSFIELD	DD 837	Bath Iron Works Corp	15 Jan 1945	27 May 1945	13 Sep 1945
*POWER (NRF)	DD 839	Bath Iron Works Corp	26 Feb 1945	30 June 1945	4 Oct 1945
*GLENNON	DD 840	Bath Iron Works Corp	12 Mar 1945	14 July 1945	28 Nov 1945
*FISKE (NRF)	DD 842	Bath Iron Works Corp	9 April 1945	8 Sep 1945	7 Feb 1947
*BAUSELL	DD 845	Bath Iron Works Corp	28 May 1945	19 Nov 1945	23 May 1946
*RICHARD E. KRAUS	DD 849 (ex-AG 151)	Bethlehem (Quincy)	31 July 1945	2 Mar 1946	28 June 1946
*LEONARD F. MASON	DD 852	Bethlehem (Staten Island)	6 Aug 1945	4 Jan 1946	28 April 1945
*VOGELGESANG (NRF)	DD 862	Bethlehem (Staten Island)	3 Aug 1944	15 Jan 1945	26 May 1945
*STEINAKER (NRF)	DD 863	Bethlehem (Staten Island)	1 Sep 1944	13 Feb 1945	23 June 1945
*HAROLD J. ELLISON (NRF)	DD 864	Bethlehem (Staten Island)	3 Oct 1944	14 Mar 1945	18 Aug 1945
*CONE (NRF)	DD 866	Bethlehem (Staten Island)	30 Nov 1944	10 May 1945	17 Nov 1945
*BROWNSON	DD 868	Bethlehem (Staten Island)	13 Feb 1945	15 Mar 1945	27 April 1946
*DAMATO (NRF)	DD 871	Consolidated Steel Corp	10 May 1945	21 Nov 1945	10 Feb 1945
*HAWKINS	DD 873	Consolidated Steel Corp	14 May 1944	7 Oct 1944	26 Mar 1945
*ROGERS (NRF)	DD 876	Consolidated Steel Corp	3 June 1944	20 Nov 1944	23 April 1945
*VESOLE	DD 878	Consolidated Steel Corp	4 July 1944	29 dec 1944	21 May 1945
*DYESS (NRF)	DD 880	Consolidated Steel Corp	17 Aug 1944	26 Jan 1945	5 June 1945
*BORDELON	DD 881	Consolidated Steel Corp	9 Sep 1944	3 Mar 1945	26 July 1945
*NEWMAN K. PERRY (NRF)	DD 883	Consolidated Steel Corp	10 Oct 1944	17 Mar 1945	20 Aug 1945
*JOHN R. CRAIG (NRF)	DD 885	Consolidated Steel Corp	17 Nov 1944	14 April 1945	15 Sep 1945
*ORLECK (NRF)	DD 886	Consolidated Steel Corp	28 Nov 1944	12 May 1945	31 Dec 1945
*MEREDITH (NRF)	DD 890	Consolidated Steel Corp	27 Jan 1945	28 June 1945	

Displacement, tons: 2 425 standard; 3 480 to 3 520 full load
Length, feet (metres): 390·5 *(119·0)* oa
Beam, feet (metres): 40·9 *(12·4)*
Draught, feet (metres): 19 *(5·8)*
Guns: 4—5 inch *(127 mm)* 38 calibre DP (Mk 38) (twin)
A/S weapons: 1 ASROC 8-tube launcher; 2 triple torpedo tubes (Mk 32)
Main engines: 2 geared turbines (General Electric or Westinghouse), 60 000 shp; 2 shafts
Boilers: 4 (Babcock & Wilcox or combination Babcock & Wilcox and Foster-Wheeler)
Speed, knots: 34
Complement: 274 (14 officers, 260 enlisted men); 307 in Naval Reserve training ships (12 officers, 176 enlisted active duty; 7 officers, 112 enlisted reserve)

These ships are the survivors under US colours of the several hundred destroyers constructed in the United States during World War II.

The *Richard E. Kraus* (ex-AG 151) and *Sarsfield* have been used for experimental work (EDD). (The former ship was designated AG 151 from 24 Aug 1949 to 11 Dec 1953).

The "Gearing" class initially covered hull numbers DD 710-721, 742, 743, 763-769, 782-791, 805-926. Forty-nine of these ships were cancelled in 1945 (DD 768, 796, 809-816, 854-856, and 891-926); four ships were never completed and were scrapped in the 1950s; *Castle* (DD 720), *Woodrow R. Thompson* (DD 721), *Lansdale* (DD 766), and *Seymour D. Owens* (DD 767).

Two similar ships completed to a modified design after World War II are listed separately as the "Carpenter" class.

All surviving ships of this class are active. Twenty-eight ships are assigned to Naval Reserve training and are manned by composite active duty-reserve crews. These ships are noted as NRF (Naval Reserve Force).

Armament-Design: As built, these ships had a pole mast and carried an armament of six 5 inch guns (twin mounts), 12—40 mm AA guns (2 quad, 2 twin), 11—20 mm AA guns (single), and 10—21 inch torpedo tubes (quin). After World War II, the after bank of tubes was replaced by an additional quad 40 mm mount. All 40 mm and 20 mm guns were replaced subsequently by six 3 inch guns (2 twin, 2 single) and a tripod mast was installed to support heavier radar antennae. The 3 inch guns and remaining anti-ship torpedo tubes were removed during FRAM modernisation.

Electronics: These ships have SPS-10 and SPS-40 or SPS-37 search radar antennae on their forward tripod mast; electronic warfare equipment fitted to most ships with an enlarged electronic "stack" atop the helicopter hangar-ASROC magazine structure. Fitted with SQS-23 sonar. *Brownson* fitted with SQQ (modified SQS-23) and *Glennon* fitted with SQS-56 (modified SQS-23) for evaluation.
Single Mk 37 gunfire control system provided.

Engineering: Range is reported at 5 800 miles at 15 knots and 4 000 miles at 20 knots.
During November 1974 the *Johnston* conducted experiments using liquified coal as fuel in one boiler (Project Seacoal).

Helicopters: These ships no longer operate drone helicopters, but rely on ASROC and tube-launched torpedoes for anti-submarine weapons. They had been fitted to operate the Drone Anti-Submarine Helicopter (DASH) during FRAM modernisation.

Modernisation: All of these ships have undergone extensive modernisation under the Fleet Rehabilitation and Modernisa-

BASILONE (DD 824)   *1975, Giorgio Arra*

POWER (DD 839)   *1973, Giorgio Arra*

"GEARING" CLASS—continued

tion (FRAM I) programme. They were stripped of all armament except two 5 inch mounts, new anti-submarine weapons were installed including facilities for operating ASW helicopters, new electronic equipment was installed, machinery was overhauled, living and working spaces were rehabilitated. For budgeting reasons FRAM I work was officially considered a "conversion". Conversions undertaken between 1961 and 1965.

There are two basic FRAM I configurations: the *Stribling*, *Agerholm*, and *Meredith* have twin 5 inch mounts in "A" and "B" positions and Mk 32 torpedo launchers abaft second funnel; others have twin 5 inch mounts in "A" and "Y" positions and Mk 32 launchers on 01 level in "B" position.

Transfers: "Gearing" class destroyers currently serve in the navies of Argentina, Brazil, Greece, South Korea, Pakistan, Spain, Taiwan and Turkey.

Photographs: In the accompanying photographs the *Basilone*, *Sarsfield*, and *Glennon* have SPS-40 radar antennae on their tripod mast; the *Power* has SPS-37. Note the special electronic van on the *Sarsfield's* helicopter deck. The *Power*, shown the same year she was assigned to the Naval Reserve Force, has less sophisticated Electronic Warfare (EW) equipment mounted on top of her helicopter hangar.

SARSFIELD (DD 837)　　　　　　　　　　1974, Stefan Terzibaschitsch

Disposals (since 1 Jan 1975): *Theodore E. Chandler* (DD 717) stricken on 1 April 1975; *Ozbourn* (DD 846) stricken on 1 June 1975; *Epperson* (DD 719) stricken on 1 Dec 1975; *Rowan* (DD 782) stricken on 18 Dec 1975 for transfer to Pakistan; *Richard B.* *Anderson* (DD 786) stricken on 20 Dec 1975; *Wiltsie* (DD 716) stricken on 23 Jan 1976 for transfer to Pakistan; *Gurke* (DD 783) stricken on 20 Jan 1976; *Stribling* (DD 867) stricken in July 1976.

GLENNON (DD 840)　　　　　　　　　　1973, United States Navy

2 DESTROYERS (DD): "CARPENTER" CLASS (FRAM I)

Name	No.	Builders	Laid down	Launched	Commissioned
*CARPENTER (NRF)	DD 825	Consolidated Steel Corp (Orange, Texas)	30 July 1945	30 Dec 1945	15 Dec 1949
*ROBERT A. OWENS (NRF)	DD 827	Bath Iron Works Corp	29 Oct 1945	15 July 1946	5 Nov 1949

Displacement, tons: 2 425 standard; 3 410 full load
Length, feet (metres): 390·5 *(119·0)* oa
Beam, feet (metres): 40·9 *(12·4)*
Draught, feet (metres): 19 *(5·8)*
Guns: 2—5 inch *(127 mm)* 38 calibre DP (Mk 38) (twin)
A/S weapons: 1 ASROC 8-tube launcher; 2 triple torpedo tubes (Mk 32)
Main engines: 2 geared turbines (Westinghouse in *Carpenter*, General Electric in *Robert A. Owens*); 60 000 shp; 2 shafts
Boilers: 4 (Babcock & Wilcox)
Speed, knots: 34
Complement: 282 (12 officers, 176 enlisted active duty; 8 officers, 86 enlisted reserve)

These ships were laid down as units of the "Gearing" class. Their construction was suspended after World War II until 1947 when they were towed to the Newport News Shipbuilding and Dry Dock Co for completion as "hunter-killer" destroyers (DDK). As specialised ASW ships they mounted 3 inch (76 mm) guns in place of 5 inch mounts and were armed with improved ahead-firing anti-submarine weapons (hedgehogs and Weapon Able/Alfa); special sonar equipment installed. The DDK and DDE classifications were merged in 1950 with both of these ships being designated DDE on 4 March 1950. Upon being modernised to the FRAM I configuration they were reclassified DD on 30 June 1962.
Both of these ships are assigned to Naval Reserve training;

they are manned by composite active duty and reserve crews.

Electronics: These ships have SPS-10 and SPS-40 search radars on their forward tripod mast and electronic warfare "pods" on a smaller tripod mast forward of their second funnel. SQS-23 sonar provided. Fitted with Mk 56 Mod 43 gunfire control system.

Photographs: The *Carpenter* and *Robert A. Owens* are distinguished as the only surviving war-built US destroyer with one 5 inch twin gun mount. Note tripod mast before second funnel; absence of extension of 01 and 02 levels aft of bridge common to "Gearing" class ships.

ROBERT A. OWENS (DD 827)　　　　　　　　　　1969, United States Navy

"ALLEN M. SUMNER" CLASS

All surviving ships of the 70-destroyer "Allen M. Sumner" class have been stricken or transferred to other navies. Between 1943 and 1945, 58 destroyers and 12 minelayers were completed to this design. See 1974-1975 and earlier editions for characteristics.
Ships of this class serve in the navies of Argentina, Brazil, Chile, Colombia, Greece, Iran, South Korea, Taiwan China, Turkey and Venezuela.

Disposals: (since 1 Jan 1975) *Laffey* (DD 724) stricken on 29 March 1975.

"FLETCHER" CLASSES

The survivors of 119 "Fletcher" and 56 "repeat Fletcher" class destroyers have been stricken or transferred to other navies. See 1975-1976 and previous editions for characteristics.

Ships of these classes serve in the navies of Argentina, Brazil, Chile, Colombia, West Germany, Greece, Italy, Japan, South Korea, Mexico, Peru, Spain, Taiwan China and Turkey.

Disposals: (since 1 Jan 1975) *Porterfield* (DD 682), *Picking* (DD 685) stricken on 1 March 1975; *Stoddard* (DD 566) stricken on 1 June 1975.

FRIGATES

SAMUEL GOMPERS (AD 37), RAMSEY (FFG 2), BARBEY (FF 1088), BRADLEY (FF 1041), and MEYERKORD (FF 1058)   *1975, courtesy Ships of the World*

The US Navy has adopted the classification "frigate" for those ships designed promarily for open-ocean escort and patrol. Previously these ships were classified as "ocean escorts" (DE/DEG) by the US Navy with the type originally being known as "destroyer escort" when developed during World War II. There are 65 frigates (FF/FFG/AGFF) in commission with another 50 ships planned for construction during the next few years. All ships now in commission have the large SQS-26 sonar, ASROC anti-submarine rockets, and a helicopter capability. However, only six have a surface-to-air missile capability for limited area defence. The planned 50 ships of the "Oliver Hazard Perry" class (FFG 7) will have the smaller SQS-56 sonar. The ASROC will be deleted but the ships will be able to operate two LAMPS (Light Airborne Multi-Purpose System) helicopters and will have a surface-to-air/surface-to-surface missile capa-

bility. The "Perry" class ships will be more versatile than the previous "Knox" class frigates and several other navies have expressed interest in the newer design. The Royal Australian Navy has ordered two of the ships as replacements for ex-British "Daring" class destroyers.

The US Navy's frigates could be supplemented in the ocean escort role by the 12 "Hamilton" class high-endurance cutters operated by the Coast Guard. The Coast Guard ships are fitted with sonar and are armed with Mk 32 torpedo tubes (as well as a single 5-inch gun). They also have facilities for operating a large helicopter.

The Coast Guard plans to construct a new class of medium endurance cutters which also will have a limited anti-submarine/escort capability.

Surface Effect Ships: The planned 2 000-ton, ocean-going Surface Effect Ship (SES) has been redesignated as the Advanced Naval Vehicles programme and is listed separately, immediately following the Frigate section of this edition.

Nomenclature: Frigates are generally named for deceased US Navy, Marine Corps, and Coast Guard personnel.

Photographs: The above photograph shows a "nest" of four frigates and a destroyer tender at San Diego, California, on New Year's Day 1975. Note the different stern configurations, the large experimental radome on the *Barbey* (subsequently removed) and the ship's large stern opening for variable-depth sonar. The *Ramsey* has a smaller stern opening for torpedo tubes and the *Meyerkord* has a Sea Sparrow multiple missile launcher on the fantail.

(50) GUIDED MISSILE FRIGATES (FFG): "OLIVER HAZARD PERRY" CLASS

Name	No.	Builders	Laid down	Launched	Commission
OLIVER HAZARD PERRY	FFG 7 (ex-PF 109)	Bath Iron Works, Bath, Maine	12 June1975	Sep 1976	Mid 1977
	FFG 8	Bath Iron Works, Bath, Maine	1978		1980
	FFG 9	Todd Shipyards Corp, San Pedro, Calif	1977		1980
	FFG 10	Todd Shipyards Corp, Seattle, Wash	1977		1980
	FFG 11	Bath Iron Works, Bath, Maine	1978		1980
	FFG 12	Todd Shipyards Corp, San Pedro, Calif	1978		1980
	FFG 13	Bath Iron Works, Bath, Maine	1978		1980
	FFG 14	Todd Shipyards Corp, San Pedro, Calif	1978		1980
	FFG 15	Bath Iron Works, Bath, Maine	1979		1981
	FFG 16	Bath Iron Works, Bath, Maine	1979		1981
Eight ships	FFG	Proposed Fiscal Year 1977 programme			
Eight ships	FFG	Planned FY 1978 programme			
Eight ships	FFG	Planned FY 1979 programme			
Eight ships	FFG	Planned FY 1980 programme			
Eight ships	FFG	Planned FY 1981 programme			

Displacement, tons: 3 605 full load
Length, feet (metres): 445 *(135·6)* oa
Beam, feet (metres): 45 *(13·7)*
Draught, feet (metres): 24·5 *(7·5)*
Missile launchers: 1 single launcher for Standard/Harpoon missiles (Mk 13 Mod 4)
Guns: 1—76 mm 62 calibre dual-purpose (Mk 75);
1—20 mm Phalanx CIWS (space reserved)
A/S weapons: 2 SH-2 LAMPS helicopters;
2 triple torpedo tubes (Mk 32)
Main engines: 2 gas turbines (General Electric); 40 000 shp; 1 shaft (controllable-pitch propeller)
Speed, knots: 28+ sustained
Complement: 176 (14 officers, 162 enlisted men)

These ships are planned to supplement existing frigates in the protection of underway replenishment groups, amphibious forces, and military and merchant shipping. They are follow-on ships to the large number of frigates (formerly DE) built in the 1960s and early 1970s, with the later ships emphasising anti-ship/aircraft/missile capabilities while the previous classes were oriented primarily against submarines (eg, larger SQS-26 sonar and ASROC).

OLIVER HAZARD PERRY (now FFG 7)   *United States Navy*

"PERRY" CLASS—continued

The lead ship (FFG 7) was authorised in the Fiscal Year 1973 shipbuilding programme; three ships (FFG 8-10) in FY 1975 programme; and six ships (FFG 11-16) in FY 1976 programme. Congress authorised nine ships in FY 1976, but cost escalation permitted the construction of only six ships.

The Navy proposes to build 40 additional ships of this class under the FY 1977-1981 programmes. However, there is strong Congressional opposition to these ships and a reduced number is expected to be procured.

Two additional ships of this class are under construction at the Todd-Seattle shipyard for the Royal Australian Navy; they are assigned US Navy hull numbers FFG 18 and FFG 19 for accounting purposes. Several other navies have expressed interest in these ships.

Classification: These ships were originally classified as "patrol frigates" (PF) at a time when the term "frigate" was used in the US Navy for the large, cruiser-size destroyer leaders (DL/DLG/DLGN). Previously the US Navy used the term frigate for a series of World War II-built escort ships (PF 1-102) and later for coastal escorts built specifically for transfer to foreign navies (PF 103-108). The *Perry* was designated PF 109 at time of keel laying and designated FFG 7 on 30 June 1975.

Design: These ships are slightly longer but lighter than the preceding "Knox" class (DE 1052) escort ships. There has been special emphasis on interior design for efficiency to reduce manning requirements and noise levels. The original single hangar (see drawing in 1973-1974 edition) has been changed to two adjacent hangars, each to house SH-2 or follow-on LAMPS (Light Airborne Multi-Purpose System) helicopters.

The engineering plant, weapons, and sensors are based largely on equipment that is already in service in US or foreign ships. Several weapon and sensor systems were evaluated at sea in the guided missile frigate *Talbot* (FFG 4).

Fin stabilisers may be fitted at a later date (space and weight reserved).

Electronics: The *Perry*-class ships have SPS-49 long-range search, SPS-55 surface search and navigation, and STIR (Separate Track and Illumination Radar) radars, the last a modification of the SPG-60 weapons control radar. The Mk 92 Mod 2 weapons control system is installed with a dome-shaped antenna atop the bridge. (The Mk 92 is the Americanised version of the WM-28 system developed by N.V. Hollandse Signaalapparaten).

Fitted with SQS-56 hull-mounted sonar (improved SQS-23). The TACTAS towed sonar system will be fitted. TACTAS will provide a passive, very-long-range detection system.

OLIVER HAZARD PERRY (now FFG 7)

United States Navy

Engineering: Each ship will be powered by two General Electric LM 2500 marine gas turbine engines, the same engine being used in the "Spruance" class (DD 963) destroyers and "Pegasus" class (PHM 1) patrol combatants.

Two auxiliary retractable propeller pods are provided in the forward hull (aft of the sonar dome) to provide "come home" power in the event of a casualty to the main engines or propeller shaft. Each pod has a 325 hp engine to provide a ship speed of 3 to 5 knots.

Range is unofficially estimated at 4 500 miles at 20 knots.

Fiscal: The design-to-cost estimate of $45 700 000 in Fiscal Year 1973 dollars based on a 49-ship programme has increased to $55 300 000 in the same dollars to design and cost estimating changes. However, adding the estimated inflation and contract escalation factors brings the estimated cost per ship in the FY 1977 programme to $143 400 000. This is approximately $21 400 000 more per ship than estimated one year earlier.

Gunnery: The principal gun on this ship is the single 76 mm OTO Melara with a 90-round-per-minute firing rate (designated Mk 75 in US service). This gun is also fitted on the "Pegasus" class patrol combatants.

Space and weight are reserved for a Close-In Weapon System (CIWS); this probably will be the 20 mm Phalanx multi-barrel, rapid-fire gun (shown at the after end of the superstructure).

These are the first US frigates/escort ships to be built since the "Bronstein" class (FF 1037) completed in 1963 which have a 3 inch gun main battery.

Missiles: The single-arm Tartar-type missile launcher will be capable of firing both Standard-MR surface-to-air and Harpoon surface-to-surface missiles; "mixed" missile magazines will be provided. These ships will have a less flexible missile capability than the earlier "Brooke" class (FFG 1) frigates because of the single Standard/Harpoon launcher, whereas the "Brookes" can be fitted to fire Harpoon anti-ship missiles from their ASROC launcher, permitting their Mk 22 launcher to remain continuously in the anti-air mode.

Nomenclature: Commodore Oliver Hazard Perry commanded the US flotilla on Lake Erie during the War of 1812, winning victory over a British force in a savage battle.

Photographs: In the two artist's concepts the *Perry* has the PF 109 hull number. The stern view shows paired LAMPS helicopter hangars. Note the three lattice antenna masts, aft of which are the STIR antenna, 76 mm OTO Melara gun, engine exhaust stack, and 20 mm Phalanx CIWS.

Below, the *Talbot* (FFG 4) is shown configured as the test platform for FFG 7 systems; visible from bow to stern are the 76 mm OTO Melara gun forward of the ASROC launcher, Mk 92 weapons control system radome adjacent to the hangar, and STIR antenna on the stern. Not visible is the SQS-56 sonar. Note the small structure installed aft of the hangar. The *Talbot* has now reverted to a "Brooke" class configuration.

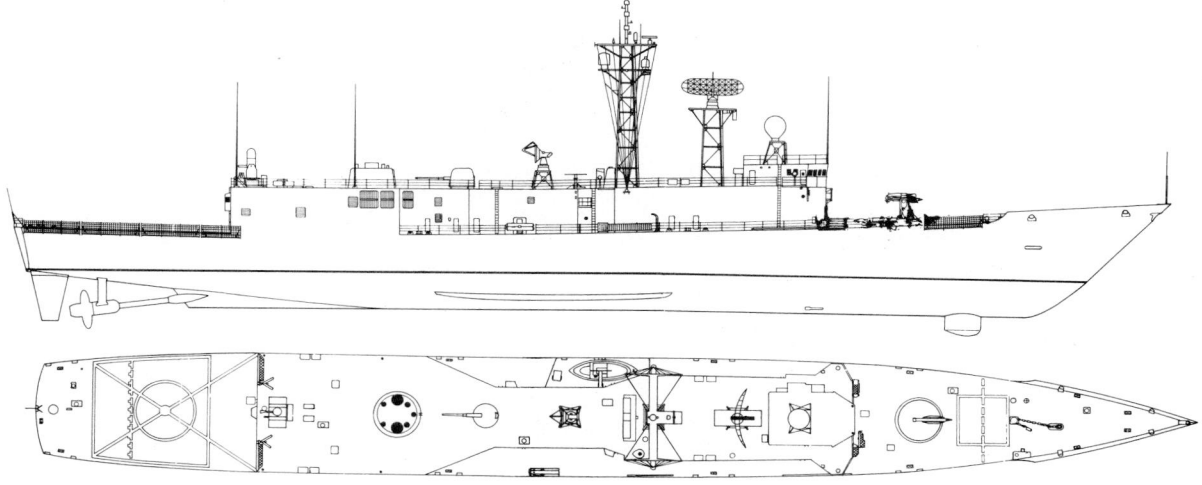

Drawing by A. D. Baker

TALBOT (FFG 4)—as test and evaluation ship for FFG 7 systems

1974, United States Navy

6 GUIDED MISSILE FRIGATES (FFG): "BROOKE" CLASS

Name	No.	Builders	Laid down	Launched	Commissioned
*BROOKE	FFG 1	Lockheed SB & Construction Co	10 Dec 1962	19 July 1963	12 Mar 1966
*RAMSEY	FFG 2	Lockheed SB & Construction Co	4 Feb 1963	15 Oct 1963	3 June1967
*SCHOFIELD	FFG 3	Lockheed SB & Construction Co	15 April1963	7 Dec 1963	20 April1968
*TALBOT	FFG 4	Bath Iron Works Corp	4 May 1964	6 Jan 1966	22 April1967
*RICHARD L. PAGE	FFG 5	Bath Iron Works Corp	4 Jan 1965	4 April1966	5 Aug 1967
*JULIUS A. FURER	FFG 6	Bath Iron Works Corp	12 July 1965	22 July 1966	11 Nov 1967

Displacement, tons: 2 640 standard; 3 245 full load
Length, feet (metres): 414·5 *(126·3)* oa
Beam, feet (metres): 44·2 *(13·5)*
Draught, feet (metres): 24 *(7·3)*
Missile launchers: 1 single Tarter/Standard-MR surface-to-air launcher (Mk 22 Mod 0)
Guns: 1—5 inch *(127 mm)* 38 calibre DP (Mk 30)
Helicopters: 1 SH-2 LAMPS helicopter
A/S weapons: 1 ASROC 8-tube launcher; 2 triple torpedo tubes (Mk 32)
Main engines: 1 geared turbine (Westinghouse); 35 000 shp; 1 shaft
Boilers: 2
Speed, knots: 27
Complement: 241 (16 officers, 225 enlisted men)

These ships are identical to the "Garcia" class escorts except for the Tarter missile system in lieu of a second 5 inch gun mount and different electronic equipment. Authorised as DEG 1-3 in the Fiscal Year 1962 new construction programme and DEG 4-6 in the FY 1963 programme. Plans for ten additional DEGs in FY 1964 and possibly three more DEGs in a later programme were dropped because of the $11 000 000 additional cost of a DEG over DE. See "Garcia" class for additional notes. In 1974-1975 the *Talbot* was reconfigured as test and evaluation ship for systems being developed for the "Oliver Hazard Perry" class (FFG 7) frigates and "Pegasus" class (PHM 7) hydrofoil missile combatants.

Classification: Built as DEG 1-6, respectively; reclassified as FFG 1-6 30 June 1975. The hull numbers DEG 7-11 were assigned for accounting purposes to guided missile frigates built in Spain with US assistance ("Baleares" class).

Electronics: SQS-26AX bow mounted sonar installed. SPS-52 three-dimensional search radar is mounted on the "mack" (combination mast and stack) and SPS-10 search radar is installed on the mast. SPG-51C missile fire control radar is installed aft of the "mack". Also provided with Mk 74 gun/missile fire control system and Mk 56 gunfire control system.
The advanced Mk 92 fire control system (Americanised version of the WM-28 radar and weapon control system) was installed in the *Talbot* in August 1974 for test and evaluation. The Mk 92 is scheduled for use in the FFG 7 class and the PHM missile combatants.
The *Talbot* served as test ship for the SQS-56 sonar planned for the FFG 7 class frigates.

Gunnery: A single 76 mm/62 calibre OTO Melara rapid-fire gun (designated Mk 75 in US service) was installed in the *Talbot* in August 1974 for test and evaluation. The gun is for use in the FFG 7 class frigates and the PHM missile combatants.

Helicopters: These ships were designed to operate Drone Anti-Submarine Helicopters (DASH), but the programme was cut back before helicopters were provided to these ships. These ships are being fitted to operate the Light Airborne Multi-purpose System (LAMPS), now the SH-2 helicopter.

Missiles: These ships have a single Tartar Mk 22 launching system which weighs 92 395 pounds. Reportedly, the system has a rate of fire similar to the larger Mk 11 and Mk 13 systems installed in guided missile destroyers, but the FFG system has a considerably smaller magazine capacity (16 missiles according to unofficial sources).
The FFG 4-6 have automatic ASROC loading system (note angled base of bridge structure aft of ASROC "pepper box" in these ships).

RICHARD L. PAGE (FFG 5)   *1973, Giorgio Arra*

BROOKE (FFG 1)   *1969, United States Navy*

RICHARD L. PAGE (FFG 5)   *1973, Giorgio Arra*

46 FRIGATES (FF): "KNOX" CLASS

Name	No.	Builders	Laid down	Launched	Commissioned
*KNOX	FF 1052	Todd Shipyards (Seattle)	5 Oct 1965	19 Nov 1966	12 April 1969
*ROARK	FF 1053	Todd Shipyards (Seattle)	2 Feb 1966	24 April 1967	22 Nov 1969
*GRAY	FF 1054	Todd Shipyards (Seattle)	19 Nov 1966	3 Nov 1967	4 April 1970
*HEPBURN	FF 1055	Todd Shipyards (San Pedro)	1 June 1966	25 Mar 1967	3 July 1969
*CONNOLE	FF 1056	Avondale Shipyards	23 Mar 1967	20 July 1968	30 Aug 1969
*RATHBURNE	FF 1057	Lockheed SB & Constn Co	8 Jan 1968	2 May 1969	16 May 1970
*MEYERKORD	FF 1058	Todd Shipyards (San Pedro)	1 Sep 1966	15 July 1967	28 Nov 1969
*W. S. SIMS	FF 1059	Avondale Shipyards	10 Apr 1967	4 Jan 1969	3 Jan 1970
*LANG	FF 1060	Todd Shipyards (San Pedro)	25 Mar 1967	17 Feb 1968	28 Mar 1970
*PATTERSON	FF 1061	Avondale Shipyards	12 Oct 1967	3 May 1969	14 Mar 1970
*WHIPPLE	FF 1062	Todd Shipyards (Seattle)	24 April 1967	12 April 1968	22 Aug 1970
*REASONER	FF 1063	Lockheed SB & Constn Co	6 Jan 1969	1 Aug 1970	31 July 1971
*LOCKWOOD	FF 1064	Todd Shipyards (Seattle)	3 Nov 1967	5 Sep 1964	5 Dec 1970
*STEIN	FF 1065	Lockheed SB & Constn Co	1 June 1970	19 Dec 1970	8 Jan 1972
*MARVIN SHIELDS	FF 1066	Todd Shipyards (Seattle)	12 Apr 1968	23 Oct 1969	10 April 1971
*FRANCIS HAMMOND	FF 1067	Todd Shipyards (San Pedro)	15 July 1967	11 May 1968	25 July 1970
*VREELAND	FF 1068	Avondale Shipyards	20 Mar 1968	14 June 1969	13 June 1970
*BAGLEY	FF 1069	Lockheed SB & Constn Co	22 Sep 1970	24 April 1971	6 May 1972
*DOWNES	FF 1070	Todd Shipyards (Seattle)	5 Sep 1968	13 Dec 1969	28 Aug 1971
*BADGER	FF 1071	Todd Shipyards (Seattle)	17 Feb 1968	7 Dec 1968	1 Dec 1970
*BLAKELY	FF 1072	Avondale Shipyards	3 June 1968	23 Aug 1969	18 July 1970
*ROBERT E. PEARY	FF 1073	Lockheed SB & Constn Co	20 Dec 1970	23 June 1971	23 Sep 1972
*HAROLD E. HOLT	FF 1074	Todd Shipyards (San Pedro)	11 May 1968	3 May 1969	26 Mar 1971
*TRIPPE	FF 1075	Avondale Shipyards	29 July 1968	1 Nov 1969	19 Sep 1970
*FANNING	FF 1076	Todd Shipyards (San Pedro)	7 Dec 1968	24 Jan 1970	23 July 1971
*OUELLET	FF 1077	Avondale Shipyards	15 Jan 1969	17 Jan 1970	12 Dec 1970
*JOSEPH HEWES	FF 1078	Avondale Shipyards	15 May 1969	7 Mar 1970	27 Feb 1971
*BOWEN	FF 1079	Avondale Shipyards	11 July 1969	2 May 1970	22 May 1971
*PAUL	FF 1080	Avondale Shipyards	12 Sep 1969	20 June 1970	14 Aug 1971
*AYLWIN	FF 1081	Avondale Shipyards	13 Nov 1969	29 Aug 1970	18 Sep 1971
*ELMER MONTGOMERY	FF 1082	Avondale Shipyards	23 Jan 1970	21 Nov 1970	30 Oct 1971
*COOK	FF 1083	Avondale Shipyards	20 Mar 1970	23 Jan 1971	18 Dec 1971
*McCANDLESS	FF 1084	Avondale Shipyards	4 June 1970	20 Mar 1971	18 Mar 1972
*DONALD B. BEARY	FF 1085	Avondale Shipyards	24 July 1970	22 May 1971	22 July 1972
*BREWTON	FF 1086	Avondale Shipyards	2 Oct 1970	24 July 1971	8 July 1972
*KIRK	FF 1087	Avondale Shipyards	4 Dec 1970	25 Sep 1971	9 Sep 1972
*BARBEY	FF 1088	Avondale Shipyards	5 Feb 1971	4 Dec 1971	11 Nov 1972
*JESSE L. BROWN	FF 1089	Avondale Shipyards	8 April 1971	18 Mar 1972	17 Feb 1973
*AINSWORTH	FF 1090	Avondale Shipyards	11 June 1971	15 Apr 1972	31 Mar 1973
*MILLER	FF 1091	Avondale Shipyards	6 Aug 1971	3 June 1972	30 June 1973
*THOMAS C. HART	FF 1092	Avondale Shipyards	8 Oct 1971	12 Aug 1972	28 July 1973
*CAPODANNO	FF 1093	Avondale Shipyards	12 Oct 1971	21 Oct 1972	17 Nov 1973
*PHARRIS	FF 1094	Avondale Shipyards	11 Feb 1972	16 Dec 1972	26 Jan 1974
*TRUETT	FF 1095	Avondale Shipyards	27 Apr 1972	3 Feb 1973	1 June 1974
*VALDEZ	FF 1096	Avondale Shipyards	30 June 1972	24 Mar 1973	27 July 1974
*MOINESTER	FF 1097	Avondale Shipyards	25 Aug 1972	12 May 1973	2 Nov 1974

Displacement, tons: 3 011 standard; 4 100 full load
Length, feet (metres): 438 (133·5) oa
Beam, feet (metres): 46·75 (14·25)
Draught, feet (metres): 24·75 (7·55)
Helicopters: 1 SH-2 LAMPS being provided
Missile launchers: 1 Sea Sparrow BPDMS multiple launcher in 30 ships (Mk 25); 1 NATO Sea Sparrow multiple launcher in *Downes* (Mk 29)
Guns: 1—5 inch (127 mm) 54 calibre (Mk 42) dual purpose
A/S weapons: 1 ASROC 8-tube launcher; 4 fixed torpedo tubes (Mk 32)
Main engines: 1 geared turbine (Westinghouse) 35 000 shp; 1 shaft
Boilers: 2
Speed, knots: 27+
Complement: 245 (17 officers, 228 enlisted men); increased to 283 (22 officers, 261 enlisted men) with BPDMS and LAMPS installation; as built 12 ships had accommodation for 2 staff officers

The 46 frigates of the "Knox" class comprise the largest group of destroyer or frigate type warships built to the same design in the West since World War II. These ships are similar to the previous "Garcia" and "Brooke" classes, but slightly larger because of the use of non-pressure-fired boilers.

Although now classified as frigates they were authorised as DE 1052-1061 (10 ships) in the Fiscal Year 1964 new construction programme, DE 1062-1077 (16 ships) in FY 1965, DE 1078-1087 (10 ships) in FY 1966, DE 1088-1097 (10 ships) in FY 1967, and DE 1098-1107 (10 ships) in FY 1968. However, construction of six ships (DE 1102-1107) was deferred in 1968 as US Navy emphasis shifted to the more versatile and faster DX/DXG ships; three additional ships (DE 1099-1101) were deferred late in 1968 to finance cost overruns of FY 1968 nuclear-powered attack submarines and to comply with a Congressional mandate to reduce expenditures; the last ship of the FY 1968 programme (DE 1098) was deferred early in 1969.

The DEG 7-11 guided missile "frigates" constructed in Spain are similar to this design.
All of these ships are active.

Classification: Originally classified as ocean escorts (DE); reclassified as frigates (FF) on 30 June 1975.

Construction: The ships built at Avondale Shipyards in Westwego, Louisiana, were assembled with mass production techniques. The hulls were built keel-up to permit downhead welding with the force of gravity allowing the molten weld to follow the contour of the hull and flow more easily between hull plates. Prefabricated, inverted hull modules were first assembled on a permanent platen, then lifted by hydraulic units and moved laterally into giant turning rings which rotated the hull into an upright position. Avondale, which also builds the "Hamilton" class cutters for the Coast Guard, side launched these ships.

Design: These ships have a very large superstructure and a distinctive, cylindrical "mack" structure combining masts and engine exhaust stacks. A 4 000-pound lightweight anchor is fitted on the port side and an 8 000-pound anchor fits into the after section of the sonar dome.

Electronics: SQS-26CX bow-mounted sonar; installation of

THOMAS C. HART (FF 1092)

1974, US Navy, PH3 Donald M. Friedman

AYLWIN (FF 1081) with BPDMS and LAMPS

1975, Giorgio Arra

"KNOX" CLASS—continued

SQS-35 Independent Variable Depth Sonar (IVDS) in 35 ships began in 1971 (not in FF 1053-1055, 1057-1062, 1072 and 1077). The SQS-26CX is fitted in a tear-drop shaped dome 20 feet wide weighing 26 tons.

These ships have SPS-40 and SPS-10 search radar antennae on their "mack" structure.

The *Downes* has SPS-58 threat detection radar with antenna on after lattice mast; the ship also has two directors fitted for the NATO Sea Sparrow (on forward lattice mast and helicopter hangar) and Improved Point Defence/Target Acquisition System (IPD/TAS) radar antenna on "mack".

The *Barbey* had an experimental radar on the hangar structure during the mid-1970s.

All ships believed fitted with Mk 68 gunfire control system and SPG-53A weapon control radar.

Engineering: DE 1101 was to have had gas turbine propulsion; construction of the ship was cancelled when decision was made to provide gas turbine propulsion in the "Spruance" class (DD 963) destroyers.

These ships can steam at 22 knots on one boiler. They have a single 5-blade, 15-foot diameter propeller.

Fiscal: These ships have cost considerably more than originally estimated. Official programme cost for the 46 ships as of January 1974 was $1·424 *billion* or an average of $30 959 000 per ship not including the LAMPS, Standard missile, VDS, or BPDMS installation.

Helicopters: These ships were designed to operate the now-discarded DASH unmanned helicopter. Beginning in 1972 they are being modified to accommodate the Light Airborne Multi-Purpose System, the SH-2D anti-submarine helicopter; hangar and flight deck are enlarged. Cost was approximately $1 000 000 per ship for LAMPS modification.

Missiles: Sea Sparrow Basic Point Defence Missile System (BPDMS) launcher installed in 30 ships from 1971-1974 (DE 1052-1067, 1069, 1071-1083); also will be installed in DE 1068 during 1975.

Modified NATO Sea Sparrow installed in *Downes* for evaluation.

In addition, some ships are being fitted with the Standard interim surface-to-surface missile which is fired from the ASROC launcher forward of the bridge.

Two of the eight "cells" in the launcher are modified to fire a single Standard. Cost was approximately $400 000 per ship for BPDMS and $750 000 for Standard missile modification.

The *Downes* and *Lockwood* have been used in at-sea firing tests and shipboard compatability for the Harpoon ship-to-ship missiles. (See photo in 1975-1976 edition).

CONNOLE (FF 1056)

1975, Giorgio Arra

Nomenclature: The lead ship of this class is named for naval historian Dudley W. Knox (the DD 742 was named for Frank Knox who was Secretary of the Navy from 1940 to 1944). The *Harold E. Holt* honours the late Prime Minister of Australia, a firm supporter of US policy in Southeast Asia during the Vietnam War. The *Jesse L. Brown* remembers the first black US naval aviator; he was killed in action during the Korean War. The DE 1073 originally was named *Conolly;* changed on 12 May 1971.

Torpedoes: Improved ASROC-torpedo reloading capability as in some ships of previous "Garcia" class (note slanting face of bridge structure immediately behind ASROC "pepper box"). Four Mk 32 torpedo tubes are fixed in the amidships structure, two to a side, angled out at 45 degrees. The arrangement provides improved loading capability over exposed triple Mk 32 torpedo tubes.

Photographs: In the photograph of the *Connole* note the small lattice mast and TACAN (Tactical Air Navigation) pod atop the hangar; expanding hangar structure and flight deck extended to full beam; Sea Sparrow BPDMS on fantail; and opening for Variable Depth Sonar (VDS).

HAROLD E. HOLT (FF 1074)

1975, United States Navy, PH3 D. J. Tyree

DOWNES (FF 1070) with NATO Sea Sparrow

1972, United States Navy

10 FRIGATES (FF): "GARCIA" CLASS

Name	No.	Builders	Laid down	Launched	Commissioned
*GARCIA	FF 1040	Bethlehem Steel (San Francisco)	16 Oct 1962	31 Oct 1963	21 Dec 1964
*BRADLEY	FF 1041	Bethlehem Steel (San Francisco)	17 Jan 1963	26 Mar 1964	15 May 1965
*EDWARD McDONNELL	FF 1043	Avondale Shipyards	1 April 1963	15 Feb 1964	15 Feb 1965
*BRUMBY	FF 1044	Avondale Shipyards	1 Aug 1963	6 June 1964	5 Aug 1965
*DAVIDSON	FF 1045	Avondale Shipyards	20 Sep 1963	2 Oct 1964	7 Dec 1965
*VOGE	FF 1047	Defoe Shipbuilding Co	21 Nov 1963	4 Feb 1965	25 Nov 1966
*SAMPLE	FF 1048	Lockheed SB & Construction Co	19 July 1963	28 Apr 1964	23 Mar 1968
*KOELSCH	FF 1049	Defoe Shipbuilding Co	19 Feb 1964	8 June 1965	10 June 1967
*ALBERT DAVID	FF 1050	Lockheed SB & Construction Co	29 April 1964	19 Dec 1964	19 Oct 1968
*O'CALLAHAN	FF 1051	Defoe Shipbuilding Co	19 Feb 1964	20 Oct 1965	13 July 1968

Displacement, tons: 2 620 standard; 3 400 full load
Length, feet (metres): 414·5 (126·3) oa
Beam, feet (metres): 44·2 (13·5)
Draught, feet (metres): 24 (7·3)
Helicopters: 1 SH-2 LAMPS helicopter
Guns: 2—5 inch (127 mm) 38 calibre (Mk 30) DP (single)
A/S weapons: 1 ASROC 8-tube launcher; 2 triple torpedo tubes (Mk 32)
Main engines: 1 geared turbine (Westinghouse); 35 000 shp; 1 shaft
Boilers: 2 (Foster Wheeler)
Speed, knots: 27
Complement: 247

These ships exceed some of the world's destroyers in size and ASW capability, but are designated as frigates by virtue of their single propeller shaft and limited speed. The FF 1040 and FF 1041 were authorised in the Fiscal Year 1961 new construction programme, FF 1043-1045 in FY 1962, and FF 1047-1051 in FY 1963.
All ten ships are active. They are expected to transfer to the Naval Reserve Force in the early 1980s.

Classification: Originally classified as ocean escorts (DE); reclassified as frigates (FF) on 30 June 1975. The hull numbers DE 1039, 1042, and 1046 were assigned to frigates built overseas for Portugal.

Design: They have a flush deck, radically raked stem, stem anchor, and mast and stack combined into a "mack" structure. Anchors are mounted at stem and on portside, just forward of 5 inch gun. Hangar structure of this class modified during the early 1970s.

Electronics: Bow-mounted SQS-26 AXR sonar in FF 1040-1045; SQS-26 BX sonar in FF 1046-1051. SPS-40 and SPS-10 search radar antennae on "mack". The Voge and Koelsch have been fitted with a specialised ASW Naval Tactical Data System (NTDS).
Also fitted with Mk 56 gunfire control system.

Helicopters: The Drone Anti-Submarine Helicopter (DASH)

O'CALLAHAN (FF 1051)   1975, United States Navy, PH1 H. J. Calligan

programme was cut back before these ships were provided with helicopters. Reportedly only the Bradley actually operated with DASH.
These ships are fitted to operate the Light Airborne Multi-Purpose System (LAMPS), now the SH-2 helicopter.

Missiles: The Bradley was fitted with a Sea Sparrow Basic Point Defense Missile System (BPDMS) in 1967-1968; removed for installation in the carrier Forrestal (CV 59). The BPDMS "pep-

perbox" was fitted between funnel and after 5 inch mount.

Torpedoes: Most of these ships were built with two Mk 25 torpedo tubes built into their transom for launching wire-guided ASW torpedoes. However, they have been removed from the earlier ships and deleted in the later ships. The Voge and later ships have automatic ASROC reload system (note angled base of bridge structure behind ASROC "pepper box" in these ships).

EDWARD McDONNELL (FF 1043) with SH-2D LAMPS helicopter   1973, United States Navy, PHC Frederick Gotauco

GARCIA (FF 1040)   1973, Giorgio Arra

1 FRIGATE RESEARCH SHIP (AGFF): "GLOVER" TYPE

Name	No.	Builders	Laid down	Launched	Commissioned
*GLOVER	AGFF 1 (ex-AGDE 1, ex-AG 163)	Bath Iron Works	29 July 1963	17 April 1965	13 Nov 1965

Displacement, tons: 2 643 standard; 3 426 full load
Length, feet (metres): 414·5 *(126·3)* oa
Beam, feet (metres): 44·2 *(13·5)*
Draught, feet (metres): 14·5 *(4·3)*
Guns: 1—5 inch *(127 mm)* 38 calibre (Mk 30) dual-purpose
A/S weapons: 1 ASROC 8-tube launcher; 2 triple torpedo tubes (Mk 32)
   facilities for small helicopter
Main engines: 1 geared turbine (Westinghouse); 35 000 shp; 1 shaft
Boilers: 2 Foster Wheeler
Speed, knots: 27
Complement: 236 plus 38 civilian technicians

The *Glover* was built to test an advanced hull design and

propulsion system, much the same as the *Albacore* (AGSS 569) embodied advanced submarine design concepts. However, unlike the *Albacore,* the *Glover* has a full combat capability. The ship was originally authorised in the Fiscal Year 1960 new construction programme, but was postponed and re-introduced in the FY 1961 programme. Estimated construction cost was $29 330 000.

Classification: The *Glover* was originally classified as a miscellaneous auxiliary (AG 163); completed as an escort research ship (AGDE 1). Subsequently changed to frigate research ship on 30 June 1975.

Design: The *Glover* has a massive bow sonar dome integral with her hull and extending well forward underwater.

No reload capability for ASROC because of space requirements for equipment and technical personnel.

Electronics: The *Glover* has bow-mounted SQS-26 AXR active sonar, hull-mounted SQR-13 Passive/Active Detection and Location (PADLOC) sonar, and SQS-35 Independent Variable Depth Sonar (IVDS) lowered from the stern.
SPS-40 and SPS-10 search radars are fitted on the "mack" structure. Also provided with Mk 56 gunfire control system. The ship has a prototype tactical assignment console that integrates signals from the three sonars and radars to present combined and coordinated tactical situation presentations in the Combat Information Centre (CIC). Reportedly, the tactical assignment console increases the combat effectiveness of the ship to a considerable extent.

GLOVER (AGFF 1)

1974, US Navy, PH1 L. M. Mackay

2 FRIGATES (FF): "BRONSTEIN" CLASS

Name	No.	Builders	Laid down	Launched	Commissioned
*BRONSTEIN	FF 1037	Avondale Shipyards	16 May 1961	31 Mar 1962	15 June 1963
*McCLOY	FF 1038	Avondale Shipyards	15 Sep 1961	9 June 1962	21 Oct 1963

Displacement, tons: 2 360 standard; 2 650 full load
Length, feet (metres): 371·5 *(113·2)* oa
Beam, feet (metres): 40·5 *(12·3)*
Draught, feet (metres): 23 *(7·0)*
Guns: 2—3 inch *(76 mm)* 50 calibre AA (Mk 33) (twin)
A/S weapons: 1 ASROC 8-tube launcher; 2 triple torpedo tubes (Mk 32)
   facilities for small helicopter
Main engines: 1 geared turbine (De Lavel); 20 000 shp; 1 shaft
Boilers: 2 (Foster Wheeler)
Speed, knots: 26
Complement: 220

These two ships may be considered the first of the "second generation" of post-World War II frigates (née escort ships) which are comparable in size and ASW capabilities to conventional destroyers. The *Bronstein* and *McCloy* have several features such as hull design, large sonar and ASW weapons that subsequently were incorporated into the mass-produced "Garcia", "Brooke", and "Knox"classes.
Both ships were built under the Fiscal Year 1960 new construction programme by Avondale Shipyards in Westwego, Louisiana.
These ships are active; they are expected to transfer to the Naval Reserve Force (NRF) about 1980.

Classification: These ships were originally classified as ocean escorts (DE); reclassified as frigates (FF) on 30 June 1975.

Design: These ships have a sharply raked stem, stem anchor, and mast and stacks combined in a "mack" structure. Position of stem anchor and portside anchor (just forward of gun mount) necessitated by large bow sonar dome.
As mast, a single 3 inch (Mk 34) open mount was aft of the helicopter deck; removed for installation of towed sonar. (These are the only US frigates with 3 inch guns) pending completion of the "Oliver Hazard Perry" class (FFG 7).

Electronics: Fitted with SPS-40 and SPS-10 search radar antennae on "mack" structure; SQS-26 bow-mounted sonar. Towed Array Surveillance System (TASS) installed in both ships in mid-1970s (see cable reel at deck break in photo of *McCloy* at right and on next page).
Also provided with Mk 56 gunfire control system.

McCLOY (FF 1038)

1971, United States Navy

Photographs: The *McCloy* is shown above while refuelling in rough seas during a NATO exercise; note the elaborate electronic antennae atop the ship's hangar structure.

RADAR PICKET ESCORTS

The surviving radar picket escorts of the converted "Edsall" class have been stricken. These ships were the last of the several hundred destroyer escorts (DE) built for the US and British navies during World War II to remain on the US Navy List. See the 1975-1976 and previous editions for characteristics as well as details of the other war programmes. The Philippine Navy has recently acquired one ship of the DER type that

had earlier served in the South Vietnamese Navy.
(The survivors of other DE classes, including several of post-World War II construction, serve in the navies of Brazil, Greece, Indonesia, Italy, South Korea, Peru, Philippines, Taiwan China, Thailand and Uruguay).

Disposals and Transfers: (since 1 Jan 1974) *Finch* (DER 328), *Lansing* (DER 388) stricken on 1 Feb 1974; *Durant* (DER 389) stricken on 1 April 1974; *Otterstetter* (DER 244), *Kirkpatrick* (DER 318), *Price* (DER 332), *Roy O. Hale* (DER 336), *Ramsden* (DER 383), *Rhodes* (DER 384) stricken on 1 Aug 1974; *Chambers* (DER 391) stricken on 1 Mar 1975; *Falgout* (DER 324), *Savage* (DER 386), *Vance* (DER 387), *Hissem* (DER 400) stricken on 1 June 1975.

ADVANCED NAVAL VEHICLES

The US Navy has applied the term Advanced Naval Vehicles (ANV) to a number of platforms being considered for future construction programmes. These include airships, Small Waterplane Area Twin Hull (SWATH) ships, hydrofoils, Surface Effect Ships (SES), Air Cushion Vehicles (ACV), and Wing-In-Ground (WIG) effect machines, among others.

Some of these concepts are relatively old, such as the airship (which the US Navy discarded in 1962) and hydrofoils; the latter now being in production for the US Navy after several years of experimentation. After successful tests of two 100-ton

SES designs (see section on Experimental, Research, and Surveying Ships), the US Navy had planned two construct prototypes of a 2 000-ton ocean-going SES combatant. Preliminary characteristics of such an Advanced Naval Vehicle are provided below and two artist's concepts are shown on this page.

Navy plans for the 2 000-ton SES were slowed in 1975 by a Department of Defense decision that the Navy should undertake a comprehensive analysis of all advanced platform con-

cepts, determine their potential roles, and relate estimated costs. Accordingly, in that year the Navy established the Advanced Naval Vehicles Concept Evaluation effort which was expected to complete the analysis in 1977.

The Navy's overall SES programme continues to be the largest ANV effort in terms of current funding, with $48 000 000 million requested for Fiscal Year 1977. Still, this is a paltry sum when compared to research and development efforts in a number of other areas.

2 000-ton SURFACE EFFECT SHIP (SES)

Weight, tons: 2 000 gross
Length, feet (metres): approx 240 (73·2)
Beam, feet (metres): approx 100 (30·5)
Helicopters: 2 large (SH-3 Sea King type)
Missile launchers: Harpoon surface-to-surface launchers; Sea Sparrow surface-to-air launchers
Main/lift engines: gas turbines
Speed, knots: 80-100

The above characteristics are those of a 2 000-ton national combat-capable surface effect ship. Contracts were awarded to the Bell Aerospace Division of Textron and to Rohr Industries to undertake the development and design of such a ship. Although the nominal weight of 2 000 tons is in general use, it has become obvious that the SES will in reality be close to 3 000 tons.

War games and analysis conducted by the Navy have indicated that the large SES, with its potential to serve as a highly mobile sensor carrier and helicopter platform, could play a valuable role in anti-submarine warfare. In A/S operations the large SES would employ the sprint-and-drift technique, whereby it would travel at high speeds—between 60 and 100 knots—to an area, slow to use its sensors to search the area, and then speed on to another area, possibly scores if not hundreds of miles away.

Classification: During the early 1970s the Navy used the classification DSX for planning purposes to indicate a large SES employed in destroyer/frigate roles.

Design: The SES concept differs from the Air Cushion Vehicle (ACV) by having rigid "sidewalls" that pentrate into the water to provide stability for high-speed operation. Flexible "skirts" forward and aft trap the air bubble under the hull.

Photographs: The two drawings on this page show the Bell design, the preliminary design for a 2 000-ton SES configured for combat operations.

2 000-ton Advanced Naval Vehicle /Surface Effect Ship design

Bell Aerospace

2 000-ton Advanced Naval Vehicle/Surface Effect Ship design

Bell Aerospace

NEW JERSEY (BB 62)—see following page

1968, United States Navy

BATTLESHIPS
4 BATTLESHIPS (BB): "IOWA" CLASS

Name	No.	Builders	Laid down	Launched	Commissioned
IOWA	BB 61	New York Navy Yard	27 June1940	27 Aug 1942	22 Feb 1943
NEW JERSEY	BB 62	Philadelphia Navy Yard	16 Sep 1940	7 Dec 1942	23 May 1943
MISSOURI	BB 63	New York Navy Yard	6 Jan 1941	29 Jan 1944	11 June 1944
WISCONSIN	BB 64	Philadelphia Navy Yard	25 Jan 1941	7 Dec 1943	16 Apr 1944

Displacement, tons: 45 000 standard; 59 000 full load
Length, feet (metres): 860 *(262·1)* wl; 887·2 *(270·4)* oa except *New Jersey* 887·6 *(270·5)*
Beam, feet (metres): 108·2 *(33·0)*
Draught, feet (metres): 38 *(11·6)*
Guns: 9—16 inch *(406 mm)* 50 cal (triple); 20—5 inch *(127 mm)* 38 cal dual purpose (twin); several 40 mm guns in all except *New Jersey*
Main engines: 4 geared turbines (General Electric in BB61 and BB 63; Westinghouse in BB 62 and BB 64); 212 000 shp; 4 shafts
Boilers: 8 (Babcock & Wilcox)
Speed, knots: 33 (all may have reached 35 knots in service)
Complement: designed complement varied, averaging 169 officers and 2 689 enlisted men in wartime; *New Jersey* was manned by 70 officers and 1 556 enlisted men (requirements reduced with removal of all light anti-aircraft weapons, float-planes, and reduced operational requirements) in 1968-1969.

These ships were the largest battleships ever built except for the Japanese *Yamato* and *Musashi* (64 170 tons standard, 863 feet overall, 9—18·1 inch guns). All four "Iowa" class ships were in action in the Pacific during World War II, primarily screening fast carriers and bombarding amphibious invasion objectives. Three were mothballed after the war with the *Missouri* being retained in service as a training ship. All four ships again were in service during the Korean War (1950-1953) as shore-bombardment ships; all mothballed 1954-1958.
The *New Jersey* began reactivation in mid-1967 at a cost of approximately $21 000 000; recommissioned on 6 Apr 1968. The *Iowa* and *Wisconsin* remained in reserve at the Philadelphia Naval Shipyard where the *New Jersey* had been berthed and reactivated; and the mothballed *Missouri* at the Puget Sound Naval Shipyard, Bremerton, Washington.
The *New Jersey* was again decommissioned on 17 Dec 1969 and mothballed at Bremerton with the *Missouri*. Two additional ships of this class were laid down, but never completed: *Illinois* (BB 65), laid down 15 Jan 1945, and *Kentucky* (BB 66), laid down 6 Dec 1944. The *Illinois* was 22 per cent complete when cancelled on 11 Aug 1945. The *Kentucky* was 69·2 per cent complete when construction was suspended late in the war; floated from its building dock on 20 Jan 1950. Conversion to a missile ship (BBG) was proposed but no work was undertaken and she was stricken on 9 June 1958 and broken up for scrap.
Approximate construction cost was $114 485 000 for *Missouri*; other ships cost slightly less.

Aircraft: As built, each ship carried three floatplanes for scouting and gunfire spotting and had two quarterdeck catapults. Catapults removed and helicopters carried during the Korean War.

Armour: These battleships are the most heavily armoured US warships ever constructed, being designed to survive ship-to-ship combat with enemy ships armed with 16 inch guns. The main armour belt consists of Class A steel armour 12·1 inches thick tapering vertically to 1·62 inches; a lower armour belt aft of Turret No. 3 to protect propeller shafts is 13·5 inches; turret faces are 17 inches; turret tops are 7·25 inches; turret backs are 12 inches; barbetts have a maximum of 11·6 inches of armour; second deck armour is 6 inches; and the three-level conning tower sides are 17·3 inches with an armoured roof 7·25 inches (the conning tower levels are pilot house navigation bridge and flag-signal bridge).

Design: These ships carried heavier armament than previous US battleships and had increased protection and larger engines accounting for additional displacement and increased speed. Design includes clipper bow and long foredeck, with graceful sheer (see photograph).
All fitted as fleet flagships with additional accommodations and bridge level for admiral and staff.

Electronics: During 1968-1969 the *New Jersey* was fitted with SPS-10 and SPS-6 search radars, and additional electronic warfare equipment.

Gunnery: The Mk VII 16 inch guns in these ships fire projectiles weighing up to 2 700 pounds *(1 225 kg)* (armour piercing) a maximum distance of 23 miles *(39 km)*. As built, these ships had 80—40 mm and 49 to 60—20 mm anti-aircraft guns (except *Iowa*, only 19 quad 40 mm mounts); all 20 mm guns removed and a reduced number of 40 mm weapons remain on the mothballed ships.
During 1968-1969 the *New Jersey* was fitted with two Mk 34 fire control directors in addition to the two Mk 56 and four Mk 37 previously installed. Mk 48 shore bombardment computer installed when reactivated.

NEW JERSEY (BB 63)   *1969, United States Navy*

NEW JERSEY (BB 63)   *1967, Norman Polmar*

Nomenclature: US battleships are generally named for states of the Union. The exception was the *Kearsarge*, BB 5 launched in 1899 (later *Crane Ship No. 1*, AB 1).
Beginning in 1969 the Navy has named frigates (now cruisers) for states and since 1976 this name source has been applied to Trident ballistic missile submarines.

Operational: The *New Jersey* made one deployment to the western Pacific during her third commission (1968-1969). During the deployment she was on the "gun line" off South Vietnam for a total of 120 days with 47 days being the longest sustained period at sea.
While on the "gun line" the *New Jersey* fired 5 688 rounds of ammunition from her 16 inch main battery guns and a total of 6 200 rounds during the commission, the additional firings being for tests and training. While off Vietnam she also fired some 15 000 rounds from her 5 inch secondary battery guns. (In comparison, during World War II the *New Jersey* fired 771 main battery rounds and during two deployments in the Korean War and midshipmen training cruises she fired 6 671 main battery rounds).

Photographs: The photograph at top shows the battleship *New Jersey* in action off the coast of South Vietnam in April 1969, firing some of the last rounds to be fired by a battleship. In the lower photograph the *New Jersey* is shown taking on ammunition from barges at Norfolk, Virginia. Her main battery guns are trained outboard and fully elevated to provide access to magazine loading hatches.
Additional photographs of "Iowa" class ships appear in the 1973-1974 and previous editions.

COMMAND SHIPS

This section describes the three US command ships configured to support national and regional command requirements. These have different functions from the amphibious command ships, listed next, which support Navy or Navy-Marine Corps operations.

The only one of the three command ships now in active service is the *La Salle*, a modified amphibious ship, which serves as flagship for the Commander US Middle East Force who represents US military interests "East of Suez" to the Straits of Malacca. The Commander US Middle East Force is generally a Rear Admiral. In reserve are two larger ships configured to serve as National Emergency Command Posts Afloat (NECPA) for the President or other national command authorities. These ships, the converted cruiser *Northampton* and the converted aircraft carrier *Wright*, when operational, steamed off the Atlantic coast of the United States, prepared to receive the President in the event of crisis or nuclear war. In the NECPA configuration the ships were not available for naval command use.

The NECPA programme was phased out in favour of employing underground command centres near Washington, DC, and airborne command posts.

Communication ships: The listings for major communication relay ships (AGMR) previously combined with the following ships has been moved to the section on Experimental, Research, and Surveying ships beginning with this edition of *Jane's Fighting Ships*. The change has been facilitated by disposal of the communications ship *Arlington* (AGMR 2), a sister ship of the command ship *Wright*.

LA SALLE (AGF 3)

1972, United States Navy

1 MISCELLANEOUS FLAGSHIP (AGF): CONVERTED AMPHIBIOUS TRANSPORT DOCK

Name	No.	Builders	Laid down	Launched	Commissioned
*LA SALLE	AGF 3 (ex-LPD 3)	New York Naval Shipyards	2 April 1962	3 Aug 1963	22 Feb 1964

Displacement, tons: 8 040 light; 13 900 full load
Length, feet (metres): 500 *(152·0)* wl; 521·8 *(158·4)* oa
Beam, feet (metres): 84 *(25·6)*
Draught, feet (metres): 21 *(6·4)*
Guns: 8—3 inch *(76 mm)* 50 cal AA (Mk 33) *(twin)*
Main engines: Steam turbines; 24 000 shp; 2 shafts
Boilers: 2
Speed, knots: 20 sustained; 23 maximum
Complement: 387 (18 officers, 369 enlisted men)
Flag accommodations: 59 (12 officers, 47 enlisted men)

The *La Salle* is a former amphibious transport dock (LPD) of the "Raleigh" class. Authorised in Fiscal Year 1961 new construction programme. The *La Salle* served as an amphibious ship from completion until 1972; the ship retains an amphibious assault capability.

The *La Salle* serves as flagship for the US commander Middle East Force, operating in the Persian Gulf, Arabian Sea, and Indian Ocean; the ship is based at Bahrain. She replaced the *Valcour* (AGF 1) in 1972.

Conversion: Converted in 1972, elaborate command and communications facilities installed; accommodations provided for admiral and staff; additional air-conditioning fitted; painted white to help retard heat of Persian Gulf area. Reclassified as a flagship and designated AGF 3 on 1 July 1972 (the designation AGF 2 not used because of ship's previous "3" hull number).

Electronics: Fitted with SPS-10 and SPS-40 search radar antennae; one Mk 56 and one Mk 70 gunfire control system.

LA SALLE (AGF 3)

1972, United States Navy

1 NATIONAL COMMAND SHIP (CC): CONVERTED HEAVY CRUISER

Name	No.	Builders	Laid down	Launched	Commissioned
NORTHAMPTON	CC 1 (ex-CLC 1, ex-CA 125)	Bethlehem Steel Co (Quincy)	31 Aug 1944	27 Jan 1951	7 Mar 1953

Displacement, tons: 14 700 standard; 17 200 full load
Length, feet (metres): 664 *(202·4)* wl; 676 *(206·0)* oa
Beam, feet (metres): 71 *(21·6)*
Draught, feet (metres): 29 *(8·8)*
Gun: 1—5 inch *(127 mm)* 54 cal dual-purpose (Mk 42) (see *Gunnery* notes)
Helicopters: 2
Main engines: 4 geared turbines (General Electric); 120 000 shp; 4 shafts
Boilers: 4 (Babcock & Wilcox)
Speed, knots: 33
Complement: 1 191 (68 officers, 1 123 enlisted men)
Flag accommodations: 328 (191 officers, 137 enlisted men)

The *Northampton* was begun as a heavy cruiser of the "Oregon City" class, numbered CA 125. She was cancelled on 11 Aug 1945 when 56·2 per cent complete. She was re-ordered as a command ship on 1 July 1948 and designated CLC 1 (Task Force Command Ship and later Tactical Command Ship). As CLC 1 she was configured for use primarily by fast carrier force commanders and fitted with an elaborate combat information

centre (CIC), electronic equipment, and flag accommodations. She was largely employed as flagship for Commander Second Fleet in the Atlantic before being made available for use by national authorities. Her designation was changed to CC (Command Ship) on 15 April 1961 and she was relieved as Second Fleet flagship in October 1961. Decommissioned on 8 April 1970 and placed in reserve.

Design. The *Northampton* is one deck higher than other US heavy cruisers to provide additional office and equipment space. Her foremast is the tallest unsupported mast afloat (125 feet). All living and working spaces are air-conditioned. Helicopter landing area aft with hangar for three UH/34 type.

Electronics: Advanced communications, electronic data processing equipment, and data displays are installed; tropospheric scatter and satellite relay communications facilities. As CLC 1 the *Northampton* carried what was believed the largest radar antenna afloat (see 1968-1969 and earlier editions); designated SPS-2; removed in 1963. Subsequently a variety of other radars installed forward; SPS-37 and SPS-8A search radar antennae on after mast.

Gunnery: As built, the *Northampton* mounted 4—5 inch and 8—3 inch weapons. The 5 inch guns were Mk 42 54 calibre weapons capable of firing up to 45 rounds per minute. (Similar weapons are installed in US destroyer-type ships built since World War II). The original 3 inch 50 calibre guns in open twin mounts were replaced by twin 3 inch/70 calibre (Mk 37) rapid-fire guns in closed mounts. The latter were removed in 1962 because of high maintenance requirements; removal of the guns and their ammunition hoists, etc, provided additional space for berthing, offices, and electronic equipment. When decommissioned, she was armed with only one 5 inch gun in the "X" position.

Operational: The *Northampton* served as flagship of the US Sixth Fleet in the Mediterranean in 1954-1955, and as flagship of the US Second Fleet in the Atlantic from 1955 to 1961.

Photographs: Note vacant "A" and "B" gun positions; single after gun is barely visible near motor launches in the view on the following page.

1 NATIONAL COMMAND SHIP (CC): CONVERTED AIRCRAFT CARRIER

Name	No.	Builders	Laid down	Launched	CVL Comm	CC Comm
WRIGHT	CC 2 (ex-AVT 7, ex-CVL 49)	New York SB Corp, Camden, NJ	21 Aug 1944	1 Sep 1945	9 Feb 1947	11 May 1963

Displacement, tons: 14 500 standard; 19 600 full load
Length, feet (metres): 664 *(202·4)* wl; 683·6 *(208·4)* oa
Beam, feet (metres): 76·8 *(23·6)*
Draught, feet (metres): 28 *(8·5)*
Flight deck width, feet (metres): 109 *(33·2)*
Guns: 8—40 mm anti-aircraft (twin)
Helicopters: 5 or 6
Main engines: 4 geared turbines (General Electric); 120 000 shp; 4 shafts
Boilers: 4 (Babcock & Wilcox)
Speed, knots: 33
Complement: 746
Flag accommodations: 522 (168 officers, 354 enlisted men)

The *Wright* was originally completed as a light aircraft carrier (CVL 49). Although her hull design is that of the "Baltimore" class heavy cruisers, she was ordered as a carrier and not changed during construction as with previous US "small" carriers. The *Wright* served for a decade as an experimental and training carrier before being mothballed in 1967. She was converted to a national emergency command ship at the Puget Sound Naval Shipyard, 1962-1963.
A sister carrier *Saipan* (CVL 48) was to have been similarly converted to the CC 3 but the programme was cut back and that ship subsequently became a major communications relay ship (*Arlington*, AGMR 2). She has now been discarded (see note below).
The *Wright* was decommissioned on 22 May 1970 and placed in reserve.

Classification: While in reserve as a carrier, the *Wright* was reclassified on 15 May 1959 as an auxiliary aircraft transport (AVT 7). She was reclassified as CC 2 on 1 Sep 1962.

Conversion: The *Wright* was converted to a command ship under the Fiscal Year 1962 authorisation at a cost of $25 000 000. Like the *Northampton*, she is fitted with elaborate communications, data processing, and display facilities for use by national authorities. The command spaces include presentation theatres similar to those at command posts ashore. The *Wright* has the most powerful transmitting antennae ever installed on a ship. They are mounted on plastic-glass masts to reduce interference with electronic transmissions. The tallest mast is 83 feet high and is designed to withstand 100-mph winds.
As a command ship hangar facilities were retained for three CH-46 and two HH-43 helicopters.

Photographs: Note the *Wright's* carrier configuration (with original open bow area) which facilitated "antenna farm" on flight deck. She has three squared-off funnels angled out on the starboard side aft of the small island structure.

"ARLINGTON" TYPE

The major communications relay ship *Arlington* (ex-*Saipan*, AGMR 2, ex-*CC 3*, ex-*AVT 6*, ex-*CVL 48*) was stricken on 15 Aug 1975. See 1975-1976 and previous editions for characteristics.

NORTHAMPTON (CC 1)   *United States Navy*

WRIGHT (CC 2)   *1968, United States Navy*

BLUE RIDGE (LCC 19) with UH-1 "Huey" helicopter on deck—see following page   *United States Navy*

AMPHIBIOUS WARFARE SHIPS

The relatively large and modern US amphibious warfare force is being improved with deliveries now under way of the five large, "Tarawa" class amphibious assault ships (LHA). These ships are the size (and configuration) of aircraft carriers, and each can embark a reinforced Marine battalion complete with equipment, trucks, landing craft, and helicopters.

The current force of 65 large amphibious ships can simultaneously lift the assault elements of slightly more than one Marine Amphibious Force (MAF) even when one includes a ship non-availability factor of 15 percent for overhauls. An MAF is a division/aircraft wing team and their supporting elements with a total of approximately 30 000 troops.

Upon completion of all five "Tarawa" class assault ships, the amphibious lift will be sufficient for one and one-third division/wing teams (excluding ships in overhaul). When the last LHA is delivered, the amphibious force will have 66 active ships and three Naval Reserve Force (NRF) ships. All are capable of 20-knot or higher sustained speeds and have helicopter facilities.

Although the MAF lift capability is used as measurement criteria for US Navy amphibious ships by defence officials, a more realistic consideration is the number of reinforced battalions which can be maintained afloat in forward areas, primarily the Mediterranean and the Western Pacific. The US Navy is now able to keep two reinforced battalions continuously afloat in "WesPac" and one in the "Med," albeit one of the former without helicopters because of a shortage of LPH/LHA-type ships. In addition, a reinforced battalion is intermittently deployed in the Atlantic, generally without helicopters. The availability of the five "Tarawa", class LHAs will alleviate the lack of helicopter ships in the deployed forces.

Landing ship (LX): The Navy plans to begin replacement of the "Thomaston" class dock landing ships (LSD) in the mid-1980s as they reach the end of their 30-year service life. Conceptual design work is now under way for a new landing ship, currently designated LX. The first LX is scheduled for construction under the Fiscal Year 1981 shipbuilding programme.

VSTOL operations: The Guam (LPH 9) operated as an interim sea control ship from 1972 to 1974, during which period she operated AV-8A Harrier VSTOL (Vertical/Short Take-Off and Landing) aircraft in the light attack and intercept role, and SH-3 Sea King helicopters in the anti-submarine role. See 1974-1975 edition for additional data.

The Guam has continued to carry a small number of Marine-flown Harriers upon return to the LPH role. Increasing VSTOL aircraft operations from the LPH/LHA ships are expected. US aircraft carriers have also deployed to the Mediterranean with Marine-piloted Harriers on board.

Minesweeping Operations: Several LPHs were used to operate RH-53D Sea Stallion helicopters in the mine countermeasures role during the 1973 sweeping of North Vietnamese ports and the 1974 sweeping of the Suez Canal.

Transport submarines: The transport submarine Grayback (SS 574, ex-LPSS 574) is in active commission and the older transport submarine Sealion (LPSS 315) is in reserve. Both submarines are listed in the Submarine section of this edition.

2 AMPHIBIOUS COMMAND SHIPS (LCC): "BLUE RIDGE" CLASS

Name	No.	Builders	Laid down	Launched	Commissioned
*BLUE RIDGE	LCC 19	Philadelphia Naval Shipyard	27 Feb 1967	4 Jan 1969	14 Nov 1970
*MOUNT WHITNEY	LCC 20	Newport News Shipbuilding & Dry Dock Co.	8 Jan 1959	8 Jan 1970	16 Jan 1971

Displacement, tons: 19 290 full load
Length, feet (metres): 620 (188·5) oa
Beam, feet (metres): 82 (25·3)
Main deck width, feet (metres): 108 (33)
Draught, feet (metres): 27 (8·2)
Missile launchers: 2 Basic Point Defence Missile System (BPDMS) launchers for Sea Sparrow missile (Mk 25)
Guns: 4—3 inch (76 mm) 50 cal AA (Mk 33) (twin)
Helicopters: Utility helicopter can be carried
Main engines: 1 geared turbine (General Electric); 22 000 shp; 1 shaft
Boilers: 2 (Foster Wheeler)
Speed, knots: 20
Complement: 720 (40 officers, 680 enlisted men)
Flag accommodations: 700 (200 officers, 500 enlisted men)

These are large amphibious force command ships of post-World War II design. They can provide integrated command and control facilities for sea, air and land commanders in amphibious operations. The Blue Ridge was authorised in the Fiscal Year 1965 new construction programme, the Mount Whitney in FY 1966. An AGC 21 was planned for the FY 1970 programme but cancelled late in 1968. It was proposed that the last ship combine fleet as well as amphibious force command-control facilities. The phasing out of the converted "Cleveland" class (CG) fleet flagships has fostered discussion of the potential use of these ships in that role. Their capabilities are greater than would be required by a fleet commander while they are considered too slow for striking fleet operations. Both ships are active, Blue Ridge in the Pacific and Mount Whitney in the Atlantic.

Classification: Originally designated Amphibious Force Flagships (AGC); redesignated Amphibious Command Ships (LCC) on 1 Jan 1969.

Design: General hull design and machinery arrangement are similar to the "Iwo Jima" class assault ships.

Electronics: Fitted with SPS-48 three-dimensional search radar, SPS-40 and SPS-10 search radars on "island" structure. After "tower" does not have large antenna sphere originally intended for these ships. (See model photo in 1970-1971 edition.) Tactical Aircraft Navigation (TACAN) pod tops mast. These ships have three computer systems to support their Naval Tactical Data System (NTDS), Amphibious Command Information System (ACIS), and Naval Intelligence Processing System (NIPS).
Each ship has two Mk 56 gunfire control systems.

Gunnery: At one stage of design two additional twin 3 inch mounts were provided on forecastle; subsequently deleted from final designs. Antennae and their supports severely restrict firing arcs of guns.

Missiles: Two BPDMS launchers installed on each ship during 1974 (on antenna deck, aft of superstructure).

Nomenclature: Amphibious command ships generally have mountain names. The Mount Whitney is named for a 14 494-foot peak in California, the highest point in the conterminous 48 states; the Mount McKinley is named for a 20 320-foot peak in Alaska, the highest point in the United States.

Personnel: The ships' complements include one Marine officer and 12 enlisted men to maintain communications equipment that would be used by a Marine general officer who would embark with his staff during amphibious operations.

Photographs: The antennae adjacent to the helicopter landing area swing out during flight operations.

BLUE RIDGE (LCC 19)   1974, United States Navy

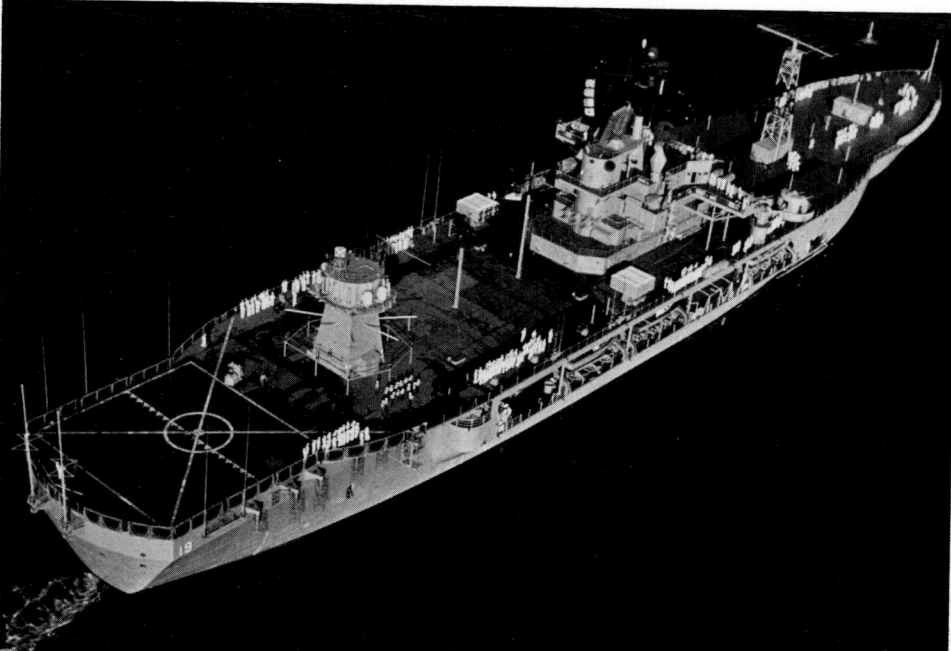

BLUE RIDGE (LCC 19)   1974, United States Navy

4 AMPHIBIOUS COMMAND SHIPS (LCC): "MOUNT McKINLEY" CLASS

Name	No.	Builders	Laid down	Launched	Commissioned
MOUNT McKINLEY	LCC 7	North Carolina SB Co, Wilmington, NC	21 Dec 1943	27 Sep 1943	1 May 1944
ESTES	LCC 12	North Carolina SB Co, Wilmington, NC	22 Feb 1944	1 Nov 1943	9 Oct 1943
POCONO	LCC 16	North Carolina SB Co, Wilmington, NC	15 Feb 1945	25 Jan 1945	29 Dec 1945
TACONIC	LCC 17	North Carolina SB Co, Wilmington, NC	6 Mar 1945	10 Feb 1945	17 Jan 1946

Displacement, tons: 7 510 light; 12 560 full load
Length, feet (metres): 435 *(132·2)* wl; 594·3 *(150·5)* oa
Beam, feet (metres): 63 *(19·2)*
Draught, feet (metres): 28·2 *(8·5)*
Guns: 1—5 inch *(127 mm)* 38 cal (Mk 37) DP; 4—40 mm AA (twin)
Helicopters: Utility helicopter carried
Main engines: 1 turbine (General Electric) 6 000 shp; 1 shaft
Boilers: 2 (Babcock & Wilcox in LCC 7; Combustion Engineering in others)
Speed, knots: 16·4
Complement: 517 (36 officers, 486 enlisted men)
Flag accommodations: 400+

Acquired by the Navy in 1943-1944 while under construction to Maritime Commission C2-S-AJ1 design. After 5 inch gun and two 40 mm twin mounts replaced by helicopter platform. The *Pocono* and *Taconic* have a single mast aft in lieu of after king post in earlier ships. All survivors transferred to Maritime Administration reserve (remain on Navy List). They were unable to provide the communication facilities or personnel accommodations required for modern amphibious operations. All are expected to be stricken in the near future.

Classification: Originally referred to as Auxiliary Combined Operations and Communications Headquarters Ships, but designated Amphibious Force Flagships (AGC); five surviving ships redesignated Amphibious Command Ships (LCC) on 1 Jan 1969.

Electronics: The *Mount McKinley* and *Estes* had an SPS-37 search radar antenna on the forward king post SPS-30 and SPS-10 antennae on the lattice mast atop the superstructure, and a TACAN antenna installed on the after king post; the *Pocono* and *Taconic* had a TACAN antenna on the forward king post, SPS-30 and SPS-10 antennae on the lattice mast atop the superstructure, and an SPS-37 antenna on the after pole mast.

MOUNT McKINLEY (LCC 7)   1969, United States Navy

5 AMPHIBIOUS ASSAULT SHIPS (LHA): "TARAWA" CLASS

Name	No.	Builders	Erection of First Module	Launched	Commission
***TARAWA**	LHA 1	Ingalls SB, Litton Industries, Pascagoula, Mississippi	15 Nov 1971	1 Dec 1973	29 May 1976
SAIPAN	LHA 2	Ingalls SB, Litton Industries, Pascagoula, Mississippi	21 July 1972	18 July 1974	Jan 1977
BELLEAU WOOD	LHA 3	Ingalls SB, Litton Industries, Pascagoula, Mississippi	5 Mar 1973	Mid 1976	Mid 1977
NASSAU	LHA 4	Ingalls SB, Litton Industries, Pascagoula, Mississippi	16 Aug 1973	Early 1977	Late 1977
DA NANG	LHA 5	Ingalls SB, Litton Industries, Pascagoula, Mississippi	June 1976	Late 1977	Mid 1978

Displacement, tons: 39 300 full load
Length, feet (metres): 778 *(237·8)* wl; 820 *(250)* oa
Beam, feet (metres): 106 *(32·3)*
Draught, feet (metres): 27·5 *(8·5)*
Aircraft: approx 30 troop helicopters or Harrier AV-8 VSTOL aircraft in place of some helicopters
Guns: 3—5 inch *(127 mm)* 54 cal DP (Mk 45) (single) 6—20 mm AA (Mk 68) (single)
Missile launchers: 2 Basic Point Defence Missile Systems (BPDMS) launchers firing Sea Sparrow missiles (Mk 25)
Main engines: Geared turbines; 70 000 shp; 2 shafts
Boilers: 2
Speed, knots: approx 22 sustained; approx 24 maximum
Complement: approx 800
Troops: 1 825 (163 officers, 1 662 enlisted men)

This is a new class of large amphibious warfare ships combining the characteristics of several previous designs including a full-length flight deck, a landing craft docking well, a large garage for trucks and armoured vehicles, and troop berthing for a reinforced battalion. The LHA 1 was authorised in the Fiscal Year 1969 new construction programme, the LHA 2 and LHA 3 in FY 1970 and LHA 4 and LHA 5 in FY 1971. The Navy announced on 20 Jan, 1971 that four additional ships of this type previously planned would not be constructed. All ships of this class are under construction by Litton Industries at a new ship production facility known as "Ingalls West". The new yard, located at Pascagoula, Mississippi, was developed specifically for multi-ship construction of the same design.

Late in 1971, the Navy announced that the LHA design work was behind schedule. Subsequently the Secretary of Defense announced that the ships will be delivered 24-44 months beyond original completion date.

Aircraft: The flight deck can operate 9 CH-53 Sea Stallion or 12 CH-46 Sea Knight helicopters; the hangar deck can accommodate 19 CH-53 Sea Stallion or 30 CH-46 Sea Knight helicopters. A mix of these and other helicopters and at times AV-8 Harriers will normally be embarked.

Contract: These ships were procured by the US Navy with the acquisition processes known as Concept Formulation, Contract Definition, and Total Package Procurement. The proposals of Litton Systems Inc, and two other shipbuilding firms were submitted in response to specific performance criteria related to the ships' mission. The firms submitted detailed designs and cost estimates for series production of not less than five ships of this type. This procurement process has subsequently been abandoned.

Design: The LHA combines the features of an amphibious assault ship (LPH), amphibious cargo ship (LKA), and amphibious transport dock (LPD) into a single hull. Beneath the flight deck is a half-length hangar deck, the two being connected by

TARAWA (LHA 1)   1975, Litton Industries

"TARAWA" CLASS—*continued*

an elevator amidships on the port side and a stern lift; beneath the after elevator is a floodable docking well measuring 268 feet in length and 78 feet in width which is capable of accommodating four LCU 1610 type landing craft.
Storage for 10 000 gallons (US) of vehicle petrol and 400 000 gallons (US) of JP-5 helicopter petrol.

Electronics: Radars in these ships are the SPS-52 three-dimensional search, and SPS-10 and SPS-40; advanced communications and helicopter navigation equipment provided. Each ship also will have an integrated Tactical Amphibious Warfare Data System (ITAWDS) to provide computerised support in control of helicopters and aircraft, shipboard weapons and sensors, navigation, landing craft control, and electronic warfare. SPN-35 aircraft navigation radar fitted on after end of "island" structure.
Provided with one Mk 86 gunfire control system in each ship; also one SPG-60 and one SPG-9A weapon control radars.

Engineering: A 900 hp fixed bow thruster is provided for holding position while unloading landing craft.

Fiscal: In early 1974 the estimated total cost to the government of the five LHAs was $1·145 *billion* or an average of $229 000 000 per ship. A cancellation fee of $109 700 000 was

due to the shipyard for cancellation of LHA 6-9. See 1973-1974 and previous editions for additional funding information.

Medical: These ships are fitted with extensive medical facilities including operating rooms, X-ray room, hospital ward, isolation ward, laboratories, pharmacy, dental operating room and medical store rooms.

Nomenclature: These ships are named for actions involving US Marines; four of the names have previously been carried by aircraft carriers. *Tarawa* (previously honoured by CV 40) and *Saipan* (CVL 48) were World War II landings in the Pacific; *Da Nang* was a battle of the Vietnam War; *Belleau Wood* (CVL 24) was a bitter World War I action in France; and *Nassau* (CVE 16) was a Marine landing during the American Revolution.

Photographs: Photographs of the *Tarawa* showing the ship being floated in a floating "launch platform" at the time of christening ceremonies appear in the 1975-1976 and previous editions. In the view at right, two 5 inch guns are evident "notched" into the forward end of the flight deck; Sea Sparrow launcher and hangar opening at the base of the "island" structure. Radio antennae along edge of flight deck swing down for air operations.

TARAWA (LHA 1) 1975, Litton Industries

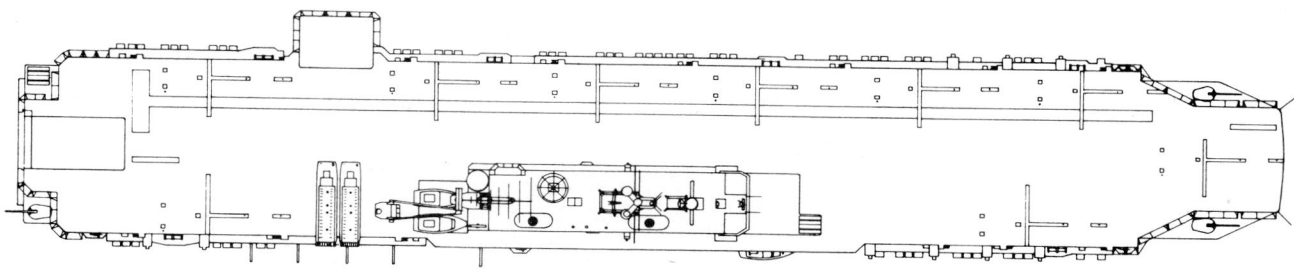

Drawing by A. D. Baker

SAIPAN (LHA 2) 1974, Litton Industries

7 AMPHIBIOUS ASSAULT SHIPS (LPH): "IWO JIMA" CLASS

Name	No.	Builders	Laid down	Launched	Commissioned
*IWO JIMA	LPH 2	Puget Sound Naval Shipyard	2 Apr 1959	17 Sep 1960	26 Aug 1961
*OKINAWA	LPH 3	Philadelphia Naval Shipyard	1 Apr 1960	14 Aug 1961	14 Apr 1962
*GUADALCANAL	LPH 7	Philadelphia Naval Shipyard	1 Sep 1961	16 Mar 1963	20 July 1963
*GUAM	LPH 9	Philadelphia Naval Shipyard	15 Nov 1962	22 Aug 1964	16 Jan 1965
*TRIPOLI	LPH 10	Ingalls Shipbuilding Corp, Pascagoula, Mississippi	15 June1964	31 July 1965	6 Aug 1966
*NEW ORLEANS	LPH 11	Philadelphia Naval Shipyard	1 Mar 1966	3 Feb 1968	16 Nov 1968
*INCHON	LPH 12	Ingalls Shipbuilding Corp, Pascagoula, Mississippi	8 Apr 1968	24 May 1969	20 June 1970

Displacement, tons: 17 000 light; 18 300 full load
Length, feet (metres): 592 *(180·0)* oa
Beam, feet (metres): 84 *(25·6)*
Draught, feet (metres): 26 *(7·9)*
Flight deck width, feet (metres): 104 *(31·9)* maximum
Aircraft: 20-24 medium (CH-46) helicopters
    4 heavy (CH-53) helicopters
    4 observation (HU-1) helicopters or AV-8 Harriers in place of
    some troop helicopters
Guns: 4—3 inch *(76 mm)* 50 cal AA (Mk 33) (twin)
Missile launchers: 2 Basic Point Defence Missile System
(BPDMS) launchers firing Sea Sparrow missiles (Mk 25)
Main engines: 1 geared turbine; 22 000 shp; 1 shaft
Boilers: 2 (Combustion Engineering or Babcock & Wilcox)
Speed, knots: 20 (sustained)
Complement: 528 (48 officers, 480 enlisted men)
Troops: 2 090 (190 officers, 1 900 enlisted men)

The *Iwo Jima* was the world's first ship designed and constructed specifically to operate helicopters. These ships correspond to Commando Ships in the Royal Navy except that the US ships do not carry landing craft save for the *Inchon* which has davits aft for two LCVPs. Each LPH can carry a Marine battalion landing team, its guns, vehicles, and equipment, plus a reinforced squadron of transport helicopters and various support personnel.

The *Iwo Jima* was authorised in the Fiscal Year 1958 new construction programme, the *Okinawa* in FY 1959, *Guadalcanal* in FY 1960, *Guam* in FY 1962, *Tripoli* in FY 1963, *New Orleans* in FY 1965, and *Inchon* in FY 1966.

Estimated cost of the *Iwo Jima* was $40 000 000.

The *Guam* was modified late in 1971 and began operations in January 1972 as an interim sea control ship. She operated Harrier AV-8 V/STOL aircraft and SH-3 Sea King A/S helicopters in convoy escort exercises; she reverted to the amphibious role in 1974. Several of these ships operated RH-53 minesweeping helicopters to clear North Vietnamese ports in 1973 and the Suez Canal in 1974.

All seven ships are active.

Aircraft: The flight decks of these ships provide for simultaneous take off or landing of seven CH-46 Sea Knight or four CH-53 Sea Stallion helicopters during normal operations. The hangar decks can accommodate 19 CH-46 Sea Knight or 11 CH-53 Sea Stallion helicopters, or various combinations of helicopters. After reverting to the amphibious role the *Guam* continues to operate Harrier AV-8 V/STOL aircraft.

Design: These ships resemble World War II-era escort carriers in size but have massive bridge structures, hull continued up to flight deck providing enclosed bows, and rounded flight decks. Each ship has two deck-edge lifts, one to port opposite the bridge and one to starboard aft of island. Full hangars are provided; no arresting wires or catapults. Two small elevators carry cargo from holds to flight deck. Storage provided for 6 500 gallons (US) of vehicle petrol and 405 000 gallons (US) of JP-5 helicopter petrol.

Electronics: These ships have SPS-40 and SPS-10 search radars, and SPN-10 navigation radar; TACAN pod tops mast; advanced electronic warfare equipment fitted. As rearmed with BPDMS these ships have two Mk 63 gunfire control systems and two SPG-50 weapon control radars.

Gunnery: As built, each ship had eight 3 inch guns in twin mounts, two forward of the island structure and two at stern "notched" into flight deck. Gun battery reduced by half with substitution of BPDMS launchers (see *Missile* notes).

Medical: These ships are fitted with extensive medical facilities including operating room, X-ray room, hospital ward, isolation ward, laboratory, pharmacy, dental operating room, and medical store rooms.

Missiles. All of these ships have been rearmed with two BPDMS launchers for the Sea Sparrow missile, one launcher forward of island structure and one on the port quarter. The *Okinawa* had one BPDMS launcher fitted in 1970 and the second in 1973; *Tripoli* and *Inchon* rearmed in 1972, *Iwo Jima* and *New Orleans* in 1973, *Guam* and *Guadalcanal* in 1974.

Nomenclature: Amphibious assault ships are named for US Marine combat actions. *Iwo Jima, Okinawa, Guadalcanal,* and *Guam* were World War II campaigns. (The name *Iwo Jima* previously was assigned to the unfinished aircraft carrier CV 46). Marines fought Barbary pirates at *Tripoli* in 1801 and helped stop the British at *New Orleans* in 1814. There was also a naval battle at *New Orleans* during the American Civil War. *Inchon* was the near-perfect 1950 amphibious assault in Korea.

Photographs: These amphibious assault ships are shown with mainly CH-53 Sea Stallion heavy and CH-46 Sea Knight medium helicopters on their flight decks; a diminutive UH-1 Huey light helicopter is parked next to the "island" structure in the view of the *Iwo Jima.* On the following page a Sea Knight hovers over the *Tripoli.* All troop-carrying helicopters are flown by Marines as are many squadrons of carrier-based tactical aircraft.

Note dome-covered approach control radar aft of funnel in these ships; the *New Orleans,* photographed prior to installation of Sea Sparrow BPDMS, has two 3 inch twin (closed) gun mounts forward of the "island"; she has since refitted with a Sea Sparrow launcher forward and a second on the port quarter.

The later "Tarawa" class LHAs are considerably larger and have broad, squared-off sterns in comparison to the sharply tapered sterns of this class.

NEW ORLEANS (LPH 11)   *1973, United States Navy, PH2 T. Ahlgrim*

IWO JIMA (LPH 2)   *1974, United States Navy*

TRIPOLI (LPH 10)   1975, United States Navy, PH1 W. H. Williams, Jr.

5 AMPHIBIOUS CARGO SHIPS (LKA): "CHARLESTON" CLASS

Name	No.	Builders	Commissioned
*CHARLESTON	LKA 113	Newport News SB & DD Co.	14 Dec 1968
*DURHAM	LKA 114	Newport News SB & DD Co.	24 May 1969
*MOBILE	LKA 115	Newport News SB & DD Co.	29 Sep 1969
*ST. LOUIS	LKA 116	Newport News SB & DD Co.	22 Nov 1969
*EL PASO	LKA 117	Newport News SB & DD Co.	17 Jan 1970

Displacement, tons: 20 700 full load
Dimensions, feet (metres): 575·5 oa × 82 × 25·5 *(175·4 × 25·0 × 7·7)*
Guns: 8—3 inch *(76 mm)* 50 cal AA (Mk 33) (twin)
Main engines: 1 steam turbine; 22 000 shp; 1 shaft = 20+ knots (sustained)
Boilers: 2 (Combustion Engineering)
Complement: 334 (24 officers, 310 enlisted men)
Troops: 226 (15 officers, 211 enlisted men)

Charleston laid down 5 Dec 1966, launched 2 Dec 1967; *Durham* laid down 10 July 1967, launched 29 March 1968; *Mobile* laid down 15 Jan 1968, launched 19 October 1968; *St. Louis* 3 April 1968 and 4 Jan 1969 and *El Paso* 22 Oct 1968 and 17 May 1969.
These ships are designed specifically for the attack cargo ship role; can carry nine landing craft (LCM) and supplies for amphibious operations. Design includes two heavy-lift cranes with a 78·4 ton capacity, two 40-ton capacity booms, and eight 15-ton capacity booms; helicopter deck aft; two Mk 56 gunfire control systems.
The LKA 113-116 were authorised in the Fiscal Year 1965 shipbuilding programme; LKA 117 in FY 1966 programme.
Cost of building was approximately $21 000 000 per ship.

Classification: Originally designated Attack Cargo Ship (AKA), *Charleston* redesignated Amphibious Cargo Ship (LKA) on 14 Dec 1968; others to LKA on 1 Jan 1969.

Engineering: These are among the first US Navy ships with a fully automated main propulsion plant; control of plant is from bridge or central machinery space console. This automation permitted a 45-man reduction in complement.

Nomenclature: Amphibious cargo ships are named for counties.

MOBILE (LKA 115)   1971, United States Navy

CHARLESTON (LKA 113) with CH-46 Sea Knight helicopter   1975, Giorgio Arra

MOBILE (LKA 115)   United States Navy

1 AMPHIBIOUS CARGO SHIP (LKA): "TULARE" TYPE

Name	No.	Builders	Commissioned
*TULARE (ex-*Evergreen Mariner*)	LKA 112	Bethlehem, San Francisco	13 Jan 1956

Displacement, tons: 12 000 light; 16 800 full load
Dimensions, feet (metres): 564 oa × 76 × 26 *(171·9 × 23·2 × 7·9)*
Guns: 12—3 inch *(76 mm)* 50 cal AA (Mk 33) (twin)
Main engines: Steam turbine (De Laval); 22 000 shp; 1 shaft = 22 knots
Boilers: 2 (Combustion Engineering)
Complement: 393 (10 officers, 154 enlisted active duty; 21 officers, 208 enlisted reserve)
Troops: 319 (18 officers, 301 enlisted men)

TULARE (LKA 112)
1969, United States Navy

Laid down on 16 Feb 1953; launched on 22 Dec 1953; acquired by Navy during construction; C4-S-1 type. Has helicopter landing platform and booms capable of lifting 60-ton landing craft. Carries 9 LCM-6 and 11 LCVP landing craft as deck cargo. Fitted with five Mk 63 gunfire control systems. Designation changed from AKA 112 to LKA 112 on 1 Jan 1969.
The *Tulare* was assigned to the Naval Reserve Force on 1 July 1975 and is partially manned by reserve personnel.

Class: Thirty-five "Mariner" design C4-S-1 merchant ships built during the early 1950s; five acquired by Navy, three for conversion to amphibious ships (AKA-APA) and two for support of Polaris-Poseidon programme (designated AG).

5 AMPHIBIOUS CARGO SHIPS (LKA): "RANKIN" CLASS

Name	No.	Builders	Commissioned	
RANKIN	LKA 103	North Carolina SB Co, Wilmington, NC	25 Feb	1945
SEMINOLE	LKA 104	North Carolina SB Co, Wilmington, NC	8 Mar	1945
UNION	LKA 106	North Carolina SB Co, Wilmington, NC	25 April	1945
VERMILION	LKA 107	North Carolina SB Co, Wilmington, NC	23 June	1945
WASHBURN	LKA 108	North Carolina SB Co, Wilmington, NC	17 May	1945

Displacement, tons: 6 546 light; 14 160 full load
Dimensions, feet (metres): 459·2 oa × 63 × 26·3 *(140·0 × 19·2 × 8·0)*
Guns: 1—5 inch *(127 mm)* 38 cal DP (removed from some ships); 8—40 mm AA (twin)
Main engines: Steam turbine (General Electric); 6 000 shp; 1 shaft = 16·5 knots
Boilers: 2 (Combustion Engineering)
Complement: 247
Troops: 138

RANKIN (LKA 103) with 5 inch gun aft
United States Navy

Union launched 23 Nov 1944, others launched in 1944 on 22 Dec, 28 Dec, 12 Dec and 12 Dec respectively. Maritime Commission C2-S-AJ3 type. These ships carry 8 LCMs and 16 LCVPs as deck cargo. Ten 20 mm AA guns removed. Designation changed from AKA to LKA on 1 Jan 1969. All of the above ships are in Maritime Administration reserve (remain on the Navy List).

SEMINOLE (LKA 104) no 5 inch gun
1970, United States Navy

7 AMPHIBIOUS CARGO SHIPS (LKA): "ANDROMEDA" CLASS

Name	No.	Builders	Commissioned
THUBAN (ex-AK 68)	LKA 19	Federal SB & Co, DD Kearney, NJ	10 June 1943
ALGOL	LKA 54	Moore DD Co, Oakland, Calif	21 July 1944
CAPRICORNUS	LKA 57	Moore DD Co, Oakland, Calif	31 May 1944
MULIPHEN	LKA 61	Federal SB & Co, DD Kearney, NJ	23 Oct 1944
YANCEY	LKA 93	Moore DD Co, Oakland, Calif	11 Oct 1944
WINSTON	LKA 94	Federal SB & Co, DD Kearney, NJ	19 Jan 1945
MERRICK	LKA 97	Federal SB & Co, DD Kearney, NJ	31 Mar 1945

Displacement, tons: 7 430 light; 14 000 full load
Dimensions, feet (metres): 435 wl; 495·2 oa × 63 × 24 *(132·6 wl; 151·4 × 19·2 × 7·3)*
Guns: 1—5 inch *(127 mm)* 38 cal (removed from some ships); 8—40 mm AA (twin) except *Thuban* 4—3 inch 50 cal AA in lieu of 40 mm
Main engines: Steam turbine (General Electric); 6 000 shp; 1 shaft = 16·5 knots
Boilers: 2 (Foster Wheeler)
Complement: 247
Troops: 414

MULIPHEN (LKA 61)
1968, United States Navy

Thuban, Algol and *Capricornus* launched on 26 April, 17 Feb and 14 Aug 1943 respectively; *Muliphen, Yancey* and *Winston* launched on 26 Aug, 8 July and 30 Nov 1944 respectively; *Merrick* launched 28 Jan 1945. C2-S-B1 type. Can carry over 5 200 tons of cargo and 2 200 tons of tanks. Designation of ships remaining on Navy List changed from AKA to LKA on 1 Jan 1969. All of the above ships are in Maritime Administration reserve (remain on the Navy List).

MULIPHEN (LKA 61)
1968, United States Navy

2 AMPHIBIOUS TRANSPORTS (LPA): "PAUL REVERE" CLASS

Name	No.	Builders	Commissioned
*PAUL REVERE (ex-*Diamond Mariner*)	LPA 248	New York SB Corp	3 Sep 1958
*FRANCIS MARION (ex-*Prairie Mariner*)	LPA 249	New York SB Corp	6 July 1961

Displacement, tons: 10 709 light; 16 838 full load
Dimensions, feet (metres): 563·5 oa × 76 × 27 *(171·8 × 23·2 × 8·2)*
Guns: 8—3 inch *(76 mm)* 50 cal AA (Mk 33) (twin)
Main engines: Steam turbine (General Electric); 22 000 shp; 1 shaft = 22 knots
Boilers: 2 (Foster Wheeler)
Complement: 307 (13 officers, 187 enlisted active duty; 15 officers, 237 enlisted reserve)
Troops: 1 657 (96 officers, 1 561 enlisted men)

Paul Revere launched 13 Feb 1954, *Francis Marion* launched 11 April 1953. "Mariner" C4-S-1 merchant ships acquired for conversion to attack transports; *Paul Revere* converted by Todd Shipyard Corp, San Pedro, California, under the Fiscal Year 1957 conversion programme; *Francis Marion* converted by Bethlehem Steel Corp, Key Highway Yard, Baltimore, Maryland, under FY 1959 programme. Helicopter platform fitted aft; 7 LCM-6 and 16 LCVP landing craft carried as deck cargo; each ship has four Mk 63 gunfire control systems. Fitted to serve as force flagships.
Designation of both ships changed from APA to LPA on 1 Jan 1969.
The *Paul Revere* was assigned to the Naval Reserve Force on 1 July 1975 and the *Francis Marion* on 1 Aug 1975; partially manned by reserve personnel.

PAUL REVERE (LPA 248)   *1969, United States Navy*

FRANCIS MARION (LPA 249)   *1975, Giorgio Arra*

7 AMPHIBIOUS TRANSPORTS (LPA): "HASKELL" CLASS

Name	No.	Builders	Commissioned
SANDOVAL	LPA 194	Kaiser Co, Vancouver	7 Oct 1944
MAGOFFIN	LPA 199	Kaiser Co, Vancouver	25 Oct 1944
TALLADEGA	LPA 208	Permanente Metals Corp, Richmond	31 Oct 1944
MOUNTRAIL	LPA 213	Permanente Metals Corp, Richmond	16 Nov 1944
NAVARRO	LPA 215	Permanente Metals Corp, Richmond	15 Nov 1944
PICKAWAY	LPA 222	Permanente Metals Corp, Richmond	12 Dec 1944
BEXAR	LPA 237	Oregon SB Corp, Portland	9 Oct 1945

Displacement, tons: 6 720 light; 10 470 full load
Dimensions, feet (metres): 435·6 wl; 455 oa × 62 × 24 *(132·8 wl; × 138·7 × 18·9 × 7·3)*
Guns: 12—40 mm AA (1 quad, 4 twin); forward quad 40 mm mount removed from some ships
Main engines: Steam turbine; 8 500 shp; 1 shaft = 17·7 knots
Boilers: 2 (Babcock & Wilcox)
Complement: 536
Troops: 1 560

The first six ships listed were launched in 1944 on 11 Sep, 4 Oct, 17 Aug, 20 Sep, 3 Oct and 5 Nov respectively. *Bexar* launched 25 July 1945. VC2-S-AP5 "Victory" cargo ships. Original 5 inch gun removed; fitted to carry 2 LCM and 20 LCVP landing craft as deck cargo.
Designation changed from APA to LPA on 1 Jan 1969. All in Maritime Administration reserve (on Navy List). *Sherburne* APA 205 converted to missile range instrumentation ship; redesignated AGM 22 (renamed *Range Sentinel*).

Nomenclature: Amphibious transports have county and parish names.

SANDOVAL (LPA 194)   *1969, United States Navy*

AMPHIBIOUS TRANSPORTS (SMALL) (LPR)

All former destroyer escorts (DE) converted or completed during World War II as transports for carrying commandoes, reconnaissance troops, or frogmen have been stricken. Fifty-six DEs were completed to this configuration and an additional 38 ships were converted after service as destroyer escorts. Originally classified as high-speed transports (APD); the 13 surviving ships on the US Navy List as of 1 Jan 1969 were changed to LPR.

Ships of this type serve in the navies of Chile, Colombia, Ecuador, Indonesia, South Korea, Mexico, and Taiwan China.

Disposals and transfers (since 1 Jan 1975): *Laning* LPR 55 (ex-DE 159) stricken on 1 Mar 1975; *Begor* LPR 127 (ex-DE 711), *Balduck* LPR 132 (ex-DE 716) transferred to Indonesia in 1976.

12 AMPHIBIOUS TRANSPORT DOCKS (LPD): "AUSTIN" CLASS

Name	No.	Builders	Commissioned
*AUSTIN	LPD 4	New York Naval Shipyard	6 Feb 1965
*OGDEN	LPD 5	New York Naval Shipyard	19 June 1965
*DULUTH	LPD 6	New York Naval Shipyard	18 Dec 1965
*CLEVELAND	LPD 7	Ingalls Shipbuilding Corp.	21 April 1967
*DUBUQUE	LPD 8	Ingalls Shipbuilding Corp.	1 Sep 1967
*DENVER	LPD 9	Lockheed Shipbuilding & Cons	26 Oct 1968
*JUNEAU	LPD 10	Lockheed Shipbuilding & Cons	12 July 1969
*CORONADO	LPD 11	Lockheed Shipbuilding & Cons	23 May 1970
*SHREVEPORT	LPD 12	Lockheed Shipbuilding & Cons	12 Dec 1970
*NASHVILLE	LPD 13	Lockheed Shipbuilding & Cons	14 Feb 1970
*TRENTON	LPD 14	Lockheed Shipbuilding & Cons	6 Mar 1971
*PONCE	LPD 15	Lockheed Shipbuilding & Cons	10 July 1971

Displacement, tons: 10 000 light; 16 900 full load
Length, feet (metres): 570 *(173·3)* oa
Beam, feet (metres): 84 *(25·6)*
Draught, feet (metres): 23 *(7·0)*
Guns: 8—3 inch *(76 mm)* 50 cal AA (Mk 33) (twin)
Helicopters: up to 6 UH-34 or CH-46
Main engines: 2 steam turbines (De Laval); 24 000 shp; 2 shafts = 20 knots sustained
Boilers: 2 Babcock & Wilcox
Complement: 490 (30 officers, 460 enlisted men)
Troops: 930 in LPD 4-6 and LPD 14-16; 840 in LPD 7-13
Flag accommodations: Approx 90 in LPD 7-13

These ships are enlarged versions of the previous "Raleigh" class; most notes for the "Raleigh" class apply to these ships. All 12 of these ships are officially considered in a single class; earlier references to separate classes were based on contract awards to builders. Fitted with one Mk 56 and two Mk 63 gunfire control systems.
The dates of laying down and launching are: *Austin* and *Ogden* 4 Feb 1963 and 27 June 1964; *Duluth* 18 Dec 1963 and 14 Aug 1965; *Cleveland* 30 Nov 1964 and 7 May 1966; *Dubuque* 25 Jan 1965 and 6 Aug 1966; *Denver* 7 Feb 1964 and 23 Jan 1965; *Juneau* 23 Jan 1965 and 12 Feb 1966; *Coronado* 3 May 1965 and 30 July 1966; *Shreveport* 27 Dec 1965 and 25 Oct 1966; *Nashville* 14 Mar 1966 and 7 Oct 1967; *Trenton* 8 Aug 1966 and 3 August 1968; *Ponce* 31 Oct 1966 and 20 May 1970.
The LPD 4-6 were authorised in the Fiscal 1962 new construction programme, LPD 7-10 in FY 1963, LPD 11-13 in FY 1964, LPD 14 and LPD 15 in FY 1965, and LPD 16 in FY 1966. LPD 16 was deferred in favour of LHA programme; officially cancelled in Feb 1969.
All ships of this class are active.

Nomenclature: Amphibious transport docks are named for American cities that honour explorers and pioneers.

Photographs: In view of *Juneau* off Queensland, Australia, the ship is ballasted down with stern gate open to float out amphibious tractors; her hangar structure is extended and a CH-53 Sea Stallion helicopter is "tucked in" on either side. The *Nashville*, also ballasted down, has a CH-46 Sea Knight on her helicopter deck.

CORONADO (LPD 11)   1975, Giorgio Arra

NASHVILLE (LPD 13)   1975, Giorgio Arra

JUNEAU (LPD 10)   1974, US Navy, PH1 John R. Sheppard

SHREVEPORT (LPD 12)   1973, Giorgio Arra

2 AMPHIBIOUS TRANSPORT DOCKS (LPD): "RALEIGH" CLASS

Name	No.	Builders	Commissioned
*RALEIGH	LPD 1	New York Naval Shipyard	8 Sep 1962
*VANCOUVER	LPD 2	New York Naval Shipyard	11 May 1963

Displacement, tons: 8 040 light; 13 900 full load
Length, feet (metres): 500 (152·0) wl; 521·8 (158·4) oa
Beam, feet (metres): 84 (25·6)
Draught, feet (metres): 21 (6·4)
Guns: 8—3 inch (76 mm) 50 cal AA (Mk 33) (twin)
Helicopters: up to 6 UH-34 or CH-46
Main engines: 2 steam turbines; (De Laval); 24 000 shp; 2 shafts = 20 knots sustained
Boilers: 2 (Babcock & Wilcox)
Complement: 490 (30 officers, 460 enlisted men)
Troops: 930

The amphibious transport dock was developed from the dock landing ship (LSD) concept but provides more versatility. The LPD replaces the amphibious transport (LPA) and, in part, the amphibious cargo ship (LKA) and dock landing ship. The LPD can carry a "balanced load"'of assault troops and their equipment, has a docking well for landing craft, a helicopter deck, cargo holds and vehicle garages. Fitted with one Mk 56 and two Mk 70 gunfire control systems. The

Raleigh was authorised in the Fiscal Year 1959 new construction programme, the *Vancouver* in FY 1960. The *Raleigh* was laid down on 23 June 1960 and launched on 17 Mar 1962; the *Vancouver* on 19 Nov 1960 and 15 Sep 1962. Approximate construction cost was $29 000 000 per ship.
A third ship of this class, *La Salle* (LPD 3), was reclassified as a command ship (AGF 3) on 1 July 1972.

Design: These ships resemble dock landing ships (LSD) but have fully enclosed docking well with the roof forming a permanent helicopter platform. The docking well is 168 feet long and 50 feet wide, less than half the length of wells in newer LSDs; the LPD design provides more space for vehicles, cargo and troops. Ramps allow vehicles to be driven between helicopter deck, parking area and docking well, side ports provide roll-on/roll-off capability when docks are available. An overhead monorail in the docking well with six cranes faciltates loading landing craft. The docking well in these ships can hold one LCU and three LCM-6s or four LCM-8s or 20 LVTs (amphibious tractors). In addition, two LCM-6s or four LCPLs are carried on the boat deck which are lowered by crane.

Helicopters: These ships are not normally assigned helicopters because they lack integral hangars and maintenance facilities. It is intended that a nearby amphibious assault ship (LHA or LPH) would provide helicopters during an amphibious operation. Telescoping hangars have been fitted (see "Austin" class notes).

RALEIGH (LPD 1)   1972, United States Navy

5 DOCK LANDING SHIPS (LSD): "ANCHORAGE" CLASS

Name	No.	Builders	Commissioned
*ANCHORAGE	LSD 36	Ingalls Shipbuilding	15 Mar 1969
*PORTLAND	LSD 37	General Dynamics, Quincy, Mass	3 Oct 1970
*PENSACOLA	LSD 38	General Dynamics, Quincy, Mass	27 Mar 1971
*MOUNT VERNON	LSD 39	General Dynamics, Quincy, Mass	13 May 1972
*FORT FISHER	LSD 40	General Dynamics, Quincy, Mass	9 Dec 1972

Displacement, tons: 8 600 light; 13 700 full load
Dimensions, feet (metres): 553·3 oa × 84 × 18·6 *(168·6 × 25·6 × 5·7)*
Guns: 8—3 inch *(76 mm)* 50 cal AA (Mk 33) (twin)
Main engines: Steam turbines (De Laval); 24 000 shp; 2 shafts = 20 knots sustained
Boilers: 2 (Foster Wheeler except Combustion Engineering in *Anchorage*)
Complement: 397 (21 officers, 376 enlisted men)
Troops: 376 (28 officers, 348 enlisted men)

PORTLAND (LSD 37)

1973, Giorgio Arra

Improved dock landing ships, slightly larger than previous class. These ships are similar in appearance to earlier classes but with a tripod mast. Helicopter platform aft with docking well partially open; helicopter platform can be removed. Fitted with one Mk 56 and two Mk 63 gunfire control systems. Docking well approximately 430 × 50 feet can accommodate three LCU-type landing craft. Space on deck for one LCM, and davits for one LCPL and one LCVP. Two 50-ton capacity cranes.
LSD 36 was authorised in Fiscal Year 1965 shipbuilding programme; LSD 37-39 in FY 1966 programme; LSD 40 in FY 1967 programme.
Anchorage was laid down on 13 Mar 1967 and launched in 5 May 1968; *Portland* on 21 Sep 1967 and 20 Dec 1969; *Pensacola* on 12 Mar 1969 and 11 July 1970; *Mount Vernon* on 29 Jan 1970 and 17 April 1971; and *Fort Fisher* on 15 July 1970 and 22 April 1972.
Estimated construction cost is $11 500 000 per ship.

Nomenclature: Dock landing ships are named for historic sites in the United States except that the *Anchorage, Portland,* and *Pensacola* primarily honour cities.

PENSACOLA (LSD 38)

1975, Giorgio Arra

8 DOCK LANDING SHIPS (LSD): "THOMASTON" CLASS

Name	No.	Builders	Commissioned
*THOMASTON	LSD 28	Ingalls SB Corp, Pascagoula	17 Sep 1954
*PLYMOUTH ROCK	LSD 29	Ingalls SB Corp, Pascagoula	24 Jan 1955
*FORT SNELLING	LSD 30	Ingalls SB Corp, Pascagoula	24 Jan 1955
*POINT DEFIANCE	LSD 31	Ingalls SB Corp, Pascagoula	31 Mar 1955
*SPIEGEL GROVE	LSD 32	Ingalls SB Corp, Pascagoula	8 June 1956
*ALAMO	LSD 33	Ingalls SB Corp, Pascagoula	24 Aug 1956
*HERMITAGE	LSD 34	Ingalls SB Corp, Pascagoula	17 Dec 1956
*MONTICELLO	LSD 35	Ingalls SB Corp, Pascagoula	29 Mar 1957

Displacement, tons: 6 880 light; 11 270 full load. *Alamo, Hermitage, Monticello, Spiegel Grove:* 12 150 full load
Dimensions, feet (metres): 510 oa × 84 × 19 *(155·5 × 25·6 × 5·8)*
Guns: 12—3 inch *(76 mm)* 50 cal AA (Mk 33) (twin)
Main engines: Steam turbines (General Electric); 24 000 shp; 2 shafts = 22·5 knots
Boilers: 2 (Babcock & Wilcox)
Complement: 400
Troops: 340

LSD 28-31 launched in 1954 on 9 Feb, 7 May, 16 July and 28 Sep respectively; LSD 32 launched on 10 Nov 1955; LSD 33-35 launched in 1956 on 20 Jan, 12 June and 10 Aug. Fitted with helicopter platform over docking well; two 5-ton capacity cranes; can carry 21 LCM-6 or 3 LCU and 6 LCM landing craft or approximately 50 LVTs (amphibious tractors) in docking well plus 30 LVTs on mezzanine and super decks (with helicopter landing area clear).
As built, each ship had 16—3 inch AA guns; twin mount on each side wall (aft of boats davits) has been removed. Fitted with two Mk 56 and two Mk 63 gunfire control systems.
Note pole mast compared to tripod mast of subsequent "Anchorage" class for rapid identification; later class has enclosed 3 inch gun mounts forward of bridge.

PLYMOUTH ROCK (LSD 29)

1975, Giorgio Arra

PLYMOUTH ROCK (LSD 29)

1975, Giorgio Arra

SPIEGEL GROVE (LSD 32)

1968, United States Navy

PLYMOUTH ROCK (LSD 29)

1975, Giorgio Arra

7 DOCK LANDING SHIPS (LSD): "CASA GRANDE" CLASS

Name	No.	Builders	Commissioned
CASA GRANDE	LSD 13	Newport News SB & DD Co	5 June 1944
RUSHMORE	LSD 14	Newport News SB & DD Co	3 July 1944
SHADWELL	LSD 15	Newport News SB & DD Co	24 July 1944
CABILDO	LSD 16	Newport News SB & DD Co	15 Mar 1945
COLONIAL	LSD 18	Newport News SB & DD Co	15 May 1945
DONNER	LSD 20	Boston Navy Yard	31 July 1945
TORTUGA	LSD 26	Boston Navy Yard	8 June 1945

Displacement, tons: 4 790 standard; 9 375 full load
Dimensions, feet (metres): 475·4 oa × 76·2 × 18 *(144·9 × 23·2 × 5·5)*
Guns: 8— or 12—40 mm AA (2 quad plus 2 twin in some ships)
Main engines: Geared turbines (Newport News except Westinghouse in *Fort Marion*); 2 shafts; 7 000 shp except 9 000 in *Fort Marion* = 15·4 knots
Boilers: 2
Complement: 265 (15 officers, 250 men)

DONNER (LSD 20)   1968, *United States Navy*

LSD 13-16 launched in 1944 on 11 April, 10 May, 24 May and 28 Dec; LSD 18, 20 and 26 launched in 1945 on 28 Feb, 6 April and 21 Jan.
Originally a class of 15 dock landing ships. *Fort Snelling* LSD 23, and *Point Defiance* LSD 24 cancelled in 1945; former ship completed for merchant service, reacquired by Navy as cargo ship *Taurus*, T-AK 273, T-AKR 8 (stricken in 1968). LSD 9-12 of this class transferred to Britain in 1943-1944.
Docking well is 392 × 44 feet; can carry 3 LCUs or 18 LSMs or 32 LVTs (amphibious tractors) in docking well. All ships are fitted with helicopter platform.
Colonial and *Donner* were modernised under the FRAM II programme in 1960-1962.
All surviving ships of this class are in Navy or Maritime Administration reserve (the latter ships remain on the Navy List).

Disposals and Transfers: *Fort Mandan* LSD 21 to Greece on 23 Jan 1971, *San Marcos* LSD 25 to Spain on 1 July 1971, *Catamount* LSD 17 stricken on 31 Oct 1974, *Fort Marion* LSD 22 transferred to South Korea in 1976, *Comstock* LSD 19 transferred to Taiwan China in 1976, *Whetstone* LSD 27 transferred to Peru in 1976. (Corrections to previous edition).

DONNER (LSD 20)   1968, *United States Navy*

DOCK LANDING SHIPS (LSD): "ASHLAND" CLASS

All ships of this class have been stricken or transferred to foreign navies; see 1972-1973 and previous editions for characteristics. One ship of this class currently serves with Argentina and Taiwan China.

20 TANK LANDING SHIPS (LST): "NEWPORT" CLASS

Name	No.	Laid down	Launched	Commissioned
*NEWPORT	LST 1179	1 Nov 1966	3 Feb 1968	7 June 1969
*MANITOWOC	LST 1180	1 Feb 1967	4 June 1969	24 Jan 1970
*SUMTER	LST 1181	14 Nov 1967	13 Dec 1969	20 June 1970
*FRESNO	LST 1182	16 Dec 1967	28 Sep 1968	22 Nov 1969
*PEORIA	LST 1183	22 Feb 1968	23 Nov 1968	21 Feb 1970
*FREDERICK	LST 1184	13 April 1968	8 Mar 1969	11 April 1970
*SCHENECTADY	LST 1185	2 Aug 1968	24 May 1969	13 June 1970
*CAYUGA	LST 1186	28 Sep 1968	12 July 1969	8 Aug 1970
*TUSCALOOSA	LST 1187	23 Nov 1968	6 Sep 1969	24 Oct 1970
*SAGINAW	LST 1188	24 May 1969	7 Feb 1970	23 Jan 1971
*SAN BERNARDINO	LST 1189	12 July 1969	28 Mar 1970	27 Mar 1971
*BOULDER	LST 1190	6 Sep 1969	22 May 1970	30 April 1971
*RACINE	LST 1191	13 Dec 1969	15 Aug 1970	9 July 1971
*SPARTANBURG COUNTY	LST 1192	7 Feb 1970	11 Nov 1970	1 Sep 1971
*FAIRFAX COUNTY	LST 1193	28 Mar 1970	19 Dec 1970	16 Oct 1971
*LA MOURE COUNTY	LST 1194	22 May 1970	13 Feb 1971	18 Dec 1971
*BARBOUR COUNTY	LST 1195	15 Aug 1970	15 May 1971	12 Feb 1972
*HARLAN COUNTY	LST 1196	7 Nov 1970	24 July 1971	8 April 1972
*BARNSTABLE COUNTY	LST 1197	19 Dec 1970	2 Oct 1971	27 May 1972
*BRISTOL COUNTY	LST 1198	13 Feb 1971	4 Dec 1971	5 Aug 1972

Displacement, tons: 8 342 full load
Dimensions, feet (metres): 522·3 hull oa × 69·5 × 17·5 (aft) *(159·2 × 21·2 × 5·3)*
Guns: 4—3 inch (76 mm) 50 cal AA (Mk 33) (twin)
Main engines: 6 diesels (Alco); 16 500 hp, 2 shafts = 20 knots (sustained)
Complement: 223 (12 officers, 211 enlisted men)
Troops: 386 (20 officers, 366 enlisted men)

SPARTANBURG COUNTY (LST 1192)   1972, *United States Navy*

These ships are of an entirely new design; larger and faster than previous tank landing ships. They operate with 20-knot amphibious squadrons to transport tanks, other heavy vehicles, engineer equipment, and supplies which cannot be readily landed by helicopters or landing craft. These are the only recent construction amphibious ships with a pole mast *vice* tripod-lattice mast. Two Mk 63 gunfire control systems are provided.
The *Newport* was authorised in the Fiscal Year 1965 new construction programme and laid down on 1 Nov 1966. LST 1180-1187 (8 ships) in FY 1966, and LST 1188-1198 (11 ships) in FY 1967. LST 1179-1181 built by Philadelphia Naval Shipyard, LST 1182-1198 built by National Steel & SB Co, San Diego, California. Seven additional ships of this type that were planned for the Fiscal Year 1971 new construction programme were deferred.
All 20 ships of this class are active; they are the only LSTs remaining in active US service. They are required to carry tanks, amphibious tractors, and other heavy equipment for amphibious landings.

Design: These ships are the first LSTs to depart from the bow-door design developed by the British early in World War II. The hull form required to achieve 20 knots would not permit bow doors, thus these ships unload by a 112-foot ramp over their bow. The ramp is supported by twin derrick arms. A ramp just forward of the superstructure connects the lower tank deck with the main deck and a vehicle passage through the superstructure provides access to the parking area amidships. A stern gate to the tank deck permits unloading of amphibious tractors into the water, or unloading of other vehicles into an LCU or onto a pier. Vehicle stowage is rated at 500 tons and 19 000 square feet (5 000 sq ft more than previous LSTs). Length over derrick arms is 562 feet; full load draught is 11·5 feet forward and 17·5 feet aft. Bow thruster fitted to hold position offshore while unloading amphibious tractors.

Nomenclature: LSTs are named for counties and parishes. In accord with the contemporary US Navy confusion over naming ships, some do not have county or parish suffix.

Photographs: Note uneven, staggered funnels, bow opening when ramp is lowered, anchors on starboard side forward and at stern, funnel opening in superstructure, and helicopter spots marked aft of funnels. Twin 3 inch closed gun mounts are difficult to distinguish in clutter atop superstructure. *Sumter* is shown in Mediterranean carrying four pontoon barges lashed amidships; her stern gate is open for unloading amphibious tractors. The *Barnstable County* is shown in Suez Canal, en route from Port Said to Ismailia during US Navy mine clearing operations.

SUMTER (LST 1181)   1975, Giorgio Arra

SUMTER (LST 1181)   1975, Giorgio Arra

SAGINAW (LST 1188) lowering ramp   1973, US Navy, PH3 J. L. Page

BARNSTABLE COUNTY (LST 1197)   1974, United States Navy

3 TANK LANDING SHIPS (LST): "SUFFOLK COUNTY" CLASS

Name	No.	Builders	Commissioned
SUFFOLK COUNTY	LST 1173	Boston Navy Yard	15 Aug 1957
LORAIN COUNTY	LST 1177	American SB Co, Lorrain, Ohio	3 Oct 1958
WOOD COUNTY	LST 1178	American SB Co, Lorrain, Ohio	5 Aug 1959

Displacement, tons: 4 164 light; 8 000 full load
Dimensions, feet (metres): 445 oa × 62 × 16·5 (138·7 × 18·9 × 5·0)
Guns: 6—3 inch (76 mm) 50 cal AA (Mk 33) (twin)
Main engines: Diesels; 14 400 bhp; 2 shafts; (controllable pitch propellers) = 17·5 knots
Complement: 184 (10 officers, 174 men)
Troops: approx 575

Originally a class of seven tank landing ships (LST 1171, 1173-1178 with LST 1172 not built). They were faster and had a greater troop capacity than earlier LSTs; considered the "ultimate" design attainable with the traditional LST bow-door configuration.
Suffolk County launched on 5 Sep 1956, *Lorain County* on 22 June 1957, and *Wood County* on 14 Dec 1957.
The surviving ships were decommissioned in 1972 and are in reserve; they probably will be transferred to foreign navies or assigned to the Military Sealift Command for use as cargo ships. The *Graham County* (LST 1176) has been converted to a gunboat support ship (AGP); see description under Fleet Support Ships.
Ships of this class serve in the navies of Brazil and Italy.

Design: High degree of habitability with all crew and troop living spaces air conditioned. Can carry 23 medium tanks or vehicles up to 75 tons on 288-foot-long (lower) tank deck. Davits for four LCVP-type landing craft. Liquid cargo capacity of 170 000 gallons (US) diesel or jet fuel plus

7 000 gallons (US) of petrol for embarked vehicles; some ships have reduced troop spaces and carry additional 250 000 gallons (US) of aviation petrol for pumping ashore or to other ships.

Engineering: All built with six Nordburg diesels. *Suffolk County* refitted with six Fairbanks Morse diesels, electric couplings and reduction gears; *Lorain County* and *Wood County* refitted with six Cooper Bessemer diesels, electric couplings and reduction gears.

Photographs: The "Suffolk County" class LSTs are identified by their twin fire control towers forward.

WOOD COUNTY (LST 1178)   1971, J. S. Kinross

WOOD COUNTY (LST 1178)   1971, United States Navy

2 TANK LANDING SHIPS (LST): "TERREBONNE PARISH" CLASS

Name	No.	Builders	Commissioned
TERRELL COUNTY	LST 1157	Bath Iron Works Corp, Maine	19 Mar 1953
WHITFIELD COUNTY	LST 1169	Christy Corp	14 Sep 1954

Displacement, tons: 2 580 light; 5 800 full load
Dimensions, feet (metres): 384 oa × 55 × 17 *(117·0 × 16·8 × 5·2)*
Guns: 6—3 inch *(76 mm)* 50 cal AA (Mk 33) (twin)
Main engines: 4 diesels (General Motors); 6 000 bhp 2 shafts (controllable pitch propellers) = 15 knots
Complement: 115
Troops: 395

Originally a class of 15 tank landing ships (LST 1156-1170). *Terrell County* launched on 6 Dec 1952. *Whitfield County* launched on 22 Aug 1953. Tank deck can accommodate 17 amphibious tractors (LVT).
Six ships were transferred from reserve to the Military Sealift Command in 1972 for use as cargo ships: *Tioga County* LST 1158, *Traverse County* LST 1160, *Wahkiakum County* LST 1162, *Waldo County* LST 1163, *Walworth County* LST 1164 and *Washoe County* LST 1165. The ships listed above were to transfer to the Military Sealift Command during 1973 but transfer delayed and they were decommissioned.
Ships of this class serve in the navies of Spain, Turkey, and Venezuela.

Photographs: In the photograph of the *Terrell County* two UH-1 "Huey" (Iroquois) helicopters are on the ship's deck during operations in Vietnam waters.

TERRELL COUNTY (LST 1157)   1969, United States Navy

"TALBOT COUNTY" CLASS

Both ships of the "Talbot County" class have been stricken; see 1973-1974 and previous editions for characteristics and photographs.
Talbot County LST 1153 stricken on 1 June 1973; *Tallahatchie County* LST 1154 converted to aviation base ship (AVB 2)—stricken in 1970.

2 TANK LANDING SHIPS (LST): 511-1152 SERIES

Name	No.	Builders	Commissioned
DUVAL COUNTY	LST 758	American Bridge Co, Pa	19 Aug 1944
SUMNER COUNTY	LST 1148	Chicago Bridge & Iron Co, Seneca, Ill	9 June 1945

Displacement, tons: 1 653 standard; 2 080 full load
Dimensions, feet (metres): 316 wl; 328 oa × 50 × 14 *(100·0 × 15·2 × 4·3)*
Guns: 8—40 mm AA (2 twin and 4 single)
Main engines: Diesels (General Motors); 1 700 bhp; 2 shafts = 11·6 knots
Complement: 119
Troops: 147

The US Navy built 1 052 LSTs during World War II in two series: LST 1-510 and LST 511-1152; an even 100 ships were cancelled: LST 85-116, 142-156, 182-196, 232-236, 248-260, 296-300, 431-445. Forty-one ships were lost during the war. Hundreds of these ships have been transferred to foreign navies or converted to auxiliary configurations.
County or Parish names were assigned to 158 LSTs on the Navy List as of 1 July 1955; 36 Japanese-manned LSTs assigned to the Military Sea Transportation Service (MSTS) at that time were not named.
The two surviving ships of this series are in reserve. Launched on 25 July 1944 and 23 May 1945, respectively.

Design: These ships are of the classical LST design developed early in World War II by the British; fitted with bow doors, tunnel-like tank deck with trucks, cargo, or landing craft carried on upper deck; small "island" structure aft with davits for two LCVP-type landing craft. Cargo capacity 2 100 tons or 14 amphibious tractors (LVT). Fitted with tripod masts during postwar period.

Transfers: Ships of this class serve in the navies of Barbados, Brazil, China, Greece, Indonesia, Japan, South Korea, Malaysia, Mexico, Philippines, Singapore, Spain, Thailand and Taiwan China.

DUVAL COUNTY (LST 758)   1968, United States Navy

LANDING CRAFT

(1) AMPHIBIOUS ASSAULT LANDING CRAFT (AALC): AEROJET-GENERAL DESIGN (JEFF-A)

Weight, tons: 85·8 empty; 166·4 gross
Dimensions, feet (metres): 96·2 oa × 48 × (height) 23 *(31·5 × 15·7 × 7·5)*
Main engines: 4 gas turbines (Avco-Lycoming T40); 11 200 hp; 4 aircraft type propellers in rotating shrouds for propulsive thrust = approx 50 knots cruise
Lift engines: 2 gas turbines (Avco-Lycoming T40); 5 600 hp; 8 horizontal fans (2 sets) for cushion lift
Complement: 6

AEROJET-GENERAL DESIGN (Model)

This is an Air Cushion Vehicle (ACV) landing craft being developed by the Aerojet-General Corp and being built by Todd Shipyards, Seattle, Washington, under Navy contract. Construction scheduled to be completed in February 1975 with one year of contractor testing before delivery to Navy in February 1976. (Construction shifted from Tacoma Boatbuilding Co after financial failure of that firm).

Above dimensions are for craft on air cushion; when at rest dimensions will be 97 × 44 × 19. Designed to carry 120 000 pound payload at a design speed of 50 knots (same as Jeff-B). Design features include aluminium construction, bow and stern ramps, cargo deck area of 2 100 square feet; two sound-insulated compartments each hold four persons; three engines housed in each side structure; two propellers in rotating shrouds provide horizontal propulsion and steering. Performance parameters include four-hour endurance (200 n mile range), four foot obstacle clearance, and capability to maintain cruise speed in Sea State 2 with 25-knot headwind. Scheduled for delivery in 1976.

Project: Aerojet-General and Bell Aerosystems were awarded contracts in January 1969 to design competitive assault landing craft employing ACV technology. Subsequently, awards were made to both companies in March 1971 to build and test one craft per company. These are air cushion or bubble craft, supported above the land or water surface by a continu-ously generated cushion or bubble of air held by flexible "skirts" that surround the base of the vehicle. According to US Navy usage, they differ from surface effect ships (SES) which have rigid sidewalls that penetrate the water surface to help hold the cushion or bubble. Official designation of these craft is Amphibious Assault Landing Craft (AALC), with the Aerojet-General design being referred to as AALC—Jeff(A) and the Bell Aerosystems craft as AALC—Jeff(B). The two SES constructed for the US Navy are listed with Experimental, Research, and Surveying Ships; also see listing for patrol Ships and Craft in this edition for additional SES programme details.

(1) AMPHIBIOUS ASSAULT LANDING CRAFT (AALC): BELL DESIGN (JEFF-B)

Weight, tons: 162·5 gross
Dimensions, feet (metres): 86·75 oa × 47 × (height) 23·5 *(28·4 × 15·4 × 7·7)*
Main/lift engines: 6 gas turbines (Avco-Lycoming T40); 16 800 hp; interconnected with 2 aircraft-type propellers in rotating shrouds for propulsive thrust and 4 horizontal fans for cushion lift = approx 50 knots cruise
Complement: 6

ACV landing craft being built by Bell Aerosystems. Above dimensions are for craft on air cushion; when at rest dimensions are 80 × 43 × 19. Aluminium construction; bow and stern ramps; cargo area of 1 738 square feet; three engines housed in each side structure with raised pilot house on starboard side. Performance parameters similar to Jeff (A).
Distinguished from Aerojet-General craft by having only two shrouded propellers for thrust and steering.
Scheduled for completion in 1976.

BELL AEROSYSTEMS DESIGN (Model)

56 UTILITY LANDING CRAFT: LCU 1610 SERIES

LCU 1613	LCU 1627	LCU 1641	LCU 1651	LCU 1661	LCU 1671
LCU 1614	LCU 1628	LCU 1644	LCU 1653	LCU 1662	LCU 1672
LCU 1616	LCU 1629	LCU 1645	LCU 1654	LCU 1663	LCU 1673
LCU 1617	LCU 1630	LCU 1646	LCU 1655	LCU 1664	LCU 1674
LCU 1618	LCU 1631	LCU 1647	LCU 1656	LCU 1665	LCU 1675
LCU 1619	LCU 1632	LCU 1648	LCU 1657	LCU 1666	LCU 1676
LCU 1621	LCU 1633	LCU 1649	LCU 1658	LCU 1667	LCU 1677
LCU 1623	LCU 1634	LCU 1650	LCU 1659	LCU 1668	LCU 1678
LCU 1624	LCU 1637	LCU 1651	LCU 1660	LCU 1669	LCU 1679
				LCU 1670	LCU 1680

Displacement, tons: 200 light; 375 full load
Dimensions, feet (metres): 134·9 oa × 29 × 6·1 *(44·2 × 9·5 × 2)*
Guns: 2—50 cal machine guns
Main engines: Diesels (Detroit); 1 000 bhp; 2 shafts = 11 knots (see *Engineering* notes)
Complement: 12 to 14 (enlisted men)

LCU 1658

1971, Defoe Shipbuilding

Improved landing craft, larger than previous series; can carry three M-103 or M-48 tanks (approx 64 tons and 48 tons respectively). Cargo capacity 170 tons.
LCU 1610-1612 built by Christy Corp, Sturgeon Bay, Wisconsin; LCU 1613-1619, 1623, 1624 built by Gunderson Bros Engineering Corp, Portland, Oregon; LCU 1620, 1621, 1625, 1626, 1629, 1630 built by Southern Shipbuilding Corp, Slidell, Louisiana; LCU 1622 built by Weaver Shipyards, Texas; LCU 1627, 1628, 1631-1636 built by General Ship and Engine Works (last six units completed in 1968). LCU 1638-1645 built by Marinette Marine Corp, Marinette, Wisconsin (completed 1969-1970); LCU 1646-1666 built by Defoe Shipbuilding Co, Bay City, Michigan (completed 1970-1971). The one-of-a-kind aluminium hull, 133·8 ft LCU 1637 built by Pacific Coast Engineering Co, Alameda, California; LCU 1667-1670 built by General Ship & Engine Works, East Boston, in 1973-1974; LCU 1671-1680 built by Marinette Marine Corp, 1974-1976. LCU 1636, 1638, 1639, 1640 reclassified as YFB 88-91 in October 1969 LCU 1620 and 1625 to YFU 92 and 93 respectively, in April 1971; LCU 1611, 1615, 1622 to YFU 97-99 in Feb 1972; LCU 1610, 1612 to YFU 100 and 101 respectively, in Aug 1972.

Engineering: These landing craft have four 250 bhp diesel engines with Kort-nozzle propellers on twin shafts except for the LCU 1620, 1621, and 1625 which have two 500-bhp diesel engines on vertical shafts fitted with vertical axis, cycloidal six-bladed propellers. The cycloidal propellers provide thrust in any horizontal direction alleviating the need for rudders. The LCU 1622 was to have been fitted with gas-turbine propulsion machinery, but this project was cancelled. Endurance is 1 200 miles at 8 knots.

Photographs: Note amidships, right-side "island" structure of LCU 1658; LCU 1625 differs with built up-structure aft. All except LCU 1621 and 1625 have stern ramps.

LCU 1658

1971, Defoe Shipbuilding

24 UTILITY LANDING CRAFT: LCU 1466 SERIES

LCU 1466	LCU 1470	LCU 1485	LCU 1490	LCU 1537
LCU 1467	LCU 1472	LCU 1486	LCU 1492	LCU 1539
LCU 1468	LCU 1477	LCU 1487	LCU 1525	LCU 1547
LCU 1469	LCU 1482	LCU 1488	LCU 1535	LCU 1548
	LCU 1484	LCU 1489	LCU 1536	LCU 1559

Displacement, tons: 180 light; 360 full load
Dimensions, feet (metres): 115 wl; 119 oa × 34 × 6 max *(37·7; 39 × 11·1 × 1·9)*
Guns: 2—20 mm
Main engines: 3 diesels (Gray Marine); 675 bhp; 3 shafts = 18 knots
Complement: 14

These are enlarged versions of the World War II-built LCTs; constructed during the early 1950s. LCU 1608 and 1609 have modified propulsion systems; LCU 1582 and later craft have Kort nozzle propellers. LCU 1496 reclassified as YFU 70 on 1 Mar 1966; LCU 1471 to YFU 88 in May 1968; LCU 1576, 1582 and 1608 to YFU 89-91, respectively, in June 1970; LCU 1488, 1491, and 1609 to YFU 94-96 on 1 June 1971; YFU 94 reverted to LCU 1488 on 1 Feb 1972.

Classification: The earlier craft of this series were initially designated as Utility Landing Ships (LSU); redesignated Utility Landing Craft (LCU) on 15 April 1952 and classified as service craft.

Transfers: (Since 1 Jan 1975) LCU 1473 to Mexico in 1975.

LCU 1468 with mast lowered   *1969, United States Navy*

LCU 1488   *1965, United States Navy*

21 UTILITY LANDING CRAFT: LCU 501 SERIES

LCU 539	LCU 660	LCU 768	LCU 1124	LCU 1430
LCU 588	LCU 666	LCU 803	LCU 1241	LCU 1451
LCU 599	LCU 667	LCU 871	LCU 1348	LCU 1462
LCU 608	LCU 674	LCU 893	LCU 1348	
LCU 654	LCU 742	LCU 1045	LCU 1387	

Displacement, tons: 143-160 light; 309 to 320 full load
Dimensions, feet (metres): 105 wl × 119 oa × 32·7 × 5 max *(34·6; 39 × 10·7 × 1·6)*
Guns: 2—20 mm
Main engines: Diesels (Gray Marine); 675 bhp; 3 shafts = 10 knots
Complement: 13 (enlisted men)

Formerly LCT(6) 501-1465 series; built in 1943-1944. Can carry four tanks or 200 tons of cargo. LCU 524, 529, 550, 562, 592, 600, 629, 664, 666, 668, 677, 686, 742, 764, 776, 788, 840, 869, 877, 960, 973, 974, 979, 980, 1056, 1082, 1086, 1124, 1136, 1156, 1159, 1162, 1195, 1224, 1236, 1250, 1283, 1286, 1363, 1376, 1378, 1384, 1386, 1398, 1411, and 1430 reclassified as YFU 1 through 46, respectively, on 18 May 1958; LCU 1040 reclassified YFB 82 on 18 May 1958; LCU 1446 reclassified YFU 53 in 1964; LCU 509, 637, 646, 709, 716, 776, 851, 916, 973, 989, 1126, 1165, 1203, 1232, 1385, and 1388 reclassified as YFU 54 through 69, respectively, on 1 Mar 1966; LCU 780 reclassified as YFU 87. YFU 9 reverted to LCU 666 on 1 Jan 1962; LCU 1459 converted to YLLC 4; LCU 1462 to YFU 102 on 1 Aug 1973. Changes reflect employment as general cargo craft assigned to shore commands (see section on Service Craft).

Classification: Originally rated as Landing Craft, Tank (LCT(6)); redesignated Utility Landing Ships (LSU) in 1949 to reflect varied employment; designation changed to Utility Landing Craft (LCU) on 15 Apr 1952 and classified as service craft.

See 1970-1971 edition for war losses, disposals, and transfers prior to 1965.

MECHANISED LANDING CRAFT: LCM 8 TYPE

Displacement, tons: 115 full load (steel) or 105 full load (aluminium)
Dimensions, feet (metres): 75·6 × 73·7 oa or 21 × 5·2 *(24·8 × 24·2 or 6·9 × 1·7)*
Main engines: 2 diesels (Detroit or General Motors); 650 bhp; 2 shafts = 9 knots
Complement: 5 (enlisted men)

Constructed of welded-steel or (later units) aluminium. Can carry one M-48 or M-60 tank (both approx 48 tons) or 60 tons cargo; range is 150 nautical miles at full load. Also operated in large numbers by the US Army.

LCM-8 carrying M-48 tank   *1970, United States Navy*

MECHANISED LANDING CRAFT: LCM 6 TYPE

Displacement, tons: 60 to 62 full load
Dimensions, feet (metres): 56·2 oa × 14 × 3·9 *(18·4 × 4·6 × 1·3)*
Main engines: Diesels; 2 shafts; 450 bhp = 9 knots

Welded-steel construction. Cargo capacity is 34 tons or 80 trops.

LANDING CRAFT VEHICLE AND PERSONNEL (LCVP)

Displacement, tons: 13·5 full load
Dimensions, feet (metres): 35·8 oa × 10·5 × 3·5 *(11·7 × 3·4 × 1·1)*
Main engines: Diesel; 325 bhp; 1 shaft = 9 knots

Constructed of wood or fibreglass-reinforced plastic. Fitted with 30-calibre machine guns when in combat areas. Cargo capacity, 8 000 lbs; range, 110 nautical miles at full load.

2 WARPING TUGS (LWT)

LWT 1   LWT 2

Displacement, tons: 61 (hoisting weight)
Dimensions, feet (metres): 85 oa × 22 × 6·75 *(27·9 × 7·2 × 2·2)*
Main engines: 2 diesels (Harbormaster); 420 bhp; 2 steerable shafts = 9 knots
Complement: 6 (enlisted men)

These craft are employed in amphibious landings to handle pontoon causeways. The LWT 1 and 2 are prototypes of a new, all-aluminium design completed in 1970. A collapsible A-frame is fitted forward to facilitate handling causeway anchors and ship-to-shore fuel lines. They can be "side loaded" on the main deck of an LST 1179 class ship or carried in an LPD/LSD type ship. The propulsion motors are similar to outboard motors, providing both steering and thrust, alleviating the need for rudders.
Built by Campbell Machine, San Diego, California.

LWT 2   *United States Navy*

WARPING TUGS (LWT)

Displacement, tons: approx 120
Dimensions, feet (metres): 92·9 oa × 23 × 6·5 *(30·4 × 7·5 × 2·1)*
Main engines: 2 outboard propulsion units = 6·5 knots

These craft are fabricated from pontoon sections and are assembled by the major amphibious commands as required.

LWT 85   *United States Navy*

PATROL SHIPS AND CRAFT

The US Navy's programme to construct a series of 30 hydrofoil missile ships has been sharply curtailed, with only six units now planned. Designated "patrol combatant missile (hydrofoil)", these PHMs are intended to operate against enemy surface ships and small craft, and conduct surveillance, screening, and special operations in coastal and inland water areas, and narrow seas.

Initial problems in the pump, gearbox, and electrical system of the prototype PHM have been overcome and the ships have demonstrated a "remarkable record of intensive operation at a pace harder than that of many fleet ships," according to defence officials.

However, the US Navy has apparently lost interest in the PHM concept, in part due to a 130 per cent growth in the estimated units procurement costs of the PHM. While much of the cost increase reflects economic factors, there were faulty initial estimates of the complexity of building this advanced-technology warship.

The six PHMs will be operated as a tactical squadron to develop tactics and gain technical experience with this type of craft. Meanwhile, the Navy has shifted additional units of the conventional-hull "Asheville" class gunboats to the Naval Reserve Force (NRF) and has relegated one of the units to an unarmed research role. Only four of the original 17 "Asheville" class ships remain in first-line Navy although the class has had less than a decade of service.

Two earlier hydrofoil craft, the *High Point* (PCH 1) and *Flagstaff* (PGH 1), are operated in a test and evaluation status. During 1974-1975 both craft were evaluated by the US Coast Guard (subsequently returned to Navy control). Finally, several patrol and riverine warfare craft are operated by the Naval Reserve Force, and two new designs (CPIC and PB) are being developed for US and foreign use. US use of these craft will be minimal; rather they are intended to compete with contemporary small craft built overseas in the foreign sales market.

Surface effect ships: The US Navy's effort to develop a 2 000-ton, 80-knot ocean-going SES as the prototype for warships of this configuration has been redesignated as the Advanced Naval Vehicles programme. This programme is described immediately after the listing for Frigates in this edition. The two 100 ton SES constructed for research and development are listed in the section on Experimental, Research and Surveying Ships.

PEGASUS (PHM 1)

1975, Boeing Co.

1 + 5 PATROL COMBATANTS—MISSILE (HYDROFOILS)

Name	No.	Builders	Commissioned
*PEGASUS	PHM 1	Boeing Co, Seattle, Wash	1976
HERCULES	PHM 2	Boeing Co, Seattle, Wash	—
	PHM 3	Boeing Co, Seattle, Wash	1979
	PHM 4	Boeing Co, Seattle, Wash	1979
	PHM 5	Boeing Co, Seattle, Wash	1979
	PHM 6	Boeing Co, Seattle, Wash	1979

Displacement, tons: 221 full load
Dimensions, feet (metres):
  foils extended: 131·2 *(40·0)* oa × 28·2 *(8·6)* hull × 23·2 *(7·1)*
  foils retracted: 147·5 *(45·0)* oa × 28·2 *(8·6)* hull × 6·2 *(1·9)*
Missile launchers: 8 launchers (quad) for Harpoon surface-to-surface missile
Guns: 1—76 mm 62 calibre AA (Mk 75)
Main engines: foil borne; 1 gas turbine (General Electric); 18 000 shp; waterjet propulsion units = 40+ knots
  hull borne; 2 diesels (Mercedes-Benz); 1 600 bhp; 2 waterjet propulsion = 12 knots
Complement: 21 (4 officers, 17 enlisted men)

The US Navy plans to construct six ships of this class. The *Pegasus* and *Hercules* were authorised in the Fiscal Year 1973 programme, and four additional ships in the FY 1975 shipbuilding programme. Planning for 24 additional units was halted in 1975. The *Pegasus* was laid down on 10 May 1973 and launched on 9 Nov 1974. The *Hercules* was laid down on 30 May 1974. The lead ship was delayed and lack of funds because of cost escalation and incorrect cost estimates caused a suspension of construction of the second ship.

The PHM design was developed in conjunction with the Italian and West German navies in an effort to produce a small combatant that would be universally acceptable to NATO navies with minor modifications. The West German Navy has advised the US government of plans to build up to 12 ships of this design in German shipyards.

Classification: The designation PHM originally was for Patrol Hydrofoil-Missile; reclassified Patrol Combatant Missile (Hydrofoil) on 30 June 1975.

Electronics: Fitted with the Mk 92 Mod 1 fire control system (Americanised version of the WM-28 radar and weapons control system developed by N. V. Hollandse Signaalapparaten). The Mk 92 will be used in the "Oliver Hazard Perry" class (FFG 7) guided missile frigates.

Engineering: The LM 2500 marine gas turbine is also used in the "Spruance" class (DD 963) destroyers and "Oliver Hazard Perry" (FFG 7) class guided missile frigates.

Gunnery: Gun armament is a single 76 mm OTO Melara rapid-fire weapon (designated Mk 75 Mod 1 in US service). The same gun will also be used in the FFG 7. No secondary gun armament is planned in US units.

Missiles: Each PHM will have two lightweight four-tube cannister launchers for the Harpoon surface-to-surface missile. No reloads will be carried. This is double the Harpoon armament originally planned.

Nomenclature: PHMs will be named for mythological terms. The PHM 1 originally was named *Delphinus;* renamed *Pegasus* on 26 April 1974.

Operational: It is planned that these ships will be "in commission" and have commanding officers *vice* being "in service" with officers-in-charge. Normally they will have an operational endurance of five days, after which they will require refuelling and resupply.

Photographs: The *Pegasus* is shown at the top of this page foilborne at high speed. When on foils the ship has a draft of 8·8 feet *(2·7 metres)*. Note the single Harpoon tube on the port side in her test configuration. The two lower photographs show the method of raising the foils for conventional hull operations. The *Pegasus* made her first foilborne "flight" on 25 Feb 1975.

PEGASUS (PHM 1)

1974, US Navy, PH2 Paul S. Burns

PEGASUS (PHM 1)

1974, US Navy, PH2 Paul S. Burns

11 PATROL COMBATANTS (PG): "ASHEVILLE" CLASS

Name	No.	Builders	Commissioned
*ASHEVILLE (NRF)	PG 84	Tacoma Boatbuilding	6 Aug 1966
*GALLUP (NRF)	PG 85	Tacoma Boatbuilding	22 Oct 1966
*ANTELOPE	PG 86	Tacoma Boatbuilding	4 Nov 1967
*READY	PG 87	Tacoma Boatbuilding	6 Jan 1968
*CROCKETT (NRF)	PG 88	Tacoma Boatbuilding	24 June 1967
*MARATHON (NRF)	PG 89	Tacoma Boatbuilding	11 May 1968
*CANON (NRF)	PG 90	Tacoma Boatbuilding	26 July 1968
*TACOMA	PG 92	Tacoma Boatbuilding	14 July 1969
*WELCH	PG 93	Peterson Builders	8 Sep 1969
*GRAND RAPIDS	PG 98	Tacoma Boatbuilding	5 Sep 1970
*DOUGLAS	PG 100	Tacoma Boatbuilding	6 Feb 1971

Displacement, tons: 225 standard; 245 full load
Dimensions, feet (metres): 164·5 oa × 23·8 × 9·5 *(50·1 × 7·3 × 2·9)*
Missile launchers: 2 launchers for Standard surface-to-surface missile in *Antelope, Ready, Grand Rapids, Douglas*
Guns: 1—3 in *(76 mm)* 50 cal (forward); 1—40 mm (aft); 4—·50 cal MG (twin) except 40 mm gun removed from ships with Standard missile
Main engines: CODAG: 2 diesels (Cummins); 1 450 shp; 2 shafts = 16 knots
1 gas turbine (General Electric); 13 300 shp; 2 shafts = 40+ knots
Complement: 25 to 29 (4 officers, 21 to 25 enlisted men) in active ships; augmented active-reserve crews in NRF ships

Originally a class of 17 patrol gunboats (PG ex-PGM) designed to perform patrol, blockade, surveillance, and support missions. No anti-submarine capability. Requirement for these craft was based on the volatile Cuban situation in the early 1960s.
PG 84 and PG 85 authorised in Fiscal Year 1963 new construction programme: PG 86 and PG 87 in FY 1964; PG 88-90 in FY 1965; PG 92-101 in FY 1966. *Asheville* was laid down on 15 April 1964 and launched on 1 May 1965; later ships approximately 18 months from keel laying to completion. Cost per ship approximately $5 000 000.
Only the four missile-armed units remain in active US Navy service. The *Tacoma* and *Welch* are at Little Creek, Virginia, involved in training Saudi Arabian naval personnel; five ships are assigned to the Naval Reserve Force (NRF) and are operated by composite active/Naval Reserve crews.
The *Chehalis* (PG 94) was stripped of armament and assigned as a research craft to the Naval Ship Research & Development Center in Annapolis, Maryland, on 21 Aug 1975; renamed *Athena* (no hull number assigned) and civilian manned.

Classification: These ships were originally classified as motor gunboats (PGM); reclassified as patrol boats (PG) with same hull numbers on 1 April 1967. This created a duplication of hull numbers used by the US Navy during World War II for designating ex-British "Arabis" or "Flower" class corvettes acquired under "reverse" lend lease in early 1942 and similar ships built in Canada with US funds (the Canadian-built ships serving in the US or Royal Navy); the first PG 101 was the Canadian-built *Asheville*, the first of the US Navy's World War II "frigates"; subsequently redesignated PF 1.
PGM 1-32 were submarine chasers modified during World War II with additional guns; PGM 33-83, 91, 102-121 assigned to gunboats built since 1955 for transfer to foreign navies.
Classification of the 14 surviving PGs changed again on 30 June 1975 to patrol combatants (PG).

Design: All-aluminium hull and aluminium-fibreglass superstructure. Because of the heat-transmitting qualities of the aluminium hull and the amount of waste heat produced by a gas turbine engine the ships are completely air conditioned.

Engineering: These ships have a Combination Diesel and Gas Turbine (CODAG) propulsion system with twin diesel engines for cruising and a gas turbine for high-speed operations. The gas turbine is an LM2500 with the gas generator essentially the same as the J-79-8 aircraft engine (used in the F-4 Phantom and other aircraft). The transfer from diesel to gas turbine propulsion (or vice versa) can be accomplished while under way with no loss of speed. From full stop these ships can attain 40 knots in one minute; manoeuvrability is excellent due in part to controllable pitch-propellers. Speed and propeller pitch is controlled directly from the pilot house console. Either JP-5 or diesel fuel can be used for both the gas turbine and the diesels. Arrangement of gas turbine intake differs on later ships.
Range is 1 700 miles at 16 knots and 325 miles at 37 knots.

Gunnery: The *Antelope* and *Ready* have the Mk 87 weapons control system for rapid acquisition and tracking of fast-moving targets; the system can also direct and fire appropriate weapons automatically. The Mk 87 can operate in a radar mode or with a stabilised optical sight on the weather decks. No further procurement of this advanced fire control system is planned in the Navy although it is being fitted to a number of foreign warships. (The Mk 87 is an American-produced copy of the Hollandse Signaalapparaten M22 weapon control system). Other ships have Mk 63 Mod 29 Gunfire Control System with SPG-50 fire control radar.
Mk 34 3 inch gun forward in closed mount with Mk 3 40 mm gun in open mount aft.

Missiles: The *Benicia* (PG 96) was experimentally fitted with a single launcher aft for the Standard interim anti-ship missile in 1971; removed prior to transfer to South Korea later that year.
During the latter part of 1971 the *Antelope* and *Ready* were provided with two standard missile launchers. The box-like missile launchers are fitted at the stern (40 mm gun removed); a reload is provided in an adjacent magazine for each launcher; subsequently *Grand Rapids* and *Douglas* fitted with missiles.

Nomenclature: Patrol gunboats are named for small American cities; however, the *Surprise* remembers several earlier US naval ships.

Transfers: *Benicia* (PG 96) transferred to South Korea on 2 Oct 1971; *Surprise* (PG 97) transfer-

ANTELOPE (PG 86)   *1972, General Dynamics*

READY (PG 87)   *1973, Giorgio Arra*

TACOMA (PG 92)   *1975, Giorgio Arra*

red to Turkey on 28 Feb 1973. *Defiance* (PG 95) transferred to Turkey on 11 June 1973; *Beacon* (PG 99), *Green Bay* (PG 101) were for transfer to Greece in June 1976 (delayed).

Photographs: Note Mk 87 antenna in *Antelope* and *Ready*. The first *Antelope* photograph shows a Standard missile raised to firing position on fantail. The gas turbine air intake is immediately aft of the bridge structure; the adjacent large funnel is the turbine exhaust with a smaller diesel exhaust stack on either side. A photograph of the *Antelope* firing a Standard missile appears in the 1974-1975 edition.

1 HYDROFOIL GUNBOAT (PGH): "FLAGSTAFF" TYPE

Name	No.	Builders	Commissioned
*FLAGSTAFF	PGH 1	Grumman Aircraft Corp, Stuart, Fla.	July 1968

Displacement, tons: 56·8 full load
Dimensions, feet (metres): 74·4 oa *(22·7)* × 21·4 *(6·2)* × 4·5 *(1·4)* (foils retracted) or 13·5 *(4·1)* (foils extended)
Guns: removed
Main engines: foil borne: 1 gas turbine (Rolls Royce); 3 620 hp; controllable pitch propeller = 40+ knots
hull borne; 2 diesels (General Motors); 300 bhp; water-jet propulsion = 8 knots
Complement: 13 (1 officer, 12 enlisted men)

The *Flagstaff* was a competitive prototype evaluated with the *Tucumcari* (PGH 2). Laid down 15 July 1966 and launched 9 Jan 1968. Construction cost was $3 600 000. The *Flagstaff* has conducted sea trials with a 152 mm howitzer (see *Gunnery* notes), foil-mounted sonars, and towed shapes representing Variable Depth Sonar (VDS). During late 1974 the *Flagstaff* was evaluated by the Coast Guard to determine possible roles for this type of craft.
The *Flagstaff* was scheduled to be laid up in reserve in the fall of 1976.

Design: The *Flagstaff* has a conventional foil arrangement with 70 per cent of the craft's weight supported by the forward set of foils and 30 per cent of the weight supported by the stern foils. Steering is accomplished by movement of the stern strut about its vertical axis. Foil-borne operation is automatically controlled by a wave-height sensing system. The foils are fully retractable for hull-borne operations. Aluminium construction.

Engineering: During foil-borne operation the propeller is driven by a geared transmission system contained in the tail strut, and in the pod located at the strut-foil connection. During hull borne operation two diesel engines drive a water-jet propulsion system. Water enters the pump inlets through openings in the hull and the thrust is exerted by water flow through nozzles in the transome. Steering in the hull-borne mode is by deflection vanes in the water stream. Rolls-Royce Tyne Mk 621 gas turbine engine.

Gunnery: Originally armed with one 40 mm gun forward, four ·50 cal MG amidships, and an 81 mm mortar aft. Rearmed in 1971 with a 152 mm gun forward. The weapon was the same used on the Army's Sheridan armoured reconnaissance vehicle; low-velocity firing a fully combustible cartridge. After firing trials in 1971 the gun was removed. See 1974-1975 and previous editions for photographs showing guns installed.

Photographs: *Flagstaff* is shown on foils in Navy and Coast Guard markings, and in the latter colours with foils retracted. Note foil configuration compared with *Pegasus*.

FLAGSTAFF (PGH 1)   *United States Navy*

FLAGSTAFF (PGH 1)   *1974, US Coast Guard*

FLAGSTAFF (PGH 1)   *1974, US Coast Guard*

1 HYDROFOIL SUBMARINE CHASER (PCH): "HIGH POINT" TYPE

Name	No.	Builders	Commissioned
*HIGH POINT	PCH 1	J. M. Martinac, Tacoma, Wash	3 Sep 1963

Displacement, tons: 100 full load
Dimensions, feet (metres): 115 *(35)* oa × 31 *(9·4)* × 6 *(1·8)* (foils retracted) or 17 *(5·2)* (foils extended)
Guns: removed
A/S weapons: removed
Main engines: foil borne; 2 gas turbines (Bristol Siddeley Marine Proteus); 6 200 shp; 2 paired counter-rotating propellers = 48 knots
   hull borne; diesel (Curtis Wright); 600 bhp; retractable outdrive with 1 propeller = 12 knots
Complement: 13 (1 officer, 12 enlisted men)

Experimental hydrofoil submarine chaser. Authorised under Fiscal Year 1960 programme. Built by Grumman Aircraft Corp at Martinac boatyard. Laid down 27 Feb 1961, launched 17 Aug 1962. Employed in experimental hydrofoil work. During early 1975 the *High Point* was evaluated by the Coast Guard.

Design: The *High Point's* forward foil is supported by a single strut and the after foil by twin struts. Twin underwater nacelles at the junction of the vertical struts and main foil housed contra-rotating, super-cavitating propellers for foil-borne propulsion. After foils modified in 1973 and nacelles repositioned to improve performance in heavy sea states. Also, forward foil strut made steerable to improve manoeuvrability. Note outboard propeller in raised position in the photographs. The twin "humps" cover the retracted hydrofoil struts.

Gunnery: A single 40 mm gun was mounted forward in 1968; subsequently removed. (Four anti-submarine torpedo tubes also have been removed).

Missiles: During 1973-1974 the *High Point* was employed as a test ship for the lightweight cannister launchers for the Harpoon surface-to-surface missile intended for the PHM.

Losses: The hydrofoil gunboat *Tucumcari* (PGH 2) ran aground on 16 Nov 1972 and wrecked; plans to restore the craft were dropped due to high costs and she was scrapped in October 1973.

HIGH POINT (PCH 1) firing Harpoon   *1973, McDonnell Douglas*

HIGH POINT (PCH 1)   *1975, US Coast Guard*

4 FAST PATROL BOATS (PTF): PTF 23 SERIES

*PTF 23   *PTF 24   *PTF 25   *PTF 26

Displacement, tons: 105 full load
Dimensions, feet (metres): 94·7 oa × 23·2 × 7 *(28·8 × 7·1 × 2·1)*
Guns: 1—81 mm mortar; 1—50 cal MG (mounted over mortar); 1—40 mm (aft); 2—20 mm (single)
Main engines: 2 diesels (Napier-Deltic); 6 200 bhp; 2 shafts = approx 40 knots
Complement: approx 20

PTF 23-26 built by Sewart Seacraft Division of Teledyne Inc of Berwick, Louisiana. First unit completed in 1967, others in 1968. Aluminium hulls. Commercial name is "Osprey".
All 17 PTFs are in service and are assigned to the Naval Reserve Force. 5 are based at San Diego, California; 5 at Norfolk, Virginia; 4 at New Orleans, Louisiana; and 3 on the Great Lakes. Conversion of these PTFs to gas turbine propulsion is being considered.

PTF 23 TYPE   *United States Navy*

6 FAST PATROL BOATS (PTF): PTF 17 SERIES

*PTF 17   *PTF 18   *PTF 19   *PTF 20   *PTF 21   *PTF 22

Displacement, tons: 85 full load
Dimensions, feet (metres): 80·3 oa × 24·5 × 6·8 *(24·5 × 7·5 × 2·1)*
Guns (may vary): 1—81 mm mortar; 1—40 mm; 2—20 mm (single); 1—·50 cal MG (mounted over mortar)
Main engines: 2 diesels (Napier-Deltic); 6 200 bhp; 2 shafts = approx 45 knots
Complement: 19 (3 officers, 16 enlisted men)

PTF 17-22 built by John Trumpy & Sons, Annapolis, Maryland; lead boat completed in late 1967, others 1968-1970. Based on "Nasty" design.
All six units are in service (PTF 21 and 22 were given "commissioned" status on 14 May 1969 but subsequently returned to "in service" on 23 Sep 1970).
PTF 22 ran aground and was severely damaged on 19 Aug 1975; future status under consideration.
These PTFs probably will be laid up or stricken in the near future.

PTF 17 Type   *1972, Courtesy Ships of the World*

7 FAST PATROL BOATS (PTF): "NASTY" CLASS

*PTF 3   *PTF 5   *PTF 6   *PTF 7   *PTF 10   *PTF 11   *PTF 12

Displacement, tons: 85 full load
Dimensions, feet (metres): 80·3 oa × 24·5 × 6·8 *(24·5 × 7·5 × 2·1)*
Guns (may vary): 1—81 mm mortar; 1—40 mm; 2—20 mm (single); 1—·50 cal MG (mounted over mortar)
Main engines: 2 diesels (Napier-Deltic); 6 200 bhp; 2 shafts = 45 knots
Complement: 19 (3 officers, 16 enlisted men)

PTF 3-16 of the "Nasty" type were built by Boatservice Ltd A/S of Mandal, Norway. Same design as the Norwegian Navy's "Tjeld" class torpedo boats. PTF 3 and PTF 4 delivered to USA in December 1962, PTF 5-8 in April 1964, and PTF 9-16 in September 1964. Hulls made of two layers of mahogany which sandwich a layer of fibreglass. British engines. Range is 450 miles at 41 knots or 600 miles at 25 knots.
These boats are expected to be laid up or stricken by 1980.

PTF 6   *1973, United States Navy*

COASTAL PATROL AND INTERDICTION CRAFT (CPIC)

The US Navy's prototype CPIC was transferred to South Korea on 1 Aug 1975. No additional craft of this type are planned for the US Navy.

5 PATROL BOATS (PB): NEW DESIGN

Two **PB** Mark I series
Three **PB** Mark III series

Displacement, tons:
  Mk I: 26·9 light; 36·3 full load
  Mk III: 31·5 light; 41·25 full load
Dimensions, feet (metres):
  Mk I: 65 oa × 16 × 4·9 *(19·8 × 4·9 × 1·5)*
  Mk III: 65 oa × 18 × 5·9 *(19·8 × 5·5 × 1·8)*
Guns: 6—20 mm or ·50 cal MG (1 twin, 4 single)
Main engines: Diesel (Detroit); 1 635 bhp; 3 shafts = 26 knots

The PB series is being developed as replacements for the "Swift" type inshore patrol craft (PCF). Mk I built by Sewart Seacraft, Berwick, Louisiana; Mk III by Peterson Builders Sturgeon Bay, Wisconsin. Two Mark I prototypes completed in 1972 and delivered to the Navy in 1973 for evaluation; assigned to Naval Reserve Force. Additional units of the Mk III design are being constructed for the Philippine Navy. Procurement of the PB Mk III for the US Navy is under consideration. (The PB Mark II design was not built).
Basic weapons arrangement provides for a twin gun mounting above the pilot house and four single mountings on the main deck. The Mk III design has the pilot house offset to starboard to provide space on port side for installation of additional weapons (see drawing).

Operational: These craft and the patrol and riverine craft listed on the following page are operated by the Naval Reserve Force.
Two Mk III units provided to Philippines.

PB Mk III (PG 99 in background)   *1975, Giorgio Arra*

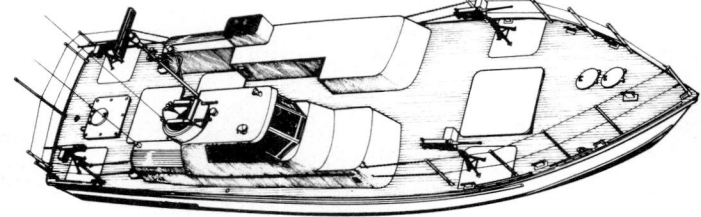

PB Mk I   *1972, Sewart Seacraft*   PB Mk III

5 PATROL CRAFT (PCF): "SWIFT" TYPE

Five PCF Mark I series

Displacement, tons: 22·5 full load
Dimensions, feet (metres): 50·1 oa × 13 × 3·5 (15·3 × 4·0 × 1·1)
Guns: 1—81 mm mortar, 3—·50 cal MG (twin MG mount atop pilot house and single MG mounted over mortar)
Main engines: 2 geared diesels (General Motors); 960 shp; 2 shafts = 28 knots
Complement: 6 (1 officer, 5 enlisted men)

The "Swift" design is adapted from the all-metal crew boat which is used to support off-shore drilling rigs in the Gulf of Mexico. Approximately 125 built since 1965. Most transferred to South Vietnam (see below).
Designation changed from Fast Patrol Craft (PCF) to Inshore Patrol Craft (PCF) on 14 Aug 1968.

Transfers: PCF 33, 34, and 83-86 transferred to the Philippines in 1966. Additional PCFs of this type constructed specifically for transfer to Thailand, the Philippines, and South Korea; not assigned US hull numbers in the PCF series; 104 PCFs formerly manned by US Navy personnel transferred to Soth Vietnam in 1968-1970.

PCF Mk I Type

1969, United States Navy

29 RIVER PATROL BOATS (PBR)

29 PBR Mk II series

Displacement, tons: 8
Dimensions, feet (metres): 32 oa × 11 × 2·6 (9·8 × 3·4 × 0·8)
Guns: 3—·50 cal MG (twin mount forward; single aft); 1—40 mm grenade launcher; 1—60 mm mortar in some boats
Main engines: 2 geared diesels (General Motors); water jets = 25+ knots
Complement: 4 or 5 (enlisted men)

Fibreglass hull river patrol boats. Approximately 500 built 1967-1973; most transferred to South Vietnam.

PBR Mk II Type

United States Navy

2 ASSAULT SUPPORT PATROL BOATS (ASPB)

Displacement, tons: 36·25 full load
Dimensions, feet (metres): 50 oa × 15·6 × 3·8 (15·2 × 4·8 × 1·1)
Guns (varies): 1 or 2—20 mm (with 2—·50 cal MG in boats with one 20 mm); 2—·30 cal MG; 2—40 mm high-velocity grenade launchers
Main engines: 2 diesels (General Motors); 2 shafts = 14 knots sustained
Complement: 6 (enlisted)

The ASPB was designed specifically for riverine operations to escort other river craft, provide mine countermeasures during river operations, and interrupt enemy river traffic. Welded-steel hulls. Armament changed to above configuration in 1968; some boats have twin—·50 cal MG "turret" forward in place of single 20 mm gun.
Note that open stern well is plated over in the ASPB pictured here (A-131-2); a view of an ASPB with 81 mm mortar/·50 cal MG aft appears in the 1968-1969 editions.

ASSAULT SUPPORT PATROL BOAT (ASPB)

1968, United States Navy

14 "MINI" ARMOURED TROOP CARRIERS (ATC)

Dimensions, feet (metres): 36 oa × 12·7 × 3·5 (11·0 × 3·9 × 1·1)
Main engines: 2 diesels (General Motors); water-jet propulsion = 28 knots except one unit with gas turbines
Complement: 2
Troops: 15 to 20

A small troop carrier for riverine and swimmer delivery operations; aluminium hull; ceramic armour. Draft is one foot when underway at high speed. The last of the Vietnam-era ATCs have been disposed of along with several hundred other riverine warfare craft.

"MINI" ATC

1974, US Navy, PH2 Terry C. Mitchell

1 COMMAND AND CONTROL BOAT (CCB)

Displacement, tons: 80 full load
Dimensions, feet (metres): 61 oa × 17·5 × 3·4 (18·6 × 5·3 × 1·0)
Guns: 3—20 mm; 2—·30 cal MG; 2—40 mm high velocity-grenade launchers
Main engines: 2 diesels (Detroit); 2 shafts = 8·5 knots max (6 knots sustained)
Complement: 11

This type of craft serves as afloat command posts providing command and communications facilities for ground force and boat group commanders. Heavily armoured. Armament changed to above configuration in 1968. Converted from LCM-6 landing craft.

COMMAND AND CONTROL BOAT (CCB)

United States Navy

SWIMMER SUPPORT CRAFT

The US Navy operates several specialised craft in support of "frogmen" (combat swimmers) assigned to SEAL (Sea-Air-Land) teams, Underwater Demolition Teams (UDT), and Explosive Ordnance Disposal (EOD) teams. Most of the craft listed in previous editions have been discarded and the primary craft in service today is the 36-foot Medium SEAL Support Craft (MSSC). Several SEAL support craft are operated by the Naval Reserve Force. A new craft for this role will probably be developed in the near future.

MEDIUM SEAL SUPPORT CRAFT (MSSC)   *United States Navy*

MINE WARFARE SHIPS

The US Navy has initiated a programme to construct ten ocean minesweepers to clear advanced Soviet mines, especially those laid in deep water.

Currently the Navy operates three active and 22 Naval Reserve Force (NRF) minesweepers. The active ships provide support to mine research and development activities at the Naval Coastal Systems Laboratory in Panama City, Florida; the NRF ships are manned by composite active-reserve crews. In addition, the Navy flies 21 specially equipped RH-53D Sea Stallion helicopters. These helicopters, which tow mine countermeasure devices, are readily deployable to aircraft carriers or amphibious ships in overseas areas. They can counter mines

laid in shallow waters but have no capability against deepwater mines.

In 1976 the Navy's mine countermeasure capability was officially estimated at about one-third that of the late 1960s. The US Navy maintains no surface ships with a minelaying capability. Rather, the Navy can plant mines by carrier-based aircraft (as was done in North Vietnam), land-based maritime patrol aircraft, and attack submarines. Although the covert nature of submarine operations makes them preferable in certain minelaying situations, modern US attack submarines have only four torpedo tubes and a limited number of reload spaces, severely restricting their capacity for tube-launched mines. The

large B-52 Stratofortress bombers of the Strategic Air Command can also plant sea mines. The use of B-52s in the minelaying role presupposes the availability of the aircraft for this purpose, the proximity of suitable air bases, the suitable location of mines, and no interference from hostile aircraft in the target area.

Photographs: A photograph of a CH-53A Sea Stallion helicopter lifting a minesweeping sled from an amphibious ship appears in the 1975-1976 edition of *Jane's Fighting Ships*.

(10) MINE COUNTERMEASURE SHIPS (MCM)

One ship	**MCM**	Planned Fiscal Year 1979 programme
Three ships	**MCM**	Planned Fiscal Year 1980 programme
Six ships	**MCM**	Planned Fiscal Year 1981 programme

These ships are planned to provide a deep-ocean capability to counter advanced Soviet mines. Specific characteristics have not yet been developed.

2 OCEAN MINESWEEPERS (MSO):"ACME" CLASS

Name	No.	Launched	Commissioned
*ADROIT (NRF)	MSO 509	20 Aug 1955	4 Mar 1957
*AFFRAY (NRF)	MSO 511	18 Dec 1956	8 Dec 1958

Displacement, tons: 720 light; 780 full load
Dimensions, feet (metres): 173 oa × 35 × 14 *(52·7 × 10·7 × 4·3)*
Guns: 1—20 mm AA or 1—40 mm AA; 2—50 cal MG
Main engines: 4 diesels (Packard), 2 800 bhp; 2 shafts (controllable pitch propellers) = 14 knots
Complement: 78 (8 officers, 70 enlisted men); 86 in NRF ships (3 officers, 36 enlisted active duty; 3 officers, 44 enlisted reserve)

This class is different from the "Agile" type but has similar basic particulars. All built by Frank L. Sample, Jnr, Inc, Boothbay Harbor, Maine. Plans to modernise these ships were cancelled (see notes under "Agile" class).
Adroit and *Affray* are assigned to Naval Reserve training, manned partially by active and partially by reserve personnel (see notes under "Agile" class).

Disposals: *Acme* (MSO 508), *Advance* (MSO 510) stricken on 15 May 1976.

Nomenclature: The ocean minesweepers are named for terms expressing action or aggressiveness.

Photographs: Note 40 mm gun in *Affray* and 20 mm gun visible in *Advance*.

AFFRAY (MSO 511)   *1969, United States Navy*

ADVANCE (MSO 510)—(now stricken)   *1968, United States Navy*

33 OCEAN MINESWEEPERS (MSO) "AGILE" CLASS

Name	No.	Launched		Commissioned	
*CONSTANT (NRF)	MSO 427	14 Feb	1952	8 Sep	1954
*DASH (NRF)	MSO 428	20 Sep	1952	14 Aug	1953
*DETECTOR (NRF)	MSO 429	5 Dec	1952	26 Jan	1954
*DIRECT (NRF)	MSO 430	27 May	1953	9 July	1954
*DOMINANT (NRF)	MSO 431	5 Nov	1953	8 Nov	1954
*ENGAGE (NRF)	MSO 433	18 June	1953	29 June	1954
*ENHANCE (NRF)	MSO 437	11 Oct	1952	16 Apr	1955
*ESTEEM (NRF)	MSO 438	20 Dec	1952	10 Sep	1955
*EXCEL (NRF)	MSO 439	25 Sep	1953	24 Feb	1955
*EXPLOIT (NRF)	MSO 440	10 Apr	1953	31 Mar	1954
*EXULTANT (NRF)	MSO 441	6 June	1953	22 June	1954
*FEARLESS (NRF)	MSO 442	17 July	1953	22 Sep	1954
*FIDELITY	MSO 443	21 Aug	1953	19 Jan	1955
*FORTIFY (NRF)	MSO 446	14 Feb	1953	16 July	1954
*ILLUSIVE	MSO 448	12 July	1952	14 Nov	1953
*IMPERVIOUS (NRF)	MSO 449	29 Aug	1952	15 July	1954
*IMPLICIT (NRF)	MSO 455	1 Aug	1953	10 Mar	1954
*INFLICT (NRF)	MSO 456	6 Oct	1953	11 May	1954
LUCID	MSO 458	14 Nov	1953	4 May	1955
NIMBLE	MSO 459	6 Aug	1954	11 May	1955
OBSERVER	MSO 461	19 Oct	1954	31 Aug	1955
PINNACLE	MSO 462	3 Jan	1955	21 Oct	1955
*PLUCK (NRF)	MSO 464	6 Feb	1954	11 Aug	1954
SKILL	MSO 471	23 Apr	1955	7 Nov	1955
VITAL	MSO 474	12 Aug	1953	9 June	1955
*CONQUEST (NRF)	MSO 488	20 May	1954	20 July	1955
*GALLANT (NRF)	MSO 489	4 June	1954	14 Sep	1955
*LEADER	MSO 490	15 Sep	1954	16 Nov	1955
*PLEDGE (NRF)	MSO 492	20 July	1955	20 Apr	1956
STURDY	MSO 494	28 Jan	1956	23 Oct	1957
SWERVE	MSO 495	1 Nov	1955	27 July	1957
VENTURE	MSO 496	27 Nov	1956	3 Feb	1958

LEADER (MSO 490)   1972, Harbor Boat Building

ENHANCE (MSO 437)   1971, Harbor Boat Building

Displacement, tons: 665 light; 750 full load
Dimensions, feet (metres): 165 wl; 172 oa × 36 × 13·6 (52·4 × 11·0 × 4·2)
Guns: 1—40 mm AA; 2—·50 cal MG (replaced by 2—20 mm AA in several ships); some modernised ships are unarmed
Main engines: 4 diesels (Packard); 2 280 bhp 2 shafts; controllable pitch propellers = 15·5 knots; *Dash, Detector, Direct* and *Dominant,* have 4 diesels (General Motors); 1 520 bhp (see *Modernisation* notes)
Complement: 78 (8 officers, 70 enlisted men); 86 in NRF ships (3 officers, 36 enlisted active duty; 3 officers, 44 enlisted reserve)

These ships were built on the basis of mine warfare experience in the Korean War (1950-1953); 58 built for US service and 35 transferred upon completion to NATO navies. (One ship cancelled, MSO 497). They have wooden hulls and non-magnetic engines and other equipment. All surviving ships were built in private shipyards.
Initially designated as minesweepers (AM); reclassified as ocean minesweepers (MSO) in Feb 1955. Originally fitted with UQS-1 mine detecting sonar.
Beginning in 1970 most of these ships have been decommissioned and placed in reserve or assigned to Naval Reserve training. Only three of these ships remain in active Navy commission: *Fidelity, Illusive,* and *Leader;* 20 others are assigned to the Naval Reserve Force and are manned by mixed active duty and reserve crews; and 10 ships are laid up in reserve.

Engineering: Diesel engines are fabricated of non-magnetic stainless steel alloy to help reduce possibility of detonating magnetic mines. Range is 2 400 miles at ten knots.

Modernisation: The 62 ocean minesweepers in commission during the mid-1960s were all to have been modernised; estimated cost and schedule per ship were $5 000 000 and ten months in shipyard. However, some of the early modernisations took as long as 26 months which, coupled with changes in mine countermeasures techniques, led to cancellation of programme after 13 ships were modernised: MSO 433, 437, 438, 441-443, 445, 446, 448, 449, 456, 488, and 490.
The modernisation provided improvements in mine detection, engines, communications, and habitability: four Waukesha Motor Co diesel engines installed (plus two or three diesel generators for sweep gear), SQQ-14 sonar with mine classification as well as detection capability provided, twin 20 mm AA in some ships (replacing single 40 mm because of space requirements for sonar hoist mechanism), habitability improved, and advanced communications equipment fitted; bridge structure in modernised ships extended around mast and aft to funnel. Complement in active modernised ships is 6 officers and 70 enlisted men.
Some MSOs have received SQQ-14 sonar but not full modernisation.

EXCEL (MSO 439)   1971, United States Navy

Transfers: Ships of this class serve in the navies of Belgium, France, Italy, Netherlands, Norway, Peru, Philippines, Portugal, Spain, Taiwan, Thailand and Uruguay.

Disposals and transfers: (since 1 Jan 1975) *Aggressive* (MSO 422), *Embattle* (MSO 434), *Prime* (MSO 466), *Reaper* (MSO 467) stricken on 28 Feb 1975; *Bold* (MSO 424), *Bulwark* (MSO 425) stricken for transfer to Taiwan. *Aggressive* and *Embattle* were to be transferred to Pakistan in 1976.

COASTAL MINESWEEPERS (MSC): NEW CONSTRUCTION

Four coastal minesweepers are under construction for transfer to Saudi Arabia; designated MSC 322-325 for accounting purposes. Contract awarded 30 Sep 1975 to Peterson Builders, Sturgeon Bay, Wisconsin; scheduled to complete March through September 1978. Hull numbers MSC 320 and MSC 321 assigned to units built in the United States for South Korea.

OCEAN MINESWEEPER (MSO): "ABILITY" CLASS

The two surviving minesweepers of this class, the *Alacrity* (MSO 520) and *Assurance* (MSO 521), have been allocated to sonar test programmes and redesignated as auxiliary ships AG 520 and AG 521, respectively. See listing under Experimental, Research, and Surveying Ships. *Ability* (MSO 519) of this class stricken on 1 Feb 1971.

COASTAL MINESWEEPERS (MSC): "BLUEBIRD" CLASS

All surviving coastal minesweepers of the 144-foot "Bluebird" class have been stricken. See 1974-1975 and previous editions for characteristics and photographs.

Transfers: Ships of this class serve in the navies of Belgium, Denmark; Fiji, France, Greece, Indonesia, Japan, South Korea, Netherlands, Norway, Pakistan, Philippines, Portugal, Spain, Taiwan, Thailand, Tunisia and Turkey.

Disposals and transfers: (since 1 Jan 1975) *Peacock* (MSC 198), *Phoebe* (MSC 199), *Shrike* (MSC 201) stricken on 1 July 1975; *Thrush* (MSC 204) leased to Virginia Institute of Marine Sciences on 1 July 1975; *Thrasher* (MSC 203), *Whippoorwill* (MSC 207) transferred to Singapore on 5 Dec 1975; *Viero* (MSC 205), *Warbler* (MSC 206), transferred to Fiji in 1976; *Bluebird* (MSC 121) was to have transferred to Thailand in 1976, but delayed indefinitely.

MINE COUNTERMEASURE CRAFT

8 MINESWEEPING BOATS (MSB)

MSB 15	MSB 25	MSB 29	MSB 51
MSB 16	MSB 28	MSB 41	MSB 52

Displacement, tons: 30 light; 39 full load except MSB 29, 80 full load
Dimensions, feet (metres): 57·2 × 15·5 × 4 except MSB 29, 82 × 19 × 5·5
Guns: several MG (Vietnam configuration)
Main engines: 2 geared diesels (Packard); 600 bhp; 2 shafts = 12 knots
Complement: 6 (enlisted)

MSB 17 (now stricken)

1966, United States Navy

Wooden-hull minesweepers intended to be carried to theatre of operations by large assault ships; however, they are too large to be easily handled by cranes and are assigned to sweeping harbours. From 1966 to 1970 they were used extensively in Vietnam for river minesweeping operations.

Of 49 minesweeping boats of this type built only eight remain in active service, all based at Charleston, South Carolina. (See 1971-1972 and previous editions for details of earlier disposals and additional data).

MSB 1-4 were ex-Army minesweepers built in 1946 (since discarded), MSB 5-54 (less MSB 24) were completed in 1952-1956. MSB 24 was not built. MSB 29 built to enlarged design by John Trumpy & Sons, Annapolis, Maryland, in an effort to improve seakeeping ability.

Normally commanded by chief petty officer or petty officer first class.

Gunnery: MSBs serving in South Vietnam were fitted with several machineguns and removable fibreglass armour. Note machineguns in tub amidships and on bow of MSB 17, shown here sweeping on the Long Tao river in South Vietnam.

INSHORE MINESWEEPERS (MSI): "COVE" CLASS

The inshore minesweepers *Cove* (MSI 1) and *Cape* (MSI 2) are employed in research activities; see listing under Experimental, Research and Surveying Ships in this edition.

SPECIAL MINESWEEPERS (MSS)

The special minesweeper *MSS 1* (ex-SS *Harry L. Gluckman*) was stricken on 10 Feb 1975. See 1973-1974 and previous editions for characteristics and photographs.

UNDERWAY REPLENISHMENT SHIPS

Underway replenishment (UNREP) ships provide fuel, munitions, provisions, spare parts, and other *matériel* to warships in forward areas.

In addition, most US Navy replenishment ships are fitted with helicopter platforms to permit helicopters to transfer supplies by vertical replenishment (VERTREP). Virtually all *matériel* except fuel oil can be transferred by helicopter, reducing, or if fuel oil is not required, alleviating the need for the replenishment ship and warship to steam in close company. Helicopters are carried specifically for this purpose by the newer ammunition ships (AE), the combat store ships (AFS), the fast combat support ships (AOE), and some replenishment oilers (AOR). Carrier-based helicopters are sometimes employed in this role when an aircraft carrier is in the area.

Planned UNREP ship force levels provide a wartime capability to support deployed carrier and amphibious task groups in up to four or five locations simultaneously. This plan is based on the availability of some storage depots on foreign territory, and the use of Military Sealift Ships to carry fuels, munitions, and the stores from the United States or overseas sources for transfer to UNREP ships in overseas areas.

During peacetime some 16 to 18 UNREP ships normally are forward deployed in the Mediterranean and western Pacific areas in support of the 6th and 7th Fleets, respectively. A few of these ships are homeported overseas.

The Navy's five-year plan for modernisation of the UNREP forces provides for six fleet oilers (AO) and one fast combat support ship (AOE) in the Fiscal Year 1977-1981 new construction programmes. This is a major reduction in the UNREP force modernisation as proposed during the past few years. For example, plans to build three new AEs in FY 1978-1980 have been dropped.

Most UNREP ships are Navy manned and armed; however, beginning in 1972, an increasing number of these ships are being operated by the Military Sealift Command (MSC) with civilian crews. The latter ships are not armed and have T-designations.

8 AMMUNITION SHIPS (AE): "KILAUEA" CLASS

Name	No.	Laid down	Launched	Commissioned
*KILAUEA	AE 26	10 Mar 1966	9 Aug 1967	10 Aug 1968
*BUTTE	AE 27	21 July 1966	9 Aug 1967	29 Nov 1968
*SANTA BARBARA	AE 28	20 Dec 1966	23 Jan 1968	11 July 1970
*MOUNT HOOD	AE 29	8 May 1967	17 July 1968	1 May 1971
*FLINT	AE 32	4 Aug 1969	9 Nov 1970	20 Nov 1971
*SHASTA	AE 33	10 Nov 1969	3 Apr 1971	26 Feb 1972
*MOUNT BAKER	AE 34	10 May 1970	23 Oct 1971	22 July 1972
*KISKA	AE 35	4 Aug 1971	11 Mar 1972	16 Dec 1972

Displacement, tons: 20 500 full load
Dimensions, feet (metres): 564 oa × 81 × 25·7 (*171·9 × 24·7 × 7·8*)
Guns: 8—3 inch (*76 mm*) 50 cal AA (twin) (Mk 33)
Helicopters: 2 UH-46 Sea Knight cargo helicopters normally embarked
Main engines: Geared turbines (General Electric); 22 000 shp; 1 shaft = 20 knots
Boilers: 3 (Foster Wheeler)
Complement: 401 (28 officers, 373 enlisted men)

KISKA (AE 35)

1972, Ingalls Shipbuilding

Ammunition ships of an advanced design. Fitted for rapid transfer of missiles and other munitions to ships alongside or with helicopters in vertical replenishment operations (VERT-REP). Helicopter platform and hangar aft. AE 26 and 27 authorised in Fiscal Year 1965 new construction programme, AE 28 and 29 in FY 1966, AE 32 and 33 in FY 1967, and AE 34 and 35 in FY 1968. AE 26 and built by General Dynamics Corp, Quincy, Massachusetts; AE 28 and 29 Bethlehem Steel Corp, Sparrows Point, Maryland; and AE 32-35 by Ingalls Shipbuilding Corp, Pascagoula, Mississippi.

The 3 inch guns are arranged in twin closed mounts forward and twin open mounts aft, atop superstructure, between funnel and after booms. Two Mk 56 gunfire control systems installed. All of these ships are active.

BUTTE (AE 27)

1972, Giorgio Arra

FLINT (AE 32)

1971, Ingalls Shipbuilding

5 AMMUNITION SHIPS (AE): "SURIBACHI" CLASS

Name	No.	Laid down	Launched	Commissioned
*SURIBACHI	AE 21	31 Jan 1955	2 Nov 1955	17 Nov 1956
*MAUNA KEA	AE 22	16 May 1955	3 May 1956	30 Mar 1957
*NITRO	AE 23	20 May 1957	25 June1958	1 May 1959
*PYRO	AE 24	21 Oct 1957	5 Nov 1958	24 July 1959
*HALEAKALA	AE 25	10 Mar 1958	17 Feb 1959	3 Nov 1959

Displacement, tons: 7 470 light; 10 000 standard; 17 500 full load
Dimensions, feet (metres): 512 oa × 72 × 29 *(156·1 × 21·9 × 8·8)*
Guns: 4—3 inch *(76 mm)* 50 cal AA (twin) (Mk 33)
Main engines: Geared turbines (Bethlehem); 16 000 shp; 1 shaft = 20·6 knots
Boilers: 2 (Combustion Engineering)
Complement: 316 (18 officers, 298 enlisted men)

Ammunition ships designed specifically for underwater replenishment. All built by Bethlehem Steel Corp, Sparrows Point, Maryland. A sixth ship of this class to have been built under the FY 1959 programme was cancelled.
All five ships were modernised in 1960s, being fitted with high-speed transfer equipment, three holds configured for stowage of missiles up to and including the 33-foot Talos, and helicopter platform fitted aft (two after twin 3 inch gun mounts removed).
Arrangements of twin 3 inch gun mounts differ, some ships have them in tandem and others side-by-side. Gunfire control systems vary.
All of these ships are active.

Nomenclature: Ammunition ships are named for volcanoes and explosives (eg *Nitro* for nitro-glycerine and *Pyro* for pyrotechnic).

PYRO (AE 24)

1971, United States Navy

NITRO (AE 23) with UH-46 Sea Knight helicopter

1975, Giorgio Arra

2 AMMUNITION SHIPS (AE): "WRANGELL" CLASS

Name	No.	Launched	Commissioned
WRANGELL (ex-*Midnight*)	AE 12	14 April1944	28 May 1944
FIREDRAKE (ex-*Winged Racer*)	AE 14	12 May 1944	27 Dec 1944

Displacement, tons: 6 350 light; 15 295 full load
Dimensions, feet (metres): 459·2 oa × 63 × 28·2 *(140·0 × 19·2 × 8·6)*
Guns: 2 or 4—3 inch *(76 mm)* 50 cal AA (single)
Main engines: Geared turbine (General Electric); 6 000 shp; 1 shaft = 16·4 knots
Boilers: 2 (Babcock & Wilcox in *Firedrake;* Combustion Engineering in *Wrangell)*
Complement: approx 265

C2 type cargo ships built by North Carolina Shipbuilding Co, Wilmington, NC. Officially the "Mount Hood" class, the *Mount Hood* (AE 11) of this class being sunk in World War II. One 5 inch gun and four 40 mm AA guns removed; the *Firedrake* has a helicopter platform installed aft in place of two after 3 inch guns. Both ships are in reserve.

WRANGELL (AE 12)

1968, United States Navy

FIREDRAKE (AE 14)

1969, United States Navy

1 AMMUNITION SHIP (AE): "LASSEN" CLASS

Name	No.	Launched	Commissioned
MAUNA LOA	AE 8	14 April 1943	27 Oct 1943

Displacement, tons: 5 220 light; 14 225 full load
Dimensions, feet (metres): 435 wl; 459 oa × 63 × 26·5 (140 × 19·2 × 8·1)
Guns: 2—3 inch (76 mm) 50 cal AA (single)
Main engines: Diesel (Nordberg); 6 000 bhp; 1 shaft = 15·3 knots
Complement: 281

Built by the Tampa Shipbuilding Co, Tampa, Florida. Modified C2 type, converted by the Navy to an ammunition ship. Original armament was one 5 inch gun, four 3 inch guns, and four 40 mm AA guns. *Mauna Loa* transferred to Maritime Administration reserve in 1960; reacquired and returned to the Navy in Sep 1961 and recommissioned on 27 Nov 1961; fitted with helicopter platform aft. Decommissioned and again placed in reserve in 1970.

MAUNA LOA (AE 8)　　　　　　　　　　　　　　　　1965, United States Navy

2 STORE SHIPS (AF): R3-S-A4 TYPE

Name	No.	Launched	Commissioned
*RIGEL	T-AF 58	15 Mar 1955	2 Sep 1955
*VEGA	AF 59	26 April 1955	10 Nov 1955

Built by Ingalls Shipbuilding Co, Pascagoula. R3-S-A4 type. Helicopter platform fitted (two after twin 3 inch mounts removed). One Mk 63 gunfire control system in *Vega*. Both of these ships are active with *Rigel* having been assigned to Military Sealift Command on 23 June 1975 (guns removed; civilian manned).

Displacement, tons: 7 950 light; 15 540 full load
Dimensions, feet (metres): 475 wl; 502 oa × 72 × 29 (153·0 × 22·0 × 8·8)
Guns: 4—3 inch (76 mm) 50 cal AA (twin (Mk 33) in *Vega*; removed from *Rigel*
Main engines: Geared turbine (General Electric); 16 000 shp; 1 shaft = 20 knots
Boilers: 2 (Combustion Engineering)
Complement: approx 350

VEGA (AF 59)　　　　　　　　　　　　　　　　1974, US Navy, PH2 John Kristoffersen

1 STORE SHIP (AF): R2-S-BV1 TYPE

Name	No.	Launched	Commissioned
ARCTURUS (ex-USNS Golden Eagle)	AF 52	15 Mar 1942	18 Nov 1961

Displacement, tons: 6 914 light; 15 500 full load
Dimensions, feet (metres): 459·2 oa × 63 × 28 (140·0 × 19·2 × 8·5)
Guns: 8—3 inch (76 mm) 50 cal AA (twin) in *Aludra*; most of others are unarmed
Main engines: Geared turbine; 6 000 shp; 1 shaft = 16 knots
Boilers: 2

All built by Moore Dry Dock Co, Oakland, California. R2-S-BV1 type refrigerated cargo ships; similar to C2-B1 design but built as "reefers".
Arcturus is formerly USNS *Golden Eagle,* transferred from Military Sea Transportation Service to active Navy; renamed on 13 Sep 1961 and commissioned as USS on 18 Nov 1961 after modification for underway replenishment at the New York Naval Shipyard. These ships have been fitted with helicopter platforms.
All have been decommissioned and are in Navy or Maritime Administration reserve fleets; last active ship was *Arcturus,* decommissioned in 1973.

Nomenclature: Stores ships are named for stars and constellations.

Disposals: (since 1 Jan 1975) *Zelima* (AF 49), *Pictor* (AF 54), *Aludra* (AF 55), *Procyon* (AF 61) stricken on 1 June 1976).

PROCYON (AF 61) (now stricken)　　　　　　　1970, United States Navy

ALUDRA (AF 55) (now stricken)　　　　　　　1967, United States Navy

1 STORE SHIP (AF): C2-S-E1 TYPE

Name	No.	Launched	Commissioned
HYADES (ex-*Iberville*)	AF 28	12 June 1943	30 Sep 1943

Displacement, tons: 6 313 light; 15 300 full load
Dimensions, feet (metres): 468·6 oa × 63 × 28 *(142·8 × 19·2 × 8·5)*
Guns: 2—3 inch *(76 mm)* 50 cal AA (single)
Main engines: Geared turbine (General Electric); 6 000 shp; 1 shaft = 15·5 knots
Boilers: 2 (Babcock & Wilcox)
Complement: 252

Built by Gulf Shipbuilding Co, Chicasaw, Alabama. Original armament included one 5 inch gun. Helicopter deck fitted aft in place of two single 3 inch guns during 1962. Decommissioned and placed in reserve in 1969.

HYADES (AF 28)   *Ing. Augusti Nani*

STORES SHIPS (AF): "VICTORY" CLASS

Disposals: (since 1 Jan 1975) *Denebola* (AF 56) stricken on 30 April 1976. (See 1975-1976 and previous editions for characteristics).

7 COMBAT STORE SHIPS (AFS): "MARS" CLASS

Name	No.	Laid down	Launched	Commissioned
*MARS	AFS 1	5 May 1962	15 June 1963	21 Dec 1963
*SYLVANIA	AFS 2	18 Aug 1962	15 Aug 1963	11 July 1964
*NIAGARA FALLS	AFS 3	22 May 1965	26 Mar 1966	29 April 1967
*WHITE PLAINS	AFS 4	2 Oct 1965	23 July 1966	23 Nov 1968
*CONCORD	AFS 5	26 Mar 1966	17 Dec 1966	27 Nov 1968
*SAN DIEGO	AFS 6	11 Mar 1967	13 April 1968	24 May 1969
*SAN JOSE	AFS 7	8 Mar 1969	13 Dec 1969	23 Oct 1970

Displacement, tons: 16 500 full load
Dimensions, feet (metres): 581 oa × 79 × 24 *(177·1 × 24·1 × 7·3)*
Guns: 8—3 inch *(76 mm)* 50 cal AA (twin) Mk 33)
Helicopters: 2 UH-46 Sea Knight helicopters normally assigned
Main engines: Steam turbines; 22 000 shp; 1 shaft = 20 knots
Boilers: 3 (Babcock & Wilcox) (one spare)
Complement: 430 (30 officers, 400 enlisted men)

NIAGARA FALLS (AFS 3)   *1975, US Navy, PH1 S. Harris*

All built by National Steel & Shipbuilding, San Diego, California. Of a new design with a completely new replenishment at sea system. "M" frames replace conventional king posts and booms, which are equipped with automatic tensioning devices to maintain transfer lines taut between the ship and the warships being replenished despite rolling and yawing. Computers provide up-to-the-minute data on stock status with data displayed by closed-circuit television. Five holds (one refrigerated). Cargo capacity 2 625 tons dry stores and 1 300 tons refrigerated stores (varies with specific loadings).
Automatic propulsion system with full controls on bridge. The large SPS-40 radar fitted in *Mars* and *Sylvania* have been removed; some ships have TACAN (tactical aircraft navigation) radar. Fitted with two Mk 56 gunfire control systems.
Mars authorised in Fiscal Year 1961 shipbuilding programme, *Sylvania* in FY 1962, *Niagara Falls* in FY 1964, *White Plains* and *Concord* in FY 1965, *San Diego* in FY 1966, *San Jose* in FY 1967. Plans to construct three additional ships of this type in the FY 1977-1978 programmes have been dropped.

Nomenclature: Combat store ships are named for American cities.

Photographs: Note the improved, smaller TACAN in the larger photograph of the *Sylvania*. The stern view shows the ship's squared-off hangar and large helicopter deck with a UH-46 Sea Knight helicopter used for vertical replenishment (VERTREP) operations.

SYLVANIA (AFS 2)   *1973, Giorgio Arra*

SYLVANIA (AFS 2)   *1973, Giorgio Arra*

(8) OILERS (AO): NEW CONSTRUCTION

	No.	
	AO 177	Fiscal Year 1976 programme
	AO 178	Fiscal Year 1976 programme
	AO 179	Proposed FY 1977 programme
One ship	AO	Planned FY 1978 programme
One ship	AO	Planned FY 1979 programme
One ship	AO	Planned FY 1980 programme
Two ships	AO	Planned FY 1981 programme

Displacement, tons: 27 500 full load
Dimensions, feet (metres): 586·5 oa × 88 × 33·5 *(178·8 × 26·8 × 10·2)*
Guns: 2—20 mm Phalanx CIWS (space reserved)
Main engines: Geared turbine; 24 000 shp; 1 shaft = 20 knots (sustained)
Boilers: 2
Complement: approx 135

This class of fleet oilers is significantly smaller than the previous built-for-the-purpose AOs of the "Neosho" class; the newer ships are "sized" to provide two complete refuellings of a fossil-fuelled aircraft carrier and six to eight accompanying destroyers. The lead ship was requested in the Fiscal Year 1975 new construction programme but was not approved by Congress. Subsequently, two ships (AO 177 and AO 178) approved in FY 1976, with six additional ships planned for FY 1977-1981.
Cargo capacity approximately 120 000 barrels of liquid fuels. Space and weight are reserved for two Phalanx 20 mm Close-In Weapons Systems (one shown forward and one aft of the superstructure in the drawing on the following page). Helicopter platform aft. With current manning practices it is anticipated that these ships will be civilian manned by the Military Sealift Command.
Estimated cost of the FY 1977 ship is $102 300 000 and the FY 1978 ship is $144 200 000.

Classification: The hull numbers AO 168-176 are assigned to the "Sealift" class tankers; listed with Sealift Ships.

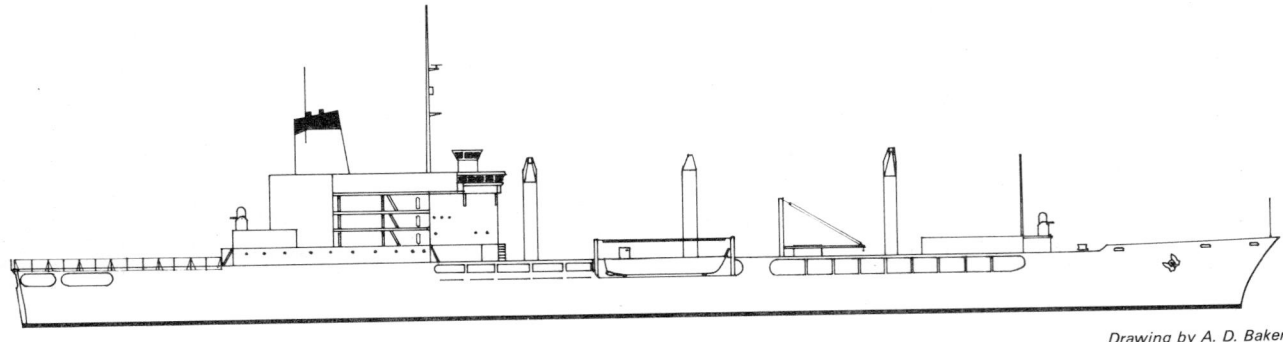

AO 177 DESIGN—see previous page

Drawing by A. D. Baker

6 OILERS (AO): "NEOSHO" CLASS

Name	No.	Launched	Commissioned
*NEOSHO	AO 143	10 Nov 1953	24 Sep 1954
*MISSISSINEWA	T-AO 144	12 June 1954	18 Jan 1955
*HASSAYAMPA	AO 145	12 Sep 1954	19 Apr 1955
*KAWISHIWI	AO 146	11 Dec 1954	6 July 1955
*TRUCKEE	AO 147	10 Mar 1955	23 Nov 1955
*PONCHATOULA	AO 148	9 July 1955	12 Jan 1956

Displacement, tons: 11 600 light; 38 000 to 40 000 full load
Dimensions, feet (metres): 640 wl; 655 oa × 86 × 35 *(199·6 × 26·2 × 10·7)*
Guns: 8 or 12—3 inch *(76 mm)* 50 cal AA (twin) (Mk 33); removed from MSC ships
Main engines: Geared turbines (General Electric); 28 000 shp; 2 shafts = 20 knots
Boilers: 2 (Babcock & Wilcox)
Complement: approx 360 (30 officers and 330 enlisted men including staff) when navy manned

Neosho built by Bethlehem Steel Co, Quincy, Massachusetts; others by New York Shipbuilding Corp, Camden, New Jersey. These are the largest "straight" fleet oilers (AO) constructed specifically for the Navy. Cargo capacity is approximately 180 000 barrels of liquid fuels. Original armament was two 5 inch DP guns and 12 3 inch AA guns; former removed in 1969. Two twin 3 inch gun mounts removed from *Neosho, Mississinewa,* and *Truckee* and helicopter platform installed. Those ships also have additional superstructure installed forward of after "island" structure. Armed ships have two Mk 56 gunfire control systems. All fitted to carry a service force commander and staff (12 officers).
Mississinewa assigned to Military Sealift Command on 2 Feb 1976 (guns removed; civilian manned); others will follow into MSC operation.

Nomenclature: Oilers are named after American rivers with Indian names.

TRUCKEE (AO 147)   *1972, Giorgio Arra*

NEOSHO (AO 143) with HARLAN COUNTY (LST 1196)   *1975, United States Navy*

5 OILERS (AO): "JUMBOISED" T3-S2-A3 TYPE

Name	No.	Launched	Commissioned
*MISPILLION	T-AO 105	10 Aug 1945	29 Dec 1945
*NAVASOTA	T-AO 106	30 Aug 1945	27 Feb 1946
*PASSUMPSIC	T-AO 107	31 Oct 1945	1 April 1946
*PAWCATUCK	T-AO 108	19 Feb 1945	10 May 1946
*WACCAMAW	T-AO 109	30 Mar 1946	25 June 1946

Displacement, tons: 11 000 light; 34 750 full load
Dimensions, feet (metres): 646 oa × 75 × 35·5 *(196·9 × 22·9 × 10·8)*
Guns: Removed
Main engines: Geared turbines (Westinghouse); 13 500 shp; 2 shafts = 16 knots
Boilers: 4 (Babcock & Wilcox)
Complement: 290 (16 officers, 274 men) when Navy manned

All built by Sun Shipbuilding & Dry Dock Co, Chester, Pennsylvania. Originally T3-S2-A-3 oilers; converted during mid-1960s under "jumbo" programme. Enlarged midsections added to increase cargo capacity to approximately 150 000 barrels. Helicopter platform fitted forward. As "jumboised" these ships had four 3 inch single gun mounts; removed in MSC service (see below). All of these ships are active.
The *Mispillion* was assigned to the Military Sealift Command in 1974 and provided with a civilian crew (guns removed); subsequently the other ships were assigned to MSC through 1975.
Note two funnels in the *Passumpsic.*

PASSUMPSIC (T-AO 107)   *1971, United States Navy*

PASSUMPSIC (T-AO 107)   *1975, United States Navy*

3 OILERS (AO): "JUMBOISED" T3-S2-A1 TYPE

Name	No.	Launched	Commissioned
*ASHTABULA	AO 51	22 May 1943	7 Aug 1943
*CALOOSAHATCHEE	AO 98	2 June1945	10 Oct 1945
*CANISTEO	AO 99	6 July 1945	3 Dec 1945

Displacement, tons: 34 750 full load
Dimensions, feet (metres): 644 oa × 75 × 31·5 *(196·3 × 22·9 × 9·6)*
Guns: 4—3 inch *(76 mm)* 50 cal AA (single) (Mk 26)
Main engines: Geared turbines; 13 500 shp; 2 shafts = 18 knots
Boilers: 4 (Foster Wheeler)
Complement: 300 (13 officers and 287 enlisted men)

All built by Bethlehem Steel Co, Sparrows Point, Maryland. Originally T3-S2-A1 oilers; converted during mid-1960s under "jumbo" programme. Enlarged midsections added to increase cargo capacity to approximately 143 000 barrels plus 175 tons of munitions and 100 tons refrigerated stores. Provided with one Mk 52 gunfire control system. No helicopter platform fitted.
All three ships are active with Navy crews.

ASHTABULA (AO 51)   *1970, United States Navy*

CANISTEO (AO 99)   *1973, Giorgio Arra*

2 OILERS (AO): T2-A TYPE

Name	No.	Launched	Commissioned
KENNEBEC (ex-*Corsicana*)	AO 36	19 Apr 1941	4 Feb 1942
TAPPAHANNOCK (ex-*Jorkay*)	AO 43	18 Apr 1942	22 June 1942

Displacement, tons: 21 580 full load
Dimensions, feet (metres): 501·4 oa × 68 × 30·75 *(152·8 × 20·7 × 9·4)*
Guns: 2 or 4—3 inch *76 mm)* 50 cal AA (single)
Main engines: Geared turbine (Westinghouse); 12 000 shp = 16·7 knots
Boilers: 2 (Foster Wheeler in *Kennebec*, Babcock & Wilcox in *Tappahannock)*

Fleet oilers of World War II construction but smaller and less capable than the contemporary T3 series. *Tappahannock* built by Sun Shipbuilding and Dry Dock Co, Chester, Pennsylvania; *Kennebec* by Bethlehem Steel Co, Sparrows Point, Maryland. Cargo capacity approximately 130 000 barrels.
Original armament for this class was one 5 inch DP gun, four 3 inch AA guns, and with 40 mm AA guns; subsequently reduced as above.
The *Tappahannock* is in Navy reserve; *Kennebec* is in Maritime Administration reserve fleet but remains on the Navy List.

KENNEBEC (AO 36)   *1965, United States Navy*

5 OILERS (AO): T3-S2-A1 TYPE

Name	No.	Launched	Commissioned
SABINE (ex-Esso Albany)	AO 25	27 Apr 1940	25 Sep 1940
CHIKASKIA	AO 54	2 Oct 1943	10 Nov 1943
AUCILLA (ex-Escanaba)	AO 56	20 Nov 1943	22 Dec 1943
*MARIAS	T-AO 57	21 Dec 1943	12 Feb 1944
*TALUGA	T-AO 62	10 July 1944	25 Aug 1944

Displacement, tons: 25 525 full load
Dimensions, feet (metres): 553 oa × 75 × 31·5
Guns: 4—3 inch (76 mm) 50 cal AA (single) in most ships; some ships retain 5 inch gun of original armament (see notes); removed from MSC ships
Main engines: Geared turbines; 13 500 shp; 2 shafts = 18 knots
Boilers: 4 (Foster Wheeler)
Complement: 274 (14 officers, 260 enlisted men)

These ships are survivors of a large number of twin-screw (S2) fleet oilers built during World War II; some converted to escort ("jeep") carriers and provided basis for the "Commencement Bay" class (CVE 105). Several ships of this type have been enlarged through the "jumbo" process and are listed separately. All above ships were built by Bethlehem Steel Co, Sparrows Point, Maryland. Original armament consisted of one 5 inch gun, four 3 inch guns, and up to eight 40 mm guns. Cargo capacity 145 000 barrels of liquid fuels.
The Marias and Taluga have been assigned to the Military Sealift Command (MSC); manned by civilian crews and guns removed. The other ships are laid up in reserve.

Disposals: (since 1 Jan 1975) Tolovana (AO 64) stricken on 15 Apr 1975; Guadalupe (AO 32) stricken on 15 May 1975.

1975, Giorgio Arra

MARIAS (T-AO 57)

4 + 1 FAST COMBAT SUPPORT SHIPS (AOE): "SACRAMENTO" CLASS

Name	No.	Laid down	Launched	Commissioned
*SACRAMENTO	AOE 1	30 June 1961	14 Sep 1963	14 Mar 1964
*CAMDEN	AOE 2	17 Feb 1964	29 May 1965	1 Apr 1967
*SEATTLE	AOE 3	1 Oct 1965	2 Mar 1968	5 Apr 1969
*DETROIT	AOE 4	29 Nov 1966	21 June 1969	28 Mar 1970
	AOE 5	Planned Fiscal Year 1981 programme		

Displacement, tons: 19 200 light; 53 600 full load
Dimensions, feet (metres): 793 oa × 107 × 39·3 (241·7 × 32·6 × 12·0)
Guns: 8—3 inch (76 mm) 50 cal AA (twin) (Mk 33)
Helicopters: 2 UH-46 Sea Knight normally assigned
Main engines: Geared turbines (General Electric); 100 000 shp; 2 shafts = 26 knots
Boilers: 4 (Combustion Engineering)
Complement: 600 (33 officers, 567 enlisted men)

These ships operate primarily with fast carrier task forces to provide rapid replenishment at sea of petroleum, munitions, provisions, and fleet freight. Fitted with helicopter platform, internal arrangements, and large hangar for vertical replenishment operations (VERTREP). Cargo capacity 177 000 barrels plus 2 150 tons munitions, 500 tons dry stores, 250 tons refrigerated stores (varies with specific loadings). One Mk 56 and one Mk 63 gunfire control systems installed in first two ships; two Mk 56 in second pair.
Built by Puget Sound Naval Shipyard except Camden by New York Shipbuilding Corp, Camden, New Jersey. Sacramento authorised in Fiscal Year 1961 new construction programme; Camden in FY 1963, Seattle in FY 1965, and Detroit in FY 1966. Construction of AOE 5 in FY 1968 was deferred and then cancelled in November 1969. No additional ships of this type were planned because of high cost, the availability of new-construction ammunition ships, and the great success of the smaller "Wichita" class replenishment oilers; however, in 1976 the Department of Defense announced plans to construct another AOE in the Fiscal Year 1981 shipbuilding programme. Approximate cost of the Camden was $70 000 000.

Engineering: Sacramento and Camden have machinery intended for the cancelled battleship Kentucky (BB 66).

SEATTLE (AOE 3)

1972, Giorgio Arra

Nomenclature: Fast combat support ships are named for American cities. This name source was previously used for cruisers. It is now used for attack submarines, continuing the confusing of US Navy ship nomenclature.

Photographs: These ships can be distinguished from the smaller "Wichita" class replenishment oilers by their larger superstructures and funnel, helicopter deck at higher level, and hangar structure aft of funnel.

1972, Giorgio Arra

SEATTLE (AOE 3)

GASOLINE TANKERS (AOG)

All of the small gasoline tankers have been stricken or transferred to other navies. See 1974-1975 and previous editions for characteristics. Ships of this type serve in the navies of Chile, Colombia, Greece, and Taiwan.

Disposals and transfers: (since 1 Jan 1975) Chewaucan (AOG 50) transferred to Colombia on 1 July 1975; Nespelen (AOG 55), Noxubee (AOG 56) stricken on 1 July 1975.

7 REPLENISHMENT OILERS (AOR): "WICHITA" CLASS

Name	No.	Laid down	Launched	Commissioned
*WICHITA	AOR 1	18 June1966	18 Mar 1968	7 June 1969
*MILWAUKEE	AOR 2	29 Nov 1966	17 Jan 1969	1 Nov 1969
*KANSAS CITY	AOR 3	20 Apr 1968	28 June1969	6 June 1970
*SAVANNAH	AOR 4	22 Jan 1969	25 Apr 1970	5 Dec 1970
*WABASH	AOR 5	21 Jan 1970	6 Feb 1971	20 Nov 1971
*KALAMAZOO	AOR 6	28 Oct 1970	11 Nov 1972	11 Aug 1973
*ROANOKE	AOR 7	19 Jan 1974	7 Dec 1974	15 Dec 1975

Displacement, tons: 38 100 full load
Dimensions, feet (metres): 659 oa × 96 × 33·3 (206·9 × 29·3 × 10·2)
Missile Launchers: 1 NATO Sea Sparrow multiple launcher (Mk 29) in *Roanoke*
Guns: 4—3 inch (76 mm) 50 cal AA (twin) (Mk 33) except *Roanoke;* removed from ships with hangar
Helicopters: 2 UH-46 Sea Knight can be embarked
Main engines: Geared turbines; 32 000 shp; 2 shafts = 20 knots (18 knots on 2 boilers)
Boilers: 3 (Foster Wheeler)
Complement: 345 (20 officers, 325 enlisted men)

MILWAUKEE (AOR 2)   1975, Giorgio Arra

These ships provide rapid replenishment at sea of petroleum and munitions with a limited capacity for provision and fleet freight. Fitted with helicopter platform and internal arrangement for vertical replenishment operations (VERTREP), but no hangar originally provided; some subsequently fitted with hangar (see *Milwaukee* photograph, below). Cargo capacity 175 000 barrels of liquid fuels plus 600 tons munitions, 425 tons dry stores, 150 tons refrigerated stores. Two Mk 56 gunfire control systems in AOR 1-6; one Mk 91 guided missile control system in *Roanoke*.
All built by General Dynamics Corp, Quincy Massachusetts except AOR 7 by National Steel and Shipbuilding Co, San Diego, California. *Wichita* and *Milwaukee* authorised in Fiscal Year 1965

new construction programme, *Kansas City* and *Savannah* in FY 1966, *Wabash* and *Kalamazoo* in FY 1967, and *Roanoke* in FY 1972. Approximate cost of *Milwaukee* was $27 700 000.

Nomenclature: Replenishment oilers are named after American cities. The port city of Savannah, Georgia, also is honoured by the world's first nuclear propelled merchant ship, the NS *Savannah*, which is now laid up out of service at that city.

Photographs: In the photograph, below the *Milwaukee* is ballasted down aft; note double hangars adjacent to helicopter deck; twin 3 inch gun mounts were removed from after superstructure. Compare with view of *Kalamazoo*.

KALAMAZOO (AOR 6)   1973, United States Navy

FLEET SUPPORT SHIPS

Fleet support ships provide primarily maintenance and related towing and salvage services at advanced bases and at ports in the United States. These ships normally do not provide fuel, munitions, or other supplies except when ships are alongside for maintenance. Three notable exceptions are the self-propelled barrack ships (APB), that can serve as semi-autonomous advanced bases for small landing craft or riverine craft in advanced areas, the dependent support ship (AH) which was refitted to provide services for US civilian dependants in overseas areas, and gun boat support ship (AGP).

Most fleet support ships operate from bases in the United States. The five Polaris/Poseidon submarine tenders (AS) are based at Holy Loch, Scotland; Rota, Spain; Charleston, South Carolina; and Apra harbour, Guam, with one ship generally in transit or overhaul. The Rota facility will be disestablished in the next few years. In addition, two support ships (AD/AR/AS type) generally are forward deployed in the Mediterranean and two in the western Pacific. Early in 1976 the Secretary of Defense proposed a five-year shipbuilding programme (1977-1981) to include three additional destroyer tenders (AD), one

submarine tender (AS), four fleet tugs (ATF), and prototypes of a repair ship (ARX) and a salvage ship (ARSX). This is a significant reduction from previous planning. (See 1975-1976 edition for previously announced programmes).
Fleet support ships are mainly Navy manned and armed; however, an increasing number are being operated by the Military Sealift Command (MSC) with civilian crews. The latter ships are not armed and have T- designations.

---

2 + 5 DESTROYER TENDERS (AD): "GOMPERS" CLASS

Name	No.	Laid down	Launched	Commissioned
*SAMUEL GOMPERS	AD 37	9 July 1964	14 May 1966	1 July 1967
*PUGET SOUND	AD 38	15 Feb 1965	16 Sep 1966	27 April 1968
	AD 41	Fiscal Year 1975 programme		1978
	AD 42	Fiscal Year 1976 programme		1979
	AD 43	Proposed FY 1977 programme		1980
	AD 44	Planned FY 1978 programme		1981
	AD 45	Planned FY 1979 programme		1982

Displacement, tons: 22 260 full load
Dimensions, feet (metres): 643 oa × 85 × 22·5 (196·0 × 25·9 × 6·9)
Guns: 1—5 inch (127 mm) 38 cal DP (Mk 30) in *Samuel Gompers* and *Puget Sound*
Missile launchers: 1 NATO Sea Sparrow system planned for AD 40 and later ships
Main engines: Steam turbines (De Laval); 20 000 shp; 1 shaft = 20 knots
Boilers: 2 (Combustion Engineering)
Complement: 1 806 (135 officers, 1 671 enlisted men)

These are the first US destroyer tenders of post-World War II design; capable of providing repair and supply services to new destroyer-type ships which have advanced missile, anti-submarine, and electronic systems. The tenders also have facilities for servicing nuclear power plants. Services can be provided simultaneously to six guided-missile destroyers moored alongside. Basic hull design similar to "L. Y. Spear" and "Simon Lake" submarine tenders. Provided with helicopter platform and hangar; two 7 000-pound capacity cranes. One Mk 56 gunfire control system in gun-armed ships.
Samuel Gompers authorised in Fiscal Year 1964 new construction programme and *Puget Sound* in FY 1965 programme. Both ships built by Puget Sound Naval Shipyard, Bremerton, Washington; AD 41 and AD 42 under construction at National Steel Shipbuilding Co, San Diego, Calif.
AD 39 of FY 1969 programme cancelled prior to start of construction to provide funds for overruns in other new ship programmes. AD 40 authorised in FY 1973 new construction programme was not built. AD 41 in FY 1975 programme and AD 42 in FY 1976 programme with

PUGET SOUND (AD 38)   1975, Giorgio Arra

three additional ships planned (AD 41 and later ships of a slightly modified design.) Estimated cost of AD 43 is $260 400 000 and estimated cost of AD 44 is $289 100 000.

Nomenclature: Destroyer tenders generally are named for geographic areas; Samuel Gompers was an American labour leader.

PUGET SOUND (AD 38)   *1972, United States Navy*

4 DESTROYER TENDERS (AD): "KLONDIKE" CLASS

Name	No.	Launched	Commissioned
EVERGLADES	AD 24	28 Jan 1945	25 May 1951
*SHENANDOAH	AD 26	29 Mar 1945	13 Aug 1945
ISLE ROYAL	AD 29	19 Sep 1945	9 June 1962
*BRYCE CANYON	AD 36	7 Mar 1946	15 Sep 1950

Displacement, tons: 8 165 standard; 16 635 to 16 900 full load
Dimensions, feet (metres): 465 wl; 492 oa × 69·5 × 27·2 *(150·0 × 21·2 × 8·3)*
Guns: 1—5 inch *(127 mm)* 38 cal DP (Mk 37); removed from some ships including *Shenandoah*
Main engines: Steam turbines; 8 500 shp 1 shaft = 18·4 knots
Boilers: 2 (Foster-Wheeler or Babcock & Wilcox)
Complement: 778 to 918

SHENANDOAH (AD 26)   *1975, US Navy, PHC A. A. Clemons*

These ships are of modified C-3 design completed as destroyer tenders. Officially considered two classes (see below). *Shenandoah* built by Todd Shipyards, Los Angeles, Calif; *Bryce Canyon* by Charleston Navy Yard; *Everglades* by Los Angeles SB & DD Co; and *Isle Royal* by Todd Pacific Shipyards, Seattle, Wash. *Isle Royal* first commissioned on 26 Mar 1946 and placed in reserve before being completely outfitted; recommissioned for service on 9 June 1962 and commenced operations in January 1963.

Originally 14 ships of two similar designs, the "Klondike" class of AD22-25 and "Shenandoah" class of AD 26-33, 35, and 36. *Great Lakes* (AD 30), *New England* (AD 32), *Canopus* (AD 33, ex-AS 27), *Arrow Head* (AD 35, ex-AV 19) cancelled before completion; *Klondike* (AD 22) reclassified AR 22; *Grand Canyon* (AD 28) reclassified AR 28.

Two ships remain in active service with two others in reserve.

Gunnery: Original armament for "Klondike" class was 1—5 in gun, 4—3 in guns, and 4—40 mm guns; for "Shenandoah" class was 2—5 in guns and 8—40 mm guns.

Modernisation: These ships have been modernised under the FRAM II programme to service modernised destroyers fitted with ASROC, improved electronics, helicopters etc.

Disposals: (since 1 Jan 1974) *Yellowstone* (AD 27) stricken on 12 Sep 1974.

ISLE ROYAL (AD 29)   *1970, United States Navy*

"CASCADE" TYPE

Cascade (AD 16) stricken on 23 Nov 1974. (See 1975-1976 and previous editions for characteristics).

5 DESTROYER TENDERS (AD): "DIXIE" CLASS

Name	No.	Builders	Commissioned
*DIXIE	AD 14	NY Shipbuilding Corp, NJ	25 April 1940
*PRAIRIE	AD 15	NY Shipbuilding Corp, NJ	5 Aug 1940
*PIEDMONT	AD 17	Tampa Shipbuilding Co, Florida	5 Jan 1944
*SIERRA	AD 18	Tampa Shipbuilding Co, Florida	20 Mar 1944
*YOSEMITE	AD 19	Tampa Shipbuilding Co, Florida	25 May 1944

Displacement, tons: 9 450 standard; 17 176 full load
Dimensions, feet (metres): 520 wl; 530·5 oa × 73·3 × 25·5 *(161·7 × 22·3 × 7·8)*
Guns: 1 or 2—5 inch *(127 mm)* 38 cal DP (Mk 30)
Main engines: Steam turbines; 11 000 shp; 2 shafts = 19·6 knots
Boilers: 4 (Babcock & Wilcox)
Complement: 1 076 to 1 698 (total accommodation)

Launched on 27 May 1939, 9 Dec 1939, 7 Dec 1942, 23 Feb 1943 and 16 May 1943 respectively. 2—5 inch guns (aft) and 8—40 mm guns removed. Parsons turbines in *Dixie* and *Prairie;* Allis Chalmers in others.

All five ships are active and are the oldest ships currently in service with the US Navy except for the sail frigate *Constitution.*

Modernisation: All of these ships have been modernised under the FRAM II programme to service destroyers fitted with ASROC, improved electronics, helicopters, etc. Two or three 5 inch guns and eight 40 mm guns removed during modernisation.

YOSEMITE (AD 19)

1968, United States Navy DIXIE (AD 14)

United States Navy

DEGAUSSING SHIPS (ADG)

The Navy's four degaussing ships were stricken on 21 Feb 1975: *Lodestone* ADG 8, *Magnet* ADG 9, *Deperm* ADG 10, *Surfbird* ADG 383. See 1974-1975 and previous editions for characteristics).

1 AUXILIARY DEEP SUBMERGENCE SUPPORT SHIP (AGDS): Ex-DOCK CARGO SHIP

Name	No.	Builders	Commissioned
*POINT LOMA	AGDS 2	Maryland SB & DD Co	28 Feb 1958
(ex-*Point Barrow*)	(ex-AKD 1)		

Displacement, tons: 9 415 standard; 14 094 full load
Dimensions, feet (metres): 475 wl; 492 oa × 78 × 22 *(150·0 × 23·8 × 6·7)*
Guns: None
Main engines: Steam turbines; 6 000 shp; 2 shafts = 18 knots
Boilers: 2
Complement: 160 (Including scientific personnel and submersible operators)

A docking or "wet" well ship designed to carry cargo, vehicles, and landing craft (originally designated AKD). Built for the Military Sea Transportation Service (now Military Sealift Command); launched on 25 May 1957 and delivered to MSTS on 29 May 1958. Maritime Administration S2-ST-23A design; winterised for arctic service. Fitted with internal ramp and garage system.
Subsequently refitted with hangar over docking well and employed in transport of large booster rockets to Cape Kennedy Space Center. Primarily used to carry the second stage of the Saturn V moon rocket and Lunar Modules. Placed out of service in reserve on 1 Jan 1971 with US space programme.
Reactivated in mid-1972 for cargo work; transferred from Military Sealift Command to Navy on 28 Feb 1974 for modification to support deep submergence vehicles, especially the bathyscaph *Trieste II*. Placed in commission "special" on 8 Mar 1974 as the AGDS 2; renamed *Point Loma* for the location of the San Diego submarine base where Submarine Development Group 1 operates most of the Navy's submersibles. The *Point Loma* was placed in commission on 30 April 1975. Aviation gas capacity increased to approximately 100 000 gallons (US) to support *Trieste II* which uses lighter-than-water avgas for flotation.

Classification: The designation AGDS was established on 3 Jan 1974; technically it is a service craft designation *vice* ship. The AGDS 1 was assigned briefly to the floating dry dock *White Sands* (ARD 20), the previous *Trieste II* support ship.

POINT LOMA (AGDS 2 as T-AKD 1) *1970, US Navy*

POINT LOMA (AGDS 2 as T-AKD 1) *1970, US Navy*

1 GUNBOAT SUPPORT SHIP (AGP): CONVERTED LST

Name	No.	Builders	Commissioned
*GRAHAM COUNTY	AGP 1176	Newport News SB & DD Co	17 Apr 1958
	(ex-LST 1176)		

Displacement, tons: approx 8 000 full load
Dimensions, feet (metres): 445 oa × 62 × 16·5 *(135·6 × 18·9 × 5·0)*
Guns: 6—3 inch *(76 mm)* 50 cal AA (twin) (Mk 33)
Main engines: Diesels (Fairbanks-Morse); 9 600 bhp; 2 shafts (controllable-pitch-propellers) = 14·5 knots

Originally an LST of the "Suffolk" County class. Launched on 19 Sep 1957. Converted in 1972 to support US patrol gunboats (PG) deployed to the Mediterranean area. Fitted with repair shops and spare parts storage.

Classification: Reclassified as a gunboat support ship (AGP) on 1 Aug 1972 with her LST hull number.
Four earlier LSTs modified to support riverine craft in Vietnam also were designated AGP (with LST hull numbers); see listing for Amphibious Warfare Ships in 1971-1972 and previous editions. AGP 1-20 were converted yachts, seaplane tenders, cargo ships, and LSTs employed during World War II to service motor torpedo boats.

GRAHAM COUNTY (AGP 1176) *1973, Giorgio Arra*

1 DEPENDENT SUPPORT SHIP (AH): "HAVEN" CLASS

Name	No.	Builders	Commissioned
SANCTUARY (ex-*Marine Owl*)	AH 17	Sun SB & DD Co, Chester	20 June 1945

Displacement, tons: 11 141 standard; 15 400 full load
Dimensions, feet (metres): 496 wl; 529 oa × 71·5 × 24 *(161·2 × 21·8 × 7·3)*
Guns: None
Main engines: Steam turbines (General Electric); 9 000 shp; 1 shaft = 18·33 knots
Boilers: 2 (Babcock & Wilcox)
Complement: 530 (70 officers, 460 enlisted)

SANCTUARY (AH 17)   1974, United States Navy

The *Sanctuary* is the survivor of six hospital ships (AH) of the "Haven" class. Built on C4-S-B2 merchant hull and launched on 15 Aug 1944. *Sanctuary* recommissioned from reserve in 1966 for service off Vietnam; decommissioned as a hospital ship on 15 Dec 1971 for modification to "dependent support ship" at Hunter's Point Naval Shipyard, San Francisco, California. Subsequently recommissioned on 18 Nov 1972.
As a dependent support ship the *Sanctuary* had special facilities for obstetrics, gynaecology, maternity, and nursery services; fitted as a 74-bed hospital which can be expanded to 300 beds in 72 hours. She was the first US Navy ship with mixed male-female crew (although previously female nurses have been assigned to hospital ships and transports). The medical personnel consisted of 50 officers and approx 120 enlisted men including several female nurse officers; the ship's company consisted of 20 officers (including two women) and approx 330 enlisted (including 60 women). The ship was modified to support US dependents of ships homeported in Pireus, Greece. However, she was not deployed to Greece, but was decommissioned on 28 Mar 1974 (correction to previous edition); laid up in Maritime Administration reserve.
Constellation (AH 15) of this class was chartered by a private group and operated under the name *Hope* as a floating hospital and medical school from 1961 to 1973; taken out of service at Philadelphia Naval Shipyard in 1974 and stripped of medical facilities.

4 SELF-PROPELLED BARRACKS SHIPS (APB/IX)

Name	No.	Builders	Commissioned
*ECHOLS	IX 504 (ex-APB 37, ex-APL 37)	Boston Navy Yard	1 Jan 1947
*MERCER	IX 502 (ex-APB 39, ex-APL 39)	Boston Navy Yard	19 Sep 1945
*NUECES	IX 503 (ex-APB 40, ex-APL 40)	Boston Navy Yard	30 Nov 1945
KINGMAN	APB 47 (ex-AKS 18, ex-LST 1113)	Missouri Valley Bridge & Iron Co, Evansville, Indiana	27 June 1945

Displacement, tons: 2 189 light; 4 080 full load
Dimensions, feet (metres): 136 wl; 328 oa × 50 × 11 *(100·0 × 15·2 × 3·4)*
Guns: Vary (see notes)
Main engines: Diesels (General Motors); 1 600 to 1 800 bhp; 2 shafts = 12 (APB 41-50) or 10 knots (APB 35-40)
Complement: 193 (13 officers, 180 enlisted men) as APB
Troops: 1 226 (26 officers, 1 200 enlisted men) as APB

MERCER (as APB 39)   1968, United States Navy

Self-propelled barracks ships (APB) built to provide support and accommodations for small craft and riverine forces. Launched on 30 July 1945, 17 Nov 1944, 6 May 1945, 17 April 1945 respectively. *Echols* placed in service *vice* commissioning in Jan 1947. All ex-LST type ships of the same basic characteristics. *Mercer* and *Nueces* recommissioned in 1968 for service in Vietnam; decommissioned in 1969-1971 as US riverine forces in South Vietnam were reduced. These most useful ships supported the joint Army-Navy Mobile Riverine Force in the Mekong Delta region of South Vietnam (Navy River Assault Flotilla 1/Task Force 117/River Support Squadron 7). Complement of each ship in this role was 12 officers and 186 enlisted men, and 900 troops and boat crew personnel were carried. Recommissioned ships had an armament of 2—3 inch guns (single), 8—40 mm guns (two quad mounts), 8—·50 cal MG, and 10—·30 cal MG. Each APB has troop berthing and messing facilities, evaporators which produce up to 40 000 gallons of fresh water per day, a 16-bed hospital, X-ray room, dental room, bacteriological laboratory, pharmacy, laundry, library, and tailor shop; living and most working spaces are air-conditioned. Most ships not activated for Vietnam have 40 mm AA guns (quad).
Mercer and *Nueces* again reactivated in 1975 to serve as barrack ships for ships in overhaul at Puget Sound Naval Shipyard, Bremerton, Washington. *Echols* (in reserve since 1947) reactivated in 1976 to provide berthing for crews of Trident missile submarines being built by General Dynamics Electric Boat Division in Groton, Connecticut. The *Kingman* remains in reserve.

Classification: *Mercer* and *Nueces* reclassified as "unclassified" (IX) on 1 Nov 1975; *Echols* changed to IX on 1 Feb 1976.

1 REPAIR SHIP (AR): Ex-DESTROYER TENDER

Name	No.	Builders	Commissioned
*GRAND CANYON	AR 28 (ex-AD 28)	Todd Shipyards Corp, Los Angeles	5 Apr 1946

Displacement, tons: 8 165 standard; 16 635 full load
Dimensions, feet (metres): 465 wl; 492 oa × 69·5 × 27·2 *(150·0 × 21·2 × 8·3)*
Guns: 1—5 inch *(127 mm)* 38 cal DP
Main engines: Steam turbines (Westinghouse); 8 500 shp; 1 shaft = 18·4 knots
Boilers: 2 (Foster-Wheeler)

GRAND CANYON (AR 28)   1971, United States Navy

The *Grand Canyon* is a modified C-3 cargo ship completed as a destroyer tender and subsequently reclassified as a repair ship; redesignated AR 28 on 10 Mar 1971. Designed armament was 2—5 inch guns and 8—40 mm guns.
Launched on 27 April 1945. Modernised; fitted with helicopter platform and hangar aft. The *Grand Canyon* is active.

Disposals: *Klondike* (AR 22, ex-AD 22) stricken on 15 Sep 1974.

Nomenclature: Repair ships normally are named for mythological characters.

REPAIR SHIPS (ARX): NEW CONSTRUCTION

Current Navy planning provides for the construction of the first of a new class of repair ships (now designated ARX) in the FY 1981 shipbuilding programme. Characteristics of the ARX have not yet been determined.

1 REPAIR SHIP (AR): Ex-DESTROYER TENDER

Name	No.	Builders	Commissioned
MARKAB	AR 23 (ex-AD 21,	Ingalls SB Co,	15 June 1941
(ex-*Mormacpenn*)	ex-AK 31)	Pascagoula	

Displacement, tons: 8 560 standard; 14 800 full load
Dimensions, feet (metres): 465 wl; 492·5 oa × 69·8 × 24·8 *(150·1 × 21·3 × 7·6)*
Guns: 4—3 inch *(76 mm)* 50 cal AA (single)
Main engines: Steam turbines (General Electric); 8 500 shp; 1 shaft = 18·4 knots
Boilers: 2 (Foster-Wheeler)

Launched on 21 Dec 1940. Completed as a destroyer tender; reclassified as repair ship on 15 April 1960 and designation changed from AD to AR. One 5 inch gun and 4—40 mm guns were removed. The *Markab* was decommissioned on 19 Dec 1969 but remains in service in reserve as station ship at Mare Island, California

MARKAB (AR 23)   *United States Navy*

2 REPAIR SHIPS (AR): "DELTA" CLASS

Name	No.	Builders	Commissioned
DELTA	AR 9 (ex-AK 29)	Newport News SB & DD Co,	16 June 1941
(ex-*Hawaiian Packer*)		Virginia	
BRIAREUS	AR 12	Newport News SB & DD Co,	16 Nov 1943
(ex-*Hawaiian Planter*)		Virginia	

Displacement, tons: 8 975 standard; 14 500 full load
Dimensions, feet (metres): 465·5 wl; 490·5 oa × 69·5 × 24·3 *(149·5 × 21·2 × 7·4)*
Guns: 4—3 inch *(76 mm)* 50 cal AA (single)
Main engines: Steam turbines (Newport News); 8 500 shp; 1 shaft = 17 knots
Boilers: 2 (Foster-Wheeler and Babcock & Wilcox, respectively)
Complement: 688 (29 officers, 559 enlisted men); 903 and 924, respectively, designed wartime

C-3 type. Both launched in 1941, with *Briareus* serving as merchant ship before being acquired by the Navy. The 5 inch and 4—40 mm guns removed. *Briareus* decommissioned in 1955 and placed in reserve; *Delta*, decommissioned in 1970, remains in service in reserve as station ship at Bremerton, Washington.

DELTA (AR 9)   *1969, United States Navy*

4 REPAIR SHIPS (AR): "VULCAN" CLASS

Name	No.	Builders	Commissioned
*****VULCAN**	AR 5	New York SB Corp	16 June 1941
*****AJAX**	AR 6	Los Angeles SB & DD Corp	30 Oct 1942
*****HECTOR**	AR 7	Los Angeles SB & DD Corp	7 Feb 1944
*****JASON**	AR 8 (ex-ARH 1)	Los Angeles SB & DD Corp	19 June 1944

Displacement, tons: 9 140 standard; 16 200 full load
Dimensions, feet (metres): 520 wl; 529·3 oa × 73·3 × 23·3 *(161·3 × 22·3 × 7·1)*
Guns: 4—5 inch *(127 mm)* 38 cal DP (single) (Mk 30); removed from some ships
Main engines: Steam turbines; 11 000 shp; 2 shafts = 19·2 knots
Boilers: 4 (Babcock & Wilcox)
Complement: 715 (23 officers, 692 enlisted men); 950 designed wartime

Vulcan was built under the 1939 programme and the other three under the 1940 programme. Launched on 14 Dec 1940, 22 Aug 1942, 11 Nov 1942 and 3 April 1943 respectively. All carry a most elaborate equipment of machine tools to undertake repairs of every description. *Jason*, originally designated ARH 1 and rated as heavy hull repair ship, was reclassified AR 8 on 9 Sep 1957. Eight 40 mm AA guns (twin) have been removed; the four 5 inch guns were the standard main battery of large fleet support ships and oilers during World War II. Gunfire control systems vary.
All of these ships are active.

VULCAN (AR 5)—four guns   *1975, Giorgio Arra*

HECTOR (AR 7)—no guns   *United States Navy*

2 CABLE SHIPS (ARC): "AEOLUS" CLASS

Name	No.	Builders	Commissioned
*AEOLUS (ex-*Turandot*)	T-ARC 3 (ex-AKA 47)	Walsh-Kaiser Co, Providence, RI	18 June 1945
THOR (ex-*Vanadis*)	T-ARC 4 (ex-AKA 49)	Walsh-Kaiser Co, Providence, RI	9 July 1945

Displacement, tons: 7 040 full load
Dimensions, feet (metres): 400 wl; 438 oa × 58·2 × 19·25 *(133·5 × 17·7 × 5·9)*
Guns: None
Main engines: Turbo-electric (Westinghouse); 6 000 shp; 2 shafts = 16·9 knots
Boilers: 2 (Wickes)

Built as S4-SE2-BE1 attack cargo ships. Transferred to Maritime Administration and laid up in reserve from 1946 until reacquired by Navy for conversion to cable ships in 1955-1956. Converted to cable ships at the Key Highway Plant of Bethlehem Steel Corp, Baltimore, Maryland, being recommissioned on 14 May 1955 and 3 Jan 1956, respectively. Fitted with cable-laying bow sheaves, cable stowage tanks, cable repair facilities, and helicopter platform aft.
Both ships have been employed in hydrographic and cable operations. They were both Navy manned until 1973 when transferred to Military Sealift Command and provided with civilian crews. *Aeolus* is again operational; *Thor* laid up in reserve on 17 July 1975.

Classification: *Portunus* (ARC 1) was the converted LSM 275; the Coast Guard *Yamacraw* (WARC 333) also served as the ACM 9 and later ARC 5.

AEOLUS (T-ARC 3)   *United States Navy*

AEOLUS (T-ARC 3)   *1970, United States Navy*

2 CABLE SHIPS (ARC): "NEPTUNE" CLASS

Name	No.	Builders	Commissioned
*NEPTUNE (ex-*William H. G. Bullard*)	T-ARC 2	Pusey & Jones Corp, Wilmington, Del	1 June 1953
*ALBERT J. MEYER	T-ARC 6	Pusey & Jones Corp, Wilmington, Del	13 May 1963

Displacement, tons: 7 400 full load
Dimensions, feet (metres): 322 wl; 370 oa × 47 × 18 *(112·8 × 14·3 × 5·5)*
Guns: Removed
Main engines: Reciprocating (Skinner); 4 800 ihp; 2 shafts = 14 knots
Boilers: 2 (Combustion Engineering)

Built as S3-S2-BP1 type cable ships for Maritime Administration.
Neptune acquired by Navy from Maritime Administration in 1953 and sister ship *Albert J. Meyer* from US Army in 1966, latter ship for operation by Military Sea Transportation Service (now Military Sealift Command). They have been fitted with electric cable handling machinery (in place of steam equipment) and precision navigation equipment; helicopter platform in *Neptune.*
Both ships are operated by the Military Sealift Command with civilian crews; *Neptune* was Navy-manned until 1973 when transferred to MSC.
The USNS *Neptune* (T-ARC 2) should not be confused with the commercial cable ship *Neptun* of the United States Undersea Cable Corp.

NEPTUNE (T-ARC 2)   *1967, United States Navy*

NEPTUNE (T-ARC 2)   *1975, Giorgio Arra*

3 LANDING CRAFT REPAIR SHIPS (ARL): CONVERTED LST TYPE

Name	No.	Builders	Commissioned
EGERIA	ARL 8 (ex-*LST 136*)	Chicago Bridge & Iron Co, Seneca, Illinois	18 Dec 1943
SPHINX	ARL 24 (ex-*LST 963*)	Bethlehem Steel Co, Higham, Mass	12 Dec 1944
INDRA	ARL 37 (ex-*LST 1147*)	Chicago Bridge & Iron Co, Seneca, Illinois	28 May 1945

Displacement, tons: 1 625 light; 4 100 full load
Dimensions, feet (metres): 316 wl; 328 oa × 50 × 11 *(100·0 × 15·2 × 3·4)*
Guns: 8—40 mm AA (quad); several 20 mm AA in some ships
Main engines: Diesels (General Motors); 1 800 bhp; 2 shafts = 11·6 knots
Complement: 251 to 286

SPHINX (ARL 24)   x968, US Navy

Tank landing ships converted during construction to landing craft repair ships (ARL). Launched on 23 Nov 1943, 18 Nov 1944 and 21 May 1945 respectively. Fitted with machine shops, *materiel* and parts storage, lifting gear, etc; 50-ton (ARL 8) and 60-ton (ARL 24 and 37) capacity booms. The ARLs cater to small amphibious, minesweeping, and riverine craft. Most units have pole masts; note tripod mast in *Sphinx,* reactivated during Vietnam War. All surviving ships are in reserve.
Photographs of ARLs active in Vietnamese waters appear in the 1972-1973 and previous editions.

Disposals: (since 1 Jan 1975) *Midas* (ARB 5), *Sarpedon* (ARB 7) on 15 Apr 1976.

Transfers. Former US Navy LSTs modified to fleet support ships (AGP-ARB-ARL-ARVE) are operated by the navies of Brazil, Chile, China, West Germany, Greece, Indonesia, Iran, South Korea, Malaysia, Mexico, Philippines, Taiwan China, Turkey, and Venezuela.

SALVAGE SHIPS (ARSX): NEW CONSTRUCTION

Current Navy planning provides for construction of the first of a new class of salvage ships (now designated ARSX) in the FY 1981 shipbuilding programme. Characteristics of the ARSX have not yet been determined.

14 SALVAGE SHIPS (ARS): "DIVER" CLASS

Name	No.	Builders	Commissioned
*ESCAPE	ARS 6	Basalt Rock Co, Napa, Calif	20 Nov 1943
*GRAPPLE	ARS 7	Basalt Rock Co, Napa, Calif	16 Dec 1943
*PRESERVER	ARS 8	Basalt Rock Co, Napa, Calif	11 Jan 1944
*DELIVER	ARS 23	Basalt Rock Co, Napa, Calif	18 July 1944
*GRASP	ARS 24	Basalt Rock Co, Napa, Calif	22 Aug 1944
*SAFEGUARD	ARS 25	Basalt Rock Co, Napa, Calif	31 Oct 1944
*CLAMP	ARS 33	Basalt Rock Co, Napa, Calif	23 Aug 1943
*GEAR	ARS 34	Basalt Rock Co, Napa, Calif	24 Sep 1943
*BOLSTER	ARS 38	Basalt Rock Co, Napa, Calif	1 May 1945
*CONSERVER	ARS 39	Basalt Rock Co, Napa, Calif	9 June 1945
*HOIST	ARS 40	Basalt Rock Co, Napa, Calif	21 July 1945
*OPPORTUNE	ARS 41	Basalt Rock Co, Napa, Calif	5 Oct 1945
*RECLAIMER	ARS 42	Basalt Rock Co, Napa, Calif	20 Dec 1945
*RECOVERY	ARS 43	Basalt Rock Co, Napa, Calif	15 May 1946

Displacement, tons: 1 530 standard; 1 900 full load
Dimensions, feet (metres): 207 wl; 213·5 oa × 39 except later ships 43 × 13 *(65·1 × 11·9 or 13·1 × 4·0)*
Guns: 1—40 mm AA (removed from some ships); 2—·50 cal MG or 2—20 mm AA fitted in some ships
Main engines: Diesel-electric (Cooper Bessemer); 3 000 shp; 2 shafts = 14·8 knots except 16 knots in later ships
Complement: 85 (120 designed wartime)

OPPORTUNE (ARS 41)—40 mm gun   1973, Giorgio Arra

SAFEGUARD (ARS 25)   1972, United States Navy

These ships are fitted for salvage and towing; equipped with compressed air diving equipment. Launched on 22 Nov 1942, 31 Dec 1942, 1 April 1943, 25 Sep 1943, 31 July 1943, 20 Nov 1943, 24 Oct 1942, 24 Oct 1942, 23 dec 1944, 27 Jan 1945, 31 Mar 1945, 31 Mar 1945, 25 June 1945 and 4 Aug 1945 respectively. Several ships retain a single 40 mm gun fitted atop the superstructure forward of the funnel; replaced in several ships by smaller weapons on bridge wings. Early ships have 8-ton and 10-ton capacity booms; later ships have 10-ton and 20-ton booms.
ARS 38 and later ships are of a slightly different design, sometimes known as the "Bolster" class; however, generally considered to be the same class.
The *Gear* is operated by a commercial firm in support of Navy activities; two additional ships are on loan to private salvage firms, the *Cable* ARS 19 and *Curb* ARS 21, and support naval requirements as needed. The *Clamp* was stricken from the Navy List in 1963 but reacquired in 1973 and returned to service.

Conversions: *Chain* ARS 20 and *Snatch* ARS 27 converted to oceanographic research ships, designated AGOR 17 and AGOR 18, respectively.

Nomenclature: Salvage ships are named for terms related to salvage activity.

Photographs: Note the McCann submarine rescue chamber on the bow of the *Safeguard;* these chambers normally are carried aboard submarine rescue ships but with reduction of the ASR force the chambers regularly are embarked in other ships. The salvage ships do not have the deep-diving capabilities of the rescue ships.

2 + 3 SUBMARINE TENDERS (AS): "L. Y. SPEAR" CLASS

Name	No.	Builders	Commissioned
*L. Y. SPEAR	AS 36	General Dynamics Corp, Quincy	28 Feb 1970
*DIXON	AS 37	General Dynamics Corp, Quincy	7 Aug 1971
EMORY S. LAND	AS 39	Lockheed SB & Cons, Co, Seattle	1978
FRANK CABLE	AS 40	Lockheed SB & Cons Co, Seattle	1979
	AS 41		1981

Displacement, tons: 13 000 standard; AS 36 and AS 37 23 350 full load; AS 39 and AS 40 24 000 full load
Dimensions, feet (metres): 643·8 oa × 85 × 28·5 *(196·2 × 25·9 × 8·7)*
Guns: 2—5 inch *(127 mm)* 38 cal DP (Mk 30) in *L. Y. Spear* and *Dixon*; 4—20 mm AA planned for AS 39 and later ships
Missile launchers: NATO Sea Sparrow missile launcher planned for AS 39 and later ships
Main engines: Steam turbines (General Electric); 20 000 shp; 1 shaft = 20 knots
Boilers: 2 (Foster Wheeler)
Complement: AS 36 and 37 1 072 (42 officers, 1 030 enlisted men); AS 39 and 40 1 158 (50 officers, 1 108 enlisted men)
Flag accommodations: 69 (25 officers, 44 enlisted men)

DIXON (AS 37)   1971, United States Navy

These ships are the first US submarine tenders designed specifically for servicing nuclear-propelled attack submarines with later ships built to a modified design to support SSN 688 class submarines. (The four previous submarine tenders of post-World War II construction are configured to support ballistic missile submarines). Basic hull design similar to "Samuel Gompers" class destroyer tenders. Provided with helicopter deck but no hangar. Each ship can simultaneously provide services to four submarines moored alongside. AS 39 and later ships are especially configured to support SSN 688 class submarines.
Spear authorised in the Fiscal Year 1965 shipbuilding programme, laid down 5 May 1966 and launched 7 Sep 1967; *Dixon* authorised in FY 1966, laid down 7 Sep 1967 and launched 20 June 1970; AS 38 of FY 1969 not built to provide funds for cost increases in other ship programmes. *Land* authorised in FY 1972, and *Cable* in FY 1973 both to be laid down in 1976 and launched in 1977. AS 41 proposed in FY 1977 programme with no additional submarine tenders planned through FY 1981.
Estimated cost of AS 41 is $260 900 000.

Nomenclature: Submarine tenders traditionally have been named for pioneers in submarine development and mythological characters. However, Rear Admiral Land was head of the US Maritime Commission and War Shipping Administration Board in the Second World War. Frank T. Cable was a key participant in submarine development at the Electric Boat Company (now Electric Boat Division of General Dynamics Corp).

1970, United States Navy

L. Y. SPEAR (AS 36)

2 SUBMARINE TENDERS (AS): "SIMON LAKE" CLASS

Name	No.	Builders	Commissioned
*SIMON LAKE	AS 33	Puget Sound Naval Shipyard	7 Nov 1964
*CANOPUS	AS 34	Ingalls SB Co, Pascagoula	4 Nov 1965

Displacement, tons: 21 500 full load
Dimensions, feet (metres): 643·7 × 85 × 30 *(196·2 × 25·9 × 9·1)*
Guns: 4—3 inch *(76 mm)* 50 cal AA (twin) (Mk 33)
Main engines: Steam turbines; 20 000 shp; 1 shaft = 18 knots
Boilers: 2 (Combustion Engineering)
Complement: 1 075 (55 officers, 1 020 men)

These ships are designed specifically to service fleet ballistic missile submarines (SSBN), with as many as three submarines alongside being supported simultaneously.
The *Simon Lake* was authorised in the Fiscal Year 1963 new construction programe, laid down on 7 Jan 1963 and launched 8 Feb 1964. The *Canopus* was authorised in FY 1964, laid down on 2 March 1964 and launched on 12 Feb 1965. AS 35 was authorised in FY 1965 programme, but her construction was deferred. The last ship would have permitted one tender to be assigned to each of five FBM submarine squadrons with a sixth ship available to rotate when another was in overhaul, however; only four SSBN squadrons were established.
Note cranes amidships, funnel location (flanked by gun mounts, and helicopter platform).

CANOPUS (AS 34)   1966, United States Navy

2 SUBMARINE TENDERS (AS): "HUNLEY" CLASS

Name	No.	Builders	Commissioned
*HUNLEY	AS 31	Newport News SB & DD Co	16 June 1962
*HOLLAND	AS 32	Ingalls SB Co, Pascagoula	7 Sep 1963

Displacement, tons: 10 500 standard; 18 300 full load
Dimensions, feet (metres): 599 × 83 × 24 (182·6 × 25·3 × 7·3)
Guns: 4—3 inch (76 mm) 50 cal AA (twin) (Mk 33)
Main engines: Diesel-electric (10 Fairbanks-Morse diesels); 15 000 bhp; 1 shaft = 19 knots
Complement: 1 081 (58 officers, 1 023 men) plus accommodation for 30 officers and 270 men from submarines

HOLLAND (AS 32) *United States Navy*

These ships are the first US submarine tenders of post-World War II construction; they are designed specifically to provide repairs and supply services to fleet ballistic missile submarines (SSBN). Provided with 52 separate workshops to provide complete support to nuclear plants, electronic and navigation systems, missiles, and other submarine systems. Helicopter platform fitted aft but no hangar. Both ships originally fitted with a 32-ton-capacity hammerhead crane (see 1972-1973 and previous editions for photographs); subsequently refitted with two amidships cranes as in "Simon Lake" class
Hunley authorised in Fiscal Year 1960 shipbuilding programme, laid down on 28 Nov 1960 and launched on 28 Sep 1961; *Holland* authorised in FY 1962 programme, laid down on 5 Mar 1962 and launched on 19 Jan 1963. Former ship cost $24 359 800.

Nomenclature: *Holland* is named after John Philip Holland, an Irish emigrant to the United States, and submarine designer and builder. One of his submarines was accepted by the US Navy in 1900 and became Submarine Torpedo Boat No 1, named *Holland*, the first officially accepted US Navy submarine (later designated SS 1).

HUNLEY (AS 31)

United States Navy

7 SUBMARINE TENDERS (AS): "FULTON" CLASS

Name	No.	Builders	Commissioned
*FULTON	AS 11	Mare Island Navy Yard	12 Sep 1941
*SPERRY	AS 12	Moore SB & DD Co, Oakland	1 May 1942
BUSHNELL	AS 15	Mare Island Navy Yard	10 April 1943
*HOWARD W. GILMORE (ex-*Neptune*)	AS 16	Mare Island Navy Yard	24 May 1944
NEREUS	AS 17	Mare Island Navy Yard	27 Oct 1945
*ORION	AS 18	Moore SB & DD Co, Oakland	30 Sep 1943
*PROTEUS	AS 19	Moore SB & DD Co, Oakland	31 Jan 1944

Displacement, tons: 9 734 standard; 18 000 full load except *Proteus:* 10 234 standard; 18 500 full load
Dimensions, feet (metres): 530·5 oa except *Proteus* 574·5 oa × 73·3 × 25·5 (161·7 *Proteus* 175·1 × 22·3 × 7·8)
Guns: 2—5 inch (127 mm) 38 cal DP (Mk 30); one gun in *Proteus;* all guns removed from some ships
Main engines: Diesel-electric (General Motors); 11 200 to 11 800 bhp; 2 shafts = 15·4 knots
Complement: 917 (34 officers, 883 enlisted men); except *Proteus* 1 121 (51 officers, 1 070 enlisted men)

HOWARD W. GILMORE (AS 16) *1971, United States Navy*

These venerable ships are contemporaries of the similar-design "Dixie" class destroyer tenders. Launched on 27 Dec 1940, 17 Dec 1941, 14 Sep 1942, 16 Sep 1943, 12 Feb 1945, 14 Oct 1942 and 12 Nov 1942 respectively. As built, they carried the then-standard large auxiliary armament of four 5 inch guns plus 8—40 mm AA guns (twin). The original 20-ton capacity cylinder cranes have been replaced in the *Howard W. Gilmore*. Five ships are active and two are in reserve.

Conversion: *Proteus* AS 19 was converted at the Charleston Naval Shipyard, under the Fiscal Year 1959 conversion programme, at a cost of $23 000 000 to service nuclear-powered fleet ballistic missile submarines (SSBN). Conversion was begun on 19 Jan 1959 and she was recommissioned on 8 July 1960. She was lengthened by adding a section amidships 44 feet in length, and the bare hull weight of this 6-deck high insertion was approximately 500 tons. Three 5 inch guns were removed and her upper decks extended aft to provide additional workshops. Storage tubes for Polaris missiles installed; bridge crane amidships loads and unloads missiles for alongside submarines.

Modernisation: All except *Proteus* have undergone FRAM II modernisation to service nuclear-powered attack submarines. Additional maintenance shops provided to service nuclear plant components and advanced electronic equipment and weapons. After two 5 inch guns and eight 40 mm guns (twin) removed.

Nomenclature: The *Howard W. Gilmore* is named for the commanding officer of a World War II submarine who, lying on the bridge wounded, ordered the boat to dive; he was posthumously awarded the Medal of Honour, the highest US military decoration.

ORION (AS 18) *1973, United States Navy, PHCS Boyd E. Spang*

2 SUBMARINE RESCUE SHIPS (ASR): "PIGEON" CLASS

Name	No.	Builders	Commissioned
*PIGEON	ASR 21	Alabama DD & SB Co, Mobile	28 Apr 1973
*ORTOLAN	ASR 22	Alabama DD & SB Co, Mobile	14 July 1973

Displacement, tons: 4 200 full load
Dimensions, feet (metres): 251 oa × 86 (see *Design* notes) × 21·25 *(76·5 × 26·2 × 6·5)*
Guns: 2—20 mm AA (single) 4—·50 cal MG
Main engines: 4 diesels; 6 000 bhp; 2 shafts = 15 knots
Complement: 115 (6 officers, 109 enlisted men)
Staff accommodation: 14 (4 officers, 10 enlisted men)
Submersible operators: 24 (4 officers, 20 enlisted men)

These are the world's first ships designed specifically for this role, all other ASR designs being adaptations of tug types. The "Pigeon" class ships serve as (1) surface support ships for the Deep Submergence Rescue Vehicles (DSRV), (2) rescue ships employing the existing McCann rescue chamber, (3) major deep-sea diving support ships and (4) operational control ships for salvage operations. Each ASR is capable of transporting, servicing, lowering, and raising two Deep Submergence Rescue Vehicles (DSRV) (see section on Deep Submergence Vehicles). The Navy had planned in the 1960s to replace the 10-ship ASR force with new construction ASRs. However, only two ships were funded, with procurement of others deferred.
Pigeon authorised in Fiscal Year 1967 new construction programme and *Ortolan* in FY 1968 programme. *Pigeon* was laid down on 17 July 1968 and launched on 13 Aug 1969; *Ortolan* was laid down on 22 Aug 1968 and launched on 10 Sep 1969; they were delayed more than two years by a shipyard strike and technical difficulties; additional delays encountered in special equipment installation.

PIGEON (ASR 21)   *1975, US Navy, PH2 Donald Westman*

Design: These ships have twin, catamaran hulls, the first ocean-going catamaran ships to be built for the US Navy since Robert Fulton's steam gunboat *Demologus* of 1812. The design provides a large deck working area, facilities for raising and lowering submersibles and underwater equipment, and improved stability when operating equipment at great depths. Each of the twin hulls is 251 feet long and 26 feet wide. The well between the hulls is 34 feet across, giving the ASR a maximum beam of 86 feet. Fitted with helicopter platform and with precision three-dimensional sonar system for tracking submersibles.

Diving: These ships have been fitted with the Mk II Deep Diving System to support conventional or saturation divers operating at depths to 850 feet. The system consists of two decompression chambers, two personnel transfer capsules to transport divers between the ship and ocean floor, and the associated controls, winches, cables, gas supplies etc. Submarine rescue ships are the US Navy's primary diving ships and the only ones fitted for helium-oxygen diving.

ORTOLAN (ASR 22)   *1973, United States Navy*

Engineering: Space and weight are reserved for future installation of a ducted thruster in each bow to enable the ship to maintain precise position while stopped or at slow speeds. Range is 8 500 miles at 13 knots.

Gunnery: As built, the *Pigeon* was armed with 2—3 inch AA guns in twin gun "tubs" forward of the bridge. She had two large mooring buoys ("spuds") forward of the bridge between the guns and two additional buoys aft, one on each stern. Subsequently the *Pigeon* was modified to the *Ortolan* configuration with four mooring buoys forward; 3 inch gun mounts removed. See 1974-1975 edition for photo of *Pigeon* with 3 inch guns.

Nomenclature: Submarine rescue ships traditionally have carried bird names (the US Navy's first six ASRs were converted "Bird" class minesweepers).

ORTOLAN (ASR 22)   *1973, United States Navy, Albert E. Flournoy*

6 SUBMARINE RESCUE SHIPS (ASR): "CHANTICLEER" CLASS

Name	No.	Builders	Commissioned
*COUCAL	ASR 8	Moore SB & DD Co, Oakland	22 Jan 1943
*FLORIKAN	ASR 9	Moore SB & DD Co, Oakland	5 Apr 1943
*KITTIWAKE	ASR 13	Savannah Machine & Foundry Co	18 July 1946
*PETREL	ASR 14	Savannah Machine & Foundry Co	24 Sep 1946
*SUNBIRD	ASR 15	Savannah Machine & Foundry Co	28 Jan 1947
*TRINGA	ASR 16	Savannah Machine & Foundry Co	28 Jan 1947

Displacement, tons: 1 653 standard; 2 290 full load
Dimensions, feet (metres): 240 wl; 251·5 oa × 42 × 14·9 *(76·7 × 12·8 × 4·5)*
Guns: 2—20 mm AA (single) in some ships
Main engines: Diesel-electric (Alco or General Motors); 3 000 bhp; 1 shaft = 14·9 knots
Complement: 85 (102 designed wartime)

Large tug-type ships equipped with powerful pumps, heavy air compressors, and rescue chambers for submarine salvage and rescue operations. Launched on 29 May 1942, 14 June 1942, 10 July 1945, 29 Sep 1945, 3 April 1945 and 25 June 1945 respectively.
Fitted for helium-oxygen diving.
As built, each ship was armed with 2—3 inch AA guns; removed 1957-1958. Some ships subsequently fitted with two 20 mm AA guns.

Transfers: Former US Navy submarine rescue ships serve in the navies of Brazil and Turkey.

Photographs: In the view of the *Florikan* note the 20 mm gun "tub" and two small mooring buoys abreast funnel; McCann submarine rescue chamber on fantail under boom; in the lower view the buoys are deployed. Note empty 3 inch gun tab forward of bridge. Fish symbol rear number is traditional diving signal for men underwater. Note different funnel caps.

SUNBIRD (ASR 15)   *1975, Giorgio Arra*

FLORIKAN (ASR 9)   *1970, United States Navy*

5 AUXILIARY TUGS (ATA): "MARICOPA" CLASS

Name	No.	Builders	Commissioned	
ACCOKEEK	ATA 181	Levingston SB Co, Orange, Texas	7 Oct	1944
SAMOSET	ATA 190	Levingston SB Co, Orange, Texas	1 Jan	1945
STALLION	ATA 193	Levingston SB Co, Orange, Texas	26 Feb	1945
TATNUCK	ATA 195	Levingston SB Co, Orange, Texas	1 Feb	1945
KEYWADIN	ATA 213	Gulfport Boiler & Welding Works, Port Arthur, Texas	1 June	1945

Displacement, tons: 534 standard; 835 full load
Dimensions, feet (metres): 134·5 wl; 143 oa × 33·9 × 13 *(43·6 × 10·3 × 4·0)*
Guns: 1—3 inch *(76 mm)* 50 cal AA or 4—20 mm AA (twin); all guns removed from some ships
Main engines: Diesel-electric (General Motors diesels); 1 500 bhp; 1 shaft = 13 knots
Complement: 45 (5 officers, 40 enlisted men)

Steel-hulled tugs formerly designated as rescue tugs (ATR); renumbered in same series as larger fleet tugs (ATF) when designation changed to ATA in 1944. Launched on 27 July 1944, 26 Oct 1944, 14 Dec 1944, 24 Nov 1944 and 9 April 1945 respectively. During 1948 they were assigned names that had been carried by discarded fleet and yard tugs.
All of the surviving ships were decommissioned in 1969-1971 and placed in reserve. Two ships of this class serve in the Coast Guard.

Transfers: Ships of this class serve with Colombia, Dominican Republic, South Korea, and Taiwan China.

Disposals: (since 1 Jan 1975) *Penobscot* (ATA 188) stricken on 28 Feb 1975.

ACCOKEEK (ATA 181)   *1970, United States Navy*

(8) FLEET TUGS (ATF): NEW CONSTRUCTION

	No,	Builders	Commission
One ship	**T-ATF 166**	Marinette Marine Corp, Wisconson	1978
Three ships	**T-ATF 167-169**	Marinette Marine Corp, Wisconson	
Four ships	**T-ATF**	Planned Fiscal Year 1978 programme	

Displacement, tons: 2 000 full load
Dimensions, feet (metres): 218 oa × 42 × 15 *(66·5 × 12·8 × 4·6)*
Guns: 2—20 mm AA; 2—·50 cal MG (space provided)
Main engines: Diesels (General Motors); 4 500 bhp; 2 shafts (controllable-pitch propellers) = 15 knots
Complement: 16 civilian plus 4 Navy communications personnel plus 20 transient diving/salvage personnel

This is a new class of fleet tugs built to commercial standards; the ships will be operated by the Military Sealift Command and manned by civilian crews. Guns will not normally be installed. A 300 hp bow thruster will be provided: 10 ton capacity crane. Range 100 000 miles at 13 knots. T-ATF 166 was to be laid down in June 1976 and launched in 1977.
Estimated cost of the lead ship is $11 500 000; an average of $15 000 000 for the FY 1976 ships and $16 000 000 for FY 1978 ships.

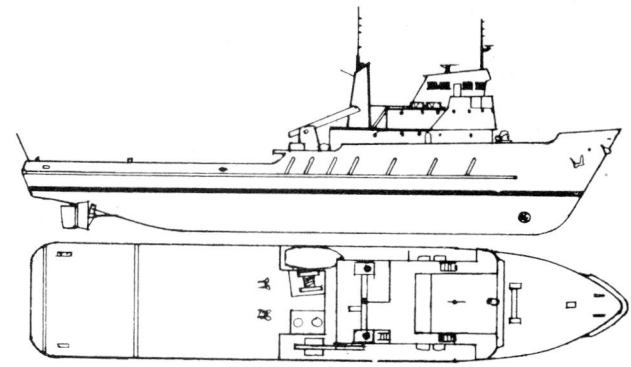

CREE (ATF 84)—large funnel   *1970, United States Navy*

21 FLEET TUGS (ATF): "APACHE" CLASS

Name	No.	Builders	Commissioned
*UTE	T-ATF 76	United Engineering Co, Alameda, Calif	31 Dec 1942
*CREE	ATF 84	United Engineering Co, Alameda, Calif	28 Mar 1943
*LIPAN	T-ATF 85	United Engineering Co, Alameda, Calif	29 Apr 1943
*MATACO	ATF 86	United Engineering Co, Alameda, Calif	29 May 1943
SENECA	ATF 91	Cramp SB Co, Philadelphia	30 Apr 1943
*ABNAKI	ATF 96	Charleston SB & DD Co, SC	15 Nov 1943
*CHOWANOC	ATF 100	Charleston SB & DD Co, SC	21 Feb 1944
*COCOPA	ATF 101	Charleston SB & DD Co, SC	25 Mar 1944
*HITCHITI	ATF 103	Charleston SB & DD Co, SC	27 May 1944
*MOCTABI	ATF 105	Charleston SB & DD Co, SC	25 July 1944
*MOLALA	ATF 106	United Engineering Co, Alameda, Calif	29 Sep 1943
*QUAPAW	ATF 110	United Engineering Co, Alameda, Calif	6 May 1944
*TAKELMA	ATF 113	United Engineering Co, Alameda, Calif	3 Aug 1944
**TAWAKONI	ATF 114	United Engineering Co, Alameda, Calif	15 Sep 1944
*ATAKAPA	T-ATF 149	Charleston SB & DD Co, SC	8 Dec 1944
*NIPMUC	ATF 157	Charleston SB & DD Co, SC	8 July 1945
*MOSOPELEA	T-ATF 158	Charleston SB & DD Co, SC	28 July 1945
*PAIUTE	ATF 159	Charleston SB & DD Co, SC	27 Aug 1945
*PAPAGO	ATF 160	Charleston SB & DD Co, SC	3 Oct 1945
*SALINAN	ATF 161	Charleston SB & DD Co, SC	9 Nov 1945
*SHAKORI	ATF 162	Charleston SB & DD Co, SC	20 Dec 1945

CHOWANOC (ATF 100)—small funnel   1973, US Navy

Displacement, tons: 1 235 standard; 1 675 full load
Dimensions, feet (metres): 195 wl; 205 oa × 38·5 × 15·5 *(62·5 × 11·7 × 4·7)*
Guns: 1—3 inch *(76 mm)* 50 cal AA (Mk 22) some ships have machineguns in "tubs" aft of bridge; guns removed from MSC ships
Main engines: Diesel-electric drive; 3 000 bhp; 1 shaft = 15 knots
Complement: 75 (5 officers, 70 enlisted men; 85 wartime) navy; 24 civilians plus 6 navy communications personnel in MSC ships.

Large ocean tugs fitted with powerful pumps and other salvage equipment. ATF 96 and later ships ("Abnaki" class) have smaller funnel. As built these ships mounted 2—40 mm guns in addition to 3 inch gun. Launched on 24 June 1942, 17 Aug 1942, 17 Sep 1942, 2 Feb 1943, 22 April 1943, 20 Aug 1943, 5 Oct 1943, 29 Jan 1944, 25 March 1944, 23 Dec 1942, 15 May 1943, 18 Sep 1943, 28 Oct 1943, 11 July 1944, 12 April 1945, 7 March 1945, 4 June 1945, 21 June 1945, 20 July 1945 and 9 August 1945 respectively.

Beginning in 1973 several fleet tugs have been assigned to the Military Sealift Command and provided with civilian crews; these ships are designated T-ATF and are unarmed. ATF 85 and ATF 158 assigned to MSC in 1973; ATF 76, and ATF 149 to MSC in 1974; additional ATFs will follow.
Three ships of this class serve with the US Coast Guard. All remaining ATFs are active except the *Seneca* which is in Maritime Administration reserve (on Navy List).

Nomenclature: US tugs of World War II construction and previous classes were named for Indian tribes and words.

Transfers: Ships of this class serve with Argentina, Chile, Dominican Republic, Peru, Turkey, Taiwan, and Venezuela.

Disposals and Transfers: (since 1 Jan 1975) *Tawasa* (ATF 92) stricken on 1 April 1975; *Luiscno* (ATF 156) transferred to Argentina on 1 July 1975.

3 SALVAGE AND RESCUE SHIPS (ATS): "EDENTON" CLASS

Name	No.	Builders	Commissioned
*EDENTON	ATS 1	Brooke Marine, Lowestoft, England	23 Jan 1971
*BEAUFORT	ATS 2	Brooke Marine, Lowestoft, England	22 Jan 1972
*BRUNSWICK	ATS 3	Brooke Marine, Lowestoft, England	10 Dec 1972

Displacement, tons: 3 117 full load
Dimensions, feet (metres): 282·6 oa × 50 × 15·1 *(86·1 × 15·2 × 4·6)*
Guns: 2—20 mm AA; 4—·50 cal MG
Main engines: 4 diesels (Paxman); 6 000 bhp; 2 shafts (controllable-pitch propellers) = 16 knots
Complement: 102 (9 officers and 93 enlisted men)

These tugs are designed specifically for salvage operations and are capable of (1) ocean towing, (2) supporting diver operations to depths of 850 feet, (3) lifting submerged objects weighing as much as 600 000 pounds from a depth of 120 feet by static tidal lift or 30 000 pounds by dynamic lift, (4) fighting ship fires, and (5) performing general salvage operations. Fitted with 10-ton capacity crane forward and 20-ton capacity crane aft.
The ATS 1 was authorised in the Fiscal Year 1966 shipbuilding programme; ATS 2 and ATS 3 in the FY 1967 programme. Laid down on 1 April 1967, 19 Feb 1968 and 5 June 1968 respectively; launched on 15 May 1968, 20 Dec 1968 and 14 Oct 1969. In service the British-made components have created severe supply problems with respect to obtaining spare parts.
ATF 4 was authorised in the FY 1972 new construction programme and ATS 5 in the FY 1973 programme, with several additional ships being planned. However, construction of these ships was deferred in 1973 with the smaller, modification of a commercial design ATF being substituted in their place.
Classification changed from salvage tug (ATS) to salvage and rescue ship (ATS) on 16 Feb 1971.

Diving: These ships can carry the air-transportable Mk 1 Deep Diving System which can support four divers working in two-man shifts at depths to 850 feet. The system consists of a double-chamber decompression chamber a personnel transfer capsule to transport divers between the ships and ocean floor and the associated controls, winches, cables, gas supplies, etc. The ships' organic diving capability is compressed air only.

Engineering: Fitted with tunnel bow thruster for precise manoeuvring.

Nomenclature: These three ships are named for small American cities with namesakes in the United Kingdom.

EDENTON (ATS 1)   1971, United States Navy

BEAUFORT (ATS 2)   1974, US Navy, PH3, J. A. Romesburg

BEAUFORT (ATS 2)   1971, Brooke Marine

SEALIFT SHIPS

Sealift ships provide ocean transportation for all components of the Department of Defense. These ships are operated by the Navy's Military Sealift Command (MSC), renamed on 1 Aug 1970 from Military Sea Transportation Service (MSTS). Sealift cargo ships and tankers carry cargoes from port to port, and are not configured to provide underway replenishment (UNREP) of other ships, or land *materiel* over the beach in amphibious landings. Four MSC-operated cargo ships are fitted to carry Submarine-Launched Ballistic Missiles (SLBM) and other supplies for US Polaris/Poseidon submarines; these ships support the Polaris/Poseidon submarine tenders.

Most US defence cargo is carried in commercial merchant ships under charter to the government (through the Military

Sealift Command).

The Commander, Deputy Commander, and Area Commanders (Atlantic, Pacific, and Far East) are flag officers of the Navy on active duty. All ships are civilian manned with most of their crews being Civil Service employees of the Navy. However, the tankers are operated under contract to commercial tanker lines and are manned by merchant seamen.

In addition to the ships listed in this section, the Military Sealift Command also operates a number of underway replenishment (UNREP) ships, fleet support ships, and special projects ships that support other defence-related activities, mostly research, surveying and missile-range support ships (see Experimental, Research and Surveying Ships listing). Other special projects

ships are the cable ships listed in the section on Fleet Support Ships.

Armament: No ships of the Military Sealift Command are armed.

Classification: Military Sealift Command ships are assigned standard US Navy hull designations with the added designation prefix "T". Ships in this category are referred to as "USNS" (United States Naval Ship) *vice* "USS" (United States Ship) which is used for Navy-manned ships.

1 HEAVY LIFT SHIP (AK): "BROSTROM" TYPE

Name	No.
PVT. LEONARD C. BROSTROM (ex-*Marine Eagle*)	T-AK 255

Displacement, tons: 13 865 deadweight
Dimensions, feet (metres): 520 oa × 71·5 × 33 *(158·5 × 21·8 × 10·1)*
Main engines: Geared turbine; 9 000 shp; 1 shaft = 15·8 knots
Boilers: 2
Complement: 57 (14 officers, 43 men)

The *Brostrom* is fitted with 150-ton capacity booms, providing the most powerful lift capability of any US ship. C4-S-B1 type built in 1943. Note the deckloaded tanks and trucks in the photograph of the *Brostrom* on previous page. Laid up in "ready reserve".

PVT LEONARD C. BROSTROM (T-AK 255)

United States Navy

4 FBM CARGO SHIPS (AK): "VICTORY" CLASS

Name	No.
*NORWALK (ex-*Norwalk Victory*)	T-AK 279
*FURMAN (ex-*Furman Victory*)	T-AK 280
*VICTORIA (ex-*Ethiopia Victory*)	T-AK 281
*MARSHFIELD (ex-*Marshfield Victory*)	T-AK 282

Displacement, tons: 6 700 light; 11 150 full load
Dimensions, feet (metres): 455·25 oa × 62 × 24 *(138·8 × 18·9 × 7·3)*
Main engines: Geared turbine; 8 500 shp; 1 shaft = 17 knots
Boilers: 2
Complement: 80 to 90 plus Navy detachment

Former merchant ships of the VC2-S-AP3 "Victory" type built during World War II. Extensively converted to supply tenders for Fleet Ballistic Missile (FBM) submarines. Fitted to carry torpedoes, spare parts, packaged petroleum products, bottled gas, black oil and diesel fuel, frozen and dry provisions, and general cargo as well as missiles. No 3 hold converted to carry 16 Polaris missiles in vertical position; tankage provided for 355 000 gallons (US) of diesel oil and 430 000 gallons (US) of fuel oil (for submarine tenders). All subsequently modified to carry Poseidon missiles. All four ships are operated by the Military Sealift Command with civilian operating crews; a small Navy detachment in each ship provides security and technical services.

Conversion: *Norwalk* converted to FBM cargo ship by Boland Machine & Manufacturing Co, and accepted for service on 30 Dec 1963; *Furman* converted by American Shipbuilding Co, and accepted in Oct 1964; *Victoria* converted by Philadelphia Naval Shipyard, and accepted in Oct 1965; and *Marshfield* converted by Boland Machine & Manufacturing Co, and accepted in June 1970.

MARSHFIELD (T-AK 282)

1970, United States Navy

1 CARGO SHIP (AK): "BLAND" TYPE

Name	No.
SCHUYLER OTIS BLAND	T-AK 277

Displacement, tons: 15 910 full load
Dimensions, feet (metres): 478 oa × 66 × 30 *(145·7 × 20·1 × 9·1)*
Main engines: Geared turbine; 13 750 shp; 1 shaft = 18·5 knots
Boilers: 2

Acquired from the Maritime Administration by the Military Sea Transportation Service in July 1961. The only ship of the type (C3-S-DX1), built in 1961; prototype of the "Mariner" cargo ship design. Laid up in "ready reserve".

SCHUYLER OTIS BLAND (T-AK 277)

United States Navy

1 CARGO SHIP (AK): "ELTANIN" TYPE

Name	No.	Builders
*MIRFAK	T-AK 271	Avondale MarineWays, New Orleans

Displacement, tons: 2 036 light; 4 942 full load
Dimensions, feet (metres): 256·8 wl; 262·2 oa × 51·5 × 18·7 *(79·9 × 15·7 × 5·7)*
Main engines: Diesel-electric (ALCO diesels with Westinghouse electric motors); 3 200 bhp; 2
 shafts = 13 knots

Built for Military Sea Transportation Service, Louisiana. Designed for Arctic operation with hull
strengthened against ice. C1-M-E2-13a type. Launched on 5 Aug 1957. Note icebreaking prow in
photo.

Conversion: Two other ships of this class converted for oceanographic research: *Eltanin*,
reclassified from T-AK 270 to T-AGOR 8 on 15 Nov 1962; *Mizar* T-AK 272 was reclassified
T-AGOR 11 on 15 Apr 1964 (see Experimental, Research and Surveying Ships).

MIRFAK (T-AK 271)   *United States Navy*

5 CARGO SHIPS (AK): "VICTORY" CLASS

Name	No.
GREENVILLE VICTORY	T-AK 237
PVT. JOHN R. TOWLE (ex-*Appleton Victory*)	T-AK 240
SGT. ANDREW MILLER (ex-*Radcliffe Victory*)	T-AK 242
SGT. TRUMAN KIMBRO	T-AK 254
LT. JAMES E. ROBINSON (ex-T-AG 170,	T-AK 274
ex-T-AK 274, ex-AKV 3, ex-*Czechoslovakia Victory*)	

Displacement, tons: 6 700 light; 12 450 full load
Dimensions, feet (metres): 455·5 oa × 62 × 28·5 *(138·9 × 18·9 × 8·9)*
Main engines: Geared turbine; 8 500 shp; 1 shaft = 17 knots except T-AK 254 15 knots
Boilers: 2

Former merchant ships of the "Victory" type built during World War II. VC2-S-AP3 type capable
of 17 knots except T-AK 254 is VC2-S-AP2 type capable of 15 knots. "Victory" type cargo ships
configured as Fleet Ballistic Missile (FBM) cargo ships are listed separately.
These ships are unarmed and civilian manned by the Military Sealift Command.
Three ships laid up in "Ready reserve"; *Miller* and *Robinson* in Maritime Administration
reserve.

Classification: The former Military Sea Transportation Service aircraft cargo and ferry ships *Lt.
James E. Robinson* AKV 3 reclassified as cargo ship on 7 May 1959. *Kingsport Victory* T-AK 239,
was renamed and reclassified *Kingsport* T-AG 164 in 1962 (see Experimental, Research and
Surveying ships).
Lt. James E. Robinson T-AK 274, was to have been transferred to the Maritime Administration,
but was modified for special project work and reclassified as T-AG 170 in 1963, and reverted to
the original classification T-AK 274 on 1 July 1964.

Disposals: (since 1 Jan 1975) *Sgt. Morris E. Crain* (T-AK 244) stricken on 11 Mar 1975 (correction
to previous edition).

GREENVILLE VICTORY (T-AK 237)   *United States Navy*

PVT. JOHN R. TOWLE (T-AK 240) in Antarctic   *1961, US Navy*

1 CARGO SHIP (AK): Ex-AKA TYPE

Name	No.	Builders	Commissioned
WYANDOT	T-AK 283 (ex-T-AKA 92)	Moore DD Co, Oakland	30 Sep 1944

Displacement, tons: 7 430 light; 14 000 full load
Dimensions, feet (metres): 435 wl; 459·2 oa × 63 × 24 *(140·0 × 19·2 × 7·3)*
Main engines: Geared turbines (General Electric); 6 000 shp; 1 shaft = 16·5 knots
Boilers: 2 (Combustion Engineering)

Former attack cargo ship (AKA) of the "Andromeda" class; C2-S-B1 type. Launched on 28 June
1944; commissioned as AKA 92. Assigned to Military Sea Transportation Service and manned
by a civilian crew since 1963. Designation changed to T-AK 283 on 1 Jan 1969. Winterised for
arctic service.
Civilian manned. Laid up in "Ready reserve."

1 VEHICLE CARGO SHIP: "CALLAGHAN" TYPE

Name	No.	Builders
ADMIRAL WM. M. CALLAGHAN	—	Sun SB & DD Co, Chester, Pennsylvania

Displacement, tons: 24 500 full load
Dimensions, feet (metres): 694 oa × 92 × 29 *(211·5 × 28·0 × 8·8)*
Main engines: 2 gas turbines (General Electric); 50 000 shp; 2 shafts = 26 knots
Complement: 33

Roll-on/roll-off vehicle cargo ship built specifically for long-term charter to the Military Sealift
Command. Launched on 17 Oct 1967. Internal parking decks and ramps for carrying some 750
vehicles on 167 537 sq ft of parking area; unloading via four side ramps and stern ramp, the
Callaghan can off load and reload full vehicle capacity in 27 hours.

Engineering: The *Callaghan* was the first Navy-sponsored all gas-turbine ship; fitted with two
GE LM 2500 engines, similar to those of the "Spruance" class destroyers (DD 963) and "Perry"
class frigates (FFG 7).

ADM. WM. M. CALLAGHAN   *United States Navy*

1 VEHICLE CARGO SHIP (AKR): "METEOR" TYPE

Name	No.	Builders
*METEOR (ex-*Sea Lift*)	T-AKR 9 (ex-LSV 9)	Puget Sound Bridge & DD Co

Displacement, tons: 11 130 light; 16 940 standard; 21 700 full load
Dimensions, feet (metres): 540 oa × 83 × 29
Main engines: Geared turbines; 19 400 shp; 2 shafts = 20 knots
Boilers: 2
Complement: 62
Passengers 12

Maritime Administration C4-ST-67a type. Roll-on/roll-off vehicle cargo ship. Built by the Puget Sound Bridge & Dry Dock Co, (now Lockheed Shipbuilding and Construction Co), Seattle, Washington. At a cost of $15 895 500. Authorised under the Fiscal Year 1963 programme. Laid down on 19 May 1964 and launched on 18 April 1965. Delivered to Military Sea Transportation Service on 19 May 1967. Designed for point-to-point sea transportation of Department of Defense self-propelled, fully loaded, wheeled, tracked and amphibious vehicles and general cargo. Internal ramps, stern ramp and side openings provide for quick loading and unloading. Designation changed from T-LSV to T-AKR on 1 Jan 1969. Originally authorised as AK-278). Civilian manned.

Nomenclature: Originally named *Sea Lift*. Renamed *Meteor* on 12 Sep 1975 to avoid confusion with "Sealift" class tankers.

METEOR (T-AKR 9)   *1966, Lockheed Shipbuilding*

METEOR (T-AKR 9)   *1966, Lockheed Shipbuilding*

1 TANKER (AO): "POTOMAC" TYPE

Name	No.
*POTOMAC (ex-*Shenandoah*)	T-AO 181

Displacement, tons: 27 467 deadweight
Dimensions, feet (metres): 620 oa × 83·5 × 34 *(189·0 × 25·5 × 10·4)*
Main engines: Geared turbine; 20 460 shp; 1 shaft = 18 knots
Boilers: 2

The merchant tanker *Shenandoah* was built from the stern of the naval tanker *Potomac* (T-AO 150) destroyed by fire on 26 Sep 1961, and new bow and mid-body sections. After being chartered by the Military Sealift Command for several years, the "new" ship was formally acquired on 12 Jan 1976, assigned the name *Potomac* and placed in MSC service. Cargo capacity 200 000 barrels. Civilian manned.

Classification: The AO hull numbers 177-180 are assigned to new construction Navy oilers (see listing with Underway Replenishment Ships).

4 TANKERS (AO): "FALCON" CLASS

Name	No.
*COLUMBIA (ex-*Falcon Lady*)	T-AO 182
*NECHES (ex-*Falcon Duchess*)	T-AO 183
*HUDSON (ex-*Falcon Princess*)	T-AO 184
*SUSQUEHANNA (ex-*Falcon Countess*)	T-AO 185

Displacement, tons: 37 276 deadweight
Dimensions, feet (metres): 672 oa × 89 × 36 *(204·8 × 27·1 × 11·0)*
Main engines: Geared turbine; 1 shaft = 16·5 knots
Boilers: 2

Former merchant tankers under charter to the Military Sealift Command. *Columbia* and *Neches* built in 1971; *Hudson* and *Susquehanna* in 1972. All four acquired for MSC service early in 1976. Cargo capacity 310 000 barrels. Civilian manned.

TALUGA (T-AO 62) and COLUMBIA (T-AO 182) (as *Falcon Lady*)

United States Navy

HUDSON (T-AO 184) (as *Falcon Princess*)

1 VEHICLE CARGO SHIP (AKR): "COMET" TYPE

Name	No.	Builders	Commissioned
*COMET	T-AKR 7 (ex-*T-LSV 7*, ex-*T-AK 269*)	Sun SB & DD Co	27 Jan 1958

Displacement, tons: 7 605 light; 18 150 full load
Dimensions, feet (metres): 465 oa; 499 oa × 78 × 28·8 (*152·1 × 23·8 × 8·8*)
Main engines: Geared turbines (General Electric); 13 200 shp; 2 shafts = 18 knots
Boilers: 2 (Babcock & Wilcox)
Complement: 73

Roll-on/roll-off vehicle carrier built for Military Sea Transportation Service C3-ST-14A type. Laid down on 15 May 1956. Launched on 31 July 1957. Maritime Administration Design includes ramp system for loading and discharging. The hull is strengthened against ice. Can accommodate 700 vehicles in two after holds; the forward holds are for general cargo. Equipped with Denny-Brown stabilisers. Reclassified from T-AK to T-LSV on 1 June 1963, and changed to T-AKR on 1 Jan 1969.

COMET (T-AKR 7)   *United States Navy*

9 TANKERS (AO): "SEALIFT" CLASS

Name	No.	Builders
*SEALIFT PACIFIC	T-AO 168	Todd Shipyards
*SEALIFT ARABIAN SEA	T-AO 169	Todd Shipyards
*SEALIFT CHINA SEA	T-AO 170	Todd Shipyards
*SEALIFT INDIAN OCEAN	T-AO 171	Todd Shipyards
*SEALIFT ATLANTIC	T-AO 172	Bath Iron Works
*SEALIFT MEDITERRANEAN	T-AO 173	Bath Iron Works
*SEALIFT CARIBBEAN	T-AO 174	Bath Iron Works
*SEALIFT ARCTIC	T-AO 175	Bath Iron Works
*SEALIFT ANTARCTIC	T-AO 176	Bath Iron Works

Displacement, tons: approx 27 000 deadweight
Dimensions, feet (metres): 587 oa × 84 × 34·4 (*178·9 × 25·6 × 10·5*)
Main engines: 2 Turbo-charged diesels; 14 000 bhp; 1 shaft (controllable-pitch propeller) = 16 knots
Complement: 30 + 2 Maritime Academy cadets

Relatively small tankers built specially for long term-charter by the Military Sealift Command. T-AO 168 launched in 1973 on 13 Oct; other launched in 1974 on 26 Jan, 20 April, 27 July, 26 Jan, 9 March, 8 June, 31 Aug and 26 Oct respectively. Commissioned 1974-1975. Operated for MSC by commercial firms with civilian crews.
Fitted with bow thruster to assist docking; automated engine room. Approximately 25 000 tons deadweight; cargo capacity 220 000 barrels. Estimated cost $146 500 000 for the nine-ship class.

SEALIFT ANTARCTIC (T-AO 176)   *1975, United States Navy*

SEALIFT PACIFIC (T-AO 168)   *1974, United States Navy*

1 TANKER (AO): "EXPLORER" TYPE

Name	No.	Builders
*AMERICAN EXPLORER	T-AO 165	Ingalls SB Co, Pascagoula

Displacement, tons: 22 525 deadweight
Dimensions, feet (metres): 615 oa × 80 × 32 (*187·5 × 24·4 × 9·8*)
Main engines: Steam turbines; 22 000 shp; 1 shaft = 20 knots

T5-S-RM2A type. Laid down on 9 July 1957; launched on 11 Apr 1958. Built for the Maritime Administration, but acquired by Military Sea Transportation Service. Cargo capacity 190 300 barrels.
Operated for Military Sealift Command by commercial firm.

AMERICAN EXPLORER (T-AO 165)   *United States Navy*

5 TANKERS (AO): "MISSION" CLASS

Name	No.	Builders	Commissioned
TALLULAH (ex-*Valley Forge*)	T-AO 50	Sun SB & DD Co, Chester	5 Sep 1942
MILLICOMA (ex-*Conastoga*, ex-*King's Mountain*)	T-AO 73	Sun SB & DD Co, Chester	5 Mar 1943
SAUGATUCK (ex-*Newton*)	T-AO 75	Sun SB & DD Co, Chester	19 Feb 1943
SCHUYLKILL (ex-*Louisburg*)	T-AO 76	Sun SB & DD Co, Chester	9 April 1943
MISSION SANTA YNEZ	T-AO 134	Marine Ship Corp, Sausalito	(see notes)

Displacement, tons: 5 730 light; 22 380 full load
Dimensions, feet (metres): 503 wl; 523·5 oa × 68 × approx 30 *(159·6 × 20·7 × 9·2)*
Main engines: Turbo-electric drive; 6 000 shp except *Mission Santa Ynez* 10 000 shp; 1 shaft = 15 knots (except *Mission Santa Ynez* 16 knots)
Boilers: 2 (Babcock & Wilcox)

T2-SE-A1 tankers begun as merchant ships but acquired by Navy and completed as fleet oilers (AO) except the *Mission Santa Ynez* of T2-SE-A2 type delivered as merchant tanker on 13 March 1944 and subsequently acquired by Navy on 22 Oct 1947. During the post World War II period, all of these ships were employed in the tanker role, carrying petroleum point-to-point. Launched on 25 June 1942, 21 Jan 1943, 7 Dec 1942, 16 Feb 1943 and 19 Dec 1943 respectively. Cargo capacity approximately 134 000 barrels.
All of these ships were laid up in reserve during 1975.

SCHUYLKILL (T-AO 76)   *United States Navy*

Photographs: The *Mission Santa Ynez* is shown at deep draft with a full cargo; the *Schuylkill*, empty of cargo, rides high in the water.

MISSION SANTA YNEZ (T-AO 134)

United States Navy

3 TANKERS (AO): "MAUMEE" CLASS

Name	No.	Builders	Commissioned
*MAUMEE	T-AO 149	Ingalls SB Co, Pascagoula	Dec 1956
*SHOSHONE	T-AO 151	Sun SB & DD Co, Chester	Apr 1957
*YUKON	T-AO 152	Ingalls SB Co, Pascagoula	May 1957

Displacement, tons: 25 000 deadweight
Dimensions, feet (metres): 591 wl; 620 oa × 83·5 × 32 *(189·0 × 25·5 × 9·8)*
Main engines: Geared turbine; 20 460 shp; 1 shaft = 18 knots

Yukon laid down 16 May 1955, launched 16 March 1956; *Maumee* laid down 8 Mar 1955, launched 16 Feb 1956; *Shoshone* laid down 15 Aug 1955, launched 17 Jan 1957, T5-S-12A type. *Potomac* T-AO 150 sank after explosion in 1961, but was rebuilt in 1963-1964; see previous listing for *Potomac* (T-AO 181). Cargo capacity 203 216 barrels.
Maumee provided with ice-strengthened bow during 1969-1970 modification at Norfolk SB & DD Co; employed in transporting petroleum products to Antarctica in support of US scientific endeavours.
These ships are operated for the Military Sealift Command by commercial firms.

SHOSHONE (T-AO 151)

United States Navy

3 GASOLINE TANKERS (AOG): "PECONIC" CLASS

Name	No.	Builders
*RINCON	T-AOG 77	Todd Shipyards, Houston
*NODAWAY (ex-*Belridge*)	T-AOG 78	Todd Shipyards, Houston
*PETALUMA (ex-*Raccoon Bend*, ex-*Tavispan*)	T-AOG 79	Todd Shipyards, Houston

Displacement, tons: 2 060 light; 6 000 full load
Dimensions, feet (metres): 325·2 oa × 48·2 × 19·1 *(99·1 × 14·7 × 5·8)*
Main engines: Diesel; 1 400 bhp; 1 shaft = 10 knots

T1-M-BT2 gasoline tankers. Launched as merchant tankers on 5 Jan 1945, 15 May 1945 and 9 Aug 1945 respectively. All acquired by Navy in 1950 and assigned to Military Sea Transportation Service and employed in point-to-point carrying of petroleum. Cargo capacity approximately 30 000 barrels.
These are the only survivors in US service of a once large number of small gasoline tankers. Several survive in foreign navies.

RINCON (T-AOG 77)   *United States Navy*

PETALUMA (T-AOG 79)   *United States Navy*

CARGO SHIPS: LST TYPE

All of the tank landing ships (LST) configured for point-to-point cargo carrying and operated by the Military Sealift Command have been stricken. In MSC service these ships generally were manned by Japanese and South Korean crews and provided logistic support for US military activities in the Western Pacific. See 1973-1974 and previous editions for T-LST lists and characteristics. Most MSC-operated LSTs were unnamed.

Disposals: (since 1 Jan 1975) LST 47, 230, 287, 491, 566, 579, 607, 613, 623, 629, 649, *Daviess County* (T-LST 692), *Harris County* (T-LST 822), *Orleans Parish* (T-LST 1069 ex-MCS 6), and LST 1072 stricken on 30 June 1975. (An earlier strike notice published for LST 566 was incorrect).T-LST 579, 613, 623, 629, and 649 were scheduled to be transferred to Singapore during 1976.

EXPERIMENTAL, RESEARCH AND SURVEYING SHIPS

1 EXPERIMENTAL SURFACE EFFECT SHIP (SES): AEROJET-GENERAL DESIGN

*SES-100A

Weight, tons: 100 gross
Dimensions, feet (metres): 81·9 oa × 41·9 *(25·0 × 12·8)*
Main/lift engines: 4 gas turbines (Avco-Lycoming) 12 000 hp; three fans for lift and two water-jet propulsion systems = 80+ knots (designed)

Surface effect ship developed by Aerojet-General Corp, and built by Tacoma Boatbuilding Co, Tacoma, Washington, to test feasibility of large SES for naval missions. Christened in July 1971; underway in mid-1972 in competition with the Bell design described below. Aluminium construction with rigid sidewalls to hold cushion or bubble of air. Cargo capacity ten tons (instrumentation during evaluation); provision for crew of four and six observers. Fitted with four TF-35 gas turbine engines, marine version of the T55-L-11A developed for the CH-47C helicopter. The SES-100A is reported to have reached 76 knots on trials.

SES-100A

1972, Aerojet General

1 EXPERIMENTAL SURFACE EFFECT SHIP (SES): BELL AEROSYSTEMS DESIGN

SES-100B

Weight, tons: 100 gross
Dimensions, feet (metres): 78 oa × 35 *(23·8 × 10·7)*
Main engines: 3 gas turbines (Pratt & Whitney); 13 500 hp; 2 semi submerged, super cavitating propellers = 80+ knots
Lift engines: 3 gas turbines (United Aircraft of Canada); 1 500 hp; eight lift fans

Surface effect ship developed by Bell Aerospace Division of the Textron Corp; built at Bell facility in Michoud, Louisiana. Christened on March 6, 1971; underway in Feb 1972 as competitive development platform for Navy.
Aluminium hull with rigid sidewalls to hold cushion or bubble of air. Cargo capacity ten tons (instrumentation during evaluation); provision for crew of four and six observers.
Fitted with three Pratt & Whitney FT-12 gas turbine engines and three United Aircraft of Canada ST-6J-70 gas turbine engines.
The SES-100B is credited with having set an SES speed record of 82·3 knots during trials in 1975.

SES-100B

1974, Bell Aerosystems

SES-100B

1974, Bell Aerosystems

2 SONAR TEST SHIPS (AG): Ex-MINESWEEPERS

Name	No.	Builders	Commissioned
*ALACRITY	AG 520 (ex-MSO 520)	Peterson Builders Inc, Wisconsin	2 Oct 1958
*ASSURANCE	AG 521 (ex-MSO 521)	Peterson Builders Inc, Wisconsin	22 Nov 1958

Displacement, tons: 810 light; 934 full load
Dimensions, feet (metres): 190 oa × 36 × 14·5 *(58·0 × 11·0 × 4·4)*
Guns: Removed
Main engines: 2 diesels (General Motors); 2 700 bhp; 2 shafts (controllable pitch propellers) = 15 knots

Former ocean minesweepers. Launched on 8 June 1957 and 31 Aug 1957. Wood-hulled with non-magnetic engines and fittings. Both ships modified for sonar test activities and redesignated as miscellaneous auxiliaries (AG) on 1 June 1973 and 1 Mar 1973, respectively. Fitted with Towed Acoustic Surveillance System (TASS).

Disposals: *Ability* MSO 519 stricken in 1 Feb 1971.

ASSURANCE (AG 521)

United States America

1 HYDROGRAPHIC RESEARCH SHIP (AG): "VICTORY" CLASS

Name	No.	Builders
*KINGSPORT (ex-*Kingsport Victory*)	T-AG 164	California SB Corp

Displacement, tons: 7 190 light; 10 680 full load
Dimensions, feet (metres): 455 oa × 62 × 22 *(138·7 × 18·9 × 6·7)*
Main engines: Geared turbines; 8 500 shp; 1 shaft = 15·2 knots
Boilers: 2
Complement: 73 (13 officers, 42 men, 15 technicians)

Maritime Administration type VC2-S-AP3. Employed as cargo ship by Military Sea Transportation Service prior to conversion. Name shortened, ship reclassified and converted in 1961-62 by Willamette Iron & Steel Co, Portland, Oregon, into the world's first satellite communications ship, for Project Advent, involving the promotion of a terminal to meet the required military capability for high capacity, world-wide radio communications using high altitude hovering satellites, and the installation of ship-to-shore communications facilities, additional electric power generating equipment, a helicopter landing platform, aerological facilities, and a 30-foot parabolic communication antenna housed in a 53-ft diameter plastic radome abaft the superstructure. Painted white for operations in the tropics. Protect Advent Syncom satellite relay operations were completed in 1966, and *Kingsport* was reassigned to hydrographic research. Antenna sphere now removed.
Note antenna mast on helicopter platform in photograph; exhaust ducts fitted to funnel.
Operated by Military Sealift Command for Naval Electronic Systems Command; civilian manned.

KINGSPORT (T-AG 164)   *United States Navy*

1 EXPERIMENTAL NAVIGATION SHIP (AG): "MARINER" CLASS

Name	No.	Builders	Commissioned
*COMPASS ISLAND (ex-*Garden Mariner*)	AG 153 (ex-YAG 56)	New York SB Corp, NJ	3 Dec 1956

Displacement, tons: 16 076 full load
Dimensions, feet (metres): 529·5 wl; 563 oa × 76 × 29 *(171·6 × 23·2 × 8·8)*
Main engines: Geared turbines (General Electric); 19 250 shp; 1 shaft = 20 knots
Boilers: 2

Originally a "Mariner" class merchant ship (C4-S-1a type). Launched on 24 Oct 1953 and acquired by the Navy on 29 Mar 1956.
Converted by New York Naval Shipyard for the development of the Fleet Ballistic Missile guidance and ship navigation systems. Her mission is to assist in the development and valuation of a navigation system independent of shore-based aids. Navy manned.

COMPASS ISLAND (AG 153)   *United States Navy*

1 POSEIDON TEST SHIP (AG): "MARINER" CLASS

Name	No.	Builders	Commissioned
OBSERVATION ISLAND (ex-*Empire State Mariner*)	AG 154 (ex-YAG 57)	New York SB Corp, NJ	5 Dec 1958

Displacement, tons: 17 600 full load
Dimensions, feet (metres): 529·5 wl; 563 oa × 76 × 29 *(171·6 × 23·2 × 8·8)*
Main engines: Geared turbines (General Electric); 19 250 shp; 1 shaft = 20 knots
Boilers: 2
Complement: 350

Built as a "Mariner" class merchant ship (C4-S-1A type); launched on 15 Aug 1953; acquired by the Navy on 10 Sep 1956 for use as a Fleet Ballistic Missile (FBM) test ship. Converted at Norfolk Naval Shipyard.
Fitted to test fire Polaris and later Poseidon missiles. Navy manned. Decommissioned on 25 Sep 1972 and placed in Maritime Administration reserve; remains in Navy List.

Missile Testing: The ship is fitted with complete missile testing, servicing and firing systems. She fired the first ship-launched Polaris missile at sea on 27 Aug 1959. Refitted to fire the improved Poseidon missile in 1969 and launched the first Poseidon test missile fired afloat on 16 Dec 1969.

Disposals: *Flyer* (T-AG 178) stricken on 17 July 1975; see 1975-1976 and previous editions for characteristics.

OBSERVATION ISLAND (AG 154)

1971, United States Navy

1 HYDROFOIL RESEARCH SHIP (AGEH): "PLAINVIEW" TYPE

Name	No.	Builders	In service
*PLAINVIEW	AGEH 1	Lockheed SB & Cons Co, Seattle	1 May 1969

Displacement, tons: 320 full load
Dimensions, feet (metres): 212 oa × 40·5 × 10 (hull borne) or 26 (with foils down) *(64·6 × 12·3 × 3·0 or 7·9)*
A/S weapons: 2 triple torpedo tubes (Mk 32)
Main engines: 2 gas turbines (General Electric); 30 000 hp; 2 diesels; 1 200 = 50 knots
Complement: 20 (6 officers, 14 men)

Aluminium hull experimental hydrofoil. Three retractable foils, 25 ft in height, each weighing 7 tons, fitted port and starboard and on stern, and used in waves up to 15 feet. Initial maximum speed of about 50 knots, with later modifications designed to raise the speed to 80 knots. Fitted with the largest titanium propellers made. The two 15 000 hp gas turbines are General Electric J-79 jet aircraft engines modified for marine use. Power plant and transmission designed to permit future investigation of various types of foils. Laid down on 8 May 1964, launched on 28 June 1965. Delayed because of engineering difficulties. In service *vice* being in commission.

Photographs: The photographs of the *Plainview* show the ship on foils and in displacement condition during experimental transfer of personnel from a CH-46A Sea Knight helicopter.

PLAINVIEW (AGEH 1)   *1972, US Navy, PH2, E. E. Murphy*

PLAINVIEW (AGEH 1)   *1972, US Navy, PH2, E. E. Murphy*

1 RANGE INSTRUMENTATION SHIP (AGM): MODIFIED "VICTORY" CLASS

Name	No.	Builders	Commissioned
*RANGE SENTINEL	T-AGM 22	Permanente Metals Corp,	20 Sep 1944
(ex-*Sherburne*)	(ex-APA 205)	Richmond, Calif	

Displacement, tons: 11 860 full load
Dimensions, feet (metres): 455 oa × 62 *(138.7 × 18.9)*
Main engines: Turbine (Westinghouse); 8 500 hp; 1 shaft = 17.7 knots
Boilers: 2 (Combustion Engineering)
Complement: 95 (14 officers, 54 men, 27 technical personnel)

Former attack transport converted specifically to serve as a range instrumentation ship in support of the Poseidon Fleet Ballistic Missile (FBM) programme. Maritime Administration VC2-S-AP5 type.
Stricken from the Navy List on 1 Oct 1958 and transferred to Maritime Administration reserve fleet; reacquired by the Navy on 22 Oct 1969 for AGM conversion.
Converted from Oct 1969 to Oct 1971; placed in service as T-AGM 22 on 14 Oct 1971. Operated by Military Sealift Command and civilian manned.

RANGE SENTINEL (T-AGM 22)   *1973, United States Navy*

2 RANGE INSTRUMENTATION SHIPS (AGM): "JUMBOISED" T2-SE-A2 TYPE

Name	No.	Builders	Completed
*VANGUARD (ex-*Muscel Shoals*,	T-AGM 19	Marine Ship Corp,	1944
ex-*Mission San Fernando*)	(ex-T-AO 122)	Sausalito, Calif	
*REDSTONE (ex-*Johnstown*,	T-AGM 20	Marine Ship Corp,	1944
ex-*Mission de Pala*)	(ex-T-AO 114)	Sausalito, Calif	

Displacement, tons: 21 626 full load
Dimensions, feet (metres): 595 oa × 75 × 25 *(181.4 × 22.9 × 7.6)*
Main engines: Turbo-electric; 10 000 shp; 1 shaft = 16 knots
Boilers: 2 (Babcock & Wilcox)
Complement: *Vanguard* 19 officers, 71 enlisted men, 108 technical personnel; *Redstone* 20 officers, 71 enlisted men, 120 technical personnel

Former "Mission" class tankers converted in 1964-1966 to serve as mid-ocean communications and tracking ships in support of the Apollo manned lunar flights. Maritime Administration T2-SE-A2 type.
Converted to range instrumentation ships by General Dynamics Corp, Quincy Division, Massachusetts; each ship was cut in half and a 72-foot mid-section was inserted, increasing length, beam, and displacement; approximately 450 tons of electronic equipment installed for support of lunar flight operations, including communications and tracking systems; balloon hangar and platform fitted aft. Cost of converting the three ships was $90 000 000. Operated by Military Sealift Command for Air Force Eastern Test Range in Atlantic *(Vanguard)* and for NASA Goddard Space Flight Center *(Redstone)*. Civilian crews.
Note different bow structure configurations and deck houses.

REDSTONE (T-AGM 20)   *1970, United States Air Force*

VANGUARD (T-AGM 19)   *1967, United States Navy*

2 RANGE INSTRUMENTATION SHIPS (AGM): C4-S-A1 TYPE

Name	No.	Builders	Commissioned
*GENERAL H. H. ARNOLD	T-AGM 9	Kaiser Co, Richmond	17 Aug 1944
(ex-USNS *General R. E. Callan*)	(ex-T-AP 139)	California	
*GENERAL HOYT S. VANDENBERG	T-AGM 10	Kaiser Co, Richmond	1 Apr 1944
(ex-USNS *General Harry Taylor*)	(ex-T-AP 145)	California	

Displacement, tons: 16 600 full load
Dimensions, feet (metres): 552.9 oa × 71.5 × 26.3 *(168.5 × 21.8 × 8.0)*
Main engines: Geared turbines (Westinghouse); 9 000 shp; 1 shaft = 16.5 knots
Boilers: 2 (Babcock & Wilcox)
Complement: 205 (21 officers, 71 men, 113 technical personnel)

Former troop transports converted in 1962-1963 for monitoring Air Force missiles firing and satellite launches. Maritime Administration C4-S-A1 type. Upon conversion to range instrumentation ships they were placed in service in 1963 under Air Force operation, however assigned to MSTS for operation on 1 July 1964 *(Arnold)* and 13 July 1964 *(Vandenberg)*.
Both ships are operated by Military Sealift Command for Air Force Eastern Test Range in Atlantic. Civilian manned.

GEN. HOYT S. VANDENBERG (T-AGM 10)   *United States Navy*

1 RANGE INSTRUMENTATION SHIP (AGM): "VICTORY" CLASS

Name	No.	Builders	Completed
*WHEELING (ex-*Seton-Hall Victory*)	T-AGM 8	Oregon SB Corp, Portland	1944

Displacement, tons: 10 680 full load
Dimensions, feet (metres): 455.3 oa × 62.2 *(138.8 × 19.0)*
Main engines: Geared turbines; 8 500 shp; 1 shaft = 17 knots
Boilers: 2
Complement: 107 (13 officers, 46 men, 48 technical personnel)

The *Wheeling* is the only survivor of a series of "Victory" type military cargo and merchant ships converted to missile range instrumentation ships during the massive US space and missile programmes of the 1960s. Maritime Administration VC2-S-AP3 type. Assigned to Military Sea Transportation Service on 28 May 1964; operated in support of Pacific Missile Range. Fitted with helicopter hangar and platform aft. Employed to test AWG-9 fire control system for use in the F-14 Tomcat fighter aircraft. Civilian manned.

Nomenclature: Range instrumentation ships have several name sources: "Range" names, as *Range Sentinel;* missile programmes, as *Vanguard;* and cities associated with space or missile programmes, as *Wheeling.* Two ships reactivated by the Air Force and briefly operated by that service before being assigned to Military Sealift Command carry the names of the Commanding General of the US Army Air Forces in World War II (Arnold) and the second Chief of Staff of the US Air Force (Vandenberg).

WHEELING (T-AGM 8)   *United States Navy*

1 MAJOR COMMUNICATIONS RELAY SHIP (AGMR): CONVERTED ESCORT CARRIER

Name	*No.*	*Builders*	*Commissioned*
ANNAPOLIS (ex-*Gilbert Islands*)	AGMR 1 (ex-AKV 39, ex-CVE 107)	Todd Shipyards, Tacoma	5 Sep 1945

Displacement, tons: 11 473 standard; 22 500 full load
Dimensions, feet (metres): 525 wl; 563 oa × 75 × 30·6 *(171·6 × 22·9 × 9·3)*
Guns: 8—3 inch *(76 mm)* 50 calibre AA (twin) (Mk 33)
Main engines: 2 turbines (Allis Chalmers); 16 000 shp; 2 shafts = 18 knots
Boilers: 4 (Combustion Engineering)
Complement: 720 (54 officers, 666 enlisted men)

The *Annapolis* was built as the escort aircraft carrier *Gilbert Islands* (CVE 107). She was decommissioned on 21 May 1946 and placed in reserve; again active as a CVE from Sep 1951 to Jan 1955 when she was again decommissioned. While in reserve on 7 May 1959 she was reclassified as a cargo ship and aircraft ferry (AKV 39). Converted into a communications ship by the New York Naval Shipyard, 1962-1964; commissioned as AGMR 1 on 7 Mar 1964. Decommissioned on 20 Dec 1969 and placed in reserve.

Conversion: During conversion the ship was fitted with elaborate communications relay equipment including approximately 30 transmitters providing frequency band coverage from low frequency to ultra-high frequency. The power outputs of the transmitters vary from 10 to 10 000 watts. Numerous radio receivers also were installed as were five large antenna towers. The ship was renamed *Annapolis* and reclassified AGMR 1 on 1 June 1963.
The former escort carrier, *Vella Gulf* (AKV 11, ex-CVHE 111, ex-CVE 111) was to have been converted to the AGMR 2; her conversion never began because of the availability of the larger carrier *Saipan* (CVL 48/AVT 6) for use in this role.

Design: The *Gilbert Islands* was one of 19 "Commencement Bay" class escort carriers built during the latter part of World War II. This ship is the last escort or "jeep" aircraft carrier on the Navy List.

Disposals: The larger *Arlington* (ex-*Saipan*) AGMR 2 (ex-CC 3, ex-AVT 6, ex-CVL 48) stricken on 15 Aug 1975.

ANNAPOLIS (AGMR 1)

1964, United States Navy

ANNAPOLIS (AGMR 1)

1966, United States Navy

2 UTILITY RESEARCH SHIPS (AGOR): "GYRE" CLASS

Name	*No.*	*Builders*	*Delivered*
*GYRE	AGOR 21	Halter Marine Service, New Orleans	14 Nov 1973
*MOANA WAVE	AGOR 22	Halter Marine Service, New Orleans	16 Jan 1974

Displacement, tons: 950 full load
Dimensions, feet (metres): 176 oa × 36 × 14·5 *(53·6 × 11·0 × 4·4)*
Main engines: Turbo-charged diesels (Caterpillar); 1 700 bhp; 2 shafts (controllable pitch propellers) = 13 knots maximum; 12 knots cruising
Complement: 21 (10 crew, 11 scientists)

Laid down on 9 Oct 1972 and 10 Oct 1972 respectively; launched on 25 May 1973 and 18 June 1973. They are based on a commercial ship design. Fitted with a 150 hp retractable propeller pod for low-speed or station keeping with main machinery shut down. Open deck aft provides space for equipment vans to permit rapid change of mission capabilities. Each ship cost approximately $1 900 000.
The Navy plans to construct several of these small, utility oceanographic research ships to replace older and obsolescent ships now operated by civilian research and educational institutions in support of Navy programmes. The above ships are assigned for operation to Texas A & M University and the University of Hawaii, respectively.

GYRE (AGOR 21)

1973, Halter Marine Services

GYRE (AGOR 21)

1973, Halter Marine Services

1 OCEANOGRAPHIC RESEARCH SHIP (AGOR): "HAYES" TYPE

Name	No.	Builders
*HAYES	T-AGOR 16	Todd Shipyards,Seattle

Displacement, tons: 3 080 full load
Dimensions, feet (metres): 220 wl; 246·5 oa × 75 (see *Design* notes) × 18·8 *(75·1 × 22·9 × 5·7)*
Main engines: Geared diesels; 5 400 bhp; 2 shafts (controllable pitch propeller) = 15 knots
Complement: 74 (11 officers, 33 men, 30 scientists)

The *Hayes* is one of two classes of modern US naval ships to have a catamaran hull, the other being the ASR 21 class submarine rescue ships. Laid down 12 Nov 1969; launched 2 July 1970, completed late in 1971. Estimated cost was $15 900 000.
Operated by the Military Sealift Command for the Office of Naval Research under the Technical control of the Oceanographer of the Navy; civilian crew.

Design: Catamaran hull design provides large deck working area, centre well for operating equipment at great depths, and removes laboratory areas from main propulsion machinery. Each hull is 246·5 feet long and 24 feet wide (maximum). There are three 36-inch diameter instrument wells in addition to the main centre well.
The T-AGOR 16 differs in appearance from the ASR 21 class ships by the oceanographic ship having a small deck working space aft of the bridge structure and the absence of stern helicopter platform of the rescue ships.

Engineering: An auxiliary 165-bhp diesel is fitted in each hull to provide "creeping" speed of 2 to 4 knots. Separation of controllable pitch propellers by catamaran hull separation provides high degree of manoeuverability eliminating the need for bow thrusters.
Range is 6 000 miles at 13·5 knots.

Nomenclature: Oceanographic research ships and surveying ships generally are named for naval oceanographers, hydrographers, and explorers. (Converted ships generally retain original names).
The AGOR 16 is named for Dr. Harvey C. Hayes of the Naval Research Laboratory, known as the "father of sonar in the US Navy".

HAYES (T-AGOR 16)　　　　　　　　　　　　　　　　　　1971, Todd Shipyards Corp

HAYES (T-AGOR 16)　　　　　　　　　　　　　　　　1971, US Navy, William Connick

2 OCEANOGRAPHIC RESEARCH SHIPS (AGOR): "MELVILLE" CLASS

Name	No.	Builders	Delivered
*MELVILLE	AGOR 14	Defoe SB Co, Bay City, Mich	27 Aug 1969
*KNORR	AGOR 15	Defoe SB Co, Bay City, Mich	14 Jan 1970

Displacement, tons: 1 915 standard; 2 080 full load
Dimensions, feet (metres): 244·9 × 46·3 × 15
Main engines: Diesel; 2 500 bhp; 2 cycloidal propellers = 12·5 knots
Complement: 50 (9 officers, 16 men, 25 scientists)

Oceanographic research ships of an advanced design. AGOR 19 and AGOR 20 of this type in FY 1968 programme, but construction of the latter ships was cancelled. These ships are fitted with internal wells for lowering equipment; underwater lights and observation ports. Range is 10 000 miles at 12 knots. Facilities for handling small research submersibles.
The *Melville* and *Knorr* laid down on 12 July 1967 and 9 Aug 1967 respectively; launched 10 July 1968 and 21 Aug 1968. *Melville* operated by Scripps Institution of Oceanography and *Knorr* by Woods Hole Oceanography Institution for the Office of Naval Research; under technical control of the Oceanographer of the Navy.

Engineering: First US Navy ocean-going ships with cycloidal propellers permitting the ships to turn 360 degrees in their own length. One propeller is fitted at each end of the ship, providing movement in any direction and optimum station keeping without use of thrusters. They have experienced engineering difficulties.

MELVILLE (AGOR 14)　　　　　　　　　　　　　　　　1969, Defoe Shipbuilding

7 OCEANOGRAPHIC RESEARCH SHIPS (AGOR): "CONRAD" CLASS

Name	No.	Builders	Delivered
*ROBERT D. CONRAD	AGOR 3	Gibbs Corp, Jacksonville	29 Nov 1962
*JAMES M. GILLISS	T-AGOR 4	Christy Corp, Sturgeon Bay	5 Nov 1962
*LYNCH	T-AGOR 7	Marinette Mfg Co, Point Pleasant	22 Oct 1965
*THOMAS G. THOMPSON	AGOR 9	Marinette Marine Corp, Wisc	4 Sep 1965
*THOMAS WASHINGTON	AGOR 10	Marinette Marine Corp, Wisc	17 Sep 1965
*DE STEIGUER	T-AGOR 12	Northwest Marine Iron Works, Portland, Oregon	28 Feb 1969
*BARTLETT	T-AGOR 13	Northwest Marine Iron Works, Portland, Oregon	15 Apr 1969

Displacement, tons: varies; approx 1 200 standard; 1 380 full load
Dimensions, feet (metres): 191·5 wl; 208·9 oa × 37·4 × 15·3 *(63·7 × 11·4 × 4·7)*
Main engines: Diesel-electric (Caterpillar Tractor Co diesels); 10 000 bhp; 1 shaft = 13·5 knots
Complement: 41 (9 officers, 17 men, 15 scientists except *De Steiguer* and *Bartlett*, 8 officers, 18 men)

This is the first class of ships designed and built by the US Navy for oceanographic research. Fitted with instrumentation and laboratories to measure the earth's gravity and magnetic fields, water temperature, sound transmission in water, and the geological profile of the ocean floor. Special features include 10 ton capacity boom and winches for handling over-the-side equipment; bow thruster propulsion unit for precise manoeuvrability and station keeping; 620 hp gas turbine (housed in funnel structure) for providing "quiet" power when conducting operations in which use of main engines would generate too high a noise level (gas turbine also can drive the ship at 6·5 knots). Range is 12 000 miles at 12 knots.

Robert D. Conrad laid down on 19 Jan 1961 and launched on 26 May 1962. Operated by Lamont Geological Observatory of Columbia University under technical control of the Oceanographer of the Navy.
James H. Gilliss laid down on 31 May 1961 and launched on 19 May 1962. Operated by the University of Miami (Florida) since 1970 in support of Navy programmes.
Lynch laid down on 7 Sep 1962 and launched on 17 Mar 1964. Operated by Military Sealift Command under the technical control of the Oceanographer of the Navy; civilian crew.
Thomas G. Thompson laid down on 12 Sep 1963 and launched on 18 July 1964. Operated by University of Washington (state) under technical control of the Oceanographer of the Navy; civilian crew.
Thomas Washington laid down on 12 Sep 1963 and launched on 1 Aug 1964. Operated by Scripps Institution of Oceanography (University of California) under technical control of the Oceanographer on the Navy; civilian crew.
De Steiguer and *Bartlett* laid down on 12 Nov 1965 and 18 Nov 1965 and launched on 21 Mar 1966 and 24 May 1966. Operated by Military Sealift Command under the technical control of the Oceanographer of the Navy; civilian crew.

Transfers: Ships of this class are in service with Brazil and New Zealand.

Photographs: Note differences in details; *Gilliss* has flat bridge face, *Thompson* has side structure amidships, and *Lynch* has tripod mast forward.

JAMES M. GILLISS (T-AGOR 4)

United States Navy

THOMAS G. THOMPSON (AGOR 9)

United States Navy

LYNCH (T-AGOR 7)

1974, Giorgio Arra

1 OCEANOGRAPHIC RESEARCH SHIP (AGOR): Ex-SALVAGE SHIP

Name	No.	Builders	Commissioned
*CHAIN	AGOR 17 (ex-ARS 20)	Basalt Rock Co, Napa	31 Mar 1944

Displacement, tons: 2 100 full load
Dimensions, feet (metres): 207 wl; 213·5 oa × 39 × 15 *(65·1 × 11·9 × 4·6)*
Main engines: Diesel-electric (4 Cooper Bessemer diesels); approx 3 000 bhp; 2 shafts = 14 knots
Complement: 29 + 26 scientists

Converted from a salvage ship for oceanographic research. Launched on 3 June 1943. Commission date as ARS. Converted to an oceanographic research ship by Savannah Machine & Foundry in 1958. Fitted with an auxiliary 250 hp outboard propulsion unit for manoeuvering at low speeds (up to 4·5 knots). The *Chain* is operated by the Woods Hole Oceanographic Institution for the Office of Naval Research under the technical control of the Oceanographer of the Navy. Civilian crew.

1 OCEANOGRAPHIC RESEARCH SHIP (AGOR): Ex-CARGO SHIP

Name	No.	Builders	Delivered
*MIZAR	T-AGOR 11 (ex-T-AK 272)	Avondale Marine Ways, New Orleans	22 Nov 1957

Displacement, tons: 2 036 light; 4 942 full load
Dimensions, feet (metres): 256·8 wl; 262·2 oa × 51·5 × 22·8 *(79·9 × 15·7 × 7·0)*
Main engines: Diesel-electric (ALCO diesels, Westinghouse electric motors) 3 200 bhp; 2 shafts = 12 knots
Complement: 56 (11 officers, 30 enlisted men, 15 scientists)

Built for Military Sea Transportation Service. Designed for Arctic operation with hull strengthened against ice. C1-ME2-13a type. Delivered as cargo ship to MSTS and subsequently converted to oceanographic research ship.
As research ship the *Mizar* is operated by the Military Sealift Command for Naval Research Laboratory, under technical control of the Oceanographer of the Navy; civilian crew. The *Eltanin* (T-AGOR 8) of this type is in Argentine service.

Conversion: *Mizar* converted in 1962 into deep sea research ship. Equipped with centre well for lowering oceanographic equipment including towed sensor platforms, fitted with laboratories and elaborate photographic facilities, hydrophone system and computer for seafloor navigation and tracking towed vehicles. The *Mizar* had key roles in the searches for the US nuclear submarines *Thresher* and *Scorpion*; the French submarine *Eurydice*; and recovery of the H-bomb lost at sea off Palomares, Spain.

Photographs: Note the enclosed crow's nest on the forward mast, a feature provided for arctic cargo operations. Compare with view of the *Mirfak* (T-AK 271) on an earlier page of this edition.

MIZAR (T-AGOR 11)

1973, Wright & Logan

OCEANOGRAPHIC RESEARCH CRAFT

The Navy also owns a number of smaller oceanographic research craft that are operated by various educational and research institutions in support of Navy programmes; under technical control of the Oceanographer of the Navy; no Navy hull numbers are assigned; all are 100 feet in length or smaller except for the *Lamb*, a converted 136-foot minesweeper (YMS/AMS type) operated by the Lamont Geophysical Laboratory.

(12) OCEAN SURVEILLANCE SHIPS (AGOS)

One ship	T-AGOS	Planned Fiscal Year 1978 programme
Two ships	T-AGOS	Planned FY 1979 programme
Five ships	T-AGOS	Planned FY 1980 programme
Four ships	T-AGOS	Planned FY 1981 programme

The Navy plans to construct 12 ocean surveillance ships to operate the new SURTASS (Surface Towed Array Surveillance System). These ships will have a hull design similar to the fleet tugs (T-ATF) now under construction, but will be specially configured for the ocean surveillance mission. They will be operated by the Military Sealift Command, apparently with civilian crews and Navy personnel to operate the classified SURTASS equipment.
Estimated cost of the lead ship in the FY 1978 shipbuilding programme is $29 100 000.

1 SURVEYING SHIP (AGS): MERCHANT TYPE

Name	No.
ex-*Canada Mail*	T-AGS 37

Displacement, tons: 14 747 deadweight
Dimensions, feet (metres): 564 oa × 76 × 32·7 *(171·9 × 23·2 × 10·0)*
Main engines: Geared turbines; 19 250 shp; 1 shaft = 20 knots
Boilers: 2

Merchant ship acquired by the Navy in 1975 for conversion to replace the "Victory" class surveying ship *Michelson* (T-AGS 23). Above data as merchant ship. As a hydrographic survey ship she will be operated by the Military Sealift Command for the Oceanographer of the Navy with a civilian crew.

ex-CANADA MAIL

1 SURVEYING SHIP (AGS): C1-M-AV1 TYPE

Name	No.	Builders
COASTAL CRUSADER	T-AGS 36 (ex-*T-AGM 16*)	Leatham D. Smith SB Co

Dimensions, feet (metres): 338·8 oa × 50·3 × 12 *(103·3 × 15·3 × 3·7)*
Main engines: Diesel; 1 750 bhp; 1 shaft = 11·5 knots

Built in 1945. Acquired for conversion to a missile range tracking ship by US Air Force; transferred to Military Sea Transportation service as T-AGM 16 on 1 July 1964.
Reclassified as a surveying ship (T-AGS 36) on 1 Dec 1969 but taken out of service and placed in reserve prior to operation as an AGS; laid up in Maritime Administration reserve but remains on the Navy List.

Conversion: The *Coastal Crusader* has been under consideration for conversion to a laser research ship. In that role she would provide a platform for fleet evaluation of high-energy lasers in the air defence role.

COASTAL CRUSADER T-AGS 36 (as T-AGM 16)   *United States Navy*

2 SURVEYING SHIPS (AGS): "CHAUVENET" CLASS

Name	No.	Builders	Delivered
*CHAUVENET	T-AGS 29	Upper Clyde Shipbuilders, Glasgow	13 Nov 1970
HARKNESS	T-AGS 32	Upper Clyde Shipbuilders, Glasgow	29 Jan 1971

Displacement, tons: 4 200 full load
Dimensions, feet (metres): 393·2 oa × 54 × 16 *(119·8 × 16·5 × 4·9)*
Main engines: Diesel (Westinghouse); 3 600 bhp; 1 shaft = 15 knots
Complement: 175 (13 officers, approx 150 men and technical personnel, 12 scientists)

These are large research ships capable of extensive military hydrographic and oceanographic surveys, supporting coastal surveying craft, amphibious survey teams and helicopters. Fitted with two helicopter hangars and platform.
Chauvenet authorised in Fiscal Year 1965 new construction programme; *Harkness* in FY 1966 programme. Laid down on 24 May 1967 and 30 June 1967 respectively; launched on 13 May 1968 and 12 June 1968
These ships are operated by the Military Sealift Command for the Oceanographer of the Navy with Navy detachments on board. Civilian crews.
Harkness laid up in ready reserve.

CHAUVENET (T-AGS 29)   *1971, United States Navy*

CHAUVENET (T-AGS 29)   *United States Navy*

4 SURVEYING SHIPS (AGS): "BENT" CLASS

Name	No.	Builders	Delivered	
*SILAS BENT	T-AGS 26	American SB Co, Lorain	23 July	1965
*KANE	T-AGS 27	Christy Corp, Sturgeon Bay	19 May	1967
WILKES	T-AGS 33	Defoe SB Co, Bay City, Mich	28 June	1971
*WYMAN	T-AGS 34	Defoe SB Co, Bay City, Mich	3 Nov	1971

Displacement, tons: 1 935 standard; *Silas Bent* and *Kane* 2 558 full load; *Wilkes* 2 540 full load; *Wyman* 2 420 full load
Dimensions, feet (metres): 285·3 oa × 48 × 15·1 *(87·0 × 14·6 × 4·6)*
Main engines: Diesel-electric (Westinghouse diesels); 3 600 bhp; 1 shaft = 14 knots
Complement: 77 to 79 (12 or 13 officers, 35 or 36 men, 30 scientists)

These ships were designed specifically for surveying operations. Special features include seafloor mapping equipment; bow propulsion unit for precise manoeuvrability and station keeping. All four ships operated by Military Sealift Command for the Oceanographer of the Navy; civilian crews.
Laid down on 2 Mar 1964, 19 Dec 1964, 18 July 1968 and 18 July 1968 respectively; launched on 16 May 1964, 20 Nov 1965, 31 July 1969 and 30 Oct 1969.
Wilkes laid up in ready reserve.

WILKES (T-AGS 33)　　　　　　　　　　1971, United States Navy

WYMAN (T-AGS 34)　　　　　　　　　　1971, United States Navy

2 SURVEYING SHIPS (AGS): "VICTORY" CLASS

Name	No.	Builders
*BOWDITCH	T-AGS 21	Oregon SB Co.
(ex-SS *South Bend Victory*)		
*DUTTON	T-AGS 22	South Coast Co, Newport Beach
(ex-SS *Tuskegee Victory*)		

Displacement, tons: 4 512 full load
Dimensions, feet (metres): 455·2 oa × 62·2 × 25 *(138·7 × 19·0 × 7·6)*
Main engines: Geared turbine; 8 500 shp; 1 shaft = 15 knots
Boilers: 2
Complement: 100 to 101 (13 or 14 officers, 47 men, approx 40 technical personnel)

VC2-S-AP3 type ships. Converted to support the Fleet Ballistic Missile Programme, *Dutton* at Philadelphia Naval Shipyard 8 Nov 1957 to 16 Nov 1958 and *Bowditch* at Charleston Naval Shipyard 10 Oct 1957 to 30 Sep 1958.
Designed to chart the ocean floor and to record magnetic fields and gravity.
Operated by Military Sealift Command for the Oceanographer of the Navy; civilian crews.

Disposals: *Michelson* (T-AGS 23) stricken on 15 April 1975.

DUTTON (T-AGS 22)　　　　　　　　　　United States Navy

1 GUIDED MISSILE SHIP (AVM): CONVERTED SEAPLANE TENDER

Name	No.	Builders	Commissioned
*NORTON SOUND	AVM 1	Los Angeles SB & DD Co,	8 Jan 1945
	(ex-AV 11)	San Pedro	

Displacement, tons: 9 106 standard; 15 170 full load
Dimensions, feet (metres): 543·25 oa × 71·6 × 23·5 *(165·6 × 21·8 × 7·2)*
Missile launchers: 1 twin Standard surface-to-air launcher (Mk 26)
Machinery: Geared turbines (Allis-Chalmers); 12 000 shp; 2 shafts = 19 knots
Boilers: 4 (Babcock & Wilcox)
Complement: approx 300

The *Norton Sound* is a seagoing laboratory and test centre for advanced weapon systems. Constructed as a seaplane tender of the "Currituck" class (AV 7); laid down 7 Sep 1942, launched 28 Nov 1943. After operating briefly in the Pacific War and afterward as a seaplane tender, in 1948 the *Norton Sound* was converted to a guided missile test ship. (See *Conversion* notes).
The *Norton Sound* has subsequently served as test ship for a number of research and weapon programmes, and is currently employed as a test platform for the Aegis advanced fleet defence system.

Classification: Changed from AV 11 to AVM 1 on 8 Aug 1951.

Conversion: The *Norton Sound* was initially fitted as a guided missile (test) ship in 1948 during a seven-month conversion at the Philadelphia Naval Shipyard; 30-ton capacity boom removed from fantail (similar boom retained on hangar structure); helicopter deck provided forward; provision for fuelling, checking out, monitoring, and firing rockets and missiles.
Converted from November 1962 to June 1964 at Maryland SB & DD Co, Baltimore, Maryland, to test ship for the Typhon advanced weapons control system (intended for a new class of nuclear-powered guided missile cruisers); Typhon system removed in July 1966.
Modified in 1974 to serve as test ship for the Aegis advanced fleet defence system. SPY-1 paired radar arrays to provide 180° coverage (12 × 12 foot, six-sided "faces") installed atop forward superstructure; Mk 110 radar control system installed (including five UYK-7 computers to control phase steering of radars). The full Aegis system, as planned in warships, would have four radar "faces" to provide 360° coverage. Twin Standard surface-to-air missile launcher fitted on stern. SPS-52 radar also fitted.

NORTON SOUND (AVM 1)　　　　　　　　1974, United States Navy

Gunnery: Fitted in 1968 with light-weight 5 inch 54 calibre gun and associated Mk 86 gunfire control system for operational test and evaluation. See 1973-1974 edition for photograph showing gun installation.
(Original armament consisted of 4—5 inch guns (two single mounts forward and two single mounts atop hangar), and 20—40 mm AA guns (three, quad, four twin). Forward guns removed to provide space or helicopter deck; all other original armament subsequently removed).

Missiles: Missiles and rockets test fired from the *Norton Sound* include the Aerobee, Loon (US version of the German V-1 "buzz bomb"), Lark, Regulus, Terrier, Tartar, and Sea Sparrow. During Project Argus in 1958 from a position south of the Falkland Islands the *Norton Sound* launched three multi-stage missiles carrying low-yield nuclear warheads which were detonated approximately 300 miles above the earth. (The ship was also used to launch high-altitude balloons in Project Skyhook during 1949).

Nomenclature: Seaplane tenders were named for bodies of water. Norton Sound is the largest Alaskan sound.

Photographs: Note mast and TACAN pod atop large crane on hangar structure; lattice radar mast atop bridge structure and pole radar mast amidships. The six-sided fixed radar antenna on the forward super-structure is "real" on the port side and a "dummy" on the starboard side. A starboard-view showing the Standard SAM launcher aft taken in 1973 appears in the 1974-1975 edition.

1 TEST RANGE SUPPORT SHIP (IX): CONVERTED LSMR

Name	No.	Builders	Commissioned
*ELK RIVER	IX 501 (ex-LSMR 501)	Brown SB Co, Houston	27 May 1945

Displacement, tons: 1 100 full load
Dimensions, feet (metres): 225 oa × 50 × 9·2 *(68·6 × 15·2 × 2·8)*
Main engines: Diesels; 1 400 bhp; 2 shafts = 11 knots
Complement: 25 + 20 technical personnel

The *Elk River* is a former rocket landing ship specifically converted to support Navy deep submergence activities on the San Clemente Island Range off the coast of southern California. Launched 21 April 1945.
The ship is capable of supporting the following activities (1) deep diving for man-in-the-sea programmes, (2) deep diving for salvage programmes, (3) submersible test and evaluation, (4) underwater equipment testing, and (5) deep mooring operations. Operated by combined Navy-civilian crew.
This is the only LSMR-type ship remaining on the Navy List.

Conversion: The *Elk River* was withdrawn from the Reserve Fleet and converted to a range support ship in 1967-1968 at Avondale Shipyards Inc, Westwego, Louisiana, and the San Francisco Bay Naval Shipyard.
The basic LSMR hull was lengthened and eight-foot sponsons were added to either side to increase deck working space and stability; superstructure added forward. An open centre well was provided to facilitate lowering and raising equipment; also fitted with 65-ton-capacity gantry crane (on tracks) to handle submersibles and active positioning mooring system to hold ship in precise location without elaborate mooring and permit shifting within the moor. Five anchors including bow anchor. Fitted with prototype Mk 2 Deep Diving System (see "Pigeon" class submarine rescue ships).

ELK RIVER (IX 501)   *1968, United States Navy*

ELK RIVER (IX 501)   *1968, United States Navy*

TORPEDO TEST SHIP (IX): Ex-CARGO SHIP

Name	No.
*NEW BEDFORD	IX 308 (ex-AKL 17, ex-FS 289)

Displacement, tons: approx 700
Dimensions, feet (metres): 176·5 oa × 32·8 × 10 *(53·8 × 10·0 × 3·1)*
Main engines: Diesel; 1 000 bhp; 1 shaft = 10 knots

Former Army cargo ship (freight and supply) acquired by Navy on 1 Mar 1950 for cargo work and subsequently converted to support torpedo testing. Operated since 1963 by Naval Torpedo Station, Keyport, Washington. Other craft serving in this role are described in the section on Service Craft (YFRT type).

NEW BEDFORD (IX 308)   *1973, United States Navy*

1 INSTRUMENTATION PLATFORM (IX): Ex-BUOY TENDER

Name	No.
*BRIER	IX 307 (ex-WLI 299)

Displacement, tons: 178
Dimensions, feet (metres): 100 × 24 × 4·5 *(30·1 × 7·3 × 1·4)*
Machinery: Diesel with electric drive; 300 bhp; 2 shafts = 8·5 knots

Former Coast Guard buoy tender built in 1943; acquired by the Navy on 10 Mar 1969 for use as instrument platform for explosive testing; redesignated IX 307 on 29 Aug 1970.

TEST AND EVALUATION SHIP (TES)

The Navy has developed the initial design for a Test and Evaluation Ship (TES) to provide a sea-going platform for the test and evaluation of future ship systems. The TES concept design sought to provide: (1) maximum flexibility in order to accept new systems with minimum modifications, (2) extensive use of modular concepts, (3) extensive use of quick-acting interface connections between the ship and test system, (4) a speed of 25 knots on two shafts plus a centreline shaft for testing prototype propulsion plants and propellers, and (5) power and other "hotel" services to meet projected requirements for the next 20 years.
Planning for future construction of a TES was halted early in 1975.

1 TORPEDO TEST SHIP (IX): Ex-CARGO SHIP

*IX 306 (ex-FS 221)

Displacement, tons: 906 full load
Dimensions, feet (metres): 179 oa × 33 × 10 *(54·6 × 10·1 × 3·1)*
Main engines: Diesel; 1 shaft = 12 knots

Former Army cargo ship (freight and supply) acquired by the Navy in January 1966 and subsequently converted to a weapon test ship, being placed in service late in 1969. Conducts research for the Naval Underwater Weapons Research and Engineering Station, Newport, Rhode Island; operates in Atlantic Underwater Test and Evaluation Centre (AUTEC) range in Caribbean. Manned by Navy and civilian RCA personnel. Note white hull with blue bow and torpedo tube opening on starboard side just aft of hull number.

IX 306

1969, United States Navy

2 RESEARCH SHIPS (MSI): Ex-MINESWEEPERS

Name	No.	Builders	In service	
*COVE	MSI 1	Bethlehem Shipyards Co, Bellingham	20 Nov	1958
*CAPE	MSI 2	Bethlehem Shipyards Co, Bellingham	27 Feb	1959

Displacement, tons: 120 light; 240 full load
Dimensions, feet (metres): 105 × 22 × 10 *(32·0 × 6·7 × 3·0)*
Guns: Removed
Main engines: Diesel (General Motors); 650 bhp; 1 shaft = 12 knots
Complement: 21 (3 officers, 18 men)

These ships were prototype inshore minesweepers (MSI) authorised under the Fiscal Year 1956 new construction programme. Both built at Bethlehem Shipyards Co, Bellingham, Washington. *Cape* laid down on 1 May 1957 and launched on 5 April 1968; *Cove* laid down 1 Feb 1957 and launched 8 Feb 1958.
The *Cape* is operated by the Naval Undersea Research Development Center, San Diego, California; neither in service nor in commission. *Cove* transferred to Johns Hopkins Applied Physics Laboratory on 31 July 1970; she remains on the Navy List. Both conduct Navy research.

CAPE (MSI 2)

1968, United States Navy

MISCELLANEOUS

1 PRESIDENTIAL YACHT (AG)

Name	No.	Builders
*SEQUOIA	AG 23	Mathias Yacht & SB Co, Camden, NJ

Displacement, tons: approx 110
Dimensions, feet (metres): 99 wl; 104 oa × 18·2 × 4·5 *(31·7 × 5·5 × 1·4)*
Main engines: Diesels (Winton); 400 bhp; 2 shafts = 11·5 knots
Complement: 21 (1 officer, 20 enlisted men; accommodation for only 14 of crew)
Passengers: accommodation for 7 under normal conditions

Small motor yacht built in 1925; acquired by the Navy on 25 Mar 1933.

SEQUOIA (AG 23)

United States Navy

1 SAIL FRIGATE

Name	No.	Launched
*CONSTITUTION	(ex-IX 21)	21 Oct 1797

The oldest ship of the US Navy remaining on the Navy List. "In service" status as a relic at Boston. Periodically she is taken out into Boston Harbor and "turned around".
The *Constitution* began an extensive, $4 200 000 overhaul in April 1973 at the Boston Naval Shipyard; completed in early 1975. The "unclassified" designation IX 21, assigned to the *Constitution* on 8 Jan 1941, was dropped on 1 Sep 1975. She is believed the only ship on the Navy List without a hull number (Military Sealift Command ships are listed separately). Characteristics and photograph appear in the 1970-1971 edition.
The sailing ship *Constellation*, which survives under private ownership at Baltimore, Maryland, is apparently the last sailing man-of-war built for the US Navy; she was constructed at the Norfolk (Virginia) Navy Yard in 1853-1854, built in part with materiél from the earlier frigate *Constellation* (launched 1797).

The classification **IX 310** has been assigned to a group of barges used at the Naval Underwater Sound Laboratory, Newport, Rhode Island.

The *Guardian* (ex-PT 809) transferred to Fleet Composite Support Squadron 6 at Little Creek, Virginia, in December 1974 for use as recovery boat for aerial targets and control boat surface target drone craft; designated DR-1 in July 1975. Formerly employed as guard boat for presidential yacht. She is the last motor torpedo boat in US Navy service (built in 1950).

The *Athena* (ex-*Chehalis*, PG 94) stripped of armament and assigned as research craft to Naval Ship Research & Development Center, Annapolis, Maryland; renamed on 21 Aug 1975 (no hull numbers assigned). See "Asheville" class (PG 86) patrol combatants for characteristics and photographs.

DR-1 (ex-GUARDIAN)

1975, Giorgio Arra

SERVICE CRAFT

The US Navy operates several hundred service craft, primarily small craft that provide services to the Fleet in harbours and ports. Only the self-propelled craft are listed here. In addition, there are hundreds of non-self-propelled barge-like craft for carrying cargo, floating cranes, dredges, workshops, power barges, berthing barges, water and fuel barges, garbage scows, et cetera. There are a few "ships" and the nuclear-propelled research submersible NR-1 officially designated as service craft. Only the Y-prefix ships and craft are listed in this section (the "Y" originally indicating yardcraft). The specific type strengths are as of March 1976. Asterisks are not used to indicate active service craft; see notes.

1 MOBILE LISTENING BARGE (YAG)

MONOB I YAG 61 (ex-IX 309, ex-YW 87)

Displacement, tons: 1 390 full load
Dimensions, feet (metres): 174 oa × 33 *(57 × 10·8)*

The *Monob I* is a mobile listening barge converted from a self-propelled water barge. Built in 1943 and converted for acoustic research in 1969, being placed in service in May 1969. Conducts research for the Naval Ship Research and Development Centre; based at Port Everglades, Florida.
Designation changed from IX 301 to YAG 61 on 1 July 1970.

MONOB I   *1969, United States Navy*

RESEARCH SHIP (YAG): "LIBERTY" CLASS

The "Liberty" ship *George Eastman* (YAG 39) employed in nuclear effects research was stricken on 1 Dec 1975. See 1975-1976 and previous editions for characteristics and details of previous YAG disposals.

2 DIVING TENDERS (YDT)

Tenders used to support shallow-water diving operations. Two self-propelled diving tenders are on the Navy List: **Phoebus** YDT 14 ex-YF 294, and **Suitland** YDT 15 ex-YF 336. (Two non-self-propelled YDTs are in service).

4 COVERED LIGHTERS (YF)

Lighters used to transport materiel in harbours; self-propelled; four are on the Navy List, three of which are named: **Lynnhaven** (YF 328), **Keyport** (YF 885), and **Kodiak** (YF 886), the two former ones being active:

6 FERRYBOATS (YFB)

Ferryboats used to transport personnel and vehicles in large harbours; self-propelled; YFB 83 and 87-91; all are active. The YFB 88-91 are the former LCU 1636, 1638-1640, all reclassified on 1 Sep 1969. The **Aquidneck** (YFB 14) transferred to State of Washington on 23 Dec 1975.

YFB 88 (ex-LCU 1636)   *United States Navy*

YFB 87   *1970, United States Navy*

1 REFRIGERATED COVERED LIGHTER (YFR)

Lighters used to store and transport food and other materials which require refrigeration. The YFR 888 remains on the Navy List in reserve.

YFR 890 (YFR 888 similar)   *United States Navy*

6 COVERED LIGHTERS (RANGE TENDER) (YFRT)

Lighters used for miscellaneous purposes; YFRT 287, 411, 451, 520, and 523 active; YFRT 418 is in reserve. Note Mk 32 torpedo tubes on YFRT 520.
Range Recoverer YFRT 524 (ex-T-AGM 2, ex-T-AG 161, ex-US Army FS 278) stricken on 15 May 1974.

YFRT 520   *United States Navy*

10 HARBOUR UTILITY CRAFT (YFU)

YFU 71	YFU 74	YFU 76	YFU 79	YFU 81
YFU 72	YFU 75	YFU 77	YFU 80	YFU 82

Dimensions, feet (metres): 125 oa × 36 × 7·5 *(40·9 × 11·8 × 2·4)*
Main engines: Diesels = 8 knots
Guns: 2—·50 cal MG

Militarised versions of a commercial lighter design. Used for off-loading large ships in harbours and ferrying cargo from one coastal port to another. Built by Pacific Coast Engineering Co, Alameda, California; completed 1967-1968. Can carry more than 300 tons cargo; considerable cruising range.
YFU 71-77 and YFU 80-82 loaned to US Army in 1970 for use in South Vietnam; returned to Navy control in 1973.

Losses and transfers: *YFU 78* sunk in Vietnam in March 1969; *YFU 73* transferred to Khmer Republic (Cambodia) on 15 Nov 1973.

YFU 75   1968, United States Navy

YFU 74   1969, United States Navy

14 HARBOUR UTILITY CRAFT (YFU): LCU TYPE

YFU 44 (ex-LCU 1398)	YFU 89 (ex-LCU 1576)	YFU 99 (ex-LCU 1622)
YFU 50 (ex-LCU 1486)	YFU 91 (ex-LCU 1608)	YFU 100 (ex-LCU 1610)
YFU 55 (ex-LCU 637)	YFU 93 (ex-LCU 1625)	YFU 101 (ex-LCU 1612)
YFU 67 (ex-LCU 1232)	YFU 97 (ex-LCU 1611)	YFU 102 (ex-LCU 1462)
YFU 83 (new; see notes)	YFU 98 (ex-LCU 1615)	

Former utility landing craft employed primarily as harbour and coastal cargo craft (see section on Landing Craft for basic characteristics). The YFU 44 has an open centre well for lowering research equipment into the water; assigned to the Naval Undersea Research and Development Centre in Long Beach, California.
YFU 83 built by Defoe Shipbuilding Co (same design as LCU 1646). Several YFUs were loaned to the US Army in 1970 for use in Vietnam after withdrawal of US Navy riverine and coastal forces.

Classifications: YFU 1-70 and 84-102 were former utility landing craft. Several reverted to LCU designations and three were modified for salvage work: YFU 2, 16, and 33 to YLLC 5, 2, and 3, respectively.

Disposals and Transfers: (since 1 Jan 1974) **YFU 4** stricken on 1 Oct 1974; **YFU 24, YFU 57** stricken on 15 Oct 1974; **YFU 96** stricken on 1 Dec 1974; **YFU 53** sricken on 1 June 1975.

YFU 83   1971, Defoe Shipbuilding

24 FUEL BARGES (YO)

Small liquid fuel carriers intended to fuel ships where no pierside fuelling facilities are available; self-propelled; 24 are on the Navy List. Two named units, **Casing Heap** (YO 47) and **Crownbrock** (YO 48), have been stricken.

YO 130   1970, United States Navy

10 GASOLINE BARGES (YOG)

Similar to the fuel barges (YO), but carry gasoline and aviation fuels; self-propelled; 10 are on the Navy List. Named unit **Lieut. Thomas W. Fowler** (YOG 107) stricken on 1 May 1975.

3 SEAMANSHIP TRAINING CRAFT (YP): NEW CONSTRUCTION

Three craft proposed in the Fiscal Year 1977 programme.

The FY 1977 shipbuilding programme proposes $6 000 000 to construct three additional YPs to replace older craft used for shiphandling training at the Surface Warfare Officers School (see below).

23 SEAMANSHIP TRAINING CRAFT (YP)

YP 587	YP 654	YP 658	YP 662	YP 666	YP 670
YP 589	YP 655	YP 659	YP 663	YP 667	YP 671
YP 590	YP 656	YP 660	YP 664	YP 668	YP 672
YP 591	YP 657	YP 661	YP 665	YP 669	

YP 584 series:

Displacement, tons: 50
Dimensions, feet (metres): 75 oa × 16 × 4·5 *(24·6 × 5·2 × 1·5)*
Main engines: 2 diesels (Superior); 400 bhp; 2 shafts = 12 knots

YP 654 series:

Displacement, tons: 69·5 full load
Dimensions, feet (metres): 80·4 oa × 18·75 × 5·3 *(26·4 × 6·1 × 1·7)*
Main engines: 4 diesels (General Motors); 660 bhp; 2 shafts = 13·5 knots

These craft are used for instruction in seamanship and navigation at the Naval Academy, Annapolis, Maryland; Naval Officer Candidate School, Newport, Rhode Island; and Surface Warfare Officers School at Newport. Fitted with surface search radar, Fathometer, gyro compass, and UHF and MF radio; the YP 655 additionally fitted for instruction in oceanographic research at the Naval Academy.
YPs numbered below 654 are older craft of a once-numerous type employed for training and utility work. YP 654-663 built by Stephens Bros, Inc, Stockton, California; completed in 1958; YP 664 and 665 built by Elizabeth City Shipbuilders, Inc, Elizabeth City, North Carolina; YP 666 and 667 built by Stephens Bros; YP 668 built by Peterson Boatbuilding Co, Tacoma, Washington, completed in 1968; YP 669-672 built by Peterson completed in 1971-1972.
These craft are of wooden construction with aluminium deck houses.

Disposals: YP 588 stricken on 1 Feb 1972; **YP 584, YP 585** stricken on 1 May 1974; **YP 586** stricken on 1 Oct 1974.

YP 669   *1971, Peterson Builders*

YP 654 type   *United States Navy*

11 SMALL HARBOUR TUGS (YTL)

Eleven of these craft are on the Navy List; unnamed. Six are active and five in reserve.

72 MEDIUM HARBOUR TUGS (YTM)

Numbered in YTM 128-779 series; several formerly designated YTB or are former US Army tugs. The YTM 659 fitted with triple Mk 32 torpedo tubes. Most have names and are active; a few are in reserve.
The photographs below show three different YTM configurations. The *Menasha* is shown being lifted by crane at the Philadelphia Naval Shipyard; note her cycloidal propellers under the hull.

MASCOUTAH (YTM 760)   *1971, United States Navy*

ETAWINA (YTM 543)   *1975, Giorgio Arra*

MENASHA (YTM 761)   *1976, US Navy, Richard Banks*

81 LARGE HARBOUR TUGS (YTB)

EDENSHAW	YTB 752	TAMAQUA	YTB 797	KITTANNING	YTB 787	CATAHECASSA	YTB 828
MARIN	YTB 753	OPELIKA	YTB 789	WAPATO	YTB 788	METACOM	YTB 829
PONTIAC	YTB 756	NATCHITOCHES	YTB 799	TOMAHAWK	YTB 789	PUSHMATHA	YTB 830
OSHKOSH	YTB 757	EUFAULA	YTB 800	MENOMINEE	YTB 790	DEKANAWIDA	YTB 831
PADUCAH	YTB 758	PALATKA	YTB 801	MARINETTE	YTB 791	PETALESHARO	YTB 832
BOGALUSA	YTB 759	CHERAW	YTB 802	ANTIGO	YTB 792	SHABONEE	YTB 833
NATICK	YTB 760	NANTICOKE	YTB 803	PIQUA	YTB 793	NEWGAGON	YTB 834
OTTUMWA	YTB 761	AHOSKIE	YTB 804	MANDAN	YTB 794	SKENANDOA	YTB 835
TUSCUMBIA	YTB 762	OCALA	YTB 805	KETCHIKAN	YTB 795	POKAGON	YTB 836
MUSKEGON	YTB 763	TUSKEGEE	YTB 806	SACO	YTB 796		
MISHAWAKA	YTB 764	MASSAPEQUA	YTB 807				
OKMULGEE	YTB 765	WENATCHEE	YTB 808				
WAPOAKINETA	YTB 766	AGAWAN	YTB 809				
APALACHICOLA	YTB 767	ANOKA	YTB 810				
ARCATA	YTB 768	HOUMA	YTB 811				
CHESANING	YTB 769	ACCONAC	YTB 812				
DAHLONEGA	YTB 770	POUGHKEEPSIE	YTB 813				
KEOKUK	YTB 771	WAXAHATCHIE	YTB 814				
NASHUA	YTB 774	NEODESHA	YTB 815				
WAUWATOSA	YTB 775	CAMPTI	YTB 816				
WEEHAWKEN	YTB 776	HAYANNIS	YTB 817				
NOGALES	YTB 777	MECOSTA	YTB 818				
APOPKA	YTB 778	IUKA	YTB 819				
MANHATTAN	YTB 779	WANAMASSA	YTB 820				
SAUGUS	YTB 780	TONTOGANY	YTB 821				
NIANTIC	YTB 781	PAWHUSKA	YTB 822				
MANISTEE	YTB 782	CANONCHET	YTB 823				
REDWING	YTB 783	SANTAQUIN	YTB 824				
KALISPELL	YTB 784	WATHENA	YTB 825				
WINNEMUCCA	YTB 785	WASHTUCNA	YTB 826				
TONKAWA	YTB 786	CHETEK	YTB 827				

Displacement, tons: 350 full load
Dimensions, feet (metres): 109 oa × 30 × 13·8 *(35·7 × 9·8 × 4·5)*
Machinery: 2 diesels; 2 000 bhp; 2 shafts
Complement: 10 to 12 (enlisted)

Large harbour tugs; 81 are in active service. YTB 752 completed in 1959, YTB 753 in 1960, YTB 756-762 in 1961, YTB 763-766 in 1963, YTB 770 and YTB 771 in 1964, YTB 767-769, 776 in 1965, YTB 774, 775, 777-789 in 1966, YTB 790-793 in 1967, YTB 794 and 795 in 1968, YTB 796-803 in 1969, and YTB 804-815 completed in 1970-1972, YTB 816-827 completed 1972-1973, YTB 828-836 completed 1974-1975. YTB 837 and YTB 838 transferred upon completion in late 1975 to Saudi Arabia.
Navy tugs have Indian names.

WATHENA (YTB 825)   1975, Giorgio Arra

PADUCAH (YTB 758) assisting JOHN F. KENNEDY (CV 67)   US Navy

11 WATER BARGES (YW)

Barges modified to carry water to ships in harbour; self-propelled; 11 of these craft are on the
Navy List with most being in reserve.

7 TORPEDO WEAPONS RETRIEVERS (TWR)

Displacement, tons: 97·4 light; 152 full load
Dimensions, feet (metres): 102 oa × 21 × 7·75 *(33·4 × 6·9 × 2·5)*
Main engines: 4 diesels; 2 shafts = 18 knots
Complement: 15 (enlisted)

These are the largest of several types of torpedo recovery craft operated by the Navy. They are
fitted to recover torpedoes and perform limited torpedo maintenance during exercises. An
internal stern ramp facilitates recovery and up to 17 tons of torpedoes can be carried. These
large TWRs also perform harbour utility duties. Range is 1 900 miles at 10 knots.

TWR 681   1969, United States Navy

SSBN in RICHLAND (AFDM 8)—see following page   1969, Robert Fudge

FLOATING DRY DOCKS

The US Navy operates a number of floating dry docks to supplement dry dock facilities at major naval activities, to support fleet ballistic missile submarines (SSBN) at advanced bases, and to provide repair capabilities in forward combat areas.

The larger floating dry docks are made sectional to facilitate movement overseas and to render them self docking. The ARD-type docks have the forward end of their docking well closed by a structure resembling the bow of a ship to facilitate towing. Berthing facilities, repair shops, and machinery are housed in sides of larger docks. None is self-propelled.

Seventeen floating dry docks are in Navy service (including two partial docks), 12 are out of service in reserve (including two partial docks), and 27 are on lease to commercial firms for private use. Several are on loan to other US services and foreign navies (including one partial dock). Asterisks indicate docks in active US service.

The ARDM 4 is under construction at the Bethlehem Steel Co, Sparrows Point, Maryland. Designed specifically to service "Los Angeles" class (SSN 688) submarines.

Figures in parenthesis indicate the number of sections for sectional docks. Each section of the AFDB docks has a lifting capacity of about 10 000 tons. Four sections of the AFDB 7 form the floating dry dock Los Alamos at Holy Loch, Scotland, one section is used at Kwajalein atoll by the US Army in support of the anti-ballistic missile project and two sections are in reserve. (The

AFDB sections each are 256 feet long, 80 feet in width, with wing walls 83 feet high; the wing walls, which contain compartments, fold down when the sections are towed).

The White Sands (ARD 20) was employed in support of the deep-diving bathyscaph Trieste II (see section on Deep Submergence Vehicles). Early in 1969 the White Sands, with Trieste II on board, was towed to the Azores to support investigation of the remains of the nuclear-powered submarine Scorpion (SSN 589). Reclassified as auxiliary deep submergence support vehicle (AGDS 1) on 1 Aug 1973; subsequently stricken.

Transfers: The following floating dry docks are on foreign loan: ARD 23 to Argentina; AFDL 39, ARD 14 to Brazil; ARD 32 to Chile; ARD 28 to Columbia; ARD 13 to Ecuador; AFDL 11 to Khmer Republic (Cambodia); ARD 15, AFDL 28 to Mexico; ARD 6 to Pakistan; AFDL 26 to Paraguay; AFDL 33, ARD 8 to Peru; AFDL 20, AFDL 44 to Philippines; ARD 9, Windsor (ARD 22) to Taiwan; ARD 13 to Venezuela; AFDL 22 to South Vietnam; ARD 12 to Turkey; Arco (ARD 29) to Iran; ARD 25 to Chile; AFDL 24 to Philippines; ARD 11 to Mexico.

Disposals: (since 1 Jan 1974): AFDB 6 stricken on 1 Jan 1974; White Sands (AGDS 1 ex-ARD 20), ARD 31 stricken on 1 Apr 1974; AFDL 42 stricken on 1 May 1974.

LARGE AUXILIARY FLOATING DRY DOCKS

Name-No.	Completed	Capacity	Construction	Notes
*AFDL 1	1943	1 000 tons	Steel	Guantanamo Bay, Cuba
AFDL 2	1943	1 000 tons	Steel	Commercial lease
*AFDL 6	1944	1 000 tons	Steel	Little Creek, Virginia
AFDL 7	1944	1 900 tons	Steel	Reserve
AFDL 8	1943	1 000 tons	Steel	Commercial lease
AFDL 9	1943	1 000 tons	Steel	Commercial lease
*AFDL 10	1943	1 000 tons	Steel	Subic Bay, Philippines
AFDL 12	1943	1 000 tons	Steel	Reserve
AFDL 15	1943	1 000 tons	Steel	Commercial lease
AFDL 16	1943	1 000 tons	Steel	Commercial lease
AFDL 19	1944	1 000 tons	Steel	Commercial lease
*AFDL 21	1944	1 000 tons	Steel	Guam, Marianas
*AFDL 23	1944	1 900 tons	Steel	Subic Bay, Philippines
AFDL 25	1944	1 000 tons	Steel	Reserve
AFDL 29	1943	1 000 tons	Steel	Commercial lease
AFDL 30	1944	1 000 tons	Steel	Commercial lease
AFDL 35	1944	2 800 tons	Concrete	Reserve
AFDL 37	1944	2 800 tons	Concrete	Commercial lease
AFDL 38	1944	2 800 tons	Concrete	Commercial lease
AFDL 40	1944	2 800 tons	Concrete	Commercial lease
AFDL 41	1944	2 800 tons	Concrete	Commercial lease

AFDL 21 under tow — 1965, United States Navy

AFDL 43	1944	2 800 tons	Concrete	Commercial lease
AFDL 45	1944	2 800 tons	Concrete	Commercial lease
AFDL 47	1946	6 500 tons	Steel	Commercial lease
*AFDL 48	1956	4 000 tons	Concrete	Long Beach Nav Shipyard

AUXILIARY REPAIR DRY DOCKS and MEDIUM AUXILIARY REPAIR DRY DOCKS

*ARD 5	1942	3 000 tons	Steel	New London, Connecticut
*ARD 7	1943	3 000 tons	Steel	New London, Connecticut
ARDM 3 (ex-ARD 18)	1944	3 000 tons	Steel	Reserve
ARDM 4	1978		Steel	Under construction
*OAK RIDGE				
ARDM 1 (ex-ARD 19)	1944	3 000 tons	Steel	Rota, Spain
ARD 24	1944	3 000 tons	Steel	Reserve
*ALAMAGORDO				
ARDM 2 (ex-ARD 26)	1944	3 000 tons	Steel	Charleston, South Carolina
*ARD 30 SAN ONOFRE	1944	3 000 tons	Steel	Pearl Harbor Nav Shipyard

SSBN in OAK RIDGE (ARDM 1) — 1964, United States Navy

SSBN in OAK RIDGE (ARDM 1) — United States Navy

LARGE AUXILIARY FLOATING DRY DOCKS

*AFDB 1 (partial)	1943	40 000 tons	Steel (4)	Subic Bay, Philippines
AFDB 1 (partial)	—	60 000 tons	Steel (6)	Reserve
AFDB 2	1944	90 000 tons	Steel (10)	Reserve
AFDB 3	1944	81 000 tons	Steel (9)	Reserve
AFDB 4	1944	55 000 tons	Steel (7)	Reserve
AFDB 5	1944	55 000 tons	Steel (7)	Reserve
AFDB 7 (partial)	1944	20 000 tons	Steel (2)	Reserve
*AFDB 7 (partial)	1945	10 000 tons	Steel (1)	US Army
*LOS ALAMOS				
AFDB 7 (partial)	—	40 000 tons	Steel (4)	Holy Loch, Scotland

MEDIUM AUXILIARY FLOATING DRY DOCKS

AFDM 1 (ex-YFD 3)	1942	15 000 tons	Steel (3)	Commercial lease
AFDM 2 (ex-YFD 4)	1942	15 000 tons	Steel (3)	Commercial lease
AFDM 3 (ex-YFD 6)	1943	18 000 tons	Steel (3)	Commercial lease
AFDM 5 (ex-YFD 21)	1943	18 000 tons	Steel (3)	Reserve
*AFDM 6 (ex-YFD 62)	1944	18 000 tons	Steel (3)	Subic Bay, Philippines
*AFDM 7 (ex-YFD 63)	1945	18 000 tons	Steel (3)	Davisville, Rhode Island
*RICHLAND AFDM 8				
(ex-YFD 64)	1944	18 000 tons	Steel (3)	Guam, Marianas
AFDM 9 (ex-YFD 65)	1945	18 000 tons	Steel (3)	Commercial lease
AFDM 10	1945	18 000 tons	Steel (3)	Commercial lease

YARD FLOATING DRY DOCKS

YFD 7	1943	18 000 tons	Steel (3)	Commercial lease
YFD 8	1942	20 000 tons	Wood	Commercial lease
YFD 9	1942	16 000 tons	Wood	Commercial lease
YFD 23	1943	10 500 tons	Wood	Commercial lease
YFD 54	1943	5 000 tons	Wood	Commercial lease
YFD 68	1945	14 000 tons	Steel (3)	Commercial lease
YFD 69	1945	14 000 tons	Steel (3)	Commercial lease
YFD 70	1945	14 000 tons	Steel (3)	Commercial lease
*YFD 71	1945	14 000 tons	Steel (3)	San Diego Naval Base
*YFD 83 (ex-AFDL 31)	1943	1 000 tons	Steel	US Coast Guard

DEEP SUBMERGENCE VEHICLES

The US Navy operates several deep submergence vehicles for scientific, military research, and operational military missions. The US Navy acquired its first deep submergence vehicle with the purchase of the bathyscaph *Trieste* in 1958. The *Trieste* was designed and constructed by Professor Auguste Piccard, the noted Swiss physicist and aeronaut. The US Navy sponsored research dives in the Mediterranean Sea with the *Trieste* in 1957 after which the bathyscaph was purchased outright and brought to the United States.

The *Trieste* reached a record depth of 35 800 feet *(10 910 metres)* in the Challenger Deep off the Marianas on 23 Jan

1960, being piloted by Lieutenant Don Walsh, USN, and Jacques Piccard (son of Auguste). Rebuilt and designated *Trieste II*, the craft was subsequently used in the search for wreckage of the nuclear-powered submarine *Thresher* (SSN 593) which was lost in 1963 and the *Scorpion* (SSN 589) lost in 1968.

After the loss of the *Thresher* the US Navy initiated an extensive deep submergence programme that led to construction of two Deep Submergence Rescue Vehicles (DSRV); however, other vehicles proposed in the recommended programme were not built because of a lack of interest, changing opera-

tional concepts, and funding limitations.

Several of these deep submergence vehicles and other craft and support ships are operated by Submarine Development Group One at San Diego, California. The Group is a major operational command that includes advanced diving equipment; divers, trained in "saturation" techniques; the DSVs *Trieste II*, *Turtle*, *Sea Cliff*, DSRV-1, DSRV-2; the submarine *Dolphin* (AGSS 555); several submarine rescue ships.

The hull of the original *Trieste* and Krupp sphere are in the Navy Yard in Washington, DC.

MIDGET SUBMARINES

The US Navy's only "midget" submarine, the 50-foot long *X-1*, was stricken on 16 Feb 1973. See 1972-1973 edition for characteristics and photographs.

NUCLEAR POWERED RESEARCH VEHICLE: PROPOSED

A second nuclear-powered submersible research vehicle has been proposed by Admiral H. G. Rickover, US Navy (Retired), Deputy Commander for Nuclear Propulsion, Naval Sea Systems Command. The craft would have a greater depth capability than the NR-1 (described below) and would employ a nuclear plant similar to that of the earlier craft. The vehicle would have a pressure hull of HY-130 steel.

Reportedly, Admiral Rickover began development of the so-called "NR-2" in 1971. The term

HTV for Hull Test Vehicle also has been used for this vehicle, reportedly to avoid critical association with the NR-1 programme.

Estimated construction time would be 2½ years; however, construction has not yet been approved. Unofficial estimates of construction costs ranged to more than $300 000 000 in Fiscal Year 1975 funding.

1 NUCLEAR POWERED OCEAN ENGINEERING AND RESEARCH VEHICLE

Name	Builders
NR-1	General Dynamics (Electric Boat)

Displacement, tons: 400 submerged
Length, feet (metres): 136·4 oa × 12·4 × 14·6 *(41·6 × 3·8 × 4·5)*
Diameter, feet (metre): 12 *(3·7)*
Machinery: Electric motors; 2 propellers; four ducted thrusters
Reactor: 1 pressurised-water cooled
Complement: 7 (2 officers, 3 enlisted men, 2 scientists)

The NR-1 was built primarily to serve as a test platform for a small nuclear propulsion plant; however, the craft additionally provides an advanced deep submergence ocean engineering and research capability. Vice-Admiral Rickover conceived and initiated the NR-1 in 1964-1965 (the craft was not proposed in a Navy research or shipbuilding budget).

Built by Electric Boat Division of General Dynamics Corp, Groton, Connecticut; laid down on 10 June 1967; launched on 25 Jan 1969; completed late in 1969. Commanded by an officer-in-charge vice commanding officer.

Describing the craft Admiral Rickover has stated: "The (NR-1) will be able to perform detailed studies and mapping of the ocean bottom, temperature, currents, and other oceanographic parameters for military, commercial, and scientific use. The development of a nuclear propulsion plant for an oceanographic research vehicle will result in greater independence from surface support ships and essentially unlimited endurance of propulsion and auxiliary power for detailed exploration of the ocean.

"The submarine (NR-1) will have viewing ports for visual observation of its surroundings and the ocean bottom. In addition, a remote grapple will be installed to permit collection of marine samples and other items. With its depth capability, the NR-1 is expected to be capable of exploring areas of the Continental Shelf, an area which appears to contain most accessible wealth in mineral and food resources in the seas. Such exploratory charting may also help the United States in establishing sovereignty over parts of the Continental Shelf".

Construction: Admiral Rickover originally planned to construct the NR-1 using "state of the art" equipment, with the cost of such a vehicle estimated to be $30 000 000 in March 1965. During detailed design of the NR-1 the Navy determined that improved, equipment had to be developed and a larger hull than originally planned would be required. Consequently, in July 1967 the Navy obtained Congressional approval to proceed with construction of the NR-1 at an estimated cost of $58 000 300. The final estimated ship construction cost at time of launching was $67 500 000 plus $19 900 000 for oceanographic equipment and sensors, and $11 800 000 for research and development (mainly related to the nuclear propulsion plant), for a total estimated cost of $99 200 000.

Design: The NR-1 is fitted with wheels beneath the hull to permit "bottom crawling". This will obviate the necessity of hovering while exploring the ocean floor. Submarine wheels, a concept proposed as early as the first decade of this century by submarine inventor Simon Lake, were tested in the small submarine *Mackerel* (SST 1).

The NR-1 is fitted with external lights, external television cameras, a remote-controlled manipulator, and various recovery devices. No periscopes, but fixed television mast. Credited with a 30 day endurance, but limited habitability makes missions of only a few days feasible. Reportedly, a surface "mother" ship is required to support the NR-1.

Engineering: The NR-1 reactor plant was designed by the Atomic Energy Commission's Knolls

Atomic Power Laboratory. She is propelled by two propellers driven by electric motors outside the pressure hull with power provided by a turbine generator within the pressure hull. Four ducted thrusters, two horizontal and two vertical, are provided for precise manoeuvring.

Photographs: No photographs of the NR-1 have been released for publication since the craft's sea trials in 1969. Note fixed TV mast at after end of sail structure in the launching view.

NR-1   *1969, General Dynamics, Electric Boat*

NR-1   *1969, General Dynamics, Electric Boat*

2 DEEP SUBMERGENCE RESCUE VEHICLES

No.	Builders
DSRV-1	Lockheed Missiles and Space Co
DSRV-2	(Sunnyvale, Calif)

Weight in air, tons: 35
Length, feet (metres): 49·2 oa *(15·0)*
Diameter, feet (metres): 8 *(2·4)*
Propulsion: Electric motors, propeller mounted in control shroud and four ducted thrusters
Speed, knots: 5 (maximum)
Endurance: 12 hours at 3 knots
Operating depth, feet (metres): 5 000 *(1 525)*
Complement: 3 (pilot, co-pilot, rescue sphere operator) +24 rescuees

The Deep Submergence Rescue Vehicle is intended to provided a quick-reaction world-wide, all-weather capability for the rescue of survivors in a disabled submarine. The DSRV will be transportable by road, aircraft (in C-141 and C-5 jet cargo aircraft), surface ship (on "Pigeon" ASR 21 class submarine rescue ships), and specially modified submarines (SSN type).

The operational effectiveness of the craft is limited severely by the lack of large numbers of ships and submarines that air transport and support the craft. They will be used for the forseeable future for evaluation and research.

Upon notification that a submarine is disabled on the ocean floor the DSRV and its support equipment (all necessary check-out equipment and spare parts being housed in a mobile van) will be loaded in cargo aircraft and flown to a port near the disabled submarine. The DSRV and van will then be towed to a pier and loaded aboard a "mother" submarine, which had proceeded to the port upon notification that a submarine was disabled.

The mother submarine, with the DSRV attached to her main deck (aft of the sail structure), will then proceed to the disabled submarine and serve as an underwater base for the DSRV which

will shuttle back and forth between the disabled submarine and the mother submarine. On each trip the DSRV will carry up to 24 survivors from the disabled submarine. The mother submarine will launch and recover the DSRV while submerged and, if necessary, while under ice. A total of six DSRVs were planned, but only two were funded. DSRV-1 was launched on 24 Jan 1970 and DSRV-2 on 1 May 1971.

Cost: The estimated construction cost for the DSRV-1 is $41 000 000 and for the DSRV-2 $23 000 000. The development, construction, test, and support of both vehicles through Fiscal Year 1975 is now estimated at $220 000 000. This expenditure includes the design and construction of both vehicles, specific research and development associated with the rescue programme, surface support equipment, modifications to "mother" submarines, test and evaluation programmes, procurement of replacement and spare parts, and training of the DSRV operators and support personnel.

Design: The DSRV outer hull is constructed of formed fibreglass. Within this outer hull are three interconnected spheres which form the main pressure capsule. Each sphere is 7·5 feet in diameter and is constructed of HY-140 steel. The forward sphere contains the vehicle's control equipment and is manned by the pilot and co-pilot, the centre and after spheres accommodate 24 passengers and a third crewman. Under the DSRVs centre sphere is a hemispherical protrusion or "skirt" which seals over the disabled submarine's hatch. During the mating operation the skirt is pumped dry to enable personnel to transfer between the DSRV and disabled or mother submarine.

Electronics: Elaborate search and navigational sonar, and closed-circuit television (supplemented by optical devices) are installed in the DSRV to determine the exact location of a disabled submarine within a given area and for pinpointing the submarine's escape hatches. Side-looking sonar can be fitted for search missions.

DSRV—*continued*

Engineering: Propulsion and control of the DSRV are achieved by a stern propeller in a movable control shroud and four ducted thrusters, two forward and two aft. These, plus a mercury trim system, permit the DSRV to manoeuvre and hover with great precision and to mate with submarines lying at angles up to 45 degrees from the horizontal. An elaborate Integrated Control and Display (ICAD) system employs computers to present sensor data to the pilots and transmit their commands to the vehicle's control and propulsion system.

Photographs: An artist's concept of a DSRV "landing" on a submarine hatch appears in the 1971-1972 edition; a view of the DSRV-1 being assembled appears in the 1970-1971 edition.

DSRV-1 on HAWKBILL (SSN 666)   *1971, United States Navy*

2 RESEARCH VEHICLES: MODIFIED "ALVIN" TYPE

Name	No.	Builders
SEA CLIFF (ex-*Autec I*)	DSV 4	General Dynamics (Electric Boat), Groton, Conn
TURTLE (ex-*Autec II*)	DSV 3	General Dynamics (Electric Boat), Groton, Conn

Weight, tons: 21
Length, feet (metres): 25 oa *(7·6)*
Beam, feet (metres): 8 *(2·4)*
Propulsion: Electric motors, trainable stern propeller; 2 rotating propeller pods
Speed, knots: 2·5
Endurance: 8 hours at 2 knots
Operating depth, feet (metres): 6 500 *(1,980)*
Complement: 2 (pilot, observer)

Intended for deep submergence research and work tasks. Designated *Autec I* and *Autec II* during construction, but assigned above names in dual launching on 11 Dec 1968. Designated DSV 4 and DSV 3, respectively, on 1 June 1971.

Construction: Three pressure spheres were fabricated for the *Alvin* submersible programme, one for installation in the *Alvin,* a spare, and one for testing. The second and third spheres subsequently were allocated to these later submersibles.

Design: Twin-arm manipulator fitted to each submersible. Propulsion by stem propeller and two smaller, manoeuvering propeller "pods" on sides of vehicles; no thrusters.

SEA CLIFF   *United States Navy*

1 RESEARCH VEHICLE: "ALVIN" TYPE

Name	No.	Builders
ALVIN	DSV 2	General Mills Inc, Minneapolis, Minn

Weight, tons: 16
Length, feet (metres): 22·5 oa *(6·9)*
Beam, feet (metres): 8·5 *(2·6)*
Propulsion: Electric motors; trainable stern propeller; 2 rotating propeller pods
Speed, knots: 2
Endurance: 8 hours at 1 knot
Operating depth, feet (metres): 12 000 *(3 658)*
Complement: 3 (1 pilot, 2 observers)

The *Alvin* was built for operation by the Woods Hole Oceanographic Institution for the Office of Naval Research. Original configuration had an operating depth of 6 000 feet. Named for Allyn C. Vine of Woods Hole Oceanographic Institution.
The *Alvin* accidentally sank in 5 051 feet of water on 16 Oct 1968; subsequently raised in August 1969; refurbished from May 1971 to Oct 1972 in essentially original configuration; subsequently refitted with titanium pressure sphere to provide increased depth capability and again operational in November 1973. See 1968-1969 edition for photographs of original configuration.

ALVIN   *1974*

1 BATHYSCAPH RESEARCH VEHICLE: "TRIESTE" TYPE

Name	No.
TRIESTE II	DSV 1 (ex-X-2)

Weight, tons: 84
Displacement, tons: 303 submerged
Length, feet (metres): 78·6 *(24·0)*
Beam, feet (metres): 15·3 *(4·7)*
Propulsion: Electric motors, 3 propellers aft, ducted thruster forward (see *Design* notes)
Speed, knots: 2
Endurance: 10-12 hours at 2 knots
Operating depth, feet (metres): 12 000 *(3 658)* (see *Design* notes)
Complement: 3 (2 operators, 1 observer)

The *Trieste II* is the extensively rebuilt *Trieste I* which the US Navy purchased in 1958 from professor Auguste Piccard. Several "modernisations" have resulted in the current vehicle being essentially a "new" craft, the third to be named *Trieste.* (The original *Trieste* was built at Castellammare, Italy; launched on 1 Aug 1953).
The vehicle is operated by Submarine Development Group One at San Diego, California, and is used primarily as a test bed for underwater equipment and to train deep submergence vehicle operators (hydronauts).
Designated as a "submersible craft" and assigned the designation X-2 on 1 Sep 1969; subsequently changed to DSV 1 on 1 June 1971.

Design: The *Trieste II* is essentially a large float with a small pressure sphere attached to the underside. The float, which is filled with aviation petrol, provides buoyancy. Designed operating depth is 20 000 feet but dives have been limited to approximately 12 000 feet. (The record-setting Challenger Deep dive was made with a Krupp sphere which has a virtually unlimited depth capability).
The bathyscaph was essentially rebuilt for a second time at the Mare Island Naval Shipyard in Sep 1965-Aug 1966 with a modified float, pressure sphere, propulsion system, and mission equipment being fitted. In the broadside view the sphere is now largely hidden by protective supports to keep the sphere clear of the welldeck when the craft rests in a floating dry dock. (Compare with photographs of the earlier *Trieste II* configuration in the 1969-1970 edition). Fitted with external television cameras and mechanical manipulator; computerised digital navigation system installed.

Photographs: Note forward "legs" to prevent pressure sphere from sinking into ocean floor when craft is resting on the bottom. Lights, manipulators, cameras, and other devices are mounted forward of the sphere, partially in view of sphere's viewpoint.

TRIESTE II   *1970, United States Navy*

Transfers: The 600-foot capability *Nemo* DSV 5 is on loan to the Southwest Research Institute, San Antonio, Texas, since 1974.

COAST GUARD

Command

Commandant: Admiral Owen W. Siler
Vice Commandant: Vice-Admiral Ellis L. Perry
Chief of Staff: Rear-Admiral Robert H. Scarborough
Commander, Atlantic Area: Vice-Admiral William F. Rea, III
Commander, Pacific Area: Vice-Admiral Austin C. Wagner

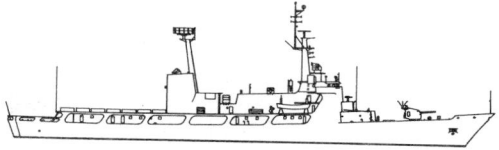
"Hamilton" Class

Establishment

The United States Coast Guard was established by an Act of Congress approved 28 Jan 1915, which consolidated the Revenue Cutter Service (founded in 1790) and the Life Saving Service (founded in 1878). The act of establishment stated the Coast Guard "shall be a military service and a branch of the armed forces of the United States at all times. The Coast Guard shall be a service in the Treasury Department except when operating as a service in the Navy".
The Congress further legislated that in time of national emergency or when the President so directs, the Coast Guard operates as a part of the Navy. The Coast Guard did operate as a part of the Navy during the First and Second World Wars.
The Lighthouse Service (founded in 1789) was transferred to the Coast Guard on 1 July 1939.
The Coast Guard was transferred to the newly established Department of Transportation on 1 April 1967.

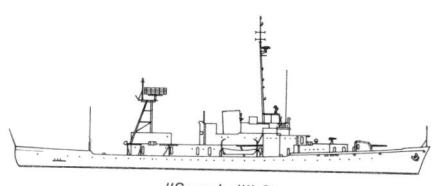
"Campbell" Class

Cutters

All Coast Guard vessels are referred to as "cutters". Cutter names are preceded by USCGC. Cutter serial numbers are prefixed with letter designations based on the US Navy classification system with the prefix letter "W". The first two digits of serial numbers for cutters less than 100 feet in length indicate their approximate length overall. All Coast Guard cutters are active unless otherwise indicated.
Approximately 600 small rescue and utility craft also are in service.

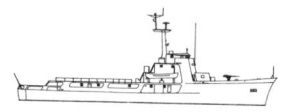
"Reliance" Class

Cutter Strength

18 High Endurance Cutters	35 Seagoing Buoy Tenders
15 Medium Endurance Cutters	66 Coastal-River-Inland Tenders
2 Oceanographic Cutters	6 Oceangoing Tugs
79 Patrol Boats	29 Harbour Tugs
7 Icebreakers	4 Lightships
4 Training Cutters	

Several of these cutters are laid up in reserve; see individual classes for status of specific cutters.

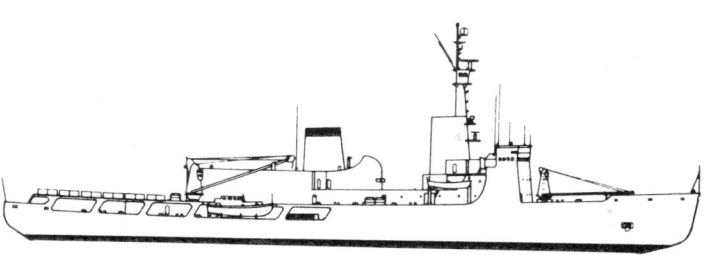
POLAR STAR

Personnel

July 1976: 4 450 officers, 1 290 warrant officers, 30 900 enlisted men.
An estimated 1 000 personnel will be added in 1976-1977 to man an increase in cutter strength to enforce a 200-mile fishing and conservation zone off the US coast.

Aviation

The Coast Guard operates a small air arm to support Coast Guard operations. Only the larger "Hamilton" class cutters and certain classes of icebreakers can support helicopters at sea. As of July 1976 the Coast Guard's aviation strength consisted of 46 fixed-wing aircraft and 112 helicopters:

1	EC-130	Hercules
20	HC-130	Hercules
23	HU-16	Albatross
1	VC-4A	Gulfstream I
1	VC-11A	Gulfstream II
38	HH-3F	Pelican
74	HH-52A	Sea Guard

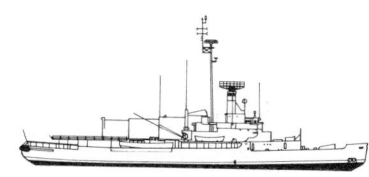
GLACIER

The Coast Guard plans to acquire approximately 40 land-based patrol and rescue aircraft in the period 1979-1983 to replace the long-serving HU-16 Albatross amphibians.

Missions

The current missions of the Coast Guard are to (1) enforce or assist in the enforcement of applicable Federal laws upon the high seas and waters subject to the jurisdiction of the United States including environmental protection; (2) administer all Federal laws regarding safety of life and property on the high seas and on waters subject to the jurisdiction of the United States, except those laws specifically entrusted to other Federal agencies; (3) develop, establish, maintain, operate, and conduct aids to maritime navigation, ocean stations, icebreaking activities, oceanographic research, and rescue facilities; and (4) maintain a state of readiness to function as a specialised service in the Navy when so directed by the President.

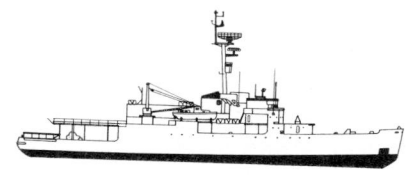
"Wind" Class

Scale: 1 inch = 150 feet (1 : 1 800)

Drawings by A. D. Baker

MELLON (WHEC 717), PONCHATOULA (AO 148), and JARVIS (WHEC 725)

1972, United States Coast Guard

HIGH ENDURANCE CUTTERS

12 HIGH ENDURANCE CUTTERS (WHEC): "HAMILTON" (378) CLASS

Name	No.	Builders	Laid down	Launched	Commissioned
HAMILTON	WHEC 715	Avondale Shipyards Inc, New Orleans, Louisiana	4 Jan 1965	18 Dec 1965	20 Feb 1967
DALLAS	WHEC 716	Avondale Shipyards Inc, New Orleans, Louisiana	7 Feb 1966	1 Oct 1966	1 Oct 1967
MELLON	WHEC 717	Avondale Shipyards Inc, New Orleans, Louisiana	25 July 1966	11 Feb 1967	22 Dec 1967
CHASE	WHEC 718	Avondale Shipyards Inc, New Orleans, Louisiana	15 Oct 1966	20 May 1967	1 Mar 1968
BOUTWELL	WHEC 719	Avondale Shipyards Inc, New Orleans, Louisiana	12 Dec 1966	17 June 1967	14 June 1968
SHERMAN	WHEC 720	Avondale Shipyards Inc, New Orleans, Louisiana	13 Feb 1967	23 Sep 1967	23 Aug 1968
GALLANTIN	WHEC 721	Avondale Shipyards Inc, New Orleans, Louisiana	17 Apr 1967	18 Nov 1967	20 Dec 1968
MORGENTHAU	WHEC 722	Avondale Shipyards Inc, New Orleans, Louisiana	17 July 1967	10 Feb 1968	14 Feb 1969
RUSH	WHEC 723	Avondale Shipyards Inc, New Orleans, Louisiana	23 Oct 1967	16 Nov 1968	3 July 1969
MUNRO	WHEC 724	Avondale Shipyards Inc, New Orleans, Louisiana	18 Feb 1970	5 Dec 1970	10 Sep 1971
JARVIS	WHEC 725	Avondale Shipyards Inc, New Orleans, Louisiana	9 Sep 1970	24 Apr 1971	30 Dec 1971
MIDGETT	WHEC 726	Avondale Shipyards Inc, New Orleans, Louisiana	5 Apr 1971	4 Sep 1971	17 Mar 1972

Displacement, tons: 2 716 standard; 3 050 full load
Length, feet (metres): 350 wl; 378 oa *(115·2)*
Beam, feet (metres): 42·8 *(13·1)*
Draught, feet (metres): 20 *(6·1)*
Guns: 1—5 inch *(127 mm)* 38 cal DP (Mk 30); 2—·50 cal machine guns
A/S weapons: 2 triple topedo tubes (Mk 32)
Helicopters: 1 HH-52 or HH-3 helicopter
Main engines: Combined Diesel and Gas turbine (CODAG): 2 diesels (Fairbanks-Morse) 7 000 bhp; 2 gas turbines (Pratt & Whitney), 28 000 shp; aggregate 35 000 hp; 2 shafts (controllable-pitch propellers)
Speed, knots: 29
Complement: 155 (15 officers, 140 enlisted men)

These are large, attractive, multi-purpose cutters. All of these ships are in active service.

Anti-submarine armament: Hedgehog anti-submarine weapons have been removed from earlier ships during overhaul and Mk 309 fire control system for Mk 32 torpedo tubes are installed. Hedgehogs deleted in later ships. *Hamilton* was first to drop hedgehogs and receive Mk 309 during 1970 overhaul.

Design: These ships have clipper bows, twin funnels enclosing a helicopter hangar, helicopter platform aft. All are fitted with oceanographic laboratories, elaborate communications equipment, and meteorological data gathering facilities. Superstructure is largely of aluminium construction. Bridge control of manoeuvring is by aircraft-type "joy stick" rather than wheel.

Electronics: Original SQS-36 sonar has been replaced by more-capable SQS-38. Fitted with SPS-29 and SPS-51 search radars; and Mk 56 gunfire control system.

Engineering: The "Hamiltons" were the largest US "military" ships with gas turbine propulsion pending completion of the Navy's "Spruance" class destroyers. The Pratt & Whitney gas turbines are FT-4A, marine variant of the J75 aircraft engine used in the Boeing 707 transport and F-105 fighter-bomber; the Fairbanks Morse diesels are 12 cylinder; variable pitch propellers fitted.
Engine and propeller pitch consoles are located in wheelhouse and at bridge wing stations as well as engine room control booth.
A retractable bow propulsion unit is provided for station keeping and precise maneouvring (Unit is located directly forward of bridge, immediately aft of sonar dome). Range is 14 000 miles at 11 knots on diesels and 2 400 miles at 29 knots on gas turbines.

Nomenclature: The first nine ships of this class were named for secretaries of the Treasury Department reflecting the Coast Guard being a part of that department from 1915 to 1967 when it was transferred to the newly formed Department of Transportation. Subsequent ships of this class honour Coast Guard

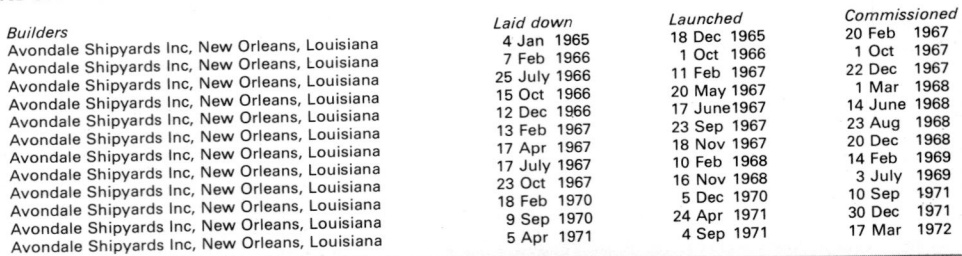

MIDGETT (WHEC 726) with HH-3F and Hovercraft   *1972, United States Coast Guard*

BOUTWELL (WHEC 719)   *1971, Giorgio Arra*

heroes.
Later ships are referred to as the "Hero" class.
Photographs: The *Midgett* has a hovercraft alongside during the Coast Guard's 1971-1973 trials with three former Navy ACVs. In the view below the *Hamilton* has machine guns

mounted in the "B" position (previously occupied by hedgehogs). The array of "E" and "hash" marks on the superstructure indicate excellence in operational competitions.
On the previous page two Honolulu-based "Hamiltons" are conducting underway replenishment from a Navy oiler.

HAMILTON (WHEC 715)   *1975, Giorgio Arra*

"OWASCO" (255) CLASS

The five surviving "Owasco" class 255-foot cutters were to be stricken during 1976: *Chautauqua* (WHEC 41), *Winona* (WHEC 65), *Minnetonka* (WHEC 67), *Mendota* (WHEC 69), and *Pontchartrain* (WHEC 70).
See 1975-1976 and previous editions for characteristics and earlier disposals.

6 HIGH ENDURANCE CUTTERS (WHEC): "CAMPBELL" (327) CLASS

Name	No.	Builders	Laid down	Launched	Commissioned
BIBB (ex-George M. Bibb)	WHEC 31	Charleston Navy Yard	18 May 1935	14 Jan 1937	19 Mar 1937
CAMPBELL (ex-George W. Campbell)	WHEC 32	Philadelphia Navy Yard	1 May 1935	3 June 1936	22 Oct 1936
DUANE (ex-William J. Duane)	WHEC 33	Philadelphia Navy Yard	1 May 1935	3 June 1936	16 Oct 1936
INGHAM (ex-Samuel D. Ingham)	WHEC 35	Philadelphia Navy Yard	1 May 1935	3 June 1936	6 Nov 1936
SPENCER (ex-John C. Spencer)	WHEC 36	New York Navy Yard	11 Sep 1935	3 Jan 1936	13 May 1937
TANEY (ex-Roger B. Taney)	WHEC 37	Philadelphia Navy Yard	1 May 1935	3 June 1936	19 Dec 1936

Displacement, tons: 2 216 standard; 2 414 full load
Length, feet (metres): 308 wl; 327 oa *(99·7)*
Beam, feet (metres): 41 *(12·5)*
Draught, feet (metres): 15 *(4·6)*
Guns: 1—5 inch *(127 mm)* 38 cal DP (Mk 30)
A/S weapons: Removed
Main engines: Geared turbines (Westinghouse); 6 200 shp; 2 shafts
Boilers: 2 (Babcock & Wilcox)
Speed, knots: 19·8
Complement: 143 (13 officers, 130 enlisted men)

Rated as 327-foot cutters. These were the Coast Guard's largest cutters until the *Hamilton* was completed in 1967.
The *Duane* served as an amphibious force flagship during the invasion of Southern France in August 1944 and was designated AGC 6 (Coast Guard manned); the other ships of this class, except the lost *Alexander Hamilton* (PG 34), were similarly employed but retained Coast Guard number with WAGC prefix (amidships structure built up and one or two additional masts installed); all reverted to gunboat configuration after war (WPG designation).
All of these cutters remain in active service except the *Spencer*, decommissioned on 23 Jan 1974 and placed in reserve at the Coast Guard Yard, Curtis Bay, Maryland. The *Spencer* was scheduled to be recommissioned during 1977.

Anti-submarine armament: During the 1960s these ships each had an ASW armament of one ahead-firing fixed hedgehog and two Mk 32 triple torpedo tube mounts; subsequently removed from all ships. Hence, no A/S capability is provided at this time.

Classification: These ships were designated as high endurance cutters (WHEC) on 1 May 1966; previously WPG.

Engineering: Range is 4 000 miles at 20 knots and 8 000 miles at 10·5 knots.

Gunnery: As built these ships had two 5 inch 51 cal guns (single mounts forward) and several smaller guns; rearmed during World War II with an additional single 5 inch 51 cal gun installed aft plus two or three 3 inch 50 cal anti-aircraft guns, and several 20 mm anti-aircraft guns (depth charge racks installed); *Taney* was experimentally armed with four 5 inch 38 cal guns in single mounts. Armament of all ships after World War II reduced to one 5 inch 38 cal gun and two 40 mm guns.

Nomenclature: Named for secretaries of the Department of Treasury; names shortened to surnames only in 1942.

Photographs: The *Taney* has a WSR-S1 storm tracking radar dome mounted on her bridge. She operates on ocean weather station "Hotel", 200 miles northeast of Norfolk, Virginia; the last of the US Coast Guard-manned ocean stations.

TANEY (WHEC 37)   1975, United States Coast Guard

BIBB (WHEC 31)   1973, United States Coast Guard

1 HIGH ENDURANCE/TRAINING CUTTER (WHEC/WTR): "CASCO" (311) CLASS

Name	No.	Builders	Laid down	Launched	Commissioned
UNIMAK	WTR 379 (ex-WHEC 379, ex-AVP 31)	Associated Shipbuilders, Seattle, Wash	15 Feb 1942	27 May 1942	31 Dec 1943

Displacement, tons: 1 766 standard; 2 800 full load
Length, feet (metres): 300 wl; 310·75 oa *(94·7)*
Beam, feet (metres): 41 *(12·5)*
Draught, feet (metres): 13·5 *(4·1)*
Guns: 1—5 inch *(127 mm)* 38 cal DP
A/S weapons: Removed
Main engines: Diesels (Fairbanks Morse); 6 080 bhp; 2 shafts
Speed, knots: 18

The *Unimak* is the sole survivor of 18 former Navy seaplane tenders (AVP) transferred to the Coast Guard in 1946-1948 (WAVP/WHEC 370-387). The *Unimak* operated as a training cutter (WTR) from 1969 until decommissioned in 1975. She was slated to be transferred to South Vietnam but with the fall of the Saigon government that year she was retained in reserve. The *Unimak* has been scheduled for commissioning in 1977. See 1974-1975 and previous editions for class disposals.
(The only other seaplane tender-type ship in US service is the *Norton Sound,* formerly AV 11, in service as a Navy weapons test ship, classified AVM 1.)

Anti-submarine armament: All A/S weapons have been removed. (The accompanying photograph, taken in 1970, shows the *Unimak* with a fixed hedgehog behind the 5 inch gun mount and triple Mk 32 torpedo tubes on the same 01 level alongside the funnel.)

Classification: The former Navy AVPs were designated WAVP by the Coast Guard until changed to high endurance cutters (WHEC) on 1 May 1966. The *Unimak* subsequently became a training cutter (WTR) on 28 Nov 1969. She is expected to be reclassified WHEC 379 upon recommissioning in 1977.

Engineering: Range is rated at 22 000 miles at 11 knots and 8 000 miles at 19 knots.

Transfers: Ships of this class (originally "Barnegat" class) serve in the navies of Ethiopia and Italy.

UNIMAK (as WTR 379)   1970, United States Coast Guard

(27) MEDIUM ENDURANCE CUTTERS (WMEC): 270-foot CLASS

WMEC 603	Proposed FY 1977 Programme
WMEC 631	Proposed FY 1977 Programme
WMEC	Planned FY 1978-1983
25 Ships	

Displacement, tons: 1 630 full load
Dimensions, feet (metres): 270 oa × 38·3 × 13 *(82·3 × 11·7 × 4·0)*
Guns: 1—76 mm 62 calibre DP (Mk 75)
Helicopters: 1 HH-52 or 1 LAMPS III
Main engines: Diesel; 7 000 bhp; 2 shafts = 19·7 knots
Complement: 103 (14 officers, 89 enlisted men)

The Coast Guard plans to construct 27 medium endurance cutters of this class over a seven-year period. They will replace older medium and high endurance cutters when they become operational from about 1980 onward.

A/S weapons: These ships will have no shipboard A/S weapons, but will rely on helicopters to deliver torpedoes against submarines detected by the ships' towed sonar array.

Design: These ships bear a superficial resemblence to the larger "Hamilton" class cutters because of the superstructure lines and the twin funnels faired into the helicopter hangar (the "Hamilton" funnels are at the after end of the hangar). They will be the only medium endurance cutters with helicopter hangars, and the first cutters with automated command and control centre. Fin stabilisers to be fitted.

Electronics: Fitted with Mk 92 weapons control system, easily identified by radome atop pilot house (as in Navy frigates and hydrofoil missile combatants). These ships will not have hull-mounted sonar, but instead the Escort Towed Array Sonar System (ETASS), capable of providing long-range targeting data for A/S helicopter attack.

Engineering: Diesels were selected over gas turbine propulsion because of the Coast Guard requirement for long on-station time at slow speeds vice high-speed naval operations. (They are slightly faster than the previous WMEC class.)

Fiscal: The Coast Guard Fiscal Year 1977 programme provides $49 000 000 for the first two ships of this class.

Gunnery: Fitted with Americanised version of the OTO Melara 76 mm guns also being provided in new Navy frigate and hydrofoil missile combatant classes.

Helicopters: The design is sized to accommodate the HH-52 Sea Guard helicopter or its Coast Guard successor, or the Navy's planned LAMPS III (Light Airborne Multi-Purpose System) helicopter. The helicopter hangar is extendable.

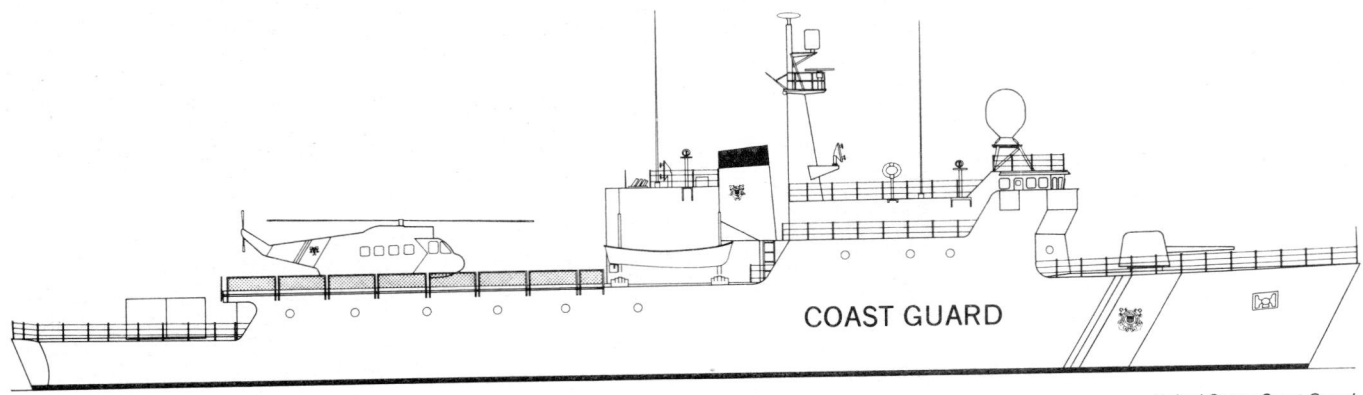

270 foot Class

United States Coast Guard

MEDIUM ENDURANCE CUTTERS

15 MEDIUM ENDURANCE CUTTERS (WMEC) } "RELIANCE" (210) CLASS
1 RESERVE TRAINING CUTTER (WTR)

Name	*No.*	*Builders*	*Commissioned*	*Name*	*No.*	*Builders*	*Commissioned*
RELIANCE	WTR 615	Todd Shipyards	20 June 1964	**STEADFAST**	WMEC 623	American Shipbuilding Co	25 Sep 1968
DILIGENCE	WMEC 616	Todd Shipyards	26 Aug 1964	**DAUNTLESS**	WMEC 624	American Shipbuilding Co	10 June 1968
VIGILANT	WMEC 617	Todd Shipyards	3 Oct 1964	**VENTUROUS**	WMEC 625	Coast Guard Yard, Curtis Bay, Baltimore	16 Aug 1968
ACTIVE	WMEC 618	Christy Corp	17 Sep 1966				
CONFIDENCE	WMEC 619	Coast Guard Yard, Curtis Bay, Baltimore	19 Feb 1966	**DEPENDABLE**	WMEC 626	American Shipbuilding Co	22 Nov 1968
				VIGOROUS	WMEC 627	American Shipbuilding Co	2 May 1969
RESOLUTE	WMEC 620	American Shipbuilding Co	8 Dec 1966	**DURABLE**	WMEC 628	Coast Guard Yard, Curtis Bay, Baltimore	8 Dec 1967
VALIANT	WMEC 621	American Shipbuilding Co	28 Oct 1967				
COURAGEOUS	WMEC 622	American Shipbuilding Co	10 Apr 1968	**DECISIVE**	WMEC 629	Coast Guard Yard, Curtis Bay, Baltimore	23 Aug 1968
				ALERT	WMEC 630	American Shipbuilding Co	4 Aug 1969

Displacement, tons: 950 standard; 1 000 full load except WMEC 615-619, 970 full load
Dimensions, feet (metres): 210·5 oa × 34 × 10·5 *(64·2 × 10·4 × 3·2)*
Guns: 1—3 inch *(76 mm)* 50 calibre AA; 2—·50 cal MG
Helicopters: 1 HH-52 helicopter embarked for missions
Main engines: 2 turbo-charged diesels; 2 shafts; 5 000 bhp = 18 knots; WMEC 615-619 also have 2 gas turbines (2 000 shp); no speed increase
Complement: 61 (7 officers, 54 enlisted men)

Rated as 210-foot cutters. Designed for search and rescue duties. Design features include 360-degree visibility from wheelhouse; helicopter flight deck (no hangar); and engine exhaust vent at stern in place of conventional funnel. Capable of towing ships up to 10 000 tons. Air-conditioned throughout except engine room; high degree of habitability.
Launched, respectively, on the following dates: 25 May 1963, 20 July 1963, 24 Dec 1963, 21 July 1965, 8 May 1965, 30 April 1966, 14 Jan 1967, 18 Mar 1967, 24 June 1967, 21 Oct 1967, 11 Nov 1967, 16 Mar 1968, 4 May 1968, 29 Apr 1967, 14 Dec 1967, 19 Oct 1968.
All of these cutters are active. The *Reliance* (ex-WMEC 615) was assigned as the Coast Guard's reserve training cutter in mid-1975, replacing the 311-foot *Unimak* (WTR 379). She is based at Yorktown, Virginia, and retains full search, rescue, and patrol capabilities.

Helicopters: The *Alert* was the first US ship fitted with the Canadian-developed "Beartrap" helicopter hauldown system. An HH-52A helicopter conducted trials late in 1969, making 30 successful landings despite winds over 40 mph. No further procurement of this system has been funded.

Designation: These ships were originally designated as patrol craft (WPC); changed to WMEC on 1 May 1966.

RELIANCE (WTR 615)

1975, United States Coast Guard

"RELIANCE" CLASS—*continued*

Engineering: Fitted with controllable-pitch propellers. The first five ships have twin Solar, 2 000 hp gas turbines in addition to the diesels common to all ships of this class. Diesels are ALCO model 251-B.
Range is 6 100 miles at 13 knots for WMEC 615-619, and 6 100 miles at 14 knots for later ships.

Photographs: At right the *Dauntless* refuels a 95-foot patrol boat off the Florida coast. An HH-52 Sea Guard helicopter rests on the deck of the larger cutter.

"ACTIVE" CLASS

All 33 of the steel patrol cutters of the 125-foot "Active" class have been stricken except the *Cuyahoga*, employed as a training ship and listed on a later page. The "Active" class boats were numbers WPC/WMEC 125-157; completed in 1926-1927.

TUG TYPE

Several tug-type cutters officially are listed as Medium Endurance Cutters. These ships are described on a later page under the heading Oceangoing Tugs.

AIR CUSHION VEHICLES

The three Coast Guard-operated Air Cushion Vehicles (ACV) have been diiscarded or lost: *Hover 02* lost operationally on Lake Michigan on 23 Nov 1971. *Hover 01* and *Hover 02* decommissioned and discarded in 1973.
All three operated by the US Navy from 1965 to 1969 as patrol Air Cushion Vehicles (PACV). See 1973-1974 and previous editions for characteristics.

DAUNTLESS (WMEC 624) and CAPE SHOALWATER (WPB 95324)

1975, US Coast Guard

PATROL BOATS

26 PATROL BOATS (WPB): "CAPE" CLASS

Plans to construct about 30 WPBs of an improved design have been cancelled in favour of modernising the existing 95-foot class.

26 PATROL BOATS (WPB): CAPE CLASS

Name	No.	Builders
"A" Series		
CAPE SMALL	95300	Coast Guard Yard, Curtis Bay, Maryland
CAPE CORAL	95301	Coast Guard Yard, Curtis Bay, Maryland
CAPE HIGGON	95302	Coast Guard Yard, Curtis Bay, Maryland
CAPE UPRIGHT	95303	Coast Guard Yard, Curtis Bay, Maryland
CAPE GULL	95304	Coast Guard Yard, Curtis Bay, Maryland
CAPE HATTERAS	95305	Coast Guard Yard, Curtis Bay, Maryland
CAPE GEORGE	95306	Coast Guard Yard, Curtis Bay, Maryland
CAPE CURRENT	95307	Coast Guard Yard, Curtis Bay, Maryland
CAPE STRAIT	95308	Coast Guard Yard, Curtis Bay, Maryland
CAPE CARTER	95309	Coast Guard Yard, Curtis Bay, Maryland
CAPE WASH	95310	Coast Guard Yard, Curtis Bay, Maryland
CAPE HEDGE	95311	Coast Guard Yard, Curtis Bay, Maryland
"B" Series		
CAPE KNOX	95312	Coast Guard Yard, Curtis Bay, Maryland
CAPE MORGAN	95313	Coast Guard Yard, Curtis Bay, Maryland
CAPE FAIRWEATHER	95314	Coast Guard Yard, Curtis Bay, Maryland
CAPE FOX	95316	Coast Guard Yard, Curtis Bay, Maryland
CAPE JELLISON	95317	Coast Guard Yard, Curtis Bay, Maryland
CAPE NEWAGEN	95318	Coast Guard Yard, Curtis Bay, Maryland
CAPE ROMAIN	95319	Coast Guard Yard, Curtis Bay, Maryland
CAPE STARR	95320	Coast Guard Yard, Curtis Bay, Maryland
"C" Series		
CAPE CROSS	95321	Coast Guard Yard, Curtis Bay, Maryland
CAPE HORN	95322	Coast Guard Yard, Curtis Bay, Maryland
CAPE SHOALWATER	95324	Coast Guard Yard, Curtis Bay, Maryland
CAPE CORWIN	95326	Coast Guard Yard, Curtis Bay, Maryland
CAPE HENLOPEN	95328	Coast Guard Yard, Curtis Bay, Maryland
CAPE YORK	95332	Coast Guard Yard, Curtis Bay, Maryland

CAPE STARR (WPB 95320)

1969, US Coast Guard

Displacement, tons: A series 106; B series 105; C series 98
Dimensions, feet (metres): 95 oa × 19 × 6 *(29·0 × 5·8 × 1·8)*
Guns: 1—81 mm mortar and 2—·50 cal MG or 2—·50 cal MG
Main engines: 4 diesels (Cummings); 2 200 bhp; 2 shafts = 20 knots
Complement: 14 (1 officer, 13 enlisted men)

Rated as 95-foot cutters. Designed and built by the Coast Guard Yard, Curtis Bay, Maryland, for port security, search, and rescue. Steel hulled; C series boats have less electronics. A series built in 1953; B series in 1955-1956, and C series in 1958-1959.
Plans to dispose of this class from 1974-1975 onward in favour of new WPB construction have been changed; instead all 26 remaining units will be modernised (see below). Several "Cape" class cutters serve in the South Korean Navy.

Engineering: Range is 2 600 miles for the A series, 3 000 miles for the B series, and 2 800 miles for the C series, all at 9 knots.

Modernisation: All 26 units will be modernised to extend their service life for an estimated ten years. Cost in 1976 was estimated at $500 000 per cutter. They will receive new engines, electronics, and deck equipment; superstructure will be modified or replaced; and habitability will be improved. The first to be modernised will be the *Cape Upright* from July 1977 to December 1977, with all 26 to be completed by 1980-1981.

53 PATROL BOATS (WPB): "POINT" CLASS

Name	No.	Builders
"A" Series		
POINT HOPE	82302	Coast Guard Yard, Curtis Bay, Maryland
POINT VERDE	82311	Coast Guard Yard, Curtis Bay, Maryland
POINT SWIFT	82312	Coast Guard Yard, Curtis Bay, Maryland
POINT THATCHER	82314	Coast Guard Yard, Curtis Bay, Maryland
"C" Series		
POINT HERRON	82318	Coast Guard Yard, Curtis Bay, Maryland
POINT ROBERTS	82332	Coast Guard Yard, Curtis Bay, Maryland
POINT HIGHLAND	82333	Coast Guard Yard, Curtis Bay, Maryland
POINT LEDGE	82334	Coast Guard Yard, Curtis Bay, Maryland
POINT COUNTESS	82335	Coast Guard Yard, Curtis Bay, Maryland
POINT GLASS	82336	Coast Guard Yard, Curtis Bay, Maryland
POINT DIVIDE	82337	Coast Guard Yard, Curtis Bay, Maryland
POINT BRIDGE	82338	Coast Guard Yard, Curtis Bay, Maryland
POINT CHICO	82339	Coast Guard Yard, Curtis Bay, Maryland
POINT BATAN	82340	Coast Guard Yard, Curtis Bay, Maryland
POINT LOOKOUT	82341	Coast Guard Yard, Curtis Bay, Maryland
POINT BAKER	82342	Coast Guard Yard, Curtis Bay, Maryland
POINT WELLS	82343	Coast Guard Yard, Curtis Bay, Maryland
POINT ESTERO	82344	Coast Guard Yard, Curtis Bay, Maryland
POINT JUDITH	82345	Martinac SB, Tacoma, Washington
POINT ARENA	82346	Martinac SB, Tacoma, Washington
POINT BONITA	82347	Martinac SB, Tacoma, Washington
POINT BARROW	82348	Martinac SB, Tacoma, Washington
POINT SPENCER	82349	Martinac SB, Tacoma, Washington
POINT FRANKLIN	82350	Coast Guard Yard, Curtis Bay, Maryland
POINT BENNETT	82351	Coast Guard Yard, Curtis Bay, Maryland
POINT SAL	82352	Coast Guard Yard, Curtis Bay, Maryland
POINT MONROE	82353	Coast Guard Yard, Curtis Bay, Maryland
POINT EVANS	82354	Coast Guard Yard, Curtis Bay, Maryland
POINT HANNON	82355	Coast Guard Yard, Curtis Bay, Maryland
POINT FRANCIS	82356	Coast Guard Yard, Curtis Bay, Maryland
POINT HURON	82357	Coast Guard Yard, Curtis Bay, Maryland
POINT STUART	82358	Coast Guard Yard, Curtis Bay, Maryland
POINT STEELE	82359	Coast Guard Yard, Curtis Bay, Maryland
POINT WINSLOW	82360	Coast Guard Yard, Curtis Bay, Maryland
POINT CHARLES	82361	Coast Guard Yard, Curtis Bay, Maryland
POINT BROWN	82362	Coast Guard Yard, Curtis Bay, Maryland
POINT NOWELL	82363	Coast Guard Yard, Curtis Bay, Maryland
POINT WHITEHORN	82364	Coast Guard Yard, Curtis Bay, Maryland
POINT TURNER	82365	Coast Guard Yard, Curtis Bay, Maryland
POINT LOBOS	82366	Coast Guard Yard, Curtis Bay, Maryland
POINT KNOLL	82367	Coast Guard Yard, Curtis Bay, Maryland
POINT WARDE	82368	Coast Guard Yard, Curtis Bay, Maryland
POINT HEYER	82369	Coast Guard Yard, Curtis Bay, Maryland
POINT RICHMOND	82370	Coast Guard Yard, Curtis Bay, Maryland
"D" Series		
POINT BARNES	82371	Coast Guard Yard, Curtis Bay, Maryland
POINT BROWER	82372	Coast Guard Yard, Curtis Bay, Maryland
POINT CAMDEN	82373	Coast Guard Yard, Curtis Bay, Maryland
POINT CARREW	82374	Coast Guard Yard, Curtis Bay, Maryland
POINT DORAN	82375	Coast Guard Yard, Curtis Bay, Maryland
POINT HARRIS	82376	Coast Guard Yard, Curtis Bay, Maryland
POINT HOBART	82377	Coast Guard Yard, Curtis Bay, Maryland
POINT JACKSON	82378	Coast Guard Yard, Curtis Bay, Maryland
POINT MARTIN	82379	Coast Guard Yard, Curtis Bay, Maryland

Displacement, tons: A series 67; C series 66; D series 69
Dimensions, feet (metres): 78·1 wl; 83 oa × 17·2 × 5·8 *(25·3 × 5·2 × 1·8)*

POINT CHARLES (WPB 82361)   *1972, US Coast Guard*

CAPE KNOX (WPB 95312) and POINT BARNES (WPB 82371)   *1972, USCG*

Guns: 1—81 mm mortar and 1—·50 cal MG or 2—·50 cal MG; some boats unarmed
Main engines: 2 diesels; 1 600 bhp; 2 shafts = 23·5 knots except D series 22·6 knots
Complement: 8 (1 officer, 7 enlisted men; see notes)

Rated as 82-foot cutters. Designed for search, rescue, and patrol. Of survivors, A series built 1960-1961; C series in 1961-1967; and D series in 1970.
Twenty-six cutters of this class were transferred to South Vietnam in 1969-1970 (see 1975-1976 and previous edition for list).

Engineering: Range is 1 500 miles at 8 knots except D series 1 200 miles at 8 knots.

Nomenclature: WPB 82301-82344 were assigned "point" names in January 1964.

Personnel: Most of these units now have an officer assigned; a few still operate with an all-enlisted crew.

ICEBREAKERS

2 ICEBREAKERS (WAGB): "POLAR" CLASS

Name	No.	Builders	Commissioned
POLAR STAR	WAGB 10	Lockheed Shipbuilding Co, Seattle, Wash	17 Jan 1976
POLAR SEA	WAGB 11	Lockheed Shipbuilding Co, Seattle, Wash	Sep 1976

Displacement, tons: 13 190 full load
Dimensions, feet (metres): 399 oa × 83·5 × 33·5 *(121·6 × 25·5 × 10·2)*
Main engines: Diesel-electric, 18 000 shp; gas turbines, 60 000 shp; 3 shafts (controllable pitch propellers) = 20 knots
Guns: None
Helicopters: 2 HH-52
Complement: 148 (13 officers, 125 enlisted men) plus 10 scientists

These ships are the first icebreakers built for US service since the *Glacier* constructed two decades earlier. The programme is intended to replace the World War II-built "Wind" class icebreakers. *Polar Star* authorised in the Fiscal Year 1971 budget of the Department of Transportation; *Polar Sea* in FY 1973 budget. *Polar Star* was laid down on 15 May 1972 and launched on 17 Nov 1973; *Polar Sea* was laid down on 27 Nov 1973 and launched on 24 June 1975. No additional ships are planned for the near future.

Design: The "Polar" class icebreakers are the largest ships operated by the US Coast Guard. Their icebreaking capability—based on total horsepower available—is greater than any other icebreaker in service except for the Soviet "Arktika" class nuclear icebreakers.
These ships have a conventional icebreaker hull form with cutaway bow configuration and well rounded body sections to prevent being trapped in ice. Two 15-ton capacity cranes fitted aft; hangar and flight deck aft; extensive research laboratories provided for arctic and oceanographic research.

Engineering: This *Polar* CODOG (Combination Diesel or Gas Turbine) design provides for conventional diesel engines for normal cruising and gas turbines for maximum power situations. The diesel engines will drive generators producing AC power; the main propulsion DC motors will draw power through rectifiers permitting absolute flexibility in the delivery of power from alternate sources. The use of controllable-pitch propellers on three shafts will permit manoeuvring in heavy ice without the risk to the propeller blades caused by stopping the shaft while going from ahead to astern.
The six Alco diesels provide a total of 18 000 bhp; the three Pratt and Whitney FT4A-12 gas turbines provide about 60 000 shp.

POLAR STAR (WAGB 10)   *1976, United States Coast Guard*

"POLAR" CLASS—continued

The Coast Guard had given consideration to the use of nuclear power for an icebreaker; however, at this time the gas turbine-diesel combination can achieve the desirable power requirements without the added cost and operating restrictions of a nuclear powerplant.

Photographs: Note pointed stern and twin funnels in overhead view. The earlier photograph shows the broad, flat superstructure front.

POLAR STAR (WAGB 10) at launching
1973, US Coast Guard

1 ICEBREAKER (WAGB): "GLACIER" TYPE

Name	No.	Builders	USN Comm.
GLACIER	WAGB 4 (ex-AGB 4)	Ingalls Shipbuilding Corp, Pascagoula, Mississippi	27 May 1955

Displacement, tons: 8 449 full load
Dimensions, feet (metres): 309·6 oa × 74 × 29 *(94·4 × 6·9 × 8·8)*
Guns: 4—·50 cal MG
Helicopters: 2 helicopters normally embarked
Main engines: Diesel-electric (10 Fairbanks-Morse diesels and 2 Westinghouse electric motors); 21 000 hp; 2 shafts = 17·6 knots
Complement: 229 (14 officers, 215 enlisted men)

The largest icebreaker in US service prior to the "Polar" class; laid down on 3 Aug 1953 and launched on 27 Aug 1954. Transferred from Navy (AGB 4) to Coast Guard on 30 June 1966. During 1972 the *Glacier* and assigned helicopters were painted red to improve visibility in Arctic regions. All other icebreakers painted red during 1973.

Engineering: When built the *Glacier* had the largest capacity single-armature DC motors ever built and installed in a ship. Range is 29 200 miles at 12 knots or 12 000 miles at 17·6 knots.

Gunnery: As built the *Glacier* was armed with two 5 inch guns (twin), six 3 inch AA guns (twin), and four 20 mm AA guns; lighter weapons removed prior to transfer to Coast Guard; 5 inch guns removed in 1969.

GLACIER (WAGB 4)
1972, US Coast Guard

3 ICEBREAKERS (WAGB): "WIND" CLASS

Name	No.	Builders	Launched
WESTWIND	WAGB 281 (ex-AGB 6)	Western Pipe & Steel Co, San Pedro, California	31 Mar 1943
NORTHWIND	WAGB 282	Western Pipe & Steel Co, San Pedro, California	25 Feb 1945
BURTON ISLAND	WAGB 283 (ex-AGB 1, ex-AG 88)	Western Pipe & Steel Co, San Pedro, California	30 April 1946

Displacement, tons: 3 500 standard; 6 515 full load
Dimensions, feet (metres): 250 wl; 269 oa × 63·5 × 29 *(82·0 × 19·4 × 8·8)*
Helicopters: 2 helicopters normally embarked
Guns: 4—·50 cal MG (see *Gunnery* notes)
Main engines: Diesel-electric; 10 000 bhp; 2 shafts = 16 knots
Complement: 135

Originally seven ships in this class built. Five ships were delivered to the US Coast Guard during World War II and two to the US Navy in 1946. The *Westwind* served in the Soviet Navy from 1945 to 1951 (named *Severni Polius* in Soviet service). The *Burton Island* was transferred from the US Navy to the Coast Guard on 15 Dec 1966.
The *Westwind* operates on the Great Lakes. The *Burton Island* was to be laid up late in 1976. Crews of *Northwind* and *Westwind* reduced from 181 to approx 135 during 1975.

Engineering: These ships were built with a bow propeller shaft in addition to the two stern shafts; bow shaft removed from all units because it would continually break in hard storis ice. Main engines are Fairbanks Morse 38D81/8. Range is 38 000 miles at 10·5 knots or 16 000 miles at 16 knots.
Westwind re-engined with four Enterprise diesels in 1973-1974, and *Northwind* in 1974-1975; same bhp and speed. Note taller funnel in photograph of *Westwind* after engine change.

Gunnery: As built the five Coast Guard ships each mounted four 5 inch guns (one twin mount forward and one twin mount aft on 01 level) and 12 40 mm anti-aircraft guns (quad); the two Navy Ships were completed with only forward twin 5 inch mount (as built a catapult and cranes were fitted immediately behind the funnel and one floatplane was carried). Armament reduced after war and helicopter platform eventually installed in all ships.
During the 1960s the *Northwind* carried two 5 inch guns (twin), and the other ships each mounted one 5 inch gun; all primary gun batteries removed in 1969-1970.

Disposals: *Eastwind* (WAGB 279) stricken in 1972; *Southwind* (WAGB 280, ex-AGB 3) stricken in 1974; *Edisto* (WAGB 284 ex-AGB 2, ex-AG 89), *Staten Island* (WAGB 278, ex-AGB 5) stricken in 1976.

BURTON ISLAND (WAGB 283)
1975, US Coast Guard

WESTWIND (WAGB 281)
1974, US Coast Guard

1 ICEBREAKER (WAGB): "MACKINAW" TYPE

Name	No.	Builders	Commissioned
MACKINAW (ex-*Manitowac*)	WAGB 83	Toledo Shipbuilding Co, Ohio	20 Dec 1944

Displacement, tons: 5 252
Dimensions, feet (metres): 290 oa × 74 × 19 *(88·4 × 22·6 × 5·8)*
Helicopters: 1 helicopter
Main engines: Diesel; with electric drive; 3 shafts (1 forward, 2 aft); 10 000 bhp = 18·7 knots
Complement: 127 (10 officers, 117 enlisted men)

Laid down on 20 Mar 1943; launched 6 Mar 1944 and completed in January 1945. Specially designed and constructed for service as icebreaker on the Great Lakes. Equipped with two 12-ton capacity cranes. Clear area for helicopter is provided on the quarterdeck.
Range is 60 000 miles at 12 knots.

MACKINAW (WAGB 83)   *United States Coast Guard*

1 ICEBREAKER (WMEC): "STORIS" TYPE

Name	No.	Builders	Commissioned
STORIS (ex-*Eskimo*)	WMEC 38 (ex-WAGB 38)	Toledo Shipbuilding Co, Ohio	30 Sep 1942

Displacement, tons: 1 715 standard; 1 925 full load
Dimensions, feet (metres): 230 oa × 43 × 15 *(70·1 × 13·1 × 4·6)*
Guns: 1—3 inch 50 cal (Mk 22); 2—50 cal MG
Main engines: Diesel-electric; 1 shaft; 1 800 bhp = 14 knots
Complement: 106 (10 officers, 96 enlisted men)

Laid down on 14 July 1941; launched on 4 Apr 1942. Ice patrol tender. Strengthened for ice navigation. Employed in Alaskan service for search, rescue and law enforcement.
Designation changed from WAG to WAGB on 1 May 1966; redesignated as medium endurance cutter (WMEC) on 1 July 1972.
Range is 22 000 miles at 8 knots or 12 000 miles at 14 knots.

STORIS (WMEC 38)   *1975, US Coast Guard*

TRAINING CUTTERS

1 TRAINING CUTTER (IX): "ACTIVE" CLASS

CUYAHOGA   WIX 157 (ex-WMEC 157, ex-WPC 157, ex-WAG 26)

Dimensions, feet (metres): 125 oa × 24 × 8 *(38·1 × 7·3 × 2·4)*
Guns: Removed
Main engines: Diesel; 2 shafts; 800 bhp = 13·2 knots
Complement: 11 (1 officer, 10 enlisted men)

Built in 1926 as one of the 33 "Active" class steel patrol boats. The *Cuyahoga* is the only cutter of this type remaining on the Coast Guard list and probably the oldest US government-owned ship in active service except the relic *Constitution*. The *Cuyahoga* is based at Yorktown, Virginia, for the training of officer candidates.

CUYAHOGA (WIX 157)   *1974, US Coast Guard*

1 TRAINING CUTTER (IX): "EAGLE" TYPE

Name	No.	Builders
EAGLE (ex-*Horst Wessel*)	WIX 327	Blohm & Voss, Hamburg

Displacement, tons: 1 816 full load
Dimensions, feet (metres): 231 wl; 295·2 oa × 39·1 × 17 *(90·0 × 11·9 × 5·2)*
Sail area, square feet: 21 350
Height of masts, feet (metres): fore and main 150·3 *(45·8)*; mizzen 132 *(40·2)*
Main engines: Auxiliary diesel (MAN); 728 bhp; 1 shaft = 10·5 knots (as high as 18 knots under full sail alone)
Complement: 245 (19 officers, 46 enlisted men, 180 cadets)

Former German training ship. Launched on 13 June 1936. Taken by the United States as part of reparations after the Second World War for employment in US Coast Guard Practice Squadron. Taken over at Bremerhaven in Jan 1946; arrived at home port of New London, Connecticut, in July 1946.
(Sister ship *Albert Leo Schlageter* was also taken by the United States in 1945 but was sold to Brazil in 1948 and re-sold to Portugal in 1962. Another ship of similar design, the *Gorch Foch*, transferred to the Soviet Union in 1946 and survives as the *Tovarisch*).

Photographs: When the Coast Guard added the orange-and-blue marking stripes to cutters in the 1960s the *Eagle* was exempted because of their affect on her graceful lines; however, in early 1976 the stripes and words "Coast Guard" were added in conjunction with the July 1976 Operation Sail in New York harbour. They detract considerably from the ship's appearance.

EAGLE (WIX 327)   *United States Coast Guard*

EAGLE (WIX 327)   *1976, US Coast Guard, Ens. Robert R. Trescott*

STORIS (WMEC 38) alongside the LAMUT, flagship of Soviet Bering Sea fishing fleet

1972, National Marine Fisheries Service

SEAGOING TENDERS

35 SEAGOING TENDERS (WLB)
1 OCEANOGRAPHIC CUTTER (WAGO) } **"BALSAM" CLASS**

Name	No.	Launched	Name	No.	Launched
BALSAM*	WLB 62	1942	BITTERSWEET	WLB 389	1944
COWSLIP	WLB 277	1942	BLACTHAW*	WLB 390	1944
GENTIAN	WLB 290	1942	BLACKTHORN	WLB 391	1944
LAUREL	WLB 291	1942	BRAMBLE*	WLB 392	1944
CLOVER	WLB 292	1942	FIREBUSH	WLB 393	1944
EVERGREEN	WAGO 295	1943	HORNBEAM	WLB 394	1944
SORREL*	WLB 296	1943	IRIS	WLB 395	1944
IRONWOOD	WLB 297	1944	MALLOW	WLB 396	1944
CITRUS*	WLB 300	1943	MARIPOSA	WLB 397	1944
CONIFER	WLB 301	1943	SAGEBRUSH	WLB 399	1944
MADRONA	WLB 302	1943	SALVIA	WLB 400	1944
TUPELO	WLB 303	1943	SASSAFRAS	WLB 401	1944
MESQUITE	WLB 305	1943	SEDGE*	WLB 402	1944
BUTTONWOOD	WLB 306	1943	SPAR*	WLB 403	1944
PLANETREE	WLB 307	1943	SUNDEW*	WLB 404	1944
PAPAW	WLB 308	1943	SWEETBRIER	WLB 405	1944
SWEETGUM	WLB 309	1943	ACACIA	WLB 406	1944
BASSWOOD	WLB 388	1944	WOODRUSH	WLB 407	1944

HORNBEAM (WLB 394) gun aft of funnel   *1969, US Coast Guard*

Displacement, tons: 935 standard; 1 025 full load
Dimensions, feet (metres): 180 oa × 37 × 13 *(59 × 12·1 × 4·2)*
Guns: 1—3 inch *(76 mm)* 50 calibre in *Citrus, Cowslip, Hornbeam,* and *Sorrel* (original armament); most others have ·50 calibre MG except *Sedge* has 2—20 mm guns; several ships are unarmed
Main engines: Diesel-electric; 1 000 bhp in tenders numbered WLB 62-303 series, except *Ironwood*; 1 shaft = 12·8 knots; others 1 200 bhp; 1 shaft = 15 knots
Complement: 53 (6 officers, 47 enlisted men)

Seagoing buoy tenders. *Ironwood* built by Coast Guard Yard at Curtis Bay, Maryland; others by Marine Iron & Shipbuilding Co, Duluth, Minnesota, or Zeneth Dredge Co, Duluth, Minnesota. Eight ships indicated by asterisks are strengthened for icebreaking. Three ships, *Cowslip, Bittersweet,* and *Hornbeam,* have controllable-pitch, bow-thrust propellers to assist in manoeuvering. All WLBs have 20-capacity booms. The *Evergreen* has been refitted as an oceanographic cutter (WAGO) and is painted white; several ships are laid up in reserve.

EVERGREEN (WAGO 295)   *1973, US Coast Guard*

COASTAL TENDERS

5 COASTAL TENDERS (WLM): "RED" CLASS

Name	No.	Launched	Name	No.	Launched
RED WOOD	WLM 685	1964	**RED CEDAR**	WLM 688	1970
RED BEECH	WLM 688	1964	**RED OAK**	WLM 689	1971
RED BIRCH	WLM 687	1965			

Displacement, tons: 471 standard; 512 full load
Dimensions, feet (metres): 157 oa × 33 × 6 *(51·5 × 10·8 × 1·9)*
Main engines: 2 diesels; 2 shafts; 1 800 hp = 12·8 knots
Complement: 31 (4 officers, 27 enlisted men)

All built by Coast Guard Yard, Curtis Bay, Maryland. Fitted with controllable-pitch propellers and bow thrusters; steel hulls strengthened for light icebreaking. Steering and engine controls on each bridge wing as well as in pilot house. Living spaces are air conditioned. Range is 3 000 miles at 11·6 knots. Fitted with 10-ton capacity boom.

RED BIRCH (WLM 687)   *1968, US Coast Guard*

3 COASTAL TENDERS (WLM): "HOLLYHOCK" CLASS

FIR WLM 212   **HOLLYHOCK** WLM 220   **WALNUT** WLM 252

Displacement, tons: 989
Dimensions, feet (metres): 175 × 34 × 12 *(57·4 × 10·9 × 3·9)*
Main engines: Diesel reduction; 2 shafts; 1 350 bhp = 12 knots
Complement: 40 (5 officers, 35 enlisted men)

Launched in 1937 *(Hollyhock)* and 1939 *(Fir and Walnut)*. *Walnut* was re-engined by Williamette Iron & Steel Co, Portland, Oregon, in 1958. Redesignated coastal tenders, (WLM), instead of buoy tenders, (WAGL) on 1 Jan 1965. Fitted with 20-ton capacity boom.

FIR (WLM 212)   *1969, US Coast Guard*

1 COASTAL TENDER (WLM): "JUNIPER" TYPE

JUNIPER WLM 224

Displacement, tons: 794
Dimensions, feet (metres): 177 × 33 × 9·2 *(58 × 10·8 × 3)*
Main engines: Diesel, with electric drive; 2 shafts; 900 bhp = 10·8 knots
Complement: 38 (4 officers, 34 enlisted men)

Launched on 18 May 1940. Redesignated WLM vice WAGL on 1 Jan 1965. Fitted with 20-ton capacity boom.

JUNIPER (WLM 224)   *1971, US Coast Guard*

7 COASTAL TENDERS (WLM): "WHITE" CLASS

WHITE BUSH	WLM 542	**WHITE PINE**	WLM 547	
WHITE HEATH	WLM 545	**WHITE SAGE**	WLM 544	
WHITE HOLLY	WLM 543	**WHITE SUMAC**	WLM 540	
WHITE LUPINE	WLM 546			

Displacement, tons: 435 standard; 600 full load
Dimensions, feet (metres): 133 oa × 31 × 9 *(43·6 × 10·1 × 2·9)*
Main engines: Diesel; 2 shafts; 600 bhp = 9·8 knots
Complement: 21 (1 officer, 20 enlisted men)

All launched in 1943. All seven ships are former US Navy YFs, adapted for the Coast Guard. The *White Alder* (WLM 541) was sunk in a collision on 7 Dec 1968. Fitted with 10-ton capacity boom.

WHITE BUSH (WLM 542)   *1969, US Coast Guard*

INLAND TENDERS

TERN WLI 80801

Displacement, tons: 168 full load
Dimensions, feet (metres): 80 oa × 25 × 5 *(26·2 × 8·2 × 1·6)*
Main engines: Diesels; 2 shafts; 450 hp = 10 knots
Complement: 7 (enlisted men)

The *Tern* is prototype for a new design of inland buoy tenders. A cutaway stern and gantry crane (the first installed in a Coast Guard tender) permit lifting buoys aboard from the stern. The crane moves on rails that extend forward to the deck house. Fitted with 125 hp bow thruster to improve manoeuvrability. Air conditioned.
Built by Coast Guard Yard at Curtis Bay, Baltimore, Maryland. Launched on 15 June 1968 and placed in service on 7 Feb 1969.

TERN (WLI 80801)   *1969, US Coast Guard*

TAMARACK WLI 248

Displacement, tons: 400 full load
Dimensions, feet (metres): 124 oa × 30 × 8 *(40·6 × 9·8 × 2·6)*
Main engines: Diesels; 1 shaft; 520 bhp = 10 knots

Launched in 1934. Fitted with 10-ton capacity boom. Out of service.

COSMOS WLI 293	**BLUEBELL** WLI 313	**PRIMROSE** WLI 316
RAMBLER WLI 298	**SMILAX** WLI 315	**VERBENA** WLI 317

Displacement, tons: 178 full load
Dimensions, feet (metres): 100 oa × 24 × 5 *(32·8 × 7·8 × 1·6)*
Main engines: Diesels; 2 shafts 600 bhp = 10·5 knots
Complement: 15 (1 officer, 14 enlisted men)

Cosmos launched in 1942, *Bluebell* in 1945, others in 1944. The *Verbena* is fitted with pile drivers.

AZALEA WLI 641

Displacement, tons: 200 full load
Dimensions, feet (metres): 100 oa × 24 × 5 *(32·8 × 7·8 × 1·6)*
Main engines: Diesels; 2 shafts; 440 bhp = 9 knots
Complement: 14 (1 officer, 13 enlisted men)

Launched in 1958. Fitted with pile driver.

BUCKTHORN WLI 642

Displacement, tons: 200 full load
Dimensions, feet (metres): 100 oa × 24 × 4 *(32·8 × 7·8 × 1·3)*
Main engines: Diesels; 2 shafts; 600 bhp = 7·3 knots
Complement: 14 (1 officer, 13 enlisted men)

Launched in 1963.

BUCKTHORN (WLI 642)   *1970, US Coast Guard*

CLEMATIS WLI 74286	**SHADBUSH** WLI 74287

Displacement, tons: 93 full load
Dimensions, feet (metres): 74 oa × 19 × 4 *(24·3 × 6·2 × 1·3)*
Main engines: Diesels; 2 shafts; 330 bhp = 8 knots
Complement: 9 (enlisted men)

Launched in 1944.

BLUEBERRY WLI 65302

Displacement, tons: 45 full load
Dimensions, feet (metres): 65 oa × 17 × 14 *(21·3 × 5·6 × 4·6)*
Main engines: Diesels; 2 shafts; 330 bhp = 10·5 knots
Complement: 5 (enlisted men)

Launched in 1942.

BLACKBERRY WLI 65303	**CHOKEBERRY** WLI 65304	**LOGANBERRY** WLI 65305

Displacement, tons: 68 full load
Dimensions, feet (metres): 65 oa × 17 × 4 *(21·3 × 5·6 × 4·6)*
Main engines: Diesels; 1 shaft; 220 hp = 9 knots
Complement: 5 (enlisted men)

Launched in 1946.

BAYBERRY WLI 65400	**ELDERBERRY** WLI 65401

Displacement, tons: 68 full load
Dimensions, feet (metres): 65 oa × 17 × 4 *(21·3 × 5·6 × 4·6)*
Main engines: Diesels; 2 shafts; 400 hp = 11·3 knots
Complement: 5 (enlisted men)

Launched in 1954.

CONSTRUCTION TENDERS

PAMLICO WLIC 800   **HUDSON** WLIC 801

Dimensions, feet (metres): 160 oa *(52·4)*
Main engines: Diesels
Complement: 13

Built in 1975-1976 at the Coast Guard Yard, Curtis Bay, Maryland.

ANVIL	WLIC 75301	**MALLET**	WLIC 75304	**WEDGE**	WLIC 75307
HAMMER	WLIC 75302	**VISE**	WLIC 75305	**SPIKE**	WLIC 75308
SLEDGE	WLIC 75303	**CLAMP**	WLIC 75306	**HATCHET**	WLIC 75309
				AXE	WLIC 75310

Displacement, tons: 145 full load
Dimensions, feet (metres): 75 oa (WLIC 75306-75310 are 76 oa) × 22 × 4 *(24·6 × 7·2 × 1·3)*
Main engines: Diesels; 2 shafts; 600 hp = 10 knots
Complement: 9 or 10 (1 officer in *Mallett, Sledge* and *Vise;* 9 enlisted men in all)

Launched 1962-1965.

SPIKE (WLIC 75308) pushing barge   *1971, US Coast Guard*

RIVER TENDERS

SUMAC WLR 311

Displacement, tons: 404 full load
Dimensions, feet (metres): 115 oa × 30 × 6 *(37·7 × 9·8 × 1·9)*
Main engines: Diesels; 3 shafts; 960 hp = 10·6 knots
Complement: 23 (1 officer, 22 enlisted men)

Built in 1943. *Fern* WLR 304 stricken.

DOGWOOD WLR 259   **FORSYTHIA** WLR 263   **SYCAMORE** WLR 268

Displacement, tons: 230 full load, except *Forsythia* 280
Dimensions, feet (metres): 114 oa × 26 × 4 *(37·4 × 8·5 × 1·3)*
Main engines: Diesels; 2 shafts; 2 800 hp = 11 knots
Complement: 21 (1 officer, 20 enlisted men)

Dogwood and *Sycamore* built in 1940; *Forsythia* in 1943.

FOXGLOVE WLR 285

Displacement, tons: 350 full load
Dimensions, feet (metres): 114 oa × 30 × 6 *(37·4 × 9·8 × 1·9)*
Main engines: Diesels; 3 shafts; 8 500 hp = 13·5 knots
Complement: 21 (1 officer, 20 enlisted men)

Built in 1945.

LANTANA WLR 80310

Displacement, tons: 235 full load
Dimensions, feet (metres): 80 oa × 30 × 6 *(26·2 × 9·8 × 1·9)*
Main engines: Diesels; 3 shafts; 10 000 hp = 10 knots
Complement: 20 (1 officer, 19 enlisted men)

Built in 1943.

GASCONADE	WLR 75401	**CHEYENNE**	WLR 75405
MUSKINGUM	WLR 75402	**KICKAPOO**	WLR 75406
WYACONDA	WLR 75403	**KANAWHA**	WLR 75407
CHIPPEWA	WLR 75404	**PATOKA**	WLR 75408
		CHENA	WLR 75409

Displacement, tons: 145 full load
Dimensions, feet (metres): 75 oa × 22 × 4 *(24·5 × 7·2 × 1·3)*
Main engines: Diesel; 2 shafts; 600 hp = 10·8 knots
Complement: 12 (enlisted men)

Built 1964-1971.

OLEANDER WLR 73264

Displacement, tons: 90 full load
Dimensions, feet (metres): 73 oa × 18 × 5 *(23·9 × 5·9 × 1·6)*
Main engines: Diesel; 2 shafts; 300 hp = 12 knots
Complement: 10 (enlisted men)

Built in 1940.

OUACHITA	WLR 65501	**SCIOTO**	WLR 65504
CIMARRON	WLR 65502	**OSAGE**	WLR 65505
OBION	WLR 65503	**SANGAMON**	WLR 65506

Displacement, tons: 139 full load
Dimensions, feet (metres): 65·6 oa × 21 × 5 *(21·5 × 6·9 × 1·6)*
Main engines: Diesel; 2 shafts; 600 hp = 12·5 knots
Complement: 10 (enlisted men)

Built in 1960-1962.

OSAGE (WLR 65505) pushing barge   *US Coast Guard*

OCEANGOING TUGS

1 MEDIUM ENDURANCE CUTTER (WMEC) } ARS TYPE
1 OCEANOGRAPHIC CUTTER (WAGO)

Name	*No.*	*Builders*	*USN Comm.*
ACUSHNET (ex-USS *Shackle*)	WAGO 167 (ex-WAT 167, ARS 9)	Basalt Rock Co, Napa, California	5 Feb 1944
YOCONA (ex-USS *Seize*)	WMEC 168 (ex-WAT 168, ARS 26)	Basalt Rock Co, Napa, California	3 Nov 1944

Displacement, tons: 1 557 standard; 1 745 full load
Dimensions, feet (metres): 213·5 oa × 39 × 15 *(70 × 12·8 × 4·9)*
Guns: Removed
Main engines: Diesels; 3 000 bhp; 2 shafts = 15·5 knots
Complement: *Acushnet* 64 (7 officers, 57 enlisted men); *Yacona* 72 (7 officers, 65 enlisted men)

Large, steel-hulled tugs transferred from the Navy to the Coast Guard after World War II. Launched 1 April 1943 and 8 April 1944 respectively. *Acushnet* modified for handling environmental data buoys and reclassified WAGO in 1969; *Yocona* reclassified as WMEC in 1969. Armament removed.

YOCONA (WMEC 168)

1970, United States Coast Guard

3 MEDIUM ENDURANCE CUTTERS (WMEC): ATF TYPE

Name	*No.*	*Builders*	*USN Comm.*
CHILULA	WMEC 153 (ex-WAT 153, ATF 153)	Charleston Shipbuilding & Drydock Co, Charleston, South Carolina	5 April1945
CHEROKEE	WMEC 165 (ex-WAT 165, ATF 66)	Bethlehem Steel Co, Staten Island, New York	26 April1940
TAMAROA (ex-*Zuni*)	WMEC 166 (ex-WAT 166, ATF 95)	Commercial Iron Works, Portland, Oregon	9 Oct 1943

Displacement, tons: 1 731 full load
Dimensions, feet (metres): 205 oa × 38·5 × 17 *(62·5 × 11·7 × 5·2)*
Guns: 1—3 inch 50 calibre; 2—·50 cal MG
Main engines: Diesel-electric (General Motors diesel); 3 000 bhp; 1 shaft = 16·2 knots
Complement: 72 (7 officers, 65 enlisted men)

Steel-hulled tugs transferred from the Navy to the Coast Guard after World War II; *Chilula* officially on loan since 9 July 1956 until stricken from the Navy List on 1 June 1969. Classification of all three ships changed to WMEC in 1969. Launched on 1 Dec 1944, 10 Nov 1939, and 13 July 1943, respectively.

CHEROKEE (WMEC 165)

1975, Giorgio Arra

2 MEDIUM ENDURANCE CUTTERS (WMEC): ATA TYPE

Name	*No.*	*Builders*	*USN Comm.*
MODOC (ex-USS *Bagaduce*)	WMEC 194 (ex-*WATA* 194, ATA 194)	Levingston Shipbuilding Co, Orange, Texas	14 Feb 1945
COMANCHE (ex-USS *Wampanoag*)	WMEC 202 (ex-*WATA* 202, ATA 202)	Gulfport Boiler & Welding Works, Port Arthur, Texas	8 Dec 1944

Displacement, tons: 534 standard; 860 full load
Dimensions, feet (metres): 143 oa × 33·8 × 14 *(46·8 × 11 × 4·9)*
Armament: 2—·50 cal MG
Main engines: Diesel-electric (General Motors diesel); 1 shaft; 1 500 hp = 13·5 knots
Complement: 47 (5 officers, 42 enlisted men)

Steel-hulled tugs. Launched on 4 Dec 1944 and 10 Oct 1944, respectively. The *Modoc* was stricken from the Navy List after World War II and transferred to Maritime Administration; transferred to Coast Guard on 15 Apr 1959. *Comanche* transferred on loan from Navy to Coast Guard from 25 Feb 1959 until stricken from Navy List on 1 June 1969. Both ships reclassified as WMEC in 1969.

COMANCHE (WMEC 202)

1969, United States Coast Guard

HARBOUR TUGS

NEW CONSTRUCTION

Displacement, tons: 660 full load
Dimensions, feet (metres): 140 oa × 30 × 12·5 *(45·9 × 9·8 × ·4)*
Main engines: Diesel-electric; 2 500 bhp; 1 shaft
Complement: 17 (3 officers, 14 enlisted men)

The Coast Guard is planning this new class of icebreaking harbour tugs to replace the ageing 110-foot harbour tugs. The initial units will operate on the Great Lakes.
The lead ship is proposed in the Fiscal Year 1977 budget. The above data reflect preliminary designs. See drawing in 1975-1976 edition.

MESSENGER WYTM 85009

Displacement, tons: 230 full load
Dimensions, feet (metres): 85 oa × 23 × 9 *(27·8 × 7·5 × 2·9)*
Main engines: Diesel; 1 shaft; 700 hp = 9·5 knots
Complement: 10 (enlisted)

Built in 1944.

MANITOU	WYTM 60	**MOHICAN**	WYTM 73	**CHINOOK**	WTYM 96
KAW	WYTM 61	**ARUNDEL**	WYTM 90	**OBJIBWA**	WYTM 97
APALACHEE	WYTM 71	**MAMONING**	WYTM 91	**SNOHOMISH**	WYTM 98
YANKTON	WYTM 72	**NAUGATUCK**	WYTM 92	**SAUK**	WYTM 99
		RARITAN	WYTM 93		

Displacement, tons: 370 full load
Dimensions, feet (metres): 110 oa × 27 × 11 *(36 × 8·8 × 3·6)*
Main engines: Diesel-electric; 1 shaft; 1 000 hp = 11·2 knots
Complement: 20 (1 officer, 19 enlisted men)

Built in 1943 except WYTM 90-93 built in 1939.

CAPSTAN	WYTL 65601	**CATENARY**	WYTL 65606	**LINE**	WYTL 65611
CHOCK	WYTL 65602	**BRIDLE**	WYTL 65607	**WIRE**	WYTL 65612
SWIVEL	WYTL 65603	**PENDANT**	WYTL 65608	**BITT**	WYTL 65613
TACKLE	WYTL 65604	**SHACKLE**	WYTL 65609	**BOLLARD**	WYTL 65614
TOWLINE	WYTL 65605	**HAWSER**	WYTL 65610	**CLEAT**	WYTL 65615

Displacement, tons: 72 full load
Dimensions, feet (metres): 65 oa × 19 × 7 *(21·3 × 6·2 × 2·3)*
Main engines: Diesel; 1 shaft; 400 hp = 9·8 knots except WYTL 65601-65606 10·5 knots
Complement: 10 (enlisted men)

Built from 1961 to 1967.

LIGHTSHIPS

LIGHTSHIP COLUMBIA WLV 604		**LIGHTSHIP NANTUCKET** WLV 612	
LIGHTSHIP RELIEF WLV 605		**LIGHTSHIP RELIEF** WLV 613	

Displacement, tons: 617 full load, except WLV 612 and 613 are 607 full load
Dimensions, feet (metres): 128 oa × 30 × 11 *(41·9 × 9·8 × 3·8)*
Main engines: Diesel; 550 bhp; 1 shaft = 10·7 knots , except WLV 612 and 613 = 11 knots

All launched 1950 except *Lightship Relief* (WLV 613) in 1952. *Lightship Columbia* assigned to Astoria, Oregon; *Lightship Relief* (605) to Seattle, Washington; *Lightship Nantucket* and *Lightship Relief* (613) to Boston, Massachusetts.
Coast Guard lightships exchange names according to assignment; hull numbers remain constant.

NATIONAL OCEANIC AND ATMOSPHERIC ADMINISTRATION

Command

Director, National Ocean Survey:
Rear-Admiral Allen L. Powell
Associate Director, Office of Fleet Operations:
Rear-Admiral Herbert R. Lippold, Jnr.
Director, Atlantic Marine Center:
Rear-Admiral Robert C. Munson
Director, Pacific Marine Center:
Rear-Admiral Eugene A. Taylor

Missions

The National Ocean Survey operates the ships of the National Oceanic and Atmospheric Administration (NOAA), a federal agency created in 1970. During 1972-1973 the National Marine Fisheries Service (formerly the Bureau of Commercial Fisheries of the Department of Interior) was consolidated into the NOAA fleet which is operated by the National Ocean Survey. Approximately 15 small ships and craft 65 feet or longer are counted in the National Marine Fisheries Service. The former National Marine Fisheries vessels are not described because of the specialised, non-military nature of their work.
The National Ocean Survey prepares nautical and aeronautical charts; conducts geodetic, geophysical, oceanographic, and marine surveys; predicts tides and currents; tests, evaluates, and calibrates sensing systems for ocean use; and conducts

the development of and eventually will operate a national system of automated ocean buoys for obtaining environmental information.
The National Ocean Survey is a civilian agency that supports national civilian and military requirements. During time of war the ships and officers of NOAA can be expected to operate with the Navy, either as a separate service or integrated into the Navy.

Establishment

The "Survey of the Coast" was established by an act of Congress on 10 Feb, 1807. Renamed US Coast Survey in 1834 and again renamed Coast and Geodetic Survey in 1878. The commissioned officer corps was established in 1917. The Coast and Geodetic Survey was made a component of the Environmental Science Services Administration on 13 July, 1965, when that agency was established within the Department of Commerce. The Environmental Science Services Administration subsequently became the National Oceanic and Atmospheric Administration in October 1970 with the Coast and Geodetic Survey being renamed National Ocean Survey and its jurisdiction expanded to include the US Lake Survey, formerly a part of the US Army Corps of Engineers; the Coast Guard's national data buoy development project; and the Navy's National Oceanographic Instrumentation Centre.

Ships

National Ocean Survey ship designations are: OSS for Ocean Survey Ship, MSS for Medium Survey Ship, CSS for Coastal Survey Ship, and ASV for Auxiliary Survey Vessel. No National Ocean Survey Ships are armed. All ships are believed active in 1976.
Most ships have Maritime Administration design designations.

Personnel

The National Ocean Survey which operates NOAA ships has approximately 225 commissioned officers and 250 officers and 2 250 civil service personnel. In addition, another 125 commissioned officers serve elsewhere in NOAA and several US Navy officers are assigned to NOAA.

Aviation

The National Ocean Survey's Coastal Mapping Division operates two aircraft for aerial photographic missions, a twin-engine de Havilland Canada Buffalo and a twin-engine North American Rockwell Aero Commander. In 1975 NOAA additionally acquired two WP-3D Orion aircraft for weather research.

SURVEY SHIPS

1 OCEANOGRAPHIC SURVEY SHIP (OSS): "RESEARCHER" TYPE

Name	No.	Builders	Commissioned
RESEARCHER	OSS 03	American Shipbuilding Co, Lorain, Ohio	8 Oct 1970

Displacement, tons: 2 875 light
Dimensions, feet (metres): 278·25 oa × 51 × 16·25 *(84·7 × 15·5 × 4·9)*
Main engines: 2 geared diesels; 3 200 hp; 2 shafts = 16 knots
Complement: 11 officers, 55 crewmen
Scientists: 13

The *Researcher* was designed specifically for deep ocean research; she is ice strengthened. Estimated cost $10 000 000. Fitted with 20-ton capacity crane, 5-ton capacity crane, four 2½-ton capacity cranes, and an A-frame with 10-ton lift capacity. Launched on 5 Oct 1968.

Design: Fitted with computerised data acquisition system that automatically samples, processes, and records oceanographic, geophysical, hydrographic, and meteorological data. The 20-ton telescoping crane is designed to handle special sampling equipment and small submersible vehicles as well as small boats. S2-MT-MA74a type.

Engineering: Controllable pitch propellers. A 450-horsepower, 360-degree retractable bow thruster provides sustained low speeds up to seven knots and permits precise positioning. Cruising speed is 14·5 knots with a range of 13 000 nautical miles.

RESEARCHER (OSS 03)   *National Ocean Survey*

2 OCEANOGRAPHIC SURVEY SHIPS (OSS): "OCEANOGRAPHER" CLASS

Name	No.	Builders	Commissioned
OCEANOGRAPHER	OSS 01	Aerojet-General Corp, Jacksonville, Florida	13 July 1966
DISCOVERER	OSS 02	Aerojet-General Corp, Jacksonville, Florida	29 April 1967

Displacement, tons: 3 959 light
Dimensions, feet (metres): 303·3 oa × 52 × 18·5 *(92·4 × 15·8 × 5·6)*
Main engines: 4 diesels with electric drive; 5 000 bhp; 2 shafts = 16+ knots
Complement: 14 Officers, 78 crewmen
Scientists: 18

Ice strengthened construction. Fitted with a 5-ton capacity crane and 3½-ton capacity crane. *Oceanographer* launched on 18 April 1964. *Discoverer* launched on 29 Oct 1964, deactivated in 1973 and placed in reserve, but subsequently reactivated.

Design: Fitted with computerised data acquisition system. Centre well 8 × 6 feet provides sheltered access to sea for SCUBA divers and for lowering research equipment. Six ports in submerged bow observation chamber. S2-MET-MA62a type.

Engineering: A 400-horsepower, through-hull thruster provides precise manoeuvring. Not equipped for silent operation. Cruising speed is 16 knots with a range of 15 200 nautical miles.

OCEANOGRAPHER (OSS 01)   *National Ocean Survey*

DISCOVERER (OSS 02)—see previous page

National Ocean Survey

DISCOVERER (OSS 02)

National Ocean Survey

2 HYDROGRAPHIC SURVEY SHIPS (CSS): "PEIRCE" CLASS

Name	No.	Builders	Commissioned
PEIRCE	CSS 28	Marietta Manufacturing Co, Point Pleasant, West Virginia	6 May 1963
WHITING	CSS 29	Marietta Manufacturing Co, Point Pleasant, West Virginia	8 July 1963

Displacement, tons: 760 light
Dimensions, feet (metres): 164 oa × 33 × 10·1 *(50·0 × 10·0 × 3·1)*
Main engines: 2 diesels; 1 600 bhp; 2 shafts = 12·5+ knots
Complement: 8 officers, 32 crewmen

Designed for nearshore operations. Ice strengthened. *Peirce* launched on 15 Oct 1962 and *Whiting* on 20 Nov 1962. S1-MT-59a type.

Engineering: Controllable-pitch propellers. Cruising speed is 12·5 knots with a range of 4 500 nautical miles.

PEIRCE (CSS 28)

National Ocean Survey

WHITING (CSS 29)

National Ocean Survey

2 HYDROGRAPHIC SURVEY SHIPS (CSS): "McARTHUR" CLASS

Name	No.	Builders	Commissioned
McARTHUR	CSS 30	Norfolk SB & DD Co, Norfolk, Virginia	15 Dec 1966
DAVIDSON	CSS 31	Norfolk SB & DD Co, Norfolk, Virginia	10 Mar 1967

Displacement, tons: 995 light
Dimensions, feet (metres): 175 oa × 38 × 11·5 *(53·0 × 11·5 × 3·5)*
Main engines: 2 diesels; 1 600 bhp; 2 shafts = 13·5+ knots
Complement: 8 officers, 32 crewmen

Designed for nearshore operations. Ice strengthened. Launched on 15 Nov 1965 and 7 May 1966 respectively. S1-MT-MA70a type.

Engineering: Controllable-pitch propellers. Cruising speed is 13·5 knots with a range of 4 500 nautical miles.

DAVIDSON (CSS 31)   *National Ocean Survey*

McARTHUR (CSS 30)   *National Ocean Survey*

1 HYDROGRAPHIC SURVEY SHIP (OSS): "SURVEYOR" TYPE

Name	No.	Builders	Commissioned
SURVEYOR	OSS 32	National Steel Co, San Diego, California	30 Apr 1960

Displacement, tons: 3 150 light
Dimensions, feet (metres): 292·3 oa × 46 × 18 *(88·8 × 14·0 × 5·5)*
Main engines: 1 steam turbine (De Laval); 3 520 shp; 1 shaft = 15 + knots
Complement: 14 officers, 106 crewmen
Scientists: 9

Specially designed for marine charting and geophysical surveys. Fitted with helicopter platform aft. Ice strengthened. Twin telescoping 2½-ton capacity cargo booms (forward) and 12½-ton capacity crane. Estimated cost $6 000 000. Launched on 25 Apr 1959. The *Surveyor* was deactivated in 1973 and placed in reserve, but subsequently reactivated.

Design: Large bilge keel (18 inches × 70 feet) permits oceanographic observations to be performed up to Sea State 6. S2-S-RM28a type.

Engineering: Retractable outboard motor mounted to stern for precision manoeuvring. Cruising speed is 15 knots with a range of 10 500 nautical miles.

Disposals: *Pathfinder* OSS 30, ex-US Navy AGS 1 decommissioned in 1972 and stricken. See 1972-1973 edition for description and photograph.

SURVEYOR (OSS 32)   *National Ocean Survey*

3 HYDROGRAPHIC SURVEY SHIPS (MSS): "FAIRWEATHER" CLASS

Name	No.	Builders	Commissioned
FAIRWEATHER	MSS 20	Aerojet-General Corp, Jacksonville, Florida	2 Oct 1968
RAINIER	MSS 21	Aerojet-General Corp, Jacksonville, Florida	2 Oct 1968
MT. MITCHELL	MSS 22	Aerojet-General Corp, Jacksonville, Florida	23 Mar 1968

Displacement, tons: 1 798 light
Dimensions, feet (metres): 231 oa × 42·07 × 13·9 *(70·2 × 12·8 × 4·2)*
Main engines: 2 diesels; 2 400 bhp; 2 shafts = 13+ knots
Complement: 12 officers, 64 crewmen
Scientists: 2

Ice strengthened. *Fairweather* and *Rainier,* launched on 15 March 1967, *Mt. Mitchell* on 29 Nov 1966. S1-MT-MA72a type.

Engineering: Fitted with a 200-horsepower, through-bow thruster for precise manoeuvring. Controllable-pitch propellers. Cruising speed is 13 knots with a range of 9 000 nautical miles.

FAIRWEATHER (MSS 20)   *National Ocean Survey*

"FAIRWEATHER" CLASS—continued

MT. MITCHELL (MSS 22)

National Ocean Survey

RAINIER (MSS 21)

National Ocean Survey

COASTAL VESSELS

2 WIRE DRAG VESSELS (ASV): "RUDE" CLASS

Name	No.	Builders	Commissioned
RUDE	ASV 90	Jacobson Shipyard Inc, Oyster Bay, New York	29 Mar 1967
HECK	ASV 91	Jacobson Shipyard Inc, Oyster Bay, New York	29 Mar 1967

Displacement, tons: 214 light
Dimensions, feet (metres): 90 oa × 22 × 7 *(27·4 × 6·7 × 2·1)*
Main engines: 2 diesels; 800 bhp; 2 shafts = 11·5+ knots
Complement: 2 officers, 8 crewmen

Designed to search out underwater navigational hazards along the coast using wire drags. Launched on 17 Aug 1966 and 1 Nov 1966 respectively. S1-MT-MA71a type. A single commanding officer is assigned to both vessels; normally he rides in one ship and the executive officer in the other.

Engineering: Propellers are guarded by shrouds similar to Kort nozzles. Auxiliary propulsion provides 50 horsepower to each propeller for dragging operations. Cruising speed is 11·5 knots with a range of 740 nautical miles (provisions carried for eight days).

RUDE (ASV 90)

National Ocean Survey

1 CURRENT SURVEY VESSEL (ASV): "FERREL" TYPE

Name	No.	Builders	Commissioned
FERREL	ASV 92	Zeigler Shipyard, Jennings, Louisiana	4 June 1968

Displacement, tons: 363 light
Dimensions, feet (metres): 133·25 × 32 × 7 *(40·5 × 9·7 × 2·1)*
Main engines: 2 diesels; 820 bhp; 2 shafts = 10+ knots
Complement: 3 officers, 13 crewmen

Specially designed to conduct nearshore and esturine current surveys. Limited surface meteorological observations are also made. Buoy workshop provided in 450-square feet of enclosed deck area with buoy stowage on open after deck. Launched on 4 April 1968. SI-MT-MA83a type.

Engineering: Fitted with 100-horsepower, electric-driven bow thruster. Cruising speed is 10 knots (provisions for 15 days carried).

FERREL (ASV 92)

National Ocean Survey

FERREL (ASV 92)

National Ocean Survey

UNION OF SOVIET SOCIALIST REPUBLICS

Flag Officers Soviet Navy

Commander-in-Chief of the Soviet Navy and First Deputy Minister of Defence:
  Admiral of the Fleet of the Soviet Union Sergei Georgiyevich Gorshkov
First Deputy Commander-in-Chief of the Soviet Navy:
  Admiral of the Fleet N. I. Smirnov
Assistant Chief of the General Staff of the Armed Forces:
  Admiral of the Fleet S. M. Lobov
Deputy Commander-in-Chief:
  Admiral N. N. Amelko
Deputy Commander-in-Chief:
  Admiral G. A. Bondarenko
Deputy Commander-in-Chief:
  Admiral V. V. Mikhaylin
Deputy Commander-in-Chief:
  Engineer Admiral P. G. Kotov
Deputy Commander-in-Chief:
  Engineer Vice-Admiral V. G. Novikov
Commander of Naval Aviation:
  Colonel-General A. A. Mironenko
Chief of the Political Directorate:
  Admiral V. M. Grishanov
Chief of Rear Services:
  Admiral L. Y. Mizin
Chief of Naval Training Establishments:
  Vice-Admiral I. M. Kuznetsov
Chief of Main Naval Staff:
  Admiral of the Fleet N. D. Sergeyev
1st Deputy Chief of the Main Naval Staff:
  Vice-Admiral P. M. Navoytsev
Chief of the Hydrographic Service:
  Admiral A. I. Rassokho

Northern Fleet

Commander-in-Chief:
  Admiral of the Fleet G. M. Yegorov
1st Deputy Commander-in-Chief:
  Vice-Admiral Ye. I. Volobuyev
Chief of Staff:
  Vice-Admiral V. N. Chernavin
In Command of the Political Department:
  Vice-Admiral A. I. Sorokin

Pacific

Commander-in-Chief:
  Admiral V. P. Maslov
1st Deputy Commander-in-Chief:
  —
Chief of Staff:
  Vice-Admiral E. N. Spiridonov
In Command of the Political Department:
  Vice-Admiral S. S. Bevz

Black Sea

Commander-in-Chief:
  Admiral N. I. Khovrin
1st Deputy Commander-in-Chief:
  Rear-Admiral V. Samoylov
Chief of Staff:
  Rear-Admiral V. Ponikarovsky
In Command of the Political Department:
  Rear-Admiral P. N. Medvedev

Baltic

Commander-in-Chief:
  Vice-Admiral A. M. Kosov
1st Deputy Commander-in-Chief:
  Rear-Admiral Ya. M. Kudelkin
Chief of Staff:
  —
In Command of the Political Department:
  Vice-Admiral N. I. Shablikov

Caspian Flotilla

Commander-in-Chief:
  Rear-Admiral L. D. Ryabtsev
In Command of the Political Department:
  Rear-Admiral V. N. Sergeyev

Leningrad Naval Base

Commanding Officer:
  Vice-Admiral V. M. Leonenkov
In Command of the Political Department:
  Rear-Admiral A. A. Plekhanov
Head of the Order of Lenin Naval Academy:
  Admiral V. S. Sysoyev
Head of Frunze Naval College:
  Rear-Admiral V. V. Platonov

Diplomatic Representation

Naval Attaché London: Captain V. Z. Khuzhokov

Personnel

(a) 1976: Approximately 500 000 officers and ratings
(b) Approximately 30% Volunteers (officers and senior ratings)—remainder 3 years National Service at sea and 2 if ashore

Mercantile Marine

Lloyd's Register of Shipping: 7 652 vessels of 19 235 973 tons gross

Main Naval Bases

North: Severomorsk (HQ), Archangelsk, Polyarny, Severodvinsk (building).
Baltic: Leningrad (Kronstadt), Tallinn, Lepaia, Baltiisk (HQ)
Black Sea: Sevastopol (HQ), Tuapse, Poti, Nikolaev (building)
Pacific: Vladivostock (HQ), Nakhodka, Sovetskaia Gavan, Magadan, Petropavlovsk.

Deletions and Conversions

Whilst it is not possible to provide an accurate estimate of total deletions and conversions during the last year the following is a guide to those estimates used in this section.

Cruisers
Deletion of *Kirov* and *Slava*.

Submarines
Decrease of 10 "Whisky" Class.
Completion of "Yankee" Class programme.

Destroyers
"Kashin" Class conversions with SSM
1 "Krupny" Class conversion to "Kanin" Class.
"Kildin" Class conversions continue.
Deletion of *Tallinn*.

Frigates
Deletion of 3 "Kola" Class.
Conversion of "Petya 1A" Class.

Corvettes
Conversion of some "Grisha" Class to all-gun ships.
Deletion of 3 "Kronstadt" Class.

Fast Attack Craft
Deletion of all "Komar" Class.
Deletion of 20 "P6, 8 and 10" Classes.
Deletion of all "P4" Class.

Mine Warfare Forces
Deletion of 5 "T 301" Class.

Pennant Numbers

The Soviet Navy has frequent changes of pennant numbers and so these are of little use in identifying individual ships. For that reason such a list has been omitted in this section.

Building Programme

The following is an abstract of the programme used in estimating force levels.

Aircraft Carriers
2 "Kiev" class building—continuing programme.

Submarines
Continuing programme for "Delta II", "Charlie", "Charlie II", "Victor", "Victor II" and "Tango" classes.

Cruisers
Continuing programme for "Kara" and "Kresta II" classes

Destroyers
"Krivak" class continues.

Corvettes
"Grisha" and "Nanuchka" classes continue.

Light Forces
"Turya" class hydrofoils continue.
"Zhuk" class coastal patrol craft—new programme.

Mine Warfare Forces
"Sonya" class (MSC) and "Natya" class continue.

Amphibious Forces
"Ropucha" class LST continues.

Air Cushion Vehicles
A large programme of unknown size.

Support and Depot Ships
"Amur" and "Ugra" classes continuing.

Service Forces

"Boris Chilikin" class continues.
"Ingul" and "Pamir" class tugs.

Subsequent types and classes have been revised from new information, not necessarily as new construction.

Overall Totals

Aircraft Carriers	1 + 2 building	Fast Attack Craft (Patrol)	65	Fishery Research Ships	192
Helicopter Cruisers	2	Fast Attack Craft (Hydrofoil)	42	Space Associated Ships	23
Submarines (SSBN)	55 + 6 building	Fast Attack Craft (Torpedo)	125	Fleet Replenishment Ships	5
Submarines (SSB)	23	River Patrol Craft	90	Tankers	26
Submarines (SSGN)	42	Coastal Patrol Craft	25	Harbour Tankers	18
Submarines (SSG)	28	Minesweepers—Ocean	185	Salvage Vessels	21
Submarines (SSN)	38	Minesweepers—Coastal	119	Rescue Ships	15
Submarines (SS)	204	Minesweepers—Inshore	100	Training Ships	27
Cruisers (CLG)	24 + 2 building	LSTs	18 + 1	Lifting Ships	15
Cruisers (Gun)	13	LCTs	60	Tenders	100 +
Destroyers (DDG)	50	LCUs	81	Icebreakers (Nuclear)	3 + 1
Destroyers (Gun)	58	LSMs	100	Icebreakers	38
Frigates	98	Depot and Repair Ships	64	Cable Ships	6 + 3
Corvettes (Missile)	32	Intelligence Collectors (AGI)	54	Large Tugs	120 +
Corvettes	175	Survey Ships	93 + 2	Transports	17
Fast Attack Craft (Missile)	120	Research Ships	35 + 1		

SOVIET NAVAL AVIATION

The Soviet Navy operates some 1 200 fixed-wing aircraft and helicopters in *Morskaya Aviatsiya*, the world's second largest naval air arm. The primary combat components are
(1) Long range and medium bombers employed in the maritime reconnaissance role.
(2) Medium bombers mostly equipped with air-to-surface missiles in the anti-ship strike role.
(3) Land based patrol aircraft, amphibians and helicopters in the anti-submarine role.
The Soviet Navy flies no fixed-wing aircraft from ships, but several medium classes of destroyers and all modern missile armed cruisers, and the cruiser-helicopter ships *Moskva* and *Leningrad* can carry helicopters. The two helicopter ships are the largest built to date by any navy specifically for anti-submarine operations and are the first Soviet warships intended primarily for aviation activities. The arrival of *Kiev* may bring the first VTOL aircraft at sea.

Bombers: The Soviet naval air arm has about 55 heavy and 550 medium bombers in the anti-shipping, strike, tanker and reconnaissance roles. The main strike force comprises about 300 "Badger" equipped with "Kipper" and "Kelt" air-to-surface missiles. The reconnaissance aircraft are about 55 "Bear D" (long range recce); 55 "Badger" and a similar number of "Blinder A". The latter and some of the "Badger" have a bombing capability.

ASW Helicopters: Over 200 anti-submarine helicopters are believed to be in the naval air arm, mostly Ka-25 "Hormone" (a twin-turbine craft known as the "Harp" in the prototype stage) and some of the older Mi-4 "Hound" helicopters. The "Hormone" anti-submarine helicopters, armed with torpedoes or other ASW weapons operate from the large helicopter cruisers *Moskva* and *Leningrad* which can each operate some 15 to 20 helicopters, servicing them in a hangar below the flight deck. They have also been seen in the "Kara". "Kresta I" and "Kresta II"

class cruisers which are the first Soviet ships of this type to be fitted with a helicopter hangar. In some of these ships the radar fitted helicopter may also have a reconnaissance role associated with the surface-to-surface missile system. The older Mi-4 "Hound" and other "Hormone" helicopters are used in the ASW role from shore bases. Other types of helicopter are also used in the transport role ashore. The presence of *Kiev* and her sisters will notably increase the seaborne helicopter capability.

ASW Patrol Aircraft: The Soviet Union is the only nation other than Japan maintaining modern military flying boats, about 100 Be-12 "Mail" (turboprop) aircraft of this type being operational. The latter aircraft, an amphibian often-photographed on runways, has an advanced anti-submarine capability evidenced by a radome extending forward, a Magnetic Anomaly Detector (MAD) boom extending aft and a weapons bay in the rear fuselage.
The "May", of which some 75 are in service, is a militarised version of the four-turboprop commercial air freighter (code name "Coot") in wide commercial service. The patrol/anti-submarine version has been lengthened and fitted with a MAD boom as well as other electronic equipment and a weapons capability similar to the US Navy's conversion of the Lockheed Electra into the P-3 "Orion" patrol aircraft.

Transports/Training Aircraft: There are also a few hundred transports, utility, and training fixed-wing aircraft and helicopters under Navy control.

*Aircraft names are NATO code names; "B" names indicate bombers, "H" names for helicopters, and "M" names for miscellaneous aircraft.

SVERDLOV

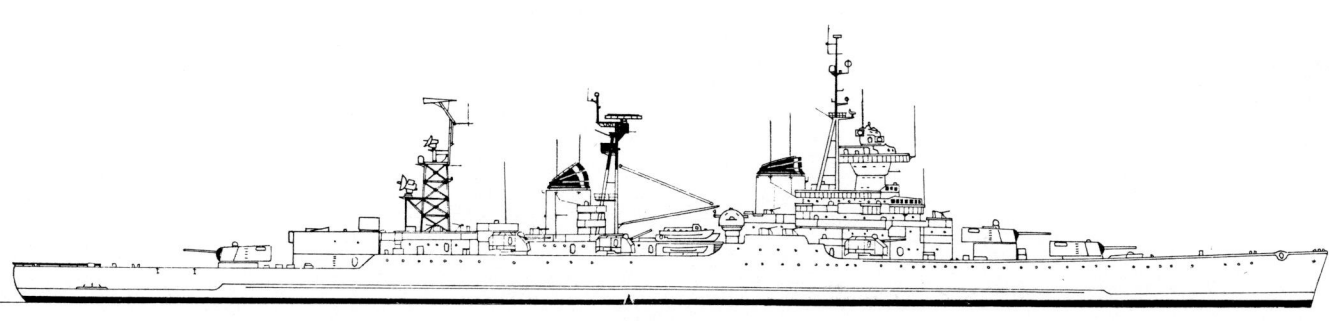

ZHDANOV

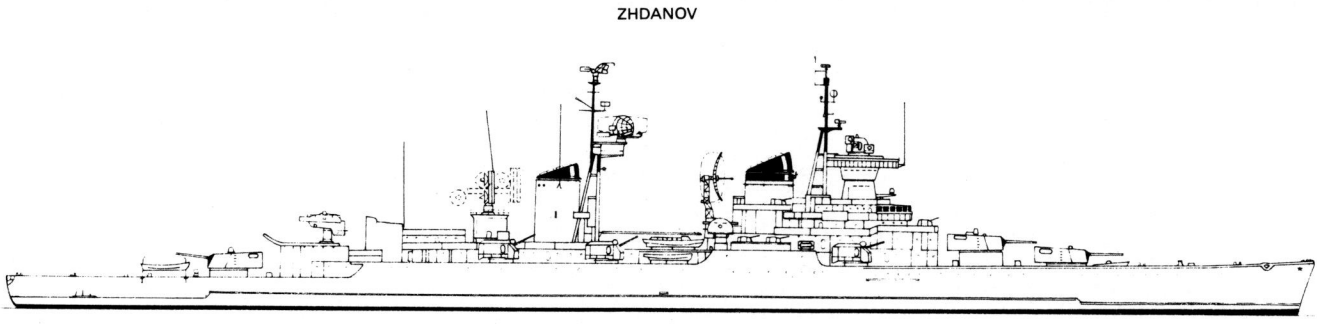

DZERZHINSKI

KARA

KRESTA II

KRESTA I

KRWAK

SAM 2

SAM 1

SAM KOTLIN

KASHIN

KOTLIN

SKORY 1

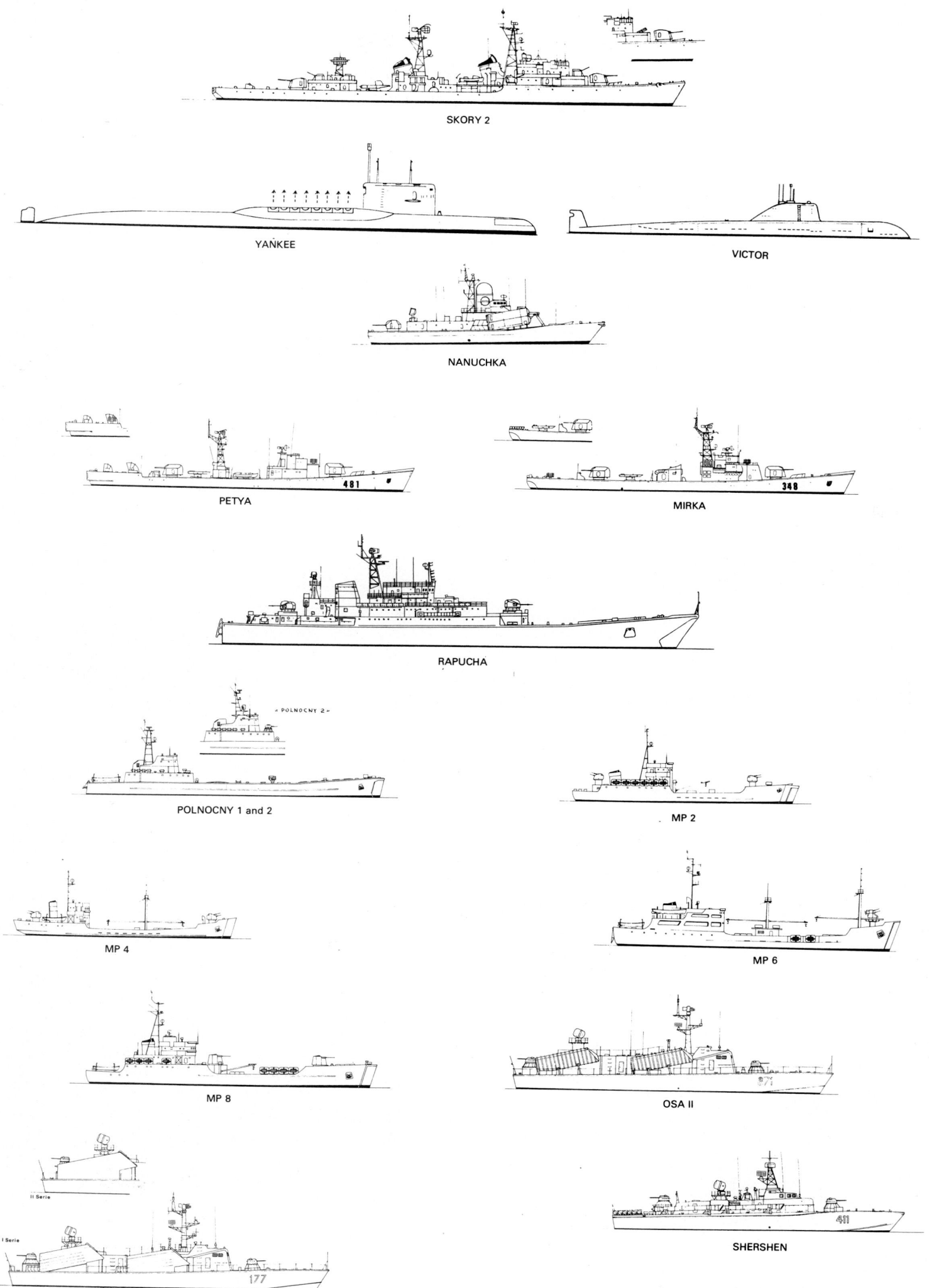

SKORY 2

YANKEE

VICTOR

NANUCHKA

PETYA 481

MIRKA 348

RAPUCHA

POLNOCNY 1 and 2

« POLNOCNY 2 »

MP 2

MP 4

MP 6

MP 8

OSA II

II Serie

I Serie

OSA I 177

SHERSHEN 411

Note: Line drawings by courtesy of Erminio Bagnasco and Siefried Breyer. Scale is 1 : 600 except for Osa I, Osa II and Shershen classes, which are 1 : 1 200.

AIRCRAFT CARRIERS

1 + 2 "KIEV" CLASS (AIRCRAFT CARRIERS)

KIEV   MINSK   —

Displacement, tons: 40 000
Length, feet (metres): 925 *(282)* oa; 880 *(268)* wl
Beam, feet (metres): 100 *(30·5)* (hull); 200 *(61)* (overall, including flight deck and sponsons)
Aircraft (estimated): 25 fixed wing (V/STOL); 25 Hormone A or modified Hind A helicopters
Missile launchers: Possibly 1 twin surface-to-surface launcher; 2 twin SAN-3; 1 SUW-N A/S launcher; 4 SAN-4 launchers
Guns: 4—76 mm; 4 Air Defence Gatling mounts
A/S weapons: 2—12 barrelled MBU 2500A launchers forward
Speed, knots: At least 30

The *Kiev*, built at Nikolayev South Yard and her sisters building at the same yard, mark an impressive and logical advance by the Soviet Navy. The arrival of these ships has been heralded by Admiral Gorshkov's support for embarked tactical air as a necessity for navies employed in extending political influence far abroad, and by a softening of previous Soviet criticisms of this class of ship.

Kiev appears to be a carrier designed for V/STOL aircraft and helicopter operations. There is no sign of steam catapults, arrester gear, mirror-landing-sights, and all the expensive gear required for fixed-wing operations. The Hormone A helicopter or a modification of the Army's Hind A helicopter could both be embarked. The type of V/STOL aircraft is currently not known, but as it is now 9 years since the first Yakovlev 36 (Freehand) appeared, and in view of the long time since the Harrier was first in service, it is not unreasonable to expect that the embarked aircraft are of a type possibly superior in perfor-

mance to the Harrier. The provision of a 550-600 ft angled flight deck in the *Kiev* will allow the V/STOL aircraft an increase of up to 25% in their take-off weight.

A rough estimate of her hangar capacity suggests that *Kiev* could carry 25 of each type simultaneously. Her forward lift appears to be adequate to accommodate a V/STOL type but until more detailed evidence is available this, with many other deductions, must remain conjectural. Her armament is of interest, her missiles being a possible twin SSN, with SAN-3 and SAN-4 surface-to-air launchers. This is the first occasion on which an aircraft carrier has mounted surface-to-surface missile armament—a multi-rôle concept which will enhance the ship's value in an intervention situation. The SAN-3 with Goblet missiles outrange the BPDMS in the larger US carriers, and the gun armament is a complete break with the latter's armament—neither *Nimitz* nor *Enterprise* carry any guns.

The provision of A/S weapons (twin A/S rocket launchers forward and an SUW-N 1 launcher) is another radical change in carrier practice. These would presuppose a sonar fit of a hull mounted set and VDS, showing the Soviets have taken the submarine threat seriously. Success with such a system depends very largely on the speed and handling of that ship and the efficiency of the A/S helicopters which, presumably, would work with the weapon launcher.

With world-wide Soviet deployments a small number of ships is clearly insufficient, allowing for maintenance and any refitting required. The design of the carrier must have been on the drawing-board before *Moskva* was commissioned in 1967. Perhaps the decision to build more of the latter was delayed until after the extensive heavy-weather operations which

Moskva and *Leningrad* carried out. It seems most likely that these were sufficiently successful to encourage the Soviet navy to proceed with the larger ships. A minimum of six would seem likely. They will be a powerful addition to the political impact of the Soviet fleet in peacetime. With ships capable of operating V/STOL strike aircraft and troop-lift helicopters their credibility in the intervention role would be increased, and their fleet would be that much more prepared for hostilities. Such ships' roles could be changed merely by alterations in the number and type of aircraft embarked. They are clearly not as enormously expensive as the US nuclear-powered carriers but will greatly enhance the manifest capability of the Soviet fleet to operate effectively world-wide in both peace and war.

Electronics: A full ECM fit similar to that in Kresta 2.

Radar: Top Sail, Head Light, Owl Screech (each end). Radome possibly for carrier-approach radar, combined with aircraft beacon.

Sonar: Possibly hull-mounted and VDS.

Soviet Type Name: Protivo Lodochny Kreyser meaning anti-submarine cruiser. This is an interesting designation for a ship of this size, continuing the Soviet practice of calling nearly all major surface units by an ASW title. It could also be aimed at circumventing the restrictions on aircraft carriers in the Montreux Convention, regulating the use of the Turkish Straits.

1976, AP

KIEV

1976, Popperfoto

KIEV

HELICOPTER CRUISERS

2 "MOSKVA" CLASS

Name	No.	Builders	Laid down	Launched	Commissioned
MOSKVA	—	Nikolayev South	1962	—	1967
LENINGRAD	—	Nikolayev South	1963	—	1968

Displacement, tons: 15 000 standard; 17 000 full load
Length, feet (metres): 624·8 (190·5); 644·8 oa (196·6)
Flight deck, feet (metres): 295·3 (90·0) aft of superstructure
Width, feet (metres): 115·0 (35·0)
Beam, feet (metres): 75·9 (23)
Draught, feet (metres): 24·9 (7·6)
Aircraft: 18 Hormone A ASW helicopters
Missile launchers: 2 SAN-3 systems of twin launchers (180 reloads)
Guns: 4—57 mm (2 twin mountings)
A/S weapons: 1 twin SUWN-1 A/S missile launcher; 2—12 tube MBU 2500A on forecastle
Torpedo tubes: 2 quintuple 21 inch
Main engines: Geared turbines; 2 shafts; 100 000 shp
Boilers: 4 watertube
Speed, knots: 30
Complement: 800

This class represented a radical change of thought in the Soviet fleet. The design must have been completed while the "November" class submarines were building and the heavy A/S armament and efficient sensors (helicopters and VDS) suggest an awareness of the problem of dealing with nuclear submarines. Alongside what is apparently a primary A/S role these ships have a capability for A/A warning and self-defence as well as a command function. With a full fit of radar and ECM equipment they clearly represent good value for money. Both ships handle well in heavy weather and are capable of helicopter-operations under adverse conditions. Why only two were built is discussed earlier in the notes on the "Kiev" class aircraft carriers.

Modification: In early 1973 *Moskva* was seen with a landing pad on the after end of the flight deck, probably for flight tests of VTOL aircraft.

Radar: Search: Top Sail 3-D and Head Net C 3-D.
Fire control: Head Light (2). Muff Cob.
Miscellaneous: Electronic warfare equipment.

Sonar: VDS and, probably, hull mounted set. In addition all helicopters have dunking-sonar.

Soviet Type Name: Protivo Lodochny Kreyser meaning Anti-Submarine Cruiser.

MOSKVA   1973, MOD (N)

LENINGRAD   11/1974, MOD (N)

MOSKVA   6/1974, MOD (N)

SUBMARINES
Ballistic Missile Classes

2 + 2 "DELTA II" CLASS
(BALLISTIC MISSILE SUBMARINES SSBNs)

Displacement, tons: ? 16 000
Dimensions, feet (metres): 500 × 36 × 34 (152·5 × 11 × 10·4)
Missiles: 16—SSN-8 tubes
Torpedo tubes: ? 8—21 in
Main machinery: Nuclear reactors; steam turbines; 2 shafts
Speed, knots: ? 25 dived

The first acknowledgement of this class was made in Nov 1973 by The US Secretary of Defense. It is now probable that this class will be built instead of the original "Delta" class.

10 "DELTA" CLASS
(BALLISTIC MISSILE SUBMARINES SSBNs)

Displacement, tons: 9 000 surfaced; 10 000 dived
Length, feet (metres): 450 (137·2)
Beam, feet (metres): 34·8 (10·6)
Draught, feet (metres): 32·8 (10·0)
Missiles: 12 SSN-8 tubes
Torpedo tubes: 8—21 in
Main machinery: Nuclear reactors; Steam turbines; 2 screws; 24 000 shp
Speed, knots: 25 dived
Complement: About 120

This advance on the "Yankee" class SSBNs was announced at the end of 1972. The missile armament is twelve SSN-8s with a range of 4 200 nautical miles, at present believed to carry single heads, rather than MRVs. As the SSN-6 has already been tested with MRV warheads, however, it is not unlikely that these missiles will in due course be similarly armed. The longer-range SSN-8 missiles are of greater length than the SSN-6s and, as this length cannot be accommodated below the keel, they stand several feet proud of the after-casing. At the same time their presumed greater diameter and the need to com-pensate for the additional top-weight would seem to be the reasons for the reduction to twelve missiles in this class. The total "Delta" class building programme depends on the final outcome of the various Strategic Arms Limitation Talks (SALT). As this is unclear and dependent on so many external influences it is unwise to forecast any figure. A building rate of 6-8 SSBNs per year is well within Soviet capabilities.

"DELTA" Class

"DELTA" Class

Submarines
Ballistic Missile Classes

34 "YANKEE" CLASS
(BALLISTIC MISSILE SUBMARINES SSBNs)

Displacement, tons: 8 000 surfaced; 9 000 dived
Length, feet (metres): 426·5 (130·0)
Beam, feet (metres): 34·8 (10·6)
Draught, feet (metres): 32·8 (10·0)
Missile launchers: 16 tubes (see note)
Torpedo tubes: 8—21 in
Main machinery: Nuclear reactors; steam turbines; 24 000 shp; 2 shafts
Speed, knots: 30 dived
Complement: About 120

The first units of this class were reported in 1968. The vertical launching tubes are arranged in two rows of eight, and the missiles have a range of 1 300 nautical miles. These missiles have been tested with MRV warheads and these, presumably, will soon be operational. At about the time that the USS *George Washington* was laid down (1 Nov 1957) as the world's first SSBN it is likely that the Soviet Navy embarked on its own major SSBN programme. With experience gained from the diesel-propelled "Golf" class and the nuclear-propelled "Hotel" class, both originally carrying three SSN-4 (300 mile) missiles in the fin, the "Yankee" design was completed mounting 16 SSN-6 missiles in the hull in two banks of 8. The first of the class was delivered late-1967 and the programme then

accelerated from 4 boats in 1968 to 8 in 1971, the last of the class being completed in 1975. Construction took place at Severodvinsk and Komsomolsk. The original deployment of this class was to the Eastern seaboard of the US giving a coverage at least as far as the Mississippi. Increase in numbers allowed a Pacific patrol to be established off California extending coverage at least as far as the Rockies. To provide greater coverage and more flexible operations a longer range missile system was needed and this is now at sea in the "Delta" class. As the numbers of "Delta" or "Delta II" classes increase there is the possibility of the alternative use of the "Yankee" class to operate in an anti-ship or anti-submarine role fitted with SSN-13 missiles.

"YANKEE" Class

1972

"YANKEE" Class

1970

"YANKEE" Class

1970

Submarines
Ballistic Missile Classes
1 "HOTEL III" CLASS
8 "HOTEL II" CLASS
(BALLISTIC MISSILE SUBMARINES SSBNs)

Displacement, tons: 4 400 surfaced; 5 150 dived
Length, feet (metres): 377·2 *(115·2)*
Beam, feet (metres): 28·2 *(8·6)*
Draught, feet (metres): 25 *(7·6)*
Missile launchers: 3 SSN-5 tubes
Torpedo tubes: 6—21 in (bow); 4—16 in (stern)
Main machinery: Nuclear reactor, steam turbine; 22 500 shp
Speed, knots: 20 (dived)
Complement: 90

Long range submarines with three vertical ballistic missile tubes in the large fin. All this class was completed between 1958 and 1962. Originally fitted with SSN-4 system with Sark missiles (300 miles). Between 1963 and 1967 this system was replaced by the SSN-5 system with Serb missiles capable of 700 mile range. Since then these boats have been deployed off both coasts of the USA and Canada. As the limitations of SALT are felt the "Hotel IIs" will probably be phased-out to allow the maximum number of "Delta" class to be built. The "Hotel III" was a single unit converted for the test firings of the SSN-8. The earlier boats of this class, which was of a similar hull and reactor design to the "Echo" class, will, by the late 1970s, be reaching their twentieth year in service.

"HOTEL II" Class damaged in North Atlantic

1972

"HOTEL II" Class

1972

Submarines
Ballistic Missile Classes

22 "GOLF I and II" CLASS
(BALLISTIC MISSILE SUBMARINES SSB)

Displacement, tons: 2 350 surfaced; 2 800 dived
Length, feet (metres): 320·0 *(97·5)*
Beam, feet (metres): 25·1 *(7·6)*
Draught, feet (metres): 22·0 *(6·7)*
Missile launchers: 3 SSN-4 (G I); 3 SSN-5 (G II)
Torpedo tubes: 10—21 in (6 bow; 4 stern)
Main machinery: 3 diesels; 3 shafts; 6 000 hp; Electric motors;
    6 000 hp
Speed, knots: 17·6 surfaced; 17 dived
Range, miles: 22 700 surfaced cruising
Complement: 86 (12 officers, 74 men)

This class has a very large fin fitted with three vertically mounted tubes and hatches for launching ballistic missiles. Built at Komsomolsk and Severodvinsk. Building started in 1958 and finished in 1961-62. After the missile conversion of the "Hotel" class was completed in 1967 about half this class ("Golf II") was converted to carry the SSN-5 system with 700 miles Serb missiles in place of the shorter range (300 mile) Sarks. One of this class has been built by China, although apparently lacking missiles.

"GOLF I" Class

1972

"GOLF I" Class (side opening hatches open)

1962, US Navy

1 "ZULU V" CLASS
(Ex-BALLISTIC MISSILE SUBMARINE SSB)

Displacement, tons: 2 100 surfaced; 2 600 dived
Length, feet (metres): 259·3 *(90·0)*
Beam, feet (metres): 24·1 *(7·3)*
Draught, feet (metres): 19·0 *(5·8)*
Missile launchers: 2 tubes for SSN-4 missiles
Torpedo tubes: 10—21 in
Main machinery: 3 diesels; 3 shafts; 10 000 bhp; 3 electric
    motors; 3 500 hp
Range, miles: 13 000 surfaced cruising
Speed, knots: 18 surfaced; 15 dived
Complement: 85

These were basically of "Zulu" class design but converted in 1955-57 to ballistic missile submarines with larger fins and two vertical tubes for launching Sark (300 mile) missiles on the surface. These were the first Soviet ballistic missile submarines. Of the six converted only one remains in the list. Three others have been converted for research duties as *Lira, Orion* and *Vega* whilst two more may have been converted back to patrol submarines.

"ZULU V" Class

1971

Submarines
Cruise Missile Classes

1 "PAPA" CLASS
(CRUISE MISSILE SUBMARINE SSGN)

A single member of an SSGN class somewhat larger than "Charlie" class.

2 "CHARLIE II" CLASS
(CRUISE MISSILE SUBMARINES SSGN)

An enlarged edition of the "Charlie" class.

12 "CHARLIE" CLASS
(CRUISE MISSILE SUBMARINES SSGN)

Displacement, tons: 4 300 surfaced; 5 100 dived
Length, feet (metres): 304·8 (94)
Beam, feet (metres): 32·8 (10·0)
Draught, feet (metres): 24·6 (7·5)
Missile launchers: 8 tubes for SSN-7 missile system
Torpedo tubes: 8—21 in
Main machinery: Nuclear reactor; steam turbines; 24 000 shp
Speed, knots: 20 surfaced; 30 approx, dived
Complement: 100

A class of cruise-missile submarines built at Gorky. The first of class was delivered in 1968, representing a very significant advance in the cruise-missile submarine field. With a speed of at least 30 knots and mounting eight missile tubes for the SSN-7 system (25 n. miles range) which has a dived launch capability, this is a great advance on the "Echo" class. These boats have an improved hull and reactor design and must be assumed to have an organic control for their missile system therefore posing a notable threat to any surface force. Their deployment to the Mediterranean, the area of the US 6th Fleet, suggests their probable employment.

"CHARLIE" Class   1974, MOD(N)

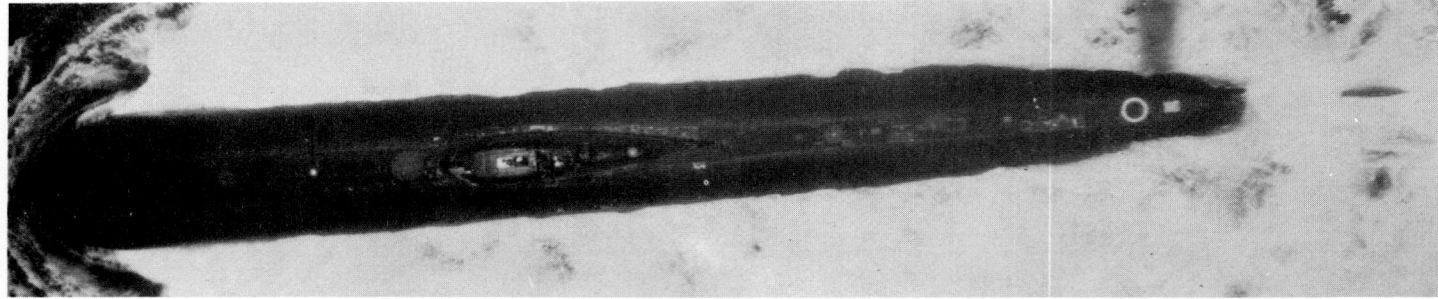

"CHARLIE" Class   1974, USN

"CHARLIE" Class   1974, MOD(N)

Submarines
Cruise Missile Classes

27 "ECHO II" CLASS
(CRUISE MISSILE SUBMARINES SSGN)

Displacement, tons: 4 800 surfaced; 5 600 dived
Length, feet (metres): 390·7 (119)
Beam, feet (metres): 28·4 (8·6)
Draught, feet (metres): 25·9 (7·9)
Missile launchers: 8 SSN-3 launching tubes
Torpedo tubes: 6—21 in (bow); 4—16 in (stern)
Main machinery: Nuclear reactor; steam turbine; 22 500 shp
Speed, knots: 20 dived
Complement: 100

The "Echo II" was the natural development of the "Echo I". With a slightly lengthened hull, a fourth pair of launchers was installed and between 1963 and 1967 twenty-seven of this class were built. They are now deployed evenly between the Pacific and Northern fleets and still provide a useful group of boats for operations such as those of the mixed task force which was in the South China Sea in June 1972. As well as surface ships this included 3 "Echo IIs" and an "Echo I".

"ECHO II" Class

1973, MOD(N)

16 "JULIET" CLASS
(CRUISE MISSILE SUBMARINES SSG)

Displacement, tons: 3 200 surfaced; 3 600 dived
Length, feet (metres): 285·4 (87)
Beam, feet (metres): 31·4 (9·5)
Draught, feet (metres): 20·0 (6·1)
Missile launchers: 4 SSN-3 tubes; 2 before and 2 abaft the fin
Torpedo tubes: 6—21 in (bow); 2 or 4—16 in (stern)
Main machinery: Diesels; 6 000 bhp. Electric motors; 6 000 hp
Speed, knots: 16 surfaced; 16 dived
Range, miles: 15 000 surfaced cruising

Completed between 1962 and 1967. An unmistakable class with a high casing to house the 4 SSN-3 launchers, one pair either end of the fin which appears to be comparatively low. This class was the logical continuation of the "Whisky" class conversions but was overtaken by the "Echo" class SSGNs. A number of this class has in the past been deployed to the Mediterranean.

"JULIET" Class

1973, MOD(N)

"JULIET" Class

1972, US Navy

Submarines
Cruise Missile Classes

7 "WHISKY LONG-BIN" CLASS
(CRUISE MISSILE SUBMARINES SSG)

Displacement, tons: 1 200 surfaced; 1 800 dived
Length, feet (metres): 275·6 *(84·0)*
Beam, feet (metres): 19·8 *(6·0)*
Draught, feet (metres): 15·7 *(4·8)*
Missile launchers: 4 SSN-3 tubes
Torpedo tubes: 6—21 in (4 bow, 2 stern)
Main machinery: Diesels; 4 000 bhp; Electric motors; 2 500 hp
Speed, knots: 17 surfaced; 15 dived
Range, miles: 13 000 surfaced, cruising

A more efficient modification of the "Whisky" class than the "Twin-Cylinder" with four SSN-3 launchers built into a remodelled fin on a hull lengthened by 26 feet. Converted between 1960-63—no organic guidance and therefore reliance must be made on aircraft or surface-ship cooperation. Must still be a very noisy boat when dived.

"WHISKY LONG BIN" Class

1975

5 "WHISKY TWIN CYLINDER" CLASS
(CRUISE MISSILE SUBMARINES SSG)

Displacement, tons: 1 100 surfaced; 1 600 dived
Length, feet (metres): 249·3 *(76)*
Beam, feet (metres): 22·0 *(6·7)*
Draught, feet (metres): 15·1 *(4·6)*
Missile launchers: 2 cylinders for SSN-3
Torpedo tubes: 6—21 in (4 bow, 2 stern)
Main machinery: Diesels; 4 000 bhp; Electric motors; 2 500 hp
Speed, knots: 17 surfaced; 15 dived
Range, miles: 13 000, surfaced, cruising

A 1958-60 modification of the conventional "Whisky" class designed to test out the SSN-3 system at sea. Probably never truly operational being a thoroughly messy conversion which must make a noise like a train if proceeding at any speed above dead slow when dived. The modification consisted of fitting a pair of launchers abaft the fin.

"WHISKY TWIN CYLINDER" Class

7/1974, Tass

Submarines
Fleet Submarine Classes

2 "ALPHA" CLASS
(FLEET SUBMARINES SSN)

Displacement, tons: 3 500 surfaced; 4 500 dived
Dimensions, feet (metres): 265 × 32·8 × 26·2 *(81 × 10 × 8)*

One unit of this class was completed in 1970. The form of propulsion of this class is by no means certain.

1 "VICTOR II" CLASS
(FLEET SUBMARINE SSN)

Displacement, tons: 4 700 surfaced; 6 000 dived
Length, feet (metres): 331·3 *(101)*

An enlargement of the "Victor" class.

"VICTOR" Class   *1974, MOD*

18 "VICTOR" CLASS
(FLEET SUBMARINES SSN)

Displacement, tons: 4 200 surfaced; 5 100 dived
Length, feet (metres): 285·4 *(87·0)*
Beam, feet (metres): 32·8 *(10·0)*
Draught, feet (metres): 26·2 *(8·0)*
Torpedo tubes: 8—21 in
Main machinery: Nuclear reactor; steam turbines; 24 000 shp
Speed, knots: 26 surfaced; 30 plus dived

Designed purely as a torpedo carrying submarine its much increased speed makes it a menace to all but the fastest ships. The first of class entered service in 1967-68 with a subsequent building rate of about two per year, which may now have been superseded by the "Victor II" programme.
The majority is deployed with the Northern Fleet, although two have joined the Pacific Fleet.

"VICTOR" Class   *1974, MOD*

"VICTOR" Class   *1974, USN*

Submarines
Fleet Submarine Classes

13 "NOVEMBER" CLASS
(FLEET SUBMARINES SSN)

Displacement, tons: 4 200 surfaced; 4 800 dived
Length, feet (metres): 360·9 *(110·0)*
Beam, feet (metres): 32·1 *(9·8)*
Draught, feet (metres): 24·3 *(7·4)*
Torpedo tubes: 6—21 in (bow)
Main machinery: Nuclear reactor; steam turbines; 22 500 shp
Speed, knots: 20 surfaced; 25 dived
Complement: 88

The first class of Soviet Fleet Submarines which entered service between 1958 and 1963. The hull form with the great number of free-flood holes in the casing suggests a noisy boat and it is surprising that greater efforts have not been made to supersede this class with the "Victors". In April 1970 one of this class sank south-west of the United Kingdom.

Class Name: Reported as *Leninsky Komsomol.*

Diving Depth: Reported as 1 650 feet *(500 metres).*

"NOVEMBER" Class foundering in Atlantic

April 1970, MOD

"NOVEMBER" Class foundering in Atlantic

April 1970, MOD

4 "ECHO I" CLASS
(FLEET SUBMARINES SSN)

Displacement, tons: 4 600 surfaced; 5 000 dived
Length, feet (metres): 380·9 *(116·0)*
Beam, feet (metres): 28·4 *(8·6)*
Draught, feet (metres): 25·9 *(7·9)*
Torpedo tubes: 6—21 in (bow); 4—16 in (stern)
Main machinery: Nuclear reactor; steam turbine; 22 500 shp
Speed, knots: 20 dived
Complement: 92 (12 officers, 80 men)

This class was completed in 1960-62. Originally mounted six SSN-3 launchers raised from the after casing.
The hull of this class is very similar to the "Hotel"/"November" type and it is probably powered by similar nuclear plant. This class was started at about the same time as the "Juliet" diesel-driven SSGs, and may have been intended as a nuclear prototype using the same SSN-3 system. Only five "Echo Is" were built, probably an adequate test for a new weapon system, being followed immediately by the "Echo IIs". In 1973-74 the "Echo I" class was converted into fleet submarines with the removal of the missile system.

"ECHO I" (Conversion) Class

1974, MOD(N)

Submarines
Patrol Submarine Classes

3 "TANGO" CLASS
(PATROL SUBMARINES SS)

Displacement, tons: 1 900 surfaced; 2 500 dived
Dimensions, feet (metres): 300 × 30 × 16 *(92 × 9·1 × 4·9)*
Complement: 60

This class was first seen at the Sevastopol review in July 1973. Notable features are the rise in the forecasing and a new shape for the snort exhaust. This class, following five years after the "Bravo", shows a continuing commitment to diesel-propelled boats which is of interest in view of the comparatively slow

Fleet Submarine building programme. If the USSR wishes to maintain a preponderance in numbers as the more elderly patrol submarines are paid off this may be the class chosen for new construction. It would also provide a modern replacement for client nations' navies.

"TANGO" Class

1975, MOD

4 "BRAVO" CLASS
(PATROL SUBMARINES SS)

Displacement, tons: 2 500 surfaced; 2 800 dived
Length, feet (metres): 229·6 *(70)*
Beam, feet (metres): 24·8 *(7·5)*
Draught, feet (metres): 14·8 *(4·5)*
Torpedo tubes: ? 6—21 in
Main machinery: Diesel-Electric
Speed, knots: 16 dived

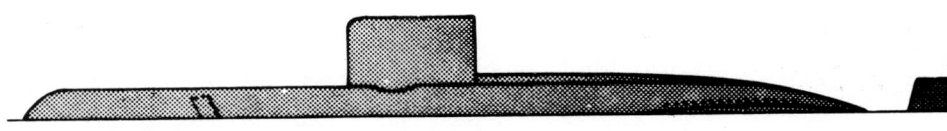

The drawing is merely an indication of the general form which this class may be expected to have. The beam-to-length ratio is larger than normal in a diesel submarine which would account in part for the large displacement for a comparatively short

hull.
First completed in 1968—built at Northern and Baltic yards. One attached to each of the main fleets, reinforcing the view that these are "padded targets" for torpedo and A/S firings.

56 "FOXTROT" CLASS
(PATROL SUBMARINES SS)

Displacement, tons: 2 000 surfaced; 2 300 dived
Length, feet (metres): 301·7 *(92)*
Beam, feet (metres): 24·1 *(7·3)*
Draught, feet (metres): 19·0 *(5·8)*
Torpedo tubes: 10—21 in (6 bow, 4 stern) (20 torpedoes carried)
Main machinery: Diesels; 3 shafts; 6 000 bhp; 3 electric motors; 6 000 hp
Speed, knots: 20 surfaced; 15 dived
Range: 20 000 miles surfaced, cruising
Complement: 70

"FOXTROT" Class

1972

Built between 1958 and 1967 at Sudomekh and Leningrad. A follow-on of the "Zulu" class with similar propulsion to the "Golf" class. A most successful class which has been deployed

world-wide, forming the bulk of the Soviet submarine force in the Mediterranean. Four transferred to India in 1968-69 with a further four new construction following.

"FOXTROT" Class

1973

Submarines
Patrol Submarine Classes

19 "ZULU IV" CLASS
(PATROL SUBMARINES SS)

Displacement, tons: 2 000 surfaced; 2 200 dived
Length, feet (metres): 259·3 *(90·0)*
Beam, feet (metres): 23·9 *(7·3)*
Draught, feet (metres): 19·0 *(5·8)*
Torpedo tubes: 10—21 in (6 bow, 4 stern); (24 torpedoes carried or 40 mines)
Main machinery: Diesel-electric; 3 shafts; 3 diesels; 10 000 bhp; 3 electric motors; 3 500 hp
Speed, knots: 18 surfaced; 15 dived
Range, miles: 20 000 surfaced, cruising
Complement: 70

The first large post-war patrol submarines built by USSR. Completed from late 1951 to 1955. General appearance is streamlined with a complete row of free-flood holes along the casing. Eighteen were built by Sudomekh Shipyard, Leningrad, in 1952-55 and others at Severodvinsk. The general external similarity to the later German U-boats of WW II suggests that this was not an entirely indigenous design. All now appear to be of the "Zulu IV" type. This class, although the majority are probably still operational, is obsolescent and will soon be disposed of.

The "Zulu V" conversions of this class provided the first Soviet ballistic missile submarines with SSN-4 systems.

"ZULU IV" Class   1974

12 "ROMEO" CLASS
(PATROL SUBMARINES SS)

Displacement, tons: 1 400 surfaced; 1 800 dived
Length, feet (metres): 249·3 *(76)*
Beam, feet (metres): 23 *(7)*
Draught, feet (metres): 18 *(5·5)*
Torpedo tubes: 8—21 in (6 bow, 2 stern) 18 torpedoes or 36 mines in place of torpedoes
Main machinery: Diesels; 4 000 bhp; Electric motors; 4 000 hp; 2 shafts
Speed, knots: 17 surfaced; 14 dived
Range, miles: 16 000 at 10 knots (surfaced)
Complement: 60

These are an improved "Whisky" class design with modernised conning tower, and sonar installation. All built in 1958 to 1961. This was presumably an interim class while the "November" class of Fleet Submarines was brought into service—an insurance against failure. Six of this class transferred to Egypt in 1966 and the Chinese are building a considerable force of the same class.

"ROMEO" Class   1974

90 "WHISKY" CLASS
(PATROL SUBMARINES SS)

Displacement, tons: 1 030 surfaced; 1 350 dived
Length, feet (metres): 249·3 *(76)*
Beam, feet (metres): 22·0 *(6·7)*
Draught, feet (metres): 15·0 *(4·6)*
Torpedo tubes: 6—21 in (4 bow, 2 stern); 18 torpedoes carried (or 40 mines)
Main machinery: Diesel-electric; 2 shafts
Diesels; 4 000 bhp
Electric motors; 2 500 hp*
Speed, knots: 17 surfaced; 15 dived
Range, miles: 13 000 at 8 knots (surfaced)
Complement: 60

This was the first post-war Soviet design for a medium-range submarine. Like its larger contemporary the "Zulu", this class shows considerable German influence. About 240 of the "Whiskys" were built between 1951 and 1957 at yards throughout the USSR. Built in six types—I and IV had guns forward of the conning tower, II had guns both ends, whilst III

"WHISKY V" Class   10/1974, MOD

Submarines
Patrol Submarine Classes

and V have no guns. V is the most common variant whilst VA has a diver's exit hatch forward of the conning tower. Now being paid-off at possibly 15-20 per year. Up to 50% are probably now in reserve.

Conversions: Two of this class, named *Severyanka* and *Slavyanka,* were converted for oceanographic and fishery research.

Foreign Transfers: Has been the most popular export model; currently in service in Albania (4), Bulgaria (2), China (21), Egypt (6), Indonesia (4), North Korea (4) and Poland (4).

"WHISKY V" Class

8/1975, MOD

3 "WHISKY CANVAS BAG" CLASS
(RADAR PICKET SUBMARINES SSR)

Displacement, tons: 1 030 surfaced; 1 350 dived
Length, feet (metres): 249·3 *(76)*
Beam, feet (metres): 22·0 *(6·7)*
Draught, feet (metres): 15·0 *(4·6)*
Torpedo tubes: 6—21 in (4 bow, 2 stern)
Main machinery: Diesels; 4 000 bhp
　Electric motors; 2 500 hp
Speed, knots: 17 surfaced; 15 dived
Range, miles: 13 000 at 8 knots surfaced
Complement: 65

Basically of same design as the "Whisky" class but with long-range Boat-Sail radar aerial mounted on the fin. The coy way in which this was covered prompted the title "Canvas Bag". Converted in 1959 to 1963.

"WHISKY CANVAS BAG" Class (with radar aerial abeam)

1975

17 "QUEBEC" CLASS
(PATROL SUBMARINES SS)

Displacement, tons: 650 surfaced; 740 dived
Length, feet (metres): 185·0 *(56·4)*
Beam, feet (metres): 18·0 *(5·5)*
Draught, feet (metres): 13·2 *(4·0)*
Torpedo tubes: 4—21 in bow
Main machinery: 1 diesel; 3 shafts; 3 000 bhp; 3 electric motors; 2 500 hp
Speed, knots: 18 surfaced; 16 dived
Oil fuel, tons: 50
Range, miles: 7 000 surfaced cruising
Complement: 42

Short range, coastal submarines. Built from 1954 to 1957. Thirteen were constructed in 1955 by Sudomekh Shipyard, Leningrad. The earlier boats of this class of 22 were fitted with what was possibly a closed-cycle propulsion, probably on the third shaft. This was more likely, however, a Walther HTP (High Test Peroxide) turbine; but, whatever it was, it is believed to have been unsuccessful and was subsequently removed. The majority of this class is now in reserve, some probably paid off.

"QUEBEC" Class

1975

CRUISERS
4 + 1 "KARA" CLASS (CLG)

NIKOLAYEV   **OCHAKOV**
KERCH   **AZOV**
      +1

Displacement, tons: 8 200 standard; 10 000 full load
Length, feet (metres): 570 *(173·8)*
Beam, feet (metres): 60 *(18·3)*
Draught, feet (metres): 20 *(6·2)*
Aircraft: 1 Hormone A helicopter (Hangar aft)
Missile Systems: 8—SSN-10 (Two mounts abreast bridge)
     4—SAN-4 (twins either side of mast)
     4—SAN-3 (twins)
Guns: 4—76 mm (2 twins abaft bridge)
     4—30 mm (abreast funnel) (see *Gunnery* note)
A/S weapons: 2—12 barrelled MBU 2500A launchers (forward)
     2—6 barrelled DC throwers
Torpedo tubes: 10—21 in (2 quintuple mountings abaft funnel)
Main engines: Gas-turbine
Speed, knots: Approximately 34

Apart from the specialised "Moskva" class this is the first class of large cruisers to join the Soviet navy since the "Sverdlovs". *Nikolayev* was first seen in public when she entered the Mediterranean from the Black Sea on 2 March 1973. Clearly capable of prolonged operations overseas.
All built or building at Nikolayev. *Azov* and the fifth ship are of a modified design.

ECM: A full oufit appears to be housed on the bridge and mast.

Gunnery: The sighting of both main and secondary armament on either beams in the waist follows the precedent of both "Kresta" classes, although the weight of the main armament is increased. The single mountings, classified above as 30 mm, appear to be some form of Gatling and are quite different from the usual twin 30 mm mountings.

Missiles: In addition to the "Kresta II" armament of eight tubes for the SSN-10 (30 n. mile) surface-to-surface system and the pair of twin launchers for SAN-3 system with Goblet missiles "Kara" mounts the new SAN-4 system in two silos, either side of the mast. The combination of such a number of systems presents a formidable capability, matched by no other ship.

Radar: Surveillance: Topsail and Headnet C.
SAN-3 control: Head Light
76 mm gun control: Owl Screech.
30 mm gun control: Drum Tilt.

Sonar and A/S: VDS is mounted below the helicopter pad and is presumably complementary to a hull-mounted set or sets. The presence of the helicopter with dipping-sonar and an A/S weapon load adds to her long-range capability.

Soviet Type Name: Bolshoy Protivo Lodochny Korabl, meaning Large Anti-Submarine Ship.

KERCH (Hull 3)   *2/1976, MOD*

OCHAKOV (Hull 2) (same pennant number as *Nikolayev* a year earlier)   *3/1975, MOD*

NIKOLAYEV (Hull 1)   *1975, MOD*

9 + 1 "KRESTA II" CLASS (CLG)

ADMIRAL ISACHENKOV
ADMIRAL ISAKOV
ADMIRAL MAKAROV
ADMIRAL NAKHIMOV
ADMIRAL OKTYABRSKY
KRONSTADT
MARSHAL TIMOSHENKO
MARSHAL VOROSHILOV
+ 2

Displacement, tons: 6 000 standard; 8 000 full load
Length, feet (metres): 519·9 *(158·5)*
Beam, feet (metres): 55·1 *(16·8)*
Draught, feet (metres): 19·7 *(6·0)*
Aircraft: 1 Hormone A
Missile launchers: 2 quadruple for SSN-10; 2 twin for SAN-3
Guns: 4—57 mm (2 twin); 8—30 mm (4 twin)
A/S weapons: 2—12 barrelled MBU 2500A (forward);
2—6 barrelled DC throwers aft
Torpedo tubes: 10—21 in (two quintuple)
Main engines: Steam turbines; 2 shafts; 100 000 shp
Boilers: 4 watertube
Speed, knots: 33
Range, miles: 5 000 at 18 knots
Complement: 500

The design was developed from that of the "Kresta I" class, but the layout is more up-to-date. The missile armament shows an advance on the "Kresta I" SAM armament and a complete change of practice in the fitting of the SS-N-10 system with 30 n. mile range missiles. This is a mach 1·2 missile and the fact that it has subsequently been fitted in the "Kara" and "Krivak" classes indicates a possible change in tactical thought. Built at Leningrad from 1968 onwards.

Flight: A flight of two helicopters could be operated, although the normal would appear to be one on the helicopter deck aft with adjacent low hangar.

New construction: One building at Zhdanov Yard Leningrad (1976).

Radar: The radar installations seems to be similar to that in the "Moskva" class with the same. Top Sail 3D and Head Net C 3D for search radar and the Head Light and Peel Group (2) fire control radar for surface to air missiles and Drum Tilt (2) for guns. Muff Cob also fitted.

Soviet Type Name: Bolshoy Protivo Lodochny Korabl, meaning Large Anti-Submarine Ship.

MARSHAL VOROSHILOV   *1974*

ADMIRAL MAKAROV   *5/1975, MOD*

ADMIRAL OKTYABRSKY   *1975, MOD*

4 "KRESTA I" CLASS (CLG)

VICE-ADMIRAL DROZD   **SEVASTOPOL**
ADMIRAL ZOZULYA   **VLADIVOSTOK**

Displacement, tons: 6 140 standard; 8 000 full load
Length, feet (metres): 510 (155·5)
Beam, feet (metres): 55·1 (16·8)
Draught, feet (metres): 18·0 (5·5)
Aircraft: 1 Hormone A helicopter with hangar aft
Missile launchers: 2 twin SSN-3 for Shaddock (no reloads); 2 twin SAN-1 for Goa
Guns: 4—57 mm (2 twin)
A/S weapons: 2—12 barrelled MBU 2 500A (60 reloads) (fw'd); 2—6 barrelled DC throwers (aft)
Torpedo tubes: 10 (two quintuple) 21 in
Main engines: Steam turbines; 2 shafts; 100 000 shp
Boilers: 4 watertube
Speed, knots: 34
Range, miles: 4 500 at 18 knots
Complement: 400

Provided with a helicopter landing deck and hangar aft for the first time in a Soviet ship. This gives an enhanced A/S capability and could certainly provide carried-on-board target-location facilities for the 250 mile SSN-3 system at a lower, possibly optimum, range. The "Kresta I" was therefore the first Soviet missile cruiser free to operate alone and distant from own aircraft.
Built at the Zhdanov Shipyard, Leningrad. The prototype ship was laid down in Sep 1964, launched in 1965 and carried out sea trials in the Baltic in Feb 1967. The second ship was launched in 1966 and the others in 1967-68.

Radar: Four pods, or radomes, are fitted to the sides of the superstructure. These are similar to those fitted in the "Moskva" class helicopter missile cruisers and probably contain passive detection and active jamming equipment.
Search: Head Net C 3D and Big Net.
Fire Control: Scoop Pair for Shaddock system and Peel Group (2) for Goa system.
Muff Cob.
Bass Tilt.

Refit: The first ship undergoing a major refit, *Vice Admiral Drozd,* was completed in 1975 with new Bass Tilt radar and Gatling guns on a new superstructure between the bridge and the tower mast.

Soviet type name: Bolshoy Protivo Lodochny Korabl, meaning Large Anti-Submarine Ship.

VICE-ADMIRAL DROZD (after 1975 refit with new Bass Tilt radar and Gatling guns)   *2/1976, MOD(N)*

SEVASTOPOL   *5/1974, MOD(N)*

VICE-ADMIRAL DROZD (see top picture)   *2/1976, MOD(N)*

4 "KYNDA" CLASS (CLG)

| ADMIRAL FOKIN | GROZNY |
| ADMIRAL GOLOVKO | VARYAG |

Displacement, tons: 4 500 standard; 6 000 full load
Length, feet (metres): 465·8 *(142·0)*
Beam, feet (metres): 51·8 *(15·8)*
Draught, feet (metres): 17·4 *(5·3)*
Aircraft: Pad for helicopter on stern
Missile launchers: 2 quadruple mounts, 1 fwd, 1 aft, for SSN-3
 system (possible reloads)
 1 twin mount on forecastle for SAN-1 system (30 reloads)
Guns: 4—3 in *(76 mm)* (2 twin)
A/S weapons: 2—12 barrelled MBUs 2 500A on forecastle
Torpedo tubes: 6—21 in *(533 mm)* (2 triple amidships)
Main engines: 2 sets geared turbines; 2 shafts; 100 000 shp
Boilers: 4 high pressure
Speed, knots: 35
Complement: 390

The first ship of this class was laid down in June 1960, launched
in Apr 1961 at Zhdanov Shipyard, Leningrad, and completed in
June 1962. The second ship was launched in Nov 1961 and
fitted out in Aug 1962. The others were completed by 1965. Two
enclosed towers, instead of masts, are stepped forward of each
raked funnel. In this class there is no helicopter embarked, so
guidance for the SS-N-3 system would be more difficult than in
later ships. She will therefore be constrained in her operations
compared with the later ships with their own helicopters.

Radar: This class showed at an early stage the Soviet ability to
match radar availability to weapon capability. The duplicated
aerials provide not only a capability for separate target
engagement but also provide a reserve in the event of damage.
Search: Head Net A.
Fire Control: Scoop Pair (2) for Shaddock systems, Peel Group
for Goa systems and Owl Screech for guns.

Soviet type name: Raketny Kreyser meaning Large Rocket
Ship.

"KYNDA" Class   4/1975, MOD(N)

"KYNDA" Class

11/1974, US Navy

"KYNDA" Class   4/1975, MOD (N)

1 "SVERDLOV" CLASS ((CG)
2 "SVERDLOV" CLASS (CC)
9 "SVERDLOV" CLASS (CA)

ADMIRAL LAZAREV	ALEKSANDR NEVSKI	DZERZHINSKI	OKTYABRSKAYA REVOLUTSIYA
ADMIRAL SENYAVIN	ALEKSANDR SUVOROV	MIKHAIL KUTUSOV	SVERDLOV
ADMIRAL USHAKOV	DMITRI POZHARSKI	MURMANSK	ZHDANOV

Displacement, tons: 15 450 standard; 18 000 full load
Length, feet (metres): 656·2 *(200·0)* pp; 689·0 *(210·0)* oa
Beam, feet (metres): 72·2 *(22·0)*
Draught, feet (metres): 24·5 *(7·5)*
Aircraft: Helicopter pad in *Zhdanov*. Pad and hangar in *Senyavin*
Armour: Belts 3·9—4·9 in *(100–125 mm)*; fwd and aft 1·6—2 in *(40–50 mm)*; turrets 4·9 in *(125 mm)*; C.T. 5·9 in *(150 mm)*; decks 1—2 in *(25—50 mm)* and 2—3 in *(50—75 mm)*
Missile launchers: Twin SAN-2 aft in *Dzerzhinski*; 2 SAN-4 in *Zhdanov* and *Senyavin* (twin) (see conversions)
Guns: 12—6 in *(152 mm)*, (4 triple) (9—6 in in *Dzerzhinski* and *Zhdanov*; 6—6 in in *Senyavin*); 12—3·9 in *(100 mm)*, (6 twin), 16—37 mm (twin), 8—30 mm (twin)
Torpedo tubes: 10—21 in *(533 mm)* 2 quintuple (see *Torpedoes*)
Mines: 150 capacity—(except *Zhdanov* and *Senyavin*)
Main engines: Geared turbines; 2 shafts; 130 000 shp
Boilers: 6 watertube
Speed, knots: 34
Oil fuel, tons: 3 800
Range, miles: 8 700 at 18 knots
Complement: 1 000 average

Of the 24 cruisers of this class originally projected, 20 keels were laid and 17 hulls were launched from 1951 onwards, but only 14 ships were completed by 1956. There were two slightly different types. *Sverdlov* and sisters had the 37 mm guns near the fore-funnel one deck higher than in later cruisers. All ships except *Zhdanov* and *Senyavin* are fitted for minelaying. Mine stowage is on the second deck. *Zhdanov* and *Senyavin* used as command ships with much increased communications capability. *Admiral Nakhimov* deleted in 1969. *Ordzhonikidze* transferred to Indonesia as *Irian* in 1962—now scrapped.

Conversions: *Dzerzhinski* has been fitted with an SAN-2 launcher aft replacing X-Turret. In 1972 *Admiral Senyavin* returned to service with both X and Y turrets removed and replaced by a helicopter pad and a hangar surmounted by four 30 mm mountings and an SAN-4 mounting. At about the same time *Zhdanov* appeared on the scene with a different outfit. She has had only X-turret removed and replaced by a high deckhouse mounting an SAN-4 launcher.

Flagships: *Admiral Senyavin* is flagship in the Pacific Fleet and *Zhdanov* is flagship in the Northern Fleet.

Names: The ship first named *Molotovsk* was renamed *Oktyabrskaya Revolutsiya* in 1957.

Torpedoes: *Oktyabrskaya Revolutsiya* and *Murmansk* no longer have tubes.

Radar: Search: Head Net A, Strut Curve and some ships fitted with Big Net. (*Dzerzhinski* only)—Fire control: Peel Group and Drum Tilt. High Lune and Fan Song E for SA-N-2 system. CCs only—Big Net and Slim Net.

Soviet Type Name: Kreyser meaning Cruiser.

SVERDLOV   5/1975, MOD(N)

ZHDANOV   4/1975, MOD(N)

ALEKSANDR NEVSKI   1974, MOD(N)

SVERDLOV

1975, J. A. Verhoog

DZERZHINSKI with twin SA-N-2 launcher in place of X turret

1972

ZHDANOV

1974

ADMIRAL SENYAVIN

1973

2 "CHAPAEV" CLASS (CA)

KOMSOMOLETS (ex-*Chkalov*)   **ZHELEZNYAKOV**

Displacement, tons: 11 300 standard; 15 000 full load
Length, feet (metres): 659·5 *(201·0)* wl; 665 *(202·8)*
Beam, feet (metres): 62 *(18·9)*
Draught, feet (metres): 24 *(7·3)*
Armour: Side 3 in *(75 mm)*; deck 2 in *(50 mm)*; gunhouses 3·9 in *(100 mm)* CT 3 in *(75 mm)*
Guns: 12—6 in *(152 mm)* 57 cal, (4 triple); 8—3·9 in *(100 mm)*; 70 cal, (4 twin); 24—37 mm (12 twin)
Mines: 200 capacity; 425 ft rails
Main engines: Geared turbines, with diesels for cruising speeds; 4 shafts; 130 000 shp
Boilers: 6 watertube
Speed, knots: 32
Range, miles: 5 400 at 15 knots
Oil fuel, tons: 2 500
Complement: 900

Originally a class of six ships of which one was never completed—shows signs of both Italian and German influence. Laid down in 1939-40. Launched during 1941-47. All work on these ships was stopped during the war, but was resumed in 1946-47. Completed in 1948-50, both in Leningrad. Catapults were removed from all ships of this type. Both remaining ships serve as training cruisers.

Gunnery: Turret guns fitting allows independent elevation to 45 degrees.

Radar: They have long range surveillance radars and gunfire control tracking radar. *Komsomolets* was fitted with modern radar in 1969-70. Surface—Low Sieve; Early warning—Slim Net and Knife Rest B; Fire control—Top Bow, Sun Visor B, Egg Cup, IFF—High Pole.

Soviet Type Name: Kreyser meaning Cruiser.

KOMSOMOLETS

1962, MOD(N)

KOMSOMOLETS refuelling astern

DESTROYERS

11 "KRIVAK" CLASS (DDG)

BDITELNY	**DOSTOYNY**	**RAZYASHCHY**	**SVIREPY**
BODRY	**DROZNY**	**SILNY**	**ZHARKI**
DOBLESTNY	**RAZUMNY**	**STOROZHEVOY**	

Displacement, tons: 3 300 standard; 3 900 full load
Length, feet (metres): 404·8 (123·4)
Beam, feet (metres): 45·9 (14·0)
Draught, feet (metres): 16·4 (5·0)
Missile launchers: 4 for SSN-10 system, in A position; (quad-
    ruple); 4 for SAN-4 system (twins)
Guns: 4—3 in (76 mm) (2 twin) in X and Y positions; 4—30 mm
A/S weapons: 2 twelve-barrelled MBU 2 500A (forward)
Torpedo tubes: 8—21 in (533 mm) (2 quads)
Main engines: 8 sets Gas turbines; 2 shafts; 112 000 shp
Speed, knots: 38

This handsome class, the first ship of which appeared in 1971,
appears to be a most successful design incorporating surface
and anti-air capability, a VDS with associated MBUs, two banks
of tubes, all in a hull designed for both speed and sea-keeping.
The use of gas-turbines gives the "Krivak" class a rapid acceleration and an availability which cannot be matched by steam
driven ships. Building continues at about 2 per year at Kaliningrad and Kerch.

Missiles: The surface-to-surface missiles of the SS-N-10 system have a range of 30 n. miles, continuing the short-range
trend of the "Kresta II" class and followed by the "Kara" class.
The SA-N-4 SAMs are of the same design which is now
mounted also in the "Kara", "Nanuchka" and "Grisha" classes.
The launcher retracts into the mounting for stowage and protection, rising to fire and retracting to reload. The two mountings are forward of the bridge and abaft the funnel.

Radar: Head Net C. Drum Tilt and Head Light.

Soviet Type Name: Bolshoy Protivo Lodochny Korabl, meaning Large Anti-Submarine Ship.

SVIREPY   5/1975, MOD(N)

SILNY   4/1975, MOD(N)

STOREZHEVOY   1975, J. A. Verhoog

SVIREPY   1975, J. A. Verhoog

19 "KASHIN" and "MODIFIED KASHIN" CLASS (DDG)

KOMSOMOLETS UKRAINY
KRASNY-KAVKAZ
KRASNY-KRIM
OBRAZTSOVY
ODARENNY
(* modified)

OGNEVOY*
PROVORNY
SKORY
RESHITELNY
SDERZHANNY*

SLAVNY*
SMELY*
SMETLIVY
SMYSHLENY*
SOOBRAZITELNY

SPOSOBNY
STEREGUSHCHY
STROGY
STROYNY

"KASHIN" Class   4/1975, MOD(N)

Displacement, tons: 3 750 standard; 4 500 full load (4 700 (mod))
Length, feet (metres): 470·9 (143·3) or 481 (146·5) (mod)
Beam, feet (metres): 52·5 (15·9)
Draught, feet (metres): 19 (5·8)
Missile launchers: 4 (2 twin) SAN-1 mounted in B and X positions for surface-to-air missiles; 4 SSN-11 in mod-class
Guns: 4—3 in (76 mm) (2 twin) in A and Y positions; 4—30 mm Gatlings in mod-class
A/S weapons: 2—12 barrelled MBU 2 500A forward; 2—6 barrelled DC throwers aft (unmodified)
Torpedo tubes: 5—21 in (533 mm) quintuple, amidships
Main engines: 8 sets gas turbines, each 12 000 hp; 2 shafts
Speed, knots: 35
Complement: 350

The first class of warships in the world to rely entirely on gas-turbine propulsion giving them the quick getaway and acceleration necessary for modern tactics. These ships were delivered from 1962 onwards from the Zhdanov Yard, Leningrad and the Nosenko Yard, Nikolayev.

Conversion: In order to bring this class up-to-date with SSM, new SAM system and VDS a conversion programme was started in 1974. This conversion consists of lengthening the hull by ten feet, shipping 4—SSN-11 launchers (SSM), 4—30 mm Gatling guns, a VDS and removing the DC throwers. By mid-1976 five had been so converted.

Loss: *Otvazhny* of this class foundered in the Black Sea in September 1974, apparently as the result of an internal explosion followed by a fire which lasted for five hours. Nearly 300 of the ship's company were lost, making this the worst peacetime naval loss for many years.

Radar: Search: Head Net C and Big Net in some ships; Head Net A (2) in others.
Fire control: Peel Group (2) for Goa system and Owl Screech (2) for guns.

Soviet type name: Bolshoy Protivo Lodochny Korabl, meaning Large Anti-Submarine Ship.

OBRAZTSOVY at Portsmouth   5/1976, C and S Taylor

SDERZHANNY (modified)   6/1975, MOD(N)

4 "KILDIN" CLASS (DDG)

BEDOVY   NEULOVIMY
NEUDERSIMY   PROZORLIVY

Displacement, tons: 3 000 standatd; 3 600 full load
Length, feet (metres): 414·9 *(126·5)*
Beam, feet (metres): 42·6 *(13·0)*
Draught, feet (metres): 16·1 *(4·9)*
Missile launchers: 4 for SSN—11 system (conversions)
A/S weapons: 2—16 barrelled MBU 2 500 on forecastle
Guns: 4—76 mm (twins aft) (conversions); 16—57 mm
  (quads—2 forward, 2 between funnels)
Torpedo tubes: 4—21 in (2 twin)
Main engines: Geared turbines: 2 shafts; 72 000 shp
Boilers: 4 high pressure
Speed, knots: 36
Range, miles: 5 500 at 16 knots
Complement: 350 officers and men

Large destroyers with the "Kotlin" type hull, but redesigned as
guided missile armed destroyers.

Conversion: In 1972 *Neulovimy* was taken in hand for modification. This was completed in mid-1973 and consisted of the
replacement of the SSN-1 on the quarterdeck by two superimposed twin 76 mm turrets, the fitting of four SSN-11 launchers abreast the after funnel and the fitting of new radar. The
substitution of the 30 n mile SSN-11 system (a modified Styx)
for the obsolescent SSN-1 system and the notable increase in
gun armament illustrate two trends in Soviet thought. *Bedovy*
has now completed this conversion.

Radar: Search: Head Net A and Slim Net.
Fire Control: New outfit at modernisation.

Soviet type name: Bolshoy Protivo Lodochny Korabl meaning
Large Anti-Submarine Ship.

"KILDIN" Class (before conversion)   *1972*

NEULOVIMY after conversion   *1974*

NEULOVIMY after conversion   *1973*

BEDOVY after conversion   *4/1975, MOD(N)*

8 "KANIN" CLASS (DDG)

BOYKY	GNEVNY	GREMYASHCHYI	ZHGUCHY
DERZKY	GORDY	UPORNY	ZORKY

Displacement, tons: 3 700 standard; 4 700 full load
Length, feet (metres): 456·9 *(139·3)*
Beam, feet (metres): 48·2 *(14·7)*
Draught, feet (metres): 16·4 *(5·0)*
Aircraft: Helicopter platform
Missile launchers: 1 twin SAN-1 mounted aft
Guns: 8—57 mm (2 quadruple forward); 8—30 mm (twin) (by after funnel)
A/S weapons: Three 12-barrelled MBU 2 500A
Torpedo tubes: 10—21 in *(533 mm)* A/S (2 quintuple)
Main engines: 2 sets geared steam turbines; 2 shafts; 80 000 shp
Boilers: 4 watertube
Speed, knots: 34
Oil fuel, tons: 900
Complement: 350

All ships of this class have been converted from "Krupnys" at Zhdanov Yard, Leningrad from 1967 onwards, being given a SAM capability instead of the latter's SSM armament.

Appearance: As compared with the "Krupny" class these ships have enlarged bridge, converted bow (probably for a new sonar) and larger helicopter platforms.

Gunnery: The four twin 30 mm abaft the after funnel were a late addition to the armament.

Radar: Search: Head Net C or Head Net A.
Fire Control: Peel Group for Goa, Hawk Screech for guns.
Drum Tilt for additional 30 mm guns.

Soviet Type Name: Bolshoy Protivo Lodochny Korabl, meaning Large Anti-Submarine Ship.

BOYKY with additional 30 mm guns   *10/1973, MOD(N)*

"KANIN" Class, Hull 2   *1972*

"KANIN" Class   *1972*

8 "SAM KOTLIN" CLASS (DDG)

BRAVY
NAKHODCIVY

NASTOYCHIVY
NESOKRUSHIMY

SKROMNY
SKRYTNY

SOZNATELNY
VOZBUZHDENNY

Displacement, tons: 2 850 standard; 3 600 full load
Length, feet (metres): 414·9 (126·5)
Beam, feet (metres): 42·6 (13·0)
Draught, feet (metres): 16·1 (4·9)
Missile launchers: 1 twin SAN-1 mounted aft
Guns: 2—3·9 in (100 mm) (1 twin); 4—57 mm (1 quadruple or twins); 8—30 mm (twins) in later ships
Torpedo tubes: 1 quintuple 21 in mounting
A/S weapons: 6 side thrown DC projectors or 2—12 barrelled MBU 2 500A (2 500 in Bravy)
Main engines: Geared turbines; 2 shafts; 72 000 shp
Boilers: 4 high pressure
Speed, knots: 36
Range, miles: 5 500 at 16 knots
Complement: 285

Converted "Kotlin" class destroyers with a surface-to-air missile launcher in place of the main twin turret aft and anti-aircraft guns reduced to one quadruple mounting.
The prototype conversion was completed about 1962 and the others since 1966. One ship transferred to Poland.

Appearance: The prototype "Kotlin" SAM class has a different after funnel and different radar pedestal from those in the standard "Kotlin" SAM class.

Radar: Search: Head Net C 3D or Head Net A.
Fire Control: Peel Group for Goa system, Hawk Screech for guns.
Drum Tilt for 30 mm in later ships.

Soviet Type Name: Esminets meaning Destroyer.

"SAM KOTLIN" Class

9/1971, USN

Later "SAM KOTLIN" (with 2 extra Drum Tilt and 8—30 mm by after funnel)

1973

"SAM KOTLIN" Class (with different design of midship radar pedestal and after funnel from the prototype)

1971, MOD

18 "KOTLIN" CLASS (DD)

BESSLEDNY
BLAGORODNY
BLESTYASHCHY
BURLIVY
BYVALY
NAPORISTY
PLAMENNY
SPESHNY
DALNEVOSTOCHNY KOMSOMOLETS
MOSKOVSKY KOMSOMOLETS

SPOKOJNY
SVEDUJSCHY
SVETLY
VDOKHNOVENNY
VESKY
VOZMUSHCHENNY
VYDERZHANNY
VYZYVAJUSCHY

Displacement, tons: 2 850 standard; 3 600 full load
Length, feet (metres): 414·9 *(126·5)*
Beam, feet (metres): 42·6 *(13·0)*
Draught, feet (metres): 16·1 *(4·9)*
Guns: 4—5·1 in *(130 mm)* (2 twin); 16—57 mm (4 quads); 8—30 mm (twin) in some, 8—25 mm (twin) in others
A/S weapons: 6 side thrown DC projectors or 2—16 barrelled MBU 2 500 or 2—6 barrelled DC throwers
Torpedo tubes: 5 or 10—21 in *(533 mm)* (quintuple)
Mines: 80 capacity
Main engines: Geared turbines; 2 shafts; 72 000 shp
Boilers: 4 high pressure
Speed, knots: 36
Range, miles: 5 500 at 16 knots
Complement: 285

Built in 1954-57. The last four hulls laid down were converted to "Kildins".

Modifications: (a) Eight converted to "Sam Kotlins" plus one transferred to Poland. (b) *Svetly* and others provided with helicopter platform on stern. (c) Some had the after torpedo-tubes replaced by a deckhouse. (d) Some ships had two 16-barrelled MBUs fitted. (e) The latest addition in some ships is the fitting of eight 30 mm either side of the after-funnel.

Radar: Search: Slim Net and Strut Curve.
Fire control: Hawk Screech (2). Hair Net. Square Head. Flat Spin in some. Don (2) in some.

Soviet Type Name: Esminets meaning Destroyer.

"KOTLIN" Class   7/1974, MOD

"KOTLIN" Class with 5 torpedo tubes and additional 30 mm guns   1973, USN

"KOTLIN" Class (helicopter platform aft)   1969, MOD

40 "SKORY" CLASS (DD)

BDITELNY
BESNERVNY
BESSMENNY
BESSMERTNY
BEZUPRETCHNY
BEZUKORIZNENNY
OGNENNY
OSTERVENELY
OSTOROZNY
OSTROGLAZY

OTCHAYANNY
OTRETOVENNY
OTVETSTVENNY
OZHESTOCHENNY
OZHIVLENNY
SERDITY
SERIOZNY
SMELY
SMOTRYASHCHY
SMYSHLYONY

SOKRUSHITELNY
SOLIDNY
SOVERSHENNY
SPOSOBNY
STATNY
STEPENNY
STOJKY
STREMITELNY
SUROVY
SVOBODNY

VAZHNY
VDUMCHIVY
VERDUSHCHY
VERNY
VIDNY
VIKHREVOY
VNESAPNY
VNIMATELNY
VOLEVOY
VRAZUMITELNY

Displacement, tons: 2 600 standard; 3 100 full load
Length, feet (metres): 395·2 *(120·5)*
Beam, feet (metres): 38·9 *(11·8)*
Draught, feet (metres): 15·1 *(4·6)*
Guns: 4—5·1 in *(130 mm)*, (2 twin); 2—3·4 in *(86 mm)*, (1 twin); 8—37 mm (4 twin), (see Modernisation Note)
A/S weapons: 4 DCT
Torpedo tubes: 10—21 in *(533 mm)* (see Modernisation Note)
Mines: 80 can be carried
Main engines: Geared turbines; 2 shafts; 60 000 shp
Boilers: 4 high pressure
Speed, knots: 33
Range, miles: 3 900 at 13 knots
Complement: 260

SVOBODNY

1968

There were to have been 85 destroyers of this class, but construction beyond 75 units was discontinued in favour of later types of destroyers, and the number has been further reduced to 40 by transfers to other countries, translations to other types and disposals.

Appearance: There were three differing types in this class, the anti-aircraft guns varying with twin and single mountings; and two types of foremast, one vertical with all scanners on top and the other with one scanner on top and one on a platform half way.

Modernisation: At least six ships, of the "Skory" class were modified from 1959 onwards including extensive alterations to anti-aircraft armament, electronic equipment and anti-submarine weapons. These now have five 57 mm single, five torpedo tubes and two 16-barrelled MBU.

Radar: Search: Strut Curve. Square Head.

Reserve: Some 50% of this class now in reserve.

Transfers: Of this class *Skory* and *Smerlivy* were transferred to the Polish Navy in 1957-58, two to the Egyptian Navy in 1956, four to the Indonesian Navy in 1959, and a further two (modernised) to Egypt in 1968.

Soviet Type Name: Esminets meaning Destroyer.

OGNENNY (modified)

5/1972, MOD(N)

"SKORY" Class Type II (unmodified)

9/1971, MOD

FRIGATES

20 "MIRKA I AND II" CLASS

Displacement, tons: 950 standard; 1 100 full load
Length, feet (metres): 269·9 *(82·3)*
Beam, feet (metres): 29·9 *(9·1)*
Draught, feet (metres): 9·8 *(3·0)*
Guns: 4—3 in *(76 mm)* (2 twin)
A/S weapons: 4—MBU 2 500A (2 forward, 2 aft) (I); 2—MBU 2 500A (forward) (II)
Torpedo tubes: 5—16 in anti-submarine (I); 10—16 in (II)
Main engines: 2 diesels; total 6 000 hp; 2 gas-turbines, total 31 000 hp; 2 shafts
Speed, knots: 30
Complement: 100

This class of ships was built in 1964-69 as improved "Petya" class. The difference between the Mark I and II is that the latter have the after MBU rocket launchers removed and an additional quintuple 16-inch torpedo mounting fitted between the bridge and the mast. At least one mounts VDS aft.

Radar: Search: Slim Net.
Fire Control: Hawk Screech.

Soviet type names: Maly Protivo Lodochny Korabl meaning Small Anti-Submarine Ship.

"MIRKA II" Class (with two torpedo mountings)   4/1975, MOD

"MIRKA II" Class

20 "PETYA I AND IA" CLASS
25 "PETYA II" CLASS

Displacement, tons: 950 standard; 1 150 full load
Length, feet (metres): 270 *(82·3)*
Beam, feet (metres): 29·9 *(9·1)*
Draught, feet (metres): 10·5 *(3·2)*
Guns: 4—3 in *(76 mm)* (2 twins)
A/S weapons: 4—MBU 2 500 (I)
2—MBU 2 500A (II)
Torpedo tubes: 5—16 in *(406 mm)* (I)
10—16 in *(406 mm)* (II)
Main engines: 2 diesels, total 6 000 hp; 2 gas-turbines; total 31 000 hp; 2 shafts
Speed, knots: 30
Complement: 100

Small freeboard with a low wide funnel. The first ship reported to have been built in 1960-61 at Kaliningrad. Construction continued until about 1964. Fitted with two mine rails. "Petya II" class mount an extra quintuple torpedo-tube in place of after MBUs.

Radar: Search: Slim Net.
Fire Control: Hawk Screech.

Soviet type name: Maly Protivo Lodochny Korabl meaning Small Anti-Submarine Ship.

VDS: In six of "Petya I" class a deck-house containing Variable Depth Sonar has replaced the after MBUs and encloses the quarter-deck. This group, part of a continuing programme, is now classified "Petya IA" class (originally "Petya III"). Some "Petya IIs" appear to have received VDS.

"PETYA II" Class (with VDS)   1973, S. Breyer

"PETYA II" Class   10/1974, USN

"PETYA I" Class   10/1970, MOD

30 "RIGA" CLASS

BARSUK	KOBCHIK	SAKAL
BUJVOL	LISA	TURMAN
BYK	MEDVED	VOLK
GEPARD	PANTERA	+18
GIENA		

Displacement, tons: 1 200 standard; 1 600 full load
Length, feet (metres): 298·8 (91·0)
Beam, feet (metres): 33·7 (10·2)
Draught, feet (metres): 11 (3·4)
Guns: 3—3·9 in (100 mm) (single); 4—37 mm (2 twin); 4—30 mm (twin) in some
A/S weapons: 2—MBU 2 500 (in some); 4 DC projectors
Torpedo tubes: 3—21 in (533 mm) (2 twin) in some
Mines: 50
Main engines: Geared turbines; 2 shafts; 25 000 shp
Boilers: 2
Speed, knots: 28
Range, miles: 2 500 at 15 knots
Complement: 150

Built from 1952 to 1959. Successors to the "Kola" class escorts, of which they are lighter and less heavily armed but improved versions. Fitted with mine rails.

Anti-submarine: The two 12-barrelled MBU rocket launchers are mounted just before the bridge abreast B gun.

Conversion: A small number of this class has been converted. Some, designed for ECM operations, have a higher funnel, more complex electronics, no torpedo tubes but with MBU launchers. Others have had the triple torpedo-tube mountings replaced by more modern twin mountings and have a twin 30 mm gun mounting on either side of the funnel.

Radar: Search: Slim Net.
Fire Control: Obsolescent type.

Soviet type name: Storozhevoy Korabl meaning Escort Ship.

Transfers: Bulgaria (2), China (4). East Germany (2), Finland (2), Indonesia (6).

"RIGA" Class   6/1974, MOD

"RIGA" Class   6/1974, MOD

3 "KOLA" CLASS

SOVIETSKY AZERBAIDJAN
SOVIETSKY DAGESTAN
SOVIETSKY TURKMENISTAN

Displacement, tons: 1 500 standard; 1 900 full load
Length, feet (metres): 315·0 (96·0) oa
Beam, feet (metres): 35·4 (10·8)
Draught, feet (metres): 10·6 (3·2)
Guns: 4—3·9 in (100 mm) single
A/S weapons: 2 MBU, 4 DC racks, 4 DC rails
Torpedo tubes: 3—21 in (533 mm)
Mines: 30
Main engines: Geared turbines; 2 shafts; 30 000 shp
Boilers: 2
Speed, knots: 30
Range, miles: 3 500 at 12 knots
Complement: 190

Built in 1950-52. In design this class of flushdecked frigates appears to be a combination of the former German "Elbing" class destroyers, with a similar hull form, and of the earlier Soviet "Birds" class escorts.

Radar: Ball Gun/Ball End, surface search; Cross Bird, air search; Wasp Head and Sun Visor, fire control; High Pole, IFF.

Soviet type name: Storozhevoy Korabl meaning Escort Ship.

"KOLA" Class

CORVETTES

18 "GRISHA I" AND 3 "GRISHA II" CLASSES

Displacement, tons: 750 standard; 900 full load
Dimensions, feet (metres): 234·8 × 32·8 × 9·2 (71·6 × 10 × 2·8)
Missile launchers: SAN-4 surface-to-air (twin) ("Grisha I" class)
Guns: 2—57 mm (1 twin) (4 in "Grisha II" class)
A/S weapons: 4—16 in A/S torpedo tubes; 2 MBU 2 500A; DCs
Mines: Fitted for minelaying
Main engines: 2 gas-turbines; 2 diesels; 24 000 shp = 30 knots

Reported to have started series production in the late 1969-70 period. Five built by end of 1972, with a continuing programme of 4 a year. SAN-4 launcher mounted on the forecastle in "Grisha I" class. This is replaced by a second twin 57 mm in "Grisha II" class.

Soviet Type Name: Maly Protivo Lodochny Korabl meaning Small Anti-Submarine Ship.

"GRISHA II" Class   7/1974, MOD

"GRISHA I" Class   7/1974

"GRISHA I" Class   1972

"GRISHA II" Class   7/1974 MOD

14 "NANUCHKA" CLASS
(MISSILE CORVETTE)

Displacement, tons: 850 full load
Length, feet (metres): 196·8 *(60·0)*
Beam, feet (metres): 39·6 *(12·0)*
Draught, feet (metres): 9·9 *(3·0)*
Missile launchers: 6 (2 triple) for SSN-9; 1—SAN-4 system forward (twin)
Guns: 2—57 mm (1 twin)
Main engines: Diesels; 28 000 shp; 2 shafts
Speed, knots: 30
Complement: 70

A new class of diesel powered craft with SSM launchers as the main armament probably mainly intended for deployment in coastal waters. Reported to have a very high beam to length ratio making her a much steadier firing platform than the "Osas" and "Komars". Built from 1969 onwards. Has received many type designations including "Missile Cutter". Building continues at rate of about 3 a year at Leningrad.

Radar: Search: Slim Net.
Fire Control: Muff Cob, Pop Group +1.
Navigation: Don.

"NANUCHKA" Class fitting out

1973, N. Polmar

"NANUCHKA" Class

1974

"NANUCHKA" Class

1974

5 "T 43/AGR" CLASS

Displacement, tons: 500 standard; 610 full load
Dimensions, feet (metres): 190·2 × 28·2 × 6·9 *(58 × 8·6 × 2·1)*
Guns: 4—37 mm; 2—25 mm
Main engines: 2 diesels; 2 shafts; 2 000 bhp = 17 knots
Range, miles: 1 600 at 10 knots
Complement: 60

Former fleet minesweepers of the "T 43" class converted into radar pickets with comprehensive electronic equipment. It is reported that there may be a dozen vessels of this type. A large Big Net-like radar is mounted on the mainmast.

"T43-AGR" Class

1973, S. Breyer

70 "POTI" CLASS

Displacement, tons: 550 standard; 600 full load
Dimensions, feet (metres): 193·5 × 26·2 × 9·2 (59 × 8 × 2·8)
Guns: 2—57 mm (1 twin mounting)
Tubes: 4—16 in anti-submarine
A/S weapons: 2 MBU 2 500A
Main engines: 2 gas turbines; 2 diesels; 4 shafts; total 20 000 hp = 28 knots

This class of ship was under series construction from 1961 to 1968. Strut Curve, Don and Muff Cob radars.

Soviet Type Name: Maly Protivo Lodochny Korabl meaning Small Anti-Submarine Ship.

Transfers: 3 to Bulgaria; 3 to Romania.

"POTI" Class   1971

"POTI" Class   1975

80 "SO I" CLASS

Displacement, tons: 215 light; 250 normal
Dimensions, feet (metres): 138·6 × 20·0 × 9·2 (42·3 × 6·1 × 2·8)
Guns: 4—25 mm (2 twin mountings) see notes
A/S weapons: 4 MBU 1 800; DCT
Torpedo tubes: 2—16 in (some)
Main engines: 3 diesels; 6 000 bhp = 29 knots
Range, miles: 1 100 at 13 knots
Complement: 30

Built since 1957. Steel hulled. Modernised boats of this class have only two 25 mm guns but also have two 16 in anti-submarine torpedo tubes. Being phased out of service.

Soviet Type Name: Maly Protivo Lodochny Korabl meaning small Anti-Submarine Ship.

Transfers: Bulgaria (6), Cuba (12), Egypt (12), East Germany (12).

"SO I" Class   1968

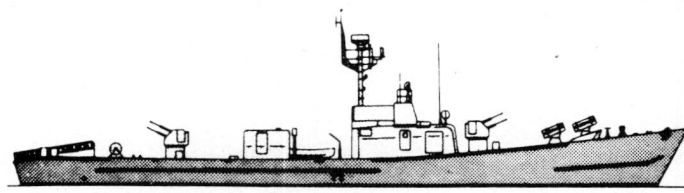

"SO I" Class

17 "KRONSTADT" CLASS

Displacement, tons: 310 standard; 380 full load
Dimensions, feet (metres): 170·6 × 21·5 × 9·0 (52 × 6·6 × 2·7)
Guns: 1—3·5 in; 2—37 mm; 6 MGs (twins)
A/S weapons: Depth charge projectors (some have 2—MBU 1 800)
Main engines: 3 diesels; 3 shafts; 3 300 hp = 24 knots
Range, miles: 1 500 at 12 knots
Complement: 65

Built in 1948-56. Flush-decked with large squat funnel, slightly raked, and massive block bridge structure. Pot Head radar. Now being phased out of service due to age. About 20 ships were rebuilt as communications relay ships of the "Libau" class. Several are de-equipped alongside in Leningrad and a considerable number have been transferred to DOSAAF (pre-military training organisation).

Soviet Type Name: Maly Protivo Lodochny Korabl meaning Small Anti-Submarine Ship.

Transfers: Bulgaria (2), China (24), Cuba (18), Indonesia (14), Poland (8), Romania (3).

"KRONSTADT" Class   1975

"KRONSTADT" Class   1972

LIGHT FORCES

120 "OSA I AND II" CLASS (65 I and 55 II)
(FAST ATTACK CRAFT—MISSILE)

Displacement, tons: 165 standard; 200 full load
Dimensions, feet (metres): 128·7 × 25·1 × 5·9 *(39·3 × 7·7 × 1·8)*
Missile launchers: 4 in two pairs abreast for SSN-2 or SSN-11
Guns: 4—30 mm; (2 twin, 1 forward, 1 aft)
Main engines: 3 diesels; 13 000 bhp = 32 knots
Range, miles: 800 at 25 knots
Complement: 25

"OSA II" Class   1970, Godfrey H. Walker

These boats, built since 1959, have a larger hull and four launchers in two pairs as compared with one pair in the "Komar" class. They have a surface-to-surface missile range of up to 23 miles. Later boats have cylindrical missile launchers, comprising the "Osa II" class.
This class was a revolution in naval shipbuilding. Although confined by their size and range to coastal operations the lethality and accuracy of the Styx missile have already been proved by the sinking of the Israeli destroyer *Eilat* on 21 Oct 1967 by an Egyptian "Komar". The operations of the Indian "Osas" in the war with Pakistan in December 1971 were equally successful: they sank *Khaibar* (destroyer) and several merchant vessels by night. These operations surely represent a most important lesson in naval operations and, in light of this, the list of transfers should be noted.

Transfers: Algeria (3), Bulgaria (3), China (17), Cuba (2), Egypt (12), East Germany (12), India (8), Iraq (5), Poland (12), Romania (5), Somalia (3), Syria (5), Yugoslavia (10).

"OSA I" Class   1970   "OSA I" (right) and "OSA II" Classes   1973, TASS

50 "STENKA" CLASS (FAST ATTACK CRAFT—PATROL)

Displacement, tons: 170 standard; 210 full load
Dimensions, feet (metres): 128·7 × 25·1 × 5·9 *(39·3 × 7·7 × 1·8)*
Guns: 4—30 mm (2 twin)
Torpedo tubes: 4—16 in *(406 mm)* anti-submarine
A/S weapons: 2 depth charge racks
Main engines: 3 diesels; 10 000 bhp = 40 knots
Complement: 25

Based on the hull design of the "Osa" class. Built from 1967-68 onwards.

Radar: Search: Square Tie. Fire Control: Drum Tilt. Pot Drum.

"STENKA" Class   1973, N. Polmar

17 "TURYA" CLASS (FAST ATTACK CRAFT—PATROL HYDROFOIL)

Displacement, tons: 220 standard; 230 full load
Dimensions, feet (metres): 134·5 × 26·2 × 6·2 *(41 × 8 × 1·9)*
Guns: 2—57 mm (twin, aft); 2—25 mm (twin, f'd)
Speed, knots: 40

A new class of hydrofoil with a naval orientation rather than the earlier "Pchela" class. Entered service from 1973—in series production, possibly 4-5 per year.

Radar: Pot Drum and Drum Tilt.

Sonar: A form of VDS is fitted on the transom. In view of this the apparent lack of A/S weapons is surprising. Could operate with shore-based helicopters.

"TURYA" Class   1974, S. Breyer

"TURYA" Class   1975, S. Breyer

25 "PCHELA" CLASS (FAST ATTACK CRAFT—PATROL HYDROFOIL)

Displacement, tons: 70 standard; 80 full load
Dimensions, feet (metres): 82·0 × 19·7 × 5·2 *(25 × 6 × 1·6)*
Guns: 4 MG (2 twin)
Main engines: 2 diesels; 6 000 bhp = 50 knots

This class of hydrofoil is reported to have been built since 1964-65. Also carry depth charges. Used for frontier guard duties by KGB.

"PCHELA" Class   1970

45 "SHERSHEN" CLASS (FAST ATTACK CRAFT—TORPEDO)

Displacement, tons: 150 standard; 160 full load
Dimensions, feet (metres): 115·5 × 23·1 × 5·0 *(35·2 × 7 × 1·5)*
Guns: 4—30 mm (2 twin)
Tubes: 4—21 in (single)
A/S weapons: 12 DC
Main engines: Diesels; 3 shafts; 13 000 bhp = 41 knots
Complement: 16

First of class produced in 1963.

Radar: Pot Drum and Drum Tilt. High Pole IFF.

Transfers: Bulgaria (4), East Germany (15), Egypt (6), Yugoslavia (13).

"SHERSHEN" Class   1970, S. Breyer

80 "P 6" "P 8" "P 10" CLASSES (FAST ATTACK CRAFT—TORPEDO)

Displacement, tons: 66 standard; 75 full load
Dimensions, feet (metres): 84·2 × 20·0 × 6·0 *(25·7 × 6·1 × 1·8)*
Guns: 4—25 mm
Tubes: 2—21 in (or mines, or depth charges)
Main engines: 4 diesels; 4 shafts; 4 800 bhp = 43 knots
    Originally gas-turbines in "P 8" and "P 10" classes
Range, miles: 450 at 30 knots
Complement: 25

The "P 6" class (Soviet Type 184 originally) was of a standard medium sized type running into series production. Launched during 1951 to 1960. Known as "MO VI" class in the submarine chaser version. The later versions, known as the "P 8" and "P 10" classes, are powered with gas-turbines, and have different bridge and funnel; "P 8" boats have hydrofoils. This class is now being deleted because of old age; some have been converted to radio-controlled target craft. Of the "P 8" and "P 10" classes the majority seem to have had their funnels removed, suggesting that the gas-turbine arrangement was not a success.

Transfers: Algeria (12), China (80, indigenous construction), Cuba (12), Egypt (24), East Germany (18), Guinea (4), Indonesia (14), Iraq (12), Nigeria (3), Poland (20), North Vietnam (6), Somalia (4).

"P 10" Class   1968, S. Breyer

"P 6" class after modernisation   1972, S. Breyer

"P 6" Class modified for target work   1975

15 "MO VI" CLASS (FAST ATTACK CRAFT—PATROL)

Displacement, tons: 64 standard; 73 full load
Dimensions, feet (metres): 84·2 × 20 × 6 *(25·7 × 6·1 × 1·8)*
Guns: 4—25 mm (2 twin)
A/S weapons: 2 depth charge mortars; 2 depth charge racks
Main engines: 4 diesels; 4 shafts; 4 800 bhp = 40 knots

Built in 1956 to 1960. Based on the hull design of the "P 6".

"MO VI" Class   1972

25 "ZHUK" CLASS (COASTAL PATROL—CRAFT)

Displacement, tons: 60
Dimensions, feet (metres): 75 × 16 × 6 *(24·6 × 5·2 × 1·9)*
Guns: 2—14·5 mm (twin forward); 1—12·7 mm (aft)
Speed, knots: 28

A new class of patrol craft mainly manned by the KGB. The after mounting may in some cases be a rocket launcher.

Transfers: Cuba (5 in 1975), Iraq (4 in 1975).

"ZHUK" Class

RIVER PATROL CRAFT

Attached to Black Sea and Pacific Fleets for operations on the Danube, Amur and Usuri Rivers, and to the Caspian Flotilla.

40 "SCHMEL" CLASS

Displacement, tons: 120
Length, feet (metres): 92 × 17·7 × 3·3 *(28·1 × 5·4 × 1)*
Guns: 1—76 mm; 2—25 mm (twin)
Speed, knots: 20
Complement: 15

Forward gun mounted in a tank-type turret. Some also mount a ten-barrelled rocket launcher amidships. Built between 1958 and 1966.

"SCHMEL" Class   *1973, J Rowe*

"SCHMEL" Class (with rocket launcher)   *1972, TASS*

30 "BK 3" CLASS

Displacement, tons: 120
Length, feet (metres): 95 *(29)*
Guns: 1—100 mm; 1—37 mm; 4 MG (twin mounts)
Speed, knots: 22
Complement: 20

Not unlike the "Schmel" class but with an additional MG mounting at after end of the waist.

"BK 3" Class   *1973, J Meister*

20 "BKL 4" CLASS

Displacement, tons: 60
Length, feet (metres): 55 *(16·8)*
Guns: 2—20 mm; 6 MG
Speed, knots: 28

1 COMMAND SHIP

PS 10

Displacement, tons: approx 250
Guns: 2—20 mm
Speed, knots: 15

Acts as Senior Officer's ship for the Danube squadron.

PS 10   *4/1975, Heinz Stockinger*

"PR" CLASS

Displacement, tons: 90
Dimensions, feet (metres): 88 × 18 × 3·3 *(26·8 × 5·5 × 1)*
Guns: 1—76 mm; 2—25 mm
Speed, knots: 25

"PR" Class   *4/1975, Heinz Stockinger*

ROK 9

Of approximately 100 tons—probably acts as support ship to Danube squadron.

ROK 9   *1973, I Meister*

MINE WARFARE FORCES

Note: The "Alesha" class (under Support and Depot Ships) probably has a primary minelaying role.

20 "NATYA" CLASS (MINESWEEPERS—OCEAN)

Displacement, tons: 650 full load
Dimensions, feet (metres): 200·1 × 34·1 × 7·2 *(61 × 10·4 × 2·2)*
Guns: 4—30 mm (2 twin); 4—25 mm (2 twin)
A/S weapons: 2 MBU 1 800
Main engines: 2 diesels; 5 000 bhp = 18 knots

A new class of fleet minesweepers first reported in 1971, evidently intended as successors to the "Yurka" class. Building rate of 3 a year.

"NATYA" Class   *1974*

45 "YURKA" CLASS (MINESWEEPERS—OCEAN)

Displacement, tons: 450 full load
Dimensions, feet (metres): 171·9 × 31 × 8·9 *(52·4 × 9·5 × 2·7)*
Guns: 4—30 mm (2 twin)
Main engines: 2 diesels; 4 000 bhp = 18 knots

A class of medium fleet minesweepers with steel hull. Built from 1963 to the late 1960s.

Transfer: 4 to Egypt.

"YURKA" Class   *1975*

20 "T 58" CLASS (MINESWEEPERS—OCEAN)

Displacement, tons: 790 standard; 900 full load
Dimensions, feet (metres): 229·9 × 29·5 × 7·9 *(70·1 × 9 × 2·4)*
A/S weapons: 2 MBU 1 800
Guns: 4—57 mm AA (2 twin)
Main engines: 2 diesels; 2 shafts; 4 000 bhp = 18 knots

Built from 1957 to 1964. Of this class 14 were converted to submarine rescue ships with armament and sweeping gear removed, see later page ("Valdai" class).

"T 58" Class (with Muff Cob)

1/1975

100 "T 43" CLASS (MINESWEEPERS—OCEAN)

Displacement, tons: 500 standard; 610 full load
Dimensions, feet (metres): 190·2 × 28·2 × 6·9 *(58 × 8·6 × 2·1)*
Guns: 2—37 mm (2 twin); 4—25 mm (2 twin)
Main engines: 2 diesels; 2 shafts; 2 000 bhp = 17 knots
Range, miles: 1 600 at 10 knots
Complement: 40

Built in 1948-57 in shipyards throughout the Soviet Union. A number of this class were converted into radar pickets. The remainder are gradually being replaced by newer types of fleet minesweepers.

Transfers: Algeria (2), Albania (2), Bulgaria (2), China (20), Egypt (6), Indonesia (6), Poland (12), Syria (2).

"T 43" Class

4/1973

6 "SONYA" CLASS (MINESWEEPERS—COASTAL)

Displacement, tons: 400
Length, feet (metres): 154·1 *(47)*
Guns: 2—30 mm (twin); 2—25 mm (twin)

A new design of MSC of similar size to the "Zhenya" class. Now in series production. First reported 1973.

Radar: Search/Navigation; Don 2.
IFF; Squarehead and High Pole B.

3 "ZHENYA" CLASS (MINESWEEPERS—COASTAL)

Displacement, tons: 320
Dimensions, feet (metres): 141 × 25 × 7 *(43 × 7·6 × 2·1)*
Guns: 2—30 mm (twin)
Main engines: 2 diesels; 2 400 shp = 18 knots

Reported to be a trial class for GRP hulls. First reported 1972.

"ZHENYA" Class

1974, S Breyer

70 "VANYA" CLASS (MINESWEEPERS—COASTAL)

Displacement, tons: 225 standard; 250 full load
Dimensions, feet (metres): 130·7 × 24 × 6·9 *(39·9 × 7·3 × 2·1)*
Guns: 2—30 mm (1 twin)
Main engines: 2 diesels; 2 200 bhp = 18 knots
Complement: 30

A coastal class with wooden hulls of a type suitable for series production built from 1961 onwards.

"VANYA" Class

1975

40 "SASHA" CLASS (MINESWEEPERS—COASTAL)

Displacement, tons: 245 standard; 280 full load
Dimensions, feet (metres): 150·9 × 20·5 × 6·6 *(46 × 6·3 × 2)*
Guns: 1—57 mm; 4—25 mm (2 twin)
Main engines: 2 diesels; 2 200 bhp = 18 knots
Complement: 25

Of steel construction. Built between 1956-60.

"SASHA" Class   1968, S Breyer

"TR 40" CLASS (MINESWEEPERS—INSHORE)

Displacement, tons: 40 standard; 60 full load
Dimensions, feet (metres): 55·8 × 11·5 × 4·0 *(17 × 3·5 × 1·2)*
Guns: 2—25 mm (twin); 2 MG (twin)
Main engines: Diesels; speed 18 knots

"K 8" CLASS (MINESWEEPERS—RIVER)

Displacement, tons: 50 standard; 70 full load
Dimensions, feet (metres): 92·0 × 13·5 × 2·3 *(28 × 4·1 × 0·7)*
Guns: 2 MG (twin)
Main engines: Diesels; 600 bhp = 14 knots

Auxiliary motor minesweeping boats of the inshore ("TR 40") and river ("K 8") types. A total of about 100 of both classes in service.

"K 8" Class   1975

AMPHIBIOUS FORCES

14 "ALLIGATOR" CLASS (LST)

ALEKSANDR TORTSEV	NIKOLAI OEBYEKOV
DONETSKY SHAKHTER	PETR ILICHEV
KRASNAYA PRESNYA	TOMSKY KOMSOMOLETS
KRYMSKY KOMSOMOLETS	VORONEZHSKY KOMSOMOLETS
	+ 6

Displacement, tons: 4 100 standard; 5 800 full load
Dimensions, feet (metres): 370·7 × 50·9 × 12·1 *(113 × 15·5 × 3·7)*
Guns: 2—57 mm; 2 rocket launchers
Main engines: Diesels; 8 000 bhp = 18 knots

Largest type of landing ship built in the USSR to date. First ship built in 1965-66 and commissioned in 1966. These ships have ramps on the bow and stern. Carrying capacity 1 700 tons. There are three variations of rig. In earlier type two or three cranes are carried—later types have only one crane. In the third type the bridge structure has been raised and the forward deck house has been considerably lengthened.

KRYMSKY KOMSOMOLETS (Type I)   10/1974, MOD

NIKOLAI OEBYEKOV (Type III) (Hull 14)   4/1976, MOD

"ALLIGATOR II" Class   1972, H. W. Van Boeijen

4 + 1 "ROPUCHA" CLASS (LST)

Displacement, tons: 2 500 standard; 4 000 full load
Dimensions, feet (metres): 360 × 49·2 × 11·5 *(110 × 15 × 3·5)*
Guns: 4—57 mm (twins)
Main engines: Diesels; 2 shafts
Speed, knots: ?18

Building at Gdansk, Poland.

"ROPUCHA" Class

10/1975

60 "POLNOCNY" CLASS (LCT)

Displacement, tons: 700 standard; 800 full load (Type IX 1 300)
Dimensions, feet (metres): 239·4 × 29·5 × 9·8 *(73 × 9 × 3)* (Type IX 285 × 27·7 × 9·8 *(86·9 × 8·4 × 3))*
Guns: 2—30 mm (twin) in all but earliest ships (see note); 2 rocket launchers
Main engines: 2 diesels; 5 000 bhp = 18 knots

Carrying capacity 350 tons. Can carry 6 tanks. Up to 9 types of this class have been built. In I to IV the mast and funnel are combined—in V onwards the mast is stepped on the bridge—in VI to VIII there is a redesign of the bow-form—IX is a completely new design of greater length with corresponding increase in tonnage and with 4—30 mm (2 twins). Muff Cob radar.

Transfers: 6 to Egypt, 3 to India, 2 to S. Yemen.

"POLNOCNY" Class with 2—30 mm before bridge and fire control radar on bridge

"POLNOCNY" Class—latest variant with higher funnel

1974, S. Breyer

"POLNOCNY" Class

1973

35 "VYDRA" CLASS (LCU)

Displacement, tons: 300 standard; 500 full load
Dimensions, feet (metres): 157·4 × 24·6 × 7·2 *(48 × 7·5 × 2·2)*
Main engines: 2 diesels; 2 shafts; 400 hp = 15 knots

Built from 1967-1969. No armament. Carrying capacity 250 tons.

Transfers: 10 to Egypt.

"VYDRA" Class

1971

8 "MP 2" CLASS (LCU)

Displacement, tons: 750
Dimensions, feet (metres): 190 × 25 × 8·2 *(58 × 7·6 × 2·5)*
Guns: 6—25 mm (twins)
Main engines: Diesels; 1 200 hp = 16 knots

Built 1956-60. Carrying capacity 200 tons.

15 "MP 4" CLASS (LCU)

Displacement, tons: 800 full load
Dimensions, feet (metres): 183·7 × 26·2 × 8·9 *(56 × 8 × 2·7)*
Guns: 4—25 mm (2 twin)
Main engines: Diesels; 2 shafts; 1 100 bhp = 12 knots

Built in 1956-58. Of the small freighter type in appearance. Two masts, one abaft the bridge and one in the waist. Gun mountings on poop and forecastle. Can carry 6 to 8 tanks. Several ships now serve as transports.

"MP 4" Class   *1973, J. Rowe*

5 "MP 8" CLASS (LCU)

Displacement, tons: 800 standard; 1 200 full load
Dimensions, feet (metres): 239·5 × 34·8 × 15·1 *(73 × 10·6 × 4·6)*
Guns: 4—57 mm (2 twin)
Main engines: Diesels; 4 000 bhp = 15 knots

Have a short and low quarter deck abaft the funnel. Can carry 6 tanks. Carrying capacity 400 tons. Built 1958-61.

"MP 8" Type   *1970, S. Breyer*

10 "MP 10" CLASS (LCU)

Displacement, tons: 200 standard; 420 full load
Dimensions, feet (metres): 157·5 × 21·3 × 6·5 *(48 × 6·5 × 2)*
Main engines: 2 diesels; 2 shafts; 400 hp = 11 knots

A type of landing craft basically similar to the German wartime type in silhouette and layout. Can carry 4 tanks. Loading capacity about 150 tons. Built 1959-66.

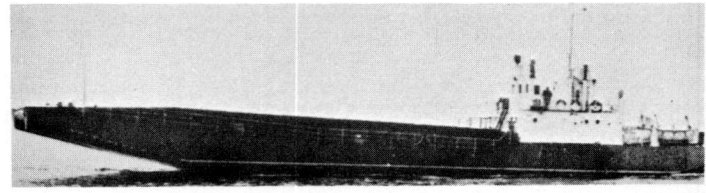

"MP 10" Class   *1971*

8 "MP 6" CLASS (LCU)

Displacement, tons: 2 000
Dimensions, feet (metres): 246 × 40 × 10·5 *(75 × 12·2 × 3·2)*
Guns: 4—45 mm (quad)
Main engines: Diesels; 2 400 hp = 14 knots

Ex-merchant ship hulls. Carrying capacity 500 tons. Built 1958-61.

100+ "T 4" CLASS (LCM)

Displacement, tons: 70
Dimensions, feet (metres): 62·3 × 14·1 × 3·3 *(19 × 4·3 × 1)*
Main engines: 2 diesels; 2 shafts = 10 knots

More than a hundred reported in service (1975).

HYDROFOIL TYPE

A small landing craft of 92 ft *(28·1 m)* length capable of carrying 2-3 tanks.

AIR CUSHION VEHICLES

(Numbers in service are not known. The following gives an indication of Soviet capability. Fuller details appear in *Jane's Surface Skimmers 1975-76).*

RESEARCH HOVERCRAFT

Operating weight: 15 tons
Dimensions, feet (metres): 70 × 30 *(21·4 × 9·2)*
Propulsion: 2—350 hp aircraft radial engines
Lift: 1—350 hp aircraft radial with centrifugal fan
Speed, knots: 50

In use in the Soviet Navy since 1967 for tests and evaluation.

Research Hovercraft   *Jane's Surface Skimmers*

"SKATE" CLASS

Operating weight: 27 tons
Dimensions, feet (metres): 67·5 × 24 *(20·6 × 7·3)*
Propulsion: 2—780 hp marine gas turbines (VP and reversible propellers)
Lift: 1—780 hp marine gas turbine
Speed, knots: 58
Range, miles: 230 cruising

This is a naval version of a 50-seat passenger carrying craft, probably in use for the Naval Infantry.

A military derivative of the "Skate" passenger ferry *Jane's Surface Skimmers*

ASSAULT CRAFT

Operating weight: 200 tons approx
Dimensions, feet (metres): 130 × 80 approx *(39·7 × 24·4)*
Speed, knots: 70 approx

Currently undergoing trials for Naval Infantry. Is the first large Soviet amphibious hovercraft. Similar to British SRN.4.

EKRANOPLAN CRAFT (WIG)

Dimensions, feet (metres): 400 × 125 (approx wing span) *(122 × 38)*
Propulsion: Ten gas turbines (two to assist take-off then eight for cruising)
Speed, knots: 300 approx

An experimental craft, a wing-in-ground-effect machine, with a carrying capacity of about 900 troops and with potential for a number of naval applications such as ASW, minesweeping or patrol. Claimed to be capable of operations in heavy weather as well as crossing marshes, ice and low obstacles.

EKRANOPLAN

Jane's Surface Skimmers

SUPPORT AND DEPOT SHIPS
9 "UGRA" CLASS (SUBMARINE DEPOT SHIPS)

BORODINO
GANGUT
IVAN KOLYSHKIN
IVAN KUCHERENKO
IVAN VADREMEEV
TOBOL
VOLGA
+2

Displacement, tons: 6 750 standard; 7 000 full load
Length, feet (metres): 463·8 *(141·4)*
Beam, feet (metres): 57·6 *(17·6)*
Draught, feet (metres): 19·8 *(6·0)*
Aircraft: 1 helicopter
Guns: 8—57 mm (twin)
Main engines: 4 diesels; 2 shafts; 14 000 bhp = 20 knots
Range, miles: 10 000 at 12 knots
Complement: 300

Improved versions of the "Don" class. Built from 1961 onwards, all in Nikolaev. Equipped with workshops. Provided with a helicopter platform and, in later versions, a hangar. Carries a large derrick to handle torpedoes. Has mooring points in hull about 100 feet apart, and has baggage ports possibly for coastal craft and submarines. The last pair of this class mount a large superstructure from the mainmast to quarter-deck and are used for training.

Radar: Search: Slim Net.
Fire Control: Hawk Screech (2), Strut Curve; Muff Cob.

Transfer: A tenth ship, *Amba,* which had four 76 mm guns, was transferred to India.

"UGRA" Class

5/1975, MOD

"UGRA" Class

5/1974, MOD

6 "DON" CLASS (SUBMARINE SUPPORT)

DMITRI GALKIN   MIKHAIL TUKAEVSKY
FEDOR VIDYAEV   NIKOLAY STOLBOV
MAGOMED GADZHIEV   VIKTOR KOTELNIKOV

Displacement, tons: 6 700 standard; 7 000 full load
Length, feet (metres): 458·9 *(139·9)*
Beam, feet (metres): 57·7 *(17·6)*
Draught, feet (metres): 22·3 *(6·8)*
Aircraft: Provision for helicopter in two ships
Guns: 4—3·9 in *(100 mm);* 8—57 mm (4 twin) (see notes)
Main engines: 4 diesels; 14 000 bhp; 2 shafts
Speed, knots: 21
Complement: 300

Support ships, all named after officers lost in WW II. Built in
1957 to 1962. Originally seven ships were built, all in Nikolaev.
Quarters for about 450 submariners.

Gunnery: In hull number III only 2—3·9 in. In IV no 3·9 in
mounted. In some of class 8—25 mm (twin) are mounted.

Radar: Search: Slim Net and probably Strut Curve.
Fire Control: Hawk Screech (2).

Transfers: 1 to Indonesia in 1962.

DMITRI GALKIN   *8/1974, MOD*

DMITRI GALKIN with new DF rig on mainmast and new trellice foremast   *8/1974, MOD*

1 "PURGA" CLASS

Displacement, tons: 2 250 standard; 3 000 full load
Length, feet (metres): 324·8 (99·0)
Beam, feet (metres): 44·3 (13·5)
Draught, feet (metres): 17·1 (5·2)
Guns: 4—3·9 in (100 mm) (singles); 2—25 mm
Mines: 50 capacity
Main engines: Diesels
Speed, knots: 18
Complement: 250

Laid down in 1939 in Leningrad and completed in 1948. Sturdy oceangoing general purpose ship equipped as icebreaker, escort, training ship and tender. Fitted with directors similar to those in the "Riga" class frigates. Modernised in 1958-60.

"PURGA" Class

6 "LAMA" CLASS (MISSILE SUPPORT)

Displacement, tons: 4 600 full load
Length, feet (metres): 370·0 (112·8) oa
Beam, feet (metres): 47·2 (14·4)
Draught, feet (metres): 19·0 (5·8)
Guns: 8—57 mm, (2 quadruple, 1 on the forecastle; 1 on the break of the quarter deck)
Main engines: Diesels; 2 shafts; 5 000 shp
Speed, knots: 15

The engines are sited aft to allow for a very large and high hangar or hold amidships for carrying missiles or weapons' spares. This is about 12 feet high above the main deck. There are doors at the forward end with rails leading in and a raised turntable gantry or travelling cranes for transferring armaments to combatant ships.
There are mooring points along the hull for ships of low freeboard such as submarines to come alongside. The well deck is about 40 feet long, enough for a missile to fit horizontally before being lifted vertically for loading.

Radar: Search: Slim Net and Strut Curve.
Fire Control: Hawk Screech, (2).

"LAMA" Class

1973, MOD

1 "AMGA" CLASS (MISSILE SUPPORT)

Displacement, tons: approx 5 500
Dimensions, feet (metres): 361 × 56 × 19 (110 × 17 × 5·8)
Guns: 4—30 mm (twins)
Main engines: Diesels; 10 000 hp = 18 knots

A single ship of similar size and duties to the "Lama" class. May be distinguished from those ships by the break at the bridge, giving a lower freeboard than that of the "Lamas". She is fitted with a large 50 ton crane forward and is thus capable of handling much larger missiles than her predecessors. Probably, therefore, designed for servicing submarines, particularly those armed with SSN-8 missiles.

"AMGA" Class

1974

10 "OSKOL" CLASS (REPAIR SHIPS)

Displacement, tons: 2 500 standard; 3 000 full load
Dimensions, feet (metres): 295·2 × 39·4 × 14·8 (90 × 12 × 4·5)
Main engines: 2 diesels; 2 shafts; speed = 16 knots

Three series: "Oskol I" class, well-decked hull, no armament; "Oskol II" class, well-decked hull, armed with 2—57 mm guns (1 twin) and 4—25 mm guns (2 twin); "Oskol III" class, flush-decked hull. General purpose tenders and repair ships. Built from 1963 to 1970 in Poland.

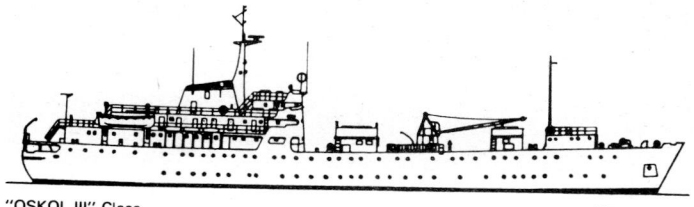

"OSKOL III" Class

1973, S. Breyer

3 "ALESHA" CLASS (MINELAYERS)

075   083   +1

Displacement, tons: 3 600 standard; 4 300 full load
Dimensions, feet (metres): 337·9 × 47·6 × 15·7 *(103 × 14·5 × 4·8)*
Guns: 4—57 mm (1 quadruple forward)
Mines: 400
Main engines: 4 diesels; 2 shafts; 8 000 bhp = 20 knots
Complement: 150

In service since 1965. Fitted with four mine tracks to provide stern launchings. Also have a capability in general support role.

"ALESHA" Class   *1972*

2 "WILHELM BAUER" CLASS (SUBMARINE TENDERS)

KUBAN (ex-*Waldemar Kophamel*)   PECHORA (ex-*Otto Wünche)*

Displacement, tons: 4 726 standard; 5 600 full load
Dimensions, feet (metres): 446·0 × 52·5 × 14·5 *(136 × 16 × 4·4)*
Main engines: 4 MAN diesels; 2 shafts; 12 400 bhp = 20 knots

Former German ships. Launched in 1939. *Kuban* was salvaged in 1950-51 after being sunk in shallow water by bombing in WW II and was rehabilitated in 1951-57.

14 "AMUR" CLASS (REPAIR SHIPS)

Displacement, tons: 6 500 full load
Dimensions, feet (metres): 377·3 × 57·4 × 18·0 *(115 × 17·5 × 5·5)*
Main engines: Diesels; 2 shafts = 18 knots

General purpose depot ships built since 1969. Successors to the "Oskol" class. In series production at a rate of about 2 a year.

"AMUR" Class   *1/1974*   "AMUR" Class   *1973*

6 "ATREK" CLASS (SUBMARINE SUPPORT)

ATREK	AYAT	BAKHMUT	DVINA	MURMATS	OSIPOV

Displacement, tons: 3 500 standard
Measurement, tons: 3 258 gross
Dimensions, feet (metres): 336 × 49 × 20 (102·5 × 14·9 × 6·1)
Main engines: Expansions and exhaust turbines; 1 shaft; 2 450 hp = 13 knots
Boilers: 2 water tube
Range, miles: 3 500 at 13 knots

Built in 1956-58, and converted to naval use from "Kolomna" class freighters. There are six of these vessels employed as submarine tenders and replenishment ships. Some may have up to 6—37 mm (twins).

BAKHMUT

1974

5 "DNEPR" CLASS (SUBMARINE TENDERS)

Displacement, tons: 4 500 standard; 5 250 full load
Dimensions, feet (metres): 370·7 × 54·1 × 14·4 (113 × 16·5 × 4·4)
Main engines: Diesels; 2 000 bhp = 12 knots

Bow lift repair ships for S/M support and maintenance. Built in 1957-66 and equipped with workshops and servicing facilities. The last two ships of this class form the "Dnepr II" Class.

"DNEPR II" Class

1974

1 "TOVDA" CLASS (REPAIR SHIP)

TOVDA

Displacement, tons: 3 000 standard; 4 000 full load
Dimensions, feet (metres): 282·1 × 39·4 × 16·0 (86 × 12 × 4·9)
Guns: 6—57 mm (3 twin mountings)
Main engines: Triple expansion; 1 300 ihp = 11 knots

Polish built ex-tanker converted in 1958.

TOVDA

1959

INTELLIGENCE COLLECTORS (AGIs)

6 "PRIMORYE" CLASS

PRIMORYE	KRYM	ZAPOROZYE
KAVKAZ	ZABAIKALYE	ZAKARPATYE

Displacement, tons: 4 000
Dimensions, feet (metres): 274 × 45 × 26·2 (83·6 × 13·7 × 8)
Main engines: Diesels

The most modern intelligence collectors in the world, apparently with built-in processing and possibly, analysis capability. Hull design is that of the "Majakowsky" class fish-factory ships. The aerials carried would seem to dispose of the contention that these are fishery research ships.

"PRIMORYE" Class

1972

ZAKARPATYE with friend (compare aerials with photograph at left)

3/1976, MOD

8 "LENTRA" CLASS

GS 34	GS 43	GS 55
GS 36	GS 46	GS 59
GS 41	GS 47	

Displacement, tons: 250
Measurement, tons: 334 gross; 186 deadweight
Dimensions, feet (metres): 143 × 25 × 12·5 (43·6 × 7·6 × 3·8)
Main engines: Diesel; 400 hp = 10·5 knots

All built in USSR 1957-63. Now have names in addition to numbers. Two known as *Neringa* and *Izvalta*.

"LENTRA" Class

1974, Michael D. J. Lennon

15 "OKEAN" CLASS

ALIDADA	EKHOLOT	REDUKTOR
AMPERMETR	GIDROFON	REPITER
BAROGRAF	KRENOMETR	TEODOLIT
BAROMETR	LINZA	TRAVERZ
DEFLEKTOR	LOTLIN	ZOND

Measurement, tons: 680 gross
Dimensions, feet (metres): 178 × 30·6 × 15·9 *(54·3 × 9·3 × 4·8)*
Main engines: Diesel; 1 shaft; 800 hp = 12 knots

Built in USSR 1965. Apparently identical to "Mayak" Class—both have the same variations in the superstructure with the port side closed in and the starboard side open.

TRAVERZ (unmodified)   3/1975, MOD

Modified "OKEAN" Class (enclosed port side)   9/1974, MOD

Modified "OKEAN" Class (open starboard side)   1975, MOD

8 "MAYAK" CLASS

ANEROID	KURSOGRAF
GIRORULEVOY	LADOGA
KHERSONES	GS 239
KURS	GS 242

Measurement, tons: 680 gross; 252 net
Dimensions, feet (metres): 178 × 30·6 × 15·9 *(54·3 × 9·3 × 4·8)*
Main engines: Diesel; 1 shaft; 800 hp = 12 knots

Built in USSR 1965. Apparently identical to "Okean" Class—see notes for that class.

"MAYAK" Class   1972

GIRORULEVOY (new aerial arrays)   9/1975, MOD(N)

4 "MIRNY" CLASS

BAKAN	VAL
LOTSMAN	VERTIKAL

Displacement, tons: 850
Dimensions, feet (metres): 208 × 31·2 × 13·8 *(63·4 × 9·5 × 4·2)*
Main engines: Diesel; 1 shaft = 15 knots

"MIRNY" Class   1972

ARKEPELAG
ILMEN
JUPITER

NAKHODKA
PELORUS
SELIGER

Displacement, tons: 1 240 standard; 1 800 full load
Dimensions, feet (metres): 219·8 × 32·8 × 13·2 (67 × 10 × 4)
Main engines: Diesels = 16 knots

6 "MOMA" CLASS

JUPITER

10/1975, MOD

GIDROGRAF   PELENG

Measurement, tons: 2 000 gross
Dimensions, feet (metres): 256 oa × 42 × 13·5 (78 × 12·8 × 4·1)
Main engines: 2—4 stroke diesels; 2 shafts; 4 200 bhp = 17 knots

Built in Sweden 1959-60. Originally salvage tugs.

2 "PAMIR" CLASS

"PAMIR" Class

1970, S. Breyer

2 "DNEPR" CLASS

IZMERITEL   PROTRAKTOR

Measurement, tons: 500 gross
Dimensions, feet (metres): 150 × 30 × 8 (45·8 × 9·2 × 2·4)
Main engines: Diesel = 11 knots

1 "T 58" CLASS

Displacement, tons: 900 full load
Dimensions, feet (metres): 229·9 × 29·5 × 7·9 (70·1 × 9 × 2·4)
Main engines: 2 diesels; 2 shafts; 4 000 bhp = 18 knots

Built in USSR 1962.

"T 58" Class

2 "ZUBOV" CLASS

GAVRIL SARYCHEV   K. LAPTEV

Displacement, tons: 3 021 full load
Dimensions, feet (metres): 295·2 × 42·7 × 15 (90 × 13 × 4·6)
Main engines: Diesels; 2 shafts = 16·5 knots

Built in Poland.

GAVRIL SARYCHEV

1973, Michael D. J. Lennon

SURVEY SHIPS

24 "MOMA" CLASS (+6 AGIs)

ALTAIR
ANADIR
ANDROMEDA
ANTARES
ANTON KTYDA
ARTIKA

ASKOLD
BEREZAN
CHELEKEN
EKVATOR
ELTON
KILDIN

KRILON
KOLGUEV
LIMAN
MARS
MORSOVIEC
OKEAN

PELORUS
RYBACHI
SEVER
TAYMYR
VEGA
ZAPOLARA

Displacement, tons: 1 240 standard; 1 800 full load
Dimensions, feet (metres): 219·8 × 32·8 × 13·2 (67 × 10 × 4)
Main engines: Diesels; 16 knots

Eight ships of this class were reported to have been built from 1967 to 1970 and the remainder since. Naval manned.

LIMAN

10/1975, MOD

9 "KAMENKA" CLASS
10 "BIYA" CLASS

Displacement, tons: 1 000 full load
Dimensions, feet (metres): 180·5 × 31·2 × 11·5 *(55·1 × 9·5 × 3·5)*
Main engines: Diesels; speed 16 knots

The ships of these classes are not named but have a number with the prefix letters "GS". All reported to have been built since 1967-68. Naval manned.

"KAMENKA" Class   1974, MOD

3 "TELNOVSK" CLASS

AYTADOR   ULYANA   GROMOVA   SVIYAGA

Displacement, tons: 1 200 standard
Measurement, tons: 1 217 gross, 448 net
Dimensions, feet (metres): 229·6 × 32·8 × 13·1 *(70 × 10 × 4)*
Main engines: Diesels; speed 10 knots

Formerly coastal freighters. Built in Hungary. Refitted and modernised for naval supply and surveying duties. Naval manned.
Sister ship *Stvor* appears under Training Ships.

AYTADOR   1974, Michael D. J. Lennon

IZUMRUD

Measurement, tons: 3 862 gross; 465 net
Main engines: Powered by diesel-electric machinery

A research and survey ship built in 1970. Civilian manned.

IZUMRUD   1972, Michael D. J. Lennon

16 "SAMARA" CLASS

AZIMUT   GLUBOMER   RUMB
DEVIATOR   GORIZONT   TROPIK
GIDROLOG   GRADUS   ZENIT
GIGROMETR   KOMPAS   VAGACH
GLOBUS   PAMYAT MERKURYIA VOSTOK
                                  YUG

Displacement, tons: 800 standard; 1 200 full load
Measurement, tons: 1 276 gross; 1 000 net
Dimensions, feet (metres): 198 × 36·3 × 10·8 *(60·4 × 11·1 × 3·3)*
Main engines: Diesels; 3 000 hp; 2 shafts = 16 knots

Built at Gdansk, Poland since 1962 for hydrographic surveying and research. Navy manned.

ZENIT   1975, J. A. Verhoog

GIGROMETR (different aerials etc from *Zenit*)   1975, J. A. Verhoog

AKADEMIK KOVALEVSKY   AKADEMIK VAVILOV

Measurement, tons: 284 gross *(Vavilov 255)*
Dimensions, feet (metres): 126·8 × 23·7 × 11·5 *(38·1 × 7·2 × 3·5)*; *(Vavilov* 119·7 × 24·1 × 11·5
(36·5 × 7·4 × 3·5)
Main engines: 1 Diesel = 10 knots

Built in E. Germany in 1949.

AKADEMIK KOVALEVSKY   *1974, Michael D. J. Lennon*

AKADEMIK ARKHANGELSKY

Measurement, tons: 416 tons gross
Dimensions, feet (metres): 132·9 × 25 × 13 *(40·5 × 7·6 × 4)*
Main engines: 1 Diesel = 10 knots

Built in USSR in 1963.

AKADEMIK ARKHANGELSKY   *1974, Michael D. J. Lennon*

MGLA

Measurement, tons: 299 gross
Dimensions, feet (metres): 129·5 × 24·3 × 11·8 *(39·5 × 7·4 × 3·6)*
Main engines: 1 diesel = 8·5 knots

MGLA   *1974, Michael D. J. Lennon*

13 + 2 "DMITRI OVSTYN" CLASS

A. SMIRNOV	PROFESSOR BOGOROV
DMITRI LAPTEV	PROFESSOR KURENTSOV
DMITRI OVSTYN	S. KRAKOV*
DMITRI STERLEGOV	STEFAN MALYGIN
E. TOLL	VALERIAN ALBANOV
N. KOLOMEYTSEV	V. SUKHOTSKY*
N. YEVGENOV*	+ 2

Displacement, tons: 1 800 full load
Dimensions, feet (metres): 220 × 39 × 15 *(67·1 × 11·9 × 4·6)*
Main engines: Diesels; 2 000 bhp = 16 knots

Built by Turku, Finland. Civilian manned. Employed largely on geological research and survey in the Arctic. Those marked *, completed Jan-Aug 1974. *P. Bogorov* launched 11 Oct 1975, *P. Kurentsov* 17 Dec 1975. Last pair laid down Oct and Dec 1975. Continuing programme.

MIKHAIL LOMONOSOV

Displacement, tons: 5 960 normal
Measurement, tons: 3 897 gross; 1 195 net
Dimensions, feet (metres): 336·0 × 47·2 × 14·0 *(102·5 × 14·4 × 4·3)*
Main engines: Triple expansion; 2 450 ihp = 13 knots

Built by Neptun, Rostock, in 1957 from the hull of a freighter of the "Kolomna" class. Operated not by the Navy but by the Academy of Sciences. Equipped with 16 laboratories. Carries a helicopter for survey. Civilian manned.

MIKHAIL LOMONOSOV   *1970, Michael D. J. Lennon*

9 "NIKOLAI ZUBOV" CLASS

A. CHIRIKOV	F. LITKE	SEJMEN DEZHNEV
A. VILKITSKY	NIKOLAI ZUBOV	T. BELLINSGAUSEN
BORIS DAVIDOV	S. CHELYUSKIN	V. GOLOVNIN

Displacement, tons: 2 674 standard; 3 021 full load
Dimensions, feet (metres): 295·2 × 42·7 × 15 *(90 × 13 × 4·6)*
Main engines: 2 diesels; speed = 16·7 knots
Complement: 108 to 120, including scientists

Oceanographic research ships built at Szczecin Shipyard, Poland in 1964. *Nikolai Zubov* visited London in 1965. Employed on survey in the Atlantic. Naval manned.

ANDREY VILKITSKY   *1973, Michael D. J. Lennon*

DOLINSK

Measurement, tons: 10 826 deadweight; 5 419 gross, 2 946 net
Dimensions, feet (metres): 456·0 × 58·0 × 15·5 *(139 × 17·7 × 4·7)*
Main engines: 2 diesels

Built at Abo in Finland in 1959. Converted for surveying. Naval manned.

DOLINSK   *1972, Michael D. J. Lennon*

ZARYA

Measurement, tons: 333 gross; 71 net

Built in 1952 for geomagnetic survey work. Civilian manned.

ZARYA   *1972, Michael D. J. Lennon*

NEREY   NOVATOR

Measurement, tons: 369 gross
Dimensions, feet (metres): 118·1 × 24·7 × 11·5 *(36 × 7·5 × 3·5)*
Main engines: 2 diesels = 11 knots

Built in USSR in 1956 and 1955. Originally fleet tugs. Converted for research. Civilian manned

NEREY   *1972, Michael D. J. Lennon*

PETRODVORETS (ex-*Bore II*)

Measurement, tons: 1 965 gross; 985 net
Dimensions, feet (metres): 254·2 × 39·4 × 24·9 *(77·5 × 12 × 7·6)*
Main engines: Diesel = 13·5 knots

Built at Abo, Finland for Finnish owners in 1938. Sold to USSR in 1950 and renamed.

ZVEZDA

Measurement, tons: 348 gross
Dimensions, feet (metres): 129 × 24·2 × 11·4 *(39·3 × 7·4 × 3·5)*
Main engines: Diesel = 10 knots

Built in East Germany in 1957. Carries winches in the chains on the quarters. Sister ships *Zarnitsa* and *Yug* are used for transporting crews to ships building outside the USSR.

ZVEZDA   *1974, Ian Brooke*

PALEH (ex-*Bratsk*)

Measurement, tons: 2 285 gross; 987 net
Dimensions, feet (metres): 239·4 × 42·6 × 22 *(73 × 13 × 6·7)*
Main engines: 1 Diesel; 1 shaft = 11 knots

Built in E. Germany in 1960 as fish-carrier of the "Evron" Class. Converted for surveying and renamed in 1966.

PALEH   *1972, Michael D. J. Lennon*

RESEARCH SHIPS

3 + 1 "AKADEMIK KRILOV" CLASS

ADMIRAL VLADIMIRSKY   **AKADEMIK KRILOV**   **LEONID SOBOLEV**   **+1**

A new class of research ships, the fourth is building in Stettin (1976).

4 "MODIFIED AKADEMIK KURCHATOV" CLASS

ABKHASIA   **ADZHARIYA**   **BASHKIRIYA**   **MOLDAVYA**

Displacement, tons: 7 500 full load
Dimensions, feet (metres): 409·2 × 56 × 21·1 (124·8 × 17·1 × 6·4)
Main engines: 2 Diesels = 20·4 knots
Range, miles: 20 000 at 15 knots
Endurance: 60 days

Fitted with helicopter platform aft. Naval manned. Completed in 1973.

BASHKIRIYA   1/1974

7 "AKADEMIK KURCHATOV" CLASS

AKADEMIK KOROLEV   **DMITRI MENDELEYEV**
AKADEMIK KURCHATOV   **PROFESSOR ZUBOV**
AKADEMIK SHIRSHOV   **PROFESSOR VIZE**
AKADEMIK VERNADSKY

Displacement, tons: 6 681 full load
Measurement, tons: 1 986 deadweight; 5 460 gross; 1 387 net
Dimensions, feet (metres): 400·3 to 406·8 × 56·1 × 15·0 (122·1 to 124·1 × 17·1 × 4·6)
Main engines: 2 Halberstadt 6-cylinder diesels; 2 shafts; 8 000 bhp = 18 to 20 knots

All built by Mathias Thesen Werft at Wismar, East Germany between 1965 and 1968. All have a hull of the same design as the "Mikhail Kalinin" class of merchant vessels. There are variations in mast and aerial rig. *Professor Vize* is similar to *A. Shirshov* whilst *A. Kurchatov, A. Vernadsky* and *D. Mendeleyev* are the same. Civilian manned.

AKADEMIK KURCHATOV   1973, Michael D. J. Lennon

AKADEMIK SHIRSHOV   1973, Michael D. J. Lennon

9 "PASSAT" CLASS

ERNST KRENKEL (ex-*Vikhr*)   **MUSSON**   **PASSAT**   **PORIV**
GEORGI USHAKOV (ex-*Schkval*) **OKEAN**   **PRIBOI**   **PRILIV**
                                                                 VOLNA

Measurement, tons: 3 280 gross
Dimensions, feet (metres): 280 × 43 × 15·5 (85·4 × 13·1 × 4·7)
Main engines: Diesels; 4 800 hp = 16 knots

Research or weather ships built at Szczecin, Poland, since 1968.

PRILIV   1973, Michael D. J. Lennon

ERNST KRENKEL   1974, J. van der Woude

2 "LEBEDEV" CLASS

PETR LEBEDEV   **SERGEI VAVILOV**

Measurement, tons: 3 561 gross; 1 180 net
Main engines: Diesels

Research vessels with comprehensive equipment and accommodation. Both built in 1954.

PETR LEBEDEV   1975, J. A. Verhoog

SERGEI VAVILOV   1973, Michael D. J. Lennon

3 "POLYUS" CLASS

BAIKAL   **BALKHASH**   **POLYUS**

Displacement, tons: 6 900 standard
Dimensions, feet (metres): 365·8 × 46·2 × 20·7 *(111·6 × 14·1 × 6·3)*
Main engines: Diesel-electric; 3 400 hp = 14 knots

These ships of the "Polyus" class were built in East Germany in 1961-64. Oceanographic research ships.

POLYUS   1972

VLADIMIR OBRUCHEV

Measurement, tons: 534 gross
Dimensions, feet (metres): 156·5 × 32·2 × 16·4 *(47·7 × 9·8 × 5)*
Main engines: 2 Diesels; = 11 knots

One of the "G" class tugs built in Romania in 1959 and subsequently converted for research duties.

VLADIMIR OBRUCHEV   1972, Michael D. J. Lennon

VITYAZ (ex-*Mars*)

Displacement, tons: 5 700 standard
Dimensions, feet (metres): 357·5 × 48·9 × 15·5 *(109 × 14·9 × 4·7)*
Main engines: Diesels; 3 000 bhp = 14·5 knots
Range, miles: 18 400 at 14 knots
Complement: 137 officers and men including 73 scientists

The first post-war Soviet oceanographic research ship. Formerly a German freighter built at Bremen in 1939. Equipped with 13 laboratories. Has now steamed over 2 million miles.

VITYAZ   1972, Michael D. J. Lennon

1 "MODIFIED DOBRINYA NIKITCH" CLASS

VLADIMIR KAVRASKY

Displacement, tons: 2 500 standard
Dimensions, feet (metres): 223·1 × 59·1 × 18·1 *(68 × 18 × 5·5)*
Main engines: 3 shafts = 13·8 knots

One of a numerous class of icebreakers built at Leningrad in the early 1960s—converted for polar research in 1972.

1 "NEVELSKOY" CLASS

NEVELSKOY

Last of a class of three research ships.

3 "ORBELI" CLASS

AKADEMIK IOSIF ORBELI
PROFESSOR NIKOLAI BARABSKI
AKADEMIK S. VAVILOV

Built in Warnemünde 1969-71. Act as Supply Ships. Civilian manned.

AKADEMIK S. VAVILOV   1972, Michael D. J. Lennon

FISHERY RESEARCH SHIPS

4 BMRT TYPE

AKADEMIK KNIPOVICH	**AKADEMIK BERG**
PROFESSOR DERYUGIN	**POSEIDON**

Measurement, tons: 3 165 gross; 1 166 net
Dimensions, feet (metres): 278 × 46 × 33 *(84·8 × 14 × 10)*
Main engines: 1 Diesel = 13 knots

Built as fishery research ships 1963-74. Civilian manned.

POSEIDON   1972, Michael D. J. Lennon

2 BMRT TYPE

Yu. M. SHOKALSKY	**A. I. VOYEYVKOV**

Measurement, tons: 3 200 gross
Dimensions, feet (metres): 278 × 46 × 33 *(84·8 × 14 × 10)*
Main engines: 1 Diesel = 13 knots

Sister ships of BMRT type fish-factory ships with freezer plant removed. Survey ships registered at Vladivostok and operated in the Pacific. Completed in 1959 at Nikolaev.

Yu. M. SHOKALSKY   1973, Michael D. J. Lennon

2 ATLANTIK TYPE

GERAKL	**PROFESSOR MESYATSYEV**

Measurement, tons: 2 242 gross
Dimensions, feet (metres): 270 × 45 × 25 *(82·4 × 13·7 × 7·6)*
Main engines: 2 8-cyl Karl Liebnecht diesels = 13 knots

Modified Atlantik type stern-trawler fish-factory ships built at Stralsund, E. Germany in 1972.

GERAKL   1973, Michael D. J. Lennon

2 SOVIET TRAWLER TYPE

ISSLEDOVATEL   **TAMANGO**

Measurement, tons: 680 gross
Dimensions, feet (metres): 178 × 30·6 × 15·9 *(54·3 × 9·3 × 4·8)*
Main engines: 1 Diesel = 12 knots

Apparently identical, except for aerials, to "Okean" and "Mayak" class AGIs. Have same different appearance of port and starboard sides of the superstructure, the former being closed in and the latter open.

TAMANGO   *1973, Michael D. J. Lennon*

3 EAST GERMAN TRAWLER TYPE

AYSBERG   **OKEANOGRAF**   **POLIARNIK**

Measurement, tons: 265 gross
Dimensions, feet (metres): 126·3 × 23·6 × 11·5 *(38·5 × 7·2 × 3·5)*
Main engines: 1 Diesel = 9·5 knots

Built in East Germany 1952-56. Civilian manned. Rigging of foremasts varies in different ships.

Note; There are also at least 180 other ships and craft, mainly of smaller size, employed on Soviet fishery research.

OKEANOGRAF   *1973, Michael D. J. Lennon*

SPACE ASSOCIATED SHIPS

Note: All civilian manned except "Baskunchak" class.

1 "GAGARIN" CLASS

KOSMONAUT YURI GAGARIN

Displacement, tons: 45 000
Measurement, tons: 32 291 gross; 5 247 net
Dimensions, feet (metres): 773·3 oa × 101·7 × 30·0 *(235·9 oa × 31 × 9·2)*
Main engines: 2 geared steam turbines; 1 shaft; 19 000 shp = 17 knots

Design based on the "Sofia" or "Akhtuba" (ex-"Hanoi") class steam tanker. Built at Leningrad in 1970, completed in 1971. Used for investigation into conditions in the upper atmosphere, and the control of space vehicles. She is the largest Soviet research vessel. Has bow and stern thrust units for ease of berthing. With all four aerials vertical and facing forward she experiences a loss in speed of 2 knots.

KOSMONAUT YURI GAGARIN   *1972, Michael D. J. Lennon*

KOSMONAUT VLADIMIR KOMAROV   *1972, Michael D. J. Lennon*

KOSMONAUT YURI GAGARIN   *1972, Michael D. J. Lennon*

1 "KOMAROV" CLASS

KOSMONAUT VLADIMIR KOMAROVO (ex-*Genichesk*)

Displacement, tons: 17 500 full load
Dimensions, feet (metres): 510·8 × 75·5 × 29·5 *(155·8 × 23 × 9)*
Main engines: Diesels; 2 shafts; 24 000 bhp = 22 knots

She was launched in 1966 at Nikolaev as *Genichesk* and operated as a merchant ship in the Black Sea for about six months. Converted to her present role at Leningrad in 1967. The ship is named in honour of the Soviet astronaut who died when his space craft crashed in 1967.

KOSMONAUT VLADIMIR KOMAROV
(with new forward aerial)   *1974, J. van der Woude*

AKADEMIK SERGEI KOROLEV

Displacement, tons: 21 250
Measurement, tons: 17 114 gross; 2 185 net
Dimensions, feet (metres): 597·1 × 82·0 × 30·0 *(182·1 × 25 × 9·2)*
Main engines: Diesels
Speed, knots: 17

Built at Nikolaev in 1970, completing in 1971. Equipped with the smaller type radome and two "saucers".

1 "KOROLEV" CLASS

AKADEMIK SERGEI KOROLEV   *1972, Michael D. J. Lennon*

AKADEMIK SERGEI KOROLEV   *1972, Michael D. J. Lennon*

BEZHITSA

Measurement, tons: 11 089 gross; 12 727 deadweight
Dimensions, feet (metres): 510·4 × 67·7 × 40·4 *(155·7 × 20·6 × 12·3)*
Main engines: Diesel = 17·5 knots

Former freighter of "Poltava" class launched at Nikolaev in 1964, and subsequently completed as a research ship. The aerial horns were fitted in 1971. Directional aerials similar to those in *Dolinsk* and *Ristna* fitted on crane stowage forward of the bridge.

1 "BEZHITSA" CLASS

BEZHITSA   *1972, Michael D. J. Lennon*

4 "SIBIR" CLASS

CHUKOTKA	SAKHALIN	SIBIR	SUCHAN

Displacement, tons: 4 000 standard; 5 000 full load
Measurement, tons: 3 767 gross (*Chukotka* 3 800, *Suchan* 3 710)
Dimensions, feet (metres): 354 × 49·2 × 20 *(108 × 15 × 6·1)*
Guns: 6—45 mm; 2 MG
Main engines: Triple expansion; 2 shafts; 3 300 ihp = 15 knots
Range, miles: 3 300 at 12 knots

Converted bulk ore carriers employed as Missile Range Ships in the Pacific. *Sakhalin* and *Sibir* have three radomes forward and aft, and carry helicopters. *Suchan* is also equipped with a helicopter flight deck. Launched in 1957-59. Formerly freighters of the Polish B 31 type. Rebuilt in 1958-59 as missile range ships in Leningrad.

7 "BASKUNCHAK" (ex-"VOSTOK") CLASS

APSHERON (ex-*Tosnoles*)   DONBASS (ex-*Kirishi*)
BASKUNCHAK (ex-*Vostok 4*)   SEVAN (ex-*Vyborgles*)
DAURIYA (ex-*Suzdal*)   TAMAN (ex-*Vostok 3*)
DIKSON (ex-*Vagales*)

Measurement, tons: 6 450 deadweight; 4 896 gross; 2 215 net
Dimensions, feet (metres): 400·3 × 55·1 × 14·0 *(122·1 × 16·8 × 4·3)*
Main engines: B & W 9-cylinder diesels; speed 15 knots

Standard timber carriers modified with helicopter flight deck. Built at Leningrad between 1963 and 1966. Entirely manned by naval personnel.

BASKUNCHAK   *1970, Michael D. J. Lennon*

TAMAN   *1972, Michael D. J. Lennon*

4 "MORZHOVETS" (ex-"VOSTOK") CLASS

BOROVICHI (ex-*Svirles*)   **KEGOSTROV** (ex-*Taimyr*)   **MORZHOVETS**   **NEVEL**

Former timber carriers but completely modified with a comprehensive array of tracking, direction finding and directional aerials. Additional laboratories built above the forward holds. Same measurements as the "Baskunchak" class, but tonnage increased to 5 277 gross

NEVEL   *1972, Michael D. J. Lennon*

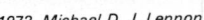

MORZHOVETS   *1972, Michael D. J. Lennon*

3 "DSHANKOY" CLASS

CHAZHMA (ex-*Dangara*)   **DSHANKOY**   **CHUMIKAN** (ex-*Dolgeschtschelje*)
Displacement, tons: 5 300 light; 14 065 full load
Dimensions, feet (metres): 457·7 × 59·0 × 25·9 *(139·6 × 18 × 7·9)*
Aircraft: 1 helicopter
Main engines: 2—7 cyl diesels = 18 knots

Formerly bulk ore-carriers of the "Dshankoy" class (7 265 tons gross).
Soviet Range Instrumentation Ships (SRIS). Active since 1963.

RISTNA

Measurement, tons: 4 200 deadweight; 3 724 gross; 1 819 net
Dimensions, feet (metres): 347·8 × 47·9 × 14·0 *(106·1 × 14·6 × 4·3)*
Main engines: MAN 6-cylinder diesels; speed = 15 knots

RISTNA   *1970, Michael D. J. lennon*

Converted from a timber carrier. Built in East Germany at Rostok by Schiffswerft—Neptun in 1963. Painted white. Fitted with directional aerials on top of bridge wings.
Serves as Missile Detection Ship.

COMMUNICATIONS RELAY SHIPS

20 "LIBAU" CLASS

Displacement, tons: 310 standard; 380 full load
Dimensions, feet (metres): 170·6 × 21·5 × 9·0 *(52 × 6·6 × 2·7)*
Main engines: 3 diesels; 2 shafts; 3 300 bhp = 24 knots
Range, miles: 1 500 at 12 knots

Converted "Kronstadt" class corvettes.

CABLE SHIPS

4 NEW CONSTRUCTION

KATYN   **+3**

Displacement, tons: 6 000

Ordered from Wärtsila, two in 1972/73 and two on 16 July 1974. *Katyn* launched 20 Mar 1974.

5 "KLASMA" CLASS

DONETZ   **INGUL**   **TSNA**   **YANA**   **ZEYA**

Displacement, tons: 6 900
Measurement, tons: 3 400 deadweight; 5 786 gross
Dimensions, feet (metres): 427·8 × 52·5 × 19 *(130·5 × 16 × 5·8)*
Main engines: 5 Wärtsila Sulzer diesels; 5 000 shp = 14 knots
Complement: 110

Ingul and *Yana* were built by Wärtsilä, Helsingforsvarvet, Finland, laid down on 10 Oct 1961 and 4 May 1962 and launched on 14 Apr 1962 and 1 Nov 1962 respectively, *Donetz* and *Tsna* were built at the Wärtsilä, Abovarvet, Abo. *Donetz* was launched on 17 Dec 1968 and completed 3 July 1969. *Tsna* was completed in summer 1968. *Zeya* was delivered on 20 Nov 1970. *Donetz, Tsna* and *Zeya* are of slightly modified design.

YANA (Type 1—no gantry aft)   *3/1976, MOD*

TSNA (Type II—with gantry aft)   *Wärtsila*

SERVICE FORCES

Note: With the Soviet merchant fleet under State control any ships of the merchant service, including tankers, may be diverted to a fleet support role at any time. Five 31 000 ton tankers (*Asheron*, *Grozny*, *Godermes*, *Makhachkaia* and *Mayrop*) recently built at Swan-Hunters are probably to be used in Soviet naval operations.

4 "BORIS CHILIKIN" CLASS (FLEET REPLENISHMENT SHIPS)

BORIS CHILIKIN	IVAN SUBNOV
DNESTR	VLADIMIR KOLECHITSKY

Displacement, tons: 23 000 full load
Dimensions, feet (metres): 531·5 × 70·2 × 28·1 *(162·1 × 21·4 × 8·6)*
Guns: 4—57 mm (2 twin) (except in *Ivan Subnov*)
Main engines: Diesel; 9 900 hp; 1 shaft = 16·5 knots

Based on the "Veliky Oktyabr" merchant ship tanker design *Boris Chilikin* was built at Leningrad completing in 1971. This is the first Soviet Navy class of purpose built underway fleet replenishment ships for the supply of both liquids and solids, indicating a growing awareness of the need for afloat support for a widely dispersed fleet.
Carry 13 000 tons fuel oil, 400 tons ammunition, 400 tons spares and 400 tons victualling stores.
A continuing programme.

DNESTR   *9/1974*

DNESTR   *9/1974, MOD*

1 "MANYCH" CLASS (FLEET REPLENISHMENT SHIP)

MANYCH

Displacement, tons: 7 500
Dimensions, feet (metres): 377·2 × 52·5 × 19·7 *(115 × 16 × 6)*
Guns: 4—57 mm (2 twin) with Muff Cob radar

Completed 1972, probably in Finland. A smaller edition of the *Boris Chilikin* but showing the new interest in custom-built replenishment ships. The high point on the single gantry is very similar to that on *Boris Chilikin's* third gantry.

MANYCH   *6/1974*

MANYCH   *2/1973*

2 "DUBNA" CLASS (REPLENISHMENT TANKERS)

ASHVA   ERKUT

Measurement, tons: 6 817 deadweight; 6 022 gross
Dimensions, feet (metres): 416·8 × 65·8 × 23·8 *(136·7 × 21·6 × 7·8)*
Main engines: Diesel; 6 000 hp = 16 knots

Erkut launched Jan 1975, completed Dec 1975 at Rauha/Repola, Finland.

1 "SOFIA" CLASS (REPLENISHMENT TANKER)

AKHTUBA (ex-*Khanoy*)

Displacement, tons: 45 000 full load
Measurement, tons: 62 000 deadweight; 32 840 gross, 16 383 net
Dimensions, feet (metres): 757·9 × 101·7 × 32·8 *(231·2 × 31 × 10)*

Built as the merchant tanker *Khanoy* in 1963 at Leningrad, she was taken over by the Navy in 1969 and renamed *Akhtuba*. The hull type was used in the construction of the space associated ship *Kosmonaut Yuri Gagarin*.

AKHTUBA   *1971, MOD*

3 "KAZBEK" CLASS (REPLENISHMENT TANKERS)

ALATYR   DESNA   VOLKHOV

Displacement, tons: 16 250 full load
Measurement, tons: 16 250 deadweight; 3 942 gross; 8 229 net
Dimensions, feet (metres): 447·4 × 63·0 × 23·0 (136·5 × 19·2 × 7)
Main engines: 2 diesels; single shaft

Former "Leningrad" class merchant fleet tankers taken over by the Navy. Built at Leningrad and Nikolaev from 1951 to 1961. Seven others—*Karl Marx, Kazbek, Dzerzhinsk, Grodno, Cheboksary, Liepaya* and *Buguzuslan* have acted in support of naval operations. The original class numbered 64. Radar—Don 2.

"KAZBEK" Class   1973, Michael D. J. Lennon

6 "ALTAY" CLASS (SUPPORT TANKERS)

ALTAY   ELYENYA   IZHORA   KOLA   TARKHANKUT   YEGORLIK

Displacement, tons: 5 500 standard
Dimensions, feet (metres): 344·5 × 49·2 × 19·7 (105·1 × 15 × 6)
Main engines: Diesels; speed = 14 knots

Building from 1967 onwards. By early 1975 over 60 of this class had been completed for naval and mercantile use.

"ALTAY" Class   1973, Michael D. J. Lennon

6 "UDA" CLASS (SUPPORT TANKERS)

DUNAY   KOIDA   LENA   SHEKSNA   TEREK   VISHERA

Displacement, tons: 5 500 standard; 7 200 full load
Dimensions, feet (metres): 400·3 × 51·8 × 20·3 (122·1 × 15·8 × 6·2)
Main engines: Diesels; 2 shafts; 8 000 bhp = 17 knots

Koida has a beam fuelling rig on starboard side abaft bridge.
Built since 1961.

LENA   1/1975, MOD

4 "PEVEK" CLASS (SUPPORT TANKERS)

IMAN   PEVEK   OLEKMA   ZOLOTOY ROG

Displacement, tons: 4 000 standard
Measurement, tons: 4 500 deadweight
Dimensions, feet (metres): 344·5 × 47·9 × 20·0 (105·1 × 14·6 × 6·1)
Main engines: Diesels; 2 900 bhp = 14 knots

Part of a class of fifty merchant tankers built by Rauma-Repola, Finland between 1955 and 1966.

"PEVEK" Class   1973, Michael D. J. Lennon

4 "KONDA" CLASS (SUPPORT TANKERS)

KONDA   ROSSOSH   SOYANNA   YAKHROMA

Displacement, tons: 1 178 standard
Dimensions, feet (metres): 226·4 × 32·8 × 13·8 (69·1 × 10 × 4·2)
Main engines: 1 100 bhp = 13 knots

15 "KHOBI" CLASS (HARBOUR TANKERS)

CHEREMSHAN	METAN	SEIMA	SOSVA
INDIGA	LOVAT	SHACHA	TUNGUSKA
KHOBI	ORSHA	SHELON	+ 4

Displacement, tons: 800 light; 2 000 approx full load
Speed, knots: 12 to 14

Built from 1957 to 1959.

3 "NERCHA" CLASS (HARBOUR TANKERS)

DORA   IRTYSH   IRBIT

SALVAGE VESSELS

1 + 1 "NEPA" CLASS

KARPATY + 1

Displacement, tons: 3 500 light; 5 000 standard
Dimensions, feet (metres): 410·1 × 52·5 × 16·4 (125·1 × 16 × 5)
Main engines: Diesels; 2 shafts

Submarine rescue and salvage ships similar to the "Prut" class but improved and enlarged and with a special high stern which extends out over the water for rescue manoeuvres. *Karpaty* completed 1969.

KARPATY   1969

10 "PRUT" CLASS

ALTAI   BRESHTAU   VLADIMIR TREFOLEV   ZHIGUILI   + 6

Displacement, tons: 2 120 standard; 3 500 full load
Dimensions, feet (metres): 296·0 × 36·1 × 13·1 (90·3 × 11 × 4)
Guns: 2—25 mm
Main engines: Diesels; 4 200 bhp = 18 knots

Large rescue vessels. Built since 1960.

"PRUT" Class   1970, S. Breyer

9 "SURA" CLASS

DIOKLAS + 8

Displacement, tons: 3 150 full load
Dimensions, feet (metres): 285·4 × 48·6 × 16·4 (87 × 14·8 × 5)
Main engines: Diesels; 1 770 bhp = 13·2 knots

Heavy lift ships built since 1965 in East Germany. Six built by 1972. Last, *Dioklas,* launched 21 Feb 1971.

"SURA" Class   6/1974

LIFTING VESSELS

15 "NEPTUN" CLASS

Displacement, tons: 700 light; 1 230 standard
Dimensions, feet (metres): 170·6 × 36·1 × 12·5 (52 × 11 × 3·8)
Main engines: Oil fuelled, speed = 12 knots

Similar to Western boom defence vessels, or netlayers. Built in 1957-60 by Neptun Rostock. Have a crane of 75 tons lifting capacity on the bow. One of this class is now based at Murmansk for the Maritime Fleet. She is acting as a diving vessel for hydrogeologists and construction personnel.

"NEPTUN" Class

SUBMARINE RESCUE SHIPS

15 "VALDAY" CLASS (Ex-"T 58" CLASS)

Displacement, tons: 725 standard; 850 full load
Dimensions, feet (metres): 229·9 × 29·5 × 7·9 *(70·1 × 9 × 2·4)*
Main engines: 2 diesels; 2 shafts; 4 000 bhp = 18 knots

Basically of similar design to that of the "T 58" class fleet minesweepers, but they were completed as emergency salvage vessels and submarine rescue ships at Leningrad. Equipped with diving bell, recompression chamber, lifting gear and emergency medical ward. It has been reported that there may be an extra six smaller rescue ships based on the "T 43" hull. One transferred to India *(Nistar)*.

"VALDAY" Class

1970, S. Breyer

TRANSPORTS

2 "KAMCHATKA" CLASS

KAMCHATKA   MONGOL

3 "CHULYM" CLASS

CHULYM   INSAR   KUZNETSKY

Displacement, tons: 5 050 full load
Dimensions, feet (metres): 311 × 44·5 × 18·3 *(101·9 × 14·6 × 6)*
Main engines: Compound 4 cyl; 1 650 hp = 14 knots
Range, miles: 5 500 at 11 knots
Complement: 40

Built by Stocznia Szczecinska, Poland from 1953-57. Nineteen others of this class operate with the merchant navy.

6 "BAIKAL" CLASS

BAIKAL   LENA   ANGARA
OB   YENISEI   INDIGIRKA

Displacement, tons: 12 400 full load
Dimensions, feet (metres): 427 oa × 61·8 × 27 *(140 × 20·3 × 8·9)*
Main engines: Diesel electric; 4 generators; 7 000 shp = 15·5 knots
Range, miles: 13 500 at 15 knots
Complement: 60

Built by Konmij de Scheldt, Flushing; three in 1954, three in 1957. Ice-strengthened. All but *Baikal* and *Ob* are civilian operated—(note *Angara* in Training Ships).

5 COASTAL TYPE

ISHIM   SHILKA   VISHERA
OLGA   USSURIJ (ex-*Okhotsk*)

Olga and *Ishim* are Coast Guard transports.

1 "LAZINKA" CLASS

KUBAN

Troop Transport of ex-"Mikhail Kalinin" class under naval command.

TORPEDO RECOVERY/PATROL CRAFT

90 "POLUCHAT I" CLASS

Displacement, tons: 100 standard
Dimensions, feet (metres): 98·4 × 19·7 × 5·9 *(30 × 6 × 1·8)*
Guns: 2—25 mm (1 twin) or 2 MG (1 twin)

Employed as specialised or dual purpose torpedo recovery vessels and/or patrol boats. They have a stern slipway. Several exported as patrol craft.

"POLUCHAT I" Class

10/1975, MOD

DIVING TENDERS/PATROL CRAFT

"NIRYAT I" CLASS

Displacement, tons: 145
Dimensions, feet (metres): 93 × 18 × 5·5 *(28·4 × 5·5 × 1·7)*
Gun: 1—12·5 MG (in some)
Main engines: Diesel; 1 shaft; 450 hp = 12·5 knots
Range, miles: 1 500 at 10 knots
Complement: 15

Built from 1955. Can operate as patrol craft.

Transfers: Cuba, Iraq (2), Yemen (North).

FIRE/PATROL BOATS

"POZHARNY I" CLASS

Displacement, tons: 180
Dimensions, feet (metres): 114·5 × 20 × 6 *(34·9 × 6·1 × 1·8)*
Guns: 4—12·7 mm or 14·5 mm (in some)
Main engines: 2 Diesels; 1 shaft; 1 800 hp = 12·5 knots

Built in USSR in mid 1950s. Harbour fire boats but can be used for patrol duties.

Transfers: Iraq (2), Yemen (North).

TRAINING SHIPS

1 "TELNOVSK" CLASS

STVOR

Displacement, tons: 1 200 standard
Dimensions, feet (metres): 229·6 × 32·8 × 13·1 *(70 × 10 × 4)*
Main engines: Diesels = 10 knots

Built in Hungary in late 1950s as a survey ship of the "Telnovsk" class. Now converted as a naval training ship with additional accommodation immediately forward of the bridge.

Note: None of the following ships is in the Navy List but their trainees are largely intended for the Navy.

STVOR

1972, Michael D. J. Lennon

ANGARA (ex-*Hela*)

Displacement, tons: 12 840 standard; 15 360 full load
Dimensions, feet (metres): 320 × 40·3 × 13 *(97·6 × 12·3 × 4)*
Guns: 2—4·1 in; 1—37 mm; 2—20 mm
Main engines: 4 MAN diesels; 2 shafts; 8 360 bhp = 21 knots
Range, miles: 2 000 at 15 knots
Complement: 250 (training)

Built by Stülcken, Hamburg. Launched in 1939. Allocated to USSR in 1946. In the Black Sea. Has prominent funnel.

3 "ZENIT" CLASS

GORIZONT	MERIDIAN	ZENIT

Measurement, tons: 4 374 gross; 986 net
Length, feet (metres): 352·6 *(107·5)*
Beam, feet (metres): 47·2 *(14·4)*
Main engines: Two 8-cylinder diesels geared to one shaft

All were built in East Germany at Rostock by Schiffswerft Neptun in 1961-62. Mercantile Cadet Training but produces officers for the Navy.

MERIDIAN·   *1972, Michael D. J. Lennon*

2 "SEDOV" CLASS

KRUZENSTERN	SEDOV

Measurement, tons: 3 064 gross

Barques. Built in 1921. Employed as sail training ships for the fishing industry.

KRUZENSTERN   *1973, Novosti*

1 Ex-GERMAN TYPE

TOVARISCH (ex-*Gorch Fock*)

Displacement, tons: 1 350
Dimensions, feet (metres): 242·8 × 39·3 × 15 *(74·1 × 12 × 4·6)*
Sail area: 19 350 sq ft
Guns: 2—20 mm
Main engines: MAN diesel; 1 shaft; 520 bhp = 8 knots
Oil fuel, tons: 25
Range, miles: 3 500 at 8 knots
Complement: 260

Barque. Ex-German training ship. Built by Blohm & Voss, Hamburg. Launched in 1933. Of mercantile attachment but produces personnel for the Navy.

TOVARISCH   *8/1974, John G. Callis*

9 "PROFESSOR ANICHKOV" CLASS

PROFESSOR ANICHKOV	PROFESSOR RYBALTOVSKI
PROFESSOR KHLYUSTIN	PROFESSOR SHCHYOGOLEV
PROFESSOR KUDREVITCH	PROFESSOR UKHOV
PROFESSOR MINYAYEV	PROFESSOR YUSHCHEKO
PROFESSOR PAVLENKO	

Measurement, tons: 5 993 gross; 1 512 net
Main engines: Diesels

Built at Szczecin, Poland between 1970-73. Used as merchant navy training ships but can operate as store transports. *Professor Rybaltovski* has a series of square ports in place of the cutaway sections below the boat-deck.

PROFESSOR KHLYUSTIN   *1972, Michael D. J. Lennon*

10 SCHOONER TYPE

ENISEJ	PRAKTIKA (ex-*Passat*)	TOBOL	UCHEBA (ex-*Mousson*)	+6

Displacement, tons: 300 approximately (ships vary)

Three masts. In the Baltic. Sailing vessels for training cadets, boys and volunteers.

DISTILLATION SHIPS

10 "VODA" CLASS

Displacement, tons: 2 100 standard
Dimensions, feet (metres): 267·3 × 37·7 × 14 *(81·5 × 11·5 × 4·3)*
Main engines: Diesels; speed = 12 knots

Water distillation ships built in 1956 onwards. No armament.

DEGAUSSING SHIP

1 "KHABAROV" CLASS

KHABAROV

Displacement, tons: 500 full load
Dimensions, feet (metres): 150·3 × 26·5 × 8 *(45·8 × 8·1 × 2·4)*
Main engines: Diesel; 1 shaft; 400 bhp = 10·5 knots
Range, miles: 1 130 at 10 knots
Complement: 30

Steel-hulled. Prominent deckhouse and stern anchors. One of class, *Kilat,* transferred to Indonesia 1961—subsequently disposed of.

ICEBREAKERS

Note: The majority of these ships is operated by V/O Sudoimport—only a small number being naval manned.

1 PROJECTED LARGE NUCLEAR POWERED

Main engines: Nuclear reactors; steam turbines; 80 000 hp

Reported as in the design stage in Oct 1974. Name possibly *Mikhail Somov*—unconfirmed.

2 NUCLEAR POWERED

ARKTIKA   SIBIR

Displacement, tons: 19 300 standard; 23 460 full load
Dimensions, feet (metres): 446·1 × 91·8 × 36·1 *(136 × 28 × 11)*
Aircraft: Helicopter with hangar
Main engines: 2 nuclear reactors; steam turbines; 75 000 shp = 21 knots

Building yard—Leningrad. *Arktika* launched summer 1973, started trials on 30 Nov 1974. Fitted with new type of reactor, the development of which may have retarded these ships' completion. *Sibir* on trials Nov 1975.

ARTIKA (Sketch)   1967

ARKTIKA   1974

1 NUCLEAR POWERED

LENIN

Displacement, tons: 15 940 standard; 19 240 full load
Dimensions, feet (metres): 406·7 × 87·9 × 34·4 *(124 × 26·8 × 0·5)*
Aircraft: 2 helicopters
Main engines: 3 pressurised water-cooled nuclear reactors, 4 steam turbines; 3 shafts; 44 000 shp = 19·7 knots
Complement: 230

The world's first nuclear powered surface ship to put to sea. Reported to have accommodation for 1 000 personnel.

Construction: Built at the Admiralty Yard, Leningrad. Launched on 5 Dec 1957. Commissioned on 15 Sep 1959.

Engineering: The original reactors, prototype submarine variety, were replaced during refit at Murmansk 1966-72. The new reactors presumably have a longer core-life than the 18 months of their predecessors. The turbines were manufactured by the Kirov plant in Leningrad. Three propellers aft, but no forward screw.

Operation: Can maintain a speed of 3-4 knots in 8 ft ice, giving a path of some 100 ft.

LENIN   1972

5 "MOSKVA" CLASS

VLADIVOSTOCK   KIEV   LENINGRAD   MOSKVA   MURMANSK

Displacement, tons: 12 840 standard; 15 360 full load
Dimensions, feet (metres): 368·8 wl; 400·7 oa × 80·3 × 34·5 *(112·5 wl; 122·2 oa × 24·5 × 10·5)*
Aircraft: 2 helicopters
Main engines: 8 Sulzer diesel-electric; 3 shafts; 22 000 shp = 18 knots
Oil fuel, tons: 3 000
Range, miles: 20 000
Complement: 145

Construction: Built by Wärtsilä Shipyard, Helsinki. *Moskva* was launched on 10 Jan 1959 and completed in June 1960. *Leningrad* was laid down in Jan 1959. Launched on 24 Oct 1959, and completed in 1962. *Kiev* was completed in 1966. *Murmansk* was launched on 14 July 1967, and *Vladivostock* on 28 May 1968.

Design: Designed to stay at sea for a year without returning to base. The concave embrasure in the ship's stern is a housing for the bow of a following vessel when additional power is required. There is a landing deck for helicopters and hangar space for two machines.

Engineering: Eight generating units of 3 250 bhp each comprising eight main diesels of the Wärtsilä-Sulzer 9 MH 51 type which together have an output of 26 000 hp. Four separate machinery compartments. Two engine rooms, four propulsion units in each. Three propellers aft. No forward propeller. Centre propeller driven by electric motors of 11 000 hp and each of the

MOSKVA   1960, Wärtsilä

side propellers by motors of 5 500 hp. Two Wärtsilä-Babcock & Wilcox boilers for heating and donkey work.

Operation: *Moskva* has four pumps which can move 480 metric tons of water from one side to the other in two minutes to rock the icebreaker and wrench her free of thick ice.

3 "ERMAK" CLASS

ERMAK   **ADMIRAL MAKAROV**   **KRASIN**

Displacement, tons: 20 241 full load
Dimensions, feet (metres): 442·8 × 85·3 × 36·1 *(135 × 26 × 11)*
Aircraft: 2 helicopters
Main engines: 9 Wärtsilä-Sulzer 12 cyl 12 ZH 40/48 diesels of 4 600 bhp each (total 41 400 hp) with Stromberg Ab generators feeding three Stromberg electric motors of total 36 000 shp; 3 shafts
Speed, knots: 19·5
Range, miles: 40 000 at 15 knots
Complement: 118 plus 28 spare berths

The Soviet Union ordered three large and powerful icebreakers on 29 April 1970 from Wärtsilä Shipyard, Helsinki, for delivery in 1974, 1975 and 1976. Six Wärtsilä auxiliary diesels, 7 200 bhp. Propelling and auxiliary machinery controlled electronically. These are the first vessels to be fitted with Wärtsilä mixed-flow air-bubbling system to decrease friction between hull and ice. *Ermak* launched 7 Sep 1973 and completed 30 June 1974. *A. Makarov* laid down 10 Sep 1973 and launched 26 April 1974, completed 2 June 1975. *Krasin* laid down 9 July 1974, launched 18 April 1975—completion Jan 1976.

KRASIN   *1976, Wärtsilä*

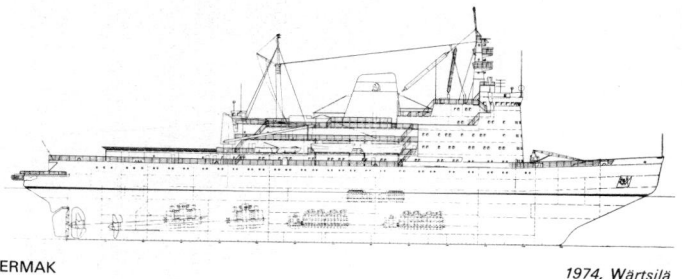

ERMAK   *1974, Wärtsilä*

3 SHALLOW-WATER TYPE NEW CONSTRUCTION

KAPITAN M. IZMAILOV
KAPITAN KOSOLAPOV
KAPITAN A. RADZABOV

Displacement, tons: 1 700
Dimensions, feet (metres): 185·3 × 51·5 × 13·8 *(56·5 × 15·7 × 4·2)*
Main engines: Diesel-electric; 3 400 shp; 2 shafts; 2 rudders
Speed, knots: 14

Contract signed with Wärtsilä, Helsinki on 22 Mar 1974 for the building of these three icebreakers for delivery in 1976. All being fitted with Wärtsilä air-bubbler system. Laid down: *K. Izmailov* 12 June 1975 (launched 11 Dec 1975), *K. Kosolapov* 19 Aug 1975, *K. Radzabov* 17 June 1975.

Shallow-water type   *1974, Wärtsilä*

3 "KAPITAN" CLASS

Name	Launched	Commissioned
KAPITAN BELOUSOV	1954	1955
KAPITAN MELECHOV	19 Oct 1956	1957
KAPITAN VORONIN	1955	1956

Displacement, tons: 4 375 to 4 415 standard; 5 350 full load
Dimensions, feet (metres): 265 wl; 273 oa × 63·7 × 23 *(80·8 wl; 83·3 oa × 19·4 × 7)*
Main engines: Diesel-electric; 6 Polar 8 cyl; 10 500 bhp = 14·9 knots
Oil fuel, tons: 740
Complement: 120

All built by Wärtsilä Shipyard, Helsinki. The ships have four screws, two forward under the forefoot and two aft.

KAPITAN BELOUSOV   *1970, Michael D. J. Lennon*

21 "DOBRINYA NIKITCH" CLASS

AFANASY NIKITIN	IVAN MOSKVITIN	SEMYON DEZHNEV
BURAN	IVAN KRUZENSHTERN	SEMEN CHELYUSHKIN
DOBRINYA NIKITCH	KHARITON LAPTEV	VASILY POYARKOV
EROFFREY KHABAROV	PERESVET	VASILY PRONCHISHCHEV
FEDOR LITKE	PETR PAKHTUSOV	VLADIMIR RUSANOV
GEORGIJ SEDOV	PLUG	YIRIY LISYANSKY
ILYA MUROMETS	SADKO	VYUGA

Displacement, tons: 2 500 standard (average)
Measurements, tons: 2 305 gross (ships vary)
Dimensions, feet (metres): 223·1 × 59·1 × 18·1 *(68 × 18 × 5·5)*
Main engines: 3 shafts; speed = 13·8 knots

All built at Leningrad between 1961 and 1965. Divided between the Baltic, Black Sea and Far East.

YIRIY LISYANSKY   *1972, Michael D. J. Lennon*

ARMED ICEBREAKERS

3 "MODIFIED DOBRINYA NIKITCH" CLASS

AISBERG   **IVAN SUSANIN**   **RUSLAN**

Of similar major characteristics to "Dobrinya Nikitch" class but lengthened by 80 feet and modified with new bridge structure, twin 76 mm forward, 2—30 mm Gatling guns aft and a helicopter platform. Classified as Arctic Survey Ships—one in each of Pacific, Northern and Baltic fleets.

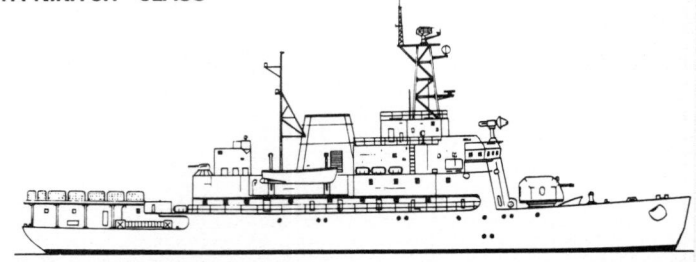

"MODIFIED DOBRINYA NIKITCH" Class   1974, S. Breyer

IVAN SUSANIN   7/1974

TUGS

2 "INGUL" CLASS

PAMIR   **MASHUK**

Displacement, tons: 3 600
Dimensions, feet (metres): 295 × 52 × 18 *(90 × 16 × 5·5)*

A new class with class-name the same as one of the "Klasma" class cable-ships.

PAMIR   4/1975, MOD(N)

2 "PAMIR" CLASS

AGATAN   **ALDAN**

Measurement, tons: 2 032 gross
Dimensions, feet (metres): 256 oa × 42 × 13·5 *(78 × 12·8 × 4·1)*
Main engines: Two 10 cyl 4 str diesels; 2 shaft; 4 200 bhp = 17 knots

Salvage tugs built at AB Gävie, Varv, Sweden, in 1959-60. Equipped with strong derricks, powerful pumps, air compressors, diving gear, fire fighting apparatus and electric generators.

ALDAN   4/1975, MOD(N)

2 DUTCH SALVAGE TUGS

DINANT   **HEKTOR**

Displacement, tons: 1 800

Launched in the Netherlands in 1974.

50 "OKHTENSKY" CLASS

Displacement, tons: 835
Dimensions, feet (metres): 134·5 wl; 143 oa × 34 × 15 *(41 wl; 43·6 × 10·4 × 4·6)*
Guns: 1—3 in; 2—20 mm
Main engines: 2 BM diesels; 2 electric motors; 2 shafts; 1 875 bhp = 14 knots
Oil fuel, tons: 187
Complement: 34

Oceangoing salvage and rescue tugs. Fitted with powerful pumps and other apparatus for salvage. Pennant numbers preceded by MB.

"OKHTENSKY" Class   1971, MOD

Measurement, tons: 828 gross
Dimensions, feet (metres): 171·5 × 37·7 × 19 *(52·3 × 11·5 × 5·8)*
Main engines: Diesel-electric = 14 knots

Built in late 1950s and early 1960s.

50 SOVIET SALVAGE TUGS

ATLANT—Soviet Salvage Tug   *1972, Michael D. J. Lennon*

5 "SORUM" CLASS

Displacement, tons: approx 800
Length, feet (metres): approx 160 *(48·8)*
Guns: 4—30 mm (twins)
Main engines: Diesels

A new class of ocean tugs first seen in 1973.

"SORUM" Class   *11/1973*

FINNISH SALVAGE TUGS

Measurement, tons: 1 070 gross
Dimensions, feet (metres): 201·2 × 39·2 × 18·1 *(61·4 × 12 × 5·5)*
Main engines: 2 Diesels = 14 knots

Class of salvage and rescue tugs normally operated by Ministry of Fisheries with the fishing fleets. Built in Finland in late 1950s and early 1960s.

STREMITELNY—Finnish Salvage Tug   *1972, Michael D. J. Lennon*

4 "OREL" CLASS

Displacement, tons: 1 300
Main engines: Diesels = 11 knots

Ocean-going tugs built between 1955 and 1958. Now being superseded.

7 "KATUN" CLASS

Displacement, tons: 950
Length, feet (metres): 210 *(64)*

Built in 1970-71.

Measurement, tons: 534 gross
Dimensions, feet (metres): 156·5 × 32·2 × 16·4 *(47·7 × 9·8 × 5)*
Main engines: 2 Diesels = 11 knots

Built in Romania in late 1950s. *Vladimir Obruchev* (see Research Ships) of same class.

15 "G" CLASS

GEROICHESKY—"G" Class   *1972, Michael D. J. Lennon*

FINNISH "530 TON" CLASS

Measurement, tons: 533 gross
Dimensions, feet (metres): 157·1 × 31·3 × 15·5 *(47·9 × 9·5 × 4·7)*
Main engines: Steam = 9·5 knots

Numerous class built in Finland in 1950s.

EAST GERMAN HARBOUR TUGS

Measurement, tons: 132 gross
Dimensions, feet (metres): 94·5 × 21·3 × 9·8 *(28·8 × 6·5 × 3)*
Main engines: 1 Diesel = 10 knots

Very numerous class built in E. Germany in 1964.

There are a large number of other tugs available in commercial service which could be directed to naval use.

EAST GERMAN BERTHING TUGS

Measurement, tons: 233 gross
Main engines: Diesels

Numerous class built in 1970 in East Germany.

URUGUAY

Headquarters Appointment

Commander-in-Chief of the Navy:
Vice-Admiral Victor González Ibargoyen

Diplomatic Representation

Naval Attaché in Washington:
Captain Jorge Laborde

Personnel

(a) 1976: Total: 3 500 officers and men (including Naval Infantry)
(b) Voluntary service

Base

Montevideo: Main naval base with a drydock and a slipway

Naval Air Arm

4 CH-34C helicopters
1 Bell 47G
2 Bell CH-13H
3 Grumman S-2A Tracker (ASW)
2 Beech SNB-5 (Training-Transport)
4 North American SNJ (Training)
1 Beech T-34 B Mentor (Training)
2 Piper PA-12 (Liaison)

Prefix to Ships' Names

R.O.U.

Mercantile Marine

Lloyd's Register of Shipping:
38 vessels of 130 998 tons gross

Strength of the Fleet

	Active	Building
Frigates	3	—
Submarines	—	?2
Corvettes	2	—
Minesweeper—Coastal	1	—
Coastal Patrol Craft	6	—
Survey Ships	2	—
Salvage Vessel	1	—
Tankers	2	—
Tenders	3	—

Deletions

Frigate

1975 *Montevideo*

Tanker

1975 *Vigilante*

Tug

1975 *General Jose Felix Rivas*

FRIGATES

2 Ex-US "CANNON" CLASS

Name		No.
ARTIGAS (ex-USS *Bronstein*, DE 189)		DE 2
URUGUAY (ex-USS *Baron*, DE 166)		DE 1

Builders	Laid down	Launched	Commissioned
Federal SB & DD Co, Pt Newark	1943	14 Nov 1943	13 Dec 1943
Federal SB & DD Co, Pt Newark	1942	9 May 1943	5 July 1943

Displacement, tons: 1 240 standard; 1 900 full load
Length, feet (metres): 306·0 *(93·3)* oa
Beam, feet (metres): 37·0 *(11·3)*
Draught, feet (metres): 17·1 *(5·2)*
Guns: 3—3 in *(76 mm)* (single); 2—40 mm (see *Gunnery* notes)
A/S weapons: Hedgehog; 8 DCT; 1 DCR (see *Torpedo Tubes* note)
Main engines: Diesel-electric; 2 shafts; 6 000 bhp
Speed, knots: 19
Oil fuel, tons: 315 (95 per cent)
Range, miles: 8 300 at 14 knots
Complement: 160

Former United States destroyer escorts of the "Cannon" class, transferred to Uruguay in 1952.

Appearance: Practically identical, but *Uruguay* can be distinguished by the absence of a mainmast, whereas *Artigas* has a small pole mast aft.

Gunnery: Formerly also mounted ten 20 mm anti-aircraft guns, but these have been removed.

Radar: Search: SPS 6.

Torpedo tubes: The three 21-inch torpedo tubes in a triple mounting, originally carried, were removed.

URUGUAY   *1975, Uruguayan Navy*

1 Ex-US "DEALEY" CLASS

Name		No.
18 DE JULIO (ex-USS *Dealey*, DE 1006)		DE 3

Builders	Laid down	Launched	Commissioned
Bath Iron Works Corpn	15 Oct 1952	8 Nov 1953	3 June 1954

Displacement, tons: 1 450 standard; 1 900 full load
Length, feet (metres): 314·5 *(95·9)* oa
Beam, feet (metres): 36·8 *(11·2)*
Draught, feet (metres): 13·6 *(4·2)*
Guns: 4—3 in *(76 mm)* (twins)
A/S weapons: 2 triple torpedo tubes (Mk 32)
Main engines: 1 De Laval geared turbine; 20 000 shp; 1 shaft
Boilers: 2 Foster Wheeler
Speed, knots: 25
Complement: 165

Purchased 28 July 1972. *Dealey* was the first US escort ship built after the war.

18 DE JULIO   *1975, Uruguayan Navy*

SUBMARINES

It is reported, though not confirmed, that two Type 209 submarines (IKL design) are building for this navy.

CORVETTES

1 Ex-US "AUK" CLASS

Name	No.	Builders	Commissioned
COMANDANTE PEDRO CAMPBELL	MS 31	Defoe B & M Works	1942
(ex-USS *Chickadee* MSF 59)			

Displacement, tons: 890 standard; 1 250 full load
Dimensions, feet (metres): 221·2 oa × 32·2 × 10·8 *(67·5 × 9·8 × 3·5)*
Guns: 1—3 in, 50 cal; 2—40 mm
Main engines: Diesel electric; 2 shafts; 3 118 bhp = 18 knots
Complement: 105

Former United States fleet minesweeper. Launched on 20 July 1942. Transferred on loan and commissioned at San Diego, Calif. on 18 Aug 1966.

COMANDANTE PEDRO CAMPBELL   1971

1 Ex-US MSO TYPE

Name	No.	Builders	Commissioned
MALDONADO	MS 33	USA	1954
(ex-*Bir Hakeim M 614*, ex-USS *MSO 451*)			

Displacement, tons: 700 standard; 795 full load
Dimensions, feet (metres): 171·0 oa × 35·0 × 10·3 *(50·3 × 10·7 × 3·2)*
Gun: 1—40 mm
Main engines: 2 GM diesels; 2 shafts; 1 600 bhp = 13·5 knots
Range, miles: 3 000 at 10 knots
Complement: 54

Former US ocean minesweeper transferred to France in Feb 1954. Returned to the US Navy and transferred to Uruguay on 9 April 1970.

MALDONADO   1975, Uruguayan Navy

COASTAL MINESWEEPER

1 Ex-US (FRENCH) MSC

Name	No.	Builders	Commissioned
RIO NEGRO	MS 32	USA	1954
(ex-*Marguerite*, ex-USS *MSC 94*)			

Displacement, tons: 370 standard; 405 full load
Dimensions, feet (metres): 141·0 oa × 26·0 × 8·3 *(43 × 8 × 2·6)*
Guns: 2—20 mm
Main engines: 2 GM diesels; 2 shafts; 1 200 bhp = 13 knots
Oil fuel, tons: 40
Range, miles: 2 500 at 10 knots
Complement: 38

Ex-US coastal minesweeper built for France under MDAP. Returned to US in 1969. She was transferred to Uruguay at Toulon on 10 Nov 1969.

RIO NEGRO   1975, Uruguayan Navy

LIGHT FORCES

1 COASTAL PATROL CRAFT

COLONIA PR 10

Displacement, tons: 25 standard; 34 full load
Dimensions, feet (metres): 63 × 15 × 3·8 *(20·6 × 4·9 × 1·2)*
Guns: 4 MGs
Main engines: 2 Hall Scott Defender; 1 260 bhp = 33·5 knots
Range, miles: 600 at 15 knots
Complement: 8

British-type rescue launch. Launched 4 July 1944.

COLONIA   1975, Uruguayan Navy

1 COASTAL PATROL CRAFT

Name	No.	Builders	Commissioned
CARMELO	PR 11	Lürssen, Vegesack	1957

Displacement, tons: 70
Dimensions, feet (metres): 93·0 × 19·0 × 7·0 (28·7 × 5·9 × 2·1)
Speed, knots: 25

CARMELO   1975, Uruguayan Navy

1 COASTAL PATROL CRAFT

Name	No.	Builders	Commissioned
PAYSANDU	PR 12	Sewart, USA	1968

Displacement, tons: 60
Dimensions, feet (metres): 83·0 × 18·0 × 6·0 (26 × 5·6 × 1·6)
Speed, knots: 22

PAYSANDU   1975, Uruguayan Navy

3 COASTAL PATROL CRAFT

701   702   703

43 ft craft transferred by USN in Feb 1970.

SURVEY SHIPS

Name	No.	Builders	Commissioned
CAPITAN MIRANDA	GS 20	Sociedad Espanola de Construccion Naval, Matagorda, Cadiz	1930

Displacement, tons: 516 standard; 549 full load
Dimensions, feet (metres): 148 pp; 179 oa × 26 × 10·5 (45; 53 × 8·4 × 3·2)
Main engines: 1 MAN diesel; 500 bhp = 11 knots
Oil fuel, tons: 37
Complement: 49

Originally a yacht with pronounced clipper bow.

CAPITAN MIRANDA (old pennant number)   1971

Name	No.	Builders	Commissioned
SALTO	GS 24	Cantieri Navali Riuniti, Ancona	1936

Displacement, tons: 150 standard; 180 full load
Dimensions, feet (metres): 137 × 18 × 10 (42·1 × 5·8 × 3)
Gun: 1—40 mm
A/S weapons: A/S grenade thrower
Main engines: 2 Germania-Krupp diesels; 2 shafts; 1 000 bhp = 17 knots
Range, miles: 4 000 at 10 knots
Complement: 26

Now used also as a buoy-tender.

SALTO (old pennant number)   1971

SALVAGE VESSEL

1 Ex-US "COHOES" CLASS

Name	No.	Builders	Commissioned
HURACAN	AM 25	Commercial Ironworks, Portland,	1945
(ex-USS *Nahant AN 83*)		Oregon	

Displacement, tons: 650 standard; 855 full load
Dimensions, feet (metres): 168·5 × 33·8 × 11·7 *(51·4 × 10·2 × 3·3)*
Guns: 3—20 mm (single)
Main engines: Diesel electric; 1 shaft; 1 200 bhp = 11·5 knots
Complement: 48

Former US netlayer, purchased in April 1969 for salvage services.

HURACAN   *1975, Uruguayan Navy*

RESCUE LAUNCH

AR 1

Displacement, tons: 25 standard; 30 full load
Dimensions, feet (metres): 63·0 × 15·0 × 3·8 *(19·2 × 4·6 × 1·2)*
Guns: 4 MG
Main engines: 2 Hall-Scott Defender; 1 260 bhp = 33·5 knots
Range, miles: 600 at 15 knots
Complement: 8

British type rescue launch. Launched on 4 July 1944.

TANKERS

Name	No.	Builders	Commissioned
PRESIDENTE ORIBE	AO 29	Ishikawajima-Harima Ltd, Japan	22 Mar 1962

Measurement, tons: 17 920 gross; 28 267 deadweight
Dimensions, feet (metres): 620 oa × 84·3 × 33 *(189 × 25·7 × 10·1)*
Main engines: 1 Ishikawajima turbine; 12 500 shp = 16·75 knots
Boilers: 2 Ishikawajima-Harima Foster Wheeler type
Range, miles: 16 100 at 16 knots
Complement: 76

PRESIDENTE ORIBE   *1971*

Name	No.	Builders	Commissioned
PRESIDENTE RIVERA	AO 28	Spain	1971

Measurement, tons: 19 350
Dimensions, feet (metres): 636·3 × 84 × 32 *(194 × 25·6 × 9·8)*
Main engines: 15 300 bhp = 15 knots

PRESIDENTE RIVERA   *1975, Uruguayan Navy*

TENDERS

VANGUARDIA AM 26

TACOMA

Training ship.

VENEZUELA

Administration

Commander General of the Navy (Chief of Naval Operations):
Rear-Admiral Armando Perez Leefmans
Chief of Naval Staff:
Rear-Admiral Enrique Dominauez Garcia

Diplomatic Representation

Naval Attaché in London:
Captain A. G. Rodriguez-Millan
Naval Attaché in Washington:
Rear-Admiral Luis Ramirez Aranda

Personnel

(a) 1976: 7 500 officers and men including 4 000 of the Marine
Corps (3 battalions)
(b) 2 years National Service

National Guard

The Fuerzas Armadas de Cooperacion, generally known as the National Guard, is a paramilitary organisation, 10 000 strong. It is concerned, amongst other things, with customs and internal security—the Maritime Wing operates the Coastal Patrol Craft listed under Light Forces, though these nominally belong to the Navy.

Mercantile Marine

Lloyd's Register of Shipping:
152 vessels of 515 661 tons gross

Naval Air Arm

2 Bell 47J helicopters
6 Grumman S-2E Trackers (ASW)
4 Grumman Hu-16A Albatros (SAR)
3 Douglas C-47 (Transports)

Strength of the Fleet

Type	Active	Building
Destroyers	4	—
Frigates	6	—
Submarines, Patrol	4	1
Fast Attack Craft—Missile/Gun	6	—
Large Patrol Craft	10	—
Coastal Patrol Craft (manned by National Guard)	43	—
LST	1	—
LSMs	4	—
Transport Landing Ship	1	—
Transports	3	—
Survey Ships and Craft	5	—
Ocean Tug	1	—
Harbour Tugs	8	—
Floating Dock	1	—

Bases

Caracas. Main HQ.

DELETION

Destroyer

1975 *Aragua*

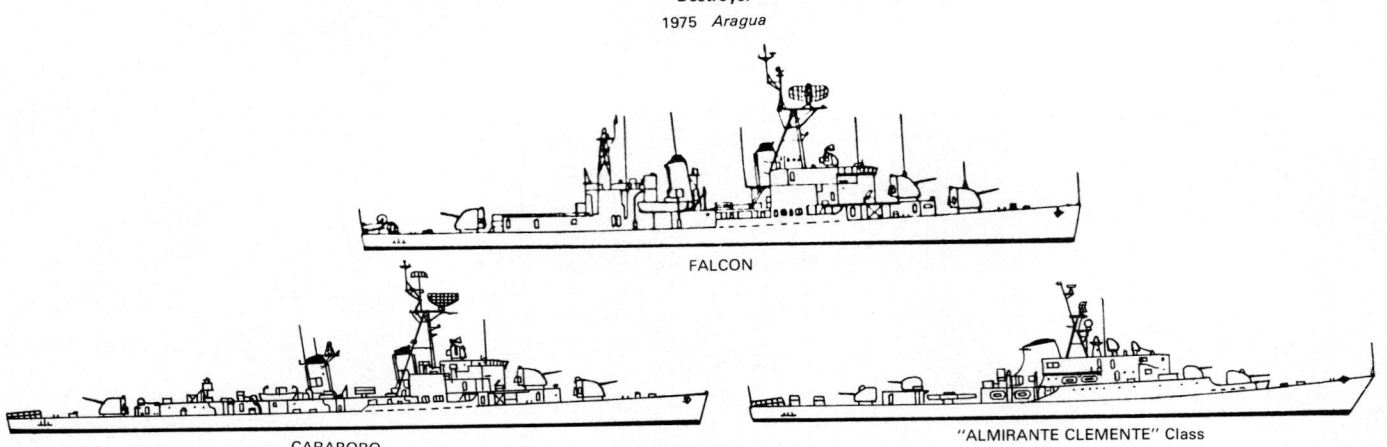

FALCON

CARABOBO

"ALMIRANTE CLEMENTE" Class

DESTROYERS

2 "ARAGUA" CLASS

Name	No.	Builders	Laid down	Launched	Commissioned
NUEVA ESPARTA	D 11	Vickers Ltd, Barrow	24 July 1951	19 Nov 1952	8 Dec 1953
ZULIA	D 21	Vickers Ltd, Barrow	24 July 1951	29 June1953	15 Sep 1954

Displacement, tons: 2 600 standard; 3 670 full load
Length, feet (metres): 384·0 *(117·0)* wl; 402·0 *(122·5)* oa
Beam, feet (metres): 43·0 *(13·1)*
Draught, feet (metres): 19·0 *(5·8)*
Missiles: 2 quadruple Seacat in D 11
Guns: 6—4·5 *(114 mm)* (twins); 16—40 mm (twins) in D 21;
4—40 mm (twins) in D 11
A/S weapons: 2 Squids; 2 DCT; 2 DC racks
Torpedo tubes: 3—21 in *(533 mm)* triple (none in D 11)

Main engines: Parsons geared turbines; 2 shafts; 50 000 shp
Boilers: 2 Yarrow
Speed, knots: 34
Range, miles: 5 000 at 10 knots
Complement: 256 (20 officers, 236 men)

Ordered in 1950 as class of three. Air conditioned. Two engine rooms and two boiler rooms served by a single uptake. The 4·5 inch guns are fully automatic.

Refits: *Nueva Esparta* and *Zulia* refitted at Palmers Hebburn Works, Vickers in 1959, and at New York Navy Yard in 1960 to improve anti-submarine and anti-aircraft capabilities. *Nueva Esparta* at Cammell Laird in 1968-69 when Seacat launchers were fitted and some 40 mm and the torpedo tubes removed.

Radar: Search: AWS 2 *(Nueva Esparta)* SPS 6 *(Zulia)*.
Fire Control: I Band.

NUEVA ESPARTA

1970, Venezuelan Navy

1 Ex- US "ALLEN M. SUMNER (FRAM II)" CLASS

Name	No.	Builders	Laid down	Launched	Commissioned
FALCON (ex-USS *Robert K. Huntington* DD 781)	D 51	Todd Pacific Shipyards	1944	5 Dec 1944	3 Mar 1945

Displacement, tons: 2 200 standard; 3 320 full load
Dimensions, feet (metres): 376·5 × 40·9 × 19 *(114·8 × 12·4 × 5·8)*
Guns: 6—5 in 38 cal (twins)
A/S weapons: 2 Hedgehogs; 2 triple torpedo tubes (Mk 32);
facilities for small helicopter
Main engines: 2 geared turbines; 60 000 shp; 2 shafts
Boilers: 4
Speed, knots: 34
Range, miles: 4 600 at 15 knots
Complement: 274

Purchase from USN 31 Oct 1973. Modernised under the FRAM II programme.

Radar: SPS 40 and SPS 10.

Sonar: Hull mounted; SQS 29 series. VDS.

"ALLEN M. SUMNER (FRAM II)" Class

USN

1 Ex-US "ALLEN M. SUMNER" CLASS

Name	No.
CARABOBO (ex-USS *Beatty*, DD 756)	D 41

Displacement, tons: 2 200 standard; 3 320 full load
Dimensions, feet (metres): 376·5 × 40·9 × 19·0 *(114·8 × 12·4 × 5·8)*
Guns: 6—5 in (twins)
A/S weapons: 2 fixed Hedgehogs, DCs; 2 triple torpedo tubes (Mk 32)
Main engines: 2 geared turbines; 60 000 shp; 2 shafts
Boilers: 4
Speed, knots: 34
Range, miles: 4 600 at 15 knots
Complement: 274

Transferred from USN 14 July 1972.

Builders	Laid down	Launched	Commissioned
Bethlehem, Staten Is.	1944	30 Nov 1944	31 Mar 1945

CARABOBO (as *Beatty*)   1965, Dr. Giorgio Arra

FRIGATES

6 "LUPO" CLASS

Displacement, tons: 2 208 standard; 2 500 full load
Dimensions, feet (metres): 366 × 39·4 × 11·8 *(111·6 × 12 × 3·6)*
Aircraft: 1 AB212 helicopter
Missiles: 4 Otomat 2 (singles); 8 cell Albatros SAM system
Guns: 1—5 in *(127 mm)* 54 cal Oto Melara; 4—40 mm 70 cal (singles)
Rocket launchers: 2 SCLAR 4·1 in multi-tube mountings
A/S weapons: 6 for A/S torpedoes (triples)
Main engines: CODAG. 2 Fiat/GELM 2 500 gas turbines; 34 400 bhp; 2 GMT A230/20M diesels; 7 800 hp; 2 shafts
Speed, knots: 35; 21 on diesels
Complement: 185

Ordered 24 Oct 1975 from Cantiere Navali Riuniti, Riva Trigoso. Delivery of first ship expected Oct 1978.

Radar: Search: Selenia MM/SPS 74. Navigation: SMA SPQ/2F. Fire Control (guns): Elsag Mark 10 Mod O Argo. Fire Control (missiles): EX 77 Mod O.

Sonar: SQS 29.

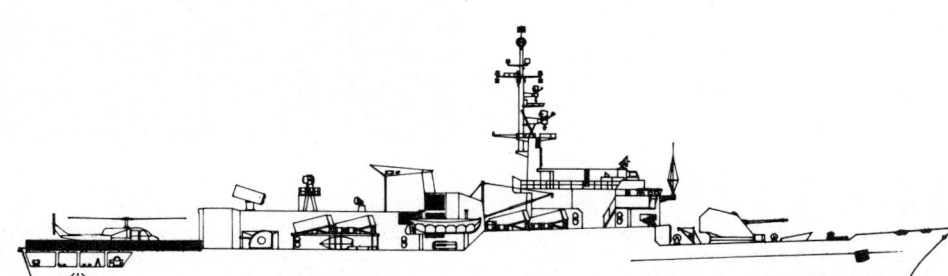
"LUPO" Class   1976, Italian Navy

6 "ALMIRANTE CLEMENTE" CLASS

Name	No.
ALMIRANTE CLEMENTE	D 12
ALMIRANTE JOSÉ GARCIA	D 33
ALMIRANTE BRION	D 23
GENERAL JOSÉ DE AUSTRIA	D 32
GENERAL JOSÉ TRINIDAD MORAN	D 22
GENERAL JUAN JOSÉ FLORES	D 13

Builders	Laid down	Launched	Commissioned
Ansaldo, Leghorn	5 May 1954	12 Dec 1954	1956
Ansaldo, Leghorn	12 Dec 1954	12 Oct 1956	1957
Ansaldo, Leghorn	12 Dec 1954	4 Sep 1955	1957
Ansaldo, Leghorn	12 Dec 1954	15 July 1956	1957
Ansaldo, Leghorn	5 May 1954	12 Dec 1954	1956
Ansaldo, Leghorn	5 May 1954	7 Feb 1955	1956

Displacement, tons: 1 300 standard; 1 500 full load
Length, feet (metres): 325·11 *(99·1)* oa
Length, feet (metres): 35·5 *(10·8)*
Draught, feet (metres): 12·2 *(3·7)*
Guns: 4—4 in *(102 mm)* (2 twin); 4—40 mm; 8—20 mm (modified group 40 mm only)
A/S weapons: 2 "Hedgehogs", 4 DCT and 2 DC racks in original group; 1 A/S Mortar, 4 DCT and 2 DC racks in modified group
Torpedo tubes: 3—21 in *(533 mm)* triple (original group only)
Main engines: 2 sets geared turbines; 2 shafts; 24 000 shp
Boilers: 2 Foster Wheeler
Speed, knots: 32
Oil fuel, tons: 350
Range, miles: 3 500 at 15 knots
Complement: 162 (12 officers, 150 men)

The first three were ordered in 1953. Three more were ordered in 1954. Aluminium alloys were widely employed in the building of all superstructure. All six ships are fitted with Denny-Brown fin stabilisers and air conditioned throughout the living and command spaces. D 32 and D 33 may soon be deleted.

Gunnery: The 4 inch anti-aircraft guns are fully automatic and radar controlled.

Modernisation: *Almirante José Garcia, Almirante Brion* and *General José de Austria* were refitted by Ansaldo, Leghorn, in 1962 to improve their anti-submarine and anti-aircraft capabilities: this group is known as "Modified Almirante Clemente" type. *Almirante Clemente* and *General José Trinidad Moran* were taken in hand for refit by Cammell Laird/Plessey group in April 1968. *Almirante Clemente* started her post-refit trials in Feb 1975 and *General Jose Moran* after trials sailed mid-Jan 1976 for Venezuela.

Radar: Search: MLA 1. Fire Control: I Band

ALMIRANTE BRION   1975, Dhr. J. Van der Woude

GENERAL JOSE DE AUSTRIA (modified group)   1972, Venezuelan Navy

SUBMARINES

2 HOWALDTSWERKE TYPE 209

Name	No.
SABALO	S 21
CONGRIO	S 22

Builders	Laid down	Launched	Commissioned
Howaldtswerke, Kiel	1973	21 Aug 1975	July 1976
Howaldtswerke, Kiel	1973	16 Dec 1975	1977

Displacement, tons: 990 surfaced; 1 350 dived
Dimensions, feet (metres): 177·1 × 20·3 × 18 *(54·0 × 6·2 × 5)*
Torpedo tubes: 8—21 in (with reloads) bow
Main machinery: Diesel-electric; 4 MTU-Siemens diesel generators; 1 Siemens electric motor 5 000 hp; 1 shaft
Speed, knots: 10 surfaced; 22 dived
Range, miles: 50 days
Complement: 31

Type 209, IK81 designed by Ingenieurkontor Lübeck for construction by Howaldtswerke, Kiel and sale by Ferrostaal, Essen, all acting as a consortium.
A single-hull design with two main ballast tanks and forward and after trim tanks. Fitted with snort and remote machinery control. Slow revving single screw. Very high capacity batteries with GRP lead-acid cells and battery-cooling—by W. Hagen and VARTA. Active and passive sonar, sonar detection set, sound-ranging equipment and underwater telephone. Have two periscopes, radar and Omega receiver. Fore-planes retract. Ordered in 1971.

SABALO   *1976, Howaldtswerke*

2 Ex-US "GUPPY II" CLASS

Name	No.
TIBURON (ex-USS *Cubera*, SS 347)	S 12
PICUDA (ex-USS *Grenadier*, SS 525)	S 13

Builders	Laid down	Launched	Commissioned
Electric Boat Co, Groton	11 May 1944	17 June1945	19 Dec 1945
Boston Navy Yard	8 Feb 1944	15 Dec 1944	10 Feb 1951

Displacement, tons: 1 870 surfaced; 2 420 dived
Length, feet (metres): 307·5 *(93·8)*
Beam, feet (metres): 27·0 *(8·2)*
Draught, feet (metres): 18·0 *(5·5)*
Torpedo tubes: 10—21 in *(533 mm)* (6 bow, 4 stern)
Main machinery: 3 diesels; 4 800 shp; 2 electric motors; 5 400 shp; 2 shafts
Speed, knots: 18 surfaced; 15 dived
Range, miles: 12 000 at 10 knots
Oil fuel, tons: 300
Complement: 80

Transferred as follows—*Tiburon* 5 Jan 1972, *Picuda* 15 May 1973.

Spares: USS *Blenny* (SS 324) was purchased for spares in early 1975.

PICUDA (as GRENADIER)   *US Navy*

1 Ex-US "BALAO" CLASS

Name	No.
CARITE (ex-USS *Tilefish*, SS 307)	S 11

Builders	Laid down	Launched	Commissioned
Mare Island Navy Yard	1943	25 Oct 1943	28 Dec 1943

Displacement, tons: 1 450 standard; 2 400 dived
Dimensions, feet (metres): 312 × 27·2 × 17·2 *(95·1 × 8·3 × 5·3)*
Torpedo tubes: 10—21 in; (6 bow, 4 stern)
Main machinery: 4 diesels; 6 400 hp; 2 electric motors; 5 400 shp; 2 shafts
Range, miles: 12 000 at 10 knots
Speed, knots: 20 surfaced; 10 dived
Complement: 85

Purchased from USN—Transfer 4 May 1960 after 4 month refit. Subsequently refitted with streamlined fin. Now used for training; non-diving.

CARITE   *1969, Venezuelan Navy*

LIGHT FORCES

6 VOSPER-THORNYCROFT 121 FT CLASS (FAST ATTACK CRAFT—MISSILE AND GUN)

Name	No.	Builders	Laid down	Launched	Commissioned
CONSITUCION	P 11	Vosper-Thornycroft Ltd	Jan 1973	1 June1973	16 Aug 1974
FEDERACION	P 14	Vosper-Thornycroft Ltd	Aug 1973	26 Feb 1974	25 Mar 1975
INDEPENDENCIA	P 12	Vosper-Thornycroft Ltd.	Feb 1973	24 July 1973	20 Sep 1974
LIBERTAD	P 15	Vosper-Thornycroft Ltd.	Sep 1973	5 Mar 1974	12 June 1975
PATRIA	P 13	Vosper-Thornycroft Ltd	Mar 1973	27 Sep 1973	9 Jan 1975
VICTORIA	P 16	Vosper-Thornycroft Ltd	Mar 1974	3 Sep 1974	22 Sep 1975

Displacement, tons: 150
Dimensions, feet (metres): 121 oa × 23·3 × 5·6 *(36·9 × 7·6 × 1·7)*
Missiles: Second 3 armed with Otomat and 1—40 mm gun
Guns: First 3 armed with Oto Melara 76 mm
Main engines: 2 MTU diesels; 7 200 hp; 2 shafts
Speed, knots: 27
Range, miles: 1 350 at 16 knots
Complement: 18

A £6m order the first laid down in Jan 1973. A new design, fitted with Elsag fire-control system NA 10 mod 1 and Selenia radar.

INDEPENDENCIA

4/1975, Vosper Thornycroft Ltd

10 Ex-US PC TYPE (LARGE PATROL CRAFT)

Name	No.	Builders	Commissioned
ALBATROS (ex-USS PC 582)	P 04	—	—
ALCATRAZ (ex-USS PC 565)	P 03	—	—
CALAMAR (ex-USS PC 566)	P 02	—	—
*CAMARON (ex-USS PC 483)	P 08	—	—
CARACOL (ex-USS PC 1077)	P 06	—	—
*GAVIOTA (ex-USS PC 619)	P 10	—	—
*PETREL (ex-USS PC 1176)	P 05	—	—
*PULPO (ex-USS PC 465)	P 07	—	—
*MEJILLON (ex-USS PC 487)	P 01	—	—
*TOGOGO (ex-USS PC 484)	P 09	—	—

(* in reserve)

Displacement, tons: 280 standard; 430 full load
Dimensions, feet (metres): 173·7 oa × 23·0 × 10·8 *(53 × 7 × 3·3)*
Guns: 1—3 in; 2—40 mm (1 twin); 2—20 mm
A/S weapons: Provision for 4 DCT
Main engines: 2 Fairbanks-Morse diesels; 2 shafts; 2 800 bhp = 19 knots
Complement: 65

ALBATROS

1972, Venezuelan Navy

Mejillon was refitted and overhauled by Diques y Astilleros Nacionalis, Venezuela, prior to commissioning in the Venezuelan Navy, and from 1962 onwards more ships of this type underwent similar preparation to join the fleet. Altogether twelve of these former United States PCs of the steel-hulled "173-ft" type were purchased from the USA in Oct 1960. *Camaron, Pulpo* and *Gaviota* were placed in reserve 1968-70 and subsequently *Petrel, Mejillon* and *Togogo.*

6 COASTAL PATROL CRAFT

RIO META	RIO PORTUGUESA
RIO ORINOCO (?)	RIO URIBANTE
	+ 2

Displacement, tons: 45
Dimensions, feet (metres): 88·6 × 16 × 4·9 *(27 × 4·9 × 1·5)*
Guns: 1—20 mm; 1 MG
Main engines: 2 diesels; 3 300 hp = 30 knots
Range, miles: 1 500 at 15 knots
Complement: 12

Built at Chantiers Navales de l'Esterel. Manned by National Guard.

8 "RIO" CLASS (COASTAL PATROL CRAFT)

Name	No.	Builders	Commissioned
RIO APURE	—	Chantiers Navales de l'Esterel, Cannes	1954
RIO ARAUCA	—	Chantiers Navales de l'Esterel, Cannes	1954
RIO CABRIALES	—	Chantiers Navales de l'Esterel, Cannes	1954
RIO CARONI	—	Chantiers Navales de l'Esterel, Cannes	1954
RIO GUARICO	—	Chantiers Navales de l'Esterel, Cannes	1954
RIO NEGRO	—	Chantiers Navales de l'Esterel, Cannes	1954
RIO NEVERI	—	Chantiers Navales de l'Esterel, Cannes	1954
RIO TUX	—	Chantiers Navales de l'Esterel, Cannes	1954

Displacement, tons: 38
Dimensions, feet (metres): 82 oa × 15 × 4 *(28 × 4·7 × 1·3)*
Main engines: 2 MTU 12 V 493 diesels; 1 400 rpm; 1 350 bhp = 27 knots

Manned by National Guard.

RIO NEGRO

1972, Venezuelan Navy

1 COASTAL PATROL CRAFT

GOLFO DE CARIACO

Displacement, tons: 37
Dimensions, feet (metres): 65 × 18 × 9 *(20 × 5·5 × 2·8)*
Main engines: Diesels; speed = 19 knots
Complement: 10

Manned by National Guard.

1 COASTAL PATROL CRAFT

RIO SANTO DOMINGO

Displacement, tons: 40
Dimensions, feet (metres): 70 × 15 × 6 *(22 × 4·6 × 1·9)*
Main engines: 2 GM diesels; 1 250 bhp = 24 knots
Complement: 10

Manned by National Guard.

21 NEW CONSTRUCTION (COASTAL PATROL CRAFT)

Name	No.	Builders	Commissioned
RIO CAPARO	C 89	Inma, La Spezia	1974
RIO ESCALANTE	C 92	Inma, La Spezia	1975
RIO LIMON	C 93	Inma, La Spezia	1975
RIO ORINOCO (?)	C 87	Inma, La Spezia	1974
RIO SAN JUAN	C 94	Inma, La Spezia	1975
RIO TORRES	C 91	Inma, La Spezia	1974
RIO TUCUYO	C 95	Inma, La Spezia	1975
RIO TURBIO	C 96	Inma, La Spezia	1975
RIO VENAMO	C 90	Inma, La Spezia	1974
RIO VENTUARI	C 88	Inma, La Spezia	1974
—	C 128-138	Iadian, Puerto Cabello	—

Displacement, tons: 65
Dimensions, feet (metres): 92·8 × 15·7 × 4·9 *(28·3 × 4·8 × 1·5)*
Main engines: 2 MTU diesels; 2 200 bhp = 25 knots

Ordered in May 1973. Assistance given in overseeing at Puerto Cabello by Inma.

AMPHIBIOUS FORCES

1 Ex-US "TERREBONNE PARISH" CLASS (LST)

Name	No.	Builders	Commissioned
AMAZONAS	T 21	Ingalls Shipbuilding Corpn	1953
(ex-USS *Vernon County* LST 1161)			

Displacement, tons: 2 590 light; 5 800 full load
Dimensions, feet (metres): 384 oa × 55 × 17 *(117·4 × 16·8 × 3·7)*
Guns: 6—3 in 50 cal (twins)
Main engines: 4 GM diesels; 2 shafts; cp propeller; 6 000 bhp = 15 knots
Complement: 116
Troops: 395

Built 1952-53. Carries four LCVP landing craft. Transferred on loan 29 June 1973.

4 Ex-US LSM TYPE

Name	No.	Builders	Commissioned
LOS FRAILES	T 15	Brown Shipbuilding Co, Houston, Texas	1945
(ex-USS *LSM 544*)			
LOS MONJES	T 13	Brown Shipbuilding Co, Houston, Texas	1945
(ex-USS *LSM 548*)			
LOS ROQUES	T 14	Brown Shipbuilding Co, Houston, Texas	1945
(ex-USS *LSM 543*)			
LOS TESTIGOS	T 16	Brown Shipbuilding Co, Houston, Texas	1945
(ex-USS *LSM 545*)			

Displacement, tons: 743 beaching; 1 095 full load
Dimensions, feet (metres): 196·5 wl; 203·5 oa × 34·5 × 8·3 *(59·9; 62·1 × 10·5 × 2·5)*
Guns: 1—40 mm; 4—20 mm
Main engines: Direct drive diesels; 2 shafts; 2 800 bhp = 12 knots
Range, miles: 9 000 at 11 knots
Complement: 59

Sold to Venezuela under MAP in Aug 1958.

LOS MONJES   *1970, Venezuelan Navy*

1 ex-US ARL TYPE

Name	No.	Builders	Commissioned
GUYANA	T 18	Chicago Bridge & Iron Co, Seneca, Illinois	1945
(ex-USS *Quirinus*, ARL 39, ex-*LST 1151*)			

Displacement, tons: 1 625 light; 4 100 full load
Dimensions, feet (metres): 316 wl; 328 oa × 50 × 11·2 *(103·6; 107·7 × 16·4 × 3·7)*
Guns: 8—40 mm AA (two quadruple mountings)
Main engines: GM diesels; 2 shafts; 1 800 bhp = 11·6 knots
Complement: 81 (11 officers, 70 men)

Former US Navy landing craft repair ship. Laid down on 3 Mar 1945. Loaned to Venezuela in June 1962 and now used as a transport.

GUYANA   *1970, Venezuelan Navy*

TRANSPORTS

1 Ex-US CI-M-AVI TYPE

MARACAIBO

Displacement, tons: 7 450 full load
Dimensions, feet (metres): 338·8 × 50·3 × 21 *(103·3 × 15·3 × 6·4)*
Main engines: Diesel; 1 shaft; 1 750 bhp = 11·5 knots

Built in USA in 1944.

PUNTA CABANA T 17

Small troop carrier of about 3 000 tons with a speed of 17 knots, built by Uraga Dockyard, Japan.

Name	No.	Builders	Commissioned
LAS AVES (ex-*Dos de Diciembre*)	T 12	Chantiers Dubigeon, Nantes-Chantenay	1955

Displacement, tons: 944
Dimensions, feet (metres): 234·2 × 33·5 × 10 *(71 × 10·2 × 3·1)*
Guns: 4—20 mm (2 twin)
Main engines: 2 diesels; 2 shafts; 1 600 bhp = 15 knots
Radius, miles: 2 600 at 11 knots

Launched in Sep 1954. Light transport for naval personnel. Renamed *Las Aves* in 1961. Can be used as Presidential Yacht.

LAS AVES   *1970, Venezuelan Navy*

SURVEY SHIPS

3 Ex-US "COHOES" CLASS

Name	No.	Builders	Commissioned
PUERTO DE NUTRIAS (ex-USS *Tunxis,* AN 90)	H 02	Zenith Bridge Co, Duluth, Minn	1945
PUERTO MIRANDA (ex-USS *Waxsaw,* AN 91)	H 03	Zenith Bridge Co, Duluth, Minn	1945
PUERTO SANTO (ex-USS *Marietta,* AN 82)	H 01	Commercial Iron Works, Portland, Oregon	1945

Displacement, tons: 650 standard; 855 full load
Dimensions, feet (metres): 168·5 oa × 33·8 × 11·7 *(51·4 × 10·2 × 3·3)*
Guns: 3—20 mm
Main engines: Bush-Sulzer diesel-electric; 1 shaft; 1 500 bhp = 12 knots
Complement: 46

Puerto Santo loaned from USA in Jan 1961 under MAP and converted into Hydrographic survey vessel and buoy tender by US Coast·Guard Yard, Curtis Bay, Maryland, in Feb 1962. All ships originally carried one 3-inch 50 cal gun. *Puerto du Nutrias* and *Puerto Miranda,* launched in 1944 were loaned to Venezuela in 1963 under MAP.

PUERTO SANTO

1970, Venezuelan Navy

2 SURVEY LAUNCHES

Name	No.	Builders	Commissioned
GABRIELA	P 119	Abeking and Rasmussen, Lemwerder	5 Feb 1974
LELY	P 121	Abeking and Rasmussen, Lemwerder	7 Feb 1974

Displacement, tons: 90
Dimensions, feet (metres): 88·6 × 18·4 × 4·9 *(27 × 5·6 × 1·5)*
Main engines: 2 diesels; 2 300 hp = 20 knots
Complement: 16

Lely laid down 28 May 1973, launched 12 Dec 1973 and *Gabriela* laid down 10 Mar 1973, launched 29 Nov 1973.

TUGS

1 OCEAN TUG

Name	No.	Builders	Commissioned
FELIPE LARRAZABAL (ex-USS *Utina,* ATF 163)	R 21	—	—

Displacement, tons: 1 235 standard; 1 675 full load
Dimensions, feet (metres): 205 oa × 38·5 × 15·5 *(61·7 × 11·6 × 4·7)*
Gun: 1—3 in 50 cal
Main engines: Diesel-electric; 3 000 bhp; 1 shaft
Speed, knots: 15
Complement: 85

Transferred 3 Sept 1972. This is the third tug of this name. The first (ex-USS *Discoverer*) was deleted in 1962. The second (ex-USS *Tolowa,* ATF 116) was deleted in 1972 after damage when grounded.

4 HARBOUR TUGS

C 139   **C 140**   **C 141**   **C 142**

Built by IADIAN, Puerto Cabello. 2 Werkspoor diesels; 2 shafts; 1 600 bhp. Ordered in 1973—C 139 launched in 1974 for completion 1975, other three completed 1976.

1 HARBOUR TUG

FERNANDO GOMEZ (ex-USS *Dudley,* YTM 744) R 12

Displacement, tons: 161
Dimensions, feet (metres): 80 × 19 × 8 *(24·5 × 5·8 × 2·5)*
Main engines: Clark diesel; 6-cyl, 315 rpm; 380 bhp = 15 knots
Complement: 10

1 HARBOUR TUG

GENERAL JOSE FELIX RIBAS (ex-USS *Oswegatchie,* YTM 778, ex-YTB 515) R 13

Large harbour tug of 450 tons. Transferred on 4 June 1965 at San Diego, Calif.

2 Ex-US MEDIUM HARBOUR TUGS

FABIO GALLIPOLI (ex-USS *Wannalancet* YTM 385) R 14
DIANA III (ex-USS *Sassacus* YTM 193)

Leased to Venezuela in Aug 1965.

5 Ex-US SMALL HARBOUR TUGS

80 feet long, leased in Jan 1963.

FLOATING DOCK

DF 1 (ex-USS *ARD 13)*

Of 3 000 tons and built of steel. Transferred on loan to Venezuela in Feb 1962.

Ex-US YR 48 (Floating Workshop) transferred 1965.

VIETNAM

Administration

Commander in Chief of the Navy: Rear Admiral Ta Xuan Thu

Strength of the Fleet

It is impossible to give an accurate estimate of this fleet—the details following refer to the known classes in 1975.

Personnel

1976: ?

CORVETTES

3 Ex-SOVIET "SO 1" CLASS

Displacement, tons: 215 light; 250 normal
Dimensions, feet (metres): 138·6 × 20 × 9·2 *(45·4 × 6·5 × 3)*
Guns: 4—25 mm (2 twin mountings)
A/S weapons: 4—5 barrelled MBU; 2 DCT
Range, miles: 1 100 at 13 knots
Main engines: 3 diesels; 6 000 hp = 29 knots
Complement: 30

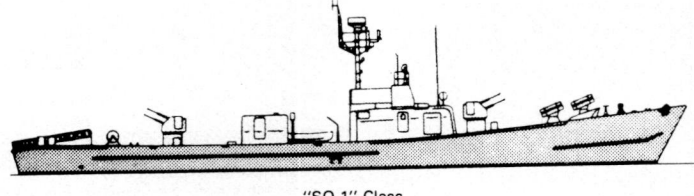

"SO 1" Class

Four of Soviet "SO 1" class were originally transferred to North Vietnam, two in 1960-61 and two in 1964-65, but one was sunk by US Navy aircraft on 1 Feb 1966.

LIGHT FORCES

2 Ex-SOVIET "KOMAR" CLASS
(FAST ATTACK CRAFT—MISSILE)

Displacement, tons: 70 standard; 80 full load
Dimensions, feet (metres): 83·7 × 19·8 × 5·0 *(27·4 × 6·5 × 1·6)*
Missiles: 2—SSN-2 launchers
Guns: 2—25 mm (twin forward)
Main engines: 4 diesels; 4 shafts; 4 800 hp = 40 knots
Range, miles: 400 at 30 knots

A sister ship was reported sunk on 19 Dec 1972.

6 Ex-SOVIET "P 4" CLASS (FAST ATTACK CRAFT—TORPEDO)

Displacement, tons: 25 standard
Dimensions, feet (metres): 62·7 × 11·6 × 5·6 *(20·5 × 3·8 × 1·8)*
Guns: 2 MG (1 twin)
Torpedo tubes: 2—18 in
Main engines: 2 diesels; 2 200 bhp = 50 knots

Approximately a dozen aluminium hulled motor torpedo boats were transferred from the Soviet Union in 1961 and 1964 and some from China. A number have been lost in action.

6 Ex-CHINESE "P 6" CLASS (FAST ATTACK CRAFT—TORPEDO)

Displacement, tons: 66 standard; 75 full load
Dimensions, feet (metres): 84·2 × 20 × 6 *(27·7 × 6·5 × 1·9)*
Guns: 4—25 mm (2 twin)
Torpedo tubes: 2—21 in (single)
Mines: 4
Main engines: 4 diesels; 4 800 bhp; 4 shafts = 43 knots
Range, miles: 450 at 30 knots
Complement: 25

Built in China and transferred in 1967. Some may have been lost in action.

"P 6" Class

8 Ex-CHINESE "SHANGHAI" CLASS
(FAST ATTACK CRAFT—GUN)

Displacement, tons: 120 full load
Dimensions, feet (metres): 128 × 18 × 5·5 *(39 × 5·5 × 1·7)*
Guns: 4—37 mm (2 twin mountings); 4—25 mm (twins)
Main engines: 4 diesels; 4 800 bhp = 30 knots
Complement: 25

Four were received from the People's Republic of China in May 1966.

"SHANGHAI II"   *1972, Aviation Fan*

14 Ex-CHINESE "SWATOW" CLASS
(FAST ATTACK CRAFT—GUN)

Displacement, tons: 80 full load
Dimensions, feet (metres): 83·5 × 19 × 6·5 *(27·4 × 6·2 × 2·1)*
Guns: 4—37 mm; 2—20 mm
A/S weapons: 8 depth charges
Main engines: 4 diesels; 4 800 bhp = 40 knots
Range, miles: 750 at 15 knots
Complement: 17

Approximately 30 "Swatow" class built in China were transferred in 1958, and 20 were delivered in 1964 to replace those lost in action. Pennant numbers run in a 600 series.

30 MOTOR LAUNCH TYPES (COASTAL PATROL CRAFT)

Some thirty motor launches were reported to have been incorporated into the North Vietnam Navy before May 1966, but not all are still in service.

4 PATROL TYPE (MSB)

Four vessels for sweeping, patrol and general purpose duties have been reported delivered in recent years.

10 GENERAL UTILITY TYPES (TENDERS)

Tenders and launches commandeered from private and commercial sources to serve the fleet and naval establishments.

AMPHIBIOUS FORCES

7 US LSM TYPE

Displacement, tons: 743 standard; 1 095 full load
Dimensions, feet (metres): 196·5 wl; 203·5 oa × 34·5 × 8·3 *(64·4; 66·7 × 11·3 × 2·7)*
Guns: 2—40 mm (1 twin mounting); 4—20 mm
Main engines: Diesels; 2 shafts; 2 800 bhp = 12 knots

One or two of these are reported to be out of operational service.

5 US LSSL TYPE

Displacement, tons: 250 standard; 430 full load
Dimensions, feet (metres): 153·0 wl; 158·5 oa × 23·7 × 5·7 *(46·7; 48·3 × 7·6 × 1·8)*
Guns: 1—3 in; 4—40 mm; 4—20 mm
Main engines: Diesels; 2 shafts; 1 800 bhp = 14 knots
Range, miles: 3 500 at 12 knots
Complement: 71

There are also reported to be five of the LCI/LSIL type, one of the LCT(6) type, and six of the LCT (7) type.

AUXILIARY PATROL CRAFT

There is a substantial number of armed junks and similarly adapted craft.

VIETNAM (Republic of)

The government of South Vietnam surrendered on 29 April 1975 following an all-out assault by North Vietnamese forces. A large number of Vietnamese naval units fled the country during the capitulation, carrying refugees to Hong Kong, Guam, and the Philippines. A few overcrowded and damaged ships were scuttled after transferring their passengers to other ships.

The Addenda to the 1975-1976 edition of *Jane's Fighting Ships* list most of the vessels that escaped from Vietnamese waters (page 658).

Most of the larger combatants as well as several amphibious and auxiliary ships reached the Philippines and have been acquired by the Philippine Navy for further service. See the Philippine section of this edition for a listing of those ships scheduled through spring 1976 for transfer.

The 1975-1976 edition contains an essentially complete listing of the South Vietnam Navy's order of battle as of April 1975.

VIRGIN ISLANDS

An area of some 40 islands, large and small.

Chief of Police:
Rex K. Jones

Base

Road Town

1 BROOKE MARINE PATROL CRAFT

VIRGIN CLIPPER

Displacement, tons: 15
Dimensions, feet (metres): 40 × 12 × 2 *(13·1 × 3·9 × 0·6)*
Gun: 1 MG
Main engines: 2 diesels; 370 hp = 22 knots
Complement: 4

Standard Brooke Marine patrol craft attached to the Royal Virgin Islands Police Force.

VIRGIN CLIPPER   1975, Virgin Islands Police Force

YEMEN—NORTH
(Arab Republic of)

Personnel

(a) 1976: 300 officers and men
(b) 3 years National Service

Base

Hodeida

Mercantile Marine

Lloyd's Register of Shipping:
3 vessels of 1 260 tons gross

4 Ex-SOVIET "P 4" CLASS (FAST ATTACK CRAFT—TORPEDO)

Displacement, tons: 25
Dimensions, feet (metres): 62·7 × 11·6 × 5·6 *(20·5 × 3·7 × 1·8)*
Guns: 2 MG
Torpedo tubes: 2—18 in
Main engines: 2 diesels; 2 shafts; 2 200 hp = 50 knots

Transferred by USSR in late 1960s.

4 Ex-SOVIET "POLUCHAT" CLASS (LARGE PATROL CRAFT)

Displacement, tons: 100 standard
Dimensions, feet (metres): 98·4 × 19 × 5·9 *(30 × 5·8 × 1·8)*
Guns: 2—25 mm

Transferred 1970.

Note: In addition a dozen smaller Patrol Craft and two small landing craft have been reported.

YEMEN—SOUTH
(People's Democratic Republic of)

Personnel	Base	Mercantile Marine
(a) 1976: 250 officers and men	Aden	*Lloyd's Register of Shipping:*
(b) Possibly 2 years National Service		13 vessels of 5 850 tons gross

CORVETTES

2 Ex-SOVIET "SO I" CLASS

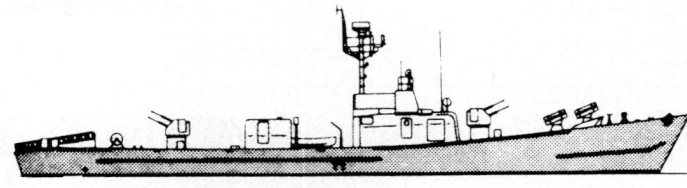

"SO 1" Class

Displacement, tons: 215 standard; 250 full load
Dimensions, feet (metres): 138·6 × 20·0 × 9·2 *(42·3 × 6·1 × 2·8)*
Guns: 4—25 mm (twins)
A/S weapons: 4—5 barrelled MBUs
Main engines: 3 diesels; 6 000 shp = 29 knots
Range, miles: 1 100 at 13 knots
Complement: 30

Transferred in late 1960's.

LIGHT FORCES

2 Ex-SOVIET "P 6" CLASS

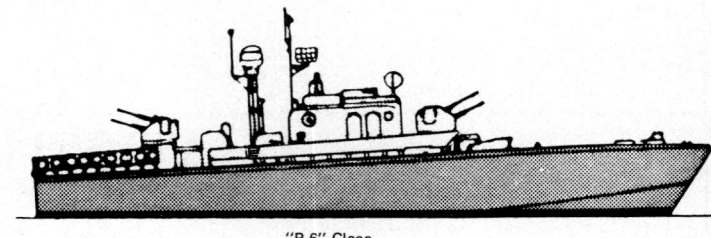

"P 6" Class

Displacement, tons: 66 standard; 75 full load
Dimensions, feet (metres): 84·2 × 20 × 6·0 *(25·7 × 6·1 × 1·8)*
Guns: 4—25 mm (twins)
Torpedo tubes: 2—21 in
Main engines: 4 diesels; 4 shafts; 4 800 bhp = 43 knots
Range, miles: 450 at 30 knots
Complement: 25

1 FAIREY MARINE "INTERCEPTOR" CLASS

Of 25 ft *(7·6 metres)* with a catamaran hull. Can carry eight 25-man liferafts or a platoon of troops. Twin 135 outboard motors = 30 knots. Delivered 27 July 1975.

3 FAIREY MARINE "SPEAR" CLASS

Dimensions, feet (metres): 29·8 × 9·2 × 2·6 *(9·1 × 2·8 × 0·8)*
Guns: 3—7·62 mm MG
Main engines: 2 diesels; 290 hp = 25 knots

Delivered 30 Sep 1975.

15 COASTAL PATROL CRAFT

Fifteen small diesel engined patrol boats were bought in the United Kingdom in 1970.

AMPHIBIOUS FORCES

2 Ex-SOVIET "POLNOCNY" CLASS (LCT)

"POLNOCNY" Class

Displacement, tons: 780 standard; 1 000 full load
Dimensions, feet (metres): 246 × 29·5 × 9·8 *(73 × 9 × 3)*
Guns: 2—30 mm (twin); 2—18 barrelled rocket launchers
Main engines: 2 diesels; 5 000 bhp = 18 knots

Can carry 6 tanks. Transferred in 1973.

1 Ex-BRITISH LCU(8)

3 Ex-SOVIET T4 (LCVPs)

Main engines: 3 diesels; 3 shafts; 3 300 bhp = 24 knots
Range, miles: 1 500 at 12 knots

INSHORE MINESWEEPERS

3 Ex-BRITISH "HAM" CLASS

JIBLA   SOCOTRA   ZINGAHAR

Displacement, tons: 120 standard; 160 full load
Dimensions, feet (metres): 106·5 oa × 21·2 × 5·5 *(32·4 × 6·5 × 1·7)*
Gun: 1—20 mm
Main engines: 2 Paxman diesels; 1 100 bhp = 14 knots
Oil fuel, tons: 15
Complement: 15 officers and men

The British inshore minesweepers *Bodenham* (renamed *Al Saqr*), *Blunham* (renamed *Al Dairak*) and *Elsenham* (renamed *Al Ghazala*) were transferred to the South Arabian Navy established by the Federal Government in 1967. All three were renamed after local islands in 1975.

YUGOSLAVIA

Administration

Assistant Secretary of State for National Defence for the Navy:
Admiral Branko Mamula

Headquarters Appointment

Commander-in-Chief of the Fleet:
Vice-Admiral Ivo Purisic

Diplomatic Representation

Defence Attaché in London:
Colonel M. Sutlan
Naval, Military and Air Attaché in Moscow:
Colonel S. Krivokapic
Naval, Military and Air Attaché in Washington:
Colonel Milan Mavric

Personnel

(a) 1976: 27 000 (2 500 officers and 24 500 men)
(b) 18 months National Service

Bases

3 Naval Zones with bases at Pula, Sibenik, Zadar and Gulf of Kotor complex.

Naval Air Arm

A number of Soviet-type Hormone helicopters now operate under naval command.

Mercantile Marine

Lloyd's Register of Shipping:
414 vessels of 1 873 482 tons gross

New Construction

As well as the new submarines, fast attack craft and LSTs it is reported that the first of a new class of surface ship, possibly of some 1 500 tons, is now in hand.

Strength of the Fleet

Type	Active	Building
Destroyer	1	—
Corvettes	3	—
Submarines—Patrol	5	?2
Fast Attack Craft—Missile	10	10
Fast Attack Craft—Gun	20	—
Fast Attack Craft—Torpedo	14	—
Large Patrol Craft	23	—
Minesweepers—Coastal	4	—
Minesweepers—Inshore	10	—
River Minesweepers	14	—
LSTs	—	?
LCTs	30+	—
Training Ships	2	—
Survey Ship	1	—
Despatch Vessels (HQ Ship)	2	—
Salvage Vessel	1	—
Tankers—Harbour	9	—
Transports	11	—
Tugs	21	—
Water Carriers	8	—
Yacht	1	—

DELETIONS

Frigates

1971 *Biokovo* (ex-*Aliseo*), *Triglav* (ex-*Indomito*)

Destroyers

1971 *Kotor* (ex-*Kempenfelt*, ex-*Valentine*)
Pula (ex-*Wager*)

Submarines

1971 *Sava* (ex-*Nautilo*)

Large Patrol Craft

1975 2 "Kraljevica" class to Bangladesh, 1 to Ethiopia

DESTROYER

1 "SPLIT" CLASS

Name	No.
SPLIT (ex-*Spalato*)	R 11

Builders	Laid down	Launched	Commissioned
Brodogradiliste, Rijeka (see note)	July 1939	1940	1959 (see note)

Displacement, tons: 2 400 standard; 3 000 full load
Length, feet (metres): 376·3 *(114·7)* pp; 393·7 *(120·0)* oa
Beam, feet (metres): 36·5 *(11·1)*
Draught, feet (metres): 12·3 *(3·8)*
Guns: 4—5 in *(127 mm)*; 12—40 mm
A/S weapons: 2 Squids, 6 DCT, 2 DC racks
Torpedo tubes: 5—21 in *(533 mm)*
Mines: Capacity 40
Main engines: Geared turbines; 2 shafts; 50 000 shp
Boilers: 2 watertube type
Speed, knots: 31·5
Oil fuel, tons: 590
Complement: 240

Built by Brodogradiliste "3 Maj", Rijeka. The original ship was laid down in July 1939 by Chantieres de Loire, Nantes, in 1939 at Split Shipyard. Completed on 4 July 1958. Ready for operational service in 1959. The original design provided for an armament of 5—5·5 inch guns, 10—40 mm guns and 6—21·7 inch torpedo tubes (tripled), but the plans were subsequently modified.

SPLIT

Commander Aldo Fraccaroli

CORVETTES

2 "MORNAR" CLASS

Name	No.
MORNAR	551
BORAC	552

Builders	Laid down	Launched	Commissioned
Yugoslavia	1957	1958	10 Sep 1959
Yugoslavia	1964	1965	1965

Displacement, tons: 330 standard; 430 full load
Dimensions, feet (metres): 170 pp; 174·8 × 23 × 6·6 *(51·8; 53·3 × 7 × 2)*
Guns: 2—3 in (single); 2—40 mm (single); 2—20 mm (single)
A/S weapons: 2 Hedgehogs; 2 DCT; 2 DC racks
Main engines: 4 SEMT-Pielstick diesels; 2 shafts; 3 240 bhp
Speed, knots: 20
Range, miles: 3 000 at 12 knots; 2 000 at 15 knots
Complement: 60

The design is an improved version of that of *Udarnik*.

BORAC

Commander Aldo Fraccaroli

Name	No.
UDARNIK (ex-*P 6*)	581

Displacement, tons: 325 standard; 400 full load
Dimensions, feet (metres): 170 pp; 174·8 oa × 23 × 6·6 *(51·8; 53·3 × 7 × 2)*
Guns: 2—40 mm; 2—20 mm
A/S weapons: 1 Hedgehog; 4 DCT; 2 DC racks
Main engines: 4 SEMT Pielstick diesels; 3 240 bhp = 18·7 knots
Range, miles: 3 000 at 12 knots; 2 000 at 15 knots
Complement: 62

USA offshore procurement.

1 FOUGUEUX TYPE

Builders	Laid down	Launched	Commissioned
F.C. Mediterranee (Le Havre)	1954	1 June 1954	1955

UDARNIK

1972, Yugoslavian Navy

SUBMARINES

2(?) NEW CONSTRUCTION

Displacement, tons: 964 dived
Length, feet (metres): 215·8 *(65·8)*
Torpedo tubes: 6—21 in *(533 mm)* (10 reloads or 20 mines)
Main machinery: Diesel-electric
Speed, knots: 16·1 dived
Complement: 35

A new class of diesel propelled submarine now under construction in Yugoslavia. Diving depth 1 000 ft.

3 "HEROJ" CLASS (PATROL SUBMARINES)

Name	No.
HEROJ	821
JUNAK	822
USKOK	823

Displacement, tons: 1 068 dived
Length, feet (metres): 210·0 *(64)*
Beam, feet (metres): 23·6 *(7·2)*
Draught, feet (metres): 16·4 *(5·0)*
Torpedo tubes: 6—21 in *(533 mm)* (bow)
Main machinery: Diesels; electric motors; 2 400 hp
Speed, knots: 16 surfaced; 10 dived
Complement: 55

Builders	Laid down	Launched	Commissioned
Uljanik Shipyard, Pula	1964	1967	1968
Uljanik Shipyard, Pula	1965	1968	1969
Uljanik Shipyard, Pula	1966	1969	1970

JUNAK

1972, S. and DE. Factory, Split

JUNAK

1972, S. and DE. Factory, Split

JUNAK

1972, S. and DE. Factory, Split

2 "SUTJESKA" CLASS (PATROL SUBMARINES)

Name	No.
NERETVA	812
SUTJESKA	811

Displacement, tons: 820 surfaced; 945 dived
Length, feet (metres): 196·8 *(60·0)*
Beam, feet (metres): 22·3 *(6·8)*
Draught, feet (metres): 16·1 *(4·9)*
Torpedo tubes: 6—21 in *(533 mm)* (bow)
Main machinery: Diesels; electric motors; 1 800 hp
Speed, knots: 14 surfaced; 9 dived
Range, miles: 4 800 at 8 knots
Complement: 38

The first class of submarines to be built in a Yugoslav yard.

Builders	Laid down	Launched	Commissioned
Uljanik Shipyard, Pula	1957	1959	1962
Uljanik Shipyard, Pula	1957	28 Sep 1958	16 Sep 1960

NERETVA

1969, Dr Giorgio Arra

"MALA" CLASS (2 MAN SUBMARINES)

Dimensions, feet (metres): 25 × 6 approx *(8·2 × 1·9 approx)*
Main motors: 1 electric motor; single screw
Complement: 2

This is a free-flood craft with the main motor, battery, navigation-pod and electronic equipment housed in separate watertight cylinders. Constructed of light aluminium it is fitted with fore- and after-hydroplanes, the tail being a conventional cruciform with a single rudder abaft the screw. Large perspex windows give a good all-round view.

"MALA" Class

1973, S. and DE. Factory, Split

LIGHT FORCES

10 NEW CONSTRUCTION
(FAST ATTACK CRAFT—MISSILE)

Displacement, tons: 240
Missiles: 2 launchers for Exocet
Dimensions, feet (metres): 147·6 × 27·6 × 15·4 *(45 × 8·4 × 4·7)*
Gun: 1 Bofors 57 mm
Main engines: 2 Rolls-Royce Proteus gas turbines; 11 600 shp; 2 MTU diesels; 7 200 shp
Speed, knots: 40
Complement: 30

Under construction in Yugoslavia. Similar to the Swedish "Spica" class.

Radar: Philips TAB in radome.

10 Ex-SOVIET "OSA" CLASS
(FAST ATTACK CRAFT—MISSILE)

M. ACEV	Z. JOVANOVIC	K. ROJC
V. BAGAT	N. MARTINOVIC	F. ROZMAN
P. DRAPSIN	J. MAZAR	V. SKORPIK
S. FILIPOVIC		

Displacement, tons: 165 standard; 200 full load
Dimensions, feet (metres): 128·7 × 25·1 × 5·9 *(39·3 × 7·7 × 1·8)*
Missile launchers: 4 for SSN-2 system
Guns: 4—30 mm (2 twin, 1 forward, 1 aft)
Main engines: 3 diesels; 13 000 bhp = 32 knots
Range, miles: 800 at 25 knots
Complement: 25

Acquired between 1965 and 1969. Pennant numbers from 301-310.

"OSA" Class

1972, Yugoslavian Navy

"OSA" Class

1972

14 Ex-SOVIET "SHERSHEN" CLASS
(FAST ATTACK CRAFT—TORPEDO)

211	213	215	217	219	221	223
212	214	216	218	220	222	224

Displacement, tons: 150 standard; 160 full load
Dimensions, feet (metres): 115·5 × 23·1 × 5·0 *(35·2 × 7 × 1·5)*
Guns: 4—31 mm (2 twin)
Torpedo tubes: 4—21 in (single)
A/S weapons: 12 DC
Main engines: 3 diesels; 3 shafts; 13 000 bhp = 41 knots
Complement: 16

Acquired between 1965 and 1971, some from the USSR whilst the remainder were built in Yugoslavia.

"SHERSHEN" Class

1972

20 "101" CLASS (FAST ATTACK CRAFT—GUN)

Displacement, tons: 55 standard; 60 full load
Dimensions, feet (metres): 69 pp; 78 oa × 21·3 × 7·8 (21; 23·8 × 6·5 × 2·4)
Guns: 1—40 mm; 4—12·7 mm MG
Torpedo tubes: 2—18 in
Main engines: 3 Packard motors; 3 shafts; 5 000 bhp = 36 knots
Complement: 14

Of the same class as US "Higgins". Built in Yugoslavia 1951-60. Some have had their torpedo tubes removed. Can be used as FAC-gun when they mount 2—40 mm and either 2 twin 50 cal MG or 2—20 mm (singles). Numbered between 102 and 201.

Transfers: 6 to Sudan in April 1970. 2 to Ethiopia in 1960 (deleted 1969).

"101" Class   *Yugoslavian Navy*

10 TYPE 131 (LARGE PATROL CRAFT)

131	133	135	137	139
132	134	136	138	140

Displacement, tons: 85 standard; 120 full load
Dimensions, feet (metres): 91·9 × 14·8 × 8·3 (28 × 4·5 × 2·5)
Guns: 2—20 mm
Main engines: 2 diesels; 900 bhp = 13 knots

Used for coastguard duties. Armament varies in individual boats. Built in Yugoslavia 1967-68.

Type 131   *1968, Yugoslavian Navy*

13 "KRALJEVICA" CLASS (LARGE PATROL CRAFT)

501, 503-4, 506-8, 510-12, 519-21 and 524

Displacement, tons: 195 standard; 250 full load
Dimensions, feet (metres): 134·5 × 20·7 × 7·2 (41 × 6·3 × 2·1)
Guns: 1—3 in; 1—40 mm; 4—20 mm
A/S weapons: DCs plus Mousetrap in some
Main engines: Diesels; 2 shafts; 3 300 bhp = 20 knots

Built in 1952-58.

Transfers: 6 to Indonesia in 1959; 2 to Sudan in 1969; 1 to Ethiopia in 1975; 2 to Bangladesh in 1975.

"KRALJEVICA" Class   *Yugoslavian Navy*

MINE WARFARE FORCES

4 "VUKOVKLANAC" CLASS (MINESWEEPERS—COASTAL)

Name	No.	Builders	Commissioned
BLITVENIC (ex-*Slobodni*)	M 153 (ex-*D 27*)	A. Normand, France	Sep 1957
PODGORA (ex-*Smeli*)	M 152 (ex-*D 26*)	A. Normand, France	Sep 1957
SNAZNI	M 161	Yugoslavia	—
VUKOYKLANAC (ex-*Hrabri*)	M 151 (ex-*D 25*)	A. Normand, France	Sep 1957

Displacement, tons: 365 standard; 424 full load
Dimensions, feet (metres): 140 pp; 152 oa × 28 × 8·2 (42·7; 46·4 × 8·6 × 2·5)
Guns: 2—20 mm
Main engines: SIGMA free piston generators; 2 shafts; 2 000 bhp = 15 knots
Oil fuel, tons: 48
Range, miles: 3 000 at 10 knots
Complement: 40

The first three were built as US "off-shore" orders, respectively. *Snazni* was built in Yugoslavia in 1960 with French assistance.

BLITVENIC (ex-*Slobodni*)   *1966, Yugoslavian Navy*

6 "M 117" CLASS (MINESWEEPERS—INSHORE)

M 117	M 118	M 119	M 121	M 122	M 123

Displacement, tons: 120 standard; 131 full load
Dimensions, feet (metres): 98·4 × 18 × 4·9 (30 × 5·5 × 1·5)
Guns: 1—40 mm; 2—12·7 mm MG
Main engines: 2 GM diesels; 1 000 bhp = 12 knots

Built in Yugoslav shipyards between 1966 and 1968.

M 121   *1968, Yugoslavian Navy*

4 BRITISH "HAM" CLASS (MINESWEEPERS—INSHORE)

M 141	M 142	M 143	M 144

Displacement, tons: 123 standard; 164 full load
Dimensions, feet (metres): 100 × 21·8 × 5·5 (32·4 × 6·3 × 1·7)
Gun: 1—40 mm or 1—20 mm
Main engines: 2 Paxman diesels; 1 100 bhp = 14 knots
Range, miles: 2 000 at 9 knots
Complement: 22

Built in Yugoslavia 1964-66 under the US Military Aid Programme. Of same design as British "Ham" class.

M 142   *1968, Yugoslavian Navy*

14 "M 301" CLASS (RIVER MINESWEEPERS)

M 301	M 303	M 305	M 307	M 309	M 311	M 313
M 302	M 304	M 306	M 308	M 310	M 312	M 314

Displacement, tons: 38
Gun: 1—20 mm
Main engines: Speed = 12 knots

All launched in 1951-53. Serve on the Danube.

AMPHIBIOUS FORCES

NEW CONSTRUCTION LST

Displacement, tons: 2 980
Dimensions, feet (metres): 334·6 × 46·6 × 10·2 *(102 × 14·2 × 3·1)*
Guns: 2—40 mm D70
Main engines: 2 diesels; 6 800 shp = 8 knots

A new class capable of carrying 6 tanks, a number of LCAs and fitted with a helicopter deck now being built in Yugoslavia.

25 DTM 230 TYPE (LCT)

DTM 230 onwards

Displacement, tons: 220 approx
Guns: 4—20 mm

Capable of carrying at least two, possibly three of the heaviest tanks. Unlike other tank landing craft in that the lower part of the bow drops to form a ramp down which the tanks go ashore, underneath the prow, which is rigid. It is reported that probably some 25 of these craft are operational. Ex-German.

DTM 230   *B. Hinchcliffe*

DTK 221 TYPE (LCT)

DTK 221

Displacement, tons: 410
Dimensions, feet (metres): 144·3 × 19·7 × 7 *(47·3 × 6·4 × 2·3)*
Guns: 1—20 mm; 2—12·7 mm
Speed, knots: 10
Complement: 15

Transfers: 2 to Sudan in 1969.

DTK 221   *Yugoslavian Navy*

2 Ex-ITALIAN MZ TYPE (LCT)

D 206 (ex-*MZ 713*)	D 219 (ex-*MZ 717*)

Displacement, tons: 225 and 239
Guns: 1—20 mm; 2 MG
Speed, knots: 11

Ex-Italian landing craft. Launched in 1942. Capable of carrying three tanks.

2 Ex-GERMAN TYPE (LCT)

D 203	D 204

Displacement, tons: 220
Guns: 1—3·4 in *(88 mm)*; 2—20 mm
Speed, knots: 10

Ex-German landing craft.

CATAMARAN TYPE (LCU)

Displacement, tons: 50 approx

A small craft consisting of two pontoons some feet apart, secured to each other by cross-girders on which stand the bridge and cabins, etc. This vessel appears to be capable of carrying one medium tank, to be put ashore by two bridge members which can be seen quite clearly, folded back on the deck. Total number unknown.

Catamaran type   *B. Hinchcliffe*

NEW CONSTRUCTION LCAs

Displacement, tons: 32
Dimensions, feet (metres): 70·2 × 15·1 × 2 *(21·4 × 4·6 × 0·6)*
Gun: 1—20 mm
Main engines: Diesels; 1 125 shp = 22 knots

A programme is under way for the construction of a considerable number of LCAs built of polyester and glass fibre. Probably to be carried in the new class of LSTs.

Note: A number of other amphibious craft of unknown types are also reported.

TRAINING SHIPS

1 "GALEB" CLASS

Name	No.	Builders	Commissioned
GALEB (ex-*Kuchuk*, ex-*Ramb III*)	M 11	Ansaldo, Genoa	1939

Displacement, tons: 5 182 standard
Measurement, tons: 3 667 gross
Length, feet (metres): 384·8 *(117·3)*
Beam, feet (metres): 51·2 *(15·6)*
Draught, feet (metres): 18·4 *(5·6)*
Main engines: 2 diesels; 2 shafts; 7 200 bhp
Speed, knots: 17

GALEB   *1972, Yugoslavian Navy*

Ex-Italian. Launched in 1938. Sunk as an auxiliary cruiser in 1944, refloated and reconstructed in 1952. Now training ship. Also Presidential Yacht. Former armament was four 3·5 inch, four 40 mm and 24—20 mm (six quadruple) guns. The guns were landed. Can act as minelayer.

JADRAN (ex-*Marco Polo*)

Displacement, tons: 720
Dimensions, feet (metres): 190 × 29·2 × 13·8 *(58 × 8·8 × 4·2)*
Sail area, sq ft (m²): 8 600 *(800)*
Main engines: 1 Linke-Hofman Diesel; 375 hp = 8 knots

Topsail schooner. Built in Italy. Launched in 1932. Accommodation for 150 Cadets.

DESPATCH VESSEL

Name	No.	Builders	Commissioned
JADRANKA (ex-*Bjeli Orao*)	—	C. R. dell Adriatico, San Marco, Trieste	Oct 1939

Displacement, tons: 567 standard; 660 full load
Dimensions, feet (metres): 213·2 oa × 26·5 × 9·3 *(60·5 × 7·9 × 2·8)*
Guns: 2—40 mm; 2 MG
Main engines: 2 Sulzer diesels; 1 900 bhp = 18 knots

JADRANKA   *1970, Yugoslavian Navy*

Launched on 3 June 1939. Was used as Admiralty and Presidential yacht. While in Italian hands was named *Alba*, for some days only, then *Zagaria*.

HQ SHIP

VIS

Built in 1956.

SURVEY SHIP

Name	No.	Builders	Commissioned
A. MOHOROVICIC	PH 33	Gdansk Shipyard, Poland	1972

Displacement, tons: 1 475
Dimensions, feet (metres): 240 × 36·3 × 10 *(73·2 × 11·1 × 3·1)*
Main engines: 2 diesels; = 17 knots
Complement: 37

A. MOHOROVICIC   *1972, Yugoslavian Navy*

Built in 1971 at the shipyard in Gdansk, Poland, and added to the Yugoslav Navy List in 1972. Of similar class to Soviet "Moma" class.

SALVAGE VESSEL

Name	No.	Builders	Commissioned
SPASILAC	PS 11	Howaldtswerke, Kiel	1930

Displacement, tons: 740
Dimensions, feet (metres): 174 × 26·2 × 13 *(52·5 × 7·9 × 4)*
Main engines: Triple expansion; 2 000 hp = 15 knots

Launched in 1929. While in Italian hands she was called *Instangabile*.

SPASILAC   *1966, Yugoslavian Navy*

TANKERS

2 PN 24 TYPE (HARBOUR TANKERS)

PN 24   **PN 25**

Built at Split in mid-1950s.

4 PN 13 TYPE (HARBOUR TANKERS)

PN 13 (ex-*Lovcen*)   **PN 14**   **PN 15**   **PN 16**

Displacement, tons: 695 standard
Speed, knots: 8·5

PN 13 (ex-*Lovcen*) was launched in 1932. PN 17 was transferred to the Sudanese Navy in 1969.

1 HARBOUR TANKER

PO 55

Of 600 tons.

2 "KIT" CLASS (HARBOUR TANKERS)

KIT   **ULJESURA**

Of 250 tons.

TRANSPORTS

5 PT 71 TYPE

PT 71—PT 75

Displacement, tons: 310 standard; 428 full load
Dimensions, feet (metres): 141·5 × 22·2 × 16 *(46·4 × 7·2 × 5·2)*
Main engines: 300 bhp = 7 knots

Built at Split and Sibenik in 1953

6 PT 61 TYPE

PT 61—6 (?)

Possibly up to 8 in service. Built at Pula and Sibenik 1951-54.

TUGS

LR 11 (ex-*Basiluzzo*)

Displacement, tons: 108
Main engines: 130 hp = 8 knots

Former Italian tug. Launched in 1915.

PR 51 (ex-*Porto Conte*)

Displacement, tons: 226

Former Italian tug. Launched in 1936.

PR 52 (ex-*San Remo*)

Displacement, tons: 170
Main engines: 350 hp = 9 knots

Former Italian tug and multi-purpose vessel. Launched in 1937.

PR 54 (ex-*Ustrajni*)

Displacement, tons: 160
Main engines: 250 hp = 9 knots

Launched in 1917.

PR 55 (ex-*Snazi*)

Displacement, tons: 100
Main engines: 300 hp = 10 knots

Launched in 1917.

PR 58 (ex-*Molara*)

Displacement, tons: 118
Main engines: 250 hp = 8 knots

Former Italian tug. Launched in 1937.

There are also in service PP1 (ex-*Marljivi*) of 130 tons, LR 67-74 new construction of 130 tons, RRM 11, BM 29, LD 21, LP 21 and RM 27—the last four being small mooring tugs—PR 28 and PR 37.

WATER CARRIERS

PV 6   **PV 11**   **PV 12**
PT 12   **PO 54**   **+3**

Of various types and of modern construction.

YACHT

ISTRANKA (ex-*Villa*, ex-*Dalmata*)

Displacement, tons: 260
Dimensions, feet (metres): 132·5 × 16·7 × 6·7 *(40·4 × 5·1 × 2·1)*
Main engines: Diesel; 235 hp = 12 knots

Built in 1896.

ZAIRE

Personnel	Bases
(a) 1976: 200 officers and men	Matadi
(b) Voluntary service	Lake Tanganyika

LIGHT FORCES

1 COASTAL PATROL CRAFT

ZAIRE (ex-*President Mobuto*, ex-*General Olsen*, ex-*Congo*)

A 70 ton craft, the first in this naval force.

3 Ex-KOREAN (N) "P 4" CLASS

Displacement, tons: 22
Dimensions, feet (metres): 62·7 × 11·6 × 5·6 *(19·1 × 3·5 × 1·7)*
Guns: 2—14·7 mm MG
Torpedo tubes: 2—18 in
Main engines: 2 diesels; 2 shafts; 2 200 hp = 50 knots
Complement: 12

Transferred 1974.

6 SEWART TYPE (COASTAL PATROL CRAFT)

Displacement, tons: 33
Length, feet (metres): 65 *(19·8)*
Guns: 6 MG
Main engines: 2 GM diesels = 26 knots
Range, miles: 1 000 at 18 knots

Purchased in USA in 1971.

12 COASTAL PATROL CRAFT

Ordered in 1974 in France.

1 COASTAL PATROL CRAFT

Of 18 tons, 25 knots and mounting 3 MG. Purchased in USA in 1968.

3 Ex-US COASTAL PATROL CRAFT

Purchased in 1974.

4 COASTAL PATROL CRAFT

Reported as transferred by China in late 1960s.

ZANZIBAR

Although part of the United Republic of Tanzania, Zanzibar retains a separate Executive and
Legislature, the President of Zanzibar being First Vice-President of Tanzania.

4 VOSPER THORNYCROFT 75 ft TYPE

Displacement, tons: 70
Dimensions, feet (metres): 75 × 19·5 × 8 *(22·9 × 6·0 × 1·5)*
Guns: 2—20 mm
Main engines: 2 diesels; 1 840 hp
Speed, knots: 24·5
Range, miles: 800 at 20 knots
Complement: 11

This is one of the first orders for the new Keith Nelson 75 ft craft. First pair delivered 6 July 1973,
second pair 1974.

75 ft Type   *1974, Vosper Thornycroft*

NAVAL AIRCRAFT

NAVAL AIRCRAFT

Notes: (a) For technical details see under country of origin   A Carrier based   B Helicopters   C Land based

Country/Manufacturer	Strength	Role	Class (See note)	Country of Origin	Max Speed	Service Ceiling	Range	Max Endurance	T/O Weight
ARGENTINA									
McDonnell Douglas									
Skyhawk (A-4Q)	15	Attack Bomber F/W	A	USA	(a)				
Grumman									
Tracker (S-2A)	6	Attack A/S, F/W	A	USA					
Grumman									
Albatross (HU-16B)	3	Amphibian, Search & Rescue, F/W	C	USA					
Aerospatiale									
Alouette III	4	Helicopter	B	France					
Sikorsky									
Sea King (S-61D-4)	4	Helicopter	B	USA					
Sikorsky									
S-61NR	2	Helicopter	B	USA					
Aermacchi									
MB 326GB	8	Trainer & F/W Light Attack	C	Italy					
Lockheed									
Neptune (P-2H)	6	Maritime F/W Patrol Bomber	C	USA					
AUSTRALIA									
McDonnell Douglas									
Skyhawk (A-4G)	14	Attack F/W	A	USA	(Plus 3 TA-4G trainers)				
Lockheed									
Orion (P-3B)	9	A/S Recce F/W	C	USA	(operated by Air Force)				
Lockheed									
Neptune (SP-2H)	10	A/S Recce F/W	C	USA	(operated by Air Force; to be replaced by P-3Cs)				
Grumman									
Tracker (S-2E)	13	A/S F/W	A	USA					
Bell									
Iroquois (UH-1D)	7	Helicopter	B	USA					
Westland									
Wessex (HAS.31B)	20	Helicopter	B	UK					
Westland									
Sea King (HAS 50)	9	Helicopter	B	UK					
BELGIUM									
Aerospatiale									
Alouette III	3	Coast Guard Helicopter	B	France					
Westland									
Sea King Mk 48	5	Helicopter	B	UK	(operated by Air Force) .				
BRAZIL									
Grumman									
Tracker (S-2E)	8	A/S F/W	A	USA	(operated by Air Force)				
Lockheed									
Neptune (P-2E)	10	Maritime F/W Patrol Bomber	C	USA	(operated by Air Force)				
Bell									
47G-2 & 47 J	2	Helicopter	B	USA					
Bell									
JetRanger II	18	Helicopter	B	USA					
Fairchild									
Hiller (FH-1100)	4	Helicopter	B	USA					
Hughes									
269/300	11	Helicopter	B	USA					
Sikorsky									
Sea King (SH-3D)	3	Helicopter	B	USA					
Sikorsky									
S.58	4	Helicopter	B	USA					
Westland									
Wasp	3	A/S Helicopter	B	UK					
Westland									
Whirlwind	5	Helicopter	B	UK					
Westland									
Lynx	9	A/S Helicopter	A	UK/France	Carried on new destroyers and operated by the Air Force				
CANADA									
Sikorsky									
CHSS-2 Sea King (CH-124)	35	Helicopter	B	USA					
Canadair									
Argus (CP-107)	13 Mk 1 20 Mk 2	F/W Maritime Reconnaissance	C	Canada	20,000 ft 274 knots	20,000 ft plus (6 100 m plus)	5 124 n. miles at 194 knots		148 000 lb (67 130 kg)
Canadair									
CL-215		F/W Amphibian	C	Canada	157 knots (cruising)	—	1 220 n. miles		Land 43 500 lb (19 731 kg) Sea 37 700 lb (17 100 kg)
Grumman									
CS2F-3 Tracker (CP-121)	40	F/W A/S	C	USA					
CHILE									
Bell									
JetRanger	4	Helicopter	B	USA					
Grumman									
Albatross (HU-16B)	5	Maritime F/W Amphibian	C	USA					
Beech									
C-45	5	F/W Transport	C	USA					
Douglas									
C-47	5	F/W Transport	C	USA					
Lockheed									
Neptune (SP-2E)	4	Maritime Recce F/W	C	USA					

Wing span Rotor diameter	Length	Height	Power Plant	Armament Capacity	Remarks
142 ft 3·5 in (43·38 m)	128 ft 9·5 in (39·25 m)	36 ft 8·5 in (11·19 m)	4 × Wright R-3350 EA-1 turbo-compound radial piston engines 3 700 hp each	15 600 lb of weapons (7 075 kg)	In service with 4 Sqdns. (Nos. 404, 405, 407 and 415)
93 ft 10 in (28·6 m)	65 ft (19·82 m)	29 ft 6 in (8·98 m)	2 × 2 100 hp Pratt & Whitney R-2800 radial piston engines		Used by Greek and Spanish Air Forces for search and rescue (Not by Canada)

Country/Manufacturer	Strength	Role	Class (See note)	Country of Origin	Max Speed	Service Ceiling	Range	Max Endurance	T/O Weight
CHINA (PEOPLE'S REPUBLIC)									
Ilyushin									
Il-28T	100	Torpedo Bomber	C	USSR (built in China)					
DENMARK									
Aerospatiale									
Alouette III	8	Helicopter	B	France	Flown from frigates				
FRANCE									
Breguet									
Br 1050 Alizé	50	A/S F/W	A	France	10 000 ft (3 050 m) 254 knots	26 250 ft (8 000 m)	Normal 1 350 n. miles	7 hrs 40 min	18 100 lb (8 200 kg)
Vought									
Crusader F-8E(FN)	36	F/W Interceptor	A	USA					
Dassault									
Etendard IV-M, IV-P	42	F/W Attack Recce	A	France	36 000 ft (11 000 m) Mach 1·02	49 000 ft (15 000 m)	at 442 knots (820 km/h) with ext tanks 1 520 n. miles		22 650 lb (10 275 kg)
Dassault									
Super Etendard	36 ordered	F/W Fighter	A	France	36 000 ft (11 000 m) Mach 1		with anti-ship missile 350 n. miles		25 350 lb (11 500 kg)
Aerospatiale									
Super Frelon SA321G	22	A/S and Minesweeping Helicopter	B	France	at S/L 148 knots	10 325 ft (3 150 m)	at S/L 442 n. miles		28 660 lb (13 000 kg)
Aerospatiale									
Alouette III	20	Gen-Purpose Helicopter	B	France	At S/L 113 knots	10 500 ft (3 200 m)	290 n. miles		4 840 lb (2 200 kg)
Breguet									
Br 1150 Atlantic	38	Long-Range F/W Maritime Patrol	C	France	High Altitude 355 knots	32 800 ft (10 000 m)	4 854 n. miles	At 169 knots 18 hours	95 900 lb (43 500 kg)
Aerospatiale									
N262	15	F/W Transport	C	France	208 knots	23 500 ft (7 160 m)	With max payload 525 n. miles		23 370 lb (10 600 kg)
Lockheed									
Neptune (P-2H)	23	F/W Maritime Patrol	C	USA					
GERMANY (FEDERAL REPUBLIC)									
Westland									
Sea King (HAS Mk 41)	22	Helicopter	B	UK					
Breguet									
Br 1150 Atlantic	20	F/W Maritime Recce	C	France					
Dornier									
Do 28D-2 Skyservant	20	F/W Gen Duty	C	Germany	10 000 ft (3 050 m) 175 knots	25 200 ft (7 680 m)	1 090 n. miles		8 470 lb (3 842 kg)
Lockheed									
Starfighter (F-104G)	120	F/W Fighter	C	USA (Built in Germany)	To be replaced by MRCA				
INDIA									
Ilyushin									
Il-38 ("May")	3	F/W Maritime Recce	C	USSR					
Breguet									
Br 1050 Alizé	5	F/W A/S	A	France					
Armstrong Whitworth									
Sea Hawk	25	F/W Fighter-Bomber	A	UK	Max cruise speed at S/L 512 knots				16 200 lb (7 355 kg)
Aerospatiale									
Alouette III	18	Helicopter	B	France					
Westland									
Sea King Mk 42	12	A/S Helicopter	B	UK					
INDONESIA									
Aerospatiale									
Alouette III	3	Helicopter	B	France					
Grumman									
Albatross (HU-16A)	5	F/W Maritime Patrol Amphibian	C	USA					
Rockwell									
OV-IOF Bronco	16	Counter-Insurgency F/W	C	USA					
ITALY									
Agusta-Sikorsky									
SH-3D	24	Helicopter	B	USA (built in Italy)					
Agusta-Bell									
204AS	30	A/S Helicopter	B	Italy	At S/L 104 knots	4 500 ft (1 370 m)	340 n. miles		9 500 lb (4 310 kg)
Agusta-Bell									
212 ASW	28	A/S Helicopter	B	Italy	At S/L 106 knots		323 n. miles	3 hrs	11 196 lb (5 079 kg)
Breguet									
Br 1150 Atlantic	18	F/W Long-Range Maritime	C	France	Operated by Air Force				
Grumman									
Tracker (S-2F)	12	F/W ASW	C	USA					
JAPAN									
Sikorsky									
Sea King (SH-3A)	80	A/S Helicopter	B	USA (built in Japan)					
Kawasaki-Boeing									
KV 107/II-3	12	Mine Countermeasures Helicopter	B	Japan USA					
Grumman									
Tracker (S-2A)	33	F/W A/S	C	USA					

Wing span Rotor diameter	Length	Height	Power Plant	Armament Capacity	Remarks
51 ft 2 in (15·6 m)	45 ft 6 in (13·86 m)	16 ft 5 in (5·00 m)	1 × 2 100 eshp Rolls-Royce Dart R.Da 21 turboprop	Depth charges, torpedo, rockets, AS.12 missiles	
					Those embarked on *Clemenceau* and *Foch* are fitted to carry 2 Matra R530 missiles each
31 ft 6 in (9·60 m)	47 ft 3 in (14·40 m)	14 ft 1 in (4·30 m)	1 × SNECMA Atar 8B turbojet	2 × 30 mm cannon, 3 000 lb *(1,360 kg)* rockets, bombs, Sidewinder missiles	
31 ft 6 in (9·60 m)	46 ft 11·5 in (14·31 m)	12 ft 8 in (3·85 m)	1 × SNECMA Atar 8K-50 turbojet	2 × 30 mm cannon, rockets, bombs, missiles	Deliveries planned to begin in 1977
62 ft 0 in (18·90 m)	Inc tail rotor 65 ft 10·75 in (20·08 m)	21 ft 10·25 in (6·66 m)	3 × 1 550 shp Turbomeca Turmo III C6 turboshaft engines	Four homing torpedoes, search radar, sonar. Provision for 27 passengers	
36 ft 1·75 in (11·02 m)	42 ft 1·5 in (12·84 m)	9 ft 10 in (3·00 m)	1 × 570 shp Turbomeca Artouste IIIB turboshaft engine	Provision for gun, missiles, torpedoes, MAD equipment	
119 ft 1 in (36·3 m)	104 ft 2 in (31·75 m)	37 ft 2 in (11·33 m)	2 × 6 106 ehp R.R. Tyne R.Ty.20 Mk 21 turboprop engines	Bombs, depth charges, homing torpedoes, rockets or ASMs	
71 ft 10 in (21·90 m)	63 ft 3 in (19·28 m)	20 ft 4 in (6·21 m)	2 × 1 080 hp Turbomeca Bastan VIC turboprop engines	Seating for 29	Used by French Navy as light transports and aircrew trainers
51 ft 0·25 in (15·55 m)	37 ft 5·25 in (11·41 m)	12 ft 9·5 in (3·90 m)	2 × 380 hp Lycoming IGSO-540-A1E piston engines	Seating for 12 or 13	
39 ft (11·89 m)	39 ft 8 in (12·09 m)	8 ft 8 in (2·64 m)	1 × R.R. Nene 103 turbojet	Cannon, bombs or rockets	Operational in carrier *Vikrant*
48 ft (14·63 m)	57 ft (17·37 m)		1 × 1 290 shp General Electric T58-GE-3 turboshaft	2 × Mk 44 torpedoes, dipping sonar	
48 ft (14·63 m)	57 ft 1 in (17·40 m)	14 ft 5 in (4·40 m)	1 × 1 290 shp Pratt & Whitney (Canada) PT6T-6 Turbo Twin Pac twin turboshaft	2 × Mk 44 or Mk 46 torpedoes, depth charges, missiles, dipping sonar	

Country/ Manufacturer	Strength	Role	Class (See note)	Country of Origin	Max Speed	Service Ceiling	Range	Max Endurance	T/O Weight
JAPAN—continued									
Kawasaki-Lockheed									
P-2J	83	F/W A/S and Maritime Patrol Bomber	C	Japan	Max cruising 217 knots	30 000 ft (9 150 m)	With max fuel 2 400 n. miles		75 000 lb (34 019 kg)
Lockheed									
Neptune (P-2H)	45	F/W A/S and Maritime Patrol Bomber	C	USA					
Shin Meiwa									
PS-1	22	A/S F/W Flying-Boat	C	Japan	Max level at 5 000 ft 295 knots	29 500 ft (9 000 m)	1 169 n. miles	15 hrs	94 800 lb (43 000 kg)
MEXICO									
Aerospatiale									
Alouette III	4	Helicopter	B	France					
Bell									
47-G	4	Helicopter	B	USA					
Bell									
47-J	1	Helicopter	B	USA					
Catalina									
PBY-5	5	F/W	C	USA					
NETHERLANDS									
Agusta-Bell									
204B A/S	7	Helicopter	B	Italy					
Westland									
Wasp (HAS Mk 1)	11	Helicopter	B	UK					
Breguet									
Br 1150 Atlantic	8	F/W A/S	C	France					
Lockheed									
Neptune (SP-2H)	14	F/W M.P.	C	USA					
NEW ZEALAND									
Westland									
Wasp (HAS Mk 1)	2	A/S Helicopter	B	UK					
Lockheed									
Orion (P-3B)	5	M.P. F/W	C	USA	Operated by R.N.Z.A.F.				
NORWAY									
Westland									
Sea King (Mk 43)	10	ASR. Helicopter	B.	UK	Operated by Norwegian Air Force				
Lockheed									
Orion (P-3B)	5	M.P. F/W	C	USA	Operated by Norwegian Air Force				
PAKISTAN									
Breguet									
Br 1150 Atlantic	3	F/W A/S	C	France					
Westland									
Sea King (Mk 45)	6	A/S Helicopter	B	UK					
PERU									
Grumman									
Tracker (S-2A)	9	F/W A/S	C	USA					
Bell									
UH-1D/H	13	Helicopter	B	USA					
Bell									
JetRanger	10	Helicopter	B	USA					
Aerospatiale									
Alouette III	2	Helicopter	B	France					
Bell									
47G	5	Helicopter	B	USA					
Grumman									
Albatross (HU-16B)	4	MP F/W	C	USA	Operated by Peruvian Air Force				
POLAND									
Mil									
Mi-4 ("Hound")	?	A/S Helicopter	B	USSR					
Ilyushin									
Il-28 ("Beagle")	10	F/W Recce & ECM	C	USSR					
PORTUGAL									
Lockheed									
Neptune (SP-2E)	6	LRMP F/W	C	USA	Operated by Portuguese Air Force				
SOUTH AFRICA									
Westland									
Wasp (HAS Mk 1)	11	A/S Helicopter	B	UK	Embarked in Destroyers: Jan Van Riebeeck; Simon van der Stel Embarked in Frigates: President Kruger; President Pretorius; President Steyn				
Avro									
Shackleton MR.3	7	LRMP F/W	C	UK	Operated by S.A.A.F.				
SPAIN									
Hawker Siddeley									
Harrier (AV-8A)	6	V/STOL F/W Strike/Recce	A	UK	Supplied via USA for operation from carrier Dedalo				
Agusta-Bell									
212AS	7	A/S Helicopter	B	Italy					
Agusta-Bell									
204AS	4	Search & Rescue Helicopter	B	Italy					
Bell									
AH-1G HueyCobra	20	Armed Helicopter	B	USA					
Sikorsky									
Sea King (SH-3D)	24	A/S Helicopter	B	USA					
Lockheed									
Orion (P-3A)	3	M.P. F/W	C	USA	Operated by Spanish Air Force				
Grumman									
Albatross (HU-16B)	11	F/W M.P. Amphibian	C	USA	Operated by Spanish Air Force				
Hughes									
500 M	12	A/S Helicopter	B	USA					

Wing span Rotor diameter	Length	Height	Power Plant	Armament Capacity	Remarks
97 ft 8·5 in (29·78 m)	95 ft 10·75 in (29·23 m)	29 ft 3·5 in (8·93 m)	2 General Electric T64-IHI/10 turboprop engines and two pod-mounted J3-IHI-7C turbojets	Classified; includes radar smoke detector and MAD	
108 ft 8·75 in (33·14 m)	109 ft 11 in (33·50 m)	31 ft 10·5 in (9·72 m)	4 Ishikawajima-built General Electric T64-IHI-10 turboprop engines each 3 060 ehp	Torpedoes, air-to-surface rockets, bombs, radar, MAD, sonobuoys	Also 3 US-1 search and rescue amphibians

Country/ Manufacturer	Strength	Role	Class (See note)	Country of Origin	Max Speed	Service Ceiling	Range	Max Endurance	T/O Weight
SWEDEN									
Agusta-Bell									
206A JetRanger	10	Search and rescue Helicopter	B	USA					
Boeing Vertol-Kawasaki									
107-II	20	A/S & Gen Duty Helicopter	B	USA Japan					
TURKEY									
Agusta-Bell									
204AS	3	A/S Helicopter	B	Italy					
Grumman									
Tracker (S-2A/E)	20	F/W A/S Attack	C	USA					
UNITED KINGDOM									
Hawker Siddeley									
Buccaneer S Mk 2	16	All weather Strike and Recce F/W	A	UK	at 200 ft Mach 0·85 approx		Tactical radius 1 000 n. miles	Strike range approx 2 000 n. miles	62 000 lb (28 123 kg)
Westland (Fairey)									
Gannet AEW Mk 3	12	AEW F/W	A	UK	220 knots approx		Approx 695 nm	5-6 hours at 120 knots	
Hawker Siddeley									
Harrier (AV-8A)	(USMC)	V/STOL F/W Strike & Recce	A	UK	Over 640 knots	over 50 000 ft (15 240 m)	over 3 000 n. miles with one flight refuelling		over 25 000 lb (11 339 kg)
McDonnell Douglas									
Phantom F.G.1 (F-4K)	16	Interceptor and Ground Attack F/W	A	USA	Mach 2+		Ferry Range 2 000 n. miles		
Westland/Aerospatiale									
Gazelle HT.2	30	Helicopter Trainer	B	UK France	At Sea Level 167 knots	16 400 ft (5 000 m)	At S/L with full fuel 361 n. miles		3 970 lb (1 800 kg)
Westland									
Lynx (HAS.2)	30 ordered	Helicopter Search and Strike	B	UK	180 knots		Mission radius 154 n. miles		9 500 lb (4 309 kg)
Westland									
Sea King (HAS.1 and HAS.2)	69	Helicopter A/S	B	UK	Normal operating 112 knots	10 000 ft (3 050 m)	664 n. miles with normal fuel		21 000 lb (9 525 kg)
Westland									
Wasp (HAS.1)	80	G/P and A/S Helicopter	B	UK	At S/L 104 knots		approx 234 n. miles		5 600 lb (2 495 kg)
Westland									
Wessex (HAS.1/3) & (HU.5)	150	A/S, Assault and GP Helicopter	B	UK	At S/L 115 knots	(HAS.1) 14 000 ft (4 300 m)	Max fuel 10% reserve 415 n. miles		13 500 lb (6 120 kg)
Westland									
Whirlwind (HAR.9)	15	Rescue and GP Helicopter	B	UK	92 knots	Service 16 000 ft (5 060 m)	260 n. miles		8 000 lb (3 630 kg)
Hawker Siddeley									
Nimrod (MR.1)	46	Long Range Maritime Recce F/W	C	UK	500 knots		Ferry 4 500-5 000 n. miles	12 hrs (typical)	177 500 lb to 192 000 lb (80 510-87 090 kg)
Avro									
Shackleton (MR.3)	(SAAF)	L R M Recce AEW F/W	C	UK	Level 152 knots		2 515 n. miles		
Hawker Siddeley (Avro)									
Shackleton (AEW.2)	12	Airborne Early Warning F/W	C	UK	226 knots			10 hrs	98 000 lb (44 452 kg)
UNITED STATES OF AMERICA									
Rockwell International									
Bronco OV-10A	114 built	Multi-purpose Counter Insurgency F/W	C	USA	At S/L W/O Weapons 244 knots		Ferry with aux. fuel 1 240 n.m.	Combat radius with max weapon load 198 n. miles	14 466 lb (6 563 kg)
Vought									
A-7E Corsair II	950 built	Single-seat Attack Aircraft F/W	A	USA	At S/L 562 knots		Ferry 2 800 n. miles		42 000 lb (19 050 kg)
F-8H Crusader	Total all versions 200	Single-seat Fighter F/W	A	USA	F-8A, B, C 868 knots + F-8D, E, H & J nearly Mach 2		F-8A 520 n. miles		34 000 lb (15 420 kg)
Grumman									
C-2A Greyhound	25	COD Transport F/W	A	USA	At 11 000 ft (3 450 m) 306 knots		At cruising speed and height 1 432 n. miles		54 830 lb (24 870 kg)
Grumman									
Hawkeye E-2B/C	90	AEW F/W	A	USA	325 knots	30 800 ft (9 390 m)	Ferry 1 394 n. miles		51 569 lb (23 391 kg)
Grumman									
A-6E Intruder	Total of 546 built	Strike and Recce F/W	A	USA	At S/L 563 knots	44 600 ft (13 600 m)	1 880 n. miles		60 400 lb (27 400 kg)
McDonnell Douglas									
F-4B Phantom II	Total built 1 189	All Weather Fighter F/W	A	USA	Mach 2·5	Combat 71 000 ft (21,640 m)	Ferry 1 997 n. miles		54 600 lb (24 765 kg)
McDonnell Douglas									
A-4M Skyhawk	500	Attack Bomber F/W	A	USA	With 4 000 lb of bombs 560 knots		Ferry 1 785 n. miles		24 500 lb (11 113 kg)
McDonnell Douglas									
EA-3B Skywarrior	60	Electronic Counter-measure F/W	A	USA	At 10 000 ft 530 knots	45 000 ft (13 780 km)	Normal 2 520 n. miles		73 000 lb (33 112 kg)
Grumman									
F-14A Tomcat	390 ordered	All Weather Fighter F/W	A	USA	Mach 2·34	Over 56 000 ft (17 070 m)			72 000 lb (32 660 kg)
Grumman									
E-1B Tracer	88 built	AEW F/W	A	USA	At S/L 230 knots			Endurance at 19 000 ft 156 knots 8 hrs	29 150 lb (13 222 kg)
Grumman									
S-2E Tracker	180	A/S Attack F/W	A	USA	At S/L 230 knots	21 000 ft (6 400 m)	Ferry 1 128 n. miles	Max endurance 9 hrs	29 150 lb (13 222 kg)

Wing span Rotor diameter	Length	Height	Power Plant	Armament Capacity	Remarks
44 ft (13·41 m)	63 ft 5 in (19·33 m)	16 ft 3 in (4·95 m)	Two RR RB 168-1A Spey Mk 101 turbofan engines	Bombs, rockets, air-to-surface missiles—camera. Max load 16 000 lb (7 257 kg)	
54 ft 6 in (16·61 m)	44 ft (13·41 m)	16 ft 10 in (5·13 m)	One Bristol Siddeley Double Mamba 102 turboprop 3 875 ehp	Electronics, early warning for long range ship and aircraft detection	
25 ft 3 in (7·70 m)	45 ft 6 in (13·87 m)	Approx 11 ft 3 in (3·43 m)	One RR Pegasus 103 vectored-thrust turbofan engine	Aden gun pods, bombs, rockets, flares, camera	In service with USMC and Spain. Total includes 8 TAV-8As. RN to operate 24 Sea Harriers from 1979
38 ft 5 in (11·71 m)	62 ft 11·75 in (19·20 m)		Two RR Spey Mk 201 turbofan engines with afterburners	Sparrow III Air-to-air missiles bombs, rockets, etc.	
34 ft 5·75 in (10·50 m)	39 ft 3·25 in (11·97 m)	10 ft 2·25 in (3·15 m)	One 590 shp Turbomeca Astazou IIIA turboshaft engine		
42 ft (12·80 m)	49 ft 9 in (15·16 m)	12 ft 0 in (3·66 m)	Two 900 shp RR BS 360.07.26 Gem turboshaft engines	Two Mk 44 or Mk 46 homing torpedoes, depth charges or missiles	
62 ft 0 in (18·90 m)	72 ft 8 in (22·15 m)	16 ft 10 in (5·13 m)	Two 1 590 shp RR Gnome H 1400-1 turboshaft engines	Dipping sonar type 195 system, radar smoke floats, AD580 doppler navigation, torpedoes, depth charges, machine gun	Data for current Mk 2 version
32 ft 3 in (9·83 m)	40 ft 4 in (12·29 m)	11 ft 8 in (3·56 m)	One RR Bristol Nimbus 503 turboshaft engine, derated to 710 shp	Two Mk 44 homing torpedoes or other stores	
56 ft 0 in (17·07 m)	65 ft 9 in (20·03 m)	16 ft 2 in (4·93 m)	One RR (Bristol) Gnome 112 and One Gnome 113 turboshaft engines, each 1 350 shp	Up to 13 troops or 7 stretchers A/S version (HAS.1) can carry weapons	
53 ft 0 in (16·15 m)	44 ft 2 in (13·46 m)	13 ft 2·5 in (4·03 m)	One RR (Bristol) Gnome H 1000 turboshaft		
114 ft 10 in (35·3 m)	126 ft 9 in (38·63 m)	29 ft 8·5 in (9·08 m)	Four RR RB168 Spey Mk 250 turbofan engines	Bombs, mines, depth charges, MAD, full range ASW detection equipment	Operated by RAF
119 ft 10 in (36·52 m)	87 ft 4 in (26·52 m)	23 ft 4 in (7·11 m)	Four RR Griffon 57A piston engines 2 455 hp each		Operated by SAAF
119 ft 10 in (36·52 m)	92 ft 6 in (28·19 m)	23 ft 4 in (7·11 m)	Four RR Griffon 67 piston engines, 2 450 hp each	Early warning electronics	Operated by RAF
40 ft 0 in (12·19 m)	41 ft 7 in (12·67 m)	15 ft 2 in (4·62 m)	Two 715 ehp Garrett AiResearch T76-G-416/417 turboprops	4 × 0·30 in machine guns, anti-aircraft missiles, bombs, rockets, etc. Max weapon load 3,600 lb (1,633 kg)	
38 ft 9 in (11·80 m)	46 ft 1·5 in (14·06 m)	16 ft 0·75 in (4·90 m)	One Allison TF41-A-2 turbofan	Air-to-air, air-to-surface missiles, guns, rockets, bombs, drop tanks	Total includes A-7A/B/C
35 ft 8 in (10·87 m)	54 ft 6 in (16·61 m)	15 ft 9 in (4·80 m)	One Pratt & Whitney J57-P-20 turbojet	Cannon, rockets, bombs, missiles	Also F-8J/K and RF-8G
80 ft 7 in (24·56 m)	56 ft 8 in (17·27 m)	15 ft 11 in (4·85 m)	Two 4 050 ehp Allison T56-A-8A turboprops	10 000 lb freight	
80 ft 7 in (24·56 m)	57 ft 7 in (17·55 m)	18 ft 4 in (5·59 m)	Two 4 910 ehp Allison T56-A-422 turboprops	Early warning and command electronics	Data for E-2C
53 ft 0 in (16·15 m)	54 ft 7 in (16·64 m)	16 ft 2 in (4·93 m)	Two Pratt & Whitney J52-P-8A turbojets	Bombs, missiles and other stores	Total includes A-6A/B/C
38 ft 5 in (11·70 m)	58 ft 0 in (17·76 m)	16 ft 0 in (4·96 m)	Two General Electric J79-GE-8 turbojets with afterburners	Missiles, bombs, rockets	Also F-4J/N and 50 RF-4Bs
27 ft 6 in (8·38 m)	40 ft 3·25 in (12·27 m)	15 ft 0 in (4·57 m)	One Pratt & Whitney J52-P-408A turbojet	Cannon, bombs, rockets, missiles	Total includes A-4C/E/F/L
72 ft 6 in (22·07 m) Unswept	76 ft 4 in (23·27 m)	22 ft 8 in (6·91 m)	Two Pratt & Whitney J57-P-10 turbojets	Provision for bombs, torpedoes, cannon	Total includes tankers
64 ft 1·5 in (19·54 m)	61 ft 11·9 in (18·89 m)	16 ft 0 in (4·88 m)	Two Pratt & Whitney TF30-P-412A turbofans with afterburners	Guns, missiles, bombs	
72 ft 7 in (22·13 m)	45 ft 4 in (13·82 m)	16 ft 10 in (5·13 m)	Two Wright R.1820-82 piston engines	Early warning and command electronics	
72 ft 7 in (22·13 m)	43 ft 6 in (13·26 m)	16 ft 7 in (5·06 m)	Two 1 525 hp Wright R-1820-82WA piston engines	Depth charges, torpedoes, rockets, sonobuoys	Total includes S-2D/G

Country/ Manufacturer	Strength	Role	Class (See note)	Country of Origin	Max Speed	Service Ceiling	Range	Max Endurance	T/O Weight
UNITED STATES—continued									
Lockheed S-3A Viking	179 ordered	A/S F/W	A	USA	450 knots	over 35 000 ft (10 670 m)	Ferry 3 000 n. miles+		42 500 lb (19 277 kg)
Rockwell International RA-5C Vigilante	100	Tactical Recce F/W	A	USA	Mach 2·1	64 000 ft (19 500 m)	2 600 n. miles		66 800 lb (30 300 kg)
Sikorsky S-58 Seabat/Seahorse		A/S and GP Helicopter	B	USA	At S/L 107 knots	9 000 ft (2 740 m)	214 n. miles +10% reserve		14 000 lb (6 350 kg)
Bell AH-1J SeaCobra	Total 79	Close Support Helicopter	B	USA	180 knots	10 550 ft (3 215 m)	310 n. miles		10 000 lb (4 535 kg)
Sikorsky SH-3A/D/G Sea King	325	ASW and Transport Helicopter	B	USA	144 knots	14 700 ft (4 480 m)	542 n. miles 10% reserve		18 626 lb (8 450 kg)
Boeing Vertol UH-46D Sea Knight	450 built	Transport and Utility Helicopter	B	USA	144 knots	14 000 ft (4 265 m)	Approx 198 n. miles		Max 23 000 lb (10 433 kg)
Kaman SH-2D/F Seasprite	75	ASW Helicopter	B	USA	At S/L 143 knots	22 500 ft (6 860 m)	367 n. miles		12 500 lb (5 670 kg)
Sikorsky CH-53A/D Sea Stallion	275	Assault Transport Helicopter	B	USA	170 knots	21 000 ft (6 400 m)	223 n. miles approx.		42 000 lb (19 050 kg)
Bell UH-1E	190	Assault Support Helicopter	B	USA	140 knots	21 000 ft (6 400 m)	248 n. miles		9 500 lb (4 309 kg)
Hawker Siddeley AV-8A Harrier	102 built	V/STOL Strike/Recce F/W	A	UK					
Grumman EA-6A/B Prowler	104	ECM/ELINT F/W	A	USA	520 knots				58 500 lb (26 535 kg)
Gyrodyne QH-50C		Pilotless Weapon Carrier Helicopter	B	USA	80 knots	16 400 ft (5 000 m)	71 n. miles		2 285 lb (1 036 kg)
Grumman HU-16 Albatross		GP Amphib F/W	C	USA	At S/L 205 knots	21 500 ft (6 550 m)	2 475 n. miles		37 500 lb (17 010 kg)
Lockheed C-130 Hercules	117	LR Transport & Recce & Tanker F/W	C	USA	335 knots	33 000 ft (10 060 m)	4 460 n. miles		155 000 lb (70 310 kg)
Lockheed SP-2H Neptune	50	LRMP F/W	C	USA	at 10 000 ft 350 knots	22 000 ft (6 700 m)	3 200 n. miles		79 895 lb (36 240 kg)
Lockheed P-3A/B/C and EP-3E Orion	400	A/S Recce F/W	C	USA	at 15 000 ft 411 knots	28 300 ft (8 625 m)	Mission radius 2 070 n. miles		142 000 lb (64 410 kg)
UNION OF SOVIET SOCIALIST REPUBLICS									
Mil Mi-4 ("Hound")		A/S Helicopter	B	USSR	113 knots	18 000 ft (5 500 m)	About 220 n. miles		17 200 lb (7 800 kg)
Kamov Ka-25 ("Hormone")		A/S and Strike Helicopter	B	USSR	119 knots	11 500 ft (3 500 m)	350 n. miles		16 100 lb (7 300 kg)
Tupolev ("Backfire")	20	V/G Recce Bomber F/W	C	USSR	Approx Mach 2·5		Approx 4 775- 5 200 n. miles		272 000 lb (123 350 kg)
Tupolev Tu-16 ("Badger")	400	L. Range Bomber Maritime Recce F/W	C	USSR	at 35 000 ft 510 knots	42 650 ft (13 000 m)	With max bomb load 2 605 n. miles		150 000 lb (68 000 kg)
Tupolev Tu-95 ("Bear")	50	L. Range Bomber Maritime Recce F/W	C	USSR	Cruising at 32 000 ft 410 knots		With max load 6 775 n. miles		340 000 lb (154 220 kg)
Tupolev Tu-22 ("Blinder")	60	Recce Bomber F/W	C	USSR	at 40 000 ft Mach 1·4	60 000 ft (18 300 m)	1 215 n. miles		185 000 lb (83 900 kg)
Beriev M-12 ("Mail")	100	A/S Recce Amphibian F/W	C	USSR	329 knots	39 977 ft (12 185 m)	2 160 n. miles		65 035 lb (29 500 kg)
Ilyushin Il-38 ("May")	60	A/S Recce F/W	C	USSR	365 knots	32 800 ft	3 900 n. miles		
URUGUAY									
Bell 47G-2	2	Helicopter	B	USA					
Grumman Tracker (S-2A)	3	A/S Patrol F/W	C	USA					
VENEZUELA									
Bell 47G	4	Helicopter	B	USA					
Grumman Tracker (S-2E)	3	A/S Patrol F/W	C	USA					

Wing span Rotor diameter	Length	Height	Power Plant	Armament Capacity	Remarks
68 ft 8 in (20·93 m)	53 ft 4 in (16·26 m)	22 ft 9 in (6·93 m)	Two General Electric TF34-GE-2 turbofan engines	Bombs, Depth bombs, rockets, missiles, mines, torpedoes, flares	
53 ft 0 in (16·15 m)	76 ft 7·25 in (23·35 m)	19 ft 5 in (5·92 m)	Two General Electric J79-GE-10 turbojets	Variety of weapons inc. thermonuclear bombs	
56 ft 0 in (17·07 m)	56 ft 8·25 in (17·27 m)	15 ft 11 in (4·85 m)	One 1 525 hp Wright R-1820-84B/D piston engine	12 passengers	
44 ft 0 in (13·41 m)	53 ft 4 in (16·26 m)	13 ft 8 in (4·15 m)	One 1 800 shp Pratt & Whitney T400-CP-400 turboshaft	Cannon and rockets	Total includes improved AH-IT
62 ft 0 in (18·90 m)	72 ft 8 in (22·15 m)	16 ft 10 in (5·13 m)	Two 1 400 shp General Electric T58-GE-10 turboshaft	Torpedoes, missiles 840 lb (381 kg) of weapons	Data for SH-3D
51 ft 0 in (15·54 m)	Fuselage 44 ft 10 in (13·66 m) Overall	16 ft 8·5 in (5·09 m)	Two 1 400 shp General Electric T58-GE-10 turboshaft	Up to 10 000 lb load	Total includes CH-46s
44 ft 0 in (13·41 m)	52 ft 7 in (16·03 m)	15 ft 6 in (4·72 m)	Two 1 350 shp GE T58-GE-8F turboshaft	LAMPS equipt. Details in JAWA	
72 ft 3 in (22·02 m)	88 ft 3 in (26·90 m)	24 ft 11 in (7·60 m)	Two 2 850 shp GE T64-GE-6 turboshaft	37 passengers or 24 stretchers with 4 attendants	Data for CH-53D
44 ft 0 in (13·41 m)	53 ft 0 in (16·15 m)	12 ft 7·25 in (3·84 m)	One Lycoming T53-L-11 shaft turbine	Machine guns, rockets, 8 passengers or 4 000 lb cargo	Total includes UH-1D/H/L
53 ft 0 in (16·15 m)	59 ft 5 in (18·11 m)		Two Pratt & Whitney J52-P-8A Turbojets	Normally unarmed ECM equipment	Data for EA-6B
20 ft 0 in (6·10 m)			One Boeing T50-BO-8A shaft turbine	2 × Mk 44 homing torpedoes	Remote control drone
96 ft 8 in (29·46 m)	62 ft 10 in (19·18 m)		Two 1 425 hp Wright R-1820-76A radial piston engines	Torpedoes, depth charges or rockets	
132 ft 7 in (40·41 m)	97 ft 9 in (29·78 m)	38 ft 3 in (11·66 m)	Four 4 508 ehp Allison T56-A-15 turboprop	Cargo up to 26 640 lb (12 080 kg) 92 troops, 64 paras or 74 stretchers	Data for late-model transport
inc. tip tanks 103 ft 10 in (31·65 m)	91 ft 8 in (27·94 m)	29 ft 4 in (8·94 m)	Two 3 500 hp Wright R-3350-32W radial piston + 2 Westinghouse J34 turbojets	8 000 lb (3 630 kg) bombs, torpedoes, depth charges and rockets	
99 ft 8 in (30·37 m)	116 ft 10 in (35·61 m)	33 ft 8·5 in (10·29 m)	Four 4 910 ehp Allison T56-A-14 turboprops	Mines, depth bombs, torpedoes	Data for P-3C
68 ft 11 in (21·0 m)	55 ft 1 in (16·8 m)	17 ft (5·18 m)	One 1 700 hp ASh-82V 18-cylinder radial piston engine	Depth charges and small stores, search radar under nose, MAD sensors in towed bird, sonobuoys	
51 ft 8 in (15·75 m)	32 ft 0 in (9·75 m)	17 ft 7·5 in (5·37 m)	Two 900 shp Glushenkov GTD-3 turboshaft	A/S torpedoes, flares, small stores	
			Possibly two Kuznetsov turbofans		
110 ft (33·5 m)	120 ft (36·5 m)	35 ft 6 in (10·8 m)	Two Mikulin AM-3M turbojets	Up to 7 × 23 mm cannon in dorsal, ventral and tail turrets and nose. 19 800 lb (9 000 kg) of bombs or missiles	
159 ft (48·5 m)	155 ft 10 in (47·5 m)	39 ft 9 in (12·12 m)	Four 14 795 ehp Kuznetsov NK-12MV turboprops	Bombs, missiles, 2 to 6 × 23 mm cannon	
90 ft 10·5 in (27·70 m)	132 ft 11·5 in (40·53 m)	17 ft 0 in (5·18 m)	Two turbojets with afterburners	Cameras. Provision for bombs and missiles	Data for "Blinder-C"
97 ft 6 in (29·70 m)	99 ft (30·20 m)	22 ft 11·5 in (7·00 m)	Two 4 000 shp Ivchenko AI-20D turboprops	Torpedoes, depth charges, sonobuoys, MAD gear, nose radome	
122 ft 8·5 in (37·4 m)	129 ft 10 in (39·6 m)	33 ft 4 in (10·15 m)	Four 4 250 ehp Ivchenko AI-20 turboprops	A/S weapons, MAD gear, undernose radar	

NAVAL MISSILES

NAVAL MISSILES

(Further details can be found in the current edition of JANE'S WEAPON SYSTEMS)

Country/ Manufacturer	Classification	Name	No.	Length ft.	Launch Weight lbs.	Power plant	Guidance	Range n. miles	Mach Speed	Warhead	Remarks
AUSTRALIA Dept of Supply	A/S	Ikara	—	11·3		Solid fuel rocket	Command link	13	—	Torpedo-HE	Acoustic homing torpedo
FRANCE Aerospatiale	Strat	MSBS	M1	34·1	39 683	Solid fuel rocket 2 stage	Inertial	1 350	—	Nuclear	In "Le Redoubtable" class SSBN
	Strat	MSBS	M2	35	44 000	as above	Inertial	1 620	—	Nuclear	In production to replace M1
	Srat	MSBS	M20	35	44 000	as above	Inertial	1 620	—	Thermonuclear MRV	First embarked mid-1976
	Strat	MSBS	M4	—	—	as above	Inertial	2 000+	—	Thermonuclear with MRV	Production by late 1970s
CNIM	SSM	—	RP14	6·5	118	Solid fuel rocket	Nil	9	—	HE	22 rocket multiple launcher
Matra (with Oto Melara)	SSM	Otomat	—	14·5	1 543	Turbojet	Autopilot Active homer	32	—	HE	Sea-skimmer for last 2 miles; can be ASM
Aerospatiale	SSM	Exocet	MM38	17	1 543	2 stage solid fuel rocket	Inertial cruise Active homer	20	1+	220 lb HE	Sea-skimmer throughout flight Variants—AM 38 and 39, air-launched; MM 39, ship-launched version of AM 39; MM 40, improved MM 38 with 40 n. mile range; SM 39, projected submarine launched MM 39
	SSM	—	SS11	3·9	66	2 stage solid fuel rocket	Wire-guided	1·6	330 knots	HE or torpedo	Same characteristics as AS-11 Harpon is very similar with improved guidance
	SSM	—	SS12	6·2	165	2 stage solid fuel rocket	Wire-guided	4·4	—	66 lb HE	Same characteristics as AS-12
Ecan Ruelle	SAM	Masurca	Mk 2	28·2 (with booster)	4 585	2 stage solid fuel rocket	Mod 2 Beam rider. Mod 3. semi active homer	22	2·5 (slant)	105 lbs HE	Mounted in *Colbert, Suffren* and *Duquesne*
	SAM	Hirondelle Super 530	—	—	—	—	—	—	—	—	Project for PDMS for small ships and craft
	SAM	Catulle	—	—	—	—	—	—	—	—	Development. Multi-barrelled rocket system firing salvoes of 40 mm shells
Matra	SAM	Crotale Navale	R440	9·5	176	Solid fuel rocket	Infra-red/ command	5	2·3 (slant)	HE	Being installed (1976) in French Navy
Matra-Hawker Siddeley	ASM	Martel	AS37/ AJ168	12 or 13·2	—	Solid fuel rocket	TV on AJ168 passive radar homing on AS37	30	—	HE	Air-to-surface weapon also in service with RAF
Aerospatiale	ASM	—	AS20	8·5	315	2 stage solid fuel rocket	Radio command	4	—	66 lb HE	In service
	ASM	—	AS30	12·4	1 100	2 stage solid fuel rocket	Radio command	6	1·5	510 lb HE	In service
Matra	AAM	Magic	R550	8·2	176	Solid fuel rocket	Infra-red	4	—	HE	In service 1975
	AAM		R530	10·8	430	Solid fuel rocket	Infra-red semi-active radar	9·5	2·7	HE	Proximity fused head
Latecoere	A/S	Malafon Mk 2	—	20·3	3 300	2 stage solid fuel rocket and booster	Radio/acoustic homing	7	450 knots	Torpedo	Torpedo dropped by parachute 875 yards from target
GERMANY Messerschmitt-Bölkow-Blöhm	ASW	Kormoran	—	14·4	1 323	3 stage solid fuel rocket	Active radar	20	0·95	350 lb HE	Suitable for all fixed and rotary-wing aircraft
ISRAEL Israel Aircraft Industries	SSM	Gabriel I	—	11·0	882	Two stage solid fuel rocket	Radar or optical with semi-active head	11 20 (Mk 2)	·9	330 lb HE (Mk 1)	Mounted in "Saar" and "Saar IV" classes. Now being exported, eg Singapore
ITALY Sistel	SSM	Sea Killer I (Nettuno)	—	12·3	375	1 stage solid fuel rocket	Beam ride/ radio-command or optical	5·4	1·9	77 lb HE	Operational for use in ships or helicopters. Five round launcher in ships
	SSM	Sea Killer II (Vulcano)	—	15·5	661	2 stage solid rocket motor	as above	10·5	1·9	155 lb HE	
	SSM	Sea Killer III	—	17·4	1 200	1 booster 2 sustainers	Active homer	24	1·9	330 lb HE	Under development
Otomat (with Matra)	SSM	Otomat (see "France")									
Sistel	SAM	Sea Indigo	—	11	266	1 stage solid fuel rocket	Radio command/ beam rider	5·5 (slant)	2·5	46 lb HE	Automatic reloading in ships over 500 tons
	ASM	Airtos	—	12·8	421	1 stage solid fuel rocket	Active radar homing	6	1·5	77 lb HE	All-weather system under development
NORWAY Kongsberg Vaapenfabrikk	SSM	Penguin	—	10	727	2 stage solid fuel rocket	Inertial/infra-red homing	14·5	—	264 lb HE	Fitted in frigates and fast attack craft
	A/S	Terne Mk 8	—	6·4	298	2 stage solid fuel rocket	Nil	1·5	—	110 lb HE depth charge	Full salvo of six can be fired in 5 seconds Reload time 40 seconds
SWEDEN Saab-Scania	SSM	—	RB 08A	18·8	1 984	Marboré turbo-jet	Radar homing	?100	0·85	HE	For ship and coast artillery use. Entered service 1967
UNITED KINGDOM	Srat	Polaris A3 (see USA)	—	—	—	—	—	—	—	UK made 1 MT Thermonuclear MIRV	Carried in "Resolution" class
Hawker Siddeley	SAM/ SSM	Sea Dart	CF 299	14·3	1 212	Solid fuel booster Liquid ramjet sustainer	Radar guidance (Type 909) semi-active radar homing	40	—	HE	Fitted in *Bristol* and Type 42 destroyers
	SAM	Sea Slug Mk 1 and 2	—	20	—	4 solid fuel boosters, solid fuel sustainer	Beam-riding (Type 901)	24(Mk 1) (approx)	—	HE Proximity fuse	Surface-to-surface capability. Mk 2 has a longer range and better low-level capability
British Aircraft Corpn.	SAM	Sea Wolf	PX 430	6·5	About 200	Solid fuel rocket	Radio command with TV or radar tracking (Type 910)	—	—	HE	Entire system GWS 25. Lightweight versions for ships smaller than frigates are Seawolf Omega and Delta. Normally to be used from 6-barrelled launcher

Country/ Manufacturer	Classifi- cation	Name	No.	Length ft.	Launch Weight, lb.	Powerplant	Guidance	Range n. mile	Mach Speed	Warhead	Remarks
Short Bros and Harland	SAM	Sea Cat	—	4·9	140	2 stage solid fuel rocket	Optical, Radar or TV	1·9	—	HE	Fitted in many systems GWS 20 (visual) GWS 22 and 24 (Radar). M4/3 (Radar), Signaal M40
	ASM	Sea Skua	CL 834	9·2	462	Solid fuel rocket	Radar/radio control radar homing	?5	—	45 lb HE	Developed for use from helicopters
Hawker-Siddeley	AAM	Firestreak	—	10·5	320	Solid fuel rocket	Infra-red homing	4·3	2+	50 lb HE	Being replaced by Red Top (below)
	AAM	Red Top	—	10·8	330	Solid fuel rocket	Infra-red homing	6	3	68 lb HE	A much improved ver- sion of Firestreak
Short Bros and Harland	SAM	Slam (Blow pipe)	—	4·6	40	2 stage solid fuel rocket	Optical with radio guidance	—	—	HE	Privately developed system. Suitable for submarines or surface ships.
USA Lockheed	Strat	Polaris A3	UGM 27C	31	35 000(3)	2 stage solid fuel rocket	Inertial	2 500(3)	10 at burn-out	Thermonuclear	See USA and UK sec- tions for fitting policy. MIRV.
	Strat	Poseidon C-3	UGM 73A	34	65 000	2 stage solid fuel rocket	Inertial	2 500	—	Thermonuclear	As above. Double A3 payload MIRV warhead
	Strat	Trident I (C-4)	—	34	65 000	3 stage solid fuel rocket	Inertial	3 750	—	Thermonuclear	MIRV. To replace Poseidon using same tubes
	Strat	Trident II	—	—	—	3 stage solid fuel rocket	Inertial	6 000 approx	—	Thermonuclear	MIRV. For fitting in "Trident" class SSBNs
McDonnell Douglas	SSM	Harpoon	RGM 84A	15	1 397	Solid fuel booster Turbojet sustainer	Pre-programmed Active radar homing	60	—	HE	For general surface-ship fitting. Submarine ver- sion under trial
	ASM	Harpoon	AGM 84A	15	1 110	As above	As above	60	—	HE	
	ASM	Condor	AGM 53A	5·5	2 130	1 solid fuel rocket	Radio control TV homing	45	11	HE (Possible nuclear)	For carrier-borne A/C particularly A6. Production 1973
Maxson	ASM	Bullpup	AGM 12B and C	10·5(B) 13·6(C)	571(B) 1 785(C)	1 liquid fuel rocket	Command	6(B) 9(C)	2	HE 250 lb(B) 1 000 lb(C)	Operational 1959
NASC/NWC	ASM	Shrike	AGM 45A	10	390	1 solid fuel rocket	Passive radar homing	8	2	HE	Production 1963
Martin, Marietta	ASM	Walleye	AGM 62A	11·3	1 100	Nil	TV guided	—	—	HE	Details are for Walleye 1 Walleye 2 is larger (2 340 lbs) with 2 000 lb HE head. Glide-bombs
GDC-Pomona	ASM	Standard ARM	AGM 78A	15	1 800	Dual-thrust solid fuel rocket	Passive Radar homing	13	2	HE	Production 1968
GDC-Pomona	SAM	Standard	RIM 66A	15	1 300	Dual thrust solid fuel rocket	Semi-active radar homing	13	—	HE	To be used with AEGIS missile system (MR)
GDC-Pomona	SAM	Standard	RIM 67A	27	3 000	2 stage solid fuel rocket	Semi-active radar homing	32	—	HE	SSM capability. Terrier replacement (ER)
Raytheon	SAM	Seasparrow	RIM 7H	12	440	1 solid fuel rocket	Semi-active radar homing	12	—	HE	Can also be used as SSM. UK version XJ 521
Bendix A/S	SAM	Talos	RIM 8F, G and H	31·3 (booster)	7 000	Solid fuel booster ram-jet sustainer	Beam rider semi-active radar homing	65+	2·5	HE/ nuclear	SSM capability. RIM H has anti-radiation housing
GDC-Pomona	SAM	Tartar	RIM 24B	15	1 300	Dual-thrust solid fuel rocket	Semi-active radar homing	14	2	HE	Ceiling 40 000 ft Replacement by Standard
GDC-Pomona	SAM	Terrier	RIM 2F	26·5 (booster)	3 000	2 stage solid-fuel rocket	Semi-active radar homing	20	2·5	HE	Ceiling 65 000 ft Operational 1963
NWC-Hughes	AAM	Agile	AIM 95	8	250	Solid fuel	Infra-red	Short	—	HE	Planned replacement for Sidewinder
Hughes	AAM	Phoenix	AIM 54A	13	838	1 solid-fuel rocket	Radar homing	90	2+	HE	In use in F14 Operational 1973
Raytheon/NWC/ Philco Ford	AAM	Sidewinder	AIM 9G, J H and L	9·5	185	1 solid fuel rocket	Infra-red	9	2	HE	Ceiling 50 000 ft+ First AIM9B entered service 1962
Raytheon	AAM	Sparrow	AIM 7E and F	12	450(E) 500(F)	1 solid fuel rocket	Semi-active radar homing	12(E) 24+(F)	3·5	HE	For carrier-borne aircraft
Honeywell	A/S	Asroc	RUR 5A	15	1 000(Mk 44) 570(Mk 46)	1 solid fuel rocket	Pre-programme	1—5	—	Mk 44 or 46 torpedo or Nuclear D/C	Fired from 8-barrelled launcher. 10 mile version under development
Goodyear	A/S or anti- surface- ship	Subroc	UUM 44A	21	4 000	2 stage solid fuel rocket	Pre-programme inertial	30	1+	Nuclear	Fired from normal 21 in torpedo tubes
USSR (NATO designa- tions used— further details at head of USSR section)	SLBM	Sark	SSN-4	37·5	—	?2 stage solid fuel rocket	Inertial	300	—	Nuclear	Operational 1958
	SLBM	Serb	SSN-5	35	—	2 stage solid fuel rocket	Inertial	700	—	Nuclear megaton	Operational 1963
	SLBM	Sawfly	SSN-6	42	—	2 stage solid fuel rocket	Inertial	1 300 (1 600)	—	Nuclear (MRV in later versions)	Operational 1967
	SLBM	—	SSN-8	45 (est)	—	?	Inertial	4 200	—	Nuclear (MRV)	Operational 1973
	SLBM	—	SSN-13	—	—	Inertial	350	—	—	Nuclear	Possibly anti-task Force. Status not certain
	SSM	Scrubber	SSN-1	22·5	—	—	Radar Infra-red homing	130	0·9	—	Operational 1958. Soon obsolete
	SSM	Styx	SSN-2	15	—	2 stage solid fuel rocket	Active radar homing	23	0·9	HE	Operational 1960
	SSM	Shaddock	SSN-3	36	—	2 boosters Turbojet sustainer	Radar, mid- course guidance Radar or IR homing	150-250	1·5	—	Operational 1961-62
	SSM	—	SSN-7	22	—	—	—	30	1·5	—	Operational 1969-70 Submarine launched from dived
	SSM	—	SSN-9	30 (est)	—	—	Radar with mid-course guidance	150	1·0+	HE or nuclear	Operational 1968-69. In "Nanuchka" class
	SSM	—	SSN-10	25 (est)	—	—	Radar	30	1·2	HE	Operational 1968
	SSM	—	SSN-11	21	—	? As in SSN-2	? Radar	29	0·9	—	Operational 1968
	SSM	—	SSN-12	—	—	—	? Radar—mid course guidance	? 250	—	—	Replacement for Shaddock

Country/ Manufacturer	Classifi-cation	Name	No.	Length ft.	Launch Weight, lb.	Powerplant	Guidance	Range n. mile	Mach Speed	Warhead	Remarks
USSR—continued											
	SAM	Goa	SAN-1	22 (booster)	—	2 stage solid fuel rocket	Beam-rider semi-active radar	17	2	HE	Operational 1961
	SAM	Guideline	SAN-2	34·7	—	Solid booster liquid sustainer	Radar	25	3·5	HE (290 lb)	
	SAM	Goblet	SAN-3	20	—	2 stage solid fuel rocket	—	20	—	HE	
	SAM	—	SAN-4	—	—	—	—	20	—	—	Probably PDMS
	ASM	Kennel	As-1	27·9	—	1 Turbojet	Command with radar homing	55	0·9	—	Obsolete
	ASM	Kipper	AS-2	31	—	1 Turbojet	Autopilot. Radar homing	115	1·0+	—	Operational 1960
	ASM	Kangaroo	AS-3	49·2	—	1 Turbojet	—	400	1·5+	—	Operational 1961
	ASM	Kitchen	AS-4	37	—	1 stage liquid fuel rocket	? Inertial guidance	185?	2+	—	Operational 1965
	ASM	Kelt	AS-5	30·8	—	1 stage liquid fuel rocket	Active radar homing	120	0·9	—	Operational 1968
	ASM	—	AS-6	—	—	1 stage	—	300	3	—	Operational 1970-71. Badger and Backfire
	A/S	—	FRAS I	—	—	—	?Pre-programme	15	—	?Nuclear	Operational 1968 in "Moskva" class on SUWN-1 mounting
	A/S	—	SSN-14	—	—	—	—	25	—	—	Operational ?1970
	A/S	—	SSN-15	—	—	—	—	20	—	?nuclear	Operational 1974? for use from submarines in A/S operations

NAVAL RADAR

NAVAL RADAR

Country/Number	Type	Transmitter frequency	Transmitter peak power	Range
DENMARK				
	I Band Navigation Radar	9 375±30 MHz	20 KW± 1dB Measured at output flange	—
FRANCE				
ELI 4	Naval IFF Interrogator	1 030± 0·5 Mcs	Selectable 0·5 or 2 kW	—
ELR 3	IFF Transponder	—	—	—
Triton	G band 5 cm air and surface surveillance radar	G Band	250 kW	—
Castor II	I Band target tracking radar	I Band (tunable)	36 kW	—
Pollux	I Band target tracking radar	I Band	200 kW	—
Pollux II	Improved version of above	—	—	—
Calypso II	TH D 1030 I Band S/M Radar	I Band (variable)	70 kW	—
Calypso III	TRS 3100 I Band S/M Radar	—	—	—
Jupiter	TH D 1077 long range surveillance			
	Radar C Band 2 MW	C/D Band 23 cm	2 MW	—
Ramses	TH D 1022 short range nav & surveillance radar	I Band	36 kW	60 nm
Lynx	TH D 1051	—	—	—
Saturne	TH D 1041	—	—	—
Sea Tiger	Surveillance radar	E/F Band	—	—
DRBC 32	Gun fire control radar	I Band	—	—
DRBI 10	Air surveillance radar	E/F Band	Between 1 and 2 mW	Between 100 and 140 nm
DRBV 13	Air search radar	E/F Band	—	—
DRBV 20	Long range search radar	—	—	—
DRBV 22	Search radar	C Band	—	—
DRBV 23	Air search radar	C Band (23 cm)	—	—
DRBR 51	Tracking and missile guidance	I Band	—	—
DRBI 23	Surveillance and target designator	C/D Band (23 cm)	—	—
INTERNATIONAL				
EX 77 Mod O	Director for NATO Sea Sparrow	Probably I Band	—	—
ITALY				
Argus 5000	Early warning radar	—	SMW	—
Orion 250	Fire control radar	I Band	—	—
Orion RTN 10X	Fire control radar	I Band	—	40 nm
Orion RTN 16X	Monopulse fire control radar	I Band	—	—
Orion RTN 20 X	Fire control radar	I Band	—	—
Orion RTN 30X	Fire control radar	I Band	—	—
RAN 2C	Surveillance radar	G Band	—	—
RAN 3L	Early warning radar	C/D Band	—	—
RAN 7S	10 cm air and surface search radar	10 cm	—	—
RAN 10S	Air and sea search on small ships	E/F Band	—	—
RAN 11L/X	Air warning and weapons control	C and I Band	28 kW C Band, 80 kW I Band	—
RAN 13X	Search radar	I Band	—	—
RAN 14X	Low altitude and surface search	I Band	—	—
Sea Hunter	Search radar	—	180 kW	—
Sea Hunter	Tracker radar	—	—	—
SPQ 2D	Search radar	I Band	—	—
NETHERLANDS				
DA 05	Naval surveillance	E/F Band	—	—
	Naval height finder	—	—	—
LW 02	Air surveillance	C/D Band	500 kW	—
LW 04	Air surveillance	C/D Band	—	100 nm
ZW 08	Surface warning and navigation	I Band	—	—
LW 08	Early warning and weapon detection	C/D Band	—	145 nm air target
ZW 06	Surface search and navigation	I Band	—	—
M 20	Fire control	I Band	—	—
3 D	Multi target tracking radar	No details released	—	—
M 40	Fire control	No details released	—	—
SWEDEN				
9 GR 600	Transmitter/receiver	I Band	200 kW	—
9 LV 200	Tracking radar	—	—	—
SUBFAR	S/M radar	—	—	—
UNITED KINGDOM				
	Naval IFF 800 series. Comprising IFF 800-825-825M	—	—	—
MRS 3/GWS 22	Fire control radar	—	—	—
AWS/2	Naval surveillance	E/F Band	—	—
PTR 461	Shipborne IFF transponder	—	—	—
S604 HN	Search radar	—	—	—
S 810	Surveillance radar	I Band	200 kW	—
RN Type 901	Missile guidance for Seaslug	?G Band	—	—
RN Type 909	Target tracking for Sea Dart	?G Band	—	—
RN Type 910	Target tracking for Sea Wolf	I Band	—	—
RN Type 912	Fire control radar	I Band	—	—
RN Type 965	Long range air search	—	—	—
RN Type 967	Air surveillance	E/F Band	—	—
RN Type 968	Surface surveillance	C/D Band	—	—
RN Type 975	Surface warning	I Band	50 kW nominal	—
RN Type 978	Navigation radar	I Band	—	—
RN Type 992Q	General purpose radar	E/F Band	—	—
RN Type 1006	High definition navigation radar	I Band	—	—

P.R.F.	Manufacturer	Remarks
Short NOM 4000 Hz±200 Hz Long NOM 2000 Hz±200 Hz	TERMA	
—	LMT	Receiver frequency: 1 090 Mc/s
—	LMT	Includes selective identification feature and side lobe suppression
—	Thompson CSF	Used with Castor or Pollux in Vega series; 200 kW
—	Thompson CSF	Used in some versions of Vega series fire control system; 20 kW
—	Thompson CSF	Used in some versions of Vega series fire control system; 200 kW
Variable	Thompson CSF	Used for surveillance and navigation; 70 kW
—	Thompson CSF	Improvement of above
—	Thompson CSF	
4·50 per sec	Thompson CSF	Naval air surveillance radar (long range)
—	Thompson CSF	
—	Thompson CSF	Dual radar. Coastal mine watching system
—	Thompson CSF	Medium range air and surface surveillance radar
—	Thompson CSF	Can be used in Thompson CSF series ship fire control systems
—	Thompson CSF	A, B, C, D, E versions fitted in various classes of French ships
—	Thompson CSF	Robinson scanner
—	Thompson CSF	Pulse doppler air search radar. Multi mode operation
—	Thompson CSF	Operates in metric wave band
—	Thompson CSF	Search radar A.C. and D versions in service on French and other vessels
—	Thompson CSF	Long range naval air search and surveillance radar
—	Thompson CSF	Part of Masurca surface-to-air missile system
—	Thompson CSF	3-Dimensional surveillance-target designator radar. Stacked beam system
—	NATO Consortium	Provides search, target designation tracking and illumination for Sea Sparrow point defence missile system
—	Selenia	High power. Ship's early warning radar
—	Selenia	Used in NA 9. System conical scan; 200 kW
—	Selenia	
—	Selenia	
—	Selenia	Used in Dardo system
—	Selenia	Used in Albatros system
—	Selenia	Dual purpose air and surface surveillance radar
—	Selenia	Digital. Signal processing
—	Selenia	Air and surface target warning
—	Selenia	Air and surface surveillance
—	Selenia	C Band air detection, I Band surface detection
—	Selenia	Surface and low flying search
—	Selenia	
Variable	Contraves	
—	Contraves	
—	SMA	Surface search and short range air search
—	HSA	Air surveillance surface warning. Target designation for fire control and weapon direction systems
—	HSA	Probably similar to SGR 109
—	HSA	Long range air surveillance
—	HSA	Long range air surveillance
—	HSA	
—	HSA	
—	HSA	
—	HSA	
—	—	IFF/SIF secondary radar integrated
—	HSA	
2-3 000 Hz	—	
Approx 2 000 Hz	—	Frequency agility naval fire control
Variable 250-3 000/sec	—	Air and surface search
—	Cossor	
—	Sperry	Control of guns MRS 3 and Seacat missiles GWS/22
400-1000 pps	Plessey	
—	Plessey	Ship identification
—	Marconi	
1 500 or 4 400 Hz	Marconi	Lightweight surveillance radars
—		Target tracking
—		
—		
—	Marconi	Also target designation for guided weapons and IFF Mk 10 facilities
—		Can be combined with Type 968 for medium range to short range defence radar
—		
—	Kelvin Hughes	
—		
—	Marconi	
—	Kelvin Hughes	

Country/Number	Type	Transmitter frequency	Transmitter peak power	Range

UNION OF SOVIET SOCIALIST REPUBLICS

Country/Number	Type	Transmitter frequency	Transmitter peak power	Range
Square Tie	Lightweight search radar	I Band	—	—
Square Head	Naval radar	—	—	—
Pop Group	Fire control radar	—	—	—
Head Net B	Air surveillance radar	Probably D or E Band	—	—
Drum Tilt	Fire control radar	Probably I Band	—	—
Sun Visor	Fire control radar	Probably I or G Band	—	—
Cylinder Head	Fire control radar	—	—	—
Big Net	Search radar	D or E Band	—	—
Fan Song E	Naval radar	G Band	—	—
Hair Net	Naval radar	—	—	—
Plinth Net	Search radar	—	—	—
Pot Drum	Naval radar	Probably I Band	—	—
Pot Head	Naval radar	Probably I Band	—	—
Scoop Pair	Surface target radar	—	—	—
Hawk Screech	Gun fire control	Probably I Band. Possibly G Band	—	—
Owl Screech	Gun fire control	Probably I Band. Possibly G Band	—	—
High Lune	Naval height finder	Probably E/F Band	—	—
Muff Cob	Fire control radar	G or I Band	—	—
Slim Net	Surface warning radar	Probably E/F Band	—	—
Flat Spin	Surveillance radar	D or E Band	—	—
Head Net C	Air surveillance radar	—	—	—
Top Sail	3D radar	Probably C/D Band	—	—
Head Light	Fire control	Probably I and G Band	—	—
Strut Curve	Search radar	Probably E/F Band	—	—
Peel Group	Fire control radar	Probably G and I Band	—	—
Head Net A	Air surveillance radar	D or E Band	—	—
Boat Sail	Submarine radar	D or E Band	—	—
Skin Head	Naval radar	Probably I Band	—	—
Top Trough	Surveillance radar	—	—	—
Knife Rest B	Early warning radar	—	—	—
High Sieve	Surface search radar	—	—	—
Top Bow	Gun fire control radar	—	—	—
Seagull	Air search	—	—	—

UNITED STATES OF AMERICA

Country/Number	Type	Transmitter frequency	Transmitter peak power	Range
RTN 10	Fire control for Sea Sparrow III	I Band	—	—
SPG 49	Guidance for Talos and Terrier. Surface-to-air	Used with SPW 2	—	120 km
SPG 51	Tartar missile guidance	I Band	—	—
SPG 55	Terrier guidance radar	G Band	Approx 50 kW	50 km
SPG 60	Doppler search and tracking	I Band	—	50 nm
SPQ 9	Lockheed MK 86 fire control system	I Band	—	20 nm
SPQ 5	Missile guidance	G Band	—	—
SPS 6	Air surveillance	C/D Band	Approx 500 kW	100-200 km
SPS 10	Surface search	G Band	—	—
SPS 12	Long range air search	—	0·1 and 1·0 mW	—
SPS 30	Long range 3D radar	—	—	—
SPS 32	Air and surface surveillance	—	—	—
SPS 33	Tracking radar	—	—	—
SPS 37	Long range air surveillance	—	—	—
SPS 39	3D radar for air surveillance	—	—	2-300 km
SPS 40	Search and surveillance for air targets	?E/F Band	?1 mW	—
SPS 43	High power very long range search radar	—	1-2 mW	—
SPS 48	Air surveillance radar	—	—	—
SPS 49	Air search radar	—	—	—
SPS 52	3D air surveillance	?E/F Band	—	—
SPS 55	Surface search and navigation	—	130 kW	—
SPS 58	Pulse Doppler air search and target acquisition radar	D Band	—	—
SPY 1	Multi function array radar	E Band	—	—

P.R.F.	Manufacturer	Remarks
—	—	Probably include target detection and tracking for anti-ship missile direction.
—	—	Possible IFF interrogator or directional array for transmission of guidance signals to surface-to-surface missiles
—	—	Associated with Soviet Navy's SAN-4 surface-to-air missile system
—	—	Air search and surveillance and in connection with fire control radars carried for direction of surface-to-air missiles and guns
—	—	
—	—	
—	—	Believed now obsolete
—	—	Very large long range air surveillance radar
—	—	Shipboard version of Guideline surface-to-air missile control and guidance radar
—	—	Medium range general purpose search and surveillance radar
—	—	Medium range general purpose search radar
—	—	Small surface search radar
—	—	Surface target detection; short range
—	—	Twin radar group for Shaddock SSM
—	—	
—	—	
—	—	
—	—	Gun fire control
—	—	High definition surface target radar
—	—	Long range air search radar
—	—	Dual V beam 3D installation of Head Net A
—	—	Long range 3D air surveillance radar
—	—	Missile fire control group
—	—	Lightweight search radar
—	—	Missile control group for Goa
—	—	Long range air surveillance radar
—	—	Air search for submarine pickets
—	—	Surface target detection radar for light forces
—	—	High definition surface target radar
—	—	Long wavelength early warning radar
—	—	Target acquisition radar for naval guns
—	—	Long range air search radar
—	Raytheon	
—	—	
—	Raytheon	Part of Mk 73 FCS
—	—	
—	—	
—	—	Now obsolescent
—	—	
—	—	
—	—	
—	—	Companion in use with SPS 33
—	—	
—	—	
—	—	
—	—	Generally carries IFF antenna
—	—	3D long range air surveillance
—	—	Narrow beam very long range for air search
—	—	
750-2 250 pps	—	Replacement for SPS 10.
—	—	Designed to operate with USN point defence Surface Missile System
—	—	Under development for US Navy Aegis fleet air defence missile system

TORPEDOES

No.	Name	Length	Dia.	Weight	Speed knots	Range	Explosive charge	Guidance	Target/Role	Carrier
FRANCE										
E 14	**Acoustic Torpedo**	4 291 mm	550 mm	900 kg	25	5 500 m	200 kg	Acoustic	A/Surface (S/M up to 20 knots)	S/M
E 15	**Acoustic Torpedo**	6 000	550 mm	1 350 kg	25	12 000 m	300 kg	Acoustic	A/Surface 0-20 knots +S/M at shallow depth	S/M
L 3	**Acoustic Torpedo**	4 300	550 mm	910 kg	25	5 500 m	200 kg	Acoustic	A/S 0-20 knots up to 300 m depth	Ship or S/M
L 4	**Acoustic Torpedo**	3·13 m inc parachute stabiliser	533 mm	540 kg	30				Acoustic	A/S up to 20 knots	Airborne
L 5 Mod 1	**Multi purpose**		533 mm	1 000 kg	35				Direct Attack or Programmed Search		Ship
L 5 Mod 3			533 mm	1 300 kg	35						S/M
Z 16		7·2 m	550 mm	1 700 kg	30	10 km	300 kg	Preset plus Pattern	A/S	S/M
FEDERAL REPUBLIC OF GERMANY										
SST 4	**Wire Guided Torpedo**	639 cm inc 46 cm wire casket	533 mm				260 kg	Wire Guide Active Passive Homing Sonar	A/Surface	Ship or S/M
ITALY										
A 184			533 mm					Active/Passive Sonar Homing Course and Depth	A/S or A/Surface	Ship or S/M
A 244		2·7 m	324 mm							Ship or Aircraft
SWEDEN										
Type 41		244 cm	400 mm	250 kg				Active Homing Sonar	A/Surface or A/S	Ship or S/M
Type 42		244 cm + 18 cm wire section	400 mm	250 kg				Active Homing Sonar or Wire Guidance	A/Surface or A/S	Ship S/M Helicopter
Type 61		702·5 cm	533 mm	1 765 kg			250 kg	Wire Guided	A/Ship	Ship or S/M
UNITED KINGDOM										
Mark 8		670 cm	533 mm	1 535 kg	45	4 500 m		Pre Set Course Angle & Depth	A/Surface	S/M
Mark 20 Improved		4·11 m	533 mm	Warshot 821 kg		Warshot 11 000 m	91 kg	Homing Passive Sonar (Depth Azimuth)	A/S with limited A/Surface capability	Some ships S/M
	Tigerfish	6·464 m	533 mm	1 550 kg	Dual high or low			Wire Guide Acoustic Homing	Primarily A/S	S/M
MW 30 Mark 44	**Drill & Practice Torpedo**	2·56 m	324 mm	233 kg				Active Acoustic Homing	A/Surface	Aircraft Ship Helicopter
UNITED STATES OF AMERICA										
Mark 14	Mod 5	525 cm	533 mm	1 780 kg	32·46	46·9 km	230 kg	Preset depth & Course Angles	A/Surface	S/M
Mark 27		3·23 m	482·6 mm					Passive Sonar Homing		S/M
Mark 37	Mod 3	3·4 m	484·5 mm	643 kg	24	—	150 kg H.E.	Free running then Sonar Auto Homing	A/S	S/M
Mark 37	Mod 2	4·09 m	484·5 mm	760 kg	24	—	150 kg H.E.	Wire Guidance Active/Passive Sonar Homing	A/S	S/M
Mark 37C	As Mark 37	Plus 40% increase speed				100% increase range		Active Passive Acoustic Homing	A/Surface, A/S	Ship or S/M
Mark 44	Mod 1	2·56 m	324 mm	195 kg				Active Acoustic Homing	A/S	Aircraft, ship (Mk 32) or Asroc or Helicopter
Mark 45	Mod 1 Astor (Mod 1)	5·76 m	484·5 mm	995·8 kg		approx 11 km	Nuclear Warhead	Wire Guided	A/S	S/M
Mark 46	Mod 0, 1 and 2	2·67 m	324 mm	257 kg 229 kg (1 and 2)		—	—	Active Passive Acoustic Homing	A/S	Ships, (Mk 32 or Asroc), Aircraft, helicopter Mod 1 and 2 have liquid propellant
Mark 46	Captor Mod 4	Mk 46 inserted in mine casing and sown in narrow seas. See J.W.S. 2541.441.								
Mark 48	Mod 1 and 3	5·8 m	533 mm	1 566 kg	93 km/h	46 km		Wire Guide and Active Passive Acoustic Homing	A/Surface A/S	S/M
—	**Freedom Torpedo**	572 cm	484·5 cm	1 237 kg	40	10 000 yds	minimum of 295 kg	Wire Guided or Long Range Homing System	A/Surface	Ship or S/M
UNION OF SOVIET SOCIALIST REPUBLICS										
—	—	—	533 mm	—	—	—	—	—	Used by surface ships, submarines and aircraft	
—	—	? 16 ft (5 m)	406 mm	—	—	—	—	—		

SONAR EQUIPMENT

Country/Designation	Description	Manufacturer	Mounting
AUSTRALIA			
Mulloka	Sonar project for Royal Australian Navy	—	—
Barra	Project Barra is RAAF/RAN project to develop advanced sonobuoy and airborne detection system	Amalgamated Wireless	—
CANADA			
HS 1000	Lightweight search and attack sonar either hull mounted or towed	Canadian Westinghouse	—
SQS 505	Medium search/attack sonar	Canadian Westinghouse	—
SQS 507 (Helen)	Lightweight variable depth towed sonar	Canadian Westinghouse	—
FRANCE			
DUBV/23D	Active surface vessel search/attack sonar	—	Bow mounted
DUBV/43B	Variable depth sonar	CIT/ALCATEL	Towed
DUUX 2A/B/C	Passive sonar. Submarine detection system	CIT/ALCATEL	—
DUBV 24/C	Low frequency panoramic search/attack sonar	CIT/ALCATEL	—
PASCAL Sonar	Surveillance and tracking sonar for small and medium ships	CIT/ALCATEL	—
DUUA 2A	Simultaneous search and attack sonar for modernised Daphne class S/M	CIT/ALCATEL	—
HS-71/DUAV-4	Helicopter Sonar	CIT/ALCATEL	—
TSM 2 400/DUBA 25	Surface vessel sonar (TARPON). Attack sonar	Thomson CSF	Hull or towed
Diodon (TSM 2314)	Submarine detection, target tracking and attack operations	Thomson CSF	—
Piranha (TSM 2140)	Attack sonar	Thomson CSF	—
DUBM 41A	Side looking sonar	Thomson CSF	Towed
DUBM 21A	Mine counter measure sonar	Thomson CSF	Hull mounted
DUBM 40B	Active mine hunting sonar	Thomson CSF	Towed
ITALY			
IP 64 MD 64	Submarine sonars	USEA	—
UNITED KINGDOM			
MS.26.27	Lightweight search/attack sonar	Plessey	Hull
Type 195	Helicopter sonar	Plessey	Dunking type
MS 32	Active panoramic sonar	Plessey	Hull
162 M	Sideways looking sonar	Kelvin Hughes	—
—	RN mine hunting system (Acoustic)	Plessey	—
193M	Solid state improved version of type 193 mine hunting sonar	Plessey	—
Type 719	Submarine sonar	EMI	—
Type 199	Variable depth towed sonar	EMI	—
Type 187	Submarine sonar	EMI	—
Type 186	Submarine sonar	EMI	—
SADE	Sensitive acoustic detection equipment. Intruder detection system	Plessey	—
Project 35	Advanced fleet escort sonar in development	Plessey	—
UNITED STATES OF AMERICA			
AQS 13	Helicopter sonar	Bendix	Dunking type
BQG 1/4	Submarine passive fire control sonars	Sperry/Raytheon	—
BQQ 1	Search and fire control sonars	Raytheon	—
BQQ 2	Sonar for Subroc system	Raytheon	—
BQQ 5	Nuclear attack submarine sonar	Hughes/GE/IBM	Hull
BQR 2	Submarine passive sonar	Raytheon	—
BQR 3	Submarine passive sonar	Raytheon	—
BQR 7	Passive sonar. Part of BQQ 2 system	Raytheon	—
BQR 15	Towed submarine sonar	Western Electric	Towed
BQR 19	Submarine sonar	Raytheon	—
BQR 21	Submarine passive detection and tracking set (DIMUS)	Honeywell	Hull
BQS 6	Active submarine sonar. Part of BQQ-2 system	Raytheon	—
BQS 8	Under ice navigation sonar	Hazeltine	—
BQS 13	Submarine search sonar. Passive/active	IBM	—
SQA 10	Variable depth sonar	Litton	—
SQA 13	Variable depth sonar	—	—
SQA 14	"Searchlight" sonar	Raytheon	—
SQA 16	"Searchlight" sonar	Raytheon	—
SQA 19	Variable depth sonar	Litton	—
SQG 1	A/S attack sonar	Raytheon	—
SQQ 14	Mine hunting and classification sonar	GE	—
SQQ 23	Sonar for A/S patrol ships	—	—
SQR 14	Surface sonar	—	—
SQS 4	Short range active sonar	Sangamo/GE	—
SQS 23	Long range active sonar	Sangamo	—
SQS 26	Bow mounted "Bottom Bounce" mode sonar to replace SQS 23	EDO/GE	—
SQS 29/32	Surface vessel active sonars. Nos relate to differing frequencies	—	—
SQS 35	Variable depth towed sonar	—	Towed
SQS 36	Medium range hull sonar	EDO	—
SQS 38	Medium range hull sonar	EDO	—
SQS 56	Lightweight sonar under development for USN PF ships	Raytheon	—
UQS 2	Mine hunting sonar	GE	—
610	Long range hull sonar	EDO	—
700 series	Medium range hull and variable depth versions	EDO	—

Frequency	Power	Ship Type	Remarks
—	—	—	
—	—	—	
—	—	—	
—	—	—	
—	—	—	
4 operating frequencies around 5 kHz, 2 of which are operational	96 kW	—	
—	—	A/S escorts T47 and T56 also C67 series and C70 series	
—	—	—	
10 and 11·5 kHz	48 kW (2 × 24 kW)	—	
8·4 kHz	5 kW	—	
	30 kW	Daphne class S/M	
—	—	Helicopter	
Selectable: 11·12 or 13 kHz	—	"Aviso" type	
8, 9 or 10 kHz	—	ASW small or medium tonnage	
	10 kVa	Small ship	
—	—	Small ship	
100 kHz mod ±10 kHz	—	Mine hunters	
730 kHz	1 kW	Mine hunters	
—	—	Small or medium size S/M	
—	—	Ships and patrol craft over 150 tons	
—	—	Westland Sea King ASW	
—	—	A/S escort ships	
—	—	—	
—	—	Vosper glassfibre 45 metre minehunter	
—	—	Minehunters	
—	—	—	
—	—	—	
—	—	Submarines	
—	—	Submarines	
—	—	Shore based	
—	—	—	
—	—	Helicopter	
—	—	S/M	
—	—	—	
—	—	S/M	
—	—	S/M	
—	—	S/M	
—	—	S/M	
—	—	—	
—	—	SSBNs	
—	—	S/M	
—	—	SSBNs and SSNs	
—	—	S/M	
—	—	S/M	
—	—	S/M	
—	—	—	
—	—	—	
—	—	—	
—	—	—	
—	—	MCM	
—	—	—	
—	—	—	
—	—	—	
—	—	—	
—	—	—	Re-designated AN/SQS 53. Specified for 30 "Spruance" Class DD 963 destroyers
—	—	—	
—	—	—	
—	—	—	
—	—	—	
—	—	—	
—	—	—	
—	—	—	

NAVAL STRENGTHS

NAVAL STRENGTHS

	Aircraft Carriers (L=light)	Cruisers and Light Cruisers	Destroyers	Frigates	Corvettes	Ballistic Missile Submarines (N=Nuclear D=Diesel)	Cruise Missile Submarines (N=Nuclear D=Diesel)	Fleet Submarines	Patrol Submarines	FAC Missile	FAC Torpedo	FAC Gun	Patrol Craft	Minelayers
ARGENTINA	1 (L)	2	9 (1)	(6)	12				4	(2)	2	2	5	
AUSTRALIA	1 (L)		5	6 (2)					4 (2)				12	
BELGIUM				(4)									6	
BRAZIL	1 (L)		12 (6)	3	10				8 (2)				14	
BULGARIA				2	2				4	2	12		6	
BURMA				2	4						5		72	
CANADA			4	19					3				7	
CHILE		2	6	6	4				2		4		5	
CHINA			8 (3)	23 (1)	35 (4)	1	1 (D)	1 (?)	60 (6)	120 (20)	240 (10)	438 (20)	39	
COLOMBIA			3	3					2+4(small)				25	
CUBA				3 Res	19					23	24		29	
DENMARK				7	3 (3)				6	4 (6)	10		38	4 (2)
DOMINION REP				3	7								15	
ECUADOR				3	2				(2)	3	3 (3)		8	
EGYPT			5	3	12				12	18	26		?	
FINLAND				1	2					4		15	46	1
FRANCE	2 (L) (1)	2	20 (4)	27 (11)	22	4 (N) 1 (D) (2N)	(1)		20 (3)	4 (1)			6	
GERMANY (DEM)				2	18					12	58		22	
GERMANY (FED)			11	6 (12)	6				24	30 (10)	10			
GREECE			11	4	5				6 (3)	10	19		7	2
INDIA	1 (L)	2	3	25 (2)	(?)				8	8			8	
INDONESIA				11	11				3	12	5		16	
IRAN			3 (4)	4	4				(3)	(12)			10	
IRAQ					3					10	12	4	26	
ISRAEL									1 (3)	18 (6)			45	
ITALY		3	8	11 (4)	13				9 (2)		6	4		
JAPAN			29 (4)	16 (1)	20				16 (2)		5 (1)		10	1
KOREA (N)				3	19				13	18	157	44	32	
KOREA (S)			7	9									48	
MALAYSIA				2						8 (10)			24	
MEXICO			2	7	18								33 (10)	
NETHERLANDS		1	12	6 (13)	11				6				6	
NEW ZEALAND				4	2								11	
NORWAY				5	2				15	26 (14)	20			5 (2)
PAKISTAN		1	4	2 (2)					3+6 small		6	12	1	
PERU		3	4	2 (4)	2				8 (2)				24 (6)	
PHILIPPINES				1	6							9	39	
POLAND			1						4	12	18		49	
PORTUGAL				17	11				3				16	
ROMANIA					6					5	12	23	26	
SOUTH AFRICA			2	7 (6)					3 (2)	(6)			5	
SPAIN	1 (L) (1)		13	16 (4+7)	4				8+2 (2)		2		22 (1)	
SWEDEN			6	6	(3)				20 (3)	1 (16)	45		23	49 (1)
TAIWAN			18	13					2		9		3	1
THAILAND				8	14					(3)			30	6
TURKEY			13	2	5				14 (3)	4 (4)	12		45 (1)	8
UNITED KINGDOM	1+2 (L)	10 (2)	3 (5+1)	61 (6)		4		9 (3+1)	19				14 (7)	1
UNITED STATES	14 (2N) +7 (2N)	27 (4) (+8 res)	100 (27)	65 (10)		41 (N) (4N)	1 res (D)	65 (27+2)	12 (3)	1 (5)			28	
USSR	1 (2)	37 (2)	108 (2)	98	207	55 (16) (N) 23 (D)	42 (N) 28 (D)	38	204	120	125	65	115+90	2
VENEZUELA			4	6					4 (1)		3	3		
YUGOSLAVIA			1		3				5 (2?)	10 (10)	14	20	23	

Ocean Mine-sweepers	Coastal Mine-sweepers/ Mine-hunters	Inshore Mine-sweepers	Mine-sweeping Boats	Assault Ships	Landing Ships	Landing Craft	Depot Repair Main-tenance Ships	Survey Research Ships (Large and Small)	Supply Ships	Large Tankers	Small Tankers	Hydrofoils and ACVs	Misc-ellaneous	
	4/2				4 (1)	20		7 (2)		1	2		18 (1)	ARGENTINA
	3					6		4 (1)	2				15	AUSTRALIA
7	9/7	12						2	2				12	BELGIUM
	8 (2)				2		2	17		1	1		16	BRAZIL
2	4	2	24			20							?	BULGARIA
								2					11	BURMA
							2	5	3		2	1	63	CANADA
					4	3	2	1		1	2		12	CHILE
16	6				48 (4)	465	1	13	16		10	70	380 +	CHINA
					1			4			1		19	COLOMBIA
								7					7	CUBA
	8						1				2		5	DENMARK
					1	1 (1)		1			2		8	DOMINICAN REP
					2			2	1				9 (1)	ECUADOR
10		2				17						(3)	6	EGYPT
	6					14							14 (1)	FINLAND
11	29/7	3		2	5	29	9	11	6	5 (1)	5		164 (2)	FRANCE
	52 (3)	10				18	4	4	4		3		53	GERMANY (DEM)
	40	18				50	14	6	13		11		44	GERMANY (FED)
	15			1	14	53	2	6			8		25	GREECE
	4	4			1	6	3	3	1	1	5		6	INDIA
6	11				9	2	5	4		1	11		22	INDONESIA
	3	2			2 (4)	1	2		2	(1)	1	14	7	IRAN
													3	IRAQ
					4	10							3	ISRAEL
4	31	10			2	60	8	3	1	1	1	1 (6)	164	ITALY
	30 (5)	4	6		4 (2)	68	4	5 (1)			1 (1)		56 (1)	JAPAN
						30							10	KOREA (N)
	12				20			1					13	KOREA (S)
	6				3		1	1					27 (3)*	MALAYSIA
17	25				3			1			2		8	MEXICO
	11/4 (15)	16				11	2	3 (1)	1 (1)				28	NETHERLANDS
	2							1 (1)					2	NEW ZEALAND
	10					7	1 (1)	1					6 (9)	NORWAY
	7							1			2		5	PAKISTAN
					4			2			5 (1)		3	PERU
4					11							4	20	PHILIPPINES
24			20			38		1			6		29+2 AGIs	POLAND
	4					12	1	5	1	1	1		5	PORTUGAL
	4	10	8										?	ROMANIA
	10							1	1				9	SOUTH AFRICA
10	12			1	5	8+93	1 (2)	6		1	13		82	SPAIN
	18 (9)	20				123 (25)		5	1		1		30 (1)	SWEDEN
2	14		9		28	22							21	TAIWAN
			10		7	41		3			6		6	THAILAND
	21	4	9 (Hunters)		2	53	5	4			5		33	TURKEY
	21/16 (+2)	6		2	7	59 (2)	4	4+9	7 (2)	17	6	5	251	UNITED KINGDOM
25 (12 res)			10 (4) (+4 res)		*47 (+4 res)	100	28 (24 res)	40 (5 res)	78 (8+21 res)	49 (2+14 res)		2	200+	UNITED STATES
185	119	100			18 (1)	60 +81	64	128 (3)	5	26	18	42+	350+ 54 AGIs	USSR
					6			5					12	VENEZUELA
	4	10	14 (river)		(1)	30+		1			9		46	YUGOSLAVIA

* Police
** In addition there are 30 Cargo and Transport Ships (amphib), of which 22 are in reserve.

ADDENDA

ADDENDA

DOMINICAN REPUBLIC

Transfer of 3 Netlayers (AN 79, 86 and 87) and Gasoline Tanker (AOG 68) from USA, 1976.

EGYPT

Contract negotiations reported in July 1976 with Vosper Thornycroft for refits of Soviet-built fast attack craft. Interest in construction of ten new craft also reported with possibility of British construction of submarines and frigates.

FRANCE

Epée (fast attack craft missile), first of class of four, launched 31 Mar 1976.

Dimensions, feet (metres): 132·5 × 19·3 × 5·2 *(40·4 × 5·9 × 1·6)*
Missiles: 6—SS 12 M
Gun: 1—12·7 mm
Speed, knots: 26·3

GREECE

Ipopliarkhos Anninos, last of four "Combattante III" class, laid down 7 Apr 1976.

IRAN

Falakhon, sixth of twelve "Kaman" class fast attack craft, laid down 15 Mar 1976.

JAPAN

Hotaka (MSC 616) and *Shikine* (MSC 613) renumbered YAS 70 and 68 respectively.

NETHERLANDS

Five Further "Kortenaer" class frigates ordered from different yard in Spring 1976.

EPÉE

M. Adam, 1976

KOREA (REPUBLIC OF)

Four 1 600-ton frigates are planned for construction in South Korea; diesel and gas turbine propulsion; armed with 5 inch gun and surface-to-surface missiles.

PERU

Second "Lupo" class frigate at Ruiniti and first at Callao laid down late 1975.

SPAIN

First pair of 22 units of new close-range weapons received early 1976 for trials. System includes two 6-barrelled 20 mm Oerlikon guns with Lockheed Sharpshooter control. To be fitted in *Dedalo,* "mod Oquendo", "Baleares" and "Descubierta" classes.

Denebola (AF 56), store ship, transferred by USA, April 1976.

UNITED STATES OF AMERICA

Fiscal Year 1977 Programme

As approved by conference of House and Senate Armed Services Committee the FY 1977 authorisation provides for:
1 Nuclear-powered FBM submarine (SSBN 726)
4 Nuclear-powered attack submarines (SSN 688)
8 Guided missile frigates (FFG 7)
1 Destroyer tender (AD 37)
1 Submarine tender (AS 36)
2 Oilers (AO 177)

In addition, long-lead time authorisation was voted for a fourth "Nimitz" class nuclear-powered aircraft carrier (CVN 71) and for conversion of the cruiser *Long Beach* (CGN 9) to be fitted with Aegis System.

Strategic Missile Submarines

"Ohio" class (SSBN 726) to be fitted with BQQ-6 sonar (improved BQQ-5). SSBN 727 named *Michigan* (for home state of incumbent president). SSBN 729 construction contract awarded to General Dynamics (Electric Boat).

Submarines

"Los Angeles" class (SSN 688) machinery: S6G reactor plant developing estimated 35 000 shp.

Cruisers

A "Mark II" strike cruiser (CSGN) has been proposed as a successor to the previously described CSGN in shipbuilding programmes of the 1980s; the later design would have vertical-launch surface-to-air missiles in place of the Mk 26 launchers and a limited flight deck for several advanced VSTOL aircraft; the VSTOLs would be hangared on deck alleviating the need for aircraft elevators and related hull redesign.

Collision damaged *Belknap* (CG 26) to be rebuilt with improved radars, missile control system, updated surface-to-air missile system, more advanced 5 inch gun; 20 mm Phalanx Close-In Weapons System (CIWS) to be provided.

Experimental, Research, and Surveying Ships

Coastal Crusader (AGS 36) stricken on 30 Apr 1976.

Underway Replenishment Ships

Firedrake (AE 14), *Kennebec* (AO 36), *Tappahannock* (AO 43) stricken on 15 July 1976.

DANIEL WEBSTER (SSBN 626)

1976, Royal Navy

Photographs: The *Daniel Webster* (SSBN 626) is the world's only modern ballistic missile submarine with bow-mounted diving planes; the *Ark Royal,* Britain's last carrier, and *Nimitz* (CVN 68), the United States' latest, are shown moored in Norfolk, Virginia; the *Tarawa* (LHA 1) is shown on sea trials.

ARK ROYAL and NIMITZ (CVN 70) at Norfolk, Virginia

US Navy, JO2, G. J. Schultz

TARAWA (LHA 1)

1976, US Navy, PH2 J. P. Arciniega

INDEXES

INDEXES

Abbreviations in brackets following the names of the ships indicate the country of origin

AbD	Abu Dhabi	Fin	Finland	Ku	Kuwait	Sau	Saudi Arabia
Al	Albania	F	France	L	Laos	Sen	Senegal
Alg	Algeria	G	Gabon	Leb	Lebanon	Sh	Sharjah
A	Argentina	Gam	Gambia	Li	Liberia	S.L.	Sierra Leone
An	Anguila	Ger	Germany (Federal Republic)	Lib	Libya	Sin	Singapore
Aus	Australia	GE	Germany (Democratic Republic)	Ma	Malagasy	Som	Somalia
Au	Austria	Gh	Ghana	Ml	Malawi	S.A.	South Africa
B	Bahamas	Gr	Greece	M	Malaysia	Sp	Spain
Bah	Bahrain	Ga	Grenada	Mal	Malta	Sri	Sri Lanka
Ba	Bangladesh	Gu	Guatemala	Mau	Mauritania	Su	Sudan
Bar	Barbados	Gui	Guinea	Ms	Mauritius	Sw	Sweden
Bel	Belgium	GB	Guinea Bissau	Mex	Mexico	Sy	Syria
Bze	Belize	Guy	Guyana	Mo	Montserrat	T	Taiwan (Republic of China)
Bo	Bolivia	H	Haiti	Mor	Morocco	Tan	Tanzania
Br	Brazil	Hon	Honduras	N	Netherlands	Th	Thailand
Bru	Brunei	HB	Honduras, British	N.Z.	New Zealand	To	Togo
Bul	Bulgaria	HK	Hong Kong	Nic	Nicaragua	Ton	Tonga
Bur	Burma	Hun	Hungary	Nig	Nigeria	T & T	Trinidad & Tobago
Cam	Cameroon	Ice	Iceland	Nor	Norway	Tu	Tunisia
Can	Canada	In	India	O	Oman (Sultanate of)	T	Turkey
Chi	Chile	Ind	Indonesia	Pak	Pakistan	U.K.	United Kingdom
C	China (People's Republic)	Ir	Iran	Pan	Panama	U.S.A.	United States of America
Col	Colombia	Ira	Iraq	PNG	Papua-New Guinea	Rus	Union of Soviet Socialist
Co	Congo	Ire	Ireland (Republic of)	Par	Paraguay		Republics
C.R.	Costa Rica	Is	Israel	P	Peru	U	Uganda
Cu	Cuba	I	Italy	Ph	Philippines	Ur	Uruguay
Cy	Cyprus	I.C.	Ivory Coast	Po	Poland	Ven	Venezuela
D	Denmark	Jam	Jamaica	Por	Portugal	V	Vietnam
Dom	Dominican Republic	J	Japan	Q	Qatar	V.I.	Virgin Islands
Ec	Ecuador	Jo	Jordan	R	Romania	Yem	Yemen
Eg	Egypt	Ke	Kenya	S	Sabah	YS	Yemen (South)
ES	El Salvador	Kh	Khmer republic	St. K	St. Kitts	Y	Yugoslavia
Et	Ethiopia	Kor	Korea (Republic of)	St. L	St. Lucia	Z	Zaire
Fi	Fiji	K.N.	Korea (North)	St. V	St. Vincent	Zan	Zanzibar

INDEX OF NAMED SHIPS

AURORA—CASTOR

DUERO—GOLIATH

J. E. BERNIER—LAKSAMANA

MORSE—PATRIA

RIGEL—SJÖHUNDEN

INDEX OF CLASSES

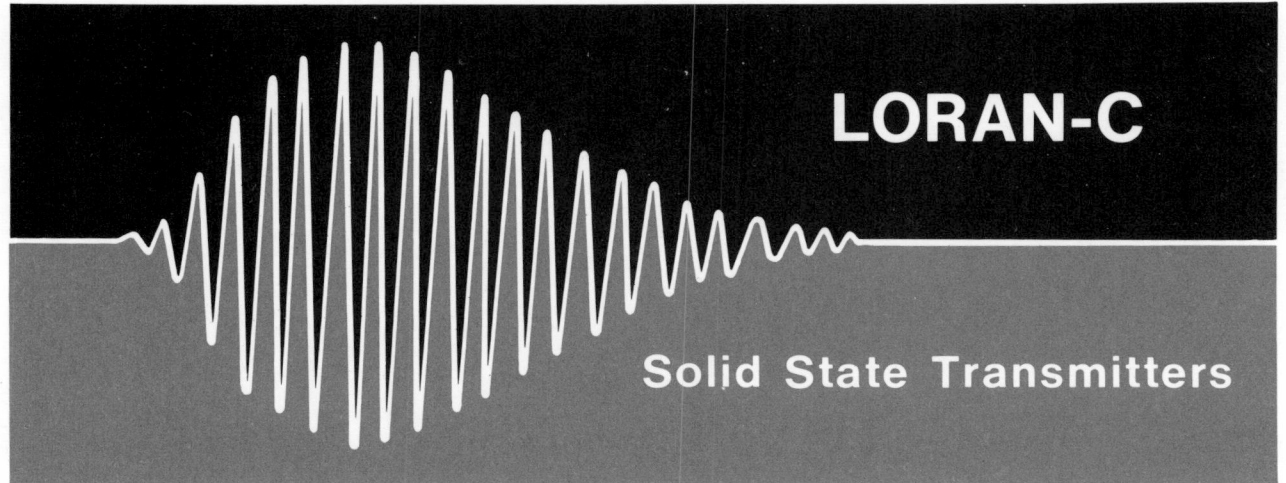

SONAR SYSTEMS FOR THE WORLD

- ☐ **Frigate and Corvette sonar**
- ☐ **Submarine sonar**
- ☐ **Helicopter sonar**
- ☐ **Minehunting sonar**
- ☐ **Passive sonar**
- ☐ **Intruder Detection sonar**

Plessey Marine is the principal sonar contractor to the Royal Navy — and to navies around the world

- ☐ **Sole UK licensee for Mark 44 Torpedo and principal sub-contractor for "Tigerfish"**

 **PLESSEY**
electronic systems

PLESSEY MARINE
Ilford Essex England IG2 6 BB
Telephone: 01-478 3040

608 P043A